The New Greek-English Interlinear New Testament

The New

ᏳᎡᎬᎬᏦ-ENGLISH

Interlinear

New Testament

A new interlinear translation of the *Greek New Testament*
United Bible Societies' Fourth, Corrected Edition
with
The New Revised Standard Version, New Testament

Translators: Robert K. Brown and Philip W. Comfort
Editor: J. D. Douglas

Editors of the *Greek New Testament,* United Bible Societies' Fourth Corrected
Edition (which has the same text as *Novum Testamentum Graece,* 26th
edition): Kurt Aland, Matthew Black, Carlo M. Martini, Bruce M. Metzger,
and Allen Wikgren in cooperation with the Institute for New Testament
Textual Research, Münster/Westphalia; under the direction of Kurt Aland and
Barbara Aland

Tyndale House Publishers, Inc., Wheaton, Illinois

CREDITS

Translators:

Robert K. Brown
Matthew, Mark, Luke, Acts, Hebrews

Philip W. Comfort
*John, Paul's Epistles, General Epistles, Revelation
and Textual Notes*

General Editor: J.D. Douglas
Tyndale House Editor: Philip W. Comfort
Tyndale House Production Editor: Elaine Showers
Graphic Designer: Timothy R. Botts
Technical Editor: Ken Petersen

Typesetters:
Ken Henley, Joan Hoyer, Judy Wireman, Sharon Baubles
with *The Typesetters,* a division of *The Complex Corporation*

Proofreaders of the Greek-English text:
Robert K. Brown, Nancy Regan

Special acknowledgments
for others who shared in making this book:

Bruce M. Metzger
*Chairperson of the Standard Bible Committee
that produced The New Revised Standard Version*

Harold P. Scanlin
*Interregional Translation Advisor,
United Bible Societies*

Arthur O. Van Eck
*Associate General Secretary
of the Division of Education and Ministry,
National Council of the Churches of Christ in the U.S.A.*

The New Greek-English Interlinear New Testament
Copyright © 1990
Tyndale House Publishers, Inc.
Wheaton, Illinois

Greek New Testament
Fourth Corrected Edition
copyright © 1966, 1968, 1975, 1983, 1993
The United Bible Societies

New Revised Standard Version
New Testament
copyright © 1990
The Division of Education and Ministry,
National Council of the Churches of Christ

Library of Congress Catalog Card Number 90-70993
ISBN 0-8423-1213-7 (standard hardcover)
ISBN 0-8423-4564-7 (personal size hardcover)
ISBN 0-8423-4565-5 (personal size bonded)
All rights reserved
Printed in the United States of America

05 04 03 02
12 11 10   9   8

CONTENTS

Introduction to
The New Greek-English Interlinear New Testament
ROBERT K. BROWN AND PHILIP W. COMFORT

New Testament Greek students all over the world recognize the superior quality of two editions of the Greek New Testament: the *Greek New Testament,* published by the United Bible Societies, and *Novum Testamentum Graece,* edited by Eberhard and Erwin Nestle, followed by Kurt Aland. These two volumes represent the best in modern textual scholarship. In the 1970s a group of international scholars, each an expert in Greek and textual criticism, worked together to produce a unified edition of these two texts. This unified edition was first displayed in the United Bible Societies' third edition of the *Greek New Testament* (1975), followed by the twenty-sixth edition of *Novum Testamentum Graece* (1979). Both editions share the same wording in the text; the two, however, differ as to punctuation, paragraph breaks, spelling (in some instances), and the critical apparatus. The United Bible Societies published a corrected edition of the *Greek New Testament* in 1983, and a fourth edition in 1993. This is the Greek text in this book.

This Greek text, with an accompanying English interlinear translation, is now made accessible to even more readers of the New Testament. Very few people learn Greek well enough to read the Greek New Testament unaided; so all Greek students (and former Greek students) can benefit from an accurate interlinear translation of the Greek New Testament. An interlinear translation also helps those who, though having very little knowledge of Greek, want the most basic, word-for-word, literal translation of the Greek text. The interlinear translation in this book should provide all such students and readers with a reliable, fresh rendering in modern English. The student can be assured that the translators used the best lexical sources in preparing this translation. The English translation of many Greek words and phrases (including idioms) very often agrees with definitions and renderings found in the second edition of *A Greek-English Lexicon of the New Testament and Other Early Christian Literature,* edited by Bauer, Ardnt, Gingrich, and Danker.

It is difficult to translate one language into another on a word-for-word basis because each language has its own syntax, grammatical constructions, and idioms that are difficult—if not impossible—to replicate literally in another language. To compensate for this difficulty, we have created special symbols and procedures for rendering certain Greek grammatical constructions and idioms that cannot be translated smoothly into English on a word-for-word basis.

The following is a concise list of some of the more commonly occurring special cases. It is, of course, impossible within the confines of an introduction to be comprehensive, particularly in regard to idioms of the Greek New Testamnet (which occur with some regularity). For further clarifications, the reader is encouraged to consult the standard Greek grammars, lexicons, and reference works.

Procedures and Symbols in the English Translation

1. Paragraph breaks are indicated by an indent in both the English and Greek lines of a couplet. (Please do not confuse this with the frequent indent of the English line due to the presence of the chapter and verse number in the Greek line beginning at the left margin.)

2. ~ shows an inversion of the Greek order into English.

3. Superior numbering ($^{1, 2, 3}$ etc.) indicates English word order.

4. ( ) indicates alternative rendering—immediately following the previous word or words.

5. [ ] indicates a supplied translation that is not found in the Greek text but is required by the context.

6. You° and your° indicates "you" and "your" plural.

7. - (the short dash) under a Greek word (frequently with definite articles) indicates that it was not necessary to translate that particular word or particle into English.

Symbols in the Greek Text

1. ⌐ ¬ indicate the beginning and ending of a textual variant; the variant readings will be shown at the bottom of the page (see John 1:18).

2. ᵀ indicates a textual addition will be shown at the bottom of the page (see John 5:3).

3. [ ] (single brackets) indicate that the enclosed words' presence in the text is disputed.

4. [[ ]] (double brackets) indicate that the enclosed words are generally regarded as later additions to the text but have been retained because of their evident antiquity and their importance in the textual tradition.

Textual Notes

The textual notes for the Greek text are of two types: (1) those that provide Scripture references for portions of the Old Testament cited in the New Testament text (indicated in the Greek text by italics), and (2) those that provide significant variant readings (designated "var.") of the Greek text. Each note includes a listing of various English translations that followed one particular variant reading over the other(s). The list also shows which translations noted a particular variant reading in the margin. In the Old Testament references, LXX is an abbreviation for the Septuagint.

Grammatical/Syntactical Constructions

1. *Genitives*

   a. genitive absolute:

   Ἀναχωρησάντων δὲ αὐτῶν
   NOW [AFTER] THEY DEPARTED
   (Matt. 2:13)

   b. objective genitive:

   ἵνα δικαιωθῶμεν ἐκ πίστεως Χριστοῦ
   THAT WE MIGHT BE JUSTIFIED BY FAITH   OF (IN) CHRIST
   (Gal. 2:16)

   c. subjective genitive:

   ἡ ἐπιθυμία τῆς σαρκὸς
   THE LUST   OF THE FLESH
   (1 John 2:16)

d. genitive of comparison:

ἰσχυρότερός μού ἐστιν
STRONGER   THAN ME IS
(Matt. 3:11)

2. *Possessives*

a. possessive pronouns:

ἐν τῇ καρδίᾳ αὐτῶν
IN THE HEART   OF THEM
(Luke 1:66)

b. plural possessives:

ὑμῶν
your° (when preceding the noun it modifies, otherwise, of you°)

c. possessive articles used before nouns indicating body parts:

καὶ ἐκτείνας   τὴν χεῖρα ἥψατο αὐτοῦ
AND   HAVING STRETCHED OUT   THE (HIS) HAND   HE TOUCHED HIM
(Matt. 8:3)

d. dative of possession:

ὄνομα αὐτῷ Ἰωάννης
NAME   TO HIM   JOHN
(John 1:6)

3. *Particles*

a. postpositive particles:

τέξεται δὲ   υἱόν
AND~SHE WILL BEAR   A SON.
(Matt. 1:21)

b. negative particles adjacent to a verb:

οὐ δύναται πόλις κρυβῆναι
A CITY~IS NOT ABLE   TO BE HIDDEN
(Matt. 5:14)

c. μὴ at the beginning of a question expecting a negative answer:

μὴ   σὺ μείζων   εἶ τοῦ πατρὸς ἡμῶν Ἰακώβ,
³[SURELY] NOT ¹YOU ⁴GREATER [THAN] ²ARE THE   FATHER   OF US,   JACOB,
(John 4:12)

d. ὅτι is not translated when it introduces direct speech or a quotation.

4. *Plurals*

a. Some nouns are singular in form but collective/plural in thought. Many of these cases have been translated into the natural English idiom without indicating their actual grammatical form. Frequently, however, the form required in natural English idiom is supplied in parentheses immediately after the correct grammatical form.

τὰ ῥήματα ἃ   ἐγὼ λελάληκα ὑμῖν πνεῦμά ἐστιν καὶ ζωή ἐστιν.
THE WORDS   WHICH I   HAVE SPOKEN   TO YOU° IS(ARE)~SPIRIT   AND   IS(ARE)~LIFE.
(John 6:63)

b. A few English words that can convey a plural meaning in a singular form are left in the singular form when translating a Greek plural, such as, bread, lightning, fish, and incense.

5. *Infinitives*

    a. the articular infinitive in the genitive case expressing purpose or result:

    μέλλει γὰρ Ἡρῴδης ζητεῖν τὸ παιδίον τοῦ ἀπολέσαι αὐτό.
    ³IS ABOUT   ¹FOR   ²HEROD   TO SEEK   THE CHILD   –   TO KILL   IT.
    (Matt. 2:13)

    b. accusative as the subject of the infinitive:

    εἰς τὸ εἶναι αὐτὸν πατέρα
    FOR   –   HIM~TO BE   A FATHER
    (Rom. 4:11)

    c. ἐν τῷ used in the temporal sense with the infinitive:

    ἐν τῷ ὑποστρέφειν αὐτοὺς
    WHEN   THEY~RETURNED
    (Luke 2:43)

    d. the infinitive translated as the main verb (rare):

    Μετὰ δὲ τὸ παραδοθῆναι τὸν Ἰωάννην
    AND~AFTER   –   ²WAS IMPRISONED   –   ¹JOHN
    (Mark 1:14)

6. *Verbs requiring their object to complete their sense are often treated as a unit:*

    σκανδαλίζει σε
    CAUSES YOU TO SIN
    (Matt. 5:29)

Some Common Idioms

1.   οὐ μὴ
    NEVER

2.   ἵνα μὴ
    LEST

3.   μὴ γένοιτο
    MAY IT NOT BE

4.   δεῖ
    IT IS NECESSARY

5.   Διὰ τοῦτο
    THEREFORE

6.   καθ' ἡμέραν
    DAILY

7.   τοῦτ' ἔστιν
    THAT IS

8.   διὰ παντὸς
    ALWAYS

9.   ἐπὶ τὸ αὐτό
    TOGETHER

Transliterations

A number of Hebrew and Aramaic words carried over into the Greek language have been transliterated rather than translated, such as "Abba" (see Gal. 4:6), "amen" (see Eph. 3:21), "Maranatha" (see 1 Cor. 16:22), and "raca" (see Matt. 5:22). Also, measurements, weights, and currency have been transliterated rather than translated, such as "stadia" (see John 11:18), "talents" (see Matt. 25:15), and "denarius" (see Matt. 18:28).

VERBS AND PARTICIPLES

Tense and Voice

We have attempted to translate verbs and participles within the strict tense guidelines listed below. However, conditional sentences, idiomatic phrases, and at times the very context of the passage, demand a less rigid approach. The paradigm below could give the impression that tense for Greek verbs and participles is primarily temporal. Therefore, it must be said that "tense" in Greek indicates kind of action more than time of action. An aorist participle, for example, may not indicate some action done in the past; rather, it could designate a present action done at a point in time. The aorist participle may function as a participle of attendant circumstance without reflecting the temporal sense at all (which is reflected in the main verb). Thus, the aorist reflects a kind of action (called "punctiliar"—referring to a point in time) more than an action done in the past.

A Paradigm of English Renderings for Greek Verbs

	ACTIVE	PASSIVE
PLUPERFECT	I had loved	I had been loved
PERFECT	I have loved	I have been loved
IMPERFECT	I was loving	I was being loved
AORIST	I loved	I was loved
PRESENT	I love/am loving	I am loved/am being loved
FUTURE	I will love	I will be loved

Note: The middle voice can rarely be distinguished from the passive voice in an English translation. Occasionally the middle voice can be seen in the use of reflexive pronouns, as in the translation of περιβεβλημένη, "having clothed herself with" (Rev. 18:16).

Mood

Subjunctive

We have used "might" or "may" whenever possible to indicate the presence of the subjunctive mood. But this was not always possible, particularly with conditional sentences (which automatically convey the subjunctive mood). Occasionally, "could" or "should" was used to indicate the subjunctive mood, especially in exhortations (technically called the "hortatory subjunctive").

Optative

The optative mood is primarily used in conjunction with certain temporal or conditional clauses; it is also used to express a wish. It is less assured in tone than the subjunctive and fairly rare in the New Testament.

Imperative

It is very difficult to make a distinction in an English translation between the tenses in the imperative mood. The only distinctive feature we have employed is the use of "constantly" or "continually" for the present imperative where such an addition seemed particularly appropriate to the context.

A Paradigm of English Renderings for Greek Participles

	ACTIVE	PASSIVE
PERFECT	having loved	having been loved
AORIST	having loved	having been loved
PRESENT	loving	being loved

Noteworthy constructions involving the participle

1. Participles with the article:

τοῖς   πιστεύουσιν
TO THE ONES   BELIEVING
(John 1:12)

2. Adjectival participle:

ἐν   τῇ   διδασκαλίᾳ   τῇ   ὑγιαινούσῃ
BY   THE   ²TEACHING   -   ¹HEALTHY
(Titus 1:9)

3. Periphrastic constructions:

Periphrastic constructions consist of a main verb (usually εἰμί) followed by a participle which together form a single verbal construction. The main verb adds only grammatical information; it does not convey semantic information.

English Equivalents of Periphrastic Constructions

1. Present

    present of εἰμί + present participle

2. Imperfect

    imperfect of εἰμί + present participle

3. Future

    future of εἰμί + present participle

4. Perfect

    present of εἰμί + perfect participle

5. Pluperfect

    imperfect of εἰμί + perfect participle

6. Future perfect

    future of εἰμί + perfect particple

We, the translators, enjoyed working with one another and with the editor, J. D. Douglas, on this book. Our labor will be rewarded if this *New Greek-English Interlinear New Testament* provides greater accessibility to the original language of the New Testament, encourages further study of the Greek text and enhances fuller knowledge of God's Word and his Son, Jesus Christ.

Introduction to
The New Revised Standard Version, New Testament
TO THE READER

This preface is addressed to you by the Committee of translators, who wish to explain, as briefly as possible, the origin and character of our work. The publication of our revision is yet another step in the long, continual process of making the Bible available in the form of the English language that is most widely current in our day. To summarize in a single sentence: the New Revised Standard Version of the Bible is an authorized revision of the Revised Standard Version, published in 1952, which was a revision of the American Standard Version, published in 1901, which, in turn, embodied earlier revisions of the King James Version, published in 1611.

The need for issuing a revision of the Revised Standard Version of the Bible arises from three circumstances: (a) the acquisition of still older biblical manuscripts, (b) further investigation of linguistic features of the text, and (c) changes in preferred English usage. Consequently, in 1974 the Policies Committee of the Revised Standard Version, which is a standing committee of the National Council of the Churches of Christ in the U.S.A., authorized the preparation of a revision of the entire RSV Bible.

For the New Testament the Committee has based its work on the most recent edition of the *Greek New Testament,* prepared by an interconfessional and international committee and published by the United Bible Societies (1966; 3rd ed. corrected, 1983; information concerning changes to be introduced into the critical apparatus of the forthcoming 4th edition was available to the Committee). As in that edition, double brackets are used to enclose a few passages that are generally regarded to be later additions to the text, but which we have retained because of their evident antiquity and their importance in the textual tradition. Only in very rare instances have we replaced the text or the punctuation of the Bible Societies' edition by an alternative that seemed to us to be superior. Here and there in the footnotes the phrase, "Other ancient authorities read," identifies alternative readings preserved by Greek manuscripts and early versions. Alternative renderings of the text are indicated by the word "Or."

As for the style of English adopted for the present revision, among the mandates given to the Committee in 1980 by the Division of Education and Ministry of the National Council of Churches of Christ (which now holds the copyright of the RSV Bible) was the directive to continue in the tradition of the King James Bible, but to introduce such changes as are warranted on the basis of accuracy, clarity, euphony, and current English usage. Within the contraints set by the original texts and by the mandates of the Division, the Committee has followed the maxim, "As literal as possible, as free as necessary." As a consequence, the New Revised Standard Version (NRSV) remains essentially a literal translation. Paraphrastic renderings have been adopted only sparingly, and then chiefly to compensate for a deficiency in the English language—the lack of a common gender third person singular pronoun.

During the almost half a century since the publication of the RSV, many in the churches have become sensitive to the danger of linguistic sexism arising from the inherent bias of the English language toward the masculine gender, a bias that in the case of the Bible has often restricted or obscured the meaning of the original text. The mandates from the Division specified that, in references to men and women, masculine oriented language should be eliminated as far as this can be done without altering passages that reflect the historical situation of ancient patriarchal culture. As can be appreciated, more than once the Committee found that the several mandates stood in tension and even in conflict. The various concerns had to be balanced case by case in order to provide a faithful and acceptable rendering without using contrived English. In the vast majority of cases, however, inclusiveness has been attained by introducing plural forms when this does not distort the meaning of the passage. Of course, in narrative and in parable no attempt was made to generalize the sex of individual persons.

It will be seen that in prayers addressed to God the archaic second person singular pronouns (*thee, thou, thine*) and verb forms (*art, hast, hadst*) are no longer used. Although some readers may regret this change, it should be pointed out that in the original languages neither the Old Testament nor the New makes any linguistic distinction between addressing a human being and addressing the Deity. Furthermore, in the tradition of the King James Bible one will not expect to find the use of capital letters for pronouns that refer to the Deity—such capitalization is an unnecessary innovation that has only recently been introduced into a few English translations of the Bible. Finally, we have left to the discretion of the licensed publishers such matters as section headings, cross-references, and clues to the pronunciation of proper names.

This new version seeks to preserve all that is best in the English Bible as it has been known and used through the years. It is intended for use in public reading and congregational worship, as well as in private study, instruction, and meditation. We have resisted the temptation to introduce terms and phrases that merely reflect current moods, and have tried to put the message of the Scriptures in simple, enduring words and expressions that are worthy to stand in the great tradition of the King James Bible and its predecessors. It is the hope and prayer of the translators that this version may continue to hold a large place in congregation life and to speak to all readers, young and old alike, helping them to understand and believe and respond to its message.

For the Committee,
Bruce M. Metzger

THE GOSPEL ACCORDING TO
MATTHEW

KATA   MAΘΘAION
ACCORDING TO MATTHEW

1.1 Βίβλος γενέσεως   Ἰησοῦ Χριστοῦ υἱοῦ Δαυὶδ
    A RECORD   OF [THE] GENEALOGY OF JESUS CHRIST   SON   OF DAVID

υἱοῦ Ἀβραάμ.
SON   OF ABRAHAM.

1.2 Ἀβραὰμ ἐγέννησεν τὸν Ἰσαάκ, Ἰσαὰκ δὲ
   ABRAHAM   FATHERED   -   ISAAC,   AND~ISAAC

ἐγέννησεν τὸν Ἰακώβ, Ἰακὼβ δὲ ἐγέννησεν τὸν Ἰούδαν
FATHERED   -   JACOB,   AND~JACOB   FATHERED   -   JUDAH

καὶ τοὺς ἀδελφοὺς αὐτοῦ, **1.3** Ἰούδας δὲ ἐγέννησεν τὸν
AND   THE   BROTHERS   OF HIM,   AND~JUDAH   FATHERED   -

Φάρες καὶ τὸν Ζάρα ἐκ τῆς Θαμάρ, Φάρες δὲ
PEREZ   AND   -   ZERAH   BY   -   TAMAR,   AND~PEREZ

ἐγέννησεν τὸν Ἐσρώμ, Ἐσρὼμ δὲ ἐγέννησεν τὸν
FATHERED   -   HEZRON,   AND~HEZRON   FATHERED   -

Ἀράμ, **1.4** Ἀρὰμ δὲ ἐγέννησεν τὸν Ἀμιναδάβ,
ARAM,   AND~ARAM   FATHERED   -   AMMINADAB,

Ἀμιναδὰβ δὲ ἐγέννησεν τὸν Ναασσών, Ναασσὼν δὲ
AND~AMMINADAB   FATHERED   -   NASHON,   AND~NASHON

ἐγέννησεν τὸν Σαλμών, **1.5** Σαλμὼν δὲ ἐγέννησεν τὸν
FATHERED   -   SALMON,   AND~SALMON   FATHERED   -

Βόες ἐκ τῆς Ῥαχάβ, Βόες δὲ ἐγέννησεν τὸν Ἰωβὴδ ἐκ
BOAZ   BY   -   RAHAB,   AND~BOAZ   FATHERED   -   OBED   BY

τῆς Ῥούθ, Ἰωβὴδ δὲ ἐγέννησεν τὸν Ἰεσσαί,
-   RUTH,   AND~OBED   FATHERED   -   JESSE,

1.6 Ἰεσσαὶ δὲ ἐγέννησεν τὸν Δαυὶδ τὸν βασιλέα.
   AND~JESSE   FATHERED   -   DAVID   THE   KING.

Δαυὶδ δὲ ἐγέννησεν τὸν Σολομῶνα ἐκ τῆς   τοῦ
AND~DAVID   FATHERED   -   SOLOMON   BY   THE [WIFE] -

Οὐρίου, **1.7** Σολομὼν δὲ ἐγέννησεν τὸν Ῥοβοάμ,
OF URIAH,   AND~SOLOMON   FATHERED   -   REHOBOAM,

Ῥοβοὰμ δὲ ἐγέννησεν τὸν Ἀβιά, Ἀβιὰ δὲ ἐγέννησεν
AND REHOBOAM   FATHERED   -   ABIJAH,   AND~ABIJAH   FATHERED

τὸν Ἀσάφ, **1.8** Ἀσὰφ δὲ ἐγέννησεν τὸν Ἰωσαφάτ,
-   ASAPH,   AND~ASAPH   FATHERED   -   JEHOSHAPHAT,

Ἰωσαφὰτ δὲ ἐγέννησεν τὸν Ἰωράμ, Ἰωρὰμ δὲ
AND~JEHOSHAPHAT   FATHERED   -   JORAM,   AND~JORAM

ἐγέννησεν τὸν Ὀζίαν, **1.9** Ὀζίας δὲ ἐγέννησεν τὸν
FATHERED   -   UZZIAH,   AND~UZZIAH   FATHERED   -

An account of the genealogy[a] of Jesus the Messiah,[b] the son of David, the son of Abraham.

2 Abraham was the father of Isaac, and Isaac the father of Jacob, and Jacob the father of Judah and his brothers, 3and Judah the father of Perez and Zerah by Tamar, and Perez the father of Hezron, and Hezron the father of Aram, 4and Aram the father of Aminadab, and Aminadab the father of Nahshon, and Nahshon the father of Salmon, 5and Salmon the father of Boaz by Rahab, and Boaz the father of Obed by Ruth, and Obed the father of Jesse, 6and Jesse the father of King David.

And David was the father of Solomon by the wife of Uriah, 7and Solomon the father of Rehoboam, and Rehoboam the father of Abijah, and Abijah the father of Asaph,[c] 8and Asaph[c] the father of Jehoshaphat, and Jehoshaphat the father of Joram, and Joram the father of Uzziah, 9and Uzziah the father of

[a] Or birth
[b] Or Jesus Christ
[c] Other ancient authorities read Asa

Jotham, and Jotham the father of Ahaz, and Ahaz the father of Hezekiah, [10]and Hezekiah the father of Manasseh, and Manasseh the father of Amos,[d] and Amos[d] the father of Josiah, [11]and Josiah the father of Jechoniah and his brothers, at the time of the deportation to Babylon.

12 And after the deportation to Babylon: Jechoniah was the father of Salathiel, and Salathiel the father of Zerubbabel, [13]and Zerubbabel the father of Abiud, and Abiud the father of Eliakim, and Eliakim the father of Azor, [14]and Azor the father of Zadok, and Zadok the father of Achim, and Achim the father of Eliud, [15]and Eliud the father of Eleazar, and Eleazar the father of Matthan, and Matthan the father of Jacob, [16]and Jacob the father of Joseph the husband of Mary, of whom Jesus was born, who is called the Messiah.[e]

17 So all the generations from Abraham to David are fourteen generations; and from David to the deportation to Babylon, fourteen generations; and from the deportation to Babylon to the Messiah,[e] fourteen generations.

18 Now the birth of Jesus the Messiah[f] took place in this way.

[d] Other ancient authorities read *Amon*
[e] Or *the Christ*
[f] Or *Jesus Christ*

'Ιωαθάμ, 'Ιωαθὰμ δὲ ἐγέννησεν τὸν 'Αχάζ, 'Αχὰζ δὲ
JOTHAM, AND~JOTHAM FATHERED - AHAZ, AND~AHAZ

ἐγέννησεν τὸν 'Εζεκίαν, **1.10** 'Εζεκίας δὲ ἐγέννησεν τὸν
FATHERED - HEZEKIAH, AND~HEZEKIAH FATHERED

Μανασσῆ, Μανασσῆς δὲ ἐγέννησεν τὸν 'Αμώς, 'Αμὼς δὲ
MANASSEH. AND~MANASSEH FATHERED - AMOS. AND~AMOS

ἐγέννησεν τὸν 'Ιωσίαν, **1.11** 'Ιωσίας δὲ ἐγέννησεν τὸν
FATHERED - JOSIAH, AND~JOSIAH FATHERED -

'Ιεχονίαν καὶ τοὺς ἀδελφοὺς αὐτοῦ ἐπὶ τῆς
JECONIAH AND THE BROTHERS OF HIM AT THE

μετοικεσίας Βαβυλῶνος.
DEPORTATION TO BABYLON.

1.12 Μετὰ δὲ τὴν μετοικεσίαν Βαβυλῶνος 'Ιεχονίας
AND~AFTER THE DEPORTATION TO BABYLON, JECONIAH

ἐγέννησεν τὸν Σαλαθιήλ, Σαλαθιὴλ δὲ ἐγέννησεν τὸν
FATHERED - SHEALTIEL, AND~SHEALTIEL FATHERED -

Ζοροβαβέλ, **1.13** Ζοροβαβὲλ δὲ ἐγέννησεν τὸν 'Αβιούδ,
ZERUBBABEL, AND~ZERUBBABEL FATHERED - ABIUD,

'Αβιοὺδ δὲ ἐγέννησεν τὸν 'Ελιακίμ, 'Ελιακὶμ δὲ
AND~ABIUD FATHERED - ELIAKIM, AND~ELIAKIM

ἐγέννησεν τὸν 'Αζώρ, **1.14** 'Αζὼρ δὲ ἐγέννησεν τὸν
FATHERED - AZOR, AND~AZOR FATHERED -

Σαδώκ, Σαδὼκ δὲ ἐγέννησεν τὸν 'Αχίμ, 'Αχὶμ δὲ
ZADOK, AND~ZADOK FATHERED - ACHIM, AND~ACHIM

ἐγέννησεν τὸν 'Ελιούδ, **1.15** 'Ελιοὺδ δὲ ἐγέννησεν τὸν
FATHERED - ELIUD, AND~ELIUD FATHERED -

'Ελεάζαρ, 'Ελεάζαρ δὲ ἐγέννησεν τὸν Ματθάν,
ELEAZAR, AND~ELEAZAR FATHERED - MATTHAN,

Ματθὰν δὲ ἐγέννησεν τὸν 'Ιακώβ, **1.16** 'Ιακὼβ δὲ
AND~MATTHAN FATHERED - JACOB, AND~JACOB

ἐγέννησεν τὸν 'Ιωσὴφ τὸν ἄνδρα Μαρίας, ἐξ ἧς
FATHERED - JOSEPH, THE HUSBAND OF MARY, FROM WHOM

ἐγεννήθη 'Ιησοῦς ὁ λεγόμενος Χριστός.
WAS BORN JESUS THE ONE BEING CALLED CHRIST.

1.17 Πᾶσαι οὖν αἱ γενεαὶ ἀπὸ 'Αβραὰμ ἕως
THUS~ALL THE GENERATIONS FROM ABRAHAM TO

Δαυὶδ γενεαὶ δεκατέσσαρες, καὶ ἀπὸ Δαυὶδ ἕως τῆς
DAVID [WERE] FOURTEEN~GENERATIONS, AND FROM DAVID TO THE

μετοικεσίας Βαβυλῶνος γενεαὶ δεκατέσσαρες, καὶ ἀπὸ
DEPORTATION TO BABYLON, FOURTEEN~GENERATIONS, AND FROM

τῆς μετοικεσίας Βαβυλῶνος ἕως τοῦ Χριστοῦ
THE DEPORTATION TO BABYLON TO THE CHRIST,

γενεαὶ δεκατέσσαρες.
FOURTEEN~GENERATIONS.

1.18 Τοῦ δὲ ⌜'Ιησοῦ Χριστοῦ⌝ ἡ γένεσις οὕτως ἦν.
NOW OF JESUS CHRIST THE BIRTH WAS~THUS.

1:18 text: KJV ASV RSV NASB NIV TEV NJB NRSV. var. Χριστου Ιησου (Christ Jesus): none. var. Ιησου (Jesus): none. var. Χριστου (Christ): NEB.

μνηστευθείσης τῆς μητρὸς αὐτοῦ Μαρίας τῷ Ἰωσήφ,
BEING ENGAGED   THE   MOTHER   OF HIM   MARY   -   TO JOSEPH,

πρὶν ἢ συνελθεῖν αὐτοὺς εὑρέθη   ἐν γαστρὶ ἔχουσα
BEFORE   THEY~CAME TOGETHER   SHE WAS FOUND PREGNANT

ἐκ πνεύματος ἁγίου. **1.19** Ἰωσὴφ δὲ ὁ ἀνὴρ αὐτῆς,
BY [THE] HOLY~SPIRIT.   NOW~JOSEPH,   THE HUSBAND OF HER,

δίκαιος ὢν καὶ μὴ θέλων αὐτὴν δειγματίσαι, ἐβουλήθη
BEING~RIGHTEOUS AND   NOT WISHING   TO DISGRACE~HER,   DECIDED

λάθρα ἀπολῦσαι αὐτήν. **1.20** ταῦτα   δὲ
SECRETLY TO DIVORCE   HER.   ³[ON] THESE THINGS ¹NOW

αὐτοῦ ἐνθυμηθέντος ἰδοὺ ἄγγελος κυρίου κατ᾽ ὄναρ
²[WHILE] HE WAS THINKING,   BEHOLD AN ANGEL   OF [THE] LORD IN   A DREAM

ἐφάνη αὐτῷ λέγων, Ἰωσὴφ υἱὸς Δαυίδ, μὴ φοβηθῇς
APPEARED TO HIM SAYING,   JOSEPH,   SON OF DAVID DO NOT BE AFRAID

παραλαβεῖν Μαρίαν τὴν γυναῖκά σου· τὸ γὰρ   ἐν
TO TAKE   MARY [TO BE] THE   WIFE   OF YOU; FOR~THE [CHILD] IN

αὐτῇ γεννηθὲν   ἐκ   πνεύματός ἐστιν ἁγίου.
HER HAVING BEEN CONCEIVED ²FROM ⁴SPIRIT   ¹IS ³[THE] HOLY.

1.21 τέξεται δὲ ⌜υἱόν⌝, καὶ καλέσεις τὸ ὄνομα αὐτοῦ
AND~SHE WILL BEAR A SON,   AND YOU WILL CALL THE NAME   OF HIM

Ἰησοῦν· αὐτὸς γὰρ σώσει τὸν λαὸν αὐτοῦ ἀπὸ τῶν
JESUS,   FOR~HE   WILL SAVE THE PEOPLE OF HIM FROM THE

ἁμαρτιῶν αὐτῶν. **1.22** Τοῦτο δὲ ὅλον γέγονεν ἵνα
SINS   OF THEM.   NOW~THIS   ALL OCCURRED THAT

πληρωθῇ   τὸ ῥηθὲν ὑπὸ κυρίου διὰ τοῦ
MIGHT BE FULFILLED THE [THING] SPOKEN BY [THE] LORD THROUGH THE

προφήτου λέγοντος,
PROPHET   SAYING,

1.23 Ἰδοὺ ἡ παρθένος ἐν γαστρὶ ἕξει καὶ τέξεται
BEHOLD THE VIRGIN   WILL BE PREGNANT   AND   SHE WILL BEAR

υἱόν,
A SON,

καὶ καλέσουσιν τὸ ὄνομα αὐτοῦ Ἐμμανουήλ,
AND THEY WILL CALL THE NAME   OF HIM   IMMANUEL,

ὅ ἐστιν μεθερμηνευόμενον· Μεθ᾽ ἡμῶν ὁ θεός.
WHICH HAVING BEEN INTERPRETED MEANS   ²WITH ³US - ¹GOD.

1.24 ἐγερθεὶς δὲ ὁ Ἰωσὴφ ἀπὸ τοῦ ὕπνου ἐποίησεν ὡς
THEN~RISING UP   - JOSEPH FROM - SLEEP HE DID   AS

προσέταξεν αὐτῷ ὁ ἄγγελος κυρίου καὶ παρέλαβεν
COMMANDED   HIM THE ANGEL   OF [THE] LORD AND   HE TOOK

τὴν γυναῖκα αὐτοῦ, **1.25** καὶ οὐκ ἐγίνωσκεν αὐτὴν
THE WIFE   OF HIM,   AND HE DID NOT KNOW   HER

ἕως οὗ ἔτεκεν ⌜υἱόν⌝· καὶ ἐκάλεσεν τὸ ὄνομα αὐτοῦ
UNTIL SHE BORE A SON; AND HE CALLED THE NAME   OF HIM

Ἰησοῦν.
JESUS.

When his mother Mary had been engaged to Joseph, but before they lived together, she was found to be with child from the Holy Spirit. [19]Her husband Joseph, being a righteous man and unwilling to expose her to public disgrace, planned to dismiss her quietly. [20]But just when he had resolved to do this, an angel of the Lord appeared to him in a dream and said, "Joseph, son of David, do not be afraid to take Mary as your wife, for the child conceived in her is from the Holy Spirit. [21]She will bear a son, and you are to name him Jesus, for he will save his people from their sins." [22]All this took place to fulfill what had been spoken by the Lord through the prophet:

[23]"Look, the virgin shall conceive and bear a son,
and they shall name him Emmanuel,"

which means, "God is with us." [24]When Joseph awoke from sleep, he did as the angel of the Lord commanded him; he took her as his wife, [25]but had no marital relations with her until she had borne a son;[g] and he named him Jesus.

[g] Other ancient authorities read *her firstborn son*

1:23a Isa. 7:14 LXX   **1:23b** Isa. 8:8, 10 LXX   **1:25** text: ASV RSV NASB NIV NEB TEV NJB NRSV. var. τον υιον αυτης τον πρωτοτοκον (her firstborn son) [see Luke 2:2]: KJV NRSVmg.

CHAPTER 2

In the time of King Herod, after Jesus was born in Bethlehem of Judea, wise men*h* from the East came to Jerusalem, ²asking, "Where is the child who has been born king of the Jews? For we observed his star at its rising,*i* and have come to pay him homage." ³When King Herod heard this, he was frightened, and all Jerusalem with him; ⁴and calling together all the chief priests and scribes of the people, he inquired of them where the Messiah*j* was to be born. ⁵They told him, "In Bethlehem of Judea; for so it has been written by the prophet:

6 'And you, Bethlehem, in the land of Judah, are by no means least among the rulers of Judah; for from you shall come a ruler who is to shepherd*k* my people Israel.' "

7 Then Herod secretly called for the wise men*h* and learned from them the exact time when the star had appeared. ⁸Then he sent them to Bethlehem, saying, "Go and search diligently for the child; and when you have found him, bring me word so that I may also go

h Or astrologers; Gk magi
i Or in the East
j Or the Christ
k Or rule

2.1 Τοῦ δὲ Ἰησοῦ γεννηθέντος ἐν Βηθλέεμ τῆς
\- NOW JESUS HAVING BEEN BORN IN BETHLEHEM -

Ἰουδαίας ἐν ἡμέραις Ἡρῴδου τοῦ βασιλέως, ἰδοὺ
OF JUDEA IN [THE] DAYS OF HEROD THE KING, BEHOLD

μάγοι ἀπὸ ἀνατολῶν παρεγένοντο εἰς Ἱεροσόλυμα
MAGI FROM [THE] EAST ARRIVED IN JERUSALEM

2.2 λέγοντες, Ποῦ ἐστιν ὁ τεχθεὶς βασιλεὺς τῶν
SAYING, WHERE IS THE ONE HAVING BEEN BORN KING OF THE

Ἰουδαίων; εἴδομεν γὰρ αὐτοῦ τὸν ἀστέρα ἐν τῇ
JEWS? FOR~WE SAW HIS - STAR IN THE

ἀνατολῇ καὶ ἤλθομεν προσκυνῆσαι αὐτῷ.
EAST AND WE CAME TO WORSHIP HIM.

2.3 ἀκούσας δὲ ὁ βασιλεὺς Ἡρῴδης ἐταράχθη καὶ
NOW~HAVING HEARD [THIS] - KING HEROD WAS TROUBLED AND

πᾶσα Ἱεροσόλυμα μετ' αὐτοῦ, **2.4** καὶ συναγαγὼν
ALL JERUSALEM WITH HIM, AND HAVING ASSEMBLED

πάντας τοὺς ἀρχιερεῖς καὶ γραμματεῖς τοῦ λαοῦ
ALL THE CHIEF PRIESTS AND SCRIBES OF THE PEOPLE

ἐπυνθάνετο παρ' αὐτῶν ποῦ ὁ Χριστὸς γεννᾶται.
HE INQUIRED FROM THEM WHERE THE CHRIST IS BEING BORN.

2.5 οἱ δὲ εἶπαν αὐτῷ, Ἐν Βηθλέεμ τῆς Ἰουδαίας·
AND~THEY SAID TO HIM, IN BETHLEHEM - OF JUDEA;

οὕτως γὰρ γέγραπται διὰ τοῦ προφήτου·
FOR~THUS IT HAS BEEN WRITTEN THROUGH THE PROPHET:

2.6 Καὶ σὺ Βηθλέεμ, γῆ Ἰούδα,
AND YOU BETHLEHEM, [IN THE] LAND OF JUDAH,

οὐδαμῶς ἐλαχίστη εἶ ἐν τοῖς ἡγεμόσιν
BY NO MEANS LEAST ARE YOU AMONG THE RULERS

Ἰούδα·
OF JUDAH.

ἐκ σοῦ γὰρ ἐξελεύσεται ἡγούμενος,
²FROM ³YOU ¹FOR WILL COME A RULER,

ὅστις ποιμανεῖ τὸν λαόν μου τὸν Ἰσραήλ.
WHO WILL SHEPHERD THE PEOPLE OF ME - ISRAEL.

2.7 Τότε Ἡρῴδης λάθρα καλέσας τοὺς μάγους
THEN HEROD SECRETLY HAVING CALLED THE MAGI

ἠκρίβωσεν παρ' αὐτῶν τὸν χρόνον τοῦ φαινομένου
ASCERTAINED FROM THEM THE TIME OF THE APPEARING

ἀστέρος, **2.8** καὶ πέμψας αὐτοὺς εἰς Βηθλέεμ εἶπεν,
OF [THE] STAR, AND HAVING SENT THEM TO BETHLEHEM HE SAID,

Πορευθέντες ἐξετάσατε ἀκριβῶς, περὶ τοῦ παιδίου·
GOING INQUIRE CAREFULLY CONCERNING THE CHILD;

ἐπὰν δὲ εὕρητε, ἀπαγγείλατέ μοι, ὅπως κἀγὼ ἐλθὼν
AND~WHEN YOU° FIND [HIM], REPORT TO ME, SO THAT I ALSO COMING

2:6 Mic. 5:2

προσκυνήσω αὐτῷ.   **2.9** οἱ δὲ ἀκούσαντες τοῦ βασιλέως
MAY WORSHIP   HIM.   SO~THEY, HAVING LISTENED   TO THE   KING,

ἐπορεύθησαν καὶ ἰδοὺ ὁ ἀστὴρ, ὃν εἶδον ἐν τῇ
DEPARTED   AND   BEHOLD THE STAR,   WHICH THEY SAW IN   THE

ἀνατολῇ, προῆγεν αὐτοὺς, ἕως ἐλθὼν ἐστάθη
EAST,   WENT BEFORE THEM,   UNTIL HAVING COME   IT STOOD

ἐπάνω   οὗ   ἦν τὸ παιδίον.   **2.10** ἰδόντες δὲ   τὸν
OVER [THE PLACE] WHERE ³WAS ¹THE ²CHILD.   AND~SEEING   THE

ἀστέρα ἐχάρησαν χαρὰν μεγάλην σφόδρα.   **2.11** καὶ
STAR,   THEY REJOICED ³JOY   ²GREAT   ¹[WITH] EXCEEDING.   AND

ἐλθόντες εἰς τὴν οἰκίαν εἶδον τὸ παιδίον μετὰ
COMING   INTO THE HOUSE   THEY SAW THE CHILD   WITH

Μαρίας τῆς μητρὸς αὐτοῦ, καὶ πεσόντες προσεκύνησαν
MARY   THE MOTHER   OF HIM,   AND   FALLING DOWN,   THEY WORSHIPED

αὐτῷ καὶ ἀνοίξαντες τοὺς θησαυροὺς αὐτῶν
HIM   AND   HAVING OPENED   THE   TREASURES   OF THEM,

προσήνεγκαν αὐτῷ δῶρα, χρυσὸν καὶ λίβανον καὶ
THEY OFFERED   TO HIM   GIFTS,   GOLD   AND   FRANKINCENSE AND

σμύρναν.   **2.12** καὶ χρηματισθέντες κατ᾽ ὄναρ μὴ
MYRRH.   AND   HAVING BEEN WARNED   IN   A DREAM NOT

ἀνακάμψαι πρὸς Ἡρῴδην, δι᾽ ἄλλης ὁδοῦ ἀνεχώρησαν
TO RETURN   TO   HEROD,   ²BY ³ANOTHER ⁴WAY   ¹THEY DEPARTED

εἰς τὴν χώραν αὐτῶν.
TO   THE   COUNTRY OF THEM.

  2.13 Ἀναχωρησάντων δὲ αὐτῶν ἰδοὺ ἄγγελος κυρίου
       NOW [AFTER] THEY DEPARTED,   BEHOLD AN ANGEL   OF [THE] LORD

φαίνεται κατ᾽ ὄναρ τῷ Ἰωσὴφ λέγων, Ἐγερθεὶς
APPEARED   IN   A DREAM -   TO JOSEPH SAYING,   RISING UP

παράλαβε τὸ παιδίον καὶ τὴν μητέρα αὐτοῦ καὶ
TAKE   THE CHILD   AND   THE MOTHER   OF HIM   AND

φεῦγε εἰς Αἴγυπτον καὶ ἴσθι ἐκεῖ ἕως ἂν εἴπω σοι·
FLEE   TO EGYPT   AND   REMAIN THERE UNTIL   I TELL   YOU;

μέλλει γὰρ Ἡρῴδης ζητεῖν τὸ παιδίον τοῦ ἀπολέσαι
³IS ABOUT ¹FOR ²HEROD   TO SEEK   THE CHILD   -   TO KILL

αὐτό.   **2.14** ὁ δὲ ἐγερθεὶς παρέλαβεν τὸ παιδίον καὶ
IT.   -   SO   HAVING ARISEN, HE TOOK   THE CHILD   AND

τὴν μητέρα αὐτοῦ νυκτὸς   καὶ ἀνεχώρησεν εἰς
THE MOTHER   OF HIM DURING [THE] NIGHT AND   DEPARTED   FOR

Αἴγυπτον, **2.15** καὶ ἦν ἐκεῖ ἕως τῆς τελευτῆς Ἡρῴδου·
EGYPT,   AND   HE WAS THERE UNTIL THE   DEATH   OF HEROD;

ἵνα   πληρωθῇ   τὸ   ῥηθὲν ὑπὸ κυρίου διὰ
IN ORDER THAT MIGHT BE FULFILLED THE [THING] SPOKEN BY   [THE] LORD THROUGH

τοῦ προφήτου λέγοντος, Ἐξ Αἰγύπτου ἐκάλεσα τὸν
THE   PROPHET   SAYING,   OUT OF EGYPT   I CALLED   THE

υἱόν μου.
SON   OF ME.

2:15 Hos. 11:1

and pay him homage." [9]When they had heard the king, they set out; and there, ahead of them, went the star that they had seen at its rising,[l] until it stopped over the place where the child was. [10]When they saw that the star had stopped,[m] they were overwhelmed with joy. [11]On entering the house, they saw the child with Mary his mother; and they knelt down and paid him homage. Then, opening their treasure chests, they offered him gifts of gold, frankincense, and myrrh. [12]And having been warned in a dream not to return to Herod, they left for their own country by another road.

13 Now after they had left, an angel of the Lord appeared to Joseph in a dream and said, "Get up, take the child and his mother, and flee to Egypt, and remain there until I tell you; for Herod is about to search for the child, to destroy him." [14]Then Joseph[n] got up, took the child and his mother by night, and went to Egypt, [15]and remained there until the death of Herod. This was to fulfill what had been spoken by the Lord through the prophet, "Out of Egypt I have called my son."

[l] Or *in the East*
[m] Gk *saw the star*
[n] Gk *he*

16 When Herod saw that he had been tricked by the wise men,*o* he was infuriated, and he sent and killed all the children in and around Bethlehem who were two years old or under, according to the time that he had learned from the wise men.*o* 17Then was fulfilled what had been spoken through the prophet Jeremiah:

18"A voice was heard in
    Ramah,
  wailing and loud
    lamentation,
  Rachel weeping for her
    children;
  she refused to be
    consoled, because
    they are no more."

19 When Herod died, an angel of the Lord suddenly appeared in a dream to Joseph in Egypt and said, 20"Get up, take the child and his mother, and go to the land of Israel, for those who were seeking the child's life are dead." 21Then Joseph*p* got up, took the child and his mother, and went to the land of Israel. 22But when he heard that Archelaus was ruling over Judea in place of his father Herod, he was afraid to go there. And after being warned in a dream, he went away to the district of Galilee.

o Or *astrologers;* Gk *magi*
p Gk *he*

2.16 Τότε Ἡρῴδης ἰδὼν ὅτι ἐνεπαίχθη ὑπὸ τῶν μάγων
THEN HEROD, SEEING THAT HE WAS DECEIVED BY THE MAGI,

ἐθυμώθη λίαν, καὶ ἀποστείλας ἀνεῖλεν πάντας τοὺς
WAS ENRAGED GREATLY, AND HAVING SENT [ORDERS] HE KILLED ALL THE

παῖδας τοὺς ἐν Βηθλέεμ καὶ ἐν πᾶσι τοῖς ὁρίοις
MALE CHILDREN - IN BETHLEHEM AND IN ALL THE DISTRICTS

αὐτῆς ἀπὸ διετοῦς καὶ κατωτέρω, κατὰ τὸν
OF IT FROM TWO YEARS OLD AND UNDER, ACCORDING TO THE

χρόνον ὃν ἠκρίβωσεν παρὰ τῶν μάγων. **2.17** τότε
TIME WHICH HE ASCERTAINED FROM THE MAGI. THEN

ἐπληρώθη τὸ ῥηθὲν διὰ Ἰερεμίου τοῦ προφήτου
WAS FULFILLED THE [THING] SPOKEN THROUGH JEREMIAH THE PROPHET

λέγοντος,
SAYING,

2.18 Φωνὴ ἐν Ῥαμὰ ἠκούσθη,
A VOICE IN RAMAH WAS HEARD,

    κλαυθμὸς καὶ ὀδυρμὸς πολύς·
    ²WEEPING ³AND ⁴MOURNING ¹GREAT;

    Ῥαχὴλ κλαίουσα τὰ τέκνα αὐτῆς,
    RACHEL WEEPING [FOR] THE CHILDREN OF HER,

    καὶ οὐκ ἤθελεν παρακληθῆναι, ὅτι
    AND SHE WOULD NOT BE COMFORTED, BECAUSE

    οὐκ εἰσίν.
    THEY ARE NOT.

2.19 Τελευτήσαντος δὲ τοῦ Ἡρῴδου ἰδοὺ ἄγγελος
NOW~HAVING DIED - HEROD, BEHOLD AN ANGEL

κυρίου φαίνεται κατ' ὄναρ τῷ Ἰωσὴφ ἐν Αἰγύπτῳ
OF [THE] LORD APPEARED IN A DREAM - TO JOSEPH IN EGYPT

2.20 λέγων, Ἐγερθεὶς παράλαβε τὸ παιδίον καὶ τὴν
SAYING, RISING UP TAKE THE CHILD AND THE

μητέρα αὐτοῦ καὶ πορεύου εἰς γῆν Ἰσραήλ·
MOTHER OF HIM AND GO INTO [THE] LAND OF ISRAEL.

τεθνήκασιν γὰρ οἱ ζητοῦντες τὴν ψυχὴν τοῦ
FOR~HAVE DIED THE ONES SEEKING THE LIFE OF THE

παιδίου. **2.21** ὁ δὲ ἐγερθεὶς παρέλαβεν τὸ παιδίον
CHILD. - SO HAVING ARISEN HE TOOK THE CHILD

καὶ τὴν μητέρα αὐτοῦ καὶ εἰσῆλθεν εἰς γῆν
AND THE MOTHER OF HIM AND ENTERED INTO [THE] LAND

Ἰσραήλ. **2.22** ἀκούσας δὲ ὅτι Ἀρχέλαος βασιλεύει
OF ISRAEL. BUT~HAVING HEARD THAT ARCHELAUS IS (WAS) REIGNING [OVER]

τῆς Ἰουδαίας ἀντὶ τοῦ πατρὸς αὐτοῦ Ἡρῴδου
- JUDEA INSTEAD OF THE FATHER OF HIM, HEROD,

ἐφοβήθη ἐκεῖ ἀπελθεῖν· χρηματισθεὶς δὲ κατ' ὄναρ
HE WAS AFRAID TO GO~THERE. AND~HAVING BEEN WARNED IN A DREAM,

ἀνεχώρησεν εἰς τὰ μέρη τῆς Γαλιλαίας,
HE DEPARTED INTO THE DISTRICTS - OF GALILEE,

2:18 Jer. 31:15

2.23 καὶ ἐλθὼν κατῴκησεν εἰς πόλιν λεγομένην
AND   HAVING COME   HE SETTLED   IN   [THE] CITY   CALLED

Ναζαρέτ· ὅπως πληρωθῇ τὸ ῥηθὲν διὰ
NAZARETH;   SO THAT   MIGHT BE FULFILLED   THE [THING]   SPOKEN   THROUGH

τῶν προφητῶν ὅτι Ναζωραῖος κληθήσεται.
THE   PROPHETS   -   A NAZARENE   HE WILL BE CALLED.

23There he made his home in a town called Nazareth, so that what had been spoken through the prophets might be fulfilled, "He will be called a Nazorean."

CHAPTER 3

3.1 Ἐν δὲ ταῖς ἡμέραις ἐκείναις παραγίνεται
NOW~IN   -   THOSE~DAYS   COMES

Ἰωάννης ὁ βαπτιστὴς κηρύσσων ἐν τῇ ἐρήμῳ τῆς
JOHN   THE   BAPTIST   PREACHING   IN   THE   WILDERNESS   -

Ἰουδαίας **3.2** [καὶ] λέγων, Μετανοεῖτε· ἤγγικεν γὰρ ἡ
OF JUDEA   -   SAYING,   REPENT;   FOR~HAS COME NEAR   THE

βασιλεία τῶν οὐρανῶν. **3.3** οὗτος γάρ ἐστιν ὁ
KINGDOM   OF THE   HEAVENS.   FOR~THIS   IS   THE ONE

ῥηθεὶς διὰ Ἡσαΐου τοῦ προφήτου λέγοντος,
SPOKEN [OF]   THROUGH   ISAIAH   THE   PROPHET   SAYING,

Φωνὴ βοῶντος ἐν τῇ ἐρήμῳ·
A VOICE   SHOUTING   IN   THE   WILDERNESS:

Ἑτοιμάσατε τὴν ὁδὸν κυρίου,
PREPARE   THE   WAY   OF [THE] LORD,

εὐθείας ποιεῖτε τὰς τρίβους αὐτοῦ.
MAKE~STRAIGHT   THE   PATHS   OF HIM.

3.4 Αὐτὸς δὲ ὁ Ἰωάννης εἶχεν τὸ ἔνδυμα αὐτοῦ ἀπὸ
3HIMSELF   1NOW   -   2JOHN   HAD   THE   CLOTHING   OF HIM   FROM

τριχῶν καμήλου καὶ ζώνην δερματίνην περὶ τὴν ὀσφὺν
[THE] HAIRS   OF A CAMEL   AND   A LEATHER~BELT   AROUND   THE   WAIST

αὐτοῦ, ἡ δὲ τροφὴ ἦν αὐτοῦ ἀκρίδες καὶ μέλι ἄγριον.
OF HIM,   AND~THE   FOOD   OF HIM~WAS   LOCUSTS   AND   WILD~HONEY.

3.5 τότε ἐξεπορεύετο πρὸς αὐτὸν Ἱεροσόλυμα καὶ πᾶσα
THEN   WENT OUT   TO   HIM   JERUSALEM   AND   ALL

ἡ Ἰουδαία καὶ πᾶσα ἡ περίχωρος τοῦ Ἰορδάνου,
-   JUDEA   AND   ALL   THE   REGION AROUND   THE   JORDAN,

3.6 καὶ ἐβαπτίζοντο ἐν τῷ Ἰορδάνῃ ποταμῷ ὑπ᾽
AND   THEY WERE BAPTIZED   IN   THE   JORDAN   RIVER   BY

αὐτοῦ ἐξομολογούμενοι τὰς ἁμαρτίας αὐτῶν.
HIM   CONFESSING   THE   SINS   OF THEM.

3.7 Ἰδὼν δὲ πολλοὺς τῶν Φαρισαίων καὶ
AND~SEEING   MANY   OF THE   PHARISEES   AND

Σαδδουκαίων ἐρχομένους ἐπὶ τὸ βάπτισμα αὐτοῦ
SADDUCEES   COMING   TO   THE   BAPTISM   OF HIM

εἶπεν αὐτοῖς, Γεννήματα ἐχιδνῶν, τίς ὑπέδειξεν ὑμῖν
HE SAID   TO THEM,   CHILDREN   OF VIPERS,   WHO   WARNED   YOU°

In those days John the Baptist appeared in the wilderness of Judea, proclaiming, 2"Repent, for the kingdom of heaven has come near."q 3This is the one of whom the prophet Isaiah spoke when he said,

"The voice of one crying out in the wilderness:
'Prepare the way of the Lord,
make his paths straight.'"

4Now John wore clothing of camel's hair with a leather belt around his waist, and his food was locusts and wild honey. 5Then the people of Jerusalem and all Judea were going out to him, and all the region along the Jordan, 6and they were baptized by him in the river Jordan, confessing their sins.

7 But when he saw many Pharisees and Sadducees coming for baptism, he said to them, "You brood of vipers! Who warned you

q Or *is at hand*

3:3 Isa. 40:3 LXX

to flee from the wrath to come? ⁸Bear fruit worthy of repentance. ⁹Do not presume to say to yourselves, 'We have Abraham as our ancestor'; for I tell you, God is able from these stones to raise up children to Abraham. ¹⁰Even now the ax is lying at the root of the trees; every tree therefore that does not bear good fruit is cut down and thrown into the fire.

11 "I baptize you withʳ water for repentance, but one who is more powerful than I is coming after me; I am not worthy to carry his sandals. He will baptize you withʳ the Holy Spirit and fire. ¹²His winnowing fork is in his hand, and he will clear his threshing floor and will gather his wheat into the granary; but the chaff he will burn with unquenchable fire."

13 Then Jesus came from Galilee to John at the Jordan, to be baptized by him. ¹⁴John would have prevented him, saying, "I need to be baptized by you, and do you come to me?" ¹⁵But Jesus answered him, "Let it be so now; for it is proper for us in this way to fulfill all righteousness." Then he consented.

ʳ Or *in*

φυγεῖν ἀπὸ τῆς μελλούσης ὀργῆς; **3.8** ποιήσατε οὖν
TO FLEE FROM THE COMING WRATH? THEREFORE~PRODUCE

καρπὸν ἄξιον τῆς μετανοίας **3.9** καὶ μὴ δόξητε λέγειν
FRUIT WORTHY - OF REPENTANCE AND DO NOT THINK TO SAY

ἐν ἑαυτοῖς, Πατέρα ἔχομεν τὸν Ἀβραάμ.
WITHIN YOURSELVES, [AS OUR] FATHER WE HAVE - ABRAHAM.

λέγω γὰρ ὑμῖν ὅτι δύναται ὁ θεὸς ἐκ τῶν
FOR~I SAY TO YOU° THAT IS ABLE - GOD FROM -

λίθων τούτων ἐγεῖραι τέκνα τῷ Ἀβραάμ.
THESE~STONES TO RAISE UP CHILDREN - TO ABRAHAM.

3.10 ἤδη δὲ ἡ ἀξίνη πρὸς τὴν ῥίζαν τῶν δένδρων
AND~ALREADY THE AXE AT THE ROOT OF THE TREES

κεῖται· πᾶν οὖν δένδρον μὴ ποιοῦν καρπὸν καλὸν
IS LAID; THEREFORE~EVERY TREE NOT PRODUCING GOOD~FRUIT

ἐκκόπτεται καὶ εἰς πῦρ βάλλεται. **3.11** ἐγὼ μὲν
IS CUT DOWN AND INTO [THE] FIRE IS THROWN. I

ὑμᾶς βαπτίζω ἐν ὕδατι εἰς μετάνοιαν, ὁ δὲ
BAPTIZE~YOU° WITH WATER [LEADING] TO REPENTANCE, BUT~THE ONE

ὀπίσω μου ἐρχόμενος ἰσχυρότερός μού ἐστιν, οὗ
AFTER ME COMING STRONGER THAN ME IS, OF WHOM

οὐκ εἰμὶ ἱκανὸς τὰ ὑποδήματα βαστάσαι· αὐτὸς
I AM NOT WORTHY THE SANDALS TO REMOVE. HE

ὑμᾶς βαπτίσει ἐν πνεύματι ἁγίῳ καὶ πυρί· **3.12** οὗ
WILL BAPTIZE~YOU° WITH [THE] HOLY~SPIRIT AND FIRE; OF WHOM

τὸ πτύον ἐν τῇ χειρὶ αὐτοῦ καὶ διακαθαριεῖ
THE WINNOWING SHOVEL [IS] IN THE HAND OF HIM AND HE WILL CLEAN OUT

τὴν ἅλωνα αὐτοῦ καὶ συνάξει τὸν σῖτον αὐτοῦ εἰς
THE THRESHING OF HIM AND HE WILL GATHER THE WHEAT OF HIM INTO

τὴν ἀποθήκην, τὸ δὲ ἄχυρον κατακαύσει
THE BARN, BUT~THE CHAFF HE WILL CONSUME

πυρὶ ἀσβέστῳ.
WITH AN INEXTINGUISHABLE~FIRE.

3.13 Τότε παραγίνεται ὁ Ἰησοῦς ἀπὸ τῆς Γαλιλαίας
THEN COMES - JESUS FROM - GALILEE

ἐπὶ τὸν Ἰορδάνην πρὸς τὸν Ἰωάννην τοῦ βαπτισθῆναι
TO THE JORDAN TO - JOHN TO BE BAPTIZED

ὑπ' αὐτοῦ. **3.14** ὁ δὲ Ἰωάννης διεκώλυεν αὐτὸν λέγων,
BY HIM. - BUT JOHN TRIED TO PREVENT HIM SAYING,

Ἐγὼ χρείαν ἔχω ὑπὸ σοῦ βαπτισθῆναι, καὶ σὺ ἔρχῃ
I HAVE~NEED BY YOU TO BE BAPTIZED, AND [YET] YOU COME

πρός με; **3.15** ἀποκριθεὶς δὲ ὁ Ἰησοῦς εἶπεν πρὸς
TO ME? BUT~ANSWERING - JESUS SAID TO

αὐτόν, Ἄφες ἄρτι, οὕτως γὰρ πρέπον ἐστὶν ἡμῖν
HIM, PERMIT [IT] NOW, FOR~THUS IT IS~PROPER FOR US

πληρῶσαι πᾶσαν δικαιοσύνην. τότε ἀφίησιν αὐτόν.
TO FULFILL ALL RIGHTEOUSNESS. THEN HE PERMITS HIM.

3.16 βαπτισθεὶς δὲ   ὁ Ἰησοῦς εὐθὺς   ἀνέβη ἀπὸ τοῦ
AND~HAVING BEEN BAPTIZED, - JESUS IMMEDIATELY CAME UP FROM THE

ὕδατος· καὶ ἰδοὺ ἠνεῴχθησαν ⌜[αὐτῷ]⌝ οἱ οὐρανοί,
WATER.   AND BEHOLD WERE OPENED   TO HIM   THE HEAVENS,

καὶ εἶδεν [τὸ] πνεῦμα [τοῦ] θεοῦ καταβαῖνον ὡσεὶ
AND HE SAW THE SPIRIT - OF GOD DESCENDING LIKE

περιστερὰν [καὶ] ἐρχόμενον ἐπ᾽ αὐτόν· **3.17** καὶ ἰδοὺ
A DOVE   AND   COMING   UPON HIM.   AND BEHOLD

φωνὴ   ἐκ τῶν οὐρανῶν λέγουσα, Οὗτός ἐστιν ὁ
A VOICE [CAME] OUT OF THE HEAVENS SAYING, THIS IS THE

υἱός μου ὁ ἀγαπητός, ἐν ᾧ   εὐδόκησα.
SON OF ME THE BELOVED, IN WHOM I AM WELL PLEASED.

3:16 text: KJV ASV RSVmg TEV NJBmg NRSV. omit: ASVmg RSV NASB NIV NEB NJB.

16And when Jesus had been baptized, just as he came up from the water, suddenly the heavens were opened to him and he saw the Spirit of God descending like a dove and alighting on him. 17And a voice from heaven said, "This is my Son, the Beloved,⁵ with whom I am well pleased."

⁵ Or *my beloved Son*

4.1 Τότε ὁ Ἰησοῦς ἀνήχθη εἰς τὴν ἔρημον ὑπὸ τοῦ
THEN - JESUS WAS LED UP INTO THE WILDERNESS BY THE

πνεύματος πειρασθῆναι ὑπὸ τοῦ διαβόλου. **4.2** καὶ
SPIRIT   TO BE TEMPTED BY THE DEVIL.   AND

νηστεύσας ἡμέρας τεσσεράκοντα καὶ
HAVING FASTED FORTY~DAYS   AND

νύκτας τεσσεράκοντα, ὕστερον ἐπείνασεν. **4.3** Καὶ
FORTY~NIGHTS,   AFTERWARDS HE HUNGERED.   AND

προσελθὼν ὁ   πειράζων εἶπεν αὐτῷ, Εἰ
HAVING APPROACHED, THE ONE TEMPTING SAID TO HIM, IF

υἱὸς εἶ   τοῦ θεοῦ, εἰπὲ ἵνα οἱ λίθοι οὗτοι
YOU ARE~[THE] SON - OF GOD, SPEAK THAT - THESE~STONES

ἄρτοι γένωνται. **4.4** ὁ δὲ   ἀποκριθεὶς εἶπεν,
MAY BECOME~BREAD.   BUT~THE ONE HAVING ANSWERED SAID,

Γέγραπται,
IT HAS BEEN WRITTEN,

        Οὐκ ἐπ᾽ ἄρτῳ μόνῳ ζήσεται ὁ ἄνθρωπος,
        NOT BY BREAD ALONE WILL LIVE - MAN,

        ἀλλ᾽ ἐπὶ παντὶ ῥήματι ἐκπορευομένῳ
        BUT BY EVERY WORD PROCEEDING

        διὰ   στόματος θεοῦ.
        THROUGH THE MOUTH OF GOD.

4.5 Τότε παραλαμβάνει αὐτὸν ὁ διάβολος εἰς τὴν
THEN TAKES   HIM   THE DEVIL   TO THE

ἁγίαν πόλιν καὶ ἔστησεν αὐτὸν ἐπὶ τὸ πτερύγιον τοῦ
HOLY CITY AND SET   HIM   UPON THE PINNACLE OF THE

4:4 Deut. 8:3

Then Jesus was led up by the Spirit into the wilderness to be tempted by the devil. ²He fasted forty days and forty nights, and afterwards he was famished. ³The tempter came and said to him, "If you are the Son of God, command these stones to become loaves of bread." ⁴But he answered, "It is written,

    'One does not live by bread alone,
    but by every word that comes from the mouth of God.'"

5 Then the devil took him to the holy city and placed him on the pinnacle of the

temple, [6]saying to him, "If you are the Son of God, throw yourself down; for it is written,

> 'He will command his angels concerning you,'
> and 'On their hands they will bear you up,
> so that you will not dash your foot against a stone.'"

[7]Jesus said to him, "Again it is written, 'Do not put the Lord your God to the test.'"

8 Again, the devil took him to a very high mountain and showed him all the kingdoms of the world and their splendor; [9]and he said to him, "All these I will give you, if you will fall down and worship me." [10]Jesus said to him, "Away with you, Satan! for it is written,

> 'Worship the Lord your God,
> and serve only him.'"

[11]Then the devil left him, and suddenly angels came and waited on him.

12 Now when Jesus[f] heard that John had been arrested, he withdrew to Galilee. [13]He left Nazareth and made his home in Capernaum by the sea, in the territory of Zebulun and Naphtali, [14]so that what had been spoken through the prophet Isaiah might be fulfilled:

[f] Gk *he*

ἱεροῦ, **4.6** καὶ λέγει αὐτῷ, Εἰ υἱὸς εἶ τοῦ θεοῦ,
TEMPLE,   AND SAYS TO HIM, IF YOU ARE~[THE] SON - OF GOD,

βάλε σεαυτὸν κάτω· γέγραπται γὰρ ὅτι
THROW YOURSELF DOWN. FOR~IT HAS BEEN WRITTEN -

Τοῖς ἀγγέλοις αὐτοῦ ἐντελεῖται περὶ σοῦ
THE ANGELS OF HIM HE WILL COMMAND CONCERNING YOU

καὶ ἐπὶ χειρῶν ἀροῦσίν σε,
AND UPON [THEIR] HANDS THEY WILL LIFT UP YOU,

μήποτε προσκόψῃς πρὸς λίθον τὸν πόδα σου.
LEST YOU STRIKE AGAINST A STONE THE FOOT OF YOU.

4.7 ἔφη αὐτῷ ὁ Ἰησοῦς, Πάλιν γέγραπται,
SAID TO HIM - JESUS, AGAIN IT HAS BEEN WRITTEN,

Οὐκ ἐκπειράσεις κύριον τὸν θεόν σου. **4.8** Πάλιν
DO NOT TEMPT [THE] LORD THE GOD OF YOU. AGAIN

παραλαμβάνει αὐτὸν ὁ διάβολος εἰς ὄρος ὑψηλὸν
TAKES HIM THE DEVIL TO [3]MOUNTAIN [2]HIGH

λίαν καὶ δείκνυσιν αὐτῷ πάσας τὰς βασιλείας τοῦ
[1]A VERY AND SHOWS TO HIM ALL THE KINGDOMS OF THE

κόσμου καὶ τὴν δόξαν αὐτῶν **4.9** καὶ εἶπεν αὐτῷ,
WORLD AND THE GLORY OF THEM AND HE SAID TO HIM,

Ταῦτά σοι πάντα δώσω, ἐὰν πεσὼν
[3]THESE THINGS [4]TO YOU [2]ALL [1]I WILL GIVE, IF FALLING DOWN

προσκυνήσῃς μοι. **4.10** τότε λέγει αὐτῷ ὁ Ἰησοῦς,
YOU MAY WORSHIP ME. THEN SAYS TO HIM - JESUS,

Ὕπαγε, Σατανᾶ· γέγραπται γάρ,
GO AWAY, SATAN, FOR~IT HAS BEEN WRITTEN,

Κύριον τὸν θεόν σου προσκυνήσεις
[THE] LORD THE GOD OF YOU YOU SHALL WORSHIP

καὶ αὐτῷ μόνῳ λατρεύσεις.
AND HIM ALONE YOU SHALL SERVE.

4.11 Τότε ἀφίησιν αὐτὸν ὁ διάβολος, καὶ ἰδοὺ
THEN LEAVES HIM THE DEVIL, AND BEHOLD

ἄγγελοι προσῆλθον καὶ διηκόνουν αὐτῷ.
ANGELS CAME AND SERVED HIM.

4.12 Ἀκούσας δὲ ὅτι Ἰωάννης παρεδόθη ἀνεχώρησεν
NOW~HAVING HEARD THAT JOHN WAS ARRESTED HE DEPARTED

εἰς τὴν Γαλιλαίαν. **4.13** καὶ καταλιπὼν τὴν Ναζαρὰ
INTO - GALILEE. AND HAVING LEFT BEHIND - NAZARETH,

ἐλθὼν κατῴκησεν εἰς Καφαρναοὺμ τὴν
HAVING COME HE SETTLED IN CAPERNAUM -

παραθαλασσίαν ἐν ὁρίοις Ζαβουλὼν καὶ Νεφθαλίμ·
BESIDE THE SEA IN [THE] DISTRICTS OF ZEBULUN AND NAPHTALI,

4.14 ἵνα πληρωθῇ τὸ ῥηθὲν διὰ Ἠσαΐου τοῦ
SO THAT MIGHT BE FULFILLED THE [THING] SPOKEN THROUGH ISAIAH THE

προφήτου λέγοντος,
PROPHET SAYING,

4:6 Ps. 91:11-12 **4:7** Deut. 6:16 **4:10** Deut. 6:13

4.15 Γῆ Ζαβουλὼν καὶ γῆ Νεφθαλίμ,
LAND OF ZEBULUN AND LAND OF NAPHTALI,

ὁδὸν θαλάσσης, πέραν τοῦ Ἰορδάνου,
ROAD TO THE SEA, BEYOND THE JORDAN,

Γαλιλαία τῶν ἐθνῶν,
GALILEE OF THE GENTILES,

4.16 ὁ λαὸς ὁ καθήμενος ἐν σκότει
THE PEOPLE - SITTING IN DARKNESS

φῶς εἶδεν μέγα,
³LIGHT ¹SAW ²A GREAT,

καὶ τοῖς καθημένοις ἐν χώρᾳ καὶ σκιᾷ
AND TO THE ONES SITTING IN [THE] LAND AND SHADOW

θανάτου
OF DEATH,

φῶς ἀνέτειλεν αὐτοῖς.
A LIGHT ROSE UP AMONG THEM.

4.17 Ἀπὸ τότε ἤρξατο ὁ Ἰησοῦς κηρύσσειν καὶ
FROM THEN BEGAN - JESUS TO PREACH AND

λέγειν, Μετανοεῖτε· ἤγγικεν γὰρ ἡ βασιλεία τῶν
TO SAY, REPENT, FOR~IS NEAR THE KINGDOM OF THE

οὐρανῶν.
HEAVENS.

4.18 Περιπατῶν δὲ παρὰ τὴν θάλασσαν τῆς Γαλιλαίας
AND~WALKING BESIDE THE SEA - OF GALILEE

εἶδεν δύο ἀδελφούς, Σίμωνα τὸν λεγόμενον Πέτρον
HE SAW TWO BROTHERS, SIMON, THE ONE BEING CALLED PETER,

καὶ Ἀνδρέαν τὸν ἀδελφὸν αὐτοῦ, βάλλοντας
AND ANDREW THE BROTHER OF HIM, CASTING

ἀμφίβληστρον εἰς τὴν θάλασσαν· ἦσαν γὰρ ἁλιεῖς.
A NET INTO THE SEA; FOR~THEY WERE FISHERMEN.

4.19 καὶ λέγει αὐτοῖς, Δεῦτε ὀπίσω μου, καὶ ποιήσω
AND HE SAYS TO THEM, COME FOLLOW ME, AND I WILL MAKE

ὑμᾶς ἁλιεῖς ἀνθρώπων. **4.20** οἱ δὲ εὐθέως ἀφέντες τὰ
YOU° FISHERMEN OF MEN. - AND IMMEDIATELY LEAVING THE

δίκτυα ἠκολούθησαν αὐτῷ. **4.21** Καὶ προβὰς ἐκεῖθεν
NETS THEY FOLLOWED HIM. AND HAVING GONE ON FROM THERE

εἶδεν ἄλλους δύο ἀδελφούς, Ἰάκωβον τὸν τοῦ
HE SAW TWO~OTHER BROTHERS, JAMES THE [SON] -

Ζεβεδαίου καὶ Ἰωάννην τὸν ἀδελφὸν αὐτοῦ, ἐν τῷ
OF ZEBEDEE AND JOHN THE BROTHER OF HIM, IN THE

πλοίῳ μετὰ Ζεβεδαίου τοῦ πατρὸς αὐτῶν καταρτίζοντας
BOAT WITH ZEBEDEE THE FATHER OF THEM, REPAIRING

τὰ δίκτυα αὐτῶν, καὶ ἐκάλεσεν αὐτούς.
THE NETS OF THEM, AND HE CALLED THEM.

4:15-16 Isa. 9:1-2

[15]"Land of Zebulun, land
of Naphtali,
on the road by the sea,
across the Jordan,
Galilee of the
Gentiles—
[16] the people who sat in
darkness
have seen a great light,
and for those who sat in
the region and
shadow of death
light has dawned."
[17] From that time Jesus began
to proclaim, "Repent, for
the kingdom of heaven has
come near."[u]
18 As he walked by the
Sea of Galilee, he saw two
brothers, Simon, who is
called Peter, and Andrew his
brother, casting a net into the
sea—for they were
fishermen. [19] And he said to
them, "Follow me, and I
will make you fish for
people." [20] Immediately they
left their nets and followed
him. [21] As he went from
there, he saw two other
brothers, James son of
Zebedee and his brother
John, in the boat with their
father Zebedee, mending
their nets, and he
called them.

[u] Or *is at hand*

²²Immediately they left the boat and their father, and followed him.

23 Jesusᵛ went throughout Galilee, teaching in their synagogues and proclaiming the good newsʷ of the kingdom and curing every disease and every sickness among the people. ²⁴So his fame spread throughout all Syria, and they brought to him all the sick, those who were afflicted with various diseases and pains, demoniacs, epileptics, and paralytics, and he cured them. ²⁵And great crowds followed him from Galilee, the Decapolis, Jerusalem, Judea, and from beyond the Jordan.

ᵛ Gk *He*
ʷ Gk *gospel*

4.22 οἱ   δὲ   εὐθέως   ἀφέντες   τὸ   πλοῖον   καὶ   τὸν   πατέρα
        -     AND   IMMEDIATELY LEAVING   THE   BOAT   AND   THE   FATHER

αὐτῶν   ἠκολούθησαν   αὐτῷ.
OF THEM THEY FOLLOWED   HIM.

4.23 Καὶ   περιῆγεν   ἐν   ὅλῃ   τῇ   Γαλιλαίᾳ   διδάσκων   ἐν
        AND   HE WENT ABOUT IN   ALL   -   GALILEE   TEACHING   IN

ταῖς   συναγωγαῖς   αὐτῶν   καὶ   κηρύσσων   τὸ   εὐαγγέλιον
THE   SYNAGOGUES   OF THEM AND   PREACHING   THE   GOOD NEWS

τῆς   βασιλείας   καὶ   θεραπεύων   πᾶσαν   νόσον   καὶ
OF THE KINGDOM   AND   HEALING   EVERY   DISEASE AND

πᾶσαν   μαλακίαν   ἐν   τῷ   λαῷ.   **4.24** καὶ   ἀπῆλθεν   ἡ
EVERY   ILLNESS   AMONG THE   PEOPLE.   AND   WENT OUT   THE

ἀκοὴ   αὐτοῦ   εἰς   ὅλην   τὴν   Συρίαν·   καὶ   προσήνεγκαν
REPORT   OF HIM   INTO   ALL   -   SYRIA;   AND   THEY BROUGHT

αὐτῷ   πάντας   τοὺς   κακῶς   ἔχοντας   ποικίλαις   νόσοις
TO HIM   ALL   THE ONES HAVING~ILLNESS   VARIOUS   DISEASES

καὶ   βασάνοις   συνεχομένους   [καὶ]   δαιμονιζομένους   καὶ
AND   SUFFERING FROM~TORMENTS   AND   BEING DEMON-POSSESSED AND

σεληνιαζομένους   καὶ   παραλυτικούς,   καὶ   ἐθεράπευσεν
EPILEPTICS   AND   PARALYTICS,   AND   HE HEALED

αὐτούς.   **4.25** καὶ   ἠκολούθησαν   αὐτῷ   ὄχλοι   πολλοὶ   ἀπὸ
THEM.   AND   FOLLOWED   HIM   MANY~CROWDS   FROM

τῆς   Γαλιλαίας   καὶ   Δεκαπόλεως   καὶ   Ἱεροσολύμων   καὶ
-      GALILEE   AND   DECAPOLIS   AND   JERUSALEM   AND

Ἰουδαίας   καὶ   πέραν   τοῦ   Ἰορδάνου.
JUDEA   AND   BEYOND   THE   JORDAN.

CHAPTER 5

When Jesusˣ saw the crowds, he went up the mountain; and after he sat down, his disciples came to him. ²Then he began to speak, and taught them, saying:

3 "Blessed are the poor in spirit, for theirs is the kingdom of heaven.

4 "Blessed are those who mourn, for they will be comforted.

ˣ Gk *he*

5.1 Ἰδὼν   δὲ   τοὺς   ὄχλους   ἀνέβη   εἰς   τὸ   ὄρος,   καὶ
        AND~HAVING SEEN THE   CROWDS   HE WENT UP TO   THE   MOUNTAIN, AND

καθίσαντος   αὐτοῦ   προσῆλθαν   αὐτῷ   οἱ   μαθηταὶ   αὐτοῦ·
[WHEN] HE SAT DOWN   CAME   TO HIM   THE   DISCIPLES   OF HIM.

5.2 καὶ   ἀνοίξας   τὸ   στόμα   αὐτοῦ   ἐδίδασκεν   αὐτοὺς
        AND   OPENING   THE   MOUTH   OF HIM   HE TAUGHT   THEM

λέγων,
SAYING,

5.3   Μακάριοι   οἱ   πτωχοὶ   τῷ   πνεύματι,
           BLESSED [ARE] THE   POOR   -   IN SPIRIT,

           ὅτι   αὐτῶν   ἐστιν   ἡ   βασιλεία   τῶν   οὐρανῶν.
           FOR   THEIRS   IS   THE KINGDOM   OF THE HEAVENS.

5.4   μακάριοι   οἱ   πενθοῦντες,
           BLESSED [ARE] THE ONES MOURNING,

           ὅτι   αὐτοὶ   παρακληθήσονται.
           FOR   THEY   WILL BE COMFORTED.

5.5 μακάριοι οἱ πραεῖς,
BLESSED [ARE] THE HUMBLE,

ὅτι αὐτοὶ κληρονομήσουσιν τὴν γῆν.
FOR THEY WILL INHERIT THE EARTH.

5.6 μακάριοι οἱ   πεινῶντες καὶ διψῶντες τὴν
BLESSED [ARE] THE ONES HUNGERING AND THIRSTING -

δικαιοσύνην,
[FOR] RIGHTEOUSNESS,

ὅτι αὐτοὶ χορτασθήσονται.
FOR THEY WILL BE SATISFIED.

5.7 μακάριοι οἱ ἐλεήμονες,
BLESSED [ARE] THE MERCIFUL,

ὅτι αὐτοὶ ἐλεηθήσονται.
FOR THEY WILL BE SHOWN MERCY.

5.8 μακάριοι οἱ καθαροὶ τῇ καρδίᾳ,
BLESSED [ARE] THE PURE - IN HEART,

ὅτι αὐτοὶ τὸν θεὸν ὄψονται.
FOR THEY - WILL SEE~GOD.

5.9 μακάριοι οἱ εἰρηνοποιοί,
BLESSED [ARE] THE PEACEMAKERS,

ὅτι αὐτοὶ υἱοὶ θεοῦ κληθήσονται.
FOR THEY SONS OF GOD WILL BE CALLED.

5.10 μακάριοι οἱ   δεδιωγμένοι ἕνεκεν δικαιοσύνης,
BLESSED [ARE] THE ONES BEING PERSECUTED BECAUSE OF RIGHTEOUSNESS,

ὅτι αὐτῶν ἐστιν ἡ βασιλεία τῶν οὐρανῶν.
FOR THEIRS IS THE KINGDOM OF THE HEAVENS.

5.11 μακάριοί ἐστε ὅταν ὀνειδίσωσιν ὑμᾶς καὶ
BLESSED ARE YOU° WHEN THEY REPROACH YOU° AND

διώξωσιν καὶ εἴπωσιν πᾶν   πονηρὸν καθ᾽ ὑμῶν
PERSECUTE [YOU°] AND SPEAK ALL [KINDS OF] EVIL AGAINST YOU°

[ψευδόμενοι] ἕνεκεν ἐμοῦ. **5.12** χαίρετε καὶ
TELLING LIES BECAUSE OF ME. REJOICE AND

ἀγαλλιᾶσθε, ὅτι ὁ μισθὸς ὑμῶν πολὺς ἐν τοῖς
BE GLAD, FOR THE REWARD OF YOU° [IS] GREAT IN THE

οὐρανοῖς· οὕτως γὰρ ἐδίωξαν τοὺς προφήτας τοὺς
HEAVENS. FOR~THUS THEY PERSECUTED THE PROPHETS -

πρὸ ὑμῶν.
BEFORE YOU°.

5.13 Ὑμεῖς ἐστε τὸ ἅλας τῆς γῆς· ἐὰν δὲ τὸ ἅλας
YOU° ARE THE SALT OF THE EARTH. BUT~IF THE SALT

μωρανθῇ, ἐν τίνι ἁλισθήσεται; εἰς οὐδὲν
BECOMES TASTELESS, IN WHAT WAY WILL IT BECOME SALTY [AGAIN]? FOR NOTHING

ἰσχύει ἔτι   εἰ μὴ βληθὲν   ἔξω καταπατεῖσθαι
IT IS GOOD [ANY] LONGER EXCEPT HAVING BEEN THROWN OUT TO BE TRAMPLED UPON

ὑπὸ τῶν ἀνθρώπων. **5.14** Ὑμεῖς ἐστε τὸ φῶς τοῦ
BY - MEN. YOU° ARE THE LIGHT OF THE

κόσμου. οὐ δύναται πόλις κρυβῆναι ἐπάνω ὄρους
WORLD. A CITY~IS NOT ABLE TO BE HIDDEN ON A MOUNTAIN

5 "Blessed are the meek, for they will inherit the earth.

6 "Blessed are those who hunger and thirst for righteousness, for they will be filled.

7 "Blessed are the merciful, for they will receive mercy.

8 "Blessed are the pure in heart, for they will see God.

9 "Blessed are the peacemakers, for they will be called children of God.

10 "Blessed are those who are persecuted for righteousness' sake, for theirs is the kingdom of heaven.

11 "Blessed are you when people revile you and persecute you and utter all kinds of evil against you falsely[y] on my account. 12 Rejoice and be glad, for your reward is great in heaven, for in the same way they persecuted the prophets who were before you.

13 "You are the salt of the earth; but if salt has lost its taste, how can its saltiness be restored? It is no longer good for anything, but is thrown out and trampled under foot.

14 "You are the light of the world. A city built on a hill cannot be hid.

[y] Other ancient authorities lack *falsely*

¹⁵No one after lighting a lamp puts it under the bushel basket, but on the lampstand, and it gives light to all in the house. ¹⁶In the same way, let your light shine before others, so that they may see your good works and give glory to your Father in heaven.

17 "Do not think that I have come to abolish the law or the prophets; I have come not to abolish but to fulfill. ¹⁸For truly I tell you, until heaven and earth pass away, not one letter,ᶻ not one stroke of a letter, will pass from the law until all is accomplished. ¹⁹Therefore, whoever breaksᵃ one of the least of these commandments, and teaches others to do the same, will be called least in the kingdom of heaven; but whoever does them and teaches them will be called great in the kingdom of heaven. ²⁰For I tell you, unless your righteousness exceeds that of the scribes and Pharisees, you will never enter the kingdom of heaven.

21 "You have heard that it was said to those of ancient times, 'You shall not murder'; and 'whoever murders shall be liable to judgment.' ²²But I say to you that if you are angry with a brother or sister,ᵇ you will be liable to judgment;

ᶻ Gk *one iota*
ᵃ Or *annuls*
ᵇ Gk *a brother*; other ancient authorities add *without cause*

κειμένη·   **5.15** οὐδὲ καίουσιν λύχνον καὶ τιθέασιν
LYING;   NOR   DO THEY LIGHT A LAMP AND PLACE

αὐτὸν ὑπὸ τὸν μόδιον   ἀλλ᾽ ἐπὶ τὴν λυχνίαν, καὶ
IT   UNDER THE GRAIN BUCKET, BUT UPON THE LAMPSTAND, AND

λάμπει πᾶσιν τοῖς   ἐν τῇ οἰκίᾳ.   **5.16** οὕτως λαμψάτω
IT LIGHTS ALL THE ONES IN THE HOUSE.   THUS LET SHINE

τὸ φῶς ὑμῶν ἔμπροσθεν τῶν ἀνθρώπων, ὅπως ἴδωσιν
THE LIGHT OF YOU° BEFORE   -   MEN,   SO THAT THEY MAY SEE

ὑμῶν τὰ καλὰ ἔργα καὶ δοξάσωσιν τὸν πατέρα ὑμῶν
YOUR° THE GOOD WORKS AND GLORIFY   THE FATHER OF YOU°

τὸν ἐν τοῖς οὐρανοῖς.
-    IN THE HEAVENS.

5.17 Μὴ νομίσητε ὅτι ἦλθον καταλῦσαι τὸν νόμον ἢ
DO NOT THINK   THAT I CAME TO ABOLISH   THE LAW   OR

τοὺς προφήτας· οὐκ ἦλθον καταλῦσαι ἀλλὰ πληρῶσαι.
THE   PROPHETS.   I DID NOT COME TO ABOLISH, BUT TO FULFILL.

5.18 ἀμὴν γὰρ λέγω ὑμῖν· ἕως ἂν παρέλθῃ ὁ οὐρανὸς
FOR~TRULY I SAY TO YOU°, UNTIL MAY PASS AWAY - HEAVEN

καὶ ἡ γῆ, ἰῶτα ἓν ἢ μία κεραία οὐ μὴ παρέλθῃ ἀπὸ
AND - EARTH, ONE~LETTER OR ONE STROKE MAY IN NO WAY PASS FROM

τοῦ νόμου, ἕως ἂν πάντα γένηται.   **5.19** ὃς ἐὰν οὖν
THE LAW,   UNTIL EVERYTHING TAKES PLACE.   THEREFORE~WHOEVER

λύσῃ μίαν τῶν ἐντολῶν   τούτων τῶν ἐλαχίστων καὶ
BREAKS ONE   -   ³COMMANDMENTS ¹OF THESE - ²LEAST   AND

διδάξῃ οὕτως τοὺς ἀνθρώπους, ἐλάχιστος κληθήσεται ἐν
TEACHES THUS   -   [TO] MEN,   HE WILL BE CALLED~LEAST IN

τῇ βασιλείᾳ τῶν οὐρανῶν· ὃς δ᾽ ἂν ποιήσῃ καὶ
THE KINGDOM OF THE HEAVENS. BUT~WHOEVER PRACTICES AND

διδάξῃ,   οὗτος μέγας κληθήσεται ἐν τῇ βασιλείᾳ
TEACHES [THEM], THIS ONE WILL BE CALLED~GREAT IN THE KINGDOM

τῶν οὐρανῶν. **5.20** λέγω γὰρ ὑμῖν ὅτι ἐὰν μὴ
OF THE HEAVENS.   FOR~I SAY TO YOU° THAT UNLESS

περισσεύσῃ ὑμῶν ἡ δικαιοσύνη πλεῖον   τῶν
EXCEEDS   YOUR° - RIGHTEOUSNESS BEYOND [THAT] OF THE

γραμματέων καὶ Φαρισαίων, οὐ μὴ εἰσέλθητε εἰς τὴν
SCRIBES   AND PHARISEES,   YOU° MAY NEVER ENTER INTO THE

βασιλείαν τῶν οὐρανῶν.
KINGDOM   OF THE HEAVENS.

5.21 Ἠκούσατε ὅτι ἐρρέθη τοῖς ἀρχαίοις,
YOU° HEARD   THAT IT WAS SAID TO THE ANCIENTS,

Οὐ φονεύσεις· ὃς δ᾽ ἂν φονεύσῃ, ἔνοχος ἔσται τῇ
YOU° SHALL NOT MURDER; AND WHOEVER MIGHT MURDER, WILL BE~SUBJECT -

κρίσει.   **5.22** ἐγὼ δὲ λέγω ὑμῖν ὅτι πᾶς ὁ ὀργιζόμενος
TO JUDGMENT.   BUT~I SAY TO YOU° - EVERYONE BEING ANGRY

τῷ   ἀδελφῷ αὐτοῦᵀ ἔνοχος ἔσται τῇ κρίσει·
WITH THE BROTHER OF HIM WILL BE~SUBJECT - TO JUDGMENT.

5:21 Exod. 20:13; Deut. 5:17   **5:22** text: ASV RSV NASB NIV NEB TEV NJB NRSV. add εικη (without cause): KJV ASVmg RSVmg NASBmg NIVmg NEBmg TEVmg NRSVmg.

ὃς δ’ ἂν εἴπῃ τῷ ἀδελφῷ αὐτοῦ, Ῥακά,
AND~WHOEVER MIGHT SAY TO THE BROTHER OF HIM, RACA,

ἔνοχος ἔσται τῷ συνεδρίῳ· ὃς δ’ ἂν εἴπῃ, Μωρέ,
WILL BE~SUBJECT TO THE SANHEDRIN; AND WHOEVER MIGHT SAY, FOOL,

ἔνοχος ἔσται εἰς τὴν γέενναν τοῦ πυρός. **5.23** ἐὰν οὖν
WILL BE~SUBJECT TO THE GEHENNA(HELL) - OF FIRE. THEREFORE~IF

προσφέρῃς τὸ δῶρόν σου ἐπὶ τὸ θυσιαστήριον κἀκεῖ
YOU MIGHT BRING THE GIFT OF YOU TO THE ALTAR AND THERE

μνησθῇς ὅτι ὁ ἀδελφός σου ἔχει τι κατὰ σοῦ,
YOU REMEMBER THAT THE BROTHER OF YOU HAS SOMETHING AGAINST YOU,

5.24 ἄφες ἐκεῖ τὸ δῶρόν σου ἔμπροσθεν τοῦ
LEAVE THERE THE GIFT OF YOU BEFORE THE

θυσιαστηρίου καὶ ὕπαγε πρῶτον διαλλάγηθι τῷ
ALTAR AND GO FIRST [AND] BE RECONCILED TO THE

ἀδελφῷ σου, καὶ τότε ἐλθὼν πρόσφερε τὸ δῶρόν σου.
BROTHER OF YOU, AND THEN COMING OFFER THE GIFT OF YOU.

5.25 ἴσθι εὐνοῶν τῷ ἀντιδίκῳ σου ταχύ, ἕως ὅτου
BE WELL-DISPOSED TO THE OPPONENT OF YOU QUICKLY, WHILE

εἶ μετ’ αὐτοῦ ἐν τῇ ὁδῷ, μήποτέ σε παραδῷ ὁ
YOU ARE WITH HIM ON THE ROAD, LEST ⁴YOU ³MIGHT DELIVER ¹THE

ἀντίδικος τῷ κριτῇ καὶ ὁ κριτὴς τῷ ὑπηρέτῃ καὶ
²OPPONENT TO THE JUDGE AND THE JUDGE, TO THE OFFICIAL, AND

εἰς φυλακὴν βληθήσῃ· **5.26** ἀμὴν λέγω σοι,
INTO PRISON YOU MAY BE THROWN. TRULY I SAY TO YOU,

οὐ μὴ ἐξέλθῃς ἐκεῖθεν, ἕως ἂν ἀποδῷς τὸν ἔσχατον
YOU MAY NEVER COME OUT [FROM] THERE UNTIL YOU REPAY THE LAST

κοδράντην.
PENNY.

5.27 Ἠκούσατε ὅτι ἐρρέθη, Οὐ μοιχεύσεις.
YOU° HAVE HEARD THAT IT WAS SAID, YOU° SHALL NOT COMMIT ADULTERY.

5.28 ἐγὼ δὲ λέγω ὑμῖν ὅτι πᾶς ὁ βλέπων γυναῖκα
BUT~I SAY TO YOU° THAT EVERYONE - LOOKING [UPON] A WOMAN

πρὸς τὸ ἐπιθυμῆσαι αὐτὴν ἤδη ἐμοίχευσεν
WITH A VIEW - TO DESIRE HER HAS COMMITTED ADULTERY~ALREADY

αὐτὴν ἐν τῇ καρδίᾳ αὐτοῦ. **5.29** εἰ δὲ ὁ ὀφθαλμός
[WITH] HER IN THE HEART OF HIM. AND~IF THE ²EYE

σου ὁ δεξιὸς σκανδαλίζει σε, ἔξελε αὐτὸν καὶ βάλε
³OF YOU - ¹RIGHT CAUSES YOU TO SIN, TEAR OUT IT AND THROW [IT]

ἀπὸ σοῦ· συμφέρει γάρ σοι ἵνα ἀπόληται ἐν τῶν
FROM YOU. FOR~IT IS BETTER FOR YOU THAT BE LOST ONE OF THE

μελῶν σου καὶ μὴ ὅλον τὸ σῶμά σου βληθῇ εἰς
MEMBERS OF YOU AND NOT [THE] WHOLE - BODY OF YOU BE THROWN INTO

γέενναν. **5.30** καὶ εἰ ἡ δεξιά σου χεὶρ
GEHENNA(HELL). AND IF THE RIGHT HAND~OF YOU

σκανδαλίζει σε, ἔκκοψον αὐτὴν καὶ βάλε ἀπὸ σοῦ·
CAUSES YOU TO SIN, CUT OFF IT AND THROW [IT] FROM YOU.

5:27 Exod. 20:14; Deut. 5:18

and if you insult[c] a brother or sister,[d] you will be liable to the council; and if you say, 'You fool,' you will be liable to the hell[e] of fire. [23]So when you are offering your gift at the altar, if you remember that your brother or sister[f] has something against you, [24]leave your gift there before the altar and go; first be reconciled to your brother or sister,[f] and then come and offer your gift. [25]Come to terms quickly with your accuser while you are on the way to court[g] with him, or your accuser may hand you over to the judge, and the judge to the guard, and you will be thrown into prison. [26]Truly I tell you, you will never get out until you have paid the last penny.

27 "You have heard that it was said, 'You shall not commit adultery.' [28]But I say to you that everyone who looks at a woman with lust has already committed adultery with her in his heart. [29]If your right eye causes you to sin, tear it out and throw it away; it is better for you to lose one of your members than for your whole body to be thrown into hell.[h] [30]And if your right hand causes you to sin, cut it off and throw it

[c] Gk *say Raca to* (an obscure term of abuse)
[d] Gk *a brother*
[e] Gk *Gehenna*
[f] Gk *your brother*
[g] Gk lacks *to court*
[h] Gk *Gehenna*

away; it is better for you to lose one of your members than for your whole body to go into hell.[h]

31 "It was also said, 'Whoever divorces his wife, let him give her a certificate of divorce.' 32But I say to you that anyone who divorces his wife, except on the ground of unchastity, causes her to commit adultery; and whoever marries a divorced woman commits adultery.

33 "Again, you have heard that it was said to those of ancient times, 'You shall not swear falsely, but carry out the vows you have made to the Lord.' 34But I say to you, Do not swear at all, either by heaven, for it is the throne of God, 35or by the earth, for it is his footstool, or by Jerusalem, for it is the city of the great King. 36And do not swear by your head, for you cannot make one hair white or black. 37Let your word be 'Yes, Yes' or 'No, No'; anything more than this comes from the evil one.[i]

38 "You have heard that it was said, 'An eye for an eye and a tooth for a tooth.' 39But I say to you, Do not resist an evildoer. But if anyone strikes you on the right cheek, turn the other also; 40and if anyone wants

[h] Gk *Gehenna*
[i] Or *evil*

συμφέρει γάρ σοι ἵνα ἀπόληται ἓν τῶν μελῶν σου
FOR~IT IS BETTER   FOR YOU   THAT   BE LOST   ONE   OF THE   MEMBERS   OF YOU

καὶ μὴ ὅλον τὸ σῶμά σου εἰς γέενναν ἀπέλθῃ.
AND   NOT [THE] WHOLE -   BODY   OF YOU   INTO   GEHENNA(HELL)   MAY GO.

5.31 Ἐρρέθη δέ, Ὃς ἂν ἀπολύσῃ τὴν γυναῖκα αὐτοῦ,
AND~IT WAS SAID,   WHOEVER   DIVORCES   THE   WIFE   OF HIM,

δότω αὐτῇ ἀποστάσιον.   **5.32** ἐγὼ δὲ λέγω ὑμῖν
LET HIM GIVE   TO HER   A CERTIFICATE OF DIVORCE.   BUT~I   SAY   TO YOU°

ὅτι πᾶς ὁ ἀπολύων τὴν γυναῖκα αὐτοῦ παρεκτὸς
THAT   EVERYONE -   DIVORCING   THE   WIFE   OF HIM   EXCEPT [FOR]

λόγου πορνείας ποιεῖ αὐτὴν μοιχευθῆναι, καὶ
[THE] MATTER   OF FORNICATION,   MAKES   HER   TO COMMIT ADULTERY,   AND

ὃς ἐὰν ἀπολελυμένην γαμήσῃ μοιχᾶται.
WHOEVER   MARRIES~A DIVORCED WOMAN   COMMITS ADULTERY.

5.33 Πάλιν ἠκούσατε ὅτι ἐρρέθη τοῖς ἀρχαίοις,
AGAIN,   YOU° HAVE HEARD   THAT   IT WAS SAID   TO THE   ANCIENTS,

Οὐκ ἐπιορκήσεις, ἀποδώσεις δὲ τῷ κυρίῳ τοὺς
YOU SHALL NOT BREAK YOUR VOWS,   BUT~YOU SHALL REPAY   TO THE   LORD   THE

ὅρκους σου.   **5.34** ἐγὼ δὲ λέγω ὑμῖν μὴ ὀμόσαι ὅλως·
VOWS   OF YOU.   BUT~I   SAY   TO YOU°   DO NOT SWEAR   AT ALL,

μήτε ἐν τῷ οὐρανῷ, ὅτι θρόνος ἐστὶν τοῦ θεοῦ,
NEITHER   BY -   HEAVEN,   FOR   IT IS~[THE] THRONE -   OF GOD,

5.35 μήτε ἐν τῇ γῇ, ὅτι ὑποπόδιόν ἐστιν τῶν ποδῶν
NOR   BY -   EARTH,   FOR   IT IS~[THE] FOOTSTOOL   OF THE   FEET

αὐτοῦ, μήτε εἰς Ἱεροσόλυμα, ὅτι πόλις ἐστὶν τοῦ
OF HIM,   NOR   BY   JERUSALEM,   FOR   IT IS~[THE] CITY   OF THE

μεγάλου βασιλέως, **5.36** μήτε ἐν τῇ κεφαλῇ σου
GREAT   KING,   NOR   BY   THE   HEAD   OF YOU

ὀμόσῃς, ὅτι οὐ δύνασαι μίαν τρίχα λευκὴν ποιῆσαι ἢ
SWEAR,   FOR   YOU ARE NOT ABLE   ONE   HAIR   WHITE   TO MAKE   OR

μέλαιναν.   **5.37** ἔστω δὲ ὁ λόγος ὑμῶν ναὶ ναί, οὒ
BLACK.   BUT~LET   THE   WORD   OF YOU° [BE]   YES,   YES [OR],   NO,

οὔ· τὸ δὲ περισσὸν τούτων ἐκ τοῦ πονηροῦ ἐστιν.
NO.   -   BUT   BEYOND   THESE   FROM -   EVIL   IS.

5.38 Ἠκούσατε ὅτι ἐρρέθη, Ὀφθαλμὸν ἀντὶ
YOU° HAVE HEARD   THAT   IT WAS SAID,   AN EYE   FOR

ὀφθαλμοῦ καὶ ὀδόντα ἀντὶ ὀδόντος.   **5.39** ἐγὼ δὲ λέγω
AN EYE   AND   A TOOTH   FOR   A TOOTH.   BUT~I   SAY

ὑμῖν μὴ ἀντιστῆναι τῷ πονηρῷ· ἀλλ᾽ ὅστις
TO YOU°   NOT   TO OPPOSE   THE   EVIL ONE,   BUT   WHOEVER

σε ῥαπίζει εἰς τὴν δεξιὰν σιαγόνα [σου], στρέψον
HITS [YOU]   ON   THE   RIGHT   CHEEK   OF YOU,   TURN

αὐτῷ καὶ τὴν ἄλλην·   **5.40** καὶ τῷ θέλοντι
TO HIM   ALSO   THE   OTHER;   AND   TO THE ONE   WISHING

5:31 Deut. 24:1   **5:33** Lev. 19:12; Num. 30:2   **5:38** Exod. 21:24; Lev. 24:20; Deut. 19:21

σοι κριθῆναι καὶ τὸν χιτῶνά σου λαβεῖν, ἄφες αὐτῷ
TO SUE~YOU AND THE SHIRT OF YOU TO TAKE, GIVE TO HIM

καὶ τὸ ἱμάτιον· **5.41** καὶ ὅστις σε ἀγγαρεύσει
ALSO THE (YOUR) COAT. AND WHOEVER WILL FORCE~YOU [TO GO]

μίλιον ἕν, ὕπαγε μετ᾽ αὐτοῦ δύο. **5.42** τῷ
ONE~MILE, GO WITH HIM TWO. [FROM] THE ONE

αἰτοῦντί σε δός, καὶ τὸν θέλοντα ἀπὸ σοῦ
ASKING YOU [TO] GIVE, AND THE ONE WISHING FROM YOU

δανίσασθαι μὴ ἀποστραφῇς.
TO BORROW DO NOT TURN AWAY.

5.43 Ἠκούσατε ὅτι ἐρρέθη, Ἀγαπήσεις τὸν πλησίον
YOU° HAVE HEARD THAT IT WAS SAID, YOU SHALL LOVE THE NEIGHBOR

σου καὶ μισήσεις τὸν ἐχθρόν σου. **5.44** ἐγὼ δὲ λέγω
OF YOU AND YOU SHALL HATE THE ENEMY OF YOU. BUT~I SAY

ὑμῖν, ἀγαπᾶτε τοὺς ἐχθροὺς⌐ ὑμῶν καὶ ⌐προσεύχεσθε
TO YOU°, LOVE THE ENEMIES OF YOU° AND PRAY

ὑπὲρ τῶν διωκόντων ὑμᾶς,⌐ **5.45** ὅπως γένησθε
FOR THE ONES PERSECUTING YOU°, SO THAT YOU° MAY BECOME

υἱοὶ τοῦ πατρὸς ὑμῶν τοῦ ἐν οὐρανοῖς, ὅτι τὸν ἥλιον
SONS OF THE FATHER OF YOU° - IN [THE] HEAVENS, FOR THE SUN

αὐτοῦ ἀνατέλλει ἐπὶ πονηροὺς καὶ ἀγαθοὺς καὶ
OF HIM HE MAKES TO RISE UPON EVIL AND GOOD AND

βρέχει ἐπὶ δικαίους καὶ ἀδίκους. **5.46** ἐὰν γὰρ
RAINS UPON [THE] JUST AND UNJUST. FOR~IF

ἀγαπήσητε τοὺς ἀγαπῶντας ὑμᾶς, τίνα μισθὸν
YOU° LOVE THE ONES LOVING YOU°, WHAT REWARD

ἔχετε; οὐχὶ καὶ οἱ τελῶναι τὸ αὐτὸ ποιοῦσιν;
DO YOU° HAVE? ²NOT ³EVEN ⁴THE ⁵TAX-COLLECTORS ⁶THE ⁷SAME ¹DO?

5.47 καὶ ἐὰν ἀσπάσησθε τοὺς ἀδελφοὺς ὑμῶν μόνον,
AND IF YOU° GREET THE BROTHERS OF YOU° ONLY,

τί περισσὸν ποιεῖτε; οὐχὶ καὶ οἱ ἐθνικοὶ τὸ
WHAT EXTRAORDINARY [THING] ARE YOU° DOING? ²NOT ³EVEN ⁴THE ⁵GENTILES ⁶THE

αὐτὸ ποιοῦσιν; **5.48** Ἔσεσθε οὖν ὑμεῖς τέλειοι ὡς ὁ
⁷SAME ¹DO? THEREFORE~WILL BE, YOU° PERFECT AS THE

πατὴρ ὑμῶν ὁ οὐράνιος τέλειός ἐστιν.
²FATHER ³OF YOU° - ¹HEAVENLY IS~PERFECT.

to sue you and take your coat, give your cloak as well; [41]and if anyone forces you to go one mile, go also the second mile. [42]Give to everyone who begs from you, and do not refuse anyone who wants to borrow from you.

43 "You have heard that it was said, 'You shall love your neighbor and hate your enemy.' [44]But I say to you, Love your enemies and pray for those who persecute you, [45]so that you may be children of your Father in heaven; for he makes his sun rise on the evil and on the good, and sends rain on the righteous and on the unrighteous. [46]For if you love those who love you, what reward do you have? Do not even the tax collectors do the same? [47]And if you greet only your brothers and sisters,[j] what more are you doing than others? Do not even the Gentiles do the same? [48]Be perfect, therefore, as your heavenly Father is perfect.

[j] Gk *your brothers*

5:43 Lev. 19:18   **5:44a** text: ASV RSV NASB NIV NEB TEV NJB NRSV. add ευλογειετε τους καταρωμενους υμας, καλως ποιειτε τοις μισουσιν υμας (bless the ones cursing you, do good to the ones hating you) [see Luke 6:27-28]: KJV NIVmg NEBmg NJBmg.   **5:44b** text: ASV RSV NASB NIV NEB TEV NJB NRSV. var. προσευχεσθε υπερ των επηρεαζοντων υμας και διωκοντων υμας (pray for the ones treating you spitefully and persecuting you) [see Luke 26:7-8]: KJV NEBmg NJBmg.

CHAPTER 6

"Beware of practicing your piety before others in order to be seen by them; for then you have no reward from your Father in heaven.

2 "So whenever you give alms, do not sound a trumpet before you, as the hypocrites do in the synagogues and in the streets, so that they may be praised by others. Truly I tell you, they have received their reward. [3]But when you give alms, do not let your left hand know what your right hand is doing, [4]so that your alms may be done in secret; and your Father who sees in secret will reward you.[k]

5 "And whenever you pray, do not be like the hypocrites; for they love to stand and pray in the synagogues and at the street corners, so that they may be seen by others. Truly I tell you, they have received their reward. [6]But whenever you pray, go into your room and shut the door and pray to your Father who is in secret; and your Father who sees in secret will reward you.[k]

[k] Other ancient authorities add openly

6.1 Προσέχετε [δὲ] τὴν δικαιοσύνην ὑμῶν μὴ
BUT~BE CAREFUL   THE   RIGHTEOUSNESS   OF YOU°   NOT

ποιεῖν   ἔμπροσθεν τῶν ἀνθρώπων πρὸς   τὸ
TO DEMONSTRATE BEFORE   -   MEN   WITH THE AIM -

θεαθῆναι αὐτοῖς·   εἰ δὲ μή γε, μισθὸν οὐκ ἔχετε παρὰ
TO BE SEEN   BY THEM;   OTHERWISE,   YOU° HAVE NO~REWARD   WITH

τῷ πατρὶ ὑμῶν τῷ ἐν τοῖς οὐρανοῖς.
THE FATHER OF YOU° -   IN   THE   HEAVENS.

6.2 Ὅταν οὖν   ποιῇς   ἐλεημοσύνην,
THEREFORE,~WHENEVER YOU DO(GIVE) ALMS,

μὴ σαλπίσῃς   ἔμπροσθέν σου, ὥσπερ οἱ ὑποκριταὶ
DO NOT SOUND A TRUMPET BEFORE   YOU,   AS   THE HYPOCRITES

ποιοῦσιν ἐν ταῖς συναγωγαῖς καὶ ἐν ταῖς ῥύμαις,
DO   IN   THE   SYNAGOGUES   AND   IN   THE   STREETS,

ὅπως δοξασθῶσιν   ὑπὸ τῶν ἀνθρώπων· ἀμὴν λέγω
SO THAT   THEY MAY BE GLORIFIED BY   -   MEN.   TRULY   I SAY

ὑμῖν, ἀπέχουσιν τὸν μισθὸν αὐτῶν. **6.3** σοῦ δὲ
TO YOU°,   THEY HAVE   THE   REWARD   OF THEM.   BUT~YOU

ποιοῦντος ἐλεημοσύνην μὴ γνώτω ἡ ἀριστερά σου
DOING(GIVING)   ALMS   DO NOT LET KNOW THE LEFT [HAND]   OF YOU

τί   ποιεῖ ἡ δεξιά   σου, **6.4** ὅπως ᾖ   σου ἡ
WHAT DOES   THE RIGHT [HAND] OF YOU,   SO THAT [3]MAY BE [1]YOUR -

ἐλεημοσύνη ἐν τῷ κρυπτῷ·   καὶ ὁ   πατήρ σου ὁ
[2]ALMS   IN   -   SECRET.   AND   THE FATHER   OF YOU THE ONE

βλέπων ἐν τῷ   κρυπτῷ ἀποδώσει σοι[T].
SEEING   IN   -   SECRET   WILL REPAY   YOU.

6.5 Καὶ ὅταν   προσεύχησθε, οὐκ ἔσεσθε ὡς οἱ
AND   WHENEVER YOU° PRAY,   DO NOT BE   AS   THE

ὑποκριταί, ὅτι φιλοῦσιν ἐν ταῖς συναγωγαῖς καὶ ἐν
HYPOCRITES,   FOR THEY LOVE IN THE   SYNAGOGUES   AND   ON

ταῖς γωνίαις τῶν πλατειῶν ἑστῶτες
THE   CORNERS   OF THE STREETS   HAVING BEEN STANDING

προσεύχεσθαι, ὅπως φανῶσιν   τοῖς ἀνθρώποις· ἀμὴν
TO PRAY,   SO THAT THEY MAY BE SEEN -   BY MEN.   TRULY

λέγω ὑμῖν, ἀπέχουσιν τὸν μισθὸν αὐτῶν. **6.6** σὺ δὲ
I SAY   TO YOU°, THEY HAVE   THE   REWARD   OF THEM.   [3]YOU [1]BUT

ὅταν   προσεύχῃ, εἴσελθε εἰς τὸ ταμεῖόν σου καὶ
[2]WHENEVER PRAY,   ENTER   INTO THE HIDDEN ROOM OF YOU AND

κλείσας τὴν θύραν σου πρόσευξαι τῷ   πατρί σου
HAVING SHUT THE   DOOR   OF YOU PRAY   TO THE FATHER   OF YOU

τῷ   ἐν τῷ κρυπτῷ·   καὶ ὁ   πατήρ σου ὁ
THE ONE IN   -   SECRET.   AND   THE FATHER   OF YOU THE ONE

βλέπων ἐν τῷ   κρυπτῷ ἀποδώσει σοι[T].
SEEING   IN   -   SECRET   WILL REPAY   YOU.

6:4, 6 text: ASV RSV NASB NIV NEB TEV NJB NRSV.   add εν τω φανερω (openly): KJV NEBmg.

6.7 Προσευχόμενοι δὲ μὴ βατταλογήσητε ὥσπερ οἱ
BUT~PRAYING   DO NOT BABBLE   AS   THE

ἐθνικοί, δοκοῦσιν γὰρ ὅτι ἐν τῇ πολυλογίᾳ αὐτῶν
GENTILES, FOR~THEY THINK THAT IN THE WORDINESS   OF THEM

εἰσακουσθήσονται. **6.8** μὴ οὖν ὁμοιωθῆτε αὐτοῖς·
THEY WILL BE HEARD.   THEREFORE~DO NOT BE LIKE THEM.

οἶδεν γὰρ ὁ πατὴρ ὑμῶν ὧν   χρείαν ἔχετε πρὸ
FOR~KNOWS THE FATHER OF YOU° OF WHAT THINGS YOU° HAVE~NEED BEFORE

τοῦ ὑμᾶς αἰτῆσαι αὐτόν. **6.9** Οὕτως οὖν προσεύχεσθε
-   YOU° ASK   HIM.   THEREFORE~THUS PRAY

ὑμεῖς·
YOU°:

Πάτερ ἡμῶν ὁ   ἐν τοῖς οὐρανοῖς·
FATHER OF US THE ONE IN THE HEAVENS,

ἁγιασθήτω τὸ ὄνομά σου·
LET BE REVERED THE NAME OF YOU,

6.10 ἐλθέτω ἡ βασιλεία σου·
LET COME THE KINGDOM OF YOU,

γενηθήτω τὸ θέλημά σου,
LET BE DONE THE WILL OF YOU,

ὡς ἐν οὐρανῷ καὶ ἐπὶ γῆς·
AS IN HEAVEN ALSO ON EARTH.

6.11 τὸν ἄρτον ἡμῶν τὸν ἐπιούσιον δὸς ἡμῖν
THE ²BREAD ³OF US -   ¹DAILY   GIVE TO US

σήμερον·
TODAY.

6.12 καὶ ἄφες ἡμῖν τὰ ὀφειλήματα ἡμῶν,
AND FORGIVE US THE DEBTS   OF US,

ὡς καὶ ἡμεῖς ἀφήκαμεν τοῖς
AS ALSO WE   HAVE FORGIVEN THE

ὀφειλέταις ἡμῶν·
DEBTORS   OF US.

6.13 καὶ μὴ εἰσενέγκῃς ἡμᾶς εἰς πειρασμόν,
AND DO NOT BRING   US   INTO TEMPTATION,

ἀλλὰ ῥῦσαι ἡμᾶς ἀπὸ τοῦ πονηροῦ⊤.
BUT RESCUE US   FROM THE EVIL ONE.

6.14 Ἐὰν γὰρ ἀφῆτε   τοῖς ἀνθρώποις τὰ
FOR~IF   YOU° FORGIVE -   MEN   THE

παραπτώματα αὐτῶν, ἀφήσει καὶ ὑμῖν ὁ πατὴρ ὑμῶν
TRESPASSES   OF THEM, WILL FORGIVE ALSO YOU° THE ²FATHER ³OF YOU°

ὁ οὐράνιος· **6.15** ἐὰν δὲ μὴ ἀφῆτε   τοῖς ἀνθρώποις,
- ¹HEAVENLY.   BUT~IF YOU° DO NOT FORGIVE -   MEN,

οὐδὲ ὁ πατὴρ ὑμῶν ἀφήσει τὰ παραπτώματα ὑμῶν.
NEITHER THE FATHER OF YOU° WILL FORGIVE THE TRESPASSES OF YOU°.

6:13 text: ASV RSV NIV NEB TEV NJB NRSV. add οτι σου εστιν η βασιλεια και η δυναμις και η δοξα εις
τους αιωνας. αμην (because yours is the kingdom and the power and the glory forever. amen) [see
1 Chron. 29:11-13]: KJV ASVmg RSVmg NASB NIVmg NEBmg TEVmg NJBmg NRSVmg.

7 "When you are praying, do not heap up empty phrases as the Gentiles do; for they think that they will be heard because of their many words. 8 Do not be like them, for your Father knows what you need before you ask him.

9 "Pray then in this way:
Our Father in heaven,
   hallowed be your
   name.
10   Your kingdom come.
   Your will be done,
   on earth as it is in
   heaven.
11   Give us this day our
   daily bread.*l*
12   And forgive us our
   debts,
   as we also have
   forgiven our
   debtors.
13   And do not bring us
   to the time of trial,*m*
   but rescue us from the
   evil one.*n*

14 For if you forgive others their trespasses, your heavenly Father will also forgive you; 15 but if you do not forgive others, neither will your Father forgive your trespasses.

l Or *our bread for tomorrow*
m Or *us into temptation*
n Or *from evil.* Other ancient authorities add, in some form, *For the kingdom and the power and the glory are yours forever. Amen.*

16 "And whenever you fast, do not look dismal, like the hypocrites, for they disfigure their faces so as to show others that they are fasting. Truly I tell you, they have received their reward. [17]But when you fast, put oil on your head and wash your face, [18]so that your fasting may be seen not by others but by your Father who is in secret; and your Father who sees in secret will reward you.*o*

19 "Do not store up for yourselves treasures on earth, where moth and rust*p* consume and where thieves break in and steal; [20]but store up for yourselves treasures in heaven, where neither moth nor rust*p* consumes and where thieves do not break in and steal. [21]For where your treasure is, there your heart will be also.

22 "The eye is the lamp of the body. So, if your eye is healthy, your whole body will be full of light; [23]but if your eye is unhealthy, your whole body will be full of darkness. If then the light in you is darkness, how great is the darkness!

24 "No one can serve two masters; for a slave will either hate the one and love

o Other ancient authorities add *openly*
p Gk *eating*

6.16 Ὅταν δὲ νηστεύητε, μὴ γίνεσθε ὡς οἱ
AND~WHENEVER YOU° FAST,   DO NOT BE   AS   THE

ὑποκριταὶ σκυθρωποί, ἀφανίζουσιν γὰρ τὰ πρόσωπα
GLOOMY~HYPOCRITES,   FOR~THEY DISFIGURE   THE FACES

αὐτῶν ὅπως φανῶσιν τοῖς ἀνθρώποις νηστεύοντες·
OF THEM SO THAT THEY MAY APPEAR - TO MEN [AS] ONES FASTING.

ἀμὴν λέγω ὑμῖν, ἀπέχουσιν τὸν μισθὸν αὐτῶν.
TRULY I SAY TO YOU°, THEY HAVE THE REWARD OF THEM.

6.17 σὺ δὲ νηστεύων ἄλειψαί σου τὴν κεφαλὴν καὶ τὸ
BUT~YOU FASTING ANOINT OF YOU THE HEAD AND THE

πρόσωπόν σου νίψαι, **6.18** ὅπως μὴ φανῇς τοῖς
FACE   OF YOU WASH,   SO THAT YOU MAY NOT APPEAR -

ἀνθρώποις νηστεύων ἀλλὰ τῷ πατρί σου τῷ ἐν
TO MEN [AS] ONES FASTING BUT TO THE FATHER OF YOU THE ONE IN

τῷ κρυφαίῳ· καὶ ὁ πατήρ σου ὁ βλέπων ἐν τῷ
-   SECRET. AND THE FATHER OF YOU THE ONE SEEING IN -

κρυφαίῳ ἀποδώσει σοι.
SECRET   WILL REPAY YOU.

6.19 Μὴ θησαυρίζετε ὑμῖν θησαυροὺς ἐπὶ τῆς γῆς,
DO NOT STORE UP FOR YOU° TREASURES UPON THE EARTH,

ὅπου σὴς καὶ βρῶσις ἀφανίζει καὶ ὅπου κλέπται
WHERE MOTH AND RUST DESTROY AND WHERE THIEVES

διορύσσουσιν καὶ κλέπτουσιν· **6.20** θησαυρίζετε δὲ
BREAK IN AND STEAL.   BUT~STORE UP

ὑμῖν θησαυροὺς ἐν οὐρανῷ, ὅπου οὔτε σὴς οὔτε
FOR YOU° TREASURES IN HEAVEN, WHERE NEITHER MOTH NOR

βρῶσις ἀφανίζει καὶ ὅπου κλέπται οὐ διορύσσουσιν
RUST   DESTROYS AND WHERE THIEVES DO NOT BREAK IN

οὐδὲ κλέπτουσιν· **6.21** ὅπου γὰρ ἐστιν ὁ θησαυρός
NOR STEAL.   FOR~WHERE IS THE TREASURE

σου, ἐκεῖ ἔσται καὶ ἡ καρδία σου.
OF YOU, THERE WILL BE ALSO THE HEART OF YOU.

6.22 Ὁ λύχνος τοῦ σώματός ἐστιν ὁ ὀφθαλμός. ἐὰν
THE LAMP OF THE BODY IS THE EYE.   IF

οὖν ᾖ ὁ ὀφθαλμός σου ἁπλοῦς, ὅλον τὸ σῶμά σου
THEREFORE IS THE EYE OF YOU HEALTHY, THE~WHOLE BODY OF YOU

φωτεινὸν ἔσται· **6.23** ἐὰν δὲ ὁ ὀφθαλμός σου
WILL BE~SHINING.   BUT~IF THE EYE OF YOU

πονηρὸς ᾖ, ὅλον τὸ σῶμά σου σκοτεινὸν ἔσται. εἰ
IS~EVIL,   THE~WHOLE BODY OF YOU WILL BE~DARKNESS.   IF

οὖν τὸ φῶς τὸ ἐν σοὶ σκότος ἐστίν, τὸ σκότος
THEREFORE THE LIGHT - IN YOU IS~DARKNESS,   2THE 3DARKNESS

πόσον.
1HOW GREAT [IS].

6.24 Οὐδεὶς δύναται δυσὶ κυρίοις δουλεύειν· ἢ γὰρ
NO ONE IS ABLE TWO MASTERS TO SERVE. FOR~EITHER

τὸν ἕνα μισήσει καὶ τὸν ἕτερον ἀγαπήσει, ἢ ἑνὸς
THE ONE HE WILL HATE AND THE OTHER HE WILL LOVE, OR ONE

ἀνθέξεται   καὶ   τοῦ   ἑτέρου   καταφρονήσει.   οὐ δύνασθε
HE WILL HOLD TO   AND   THE   OTHER   HE WILL DESPISE.   YOU° ARE NOT ABLE

θεῷ δουλεύειν   καὶ   μαμωνᾷ.
TO SERVE~GOD   AND   MAMMON.

6.25 Διὰ τοῦτο   λέγω   ὑμῖν,   μὴ μεριμνᾶτε   τῇ ψυχῇ
THEREFORE   I SAY   TO YOU°,   DO NOT BE ANXIOUS [ABOUT]   THE LIFE

ὑμῶν   τί   φάγητε   [ἢ τί   πίητε],   μηδὲ τῷ
OF YOU°   WHAT   YOU MIGHT EAT   OR   WHAT   YOU° MIGHT DRINK,   NOR   FOR THE

σώματι ὑμῶν   τί   ἐνδύσησθε.   οὐχὶ ἡ ψυχὴ πλεῖόν
BODY   OF YOU°   WHAT   YOU° MIGHT PUT ON.   ²NOT   - ³LIFE   ⁴MORE THAN

ἐστιν   τῆς   τροφῆς   καὶ   τὸ   σῶμα   τοῦ ἐνδύματος;
¹IS   -   FOOD   AND   THE   BODY [MORE THAN]   -   CLOTHING?

6.26 ἐμβλέψατε   εἰς   τὰ   πετεινὰ   τοῦ   οὐρανοῦ ὅτι
LOOK   TO   THE   BIRDS   -   OF HEAVEN   FOR

οὐ σπείρουσιν   οὐδὲ   θερίζουσιν   οὐδὲ   συνάγουσιν   εἰς
THEY DO NOT SOW   NOR   REAP   NOR   GATHER   INTO

ἀποθήκας,   καὶ   ὁ   πατὴρ   ὑμῶν   ὁ   οὐράνιος   τρέφει
BARNS,   AND   THE   ²FATHER   ³OF YOU°   -   ¹HEAVENLY   FEEDS

αὐτά·   οὐχ ὑμεῖς   μᾶλλον διαφέρετε   αὐτῶν;
THEM.   ³NOT   ²YOURSELVES   ⁴MORE   ¹ARE YOU° WORTH   [THAN] THEY?

6.27 τίς   δὲ   ἐξ   ὑμῶν μεριμνῶν   δύναται   προσθεῖναι   ἐπὶ
AND~WHO   AMONG   YOU°   BEING ANXIOUS   IS ABLE   TO ADD   TO

τὴν ἡλικίαν   αὐτοῦ   πῆχυν ἕνα;   **6.28** καὶ   περὶ
THE   LIFE SPAN   OF HIM   ONE~CUBIT?   AND   CONCERNING

ἐνδύματος   τί   μεριμνᾶτε;   καταμάθετε   τὰ   κρίνα   τοῦ
CLOTHING   WHY   BE ANXIOUS?   OBSERVE   THE   LILIES   OF THE

ἀγροῦ   πῶς αὐξάνουσιν·   οὐ κοπιῶσιν   οὐδὲ   νήθουσιν·
FIELD   HOW   THEY GROW.   THEY DO NOT LABOR   NOR   SPIN.

6.29 λέγω   δὲ   ὑμῖν   ὅτι   οὐδὲ   Σολομὼν ἐν   πάσῃ   τῇ
BUT~I SAY   TO YOU°   THAT   NOT [EVEN]   SOLOMON   IN   ALL   THE

δόξῃ   αὐτοῦ περιεβάλετο   ὡς   ἓν   τούτων.   **6.30** εἰ δὲ   τὸν
GLORY   OF HIM   WAS CLOTHED   AS   ONE   OF THESE.   AND~IF   THE

χόρτον   τοῦ   ἀγροῦ   σήμερον ὄντα   καὶ   αὔριον   εἰς
GRASS   OF THE FIELD   TODAY   BEING   AND   TOMORROW   INTO

κλίβανον   βαλλόμενον ὁ   θεὸς οὕτως ἀμφιέννυσιν,
AN OVEN   BEING THROWN   -   GOD   THUS   CLOTHES,

οὐ   πολλῷ   μᾶλλον   ὑμᾶς, ὀλιγόπιστοι;
[WILL HE] NOT   MUCH   MORE [CLOTHE]   YOU°,   ONES OF LITTLE FAITH?

6.31 μὴ   οὖν μεριμνήσητε λέγοντες,   Τί   φάγωμεν;   ἤ,
THEREFORE~DO NOT BE ANXIOUS   SAYING,   WHAT   MIGHT WE EAT?   OR,

Τί   πίωμεν;   ἤ,   Τί   περιβαλώμεθα;
WHAT   MIGHT WE DRINK?   OR,   WHAT   MIGHT WE CLOTHE OURSELVES [WITH]?

6.32 πάντα γὰρ   ταῦτα   τὰ ἔθνη   ἐπιζητοῦσιν·
FOR~ALL   THESE THINGS   THE   GENTILES   STRIVE FOR.

οἶδεν γὰρ   ὁ   πατὴρ   ὑμῶν   ὁ   οὐράνιος   ὅτι   χρῄζετε
FOR~HAS KNOWN   THE   ²FATHER   ³OF YOU°   -   ¹HEAVENLY   THAT   YOU° NEED

τούτων ἀπάντων.   **6.33** ζητεῖτε   δὲ   πρῶτον   τὴν   βασιλείαν
ALL~THESE THINGS.   BUT~SEEK   FIRST   THE   KINGDOM

the other, or be devoted to the one and despise the other. You cannot serve God and wealth.*q*

25 "Therefore I tell you, do not worry about your life, what you will eat or what you will drink,*r* or about your body, what you will wear. Is not life more than food, and the body more than clothing? ²⁶Look at the birds of the air; they neither sow nor reap nor gather into barns, and yet your heavenly Father feeds them. Are you not of more value than they? ²⁷And can any of you by worrying add a single hour to your span of life?*s* ²⁸And why do you worry about clothing? Consider the lilies of the field, how they grow; they neither toil nor spin, ²⁹yet I tell you, even Solomon in all his glory was not clothed like one of these. ³⁰But if God so clothes the grass of the field, which is alive today and tomorrow is thrown into the oven, will he not much more clothe you— you of little faith? ³¹Therefore do not worry, saying, 'What will we eat?' or 'What will we drink?' or 'What will we wear?' ³²For it is the Gentiles who strive for all these things; and indeed your heavenly Father knows that you need all these things. ³³But strive first for the kingdom

q Gk *mammon*
r Other ancient authorities lack *or what you will drink*
s Or *add one cubit to your height*

of God[t] and his[u] righteousness, and all these things will be given to you as well.

34 "So do not worry about tomorrow, for tomorrow will bring worries of its own. Today's trouble is enough for today.

[t] Other ancient authorities lack *of God*
[u] Or *its*

[τοῦ θεοῦ] καὶ τὴν δικαιοσύνην αὐτοῦ, καὶ
-           OF GOD AND THE RIGHTEOUSNESS OF HIM, AND

ταῦτα πάντα προστεθήσεται ὑμῖν.
ALL~THESE THINGS WILL BE ADDED TO YOU°.

6.34 μὴ οὖν μεριμνήσητε εἰς τὴν αὔριον, ἡ γὰρ αὔριον
THEREFORE~DO NOT BE ANXIOUS FOR - TOMORROW, - FOR TOMORROW

μεριμνήσει ἑαυτῆς· ἀρκετὸν τῇ ἡμέρᾳ ἡ κακία
WILL BE ANXIOUS FOR ITSELF. SUFFICIENT FOR THE DAY [IS] THE EVIL

αὐτῆς.
OF IT.

CHAPTER 7

"Do not judge, so that you may not be judged. [2]For with the judgment you make you will be judged, and the measure you give will be the measure you get. [3]Why do you see the speck in your neighbor's[v] eye, but do not notice the log in your own eye? [4]Or how can you say to your neighbor,[w] 'Let me take the speck out of your eye,' while the log is in your own eye? [5]You hypocrite, first take the log out of your own eye, and then you will see clearly to take the speck out of your neighbor's[v] eye.

6 "Do not give what is holy to dogs; and do not throw your pearls before swine, or they will trample them under foot and turn and maul you.

7 "Ask, and it will be given you; search, and you will find; knock, and the door will be opened for you. [8]For everyone who asks receives, and everyone who searches finds, and for everyone who knocks,

[v] Gk *brother's*
[w] Gk *brother*

7.1 Μὴ κρίνετε, ἵνα μὴ κριθῆτε· **7.2** ἐν ᾧ γὰρ
DO NOT JUDGE LEST YOU° BE JUDGED. [2]WITH [3]WHAT [1]FOR

κρίματι κρίνετε κριθήσεσθε, καὶ ἐν ᾧ μέτρῳ
JUDGMENT YOU° JUDGE YOU° WILL BE JUDGED, AND WITH WHAT MEASURE

μετρεῖτε μετρηθήσεται ὑμῖν. **7.3** τί δὲ βλέπεις τὸ
YOU° MEASURE IT WILL BE MEASURED TO YOU°. AND~WHY DO YOU SEE THE

κάρφος τὸ ἐν τῷ ὀφθαλμῷ τοῦ ἀδελφοῦ σου, τὴν δὲ
SPECK - IN THE EYE OF THE BROTHER OF YOU, BUT~THE

ἐν τῷ σῷ ὀφθαλμῷ δοκὸν οὐ κατανοεῖς; **7.4** ἢ πῶς
[2]IN - [3]YOUR [4]EYE [1]BEAM YOU DO NOT CONSIDER? OR HOW

ἐρεῖς τῷ ἀδελφῷ σου, Ἄφες ἐκβάλω τὸ κάρφος
WILL YOU SAY TO THE BROTHER OF YOU, LET [ME] TAKE OUT THE SPECK

ἐκ τοῦ ὀφθαλμοῦ σου, καὶ ἰδοὺ ἡ δοκὸς ἐν τῷ
FROM THE EYE OF YOU, AND BEHOLD THE BEAM [IS] IN THE

ὀφθαλμῷ σοῦ; **7.5** ὑποκριτά, ἔκβαλε πρῶτον ἐκ τοῦ
EYE OF YOU? HYPOCRITE, FIRST~TAKE OUT FROM THE

ὀφθαλμοῦ σοῦ τὴν δοκόν καὶ τότε διαβλέψεις
EYE OF YOU THE BEAM AND THEN YOU WILL SEE CLEARLY [ENOUGH]

ἐκβαλεῖν τὸ κάρφος ἐκ τοῦ ὀφθαλμοῦ τοῦ ἀδελφοῦ
TO TAKE OUT THE SPECK FROM THE EYE OF THE BROTHER

σου. **7.6** Μὴ δῶτε τὸ ἅγιον τοῖς κυσὶν μηδὲ βάλητε
OF YOU. DO NOT GIVE - HOLY THINGS - TO DOGS, NOR THROW

τοὺς μαργαρίτας ὑμῶν ἔμπροσθεν τῶν χοίρων, μήποτε
THE PEARLS OF YOU° BEFORE THE PIGS, LEST

καταπατήσουσιν αὐτοὺς ἐν τοῖς ποσὶν αὐτῶν καὶ
THEY WILL TRAMPLE THEM WITH THE FEET OF THEM AND

στραφέντες ῥήξωσιν ὑμᾶς.
HAVING TURNED, THEY WILL TEAR [INTO PIECES] YOU°.

7.7 Αἰτεῖτε καὶ δοθήσεται ὑμῖν, ζητεῖτε καὶ
ASK AND IT WILL BE GIVEN TO YOU°, SEEK AND

εὑρήσετε, κρούετε καὶ ἀνοιγήσεται ὑμῖν· **7.8** πᾶς γὰρ
YOU° WILL FIND, KNOCK AND IT WILL BE OPENED TO YOU°. FOR~EVERYONE

ὁ αἰτῶν λαμβάνει καὶ ὁ ζητῶν εὑρίσκει καὶ τῷ
- ASKING RECEIVES AND THE ONE SEEKING FINDS AND TO THE ONE

κρούοντι ἀνοιγήσεται. **7.9** ἢ τίς ἐστιν ἐξ ὑμῶν
KNOCKING   IT WILL BE OPENED.   OR ¹WHAT ³IS THERE ⁴AMONG ⁵YOU°

ἄνθρωπος, ὃν αἰτήσει ὁ υἱὸς αὐτοῦ ἄρτον, μὴ
²MAN,   WHOM WILL ASK THE SON OF HIM [FOR] BREAD, [SURELY] NOT

λίθον ἐπιδώσει αὐτῷ; **7.10** ἢ καὶ ἰχθὺν αἰτήσει,
A STONE WILL HE GIVE TO HIM?   OR [IF] ALSO [FOR] A FISH HE ASKS,

μὴ   ὄφιν ἐπιδώσει αὐτῷ; **7.11** εἰ οὖν ὑμεῖς
[SURELY] NOT A SNAKE WILL HE GIVE TO HIM?   IF THEREFORE YOU°

πονηροὶ ὄντες οἴδατε δόματα ἀγαθὰ διδόναι τοῖς
BEING~EVIL   KNOW GOOD~GIFTS   TO GIVE TO THE

τέκνοις ὑμῶν, πόσῳ μᾶλλον ὁ πατὴρ ὑμῶν ὁ ἐν
CHILDREN OF YOU°, HOW MUCH MORE THE FATHER OF YOU°, THE ONE IN

τοῖς οὐρανοῖς δώσει ἀγαθὰ τοῖς αἰτοῦσιν αὐτόν.
THE HEAVENS,   WILL GIVE GOOD THINGS TO THE ONES ASKING HIM.

7.12 Πάντα οὖν ὅσα ἐὰν θέλητε ἵνα ποιῶσιν ὑμῖν
       THEREFORE~EVERYTHING THAT YOU° WISH THAT ²DO   ³FOR YOU°

οἱ ἄνθρωποι, οὕτως καὶ ὑμεῖς ποιεῖτε αὐτοῖς·
- ¹MEN,   THUS ALSO YOU° DO   FOR THEM.

οὗτος γάρ ἐστιν ὁ νόμος καὶ οἱ προφῆται.
FOR~THIS IS   THE LAW AND THE PROPHETS.

7.13 Εἰσέλθατε διὰ τῆς στενῆς πύλης· ὅτι πλατεῖα
        ENTER   THROUGH THE NARROW GATE·   FOR WIDE [IS]

⌐ἡ πύλη⌐ καὶ εὐρύχωρος ἡ ὁδὸς ἡ ἀπάγουσα εἰς τὴν
THE GATE AND BROAD [IS] THE WAY - LEADING   TO -

ἀπώλειαν καὶ πολλοί εἰσιν οἱ εἰσερχόμενοι δι᾽
DESTRUCTION AND MANY ARE THE ONES ENTERING   THROUGH

αὐτῆς· **7.14** τί στενὴ ἡ πύλη καὶ τεθλιμμένη ἡ
IT.   HOW NARROW [IS] THE GATE AND CONSTRICTED THE

ὁδὸς ἡ ἀπάγουσα εἰς τὴν ζωὴν καὶ ὀλίγοι εἰσὶν
ROAD - LEADING   TO - LIFE AND FEW   ARE

οἱ εὑρίσκοντες αὐτήν.
THE ONES FINDING   IT.

7.15 Προσέχετε ἀπὸ τῶν ψευδοπροφητῶν, οἵτινες
        BEWARE   OF -   FALSE PROPHETS,   WHO

ἔρχονται πρὸς ὑμᾶς ἐν ἐνδύμασιν προβάτων, ἔσωθεν δέ
COME   TO   YOU° IN CLOTHING   OF SHEEP,   BUT~WITHIN

εἰσιν λύκοι ἅρπαγες. **7.16** ἀπὸ τῶν καρπῶν αὐτῶν
ARE   RAVENOUS~WOLVES.   BY   THE FRUITS OF THEM

ἐπιγνώσεσθε αὐτούς. μήτι συλλέγουσιν ἀπὸ ἀκανθῶν
YOU° WILL KNOW THEM. ²ARE NOT GATHERED ³FROM ⁴THORNS

σταφυλὰς ἢ ἀπὸ τριβόλων σῦκα; **7.17** οὕτως πᾶν
¹[SURELY] GRAPES ⁵OR ⁷FROM ⁸THISTLES ⁶FIGS?   SO   EVERY

δένδρον ἀγαθὸν καρποὺς καλοὺς ποιεῖ, τὸ δὲ σαπρὸν
GOOD~TREE   GOOD~FRUITS   PRODUCES, BUT~THE ROTTEN

δένδρον καρποὺς πονηροὺς ποιεῖ. **7.18** οὐ δύναται
TREE   BAD~FRUIT   PRODUCES.   IS NOT ABLE

the door will be opened. ⁹Is there anyone among you who, if your child asks for bread, will give a stone? ¹⁰Or if the child asks for a fish, will give a snake? ¹¹If you then, who are evil, know how to give good gifts to your children, how much more will your Father in heaven give good things to those who ask him!

12 "In everything do to others as you would have them do to you; for this is the law and the prophets.

13 "Enter through the narrow gate; for the gate is wide and the road is easy^x that leads to destruction, and there are many who take it. ¹⁴For the gate is narrow and the road is hard that leads to life, and there are few who find it.

15 "Beware of false prophets, who come to you in sheep's clothing but inwardly are ravenous wolves. ¹⁶You will know them by their fruits. Are grapes gathered from thorns, or figs from thistles? ¹⁷In the same way, every good tree bears good fruit, but the bad tree bears bad fruit. ¹⁸A good tree cannot

x Other ancient authorities read *for the road is wide and easy*

7:13 text: KJV ASV RSV NASB NIV NEB TEV NJB NRSV. omit: ASVmg RSVmg NEBmg NJBmg NRSVmg.

bear bad fruit, nor can a bad tree bear good fruit. 19Every tree that does not bear good fruit is cut down and thrown into the fire. 20Thus you will know them by their fruits.

21 "Not everyone who says to me, 'Lord, Lord,' will enter the kingdom of heaven, but only the one who does the will of my Father in heaven. 22On that day many will say to me, 'Lord, Lord, did we not prophesy in your name, and cast out demons in your name, and do many deeds of power in your name?' 23Then I will declare to them, 'I never knew you; go away from me, you evildoers.'

24 "Everyone then who hears these words of mine and acts on them will be like a wise man who built his house on rock. 25The rain fell, the floods came, and the winds blew and beat on that house, but it did not fall, because it had been founded on rock. 26And everyone who hears these words of mine and does not act on them will be like a foolish man who built his house on sand.

δένδρον ἀγαθὸν καρποὺς πονηροὺς ποιεῖν οὐδὲ
A GOOD~TREE   BAD~FRUIT   TO PRODUCE   NOR [IS]

δένδρον σαπρὸν καρποὺς καλοὺς ποιεῖν. 7.19 πᾶν
A ROTTEN~TREE [ABLE]   GOOD~FRUIT   TO PRODUCE.   EVERY

δένδρον μὴ ποιοῦν καρπὸν καλὸν ἐκκόπτεται καὶ εἰς
TREE   NOT   PRODUCING   GOOD~FRUIT   IS CUT OFF   AND   INTO

πῦρ βάλλεται. 7.20 ἄρα γε ἀπὸ τῶν καρπῶν αὐτῶν
[THE] FIRE   IS THROWN.   THEREFORE,   BY   THE   FRUITS   OF THEM

ἐπιγνώσεσθε αὐτούς.
YOU° WILL KNOW   THEM.

7.21 Οὐ πᾶς ὁ λέγων μοι, Κύριε κύριε,
NOT   ALL   THE ONES   SAYING   TO ME,   LORD,   LORD,

εἰσελεύσεται εἰς τὴν βασιλείαν τῶν οὐρανῶν, ἀλλ᾽
WILL ENTER   INTO   THE   KINGDOM   OF THE HEAVENS,   BUT

ὁ ποιῶν τὸ θέλημα τοῦ πατρός μου τοῦ ἐν τοῖς
THE ONE DOING   THE WILL   OF THE FATHER   OF ME, THE ONE IN   THE

οὐρανοῖς. 7.22 πολλοὶ ἐροῦσίν μοι ἐν ἐκείνῃ τῇ
HEAVENS.   MANY   WILL SAY   TO ME ON   THAT   -

ἡμέρᾳ, Κύριε κύριε, οὐ τῷ σῷ ὀνόματι
DAY,   LORD,   LORD,   NOT - IN YOUR NAME

ἐπροφητεύσαμεν, καὶ τῷ σῷ ὀνόματι
DID WE PROPHESY   AND - IN YOUR NAME

δαιμόνια ἐξεβάλομεν, καὶ τῷ σῷ ὀνόματι
CAST OUT~DEMONS,   AND - IN YOUR NAME

δυνάμεις πολλὰς ἐποιήσαμεν; 7.23 καὶ τότε ὁμολογήσω
MANY~MIGHTY WORKS   PERFORM?   AND   THEN   I WILL DECLARE

αὐτοῖς ὅτι Οὐδέποτε ἔγνων ὑμᾶς· ἀποχωρεῖτε ἀπ᾽
TO THEM - I NEVER KNEW   YOU°.   DEPART   FROM

ἐμοῦ οἱ ἐργαζόμενοι τὴν ἀνομίαν.
ME   THE ONES WORKING   -   LAWLESSNESS.

7.24 Πᾶς οὖν ὅστις ἀκούει μου τοὺς λόγους τούτους
THEREFORE,~EVERYONE WHO   HEARS   OF ME - THESE~WORDS

καὶ ποιεῖ αὐτούς, ὁμοιωθήσεται ἀνδρὶ φρονίμῳ, ὅστις
AND   DOES   THEM,   WILL BE COMPARED   TO A WISE~MAN,   WHO

ᾠκοδόμησεν αὐτοῦ τὴν οἰκίαν ἐπὶ τὴν πέτραν·
BUILT   HIS   -   HOUSE   UPON   THE   ROCK.

7.25 καὶ κατέβη ἡ βροχὴ καὶ ἦλθον οἱ ποταμοὶ καὶ
AND   CAME DOWN THE RAIN   AND   CAME   THE   RIVERS   AND

ἔπνευσαν οἱ ἄνεμοι καὶ προσέπεσαν τῇ οἰκίᾳ ἐκείνῃ,
BLEW   THE WINDS   AND   BEAT AGAINST   - THAT~HOUSE,

καὶ οὐκ ἔπεσεν, τεθεμελίωτο γὰρ ἐπὶ τὴν πέτραν.
AND   IT DID NOT FALL,   FOR~IT HAD BEEN FOUNDED   UPON   THE   ROCK.

7.26 καὶ πᾶς ὁ ἀκούων μου τοὺς λόγους τούτους καὶ
AND   EVERYONE - HEARING   OF ME - THESE~WORDS   AND

μὴ ποιῶν αὐτοὺς ὁμοιωθήσεται ἀνδρὶ μωρῷ, ὅστις
NOT DOING   THEM   WILL BE COMPARED   TO A FOOLISH~MAN,   WHO

ᾠκοδόμησεν αὐτοῦ τὴν οἰκίαν ἐπὶ τὴν ἄμμον·
BUILT   HIS   -   HOUSE   UPON   THE   SAND.

7.27 καὶ   κατέβη   ἡ   βροχὴ   καὶ   ἦλθον   οἱ   ποταμοὶ   καὶ
AND   CAME DOWN   THE   RAIN   AND   CAME   THE   RIVERS   AND

ἔπνευσαν   οἱ   ἄνεμοι   καὶ   προσέκοψαν   τῇ   οἰκίᾳ   ἐκείνῃ,
BLEW   THE   WINDS   AND   BEAT AGAINST   -   THAT~HOUSE,

καὶ   ἔπεσεν   καὶ   ἦν   ἡ   πτῶσις αὐτῆς   μεγάλη.
AND   IT FELL   AND   ⁴WAS   ¹THE   ²FALL   ³OF IT   ⁵GREAT.

7.28 Καὶ   ἐγένετο   ὅτε   ἐτέλεσεν   ὁ   Ἰησοῦς   τοὺς
AND   IT CAME ABOUT   WHEN   FINISHED   -   JESUS   -

λόγους τούτους,   ἐξεπλήσσοντο   οἱ   ὄχλοι   ἐπὶ   τῇ   διδαχῇ
THESE~WORDS,   WERE AMAZED   THE   CROWDS   AT   THE   TEACHING

αὐτοῦ·   **7.29** ἦν   γὰρ   διδάσκων   αὐτοὺς   ὡς
OF HIM.   FOR~HE WAS   TEACHING   THEM   AS

ἐξουσίαν ἔχων   καὶ   οὐχ   ὡς   οἱ   γραμματεῖς   αὐτῶν.
HAVING~AUTHORITY   AND   NOT   AS   THE   SCRIBES   OF THEM.

²⁷The rain fell, and the floods came, and the winds blew and beat against that house, and it fell—and great was its fall!"

28 Now when Jesus had finished saying these things, the crowds were astounded at his teaching, ²⁹for he taught them as one having authority, and not as their scribes.

8.1 Καταβάντος   δὲ   αὐτοῦ   ἀπὸ   τοῦ   ὄρους   ἠκολούθησαν
AND~[WHEN] HE CAME DOWN   FROM   THE   MOUNTAIN   FOLLOWED

αὐτῷ   ὄχλοι πολλοί.   **8.2** καὶ   ἰδοὺ   λεπρὸς   προσελθὼν
HIM   MANY~CROWDS.   AND   BEHOLD   A LEPER   HAVING APPROACHED

προσεκύνει   αὐτῷ   λέγων,   Κύριε,   ἐὰν   θέλῃς   δύνασαί
WORSHIPED   HIM   SAYING,   LORD,   IF   YOU ARE WILLING   YOU ARE ABLE

με καθαρίσαι.   **8.3** καὶ   ἐκτείνας   τὴν   χεῖρα
TO CLEANSE~ME.   AND   HAVING STRETCHED OUT   THE (HIS)   HAND

ἥψατο   αὐτοῦ   λέγων,   Θέλω,   καθαρίσθητι·   καὶ
HE TOUCHED   HIM   SAYING,   I AM WILLING,   BE CLEANSED.   AND

εὐθέως   ἐκαθαρίσθη   αὐτοῦ   ἡ   λέπρα.   **8.4** καὶ   λέγει
IMMEDIATELY   WAS CLEANSED   HIS   -   LEPROSY.   AND   SAYS

αὐτῷ   ὁ   Ἰησοῦς,   Ὅρα   μηδενὶ   εἴπῃς,   ἀλλὰ   ὕπαγε
TO HIM   -   JESUS,   SEE [THAT]   YOU TELL~NO ONE,   BUT   GO [AND]

σεαυτὸν δεῖξον   τῷ   ἱερεῖ   καὶ   προσένεγκον   τὸ   δῶρον
SHOW~YOURSELF   TO THE   PRIEST   AND   OFFER   THE   GIFT

ὃ   προσέταξεν Μωϋσῆς,   εἰς   μαρτύριον   αὐτοῖς.
WHICH   MOSES~COMMANDED,   FOR   A TESTIMONY   TO THEM.

8.5 Εἰσελθόντος   δὲ   αὐτοῦ   εἰς   Καφαρναοὺμ   προσῆλθεν
NOW~[WHEN] HE ENTERED   INTO   CAPERNAUM,   APPROACHED

αὐτῷ   ἑκατόνταρχος   παρακαλῶν αὐτὸν   **8.6** καὶ   λέγων,
HIM   A CENTURION   BEGGING   HIM   AND   SAYING,

Κύριε, ὁ   παῖς   μου   βέβληται   ἐν   τῇ   οἰκίᾳ
LORD,   THE   CHILD   OF ME   HAS BEEN BEDRIDDEN   IN   THE   HOUSE

παραλυτικός,   δεινῶς   βασανιζόμενος.   **8.7** καὶ   λέγει   αὐτῷ,
PARALYZED,   BEING TORTURED~TERRIBLY.   AND   HE SAYS   TO HIM,

Ἐγὼ ἐλθὼν θεραπεύσω αὐτόν.   **8.8** καὶ   ἀποκριθεὶς   ὁ
I   COMING   WILL HEAL   HIM.   AND   HAVING ANSWERED   THE

ἑκατόνταρχος   ἔφη,   Κύριε,   οὐκ   εἰμὶ   ἱκανὸς   ἵνα   μου
CENTURION   SAID,   LORD,   I AM NOT   WORTHY   THAT   ⁴OF ME

When Jesusʸ had come down from the mountain, great crowds followed him; ²and there was a leperᶻ who came to him and knelt before him, saying, "Lord, if you choose, you can make me clean." ³He stretched out his hand and touched him, saying, "I do choose. Be made clean!" Immediately his leprosyᶻ was cleansed. ⁴Then Jesus said to him, "See that you say nothing to anyone; but go, show yourself to the priest, and offer the gift that Moses commanded, as a testimony to them."

5 When he entered Capernaum, a centurion came to him, appealing to him ⁶and saying, "Lord, my servant is lying at home paralyzed, in terrible distress." ⁷And he said to him, "I will come and cure him." ⁸The centurion answered, "Lord, I am not worthy

ʸ Gk *he*
ᶻ The terms *leper* and *leprosy* can refer to several diseases

to have you come under my roof; but only speak the word, and my servant will be healed. 9For I also am a man under authority, with soldiers under me; and I say to one, 'Go,' and he goes, and to another, 'Come,' and he comes, and to my slave, 'Do this,' and the slave does it." 10When Jesus heard him, he was amazed and said to those who followed him, "Truly I tell you, in no one*a* in Israel have I found such faith. 11I tell you, many will come from east and west and will eat with Abraham and Isaac and Jacob in the kingdom of heaven, 12while the heirs of the kingdom will be thrown into the outer darkness, where there will be weeping and gnashing of teeth." 13And to the centurion Jesus said, "Go; let it be done for you according to your faith." And the servant was healed in that hour.

14 When Jesus entered Peter's house, he saw his mother-in-law lying in bed with a fever; 15he touched her hand, and the fever left her, and she got up and began to serve him. 16That evening they brought to him many who were possessed with demons; and he cast out the spirits

a Other ancient authorities read *Truly I tell you, not even*

ὑπὸ   τὴν   στέγην   εἰσέλθῃς,   ἀλλὰ   μόνον   εἰπὲ   λόγῳ,
¹UNDER   ²THE   ³ROOF   YOU MIGHT COME,   BUT   ONLY   SAY   IN A WORD,

καὶ   ἰαθήσεται   ὁ   παῖς   μου.   **8.9** καὶ   γὰρ   ἐγὼ
AND   WILL BE HEALED   THE   CHILD   OF ME.   FOR~ALSO   I

ἄνθρωπός   εἰμι   ὑπὸ   ἐξουσίαν,   ἔχων   ὑπ'   ἐμαυτὸν
AM~A MAN   UNDER AUTHORITY,   HAVING   UNDER   MYSELF

στρατιώτας,   καὶ   λέγω   τούτῳ,   Πορεύθητι,   καὶ   πορεύεται,
SOLDIERS,   AND   I SAY   TO THIS ONE,   GO,   AND   HE GOES,

καὶ   ἄλλῳ,   Ἔρχου,   καὶ   ἔρχεται,   καὶ   τῷ   δούλῳ μου,
AND   TO ANOTHER,   COME,   AND   HE COMES,   AND   TO THE   SLAVE   OF ME,

Ποίησον   τοῦτο,   καὶ   ποιεῖ.   **8.10** ἀκούσας   δὲ   ὁ
DO   THIS,   AND   HE DOES [IT].   AND~HAVING HEARD [THIS] -

Ἰησοῦς   ἐθαύμασεν   καὶ   εἶπεν   τοῖς   ἀκολουθοῦσιν,
JESUS   MARVELED   AND   SAID   TO THE ONES   FOLLOWING,

Ἀμὴν   λέγω   ὑμῖν,   ⌜παρ'⌝   οὐδενὶ   τοσαύτην   πίστιν   ἐν
TRULY   I SAY   TO YOU°,   WITH   NO ONE   SUCH GREAT   FAITH   IN

τῷ   Ἰσραὴλ   εὗρον⌝.   **8.11** λέγω   δὲ   ὑμῖν   ὅτι   πολλοὶ
-    ISRAEL   I HAVE FOUND.   AND~I SAY   TO YOU°   THAT   MANY

ἀπὸ   ἀνατολῶν   καὶ   δυσμῶν   ἥξουσιν   καὶ   ἀνακλιθήσονται
FROM   EAST   AND   WEST   WILL COME   AND   WILL RECLINE AT TABLE

μετὰ   Ἀβραὰμ   καὶ   Ἰσαὰκ   καὶ   Ἰακὼβ   ἐν   τῇ   βασιλείᾳ
WITH   ABRAHAM   AND   ISAAC   AND   JACOB   IN   THE   KINGDOM

τῶν   οὐρανῶν,   **8.12** οἱ   δὲ   υἱοὶ   τῆς   βασιλείας
OF THE   HEAVENS,   BUT~THE   SONS   OF THE   KINGDOM

ἐκβληθήσονται   εἰς   τὸ   σκότος   τὸ   ἐξώτερον·   ἐκεῖ   ἔσται
WILL BE THROWN OUT   INTO   THE   ²DARKNESS -   ¹EXTREME.   THERE   WILL BE

ὁ   κλαυθμὸς   καὶ   ὁ   βρυγμὸς   τῶν   ὀδόντων.   **8.13** καὶ
-   WEEPING   AND   -   GRINDING   OF THE   TEETH.   AND

εἶπεν   ὁ   Ἰησοῦς   τῷ   ἑκατοντάρχῃ,   Ὕπαγε,   ὡς
SAID   -   JESUS   TO THE   CENTURION,   GO,   AS

ἐπίστευσας   γενηθήτω   σοι.   καὶ   ἰάθη   ὁ   παῖς
YOU BELIEVED   LET IT BE   FOR YOU.   AND   WAS HEALED   THE   CHILD

[αὐτοῦ]   ἐν   τῇ   ὥρᾳ   ἐκείνῃ.
OF HIM   AT   -   THAT~HOUR.

8.14 Καὶ   ἐλθὼν   ὁ   Ἰησοῦς   εἰς   τὴν   οἰκίαν   Πέτρου   εἶδεν
   AND   COMING   -   JESUS   INTO   THE   HOUSE   OF PETER,   HE SAW

τὴν   πενθερὰν   αὐτοῦ   βεβλημένην   καὶ   πυρέσσουσαν·
THE   MOTHER-IN-LAW   OF HIM   HAVING BEEN BEDRIDDEN   AND   FEVER-STRICKEN.

8.15 καὶ   ἥψατο   τῆς   χειρὸς   αὐτῆς,   καὶ   ἀφῆκεν   αὐτὴν
   AND   HE TOUCHED   THE   HAND   OF HER,   AND   LEFT   HER

ὁ   πυρετός,   καὶ   ἠγέρθη   καὶ   διηκόνει   αὐτῷ.
THE   FEVER,   AND   SHE AROSE   AND   WAS SERVING   HIM.

8.16 Ὀψίας   δὲ   γενομένης   προσήνεγκαν   αὐτῷ
   AND~[WHEN] EVENING HAD COME   THEY BROUGHT   TO HIM

δαιμονιζομένους   πολλούς·   καὶ   ἐξέβαλεν   τὰ   πνεύματα
MANY~DEMON-POSSESSED [PEOPLE].   AND   HE CAST OUT   THE   SPIRITS

8:10 text: ASVmg RSVmg NASB NIV TEV NJB NRSV.   var. ουδε εν τω Ισραηλ τοσαυτην πιστιν ευρον (not even in Israel I found such faith) [see Luke 7:9]: KJV ASV RSV NASBmg NEB NRSVmg.

λόγῳ   καὶ πάντας τοὺς   κακῶς ἔχοντας ἐθεράπευσεν,
WITH A WORD, AND   ALL   THE ONES ILLNESS HAVING   HE HEALED.

8.17 ὅπως πληρωθῇ τὸ   ῥηθὲν διὰ Ἡσαΐου τοῦ
THUS   WAS FULFILLED THE [THING] SPOKEN THROUGH ISAIAH   THE

προφήτου λέγοντος,
PROPHET   SAYING,

Αὐτὸς τὰς ἀσθενείας ἡμῶν ἔλαβεν
HE   THE   WEAKNESSES   OF US   TOOK

καὶ τὰς νόσους   ἐβάστασεν.
AND THE   DISEASES [OF US] HE REMOVED.

8.18 Ἰδὼν δὲ ὁ Ἰησοῦς ὄχλον περὶ αὐτὸν ἐκέλευσεν
³SEEING ¹AND - ²JESUS A CROWD AROUND HIM   COMMANDED

ἀπελθεῖν εἰς τὸ πέραν. **8.19** καὶ προσελθὼν εἷς
TO GO   TO   THE OTHER SIDE.   AND   HAVING APPROACHED ONE

γραμματεὺς εἶπεν αὐτῷ, Διδάσκαλε, ἀκολουθήσω σοι
SCRIBE   SAID   TO HIM, TEACHER,   I WILL FOLLOW   YOU

ὅπου ἐὰν ἀπέρχῃ. **8.20** καὶ λέγει αὐτῷ ὁ Ἰησοῦς, Αἱ
WHEREVER YOU GO.   AND   SAYS   TO HIM - JESUS,   THE

ἀλώπεκες φωλεοὺς ἔχουσιν καὶ τὰ πετεινὰ τοῦ οὐρανοῦ
FOXES   HAVE~HOLES   AND THE BIRDS   -   OF HEAVEN,

κατασκηνώσεις, ὁ δὲ υἱὸς τοῦ ἀνθρώπου οὐκ ἔχει
NESTS,   BUT~THE SON - OF MAN   DOES NOT HAVE [A PLACE]

ποῦ τὴν κεφαλὴν κλίνῃ. **8.21** ἕτερος δὲ τῶν μαθητῶν
WHERE THE(HIS) HEAD   HE MAY LAY.   AND~ANOTHER OF THE DISCIPLES

[αὐτοῦ] εἶπεν αὐτῷ, Κύριε, ἐπίτρεψόν μοι πρῶτον
OF HIM   SAID   TO HIM, LORD,   ALLOW   ME   FIRST

ἀπελθεῖν καὶ θάψαι τὸν πατέρα μου. **8.22** ὁ δὲ
TO GO   AND BURY   THE FATHER OF ME.   - BUT

Ἰησοῦς λέγει αὐτῷ, Ἀκολούθει μοι καὶ ἄφες τοὺς
JESUS   SAYS   TO HIM, FOLLOW   ME   AND PERMIT THE

νεκροὺς θάψαι τοὺς ἑαυτῶν νεκρούς.
DEAD   TO BURY THE   DEAD~OF THEMSELVES.

8.23 Καὶ ἐμβάντι αὐτῷ εἰς τὸ πλοῖον ἠκολούθησαν
AND   HE~HAVING EMBARKED INTO THE BOAT,   FOLLOWED

αὐτῷ οἱ μαθηταὶ αὐτοῦ. **8.24** καὶ ἰδοὺ σεισμὸς μέγας
HIM   THE DISCIPLES OF HIM.   AND   BEHOLD A GREAT~STORM

ἐγένετο ἐν τῇ θαλάσσῃ, ὥστε τὸ πλοῖον
CAME ABOUT ON THE LAKE,   SO THAT THE BOAT

καλύπτεσθαι ὑπὸ τῶν κυμάτων, αὐτὸς δὲ ἐκάθευδεν.
[WAS ABOUT] TO BE COVERED BY THE WAVES,   BUT~HE   WAS SLEEPING.

8.25 καὶ προσελθόντες ἤγειραν αὐτὸν λέγοντες, Κύριε,
AND   HAVING APPROACHED THEY AROUSED HIM   SAYING,   LORD,

σῶσον, ἀπολλύμεθα. **8.26** καὶ λέγει αὐτοῖς, Τί
SAVE [US], WE ARE PERISHING.   AND   HE SAYS TO THEM, WHY

δειλοί ἐστε, ὀλιγόπιστοι; τότε ἐγερθεὶς ἐπετίμησεν
ARE YOU°~FEARFUL, ONES OF LITTLE FAITH? THEN ARISING   HE REBUKED

with a word, and cured all who were sick. ¹⁷This was to fulfill what had been spoken through the prophet Isaiah, "He took our infirmities and bore our diseases."

18 Now when Jesus saw great crowds around him, he gave orders to go over to the other side. ¹⁹A scribe then approached and said, "Teacher, I will follow you wherever you go." ²⁰And Jesus said to him, "Foxes have holes, and birds of the air have nests; but the Son of Man has nowhere to lay his head." ²¹Another of his disciples said to him, "Lord, first let me go and bury my father." ²²But Jesus said to him, "Follow me, and let the dead bury their own dead."

23 And when he got into the boat, his disciples followed him. ²⁴A windstorm arose on the sea, so great that the boat was being swamped by the waves; but he was asleep. ²⁵And they went and woke him up, saying, "Lord, save us! We are perishing!" ²⁶And he said to them, "Why are you afraid, you of little faith?" Then he got up and rebuked

8:17 Isa. 53:4

the winds and the sea; and there was a dead calm. [27]They were amazed, saying, "What sort of man is this, that even the winds and the sea obey him?"

28 When he came to the other side, to the country of the Gadarenes,[b] two demoniacs coming out of the tombs met him. They were so fierce that no one could pass that way. [29]Suddenly they shouted, "What have you to do with us, Son of God? Have you come here to torment us before the time?" [30]Now a large herd of swine was feeding at some distance from them. [31]The demons begged him, "If you cast us out, send us into the herd of swine." [32]And he said to them, "Go!" So they came out and entered the swine; and suddenly, the whole herd rushed down the steep bank into the sea and perished in the water. [33]The swineherds ran off, and on going into the town, they told the whole story about what had happened to the demoniacs. [34]Then the whole town came out to meet Jesus; and when they saw him, they begged him to leave their neighborhood.

[b] Other ancient authorities read Gergesenes; others, Gerasenes

τοῖς ἀνέμοις καὶ τῇ θαλάσσῃ, καὶ ἐγένετο
THE WINDS AND THE LAKE, AND THERE WAS

γαλήνη μεγάλη. **8.27** οἱ δὲ ἄνθρωποι ἐθαύμασαν
GREAT~CALM. AND~THE MEN WERE AMAZED

λέγοντες, Ποταπός ἐστιν οὗτος ὅτι καὶ οἱ ἄνεμοι
SAYING, OF WHAT SORT IS THIS [MAN] THAT EVEN THE WINDS

καὶ ἡ θάλασσα αὐτῷ ὑπακούουσιν;
AND THE LAKE OBEY~HIM?

8.28 Καὶ ἐλθόντος αὐτοῦ εἰς τὸ πέραν εἰς τὴν χώραν
AND HE~HAVING COME TO THE OTHER SIDE TO THE COUNTRY

τῶν ⌜Γαδαρηνῶν⌝ ὑπήντησαν αὐτῷ δύο δαιμονιζόμενοι
OF THE GADARENES, MET HIM TWO DEMON-POSSESSED [MEN]

ἐκ τῶν μνημείων ἐξερχόμενοι, χαλεποὶ λίαν, ὥστε
OUT OF THE TOMBS COMING OUT [WHO WERE] VERY~DANGEROUS, SO THAT

μὴ ἰσχύειν τινὰ παρελθεῖν διὰ τῆς ὁδοῦ ἐκείνης.
SOME~WERE NOT ABLE TO PASS BY THROUGH - THAT~WAY.

8.29 καὶ ἰδοὺ ἔκραξαν λέγοντες, Τί ἡμῖν καὶ σοί,
AND BEHOLD THEY CALLED OUT SAYING, WHAT TO US AND TO YOU,

υἱὲ τοῦ θεοῦ; ἦλθες ὧδε πρὸ καιροῦ βασανίσαι
SON - OF GOD? HAVE YOU COME HERE BEFORE [THE] TIME TO TORTURE

ἡμᾶς; **8.30** ἦν δὲ μακρὰν ἀπ᾽ αὐτῶν ἀγέλη
US? NOW~THERE WAS FAR AWAY FROM THEM A HERD

χοίρων πολλῶν βοσκομένη. **8.31** οἱ δὲ δαίμονες
OF MANY~PIGS FEEDING. AND~THE DEMONS

παρεκάλουν αὐτὸν λέγοντες, Εἰ ἐκβάλλεις ἡμᾶς,
BEGGED HIM SAYING, IF YOU CAST OUT US,

ἀπόστειλον ἡμᾶς εἰς τὴν ἀγέλην τῶν χοίρων. **8.32** καὶ
SEND US INTO THE HERD - OF PIGS. AND

εἶπεν αὐτοῖς, Ὑπάγετε. οἱ δὲ ἐξελθόντες ἀπῆλθον
HE SAID TO THEM, GO AWAY. SO~THE ONES COMING OUT WENT AWAY

εἰς τοὺς χοίρους· καὶ ἰδοὺ ὥρμησεν πᾶσα ἡ ἀγέλη
INTO THE PIGS. AND BEHOLD RUSHED ALL THE HERD

κατὰ τοῦ κρημνοῦ εἰς τὴν θάλασσαν καὶ ἀπέθανον ἐν
DOWN THE BANK INTO THE LAKE AND THEY DIED IN

τοῖς ὕδασιν. **8.33** οἱ δὲ βόσκοντες ἔφυγον, καὶ
THE WATERS. BUT~THE ONES FEEDING FLED, AND

ἀπελθόντες εἰς τὴν πόλιν ἀπήγγειλαν πάντα καὶ
HAVING GONE AWAY INTO THE CITY, THEY REPORTED EVERYTHING AND

τὰ τῶν δαιμονιζομένων. **8.34** καὶ ἰδοὺ πᾶσα
THE [THINGS] OF THE ONES DEMON-POSSESSED. AND BEHOLD ALL

ἡ πόλις ἐξῆλθεν εἰς ὑπάντησιν τῷ Ἰησοῦ, καὶ
THE CITY CAME OUT TO A MEETING - WITH JESUS, AND

ἰδόντες αὐτὸν παρεκάλεσαν ὅπως μεταβῇ ἀπὸ τῶν
SEEING HIM THEY BEGGED THAT HE MIGHT PASS OVER FROM THE

ὁρίων αὐτῶν.
BOUNDARIES OF THEM.

8:28 text [see Mark 5:1; Luke 8:26]: ASV RSV NASB NIV NEB TEV NJB NRSV. var. Γεργεσηνων (Gergesenes) KJV RSVmg NIVmg NJBmg NRSVmg. var. Γερασηνων (Gerasenes): RSVmg NIVmg NJBmg NRSVmg.

9.1 Καὶ   ἐμβὰς   εἰς πλοῖον διεπέρασεν καὶ   ἦλθεν
AND   HAVING EMBARKED INTO A BOAT   HE CROSSED OVER AND   CAME

εἰς τὴν   ἰδίαν πόλιν. **9.2** καὶ ἰδοὺ προσέφερον αὐτῷ
INTO THE(HIS) OWN CITY.   AND BEHOLD THEY BROUGHT TO HIM

παραλυτικὸν ἐπὶ κλίνης βεβλημένον. καὶ ἰδὼν   ὁ
A PARALYTIC   UPON A STRETCHER LYING.   AND   HAVING SEEN -

Ἰησοῦς τὴν πίστιν αὐτῶν εἶπεν τῷ   παραλυτικῷ,
JESUS   THE FAITH OF THEM, HE SAID TO THE PARALYTIC,

Θάρσει, τέκνον, ἀφίενταί σου αἱ ἁμαρτίαι. **9.3** καὶ
CHEER UP, CHILD, ARE FORGIVEN OF YOU THE SINS.   AND

ἰδού τινες τῶν γραμματέων εἶπαν ἐν   ἑαυτοῖς, Οὗτος
BEHOLD SOME OF THE SCRIBES   SAID AMONG THEMSELVES, THIS ONE

βλασφημεῖ. **9.4** καὶ ἰδὼν   ὁ Ἰησοῦς τὰς ἐνθυμήσεις
BLASPHEMES.   AND HAVING SEEN - JESUS THE THOUGHTS

αὐτῶν εἶπεν, Ἰνατί ἐνθυμεῖσθε πονηρὰ ἐν ταῖς
OF THEM SAID, WHY ARE YOU° THINKING EVIL   IN THE

καρδίαις ὑμῶν; **9.5** τί γάρ ἐστιν εὐκοπώτερον, εἰπεῖν,
HEARTS   OF YOU°?   FOR~WHICH IS EASIER   TO SAY,

Ἀφίενταί σου αἱ ἁμαρτίαι, ἢ εἰπεῖν, Ἔγειρε καὶ
ARE FORGIVEN OF YOU THE SINS, OR TO SAY, RISE UP   AND

περιπάτει; **9.6** ἵνα δὲ   εἰδῆτε   ὅτι ἐξουσίαν ἔχει
WALK?   BUT~IN ORDER THAT YOU° MAY KNOW THAT AUTHORITY HAS

ὁ υἱὸς τοῦ ἀνθρώπου ἐπὶ τῆς γῆς ἀφιέναι
THE SON - OF MAN   ON - EARTH TO FORGIVE

ἁμαρτίας—τότε λέγει τῷ   παραλυτικῷ, Ἐγερθεὶς ἆρόν
SINS—THEN   HE SAID TO THE PARALYTIC,   RISING UP, TAKE

σου τὴν κλίνην καὶ ὕπαγε εἰς τὸν οἶκόν σου.
OF YOU THE STRETCHER AND GO TO THE HOUSE OF YOU.

9.7 καὶ ἐγερθεὶς ἀπῆλθεν εἰς τὸν οἶκον αὐτοῦ.
AND RISING UP HE WENT AWAY TO THE HOUSE OF HIM.

9.8 ἰδόντες δὲ   οἱ ὄχλοι ἐφοβήθησαν καὶ   ἐδόξασαν
AND~HAVING SEEN [THIS], THE CROWDS WERE AFRAID AND   GLORIFIED

τὸν θεὸν τὸν   δόντα   ἐξουσίαν τοιαύτην τοῖς
-   GOD, THE ONE HAVING GIVEN SUCH~AUTHORITY -

ἀνθρώποις.
TO MEN.

9.9 Καὶ   παράγων ὁ Ἰησοῦς ἐκεῖθεν εἶδεν ἄνθρωπον
AND   GOING AWAY - ²JESUS ¹FROM THERE ³SAW A MAN

καθήμενον ἐπὶ τὸ τελώνιον, Μαθθαῖον λεγόμενον, καὶ
SITTING   IN   THE TAX OFFICE, BEING CALLED~MATTHEW, AND

λέγει αὐτῷ, Ἀκολούθει μοι. καὶ ἀναστὰς ἠκολούθησεν
HE SAYS TO HIM, FOLLOW ME.   AND RISING HE FOLLOWED

αὐτῷ. **9.10** Καὶ ἐγένετο   αὐτοῦ ἀνακειμένου ἐν
HIM.   AND IT CAME ABOUT [WHILE] HE WAS RECLINING AT TABLE IN

τῇ οἰκίᾳ, καὶ ἰδοὺ πολλοὶ τελῶναι   καὶ ἁμαρτωλοὶ
THE HOUSE, AND BEHOLD MANY   TAX COLLECTORS AND SINNERS

And after getting into a boat he crossed the sea and came to his own town.

2 And just then some people were carrying a paralyzed man lying on a bed. When Jesus saw their faith, he said to the paralytic, "Take heart, son; your sins are forgiven." [3]Then some of the scribes said to themselves, "This man is blaspheming." [4]But Jesus, perceiving their thoughts, said, "Why do you think evil in your hearts? [5]For which is easier, to say, 'Your sins are forgiven,' or to say, 'Stand up and walk'? [6]But so that you may know that the Son of Man has authority on earth to forgive sins"—he then said to the paralytic— "Stand up, take your bed and go to your home." [7]And he stood up and went to his home. [8]When the crowds saw it, they were filled with awe, and they glorified God, who had given such authority to human beings.

9 As Jesus was walking along, he saw a man called Matthew sitting at the tax booth; and he said to him, "Follow me." And he got up and followed him.

10 And as he sat at dinner[c] in the house, many tax collectors and sinners

[c] Gk *reclined*

came and were sitting*d* with him and his disciples. ¹¹When the Pharisees saw this, they said to his disciples, "Why does your teacher eat with tax collectors and sinners?" ¹²But when he heard this, he said, "Those who are well have no need of a physician, but those who are sick. ¹³Go and learn what this means, 'I desire mercy, not sacrifice.' For I have come to call not the righteous but sinners."

14 Then the disciples of John came to him, saying, "Why do we and the Pharisees fast often,*e* but your disciples do not fast?" ¹⁵And Jesus said to them, "The wedding guests cannot mourn as long as the bridegroom is with them, can they? The days will come when the bridegroom is taken away from them, and then they will fast. ¹⁶No one sews a piece of unshrunk cloth on an old cloak, for the patch pulls away from the cloak, and a worse tear is made. ¹⁷Neither is new wine put into old wineskins; otherwise, the skins burst, and the wine is spilled, and the skins are destroyed; but new wine is put

d Gk *were reclining*
e Other ancient authorities lack *often*

ἐλθόντες συνανέκειντο τῷ Ἰησοῦ καὶ τοῖς μαθηταῖς
HAVING COME   RECLINED AT TABLE WITH -   JESUS   AND   WITH THE   DISCIPLES

αὐτοῦ. 9.11 καὶ ἰδόντες οἱ Φαρισαῖοι ἔλεγον τοῖς
OF HIM.   AND HAVING SEEN [THIS] THE PHARISEES WERE SAYING TO THE

μαθηταῖς αὐτοῦ, Διὰ τί μετὰ τῶν τελωνῶν καὶ
DISCIPLES   OF HIM,   WHY WITH - TAX COLLECTORS AND

ἁμαρτωλῶν ἐσθίει ὁ διδάσκαλος ὑμῶν; 9.12 ὁ δὲ
SINNERS   EATS   THE   TEACHER   OF YOU°?   BUT~THE ONE

ἀκούσας εἶπεν, Οὐ χρείαν ἔχουσιν οἱ ἰσχύοντες
HAVING HEARD SAID,   NO NEED HAVE THE ONES BEING STRONG

ἰατροῦ ἀλλ᾽ οἱ κακῶς ἔχοντες. 9.13 πορευθέντες δὲ
OF A PHYSICIAN BUT THE ONES HAVING~ILLNESS.   BUT~GOING

μάθετε τί ἐστιν, Ἔλεος θέλω καὶ οὐ
LEARN   WHAT IS [THE MEANING OF THIS], I DESIRE~MERCY AND NOT

θυσίαν· οὐ γὰρ ἦλθον καλέσαι δικαίους ἀλλὰ
SACRIFICE.   FOR~I HAVE NOT COME TO CALL [THE] RIGHTEOUS, BUT

ἁμαρτωλούς.
SINNERS.

9.14 Τότε προσέρχονται αὐτῷ οἱ μαθηταὶ Ἰωάννου
THEN APPROACHED HIM THE DISCIPLES OF JOHN

λέγοντες, Διὰ τί ἡμεῖς καὶ οἱ Φαρισαῖοι νηστεύομεν
SAYING,   WHY [DO] WE AND THE PHARISEES FAST

[πολλά], οἱ δὲ μαθηταί σου οὐ νηστεύουσιν; 9.15 καὶ
OFTEN,   BUT~THE DISCIPLES OF YOU DO NOT FAST?   AND

εἶπεν αὐτοῖς ὁ Ἰησοῦς, Μὴ δύνανται οἱ
SAID TO THEM - JESUS, ³ARE NOT ABLE ¹[SURELY] THE

υἱοὶ τοῦ νυμφῶνος πενθεῖν ἐφ᾽ ὅσον μετ᾽ αὐτῶν
²SONS (RELATIVES) FOR THE BRIDEGROOM TO MOURN AS LONG AS WITH THEM

ἐστιν ὁ νυμφίος; ἐλεύσονται δὲ ἡμέραι ὅταν ἀπαρθῇ
IS THE BRIDEGROOM? BUT~WILL COME DAYS WHEN IS TAKEN AWAY

ἀπ᾽ αὐτῶν ὁ νυμφίος, καὶ τότε νηστεύσουσιν.
FROM THEM THE BRIDEGROOM, AND THEN THEY WILL FAST.

9.16 οὐδεὶς δὲ ἐπιβάλλει ἐπίβλημα ῥάκους ἀγνάφου ἐπὶ
BUT~NO ONE SEWS A PATCH OF UNSHRUNK~CLOTH ON

ἱματίῳ παλαιῷ· αἴρει γὰρ τὸ πλήρωμα αὐτοῦ ἀπὸ
AN OLD~GARMENT. FOR~IT TAKES AWAY THE FULLNESS OF IT FROM

τοῦ ἱματίου καὶ χεῖρον σχίσμα γίνεται. 9.17 οὐδὲ
THE GARMENT, AND A WORSE TEAR RESULTS.   NO ONE

βάλλουσιν οἶνον νέον εἰς ἀσκοὺς παλαιούς·
PUTS   NEW~WINE   INTO OLD~WINESKINS.

εἰ δὲ μή γε, ῥήγνυνται οἱ ἀσκοὶ καὶ ὁ οἶνος
OTHERWISE,   ARE TORN THE WINESKINS AND THE WINE

ἐκχεῖται καὶ οἱ ἀσκοὶ ἀπόλλυνται· ἀλλὰ βάλλουσιν
IS POURED OUT AND THE WINESKINS ARE RUINED.   BUT THEY POUR

9:13 Hos. 6:6

οἶνον νέον εἰς ἀσκοὺς καινούς, καὶ ἀμφότεροι
NEW WINE   INTO FRESH~WINESKINS,   AND   BOTH

συντηροῦνται.
ARE PRESERVED.

9.18 Ταῦτα αὐτοῦ λαλοῦντος   αὐτοῖς ἰδοὺ ἄρχων εἷς
[WHILE] HE WAS SPEAKING~THESE THINGS TO THEM BEHOLD ONE~RULER

ἐλθὼν προσεκύνει αὐτῷ λέγων ὅτι Ἡ θυγάτηρ μου
COMING WORSHIPED   HIM   SAYING   -   THE DAUGHTER OF ME

ἄρτι ἐτελεύτησεν· ἀλλὰ ἐλθὼν ἐπίθες τὴν χεῖρά σου
DIED~JUST NOW;   BUT   COMING LAY   THE HAND OF YOU

ἐπ᾽ αὐτήν, καὶ ζήσεται. **9.19** καὶ ἐγερθεὶς ὁ Ἰησοῦς
UPON HER,   AND SHE WILL LIVE.   AND   HAVING ARISEN - JESUS

ἠκολούθησεν αὐτῷ καὶ οἱ μαθηταὶ αὐτοῦ. **9.20** Καὶ
FOLLOWED   HIM   ALSO THE DISCIPLES OF HIM.   AND

ἰδοὺ γυνὴ αἱμορροοῦσα δώδεκα ἔτη προσελθοῦσα
BEHOLD A WOMAN HEMORRHAGING TWELVE YEARS HAVING APPROACHED

ὄπισθεν ἥψατο τοῦ κρασπέδου τοῦ ἱματίου αὐτοῦ·
BEHIND   TOUCHED THE EDGE   OF THE GARMENT OF HIM.

9.21 ἔλεγεν γὰρ ἐν ἑαυτῇ, Ἐὰν μόνον ἅψωμαι τοῦ
FOR~SHE WAS SAYING TO HERSELF, IF   ONLY   I MIGHT TOUCH THE

ἱματίου αὐτοῦ σωθήσομαι. **9.22** ὁ δὲ Ἰησοῦς στραφεὶς
GARMENT   OF HIM I WILL BE HEALED.   - AND JESUS   TURNING

καὶ ἰδὼν αὐτὴν εἶπεν, Θάρσει, θύγατερ· ἡ πίστις
AND SEEING HER   SAID, CHEER UP, DAUGHTER; THE FAITH

σου σέσωκέν σε. καὶ ἐσώθη ἡ γυνὴ ἀπὸ τῆς
OF YOU HAS HEALED YOU. AND WAS HEALED THE WOMAN FROM -

ὥρας ἐκείνης. **9.23** Καὶ ἐλθὼν ὁ Ἰησοῦς εἰς τὴν
THAT~HOUR.   AND   HAVING COME - JESUS   INTO THE

οἰκίαν τοῦ ἄρχοντος καὶ ἰδὼν τοὺς αὐλητὰς καὶ
HOUSE   OF THE RULER   AND HAVING SEEN THE FLUTE PLAYERS AND

τὸν ὄχλον θορυβούμενον **9.24** ἔλεγεν, Ἀναχωρεῖτε,
THE DISORDERLY~CROWD   HE WAS SAYING, GO AWAY,

οὐ γὰρ ἀπέθανεν τὸ κοράσιον ἀλλὰ καθεύδει. καὶ
FOR~NOT DIED   THE GIRL   BUT   SHE SLEEPS. AND

κατεγέλων αὐτοῦ. **9.25** ὅτε δὲ ἐξεβλήθη ὁ ὄχλος
THEY WERE RIDICULING HIM.   BUT~WHEN WAS PUT OUT THE CROWD,

εἰσελθὼν ἐκράτησεν τῆς χειρὸς αὐτῆς, καὶ ἠγέρθη τὸ
HAVING ENTERED HE GRASPED THE HAND OF HER, AND WAS RAISED THE

κοράσιον. **9.26** καὶ ἐξῆλθεν ἡ φήμη αὕτη εἰς ὅλην τὴν
GIRL.   AND WENT OUT - THIS~REPORT INTO ALL   -

γῆν ἐκείνην.
THAT~REGION.

9.27 Καὶ παράγοντι ἐκεῖθεν τῷ Ἰησοῦ ἠκολούθησαν
AND   ²GOING AWAY ³FROM THERE - ¹JESUS FOLLOWED

[αὐτῷ] δύο τυφλοὶ κράζοντες καὶ λέγοντες, Ἐλέησον
HIM   TWO BLIND [MEN] CRYING OUT AND SAYING, HAVE MERCY

into fresh wineskins, and so both are preserved."

18 While he was saying these things to them, suddenly a leader of the synagogue⨍ came in and knelt before him, saying, "My daughter has just died; but come and lay your hand on her, and she will live." [19]And Jesus got up and followed him, with his disciples. [20]Then suddenly a woman who had been suffering from hemorrhages for twelve years came up behind him and touched the fringe of his cloak, [21]for she said to herself, "If I only touch his cloak, I will be made well." [22]Jesus turned, and seeing her he said, "Take heart, daughter; your faith has made you well." And instantly the woman was made well. [23]When Jesus came to the leader's house and saw the flute players and the crowd making a commotion, [24]he said, "Go away; for the girl is not dead but sleeping." And they laughed at him. [25]But when the crowd had been put outside, he went in and took her by the hand, and the girl got up. [26]And the report of this spread throughout that district.

27 As Jesus went on from there, two blind men followed him, crying loudly, "Have mercy

⨍ Gk lacks *of the synagogue*

on us, Son of David!"
28When he entered the
house, the blind men came
to him; and Jesus said to
them, "Do you believe that I
am able to do this?" They
said to him, "Yes, Lord."
29Then he touched their eyes
and said, "According to your
faith let it be done to you."
30And their eyes were
opened. Then Jesus sternly
ordered them, "See that no
one knows of this." 31But
they went away and spread
the news about him
throughout that district.

32 After they had gone
away, a demoniac who was
mute was brought to him.
33And when the demon had
been cast out, the one who
had been mute spoke; and
the crowds were amazed and
said, "Never has anything
like this been seen in Israel."
34But the Pharisees said,
"By the ruler of the demons
he casts out the demons."g

35 Then Jesus went about
all the cities and villages,
teaching in their syna-
gogues, and proclaiming the
good news of the kingdom,
and curing every disease and
every sickness. 36When he
saw the crowds, he had
compassion for them,
because they were harassed
and helpless, like sheep
without a shepherd. 37Then
he said to his disciples, "The
harvest is plentiful, but the
laborers are few;

g Other ancient authorities lack this
  verse

ἡμᾶς, υἱὸς Δαυίδ. **9.28** ἐλθόντι δὲ εἰς τὴν οἰκίαν
[ON] US, SON OF DAVID.   AND~HAVING COME INTO THE HOUSE,

προσῆλθον αὐτῷ οἱ τυφλοί, καὶ λέγει αὐτοῖς ὁ
APPROACHED HIM THE BLIND [MEN], AND SAYS TO THEM -

Ἰησοῦς, Πιστεύετε ὅτι δύναμαι τοῦτο ποιῆσαι;
JESUS,   DO YOU° BELIEVE THAT I AM ABLE TO DO~THIS?

λέγουσιν αὐτῷ, Ναί κύριε. **9.29** τότε ἥψατο τῶν
THEY SAY TO HIM, YES, LORD.   THEN HE TOUCHED THE

ὀφθαλμῶν αὐτῶν λέγων, Κατὰ τὴν πίστιν ὑμῶν
EYES   OF THEM SAYING, ACCORDING TO THE FAITH OF YOU°

γενηθήτω ὑμῖν. **9.30** καὶ ἠνεῴχθησαν αὐτῶν οἱ
LET IT BE DONE TO YOU°. AND WERE OPENED THEIR -

ὀφθαλμοί. καὶ ἐνεβριμήθη αὐτοῖς ὁ Ἰησοῦς λέγων,
EYES.   AND STERNLY WARNED THEM - JESUS SAYING,

Ὁρᾶτε μηδεὶς γινωσκέτω. **9.31** οἱ δὲ ἐξελθόντες
TAKE CARE, LET NO ONE KNOW.   BUT~THE ONES HAVING GONE OUT

διεφήμισαν αὐτὸν ἐν ὅλῃ τῇ γῇ ἐκείνῃ.
MADE HIM KNOWN   IN ²ENTIRE - ³REGION ¹THAT.

9.32 Αὐτῶν δὲ ἐξερχομένων ἰδοὺ προσήνεγκαν αὐτῷ
AND~THEY GOING OUT, BEHOLD THEY BROUGHT TO HIM

ἄνθρωπον κωφὸν δαιμονιζόμενον. **9.33** καὶ ἐκβληθέντος
A MUTE~MAN   BEING DEMON-POSSESSED.   AND CASTING OUT

τοῦ δαιμονίου ἐλάλησεν ὁ κωφός. καὶ ἐθαύμασαν
THE DEMONS,   SPOKE   THE MUTE [MAN]. AND WERE AMAZED

οἱ ὄχλοι λέγοντες, Οὐδέποτε ἐφάνη οὕτως ἐν τῷ
THE CROWDS SAYING, NEVER HAPPENED THUS IN -

Ἰσραήλ. ⌐**9.34** οἱ δὲ Φαρισαῖοι ἔλεγον, Ἐν τῷ
ISRAEL.   BUT~THE PHARISEES WERE SAYING, BY THE

ἄρχοντι τῶν δαιμονίων ἐκβάλλει τὰ δαιμόνια.⌐
RULER   OF THE DEMONS HE CASTS OUT - DEMONS.

9.35 Καὶ περιῆγεν ὁ Ἰησοῦς τὰς πόλεις πάσας
AND WENT ABOUT - JESUS [THROUGH] ²THE ³CITIES ¹ALL

καὶ τὰς κώμας διδάσκων ἐν ταῖς συναγωγαῖς αὐτῶν
AND THE VILLAGES TEACHING IN THE SYNAGOGUES OF THEM

καὶ κηρύσσων τὸ εὐαγγέλιον τῆς βασιλείας καὶ
AND PREACHING THE GOOD NEWS OF THE KINGDOM AND

θεραπεύων πᾶσαν νόσον καὶ πᾶσαν μαλακίαν.
HEALING   EVERY DISEASE AND EVERY ILLNESS.

9.36 Ἰδὼν δὲ τοὺς ὄχλους ἐσπλαγχνίσθη περὶ αὐτῶν,
AND~HAVING SEEN THE CROWDS, HE FELT SYMPATHY FOR THEM,

ὅτι ἦσαν ἐσκυλμένοι καὶ ἐρριμμένοι ὡσεὶ πρόβατα
FOR THEY WERE DISTRESSED AND WEARY AS SHEEP

μὴ ἔχοντα ποιμένα. **9.37** τότε λέγει τοῖς μαθηταῖς
NOT HAVING A SHEPHERD. THEN HE SAYS TO THE DISCIPLES

αὐτοῦ, Ὁ μὲν θερισμὸς πολύς, οἱ δὲ ἐργάται ὀλίγοι·
OF HIM, INDEED~THE HARVEST [IS] GREAT, BUT~THE WORKERS [ARE] FEW.

9:34 text: KJV ASV RSV NASB NIV NEBmg TEV NJB NRSV. omit: RSVmg NEB NJBmg NRSVmg.

9.38 δεήθητε οὖν τοῦ κυρίου τοῦ θερισμοῦ ὅπως
THEREFORE~ASK THE LORD OF THE HARVEST SO THAT

ἐκβάλῃ ἐργάτας εἰς τὸν θερισμὸν αὐτοῦ.
HE MAY SEND OUT WORKERS INTO THE HARVEST OF HIM.

[38]therefore ask the Lord of the harvest to send out laborers into his harvest."

CHAPTER 10

10.1 Καὶ προσκαλεσάμενος τοὺς δώδεκα μαθητὰς
AND SUMMONING THE TWELVE DISCIPLES

αὐτοῦ ἔδωκεν αὐτοῖς ἐξουσίαν πνευμάτων ἀκαθάρτων
OF HIM, HE GAVE TO THEM AUTHORITY [OVER] UNCLEAN~SPIRITS

ὥστε ἐκβάλλειν αὐτὰ καὶ θεραπεύειν πᾶσαν νόσον καὶ
SO AS TO CAST OUT THEM AND TO HEAL EVERY DISEASE AND

πᾶσαν μαλακίαν. **10.2** Τῶν δὲ δώδεκα ἀποστόλων τὰ
EVERY ILLNESS. NOW~OF THE TWELVE APOSTLES THE

ὀνόματά ἐστιν ταῦτα· πρῶτος Σίμων ὁ λεγόμενος
NAMES ARE THESE: FIRST, SIMON, THE ONE BEING CALLED

Πέτρος καὶ Ἀνδρέας ὁ ἀδελφὸς αὐτοῦ, καὶ Ἰάκωβος
PETER AND ANDREW THE BROTHER OF HIM, AND JAMES

ὁ τοῦ Ζεβεδαίου καὶ Ἰωάννης ὁ ἀδελφὸς αὐτοῦ,
THE [SON] - OF ZEBEDEE AND JOHN THE BROTHER OF HIM,

10.3 Φίλιππος καὶ Βαρθολομαῖος, Θωμᾶς καὶ
PHILIP AND BARTHOLOMEW, THOMAS AND

Μαθθαῖος ὁ τελώνης, Ἰάκωβος ὁ τοῦ Ἁλφαίου
MATTHEW, THE TAX COLLECTOR, JAMES THE [SON] - OF ALPHAEUS

καὶ Θαδδαῖος, **10.4** Σίμων ὁ Καναναῖος καὶ Ἰούδας ὁ
AND THADDAEUS, SIMON THE CANANAEAN AND JUDAS -

Ἰσκαριώτης ὁ καὶ παραδοὺς αὐτόν.
ISCARIOT THE ONE ALSO BETRAYING HIM.

10.5 Τούτους τοὺς δώδεκα ἀπέστειλεν ὁ Ἰησοῦς
THESE - TWELVE [2]SENT OUT - [1]JESUS

παραγγείλας αὐτοῖς λέγων, Εἰς ὁδὸν ἐθνῶν
COMMANDING THEM SAYING, IN [THE] WAY OF THE GENTILES

μὴ ἀπέλθητε καὶ εἰς πόλιν Σαμαριτῶν μὴ εἰσέλθητε·
DO NOT GO AND INTO A CITY OF SAMARITANS DO NOT ENTER.

10.6 πορεύεσθε δὲ μᾶλλον πρὸς τὰ πρόβατα τὰ
BUT~GO INSTEAD TO - [3]SHEEP [1]THE

ἀπολωλότα οἴκου Ἰσραήλ. **10.7** πορευόμενοι δὲ
[2]LOST OF [THE] HOUSE OF ISRAEL. AND~[WHILE] GOING

κηρύσσετε λέγοντες ὅτι Ἤγγικεν ἡ βασιλεία τῶν
PREACH SAYING - IS NEAR THE KINGDOM OF THE

οὐρανῶν. **10.8** ἀσθενοῦντας θεραπεύετε, νεκροὺς ἐγείρετε,
HEAVENS. HEAL~[THE] AILING, RAISE~[THE] DEAD,

λεπροὺς καθαρίζετε, δαιμόνια ἐκβάλλετε· δωρεὰν
CLEANSE~[THE] LEPERS, CAST OUT~DEMONS. FREELY

ἐλάβετε, δωρεὰν δότε. **10.9** Μὴ κτήσησθε χρυσὸν μηδὲ
YOU° RECEIVED, FREELY GIVE. DO NOT ACQUIRE GOLD, NOR

Then Jesus[h] summoned his twelve disciples and gave them authority over unclean spirits, to cast them out, and to cure every disease and every sickness. [2]These are the names of the twelve apostles: first, Simon, also known as Peter, and his brother Andrew; James son of Zebedee, and his brother John; [3]Philip and Bartholomew; Thomas and Matthew the tax collector; James son of Alphaeus, and Thaddaeus;[i] [4]Simon the Cananaean, and Judas Iscariot, the one who betrayed him.

5 These twelve Jesus sent out with the following instructions: "Go nowhere among the Gentiles, and enter no town of the Samaritans, [6]but go rather to the lost sheep of the house of Israel. [7]As you go, proclaim the good news, 'The kingdom of heaven has come near.'[j] [8]Cure the sick, raise the dead, cleanse the lepers,[k] cast out demons. You received without payment; give without payment. [9]Take no gold, or

[h] Gk *he*
[i] Other ancient authorities read *Lebbaeus*, or *Lebbaeus called Thaddaeus*
[j] Or *is at hand*
[k] The terms *leper* and *leprosy* can refer to several diseases

silver, or copper in your belts, [10]no bag for your journey, or two tunics, or sandals, or a staff; for laborers deserve their food. [11]Whatever town or village you enter, find out who in it is worthy, and stay there until you leave. [12]As you enter the house, greet it. [13]If the house is worthy, let your peace come upon it; but if it is not worthy, let your peace return to you. [14]If anyone will not welcome you or listen to your words, shake off the dust from your feet as you leave that house or town. [15]Truly I tell you, it will be more tolerable for the land of Sodom and Gomorrah on the day of judgment than for that town.

[16]"See, I am sending you out like sheep into the midst of wolves; so be wise as serpents and innocent as doves. [17]Beware of them, for they will hand you over to councils and flog you in their synagogues; [18]and you will be dragged before governors and kings because of me, as a testimony to them and the Gentiles. [19]When they hand you over, do not worry about how you are to speak or what you are to say;

ἄργυρον μηδὲ χαλκὸν εἰς τὰς ζώνας ὑμῶν, **10.10** μὴ
SILVER   NOR   COPPER IN THE BELTS OF YOU°,   NOR

πήραν εἰς ὁδὸν μηδὲ δύο χιτῶνας μηδὲ ὑποδήματα
A KNAPSACK FOR [THE] ROAD NOR TWO SHIRTS NOR SANDALS,

μηδὲ ῥάβδον· ἄξιος γὰρ ὁ ἐργάτης τῆς τροφῆς
NOR A STAFF. FOR~[IS] WORTHY THE WORKER OF THE FOOD

αὐτοῦ. **10.11** εἰς ἣν δ' ἂν πόλιν ἢ κώμην εἰσέλθητε,
OF HIM.   AND~INTO WHICHEVER CITY OR VILLAGE YOU° ENTER,

ἐξετάσατε τίς ἐν αὐτῇ ἄξιός ἐστιν· κἀκεῖ μείνατε
INQUIRE   WHO IN IT   IS~WORTHY.   AND THERE REMAIN

ἕως ἂν ἐξέλθητε. **10.12** εἰσερχόμενοι δὲ εἰς τὴν οἰκίαν
UNTIL   YOU° LEAVE.   AND~ENTERING   INTO THE HOUSE,

ἀσπάσασθε αὐτήν· **10.13** καὶ ἐὰν μὲν ᾖ ἡ οἰκία
GREET   IT.   AND IF INDEED ³IS ¹THE ²HOUSE

ἀξία, ἐλθάτω ἡ εἰρήνη ὑμῶν ἐπ' αὐτήν, ἐὰν δὲ μὴ ᾖ
WORTHY, LET COME THE PEACE OF YOU° UPON IT; BUT~IF IT IS NOT

ἀξία, ἡ εἰρήνη ὑμῶν πρὸς ὑμᾶς ἐπιστραφήτω.
WORTHY, THE PEACE OF YOU° TO YOU° LET RETURN.

10.14 καὶ ὃς ἂν μὴ δέξηται ὑμᾶς μηδὲ ἀκούσῃ τοὺς
AND WHOEVER DOES NOT RECEIVE YOU° NOR LISTEN TO THE

λόγους ὑμῶν, ἐξερχόμενοι ἔξω τῆς οἰκίας ἢ τῆς
WORDS OF YOU°, GOING OUT OUTSIDE OF THE HOUSE OR -

πόλεως ἐκείνης ἐκτινάξατε τὸν κονιορτὸν τῶν ποδῶν
THAT~CITY,   SHAKE OFF THE DUST OF THE FEET

ὑμῶν. **10.15** ἀμὴν λέγω ὑμῖν, ἀνεκτότερον ἔσται
OF YOU°.   TRULY I SAY TO YOU°, IT WILL BE~MORE TOLERABLE

γῇ Σοδόμων καὶ Γομόρρων ἐν ἡμέρᾳ κρίσεως
[FOR THE] LAND OF SODOM AND GOMORRAH ON [THE] DAY OF JUDGMENT

ἢ τῇ πόλει ἐκείνῃ.
THAN - [FOR] THAT~CITY.

10.16 Ἰδοὺ ἐγὼ ἀποστέλλω ὑμᾶς ὡς πρόβατα ἐν
BEHOLD I SEND YOU° AS SHEEP IN

μέσῳ λύκων· γίνεσθε οὖν φρόνιμοι ὡς οἱ ὄφεις
[THE] MIDST OF WOLVES. THEREFORE~BE WISE AS - SERPENTS

καὶ ἀκέραιοι ὡς αἱ περιστεραί. **10.17** προσέχετε δὲ
AND INNOCENT AS - DOVES.   AND~BEWARE

ἀπὸ τῶν ἀνθρώπων· παραδώσουσιν γὰρ ὑμᾶς εἰς
OF - MEN.   FOR~THEY WILL DELIVER UP YOU° TO

συνέδρια καὶ ἐν ταῖς συναγωγαῖς αὐτῶν
[THE] COUNCILS, AND IN THE SYNAGOGUES OF THEM

μαστιγώσουσιν ὑμᾶς· **10.18** καὶ ἐπὶ ἡγεμόνας δὲ καὶ
THEY WILL SCOURGE YOU°,   AND BEFORE GOVERNORS AND ALSO

βασιλεῖς ἀχθήσεσθε ἕνεκεν ἐμοῦ εἰς μαρτύριον
KINGS   YOU° WILL BE LED FOR [THE] SAKE OF ME AS A TESTIMONY

αὐτοῖς καὶ τοῖς ἔθνεσιν. **10.19** ὅταν δὲ παραδῶσιν
TO THEM AND TO THE GENTILES.   BUT~WHEN THEY DELIVER UP

ὑμᾶς, μὴ μεριμνήσητε πῶς ἢ τί λαλήσητε·
YOU°, DO NOT BE ANXIOUS [ABOUT] HOW OR WHAT YOU° MAY SAY,

δοθήσεται γὰρ ὑμῖν ἐν ἐκείνῃ τῇ ὥρᾳ τί λαλήσητε·
FOR~IT WILL BE GIVEN   TO YOU° IN   THAT   -   HOUR WHAT YOU° MAY SAY.

10.20 οὐ γὰρ ὑμεῖς ἐστε οἱ λαλοῦντες ἀλλὰ τὸ
FOR~NOT YOU°   ARE THE ONES SPEAKING   BUT   THE

πνεῦμα τοῦ πατρὸς ὑμῶν τὸ λαλοῦν ἐν ὑμῖν.
SPIRIT OF THE FATHER OF YOU° [WILL BE] THE ONE SPEAKING IN YOU°.

10.21 παραδώσει δὲ ἀδελφὸς ἀδελφὸν εἰς θάνατον καὶ
³WILL DELIVER UP ¹AND ²BROTHER BROTHER   TO DEATH   AND

πατὴρ   τέκνον, καὶ ἐπαναστήσονται τέκνα
A FATHER [WILL DELIVER UP HIS] CHILD, AND CHILDREN~WILL RISE UP

ἐπὶ   γονεῖς καὶ θανατώσουσιν αὐτούς. **10.22** καὶ
AGAINST [THEIR] PARENTS AND PUT TO DEATH   THEM.   AND

ἔσεσθε μισούμενοι ὑπὸ πάντων διὰ   τὸ ὄνομά
YOU° WILL BE HATED   BY   ALL   ON ACCOUNT OF THE NAME

μου· ὁ δὲ ὑπομείνας εἰς τέλος οὗτος σωθήσεται.
OF ME. BUT~THE ONE HAVING ENDURED TO [THE] END, THIS ONE WILL BE SAVED.

10.23 ὅταν δὲ διώκωσιν ὑμᾶς ἐν τῇ πόλει ταύτῃ,
AND~WHEN THEY PERSECUTE YOU°   IN -   THIS~CITY,

φεύγετε εἰς τὴν ἑτέραν· ἀμὴν γὰρ λέγω ὑμῖν,
FLEE   TO   ANOTHER. FOR~TRULY I SAY TO YOU°,

οὐ μὴ τελέσητε   τὰς πόλεις τοῦ Ἰσραὴλ
YOU° WILL BY NO MEANS FINISH [GOING THROUGH] THE CITIES   -   OF ISRAEL

ἕως ἂν ἔλθῃ ὁ υἱὸς τοῦ ἀνθρώπου.
UNTIL   COMES THE SON   -   OF MAN.

10.24 Οὐκ ἔστιν μαθητὴς ὑπὲρ τὸν διδάσκαλον οὐδὲ
A DISCIPLE~IS NOT   ABOVE THE TEACHER   NEITHER [IS]

δοῦλος ὑπὲρ τὸν κύριον αὐτοῦ. **10.25** ἀρκετὸν τῷ
A SLAVE ABOVE THE MASTER OF HIM.   [IT IS] ENOUGH FOR THE

μαθητῇ ἵνα γένηται ὡς ὁ διδάσκαλος αὐτοῦ καὶ
DISCIPLE THAT HE BE   LIKE THE TEACHER   OF HIM   AND

ὁ δοῦλος ὡς ὁ κύριος αὐτοῦ. εἰ τὸν
[FOR] THE SLAVE [TO BE] LIKE THE MASTER OF HIM. IF THE

οἰκοδεσπότην Βεελζεβοὺλ ἐπεκάλεσαν, πόσῳ μᾶλλον
HOUSE MASTER   THEY CALLED~BEELZEBOUL,   HOW MUCH MORE

τοὺς οἰκιακοὺς   αὐτοῦ.
THE   MEMBERS OF THE HOUSEHOLD OF HIM.

10.26 Μὴ οὖν φοβηθῆτε αὐτούς· οὐδὲν γάρ
THEREFORE,~DO NOT BE AFRAID OF THEM. FOR~NOTHING

ἐστιν κεκαλυμμένον ὃ οὐκ ἀποκαλυφθήσεται καὶ
HAS BEEN VEILED   WHICH WILL NOT BE REVEALED,   AND [NOTHING]

κρυπτὸν ὃ οὐ γνωσθήσεται. **10.27** ὃ λέγω ὑμῖν ἐν
HIDDEN WHICH WILL NOT BE MADE KNOWN.   WHAT I SAY TO YOU° IN

τῇ σκοτίᾳ εἴπατε ἐν τῷ φωτί, καὶ ὃ εἰς τὸ οὖς
THE DARKNESS SPEAK IN THE LIGHT, AND WHAT IN YOUR EAR

ἀκούετε κηρύξατε ἐπὶ τῶν δωμάτων. **10.28** καὶ
YOU° HEAR PREACH   ON   THE HOUSETOPS.   AND

μὴ φοβεῖσθε ἀπὸ τῶν ἀποκτεννόντων τὸ σῶμα, τὴν δὲ
DO NOT BE AFRAID OF   THE ONES KILLING   THE BODY,   BUT~THE

for what you are to say will be given to you at that time; [20]for it is not you who speak, but the Spirit of your Father speaking through you. [21]Brother will betray brother to death, and a father his child, and children will rise against parents and have them put to death; [22]and you will be hated by all because of my name. But the one who endures to the end will be saved. [23]When they persecute you in one town, flee to the next; for truly I tell you, you will not have gone through all the towns of Israel before the Son of Man comes.

24 "A disciple is not above the teacher, nor a slave above the master; [25]it is enough for the disciple to be like the teacher, and the slave like the master. If they have called the master of the house Beelzebul, how much more will they malign those of his household!

26 "So have no fear of them; for nothing is covered up that will not be uncovered, and nothing secret that will not become known. [27]What I say to you in the dark, tell in the light; and what you hear whispered, proclaim from the housetops. [28]Do not fear those who kill the body but

cannot kill the soul; rather fear him who can destroy both soul and body in hell.[l] [29]Are not two sparrows sold for a penny? Yet not one of them will fall to the ground apart from your Father. [30]And even the hairs of your head are all counted. [31]So do not be afraid; you are of more value than many sparrows.

[32] "Everyone therefore who acknowledges me before others, I also will acknowledge before my Father in heaven; [33]but whoever denies me before others, I also will deny before my Father in heaven.

[34] "Do not think that I have come to bring peace to the earth; I have not come to bring peace, but a sword. [35]For I have come to set a man against his father, and a daughter against her mother, and a daughter-in-law against her mother-in-law; [36]and one's foes will be members of one's own household. [37]Whoever loves father or mother more than me

[l] Gk *Gehenna*

ψυχὴν μὴ δυναμένων ἀποκτεῖναι· φοβεῖσθε δὲ μᾶλλον
SOUL   NOT BEING ABLE   TO KILL.   BUT~FEAR   INSTEAD

τὸν δυνάμενον καὶ ψυχὴν καὶ σῶμα ἀπολέσαι ἐν
THE ONE BEING ABLE BOTH SOUL AND BODY TO DESTROY IN

γεέννῃ.   10.29 οὐχὶ δύο στρουθία ἀσσαρίου πωλεῖται;
GEHENNA(HELL).   ARE NOT TWO SPARROWS   SOLD~FOR A PENNY?

καὶ ἓν ἐξ αὐτῶν οὐ πεσεῖται ἐπὶ τὴν γῆν
AND ONE OF THEM WILL NOT FALL   ON THE EARTH

ἄνευ   του πατρὸς ὑμῶν. 10.30 ὑμῶν δὲ καὶ
WITHOUT [THE KNOWLEDGE OF] THE FATHER OF YOU°.   AND~OF YOU° EVEN

αἱ τρίχες τῆς κεφαλῆς πᾶσαι ἠριθμημέναι εἰσίν.
THE HAIRS OF THE HEAD ALL NUMBERED   ARE.

10.31 μὴ οὖν φοβεῖσθε·   πολλῶν στρουθίων διαφέρετε
      THEREFORE,~DO NOT BE AFRAID. ³THAN MANY ⁴SPARROWS ²ARE WORTH MORE

ὑμεῖς.
¹YOU°.

10.32 Πᾶς οὖν   ὅστις ὁμολογήσει ἐν ἐμοὶ
      THEREFORE~EVERYONE WHO · CONFESSES   -   ME

ἔμπροσθεν τῶν ἀνθρώπων, ὁμολογήσω κἀγὼ ἐν αὐτῷ
BEFORE   -   MEN,   I ALSO~WILL CONFESS   -   HIM

ἔμπροσθεν τοῦ πατρός μου τοῦ ἐν [τοῖς] οὐρανοῖς·
BEFORE   THE FATHER OF ME, THE ONE IN THE   HEAVENS.

10.33 ὅστις δ' ἂν ἀρνήσηταί με ἔμπροσθεν τῶν
      AND~WHOEVER WILL DENY ME BEFORE   -

ἀνθρώπων, ἀρνήσομαι κἀγὼ αὐτὸν ἔμπροσθεν τοῦ
MEN,   I ALSO~WILL DENY HIM BEFORE   THE

πατρός μου τοῦ ἐν [τοῖς] οὐρανοῖς.
FATHER OF ME, THE ONE IN THE   HEAVENS.

10.34 Μὴ νομίσητε ὅτι ἦλθον βαλεῖν εἰρήνην ἐπὶ τὴν
      DO NOT THINK THAT I CAME TO BRING PEACE   ON THE

γῆν· οὐκ ἦλθον βαλεῖν εἰρήνην ἀλλὰ μάχαιραν.
EARTH. I HAVE NOT COME TO BRING PEACE   BUT   A SWORD.

10.35 ἦλθον γὰρ διχάσαι
      FOR~I CAME TO DIVIDE

        ἄνθρωπον κατὰ τοῦ πατρὸς αὐτοῦ
        A MAN   AGAINST THE FATHER OF HIM,

          καὶ θυγατέρα κατὰ τῆς μητρὸς αὐτῆς
          AND A DAUGHTER AGAINST THE MOTHER OF HER,

        καὶ νύμφην   κατὰ τῆς πενθερᾶς αὐτῆς,
        AND A DAUGHTER-IN-LAW AGAINST THE MOTHER-IN-LAW OF HER,

10.36   καὶ ἐχθροὶ τοῦ ἀνθρώπου οἱ
           AND [THE] ENEMIES OF THE MAN [WILL BE] THE

              οἰκιακοὶ   αὐτοῦ.
              MEMBERS OF THE HOUSEHOLD OF HIM.

10.37 Ὁ φιλῶν πατέρα ἢ μητέρα ὑπὲρ ἐμὲ
      THE ONE LOVING A FATHER OR MOTHER MORE THAN ME

10:35-36 Mic. 7:6

οὐκ ἔστιν μου ἄξιος, καὶ ὁ   φιλῶν υἱὸν ἢ θυγατέρα
IS NOT   WORTHY~OF ME, AND THE ONE LOVING A SON OR A DAUGHTER

ὑπὲρ ἐμὲ οὐκ ἔστιν μου ἄξιος· 10.38 καὶ   ὃς
MORE THAN ME IS NOT   WORTHY~OF ME.   AND [THE ONE] WHO

οὐ λαμβάνει τὸν σταυρὸν αὐτοῦ καὶ ἀκολουθεῖ ὀπίσω
DOES NOT TAKE UP THE CROSS   OF HIM AND FOLLOW   AFTER

μου, οὐκ ἔστιν μου ἄξιος. 10.39 ὁ   εὑρὼν   τὴν
ME, IS NOT   WORTHY~OF ME.   THE ONE HAVING FOUND THE

ψυχὴν αὐτοῦ ἀπολέσει αὐτήν, καὶ ὁ   ἀπολέσας τὴν
LIFE   OF HIM WILL LOSE IT,   AND THE ONE HAVING LOST THE

ψυχὴν αὐτοῦ ἕνεκεν ἐμοῦ εὑρήσει αὐτήν.
LIFE   OF HIM BECAUSE OF ME WILL FIND IT.

10.40 Ὁ   δεχόμενος ὑμᾶς ἐμὲ δέχεται, καὶ ὁ
      THE ONE RECEIVING YOU°, RECEIVES~ME AND THE ONE

ἐμὲ δεχόμενος δέχεται τὸν   ἀποστείλαντά με.
RECEIVING~ME   RECEIVES THE ONE HAVING SENT ME.

10.41 ὁ   δεχόμενος προφήτην εἰς ὄνομα προφήτου
      THE ONE RECEIVING A PROPHET IN [THE] NAME OF A PROPHET

μισθὸν   προφήτου λήμψεται, καὶ ὁ   δεχόμενος
[THE] REWARD OF A PROPHET WILL RECEIVE, AND THE ONE RECEIVING

δίκαιον   εἰς ὄνομα δικαίου   μισθὸν
A RIGHTEOUS PERSON IN [THE] NAME OF A RIGHTEOUS PERSON [THE] REWARD

δικαίου   λήμψεται. 10.42 καὶ ὃς ἂν ποτίσῃ   ἕνα
OF A RIGHTEOUS PERSON WILL RECEIVE.   AND WHOEVER GIVES TO DRINK ONE

τῶν μικρῶν τούτων ποτήριον ψυχροῦ   μόνον εἰς ὄνομα
-    OF THESE~LITTLE ONES A CUP OF COLD WATER ONLY IN [THE] NAME

μαθητοῦ, ἀμὴν λέγω ὑμῖν, οὐ μὴ ἀπολέσῃ τὸν μισθὸν
OF A DISCIPLE, TRULY I SAY TO YOU°, HE WILL BY NO MEANS LOSE THE REWARD

αὐτοῦ.
OF HIM.

is not worthy of me; and whoever loves son or daughter more than me is not worthy of me; [38]and whoever does not take up the cross and follow me is not worthy of me. [39]Those who find their life will lose it, and those who lose their life for my sake will find it.

[40] "Whoever welcomes you welcomes me, and whoever welcomes me welcomes the one who sent me. [41]Whoever welcomes a prophet in the name of a prophet will receive a prophet's reward; and whoever welcomes a righteous person in the name of a righteous person will receive the reward of the righteous; [42]and whoever gives even a cup of cold water to one of these little ones in the name of a disciple—truly I tell you, none of these will lose their reward."

CHAPTER 11

11.1 Καὶ ἐγένετο ὅτε ἐτέλεσεν ὁ Ἰησοῦς διατάσσων
     AND IT CAME ABOUT WHEN FINISHED - JESUS   GIVING ORDERS

τοῖς δώδεκα μαθηταῖς αὐτοῦ, μετέβη ἐκεῖθεν τοῦ
TO THE TWELVE DISCIPLES OF HIM, HE MOVED ON FROM THERE -

διδάσκειν καὶ κηρύσσειν ἐν ταῖς πόλεσιν αὐτῶν.
TO TEACH   AND TO PREACH IN THE CITIES   OF THEM.

11.2 Ὁ δὲ Ἰωάννης ἀκούσας ἐν τῷ δεσμωτηρίῳ τὰ
     - NOW JOHN   HAVING HEARD IN THE PRISON   THE

ἔργα τοῦ Χριστοῦ πέμψας διὰ   τῶν μαθητῶν αὐτοῦ
WORKS OF THE CHRIST HAVING SENT BY WAY OF THE DISCIPLES OF HIM

11.3 εἶπεν αὐτῷ, Σὺ εἶ ὁ   ἐρχόμενος ἢ
     SAID TO HIM, ARE~YOU THE ONE COMING   OR

ἕτερον προσδοκῶμεν; 11.4 καὶ ἀποκριθεὶς ὁ Ἰησοῦς
SHOULD WE EXPECT~ANOTHER? AND ANSWERING   - JESUS

Now when Jesus had finished instructing his twelve disciples, he went on from there to teach and proclaim his message in their cities.

2 When John heard in prison what the Messiah[m] was doing, he sent word by his[n] disciples [3]and said to him, "Are you the one who is to come, or are we to wait for another?" [4]Jesus answered

[m] Or *the Christ*
[n] Other ancient authorities read *two of his*

them, "Go and tell John what you hear and see: ⁵the blind receive their sight, the lame walk, the lepers° are cleansed, the deaf hear, the dead are raised, and the poor have good news brought to them. ⁶And blessed is anyone who takes no offense at me."

7 As they went away, Jesus began to speak to the crowds about John: "What did you go out into the wilderness to look at? A reed shaken by the wind? ⁸What then did you go out to see? Someone^p dressed in soft robes? Look, those who wear soft robes are in royal palaces. ⁹What then did you go out to see? A prophet?^q Yes, I tell you, and more than a prophet. ¹⁰This is the one about whom it is written,

'See, I am sending my messenger ahead of you,
who will prepare your way before you.'

¹¹Truly I tell you, among those born of women no one has arisen greater than John the Baptist; yet the least in the kingdom of heaven is greater than he. ¹²From the days of John the Baptist until now the kingdom of heaven

° The terms *leper* and *leprosy* can refer to several diseases
^p Or *Why then did you go out? To see someone*
^q Other ancient authorities read *Why then did you go out? To see a prophet?*

εἶπεν αὐτοῖς, Πορευθέντες ἀπαγγείλατε Ἰωάννῃ ἃ
SAID TO THEM, GOING REPORT TO JOHN WHAT

ἀκούετε καὶ βλέπετε· **11.5** τυφλοὶ ἀναβλέπουσιν καὶ
YOU° HEAR AND SEE. [THE] BLIND RECEIVE SIGHT AND

χωλοὶ περιπατοῦσιν, λεπροὶ καθαρίζονται καὶ
[THE] CRIPPLED WALK, LEPERS ARE CLEANSED AND

κωφοὶ ἀκούουσιν, καὶ νεκροὶ ἐγείρονται καὶ πτωχοὶ
[THE] DEAF HEAR, AND [THE] DEAD ARE RAISED AND [THE] POOR

εὐαγγελίζονται· **11.6** καὶ μακάριός ἐστιν ὃς ἐὰν
ARE EVANGELIZED. AND BLESSED IS WHOEVER

μὴ σκανδαλισθῇ ἐν ἐμοί. **11.7** Τούτων δὲ πορευομένων
DOES NOT TAKE OFFENSE AT ME. AND~[AS] THESE ONES WERE LEAVING,

ἤρξατο ὁ Ἰησοῦς λέγειν τοῖς ὄχλοις περὶ Ἰωάννου,
BEGAN - JESUS TO SAY TO THE CROWDS CONCERNING JOHN,

Τί ἐξήλθατε εἰς τὴν ἔρημον θεάσασθαι; κάλαμον
WHAT DID YOU° GO OUT INTO THE WILDERNESS TO SEE? A REED

ὑπὸ ἀνέμου σαλευόμενον; **11.8** ἀλλὰ τί ἐξήλθατε
BY [THE] WIND BEING SHAKEN? BUT WHAT DID YOU° GO OUT

ἰδεῖν; ἄνθρωπον ἐν μαλακοῖς ἠμφιεσμένον; ἰδοὺ
TO SEE? A MAN IN SOFT CLOTHES DRESSED? BEHOLD

οἱ τὰ μαλακὰ φοροῦντες ἐν τοῖς οἴκοις τῶν
THE ONES - WEARING~SOFT CLOTHES IN THE HOUSES -

βασιλέων εἰσίν. **11.9** ἀλλὰ τί ἐξήλθατε ἰδεῖν;
OF KINGS ARE. BUT WHAT DID YOU° GO OUT TO SEE?

προφήτην; ναί λέγω ὑμῖν, καὶ περισσότερον
A PROPHET? YES, I TELL YOU°, AND [ONE] GREATER THAN

προφήτου. **11.10** οὗτός ἐστιν περὶ οὗ γέγραπται,
A PROPHET. THIS IS [HE] ABOUT WHOM IT HAS BEEN WRITTEN,

Ἰδοὺ ἐγὼ ἀποστέλλω τὸν ἄγγελόν μου πρὸ
BEHOLD I SEND THE MESSENGER OF ME BEFORE

προσώπου σου,
[THE] FACE OF YOU,

ὃς κατασκευάσει τὴν ὁδόν σου ἔμπροσθέν
WHO WILL PREPARE THE WAY OF YOU IN FRONT OF

σου.
YOU.

11.11 ἀμὴν λέγω ὑμῖν· οὐκ ἐγήγερται ἐν
TRULY I SAY TO YOU°, THERE HAS NOT ARISEN AMONG [THOSE]

γεννητοῖς γυναικῶν μείζων Ἰωάννου τοῦ βαπτιστοῦ·
BORN OF WOMEN [ONE] GREATER THAN JOHN THE BAPTIST.

ὁ δὲ μικρότερος ἐν τῇ βασιλείᾳ τῶν οὐρανῶν μείζων
BUT~THE LEAST IMPORTANT IN THE KINGDOM OF THE HEAVENS GREATER THAN

αὐτοῦ ἐστιν. **11.12** ἀπὸ δὲ τῶν ἡμερῶν Ἰωάννου τοῦ
HIM IS. AND~FROM THE DAYS OF JOHN THE

βαπτιστοῦ ἕως ἄρτι ἡ βασιλεία τῶν οὐρανῶν
BAPTIST UNTIL NOW, THE KINGDOM OF THE HEAVENS

11:10 Mal. 3:1

βιάζεται καὶ βιασταὶ ἁρπάζουσιν αὐτήν.
IS FORCIBLY ENTERED, AND VIOLENT MEN SEIZE IT.

11.13 πάντες γὰρ οἱ προφῆται καὶ ὁ νόμος ἕως
FOR~ALL THE PROPHETS AND THE LAW UNTIL

Ἰωάννου ἐπροφήτευσαν· **11.14** καὶ εἰ θέλετε
JOHN PROPHESIED. AND IF YOU° ARE WILLING

δέξασθαι, αὐτός ἐστιν Ἡλίας ὁ μέλλων ἔρχεσθαι.
TO ACCEPT [IT], HE IS ELIJAH, THE ONE ABOUT TO COME.

11.15 ὁ ἔχων ὦτα ἀκουέτω.
THE ONE HAVING EARS, LET THAT ONE HEAR.

11.16 Τίνι δὲ ὁμοιώσω τὴν γενεὰν ταύτην;
BUT~TO WHAT WILL I COMPARE - THIS~GENERATION?

ὁμοία ἐστὶν παιδίοις καθημένοις ἐν ταῖς ἀγοραῖς
IT IS~LIKE CHILDREN SITTING IN THE MARKETPLACES

ἃ προσφωνοῦντα τοῖς ἑτέροις **11.17** λέγουσιν,
WHO, CALLING TO THE OTHERS SAY,

Ηὐλήσαμεν ὑμῖν καὶ οὐκ ὠρχήσασθε,
WE PLAYED THE FLUTE FOR YOU° AND YOU° DID NOT DANCE;

ἐθρηνήσαμεν καὶ οὐκ ἐκόψασθε.
WE SANG A DIRGE AND YOU° DID NOT MOURN.

11.18 ἦλθεν γὰρ Ἰωάννης μήτε ἐσθίων μήτε πίνων,
FOR~CAME JOHN NEITHER EATING NOR DRINKING,

καὶ λέγουσιν, Δαιμόνιον ἔχει. **11.19** ἦλθεν ὁ υἱὸς τοῦ
AND THEY SAY, HE HAS~A DEMON. CAME THE SON -

ἀνθρώπου ἐσθίων καὶ πίνων, καὶ λέγουσιν, Ἰδοὺ
OF MAN EATING AND DRINKING, AND THEY SAY, BEHOLD

ἄνθρωπος φάγος καὶ οἰνοπότης, τελωνῶν φίλος
A MAN GLUTTONOUS AND WINE-DRINKING, A FRIEND~OF TAX COLLECTORS

καὶ ἁμαρτωλῶν. καὶ ἐδικαιώθη ἡ σοφία ἀπὸ τῶν
AND SINNERS. AND IS JUSTIFIED - WISDOM BY THE

⌜ἔργων⌝ αὐτῆς.
WORKS OF HER.

11.20 Τότε ἤρξατο ὀνειδίζειν τὰς πόλεις ἐν αἷς
THEN HE BEGAN TO REPROACH THE CITIES IN WHICH

ἐγένοντο αἱ πλεῖσται δυνάμεις αὐτοῦ, ὅτι
WERE PERFORMED THE MAJORITY [OF THE] MIRACLES OF HIM, BECAUSE

οὐ μετενόησαν· **11.21** Οὐαί σοι, Χοραζίν, οὐαί σοι,
THEY DID NOT REPENT. WOE TO YOU, CHORAZIN, WOE TO YOU,

Βηθσαϊδά· ὅτι εἰ ἐν Τύρῳ καὶ Σιδῶνι ἐγένοντο αἱ
BETHSAIDA. FOR IF IN TYRE AND SIDON WERE PERFORMED THE

δυνάμεις αἱ γενόμεναι ἐν ὑμῖν, πάλαι ἂν ἐν
MIRACLES, THE ONES HAVING BEEN PERFORMED AMONG YOU°, LONG AGO - IN

σάκκῳ καὶ σποδῷ μετενόησαν. **11.22** πλὴν
SACKCLOTH AND ASHES THEY WOULD HAVE REPENTED. NEVERTHELESS,

λέγω ὑμῖν, Τύρῳ καὶ Σιδῶνι ἀνεκτότερον ἔσται ἐν
I SAY YOU°, FOR TYRE AND SIDON IT WILL BE~MORE BEARABLE IN

has suffered violence,[r] and the violent take it by force. [13]For all the prophets and the law prophesied until John came; [14]and if you are willing to accept it, he is Elijah who is to come. [15]Let anyone with ears[s] listen!

16 "But to what will I compare this generation? It is like children sitting in the marketplaces and calling to one another,

[17]'We played the flute for
you, and you did not
dance;
we wailed, and you did
not mourn.'

[18]For John came neither eating nor drinking, and they say, 'He has a demon'; [19]the Son of Man came eating and drinking, and they say, 'Look, a glutton and a drunkard, a friend of tax collectors and sinners!' Yet wisdom is vindicated by her deeds."[t]

20 Then he began to reproach the cities in which most of his deeds of power had been done, because they did not repent. [21]"Woe to you, Chorazin! Woe to you, Bethsaida! For if the deeds of power done in you had been done in Tyre and Sidon, they would have repented long ago in sackcloth and ashes. [22]But I tell you, on the day of judgment it will be more tolerable for Tyre and Sidon

[r] Or *has been coming violently*
[s] Other ancient authorities add *to hear*
[t] Other ancient authorities read *children*

11:19 text: ASV RSV NASB NIV NEB TEV NJB NRSV. var. τεκνων (children) [see Luke 7:35]: KJV ASVmg RSVmg NJBmg NRSVmg.

than for you. ²³And you, Capernaum,
　　will you be exalted to heaven?
　　No, you will be brought down to Hades.
For if the deeds of power done in you had been done in Sodom, it would have remained until this day. ²⁴But I tell you that on the day of judgment it will be more tolerable for the land of Sodom than for you."
　　25 At that time Jesus said, "I thank[u] you, Father, Lord of heaven and earth, because you have hidden these things from the wise and the intelligent and have revealed them to infants; ²⁶yes, Father, for such was your gracious will.[v] ²⁷All things have been handed over to me by my Father; and no one knows the Son except the Father, and no one knows the Father except the Son and anyone to whom the Son chooses to reveal him.
　　28 "Come to me, all you that are weary and are carrying heavy burdens, and I will give you rest. ²⁹Take my yoke upon you, and learn from me; for I am gentle and humble in heart, and you will find rest for your souls. ³⁰For my yoke is easy, and my burden is light."

[u] Or *praise*
[v] Or *for so it was well-pleasing in your sight*

ἡμέρα κρίσεως ἢ ὑμῖν. **11.23** καὶ σύ, Καφαρναούμ,
[THE] DAY OF JUDGMENT THAN FOR YOU°. AND YOU, CAPERNAUM,

μὴ ἕως οὐρανοῦ ὑψωθήσῃ;
²NOT ⁴AS FAR AS ⁵HEAVEN ¹WERE YOU ³LIFTED UP?

ἕως ᾅδου καταβήσῃ·
AS FAR AS HADES YOU WILL BE BROUGHT DOWN.

ὅτι εἰ ἐν Σοδόμοις ἐγενήθησαν αἱ δυνάμεις αἱ
FOR IF IN SODOM HAD BEEN PERFORMED THE MIRACLES, THE ONES

γενόμεναι ἐν σοί, ἔμεινεν ἂν μέχρι τῆς
HAVING BEING PERFORMED AMONG YOU, IT WOULD HAVE REMAINED - UNTIL -

σήμερον. **11.24** πλὴν λέγω ὑμῖν ὅτι γῇ
TODAY. NEVERTHELESS, I SAY TO YOU°, THAT FOR [THE] LAND

Σοδόμων ἀνεκτότερον ἔσται ἐν ἡμέρᾳ κρίσεως ἢ
OF SODOM IT WILL BE~MORE TOLERABLE IN [THE] DAY OF JUDGMENT THAN

σοί.
FOR YOU.

11.25 Ἐν ἐκείνῳ τῷ καιρῷ ἀποκριθεὶς ὁ Ἰησοῦς
AT THAT - TIME HAVING ANSWERED - JESUS

εἶπεν, Ἐξομολογοῦμαί σοι, πάτερ, κύριε τοῦ οὐρανοῦ
SAID, I PRAISE YOU, FATHER, LORD - OF HEAVEN

καὶ τῆς γῆς, ὅτι ἔκρυψας ταῦτα ἀπὸ σοφῶν καὶ
AND - EARTH, BECAUSE YOU HID THESE THINGS FROM [THE] WISE AND

συνετῶν καὶ ἀπεκάλυψας αὐτὰ νηπίοις· **11.26** ναὶ ὁ
INTELLIGENT AND REVEALED THEM TO INFANTS. YES, -

πατήρ, ὅτι οὕτως εὐδοκία ἐγένετο ἔμπροσθέν σου.
FATHER, FOR THUS IT WAS~PLEASING BEFORE YOU.

11.27 Πάντα μοι παρεδόθη ὑπὸ τοῦ πατρός μου, καὶ
ALL THINGS WERE GIVEN~TO ME BY THE FATHER OF ME, AND

οὐδεὶς ἐπιγινώσκει τὸν υἱὸν εἰ μὴ ὁ πατήρ, οὐδὲ τὸν
NO ONE KNOWS THE SON EXCEPT THE FATHER, NOR THE

πατέρα τις ἐπιγινώσκει εἰ μὴ ὁ υἱὸς καὶ
FATHER [DOES] ANYONE KNOW EXCEPT THE SON AND

ᾧ ἐὰν βούληται ὁ υἱὸς ἀποκαλύψαι.
[THOSE] TO WHOM IF ³WISHES ¹THE ²SON TO REVEAL.

11.28 Δεῦτε πρός με πάντες οἱ κοπιῶντες καὶ
COME TO ME ALL THE ONES BECOMING WEARY AND

πεφορτισμένοι, κἀγὼ ἀναπαύσω ὑμᾶς. **11.29** ἄρατε τὸν
BEING BURDENED, AND I WILL GIVE REST TO YOU°. TAKE UP THE

ζυγόν μου ἐφ' ὑμᾶς καὶ μάθετε ἀπ' ἐμοῦ, ὅτι
YOKE OF ME UPON YOU° AND LEARN FROM ME, FOR

πραΰς εἰμι καὶ ταπεινὸς τῇ καρδίᾳ, καὶ εὑρήσετε
I AM~HUMBLE AND LOWLY IN HEART, AND YOU° WILL FIND

ἀνάπαυσιν ταῖς ψυχαῖς ὑμῶν· **11.30** ὁ γὰρ ζυγός μου
REST FOR THE SOULS OF YOU°. FOR~THE YOKE OF ME [IS]

χρηστὸς καὶ τὸ φορτίον μου ἐλαφρόν ἐστιν.
EASY AND THE LOAD OF ME IS~LIGHT.

12.1 Ἐν ἐκείνῳ τῷ καιρῷ ἐπορεύθη ὁ Ἰησοῦς τοῖς
AT   THAT - TIME WENT - JESUS ON THE

σάββασιν διὰ τῶν σπορίμων· οἱ δὲ μαθηταὶ αὐτοῦ
SABBATH THROUGH THE GRAINFIELDS. AND~THE DISCIPLES OF HIM

ἐπείνασαν καὶ ἤρξαντο τίλλειν στάχυας καὶ
HUNGERED AND THEY BEGAN TO PICK [THE] HEADS OF WHEAT AND

ἐσθίειν. **12.2** οἱ δὲ Φαρισαῖοι ἰδόντες εἶπαν αὐτῷ,
TO EAT [THEM]. BUT~THE PHARISEES, SEEING [THIS] SAID TO HIM,

Ἰδοὺ οἱ μαθηταί σου ποιοῦσιν ὃ οὐκ ἔξεστιν ποιεῖν
BEHOLD THE DISCIPLES OF YOU ARE DOING WHAT IS NOT PERMITTED TO DO

ἐν σαββάτῳ. **12.3** ὁ δὲ εἶπεν αὐτοῖς, Οὐκ ἀνέγνωτε τί
ON [THE] SABBATH. BUT~HE SAID TO THEM, HAVE YOU° NOT READ WHAT

ἐποίησεν Δαυὶδ ὅτε ἐπείνασεν καὶ οἱ μετ' αὐτοῦ,
DAVID~DID WHEN HE HUNGERED AND THE ONES WITH HIM,

12.4 πῶς εἰσῆλθεν εἰς τὸν οἶκον τοῦ θεοῦ καὶ τοὺς
HOW HE ENTERED INTO THE HOUSE - OF GOD AND THE

ἄρτους τῆς προθέσεως ἔφαγον, ὃ οὐκ ἐξὸν ἦν
BREAD OF THE PRESENTATION ATE, WHICH WAS~NOT PERMISSIBLE

αὐτῷ φαγεῖν οὐδὲ τοῖς μετ' αὐτοῦ εἰ μὴ τοῖς
FOR HIM TO EAT NOR FOR THE ONES WITH HIM, EXCEPT FOR THE

ἱερεῦσιν μόνοις; **12.5** ἢ οὐκ ἀνέγνωτε ἐν τῷ νόμῳ ὅτι
PRIESTS ALONE? OR HAVE YOU° NOT READ IN THE LAW THAT

τοῖς σάββασιν οἱ ἱερεῖς ἐν τῷ ἱερῷ τὸ σάββατον
ON THE SABBATHS THE PRIESTS IN THE TEMPLE THE SABBATH

βεβηλοῦσιν καὶ ἀναίτιοί εἰσιν; **12.6** λέγω δὲ ὑμῖν ὅτι
DESECRATE AND INNOCENT ARE? BUT~I SAY TO YOU° THAT

τοῦ ἱεροῦ μεῖζόν ἐστιν ὧδε. **12.7** εἰ δὲ
²THE ³TEMPLE ¹[SOMETHING] GREATER THAN IS HERE. BUT~IF

ἐγνώκειτε τί ἐστιν, Ἔλεος θέλω καὶ οὐ θυσίαν,
YOU HAD KNOWN WHAT THIS MEANS, I DESIRE~MERCY AND NOT SACRIFICE,

οὐκ ἂν κατεδικάσατε τοὺς ἀναιτίους. **12.8** κύριος γάρ
YOU° WOULD NOT HAVE CONDEMNED THE INNOCENT. ⁶LORD ¹FOR

ἐστιν τοῦ σαββάτου ὁ υἱὸς τοῦ ἀνθρώπου.
⁵IS ⁷OF THE ⁸SABBATH ²THE ³SON - ⁴OF MAN.

12.9 Καὶ μεταβὰς ἐκεῖθεν ἦλθεν εἰς τὴν συναγωγὴν
AND HAVING GONE FROM THERE HE CAME INTO THE SYNAGOGUE

αὐτῶν· **12.10** καὶ ἰδοὺ ἄνθρωπος χεῖρα ἔχων ξηράν.
OF THEM. AND BEHOLD A MAN ³HAND ¹HAVING ²A WITHERED.

καὶ ἐπηρώτησαν αὐτὸν λέγοντες, Εἰ ἔξεστιν τοῖς
AND THEY QUESTIONED HIM ASKING, IF IT IS PERMISSIBLE ON THE

σάββασιν θεραπεῦσαι; ἵνα κατηγορήσωσιν αὐτοῦ.
SABBATHS TO HEAL? IN ORDER THAT THEY MIGHT ACCUSE HIM.

12.11 ὁ δὲ εἶπεν αὐτοῖς, Τίς ἔσται ἐξ ὑμῶν
BUT~HE SAID TO THEM, WHAT ²WILL THERE BE ³AMONG ⁴YOU°

12:7 Hds. 6:6

At that time Jesus went through the grainfields on the sabbath; his disciples were hungry, and they began to pluck heads of grain and to eat. ²When the Pharisees saw it, they said to him, "Look, your disciples are doing what is not lawful to do on the sabbath." ³He said to them, "Have you not read what David did when he and his companions were hungry? ⁴He entered the house of God and ate the bread of the Presence, which it was not lawful for him or his companions to eat, but only for the priests? ⁵Or have you not read in the law that on the sabbath the priests in the temple break the sabbath and yet are guiltless? ⁶I tell you, something greater than the temple is here. ⁷But if you had known what this means, 'I desire mercy and not sacrifice,' you would not have condemned the guiltless. ⁸For the Son of Man is lord of the sabbath."

9 He left that place and entered their synagogue; ¹⁰a man was there with a withered hand, and they asked him, "Is it lawful to cure on the sabbath?" so that they might accuse him. ¹¹He said to them, "Suppose one

of you has only one sheep and it falls into a pit on the sabbath; will you not lay hold of it and lift it out? [12]How much more valuable is a human being than a sheep! So it is lawful to do good on the sabbath." [13]Then he said to the man, "Stretch out your hand." He stretched it out, and it was restored, as sound as the other. [14]But the Pharisees went out and conspired against him, how to destroy him.

15 When Jesus became aware of this, he departed. Many crowds[w] followed him, and he cured all of them, [16]and he ordered them not to make him known. [17]This was to fulfill what had been spoken through the prophet Isaiah:

[18]"Here is my servant,
  whom I have chosen,
 my beloved, with
  whom my soul is
  well pleased.
 I will put my Spirit upon
  him,
  and he will proclaim
  justice to the
  Gentiles.
[19]He will not wrangle or
  cry aloud,

[w] Other ancient authorities lack *crowds*

ἄνθρωπος ὃς ἕξει πρόβατον ἕν καὶ ἐὰν
[1]MAN   WHO   WILL HAVE   ONE~SHEEP,   AND   IF

ἐμπέσῃ τοῦτο τοῖς σάββασιν εἰς βόθυνον,
THIS ONE~FALLS   ON THE   SABBATHS   INTO   A PIT,

οὐχὶ κρατήσει αὐτὸ καὶ ἐγερεῖ;
WILL NOT TAKE HOLD OF   IT   AND   RAISE [IT] UP?

12.12 πόσῳ οὖν   διαφέρει ἄνθρωπος προβάτου.
THEREFORE,~HOW MUCH MORE   VALUABLE IS   A MAN   THAN A SHEEP.

ὥστε   ἔξεστιν τοῖς σάββασιν καλῶς ποιεῖν.
FOR THIS REASON   IT IS PERMISSIBLE   ON THE   SABBATHS   TO DO~GOOD.

12.13 τότε λέγει τῷ ἀνθρώπῳ, Ἔκτεινόν σου τὴν χεῖρα.
THEN   HE SAYS   TO THE   MAN,   STRETCH OUT   YOUR -   HAND.

καὶ ἐξέτεινεν καὶ ἀπεκατεστάθη ὑγιὴς ὡς ἡ
AND   HE STRETCHED [IT] OUT   AND   IT WAS RESTORED   HEALTHY   AS   THE

ἄλλη. **12.14** ἐξελθόντες δὲ οἱ Φαρισαῖοι
OTHER.   AND~HAVING GONE   THE   PHARISEES

συμβούλιον ἔλαβον κατ' αὐτοῦ ὅπως
TOOK~COUNSEL   AGAINST   HIM   SO THAT

αὐτὸν ἀπολέσωσιν.
THEY MIGHT DESTROY~HIM.

12.15 Ὁ δὲ Ἰησοῦς γνοὺς ἀνεχώρησεν ἐκεῖθεν.
 -   BUT   JESUS   KNOWING [THIS]   DEPARTED   FROM THERE.

καὶ ἠκολούθησαν αὐτῷ [ὄχλοι] πολλοί, καὶ
AND   FOLLOWED   HIM   MANY~CROWDS   AND

ἐθεράπευσεν αὐτοὺς πάντας **12.16** καὶ ἐπετίμησεν
HE HEALED   THEM   ALL   AND   HE WARNED

αὐτοῖς ἵνα μὴ φανερὸν αὐτὸν ποιήσωσιν, **12.17** ἵνα
THEM   THAT   [2]NOT   [3]MANIFEST   [4]HIM   [1]THEY SHOULD MAKE,   THAT

πληρωθῇ τὸ ῥηθὲν διὰ Ἠσαΐου τοῦ προφήτου
MIGHT BE FULFILLED   THE THING   SPOKEN   THROUGH   ISAIAH   THE   PROPHET

λέγοντος,
SAYING,

12.18 Ἰδοὺ ὁ παῖς μου ὃν ᾑρέτισα,
BEHOLD   THE   SERVANT   OF ME   WHOM   I CHOSE,

ὁ ἀγαπητός μου εἰς ὃν εὐδόκησεν ἡ
THE   BELOVED   OF ME   IN   WHOM   WAS WELL PLEASED   THE

ψυχή μου·
SOUL   OF ME.

θήσω τὸ πνεῦμά μου ἐπ' αὐτόν,
I WILL PUT   THE   SPIRIT   OF ME   UPON   HIM,

καὶ κρίσιν τοῖς ἔθνεσιν ἀπαγγελεῖ.
AND   JUDGMENT   TO THE   NATIONS   HE WILL PROCLAIM.

12.19 οὐκ ἐρίσει οὐδὲ κραυγάσει,
HE WILL NOT QUARREL   NOR   SHOUT,

12:18-20 Isa. 42:1-3

οὐδὲ   ἀκούσει τις   ἐν ταῖς πλατείαις   τὴν
NOR   WILL HEAR ANYONE IN THE   STREETS   THE

φωνὴν αὐτοῦ.
VOICE OF HIM.

12.20 κάλαμον συντετριμμένον οὐ κατεάξει
A REED   BEING CRUSHED   HE WILL NOT BREAK

καὶ   λίνον τυφόμενον   οὐ σβέσει,
AND   A SMOKING~LAMP WICK HE WILL NOT EXTINGUISH,

ἕως ἂν ἐκβάλῃ εἰς νῖκος τὴν κρίσιν.
UNTIL   HE LEADS ²TO ³VICTORY - ¹JUSTICE.

12.21   καὶ τῷ ὀνόματι αὐτοῦ ἔθνη   ἐλπιοῦσιν.
AND   IN THE NAME   OF HIM [THE] GENTILES WILL HOPE.

12.22 Τότε προσηνέχθη αὐτῷ δαιμονιζόμενος
THEN WAS BROUGHT   TO HIM A DEMON-POSSESSED [MAN WHO WAS]

τυφλὸς καὶ κωφός, καὶ ἐθεράπευσεν αὐτόν, ὥστε τὸν
BLIND   AND MUTE,   AND HE HEALED   HIM,   SO THAT THE

κωφὸν   λαλεῖν καὶ βλέπειν. **12.23** καὶ ἐξίσταντο
MUTE [MAN WAS ABLE] TO SPEAK AND TO SEE.   AND   WERE AMAZED

πάντες οἱ ὄχλοι καὶ ἔλεγον, Μήτι οὗτός ἐστιν ὁ
ALL   THE CROWDS AND THEY WERE SAYING, SURELY THIS ONE IS [NOT] THE

υἱὸς Δαυίδ;   **12.24** οἱ δὲ Φαρισαῖοι ἀκούσαντες
SON OF DAVID [IS HE]?   BUT~THE PHARISEES   HAVING HEARD [THIS]

εἶπον, Οὗτος οὐκ ἐκβάλλει τὰ δαιμόνια εἰ μὴ ἐν τῷ
SAID,   THIS ONE DOES NOT CAST OUT - DEMONS   EXCEPT BY -

Βεελζεβοὺλ ἄρχοντι τῶν δαιμονίων. **12.25** εἰδὼς δὲ τὰς
BEELZEBOUL [THE] RULER OF THE DEMONS.   BUT~KNOWING THE

ἐνθυμήσεις αὐτῶν εἶπεν αὐτοῖς, Πᾶσα βασιλεία
THOUGHTS   OF THEM HE SAID TO THEM, EVERY KINGDOM

μερισθεῖσα   καθ' ἑαυτῆς ἐρημοῦται καὶ πᾶσα πόλις
HAVING BEEN DIVIDED AGAINST ITSELF IS LAID WASTE, AND EVERY   CITY

ἢ οἰκία μερισθεῖσα   καθ' ἑαυτῆς οὐ σταθήσεται.
OR HOUSE HAVING BEEN DIVIDED AGAINST ITSELF WILL NOT STAND.

12.26 καὶ εἰ ὁ Σατανᾶς τὸν Σατανᾶν ἐκβάλλει, ἐφ'
AND IF - SATAN   - CASTS OUT~SATAN,   AGAINST

ἑαυτὸν ἐμερίσθη· πῶς οὖν   σταθήσεται ἡ βασιλεία
HIMSELF HE IS DIVIDED. HOW THEREFORE WILL STAND   THE KINGDOM

αὐτοῦ; **12.27** καὶ εἰ ἐγὼ ἐν Βεελζεβοὺλ ἐκβάλλω τὰ
OF HIM?   AND IF I BY BEELZEBOUL   CAST OUT   THE

δαιμόνια, οἱ   υἱοὶ ὑμῶν ἐν τίνι ἐκβάλλουσιν;
DEMONS,   ³[DO] THE ⁴SONS ⁵OF YOU° ¹BY ²WHOM CAST [THEM] OUT?

διὰ τοῦτο αὐτοὶ κριταὶ ἔσονται ὑμῶν. **12.28** εἰ δὲ ἐν
THEREFORE, THEY WILL BE~JUDGES   OF YOU°.   BUT~IF BY

πνεύματι θεοῦ ἐγὼ ἐκβάλλω τὰ δαιμόνια, ἄρα ἔφθασεν
[THE] SPIRIT OF GOD I   CAST OUT   THE DEMONS,   THEN HAS ARRIVED

ἐφ' ὑμᾶς ἡ βασιλεία τοῦ θεοῦ. **12.29** ἢ πῶς δύναταί
UPON YOU° THE KINGDOM - OF GOD.   OR HOW IS ABLE

nor will anyone hear
his voice in the
streets.
²⁰He will not break a
bruised reed
or quench a smoldering
wick
until he brings justice to
victory.
²¹   And in his name the
Gentiles will hope."
²² Then they brought to
him a demoniac who was
blind and mute; and he cured
him, so that the one who had
been mute could speak and
see. ²³All the crowds were
amazed and said, "Can this
be the Son of David?" ²⁴But
when the Pharisees heard it,
they said, "It is only by
Beelzebul, the ruler of the
demons, that this fellow
casts out the demons." ²⁵He
knew what they were
thinking and said to them,
"Every kingdom divided
against itself is laid waste,
and no city or house divided
against itself will stand. ²⁶If
Satan casts out Satan, he is
divided against himself; how
then will his kingdom stand?
²⁷If I cast out demons by
Beelzebul, by whom do
your own exorcistsˣ cast
them out? Therefore they
will be your judges. ²⁸But if
it is by the Spirit of God that
I cast out demons, then the
kingdom of God has come
to you. ²⁹Or how can one

ˣ Gk sons

12:21 Isa. 42:4 LXX

enter a strong man's house and plunder his property, without first tying up the strong man? Then indeed the house can be plundered. ³⁰Whoever is not with me is against me, and whoever does not gather with me scatters. ³¹Therefore I tell you, people will be forgiven for every sin and blasphemy, but blasphemy against the Spirit will not be forgiven. ³²Whoever speaks a word against the Son of Man will be forgiven, but whoever speaks against the Holy Spirit will not be forgiven, either in this age or in the age to come.

33 "Either make the tree good, and its fruit good; or make the tree bad, and its fruit bad; for the tree is known by its fruit. ³⁴You brood of vipers! How can you speak good things, when you are evil? For out of the abundance of the heart the mouth speaks. ³⁵The good person brings good things out of a good treasure, and the evil person brings evil things out of an evil treasure. ³⁶I tell you, on the day of judgment you will have to give an account for every careless word you utter; ³⁷for by your words

τις εἰσελθεῖν εἰς τὴν οἰκίαν τοῦ ἰσχυροῦ καὶ τὰ
SOMEONE TO ENTER INTO THE HOUSE OF THE STONG ONE AND THE

σκεύη αὐτοῦ ἁρπάσαι, ἐὰν μὴ πρῶτον δήσῃ τὸν
FURNISHINGS OF HIM STEAL, UNLESS FIRST HE BINDS THE

ἰσχυρόν; καὶ τότε τὴν οἰκίαν αὐτοῦ διαρπάσει.
STONG ONE? AND THEN THE HOUSE OF HIM HE WILL PLUNDER.

12.30 ὁ μὴ ὢν μετ' ἐμοῦ κατ' ἐμοῦ ἐστιν, καὶ
THE ONE NOT BEING WITH ME AGAINST ME IS, AND

ὁ μὴ συνάγων μετ' ἐμοῦ σκορπίζει. **12.31** Διὰ τοῦτο
THE ONE NOT GATHERING WITH ME SCATTERS. THEREFORE,

λέγω ὑμῖν, πᾶσα ἁμαρτία καὶ βλασφημία
I SAY TO YOU°, EVERY SIN AND BLASPHEMY

ἀφεθήσεται τοῖς ἀνθρώποις, ἡ δὲ τοῦ πνεύματος
WILL BE FORGIVEN - MEN, - BUT ²THE ³SPIRIT

βλασφημία οὐκ ἀφεθήσεται. **12.32** καὶ ὃς ἐὰν εἴπῃ
¹BLASPHEMY [AGAINST] WILL NOT BE FORGIVEN. AND WHOEVER SPEAKS

λόγον κατὰ τοῦ υἱοῦ τοῦ ἀνθρώπου, ἀφεθήσεται αὐτῷ·
A WORD AGAINST THE SON - OF MAN, IT WILL BE FORGIVEN HIM.

ὃς δ' ἂν εἴπῃ κατὰ τοῦ πνεύματος τοῦ ἁγίου,
BUT~WHOEVER SPEAKS AGAINST - ³SPIRIT ¹THE ²HOLY,

οὐκ ἀφεθήσεται αὐτῷ οὔτε ἐν τούτῳ τῷ αἰῶνι οὔτε ἐν
IT WILL NOT BE FORGIVEN HIM NEITHER IN THIS - AGE NOR IN

τῷ μέλλοντι.
THE ONE COMING.

12.33 Ἢ ποιήσατε τὸ δένδρον καλὸν καὶ τὸν
EITHER MAKE THE TREE GOOD AND THE

καρπὸν αὐτοῦ καλόν, ἢ ποιήσατε τὸ δένδρον
FRUIT OF IT [WILL BE] GOOD, OR MAKE THE TREE

σαπρὸν καὶ τὸν καρπὸν αὐτοῦ σαπρόν· ἐκ γὰρ τοῦ
ROTTEN AND THE FRUIT OF IT [WILL BE] ROTTEN. FOR~BY THE

καρποῦ τὸ δένδρον γινώσκεται. **12.34** γεννήματα
FRUIT THE TREE IS KNOWN. [YOU°] OFFSPRING

ἐχιδνῶν, πῶς δύνασθε ἀγαθὰ λαλεῖν πονηροὶ ὄντες;
OF VIPERS, HOW ARE YOU° ABLE TO SPEAK~GOOD BEING~EVIL?

ἐκ γὰρ τοῦ περισσεύματος τῆς καρδίας τὸ στόμα
FOR~OUT OF THE ABUNDANCE OF THE HEART THE MOUTH

λαλεῖ. **12.35** ὁ ἀγαθὸς ἄνθρωπος ἐκ τοῦ ἀγαθοῦ
SPEAKS. THE GOOD MAN OUT OF THE GOOD

θησαυροῦ ἐκβάλλει ἀγαθά, καὶ ὁ πονηρὸς ἄνθρωπος
TREASURE BRINGS FORTH GOOD, AND THE EVIL MAN

ἐκ τοῦ πονηροῦ θησαυροῦ ἐκβάλλει πονηρά.
OUT OF THE EVIL TREASURE BRINGS FORTH EVIL.

12.36 λέγω δὲ ὑμῖν ὅτι πᾶν ῥῆμα ἀργὸν ὃ
BUT~I SAY TO YOU° THAT EVERY CARELESS~WORD WHICH

λαλήσουσιν οἱ ἄνθρωποι ἀποδώσουσιν περὶ αὐτοῦ
SPEAK - MEN THEY WILL GIVE CONCERNING IT

λόγον ἐν ἡμέρᾳ κρίσεως· **12.37** ἐκ γὰρ τῶν λόγων
AN ACCOUNT ON [THE] DAY OF JUDGMENT; FOR~BY THE WORDS

σου   δικαιωθήσῃ,   καὶ   ἐκ   τῶν   λόγων   σου
OF YOU   YOU WILL BE JUSTIFIED,   AND   BY   THE   WORDS   OF YOU

καταδικασθήσῃ.
YOU WILL BE CONDEMNED.

12.38 Τότε   ἀπεκρίθησαν   αὐτῷ   τινες   τῶν   γραμματέων
THEN   ANSWERED   HIM   SOME   OF THE SCRIBES

καὶ   Φαρισαίων   λέγοντες,   Διδάσκαλε,   θέλομεν   ἀπὸ   σοῦ
AND   PHARISEES   SAYING,   TEACHER,   WE DESIRE   FROM   YOU

σημεῖον ἰδεῖν.   **12.39** ὁ   δὲ   ἀποκριθεὶς   εἶπεν   αὐτοῖς,
TO SEE~A SIGN.   -   BUT   HAVING ANSWERED   HE SAID   TO THEM,

Γενεὰ   πονηρὰ   καὶ   μοιχαλὶς   σημεῖον ἐπιζητεῖ,   καὶ
A GENERATION   EVIL   AND   ADULTEROUS   SEEKS~A SIGN,   AND

σημεῖον   οὐ   δοθήσεται   αὐτῇ   εἰ   μὴ   τὸ   σημεῖον   Ἰωνᾶ
A SIGN   WILL NOT BE GIVEN   TO IT   EXCEPT   THE   SIGN   OF JONAH

τοῦ   προφήτου.   **12.40** ὥσπερ   γὰρ   ἦν   Ἰωνᾶς   ἐν   τῇ   κοιλίᾳ
THE   PROPHET.   FOR~JUST AS   JONAH~WAS   IN   THE   BELLY

τοῦ   κήτους   τρεῖς   ἡμέρας   καὶ   τρεῖς   νύκτας,   οὕτως
OF THE   SEA MONSTER   THREE   DAYS   AND   THREE   NIGHTS,   SO

ἔσται   ὁ   υἱὸς   τοῦ   ἀνθρώπου   ἐν   τῇ   καρδίᾳ   τῆς   γῆς
WILL BE   THE   SON   -   OF MAN   IN   THE   HEART   OF THE   EARTH

τρεῖς   ἡμέρας   καὶ   τρεῖς   νύκτας.   **12.41** ἄνδρες   Νινευῖται
THREE   DAYS   AND   THREE   NIGHTS.   [THE] MEN   OF NINEVEH

ἀναστήσονται   ἐν   τῇ   κρίσει   μετὰ   τῆς   γενεᾶς ταύτης   καὶ
WILL STAND UP   AT   THE   JUDGMENT   WITH   -   THIS~GENERATION   AND

κατακρινοῦσιν   αὐτήν,   ὅτι   μετενόησαν   εἰς   τὸ   κήρυγμα
THEY WILL CONDEMN   IT,   FOR   THEY REPENTED   AT   THE   PREACHING

Ἰωνᾶ,   καὶ   ἰδοὺ   πλεῖον   Ἰωνᾶ   ὧδε.
OF JONAH,   AND   BEHOLD   [SOMETHING] MUCH GREATER THAN   JONAH [IS]   HERE.

12.42 βασίλισσα   νότου   ἐγερθήσεται   ἐν   τῇ   κρίσει
[THE] QUEEN   OF [THE] SOUTH   WILL BE RAISED   AT   THE   JUDGMENT

μετὰ   τῆς   γενεᾶς ταύτης   καὶ   κατακρινεῖ   αὐτήν,   ὅτι
WITH   -   THIS~GENERATION   AND   WILL CONDEMN   IT,   FOR

ἦλθεν   ἐκ   τῶν περάτων   τῆς   γῆς   ἀκοῦσαι   τὴν   σοφίαν
SHE CAME   FROM   THE   ENDS   OF THE   EARTH   TO LISTEN TO   THE   WISDOM

Σολομῶνος,   καὶ   ἰδοὺ   πλεῖον   Σολομῶνος
OF SOLOMON   AND   BEHOLD   [SOMETHING] MUCH GREATER THAN   SOLOMON [IS]

ὧδε.
HERE.

12.43 Ὅταν   δὲ   τὸ   ἀκάθαρτον   πνεῦμα   ἐξέλθῃ   ἀπὸ   τοῦ
NOW~WHEN   THE   UNCLEAN   SPIRIT   GOES OUT   FROM   THE

ἀνθρώπου,   διέρχεται   δι'   ἀνύδρων   τόπων   ζητοῦν
MAN,   IT GOES   THROUGH   DRY   PLACES   SEEKING

ἀνάπαυσιν   καὶ   οὐχ   εὑρίσκει.   **12.44** τότε   λέγει,   Εἰς   τὸν
A RESTING PLACE   AND   IT DOES NOT FIND [ONE].   THEN   IT SAYS,   INTO   THE

οἶκόν   μου   ἐπιστρέψω   ὅθεν   ἐξῆλθον·   καὶ   ἐλθὸν
HOUSE   OF ME   I WILL RETURN   FROM WHERE   I CAME OUT.   AND   HAVING COME

12:40 Jonah 1:17

you will be justified, and by your words you will be condemned."

38 Then some of the scribes and Pharisees said to him, "Teacher, we wish to see a sign from you." [39]But he answered them, "An evil and adulterous generation asks for a sign, but no sign will be given to it except the sign of the prophet Jonah. [40]For just as Jonah was three days and three nights in the belly of the sea monster, so for three days and three nights the Son of Man will be in the heart of the earth. [41]The people of Nineveh will rise up at the judgment with this generation and condemn it, because they repented at the proclamation of Jonah, and see, something greater than Jonah is here! [42]The queen of the South will rise up at the judgment with this generation and condemn it, because she came from the ends of the earth to listen to the wisdom of Solomon, and see, something greater than Solomon is here!

43 "When the unclean spirit has gone out of a person, it wanders through waterless regions looking for a resting place, but it finds none. [44]Then it says, 'I will return to my house from which I came.' When it comes,

it finds it empty, swept, and put in order. 45Then it goes and brings along seven other spirits more evil than itself, and they enter and live there; and the last state of that person is worse than the first. So will it be also with this evil generation."

46 While he was still speaking to the crowds, his mother and his brothers were standing outside, wanting to speak to him. 47Someone told him, "Look, your mother and your brothers are standing outside, wanting to speak to you."y 48But to the one who had told him this, Jesusz replied, "Who is my mother, and who are my brothers?" 49And pointing to his disciples, he said, "Here are my mother and my brothers! 50For whoever does the will of my Father in heaven is my brother and sister and mother."

y Other ancient authorities lack verse 47
z Gk he

εὑρίσκει σχολάζοντα σεσαρωμένον καὶ
IT FINDS [THE HOUSE]　STANDING EMPTY　HAVING BEEN SWEPT　AND

κεκοσμημένον. **12.45** τότε πορεύεται καὶ
HAVING BEEN PUT IN ORDER.　THEN　IT GOES　AND

παραλαμβάνει μεθ᾽ ἑαυτοῦ ἑπτὰ ἕτερα πνεύματα
TAKES ALONG　WITH　ITSELF　SEVEN　OTHER　SPIRITS

πονηρότερα ἑαυτοῦ καὶ εἰσελθόντα κατοικεῖ
MORE EVIL THAN　ITSELF　AND　HAVING ENTERED [THE HOUSE]　IT SETS UP RESIDENCE

ἐκεῖ· καὶ γίνεται τὰ ἔσχατα τοῦ ἀνθρώπου ἐκείνου
THERE.　AND　BECOMES　THE　LAST [STATE]　-　OF THAT~MAN

χείρονα τῶν πρώτων. οὕτως ἔσται καὶ τῇ γενεᾷ
WORSE　THAN THE FIRST.　THUS　IT WILL BE　AS WELL　-　³GENERATION

ταύτῃ τῇ πονηρᾷ.
¹WITH THIS　-　²EVIL.

12.46 Ἔτι αὐτοῦ λαλοῦντος τοῖς ὄχλοις ἰδοὺ ἡ μήτηρ
WHILE HE WAS STILL SPEAKING　TO THE　CROWDS　BEHOLD　THE　MOTHER

καὶ οἱ ἀδελφοὶ αὐτοῦ εἰστήκεισαν ἔξω ζητοῦντες
AND　THE　BROTHERS　OF HIM　STOOD　OUTSIDE　SEEKING

αὐτῷ λαλῆσαι. ⌜**12.47** [εἶπεν δέ τις αὐτῷ, Ἰδοὺ ἡ
TO SPEAK~WITH HIM.　AND~SAID　SOMEONE　TO HIM,　BEHOLD　THE

μήτηρ σου καὶ οἱ ἀδελφοί σου ἔξω ἑστήκασιν
MOTHER　OF YOU　AND　THE　BROTHERS　OF YOU　HAVE STOOD~OUTSIDE

ζητοῦντές σοι λαλῆσαι.]⌝ **12.48** ὁ δὲ ἀποκριθεὶς εἶπεν
SEEKING　TO SPEAK~WITH YOU.　-　AND　HAVING ANSWERED　HE SAID

τῷ λέγοντι αὐτῷ, Τίς ἐστιν ἡ μήτηρ μου καὶ
TO THE ONE　SPEAKING　WITH HIM,　WHO　IS　THE　MOTHER　OF ME　AND

τίνες εἰσὶν οἱ ἀδελφοί μου; **12.49** καὶ ἐκτείνας τὴν
WHO　ARE　THE　BROTHERS　OF ME?　AND　STRETCHING OUT　THE

χεῖρα αὐτοῦ ἐπὶ τοὺς μαθητὰς αὐτοῦ εἶπεν, Ἰδοὺ ἡ
HAND　OF HIM　UPON　THE　DISCIPLES　OF HIM　HE SAID,　BEHOLD　THE

μήτηρ μου καὶ οἱ ἀδελφοί μου. **12.50** ὅστις γὰρ ἂν
MOTHER　OF ME　AND　THE　BROTHERS　OF ME.　FOR~WHOEVER

ποιήσῃ τὸ θέλημα τοῦ πατρός μου τοῦ ἐν οὐρανοῖς
DOES　THE　WILL　OF THE　FATHER　OF ME,　THE ONE IN　[THE] HEAVENS,

αὐτός μου ἀδελφὸς καὶ ἀδελφὴ καὶ μήτηρ ἐστίν.
HE　MY　BROTHER　AND　SISTER　AND　MOTHER　IS.

12:47 text: KJV ASV RSVmg NASB NIV NEB TEV NJBmg NRSV. omit: ASVmg RSV NIVmg TEVmg NJB NRSVmg.

CHAPTER 13

That same day Jesus went out of the house and sat beside the sea. 2Such

13.1 Ἐν τῇ ἡμέρᾳ ἐκείνῃ ἐξελθὼν ὁ Ἰησοῦς τῆς
ON　-　THAT~DAY　HAVING GONE OUT　-　JESUS　OF THE

οἰκίας ἐκάθητο παρὰ τὴν θάλασσαν· **13.2** καὶ
HOUSE,　HE SAT　BESIDE　THE　LAKE.　AND

συνήχθησαν πρὸς αὐτὸν ὄχλοι πολλοί, ὥστε αὐτὸν εἰς
GATHERED TOGETHER TO HIM MANY~CROWDS, SO THAT HE INTO

πλοῖον ἐμβάντα καθῆσθαι, καὶ πᾶς ὁ ὄχλος ἐπὶ τὸν
A BOAT GOT IN TO SIT DOWN, AND THE~ENTIRE CROWD ALONG THE

αἰγιαλὸν εἱστήκει. **13.3** καὶ ἐλάλησεν αὐτοῖς πολλὰ
SHORE STOOD. AND HE TOLD THEM MANY THINGS

ἐν παραβολαῖς λέγων, Ἰδοὺ ἐξῆλθεν ὁ σπείρων τοῦ
IN PARABLES SAYING, BEHOLD WENT OUT THE SOWER -

σπείρειν. **13.4** καὶ ἐν τῷ σπείρειν αὐτὸν ἃ
TO SOW [SEEDS]. AND WHILE HE SOWED THIS ONE

μὲν ἔπεσεν παρὰ τὴν ὁδόν, καὶ ἐλθόντα τὰ
ON THE ONE HAND FELL ALONG THE ROAD, AND HAVING COME THE

πετεινὰ κατέφαγεν αὐτά. **13.5** ἄλλα δὲ ἔπεσεν ἐπὶ τὰ
BIRDS DEVOURED THEM. BUT~OTHERS FELL UPON THE

πετρώδη ὅπου οὐκ εἶχεν γῆν πολλήν, καὶ εὐθέως
ROCKY PLACES WHERE IT DOES NOT HAVE MUCH~SOIL, AND IMMEDIATELY

ἐξανέτειλεν διὰ τὸ μὴ ἔχειν βάθος γῆς·
IT SPRANG UP ON ACCOUNT OF THE NOT HAVING DEPTH OF SOIL.

13.6 ἡλίου δὲ ἀνατείλαντος ἐκαυματίσθη καὶ διὰ τὸ
AND~[THE] SUN HAVING ARISEN IT WAS SCORCHED AND BECAUSE

μὴ ἔχειν ῥίζαν ἐξηράνθη. **13.7** ἄλλα δὲ ἔπεσεν ἐπὶ
IT DID NOT HAVE A ROOT IT WITHERED. AND~OTHERS FELL AMONG

τὰς ἀκάνθας, καὶ ἀνέβησαν αἱ ἄκανθαι καὶ ἔπνιξαν
THE THORNS, AND GREW UP THE THORNS AND CHOKED

αὐτά. **13.8** ἄλλα δὲ ἔπεσεν ἐπὶ τὴν γῆν τὴν καλὴν
THEM. BUT~OTHERS FELL ON THE ²EARTH - ¹GOOD

καὶ ἐδίδου καρπόν, ὃ μὲν ἑκατόν, ὃ δὲ ἑξήκοντα,
AND THEY YIELDED FRUIT, THE ONE ONE HUNDRED, THE OTHER SIXTY,

ὃ δὲ τριάκοντα. **13.9** ὁ ἔχων ὦτα ἀκουέτω.
THE OTHER THIRTY. THE ONE HAVING EARS LET THAT ONE HEAR.

13.10 Καὶ προσελθόντες οἱ μαθηταὶ εἶπαν αὐτῷ,
AND APPROACHING THE DISCIPLES SAID TO HIM,

Διὰ τί ἐν παραβολαῖς λαλεῖς αὐτοῖς; **13.11** ὁ δὲ
WHY IN PARABLES ARE YOU SPEAKING TO THEM? - AND

ἀποκριθεὶς εἶπεν αὐτοῖς, Ὅτι ὑμῖν δέδοται
HAVING ANSWERED HE SAID TO THEM, BECAUSE TO YOU° IT HAS BEEN GRANTED

γνῶναι τὰ μυστήρια τῆς βασιλείας τῶν οὐρανῶν,
TO KNOW THE MYSTERIES OF THE KINGDOM OF THE HEAVENS,

ἐκείνοις δὲ οὐ δέδοται. **13.12** ὅστις γὰρ ἔχει,
BUT~TO THOSE IT HAS NOT BEEN GRANTED. FOR~WHOEVER HAS,

δοθήσεται αὐτῷ καὶ περισσευθήσεται· ὅστις δὲ
[MORE] WILL BE GIVEN TO HIM AND HE WILL HAVE AN ABUNDANCE. BUT~WHOEVER

οὐκ ἔχει, καὶ ὃ ἔχει ἀρθήσεται ἀπ' αὐτοῦ.
DOES NOT HAVE, EVEN WHAT HE HAS WILL BE TAKEN FROM HIM.

13.13 διὰ τοῦτο ἐν παραβολαῖς αὐτοῖς λαλῶ, ὅτι
FOR THIS REASON IN PARABLES I AM SPEAKING~TO THEM, FOR

βλέποντες οὐ βλέπουσιν καὶ ἀκούοντες οὐκ ἀκούουσιν
[WHILE] SEEING THEY DO NOT SEE AND [WHILE] HEARING THEY DO NOT HEAR

great crowds gathered around him that he got into a boat and sat there, while the whole crowd stood on the beach. ³And he told them many things in parables, saying: "Listen! A sower went out to sow. ⁴And as he sowed, some seeds fell on the path, and the birds came and ate them up. ⁵Other seeds fell on rocky ground, where they did not have much soil, and they sprang up quickly, since they had no depth of soil. ⁶But when the sun rose, they were scorched; and since they had no root, they withered away. ⁷Other seeds fell among thorns, and the thorns grew up and choked them. ⁸Other seeds fell on good soil and brought forth grain, some a hundredfold, some sixty, some thirty. ⁹Let anyone with ears[a] listen!"

10 Then the disciples came and asked him, "Why do you speak to them in parables?" ¹¹He answered, "To you it has been given to know the secrets[b] of the kingdom of heaven, but to them it has not been given. ¹²For to those who have, more will be given, and they will have an abundance; but from those who have nothing, even what they have will be taken away. ¹³The reason I speak to them in parables is that 'seeing they do not perceive, and hearing they do not listen,

[a] Other ancient authorities add *to hear*
[b] Or *mysteries*

nor do they understand.'
¹⁴With them indeed is
fulfilled the prophecy of
Isaiah that says:
　'You will indeed listen,
　　but never
　　understand,
　and you will indeed
　　look, but never
　　perceive.
¹⁵For this people's heart
　　has grown dull,
　and their ears are hard
　　of hearing,
　and they have shut
　　their eyes;
　so that they might not
　　look with their
　　eyes,
　and listen with their
　　ears,
　and understand with their
　　heart and turn—
　and I would heal
　　them.'
¹⁶But blessed are your eyes,
for they see, and your ears,
for they hear. ¹⁷Truly I tell
you, many prophets and
righteous people longed to
see what you see, but did not
see it, and to hear what you
hear, but did not hear it.
　18 "Hear then the parable
of the sower. ¹⁹When
anyone hears the word of the
kingdom and does not
understand it, the evil one
comes away and snatches away
what is sown in the heart;
this is what was sown on the
path. ²⁰As for what was
sown on rocky ground, this
is the one who hears the
word and immediately

οὐδὲ συνίουσιν, **13.14** καὶ ἀναπληροῦται αὐτοῖς ἡ
NOR　　DO THEY UNDERSTAND,　　AND　　IS FULFILLED　　IN THEM　　THE

προφητεία Ἠσαΐου ἡ λέγουσα,
PROPHECY　OF ISAIAH　-　SAYING,

Ἀκοῇ ἀκούσετε καὶ οὐ μὴ συνῆτε,
IN HEARING　YOU° WILL HEAR　AND　BY NO MEANS UNDERSTAND,

καὶ βλέποντες βλέψετε καὶ οὐ μὴ ἴδητε.
AND　[WHILE] SEEING　YOU° WILL SEE　AND　BY NO MEANS PERCEIVE.

13.15 ἐπαχύνθη γὰρ ἡ καρδία τοῦ λαοῦ τούτου,
FOR~HAS BEEN MADE DULL THE HEART　-　OF THIS~PEOPLE,

καὶ τοῖς ὠσὶν βαρέως ἤκουσαν
AND　WITH　[THEIR] EARS　THEY HEAR~WITH DIFFICULTY

καὶ τοὺς ὀφθαλμοὺς αὐτῶν ἐκάμμυσαν,
AND　THE　EYES　OF THEM　ARE CLOSED,

μήποτε ἴδωσιν τοῖς ὀφθαλμοῖς
LEST　THEY SEE　WITH THE(THEIR) EYES

καὶ τοῖς ὠσὶν ἀκούσωσιν
AND　WITH THE(THEIR) EARS　THEY HEAR

καὶ τῇ καρδίᾳ συνῶσιν καὶ ἐπιστρέψωσιν
AND　WITH THE HEART　THEY UNDERSTAND AND　THEY TURN

καὶ ἰάσομαι αὐτούς.
AND　I WILL HEAL　THEM.

13.16 ὑμῶν δὲ μακάριοι οἱ ὀφθαλμοὶ ὅτι βλέπουσιν
BUT~OF YOU°　[ARE] BLESSED　THE EYES　FOR　THEY SEE

καὶ τὰ ὦτα ὑμῶν ὅτι ἀκούουσιν. **13.17** ἀμὴν γὰρ λέγω
AND　THE EARS OF YOU°　FOR　THEY HEAR.　　FOR~TRULY　I SAY

ὑμῖν ὅτι πολλοὶ προφῆται καὶ δίκαιοι ἐπεθύμησαν
TO YOU° THAT MANY　PROPHETS　AND　RIGHTEOUS ONES　DESIRED

ἰδεῖν ἃ βλέπετε καὶ οὐκ εἶδαν, καὶ ἀκοῦσαι ἃ
TO SEE　WHAT YOU° SEE　AND　THEY DID NOT SEE [IT],　AND　TO HEAR　WHAT

ἀκούετε καὶ οὐκ ἤκουσαν.
YOU° HEAR　AND　THEY DID NOT HEAR [IT].

13.18 Ὑμεῖς οὖν ἀκούσατε τὴν παραβολὴν τοῦ
YOU°　THEREFORE　LISTEN TO　THE　PARABLE　OF THE

σπείραντος. **13.19** παντὸς ἀκούοντος τὸν λόγον τῆς
SOWER.　　[WHEN] ANYONE　HEARING　THE　WORD　OF THE

βασιλείας καὶ μὴ συνιέντος ἔρχεται ὁ πονηρὸς καὶ
KINGDOM　AND　NOT UNDERSTANDING [IT],　COMES　THE EVIL ONE　AND

ἁρπάζει τὸ ἐσπαρμένον ἐν τῇ καρδίᾳ αὐτοῦ,
SEIZES　THE [THING]　HAVING BEEN SOWN　IN　THE HEART　OF HIM,

οὗτός ἐστιν ὁ παρὰ τὴν ὁδὸν σπαρείς.
THIS ONE　IS [LIKE]　THE [SEED]　ALONG　THE　PATH　BEING SOWN.

13.20 ὁ δὲ ἐπὶ τὰ πετρώδη σπαρείς, οὗτός ἐστιν
AND~THE [SEED] UPON　THE　ROCKY PLACES　BEING SOWN,　THIS ONE　IS [LIKE]

ὁ τὸν λόγον ἀκούων καὶ εὐθὺς μετὰ χαρᾶς
THE ONE　²THE　³WORD　¹LISTENING TO　AND　IMMEDIATELY WITH　JOY

13:14-15 Isa. 6:9-10 LXX

λαμβάνων αὐτόν, **13.21** οὐκ ἔχει δὲ ῥίζαν ἐν ἑαυτῷ
RECEIVING   IT,   BUT~HE HAS NO   ROOT   IN   HIMSELF,

ἀλλὰ πρόσκαιρός ἐστιν, γενομένης δὲ θλίψεως ἢ
BUT   IS~TRANSITORY,   BUT~[WHEN] COMING   TRIBULATION OR

διωγμοῦ διὰ   τὸν λόγον εὐθὺς   σκανδαλίζεται.
PERSECUTION ON ACCOUNT OF THE WORD, IMMEDIATELY HE FALLS AWAY.

13.22 ὁ δὲ   εἰς τὰς ἀκάνθας σπαρείς, οὗτός ἐστιν
AND~THE [SEED] AMONG THE THORNS   BEING SOWN, THIS ONE IS

ὁ   τὸν λόγον ἀκούων, καὶ ἡ μέριμνα τοῦ αἰῶνος
THE ONE ²THE ³WORD ¹LISTENING TO, AND THE ANXIETY OF THE AGE

καὶ ἡ ἀπάτη τοῦ πλούτου συμπνίγει τὸν λόγον καὶ
AND THE DECEIT -   OF RICHES CHOKE   THE WORD AND

ἄκαρπος γίνεται. **13.23** ὁ δὲ   ἐπὶ τὴν καλὴν γῆν
IT BECOMES~UNFRUITFUL.   BUT~THE [SEED] UPON THE GOOD SOIL

σπαρείς, οὗτός ἐστιν ὁ   τὸν λόγον ἀκούων καὶ
BEING SOWN, THIS ONE IS THE ONE ²THE ³WORD ¹LISTENING TO AND

συνιείς,   ὃς δὴ καρποφορεῖ καὶ ποιεῖ ὃ μὲν
UNDERSTANDING [IT], WHO INDEED BEARS FRUIT AND THE ONE~PRODUCES

ἑκατόν, ὃ δὲ ἑξήκοντα, ὃ δὲ   τριάκοντα.
A HUNDRED, THE OTHER SIXTY,   THE OTHER THIRTY.

13.24 Ἄλλην παραβολὴν παρέθηκεν αὐτοῖς λέγων,
      ANOTHER   PARABLE   HE PLACED BEFORE THEM   SAYING,

Ὡμοιώθη ἡ βασιλεία τῶν οὐρανῶν ἀνθρώπῳ
⁵IS LIKE ¹THE ²KINGDOM ³OF THE ⁴HEAVENS A MAN

σπείραντι καλὸν σπέρμα ἐν τῷ ἀγρῷ αὐτοῦ.
HAVING SOWN GOOD SEED   IN THE FIELD OF HIM.

13.25 ἐν δὲ τῷ καθεύδειν τοὺς ἀνθρώπους ἦλθεν αὐτοῦ
       BUT~WHILE SLEPT   THE   MEN   ⁴CAME ³OF HIM

ὁ ἐχθρὸς καὶ ἐπέσπειρεν ζιζάνια ἀνὰ μέσον τοῦ
¹THE ²ENEMY AND SOWED AFTERWARD WEEDS IN THE MIDST OF THE

σίτου καὶ ἀπῆλθεν. **13.26** ὅτε δὲ ἐβλάστησεν ὁ
WHEAT AND WENT AWAY.   AND~WHEN SPROUTED   THE

χόρτος καὶ καρπὸν ἐποίησεν, τότε ἐφάνη καὶ τὰ
GRASS AND IT PRODUCED~FRUIT,   THEN APPEARED ALSO THE

ζιζάνια. **13.27** προσελθόντες δὲ οἱ δοῦλοι τοῦ
WEEDS.   AND~HAVING APPROACHED THE SLAVES OF THE

οἰκοδεσπότου εἶπον αὐτῷ, Κύριε, οὐχὶ καλὸν σπέρμα
MASTER OF THE HOUSE SAID TO HIM, LORD, ²NOT ⁴GOOD ⁵SEED

ἔσπειρας ἐν τῷ σῷ ἀγρῷ; πόθεν οὖν   ἔχει
¹DID YOU ³SOW IN - YOUR FIELD? THEN~FROM WHERE HAVE

ζιζάνια; **13.28** ὁ δὲ ἔφη αὐτοῖς, Ἐχθρὸς ἄνθρωπος
[THE] WEEDS [COME]?   AND~HE SAID TO THEM, AN ENEMY MAN

τοῦτο ἐποίησεν. οἱ δὲ δοῦλοι λέγουσιν αὐτῷ, Θέλεις
DID~THIS.   SO~THE SLAVES SAY   TO HIM, DO YOU WANT

οὖν ἀπελθόντες συλλέξωμεν αὐτά; **13.29** ὁ δέ φησιν,
THEN [AS] WE GO [THAT] WE COLLECT THEM?   BUT~HE SAID,

Οὔ, μήποτε συλλέγοντες τὰ ζιζάνια ἐκριζώσητε ἅμα
NO, LEST [WHILE] GATHERING THE WEEDS   YOU° UPROOT TOGETHER

receives it with joy; [21]yet such a person has no root, but endures only for a while, and when trouble or persecution arises on account of the word, that person immediately falls away.[c] [22]As for what was sown among thorns, this is the one who hears the word, but the cares of the world and the lure of wealth choke the word, and it yields nothing. [23]But as for what was sown on good soil, this is the one who hears the word and understands it, who indeed bears fruit and yields, in one case a hundredfold, in another sixty, and in another thirty."

24 He put before them another parable: "The kingdom of heaven may be compared to someone who sowed good seed in his field; [25]but while everybody was asleep, an enemy came and sowed weeds among the wheat, and then went away. [26]So when the plants came up and bore grain, then the weeds appeared as well. [27]And the slaves of the householder came and said to him, 'Master, did you not sow good seed in your field? Where, then, did these weeds come from?' [28]He answered, 'An enemy has done this.' The slaves said to him, 'Then do you want us to go and gather them?' [29]But he replied, 'No; for in gathering the weeds you would uproot

[c] Gk *stumbles*

the wheat along with them. [30]Let both of them grow together until the harvest; and at harvest time I will tell the reapers, Collect the weeds first and bind them in bundles to be burned, but gather the wheat into my barn.' "

31 He put before them another parable: "The kingdom of heaven is like a mustard seed that someone took and sowed in his field; [32]it is the smallest of all the seeds, but when it has grown it is the greatest of shrubs and becomes a tree, so that the birds of the air come and make nests in its branches."

33 He told them another parable: "The kingdom of heaven is like yeast that a woman took and mixed in with[d] three measures of flour until all of it was leavened."

34 Jesus told the crowds all these things in parables; without a parable he told them nothing. [35]This was to fulfill what had been spoken through the prophet:[e]

"I will open my mouth to speak in parables;

[d] Gk *hid in*
[e] Other ancient authorities read *the prophet Isaiah*

αὐτοῖς τὸν σῖτον. **13.30** ἄφετε συναυξάνεσθαι ἀμφότερα
WITH THEM THE WHEAT. PERMIT TO GROW TOGETHER BOTH

ἕως τοῦ θερισμοῦ, καὶ ἐν καιρῷ τοῦ θερισμοῦ ἐρῶ
UNTIL THE HARVEST, AND AT [THE] TIME OF THE HARVEST I WILL SAY

τοῖς θερισταῖς, Συλλέξατε πρῶτον τὰ ζιζάνια καὶ
TO THE REAPERS, COLLECT FIRST THE WEEDS AND

δήσατε αὐτὰ εἰς δέσμας πρὸς τὸ κατακαῦσαι αὐτά,
TIE THEM INTO BUNDLES IN ORDER TO BURN THEM,

τὸν δὲ σῖτον συναγάγετε εἰς τὴν ἀποθήκην μου.
BUT~THE WHEAT GATHER INTO THE STOREHOUSE OF ME.

13.31 Ἄλλην παραβολὴν παρέθηκεν αὐτοῖς λέγων,
ANOTHER PARABLE HE PLACED BEFORE THEM SAYING,

Ὁμοία ἐστὶν ἡ βασιλεία τῶν οὐρανῶν
[6]LIKE [5]IS [1]THE [2]KINGDOM [3]OF THE [4]HEAVENS

κόκκῳ σινάπεως, ὃν λαβὼν ἄνθρωπος ἔσπειρεν ἐν τῷ
A MUSTARD~SEED, WHICH TAKING A MAN PLANTED IN THE

ἀγρῷ αὐτοῦ· **13.32** ὃ μικρότερον μέν ἐστιν πάντων
FIELD OF HIM, WHICH [3]SMALLER THAN [2]INDEED [1]IS ALL

τῶν σπερμάτων, ὅταν δὲ αὐξηθῇ μεῖζον τῶν
OF THE SEEDS, BUT~WHEN IT GROWS, LARGER THAN THE

λαχάνων ἐστὶν καὶ γίνεται δένδρον, ὥστε ἐλθεῖν
GARDEN VEGETABLES IT IS AND IT BECOMES A TREE, SO THAT TO COME

τὰ πετεινὰ τοῦ οὐρανοῦ καὶ κατασκηνοῦν ἐν τοῖς
THE BIRDS - OF HEAVEN AND TO LIVE IN THE

κλάδοις αὐτοῦ.
BRANCHES OF IT.

13.33 Ἄλλην παραβολὴν ἐλάλησεν αὐτοῖς· Ὁμοία
ANOTHER PARABLE HE PLACED BEFORE THEM: [6]LIKE

ἐστὶν ἡ βασιλεία τῶν οὐρανῶν ζύμῃ, ἣν λαβοῦσα
[5]IS [1]THE [2]KINGDOM [3]OF THE [4]HEAVENS LEAVEN, WHICH HAVING TAKEN

γυνὴ ἐνέκρυψεν εἰς ἀλεύρου σάτα τρία ἕως οὗ
A WOMAN HID IN [3]OF WHEAT FLOUR [2]MEASURES [1]THREE UNTIL

ἐζυμώθη ὅλον.
IT LEAVENED [THE] WHOLE.

13.34 Ταῦτα πάντα ἐλάλησεν ὁ Ἰησοῦς ἐν
ALL~THESE THINGS SPOKE - JESUS IN

παραβολαῖς τοῖς ὄχλοις καὶ χωρὶς παραβολῆς
PARABLES TO THE CROWDS AND APART FROM PARABLES

οὐδὲν ἐλάλει αὐτοῖς, **13.35** ὅπως πληρωθῇ τὸ
HE DID NOT SPEAK TO THEM, SO THAT MIGHT BE FULFILLED THE [THING]

ῥηθὲν διὰ᾽ τοῦ προφήτου λέγοντος,
SPOKEN THROUGH THE PROPHET SAYING,

Ἀνοίξω ἐν παραβολαῖς τὸ στόμα μου,
I WILL OPEN WITH PARABLES THE MOUTH OF ME,

13:35a text: KJV ASV RSV NASB NIV NEBmg TEV NJB NRSV. add Ἡσαιου (Isaiah): RSVmg NEB NRSVmg.

ἐρεύξομαι κεκρυμμένα   ἀπὸ καταβολῆς
I WILL UTTER THINGS HAVING BEEN HIDDEN FROM [THE] FOUNDATION

[κόσμου].
OF [THE] WORLD.

13.36 Τότε ἀφεὶς   τοὺς ὄχλους ἦλθεν εἰς τὴν
THEN HAVING SENT AWAY THE CROWDS HE CAME INTO THE

οἰκίαν. καὶ προσῆλθον αὐτῷ οἱ μαθηταὶ αὐτοῦ
HOUSE.   AND APPROACHED HIM THE DISCIPLES OF HIM

λέγοντες, Διασάφησον ἡμῖν τὴν παραβολὴν τῶν
SAYING,   EXPLAIN   TO US THE   PARABLE   OF THE

ζιζανίων τοῦ ἀγροῦ. **13.37** ὁ δὲ ἀποκριθεὶς εἶπεν,
WEEDS   OF THE FIELD.   AND~HE HAVING ANSWERED SAID,

Ὁ   σπείρων τὸ καλὸν σπέρμα ἐστὶν ὁ υἱὸς τοῦ
THE ONE SOWING THE GOOD SEED   IS   THE SON   -

ἀνθρώπου, **13.38** ὁ δὲ ἀγρός ἐστιν ὁ κόσμος, τὸ δὲ
OF MAN,   AND~THE FIELD IS   THE WORLD,   AND~THE

καλὸν σπέρμα οὗτοί εἰσιν οἱ υἱοὶ τῆς βασιλείας·
GOOD   SEED   THESE ARE THE SONS OF THE KINGDOM.

τὰ δὲ ζιζάνιά εἰσιν οἱ υἱοὶ τοῦ πονηροῦ, **13.39** ὁ δὲ
BUT~THE WEEDS ARE THE SONS OF THE EVIL [ONE],   AND~THE

ἐχθρὸς ὁ σπείρας αὐτά ἐστιν ὁ διάβολος, ὁ δὲ
ENEMY—THE ONE HAVING SOWN THEM—IS THE DEVIL,   AND~THE

θερισμὸς συντέλεια αἰῶνός ἐστιν, οἱ δὲ θερισταὶ
HARVEST   [THE] END OF [THE] AGE IS,   AND~THE REAPERS

ἄγγελοί εἰσιν. **13.40** ὥσπερ οὖν συλλέγεται   τὰ
ARE~ANGELS.   THEREFORE,~JUST AS ARE GATHERED TOGETHER THE

ζιζάνια καὶ πυρὶ [κατα]καίεται, οὕτως ἔσται ἐν τῇ
WEEDS   -   TO BE CONSUMED~BY FIRE,   SO ALSO IT WILL BE AT THE

συντελείᾳ τοῦ αἰῶνος· **13.41** ἀποστελεῖ ὁ υἱὸς τοῦ
END   OF THE AGE.   WILL SEND OUT THE SON   -

ἀνθρώπου τοὺς ἀγγέλους αὐτοῦ, καὶ συλλέξουσιν
OF MAN   THE   ANGELS   OF HIM, AND THEY WILL GATHER TOGETHER

ἐκ τῆς βασιλείας αὐτοῦ πάντα τὰ σκάνδαλα καὶ
FROM THE KINGDOM   OF HIM ALL THE OFFENSIVE THINGS AND

τοὺς ποιοῦντας τὴν ἀνομίαν **13.42** καὶ βαλοῦσιν
THE ONES PRACTICING -   LAWLESSNESS   AND THEY WILL THROW

αὐτοὺς εἰς τὴν κάμινον τοῦ πυρός· ἐκεῖ ἔσται
THEM   INTO THE FURNACE   - OF FIRE. IN THAT PLACE THERE WILL BE

ὁ κλαυθμὸς καὶ ὁ βρυγμὸς τῶν ὀδόντων. **13.43** Τότε
- WEEPING   AND - GRINDING OF THE TEETH.   THEN

οἱ δίκαιοι ἐκλάμψουσιν ὡς ὁ ἥλιος ἐν τῇ
THE RIGHTEOUS ONES WILL SHINE AS THE SUN   IN THE

βασιλείᾳ τοῦ πατρὸς αὐτῶν. ὁ ἔχων ὦτα
KINGDOM   OF THE FATHER OF THEM. THE ONE HAVING EARS

ἀκουέτω.
LET THAT ONE HEAR.

13:35b Ps. 78:2

I will proclaim what has been hidden from the foundation of the world.'[f]

36 Then he left the crowds and went into the house. And his disciples approached him, saying, "Explain to us the parable of the weeds of the field." [37]He answered, "The one who sows the good seed is the Son of Man; [38]the field is the world, and the good seed are the children of the kingdom; the weeds are the children of the evil one, [39]and the enemy who sowed them is the devil; the harvest is the end of the age, and the reapers are angels. [40]Just as the weeds are collected and burned up with fire, so will it be at the end of the age. [41]The Son of Man will send his angels, and they will collect out of his kingdom all causes of sin and all evildoers, [42]and they will throw them into the furnace of fire, where there will be weeping and gnashing of teeth. [43]Then the righteous will shine like the sun in the kingdom of their Father. Let anyone with ears[g] listen!

[f] Other ancient authorities lack *of the world*

[g] Other ancient authorities add *to hear*

44 "The kingdom of heaven is like treasure hidden in a field, which someone found and hid; then in his joy he goes and sells all that he has and buys that field.

45 "Again, the kingdom of heaven is like a merchant in search of fine pearls; ⁴⁶on finding one pearl of great value, he went and sold all that he had and bought it.

47 "Again, the kingdom of heaven is like a net that was thrown into the sea and caught fish of every kind; ⁴⁸when it was full, they drew it ashore, sat down, and put the good into baskets but threw out the bad. ⁴⁹So it will be at the end of the age. The angels will come out and separate the evil from the righteous ⁵⁰and throw them into the furnace of fire, where there will be weeping and gnashing of teeth.

51 "Have you understood all this?" They answered, "Yes." ⁵²And he said to them, "Therefore every scribe who has been trained for the kingdom of heaven

13.44 Ὁμοία ἐστὶν ἡ βασιλεία τῶν οὐρανῶν
⁶LIKE   ⁵IS   ¹THE ²KINGDOM ³OF THE ⁴HEAVENS

θησαυρῷ κεκρυμμένῳ ἐν τῷ ἀγρῷ, ὃν εὑρὼν
A HAVING BEEN HIDDEN~TREASURE IN THE FIELD; WHICH HAVING FOUND

ἄνθρωπος ἔκρυψεν, καὶ ἀπὸ τῆς χαρᾶς αὐτοῦ ὑπάγει
A MAN   HID,   AND FROM THE JOY   OF HIM   GOES AWAY

καὶ πωλεῖ πάντα ὅσα ἔχει καὶ ἀγοράζει τὸν
AND SELLS EVERYTHING WHICH HE HAS AND BUYS   -

ἀγρὸν ἐκεῖνον.
THAT~FIELD.

13.45 Πάλιν ὁμοία ἐστὶν ἡ βασιλεία τῶν οὐρανῶν
AGAIN ⁶LIKE ⁵IS ¹THE ²KINGDOM ³OF THE ⁴HEAVENS

ἀνθρώπῳ ἐμπόρῳ ζητοῦντι καλοὺς μαργαρίτας·
A MERCHANT~MAN   SEEKING   FINE   PEARLS.

13.46 εὑρὼν δὲ   ἕνα πολύτιμον μαργαρίτην
AND~HAVING FOUND ONE VALUABLE   PEARL,

ἀπελθὼν   πέπρακεν πάντα ὅσα εἶχεν καὶ ἡγόρασεν
HAVING GONE AWAY SOLD   EVERYTHING WHICH HE HAD AND BOUGHT

αὐτόν.
IT.

13.47 Πάλιν ὁμοία ἐστὶν ἡ βασιλεία τῶν οὐρανῶν
AGAIN ⁶LIKE ⁵IS ¹THE ²KINGDOM ³OF THE ⁴HEAVENS

σαγήνῃ βληθείσῃ εἰς τὴν θάλασσαν καὶ ἐκ παντὸς
A NET   HAVING BEEN CAST INTO THE LAKE   AND FROM EVERY

γένους συναγαγούσῃ· **13.48** ἦν ὅτε ἐπληρώθη
KIND   IT GATHERED.   WHICH WHEN IT WAS FILLED

ἀναβιβάσαντες ἐπὶ τὸν αἰγιαλὸν καὶ καθίσαντες
HAVING BEEN PULLED UP ON THE SHORE   AND HAVING SAT DOWN

συνέλεξαν τὰ καλὰ εἰς ἄγγη, τὰ δὲ σαπρὰ
THEY COLLECTED THE GOOD THINGS INTO A CONTAINER, AND~THE ROTTEN THINGS

ἔξω ἔβαλον. **13.49** οὕτως ἔσται ἐν τῇ συντελείᾳ τοῦ
THEY THREW~OUT.   THUS   IT WILL BE AT THE END   OF THE

αἰῶνος· ἐξελεύσονται οἱ ἄγγελοι καὶ ἀφοριοῦσιν τοὺς
AGE.   WILL GO OUT   THE ANGELS AND THEY WILL SEPARATE THE

πονηροὺς ἐκ μέσου τῶν δικαίων **13.50** καὶ
EVIL [ONES] FROM AMONG THE RIGHTEOUS [ONES]   AND

βαλοῦσιν αὐτοὺς εἰς τὴν κάμινον τοῦ πυρός·
THEY WILL THROW THEM INTO THE FURNACE - OF FIRE.

ἐκεῖ ἔσται ὁ κλαυθμὸς καὶ ὁ βρυγμὸς τῶν
IN THAT PLACE THERE WILL BE - WEEPING AND - GRINDING OF THE

ὀδόντων.
TEETH.

13.51 Συνήκατε ταῦτα πάντα; λέγουσιν αὐτῷ, Ναί.
DID YOU° UNDERSTAND ALL~THESE THINGS? THEY SAY TO HIM, YES.

13.52 ὁ δὲ εἶπεν αὐτοῖς, Διὰ τοῦτο πᾶς γραμματεὺς
SO~HE SAID TO THEM, THEREFORE EVERY SCRIBE

μαθητευθεὶς τῇ βασιλείᾳ τῶν οὐρανῶν
HAVING BECOME A DISCIPLE OF THE KINGDOM OF THE HEAVENS

ὅμοιός ἐστιν ἀνθρώπῳ οἰκοδεσπότῃ, ὅστις ἐκβάλλει ἐκ
IS~LIKE   A MAN [WHO IS]   A HOUSE MASTER,   WHO   TAKES OUT   OF

τοῦ θησαυροῦ αὐτοῦ καινὰ καὶ παλαιά.
THE   TREASURE   OF HIM   NEW   AND   OLD.

13.53 Καὶ ἐγένετο ὅτε ἐτέλεσεν ὁ Ἰησοῦς τὰς
     AND   IT CAME ABOUT   WHEN   FINISHED   -   JESUS   -

παραβολὰς ταύτας, μετῆρεν ἐκεῖθεν. **13.54** καὶ
THESE~PARABLES, [THAT]   HE WENT AWAY   FROM THERE.   AND

ἐλθὼν εἰς τὴν πατρίδα αὐτοῦ ἐδίδασκεν αὐτοὺς ἐν
HAVING COME   INTO   THE   HOMETOWN   OF HIM   HE TAUGHT   THEM   IN

τῇ συναγωγῇ αὐτῶν, ὥστε ἐκπλήσσεσθαι αὐτοὺς καὶ
THE SYNAGOGUE   OF THEM,   SO AS   TO BE AMAZED   THEM   AND

λέγειν, Πόθεν   τούτῳ ἡ σοφία αὕτη καὶ αἱ
TO SAY,   FROM WHERE [DID IT COME]   TO THIS ONE   -   THIS~WISDOM   AND   THE

δυνάμεις; **13.55** οὐχ οὗτός ἐστιν ὁ τοῦ τέκτονος υἱός;
MIRACLES?   IS THIS NOT   THE   -   CARPENTER'S   SON?

οὐχ ἡ μήτηρ αὐτοῦ λέγεται Μαριὰμ καὶ οἱ ἀδελφοὶ
[IS] NOT   THE   MOTHER   OF HIM   CALLED   MARY   AND   THE BROTHERS

αὐτοῦ Ἰάκωβος καὶ Ἰωσὴφ καὶ Σίμων καὶ Ἰούδας;
OF HIM   JAMES   AND   JOSEPH   AND   SIMON   AND   JUDAS?

13.56 καὶ αἱ ἀδελφαὶ αὐτοῦ οὐχὶ πᾶσαι πρὸς ἡμᾶς
     AND   THE   SISTERS   OF HIM   NOT   ALL   WITH   US

εἰσιν; πόθεν οὖν   τούτῳ ταῦτα πάντα;
ARE?   FROM WHERE   THEREFORE [CAME]   TO THIS ONE   ALL~THESE THINGS?

13.57 καὶ ἐσκανδαλίζοντο ἐν αὐτῷ. ὁ δὲ Ἰησοῦς
     AND   THEY WERE TAKING OFFENSE   AT   HIM.   -   BUT   JESUS

εἶπεν αὐτοῖς, Οὐκ ἔστιν προφήτης ἄτιμος εἰ μὴ ἐν τῇ
SAID   TO THEM,   A PROPHET~IS NOT   DISHONORED   EXCEPT   IN   HIS

πατρίδι καὶ ἐν τῇ οἰκίᾳ αὐτοῦ. **13.58** καὶ
COUNTRY   AND   IN   THE   HOUSE   OF HIM.   AND

οὐκ ἐποίησεν ἐκεῖ   δυνάμεις πολλὰς διὰ   τὴν
HE DID NOT PERFORM   IN THAT PLACE   MANY~MIRACLES   BECAUSE OF   THE

ἀπιστίαν αὐτῶν.
UNBELIEF   OF THEM.

---

is like the master of a household who brings out of his treasure what is new and what is old." [53]When Jesus had finished these parables, he left that place.

54 He came to his hometown and began to teach the people[h] in their synagogue, so that they were astounded and said, "Where did this man get this wisdom and these deeds of power? [55]Is not this the carpenter's son? Is not his mother called Mary? And are not his brothers James and Joseph and Simon and Judas? [56]And are not all his sisters with us? Where then did this man get all this?" [57]And they took offense at him. But Jesus said to them, "Prophets are not without honor except in their own country and in their own house." [58]And he did not do many deeds of power there, because of their unbelief.

[h] Gk *them*

14.1 Ἐν ἐκείνῳ τῷ καιρῷ ἤκουσεν Ἡρῴδης ὁ
     AT   THAT   -   TIME   HEARD   HEROD   THE

τετραάρχης τὴν ἀκοὴν Ἰησοῦ, **14.2** καὶ εἶπεν τοῖς
TETRARCH   THE   REPORT   OF JESUS,   AND   HE SAID   TO THE

παισὶν αὐτοῦ, Οὗτός ἐστιν Ἰωάννης ὁ βαπτιστής·
SERVANTS   OF HIM,   THIS ONE   IS   JOHN   THE   BAPTIST.

αὐτὸς ἠγέρθη ἀπὸ τῶν νεκρῶν καὶ διὰ τοῦτο αἱ
HE   HAS RISEN   FROM   THE   DEAD   AND   FOR THIS REASON   THE

δυνάμεις ἐνεργοῦσιν ἐν αὐτῷ. **14.3** Ὁ γὰρ Ἡρῴδης
POWERS   ARE WORKING   IN   HIM.   -   FOR   HEROD

At that time Herod the ruler[i] heard reports about Jesus; [2]and he said to his servants, "This is John the Baptist; he has been raised from the dead, and for this reason these powers are at work in him." [3]For Herod

[i] Gk *tetrarch*

had arrested John, bound him, and put him in prison on account of Herodias, his brother Philip's wife,[j] [4]because John had been telling him, "It is not lawful for you to have her." [5]Though Herod[k] wanted to put him to death, he feared the crowd, because they regarded him as a prophet. [6]But when Herod's birthday came, the daughter of Herodias danced before the company, and she pleased Herod [7]so much that he promised on oath to grant her whatever she might ask. [8]Prompted by her mother, she said, "Give me the head of John the Baptist here on a platter." [9]The king was grieved, yet out of regard for his oaths and for the guests, he commanded it to be given; [10]he sent and had John beheaded in the prison. [11]The head was brought on a platter and given to the girl, who brought it to her mother. [12]His disciples came and took the body and buried it; then they went and told Jesus.

13 Now when Jesus heard this, he withdrew from there in a boat to a deserted place by himself. But when the crowds heard it, they followed him on foot from the towns. [14]When he went ashore, he saw a great crowd; and he had compassion for them and cured their sick.

[j] Other ancient authorities read *his brother's wife*
[k] Gk *he*

κρατήσας   τὸν   Ἰωάννην   ἔδησεν   [αὐτὸν]   καὶ   ἐν   φυλακῇ
HAVING ARRESTED -   JOHN   BOUND   HIM   AND   IN   PRISON

ἀπέθετο   διὰ   Ἡρῳδιάδα τὴν   γυναῖκα   Φιλίππου   τοῦ
HE PUT [HIM] AWAY BECAUSE HERODIAS   THE   WIFE   OF PHILIP,   THE

ἀδελφοῦ   αὐτοῦ·   **14.4** ἔλεγεν γὰρ   ὁ   Ἰωάννης   αὐτῷ,
BROTHER   OF HIM.   FOR~WAS SAYING   -   JOHN   TO HIM,

Οὐκ   ἔξεστίν   σοι   ἔχειν   αὐτήν.   **14.5** καὶ   θέλων
IT IS NOT PERMISSIBLE FOR YOU TO HAVE HER.   AND [ALTHOUGH] DESIRING

αὐτὸν   ἀποκτεῖναι   ἐφοβήθη   τὸν   ὄχλον,   ὅτι   ὡς
TO KILL~HIM,   HE FEARED THE   CROWD,   BECAUSE AS

προφήτην   αὐτὸν   εἶχον.   **14.6** γενεσίοις   δὲ
A PROPHET THEY CONSIDERED~HIM.   NOW~AT THE BIRTHDAY CELEBRATION

γενομένοις   τοῦ   Ἡρῴδου ὠρχήσατο ἡ   θυγάτηρ τῆς
[IT CAME ABOUT [THAT] -   ¹OF HEROD DANCED   THE DAUGHTER   -

Ἡρῳδιάδος ἐν   τῷ   μέσῳ   καὶ   ἤρεσεν τῷ   Ἡρῴδῃ,
OF HERODIAS IN THE   MIDST [OF THEM] AND IT PLEASED -   HEROD,

14.7 ὅθεν   μεθ'   ὅρκου   ὡμολόγησεν   αὐτῇ δοῦναι ὃ ἐὰν
THEREFORE WITH   AN OATH HE PROMISED   TO GIVE~TO HER   WHATEVER

αἰτήσηται.   **14.8** ἡ δὲ   προβιβασθεῖσα   ὑπὸ τῆς μητρὸς
SHE WISHED.   SO~SHE HAVING BEEN PROMPTED   BY   THE MOTHER

αὐτῆς,   Δός μοι, φησίν,   ὧδε ἐπὶ πίνακι τὴν κεφαλὴν
OF HER, GIVE TO ME, SHE SAID, HERE UPON A PLATTER THE HEAD

Ἰωάννου   τοῦ   βαπτιστοῦ.   **14.9** καὶ λυπηθεὶς   ὁ
OF JOHN   THE   BAPTIST.   AND [ALTHOUGH] GRIEVING THE

βασιλεὺς διὰ   τοὺς ὅρκους καὶ τοὺς
KING   ON ACCOUNT OF THE OATHS   AND THE

συνανακειμένους ἐκέλευσεν   δοθῆναι, **14.10** καὶ   πέμψας
FELLOW GUESTS   HE COMMANDED [IT] TO BE GIVEN,   AND HAVING SENT

ἀπεκεφάλισεν [τὸν] Ἰωάννην ἐν τῇ φυλακῇ.   **14.11** καὶ
HE BEHEADED   -   JOHN   IN   -   PRISON.   AND

ἠνέχθη   ἡ   κεφαλὴ αὐτοῦ ἐπὶ πίνακι καὶ ἐδόθη
WAS BROUGHT THE HEAD   OF HIM   UPON A PLATTER AND IT WAS GIVEN

τῷ   κορασίῳ, καὶ ἤνεγκεν τῇ   μητρὶ αὐτῆς.   **14.12** καὶ
TO THE GIRL,   AND SHE GAVE [IT] TO THE MOTHER OF HER.   AND

προσελθόντες οἱ μαθηταὶ αὐτοῦ ἦραν   τὸ πτῶμα καὶ
HAVING APPROACHED THE DISCIPLES OF HIM THEY CARRIED THE CORPSE   AND

ἔθαψαν αὐτό[ν] καὶ ἐλθόντες   ἀπήγγειλαν τῷ   Ἰησοῦ.
BURIED   HIM   AND HAVING COME THEY REPORTED [IT] -   TO JESUS.

14.13 Ἀκούσας δὲ   ὁ Ἰησοῦς ἀνεχώρησεν ἐκεῖθεν
AND~HAVING HEARD [THIS] - JESUS   WITHDREW   FROM THERE

ἐν   πλοίῳ εἰς ἔρημον τόπον κατ' ἰδίαν·   καὶ
IN   A BOAT   TO   A DESOLATE PLACE BY HIMSELF.   AND

ἀκούσαντες οἱ ὄχλοι ἠκολούθησαν αὐτῷ πεζῇ ἀπὸ τῶν
HAVING HEARD [THIS] THE CROWDS FOLLOWED   HIM   BY LAND FROM THE

πόλεων. **14.14** καὶ ἐξελθὼν   εἶδεν   πολὺν ὄχλον καὶ
CITIES.   AND HAVING GONE OUT HE SAW A GREAT CROWD AND

ἐσπλαγχνίσθη ἐπ' αὐτοῖς καὶ ἐθεράπευσεν τοὺς
HE FELT COMPASSION FOR THEM   AND HEALED   -

ἀρρώστους αὐτῶν. **14.15** ὀψίας δὲ γενομένης   προσῆλθον
THEIR~SICK.   NOW~[WHEN] EVENING HAVING COME, CAME

αὐτῷ οἱ μαθηταὶ λέγοντες, Ἔρημός ἐστιν ὁ τόπος
TO HIM THE DISCIPLES SAYING,   DESOLATE IS   THE PLACE

καὶ ἡ ὥρα ἤδη παρῆλθεν· ἀπόλυσον τοὺς ὄχλους,
AND THE HOUR HAS PASSED~ALREADY. DISMISS   THE   CROWDS,

ἵνα ἀπελθόντες εἰς τὰς κώμας ἀγοράσωσιν ἑαυτοῖς
SO THAT HAVING GONE OUT INTO THE VILLAGES THEY MAY BUY FOR THEMSELVES

βρώματα. **14.16** ὁ δὲ [Ἰησοῦς] εἶπεν αὐτοῖς,
FOOD.   - BUT JESUS   SAID   TO THEM,

Οὐ χρείαν ἔχουσιν ἀπελθεῖν, δότε αὐτοῖς
THEY HAVE NO NEED   TO GO OUT,   GIVE TO THEM

ὑμεῖς   φαγεῖν. **14.17** οἱ δὲ λέγουσιν αὐτῷ,
YOURSELVES [SOMETHING] TO EAT.   BUT~THEY SAY   TO HIM,

Οὐκ ἔχομεν ὧδε εἰ μὴ πέντε ἄρτους καὶ δύο ἰχθύας.
WE DO NOT HAVE HERE EXCEPT FIVE LOAVES AND TWO FISH.

14.18 ὁ δὲ εἶπεν, Φέρετέ μοι ὧδε αὐτούς. **14.19** καὶ
BUT~HE SAID, BRING ³TO ME ²HERE ¹THEM.   AND

κελεύσας τοὺς ὄχλους ἀνακλιθῆναι ἐπὶ τοῦ χόρτου,
HAVING COMMANDED THE CROWDS TO RECLINE ON THE GRASS,

λαβὼν τοὺς πέντε ἄρτους καὶ τοὺς δύο ἰχθύας,
[AND] HAVING TAKEN THE FIVE LOAVES AND THE TWO FISH,

ἀναβλέψας   εἰς τὸν οὐρανὸν εὐλόγησεν καὶ
[AND] HAVING LOOKED UP TO - HEAVEN   HE BLESSED [THEM] AND

κλάσας   ἔδωκεν τοῖς μαθηταῖς τοὺς ἄρτους, οἱ δὲ
HAVING BROKEN [THEM] HE GAVE TO THE DISCIPLES THE LOAVES, AND~THE

μαθηταὶ   τοῖς ὄχλοις. **14.20** καὶ ἔφαγον πάντες
DISCIPLES [GAVE THEM] TO THE CROWDS. AND EVERYONE~ATE

καὶ ἐχορτάσθησαν, καὶ ἦραν   τὸ περισσεῦον τῶν
AND THEY WERE SATISFIED, AND THEY CARRIED UP THE LEFTOVERS OF THE

κλασμάτων δώδεκα κοφίνους πλήρεις. **14.21** οἱ δὲ
FRAGMENTS, TWELVE BASKETS FULL.   AND~THE ONES

ἐσθίοντες ἦσαν ἄνδρες ὡσεὶ πεντακισχίλιοι χωρὶς
EATING   WERE MEN   ABOUT FIVE THOUSAND   APART FROM

γυναικῶν καὶ παιδίων.
[THE] WOMEN AND CHILDREN.

14.22 Καὶ εὐθέως ἠνάγκασεν τοὺς μαθητὰς ἐμβῆναι
AND IMMEDIATELY HE COMPELLED THE DISCIPLES TO ENTER

εἰς τὸ πλοῖον καὶ προάγειν αὐτὸν εἰς τὸ πέραν,
INTO THE BOAT AND TO GO BEFORE HIM TO THE OTHER SIDE,

ἕως οὗ ἀπολύσῃ   τοὺς ὄχλους. **14.23** καὶ ἀπολύσας
UNTIL HE MIGHT SEND AWAY THE CROWDS. AND HAVING SENT AWAY

τοὺς ὄχλους ἀνέβη εἰς τὸ ὄρος κατ' ἰδίαν
THE CROWDS HE WENT UP TO THE MOUNTAIN BY HIMSELF

προσεύξασθαι. ὀψίας δὲ γενομένης μόνος ἦν ἐκεῖ.
TO PRAY.   NOW~[WHEN] EVENING HAVING COME HE WAS~ALONE THERE.

14.24 τὸ δὲ πλοῖον ἤδη σταδίους πολλοὺς ἀπὸ τῆς
NOW~THE BOAT BY THIS TIME MANY~STADIA   FROM THE

[15]When it was evening, the disciples came to him and said, "This is a deserted place, and the hour is now late; send the crowds away so that they may go into the villages and buy food for themselves." [16]Jesus said to them, "They need not go away; you give them something to eat." [17]They replied, "We have nothing here but five loaves and two fish." [18]And he said, "Bring them here to me." [19]Then he ordered the crowds to sit down on the grass. Taking the five loaves and the two fish, he looked up to heaven, and blessed and broke the loaves, and gave them to the disciples, and the disciples gave them to the crowds. [20]And all ate and were filled; and they took up what was left over of the broken pieces, twelve baskets full. [21]And those who ate were about five thousand men, besides women and children.

[22] Immediately he made the disciples get into the boat and go on ahead to the other side, while he dismissed the crowds. [23]And after he had dismissed the crowds, he went up the mountain by himself to pray. When evening came, he was there alone, [24]but by this time the boat, battered by the waves, was far from the

land,[l] for the wind was against them. [25]And early in the morning he came walking toward them on the sea. [26]But when the disciples saw him walking on the sea, they were terrified, saying, "It is a ghost!" And they cried out in fear. [27]But immediately Jesus spoke to them and said, "Take heart, it is I; do not be afraid."

28 Peter answered him, "Lord, if it is you, command me to come to you on the water." [29]He said, "Come." So Peter got out of the boat, started walking on the water, and came toward Jesus. [30]But when he noticed the strong wind,[m] he became frightened, and beginning to sink, he cried out, "Lord, save me!" [31]Jesus immediately reached out his hand and caught him, saying to him, "You of little faith, why did you doubt?" [32]When they got into the boat, the wind ceased. [33]And those in the boat worshiped him, saying, "Truly you are the Son of God."

34 When they had crossed over, they came to land at Gennesaret. [35]After the people of that place recognized him, they sent word throughout the region and brought all

[l] Other ancient authorities read *was out on the sea*
[m] Other ancient authorities read *the wind*

γῆς ἀπεῖχεν βασανιζόμενον ὑπὸ τῶν κυμάτων, ἦν γὰρ
LAND WAS DISTANT, BEING TOSSED   BY   THE   WAVES,   FOR~WAS

ἐναντίος ὁ ἄνεμος. **14.25** τετάρτῃ δὲ φυλακῇ τῆς
CONTRARY   THE WIND.   NOW~IN [THE] FOURTH WATCH   OF THE

νυκτὸς ἦλθεν πρὸς αὐτοὺς περιπατῶν ἐπὶ τὴν
NIGHT   HE CAME TOWARDS THEM   WALKING   ON   THE

θάλασσαν. **14.26** οἱ δὲ μαθηταὶ ἰδόντες αὐτὸν ἐπὶ τῆς
LAKE.   BUT~THE DISCIPLES HAVING SEEN HIM   ON   THE

θαλάσσης περιπατοῦντα ἐταράχθησαν λέγοντες ὅτι
LAKE   WALKING ABOUT   WERE TROUBLED   SAYING

Φάντασμά ἐστιν, καὶ ἀπὸ τοῦ φόβου ἔκραξαν.
IT IS~AN APPARITION, AND FROM -   FEAR   THEY CRIED OUT.

14.27 εὐθὺς δὲ ἐλάλησεν [ὁ Ἰησοῦς] αὐτοῖς λέγων,
        AND~IMMEDIATELY SPOKE   -   JESUS   TO THEM   SAYING,

Θαρσεῖτε, ἐγώ εἰμι· μὴ φοβεῖσθε.
HAVE COURAGE, I AM [HERE]. DO NOT BE AFRAID.

14.28 ἀποκριθεὶς δὲ αὐτῷ ὁ Πέτρος εἶπεν, Κύριε, εἰ
        AND~HAVING ANSWERED HIM   -   PETER   SAID,   LORD,   IF

σὺ εἶ, κέλευσόν με ἐλθεῖν πρὸς σὲ ἐπὶ τὰ ὕδατα.
IT IS [REALLY]~YOU, COMMAND ME TO COME TO   YOU ON   THE WATERS.

14.29 ὁ δὲ εἶπεν, Ἐλθέ. καὶ καταβὰς ἀπὸ τοῦ
        - AND HE SAID,   COME.   AND HAVING GONE DOWN FROM THE

πλοίου [ὁ] Πέτρος περιεπάτησεν ἐπὶ τὰ ὕδατα καὶ
BOAT   -   PETER   WALKED   ON THE WATERS AND

ἦλθεν πρὸς τὸν Ἰησοῦν. **14.30** βλέπων δὲ τὸν
HE CAME TOWARDS -   JESUS.   AND~SEEING   THE

ἄνεμον [ἰσχυρὸν] ἐφοβήθη καὶ ἀρξάμενος
STRONG~WIND   HE WAS AFRAID AND HAVING BEGUN

καταποντίζεσθαι ἔκραξεν λέγων, Κύριε, σῶσόν με.
TO SINK   HE CRIED OUT SAYING, LORD,   SAVE   ME.

14.31 εὐθέως δὲ ὁ Ἰησοῦς ἐκτείνας τὴν χεῖρα
        AND~IMMEDIATELY - JESUS,   HAVING STRETCHED OUT THE(HIS) HAND,

ἐπελάβετο αὐτοῦ καὶ λέγει αὐτῷ, Ὀλιγόπιστε, εἰς τί
TOOK HOLD   OF HIM AND HE SAYS TO HIM, ONE OF LITTLE FAITH, WHY

ἐδίστασας; **14.32** καὶ ἀναβάντων αὐτῶν εἰς τὸ πλοῖον
DID YOU DOUBT?   AND   AS THEY~WERE GOING UP   INTO THE BOAT,

ἐκόπασεν ὁ ἄνεμος. **14.33** οἱ δὲ ἐν τῷ πλοίῳ
CEASED   THE WIND.   AND~THE ONES IN THE BOAT

προσεκύνησαν αὐτῷ λέγοντες, Ἀληθῶς θεοῦ υἱὸς εἶ.
WORSHIPED   HIM   SAYING,   TRULY   GOD'S SON YOU ARE.

14.34 Καὶ διαπεράσαντες ἦλθον ἐπὶ τὴν γῆν εἰς
        AND HAVING CROSSED OVER THEY CAME ONTO THE LAND AT

Γεννησαρέτ. **14.35** καὶ ἐπιγνόντες αὐτὸν οἱ ἄνδρες
GENNESARET.   AND HAVING RECOGNIZED HIM,   THE MEN

τοῦ τόπου ἐκείνου ἀπέστειλαν εἰς ὅλην τὴν
-   OF THAT~AREA   SENT   INTO ALL   -

περίχωρον ἐκείνην καὶ προσήνεγκαν αὐτῷ πάντας
THAT~REGION AROUND AND THEY BROUGHT   TO HIM ALL

τοὺς   κακῶς ἔχοντας **14.36** καὶ   παρεκάλουν   αὐτὸν   ἵνα
THE ONES HAVING~ILLNESS   AND   THEY WERE APPEALING TO HIM   THAT

μόνον ἅψωνται τοῦ κρασπέδου τοῦ ἱματίου αὐτοῦ·
THEY MIGHT TOUCH~ONLY THE FRINGE   OF THE GARMENT OF HIM.

καὶ ὅσοι   ἥψαντο διεσώθησαν.
AND AS MANY AS HE TOUCHED THEY WERE CURED.

---

who were sick to him, [36]and
begged him that they might
touch even the fringe of his
cloak; and all who touched it
were healed.

15.1 Τότε προσέρχονται τῷ Ἰησοῦ ἀπὸ Ἱεροσολύμων
THEN APPROACHES   -   JESUS FROM JERUSALEM

Φαρισαῖοι καὶ γραμματεῖς λέγοντες, **15.2** Διὰ τί οἱ
PHARISEES AND   SCRIBES   SAYING,   WHY [DO] THE

μαθηταί σου παραβαίνουσιν τὴν παράδοσιν τῶν
DISCIPLES OF YOU TRANSGRESS   THE   TRADITION OF THE

πρεσβυτέρων; οὐ γὰρ νίπτονται τὰς χεῖρας [αὐτῶν]
ELDERS?   FOR~THEY DO NOT WASH THE HANDS OF THEM

ὅταν ἄρτον ἐσθίωσιν. **15.3** ὁ δὲ ἀποκριθεὶς εἶπεν
WHEN THEY EAT~BREAD.   BUT~HE HAVING ANSWERED SAID

αὐτοῖς, Διὰ τί καὶ ὑμεῖς παραβαίνετε τὴν ἐντολὴν
TO THEM, WHY [DO] ALSO YOU° TRANSGRESS   THE COMMANDMENT

τοῦ θεοῦ διὰ   τὴν παράδοσιν ὑμῶν; **15.4** ὁ γὰρ
-    OF GOD ON ACCOUNT OF THE TRADITION OF YOU°?   -   FOR

θεὸς εἶπεν, Τίμα τὸν πατέρα καὶ τὴν μητέρα,
GOD SAID,   HONOR THE(YOUR) FATHER AND THE(YOUR) MOTHER,

καί, Ὁ   κακολογῶν πατέρα ἢ μητέρα θανάτῳ
AND, THE ONE SPEAKING EVIL OF FATHER OR MOTHER BY DEATH

τελευτάτω. **15.5** ὑμεῖς δὲ λέγετε, Ὃς ἂν εἴπῃ τῷ
LET HIM DIE.   BUT~YOU° SAY,   WHOEVER SAYS TO THE (HIS)

πατρὶ ἢ τῇ   μητρί, Δῶρον ὃ ἐὰν ἐξ ἐμοῦ
FATHER OR THE(HIS) MOTHER, [IT IS] A GIFT, WHATEVER FROM ME

ὠφεληθῇς, **15.6** οὐ μὴ τιμήσει   τὸν πατέρα
YOU MIGHT HAVE BENEFITED FROM, BY NO MEANS DOES HE HONOR THE FATHER

αὐτοῦ·   καὶ ἠκυρώσατε ⌜τὸν λόγον⌝ τοῦ θεοῦ
OF HIM.   AND YOU° NULLIFY   THE WORD   -   OF GOD

διὰ   τὴν παράδοσιν ὑμῶν. **15.7** ὑποκριταί, καλῶς
ON ACCOUNT OF THE TRADITION OF YOU°. HYPOCRITES,   WELL

ἐπροφήτευσεν περὶ   ὑμῶν Ἡσαΐας λέγων,
PROPHESIED   CONCERNING YOU° ISAIAH   SAYING,

15.8 Ὁ λαὸς οὗτος τοῖς   χείλεσίν με τιμᾷ,
-    THIS~PEOPLE WITH THE(THEIR) LIPS   HONOR~ME,

ἡ δὲ καρδία αὐτῶν πόρρω ἀπέχει ἀπ᾽ ἐμοῦ·
BUT~THE HEART OF THEM FAR   IS AWAY FROM ME

15.9 μάτην δὲ σέβονταί με
AND~IN VAIN DO THEY WORSHIP ME

Then Pharisees and scribes
came to Jesus from Jeru-
salem and said, [2]"Why do
your disciples break the
tradition of the elders? For
they do not wash their hands
before they eat." [3]He
answered them, "And why
do you break the command-
ment of God for the sake of
your tradition? [4]For God
said,[n] 'Honor your father
and your mother,' and,
'Whoever speaks evil of
father or mother must surely
die.' [5]But you say that
whoever tells father or
mother, 'Whatever support
you might have had from me
is given to God,'[o] then that
person need not honor the
father.[p] [6]So, for the sake of
your tradition, you make
void the word[q] of God.
[7]You hypocrites! Isaiah
prophesied rightly about you
when he said:

[8] 'This people honors me
        with their lips,
      but their hearts are far
        from me;
[9] in vain do they worship
        me,

[n] Other ancient authorities read
    commanded, saying
[o] Or *is an offering*
[p] Other ancient authorities add *or the
    mother*
[q] Other ancient authorities read *law;*
    others, *commandment*

15:4a Exod. 20:12; Deut. 5:16   **15:4b** Exod. 21:17   **15:6a** text: ASV RSV NASBmg NIV TEV NRSV.
add η την μητερα αυτου (or his mother): KJV ASVmg NASB NIVmg NEB TEVmg NJB NRSVmg.
15:6b text [see Mark 7:13]: ASV RSV NASB NJB (TEV) NRSV. var. τον νομον (the law): ASVmg RSVmg
NASBmg NEB NRSVmg. var. την εντολην (the commandment): KJV.   **15:8-9** Isa. 29:13 LXX

teaching human precepts as doctrines.'"

10 Then he called the crowd to him and said to them, "Listen and understand: [11]it is not what goes into the mouth that defiles a person, but it is what comes out of the mouth that defiles." [12]Then the disciples approached and said to him, "Do you know that the Pharisees took offense when they heard what you said?" [13]He answered, "Every plant that my heavenly Father has not planted will be uprooted. [14]Let them alone; they are blind guides of the blind.[r] And if one blind person guides another, both will fall into a pit." [15]But Peter said to him, "Explain this parable to us." [16]Then he said, "Are you also still without understanding? [17]Do you not see that whatever goes into the mouth enters the stomach, and goes out into the sewer? [18]But what comes out of the mouth proceeds from the heart, and this is what defiles. [19]For out of the heart come evil intentions, murder, adultery, fornication, theft, false witness, slander. [20]These are what defile a person, but to eat with unwashed

[r] Other ancient authorities lack *of the blind*

διδάσκοντες διδασκαλίας ἐντάλματα
TEACHING [AS]   TEACHINGS   COMMANDMENTS

ἀνθρώπων.
OF MEN.

15.10 Καὶ προσκαλεσάμενος τὸν ὄχλον εἶπεν αὐτοῖς,
AND HAVING SUMMONED   THE   CROWD   HE SAID   TO THEM,

Ἀκούετε καὶ συνίετε· **15.11** οὐ τὸ εἰσερχόμενον
LISTEN   AND   UNDERSTAND.   [IT IS] NOT   THE THING   ENTERING

εἰς τὸ στόμα κοινοῖ τὸν ἄνθρωπον, ἀλλὰ τὸ
INTO   THE   MOUTH [WHICH]   DEFILES   THE   MAN,   BUT   THE THING

ἐκπορευόμενον ἐκ τοῦ στόματος τοῦτο κοινοῖ τὸν
GOING OUT   FROM   THE   MOUTH   THIS   DEFILES   THE

ἄνθρωπον. **15.12** Τότε προσελθόντες οἱ μαθηταὶ
MAN.   THEN   HAVING APPROACHED   THE   DISCIPLES

λέγουσιν αὐτῷ, Οἶδας ὅτι οἱ Φαρισαῖοι ἀκούσαντες
SAY   TO HIM,   DO YOU KNOW   THAT   THE   PHARISEES   HAVING HEARD

τὸν λόγον ἐσκανδαλίσθησαν; **15.13** ὁ δὲ ἀποκριθεὶς
THE   WORD   HAVE TAKEN OFFENSE?   BUT~HE   HAVING ANSWERED

εἶπεν, Πᾶσα φυτεία ἣν οὐκ ἐφύτευσεν ὁ πατήρ μου
SAID,   EVERY   PLANT   WHICH   DID NOT PLANT   THE   [2]FATHER   [3]OF ME

ὁ οὐράνιος ἐκριζωθήσεται. **15.14** ἄφετε αὐτούς·
-   [1]HEAVENLY   WILL BE UPROOTED.   LEAVE   THEM.

τυφλοί εἰσιν ὁδηγοὶ [τυφλῶν]· τυφλὸς δὲ τυφλὸν ἐὰν
THEY ARE~BLIND   GUIDES   OF [THE] BLIND.   [3][THE] BLIND   [1]AND   [5][THE] BLIND   [2]IF

ὁδηγῇ, ἀμφότεροι εἰς βόθυνον πεσοῦνται.
[4]LEAD,   BOTH   INTO   A PIT   WILL FALL.

15.15 Ἀποκριθεὶς δὲ ὁ Πέτρος εἶπεν αὐτῷ, Φράσον
AND~HAVING ANSWERED   -   PETER   SAID   TO HIM,   EXPLAIN

ἡμῖν τὴν παραβολήν [ταύτην]. **15.16** ὁ δὲ εἶπεν, Ἀκμὴν
TO US   -   THIS~PARABLE.   AND~HE SAID,   STILL

καὶ ὑμεῖς ἀσύνετοί ἐστε; **15.17** οὐ νοεῖτε ὅτι
ALSO   YOU°   WITHOUT UNDERSTANDING   ARE?   DO YOU° NOT KNOW   THAT

πᾶν τὸ εἰσπορευόμενον εἰς τὸ στόμα εἰς τὴν
EVERY   THING [WHICH]   ENTERING   INTO   THE MOUTH   INTO   THE

κοιλίαν χωρεῖ καὶ εἰς ἀφεδρῶνα ἐκβάλλεται;
STOMACH   GOES   AND   INTO   A LATRINE   PASSES?

15.18 τὰ δὲ ἐκπορευόμενα ἐκ τοῦ στόματος ἐκ τῆς
BUT~THE THINGS   COMING OUT   FROM   THE   MOUTH   FROM   THE

καρδίας ἐξέρχεται, κἀκεῖνα κοινοῖ τὸν ἄνθρωπον.
HEART   COME OUT,   AND THAT   DEFILES   THE   MAN.

15.19 ἐκ γὰρ τῆς καρδίας ἐξέρχονται
FOR~OUT OF   THE   HEART   COMES FORTH

διαλογισμοὶ πονηροί, φόνοι, μοιχεῖαι, πορνεῖαι,
EVIL~THOUGHTS,   MURDERS,   ADULTERIES,   FORNICATIONS,

κλοπαί, ψευδομαρτυρίαι, βλασφημίαι. **15.20** ταῦτά
THEFTS,   FALSE TESTIMONIES, [AND]   BLASPHEMIES.   THESE

ἐστιν τὰ κοινοῦντα τὸν ἄνθρωπον, τὸ δὲ ἀνίπτοις
ARE   THE THINGS   DEFILING   THE   MAN,   -   BUT   WITH UNWASHED

χερσὶν φαγεῖν οὐ κοινοῖ τὸν ἄνθρωπον.
HANDS   TO EAT   DOES NOT DEFILE THE   MAN.

15.21 Καὶ ἐξελθὼν ἐκεῖθεν ὁ Ἰησοῦς ἀνεχώρησεν εἰς
AND HAVING GONE OUT FROM THERE - JESUS   WITHDREW   INTO

τὰ μέρη Τύρου καὶ Σιδῶνος. **15.22** καὶ ἰδοὺ
THE DISTRICTS OF TYRE AND SIDON.   AND BEHOLD

γυνὴ Χαναναία ἀπὸ τῶν ὁρίων ἐκείνων ἐξελθοῦσα
A CANAANITE~WOMAN FROM - THOSE~BORDERS HAVING COME OUT

ἔκραζεν λέγουσα, Ἐλέησόν με, κύριε υἱὸς Δαυίδ·
WAS CRYING OUT SAYING, HAVE MERCY ON ME, LORD, SON OF DAVID.

ἡ θυγάτηρ μου κακῶς δαιμονίζεται. **15.23** ὁ δὲ
THE DAUGHTER OF ME SEVERELY IS DEMON-POSSESSED.   BUT~HE

οὐκ ἀπεκρίθη αὐτῇ λόγον. καὶ προσελθόντες οἱ
DID NOT ANSWER HER A WORD.   AND HAVING APPROACHED THE

μαθηταὶ αὐτοῦ ἠρώτουν αὐτὸν λέγοντες, Ἀπόλυσον
DISCIPLES OF HIM WERE ASKING HIM SAYING,   SEND AWAY

αὐτήν, ὅτι κράζει ὄπισθεν ἡμῶν. **15.24** ὁ δὲ
HER, FOR SHE CRIES OUT AFTER US.   BUT~HE

ἀποκριθεὶς εἶπεν, Οὐκ ἀπεστάλην εἰ μὴ εἰς τὰ
HAVING ANSWERED SAID, I WAS NOT SENT   EXCEPT TO THE

πρόβατα τὰ ἀπολωλότα οἴκου Ἰσραήλ. **15.25** ἡ δὲ
²SHEEP - ¹LOST   OF [THE] HOUSE OF ISRAEL.   BUT~SHE

ἐλθοῦσα προσεκύνει αὐτῷ λέγουσα, Κύριε, βοήθει μοι.
HAVING COME WAS WORSHIPING HIM SAYING, LORD,   HELP   ME.

15.26 ὁ δὲ ἀποκριθεὶς εἶπεν, Οὐκ ἔστιν καλὸν λαβεῖν
BUT~HE HAVING ANSWERED SAID,   IT IS NOT   GOOD   TO TAKE

τὸν ἄρτον τῶν τέκνων καὶ βαλεῖν τοῖς κυναρίοις.
THE BREAD OF THE CHILDREN AND TO THROW [IT] TO THE DOGS.

15.27 ἡ δὲ εἶπεν, Ναί κύριε, καὶ γὰρ τὰ κυνάρια
BUT~SHE SAID, YES LORD, FOR~EVEN THE DOGS

ἐσθίει ἀπὸ τῶν ψιχίων τῶν πιπτόντων ἀπὸ τῆς
EAT   FROM THE CRUMBS - FALLING   FROM THE

τραπέζης τῶν κυρίων αὐτῶν. **15.28** τότε ἀποκριθεὶς ὁ
TABLE   OF THE MASTERS OF THEM.   THEN HAVING ANSWERED -

Ἰησοῦς εἶπεν αὐτῇ, Ὦ γύναι, μεγάλη σου ἡ πίστις·
JESUS SAID TO HER, O WOMAN, GREAT [IS] YOUR - FAITH.

γενηθήτω σοι ὡς θέλεις. καὶ ἰάθη ἡ θυγάτηρ
LET IT BE DONE FOR YOU AS YOU DESIRE. AND WAS HEALED THE DAUGHTER

αὐτῆς ἀπὸ τῆς ὥρας ἐκείνης.
OF HER FROM - THAT~HOUR.

15.29 Καὶ μεταβὰς ἐκεῖθεν ὁ Ἰησοῦς ἦλθεν παρὰ
AND HAVING PASSED OVER FROM THERE - JESUS   CAME BESIDE

τὴν θάλασσαν τῆς Γαλιλαίας, καὶ ἀναβὰς εἰς τὸ
THE LAKE   - OF GALILEE, AND HAVING GONE UP TO THE

ὄρος ἐκάθητο ἐκεῖ. **15.30** καὶ προσῆλθον αὐτῷ
MOUNTAIN HE WAS SITTING THERE.   AND APPROACHED HIM

ὄχλοι πολλοὶ ἔχοντες μεθ᾽ ἑαυτῶν χωλούς, τυφλούς,
GREAT~CROWDS HAVING WITH THEM LAME,   BLIND,

hands does not defile."
21 Jesus left that place and went away to the district of Tyre and Sidon. 22Just then a Canaanite woman from that region came out and started shouting, "Have mercy on me, Lord, Son of David; my daughter is tormented by a demon." 23But he did not answer her at all. And his disciples came and urged him, saying, "Send her away, for she keeps shouting after us." 24He answered, "I was sent only to the lost sheep of the house of Israel." 25But she came and knelt before him, saying, "Lord, help me." 26He answered, "It is not fair to take the children's food and throw it to the dogs." 27She said, "Yes, Lord, yet even the dogs eat the crumbs that fall from their masters' table." 28Then Jesus answered her, "Woman, great is your faith! Let it be done for you as you wish." And her daughter was healed instantly.

29 After Jesus had left that place, he passed along the Sea of Galilee, and he went up the mountain, where he sat down. 30Great crowds came to him, bringing with them the lame, the maimed, the blind,

the mute, and many others. They put them at his feet, and he cured them, ³¹so that the crowd was amazed when they saw the mute speaking, the maimed whole, the lame walking, and the blind seeing. And they praised the God of Israel.

32 Then Jesus called his disciples to him and said, "I have compassion for the crowd, because they have been with me now for three days and have nothing to eat; and I do not want to send them away hungry, for they might faint on the way." ³³The disciples said to him, "Where are we to get enough bread in the desert to feed so great a crowd?" ³⁴Jesus asked them, "How many loaves have you?" They said, "Seven, and a few small fish." ³⁵Then ordering the crowd to sit down on the ground, ³⁶he took the seven loaves and the fish; and after giving thanks he broke them and gave them to the disciples, and the disciples gave them to the crowds. ³⁷And all of them ate and were filled; and they took up the broken pieces left over, seven baskets full. ³⁸Those who had eaten were four thousand men, besides women and children.

κυλλούς, κωφούς, καὶ ἑτέρους πολλοὺς καὶ ἔρριψαν
CRIPPLED,   MUTE,   AND   MANY~OTHERS   AND   THEY LAID

αὐτοὺς παρὰ τοὺς πόδας αὐτοῦ, καὶ ἐθεράπευσεν
THEM   AT   THE   FEET   OF HIM,   AND   HE HEALED

αὐτούς· **15.31** ὥστε τὸν ὄχλον θαυμάσαι βλέποντας
THEM,   SO AS ²THE ³CROWD ¹TO AMAZE   SEEING

κωφοὺς λαλοῦντας, κυλλοὺς ὑγιεῖς καὶ χωλοὺς
MUTES   SPEAKING,   CRIPPLES   HEALTHY   AND   LAME

περιπατοῦντας καὶ τυφλοὺς βλέποντας· καὶ ἐδόξασαν
WALKING AROUND   AND   BLIND   SEEING.   AND   THEY GLORIFIED

τὸν θεὸν Ἰσραήλ.
THE   GOD   OF ISRAEL.

15.32 Ὁ δὲ Ἰησοῦς προσκαλεσάμενος τοὺς μαθητὰς
-   AND   JESUS   HAVING SUMMONED   THE   DISCIPLES

αὐτοῦ εἶπεν, Σπλαγχνίζομαι ἐπὶ τὸν ὄχλον, ὅτι ἤδη
OF HIM   SAID,   I FEEL COMPASSION   FOR   THE   CROWD,   FOR   ALREADY

ἡμέραι τρεῖς προσμένουσίν μοι καὶ οὐκ ἔχουσιν
THREE~DAYS   THEY REMAIN   WITH ME   AND   THEY DO NOT HAVE

τί φάγωσιν· καὶ ἀπολῦσαι αὐτοὺς νήστεις
ANYTHING   THEY MAY EAT.   AND   TO SEND AWAY   THEM   HUNGRY

οὐ θέλω, μήποτε ἐκλυθῶσιν ἐν τῇ ὁδῷ. **15.33** καὶ
I DO NOT WISH,   LEST   THEY BECOME WEARY   ON   THE   WAY.   AND

λέγουσιν αὐτῷ οἱ μαθηταί, Πόθεν ἡμῖν ἐν
SAY   TO HIM   THE DISCIPLES,   FROM WHERE   [IS THERE TO COME] TO US   IN

ἐρημίᾳ ἄρτοι τοσοῦτοι ὥστε χορτάσαι
[THE] WILDERNESS   SO MANY~LOAVES   SO AS   TO FEED

ὄχλον τοσοῦτον; **15.34** καὶ λέγει αὐτοῖς ὁ Ἰησοῦς,
SUCH A GREAT~CROWD?   AND   SAYS   TO THEM   -   JESUS,

Πόσους ἄρτους ἔχετε; οἱ δὲ εἶπαν, Ἑπτὰ καὶ
HOW MANY   LOAVES   DO YOU° HAVE?   -   AND   THEY SAID,   SEVEN   AND

ὀλίγα ἰχθύδια. **15.35** καὶ παραγγείλας τῷ ὄχλῳ
A FEW   FISH.   AND   HAVING GIVEN ORDERS   TO THE   CROWD

ἀναπεσεῖν ἐπὶ τὴν γῆν **15.36** ἔλαβεν τοὺς ἑπτὰ
TO RECLINE   ON   THE   GROUND,   HE TOOK   THE   SEVEN

ἄρτους καὶ τοὺς ἰχθύας καὶ εὐχαριστήσας ἔκλασεν
LOAVES   AND   THE   FISH   AND   HAVING GIVEN THANKS   HE BROKE [THEM]

καὶ ἐδίδου τοῖς μαθηταῖς, οἱ δὲ μαθηταὶ τοῖς
AND   GAVE [THEM]   TO THE   DISCIPLES,   AND~THE   DISCIPLES [GAVE THEM]   TO THE

ὄχλοις. **15.37** καὶ ἔφαγον πάντες καὶ ἐχορτάσθησαν.
CROWDS.   AND   EVERYONE~ATE   AND   THEY WERE SATISFIED.

καὶ τὸ περισσεῦον τῶν κλασμάτων ἦραν ἑπτὰ
AND   THE   LEFTOVERS   OF THE   FRAGMENTS   WERE   SEVEN

σπυρίδας πλήρεις. **15.38** οἱ δὲ ἐσθίοντες ἦσαν
BASKETS   FULL.   AND~THE ONES   EATING   WERE

τετρακισχίλιοι ἄνδρες χωρὶς γυναικῶν καὶ παιδίων.
FOUR THOUSAND   MEN   APART FROM   [THE] WOMEN   AND   CHILDREN.

15.39 Καὶ   ἀπολύσας   τοὺς   ὄχλους   ἐνέβη   εἰς   τὸ
AND   HAVING SENT AWAY   THE   CROWDS   HE ENTERED   INTO   THE

πλοῖον   καὶ   ἦλθεν   εἰς   τὰ   ὅρια   Μαγαδάν.
BOAT   AND   CAME   INTO   THE   BORDERS   OF MAGADAN.

[39]After sending away the crowds, he got into the boat and went to the region of Magadan.[s]

[s] Other ancient authorities read *Magdala* or *Magdalan*

16.1 Καὶ   προσελθόντες   οἱ   Φαρισαῖοι   καὶ
AND   HAVING APPROACHED   THE   PHARISEES   AND

Σαδδουκαῖοι   πειράζοντες   ἐπηρώτησαν   αὐτὸν   σημεῖον
SADDUCEES   TESTING   ASKED   HIM   A SIGN

ἐκ   τοῦ   οὐρανοῦ   ἐπιδεῖξαι   αὐτοῖς.   **16.2** ὁ   δὲ
FROM   -   HEAVEN   TO SHOW   THEM.   BUT~HE

ἀποκριθεὶς   εἶπεν   αὐτοῖς,   ⌈['Οψίας   γενομένης   λέγετε,
HAVING ANSWERED   SAID   TO THEM,   [WHEN] EVENING HAVING COME   YOU° SAY,

Εὐδία,   πυρράζει   γὰρ   ὁ   οὐρανός·   **16.3** καὶ   πρωΐ,
FAIR WEATHER,   FOR~IS FIERY RED   THE   SKY.   AND   IN THE MORNING,

Σήμερον   χειμών,   πυρράζει   γὰρ   στυγνάζων   ὁ
TODAY   STORMY WEATHER,   FOR~IS FIERY RED   BEING OVERCAST   THE

οὐρανός.   τὸ   μὲν   πρόσωπον   τοῦ   οὐρανοῦ   γινώσκετε
SKY.   THE   -   APPEARANCE   OF THE   SKY   YOU° KNOW [ENOUGH]

διακρίνειν,   τὰ   δὲ   σημεῖα   τῶν   καιρῶν   οὐ   δύνασθε;]⌉
TO DISTINGUISH,   BUT THE   SIGNS   OF THE   TIMES   CAN'T YOU° MAKE OUT?

16.4 Γενεὰ   πονηρὰ   καὶ   μοιχαλὶς   σημεῖον   ἐπιζητεῖ,
A GENERATION   EVIL   AND   ADULTEROUS   DEMANDS~A SIGN,

καὶ   σημεῖον   οὐ   δοθήσεται   αὐτῇ   εἰ   μὴ   τὸ   σημεῖον
AND   A SIGN   WILL NOT BE GIVEN   TO IT   EXCEPT   THE   SIGN

'Ιωνᾶ.   καὶ   καταλιπὼν   αὐτοὺς   ἀπῆλθεν.
OF JONAH.   AND   HAVING LEFT   THEM   HE WENT AWAY.

16.5 Καὶ   ἐλθόντες   οἱ   μαθηταὶ   εἰς   τὸ   πέραν
AND   HAVING COME   THE   DISCIPLES   TO   THE   OTHER SIDE,

ἐπελάθοντο   ἄρτους   λαβεῖν.   **16.6** ὁ   δὲ   'Ιησοῦς   εἶπεν
THEY FORGOT   TO TAKE~LOAVES.   -   BUT   JESUS   SAID

αὐτοῖς,   'Ορᾶτε   καὶ   προσέχετε   ἀπὸ   τῆς   ζύμης   τῶν
TO THEM,   TAKE CARE   AND   BEWARE   OF   THE   LEAVEN   OF THE

Φαρισαίων   καὶ   Σαδδουκαίων.   **16.7** οἱ   δὲ   διελογίζοντο
PHARISEES   AND   THE SADDUCEES.   BUT~THEY   WERE REASONING

ἐν   ἑαυτοῖς   λέγοντες   ὅτι   "Αρτους   οὐκ   ἐλάβομεν.
AMONG   THEMSELVES   SAYING   -   WE DID NOT TAKE~BREAD.

16.8 γνοὺς   δὲ   ὁ   'Ιησοῦς   εἶπεν,   Τί
BUT~HAVING KNOWN [THEIR THOUGHTS]   -   JESUS   SAID,   WHY

διαλογίζεσθε   ἐν   ἑαυτοῖς,   ὀλιγόπιστοι,   ὅτι
ARE YOU° REASONING   AMONG   YOURSELVES,   ONES OF LITTLE FAITH, [SAYING]   -

ἄρτους   οὐκ   ἔχετε;   **16.9** οὔπω   νοεῖτε,   οὐδὲ
YOU° HAVE NO~BREAD?   DO YOU° NOT YET UNDERSTAND,   NOR

The Pharisees and Sadducees came, and to test Jesus[t] they asked him to show them a sign from heaven. [2]He answered them, "When it is evening, you say, 'It will be fair weather, for the sky is red.' [3]And in the morning, 'It will be stormy today, for the sky is red and threatening.' You know how to interpret the appearance of the sky, but you cannot interpret the signs of the times.[u] [4]An evil and adulterous generation asks for a sign, but no sign will be given to it except the sign of Jonah." Then he left them and went away.

5 When the disciples reached the other side, they had forgotten to bring any bread. [6]Jesus said to them, "Watch out, and beware of the yeast of the Pharisees and Sadducees." [7]They said to one another, "It is because we have brought no bread." [8]And becoming aware of it, Jesus said, "You of little faith, why are you talking about having no bread? [9]Do you still not perceive?

[t] Gk *him*
[u] Other ancient authorities lack [2]*When it is . . . of the times*

16:2b-3 text: KJV ASV RSV NASB NIV NEBmg TEV NJB NRSV.   omit: ASVmg RSVmg NASBmg NIVmg NEB TEVmg NJBmg NRSVmg.

Do you not remember the five loaves for the five thousand, and how many baskets you gathered? [10]Or the seven loaves for the four thousand, and how many baskets you gathered? [11]How could you fail to perceive that I was not speaking about bread? Beware of the yeast of the Pharisees and Sadducees!" [12]Then they understood that he had not told them to beware of the yeast of bread, but of the teaching of the Pharisees and Sadducees.

13 Now when Jesus came into the district of Caesarea Philippi, he asked his disciples, "Who do people say that the Son of Man is?" [14]And they said, "Some say John the Baptist, but others Elijah, and still others Jeremiah or one of the prophets." [15]He said to them, "But who do you say that I am?" [16]Simon Peter answered, "You are the Messiah,[y] the Son of the living God." [17]And Jesus answered him, "Blessed are you, Simon son of Jonah! For flesh and blood has not revealed this to you, but my Father in heaven. [18]And I tell you, you are Peter,[w] and on this rock[x] I will build my church, and the gates of Hades will not prevail against it. [19]I will give you the keys of the kingdom of

[y] Or *the Christ*
[w] Gk *Petros*
[x] Gk *petra*

μνημονεύετε τοὺς πέντε ἄρτους τῶν πεντακισχιλίων
REMEMBER THE FIVE LOAVES OF THE FIVE THOUSAND

καὶ πόσους κοφίνους ἐλάβετε; **16.10** οὐδὲ τοὺς ἑπτὰ
AND HOW MANY BASKETS YOU° TOOK [UP]? NOR THE SEVEN

ἄρτους τῶν τετρακισχιλίων καὶ πόσας σπυρίδας
LOAVES OF THE FOUR THOUSAND AND HOW MANY BASKETS

ἐλάβετε; **16.11** πῶς οὐ νοεῖτε ὅτι οὐ περὶ
YOU° TOOK [UP]? HOW CAN YOU° NOT UNDERSTAND THAT NOT CONCERNING

ἄρτων εἶπον ὑμῖν; προσέχετε δὲ ἀπὸ τῆς ζύμης τῶν
LOAVES I SPOKE TO YOU°? BUT~BEWARE OF THE LEAVEN OF THE

Φαρισαίων καὶ Σαδδουκαίων. **16.12** τότε συνῆκαν
PHARISEES AND SADDUCEES. THEN THEY UNDERSTOOD

ὅτι οὐκ εἶπεν προσέχειν ἀπὸ τῆς ζύμης τῶν ἄρτων
THAT HE DID NOT SAY TO BEWARE OF THE LEAVEN OF THE LOAVES,

ἀλλὰ ἀπὸ τῆς διδαχῆς τῶν Φαρισαίων καὶ
BUT OF THE TEACHING OF THE PHARISEES AND

Σαδδουκαίων.
SADDUCEES.

16.13 Ἐλθὼν δὲ ὁ Ἰησοῦς εἰς τὰ μέρη Καισαρείας
AND~HAVING COME - JESUS INTO THE REGION OF CAESAREA

τῆς Φιλίππου ἠρώτα τοὺς μαθητὰς αὐτοῦ λέγων,
- PHILIPPI HE WAS QUESTIONING THE DISCIPLES OF HIM SAYING,

Τίνα λέγουσιν οἱ ἄνθρωποι εἶναι τὸν υἱὸν τοῦ
WHOM SAY THE MEN TO BE THE SON -

ἀνθρώπου; **16.14** οἱ δὲ εἶπαν, Οἱ μὲν Ἰωάννην
OF MAN? - AND THEY SAID, SOME [SAY] - JOHN

τὸν βαπτιστήν, ἄλλοι δὲ Ἠλίαν, ἕτεροι δὲ Ἰερεμίαν ἢ
THE BAPTIST, BUT~OTHERS ELIJAH, AND~OTHERS JEREMIAH OR

ἕνα τῶν προφητῶν. **16.15** λέγει αὐτοῖς, Ὑμεῖς δὲ τίνα
ONE OF THE PROPHETS. HE SAYS TO THEM, BUT~YOU° WHO

με λέγετε εἶναι; **16.16** ἀποκριθεὶς δὲ Σίμων Πέτρος
DO YOU° CONSIDER~ME TO BE? AND~HAVING ANSWERED SIMON PETER

εἶπεν, Σὺ εἶ ὁ Χριστὸς ὁ υἱὸς τοῦ θεοῦ τοῦ ζῶντος.
SAID, YOU ARE THE CHRIST, THE SON - [3]GOD [1]OF THE [2]LIVING.

16.17 ἀποκριθεὶς δὲ ὁ Ἰησοῦς εἶπεν αὐτῷ, Μακάριος
AND~HAVING ANSWERED - JESUS SAID TO HIM, BLESSED

εἶ, Σίμων Βαριωνᾶ, ὅτι σὰρξ καὶ αἷμα
ARE YOU, SIMON BAR-JONA, FOR FLESH AND BLOOD

οὐκ ἀπεκάλυψέν σοι ἀλλ᾽ ὁ πατήρ μου ὁ ἐν τοῖς
DID NOT REVEAL [THIS] TO YOU BUT THE FATHER OF ME THE ONE IN THE

οὐρανοῖς. **16.18** κἀγὼ δέ σοι λέγω ὅτι σὺ εἶ Πέτρος,
HEAVENS. AND~I ALSO SAY~TO YOU THAT YOU ARE PETER (ROCK),

καὶ ἐπὶ ταύτῃ τῇ πέτρᾳ οἰκοδομήσω μου τὴν
AND UPON THIS - ROCK I WILL BUILD OF ME THE

ἐκκλησίαν καὶ πύλαι ᾅδου οὐ κατισχύσουσιν αὐτῆς.
CHURCH AND [THE] GATES OF HADES WILL NOT OVERCOME IT.

16.19 δώσω σοι τὰς κλεῖδας τῆς βασιλείας τῶν
I WILL GIVE TO YOU THE KEYS OF THE KINGDOM OF THE

οὐρανῶν, καὶ ὃ ἐὰν δήσῃς ἐπὶ τῆς γῆς
HEAVENS, AND WHATEVER YOU MAY HAVE BOUND UPON THE EARTH

ἔσται δεδεμένον ἐν τοῖς οὐρανοῖς, καὶ ὃ ἐὰν
IT WILL HAVE BEEN BOUND IN THE HEAVENS, AND WHATEVER

λύσῃς ἐπὶ τῆς γῆς ἔσται λελυμένον ἐν τοῖς
YOU MAY HAVE ABOLISHED UPON THE EARTH IT WILL HAVE BEEN ABOLISHED IN THE

οὐρανοῖς. **16.20** τότε διεστείλατο τοῖς μαθηταῖς ἵνα
HEAVENS. THEN HE GAVE ORDERS TO THE DISCIPLES THAT

μηδενὶ εἴπωσιν ὅτι αὐτός ἐστιν ὁ Χριστός.
THEY SHOULD TELL~NO ONE THAT HE IS THE CHRIST.

16.21 Ἀπὸ τότε ἤρξατο ὁ Ἰησοῦς δεικνύειν τοῖς
FROM THAT POINT BEGAN - JESUS TO EXPLAIN TO THE

μαθηταῖς αὐτοῦ ὅτι δεῖ αὐτὸν εἰς Ἱεροσόλυμα
DISCIPLES OF HIM THAT IT IS NECESSARY FOR HIM TO JERUSALEM

ἀπελθεῖν καὶ πολλὰ παθεῖν ἀπὸ τῶν πρεσβυτέρων καὶ
TO GO AND TO SUFFER~MANY THINGS FROM THE ELDERS AND

ἀρχιερέων καὶ γραμματέων καὶ ἀποκτανθῆναι καὶ
CHIEF PRIESTS AND SCRIBES AND TO BE KILLED AND

τῇ τρίτῃ ἡμέρᾳ ἐγερθῆναι. **16.22** καὶ προσλαβόμενος
ON THE THIRD DAY TO BE RAISED. AND HAVING TAKEN

αὐτὸν ὁ Πέτρος ἤρξατο ἐπιτιμᾶν αὐτῷ λέγων,
HIM [ASIDE] - PETER BEGAN TO REBUKE HIM SAYING,

Ἵλεώς σοι, κύριε· οὐ μὴ ἔσται σοι τοῦτο.
MAY [GOD] BE GRACIOUS TO YOU, LORD. WILL NEVER HAPPEN TO YOU THIS.

16.23 ὁ δὲ στραφεὶς εἶπεν τῷ Πέτρῳ, Ὕπαγε
BUT~HE HAVING TURNED AROUND SAID - TO PETER, GET

ὀπίσω μου, Σατανᾶ· σκάνδαλον εἶ ἐμοῦ, ὅτι
BEHIND ME, SATAN. YOU ARE~A STUMBLING BLOCK TO ME, FOR

οὐ φρονεῖς τὰ τοῦ θεοῦ ἀλλὰ τὰ τῶν
YOU ARE NOT THINKING THE THINGS - OF GOD BUT THE THINGS -

ἀνθρώπων. **16.24** Τότε ὁ Ἰησοῦς εἶπεν τοῖς μαθηταῖς
OF MEN. THEN - JESUS SAID TO THE DISCIPLES

αὐτοῦ, Εἴ τις θέλει ὀπίσω μου ἐλθεῖν,
OF HIM, IF SOMEONE WISHES AFTER ME TO COME,

ἀπαρνησάσθω ἑαυτὸν καὶ ἀράτω τὸν σταυρὸν αὐτοῦ
LET HIM DENY HIMSELF AND TAKE UP THE CROSS OF HIM

καὶ ἀκολουθείτω μοι. **16.25** ὃς γὰρ ἐὰν θέλῃ τὴν ψυχὴν
AND LET [HIM] FOLLOW ME. FOR~WHOEVER DESIRES THE SOUL

αὐτοῦ σῶσαι ἀπολέσει αὐτήν· ὃς δ' ἂν ἀπολέσῃ τὴν
OF HIM TO SAVE WILL LOSE IT. BUT~WHOEVER LOSES THE

ψυχὴν αὐτοῦ ἕνεκεν ἐμοῦ εὑρήσει αὐτήν. **16.26** τί γὰρ
SOUL OF HIM ON ACCOUNT OF ME WILL FIND IT. FOR~WHAT

ὠφεληθήσεται ἄνθρωπος ἐὰν τὸν κόσμον ὅλον κερδήσῃ
WILL BE BENEFITED A MAN IF THE WHOLE~WORLD HE ACQUIRES

τὴν δὲ ψυχὴν αὐτοῦ ζημιωθῇ; ἢ τί δώσει ἄνθρωπος
BUT~THE SOUL OF HIM HE FORFEITS? OR WHAT WILL GIVE A MAN

ἀντάλλαγμα τῆς ψυχῆς αὐτοῦ; **16.27** μέλλει γὰρ ὁ υἱὸς
IN EXCHANGE FOR THE SOUL OF HIM? FOR~IS ABOUT THE SON

heaven, and whatever you bind on earth will be bound in heaven, and whatever you loose on earth will be loosed in heaven." [20]Then he sternly ordered the disciples not to tell anyone that he was[y] the Messiah.[z]

21 From that time on, Jesus began to show his disciples that he must go to Jerusalem and undergo great suffering at the hands of the elders and chief priests and scribes, and be killed, and on the third day be raised. [22]And Peter took him aside and began to rebuke him, saying, "God forbid it, Lord! This must never happen to you." [23]But he turned and said to Peter, "Get behind me, Satan! You are a stumbling block to me; for you are setting your mind not on divine things but on human things."

24 Then Jesus told his disciples, "If any want to become my followers, let them deny themselves and take up their cross and follow me. [25]For those who want to save their life will lose it, and those who lose their life for my sake will find it. [26]For what will it profit them if they gain the whole world but forfeit their life? Or what will they give in return for their life?

27 "For the Son of Man is

[y] Other ancient authorities add *Jesus*
[z] Or *the Christ*

to come with his angels in the glory of his Father, and then he will repay everyone for what has been done. ²⁸Truly I tell you, there are some standing here who will not taste death before they see the Son of Man coming in his kingdom."

τοῦ ἀνθρώπου ἔρχεσθαι ἐν τῇ δόξῃ τοῦ πατρὸς αὐτοῦ
- OF MAN   TO COME   IN   THE GLORY OF THE FATHER   OF HIM

μετὰ τῶν ἀγγέλων αὐτοῦ, καὶ τότε ἀποδώσει ἑκάστῳ
WITH THE ANGELS   OF HIM, AND THEN HE WILL RECOMPENSE EACH ONE

κατὰ τὴν πρᾶξιν αὐτοῦ. 16.28 ἀμὴν λέγω ὑμῖν ὅτι
ACCORDING TO THE ACTIONS OF HIM.   TRULY I SAY TO YOU° THAT

εἰσίν τινες τῶν   ὧδε ἑστώτων οἵτινες οὐ μὴ γεύσωνται
THERE ARE SOME OF THE ONES STANDING~HERE WHO   WILL IN NO WAY TASTE

θανάτου ἕως ἂν ἴδωσιν τὸν υἱὸν τοῦ ἀνθρώπου
DEATH   UNTIL   THEY SEE THE SON   - OF MAN

ἐρχόμενον ἐν τῇ βασιλείᾳ αὐτοῦ.
COMING   WITH THE KINGDOM   OF HIM.

CHAPTER 17

Six days later, Jesus took with him Peter and James and his brother John and led them up a high mountain, by themselves. ²And he was transfigured before them, and his face shone like the sun, and his clothes became dazzling white. ³Suddenly there appeared to them Moses and Elijah, talking with him. ⁴Then Peter said to Jesus, "Lord, it is good for us to be here; if you wish, Iᵃ will make three dwellingsᵇ here, one for you, one for Moses, and one for Elijah." ⁵While he was still speaking, suddenly a bright cloud overshadowed them, and from the cloud a voice said, "This is my Son, the Beloved;ᶜ with him I am well pleased; listen to him!" ⁶When the disciples heard this, they fell to the ground and were overcome by fear. ⁷But Jesus came and

ᵃ Other ancient authorities read we
ᵇ Or tents
ᶜ Or my beloved Son

17.1 Καὶ μεθ' ἡμέρας ἓξ παραλαμβάνει ὁ Ἰησοῦς τὸν
     AND AFTER SIX~DAYS   TOOK   - JESUS   -

Πέτρον καὶ Ἰάκωβον καὶ Ἰωάννην τὸν ἀδελφὸν αὐτοῦ
PETER   AND JAMES   AND JOHN   THE BROTHER   OF HIM

καὶ ἀναφέρει αὐτοὺς εἰς ὄρος ὑψηλὸν κατ' ἰδίαν.
AND HE BRINGS UP THEM TO A HIGH~MOUNTAIN PRIVATELY.

17.2 καὶ μετεμορφώθη ἔμπροσθεν αὐτῶν, καὶ ἔλαμψεν
     AND HE WAS TRANSFIGURED BEFORE   THEM,   AND   SHONE

τὸ πρόσωπον αὐτοῦ ὡς ὁ ἥλιος, τὰ δὲ ἱμάτια αὐτοῦ
THE FACE   OF HIM LIKE THE SUN, AND~THE GARMENTS OF HIM

ἐγένετο λευκὰ ὡς τὸ φῶς. 17.3 καὶ ἰδοὺ ὤφθη αὐτοῖς
BECAME BRILLIANT AS THE LIGHT.   AND BEHOLD APPEARED TO THEM

Μωϋσῆς καὶ Ἠλίας συλλαλοῦντες μετ' αὐτοῦ.
MOSES   AND ELIJAH   TALKING   WITH HIM.

17.4 ἀποκριθεὶς δὲ ὁ Πέτρος εἶπεν τῷ Ἰησοῦ, Κύριε,
     AND~HAVING ANSWERED - PETER SAID - TO JESUS, LORD,

καλόν ἐστιν ἡμᾶς ὧδε εἶναι· εἰ θέλεις, ποιήσω ὧδε
IT IS~GOOD   FOR US TO BE~HERE. IF YOU WISH, I WILL MAKE HERE

τρεῖς σκηνάς, σοὶ μίαν καὶ Μωϋσεῖ μίαν καὶ
THREE TENTS, ONE~FOR YOU AND ONE~FOR MOSES AND

Ἠλίᾳ μίαν. 17.5 ἔτι αὐτοῦ λαλοῦντος ἰδοὺ
ONE~FOR ELIJAH.   WHILE HE IS SPEAKING BEHOLD

νεφέλη φωτεινὴ ἐπεσκίασεν αὐτούς, καὶ ἰδοὺ φωνὴ ἐκ
A SHINING~CLOUD OVERSHADOWED THEM,   AND BEHOLD A VOICE FROM

τῆς νεφέλης λέγουσα, Οὗτός ἐστιν ὁ υἱός μου ὁ
THE CLOUD   SPEAKING,   THIS   IS   THE SON OF ME, THE

ἀγαπητός, ἐν ᾧ εὐδόκησα· ἀκούετε αὐτοῦ. 17.6 καὶ
BELOVED,   IN WHOM I AM WELL PLEASED. LISTEN TO HIM.   AND

ἀκούσαντες οἱ μαθηταὶ ἔπεσαν ἐπὶ πρόσωπον αὐτῶν
HAVING HEARD [THIS] THE DISCIPLES FELL UPON [THE] FACE[S] OF THEM

καὶ ἐφοβήθησαν σφόδρα. 17.7 καὶ προσῆλθεν ὁ Ἰησοῦς
AND THEY WERE TERRIFIED GREATLY.   AND APPROACHED   - JESUS

καὶ ἁψάμενος αὐτῶν εἶπεν, Ἐγέρθητε καὶ μὴ φοβεῖσθε.
AND   HAVING TOUCHED   THEM   HE SAID,   ARISE   AND   DO NOT BE AFRAID.

17.8 ἐπάραντες δὲ τοὺς ὀφθαλμοὺς αὐτῶν οὐδένα εἶδον
AND~HAVING LIFTED   THE   EYES   OF THEM   THEY SAW~NO ONE

εἰ μὴ αὐτὸν Ἰησοῦν μόνον.
EXCEPT   JESUS~HIMSELF   ONLY.

17.9 Καὶ καταβαινόντων αὐτῶν ἐκ τοῦ ὄρους
AND   [AS] THEY~[WERE] COMING DOWN   FROM   THE   MOUNTAIN

ἐνετείλατο αὐτοῖς ὁ Ἰησοῦς λέγων, Μηδενὶ εἴπητε τὸ
COMMANDED   THEM   -   JESUS   SAYING,   TELL~NO ONE   THE

ὅραμα ἕως οὗ ὁ υἱὸς τοῦ ἀνθρώπου ἐκ νεκρῶν
VISION   UNTIL   THE SON   -   OF MAN   FROM   [THE] DEAD

ἐγερθῇ.   **17.10** καὶ ἐπηρώτησαν αὐτὸν οἱ μαθηταὶ
HAS BEEN RAISED.   AND   ASKED   HIM   THE DISCIPLES

λέγοντες, Τί οὖν οἱ γραμματεῖς λέγουσιν ὅτι
SAYING,   WHY   THEREFORE [DO] THE   SCRIBES   SAY   THAT

Ἠλίαν δεῖ ἐλθεῖν πρῶτον; **17.11** ὁ δὲ ἀποκριθεὶς
IT IS NECESSARY~FOR ELIJAH TO COME   FIRST?   AND~HE HAVING ANSWERED

εἶπεν, Ἠλίας μὲν ἔρχεται καὶ ἀποκαταστήσει πάντα·
SAID,   ELIJAH   INDEED   IS COMING   AND   WILL RESTORE   ALL THINGS.

17.12 λέγω δὲ ὑμῖν ὅτι Ἠλίας ἤδη ἦλθεν, καὶ
BUT~I SAY   TO YOU°   THAT   ELIJAH   ALREADY   CAME,   AND

οὐκ ἐπέγνωσαν αὐτὸν ἀλλὰ ἐποίησαν ἐν αὐτῷ ὅσα
THEY DID NOT RECOGNIZE   HIM   BUT   DID   WITH   HIM   WHATEVER

ἠθέλησαν· οὕτως καὶ ὁ υἱὸς τοῦ ἀνθρώπου μέλλει
THEY WISHED.   THUS   ALSO   THE SON   -   OF MAN   IS ABOUT

πάσχειν ὑπ᾽ αὐτῶν. **17.13** τότε συνῆκαν οἱ μαθηταὶ ὅτι
TO SUFFER   BY   THEM.   THEN   UNDERSTOOD THE DISCIPLES   THAT

περὶ Ἰωάννου τοῦ βαπτιστοῦ εἶπεν αὐτοῖς.
ABOUT   JOHN   THE   BAPTIST   HE SPOKE TO THEM.

17.14 Καὶ ἐλθόντων πρὸς τὸν ὄχλον προσῆλθεν αὐτῷ
AND   HAVING COME   TO   THE   CROWD,   CAME   TO HIM

ἄνθρωπος γονυπετῶν αὐτὸν **17.15** καὶ λέγων, Κύριε,
A MAN   KNEELING DOWN [BEFORE] HIM   AND   SAYING,   LORD,

ἐλέησόν μου τὸν υἱόν, ὅτι σεληνιάζεται καὶ
HAVE MERCY ON   MY   -   SON,   FOR   HE IS AN EPILEPTIC   AND

κακῶς πάσχει· πολλάκις γὰρ πίπτει εἰς τὸ πῦρ καὶ
SUFFERS~TERRIBLY.   FOR~OFTEN   HE FALLS   INTO   THE   FIRE   AND

πολλάκις εἰς τὸ ὕδωρ. **17.16** καὶ προσήνεγκα αὐτὸν
OFTEN   INTO   THE   WATER.   AND   I BROUGHT   HIM

τοῖς μαθηταῖς σου, καὶ οὐκ ἠδυνήθησαν
TO THE   DISCIPLES   OF YOU,   AND   THEY WERE NOT ABLE

αὐτὸν θεραπεῦσαι. **17.17** ἀποκριθεὶς δὲ ὁ Ἰησοῦς εἶπεν,
TO HEAL~HIM.   AND~HAVING ANSWERED   -   JESUS   SAID

Ὦ γενεὰ ἄπιστος καὶ διεστραμμένη, ἕως πότε μεθ᾽
O   ⁴GENERATION ¹FAITHLESS   ²AND ³DEPRAVED,   HOW LONG   WITH

ὑμῶν ἔσομαι; ἕως πότε ἀνέξομαι ὑμῶν; φέρετέ μοι
YOU°   WILL I BE?   HOW LONG   WILL I ENDURE   YOU°?   BRING   TO ME

touched them, saying, "Get up and do not be afraid." [8]And when they looked up, they saw no one except Jesus himself alone.

9 As they were coming down the mountain, Jesus ordered them, "Tell no one about the vision until after the Son of Man has been raised from the dead." [10]And the disciples asked him, "Why, then, do the scribes say that Elijah must come first?" [11]He replied, "Elijah is indeed coming and will restore all things; [12]but I tell you that Elijah has already come, and they did not recognize him, but they did to him whatever they pleased. So also the Son of Man is about to suffer at their hands." [13]Then the disciples understood that he was speaking to them about John the Baptist.

14 When they came to the crowd, a man came to him, knelt before him, [15]and said, "Lord, have mercy on my son, for he is an epileptic and he suffers terribly; he often falls into the fire and often into the water. [16]And I brought him to your disciples, but they could not cure him." [17]Jesus answered, "You faithless and perverse generation, how much longer must I be with you? How much longer must I put up with you? Bring him

here to me." [18]And Jesus rebuked the demon,[d] and it[e] came out of him, and the boy was cured instantly. [19]Then the disciples came to Jesus privately and said, "Why could we not cast it out?" [20]He said to them, "Because of your little faith. For truly I tell you, if you have faith the size of a[f] mustard seed, you will say to this mountain, 'Move from here to there,' and it will move; and nothing will be impossible for you."[g]

[22] As they were gathering[h] in Galilee, Jesus said to them, "The Son of Man is going to be betrayed into human hands, [23]and they will kill him, and on the third day he will be raised." And they were greatly distressed.

[24] When they reached Capernaum, the collectors of the temple tax[i] came to Peter and said, "Does your teacher not pay the temple tax?"[i] [25]He said, "Yes, he does." And when he came home, Jesus spoke of it first, asking, "What do you think, Simon? From whom do kings of the earth take toll or tribute? From their children or from others?" [26]When Peter[j] said, "From others," Jesus said to him, "Then

[d] Gk it or him
[e] Gk the demon
[f] Gk faith as a grain of
[g] Other ancient authorities add verse 21, But this kind does not come out except by prayer and fasting
[h] Other ancient authorities read living
[i] Gk didrachma
[j] Gk he

αὐτὸν ὧδε. **17.18** καὶ ἐπετίμησεν αὐτῷ ὁ Ἰησοῦς καὶ
HIM HERE. AND REBUKED IT - JESUS AND

ἐξῆλθεν ἀπ᾽ αὐτοῦ τὸ δαιμόνιον καὶ ἐθεραπεύθη ὁ
CAME OUT FROM HIM THE DEMON AND WAS HEALED THE

παῖς ἀπὸ τῆς ὥρας ἐκείνης. **17.19** Τότε προσελθόντες
CHILD FROM - THAT~HOUR. THEN HAVING APPROACHED

οἱ μαθηταὶ τῷ Ἰησοῦ κατ᾽ ἰδίαν εἶπον, Διὰ τί ἡμεῖς
THE DISCIPLES - TO JESUS PRIVATELY THEY SAID, WHY [WERE] WE

οὐκ ἠδυνήθημεν ἐκβαλεῖν αὐτό; **17.20** ὁ δὲ λέγει
NOT ABLE TO CAST OUT IT? AND~HE SAYS

αὐτοῖς, Διὰ τὴν ὀλιγοπιστίαν ὑμῶν· ἀμὴν γὰρ
TO THEM, ON ACCOUNT OF THE LITTLE FAITH OF YOU°. FOR~TRULY

λέγω ὑμῖν, ἐὰν ἔχητε πίστιν ὡς κόκκον σινάπεως,
I SAY TO YOU°, IF YOU° HAVE FAITH LIKE A MUSTARD~SEED,

ἐρεῖτε τῷ ὄρει τούτῳ, Μετάβα ἔνθεν ἐκεῖ, καὶ
YOU° WILL SAY - TO THIS~MOUNTAIN, MOVE FROM THERE, AND

μεταβήσεται· καὶ οὐδὲν ἀδυνατήσει ὑμῖν[T].
IT WILL BE MOVED. AND NOTHING WILL BE IMPOSSIBLE FOR YOU°.

17.22 Συστρεφομένων δὲ αὐτῶν ἐν τῇ Γαλιλαίᾳ εἶπεν
AND~[AFTER] COMING TOGETHER THEY IN - GALILEE, SAID

αὐτοῖς ὁ Ἰησοῦς, Μέλλει ὁ υἱὸς τοῦ ἀνθρώπου
TO THEM - JESUS, IS ABOUT THE SON - OF MAN

παραδίδοσθαι εἰς χεῖρας ἀνθρώπων, **17.23** καὶ
TO BE BETRAYED INTO [THE] HANDS OF MEN, AND

ἀποκτενοῦσιν αὐτόν, καὶ τῇ τρίτῃ ἡμέρᾳ ἐγερθήσεται.
THEY WILL KILL HIM, AND ON THE THIRD DAY HE WILL BE RAISED.

καὶ ἐλυπήθησαν σφόδρα.
AND THEY GRIEVED GREATLY.

17.24 Ἐλθόντων δὲ αὐτῶν εἰς Καφαρναοὺμ προσῆλθον
AND~HAVING COME THEY INTO CAPERNAUM, APPROACHED

οἱ τὰ δίδραχμα λαμβάνοντες τῷ Πέτρῳ καὶ
THE ONES THE TWO-DRACHMA PIECE RECEIVING - TO PETER AND

εἶπαν, Ὁ διδάσκαλος ὑμῶν οὐ τελεῖ [τὰ]
THEY SAID, THE TEACHER OF YOU°, DOES HE NOT PAY THE

δίδραχμα; **17.25** λέγει, Ναί. καὶ ἐλθόντα εἰς
TWO-DRACHMA PIECE [TAX]? HE SAYS, YES. AND HAVING COME INTO

τὴν οἰκίαν προέφθασεν αὐτὸν ὁ Ἰησοῦς λέγων, Τί
THE HOUSE ANTICIPATED HIM - JESUS SAYING, WHAT

σοι δοκεῖ, Σίμων; οἱ βασιλεῖς τῆς γῆς ἀπὸ
SEEMS [RIGHT]~TO YOU, SIMON? THE KINGS OF THE EARTH, FROM

τίνων λαμβάνουσιν τέλη ἢ κῆνσον; ἀπὸ τῶν υἱῶν
WHOM DO THEY RECEIVE A TAX OR [THE] POLL TAX? FROM THE SONS

αὐτῶν ἢ ἀπὸ τῶν ἀλλοτρίων; **17.26** εἰπόντος δέ, Ἀπὸ
OF THEM OR FROM - STRANGERS? AND~HAVING SPOKEN, FROM

τῶν ἀλλοτρίων, ἔφη αὐτῷ ὁ Ἰησοῦς, Ἄρα γε ἐλεύθεροί
THE STRANGERS. SAID TO HIM - JESUS, THEN EXEMPT

17:20 text: ASV RSV NASB NIV NEB TEV NJB NRSV. add v. 21 τουτο δε το γενος ουκ εκπορευεται ει μη εν προσευξη και νηστεια (but this kind does not come out except by prayer and fasting) [see Mark 9:29]: KJV ASVmg RSVmg NASBmg NIVmg NEBmg TEVmg NJBmg.

εἰσιν οἱ υἱοί. **17.27** ἵνα δὲ   μὴ σκανδαλίσωμεν
ARE   THE SONS.   BUT~IN ORDER THAT WE MAY NOT OFFEND

αὐτούς, πορευθεὶς εἰς θάλασσαν βάλε ἄγκιστρον καὶ
THEM,   HAVING GONE   TO [THE] LAKE   CAST A FISHOOK   AND

τὸν ἀναβάντα πρῶτον ἰχθὺν ἆρον, καὶ ἀνοίξας   τὸ
THE ²HAVING COME UP ³FIRST ¹FISH TAKE,   AND HAVING OPENED THE

στόμα αὐτοῦ εὑρήσεις στατῆρα·   ἐκεῖνον λαβὼν δὸς
MOUTH OF IT   YOU WILL FIND A STATER.   HAVING TAKEN~THAT   GIVE

αὐτοῖς ἀντὶ ἐμοῦ καὶ σοῦ.
TO THEM ON BEHALF OF ME   AND YOU.

the children are free.
²⁷However, so that we do not
give offense to them, go to
the sea and cast a hook; take
the first fish that comes up;
and when you open its
mouth, you will find a coin;[k]
take that and give it to them
for you and me."

18.1 Ἐν ἐκείνῃ τῇ ὥρᾳ προσῆλθον οἱ μαθηταὶ τῷ
       AT   THAT   - HOUR APPROACHED   THE DISCIPLES -

Ἰησοῦ λέγοντες, Τίς ἄρα μείζων ἐστὶν ἐν τῇ
TO JESUS SAYING,   WHO THEN IS~GREATEST   IN THE

βασιλείᾳ τῶν οὐρανῶν; **18.2** καὶ προσκαλεσάμενος
KINGDOM   OF THE HEAVENS?   AND   HAVING CALLED

παιδίον ἔστησεν αὐτὸ ἐν μέσῳ   αὐτῶν **18.3** καὶ εἶπεν,
A CHILD HE SET   HIM IN [THE] MIDST OF THEM   AND SAID,

Ἀμὴν λέγω ὑμῖν, ἐὰν μὴ στραφῆτε καὶ γένησθε ὡς
TRULY I SAY TO YOU°, UNLESS YOU° CHANGE AND YOU° BECOME LIKE

τὰ παιδία, οὐ μὴ εἰσέλθητε εἰς τὴν βασιλείαν τῶν
- CHILDREN, YOU° WILL NEVER ENTER INTO THE   KINGDOM   OF THE

οὐρανῶν. **18.4** ὅστις οὖν   ταπεινώσει ἑαυτὸν ὡς τὸ
HEAVENS.   THEREFORE~WHOEVER WILL HUMBLE HIMSELF   LIKE -

παιδίον τοῦτο, οὗτός ἐστιν ὁ μείζων ἐν τῇ βασιλείᾳ
THIS~CHILD,   THIS ONE IS   THE GREATEST IN THE KINGDOM

τῶν οὐρανῶν. **18.5** καὶ ὃς ἐὰν δέξηται ἐν παιδίον τοιοῦτο
OF THE HEAVENS.   AND WHOEVER MAY RECEIVE ONE SUCH~CHILD

ἐπὶ τῷ ὀνόματί μου, ἐμὲ δέχεται.
IN   THE   NAME   OF ME, RECEIVES~ME.

18.6 Ὃς δ᾽ ἂν σκανδαλίσῃ ἕνα τῶν μικρῶν τούτων τῶν
       AND~WHOEVER CAUSES TO FALL ONE   -   OF THESE~LITTLE ONES -

πιστευόντων εἰς ἐμέ, συμφέρει αὐτῷ ἵνα κρεμασθῇ
BELIEVING   IN   ME, IT IS BETTER FOR HIM THAT BE HUNG

μύλος   ὀνικὸς περὶ τὸν τράχηλον αὐτοῦ καὶ
[THE] MILLSTONE OF A DONKEY AROUND THE   NECK   OF HIM   AND

καταποντισθῇ ἐν τῷ πελάγει τῆς θαλάσσης.
HE BE DROWNED   IN   THE DEPTH   OF THE SEA.

18.7 οὐαὶ τῷ κόσμῳ ἀπὸ   τῶν σκανδάλων·
       WOE TO THE WORLD · BECAUSE OF THE OFFENSES.

ἀνάγκη γὰρ ἐλθεῖν τὰ σκάνδαλα, πλὴν οὐαὶ τῷ
FOR~[IT IS] NECESSARY TO COME THE OFFENSES,   BUT   WOE TO THE

ἀνθρώπῳ δι᾽ οὗ τὸ σκάνδαλον ἔρχεται.
MAN   THROUGH WHOM THE OFFENSE   COMES.

At that time the disciples
came to Jesus and asked,
"Who is the greatest in the
kingdom of heaven?" ²He
called a child, whom he put
among them, ³and said,
"Truly I tell you, unless you
change and become like
children, you will never
enter the kingdom of
heaven. ⁴Whoever becomes
humble like this child is the
greatest in the kingdom of
heaven. ⁵Whoever
welcomes one such child in
my name welcomes me.

6 "If any of you put a
stumbling block before one
of these little ones who
believe in me, it would be
better for you if a great
millstone were fastened
around your neck and you
were drowned in the depth of
the sea. ⁷Woe to the world
because of stumbling
blocks! Occasions for
stumbling are bound to
come, but woe to the one by
whom the stumbling block
comes!

k Gk *stater;* the stater was worth two
   didrachmas

8 "If your hand or your foot causes you to stumble, cut it off and throw it away; it is better for you to enter life maimed or lame than to have two hands or two feet and to be thrown into the eternal fire. 9And if your eye causes you to stumble, tear it out and throw it away; it is better for you to enter life with one eye than to have two eyes and to be thrown into the hell[l] of fire.

10 "Take care that you do not despise one of these little ones; for, I tell you, in heaven their angels continually see the face of my Father in heaven.[m] 12What do you think? If a shepherd has a hundred sheep, and one of them has gone astray, does he not leave the ninety-nine on the mountains and go in search of the one that went astray? 13And if he finds it, truly I tell you, he rejoices over it more than over the ninety-nine that never went astray. 14So it is not the will of your[n] Father in heaven that one of these little ones should be lost.

15 "If another member of the church[o] sins against you,[p]

[l] Gk Gehenna
[m] Other ancient authorities add verse 11, For the Son of Man came to save the lost
[n] Other ancient authorities read my
[o] Gk If your brother
[p] Other ancient authorities lack against you

18.8 Εἰ δὲ ἡ χείρ σου ἢ ὁ πούς σου σκανδαλίζει σε,
AND~IF THE HAND OF YOU OR THE FOOT OF YOU CAUSES YOU TO FALL

ἔκκοψον αὐτὸν καὶ βάλε ἀπὸ σοῦ· καλόν σοί ἐστιν
CUT OFF IT AND THROW [IT] FROM YOU. BETTER FOR YOU IT IS

εἰσελθεῖν εἰς τὴν ζωὴν κυλλὸν ἢ χωλὸν ἢ δύο
TO ENTER INTO - LIFE CRIPPLED OR LAME THAN TWO

χεῖρας ἢ δύο πόδας ἔχοντα βληθῆναι εἰς τὸ πῦρ τὸ
HANDS OR TWO FEET HAVING TO BE THROWN INTO THE FIRE -

αἰώνιον. **18.9** καὶ εἰ ὁ ὀφθαλμός σου σκανδαλίζει σε,
ETERNAL. AND IF THE EYE OF YOU CAUSES YOU TO FALL,

ἔξελε αὐτὸν καὶ βάλε ἀπὸ σοῦ· καλόν σοί ἐστιν
TAKE OUT IT AND THROW [IT] FROM YOU. BETTER FOR YOU IT IS

μονόφθαλμον εἰς τὴν ζωὴν εἰσελθεῖν ἢ δύο
ONE-EYED INTO - LIFE TO ENTER THAN TWO

ὀφθαλμοὺς ἔχοντα βληθῆναι εἰς τὴν γέενναν τοῦ
EYES HAVING TO BE CAST INTO THE GEHENNA(HELL) -

πυρός.
OF FIRE.

18.10 Ὁρᾶτε μὴ καταφρονήσητε ἑνὸς τῶν
SEE [TO IT THAT] YOU° DO NOT LOOK DOWN UPON ONE -

μικρῶν τούτων· λέγω γὰρ ὑμῖν ὅτι οἱ ἄγγελοι αὐτῶν
OF THESE~LITTLE ONES. FOR~I SAY TO YOU° THAT THE ANGELS OF THEM

ἐν οὐρανοῖς διὰ παντὸς βλέπουσι τὸ πρόσωπον τοῦ
IN [THE] HEAVENS CONTINUALLY SEE THE FACE OF THE

πατρός μου τοῦ ἐν οὐρανοῖς⊤. **18.12** Τί ὑμῖν δοκεῖ;
FATHER OF ME, THE ONE IN [THE] HEAVENS. WHAT SEEMS [RIGHT]~TO YOU°?

ἐὰν γένηταί τινι ἀνθρώπῳ ἑκατὸν πρόβατα
IF BELONGED TO ANY MAN ONE HUNDRED SHEEP

καὶ πλανηθῇ ἓν ἐξ αὐτῶν, οὐχὶ ἀφήσει τὰ
AND WANDERED ONE OF THEM, WILL HE NOT LEAVE THE

ἐνενήκοντα ἐννέα ἐπὶ τὰ ὄρη καὶ πορευθεὶς ζητεῖ
NINETY-NINE ON THE HILLSIDES AND HAVING GONE SEEK

τὸ πλανώμενον; **18.13** καὶ ἐὰν γένηται εὑρεῖν αὐτό,
THE ONE HAVING WANDERED? AND IF HE HAPPENS TO FIND IT,

ἀμὴν λέγω ὑμῖν ὅτι χαίρει ἐπ' αὐτῷ μᾶλλον ἢ
TRULY I SAY TO YOU° THAT HE REJOICES OVER IT MORE THAN

ἐπὶ τοῖς ἐνενήκοντα ἐννέα τοῖς μὴ πεπλανημένοις.
OVER THE NINETY-NINE WHICH HAVE NOT BEEN WANDERING.

18.14 οὕτως οὐκ ἔστιν θέλημα ἔμπροσθεν τοῦ πατρὸς
THUS IT IS NOT [THE] WILL BEFORE THE FATHER

ὑμῶν τοῦ ἐν οὐρανοῖς ἵνα ἀπόληται ἓν τῶν
OF YOU° THE ONE IN [THE] HEAVENS THAT SHOULD PERISH ONE -

μικρῶν τούτων.
OF THESE~LITTLE ONES.

18.15 Ἐὰν δὲ ἁμαρτήσῃ [εἰς σὲ] ὁ ἀδελφός σου,
AND~IF SINS AGAINST YOU THE BROTHER OF YOU,

18:10 text: ASV RSV NASBmg NIV NEB TEV NJB NRSV. add v. 11 ηλθεν γαρ ο υιος του ανθρωπου σωσαι το απολωλος (for the Son of Man came to save the lost) [see Luke 19:10]: KJV ASVmg RSVmg NASB NIVmg NEBmg TEVmg NJBmg NRSVmg.

ὕπαγε ἔλεγξον αὐτὸν μεταξὺ σοῦ καὶ αὐτοῦ μόνου.
GO [AND] REPROVE HIM BETWEEN YOU AND HE ALONE.

ἐάν σου ἀκούσῃ, ἐκέρδησας τὸν ἀδελφόν σου·
IF HE HEARS~YOU, YOU GAINED THE BROTHER OF YOU.

18.16 ἐὰν δὲ μὴ ἀκούσῃ, παράλαβε μετὰ σοῦ ἔτι ἕνα
BUT~IF HE DOES NOT LISTEN, TAKE WITH YOU STILL ONE

ἢ δύο, ἵνα ἐπὶ στόματος δύο μαρτύρων ἢ τριῶν
OR TWO, THAT BY [THE] MOUTH OF TWO WITNESSES OR THREE

σταθῇ   πᾶν ῥῆμα· **18.17** ἐὰν δὲ παρακούσῃ
MAY BE ESTABLISHED EVERY WORD.   BUT~IF HE REFUSES TO HEAR

αὐτῶν, εἰπὲ τῇ ἐκκλησίᾳ· ἐὰν δὲ καὶ τῆς ἐκκλησίας
THEM, SPEAK TO THE CHURCH. AND~IF EVEN THE CHURCH

παρακούσῃ, ἔστω σοι ὥσπερ ὁ ἐθνικὸς καὶ ὁ
HE REFUSES TO HEAR, LET HIM BE TO YOU AS THE GENTILE AND THE

τελώνης.
TAX COLLECTOR.

18.18 Ἀμὴν λέγω ὑμῖν· ὅσα ἐὰν δήσητε ἐπὶ τῆς
TRULY I SAY TO YOU°: WHATEVER YOU° BIND ON THE

γῆς ἔσται δεδεμένα ἐν οὐρανῷ, καὶ ὅσα ἐὰν λύσητε
EARTH WILL HAVE BEEN BOUND IN HEAVEN, AND WHATEVER YOU° ABOLISH

ἐπὶ τῆς γῆς ἔσται λελυμένα ἐν οὐρανῷ. **18.19** Πάλιν
UPON THE EARTH WILL HAVE BEEN ABOLISHED IN HEAVEN.   AGAIN

[ἀμὴν] λέγω ὑμῖν ὅτι ἐὰν δύο συμφωνήσωσιν ἐξ ὑμῶν
TRULY I SAY TO YOU° THAT IF TWO ³WILL BE IN AGREEMENT ¹OF ²YOU°

ἐπὶ τῆς γῆς περὶ παντὸς πράγματος οὗ ἐὰν
UPON THE EARTH CONCERNING EVERY MATTER WHATEVER

αἰτήσωνται, γενήσεται αὐτοῖς παρὰ τοῦ πατρός μου
THEY WILL ASK, IT WILL BE DONE FOR THEM BY THE FATHER OF ME

τοῦ ἐν οὐρανοῖς. **18.20** οὗ γὰρ εἰσιν δύο ἢ τρεῖς
THE ONE IN [THE] HEAVENS.   FOR~WHERE THERE ARE TWO OR THREE

συνηγμένοι εἰς τὸ ἐμὸν ὄνομα, ἐκεῖ εἰμι ἐν μέσῳ
HAVING BEEN GATHERED IN - MY NAME, THERE I AM IN [THE] MIDST

αὐτῶν.
OF THEM.

18.21 Τότε προσελθὼν ὁ Πέτρος εἶπεν αὐτῷ, Κύριε,
THEN HAVING APPROACHED - PETER SAID TO HIM, LORD,

ποσάκις ἁμαρτήσει εἰς ἐμὲ ὁ ἀδελφός μου καὶ
HOW OFTEN WILL SIN AGAINST ME THE BROTHER OF ME AND

ἀφήσω αὐτῷ; ἕως ἑπτάκις; **18.22** λέγει αὐτῷ ὁ
I WILL FORGIVE HIM? AS MANY AS SEVEN TIMES? SAYS TO HIM -

Ἰησοῦς, Οὐ λέγω σοι ἕως ἑπτάκις ἀλλὰ ἕως
JESUS, I DO NOT SAY TO YOU AS MANY AS SEVEN BUT AS MANY AS

ἑβδομηκοντάκις ἑπτά. **18.23** Διὰ τοῦτο ὡμοιώθη ἡ
SEVENTY TIMES SEVEN. THEREFORE, ⁵IS LIKE ¹THE

βασιλεία τῶν οὐρανῶν ἀνθρώπῳ βασιλεῖ, ὃς ἠθέλησεν
²KINGDOM ³OF THE ⁴HEAVENS A MAN, A KING, WHO WISHED

go and point out the fault when the two of you are alone. If the member listens to you, you have regained that one.[q] [16]But if you are not listened to, take one or two others along with you, so that every word may be confirmed by the evidence of two or three witnesses. [17]If the member refuses to listen to them, tell it to the church; and if the offender refuses to listen even to the church, let such a one be to you as a Gentile and a tax collector. [18]Truly I tell you, whatever you bind on earth will be bound in heaven, and whatever you loose on earth will be loosed in heaven. [19]Again, truly I tell you, if two of you agree on earth about anything you ask, it will be done for you by my Father in heaven. [20]For where two or three are gathered in my name, I am there among them."

21 Then Peter came and said to him, "Lord, if another member of the church[r] sins against me, how often should I forgive? As many as seven times?" [22]Jesus said to him, "Not seven times, but, I tell you, seventy-seven[s] times.

23 "For this reason the kingdom of heaven may be compared to a king who wished

[q] Gk *the brother*
[r] Gk *if my brother*
[s] Or *seventy times seven*

to settle accounts with his slaves. 24When he began the reckoning, one who owed him ten thousand talents[t] was brought to him; 25and, as he could not pay, his lord ordered him to be sold, together with his wife and children and all his possessions, and payment to be made. 26So the slave fell on his knees before him, saying, 'Have patience with me, and I will pay you everything.' 27And out of pity for him, the lord of that slave released him and forgave him the debt. 28But that same slave, as he went out, came upon one of his fellow slaves who owed him a hundred denarii;[u] and seizing him by the throat, he said, 'Pay what you owe.' 29Then his fellow slave fell down and pleaded with him, 'Have patience with me, and I will pay you.' 30But he refused; then he went and threw him into prison until he would pay the debt. 31When his fellow slaves saw what had happened, they were greatly distressed, and they went and reported to their lord all that had taken place. 32Then his lord summoned him and said to him, 'You wicked slave! I forgave you all that debt because you pleaded with me. 33Should you not have had mercy on

[t] A talent was worth more than fifteen years' wages of a laborer
[u] The denarius was the usual day's wage for a laborer

συνᾶραι λόγον μετὰ τῶν δούλων αὐτοῦ.
TO SETTLE ACCOUNTS   WITH   THE   SLAVES   OF HIM.

18.24 ἀρξαμένου δὲ αὐτοῦ συναίρειν προσηνέχθη
AND~HAVING BEGUN   HE   TO SETTLE [ACCOUNTS]   WAS BROUGHT

αὐτῷ εἷς ὀφειλέτης μυρίων ταλάντων.
TO HIM   ONE   DEBTOR   OF TEN THOUSAND   TALENTS.

18.25 μὴ ἔχοντος δὲ αὐτοῦ ἀποδοῦναι ἐκέλευσεν αὐτὸν
BUT~NOT HAVING   HIM   TO REPAY   COMMANDED   HIM

ὁ κύριος πραθῆναι καὶ τὴν γυναῖκα καὶ τὰ τέκνα
THE   LORD   TO BE SOLD   AND   THE   WIFE   AND   THE   CHILDREN

καὶ πάντα ὅσα ἔχει, καὶ ἀποδοθῆναι.
AND   EVERYTHING   WHICH   HE HAS,   AND   TO BE REPAID.

18.26 πεσὼν οὖν ὁ δοῦλος προσεκύνει αὐτῷ λέγων,
THEREFORE~FALLING   THE   SLAVE   DID HOMAGE BEFORE   HIM   SAYING,

Μακροθύμησον ἐπ' ἐμοί, καὶ πάντα ἀποδώσω σοι.
HAVE PATIENCE   WITH   ME   AND   EVERYTHING   I WILL PAY BACK   TO YOU.

18.27 σπλαγχνισθεὶς δὲ ὁ κύριος τοῦ δούλου ἐκείνου
AND~HAVING HAD COMPASSION   THE   LORD   -   OF THAT~SLAVE

ἀπέλυσεν αὐτόν καὶ τὸ δάνειον ἀφῆκεν αὐτῷ.
PARDONED   HIM   AND   THE   LOAN   FORGAVE   HIM.

18.28 ἐξελθὼν δὲ ὁ δοῦλος ἐκεῖνος εὗρεν ἕνα τῶν
AND~HAVING GONE OUT   -   THAT~SLAVE   FOUND   ONE   OF THE

συνδούλων αὐτοῦ, ὃς ὤφειλεν αὐτῷ ἑκατὸν δηνάρια,
FELLOW SLAVES   OF HIM,   WHO   OWED   HIM   ONE HUNDRED   DENARII,

καὶ κρατήσας αὐτὸν ἔπνιγεν λέγων, Ἀπόδος εἴ
AND   HAVING SEIZED   HIM   WAS CHOKING [HIM]   SAYING,   REPAY   IF

τι ὀφείλεις. **18.29** πεσὼν οὖν ὁ σύνδουλος
YOU OWE [ME]~SOMETHING.   THEREFORE~HAVING FALLEN   THE   FELLOW SLAVE

αὐτοῦ παρεκάλει αὐτὸν λέγων, Μακροθύμησον ἐπ'
OF HIM   BEGGED   HIM   SAYING,   HAVE PATIENCE   WITH

ἐμοί, καὶ ἀποδώσω σοι. **18.30** ὁ δὲ οὐκ ἤθελεν ἀλλὰ
ME,   AND   I WILL REPAY   YOU.   BUT~HE   WAS NOT WILLING   BUT

ἀπελθὼν ἔβαλεν αὐτὸν εἰς φυλακὴν ἕως ἀποδῷ
HAVING LEFT   HE THREW   HIM   INTO   PRISON   UNTIL   HE SHOULD REPAY

τὸ ὀφειλόμενον. **18.31** ἰδόντες οὖν οἱ σύνδουλοι
THAT WHICH   IS OWING.   THEREFORE~HAVING SEEN   THE   FELLOW SLAVES

αὐτοῦ τὰ γενόμενα ἐλυπήθησαν σφόδρα καὶ
OF HIM   THE THINGS   HAVING TAKEN PLACE   THEY GRIEVED   GREATLY   AND

ἐλθόντες διεσάφησαν τῷ κυρίῳ ἑαυτῶν πάντα τὰ
HAVING COME   THEY REPORTED   TO THE   LORD   OF THEM   ALL   THE THINGS

γενόμενα. **18.32** τότε προσκαλεσάμενος αὐτὸν ὁ
HAVING TAKEN PLACE.   THEN   HAVING CALLED   HIM   THE

κύριος αὐτοῦ λέγει αὐτῷ, Δοῦλε πονηρέ, πᾶσαν τὴν
LORD   OF HIM   SAYS   TO HIM,   WICKED~SLAVE,   ALL   -

ὀφειλὴν ἐκείνην ἀφῆκά σοι, ἐπεὶ παρεκάλεσάς με·
THAT~DEBT   I FORGAVE   YOU,   BECAUSE   YOU BEGGED   ME.

18.33 οὐκ ἔδει καὶ σὲ ἐλεῆσαι τὸν
WAS IT NOT NECESSARY   ALSO   FOR YOU   TO HAVE MERCY UPON   THE

σύνδουλόν σου, ὡς κἀγὼ σὲ ἠλέησα;   **18.34** καὶ
FELLOW SLAVE   OF YOU   AS   I ALSO   HAD MERCY~ON YOU?   AND

ὀργισθεὶς   ὁ   κύριος αὐτοῦ παρέδωκεν αὐτὸν τοῖς
HAVING BEEN ANGRY   THE   LORD   OF HIM   HANDED OVER   HIM   TO THE

βασανισταῖς ἕως οὗ ἀποδῷ   πᾶν   τὸ ὀφειλόμενον.
JAILERS   UNTIL   HE SHOULD REPAY EVERYTHING -   OWING.

18.35 Οὕτως καὶ ὁ   πατήρ μου ὁ οὐράνιος ποιήσει
         THUS   ALSO   THE ²FATHER   ³OF ME   -   ¹HEAVENLY   WILL DO

ὑμῖν, ἐὰν μὴ ἀφῆτε   ἕκαστος τῷ ἀδελφῷ αὐτοῦ ἀπὸ
TO YOU°, UNLESS   YOU° FORGIVE EACH ONE   THE   BROTHER   OF HIM   FROM

τῶν καρδιῶν ὑμῶν.
THE   HEARTS   OF YOU°.

your fellow slave, as I had mercy on you?' ³⁴And in anger his lord handed him over to be tortured until he would pay his entire debt. ³⁵So my heavenly Father will also do to every one of you, if you do not forgive your brother or sister[v] from your heart."

[v] Gk *brother*

19.1 Καὶ ἐγένετο   ὅτε ἐτέλεσεν ὁ Ἰησοῦς τοὺς
        AND   IT CAME TO PASS   WHEN FINISHED   -   JESUS   -

λόγους τούτους, μετῆρεν ἀπὸ τῆς Γαλιλαίας καὶ ἦλθεν
THESE~WORDS,   HE DEPARTED FROM   -   GALILEE   AND   CAME

εἰς τὰ ὅρια   τῆς Ἰουδαίας πέραν τοῦ Ἰορδάνου.
INTO THE REGIONS   -   OF JUDEA   BEYOND   THE   JORDAN.

19.2 καὶ ἠκολούθησαν αὐτῷ ὄχλοι πολλοί, καὶ
        AND   FOLLOWED   HIM   A GREAT~CROWD,   AND

ἐθεράπευσεν αὐτοὺς ἐκεῖ.
HE HEALED   THEM   THERE.

19.3 Καὶ προσῆλθον αὐτῷ Φαρισαῖοι πειράζοντες
        AND   APPROACHED   HIM   [THE] PHARISEES   TEMPTING

αὐτὸν καὶ λέγοντες, Εἰ ἔξεστιν   ἀνθρώπῳ ἀπολῦσαι
HIM   AND   SAYING,   IF   IT IS PERMISSIBLE FOR A MAN   TO DIVORCE

τὴν γυναῖκα αὐτοῦ κατὰ πᾶσαν   αἰτίαν;   **19.4** ὁ δὲ
THE   WIFE   OF HIM   FOR   [ANY AND] EVERY REASON?   BUT~HE

ἀποκριθεὶς εἶπεν, Οὐκ ἀνέγνωτε ὅτι ὁ   κτίσας
HAVING ANSWERED SAID,   HAVE YOU° NOT READ   THAT THE ONE HAVING CREATED

ἀπ' ἀρχῆς   ἄρσεν καὶ θῆλυ ἐποίησεν αὐτούς;
FROM [THE] BEGINNING MALE   AND   FEMALE MADE   THEM?

19.5 καὶ εἶπεν, Ἕνεκα τούτου καταλείψει ἄνθρωπος
        AND   HE SAID,   BECAUSE OF THIS   A MAN~WILL LEAVE

τὸν   πατέρα καὶ τὴν   μητέρα καὶ κολληθήσεται τῇ
THE(HIS) FATHER   AND   THE(HIS) MOTHER   AND   WILL BE JOINED   TO THE

γυναικὶ αὐτοῦ, καὶ ἔσονται οἱ δύο εἰς σάρκα μίαν.
WIFE   OF HIM,   AND   WILL BE   THE TWO   -   ONE~FLESH.

19.6 ὥστε οὐκέτι εἰσὶν   δύο ἀλλὰ σὰρξ μία.
        SO   THEY ARE~NO LONGER TWO   BUT   ONE~FLESH.

ὃ οὖν   ὁ θεὸς συνέζευξεν ἄνθρωπος μὴ χωριζέτω.
THEREFORE~WHATEVER   -   GOD   JOINED TOGETHER   A MAN   LET NOT DIVIDE.

When Jesus had finished saying these things, he left Galilee and went to the region of Judea beyond the Jordan. ²Large crowds followed him, and he cured them there.

3 Some Pharisees came to him, and to test him they asked, "Is it lawful for a man to divorce his wife for any cause?" ⁴He answered, "Have you not read that the one who made them at the beginning 'made them male and female,' ⁵and said, 'For this reason a man shall leave his father and mother and be joined to his wife, and the two shall become one flesh'? ⁶So they are no longer two, but one flesh. Therefore what God has joined together, let no one separate."

19:4 Gen. 1:27; 5:2   **19:5** Gen. 2:24

7They said to him, "Why then did Moses command us to give a certificate of dismissal and to divorce her?" 8He said to them, "It was because you were so hard-hearted that Moses allowed you to divorce your wives, but from the beginning it was not so. 9And I say to you, whoever divorces his wife, except for unchastity, and marries another commits adultery."w

10 His disciples said to him, "If such is the case of a man with his wife, it is better not to marry." 11But he said to them, "Not everyone can accept this teaching, but only those to whom it is given. 12For there are eunuchs who have been so from birth, and there are eunuchs who have been made eunuchs by others, and there are eunuchs who have made themselves eunuchs for the sake of the kingdom of heaven. Let anyone accept this who can."

13 Then little children were being brought to him in order that he might lay his hands on them and pray. The disciples spoke sternly to those who brought them; 14but Jesus said, "Let the little children come to me, and do not stop them; for it is to such as these that the king-dom of heaven belongs."

w Other ancient authorities read *except on the ground of unchastity, causes her to commit adultery;* others add at the end of the verse *and he who marries a divorced woman commits adultery*

19.7 λέγουσιν αὐτῷ, Τί οὖν Μωϋσῆς ἐνετείλατο δοῦναι
THEY SAY TO HIM, WHY THEN DID COMMAND~MOSES TO GIVE

βιβλίον ἀποστασίου καὶ ἀπολῦσαι [αὐτήν]; **19.8** λέγει
A CERTIFICATE OF DIVORCE AND TO DIVORCE HER? HE SAYS

αὐτοῖς ὅτι Μωϋσῆς πρὸς τὴν σκληροκαρδίαν ὑμῶν
TO THEM THAT MOSES BECAUSE OF THE HARDNESS OF HEART OF YOU°

ἐπέτρεψεν ὑμῖν ἀπολῦσαι τὰς γυναῖκας ὑμῶν, ἀπ'
PERMITTED YOU TO DIVORCE THE WIVES OF YOU°, FROM

ἀρχῆς δὲ οὐ γέγονεν οὕτως. **19.9** λέγω δὲ ὑμῖν
THE BEGINNING HOWEVER IT WAS NOT THUS. BUT~I SAY TO YOU°

ὅτι ὃς ἂν ἀπολύσῃ τὴν γυναῖκα αὐτοῦ μὴ ἐπὶ
THAT WHOEVER DIVORCES THE WIFE OF HIM NOT BASED ON

πορνείᾳ⊤ ⌜καὶ γαμήσῃ ἄλλην μοιχᾶται⌝.
FORNICATION AND MARRIES ANOTHER COMMITS ADULTERY.

19.10 λέγουσιν αὐτῷ οἱ μαθηταὶ [αὐτοῦ], Εἰ οὕτως
SAY TO HIM THE DISCIPLES OF HIM, IF THUS

ἐστὶν ἡ αἰτία τοῦ ἀνθρώπου μετὰ τῆς γυναικός,
IS THE CASE OF THE MAN WITH THE WIFE,

οὐ συμφέρει γαμῆσαι. **19.11** ὁ δὲ εἶπεν αὐτοῖς, Οὐ
IT IS NOT ADVANTAGEOUS TO MARRY. BUT~HE SAID TO THEM, NOT

πάντες χωροῦσιν τὸν λόγον [τοῦτον] ἀλλ' οἷς
EVERYONE IS ABLE TO COMPREHEND - THIS~WORD BUT [THOSE] TO WHOM

δέδοται. **19.12** εἰσὶν γὰρ εὐνοῦχοι οἵτινες ἐκ
IT HAS BEEN GIVEN. FOR~THERE ARE EUNUCHS WHO FROM

κοιλίας μητρὸς ἐγεννήθησαν οὕτως, καὶ εἰσὶν
[THE] WOMB OF [THEIR] MOTHER WERE BORN THUS, AND THERE ARE

εὐνοῦχοι οἵτινες εὐνουχίσθησαν ὑπὸ τῶν ἀνθρώπων, καὶ
EUNUCHS WHO WERE MADE EUNUCHS BY - MEN, AND

εἰσὶν εὐνοῦχοι οἵτινες εὐνούχισαν ἑαυτοὺς διὰ
THERE ARE EUNUCHS WHO MAKE EUNUCHS OF THEMSELVES ON ACCOUNT

τὴν βασιλείαν τῶν οὐρανῶν. ὁ δυνάμενος
OF THE KINGDOM OF THE HEAVENS. THE ONE BEING ABLE

χωρεῖν χωρείτω.
TO COMPREHEND [THIS] LET HIM COMPREHEND.

19.13 Τότε προσηνέχθησαν αὐτῷ παιδία ἵνα τὰς
THEN WAS BROUGHT TO HIM CHILDREN THAT THE(HIS)

χεῖρας ἐπιθῇ αὐτοῖς καὶ προσεύξηται· οἱ δὲ
HANDS HE MIGHT PUT ON THEM AND TO PRAY. HOWEVER~THE

μαθηταὶ ἐπετίμησαν αὐτοῖς. **19.14** ὁ δὲ Ἰησοῦς εἶπεν,
DISCIPLES REBUKED THEM. - BUT JESUS SAID,

Ἄφετε τὰ παιδία καὶ μὴ κωλύετε αὐτὰ ἐλθεῖν πρός
PERMIT THE CHILDREN AND DO NOT FORBID THEM TO COME TO

με, τῶν γὰρ τοιούτων ἐστὶν ἡ βασιλεία τῶν οὐρανῶν.
ME, - FOR OF SUCH ONES IS THE KINGDOM OF THE HEAVENS.

19:7 Deut. 24:1 **19:9a** text: all. add ποιει αυτην μοιχευθηναι (makes her commit adultery): ASVmg RSVmg NASBmg NRSVmg. **19:9b** text: ASVmg RSV NASB NIV NEB TEV NJB. var. και ο απολελυμενην γαμων [γαμησας in some MSS] μοιξαται (and the one marrying a divorced woman commits adultery): KJV ASV RSVmg NASBmg NEBmg NRSVmg.

19.15 καὶ   ἐπιθεὶς   τὰς   χεῖρας   αὐτοῖς ἐπορεύθη
AND   HAVING PLACED THE(HIS) HANDS   ON THEM   HE DEPARTED

ἐκεῖθεν.
FROM THERE.

19.16 Καὶ ἰδοὺ εἷς προσελθὼν   αὐτῷ εἶπεν,
AND   BEHOLD ONE HAVING APPROACHED TO HIM SAID,

Διδάσκαλε, τί   ἀγαθὸν ποιήσω ἵνα σχῶ
TEACHER,   WHAT GOOD   MAY I DO   THAT I MAY HAVE

ζωὴν αἰώνιον; **19.17** ὁ δὲ εἶπεν αὐτῷ, Τί με ἐρωτᾷς
ETERNAL~LIFE?   AND~HE SAID TO HIM, WHY DO YOU ASK~ME

περὶ τοῦ ἀγαθοῦ; εἷς ἐστιν ὁ ἀγαθός· εἰ δὲ θέλεις
ABOUT THE   GOOD?   ONE IS   -   GOOD.   BUT~IF YOU WISH

εἰς τὴν ζωὴν εἰσελθεῖν, τήρησον τὰς ἐντολάς.
INTO -   LIFE   TO ENTER,   KEEP   THE   COMMANDMENTS.

19.18 λέγει αὐτῷ, Ποίας; ὁ δὲ Ἰησοῦς εἶπεν, Τὸ
HE SAYS TO HIM, WHICH?   - AND JESUS   SAID,   -

Οὐ φονεύσεις,   Οὐ μοιχεύσεις,   Οὐ κλέψεις,
YOU SHALL NOT MURDER, YOU SHALL NOT COMMIT ADULTERY, YOU SHALL NOT STEAL,

Οὐ ψευδομαρτυρήσεις, **19.19** Τίμα τὸν   πατέρα καὶ
YOU SHALL NOT BEAR FALSE WITNESS, HONOR THE(YOUR) FATHER   AND

τὴν   μητέρα, καί, Ἀγαπήσεις τὸν πλησίον σου ὡς
THE(YOUR) MOTHER, AND, YOU SHALL LOVE THE   NEIGHBOR   OF YOU AS

σεαυτόν. **19.20** λέγει αὐτῷ ὁ νεανίσκος, Πάντα
YOURSELF.   SAYS   TO HIM THE YOUNG MAN,   ALL

ταῦτα   ἐφύλαξα· τί ἔτι ὑστερῶ; **19.21** ἔφη αὐτῷ
THESE THINGS I FOLLOWED. WHAT STILL AM I LACKING?   SAID TO HIM

ὁ Ἰησοῦς, Εἰ θέλεις τέλειος εἶναι, ὕπαγε πώλησόν σου
-   JESUS,   IF YOU WISH TO BE~PERFECT, GO [AND] SELL   YOUR

τὰ ὑπάρχοντα καὶ δὸς [τοῖς] πτωχοῖς, καὶ ἕξεις
-   POSSESSIONS   AND GIVE TO THE   POOR,   AND YOU WILL HAVE

θησαυρὸν ἐν οὐρανοῖς, καὶ δεῦρο ἀκολούθει μοι.
TREASURE   IN [THE] HEAVENS, AND COME   FOLLOW   ME.

19.22 ἀκούσας δὲ ὁ νεανίσκος τὸν λόγον ἀπῆλθεν
BUT~HAVING HEARD ³THE ⁴YOUNG MAN ¹THE ²WORD WENT AWAY

λυπούμενος· ἦν γὰρ ἔχων κτήματα πολλά.
GRIEVING,   FOR~HE WAS HAVING MANY~POSSESSIONS.

19.23 Ὁ δὲ Ἰησοῦς εἶπεν τοῖς μαθηταῖς αὐτοῦ,
-    AND JESUS   SAID   TO THE DISCIPLES   OF HIM,

Ἀμὴν λέγω ὑμῖν ὅτι πλούσιος δυσκόλως εἰσελεύσεται
TRULY   I SAY TO YOU° THAT A RICH PERSON WITH DIFFICULTY WILL ENTER

εἰς τὴν βασιλείαν τῶν οὐρανῶν. **19.24** πάλιν δὲ λέγω
INTO THE   KINGDOM   OF THE HEAVENS.   AND~AGAIN I SAY

ὑμῖν, εὐκοπώτερόν ἐστιν κάμηλον διὰ   τρυπήματος
TO YOU°, IT IS~EASIER   [FOR] A CAMEL THROUGH [THE] EYE

ῥαφίδος διελθεῖν ἢ πλούσιον εἰσελθεῖν εἰς τὴν
OF A NEEDLE TO GO THROUGH THAN [FOR] A RICH PERSON TO ENTER INTO THE

19:18-19 Exod. 20:12-16; Deut. 5:16-20   **19:19** Lev. 19:18

¹⁵And he laid his hands on them and went on his way.

16 Then someone came to him and said, "Teacher, what good deed must I do to have eternal life?" ¹⁷And he said to him, "Why do you ask me about what is good? There is only one who is good. If you wish to enter into life, keep the commandments." ¹⁸He said to him, "Which ones?" And Jesus said, "You shall not murder; You shall not commit adultery; You shall not steal; You shall not bear false witness; ¹⁹Honor your father and mother; also, You shall love your neighbor as yourself." ²⁰The young man said to him, "I have kept all these;ˣ what do I still lack?" ²¹Jesus said to him, "If you wish to be perfect, go, sell your possessions, and give the moneyʸ to the poor, and you will have treasure in heaven; then come, follow me." ²²When the young man heard this word, he went away grieving, for he had many possessions.

23 Then Jesus said to his disciples, "Truly I tell you, it will be hard for a rich person to enter the kingdom of heaven. ²⁴Again I tell you, it is easier for a camel to go through the eye of a needle than for someone who is rich to enter the

ˣ Other ancient authorities add *from my youth*
ʸ Gk lacks *the money*

kingdom of God." 25When the disciples heard this, they were greatly astounded and said, "Then who can be saved?" 26But Jesus looked at them and said, "For mortals it is impossible, but for God all things are possible."

27 Then Peter said in reply, "Look, we have left everything and followed you. What then will we have?" 28Jesus said to them, "Truly I tell you, at the renewal of all things, when the Son of Man is seated on the throne of his glory, you who have followed me will also sit on twelve thrones, judging the twelve tribes of Israel. 29And everyone who has left houses or brothers or sisters or father or mother or children or fields, for my name's sake, will receive a hundredfold,z and will inherit eternal life. 30But many who are first will be last, and the last will be first.

βασιλείαν   τοῦ   θεοῦ.   **19.25** ἀκούσαντες   δὲ   οἱ   μαθηταὶ
KINGDOM   -   OF GOD.   AND~HAVING HEARD [THIS]   THE   DISCIPLES

ἐξεπλήσσοντο   σφόδρα   λέγοντες,   Τίς   ἄρα   δύναται
WERE AMAZED   GREATLY   SAYING,   WHO   THEN   IS ABLE

σωθῆναι;   **19.26** ἐμβλέψας   δὲ   ὁ   Ἰησοῦς   εἶπεν
TO BE SAVED?   AND~HAVING LOOKED UPON [THEM]   -   JESUS   SAID

αὐτοῖς,   Παρὰ   ἀνθρώποις   τοῦτο   ἀδύνατόν ἐστιν,   παρὰ δὲ
TO THEM,   WITH   MEN   THIS   IS~IMPOSSIBLE,   BUT~WITH

θεῷ   πάντα   δυνατά.   **19.27** Τότε   ἀποκριθεὶς   ὁ
GOD   ALL THINGS [ARE]   POSSIBLE.   THEN   HAVING ANSWERED   -

Πέτρος   εἶπεν   αὐτῷ,   Ἰδοὺ   ἡμεῖς   ἀφήκαμεν   πάντα
PETER   SAID   TO HIM,   BEHOLD   WE   LEFT   EVERYTHING

καὶ   ἠκολουθήσαμέν σοι·   τί   ἄρα   ἔσται ἡμῖν;   **19.28** ὁ
AND   FOLLOWED   YOU.   WHAT THEN   WILL BE   TO US?   -

δὲ   Ἰησοῦς   εἶπεν   αὐτοῖς,   Ἀμὴν   λέγω   ὑμῖν   ὅτι   ὑμεῖς
AND JESUS   SAID   TO THEM,   TRULY   I SAY   TO YOU°   THAT   YOU°

οἱ   ἀκολουθήσαντές   μοι   ἐν   τῇ   παλιγγενεσίᾳ,   ὅταν
THE ONES   HAVING FOLLOWED   ME,   IN   THE   NEW WORLD,   WHEN

καθίσῃ   ὁ   υἱὸς   τοῦ   ἀνθρώπου ἐπὶ   θρόνου   δόξης
SITS   THE   SON   -   OF MAN   UPON   [THE] THRONE   OF GLORY

αὐτοῦ,   καθήσεσθε   καὶ   ὑμεῖς   ἐπὶ   δώδεκα   θρόνους
OF HIM,   WILL SIT   ALSO   YOU°   UPON   TWELVE   THRONES

κρίνοντες   τὰς   δώδεκα   φυλὰς   τοῦ   Ἰσραήλ.   **19.29** καὶ
JUDGING   THE   TWELVE   TRIBES   -   OF ISRAEL.   AND

πᾶς   ὅστις   ἀφῆκεν   οἰκίας   ἢ   ἀδελφοὺς   ἢ   ἀδελφὰς   ἢ
ANYONE   WHO   LEFT   HOME   OR   BROTHERS   OR   SISTERS   OR

πατέρα   ἢ   μητέρα   ἢ   τέκνα   ἢ   ἀγροὺς   ἕνεκεν   τοῦ
FATHER   OR   MOTHER   OR   CHILDREN OR   LANDS   ON ACCOUNT OF   THE

ὀνόματός   μου,   ἑκατονταπλασίονα λήμψεται   καὶ   ζωὴν
NAME   OF ME,   WILL RECEIVE~A HUNDRED TIMES   AND   LIFE

αἰώνιον   κληρονομήσει.   **19.30** Πολλοὶ δὲ   ἔσονται πρῶτοι
ETERNAL   WILL INHERIT.   AND~MANY   [WHO ARE] FIRST~WILL BE

ἔσχατοι   καὶ   ἔσχατοι   πρῶτοι.
LAST   AND   [THE] LAST   FIRST.

CHAPTER 20

"For the kingdom of heaven is like a landowner who went out early in the morning to hire laborers for his vineyard. 2After agreeing with the laborers for the usual daily wage,a he sent them into his vineyard.

a Gk a denarius

20.1 Ὁμοία   γὰρ   ἐστιν   ἡ   βασιλεία   τῶν   οὐρανῶν
      7LIKE   1FOR   6IS   2THE   3KINGDOM   4OF THE   5HEAVENS

ἀνθρώπῳ   οἰκοδεσπότῃ,   ὅστις   ἐξῆλθεν   ἅμα πρωῒ
A MAN   A MASTER OF THE HOUSE,   WHO   WENT OUT   EARLY IN THE MORNING

μισθώσασθαι ἐργάτας   εἰς   τὸν   ἀμπελῶνα αὐτοῦ.
TO HIRE   WORKERS   FOR   THE   VINEYARD   OF HIM.

20.2 συμφωνήσας   δὲ   μετὰ   τῶν   ἐργατῶν ἐκ   δηναρίου
          AND~HAVING AGREED   WITH   THE   WORKERS   FOR   A DENARIUS

τὴν   ἡμέραν   ἀπέστειλεν   αὐτοὺς   εἰς   τὸν   ἀμπελῶνα
[FOR] THE   DAY,   HE SENT   THEM   INTO   THE   VINEYARD

αὐτοῦ. **20.3** καὶ ἐξελθὼν περὶ τρίτην ὥραν εἶδεν
OF HIM.   AND   HAVING GONE OUT AROUND [THE] THIRD HOUR HE SAW

ἄλλους ἑστῶτας ἐν τῇ ἀγορᾷ ἀργούς **20.4** καὶ
OTHERS   HAVING STOOD IN THE MARKETPLACE IDLE,   AND

ἐκείνοις εἶπεν, Ὑπάγετε καὶ ὑμεῖς εἰς τὸν ἀμπελῶνα,
TO THOSE HE SAID,   GO   ALSO YOU°   INTO THE VINEYARD,

καὶ ὃ ἐὰν ᾖ   δίκαιον δώσω ὑμῖν. **20.5** οἱ
AND WHATEVER MAY BE [CONSIDERED] RIGHT I WILL GIVE TO YOU°.

δὲ ἀπῆλθον. πάλιν [δὲ] ἐξελθὼν περὶ ἕκτην καὶ
AND THEY LEFT.   AND~AGAIN HAVING GONE OUT AROUND [THE] SIXTH AND

ἐνάτην ὥραν ἐποίησεν ὡσαύτως. **20.6** περὶ δὲ τὴν
[THE] NINTH HOUR HE DID   LIKEWISE.   AND~AROUND THE

ἑνδεκάτην ἐξελθὼν εὗρεν ἄλλους ἑστῶτας καὶ λέγει
ELEVENTH [HOUR] HAVING GONE OUT HE FOUND OTHERS HAVING STOOD AND HE SAYS

αὐτοῖς, Τί ὧδε ἑστήκατε   ὅλην τὴν ἡμέραν ἀργοί;
TO THEM, WHY HAVE YOU° BEEN STANDING~HERE ALL THE DAY   IDLE?

20.7 λέγουσιν αὐτῷ, Ὅτι οὐδεὶς ἡμᾶς ἐμισθώσατο.
THEY SAY TO HIM, BECAUSE NO ONE HIRED~US.

λέγει αὐτοῖς, Ὑπάγετε καὶ ὑμεῖς εἰς τὸν ἀμπελῶνα.
HE SAYS TO THEM,   GO   ALSO YOU°   INTO THE VINEYARD.

20.8 ὀψίας δὲ γενομένης λέγει ὁ κύριος τοῦ
AND~[WHEN] EVENING HAVING COME SAYS THE OWNER OF THE

ἀμπελῶνος τῷ ἐπιτρόπῳ αὐτοῦ, Κάλεσον τοὺς ἐργάτας
VINEYARD   TO THE FOREMAN OF HIM, CALL   THE WORKERS

καὶ ἀπόδος αὐτοῖς τὸν μισθὸν ἀρξάμενος ἀπὸ τῶν
AND GIVE   TO THEM THE WAGE HAVING BEGUN WITH THE

ἐσχάτων ἕως τῶν πρώτων. **20.9** καὶ ἐλθόντες οἱ
LAST ONES UNTIL THE FIRST.   AND HAVING COME THE ONES

περὶ τὴν ἑνδεκάτην ὥραν ἔλαβον ἀνὰ δηνάριον.
AROUND THE ELEVENTH   HOUR THEY RECEIVED EACH A DENARIUS.

20.10 καὶ ἐλθόντες οἱ πρῶτοι ἐνόμισαν ὅτι
AND HAVING COME THE FIRST ONES THEY THOUGHT THAT

πλεῖον λήμψονται· καὶ ἔλαβον [τὸ] ἀνὰ δηνάριον
THEY WOULD RECEIVE~A LARGER SUM; AND THEY RECEIVED -   EACH A DENARIUS

καὶ αὐτοί. **20.11** λαβόντες δὲ
ALSO THEMSELVES.   AND~HAVING RECEIVED [THE DENARIUS]

ἐγόγγυζον   κατὰ τοῦ οἰκοδεσπότου **20.12** λέγοντες,
THEY WERE COMPLAINING AGAINST THE HOUSE MASTER   SAYING,

Οὗτοι οἱ ἔσχατοι μίαν ὥραν ἐποίησαν, καὶ ἴσους
THESE   -   LAST ONES ONE HOUR WORKED,   AND EQUAL

ἡμῖν αὐτοὺς ἐποίησας τοῖς βαστάσασι τὸ βάρος τῆς
TO US   YOU MADE~THEM,   THE ONES HAVING ENDURED THE BURDEN OF THE

ἡμέρας καὶ τὸν καύσωνα. **20.13** ὁ δὲ ἀποκριθεὶς ἑνὶ
DAY   AND THE HEAT.   BUT~HE HAVING ANSWERED ONE

αὐτῶν εἶπεν, Ἑταῖρε, οὐκ ἀδικῶ σε· οὐχὶ
OF THEM SAID,   FRIEND, I AM NOT CHEATING YOU.   [DID YOU] NOT

δηναρίου συνεφώνησάς μοι; **20.14** ἆρον τὸ
FOR A DENARIUS MAKE AN AGREEMENT WITH ME?   TAKE THE [DENARIUS WHICH IS]

[3]When he went out about nine o'clock, he saw others standing idle in the marketplace; [4]and he said to them, 'You also go into the vineyard, and I will pay you whatever is right.' So they went. [5]When he went out again about noon and about three o'clock, he did the same. [6]And about five o'clock he went out and found others standing around; and he said to them, 'Why are you standing here idle all day?' [7]They said to him, 'Because no one has hired us.' He said to them, 'You also go into the vineyard.' [8]When evening came, the owner of the vineyard said to his manager, 'Call the laborers and give them their pay, beginning with the last and then going to the first.' [9]When those hired about five o'clock came, each of them received the usual daily wage.[b] [10]Now when the first came, they thought they would receive more; but each of them also received the usual daily wage.[b] [11]And when they received it, they grumbled against the landowner, [12]saying, 'These last worked only one hour, and you have made them equal to us who have borne the burden of the day and the scorching heat.' [13]But he replied to one of them, 'Friend, I am doing you no wrong; did you not agree with me for the usual daily wage?[b] [14]Take what

[b] Gk a denarius

belongs to you and go; I choose to give to this last the same as I give to you. ¹⁵Am I not allowed to do what I choose with what belongs to me? Or are you envious because I am generous?"ᶜ ¹⁶So the last will be first, and the first will be last."ᵈ

17 While Jesus was going up to Jerusalem, he took the twelve disciples aside by themselves, and said to them on the way, ¹⁸"See, we are going up to Jerusalem, and the Son of Man will be handed over to the chief priests and scribes, and they will condemn him to death; ¹⁹then they will hand him over to the Gentiles to be mocked and flogged and crucified; and on the third day he will be raised."

20 Then the mother of the sons of Zebedee came to him with her sons, and kneeling before him, she asked a favor of him. ²¹And he said to her, "What do you want?" She said to him, "Declare that these two sons of mine will sit, one at your right hand and one at your left, in your kingdom." ²²But Jesus answered, "You do not know what you are asking. Are you able to drink the cup that I am about to drink?"ᵉ They said to him, "We are able." ²³He said to them, "You will indeed drink my cup, but to sit at my right hand and at my left, this is not mine to grant, but it is for those for whom

ᶜ Gk is your eye evil because I am good?
ᵈ Other ancient authorities add for many are called but few are chosen
ᵉ Other ancient authorities add or to be baptized with the baptism that I am baptized with?

σὸν καὶ ὕπαγε. θέλω δὲ τούτῳ τῷ ἐσχάτῳ δοῦναι ὡς
YOURS AND GO.   BUT~I WISH TO THIS - LAST ONE TO GIVE AS

καὶ   σοί· **20.15** [ἢ] οὐκ ἔξεστίν μοι ὃ θέλω
ALSO [I GAVE] TO YOU.   OR   IS IT NOT PERMISSIBLE FOR ME WHAT I WISH

ποιῆσαι ἐν τοῖς   ἐμοῖς; ἢ ὁ ὀφθαλμός
TO DO WITH THE THINGS [WHICH ARE] MINE? OR THE EYE

σου πονηρός ἐστιν ὅτι ἐγὼ ἀγαθός εἰμι; **20.16** Οὕτως
OF YOU ENVIOUS IS   THAT I   AM~GOOD?   THUS

ἔσονται οἱ ἔσχατοι πρῶτοι καὶ οἱ πρῶτοι ἔσχατοι.
WILL BE THE LAST ONES FIRST AND THE FIRST ONES LAST.

20.17 Καὶ ἀναβαίνων ὁ Ἰησοῦς εἰς Ἱεροσόλυμα
          AND GOING UP - JESUS TO JERUSALEM

παρέλαβεν τοὺς δώδεκα [μαθητὰς] κατ' ἰδίαν καὶ ἐν
HE TOOK   THE TWELVE DISCIPLES PRIVATELY AND ON

τῇ ὁδῷ εἶπεν αὐτοῖς, **20.18** Ἰδοὺ ἀναβαίνομεν εἰς
THE WAY HE SAID TO THEM,   BEHOLD WE ARE GOING UP TO

Ἱεροσόλυμα, καὶ ὁ υἱὸς τοῦ ἀνθρώπου παραδοθήσεται
JERUSALEM,   AND THE SON - OF MAN   WILL BE HANDED OVER

τοῖς ἀρχιερεῦσιν καὶ γραμματεῦσιν, καὶ κατακρινοῦσιν
TO THE CHIEF PRIESTS AND SCRIBES,   AND THEY WILL CONDEMN

αὐτὸν θανάτῳ **20.19** καὶ παραδώσουσιν αὐτὸν τοῖς
HIM   TO DEATH   AND THEY WILL HAND OVER HIM   TO THE

ἔθνεσιν εἰς τὸ ἐμπαῖξαι καὶ μαστιγῶσαι καὶ
GENTILES IN ORDER TO MOCK AND TO WHIP   AND

σταυρῶσαι, καὶ τῇ τρίτῃ ἡμέρᾳ ἐγερθήσεται.
TO CRUCIFY, AND ON THE THIRD DAY HE WILL BE RAISED.

20.20 Τότε προσῆλθεν αὐτῷ ἡ μήτηρ τῶν υἱῶν
          THEN APPROACHED HIM THE MOTHER OF THE SONS

Ζεβεδαίου μετὰ τῶν υἱῶν αὐτῆς προσκυνοῦσα καὶ
OF ZEBEDEE ALONG WITH THE SONS OF HER WORSHIPING AND

αἰτοῦσά τι   ἀπ' αὐτοῦ. **20.21** ὁ δὲ εἶπεν αὐτῇ, Τί
REQUESTING SOMETHING FROM HIM.   AND~HE SAID TO HER, WHAT

θέλεις; λέγει αὐτῷ, Εἰπὲ ἵνα καθίσωσιν οὗτοι οἱ
DO YOU° WISH? SHE SAYS TO HIM, SAY THAT THESE~MAY SIT THE

δύο υἱοί μου εἷς ἐκ δεξιῶν σου καὶ εἷς ἐξ εὐωνύμων
TWO SONS OF ME ONE ON [THE] RIGHT OF YOU AND ONE ON [THE] LEFT

σου ἐν τῇ βασιλείᾳ σου. **20.22** ἀποκριθεὶς δὲ ὁ
OF YOU IN THE KINGDOM OF YOU.   AND~HAVING ANSWERED -

Ἰησοῦς εἶπεν, Οὐκ οἴδατε τί αἰτεῖσθε. δύνασθε
JESUS SAID, YOU° DO NOT KNOW WHAT YOU° ARE ASKING. ARE YOU° ABLE

πιεῖν τὸ ποτήριον ὃ ἐγὼ μέλλω πίνειν; λέγουσιν
TO DRINK THE CUP WHICH I AM ABOUT TO DRINK? THEY SAY

αὐτῷ, Δυνάμεθα. **20.23** λέγει αὐτοῖς, Τὸ μὲν ποτήριόν
TO HIM, WE ARE ABLE.   HE SAYS TO THEM, INDEED~THE CUP

μου πίεσθε, τὸ δὲ καθίσαι ἐκ δεξιῶν μου καὶ ἐξ
OF ME YOU° WILL DRINK, - BUT TO SIT ON [THE] RIGHT OF ME AND ON

εὐωνύμων οὐκ ἔστιν ἐμὸν [τοῦτο] δοῦναι, ἀλλ' οἷς
[THE] LEFT IT IS NOT MINE TO GRANT~THIS, BUT FOR WHOM

ἡτοίμασται   ὑπὸ τοῦ πατρός μου.   **20.24** Καὶ
IT HAS BEEN PREPARED   BY   THE   FATHER   OF ME.   AND

ἀκούσαντες   οἱ δέκα   ἠγανάκτησαν περὶ   τῶν δύο
HAVING HEARD [THIS] THE   TEN   WERE INDIGNANT ABOUT   THE   TWO

ἀδελφῶν.   **20.25** ὁ δὲ Ἰησοῦς προσκαλεσάμενος αὐτοὺς
BROTHERS.   - BUT JESUS   HAVING SUMMONED   THEM

εἶπεν, Οἴδατε ὅτι   οἱ   ἄρχοντες τῶν   ἐθνῶν
SAID,   YOU° KNOW THAT THE RULERS   OF THE GENTILES

κατακυριεύουσιν αὐτῶν καὶ οἱ μεγάλοι κατεξουσιάζουσιν
LORD IT OVER   THEM AND THE GREAT ONES EXERCISE AUTHORITY OVER

αὐτῶν. **20.26** οὐχ οὕτως ἔσται ἐν   ὑμῖν, ἀλλ᾽ ὃς ἐὰν
THEM.   NOT THUS   WILL IT BE AMONG YOU°,   BUT   WHOEVER

θέλῃ ἐν   ὑμῖν   μέγας γενέσθαι ἔσται ὑμῶν διάκονος,
WISHES AMONG YOU°   TO BECOME~GREAT   WILL BE   [THE] SERVANT~OF YOU°,

20.27 καὶ ὃς ἂν θέλῃ ἐν   ὑμῖν εἶναι πρῶτος ἔσται
         AND WHOEVER WISHES AMONG YOU° TO BE   FIRST   WILL BE

ὑμῶν δοῦλος· **20.28** ὥσπερ ὁ   υἱὸς τοῦ ἀνθρώπου
[THE] SLAVE~OF YOU°.   JUST AS THE SON   -   OF MAN

οὐκ ἦλθεν διακονηθῆναι ἀλλὰ διακονῆσαι καὶ δοῦναι
DID NOT COME TO BE SERVED   BUT   TO SERVE   AND   TO GIVE

τὴν ψυχὴν αὐτοῦ λύτρον   ἀντὶ πολλῶν.
THE LIFE   OF HIM [AS] A RANSOM FOR   MANY.

20.29 Καὶ ἐκπορευομένων αὐτῶν ἀπὸ Ἰεριχὼ
         AND   [AS] THEY [WERE] GOING OUT   FROM   JERICHO

ἠκολούθησεν αὐτῷ ὄχλος πολύς. **20.30** καὶ ἰδοὺ δύο
FOLLOWED   HIM   A GREAT~CROWD.   AND BEHOLD TWO

τυφλοὶ καθήμενοι παρὰ τὴν ὁδὸν ἀκούσαντες ὅτι
BLIND MEN SITTING   BESIDE THE ROAD, HAVING HEARD   THAT

Ἰησοῦς παράγει, ἔκραξαν λέγοντες, Ἐλέησον ἡμᾶς,
JESUS   IS PASSING BY, CRIED OUT SAYING,   HAVE MERCY ON US,

[κύριε], υἱὸς Δαυίδ. **20.31** ὁ δὲ ὄχλος ἐπετίμησεν
LORD,   SON OF DAVID.   BUT~THE CROWD REBUKED

αὐτοῖς ἵνα σιωπήσωσιν· οἱ δὲ   μεῖζον ἔκραξαν
THEM   THAT THEY MIGHT BE SILENT. BUT~THEY CRIED OUT~MORE

λέγοντες, Ἐλέησον ἡμᾶς, κύριε, υἱὸς Δαυίδ. **20.32** καὶ
SAYING,   HAVE MERCY ON US, LORD, SON OF DAVID.   AND

στὰς   ὁ Ἰησοῦς ἐφώνησεν αὐτοὺς καὶ εἶπεν, Τί
HAVING STOOD - JESUS   CALLED   THEM   AND SAID,   WHAT

θέλετε   ποιήσω ὑμῖν; **20.33** λέγουσιν αὐτῷ,
DO YOU° WISH [THAT] I SHOULD DO FOR YOU°?   THEY SAY   TO HIM,

Κύριε, ἵνα ἀνοιγῶσιν οἱ ὀφθαλμοὶ ἡμῶν.
LORD,   THAT MAY BE OPENED THE EYES   OF US.

20.34 σπλαγχνισθεὶς δὲ   ὁ Ἰησοῦς ἥψατο τῶν
         AND~HAVING BEEN FILLED WITH COMPASSION - JESUS   TOUCHED THE

ὀμμάτων αὐτῶν, καὶ εὐθέως ἀνέβλεψαν καὶ
EYES   OF THEM, AND IMMEDIATELY THEY SAW AGAIN   AND

ἠκολούθησαν αὐτῷ.
THEY FOLLOWED   HIM.

it has been prepared by my Father."

24 When the ten heard it, they were angry with the two brothers. 25But Jesus called them to him and said, "You know that the rulers of the Gentiles lord it over them, and their great ones are tyrants over them. 26It will not be so among you; but whoever wishes to be great among you must be your servant, 27and whoever wishes to be first among you must be your slave; 28just as the Son of Man came not to be served but to serve, and to give his life a ransom for many."

29 As they were leaving Jericho, a large crowd followed him. 30There were two blind men sitting by the roadside. When they heard that Jesus was passing by, they shouted, "Lord,ᶠ have mercy on us, Son of David!" 31The crowd sternly ordered them to be quiet; but they shouted even more loudly, "Have mercy on us, Lord, Son of David!" 32Jesus stood still and called them, saying, "What do you want me to do for you?" 33They said to him, "Lord, let our eyes be opened." 34Moved with compassion, Jesus touched their eyes. Immediately they regained their sight and followed him.

ᶠ Other ancient authorities lack *Lord*

CHAPTER 21

When they had come near Jerusalem and had reached Bethphage, at the Mount of Olives, Jesus sent two disciples, ²saying to them, "Go into the village ahead of you, and immediately you will find a donkey tied, and a colt with her; untie them and bring them to me. ³If anyone says anything to you, just say this, 'The Lord needs them.' And he will send them immediately."ᵍ ⁴This took place to fulfill what had been spoken through the prophet, saying,

⁵ "Tell the daughter of
    Zion,
   Look, your king is
     coming to you,
   humble, and mounted
    on a donkey,
   and on a colt, the foal
    of a donkey."

⁶The disciples went and did as Jesus had directed them; ⁷they brought the donkey and the colt, and put their cloaks on them, and he sat on them. ⁸A very large crowdʰ spread their cloaks on the road, and others cut branches from the trees and spread them on the road. ⁹The crowds

ᵍ Or 'The Lord needs them and will
  send them back immediately.'
ʰ Or Most of the crowd

21.1 Καὶ ὅτε ἤγγισαν εἰς Ἱεροσόλυμα καὶ ἦλθον
AND WHEN THEY CAME NEAR TO JERUSALEM AND CAME

εἰς Βηθφαγὴ εἰς τὸ Ὄρος τῶν Ἐλαιῶν, τότε Ἰησοῦς
TO BETHPHAGE, TO THE MOUNT - OF OLIVES, THEN JESUS

ἀπέστειλεν δύο μαθητὰς **21.2** λέγων αὐτοῖς, Πορεύεσθε
SENT TWO DISCIPLES SAYING TO THEM, GO

εἰς τὴν κώμην τὴν κατέναντι ὑμῶν, καὶ εὐθέως
INTO THE VILLAGE - OPPOSITE YOU°, AND IMMEDIATELY

εὑρήσετε ὄνον δεδεμένην καὶ πῶλον μετ' αὐτῆς·
YOU° WILL FIND A DONKEY HAVING BEEN TIED AND A COLT WITH HER;

λύσαντες ἀγάγετέ μοι. **21.3** καὶ ἐάν τις
HAVING UNTIED [THEM] BRING [THEM] TO ME. AND IF ANYONE

ὑμῖν εἴπῃ τι, ἐρεῖτε ὅτι Ὁ κύριος αὐτῶν χρείαν
SHOULD SAY~TO YOU° ANYTHING, YOU° SAY, - THE LORD ³OF THEM ²NEED

ἔχει· εὐθὺς δὲ ἀποστελεῖ αὐτούς. **21.4** Τοῦτο δὲ
¹HAS. AND~IMMEDIATELY HE WILL SEND THEM. AND~THIS

γέγονεν ἵνα πληρωθῇ τὸ ῥηθὲν διὰ τοῦ
TOOK PLACE IN ORDER THAT MIGHT BE FULFILLED THE [THING] SPOKEN THROUGH THE

προφήτου λέγοντος,
PROPHET SAYING,

21.5 Εἴπατε τῇ θυγατρὶ Σιών,
TELL THE DAUGHTER OF ZION,

  Ἰδοὺ ὁ βασιλεύς σου ἔρχεταί σοι
  BEHOLD THE KING OF YOU COMES TO YOU

    πραῢς καὶ ἐπιβεβηκὼς ἐπὶ ὄνον
    HUMBLE AND HAVING MOUNTED ON A DONKEY

    καὶ ἐπὶ πῶλον υἱὸν ὑποζυγίου.
    AND UPON A COLT [THE] FOAL OF A DONKEY.

21.6 πορευθέντες δὲ οἱ μαθηταὶ καὶ ποιήσαντες καθὼς
AND~HAVING GONE THE DISCIPLES AND HAVING DONE JUST AS

συνέταξεν αὐτοῖς ὁ Ἰησοῦς **21.7** ἤγαγον τὴν ὄνον καὶ
COMMANDED THEM - JESUS THEY BROUGHT THE DONKEY AND

τὸν πῶλον καὶ ἐπέθηκαν ἐπ' αὐτῶν τὰ ἱμάτια,
THE COLT AND THEY PUT UPON THEM THE(THEIR) GARMENTS,

καὶ ἐπεκάθισεν ἐπάνω αὐτῶν. **21.8** ὁ δὲ πλεῖστος
AND HE SAT ON THEM. AND~THE VERY LARGE

ὄχλος ἔστρωσαν ἑαυτῶν τὰ ἱμάτια ἐν τῇ ὁδῷ,
CROWD SPREAD OUT THEIR - GARMENTS ON THE ROAD,

ἄλλοι δὲ ἔκοπτον κλάδους ἀπὸ τῶν δένδρων καὶ
AND~OTHERS WERE CUTTING BRANCHES FROM THE TREES AND

ἐστρώννυον ἐν τῇ ὁδῷ. **21.9** οἱ δὲ ὄχλοι οἱ
WERE SPREADING [THEM] OUT ON THE ROAD. AND~THE CROWDS THE ONES

21:5 Isa. 62:11; Zech. 9:9

προάγοντες αὐτὸν καὶ οἱ ἀκολουθοῦντες ἔκραζον
GOING BEFORE HIM AND THE ONES FOLLOWING WERE CRYING OUT

λέγοντες,
SAYING,

Ὡσαννὰ τῷ υἱῷ Δαυίδ·
HOSANNA TO THE SON OF DAVID;

Εὐλογημένος ὁ ἐρχόμενος ἐν ὀνόματι
HAVING BEEN BLESSED [IS] THE ONE COMING IN [THE] NAME

κυρίου·
OF [THE] LORD;

Ὡσαννὰ ἐν τοῖς ὑψίστοις.
HOSANNA IN THE HIGHEST.

21.10 καὶ εἰσελθόντος αὐτοῦ εἰς Ἱεροσόλυμα ἐσείσθη
AND HE~HAVING ENTERED INTO JERUSALEM, WAS STIRRED

πᾶσα ἡ πόλις λέγουσα, Τίς ἐστιν οὗτος; **21.11** οἱ δὲ
ALL THE CITY SAYING, WHO IS THIS? AND~THE

ὄχλοι ἔλεγον, Οὗτός ἐστιν ὁ προφήτης Ἰησοῦς ὁ ἀπὸ
CROWDS WERE SAYING, THIS IS THE PROPHET JESUS - FROM

Ναζαρὲθ τῆς Γαλιλαίας.
NAZARETH - OF GALILEE.

21.12 Καὶ εἰσῆλθεν Ἰησοῦς εἰς τὸ ἱερόν καὶ
AND JESUS~ENTERED INTO THE TEMPLE AND

ἐξέβαλεν πάντας τοὺς πωλοῦντας καὶ ἀγοράζοντας ἐν
THREW OUT ALL THE ONES SELLING AND BUYING IN

τῷ ἱερῷ, καὶ τὰς τραπέζας τῶν κολλυβιστῶν
THE TEMPLE, AND THE TABLES OF THE MONEY-CHANGERS

κατέστρεψεν καὶ τὰς καθέδρας τῶν πωλούντων τὰς
HE OVERTURNED AND THE CHAIRS OF THE ONES SELLING THE

περιστεράς, **21.13** καὶ λέγει αὐτοῖς, Γέγραπται,
DOVES, AND HE SAYS TO THEM, IT HAS BEEN WRITTEN,

Ὁ οἶκός μου οἶκος προσευχῆς κληθήσεται,
THE HOUSE OF ME A HOUSE OF PRAYER IS TO BE CALLED,

ὑμεῖς δὲ αὐτὸν ποιεῖτε σπήλαιον λῃστῶν.
BUT~YOU° ARE MAKING~IT A DEN OF ROBBERS.

21.14 Καὶ προσῆλθον αὐτῷ τυφλοὶ καὶ χωλοὶ
AND APPROACHED HIM BLIND PERSONS AND LAME PERSONS

ἐν τῷ ἱερῷ, καὶ ἐθεράπευσεν αὐτούς. **21.15** ἰδόντες δὲ
IN THE TEMPLE, AND HE HEALED THEM. BUT~HAVING SEEN

οἱ ἀρχιερεῖς καὶ οἱ γραμματεῖς τὰ θαυμάσια ἃ
THE CHIEF PRIESTS AND THE SCRIBES THE WONDERS WHICH

ἐποίησεν καὶ τοὺς παῖδας τοὺς κράζοντας ἐν τῷ
HE PERFORMED AND THE CHILDREN - CRYING OUT IN THE

ἱερῷ καὶ λέγοντας, Ὡσαννὰ τῷ υἱῷ Δαυίδ,
TEMPLE AND SAYING, HOSANNA TO THE SON OF DAVID,

ἠγανάκτησαν **21.16** καὶ εἶπαν αὐτῷ, Ἀκούεις τί
THEY WERE INDIGNANT AND THEY SAID TO HIM, DO YOU HEAR WHAT

that went ahead of him and that followed were shouting, "Hosanna to the Son of David! Blessed is the one who comes in the name of the Lord! Hosanna in the highest heaven!" [10]When he entered Jerusalem, the whole city was in turmoil, asking, "Who is this?" [11]The crowds were saying, "This is the prophet Jesus from Nazareth in Galilee."

12 Then Jesus entered the temple[i] and drove out all who were selling and buying in the temple, and he overturned the tables of the money changers and the seats of those who sold doves. [13]He said to them, "It is written, 'My house shall be called a house of prayer'; but you are making it a den of robbers."

14 The blind and the lame came to him in the temple, and he cured them. [15]But when the chief priests and the scribes saw the amazing things that he did, and heard[j] the children crying out in the temple, "Hosanna to the Son of David," they became angry [16]and said to him, "Do you hear what

[i] Other ancient authorities add of God
[j] Gk lacks heard

21:9 Ps. 118:25-26   **21:13** Isa. 56:7   **21:16** Ps. 8:3 LXX

these are saying?" Jesus said to them, "Yes; have you never read,

'Out of the mouths of
infants and nursing
babies
you have prepared
praise for
yourself'?"

[17]He left them, went out of the city to Bethany, and spent the night there.

18 In the morning, when he returned to the city, he was hungry. [19]And seeing a fig tree by the side of the road, he went to it and found nothing at all on it but leaves. Then he said to it, "May no fruit ever come from you again!" And the fig tree withered at once. [20]When the disciples saw it, they were amazed, saying, "How did the fig tree wither at once?" [21]Jesus answered them, "Truly I tell you, if you have faith and do not doubt, not only will you do what has been done to the fig tree, but even if you say to this mountain, 'Be lifted up and thrown into the sea,' it will be done. [22]Whatever you ask for in prayer with faith, you will receive."

23 When he entered the temple, the chief priests and the elders of the people came to him as he was teaching, and said, "By what authority are you doing these things, and who gave you this authority?" [24]Jesus said to them, "I will also ask you

οὗτοι λέγουσιν; ὁ δὲ Ἰησοῦς λέγει αὐτοῖς, Ναί.
THESE ONES ARE SAYING? - AND JESUS SAYS TO THEM, YES.

οὐδέποτε ἀνέγνωτε ὅτι Ἐκ στόματος νηπίων καὶ
HAVE YOU° NEVER READ - OUT OF [THE] MOUTH OF CHILDREN AND

θηλαζόντων κατηρτίσω αἶνον; 21.17 Καὶ
NURSING BABIES YOU PREPARED FOR YOURSELF PRAISE? AND

καταλιπὼν αὐτοὺς ἐξῆλθεν ἔξω τῆς πόλεως εἰς
HAVING LEFT THEM HE WENT OUT OF THE CITY TO

Βηθανίαν καὶ ηὐλίσθη ἐκεῖ.
BETHANY AND SPENT THE NIGHT THERE.

21.18 Πρωῒ δὲ ἐπανάγων εἰς τὴν πόλιν ἐπείνασεν.
NOW~EARLY GOING UP INTO THE CITY HE HUNGERED.

21.19 καὶ ἰδὼν συκῆν μίαν ἐπὶ τῆς ὁδοῦ ἦλθεν ἐπ'
AND HAVING SEEN ONE~FIG TREE ON THE WAY HE WENT UP TO

αὐτήν καὶ οὐδὲν εὗρεν ἐν αὐτῇ εἰ μὴ φύλλα μόνον, καὶ
IT AND FOUND NOTHING ON IT EXCEPT LEAVES ONLY, AND

λέγει αὐτῇ, Μηκέτι ἐκ σοῦ καρπὸς γένηται εἰς τὸν
HE SAYS TO IT, NO LONGER FROM YOU MAY THERE BE~FRUIT TO THE

αἰῶνα. καὶ ἐξηράνθη παραχρῆμα ἡ συκῆ. 21.20 καὶ
AGE. AND WAS WITHERED AT ONCE THE FIG TREE. AND

ἰδόντες οἱ μαθηταὶ ἐθαύμασαν λέγοντες, Πῶς
HAVING SEEN [THIS] THE DISCIPLES WERE AMAZED SAYING, HOW [DID]

παραχρῆμα ἐξηράνθη ἡ συκῆ; 21.21 ἀποκριθεὶς δὲ ὁ
INSTANTLY WITHER THE FIG TREE? AND~HAVING ANSWERED -

Ἰησοῦς εἶπεν αὐτοῖς, Ἀμὴν λέγω ὑμῖν, ἐὰν ἔχητε
JESUS SAID TO THEM, TRULY I SAY TO YOU°, IF YOU° HAVE

πίστιν καὶ μὴ διακριθῆτε, οὐ μόνον
FAITH AND DO NOT DOUBT, NOT ONLY

τὸ τῆς συκῆς ποιήσετε, ἀλλὰ κἂν
THE [THING WHICH HAS BEEN DONE TO] THE FIG TREE WILL YOU° DO, BUT ALSO IF

τῷ ὄρει τούτῳ εἴπητε, Ἄρθητι καὶ βλήθητι εἰς τὴν
- TO THIS~MOUNTAIN YOU° SAY, BE LIFTED UP AND THROWN INTO THE

θάλασσαν, γενήσεται· 21.22 καὶ πάντα ὅσα ἂν
SEA, [AND] IT WILL HAPPEN. AND ALL THINGS WHATEVER

αἰτήσητε ἐν τῇ προσευχῇ πιστεύοντες λήμψεσθε.
YOU° MAY ASK IN - PRAYER BELIEVING YOU° WILL RECEIVE.

21.23 Καὶ ἐλθόντος αὐτοῦ εἰς τὸ ἱερὸν προσῆλθον αὐτῷ
AND [AFTER] HE HAD GONE INTO THE TEMPLE, [8]APPROACHED [9]HIM

διδάσκοντι οἱ ἀρχιερεῖς καὶ οἱ πρεσβύτεροι τοῦ
[10][WHILE HE WAS] TEACHING [1]THE [2]CHIEF PRIESTS [3]AND [4]THE [5]ELDERS [6]OF THE

λαοῦ λέγοντες, Ἐν ποίᾳ ἐξουσίᾳ ταῦτα ποιεῖς; καὶ
[7]PEOPLE SAYING, BY WHAT AUTHORITY DO YOU° DO~THESE THINGS? AND

τίς σοι ἔδωκεν τὴν ἐξουσίαν ταύτην; 21.24 ἀποκριθεὶς δὲ
WHO GAVE~TO YOU - THIS~AUTHORITY? AND~HAVING ANSWERED

ὁ Ἰησοῦς εἶπεν αὐτοῖς, Ἐρωτήσω ὑμᾶς κἀγὼ
- JESUS SAID TO THEM, [2]WILL ASK [3]YOU° [1]I ALSO

λόγον ἕνα, ὃν ἐὰν εἴπητέ μοι κἀγὼ ὑμῖν ἐρῶ ἐν
ONE~QUESTION, WHICH IF YOU° TELL ME I ALSO WILL TELL~YOU° BY

ποίᾳ ἐξουσίᾳ ταῦτα ποιῶ· **21.25** τὸ βάπτισμα τὸ
WHAT AUTHORITY I DO~THESE THINGS. THE BAPTISM -

Ἰωάννου πόθεν ἦν; ἐξ οὐρανοῦ ἢ ἐξ ἀνθρώπων;
OF JOHN FROM WHERE WAS IT? FROM HEAVEN OR FROM MEN?

οἱ δὲ διελογίζοντο ἐν ἑαυτοῖς λέγοντες, Ἐὰν
AND~THEY WERE DISCUSSING [IT] AMONG THEMSELVES SAYING, IF

εἴπωμεν, Ἐξ οὐρανοῦ, ἐρεῖ ἡμῖν, Διὰ τί οὖν
WE SAY, FROM HEAVEN, HE WILL SAY TO US, WHY THEN

οὐκ ἐπιστεύσατε αὐτῷ; **21.26** ἐὰν δὲ εἴπωμεν, Ἐξ
DID YOU° NOT BELIEVE HIM? BUT~IF WE SAY, FROM

ἀνθρώπων, φοβούμεθα τὸν ὄχλον, πάντες γὰρ ὡς
MEN, WE FEAR THE CROWD, FOR~EVERYONE AS

προφήτην ἔχουσιν τὸν Ἰωάννην. **21.27** καὶ
A PROPHET CONSIDERS - JOHN. AND

ἀποκριθέντες τῷ Ἰησοῦ εἶπαν, Οὐκ οἴδαμεν. ἔφη
HAVING ANSWERED - JESUS THEY SAID, WE DO NOT KNOW. SAID

αὐτοῖς καὶ αὐτός, Οὐδὲ ἐγὼ λέγω ὑμῖν ἐν ποίᾳ
TO THEM ALSO HE, NEITHER I TELL YOU° BY WHAT

ἐξουσίᾳ ταῦτα ποιῶ.
AUTHORITY I DO~THESE THINGS.

21.28 Τί δὲ ὑμῖν δοκεῖ; ἄνθρωπος εἶχεν τέκνα δύο.
AND~WHAT DOES IT SEEM~TO YOU°? A MAN HAD TWO~CHILDREN.

καὶ προσελθὼν τῷ πρώτῳ εἶπεν, Τέκνον, ὕπαγε
AND HAVING APPROACHED THE FIRST HE SAID, CHILD, GO

σήμερον ἐργάζου ἐν τῷ ἀμπελῶνι. **21.29** ὁ δὲ
TODAY [AND] WORK IN THE VINEYARD. BUT~HE

ἀποκριθεὶς εἶπεν, Οὐ θέλω, ὕστερον δὲ
HAVING ANSWERED SAID, I DO NOT WANT TO, BUT~LATER

μεταμεληθεὶς ἀπῆλθεν. **21.30** προσελθὼν δὲ τῷ
HAVING CHANGED HIS MIND HE WENT. AND~HAVING APPROACHED THE

ἑτέρῳ εἶπεν ὡσαύτως. ὁ δὲ ἀποκριθεὶς εἶπεν, Ἐγώ,
OTHER HE SPOKE SIMILARLY. AND~HE HAVING ANSWERED SAID, I [WILL GO],

κύριε, καὶ οὐκ ἀπῆλθεν. **21.31** τίς ἐκ τῶν δύο
LORD, AND HE DID NOT GO. WHICH OF THE TWO

ἐποίησεν τὸ θέλημα τοῦ πατρός; λέγουσιν, Ὁ
DID THE WILL OF THE(THEIR) FATHER? THEY SAY, THE

πρῶτος. λέγει αὐτοῖς ὁ Ἰησοῦς, Ἀμὴν λέγω ὑμῖν ὅτι
FIRST. SAYS TO THEM - JESUS, TRULY I SAY TO YOU°, THAT

οἱ τελῶναι καὶ αἱ πόρναι προάγουσιν ὑμᾶς εἰς
THE TAX-COLLECTORS AND THE PROSTITUTES ARE GOING AHEAD OF YOU° INTO

τὴν βασιλείαν τοῦ θεοῦ. **21.32** ἦλθεν γὰρ Ἰωάννης
THE KINGDOM - OF GOD. FOR~CAME JOHN

πρὸς ὑμᾶς ἐν ὁδῷ δικαιοσύνης, καὶ οὐκ ἐπιστεύσατε
TO YOU° IN [THE] WAY OF RIGHTEOUSNESS, AND YOU° DID NOT BELIEVE

one question; if you tell me the answer, then I will also tell you by what authority I do these things. 25Did the baptism of John come from heaven, or was it of human origin?" And they argued with one another, "If we say, 'From heaven,' he will say to us, 'Why then did you not believe him?' 26But if we say, 'Of human origin,' we are afraid of the crowd; for all regard John as a prophet." 27So they answered Jesus, "We do not know." And he said to them, "Neither will I tell you by what authority I am doing these things.

28 "What do you think? A man had two sons; he went to the first and said, 'Son, go and work in the vineyard today.' 29He answered, 'I will not'; but later he changed his mind and went. 30The father[k] went to the second and said the same; and he answered, 'I go, sir'; but he did not go. 31Which of the two did the will of his father?" They said, "The first." Jesus said to them, "Truly I tell you, the tax collectors and the prostitutes are going into the kingdom of God ahead of you. 32For John came to you in the way of righteousness and you did not believe

[k] Gk *He*

him, but the tax collectors
and the prostitutes believed
him; and even after you saw
it, you did not change your
minds and believe him.

33 "Listen to another
parable. There was a
landowner who planted a
vineyard, put a fence around
it, dug a wine press in it, and
built a watchtower. Then he
leased it to tenants and went
to another country. 34When
the harvest time had come,
he sent his slaves to the
tenants to collect his
produce. 35But the tenants
seized his slaves and beat
one, killed another, and
stoned another. 36Again he
sent other slaves, more than
the first; and they treated
them in the same way.
37Finally he sent his son to
them, saying, 'They will
respect my son.' 38But when
the tenants saw the son, they
said to themselves, 'This is
the heir; come, let us kill him
and get his inheritance.' 39So
they seized him, threw him
out of the vineyard, and
killed him. 40Now when the
owner of the vineyard
comes, what will he do to
those tenants?" 41They said
to him, "He will put those
wretches to a miserable
death, and lease the vineyard
to other tenants who

αὐτῷ,   οἱ δὲ   τελῶναι   καὶ   αἱ   πόρναι   ἐπίστευσαν
HIM,   BUT~THE TAX-COLLECTORS AND   THE   PROSTITUTES BELIEVED

αὐτῷ·   ὑμεῖς δὲ   ἰδόντες   οὐδὲ   μετεμελήθητε   ὕστερον
IN HIM.   BUT~YOU   HAVING SEEN DID NOT REPENT   LATER

τοῦ   πιστεῦσαι   αὐτῷ.
-      TO BELIEVE   IN HIM.

21.33 Ἄλλην   παραβολὴν   ἀκούσατε.   Ἄνθρωπος   ἦν
         ²ANOTHER   ³PARABLE   ¹LISTEN TO.   THERE WAS~A MAN,

οἰκοδεσπότης   ὅστις   ἐφύτευσεν   ἀμπελῶνα καὶ   φραγμὸν
A HOUSE MASTER   WHO   PLANTED   A VINEYARD   AND   A FENCE

αὐτῷ   περιέθηκεν   καὶ   ὤρυξεν ἐν   αὐτῷ   ληνὸν   καὶ
HE PUT AROUND~IT   AND   DUG   IN   IT   A WINE PRESS AND

ᾠκοδόμησεν   πύργον   καὶ   ἐξέδετο   αὐτὸν   γεωργοῖς   καὶ
BUILT   A TOWER   AND   LEASED   IT   TO FARMERS   AND

ἀπεδήμησεν.   **21.34** ὅτε δὲ   ἤγγισεν ὁ   καιρὸς   τῶν
DEPARTED.   AND~WHEN CAME NEAR THE TIME   OF THE

καρπῶν,   ἀπέστειλεν   τοὺς   δούλους   αὐτοῦ   πρὸς   τοὺς
FRUITS,   HE SENT   THE   SLAVES   OF HIM   TO   THE

γεωργοὺς   λαβεῖν   τοὺς   καρποὺς   αὐτοῦ.   **21.35** καὶ
FARMERS   TO RECEIVE THE   FRUITS   OF IT.   AND

λαβόντες   οἱ   γεωργοὶ   τοὺς   δούλους   αὐτοῦ   ὃν μὲν
³HAVING TAKEN ¹THE ²FARMERS THE   SLAVES   OF HIM,   THIS ONE

ἔδειραν,   ὃν δὲ   ἀπέκτειναν,   ὃν δὲ   ἐλιθοβόλησαν.
THEY BEAT, ANOTHER THEY KILLED,   AND ANOTHER THEY STONED.

21.36 πάλιν   ἀπέστειλεν   ἄλλους   δούλους   πλείονας   τῶν
          AGAIN   HE SENT   OTHER   SLAVES   MORE THAN   THE

πρώτων, καὶ   ἐποίησαν   αὐτοῖς   ὡσαύτως.
FIRST ONES, AND THEY DID   TO THEM SIMILARLY.

21.37 ὕστερον   δὲ   ἀπέστειλεν   πρὸς   αὐτοὺς   τὸν   υἱὸν   αὐτοῦ
          AND~FINALLY   HE SENT   TO   THEM   THE   SON   OF HIM

λέγων,   Ἐντραπήσονται   τὸν   υἱόν   μου.   **21.38** οἱ δὲ
SAYING,   THEY WILL RESPECT THE   SON   OF ME.   BUT~THE

γεωργοὶ   ἰδόντες   τὸν   υἱὸν   εἶπον   ἐν   ἑαυτοῖς,   Οὗτός
FARMERS   HAVING SEEN THE   SON   SAID   AMONG THEMSELVES, THIS

ἐστιν   ὁ   κληρονόμος·   δεῦτε   ἀποκτείνωμεν   αὐτὸν   καὶ
IS   THE HEIR.   COME   LET US KILL   HIM   AND

σχῶμεν   τὴν   κληρονομίαν   αὐτοῦ,   **21.39** καὶ
LET US TAKE POSSESSION OF THE INHERITANCE OF HIM,   AND

λαβόντες   αὐτὸν   ἐξέβαλον   ἔξω   τοῦ   ἀμπελῶνος   καὶ
HAVING TAKEN HIM   THEY THREW HIM OUT   OF THE VINEYARD   AND

ἀπέκτειναν.   **21.40** ὅταν   οὖν   ἔλθῃ ὁ   κύριος   τοῦ
KILLED [HIM].   THEREFORE~WHEN CAME THE LORD   OF THE

ἀμπελῶνος, τί   ποιήσει   τοῖς   γεωργοῖς   ἐκείνοις;
VINEYARD,   WHAT WILL HE DO -   TO THOSE~FARMERS?

21.41 λέγουσιν   αὐτῷ,   Κακοὺς   κακῶς ἀπολέσει αὐτοὺς
          THEY SAY   TO HIM,   [THOSE] EVILDOERS HE WILL BRING THEM TO A TERRIBLE END

καὶ   τὸν   ἀμπελῶνα   ἐκδώσεται   ἄλλοις   γεωργοῖς,   οἵτινες
AND   THE   VINEYARD   HE WILL LEASE TO OTHER FARMERS,   WHO

ἀποδώσουσιν αὐτῷ τοὺς καρποὺς ἐν τοῖς καιροῖς αὐτῶν.
WILL GIVE BACK   TO HIM   THE   FRUITS   IN -   THEIR~SEASONS.

21.42 λέγει αὐτοῖς ὁ Ἰησοῦς, Οὐδέποτε ἀνέγνωτε ἐν
SAYS   TO THEM - JESUS,   HAVE YOU° NEVER READ   IN

ταῖς γραφαῖς,
THE   SCRIPTURES,

Λίθον ὃν ἀπεδοκίμασαν οἱ οἰκοδομοῦντες,
[THE] STONE WHICH ³REJECTED   ¹THE ONES ²BUILDING,

οὗτος ἐγενήθη εἰς κεφαλὴν γωνίας·
THIS ONE BECAME - HEAD   OF [THE] CORNER.

παρὰ κυρίου ἐγένετο αὕτη
FROM [THE] LORD CAME ABOUT THIS

καὶ ἔστιν θαυμαστὴ ἐν ὀφθαλμοῖς ἡμῶν;
AND IT IS MARVELOUS IN OUR~EYES?

21.43 διὰ τοῦτο λέγω ὑμῖν ὅτι ἀρθήσεται ἀφ᾽ ὑμῶν
FOR THIS REASON I SAY TO YOU° - WILL BE TAKEN FROM YOU°

ἡ βασιλεία τοῦ θεοῦ καὶ δοθήσεται ἔθνει ποιοῦντι
THE KINGDOM - OF GOD AND IT WILL BE GIVEN TO A NATION PRODUCING

τοὺς καρποὺς αὐτῆς. ⌜**[21.44** Καὶ ὁ πεσὼν ἐπὶ
THE   FRUIT   OF IT.   AND THE ONE HAVING FALLEN ON

τὸν λίθον τοῦτον συνθλασθήσεται· ἐφ᾽ ὃν δ᾽ ἂν πέσῃ
-   THIS~STONE   WILL BE CRUSHED.   AND~ON WHOMEVER IT FALLS

λικμήσει αὐτόν.]⌝
IT WILL CRUSH HIM.

21.45 Καὶ ἀκούσαντες οἱ ἀρχιερεῖς καὶ οἱ Φαρισαῖοι
AND HAVING HEARD   THE CHIEF PRIESTS AND THE PHARISEES

τὰς παραβολὰς αὐτοῦ ἔγνωσαν ὅτι περὶ αὐτῶν
THE PARABLES OF HIM THEY UNDERSTOOD THAT ABOUT THEM

λέγει· **21.46** καὶ ζητοῦντες αὐτὸν κρατῆσαι ἐφοβήθησαν
HE SPOKE.   AND SEEKING TO ARREST~HIM THEY WERE AFRAID

τοὺς ὄχλους, ἐπεὶ εἰς προφήτην αὐτὸν εἶχον.
OF THE CROWDS, SINCE AS A PROPHET THEY CONSIDERED~HIM.

21:42 Ps. 118:22-23   **21:44** text [see Luke 20:18]: KJV ASV RSVmg NASB NIV NEBmg TEVmg NJBmg NRSV. omit: ASVmg RSV NIVmg NEB TEV NJB NRSVmg.

22.1 Καὶ ἀποκριθεὶς ὁ Ἰησοῦς πάλιν εἶπεν ἐν
AND HAVING ANSWERED - JESUS   AGAIN SPOKE IN

παραβολαῖς αὐτοῖς λέγων, **22.2** Ὡμοιώθη ἡ βασιλεία
PARABLES   TO THEM SAYING,   ⁵IS LIKE ¹THE ²KINGDOM

τῶν οὐρανῶν ἀνθρώπῳ βασιλεῖ, ὅστις ἐποίησεν
³OF THE ⁴HEAVENS A MAN,   A KING, WHO PREPARED

γάμους τῷ υἱῷ αὐτοῦ. **22.3** καὶ ἀπέστειλεν τοὺς
A WEDDING FEAST FOR THE SON OF HIM.   AND HE SENT OUT THE

δούλους αὐτοῦ καλέσαι τοὺς κεκλημένους εἰς τοὺς
SLAVES   OF HIM TO CALL THE ONES HAVING BEEN INVITED TO THE

---

will give him the produce at the harvest time."

42 Jesus said to them, "Have you never read in the scriptures:

'The stone that the builders rejected has become the cornerstone;[l] this was the Lord's doing, and it is amazing in our eyes'?

43Therefore I tell you, the kingdom of God will be taken away from you and given to a people that produces the fruits of the kingdom.[m] 44The one who falls on this stone will be broken to pieces; and it will crush anyone on whom it falls."[n]

45 When the chief priests and the Pharisees heard his parables, they realized that he was speaking about them. 46They wanted to arrest him, but they feared the crowds, because they regarded him as a prophet.

[l] Or keystone
[m] Gk the fruits of it
[n] Other ancient authorities lack verse 44

Once more Jesus spoke to them in parables, saying: 2"The kingdom of heaven may be compared to a king who gave a wedding banquet for his son. 3He sent his slaves to call those who had been invited to the wedding banquet, but they would not come. [4]Again he sent other slaves, saying, 'Tell those who have been invited: Look, I have prepared my dinner, my oxen and my fat calves have been slaughtered, and everything is ready; come to the wedding banquet.' [5]But they made light of it and went away, one to his farm, another to his business, [6]while the rest seized his slaves, mistreated them, and killed them. [7]The king was enraged. He sent his troops, destroyed those murderers, and burned their city. [8]Then he said to his slaves, 'The wedding is ready, but those invited were not worthy. [9]Go therefore into the main streets, and invite everyone you find to the wedding banquet.' [10]Those slaves went out into the streets and gathered all whom they found, both good and bad; so the wedding hall was filled with guests.

11 "But when the king came in to see the guests, he noticed a man there who was not wearing a wedding robe, [12]and he said to him, 'Friend, how did you get in here without a wedding robe?' And he was speechless. [13]Then the king said to the attendants, 'Bind him hand and foot, and throw him into the outer darkness, where there will

γάμους,   καὶ οὐκ ἤθελον ἐλθεῖν.   **22.4** πάλιν
WEDDING FEAST,   AND   THEY DID NOT WANT   TO COME.   AGAIN

ἀπέστειλεν ἄλλους δούλους λέγων, Εἴπατε τοῖς
HE SENT OUT   OTHER   SLAVES   SAYING,   TELL   THE ONES

κεκλημένοις, Ἰδοὺ τὸ ἄριστόν μου ἡτοίμακα, οἱ ταῦροί
HAVING BEEN INVITED, BEHOLD THE DINNER   OF ME I HAVE PREPARED, THE BULLS

μου καὶ τὰ σιτιστὰ   τεθυμένα   καὶ πάντα
OF ME AND   THE FATTENED CATTLE   HAVE BEEN SLAUGHTERED AND   EVERYTHING

ἕτοιμα·   δεῦτε εἰς τοὺς γάμους.   **22.5** οἱ δὲ
IS READY,   COME TO THE   WEDDING FEAST.   BUT~THEY

ἀμελήσαντες   ἀπῆλθον, ὃς μὲν εἰς τὸν ἴδιον ἀγρόν,
HAVING PAID NO ATTENTION   LEFT,   THE ONE TO HIS OWN   FIELD,

ὃς δὲ   ἐπὶ τὴν ἐμπορίαν αὐτοῦ·   **22.6** οἱ δὲ λοιποὶ
THE OTHER TO   THE   BUSINESS   OF HIM.   AND~THE OTHERS

κρατήσαντες τοὺς δούλους αὐτοῦ ὕβρισαν καὶ
HAVING CALLED   THE   SLAVES   OF HIM,   MISTREATED AND

ἀπέκτειναν.   **22.7** ὁ δὲ βασιλεὺς ὠργίσθη καὶ πέμψας
KILLED [THEM].   SO~THE KING   WAS ANGRY   AND   HAVING SENT

τὰ στρατεύματα αὐτοῦ ἀπώλεσεν τοὺς φονεῖς ἐκείνους
THE ARMIES   OF HIM,   HE DESTROYED   -   THOSE~MURDERERS

καὶ τὴν πόλιν αὐτῶν ἐνέπρησεν.   **22.8** τότε λέγει τοῖς
AND THE CITY   OF THEM HE BURNED.   THEN   HE SAYS TO THE

δούλοις αὐτοῦ, Ὁ μὲν γάμος   ἕτοιμός ἐστιν, οἱ δὲ
SLAVES   OF HIM,   THE -   WEDDING FEAST IS~READY,   BUT~THE ONES

κεκλημένοι   οὐκ ἦσαν ἄξιοι·   **22.9** πορεύεσθε οὖν   ἐπὶ
HAVING BEEN INVITED WERE NOT   WORTHY.   GO   THEREFORE TO

τὰς διεξόδους τῶν ὁδῶν καὶ ὅσους ἐὰν εὕρητε καλέσατε
THE CROSSINGS   OF THE STREETS AND   WHOEVER   YOU° FIND   INVITE

εἰς τοὺς γάμους.   **22.10** καὶ ἐξελθόντες οἱ
TO THE   WEDDING FEAST.   AND   HAVING GONE OUT -

δοῦλοι ἐκεῖνοι εἰς τὰς ὁδοὺς   συνήγαγον   πάντας
THOSE~SLAVES   TO THE   ROADWAYS, THEY GATHERED TOGETHER EVERYONE

οὓς εὗρον,   πονηρούς τε καὶ ἀγαθούς· καὶ ἐπλήσθη
WHOM THEY FOUND,   BOTH~BAD   AND   GOOD.   AND   WAS FILLED

ὁ γάμος   ἀνακειμένων.   **22.11** εἰσελθὼν δὲ   ὁ
THE WEDDING FEAST [WITH] GUESTS.   AND~HAVING ENTERED THE

βασιλεὺς θεάσασθαι τοὺς   ἀνακειμένους εἶδεν ἐκεῖ
KING   TO SEE   THE ONES RECLINING AT TABLE HE SAW THERE

ἄνθρωπον οὐκ ἐνδεδυμένον ἔνδυμα γάμου,   **22.12** καὶ
A MAN   NOT HAVING BEEN CLOTHED WITH WEDDING~GARMENTS,   AND

λέγει αὐτῷ, Ἑταῖρε, πῶς εἰσῆλθες ὧδε μὴ ἔχων
HE SAYS TO HIM,   FRIEND,   HOW   DID YOU ENTER HERE NOT HAVING

ἔνδυμα γάμου; ὁ δὲ ἐφιμώθη.   **22.13** τότε ὁ βασιλεὺς
WEDDING~GARMENTS?   BUT~HE WAS SPEECHLESS.   THEN THE KING

εἶπεν τοῖς διακόνοις, Δήσαντες αὐτοῦ πόδας καὶ χεῖρας
SAID   TO THE SERVANTS,   HAVING BOUND HIM   FEET   AND   HANDS

ἐκβάλετε αὐτὸν εἰς τὸ σκότος ⸀τὸ ἐξώτερον· ἐκεῖ ἔσται
THROW OUT   HIM   INTO THE ²DARKNESS - ¹OUTER.   THERE   WILL BE

ὁ κλαυθμὸς καὶ ὁ βρυγμὸς τῶν ὀδόντων.
- WEEPING   AND   - GRINDING   OF THE TEETH.

22.14 πολλοὶ γάρ εἰσιν κλητοὶ, ὀλίγοι δὲ ἐκλεκτοί.
FOR~MANY   ARE   CALLED,   BUT~FEW   CHOSEN.

22.15 Τότε πορευθέντες οἱ Φαρισαῖοι
THEN   HAVING DEPARTED   THE PHARISEES

συμβούλιον ἔλαβον ὅπως αὐτὸν παγιδεύσωσιν ἐν
TOOK~COUNSEL TOGETHER   SO THAT FOR HIM   THEY MIGHT SET A TRAP IN

λόγῳ.   **22.16** καὶ ἀποστέλλουσιν αὐτῷ τοὺς μαθητὰς
A STATEMENT.   AND   THEY ARE SENDING   TO HIM   THE   DISCIPLES

αὐτῶν μετὰ τῶν Ἡρῳδιανῶν λέγοντες, Διδάσκαλε,
OF THEM WITH THE HERODIANS   SAYING,   TEACHER,

οἴδαμεν ὅτι ἀληθὴς εἶ καὶ τὴν ὁδὸν τοῦ θεοῦ ἐν
WE KNOW   THAT YOU ARE~GOOD AND THE WAY   -   OF GOD IN

ἀληθείᾳ διδάσκεις καὶ οὐ μέλει   σοι περὶ οὐδενός·
TRUTH   YOU TEACH,   AND IT IS NOT A CONCERN TO YOU ABOUT ANYBODY,

οὐ γὰρ βλέπεις εἰς πρόσωπον ἀνθρώπων, **22.17** εἰπὲ οὖν
FOR~YOU DO NOT LOOK INTO [THE] FACE   OF MEN.   THEREFORE~TELL

ἡμῖν τί σοι δοκεῖ· ἔξεστιν δοῦναι κῆνσον
US WHAT TO YOU SEEMS RIGHT. IS IT PERMISSIBLE TO GIVE   POLL TAX

Καίσαρι ἢ οὔ; **22.18** γνοὺς δὲ ὁ Ἰησοῦς τὴν
TO CAESAR OR NOT?   BUT~HAVING KNOWN - JESUS THE

πονηρίαν αὐτῶν εἶπεν, Τί με πειράζετε, ὑποκριταί;
EVIL   OF THEM HE SAID, WHY DO YOU° TEST~ME, HYPOCRITES?

22.19 ἐπιδείξατέ μοι τὸ νόμισμα τοῦ κήνσου. οἱ δὲ
SHOW   ME   THE COIN   OF THE POLL TAX.   AND~THEY

προσήνεγκαν αὐτῷ δηνάριον. **22.20** καὶ λέγει αὐτοῖς,
BROUGHT   TO HIM A DENARIUS.   AND HE SAYS TO THEM,

Τίνος ἡ εἰκὼν αὕτη καὶ ἡ ἐπιγραφή; **22.21** λέγουσιν
WHOSE - IMAGE [IS] THIS AND THE INSCRIPTION?   THEY SAY

αὐτῷ, Καίσαρος. τότε λέγει αὐτοῖς, Ἀπόδοτε οὖν
TO HIM, CAESAR'S.   THEN HE SAYS TO THEM,   GIVE   THEREFORE

τὰ   Καίσαρος Καίσαρι καὶ τὰ   τοῦ θεοῦ τῷ
THE THINGS OF CAESAR'S TO CAESAR AND THE THINGS - OF GOD -

θεῷ. **22.22** καὶ ἀκούσαντες ἐθαύμασαν, καὶ ἀφέντες
TO GOD.   AND HAVING HEARD [THIS] THEY WERE AMAZED, AND HAVING LEFT

αὐτὸν ἀπῆλθαν.
HIM   THEY WENT AWAY.

22.23 Ἐν ἐκείνῃ τῇ ἡμέρᾳ προσῆλθον αὐτῷ
ON   THAT   -   DAY   APPROACHED   HIM

Σαδδουκαῖοι, λέγοντες μὴ εἶναι ἀνάστασιν, καὶ
SADDUCEES,   SAYING   NOT TO BE A RESURRECTION, AND

ἐπηρώτησαν αὐτὸν **22.24** λέγοντες, Διδάσκαλε, Μωϋσῆς
THEY QUESTIONED HIM   SAYING,   TEACHER,   MOSES

εἶπεν, Ἐάν τις ἀποθάνῃ μὴ ἔχων τέκνα,
SAID, IF   SOMEONE DIES   NOT HAVING CHILDREN,

22:24 Deut. 25:5

be weeping and gnashing of teeth.' [14]For many are called, but few are chosen."

15 Then the Pharisees went and plotted to entrap him in what he said. [16]So they sent their disciples to him, along with the Herodians, saying, "Teacher, we know that you are sincere, and teach the way of God in accordance with truth, and show deference to no one; for you do not regard people with partiality. [17]Tell us, then, what you think. Is it lawful to pay taxes to the emperor, or not?" [18]But Jesus, aware of their malice, said, "Why are you putting me to the test, you hypocrites? [19]Show me the coin used for the tax." And they brought him a denarius. [20]Then he said to them, "Whose head is this, and whose title?" [21]They answered, "The emperor's." Then he said to them, "Give therefore to the emperor the things that are the emperor's, and to God the things that are God's." [22]When they heard this, they were amazed; and they left him and went away.

23 The same day some Sadducees came to him, saying there is no resurrection;[o] and they asked him a question, saying, [24]"Teacher, Moses said, 'If a man dies childless,

[o] Other ancient authorities read *who say that there is no resurrection*

his brother shall marry the widow, and raise up children for his brother.' ²⁵Now there were seven brothers among us; the first married, and died childless, leaving the widow to his brother. ²⁶The second did the same, so also the third, down to the seventh. ²⁷Last of all, the woman herself died. ²⁸In the resurrection, then, whose wife of the seven will she be? For all of them had married her."

29 Jesus answered them, "You are wrong, because you know neither the scriptures nor the power of God. ³⁰For in the resurrection they neither marry nor are given in marriage, but are like angels*p* in heaven. ³¹And as for the resurrection of the dead, have you not read what was said to you by God, ³²'I am the God of Abraham, the God of Isaac, and the God of Jacob'? He is God not of the dead, but of the living." ³³And when the crowd heard it, they were astounded at his teaching.

34 When the Pharisees heard that he had silenced the Sadducees, they gathered together, ³⁵and one of them, a lawyer, asked him a question to test him. ³⁶"Teacher, which commandment in the law is the greatest?"

p Other ancient authorities add of God

ἐπιγαμβρεύσει ὁ ἀδελφὸς αὐτοῦ τὴν γυναῖκα αὐτοῦ
SHALL MARRY   THE   BROTHER   OF HIM   THE   WIFE   OF HIM

καὶ ἀναστήσει σπέρμα τῷ ἀδελφῷ αὐτοῦ.
AND   RAISE UP   SEED   FOR THE BROTHER   OF HIM.

22.25 ἦσαν δὲ παρ' ἡμῖν ἑπτὰ ἀδελφοί· καὶ ὁ
NOW~THERE WERE WITH US   SEVEN BROTHERS.   AND THE

πρῶτος γήμας ἐτελεύτησεν, καὶ μὴ ἔχων σπέρμα
FIRST   HAVING MARRIED DIED,   AND NOT HAVING OFFSPRING

ἀφῆκεν τὴν γυναῖκα αὐτοῦ τῷ ἀδελφῷ αὐτοῦ·
LEFT   THE   WIFE   OF HIM TO THE BROTHER   OF HIM.

22.26 ὁμοίως καὶ ὁ δεύτερος καὶ ὁ τρίτος ἕως τῶν
LIKEWISE ALSO THE SECOND   AND THE THIRD UP TO THE

ἑπτά. **22.27** ὕστερον δὲ πάντων ἀπέθανεν ἡ γυνή.
SEVENTH.   AND~LAST   OF ALL   DIED   THE WOMAN.

22.28 ἐν τῇ ἀναστάσει οὖν τίνος τῶν ἑπτὰ ἔσται
IN THE RESURRECTION THEREFORE WHICH OF THE SEVEN WILL SHE BE

γυνή; πάντες γὰρ ἔσχον αὐτήν· **22.29** ἀποκριθεὶς δὲ
[THE] WIFE? FOR~ALL   HAD   HER.   AND~HAVING ANSWERED

ὁ Ἰησοῦς εἶπεν αὐτοῖς, Πλανᾶσθε μὴ εἰδότες τὰς
- JESUS   SAID TO THEM, YOU° ARE MISTAKEN NOT HAVING KNOWN THE

γραφὰς μηδὲ τὴν δύναμιν τοῦ θεοῦ· **22.30** ἐν γὰρ τῇ
SCRIPTURES NOR THE POWER   - OF GOD.   FOR~IN THE

ἀναστάσει οὔτε γαμοῦσιν οὔτε γαμίζονται, ἀλλ' ὡς
RESURRECTION NEITHER THEY MARRY NOR ARE GIVEN IN MARRIAGE, BUT LIKE

ἄγγελοι ἐν τῷ οὐρανῷ εἰσιν. **22.31** περὶ δὲ τῆς
ANGELS   IN - HEAVEN   THEY ARE.   BUT~CONCERNING THE

ἀναστάσεως τῶν νεκρῶν οὐκ ἀνέγνωτε τὸ ῥηθὲν
RESURRECTION OF THE DEAD HAVE YOU° NOT READ THE THING SPOKEN

ὑμῖν ὑπὸ τοῦ θεοῦ λέγοντος, **22.32** Ἐγώ εἰμι ὁ θεὸς
TO YOU° BY   -   GOD SAYING,   I   AM THE GOD

Ἀβραὰμ καὶ ὁ θεὸς Ἰσαὰκ καὶ ὁ θεὸς Ἰακώβ;
OF ABRAHAM AND THE GOD OF ISAAC AND THE GOD OF JACOB?

οὐκ ἔστιν [ὁ] θεὸς νεκρῶν ἀλλὰ ζώντων.
²IS NOT   -   ¹GOD OF THE DEAD ONES BUT OF THE LIVING ONES.

22.33 καὶ ἀκούσαντες οἱ ὄχλοι ἐξεπλήσσοντο ἐπὶ τῇ
AND   HAVING HEARD [THIS] THE CROWDS WERE BEING AMAZED AT THE

διδαχῇ αὐτοῦ.
TEACHING OF HIM.

22.34 Οἱ δὲ Φαρισαῖοι ἀκούσαντες ὅτι ἐφίμωσεν τοὺς
BUT~THE PHARISEES HAVING HEARD   THAT HE SILENCED THE

Σαδδουκαίους συνήχθησαν ἐπὶ τὸ αὐτό, **22.35** καὶ
SADDUCEES,   ASSEMBLED   TOGETHER,   AND

ἐπηρώτησεν εἷς ἐξ αὐτῶν [νομικὸς] πειράζων αὐτόν,
⁵QUESTIONED [HIM] ¹ONE ²OF ³THEM, ⁴A LAWYER, TESTING HIM.

22.36 Διδάσκαλε, ποία ἐντολὴ μεγάλη ἐν τῷ νόμῳ;
TEACHER,   WHICH COMMANDMENT [IS] GREAT IN THE LAW?

22:32 Exod. 3:6, 15

22.37 ὁ δὲ ἔφη αὐτῷ, Ἀγαπήσεις κύριον τὸν θεόν σου
AND~HE SAID TO HIM, YOU SHALL LOVE [THE] LORD THE GOD OF YOU

ἐν ὅλῃ τῇ καρδίᾳ σου καὶ ἐν ὅλῃ τῇ ψυχῇ σου καὶ
WITH ALL THE HEART OF YOU AND WITH ALL THE SOUL OF YOU AND

ἐν ὅλῃ τῇ διανοίᾳ σου· **22.38** αὕτη ἐστὶν ἡ
WITH ALL THE UNDERSTANDING OF YOU. THIS IS THE

μεγάλη καὶ πρώτη ἐντολή. **22.39** δευτέρα δὲ
GREAT AND FIRST COMMANDMENT. AND~[THE] SECOND [IS]

ὁμοία αὐτῇ, Ἀγαπήσεις τὸν πλησίον σου ὡς σεαυτόν.
LIKE IT, LOVE THE NEIGHBOR OF YOU AS YOURSELF.

22.40 ἐν ταύταις ταῖς δυσὶν ἐντολαῖς ὅλος ὁ νόμος
ON THESE - TWO COMMANDMENTS [THE] ENTIRE - LAW

κρέμαται καὶ οἱ προφῆται.
HANGS AND THE PROPHETS.

22.41 Συνηγμένων δὲ τῶν Φαρισαίων ἐπηρώτησεν
AND~HAVING BEEN ASSEMBLED THE PHARISEES, ²QUESTIONED

αὐτοὺς ὁ Ἰησοῦς **22.42** λέγων, Τί ὑμῖν δοκεῖ περὶ
³THEM - ¹JESUS SAYING, WHAT SEEMS RIGHT~TO YOU° CONCERNING

τοῦ Χριστοῦ; τίνος υἱός ἐστιν; λέγουσιν αὐτῷ, Τοῦ
THE CHRIST? WHOSE SON IS HE? THEY SAY TO HIM, THE [SON]

Δαυίδ. **22.43** λέγει αὐτοῖς, Πῶς οὖν Δαυὶδ ἐν
OF DAVID. HE SAYS TO THEM, HOW THEN [CAN] DAVID IN

πνεύματι καλεῖ αὐτὸν κύριον λέγων,
[THE] SPIRIT CALL HIM LORD SAYING,

22.44 Εἶπεν κύριος τῷ κυρίῳ μου,
[THE] LORD~SAID - TO MY~LORD,

Κάθου ἐκ δεξιῶν μου,
SIT ON [THE] RIGHT OF ME,

ἕως ἂν θῶ τοὺς ἐχθρούς σου ὑποκάτω τῶν
UNTIL I PUT THE ENEMIES OF YOU UNDER THE

ποδῶν σου;
FEET OF YOU?

22.45 εἰ οὖν Δαυὶδ καλεῖ αὐτὸν κύριον, πῶς υἱὸς
THEREFORE~IF DAVID CALLS HIM LORD, HOW [THE] SON

αὐτοῦ ἐστιν; **22.46** καὶ οὐδεὶς ἐδύνατο ἀποκριθῆναι αὐτῷ
OF HIM IS HE? AND NO ONE WAS ABLE TO ANSWER HIM

λόγον οὐδὲ ἐτόλμησέν τις ἀπ' ἐκείνης τῆς ἡμέρας
A WORD NOR DID ANYONE~DARE FROM THAT - DAY

ἐπερωτῆσαι αὐτὸν οὐκέτι.
TO ASK HIM ANY MORE [QUESTIONS].

22:37 Deut. 6:5　**22:39** Lev. 19:18　**22:44** Ps. 110:1

[37]He said to him, "'You shall love the Lord your God with all your heart, and with all your soul, and with all your mind.' [38]This is the greatest and first commandment. [39]And a second is like it: 'You shall love your neighbor as yourself.' [40]On these two commandments hang all the law and the prophets."

41 Now while the Pharisees were gathered together, Jesus asked them this question: [42]"What do you think of the Messiah?[q] Whose son is he?" They said to him, "The son of David." [43]He said to them, "How is it then that David by the Spirit[r] calls him Lord, saying,

[44] 'The Lord said to my Lord,
"Sit at my right hand,
until I put your enemies
under your feet"'?

[45]If David thus calls him Lord, how can he be his son?" [46]No one was able to give him an answer, nor from that day did anyone dare to ask him any more questions.

[q] Or *Christ*
[r] Gk *in spirit*

CHAPTER 23

Then Jesus said to the crowds and to his disciples, [2]"The scribes and the Pharisees sit on Moses' seat; [3]therefore, do whatever they teach you and follow it; but do not do as they do, for they do not practice what they teach. [4]They tie up heavy burdens, hard to bear,[s] and lay them on the shoulders of others; but they themselves are unwilling to lift a finger to move them. [5]They do all their deeds to be seen by others; for they make their phylacteries broad and their fringes long. [6]They love to have the place of honor at banquets and the best seats in the synagogues, [7]and to be greeted with respect in the marketplaces, and to have people call them rabbi. [8]But you are not to be called rabbi, for you have one teacher, and you are all students.[t] [9]And call no one your father on earth, for you have one Father—the one in heaven. [10]Nor are you to be called instructors, for you have one instructor, the Messiah.[u] [11]The greatest among you will be your servant. [12]All who exalt themselves will be humbled, and all who humble themselves will be exalted.

[s] Other ancient authorities lack *hard to bear*
[t] Gk *brothers*
[u] Or *the Christ*

23.1 Τότε ὁ Ἰησοῦς ἐλάλησεν τοῖς ὄχλοις καὶ τοῖς
THEN - JESUS SPOKE TO THE CROWDS AND TO THE

μαθηταῖς αὐτοῦ **23.2** λέγων, Ἐπὶ τῆς Μωϋσέως καθέδρας
DISCIPLES OF HIM SAYING, UPON THE SEAT~OF MOSES

ἐκάθισαν οἱ γραμματεῖς καὶ οἱ Φαρισαῖοι.
SAT THE SCRIBES AND THE PHARISEES.

23.3 πάντα οὖν ὅσα ἐὰν εἴπωσιν ὑμῖν ποιήσατε
THEREFORE~EVERYTHING WHATEVER THEY MAY TELL YOU° DO

καὶ τηρεῖτε, κατὰ δὲ τὰ ἔργα αὐτῶν μὴ ποιεῖτε·
AND KEEP, BUT~ACCORDING TO THE WORKS OF THEM DO NOT DO.

λέγουσιν γὰρ καὶ οὐ ποιοῦσιν. **23.4** δεσμεύουσιν δὲ
FOR~THEY SAY AND DO NOT DO. AND~THEY TIE UP

φορτία βαρέα [καὶ δυσβάστακτα] καὶ ἐπιτιθέασιν ἐπὶ
LOADS HEAVY AND HARD TO BEAR AND THEY PLACE [THEM] UPON

τοὺς ὤμους τῶν ἀνθρώπων, αὐτοὶ δὲ τῷ δακτύλῳ
THE SHOULDERS - OF MEN, BUT~THEY WITH THE FINGER

αὐτῶν οὐ θέλουσιν κινῆσαι αὐτά. **23.5** πάντα δὲ τὰ
OF THEM ARE NOT WILLING TO MOVE THEM. AND~ALL THE

ἔργα αὐτῶν ποιοῦσιν πρὸς τὸ θεαθῆναι τοῖς ἀνθρώποις·
WORKS OF THEM THEY DO IN ORDER TO BE SEEN - BY MEN.

πλατύνουσιν γὰρ τὰ φυλακτήρια αὐτῶν καὶ
FOR~THEY ENLARGE THE PHYLACTERIES OF THEM AND

μεγαλύνουσιν τὰ κράσπεδα, **23.6** φιλοῦσιν δὲ τὴν
MAKE LARGE THE TASSELS, AND~THEY LOVE THE

πρωτοκλισίαν ἐν τοῖς δείπνοις καὶ τὰς πρωτοκαθεδρίας
PLACES OF HONOR AT THE BANQUETS AND THE SEATS OF HONOR

ἐν ταῖς συναγωγαῖς **23.7** καὶ τοὺς ἀσπασμοὺς ἐν ταῖς
IN THE SYNAGOGUES AND THE GREETINGS IN THE

ἀγοραῖς καὶ καλεῖσθαι ὑπὸ τῶν ἀνθρώπων, Ῥαββί.
MARKET PLACES AND TO BE CALLED BY - MEN, RABBI.

23.8 ὑμεῖς δὲ μὴ κληθῆτε, Ῥαββί· εἷς γάρ ἐστιν ὑμῶν
BUT~YOU° ARE NOT TO BE CALLED, RABBI, FOR~ONE IS YOUR°

ὁ διδάσκαλος, πάντες δὲ ὑμεῖς ἀδελφοί ἐστε. **23.9** καὶ
- TEACHER, AND~ALL [OF] YOU° ARE~BROTHERS. AND

πατέρα μὴ καλέσητε ὑμῶν ἐπὶ τῆς γῆς, εἷς γάρ ἐστιν
[5]FATHER [1]DO NOT CALL [ANYONE] [4]YOUR° [2]ON - [3]EARTH, FOR~ONE IS

ὑμῶν ὁ πατὴρ ὁ οὐράνιος. **23.10** μηδὲ κληθῆτε
YOUR° - [2]FATHER - [1]HEAVENLY. NEITHER BE CALLED

καθηγηταί, ὅτι καθηγητὴς ὑμῶν ἐστιν εἷς ὁ Χριστός.
TEACHERS, FOR [THE] TEACHER OF YOU° IS ONE—THE CHRIST.

23.11 ὁ δὲ μείζων ὑμῶν ἔσται ὑμῶν διάκονος.
AND~THE GREATEST OF YOU° WILL BE OF YOU° [THE] SERVANT.

23.12 ὅστις δὲ ὑψώσει ἑαυτὸν ταπεινωθήσεται καὶ
BUT~WHOEVER WILL LIFT UP HIMSELF WILL BE HUMBLED AND

ὅστις ταπεινώσει ἑαυτὸν ὑψωθήσεται.
WHOEVER WILL HUMBLE HIMSELF WILL BE LIFTED UP.

23.13 Οὐαὶ δὲ ὑμῖν, γραμματεῖς καὶ Φαρισαιοι
BUT~WOE   TO YOU°, SCRIBES   AND   PHARISEES,

ὑποκριταί, ὅτι κλείετε τὴν βασιλείαν τῶν οὐρανῶν
HYPOCRITES,   FOR YOU° SHUT THE KINGDOM   OF THE HEAVENS

ἔμπροσθεν τῶν ἀνθρώπων· ὑμεῖς γὰρ οὐκ εἰσέρχεσθε
IN FRONT OF   -   MEN.   FOR~YOU°   DO NOT ENTER

οὐδὲ τοὺς εἰσερχομένους ἀφίετε εἰσελθεῖν.ᵀ
NOR THE ONES ENTERING   DO YOU° PERMIT TO ENTER.

23.15 Οὐαὶ ὑμῖν, γραμματεῖς καὶ Φαρισαιοι ὑποκριταί,
        WOE TO YOU°, SCRIBES   AND   PHARISEES,   HYPOCRITES,

ὅτι περιάγετε τὴν θάλασσαν καὶ τὴν ξηρὰν ποιῆσαι
FOR YOU° TRAVEL ABOUT THE SEA   AND THE DRY [LAND] TO MAKE

ἕνα προσήλυτον, καὶ ὅταν γένηται ποιεῖτε αὐτὸν
ONE PROSELYTE,   AND WHEN HE BECOMES [ONE] YOU° MAKE HIM

υἱὸν γεέννης διπλότερον ὑμῶν.
A SON OF GEHENNA(HELL) TWICE AS MUCH AS YOU°.

23.16 Οὐαὶ ὑμῖν, ὁδηγοὶ τυφλοὶ οἱ λέγοντες,
        WOE TO YOU°, BLIND~LEADERS,   THE ONES SAYING,

Ὃς ἂν ὀμόσῃ ἐν τῷ ναῷ, οὐδέν ἐστιν· ὃς δ' ἂν
WHOEVER SWEARS BY THE TEMPLE, IT IS~WORTHLESS; BUT~WHOEVER

ὀμόσῃ ἐν τῷ χρυσῷ τοῦ ναοῦ, ὀφείλει.   **23.17** μωροὶ
SWEARS BY THE GOLD OF THE TEMPLE, HE IS OBLIGATED.   FOOLS

καὶ τυφλοί, τίς γὰρ μείζων ἐστίν, ὁ χρυσὸς ἢ ὁ ναὸς
AND BLIND MEN, FOR~WHICH IS~GREATER, THE GOLD OR THE TEMPLE

ὁ ἁγιάσας τὸν χρυσόν; **23.18** καί, Ὃς ἂν ὀμόσῃ ἐν
- HAVING SANCTIFIED THE GOLD?   AND WHOEVER SWEARS BY

τῷ θυσιαστηρίῳ, οὐδέν ἐστιν· ὃς δ' ἂν ὀμόσῃ ἐν τῷ
THE ALTAR,   IT IS~WORTHLESS; BUT~WHOEVER SWEARS BY THE

δώρῳ τῷ ἐπάνω αὐτοῦ, ὀφείλει.   **23.19** τυφλοί,
GIFT   -   UPON   IT,   HE IS OBLIGATED.   BLIND MEN,

τί γὰρ μεῖζον, τὸ δῶρον ἢ τὸ θυσιαστήριον τὸ
FOR~WHICH [IS] GREATER, THE GIFT OR THE ALTAR   -

ἁγιάζον τὸ δῶρον; **23.20** ὁ οὖν ὀμόσας ἐν τῷ
SANCTIFYING THE GIFT?   THEREFORE~THE ONE HAVING SWORN BY THE

θυσιαστηρίῳ ὀμνύει ἐν αὐτῷ καὶ ἐν πᾶσι τοῖς ἐπάνω
ALTAR   SWEARS BY IT AND ON EVERYTHING -   UPON

αὐτοῦ· **23.21** καὶ ὁ ὀμόσας ἐν τῷ ναῷ ὀμνύει ἐν
IT.   AND THE ONE HAVING SWORN BY THE TEMPLE SWEARS BY

αὐτῷ καὶ ἐν τῷ κατοικοῦντι αὐτόν, **23.22** καὶ ὁ
IT   AND BY THE ONE INHABITING   IT,   AND THE ONE

ὀμόσας ἐν τῷ οὐρανῷ ὀμνύει ἐν τῷ θρόνῳ τοῦ θεοῦ
HAVING SWORN BY - HEAVEN SWEARS BY THE THRONE - OF GOD

καὶ ἐν τῷ καθημένῳ ἐπάνω αὐτοῦ.
AND BY THE ONE SITTING   UPON   IT.

13 "But woe to you, scribes and Pharisees, hypocrites! For you lock people out of the kingdom of heaven. For you do not go in yourselves, and when others are going in, you stop them.ᵛ ¹⁵Woe to you, scribes and Pharisees, hypocrites! For you cross sea and land to make a single convert, and you make the new convert twice as much a child of hellʷ as yourselves.

16 "Woe to you, blind guides, who say, 'Whoever swears by the sanctuary is bound by nothing, but whoever swears by the gold of the sanctuary is bound by the oath.' ¹⁷You blind fools! For which is greater, the gold or the sanctuary that has made the gold sacred? ¹⁸And you say, 'Whoever swears by the altar is bound by nothing, but whoever swears by the gift that is on the altar is bound by the oath.' ¹⁹How blind you are! For which is greater, the gift or the altar that makes the gift sacred? ²⁰So whoever swears by the altar, swears by it and by everything on it; ²¹and whoever swears by the sanctuary, swears by it and by the one who dwells in it; ²²and whoever swears by heaven, swears by the throne of God and by the one who is seated upon it.

ᵛ Other authorities add here (or after verse 12) verse 14, *Woe to you, scribes and Pharisees, hypocrites! For you devour widows' houses and for the sake of appearance you make long prayers; therefore you will receive the greater condemnation.*
ʷ Gk *Gehenna*

23:13 text: ASV RSV NASBmg NIV NEB TEV NJB NRSV.   add v. 14 Οὐαι δε υμιν, γραμματεις και Φαρισαιοι υποκριται, οτι κατεσθιετε τας οικιας των χηρων και προφασει μακρα προσευχομενοι· δια τουτο λημψεσθε περισσοτερον κριμα (Woe to you, scribes and Pharisees, hypocrites, because you devour widows' houses and for a pretense make long prayers; therefore, you will receive the greater judgment) [see Mark 12:40; Luke 20:47]: KJV ASVmg RSVmg NASB NIVmg NEBmg TEVmg NJBmg NRSVmg.

23 "Woe to you, scribes and Pharisees, hypocrites! For you tithe mint, dill, and cummin, and have neglected the weightier matters of the law: justice and mercy and faith. It is these you ought to have practiced without neglecting the others. 24You blind guides! You strain out a gnat but swallow a camel!

25 "Woe to you, scribes and Pharisees, hypocrites! For you clean the outside of the cup and of the plate, but inside they are full of greed and self-indulgence. 26You blind Pharisee! First clean the inside of the cup,ˣ so that the outside also may become clean.

27 "Woe to you, scribes and Pharisees, hypocrites! For you are like white-washed tombs, which on the outside look beautiful, but inside they are full of the bones of the dead and of all kinds of filth. 28So you also on the outside look righteous to others, but inside you are full of hypocrisy and lawlessness.

29 "Woe to you, scribes and Pharisees, hypocrites! For you build the tombs of the prophets and decorate the graves of the righteous, 30and you say, 'If we had lived in the days of our ancestors,

ˣ Other ancient authorities add *and of the plate*

23.23 Οὐαὶ ὑμῖν, γραμματεῖς καὶ Φαρισαῖοι ὑποκριταί,
WOE TO YOU°, SCRIBES AND PHARISEES, HYPOCRITES,

ὅτι ἀποδεκατοῦτε τὸ ἡδύοσμον καὶ τὸ ἄνηθον καὶ τὸ
FOR YOU° TITHE THE MINT AND THE DILL AND THE

κύμινον καὶ ἀφήκατε τὰ βαρύτερα τοῦ
CUMIN AND YOU° HAVE NEGLECTED THE MORE IMPORTANT [THINGS] OF THE

νόμου, τὴν κρίσιν καὶ τὸ ἔλεος καὶ τὴν πίστιν·
LAW, - JUSTICE AND - MERCY AND - FAITH.

ταῦτα [δὲ] ἔδει ποιῆσαι κἀκεῖνα μὴ ἀφιέναι.
BUT~THESE THINGS IT WAS NECESSARY TO DO AND THOSE NOT TO NEGLECT.

23.24 ὁδηγοὶ τυφλοί, οἱ διϋλίζοντες τὸν κώνωπα,
BLIND~LEADERS, THE ONES FILTERING OUT THE GNAT,

τὴν δὲ κάμηλον καταπίνοντες.
BUT~THE CAMEL SWALLOWING.

23.25 Οὐαὶ ὑμῖν, γραμματεῖς καὶ Φαρισαῖοι ὑποκριταί,
WOE TO YOU°, SCRIBES AND PHARISEES, HYPOCRITES,

ὅτι καθαρίζετε τὸ ἔξωθεν τοῦ ποτηρίου καὶ τῆς
FOR YOU° CLEANSE THE OUTSIDE OF THE CUP AND THE

παροψίδος, ἔσωθεν δὲ γέμουσιν ἐξ ἁρπαγῆς καὶ
DISH, BUT~INSIDE THEY ARE FULL OF GREED AND

ἀκρασίας. **23.26** Φαρισαῖε τυφλέ, καθάρισον πρῶτον τὸ
SELF-INDULGENCE. BLIND~PHARISEE, FIRST~CLEANSE THE

ἐντὸς τοῦ ποτηρίου, ἵνα γένηται καὶ τὸ ἐκτὸς αὐτοῦ
INSIDE OF THE CUP, THAT MAY BE ALSO THE OUTSIDE OF IT

καθαρόν.
CLEAN.

23.27 Οὐαὶ ὑμῖν, γραμματεῖς καὶ Φαρισαῖοι ὑποκριταί,
WOE TO YOU°, SCRIBES AND PHARISEES, HYPOCRITES,

ὅτι παρομοιάζετε τάφοις κεκονιαμένοις, οἵτινες
FOR YOU° ARE LIKE GRAVES HAVING BEEN WHITEWASHED, WHICH

ἔξωθεν μὲν φαίνονται ὡραῖοι, ἔσωθεν δὲ γέμουσιν
ON THE OUTSIDE INDEED APPEAR BEAUTIFUL, BUT~ON THE INSIDE ARE FULL

ὀστέων νεκρῶν καὶ πάσης ἀκαθαρσίας. **23.28** οὕτως
OF [THE] BONES OF DEAD PERSONS AND EVERY KIND OF IMPURITY. THUS

καὶ ὑμεῖς ἔξωθεν μὲν φαίνεσθε τοῖς ἀνθρώποις
ALSO YOU° ON THE OUTSIDE INDEED APPEAR - TO MEN

δίκαιοι, ἔσωθεν δέ ἐστε μεστοὶ ὑποκρίσεως καὶ
RIGHTEOUS, BUT~ON THE INSIDE YOU° ARE FULL OF HYPOCRISY AND

ἀνομίας.
LAWLESSNESS.

23.29 Οὐαὶ ὑμῖν, γραμματεῖς καὶ Φαρισαῖοι ὑποκριταί,
WOE TO YOU°, SCRIBES AND PHARISEES HYPOCRITES,

ὅτι οἰκοδομεῖτε τοὺς τάφους τῶν προφητῶν καὶ
FOR YOU° BUILD THE GRAVES OF THE PROPHETS AND

κοσμεῖτε τὰ μνημεῖα τῶν δικαίων, **23.30** καὶ λέγετε,
DECORATE THE MONUMENTS OF THE RIGHTEOUS ONES, AND YOU° SAY,

Εἰ ἤμεθα ἐν ταῖς ἡμέραις τῶν πατέρων ἡμῶν,
IF WE WERE IN THE DAYS OF THE FATHERS OF US,

οὐκ ἂν ἤμεθα   αὐτῶν κοινωνοὶ ἐν τῷ αἵματι τῶν
WE WOULD NOT HAVE BEEN   PARTNERS~WITH THEM   IN   THE   BLOOD   OF THE

προφητῶν.   **23.31** ὥστε   μαρτυρεῖτε ἑαυτοῖς   ὅτι
PROPHETS.   THEREFORE   YOU° TESTIFY   TO YOURSELVES   THAT

υἱοί ἐστε   τῶν   φονευσάντων τοὺς προφήτας.
YOU° ARE~[THE] SONS OF THE ONES HAVING MURDERED   THE   PROPHETS.

23.32 καὶ ὑμεῖς πληρώσατε τὸ μέτρον τῶν πατέρων
AND   YOU°   FILL   THE MEASURE OF THE FATHERS

ὑμῶν.   **23.33** ὄφεις, γεννήματα ἐχιδνῶν, πῶς φύγητε
OF YOU°.   SNAKES, OFFSPRING   OF VIPERS,   HOW [CAN] YOU ESCAPE

ἀπὸ τῆς κρίσεως τῆς γεέννης;   **23.34** διὰ τοῦτο ἰδοὺ
FROM THE JUDGMENT   -   OF GEHENNA(HELL)?   FOR THIS REASON BEHOLD

ἐγὼ ἀποστέλλω πρὸς ὑμᾶς προφήτας καὶ σοφοὺς καὶ
I   SEND   TO   YOU°   PROPHETS   AND WISE MEN   AND

γραμματεῖς· ἐξ αὐτῶν ἀποκτενεῖτε καὶ σταυρώσετε καὶ
SCRIBES.   OF THEM   YOU° WILL KILL   AND   YOU° WILL CRUCIFY AND

ἐξ αὐτῶν μαστιγώσετε ἐν ταῖς συναγωγαῖς ὑμῶν καὶ
OF THEM   YOU° WILL WHIP   IN   THE   SYNAGOGUES   OF YOU°   AND

διώξετε   ἀπὸ πόλεως εἰς πόλιν·   **23.35** ὅπως
YOU° WILL DRIVE [THEM] OUT   FROM CITY   TO CITY.   SO

ἔλθῃ ἐφ' ὑμᾶς πᾶν αἷμα δίκαιον   ἐκχυννόμενον ἐπὶ
CAME   UPON YOU°   ALL [THE] RIGHTEOUS~BLOOD BEING SHED   UPON

τῆς γῆς ἀπὸ τοῦ αἵματος Ἅβελ τοῦ δικαίου ἕως τοῦ
THE EARTH FROM THE   BLOOD   OF ABEL   THE   RIGHTEOUS   TO   THE

αἵματος Ζαχαρίου υἱοῦ Βαραχίου, ὃν   ἐφονεύσατε
BLOOD   OF ZECHARIAH SON OF BARACHIAH, WHOM YOU° MURDERED

μεταξὺ τοῦ ναοῦ καὶ τοῦ θυσιαστηρίου.   **23.36** ἀμὴν
BETWEEN   THE TEMPLE AND THE ALTAR.   TRULY

λέγω ὑμῖν, ἥξει   ταῦτα πάντα ἐπὶ τὴν γενεὰν ταύτην.
I SAY TO YOU°, WILL COME ALL~THESE THINGS UPON   -   THIS~GENERATION.

23.37 Ἰερουσαλὴμ Ἰερουσαλήμ, ἡ   ἀποκτείνουσα
JERUSALEM   JERUSALEM,   THE ONE KILLING

τοὺς προφήτας καὶ λιθοβολοῦσα τοὺς   ἀπεσταλμένους
THE   PROPHETS   AND STONING   THE ONES HAVING BEEN SENT

πρὸς αὐτήν, ποσάκις ἠθέλησα ἐπισυναγαγεῖν τὰ τέκνα
TO   HER,   HOW OFTEN I WANTED TO GATHER   THE CHILDREN

σου, ὃν τρόπον ὄρνις ἐπισυνάγει τὰ νοσσία αὐτῆς
OF YOU, IN THE SAME WAY A HEN GATHERS   THE YOUNG ONES OF HER

ὑπὸ τὰς   πτέρυγας, καὶ οὐκ ἠθελήσατε.   **23.38** ἰδοὺ
UNDER THE(HER) WINGS,   AND YOU° WERE NOT WILLING.   BEHOLD

ἀφίεται ὑμῖν ὁ οἶκος ὑμῶν ⌜ἔρημος⌝.   **23.39** λέγω γὰρ
IS LEFT TO YOU° THE HOUSE OF YOU° DESOLATE.   FOR~I SAY

ὑμῖν, οὐ μή με ἴδητε   ἀπ' ἄρτι ἕως ἂν εἴπητε,
TO YOU°, BY NO MEANS [WILL] YOU° SEE~ME FROM NOW UNTIL   YOU° SAY,

Εὐλογημένος   ὁ   ἐρχόμενος ἐν ὀνόματι κυρίου.
HAVING BEEN BLESSED [IS] THE ONE COMING   IN [THE] NAME OF [THE] LORD.

we would not have taken part with them in shedding the blood of the prophets.' [31]Thus you testify against yourselves that you are descendants of those who murdered the prophets. [32]Fill up, then, the measure of your ancestors. [33]You snakes, you brood of vipers! How can you escape being sentenced to hell?[y] [34]Therefore I send you prophets, sages, and scribes, some of whom you will kill and crucify, and some you will flog in your synagogues and pursue from town to town, [35]so that upon you may come all the righteous blood shed on earth, from the blood of righteous Abel to the blood of Zechariah son of Barachiah, whom you murdered between the sanctuary and the altar. [36]Truly I tell you, all this will come upon this generation.

37 "Jerusalem, Jerusalem, the city that kills the prophets and stones those who are sent to it! How often have I desired to gather your children together as a hen gathers her brood under her wings, and you were not willing! [38]See, your house is left to you, desolate.[z] [39]For I tell you, you will not see me again until you say, 'Blessed is the one who comes in the name of the Lord.'"

[y] Gk *Gehenna*
[z] Other ancient authorities lack *desolate*

23:38 text [see Jer. 22:5]: KJV ASV RSV NASB NIV NEBmg TEV NJB NRSV. omit: ASVmg RSVmg NASBmg NEB NRSVmg.   **23:39** Ps. 118:26

CHAPTER 24

As Jesus came out of the temple and was going away, his disciples came to point out to him the buildings of the temple. ²Then he asked them, "You see all these, do you not? Truly I tell you, not one stone will be left here upon another; all will be thrown down."

3 When he was sitting on the Mount of Olives, the disciples came to him privately, saying, "Tell us, when will this be, and what will be the sign of your coming and of the end of the age?" ⁴Jesus answered them, "Beware that no one leads you astray. ⁵For many will come in my name, saying, 'I am the Messiah!'ᵃ and they will lead many astray. ⁶And you will hear of wars and rumors of wars; see that you are not alarmed; for this must take place, but the end is not yet. ⁷For nation will rise against nation, and kingdom against kingdom, and there will be faminesᵇ and earthquakes in various places; ⁸all this is but the beginning of the birth pangs.

9 "Then they will hand you over to be tortured and will put you to death, and you will be hated by all nations because of my name. ¹⁰Then many will fall away,ᶜ and they will betray one another

ᵃ Or the Christ
ᵇ Other ancient authorities add and pestilences
ᶜ Or stumble

24.1 Καὶ   ἐξελθὼν   ὁ Ἰησοῦς ἀπὸ τοῦ ἱεροῦ
AND   HAVING GONE OUT -   JESUS   FROM THE TEMPLE

ἐπορεύετο, καὶ προσῆλθον οἱ μαθηταὶ αὐτοῦ ἐπιδεῖξαι
HE WENT,   AND APPROACHED THE DISCIPLES OF HIM TO SHOW

αὐτῷ τὰς οἰκοδομὰς τοῦ ἱεροῦ. **24.2** ὁ δὲ ἀποκριθεὶς
HIM THE BUILDINGS OF THE TEMPLE.   BUT~HE HAVING ANSWERED

εἶπεν αὐτοῖς, Οὐ βλέπετε ταῦτα πάντα; ἀμὴν λέγω
SAID   TO THEM, DO YOU° NOT SEE ALL~THESE THINGS? TRULY I SAY

ὑμῖν, οὐ μὴ ἀφεθῇ   ὧδε λίθος ἐπὶ λίθον ὃς
TO YOU°, BY NO MEANS WILL BE LEFT HERE A STONE UPON A STONE WHICH

οὐ καταλυθήσεται.
WILL NOT BE DEMOLISHED.

24.3 Καθημένου δὲ αὐτοῦ ἐπὶ τοῦ Ὄρους τῶν Ἐλαιῶν
AND~[WHILE] HE WAS SITTING ON THE MOUNT - OF OLIVES

προσῆλθον αὐτῷ οἱ μαθηταὶ κατ' ἰδίαν λέγοντες, Εἰπὲ
APPROACHED HIM THE DISCIPLES PRIVATELY SAYING, TELL

ἡμῖν πότε ταῦτα   ἔσται καὶ τί   τὸ σημεῖον τῆς
US   WHEN THESE THINGS WILL BE AND WHAT THE SIGN   -

σῆς παρουσίας καὶ συντελείας τοῦ αἰῶνος; **24.4** καὶ
OF YOUR COMING   AND OF [THE] CLOSING OF THE AGE?   AND

ἀποκριθεὶς ὁ Ἰησοῦς εἶπεν αὐτοῖς, Βλέπετε
HAVING ANSWERED - JESUS   SAID   TO THEM, SEE TO IT [THAT]

μή τις   ὑμᾶς πλανήσῃ· **24.5** πολλοὶ γὰρ ἐλεύσονται
SOMEONE~[DOES] NOT DECEIVE~YOU°,   FOR~MANY   WILL COME

ἐπὶ τῷ ὀνόματί μου λέγοντες, Ἐγώ εἰμι ὁ Χριστός,
IN   THE NAME   OF ME SAYING,   I   AM THE CHRIST,

καὶ πολλοὺς πλανήσουσιν. **24.6** μελλήσετε δὲ ἀκούειν
AND THEY WILL DECEIVE~MANY.   BUT~YOU° ARE ABOUT TO HEAR

πολέμους καὶ ἀκοὰς πολέμων· ὁρᾶτε   μὴ θροεῖσθε·
OF WARS   AND RUMORS OF WARS.   SEE TO IT [THAT] YOU° ARE NOT ALARMED.

δεῖ γὰρ   γενέσθαι, ἀλλ' οὔπω ἐστὶν τὸ τέλος.
FOR~IT IS NECESSARY [FOR THIS] TO HAPPEN, BUT IT IS~NOT YET THE END.

24.7 ἐγερθήσεται γὰρ ἔθνος ἐπὶ ἔθνος καὶ βασιλεία
FOR~WILL BE RAISED UP NATION AGAINST NATION AND KINGDOM

ἐπὶ βασιλείαν καὶ ἔσονται λιμοὶ καὶ σεισμοὶ
AGAINST KINGDOM   AND THERE WILL BE FAMINES AND EARTHQUAKES

κατὰ τόπους· **24.8** πάντα δὲ ταῦτα   ἀρχὴ
IN PLACE AFTER PLACE.   BUT~ALL   THESE THINGS [ARE] [THE] BEGINNING

ὠδίνων.   **24.9** τότε παραδώσουσιν ὑμᾶς εἰς θλῖψιν καὶ
OF BIRTH PAINS.   THEN THEY WILL HAND OVER YOU° TO AFFLICTION AND

ἀποκτενοῦσιν ὑμᾶς, καὶ ἔσεσθε μισούμενοι ὑπὸ πάντων
THEY WILL KILL YOU°,   AND YOU WILL BE HATED   BY   ALL

τῶν ἐθνῶν διὰ   τὸ ὄνομά μου. **24.10** καὶ τότε
THE NATIONS ON ACCOUNT OF THE NAME OF ME.   AND THEN

σκανδαλισθήσονται πολλοὶ καὶ ἀλλήλους παραδώσουσιν
MANY~WILL BE LED INTO SIN   AND OTHERS   THEY WILL HAND OVER

καὶ μισήσουσιν ἀλλήλους· **24.11** καὶ πολλοὶ
AND   THEY WILL HATE   OTHERS.   AND   MANY

ψευδοπροφῆται ἐγερθήσονται καὶ πλανήσουσιν πολλούς·
FALSE PROPHETS   WILL ARISE   AND   THEY WILL DECEIVE   MANY.

24.12 καὶ διὰ   τὸ πληθυνθῆναι τὴν ἀνομίαν
AND   BECAUSE OF THE   INCREASED   -   LAWLESSNESS

ψυγήσεται ἡ ἀγάπη τῶν πολλῶν. **24.13** ὁ δὲ
WILL BECOME COLD THE LOVE   -   OF MANY.   BUT~THE ONE

ὑπομείνας εἰς τέλος οὗτος σωθήσεται. **24.14** καὶ
HAVING ENDURED TO [THE] END, THIS ONE WILL BE SAVED.   AND

κηρυχθήσεται τοῦτο τὸ εὐαγγέλιον τῆς βασιλείας ἐν
WILL BE ANNOUNCED THIS   -   GOOD NEWS   OF THE   KINGDOM   IN

ὅλῃ τῇ οἰκουμένῃ εἰς μαρτύριον πᾶσιν τοῖς ἔθνεσιν,
ALL   THE WORLD   AS A TESTIMONY TO ALL   THE   NATIONS,

καὶ τότε ἥξει τὸ τέλος.
AND   THEN WILL COME THE END.

24.15 Ὅταν οὖν ἴδητε τὸ βδέλυγμα τῆς ἐρημώσεως
THEREFORE~WHEN YOU° SEE THE ABOMINATION   -   OF DESOLATION

τὸ   ῥηθὲν διὰ   Δανιὴλ τοῦ προφήτου ἑστὸς   ἐν
THE THING SPOKEN THROUGH DANIEL   THE   PROPHET,   HAVING STOOD IN

τόπῳ ἁγίῳ, ὁ   ἀναγινώσκων νοείτω,   **24.16** τότε
[THE] HOLY~PLACE, THE ONE READING   LET HIM UNDERSTAND,   THEN

οἱ   ἐν τῇ Ἰουδαίᾳ φευγέτωσαν εἰς τὰ ὄρη,
THE ONES IN   -   JUDEA   LET THEM FLEE   TO   THE MOUNTAINS,

24.17 ὁ   ἐπὶ τοῦ δώματος μὴ καταβάτω   ἆραι
THE ONE UPON THE   ROOF   LET HIM NOT COME DOWN TO CARRY AWAY

τὰ   ἐκ τῆς οἰκίας αὐτοῦ, **24.18** καὶ ὁ   ἐν τῷ
THE THINGS FROM THE HOUSE   OF HIM,   AND   THE ONE IN   THE

ἀγρῷ μὴ ἐπιστρεψάτω ὀπίσω ἆραι   τὸ ἱμάτιον
FIELD   DO NOT LET HIM TURN BACK BEHIND TO CARRY AWAY THE GARMENT

αὐτοῦ. **24.19** οὐαὶ δὲ ταῖς   ἐν γαστρὶ ἐχούσαις καὶ
OF HIM.   BUT~WOE TO THE ONES   [WHO ARE] PREGNANT   AND

ταῖς θηλαζούσαις ἐν ἐκείναις ταῖς ἡμέραις.
THE ONES WITH NURSING BABIES IN THOSE   -   DAYS.

24.20 προσεύχεσθε δὲ ἵνα μὴ γένηται ἡ φυγὴ ὑμῶν
BUT~PRAY   THAT MAY NOT BE   THE ESCAPE OF YOU°

χειμῶνος μηδὲ σαββάτῳ. **24.21** ἔσται γὰρ τότε
IN WINTER   NOR   ON [THE] SABBATH.   FOR~WILL BE   THEN

θλῖψις μεγάλη οἵα   οὐ γέγονεν ἀπ᾽ ἀρχῆς
GREAT~TRIBULATION   SUCH AS HAS NOT BEEN   FROM [THE] BEGINNING

κόσμου   ἕως τοῦ νῦν οὐδ᾽ οὐ μὴ γένηται.
OF [THE] WORLD UNTIL   -   NOW   NOR   WILL IT BY ANY MEANS HAPPEN AGAIN.

24.22 καὶ εἰ μὴ ἐκολοβώθησαν αἱ ἡμέραι ἐκεῖναι,
AND   IF WERE NOT CUT SHORT   -   THOSE~DAYS

οὐκ ἂν ἐσώθη πᾶσα σάρξ· διὰ δὲ   τοὺς ἐκλεκτοὺς
NOT WOULD BE SAVED ALL   FLESH.   BUT~ON ACCOUNT OF THE CHOSEN ONES

κολοβωθήσονται αἱ ἡμέραι ἐκεῖναι. **24.23** τότε ἐάν
WILL BE CUT SHORT   -   THOSE~DAYS.   THEN   IF

and hate one another. [11]And
many false prophets will
arise and lead many astray.
[12]And because of the
increase of lawlessness, the
love of many will grow cold.
[13]But the one who endures to
the end will be saved. [14]And
this good news[d] of the
kingdom will be proclaimed
throughout the world, as a
testimony to all the nations;
and then the end will come.

15 "So when you see the
desolating sacrilege standing
in the holy place, as was
spoken of by the prophet
Daniel (let the reader
understand), [16]then those in
Judea must flee to the
mountains; [17]the one on the
housetop must not go down
to take what is in the house;
[18]the one in the field must
not turn back to get a coat.
[19]Woe to those who are
pregnant and to those who
are nursing infants in those
days! [20]Pray that your flight
may not be in winter or on a
sabbath. [21]For at that time
there will be great suffering,
such as has not been from
the beginning of the world
until now, no, and never will
be. [22]And if those days had
not been cut short, no one
would be saved; but for the
sake of the elect those days
will be cut short. [23]Then if

[d] Or gospel

anyone says to you, 'Look! Here is the Messiah!'*e* or 'There he is!'—do not believe it. [24]For false messiahs*f* and false prophets will appear and produce great signs and omens, to lead astray, if possible, even the elect. [25]Take note, I have told you beforehand. [26]So, if they say to you, 'Look! He is in the wilderness,' do not go out. If they say, 'Look! He is in the inner rooms,' do not believe it. [27]For as the lightning comes from the east and flashes as far as the west, so will be the coming of the Son of Man. [28]Wherever the corpse is, there the vultures will gather.

29 "Immediately after the suffering of those days

the sun will be darkened,
and the moon will not
give its light;
the stars will fall from
heaven,
and the powers of
heaven will be
shaken.

[30]Then the sign of the Son of Man will appear in heaven, and then all the tribes of the earth will mourn, and they will see 'the Son of Man coming on the clouds of heaven' with power and great glory. [31]And he will send out his angels with a loud trumpet call, and they

e Or *the Christ*
f Or *christs*

τις   ὑμῖν εἴπῃ, Ἰδοὺ ὧδε   ὁ Χριστός, ἤ, Ὧδε,
SOMEONE SAYS~TO YOU°, BEHOLD HERE [IS] THE CHRIST,   OR, HERE,

μὴ πιστεύσητε·   **24.24** ἐγερθήσονται γὰρ ψευδόχριστοι
DO NOT BELIEVE [THEM].   FOR~WILL ARISE   FALSE CHRISTS

καὶ ψευδοπροφῆται καὶ δώσουσιν σημεῖα μεγάλα καὶ
AND   FALSE PROPHETS   AND THEY WILL GIVE GREAT~SIGNS   AND

τέρατα ὥστε πλανῆσαι, εἰ δυνατόν, καὶ τοὺς ἐκλεκτούς.
WONDERS SO AS TO DECEIVE,   IF POSSIBLE, EVEN THE CHOSEN ONES.

24.25 ἰδοὺ προείρηκα   ὑμῖν. **24.26** ἐὰν οὖν
     BEHOLD I HAVE TOLD BEFOREHAND YOU°.   IF   THEREFORE

εἴπωσιν ὑμῖν, Ἰδοὺ ἐν τῇ ἐρήμῳ ἐστίν, μὴ ἐξέλθητε·
THEY SAY TO YOU°, BEHOLD IN THE DESERT HE IS, DO NOT GO OUT [THERE].

Ἰδοὺ ἐν τοῖς ταμείοις, μὴ πιστεύσητε· **24.27** ὥσπερ γὰρ
BEHOLD IN THE INNER ROOMS, DO NOT BELIEVE [THEM].   FOR~AS

ἡ ἀστραπὴ ἐξέρχεται ἀπὸ ἀνατολῶν καὶ φαίνεται
THE LIGHTNING   GOES OUT   FROM   [THE] EAST   AND   SHINES

ἕως   δυσμῶν, οὕτως ἔσται ἡ παρουσία τοῦ υἱοῦ τοῦ
AS FAR AS [THE] WEST, THUS WILL BE THE COMING   OF THE SON   -

ἀνθρώπου· **24.28** ὅπου ἐὰν ᾖ   τὸ πτῶμα, ἐκεῖ
OF MAN.   WHEREVER MAY BE THE CORPSE, THERE

συναχθήσονται   οἱ ἀετοί.
WILL BE GATHERED TOGETHER THE VULTURES.

24.29 Εὐθέως δὲ   μετὰ τὴν θλῖψιν τῶν
          AND~IMMEDIATELY AFTER THE TRIBULATION -

ἡμερῶν ἐκείνων
OF THOSE~DAYS

ὁ ἥλιος σκοτισθήσεται,
THE SUN   WILL BE DARKENED,

καὶ ἡ σελήνη οὐ δώσει τὸ φέγγος αὐτῆς,
AND THE MOON WILL NOT GIVE THE LIGHT OF IT,

καὶ οἱ ἀστέρες πεσοῦνται ἀπὸ τοῦ οὐρανοῦ,
AND THE STARS WILL FALL FROM   -   HEAVEN,

καὶ αἱ δυνάμεις τῶν οὐρανῶν σαλευθήσονται.
AND THE POWERS OF THE HEAVENS WILL BE SHAKEN.

24.30 καὶ τότε φανήσεται τὸ σημεῖον τοῦ υἱοῦ τοῦ
        AND THEN WILL APPEAR THE SIGN   OF THE SON -

ἀνθρώπου ἐν οὐρανῷ, καὶ τότε κόψονται πᾶσαι αἱ
OF MAN   IN HEAVEN,   AND THEN WILL MOURN ALL   THE

φυλαὶ τῆς γῆς καὶ ὄψονται τὸν υἱὸν τοῦ ἀνθρώπου
TRIBES OF THE EARTH AND THEY WILL SEE THE SON   -   OF MAN

ἐρχόμενον ἐπὶ τῶν νεφελῶν τοῦ οὐρανοῦ μετὰ δυνάμεως
COMING   ON THE CLOUDS   -   OF HEAVEN WITH   POWER

καὶ δόξης πολλῆς· **24.31** καὶ ἀποστελεῖ τοὺς ἀγγέλους
AND GREAT~GLORY·   AND HE WILL SEND THE ANGELS

αὐτοῦ μετὰ σάλπιγγος μεγάλης, καὶ ἐπισυνάξουσιν
OF HIM WITH   A LOUD~TRUMPET CALL,   AND THEY WILL GATHER TOGETHER

24:30 Dan. 7:13

τοὺς ἐκλεκτοὺς αὐτοῦ ἐκ τῶν τεσσάρων ἀνέμων ἀπ'
THE CHOSEN ONES OF HIM FROM THE FOUR   WINDS   FROM

ἄκρων οὐρανῶν   ἕως [τῶν] ἄκρων αὐτῶν.
[ONE] END OF [THE] HEAVENS TO THE [OTHER] END OF IT.

24.32 Ἀπὸ δὲ τῆς συκῆς μάθετε τὴν παραβολήν· ὅταν
AND~FROM THE FIG TREE LEARN   THE PARABLE: WHEN

ἤδη ὁ κλάδος αὐτῆς γένηται ἀπαλὸς καὶ τὰ
ALREADY THE BRANCH OF IT HAS BECOME TENDER AND -

φύλλα ἐκφύῃ, γινώσκετε ὅτι ἐγγὺς τὸ θέρος·
IT SPROUTS~LEAVES, YOU° KNOW THAT ²[IS] NEAR - ¹SUMMER.

24.33 οὕτως καὶ ὑμεῖς, ὅταν ἴδητε πάντα ταῦτα
THUS   ALSO YOU°, WHEN YOU° SEE ALL   THESE THINGS

γινώσκετε ὅτι ἐγγύς ἐστιν ἐπὶ θύραις. **24.34** ἀμὴν
YOU° KNOW THAT IT IS~NEAR AT [THE] DOORS.   TRULY

λέγω ὑμῖν ὅτι οὐ μὴ παρέλθῃ   ἡ γενεὰ αὕτη ἕως ἂν
I SAY TO YOU° - WILL BY NO MEANS PASS AWAY - THIS~GENERATION UNTIL

πάντα ταῦτα   γένεται. **24.35** ὁ οὐρανὸς καὶ ἡ γῆ
ALL   THESE THINGS COME ABOUT.   - HEAVEN   AND - EARTH

παρελεύσεται, οἱ δὲ λόγοι μου οὐ μὴ παρέλθωσιν.
WILL PASS AWAY, BUT~THE WORDS OF ME WILL BY NO MEANS PASS AWAY.

24.36 Περὶ δὲ   τῆς ἡμέρας ἐκείνης καὶ ὥρας οὐδεὶς
BUT~CONCERNING - THAT~DAY   AND HOUR NO ONE

οἶδεν, οὐδὲ οἱ ἄγγελοι τῶν οὐρανῶν ⌐οὐδὲ ὁ υἱός⌐,
KNOWS, NEITHER THE ANGELS OF THE HEAVENS NOR THE SON,

εἰ μὴ ὁ πατὴρ μόνος. **24.37** ὥσπερ γὰρ αἱ ἡμέραι
EXCEPT THE FATHER ALONE.   FOR~AS   IN THE DAYS

τοῦ Νῶε, οὕτως ἔσται ἡ παρουσία τοῦ υἱοῦ τοῦ
- OF NOAH, THUS WILL BE THE COMING OF THE SON -

ἀνθρώπου. **24.38** ὡς γὰρ ἦσαν ἐν ταῖς
OF MAN.   FOR~AS THEY WERE IN -

ἡμέραις [ἐκείναις] ταῖς πρὸ τοῦ κατακλυσμοῦ
THOSE~DAYS   -   BEFORE THE FLOOD

τρώγοντες καὶ πίνοντες, γαμοῦντες καὶ γαμίζοντες,
EATING   AND DRINKING, AND~MARRYING AND BEING GIVEN IN MARRIAGE,

ἄχρι ἧς ἡμέρας εἰσῆλθεν Νῶε εἰς τὴν κιβωτόν,
UNTIL [THE] DAY [WHEN] ENTERED NOAH INTO THE ARK,

24.39 καὶ οὐκ ἔγνωσαν ἕως ἦλθεν ὁ κατακλυσμὸς καὶ
AND THEY DID NOT KNOW UNTIL CAME THE FLOOD   AND

ἦρεν ἅπαντας, οὕτως ἔσται [καὶ] ἡ παρουσία τοῦ
TOOK AWAY EVERYTHING, THUS WILL BE ALSO THE COMING OF THE

υἱοῦ τοῦ ἀνθρώπου. **24.40** τότε δύο ἔσονται ἐν τῷ
SON -   OF MAN.   THEN TWO MEN WILL BE IN THE

ἀγρῷ, εἷς παραλαμβάνεται καὶ εἷς ἀφίεται·
FIELD, ONE IS TAKEN   AND ONE IS LEFT.

24.41 δύο   ἀλήθουσαι ἐν τῷ μύλῳ, μία
TWO WOMEN ARE GRINDING IN THE MILL HOUSE, ONE

---

will gather his elect from the four winds, from one end of heaven to the other.

32 "From the fig tree learn its lesson: as soon as its branch becomes tender and puts forth its leaves, you know that summer is near. ³³So also, when you see all these things, you know that he[g] is near, at the very gates. ³⁴Truly I tell you, this generation will not pass away until all these things have taken place. ³⁵Heaven and earth will pass away, but my words will not pass away.

36 "But about that day and hour no one knows, neither the angels of heaven, nor the Son,[h] but only the Father. ³⁷For as the days of Noah were, so will be the coming of the Son of Man. ³⁸For as in those days before the flood they were eating and drinking, marrying and giving in marriage, until the day Noah entered the ark, ³⁹and they knew nothing until the flood came and swept them all away, so too will be the coming of the Son of Man. ⁴⁰Then two will be in the field; one will be taken and one will be left. ⁴¹Two women will be grinding meal together; one

[g] Or it
[h] Other ancient authorities lack nor the Son

24:36 text [see Mark 13:32]: ASV RSV NASB NIV NEB TEV NJB NRSV. omit: KJV ASVmg RSVmg NIVmg TEVmg NJBmg NRSVmg.

will be taken and one will be left. [42]Keep awake therefore, for you do not know on what day[i] your Lord is coming. [43]But understand this: if the owner of the house had known in what part of the night the thief was coming, he would have stayed awake and would not have let his house be broken into. [44]Therefore you also must be ready, for the Son of Man is coming at an unexpected hour.

[45]"Who then is the faithful and wise slave, whom his master has put in charge of his household, to give the other slaves[j] their allowance of food at the proper time? [46]Blessed is that slave whom his master will find at work when he arrives. [47]Truly I tell you, he will put that one in charge of all his possessions. [48]But if that wicked slave says to himself, 'My master is delayed,' [49]and he begins to beat his fellow slaves, and eats and drinks with drunkards, [50]the master of that slave will come on a day when he does not expect him and at an hour that he does not know. [51]He will cut him in pieces[k] and put him with the hypocrites, where there will be weeping and gnashing of teeth.

[i] Other ancient authorities read *at what hour*
[j] Gk. *to give them*
[k] Or *cut him off*

παραλαμβάνεται καὶ μία ἀφίεται. **24.42** γρηγορεῖτε οὖν,
IS TAKEN   AND   ONE   IS LEFT.   SO~BE ON GUARD,

ὅτι   οὐκ οἴδατε   ποίᾳ   ἡμέρᾳ ὁ   κύριος ὑμῶν
BECAUSE   YOU° DO NOT KNOW ON WHICH DAY   THE LORD   OF YOU°

ἔρχεται. **24.43** ἐκεῖνο δὲ γινώσκετε ὅτι   εἰ ᾔδει   ὁ
COMES.   AND~THAT   YOU° KNOW   SO THAT IF HAD KNOWN THE

οἰκοδεσπότης ποίᾳ   φυλακῇ ὁ   κλέπτης ἔρχεται,
HOUSE MASTER   IN WHICH WATCH   THE THIEF   IS COMING,

ἐγρηγόρησεν ἂν   καὶ οὐκ ἂν εἴασεν   διορυχθῆναι τὴν
HE WOULD HAVE STAYED AWAKE AND   WOULD NOT HAVE ALLOWED TO BE DUG THROUGH THE

οἰκίαν αὐτοῦ. **24.44** διὰ τοῦτο   καὶ ὑμεῖς γίνεσθε
HOUSE   OF HIM.   FOR THIS REASON ALSO   YOU°   BE

ἕτοιμοι, ὅτι ᾗ   οὐ δοκεῖτε   ὥρᾳ   ὁ υἱὸς τοῦ
READY,   FOR ²WHEN ³YOU° DO NOT THINK ¹IN [THE] HOUR THE SON   -

ἀνθρώπου ἔρχεται.
OF MAN   COMES.

24.45 Τίς ἄρα ἐστὶν ὁ   πιστὸς δοῦλος καὶ φρόνιμος
          WHO THEN IS   THE FAITHFUL   SLAVE   AND WISE

ὃν   κατέστησεν ὁ   κύριος ἐπὶ τῆς οἰκετείας
WHOM APPOINTED   THE   MASTER   OVER THE   SLAVE OF THE HOUSEHOLD

αὐτοῦ τοῦ δοῦναι αὐτοῖς τὴν τροφὴν ἐν καιρῷ;
OF HIM - TO GIVE   TO THEM   -   FOOD   AT [THE] PROPER TIME?

24.46 μακάριος ὁ   δοῦλος ἐκεῖνος ὃν   ἐλθὼν   ὁ
          BLESSED [IS]   -   THAT~SLAVE   WHOM [WHEN] HAVING COME THE

κύριος αὐτοῦ εὑρήσει οὕτως ποιοῦντα· **24.47** ἀμὴν λέγω
MASTER   OF HIM   FINDS   SO   DOING.   TRULY I SAY

ὑμῖν ὅτι ἐπὶ πᾶσιν τοῖς ὑπάρχουσιν αὐτοῦ καταστήσει
TO YOU° THAT OVER ALL   THE   POSSESSIONS   OF HIM   HE WILL APPOINT

αὐτόν. **24.48** ἐὰν δὲ εἴπῃ ὁ κακὸς δοῦλος ἐκεῖνος ἐν τῇ
HIM.   BUT~IF ⁴SAYS - ²WICKED ³SLAVE ¹THAT   IN   THE

καρδίᾳ αὐτοῦ, Χρονίζει μου ὁ κύριος, **24.49** καὶ ἄρξηται
HEART   OF HIM,   IS LINGERING MY - MASTER,   AND   HE BEGINS

τύπτειν τοὺς συνδούλους αὐτοῦ, ἐσθίῃ δὲ καὶ πίνῃ μετὰ
TO BEAT   THE   FELLOW SLAVES   OF HIM,   AND~HE EATS AND   DRINKS WITH

τῶν   μεθυόντων, **24.50** ἥξει   ὁ   κύριος τοῦ
THE ONES BEING DRUNK,   WILL COME THE MASTER   -

δούλου ἐκείνου ἐν ἡμέρᾳ ᾗ   οὐ προσδοκᾷ καὶ ἐν ὥρᾳ
OF THAT~SLAVE   ON   A DAY   WHICH HE DOES NOT EXPECT AND   AT   AN HOUR

ᾗ   οὐ γινώσκει, **24.51** καὶ διχοτομήσει αὐτὸν καὶ τὸ
WHICH HE DOES NOT KNOW,   AND   HE WILL CUT IN TWO HIM   AND   THE

μέρος αὐτοῦ μετὰ τῶν ὑποκριτῶν θήσει· ἐκεῖ ἔσται ὁ
PORTION OF HIM WITH   THE   HYPOCRITES   HE WILL PUT.   THERE WILL BE   -

κλαυθμὸς καὶ ὁ βρυγμὸς τῶν ὀδόντων.
WEEPING   AND   - GRINDING   OF THE TEETH.

25.1 Τότε ὁμοιωθήσεται ἡ βασιλεία τῶν οὐρανῶν
　　　　THEN　WILL BE COMPARED　THE　KINGDOM　OF THE　HEAVENS

δέκα παρθένοις, αἵτινες λαβοῦσαι τὰς λαμπάδας
TO TEN　VIRGINS,　　　WHO　　HAVING TAKEN　THE　LAMPS

ἑαυτῶν ἐξῆλθον εἰς ὑπάντησιν τοῦ νυμφίου.
OF THEM　WENT OUT　TO　MEET　　　　THE　BRIDEGROOM.

25.2 πέντε δὲ ἐξ αὐτῶν ἦσαν μωραὶ καὶ πέντε
　　　　NOW~FIVE　OF THEM　WERE　FOOLISH　AND　FIVE [WERE]

φρόνιμοι. **25.3** αἱ γὰρ μωραὶ λαβοῦσαι τὰς λαμπάδας
WISE.　　　　　FOR~THE　FOOLISH　HAVING TAKEN　-　LAMPS

αὐτῶν οὐκ ἔλαβον μεθ᾽ ἑαυτῶν ἔλαιον. **25.4** αἱ δὲ
OF THEM　DID NOT TAKE　WITH　THEM　OIL.　　　　　　BUT~THE

φρόνιμοι ἔλαβον ἔλαιον ἐν τοῖς ἀγγείοις μετὰ τῶν
WISE ONES　TOOK　OIL　IN　-　CONTAINERS　WITH　THE

λαμπάδων ἑαυτῶν. **25.5** χρονίζοντος δὲ τοῦ νυμφίου
LAMPS　　　OF THEM.　　　NOW~BEING DELAYED　THE　BRIDEGROOM,

ἐνύσταξαν πᾶσαι καὶ ἐκάθευδον.
ALL [OF THE VIRGINS]~BECAME DROWSY AND　WERE SLEEPING.

25.6 μέσης δὲ νυκτὸς κραυγὴ γέγονεν, Ἰδοὺ ὁ νυμφίος,
AND~AT MIDNIGHT　　　THERE WAS~A SHOUT,　　BEHOLD THE BRIDEGROOM,

ἐξέρχεσθε εἰς ἀπάντησιν [αὐτοῦ]. **25.7** τότε ἠγέρθησαν
GO OUT　　　TO　MEET　　　　HIM.　　　　　THEN　AWAKENED

πᾶσαι αἱ παρθένοι ἐκεῖναι καὶ ἐκόσμησαν τὰς
ALL　-　THOSE~VIRGINS　　AND　THEY TRIMMED　THE

λαμπάδας ἑαυτῶν. **25.8** αἱ δὲ μωραὶ ταῖς φρονίμοις
LAMPS　　　OF THEM.　　　BUT~THE FOOLISH　TO THE　WISE

εἶπαν, Δότε ἡμῖν ἐκ τοῦ ἐλαίου ὑμῶν, ὅτι αἱ
SAID,　GIVE　US　FROM THE　OIL　　OF YOU°, FOR　THE

λαμπάδες ἡμῶν σβέννυνται. **25.9** ἀπεκρίθησαν δὲ αἱ
LAMPS　　　OF US　ARE GOING OUT.　　BUT~ANSWERED　　THE

φρόνιμοι λέγουσαι, Μήποτε οὐ μὴ ἀρκέσῃ ἡμῖν καὶ
WISE ONES　SAYING,　　CERTAINLY　THERE WOULD NOT BE ENOUGH FOR US　AND

ὑμῖν· πορεύεσθε μᾶλλον πρὸς τοὺς πωλοῦντας καὶ
FOR YOU°.　INSTEAD~GO　　　TO　THE ONES SELLING　　AND

ἀγοράσατε ἑαυταῖς. **25.10** ἀπερχομένων δὲ αὐτῶν
BUY　　　　FOR YOURSELVES.　　AND~[AS] THEY WERE GOING AWAY

ἀγοράσαι ἦλθεν ὁ νυμφίος, καὶ αἱ ἕτοιμοι
TO BUY,　　CAME　THE BRIDEGROOM, AND　THE ONES PREPARED

εἰσῆλθον μετ᾽ αὐτοῦ εἰς τοὺς γάμους καὶ
ENTERED　WITH　HIM　INTO THE　WEDDING CELEBRATION AND

ἐκλείσθη ἡ θύρα. **25.11** ὕστερον δὲ ἔρχονται καὶ αἱ
WAS SHUT　THE DOOR.　　　AND~LATER　COME　　ALSO　THE

λοιπαὶ παρθένοι λέγουσαι, Κύριε κύριε, ἄνοιξον
OTHER　VIRGINS　SAYING,　　LORD,　LORD,　OPEN [THE DOOR]

ἡμῖν. **25.12** ὁ δὲ ἀποκριθεὶς εἶπεν, Ἀμὴν λέγω ὑμῖν,
FOR US.　　　BUT~HE HAVING ANSWERED SAID,　TRULY　I SAY　TO YOU°,

"Then the kingdom of heaven will be like this. Ten bridesmaids[l] took their lamps and went to meet the bridegroom.[m] 2Five of them were foolish, and five were wise. 3When the foolish took their lamps, they took no oil with them; 4but the wise took flasks of oil with their lamps. 5As the bridegroom was delayed, all of them became drowsy and slept. 6But at midnight there was a shout, 'Look! Here is the bridegroom! Come out to meet him.' 7Then all those bridesmaids[l] got up and trimmed their lamps. 8The foolish said to the wise, 'Give us some of your oil, for our lamps are going out.' 9But the wise replied, 'No! there will not be enough for you and for us; you had better go to the dealers and buy some for yourselves.' 10And while they went to buy it, the bridegroom came, and those who were ready went with him into the wedding banquet; and the door was shut. 11Later the other bridesmaids[l] came also, saying, 'Lord, lord, open to us.' 12But he replied, 'Truly I tell you,

[l] Gk virgins
[m] Other ancient authorities add and the bride

I do not know you.' ¹³Keep awake therefore, for you know neither the day nor the hour.ⁿ

14 "For it is as if a man, going on a journey, summoned his slaves and entrusted his property to them; ¹⁵to one he gave five talents,ᵒ to another two, to another one, to each according to his ability. Then he went away. ¹⁶The one who had received the five talents went off at once and traded with them, and made five more talents. ¹⁷In the same way, the one who had the two talents made two more talents. ¹⁸But the one who had received the one talent went off and dug a hole in the ground and hid his master's money. ¹⁹After a long time the master of those slaves came and settled accounts with them. ²⁰Then the one who had received the five talents came forward, bringing five more talents, saying, 'Master, you handed over to me five talents; see, I have made five more talents.' ²¹His master said to him, 'Well done, good and trustworthy slave; you have been trustworthy in a few things, I will put you in charge of many things; enter into the joy of your master.' ²²And the one with the two talents also came forward, saying, 'Master, you handed over to me two talents; see, I have made two more talents.' ²³His master said to him, 'Well done, good

ⁿ Other ancient authorities add *in which the Son of Man is coming*
ᵒ A talent was worth more than fifteen years' wages of a laborer

---

οὐκ οἶδα ὑμᾶς.　**25.13** Γρηγορεῖτε οὖν,　ὅτι
I DO NOT KNOW YOUᵒ.　　　　　BE ON THE ALERT　THEREFORE,　FOR

οὐκ οἴδατε　τὴν ἡμέραν οὐδὲ τὴν ὥραν.
YOUᵒ DO NOT KNOW　THE　DAY　　NOR　THE　HOUR.

25.14 Ὥσπερ γὰρ ἄνθρωπος ἀποδημῶν　ἐκάλεσεν
　　　　　FOR~AS　　A MAN　　GOING ON A JOURNEY　CALLED

τοὺς ἰδίους δούλους καὶ παρέδωκεν αὐτοῖς τὰ
TO HIS OWN　SLAVES　AND　HANDED OVER　TO THEM　THE

ὑπάρχοντα αὐτοῦ,　**25.15** καὶ　ᾧ μὲν　ἔδωκεν πέντε
POSSESSIONS　OF HIM,　　　AND　TO THIS ONE HE GAVE　FIVE

τάλαντα, ᾧ δὲ　　δύο, ᾧ δὲ　　ἓν, ἑκάστῳ κατὰ
TALENTS,　AND~TO THIS ONE TWO,　AND~TO THIS ONE ONE,　EACH　ACCORDING TO

τὴν ἰδίαν δύναμιν, καὶ ἀπεδήμησεν.　εὐθέως
-　HIS OWN ABILITY,　AND　WENT ON [HIS] JOURNEY.　IMMEDIATELY

25.16 πορευθεὶς ὁ　τὰ πέντε τάλαντα λαβὼν
　　　　HAVING GONE　THE ONE THE FIVE　TALENTS　HAVING RECEIVED

ἠργάσατο ἐν αὐτοῖς καὶ ἐκέρδησεν ἄλλα πέντε·
WORKED　WITH THEM　AND　GAINED　　FIVE~OTHERS.

25.17 ὡσαύτως ὁ　　　　τὰ δύο ἐκέρδησεν
　　　　LIKEWISE　THE ONE [HAVING RECEIVED] THE TWO GAINED

ἄλλα δύο.　**25.18** ὁ δὲ　τὸ ἓν　λαβὼν
TWO~OTHERS.　　　　BUT~THE ONE THE ONE [TALENT] HAVING RECEIVED,

ἀπελθὼν ὤρυξεν γῆν　καὶ ἔκρυψεν τὸ ἀργύριον
HAVING GONE OUT DUG　IN [THE] GROUND AND　HID　　THE MONEY

τοῦ κυρίου αὐτοῦ.　**25.19** μετὰ δὲ πολὺν χρόνον ἔρχεται
OF THE MASTER OF HIM.　　　AND~AFTER MUCH TIME　COMES

ὁ κύριος τῶν δούλων ἐκείνων καὶ συναίρει λόγον μετ᾽
THE MASTER　-　OF THOSE~SLAVES　AND SETTLES ACCOUNTS WITH

αὐτῶν.　**25.20** καὶ προσελθὼν ὁ　τὰ πέντε τάλαντα
THEM.　　　AND　HAVING APPROACHED THE ONE THE FIVE　TALENTS

λαβὼν　προσήνεγκεν ἄλλα πέντε τάλαντα λέγων,
HAVING RECEIVED BROUGHT　　FIVE~MORE　TALENTS　SAYING,

Κύριε, πέντε τάλαντά μοι παρέδωκας·　ἴδε ἄλλα πέντε
MASTER, FIVE　TALENTS YOU GAVE~TO ME.　　SEE,　FIVE~MORE

τάλαντα ἐκέρδησα.　**25.21** ἔφη αὐτῷ ὁ κύριος αὐτοῦ,
TALENTS　I GAINED.　　　SAID TO HIM THE MASTER OF HIM,

Εὖ,　δοῦλε ἀγαθὲ καὶ πιστέ, ἐπὶ ὀλίγα　ἦς
WELL DONE, SLAVE GOOD　AND FAITHFUL, OVER A FEW THINGS YOU WERE

πιστός, ἐπὶ πολλῶν σε καταστήσω·　εἴσελθε εἰς τὴν
FAITHFUL, OVER MANY THINGS I WILL APPOINT~YOU.　ENTER　INTO THE

χαρὰν τοῦ κυρίου σου.　**25.22** προσελθὼν [δὲ] καὶ
JOY　OF THE MASTER OF YOU.　　AND~HAVING APPROACHED ALSO

ὁ　τὰ δύο τάλαντα　εἶπεν, Κύριε, δύο τάλαντά
THE ONE THE TWO TALENTS [HAVING RECEIVED] SAID,　MASTER, TWO TALENTS

μοι παρέδωκας·　ἴδε ἄλλα δύο τάλαντα ἐκέρδησα.
YOU GAVE~TO ME.　SEE, TWO~MORE　TALENTS　I GAINED.

25.23 ἔφη αὐτῷ ὁ κύριος αὐτοῦ, Εὖ,　δοῦλε ἀγαθὲ
　　　　SAID TO HIM THE MASTER OF HIM, WELL DONE, SLAVE GOOD

καὶ   πιστέ,   ἐπὶ   ὀλίγα   ἧς   πιστός,   ἐπὶ   πολλῶν
AND   FAITHFUL,   OVER   A FEW THINGS   YOU WERE   FAITHFUL,   OVER   MANY THINGS

σε   καταστήσω·   εἴσελθε   εἰς   τὴν   χαρὰν   τοῦ   κυρίου
I WILL APPOINT~YOU.   ENTER   INTO   THE   JOY   OF THE   MASTER

σου.   **25.24** προσελθὼν δὲ   καὶ   ὁ   τὸ   ἓν   τάλαντον
OF YOU.   AND~HAVING APPROACHED   ALSO   THE ONE   THE   ONE   TALENT

εἰληφὼς   εἶπεν,   Κύριε,   ἔγνων   σε   ὅτι   σκληρὸς   εἶ
HAVING RECEIVED   SAID,   MASTER,   I KNEW   THAT~YOU   ARE~A HARD

ἄνθρωπος,   θερίζων   ὅπου   οὐκ   ἔσπειρας   καὶ   συνάγων
MAN,   REAPING   WHERE   YOU DID NOT SOW   AND   GATHERING

ὅθεν   οὐ   διεσκόρπισας,   **25.25** καὶ   φοβηθεὶς
FROM WHICH   YOU DID NOT SCATTER,   AND   HAVING BEEN AFRAID [AND]

ἀπελθὼν   ἔκρυψα   τὸ   τάλαντόν   σου   ἐν   τῇ   γῇ·   ἴδε
HAVING GONE AWAY   I HID   THE   TALENT   OF YOU   IN   THE   GROUND.   SEE,

ἔχεις   τὸ   σόν.   **25.26** ἀποκριθεὶς δὲ   ὁ   κύριος
YOU HAVE   THAT WHICH [IS]   YOURS.   AND~HAVING ANSWERED,   THE   MASTER

αὐτοῦ   εἶπεν   αὐτῷ,   Πονηρὲ   δοῦλε   καὶ   ὀκνηρέ,
OF HIM   SAID   TO HIM,   WICKED   SLAVE   AND   LAZY,

ᾔδεις   ὅτι   θερίζω   ὅπου   οὐκ   ἔσπειρα   καὶ   συνάγω
[SO] YOU KNEW   THAT   I REAP   WHERE   I DID NOT SOW   AND   I GATHER

ὅθεν   οὐ   διεσκόρπισα;   **25.27** ἔδει   σε   οὖν
FROM WHICH   I DID NOT SCATTER?   IT WAS NECESSARY   FOR YOU   THEN

βαλεῖν   τὰ   ἀργύριά   μου   τοῖς   τραπεζίταις,   καὶ
TO DEPOSIT   THE   MONEY   OF ME   WITH THE   BANKERS,   AND

ἐλθὼν   ἐγὼ   ἐκομισάμην   ἂν   τὸ   ἐμὸν   σὺν
HAVING COME   I   WOULD HAVE RECEIVED BACK   THAT WHICH [WAS]   MINE   WITH

τόκῳ.   **25.28** ἄρατε   οὖν   ἀπ᾽   αὐτοῦ   τὸ   τάλαντον   καὶ
INTEREST.   TAKE   THEREFORE   FROM   HIM   THE   TALENT   AND

δότε   τῷ   ἔχοντι   τὰ   δέκα   τάλαντα·   **25.29** τῷ   γὰρ
GIVE [IT]   TO THE ONE   HAVING   THE   TEN   TALENTS.   FOR~TO

ἔχοντι   παντὶ   δοθήσεται   καὶ   περισσευθήσεται,
EVERYONE~HAVING   IT WILL BE GIVEN   AND   HE WILL HAVE AN ABUNDANCE,

τοῦ δὲ   μὴ   ἔχοντος   καὶ   ὃ   ἔχει   ἀρθήσεται   ἀπ᾽
BUT~FROM THE ONE   NOT HAVING   EVEN   WHAT   HE HAS   WILL BE TAKEN   FROM

αὐτοῦ.   **25.30** καὶ   τὸν   ἀχρεῖον   δοῦλον   ἐκβάλετε   εἰς   τὸ
HIM.   AND   THE   USELESS   SLAVE   THROW   INTO   THE

σκότος   τὸ   ἐξώτερον·   ἐκεῖ   ἔσται   ὁ   κλαυθμὸς   καὶ   ὁ
²DARKNESS   -   ¹OUTER.   THERE   WILL BE   -   WEEPING   AND   -

βρυγμὸς   τῶν   ὀδόντων.
GRINDING   OF THE   TEETH.

25.31 Ὅταν   δὲ   ἔλθῃ   ὁ   υἱὸς   τοῦ   ἀνθρώπου   ἐν   τῇ   δόξῃ
AND~WHEN   COMES   THE   SON   -   OF MAN   IN   THE   GLORY

αὐτοῦ   καὶ   πάντες   οἱ   ἄγγελοι   μετ᾽   αὐτοῦ,   τότε   καθίσει
OF HIM   AND   ALL   THE   ANGELS   WITH   HIM,   THEN   HE WILL SIT

ἐπὶ   θρόνου   δόξης   αὐτοῦ·   **25.32** καὶ   συναχθήσονται
UPON   [THE] THRONE   OF GLORY   OF HIM.   AND   WILL BE ASSEMBLED

ἔμπροσθεν   αὐτοῦ   πάντα   τὰ   ἔθνη,   καὶ   ἀφορίσει
BEFORE   HIM   ALL   THE   NATIONS,   AND   HE WILL SEPARATE

and trustworthy slave; you have been trustworthy in a few things, I will put you in charge of many things; enter into the joy of your master.' [24]Then the one who had received the one talent also came forward, saying, 'Master, I knew that you were a harsh man, reaping where you did not sow, and gathering where you did not scatter seed; [25]so I was afraid, and I went and hid your talent in the ground. Here you have what is yours.' [26]But his master replied, 'You wicked and lazy slave! You knew, did you, that I reap where I did not sow, and gather where I did not scatter? [27]Then you ought to have invested my money with the bankers, and on my return I would have received what was my own with interest. [28]So take the talent from him, and give it to the one with the ten talents. [29]For to all those who have, more will be given, and they will have an abundance; but from those who have nothing, even what they have will be taken away. [30]As for this worthless slave, throw him into the outer darkness, where there will be weeping and gnashing of teeth.'

31 "When the Son of Man comes in his glory, and all the angels with him, then he will sit on the throne of his glory. [32]All the nations will be gathered before him, and he will separate

people one from another as a shepherd separates the sheep from the goats, 33and he will put the sheep at his right hand and the goats at the left. 34Then the king will say to those at his right hand, 'Come, you that are blessed by my Father, inherit the kingdom prepared for you from the foundation of the world; 35for I was hungry and you gave me food, I was thirsty and you gave me something to drink, I was a stranger and you welcomed me, 36I was naked and you gave me clothing, I was sick and you took care of me, I was in prison and you visited me.' 37Then the righteous will answer him, 'Lord, when was it that we saw you hungry and gave you food, or thirsty and gave you something to drink? 38And when was it that we saw you a stranger and welcomed you, or naked and gave you clothing? 39And when was it that we saw you sick or in prison and visited you?' 40And the king will answer them, 'Truly I tell you, just as you did it to one of the least of these who are members of my family,p you did it to me.' 41Then he will say to those at his left hand, 'You that are accursed, depart from me into the eternal fire prepared for the devil and his angels; 42for I was hungry and you gave me no food, I was thirsty and you gave me nothing to drink,

p Gk these my brothers

αὐτοὺς ἀπ' ἀλλήλων, ὥσπερ ὁ ποιμὴν ἀφορίζει τὰ
THEM   FROM EACH OTHER, AS THE SHEPHERD SEPARATES THE

πρόβατα ἀπὸ τῶν ἐρίφων, 25.33 καὶ στήσει τὰ μὲν
SHEEP   FROM THE GOATS,   AND HE WILL PUT THE -

πρόβατα ἐκ δεξιῶν αὐτοῦ, τὰ δὲ ἐρίφια ἐξ εὐωνύμων.
SHEEP ON [THE] RIGHT OF HIM, BUT~THE GOATS ON [THE] LEFT.

25.34 τότε ἐρεῖ ὁ βασιλεὺς τοῖς ἐκ δεξιῶν αὐτοῦ,
    THEN WILL SAY THE KING TO THE ONES ON [THE] RIGHT OF HIM,

Δεῦτε οἱ εὐλογημένοι τοῦ πατρός μου,
COME THE ONES HAVING BEEN BLESSED OF THE FATHER OF ME,

κληρονομήσατε τὴν ἡτοιμασμένην ὑμῖν βασιλείαν ἀπὸ
INHERIT   THE HAVING BEEN PREPARED FOR YOU° KINGDOM FROM

καταβολῆς κόσμου. 25.35 ἐπείνασα γὰρ καὶ ἐδώκατέ
[THE] FOUNDATION OF [THE] WORLD.   FOR~I HUNGERED AND YOU° GAVE

μοι φαγεῖν, ἐδίψησα καὶ ἐποτίσατέ με, ξένος ἤμην
TO ME TO EAT, I THIRSTED AND YOU° GAVE DRINK TO ME, I WAS~A STRANGER

καὶ συνηγάγετέ με, 25.36 γυμνὸς καὶ περιεβάλετέ με,
AND YOU° INVITED IN ME,   NAKED AND YOU° CLOTHED ME,

ἠσθένησα καὶ ἐπεσκέψασθέ με, ἐν φυλακῇ ἤμην καὶ
I WAS SICK AND YOU° VISITED ME, IN PRISON I WAS AND

ἤλθατε πρός με. 25.37 τότε ἀποκριθήσονται αὐτῷ οἱ
YOU° CAME TO ME.   THEN ANSWERED HIM THE

δίκαιοι λέγοντες, Κύριε, πότε σε εἴδομεν πεινῶντα
RIGHTEOUS ONES SAYING, MASTER, WHEN DID WE SEE~YOU HUNGERING

καὶ ἐθρέψαμεν, ἢ διψῶντα καὶ ἐποτίσαμεν;
AND WE FED [YOU], OR THIRSTING AND WE GAVE [YOU] DRINK?

25.38 πότε δέ σε εἴδομεν ξένον καὶ συνηγάγομεν, ἢ
    AND~WHEN DID WE SEE~YOU A STRANGER AND INVITE [YOU] IN, OR

γυμνὸν καὶ περιεβάλομεν; 25.39 πότε δέ σε εἴδομεν
NAKED AND WE CLOTHED [YOU]?   AND~WHEN DID WE SEE~YOU

ἀσθενοῦντα ἢ ἐν φυλακῇ καὶ ἤλθομεν πρός σε;
HAVING SICKNESS OR IN PRISON AND WE CAME TO YOU?

25.40 καὶ ἀποκριθεὶς ὁ βασιλεὺς ἐρεῖ αὐτοῖς, Ἀμὴν
    AND HAVING ANSWERED THE KING WILL SAY TO THEM, TRULY

λέγω ὑμῖν, ἐφ' ὅσον ἐποιήσατε ἑνὶ τούτων τῶν
I SAY TO YOU°, IN AS MUCH AS YOU° DID [IT] TO ONE OF THESE OF THE

ἀδελφῶν μου τῶν ἐλαχίστων, ἐμοὶ ἐποιήσατε.
BROTHERS OF ME THE LEAST, YOU° DID [IT]~TO ME.

25.41 Τότε ἐρεῖ καὶ τοῖς ἐξ εὐωνύμων,
    THEN HE WILL SAY ALSO TO THE ONES ON [THE] LEFT [OF HIM],

Πορεύεσθε ἀπ' ἐμοῦ [οἱ] κατηραμένοι εἰς τὸ πῦρ τὸ
GO   FROM ME THE ONES HAVING BEEN CURSED INTO THE FIRE -

αἰώνιον τὸ ἡτοιμασμένον τῷ διαβόλῳ καὶ τοῖς
ETERNAL - HAVING BEEN PREPARED FOR THE DEVIL AND THE

ἀγγέλοις αὐτοῦ. 25.42 ἐπείνασα γὰρ καὶ οὐκ ἐδώκατέ
ANGELS OF HIM.   FOR~I HUNGERED AND YOU° DID NOT GIVE

μοι φαγεῖν, ἐδίψησα καὶ οὐκ ἐποτίσατέ με,
TO ME TO EAT, I THIRSTED AND YOU° DID NOT GIVE DRINK TO ME,

25.43 ξένος ἤμην καὶ οὐ συνηγάγετέ με, γυμνὸς καὶ
I WAS~A STRANGER AND YOU° DID NOT INVITE IN ME, NAKED AND

οὐ περιεβάλετέ με, ἀσθενὴς καὶ ἐν φυλακῇ καὶ
YOU° DID NOT CLOTHE ME, SICK AND IN PRISON AND

οὐκ ἐπεσκέψασθέ με. **25.44** τότε ἀποκριθήσονται καὶ
YOU° DID NOT VISIT ME. THEN WILL ANSWER ALSO

αὐτοὶ λέγοντες, Κύριε, πότε σε εἴδομεν πεινῶντα ἢ
THEY SAYING, LORD, WHEN DID WE SEE~YOU HUNGERING OR

διψῶντα ἢ ξένον ἢ γυμνὸν ἢ ἀσθενῆ ἢ ἐν φυλακῇ
THIRSTING OR A STRANGER OR NAKED OR SICK OR IN PRISON

καὶ οὐ διηκονήσαμέν σοι; **25.45** τότε ἀποκριθήσεται
AND WE DID NOT HELP YOU? THEN HE WILL ANSWER

αὐτοῖς λέγων, Ἀμὴν λέγω ὑμῖν, ἐφ᾽ ὅσον
THEM SAYING, TRULY I SAY TO YOU°, IN AS MUCH AS

οὐκ ἐποιήσατε ἑνὶ τούτων τῶν ἐλαχίστων, οὐδὲ ἐμοὶ
YOU° DID NOT DO [IT] FOR ONE OF THESE THE LEAST ONES, NEITHER FOR ME

ἐποιήσατε. **25.46** καὶ ἀπελεύσονται οὗτοι εἰς
DID YOU° DO [IT]. AND WILL GO AWAY THESE INTO

κόλασιν αἰώνιον, οἱ δὲ δίκαιοι εἰς ζωὴν αἰώνιον.
ETERNAL~PUNISHMENT, BUT~THE RIGHTEOUS ONES INTO ETERNAL~LIFE.

[43]I was a stranger and you did not welcome me, naked and you did not give me clothing, sick and in prison and you did not visit me.' [44]Then they also will answer, 'Lord, when was it that we saw you hungry or thirsty or a stranger or naked or sick or in prison, and did not take care of you?' [45]Then he will answer them, 'Truly I tell you, just as you did not do it to one of the least of these, you did not do it to me.' [46]And these will go away into eternal punishment, but the righteous into eternal life."

CHAPTER 26

26.1 Καὶ ἐγένετο ὅτε ἐτέλεσεν ὁ Ἰησοῦς πάντας
AND IT CAME ABOUT WHEN FINISHED - JESUS ALL

τοὺς λόγους τούτους, εἶπεν τοῖς μαθηταῖς αὐτοῦ,
- THESE~WORDS, HE SAID TO THE DISCIPLES OF HIM,

26.2 Οἴδατε ὅτι μετὰ δύο ἡμέρας τὸ πάσχα γίνεται,
YOU° KNOW THAT AFTER TWO DAYS THE PASSOVER TAKES PLACE,

καὶ ὁ υἱὸς τοῦ ἀνθρώπου παραδίδοται
AND THE SON - OF MAN IS HANDED OVER

εἰς τὸ σταυρωθῆναι. **26.3** Τότε συνήχθησαν οἱ ἀρχιερεῖς
TO BE CRUCIFIED. THEN WERE ASSEMBLED THE CHIEF PRIESTS

καὶ οἱ πρεσβύτεροι τοῦ λαοῦ εἰς τὴν αὐλὴν τοῦ
AND THE ELDERS OF THE PEOPLE IN THE PALACE OF THE

ἀρχιερέως τοῦ λεγομένου Καϊάφα **26.4** καὶ
HIGH PRIEST, THE ONE BEING CALLED CAIAPHAS, AND

συνεβουλεύσαντο ἵνα τὸν Ἰησοῦν δόλῳ κρατήσωσιν
THEY TOOK COUNSEL TOGETHER THAT - JESUS BY A TRAP THEY MIGHT ARREST

καὶ ἀποκτείνωσιν· **26.5** ἔλεγον δέ, Μὴ ἐν τῇ
AND MIGHT KILL. BUT~THEY WERE SAYING, NOT DURING THE

ἑορτῇ, ἵνα μὴ θόρυβος γένηται ἐν τῷ λαῷ.
FEAST, LEST A DISTURBANCE OCCURS AMONG THE PEOPLE.

26.6 Τοῦ δὲ Ἰησοῦ γενομένου ἐν Βηθανίᾳ ἐν οἰκίᾳ
- AND JESUS BEING IN BETHANY IN [THE] HOUSE

Σίμωνος τοῦ λεπροῦ, **26.7** προσῆλθεν αὐτῷ γυνὴ
OF SIMON THE LEPER, APPROACHED HIM A WOMAN

When Jesus had finished saying all these things, he said to his disciples, [2]"You know that after two days the Passover is coming, and the Son of Man will be handed over to be crucified."

3 Then the chief priests and the elders of the people gathered in the palace of the high priest, who was called Caiaphas, [4]and they conspired to arrest Jesus by stealth and kill him. [5]But they said, "Not during the festival, or there may be a riot among the people."

6 Now while Jesus was at Bethany in the house of Simon the leper,[q] [7]a woman came to him

[q] The terms leper and leprosy can refer to several diseases

with an alabaster jar of very costly ointment, and she poured it on his head as he sat at the table. ⁸But when the disciples saw it, they were angry and said, "Why this waste? ⁹For this ointment could have been sold for a large sum, and the money given to the poor." ¹⁰But Jesus, aware of this, said to them, "Why do you trouble the woman? She has performed a good service for me. ¹¹For you always have the poor with you, but you will not always have me. ¹²By pouring this ointment on my body she has prepared me for burial. ¹³Truly I tell you, wherever this good news* is proclaimed in the whole world, what she has done will be told in remembrance of her."

14 Then one of the twelve, who was called Judas Iscariot, went to the chief priests ¹⁵and said, "What will you give me if I betray him to you?" They paid him thirty pieces of silver. ¹⁶And from that moment he began to look for an opportunity to betray him.

17 On the first day of Unleavened Bread the disciples came to Jesus, saying, "Where do you want us to make the preparations for you to eat the Passover?" ¹⁸He said, "Go into the city to a certain man, and say to him, 'The Teacher says,

ʳ Or *gospel*

ἔχουσα ἀλάβαστρον μύρου βαρυτίμου καὶ κατέχεεν
HAVING   AN ALABASTER [FLASK] OF EXPENSIVE~OINTMENT AND SHE POURED [IT] OUT

ἐπὶ τῆς κεφαλῆς αὐτοῦ ἀνακειμένου.
UPON THE HEAD   OF HIM RECLINING AT THE TABLE.

26.8 ἰδόντες δὲ   οἱ μαθηταὶ ἠγανάκτησαν λέγοντες,
AND~HAVING SEEN [THIS] THE DISCIPLES WERE ANGRY   SAYING,

Εἰς τί   ἡ ἀπώλεια αὕτη; **26.9** ἐδύνατο γὰρ
FOR WHAT - THIS~WASTE?   FOR~IT WOULD HAVE BEEN POSSIBLE

τοῦτο πραθῆναι πολλοῦ καὶ δοθῆναι πτωχοῖς.
TO SELL~THIS   FOR MUCH AND TO GIVE [IT] TO [THE] POOR.

26.10 γνοὺς δὲ   ὁ Ἰησοῦς εἶπεν αὐτοῖς, Τί
AND~HAVING KNOWN [THIS] - JESUS   SAID TO THEM, WHY

κόπους παρέχετε τῇ   γυναικί; ἔργον γὰρ καλὸν
ARE YOU° CAUSING~TROUBLE FOR THE WOMAN? ³WORK ¹FOR ²A GOOD

ἠργάσατο εἰς ἐμέ· **26.11** πάντοτε γὰρ τοὺς πτωχοὺς
SHE DOES   TO ME.   FOR~ALWAYS   THE   POOR

ἔχετε μεθ' ἑαυτῶν, ἐμὲ δὲ οὐ πάντοτε ἔχετε·
YOU° HAVE WITH YOURSELVES, BUT~ME NOT ALWAYS DO YOU° HAVE.

26.12 βαλοῦσα γὰρ αὕτη   τὸ μύρον τοῦτο ἐπὶ τοῦ
³HAVING PUT ¹FOR ²THIS WOMAN - THIS~OINTMENT UPON THE

σώματός μου πρὸς τὸ ἐνταφιάσαι με ἐποίησεν.
BODY   OF ME IN ORDER TO PREPARE FOR BURIAL ME SHE DID [IT].

26.13 ἀμὴν λέγω ὑμῖν, ὅπου ἐὰν κηρυχθῇ τὸ
TRULY, I SAY TO YOU°, WHEREVER   IS PREACHED -

εὐαγγέλιον τοῦτο ἐν ὅλῳ   τῷ κόσμῳ, λαληθήσεται
THIS~GOOD NEWS   IN [THE] WHOLE - WORLD, IT WILL BE SPOKEN

καὶ ὃ ἐποίησεν αὕτη εἰς μνημόσυνον αὐτῆς.
ALSO WHAT THIS WOMAN~DID IN MEMORY   OF HER.

26.14 Τότε πορευθεὶς εἷς τῶν δώδεκα, ὁ λεγόμενος
THEN HAVING GONE ONE OF THE TWELVE, THE ONE BEING CALLED

Ἰούδας Ἰσκαριώτης, πρὸς τοὺς ἀρχιερεῖς **26.15** εἶπεν,
JUDAS ISCARIOT,   TO THE CHIEF PRIESTS   SAID,

Τί θέλετέ   μοι δοῦναι, κἀγὼ ὑμῖν παραδώσω αὐτόν;
WHAT ARE YOU° WILLING TO GIVE~ME, AND I TO YOU° WILL HAND OVER HIM?

οἱ δὲ ἔστησαν αὐτῷ τριάκοντα ἀργύρια. **26.16** καὶ
AND~THEY WEIGHED OUT FOR HIM THIRTY   PIECES OF SILVER.   AND

ἀπὸ τότε ἐζήτει   εὐκαιρίαν ἵνα αὐτὸν παραδῷ.
FROM THEN [ON] HE WAS SEEKING AN OPPORTUNITY THAT HE MIGHT HAND OVER~HIM.

26.17 Τῇ δὲ πρώτῃ τῶν ἀζύμων
BUT~ON THE FIRST [DAY] OF THE [FEAST] OF UNLEAVENED BREAD

προσῆλθον οἱ μαθηταὶ τῷ Ἰησοῦ λέγοντες, Ποῦ
APPROACHED THE DISCIPLES TO JESUS SAYING,   WHERE

θέλεις ἑτοιμάσωμέν σοι   φαγεῖν τὸ πάσχα;
DO YOU WISH WE SHOULD PREPARE FOR YOU TO EAT THE PASSOVER?

26.18 ὁ δὲ εἶπεν, Ὑπάγετε εἰς τὴν πόλιν πρὸς
AND~HE SAID,   GO   INTO THE CITY TO

τὸν δεῖνα καὶ εἴπατε αὐτῷ, Ὁ διδάσκαλος λέγει, Ὁ
SUCH A ONE AND SAY   TO HIM, THE TEACHER   SAYS, THE

καιρός μου ἐγγύς ἐστιν, πρὸς σὲ ποιῶ τὸ πάσχα
TIME   OF ME IS~NEAR,   WITH YOU I AM MAKING THE PASSOVER

μετὰ τῶν μαθητῶν μου. 26.19 καὶ ἐποίησαν οἱ
WITH THE DISCIPLES OF ME.   AND   DID   THE

μαθηταὶ ὡς συνέταξεν αὐτοῖς ὁ Ἰησοῦς καὶ
DISCIPLES AS COMMANDED THEM   - JESUS   AND

ἡτοίμασαν τὸ πάσχα. 26.20 Ὀψίας δὲ γενομένης
THEY PREPARED THE PASSOVER MEAL.   AND~[WHEN] EVENING CAME

ἀνέκειτο   μετὰ τῶν δώδεκα. 26.21 καὶ
HE WAS RECLINING AT TABLE WITH THE TWELVE.   AND

ἐσθιόντων αὐτῶν εἶπεν, Ἀμὴν λέγω ὑμῖν ὅτι εἷς ἐξ
[AS] THEY~WERE EATING HE SAID, TRULY I SAY TO YOU° THAT ONE OF

ὑμῶν παραδώσει με. 26.22 καὶ λυπούμενοι σφόδρα
YOU° WILL BETRAY ME.   AND   GRIEVING   GREATLY

ἤρξαντο λέγειν αὐτῷ εἷς ἕκαστος, Μήτι ἐγώ εἰμι,
THEY BEGAN TO SAY TO HIM EACH~ONE,   SURELY NOT I AM [THE ONE],

κύριε; 26.23 ὁ δὲ ἀποκριθεὶς εἶπεν, Ὁ ἐμβάψας
LORD?   BUT~HE HAVING ANSWERED SAID, THE ONE HAVING DIPPED

μετ᾽ ἐμοῦ τὴν χεῖρα ἐν τῷ τρυβλίῳ οὗτός
WITH ME   THE HAND IN THE BOWL   THIS ONE

με παραδώσει. 26.24 ὁ μὲν υἱὸς τοῦ ἀνθρώπου ὑπάγει
WILL BETRAY~ME.   INDEED~THE SON - OF MAN   IS GOING

καθὼς γέγραπται περὶ αὐτοῦ, οὐαὶ δὲ τῷ
JUST AS IT HAS BEEN WRITTEN CONCERNING HIM,   BUT~WOE -

ἀνθρώπῳ ἐκείνῳ δι᾽ οὗ ὁ υἱὸς τοῦ ἀνθρώπου
TO THAT~MAN   THROUGH WHOM THE SON - OF MAN

παραδίδοται· καλὸν ἦν αὐτῷ εἰ οὐκ ἐγεννήθη
IS BETRAYED.   IT WOULD HAVE BEEN~BETTER FOR HIM IF HAD NOT BEEN BORN

ὁ ἄνθρωπος ἐκεῖνος. 26.25 ἀποκριθεὶς δὲ Ἰούδας ὁ
- THAT~MAN.   AND~HAVING ANSWERED JUDAS THE ONE

παραδιδοὺς αὐτὸν εἶπεν, Μήτι ἐγώ εἰμι, ῥαββί;
BETRAYING   HIM   SAID, SURELY NOT I AM [THE ONE], RABBI?

λέγει αὐτῷ, Σὺ εἶπας.
HE SAYS TO HIM, YOU HAVE SAID [IT].

26.26 Ἐσθιόντων δὲ αὐτῶν λαβὼν ὁ Ἰησοῦς ἄρτον
      AND~[AS] THEY WERE EATING, ²HAVING TAKEN - ¹JESUS BREAD

καὶ εὐλογήσας ἔκλασεν καὶ δοὺς τοῖς μαθηταῖς
AND HAVING GIVEN THANKS HE BROKE [IT] AND GIVING [IT] TO THE DISCIPLES [AND]

εἶπεν, Λάβετε φάγετε, τοῦτό ἐστιν τὸ σῶμά μου.
SAID,   TAKE [AND] EAT,   THIS   IS   THE BODY OF ME.

26.27 καὶ λαβὼν ποτήριον καὶ εὐχαριστήσας ἔδωκεν
      AND HAVING TAKEN [THE] CUP AND HAVING GIVEN THANKS HE GAVE

αὐτοῖς λέγων, Πίετε ἐξ αὐτοῦ πάντες,
TO THEM SAYING, DRINK FROM IT   ALL [OF YOU°],

26.28 τοῦτο γάρ ἐστιν τὸ αἷμά μου τῆς ᵀ διαθήκης
      FOR~THIS   IS   THE BLOOD OF ME OF THE COVENANT

26:28 text [see Mark 14:24]: ASV RSV NASB NIV NEB TEV NJB NRSV. add καινης (new) [see Luke 22:20]: KJV ASVmg RSVmg NIVmg NJBmg NRSVmg.

My time is near; I will keep the Passover at your house with my disciples.' " [19]So the disciples did as Jesus had directed them, and they prepared the Passover meal.

20 When it was evening, he took his place with the twelve;[s] [21]and while they were eating, he said, "Truly I tell you, one of you will betray me." [22]And they became greatly distressed and began to say to him one after another, "Surely not I, Lord?" [23]He answered, "The one who has dipped his hand into the bowl with me will betray me. [24]The Son of Man goes as it is written of him, but woe to that one by whom the Son of Man is betrayed! It would have been better for that one not to have been born." [25]Judas, who betrayed him, said, "Surely not I, Rabbi?" He replied, "You have said so."

26 While they were eating, Jesus took a loaf of bread, and after blessing it he broke it, gave it to the disciples, and said, "Take, eat; this is my body." [27]Then he took a cup, and after giving thanks he gave it to them, saying, "Drink from it, all of you; [28]for this is my blood of the[t] covenant,

[s] Other ancient authorities add *disciples*

[t] Other ancient authorities add *new*

which is poured out for many for the forgiveness of sins. 29I tell you, I will never again drink of this fruit of the vine until that day when I drink it new with you in my Father's kingdom."

30 When they had sung the hymn, they went out to the Mount of Olives.

31 Then Jesus said to them, "You will all become deserters because of me this night; for it is written,

'I will strike the
    shepherd,
  and the sheep of the
    flock will be
    scattered.'

32But after I am raised up, I will go ahead of you to Galilee." 33Peter said to him, "Though all become deserters because of you, I will never desert you." 34Jesus said to him, "Truly I tell you, this very night, before the cock crows, you will deny me three times." 35Peter said to him, "Even though I must die with you, I will not deny you." And so said all the disciples.

36 Then Jesus went with them to a place called Gethsemane; and he said to his disciples,

τὸ   περὶ   πολλῶν ἐκχυννόμενον εἰς ἄφεσιν
THAT WHICH FOR   MANY   IS BEING SHED   FOR FORGIVENESS

ἁμαρτιῶν. **26.29** λέγω δὲ ὑμῖν,   οὐ μὴ πίω   ἀπ'
OF SINS.   AND~I SAY TO YOU°, I WILL BY NO MEANS DRINK FROM

ἄρτι ἐκ τούτου τοῦ γενήματος τῆς ἀμπέλου ἕως τῆς
NOW [ON] OF THIS   -   FRUIT   OF THE VINE   UNTIL -

ἡμέρας ἐκείνης ὅταν αὐτὸ πίνω μεθ' ὑμῶν καινὸν ἐν
THAT~DAY   WHEN I DRINK~IT WITH YOU°   NEW   IN

τῇ βασιλείᾳ τοῦ πατρός μου. **26.30** Καὶ ὑμνήσαντες
THE KINGDOM   OF THE FATHER OF ME.   AND HAVING SUNG A HYMN

ἐξῆλθον εἰς τὸ Ὄρος τῶν Ἐλαιῶν.
THEY WENT OUT TO THE MOUNT   -   OF OLIVES.

26.31 Τότε λέγει αὐτοῖς ὁ Ἰησοῦς, Πάντες ὑμεῖς
       THEN   SAYS   TO THEM - JESUS,   ALL   OF YOU°

σκανδαλισθήσεσθε ἐν ἐμοὶ ἐν   τῇ νυκτὶ ταύτῃ,
WILL BE OFFENDED   AT ME   DURING - THIS~NIGHT,

γέγραπται γάρ,
FOR~IT HAS BEEN WRITTEN,

     Πατάξω   τὸν ποιμένα,
     I WILL STRIKE DOWN THE SHEPHERD,

          καὶ διασκορπισθήσονται τὰ πρόβατα τῆς
          AND WILL BE SCATTERED   THE SHEEP   OF THE

          ποίμνης.
          FLOCK.

26.32 μετὰ δὲ τὸ ἐγερθῆναί με προάξω   ὑμᾶς εἰς
       BUT~AFTER I AM RAISED   I WILL GO AHEAD OF YOU° TO

τὴν Γαλιλαίαν. **26.33** ἀποκριθεὶς δὲ ὁ Πέτρος εἶπεν
 -   GALILEE.   AND~HAVING ANSWERED - PETER   SAID

αὐτῷ, Εἰ πάντες σκανδαλισθήσονται ἐν σοί, ἐγὼ
TO HIM, IF EVERYONE WILL BE OFFENDED   AT YOU,   I

οὐδέποτε σκανδαλισθήσομαι. **26.34** ἔφη αὐτῷ ὁ
NEVER   WILL BE OFFENDED.   SAID TO HIM -

Ἰησοῦς, Ἀμὴν λέγω σοι ὅτι ἐν   ταύτῃ τῇ νυκτὶ
JESUS,   TRULY I SAY TO YOU THAT DURING THIS - NIGHT

πρὶν ἀλέκτορα φωνῆσαι τρὶς   ἀπαρνήσῃ με.
BEFORE A COCK   CROWS   THREE TIMES YOU WILL DENY ME.

26.35 λέγει αὐτῷ ὁ Πέτρος, Κἂν δέῃ   με   σὺν
       SAYS TO HIM - PETER, EVEN IF IT IS NECESSARY FOR ME WITH

σοὶ ἀποθανεῖν, οὐ μὴ σε ἀπαρνήσομαι. ὁμοίως καὶ
YOU TO DIE,   BY NO MEANS WILL I DENY~YOU.   LIKEWISE ALSO

πάντες οἱ μαθηταὶ εἶπαν.
ALL   THE DISCIPLES SPOKE.

26.36 Τότε ἔρχεται μετ' αὐτῶν ὁ Ἰησοῦς εἰς χωρίον
       THEN COMES   WITH THEM   - JESUS   TO A PLACE

λεγόμενον Γεθσημανί καὶ λέγει τοῖς μαθηταῖς,
BEING CALLED GETHSEMANE AND HE SAYS TO THE DISCIPLES,

26:31 Zech. 13:7

Καθίσατε αὐτοῦ ἕως [οὗ] ἀπελθὼν ἐκεῖ προσεύξωμαι.
SIT HERE UNTIL HAVING LEFT THERE I MAY PRAY.

26.37 καὶ παραλαβὼν τὸν Πέτρον καὶ τοὺς δύο υἱοὺς
AND HAVING TAKEN - PETER AND THE TWO SONS

Ζεβεδαίου ἤρξατο λυπεῖσθαι καὶ ἀδημονεῖν. **26.38** τότε
OF ZEBEDEE HE BEGAN TO BE GRIEVED AND TO BE DISTRESSED. THEN

λέγει αὐτοῖς, Περίλυπός ἐστιν ἡ ψυχή μου ἕως
HE SAYS TO THEM, VERY SAD IS THE SOUL OF ME TO THE POINT OF

θανάτου· μείνατε ὧδε καὶ γρηγορεῖτε μετ' ἐμοῦ.
DEATH. REMAIN HERE AND KEEP AWAKE WITH ME.

26.39 καὶ προελθὼν μικρὸν ἔπεσεν ἐπὶ
AND HAVING GONE FORWARD A LITTLE HE FELL UPON

πρόσωπον αὐτοῦ προσευχόμενος καὶ λέγων, Πάτερ μου,
HIS FACE PRAYING AND SAYING, FATHER OF ME,

εἰ δυνατόν ἐστιν, παρελθάτω ἀπ' ἐμοῦ τὸ
IF IT IS~POSSIBLE, LET PASS FROM ME -

ποτήριον τοῦτο· πλὴν οὐχ ὡς ἐγὼ θέλω ἀλλ' ὡς
THIS~CUP. BUT NOT AS I WISH BUT AS

σύ. **26.40** καὶ ἔρχεται πρὸς τοὺς μαθητὰς καὶ
YOU [WISH]. AND HE COMES TO THE DISCIPLES AND

εὑρίσκει αὐτοὺς καθεύδοντας, καὶ λέγει τῷ Πέτρῳ,
HE FINDS THEM SLEEPING, AND HE SAYS - TO PETER,

Οὕτως οὐκ ἰσχύσατε μίαν ὥραν γρηγορῆσαι μετ'
SO WERE YOU° NOT STRONG ENOUGH [FOR] ONE HOUR TO BE AWAKE WITH

ἐμοῦ; **26.41** γρηγορεῖτε καὶ προσεύχεσθε, ἵνα μὴ
ME? STAY AWAKE AND PRAY, LEST

εἰσέλθητε εἰς πειρασμόν· τὸ μὲν πνεῦμα πρόθυμον
YOU° ENTER INTO TEMPTATION. INDEED~THE SPIRIT [IS] READY

ἡ δὲ σὰρξ ἀσθενής. **26.42** πάλιν ἐκ δευτέρου
BUT~THE FLESH [IS] WEAK. AGAIN FOR A SECOND [TIME]

ἀπελθὼν προσηύξατο λέγων, Πάτερ μου, εἰ
HAVING LEFT HE PRAYED SAYING, FATHER OF ME, IF

οὐ δύναται τοῦτο παρελθεῖν ἐὰν μὴ αὐτὸ πίω,
IT IS NOT POSSIBLE [FOR] THIS TO PASS AWAY EXCEPT I DRINK~IT,

γενηθήτω τὸ θέλημά σου. **26.43** καὶ ἐλθὼν πάλιν
LET BE DONE THE WILL OF YOU. AND HAVING COME AGAIN

εὗρεν αὐτοὺς καθεύδοντας, ἦσαν γὰρ αὐτῶν οἱ
HE FOUND THEM SLEEPING, FOR~WERE OF THEM THE

ὀφθαλμοὶ βεβαρημένοι. **26.44** καὶ ἀφεὶς αὐτοὺς
EYES HAVING BEEN WEIGHED DOWN. AND HAVING LEFT THEM

πάλιν ἀπελθὼν προσηύξατο ἐκ τρίτου τὸν
AGAIN [AND] HAVING GONE AWAY HE WAS PRAYING FOR [THE] THIRD [TIME] THE

αὐτὸν λόγον εἰπὼν πάλιν. **26.45** τότε ἔρχεται πρὸς
SAME THING HAVING SAID AGAIN. THEN HE COMES TO

τοὺς μαθητὰς καὶ λέγει αὐτοῖς, Καθεύδετε [τὸ]
THE DISCIPLES AND HE SAYS TO THEM, SLEEP -

λοιπὸν καὶ ἀναπαύεσθε· ἰδοὺ ἤγγικεν ἡ ὥρα καὶ
FROM NOW ON AND REST. BEHOLD HAS DRAWN NEAR THE HOUR AND

"Sit here while I go over there and pray." [37]He took with him Peter and the two sons of Zebedee, and began to be grieved and agitated. [38]Then he said to them, "I am deeply grieved, even to death; remain here, and stay awake with me." [39]And going a little farther, he threw himself on the ground and prayed, "My Father, if it is possible, let this cup pass from me; yet not what I want but what you want." [40]Then he came to the disciples and found them sleeping; and he said to Peter, "So, could you not stay awake with me one hour? [41]Stay awake and pray that you may not come into the time of trial;[u] the spirit indeed is willing, but the flesh is weak." [42]Again he went away for the second time and prayed, "My Father, if this cannot pass unless I drink it, your will be done." [43]Again he came and found them sleeping, for their eyes were heavy. [44]So leaving them again, he went away and prayed for the third time, saying the same words. [45]Then he came to the disciples and said to them, "Are you still sleeping and taking your rest? See, the hour is at hand, and

[u] Or *into temptation*

the Son of Man is betrayed into the hands of sinners. [46]Get up, let us be going. See, my betrayer is at hand."

47 While he was still speaking, Judas, one of the twelve, arrived; with him was a large crowd with swords and clubs, from the chief priests and the elders of the people. [48]Now the betrayer had given them a sign, saying, "The one I will kiss is the man; arrest him." [49]At once he came up to Jesus and said, "Greetings, Rabbi!" and kissed him. [50]Jesus said to him, "Friend, do what you are here to do." Then they came and laid hands on Jesus and arrested him. [51]Suddenly, one of those with Jesus put his hand on his sword, drew it, and struck the slave of the high priest, cutting off his ear. [52]Then Jesus said to him, "Put your sword back into its place; for all who take the sword will perish by the sword. [53]Do you think that I cannot appeal to my Father, and he will at once send me more than twelve legions of angels? [54]But how then would the scriptures be fulfilled, which say

ὁ υἱὸς τοῦ ἀνθρώπου παραδίδοται εἰς χεῖρας
THE SON - OF MAN IS BEING BETRAYED INTO [THE] HANDS

ἁμαρτωλῶν. **26.46** ἐγείρεσθε ἄγωμεν· ἰδοὺ ἤγγικεν
OF SINNERS. RISE UP [AND] LET US GO. BEHOLD HAS DRAWN NEAR

ὁ παραδιδούς με.
THE ONE BETRAYING ME.

26.47 Καὶ ἔτι αὐτοῦ λαλοῦντος ἰδοὺ Ἰούδας εἷς τῶν
AND YET [WHILE] HE [WAS] SPEAKING, BEHOLD JUDAS ONE OF THE

δώδεκα ἦλθεν καὶ μετ᾽ αὐτοῦ ὄχλος πολὺς μετὰ
TWELVE CAME AND WITH HIM A GREAT~CROWD WITH

μαχαιρῶν καὶ ξύλων ἀπὸ τῶν ἀρχιερέων καὶ
SWORDS AND CLUBS FROM THE CHIEF PRIESTS AND

πρεσβυτέρων τοῦ λαοῦ. **26.48** ὁ δὲ παραδιδοὺς
ELDERS OF THE PEOPLE. AND~THE ONE BETRAYING

αὐτὸν ἔδωκεν αὐτοῖς σημεῖον λέγων, Ὃν ἂν φιλήσω
HIM GAVE THEM A SIGN SAYING, WHOMEVER I MAY KISS

αὐτός ἐστιν, κρατήσατε αὐτόν. **26.49** καὶ εὐθέως
HE IS [THE ONE], ARREST HIM. AND IMMEDIATELY

προσελθὼν τῷ Ἰησοῦ εἶπεν, Χαῖρε, ῥαββί, καὶ
HAVING APPROACHED - JESUS HE SAID, HELLO, RABBI, AND

κατεφίλησεν αὐτόν. **26.50** ὁ δὲ Ἰησοῦς εἶπεν αὐτῷ,
HE KISSED HIM. - AND JESUS SAID TO HIM,

Ἑταῖρε, ἐφ᾽ ὃ πάρει. τότε προσελθόντες
FRIEND, [DO THAT] FOR WHICH YOU ARE COMING. THEN HAVING APPROACHED

ἐπέβαλον τὰς χεῖρας ἐπὶ τὸν Ἰησοῦν καὶ
THEY LAID THE (THEIR) HANDS ON - JESUS AND

ἐκράτησαν αὐτόν. **26.51** καὶ ἰδοὺ εἷς τῶν μετὰ
THEY ARRESTED HIM. AND BEHOLD ONE OF THE ONES WITH

Ἰησοῦ ἐκτείνας τὴν χεῖρα ἀπέσπασεν τὴν
JESUS HAVING STRETCHED OUT THE (HIS) HAND DREW THE

μάχαιραν αὐτοῦ καὶ πατάξας τὸν δοῦλον τοῦ
SWORD OF HIM AND HAVING STRUCK THE SERVANT OF THE

ἀρχιερέως ἀφεῖλεν αὐτοῦ τὸ ὠτίον. **26.52** τότε λέγει
HIGH PRIEST HE CUT OFF OF HIM THE EAR. THEN SAYS

αὐτῷ ὁ Ἰησοῦς, Ἀπόστρεψον τὴν μάχαιράν σου εἰς
TO HIM - JESUS, RETURN THE SWORD OF YOU INTO

τὸν τόπον αὐτῆς· πάντες γὰρ οἱ λαβόντες
THE PLACE OF IT, FOR~ALL THE ONES HAVING TAKEN

μάχαιραν ἐν μαχαίρῃ ἀπολοῦνται. **26.53** ἢ δοκεῖς
[THE] SWORD BY [THE] SWORD WILL DIE. OR DO YOU THINK

ὅτι οὐ δύναμαι παρακαλέσαι τὸν πατέρα μου, καὶ
THAT I AM NOT ABLE TO CALL UPON THE FATHER OF ME, AND

παραστήσει μοι ἄρτι πλείω δώδεκα λεγιῶνας ἀγγέλων;
HE WILL PROVIDE ME NOW MORE THAN TWELVE LEGIONS OF ANGELS?

26.54 πῶς οὖν πληρωθῶσιν αἱ γραφαὶ ὅτι οὕτως
HOW THEN MAY BE FULFILLED THE SCRIPTURES THAT [SAY] THUS

δεῖ   γενέσθαι; **26.55** Ἐν ἐκείνῃ τῇ ὥρᾳ εἶπεν ὁ
IT IS NECESSARY TO HAPPEN?   AT THAT   - TIME SAID -

Ἰησοῦς τοῖς ὄχλοις, Ὡς ἐπὶ λῃστὴν ἐξήλθατε
JESUS TO THE CROWDS, AS AGAINST A REVOLUTIONARY HAVE YOU° COME OUT

μετὰ μαχαιρῶν καὶ ξύλων συλλαβεῖν με; καθ' ἡμέραν
WITH SWORDS AND CLUBS TO ARREST ME? DAILY

ἐν τῷ ἱερῷ ἐκαθεζόμην διδάσκων καὶ οὐκ ἐκρατήσατέ
IN THE TEMPLE I WAS SITTING TEACHING AND YOU° DID NOT ARREST

με. **26.56** τοῦτο δὲ ὅλον γέγονεν ἵνα πληρωθῶσιν αἱ
ME.   BUT~THIS ALL HAPPENED THAT MIGHT BE FULFILLED THE

γραφαὶ τῶν προφητῶν. Τότε οἱ μαθηταὶ πάντες
SCRIPTURES OF THE PROPHETS. THEN THE DISCIPLES ALL

ἀφέντες αὐτὸν ἔφυγον.
HAVING LEFT HIM   FLED.

26.57 Οἱ δὲ κρατήσαντες τὸν Ἰησοῦν ἀπήγαγον
       BUT~THE ONES HAVING ARRESTED - JESUS LED [HIM] AWAY

πρὸς Καϊάφαν τὸν ἀρχιερέα, ὅπου οἱ γραμματεῖς
TO CAIAPHAS THE HIGH PRIEST, WHERE THE SCRIBES

καὶ οἱ πρεσβύτεροι συνήχθησαν. **26.58** ὁ δὲ Πέτρος
AND THE ELDERS WERE GATHERED TOGETHER.   - AND PETER

ἠκολούθει αὐτῷ ἀπὸ μακρόθεν ἕως τῆς αὐλῆς τοῦ
WAS FOLLOWING HIM FROM FAR AWAY AS FAR AS THE COURTYARD OF THE

ἀρχιερέως καὶ εἰσελθὼν ἔσω ἐκάθητο μετὰ τῶν
HIGH PRIEST AND HAVING ENTERED INSIDE HE WAS SITTING DOWN WITH THE

ὑπηρετῶν ἰδεῖν τὸ τέλος. **26.59** οἱ δὲ ἀρχιερεῖς καὶ τὸ
SERVANTS TO SEE THE OUTCOME.   AND~THE CHIEF PRIESTS AND THE

συνέδριον ὅλον ἐζήτουν ψευδομαρτυρίαν κατὰ τοῦ
SANHEDRIN ALL WERE SEEKING FALSE WITNESS AGAINST -

Ἰησοῦ ὅπως αὐτὸν θανατώσωσιν, **26.60** καὶ
JESUS SO THAT HIM THEY MIGHT PUT TO DEATH, AND

οὐχ εὗρον πολλῶν προσελθόντων ψευδομαρτύρων.
THEY DID NOT FIND MANY FALSE WITNESSES~HAVING APPROACHED.

ὕστερον δὲ προσελθόντες δύο **26.61** εἶπαν, Οὗτος ἔφη,
BUT~LATER HAVING APPROACHED TWO SAID, THIS ONE SAID,

Δύναμαι καταλῦσαι τὸν ναὸν τοῦ θεοῦ καὶ διὰ τριῶν
I AM ABLE TO DESTROY THE TEMPLE - OF GOD AND WITHIN THREE

ἡμερῶν οἰκοδομῆσαι. **26.62** καὶ ἀναστὰς ὁ ἀρχιερεὺς
DAYS TO BUILD [IT].   AND HAVING ARISEN THE HIGH PRIEST

εἶπεν αὐτῷ, Οὐδὲν ἀποκρίνῃ τί οὗτοί
SAID TO HIM, DO YOU ANSWER~NOTHING WHAT THESE MEN

σου καταμαρτυροῦσιν; **26.63** ὁ δὲ Ἰησοῦς ἐσιώπα. καὶ
TESTIFY AGAINST~YOU?   - BUT JESUS WAS SILENT. AND

ὁ ἀρχιερεὺς εἶπεν αὐτῷ, Ἐξορκίζω σε κατὰ τοῦ θεοῦ
THE HIGH PRIEST SAID TO HIM, I ADJURE YOU BY - GOD

τοῦ ζῶντος ἵνα ἡμῖν εἴπῃς εἰ σὺ εἶ ὁ Χριστὸς
THE ONE LIVING THAT TO US YOU TELL IF YOU ARE THE CHRIST,

it must happen in this way?" [55]At that hour Jesus said to the crowds, "Have you come out with swords and clubs to arrest me as though I were a bandit? Day after day I sat in the temple teaching, and you did not arrest me. [56]But all this has taken place, so that the scriptures of the prophets may be fulfilled." Then all the disciples deserted him and fled.

57 Those who had arrested Jesus took him to Caiaphas the high priest, in whose house the scribes and the elders had gathered. [58]But Peter was following him at a distance, as far as the courtyard of the high priest; and going inside, he sat with the guards in order to see how this would end. [59]Now the chief priests and the whole council were looking for false testimony against Jesus so that they might put him to death, [60]but they found none, though many false witnesses came forward. At last two came forward [61]and said, "This fellow said, 'I am able to destroy the temple of God and to build it in three days.'" [62]The high priest stood up and said, "Have you no answer? What is it that they testify against you?" [63]But Jesus was silent. Then the high priest said to him, "I put you under oath before the living God, tell us if you are the Messiah,[v]

[v] Or Christ

the Son of God." ⁶⁴Jesus said to him, "You have said so. But I tell you,

From now on you will see the Son of Man seated at the right hand of Power and coming on the clouds of heaven."

⁶⁵Then the high priest tore his clothes and said, "He has blasphemed! Why do we still need witnesses? You have now heard his blasphemy. ⁶⁶What is your verdict?" They answered, "He deserves death." ⁶⁷Then they spat in his face and struck him; and some slapped him, ⁶⁸saying, "Prophesy to us, you Messiah!^w Who is it that struck you?"

69 Now Peter was sitting outside in the courtyard. A servant-girl came to him and said, "You also were with Jesus the Galilean." ⁷⁰But he denied it before all of them, saying, "I do not know what you are talking about." ⁷¹When he went out to the porch, another servant-girl saw him, and she said to the bystanders, "This man was with Jesus of Nazareth."^x ⁷²Again he denied it with an oath, "I do not know the man." ⁷³After a little while the bystanders came up and said to Peter, "Certainly you are also one of them, for your accent

^w Or *Christ*
^x Gk *the Nazorean*

ὁ   υἱὸς   τοῦ   θεοῦ.   **26.64** λέγει   αὐτῷ   ὁ   Ἰησοῦς,   Σὺ
THE   SON   -   OF GOD.   SAYS   TO HIM   -   JESUS,   YOU

εἶπας.   πλὴν   λέγω   ὑμῖν,
SAID [IT].   BUT   I SAY   TO YOU°,

ἀπ' ἄρτι   ὄψεσθε   τὸν   υἱὸν   τοῦ   ἀνθρώπου
FROM   NOW ON   YOU° WILL SEE   THE   SON   -   OF MAN

καθήμενον   ἐκ   δεξιῶν   τῆς   δυνάμεως
SITTING   AT   [THE] RIGHT [HAND]   OF THE   POWER

καὶ   ἐρχόμενον   ἐπὶ   τῶν   νεφελῶν   τοῦ   οὐρανοῦ.
AND   COMING   UPON   THE   CLOUDS   -   OF HEAVEN.

26.65 τότε   ὁ   ἀρχιερεὺς   διέρρηξεν   τὰ   ἱμάτια   αὐτοῦ
THEN   THE   HIGH PRIEST   TORE   THE   GARMENTS   OF HIM

λέγων,   Ἐβλασφήμησεν·   τί   ἔτι   χρείαν   ἔχομεν
SAYING,   HE HAS BLASPHEMED.   WHAT   FURTHER   NEED   DO WE HAVE

μαρτύρων;   ἴδε   νῦν   ἠκούσατε   τὴν   βλασφημίαν·
OF WITNESSES?   SEE,   NOW   YOU° HAVE HEARD   THE   BLASPHEMY.

26.66 τί   ὑμῖν   δοκεῖ;   οἱ   δὲ   ἀποκριθέντες   εἶπαν,
WHAT   DOES [IT] SEEM~TO YOU°?   AND~THEY   HAVING ANSWERED   SAID,

Ἔνοχος   θανάτου   ἐστίν.   **26.67** Τότε   ἐνέπτυσαν   εἰς   τὸ
DESERVING   OF DEATH   HE IS.   THEN   THEY SPAT   INTO   THE

πρόσωπον   αὐτοῦ   καὶ   ἐκολάφισαν   αὐτόν,   οἱ   δὲ
FACE   OF HIM   AND   THEY STRUCK   HIM,   AND~THEY

ἐράπισαν   **26.68** λέγοντες,   Προφήτευσον   ἡμῖν,   Χριστέ,
SLAPPED [HIM]   SAYING,   PROPHESY   TO US,   CHRIST,

τίς   ἐστιν   ὁ   παίσας   σε;
WHO   IS   THE ONE   HAVING HIT   YOU?

26.69 Ὁ   δὲ   Πέτρος   ἐκάθητο   ἔξω   ἐν   τῇ   αὐλῇ·
-   NOW   PETER   WAS SITTING   OUTSIDE   IN   THE   COURTYARD.

καὶ   προσῆλθεν   αὐτῷ   μία   παιδίσκη   λέγουσα,   Καὶ   σὺ
AND   APPROACHED   HIM   ONE   MAID   SAYING,   AND   YOU

ἦσθα   μετὰ   Ἰησοῦ   τοῦ   Γαλιλαίου.   **26.70** ὁ   δὲ   ἠρνήσατο
WERE   WITH   JESUS   -   OF GALILEE.   BUT~HE   DENIED [IT]

ἔμπροσθεν   πάντων   λέγων,   Οὐκ   οἶδα   τί   λέγεις.
BEFORE   EVERYONE   SAYING,   I DO NOT KNOW   WHAT   YOU ARE SAYING.

26.71 ἐξελθόντα   δὲ   εἰς   τὸν   πυλῶνα   εἶδεν   αὐτὸν   ἄλλη
AND~HAVING GONE OUT   TO   THE   GATE   SAW   HIM   ANOTHER

καὶ   λέγει   τοῖς   ἐκεῖ,   Οὗτος   ἦν   μετὰ   Ἰησοῦ   τοῦ
AND   SHE SAYS   TO THE ONES   THERE,   THIS ONE   WAS   WITH   JESUS   -

Ναζωραίου.   **26.72** καὶ   πάλιν   ἠρνήσατο   μετὰ   ὅρκου   ὅτι
OF NAZARETH.   AND   AGAIN   HE DENIED [IT]   WITH   AN OATH   -

Οὐκ   οἶδα   τὸν   ἄνθρωπον.   **26.73** μετὰ   μικρὸν   δὲ
I DO NOT KNOW   THE   MAN.   ²AFTER   ³A LITTLE [WHILE]   ¹AND

προσελθόντες   οἱ   ἑστῶτες   εἶπον   τῷ   Πέτρῳ,   Ἀληθῶς
HAVING APPROACHED   THE ONES   HAVING STOOD   SAID   -   TO PETER,   TRULY

καὶ   σὺ   ἐξ   αὐτῶν   εἶ,   καὶ   γὰρ   ἡ   λαλιά   σου   δῆλόν   σε
ALSO   YOU   OF   THEM   ARE,   FOR~EVEN   THE   ACCENT   OF YOU   ³MANIFEST   ²YOU

26:64a Ps. 110:1   **26:64b** Dan. 7:13

ποιεῖ. **26.74** τότε ἤρξατο καταθεματίζειν καὶ
¹MAKES.   THEN   HE BEGAN   TO CURSE   AND

ὀμνύειν   ὅτι Οὐκ οἶδα   τὸν ἄνθρωπον.   καὶ εὐθέως
TO SWEAR [SAYING] - I DO NOT KNOW THE   MAN.   AND IMMEDIATELY

ἀλέκτωρ ἐφώνησεν. **26.75** καὶ ἐμνήσθη ὁ Πέτρος τοῦ
A COCK   CROWED.   AND REMEMBERED - PETER   THE

ῥήματος Ἰησοῦ εἰρηκότος ὅτι Πρὶν ἀλέκτορα φωνῆσαι
WORD   OF JESUS HAVING SPOKEN - BEFORE A COCK   CROWS

τρὶς   ἀπαρνήσῃ με· καὶ ἐξελθὼν ἔξω ἔκλαυσεν
THREE TIMES YOU WILL DENY ME. AND HAVING GONE OUTSIDE HE WEPT

πικρῶς.
BITTERLY.

betrays you." ⁷⁴Then he began to curse, and he swore an oath, "I do not know the man!" At that moment the cock crowed. ⁷⁵Then Peter remembered what Jesus had said: "Before the cock crows, you will deny me three times." And he went out and wept bitterly.

27.1 Πρωΐας δὲ γενομένης συμβούλιον ἔλαβον πάντες
       AND~[WHEN] EARLY MORNING CAME TOOK~COUNSEL TOGETHER   ALL

οἱ ἀρχιερεῖς καὶ οἱ πρεσβύτεροι τοῦ λαοῦ κατὰ τοῦ
THE CHIEF PRIESTS AND THE ELDERS   OF THE PEOPLE AGAINST -

Ἰησοῦ ὥστε θανατῶσαι αὐτόν· **27.2** καὶ δήσαντες
JESUS SO AS TO PUT TO DEATH HIM.   AND HAVING BOUND

αὐτὸν ἀπήγαγον   καὶ παρέδωκαν Πιλάτῳ τῷ
HIM   THEY LED [HIM] AWAY AND HANDED [HIM] OVER TO PILATE THE

ἡγεμόνι.
GOVERNOR.

27.3 Τότε ἰδὼν   Ἰούδας ὁ   παραδιδοὺς αὐτὸν ὅτι
       THEN HAVING SEEN JUDAS, THE ONE BETRAYING   HIM,   THAT

κατεκρίθη,   μεταμεληθεὶς ἔστρεψεν τὰ τριάκοντα
HE WAS CONDEMNED [TO DIE], HAVING REPENTED HE RETURNED THE THIRTY

ἀργύρια   τοῖς ἀρχιερεῦσιν καὶ πρεσβυτέροις
PIECES OF SILVER TO THE CHIEF PRIESTS AND [THE] ELDERS

27.4 λέγων, Ἥμαρτον παραδοὺς αἷμα ἀθῷον. οἱ δὲ
       SAYING, I SINNED HAVING BETRAYED INNOCENT~BLOOD. BUT~THEY

εἶπαν, Τί   πρὸς ἡμᾶς; σὺ ὄψῃ.   **27.5** καὶ
SAID, WHAT [IS THAT] TO US? YOU SEE [TO IT].   AND

ῥίψας   τὰ ἀργύρια εἰς τὸν ναὸν ἀνεχώρησεν, καὶ
HAVING THROWN THE SILVER [COINS] INTO THE TEMPLE HE DEPARTED,   AND

ἀπελθὼν ἀπήγξατο. **27.6** οἱ δὲ ἀρχιερεῖς λαβόντες
HAVING GONE AWAY HE HANGED HIMSELF. BUT~THE CHIEF PRIESTS HAVING TAKEN

τὰ ἀργύρια εἶπαν, Οὐκ ἔξεστιν βαλεῖν αὐτὰ εἰς τὸν
THE SILVER [COINS] SAID, IT IS NOT PERMISSIBLE TO PUT THESE INTO THE

κορβανᾶν, ἐπεὶ τιμὴ   αἵματός ἐστιν.
TEMPLE TREASURY, SINCE [THE] PRICE OF BLOOD IT IS.

27.7 συμβούλιον δὲ λαβόντες ἠγόρασαν ἐξ αὐτῶν τὸν
       SO~HAVING TAKEN COUNSEL TOGETHER THEY BOUGHT WITH THEM THE

ἀγρὸν τοῦ κεραμέως εἰς ταφὴν τοῖς ξένοις.
FIELD   OF THE POTTER FOR A BURIAL PLACE - FOR STRANGERS.

When morning came, all the chief priests and the elders of the people conferred together against Jesus in order to bring about his death. ²They bound him, led him away, and handed him over to Pilate the governor.

3 When Judas, his betrayer, saw that Jesusʸ was condemned, he repented and brought back the thirty pieces of silver to the chief priests and the elders. ⁴He said, "I have sinned by betraying innocentᶻ blood." But they said, "What is that to us? See to it yourself." ⁵Throwing down the pieces of silver in the temple, he departed; and he went and hanged himself. ⁶But the chief priests, taking the pieces of silver, said, "It is not lawful to put them into the treasury, since they are blood money." ⁷After conferring together, they used them to buy the potter's field as a place to bury foreigners.

ʸ Gk *he*
ᶻ Other ancient authorities read *righteous*

8For this reason that field has been called the Field of Blood to this day. 9Then was fulfilled what had been spoken through the prophet Jeremiah,*a* "And they took*b* the thirty pieces of silver, the price of the one on whom a price had been set,*c* on whom some of the people of Israel had set a price, 10and they gave*d* them for the potter's field, as the Lord commanded me."

11 Now Jesus stood before the governor; and the governor asked him, "Are you the King of the Jews?" Jesus said, "You say so." 12But when he was accused by the chief priests and elders, he did not answer. 13Then Pilate said to him, "Do you not hear how many accusations they make against you?" 14But he gave him no answer, not even to a single charge, so that the governor was greatly amazed.

15 Now at the festival the governor was accustomed to release a prisoner for the crowd, anyone whom they wanted. 16At that time they had a notorious prisoner, called Jesus*e* Barabbas. 17So after they had gathered, Pilate said to them, "Whom do you want me to release for you, Jesus*e* Barabbas or Jesus who is called the Messiah?"*f* 18For he realized that it was

a Other ancient authorities read *Zechariah* or *Isaiah*
b Or *I took*
c Or *the price of the precious One*
d Other ancient authorities read *I gave*
e Other ancient authorities lack *Jesus*
f Or *the Christ*

27.8 διὸ   ἐκλήθη ὁ ἀγρὸς ἐκεῖνος Ἀγρὸς Αἵματος
THEREFORE WAS CALLED - THAT~FIELD   [THE] FIELD OF BLOOD

ἕως τῆς σήμερον. **27.9** τότε ἐπληρώθη τὸ   ῥηθὲν
UP TO - TODAY.   THEN WAS FULFILLED THE [THING] SPOKEN

διὰ Ἰερεμίου τοῦ προφήτου λέγοντος, Καὶ ἔλαβον
THROUGH JEREMIAH THE PROPHET SAYING,   AND THEY TOOK

τὰ τριάκοντα ἀργύρια,   τὴν τιμὴν τοῦ   τετιμημένου
THE THIRTY PIECES OF SILVER, THE PRICE OF THE ONE HAVING BEEN VALUED

ὃν ἐτιμήσαντο ἀπὸ υἱῶν   Ἰσραήλ, **27.10** καὶ ἔδωκαν
WHICH THEY ESTIMATED FROM [THE] SONS OF ISRAEL,   AND THEY GAVE

αὐτὰ εἰς τὸν ἀγρὸν τοῦ κεραμέως, καθὰ συνέταξέν
THEM FOR THE FIELD OF THE POTTER,   JUST AS COMMANDED

μοι κύριος.
ME [THE] LORD.

27.11 Ὁ δὲ Ἰησοῦς ἐστάθη ἔμπροσθεν τοῦ ἡγεμόνος·
      - NOW JESUS STOOD BEFORE   THE GOVERNOR.

καὶ ἐπηρώτησεν αὐτὸν ὁ ἡγεμὼν λέγων, Σὺ εἶ ὁ
AND ASKED   HIM THE GOVERNOR SAYING, ARE YOU THE

βασιλεὺς τῶν Ἰουδαίων; ὁ δὲ Ἰησοῦς ἔφη, Σὺ
KING   OF THE JEWS?   - AND JESUS SAID, YOU

λέγεις. **27.12** καὶ ἐν τῷ κατηγορεῖσθαι αὐτὸν ὑπὸ
ARE SAYING [IT].   AND WHEN HE WAS ACCUSED   BY

τῶν ἀρχιερέων καὶ πρεσβυτέρων οὐδὲν ἀπεκρίνατο.
THE CHIEF PRIESTS AND ELDERS   HE ANSWERED~NOTHING.

27.13 τότε λέγει αὐτῷ ὁ Πιλᾶτος, Οὐκ ἀκούεις
      THEN SAYS TO HIM - PILATE,   DO YOU NOT HEAR

πόσα   σου καταμαρτυροῦσιν; **27.14** καὶ
HOW MANY THINGS THEY TESTIFY AGAINST~YOU?   AND

οὐκ ἀπεκρίθη αὐτῷ πρὸς οὐδὲ ἓν ῥῆμα, ὥστε
HE DID NOT ANSWER HIM WITH EVEN ONE WORD, SO AS

θαυμάζειν τὸν ἡγεμόνα λίαν.
TO AMAZE THE GOVERNOR GREATLY.

27.15 Κατὰ δὲ ἑορτὴν εἰώθει   ὁ ἡγεμὼν
       AND~ACCORDING TO [THE] FESTIVAL WAS ACCUSTOMED THE GOVERNOR

ἀπολύειν ἕνα τῷ ὄχλῳ δέσμιον ὃν ἤθελον.
TO RELEASE ONE 2TO THE 3CROWD 1PRISONER WHOM[EVER] THEY WISHED.

27.16 εἶχον δὲ τότε δέσμιον ἐπίσημον λεγόμενον
       AND~THEY HAD THEN A NOTORIOUS~PRISONER BEING CALLED

[Ἰησοῦν] Βαραββᾶν. **27.17** συνηγμένων οὖν
JESUS   BARABBAS.   THEREFORE 2[AS] WERE GATHERING

αὐτῶν εἶπεν αὐτοῖς ὁ Πιλᾶτος, Τίνα θέλετε
1THEY, SAID TO THEM - PILATE,   WHOM DO YOU WISH [THAT]

ἀπολύσω ὑμῖν, [Ἰησοῦν τὸν] Βαραββᾶν ἢ Ἰησοῦν
I MAY RELEASE TO YOU°, JESUS - BARABBAS OR JESUS

τὸν λεγόμενον Χριστόν; **27.18** ᾔδει γὰρ ὅτι διὰ
THE ONE BEING CALLED CHRIST?   FOR~HE HAD KNOWN THAT ON ACCOUNT

27:9-10 Zech.11:12-13

φθόνον παρέδωκαν αὐτόν. **27.19** Καθημένου δὲ αὐτοῦ
OF ENVY   THEY HANDED OVER HIM.   AND~[WHILE] HE WAS SITTING

ἐπὶ τοῦ βήματος ἀπέστειλεν πρὸς αὐτὸν ἡ γυνὴ
ON THE JUDGMENT SEAT SENT   TO HIM   THE WIFE

αὐτοῦ λέγουσα, Μηδὲν   σοὶ καὶ τῷ
OF HIM SAYING, [LET THERE BE] NOTHING [BETWEEN] YOU AND -

δικαίῳ ἐκείνῳ· πολλὰ γὰρ ἔπαθον σήμερον κατ' ὄναρ
THAT~RIGHTEOUS [MAN], FOR~MUCH I SUFFERED TODAY   IN A DREAM

δι'   αὐτόν. **27.20** Οἱ δὲ ἀρχιερεῖς καὶ οἱ
ON ACCOUNT OF HIM.   BUT~THE CHIEF PRIESTS AND THE

πρεσβύτεροι ἔπεισαν τοὺς ὄχλους ἵνα αἰτήσωνται   τὸν
ELDERS   PERSUADED THE CROWDS THAT THEY SHOULD ASK FOR -

Βαραββᾶν, τὸν δὲ Ἰησοῦν ἀπολέσωσιν.
BARABBAS,   - BUT JESUS   THEY SHOULD DESTROY.

27.21 ἀποκριθεὶς δὲ ὁ ἡγεμὼν εἶπεν αὐτοῖς, Τίνα
        AND~HAVING ANSWERED, THE GOVERNOR SAID TO THEM, WHOM

θέλετε   ἀπὸ τῶν δύο   ἀπολύσω ὑμῖν; οἱ δὲ εἶπαν,
DO YOU° WISH FROM THE TWO [THAT] I MAY RELEASE TO YOU°? AND~THEY SAID,

Τὸν Βαραββᾶν. **27.22** λέγει αὐτοῖς ὁ Πιλᾶτος, Τί
-   BARABBAS.   SAYS TO THEM - PILATE,   WHAT

οὖν   ποιήσω Ἰησοῦν τὸν λεγόμενον Χριστόν;
THEREFORE MAY I DO [WITH] JESUS THE ONE BEING CALLED CHRIST?

λέγουσιν πάντες, Σταυρωθήτω. **27.23** ὁ δὲ ἔφη, Τί
SAYS   EVERYONE, LET [HIM] BE CRUCIFIED.   BUT~HE SAID, WHY

γὰρ κακὸν ἐποίησεν; οἱ δὲ περισσῶς ἔκραζον
WHAT EVIL THING HAS HE DONE? BUT~THEY WERE CRYING OUT~MORE

λέγοντες, Σταυρωθήτω. **27.24** ἰδὼν δὲ   ὁ Πιλᾶτος ὅτι
SAYING,   LET [HIM] BE CRUCIFIED.   AND~HAVING SEEN - PILATE   THAT

οὐδὲν ὠφελεῖ   ἀλλὰ μᾶλλον θόρυβος γίνεται,
NOTHING HE IS ACCOMPLISHING BUT RATHER AN UPROAR IS STARTING,

λαβὼν ὕδωρ ἀπενίψατο τὰς χεῖρας ἀπέναντι τοῦ
HAVING TAKEN WATER HE WASHED THE (HIS) HANDS BEFORE   THE

ὄχλου λέγων, Ἀθῷός εἰμι ἀπὸ τοῦ αἵματος τούτου·
CROWD SAYING, I AM~INNOCENT OF THE BLOOD   OF THIS [MAN].

ὑμεῖς ὄψεσθε. **27.25** καὶ ἀποκριθεὶς πᾶς ὁ λαὸς
YOU   WILL SEE [TO THAT].   AND HAVING ANSWERED ALL THE PEOPLE

εἶπεν, Τὸ αἷμα αὐτοῦ ἐφ' ἡμᾶς καὶ ἐπὶ τὰ τέκνα
SAID, THE BLOOD OF HIM [BE] UPON US AND UPON THE CHILDREN

ἡμῶν. **27.26** τότε ἀπέλυσεν αὐτοῖς τὸν Βαραββᾶν, τὸν
OF US.   THEN HE RELEASED TO THEM - BARABBAS,   -

δὲ Ἰησοῦν φραγελλώσας παρέδωκεν ἵνα σταυρωθῇ.
BUT JESUS   HAVING SCOURGED HE HANDED OVER THAT HE MIGHT BE CRUCIFIED.

27.27 Τότε οἱ στρατιῶται τοῦ ἡγεμόνος παραλαβόντες
        THEN THE SOLDIERS   OF THE GOVERNOR HAVING TAKEN

τὸν Ἰησοῦν εἰς τὸ πραιτώριον συνήγαγον ἐπ'   αὐτὸν
-   JESUS   INTO THE PRAETORIUM GATHERED TOGETHER AGAINST HIM

ὅλην   τὴν σπεῖραν. **27.28** καὶ ἐκδύσαντες αὐτὸν
[THE] ENTIRE - COHORT.   AND HAVING STRIPPED HIM

out of jealousy that they had handed him over. [19]While he was sitting on the judgment seat, his wife sent word to him, "Have nothing to do with that innocent man, for today I have suffered a great deal because of a dream about him." [20]Now the chief priests and the elders persuaded the crowds to ask for Barabbas and to have Jesus killed. [21]The governor again said to them, "Which of the two do you want me to release for you?" And they said, "Barabbas." [22]Pilate said to them, "Then what should I do with Jesus who is called the Messiah?"[g] All of them said, "Let him be crucified!" [23]Then he asked, "Why, what evil has he done?" But they shouted all the more, "Let him be crucified!"

24 So when Pilate saw that he could do nothing, but rather that a riot was beginning, he took some water and washed his hands before the crowd, saying, "I am innocent of this man's blood;[h] see to it yourselves." [25]Then the people as a whole answered, "His blood be on us and on our children!" [26]So he released Barabbas for them; and after flogging Jesus, he handed him over to be crucified.

27 Then the soldiers of the governor took Jesus into the governor's headquarters,[i] and they gathered the whole cohort around him. [28]They stripped him

[g] Or the Christ
[h] Other ancient authorities read this righteous blood, or this righteous man's blood
[i] Gk the praetorium

and put a scarlet robe on him, [29]and after twisting some thorns into a crown, they put it on his head. They put a reed in his right hand and knelt before him and mocked him, saying, "Hail, King of the Jews!" [30]They spat on him, and took the reed and struck him on the head. [31]After mocking him, they stripped him of the robe and put his own clothes on him. Then they led him away to crucify him.

32 As they went out, they came upon a man from Cyrene named Simon; they compelled this man to carry his cross. [33]And when they came to a place called Golgotha (which means Place of a Skull), [34]they offered him wine to drink, mixed with gall; but when he tasted it, he would not drink it. [35]And when they had crucified him, they divided his clothes among themselves by casting lots;[j] [36]then they sat down there and kept watch over him. [37]Over his head they put the charge against him, which read, "This is Jesus, the King of the Jews."

38 Then two bandits were crucified with him, one on his right and one on his left. [39]Those who passed by derided[k] him, shaking their heads

[j] Other ancient authorities add in order that what had been spoken through the prophet might be fulfilled, "They divided my clothes among themselves, and for my clothing they cast lots."
[k] Or blasphemed

χλαμύδα κοκκίνην περιέθηκαν αὐτῷ, **27.29** καὶ
A SCARLET~ROBE THEY PLACED AROUND HIM, AND

πλέξαντες στέφανον ἐξ ἀκανθῶν ἐπέθηκαν ἐπὶ τῆς
HAVING WOVEN A CROWN OF THORNS THEY PLACED [IT] UPON THE

κεφαλῆς αὐτοῦ καὶ κάλαμον ἐν τῇ δεξιᾷ αὐτοῦ,
HEAD OF HIM AND [PUT] A STAFF IN THE RIGHT [HAND] OF HIM,

καὶ γονυπετήσαντες ἔμπροσθεν αὐτοῦ ἐνέπαιξαν αὐτῷ
AND HAVING KNELT BEFORE HIM THEY RIDICULED HIM

λέγοντες, Χαῖρε, βασιλεῦ τῶν Ἰουδαίων, **27.30** καὶ
SAYING, HAIL, KING OF THE JEWS, AND

ἐμπτύσαντες εἰς αὐτὸν ἔλαβον τὸν κάλαμον καὶ
HAVING SPAT AT HIM THEY TOOK THE STAFF AND

ἔτυπτον εἰς τὴν κεφαλὴν αὐτοῦ. **27.31** καὶ ὅτε
WERE STRIKING AT THE HEAD OF HIM. AND WHEN

ἐνέπαιξαν αὐτῷ, ἐξέδυσαν αὐτὸν τὴν χλαμύδα καὶ
THEY RIDICULED HIM, THEY TOOK OFF HIS - SCARLET [ROBE] AND

ἐνέδυσαν αὐτὸν τὰ ἱμάτια αὐτοῦ καὶ ἀπήγαγον
DRESSED HIM IN THE GARMENTS OF HIM AND LED AWAY

αὐτὸν εἰς τὸ σταυρῶσαι.
HIM TO BE CRUCIFIED.

27.32 Ἐξερχόμενοι δὲ εὗρον ἄνθρωπον Κυρηναῖον
AND~COMING OUT THEY FOUND A MAN A CYRENIAN

ὀνόματι Σίμωνα, τοῦτον ἠγγάρευσαν ἵνα
BY [THE] NAME OF SIMON, THIS [MAN] THEY PRESSED INTO SERVICE THAT

ἄρῃ τὸν σταυρὸν αὐτοῦ. **27.33** Καὶ ἐλθόντες εἰς
HE MIGHT CARRY THE CROSS OF HIM. AND HAVING COME TO

τόπον λεγόμενον Γολγοθᾶ, ὅ ἐστιν Κρανίου Τόπος
[THE] PLACE BEING CALLED GOLGOTHA, WHICH IS [THE] PLACE~OF [THE] SKULL

λεγόμενος, **27.34** ἔδωκαν αὐτῷ πιεῖν οἶνον μετὰ χολῆς
BEING CALLED, THEY GAVE TO HIM TO DRINK WINE WITH GALL

μεμιγμένον· καὶ γευσάμενος οὐκ ἠθέλησεν πιεῖν.
HAVING BEEN MIXED [IN]. AND TASTING [IT] HE DID NOT WISH TO DRINK.

27.35 σταυρώσαντες δὲ αὐτὸν διεμερίσαντο τὰ ἱμάτια
AND~HAVING CRUCIFIED HIM THEY DIVIDED THE GARMENTS

αὐτοῦ βάλλοντες κλῆρον, **27.36** καὶ καθήμενοι ἐτήρουν
OF HIM CASTING A LOT, AND SITTING THEY GUARDED

αὐτὸν ἐκεῖ. **27.37** καὶ ἐπέθηκαν ἐπάνω τῆς κεφαλῆς
HIM THERE. AND THEY PLACED ABOVE THE HEAD

αὐτοῦ τὴν αἰτίαν αὐτοῦ γεγραμμένην· Οὗτός ἐστιν
OF HIM THE CHARGE OF HIM HAVING BEEN WRITTEN: THIS IS

Ἰησοῦς ὁ βασιλεῦς τῶν Ἰουδαίων. **27.38** Τότε
JESUS THE KING OF THE JEWS. THEN

σταυροῦνται σὺν αὐτῷ δύο λῃσταί, εἷς ἐκ δεξιῶν καὶ
WERE CRUCIFIED WITH HIM TWO THIEVES, ONE ON [THE] RIGHT AND

εἷς ἐξ εὐωνύμων. **27.39** Οἱ δὲ παραπορευόμενοι
ONE ON [THE] LEFT. AND~THE ONES PASSING BY

ἐβλασφήμουν αὐτὸν κινοῦντες τὰς κεφαλὰς αὐτῶν
BLASPHEMED HIM SHAKING THE HEADS OF THEM

27.40 καὶ λέγοντες, Ὁ καταλύων τὸν ναὸν καὶ
AND SAYING, THE ONE DESTROYING THE TEMPLE AND

ἐν τρισὶν ἡμέραις οἰκοδομῶν, σῶσον σεαυτόν, εἰ
IN THREE DAYS [AND] BUILDING [IT], SAVE YOURSELF, IF

υἱὸς εἶ τοῦ θεοῦ, [καὶ] κατάβηθι ἀπὸ τοῦ σταυροῦ.
YOU ARE~[THE] SON - OF GOD, AND COME DOWN FROM THE CROSS.

27.41 ὁμοίως καὶ οἱ ἀρχιερεῖς ἐμπαίζοντες μετὰ
LIKEWISE ALSO THE CHIEF PRIESTS MOCKING WITH

τῶν γραμματέων καὶ πρεσβυτέρων ἔλεγον,
THE SCRIBES AND ELDERS SAID,

27.42 Ἄλλους ἔσωσεν, ἑαυτὸν οὐ δύναται σῶσαι·
HE SAVED~OTHERS, [YET] HIMSELF HE IS NOT ABLE TO SAVE.

βασιλεὺς Ἰσραήλ ἐστιν, καταβάτω νῦν ἀπὸ τοῦ
[SOME] KING OF ISRAEL HE IS, LET [HIM] COME DOWN NOW FROM THE

σταυροῦ καὶ πιστεύσομεν ἐπ' αὐτόν. **27.43** πέποιθεν
CROSS AND WE WILL BELIEVE ON HIM. HE HAS TRUSTED

ἐπὶ τὸν θεόν, ῥυσάσθω νῦν εἰ θέλει αὐτόν·
IN - GOD, LET HIM RESCUE NOW IF HE WANTS HIM.

εἶπεν γὰρ ὅτι Θεοῦ εἰμι υἱός. **27.44** τὸ δ' αὐτὸ
FOR~HE SAID - OF GOD I AM [THE] SON. AND~THE SAME

καὶ οἱ λῃσταὶ οἱ συσταυρωθέντες σὺν αὐτῷ
ALSO [SPOKE] THE THIEVES, THE ONES HAVING BEEN CRUCIFIED WITH HIM

ὠνείδιζον αὐτόν.
THEY WERE REPROACHING HIM.

27.45 Ἀπὸ δὲ ἕκτης ὥρας σκότος ἐγένετο ἐπὶ πᾶσαν
NOW~FROM [THE] SIXTH HOUR DARKNESS WAS OVER ALL

τὴν γῆν ἕως ὥρας ἐνάτης. **27.46** περὶ δὲ τὴν ἐνάτην
THE LAND UNTIL [THE] NINTH~HOUR. AND~ABOUT THE NINTH

ὥραν ἀνεβόησεν ὁ Ἰησοῦς φωνῇ μεγάλῃ λέγων, Ηλι
HOUR CRIED OUT - JESUS WITH A LOUD~VOICE SAYING, ELI,

ηλι λεμα σαβαχθανι; τοῦτ' ἔστιν, Θεέ μου θεέ μου,
ELI LEMA SABACHTHANI? THIS MEANS, MY~GOD, MY~GOD,

ἱνατί με ἐγκατέλιπες; **27.47** τινὲς δὲ τῶν
WHY HAVE YOU FORSAKEN~ME? AND~SOME OF THE ONES

ἐκεῖ ἑστηκότων ἀκούσαντες ἔλεγον ὅτι Ἠλίαν φωνεῖ
HAVING STOOD~THERE [AND] HAVING LISTENED SAID - ³ELIJAH ²CALLS FOR

οὗτος. **27.48** καὶ εὐθέως δραμὼν εἷς ἐξ αὐτῶν καὶ
¹THIS ONE. AND IMMEDIATELY RUNNING ONE OF THEM AND

λαβὼν σπόγγον πλήσας τε ὄξους καὶ
HAVING TAKEN A SPONGE AND~HAVING FILLED [IT] WITH VINEGAR AND

περιθεὶς καλάμῳ ἐπότιζεν αὐτόν. **27.49** οἱ δὲ
HAVING PLACED [IT] ON A STICK HE GAVE TO DRINK HIM. BUT~THE

λοιποὶ ἔλεγον, Ἄφες ἴδωμεν εἰ ἔρχεται Ἠλίας
OTHERS SAID, LEAVE [HIM ALONE AND] LET US SEE IF ELIJAH~COMES

σώσων αὐτόν.ᵀ **27.50** ὁ δὲ Ἰησοῦς πάλιν κράξας
SAVING HIM. - AND JESUS AGAIN HAVING CRIED OUT

[40]and saying, "You who would destroy the temple and build it in three days, save yourself! If you are the Son of God, come down from the cross." [41]In the same way the chief priests also, along with the scribes and elders, were mocking him, saying, [42]"He saved others; he cannot save himself.*l* He is the King of Israel; let him come down from the cross now, and we will believe in him. [43]He trusts in God; let God deliver him now, if he wants to; for he said, 'I am God's Son.'" [44]The bandits who were crucified with him also taunted him in the same way.

[45]From noon on, darkness came over the whole land*m* until three in the afternoon. [46]And about three o'clock Jesus cried with a loud voice, "Eli, Eli, lema sabachthani?" that is, "My God, my God, why have you forsaken me?" [47]When some of the bystanders heard it, they said, "This man is calling for Elijah." [48]At once one of them ran and got a sponge, filled it with sour wine, put it on a stick, and gave it to him to drink. [49]But the others said, "Wait, let us see whether Elijah will come to save him."*n* [50]Then Jesus cried again

l Or *is he unable to save himself?*
m Or *earth*
n Other ancient authorities add *And another took a spear and pierced his side, and out came water and blood*

27:46 Ps. 22:1   **27:49** text: all. add αλλος δε λαβων λογχην ενυξεν αυτου την πλευραν, και εξηλθεν ὑδωρ και αιμα (and another took his spear and pierced his side, and out came water and blood) [see John 19:34]: ASVmg RSVmg NASBmg NRSVmg.

with a loud voice and breathed his last.[o] 51At that moment the curtain of the temple was torn in two, from top to bottom. The earth shook, and the rocks were split. 52The tombs also were opened, and many bodies of the saints who had fallen asleep were raised. 53After his resurrection they came out of the tombs and entered the holy city and appeared to many. 54Now when the centurion and those with him, who were keeping watch over Jesus, saw the earthquake and what took place, they were terrified and said, "Truly this man was God's Son!"[p]

55 Many women were also there, looking on from a distance; they had followed Jesus from Galilee and had provided for him. 56Among them were Mary Magdalene, and Mary the mother of James and Joseph, and the mother of the sons of Zebedee.

57 When it was evening, there came a rich man from Arimathea, named Joseph, who was also a disciple of Jesus. 58He went to Pilate and asked for the body of Jesus; then Pilate ordered it to be given to him. 59So Joseph took the body and wrapped it in a clean linen cloth 60and laid it in his own new tomb, which he had hewn in the rock. He then rolled

[o] Or *gave up his spirit*
[p] Or *a son of God*

φωνῇ μεγάλῃ ἀφῆκεν τὸ πνεῦμα. **27.51** Καὶ ἰδοὺ τὸ
WITH A LOUD VOICE GAVE UP THE(HIS) SPIRIT. AND BEHOLD THE

καταπέτασμα τοῦ ναοῦ ἐσχίσθη ἀπ᾽ ἄνωθεν ἕως
CURTAIN OF THE TEMPLE WAS TORN FROM ABOVE TO

κάτω εἰς δύο καὶ ἡ γῆ ἐσείσθη καὶ αἱ πέτραι
BELOW IN TWO AND THE EARTH WAS SHAKEN AND THE ROCKS

ἐσχίσθησαν, **27.52** καὶ τὰ μνημεῖα ἀνεῴχθησαν καὶ
WERE SPLIT, AND THE TOMBS WERE OPENED AND

πολλὰ σώματα τῶν κεκοιμημένων ἁγίων ἠγέρθησαν,
MANY BODIES OF THE SAINTS~HAVING FALLEN ASLEEP WERE RAISED,

27.53 καὶ ἐξελθόντες ἐκ τῶν μνημείων μετὰ τὴν
AND HAVING GONE OUT FROM THE TOMBS AFTER THE

ἔγερσιν αὐτοῦ εἰσῆλθον εἰς τὴν ἁγίαν πόλιν καὶ
RESURRECTION OF HIM THEY ENTERED INTO THE HOLY CITY AND

ἐνεφανίσθησαν πολλοῖς. **27.54** Ὁ δὲ ἑκατόνταρχος καὶ
THEY APPEARED TO MANY. AND~THE CENTURION AND

οἱ μετ᾽ αὐτοῦ τηροῦντες τὸν Ἰησοῦν ἰδόντες τὸν
THE ONES WITH HIM GUARDING - JESUS SEEING THE

σεισμὸν καὶ τὰ γενόμενα ἐφοβήθησαν σφόδρα,
EARTHQUAKE AND THE THINGS TAKING PLACE WERE AFRAID GREATLY,

λέγοντες, Ἀληθῶς θεοῦ υἱὸς ἦν οὗτος. **27.55** Ἦσαν δὲ
SAYING, TRULY GOD'S SON WAS THIS ONE. AND~THERE WERE

ἐκεῖ γυναῖκες πολλαὶ ἀπὸ μακρόθεν θεωροῦσαι,
THERE MANY~WOMEN FROM A DISTANCE OBSERVING,

αἵτινες ἠκολούθησαν τῷ Ἰησοῦ ἀπὸ τῆς Γαλιλαίας
WHO FOLLOWED - JESUS FROM - GALILEE

διακονοῦσαι αὐτῷ· **27.56** ἐν αἷς ἦν Μαρία ἡ
SERVING HIM. AMONG WHOM WAS MARY -

Μαγδαληνὴ καὶ Μαρία ἡ τοῦ Ἰακώβου καὶ Ἰωσὴφ
MAGDALENE AND MARY THE - [2]OF JAMES [3]AND [4]JOSEPH

μήτηρ καὶ ἡ μήτηρ τῶν υἱῶν Ζεβεδαίου.
[1]MOTHER AND THE MOTHER OF THE SONS OF ZEBEDEE.

27.57 Ὀψίας δὲ γενομένης ἦλθεν ἄνθρωπος πλούσιος
NOW [WHEN] EVENING CAME, [5]CAME [2]MAN [1]A RICH

ἀπὸ Ἀριμαθαίας, τοὔνομα Ἰωσήφ, ὃς καὶ αὐτὸς
[3]FROM [4]ARIMATHEA, BY NAME JOSEPH, WHO ALSO HIMSELF

ἐμαθητεύθη τῷ Ἰησοῦ· **27.58** οὗτος προσελθὼν τῷ
WAS A DISCIPLE - OF JESUS. THIS ONE HAVING APPROACHED -

Πιλάτῳ ᾐτήσατο τὸ σῶμα τοῦ Ἰησοῦ. τότε ὁ Πιλᾶτος
PILATE ASKED FOR THE BODY - OF JESUS. THEN - PILATE

ἐκέλευσεν ἀποδοθῆναι. **27.59** καὶ λαβὼν τὸ σῶμα ὁ
COMMANDED [IT] TO BE GIVEN. AND HAVING TAKEN THE BODY -

Ἰωσὴφ ἐνετύλιξεν αὐτὸ [ἐν] σινδόνι καθαρᾷ **27.60** καὶ
JOSEPH WRAPPED IT IN CLEAN~LINEN AND

ἔθηκεν αὐτὸ ἐν τῷ καινῷ αὐτοῦ μνημείῳ ὃ
PLACED IT IN THE NEW TOMB~OF HIM WHICH

ἐλατόμησεν ἐν τῇ πέτρᾳ καὶ προσκυλίσας
HE CUT IN THE ROCK AND HAVING ROLLED

λίθον μέγαν   τῇ θύρᾳ τοῦ   μνημείου   ἀπῆλθεν.
A LARGE~STONE [OVER] THE DOOR OF THE TOMB   HE LEFT.

27.61 ἦν δὲ ἐκεῖ Μαριὰμ ἡ Μαγδαληνὴ καὶ ἡ   ἄλλη
AND~WAS THERE MARY   -   MAGDALENE   AND   THE   OTHER

Μαρία   καθήμεναι ἀπέναντι τοῦ τάφου.
MARY   SITTING   OPPOSITE   THE GRAVE.

27.62 Τῇ δὲ ἐπαύριον, ἥτις ἐστὶν μετὰ τὴν
NOW~ON THE NEXT DAY, WHICH IS   AFTER   THE

παρασκευήν, συνήχθησαν   οἱ ἀρχιερεῖς καὶ οἱ
PREPARATION [DAY], WERE GATHERED TOGETHER THE CHIEF PRIESTS AND   THE

Φαρισαῖοι πρὸς Πιλᾶτον **27.63** λέγοντες, Κύριε,
PHARISEES TO   PILATE   SAYING,   SIR,

ἐμνήσθημεν ὅτι ἐκεῖνος ὁ πλάνος εἶπεν ἔτι   ζῶν,
WE REMEMBERED THAT THAT   - DECEIVER SAID WHILE LIVING,

Μετὰ τρεῖς ἡμέρας ἐγείρομαι. **27.64** κέλευσον οὖν
AFTER THREE   DAYS   I WILL BE RAISED.   THEREFORE~COMMAND

ἀσφαλισθῆναι τὸν τάφον ἕως τῆς τρίτης ἡμέρας,
TO BE GUARDED   THE GRAVE UNTIL THE THIRD   DAY,

μήποτε ἐλθόντες οἱ μαθηταὶ αὐτοῦ κλέψωσιν αὐτὸν
LEST   HAVING COME THE DISCIPLES OF HIM MIGHT STEAL   IT

καὶ εἴπωσιν τῷ   λαῷ, Ἠγέρθη   ἀπὸ τῶν νεκρῶν,
AND SAY   TO THE PEOPLE, HE HAS BEEN RAISED FROM THE   DEAD,

καὶ ἔσται ἡ ἐσχάτη πλάνη χείρων τῆς   πρώτης.
AND WILL BE THE LAST   DECEPTION WORSE THAN THE FIRST.

27.65 ἔφη αὐτοῖς ὁ Πιλᾶτος, Ἔχετε κουστωδίαν·
SAID TO THEM - PILATE,   YOU° HAVE A GUARD.

ὑπάγετε ἀσφαλίσασθε ὡς οἴδατε. **27.66** οἱ δὲ
GO AWAY [AND] GUARD [IT]   AS   YOU° KNOW.   AND~THE ONES

πορευθέντες ἠσφαλίσαντο τὸν τάφον σφραγίσαντες τὸν
HAVING GONE   GUARDED   THE GRAVE HAVING SEALED   THE

λίθον μετὰ τῆς κουστωδίας.
STONE WITH THE GUARD.

a great stone to the door of
the tomb and went away.
[61]Mary Magdalene and the
other Mary were there,
sitting opposite the tomb.

62 The next day, that is,
after the day of Preparation,
the chief priests and the
Pharisees gathered before
Pilate [63]and said, "Sir, we
remember what that
impostor said while he was
still alive, 'After three days I
will rise again.' [64]Therefore
command the tomb to be
made secure until the third
day; otherwise his disciples
may go and steal him away,
and tell the people, 'He has
been raised from the dead,'
and the last deception would
be worse than the first."
[65]Pilate said to them, "You
have a guard[q] of soldiers; go,
make it as secure as you
can."[r] [66]So they went with
the guard and made the tomb
secure by sealing the stone.

[q] Or *Take a guard*
[r] Gk *you know how*

28.1 Ὀψὲ δὲ σαββάτων, τῇ   ἐπιφωσκούσῃ εἰς
NOW~AFTER [THE] SABBATH IN THE DAWNING   TOWARDS

μίαν   σαββάτων ἦλθεν Μαριὰμ ἡ Μαγδαληνὴ καὶ ἡ
[THE] FIRST OF [THE] WEEK, CAME MARY   -   MAGDALENE   AND THE

ἄλλη Μαρία θεωρῆσαι τὸν τάφον. **28.2** καὶ ἰδοὺ
OTHER MARY   TO LOOK AT   THE GRAVE.   AND   BEHOLD

σεισμὸς ἐγένετο μέγας· ἄγγελος γὰρ κυρίου
[3]EARTHQUAKE [1]THERE WAS [2]A GREAT. FOR~AN ANGEL OF [THE] LORD

καταβὰς ἐξ οὐρανοῦ καὶ προσελθὼν ἀπεκύλισεν
HAVING COME DOWN FROM HEAVEN AND HAVING APPROACHED ROLLED AWAY

τὸν λίθον καὶ ἐκάθητο ἐπάνω αὐτοῦ. **28.3** ἦν δὲ ἡ
THE STONE AND WAS SITTING ABOVE   IT.   AND~WAS THE

After the sabbath, as the first
day of the week was
dawning, Mary Magdalene
and the other Mary went to
see the tomb. [2]And suddenly
there was a great earthquake;
for an angel of the Lord,
descending from heaven,
came and rolled back the
stone and sat on it. [3]His

appearance was like lightning, and his clothing white as snow. ⁴For fear of him the guards shook and became like dead men. ⁵But the angel said to the women, "Do not be afraid; I know that you are looking for Jesus who was crucified. ⁶He is not here; for he has been raised, as he said. Come, see the place where heˢ lay. ⁷Then go quickly and tell his disciples, 'He has been raised from the dead,ᵗ and indeed he is going ahead of you to Galilee; there you will see him.' This is my message for you." ⁸So they left the tomb quickly with fear and great joy, and ran to tell his disciples. ⁹Suddenly Jesus met them and said, "Greetings!" And they came to him, took hold of his feet, and worshiped him. ¹⁰Then Jesus said to them, "Do not be afraid; go and tell my brothers to go to Galilee; there they will see me."

11 While they were going, some of the guard went into the city and told the chief priests everything that had happened. ¹²After the priestsᵘ had assembled with the elders, they devised a plan to give a large sum of money to the soldiers,

ˢ Other ancient authorities read the Lord
ᵗ Other ancient authorities lack from the dead
ᵘ Gk they

εἰδέα   αὐτοῦ   ὡς   ἀστραπὴ   καὶ   τὸ   ἔνδυμα   αὐτοῦ
APPEARANCE   OF HIM   LIKE LIGHTNING   AND   THE GARMENT OF HIM

λευκὸν   ὡς   χιών.   **28.4** ἀπὸ   δὲ   τοῦ   φόβου   αὐτοῦ
WHITE   AS   SNOW.   AND~FROM   -   FEAR   OF HIM

ἐσείσθησαν   οἱ   τηροῦντες   καὶ   ἐγενήθησαν   ὡς
WERE SHAKEN THE ONES GUARDING   AND   THEY BECAME   AS

νεκροί.   **28.5** ἀποκριθεὶς   δὲ   ὁ   ἄγγελος   εἶπεν   ταῖς
DEAD [PERSONS].   BUT~HAVING ANSWERED   THE ANGEL   SAID   TO THE

γυναιξίν,   Μὴ   φοβεῖσθε   ὑμεῖς,   οἶδα   γὰρ   ὅτι   Ἰησοῦν
WOMEN,   YOU°~DO NOT BE AFRAID   FOR~I KNOW   THAT   JESUS,

τὸν   ἐσταυρωμένον   ζητεῖτε·   **28.6** οὐκ   ἔστιν   ὧδε,
THE ONE   HAVING BEEN CRUCIFIED,   YOU° ARE SEEKING;   HE IS NOT   HERE,

ἠγέρθη   γὰρ   καθὼς   εἶπεν·   δεῦτε   ἴδετε   τὸν   τόπον   ὅπου
FOR~HE WAS RAISED   JUST AS   HE SAID.   COME   SEE   THE   PLACE   WHERE

ἔκειτο.   **28.7** καὶ   ταχὺ   πορευθεῖσαι   εἴπατε   τοῖς
HE WAS LYING.   AND   QUICKLY   HAVING GONE   TELL   THE

μαθηταῖς   αὐτοῦ   ὅτι   Ἠγέρθη   ἀπὸ   τῶν   νεκρῶν,   καὶ
DISCIPLES   OF HIM,   -   HE WAS RAISED   FROM   THE   DEAD,   AND

ἰδοὺ   προάγει   ὑμᾶς   εἰς   τὴν   Γαλιλαίαν,   ἐκεῖ
BEHOLD   HE IS GOING AHEAD   OF YOU°   TO   -   GALILEE,   THERE

αὐτὸν   ὄψεσθε·   ἰδοὺ   εἶπον   ὑμῖν.   **28.8** καὶ   ἀπελθοῦσαι
YOU° WILL SEE~HIM.   BEHOLD   I TOLD   YOU°.   AND   HAVING DEPARTED

ταχὺ   ἀπὸ   τοῦ   μνημείου   μετὰ   φόβου   καὶ
QUICKLY   FROM   THE   TOMB   WITH   FEAR   AND

χαρᾶς   μεγάλης   ἔδραμον   ἀπαγγεῖλαι   τοῖς   μαθηταῖς
GREAT~JOY   THEY RAN   TO REPORT   TO THE   DISCIPLES

αὐτοῦ.   **28.9** καὶ   ἰδοὺ   Ἰησοῦς   ὑπήντησεν   αὐταῖς   λέγων,
OF HIM.   AND   BEHOLD   JESUS   MET   THEM   SAYING,

Χαίρετε.   αἱ   δὲ   προσελθοῦσαι   ἐκράτησαν   αὐτοῦ   τοὺς
HELLO.   AND~THEY   HAVING APPROACHED   GRASPED   HIS   -

πόδας   καὶ   προσεκύνησαν   αὐτῷ.   **28.10** τότε   λέγει
FEET   AND   THEY WORSHIPED   HIM.   THEN   SAID

αὐταῖς   ὁ   Ἰησοῦς,   Μὴ   φοβεῖσθε·   ὑπάγετε   ἀπαγγείλατε
TO THEM   -   JESUS,   DO NOT BE AFRAID.   GO [AND]   REPORT

τοῖς   ἀδελφοῖς   μου   ἵνα   ἀπέλθωσιν   εἰς   τὴν   Γαλιλαίαν,
TO THE   BROTHERS   OF ME   THAT   THEY MAY GO AWAY   INTO   -   GALILEE,

κἀκεῖ   με   ὄψονται.
AND THERE   THEY WILL SEE~ME.

28.11 Πορευομένων   δὲ   αὐτῶν   ἰδοὺ   τινες   τῆς
          AND~[AS] THEY WERE GOING   BEHOLD   SOME   OF THE

κουστωδίας   ἐλθόντες   εἰς   τὴν   πόλιν   ἀπήγγειλαν   τοῖς
GUARD   HAVING COME   INTO   THE   CITY   REPORTED   TO THE

ἀρχιερεῦσιν   ἄπαντα   τὰ   γενόμενα.   **28.12** καὶ
CHIEF PRIESTS   ALL THE THINGS   HAVING HAPPENED.   AND

συναχθέντες   μετὰ   τῶν   πρεσβυτέρων   συμβούλιόν   τε
HAVING GATHERED TOGETHER   WITH   THE   ELDERS   ³COUNSEL   ¹AND

λαβόντες   ἀργύρια   ἱκανὰ   ἔδωκαν   τοῖς   στρατιώταις
²HAVING TAKEN,   ⁶SILVER   ⁵SUFFICIENT   ⁴THEY GAVE   TO THE   SOLDIERS

28.13 λέγοντες, Εἴπατε Οἱ μαθηταὶ αὐτοῦ νυκτὸς
SAYING, SAY [THAT] THE DISCIPLES OF HIM DURING [THE] NIGHT

ἐλθόντες ἔκλεψαν αὐτὸν ἡμῶν κοιμωμένων. **28.14** καὶ
HAVING COME STOLE HIM [WHILE] WE ARE (WERE) SLEEPING. AND

ἐὰν ἀκουσθῇ τοῦτο ἐπὶ τοῦ ἡγεμόνος, ἡμεῖς πείσομεν
IF THIS~IS HEARD BEFORE THE GOVERNOR, WE WILL PERSUADE

[αὐτὸν] καὶ ὑμᾶς ἀμερίμνους ποιήσομεν. **28.15** οἱ δὲ
HIM AND YOU° WE WILL KEEP~OUT OF TROUBLE. AND~THE ONES

λαβόντες τὰ ἀργύρια ἐποίησαν ὡς ἐδιδάχθησαν.
HAVING RECEIVED THE SILVER DID AS THEY WERE TAUGHT.

Καὶ διεφημίσθη ὁ λόγος οὗτος παρὰ Ἰουδαίοις μέχρι
AND WAS MADE KNOWN - THIS~WORD AMONG [THE] JEWS UP TO

τῆς σήμερον [ἡμέρας].
THE DAY~TODAY.

28.16 Οἱ δὲ ἕνδεκα μαθηταὶ ἐπορεύθησαν εἰς τὴν
NOW~THE ELEVEN DISCIPLES WENT TO -

Γαλιλαίαν εἰς τὸ ὄρος οὗ ἐτάξατο αὐτοῖς ὁ
GALILEE TO THE MOUNTAIN WHERE COMMANDED THEM -

Ἰησοῦς, **28.17** καὶ ἰδόντες αὐτὸν προσεκύνησαν, οἱ δὲ
JESUS, AND HAVING SEEN HIM THEY WORSHIPED [HIM], BUT~SOME

ἐδίστασαν. **28.18** καὶ προσελθὼν ὁ Ἰησοῦς ἐλάλησεν
DOUBTED. AND HAVING APPROACHED - JESUS SPOKE

αὐτοῖς λέγων, Ἐδόθη μοι πᾶσα ἐξουσία ἐν οὐρανῷ
TO THEM SAYING, WAS GIVEN TO ME ALL AUTHORITY IN HEAVEN

καὶ ἐπὶ [τῆς] γῆς. **28.19** πορευθέντες οὖν μαθητεύσατε
AND ON THE EARTH. THEREFORE~HAVING GONE MAKE DISCIPLES

πάντα τὰ ἔθνη, βαπτίζοντες αὐτοὺς εἰς τὸ ὄνομα τοῦ
OF ALL THE NATIONS, BAPTIZING THEM IN THE NAME OF THE

πατρὸς καὶ τοῦ υἱοῦ καὶ τοῦ ἁγίου πνεύματος,
FATHER AND THE SON AND THE HOLY SPIRIT,

28.20 διδάσκοντες αὐτοὺς τηρεῖν πάντα ὅσα
TEACHING THEM TO KEEP ALL THINGS WHATSOEVER

ἐνετειλάμην ὑμῖν· καὶ ἰδοὺ ἐγὼ μεθ' ὑμῶν εἰμι
I COMMANDED YOU°. AND BEHOLD I WITH YOU° AM

πάσας τὰς ἡμέρας ἕως τῆς συντελείας τοῦ αἰῶνος.
ALL THE DAYS UNTIL THE COMPLETION OF THE AGE.

[13]telling them, "You must say, 'His disciples came by night and stole him away while we were asleep.' [14]If this comes to the governor's ears, we will satisfy him and keep you out of trouble." [15]So they took the money and did as they were directed. And this story is still told among the Jews to this day.

16 Now the eleven disciples went to Galilee, to the mountain to which Jesus had directed them. [17]When they saw him, they worshiped him; but some doubted. [18]And Jesus came and said to them, "All authority in heaven and on earth has been given to me. [19]Go therefore and make disciples of all nations, baptizing them in the name of the Father and of the Son and of the Holy Spirit, [20]and teaching them to obey everything that I have commanded you. And remember, I am with you always, to the end of the age."[v]

[v] Other ancient authorities add *Amen*

THE GOSPEL ACCORDING TO
MARK

ΚΑΤΑ   ΜΑΡΚΟΝ
ACCORDING TO MARK

1.1 Ἀρχὴ   τοῦ εὐαγγελίου Ἰησοῦ Χριστοῦ ⌐[υἱοῦ
[THE] BEGINNING OF THE GOOD NEWS OF JESUS CHRIST [THE] SON

θεοῦ]⌐.
OF GOD.

1.2 Καθὼς γέγραπται ⌐ἐν τῷ Ἡσαΐᾳ τῷ προφήτῃ⌐,
JUST AS IT HAS BEEN WRITTEN IN - ISAIAH THE PROPHET,

Ἰδοὺ ἀποστέλλω τὸν ἄγγελόν μου πρὸ προσώπου
BEHOLD I SEND THE MESSENGER OF ME BEFORE [THE] FACE

σου,
OF YOU,

ὃς κατασκευάσει τὴν ὁδόν σου·
WHO WILL PREPARE THE WAY OF YOU;

1.3 φωνὴ βοῶντος ἐν τῇ ἐρήμῳ,
A VOICE CRYING OUT IN THE WILDERNESS,

Ἑτοιμάσατε τὴν ὁδὸν κυρίου,
PREPARE THE WAY OF [THE] LORD,

εὐθείας ποιεῖτε τὰς τρίβους αὐτοῦ,
MAKE~STRAIGHT THE PATHS OF HIM,

1.4 ἐγένετο Ἰωάννης [ὁ] βαπτίζων ἐν τῇ ἐρήμῳ καὶ
JOHN~CAME - BAPTIZING IN THE WILDERNESS AND

κηρύσσων βάπτισμα μετανοίας εἰς ἄφεσιν
PREACHING A BAPTISM OF REPENTANCE FOR [THE] FORGIVENESS

ἁμαρτιῶν. **1.5** καὶ ἐξεπορεύετο πρὸς αὐτὸν πᾶσα ἡ
OF SINS. AND ⁸WERE GOING OUT ⁹TO ¹⁰HIM ¹[THE] ENTIRE -

Ἰουδαία χώρα καὶ οἱ Ἱεροσολυμῖται πάντες, καὶ
²JUDEAN ³COUNTRY ⁴AND ⁶THE ⁷JERUSALEMITES ⁵ALL, AND

ἐβαπτίζοντο ὑπ᾽ αὐτοῦ ἐν τῷ Ἰορδάνῃ ποταμῷ
THEY WERE BEING BAPTIZED BY HIM IN THE JORDAN RIVER,

ἐξομολογούμενοι τὰς ἁμαρτίας αὐτῶν. **1.6** καὶ ἦν   ὁ
CONFESSING THE SINS OF THEM. AND ²HAD BEEN -

Ἰωάννης ἐνδεδυμένος τρίχας καμήλου καὶ
¹JOHN CLOTHED [IN] CAMEL~HAIRS AND

ζώνην δερματίνην περὶ τὴν ὀσφὺν αὐτοῦ, καὶ ἐσθίων
A LEATHER~BELT AROUND THE WAIST OF HIM, AND EATING

ἀκρίδας καὶ μέλι ἄγριον. **1.7** καὶ ἐκήρυσσεν λέγων,
LOCUSTS AND WILD~HONEY. AND HE WAS PREACHING SAYING,

Ἔρχεται ὁ ἰσχυρότερός μου ὀπίσω μου, οὗ
³IS COMING ⁴THE ONE ⁵STRONGER ⁶THAN ME, ¹AFTER ²ME, OF WHOM

The beginning of the good news[a] of Jesus Christ, the Son of God.[b] 2 As it is written in the prophet Isaiah,[c]

"See, I am sending my messenger ahead of you,[d] who will prepare your way;

³ the voice of one crying out in the wilderness: 'Prepare the way of the Lord, make his paths straight,'"

⁴John the baptizer appeared[e] in the wilderness, proclaiming a baptism of repentance for the forgiveness of sins. ⁵And people from the whole Judean countryside and all the people of Jerusalem were going out to him, and were baptized by him in the river Jordan, confessing their sins. ⁶Now John was clothed with camel's hair, with a leather belt around his waist, and he ate locusts and wild honey. ⁷He proclaimed, "The one who is more powerful than I is coming after me;

[a] Or *gospel*
[b] Other ancient authorities lack *the Son of God*
[c] Other ancient authorities read *in the prophets*
[d] Gk *before your face*
[e] Other ancient authorities read *John was baptizing*

1:1 text: all. omit: ASVmg RSVmg NASBmg NIVmg NEBmg TEVmg NJBmg NRSVmg. **1:2a** text: all. var. εν τοις προφηταις (in the prophets): ASVmg RSVmg NRSVmg. **1:2b** Mal. 3:1 **1:3** Isa. 40:3 LXX

I am not worthy to stoop down and untie the thong of his sandals. [8]I have baptized you with[f] water; but he will baptize you with[f] the Holy Spirit."

9 In those days Jesus came from Nazareth of Galilee and was baptized by John in the Jordan. [10]And just as he was coming up out of the water, he saw the heavens torn apart and the Spirit descending like a dove on him. [11]And a voice came from heaven, "You are my Son, the Beloved;[g] with you I am well pleased."

12 And the Spirit immediately drove him out into the wilderness. [13]He was in the wilderness forty days, tempted by Satan; and he was with the wild beasts; and the angels waited on him.

14 Now after John was arrested, Jesus came to Galilee, proclaiming the good news[h] of God,[i] [15]and saying, "The time is fulfilled, and the kingdom of God has come near;[j] repent, and believe in the good news."[h]

16 As Jesus passed along the Sea of Galilee, he saw Simon and his brother Andrew casting a net into the sea—for they were fishermen. [17]And Jesus said to them, "Follow

[f] Or in
[g] Or my beloved Son
[h] Or gospel
[i] Other ancient authorities read of the kingdom
[j] Or is at hand

οὐκ εἰμὶ ἱκανὸς κύψας λῦσαι τὸν ἱμάντα τῶν
I AM NOT   QUALIFIED, STOOPING, TO UNTIE THE STRAP OF THE

ὑποδημάτων αὐτοῦ. **1.8** ἐγὼ ἐβάπτισα ὑμᾶς ὕδατι,
SANDALS   OF HIM.   I   BAPTIZED   YOU°   IN WATER,

αὐτὸς δὲ βαπτίσει ὑμᾶς ἐν πνεύματι ἁγίῳ.
BUT~HE   WILL BAPTIZE YOU°   IN   [THE] HOLY~SPIRIT.

1.9 Καὶ ἐγένετο ἐν ἐκείναις ταῖς ἡμέραις
AND   IT CAME ABOUT IN   THOSE   -   DAYS [THAT]

ἦλθεν Ἰησοῦς ἀπὸ Ναζαρὲτ τῆς Γαλιλαίας καὶ
JESUS~CAME   FROM   NAZARETH - OF GALILEE   AND

ἐβαπτίσθη εἰς τὸν Ἰορδάνην ὑπὸ Ἰωάννου. **1.10** καὶ
WAS BAPTIZED IN THE JORDAN [RIVER] BY   JOHN.   AND

εὐθὺς ἀναβαίνων ἐκ τοῦ ὕδατος εἶδεν σχιζομένους
IMMEDIATELY COMING UP OUT OF THE WATER HE SAW BEING OPENED

τοὺς οὐρανοὺς καὶ τὸ πνεῦμα ὡς περιστερὰν
THE   HEAVENS   AND THE SPIRIT   AS   A DOVE

καταβαῖνον εἰς αὐτόν· **1.11** καὶ φωνὴ ἐγένετο ἐκ
DESCENDING TOWARDS HIM.   AND THERE WAS~A VOICE OUT OF

τῶν οὐρανῶν, Σὺ εἶ ὁ υἱός μου ὁ ἀγαπητός, ἐν σοὶ
THE HEAVENS, YOU ARE THE SON OF ME, THE BELOVED,   WITH YOU

εὐδόκησα.
I AM WELL PLEASED.

1.12 Καὶ εὐθὺς τὸ πνεῦμα αὐτὸν ἐκβάλλει εἰς τὴν
AND   IMMEDIATELY THE SPIRIT   DRIVES HIM OUT   INTO THE

ἔρημον. **1.13** καὶ ἦν ἐν τῇ ἐρήμῳ τεσσεράκοντα
WILDERNESS.   AND HE HAD BEEN [4]IN [5]THE [6]WILDERNESS [7]FORTY

ἡμέρας πειραζόμενος ὑπὸ τοῦ Σατανᾶ, καὶ ἦν μετὰ
[8]DAYS [1]TEMPTED   [2]BY - [3]SATAN,   AND HE WAS AMONG

τῶν θηρίων, καὶ οἱ ἄγγελοι διηκόνουν αὐτῷ.
-    WILD BEASTS, AND THE ANGELS WERE MINSTERING TO HIM.

1.14 Μετὰ δὲ τὸ παραδοθῆναι τὸν Ἰωάννην ἦλθεν ὁ
AND~AFTER - [2]WAS IMPRISONED - [1]JOHN   [4]CAME -

Ἰησοῦς εἰς τὴν Γαλιλαίαν κηρύσσων τὸ εὐαγγέλιον
[3]JESUS TO -   GALILEE   PREACHING   THE GOOD NEWS

τοῦ θεοῦ **1.15** καὶ λέγων ὅτι Πεπλήρωται ὁ καιρὸς
-   OF GOD   AND SAYING - [3]HAS BEEN FULFILLED [1]THE [2]TIME

καὶ ἤγγικεν ἡ βασιλεία τοῦ θεοῦ· μετανοεῖτε καὶ
AND HAS APPROACHED THE KINGDOM - OF GOD. REPENT   AND

πιστεύετε ἐν τῷ εὐαγγελίῳ.
BELIEVE   IN THE GOOD NEWS.

1.16 Καὶ παράγων παρὰ τὴν θάλασσαν τῆς
AND   PASSING BY ALONGSIDE THE LAKE   -

Γαλιλαίας εἶδεν Σίμωνα καὶ Ἀνδρέαν τὸν ἀδελφὸν
OF GALILEE HE SAW SIMON   AND   ANDREW,   THE   BROTHER

Σίμωνος ἀμφιβάλλοντας ἐν τῇ θαλάσσῃ· ἦσαν γὰρ
OF SIMON,   CASTING [THEIR NETS] INTO THE LAKE;   FOR~THEY WERE

ἁλιεῖς. **1.17** καὶ εἶπεν αὐτοῖς ὁ Ἰησοῦς, Δεῦτε ὀπίσω
FISHERMEN.   AND [2]SAID [3]TO THEM - [1]JESUS,   COME   AFTER

μου, καὶ ποιήσω ὑμᾶς γενέσθαι ἁλιεῖς ἀνθρώπων.
ME, AND I WILL MAKE YOU° TO BECOME FISHERMEN OF MEN.

1.18 καὶ εὐθὺς ἀφέντες τὰ δίκτυα ἠκολούθησαν
AND IMMEDIATELY LEAVING THE(THEIR) NETS THEY FOLLOWED

αὐτῷ. **1.19** Καὶ προβὰς ὀλίγον εἶδεν Ἰάκωβον
HIM. AND HAVING GONE ON A LITTLE, HE SAW JAMES

τὸν τοῦ Ζεβεδαίου καὶ Ἰωάννην τὸν ἀδελφὸν αὐτοῦ
THE [SON] - OF ZEBEDEE AND JOHN THE BROTHER OF HIM

καὶ αὐτοὺς ἐν τῷ πλοίῳ καταρτίζοντας τὰ
AND THEY [WERE] IN THE(THEIR) BOAT MENDING THE(THEIR)

δίκτυα, **1.20** καὶ εὐθὺς ἐκάλεσεν αὐτούς. καὶ
NETS, AND IMMEDIATELY HE CALLED THEM. AND

ἀφέντες τὸν πατέρα αὐτῶν Ζεβεδαῖον ἐν τῷ πλοίῳ
LEAVING - THEIR~FATHER ZEBEDEE IN THE BOAT

μετὰ τῶν μισθωτῶν ἀπῆλθον ὀπίσω αὐτοῦ.
WITH THE HIRED SERVANTS [AND] DEPARTED AFTER HIM.

1.21 Καὶ εἰσπορεύονται εἰς Καφαρναούμ· καὶ
AND THEY ENTER INTO CAPERNAUM. AND

εὐθὺς τοῖς σάββασιν εἰσελθὼν εἰς τὴν συναγωγὴν
IMMEDIATELY ON THE SABBATHS ENTERING INTO THE SYNAGOGUE

ἐδίδασκεν. **1.22** καὶ ἐξεπλήσσοντο ἐπὶ τῇ
HE WAS TEACHING [THEM]. AND THEY WERE AMAZED AT -

διδαχῇ αὐτοῦ· ἦν γὰρ διδάσκων αὐτοὺς ὡς
HIS~TEACHING; FOR~HE WAS TEACHING THEM AS

ἐξουσίαν ἔχων καὶ οὐχ ὡς οἱ γραμματεῖς. **1.23** καὶ
[ONE] HAVING~AUTHORITY AND NOT AS THE SCRIBES. AND

εὐθὺς ἦν ἐν τῇ συναγωγῇ αὐτῶν ἄνθρωπος ἐν
IMMEDIATELY THERE WAS IN - THEIR~SYNAGOGUE A MAN WITH

πνεύματι ἀκαθάρτῳ καὶ ἀνέκραξεν **1.24** λέγων, Τί ἡμῖν
AN UNCLEAN~SPIRIT AND HE CRIED OUT SAYING, WHAT TO US

καὶ σοί, Ἰησοῦ Ναζαρηνέ; ἦλθες ἀπολέσαι ἡμᾶς;
AND TO YOU, JESUS [THE] NAZARENE? HAVE YOU COME TO DESTROY US?

οἶδά σε τίς εἶ, ὁ ἅγιος τοῦ θεοῦ. **1.25** καὶ
I KNOW YOU, WHO YOU ARE, THE HOLY ONE - OF GOD. AND

ἐπετίμησεν αὐτῷ ὁ Ἰησοῦς λέγων, Φιμώθητι καὶ
REBUKED HIM - JESUS SAYING, BE QUIET AND

ἔξελθε ἐξ αὐτοῦ. **1.26** καὶ σπαράξαν αὐτὸν τὸ
COME OUT OF HIM. AND ⁴HAVING CONVULSED ⁵HIM, ¹THE

πνεῦμα τὸ ἀκάθαρτον καὶ φωνῆσαν φωνῇ μεγάλῃ
³SPIRIT - ²UNCLEAN AND HAVING CRIED OUT WITH A LOUD~VOICE,

ἐξῆλθεν ἐξ αὐτοῦ. **1.27** καὶ ἐθαμβήθησαν ἅπαντες ὥστε
IT CAME OUT OF HIM. AND EVERYONE~WAS AMAZED SO AS

συζητεῖν πρὸς ἑαυτοὺς λέγοντας, Τί ἐστιν τοῦτο;
[TO BEGIN] TO DISCUSS WITH EACH OTHER SAYING, WHAT IS THIS?

διδαχὴ καινὴ κατ' ἐξουσίαν· καὶ τοῖς πνεύμασι τοῖς
A NEW~TEACHING WITH AUTHORITY; - ²THE ⁴SPIRITS -

ἀκαθάρτοις ἐπιτάσσει, καὶ ὑπακούουσιν αὐτῷ. **1.28** καὶ
³UNCLEAN ¹HE COMMANDS AND THEY OBEY HIM. AND

me and I will make you fish for people." [18]And immediately they left their nets and followed him. [19]As he went a little farther, he saw James son of Zebedee and his brother John, who were in their boat mending the nets. [20]Immediately he called them; and they left their father Zebedee in the boat with the hired men, and followed him.

21 They went to Capernaum; and when the sabbath came, he entered the synagogue and taught. [22]They were astounded at his teaching, for he taught them as one having authority, and not as the scribes. [23]Just then there was in their synagogue a man with an unclean spirit, [24]and he cried out, "What have you to do with us, Jesus of Nazareth? Have you come to destroy us? I know who you are, the Holy One of God." [25]But Jesus rebuked him, saying, "Be silent, and come out of him!" [26]And the unclean spirit, convulsing him and crying with a loud voice, came out of him. [27]They were all amazed, and they kept on asking one another, "What is this? A new teaching—with authority! He[k] commands even the unclean spirits, and they obey him." [28]At once

[k] Or *A new teaching! With authority he*

his fame began to spread throughout the surrounding region of Galilee.

29 As soon as they[l] left the synagogue, they entered the house of Simon and Andrew, with James and John. [30]Now Simon's mother-in-law was in bed with a fever, and they told him about her at once. [31]He came and took her by the hand and lifted her up. Then the fever left her, and she began to serve them.

32 That evening, at sundown, they brought to him all who were sick or possessed with demons. [33]And the whole city was gathered around the door. [34]And he cured many who were sick with various diseases, and cast out many demons; and he would not permit the demons to speak, because they knew him.

35 In the morning, while it was still very dark, he got up and went out to a deserted place, and there he prayed. [36]And Simon and his companions hunted for him. [37]When they found him, they said to him, "Everyone is searching for you." [38]He answered, "Let us go on to the neighboring towns, so that I may proclaim the message there also; for that is what I came out to do." [39]And he went throughout Galilee, proclaiming the message in their synagogues

[l] Other ancient authorities read he

ἐξῆλθεν ἡ ἀκοὴ αὐτοῦ εὐθὺς πανταχοῦ εἰς ὅλην τὴν
WENT OUT   THE   REPORT   OF HIM   IMMEDIATELY   EVERYWHERE   INTO   ALL   THE

περίχωρον   τῆς Γαλιλαίας.
SURROUNDING COUNTRYSIDE -   OF GALILEE.

1.29 Καὶ εὐθὺς ἐκ τῆς συναγωγῆς ἐξελθόντες
AND IMMEDIATELY OUT OF THE SYNAGOGUE   COMING

ἦλθον εἰς τὴν οἰκίαν Σίμωνος καὶ Ἀνδρέου μετὰ
THEY WENT INTO THE HOUSE   OF SIMON   AND   ANDREW   WITH

Ἰακώβου καὶ Ἰωάννου. **1.30** ἡ δὲ πενθερὰ Σίμωνος
JAMES   AND   JOHN.   AND~THE MOTHER-IN-LAW OF SIMON

κατέκειτο πυρέσσουσα, καὶ εὐθὺς λέγουσιν αὐτῷ
WAS LYING DOWN HAVING A FEVER, AND RIGHT AWAY THEY SPEAK TO HIM

περὶ   αὐτῆς. **1.31** καὶ προσελθὼν ἤγειρεν αὐτὴν
CONCERNING HER.   AND HAVING APPROACHED, HE RAISED HER

κρατήσας τῆς χειρός· καὶ ἀφῆκεν αὐτὴν ὁ πυρετός,
TAKING [HER]   BY THE HAND;   AND   LEFT   HER   THE   FEVER,

καὶ διηκόνει αὐτοῖς. **1.32** Ὀψίας δὲ γενομένης, ὅτε
AND SHE WAS SERVING THEM.   AND~EVENING HAVING COME, WHEN

ἔδυ ὁ ἥλιος, ἔφερον   πρὸς αὐτὸν πάντας τοὺς
SET THE SUN, THEY WERE BRINGING TO   HIM   ALL   THE ONES

κακῶς ἔχοντας καὶ τοὺς δαιμονιζομένους· **1.33** καὶ
HAVING~ILLNESS AND THE ONES BEING DEMON-POSSESSED.   AND

ἦν ὅλη ἡ πόλις ἐπισυνηγμένη πρὸς τὴν θύραν.
[4]WAS [2]WHOLE [1]THE [3]CITY GATHERED TOGETHER AT THE DOOR.

1.34 καὶ ἐθεράπευσεν πολλοὺς κακῶς ἔχοντας ποικίλαις
AND HE HEALED   MANY   HAVING~ILLNESS WITH VARIOUS

νόσοις καὶ δαιμόνια πολλὰ ἐξέβαλεν καὶ οὐκ ἤφιεν
DISEASES AND MANY~DEMONS   HE CAST OUT AND HE DID NOT PERMIT

λαλεῖν τὰ δαιμόνια, ὅτι ᾔδεισαν αὐτόν[*].
[3]TO SPEAK [1]THE [2]DEMONS, BECAUSE THEY HAD KNOWN HIM.

1.35 Καὶ πρωῒ ἔννυχα λίαν ἀναστὰς ἐξῆλθεν καὶ
AND [3]EARLY [4]AT NIGHT [2]VERY [1]HAVING ARISEN, HE WENT OUT AND

ἀπῆλθεν εἰς ἔρημον τόπον κἀκεῖ προσηύχετο. **1.36** καὶ
WENT AWAY TO A DESOLATE PLACE AND THERE HE WAS PRAYING.   AND

κατεδίωξεν αὐτὸν Σίμων καὶ οἱ μετ᾽ αὐτοῦ,
SEARCHED [FOR] HIM SIMON AND THE ONES WITH HIM,

1.37 καὶ εὗρον αὐτὸν καὶ λέγουσιν αὐτῷ ὅτι Πάντες
AND THEY FOUND HIM AND THEY SAY TO HIM - EVERYONE

ζητοῦσίν σε. **1.38** καὶ λέγει αὐτοῖς, Ἄγωμεν
IS(ARE) LOOKING FOR YOU. AND HE SAYS TO THEM, LET US GO

ἀλλαχοῦ εἰς τὰς ἐχομένας κωμοπόλεις, ἵνα καὶ ἐκεῖ
ELSEWHERE INTO THE NEIGHBORING VILLAGES, SO THAT ALSO THERE

κηρύξω· εἰς τοῦτο   γὰρ ἐξῆλθον. **1.39** καὶ ἦλθεν
I MAY PREACH. [3]FOR [4]THIS [PURPOSE] [1]FOR [2]I CAME. AND HE CAME

κηρύσσων εἰς τὰς συναγωγὰς αὐτῶν εἰς ὅλην
PREACHING IN THE SYNAGOGUES OF THEM IN [THE] WHOLE [REGION OF]

1:34 text: all. add Χριστον ειναι (knew [him] to be Christ) [see Luke 4:41]: ASVmg NASBmg.

τὴν Γαλιλαίαν καὶ τὰ δαιμόνια ἐκβάλλων.
\-   GALILEE   AND   ²THE   ³DEMONS   ¹CASTING OUT.

1.40 Καὶ ἔρχεται πρὸς αὐτὸν λεπρὸς παρακαλῶν
AND   COMES   TO   HIM   A LEPER   BEGGING

αὐτὸν [καὶ γονυπετῶν] καὶ λέγων αὐτῷ ὅτι Ἐὰν
HIM   AND   KNEELING DOWN   AND   SAYING   TO HIM   -   IF

θέλῃς δύνασαί με καθαρίσαι. **1.41** καὶ
YOU ARE WILLING   YOU ARE ABLE   TO CLEANSE~ME.   AND

⌜σπλαγχνισθεὶς⌝ ἐκτείνας τὴν χεῖρα αὐτοῦ
BEING FILLED WITH COMPASSION   [AND] STRETCHING OUT   THE   HAND   OF HIM

ἥψατο καὶ λέγει αὐτῷ, Θέλω, καθαρίσθητι·
HE TOUCHED [THE MAN]   AND   SAYS   TO HIM,   I AM WILLING,   BE CLEANSED.

1.42 καὶ εὐθὺς ἀπῆλθεν ἀπ᾽ αὐτοῦ ἡ λέπρα, καὶ
AND   IMMEDIATELY   WENT AWAY   FROM   HIM   THE   LEPER,   AND

ἐκαθαρίσθη. **1.43** καὶ ἐμβριμησάμενος αὐτῷ εὐθὺς
HE WAS CLEANSED.   AND   HAVING STERNLY WARNED   HIM,   IMMEDIATELY

ἐξέβαλεν αὐτόν **1.44** καὶ λέγει αὐτῷ, Ὅρα μηδενὶ
HE SENT OUT   HIM   AND   HE SAYS   TO HIM,   SEE [THAT]   TO NO ONE

μηδὲν εἴπῃς, ἀλλὰ ὕπαγε σεαυτὸν δεῖξον τῷ ἱερεῖ
YOU SAY~NOTHING,   BUT RATHER   GO   SHOW~YOURSELF   TO THE   PRIEST

καὶ προσένεγκε περὶ τοῦ καθαρισμοῦ σου ἃ
AND   OFFER [THE SACRIFICES]   FOR   THE   CLEANSING   OF YOU   WHICH

προσέταξεν Μωϋσῆς, εἰς μαρτύριον αὐτοῖς. **1.45** ὁ δὲ
MOSES~COMMANDED,   FOR   A TESTIMONY   TO THEM.   BUT~THE ONE

ἐξελθὼν ἤρξατο κηρύσσειν πολλὰ καὶ διαφημίζειν
HAVING GONE OUT   BEGAN   TO PREACH   MANY THINGS   AND   TO SPREAD

τὸν λόγον, ὥστε μηκέτι αὐτὸν δύνασθαι φανερῶς
THE   WORD,   SO THAT   ³NO LONGER   ¹HE   ²WAS ABLE   OPENLY

εἰς πόλιν εἰσελθεῖν, ἀλλ᾽ ἔξω ἐπ᾽ ἐρήμοις τόποις
INTO [THE] CITY   TO ENTER,   BUT   OUTSIDE   IN   DESOLATE   PLACES

ἦν· καὶ ἤρχοντο πρὸς αὐτὸν πάντοθεν.
HE WAS.   AND   THEY WERE COMING   TO   HIM   FROM EVERY DIRECTION.

1:41 text: KJV ASV RSV NASB NIV NEBmg TEV NJB NRSV. var. οργισθεις (was angry): NEB TEVmg NRSVmg.

and casting out demons.

40 A leper[m] came to him begging him, and kneeling[n] he said to him, "If you choose, you can make me clean." [41]Moved with pity,[o] Jesus[p] stretched out his hand and touched him, and said to him, "I do choose. Be made clean!" [42]Immediately the leprosy[m] left him, and he was made clean. [43]After sternly warning him he sent him away at once, [44]saying to him, "See that you say nothing to anyone; but go, show yourself to the priest, and offer for your cleansing what Moses commanded, as a testimony to them." [45]But he went out and began to proclaim it freely, and to spread the word, so that Jesus[p] could no longer go into a town openly, but stayed out in the country; and people came to him from every quarter.

[m] The terms *leper* and *leprosy* can refer to several diseases
[n] Other ancient authorities lack *kneeling*
[o] Other ancient authorities read *anger*
[p] Gk *he*

CHAPTER 2

2.1 Καὶ εἰσελθὼν πάλιν εἰς Καφαρναοὺμ δι᾽
AND   HAVING ENTERED   AGAIN   INTO   CAPERNAUM   AFTER [MANY]

ἡμερῶν ἠκούσθη ὅτι ἐν οἴκῳ ἐστίν. **2.2** καὶ
DAYS,   IT WAS HEARD   THAT   AT   HOME   HE IS.   AND

συνήχθησαν πολλοὶ ὥστε μηκέτι χωρεῖν μηδὲ τὰ
MANY~WERE GATHERED TOGETHER   SO AS   NO LONGER   TO HAVE ROOM   -   -

πρὸς τὴν θύραν, καὶ ἐλάλει αὐτοῖς τὸν λόγον.
AT   THE   DOOR,   AND   HE WAS SPEAKING   TO THEM   THE   WORD.

2.3 καὶ ἔρχονται φέροντες πρὸς αὐτὸν παραλυτικὸν
AND   THEY COME   CARRYING   TO   HIM   A PARALYTIC

When he returned to Capernaum after some days, it was reported that he was at home. [2]So many gathered around that there was no longer room for them, not even in front of the door; and he was speaking the word to them. [3]Then some people[q] came, bringing to him a paralyzed man,

[q] Gk *they*

carried by four of them.
⁴And when they could not
bring him to Jesus because
of the crowd, they removed
the roof above him; and after
having dug through it, they
let down the mat on which
the paralytic lay. ⁵When
Jesus saw their faith, he said
to the paralytic, "Son, your
sins are forgiven." ⁶Now
some of the scribes were
sitting there, questioning in
their hearts, ⁷"Why does this
fellow speak in this way? It
is blasphemy! Who can
forgive sins but God alone?"
⁸At once Jesus perceived in
his spirit that they were
discussing these questions
among themselves; and he
said to them, "Why do you
raise such questions in your
hearts? ⁹Which is easier, to
say to the paralytic, 'Your
sins are forgiven,' or to say,
'Stand up and take your mat
and walk'? ¹⁰But so that you
may know that the Son of
Man has authority on earth
to forgive sins"—he said to
the paralytic— ¹¹"I say to
you, stand up, take your mat
and go to your home."
¹²And he stood up, and
immediately took the mat
and went out before all of
them; so that they were all
amazed and glorified God,
saying, "We have never seen
anything like this!"

αἰρόμενον   ὑπὸ   τεσσάρων. **2.4** καὶ   μὴ   δυνάμενοι
BEING CARRIED ALONG   BY   FOUR [MEN].   AND   NOT   BEING ABLE

προσενέγκαι   αὐτῷ   διὰ   τὸν   ὄχλον
TO BRING [THE PARALYTIC] TO HIM ON ACCOUNT OF THE   CROWD,

ἀπεστέγασαν   τὴν   στέγην   ὅπου   ἦν,   καὶ
THEY REMOVED   THE   ROOF   WHERE HE WAS, AND

ἐξορύξαντες   χαλῶσι   τὸν   κράβαττον ὅπου   ὁ
HAVING MADE AN OPENING THEY LOWERED THE   MATTRESS   UPON WHICH THE

παραλυτικὸς   κατέκειτο. **2.5** καὶ   ἰδὼν   ὁ   Ἰησοῦς τὴν
PARALYTIC   WAS LYING.   AND   ²HAVING SEEN - ¹JESUS   THE

πίστιν   αὐτῶν λέγει τῷ   παραλυτικῷ, Τέκνον,
FAITH   OF THEM SAYS   TO THE PARALYTIC,   CHILD,

ἀφίενταί σου αἱ   ἁμαρτίαι. **2.6** ἦσαν δέ   τινες τῶν
ARE FORGIVEN YOUR - SINS.   AND~THERE WERE SOME   OF THE

γραμματέων ἐκεῖ καθήμενοι καὶ   διαλογιζόμενοι   ἐν
SCRIBES   SITTING~THERE AND   THINKING ABOUT [THESE THINGS] IN

ταῖς   καρδίαις αὐτῶν, **2.7** Τί   οὗτος οὕτως λαλεῖ;
THE   HEARTS   OF THEM,   WHY [IS] THIS ONE SPEAKING~THUS?

βλασφημεῖ· τίς δύναται ἀφιέναι ἁμαρτίας εἰ μὴ
HE BLASPHEMES. WHO IS ABLE   TO FORGIVE SINS   EXCEPT

εἷς   ὁ θεός; **2.8** καὶ   εὐθὺς   ἐπιγνοὺς ὁ Ἰησοῦς
[THE] ONE, - GOD?   AND   IMMEDIATELY HAVING KNOWN - JESUS

τῷ   πνεύματι αὐτοῦ ὅτι οὕτως   διαλογίζονται ἐν
IN THE SPIRIT   OF HIM   THAT IN THIS MANNER THEY ARE DIALOGUING AMONG

ἑαυτοῖς λέγει αὐτοῖς, Τί   ταῦτα διαλογίζεσθε   ἐν
THEMSELVES HE SAYS TO THEM,   WHY ARE YOU° CONSIDERING~THESE THINGS IN

ταῖς   καρδίαις ὑμῶν; **2.9** τί   ἐστιν εὐκοπώτερον, εἰπεῖν
THE   HEARTS   OF YOU°?   WHICH IS   EASIER,   TO SAY

τῷ   παραλυτικῷ, Ἀφίενταί σου αἱ   ἁμαρτίαι, ἢ
TO THE PARALYTIC,   ARE FORGIVEN YOUR - SINS,   OR

εἰπεῖν, Ἔγειρε καὶ   ἆρον τὸν   κράβαττόν σου καὶ
TO SAY,   STAND   AND   PICK UP THE   MATTRESS   OF YOU AND

περιπάτει; **2.10** ἵνα δὲ   εἰδῆτε   ὅτι ἐξουσίαν ἔχει
WALK?   BUT~IN ORDER THAT YOU° MAY KNOW THAT HAS~AUTHORITY

ὁ   υἱὸς τοῦ ἀνθρώπου ἀφιέναι ἁμαρτίας ἐπὶ τῆς γῆς—
THE SON -   OF MAN   TO FORGIVE SINS   UPON -   EARTH—

λέγει τῷ   παραλυτικῷ, **2.11** Σοὶ λέγω, ἔγειρε ἆρον
HE SAYS TO THE PARALYTIC,   TO YOU I SAY, STAND,   PICK UP

τὸν   κράβαττόν σου καὶ   ὕπαγε εἰς τὸν   οἶκόν σου.
THE   MATTRESS   OF YOU AND   GO   TO   THE   HOME   OF YOU.

2.12 καὶ   ἠγέρθη καὶ   εὐθὺς   ἄρας τὸν   κράβαττον
       AND   HE AROSE AND   IMMEDIATELY TAKING THE   MATTRESS

ἐξῆλθεν   ἔμπροσθεν πάντων, ὥστε ἐξίστασθαι   πάντας
WENT OUTSIDE IN FRONT OF   EVERYONE,   SO AS   TO ASTONISH   EVERYONE

καὶ   δοξάζειν τὸν   θεὸν λέγοντας ὅτι Οὕτως οὐδέποτε
AND   TO GLORIFY -   GOD   SAYING,   -   THUS   NEVER

εἴδομεν.
HAVE WE SEEN.

2.13 Καὶ   ἐξῆλθεν   πάλιν   παρὰ   τὴν   θάλασσαν·   καὶ
AND   HE WENT OUT   AGAIN   BESIDE   THE   LAKE;   AND

πᾶς ὁ   ὄχλος   ἤρχετο   πρὸς   αὐτόν,   καὶ   ἐδίδασκεν
ALL   THE   CROWD   WAS COMING   TO   HIM,   AND   HE WAS TEACHING

αὐτούς.   **2.14** καὶ   παράγων   εἶδεν   Λευὶν   τὸν   τοῦ
THEM.   AND   PASSING BY   HE SAW   LEVI   THE [SON]   -

Ἀλφαίου   καθήμενον   ἐπὶ   τὸ   τελώνιον,   καὶ   λέγει   αὐτῷ,
OF ALPHAEUS   SITTING   IN   THE   TAX OFFICE,   AND   HE SAYS   TO HIM,

Ἀκολούθει   μοι.   καὶ   ἀναστὰς   ἠκολούθησεν   αὐτῷ.
FOLLOW   ME.   AND   RISING UP   HE FOLLOWED   HIM.

2.15 Καὶ   γίνεται   κατακεῖσθαι   αὐτὸν   ἐν   τῇ   οἰκίᾳ
AND   IT CAME TO PASS   [THAT] HE RECLINED   IN   THE   HOUSE

αὐτοῦ,   καὶ   πολλοὶ   τελῶναι   καὶ   ἁμαρτωλοὶ
OF HIM,   AND   MANY   TAX COLLECTORS   AND   SINNERS

συνανέκειντο   τῷ   Ἰησοῦ   καὶ   τοῖς   μαθηταῖς   αὐτοῦ·
WERE RECLINING   -   WITH JESUS   AND   WITH THE   DISCIPLES   OF HIM.

ἦσαν   γὰρ   πολλοὶ   καὶ   ἠκολούθουν   αὐτῷ.   **2.16** καὶ
FOR~THERE WERE   MANY   AND   THEY WERE FOLLOWING   HIM.   AND

⌐οἱ   γραμματεῖς   τῶν   Φαρισαίων⌐   ἰδόντες   ὅτι   ἐσθίει⊤
THE   SCRIBES   OF THE   PHARISEES   SEEING   THAT   HE EATS

μετὰ   τῶν   ἁμαρτωλῶν   καὶ   τελωνῶν   ἔλεγον   τοῖς
WITH   -   SINNERS   AND   TAX COLLECTORS   WERE SAYING   TO THE

μαθηταῖς   αὐτοῦ,   Ὅτι   μετὰ   τῶν   τελωνῶν   καὶ
DISCIPLES   OF HIM   -   2WITH   -   3TAX COLLECTORS   4AND

ἁμαρτωλῶν   ἐσθίει;   **2.17** καὶ   ἀκούσας   ὁ   Ἰησοῦς
5SINNERS   1DOES HE EAT?   AND   HAVING HEARD [THIS]   -   JESUS

λέγει   αὐτοῖς   [ὅτι]   Οὐ   χρείαν   ἔχουσιν   οἱ   ἰσχύοντες
SAYS   TO THEM   -   4NO NEED   3HAVE   1THE   2STRONG ONES

ἰατροῦ   ἀλλ'   οἱ   κακῶς   ἔχοντες·   οὐκ   ἦλθον
OF A PHYSICIAN   BUT RATHER   THE ONES   HAVING~ILLNESS.   I DID NOT COME

καλέσαι   δικαίους   ἀλλὰ   ἁμαρτωλούς.
TO CALL   [THE] RIGHTEOUS   BUT   SINNERS.

2.18 Καὶ   ἦσαν   οἱ   μαθηταὶ   Ἰωάννου   καὶ   οἱ
AND   CAME   THE   DISCIPLES   OF JOHN   AND   THE

Φαρισαῖοι   νηστεύοντες.   καὶ   ἔρχονται   καὶ   λέγουσιν
PHARISEES   FASTING.   AND   THEY COME   AND   SAY

αὐτῷ,   Διὰ   τί   οἱ   μαθηταὶ   Ἰωάννου   καὶ   οἱ   μαθηταὶ
TO HIM,   WHY [DO]   THE   DISCIPLES   OF JOHN   AND   THE   DISCIPLES

τῶν   Φαρισαίων   νηστεύουσιν,   οἱ   δὲ   σοὶ   μαθηταὶ
OF THE   PHARISEES   FAST,   -   BUT   YOUR   DISCIPLES

οὐ   νηστεύουσιν;   **2.19** καὶ   εἶπεν   αὐτοῖς   ὁ   Ἰησοῦς,
DO NOT FAST?   AND   SAID   TO THEM   -   JESUS,

Μὴ   δύνανται   οἱ   υἱοὶ   τοῦ   νυμφῶνος ἐν   ᾧ   ὁ
5ARE NOT ABLE   1[SURELY] THE   2ATTENDANTS   3OF THE   4GROOM   7WHILE   8THE

νυμφίος   μετ'   αὐτῶν   ἐστιν   νηστεύειν;   ὅσον   χρόνον
9GROOM   11WITH   12THEM   10IS   6TO FAST?   AS LONG AS

13 Jesus[r] went out again beside the sea; the whole crowd gathered around him, and he taught them. 14As he was walking along, he saw Levi son of Alphaeus sitting at the tax booth, and he said to him, "Follow me." And he got up and followed him.

15 And as he sat at dinner[s] in Levi's[t] house, many tax collectors and sinners were also sitting[u] with Jesus and his disciples—for there were many who followed him. 16When the scribes of[v] the Pharisees saw that he was eating with sinners and tax collectors, they said to his disciples, "Why does he eat[w] with tax collectors and sinners?" 17When Jesus heard this, he said to them, "Those who are well have no need of a physician, but those who are sick; I have come to call not the righteous but sinners."

18 Now John's disciples and the Pharisees were fasting; and people[x] came and said to him, "Why do John's disciples and the disciples of the Pharisees fast, but your disciples do not fast?" 19Jesus said to them, "The wedding guests cannot fast while the bridegroom is with them, can they? As long as

[r] Gk *He*
[s] Gk *reclined*
[t] Gk *his*
[u] Gk *reclining*
[v] Other ancient authorities read *and*
[w] Other ancient authorities add *and drink*
[x] Gk *they*

2:16a text: ASV RSV NASB NIV NEB TEV NJB NRSV.   var. οι γραμματεις και οι Φαρισαιοι (the scribes and the Pharisees): KJV ASVmg RSVmg NRSVmg.   **2:16b** text [see Matt. 9:11]: ASV RSV NIV NEB TEV NJB NRSV.   add και πινει (and drink): ASV RSVmg NASB NRSVmg.

they have the bridegroom with them, they cannot fast. [20]The days will come when the bridegroom is taken away from them, and then they will fast on that day.

21 "No one sews a piece of unshrunk cloth on an old cloak; otherwise, the patch pulls away from it, the new from the old, and a worse tear is made. [22]And no one puts new wine into old wineskins; otherwise, the wine will burst the skins, and the wine is lost, and so are the skins; but one puts new wine into fresh wineskins."[y]

23 One sabbath he was going through the grainfields; and as they made their way his disciples began to pluck heads of grain. [24]The Pharisees said to him, "Look, why are they doing what is not lawful on the sabbath?" [25]And he said to them, "Have you never read what David did when he and his companions were hungry and in need of food? [26]He entered the house of God, when Abiathar was high priest, and ate the bread of the Presence, which it is not lawful for any but the priests to eat, and he gave some to his companions." [27]Then he said to them, "The sabbath was made for humankind, and not humankind for the

[y] Other ancient authorities lack *but one puts new wine into fresh wineskins*

ἔχουσιν τὸν νυμφίον μετ' αὐτῶν οὐ δύνανται νηστεύειν.
THEY HAVE   THE   GROOM   WITH   THEM   THEY ARE NOT ABLE   TO FAST.

2.20 ἐλεύσονται δὲ ἡμέραι ὅταν ἀπαρθῇ ἀπ' αὐτῶν ὁ
BUT~WILL COME   DAYS   WHEN   IS TAKEN AWAY   FROM   THEM   THE

νυμφίος, καὶ τότε νηστεύσουσιν ἐν ἐκείνῃ τῇ ἡμέρᾳ.
GROOM,   AND   THEN   THEY WILL FAST   IN   THAT   -   DAY.

2.21 Οὐδεὶς ἐπίβλημα ῥάκους ἀγνάφου ἐπιράπτει
NO ONE   ²A PATCH   ⁴CLOTH   ³OF UNSHRUNK   ¹SEWS

ἐπὶ ἱμάτιον παλαιόν· εἰ δὲ μή, αἴρει τὸ πλήρωμα
ON   AN OLD~GARMENT;   OTHERWISE,   ³WILL PULL AWAY   ¹THE   ²PATCH

ἀπ' αὐτοῦ τὸ καινὸν τοῦ παλαιοῦ καὶ χεῖρον
FROM IT,   THE NEW   FROM THE OLD   AND   A WORSE

σχίσμα γίνεται. **2.22** καὶ οὐδεὶς βάλλει οἶνον νέον εἰς
TEAR   RESULTS.   AND   NO ONE   PUTS   NEW~WINE   INTO

ἀσκοὺς παλαιούς· εἰ δὲ μή, ῥήξει ὁ οἶνος τοὺς
OLD~WINESKINS;   OTHERWISE,   ³WILL TEAR   ¹THE   ²WINE   THE

ἀσκούς καὶ ὁ οἶνος ἀπόλλυται καὶ οἱ ἀσκοί· ἀλλὰ
WINESKINS   AND   THE   WINE   IS RUINED   AND   THE   WINESKINS.   INSTEAD,

οἶνον νέον εἰς ἀσκοὺς καινούς.
NEW~WINE [IS PUT]   INTO   NEW~WINESKINS.

2.23 Καὶ ἐγένετο αὐτὸν ἐν τοῖς σάββασιν
AND   IT CAME ABOUT [THAT]   HE   ON THE   SABBATH(S)

παραπορεύεσθαι διὰ τῶν σπορίμων, καὶ οἱ μαθηταὶ
WAS PASSING   THROUGH   THE   GRAINFIELDS,   AND   THE   DISCIPLES

αὐτοῦ ἤρξαντο ὁδὸν ποιεῖν τίλλοντες τοὺς στάχυας.
OF HIM   BEGAN   TO MAKE~[THEIR] WAY   PICKING   THE   HEADS OF GRAIN.

2.24 καὶ οἱ Φαρισαῖοι ἔλεγον αὐτῷ, Ἴδε τί ποιοῦσιν
AND   THE   PHARISEES   SAID   TO HIM,   LOOK,   WHY   ARE THEY DOING

τοῖς σάββασιν ὃ οὐκ ἔξεστιν; **2.25** καὶ λέγει αὐτοῖς,
ON THE   SABBATHS   WHAT   IS NOT PERMITTED?   AND   HE SAYS   TO THEM,

Οὐδέποτε ἀνέγνωτε τί ἐποίησεν Δαυίδ ὅτε
HAVE YOU° NEVER READ   WHAT   DAVID~DID   WHEN

χρείαν ἔσχεν καὶ ἐπείνασεν αὐτὸς καὶ οἱ μετ'
HE HAD~NEED   AND   HE WAS HUNGRY,   HE   AND   THE ONES   WITH

αὐτοῦ, **2.26** πῶς εἰσῆλθεν εἰς τὸν οἶκον τοῦ θεοῦ
HIM,   HOW   HE ENTERED   INTO THE   HOUSE   -   OF GOD

ἐπὶ Ἀβιαθὰρ ἀρχιερέως καὶ τοὺς ἄρτους τῆς
DURING [THE DAYS OF]   ABIATHAR   [THE] HIGH PRIEST   AND   THE   LOAVES   OF THE

προθέσεως ἔφαγεν, οὓς οὐκ ἔξεστιν φαγεῖν εἰ μὴ τοὺς
PRESENTATION   HE ATE,   WHICH   IS NOT PERMITTED   TO BE EATEN   EXCEPT   BY THE

ἱερεῖς, καὶ ἔδωκεν καὶ τοῖς σὺν αὐτῷ οὖσιν;
PRIESTS,   AND   HE GAVE [SOME]   ALSO   TO THE ONES   WITH   HIM   BEING?

2.27 καὶ ἔλεγεν αὐτοῖς, Τὸ σάββατον διὰ τὸν
AND   HE SAID   TO THEM,   THE   SABBATH   ON ACCOUNT OF   -

ἄνθρωπον ἐγένετο καὶ οὐχ ὁ ἄνθρωπος διὰ τὸ
MAN   WAS CREATED   AND   NOT   -   MAN   ON ACCOUNT   OF THE

σάββατον· **2.28** ὥστε κύριός ἐστιν ὁ υἱὸς τοῦ
SABBATH.   SO THAT ⁵LORD ⁴IS ¹THE ²SON -

ἀνθρώπου καὶ τοῦ σαββάτου.
³OF MAN   EVEN   OF THE   SABBATH.

sabbath; 28so the Son of Man is lord even of the sabbath."

3.1 Καὶ εἰσῆλθεν πάλιν εἰς τὴν συναγωγήν. καὶ
AND   HE ENTERED   AGAIN   INTO THE   SYNAGOGUE.   AND

ἦν ἐκεῖ ἄνθρωπος ἐξηραμμένην ἔχων τὴν χεῖρα.
THERE WAS   THERE   A MAN   HAVING~A WITHERED   -   HAND.

3.2 καὶ παρετήρουν αὐτὸν εἰ τοῖς σάββασιν
AND   THEY WERE WATCHING   HIM   [TO SEE] IF   ON THE   SABBATHS

θεραπεύσει αὐτόν, ἵνα κατηγορήσωσιν αὐτοῦ.
HE WILL HEAL   HIM,   IN ORDER THAT   THEY MIGHT ACCUSE   HIM.

3.3 καὶ λέγει τῷ ἀνθρώπῳ τῷ τὴν ξηρὰν χεῖρα
AND   HE SAYS   TO THE   MAN,   THE ONE   WITH THE   WITHERED   HAND

ἔχοντι, Ἔγειρε εἰς τὸ μέσον. **3.4** καὶ λέγει αὐτοῖς,
HAVING,   STAND UP   IN   THE   MIDDLE.   AND   HE SAYS   TO THEM,

Ἔξεστιν τοῖς σάββασιν ἀγαθὸν ποιῆσαι ἢ
IS IT PERMITTED   ON THE   SABBATHS   TO DO~GOOD   OR

κακοποιῆσαι, ψυχὴν σῶσαι ἢ ἀποκτεῖναι; οἱ δὲ
TO DO EVIL,   TO RESTORE~LIFE   OR   TO DESTROY [IT]?   BUT~THEY

ἐσιώπων. **3.5** καὶ περιβλεψάμενος αὐτοὺς μετ᾽ ὀργῆς,
WERE SILENT.   AND   HAVING LOOKED   [AT] THEM   WITH   ANGER,

συλλυπούμενος ἐπὶ τῇ πωρώσει τῆς καρδίας αὐτῶν
BEING DEEPLY GRIEVED   AT   THE   HARDNESS   -   OF THEIR~HEART

λέγει τῷ ἀνθρώπῳ, Ἔκτεινον τὴν χεῖρα. καὶ
HE SAYS   TO THE   MAN,   STRETCH OUT   THE(YOUR)   HAND.   AND

ἐξέτεινεν καὶ ἀπεκατεστάθη ἡ χεὶρ αὐτοῦ.
HE STRETCHED [IT] OUT   AND   WAS RESTORED   THE   HAND   OF HIM.

3.6 καὶ ἐξελθόντες οἱ Φαρισαῖοι εὐθὺς μετὰ τῶν
AND   GOING OUT   THE PHARISEES   IMMEDIATELY   WITH   THE

Ἡρῳδιανῶν συμβούλιον ἐδίδουν κατ᾽ αὐτοῦ ὅπως
HERODIANS   HELD~CONSULTATION   AGAINST   HIM   AS TO HOW

αὐτὸν ἀπολέσωσιν.
THEY MIGHT DESTROY~HIM.

3.7 Καὶ ὁ Ἰησοῦς μετὰ τῶν μαθητῶν αὐτοῦ
AND   -   JESUS   WITH   THE   DISCIPLES   OF HIM

ἀνεχώρησεν πρὸς τὴν θάλασσαν, καὶ πολὺ πλῆθος ἀπὸ
WENT AWAY   TO   THE   LAKE,   AND   A GREAT   MULTITUDE   FROM

τῆς Γαλιλαίας [ἠκολούθησεν], καὶ ἀπὸ τῆς Ἰουδαίας
-    GALILEE   FOLLOWED [HIM],   ALSO   FROM   -   JUDEA

3.8 καὶ ἀπὸ Ἱεροσολύμων καὶ ἀπὸ τῆς Ἰδουμαίας καὶ
AND   FROM   JERUSALEM   AND   FROM   -   IDUMEA   AND

Again he entered the synagogue, and a man was there who had a withered hand. 2They watched him to see whether he would cure him on the sabbath, so that they might accuse him. 3And he said to the man who had the withered hand, "Come forward." 4Then he said to them, "Is it lawful to do good or to do harm on the sabbath, to save life or to kill?" But they were silent. 5He looked around at them with anger; he was grieved at their hardness of heart and said to the man, "Stretch out your hand." He stretched it out, and his hand was restored. 6The Pharisees went out and immediately conspired with the Herodians against him, how to destroy him.

7 Jesus departed with his disciples to the sea, and a great multitude from Galilee followed him; 8hearing all that he was doing, they came to him in great numbers from Judea, Jerusalem, Idumea,

beyond the Jordan, and the region around Tyre and Sidon. [9]He told his disciples to have a boat ready for him because of the crowd, so that they would not crush him; [10]for he had cured many, so that all who had diseases pressed upon him to touch him. [11]Whenever the unclean spirits saw him, they fell down before him and shouted, "You are the Son of God!" [12]But he sternly ordered them not to make him known.

[13] He went up the mountain and called to him those whom he wanted, and they came to him. [14]And he appointed twelve, whom he also named apostles,[z] to be with him, and to be sent out to proclaim the message, [15]and to have authority to cast out demons. [16]So he appointed the twelve:[a] Simon (to whom he gave the name Peter); [17]James son of Zebedee and John the brother of James (to whom he gave the name Boanerges, that is, Sons of Thunder); [18]and Andrew, and Philip, and Bartholomew, and Matthew, and Thomas, and James son

[z] Other ancient authorities lack *whom he also named apostles*
[a] Other ancient authorities lack *So he appointed the twelve*

πέραν   τοῦ   Ἰορδάνου καὶ περὶ Τύρον καὶ Σιδῶνα
ON THE OTHER SIDE OF THE JORDAN   AND AROUND TYRE   AND   SIDON,

πλῆθος πολὺ   ἀκούοντες ὅσα   ἐποίει
A GREAT~MULTITUDE [FOLLOWED], HEARING   EVERYTHING THAT HE WAS DOING,

ἦλθον πρὸς αὐτόν.   **3.9** καὶ εἶπεν τοῖς μαθηταῖς
THEY CAME TO   HIM.   AND   HE SAID TO THE DISCIPLES

αὐτοῦ ἵνα πλοιάριον προσκαρτερῇ αὐτῷ διὰ   τὸν
OF HIM THAT A BOAT   SHOULD STAND READY FOR HIM BECAUSE OF THE

ὄχλον ἵνα μὴ θλίβωσιν   αὐτόν· **3.10** πολλοὺς γὰρ
CROWD LEST THEY CROWD AROUND HIM.   ³MANY   ¹FOR

ἐθεράπευσεν, ὥστε ἐπιπίπτειν αὐτῷ ἵνα αὐτοῦ ἅψωνται
²HE HEALED,   SO AS TO FALL UPON HIM   THAT HE   MIGHT TOUCH

ὅσοι   εἶχον μάστιγας. **3.11** καὶ τὰ πνεύματα τὰ
AS MANY AS HAD   AFFLICTIONS.   AND THE ²SPIRITS   -

ἀκάθαρτα, ὅταν   αὐτὸν ἐθεώρουν, προσέπιπτον αὐτῷ
¹UNCLEAN, WHENEVER THEY SAW~HIM,   WERE FALLING BEFORE HIM

καὶ ἔκραζον λέγοντες ὅτι Σὺ εἶ ὁ υἱὸς τοῦ θεοῦ.
AND WERE CRYING OUT SAYING - YOU ARE THE SON - OF GOD.

3.12 καὶ πολλὰ ἐπετίμα αὐτοῖς ἵνα μὴ αὐτὸν
       AND   ³STERNLY ¹HE REBUKED ²THEM LEST   HIM

φανερὸν ποιήσωσιν.
THEY SHOULD MAKE~MANIFEST.

3.13 Καὶ ἀναβαίνει εἰς τὸ ὄρος καὶ
       AND   HE GOES UP   TOWARD THE MOUNTAIN AND

προσκαλεῖται οὓς ἤθελεν αὐτός, καὶ ἀπῆλθον πρὸς
SUMMONS   WHOM HE~WANTED,   AND THEY CAME TO

αὐτόν. **3.14** καὶ ἐποίησεν δώδεκα ⌐οὓς καὶ
HIM.   AND   HE APPOINTED TWELVE WHOM ALSO

ἀποστόλους ὠνόμασεν⌐ ἵνα ὦσιν   μετ᾽ αὐτοῦ καὶ
HE DESIGNATED~APOSTLES   THAT THEY MIGHT BE WITH HIM   AND

ἵνα ἀποστέλλῃ αὐτοὺς κηρύσσειν **3.15** καὶ ἔχειν
THAT HE MIGHT SEND THEM   TO PREACH   AND   TO HAVE

ἐξουσίαν ἐκβάλλειν τὰ δαιμόνια· **3.16** [καὶ ἐποίησεν
AUTHORITY TO CAST OUT - DEMONS.   AND   HE APPOINTED

τοὺς δώδεκα,] καὶ ἐπέθηκεν ὄνομα τῷ Σίμωνι Πέτρον,
THE TWELVE,   AND HE GAVE [THE] NAME - PETER~TO SIMON,

3.17 καὶ Ἰάκωβον τὸν   τοῦ Ζεβεδαίου καὶ Ἰωάννην
        AND   JAMES   THE [SON] - OF ZEBEDEE   AND   JOHN

τὸν ἀδελφὸν τοῦ Ἰακώβου καὶ ἐπέθηκεν αὐτοῖς
THE BROTHER   - OF JAMES   AND HE GAVE   TO THEM

ὀνόμα[τα] Βοανηργές, ὅ ἐστιν Υἱοὶ Βροντῆς·
[THE] NAME[S] BOANERGES WHICH MEANS SONS OF THUNDER.

3.18 καὶ Ἀνδρέαν καὶ Φίλιππον καὶ Βαρθολομαῖον
        AND   ANDREW   AND   PHILIP   AND   BARTHOLOMEW

καὶ Μαθθαῖον καὶ Θωμᾶν καὶ Ἰάκωβον τὸν   τοῦ
AND MATTHEW   AND   THOMAS AND   JAMES   THE [SON] -

3:14 text [see Luke 6:13]: ASVmg RSVmg NASBmg NIV TEV NRSV. omit: KJV ASV RSV NASB NIVmg NEB NJB NRSVmg.

Ἀλφαίου   καὶ   Θαδδαῖον   καὶ   Σίμωνα   τὸν   Καναναῖον
OF ALPHAEUS   AND   THADDAEUS   AND   SIMON   THE   CANANAEAN

3.19 καὶ   Ἰούδαν   Ἰσκαριώθ,   ὃς   καὶ   παρέδωκεν   αὐτόν.
AND   JUDAS   ISCARIOT,   WHO   ALSO   BETRAYED   HIM.

3.20 Καὶ   ἔρχεται   εἰς   οἶκον·   καὶ   συνέρχεται   πάλιν
AND   HE GOES   INTO   A HOUSE;   AND   ASSEMBLES   AGAIN

[ὁ]   ὄχλος,   ὥστε   μὴ   δύνασθαι   αὐτοὺς   μηδὲ   ἄρτον   φαγεῖν.
THE   CROWD,   SO THAT   THEY~WERE NOT ABLE   -   TO EAT~BREAD.

3.21 καὶ   ἀκούσαντες   οἱ   παρ᾽   αὐτοῦ   ἐξῆλθον   κρατῆσαι
AND   HAVING HEARD [THIS]   HIS~FAMILY   WENT OUT   TO TAKE HOLD OF

αὐτόν·   ἔλεγον   γὰρ   ὅτι   ἐξέστη.   **3.22** καὶ   οἱ
HIM.   FOR~THEY WERE SAYING   -   HE HAS LOST HIS MIND.   AND   THE

γραμματεῖς   οἱ   ἀπὸ   Ἱεροσολύμων   καταβάντες
SCRIBES,   THE ONES FROM   JERUSALEM   HAVING COME DOWN

ἔλεγον   ὅτι   Βεελζεβοὺλ   ἔχει   καὶ   ὅτι   ἐν   τῷ   ἄρχοντι
WERE SAYING   -   HE HAS~BEELZEBUL   -   FOR   BY   THE   RULER

τῶν   δαιμονίων   ἐκβάλλει   τὰ   δαιμόνια.   **3.23** καὶ
OF THE   DEMONS   HE CASTS OUT   -   DEMONS.   AND

προσκαλεσάμενος   αὐτοὺς   ἐν   παραβολαῖς   ἔλεγεν
HAVING CALLED   THEM,   IN   PARABLES   HE WAS SPEAKING

αὐτοῖς,   Πῶς   δύναται   Σατανᾶς   Σατανᾶν   ἐκβάλλειν;
TO THEM,   HOW   IS IT POSSIBLE [FOR]   SATAN   TO CAST OUT~SATAN?

3.24 καὶ   ἐὰν   βασιλεία   ἐφ᾽   ἑαυτὴν   μερισθῇ,
AND   IF   A KINGDOM   AGAINST   ITSELF   IS DIVIDED,

οὐ   δύναται   σταθῆναι   ἡ   βασιλεία   ἐκείνη·   **3.25** καὶ
IT IS NOT POSSIBLE [FOR]   ³TO STAND   -   ²KINGDOM   ¹THAT.   AND

ἐὰν   οἰκία   ἐφ᾽   ἑαυτὴν   μερισθῇ,   οὐ   δυνήσεται   ἡ
IF   A HOUSE   AGAINST   ITSELF   IS DIVIDED,   IT WILL NOT BE POSSIBLE [FOR]   -

οἰκία   ἐκείνη   σταθῆναι.   **3.26** καὶ   εἰ   ὁ   Σατανᾶς   ἀνέστη
THAT~HOUSE   TO STAND.   AND   IF   -   SATAN   STOOD UP

ἐφ᾽   ἑαυτὸν   καὶ   ἐμερίσθη,   οὐ   δύναται   στῆναι
AGAINST   HIMSELF   AND   WAS DIVIDED,   IT IS NOT POSSIBLE [FOR HIM]   TO STAND

ἀλλὰ   τέλος   ἔχει.   **3.27** ἀλλ᾽   οὐ   δύναται   οὐδεὶς   εἰς   τὴν
BUT   HE HAS~AN END.   BUT   NO ONE IS ABLE   INTO   THE

οἰκίαν   τοῦ   ἰσχυροῦ   εἰσελθὼν   τὰ   σκεύη   αὐτοῦ
HOUSE   OF THE   STRONG MAN   HAVING ENTERED   THE   POSSESSIONS   OF HIM

διαρπάσαι,   ἐὰν   μὴ   πρῶτον   τὸν   ἰσχυρὸν   δήσῃ,   καὶ   τότε
TO PLUNDER,   UNLESS   FIRST,   THE   STRONG MAN   HE BINDS,   AND   THEN

τὴν   οἰκίαν   αὐτοῦ   διαρπάσει.   **3.28** Ἀμὴν   λέγω   ὑμῖν
THE   HOUSE   OF HIM   HE WILL PLUNDER.   TRULY   I SAY   TO YOU°

ὅτι   πάντα   ἀφεθήσεται   τοῖς   υἱοῖς   τῶν   ἀνθρώπων
THAT   EVERYTHING   WILL BE FORGIVEN   THE   SONS   -   OF MEN

τὰ   ἁμαρτήματα   καὶ   αἱ   βλασφημίαι   ὅσα   ἐὰν
THE   SINS   AND   THE   BLASPHEMIES   WHATEVER

βλασφημήσωσιν·   **3.29** ὃς   δ᾽   ἂν   βλασφημήσῃ   εἰς   τὸ
THEY MAY BLASPHEME.   BUT~WHOEVER   BLASPHEMES   AGAINST   THE

πνεῦμα   τὸ   ἅγιον,   οὐκ   ἔχει   ἄφεσιν   εἰς   τὸν   αἰῶνα,
²SPIRIT   -   ¹HOLY,   DOES NOT HAVE   FORGIVENESS   INTO   THE   AGE,

of Alphaeus, and Thaddaeus, and Simon the Cananaean, [19]and Judas Iscariot, who betrayed him.

Then he went home; [20]and the crowd came together again, so that they could not even eat. [21]When his family heard it, they went out to restrain him, for people were saying, "He has gone out of his mind." [22]And the scribes who came down from Jerusalem said, "He has Beelzebul, and by the ruler of the demons he casts out demons." [23]And he called them to him, and spoke to them in parables, "How can Satan cast out Satan? [24]If a kingdom is divided against itself, that kingdom cannot stand. [25]And if a house is divided against itself, that house will not be able to stand. [26]And if Satan has risen up against himself and is divided, he cannot stand, but his end has come. [27]But no one can enter a strong man's house and plunder his property without first tying up the strong man; then indeed the house can be plundered.

[28]"Truly I tell you, people will be forgiven for their sins and whatever blasphemies they utter; [29]but whoever blasphemes against the Holy Spirit can never have forgiveness,

but is guilty of an eternal sin"— [30]for they had said, "He has an unclean spirit."

31 Then his mother and his brothers came; and standing outside, they sent to him and called him. [32]A crowd was sitting around him; and they said to him, "Your mother and your brothers and sisters[b] are outside, asking for you." [33]And he replied, "Who are my mother and my brothers?" [34]And looking at those who sat around him, he said, "Here are my mother and my brothers! [35]Whoever does the will of God is my brother and sister and mother."

[b] Other ancient authorities lack *and sisters*

ἀλλὰ ἔνοχός ἐστιν αἰωνίου ἁμαρτήματος. **3.30** ὅτι
BUT IS~GUILTY OF AN ETERNAL SIN. FOR

ἔλεγον, Πνεῦμα ἀκάθαρτον ἔχει.
THEY WERE SAYING, ³SPIRIT ²AN UNCLEAN ¹HE HAS.

3.31 Καὶ ἔρχεται ἡ μήτηρ αὐτοῦ καὶ οἱ ἀδελφοὶ
AND COMES THE MOTHER OF HIM AND THE BROTHERS

αὐτοῦ καὶ ἔξω στήκοντες ἀπέστειλαν πρὸς αὐτὸν
OF HIM AND STANDING~OUTSIDE THEY SENT TO HIM

καλοῦντες αὐτόν. **3.32** καὶ ἐκάθητο περὶ αὐτὸν ὄχλος,
CALLING HIM. AND WERE SITTING AROUND HIM A CROWD,

καὶ λέγουσιν αὐτῷ, Ἰδοὺ ἡ μήτηρ σου καὶ οἱ
AND THEY ARE SAYING TO HIM, BEHOLD THE MOTHER OF YOU AND THE

ἀδελφοί σου ⌜[καὶ αἱ ἀδελφαι σου]⌝ ἔξω
BROTHERS OF YOU AND THE SISTERS OF YOU [ARE] OUTSIDE

ζητοῦσίν σε. **3.33** καὶ ἀποκριθεὶς αὐτοῖς λέγει, Τίς
LOOKING FOR YOU. AND HAVING ANSWERED THEM HE SAYS, WHO

ἐστιν ἡ μήτηρ μου καὶ οἱ ἀδελφοί [μου]; **3.34** καὶ
IS THE MOTHER OF ME AND THE BROTHERS OF ME? AND

περιβλεψάμενος τοὺς περὶ αὐτὸν κύκλῳ καθημένους
HAVING LOOKED AROUND AT THE ONES AROUND HIM SITTING~IN A CIRCLE

λέγει, Ἴδε ἡ μήτηρ μου καὶ οἱ ἀδελφοί μου.
HE SAYS, BEHOLD THE MOTHER OF ME AND THE BROTHERS OF ME.

3.35 ὃς [γὰρ] ἂν ποιήσῃ τὸ θέλημα τοῦ θεοῦ, οὗτος
FOR~WHOEVER DOES THE WILL - OF GOD, THIS ONE

ἀδελφός μου καὶ ἀδελφὴ καὶ μήτηρ ἐστίν.
[THE] BROTHER OF ME AND SISTER AND MOTHER IS.

3:32 text: RSVmg NASBmg TEV NJB NRSV. omit [see Matt. 12:47; Luke 8:20]: KJV ASV RSV NASB NIV NEB NRSVmg.

CHAPTER 4

Again he began to teach beside the sea. Such a very large crowd gathered around him that he got into a boat on the sea and sat there, while the whole crowd was beside the sea on the land. [2]He began to teach them many things in parables, and in his teaching he said to them: [3]"Listen! A sower went out to sow. [4]And as he sowed, some seed fell on the path,

[b] Other ancient authorities lack *and sisters*

4.1 Καὶ πάλιν ἤρξατο διδάσκειν παρὰ τὴν θάλασσαν·
AND AGAIN HE BEGAN TO TEACH BESIDE THE LAKE.

καὶ συνάγεται πρὸς αὐτὸν ὄχλος πλεῖστος, ὥστε
AND GATHERED TOGETHER TO HIM A HUGE~CROWD SO THAT

αὐτὸν εἰς πλοῖον ἐμβάντα καθῆσθαι ἐν τῇ θαλάσσῃ,
HE INTO A BOAT HAVING GOTTEN IN TO SIT IN THE LAKE,

καὶ πᾶς ὁ ὄχλος πρὸς τὴν θάλασσαν ἐπὶ τῆς γῆς
AND ALL THE CROWD NEAR THE LAKE ON THE LAND

ἦσαν. **4.2** καὶ ἐδίδασκεν αὐτοὺς ἐν παραβολαῖς πολλὰ
WERE. AND HE WAS TEACHING THEM WITH MANY~PARABLES

καὶ ἔλεγεν αὐτοῖς ἐν τῇ διδαχῇ αὐτοῦ, **4.3** Ἀκούετε.
AND HE WAS SAYING TO THEM IN THE TEACHING OF HIM, LISTEN.

ἰδοὺ ἐξῆλθεν ὁ σπείρων σπεῖραι. **4.4** καὶ ἐγένετο
BEHOLD WENT OUT THE ONE SOWING TO SOW [SEED]. AND IT CAME ABOUT

ἐν τῷ σπείρειν ὃ μὲν ἔπεσεν παρὰ τὴν ὁδόν,
WHILE - [HE WENT] TO SOW [THAT] SOME [SEED] FELL BESIDE THE ROAD,

καὶ ἦλθεν τὰ πετεινὰ καὶ κατέφαγεν αὐτό. **4.5** καὶ
AND   CAME   THE BIRDS   AND   DEVOURED   IT.   AND

ἄλλο   ἔπεσεν ἐπὶ τὸ πετρῶδες ὅπου οὐκ εἶχεν
OTHER [SEED] FELL   UPON THE ROCKY PLACE WHERE IT DID NOT HAVE

γῆν πολλήν, καὶ εὐθὺς   ἐξανέτειλεν διὰ   τὸ
MUCH~SOIL,   AND   IMMEDIATELY IT SPRANG UP   BECAUSE   -

μὴ ἔχειν βάθος γῆς· **4.6** καὶ ὅτε ἀνέτειλεν ὁ ἥλιος
IT DID NOT HAVE DEPTH OF SOIL.   AND WHEN ROSE   THE SUN

ἐκαυματίσθη καὶ διὰ   τὸ μὴ ἔχειν ῥίζαν ἐξηράνθη.
IT WAS SCORCHED   AND BECAUSE - IT DID NOT HAVE A ROOT   IT WITHERED.

4.7 καὶ ἄλλο   ἔπεσεν εἰς τὰς ἀκάνθας, καὶ
AND   OTHER [SEED] FELL   INTO THE   THORN BUSHES, AND

ἀνέβησαν αἱ ἄκανθαι καὶ συνέπνιξαν αὐτό, καὶ
CAME UP   THE THORNS   AND   CHOKED   IT,   AND

καρπὸν οὐκ ἔδωκεν. **4.8** καὶ ἄλλα ἔπεσεν εἰς τὴν γῆν
FRUIT   IT DID NOT GIVE.   AND OTHERS FELL   INTO THE ²SOIL

τὴν καλὴν καὶ ἐδίδου   καρπὸν ἀναβαίνοντα καὶ
-    ¹GOOD   AND IT WAS GIVING FRUIT   RISING UP   AND

αὐξανόμενα καὶ ἔφερεν   ἐν τριάκοντα καὶ ἐν
GROWING   AND IT WAS BEARING [FRUIT], ONE THIRTY   AND ONE

ἑξήκοντα καὶ ἐν ἑκατόν. **4.9** καὶ ἔλεγεν,   Ὃς ἔχει
SIXTY   AND ONE ONE HUNDRED. AND HE WAS SAYING, WHO HAS

ὦτα ἀκούειν ἀκουέτω.
EARS TO HEAR   LET HIM HEAR.

4.10 Καὶ ὅτε ἐγένετο κατὰ μόνας, ἠρώτων αὐτὸν
AND WHEN HE WAS   BY HIMSELF,   WERE ASKING HIM

οἱ   περὶ αὐτὸν σὺν τοῖς δώδεκα τὰς
THE ONES AROUND HIM   WITH THE   TWELVE   THE [MEANING OF THE]

παραβολάς. **4.11** καὶ ἔλεγεν   αὐτοῖς, Ὑμῖν τὸ
PARABLES.   AND   HE WAS SAYING TO THEM, TO YOU° THE

μυστήριον δέδοται   τῆς βασιλείας τοῦ θεοῦ·
MYSTERY   HAS BEEN GIVEN OF THE KINGDOM   -   OF GOD.

ἐκείνοις δὲ τοῖς ἔξω   ἐν παραβολαῖς τὰ πάντα
BUT~TO THOSE   -   OUTSIDE ³IN ⁴PARABLES   -   ¹EVERYTHING

γίνεται, **4.12** ἵνα   βλέποντες βλέπωσιν καὶ
²COMES,   IN ORDER THAT SEEING   THEY MAY SEE   AND

μὴ ἴδωσιν,
THEY MAY NOT PERCEIVE,

καὶ ἀκούοντες ἀκούωσιν καὶ μὴ συνιῶσιν,
AND   HEARING   THEY MAY HEAR AND THEY MAY NOT UNDERSTAND,

μήποτε ἐπιστρέψωσιν καὶ ἀφεθῇ   αὐτοῖς.
LEST   THEY SHOULD TURN   AND IT SHOULD BE FORGIVEN THEM.

4.13 Καὶ λέγει αὐτοῖς, Οὐκ οἴδατε   τὴν
AND   HE SAYS TO THEM, DO YOU° NOT KNOW [THE MEANING OF] -

παραβολὴν ταύτην, καὶ πῶς πάσας τὰς παραβολὰς
THIS~PARABLE,   AND HOW   ALL   THE PARABLES

4:12 Isa. 6:9-10 LXX

and the birds came and ate it up. ⁵Other seed fell on rocky ground, where it did not have much soil, and it sprang up quickly, since it had no depth of soil. ⁶And when the sun rose, it was scorched; and since it had no root, it withered away. ⁷Other seed fell among thorns, and the thorns grew up and choked it, and it yielded no grain. ⁸Other seed fell into good soil and brought forth grain, growing up and increasing and yielding thirty and sixty and a hundredfold." ⁹And he said, "Let anyone with ears to hear listen!"

10 When he was alone, those who were around him along with the twelve asked him about the parables. ¹¹And he said to them, "To you has been given the secretᶜ of the kingdom of God, but for those outside, everything comes in parables; ¹²in order that

'they may indeed look,
    but not perceive,
and may indeed listen,
    but not understand;
so that they may not turn
    again and be
    forgiven.'"

13 And he said to them, "Do you not understand this parable? Then how will you understand all

ᶜ Or *mystery*

the parables? [14]The sower sows the word. [15]These are the ones on the path where the word is sown: when they hear, Satan immediately comes and takes away the word that is sown in them. [16]And these are the ones sown on rocky ground: when they hear the word, they immediately receive it with joy. [17]But they have no root, and endure only for a while; then, when trouble or persecution arises on account of the word, immediately they fall away.[d] [18]And others are those sown among the thorns: these are the ones who hear the word, [19]but the cares of the world, and the lure of wealth, and the desire for other things come in and choke the word, and it yields nothing. [20]And these are the ones sown on the good soil: they hear the word and accept it and bear fruit, thirty and sixty and a hundredfold."

21 He said to them, "Is a lamp brought in to be put under the bushel basket, or under the bed, and not on the lampstand? [22]For there is nothing hidden, except to be disclosed; nor is anything secret, except to come to light.

[d] Or　stumble

γνώσεσθε;　　　**4.14** ὁ　　σπείρων τὸν λόγον σπείρει.
WILL YOU° COME TO KNOW?　　THE ONE SOWING　²THE ³WORD ¹SOWS.

4.15 οὗτοι δέ εἰσιν οἱ　　παρὰ τὴν ὁδόν· ὅπου
AND~THESE ARE THE ONES BESIDE THE ROAD, WHERE

σπείρεται ὁ λόγος καὶ ὅταν ἀκούσωσιν, εὐθὺς
IS SOWN THE WORD, AND WHEN THEY HEAR [IT], IMMEDIATELY

ἔρχεται ὁ Σατανᾶς καὶ αἴρει τὸν λόγον τὸν
COMES - SATAN AND TAKES THE WORD -

ἐσπαρμένον εἰς αὐτούς. **4.16** καὶ οὗτοί εἰσιν οἱ　ἐπὶ
HAVING BEEN SOWN IN THEM. AND THESE ARE THE ONES UPON

τὰ πετρώδη σπειρόμενοι, οἳ ὅταν ἀκούσωσιν τὸν
THE ROCKY PLACES BEING SOWN, WHO WHEN THEY HEAR THE

λόγον εὐθὺς　μετὰ χαρᾶς λαμβάνουσιν αὐτόν,
WORD IMMEDIATELY WITH JOY RECEIVE IT,

4.17 καὶ οὐκ ἔχουσιν ῥίζαν ἐν ἑαυτοῖς ἀλλὰ
AND THEY DO NOT HAVE A ROOT IN THEMSELVES BUT

πρόσκαιροί εἰσιν, εἶτα γενομένης θλίψεως ἢ διωγμοῦ
ARE~TRANSITORY, THEN [WHEN] TRIBULATION~COMES ABOUT OR PERSECUTION

διὰ　　τὸν λόγον εὐθὺς　σκανδαλίζονται. **4.18** καὶ
ON ACCOUNT OF THE WORD IMMEDIATELY THEY FALL AWAY. AND

ἄλλοι εἰσὶν οἱ　εἰς τὰς ἀκάνθας σπειρόμενοι·
OTHERS ARE THE ONES AMONG THE THORNS BEING SOWN.

οὗτοί εἰσιν οἱ　τὸν λόγον ἀκούσαντες, **4.19** καὶ αἱ
THESE ARE THE ONES THE WORD HAVING HEARD, AND THE

μέριμναι τοῦ αἰῶνος καὶ ἡ ἀπάτη τοῦ πλούτου καὶ
WORRIES OF THE AGE AND THE SEDUCTION - OF WEALTH AND

αἱ περὶ τὰ λοιπὰ　ἐπιθυμίαι εἰσπορευόμεναι
THE ²FOR ³THE ⁴REMAINING THINGS ¹DESIRES COMING IN

συμπνίγουσιν τὸν λόγον καὶ ἄκαρπος γίνεται.
CHOKE THE WORD AND IT BECOMES~UNFRUITFUL.

4.20 καὶ ἐκεῖνοί εἰσιν οἱ　ἐπὶ τὴν γῆν τὴν καλὴν
AND THOSE ARE THE ONES UPON THE ²SOIL - ¹GOOD

σπαρέντες, οἵτινες ἀκούουσιν τὸν λόγον καὶ
HAVING BEEN SOWN, WHO HEAR THE WORD AND

παραδέχονται καὶ καρποφοροῦσιν ἐν τριάκοντα καὶ ἐν
RECEIVE [IT] AND BEAR FRUIT ONE THIRTY AND ONE

ἑξήκοντα καὶ ἐν ἑκατόν.
SIXTY AND ONE ONE HUNDRED.

4.21 Καὶ ἔλεγεν αὐτοῖς, Μήτι ἔρχεται　ὁ
AND HE WAS SAYING TO THEM, SURELY ³IS [NOT] BROUGHT [OUT] ¹THE

λύχνος ἵνα　ὑπὸ τὸν μόδιον τεθῇ　ἢ
²LAMP IN ORDER THAT UNDER THE MEASURING BUCKET IT MAY BE PLACED OR

ὑπὸ τὴν κλίνην; οὐχ ἵνα ἐπὶ τὴν λυχνίαν τεθῇ;
UNDER THE COUCH? NOR THAT UPON THE LAMPSTAND IT MAY BE PLACED?

4.22 οὐ γάρ ἐστιν　κρυπτὸν ἐὰν μὴ ἵνα φανερωθῇ,
FOR THERE IS NOT [ANYTHING] HIDDEN EXCEPT THAT IT MAY BE REVEALED

οὐδὲ ἐγένετο ἀπόκρυφον ἀλλ᾽ ἵνα ἔλθη εἰς
NOR HAS IT BECOME HIDDEN BUT THAT IT MAY COME INTO

φανερόν. **4.23** εἴ τις   ἔχει ὦτα ἀκούειν ἀκουέτω.
[THE] OPEN.   IF ANYONE HAS   EARS TO HEAR LET HIM HEAR.

4.24 Καὶ ἔλεγεν αὐτοῖς, Βλέπετε τί   ἀκούετε. ἐν
      AND HE WAS SAYING TO THEM, CONSIDER WHAT YOU° HEAR. BY

ᾧ   μέτρῳ μετρεῖτε μετρηθήσεται ὑμῖν καὶ
WHAT MEASURE YOU° MEASURE IT WILL BE MEASURED TO YOU° AND

προστεθήσεται ὑμῖν. **4.25** ὃς γὰρ   ἔχει, δοθήσεται
IT WILL BE ADDED TO YOU°.   FOR~WHO[EVER] HAS, IT WILL BE GIVEN

αὐτῷ· καὶ ὃς   οὐκ ἔχει, καὶ ὃ   ἔχει
TO HIM. AND WHO[EVER] DOES NOT HAVE, EVEN WHAT HE HAS

ἀρθήσεται ἀπ' αὐτοῦ.
WILL BE TAKEN AWAY FROM HIM.

4.26 Καὶ ἔλεγεν,   Οὕτως ἐστὶν ἡ βασιλεία τοῦ
      AND HE WAS SAYING, THUS IS   THE KINGDOM   -

θεοῦ ὡς ἄνθρωπος βάλῃ   τὸν σπόρον ἐπὶ τῆς γῆς
OF GOD AS A MAN   MIGHT THROW THE SEED UPON THE SOIL

4.27 καὶ καθεύδῃ   καὶ ἐγείρηται νύκτα καὶ ἡμέραν,
      AND HE MIGHT SLEEP AND RISE   NIGHT AND DAY,

καὶ ὁ σπόρος βλαστᾷ καὶ μηκύνηται ὡς
AND THE SEED SPROUTS AND GROWS UP IN SUCH A WAY SO THAT

οὐκ οἶδεν   αὐτός. **4.28** αὐτομάτη ἡ γῆ καρποφορεῖ,
HE DOES NOT KNOW IT.   ON ITS OWN THE SOIL BEARS FRUIT,

πρῶτον χόρτον εἶτα στάχυν   εἶτα πλήρη[ς] σῖτον ἐν
FIRST GRASS THEN A HEAD OF GRAIN THEN FULL   WHEAT IN

τῷ στάχυϊ. **4.29** ὅταν δὲ παραδοῖ ὁ καρπός, εὐθὺς
THE HEAD.   BUT~WHEN PERMITS THE CROP,   IMMEDIATELY

ἀποστέλλει τὸ δρέπανον, ὅτι παρέστηκεν ὁ   θερισμός.
HE PUTS FORTH THE SICKLE,   FOR ³HAS COME ¹THE ²HARVEST.

4.30 Καὶ ἔλεγεν,   Πῶς ὁμοιώσωμεν τὴν βασιλείαν
      AND HE WAS SAYING, TO WHAT SHOULD WE COMPARE THE KINGDOM

τοῦ θεοῦ ἢ ἐν τίνι αὐτὴν παραβολῇ θῶμεν;
 - OF GOD OR BY WHAT ³IT   ¹PARABLE ²MAY WE PRESENT?

4.31 ὡς κόκκῳ σινάπεως, ὃς   ὅταν σπαρῇ ἐπὶ τῆς
      AS A MUSTARD~SEED,   WHICH WHEN IT IS SOWN ON THE

γῆς, μικρότερον ὂν πάντων τῶν σπερμάτων τῶν ἐπὶ
EARTH, BEING~SMALLER [THAN] ALL OF THE SEEDS   -   ON

τῆς γῆς, **4.32** καὶ ὅταν σπαρῇ, ἀναβαίνει καὶ γίνεται
THE EARTH,   AND WHEN IT IS SOWN, IT GROWS UP AND BECOMES

μεῖζον πάντων τῶν λαχάνων καὶ ποιεῖ
GREATER [THAN] ALL OF THE VEGETABLES AND MAKES

κλάδους μεγάλους, ὥστε δύνασθαι   ὑπὸ τὴν σκιὰν
LARGE~BRANCHES,   SO AS TO MAKE [IT] POSSIBLE [FOR] ⁵UNDER ⁶THE ⁷SHADE

αὐτοῦ τὰ πετεινὰ τοῦ οὐρανοῦ κατασκηνοῦν.
⁸OF IT ¹THE ²BIRDS   -   ³OF HEAVEN ⁴TO NEST.

4.33 Καὶ τοιαύταις παραβολαῖς πολλαῖς ἐλάλει
      AND ²SIMILAR   ³PARABLES   ¹WITH MANY HE WAS SPEAKING

αὐτοῖς τὸν λόγον καθὼς ἠδύναντο   ἀκούειν·
TO THEM THE WORD AS   THEY WERE ABLE TO HEAR.

[23]Let anyone with ears to hear listen!" [24]And he said to them, "Pay attention to what you hear; the measure you give will be the measure you get, and still more will be given you. [25]For to those who have, more will be given; and from those who have nothing, even what they have will be taken away."

26 He also said, "The kingdom of God is as if someone would scatter seed on the ground, [27]and would sleep and rise night and day, and the seed would sprout and grow, he does not know how. [28]The earth produces of itself, first the stalk, then the head, then the full grain in the head. [29]But when the grain is ripe, at once he goes in with his sickle, because the harvest has come."

30 He also said, "With what can we compare the kingdom of God, or what parable will we use for it? [31]It is like a mustard seed, which, when sown upon the ground, is the smallest of all the seeds on earth; [32]yet when it is sown it grows up and becomes the greatest of all shrubs, and puts forth large branches, so that the birds of the air can make nests in its shade."

33 With many such parables he spoke the word to them, as they were able to hear it;

³⁴he did not speak to them except in parables, but he explained everything in private to his disciples.

35 On that day, when evening had come, he said to them, "Let us go across to the other side." ³⁶And leaving the crowd behind, they took him with them in the boat, just as he was. Other boats were with him. ³⁷A great windstorm arose, and the waves beat into the boat, so that the boat was already being swamped. ³⁸But he was in the stern, asleep on the cushion; and they woke him up and said to him, "Teacher, do you not care that we are perishing?" ³⁹He woke up and rebuked the wind, and said to the sea, "Peace! Be still!" Then the wind ceased, and there was a dead calm. ⁴⁰He said to them, "Why are you afraid? Have you still no faith?" ⁴¹And they were filled with great awe and said to one another, "Who then is this, that even the wind and the sea obey him?"

4.34 χωρὶς δὲ παραβολῆς οὐκ ἐλάλει αὐτοῖς,
BUT~APART FROM PARABLES HE WAS NOT SPEAKING TO THEM,

κατ᾽ ἰδίαν δὲ τοῖς ἰδίοις μαθηταῖς ἐπέλυεν
PRIVATELY HOWEVER - TO [HIS] OWN DISCIPLES HE WAS EXPLAINING

πάντα.
EVERYTHING.

4.35 Καὶ λέγει αὐτοῖς ἐν ἐκείνῃ τῇ ἡμέρᾳ
AND HE SAYS TO THEM ON THAT - DAY

ὀψίας γενομένης, Διέλθωμεν εἰς τὸ πέραν. **4.36** καὶ
AS IT HAD BECOME~EVENING, LET US GO OVER TO THE OTHER SIDE. AND

ἀφέντες τὸν ὄχλον παραλαμβάνουσιν αὐτὸν ὡς ἦν
LEAVING THE CROWD THEY TAKE HIM AS HE WAS

ἐν τῷ πλοίῳ, καὶ ἄλλα πλοῖα ἦν μετ᾽ αὐτοῦ.
IN THE BOAT, AND OTHER BOATS WERE WITH HIM.

4.37 καὶ γίνεται λαῖλαψ μεγάλη ἀνέμου καὶ τὰ
AND THERE CAME ABOUT A FIERCE~GUST OF WIND AND THE

κύματα ἐπέβαλλεν εἰς τὸ πλοῖον, ὥστε ἤδη
WAVES WERE BEATING AGAINST THE BOAT, SO THAT ALREADY

γεμίζεσθαι τὸ πλοῖον. **4.38** καὶ αὐτὸς ἦν ἐν τῇ
TO BE FILLED THE BOAT. AND HE WAS IN THE

πρύμνῃ ἐπὶ τὸ προσκεφάλαιον καθεύδων. καὶ
STERN ON THE CUSHION SLEEPING. AND

ἐγείρουσιν αὐτὸν καὶ λέγουσιν αὐτῷ, Διδάσκαλε,
THEY ROUSE HIM AND THEY SAY TO HIM, TEACHER,

οὐ μέλει σοι ὅτι ἀπολλύμεθα; **4.39** καὶ
DOES IT NOT MATTER TO YOU THAT WE ARE PERISHING? AND

διεγερθεὶς ἐπετίμησεν τῷ ἀνέμῳ καὶ εἶπεν τῇ
HAVING BEEN AROUSED HE REBUKED THE WIND AND HE SPOKE TO THE

θαλάσσῃ, Σιώπα, πεφίμωσο. καὶ ἐκόπασεν ὁ ἄνεμος
LAKE, BE STILL, BE SILENCED. AND DIED DOWN THE WIND

καὶ ἐγένετο γαλήνη μεγάλη. **4.40** καὶ εἶπεν αὐτοῖς,
AND THERE WAS A GREAT~CALM. AND HE SAID TO THEM,

Τί δειλοί ἐστε; οὔπω ἔχετε πίστιν; **4.41** καὶ
WHY ARE YOU°~COWARDLY? DO YOU° STILL NOT HAVE FAITH? AND

ἐφοβήθησαν φόβον μέγαν καὶ ἔλεγον πρὸς
THEY WERE AFRAID WITH A TERRIBLE~FEAR AND THEY WERE SAYING TO

ἀλλήλους, Τίς ἄρα οὗτός ἐστιν ὅτι καὶ ὁ ἄνεμος καὶ
ONE ANOTHER, WHO THEN IS~THIS THAT EVEN THE WIND AND

ἡ θάλασσα ὑπακούει αὐτῷ;
THE LAKE OBEY HIM?

5.1 Καὶ ἦλθον εἰς τὸ πέραν τῆς θαλάσσης εἰς τὴν
AND THEY CAME TO THE OTHER SIDE OF THE LAKE TO THE

χώραν τῶν ⌐Γερασηνῶν⌐. **5.2** καὶ ἐξελθόντος αὐτοῦ ἐκ
COUNTRY OF THE GERASENES. AND HE~HAVING COME OUT

τοῦ πλοίου εὐθὺς ὑπήντησεν αὐτῷ ἐκ τῶν
OF THE BOAT IMMEDIATELY MET HIM OUT OF THE

μνημείων ἄνθρωπος ἐν πνεύματι ἀκαθάρτῳ, **5.3** ὃς
TOMBS A MAN WITH AN UNCLEAN~SPIRIT, WHO

τὴν κατοίκησιν εἶχεν ἐν τοῖς μνήμασιν, καὶ
THE(HIS) DWELLING HAD IN THE TOMBS, AND

οὐδὲ ἁλύσει οὐκέτι οὐδεὶς ἐδύνατο αὐτὸν δῆσαι
NOT [EVEN] WITH A CHAIN ANY LONGER WAS ANY ONE ABLE TO BIND~HIM

5.4 διὰ τὸ αὐτὸν πολλάκις πέδαις καὶ ἁλύσεσιν
BECAUSE - HE OFTEN WITH SHACKLES AND CHAINS

δεδέσθαι καὶ διεσπάσθαι ὑπ' αὐτοῦ τὰς ἁλύσεις
HAD BEEN BOUND AND HAD BEEN TORN APART BY HIM THE CHAINS

καὶ τὰς πέδας συντετρῖφθαι, καὶ οὐδεὶς ἴσχυεν
AND THE SHACKLES HAD BEEN SMASHED, AND NO ONE WAS STRONG [ENOUGH]

αὐτὸν δαμάσαι· **5.5** καὶ διὰ παντὸς νυκτὸς καὶ ἡμέρας
TO SUBDUE~HIM. AND CONSTANTLY NIGHT AND DAY

ἐν τοῖς μνήμασιν καὶ ἐν τοῖς ὄρεσιν ἦν κράζων
AMONG THE TOMBS AND IN THE MOUNTAINS HE WAS CRYING OUT

καὶ κατακόπτων ἑαυτὸν λίθοις. **5.6** καὶ ἰδὼν τὸν
AND BEATING HIMSELF WITH STONES. AND HAVING SEEN -

Ἰησοῦν ἀπὸ μακρόθεν ἔδραμεν καὶ προσεκύνησεν
JESUS FROM AFAR HE RAN AND BOWED DOWN BEFORE

αὐτῷ **5.7** καὶ κράξας φωνῇ μεγάλῃ λέγει, Τί ἐμοὶ
HIM AND HAVING CRIED OUT WITH A LOUD~VOICE HE SAYS, WHAT TO ME

καὶ σοί, Ἰησοῦ υἱὲ τοῦ θεοῦ τοῦ ὑψίστου; ὁρκίζω
AND TO YOU, JESUS SON - OF GOD - MOST HIGH? I IMPLORE

σε τὸν θεόν, μή με βασανίσῃς. **5.8** ἔλεγεν γὰρ
YOU - BY GOD, [DO] NOT TORMENT~ME. FOR~HE WAS SAYING

αὐτῷ, Ἔξελθε τὸ πνεῦμα τὸ ἀκάθαρτον ἐκ τοῦ
TO HIM, COME OUT, - ²SPIRIT - ¹UNCLEAN FROM THE

ἀνθρώπου. **5.9** καὶ ἐπηρώτα αὐτόν, Τί
MAN. AND HE WAS QUESTIONING HIM, WHAT [IS]

ὄνομά σοι; καὶ λέγει αὐτῷ, Λεγιὼν ὄνομά μοι, ὅτι
YOUR~NAME? AND HE SAYS TO HIM, LEGION [IS] MY~NAME, FOR

πολλοί ἐσμεν. **5.10** καὶ παρεκάλει αὐτὸν πολλὰ ἵνα
WE ARE~MANY. AND HE WAS IMPLORING HIM GREATLY THAT

μὴ αὐτὰ ἀποστείλῃ ἔξω τῆς χώρας.
²NOT ³THEM ¹HE SEND OUT OF THE COUNTRY.

They came to the other side of the sea, to the country of the Gerasenes.[e] [2]And when he had stepped out of the boat, immediately a man out of the tombs with an unclean spirit met him. [3]He lived among the tombs; and no one could restrain him any more, even with a chain; [4]for he had often been restrained with shackles and chains, but the chains he wrenched apart, and the shackles he broke in pieces; and no one had the strength to subdue him. [5]Night and day among the tombs and on the mountains he was always howling and bruising himself with stones. [6]When he saw Jesus from a distance, he ran and bowed down before him; [7]and he shouted at the top of his voice, "What have you to do with me, Jesus, Son of the Most High God? I adjure you by God, do not torment me." [8]For he had said to him, "Come out of the man, you unclean spirit!" [9]Then Jesus[f] asked him, "What is your name?" He replied, "My name is Legion; for we are many." [10]He begged him earnestly not to send them out of the country.

[e] Other ancient authorities read *Gergesenes*; others, *Gadarenes*
[f] Gk *he*

5:1 text [see Luke 8:26]: ASV RSV NASB NIV NEB TEV NJB NRSV. var. Γαδαρηνων (Gadarenes) [see Matt. 8:28]: KJV RSVmg NIVmg NJBmg NRSVmg. var. Γεργεσηνων (Gergesenes): RSVmg NIVmg NJBmg NRSVmg.

¹¹Now there on the hillside a great herd of swine was feeding; ¹²and the unclean spirits[g] begged him, "Send us into the swine; let us enter them." ¹³So he gave them permission. And the unclean spirits came out and entered the swine; and the herd, numbering about two thousand, rushed down the steep bank into the sea, and were drowned in the sea.

14 The swineherds ran off and told it in the city and in the country. Then people came to see what it was that had happened. ¹⁵They came to Jesus and saw the demoniac sitting there, clothed and in his right mind, the very man who had had the legion; and they were afraid. ¹⁶Those who had seen what had happened to the demoniac and to the swine reported it. ¹⁷Then they began to beg Jesus[h] to leave their neighborhood. ¹⁸As he was getting into the boat, the man who had been possessed by demons begged him that he might be with him. ¹⁹But Jesus[i] refused, and said to him, "Go home to your friends, and tell them how much the Lord has done for you, and what mercy he has shown you." ²⁰And he went away

[g] Gk *they*
[h] Gk *him*
[i] Gk *he*

5.11 ῏Ην δὲ ἐκεῖ πρὸς τῷ ὄρει ἀγέλη χοίρων
NOW~THERE WAS THERE NEAR THE MOUNTAIN ²HERD ³OF PIGS

μεγάλη βοσκομένη· **5.12** καὶ παρεκάλεσαν αὐτὸν
¹A GREAT FEEDING; AND THEY IMPLORED HIM

λέγοντες, Πέμψον ἡμᾶς εἰς τοὺς χοίρους, ἵνα εἰς
SAYING, SEND US INTO THE PIGS, SO THAT INTO

αὐτοὺς εἰσέλθωμεν. **5.13** καὶ ἐπέτρεψεν αὐτοῖς. καὶ
THEM WE MAY ENTER. AND HE PERMITTED THEM. AND

ἐξελθόντα τὰ πνεύματα τὰ ἀκάθαρτα εἰσῆλθον εἰς
HAVING COME OUT, THE ²SPIRITS - ¹UNCLEAN ENTERED INTO

τοὺς χοίρους, καὶ ὥρμησεν ἡ ἀγέλη κατὰ τοῦ
THE PIGS, AND RUSHED THE HERD DOWN THE

κρημνοῦ εἰς τὴν θάλασσαν, ὡς δισχίλιοι, καὶ
SLOPE INTO THE LAKE, ABOUT TWO THOUSAND, AND

ἐπνίγοντο ἐν τῇ θαλάσσῃ. **5.14** καὶ οἱ βόσκοντες
WERE DROWNED IN THE LAKE. AND THE ONES FEEDING

αὐτοὺς ἔφυγον καὶ ἀπήγγειλαν εἰς τὴν πόλιν καὶ εἰς
THEM FLED AND REPORTED [IT] IN THE CITY AND IN

τοὺς ἀγρούς· καὶ ἦλθον ἰδεῖν τί ἐστιν τὸ
THE FARMS. AND THEY CAME TO SEE WHAT IS THE [THING]

γεγονὸς **5.15** καὶ ἔρχονται πρὸς τὸν Ἰησοῦν
HAVING COME TO PASS AND THEY COME TO - JESUS

καὶ θεωροῦσιν τὸν δαιμονιζόμενον καθήμενον
AND THEY SEE THE ONE BEING DEMON-POSSESSED SITTING

ἱματισμένον καὶ σωφρονοῦντα, τὸν ἐσχηκότα τὸν
HAVING BEEN CLOTHED AND BEING OF SOUND MIND, THE ONE HAVING HAD THE

λεγιῶνα, καὶ ἐφοβήθησαν. **5.16** καὶ διηγήσαντο αὐτοῖς
LEGION, AND THEY WERE AFRAID. AND THEY DESCRIBED TO THEM

οἱ ἰδόντες πῶς ἐγένετο τῷ δαιμονιζομένῳ καὶ
THE ONES HAVING SEEN HOW IT HAPPENED TO THE DEMON-POSSESSED [MAN] AND

περὶ τῶν χοίρων. **5.17** καὶ ἤρξαντο παρακαλεῖν
ABOUT THE PIGS. AND THEY BEGAN TO IMPLORE

αὐτὸν ἀπελθεῖν ἀπὸ τῶν ὁρίων αὐτῶν. **5.18** καὶ
HIM TO LEAVE FROM THE REGION OF THEM. AND

ἐμβαίνοντος αὐτοῦ εἰς τὸ πλοῖον παρεκάλει αὐτὸν
WHILE HE IS EMBARKING INTO THE BOAT, ³WAS BEGGING ⁴HIM

ὁ δαιμονισθεὶς ἵνα μετ' αὐτοῦ ᾖ.
¹THE ONE ²HAVING BEEN DEMON-POSSESSED THAT WITH HIM HE MIGHT BE.

5.19 καὶ οὐκ ἀφῆκεν αὐτόν, ἀλλὰ λέγει αὐτῷ, Ὕπαγε
AND HE DID NOT PERMIT HIM, BUT SAYS TO HIM, GO

εἰς τὸν οἶκόν σου πρὸς τοὺς σοὺς καὶ
TO THE HOUSE OF YOU TO THE ONES [WHO ARE] YOURS AND

ἀπάγγειλον αὐτοῖς ὅσα ὁ κύριός σοι πεποίηκεν
REPORT TO THEM EVERYTHING THAT THE LORD HAS DONE~FOR YOU

καὶ ἠλέησέν σε. **5.20** καὶ ἀπῆλθεν καὶ ἤρξατο
AND [THAT] HE HAD MERCY UPON YOU. AND HE LEFT AND BEGAN

κηρύσσειν ἐν τῇ Δεκαπόλει ὅσα   ἐποίησεν αὐτῷ
TO PREACH   IN THE DECAPOLIS EVERYTHING THAT ²DID   ³FOR HIM

ὁ Ἰησοῦς, καὶ πάντες ἐθαύμαζον.
- ¹JESUS,   AND EVERYONE WAS AMAZED.

5.21 Καὶ διαπεράσαντος τοῦ Ἰησοῦ [ἐν τῷ πλοίῳ]
AND   ²HAVING CROSSED OVER   -   ¹JESUS   IN THE BOAT

πάλιν εἰς τὸ πέραν συνήχθη   ὄχλος πολὺς ἐπ'
AGAIN TO THE OTHER SIDE WAS GATHERED TOGETHER A LARGE~CROWD TO

αὐτόν, καὶ ἦν παρὰ τὴν θάλασσαν. **5.22** καὶ ἔρχεται
HIM,   AND HE WAS BESIDE THE LAKE.   AND COMES

εἷς τῶν ἀρχισυναγώγων, ὀνόματι Ἰάϊρος, καὶ ἰδὼν
ONE OF THE SYNAGOGUE LEADERS,   BY NAME JAIRUS,   AND HAVING SEEN

αὐτὸν πίπτει   πρὸς τοὺς πόδας αὐτοῦ **5.23** καὶ
HIM   HE FALLS DOWN AT THE FEET OF HIM   AND

παρακαλεῖ αὐτὸν πολλὰ λέγων ὅτι Τὸ θυγάτριόν μου
HE BEGS   HIM   EARNESTLY SAYING, -   MY~DAUGHTER

ἐσχάτως ἔχει, ἵνα ἐλθὼν ἐπιθῇς τὰς χεῖρας
IS AT THE POINT OF DEATH, THAT HAVING COME YOU MAY PUT THE(YOUR) HAND

αὐτῇ ἵνα σωθῇ   καὶ ζήσῃ. **5.24** καὶ ἀπῆλθεν
ON HER THAT SHE MAY BE HEALED AND MAY LIVE.   AND HE WENT

μετ' αὐτοῦ.
WITH HIM.

Καὶ ἠκολούθει αὐτῷ ὄχλος πολὺς καὶ
AND WERE FOLLOWING HIM A LARGE~CROWD AND

συνέθλιβον   αὐτόν. **5.25** καὶ   γυνὴ οὖσα
THEY WERE PRESSING AGAINST HIM.   AND [THERE WAS] A WOMAN BEING

ἐν ῥύσει αἵματος δώδεκα ἔτη **5.26** καὶ πολλὰ παθοῦσα
WITH A FLOW OF BLOOD TWELVE YEARS   AND HAVING SUFFERED~MUCH

ὑπὸ πολλῶν ἰατρῶν καὶ δαπανήσασα τὰ παρ' αὐτῆς
BY MANY   PHYSICIANS AND HAVING SPENT   -   ²WITH ³HER

πάντα καὶ μηδὲν ὠφεληθεῖσα ἀλλὰ μᾶλλον εἰς τὸ
¹EVERYTHING AND HAVING BENEFITED~NOTHING BUT RATHER INTO -

χεῖρον   ἐλθοῦσα, **5.27** ἀκούσασα περὶ τοῦ Ἰησοῦ,
A WORSE [CONDITION] HAVING COME,   HAVING HEARD ABOUT - JESUS,

ἐλθοῦσα ἐν τῷ ὄχλῳ ὄπισθεν ἥψατο   τοῦ ἱματίου
HAVING COME IN THE CROWD BEHIND SHE TOUCHED THE GARMENT

αὐτοῦ· **5.28** ἔλεγεν γὰρ ὅτι Ἐὰν ἅψωμαι κἂν τῶν
OF HIM.   FOR~SHE WAS SAYING - IF I MAY TOUCH EVEN THE

ἱματίων αὐτοῦ σωθήσομαι. **5.29** καὶ εὐθὺς ἐξηράνθη
GARMENTS OF HIM I WILL BE HEALED.   AND IMMEDIATELY WAS DRIED UP

ἡ πηγὴ τοῦ αἵματος αὐτῆς καὶ ἔγνω τῷ
THE FOUNTAIN OF THE BLOOD OF HER AND SHE KNEW IN THE(HER)

σώματι ὅτι ἴαται   ἀπὸ τῆς μάστιγος. **5.30** καὶ
BODY   THAT SHE HAS BEEN CURED FROM THE TERRIBLE AFFLICTION. AND

εὐθὺς   ὁ Ἰησοῦς ἐπιγνοὺς ἐν ἑαυτῷ τὴν ἐξ
IMMEDIATELY - JESUS HAVING KNOWN WITHIN HIMSELF THE ³FROM

and began to proclaim in the Decapolis how much Jesus had done for him; and everyone was amazed.

21 When Jesus had crossed again in the boat[j] to the other side, a great crowd gathered around him; and he was by the sea. 22Then one of the leaders of the synagogue named Jairus came and, when he saw him, fell at his feet 23and begged him repeatedly, "My little daughter is at the point of death. Come and lay your hands on her, so that she may be made well, and live." 24So he went with him.

And a large crowd followed him and pressed in on him. 25Now there was a woman who had been suffering from hemorrhages for twelve years. 26She had endured much under many physicians, and had spent all that she had; and she was no better, but rather grew worse. 27She had heard about Jesus, and came up behind him in the crowd and touched his cloak, 28for she said, "If I but touch his clothes, I will be made well." 29Immediately her hemorrhage stopped; and she felt in her body that she was healed of her disease. 30Immediately aware that power had gone forth from

[j] Other ancient authorities lack *in the boat*

him, Jesus turned about in the crowd and said, "Who touched my clothes?" ³¹And his disciples said to him, "You see the crowd pressing in on you; how can you say, 'Who touched me?'" ³²He looked all around to see who had done it. ³³But the woman, knowing what had happened to her, came in fear and trembling, fell down before him, and told him the whole truth. ³⁴He said to her, "Daughter, your faith has made you well; go in peace, and be healed of your disease."

35 While he was still speaking, some people came from the leader's house to say, "Your daughter is dead. Why trouble the teacher any further?" ³⁶But overhearing*ᵏ* what they said, Jesus said to the leader of the synagogue, "Do not fear, only believe." ³⁷He allowed no one to follow him except Peter, James, and John, the brother of James. ³⁸When they came to the house of the leader of the synagogue, he saw a commotion, people weeping and wailing loudly. ³⁹When he had entered, he said to them, "Why do you make a commotion and weep? The child is not dead but sleeping." ⁴⁰And they laughed at him. Then he put them all outside, and took the child's father and mother and those who were with

ᵏ Or *ignoring;* other ancient authorities read *hearing*

αὐτοῦ δύναμιν ἐξελθοῦσαν ἐπιστραφεὶς ἐν τῷ ὄχλῳ
⁴HIM   ¹POWER   ²HAVING GONE OUT   HAVING TURNED AROUND   IN   THE   CROWD

ἔλεγεν, Τίς μου ἥψατο τῶν ἱματίων; **5.31** καὶ
HE WAS SAYING,   WHO   TOUCHED~MY   -   GARMENTS?   AND

ἔλεγον αὐτῷ οἱ μαθηταὶ αὐτοῦ, Βλέπεις τὸν ὄχλον
WERE SAYING   TO HIM   THE   DISCIPLES   OF HIM,   YOU SEE   THE   CROWD

συνθλίβοντά σε, καὶ λέγεις, Τίς μου ἥψατο; **5.32** καὶ
PRESSING AGAINST   YOU,   AND   YOU SAY,   WHO   TOUCHED~ME?   AND

περιεβλέπετο ἰδεῖν τὴν τοῦτο ποιήσασαν. **5.33** ἡ δὲ
HE WAS LOOKING AROUND   TO SEE   THE ONE   HAVING DONE~THIS.   NOW~THE

γυνὴ φοβηθεῖσα καὶ τρέμουσα, εἰδυῖα ὃ γέγονεν
WOMAN   WAS FEARING   AND   TREMBLING,   HAVING KNOWN   WHAT   HAD HAPPENED

αὐτῇ, ἦλθεν καὶ προσέπεσεν αὐτῷ καὶ εἶπεν αὐτῷ
TO HER,   SHE CAME   AND   FELL DOWN BEFORE   HIM   AND   SAID   TO HIM

πᾶσαν τὴν ἀλήθειαν. **5.34** ὁ δὲ εἶπεν αὐτῇ, Θυγάτηρ,
²WHOLE   ¹THE   ³TRUTH.   -   AND   HE SAID   TO HER,   DAUGHTER,

ἡ πίστις σου σέσωκέν σε· ὕπαγε εἰς εἰρήνην καὶ
THE   FAITH   OF YOU   HAS HEALED   YOU.   GO   IN   PEACE   AND

ἴσθι ὑγιὴς ἀπὸ τῆς μάστιγός σου.
BE   HEALED   FROM   THE   AFFLICTION   OF YOU.

5.35 Ἔτι αὐτοῦ λαλοῦντος ἔρχονται ἀπὸ τοῦ
WHILE   HE   WAS SPEAKING   THEY COME   FROM   THE [HOUSE OF THE]

ἀρχισυναγώγου λέγοντες ὅτι Ἡ θυγάτηρ σου ἀπέθανεν·
SYNAGOGUE LEADER   SAYING   -   YOUR~DAUGHTER   DIED.

τί ἔτι σκύλλεις τὸν διδάσκαλον; **5.36** ὁ δὲ Ἰησοῦς
WHY   STILL   ARE YOU BOTHERING   THE   TEACHER?   -   BUT   JESUS

παρακούσας τὸν λόγον λαλούμενον λέγει τῷ
HAVING OVERHEARD   THE   WORD   BEING SPOKEN   SAYS   TO THE

ἀρχισυναγώγῳ, Μὴ φοβοῦ, μόνον πίστευε. **5.37** καὶ
SYNAGOGUE LEADER,   DO NOT BE AFRAID,   ONLY   BELIEVE.   AND

οὐκ ἀφῆκεν οὐδένα μετ' αὐτοῦ συνακολουθῆσαι εἰ μὴ
HE DID NOT PERMIT   ANYONE   ²AFTER   ³HIM   ¹TO FOLLOW   EXCEPT

τὸν Πέτρον καὶ Ἰάκωβον καὶ Ἰωάννην τὸν ἀδελφὸν
-   PETER   AND   JAMES   AND   JOHN   THE   BROTHER

Ἰακώβου. **5.38** καὶ ἔρχονται εἰς τὸν οἶκον τοῦ
OF JAMES.   AND   THEY COME   INTO THE   HOUSE   OF THE

ἀρχισυναγώγου, καὶ θεωρεῖ θόρυβον καὶ κλαίοντας καὶ
SYNAGOGUE LEADER,   AND   HE SEES   AN UPROAR   AND   WEEPING   AND

ἀλαλάζοντας πολλά, **5.39** καὶ εἰσελθὼν λέγει αὐτοῖς,
LOUD WAILING,   AND   HAVING ENTERED   HE SAYS   TO THEM,

Τί θορυβεῖσθε καὶ κλαίετε; τὸ παιδίον
WHY   ARE YOU° DISTRESSED   AND   WEEPING?   THE   CHILD

οὐκ ἀπέθανεν ἀλλὰ καθεύδει. **5.40** καὶ κατεγέλων
DID NOT DIE   BUT   IS SLEEPING.   AND   THEY WERE LAUGHING AT

αὐτοῦ. αὐτὸς δὲ ἐκβαλὼν πάντας παραλαμβάνει τὸν
HIM.   BUT~HE   HAVING PUT OUT   EVERYONE   TAKES   THE

πατέρα τοῦ παιδίου καὶ τὴν μητέρα καὶ τοὺς μετ'
FATHER   OF THE   CHILD   AND   THE   MOTHER   AND   THE ONES WITH

αὐτοῦ καὶ εἰσπορεύεται ὅπου ἦν τὸ παιδίον. **5.41** καὶ
HIM, AND GOES INTO WHERE ³WAS ¹THE ²CHILD. AND

κρατήσας τῆς χειρὸς τοῦ παιδίου λέγει αὐτῇ, Ταλιθα
HAVING GRASPED THE HAND OF THE CHILD HE SAYS TO HER, TALITHA

κουμ, ὅ ἐστιν μεθερμηνευόμενον Τὸ κοράσιον, σοὶ
KOUM, WHICH BEING TRANSLATED MEANS - LITTLE GIRL, TO YOU

λέγω, ἔγειρε. **5.42** καὶ εὐθὺς ἀνέστη τὸ κοράσιον
I SAY, ARISE. AND IMMEDIATELY AROSE THE LITTLE GIRL

καὶ περιεπάτει· ἦν γὰρ ἐτῶν δώδεκα. καὶ
AND SHE WAS WALKING AROUND. FOR~SHE WAS TWELVE~YEARS OLD. AND

ἐξέστησαν [εὐθὺς] ἐκστάσει μεγάλῃ. **5.43** καὶ
IMMEDIATELY~THEY WERE AMAZED WITH GREAT~AMAZEMENT. AND

διεστείλατο αὐτοῖς πολλὰ ἵνα μηδεὶς γνοῖ τοῦτο,
HE GAVE ORDERS TO THEM EARNESTLY THAT NO ONE SHOULD KNOW THIS,

καὶ εἶπεν δοθῆναι αὐτῇ φαγεῖν.
AND HE SAID TO GIVE HER [SOMETHING] TO EAT.

him, and went in where the child was. ⁴¹He took her by the hand and said to her, "Talitha cum," which means, "Little girl, get up!" ⁴²And immediately the girl got up and began to walk about (she was twelve years of age). At this they were overcome with amazement. ⁴³He strictly ordered them that no one should know this, and told them to give her something to eat.

CHAPTER 6

6.1 Καὶ ἐξῆλθεν ἐκεῖθεν καὶ ἔρχεται εἰς τὴν
AND HE CAME OUT FROM THERE AND COMES INTO THE

πατρίδα αὐτοῦ, καὶ ἀκολουθοῦσιν αὐτῷ οἱ μαθηταὶ
HOMETOWN OF HIM, AND FOLLOW HIM THE DISCIPLES

αὐτοῦ. **6.2** καὶ γενομένου σαββάτου ἤρξατο διδάσκειν
OF HIM. AND HAVING BECOME [THE] SABBATH HE BEGAN TO TEACH

ἐν τῇ συναγωγῇ, καὶ πολλοὶ ἀκούοντες ἐξεπλήσσοντο
IN THE SYNAGOGUE, AND MANY LISTENING WERE AMAZED

λέγοντες, Πόθεν τούτῳ ταῦτα, καὶ τίς ἡ
SAYING, FROM WHERE [DID] THIS ONE [LEARN] THESE THINGS, AND WHAT [IS] THE

σοφία ἡ δοθεῖσα τούτῳ, καὶ αἱ δυνάμεις τοιαῦται
WISDOM - HAVING BEEN GIVEN TO THIS ONE, AND - SUCH~MIRACLES

διὰ τῶν χειρῶν αὐτοῦ γινόμεναι; **6.3** οὐχ οὗτός ἐστιν ὁ
BY THE HANDS OF HIM COMING ABOUT? ³NOT ²THIS ONE ¹IS THE

τέκτων, ὁ υἱὸς τῆς Μαρίας καὶ ἀδελφὸς Ἰακώβου καὶ
CARPENTER, THE SON - OF MARY, AND BROTHER OF JAMES AND

Ἰωσῆτος καὶ Ἰούδα καὶ Σίμωνος; καὶ οὐκ εἰσὶν αἱ
JOSES AND JUDAS AND SIMON? AND ARE NOT THE

ἀδελφαὶ αὐτοῦ ὧδε πρὸς ἡμᾶς; καὶ ἐσκανδαλίζοντο
SISTERS OF HIM HERE WITH US? AND THEY WERE TAKING OFFENSE

ἐν αὐτῷ. **6.4** καὶ ἔλεγεν αὐτοῖς ὁ Ἰησοῦς ὅτι
AT HIM. AND WAS SAYING TO THEM - JESUS -

Οὐκ ἔστιν προφήτης ἄτιμος εἰ μὴ ἐν τῇ πατρίδι αὐτοῦ
A PROPHET~IS NOT DISHONORED EXCEPT IN THE HOMETOWN OF HIM

καὶ ἐν τοῖς συγγενεῦσιν αὐτοῦ καὶ ἐν τῇ οἰκίᾳ
AND AMONG THE RELATIVES OF HIM AND IN THE HOUSE

αὐτοῦ. **6.5** καὶ οὐκ ἐδύνατο ἐκεῖ ποιῆσαι οὐδεμίαν
OF HIM. AND HE WAS NOT ABLE THERE TO DO ANY

He left that place and came to his hometown, and his disciples followed him. ²On the sabbath he began to teach in the synagogue, and many who heard him were astounded. They said, "Where did this man get all this? What is this wisdom that has been given to him? What deeds of power are being done by his hands! ³Is not this the carpenter, the son of Mary*l* and brother of James and Joses and Judas and Simon, and are not his sisters here with us?" And they took offense*m* at him. ⁴Then Jesus said to them, "Prophets are not without honor, except in their hometown, and among their own kin, and in their own house." ⁵And he could do no

l Other ancient authorities read *son of the carpenter and of Mary*
m Or *stumbled*

deed of power there, except that he laid his hands on a few sick people and cured them. [6]And he was amazed at their unbelief.

Then he went about among the villages teaching. [7]He called the twelve and began to send them out two by two, and gave them authority over the unclean spirits. [8]He ordered them to take nothing for their journey except a staff; no bread, no bag, no money in their belts; [9]but to wear sandals and not to put on two tunics. [10]He said to them, "Wherever you enter a house, stay there until you leave the place. [11]If any place will not welcome you and they refuse to hear you, as you leave, shake off the dust that is on your feet as a testimony against them." [12]So they went out and proclaimed that all should repent. [13]They cast out many demons, and anointed with oil many who were sick and cured them.

14 King Herod heard of it, for Jesus'[n] name had become known. Some were[o] saying, "John the baptizer has been raised from the dead; and

[n] Gk his
[o] Other ancient authorities read He was

δύναμιν, εἰ μὴ ὀλίγοις ἀρρώστοις ἐπιθεὶς τὰς
MIRACLES,   EXCEPT   ON A FEW   SICK PERSONS   HAVING LAID ON   THE(HIS)

χεῖρας ἐθεράπευσεν. **6.6** καὶ ἐθαύμαζεν διὰ τὴν
HANDS   HE HEALED [THEM].   AND   HE WAS AMAZED   ON ACCOUNT OF   THE

ἀπιστίαν αὐτῶν.
UNBELIEF   OF THEM.

Καὶ περιῆγεν τὰς κώμας κύκλῳ διδάσκων.
AND   HE WAS GOING AROUND   THE   VILLAGES   IN A CIRCUIT   TEACHING.

6.7 καὶ προσκαλεῖται τοὺς δώδεκα καὶ ἤρξατο
AND   HE SUMMONS   THE   TWELVE   AND   HE BEGAN

αὐτοὺς ἀποστέλλειν δύο δύο καὶ ἐδίδου αὐτοῖς
TO SEND THEM OUT   TWO [BY]   TWO   AND   HE WAS GIVING   TO THEM

ἐξουσίαν τῶν πνευμάτων τῶν ἀκαθάρτων, **6.8** καὶ
AUTHORITY [OVER]   THE   ²SPIRITS   -   ¹UNCLEAN,   AND

παρήγγειλεν αὐτοῖς ἵνα μηδὲν αἴρωσιν εἰς ὁδὸν
HE GAVE ORDERS   TO THEM   THAT   THEY SHOULD TAKE~NOTHING   ON   [THE] ROAD

εἰ μὴ ῥάβδον μόνον, μὴ ἄρτον, μὴ πήραν, μὴ
EXCEPT   A WALKING STICK   ONLY,   NOT   BREAD,   NOT   A KNAPSACK,   NOR [TO CARRY]

εἰς τὴν ζώνην χαλκόν, **6.9** ἀλλὰ ὑποδεδεμένους
IN   THE   BELT   COPPER [COINS],   BUT   HAVING HAD TIED ON

σανδάλια, καὶ μὴ ἐνδύσησθε δύο χιτῶνας. **6.10** καὶ
SANDALS,   AND   DO NOT DRESS [WITH]   TWO   SHIRTS.   AND

ἔλεγεν αὐτοῖς, Ὅπου ἐὰν εἰσέλθητε εἰς οἰκίαν,
HE WAS SAYING   TO THEM,   WHEREVER   YOU° ENTER   INTO   A HOUSE,

ἐκεῖ μένετε ἕως ἂν ἐξέλθητε ἐκεῖθεν. **6.11** καὶ ὃς ἂν
STAY~THERE   UNTIL   YOU° LEAVE   FROM THERE.   AND   WHATEVER

τόπος μὴ δέξηται ὑμᾶς μηδὲ ἀκούσωσιν ὑμῶν,
PLACE   DOES NOT WELCOME   YOU°   NOR   LISTEN   TO YOU°,

ἐκπορευόμενοι ἐκεῖθεν ἐκτινάξατε τὸν χοῦν τὸν
GOING OUT   FROM THERE   SHAKE OFF   THE   DUST   -

ὑποκάτω τῶν ποδῶν ὑμῶν εἰς μαρτύριον αὐτοῖς.
UNDER   THE   FEET   OF YOU°   FOR   A TESTIMONY   TO THEM.

6.12 Καὶ ἐξελθόντες ἐκήρυξαν ἵνα μετανοῶσιν,
AND   HAVING GONE OUT   THEY PREACHED   THAT   THEY SHOULD REPENT,

6.13 καὶ δαιμόνια πολλὰ ἐξέβαλλον, καὶ
AND   MANY~DEMONS   THEY WERE CASTING OUT,   AND

ἤλειφον ἐλαίῳ πολλοὺς ἀρρώστους καὶ
THEY WERE ANOINTING   WITH OIL   MANY   SICK PERSONS   AND

ἐθεράπευον.
THEY WERE HEALING [THEM].

6.14 Καὶ ἤκουσεν ὁ βασιλεὺς Ἡρῴδης, φανερὸν γὰρ
AND   ³HEARD [THIS]   -   ¹KING   ²HEROD,   ⁹WELL KNOWN   ⁴FOR

ἐγένετο τὸ ὄνομα αὐτοῦ, καὶ ⌜ἔλεγον⌝ ὅτι Ἰωάννης
⁸BECAME   ⁵THE   ⁶NAME   ⁷OF HIM,   AND   THEY WERE SAYING   -   JOHN

ὁ βαπτίζων ἐγήγερται ἐκ νεκρῶν καὶ
THE ONE   BAPTIZING   HAS BEEN RASIED   FROM AMONG   [THE] DEAD   AND

6:14 text: ASV RSV NASB.NIV NEB TEV NJB NRSV.   var. ελεγεν (he was saying): KJV ASVmg RSVmg NIVmg NEBmg NJBmg NRSVmg.

διὰ τοῦτο ἐνεργοῦσιν αἱ δυνάμεις ἐν αὐτῷ.
FOR THIS REASON ²ARE AT WORK - ¹MIRACLES IN HIM.

6.15 ἄλλοι δὲ ἔλεγον ὅτι Ἠλίας ἐστίν· ἄλλοι δὲ
BUT~OTHERS WERE SAYING - IT IS~ELIJAH. AND~OTHERS

ἔλεγον ὅτι προφήτης ὡς εἷς τῶν προφητῶν.
WERE SAYING - A PROPHET LIKE ONE OF THE [OLD] PROPHETS.

6.16 ἀκούσας δὲ ὁ Ἡρῴδης ἔλεγεν, Ὃν ἐγὼ
AND~HAVING HEARD [THESE THINGS] - HEROD WAS SAYING, ²WHOM ³I

ἀπεκεφάλισα Ἰωάννην, οὗτος ἠγέρθη. **6.17** Αὐτὸς γὰρ
⁴BEHEADED ¹JOHN, THIS ONE WAS RAISED. ³HIMSELF ¹FOR

ὁ Ἡρῴδης ἀποστείλας ἐκράτησεν τὸν Ἰωάννην καὶ
- ²HEROD HAVING SENT ARRESTED - JOHN AND

ἔδησεν αὐτὸν ἐν φυλακῇ διὰ Ἡρῳδιάδα τὴν
BOUND HIM IN PRISON ON ACCOUNT OF HERODIAS THE

γυναῖκα Φιλίππου τοῦ ἀδελφοῦ αὐτοῦ, ὅτι
WIFE OF PHILIP THE BROTHER OF HIM, FOR

αὐτὴν ἐγάμησεν· **6.18** ἔλεγεν γὰρ ὁ Ἰωάννης τῷ
HE MARRIED~HER. FOR~WAS SAYING - JOHN

Ἡρῴδῃ ὅτι Οὐκ ἔξεστίν σοι ἔχειν τὴν γυναῖκα τοῦ
TO HEROD - IT IS NOT PERMISSIBLE FOR YOU TO HAVE THE WIFE OF THE

ἀδελφοῦ σου. **6.19** ἡ δὲ Ἡρῳδιὰς ἐνεῖχεν αὐτῷ
BROTHER OF YOU. - AND HERODIAS BORE A GRUDGE AGAINST HIM

καὶ ἤθελεν αὐτὸν ἀποκτεῖναι, καὶ οὐκ ἠδύνατο· **6.20** ὁ
AND DESIRED TO KILL~HIM, AND SHE COULD NOT; -

γὰρ Ἡρῴδης ἐφοβεῖτο τὸν Ἰωάννην, εἰδὼς αὐτὸν
FOR HEROD FEARED - JOHN, HAVING KNOWN HIM [TO BE]

ἄνδρα δίκαιον καὶ ἅγιον, καὶ συνετήρει αὐτόν, καὶ
⁴MAN ¹A RIGHTEOUS ²AND ³HOLY, AND HE WAS PROTECTING HIM, AND

ἀκούσας αὐτοῦ πολλὰ ἠπόρει, καὶ ἡδέως
HAVING HEARD HIM HE WAS DISTURBED~GREATLY, AND [YET] GLADLY

αὐτοῦ ἤκουεν. **6.21** Καὶ γενομένης ἡμέρας εὐκαίρου
HE WAS LISTENING~TO HIM. AND HAVING COME ABOUT A SUITABLE~DAY

ὅτε Ἡρῴδης τοῖς γενεσίοις αὐτοῦ
WHEN HEROD ON THE BIRTHDAY CELEBRATIONS OF HIM

δεῖπνον ἐποίησεν τοῖς μεγιστᾶσιν αὐτοῦ καὶ τοῖς
MADE~A DINNER FOR THE COURT NOBLES OF HIM AND THE

χιλιάρχοις καὶ τοῖς πρώτοις τῆς Γαλιλαίας,
MILITARY COMMANDERS AND THE MOST PROMINENT PERSONS - OF GALILEE,

6.22 καὶ εἰσελθούσης ⌜τῆς θυγατρὸς αὐτοῦ Ἡρῳδιάδος⌝
AND HAVING ENTERED THE DAUGHTER OF HIM, HERODIAS,

καὶ ὀρχησαμένης ἤρεσεν τῷ Ἡρῴδῃ καὶ τοῖς
AND HAVING DANCED SHE PLEASED - HEROD AND THE ONES

συνανακειμένοις. εἶπεν ὁ βασιλεὺς τῷ κορασίῳ,
RECLINING AT TABLE WITH [HIM]. SAID THE KING TO THE YOUNG GIRL,

Αἴτησόν με ὃ ἐὰν θέλῃς, καὶ δώσω σοι· **6.23** καὶ
ASK ME WHATEVER YOU WISH AND I WILL GIVE [IT] TO YOU. AND

for this reason these powers are at work in him." [15]But others said, "It is Elijah." And others said, "It is a prophet, like one of the prophets of old." [16]But when Herod heard of it, he said, "John, whom I beheaded, has been raised."

17 For Herod himself had sent men who arrested John, bound him, and put him in prison on account of Herodias, his brother Philip's wife, because Herod[p] had married her. [18]For John had been telling Herod, "It is not lawful for you to have your brother's wife." [19]And Herodias had a grudge against him, and wanted to kill him. But she could not, [20]for Herod feared John, knowing that he was a righteous and holy man, and he protected him. When he heard him, he was greatly perplexed;[q] and yet he liked to listen to him. [21]But an opportunity came when Herod on his birthday gave a banquet for his courtiers and officers and for the leaders of Galilee. [22]When his daughter Herodias[r] came in and danced, she pleased Herod and his guests; and the king said to the girl, "Ask me for whatever you wish, and I will give it." [23]And

[p] Gk *he*
[q] Other ancient authorities read *he did many things*
[r] Other ancient authorities read *the daughter of Herodias herself*

6:22 text: ASVmg TEVmg NRSV. var. της θυγατρος αυτης της Ηρωδιαδος (the daughter of Herodias herself): KJV ASV RSV NASB NIV NEB TEV NJB NRSVmg.

he solemnly swore to her, "Whatever you ask me, I will give you, even half of my kingdom." 24She went out and said to her mother, "What should I ask for?" She replied, "The head of John the baptizer." 25Immediately she rushed back to the king and requested, "I want you to give me at once the head of John the Baptist on a platter. 26The king was deeply grieved; yet out of regard for his oaths and for the guests, he did not want to refuse her. 27Immediately the king sent a soldier of the guard with orders to bring John's⁵ head. He went and beheaded him in the prison, 28brought his head on a platter, and gave it to the girl. Then the girl gave it to her mother. 29When his disciples heard about it, they came and took his body, and laid it in a tomb.

30 The apostles gathered around Jesus, and told him all that they had done and taught. 31He said to them, "Come away to a deserted place all by yourselves and rest a while." For many were coming and going, and they had no leisure even to eat. 32And

⁵ Gk *his*

ὤμοσεν αὐτῇ [πολλά], Ὅ τι ἐάν με αἰτήσῃς δώσω
HE MADE A PROMISE TO HER SOLEMNLY, WHATEVER YOU ASK~ME I WILL GIVE

σοι ἕως ἡμίσους τῆς βασιλείας μου. 6.24 καὶ
TO YOU UP TO HALF OF THE KINGDOM OF ME. AND

ἐξελθοῦσα εἶπεν τῇ μητρὶ αὐτῆς, Τί αἰτήσωμαι; ἡ
HAVING GONE OUT SHE SAID TO THE MOTHER OF HER, WHAT SHOULD I ASK [FOR]? -

δὲ εἶπεν, Τὴν κεφαλὴν Ἰωάννου τοῦ βαπτίζοντος.
AND SHE SAID, THE HEAD OF JOHN THE ONE BAPTIZING.

6.25 καὶ εἰσελθοῦσα εὐθὺς μετὰ σπουδῆς πρὸς τὸν
AND HAVING ENTERED IMMEDIATELY WITH HASTE TO THE

βασιλέα ᾐτήσατο λέγουσα, Θέλω ἵνα ἐξαυτῆς
KING SHE MADE [HER] REQUEST SAYING, I DESIRE THAT AT ONCE

δῷς μοι ἐπὶ πίνακι τὴν κεφαλὴν Ἰωάννου τοῦ
YOU MAY GIVE TO ME UPON A PLATTER THE HEAD OF JOHN THE

βαπτιστοῦ. 6.26 καὶ περίλυπος γενόμενος ὁ βασιλεὺς
BAPTIST. AND HAVING BECOME VERY SAD, THE KING

διὰ τοὺς ὅρκους καὶ τοὺς ἀνακειμένους
ON ACCOUNT OF THE PROMISE AND THE ONES RECLINING AT TABLE [WITH HIM]

οὐκ ἠθέλησεν ἀθετῆσαι αὐτήν· 6.27 καὶ εὐθὺς
HE DID NOT WANT TO REFUSE HER. AND IMMEDIATELY

ἀποστείλας ὁ βασιλεὺς σπεκουλάτορα ἐπέταξεν
³HAVING SENT ¹THE ²KING AN EXECUTIONER HE COMMANDED

ἐνέγκαι τὴν κεφαλὴν αὐτοῦ. καὶ ἀπελθὼν
TO BRING THE HEAD OF HIM. AND HAVING LEFT

ἀπεκεφάλισεν αὐτὸν ἐν τῇ φυλακῇ 6.28 καὶ ἤνεγκεν
HE BEHEADED HIM IN THE PRISON AND HE BROUGHT

τὴν κεφαλὴν αὐτοῦ ἐπὶ πίνακι καὶ ἔδωκεν αὐτὴν τῷ
THE HEAD OF HIM UPON A PLATTER AND GAVE IT TO THE

κορασίῳ, καὶ τὸ κοράσιον ἔδωκεν αὐτὴν τῇ μητρὶ
YOUNG GIRL, AND THE YOUNG GIRL GAVE IT TO THE MOTHER

αὐτῆς. 6.29 καὶ ἀκούσαντες οἱ μαθηταὶ αὐτοῦ ἦλθον
OF HER. AND HAVING HEARD [THIS] THE DISCIPLES OF HIM CAME

καὶ ἦραν τὸ πτῶμα αὐτοῦ καὶ ἔθηκαν αὐτὸ ἐν
AND CARRIED AWAY THE CORPSE OF HIM AND PLACED IT IN

μνημείῳ.
A TOMB.

6.30 Καὶ συνάγονται οἱ ἀπόστολοι πρὸς τὸν Ἰησοῦν
AND GATHERED TOGETHER THE APOSTLES TO - JESUS

καὶ ἀπήγγειλαν αὐτῷ πάντα ὅσα ἐποίησαν καὶ ὅσα
AND REPORTED TO HIM EVERYTHING WHICH THEY DID AND WHICH

ἐδίδαξαν. 6.31 καὶ λέγει αὐτοῖς, Δεῦτε ὑμεῖς αὐτοὶ
THEY TAUGHT. AND HE SAYS TO THEM, COME YOU° YOURSELVES

κατ᾽ ἰδίαν εἰς ἔρημον τόπον καὶ ἀναπαύσασθε ὀλίγον.
PRIVATELY TO A DESOLATE PLACE AND REST A LITTLE.

ἦσαν γὰρ οἱ ἐρχόμενοι καὶ οἱ ὑπάγοντες
⁷WERE ¹FOR ²THE ONES ³COMING ⁴AND ⁵THE ONES ⁶GOING

πολλοί, καὶ οὐδὲ φαγεῖν εὐκαίρουν. 6.32 καὶ
⁸MANY, ⁹AND ¹⁰[DID] NOT ¹²TO EAT ¹¹HAVE OPPORTUNITY. AND

ἀπῆλθον ἐν τῷ πλοίῳ εἰς ἔρημον τόπον κατ᾽ ἰδίαν.
THEY DEPARTED IN THE BOAT TO A DESOLATE PLACE PRIVATELY.

6.33 καὶ εἶδον αὐτοὺς ὑπάγοντας καὶ
AND ²SAW ³THEM ⁴GOING ⁵AND

ἐπέγνωσαν πολλοί καὶ πεζῇ ἀπὸ πασῶν τῶν
⁶KNEW [WHERE THEY WERE GOING] ¹MANY AND ON FOOT FROM ALL OF THE

πόλεων συνέδραμον ἐκεῖ καὶ προῆλθον αὐτούς.
TOWNS THEY RAN THERE AND THEY ARRIVED AHEAD OF THEM.

6.34 καὶ ἐξελθὼν εἶδεν πολὺν ὄχλον καὶ
AND HAVING GOTTEN OUT [OF THE BOAT] HE SAW A LARGE CROWD AND

ἐσπλαγχνίσθη ἐπ᾽ αὐτούς, ὅτι ἦσαν ὡς πρόβατα
HE HAD COMPASSION ON THEM, FOR THEY WERE LIKE SHEEP

μὴ ἔχοντα ποιμένα, καὶ ἤρξατο διδάσκειν αὐτοὺς
NOT HAVING A SHEPHERD, AND HE BEGAN TO TEACH THEM

πολλά. **6.35** Καὶ ἤδη ὥρας πολλῆς γενομένης
MANY THINGS. AND ALREADY A LATE HOUR WAS COMING [AND]

προσελθόντες αὐτῷ οἱ μαθηταὶ αὐτοῦ ἔλεγον ὅτι
WAS APPROACHING HIM THE DISCIPLES OF HIM WERE SAYING -

Ἔρημός ἐστιν ὁ τόπος καὶ ἤδη ὥρα πολλή·
DESOLATE IS THE PLACE AND ALREADY [IT IS] A LATE HOUR.

6.36 ἀπόλυσον αὐτούς, ἵνα ἀπελθόντες εἰς τοὺς
SEND AWAY THEM, IN ORDER THAT HAVING DEPARTED TO THE

κύκλῳ ἀγροὺς καὶ κώμας ἀγοράσωσιν ἑαυτοῖς τί
SURROUNDING FARMS AND VILLAGES THEY MAY BUY FOR THEMSELVES WHAT

φάγωσιν. **6.37** ὁ δὲ ἀποκριθεὶς εἶπεν αὐτοῖς, Δότε
THEY MAY EAT. - BUT HAVING ANSWERED HE SAID TO THEM, GIVE

αὐτοῖς ὑμεῖς φαγεῖν. καὶ λέγουσιν αὐτῷ,
TO THEM YOURSELVES [SOMETHING] TO EAT. AND THEY SAY TO HIM,

Ἀπελθόντες ἀγοράσωμεν δηναρίων διακοσίων ἄρτους
HAVING DEPARTED MAY WE BUY FOR TWO HUNDRED~DENARII LOAVES

καὶ δώσομεν αὐτοῖς φαγεῖν; **6.38** ὁ δὲ λέγει αὐτοῖς,
AND WILL WE GIVE TO THEM TO EAT? - AND HE SAYS TO THEM,

Πόσους ἄρτους ἔχετε; ὑπάγετε ἴδετε. καὶ γνόντες
HOW MANY LOAVES DO YOU° HAVE? GO [AND] SEE. AND HAVING KNOWN

λέγουσιν, Πέντε, καὶ δύο ἰχθύας. **6.39** καὶ ἐπέταξεν
THEY SAY, FIVE, AND TWO FISH. AND HE COMMANDED

αὐτοῖς ἀνακλῖναι πάντας συμπόσια συμπόσια ἐπὶ τῷ
THEM TO LIE DOWN EVERYONE GROUP BY GROUP ON THE

χλωρῷ χόρτῳ. **6.40** καὶ ἀνέπεσαν πρασιαὶ πρασιαὶ
GREEN GRASS. AND THEY RECLINED GROUP BY GROUP

κατὰ ἑκατὸν καὶ κατὰ πεντήκοντα. **6.41** καὶ λαβὼν
IN HUNDREDS AND IN FIFTIES. AND HAVING TAKEN

τοὺς πέντε ἄρτους καὶ τοὺς δύο ἰχθύας ἀναβλέψας εἰς
THE FIVE LOAVES AND THE TWO FISH HAVING LOOKED UP TO

τὸν οὐρανὸν εὐλόγησεν καὶ κατέκλασεν τοὺς ἄρτους
- HEAVEN HE BLESSED AND BROKE THE LOAVES

καὶ ἐδίδου τοῖς μαθηταῖς [αὐτοῦ] ἵνα
AND HE WAS GIVING [THEM] TO THE DISCIPLES OF HIM IN ORDER THAT

they went away in the boat to a deserted place by themselves. ³³Now many saw them going and recognized them, and they hurried there on foot from all the towns and arrived ahead of them. ³⁴As he went ashore, he saw a great crowd; and he had compassion for them, because they were like sheep without a shepherd; and he began to teach them many things. ³⁵When it grew late, his disciples came to him and said, "This is a deserted place, and the hour is now very late; ³⁶send them away so that they may go into the surrounding country and villages and buy something for themselves to eat." ³⁷But he answered them, "You give them something to eat." They said to him, "Are we to go and buy two hundred denarii*f* worth of bread, and give it to them to eat?" ³⁸And he said to them, "How many loaves have you? Go and see." When they had found out, they said, "Five, and two fish." ³⁹Then he ordered them to get all the people to sit down in groups on the green grass. ⁴⁰So they sat down in groups of hundreds and of fifties. ⁴¹Taking the five loaves and the two fish, he looked up to heaven, and blessed and broke the loaves, and gave them to his disciples to

f The denarius was the usual day's wage for a laborer

set before the people; and he divided the two fish among them all. ⁴²And all ate and were filled; ⁴³and they took up twelve baskets full of broken pieces and of the fish. ⁴⁴Those who had eaten the loaves numbered five thousand men.

45 Immediately he made his disciples get into the boat and go on ahead to the other side, to Bethsaida, while he dismissed the crowd. ⁴⁶After saying farewell to them, he went up on the mountain to pray.

47 When evening came, the boat was out on the sea, and he was alone on the land. ⁴⁸When he saw that they were straining at the oars against an adverse wind, he came towards them early in the morning, walking on the sea. He intended to pass them by. ⁴⁹But when they saw him walking on the sea, they thought it was a ghost and cried out; ⁵⁰for they all saw him and were terrified. But immediately he spoke to them and said, "Take heart, it is I; do not be afraid." ⁵¹Then he got into the boat with them and the wind ceased. And they were utterly astounded, ⁵²for they did not understand about

παρατιθῶσιν   αὐτοῖς,   καὶ   τοὺς   δύο   ἰχθύας   ἐμέρισεν
THEY MIGHT SET BEFORE   THEM,   AND   THE   TWO   FISH   HE DIVIDED

πᾶσιν.   **6.42** καὶ   ἔφαγον πάντες   καὶ   ἐχορτάσθησαν,
TO ALL.   AND   EVERYONE~ATE   AND   THEY WERE SATISFIED,

6.43 καὶ   ἦραν   κλάσματα   δώδεκα
AND   THEY PICKED UP   FRAGMENTS   TWELVE

κοφίνων   πληρώματα   καὶ   ἀπὸ   τῶν   ἰχθύων.   **6.44** καὶ
FULL~BASKETS   AND   FROM   THE   FISH.   AND

ἦσαν οἱ   φαγόντες   [τοὺς ἄρτους]   πεντακισχίλιοι
⁵WERE   ¹THE ONES   ²HAVING EATEN   ³THE   ⁴LOAVES   ⁶FIVE THOUSAND

ἄνδρες.
MEN.

6.45 Καὶ   εὐθὺς   ἠνάγκασεν   τοὺς   μαθητὰς   αὐτοῦ
AND   IMMEDIATELY   HE COMPELLED   THE   DISCIPLES   OF HIM

ἐμβῆναι   εἰς   τὸ   πλοῖον   καὶ   προάγειν   εἰς   τὸ   πέραν
TO EMBARK   INTO   THE   BOAT   AND   TO GO BEFORE [HIM]   TO   THE   OTHER SIDE

πρὸς   Βηθσαϊδάν,   ἕως   αὐτὸς   ἀπολύει   τὸν   ὄχλον.
TO   BETHSAIDA,   UNTIL   HE   DISMISSES   THE   CROWD.

6.46 καὶ   ἀποταξάμενος   αὐτοῖς   ἀπῆλθεν   εἰς   τὸ   ὄρος
AND   HAVING SAID FAREWELL   TO THEM   HE DEPARTED   TO   THE   MOUNTAIN

προσεύξασθαι.   **6.47** καὶ   ὀψίας   γενομένης   ἦν   τὸ
TO PRAY.   AND   EVENING   HAVING COME   ³WAS   ¹THE

πλοῖον   ἐν   μέσῳ   τῆς   θαλάσσης,   καὶ   αὐτὸς   μόνος
²BOAT   IN   [THE] MIDDLE   OF THE   LAKE,   AND   HE   ALONE [WAS]

ἐπὶ   τῆς   γῆς.   **6.48** καὶ   ἰδὼν   αὐτοὺς   βασανιζομένους
ON   THE   LAND.   AND   HAVING SEEN   THEM   STRAINING

ἐν   τῷ   ἐλαύνειν,   ἦν   γὰρ   ὁ   ἄνεμος   ἐναντίος   αὐτοῖς,
IN   THE   ROWING,   ⁴WAS   ¹FOR   ²THE   ³WIND   AGAINST   THEM,

περὶ   τετάρτην   φυλακὴν   τῆς   νυκτὸς   ἔρχεται   πρὸς
ABOUT   [THE] FOURTH   WATCH   OF THE   NIGHT   HE COMES   TO

αὐτοὺς   περιπατῶν ἐπὶ   τῆς   θαλάσσης   καὶ   ἤθελεν
THEM   WALKING   ON   THE   LAKE.   AND   HE WANTED

παρελθεῖν   αὐτούς.   **6.49** οἱ   δὲ   ἰδόντες   αὐτὸν   ἐπὶ   τῆς
TO GO BY   THEM.   -   BUT   HAVING SEEN   HIM   ON   THE

θαλάσσης   περιπατοῦντα   ἔδοξαν   ὅτι   φάντασμά ἐστιν,
LAKE   WALKING   THEY THOUGHT   THAT   IT IS~AN APPARITION,

καὶ   ἀνέκραξαν·   **6.50** πάντες   γὰρ   αὐτὸν   εἶδον   καὶ
AND   THEY CRIED OUT;   FOR~EVERYONE   SAW~HIM   AND

ἐταράχθησαν.   ὁ   δὲ   εὐθὺς   ἐλάλησεν   μετ'   αὐτῶν, καὶ
THEY WERE TERRIFIED.   -   AND   IMMEDIATELY   HE SPOKE   WITH   THEM,   AND

λέγει   αὐτοῖς,   Θαρσεῖτε,   ἐγώ εἰμι·   μὴ   φοβεῖσθε.
HE SAYS   TO THEM,   HAVE COURAGE,   I   AM;   DO NOT BE AFRAID.

6.51 καὶ   ἀνέβη   πρὸς   αὐτοὺς   εἰς   τὸ   πλοῖον   καὶ
AND   HE WENT UP   TO   THEM   IN   THE   BOAT   AND

ἐκόπασεν   ὁ   ἄνεμος,   καὶ   λίαν   [ἐκ περισσοῦ]   ἐν
DIED DOWN   THE   WIND,   AND   VERY MUCH   EXCEEDINGLY   IN

ἑαυτοῖς   ἐξίσταντο·   **6.52** οὐ   γὰρ   συνῆκαν   ἐπὶ
THEMSELVES   THEY WERE AMAZED.   FOR~THEY DID NOT UNDERSTAND   CONCERNING

τοῖς ἄρτοις, ἀλλ᾽ ἦν αὐτῶν ἡ καρδία πεπωρωμένη.
THE LOAVES, BUT ³HAD BEEN ¹THEIR - ²HEART ⁴HARDENED.

6.53 Καὶ διαπεράσαντες ἐπὶ τὴν γῆν ἦλθον εἰς
AND HAVING CROSSED OVER ONTO THE LAND THEY CAME TO

Γεννησαρὲτ καὶ προσωρμίσθησαν. **6.54** καὶ
GENNESARET AND ANCHORED [THERE]. AND

ἐξελθόντων αὐτῶν ἐκ τοῦ πλοίου εὐθὺς ἐπιγνόντες
THEY~HAVING COME OUT FROM THE BOAT, IMMEDIATELY HAVING RECOGNIZED

αὐτὸν **6.55** περιέδραμον ὅλην τὴν χώραν ἐκείνην καὶ
HIM, THEY RAN AROUND ²WHOLE - ³REGION ¹THAT ⁴AND

ἤρξαντο ἐπὶ τοῖς κραβάττοις τοὺς κακῶς ἔχοντας
⁵THEY BEGAN ⁷UPON - ⁸MATTRESSES ⁹THE ONES ¹¹ILLNESS ¹⁰HAVING

περιφέρειν ὅπου ἤκουον ὅτι ἐστίν. **6.56** καὶ ὅπου ἂν
⁶TO CARRY WHERE THEY HEARD THAT HE IS(WAS). AND WHEREVER

εἰσεπορεύετο εἰς κώμας ἢ εἰς πόλεις ἢ εἰς ἀγρούς, ἐν
HE WAS ENTERING INTO VILLAGES OR INTO CITIES OR INTO COUNTRYSIDE, IN

ταῖς ἀγοραῖς ἐτίθεσαν τοὺς ἀσθενοῦντας καὶ
THE MARKETPLACES THEY WERE PUTTING THE ONES HAVING SICKNESS AND

παρεκάλουν αὐτὸν ἵνα κἂν τοῦ κρασπέδου τοῦ
THEY WERE BEGGING HIM THAT EVEN IF THE EDGE OF THE

ἱματίου αὐτοῦ ἅψωνται· καὶ ὅσοι ἂν ἥψαντο αὐτοῦ
GARMENT OF HIM THEY MIGHT TOUCH. AND AS MANY AS TOUCHED HIM

ἐσῴζοντο.
THEY WERE BEING HEALED.

the loaves, but their hearts were hardened. 53 When they had crossed over, they came to land at Gennesaret and moored the boat. ⁵⁴When they got out of the boat, people at once recognized him, ⁵⁵and rushed about that whole region and began to bring the sick on mats to wherever they heard he was. ⁵⁶And wherever he went, into villages or cities or farms, they laid the sick in the marketplaces, and begged him that they might touch even the fringe of his cloak; and all who touched it were healed.

CHAPTER 7

7.1 Καὶ συνάγονται πρὸς αὐτὸν οἱ Φαρισαῖοι καί
AND COMES TOGETHER TO HIM THE PHARISEES AND

τινες τῶν γραμματέων ἐλθόντες ἀπὸ Ἱεροσολύμων.
SOME OF THE SCRIBES HAVING COME FROM JERUSALEM.

7.2 καὶ ἰδόντες τινὰς τῶν μαθητῶν αὐτοῦ ὅτι κοιναῖς
AND HAVING SEEN SOME OF THE DISCIPLES OF HIM THAT WITH IMPURE

χερσίν, τοῦτ᾽ ἔστιν ἀνίπτοις, ἐσθίουσιν τοὺς ἄρτους
HANDS, THAT IS, UNWASHED, THEY ARE EATING THE LOAVES

7.3 — οἱ γὰρ Φαρισαῖοι καὶ πάντες οἱ Ἰουδαῖοι
— FOR~THE PHARISEES AND ALL THE JEWS,

ἐὰν μὴ πυγμῇ νίψωνται τὰς χεῖρας οὐκ ἐσθίουσιν,
UNLESS WITH A FIST THEY WASH THE(THEIR) HANDS THEY DO NOT EAT,

κρατοῦντες τὴν παράδοσιν τῶν πρεσβυτέρων, **7.4** καὶ
HOLDING TO THE TRADITION OF THE ELDERS, AND

ἀπ᾽ ἀγορᾶς ἐὰν μὴ ⌐βαπτίσωνται⌐ οὐκ ἐσθίουσιν,
FROM [THE] MARKETPLACE UNLESS THEY WASH THEMSELVES THEY DO NOT EAT,

καὶ ἄλλα πολλά ἐστιν ἃ παρέλαβον κρατεῖν,
AND MANY~OTHER THINGS THERE IS(ARE) WHICH THEY RECEIVED TO HOLD TO,

Now when the Pharisees and some of the scribes who had come from Jerusalem gathered around him, ²they noticed that some of his disciples were eating with defiled hands, that is, without washing them. ³(For the Pharisees, and all the Jews, do not eat unless they thoroughly wash their hands,ᵘ thus observing the tradition of the elders; ⁴and they do not eat anything from the market unless they wash it;ᵛ and there are also many other traditions that they observe,

ᵘ Meaning of Gk uncertain
ᵛ Other ancient authorities read *and when they come from the marketplace, they do not eat unless they purify themselves*

7:4a text: KJV ASV RSVmg NIV NEB TEVmg NJBmg NRSV. var. βαπτιζονται (immerse [themselves]): RSVmg TEV NJBmg. var. ραντισωνται (sprinkle [themselves]): ASVmg (RSV) NJB (NRSVmg).

the washing of cups, pots, and bronze kettles.ʷ) ⁵So the Pharisees and the scribes asked him, "Why do your disciples not liveˣ according to the tradition of the elders, but eat with defiled hands?" ⁶He said to them, "Isaiah prophesied rightly about you hypocrites, as it is written,

'This people honors me
with their lips,
but their hearts are far
from me;
⁷ in vain do they worship
me,
teaching human
precepts as
doctrines.'

⁸You abandon the commandment of God and hold to human tradition."

9 Then he said to them, "You have a fine way of rejecting the commandment of God in order to keep your tradition! ¹⁰For Moses said, 'Honor your father and your mother'; and, 'Whoever speaks evil of father or mother must surely die.' ¹¹But you say that if anyone tells father or mother, 'Whatever support you might have had from me is Corban' (that is, an offering to Godʸ)— ¹²then you no longer permit doing anything for

ʷ Other ancient authorities add *and beds*
ˣ Gk *walk*
ʸ Gk *lacks to God*

βαπτισμοὺς ποτηρίων καὶ ξεστῶν καὶ χαλκίων ⌜[καὶ
WASHING   OF CUPS   AND PITCHERS AND KETTLES   AND

κλινῶν]⌝— **7.5** καὶ ἐπερωτῶσιν αὐτὸν οἱ Φαρισαῖοι
DINING COUCHES— AND QUESTION   HIM   THE PHARISEES

καὶ οἱ γραμματεῖς, Διὰ τί οὐ περιπατοῦσιν οἱ
AND THE SCRIBES,   WHY DO NOT WALK   THE

μαθηταί σου κατὰ τὴν παράδοσιν τῶν
DISCIPLES OF YOU ACCORDING TO THE TRADITION OF THE

πρεσβυτέρων, ἀλλὰ κοιναῖς χερσὶν ἐσθίουσιν τὸν
ELDERS,   BUT WITH IMPURE HANDS EAT   THE

ἄρτον; **7.6** ὁ δὲ εἶπεν αὐτοῖς, Καλῶς ἐπροφήτευσεν
BREAD? - AND HE SAID TO THEM, WELL PROPHESIED

Ἠσαΐας περὶ ὑμῶν τῶν ὑποκριτῶν, ὡς γέγραπται
ISAIAH CONCERNING YOU° - HYPOCRITES, AS IT HAS BEEN WRITTEN

[ὅτι]

Οὗτος ὁ λαὸς τοῖς χείλεσίν με τιμᾷ,
THIS - PEOPLE WITH THE(THEIR) LIPS HONOR~ME,

ἡ δὲ καρδία αὐτῶν πόρρω ἀπέχει ἀπ' ἐμοῦ·
BUT~THE HEART OF THEM IS REMOVED~FAR AWAY FROM ME.

7.7 μάτην δὲ σέβονταί με
AND~IN VAIN THEY WORSHIP ME

διδάσκοντες διδασκαλίας ἐντάλματα
TEACHING [AS] TEACHINGS [THE] COMMANDMENTS

ἀνθρώπων.
OF MEN.

7.8 ἀφέντες τὴν ἐντολὴν τοῦ θεοῦ κρατεῖτε
HAVING ABANDONED THE COMMANDMENT - OF GOD YOU° ARE HOLDING TO

τὴν παράδοσιν τῶν ἀνθρώπων. **7.9** Καὶ ἔλεγεν
THE TRADITIONS - OF MEN. AND HE WAS SAYING

αὐτοῖς, Καλῶς ἀθετεῖτε τὴν ἐντολὴν τοῦ
TO THEM, YOU° HAVE SET ASIDE~WELL ENOUGH THE COMMANDMENT -

θεοῦ, ἵνα τὴν παράδοσιν ὑμῶν στήσητε.
OF GOD, IN ORDER THAT THE TRADITIONS OF YOU° MIGHT STAND.

7.10 Μωϋσῆς γὰρ εἶπεν, Τίμα τὸν πατέρα σου καὶ τὴν
FOR~MOSES SAID, HONOR THE FATHER OF YOU AND THE

μητέρα σου, καί, Ὁ κακολογῶν πατέρα ἢ μητέρα
MOTHER OF YOU, AND, THE ONE REVILING FATHER OR MOTHER

θανάτῳ τελευτάτω. **7.11** ὑμεῖς δὲ λέγετε, Ἐὰν
BY DEATH LET HIM DIE. BUT~YOU° SAY, IF

εἴπῃ ἄνθρωπος τῷ πατρὶ ἢ τῇ μητρί, Κορβᾶν,
A MAN~SAYS TO THE(HIS) FATHER OR TO THE(HIS) MOTHER, KORBAN,

ὅ ἐστιν, Δῶρον, ὃ ἐὰν ἐξ ἐμοῦ ὠφεληθῇς,
WHICH MEANS, GIFT, WHATEVER BY ME YOU MIGHT HAVE BENEFITED,

7.12 οὐκέτι ἀφίετε αὐτὸν οὐδὲν ποιῆσαι τῷ
NO LONGER DO YOU° PERMIT HIM TO DO~ANYTHING FOR THE(HIS)

7:4b text: ASVmg RSVmg NIVmg TEV NRSVmg. omit: ASV RSV NIV NEB TEVmg NRSV.
7:6-7 Isa. 29:13 LXX **7:10a** Exod. 20:12; Deut. 5:16 **7:10b** Exod. 21:17

πατρὶ ἢ τῇ μητρί, **7.13** ἀκυροῦντες τὸν λόγον τοῦ
FATHER OR THE(HIS) MOTHER, NULLIFYING THE WORD -

θεοῦ τῇ παραδόσει ὑμῶν ἧ παρεδώκατε· καὶ
OF GOD BY THE TRADITION OF YOU° WHICH YOU° RECEIVED. AND

παρόμοια τοιαῦτα πολλὰ ποιεῖτε.
⁴SIMILAR THINGS ³SUCH ²MANY ¹YOU° DO.

7.14 Καὶ προσκαλεσάμενος πάλιν τὸν ὄχλον ἔλεγεν
AND HAVING SUMMONED AGAIN THE CROWD HE WAS SAYING

αὐτοῖς, Ἀκούσατέ μου πάντες καὶ σύνετε.
TO THEM, LISTEN TO ME EVERYONE AND UNDERSTAND.

7.15 οὐδέν ἐστιν ἔξωθεν τοῦ ἀνθρώπου εἰσπορευόμενον
THERE IS~NOTHING OUTSIDE OF THE MAN ENTERING

εἰς αὐτὸν ὃ δύναται κοινῶσαι αὐτόν, ἀλλὰ τὰ
INTO HIM WHICH IS ABLE TO DEFILE HIM, BUT THE THINGS

ἐκ τοῦ ἀνθρώπου ἐκπορευόμενά ἐστιν τὰ
FROM THE MAN COMING OUT ARE THE THINGS

κοινοῦντα τὸν ἄνθρωπον.ᵀ **7.17** Καὶ ὅτε εἰσῆλθεν εἰς
DEFILING THE MAN. AND WHEN HE ENTERED INTO

οἶκον ἀπὸ τοῦ ὄχλου, ἐπηρώτων αὐτὸν οἱ μαθηταὶ
A HOUSE FROM THE CROWD, WERE ASKING HIM THE DISCIPLES

αὐτοῦ τὴν παραβολήν. **7.18** καὶ λέγει αὐτοῖς, Οὕτως
OF HIM [ABOUT] THE PARABLE. AND HE SAYS TO THEM, THUS

καὶ ὑμεῖς ἀσύνετοί ἐστε; οὐ νοεῖτε ὅτι
ALSO ²YOU° ³WITHOUT UNDERSTANDING ¹ARE? DO YOU° NOT UNDERSTAND THAT

πᾶν τὸ ἔξωθεν εἰσπορευόμενον εἰς τὸν ἄνθρωπον
EVERYTHING OUTSIDE ENTERING INTO THE MAN

οὐ δύναται αὐτὸν κοινῶσαι **7.19** ὅτι οὐκ εἰσπορεύεται
IS NOT ABLE TO DEFILE~HIM BECAUSE IT DOES NOT ENTER

αὐτοῦ εἰς τὴν καρδίαν ἀλλ᾽ εἰς τὴν κοιλίαν, καὶ εἰς
⁴OF HIM ¹INTO ²THE ³HEART BUT INTO THE STOMACH, AND INTO

τὸν ἀφεδρῶνα ἐκπορεύεται, καθαρίζων πάντα τὰ
THE LATRINE GOES OUT, CLEANSING ALL -

βρώματα; **7.20** ἔλεγεν δὲ ὅτι Τὸ ἐκ τοῦ
FOODS? AND~HE WAS SAYING - THE THING OUT OF THE

ἀνθρώπου ἐκπορευόμενον, ἐκεῖνο κοινοῖ τὸν ἄνθρωπον.
MAN GOING OUT, THAT DEFILES THE MAN.

7.21 ἔσωθεν γὰρ ἐκ τῆς καρδίας τῶν ἀνθρώπων οἱ
FOR~FROM WITHIN OUT OF THE HEART OF THE MAN THE

διαλογισμοὶ οἱ κακοὶ ἐκπορεύονται, πορνεῖαι, κλοπαί,
³THOUGHTS - ²EVIL ¹COME FORTH, FORNICATIONS, THEFTS,

φόνοι, **7.22** μοιχεῖαι, πλεονεξίαι, πονηρίαι, δόλος,
MURDERS, ADULTERIES, GREEDINESSES, WICKEDNESSES, DECEIT,

ἀσέλγεια, ὀφθαλμὸς πονηρός, βλασφημία, ὑπερηφανία,
LEWDNESS, AN EVIL~EYE, BLASPHEMY, PRIDE, [AND]

a father or mother, [13]thus making void the word of God through your tradition that you have handed on. And you do many things like this."

14 Then he called the crowd again and said to them, "Listen to me, all of you, and understand: [15]there is nothing outside a person that by going in can defile, but the things that come out are what defile."[z]

17 When he had left the crowd and entered the house, his disciples asked him about the parable. [18]He said to them, "Then do you also fail to understand? Do you not see that whatever goes into a person from outside cannot defile, [19]since it enters, not the heart but the stomach, and goes out into the sewer?" (Thus he declared all foods clean.) [20]And he said, "It is what comes out of a person that defiles. [21]For it is from within, from the human heart, that evil intentions come: fornication, theft, murder, [22]adultery, avarice, wickedness, deceit, licentiousness, envy, slander, pride,

[z] Other ancient authorities add verse 16, *"Let anyone with ears to hear listen"*

7:15 text: ASV RSV NASB NIV NEB TEV NJBmg NRSV. add v. 16 Ει τις εχει ωτα ακουειν, ακουετω (If any one has ears to hear, let him hear) [see Mark 4:9, 23]: KJV ASVmg RSVmg NIVmg NEBmg TEVmg NJB NRSVmg.

folly. ²³All these evil things come from within, and they defile a person."

24 From there he set out and went away to the region of Tyre.ᵃ He entered a house and did not want anyone to know he was there. Yet he could not escape notice, ²⁵but a woman whose little daughter had an unclean spirit immediately heard about him, and she came and bowed down at his feet. ²⁶Now the woman was a Gentile, of Syrophoenician origin. She begged him to cast the demon out of her daughter. ²⁷He said to her, "Let the children be fed first, for it is not fair to take the children's food and throw it to the dogs." ²⁸But she answered him, "Sir,ᵇ even the dogs under the table eat the children's crumbs." ²⁹Then he said to her, "For saying that, you may go— the demon has left your daughter." ³⁰So she went home, found the child lying on the bed, and the demon gone.

31 Then he returned from the region of Tyre, and went by way of Sidon towards the Sea of Galilee,

ᵃ Other ancient authorities add *and Sidon*
ᵇ Or *Lord*; other ancient authorities prefix *Yes*

ἀφροσύνη· **7.23** πάντα ταῦτα τὰ πονηρὰ ἔσωθεν
FOOLISHNESS;   ALL   THESE   -   EVIL THINGS FROM WITHIN

ἐκπορεύεται καὶ κοινοῖ τὸν ἄνθρωπον.
COMES FORTH   AND DEFILES THE MAN.

7.24 Ἐκεῖθεν δὲ ἀναστὰς ἀπῆλθεν εἰς τὰ ὅρια
AND~FROM THERE HAVING ARISEN HE DEPARTED TO THE DISTRICT

Τύρουᵀ. καὶ εἰσελθὼν εἰς οἰκίαν οὐδένα ἤθελεν
OF TYRE. AND HAVING ENTERED INTO A HOUSE HE WANTED~NO ONE

γνῶναι, καὶ οὐκ ἠδυνήθη λαθεῖν· **7.25** ἀλλ'
TO KNOW, AND [YET] HE WAS NOT ABLE TO ESCAPE NOTICE. BUT

εὐθὺς ἀκούσασα γυνὴ περὶ αὐτοῦ, ἧς εἶχεν τὸ
IMMEDIATELY A WOMAN~HAVING HEARD ABOUT HIM, OF WHOM WAS HAVING THE

θυγάτριον αὐτῆς πνεῦμα ἀκάθαρτον, ἐλθοῦσα
DAUGHTER OF HER AN UNCLEAN~SPIRIT, HAVING COME

προσέπεσεν πρὸς τοὺς πόδας αὐτοῦ· **7.26** ἡ δὲ γυνὴ
SHE FELL DOWN AT THE FEET OF HIM. AND~THE WOMAN

ἦν Ἑλληνίς, Συροφοινίκισσα τῷ γένει· καὶ
WAS A GREEK, A SYROPHOENICIAN - BY RACE. AND

ἠρώτα αὐτὸν ἵνα τὸ δαιμόνιον ἐκβάλη ἐκ τῆς
SHE WAS ASKING HIM THAT THE DEMON HE MIGHT CAST OUT FROM THE

θυγατρὸς αὐτῆς.
DAUGHTER OF HER.

7.27 καὶ ἔλεγεν αὐτῇ, Ἄφες πρῶτον χορτασθῆναι τὰ
AND HE WAS SAYING TO HER, FIRST~ALLOW TO BE SATISFIED THE

τέκνα, οὐ γάρ ἐστιν καλὸν λαβεῖν τὸν ἄρτον τῶν
CHILDREN, ³NOT ¹FOR ²IT IS GOOD TO TAKE THE BREAD OF THE

τέκνων καὶ τοῖς κυναρίοις βαλεῖν. **7.28** ἡ δὲ
CHILDREN AND TO THE DOGS TO THROW [IT]. - BUT

ἀπεκρίθη καὶ λέγει αὐτῷ, Κύριε· καὶ τὰ κυνάρια
SHE ANSWERED AND SAYS TO HIM, LORD, EVEN THE DOGS

ὑποκάτω τῆς τραπέζης ἐσθίουσιν ἀπὸ τῶν ψιχίων τῶν
UNDER THE TABLE EAT FROM THE CRUMBS OF THE

παιδίων. **7.29** καὶ εἶπεν αὐτῇ, Διὰ τοῦτον τὸν
CHILDREN. AND HE SAID TO HER, BECAUSE OF THIS -

λόγον ὕπαγε, ἐξελήλυθεν ἐκ τῆς θυγατρός σου τὸ
WORD, GO, HAS GONE OUT FROM THE DAUGHTER OF YOU THE

δαιμόνιον. **7.30** καὶ ἀπελθοῦσα εἰς τὸν οἶκον αὐτῆς,
DEMON. AND HAVING DEPARTED TO THE HOUSE OF HER

εὗρεν τὸ παιδίον βεβλημένον ἐπὶ τὴν κλίνην καὶ τὸ
SHE FOUND THE CHILD HAVING BEEN LYING ON THE COUCH AND THE

δαιμόνιον ἐξεληλυθός.
DEMON HAVING GONE OUT.

7.31 Καὶ πάλιν ἐξελθὼν ἐκ τῶν ὁρίων Τύρου
AND AGAIN HAVING COME OUT FROM THE REGION OF TYRE,

ἦλθεν διὰ Σιδῶνος εἰς τὴν θάλασσαν τῆς Γαλιλαίας
HE CAME THROUGH SIDON TO THE LAKE - OF GALILEE

7:24 text: ASVmg RSVmg NASB NIV NEB TEV NJB NRSV. add καὶ Σιδῶνος (and Sidon) [see Matt. 15:21]: KJV ASV RSV NASBmg NIVmg NJBmg NRSVmg.

ἀνὰ μέσον τῶν ὁρίων Δεκαπόλεως. **7.32** καὶ φέρουσιν
IN　THE MIDST OF THE REGION　OF DECAPOLIS.　　AND　THEY BRING

αὐτῷ　　　　κωφὸν καὶ μογιλάλον καὶ
TO HIM [A MAN WHO WAS] DEAF　AND　MUTE　　AND

παρακαλοῦσιν αὐτὸν ἵνα ἐπιθῇ　αὐτῷ τὴν
THEY BEG　　　HIM　THAT　HE MIGHT PUT UPON HIM　THE(HIS)

χεῖρα. **7.33** καὶ ἀπολαβόμενος αὐτὸν ἀπὸ τοῦ ὄχλου
HAND.　　　AND　HAVING TAKEN ASIDE　HIM　FROM THE CROWD

κατ' ἰδίαν ἔβαλεν τοὺς δακτύλους αὐτοῦ εἰς τὰ ὦτα
PRIVATELY　HE PUT　THE　FINGERS　OF HIM　INTO THE EARS

αὐτοῦ καὶ πτύσας ἥψατο τῆς γλώσσης αὐτοῦ, **7.34** καὶ
OF HIM　AND HAVING SPIT HE TOUCHED THE TONGUE　OF HIM,　　AND

ἀναβλέψας εἰς τὸν οὐρανὸν ἐστέναξεν καὶ λέγει
HAVING LOOKED UP TO　-　HEAVEN　HE SIGHED　AND　SAYS

αὐτῷ, Εφφαθα, ὅ ἐστιν, Διανοίχθητι. **7.35** καὶ
TO HIM　EPHPHATHA, WHICH MEANS,　BE OPENED.　　　AND

[εὐθέως] ἠνοίγησαν αὐτοῦ αἱ ἀκοαί, καὶ ἐλύθη
IMMEDIATELY WAS OPENED　HIS　-　EARS,　AND　WAS LOOSENED

ὁ δεσμὸς τῆς γλώσσης αὐτοῦ καὶ ἐλάλει
THE BOND　OF THE TONGUE　OF HIM　AND　HE WAS SPEAKING

ὀρθῶς. **7.36** καὶ διεστείλατο αὐτοῖς ἵνα
PROPERLY.　　AND　HE WAS ORDERING THEM　　THAT

μηδενὶ λέγωσιν· ὅσον δὲ αὐτοῖς διεστέλλετο,
THEY SHOULD TELL~NO ONE. BUT~AS MUCH AS HE ORDERED~THEM

αὐτοὶ μᾶλλον περισσότερον ἐκήρυσσον. **7.37** καὶ
THEY　ˉ ALL THE MORE　　WERE PROCLAIMING [IT].　　AND

ὑπερπερισσῶς ἐξεπλήσσοντο λέγοντες, Καλῶς πάντα
THEY WERE AMAZED~BEYOND ALL MEASURE　SAYING,　　³WELL　²ALL THINGS

πεποίηκεν, καὶ τοὺς κωφοὺς ποιεῖ ἀκούειν καὶ [τοὺς]
¹HE HAS DONE,　AND　THE　DEAF　HE MAKES TO HEAR　AND　THE

ἀλάλους λαλεῖν.
MUTE　　TO SPEAK.

in the region of the Decapolis. ³²They brought to him a deaf man who had an impediment in his speech; and they begged him to lay his hand on him. ³³He took him aside in private, away from the crowd, and put his fingers into his ears, and he spat and touched his tongue. ³⁴Then looking up to heaven, he sighed and said to him, "Ephphatha," that is, "Be opened." ³⁵And immediately his ears were opened, his tongue was released, and he spoke plainly. ³⁶Then Jesus[c] ordered them to tell no one; but the more he ordered them, the more zealously they proclaimed it. ³⁷They were astounded beyond measure, saying, "He has done everything well; he even makes the deaf to hear and the mute to speak."

[c] Gk *he*

CHAPTER 8

8.1 Ἐν ἐκείναις ταῖς ἡμέραις πάλιν πολλοῦ ὄχλου
IN　THOSE　-　DAYS　AGAIN A LARGE CROWD

ὄντος καὶ μὴ ἐχόντων τί φάγωσιν,
BEING　AND　NOT HAVING　ANYTHING THEY MIGHT EAT,

προσκαλεσάμενος τοὺς μαθητὰς λέγει αὐτοῖς,
HAVING CALLED　　THE　DISCIPLES　HE SAYS TO THEM,

8.2 Σπλαγχνίζομαι ἐπὶ τὸν ὄχλον, ὅτι ἤδη
I HAVE COMPASSION　ON　THE CROWD,　BECAUSE ALREADY

ἡμέραι τρεῖς προσμένουσίν μοι καὶ οὐκ ἔχουσιν
THREE~DAYS　THEY HAVE REMAINED WITH ME　AND　THEY DO NOT HAVE

τί φάγωσιν· **8.3** καὶ ἐὰν ἀπολύσω αὐτοὺς νήστεις
ANYTHING THEY MAY EAT.　AND　IF　I SEND AWAY THEM　HUNGRY

In those days when there was again a great crowd without anything to eat, he called his disciples and said to them, ²"I have compassion for the crowd, because they have been with me now for three days and have nothing to eat. ³If I send them away hungry to their homes, they will faint on the way—and some of them have come from a great distance." [4]His disciples replied, "How can one feed these people with bread here in the desert?" [5]He asked them, "How many loaves do you have?" They said, "Seven." [6]Then he ordered the crowd to sit down on the ground; and he took the seven loaves, and after giving thanks he broke them and gave them to his disciples to distribute; and they distributed them to the crowd. [7]They had also a few small fish; and after blessing them, he ordered that these too should be distributed. [8]They ate and were filled; and they took up the broken pieces left over, seven baskets full. [9]Now there were about four thousand people. And he sent them away. [10]And immediately he got into the boat with his disciples and went to the district of Dalmanutha.[d]

11 The Pharisees came and began to argue with him, asking him for a sign from heaven, to test him. [12]And he sighed deeply in his spirit and said, "Why does this generation ask for a sign? Truly I tell you, no sign will be given to this generation." [13]And he left, them, and getting into the boat again, he went across to the other side.

[d] Other ancient authorities read *Mageda* or *Magdala*

εἰς οἶκον αὐτῶν, ἐκλυθήσονται ἐν τῇ ὁδῷ· καί τινες
TO [THE] HOUSE OF THEM, THEY WILL GIVE OUT ON THE WAY; AND SOME

αὐτῶν ἀπὸ μακρόθεν ἥκασιν. **8.4** καὶ ἀπεκρίθησαν
OF THEM FROM FAR AWAY HAVE COME. AND ANSWERED

αὐτῷ οἱ μαθηταὶ αὐτοῦ ὅτι Πόθεν τούτους
HIM THE DISCIPLES OF HIM - FROM WHERE [4]THESE ONES

δυνήσεταί τις ὧδε χορτάσαι ἄρτων ἐπ᾽ ἐρημίας;
[1]WILL BE ABLE [2]ANYONE [6]HERE [3]TO FEED [5]LOAVES IN A DESOLATE PLACE?

8.5 καὶ ἠρώτα αὐτούς, Πόσους ἔχετε ἄρτους; οἱ δὲ
AND HE WAS ASKING THEM, HOW MANY LOAVES~DO YOU HAVE? - AND

εἶπαν, Ἑπτά. **8.6** καὶ παραγγέλλει τῷ ὄχλῳ
THEY SAID, SEVEN. AND HE GIVES ORDERS TO THE CROWD

ἀναπεσεῖν ἐπὶ τῆς γῆς· καὶ λαβὼν τοὺς ἑπτὰ
TO RECLINE ON THE GROUND. AND HAVING TAKEN THE SEVEN

ἄρτους εὐχαριστήσας ἔκλασεν καὶ ἐδίδου τοῖς
LOAVES [AND] HAVING GIVEN THANKS HE BROKE [THEM] AND WAS GIVING [THEM] TO THE

μαθηταῖς αὐτοῦ ἵνα παρατιθῶσιν, καὶ παρέθηκαν τῷ
DISCIPLES OF HIM SO THAT THEY MIGHT SERVE, AND THEY SERVED THE

ὄχλῳ. **8.7** καὶ εἶχον ἰχθύδια ὀλίγα· καὶ
CROWD. AND THEY WERE HAVING A FEW~FISH. AND

εὐλογήσας αὐτὰ εἶπεν καὶ ταῦτα παρατιθέναι.
HAVING BLESSED THEM HE SAID ALSO THESE [ARE] TO BE SERVED.

8.8 καὶ ἔφαγον καὶ ἐχορτάσθησαν, καὶ ἦραν
AND THEY ATE AND WERE SATISFIED, AND THERE WAS

περισσεύματα κλασμάτων ἑπτὰ σπυρίδας.
AN ABUNDANCE OF PIECES, SEVEN BASKETS [FULL].

8.9 ἦσαν δὲ ὡς τετρακισχίλιοι. καὶ ἀπέλυσεν
AND~THERE WERE APPROXIMATELY FOUR THOUSAND [PEOPLE]. AND HE SENT AWAY

αὐτούς. **8.10** Καὶ εὐθὺς ἐμβὰς εἰς τὸ πλοῖον
THEM. AND IMMEDIATELY HAVING EMBARKED INTO THE BOAT

μετὰ τῶν μαθητῶν αὐτοῦ ἦλθεν εἰς τὰ μέρη
WITH THE DISCIPLES OF HIM HE CAME INTO THE REGION

Δαλμανουθά.
OF DALMANUTHA.

8.11 Καὶ ἐξῆλθον οἱ Φαρισαῖοι καὶ ἤρξαντο συζητεῖν
AND CAME OUT THE PHARISEES AND THEY BEGAN TO ARGUE

αὐτῷ, ζητοῦντες παρ᾽ αὐτοῦ σημεῖον ἀπὸ τοῦ οὐρανοῦ,
WITH HIM, SEEKING FROM HIM A SIGN FROM - HEAVEN,

πειράζοντες αὐτόν. **8.12** καὶ ἀναστενάξας τῷ
TRYING HIM. AND HAVING SIGHED DEEPLY IN THE

πνεύματι αὐτοῦ λέγει, Τί ἡ γενεὰ αὕτη ζητεῖ
SPIRIT OF HIM HE SAYS, WHY - [3]GENERATION [2]THIS [1]DOES SEEK

σημεῖον; ἀμὴν λέγω ὑμῖν, εἰ δοθήσεται τῇ
A SIGN? TRULY I SAY TO YOU°, IN NO WAY WILL BE GIVEN -

γενεᾷ ταύτῃ σημεῖον. **8.13** καὶ ἀφεὶς αὐτοὺς πάλιν
TO THIS~GENERATION A SIGN. AND HAVING LEFT THEM AGAIN

ἐμβὰς ἀπῆλθεν εἰς τὸ πέραν.
HAVING EMBARKED HE DEPARTED TO THE OTHER SIDE.

8.14 Καὶ ἐπελάθοντο λαβεῖν ἄρτους καὶ εἰ μὴ ἕνα
AND THEY FORGOT TO TAKE LOAVES AND EXCEPT ONE

ἄρτον οὐκ εἶχον μεθ᾽ ἑαυτῶν ἐν τῷ πλοίῳ.
LOAF THEY DID NOT HAVE [ANYTHING] WITH THEMSELVES IN THE BOAT.

8.15 καὶ διεστέλλετο αὐτοῖς λέγων, Ὁρᾶτε, βλέπετε
AND HE WAS GIVING ORDERS TO THEM SAYING, TAKE CARE, BEWARE

ἀπὸ τῆς ζύμης τῶν Φαρισαίων καὶ τῆς ζύμης Ἡρῴδου.
OF THE LEAVEN OF THE PHARISEES AND THE LEAVEN OF HEROD.

8.16 καὶ διελογίζοντο πρὸς ἀλλήλους ὅτι
AND THEY WERE ARGUING AMONG THEMSELVES -

ἄρτους οὐκ ἔχουσιν. **8.17** καὶ γνοὺς λέγει
THEY DO NOT HAVE [ANY]~LOAVES. AND HAVING KNOWN [THIS] HE SAYS

αὐτοῖς, Τί διαλογίζεσθε ὅτι ἄρτους οὐκ ἔχετε;
TO THEM, WHY ARE YOU° DISCUSSING THAT YOU° DO NOT HAVE~LOAVES?

οὔπω νοεῖτε οὐδὲ συνίετε;
DO YOU° NOT YET UNDERSTAND NOR COMPREHEND?

πεπωρωμένην ἔχετε τὴν καρδίαν ὑμῶν;
HAVE YOU°~HAVING BECOME HARDENED THE HEART OF YOU°?

8.18 ὀφθαλμοὺς ἔχοντες οὐ βλέπετε καὶ ὦτα ἔχοντες
HAVING~EYES DO YOU° NOT SEE AND HAVING~EARS

οὐκ ἀκούετε; καὶ οὐ μνημονεύετε, **8.19** ὅτε τοὺς πέντε
DO YOU° NOT HEAR? AND DO YOU° NOT REMEMBER. WHEN THE FIVE

ἄρτους ἔκλασα εἰς τοὺς πεντακισχιλίους, πόσους
LOAVES I BROKE FOR THE FIVE THOUSAND, HOW MANY

κοφίνους κλασμάτων πλήρεις ἤρατε; λέγουσιν
BASKETS OF PIECES FULL YOU° PICKED UP? THEY SAY

αὐτῷ, Δώδεκα. **8.20** Ὅτε τοὺς ἑπτὰ εἰς τοὺς
TO HIM, TWELVE. WHEN THE SEVEN FOR THE

τετρακισχιλίους, πόσων σπυρίδων πληρώματα
FOUR THOUSAND, HOW MANY BASKETS FULL

κλασμάτων ἤρατε; καὶ λέγουσιν [αὐτῷ], Ἑπτά.
OF PIECES YOU° PICKED UP? AND THEY SAY TO HIM, SEVEN.

8.21 καὶ ἔλεγεν αὐτοῖς, Οὔπω συνίετε;
AND HE WAS SAYING TO THEM, DO YOU° NOT YET COMPREHEND?

8.22 Καὶ ἔρχονται εἰς Βηθσαϊδάν. καὶ φέρουσιν
AND THEY COME TO BETHSAIDA. AND THEY BRING

αὐτῷ τυφλὸν καὶ παρακαλοῦσιν αὐτὸν ἵνα
TO HIM A BLIND [MAN] AND THEY BEG HIM THAT

αὐτοῦ ἅψηται. **8.23** καὶ ἐπιλαβόμενος τῆς χειρὸς τοῦ
HE MIGHT TOUCH~HIM. AND HAVING GRASPED THE HAND OF THE

τυφλοῦ ἐξήνεγκεν αὐτὸν ἔξω τῆς κώμης καὶ πτύσας
BLIND [MAN] HE TOOK HIM OUTSIDE THE VILLAGE AND HAVING SPIT

εἰς τὰ ὄμματα αὐτοῦ, ἐπιθεὶς τὰς χεῖρας αὐτῷ
IN THE EYES OF HIM, [AND] HAVING PUT THE(HIS) HANDS [ON] HIM

ἐπηρώτα αὐτόν, Εἴ τι βλέπεις; **8.24** καὶ
HE WAS QUESTIONING HIM, IF YOU SEE~ANYTHING? AND

ἀναβλέψας ἔλεγεν, Βλέπω τοὺς ἀνθρώπους ὅτι ὡς
HAVING LOOKED UP HE WAS SAYING, I SEE - MEN THAT AS

14 Now the disciples[e] had forgotten to bring any bread; and they had only one loaf with them in the boat. [15]And he cautioned them, saying, "Watch out—beware of the yeast of the Pharisees and the yeast of Herod."[f] [16]They said to one another, "It is because we have no bread." [17]And becoming aware of it, Jesus said to them, "Why are you talking about having no bread? Do you still not perceive or understand? Are your hearts hardened? [18]Do you have eyes, and fail to see? Do you have ears, and fail to hear? And do you not remember? [19]When I broke the five loaves for the five thousand, how many baskets full of broken pieces did you collect?" They said to him, "Twelve." [20]"And the seven for the four thousand, how many baskets full of broken pieces did you collect?" And they said to him, "Seven." [21]Then he said to them, "Do you not yet understand?"

22 They came to Bethsaida. Some people[g] brought a blind man to him and begged him to touch him. [23]He took the blind man by the hand and led him out of the village; and when he had put saliva on his eyes and laid his hands on him, he asked him, "Can you see anything?" [24]And the man[h] looked up and said, "I can see people,

[e] Gk *they*
[f] Other ancient authorities read *the Herodians*
[g] Gk *They*
[h] Gk *he*

but they look like trees, walking." [25]Then Jesus[i] laid his hands on his eyes again; and he looked intently and his sight was restored, and he saw everything clearly. [26]Then he sent him away to his home, saying, "Do not even go into the village."[j]

27 Jesus went on with his disciples to the villages of Caesarea Philippi; and on the way he asked his disciples, "Who do people say that I am?" [28]And they answered him, "John the Baptist; and others, Elijah; and still others, one of the prophets." [29]He asked them, "But who do you say that I am?" Peter answered him, "You are the Messiah."[k] [30]And he sternly ordered them not to tell anyone about him.

31 Then he began to teach them that the Son of Man must undergo great suffering, and be rejected by the elders, the chief priests, and the scribes, and be killed, and after three days rise again. [32]He said all this quite openly. And Peter took him aside and began to rebuke him. [33]But turning and looking at his disciples, he rebuked Peter and said, "Get behind me, Satan! For you are setting your mind

[i] Gk he
[j] Other ancient authorities add or tell anyone in the village
[k] Or the Christ

δένδρα ὁρῶ περιπατοῦντας. **8.25** εἶτα πάλιν ἐπέθηκεν
TREES I SEE WALKING. THEN AGAIN HE PLACED

τὰς χεῖρας ἐπὶ τοὺς ὀφθαλμοὺς αὐτοῦ, καὶ
THE(HIS) HANDS ON THE EYES OF HIM, AND

διέβλεψεν καὶ ἀπεκατέστη καὶ ἐνέβλεπεν
HE OPENED HIS EYES AND HE WAS RESTORED AND HE WAS SEEING

τηλαυγῶς ἅπαντα. **8.26** καὶ ἀπέστειλεν αὐτὸν εἰς
EVERYTHING~CLEARLY. AND HE SENT HIM TO

οἶκον αὐτοῦ λέγων, Μηδὲ εἰς τὴν κώμην εἰσέλθῃς.
[THE] HOUSE OF HIM SAYING, NOT INTO THE VILLAGE YOU MAY GO.

8.27 Καὶ ἐξῆλθεν ὁ Ἰησοῦς καὶ οἱ μαθηταὶ αὐτοῦ
AND WENT OUT - JESUS AND THE DISCIPLES OF HIM

εἰς τὰς κώμας Καισαρείας τῆς Φιλίππου· καὶ ἐν τῇ
TO THE VILLAGES OF CAESAREA - OF PHILIP. AND ON THE

ὁδῷ ἐπηρώτα τοὺς μαθητὰς αὐτοῦ λέγων αὐτοῖς,
WAY HE WAS QUESTIONING THE DISCIPLES OF HIM SAYING TO THEM,

Τίνα με λέγουσιν οἱ ἄνθρωποι εἶναι; **8.28** οἱ δὲ
WHOM ME SAY - MEN TO BE? - AND

εἶπαν αὐτῷ λέγοντες [ὅτι] Ἰωάννην τὸν βαπτιστήν,
THEY SPOKE TO HIM SAYING - JOHN THE BAPTIST,

καὶ ἄλλοι, Ἡλίαν, ἄλλοι δὲ ὅτι εἷς τῶν προφητῶν.
AND OTHERS, ELIJAH, BUT~OTHERS THAT ONE OF THE PROPHETS.

8.29 καὶ αὐτὸς ἐπηρώτα αὐτούς, Ὑμεῖς δὲ τίνα
AND HE QUESTIONED THEM, BUT~YOU° WHOM

με λέγετε εἶναι; ἀποκριθεὶς ὁ Πέτρος λέγει αὐτῷ, Σὺ
DO YOU° SAY~ME TO BE? HAVING ANSWERED - PETER SAYS TO HIM, YOU

εἶ ὁ Χριστός. **8.30** καὶ ἐπετίμησεν αὐτοῖς ἵνα
ARE THE CHRIST. AND HE WARNED THEM THAT

μηδενὶ λέγωσιν περὶ αὐτοῦ.
NO ONE THEY SHOULD TELL ABOUT HIM.

8.31 Καὶ ἤρξατο διδάσκειν αὐτοὺς ὅτι δεῖ
AND HE BEGAN TO TEACH THEM THAT IT IS NECESSARY [FOR]

τὸν υἱὸν τοῦ ἀνθρώπου πολλὰ παθεῖν καὶ
THE SON - OF MAN TO SUFFER~MANY THINGS AND

ἀποδοκιμασθῆναι ὑπὸ τῶν πρεσβυτέρων καὶ τῶν
TO BE REJECTED BY THE ELDERS AND THE

ἀρχιερέων καὶ τῶν γραμματέων καὶ ἀποκτανθῆναι καὶ
CHIEF PRIESTS AND THE SCRIBES AND TO BE KILLED AND

μετὰ τρεῖς ἡμέρας ἀναστῆναι· **8.32** καὶ παρρησίᾳ τὸν
AFTER THREE DAYS TO RISE. AND WITH PLAINNESS ²THE

λόγον ἐλάλει. καὶ προσλαβόμενος ὁ Πέτρος αὐτὸν
³WORD ¹HE WAS SPEAKING. AND ²HAVING TAKEN ASIDE - ¹PETER ³HIM

ἤρξατο ἐπιτιμᾶν αὐτῷ. **8.33** ὁ δὲ ἐπιστραφεὶς καὶ
BEGAN TO REBUKE HIM. - AND HAVING TURNED AROUND AND

ἰδὼν τοὺς μαθητὰς αὐτοῦ ἐπετίμησεν Πέτρῳ καὶ
HAVING SEEN THE DISCIPLES OF HIM HE REBUKED PETER AND

λέγει, Ὕπαγε ὀπίσω μου, Σατανᾶ, ὅτι οὐ φρονεῖς
SAYS, GO AWAY BEHIND ME, SATAN, BECAUSE YOU ARE NOT THINKING

τὰ   τοῦ θεοῦ ἀλλὰ τὰ   τῶν ἀνθρώπων. **8.34** Καὶ
THE THINGS -   OF GOD BUT THE THINGS -   OF MEN.   AND

προσκαλεσάμενος τὸν ὄχλον σὺν   τοῖς μαθηταῖς
HAVING CALLED TOGETHER THE CROWD ALONG WITH THE   DISCIPLES

αὐτοῦ εἶπεν αὐτοῖς, Εἴ τις   θέλει ὀπίσω μου
OF HIM HE SAID TO THEM, IF SOMEONE DESIRES AFTER   ME

ἀκολουθεῖν, ἀπαρνησάσθω ἑαυτὸν καὶ ἀράτω   τὸν
TO FOLLOW,   LET HIM DENY   HIMSELF AND LET HIM TAKE UP THE

σταυρὸν αὐτοῦ καὶ ἀκολουθείτω μοι. **8.35** ὃς γὰρ ἐὰν
CROSS   OF HIM AND LET HIM FOLLOW ME.   FOR~WHOEVER

θέλῃ τὴν ψυχὴν αὐτοῦ σῶσαι ἀπολέσει αὐτήν·
DESIRES THE LIFE OF HIM TO SAVE HE WILL LOSE IT.

ὃς δ' ἂν ἀπολέσει τὴν ψυχὴν αὐτοῦ ἕνεκεν   ἐμοῦ καὶ
BUT~WHOEVER LOSES   THE LIFE   OF HIM FOR THE SAKE OF ME AND

τοῦ εὐαγγελίου σώσει αὐτήν. **8.36** τί γὰρ ὠφελεῖ
THE GOOD NEWS WILL SAVE IT.   FOR~WHAT DOES IT BENEFIT

ἄνθρωπον κερδῆσαι τὸν κόσμον ὅλον καὶ ζημιωθῆναι
A MAN   TO GAIN   THE WHOLE~WORLD AND TO FORFEIT

τὴν ψυχὴν αὐτοῦ; **8.37** τί γὰρ δοῖ   ἄνθρωπος
THE LIFE   OF HIM?   FOR~WHAT MAY GIVE A MAN

ἀντάλλαγμα τῆς ψυχῆς αὐτοῦ; **8.38** ὃς γὰρ ἐὰν
IN EXCHANGE [FOR] THE LIFE   OF HIM?   FOR~WHOEVER

ἐπαισχυνθῇ με καὶ τοὺς ἐμοὺς λόγους ἐν τῇ γενεᾷ
IS ASHAMED OF ME AND -   MY WORDS   IN - 5GENERATION

ταύτῃ τῇ μοιχαλίδι καὶ ἁμαρτωλῷ, καὶ ὁ υἱὸς τοῦ
1THIS - 2ADULTEROUS 3AND 4SINFUL,   ALSO THE SON -

ἀνθρώπου ἐπαισχυνθήσεται αὐτόν, ὅταν ἔλθῃ ἐν τῇ
OF MAN   WILL BE ASHAMED OF HIM,   WHEN HE COMES IN THE

δόξῃ τοῦ πατρὸς αὐτοῦ μετὰ τῶν ἀγγέλων τῶν ἁγίων.
GLORY OF THE FATHER OF HIM WITH THE 2ANGELS   - 1HOLY.

not on divine things but on human things."

34 He called the crowd with his disciples, and said to them, "If any want to become my followers, let them deny themselves and take up their cross and follow me. [35]For those who want to save their life will lose it, and those who lose their life for my sake, and for the sake of the gospel,[l] will save it. [36]For what will it profit them to gain the whole world and forfeit their life? [37]Indeed, what can they give in return for their life? [38]Those who are ashamed of me and of my words[m] in this adulterous and sinful generation, of them the Son of Man will also be ashamed when he comes in the glory of his Father with the holy angels."

[l] Other ancient authorities read *lose their life for the sake of the gospel*
[m] Other ancient authorities read *and of mine*

9.1 Καὶ ἔλεγεν   αὐτοῖς, Ἀμὴν λέγω ὑμῖν ὅτι
      AND HE WAS SAYING TO THEM, TRULY I SAY TO YOU° THAT

εἰσίν τινες ὧδε τῶν   ἑστηκότων οἵτινες
THERE ARE SOME HERE OF THE ONES HAVING STOOD WHO

οὐ μὴ γεύσωνται θανάτου ἕως ἂν ἴδωσιν τὴν βασιλείαν
WILL BY NO MEANS TASTE DEATH UNTIL THEY SEE THE KINGDOM

τοῦ θεοῦ ἐληλυθυῖαν ἐν δυνάμει.
 - OF GOD HAVING COME   IN POWER.

9.2 Καὶ μετὰ ἡμέρας ἓξ παραλαμβάνει ὁ Ἰησοῦς τὸν
      AND AFTER SIX~DAYS TAKES   - JESUS   -

Πέτρον καὶ τὸν Ἰάκωβον καὶ τὸν Ἰωάννην καὶ
PETER   AND - JAMES   AND - JOHN   AND

ἀναφέρει αὐτοὺς εἰς ὄρος ὑψηλὸν κατ' ἰδίαν μόνους.
LEADS   THEM TO A HIGH~MOUNTAIN PRIVATELY ALONE.

[1]And he said to them, "Truly I tell you, there are some standing here who will not taste death until they see that the kingdom of God has come with[n] power."

2 Six days later, Jesus took with him Peter and James and John, and led them up a high mountain apart, by themselves.

[n] Or *in*

And he was transfigured before them, [3]and his clothes became dazzling white, such as no one[o] on earth could bleach them. [4]And there appeared to them Elijah with Moses, who were talking with Jesus. [5]Then Peter said to Jesus, "Rabbi, it is good for us to be here; let us make three dwellings,[p] one for you, one for Moses, and one for Elijah." [6]He did not know what to say, for they were terrified. [7]Then a cloud overshadowed them, and from the cloud there came a voice, "This is my Son, the Beloved;[q] listen to him!" [8]Suddenly when they looked around, they saw no one with them any more, but only Jesus.

9 As they were coming down the mountain, he ordered them to tell no one about what they had seen, until after the Son of Man had risen from the dead. [10]So they kept the matter to themselves, questioning what this rising from the dead could mean. [11]Then they asked him, "Why do the scribes say that Elijah must come first?" [12]He said to them, "Elijah is indeed coming first to restore all things. How then is it written about the Son of Man, that he is to go through many sufferings and

[o] Gk no fuller
[p] Or tents
[q] Or my beloved Son

καὶ μετεμορφώθη ἔμπροσθεν αὐτῶν, **9.3** καὶ τὰ ἱμάτια
AND   HE WAS TRANSFIGURED   BEFORE   THEM,   AND   THE   GARMENTS

αὐτοῦ ἐγένετο στίλβοντα λευκὰ λίαν, οἷα
OF HIM   BECAME   SHINING   EXCEEDINGLY~WHITE OF SUCH A KIND

γναφεὺς ἐπὶ τῆς γῆς οὐ δύναται οὕτως λευκᾶναι.
A BLEACHER ON   — EARTH IS NOT ABLE THUS   TO WHITEN.

9.4 καὶ ὤφθη αὐτοῖς Ἡλίας σὺν Μωϋσεῖ καὶ
     AND   APPEARED TO THEM ELIJAH ALONG WITH MOSES,   AND

ἦσαν συλλαλοῦντες τῷ Ἰησοῦ. **9.5** καὶ ἀποκριθεὶς ὁ
THEY WERE TALKING WITH   —   JESUS.   AND   HAVING ANSWERED —

Πέτρος λέγει τῷ Ἰησοῦ, Ῥαββί, καλόν ἐστιν ἡμᾶς
PETER   SAYS   — TO JESUS, RABBI, IT IS~GOOD [FOR] US

ὧδε εἶναι, καὶ ποιήσωμεν τρεῖς σκηνάς, σοὶ μίαν καὶ
TO BE~HERE,   AND   LET US MAKE   THREE   TENTS,   ONE~FOR YOU AND

Μωϋσεῖ μίαν καὶ Ἡλίᾳ μίαν. **9.6** οὐ γὰρ ᾔδει τί
ONE~FOR MOSES AND   ONE~FOR ELIJAH.   FOR~HE HAD NOT KNOWN WHAT

ἀποκριθῇ ἔκφοβοι γὰρ ἐγένοντο. **9.7** καὶ ἐγένετο
HE ANSWERED, [3]TERRIFIED [1]FOR   [2]THEY WERE.   AND   THERE CAME

νεφέλη ἐπισκιάζουσα αὐτοῖς, καὶ ἐγένετο φωνὴ ἐκ
A CLOUD   OVERSHADOWING   THEM,   AND THERE CAME A VOICE OUT FROM

τῆς νεφέλης, Οὗτός ἐστιν ὁ υἱός μου ὁ ἀγαπητός,
THE CLOUD,   THIS   IS   THE SON OF ME THE BELOVED,

ἀκούετε αὐτοῦ. **9.8** καὶ ἐξάπινα περιβλεψάμενοι οὐκέτι
LISTEN   TO HIM.   AND   SUDDENLY   HAVING LOOKED AROUND   NO LONGER

οὐδένα εἶδον ἀλλὰ τὸν Ἰησοῦν μόνον μεθ᾽ ἑαυτῶν.
ANYONE THEY SAW BUT   —   JESUS   ALONE WITH THEMSELVES.

9.9 Καὶ καταβαινόντων αὐτῶν ἐκ τοῦ ὄρους
     AND   [AS] THEY WERE~COMING DOWN   FROM THE MOUNTAIN

διεστείλατο αὐτοῖς ἵνα μηδενὶ ἃ εἶδον διηγήσωνται,
HE GAVE ORDERS TO THEM THAT NO ONE   WHAT THEY SAW THEY SHOULD TELL,

εἰ μὴ ὅταν ὁ υἱὸς τοῦ ἀνθρώπου ἐκ νεκρῶν ἀναστῇ.
EXCEPT WHEN THE SON   —   OF MAN   FROM [THE] DEAD SHOULD ARISE.

9.10 καὶ τὸν λόγον ἐκράτησαν πρὸς ἑαυτοὺς
      AND THE WORD   THEY KEPT   TO   THEMSELVES

συζητοῦντες τί ἐστιν τὸ ἐκ νεκρῶν ἀναστῆναι.
DISCUSSING   WHAT [4]MEANS — [2]FROM [3][THE] DEAD [1]TO RISE.

9.11 καὶ ἐπηρώτων αὐτὸν λέγοντες, Ὅτι λέγουσιν
      AND THEY WERE QUESTIONING HIM   SAYING,   WHY   SAY

οἱ γραμματεῖς ὅτι Ἡλίαν δεῖ ἐλθεῖν πρῶτον;
THE SCRIBES   THAT IT IS NECESSARY FOR~ELIJAH TO COME   FIRST?

9.12 ὁ δὲ ἔφη αὐτοῖς, Ἡλίας μὲν ἐλθὼν πρῶτον
       — AND HE SAID TO THEM, ELIJAH INDEED HAVING COME FIRST

ἀποκαθιστάνει πάντα· καὶ πῶς γέγραπται ἐπὶ
RESTORES   EVERYTHING. AND   HOW HAS IT BEEN WRITTEN CONCERNING

τὸν υἱὸν τοῦ ἀνθρώπου ἵνα πολλὰ πάθη καὶ
THE SON   —   OF MAN   THAT HE MUST SUFFER~MANY THINGS AND

ἐξουδενηθῇ; **9.13** ἀλλὰ λέγω ὑμῖν ὅτι καὶ Ἡλίας
BE REJECTED?   BUT   I SAY   TO YOU°   THAT   INDEED   ELIJAH

ἐλήλυθεν, καὶ ἐποίησαν αὐτῷ ὅσα ἤθελον,
HAS COME,   AND   THEY DID   TO HIM   WHATEVER THEY WERE DESIRING,

καθὼς γέγραπται ἐπ᾽ αὐτόν.
JUST AS   IT HAS BEEN WRITTEN   CONCERNING   HIM.

9.14 Καὶ ἐλθόντες πρὸς τοὺς μαθητὰς εἶδον
        AND   HAVING COME TO   THE   DISCIPLES   THEY SAW

ὄχλον πολὺν περὶ αὐτοὺς καὶ γραμματεῖς συζητοῦντας
A GREAT~CROWD AROUND THEM   AND   [THE] SCRIBES   ARGUING

πρὸς αὐτούς. **9.15** καὶ εὐθὺς πᾶς ὁ ὄχλος ἰδόντες
WITH   THEM.   AND IMMEDIATELY ALL   THE CROWD   HAVING SEEN

αὐτὸν ἐξεθαμβήθησαν καὶ προστρέχοντες ἠσπάζοντο
HIM   WERE AMAZED   AND   RUNNING UP TO [HIM]   THEY WERE GREETING

αὐτόν. **9.16** καὶ ἐπηρώτησεν αὐτούς, Τί συζητεῖτε
HIM.   AND   HE QUESTIONED   THEM,   WHAT ARE YOU° ARGUING

πρὸς αὐτούς; **9.17** καὶ ἀπεκρίθη αὐτῷ εἷς ἐκ τοῦ
WITH   THEM?   AND   ANSWERED   HIM   ONE   OF   THE

ὄχλου, Διδάσκαλε, ἤνεγκα τὸν υἱόν μου πρὸς σέ,
CROWD,   TEACHER,   I BROUGHT   THE   SON   OF ME   TO   YOU,

ἔχοντα πνεῦμα ἄλαλον· **9.18** καὶ ὅπου ἐὰν
HAVING   A MUTE~SPIRIT.   AND   WHEREVER

αὐτὸν καταλάβῃ ῥήσσει αὐτόν, καὶ ἀφρίζει
IT SEIZES~HIM   IT THROWS DOWN   HIM,   AND   HE FOAMS AT THE MOUTH

καὶ τρίζει τοὺς ὀδόντας καὶ ξηραίνεται· καὶ εἶπα
AND   GNASHES THE(HIS) TEETH   AND   HE BECOMES STIFF.   AND   I TOLD

τοῖς μαθηταῖς σου ἵνα αὐτὸ ἐκβάλωσιν, καὶ
THE   DISCIPLES   OF YOU IN ORDER THAT IT   THEY MIGHT CAST OUT,   AND

οὐκ ἴσχυσαν. **9.19** ὁ δὲ ἀποκριθεὶς αὐτοῖς λέγει,
THEY WERE NOT STRONG ENOUGH.   -   AND   HAVING ANSWERED   THEM   HE SAYS,

Ὦ γενεὰ ἄπιστος, ἕως πότε πρὸς ὑμᾶς ἔσομαι;
O   FAITHLESS~GENERATION, HOW LONG   ²WITH   ³YOU°   ¹WILL I BE?

ἕως πότε ἀνέξομαι ὑμῶν; φέρετε αὐτὸν πρός με.
HOW LONG   WILL I PUT UP WITH   YOU°?   BRING   HIM   TO   ME.

9.20 καὶ ἤνεγκαν αὐτὸν πρὸς αὐτόν. καὶ ἰδὼν
        AND   THEY BROUGHT HIM   TO   HIM.   AND   HAVING SEEN

αὐτὸν τὸ πνεῦμα εὐθὺς συνεσπάραξεν αὐτόν, καὶ
HIM   THE   SPIRIT   IMMEDIATELY CONVULSED   HIM,   AND

πεσὼν ἐπὶ τῆς γῆς ἐκυλίετο ἀφρίζων.
HAVING FALLEN ON   THE   GROUND HE WAS ROLLING AROUND FOAMING AT THE MOUTH.

9.21 καὶ ἐπηρώτησεν τὸν πατέρα αὐτοῦ, Πόσος
        AND   HE QUESTIONED   THE   FATHER   OF HIM,   HOW LONG [IN]

χρόνος ἐστὶν ὡς τοῦτο γέγονεν αὐτῷ; ὁ δὲ εἶπεν,
TIME   IS IT   WHILE THIS   HAS HAPPENED   TO HIM?   -   AND HE SAID,

Ἐκ παιδιόθεν· **9.22** καὶ πολλάκις καὶ εἰς πῦρ
FROM CHILDHOOD.   AND   OFTEN   ALSO   INTO [THE] FIRE

be treated with contempt? [13]But I tell you that Elijah has come, and they did to him whatever they pleased, as it is written about him."

14 When they came to the disciples, they saw a great crowd around them, and some scribes arguing with them. [15]When the whole crowd saw him, they were immediately overcome with awe, and they ran forward to greet him. [16]He asked them, "What are you arguing about with them?" [17]Someone from the crowd answered him, "Teacher, I brought you my son; he has a spirit that makes him unable to speak; [18]and whenever it seizes him, it dashes him down; and he foams and grinds his teeth and becomes rigid; and I asked your disciples to cast it out, but they could not do so." [19]He answered them, "You faithless generation, how much longer must I be among you? How much longer must I put up with you? Bring him to me." [20]And they brought the boy[r] to him. When the spirit saw him, immediately it convulsed the boy,[r] and he fell on the ground and rolled about, foaming at the mouth. [21]Jesus[s] asked the father, "How long has this been happening to him?" And he said, "From childhood. [22]It has often cast him into the fire

[r] Gk *him*
[s] Gk *He*

and into the water, to destroy him; but if you are able to do anything, have pity on us and help us." 23Jesus said to him, "If you are able!—All things can be done for the one who believes." 24Immediately the father of the child cried out,[t] "I believe; help my unbelief!" 25When Jesus saw that a crowd came running together, he rebuked the unclean spirit, saying to it, "You spirit that keeps this boy from speaking and hearing, I command you, come out of him, and never enter him again!" 26After crying out and convulsing him terribly, it came out, and the boy was like a corpse, so that most of them said, "He is dead." 27But Jesus took him by the hand and lifted him up, and he was able to stand. 28When he had entered the house, his disciples asked him privately, "Why could we not cast it out?" 29He said to them, "This kind can come out only through prayer."[u]

30 They went on from there and passed through Galilee. He did not want anyone to know it; 31for he was teaching his disciples, saying to them, "The Son of Man is to be betrayed into human hands, and

[t] Other ancient authorities add *with tears*

[u] Other ancient authorities add *and fasting*

αὐτὸν ἔβαλεν καὶ εἰς ὕδατα ἵνα ἀπολέσῃ αὐτόν·
IT THREW~HIM AND INTO [THE] WATERS THAT IT MIGHT DESTROY HIM.

ἀλλ᾽ εἴ τι δύνῃ, βοήθησον ἡμῖν σπλαγχνισθεὶς
BUT IF YOU CAN DO~ANYTHING, HELP US HAVING COMPASSION

ἐφ᾽ ἡμᾶς. **9.23** ὁ δὲ Ἰησοῦς εἶπεν αὐτῷ, Τὸ Εἰ
UPON US. - AND JESUS SAID TO HIM, - IF

δύνῃ, πάντα δυνατὰ τῷ πιστεύοντι.
YOU ARE ABLE, ALL THINGS ARE POSSIBLE FOR THE ONE BELIEVING.

9.24 εὐθὺς κράξας ὁ πατὴρ τοῦ παιδίου ἔλεγεν,
HAVING CRIED OUT~IMMEDIATELY THE FATHER OF THE CHILD WAS SAYING,

Πιστεύω· βοήθει μου τῇ ἀπιστίᾳ. **9.25** ἰδὼν δὲ ὁ
I BELIEVE. HELP MY - UNBELIEF. ³HAVING SEEN ¹AND -

Ἰησοῦς ὅτι ἐπισυντρέχει ὄχλος, ἐπετίμησεν τῷ
²JESUS THAT A CROWD~IS RUNNING TOGETHER, COMMANDED THE

πνεύματι τῷ ἀκαθάρτῳ λέγων αὐτῷ, Τὸ ἄλαλον καὶ
²SPIRIT ¹UNCLEAN SAYING TO IT, - MUTE AND

κωφὸν πνεῦμα, ἐγὼ ἐπιτάσσω σοι, ἔξελθε ἐξ αὐτοῦ
DEAF SPIRIT, I COMMAND YOU, COME OUT FROM HIM

καὶ μηκέτι εἰσέλθῃς εἰς αὐτόν. **9.26** καὶ κράξας
AND NO MORE MAY YOU ENTER INTO HIM. AND HAVING CRIED OUT

καὶ πολλὰ σπαράξας ἐξῆλθεν· καὶ ἐγένετο ὡσεὶ
AND HAVING CONVULSED [HIM]~GREATLY IT CAME OUT. AND HE WAS LIKE

νεκρός, ὥστε τοὺς πολλοὺς λέγειν ὅτι ἀπέθανεν.
A DEAD [PERSON], SO THAT - MANY [WERE LED] TO SAY THAT HE DIED.

9.27 ὁ δὲ Ἰησοῦς κρατήσας τῆς χειρὸς αὐτοῦ ἤγειρεν
- BUT JESUS HAVING GRASPED THE HAND OF HIM LIFTED UP

αὐτόν, καὶ ἀνέστη. **9.28** καὶ εἰσελθόντος αὐτοῦ εἰς
HIM, AND HE STOOD UP. AND HE~HAVING ENTERED INTO

οἶκον οἱ μαθηταὶ αὐτοῦ κατ᾽ ἰδίαν ἐπηρώτων αὐτόν,
A HOUSE, THE DISCIPLES OF HIM PRIVATELY WERE QUESTIONING HIM,

Ὅτι ἡμεῖς οὐκ ἠδυνήθημεν ἐκβαλεῖν αὐτό; **9.29** καὶ
WHY WE WERE NOT ABLE TO CAST OUT IT? AND

εἶπεν αὐτοῖς, Τοῦτο τὸ γένος ἐν οὐδενὶ δύναται
HE SAID TO THEM, THIS - KIND BY NOTHING IS ABLE

ἐξελθεῖν εἰ μὴ ἐν προσευχῇᵀ.
TO BE CAST OUT EXCEPT BY PRAYER.

9.30 Κἀκεῖθεν ἐξελθόντες παρεπορεύοντο διὰ τῆς
AND FROM THERE HAVING GONE FORTH THEY WERE PASSING THROUGH -

Γαλιλαίας, καὶ οὐκ ἤθελεν ἵνα τις γνοῖ·
GALILEE, AND HE DID NOT WANT THAT ANYONE SHOULD KNOW.

9.31 ἐδίδασκεν γὰρ τοὺς μαθητὰς αὐτοῦ καὶ ἔλεγεν
FOR~HE WAS TEACHING THE DISCIPLES OF HIM AND WAS SAYING

αὐτοῖς ὅτι Ὁ υἱὸς τοῦ ἀνθρώπου παραδίδοται εἰς
TO THEM - THE SON - OF MAN IS BETRAYED INTO

χεῖρας ἀνθρώπων, καὶ ἀποκτενοῦσιν αὐτόν, καὶ
[THE] HANDS OF MEN, AND THEY WILL KILL HIM, AND

9:29 text: ASV RSV NASB NIV NEB TEV NJB NRSV. add καὶ νηστεία (and fasting): KJV ASVmg RSVmg NASBmg NIVmg NEBmg NJBmg NRSVmg.

ἀποκτανθεὶς   μετὰ   τρεῖς   ἡμέρας   ἀναστήσεται.
HAVING BEEN KILLED,   AFTER   THREE   DAYS   HE WILL ARISE.

9.32 οἱ δὲ   ἠγνόουν   τὸ   ῥῆμα,   καὶ   ἐφοβοῦντο
BUT~THEY   WERE NOT UNDERSTANDING   THE   WORD,   AND   THEY WERE AFRAID

αὐτὸν   ἐπερωτῆσαι.
TO ASK~HIM.

9.33 Καὶ   ἦλθον   εἰς   Καφαρναούμ.   καὶ   ἐν   τῇ   οἰκίᾳ
AND   THEY CAME   INTO   CAPERNAUM.   AND   IN   THE   HOUSE

γενόμενος   ἐπηρώτα   αὐτούς,   Τί   ἐν   τῇ   ὁδῷ
BEING   HE WAS QUESTIONING   THEM,   WHAT   ON   THE   WAY

διελογίζεσθε;   **9.34** οἱ δὲ   ἐσιώπων·   πρὸς   ἀλλήλους
WERE YOU° ARGUING ABOUT?   BUT~THEY   WERE BEING SILENT,   ²WITH   ³ONE ANOTHER

γὰρ   διελέχθησαν   ἐν   τῇ   ὁδῷ   τίς   μείζων.
¹FOR   THEY ARGUED   ON   THE   WAY [ABOUT]   WHO [WAS]   GREATER.

9.35 καὶ   καθίσας   ἐφώνησεν   τοὺς   δώδεκα   καὶ   λέγει
AND   HAVING SAT DOWN   HE CALLED   THE   TWELVE   AND   HE SAYS

αὐτοῖς,   Εἴ   τις   θέλει   πρῶτος   εἶναι, ἔσται
TO THEM,   IF   SOMEONE   DESIRES   TO BECOME~FIRST,   HE WILL BE

πάντων   ἔσχατος   καὶ   πάντων   διάκονος.   **9.36** καὶ
LAST~OF ALL   AND   A SERVANT~OF ALL.   AND

λαβὼν   παιδίον   ἔστησεν   αὐτὸ   ἐν   μέσῳ   αὐτῶν   καὶ
HAVING TAKEN   A CHILD   HE SET   HIM   IN   [THE] MIDDLE   OF THEM   AND

ἐναγκαλισάμενος   αὐτὸ   εἶπεν   αὐτοῖς,   **9.37** Ὃς   ἂν   ἓν   τῶν
HAVING TAKEN INTO HIS ARMS   HIM   HE SAID   TO THEM,   WHOEVER   ONE   -

τοιούτων   παιδίων   δέξηται   ἐπὶ   τῷ   ὀνόματί   μου,
OF SUCH AS THESE   CHILDREN   RECEIVES   IN   THE   NAME   OF ME,

ἐμὲ   δέχεται·   καὶ   ὃς   ἂν   ἐμὲ   δέχηται,   οὐκ
RECEIVES~ME.   AND   WHOEVER   RECEIVES~ME,   NOT [ONLY]

ἐμὲ   δέχεται   ἀλλὰ   τὸν   ἀποστείλαντά   με.
RECEIVES~ME   BUT [ALSO]   THE ONE   HAVING SENT   ME.

9.38 Ἔφη   αὐτῷ   ὁ   Ἰωάννης,   Διδάσκαλε,   εἴδομέν
SAID   TO HIM   -   JOHN,   TEACHER,   WE SAW

τινα   ἐν   τῷ   ὀνόματί   σου   ἐκβάλλοντα   δαιμόνια,   καὶ
SOMEONE   IN   THE   NAME   OF YOU   CASTING OUT   DEMONS,   AND

ἐκωλύομεν   αὐτόν,   ὅτι   οὐκ   ἠκολούθει   ἡμῖν.   **9.39** ὁ
WE WERE PREVENTING   HIM,   BECAUSE   HE WAS NOT FOLLOWING   US.   -

δὲ   Ἰησοῦς   εἶπεν,   Μὴ   κωλύετε   αὐτόν.   οὐδεὶς   γάρ   ἐστιν
BUT   JESUS   SAID,   DO NOT PREVENT   HIM.   FOR~NO ONE   THERE IS

ὃς   ποιήσει   δύναμιν   ἐπὶ   τῷ   ὀνόματί   μου   καὶ
WHO   WILL DO   A MIGHTY WORK   IN   THE   NAME   OF ME   AND

δυνήσεται   ταχὺ   κακολογῆσαί   με·   **9.40** ὃς   γὰρ
WILL BE ABLE   QUICKLY   TO SPEAK EVIL OF   ME.   FOR~WHOEVER

οὐκ   ἔστιν   καθ᾽   ἡμῶν,   ὑπὲρ   ἡμῶν   ἐστιν.
IS NOT   AGAINST   US,   ²FOR   ³US   ¹IS.

9.41 Ὃς   γὰρ   ἂν   ποτίσῃ   ὑμᾶς   ποτήριον   ὕδατος   ἐν
FOR~WHOEVER   GIVES TO DRINK   YOU°   A CUP   OF WATER   IN

they will kill him, and three days after being killed, he will rise again." ³²But they did not understand what he was saying and were afraid to ask him.

33 Then they came to Capernaum; and when he was in the house he asked them, "What were you arguing about on the way?" ³⁴But they were silent, for on the way they had argued with one another who was the greatest. ³⁵He sat down, called the twelve, and said to them, "Whoever wants to be first must be last of all and servant of all." ³⁶Then he took a little child and put it among them; and taking it in his arms, he said to them, ³⁷"Whoever welcomes one such child in my name welcomes me, and whoever welcomes me welcomes not me but the one who sent me."

38 John said to him, "Teacher, we saw someoneᵛ casting out demons in your name, and we tried to stop him, because he was not following us." ³⁹But Jesus said, "Do not stop him; for no one who does a deed of power in my name will be able soon afterward to speak evil of me. ⁴⁰Whoever is not against us is for us. ⁴¹For truly I tell you, whoever gives you a cup of water to

ᵛ Other ancient authorities add *who does not follow us*

drink because you bear the name of Christ will by no means lose the reward.

42 "If any of you put a stumbling block before one of these little ones who believe in me,[w] it would be better for you if a great millstone were hung around your neck and you were thrown into the sea. [43]If your hand causes you to stumble, cut it off; it is better for you to enter life maimed than to have two hands and to go to hell,[x] to the unquenchable fire.[y] [45]And if your foot causes you to stumble, cut it off; it is better for you to enter life lame than to have two feet and to be thrown into hell.[x, y] [47]And if your eye causes you to stumble, tear it out; it is better for you to enter the kingdom of God with one eye than to have two eyes and to be thrown into hell,[x] [48]where their worm never dies, and the fire is never quenched.

49 "For everyone will be salted with fire.[z] [50]Salt is good; but if salt has lost its saltiness, how can you season it?[a] Have salt in yourselves, and be at peace with one another."

[w] Other ancient authorities lack *in me*
[x] Gk *Gehenna*
[y] Verses 44 and 46 (which are identical with verse 48) are lacking in the best ancient authorities
[z] Other ancient authorities either add or substitute *and every sacrifice will be salted with salt*
[a] Or *how can you restore its saltiness?*

ὀνόματι ὅτι   Χριστοῦ ἐστε, ἀμὴν λέγω ὑμῖν ὅτι
[MY] NAME BECAUSE   YOU° ARE~CHRIST'S,   TRULY   I SAY   TO YOU°   THAT

οὐ μὴ ἀπολέσῃ τὸν μισθὸν αὐτοῦ.
HE WILL IN NO WAY LOSE   THE   REWARD   OF HIM.

9.42 Καὶ ὃς ἂν σκανδαλίσῃ ἕνα τῶν μικρῶν τούτων
     AND   WHOEVER CAUSES TO STUMBLE   ONE   -   OF THESE~LITTLE ONES

τῶν   πιστευόντων [εἰς ἐμέ], καλόν ἐστιν αὐτῷ μᾶλλον
THE ONES   BELIEVING   IN   ME,   IT IS~BETTER   FOR HIM   RATHER

εἰ περίκειται μύλος ὀνικὸς περὶ τὸν τράχηλον
IF   HANGS AROUND   A MILLSTONE   OF A DONKEY   AROUND   THE   NECK

αὐτοῦ καὶ βέβληται εἰς τὴν θάλασσαν. **9.43** Καὶ ἐὰν
OF HIM   AND   HE BE CAST   INTO   THE   LAKE.   AND   IF

σκανδαλίζῃ σε ἡ χείρ σου, ἀπόκοψον αὐτήν·
CAUSES YOU TO STUMBLE   THE   HAND   OF YOU,   CUT OFF   IT;

καλόν ἐστίν σε   κυλλὸν εἰσελθεῖν εἰς τὴν ζωὴν ἢ
IT IS~BETTER   FOR YOU   TO ENTER~CRIPPLED   INTO   -   LIFE   THAN

τὰς δύο χεῖρας ἔχοντα ἀπελθεῖν εἰς τὴν γέενναν, εἰς
THE   TWO   HANDS   HAVING   TO GO AWAY   INTO   -   GEHENNA,   INTO

τὸ πῦρ τὸ ἄσβεστον.ᵀ **9.45** καὶ ἐὰν ὁ πούς σου
THE   ²FIRE   -   ¹INEXTINGUISHABLE.   AND   IF   THE   FOOT   OF YOU

σκανδαλίζῃ σε, ἀπόκοψον αὐτόν· καλόν ἐστίν σε
CAUSES YOU TO STUMBLE   CUT OFF   IT;   IT IS~BETTER   FOR YOU

εἰσελθεῖν εἰς τὴν ζωὴν χωλὸν ἢ   τοὺς δύο πόδας
TO ENTER   INTO   -   LIFE   LAME   THAN THE   TWO   FEET

ἔχοντα βληθῆναι εἰς τὴν γέενναν.ᵀ **9.47** καὶ ἐὰν ὁ
HAVING   TO BE CAST   INTO   -   GEHENNA.   AND   IF   THE

ὀφθαλμός σου σκανδαλίζῃ σε, ἔκβαλε αὐτόν· καλόν
EYE   OF YOU   CAUSES YOU TO STUMBLE,   TAKE OUT   IT;   ²BETTER

σέ   ἐστιν μονόφθαλμον εἰσελθεῖν εἰς τὴν βασιλείαν
³FOR YOU ¹IT IS   ⁵ONE EYED   ⁴TO ENTER   INTO   THE   KINGDOM

τοῦ θεοῦ ἢ   δύο ὀφθαλμοὺς ἔχοντα βληθῆναι εἰς τὴν
-   OF GOD   THAN   TWO   EYES   HAVING   TO BE CAST   INTO   -

γέενναν, **9.48** ὅπου ὁ σκώληξ αὐτῶν οὐ τελευτᾷ καὶ τὸ
GEHENNA,   WHERE   THE   WORM   OF THEM   DOES NOT DIE   AND   THE

πῦρ οὐ σβέννυται. **9.49** πᾶς γὰρ πυρὶ ἀλισθήσεται.ᵀ
FIRE   IS NOT EXTINGUISHED.   FOR~EVERYONE   WITH FIRE   WILL BE SALTED.

9.50 Καλὸν τὸ ἅλας· ἐὰν δὲ τὸ ἅλας ἄναλον γένηται,
     ²GOOD   -   ¹SALT [IS].   BUT~IF   THE   SALT   BECOMES~UNSALTY,

ἐν τίνι   αὐτὸ ἀρτύσετε; ἔχετε ἐν ἑαυτοῖς ἅλα καὶ
BY   WHAT [MEANS]   WILL YOU° SEASON~IT?   HAVE   IN   YOURSELVES   SALT   AND

εἰρηνεύετε ἐν ἀλλήλοις.
BE AT PEACE   WITH   ONE ANOTHER.

9:43, 45 text: ASV RSV NASB NIV NEB TEV NJB NRSV. add vv. 44 and 46 [which are identical to Mark 9:48]: KJV ASVmg RSVmg NASBmg NIVmg NEBmg TEVmg NJBmg NRSVmg.   **9:49** text: ASV RSV NASB NIV NEB NJB NRSV. add καὶ πασα θυιτα αλι αλισθησεται (and every sacrifice with salt will be salted) [see Lev. 2:13]: KJV RSVmg (TEV) NJBmg NRSVmg.

10.1 Καὶ   ἐκεῖθεν   ἀναστὰς   ἔρχεται   εἰς   τὰ   ὅρια   τῆς
AND   FROM THERE   HAVING ARISEN   HE COMES   INTO   THE   REGION   -

Ἰουδαίας   [καὶ]   πέραν   τοῦ   Ἰορδάνου,   καὶ
OF JUDEA   AND   ON THE OTHER SIDE OF   THE   JORDAN,   AND

συμπορεύονται   πάλιν   ὄχλοι   πρὸς   αὐτόν,   καὶ   ὡς
COMES TOGETHER   AGAIN   CROWDS   TO   HIM,   AND   AS

εἰώθει   πάλιν   ἐδίδασκεν   αὐτούς.   **10.2** καὶ
HE WAS ACCUSTOMED   AGAIN   HE WAS TEACHING   THEM.   AND

προσελθόντες   Φαρισαῖοι   ἐπηρώτων   αὐτὸν   εἰ
HAVING APPROACHED   PHARISEES,   THEY WERE ASKING   HIM   IF

ἔξεστιν   ἀνδρὶ   γυναῖκα   ἀπολῦσαι,   πειράζοντες
IT IS PERMISSIBLE FOR   A HUSBAND   TO DIVORCE~[HIS] WIFE,   TESTING

αὐτόν.   **10.3** ὁ   δὲ   ἀποκριθεὶς   εἶπεν   αὐτοῖς,   Τί   ὑμῖν
HIM.   -   BUT   HAVING ANSWERED   HE SAID   TO THEM,   WHAT [DID]   ³YOU°

ἐνετείλατο   Μωϋσῆς;   **10.4** οἱ   δὲ   εἶπαν,
²COMMAND   ¹MOSES?   AND~THEY   SAID,

Ἐπέτρεψεν   Μωϋσῆς   βιβλίον   ἀποστασίου   γράψαι   καὶ
MOSES~PERMITTED [A MAN]   A CERTIFICATE   OF DIVORCE   TO WRITE   AND

ἀπολῦσαι.   **10.5** ὁ   δὲ   Ἰησοῦς   εἶπεν   αὐτοῖς,   Πρὸς
TO DIVORCE [HIS WIFE].   -   BUT   JESUS   SAID   TO THEM,   BECAUSE OF

τὴν   σκληροκαρδίαν   ὑμῶν   ἔγραψεν   ὑμῖν   τὴν
THE   HARDHEARTEDNESS   OF YOU°   HE WROTE   TO YOU°   -

ἐντολὴν   ταύτην.   **10.6** ἀπὸ   δὲ   ἀρχῆς   κτίσεως   ἄρσεν
THIS~COMMANDMENT.   BUT~FROM [THE]   BEGINNING   OF CREATION   MALE

καὶ   θῆλυ   ἐποίησεν   αὐτούς·   **10.7** ἕνεκεν   τούτου
AND   FEMALE   HE MADE   THEM.   ON ACCOUNT OF   THIS

καταλείψει   ἄνθρωπος   τὸν   πατέρα   αὐτοῦ   καὶ   τὴν
A MAN~WILL LEAVE   THE   FATHER   OF HIM   AND   THE

μητέρα   ⌐[καὶ   προσκολληθήσεται   πρὸς   τὴν   γυναῖκα
MOTHER   AND   HE WILL BE JOINED   TO   THE   WIFE

αὐτοῦ]⌐,   **10.8** καὶ   ἔσονται   οἱ   δύο   εἰς   σάρκα   μίαν·
OF HIM,   AND   ³WILL BE   ¹THE   ²TWO   -   ⁵FLESH   ⁴ONE.

ὥστε   οὐκέτι   εἰσὶν   δύο   ἀλλὰ   μία   σάρξ.
FOR THIS REASON   THEY ARE~NO LONGER   TWO   BUT   ONE   FLESH.

10.9 ὃ   οὖν   ὁ   θεὸς   συνέζευξεν
THEREFORE~WHAT   -   GOD   JOINED TOGETHER,

ἄνθρωπος   μὴ   χωριζέτω.   **10.10** Καὶ   εἰς   τὴν   οἰκίαν   πάλιν
DO NOT LET MAN SEPARATE.   AND   INTO   THE   HOUSE   AGAIN

οἱ   μαθηταὶ   περὶ   τούτου   ἐπηρώτων   αὐτόν.   **10.11** καὶ
THE   DISCIPLES   ABOUT   THIS   WERE ASKING   HIM.   AND

λέγει   αὐτοῖς,   Ὃς   ἂν   ἀπολύσῃ   τὴν   γυναῖκα   αὐτοῦ   καὶ
HE SAYS   TO THEM,   WHOEVER   DIVORCES   THE   WIFE   OF HIM   AND

γαμήσῃ   ἄλλην   μοιχᾶται   ἐπ᾽   αὐτήν·   **10.12** καὶ   ἐὰν
MARRIES   ANOTHER   COMMITS ADULTERY   WITH   HER.   AND   IF

He left that place and went to the region of Judea and[b] beyond the Jordan. And crowds again gathered around him; and, as was his custom, he again taught them.

2 Some Pharisees came, and to test him they asked, "Is it lawful for a man to divorce his wife?" ³He answered them, "What did Moses command you?" ⁴They said, "Moses allowed a man to write a certificate of dismissal and to divorce her." ⁵But Jesus said to them, "Because of your hardness of heart he wrote this commandment for you. ⁶But from the beginning of creation, 'God made them male and female.' ⁷'For this reason a man shall leave his father and mother and be joined to his wife,[c] ⁸and the two shall become one flesh.' So they are no longer two, but one flesh. ⁹Therefore what God has joined together, let no one separate."

10 Then in the house the disciples asked him again about this matter. ¹¹He said to them, "Whoever divorces his wife and marries another commits adultery against her; ¹²and if

[b] Other ancient authorities lack *and*
[c] Other ancient authorities lack *and be joined to his wife*

10:4 Deut. 24:1, 3   **10:6** Gen. 1:27; 5:2   **10:7** text [see Gen. 2:24]: KJV ASV RSV NASBmg NIV NEB TEV NJBmg NRSV. omit: ASVmg RSVmg NASB NIVmg NEBmg NIVmg TEVmg NJB NRSVmg.
10:7-8 Gen. 2:24

she divorces her husband and marries another, she commits adultery."

13 People were bringing little children to him in order that he might touch them; and the disciples spoke sternly to them. ¹⁴But when Jesus saw this, he was indignant and said to them, "Let the little children come to me; do not stop them; for it is to such as these that the kingdom of God belongs. ¹⁵Truly I tell you, whoever does not receive the kingdom of God as a little child will never enter it." ¹⁶And he took them up in his arms, laid his hands on them, and blessed them.

17 As he was setting out on a journey, a man ran up and knelt before him, and asked him, "Good Teacher, what must I do to inherit eternal life?" ¹⁸Jesus said to him, "Why do you call me good? No one is good but God alone. ¹⁹You know the commandments: 'You shall not murder; You shall not commit adultery; You shall not steal; You shall not bear false witness; You shall not defraud; Honor your father and mother.'" ²⁰He said to him, "Teacher, I have kept all these since my youth." ²¹Jesus, looking at him, loved him and said, "You lack one thing; go, sell what

αὐτὴ ἀπολύσασα τὸν ἄνδρα αὐτῆς γαμήσῃ ἄλλον
SHE   DIVORCES   THE HUSBAND OF HER [AND] MARRIES ANOTHER

μοιχᾶται.
SHE COMMITS ADULTERY.

10.13 Καὶ προσέφερον αὐτῷ παιδία ἵνα
          AND   THEY BROUGHT TO HIM CHILDREN THAT

αὐτῶν ἅψηται· οἱ δὲ μαθηταὶ ἐπετίμησαν αὐτοῖς.
HE MIGHT TOUCH~THEM. BUT~THE DISCIPLES REBUKED THEM.

10.14 ἰδὼν δὲ   ὁ Ἰησοῦς ἠγανάκτησεν καὶ εἶπεν
          AND~HAVING SEEN [THIS] - JESUS BECAME ANGRY AND SAID

αὐτοῖς, Ἄφετε τὰ παιδία ἔρχεσθαι πρός με,
TO THEM, PERMIT THE CHILDREN TO COME TO ME,

μὴ κωλύετε αὐτά, τῶν γὰρ τοιούτων ἐστὶν ἡ
DO NOT HINDER THEM, - FOR OF SUCH AS THESE IS THE

βασιλεία τοῦ θεοῦ. **10.15** ἀμὴν λέγω ὑμῖν, ὃς ἂν
KINGDOM - OF GOD.   TRULY I SAY TO YOU°, WHOEVER

μὴ δέξηται τὴν βασιλείαν τοῦ θεοῦ ὡς παιδίον,
DOES NOT RECEIVE THE KINGDOM - OF GOD AS A CHILD,

οὐ μὴ εἰσέλθῃ εἰς αὐτήν. **10.16** καὶ ἐναγκαλισάμενος
MAY BY NO MEANS ENTER INTO IT.   AND HAVING TAKEN INTO HIS ARMS

αὐτὰ κατευλόγει τιθεὶς τὰς χεῖρας ἐπ᾽ αὐτά.
THEM, HE BLESSES PLACING THE (HIS) HANDS ON THEM.

10.17 Καὶ ἐκπορευομένου αὐτοῦ εἰς ὁδὸν
          AND   [AS] HE~GOING FORTH ON [THE] ROAD,

προσδραμὼν εἷς καὶ γονυπετήσας αὐτὸν ἐπηρώτα
ONE~HAVING RUN AND HAVING KNELT BEFORE HIM WAS ASKING

αὐτόν, Διδάσκαλε ἀγαθέ, τί ποιήσω ἵνα ζωὴν αἰώνιον
HIM,   GOOD~TEACHER, WHAT MAY I DO THAT LIFE ETERNAL

κληρονομήσω; **10.18** ὁ δὲ Ἰησοῦς εἶπεν αὐτῷ, Τί
I MAY INHERIT?   - AND JESUS SAID TO HIM, WHY

με λέγεις ἀγαθόν; οὐδεὶς ἀγαθὸς εἰ μὴ εἷς ὁ θεός.
DO YOU CALL~ME GOOD? NO ONE [IS] GOOD EXCEPT ONE - GOD.

10.19 τὰς ἐντολὰς οἶδας· Μὴ φονεύσῃς,
          ²THE ³COMMANDMENTS ¹YOU KNOW. DO NOT MURDER,

Μὴ μοιχεύσῃς, Μὴ κλέψῃς, Μὴ ψευδομαρτυρήσῃς,
DO NOT COMMIT ADULTERY, DO NOT STEAL, DO NOT BEAR FALSE WITNESS,

Μὴ ἀποστερήσῃς, Τίμα τὸν πατέρα σου καὶ τὴν
DO NOT DEFRAUD, HONOR THE FATHER OF YOU AND THE

μητέρα. **10.20** ὁ δὲ ἔφη   αὐτῷ, Διδάσκαλε,
MOTHER.   - AND HE WAS SAYING TO HIM, TEACHER,

ταῦτα πάντα ἐφυλαξάμην ἐκ νεότητός μου. **10.21** ὁ δὲ
ALL~THESE THINGS I HAVE KEPT FROM MY~YOUTH.   - AND

Ἰησοῦς ἐμβλέψας αὐτῷ ἠγάπησεν αὐτὸν καὶ εἶπεν
JESUS   HAVING LOOKED AT HIM LOVED HIM AND SAID

αὐτῷ, Ἕν σε ὑστερεῖ· ὕπαγε, ὅσα ἔχεις
TO HIM, ONE THING YOU LACK; GO, AS MUCH AS YOU HAVE

10:19 Exod. 20:12-16; Deut. 5:16-20

πώλησον καὶ δὸς [τοῖς] πτωχοῖς, καὶ ἕξεις
SELL   AND   GIVE TO THE POOR,   AND   YOU WILL HAVE

θησαυρὸν ἐν οὐρανῷ, καὶ δεῦρο ἀκολούθει μοι.
TREASURE   IN HEAVEN,   AND COME FOLLOW   ME.

10.22 ὁ δὲ στυγνάσας ἐπὶ τῷ λόγῳ ἀπῆλθεν
BUT~HE HAVING BECOME GLOOMY AT   THE WORD HE LEFT

λυπούμενος· ἦν γὰρ ἔχων κτήματα πολλά.
GRIEVING.   FOR~HE HAD   MANY~POSSESSIONS.

10.23 Καὶ περιβλεψάμενος ὁ Ἰησοῦς λέγει τοῖς
      AND   HAVING LOOKED AROUND   -   JESUS   SAYS   TO THE

μαθηταῖς αὐτοῦ, Πῶς δυσκόλως οἱ   τὰ
DISCIPLES OF HIM, HOW DIFFICULTLY THE ONES -

χρήματα ἔχοντες εἰς τὴν βασιλείαν τοῦ θεοῦ
HAVING~RICHES   INTO THE KINGDOM   -   OF GOD

εἰσελεύσονται. **10.24** οἱ δὲ μαθηταὶ ἐθαμβοῦντο ἐπὶ
WILL ENTER.   AND~THE DISCIPLES WERE AMAZED   AT

τοῖς λόγοις αὐτοῦ. ὁ δὲ Ἰησοῦς πάλιν ἀποκριθεὶς
THE WORDS OF HIM. - BUT JESUS AGAIN HAVING ANSWERED

λέγει αὐτοῖς, Τέκνα, πῶς δύσκολόν ἐστιν᭐ εἰς τὴν
SAYS   TO THEM, CHILDREN, HOW DIFFICULT IT IS   INTO THE

βασιλείαν τοῦ θεοῦ εἰσελθεῖν· **10.25** εὐκοπώτερόν ἐστιν
KINGDOM   -   OF GOD TO ENTER.   IT IS~EASIER [FOR]

κάμηλον διὰ [τῆς] τρυμαλιᾶς [τῆς] ῥαφίδος διελθεῖν
A CAMEL   THROUGH THE   EYE   OF THE NEEDLE   TO GO

ἢ   πλούσιον εἰς τὴν βασιλείαν τοῦ θεοῦ εἰσελθεῖν.
THAN [FOR] A RICH PERSON INTO THE KINGDOM   -   OF GOD TO ENTER.

10.26 οἱ δὲ περισσῶς ἐξεπλήσσοντο λέγοντες πρὸς
      AND~THEY [EVEN] MORE WERE AMAZED,   SAYING   TO

ἑαυτούς, Καὶ τίς δύναται σωθῆναι; **10.27** ἐμβλέψας
THEMSELVES, AND WHO IS ABLE   TO BE SAVED?   HAVING LOOKED AT

αὐτοῖς ὁ Ἰησοῦς λέγει, Παρὰ ἀνθρώποις ἀδύνατον,
THEM   - JESUS   SAYS, WITH   MEN [THIS IS] IMPOSSIBLE,

ἀλλ᾽ οὐ παρὰ θεῷ· πάντα γὰρ δυνατὰ παρὰ τῷ
BUT   NOT WITH GOD. FOR~ALL THINGS ARE POSSIBLE WITH   -

θεῷ. **10.28** Ἤρξατο λέγειν ὁ Πέτρος αὐτῷ, Ἰδοὺ
GOD.   ²BEGAN   ³TO SAY - ¹PETER TO HIM, BEHOLD

ἡμεῖς ἀφήκαμεν πάντα καὶ ἠκολουθήκαμέν σοι.
WE   LEFT   EVERYTHING AND HAVE FOLLOWED   YOU.

10.29 ἔφη ὁ Ἰησοῦς, Ἀμὴν λέγω ὑμῖν, οὐδείς ἐστιν ὃς
      ²SAID - ¹JESUS,   TRULY, I SAY TO YOU°, THERE IS~NO ONE WHO

ἀφῆκεν οἰκίαν ἢ ἀδελφοὺς ἢ ἀδελφὰς ἢ μητέρα ἢ
LEFT   HOUSE   OR BROTHERS OR SISTERS   OR MOTHER OR

πατέρα ἢ τέκνα ἢ ἀγροὺς ἕνεκεν ἐμοῦ καὶ
FATHER   OR CHILDREN OR FIELDS FOR THE SAKE OF ME AND

ἕνεκεν τοῦ εὐαγγελίου, **10.30** ἐὰν μὴ λάβῃ
FOR THE SAKE OF THE GOOD NEWS,   BUT   RECEIVES

you own, and give the money[d] to the poor, and you will have treasure in heaven; then come, follow me." [22]When he heard this, he was shocked and went away grieving, for he had many possessions.

23 Then Jesus looked around and said to his disciples, "How hard it will be for those who have wealth to enter the kingdom of God!" [24]And the disciples were perplexed at these words. But Jesus said to them again, "Children, how hard it is[e] to enter the kingdom of God! [25]It is easier for a camel to go through the eye of a needle than for someone who is rich to enter the kingdom of God." [26]They were greatly astounded and said to one another,[f] "Then who can be saved?" [27]Jesus looked at them and said, "For mortals it is impossible, but not for God; for God all things are possible."

28 Peter began to say to him, "Look, we have left everything and followed you." [29]Jesus said, "Truly I tell you, there is no one who has left house or brothers or sisters or mother or father or children or fields, for my sake and for the sake of the good news,[g] [30]who will not receive

[d] Gk lacks *the money*
[e] Other ancient authorities add *for those who trust in riches*
[f] Other ancient authorities read *to him*
[g] Or *gospel*

10:24 text: ASVmg RSV NASB NIV NEB TEV NJB NRSV.   add τους πεποιθοτας επι χρημασιν (for those having trusted in riches): KJV ASV RSVmg NASBmg NIVmg NJBmg NRSVmg.

a hundredfold now in this age—houses, brothers and sisters, mothers and children, and fields, with persecutions—and in the age to come eternal life. [31]But many who are first will be last, and the last will be first."

32 They were on the road, going up to Jerusalem, and Jesus was walking ahead of them; they were amazed, and those who followed were afraid. He took the twelve aside again and began to tell them what was to happen to him, [33]saying, "See, we are going up to Jerusalem, and the Son of Man will be handed over to the chief priests and the scribes, and they will condemn him to death; then they will hand him over to the Gentiles; [34]they will mock him, and spit upon him, and flog him, and kill him; and after three days he will rise again."

35 James and John, the sons of Zebedee, came forward to him and said to him, "Teacher, we want you to do for us whatever we ask of you." [36]And he said to them, "What is it you want me to do for you?" [37]And they said to him, "Grant us to sit, one at your right hand and one at your left, in your glory." [38]But Jesus said to them,

ἑκατονταπλασίονα νῦν ἐν τῷ καιρῷ τούτῳ οἰκίας καὶ
A HUNDREDFOLD NOW IN - THIS~AGE, HOUSES AND

ἀδελφοὺς καὶ ἀδελφὰς καὶ μητέρας καὶ τέκνα καὶ
BROTHERS AND SISTERS AND MOTHERS AND CHILDREN AND

ἀγροὺς μετὰ διωγμῶν, καὶ ἐν τῷ αἰῶνι τῷ ἐρχομένῳ
FIELDS WITH PERSECUTIONS, AND IN THE AGE THE ONE COMING,

ζωὴν αἰώνιον. 10.31 πολλοὶ δὲ ἔσονται πρῶτοι ἔσχατοι
LIFE ETERNAL. AND~MANY FIRST~WILL BE LAST

καὶ [οἱ] ἔσχατοι πρῶτοι.
AND THE LAST FIRST.

10.32 Ἦσαν δὲ ἐν τῇ ὁδῷ ἀναβαίνοντες εἰς
AND~THEY WERE ON THE ROAD GOING UP TO

Ἱεροσόλυμα, καὶ ἦν προάγων αὐτοὺς ὁ Ἰησοῦς, καὶ
JERUSALEM, AND ²WAS LEADING ³THEM - ¹JESUS, AND

ἐθαμβοῦντο, οἱ δὲ ἀκολουθοῦντες ἐφοβοῦντο. καὶ
THEY WERE ASTOUNDED, AND~THE ONES FOLLOWING WERE AFRAID. AND

παραλαβὼν πάλιν τοὺς δώδεκα ἤρξατο αὐτοῖς λέγειν
HAVING TAKEN AGAIN THE TWELVE HE BEGAN TO TELL~TO THEM

τὰ μέλλοντα αὐτῷ συμβαίνειν 10.33 ὅτι Ἰδοὺ
THE THINGS ABOUT TO HAPPEN~TO HIM, - BEHOLD

ἀναβαίνομεν εἰς Ἱεροσόλυμα, καὶ ὁ υἱὸς τοῦ
I GO UP TO JERUSALEM, AND THE SON -

ἀνθρώπου παραδοθήσεται τοῖς ἀρχιερεῦσιν καὶ τοῖς
OF MAN WILL BE BETRAYED TO THE CHIEF PRIESTS AND THE

γραμματεῦσιν καὶ κατακρινοῦσιν αὐτὸν θανάτῳ καὶ
SCRIBES AND THEY WILL CONDEMN HIM TO DEATH AND

παραδώσουσιν αὐτὸν τοῖς ἔθνεσιν 10.34 καὶ
WILL DELIVER HIM TO THE GENTILES AND

ἐμπαίξουσιν αὐτῷ καὶ ἐμπτύσουσιν αὐτῷ καὶ
THEY WILL RIDICULE HIM AND SPIT ON HIM AND

μαστιγώσουσιν αὐτὸν καὶ ἀποκτενοῦσιν, καὶ μετὰ
WHIP HIM AND WILL KILL [HIM], AND AFTER

τρεῖς ἡμέρας ἀναστήσεται.
THREE DAYS HE WILL RISE AGAIN.

10.35 Καὶ προσπορεύονται αὐτῷ Ἰάκωβος καὶ
AND APPROACHED HIM JAMES AND

Ἰωάννης οἱ υἱοὶ Ζεβεδαίου λέγοντες αὐτῷ,
JOHN, THE SONS OF ZEBEDEE, SAYING TO HIM,

Διδάσκαλε, θέλομεν ἵνα ὃ ἐὰν αἰτήσωμέν σε ποιήσῃς
TEACHER, WE WISH THAT WHATEVER WE MAY ASK YOU YOU MAY DO

ἡμῖν. 10.36 ὁ δὲ εἶπεν αὐτοῖς, Τί θέλετέ [με]
FOR US. - AND HE SAID TO THEM, WHAT DO YOU° WISH ME [THAT]

ποιήσω ὑμῖν; 10.37 οἱ δὲ εἶπαν αὐτῷ, Δὸς ἡμῖν ἵνα
I MAY DO FOR YOU°? - AND THEY SAID TO HIM, GRANT TO US THAT

εἷς σου ἐκ δεξιῶν καὶ εἷς ἐξ ἀριστερῶν καθίσωμεν
ONE ON~YOUR RIGHT AND ONE ON [YOUR] LEFT WE MAY SIT

ἐν τῇ δόξῃ σου. 10.38 ὁ δὲ Ἰησοῦς εἶπεν αὐτοῖς,
IN THE GLORY OF YOU. - BUT JESUS SAID TO THEM,

Οὐκ οἴδατε τί αἰτεῖσθε. δύνασθε πιεῖν τὸ ποτήριον
YOU° DO NOT KNOW WHAT YOU° ASK.   ARE YOU° ABLE TO DRINK THE CUP

ὃ ἐγὼ πίνω ἢ τὸ βάπτισμα ὃ ἐγὼ βαπτίζομαι
WHICH I DRINK OR THE BAPTISM   WHICH I AM BAPTIZED

βαπτισθῆναι; **10.39** οἱ δὲ εἶπαν αὐτῷ, Δυνάμεθα. ὁ
TO BE BAPTIZED [WITH]?   - AND THEY SAID TO HIM, WE ARE ABLE.   -

δὲ Ἰησοῦς εἶπεν αὐτοῖς, Τὸ ποτήριον ὃ ἐγὼ πίνω
AND JESUS   SAID TO THEM, THE CUP   WHICH I DRINK

πίεσθε καὶ τὸ βάπτισμα ὃ ἐγὼ βαπτίζομαι
YOU° WILL DRINK AND THE BAPTISM WHICH I AM BAPTIZED [WITH]

βαπτισθήσεσθε, **10.40** τὸ δὲ καθίσαι ἐκ δεξιῶν μου ἢ
YOU° WILL BE BAPTIZED [WITH]   - BUT TO SIT ON MY~RIGHT   OR

ἐξ εὐωνύμων οὐκ ἔστιν ἐμὸν δοῦναι, ἀλλ᾽ οἷς
ON [MY] LEFT   IS NOT [FOR] ME TO GRANT, BUT FOR THE ONES

ἡτοίμασται. **10.41** Καὶ ἀκούσαντες οἱ δέκα ἤρξαντο
IT HAS BEEN PREPARED.   AND HAVING HEARD THE TEN BECAME

ἀγανακτεῖν περὶ Ἰακώβου καὶ Ἰωάννου. **10.42** καὶ
ANGRY   WITH JAMES   AND JOHN.   AND

προσκαλεσάμενος αὐτοὺς ὁ Ἰησοῦς λέγει αὐτοῖς,
HAVING SUMMONED   THEM   - JESUS SAYS TO THEM,

Οἴδατε ὅτι οἱ δοκοῦντες ἄρχειν τῶν ἐθνῶν
YOU° KNOW THAT THE ONES HAVING A REPUTATION TO RULE THE GENTILES

κατακυριεύουσιν αὐτῶν καὶ οἱ μεγάλοι αὐτῶν
LORD IT OVER   THEM AND THE GREAT ONES OF THEM

κατεξουσιάζουσιν αὐτῶν. **10.43** οὐχ οὕτως δέ ἔστιν
EXERCISE AUTHORITY OVER THEM.   ³NOT ⁴SO ¹HOWEVER, ²IT IS

ἐν ὑμῖν, ἀλλ᾽ ὃς ἂν θέλῃ μέγας γενέσθαι ἐν ὑμῖν
WITH YOU°, BUT WHOEVER WISHES TO BECOME~GREAT AMONG YOU°,

ἔσται ὑμῶν διάκονος, **10.44** καὶ ὃς ἂν θέλῃ ἐν
HE MUST BE [THE] SERVANT~OF YOU°,   AND WHOEVER WISHES AMONG

ὑμῖν εἶναι πρῶτος ἔσται πάντων δοῦλος·
YOU° TO BE FIRST HE MUST BE [THE] SLAVE~OF ALL.

10.45 καὶ γὰρ ὁ υἱὸς τοῦ ἀνθρώπου οὐκ ἦλθεν
        FOR~EVEN THE SON - OF MAN DID NOT COME

διακονηθῆναι ἀλλὰ διακονῆσαι καὶ δοῦναι τὴν ψυχὴν
TO BE SERVED   BUT TO SERVE   AND TO GIVE THE LIFE

αὐτοῦ λύτρον ἀντὶ πολλῶν.
OF HIM [AS] A RANSOM ON BEHALF OF MANY.

10.46 Καὶ ἔρχονται εἰς Ἰεριχώ. καὶ
        AND THEY COME TO JERICHO. AND

ἐκπορευομένου αὐτοῦ ἀπὸ Ἰεριχὼ καὶ τῶν μαθητῶν
HE~GOING FORTH   FROM JERICHO AND THE DISCIPLES

αὐτοῦ καὶ ὄχλου ἱκανοῦ ὁ υἱὸς Τιμαίου Βαρτιμαῖος,
OF HIM AND A LARGE~CROWD, THE SON OF TIMAEUS BARTIMAEUS,

τυφλὸς προσαίτης, ἐκάθητο παρὰ τὴν ὁδόν.
A BLIND BEGGAR,   WAS SITTING DOWN BESIDE THE ROAD.

10.47 καὶ ἀκούσας ὅτι Ἰησοῦς ὁ Ναζαρηνός
        AND HAVING HEARD THAT JESUS THE NAZARENE

"You do not know what you are asking. Are you able to drink the cup that I drink, or be baptized with the baptism that I am baptized with?" ³⁹They replied, "We are able." Then Jesus said to them, "The cup that I drink you will drink; and with the baptism with which I am baptized, you will be baptized; ⁴⁰but to sit at my right hand or at my left is not mine to grant, but it is for those for whom it has been prepared."

41 When the ten heard this, they began to be angry with James and John. ⁴²So Jesus called them and said to them, "You know that among the Gentiles those whom they recognize as their rulers lord it over them, and their great ones are tyrants over them. ⁴³But it is not so among you; but whoever wishes to become great among you must be your servant, ⁴⁴and whoever wishes to be first among you must be slave of all. ⁴⁵For the Son of Man came not to be served but to serve, and to give his life a ransom for many."

46 They came to Jericho. As he and his disciples and a large crowd were leaving Jericho, Bartimaeus son of Timaeus, a blind beggar, was sitting by the roadside. ⁴⁷When he heard that it was Jesus of Nazareth,

he began to shout out and say, "Jesus, Son of David, have mercy on me!" ⁴⁸Many sternly ordered him to be quiet, but he cried out even more loudly, "Son of David, have mercy on me!" ⁴⁹Jesus stood still and said, "Call him here." And they called the blind man, saying to him, "Take heart; get up, he is calling you." ⁵⁰So throwing off his cloak, he sprang up and came to Jesus. ⁵¹Then Jesus said to him, "What do you want me to do for you?" The blind man said to him, "My teacher,ʰ let me see again." ⁵²Jesus said to him, "Go; your faith has made you well." Immediately he regained his sight and followed him on the way.

ʰ Aramaic *Rabbouni*

ἔστιν	ἤρξατο	κράζειν	καὶ	λέγειν,	Υἱὲ	Δαυὶδ
IS(WAS) [COMING]	HE BEGAN	TO CRY OUT	AND	TO SAY,	SON	OF DAVID

Ἰησοῦ,	ἐλέησόν	με.	**10.48** καὶ	ἐπετίμων	αὐτῷ
JESUS,	HAVE MERCY ON	ME.	AND	WERE REBUKING	HIM

πολλοὶ	ἵνα	σιωπήσῃ·	ὁ δὲ	πολλῷ	μᾶλλον
MANY	THAT	HE SHOULD BE SILENT.	- BUT	MUCH	MORE

ἔκραζεν,	Υἱὲ	Δαυίδ,	ἐλέησόν	με.	**10.49** καὶ
HE WAS CRYING OUT,	SON	OF DAVID,	HAVE MERCY ON	ME.	AND

στὰς	ὁ Ἰησοῦς	εἶπεν,	Φωνήσατε αὐτόν.	καὶ
HAVING STOOD	- JESUS	SAID,	CALL HIM.	AND

φωνοῦσιν	τὸν	τυφλὸν	λέγοντες αὐτῷ,	Θάρσει,	ἔγειρε,
THEY CALLED	THE	BLIND MAN	SAYING TO HIM,	BE CHEERFUL,	STAND UP,

φωνεῖ	σε.	**10.50** ὁ δὲ	ἀποβαλὼν	τὸ ἱμάτιον
HE IS CALLING	YOU.	- AND	HAVING TOSSED ASIDE	THE GARMENT

αὐτοῦ	ἀναπηδήσας	ἦλθεν	πρὸς	τὸν	Ἰησοῦν.
OF HIM [AND]	HAVING JUMPED UP	HE CAME	TO	-	JESUS.

10.51 καὶ	ἀποκριθεὶς	αὐτῷ	ὁ Ἰησοῦς	εἶπεν,	Τί	σοι
AND	HAVING ANSWERED	HIM	- JESUS	SAID,	WHAT	FOR YOU

θέλεις	ποιήσω;	ὁ δὲ	τυφλὸς	εἶπεν	αὐτῷ,
DO YOU WISH	THAT I MAY DO?	AND~THE	BLIND MAN	SAID	TO HIM,

Ραββουνι,	ἵνα	ἀναβλέψω.	**10.52** καὶ	ὁ Ἰησοῦς	εἶπεν
RABBONI,	THAT	I MAY SEE.	AND	- JESUS	SAID

αὐτῷ,	Ὕπαγε,	ἡ	πίστις	σου	σέσωκέν	σε.	καὶ
TO HIM,	GO,	THE	FAITH	OF YOU	HAS RESTORED	YOU.	AND

εὐθὺς	ἀνέβλεψεν	καὶ	ἠκολούθει	αὐτῷ	ἐν	τῇ	ὁδῷ.
IMMEDIATELY	HE SAW AGAIN	AND	HE WAS FOLLOWING	HIM	ON	THE	ROAD.

CHAPTER 11

When they were ap - proaching Jerusalem, at Bethphage and Bethany, near the Mount of Olives, he sent two of his disciples ²and said to them, "Go into the village ahead of you, and immediately as you enter it, you will find tied there a colt that has never been ridden; untie it and bring it. ³If anyone says to you, 'Why are you doing this?' just say this, 'The Lord needs it and will send it

11.1 Καὶ	ὅτε	ἐγγίζουσιν	εἰς	Ἱεροσόλυμα	εἰς
AND	WHEN	THEY DRAW NEAR	TO	JERUSALEM	TO

Βηθφαγὴ	καὶ	Βηθανίαν	πρὸς	τὸ	Ὄρος	τῶν Ἐλαιῶν,
BETHPHAGE	AND	BETHANY	TO	THE	MOUNT	- OF OLIVES,

ἀποστέλλει	δύο	τῶν	μαθητῶν	αὐτοῦ	**11.2** καὶ	λέγει
HE SENDS	TWO	OF THE	DISCIPLES	OF HIM	AND	HE SAYS

αὐτοῖς,	Ὑπάγετε	εἰς	τὴν	κώμην	τὴν	κατέναντι	ὑμῶν,
TO THEM,	GO	INTO	THE	VILLAGE	-	OPPOSITE	OF YOU°,

καὶ	εὐθὺς	εἰσπορευόμενοι	εἰς	αὐτὴν	εὑρήσετε	πῶλον
AND	IMMEDIATELY	ENTERING	INTO	IT	YOU° WILL FIND	A COLT

δεδεμένον	ἐφ'	ὃν	οὐδεὶς	οὔπω	ἀνθρώπων	ἐκάθισεν·
HAVING BEEN TIED,	UPON	WHICH	NO ONE	NOT YET	OF MEN	SAT.

λύσατε	αὐτὸν	καὶ	φέρετε.	**11.3** καὶ	ἐάν	τις
UNTIE	IT	AND	BRING [IT].	AND	IF	SOMEONE

ὑμῖν	εἴπῃ,	Τί	ποιεῖτε	τοῦτο;	εἴπατε,	Ὁ	κύριος
SAYS~TO YOU°		WHY	ARE YOU° DOING	THIS?	SAY,	THE	LORD

αὐτοῦ	χρείαν	ἔχει,	καὶ	εὐθὺς	αὐτὸν	ἀποστέλλει
³OF IT	²NEED	¹HAS,	AND	IMMEDIATELY		HE SENDS~IT

πάλιν ὧδε. **11.4** καὶ ἀπῆλθον καὶ εὗρον πῶλον
AGAIN HERE.   AND THEY LEFT AND FOUND A COLT

δεδεμένον πρὸς θύραν ἔξω ἐπὶ τοῦ ἀμφόδου καὶ
HAVING BEEN TIED TO A DOOR OUT ON THE STREET   AND

λύουσιν αὐτόν. **11.5** καί τινες τῶν   ἐκεῖ ἑστηκότων
THEY UNTIE HIM.   AND SOME OF THE ONES HAVING BEEN STANDING~THERE

ἔλεγον αὐτοῖς, Τί ποιεῖτε λύοντες τὸν πῶλον;
WERE SAYING TO THEM, WHAT ARE YOU° DOING UNTYING THE COLT?

11.6 οἱ δὲ εἶπαν αὐτοῖς καθὼς εἶπεν ὁ Ἰησοῦς,
-    AND THEY SPOKE TO THEM JUST AS ²TOLD [THEM] - ¹JESUS,

καὶ ἀφῆκαν αὐτούς. **11.7** καὶ φέρουσιν τὸν πῶλον
AND THEY PERMITTED THEM.   AND THEY BRING THE COLT

πρὸς τὸν Ἰησοῦν καὶ ἐπιβάλλουσιν αὐτῷ τὰ ἱμάτια
TO - JESUS   AND THEY LAY UPON   IT   THE GARMENTS

αὐτῶν, καὶ ἐκάθισεν ἐπ' αὐτόν. **11.8** καὶ πολλοὶ τὰ
OF THEM, AND HE SAT   UPON IT.   AND MANY   ²THE

ἱμάτια αὐτῶν ἔστρωσαν εἰς τὴν ὁδόν, ἄλλοι δὲ
³GARMENTS ⁴OF THEM ¹SPREAD ON THE ROAD, BUT~OTHERS

στιβάδας κόψαντες ἐκ τῶν ἀγρῶν. **11.9** καὶ οἱ
LEAFY BRANCHES HAVING CUT FROM THE FIELDS.   AND THE ONES

προάγοντες καὶ οἱ   ἀκολουθοῦντες ἔκραζον,
LEADING THE WAY AND THE ONES FOLLOWING   WERE CRYING OUT,

    Ὡσαννά·
    HOSANNA!

    Εὐλογημένος ὁ   ἐρχόμενος ἐν   ὀνόματι
    HAVING BEEN BLESSED THE ONE COMING IN [THE] NAME

    κυρίου·
    OF [THE] LORD.

11.10   Εὐλογημένη ἡ ἐρχομένη βασιλεία τοῦ
        HAVING BEEN BLESSED THE COMING KINGDOM OF THE

    πατρὸς ἡμῶν Δαυίδ·
    FATHER OF US DAVID.

    Ὡσαννὰ ἐν τοῖς ὑψίστοις.
    HOSANNA IN THE HIGHEST.

11.11 Καὶ εἰσῆλθεν εἰς Ἰεροσόλυμα εἰς τὸ ἱερόν καὶ
    AND HE ENTERED INTO JERUSALEM INTO THE TEMPLE AND

περιβλεψάμενος πάντα, ὀψίας ἤδη οὔσης τῆς ὥρας,
HAVING LOOKED AROUND EVERYWHERE, LATE NOW BEING THE HOUR,

ἐξῆλθεν εἰς Βηθανίαν μετὰ τῶν δώδεκα.
HE WENT OUT TO BETHANY WITH THE TWELVE.

11.12 Καὶ τῇ ἐπαύριον ἐξελθόντων αὐτῶν ἀπὸ
      AND ON THE NEXT DAY THEY~HAVING GONE OUT FROM

Βηθανίας ἐπείνασεν. **11.13** καὶ ἰδὼν   συκῆν ἀπὸ
BETHANY, HE WAS HUNGRY.   AND HAVING SEEN A FIG TREE FROM

μακρόθεν ἔχουσαν φύλλα ἦλθεν,   εἰ ἄρα
A DISTANCE HAVING LEAVES HE CAME [TO SEE], WHETHER

11:9-10 Ps. 118:25-26

back here immediately.'"
[4]They went away and found
a colt tied near a door,
outside in the street. As they
were untying it, [5]some of the
bystanders said to them,
"What are you doing,
untying the colt?" [6]They told
them what Jesus had said;
and they allowed them to
take it. [7]Then they brought
the colt to Jesus and threw
their cloaks on it; and he sat
on it. [8]Many people spread
their cloaks on the road, and
others spread leafy branches
that they had cut in the
fields. [9]Then those who
went ahead and those who
followed were shouting,
    "Hosanna!
    Blessed is the one who
        comes in the name
        of the Lord!
[10]   Blessed is the coming
        kingdom of our
        ancestor David!
    Hosanna in the highest
        heaven!"
    11 Then he entered
Jerusalem and went into the
temple; and when he had
looked around at everything,
as it was already late, he
went out to Bethany with the
twelve.
    12 On the following day,
when they came from
Bethany, he was hungry.
[13]Seeing in the distance a
fig tree in leaf, he went
to see whether perhaps

he would find anything on it.
When he came to it, he
found nothing but leaves, for
it was not the season for figs.
¹⁴He said to it, "May no one
ever eat fruit from you
again." And his disciples
heard it.

15 Then they came to
Jerusalem. And he entered
the temple and began to
drive out those who were
selling and those who were
buying in the temple, and he
overturned the tables of the
money changers and the
seats of those who sold
doves; ¹⁶and he would not
allow anyone to carry
anything through the temple.
¹⁷He was teaching and
saying, "Is it not written,
    'My house shall be
        called a house of
        prayer for all the
        nations'?
    But you have made it a
        den of robbers."
¹⁸And when the chief priests
and the scribes heard it, they
kept looking for a way to kill
him; for they were afraid of
him, because the whole
crowd was spellbound by his
teaching. ¹⁹And when
evening came, Jesus and his
disciples' went out of the
city.

20 In the morning as
they passed by, they saw
the fig tree withered
away to its roots. ²¹Then
Peter remembered and
said to him, "Rabbi,
look! The fig tree that

ⁱ Gk they: other ancient authorities
read he

τι εὑρήσει   ἐν αὐτῇ, καὶ ἐλθὼν   ἐπ' αὐτὴν
HE MIGHT FIND~SOMETHING ON IT,   AND   HAVING COME UPON IT

οὐδὲν εὗρεν εἰ μὴ φύλλα· ὁ γὰρ καιρὸς οὐκ ἦν
HE FOUND~NOTHING EXCEPT LEAVES.   FOR~THE SEASON WAS NOT [FOR]

σύκων. **11.14** καὶ ἀποκριθεὶς εἶπεν αὐτῇ, Μηκέτι εἰς
FIGS.   AND   HAVING ANSWERED HE SAID TO IT, NO LONGER INTO

τὸν αἰῶνα ἐκ σοῦ μηδεὶς καρπὸν φάγοι. καὶ
THE AGE FROM YOU NO ONE MAY EAT [THE]~FRUIT. AND

ἤκουον οἱ μαθηταὶ αὐτοῦ. **11.15** Καὶ ἔρχονται εἰς
WERE LISTENING THE DISCIPLES OF HIM.   AND THEY COME TO

Ἱεροσόλυμα. καὶ εἰσελθὼν εἰς τὸ ἱερὸν ἤρξατο
JERUSALEM. AND HAVING ENTERED INTO THE TEMPLE, HE BEGAN

ἐκβάλλειν τοὺς πωλοῦντας καὶ τοὺς ἀγοράζοντας ἐν
TO DRIVE OUT THE ONES SELLING AND THE ONES BUYING IN

τῷ ἱερῷ, καὶ τὰς τραπέζας τῶν κολλυβιστῶν καὶ τὰς
THE TEMPLE, AND THE TABLES OF THE MONEY CHANGERS AND THE

καθέδρας τῶν πωλούντων τὰς περιστερὰς
CHAIRS OF THE ONES SELLING THE DOVES

κατέστρεψεν, **11.16** καὶ οὐκ ἤφιεν ἵνα τις
HE OVERTURNED,   AND HE WAS NOT ALLOWING THAT ANYONE

διενέγκῃ σκεῦος διὰ τοῦ ἱεροῦ. **11.17** καὶ ἐδίδασκεν
SHOULD CARRY THINGS THROUGH THE TEMPLE.   AND HE WAS TEACHING

καὶ ἔλεγεν αὐτοῖς, Οὐ γέγραπται ὅτι
AND HE WAS SAYING TO THEM, HAS IT NOT BEEN WRITTEN -

Ὁ οἶκός μου οἶκος προσευχῆς κληθήσεται πᾶσιν
THE HOUSE OF ME A HOUSE OF PRAYER WILL BE CALLED [FOR] ALL

τοῖς ἔθνεσιν;
THE GENTILES?

ὑμεῖς δὲ πεποιήκατε αὐτὸν σπήλαιον λῃστῶν.
BUT~YOU° HAVE MADE IT A REFUGE OF ROBBERS.

11.18 καὶ ἤκουσαν οἱ ἀρχιερεῖς καὶ οἱ γραμματεῖς
AND HEARD [THIS] THE CHIEF PRIESTS AND THE SCRIBES

καὶ ἐζήτουν πῶς αὐτὸν ἀπολέσωσιν· ἐφοβοῦντο γὰρ
AND THEY WERE SEEKING HOW THEY MIGHT DESTROY~HIM FOR~THEY WERE AFRAID

αὐτόν, πᾶς γὰρ ὁ ὄχλος ἐξεπλήσσετο ἐπὶ τῇ διδαχῇ
OF HIM, FOR~ALL THE CROWD WERE AMAZED AT THE TEACHING

αὐτοῦ. **11.19** Καὶ ὅταν ὀψὲ ἐγένετο, ἐξεπορεύοντο
OF HIM.   AND WHEN IT BECAME~LATE, THEY WERE GOING FORTH

ἔξω τῆς πόλεως.
OUTSIDE THE CITY.

11.20 Καὶ παραπορευόμενοι πρωῒ εἶδον τὴν συκῆν
AND PASSING BY EARLY THEY SAW THE FIG TREE

ἐξηραμμένην ἐκ ῥιζῶν. **11.21** καὶ ἀναμνησθεὶς ὁ
HAVING BEEN WITHERED FROM [THE] ROOTS. AND HAVING REMEMBERED -

Πέτρος λέγει αὐτῷ, Ῥαββί, ἴδε ἡ συκῆ ἦν
PETER SAYS TO HIM, RABBI, LOOK, THE FIG TREE WHICH

11:17 Isa. 56:7

κατηράσω ἐξήρανται.   **11.22** καὶ   ἀποκριθεὶς ὁ Ἰησοῦς
YOU CURSED   HAS BEEN WITHERED.   AND   HAVING ANSWERED - JESUS

λέγει αὐτοῖς, Ἔχετε πίστιν θεοῦ.   **11.23** ἀμὴν λέγω
SAYS   TO THEM,   HAVE   FAITH   IN GOD.   TRULY   I SAY

ὑμῖν ὅτι ὃς ἂν εἴπῃ τῷ ὄρει τούτῳ, Ἄρθητι καὶ
TO YOU° THAT WHOEVER SAYS - TO THIS~MOUNTAIN, BE LIFTED UP AND

βλήθητι εἰς τὴν θάλασσαν, καὶ μὴ διακριθῇ ἐν τῇ
BE THROWN   INTO THE   SEA,   AND   DOES NOT WAVER   IN   THE

καρδίᾳ αὐτοῦ ἀλλὰ πιστεύῃ ὅτι ὃ λαλεῖ γίνεται,
HEART   OF HIM   BUT   BELIEVES   THAT WHAT HE SAYS HAPPENS,

ἔσται αὐτῷ.   **11.24** διὰ τοῦτο λέγω ὑμῖν, πάντα
IT WILL BE [SO] FOR HIM.   FOR THIS REASON I SAY TO YOU°, EVERYTHING

ὅσα προσεύχεσθε καὶ αἰτεῖσθε, πιστεύετε ὅτι
WHICH YOU° PRAY   AND   ASK,   BELIEVE   THAT

ἐλάβετε, καὶ ἔσται ὑμῖν.   **11.25** καὶ ὅταν
YOU° RECEIVED [IT], AND   IT WILL BE [SO]   FOR YOU°.   AND   WHEN

στήκετε προσευχόμενοι, ἀφίετε εἴ τι ἔχετε κατά
YOU° STAND PRAYING,   FORGIVE IF SOMETHING YOU° HAVE AGAINST

τινος, ἵνα καὶ ὁ πατὴρ ὑμῶν ὁ ἐν τοῖς
SOMEONE, IN ORDER THAT ALSO THE FATHER OF YOU°, THE ONE IN   THE

οὐρανοῖς ἀφῇ ὑμῖν τὰ παραπτώματα ὑμῶν.ᵀ
HEAVENS,   MAY FORGIVE YOU°   THE   TRANSGRESSIONS   OF YOU.

11.27 Καὶ ἔρχονται πάλιν εἰς Ἱεροσόλυμα. καὶ ἐν
AND   THEY COME   AGAIN   INTO JERUSALEM.   AND IN

τῷ ἱερῷ περιπατοῦντος αὐτοῦ ἔρχονται πρὸς αὐτὸν οἱ
THE TEMPLE [WHEN] HE~WALKING ABOUT,   COME   TO   HIM   THE

ἀρχιερεῖς καὶ οἱ γραμματεῖς καὶ οἱ πρεσβύτεροι
CHIEF PRIESTS AND   THE SCRIBES   AND   THE ELDERS

11.28 καὶ ἔλεγον αὐτῷ, Ἐν ποίᾳ ἐξουσίᾳ
AND   THEY WERE SAYING TO HIM,   BY   WHAT KIND OF AUTHORITY

ταῦτα ποιεῖς; ἢ τίς σοι ἔδωκεν τὴν ἐξουσίαν ταύτην
DO YOU DO~THESE THINGS? OR WHO GAVE~TO YOU - THIS~AUTHORITY

ἵνα ταῦτα ποιῇς;   **11.29** ὁ δὲ Ἰησοῦς εἶπεν αὐτοῖς,
THAT YOU MAY DO~THESE THINGS?   - BUT JESUS   SAID   TO THEM,

Ἐπερωτήσω ὑμᾶς ἕνα λόγον, καὶ ἀποκρίθητέ μοι
I WILL ASK   YOU°   ONE WORD(QUESTION), AND YOU° ANSWER ME

καὶ ἐρῶ ὑμῖν ἐν ποίᾳ ἐξουσίᾳ ταῦτα ποιῶ·
AND I WILL TELL YOU   BY WHAT KIND OF AUTHORITY I DO~THESE THINGS.

11.30 τὸ βάπτισμα τὸ Ἰωάννου ἐξ οὐρανοῦ ἦν ἢ
THE BAPTISM   - OF JOHN ²FROM ³HEAVEN ¹WAS IT OR

ἐξ ἀνθρώπων; ἀποκρίθητέ μοι.   **11.31** καὶ
FROM MEN?   ANSWER   ME.   AND

διελογίζοντο πρὸς ἑαυτοὺς λέγοντες, Ἐὰν εἴπωμεν,
THEY WERE DISCUSSING WITH THEMSELVES SAYING,   IF   WE SAY,

Ἐξ οὐρανοῦ, ἐρεῖ, Διὰ τί [οὖν] οὐκ ἐπιστεύσατε
FROM HEAVEN,   HE WILL SAY, WHY   THEN   DID YOU° NOT BELIEVE

you cursed has withered."
²²Jesus answered them,
"Have[j] faith in God. ²³Truly
I tell you, if you say to this
mountain, 'Be taken up and
thrown into the sea,' and if
you do not doubt in your
heart, but believe that what
you say will come to pass, it
will be done for you. ²⁴So I
tell you, whatever you ask
for in prayer, believe that
you have received[k] it, and it
will be yours.

25 "Whenever you stand
praying, forgive, if you have
anything against anyone; so
that your Father in heaven
may also forgive you your
trespasses."[l]

27 Again they came to
Jerusalem. As he was
walking in the temple, the
chief priests, the scribes, and
the elders came to him ²⁸and
said, "By what authority are
you doing these things? Who
gave you this authority to do
them?" ²⁹Jesus said to them,
"I will ask you one question;
answer me, and I will tell
you by what authority I do
these things. ³⁰Did the
baptism of John come from
heaven, or was it of human
origin? Answer me." ³¹They
argued with one another,
"If we say, 'From heaven,'
he will say, 'Why then
did you not believe

[j] Other ancient authorities read *"If you
have*

[k] Other ancient authorities read *are
receiving*

[l] Other ancient authorities add verse
26, *"But if you do not forgive,
neither will your Father in heaven
forgive your trespasses."*

11:25 text: ASV RSV NASB NIV NEB TEV NJB NRSV.   add v. 26 ει δε υμεις ουκ αφιετε, ουδε ο πατηρ υμων ο
εν τοις ουρανοις αφησει τα παραπτωματα υμων (But if you do not forgive, neither will your Father in
heaven forgive your trespasses): KJV ASVmg RSVmg NASBmg NIVmg NEBmg TEVmg NJBmg NRSVmg.

him?' ³²But shall we say, 'Of human origin'?"—they were afraid of the crowd, for all regarded John as truly a prophet. ³³So they answered Jesus, "We do not know." And Jesus said to them, "Neither will I tell you by what authority I am doing these things."

αὐτῷ;   **11.32** ἀλλὰ εἴπωμεν, Ἐξ ἀνθρώπων;—ἐφοβοῦντο
HIM?   BUT [IF] WE SAY   FROM MEN?—THEY WERE AFRAID OF

τὸν ὄχλον· ἅπαντες γὰρ εἶχον   τὸν Ἰωάννην
THE CROWD. FOR~EVERYONE WAS CONSIDERING -   JOHN

ὄντως ὅτι προφήτης ἦν. **11.33** καὶ ἀποκριθέντες τῷ
REALLY THAT HE WAS~A PROPHET.   AND HAVING ANSWERED   -

Ἰησοῦ λέγουσιν, Οὐκ οἴδαμεν. καὶ ὁ Ἰησοῦς λέγει
JESUS THEY SAY,   WE DO NOT KNOW. AND - JESUS   SAYS

αὐτοῖς, Οὐδὲ ἐγὼ λέγω ὑμῖν ἐν ποίᾳ   ἐξουσίᾳ
TO THEM, NEITHER I   TELL YOU° BY WHAT KIND OF AUTHORITY

ταῦτα ποιῶ.
I DO~THESE THINGS.

CHAPTER 12

Then he began to speak to them in parables. "A man planted a vineyard, put a fence around it, dug a pit for the winepress, and built a watchtower; then he leased it to tenants and went to another country. ²When the season came, he sent a slave to the tenants to collect from them his share of the produce of the vineyard. ³But they seized him, and beat him, and sent him away empty-handed. ⁴And again he sent another slave to them; this one they beat over the head and insulted. ⁵Then he sent another, and that one they killed. And so it was with many others; some they beat, and others they killed. ⁶He had still one other, a beloved son. Finally he sent him to them, saying, 'They will respect my son.' ⁷But those tenants said to one another, 'This is the heir;

12.1 Καὶ ἤρξατο αὐτοῖς ἐν παραβολαῖς λαλεῖν,
        AND HE BEGAN ²TO THEM ³IN ⁴PARABLES   ¹TO SPEAK,

Ἀμπελῶνα ἄνθρωπος ἐφύτευσεν καὶ περιέθηκεν
³A VINEYARD ¹A MAN   ²PLANTED   AND HE PUT AROUND [IT]

φραγμὸν καὶ ὤρυξεν ὑπολήνιον καὶ ᾠκοδόμησεν πύργον
A FENCE   AND   DUG   A TROUGH   AND   BUILT   A TOWER

καὶ ἐξέδετο αὐτὸν γεωργοῖς καὶ ἀπεδήμησεν.
AND HE LEASED IT   TO FARMERS AND HE WENT ON A JOURNEY.

12.2 καὶ ἀπέστειλεν πρὸς τοὺς γεωργοὺς τῷ
        AND HE SENT   TO   THE   FARMERS   IN THE

καιρῷ   δοῦλον ἵνα   παρὰ τῶν γεωργῶν
SEASON [OF HARVEST] A SLAVE IN ORDER THAT FROM THE FARMERS

λάβῃ   ἀπὸ τῶν καρπῶν τοῦ ἀμπελῶνος· **12.3** καὶ
HE MIGHT RECEIVE FROM THE FRUITS OF THE VINEYARD.   AND

λαβόντες αὐτὸν ἔδειραν καὶ ἀπέστειλαν κενόν.
HAVING TAKEN HIM   THEY BEAT [HIM] AND SENT [HIM] AWAY EMPTY.

12.4 καὶ πάλιν ἀπέστειλεν πρὸς αὐτοὺς ἄλλον δοῦλον·
        AND AGAIN HE SENT   TO   THEM   ANOTHER SLAVE;

κἀκεῖνον ἐκεφαλίωσαν   καὶ ἠτίμασαν. **12.5** καὶ
AND THAT ONE THEY STRUCK ON THE HEAD AND INSULTED.   AND

ἄλλον ἀπέστειλεν· κἀκεῖνον ἀπέκτειναν, καὶ πολλοὺς
HE SENT~ANOTHER;   AND THAT ONE THEY KILLED,   AND MANY

ἄλλους, οὓς μὲν δέροντες, οὓς δὲ ἀποκτέννοντες.
OTHERS, SOME   BEATING, AND~OTHERS KILLING.

12.6 ἔτι ἕνα εἶχεν υἱὸν ἀγαπητόν· ἀπέστειλεν αὐτὸν
        STILL HE HAD~ONE BELOVED~SON.   HE SENT   HIM

ἔσχατον πρὸς αὐτοὺς λέγων ὅτι Ἐντραπήσονται τὸν
FINALLY   TO   THEM   SAYING - THEY WILL RESPECT THE

υἱόν μου. **12.7** ἐκεῖνοι δὲ οἱ γεωργοὶ πρὸς ἑαυτοὺς
SON OF ME.   BUT~THOSE - FARMERS   TO   THEMSELVES

εἶπαν ὅτι Οὗτός ἐστιν ὁ κληρονόμος· δεῦτε
SAID   - THIS ONE IS   THE HEIR.   COME

ἀποκτείνωμεν αὐτόν, καὶ ἡμῶν ἔσται ἡ κληρονομία.
LET US KILL HIM, AND ⁴OURS ³WILL BE ¹THE ²INHERITANCE.

12.8 καὶ λαβόντες ἀπέκτειναν αὐτόν καὶ ἐξέβαλον
AND HAVING SEIZED [HIM] THEY KILLED HIM AND THREW OUT

αὐτὸν ἔξω τοῦ ἀμπελῶνος. **12.9** τί [οὖν] ποιήσει ὁ
HIM OUTSIDE OF THE VINEYARD. WHAT THEN WILL DO THE

κύριος τοῦ ἀμπελῶνος; ἐλεύσεται καὶ ἀπολέσει τοὺς
MASTER OF THE VINEYARD? HE WILL COME AND DESTROY THE

γεωργούς καὶ δώσει τὸν ἀμπελῶνα ἄλλοις.
FARMERS AND WILL GIVE THE VINEYARD TO OTHERS.

12.10 οὐδὲ τὴν γραφὴν ταύτην ἀνέγνωτε,
[HAVE YOU°] NOT - ³SCRIPTURE ²THIS ¹READ,

Λίθον ὃν ἀπεδοκίμασαν οἱ οἰκοδομοῦντες,
A STONE WHICH ³REJECTED ¹THE ONES ²BUILDING,

οὗτος ἐγενήθη εἰς κεφαλὴν γωνίας·
THIS ONE HAS COME TO BE FOR [THE] CAPSTONE OF [THE] CORNER.

12.11 παρὰ κυρίου ἐγένετο αὕτη
FROM [THE] LORD THIS~CAME TO BE

καὶ ἔστιν θαυμαστὴ ἐν ὀφθαλμοῖς ἡμῶν;
AND IT IS WONDERFUL IN [THE] EYES OF US?

12.12 Καὶ ἐζήτουν αὐτὸν κρατῆσαι, καὶ
AND THEY WERE SEEKING TO SEIZE~HIM, AND

ἐφοβήθησαν τὸν ὄχλον, ἔγνωσαν γὰρ ὅτι πρὸς αὐτοὺς
THEY WERE AFRAID OF THE CROWD, FOR~THEY KNEW THAT TO THEM

τὴν παραβολὴν εἶπεν. καὶ ἀφέντες αὐτὸν ἀπῆλθον.
THE PARABLE HE TOLD. AND LEAVING HIM THEY WENT AWAY.

12.13 Καὶ ἀποστέλλουσιν πρὸς αὐτόν τινας τῶν
AND THEY SEND TO HIM SOME OF THE

Φαρισαίων καὶ τῶν Ἡρῳδιανῶν ἵνα
PHARISEES AND THE HERODIANS IN ORDER THAT

αὐτὸν ἀγρεύσωσιν λόγῳ. **12.14** καὶ ἐλθόντες λέγουσιν
THEY MIGHT CATCH~HIM IN A WORD. AND HAVING COME THEY SAY

αὐτῷ, Διδάσκαλε, οἴδαμεν ὅτι ἀληθὴς εἶ καὶ
TO HIM, TEACHER, WE KNOW THAT YOU ARE~TRUTHFUL AND

οὐ μέλει σοι περὶ οὐδενός· οὐ γὰρ βλέπεις εἰς
IT IS NOT A CONCERN TO YOU ABOUT ANYONE. FOR~YOU DO NOT LOOK AT

πρόσωπον ἀνθρώπων, ἀλλ᾽ ἐπ᾽ ἀληθείας τὴν
[THE] FACE OF MEN, BUT RATHER ON THE BASIS OF TRUTH THE

ὁδὸν τοῦ θεοῦ διδάσκεις· ἔξεστιν δοῦναι κῆνσον
WAY - OF GOD YOU TEACH. IS IT PERMISSIBLE TO GIVE A POLL TAX

Καίσαρι ἢ οὔ; δῶμεν ἢ μὴ δῶμεν; **12.15** ὁ δὲ
TO CAESAR OR NOT? SHOULD WE GIVE OR SHOULD WE NOT GIVE? BUT~HE

εἰδὼς αὐτῶν τὴν ὑπόκρισιν εἶπεν αὐτοῖς, Τί
HAVING SEEN THEIR - HYPOCRISY SAID TO THEM, WHY

με πειράζετε; φέρετέ μοι δηνάριον ἵνα ἴδω.
ARE YOU° TESTING~ME? BRING ME A DENARIUS THAT I MAY LOOK [AT IT].

12:10-11 Ps. 118:22-23

come, let us kill him, and the inheritance will be ours.' ⁸So they seized him, killed him, and threw him out of the vineyard. ⁹What then will the owner of the vineyard do? He will come and destroy the tenants and give the vineyard to others. ¹⁰Have you not read this scripture:

'The stone that the builders rejected has become the cornerstone;ᵐ ¹¹ this was the Lord's doing, and it is amazing in our eyes'?"

12 When they realized that he had told this parable against them, they wanted to arrest him, but they feared the crowd. So they left him and went away.

13 Then they sent to him some Pharisees and some Herodians to trap him in what he said. ¹⁴And they came and said to him, "Teacher, we know that you are sincere, and show deference to no one; for you do not regard people with partiality, but teach the way of God in accordance with truth. Is it lawful to pay taxes to the emperor, or not? ¹⁵Should we pay them, or should we not?" But knowing their hypocrisy, he said to them, "Why are you putting me to the test? Bring me a denarius and let me see it."

ᵐ Or *keystone*

16And they brought one. Then he said to them, "Whose head is this, and whose title?" They answered, "The emperor's." 17Jesus said to them, "Give to the emperor the things that are the emperor's, and to God the things that are God's." And they were utterly amazed at him.

18 Some Sadducees, who say there is no resurrection, came to him and asked him a question, saying, 19"Teacher, Moses wrote for us that if a man's brother dies, leaving a wife but no child, the man[n] shall marry the widow and raise up children for his brother. 20There were seven brothers; the first married and, when he died, left no children; 21and the second married the widow[o] and died, leaving no children; and the third likewise; 22none of the seven left children. Last of all the woman herself died. 23In the resurrection[p] whose wife will she be? For the seven had married her."

24 Jesus said to them, "Is not this the reason you are wrong, that you know neither the scriptures nor the power of God? 25For when they rise from the dead, they neither marry nor are given in marriage, but are like angels in

n Gk his brother
o Gk her
p Other ancient authorities add when they rise

12.16 οἱ δὲ ἤνεγκαν.   καὶ λέγει αὐτοῖς, Τίνος ἡ
\- AND THEY BROUGHT [ONE]. AND HE SAYS TO THEM, WHOSE -

εἰκὼν αὕτη καὶ   ἡ ἐπιγραφή; οἱ δὲ εἶπαν αὐτῷ,
IMAGE [IS] THIS AND [WHOSE] - INSCRIPTION? - AND THEY SAID TO HIM,

Καίσαρος. **12.17** ὁ δὲ Ἰησοῦς εἶπεν αὐτοῖς, Τὰ
CAESAR'S. - AND JESUS SAID TO THEM, THE THINGS

Καίσαρος ἀπόδοτε Καίσαρι καὶ τὰ   τοῦ θεοῦ
OF CAESAR GIVE TO CAESAR AND THE THINGS - OF GOD [GIVE]

τῷ θεῷ. καὶ ἐξεθαύμαζον ἐπ' αὐτῷ.
- TO GOD. AND THEY WERE AMAZED AT HIM.

12.18 Καὶ ἔρχονται Σαδδουκαῖοι πρὸς αὐτόν, οἵτινες
AND [THE] SADDUCEES~COME TO HIM, WHO

λέγουσιν ἀνάστασιν μὴ εἶναι, καὶ ἐπηρώτων
SAY A RESURRECTION [IS] NOT TO BE, AND THEY WERE QUESTIONING

αὐτὸν λέγοντες, **12.19** Διδάσκαλε, Μωϋσῆς ἔγραψεν ἡμῖν
HIM SAYING, TEACHER, MOSES WROTE TO US

ὅτι ἐάν τινος ἀδελφὸς ἀποθάνῃ καὶ καταλίπῃ
THAT IF OF SOMEONE A BROTHER SHOULD DIE AND LEAVE BEHIND

γυναῖκα καὶ μὴ ἀφῇ τέκνον, ἵνα λάβῃ ὁ ἀδελφὸς
A WIFE AND NOT LEAVE A CHILD, - 4MAY TAKE 1THE 2BROTHER

αὐτοῦ τὴν γυναῖκα καὶ ἐξαναστήσῃ σπέρμα τῷ
3OF HIM THE WIFE AND MAY RAISE UP SEED FOR THE

ἀδελφῷ αὐτοῦ. **12.20** ἑπτὰ ἀδελφοὶ ἦσαν· καὶ ὁ
BROTHER OF HIM. 2SEVEN 3BROTHERS 1THERE WERE. AND THE

πρῶτος ἔλαβεν γυναῖκα καὶ ἀποθνήσκων οὐκ ἀφῆκεν
FIRST TOOK A WIFE AND DYING DID NOT LEAVE

σπέρμα· **12.21** καὶ ὁ δεύτερος ἔλαβεν αὐτὴν καὶ
A DESCENDANT. AND THE SECOND TOOK HER AND

ἀπέθανεν μὴ καταλιπὼν σπέρμα· καὶ ὁ τρίτος
HE DIED NOT HAVING LEFT BEHIND A DESCENDANT. AND THE THIRD

ὡσαύτως· **12.22** καὶ οἱ ἑπτὰ οὐκ ἀφῆκαν σπέρμα.
LIKEWISE. AND THE SEVEN DID NOT LEAVE A DESCENDANT.

ἔσχατον πάντων καὶ ἡ γυνὴ ἀπέθανεν. **12.23** ἐν τῇ
LAST OF ALL ALSO THE WOMAN DIED. IN THE

ἀναστάσει ⌜[ὅταν ἀναστῶσιν]⌝ τίνος αὐτῶν ἔσται
RESURRECTION WHEN THEY ARE RAISED OF WHICH OF THEM WILL SHE BE

γυνή; οἱ γὰρ ἑπτὰ ἔσχον αὐτὴν γυναῖκα. **12.24** ἔφη
[THE] WIFE? - FOR SEVEN HAD HER [AS] WIFE. SAID

αὐτοῖς ὁ Ἰησοῦς, Οὐ διὰ τοῦτο πλανᾶσθε
TO THEM - JESUS, [IS IT] NOT FOR THIS REASON [THAT] YOU° ARE MISTAKEN

μὴ εἰδότες τὰς γραφὰς μηδὲ τὴν δύναμιν τοῦ θεοῦ;
NOT HAVING KNOWN THE SCRIPTURES NOR THE POWER - OF GOD?

12.25 ὅταν γὰρ ἐκ νεκρῶν ἀναστῶσιν οὔτε γαμοῦσιν
FOR~WHEN FROM [THE] DEAD THEY RISE THEY DO NOT MARRY

οὔτε γαμίζονται, ἀλλ' εἰσὶν ὡς ἄγγελοι ἐν τοῖς
NOR ARE THEY GIVEN IN MARRIAGE, BUT THEY ARE LIKE ANGELS IN THE

12:19 Deut. 25:5   **12:23** text: KJV NASB NIVmg TEV NJB NRSVmg. omit: ASV RSV NASBmg NIV NEB NRSV.

201

2111 MARK 12:33

οὐρανοῖς. **12.26** περὶ δὲ τῶν νεκρῶν ὅτι ἐγείρονται
HEAVENS. BUT~CONCERNING THE DEAD THAT THEY ARE RAISED

οὐκ ἀνέγνωτε ἐν τῇ βίβλῳ Μωϋσέως ἐπὶ τοῦ βάτου
HAVE YOU° NOT READ IN THE BOOK OF MOSES AT THE THORNBUSH

πῶς εἶπεν αὐτῷ ὁ θεὸς λέγων, Ἐγὼ ὁ θεὸς Ἀβραὰμ
HOW ²SPOKE ³TO HIM - ¹GOD SAYING, I [AM] THE GOD OF ABRAHAM

καὶ [ὁ] θεὸς Ἰσαὰκ καὶ [ὁ] θεὸς Ἰακώβ;
AND THE GOD OF ISAAC AND THE GOD OF JACOB?

12.27 οὐκ ἔστιν θεὸς νεκρῶν ἀλλὰ ζώντων·
HE IS NOT [THE] GOD OF DEAD [PERSONS] BUT OF LIVING [ONES].

πολὺ πλανᾶσθε.
YOU ARE MISTAKEN~GREATLY.

12.28 Καὶ προσελθὼν εἷς τῶν γραμματέων ἀκούσας
AND HAVING APPROACHED ONE OF THE SCRIBES HAVING HEARD

αὐτῶν συζητούντων, ἰδὼν ὅτι καλῶς ἀπεκρίθη αὐτοῖς
THEM DEBATING, HAVING SEEN THAT ³WELL ¹HE ANSWERED ²THEM

ἐπηρώτησεν αὐτόν, Ποία ἐστὶν ἐντολὴ πρώτη
ASKED HIM, WHICH IS [THE] FIRST~COMMANDMENT

πάντων; **12.29** ἀπεκρίθη ὁ Ἰησοῦς ὅτι Πρώτη ἐστίν,
OF ALL? ²ANSWERED - ¹JESUS - [THE] FIRST IS,

Ἄκουε, Ἰσραήλ, κύριος ὁ θεὸς ἡμῶν κύριος εἷς ἐστιν,
HEAR, [O] ISRAEL, [THE] LORD - GOD OF US, ONE~LORD IS,

12.30 καὶ ἀγαπήσεις κύριον τὸν θεόν σου ἐξ ὅλης
AND YOU° SHALL LOVE [THE] LORD THE GOD OF YOU FROM [THE] WHOLE

τῆς καρδίας σου καὶ ἐξ ὅλης τῆς ψυχῆς σου
OF THE HEART OF YOU AND FROM [THE] WHOLE OF THE SOUL OF YOU

καὶ ἐξ ὅλης τῆς διανοίας σου καὶ ἐξ ὅλης
AND FROM [THE] WHOLE OF THE MIND OF YOU AND FROM [THE] WHOLE

τῆς ἰσχύος σου. **12.31** δευτέρα αὕτη, Ἀγαπήσεις τὸν
OF THE STRENGTH OF YOU. [THE] SECOND [IS]~THIS, YOU° SHALL LOVE THE

πλησίον σου ὡς σεαυτόν. μείζων τούτων ἄλλη
NEIGHBOR OF YOU AS YOURSELF. GREATER [THAN] THESE ²ANOTHER

ἐντολὴ οὐκ ἔστιν. **12.32** καὶ εἶπεν αὐτῷ ὁ
³COMMANDMENT ¹THERE IS NOT. AND SAID TO HIM THE

γραμματεύς, Καλῶς, διδάσκαλε, ἐπ' ἀληθείας
SCRIBE, WELL, TEACHER, ON THE BASIS OF TRUTH

εἶπες ὅτι εἷς ἐστιν καὶ οὐκ ἔστιν ἄλλος πλὴν αὐτοῦ·
YOU SAY THAT THERE IS~ONE AND THERE IS NOT ANOTHER EXCEPT HIM.

12.33 καὶ τὸ ἀγαπᾶν αὐτὸν ἐξ ὅλης τῆς καρδίας
AND - TO LOVE HIM FROM [THE] WHOLE OF THE HEART

καὶ ἐξ ὅλης τῆς συνέσεως καὶ ἐξ ὅλης τῆς
AND FROM [THE] WHOLE OF THE INTELLIGENCE AND FROM [THE] WHOLE OF THE

ἰσχύος καὶ τὸ ἀγαπᾶν τὸν πλησίον ὡς ἑαυτὸν
STRENGTH AND - TO LOVE THE NEIGHBOR AS HIMSELF

περισσότερόν ἐστιν πάντων τῶν ὁλοκαυτωμάτων καὶ
IS~GREATER [THAN] ALL OF THE BURNT OFFERINGS AND

heaven. ²⁶And as for the dead being raised, have you not read in the book of Moses, in the story about the bush, how God said to him, 'I am the God of Abraham, the God of Isaac, and the God of Jacob'? ²⁷He is God not of the dead, but of the living; you are quite wrong."

²⁸ One of the scribes came near and heard them disputing with one another, and seeing that he answered them well, he asked him, "Which commandment is the first of all?" ²⁹Jesus answered, "The first is, 'Hear, O Israel: the Lord our God, the Lord is one; ³⁰you shall love the Lord your God with all your heart, and with all your soul, and with all your mind, and with all your strength.' ³¹The second is this, 'You shall love your neighbor as yourself.' There is no other commandment greater than these." ³²Then the scribe said to him, "You are right, Teacher; you have truly said that 'he is one, and besides him there is no other'; ³³and 'to love him with all the heart, and with all the understanding, and with all the strength,' and 'to love one's neighbor as oneself,'—this is much more important than all whole burnt offerings and

12:26 Exod. 3:6, 15 **12:29-30** Deut. 6:4-5 **12:31** Lev. 19:18 **12:32a** Deut. 6:4 **12:32b** Deut. 4:35; Isa. 45:21 **12:33a** Deut. 6:5 **12:33b** Lev. 19:18

sacrifices." ³⁴When Jesus saw that he answered wisely, he said to him, "You are not far from the kingdom of God." After that no one dared to ask him any question.

35 While Jesus was teaching in the temple, he said, "How can the scribes say that the Messiah*ᵖ* is the son of David? ³⁶David himself, by the Holy Spirit, declared,

'The Lord said to my Lord,

"Sit at my right hand, until I put your enemies under your feet." '

³⁷David himself calls him Lord; so how can he be his son?" And the large crowd was listening to him with delight.

38 As he taught, he said, "Beware of the scribes, who like to walk around in long robes, and to be greeted with respect in the marketplaces, ³⁹and to have the best seats in the synagogues and places of honor at banquets! ⁴⁰They devour widows' houses and for the sake of appearance say long prayers. They will receive the greater condemnation."

41 He sat down opposite the treasury, and

ᵖ Or *the Christ*

θυσιῶν. **12.34** καὶ ὁ Ἰησοῦς ἰδὼν [αὐτὸν] ὅτι
SACRIFICES.   AND - JESUS HAVING SEEN HIM   THAT

νουνεχῶς ἀπεκρίθη εἶπεν αὐτῷ, Οὐ μακρὰν εἶ ἀπὸ
HE ANSWERED~WISELY SAID TO HIM, ²NOT ³FAR ¹YOU ARE FROM

τῆς βασιλείας τοῦ θεοῦ. καὶ οὐδεὶς οὐκέτι ἐτόλμα
THE KINGDOM   - OF GOD. AND NO ONE ANY LONGER WAS DARING

αὐτὸν ἐπερωτῆσαι.
TO QUESTION~HIM.

12.35 Καὶ ἀποκριθεὶς ὁ Ἰησοῦς ἔλεγεν διδάσκων ἐν
      AND HAVING ANSWERED - JESUS WAS SAYING [WHEN] TEACHING IN

τῷ ἱερῷ, Πῶς λέγουσιν οἱ γραμματεῖς ὅτι ὁ Χριστὸς
THE TEMPLE, HOW SAY   THE SCRIBES   THAT THE CHRIST

υἱὸς Δαυὶδ ἐστιν; **12.36** αὐτὸς Δαυὶδ εἶπεν ἐν τῷ
[THE] SON OF DAVID IS?   DAVID~HIMSELF SAID BY THE

πνεύματι τῷ ἁγίῳ,
²SPIRIT   - ¹HOLY,

Εἶπεν κύριος τῷ κυρίῳ μου,
[THE] LORD~SAID TO THE LORD OF ME,

Κάθου ἐκ δεξιῶν μου,
SIT   AT [THE] RIGHT OF ME,

ἕως ἂν θῶ τοὺς ἐχθρούς σου ὑποκάτω τῶν
UNTIL I PUT THE ENEMIES OF YOU UNDER   THE

ποδῶν σου.
FEET OF YOU.

12.37 αὐτὸς Δαυὶδ λέγει αὐτὸν κύριον, καὶ πόθεν
      DAVID~HIMSELF CALLS HIM LORD,   AND HOW

αὐτοῦ ἐστιν υἱός; καὶ [ὁ] πολὺς ὄχλος ἤκουεν
IS~HE   [HIS] SON? AND THE HUGE CROWD WAS LISTENING

αὐτοῦ ἡδέως.
HIM   GLADLY.

12.38 Καὶ ἐν τῇ διδαχῇ αὐτοῦ ἔλεγεν, Βλέπετε
      AND IN THE TEACHING OF HIM HE WAS SAYING, BEWARE

ἀπὸ τῶν γραμματέων τῶν θελόντων ἐν στολαῖς
OF   THE SCRIBES,   THE ONES DESIRING IN LONG ROBES

περιπατεῖν καὶ ἀσπασμοὺς ἐν ταῖς ἀγοραῖς **12.39** καὶ
TO WALK ABOUT AND GREETINGS IN THE MARKETPLACES   AND

πρωτοκαθεδρίας ἐν ταῖς συναγωγαῖς καὶ πρωτοκλισίας
CHIEF SEATS   IN THE SYNAGOGUES   AND PLACES OF HONOR

ἐν τοῖς δείπνοις, **12.40** οἱ κατεσθίοντες τὰς οἰκίας
AT THE BANQUETS,   THE ONES DEVOURING THE HOUSES

τῶν χηρῶν καὶ προφάσει μακρὰ προσευχόμενοι·
OF THE WIDOWS AND FOR SHOW PRAYING~LONG [PRAYERS].

οὗτοι λήμψονται περισσότερον κρίμα.
THESE ONES WILL RECEIVE GREATER   JUDGMENT.

12.41 Καὶ καθίσας κατέναντι τοῦ γαζοφυλακίου
      AND HAVING SAT [DOWN] OPPOSITE THE TREASURY

12:36 Ps. 110:1

ἐθεώρει   πῶς ὁ   ὄχλος βάλλει χαλκὸν   εἰς τὸ
HE WAS OBSERVING HOW THE CROWD THROWS COPPER [COINS] INTO THE

γαζοφυλάκιον.   καὶ   πολλοὶ πλούσιοι ἔβαλλον
TREASURY.   AND   MANY   RICH PEOPLE WERE THROWING [IN]

πολλά·   **12.42** καὶ ἐλθοῦσα μία χήρα πτωχὴ ἔβαλεν
MUCH.   AND HAVING COME ONE POOR~WIDOW, SHE THREW [IN]

λεπτὰ δύο, ὅ   ἐστιν κοδράντης.   **12.43** καὶ
TWO~LEPTAS, WHICH IS A KODRANTES.   AND

προσκαλεσάμενος τοὺς μαθητὰς αὐτοῦ εἶπεν αὐτοῖς,
HAVING SUMMONED   THE DISCIPLES OF HIM HE SAID TO THEM,

Ἀμὴν λέγω ὑμῖν ὅτι ἡ χήρα αὕτη ἡ πτωχὴ πλεῖον
TRULY I SAY TO YOU° THAT - 3WIDOW 1THIS - 2POOR 5MORE [THAN]

πάντων ἔβαλεν τῶν   βαλλόντων εἰς τὸ γαζοφυλάκιον·
6ALL   4THREW [IN] THE ONES THROWING INTO THE TREASURY.

12.44 πάντες γὰρ ἐκ   τοῦ περισσεύοντος αὐτοῖς ἔβαλον,
         FOR~EVERYONE FROM THE ABOUNDING   TO THEM THREW [IN],

αὕτη δὲ   ἐκ   τῆς ὑστερήσεως αὐτῆς πάντα ὅσα
BUT~THIS [WIDOW] FROM THE NEED   OF HER EVERYTHING AS MUCH AS

εἶχεν ἔβαλεν ὅλον τὸν βίον αὐτῆς.
SHE HAD SHE PUT [IN] ALL THE LIVING OF HER.

watched the crowd putting money into the treasury. [42]A poor widow came and put in two small copper coins, which are worth a penny. [43]Then he called his disciples and said to them, "Truly I tell you, this poor widow has put in more than all those who are contributing to the treasury. [44]For all of them have contributed out of their abundance; but she out of her poverty has put in everything she had, all she had to live on."

CHAPTER 13

13.1 Καὶ ἐκπορευωμένου αὐτοῦ ἐκ   τοῦ ἱεροῦ λέγει
        AND HE~GOING OUT   FROM THE TEMPLE SAYS

αὐτῷ εἷς τῶν μαθητῶν αὐτοῦ, Διδάσκαλε, ἴδε ποταποὶ
TO HIM ONE OF THE DISCIPLES OF HIM, TEACHER,   LOOK WHAT SORT OF

λίθοι καὶ ποταπαὶ οἰκοδομαί.   **13.2** καὶ ὁ Ἰησοῦς
STONES AND WHAT SORT OF BUILDINGS.   AND - JESUS

εἶπεν αὐτῷ, Βλέπεις ταύτας τὰς μεγάλας οἰκοδομάς;
SAID   TO HIM, DO YOU SEE THESE   -   GREAT BUILDINGS?

οὐ μὴ ἀφεθῇ   ὧδε λίθος ἐπὶ λίθον ὃς
BY NO MEANS WILL BE LEFT HERE A STONE ON A STONE WHICH

οὐ μὴ καταλυθῇ.
WILL NOT BE THROWN DOWN.

13.3 Καὶ καθημένου αὐτοῦ εἰς τὸ Ὄρος τῶν Ἐλαιῶν
        AND HE~SITTING   ON THE MOUNT - OF OLIVES

κατέναντι τοῦ ἱεροῦ ἐπηρώτα   αὐτὸν κατ᾽ ἰδίαν
OPPOSITE   THE TEMPLE WERE QUESTIONING HIM   PRIVATELY

Πέτρος καὶ Ἰάκωβος καὶ Ἰωάννης καὶ Ἀνδρέας,
PETER   AND JAMES   AND JOHN   AND ANDREW,

13.4 Εἰπὸν ἡμῖν, πότε ταῦτα   ἔσται καὶ τί   τὸ
        TELL   US   WHEN THESE THINGS WILL BE AND WHAT [WILL BE] THE

σημεῖον ὅταν μέλλῃ   ταῦτα   συντελεῖσθαι πάντα;
SIGN   WHEN 3ARE ABOUT 2THESE THINGS 4TO BE COMPLETE 1ALL?

13.5 ὁ δὲ Ἰησοῦς ἤρξατο λέγειν αὐτοῖς, Βλέπετε μή
        - AND JESUS   BEGAN   TO SAY TO THEM, BEWARE   LEST

As he came out of the temple, one of his disciples said to him, "Look, Teacher, what large stones and what large buildings!" [2]Then Jesus asked him, "Do you see these great buildings? Not one stone will be left here upon another; all will be thrown down."

3 When he was sitting on the Mount of Olives opposite the temple, Peter, James, John, and Andrew asked him privately, [4]"Tell us, when will this be, and what will be the sign that all these things are about to be accomplished?" [5]Then Jesus began to say to them, "Beware that

no one leads you astray. ⁶Many will come in my name and say, 'I am he!'*q* and they will lead many astray. ⁷When you hear of wars and rumors of wars, do not be alarmed; this must take place, but the end is still to come. ⁸For nation will rise against nation, and kingdom against kingdom; there will be earthquakes in various places; there will be famines. This is but the beginning of the birth pangs.

9 "As for yourselves, beware; for they will hand you over to councils; and you will be beaten in synagogues; and you will stand before governors and kings because of me, as a testimony to them. ¹⁰And the good news*r* must first be proclaimed to all nations. ¹¹When they bring you to trial and hand you over, do not worry beforehand about what you are to say; but say whatever is given you at that time, for it is not you who speak, but the Holy Spirit. ¹²Brother will betray brother to death, and a father his child, and children will rise against parents and have them put to death; ¹³and you will be hated by all because of my name. But the one who endures to the end will be saved.

14 "But when you see the desolating sacrilege

q Gk *I am*
r Gk *gospel*

τις   ὑμᾶς πλανήσῃ· **13.6** πολλοὶ ἐλεύσονται ἐπὶ τῷ
SOMEONE DECEIVE~YOU°.   MANY   WILL COME   IN THE

ὀνόματί μου λέγοντες ὅτι Ἐγώ εἰμι,   καὶ
NAME   OF ME SAYING   -   I AM [HERE], AND

πολλοὺς πλανήσουσιν. **13.7** ὅταν δὲ ἀκούσητε πολέμους
THEY WILL DECEIVE~MANY.   BUT~WHEN YOU° HEAR OF WARS

καὶ ἀκοὰς πολέμων, μὴ θροεῖσθε·
AND REPORTS OF WARS,   DO NOT BE TROUBLED.

δεῖ   γενέσθαι, ἀλλ᾽ οὔπω τὸ τέλος.
IT IS NECESSARY [FOR THESE THINGS] TO OCCUR, BUT ³NOT YET ¹THE ²END [IS].

13.8 ἐγερθήσεται γὰρ ἔθνος ἐπ᾽ ἔθνος καὶ βασιλεία
³WILL BE RAISED   ¹FOR ²NATION AGAINST NATION AND KINGDOM

ἐπὶ βασιλείαν, ἔσονται σεισμοὶ κατὰ τόπους,
AGAINST KINGDOM, THERE WILL BE EARTHQUAKES IN PLACE AFTER PLACE, [AND]

ἔσονται λιμοί· ἀρχὴ   ὠδίνων   ταῦτα.
THERE WILL BE FAMINES. ²[THE] BEGINNING ³OF THE BIRTH PANGS ¹THESE THINGS [ARE].

13.9 βλέπετε δὲ ὑμεῖς ἑαυτούς· παραδώσουσιν ὑμᾶς
³TAKE HEED ¹BUT ²YOU° TO YOURSELVES. THEY WILL HAND OVER YOU°

εἰς συνέδρια καὶ εἰς συναγωγὰς δαρήσεσθε καὶ
TO [THE] SANHEDRIN AND IN SYNAGOGUES YOU° WILL BE BEATEN AND

ἐπὶ ἡγεμόνων καὶ βασιλέων σταθήσεσθε ἕνεκεν
BEFORE GOVERNORS AND KINGS YOU° WILL STAND FOR THE SAKE OF

ἐμοῦ εἰς μαρτύριον αὐτοῖς. **13.10** καὶ εἰς πάντα τὰ
ME AS A TESTIMONY TO THEM.   AND TO ALL THE

ἔθνη πρῶτον δεῖ   κηρυχθῆναι τὸ εὐαγγέλιον.
NATIONS FIRST IT IS NECESSARY [FOR] ³TO BE PREACHED ¹THE ²GOOD NEWS.

13.11 καὶ ὅταν ἄγωσιν ὑμᾶς παραδιδόντες,
AND WHEN THEY LEAD YOU° HANDING [YOU°] OVER,

μὴ προμεριμνᾶτε τί λαλήσητε, ἀλλ᾽ ὃ ἐὰν δοθῇ
DO NOT BE WORRIED BEFOREHAND WHAT YOU° MIGHT SAY, BUT WHATEVER IS GIVEN

ὑμῖν ἐν ἐκείνῃ τῇ ὥρᾳ τοῦτο λαλεῖτε· οὐ γάρ ἐστε
TO YOU° IN THAT - HOUR THIS YOU° SHALL SAY. FOR~YOU° ARE NOT

ὑμεῖς οἱ λαλοῦντες ἀλλὰ τὸ πνεῦμα τὸ ἅγιον.
YOURSELVES THE ONES SPEAKING BUT THE ²SPIRIT - ¹HOLY.

13.12 καὶ παραδώσει ἀδελφὸς ἀδελφὸν εἰς θάνατον καὶ
AND BROTHER~WILL HAND OVER BROTHER TO DEATH AND

πατὴρ τέκνον, καὶ ἐπαναστήσονται τέκνα ἐπὶ γονεῖς
FATHER [HIS] CHILD, AND CHILDREN~WILL RISE UP AGAINST PARENTS

καὶ θανατώσουσιν αὐτούς· **13.13** αἱ ἔσεσθε μισούμενοι
AND PUT TO DEATH THEM.   AND YOU° WILL BE HATED

ὑπὸ πάντων διὰ τὸ ὄνομά μου. ὁ δὲ ὑπομείνας
BY EVERYONE BECAUSE OF THE NAME OF ME. BUT~THE ONE HAVING ENDURED

εἰς τέλος οὗτος σωθήσεται.
TO [THE] END THIS ONE WILL BE SAVED.

13.14 Ὅταν δὲ ἴδητε τὸ βδέλυγμα τῆς ἐρημώσεως
AND~WHEN YOU° SEE THE ABOMINATION - OF DESOLATION

ἑστηκότα ὅπου οὐ δεῖ, ὁ ἀναγινώσκων νοείτω,
HAVING STOOD WHERE IT OUGHT NOT, THE ONE READING TAKE NOTE,

τότε οἱ ἐν τῇ Ἰουδαίᾳ φευγέτωσαν εἰς τὰ ὄρη,
THEN THE ONES IN - JUDEA LET THEM FLEE TO THE MOUNTAINS,

13.15 ὁ [δὲ] ἐπὶ τοῦ δώματος μὴ καταβάτω μηδὲ
AND~THE ONE ON THE ROOF LET HIM NOT COME DOWN NOR

εἰσελθάτω ἆραί τι ἐκ τῆς οἰκίας αὐτοῦ, **13.16** καὶ
LET HIM ENTER TO TAKE ANYTHING FROM THE HOUSE OF HIM, AND

ὁ εἰς τὸν ἀγρὸν μὴ ἐπιστρεψάτω εἰς τὰ ὀπίσω
THE ONE IN THE FIELD LET HIM NOT RETURN TO THE THINGS BEHIND

ἆραι τὸ ἱμάτιον αὐτοῦ. **13.17** οὐαὶ δὲ ταῖς
TO TAKE THE GARMENT OF HIM. AND~WOE TO THE ONES

ἐν γαστρὶ ἐχούσαις καὶ ταῖς θηλαζούσαις ἐν ἐκείναις
PREGNANT AND THE ONES NURSING IN THOSE

ταῖς ἡμέραις. **13.18** προσεύχεσθε δὲ ἵνα μὴ γένηται
- DAYS. BUT~PRAY THAT IT MAY NOT COME

χειμῶνος· **13.19** ἔσονται γὰρ αἱ ἡμέραι ἐκεῖναι
IN WINTER. 4WILL BE 1FOR - 3DAYS 2IN THOSE

θλῖψις οἵα οὐ γέγονεν τοιαύτη ἀπ᾽ ἀρχῆς
TRIBULATION OF SUCH A KIND AS~HAS NOT HAPPENED FROM [THE] BEGINNING

κτίσεως ἣν ἔκτισεν ὁ θεὸς ἕως τοῦ νῦν καὶ
OF CREATION WHICH 2CREATED - 1GOD UNTIL - NOW AND

οὐ μὴ γένηται. **13.20** καὶ εἰ μὴ ἐκολόβωσεν κύριος τὰς
BY NO MEANS SHALL BE. AND UNLESS [THE] LORD~SHORTENS THE

ἡμέρας, οὐκ ἂν ἐσώθη πᾶσα σάρξ· ἀλλὰ διὰ
DAYS, WOULD NOT BE SAVED ALL FLESH. BUT ON ACCOUNT OF

τοὺς ἐκλεκτοὺς οὓς ἐξελέξατο ἐκολόβωσεν τὰς ἡμέρας.
THE CHOSEN WHOM HE CHOSE HE SHORTENED THE DAYS.

13.21 καὶ τότε ἐάν τις ὑμῖν εἴπῃ, Ἴδε ὧδε ὁ
AND THEN IF SOMEONE TO YOU° SAYS, LOOK, HERE [IS] THE

Χριστός, Ἴδε ἐκεῖ, μὴ πιστεύετε· **13.22** ἐγερθήσονται
CHRIST, LOOK, THERE, DO NOT BELIEVE [THEM]. 5WILL BE RAISED UP

γὰρ ψευδόχριστοι καὶ ψευδοπροφῆται καὶ δώσουσιν
1FOR 2FALSE CHRISTS 3AND 4FALSE PROPHETS AND THEY WILL PERFORM

σημεῖα καὶ τέρατα πρὸς τὸ ἀποπλανᾶν, εἰ δυνατόν,
SIGNS AND WONDERS SO AS - TO DECEIVE, IF POSSIBLE,

τοὺς ἐκλεκτούς. **13.23** ὑμεῖς δὲ βλέπετε· προείρηκα
THE CHOSEN. BUT~YOU° BEWARE. I HAVE FOREWARNED

ὑμῖν πάντα.
YOU° [CONCERNING] ALL THINGS.

13.24 Ἀλλὰ ἐν ἐκείναις ταῖς ἡμέραις μετὰ τὴν
BUT IN THOSE - DAYS AFTER -

θλῖψιν ἐκείνην
THAT~TRIBULATION

ὁ ἥλιος σκοτισθήσεται,
THE SUN WILL BE DARKENED,

set up where it ought not to be (let the reader understand), then those in Judea must flee to the mountains; [15]the one on the housetop must not go down or enter the house to take anything away; [16]the one in the field must not turn back to get a coat. [17]Woe to those who are pregnant and to those who are nursing infants in those days! [18]Pray that it may not be in winter. [19]For in those days there will be suffering, such as has not been from the beginning of the creation that God created until now, no, and never will be. [20]And if the Lord had not cut short those days, no one would be saved; but for the sake of the elect, whom he chose, he has cut short those days. [21]And if anyone says to you at that time, 'Look! Here is the Messiah!'[s] or 'Look! There he is!'—do not believe it. [22]False messiahs[t] and false prophets will appear and produce signs and omens, to lead astray, if possible, the elect. [23]But be alert; I have already told you everything.

24 "But in those days, after that suffering,
the sun will be darkened,

[s] Or *the Christ*
[t] Or *christs*

and the moon will not give its light, ²⁵and the stars will be falling from heaven, and the powers in the heavens will be shaken. ²⁶Then they will see 'the Son of Man coming in clouds' with great power and glory. ²⁷Then he will send out the angels, and gather his elect from the four winds, from the ends of the earth to the ends of heaven.

28 "From the fig tree learn its lesson: as soon as its branch becomes tender and puts forth its leaves, you know that summer is near. ²⁹So also, when you see these things taking place, you know that he*ᵘ* is near, at the very gates. ³⁰Truly I tell you, this generation will not pass away until all these things have taken place. ³¹Heaven and earth will pass away, but my words will not pass away.

32 "But about that day or hour no one knows, neither the angels in heaven, nor the Son, but only the Father. ³³Beware, keep alert;ᵛ

ᵘ Or *it*
ᵛ Other ancient authorities add *and pray*

καὶ ἡ σελήνη οὐ δώσει τὸ φέγγος αὐτῆς,
AND THE MOON WILL NOT GIVE THE LIGHT OF IT,

13.25 καὶ οἱ ἀστέρες ἔσονται ἐκ τοῦ οὐρανοῦ
AND THE STARS WILL BE ²OUT - ³OF HEAVEN

πίπτοντες,
¹FALLING,

καὶ αἱ δυνάμεις αἱ ἐν τοῖς οὐρανοῖς
AND THE POWERS, THE ONES IN THE HEAVENS

σαλευθήσονται.
WILL BE SHAKEN.

13.26 καὶ τότε ὄψονται τὸν υἱὸν τοῦ ἀνθρώπου
AND THEN YOU° WILL SEE THE SON - OF MAN

ἐρχόμενον ἐν νεφέλαις μετὰ δυνάμεως πολλῆς καὶ
COMING ON CLOUDS WITH GREAT~POWER AND

δόξης. **13.27** καὶ τότε ἀποστελεῖ τοὺς ἀγγέλους καὶ
GLORY. AND THEN HE WILL SEND THE ANGELS AND

ἐπισυνάξει τοὺς ἐκλεκτοὺς [αὐτοῦ] ἐκ τῶν
HE WILL GATHER TOGETHER THE CHOSEN OF HIM FROM THE

τεσσάρων ἀνέμων ἀπ' ἄκρου γῆς ἕως ἄκρου
FOUR WINDS FROM [THE] ENDS OF [THE] EARTH TO [THE] ENDS

οὐρανοῦ.
OF HEAVEN.

13.28 Ἀπὸ δὲ τῆς συκῆς μάθετε τὴν παραβολήν·
AND~FROM THE FIG TREE LEARN THE PARABLE.

ὅταν ἤδη ὁ κλάδος αὐτῆς ἀπαλὸς γένηται καὶ
WHEN BY THAT TIME THE BRANCH OF IT HAS BECOME~TENDER AND

ἐκφύῃ τὰ φύλλα, γινώσκετε ὅτι ἐγγὺς τὸ θέρος
IT PUTS FORTH THE LEAVES, YOU° KNOW THAT ³NEAR - ¹SUMMER

ἐστίν· **13.29** οὕτως καὶ ὑμεῖς, ὅταν ἴδητε ταῦτα
²IS. SO ALSO YOU°, WHEN YOU° SEE THESE THINGS

γινόμενα, γινώσκετε ὅτι ἐγγύς ἐστιν ἐπὶ θύραις.
HAPPENING, KNOW THAT IT IS~NEAR AT [THE] DOORS.

13.30 ἀμὴν λέγω ὑμῖν ὅτι οὐ μὴ παρέλθῃ ἡ γενεὰ
TRULY I SAY TO YOU° THAT ³BY NO MEANS PASSES AWAY - ²GENERATION

αὕτη μέχρις οὗ ταῦτα πάντα γένηται. **13.31** ὁ οὐρανὸς
¹THIS UNTIL ALL~THESE THINGS HAPPEN. - HEAVEN

καὶ ἡ γῆ παρελεύσονται, οἱ δὲ λόγοι μου
AND - EARTH WILL PASS AWAY, BUT~THE WORDS OF ME

οὐ μὴ παρελεύσονται.
WILL BY NO MEANS PASS AWAY.

13.32 Περὶ δὲ τῆς ἡμέρας ἐκείνης ἢ τῆς ὥρας
BUT~CONCERNING - THAT~DAY OR THE HOUR

οὐδεὶς οἶδεν, οὐδὲ οἱ ἄγγελοι ἐν οὐρανῷ οὐδὲ ὁ
NO ONE KNOWS, NEITHER THE ANGELS IN HEAVEN NOR THE

υἱός, εἰ μὴ ὁ πατήρ. **13.33** βλέπετε, ἀγρυπνεῖτεᵀ·
SON, EXCEPT THE FATHER. BEWARE, BE AWAKE.

13:26 Dan. 7:13   **13:33** text: ASVmg HSV NASB NIV NEB TEV NJB NRSV. add καὶ προσεύχεσθε (and pray): KJV ASV RSVmg NIVmg NEBmg NRSVmg.

οὐκ οἴδατε γὰρ πότε ὁ καιρός ἐστιν. **13.34** ὡς
FOR~YOU° DO NOT KNOW   WHEN THE TIME IS.   AS

ἄνθρωπος ἀπόδημος ἀφεὶς   τὴν οἰκίαν αὐτοῦ καὶ
A MAN   HAVING LEFT~ON A JOURNEY [LEFT] THE HOUSE OF HIM AND

δοὺς   τοῖς δούλοις αὐτοῦ τὴν ἐξουσίαν ἑκάστῳ τὸ
HAVING GIVEN TO THE SLAVES OF HIM -   AUTHORITY, TO EACH THE

ἔργον αὐτοῦ καὶ τῷ   θυρωρῷ   ἐνετείλατο ἵνα
WORK OF HIM AND TO THE DOORKEEPER HE COMMANDED THAT

γρηγορῇ.   **13.35** γρηγορεῖτε οὖν·   οὐκ οἴδατε γὰρ
HE SHOULD BE ALERT.   THEREFORE~YOU° BE ALERT. FOR~YOU° DO NOT KNOW

πότε ὁ . κύριος τῆς οἰκίας ἔρχεται, ἢ   ὀψὲ   ἢ
WHEN THE LORD OF THE HOUSE COMES, EITHER LATE IN THE DAY OR

μεσονύκτιον ἢ ἀλεκτοροφωνίας ἢ πρωΐ, **13.36** μὴ
MIDNIGHT   OR [AT THE] CROWING OR EARLY,   LEST

ἐλθὼν   ἐξαίφνης εὕρῃ ὑμᾶς καθεύδοντας.
HAVING COME SUDDENLY HE FINDS YOU° SLEEPING.

13.37 ὃ δὲ   ὑμῖν λέγω πᾶσιν λέγω, γρηγορεῖτε.
AND~WHAT I SAY~TO YOU° I SAY~TO EVERYONE, BE ON THE ALERT.

for you do not know when the time will come. [34]It is like a man going on a journey, when he leaves home and puts his slaves in charge, each with his work, and commands the doorkeeper to be on the watch. [35]Therefore, keep awake—for you do not know when the master of the house will come, in the evening, or at midnight, or at cockcrow, or at dawn, [36]or else he may find you asleep when he comes suddenly. [37]And what I say to you I say to all: Keep awake."

14.1 Ἦν δὲ τὸ πάσχα καὶ τὰ   ἄζυμα
NOW~IT WAS THE PASSOVER AND THE [FEAST OF] UNLEAVENED BREAD

μετὰ δύο ἡμέρας. καὶ ἐζήτουν οἱ ἀρχιερεῖς καὶ οἱ
AFTER TWO DAYS.   AND WERE SEEKING THE CHIEF PRIESTS AND THE

γραμματεῖς πῶς αὐτὸν ἐν δόλῳ κρατήσαντες
SCRIBES   HOW HIM   BY DECEIT HAVING SEIZED

ἀποκτείνωσιν· **14.2** ἔλεγον γάρ, Μὴ ἐν τῇ ἑορτῇ,
THEY MIGHT KILL.   FOR~THEY WERE SAYING, NOT AT THE FEAST,

μήποτε ἔσται   θόρυβος τοῦ λαοῦ.
LEST   THERE WILL BE A DISTURBANCE OF THE PEOPLE.

14.3 Καὶ ὄντος αὐτοῦ ἐν Βηθανίᾳ ἐν τῇ οἰκίᾳ
AND   HE~BEING   IN BETHANY AT THE HOUSE

Σίμωνος τοῦ λεπροῦ, κατακειμένου αὐτοῦ ἦλθεν γυνὴ
OF SIMON THE LEPER,   HE~RECLINING,   CAME A WOMAN

ἔχουσα ἀλάβαστρον μύρου   νάρδου πιστικῆς
HAVING AN ALABASTER [JAR] OF OINTMENT, PURE~NARD [WHICH WAS]

πολυτελοῦς, συντρίψασα τὴν ἀλάβαστρον κατέχεεν
EXPENSIVE, HAVING BROKEN THE ALABASTER [JAR] SHE POURED [IT ON]

αὐτοῦ τῆς κεφαλῆς. **14.4** ἦσαν δὲ τινες ἀγανακτοῦντες
HIS   -   HEAD.   ³WERE ¹NOW ²SOME BEING ANGRY

πρὸς ἑαυτούς, Εἰς τί   ἡ ἀπώλεια αὕτη τοῦ
WITH THEMSELVES, FOR WHAT [REASON HAS] - THIS~WASTE -

μύρου   γέγονεν; **14.5** ἠδύνατο γὰρ τοῦτο τὸ μύρον
OF OINTMENT TAKEN PLACE? ⁴WAS ABLE ¹FOR ²THIS - ³OINTMENT

πραθῆναι ἐπάνω δηναρίων τριακοσίων καὶ δοθῆναι
TO BE SOLD [FOR] MORE THAN THREE HUNDRED~DENARII AND TO BE GIVEN

It was two days before the Passover and the festival of Unleavened Bread. The chief priests and the scribes were looking for a way to arrest Jesus[w] by stealth and kill him; [2]for they said, "Not during the festival, or there may be a riot among the people."

3 While he was at Bethany in the house of Simon the leper,[x] as he sat at the table, a woman came with an alabaster jar of very costly ointment of nard, and she broke open the jar and poured the ointment on his head. [4]But some were there who said to one another in anger, "Why was the ointment wasted in this way? [5]For this ointment could have been sold for more than three hundred denarii,[y] and the money

[w] Gk *him*
[x] The terms *leper* and *leprosy* can refer to several diseases
[y] The *denarius* was the usual day's wage for a laborer

given to the poor." And they
scolded her. 6But Jesus said,
"Let her alone; why do you
trouble her? She has
performed a good service
for me. 7For you always
have the poor with you, and
you can show kindness to
them whenever you wish;
but you will not always have
me. 8She has done what she
could; she has anointed my
body beforehand for its
burial. 9Truly I tell you,
wherever the good news[z] is
proclaimed in the whole
world, what she has done
will be told in remembrance
of her."

10 Then Judas Iscariot,
who was one of the twelve,
went to the chief priests in
order to betray him to them.
11When they heard it, they
were greatly pleased, and
promised to give him
money. So he began to look
for an opportunity to betray
him.

12 On the first day of
Unleavened Bread, when
the Passover lamb is
sacrificed, his disciples said
to him, "Where do you want
us to go and make the
preparations for you to eat
the Passover?" 13So he sent
two of his disciples, saying
to them, "Go into the city,
and a man carrying a jar
of water will meet you;
follow him, 14and wher-
ever he enters, say to
the owner of the house,
'The Teacher asks, Where
is my guest room where

[z] Or gospel

τοῖς   πτωχοῖς·   καὶ   ἐνεβριμῶντο   αὐτῇ.   **14.6** ὁ   δὲ
TO THE   POOR.   AND   THEY WERE REPROACHING HER.   - BUT

Ἰησοῦς   εἶπεν,   Ἄφετε   αὐτήν·   τί   αὐτῇ   κόπους
JESUS   SAID,   LEAVE   HER [ALONE]. WHY 2HER   3TROUBLE

παρέχετε;   καλὸν   ἔργον   ἠργάσατο   ἐν   ἐμοί.
1DO YOU° CAUSE? A GOOD   WORK   SHE HAS PERFORMED ON   ME.

14.7 πάντοτε   γὰρ   τοὺς   πτωχοὺς   ἔχετε   μεθ᾽   ἑαυτῶν   καὶ
FOR~ALWAYS   THE   POOR   YOU° HAVE   WITH   YOURSELVES   AND

ὅταν   θέλητε   δύνασθε   αὐτοῖς   εὖ   ποιῆσαι,   ἐμὲ   δὲ   οὐ
WHEN   YOU° WISH   YOU° ARE ABLE FOR THEM TO DO~GOOD, BUT~ME   NOT

πάντοτε   ἔχετε.   **14.8** ὃ   ἔσχεν   ἐποίησεν·
ALWAYS   DO YOU° HAVE.   WHAT   SHE HAD   SHE DID.

προέλαβεν   μυρίσαι   τὸ   σῶμά   μου   εἰς   τὸν
SHE PREPARED AHEAD OF TIME TO ANOINT THE BODY   OF ME FOR   THE

ἐνταφιασμόν.   **14.9** ἀμὴν   δὲ   λέγω   ὑμῖν,   ὅπου   ἐὰν
BURIAL.   AND~TRULY   I SAY   TO YOU°, WHEREVER

κηρυχθῇ   τὸ   εὐαγγέλιον   εἰς   ὅλον   τὸν   κόσμον,   καὶ   ὃ
IS PREACHED THE GOOD NEWS   IN [THE] WHOLE -   WORLD,   ALSO   WHAT

ἐποίησεν   αὕτη   λαληθήσεται   εἰς   μνημόσυνον   αὐτῆς.
THIS [WOMAN]~DID   WILL BE SPOKEN   IN   MEMORY   OF HER.

14.10 Καὶ   Ἰούδας   Ἰσκαριὼθ   ὁ   εἷς   τῶν   δώδεκα
AND   JUDAS   ISCARIOT   -   ONE   OF THE TWELVE

ἀπῆλθεν   πρὸς   τοὺς   ἀρχιερεῖς   ἵνα   αὐτὸν   παραδοῖ
WENT   TO   THE   CHIEF PRIESTS IN ORDER THAT HE MIGHT BETRAY~HIM

αὐτοῖς.   **14.11** οἱ   δὲ   ἀκούσαντες   ἐχάρησαν   καὶ
TO THEM.   AND~THE ONES HAVING HEARD   REJOICED   AND

ἐπηγγείλαντο   αὐτῷ   ἀργύριον   δοῦναι.   καὶ   ἐζήτει
PROMISED   2HIM   3MONEY   1TO GIVE.   AND   HE WAS SEEKING

πῶς   αὐτὸν   εὐκαίρως   παραδοῖ.
HOW   2HIM   3CONVENIENTLY 1HE MIGHT BETRAY.

14.12 Καὶ   τῇ   πρώτῃ   ἡμέρᾳ   τῶν   ἀζύμων,
AND   ON THE FIRST   DAY   OF THE [FEAST OF] UNLEAVENED BREAD,

ὅτε   τὸ   πάσχα   ἔθυον,   λέγουσιν   αὐτῷ   οἱ
WHEN THE   PASSOVER [LAMB] WAS BEING SACRIFICED, SAY   TO HIM   THE

μαθηταὶ   αὐτοῦ,   Ποῦ   θέλεις   ἀπελθόντες   ἑτοιμάσωμεν
DISCIPLES   OF HIM,   WHERE   DO YOU WISH HAVING GONE   WE MAY PREPARE

ἵνα   φάγῃς   τὸ   πάσχα;   **14.13** καὶ   ἀποστέλλει   δύο
THAT   YOU MAY EAT THE PASSOVER [LAMB]?   AND   HE SENDS   TWO

τῶν   μαθητῶν   αὐτοῦ   καὶ   λέγει   αὐτοῖς,   Ὑπάγετε   εἰς
OF THE DISCIPLES   OF HIM   AND   HE SAYS   TO THEM,   GO   INTO

τὴν   πόλιν,   καὶ   ἀπαντήσει   ὑμῖν   ἄνθρωπος   κεράμιον
THE   CITY,   AND   WILL MEET   YOU°   A MAN   2A JAR

ὕδατος   βαστάζων·   ἀκολουθήσατε   αὐτῷ   **14.14** καὶ
3OF WATER 1CARRYING;   FOLLOW   HIM   AND

ὅπου   ἐὰν   εἰσέλθῃ   εἴπατε   τῷ   οἰκοδεσπότῃ   ὅτι   Ὁ
WHEREVER HE ENTERS   TELL   THE   MASTER OF THE HOUSE THAT   THE

διδάσκαλος   λέγει,   Ποῦ   ἐστιν   τὸ   κατάλυμά   μου   ὅπου
TEACHER   SAYS,   WHERE   IS   THE   GUEST ROOM   OF ME WHERE

τὸ πάσχα μετὰ τῶν μαθητῶν μου φάγω; **14.15** καὶ
THE PASSOVER WITH THE DISCIPLES OF ME I MAY EAT? AND

αὐτὸς ὑμῖν δείξει ἀνάγαιον μέγα ἐστρωμένον
HE WILL SHOW~YOU° A LARGE~ UPSTAIRS ROOM HAVING BEEN FURNISHED [AND]

ἕτοιμον· καὶ ἐκεῖ ἑτοιμάσατε ἡμῖν. **14.16** καὶ
READY. AND THERE PREPARE [THE MEAL] FOR US. AND

ἐξῆλθον οἱ μαθηταὶ καὶ ἦλθον εἰς τὴν πόλιν καὶ
WENT OUT THE DISCIPLES AND THEY CAME INTO THE CITY AND

εὗρον καθὼς εἶπεν αὐτοῖς καὶ ἡτοίμασαν τὸ
FOUND [THINGS] JUST AS HE TOLD THEM AND THEY PREPARED THE

πάσχα. **14.17** Καὶ ὀψίας γενομένης ἔρχεται μετὰ
PASSOVER [LAMB]. AND EVENING HAVING COME HE COMES WITH

τῶν δώδεκα. **14.18** καὶ ἀνακειμένων αὐτῶν καὶ
THE TWELVE. AND THEY~RECLINING AND

ἐσθιόντων ὁ Ἰησοῦς εἶπεν, Ἀμὴν λέγω ὑμῖν ὅτι εἷς
EATING - JESUS SAID, TRULY I SAY TO YOU° THAT ONE

ἐξ ὑμῶν παραδώσει με ὁ ἐσθίων μετ' ἐμοῦ.
OF YOU° WILL BETRAY ME THE ONE EATING WITH ME.

14.19 ἤρξαντο λυπεῖσθαι καὶ λέγειν αὐτῷ εἷς κατὰ
THEY BEGAN TO BE SORROWFUL AND TO SAY TO HIM ONE BY

εἷς, Μήτι ἐγώ; **14.20** ὁ δὲ εἶπεν αὐτοῖς, Εἷς τῶν
ONE, [SURELY] NOT I? - AND HE SAID TO THEM, ONE OF THE

δώδεκα, ὁ ἐμβαπτόμενος μετ' ἐμοῦ εἰς τὸ τρύβλιον.
TWELVE, THE ONE DIPPING WITH ME INTO THE BOWL.

14.21 ὅτι ὁ μὲν υἱὸς τοῦ ἀνθρώπου ὑπάγει καθὼς
FOR THE - SON - OF MAN GOES JUST AS

γέγραπται περὶ αὐτοῦ, οὐαὶ δὲ τῷ ἀνθρώπῳ ἐκείνῳ
IT HAS BEEN WRITTEN CONCERNING HIM, BUT~WOE - TO THAT~MAN

δι' οὗ ὁ υἱὸς τοῦ ἀνθρώπου παραδίδοται·
THROUGH WHOM THE SON - OF MAN IS BETRAYED.

καλὸν αὐτῷ εἰ οὐκ ἐγεννήθη ὁ
[IT WOULD HAVE BEEN] BETTER FOR HIM IF HAD NOT BEEN BORN -

ἄνθρωπος ἐκεῖνος.
THAT~MAN.

14.22 Καὶ ἐσθιόντων αὐτῶν λαβὼν ἄρτον
AND THEY~EATING HAVING TAKEN BREAD [AND]

εὐλογήσας ἔκλασεν καὶ ἔδωκεν αὐτοῖς καὶ εἶπεν,
HAVING BLESSED [IT] HE BROKE [IT] AND GAVE [IT] TO THEM AND SAID,

Λάβετε, τοῦτό ἐστιν τὸ σῶμά μου. **14.23** καὶ λαβὼν
TAKE [IT] THIS IS THE BODY OF ME. AND HAVING TAKEN

ποτήριον εὐχαριστήσας ἔδωκεν αὐτοῖς, καὶ ἔπιον ἐξ
A CUP [AND] HAVING GIVEN THANKS HE GAVE [IT] TO THEM, AND DRANK OF

αὐτοῦ πάντες. **14.24** καὶ εἶπεν αὐτοῖς, Τοῦτό ἐστιν τὸ
IT EVERYONE. AND HE SAID TO THEM, THIS IS THE

αἷμά μου τῆς ⌐διαθήκης τὸ ἐκχυννόμενον
BLOOD OF ME OF THE COVENANT THE [BLOOD WHICH] IS BEING POURED OUT

I may eat the Passover with my disciples?' [15]He will show you a large room upstairs, furnished and ready. Make preparations for us there." [16]So the disciples set out and went to the city, and found everything as he had told them; and they prepared the Passover meal.

17 When it was evening, he came with the twelve. [18]And when they had taken their places and were eating, Jesus said, "Truly I tell you, one of you will betray me, one who is eating with me." [19]They began to be distressed and to say to him one after another, "Surely, not I?" [20]He said to them, "It is one of the twelve, one who is dipping bread[a] into the bowl[b] with me. [21]For the Son of Man goes as it is written of him, but woe to that one by whom the Son of Man is betrayed! It would have been better for that one not to have been born."

22 While they were eating, he took a loaf of bread, and after blessing it he broke it, gave it to them, and said, "Take; this is my body." [23]Then he took a cup, and after giving thanks he gave it to them, and all of them drank from it. [24]He said to them, "This is my blood of the[c] covenant, which is poured out

[a] Gk lacks *bread*
[b] Other ancient authorities read *same bowl*
[c] Other ancient authorities add *new*

14:24 text: ASV RSV NASB NIV NEB TEV NJB NRSV. add καινης (new) [see Luke 22:20; 1 Cor. 11:25]: KJV ASVmg RSVmg NIVmg NRSVmg.

for many. ²⁵Truly I tell you, I will never again drink of the fruit of the vine until that day when I drink it new in the kingdom of God."

26 When they had sung the hymn, they went out to the Mount of Olives. ²⁷And Jesus said to them, "You will all become deserters; for it is written,

'I will strike the shepherd,
and the sheep will be scattered.'

²⁸But after I am raised up, I will go before you to Galilee." ²⁹Peter said to him, "Even though all become deserters, I will not." ³⁰Jesus said to him, "Truly I tell you, this day, this very night, before the cock crows twice, you will deny me three times." ³¹But he said vehemently, "Even though I must die with you, I will not deny you." And all of them said the same.

32 They went to a place called Gethsemane; and he said to his disciples, "Sit here while I pray." ³³He took with him Peter and James and John, and began to be distressed and agitated.

· ὑπὲρ πολλῶν. **14.25** ἀμὴν λέγω ὑμῖν ὅτι οὐκέτι
FOR MANY. TRULY I SAY TO YOU° THAT NO LONGER

οὐ μὴ πίω ἐκ τοῦ γενήματος τῆς ἀμπέλου ἕως
WILL I BY ANY MEANS DRINK OF THE FRUIT OF THE VINE UNTIL

τῆς ἡμέρας ἐκείνης ὅταν αὐτὸ πίνω καινὸν ἐν τῇ
- THAT~DAY WHEN I DRINK~IT NEW IN THE

βασιλείᾳ τοῦ θεοῦ. **14.26** Καὶ ὑμνήσαντες ἐξῆλθον
KINGDOM - OF GOD. AND HAVING SUNG A HYMN THEY WENT OUT

εἰς τὸ Ὄρος τῶν Ἐλαιῶν.
TO THE MOUNT - OF OLIVES.

14.27 Καὶ λέγει αὐτοῖς ὁ Ἰησοῦς ὅτι Πάντες
AND SAYS TO THEM - JESUS - EVERY [ONE OF]

σκανδαλισθήσεσθε, ὅτι γέγραπται,
YOU° WILL FALL AWAY, FOR IT HAS BEEN WRITTEN,

Πατάξω τὸν ποιμένα,
I WILL STRIKE DOWN THE SHEPHERD,

καὶ τὰ πρόβατα διασκορπισθήσονται.
AND THE SHEEP WILL BE SCATTERED.

14.28 ἀλλὰ μετὰ τὸ ἐγερθῆναί με προάξω ὑμᾶς εἰς
BUT AFTER I~AM RAISED I WILL GO BEFORE YOU° INTO

τὴν Γαλιλαίαν. **14.29** ὁ δὲ Πέτρος ἔφη αὐτῷ, Εἰ καὶ
- GALILEE. - BUT PETER SAID TO HIM, EVEN~IF

πάντες σκανδαλισθήσονται, ἀλλ᾽ οὐκ ἐγώ. **14.30** καὶ
EVERYONE WILL FALL AWAY, YET I [WILL] NOT. AND

λέγει αὐτῷ ὁ Ἰησοῦς, Ἀμὴν λέγω σοι ὅτι σὺ
SAYS TO HIM - JESUS, TRULY I SAY TO YOU THAT YOU

σήμερον ταύτῃ τῇ νυκτὶ πρὶν ἢ δὶς ἀλέκτορα φωνῆσαι
TODAY THIS - NIGHT BEFORE ³TWICE ¹A ROOSTER ²CROWS

τρίς με ἀπαρνήσῃ. **14.31** ὁ δὲ ἐκπερισσῶς
⁶THREE [TIMES] ⁵ME ⁴YOU WILL DENY. - BUT WITH GREAT EMPHASIS

ἐλάλει, Ἐὰν δέῃ με συναποθανεῖν σοι,
HE WAS SAYING, IF IT IS NECCESSARY [FOR] ME TO DIE FOR YOU,

οὐ μὴ σε ἀπαρνήσομαι. ὡσαύτως δὲ καὶ πάντες
BY NO MEANS WILL I DENY~YOU. AND~LIKEWISE ALSO EVERYONE

ἔλεγον.
SPOKE.

14.32 Καὶ ἔρχονται εἰς χωρίον οὗ τὸ ὄνομα
AND THEY COME TO A PLACE OF WHICH THE NAME [WAS]

Γεθσημανὶ καὶ λέγει τοῖς μαθηταῖς αὐτοῦ, Καθίσατε
GETHSEMANE AND HE SAYS TO THE DISCIPLES OF HIM, SIT DOWN

ὧδε ἕως προσεύξωμαι. **14.33** καὶ παραλαμβάνει τὸν
HERE WHILE I PRAY. AND HE TAKES -

Πέτρον καὶ [τὸν] Ἰάκωβον καὶ [τὸν] Ἰωάννην μετ᾽
PETER AND - JAMES AND - JOHN WITH

αὐτοῦ καὶ ἤρξατο ἐκθαμβεῖσθαι καὶ ἀδημονεῖν
HIM AND HE BEGAN TO BE DISTRESSED AND TO BE TROUBLED

14:27 Zech. 13:7

14.34 καὶ   λέγει   αὐτοῖς,   Περίλυπός   ἐστιν   ἡ   ψυχή   μου
AND   HE SAYS   TO THEM,   ⁵VERY SAD   ⁴IS   ¹THE   ²SOUL   ³OF ME

ἕως   θανάτου·   μείνατε   ὧδε   καὶ   γρηγορεῖτε.   **14.35** καὶ
UNTO   DEATH.   REMAIN   HERE   AND   STAY AWAKE.   AND

προελθὼν   μικρὸν   ἔπιπτεν   ἐπὶ   τῆς   γῆς   καὶ
HAVING GONE FORTH   A LITTLE   HE WAS FALLING   ON   THE   GROUND   AND

προσηύχετο   ἵνα   εἰ   δυνατόν   ἐστιν   παρέλθῃ   ἀπ'   αὐτοῦ
WAS PRAYING   THAT   IF   IT IS~POSSIBLE   ³MIGHT PASS AWAY   ⁴FROM   ⁵HIM

ἡ   ὥρα,   **14.36** καὶ   ἔλεγεν,   Αββα ὁ   πατήρ,   πάντα
¹THE   ²HOUR,   AND   HE WAS SAYING,   ABBA   -   FATHER,   ALL THINGS [ARE]

δυνατά   σοι·   παρένεγκε   τὸ   ποτήριον   τοῦτο   ἀπ'   ἐμοῦ·
POSSIBLE   FOR YOU.   TAKE AWAY   -   THIS~CUP   FROM   ME.

ἀλλ'   οὐ   τί   ἐγὼ   θέλω   ἀλλὰ   τί   σύ.   **14.37** καὶ
BUT   NOT   WHAT   I   WILL   BUT   WHAT   YOU [WILL].   AND

ἔρχεται   καὶ   εὑρίσκει   αὐτοὺς   καθεύδοντας,   καὶ   λέγει
HE COMES   AND   FINDS   THEM   SLEEPING,   AND   HE SAYS

τῷ   Πέτρῳ,   Σίμων,   καθεύδεις;   οὐκ   ἴσχυσας
-   TO PETER,   SIMON,   ARE YOU SLEEPING?   WERE YOU NOT STRONG [ENOUGH]

μίαν   ὥραν   γρηγορῆσαι;   **14.38** γρηγορεῖτε   καὶ
²ONE   ³HOUR   ¹TO STAY AWAKE?   STAY AWAKE   AND

προσεύχεσθε,   ἵνα   μὴ   ἔλθητε   εἰς   πειρασμόν·   τὸ   μὲν
PRAY   THAT   YOU° MAY NOT COME   INTO   TEMPTATION.   INDEED~THE

πνεῦμα   πρόθυμον   ἡ   δὲ   σὰρξ   ἀσθενής.   **14.39** καὶ
SPIRIT [IS]   READY   BUT~THE   FLESH [IS]   WEAK.   AND

πάλιν   ἀπελθὼν   προσηύξατο   τὸν   αὐτὸν   λόγον
AGAIN   HAVING GONE AWAY   HE PRAYED   ²THE   ³SAME   ⁴WORD

εἰπών.   **14.40** καὶ   πάλιν   ἐλθὼν   εὗρεν   αὐτοὺς
¹HAVING SAID.   AND   AGAIN   HAVING COME   HE FOUND   THEM

καθεύδοντας,   ἦσαν   γὰρ   αὐτῶν   οἱ   ὀφθαλμοὶ
SLEEPING,   ⁵WERE   ¹FOR   ⁴OF THEM   ²THE   ³EYES

καταβαρυνόμενοι,   καὶ   οὐκ   ᾔδεισαν   τί   ἀποκριθῶσιν
FALLING SHUT   AND   THEY DID NOT KNOW   WHAT   THEY MIGHT ANSWER

αὐτῷ.   **14.41** καὶ   ἔρχεται   τὸ   τρίτον   καὶ   λέγει
HIM.   AND   HE COMES   -   A THIRD [TIME]   AND   SAYS

αὐτοῖς,   Καθεύδετε   τὸ   λοιπὸν   καὶ   ἀναπαύεσθε·   ἀπέχει·
TO THEM,   SLEEP [FOR]   THE   REMAINDER   AND   REST.   IT IS ENOUGH.

ἦλθεν   ἡ   ὥρα,   ἰδοὺ   παραδίδοται   ὁ   υἱὸς   τοῦ
HAS COME   THE   HOUR,   BEHOLD   ⁴IS BETRAYED   ¹THE   ²SON   -

ἀνθρώπου   εἰς   τὰς   χεῖρας   τῶν   ἁμαρτωλῶν.
³OF MAN   INTO   THE   HANDS   -   OF SINNERS.

14.42 ἐγείρεσθε   ἄγωμεν·   ἰδοὺ   ὁ   παραδιδούς   με
GET UP,   LET US GO.   BEHOLD   THE   ONE BETRAYING   ME

ἤγγικεν.
HAS DRAWN NEAR.

14.43 Καὶ   εὐθὺς   ἔτι   αὐτοῦ   λαλοῦντος   παραγίνεται
AND   IMMEDIATELY   WHILE   HE   IS SPEAKING   ARRIVES

Ἰούδας   εἷς   τῶν   δώδεκα   καὶ   μετ'   αὐτοῦ   ὄχλος   μετὰ
JUDAS,   ONE   OF THE TWELVE,   AND   WITH   HIM   A CROWD   WITH

34And he said to them, "I am deeply grieved, even to death; remain here, and keep awake." 35And going a little farther, he threw himself on the ground and prayed that, if it were possible, the hour might pass from him. 36He said, "Abba,ᵈ Father, for you all things are possible; remove this cup from me; yet, not what I want, but what you want." 37He came and found them sleeping; and he said to Peter, "Simon, are you asleep? Could you not keep awake one hour? 38Keep awake and pray that you may not come into the time of trial;ᵉ the spirit indeed is willing, but the flesh is weak." 39And again he went away and prayed, saying the same words. 40And once more he came and found them sleeping, for their eyes were very heavy; and they did not know what to say to him. 41He came a third time and said to them, "Are you still sleeping and taking your rest? Enough! The hour has come; the Son of Man is betrayed into the hands of sinners. 42Get up, let us be going. See, my betrayer is at hand."

43 Immediately, while he was still speaking, Judas, one of the twelve, arrived; and with him there was a crowd with

ᵈ Aramaic for *Father*
ᵉ Or *into temptation*

swords and clubs, from the chief priests, the scribes, and the elders. ⁴⁴Now the betrayer had given them a sign, saying, "The one I will kiss is the man; arrest him and lead him away under guard." ⁴⁵So when he came, he went up to him at once and said, "Rabbi!" and kissed him. ⁴⁶Then they laid hands on him and arrested him. ⁴⁷But one of those who stood near drew his sword and struck the slave of the high priest, cutting off his ear. ⁴⁸Then Jesus said to them, "Have you come out with swords and clubs to arrest me as though I were a bandit? ⁴⁹Day after day I was with you in the temple teaching, and you did not arrest me. But let the scriptures be fulfilled." ⁵⁰All of them deserted him and fled.

51 A certain young man was following him, wearing nothing but a linen cloth. They caught hold of him, ⁵²but he left the linen cloth and ran off naked.

53 They took Jesus to the high priest; and all the chief priests, the elders, and the scribes were assembled. ⁵⁴Peter

μαχαιρῶν καὶ ξύλων παρὰ τῶν ἀρχιερέων καὶ τῶν
SWORDS AND CLUBS WITH THE CHIEF PRIESTS AND THE

γραμματέων καὶ τῶν πρεσβυτέρων. **14.44** δεδώκει δὲ
SCRIBES AND THE ELDERS. ⁵HAD GIVEN ¹NOW

ὁ παραδιδοὺς αὐτὸν σύσσημον αὐτοῖς λέγων,
²THE ONE ³BETRAYING ⁴HIM A SIGNAL TO THEM SAYING,

῝Ον ἂν φιλήσω αὐτός ἐστιν, κρατήσατε αὐτὸν καὶ
WHOMEVER I MAY KISS HE IS [THE ONE], SEIZE HIM, AND

ἀπάγετε ἀσφαλῶς. **14.45** καὶ ἐλθὼν εὐθὺς
LEAD [HIM] AWAY UNDER GUARD. AND HAVING COME IMMEDIATELY

προσελθὼν αὐτῷ λέγει, ᾿Ραββί, καὶ κατεφίλησεν
HAVING APPROACHED HIM HE SAYS, RABBI, AND HE KISSED

αὐτόν· **14.46** οἱ δὲ ἐπέβαλον τὰς χεῖρας αὐτῷ καὶ
HIM. - AND THEY LAID ON THE (THEIR) HANDS ON HIM AND

ἐκράτησαν αὐτόν. **14.47** εἷς δέ [τις] τῶν
ARRESTED HIM. ³ONE ¹BUT ²A CERTAIN OF THE ONES

παρεστηκότων σπασάμενος τὴν μάχαιραν ἔπαισεν τὸν
HAVING STOOD BY HAVING DRAWN THE SWORD, STRUCK THE

δοῦλον τοῦ ἀρχιερέως καὶ ἀφεῖλεν αὐτοῦ τὸ ὠτάριον.
SLAVE OF THE HIGH PRIEST AND CUT OFF HIS - EAR.

14.48 καὶ ἀποκριθεὶς ὁ ᾿Ιησοῦς εἶπεν αὐτοῖς, ῾Ως ἐπὶ
AND HAVING ANSWERED - JESUS SAID TO THEM, AS AGAINST

λῃστὴν ἐξήλθατε μετὰ μαχαιρῶν καὶ ξύλων
A THIEF DO YOU° COME OUT WITH SWORDS AND CLUBS

συλλαβεῖν με; **14.49** καθ᾿ ἡμέραν ἤμην πρὸς ὑμᾶς ἐν
TO SEIZE ME? EVERY DAY I WAS WITH YOU° IN

τῷ ἱερῷ διδάσκων καὶ οὐκ ἐκρατήσατέ με· ἀλλ᾿
THE TEMPLE TEACHING AND YOU° DID NOT ARREST ME; BUT

ἵνα πληρωθῶσιν αἱ γραφαί. **14.50** καὶ ἀφέντες
IN ORDER THAT ³MIGHT BE FULFILLED ¹THE ²SCRIPTURES. AND HAVING LEFT

αὐτὸν ἔφυγον πάντες.
HIM EVERYONE~FLED.

14.51 Καὶ νεανίσκος τις συνηκολούθει αὐτῷ
AND A CERTAIN~YOUNG MAN WAS FOLLOWING ALONG WITH HIM

περιβεβλημένος σινδόνα ἐπὶ γυμνοῦ, καὶ
HAVING BEEN CLOTHED WITH A LINEN GARMENT OVER [HIS] NAKED [BODY], AND

κρατοῦσιν αὐτόν· **14.52** ὁ δὲ καταλιπὼν τὴν σινδόνα
THEY SEIZE HIM. BUT~HE HAVING LEFT BEHIND THE LINEN GARMENT

γυμνὸς ἔφυγεν.
FLED~NAKED.

14.53 Καὶ ἀπήγαγον τὸν ᾿Ιησοῦν πρὸς τὸν ἀρχιερέα,
AND THEY LED AWAY - JESUS TO THE HIGH PRIEST,

καὶ συνέρχονται πάντες οἱ ἀρχιερεῖς καὶ οἱ
AND GATHER TOGETHER ALL THE CHIEF PRIESTS AND THE

πρεσβύτεροι καὶ οἱ γραμματεῖς. **14.54** καὶ ὁ Πέτρος
ELDERS AND THE SCRIBES. AND - PETER

ἀπὸ μακρόθεν ἠκολούθησεν αὐτῷ ἕως ἕσω εἰς τὴν
FROM   A DISTANCE   FOLLOWED   HIM   UNTIL INSIDE IN   THE

αὐλὴν τοῦ ἀρχιερέως καὶ ἦν συγκαθήμενος μετὰ τῶν
COURTYARD OF THE HIGH PRIEST AND HE WAS SITTING TOGETHER WITH THE

ὑπηρετῶν καὶ θερμαινόμενος πρὸς τὸ φῶς.
SERVANTS   AND   WARMING HIMSELF   NEAR   THE LIGHT [OF THE FIRE].

14.55 οἱ δὲ ἀρχιερεῖς καὶ ὅλον   τὸ συνέδριον ἐζήτουν
       AND~THE CHIEF PRIESTS AND [THE] ENTIRE - COUNCIL   WERE SEEKING

κατὰ τοῦ Ἰησοῦ μαρτυρίαν εἰς   τὸ θανατῶσαι
AGAINST - JESUS   A WITNESS IN ORDER TO - PUT TO DEATH

αὐτόν, καὶ οὐχ ηὕρισκον·   **14.56** πολλοὶ γὰρ
HIM,   AND THEY WERE NOT FINDING [ANY].   FOR~MANY

ἐψευδομαρτύρουν κατ' αὐτοῦ, καὶ ἴσαι   αἱ μαρτυρίαι
WERE TESTIFYING FALSELY AGAINST HIM, AND 4IDENTICAL 1THE 2TESTIMONIES

οὐκ ἦσαν. **14.57** καὶ τινες ἀναστάντες ἐψευδομαρτύρουν
3WERE NOT.   AND SOME HAVING STOOD UP WERE TESTIFYING FALSELY

κατ' αὐτοῦ λέγοντες **14.58** ὅτι Ἡμεῖς ἠκούσαμεν αὐτοῦ
AGAINST HIM SAYING   -   WE   HEARD   HIM

λέγοντος ὅτι Ἐγὼ καταλύσω τὸν ναὸν τοῦτον τὸν
SAYING   -   I WILL DESTROY - THIS~TEMPLE   -

χειροποίητον   καὶ διὰ τριῶν ἡμερῶν ἄλλον
MADE WITH HUMAN HANDS AND AFTER THREE DAYS ANOTHER

ἀχειροποίητον οἰκοδομήσω **14.59** καὶ οὐδὲ οὕτως ἴση
NOT MADE WITH HANDS I WILL BUILD   AND 6NOT 1SO 7IDENTICAL

ἦν ἡ μαρτυρία αὐτῶν. **14.60** καὶ ἀναστὰς ὁ
5WAS 2THE 3TESTIMONY 4OF THEM.   AND HAVING STOOD UP THE

ἀρχιερεὺς εἰς μέσον ἐπηρώτησεν τὸν Ἰησοῦν λέγων,
HIGH PRIEST IN [THE] MIDST QUESTIONED -   JESUS   SAYING,

Οὐκ ἀποκρίνῃ οὐδέν   τί οὗτοί σου καταμαρτυροῦσιν;
DO YOU NOT ANSWER ANYTHING [TO] WHAT THESE TESTIFY AGAINST~YOU?

14.61 ὁ δὲ ἐσιώπα καὶ οὐκ ἀπεκρίνατο οὐδέν.   πάλιν
       - BUT HE WAS SILENT AND DID NOT ANSWER ANYTHING. AGAIN

ὁ ἀρχιερεὺς ἐπηρώτα αὐτὸν καὶ λέγει αὐτῷ, Σὺ εἶ
THE HIGH PRIEST WAS QUESTIONING HIM AND HE SAYS TO HIM, ARE~YOU

ὁ Χριστὸς ὁ υἱὸς τοῦ εὐλογητοῦ; **14.62** ὁ δὲ Ἰησοῦς
THE CHRIST THE SON OF THE BLESSED ONE?   - AND JESUS

εἶπεν, Ἐγώ εἰμι,
SAID   I   AM,

    καὶ ὄψεσθε τὸν υἱὸν τοῦ ἀνθρώπου
    AND YOU° WILL SEE THE SON - OF MAN

    ἐκ δεξιῶν καθήμενον τῆς δυνάμεως
    2AT [THE] 3RIGHT [HAND] 1SITTING OF THE POWER

    καὶ ἐρχόμενον μετὰ τῶν νεφελῶν τοῦ
    AND COMING   WITH THE CLOUDS   -

    οὐρανοῦ.
    OF HEAVEN.

14:62a Ps. 110:1   **14:62b** Dan. 7:13

had followed him at a distance, right into the courtyard of the high priest; and he was sitting with the guards, warming himself at the fire. 55Now the chief priests and the whole council were looking for testimony against Jesus to put him to death; but they found none. 56For many gave false testimony against him, and their testimony did not agree. 57Some stood up and gave false testimony against him, saying, 58"We heard him say, 'I will destroy this temple that is made with hands, and in three days I will build another, not made with hands.' " 59But even on this point their testimony did not agree. 60Then the high priest stood up before them and asked Jesus, "Have you no answer? What is it that they testify against you?" 61But he was silent and did not answer. Again the high priest asked him, "Are you the Messiah, *f* the Son of the Blessed One?" 62Jesus said, "I am; and

'you will see the Son of
        Man
seated at the right hand of
        the Power,'
and 'coming with the
        clouds of heaven.' "

f Or *the Christ*

⁶³Then the high priest tore his clothes and said, "Why do we still need witnesses? ⁶⁴You have heard his blasphemy! What is your decision?" All of them condemned him as deserving death. ⁶⁵Some began to spit on him, to blindfold him, and to strike him, saying to him, "Prophesy!" The guards also took him over and beat him.

66 While Peter was below in the courtyard, one of the servant-girls of the high priest came by. ⁶⁷When she saw Peter warming himself, she stared at him and said, "You also were with Jesus, the man from Nazareth." ⁶⁸But he denied it, saying, "I do not know or understand what you are talking about." And he went out into the forecourt.ᵍ Then the cock crowed.ʰ ⁶⁹And the servant-girl, on seeing him, began again to say to the bystanders, "This man is one of them." ⁷⁰But again he denied it. Then after a little while the bystanders again said to Peter, "Certainly you are one of them; for you are a Galilean." ⁷¹But he began to curse, and he swore an oath, "I do not know this man you are talking about." ⁷²At that moment the cock crowed for the second time. Then Peter remembered

ᵍ Or *gateway*
ʰ Other ancient authorities lack *Then the cock crowed*

14.63 ὁ δὲ   ἀρχιερεὺς διαρρήξας τοὺς χιτῶνας αὐτοῦ
AND~THE HIGH PRIEST HAVING TORN   THE   TUNIC   OF HIM

λέγει, Τί   ἔτι   χρείαν ἔχομεν μαρτύρων;
SAYS,   WHAT FURTHER NEED   DO WE HAVE OF WITNESSES?

14.64 ἠκούσατε τῆς βλασφημίας·   τί ὑμῖν φαίνεται;
YOU° HEARD   THE BLASPHEMY.   HOW DOES IT SEEM~TO YOU°?

οἱ δὲ   πάντες κατέκριναν αὐτὸν ἔνοχον εἶναι   θανάτου.
AND~THEY ALL   CONDEMNED   HIM   TO BE~DESERVING OF DEATH.

14.65 Καὶ ἤρξαντό τινες ἐμπτύειν αὐτῷ καὶ
AND   SOME~BEGAN   TO SPIT ON HIM   AND

περικαλύπτειν αὐτοῦ τὸ πρόσωπον καὶ κολαφίζειν
TO COVER   HIS   -   FACE   AND STRIKE

αὐτὸν καὶ λέγειν αὐτῷ, Προφήτευσον, καὶ οἱ
HIM   AND TO SAY TO HIM, PROPHESY,   AND THE

ὑπηρέται ῥαπίσμασιν αὐτὸν ἔλαβον.
SERVANTS ³WITH SLAPS ²HIM ¹RECEIVED.

14.66 Καὶ ὄντος τοῦ Πέτρου κάτω ἐν τῇ αὐλῇ
AND ²BEING - ¹PETER   BELOW IN THE COURTYARD,

ἔρχεται μία τῶν παιδισκῶν τοῦ ἀρχιερέως **14.67** καὶ
COMES   ONE OF THE MAIDS   OF THE HIGH PRIEST   AND

ἰδοῦσα   τὸν Πέτρον θερμαινόμενον ἐμβλέψασα αὐτῷ
HAVING SEEN -   PETER WARMING HIMSELF, HAVING LOOKED AT HIM

λέγει, Καὶ σὺ μετὰ τοῦ Ναζαρηνοῦ ἦσθα τοῦ Ἰησοῦ.
SHE SAYS, YOU~ALSO ²WITH ⁴THE ⁵NAZARENE ¹WERE - ³JESUS.

14.68 ὁ δὲ ἠρνήσατο λέγων, Οὔτε οἶδα   οὔτε ἐπίσταμαι
- BUT HE DENIED [IT] SAYING, I DO NOT KNOW NOR UNDERSTAND

σὺ τί   λέγεις. καὶ ἐξῆλθεν ἔξω   εἰς τὸ προαύλιον
WHAT~YOU ARE SAYING. AND HE WENT OUT OUTSIDE INTO THE ENTRYWAY

⌐[καὶ ἀλέκτωρ ἐφώνησεν].⌐ **14.69** καὶ ἡ παιδίσκη
AND A ROOSTER CROWED.   AND THE MAID

ἰδοῦσα   αὐτὸν ἤρξατο πάλιν λέγειν τοῖς   παρεστῶσιν
HAVING SEEN HIM BEGAN   AGAIN TO SAY TO THE ONES HAVING STOOD BY

ὅτι Οὗτος ἐξ αὐτῶν ἐστιν. **14.70** ὁ δὲ πάλιν
- THIS ONE ²OF ³THEM ¹IS [ONE].   - BUT AGAIN

ἠρνεῖτο.   καὶ μετὰ μικρὸν   πάλιν οἱ
HE WAS DENYING [IT]. AND AFTER A LITTLE [WHILE] AGAIN THE ONES

παρεστῶτες ἔλεγον τῷ Πέτρῳ, Ἀληθῶς ἐξ αὐτῶν
HAVING STOOD BY WERE SAYING - TO PETER, TRULY   ²OF ³THEM

εἶ,   καὶ γὰρ Γαλιλαῖος εἶ. **14.71** ὁ δὲ ἤρξατο
¹YOU ARE [ONE], FOR~INDEED YOU ARE~A GALILEAN.   - AND HE BEGAN

ἀναθεματίζειν καὶ ὀμνύναι ὅτι Οὐκ οἶδα   τὸν
TO CURSE   AND TO SWEAR - I DO NOT KNOW -

ἄνθρωπον τοῦτον ὃν λέγετε. **14.72** καὶ εὐθὺς ἐκ
THIS~MAN   OF WHOM YOU° SPEAK. AND IMMEDIATELY FOR

δευτέρου ἀλέκτωρ ἐφώνησεν. καὶ ἀνεμνήσθη ὁ Πέτρος
A SECOND TIME A ROOSTER CROWED. AND REMEMBERED - PETER

14:68 text: KJV ASV RSVmg NASBmg NIVmg NEBmg TEV NJB NRSV.   omit [see Matt. 26:71; Luke 22:57; John 18:25]: ASVmg RSV NASB NIV NEB TEVmg NRSVmg.

τὸ ῥῆμα ὡς εἶπεν αὐτῷ ὁ Ἰησοῦς ὅτι Πρὶν ἀλέκτορα
THE WORD AS SPOKE TO HIM - JESUS - BEFORE A ROOSTER

φωνῆσαι δὶς τρίς με ἀπαρνήσῃ· καὶ
CROWS TWICE, THREE [TIMES] YOU WILL DENY~ME. AND

ἐπιβαλὼν ἔκλαιεν.
HAVING BROKEN DOWN HE WAS CRYING.

that Jesus had said to him, "Before the cock crows twice, you will deny me three times." And he broke down and wept.

CHAPTER 15

15.1 Καὶ εὐθὺς πρωῒ συμβούλιον ποιήσαντες οἱ
AND IMMEDIATELY EARLY HAVING PREPARED~A COUNCIL, THE

ἀρχιερεῖς μετὰ τῶν πρεσβυτέρων καὶ γραμματέων
CHIEF PRIESTS WITH THE ELDERS AND SCRIBES

καὶ ὅλον τὸ συνέδριον, δήσαντες τὸν Ἰησοῦν
AND [THE] ENTIRE - COUNCIL, HAVING BOUND - JESUS

ἀπήνεγκαν καὶ παρέδωκαν Πιλάτῳ. **15.2** καὶ
THEY LED [HIM] AWAY AND HANDED [HIM] OVER TO PILATE. AND

ἐπηρώτησεν αὐτὸν ὁ Πιλᾶτος, Σὺ εἶ ὁ βασιλεὺς
²QUESTIONED ³HIM - ¹PILATE, ARE~YOU THE KING

τῶν Ἰουδαίων; ὁ δὲ ἀποκριθεὶς αὐτῷ λέγει,
OF THE JEWS? - AND HAVING ANSWERED HIM HE SAYS,

Σὺ λέγεις. **15.3** καὶ κατηγόρουν αὐτοῦ οἱ ἀρχιερεῖς
YOU SAY [SO]~YOURSELF. AND WERE ACCUSING HIM THE CHIEF PRIESTS

πολλά. **15.4** ὁ δὲ Πιλᾶτος πάλιν ἐπηρώτα αὐτὸν
[OF] MANY THINGS. - AND PILATE AGAIN QUESTIONED HIM

λέγων, Οὐκ ἀποκρίνῃ οὐδέν; ἴδε πόσα
SAYING, DO YOU NOT ANSWER ANYTHING? LOOK HOW MANY THINGS

σου κατηγοροῦσιν. **15.5** ὁ δὲ Ἰησοῦς οὐκέτι
THEY ACCUSE~YOU [OF]. - BUT JESUS NO LONGER

οὐδὲν ἀπεκρίθη, ὥστε θαυμάζειν τὸν Πιλᾶτον.
ANSWERED~ANYTHING, SO AS TO AMAZE - PILATE.

15.6 Κατὰ δὲ ἑορτὴν ἀπέλυεν αὐτοῖς ἕνα
NOW~[AT] EVERY FESTIVAL HE WAS RELEASING TO THEM ONE

δέσμιον ὃν παρῃτοῦντο. **15.7** ἦν δὲ ὁ
PRISONER [FOR] WHOM THEY WERE BEGGING. NOW~THERE WAS THE ONE

λεγόμενος Βαραββᾶς μετὰ τῶν στασιαστῶν
BEING CALLED BARABBAS WITH THE FELLOW INSURRECTIONISTS

δεδεμένος οἵτινες ἐν τῇ στάσει φόνον πεποιήκεισαν.
HAVING BEEN BOUND, WHO IN THE UPRISING HAD COMMITTED~MURDER.

15.8 καὶ ἀναβὰς ὁ ὄχλος ἤρξατο αἰτεῖσθαι καθὼς
AND HAVING GONE UP THE CROWD BEGAN TO ASK JUST AS

ἐποίει αὐτοῖς. **15.9** ὁ δὲ Πιλᾶτος ἀπεκρίθη αὐτοῖς
HE USED TO DO FOR THEM. - BUT PILATE ANSWERED THEM

λέγων, Θέλετε ἀπολύσω ὑμῖν τὸν βασιλέα τῶν
SAYING, DO YOU° WISH [THAT] I SHOULD RELEASE TO YOU° THE KING OF THE

As soon as it was morning, the chief priests held a consultation with the elders and scribes and the whole council. They bound Jesus, led him away, and handed him over to Pilate. ²Pilate asked him, "Are you the King of the Jews?" He answered him, "You say so." ³Then the chief priests accused him of many things. ⁴Pilate asked him again, "Have you no answer? See how many charges they bring against you." ⁵But Jesus made no further reply, so that Pilate was amazed.

6 Now at the festival he used to release a prisoner for them, anyone for whom they asked. ⁷Now a man called Barabbas was in prison with the rebels who had committed murder during the insurrection. ⁸So the crowd came and began to ask Pilate to do for them according to his custom. ⁹Then he answered them, "Do you want me to release for you the King of the

Jews?" [10]For he realized that it was out of jealousy that the chief priests had handed him over. [11]But the chief priests stirred up the crowd to have him release Barabbas for them instead. [12]Pilate spoke to them again, "Then what do you wish me to do[i] with the man you call[j] the King of the Jews?" [13]They shouted back, "Crucify him!" [14]Pilate asked them, "Why, what evil has he done?" But they shouted all the more, "Crucify him!" [15]So Pilate, wishing to satisfy the crowd, released Barabbas for them; and after flogging Jesus, he handed him over to be crucified.

16 Then the soldiers led him into the courtyard of the palace (that is, the governor's headquarters[k]); and they called together the whole cohort. [17]And they clothed him in a purple cloak; and after twisting some thorns into a crown, they put it on him. [18]And they began saluting him, "Hail, King of the Jews!" [19]They struck his head with a reed, spat upon him, and knelt down in homage to him. [20]After mocking him, they stripped him of the purple cloak and put

[i] Other ancient authorities read *what should I do*
[j] Other ancient authorities lack *the man you call*
[k] Gk *the praetorium*

Ἰουδαίων; **15.10** ἐγίνωσκεν γὰρ ὅτι διὰ φθόνον
JEWS?   FOR~HE KNEW   THAT BECAUSE OF ENVY

παραδεδώκεισαν αὐτὸν οἱ ἀρχιερεῖς. **15.11** οἱ δὲ
[3]HAD HANDED [HIM] OVER [4]TO HIM [1]THE [2]CHIEF PRIESTS.   BUT~THE

ἀρχιερεῖς ἀνέσεισαν τὸν ὄχλον ἵνα μᾶλλον τὸν
CHIEF PRIESTS INCITED   THE CROWD THAT RATHER   -

Βαραββᾶν ἀπολύσῃ αὐτοῖς. **15.12** ὁ δὲ Πιλᾶτος πάλιν
HE SHOULD RELEASE~BARABBAS TO THEM.   - BUT PILATE   AGAIN

ἀποκριθεὶς ἔλεγεν αὐτοῖς, Τί οὖν [θέλετε]
HAVING ANSWERED WAS SAYING TO THEM, WHAT THEN DO YOU° WISH [THAT]

ποιήσω   [ὃν λέγετε] τὸν βασιλέα τῶν
I SHOULD DO [WITH THE ONE] WHOM YOU° CALL THE KING   OF THE

Ἰουδαίων; **15.13** οἱ δὲ πάλιν ἔκραξαν, Σταύρωσον
JEWS?   - AND AGAIN THEY CRIED OUT, CRUCIFY

αὐτόν. **15.14** ὁ δὲ Πιλᾶτος ἔλεγεν αὐτοῖς, Τί γὰρ
HIM.   - BUT PILATE   WAS SAYING TO THEM, FOR~WHAT

ἐποίησεν κακόν; οἱ δὲ περισσῶς ἔκραξαν, Σταύρωσον
EVIL~DID HE COMMIT? BUT~THEY ALL THE MORE CRIED OUT, CRUCIFY

αὐτόν. **15.15** ὁ δὲ Πιλᾶτος βουλόμενος τῷ ὄχλῳ
HIM.   - SO PILATE,   DESIRING   [2]THE [3]CROWD

τὸ ἱκανὸν ποιῆσαι ἀπέλυσεν αὐτοῖς τὸν Βαραββᾶν,
[1]TO SATISFY   RELEASED TO THEM - BARABBAS,

καὶ παρέδωκεν τὸν Ἰησοῦν φραγελλώσας ἵνα
AND HANDED OVER - JESUS   HAVING SCOURGED [HIM] THAT

σταυρωθῇ.
HE MIGHT BE CRUCIFIED.

15.16 Οἱ δὲ στρατιῶται ἀπήγαγον αὐτὸν ἔσω τῆς
        AND~THE SOLDIERS   LED AWAY   HIM INTO THE

αὐλῆς, ὅ ἐστιν πραιτώριον, καὶ συγκαλοῦσιν
COURTYARD, WHICH IS [THE] PRAETORIUM, AND THEY CALL TOGETHER [THE]

ὅλην τὴν σπεῖραν. **15.17** καὶ ἐνδιδύσκουσιν αὐτὸν
WHOLE - COHORT.   AND THEY CLOTHE   HIM [IN]

πορφύραν καὶ περιτιθέασιν αὐτῷ πλέξαντες
PURPLE   AND PLACE UPON   HIM HAVING BEEN WOVEN

ἀκάνθινον στέφανον· **15.18** καὶ ἤρξαντο ἀσπάζεσθαι
A THORNY   CROWN.   AND THEY BEGAN TO GREET

αὐτόν, Χαῖρε, βασιλεῦ τῶν Ἰουδαίων· **15.19** καὶ
HIM,   HAIL,   KING   OF THE JEWS.   AND

ἔτυπτον αὐτοῦ τὴν κεφαλὴν καλάμῳ καὶ
THEY WERE STRIKING HIM [ON] THE HEAD WITH A STAFF AND

ἐνέπτυον αὐτῷ καὶ τιθέντες τὰ γόνατα
THEY WERE SPITTING ON HIM AND BENDING THE(THEIR) KNEES

προσεκύνουν αὐτῷ. **15.20** καὶ ὅτε ἐνέπαιξαν
THEY WERE BOWING DOWN BEFORE HIM.   AND WHEN THEY RIDICULED

αὐτῷ, ἐξέδυσαν αὐτὸν τὴν πορφύραν καὶ ἐνέδυσαν
HIM,   THEY STRIPPED HIM [OF] THE PURPLE   AND CLOTHED

αὐτὸν τὰ ἱμάτια αὐτοῦ. καὶ ἐξάγουσιν αὐτὸν ἵνα
HIM [IN] THE GARMENTS OF HIM.   AND   THEY LEAD OUT HIM   THAT

σταυρώσωσιν αὐτόν.
THEY MIGHT CRUCIFY HIM.

15.21 Καὶ ἀγγαρεύουσιν παράγοντά τινα   Σίμωνα
     AND   THEY REQUISITION PASSING BY   A CERTAIN SIMON,

Κυρηναῖον ἐρχόμενον ἀπ'   ἀγροῦ,   τὸν πατέρα
A CYRENIAN   COMING   FROM [THE] COUNTRYSIDE, THE   FATHER

'Αλεξάνδρου καὶ 'Ρούφου, ἵνα   ἄρῃ   τὸν
OF ALEXANDER AND RUFUS, IN ORDER THAT HE MIGHT CARRY THE

σταυρὸν αὐτοῦ. **15.22** καὶ φέρουσιν αὐτὸν ἐπὶ τὸν
CROSS   OF HIM.   AND   THEY BRING HIM   TO THE

Γολγοθᾶν τόπον,   ὅ   ἐστιν μεθερμηνευόμενον
²GOLGOTHA ¹PLACE [CALLED], WHICH MEANS BEING INTERPRETED

Κρανίου Τόπος. **15.23** καὶ ἐδίδουν   αὐτῷ
PLACE~OF [THE] SKULL.   AND   THEY WERE GIVING TO HIM

ἐσμυρνισμένον οἶνον·   ὃς δὲ   οὐκ ἔλαβεν. **15.24** καὶ
WINE~HAVING BEEN MIXED WITH MYRRH. BUT~THIS ONE DID NOT TAKE [IT].   AND

σταυροῦσιν αὐτὸν
THEY CRUCIFY HIM

     καὶ διαμερίζονται τὰ ἱμάτια αὐτοῦ,
     AND DIVIDE   THE GARMENTS OF HIM,

     βάλλοντες κλῆρον ἐπ' αὐτὰ τίς τί
     CASTING   A LOT FOR THEM, WHICH~ONE

     ἄρῃ.
     MIGHT TAKE [THEM].

15.25 ἦν δὲ   ὥρα τρίτη καὶ ἐσταύρωσαν αὐτόν.
NOW~IT WAS [THE] THIRD~HOUR AND THEY CRUCIFIED HIM.

15.26 καὶ ἦν ἡ ἐπιγραφὴ τῆς αἰτίας   αὐτοῦ
     AND ⁶HAD ¹THE ²INSCRIPTION ³OF THE ⁴CHARGE [AGAINST] ⁵HIM

ἐπιγεγραμμένη, Ὁ βασιλεὺς τῶν Ἰουδαίων. **15.27** Καὶ
⁷BEEN WRITTEN OVER [HIM], THE KING OF THE JEWS.   AND

σὺν αὐτῷ σταυροῦσιν δύο λῃστάς, ἕνα ἐκ   δεξιῶν
WITH HIM THEY CRUCIFY TWO THIEVES, ONE ON [THE] RIGHT

καὶ ἕνα ἐξ   εὐωνύμων αὐτοῦ.ᵀ **15.29** Καὶ οἱ
AND ONE ON [THE] LEFT   OF HIM.   AND THE ONES

παραπορευόμενοι ἐβλασφήμουν αὐτὸν κινοῦντες τὰς
PASSING BY   WERE REVILING HIM   SHAKING   THE

κεφαλὰς αὐτῶν καὶ λέγοντες, Οὐὰ ὁ   καταλύων τὸν
HEADS   OF THEM AND SAYING, HA! THE ONE DESTROYING THE

ναὸν καὶ οἰκοδομῶν ἐν τρισὶν ἡμέραις, **15.30** σῶσον
TEMPLE AND BUILDING [IT] IN THREE   DAYS,   SAVE

σεαυτὸν καταβὰς   ἀπὸ τοῦ σταυροῦ. **15.31** ὁμοίως
YOURSELF HAVING COME DOWN FROM THE CROSS.   LIKEWISE

his own clothes on him.
Then they led him out to
crucify him.

21 They compelled a
passer-by, who was coming
in from the country, to carry
his cross; it was Simon of
Cyrene, the father of
Alexander and Rufus.
²²Then they brought Jesus*ˡ* to
the place called Golgotha
(which means the place of a
skull). ²³And they offered
him wine mixed with myrrh;
but he did not take it. ²⁴And
they crucified him, and
divided his clothes among
them, casting lots to decide
what each should take.

25 It was nine o'clock in
the morning when they
crucified him. ²⁶The
inscription of the charge
against him read, "The King
of the Jews." ²⁷And with
him they crucified two
bandits, one on his right and
one on his left.*ᵐ* ²⁹Those
who passed by derided*ⁿ*
him, shaking their heads and
saying, "Aha! You who
would destroy the temple
and build it in three days,
³⁰save yourself, and come
down from the cross!"
³¹In the same way

ˡ Gk *him*
ᵐ Other ancient authorities add verse
28, *And the scripture was fulfilled
that says, "And he was counted
among the lawless."*
ⁿ Or *blasphemed*

15:27 text: ASV RSV NASB NIV NEB TEV NJB NRSV.   add v. 28 καὶ ἐπληρώθη ἡ γραφὴ ἡ λέγουσα, Καὶ
μετὰ ἀνομων ἐλογισθη (And the scripture was fulfilled which says, He was counted with the lawless
ones—NIVmg) [see Luke 22:37; Isa. 53:12]: KJV ASVmg RSVmg NASBmg NIVmg NEBmg TEVmg
NJBmg NRSVmg.

the chief priests, along with
the scribes, were also
mocking him among
themselves and saying, "He
saved others; he cannot save
himself. [32]Let the Messiah,[o]
the King of Israel, come
down from the cross now,
so that we may see and
believe." Those who were
crucified with him also
taunted him.

33 When it was noon,
darkness came over the
whole land[p] until three in the
afternoon. [34]At three o'clock
Jesus cried out with a loud
voice, "Eloi, Eloi, lema
sabachthani?" which means,
"My God, my God, why
have you forsaken me?"[q]
[35]When some of the
bystanders heard it, they
said, "Listen, he is calling
for Elijah." [36]And someone
ran, filled a sponge with sour
wine, put it on a stick, and
gave it to him to drink,
saying, "Wait, let us see
whether Elijah will come to
take him down." [37]Then
Jesus gave a loud cry and
breathed his last. [38]And the
curtain of the temple was
torn in two, from top to
bottom. [39]Now when the
centurion, who stood facing
him, saw that in this way he[r]
breathed his last, he said,
"Truly this man was God's
Son!"[s]

40 There were also
women looking on from a
distance; among them were
Mary Magdalene, and Mary

[o] Or *the Christ*
[p] Or *earth*
[q] Other ancient authorities read *made
me a reproach*
[r] Other ancient authorities add *cried
out and*
[s] Or *a son of God*

καὶ οἱ ἀρχιερεῖς ἐμπαίζοντες πρὸς ἀλλήλους μετὰ
ALSO THE CHIEF PRIESTS MOCKING TO ONE ANOTHER WITH

τῶν γραμματέων ἔλεγον, Ἄλλους ἔσωσεν, ἑαυτὸν
THE SCRIBES WERE SAYING, HE SAVED~OTHERS, [BUT] HIMSELF

οὐ δύναται σῶσαι· **15.32** ὁ Χριστὸς ὁ βασιλεὺς
HE IS NOT ABLE TO SAVE. THE CHRIST THE KING

Ἰσραὴλ καταβάτω νῦν ἀπὸ τοῦ σταυροῦ, ἵνα
OF ISRAEL LET [HIM] COME DOWN NOW FROM THE CROSS, IN ORDER THAT

ἴδωμεν καὶ πιστεύσωμεν. καὶ οἱ συνεσταυρωμένοι
WE MAY SEE AND BELIEVE. AND THE ONES HAVING BEEN CRUCIFIED

σὺν αὐτῷ ὠνείδιζον αὐτόν.
WITH HIM WERE REPROACHING HIM.

15.33 Καὶ γενομένης ὥρας ἕκτης σκότος ἐγένετο
AND HAVING BECOME [THE] SIXTH~HOUR IT BECAME~DARK

ἐφ' ὅλην τὴν γῆν ἕως ὥρας ἐνάτης. **15.34** καὶ
OVER [THE] WHOLE - LAND UNTIL [THE] NINTH~HOUR. AND

τῇ ἐνάτῃ ὥρᾳ ἐβόησεν ὁ Ἰησοῦς φωνῇ μεγάλῃ, Ελωι
AT THE NINTH HOUR CRIED OUT - JESUS IN A LOUD~VOICE, ELOI,

ελωι λεμα σαβαχθανι; ὅ ἐστιν μεθερμηνευόμενον
ELOI LEMA SABACHTHANI? WHICH MEANS BEING INTERPRETED

Ὁ θεός μου ὁ θεός μου, εἰς τί ἐγκατέλιπές με;
- GOD OF ME - GOD OF ME, WHY DID YOU FORSAKE ME?

15.35 καὶ τινες τῶν παρεστηκότων ἀκούσαντες
AND SOME OF THE ONES HAVING BEEN STANDING NEARBY HAVING HEARD

ἔλεγον, Ἴδε Ἡλίαν φωνεῖ. **15.36** δραμὼν δέ τις
WERE SAYING, LOOK HE CALLS~FOR ELIJAH. [3]HAVING RUN [1]AND [2]SOMEONE

[καὶ] γεμίσας σπόγγον ὄξους περιθεὶς καλάμῳ
AND HAVING FILLED A SPONGE WITH VINEGAR HAVING BEEN PLACED ON A STAFF

ἐπότιζεν αὐτόν λέγων, Ἄφετε ἴδωμεν εἰ
HE GAVE DRINK TO HIM SAYING, LEAVE [HIM ALONE] LET US SEE IF

ἔρχεται Ἡλίας καθελεῖν αὐτόν. **15.37** ὁ δὲ Ἰησοῦς
ELIJAH~COMES TO TAKE DOWN HIM. - AND JESUS,

ἀφεὶς φωνὴν μεγάλην ἐξέπνευσεν. **15.38** Καὶ τὸ
HAVING UTTERED A LOUD~CRY EXPIRED. AND THE

καταπέτασμα τοῦ ναοῦ ἐσχίσθη εἰς δύο ἀπ' ἄνωθεν
CURTAIN OF THE TEMPLE WAS TORN IN TWO FROM TOP

ἕως κάτω. **15.39** Ἰδὼν δὲ ὁ κεντυρίων ὁ
TO BOTTOM. [7]HAVING SEEN [1]AND [2]THE [3]CENTURION -

παρεστηκὼς ἐξ ἐναντίας αὐτοῦ ὅτι οὕτως[τ] ἐξέπνευσεν
[4]HAVING STOOD NEARBY [5]OPPOSITE [6]HIM THAT HE EXPIRED~THIS WAY

εἶπεν, Ἀληθῶς οὗτος ὁ ἄνθρωπος υἱὸς θεοῦ ἦν.
SAID, TRULY, THIS - MAN [2]SON [3]OF GOD [1]WAS [THE].

15.40 Ἦσαν δὲ καὶ γυναῖκες ἀπὸ μακρόθεν θεωροῦσαι,
AND~THERE WERE ALSO WOMEN FROM A DISTANCE LOOKING ON,

ἐν αἷς καὶ Μαρία ἡ Μαγδαληνὴ καὶ Μαρία
AMONG WHOM [WERE] BOTH MARY - MAGDALENE AND MARY

15:34 Ps. 22:1 **15:39** text: ASV RSV NASB NIVmg NEB TEV NJB NRSV. add κραξας (crying out): KJV
ASVmg RSVmg NIV NEBmg TEVmg NRSVmg.

ἡ   Ἰακώβου τοῦ μικροῦ καὶ   Ἰωσῆτος μήτηρ καὶ
THE ²OF JAMES ³THE ⁴YOUNGER ⁵AND ⁶OF JOSES ¹MOTHER AND

Σαλώμη, **15.41** αἳ   ὅτε   ἦν   ἐν τῇ Γαλιλαίᾳ ἠκολούθουν
SALOME,   WHO WHEN HE WAS IN - GALILEE WERE FOLLOWING

αὐτῷ   καὶ διηκόνουν αὐτῷ,   καὶ ἄλλαι πολλαὶ αἱ
HIM   AND WERE SERVING HIM,   AND MANY~OTHERS   -

συναναβᾶσαι αὐτῷ   εἰς Ἱεροσόλυμα.
HAVING GONE UP WITH HIM TO JERUSALEM.

15.42 Καὶ ἤδη ὀψίας γενομένης, ἐπεὶ ἦν
       AND ALREADY HAVING BECOME~EVENING, SINCE IT WAS [THE]

παρασκευή ὅ   ἐστιν προσάββατον,   **15.43** ἐλθὼν
PREPARATION WHICH IS THE DAY BEFORE THE SABBATH,   HAVING COME

Ἰωσὴφ [ὁ]   ἀπὸ Ἀριμαθαίας εὐσχήμων
JOSEPH THE ONE FROM ARIMATHEA,   A PROMINENT

βουλευτής,   ὃς καὶ αὐτὸς ἦν προσδεχόμενος τὴν
MEMBER OF THE COUNCIL, WHO ALSO HIMSELF WAS LOOKING FORWARD TO THE

βασιλείαν τοῦ θεοῦ, τολμήσας εἰσῆλθεν πρὸς τὸν
KINGDOM   - OF GOD, HAVING BOLDNESS HE WENT IN TO   -

Πιλᾶτον καὶ ἠτήσατο τὸ σῶμα τοῦ Ἰησοῦ. **15.44** ὁ δὲ
PILATE   AND ASKED [FOR] THE BODY - OF JESUS.   - AND

Πιλᾶτος ἐθαύμασεν εἰ   ἤδη τέθνηκεν καὶ
PILATE   WAS AMAZED THAT HE HAD DIED~ALREADY AND

προσκαλεσάμενος τὸν κεντυρίωνα ἐπηρώτησεν αὐτὸν
HAVING SUMMONED THE CENTURION HE QUESTIONED HIM [TO SEE]

εἰ   πάλαι ἀπέθανεν· **15.45** καὶ γνοὺς   ἀπὸ τοῦ
WHETHER HE DIED~ALREADY.   AND HAVING FOUND OUT FROM THE

κεντυρίωνος ἐδωρήσατο τὸ πτῶμα τῷ   Ἰωσήφ.
CENTURION,   HE GAVE   THE CORPSE - TO JOSEPH.

15.46 καὶ ἀγοράσας σινδόνα   καθελὼν   αὐτὸν
     AND HAVING BOUGHT A LINEN CLOTH [AND] HAVING TAKEN DOWN HIM,

ἐνείλησεν τῇ   σινδόνι καὶ ἔθηκεν αὐτὸν ἐν μνημείῳ
HE WRAPPED [HIM] IN THE LINEN CLOTH AND PLACED HIM IN A TOMB

ὃ   ἦν λελατομημένον ἐκ πέτρας καὶ προσεκύλισεν
WHICH HAD BEEN CUT   FROM ROCK AND HE ROLLED

λίθον ἐπὶ   τὴν θύραν τοῦ μνημείου. **15.47** ἡ δὲ
A STONE AGAINST THE ENTRANCE OF THE TOMB.   - AND

Μαρία ἡ Μαγδαληνὴ καὶ Μαρία ἡ   Ἰωσῆτος
MARY - MAGDALENE AND MARY THE [MOTHER] OF JOSES

ἐθεώρουν ποῦ τέθειται.
WERE OBSERVING WHERE HE HAS BEEN LAID.

the mother of James the younger and of Joses, and Salome. [41]These used to follow him and provided for him when he was in Galilee; and there were many other women who had come up with him to Jerusalem.

42 When evening had come, and since it was the day of Preparation, that is, the day before the sabbath, [43]Joseph of Arimathea, a respected member of the council, who was also himself waiting expectantly for the kingdom of God, went boldly to Pilate and asked for the body of Jesus. [44]Then Pilate wondered if he were already dead; and summoning the centurion, he asked him whether he had been dead for some time. [45]When he learned from the centurion that he was dead, he granted the body to Joseph. [46]Then Joseph[t] bought a linen cloth, and taking down the body,[u] wrapped it in the linen cloth, and laid it in a tomb that had been hewn out of the rock. He then rolled a stone against the door of the tomb. [47]Mary Magdalene and Mary the mother of Joses saw where the body[u] was laid.

[t] Gk he
[u] Gk it

CHAPTER 16

When the sabbath was over, Mary Magdalene, and Mary the mother of James, and Salome bought spices, so that they might go and anoint him. [2]And very early on the first day of the week, when the sun had risen, they went to the tomb. [3]They had been saying to one another, "Who will roll away the stone for us from the entrance to the tomb?" [4]When they looked up, they saw that the stone, which was very large, had already been rolled back. [5]As they entered the tomb, they saw a young man, dressed in a white robe, sitting on the right side; and they were alarmed. [6]But he said to them, "Do not be alarmed; you are looking for Jesus of Nazareth, who was crucified. He has been raised; he is not here. Look, there is the place they laid him. [7]But go, tell his disciples and Peter that he is going ahead of you to Galilee; there you will see him, just as he told you." [8]So they went out and fled from the tomb, for terror and amazement had seized them; and they said nothing to anyone, for they were afraid.[v]

[v] Some of the most ancient authorities bring the book to a close at the end of verse 8. One authority concludes the book with the shorter ending; others include the shorter ending and then continue with verses 9-20. In most authorities verses 9-20 follow immediately after verse 8, though in some of these authorities the passage is marked as being doubtful.

16.1 Καὶ διαγενομένου τοῦ σαββάτου Μαρία ἡ
AND ³HAVING PASSED ¹THE ²SABBATH, MARY -

Μαγδαληνὴ καὶ Μαρία ἡ [τοῦ] Ἰακώβου καὶ
MAGDALENE AND MARY, THE [MOTHER] - OF JAMES, AND

Σαλώμη ἠγόρασαν ἀρώματα ἵνα ἐλθοῦσαι
SALOME BOUGHT SPICES IN ORDER THAT HAVING COME

ἀλείψωσιν αὐτόν. **16.2** καὶ λίαν πρωῒ τῇ μιᾷ
THEY MIGHT ANOINT HIM. AND VERY EARLY ON THE FIRST [DAY]

τῶν σαββάτων ἔρχονται ἐπὶ τὸ μνημεῖον
OF THE WEEK THEY COME UPON THE TOMB,

ἀνατείλαντος τοῦ ἡλίου. **16.3** καὶ ἔλεγον πρὸς
HAVING ARISEN THE SUN. AND THEY WERE SAYING TO

ἑαυτάς, Τίς ἀποκυλίσει ἡμῖν τὸν λίθον ἐκ τῆς
THEMSELVES WHO WILL ROLL AWAY FOR US THE STONE FROM THE

θύρας τοῦ μνημείου; **16.4** καὶ ἀναβλέψασαι θεωροῦσιν
ENTRANCE OF THE TOMB? AND HAVING LOOKED UP THEY SEE

ὅτι ἀποκεκύλισται ὁ λίθος· ἦν γὰρ μέγας σφόδρα.
THAT HAS BEEN ROLLED AWAY THE STONE. FOR~IT WAS EXTREMELY~LARGE.

16.5 καὶ εἰσελθοῦσαι εἰς τὸ μνημεῖον εἶδον νεανίσκον
AND HAVING ENTERED INTO THE TOMB, THEY SAW A YOUNG MAN

καθήμενον ἐν τοῖς δεξιοῖς περιβεβλημένον
SITTING ON THE RIGHT HAVING BEEN CLOTHED [IN]

στολὴν λευκήν, καὶ ἐξεθαμβήθησαν. **16.6** ὁ δὲ λέγει
A WHITE~ROBE, AND THEY WERE UTTERLY AMAZED. - BUT HE SAYS

αὐταῖς, Μὴ ἐκθαμβεῖσθε· Ἰησοῦν ζητεῖτε τὸν
TO THEM, DO NOT BE AMAZED. YOU° SEEK~JESUS THE

Ναζαρηνὸν τὸν ἐσταυρωμένον· ἠγέρθη, οὐκ ἔστιν
NAZARENE THE ONE HAVING BEEN CRUCIFIED. HE WAS RAISED, HE IS NOT

ὧδε· ἴδε ὁ τόπος ὅπου ἔθηκαν αὐτόν. **16.7** ἀλλὰ
HERE. LOOK, THE PLACE WHERE THEY LAID HIM. BUT

ὑπάγετε εἴπατε τοῖς μαθηταῖς αὐτοῦ καὶ τῷ Πέτρῳ
GO TELL THE DISCIPLES OF HIM AND - PETER

ὅτι Προάγει ὑμᾶς εἰς τὴν Γαλιλαίαν· ἐκεῖ
- HE GOES BEFORE YOU° INTO - GALILEE. THERE

αὐτὸν ὄψεσθε, καθὼς εἶπεν ὑμῖν. **16.8** καὶ ἐξελθοῦσαι
YOU° WILL SEE~HIM, JUST AS HE TOLD YOU°. AND HAVING GONE OUT

ἔφυγον ἀπὸ τοῦ μνημείου, εἶχεν γὰρ αὐτὰς τρόμος
THEY FLED FROM THE TOMB, ⁵SEIZED ¹FOR ⁶THEM ²TREMBLING

καὶ ἔκστασις· καὶ οὐδενὶ οὐδὲν εἶπαν·
³AND ⁴AMAZEMENT. AND ²NO ONE ³NOTHING ¹THEY TOLD,

ἐφοβοῦντα γάρ.
FOR~THEY WERE AFRAID.

THE SHORTER ENDING OF MARK

[[Πάντα δὲ τὰ   παρηγγελμένα τοῖς   περὶ τὸν
AND ALL   THE THINGS HAVING BEEN TOLD [THEM] ³TO THE ONES ⁴WITH -

Πέτρον συντόμως ἐξήγγειλαν. Μετὰ δὲ ταῦτα   καὶ
⁵PETER   ²BRIEFLY   ¹THEY REPORTED.   AND~AFTER   THESE THINGS ALSO

αὐτὸς ὁ Ἰησοῦς ἀπὸ ἀνατολῆς καὶ ἄχρι   δύσεως
²HIMSELF - ¹JESUS   FROM [THE] EAST   AND   AS FAR AS [THE] WEST

ἐξαπέστειλεν δι'   αὐτῶν τὸ ἱερὸν καὶ ἄφθαρτον
SENT OUT   THROUGH THEM   THE SACRED AND IMPERISHABLE

κήρυγμα τῆς αἰωνίου σωτηρίας. ἀμήν.]]
PROCLAMATION -   OF ETERNAL SALVATION.   AMEN.

THE SHORTER ENDING OF MARK

[[And all that had been commanded them they told briefly to those around Peter. And afterward Jesus himself sent out through them, from east to west, the sacred and imperishable proclamation of eternal salvation.ʷ]]

THE LONGER ENDING OF MARK

[[**16.9** Ἀναστὰς δὲ πρωῒ πρώτῃ   σαββάτου
AND~HAVING ARISEN   EARLY   ON [THE] FIRST [DAY OF THE] WEEK

ἐφάνη   πρῶτον Μαρίᾳ τῇ Μαγδαληνῇ, παρ' ἧς
HE APPEARED FIRST   TO MARY -   MAGDALENE,   FROM WHOM

ἐκβεβλήκει ἑπτὰ δαιμόνια. **16.10** ἐκείνη   πορευθεῖσα
HE HAD CAST OUT SEVEN DEMONS.   THAT ONE   HAVING GONE

ἀπήγγειλεν τοῖς   μετ' αὐτοῦ γενομένοις πενθοῦσι
ANNOUNCED   TO THE ONES ²WITH ³HIM   ¹HAVING BEEN   MOURNING

καὶ κλαίουσιν· **16.11** κἀκεῖνοι ἀκούσαντες ὅτι ζῇ
AND   CRYING.   AND THOSE   HAVING HEARD   THAT HE LIVES

καὶ ἐθεάθη ὑπ' αὐτῆς ἠπίστησαν.
AND   HE WAS SEEN BY HER,   REFUSED TO BELIEVE.

16.12 Μετὰ δὲ ταῦτα   δυσὶν ἐξ αὐτῶν περιπατοῦσιν
AND~AFTER   THESE THINGS, ⁵TO TWO ⁶OF ⁷THEM ⁸WALKING ALONG

ἐφανερώθη ἐν ἑτέρᾳ μορφῇ πορευομένοις εἰς   ἀγρόν·
¹HE APPEARED ²IN ³ANOTHER ⁴FORM   GOING   INTO [THE] COUNTRY.

16.13 κἀκεῖνοι ἀπελθόντες ἀπήγγειλαν τοῖς λοιποῖς·
AND THOSE   HAVING GONE   REPORTED   TO THE REST.

οὐδὲ   ἐκείνοις ἐπίστευσαν.
NEITHER [DID] THOSE   BELIEVE.

16.14 Ὕστερον [δὲ] ἀνακειμένοις αὐτοῖς   τοῖς ἕνδεκα
BUT~LATER   ⁵RECLINING AT TABLE ⁴THEMSELVES ²TO THE ³ELEVEN

ἐφανερώθη καὶ ὠνείδισεν τὴν ἀπιστίαν αὐτῶν καὶ
¹HE WAS REVEALED AND HE REPROACHED THE UNBELIEF   OF THEM AND [THEIR]

σκληροκαρδίαν ὅτι   τοῖς   θεασαμένοις αὐτὸν
HARDNESS OF HEART BECAUSE THE ONES HAVING SEEN   HIM

THE LONGER ENDING OF MARK

9 [[Now after he rose early on the first day of the week, he appeared first to Mary Magdalene, from whom he had cast out seven demons. ¹⁰She went out and told those who had been with him, while they were mourning and weeping. ¹¹But when they heard that he was alive and had been seen by her, they would not believe it.

12 After this he appeared in another form to two of them, as they were walking into the country. ¹³And they went back and told the rest, but they did not believe them.

14 Later he appeared to the eleven themselves as they were sitting at the table; and he upbraided them for their lack of faith and stubbornness, because they

ʷ Other ancient authorities add *Amen*

The Shorter Ending of Mark is included in NEB, TEV, NASB and NRSV, and is noted in RSVmg and NJBmg. **16:9-20** The two earliest MSS (Codex Vaticanus and Codex Sinaiticus) stop at Mark 16:8; this is indicated (in some form or another) in ASVmg RSVmg NASBmg NIVmg NEBmg TEVmg NJBmg NRSVmg. Many MSS contain the text as printed above in 16:9-20; this portion is included in the text of all the translations. Some MSS contain a shorter ending to Mark, and one MS (the Freer Gospels) contains the longer ending of Mark with a major addition after 16:14, see NRSVmg for a rendering of this text (cf. NJBmg).

had not believed those who saw him after he had risen.[x] [15]And he said to them, "Go into all the world and proclaim the good news[y] to the whole creation. [16]The one who believes and is baptized will be saved; but the one who does not believe will be condemned. [17]And these signs will accompany those who believe: by using my name they will cast out demons; they will speak in new tongues; [18]they will pick up snakes in their hands,[z] and if they drink any deadly thing, it will not hurt them; they will lay their hands on the sick, and they will recover."

19 So then the Lord Jesus, after he had spoken to them, was taken up into heaven and sat down at the right hand of God. [20]And they went out and proclaimed the good news everywhere, while the Lord worked with them and confirmed the message by the signs that accompanied it.[a]]]

[x] Other ancient authorities add, in whole or in part, *And they excused themselves, saying, "This age of lawlessness and unbelief is under Satan, who does not allow the truth and power of God to prevail over the unclean things of the spirits. Therefore reveal your righteousness now"—thus they spoke to Christ. And Christ replied to them, "The term of years of Satan's power has been fulfilled, but other terrible things draw near. And for those who have sinned I was handed over to death, that they may return to the truth and sin no more, that they may inherit the spiritual and imperishable glory of righteousness that is in heaven."*

[y] Or *gospel*

[z] Other ancient authorities lack *in their hands*

[a] Other ancient authorities add *Amen*

ἐγηγερμένον οὐκ ἐπίστευσαν. **16.15** καὶ εἶπεν αὐτοῖς,
HAVING BEEN RAISED   THEY DID NOT BELIEVE.   AND   HE SAID   TO THEM,

Πορευθέντες εἰς τὸν κόσμον ἅπαντα κηρύξατε τὸ
HAVING GONE   INTO   [2]THE   [3]WORLD   [1]ALL   PREACH   THE

εὐαγγέλιον πάσῃ τῇ κτίσει. **16.16** ὁ   πιστεύσας καὶ
GOOD NEWS   TO ALL   -   CREATION.   THE ONE HAVING BELIEVED AND

βαπτισθεὶς   σωθήσεται, ὁ δὲ   ἀπιστήσας
HAVING BEEN BAPTIZED   WILL BE SAVED,   BUT~THE ONE   NOT HAVING BELIEVED

κατακριθήσεται. **16.17** σημεῖα δὲ τοῖς   πιστεύσασιν
WILL BE CONDEMNED.   [3]SIGNS   [1]AND [5]THE ONES [6]HAVING BELIEVED

ταῦτα παρακολουθήσει· ἐν τῷ ὀνόματί μου
[2]THESE   [4]WILL ACCOMPANY: IN   THE   NAME   OF ME

δαιμόνια ἐκβαλοῦσιν, γλώσσαις λαλήσουσιν καιναῖς,
THEY WILL CAST OUT~DEMONS,   [3]TONGUES   [1]THEY WILL SPEAK   [2]WITH NEW,

16.18 [καὶ ἐν ταῖς   χερσὶν] ὄφεις ἀροῦσιν   κἂν
AND   WITH   THE(THEIR) HANDS   THEY WILL PICK UP~SNAKES   AND IF

θανάσιμόν τι πίωσιν οὐ μὴ αὐτοὺς βλάψῃ, ἐπὶ
ANY~DEADLY POISON   THEY DRINK   IN NO WAY   WILL IT HARM~THEM,   UPON [THE]

ἀρρώστους χεῖρας ἐπιθήσουσιν καὶ καλῶς ἕξουσιν.
SICK   THEY WILL LAY~[THEIR] HANDS   AND   THEY WILL BE~HEALTHY.

16.19 Ὁ μὲν οὖν κύριος Ἰησοῦς μετὰ τὸ λαλῆσαι
[2]THE -   [1]THEN LORD   JESUS   AFTER   -   SPEAKING

αὐτοῖς ἀνελήμφθη εἰς τὸν οὐρανὸν καὶ ἐκάθισεν ἐκ
TO THEM   WAS TAKEN UP   INTO   -   HEAVEN   AND   SAT DOWN   AT [THE]

δεξιῶν τοῦ θεοῦ. **16.20** ἐκεῖνοι δὲ ἐξελθόντες
RIGHT [HAND] -   OF GOD.   AND~THOSE   HAVING GONE FORTH

ἐκήρυξαν πανταχοῦ, τοῦ κυρίου συνεργοῦντος καὶ
PREACHED   EVERYWHERE, [WHILE]   THE   LORD   WORKING WITH [THEM]   AND

τὸν λόγον βεβαιοῦντος διὰ τῶν ἐπακολουθούντων
[2]THE [3]WORD   [1]CONFIRMING   THROUGH THE   ACCOMPANYING

σημείων.]]
SIGNS.

THE GOSPEL ACCORDING TO
LUKE

ΚΑΤΑ   ΛΟΥΚΑΝ
ACCORDING TO   LUKE

1.1 Ἐπειδήπερ πολλοὶ ἐπεχείρησαν ἀνατάξασθαι
SINCE   MANY   ATTEMPTED   TO COMPILE

διήγησιν περὶ τῶν πεπληροφορημένων ἐν   ἡμῖν
A NARRATIVE ABOUT ¹THE ³HAVING BEEN FULFILLED ⁴AMONG ⁵US

πραγμάτων, **1.2** καθὼς παρέδοσαν ἡμῖν οἱ
²EVENTS,   JUST AS DELIVERED TO US THE ONES [WHO]

ἀπ'   ἀρχῆς αὐτόπται καὶ ὑπηρέται γενόμενοι
FROM [THE] BEGINNING ²EYEWITNESSES ³AND ⁴SERVANTS ¹HAVING BECOME

τοῦ λόγου, **1.3** ἔδοξε   κἀμοὶ παρηκολουθηκότι
OF THE WORD,   IT SEEMED GOOD TO ME ALSO HAVING INVESTIGATED

ἄνωθεν   πᾶσιν ἀκριβῶς καθεξῆς   σοι   γράψαι,
FROM [THE] BEGINNING EVERYTHING CAREFULLY, ³IN AN ORDERLY WAY ²TO YOU ¹TO WRITE,

κράτιστε Θεόφιλε, **1.4** ἵνα ἐπιγνῷς περὶ ὧν
MOST NOBLE THEOPHILUS,   THAT YOU MAY KNOW ⁴ABOUT ⁵WHICH

κατηχήθης λόγων   τὴν ἀσφάλειαν.
⁶YOU WERE TAUGHT ³OF [THE] WORDS ¹THE ²CERTAINTY.

1.5 Ἐγένετο ἐν ταῖς ἡμέραις Ἡρῴδου βασιλέως τῆς
THERE WAS IN THE DAYS   OF KING~HEROD   -

Ἰουδαίας ἱερεύς τις ὀνόματι Ζαχαρίας ἐξ
OF JUDEA, A CERTAIN~PRIEST BY NAME ZECHARIAH, OF [THE]

ἐφημερίας Ἀβιά, καὶ   γυνὴ αὐτῷ ἐκ τῶν θυγατέρων
DIVISION   OF ABIJAH, AND [THE] WIFE TO HIM OF THE DAUGHTERS

Ἀαρὼν καὶ τὸ ὄνομα αὐτῆς   Ἐλισάβετ.
OF AARON AND THE NAME OF HER [WAS] ELIZABETH.

1.6 ἦσαν δὲ   δίκαιοι ἀμφότεροι ἐναντίον τοῦ θεοῦ,
AND~THEY WERE BOTH~RIGHTEOUS   BEFORE   -   GOD,

πορευόμενοι ἐν πάσαις ταῖς ἐντολαῖς   καὶ
WALKING   IN ALL   THE COMMANDMENTS AND

δικαιώμασιν τοῦ κυρίου ἄμεμπτοι. **1.7** καὶ οὐκ ἦν
REGULATIONS OF THE LORD BLAMELESS.   AND THERE WAS NOT

αὐτοῖς τέκνον, καθότι ἦν ἡ Ἐλισάβετ στεῖρα, καὶ
TO THEM A CHILD, BECAUSE ²WAS - ¹ELIZABETH BARREN, AND

ἀμφότεροι προβεβηκότες ἐν ταῖς ἡμέραις αὐτῶν ἦσαν.
BOTH   HAVING BEEN ADVANCED IN THE DAYS OF THEM WERE.

1.8 Ἐγένετο δὲ ἐν τῷ ἱερατεύειν αὐτὸν   ἐν τῇ
AND~IT CAME TO PASS IN - HIS~PERFORMING OF DUTIES AS PRIEST IN THE

τάξει   τῆς ἐφημερίας αὐτοῦ ἔναντι τοῦ θεοῦ,
SUCCESSION OF THE DIVISION OF HIM BEFORE - GOD,

Since many have undertaken to set down an orderly account of the events that have been fulfilled among us, ²just as they were handed on to us by those who from the beginning were eyewitnesses and servants of the word, ³I too decided, after investigating everything carefully from the very first,ᵃ to write an orderly account for you, most excellent Theophilus, ⁴so that you may know the truth concerning the things about which you have been instructed.

5 In the days of King Herod of Judea, there was a priest named Zechariah, who belonged to the priestly order of Abijah. His wife was a descendant of Aaron, and her name was Elizabeth. ⁶Both of them were righteous before God, living blamelessly according to all the commandments and regulations of the Lord. ⁷But they had no children, because Elizabeth was barren, and both were getting on in years.

8 Once when he was serving as priest before God and his section was on duty,

ᵃ Or *for a long time*

⁹he was chosen by lot, according to the custom of the priesthood, to enter the sanctuary of the Lord and offer incense. ¹⁰Now at the time of the incense offering, the whole assembly of the people was praying outside. ¹¹Then there appeared to him an angel of the Lord, standing at the right side of the altar of incense. ¹²When Zechariah saw him, he was terrified; and fear overwhelmed him. ¹³But the angel said to him, "Do not be afraid, Zechariah, for your prayer has been heard. Your wife Elizabeth will bear you a son, and you will name him John. ¹⁴You will have joy and gladness, and many will rejoice at his birth, ¹⁵for he will be great in the sight of the Lord. He must never drink wine or strong drink; even before his birth he will be filled with the Holy Spirit. ¹⁶He will turn many of the people of Israel to the Lord their God. ¹⁷With the spirit and power of Elijah he will go before him, to turn the hearts of parents to their children, and the disobedient to the wisdom of the righteous, to make ready a people prepared for the Lord." ¹⁸Zechariah said to the angel, "How will I know that this is so? For I am an old man, and my wife is getting on in years." ¹⁹The

1.9 κατὰ τὸ ἔθος τῆς ἱερατείας ἔλαχε τοῦ
ACCORDING TO THE CUSTOM OF THE PRIESTLY OFFICE, HE WAS CHOSEN BY LOT -

θυμιᾶσαι εἰσελθὼν εἰς τὸν ναὸν τοῦ κυρίου, **1.10** καὶ
TO BURN INCENSE HAVING ENTERED INTO THE TEMPLE OF THE LORD, AND

πᾶν τὸ πλῆθος ἦν τοῦ λαοῦ προσευχόμενον ἔξω
ALL THE MULTITUDE ³WERE ¹OF THE ²PEOPLE PRAYING OUTSIDE

τῇ ὥρᾳ τοῦ θυμιάματος. **1.11** ὤφθη δὲ αὐτῷ
AT THE HOUR OF THE INCENSE OFFERING. AND~THERE APPEARED TO HIM

ἄγγελος κυρίου ἑστὼς ἐκ δεξιῶν τοῦ
AN ANGEL OF [THE] LORD HAVING STOOD ON [THE] RIGHT SIDE OF THE

θυσιαστηρίου τοῦ θυμιάματος. **1.12** καὶ ἐταράχθη
ALTAR - OF INCENSE. AND WAS TERRIFIED

Ζαχαρίας ἰδὼν καὶ φόβος ἐπέπεσεν ἐπ᾿ αὐτόν.
ZECHARIAH SEEING [THE ANGEL] AND FEAR FELL UPON HIM.

1.13 εἶπεν δὲ πρὸς αὐτὸν ὁ ἄγγελος, Μὴ φοβοῦ,
BUT~SAID TO HIM THE ANGEL, DO NOT BE AFRAID,

Ζαχαρία, διότι εἰσηκούσθη ἡ δέησίς σου, καὶ ἡ
ZECHARIAH, FOR WAS HEARD THE PRAYER OF YOU, AND THE

γυνή σου Ἐλισάβετ γεννήσει υἱόν σοι καὶ καλέσεις
WIFE OF YOU, ELIZABETH, WILL BEAR A SON TO YOU AND YOU WILL CALL

τὸ ὄνομα αὐτοῦ Ἰωάννην. **1.14** καὶ ἔσται χαρά σοι
THE NAME OF HIM JOHN. AND HE WILL BE A JOY TO YOU

καὶ ἀγαλλίασις καὶ πολλοὶ ἐπὶ τῇ γενέσει αὐτοῦ
AND GLADNESS, AND MANY AT THE BIRTH OF HIM

χαρήσονται. **1.15** ἔσται γὰρ μέγας ἐνώπιον [τοῦ] κυρίου,
WILL REJOICE. FOR~HE WILL BE GREAT BEFORE THE LORD,

καὶ οἶνον καὶ σίκερα οὐ μὴ πίῃ, καὶ πνεύματος
AND WINE AND STRONG DRINK IN NO WAY WILL HE DRINK, AND ³SPIRIT

ἁγίου πλησθήσεται ἔτι ἐκ κοιλίας μητρὸς
²[THE] HOLY ¹HE WILL BE FILLED [WITH] WHILE IN [THE] WOMB OF [THE] MOTHER

αὐτοῦ, **1.16** καὶ πολλοὺς τῶν υἱῶν Ἰσραὴλ ἐπιστρέψει
OF HIM, AND MANY OF THE SONS OF ISRAEL HE WILL TURN BACK

ἐπὶ κύριον τὸν θεὸν αὐτῶν. **1.17** καὶ αὐτὸς
TO [THE] LORD THE GOD OF THEM. AND HE

προελεύσεται ἐνώπιον αὐτοῦ ἐν πνεύματι καὶ δυνάμει
WILL GO FORWARD BEFORE HIM IN [THE] SPIRIT AND POWER

Ἡλίου, ἐπιστρέψαι καρδίας πατέρων ἐπὶ τέκνα
OF ELIJAH, TO TURN BACK [THE] HEARTS OF [THE] FATHERS TO [THEIR] CHILDREN

καὶ ἀπειθεῖς ἐν φρονήσει δικαίων, ἑτοιμάσαι
AND [THE] DISOBEDIENT TO [THE] WISDOM OF [THE] RIGHTEOUS, TO PREPARE

κυρίῳ λαὸν κατεσκευασμένον. **1.18** Καὶ
FOR [THE] LORD A PEOPLE HAVING BEEN MADE READY. AND

εἶπεν Ζαχαρίας πρὸς τὸν ἄγγελον, Κατὰ τί γνώσομαι
ZECHARIAH~SAID TO THE ANGEL, BY WHAT WILL I KNOW

τοῦτο; ἐγὼ γὰρ εἰμι πρεσβύτης καὶ ἡ γυνή μου
THIS? FOR~I AM OLD AND THE WIFE OF ME

προβεβηκυῖα ἐν ταῖς ἡμέραις αὐτῆς. **1.19** καὶ
HAVING ADVANCED IN THE DAYS OF HER. AND

ἀποκριθεὶς ὁ   ἄγγελος εἶπεν αὐτῷ, Ἐγώ εἰμι Γαβριὴλ
HAVING ANSWERED THE ANGEL   SAID   TO HIM, I   AM   GABRIEL

ὁ   παρεστηκὼς ἐνώπιον τοῦ θεοῦ καὶ ἀπεστάλην
THE ONE HAVING STOOD   BEFORE   -   GOD   AND   I WAS SENT

λαλῆσαι πρὸς σὲ καὶ εὐαγγελίσασθαί σοι ταῦτα·
TO SPEAK   TO   YOU AND   TO ANNOUNCE   THESE THINGS~TO YOU.

1.20 καὶ ἰδοὺ ἔσῃ   σιωπῶν καὶ μὴ δυνάμενος
    AND LOOK, YOU WILL BE MUTE   AND NOT BEING ABLE

λαλῆσαι ἄχρι ἧς   ἡμέρας γένηται ταῦτα, ἀνθ’ ὧν
TO SPEAK   UNTIL WHICH DAY   THESE THINGS~HAPPEN, BECAUSE

οὐκ ἐπίστευσας τοῖς λόγοις μου, οἵτινες πληρωθήσονται
YOU DID NOT BELIEVE IN THE WORDS OF ME, WHICH   WILL BE FULFILLED

εἰς τὸν καιρὸν αὐτῶν.
IN   THE   TIME   OF THEM.

1.21 Καὶ ἦν ὁ   λαὸς προσδοκῶν τὸν Ζαχαρίαν καὶ
      AND WERE THE PEOPLE EXPECTING   -   ZECHARIAH   AND

ἐθαύμαζον ἐν τῷ χρονίζειν ἐν τῷ ναῷ αὐτόν.
THEY WERE AMAZED AT -   ²DELAY   ³IN ⁴THE ⁵TEMPLE ¹HIS.

1.22 ἐξελθὼν δὲ   οὐκ ἐδύνατο λαλῆσαι αὐτοῖς, καὶ
      AND~HAVING COME OUT HE WAS NOT ABLE TO SPEAK   TO THEM,   AND

ἐπέγνωσαν ὅτι ὀπτασίαν ἑώρακεν ἐν τῷ ναῷ· καὶ
THEY KNEW   THAT HE HAS SEEN~A VISION   IN THE TEMPLE. AND

αὐτὸς ἦν διανεύων αὐτοῖς καὶ διέμενεν κωφός.
HE   KEPT MOTIONING TO THEM AND HE REMAINED MUTE.

1.23 καὶ ἐγένετο ὡς ἐπλήσθησαν αἱ ἡμέραι τῆς
      AND IT CAME ABOUT AS WERE FULFILLED   THE DAYS   OF THE

λειτουργίας αὐτοῦ, ἀπῆλθεν εἰς τὸν οἶκον αὐτοῦ.
SERVICE   OF HIM,   HE WENT   TO   THE HOUSE OF HIM.

1.24 Μετὰ δὲ ταύτας τὰς ἡμέρας συνέλαβεν Ἐλισάβετ
      AND~AFTER THESE   -   DAYS   BECAME PREGNANT ELIZABETH,

ἡ γυνὴ αὐτοῦ καὶ περιέκρυβεν ἑαυτὴν   μῆνας πέντε
THE WIFE OF HIM AND   SHE WAS HIDING   HERSELF [FOR] FIVE~MONTHS

λέγουσα **1.25** ὅτι Οὕτως μοι πεποίηκεν κύριος ἐν
SAYING   -   THUS   TO ME HAS DONE   [THE] LORD IN

ἡμέραις αἷς ἐπεῖδεν   ἀφελεῖν ὄνειδός μου ἐν
DAYS   IN WHICH HE LOOKED WITH FAVOR TO TAKE AWAY MY~REPROACH AMONG

ἀνθρώποις.
MEN.

1.26 Ἐν δὲ τῷ μηνὶ τῷ ἕκτῳ ἀπεστάλη ὁ ἄγγελος
      NOW~IN THE ²MONTH - ¹SIXTH, WAS SENT   THE ANGEL

Γαβριὴλ ἀπὸ τοῦ θεοῦ εἰς πόλιν τῆς Γαλιλαίας
GABRIEL   FROM   -   GOD   TO A CITY   -   OF GALILEE

ᾗ   ὄνομα Ναζαρὲθ **1.27** πρὸς παρθένον
TO WHICH [IS THE] NAME,   NAZARETH,   TO   A VIRGIN

ἐμνηστευμένην ἀνδρὶ ᾧ   ὄνομα Ἰωσὴφ ἐξ
HAVING BEEN ENGAGED TO A MAN TO WHOM [IS THE] NAME   JOSEPH OF

οἴκου Δαυὶδ, καὶ τὸ ὄνομα τῆς παρθένου Μαριάμ.
[THE] HOUSE OF DAVID, AND THE NAME   OF THE VIRGIN [WAS]   MARY.

angel replied, "I am Gabriel. I stand in the presence of God, and I have been sent to speak to you and to bring you this good news. ²⁰But now, because you did not believe my words, which will be fulfilled in their time, you will become mute, unable to speak, until the day these things occur."

21 Meanwhile the people were waiting for Zechariah, and wondered at his delay in the sanctuary. ²²When he did come out, he could not speak to them, and they realized that he had seen a vision in the sanctuary. He kept motioning to them and remained unable to speak. ²³When his time of service was ended, he went to his home.

24 After those days his wife Elizabeth conceived, and for five months she remained in seclusion. She said, ²⁵"This is what the Lord has done for me when he looked favorably on me and took away the disgrace I have endured among my people."

26 In the sixth month the angel Gabriel was sent by God to a town in Galilee called Nazareth, ²⁷to a virgin engaged to a man whose name was Joseph, of the house of David. The virgin's name was Mary.

28And he came to her and said, "Greetings, favored one! The Lord is with you."*b* 29But she was much perplexed by his words and pondered what sort of greeting this might be. 30The angel said to her, "Do not be afraid, Mary, for you have found favor with God. 31And now, you will conceive in your womb and bear a son, and you will name him Jesus. 32He will be great, and will be called the Son of the Most High, and the Lord God will give to him the throne of his ancestor David. 33He will reign over the house of Jacob forever, and of his kingdom there will be no end." 34Mary said to the angel, "How can this be, since I am a virgin?"*c* 35The angel said to her, "The Holy Spirit will come upon you, and the power of the Most High will overshadow you; therefore the child to be born*d* will be holy; he will be called Son of God. 36And now, your relative Elizabeth in her old age has also conceived a son; and this is the sixth month for her who was said to be barren. 37For nothing will be impossible with God." 38Then Mary said, "Here am I, the servant of the Lord;

b Other ancient authorities add *Blessed are you among women*
c Gk *I do not know a man*
d Other ancient authorities add *of you*

1.28 καὶ   εἰσελθὼν   πρὸς   αὐτὴν   εἶπεν,   Χαῖρε,
AND   HAVING APPROACHED   TOWARD   HER   HE SAID   HAIL,

κεχαριτωμένη,   ὁ   κύριος   μετὰ   σοῦ.⊤   **1.29** ἡ   δὲ   ἐπὶ
[ONE] HAVING BEEN FAVORED,   THE   LORD [IS]   WITH   YOU.   BUT~SHE   AT

τῷ   λόγῳ   διεταράχθη   καὶ   διελογίζετο   ποταπὸς
THE   MESSAGE   WAS GREATLY PERPLEXED   AND   KEPT PONDERING   OF WHAT SORT

εἴη   ὁ   ἀσπασμὸς   οὗτος.   **1.30** καὶ   εἶπεν   ὁ   ἄγγελος
MIGHT BE   -   THIS~GREETING.   AND   SAID   THE   ANGEL

αὐτῇ,   Μὴ   φοβοῦ,   Μαριάμ,   εὗρες   γὰρ   χάριν   παρὰ   τῷ
TO HER,   DO NOT FEAR,   MARY,   FOR~YOU FOUND   FAVOR   WITH   -

θεῷ.   **1.31** καὶ   ἰδοὺ   συλλήμψῃ   ἐν   γαστρὶ   καὶ
GOD.   AND   BEHOLD   YOU WILL CONCEIVE   IN [YOUR]   WOMB   AND

τέξῃ   υἱὸν   καὶ   καλέσεις   τὸ   ὄνομα   αὐτοῦ   Ἰησοῦν.
WILL BEAR   A SON   AND   YOU WILL CALL   THE   NAME   OF HIM   JESUS.

1.32 οὗτος   ἔσται   μέγας   καὶ   υἱὸς   ὑψίστου
THIS ONE   WILL BE   GREAT   AND [THE]   SON   OF [THE] MOST HIGH

κληθήσεται   καὶ   δώσει   αὐτῷ   κύριος   ὁ   θεὸς   τὸν   θρόνον
HE WILL BE CALLED   AND   WILL GIVE   HIM [THE]   LORD   -   GOD,   THE   THRONE

Δαυὶδ   τοῦ   πατρὸς   αὐτοῦ,   **1.33** καὶ   βασιλεύσει   ἐπὶ   τὸν
OF DAVID   THE   FATHER   OF HIM,   AND   HE WILL RULE   OVER   THE

οἶκον   Ἰακὼβ   εἰς   τοὺς   αἰῶνας   καὶ   τῆς   βασιλείας
HOUSE   OF JACOB   INTO   THE   AGES   AND   OF THE   KINGDOM

αὐτοῦ   οὐκ   ἔσται   τέλος.   **1.34** εἶπεν   δὲ   Μαριὰμ   πρὸς
OF HIM   THERE WILL NOT BE   AN END.   BUT~SAID   MARY   TO

τὸν   ἄγγελον,   Πῶς   ἔσται   τοῦτο,   ἐπεὶ   ἄνδρα   οὐ   γινώσκω;
THE   ANGEL,   HOW   WILL BE   THIS,   SINCE   I DO NOT KNOW~A MAN?

1.35 καὶ   ἀποκριθεὶς   ὁ   ἄγγελος   εἶπεν   αὐτῇ,
AND   ANSWERING   THE   ANGEL   SAID   TO HER,

Πνεῦμα   ἅγιον   ἐπελεύσεται   ἐπὶ   σὲ   καὶ   δύναμις
[THE] HOLY~SPIRIT   WILL COME   UPON   YOU   AND   [THE] POWER

ὑψίστου   ἐπισκιάσει   σοι·   διὸ   καὶ   τὸ
OF [THE] MOST HIGH   WILL OVERSHADOW   YOU.   THEREFORE   ALSO   THE ONE

γεννώμενον⊤   ἅγιον   κληθήσεται   υἱὸς   θεοῦ.   **1.36** καὶ
BEING BORN   WILL BE CALLED~HOLY,   [THE] SON   OF GOD.   AND

ἰδοὺ   Ἐλισάβετ   ἡ   συγγενίς   σου   καὶ   αὐτὴ   συνείληφεν
BEHOLD   ELIZABETH   THE   RELATIVE   OF YOU   ALSO   SHE   HAS CONCEIVED

υἱὸν   ἐν   γήρει   αὐτῆς   καὶ   οὗτος   μὴν   ἕκτος   ἐστὶν
A SON   IN   [THE] OLD AGE   OF HER   AND   THIS   MONTH   IS~[THE] SIXTH

αὐτῇ   τῇ   καλουμένῃ   στείρᾳ·   **1.37** ὅτι
[FOR] HER   THE ONE   BEING CALLED   BARREN;   BECAUSE

⌜οὐκ   ἀδυνατήσει   παρὰ   τοῦ   θεοῦ   πᾶν   ῥῆμα⌝.
WILL NOT BE IMPOSSIBLE   WITH   -   GOD   EVERY   WORD.

1.38 εἶπεν   δὲ   Μαριάμ,   Ἰδοὺ   ἡ   δούλη   κυρίου·
AND~SAID   MARY,   BEHOLD   THE   BONDMAID   OF [THE] LORD;

1:28 text: ASV RSV NASB NIV NEB TEV NJB NRSV.   add ευλογημενη συ εν γυναιξιν (blessed are you among women) [see Luke 1:42]: KJV ASVmg RSVmg NASBmg NJBmg NRSVmg.   **1:35** text: ASV RSV NASB NIV NEB TEV NJB NRSV.   add εκ σου (of you): KJV ASVmg RSVmg NRSVmg.   **1:37** text: ASV NEB NRSV.   var. ουκ αδυνατησει παρα τω θεω παν ρημα (with God nothing will be impossible): KJV RSV NASB NIV NEBmg TEV NJB.

γένοιτό   μοι   κατὰ   τὸ ῥῆμά σου.   καὶ   ἀπῆλθεν
MAY IT BE DONE   TO ME   ACCORDING TO   THE   WORD   OF YOU.   AND   DEPARTED

ἀπ' αὐτῆς ὁ   ἄγγελος.
FROM HER   THE ANGEL.

1.39 Ἀναστᾶσα δὲ   Μαριὰμ ἐν ταῖς ἡμέραις ταύταις
AND~HAVING ARISEN   MARY   IN -   THESE~DAYS

ἐπορεύθη εἰς τὴν ὀρεινὴν   μετὰ σπουδῆς εἰς πόλιν
TRAVELED   INTO THE   HILL COUNTRY   WITH   HASTE   TO   A CITY

Ἰούδα, **1.40** καὶ   εἰσῆλθεν εἰς τὸν οἶκον Ζαχαρίου καὶ
OF JUDAH,   AND   SHE ENTERED   INTO THE   HOUSE   OF ZECHARIAH   AND

ἠσπάσατο τὴν Ἐλισάβετ. **1.41** καὶ ἐγένετο   ὡς
GREETED -   ELIZABETH.   AND   IT CAME ABOUT   WHEN

ἤκουσεν τὸν ἀσπασμὸν τῆς Μαρίας ἡ Ἐλισάβετ,
²HEARD   ³THE   ⁴GREETING -   ⁵OF MARY, -   ¹ELIZABETH,

ἐσκίρτησεν τὸ βρέφος ἐν τῇ κοιλίᾳ αὐτῆς, καὶ
LEAPED   THE BABY   IN   THE WOMB   OF HER,   AND

ἐπλήσθη πνεύματος ἁγίου ἡ Ἐλισάβετ, **1.42** καὶ
WAS FILLED   [WITH THE] HOLY~SPIRIT, -   ELIZABETH,   AND

ἀνεφώνησεν κραυγῇ μεγάλῃ καὶ εἶπεν,   Εὐλογημένη
SHE CRIED OUT   WITH A LOUD~CRY   AND   SAID,   HAVING BEEN BLESSED [ARE]

σὺ ἐν   γυναιξὶν καὶ εὐλογημένος   ὁ καρπὸς τῆς
YOU AMONG   WOMEN   AND   HAVING BEEN BLESSED [IS]   THE   FRUIT   OF THE

κοιλίας σου. **1.43** καὶ   πόθεν   μοι τοῦτο ἵνα
WOMB   OF YOU.   AND   WHY [HAS HAPPENED]   THIS~TO ME   THAT

ἔλθῃ   ἡ μήτηρ τοῦ κυρίου μου πρὸς ἐμέ;
SHOULD COME   THE MOTHER   OF THE LORD   OF ME TO   ME?

1.44 ἰδοὺ γὰρ ὡς   ἐγένετο ἡ φωνὴ τοῦ ἀσπασμοῦ
FOR~BEHOLD   WHEN   CAME   THE SOUND   OF THE GREETING

σου εἰς τὰ ὦτά μου, ἐσκίρτησεν ἐν ἀγαλλιάσει τὸ
OF YOU INTO THE EARS OF ME,   LEAPED   WITH JOY   THE

βρέφος ἐν τῇ κοιλίᾳ μου. **1.45** καὶ μακαρία ἡ
BABY   IN   THE WOMB   OF ME.   AND   BLESSED [IS]   THE ONE

πιστεύσασα ὅτι ἔσται   τελείωσις τοῖς
HAVING BELIEVED   THAT   THERE WILL BE   A FULFILLMENT   TO THE THINGS

λελαλημένοις αὐτῇ παρὰ κυρίου.
HAVING BEEN SPOKEN   TO HER   BY   [THE] LORD.

1.46 Καὶ   εἶπεν Μαριάμ,
AND   MARY~SAID,

1.47 Μεγαλύνει ἡ ψυχή μου τὸν κύριον,
EXALTS   THE SOUL   OF ME,   THE LORD,

καὶ ἠγαλλίασεν τὸ πνεῦμά μου ἐπὶ τῷ
AND   REJOICED   THE SPIRIT   OF ME IN -

θεῷ τῷ σωτῆρί μου,
GOD   THE   SAVIOR   OF ME,

1.48 ὅτι ἐπέβλεψεν ἐπὶ τὴν ταπείνωσιν τῆς δούλης
FOR   HE LOOKED   UPON THE   HUMBLE STATE   OF THE BONDMAID

αὐτοῦ.
OF HIM.

let it be with me according to your word." Then the angel departed from her.

39 In those days Mary set out and went with haste to a Judean town in the hill country, ⁴⁰where she entered the house of Zechariah and greeted Elizabeth. ⁴¹When Elizabeth heard Mary's greeting, the child leaped in her womb. And Elizabeth was filled with the Holy Spirit ⁴²and exclaimed with a loud cry, "Blessed are you among women, and blessed is the fruit of your womb. ⁴³And why has this happened to me, that the mother of my Lord comes to me? ⁴⁴For as soon as I heard the sound of your greeting, the child in my womb leaped for joy. ⁴⁵And blessed is she who believed that there would be*e* a fulfillment of what was spoken to her by the Lord."

46 And Mary*f* said,
"My soul magnifies the Lord,
47   and my spirit rejoices
in God my Savior,
⁴⁸ for he has looked with favor on the lowliness of his servant.

e Or *believed, for there will be*
f Other ancient authorities read *Elizabeth*

Surely, from now on all
generations will call
me blessed;
⁴⁹for the Mighty One has
done great things
for me,
and holy is his name.
⁵⁰His mercy is for those
who fear him
from generation to
generation.
⁵¹He has shown strength
with his arm;
he has scattered the
proud in the
thoughts of their
hearts.
⁵²He has brought down the
powerful from their
thrones,
and lifted up the lowly;
⁵³he has filled the hungry
with good things,
and sent the rich away
empty.
⁵⁴He has helped his servant
Israel,
in remembrance of his
mercy,
⁵⁵according to the promise
he made to our
ancestors,
to Abraham and to his
descendants
forever."
56 And Mary remained
with her about three months
and then returned to her
home.
57 Now the time came for
Elizabeth to give birth, and
she bore a son. ⁵⁸Her neighbors and relatives heard that
the Lord had shown his
great mercy to her, and

ἰδοὺ γὰρ ἀπὸ τοῦ νῦν
FOR~BEHOLD FROM - NOW [ON]

μακαριοῦσίν   με πᾶσαι αἱ γενεαί,
WILL CONSIDER BLESSED ME, ALL - GENERATIONS,

1.49 ὅτι ἐποίησέν μοι μεγάλα ὁ δυνατός.
FOR DID TO ME GREAT THINGS THE MIGHTY ONE.

καὶ ἅγιον τὸ ὄνομα αὐτοῦ,
AND HOLY [IS] THE NAME OF HIM,

1.50 καὶ τὸ ἔλεος αὐτοῦ εἰς γενεὰς καὶ γενεὰς
AND THE MERCY OF HIM TO GENERATIONS AND GENERATIONS

τοῖς   φοβουμένοις αὐτόν.
TO THE ONES FEARING HIM.

1.51 Ἐποίησεν κράτος ἐν βραχίονι αὐτοῦ,
HE DID A MIGHTY DEED WITH [THE] ARM OF HIM,

διεσκόρπισεν ὑπερηφάνους διανοίᾳ
HE SCATTERED [THE] PROUD IN [THE] THOUGHTS

καρδίας αὐτῶν·
OF THEIR~HEART.

1.52 καθεῖλεν   δυνάστας ἀπὸ θρόνων
HE BROUGHT DOWN RULERS FROM [THEIR] THRONES

καὶ ὕψωσεν ταπεινούς,
AND LIFTED UP [THE] HUMBLE,

1.53 πεινῶντας   ἐνέπλησεν ἀγαθῶν
[THE ONES] HUNGERING HE FILLED WITH GOOD THINGS

καὶ πλουτοῦντας ἐξαπέστειλεν κενούς.
AND RICH [ONES] HE SENT AWAY EMPTY.

1.54 ἀντελάβετο Ἰσραὴλ παιδὸς αὐτοῦ,
HE HELPED ISRAEL HIS~SERVANT,

μνησθῆναι ἐλέους,
TO REMEMBER MERCY,

1.55 καθὼς ἐλάλησεν πρὸς τοὺς πατέρας ἡμῶν,
JUST AS HE SPOKE TO THE FATHERS OF US,

τῷ Ἀβραὰμ καὶ τῷ σπέρματι
- TO ABRAHAM AND THE OFFSPRING

αὐτοῦ εἰς τὸν αἰῶνα.
OF HIM INTO THE AGE.

1.56 Ἔμεινεν δὲ Μαριὰμ σὺν αὐτῇ ὡς μῆνας τρεῖς,
AND~REMAINED MARY WITH HER ABOUT THREE~MONTHS,

καὶ ὑπέστρεψεν εἰς τὸν οἶκον αὐτῆς.
AND SHE RETURNED TO THE HOUSE OF HER.

1.57 Τῇ δὲ Ἐλισάβετ ἐπλήσθη ὁ χρόνος τοῦ
- NOW FOR ELIZABETH WAS FULFILLED THE TIME -

τεκεῖν αὐτὴν   καὶ ἐγέννησεν υἱόν. **1.58** καὶ ἤκουσαν
[FOR] HER~TO GIVE BIRTH, AND SHE BORE A SON. AND HEARD

οἱ περίοικοι καὶ οἱ συγγενεῖς αὐτῆς ὅτι
THE NEIGHBORS AND THE RELATIVES OF HER THAT

ἐμεγάλυνεν κύριος   τὸ ἔλεος αὐτοῦ μετ' αὐτῆς καὶ
[THE] LORD~GREATLY DEMONSTRATED THE MERCY OF HIM TO HER AND

συνέχαιρον αὐτῇ. **1.59** Καὶ ἐγένετο ἐν τῇ ἡμέρᾳ τῇ
THEY WERE REJOICING WITH HER. AND IT CAME ABOUT ON THE ²DAY -

ὀγδόῃ ἦλθον περιτεμεῖν τὸ παιδίον καὶ ἐκάλουν
¹EIGHTH THEY CAME TO CIRCUMCISE THE CHILD AND THEY WERE CALLING

αὐτὸ ἐπὶ τῷ ὀνόματι τοῦ πατρὸς αὐτοῦ Ζαχαρίαν.
IT(HIM) BY THE NAME OF THE FATHER OF HIM, ZECHARIAH.

1.60 καὶ ἀποκριθεῖσα ἡ μήτηρ αὐτοῦ εἶπεν, Οὐχί,
AND HAVING ANSWERED THE MOTHER OF HIM SAID, NO,

ἀλλὰ κληθήσεται Ἰωάννης. **1.61** καὶ εἶπαν πρὸς αὐτὴν
BUT HE WILL BE CALLED JOHN. AND THEY SAID TO HER

ὅτι Οὐδείς ἐστιν ἐκ τῆς συγγενείας σου ὃς καλεῖται
- THERE IS~NO ONE FROM THE RELATIVES OF YOU WHO IS CALLED

τῷ ὀνόματι τούτῳ. **1.62** ἐνένευον δὲ τῷ πατρὶ
- BY THIS~NAME. AND~THEY WERE MOTIONING TO THE FATHER

αὐτοῦ τὸ τί ἂν θέλοι καλεῖσθαι αὐτό. **1.63** καὶ
OF HIM - WHATEVER HE MIGHT WISH IT(HIM)~TO BE CALLED. AND

αἰτήσας πινακίδιον ἔγραψεν λέγων, Ἰωάννης ἐστὶν
HAVING ASKED [FOR] A TABLET HE WROTE SAYING, JOHN IS

ὄνομα αὐτοῦ. καὶ ἐθαύμασαν πάντες. **1.64** ἀνεῴχθη δὲ
[THE] NAME OF HIM. AND EVERYONE~WAS AMAZED. AND~WAS OPENED

τὸ στόμα αὐτοῦ παραχρῆμα καὶ ἡ γλῶσσα αὐτοῦ, καὶ
THE MOUTH OF HIM AT ONCE AND THE TONGUE OF HIM, AND

ἐλάλει εὐλογῶν τὸν θεόν. **1.65** καὶ ἐγένετο ἐπὶ
HE WAS SPEAKING PRAISING - GOD. AND ²CAME ³UPON

πάντας φόβος τοὺς περιοικοῦντας αὐτούς, καὶ
⁴ALL ¹FEAR THE ONES LIVING AROUND THEM, AND

ἐν ὅλῃ τῇ ὀρεινῇ τῆς Ἰουδαίας
IN [THE] ENTIRE - MOUNTAIN COUNTRY - OF JUDEA

διελαλεῖτο πάντα τὰ ῥήματα ταῦτα, **1.66** καὶ
EVERYONE~WAS TALKING ABOUT - THESE~MATTERS, AND

ἔθεντο πάντες οἱ ἀκούσαντες ἐν τῇ καρδίᾳ αὐτῶν
³KEPT [THESE THINGS] ¹EVERYONE - ²HAVING LISTENED IN THE HEART OF THEM,

λέγοντες, Τί ἄρα τὸ παιδίον τοῦτο ἔσται; καὶ γὰρ
SAYING, WHAT THEN - ³CHILD ²THIS ¹WILL BE? FOR~INDEED

χεὶρ κυρίου ἦν μετ᾽ αὐτοῦ.
[THE] HAND OF [THE] LORD WAS WITH HIM.

1.67 Καὶ Ζαχαρίας ὁ πατὴρ αὐτοῦ ἐπλήσθη
AND ZECHARIAH, THE FATHER OF HIM, WAS FILLED

πνεύματος ἁγίου καὶ ἐπροφήτευσεν λέγων,
[WITH THE] HOLY~SPIRIT AND PROPHESIED, SAYING,

1.68 Εὐλογητὸς κύριος ὁ θεὸς τοῦ Ἰσραήλ,
BLESSED [IS] [THE] LORD, THE GOD - OF ISRAEL,

ὅτι ἐπεσκέψατο καὶ ἐποίησεν
BECAUSE HE VISITED AND ACCOMPLISHED

λύτρωσιν τῷ λαῷ αὐτοῦ,
REDEMPTION FOR THE PEOPLE OF HIM,

1.69 καὶ ἤγειρεν κέρας σωτηρίας ἡμῖν
AND HE RAISED UP A HORN OF SALVATION FOR US

they rejoiced with her.

59 On the eighth day they came to circumcise the child, and they were going to name him Zechariah after his father. ⁶⁰But his mother said, "No; he is to be called John." ⁶¹They said to her, "None of your relatives has this name." ⁶²Then they began motioning to his father to find out what name he wanted to give him. ⁶³He asked for a writing tablet and wrote, "His name is John." And all of them were amazed. ⁶⁴Immediately his mouth was opened and his tongue freed, and he began to speak, praising God. ⁶⁵Fear came over all their neighbors, and all these things were talked about throughout the entire hill country of Judea. ⁶⁶All who heard them pondered them and said, "What then will this child become?" For, indeed, the hand of the Lord was with him.

67 Then his father Zechariah was filled with the Holy Spirit and spoke this prophecy:
⁶⁸ "Blessed be the Lord
    God of Israel,
  for he has looked
    favorably on his
    people and
    redeemed them.
⁶⁹ He has raised up a mighty
    Savior⁸ for us

⁸ Gk *a horn of salvation*

in the house of his
servant David,
70 as he spoke through the
mouth of his holy
prophets from of
old,
71   that we would be
saved from our
enemies and from
the hand of all who
hate us.
72 Thus he has shown the
mercy promised to
our ancestors,
and has remembered
his holy covenant,
73 the oath that he swore to
our ancestor
Abraham,
to grant us
74 that we, being rescued
from the hands of
our enemies,
might serve him
without fear,
75 in holiness and
righteousness
before him all our days.
76 And you, child, will be
called the prophet
of the Most High;
for you will go before
the Lord to prepare
his ways,
77 to give knowledge of
salvation to his
people
by the forgiveness of
their sins.
78 By the tender mercy of
our God,
the dawn from on high
will break upon[h] us,

[h] Other ancient authorities read *has broken upon*

ἐν οἴκῳ   Δαυὶδ   παιδὸς   αὐτοῦ,
IN [THE] HOUSE OF DAVID, [THE] SERVANT OF HIM,

1.70 καθὼς ἐλάλησεν διὰ   στόματος τῶν ἁγίων
JUST AS HE SPOKE   THROUGH [THE] MOUTH OF THE HOLY

ἀπ᾽ αἰῶνος προφητῶν αὐτοῦ,
³FROM ⁴[THE] AGE ¹PROPHETS ²OF HIM,

1.71 σωτηρίαν ἐξ ἐχθρῶν ἡμῶν καὶ ἐκ
SALVATION FROM OUR~ENEMIES AND FROM

χειρὸς πάντων τῶν   μισούντων ἡμᾶς,
[THE] HAND OF ALL OF THE ONES HATING US,

1.72 ποιῆσαι   ἔλεος μετὰ τῶν πατέρων ἡμῶν
TO DEMONSTRATE MERCY TO THE FATHERS OF US

καὶ μνησθῆναι διαθήκης ἁγίας αὐτοῦ,
AND TO REMEMBER [THE] HOLY~COVENANT OF HIM,

1.73 ὅρκον ὃν ὤμοσεν πρὸς ᾽Αβραὰμ τὸν πατέρα
[THE] OATH WHICH HE SWORE TO ABRAHAM THE FATHER

ἡμῶν,
OF US,

τοῦ δοῦναι ἡμῖν **1.74** ἀφόβως ἐκ   χειρὸς
-   TO GRANT US,   ⁷FEARLESSLY ²FROM ³[THE] HAND

ἐχθρῶν   ῥυσθέντας
⁴OF [OUR] ENEMIES, ¹HAVING BEEN DELIVERED

λατρεύειν αὐτῷ **1.75** ἐν ὁσιότητι καὶ δικαιοσύνῃ
⁵TO SERVE ⁶HIM   IN HOLINESS AND RIGHTEOUSNESS

ἐνώπιον αὐτοῦ πάσαις ταῖς ἡμέραις ἡμῶν.
BEFORE HIM ALL THE DAYS OF US.

1.76 Καὶ σὺ δέ, παιδίον, προφήτης ὑψίστου
AND YOU ALSO, CHILD, A PROPHET OF [THE] MOST HIGH

κληθήσῃ·
WILL BE CALLED;

προπορεύσῃ γὰρ ἐνώπιον κυρίου
FOR~YOU WILL GO BEFORE [THE] LORD

ἑτοιμάσαι ὁδοὺς αὐτοῦ,
TO PREPARE HIS~WAYS,

1.77 τοῦ δοῦναι γνῶσιν σωτηρίας τῷ λαῷ αὐτοῦ
-   TO GIVE KNOWLEDGE OF SALVATION TO THE PEOPLE OF HIM

ἐν ἀφέσει   ἁμαρτιῶν αὐτῶν,
BY A FORGIVENESS OF [THE] SINS OF THEM

1.78 διὰ   σπλάγχνα ἐλέους θεοῦ   ἡμῶν,
THROUGH [THE] TENDER MERCIES OF [THE] GOD OF US,

ἐν οἷς ⌜ἐπισκέψεται⌝ ἡμᾶς ἀνατολὴ ἐξ
BY WHICH WILL VISIT US [THE] RISING [SUN] FROM

ὕψους,
HEAVEN,

1:78 text: ASV RSV NASB NIV NEB TEV NRSV. var. επεσκεψατο (visited): KJV ASVmg RSVmg NEBmg NJB NRSVmg.

1.79 ἐπιφᾶναι τοῖς   ἐν σκότει καὶ σκιᾷ
TO APPEAR   TO THE ONES ²IN ³DARKNESS ⁴AND ⁵IN [THE] SHADOW

θανάτου   καθημένοις,
⁶OF DEATH ¹SITTING,

τοῦ κατευθῦναι τοὺς πόδας ἡμῶν
-      TO DIRECT   THE   FEET   OF US

εἰς ὁδὸν   εἰρήνης.
INTO [THE] WAY OF PEACE.

1.80 Τὸ δὲ παιδίον ηὔξανεν   καὶ ἐκραταιοῦτο
AND [THE] CHILD WAS GROWING AND WAS BEING STRENGTHENED

πνεύματι, καὶ ἦν   ἐν ταῖς ἐρήμοις   ἕως ἡμέρας
IN SPIRIT,   AND HE WAS IN THE   DESOLATE PLACES UNTIL [THE] DAY

ἀναδείξεως   αὐτοῦ πρὸς τὸν Ἰσραήλ.
OF [THE] MANIFESTATION OF HIM TO   -   ISRAEL.

⁷⁹to give light to those who sit in darkness and in the shadow of death, to guide our feet into the way of peace."
80 The child grew and became strong in spirit, and he was in the wilderness until the day he appeared publicly to Israel.

2.1 Ἐγένετο δὲ ἐν ταῖς ἡμέραις ἐκείναις
AND~IT CAME ABOUT IN   -   THOSE~DAYS

ἐξῆλθεν δόγμα   παρὰ Καίσαρος Αὐγούστου
[THAT] A DECREE~WAS SENT OUT FROM CAESAR   AUGUSTUS

ἀπογράφεσθαι πᾶσαν τὴν οἰκουμένην. **2.2** αὕτη
TO REGISTER   ALL   THE   WORLD.   THIS

ἀπογραφὴ πρώτη ἐγένετο   ἡγεμονεύοντος τῆς Συρίας
CENSUS   WAS~[THE] FIRST [TAKEN WHILE] ²IS GOVERNING   -   ³SYRIA

Κυρηνίου. **2.3** καὶ ἐπορεύοντο πάντες ἀπογράφεσθαι,
¹QUIRINIUS.   AND EVERYONE~WAS TRAVELING   TO REGISTER,

ἕκαστος εἰς τὴν ἑαυτοῦ πόλιν. **2.4** Ἀνέβη δὲ καὶ
EACH   TO   -   HIS OWN   CITY.   NOW~WENT UP ALSO

Ἰωσὴφ ἀπὸ τῆς Γαλιλαίας ἐκ πόλεως Ναζαρὲθ εἰς
JOSEPH FROM -   GALILEE   FROM [THE] CITY OF NAZARETH TO

τὴν Ἰουδαίαν εἰς πόλιν Δαυὶδ ἥτις καλεῖται Βηθλέεμ,
-      JUDEA   TO [THE] CITY OF DAVID WHICH IS CALLED   BETHLEHEM,

διὰ   τὸ εἶναι αὐτὸν ἐξ οἴκου   καὶ πατριᾶς Δαυίδ,
BECAUSE -   HE~WAS   OF [THE] HOUSE AND LINEAGE   OF DAVID,

2.5 ἀπογράψασθαι σὺν Μαριὰμ τῇ   ἐμνηστευμένῃ
TO REGISTER   WITH MARY,   THE ONE HAVING BEEN ENGAGED

αὐτῷ,   οὔσῃ ἐγκύῳ. **2.6** ἐγένετο δὲ ἐν τῷ
TO HIM, BEING PREGNANT.   AND~IT CAME ABOUT WHILE -

εἶναι αὐτοὺς ἐκεῖ ἐπλήσθησαν αἱ ἡμέραι τοῦ
THEY~WERE THERE WERE FULFILLED THE DAYS   -

τεκεῖν αὐτήν, **2.7** καὶ ἔτεκεν τὸν υἱὸν αὐτῆς τὸν
[FOR] HER~TO BEAR,   AND SHE BORE THE SON   OF HER THE

πρωτότοκον, καὶ ἐσπαργάνωσεν αὐτὸν καὶ ἀνέκλινεν
FIRSTBORN,   AND SHE WRAPPED IN CLOTHS HIM   AND LAID

In those days a decree went out from Emperor Augustus that all the world should be registered. ²This was the first registration and was taken while Quirinius was governor of Syria. ³All went to their own towns to be registered. ⁴Joseph also went from the town of Nazareth in Galilee to Judea, to the city of David called Bethlehem, because he was descended from the house and family of David. ⁵He went to be registered with Mary, to whom he was engaged and who was expecting a child. ⁶While they were there, the time came for her to deliver her child. ⁷And she gave birth to her firstborn son and wrapped him in bands of cloth, and laid him in a manger, because there was no place for them in the inn.

8 In that region there were shepherds living in the fields, keeping watch over their flock by night. [9]Then an angel of the Lord stood before them, and the glory of the Lord shone around them, and they were terrified. [10]But the angel said to them, "Do not be afraid; for see—I am bringing you good news of great joy for all the people: [11]to you is born this day in the city of David a Savior, who is the Messiah,[i] the Lord. [12]This will be a sign for you: you will find a child wrapped in bands of cloth and lying in a manger." [13]And suddenly there was with the angel a multitude of the heavenly host,[j] praising God and saying,

[14]"Glory to God in the
  highest heaven,
 and on earth peace
  among those whom
  he favors!"[k]

15 When the angels had left them and gone into heaven, the shepherds said to one another, "Let us go now to Bethlehem and see this thing that has taken place, which the Lord has made known to us." [16]So they went with haste and found

[i] Or *the Christ*
[j] Gk *army*
[k] Other ancient authorities read *peace,*
 goodwill among people

αὐτὸν ἐν φάτνῃ, διότι οὐκ ἦν αὐτοῖς τόπος ἐν τῷ
HIM IN A MANGER, BECAUSE THERE WAS NOT FOR THEM A PLACE IN THE

καταλύματι.
INN.

2.8 Καὶ ποιμένες ἦσαν ἐν τῇ χώρᾳ τῇ αὐτῇ
  AND SHEPHERDS WERE IN THE [2]REGION - [1]SAME

ἀγραυλοῦντες καὶ φυλάσσοντες φυλακὰς τῆς νυκτὸς
LIVING OUTSIDE AND KEEPING WATCH [DURING] THE NIGHT

ἐπὶ τὴν ποίμνην αὐτῶν. **2.9** καὶ ἄγγελος κυρίου
OVER THE FLOCK OF THEM. AND AN ANGEL OF [THE] LORD

ἐπέστη αὐτοῖς καὶ δόξα κυρίου περιέλαμψεν
APPEARED TO THEM AND [THE] GLORY OF [THE] LORD SHONE AROUND

αὐτούς, καὶ ἐφοβήθησαν φόβον μέγαν. **2.10** καὶ
THEM, AND THEY WERE AFRAID [WITH] A GREAT~FEAR. AND

εἶπεν αὐτοῖς ὁ ἄγγελος, Μὴ φοβεῖσθε, ἰδοὺ γὰρ
SAID TO THEM THE ANGEL, DO NOT BE AFRAID, FOR~BEHOLD

εὐαγγελίζομαι ὑμῖν χαρὰν μεγάλην ἥτις ἔσται παντὶ
I ANNOUNCE GOOD NEWS TO YOU° [OF] GREAT~JOY WHICH WILL BE TO ALL

τῷ λαῷ, **2.11** ὅτι ἐτέχθη ὑμῖν σήμερον σωτὴρ ὅς
THE PEOPLE, BECAUSE WAS BORN TO YOU° TODAY A SAVIOR, WHO

ἐστιν Χριστὸς κύριος ἐν πόλει Δαυίδ. **2.12** καὶ
IS CHRIST [THE] LORD IN [THE] CITY OF DAVID. AND

τοῦτο ὑμῖν τὸ σημεῖον, εὑρήσετε βρέφος
THIS [WILL BE] TO YOU° THE SIGN, YOU° WILL FIND AN INFANT

ἐσπαργανωμένον καὶ κείμενον ἐν φάτνῃ. **2.13** καὶ
HAVING BEEN WRAPPED IN CLOTHS AND LYING IN A MANGER. AND

ἐξαίφνης ἐγένετο σὺν τῷ ἀγγέλῳ πλῆθος
SUDDENLY THERE WAS WITH THE ANGEL A MULTITUDE

στρατιᾶς οὐρανίου αἰνούντων τὸν θεὸν καὶ λεγόντων,
OF [THE] HEAVENLY~ARMY PRAISING - GOD AND SAYING,

2.14 Δόξα ἐν ὑψίστοις θεῷ
  GLORY IN [THE] HIGHEST TO GOD

καὶ ⌐ἐπὶ γῆς εἰρήνη ἐν ἀνθρώποις
AND ON EARTH PEACE AMONG MEN

εὐδοκίας⌐.
OF GOODWILL.

2.15 Καὶ ἐγένετο ὡς ἀπῆλθον ἀπ᾽ αὐτῶν εἰς τὸν
  AND IT CAME ABOUT WHEN DEPARTED FROM THEM TO -

οὐρανὸν οἱ ἄγγελοι, οἱ ποιμένες ἐλάλουν πρὸς
HEAVEN THE ANGELS, THE SHEPHERDS WERE SAYING TO

ἀλλήλους, Διέλθωμεν δὴ ἕως Βηθλέεμ καὶ ἴδωμεν τὸ
ONE ANOTHER, LET US GO NOW UP TO BETHLEHEM AND LET US SEE -

ῥῆμα τοῦτο τὸ γεγονὸς ὃ ὁ κύριος ἐγνώρισεν
THIS~THING - HAVING COME ABOUT WHICH THE LORD MADE KNOWN

ἡμῖν. **2.16** καὶ ἦλθαν σπεύσαντες καὶ ἀνεῦραν τήν
TO US. AND THEY CAME HAVING MADE HASTE AND THEY FOUND -

2:14 text: ASV RSV NASB NIV NEB TEV NJB NRSV. var. επι γης ειρηνη εν ανθρωποις ευδοκια (peace on earth, good pleasure toward men): KJV ASVmg RSVmg NEBmg NJBmg NRSVmg.

τε Μαριὰμ καὶ τὸν Ἰωσὴφ καὶ τὸ βρέφος κείμενον
BOTH MARY AND - JOSEPH AND THE INFANT LYING

ἐν τῇ φάτνῃ· **2.17** ἰδόντες δὲ ἐγνώρισαν περὶ
IN THE MANGER. AND~HAVING SEEN [THEM] THEY MADE KNOWN CONCERNING

τοῦ ῥήματος τοῦ λαληθέντος αὐτοῖς περὶ τοῦ
THE WORD - HAVING BEEN MADE KNOWN TO THEM ABOUT -

παιδίου τούτου. **2.18** καὶ πάντες οἱ ἀκούσαντες
THIS~CHILD. AND ALL THE ONES HAVING HEARD

ἐθαύμασαν περὶ τῶν λαληθέντων ὑπὸ τῶν ποιμένων
WERE AMAZED ABOUT THE THINGS HAVING BEEN SPOKEN BY THE SHEPHERDS

πρὸς αὐτούς· **2.19** ἡ δὲ Μαριὰμ πάντα συνετήρει τὰ
TO THEM. - BUT MARY WAS KEEPING [IN MIND]~ALL -

ῥήματα ταῦτα συμβάλλουσα ἐν τῇ καρδίᾳ αὐτῆς.
THESE~THINGS PONDERING [THEM] IN THE HEART OF HER.

2.20 καὶ ὑπέστρεψαν οἱ ποιμένες δοξάζοντες καὶ
AND RETURNED THE SHEPHERDS GLORIFYING AND

αἰνοῦντες τὸν θεὸν ἐπὶ πᾶσιν οἷς ἤκουσαν καὶ εἶδον
PRAISING - GOD FOR ALL WHICH THEY HEARD AND SAW

καθὼς ἐλαλήθη πρὸς αὐτούς.
JUST AS WAS SPOKEN TO THEM.

2.21 Καὶ ὅτε ἐπλήσθησαν ἡμέραι ὀκτὼ τοῦ
AND WHEN WERE COMPLETED EIGHT~DAYS, -

περιτεμεῖν αὐτὸν καὶ ἐκλήθη τὸ ὄνομα αὐτοῦ Ἰησοῦς,
FOR HIM~TO BE CIRCUMCISED - WAS CALLED THE NAME OF HIM JESUS,

τὸ κληθὲν ὑπὸ τοῦ ἀγγέλου πρὸ τοῦ
THE [NAME] CALLED BY THE ANGEL BEFORE -

συλλημφθῆναι αὐτὸν ἐν τῇ κοιλίᾳ.
HE~WAS CONCEIVED IN THE WOMB.

2.22 Καὶ ὅτε ἐπλήσθησαν αἱ ἡμέραι τοῦ
AND WHEN WERE COMPLETED THE DAYS OF THE

καθαρισμοῦ αὐτῶν κατὰ τὸν νόμον Μωϋσέως,
PURIFICATION OF THEM ACCORDING TO THE LAW OF MOSES,

ἀνήγαγον αὐτὸν εἰς Ἱεροσόλυμα παραστῆσαι τῷ
THEY BROUGHT HIM [UP] TO JERUSALEM TO PRESENT [HIM] TO THE

κυρίῳ, **2.23** καθὼς γέγραπται ἐν νόμῳ κυρίου ὅτι
LORD, JUST AS IT HAS BEEN WRITTEN IN [THE] LAW OF [THE] LORD -

Πᾶν ἄρσεν διανοῖγον μήτραν ἅγιον τῷ κυρίῳ
EVERY MALE OPENING [THE] WOMB HOLY TO THE LORD

κληθήσεται, **2.24** καὶ τοῦ δοῦναι θυσίαν κατὰ
WILL BE CALLED, AND - TO OFFER A SACRIFICE ACCORDING TO

τὸ εἰρημένον ἐν τῷ νόμῳ κυρίου, ζεῦγος
THE THING HAVING BEEN SAID IN THE LAW OF [THE] LORD, A PAIR

τρυγόνων ἢ δύο νοσσοὺς περιστερῶν.
OF TURTLE DOVES OR TWO YOUNG PIGEONS.

2.25 Καὶ ἰδοὺ ἄνθρωπος ἦν ἐν Ἱερουσαλὴμ
AND BEHOLD A MAN WAS IN JERUSALEM

Mary and Joseph, and the child lying in the manger. [17]When they saw this, they made known what had been told them about this child; [18]and all who heard it were amazed at what the shepherds told them. [19]But Mary treasured all these words and pondered them in her heart. [20]The shepherds returned, glorifying and praising God for all they had heard and seen, as it had been told them.

21 After eight days had passed, it was time to circumcise the child; and he was called Jesus, the name given by the angel before he was conceived in the womb.

22 When the time came for their purification according to the law of Moses, they brought him up to Jerusalem to present him to the Lord [23](as it is written in the law of the Lord, "Every firstborn male shall be designated as holy to the Lord"), [24]and they offered a sacrifice according to what is stated in the law of the Lord, "a pair of turtledoves or two young pigeons."

25 Now there was a man in Jerusalem

2:23 Exod. 13:2, 12, 15   **2:24** Lev. 12:8

whose name was Simeon;*l* this man was righteous and devout, looking forward to the consolation of Israel, and the Holy Spirit rested on him. 26It had been revealed to him by the Holy Spirit that he would not see death before he had seen the Lord's Messiah.*m* 27Guided by the Spirit, Simeon*n* came into the temple; and when the parents brought in the child Jesus, to do for him what was customary under the law, 28Simeon*o* took him in his arms and praised God, saying,

29"Master, now you are dismissing your servant*p* in peace, according to your word;

30for my eyes have seen your salvation,

31 which you have prepared in the presence of all peoples,

32a light for revelation to the Gentiles and for glory to your people Israel."

33 And the child's father and mother were amazed at what was being said about him. 34Then Simeon*l* blessed them and said to his mother Mary, "This child is destined for the falling and the rising of many in Israel, and to be a sign that will be opposed 35so that the

l Gk *Symeon*
m Or *the Lord's Christ*
n Gk *In the Spirit, he*
o Gk *he*
p Gk *slave*

ᾧ ὄνομα Συμεὼν καὶ ὁ ἄνθρωπος οὗτος
TO WHOM [WAS THE] NAME SIMEON AND - THIS~MAN [WAS]

δίκαιος καὶ εὐλαβὴς προσδεχόμενος παράκλησιν τοῦ
RIGHTEOUS AND DEVOUT, WAITING FOR [THE] CONSOLATION -

Ἰσραήλ, καὶ πνεῦμα ἦν ἅγιον ἐπ᾽ αὐτόν· 2.26 καὶ
OF ISRAEL, AND 2SPIRIT 3WAS 1[THE] HOLY UPON HIM. AND

ἦν αὐτῷ κεχρηματισμένον ὑπὸ τοῦ πνεύματος τοῦ
IT HAD TO HIM BEEN REVEALED BY THE 2SPIRIT -

ἁγίου μὴ ἰδεῖν θάνατον πρὶν [ἢ] ἂν ἴδῃ τὸν
1HOLY [THAT HE WAS] NOT TO SEE DEATH UNTIL HE MIGHT SEE THE

Χριστὸν κυρίου. 2.27 καὶ ἦλθεν ἐν τῷ πνεύματι εἰς
CHRIST OF [THE] LORD. AND HE CAME BY THE SPIRIT INTO

τὸ ἱερόν· καὶ ἐν τῷ εἰσαγαγεῖν τοὺς γονεῖς τὸ
THE TEMPLE. AND WHEN 3BROUGHT IN 1THE 2PARENTS THE

παιδίον Ἰησοῦν τοῦ ποιῆσαι αὐτοὺς κατὰ τὸ
CHILD, JESUS - [FOR] THEM~TO DO ACCORDING TO THE THING

εἰθισμένον τοῦ νόμου περὶ αὐτοῦ 2.28 καὶ
HAVING BEEN CUSTOMARY [IN] THE LAW CONCERNING HIM AND

αὐτὸς ἐδέξατο αὐτὸ εἰς τὰς ἀγκάλας καὶ εὐλόγησεν
HE RECEIVED IT(HIM) IN THE(HIS) ARMS AND BLESSED

τὸν θεὸν καὶ εἶπεν,
- GOD AND SAID,

2.29 Νῦν ἀπολύεις τὸν δοῦλόν σου, δέσποτα,
NOW YOU DISMISS THE SERVANT OF YOU, MASTER,

κατὰ τὸ ῥῆμά σου ἐν εἰρήνῃ·
ACCORDING TO THE WORD OF YOU IN PEACE;

2.30 ὅτι εἶδον οἱ ὀφθαλμοί μου τὸ σωτήριόν σου,
BECAUSE SAW THE EYES OF ME THE SALVATION OF YOU,

2.31 ὃ ἡτοίμασας κατὰ πρόσωπον πάντων τῶν
WHICH YOU PREPARED BEFORE [THE] FACE OF ALL THE

λαῶν,
PEOPLE,

2.32 φῶς εἰς ἀποκάλυψιν ἐθνῶν
A LIGHT FOR REVELATION [TO THE] GENTILES

καὶ δόξαν λαοῦ σου Ἰσραήλ.
AND GLORY OF YOUR~PEOPLE ISRAEL.

2.33 καὶ ἦν ὁ πατὴρ αὐτοῦ καὶ ἡ μήτηρ
AND WERE THE FATHER OF HIM AND THE MOTHER

θαυμάζοντες ἐπὶ τοῖς λαλουμένοις περὶ αὐτοῦ.
BEING AMAZED AT THE THINGS BEING SPOKEN ABOUT HIM.

2.34 καὶ εὐλόγησεν αὐτοὺς Συμεὼν καὶ εἶπεν πρὸς
AND BLESSED THEM SIMEON AND SAID TO

Μαριὰμ τὴν μητέρα αὐτοῦ, Ἰδοὺ οὗτος κεῖται εἰς
MARY THE MOTHER OF HIM, BEHOLD THIS ONE IS DESTINED FOR

πτῶσιν καὶ ἀνάστασιν πολλῶν ἐν τῷ Ἰσραὴλ καὶ εἰς
[THE] FALL AND RISING OF MANY IN - ISRAEL AND FOR

σημεῖον ἀντιλεγόμενον 2.35 —καὶ σοῦ [δὲ] αὐτῆς τὴν
A SIGN BEING OPPOSED —AND 5OF YOU 7ALSO 6YOURSELF 3THE

ψυχὴν διελεύσεται ῥομφαία—, ὅπως ἂν ἀποκαλυφθῶσιν
⁴SOUL   ²WILL PIERCE   ¹A SWORD—SO THAT   MAY BE REVEALED

ἐκ πολλῶν καρδιῶν διαλογισμοί.
FROM MANY   HEARTS   [THE] THOUGHTS.

2.36 Καὶ ἦν   Ἄννα προφῆτις, θυγάτηρ Φανουήλ,
AND   THERE WAS ANNA, A PROPHETESS, A DAUGHTER OF PHANUEL,

ἐκ φυλῆς Ἀσήρ· αὕτη   προβεβηκυῖα   ἐν
FROM [THE] TRIBE OF ASHER; THIS [WOMAN], HAVING BECOME ADVANCED IN

ἡμέραις πολλαῖς, ζήσασα μετὰ ἀνδρὸς ἔτη ἑπτὰ ἀπὸ
MANY~DAYS,   HAVING LIVED WITH [HER] HUSBAND SEVEN~YEARS FROM

τῆς παρθενίας αὐτῆς **2.37** καὶ αὐτὴ χήρα ἕως ἐτῶν
THE VIRGINITY   OF HER   AND SHE [WAS] A WIDOW UNTIL YEARS

ὀγδοήκοντα τεσσάρων, ἡ οὐκ ἀφίστατο τοῦ ἱεροῦ
EIGHTY-FOUR,   WHO WAS NOT DEPARTING [FROM] THE TEMPLE,

νηστείαις καὶ δεήσεσιν λατρεύουσα νύκτα καὶ ἡμέραν.
WITH FASTINGS AND PRAYERS   SERVING   NIGHT AND DAY.

2.38 καὶ αὐτῇ τῇ ὥρᾳ ἐπιστᾶσα ἀνθωμολογεῖτο τῷ
AND   AT THAT VERY HOUR HAVING STOOD NEARBY SHE WAS PRAISING -

θεῷ καὶ ἐλάλει   περὶ αὐτοῦ πᾶσιν τοῖς
GOD   AND SHE WAS SPEAKING ABOUT HIM   TO ALL THE ONES

προσδεχομένοις λύτρωσιν Ἰερουσαλήμ.
ANTICIPATING   [THE] REDEMPTION OF JERUSALEM.

2.39 Καὶ ὡς ἐτέλεσαν πάντα τὰ κατὰ   τὸν
AND   WHEN COMPLETED EVERYTHING -   ACCORDING TO THE

νόμον κυρίου, ἐπέστρεψαν εἰς τὴν Γαλιλαίαν εἰς
LAW   OF [THE] LORD, THEY RETURNED TO -   GALILEE   TO

πόλιν ἑαυτῶν Ναζαρέθ. **2.40** Τὸ δὲ παιδίον ηὔξανεν
[THE] CITY OF THEM, NAZARETH.   AND~THE CHILD   WAS GROWING

καὶ ἐκραταιοῦτο   πληρούμενον σοφίᾳ, καὶ χάρις
AND WAS BEING STRENGTHENED, BEING FILLED WITH WISDOM, AND [THE] GRACE

θεοῦ ἦν ἐπ᾽ αὐτό.
OF GOD WAS UPON IT(HIM).

2.41 Καὶ ἐπορεύοντο οἱ γονεῖς αὐτοῦ κατ᾽ ἔτος εἰς
AND   WERE TRAVELING THE PARENTS OF HIM EVERY YEAR TO

Ἰερουσαλὴμ τῇ   ἑορτῇ τοῦ πάσχα. **2.42** καὶ ὅτε
JERUSALEM   FOR THE FEAST OF THE PASSOVER.   AND WHEN

ἐγένετο ἐτῶν δώδεκα, ἀναβαινόντων αὐτῶν κατὰ
HE BECAME OF YEARS TWELVE, GOING UP   [WITH] THEM ACCORDING TO

τὸ ἔθος τῆς ἑορτῆς **2.43** καὶ τελειωσάντων τὰς
THE CUSTOM OF THE FEAST   AND HAVING FULFILLED   THE

ἡμέρας, ἐν τῷ ὑποστρέφειν αὐτοὺς ὑπέμεινεν Ἰησοῦς
DAYS,   WHEN THEY~RETURNED,   REMAINED   JESUS

ὁ παῖς ἐν Ἰερουσαλήμ, καὶ οὐκ ἔγνωσαν οἱ γονεῖς
THE BOY IN JERUSALEM,   AND DID NOT KNOW THE PARENTS

αὐτοῦ. **2.44** νομίσαντες δὲ αὐτὸν εἶναι ἐν τῇ συνοδίᾳ
OF HIM.   AND~HAVING SUPPOSED HIM   TO BE IN THE CARAVAN

ἦλθον ἡμέρας ὁδὸν καὶ ἀνεζήτουν   αὐτὸν ἐν τοῖς
THEY WENT A JOURNEY~OF A DAY AND THEY WERE LOOKING FOR HIM   AMONG THE

inner thoughts of many will
be revealed—and a sword
will pierce your own soul
too."

36 There was also a
prophet, Anna[q] the daughter
of Phanuel, of the tribe of
Asher. She was of a great
age, having lived with her
husband seven years after
her marriage, [37]then as a
widow to the age of eighty-
four. She never left the
temple but worshiped there
with fasting and prayer night
and day. [38]At that moment
she came, and began to
praise God and to speak
about the child[r] to all who
were looking for the
redemption of Jerusalem.

39 When they had
finished everything required
by the law of the Lord, they
returned to Galilee, to their
own town of Nazareth.
[40]The child grew and
became strong, filled with
wisdom; and the favor of
God was upon him.

41 Now every year his
parents went to Jerusalem
for the festival of the
Passover. [42]And when he
was twelve years old, they
went up as usual for the
festival. [43]When the festival
was ended and they started
to return, the boy Jesus
stayed behind in Jerusalem,
but his parents did not know
it. [44]Assuming that he was
in the group of travelers,
they went a day's journey.
Then they started to look
for him among their

[q] Gk Hanna
[r] Gk him

relatives and friends.
45When they did not find him, they returned to Jerusalem to search for him. 46After three days they found him in the temple, sitting among the teachers, listening to them and asking them questions. 47And all who heard him were amazed at his understanding and his answers. 48When his parents[s] saw him they were astonished; and his mother said to him, "Child, why have you treated us like this? Look, your father and I have been searching for you in great anxiety." 49He said to them, "Why were you searching for me? Did you not know that I must be in my Father's house?"[t] 50But they did not understand what he said to them. 51Then he went down with them and came to Nazareth, and was obedient to them. His mother treasured all these things in her heart.

52 And Jesus increased in wisdom and in years,[u] and in divine and human favor.

[s] Gk they
[t] Or be about my Father's interests?
[u] Or in stature

συγγενεῦσιν	καὶ	τοῖς	γνωστοῖς,	**2.45** καὶ	μὴ
RELATIVES	AND	THE	ACQUAINTANCES,	AND	NOT

εὑρόντες	ὑπέστρεψαν	εἰς	Ἰερουσαλὴμ	ἀναζητοῦντες
HAVING FOUND [HIM]	THEY RETURNED	TO	JERUSALEM	LOOKING FOR

αὐτόν.	**2.46** καὶ	ἐγένετο	μετὰ	ἡμέρας	τρεῖς	εὗρον
HIM.	AND	IT CAME ABOUT	AFTER	THREE~DAYS		THEY FOUND

αὐτὸν	ἐν	τῷ	ἱερῷ	καθεζόμενον	ἐν	μέσῳ	τῶν
HIM	IN	THE	TEMPLE	SITTING	IN	[THE] MIDST	OF THE

διδασκάλων	καὶ	ἀκούοντα	αὐτῶν	καὶ	ἐπερωτῶντα
TEACHERS	AND	LISTENING	TO THEM	AND	QUESTIONING

αὐτούς·	**2.47** ἐξίσταντο	δὲ	πάντες	οἱ	ἀκούοντες
THEM.	AND~WERE AMAZED		ALL	THE ONES	LISTENING

αὐτοῦ	ἐπὶ	τῇ	συνέσει	καὶ	ταῖς	ἀποκρίσεσιν	αὐτοῦ.
TO HIM	AT	THE	INTELLIGENCE	AND	THE	ANSWERS	OF HIM.

2.48 καὶ	ἰδόντες	αὐτὸν	ἐξεπλάγησαν,	καὶ	εἶπεν	πρὸς
AND	HAVING SEEN	HIM	THEY WERE ASTOUNDED,	AND	SAID	TO

αὐτὸν	ἡ	μήτηρ	αὐτοῦ,	Τέκνον,	τί	ἐποίησας
HIM	THE	MOTHER	OF HIM,	SON,	WHY	DID YOU DO

ἡμῖν	οὕτως;	ἰδοὺ	ὁ	πατήρ	σου	κἀγὼ	ὀδυνώμενοι
THUS~TO US?		BEHOLD	THE	FATHER	OF YOU	AND I	BEING ANXIOUS

ἐζητοῦμέν	σε.	**2.49** καὶ	εἶπεν	πρὸς	αὐτούς,	Τί	ὅτι
WERE LOOKING FOR	YOU.	AND	HE SAID	TO	THEM,	WHY [IS IT]	THAT

ἐζητεῖτέ	με;	οὐκ	ᾔδειτε	ὅτι	ἐν	τοῖς	τοῦ
YOU° WERE LOOKING FOR	ME?	HAD YOU°	NOT KNOWN	THAT	IN	THE THINGS	OF THE

πατρός	μου	δεῖ	εἶναί	με;	**2.50** καὶ	αὐτοὶ
FATHER	OF ME	IT IS NECESSARY [FOR]	ME~TO BE?		AND	THEY

οὐ συνῆκαν	τὸ	ῥῆμα	ὃ	ἐλάλησεν	αὐτοῖς.	**2.51** καὶ
DID NOT UNDERSTAND	THE	WORD	WHICH	HE SPOKE	TO THEM.	AND

κατέβη	μετ'	αὐτῶν	καὶ	ἦλθεν	εἰς	Ναζαρὲθ	καὶ
HE WENT DOWN	WITH	THEM	AND	THEY CAME	TO	NAZARETH	AND

ἦν	ὑποτασσόμενος	αὐτοῖς.	καὶ	ἡ	μήτηρ	αὐτοῦ
HE WAS BEING SUBJECT		TO THEM.	AND	THE	MOTHER	OF HIM

διετήρει	πάντα	τὰ	ῥήματα	ἐν	τῇ	καρδίᾳ	αὐτῆς.
WAS TREASURING	ALL	THE	MATTERS	IN	THE	HEART	OF HER.

2.52 Καὶ	Ἰησοῦς	προέκοπτεν	[ἐν τῇ]	σοφίᾳ	καὶ	ἡλικίᾳ
AND	JESUS	WAS INCREASING	IN -	WISDOM	AND	STATURE

καὶ	χάριτι	παρὰ	θεῷ	καὶ	ἀνθρώποις.
AND	IN FAVOR	WITH	GOD	AND	MEN.

CHAPTER 3

In the fifteenth year of the reign of Emperor Tiberius, when Pontius Pilate was governor of Judea, and Herod was ruler[v] of Galilee,

[v] Gk tetrarch

3.1 Ἐν	ἔτει	δὲ	πεντεκαιδεκάτῳ	τῆς	ἡγεμονίας
²IN	³[THE] YEAR	¹NOW	FIFTEENTH	OF THE	REIGN

Τιβερίου	Καίσαρος,	ἡγεμονεύοντος	Ποντίου	Πιλάτου	τῆς
OF TIBERIUS	CAESAR,	[WHILE] GOVERNING	PONTIUS	PILATE	-

Ἰουδαίας,	καὶ	τετρααρχοῦντος	τῆς	Γαλιλαίας	Ἡρῴδου,
OF JUDEA,	AND	BEING TETRARCH	-	OF GALILEE [WAS]	HEROD,

Φιλίππου δὲ τοῦ ἀδελφοῦ αὐτοῦ τετρααρχοῦντος τῆς
AND~PHILIP   THE   BROTHER   OF HIM   BEING TETRARCH   -

'Ιτουραίας καὶ Τραχωνίτιδος χώρας,   καὶ Λυσανίου
2OF ITUREA   3AND   4OF TRACHONITIS   1OF [THE] COUNTRY,   AND   LYSANIAS

τῆς 'Αβιληνῆς τετρααρχοῦντος, 3.2 ἐπὶ
-    OF ABILENE   BEING TETRARCH,   AT THE TIME OF

ἀρχιερέως   ''Αννα καὶ Καϊάφα,   ἐγένετο ῥῆμα
[THE] HIGH PRIEST[HOOD]   OF ANNA   AND   CAIAPHAS,   CAME   [THE] WORD

θεοῦ ἐπὶ 'Ιωάννην τὸν Ζαχαρίου υἱὸν ἐν τῇ ἐρήμῳ.
OF GOD   TO   JOHN   THE   SON~OF ZECHARIAH   IN   THE   WILDERNESS.

3.3 καὶ ἦλθεν εἰς πᾶσαν [τὴν] περίχωρον   τοῦ
AND   HE CAME   TO   ALL   THE   SURROUNDING REGION   OF THE

'Ιορδάνου κηρύσσων βάπτισμα μετανοίας εἰς
JORDAN   PREACHING   A BAPTISM   OF REPENTANCE   FOR

ἄφεσιν   ἁμαρτιῶν, 3.4 ὡς   γέγραπται   ἐν βίβλῳ
[THE] FORGIVENESS   OF SINS,   AS   IT HAS BEEN WRITTEN   IN   [THE] BOOK

λόγων   'Ησαΐου τοῦ προφήτου,
OF [THE] WORDS   OF ISAIAH   THE   PROPHET,

     Φωνὴ βοῶντος ἐν τῇ ἐρήμῳ,
     A VOICE   CRYING   IN   THE   WILDERNESS,

     'Ετοιμάσατε τὴν ὁδὸν κυρίου,
     PREPARE   THE   WAY   OF [THE] LORD,

          εὐθείας ποιεῖτε τὰς τρίβους αὐτοῦ·
          MAKE~STRAIGHT   THE   PATHS   OF HIM;

3.5   πᾶσα φάραγξ πληρωθήσεται
      EVERY   VALLEY   WILL BE FILLED IN

          καὶ πᾶν ὄρος καὶ βουνὸς ταπεινωθήσεται,
          AND   EVERY   MOUNTAIN   AND   HILL   WILL BE LEVELED OFF,

     καὶ ἔσται τὰ σκολιὰ   εἰς εὐθείαν
     AND   WILL BE   THE   CROOKED [MADE]   INTO   STRAIGHT

          καὶ αἱ τραχεῖαι   εἰς ὁδοὺς λείας·
          AND   THE   ROUGH [PATHS MADE]   INTO   SMOOTH~ROADS;

3.6   καὶ ὄψεται πᾶσα σὰρξ τὸ σωτήριον τοῦ θεοῦ.
      AND   WILL SEE   ALL   FLESH   THE   SALVATION   -   OF GOD.

3.7 'Ελεγεν οὖν   τοῖς ἐκπορευομένοις ὄχλοις
    THEREFORE~HE WAS SAYING   TO THE   CROWDS~COMING OUT

βαπτισθῆναι ὑπ' αὐτοῦ, Γεννήματα ἐχιδνῶν, τίς
TO BE BAPTIZED   BY   HIM,   CHILDREN   OF VIPERS,   WHO

ὑπέδειξεν ὑμῖν φυγεῖν ἀπὸ τῆς μελλούσης ὀργῆς;
WARNED   YOU°   TO FLEE   FROM   THE   COMING   WRATH?

3.8 ποιήσατε οὖν καρποὺς ἀξίους τῆς μετανοίας καὶ
    THEREFORE~PRODUCE   FRUITS   WORTHY   -   OF REPENTANCE   AND

μὴ ἄρξησθε λέγειν ἐν ἑαυτοῖς, Πατέρα ἔχομεν τὸν
DO NOT BEGIN   TO SAY   WITHIN   YOURSELVES,   WE HAVE~FATHER   -

'Αβραάμ. λέγω γὰρ ὑμῖν ὅτι δύναται ὁ θεὸς ἐκ τῶν
ABRAHAM.   FOR~I SAY   TO YOU°   THAT   IS ABLE   -   GOD   FROM   -

3:4-6 Isa. 40:3-5 LXX

and his brother Philip ruler[w] of the region of Ituraea and Trachonitis, and Lysanias ruler[w] of Abilene, [2]during the high priesthood of Annas and Caiaphas, the word of God came to John son of Zechariah in the wilderness. [3]He went into all the region around the Jordan, proclaiming a baptism of repentance for the forgiveness of sins, [4]as it is written in the book of the words of the prophet Isaiah,

"The voice of one crying
    out in the
    wilderness:
'Prepare the way of
    the Lord,
    make his paths straight.
[5] Every valley shall
    be filled,
    and every mountain
    and hill shall be
    made low,
    and the crooked shall be
    made straight,
    and the rough ways
    made smooth;
[6] and all flesh shall see the
    salvation of God.' "

7 John said to the crowds that came out to be baptized by him, "You brood of vipers! Who warned you to flee from the wrath to come? [8]Bear fruits worthy of repentance. Do not begin to say to yourselves, 'We have Abraham as our ancestor'; for I tell you, God is able from

[w] Gk tetrarch

these stones to raise up children to Abraham. ⁹Even now the ax is lying at the root of the trees; every tree therefore that does not bear good fruit is cut down and thrown into the fire."

10 And the crowds asked him, "What then should we do?" ¹¹In reply he said to them, "Whoever has two coats must share with anyone who has none; and whoever has food must do likewise." ¹²Even tax collectors came to be baptized, and they asked him, "Teacher, what should we do?" ¹³He said to them, "Collect no more than the amount prescribed for you." ¹⁴Soldiers also asked him, "And we, what should we do?" He said to them, "Do not extort money from anyone by threats or false accusation, and be satisfied with your wages."

15 As the people were filled with expectation, and all were questioning in their hearts concerning John, whether he might be the Messiah,ˣ ¹⁶John answered all of them by saying, "I baptize you with water; but one who is more powerful than I is coming; I am not worthy to untie the thong of his sandals. He will baptize you withʸ the Holy Spirit and fire. ¹⁷His winnowing fork is in his hand, to clear his threshing floor

ˣ Or *the Christ*
ʸ Or *in*

λίθων τούτων ἐγεῖραι τέκνα τῷ Ἀβραάμ. **3.9** ἤδη δὲ
THESE~STONES   TO RAISE UP   CHILDREN   -   TO ABRAHAM.   AND~ALREADY

καὶ ἡ ἀξίνη πρὸς τὴν ῥίζαν τῶν δένδρων κεῖται·
EVEN   THE   AX   TO   THE   ROOT   OF THE   TREES   IS LAID.

πᾶν οὖν δένδρον μὴ ποιοῦν καρπὸν καλὸν ἐκκόπτεται
THEREFORE~EVERY   TREE   NOT PRODUCING   GOOD~FRUIT   IS CUT DOWN

καὶ εἰς πῦρ βάλλεται. **3.10** Καὶ ἐπηρώτων αὐτὸν
AND   INTO   [THE] FIRE   IS THROWN.   AND   WERE QUESTIONING   HIM

οἱ ὄχλοι λέγοντες, Τί οὖν ποιήσωμεν;
THE   CROWDS   SAYING,   WHAT   THEN   SHOULD WE DO?

3.11 ἀποκριθεὶς δὲ ἔλεγεν αὐτοῖς, Ὁ ἔχων δύο
AND~HAVING ANSWERED   HE WAS SAYING   TO THEM,   THE ONE   HAVING   TWO

χιτῶνας μεταδότω τῷ μὴ ἔχοντι, καὶ ὁ ἔχων
COATS   LET HIM SHARE   WITH THE ONE   NOT   HAVING [ONE],   AND   THE ONE HAVING

βρώματα ὁμοίως ποιείτω. **3.12** ἦλθον δὲ καὶ τελῶναι
FOOD   LET HIM DO~LIKEWISE.   NOW~CAME   ALSO   TAX COLLECTORS

βαπτισθῆναι καὶ εἶπαν πρὸς αὐτόν, Διδάσκαλε, τί
TO BE BAPTIZED   AND   THEY SAID   TO   HIM,   TEACHER,   WHAT

ποιήσωμεν; **3.13** ὁ δὲ εἶπεν πρὸς αὐτούς, Μηδὲν πλέον
SHOULD WE DO?   -   AND   HE SAID   TO   THEM,   NOTHING   MORE

παρὰ τὸ διατεταγμένον ὑμῖν πράσσετε.
THAN   THE [AMOUNT]   HAVING BEEN COMMANDED   YOU°   COLLECT.

3.14 ἐπηρώτων δὲ αὐτὸν καὶ στρατευόμενοι λέγοντες,
AND~WERE ASKING   HIM   ALSO   SOLDIERS   SAYING,

Τί ποιήσωμεν καὶ ἡμεῖς; καὶ εἶπεν αὐτοῖς,
WHAT   SHOULD DO   ALSO   WE?   AND   HE SAID   TO THEM,

Μηδένα διασείσητε μηδὲ συκοφαντήσητε καὶ ἀρκεῖσθε
EXTORT MONEY~[FROM] NO ONE   NOR   SLANDER   AND   BE SATISFIED

τοῖς ὀψωνίοις ὑμῶν.
WITH THE   WAGES   OF YOU°.

3.15 Προσδοκῶντος δὲ τοῦ λαοῦ καὶ διαλογιζομένων
AND~BEING EXPECTANT   THE   PEOPLE   AND   ²WONDERING

πάντων ἐν ταῖς καρδίαις αὐτῶν περὶ τοῦ
¹EVERYONE   IN   THE   HEARTS   OF THEM   CONCERNING   -

Ἰωάννου, μήποτε αὐτὸς εἴη ὁ Χριστός,
JOHN,   WHETHER PERHAPS   HE   MIGHT BE   THE   CHRIST,

3.16 ἀπεκρίνατο λέγων πᾶσιν ὁ Ἰωάννης, Ἐγὼ μὲν
²ANSWERED   ⁴SAYING   ³EVERYONE   -   ¹JOHN,   I   -

ὕδατι βαπτίζω ὑμᾶς· ἔρχεται δὲ ὁ ἰσχυρότερός
WITH WATER   BAPTIZE   YOU°.   BUT~IS COMING   THE ONE   STRONGER

μου, οὗ οὐκ εἰμὶ ἱκανὸς λῦσαι τὸν ἱμάντα τῶν
THAN ME(I),   OF WHOM   I AM NOT   WORTHY   TO UNTIE   THE   STRAP   OF THE

ὑποδημάτων αὐτοῦ· αὐτὸς ὑμᾶς βαπτίσει ἐν
SANDALS   OF HIM.   HE   WILL BAPTIZE~YOU°   WITH

πνεύματι ἁγίῳ καὶ πυρί· **3.17** οὗ τὸ πτύον
[THE] HOLY~SPIRIT   AND   WITH FIRE;   OF WHOM   THE   WINNOWING FORK [IS]

ἐν τῇ χειρὶ αὐτοῦ διακαθᾶραι τὴν ἅλωνα αὐτοῦ
IN   THE   HAND   OF HIM   TO CLEAN OUT   THE   THRESHING FLOOR   OF HIM

καὶ   συναγαγεῖν   τὸν   σῖτον   εἰς   τὴν   ἀποθήκην   αὐτοῦ,
AND   TO GATHER   THE   WHEAT   INTO THE   BARN   OF HIM,

τὸ δὲ   ἄχυρον   κατακαύσει   πυρὶ   ἀσβέστῳ.
BUT~THE CHAFF   HE WILL BURN UP   WITH AN INEXTINGUISHABLE~FIRE.

3.18 Πολλὰ   μὲν   οὖν   καὶ   ἕτερα   παρακαλῶν
[3][WITH] MANY   -   [2]THEREFORE   [1]AND OTHER [WORDS]   EXHORTING

εὐηγγελίζετο   τὸν   λαόν.   **3.19** ὁ   δὲ   Ἡρῴδης   ὁ
HE WAS PREACHING THE GOOD NEWS   TO THE   PEOPLE.   -   NOW HEROD   THE

τετραάρχης,   ἐλεγχόμενος   ὑπ'   αὐτοῦ   περὶ   Ἡρῳδιάδος
TETRARCH,   BEING REPROVED   BY   HIM   ABOUT HERODIAS,

τῆς   γυναικὸς   τοῦ   ἀδελφοῦ   αὐτοῦ   καὶ   περὶ   πάντων
THE   WIFE   OF THE BROTHER   OF HIM   AND   ABOUT ALL

ὧν   ἐποίησεν   πονηρῶν   ὁ   Ἡρῴδης,   **3.20** προσέθηκεν
[2]WHICH [4]DID   [1][THE] EVIL [THINGS]   -   [3]HEROD,   HE ADDED

καὶ τοῦτο   ἐπὶ   πᾶσιν   [καὶ]   κατέκλεισεν   τὸν
THIS~ALSO   ON TOP OF   EVERYTHING [ELSE]   AND   LOCKED UP   -

Ἰωάννην   ἐν   φυλακῇ.
JOHN   IN   PRISON.

3.21 Ἐγένετο   δὲ   ἐν τῷ   βαπτισθῆναι   ἅπαντα   τὸν
AND~IT CAME ABOUT   WHILE   WERE BAPTIZED   ALL   THE

λαὸν   καὶ   Ἰησοῦ   βαπτισθέντος   καὶ   προσευχομένου
PEOPLE ALSO   JESUS   HAVING BEEN BAPTIZED   AND   PRAYING,

ἀνεῳχθῆναι   τὸν   οὐρανὸν   **3.22** καὶ   καταβῆναι   τὸ   πνεῦμα
TO BE OPENED   -   HEAVEN   AND   TO DESCEND   THE [2]SPIRIT

τὸ   ἅγιον   σωματικῷ   εἴδει   ὡς   περιστερὰν   ἐπ'   αὐτόν,
-    [1]HOLY   IN BODILY   FORM   AS   A DOVE   UPON HIM,

καὶ   φωνὴν   ἐξ   οὐρανοῦ   γενέσθαι,   Σὺ   εἶ   ὁ   υἱός   μου
AND   A VOICE   OUT OF HEAVEN   TO COME,   YOU ARE THE SON   OF ME,

ὁ   ἀγαπητός,   ⌜ἐν   σοὶ   εὐδόκησα⌝.
THE   BELOVED [ONE],   WITH   YOU   I AM WELL PLEASED.

3.23 Καὶ   αὐτὸς   ἦν   Ἰησοῦς   ἀρχόμενος   ὡσεὶ
AND   [2]HIMSELF   [3]WAS   [1]JESUS   BEGINNING   ABOUT

ἐτῶν   τριάκοντα,   ὢν   υἱός,   ὡς   ἐνομίζετο,   Ἰωσὴφ
THIRTY~YEARS [OF AGE],   BEING   [THE] SON,   AS   IT WAS BEING THOUGHT,   OF JOSEPH,

τοῦ   Ἡλὶ   **3.24** τοῦ Ματθὰτ   τοῦ Λευὶ   τοῦ
THE [SON]   OF HELI,   THE   [SON] OF MATTHAT,   THE   [SON] OF LEVI,   THE

Μελχὶ   τοῦ   Ἰανναὶ   τοῦ   Ἰωσὴφ   **3.25** τοῦ
[SON] OF MELCHI,   THE   [SON] OF JANNAI,   THE   [SON] OF JOSEPH,   THE

Ματταθίου   τοῦ   Ἀμὼς   τοῦ   Ναοὺμ   τοῦ   Ἐσλὶ
[SON] OF MATTATHIAS,   THE   [SON] OF AMOS,   THE   [SON] OF NAHUM,   THE   [SON] OF ESLI,

τοῦ Ναγγαὶ   **3.26** τοῦ Μάαθ   τοῦ   Ματταθίου   τοῦ
THE   [SON] OF NAGGAI,   THE   [SON] OF MAATH,   THE   [SON] OF MATTATHIAS,   THE

Σεμεῒν   τοῦ   Ἰωσὴχ   τοῦ   Ἰωδὰ   **3.27** τοῦ
[SON] OF SEMEIN,   THE   [SON] OF JOSECH,   THE   [SON] OF JODA,   THE

Ἰωανὰν   τοῦ   Ῥησὰ   τοῦ   Ζοροβαβὲλ   τοῦ
[SON] OF JOANAN,   THE   [SON] OF RHESA,   THE   [SON] OF ZERUBBABEL,   THE

and to gather the wheat into his granary; but the chaff he will burn with unquenchable fire."

18 So, with many other exhortations, he proclaimed the good news to the people. [19]But Herod the ruler,[z] who had been rebuked by him because of Herodias, his brother's wife, and because of all the evil things that Herod had done, [20]added to them all by shutting up John in prison.

21 Now when all the people were baptized, and when Jesus also had been baptized and was praying, the heaven was opened, [22]and the Holy Spirit descended upon him in bodily form like a dove. And a voice came from heaven, "You are my Son, the Beloved;[a] with you I am well pleased."[b]

23 Jesus was about thirty years old when he began his work. He was the son (as was thought) of Joseph son of Heli, [24]son of Matthat, son of Levi, son of Melchi, son of Jannai, son of Joseph, [25]son of Mattathias, son of Amos, son of Nahum, son of Esli, son of Naggai, [26]son of Maath, son of Mattathias, son of Semein, son of Josech, son of Joda, [27]son of Joanan, son of Rhesa, son of Zerubbabel,

---

[z] Gk *tetrarch*
[a] Or *my beloved Son*
[b] Other ancient authorities read *You are my Son, today I have begotten you*

3:22 text [see Mark 1:11; Luke 9:35]: KJV ASV RSV NASB NIV NEB TEV NJBmg NRSV.   var. ἐγω σημερον γεγεννηκα σε (this day I have begotten you) [see Ps. 2:7]: RSVmg NEBmg NJB NRSVmg.

son of Shealtiel,^{c} son of
Neri, ^{28}son of Melchi, son of
Addi, son of Cosam, son of
Elmadam, son of Er, ^{29}son
of Joshua, son of Eliezer,
son of Jorim, son of Matthat,
son of Levi, ^{30}son of
Simeon, son of Judah, son
of Joseph, son of Jonam,
son of Eliakim, ^{31}son of
Melea, son of Menna, son of
Mattatha, son of Nathan,
son of David, ^{32}son of Jesse,
son of Obed, son of Boaz,
son of Sala,^{d} son of
Nahshon, ^{33}son of
Amminadab, son of Admin,
son of Arni,^{e} son of Hezron,
son of Perez, son of Judah,
^{34}son of Jacob, son of Isaac,
son of Abraham, son of
Terah, son of Nahor, ^{35}son of
Serug, son of Reu, son of
Peleg, son of Eber, son of
Shelah, ^{36}son of Cainan, son
of Arphaxad, son of Shem,
son of Noah, son of
Lamech, ^{37}son of
Methuselah, son of Enoch,
son of Jared, son of
Mahalaleel, son of Cainan,
^{38}son of Enos, son of Seth,
son of Adam, son of God.

^{c} Gk *Salathiel*
^{d} Other ancient authorities read
Salmon
^{e} Other ancient authorities read
Amminadab, son of Aram; others
vary widely

Σαλαθιὴλ   τοῦ   Νηρὶ   **3.28** τοῦ   Μελχὶ   τοῦ
[SON] OF SHEALTIEL,   THE   [SON] OF NERI,   THE   [SON] OF MELCHI,   THE

Ἀδδὶ   τοῦ   Κωσὰμ   τοῦ   Ἐλμαδὰμ   τοῦ   Ἢρ
[SON] OF ADDI,   THE   [SON] OF COSAM,   THE   [SON] OF ELMADAM,   THE   [SON] OF ER,

3.29 τοῦ   Ἰησοῦ   τοῦ   Ἐλιέζερ   τοῦ   Ἰωρὶμ   τοῦ
THE   [SON] OF JOSHUA,   THE   [SON] OF ELIEZER,   THE   [SON] OF JORIM,   THE

Ματθὰτ   τοῦ   Λευὶ   **3.30** τοῦ   Συμεὼν   τοῦ
[SON] OF MATTHAT,   THE   [SON] OF LEVI,   THE   [SON] OF SIMEON,   THE

Ἰούδα   τοῦ   Ἰωσὴφ   τοῦ   Ἰωνὰμ   τοῦ   Ἐλιακὶμ
[SON] OF JUDAH,   THE   [SON] OF JOSEPH,   THE   [SON] OF JONAM,   THE   [SON] OF ELIAKIM,

3.31 τοῦ   Μελεὰ   τοῦ   Μεννὰ   τοῦ   Ματταθὰ   τοῦ
THE   [SON] OF MELEA,   THE   [SON] OF MENNA,   THE   [SON] OF MATTATHA,   THE

Ναθὰμ   τοῦ   Δαυὶδ   **3.32** τοῦ   Ἰεσσαὶ   τοῦ
[SON] OF NATHAN,   THE   [SON] OF DAVID,   THE   [SON] OF JESSE,   THE

Ἰωβὴδ   τοῦ   Βόος   τοῦ   Σαλὰ   τοῦ   Ναασσὼν
[SON] OF OBED,   THE   [SON] OF BOAZ,   THE   [SON] OF SALA,   THE   [SON] OF NAHSHON,

3.33 τοῦ   Ἀμιναδὰβ   τοῦ   Ἀδμὶν   τοῦ   Ἀρνὶ   τοῦ
THE   [SON] OF AMMINADAB,   THE   [SON] OF ADMIN,   THE   [SON] OF ARNI,   THE

Ἐσρὼμ   τοῦ   Φάρες   τοῦ   Ἰούδα   **3.34** τοῦ
[SON] OF HEZROM,   THE   [SON] OF PEREZ,   THE   [SON] OF JUDAH,   THE

Ἰακὼβ   τοῦ   Ἰσαὰκ   τοῦ   Ἀβραὰμ   τοῦ   Θάρα
[SON] OF JACOB,   THE   [SON] OF ISAAC,   THE   [SON] OF ABRAHAM,   THE   [SON] OF TERAH,

τοῦ   Ναχὼρ   **3.35** τοῦ   Σεροὺχ   τοῦ   Ῥαγαὺ   τοῦ
THE   [SON] OF NAHOR,   THE   [SON] OF SERUG,   THE   [SON] OF REU,   THE

Φάλεκ   τοῦ   Ἔβερ   τοῦ   Σαλὰ   **3.36** τοῦ
[SON] OF PELEG,   THE   [SON] OF EBER,   THE   [SON] OF SHELAH,   THE

Καϊνὰμ   τοῦ   Ἀρφαξὰδ   τοῦ   Σὴμ   τοῦ   Νῶε
[SON] OF CAINAN,   THE   [SON] OF ARPHAXAD,   THE   [SON] OF SHEM,   THE   [SON] OF NOAH,

τοῦ   Λάμεχ   **3.37** τοῦ   Μαθουσαλὰ   τοῦ   Ἐνὼχ   τοῦ
THE   [SON] OF LAMECH,   THE   [SON] OF METHUSELAH,   THE   [SON] OF ENOCH,   THE

Ἰάρετ   τοῦ   Μαλελεὴλ   τοῦ   Καϊνὰμ   **3.38** τοῦ
[SON] OF JARED,   THE   [SON] OF MAHALALEEL,   THE   [SON] OF CAINAN,   THE

Ἐνὼς   τοῦ   Σὴθ   τοῦ   Ἀδὰμ   τοῦ   θεοῦ.
[SON] OF ENOS,   THE   [SON] OF SETH,   THE   [SON] OF ADAM,   THE   [SON] OF GOD.

CHAPTER 4

Jesus, full of the Holy Spirit,
returned from the Jordan and
was led by the Spirit in the
wilderness, ^{2}where for forty
days he was tempted by the
devil. He ate nothing at all

4.1 Ἰησοῦς   δὲ   πλήρης   πνεύματος   ἁγίου   ὑπέστρεψεν
NOW~JESUS,   FULL   OF [THE] HOLY~SPIRIT,   RETURNED

ἀπὸ   τοῦ   Ἰορδάνου   καὶ   ἤγετο   ἐν   τῷ   πνεύματι   ἐν
FROM   THE   JORDAN   AND   WAS BEING LED   BY   THE   SPIRIT   IN

τῇ   ἐρήμῳ   **4.2** ἡμέρας   τεσσεράκοντα   πειραζόμενος   ὑπὸ
THE   DESERT   FORTY~DAYS   BEING TEMPTED   BY

τοῦ   διαβόλου.   καὶ   οὐκ   ἔφαγεν   οὐδὲν   ἐν   ταῖς
THE   DEVIL.   AND   HE DID NOT EAT   ANYTHING   IN   -

ἡμέραις ἐκείναις καὶ συντελεσθεισῶν αὐτῶν
THOSE~DAYS   AND   THEY(THE DAYS)~HAVING BEEN COMPLETED

ἐπείνασεν.   **4.3** Εἶπεν δὲ αὐτῷ ὁ διάβολος, Εἰ
HE HUNGERED.   AND~SAID   TO HIM   THE DEVIL,   IF

υἱὸς εἶ   τοῦ θεοῦ, εἰπὲ τῷ λίθῳ τούτῳ ἵνα
YOU ARE~[THE] SON   -   OF GOD, TELL   -   THIS~STONE   THAT

γένηται   ἄρτος.   **4.4** καὶ ἀπεκρίθη πρὸς αὐτὸν ὁ
IT MIGHT BECOME A LOAF [OF BREAD]. AND ANSWERED   TO   HIM   -

Ἰησοῦς, Γέγραπται ὅτι Οὐκ ἐπ᾿ ἄρτῳ μόνῳ ζήσεται ὁ
JESUS,   IT HAS BEEN WRITTEN -   NOT BY BREAD ALONE WILL LIVE -

ἄνθρωπος.   **4.5** Καὶ ἀναγαγὼν αὐτὸν ἔδειξεν αὐτῷ
MAN.   AND   HAVING LED UP HIM   HE SHOWED TO HIM

πάσας τὰς βασιλείας τῆς οἰκουμένης ἐν στιγμῇ
ALL   THE   KINGDOMS   OF THE WORLD   IN   A MOMENT

χρόνου **4.6** καὶ εἶπεν αὐτῷ ὁ διάβολος, Σοὶ δώσω
OF TIME;   AND   SAID TO HIM THE DEVIL,   TO YOU I WILL GIVE

τὴν ἐξουσίαν ταύτην ἅπασαν καὶ τὴν δόξαν αὐτῶν,
-    ³AUTHORITY ²THIS   ¹ALL   AND   THE GLORY OF THEM,

ὅτι   ἐμοὶ παραδέδοται καὶ ᾧ ἐὰν   θέλω δίδωμι
BECAUSE IT HAS BEEN GIVEN~TO ME AND TO WHOMEVER I DESIRE, I GIVE

αὐτήν· **4.7** σὺ οὖν   ἐὰν προσκυνήσῃς ἐνώπιον ἐμοῦ,
IT.   ³YOU ¹THEREFORE ²IF BOW DOWN IN WORSHIP BEFORE   ME,

ἔσται σοῦ πᾶσα.   **4.8** καὶ ἀποκριθεὶς ὁ Ἰησοῦς
WILL BE YOURS EVERYTHING.   AND HAVING ANSWERED -   JESUS

εἶπεν αὐτῷ, Γέγραπται,
SAID   TO HIM,   IT HAS BEEN WRITTEN,

    Κύριον τὸν θεόν σου προσκυνήσεις
    [THE] LORD THE GOD OF YOU YOU SHALL WORSHIP

        καὶ αὐτῷ μόνῳ λατρεύσεις.
        AND   HIM   ALONE   YOU SHALL SERVE.

4.9 Ἤγαγεν δὲ αὐτὸν εἰς Ἰερουσαλὴμ καὶ ἔστησεν
AND~HE LED   HIM   TO   JERUSALEM   AND   SET [HIM]

ἐπὶ τὸ πτερύγιον τοῦ ἱεροῦ καὶ εἶπεν αὐτῷ, Εἰ
UPON THE PINNACLE OF THE TEMPLE AND SAID   TO HIM, IF

υἱὸς εἶ   τοῦ θεοῦ, βάλε σεαυτὸν ἐντεῦθεν κάτω·
YOU ARE~[THE] SON   -   OF GOD, THROW YOURSELF DOWN~FROM HERE;

4.10 γέγραπται γὰρ ὅτι
FOR~IT HAS BEEN WRITTEN -

    Τοῖς ἀγγέλοις αὐτοῦ ἐντελεῖται   περὶ   σοῦ
    TO THE ANGELS   OF HIM HE WILL GIVE ORDERS CONCERNING YOU

        τοῦ διαφυλάξαι σε,
        -    TO PROTECT   YOU,

4.11 καὶ ὅτι
AND   -

    Ἐπὶ   χειρῶν ἀροῦσίν   σε,
    UPON [THEIR] HANDS THEY WILL LIFT UP YOU,

4:4 Deut. 8:3   **4:8** Deut. 6:13   **4:10-11** Ps. 91:11-12

during those days, and when they were over, he was famished. ³The devil said to him, "If you are the Son of God, command this stone to become a loaf of bread." ⁴Jesus answered him, "It is written, 'One does not live by bread alone.'"

5 Then the devil[f] led him up and showed him in an instant all the kingdoms of the world. ⁶And the devil[f] said to him, "To you I will give their glory and all this authority; for it has been given over to me, and I give it to anyone I please. ⁷If you, then, will worship me, it will all be yours." ⁸Jesus answered him, "It is written,

'Worship the Lord
    your God,
    and serve only him.'"

9 Then the devil[f] took him to Jerusalem, and placed him on the pinnacle of the temple, saying to him, "If you are the Son of God, throw yourself down from here, ¹⁰for it is written,

'He will command his
    angels concerning
    you,
    to protect you,'
¹¹and
'On their hands they will
    bear you up,

[f] Gk *he*

so that you will not
dash your foot
against a stone.' "
[12]Jesus answered him, "It is
said, 'Do not put the Lord
your God to the test.' "
[13]When the devil had
finished every test, he
departed from him until an
opportune time.

14 Then Jesus, filled with
the power of the Spirit,
returned to Galilee, and a
report about him spread
through all the surrounding
country. [15]He began to teach
in their synagogues and was
praised by everyone.

16 When he came to
Nazareth, where he had
been brought up, he went
to the synagogue on the
sabbath day, as was his
custom. He stood up to
read, [17]and the scroll of the
prophet Isaiah was given to
him. He unrolled the scroll
and found the place where it
was written:
[18] "The Spirit of the Lord is
upon me,
because he has
anointed me
to bring good news to
the poor.
He has sent me to
proclaim release to
the captives
and recovery of sight to
the blind,

μήποτε προσκόψῃς πρὸς λίθον τὸν πόδα
LEST   YOU STRIKE   AGAINST A STONE THE FOOT

σου.
OF YOU.

4.12 καὶ ἀποκριθεὶς εἶπεν αὐτῷ ὁ Ἰησοῦς ὅτι
AND   HAVING ANSWERED SAID TO HIM - JESUS -

Εἴρηται, Οὐκ ἐκπειράσεις κύριον τὸν θεόν σου.
IT HAS BEEN SAID, YOU SHALL NOT PUT TO THE TEST [THE] LORD, THE GOD OF YOU.

4.13 Καὶ συντελέσας πάντα πειρασμὸν ὁ διάβολος
AND HAVING COMPLETED EVERY TEMPTATION THE DEVIL

ἀπέστη ἀπ' αὐτοῦ ἄχρι καιροῦ.
WENT AWAY FROM HIM   UNTIL [AN OPPORTUNE] TIME.

4.14 Καὶ ὑπέστρεψεν ὁ Ἰησοῦς ἐν τῇ δυνάμει τοῦ
AND RETURNED - JESUS IN THE POWER OF THE

πνεύματος εἰς τὴν Γαλιλαίαν. καὶ φήμη ἐξῆλθεν
SPIRIT   TO - GALILEE.   AND A REPORT WENT OUT

καθ' ὅλης τῆς περιχώρου περὶ αὐτοῦ.
THROUGHOUT ALL THE SURROUNDING COUNTRYSIDE ABOUT HIM.

4.15 καὶ αὐτὸς ἐδίδασκεν ἐν ταῖς συναγωγαῖς αὐτῶν
AND HE WAS TEACHING IN THE SYNAGOGUES OF THEM

δοξαζόμενος ὑπὸ πάντων.
BEING PRAISED BY ALL.

4.16 Καὶ ἦλθεν εἰς Ναζαρά, οὗ ἦν τεθραμμένος καὶ
AND HE CAME TO NAZARETH, WHERE HE HAD BEEN BROUGHT UP AND

εἰσῆλθεν κατὰ τὸ εἰωθὸς αὐτῷ ἐν τῇ ἡμέρᾳ τῶν
HE ENTERED ACCORDING TO - HIS~CUSTOM ON THE DAY OF THE

σαββάτων εἰς τὴν συναγωγὴν καὶ ἀνέστη ἀναγνῶναι.
SABBATH INTO THE SYNAGOGUE AND STOOD UP TO READ.

4.17 καὶ ἐπεδόθη αὐτῷ βιβλίον τοῦ προφήτου Ἠσαΐου
AND WAS GIVEN TO HIM [THE] BOOK OF THE PROPHET ISAIAH

καὶ ἀναπτύξας τὸ βιβλίον εὗρεν τὸν τόπον οὗ
AND HAVING UNROLLED THE SCROLL HE FOUND THE PLACE WHERE

ἦν γεγραμμένον,
IT HAD BEEN WRITTEN,

4.18 Πνεῦμα κυρίου ἐπ' ἐμὲ
[THE] SPIRIT OF [THE] LORD [IS] UPON ME

οὗ εἵνεκεν ἔχρισέν με
ON ACCOUNT~OF WHICH HE ANOINTED ME

εὐαγγελίσασθαι πτωχοῖς,
TO PREACH GOOD NEWS TO [THE] POOR,

ἀπέσταλκέν με, κηρύξαι αἰχμαλώτοις ἄφεσιν
HE HAS SENT ME TO PREACH TO [THE] CAPTIVES RELEASE

καὶ τυφλοῖς ἀνάβλεψιν,
AND TO [THE] BLIND [THE] RECOVERY OF SIGHT,

4:12 Deut. 6:16   **4:18-19** Isa. 61:1-2 LXX

ἀποστεῖλαι τεθραυσμένους   ἐν
TO SEND FORTH   ONES HAVING BEEN OPPRESED   IN [TO]

ἀφέσει,
FREEDOM,

4.19 κηρύξαι ἐνιαυτὸν κυρίου   δεκτόν.
TO PREACH [THE] YEAR   OF [THE] LORD'S FAVOR.

4.20 καὶ πτύξας   τὸ βιβλίον ἀποδοὺς   τῷ
AND   HAVING ROLLED UP THE SCROLL [AND] HAVING GIVEN [IT] BACK TO THE

ὑπηρέτῃ ἐκάθισεν· καὶ πάντων οἱ ὀφθαλμοὶ ἐν τῇ
ATTENDANT HE SAT DOWN.   AND ³OF ALL ¹THE ²EYES   IN   THE

συναγωγῇ ἦσαν ἀτενίζοντες αὐτῷ.   **4.21** ἤρξατο δὲ
SYNAGOGUE WERE FOCUSED   ON HIM.   AND~HE BEGAN

λέγειν πρὸς αὐτοὺς ὅτι Σήμερον πεπλήρωται ἡ
TO SPEAK TO   THEM   -   TODAY   HAS BEEN FULFILLED -

γραφὴ αὕτη ἐν τοῖς ὠσὶν ὑμῶν. **4.22** Καὶ πάντες
THIS~SCRIPTURE IN THE EARS OF YOU°.   AND   EVERYONE

ἐμαρτύρουν   αὐτῷ καὶ ἐθαύμαζον ἐπὶ τοῖς λόγοις
WAS SPEAKING WELL [OF] HIM   AND THEY WERE AMAZED AT   THE   ²WORDS

τῆς χάριτος τοῖς ἐκπορευομένοις ἐκ τοῦ στόματος
-   ¹GRACIOUS -   COMING OUT   FROM THE MOUTH

αὐτοῦ καὶ ἔλεγον,   Οὐχὶ υἱός   ἐστιν Ἰωσὴφ
OF HIM AND THEY WERE SAYING, ³NOT ⁴[THE] SON ¹IS   ⁵OF JOSEPH

οὗτος; **4.23** καὶ εἶπεν πρὸς αὐτούς, Πάντως ἐρεῖτέ
²THIS ONE?   AND   HE SAID TO   THEM,   NO DOUBT YOU° WILL SPEAK

μοι τὴν παραβολὴν ταύτην· Ἰατρέ, θεράπευσον
TO ME -   THIS~PARABLE: PHYSICIAN, HEAL

σεαυτόν· ὅσα   ἠκούσαμεν γενόμενα εἰς τὴν
YOURSELF. EVERYTHING WHICH WE HEARD   HAVING HAPPENED IN   -

Καφαρναοὺμ ποίησον καὶ ὧδε ἐν τῇ πατρίδι σου.
CAPERNAUM   DO   ALSO HERE IN THE HOMETOWN OF YOU.

4.24 εἶπεν δέ, Ἀμὴν λέγω ὑμῖν ὅτι οὐδεὶς προφήτης
BUT~HE SAID, TRULY I SAY TO YOU° THAT NO   PROPHET

δεκτός ἐστιν ἐν τῇ πατρίδι αὐτοῦ. **4.25** ἐπ᾽ ἀληθείας
IS~WELCOME IN THE HOMETOWN OF HIM.   ²IN ³TRUTH

δὲ λέγω ὑμῖν, πολλαὶ χῆραι ἦσαν ἐν ταῖς ἡμέραις
¹AND I TELL YOU°, MANY WIDOWS WERE IN THE   DAYS

Ἠλίου ἐν τῷ Ἰσραήλ, ὅτε ἐκλείσθη ὁ οὐρανὸς ἐπὶ
OF ELIJAH IN - ISRAEL, WHEN WAS SHUT UP - HEAVEN   FOR

ἔτη τρία καὶ μῆνας ἕξ, ὡς ἐγένετο λιμὸς μέγας ἐπὶ
THREE~YEARS AND SIX~MONTHS, WHEN OCCURRED A GREAT~FAMINE OVER

πᾶσαν τὴν γῆν, **4.26** καὶ πρὸς οὐδεμίαν αὐτῶν ἐπέμφθη
ALL   THE LAND,   AND TO   NOT ONE   OF THEM WAS SENT

Ἠλίας εἰ μὴ εἰς Σάρεπτα τῆς Σιδωνίας πρὸς γυναῖκα
ELIJAH EXCEPT TO ZAREPHATH   - OF SIDON   TO   A WOMAN,

χήραν. **4.27** καὶ πολλοὶ λεπροὶ ἦσαν ἐν τῷ Ἰσραὴλ
A WIDOW.   AND MANY   LEPERS WERE IN -   ISRAEL

to let the oppressed
go free,
[19]to proclaim the year of
the Lord's favor."
[20]And he rolled up the scroll,
gave it back to the attendant,
and sat down. The eyes of all
in the synagogue were fixed
on him. [21]Then he began to
say to them, "Today this
scripture has been fulfilled in
your hearing." [22]All spoke
well of him and were
amazed at the gracious
words that came from his
mouth. They said, "Is not
this Joseph's son?" [23]He said
to them, "Doubtless you will
quote to me this proverb,
'Doctor, cure yourself!' And
you will say, 'Do here also in
your hometown the things
that we have heard you did at
Capernaum.'" [24]And he
said, "Truly I tell you, no
prophet is accepted in the
prophet's hometown. [25]But
the truth is, there were many
widows in Israel in the time
of Elijah, when the heaven
was shut up three years and
six months, and there was a
severe famine over all the
land; [26]yet Elijah was sent to
none of them except to a
widow at Zarephath in
Sidon. [27]There were also
many lepers[g] in Israel

[g] The terms *leper* and *leprosy* can
refer to several diseases

in the time of the prophet Elisha, and none of them was cleansed except Naaman the Syrian." 28When they heard this, all in the synagogue were filled with rage. 29They got up, drove him out of the town, and led him to the brow of the hill on which their town was built, so that they might hurl him off the cliff. 30But he passed through the midst of them and went on his way.

31 He went down to Capernaum, a city in Galilee, and was teaching them on the sabbath. 32They were astounded at his teaching, because he spoke with authority. 33In the synagogue there was a man who had the spirit of an unclean demon, and he cried out with a loud voice, 34"Let us alone! What have you to do with us, Jesus of Nazareth? Have you come to destroy us? I know who you are, the Holy One of God." 35But Jesus rebuked him, saying, "Be silent, and come out of him!" When the demon had thrown him down before them, he came out of him without having done him any harm. 36They were all amazed and kept saying to one another, "What kind of utterance is this? For with authority and power he commands the unclean spirits, and out they come!"

ἐπὶ   Ἐλισαίου τοῦ προφήτου, καὶ οὐδεὶς αὐτῶν
DURING [THE TIME OF] ELISHA   THE   PROPHET,   AND NOT ONE OF THEM

ἐκαθαρίσθη εἰ μὴ Ναιμὰν ὁ Σύρος. **4.28** καὶ
WAS CLEANSED EXCEPT NAAMAN THE SYRIAN.   AND

ἐπλήσθησαν πάντες θυμοῦ ἐν τῇ συναγωγῇ ἀκούοντες
ALL~WERE FILLED   WITH ANGER IN THE SYNAGOGUE, HEARING

ταῦτα   **4.29** καὶ ἀναστάντες ἐξέβαλον αὐτὸν ἔξω τῆς
THESE THINGS   AND HAVING ARISEN THEY DROVE OUT HIM OUTSIDE THE

πόλεως καὶ ἤγαγον αὐτὸν ἕως ὀφρύος τοῦ ὄρους ἐφ'
CITY   AND THEY LED HIM UP TO [THE] TOP OF THE HILL UPON

οὗ ἡ πόλις ᾠκοδόμητο αὐτῶν ὥστε κατακρημνίσαι
WHICH THE CITY OF THEM~HAD BEEN BUILT IN ORDER TO THROW DOWN

αὐτόν· **4.30** αὐτὸς δὲ διελθὼν διὰ μέσου αὐτῶν
HIM.   BUT~HE, HAVING GONE THROUGH [THE] MIDST OF THEM,

ἐπορεύετο.
WAS WALKING AWAY.

4.31 Καὶ κατῆλθεν εἰς Καφαρναοὺμ πόλιν τῆς
AND HE WENT DOWN TO CAPERNAUM, A CITY -

Γαλιλαίας. καὶ ἦν διδάσκων αὐτοὺς ἐν τοῖς
OF GALILEE. AND HE WAS TEACHING THEM ON THE

σάββασιν· **4.32** καὶ ἐξεπλήσσοντο ἐπὶ τῇ διδαχῇ
SABBATHS.   AND THEY WERE AMAZED   AT THE TEACHING

αὐτοῦ, ὅτι ἐν ἐξουσίᾳ ἦν ὁ λόγος αὐτοῦ. **4.33** καὶ
OF HIM, BECAUSE WITH AUTHORITY WAS THE WORD OF HIM.   AND

ἐν τῇ συναγωγῇ ἦν ἄνθρωπος ἔχων πνεῦμα
IN THE SYNAGOGUE THERE WAS A MAN HAVING A SPIRIT

δαιμονίου ἀκαθάρτου καὶ ἀνέκραξεν φωνῇ μεγάλῃ,
OF AN UNCLEAN~DEMON   AND HE CRIED OUT [WITH] A LOUD~VOICE,

4.34 Ἔα, τί   ἡμῖν καὶ σοί, Ἰησοῦ Ναζαρηνέ;
AH, WHAT [IS THIS] TO US AND TO YOU, JESUS OF NAZARETH?

ἦλθες ἀπολέσαι ἡμᾶς; οἶδά σε τίς εἶ, ὁ ἅγιος
DID YOU COME TO DESTROY US?   I KNOW WHO~YOU ARE, THE HOLY ONE

τοῦ θεοῦ. **4.35** καὶ ἐπετίμησεν αὐτῷ ὁ Ἰησοῦς λέγων,
- OF GOD.   AND REBUKED   HIM - JESUS   SAYING,

Φιμώθητι καὶ ἔξελθε ἀπ' αὐτοῦ. καὶ ῥίψαν
BE SILENT AND COME OUT FROM HIM.   AND 3HAVING THROWN [DOWN]

αὐτὸν τὸ δαιμόνιον εἰς τὸ μέσον ἐξῆλθεν ἀπ'
4HIM 1THE 2DEMON INTO THE MIDST [OF THEM] HE CAME OUT FROM

αὐτοῦ μηδὲν βλάψαν αὐτόν. **4.36** καὶ ἐγένετο θάμβος
HIM WITHOUT HAVING HARMED HIM.   AND FEAR~CAME

ἐπὶ πάντας καὶ συνελάλουν πρὸς ἀλλήλους λέγοντες,
UPON EVERYONE AND THEY WERE TALKING TO ONE ANOTHER SAYING,

Τίς   ὁ λόγος οὗτος ὅτι ἐν ἐξουσίᾳ καὶ δυνάμει
WHAT [IS] - THIS~WORD, FOR WITH AUTHORITY AND POWER

ἐπιτάσσει τοῖς ἀκαθάρτοις πνεύμασιν καὶ ἐξέρχονται;
HE COMMANDS THE UNCLEAN   SPIRITS   AND THEY COME OUT?

4.37 καὶ   ἐξεπορεύετο ἦχος περὶ   αὐτοῦ εἰς πάντα τόπον
AND   A REPORT~WAS GOING OUT   ABOUT   HIM   INTO EVERY   PLACE

τῆς   περιχώρου.
OF THE   SURROUNDING REGION.

4.38 Ἀναστὰς δὲ   ἀπὸ τῆς συναγωγῆς εἰσῆλθεν εἰς τὴν
AND~HAVING ARISEN   FROM   THE   SYNAGOGUE   HE ENTERED   INTO THE

οἰκίαν Σίμωνος.   πενθερὰ δὲ   τοῦ Σίμωνος
HOUSE   OF SIMON.   AND~[THE] MOTHER-IN-LAW -   OF SIMON

ἦν συνεχομένη πυρετῷ μεγάλῳ καὶ   ἠρώτησαν αὐτὸν
WAS SUFFERING WITH   A HIGH~FEVER   AND   THEY ASKED   HIM

περὶ   αὐτῆς. **4.39** καὶ   ἐπιστὰς   ἐπάνω αὐτῆς
ABOUT   HER.   AND   HAVING STOOD   OVER   HER,

ἐπετίμησεν τῷ   πυρετῷ καὶ   ἀφῆκεν αὐτήν·
HE REBUKED   THE   FEVER   AND   IT LEFT   HER.

παραχρῆμα δὲ ἀναστᾶσα διηκόνει   αὐτοῖς.
AND~AT ONCE   HAVING ARISEN   SHE WAS SERVING   THEM.

4.40 Δύνοντος δὲ   τοῦ ἡλίου ἅπαντες ὅσοι εἶχον
AND~[WHILE] SETTING   THE SUN,   ALL   WHO   HAD

ἀσθενοῦντας νόσοις ποικίλαις ἤγαγον   αὐτοὺς πρὸς
AILING ONES   WITH VARIOUS~DISEASES,   THEY BROUGHT   THEM   TO

αὐτόν·   ὁ δὲ ἑνὶ ἑκάστῳ αὐτῶν τὰς   χεῖρας ἐπιτιθεὶς
HIM.   AND~HE, [UPON] EACH~ONE   OF THEM   THE(HIS) HANDS   LAYING,

ἐθεράπευεν αὐτούς. **4.41** ἐξήρχετο δὲ   καὶ δαιμόνια
HE WAS HEALING   THEM.   AND~WERE COMING OUT   ALSO   DEMONS

ἀπὸ πολλῶν κρ[αυγ]άζοντα καὶ λέγοντα ὅτι Σὺ εἶ ὁ
FROM MANY   CRYING OUT   AND   SAYING   -   YOU ARE THE

υἱὸς τοῦ θεοῦ. καὶ ἐπιτιμῶν   οὐκ εἴα   αὐτὰ
SON   - OF GOD.   AND   REBUKING [THEM],   HE WAS NOT ALLOWING   THEM

λαλεῖν, ὅτι   ᾔδεισαν   τὸν Χριστὸν αὐτὸν εἶναι.
TO SPEAK,   BECAUSE   THEY HAD KNOWN   3THE   4CHRIST   1HIM   2TO BE.

4.42 Γενομένης δὲ ἡμέρας ἐξελθὼν   ἐπορεύθη εἰς
AND~HAVING COME   DAY,   HAVING GONE FORTH   HE WENT OUT   TO

ἔρημον τόπον·   καὶ οἱ ὄχλοι ἐπεζήτουν αὐτὸν καὶ
A DESOLATE   PLACE.   AND   THE CROWDS   WERE SEEKING   HIM   AND

ἦλθον ἕως αὐτοῦ καὶ κατεῖχον   αὐτὸν τοῦ
THEY CAME UP TO HIM   AND   THEY WERE HINDERING   HIM [SO AS]   -

μὴ   πορεύεσθαι ἀπ' αὐτῶν. **4.43** ὁ δὲ εἶπεν
NOT [TO ALLOW HIM]   TO DEPART   FROM THEM.   -   BUT   HE SAID

πρὸς αὐτοὺς ὅτι Καὶ ταῖς ἑτέραις πόλεσιν
TO   THEM   - ALSO TO THE   OTHER   CITIES

εὐαγγελίσασθαί με   δεῖ   τὴν βασιλείαν τοῦ
3TO PREACH   2[FOR] ME   1IT IS NECESSARY THE   KINGDOM   -

θεοῦ, ὅτι   ἐπὶ τοῦτο ἀπεστάλην. **4.44** καὶ
OF GOD,   BECAUSE   FOR THIS PURPOSE   I WAS SENT.   AND

ἦν κηρύσσων εἰς τὰς συναγωγὰς τῆς ⌜Ἰουδαίας.⌝
HE WAS PREACHING   IN   THE   SYNAGOGUES   -   OF JUDEA.

4:44 text: ASVmg RSV NASB NIV NEB NJB NRSV.   var. Γαλιλαιας (of Galilee) [see Matt. 4:23; Mark 1:39]:
KJV ASV RSVmg NASBmg NIVmg NEBmg NRSVmg.

[37]And a report about him began to reach every place in the region.

38 After leaving the synagogue he entered Simon's house. Now Simon's mother-in-law was suffering from a high fever, and they asked him about her. [39]Then he stood over her and rebuked the fever, and it left her. Immediately she got up and began to serve them.

40 As the sun was setting, all those who had any who were sick with various kinds of diseases brought them to him; and he laid his hands on each of them and cured them. [41]Demons also came out of many, shouting, "You are the Son of God!" But he rebuked them and would not allow them to speak, because they knew that he was the Messiah.[h]

42 At daybreak he departed and went into a deserted place. And the crowds were looking for him; and when they reached him, they wanted to prevent him from leaving them. [43]But he said to them, "I must proclaim the good news of the kingdom of God to the other cities also; for I was sent for this purpose." [44]So he continued proclaiming the message in the synagogues of Judea.[i]

[h] Or the Christ
[i] Other ancient authorities read Galilee

CHAPTER 5

Once while Jesus[j] was standing beside the lake of Gennesaret, and the crowd was pressing in on him to hear the word of God, [2]he saw two boats there at the shore of the lake; the fishermen had gone out of them and were washing their nets. [3]He got into one of the boats, the one belonging to Simon, and asked him to put out a little way from the shore. Then he sat down and taught the crowds from the boat. [4]When he had finished speaking, he said to Simon, "Put out into the deep water and let down your nets for a catch." [5]Simon answered, "Master, we have worked all night long but have caught nothing. Yet if you say so, I will let down the nets." [6]When they had done this, they caught so many fish that their nets were beginning to break. [7]So they signaled their partners in the other boat to come and help them. And they came and filled both boats, so that they began to sink. [8]But when Simon Peter saw it, he fell down at Jesus' knees, saying, "Go away from me, Lord, for I am a sinful man!" [9]For he and all who were with him were amazed at the catch of fish that they had taken;

[j] Gk he

5.1 Ἐγένετο δὲ ἐν τῷ τὸν ὄχλον ἐπικεῖσθαι
NOW~IT CAME ABOUT [THAT] WHILE THE CROWD WAS PRESSING UPON

αὐτῷ καὶ ἀκούειν τὸν λόγον τοῦ θεοῦ καὶ αὐτὸς
HIM AND LISTENING TO THE WORD - OF GOD, - HE

ἦν ἑστὼς παρὰ τὴν λίμνην Γεννησαρὲτ, **5.2** καὶ
HAD BEEN STANDING BESIDE THE LAKE OF GENNESARET, AND

εἶδεν δύο πλοῖα ἑστῶτα παρὰ τὴν λίμνην· οἱ δὲ
HE SAW TWO BOATS HAVING BEEN BESIDE THE LAKE. BUT~THE

ἁλιεῖς ἀπ' αὐτῶν ἀποβάντες ἔπλυνον τὰ δίκτυα.
FISHERMEN FROM THEM HAVING GONE AWAY WERE WASHING THE NETS.

5.3 ἐμβὰς δὲ εἰς ἓν τῶν πλοίων, ὃ ἦν Σίμωνος,
AND~EMBARKING INTO ONE OF THE BOATS, WHICH WAS SIMON'S,

ἠρώτησεν αὐτὸν ἀπὸ τῆς γῆς ἐπαναγαγεῖν ὀλίγον,
HE ASKED HIM FROM THE LAND TO PUT OUT A LITTLE,

καθίσας δὲ ἐκ τοῦ πλοίου ἐδίδασκεν τοὺς ὄχλους.
AND~HAVING SAT DOWN, FROM THE BOAT HE WAS TEACHING THE CROWDS.

5.4 ὡς δὲ ἐπαύσατο λαλῶν, εἶπεν πρὸς τὸν Σίμωνα,
AND~WHEN HE STOPPED SPEAKING, HE SAID TO - SIMON,

Ἐπανάγαγε εἰς τὸ βάθος καὶ χαλάσατε τὰ δίκτυα
PUT OUT INTO THE DEEP [WATER] AND LET DOWN THE NETS

ὑμῶν εἰς ἄγραν. **5.5** καὶ ἀποκριθεὶς Σίμων εἶπεν,
OF YOU° FOR A CATCH. AND HAVING ANSWERED, SIMON SAID,

Ἐπιστάτα, δι' ὅλης νυκτὸς κοπιάσαντες
MASTER, THROUGHOUT [THE] WHOLE NIGHT HAVING LABORED

οὐδὲν ἐλάβομεν· ἐπὶ δὲ τῷ ῥήματί σου
WE CAUGHT~NOTHING. BUT~ON ACCOUNT OF THE WORD OF YOU

χαλάσω τὰ δίκτυα. **5.6** καὶ τοῦτο ποιήσαντες
I WILL LET DOWN THE NETS. AND HAVING DONE~THIS

συνέκλεισαν πλῆθος ἰχθύων πολύ, διερρήσσετο δὲ τὰ
THEY ENCLOSED [2]MULTITUDE [3]OF FISH [1]A GREAT, AND~WERE BEING TORN THE

δίκτυα αὐτῶν. **5.7** καὶ κατένευσαν τοῖς μετόχοις ἐν
NETS OF THEM. AND THEY SIGNALED FOR THE PARTNERS IN

τῷ ἑτέρῳ πλοίῳ τοῦ ἐλθόντας συλλαβέσθαι αὐτοῖς·
THE OTHER BOAT [THAT] - HAVING COME TO HELP THEM.

καὶ ἦλθον καὶ ἔπλησαν ἀμφότερα τὰ πλοῖα ὥστε
AND THEY CAME AND THEY FILLED BOTH - BOATS SO AS

βυθίζεσθαι αὐτά. **5.8** ἰδὼν δὲ Σίμων Πέτρος
TO BE SINKING THEM. AND~HAVING SEEN [THIS], SIMON PETER

προσέπεσεν τοῖς γόνασιν Ἰησοῦ λέγων, Ἔξελθε ἀπ'
FELL DOWN AT THE KNEES OF JESUS SAYING, DEPART FROM

ἐμοῦ, ὅτι ἀνὴρ ἁμαρτωλός εἰμι, κύριε. **5.9** θάμβος γὰρ
ME, FOR A SINFUL~MAN I AM, LORD. FOR~ASTONISHMENT

περιέσχεν αὐτὸν καὶ πάντας τοὺς σὺν αὐτῷ
SEIZED HIM AND ALL THE ONES WITH HIM

ἐπὶ τῇ ἄγρᾳ τῶν ἰχθύων ὧν συνέλαβον,
ON ACCOUNT OF THE CATCH - OF FISH WHICH THEY TOOK,

5.10 ὁμοίως δὲ καὶ Ἰάκωβον καὶ Ἰωάννην υἱοὺς
AND~LIKEWISE ALSO JAMES AND JOHN [THE] SONS

Ζεβεδαίου, οἳ ἦσαν κοινωνοὶ τῷ Σίμωνι. καὶ εἶπεν
OF ZEBEDEE, WHO WERE PARTNERS - WITH SIMON. AND ²SAID

πρὸς τὸν Σίμωνα ὁ Ἰησοῦς, Μὴ φοβοῦ· ἀπὸ τοῦ
³TO - ⁴SIMON - ¹JESUS, DO NOT BE AFRAID. FROM -

νῦν ἀνθρώπους ἔσῃ ζωγρῶν. **5.11** καὶ καταγαγόντες τὰ
NOW [ON] ²MEN ¹YOU WILL CATCH. AND HAVING LEFT BEHIND THE

πλοῖα ἐπὶ τὴν γῆν ἀφέντες πάντα ἠκολούθησαν
BOATS ON THE LAND [AND], HAVING LEFT EVERYTHING, THEY FOLLOWED

αὐτῷ.
HIM.

5.12 Καὶ ἐγένετο ἐν τῷ εἶναι αὐτὸν ἐν μιᾷ τῶν
AND IT CAME ABOUT WHILE HE [WAS]~TO BE IN ONE OF THE

πόλεων καὶ ἰδοὺ ἀνὴρ πλήρης λέπρας·
CITIES AND BEHOLD [THERE WAS] A MAN FULL OF LEPROSY.

ἰδὼν δὲ τὸν Ἰησοῦν, πεσὼν ἐπὶ πρόσωπον
AND~HAVING SEEN - JESUS, HAVING FALLEN ON [HIS] FACE

ἐδεήθη αὐτοῦ λέγων, Κύριε, ἐὰν θέλῃς δύνασαί
HE BEGGED HIM SAYING, LORD, IF YOU ARE WILLING YOU ARE ABLE

με καθαρίσαι. **5.13** καὶ ἐκτείνας τὴν χεῖρα
TO CLEANSE~ME. AND HAVING STRETCHED OUT THE(HIS) HAND,

ἥψατο αὐτοῦ λέγων, Θέλω, καθαρίσθητι· καὶ
HE TOUCHED HIM SAYING, I AM WILLING, BE CLEANSED. AND

εὐθέως ἡ λέπρα ἀπῆλθεν ἀπ᾽ αὐτοῦ. **5.14** καὶ αὐτὸς
IMMEDIATELY THE LEPROSY DEPARTED FROM HIM. AND HE

παρήγγειλεν αὐτῷ μηδενὶ εἰπεῖν, ἀλλὰ ἀπελθὼν
GAVE ORDERS TO HIM TO TELL~NO ONE, BUT HAVING DEPARTED

δεῖξον σεαυτὸν τῷ ἱερεῖ καὶ προσένεγκε περὶ τοῦ
SHOW YOURSELF TO THE PRIEST AND MAKE AN OFFERING FOR THE

καθαρισμοῦ σου καθὼς προσέταξεν Μωϋσῆς, εἰς
CLEANSING OF YOU AS MOSES~COMMANDED, FOR

μαρτύριον αὐτοῖς. **5.15** διήρχετο δὲ μᾶλλον ὁ λόγος
A TESTIMONY TO THEM. BUT~HE WAS SPREADING [EVEN] MORE THE WORD

περὶ αὐτοῦ, καὶ συνήρχοντο ὄχλοι πολλοὶ ἀκούειν καὶ
ABOUT HIM, AND WERE ASSEMBLING MANY~CROWDS TO LISTEN AND

θεραπεύεσθαι ἀπὸ τῶν ἀσθενειῶν αὐτῶν· **5.16** αὐτὸς δὲ
TO BE HEALED FROM THE SICKNESSES OF THEM. BUT~HE

ἦν ὑποχωρῶν ἐν ταῖς ἐρήμοις καὶ προσευχόμενος.
WAS WITHDRAWING IN THE WILDERNESS PLACES AND WAS PRAYING.

5.17 Καὶ ἐγένετο ἐν μιᾷ τῶν ἡμερῶν καὶ αὐτὸς
AND IT CAME ABOUT ON ONE OF THE DAYS - HE

ἦν διδάσκων, καὶ ἦσαν καθήμενοι Φαρισαῖοι καὶ
WAS TEACHING, AND WERE SITTING DOWN PHARISEES AND

νομοδιδάσκαλοι οἳ ἦσαν ἐληλυθότες ἐκ πάσης κώμης
TEACHERS OF THE LAW WHO HAD COME FROM EVERY VILLAGE

τῆς Γαλιλαίας καὶ Ἰουδαίας καὶ Ἰερουσαλήμ· καὶ
- OF GALILEE AND JUDEA AND JERUSALEM. AND

[10]and so also were James and John, sons of Zebedee, who were partners with Simon. Then Jesus said to Simon, "Do not be afraid; from now on you will be catching people." [11]When they had brought their boats to shore, they left everything and followed him.

[12] Once, when he was in one of the cities, there was a man covered with leprosy.[k] When he saw Jesus, he bowed with his face to the ground and begged him, "Lord, if you choose, you can make me clean." [13]Then Jesus[l] stretched out his hand, touched him, and said, "I do choose. Be made clean." Immediately the leprosy[k] left him. [14]And he ordered him to tell no one. "Go," he said, "and show yourself to the priest, and, as Moses commanded, make an offering for your cleansing, for a testimony to them." [15]But now more than ever the word about Jesus[m] spread abroad; many crowds would gather to hear him and to be cured of their diseases. [16]But he would withdraw to deserted places and pray.

[17] One day, while he was teaching, Pharisees and teachers of the law were sitting near by (they had come from every village of Galilee and Judea and from Jerusalem); and the

[k] The terms *leper* and *leprosy* can refer to several diseases
[l] Gk *he*
[m] Gk *him*

power of the Lord was with him to heal.*n* 18Just then some men came, carrying a paralyzed man on a bed. They were trying to bring him in and lay him before Jesus;*o* 19but finding no way to bring him in because of the crowd, they went up on the roof and let him down with his bed through the tiles into the middle of the crowd*p* in front of Jesus. 20When he saw their faith, he said, "Friend,*q* your sins are forgiven you." 21Then the scribes and the Pharisees began to question, "Who is this who is speaking blasphemies? Who can forgive sins but God alone?" 22When Jesus perceived their questionings, he answered them, "Why do you raise such questions in your hearts? 23Which is easier, to say, 'Your sins are forgiven you,' or to say, 'Stand up and walk'? 24But so that you may know that the Son of Man has authority on earth to forgive sins"— he said to the one who was paralyzed—"I say to you, stand up and take your bed and go to your home." 25Immediately he stood up before them, took what he had been lying on, and went to his home, glorifying

n Other ancient authorities read *was present to heal them*
o Gk *him*
p Gk *into the midst*
q Gk *Man*

⌜δύναμις κυρίου ἦν εἰς τὸ ἰᾶσθαι αὐτόν.⌝ **5.18** καὶ
[THE] POWER OF [THE] LORD WAS IN - HIM~TO CURE. AND

ἰδοὺ ἄνδρες φέροντες ἐπὶ κλίνης ἄνθρωπον ὃς
BEHOLD MEN CARRYING ON A PALLET A MAN WHO

ἦν παραλελυμένος καὶ ἐζήτουν αὐτὸν εἰσενεγκεῖν καὶ
HAD BEEN PARALYZED AND WERE SEEKING TO CARRY IN~HIM AND

θεῖναι [αὐτὸν] ἐνώπιον αὐτοῦ. **5.19** καὶ μὴ εὑρόντες
TO PLACE HIM BEFORE HIM. AND NOT HAVING FOUND

ποίας εἰσενέγκωσιν αὐτὸν διὰ τὸν ὄχλον,
BY WHAT WAY THEY MIGHT CARRY HIM BECAUSE OF THE CROWD,

ἀναβάντες ἐπὶ τὸ δῶμα διὰ τῶν κεράμων καθῆκαν
HAVING GONE UP ONTO THE ROOF, THROUGH THE TILES THEY LET DOWN

αὐτὸν σὺν τῷ κλινιδίῳ εἰς τὸ μέσον ἔμπροσθεν τοῦ
HIM WITH THE PALLET INTO THE MIDST IN FRONT OF -

Ἰησοῦ. **5.20** καὶ ἰδὼν τὴν πίστιν αὐτῶν εἶπεν,
JESUS. AND HAVING SEEN THE FAITH OF THEM HE SAID,

Ἄνθρωπε, ἀφέωνταί σοι αἱ ἁμαρτίαι σου. **5.21** καὶ
MAN, HAVE BEEN FORGIVEN YOU THE SINS OF YOU. AND

ἤρξαντο διαλογίζεσθαι οἱ γραμματεῖς καὶ οἱ
BEGAN TO REASON THE SCRIBES AND THE

Φαρισαῖοι λέγοντες, Τίς ἐστιν οὗτος ὃς λαλεῖ
PHARISEES SAYING, WHO IS THIS WHO IS SPEAKING

βλασφημίας; τίς δύναται ἁμαρτίας ἀφεῖναι εἰ μὴ
BLASPHEMIES? WHO IS ABLE TO FORGIVE~SINS EXCEPT

μόνος ὁ θεός; **5.22** ἐπιγνοὺς δὲ ὁ Ἰησοῦς τοὺς
2ALONE - 1GOD? BUT~HAVING KNOWN - JESUS THE

διαλογισμοὺς αὐτῶν ἀποκριθεὶς εἶπεν πρὸς αὐτούς, Τί
THOUGHTS OF THEM, HAVING ANSWERED HE SAID TO THEM, WHY

διαλογίζεσθε ἐν ταῖς καρδίαις ὑμῶν; **5.23** τί ἐστιν
ARE YOU° REASONING IN THE HEARTS OF YOU°? WHICH IS

εὐκοπώτερον, εἰπεῖν, Ἀφέωνταί σοι αἱ ἁμαρτίαι
EASIER, TO SAY, HAVE BEEN FORGIVEN YOU THE SINS

σου, ἢ εἰπεῖν, Ἔγειρε καὶ περιπάτει; **5.24** ἵνα δὲ
OF YOU, OR TO SAY GET UP AND WALK? BUT~IN ORDER THAT

εἰδῆτε ὅτι ὁ υἱὸς τοῦ ἀνθρώπου ἐξουσίαν ἔχει
YOU° MAY KNOW THAT THE SON - OF MAN HAS~AUTHORITY

ἐπὶ τῆς γῆς ἀφιέναι ἁμαρτίας—εἶπεν τῷ
ON - EARTH TO FORGIVE SINS—HE SAID TO THE ONE

παραλελυμένῳ, Σοὶ λέγω, ἔγειρε καὶ ἄρας τὸ
HAVING BEEN PARALYZED, TO YOU I SAY, GET UP AND HAVING PICKED UP THE

κλινίδιόν σου πορεύου εἰς τὸν οἶκόν σου. **5.25** καὶ
PALLET OF YOU [AND] GO TO THE HOUSE OF YOU. AND

παραχρῆμα ἀναστὰς ἐνώπιον αὐτῶν, ἄρας ἐφ᾽
AT ONCE HAVING ARISEN IN FRONT OF THEM, HAVING PICKED UP [THAT] UPON

ὃ κατέκειτο, ἀπῆλθεν εἰς τὸν οἶκον αὐτοῦ δοξάζων
WHICH HE WAS LYING, HE DEPARTED TO THE HOUSE OF HIM GLORIFYING

5:17 text: ASV RSV NASB (NIV) (NEB) (TEV) NJB NRSV. var. δυναμις κυριου ην εις το ιασθαι αυτους ([the] power of [the] Lord was [present] to heal them): KJV ASVmg RSVmg NRSVmg.

τὸν θεόν. **5.26** καὶ ἔκστασις ἔλαβεν ἅπαντας καὶ
- GOD.   AND   TERROR   SEIZED   EVERYONE   AND

ἐδόξαζον   τὸν θεὸν καὶ ἐπλήσθησαν φόβου
THEY WERE GLORIFYING -   GOD   AND   THEY WERE FILLED   WITH FEAR

λέγοντες ὅτι Εἴδομεν παράδοξα   σήμερον.
SAYING,   -   WE SAW   REMARKABLE THINGS TODAY.

5.27 Καὶ μετὰ ταῦτα   ἐξῆλθεν καὶ ἐθεάσατο
        AND   AFTER   THESE THINGS   HE WENT OUT AND   SAW

τελώνην   ὀνόματι Λευὶν καθήμενον ἐπὶ τὸ τελώνιον,
A TAX COLLECTOR   BY NAME   LEVI   SITTING   IN   THE TAX OFFICE,

καὶ εἶπεν αὐτῷ, Ἀκολούθει μοι. **5.28** καὶ καταλιπὼν
AND HE SAID TO HIM,   FOLLOW   ME.   AND   HAVING LEFT BEHIND

πάντα   ἀναστὰς ἠκολούθει αὐτῷ. **5.29** Καὶ
EVERYTHING [AND] HAVING ARISEN HE WAS FOLLOWING HIM.   AND

ἐποίησεν δοχὴν μεγάλην Λευὶς αὐτῷ ἐν τῇ οἰκίᾳ
ARRANGED   A GREAT~BANQUET   LEVI   FOR HIM   IN   THE HOUSE

αὐτοῦ, καὶ ἦν   ὄχλος πολὺς τελωνῶν   καὶ ἄλλων
OF HIM,   AND THERE WAS A GREAT~CROWD OF TAX COLLECTORS AND OTHERS

οἳ ἦσαν μετ' αὐτῶν κατακείμενοι. **5.30** καὶ ἐγόγγυζον
WHO WERE   WITH   THEM   RECLINING.   AND   WERE MURMURING

οἱ Φαρισαῖοι καὶ οἱ γραμματεῖς αὐτῶν πρὸς τοὺς
THE PHARISEES   AND   THE   SCRIBES   OF THEM   AGAINST THE

μαθητὰς αὐτοῦ λέγοντες, Διὰ τί μετὰ τῶν τελωνῶν
DISCIPLES   OF HIM   SAYING,   WHY   WITH   THE   TAX COLLECTORS

καὶ ἁμαρτωλῶν ἐσθίετε   καὶ πίνετε; **5.31** καὶ
AND   SINNERS   ARE YOU° EATING AND   DRINKING?   AND

ἀποκριθεὶς ὁ Ἰησοῦς εἶπεν πρὸς αὐτούς, Οὐ χρείαν
HAVING ANSWERED -   JESUS   SAID   TO   THEM,   NO   NEED

ἔχουσιν οἱ   ὑγιαίνοντες ἰατροῦ   ἀλλὰ οἱ
HAVE   THE ONES BEING HEALTHY   OF A PHYSICIAN BUT   THE ONES

κακῶς ἔχοντες· **5.32** οὐκ ἐλήλυθα καλέσαι δικαίους
HAVING~ILLNESS.   I HAVE NOT COME   TO CALL   [THE] RIGHTEOUS

ἀλλὰ ἁμαρτωλοὺς εἰς μετάνοιαν.
BUT   SINNERS   TO   REPENTANCE.

5.33 Οἱ δὲ εἶπαν πρὸς αὐτόν, Οἱ μαθηταὶ Ἰωάννου
        -   BUT THEY SAID TO   HIM,   THE DISCIPLES   OF JOHN

νηστεύουσιν πυκνὰ καὶ δεήσεις ποιοῦνται ὁμοίως καὶ
FAST   OFTEN   AND   OFFER~PRAYERS   LIKEWISE ALSO

οἱ   τῶν Φαρισαίων, οἱ δὲ   σοὶ ἐσθίουσιν καὶ
THE ONES OF THE PHARISEES,   BUT~THE ONES TO YOU EAT   AND

πίνουσιν. **5.34** ὁ δὲ Ἰησοῦς εἶπεν πρὸς αὐτούς,
DRINK.   -   BUT JESUS   SAID   TO   THEM,

Μὴ δύνασθε τοὺς υἱοὺς τοῦ νυμφῶνος   ἐν ᾧ ὁ
YOU° ARE NOT ABLE THE   SONS   OF THE WEDDING ATTENDANTS WHILE THE

νυμφίος μετ' αὐτῶν ἐστιν ποιῆσαι νηστεῦσαι;
BRIDEGROOM ²WITH   ³THEM   ¹IS   TO MAKE   TO FAST [ARE YOU°]?

5.35 ἐλεύσονται δὲ ἡμέραι, καὶ ὅταν ἀπαρθῇ ἀπ' αὐτῶν
        BUT~WILL COME   DAYS,   ALSO WHEN   IS TAKEN AWAY FROM THEM

God. 26Amazement seized all of them, and they glorified God and were filled with awe, saying, "We have seen strange things today."

27 After this he went out and saw a tax collector named Levi, sitting at the tax booth; and he said to him, "Follow me." 28And he got up, left everything, and followed him.

29 Then Levi gave a great banquet for him in his house; and there was a large crowd of tax collectors and others sitting at the table[r] with them. 30The Pharisees and their scribes were complaining to his disciples, saying, "Why do you eat and drink with tax collectors and sinners?" 31Jesus answered, "Those who are well have no need of a physician, but those who are sick; 32I have come to call not the righteous but sinners to repentance."

33 Then they said to him, "John's disciples, like the disciples of the Pharisees, frequently fast and pray, but your disciples eat and drink." 34Jesus said to them, "You cannot make wedding guests fast while the bridegroom is with them, can you? 35The days will come when the bridegroom will be taken away from them,

[r] Gk *reclining*

and then they will fast in those days." [36]He also told them a parable: "No one tears a piece from a new garment and sews it on an old garment; otherwise the new will be torn, and the piece from the new will not match the old. [37]And no one puts new wine into old wineskins; otherwise the new wine will burst the skins and will be spilled, and the skins will be destroyed. [38]But new wine must be put into fresh wineskins. [39]And no one after drinking old wine desires new wine, but says, 'The old is good.'"[s]

[s] Other ancient authorities read better; others lack verse 39

ὁ   νυμφίος,   τότε   νηστεύσουσιν ἐν   ἐκείναις ταῖς
THE   BRIDEGROOM,   THEN   THEY WILL FAST   IN   THOSE   -

ἡμέραις.   **5.36** Ἔλεγεν δὲ   καὶ   παραβολὴν πρὸς αὐτοὺς
DAYS.   NOW~HE WAS TELLING ALSO   A PARABLE   TO   THEM:

ὅτι Οὐδεὶς ἐπίβλημα ἀπὸ ἱματίου καινοῦ σχίσας
-    NO ONE   A PATCH   FROM A NEW~GARMENT   HAVING TORN

ἐπιβάλλει ἐπὶ ἱμάτιον παλαιόν·   εἰ δὲ μή γε, καὶ τὸ
PUTS [IT]   ON   AN OLD~GARMENT.   OTHERWISE,   BOTH THE

καινὸν σχίσει καὶ τῷ   παλαιῷ   οὐ συμφωνήσει τὸ
NEW   WILL TEAR   AND   WITH THE OLD   WILL NOT MATCH   THE

ἐπίβλημα τὸ ἀπὸ τοῦ καινοῦ.   **5.37** καὶ οὐδεὶς βάλλει
PATCH   -   FROM THE   NEW.   AND   NO ONE   PUTS

οἶνον νέον εἰς ἀσκοὺς παλαιούς·   εἰ δὲ μή γε, ῥήξει
NEW~WINE   INTO OLD~WINESKINS.   OTHERWISE,   [4]WILL BURST

ὁ οἶνος ὁ νέος τοὺς ἀσκοὺς καὶ αὐτὸς ἐκχυθήσεται
[1]THE [3]WINE - [2]NEW THE   WINESKINS   AND   IT   WILL BE SPILLED

καὶ οἱ ἀσκοὶ ἀπολοῦνται·   **5.38** ἀλλὰ οἶνον νέον εἰς
AND   THE WINESKINS WILL BE DESTROYED.   RATHER,   NEW~WINE   INTO

ἀσκοὺς καινοὺς βλητέον.   **5.39** [καὶ] οὐδεὶς πιὼν
NEW~WINESKINS   MUST BE PUT.   AND   NO ONE HAVING DRUNK

παλαιὸν θέλει νέον·   λέγει γάρ, Ὁ παλαιὸς
[THE] OLD   DESIRES   [THE] NEW.   FOR~HE SAYS,   THE OLD

χρηστός ἐστιν.
IS~GOOD [ENOUGH].

CHAPTER 6

One sabbath[t] while Jesus[u] was going through the grainfields, his disciples plucked some heads of grain, rubbed them in their hands, and ate them. [2]But some of the Pharisees said, "Why are you doing what is not lawful[v] on the sabbath?" [3]Jesus answered, "Have you not read what David did when he and his companions were hungry? [4]He entered the house of God and took and ate the bread of the

[t] Other ancient authorities read On the second first sabbath
[u] Gk he
[v] Other ancient authorities add to do

6.1 Ἐγένετο δὲ ἐν ⌐σαββάτῳ⌐ διαπορεύεσθαι αὐτὸν
AND~IT CAME ABOUT   ON   [THE] SABBATH   [THAT] HE~IS PASSING

διὰ   σπορίμων, καὶ ἔτιλλον οἱ μαθηταὶ αὐτοῦ καὶ
THROUGH   GRAIN FIELDS,   AND   WERE PLUCKING THE DISCIPLES   OF HIM   AND

ἤσθιον τοὺς στάχυας   ψώχοντες ταῖς   χερσίν.
EATING   THE   HEADS [OF GRAIN AND] RUBBING [THEM] IN THE(THEIR) HANDS.

6.2 τινὲς δὲ τῶν Φαρισαίων εἶπαν, Τί ποιεῖτε ὃ
NOW~SOME   OF THE   PHARISEES   SAID,   WHY ARE YOU[v] DOING WHAT

οὐκ ἔξεστιν τοῖς σάββασιν;   **6.3** καὶ ἀποκριθεὶς πρὸς
IS NOT PERMISSIBLE ON THE SABBATHS?   AND   HAVING ANSWERED   TO

αὐτοὺς εἶπεν ὁ Ἰησοῦς, Οὐδὲ τοῦτο ἀνέγνωτε ὃ
THEM   SAID   -   JESUS,   [2]NOT   [3]THIS   [1]HAVE YOU[v] READ   WHAT

ἐποίησεν Δαυὶδ ὅτε ἐπείνασεν αὐτὸς καὶ οἱ   μετ'
DAVID~DID   WHEN   HE~WAS HUNGRY   AND   THE ONES WITH

αὐτοῦ [ὄντες],   **6.4** [ὡς] εἰσῆλθεν εἰς τὸν οἶκον τοῦ
HIM   BEING [HUNGRY],   HOW   HE ENTERED   INTO THE   HOUSE   -

θεοῦ καὶ τοὺς ἄρτους τῆς προθέσεως λαβὼν ἔφαγεν
OF GOD   AND   THE   LOAVES   OF THE PRESENTATION HAVING TAKEN HE ATE

6:1 text: KJV ASVmg RSVmg NRSV. var. σαββατω δευτεροπρωτω (second-first sabbath—i.e., the second sabbath after the first): ASV RSV NASB NIV NEB TEV NJB NRSVmg.

καὶ ἔδωκεν τοῖς μετ' αὐτοῦ, οὓς οὐκ ἔξεστιν
AND GAVE TO THE ONES WITH HIM, WHICH IS NOT PERMISSIBLE

φαγεῖν εἰ μὴ μόνους τοὺς ἱερεῖς; **6.5** καὶ ἔλεγεν
TO EAT EXCEPT ONLY THE PRIESTS? AND HE WAS SAYING

αὐτοῖς, Κύριός ἐστιν τοῦ σαββάτου ὁ υἱὸς τοῦ
TO THEM, LORD IS OF THE SABBATH THE SON -

ἀνθρώπου.
OF MAN.

6.6 Ἐγένετο δὲ ἐν ἑτέρῳ σαββάτῳ εἰσελθεῖν αὐτὸν εἰς
AND~IT CAME ABOUT ON ANOTHER SABBATH [THAT] HE~ENTERED INTO

τὴν συναγωγὴν καὶ διδάσκειν. καὶ ἦν ἄνθρωπος
THE SYNAGOGUE AND TAUGHT. AND THERE WAS A MAN

ἐκεῖ καὶ ἡ χεὶρ αὐτοῦ ἡ δεξιὰ ἦν ξηρά.
THERE ALSO THE HAND OF HIM THE RIGHT [ONE] WAS WITHERED.

6.7 παρετηροῦντο δὲ αὐτὸν οἱ γραμματεῖς καὶ οἱ
NOW~WERE WATCHING HIM THE SCRIBES AND THE

Φαρισαῖοι εἰ ἐν τῷ σαββάτῳ θεραπεύει, ἵνα
PHARISEES IF ON THE SABBATH HE HEALS, IN ORDER THAT

εὕρωσιν κατηγορεῖν αὐτοῦ. **6.8** αὐτὸς δὲ ᾔδει
THEY MIGHT FIND [SOMETHING] TO ACCUSE HIM. BUT~HE KNEW

τοὺς διαλογισμοὺς αὐτῶν, εἶπεν δὲ τῷ ἀνδρὶ τῷ
THE THOUGHTS OF THEM, AND~SAID TO THE MAN -

ξηρὰν ἔχοντι τὴν χεῖρα, Ἔγειρε καὶ στῆθι εἰς τὸ
³WITHERED ¹HAVING ²THE ⁴HAND, RISE AND STAND IN THE

μέσον· καὶ ἀναστὰς ἔστη. **6.9** εἶπεν δὲ ὁ Ἰησοῦς
MIDST. AND HAVING ARISEN HE STOOD. AND~SAID - JESUS

πρὸς αὐτούς, Ἐπερωτῶ ὑμᾶς εἰ ἔξεστιν τῷ
TO THEM, I ASK YOU° WHETHER IT IS PERMISSIBLE ON THE

σαββάτῳ ἀγαθοποιῆσαι ἢ κακοποιῆσαι, ψυχὴν σῶσαι ἢ
SABBATH TO DO GOOD OR TO DO EVIL, TO SAVE~LIFE OR

ἀπολέσαι; **6.10** καὶ περιβλεψάμενος πάντας αὐτοὺς
DESTROY [IT]? AND HAVING LOOKED AROUND [AT] ALL OF THEM

εἶπεν αὐτῷ, Ἔκτεινον τὴν χεῖρά σου. ὁ δὲ ἐποίησεν
HE SAID TO HIM, STRETCH OUT THE HAND OF YOU. - AND HE DID,

καὶ ἀπεκατεστάθη ἡ χεὶρ αὐτοῦ. **6.11** αὐτοὶ δὲ
AND WAS RESTORED THE HAND OF HIM. BUT~THEY

ἐπλήσθησαν ἀνοίας καὶ διελάλουν πρὸς ἀλλήλους
WERE FILLED WITH FURY AND THEY WERE DISCUSSING WITH ONE ANOTHER

τί ἂν ποιήσαιεν τῷ Ἰησοῦ.
WHAT THEY MIGHT DO - TO JESUS.

6.12 Ἐγένετο δὲ ἐν ταῖς ἡμέραις ταύταις
NOW~IT CAME ABOUT IN - THESE~DAYS

ἐξελθεῖν αὐτὸν εἰς τὸ ὄρος προσεύξασθαι, καὶ
[THAT] HE~WENT FORTH TO THE MOUNTAIN TO PRAY, AND

ἦν διανυκτερεύων ἐν τῇ προσευχῇ τοῦ θεοῦ.
HE WAS SPENDING THE WHOLE NIGHT IN - PRAYER - TO GOD.

6.13 καὶ ὅτε ἐγένετο ἡμέρα, προσεφώνησεν τοὺς
AND WHEN DAY~CAME, HE SUMMONED THE

Presence, which it is not lawful for any but the priests to eat, and gave some to his companions?" [5]Then he said to them, "The Son of Man is lord of the sabbath."

6 On another sabbath he entered the synagogue and taught, and there was a man there whose right hand was withered. [7]The scribes and the Pharisees watched him to see whether he would cure on the sabbath, so that they might find an accusation against him. [8]Even though he knew what they were thinking, he said to the man who had the withered hand, "Come and stand here." He got up and stood there. [9]Then Jesus said to them, "I ask you, is it lawful to do good or to do harm on the sabbath, to save life or to destroy it?" [10]After looking around at all of them, he said to him, "Stretch out your hand." He did so, and his hand was restored. [11]But they were filled with fury and discussed with one another what they might do to Jesus.

12 Now during those days he went out to the mountain to pray; and he spent the night in prayer to God. [13]And when day came, he

called his disciples and chose twelve of them, whom he also named apostles: [14]Simon, whom he named Peter, and his brother Andrew, and James, and John, and Philip, and Bartholomew, [15]and Matthew, and Thomas, and James son of Alphaeus, and Simon, who was called the Zealot, [16]and Judas son of James, and Judas Iscariot, who became a traitor.

[17] He came down with them and stood on a level place, with a great crowd of his disciples and a great multitude of people from all Judea, Jerusalem, and the coast of Tyre and Sidon. [18]They had come to hear him and to be healed of their diseases; and those who were troubled with unclean spirits were cured. [19]And all in the crowd were trying to touch him, for power came out from him and healed all of them.

[20] Then he looked up at his disciples and said:

"Blessed are you who
    are poor,
    for yours is the
        kingdom of God.
[21] "Blessed are you who are
    hungry now,
    for you will be filled.

μαθητὰς αὐτοῦ, καὶ ἐκλεξάμενος ἀπ᾽ αὐτῶν δώδεκα,
DISCIPLES   OF HIM,   AND   HAVING CHOSEN   FROM   THEM   TWELVE,

οὓς καὶ ἀποστόλους ὠνόμασεν, 6.14 Σίμωνα ὃν καὶ
WHOM ALSO   HE NAMED~APOSTLES,   SIMON,   WHO ALSO

ὠνόμασεν Πέτρον, καὶ ᾽Ανδρέαν τὸν ἀδελφὸν αὐτοῦ,
HE CALLED   PETER,   AND   ANDREW,   THE   BROTHER   OF HIM,

καὶ ᾽Ιάκωβον καὶ ᾽Ιωάννην καὶ Φίλιππον καὶ
AND   JAMES   AND   JOHN   AND   PHILIP   AND

Βαρθολομαῖον 6.15 καὶ Ματθαῖον καὶ Θωμᾶν καὶ
BARTHOLOMEW   AND   MATTHEW   AND   THOMAS   AND

᾽Ιάκωβον ᾽Αλφαίου   καὶ Σίμωνα τὸν καλούμενον
JAMES,   [THE SON OF] ALPHAEUS,   AND   SIMON,   THE ONE   BEING CALLED

Ζηλωτὴν 6.16 καὶ ᾽Ιούδαν ᾽Ιακώβου   καὶ ᾽Ιούδαν
A ZEALOT,   AND   JUDAS,   [THE SON OF] JAMES,   AND   JUDAS

᾽Ισκαριώθ, ὃς ἐγένετο προδότης.
ISCARIOT,   WHO BECAME   A TRAITOR.

6.17 Καὶ καταβὰς   μετ᾽ αὐτῶν ἔστη ἐπὶ
AND   HAVING COME DOWN   WITH   THEM   HE STOOD   ON

τόπου πεδινοῦ, καὶ ὄχλος πολὺς μαθητῶν αὐτοῦ, καὶ
A LEVEL~PLACE,   AND   A GREAT~CROWD   OF DISCIPLES   OF HIM,   AND

πλῆθος πολὺ τοῦ λαοῦ ἀπὸ πάσης τῆς ᾽Ιουδαίας καὶ
A GREAT~MULTITUDE   OF THE   PEOPLE   FROM   ALL   -   JUDEA   AND

᾽Ιερουσαλὴμ καὶ τῆς παραλίου Τύρου καὶ Σιδῶνος,
JERUSALEM   AND   THE   COASTAL REGION   OF TYRE   AND   SIDON,

6.18 οἳ ἦλθον ἀκοῦσαι αὐτοῦ καὶ ἰαθῆναι ἀπὸ τῶν
WHO   CAME   TO HEAR   HIM   AND   TO BE HEALED   FROM   THE

νόσων αὐτῶν· καὶ οἱ   ἐνοχλούμενοι ἀπὸ
DISEASES   OF THEM.   AND   THE ONES   BEING TROUBLED   BY

πνευμάτων ἀκαθάρτων ἐθεραπεύοντο, 6.19 καὶ πᾶς ὁ
UNCLEAN~SPIRITS   WERE BEING HEALED,   AND   ALL   THE

ὄχλος ἐζήτουν ἅπτεσθαι αὐτοῦ, ὅτι δύναμις παρ᾽
CROWD   WERE SEEKING   TO TOUCH   HIM,   BECAUSE   POWER   FROM

αὐτοῦ ἐξήρχετο καὶ ἰᾶτο πάντας.
HIM   WAS GOING OUT   AND   HE WAS HEALING   EVERYONE.

6.20 Καὶ αὐτὸς ἐπάρας   τοὺς ὀφθαλμοὺς αὐτοῦ εἰς
AND   HE   HAVING LIFTED UP   THE   EYES   OF HIM   TO

τοὺς μαθητὰς αὐτοῦ ἔλεγεν,
THE   DISCIPLES   OF HIM   WAS SAYING,

Μακάριοι οἱ πτωχοί,
BLESSED [ARE]   THE   POOR,

ὅτι ὑμετέρα ἐστὶν ἡ βασιλεία τοῦ θεοῦ.
FOR   YOURS   IS   THE   KINGDOM   -   OF GOD.

6.21 μακάριοι οἱ   πεινῶντες νῦν,
BLESSED [ARE]   THE ONES   HUNGERING   NOW,

ὅτι χορτασθήσεσθε.
FOR   YOU° WILL EAT YOUR FILL.

μακάριοι οἱ   κλαίοντες νῦν,
BLESSED [ARE] THE ONES WEEPING   NOW,

ὅτι γελάσετε.
FOR   YOU° WILL LAUGH.

6.22 μακάριοί ἐστε   ὅταν μισήσωσιν ὑμᾶς οἱ
BLESSED   ARE YOU° WHEN ²HATE   ³YOU° -

ἄνθρωποι καὶ ὅταν ἀφορίσωσιν ὑμᾶς καὶ
¹MEN   AND WHEN THEY OSTRACIZE YOU° AND

ὀνειδίσωσιν   καὶ ἐκβάλωσιν τὸ ὄνομα ὑμῶν ὡς
THEY REPROACH [YOU°] AND CAST OUT   THE NAME OF YOU° AS

πονηρὸν ἕνεκα τοῦ υἱοῦ τοῦ ἀνθρώπου· **6.23** χάρητε ἐν
EVIL   BECAUSE OF THE SON -   OF MAN.   REJOICE IN

ἐκείνῃ τῇ ἡμέρᾳ καὶ σκιρτήσατε, ἰδοὺ γὰρ ὁ   μισθὸς
THAT   - DAY   AND LEAP FOR JOY,   FOR~BEHOLD THE REWARD

ὑμῶν   πολὺς ἐν τῷ οὐρανῷ· κατὰ   τὰ αὐτὰ
OF YOU° [IS] GREAT IN - HEAVEN.   ²ACCORDING TO ³THE ⁴SAME THINGS

γὰρ ἐποίουν τοῖς προφήταις οἱ πατέρες αὐτῶν.
¹FOR WERE DOING TO THE PROPHETS   THE FATHERS OF THEM.

6.24 Πλὴν οὐαὶ ὑμῖν τοῖς πλουσίοις,
BUT   WOE   TO YOU° THE   RICH ONES,

ὅτι ἀπέχετε   τὴν παράκλησιν ὑμῶν.
FOR YOU° ARE RECEIVING IN FULL THE COMFORT   OF YOU°.

6.25 οὐαὶ ὑμῖν, οἱ   ἐμπεπλησμένοι νῦν,
WOE   TO YOU°, THE ONES HAVING BEEN WELL FED NOW,

ὅτι πεινάσετε.
FOR YOU° WILL HUNGER.

οὐαί, οἱ   γελῶντες νῦν,
WOE, THE ONES LAUGHING NOW,

ὅτι πενθήσετε καὶ κλαύσετε.
FOR YOU° WILL MOURN AND WEEP.

6.26 οὐαὶ ὅταν ὑμᾶς καλῶς εἴπωσιν πάντες οἱ
WOE   WHEN WELL~OF YOU° SPEAK   ALL   -

ἄνθρωποι· κατὰ   τὰ αὐτὰ   γὰρ ἐποίουν τοῖς
MEN.   ²ACCORDING ³TO THE ⁴SAME THINGS ¹FOR WERE DOING TO THE

ψευδοπροφήταις οἱ πατέρες αὐτῶν.
FALSE PROPHETS   THE FATHERS OF THEM.

6.27 Ἀλλὰ ὑμῖν λέγω τοῖς   ἀκούουσιν, Ἀγαπᾶτε
BUT   TO YOU° I SAY TO THE ONES LISTENING,   LOVE

τοὺς ἐχθροὺς ὑμῶν, καλῶς ποιεῖτε τοῖς   μισοῦσιν
THE ENEMIES OF YOU°, DO~GOOD   TO THE ONES HATING

ὑμᾶς, **6.28** εὐλογεῖτε τοὺς   καταρωμένους ὑμᾶς,
YOU°,   BLESS   THE ONES CURSING   YOU°,

προσεύχεσθε περὶ τῶν ἐπηρεαζόντων ὑμᾶς.
PRAY   FOR THE ONES MISTREATING   YOU°.

6.29 τῷ   τύπτοντί σε ἐπὶ τὴν σιαγόνα πάρεχε καὶ
TO THE ONE HITTING   YOU ON THE CHEEK,   OFFER ALSO

"Blessed are you who
   weep now,
   for you will laugh.
22 "Blessed are you when
people hate you, and when
they exclude you, revile you,
and defame you[w] on account
of the Son of Man. 23Rejoice
in that day and leap for joy,
for surely your reward is
great in heaven; for that is
what their ancestors did to
the prophets.
   24 "But woe to you who
      are rich,
      for you have received
      your consolation.
   25 "Woe to you who are
      full now,
      for you will be hungry.
   "Woe to you who are
      laughing now,
      for you will mourn
      and weep.
26 "Woe to you when all
speak well of you, for that is
what their ancestors did to
the false prophets.
   27 "But I say to you that
listen, Love your enemies,
do good to those who hate
you, 28bless those who curse
you, pray for those who
abuse you. 29If anyone
strikes you on the cheek,

[w] Gk *cast out your name as evil*

offer the other also; and from anyone who takes away your coat do not withhold even your shirt. ³⁰Give to everyone who begs from you; and if anyone takes away your goods, do not ask for them again. ³¹Do to others as you would have them do to you.

32 "If you love those who love you, what credit is that to you? For even sinners love those who love them. ³³If you do good to those who do good to you, what credit is that to you? For even sinners do the same. ³⁴If you lend to those from whom you hope to receive, what credit is that to you? Even sinners lend to sinners, to receive as much again. ³⁵But love your enemies, do good, and lend, expecting nothing in return.ˣ Your reward will be great, and you will be children of the Most High; for he is kind to the ungrateful and the wicked. ³⁶Be merciful, just as your Father is merciful.

37 "Do not judge, and you will not be judged; do not condemn, and you will not be condemned. Forgive, and you will be forgiven; ³⁸give, and it will be given to you. A good measure, pressed down, shaken together, running over, will be put into your lap;

ˣ Other ancient authorities read *despairing of no one*

τὴν ἄλλην, καὶ ἀπὸ τοῦ αἴροντός σου τὸ ἱμάτιον
THE OTHER, AND FROM THE ONE TAKING AWAY YOUR - COAT,

καὶ τὸν χιτῶνα μὴ κωλύσῃς. **6.30** παντὶ αἰτοῦντί
ALSO THE SHIRT DO NOT WITHHOLD. TO EVERYONE ASKING

σε δίδου, καὶ ἀπὸ τοῦ αἴροντος τὰ σὰ
YOU, GIVE; AND FROM THE ONE TAKING AWAY YOUR~THINGS

μὴ ἀπαίτει. **6.31** καὶ καθὼς θέλετε ἵνα ποιῶσιν
DO NOT DEMAND [THEM] BACK. AND JUST AS YOU° WANT THAT MAY DO

ὑμῖν οἱ ἄνθρωποι ποιεῖτε αὐτοῖς ὁμοίως. **6.32** καὶ εἰ
TO YOU° - MEN, DO TO THEM SIMILARLY. AND IF

ἀγαπᾶτε τοὺς ἀγαπῶντας ὑμᾶς, ποία ὑμῖν χάρις
YOU° LOVE THE ONES LOVING YOU°, WHAT KIND OF ³TO YOU° ¹CREDIT

ἐστίν; καὶ γὰρ οἱ ἁμαρτωλοὶ τοὺς ἀγαπῶντας
²IS [THAT]? FOR~EVEN THE SINNERS ²THE ONES ³LOVING

αὐτοὺς ἀγαπῶσιν. **6.33** καὶ [γὰρ] ἐὰν ἀγαθοποιῆτε
⁴THEM ¹LOVE. FOR~EVEN IF YOU° DO GOOD

τοὺς ἀγαθοποιοῦντας ὑμᾶς, ποία ὑμῖν χάρις
TO THE ONES DOING GOOD TO YOU°, WHAT KIND OF ³TO YOU° ¹CREDIT

ἐστίν; καὶ οἱ ἁμαρτωλοὶ τὸ αὐτὸ ποιοῦσιν. **6.34** καὶ
²IS [THAT]? EVEN - SINNERS THE SAME DO. AND

ἐὰν δανίσητε παρ' ὧν ἐλπίζετε λαβεῖν, ποία
IF YOU° LEND FROM WHOM YOU° HOPE TO RECEIVE, WHAT KIND OF

ὑμῖν χάρις [ἐστίν]; καὶ ἁμαρτωλοὶ
³TO YOU° ¹CREDIT ²IS [THAT]? EVEN SINNERS

ἁμαρτωλοῖς δανίζουσιν ἵνα ἀπολάβωσιν
LEND~TO SINNERS THAT THEY MAY RECEIVE IN RETURN

τὰ ἴσα. **6.35** πλὴν ἀγαπᾶτε τοὺς ἐχθροὺς ὑμῶν καὶ
THE SAME AMOUNT. BUT LOVE THE ENEMIES OF YOU° AND

ἀγαθοποιεῖτε καὶ δανίζετε μηδὲν ἀπελπίζοντες· καὶ
DO GOOD AND LOAN EXPECTING IN RETURN~NOTHING. AND

ἔσται ὁ μισθὸς ὑμῶν πολύς, καὶ ἔσεσθε υἱοὶ
WILL BE THE REWARD OF YOU° GREAT, AND YOU° WILL BE SONS

ὑψίστου, ὅτι αὐτὸς χρηστός ἐστιν ἐπὶ τοὺς
OF [THE] MOST HIGH, BECAUSE HE IS~KIND TO THE

ἀχαρίστους καὶ πονηρούς. **6.36** Γίνεσθε οἰκτίρμονες
UNGRATEFUL AND EVIL [ONES]. BE COMPASSIONATE

καθὼς [καὶ] ὁ πατὴρ ὑμῶν οἰκτίρμων ἐστίν.
JUST AS ALSO THE FATHER OF YOU° IS~COMPASSIONATE.

6.37 Καὶ μὴ κρίνετε, καὶ οὐ μὴ κριθῆτε· καὶ
AND DO NOT~JUDGE, AND BY NO MEANS MAY YOU° BE JUDGED. AND

μὴ καταδικάζετε, καὶ οὐ μὴ καταδικασθῆτε. ἀπολύετε,
DO NOT CONDEMN, AND BY NO MEANS MAY YOU° BE CONDEMNED. FORGIVE,

καὶ ἀπολυθήσεσθε· **6.38** δίδοτε, καὶ δοθήσεται ὑμῖν·
AND YOU° WILL BE FORGIVEN. GIVE, AND IT WILL BE GIVEN TO YOU°.

μέτρον καλὸν πεπιεσμένον σεσαλευμένον
A GOOD~MEASURE HAVING BEEN PRESSED DOWN [AND] HAVING BEEN SHAKEN,

ὑπερεκχυννόμενον δώσουσιν εἰς τὸν κόλπον ὑμῶν·
OVERFLOWING WILL BE PUT INTO THE LAP OF YOU°.

ᾧ γὰρ   μέτρῳ μετρεῖτε ἀντιμετρηθήσεται   ὑμῖν.
FOR~BY WHAT MEASURE YOU° MEASURE IT WILL BE MEASURED IN RETURN TO YOU°.

6.39 Εἶπεν δὲ καὶ   παραβολὴν αὐτοῖς·   Μήτι
NOW~HE TOLD ALSO A PARABLE TO THEM.   SURELY

δύναται τυφλὸς   τυφλὸν ὁδηγεῖν; οὐχὶ   ἀμφότεροι
A BLIND PERSON~IS [NOT] ABLE TO LEAD~A BLIND PERSON? [WILL] NOT BOTH

εἰς βόθυνον ἐμπεσοῦνται; **6.40** οὐκ ἔστιν μαθητὴς ὑπὲρ
INTO A PIT   FALL IN?   A PUPIL~IS NOT   ABOVE

τὸν διδάσκαλον·   κατηρτισμένος δὲ   πᾶς   ἔσται ὡς
THE TEACHER.   BUT~HAVING BEEN FULLY TRAINED EVERYONE WILL BE LIKE

ὁ διδάσκαλος αὐτοῦ. **6.41** Τί δὲ βλέπεις τὸ κάρφος τὸ
THE TEACHER   OF HIM.   AND~WHY DO YOU SEE THE SPECK   -

ἐν τῷ ὀφθαλμῷ τοῦ ἀδελφοῦ σου,   τὴν δὲ δοκὸν τὴν
IN THE EYE   OF THE BROTHER OF YOU, BUT~THE LOG   -

ἐν τῷ ἰδίῳ ὀφθαλμῷ οὐ κατανοεῖς; **6.42** πῶς δύνασαι
IN YOUR OWN EYE   YOU DO NOT NOTICE?   HOW ARE YOU ABLE

λέγειν τῷ ἀδελφῷ σου, Ἀδελφέ, ἄφες   ἐκβάλω
TO SAY TO THE BROTHER OF YOU, BROTHER, LET ME [THAT] I MAY REMOVE

τὸ κάρφος τὸ ἐν τῷ ὀφθαλμῷ σου, αὐτὸς   τὴν
THE SPECK   - IN THE EYE   OF YOU, [WHILE] YOURSELF -

ἐν τῷ ὀφθαλμῷ σοῦ δοκὸν οὐ βλέπων; ὑποκριτά,
IN THE EYE   OF YOU, [THE] LOG NOT SEEING? HYPOCRITE,

ἔκβαλε πρῶτον τὴν δοκὸν ἐκ τοῦ ὀφθαλμοῦ σου, καὶ
REMOVE FIRST   THE LOG FROM THE EYE   OF YOU, AND

τότε διαβλέψεις   τὸ κάρφος τὸ ἐν τῷ ὀφθαλμῷ τοῦ
THEN YOU WILL SEE CLEARLY THE SPECK   - IN THE EYE   OF THE

ἀδελφοῦ σου ἐκβαλεῖν.
BROTHER OF YOU TO TAKE OUT.

6.43 Οὐ γὰρ ἔστιν δένδρον καλὸν ποιοῦν
³NO ¹FOR ²THERE IS ⁵TREE ⁴GOOD PRODUCING

καρπὸν σαπρόν, οὐδὲ πάλιν δένδρον σαπρὸν ποιοῦν
BAD~FRUIT,   NOR AGAIN A BAD~TREE   PRODUCING

καρπὸν καλόν. **6.44** ἕκαστον γὰρ δένδρον ἐκ τοῦ ἰδίου
GOOD~FRUIT.   FOR~EACH   TREE   BY ITS OWN

καρποῦ γινώσκεται· οὐ γὰρ ἐξ ἀκανθῶν συλλέγουσιν
FRUIT   WILL BE KNOWN. FOR~NOT FROM THORNS DO THEY GATHER

σῦκα οὐδὲ ἐκ βάτου   σταφυλὴν τρυγῶσιν. **6.45** ὁ
FIGS NOR FROM A THORN BUSH DO THEY PICK~GRAPES.   THE

ἀγαθὸς ἄνθρωπος ἐκ τοῦ ἀγαθοῦ θησαυροῦ τῆς
GOOD   MAN   FROM THE GOOD   STOREHOUSE OF THE

καρδίας προφέρει τὸ ἀγαθόν, καὶ ὁ πονηρὸς ἐκ τοῦ
HEART PRODUCES - GOOD, AND THE EVIL FROM -

πονηροῦ προφέρει τὸ πονηρόν· ἐκ γὰρ περισσεύματος
EVIL   PRODUCES - EVIL. FOR~FROM [THE] ABUNDANCE

καρδίας λαλεῖ τὸ στόμα αὐτοῦ.
OF [THE] HEART SPEAKS THE MOUTH OF HIM.

6.46 Τί δέ με καλεῖτε, Κύριε κύριε, καὶ οὐ ποιεῖτε
AND~WHY .DO YOU° CALL~ME, LORD LORD, AND [YET] YOU° DO NOT DO

for the measure you give
will be the measure you get
back."

39 He also told them a
parable: "Can a blind person
guide a blind person? Will
not both fall into a pit? 40 A
disciple is not above the
teacher, but everyone who is
fully qualified will be like
the teacher. 41 Why do you
see the speck in your
neighbor's[y] eye, but do not
notice the log in your own
eye? 42 Or how can you say
to your neighbor,[z] 'Friend,[z]
let me take out the speck
in your eye,' when you
yourself do not see the log
in your own eye? You
hypocrite, first take the log
out of your own eye, and
then you will see clearly to
take the speck out of your
neighbor's[y] eye.

43 "No good tree bears
bad fruit, nor again does a
bad tree bear good fruit; 44 for
each tree is known by its
own fruit. Figs are not
gathered from thorns, nor
are grapes picked from a
bramble bush. 45 The good
person out of the good
treasure of the heart
produces good, and the evil
person out of evil treasure
produces evil; for it is out of
the abundance of the heart
that the mouth speaks.

46 "Why do you call me
'Lord, Lord,' and do not do

[y] Gk brother's
[z] Gk brother

what I tell you? [47]I will show you what someone is like who comes to me, hears my words, and acts on them. [48]That one is like a man building a house, who dug deeply and laid the foundation on rock; when a flood arose, the river burst against that house but could not shake it, because it had been well built.[a] [49]But the one who hears and does not act is like a man who built a house on the ground without a foundation. When the river burst against it, immediately it fell, and great was the ruin of that house."

[a] Other ancient authorities read founded upon the rock

ἃ λέγω; **6.47** πᾶς ὁ ἐρχόμενος πρός με καὶ
WHAT I SAY?   EVERYONE - COMING   TO   ME AND

ἀκούων μου τῶν λόγων καὶ ποιῶν αὐτούς, ὑποδείξω
HEARING MY - WORDS AND DOING THEM, I WILL SHOW

ὑμῖν τίνι ἐστὶν ὅμοιος· **6.48** ὅμοιός ἐστιν ἀνθρώπῳ
YOU° TO WHOM HE IS LIKENED.   HE IS~LIKENED TO [THE] MAN

οἰκοδομοῦντι οἰκίαν ὃς ἔσκαψεν καὶ ἐβάθυνεν καὶ
BUILDING   A HOUSE WHO DUG   AND WENT DOWN DEEP AND

ἔθηκεν θεμέλιον ἐπὶ τὴν πέτραν· πλημμύρης δὲ
LAID   A FOUNDATION UPON THE ROCK.   AND~A FLOOD

γενομένης προσέρηξεν ὁ ποταμὸς τῇ οἰκίᾳ ἐκείνῃ,
HAVING COME, [3]STRUCK AGAINST [1]THE [2]RIVER - THAT~HOUSE,

καὶ οὐκ ἴσχυσεν σαλεῦσαι αὐτὴν ⌜διὰ τὸ καλῶς
AND IT WAS NOT STRONG [ENOUGH] TO SHAKE IT   BECAUSE - WELL

οἰκοδομῆσθαι αὐτήν.⌝ **6.49** ὁ δὲ ἀκούσας καὶ
IT~TO HAVE BEEN BUILT.   NOW~THE ONE HAVING HEARD AND

μὴ ποιήσας ὅμοιός ἐστιν ἀνθρώπῳ οἰκοδομήσαντι οἰκίαν
NOT HAVING DONE IS~LIKE   A MAN   HAVING BUILT   A HOUSE

ἐπὶ τὴν γῆν χωρὶς θεμελίου, ᾗ προσέρηξεν ὁ
UPON THE GROUND WITHOUT A FOUNDATION, WHICH [3]STRUCK AGAINST [1]THE

ποταμός, καὶ εὐθὺς συνέπεσεν καὶ ἐγένετο τὸ
[2]RIVER,   AND IMMEDIATELY IT COLLAPSED AND WAS   THE

ῥῆγμα τῆς οἰκίας ἐκείνης μέγα.
RUIN   - OF THAT~HOUSE   GREAT.

6:48 text: ASV RSV NASB NIV NEB TEV NJB NRSV. var. τεθεμελιωτο γαρ επι την πετραν (for it was founded upon the rock): KJV RSVmg NRSVmg.

CHAPTER 7

After Jesus[b] had finished all his sayings in the hearing of the people, he entered Capernaum. [2]A centurion there had a slave whom he valued highly, and who was ill and close to death. [3]When he heard about Jesus, he sent some Jewish elders to him, asking him to come and heal his slave. [4]When they came to Jesus, they appealed to him earnestly, saying, "He is worthy of having you do this for him,

[b] Gk he

7.1 Ἐπειδὴ ἐπλήρωσεν πάντα τὰ ῥήματα αὐτοῦ εἰς
WHEN HE FINISHED   ALL THE WORDS OF HIM IN

τὰς ἀκοὰς τοῦ λαοῦ, εἰσῆλθεν εἰς Καφαρναούμ.
THE EARS OF THE PEOPLE, HE ENTERED INTO CAPERNAUM.

7.2 Ἑκατοντάρχου δέ τινος δοῦλος κακῶς ἔχων
[4]OF A CENTURION [1]NOW [2]A CERTAIN [3]SLAVE HAVING~AN ILLNESS

ἤμελλεν τελευτᾶν, ὃς ἦν αὐτῷ ἔντιμος.
WAS ABOUT TO DIE, WHO WAS BY HIM HIGHLY REGARDED.

7.3 ἀκούσας δὲ περὶ τοῦ Ἰησοῦ ἀπέστειλεν πρὸς αὐτὸν
AND~HAVING HEARD ABOUT - JESUS, HE SENT   TO   HIM

πρεσβυτέρους τῶν Ἰουδαίων ἐρωτῶν αὐτὸν ὅπως
ELDERS   OF THE JEWS   ASKING HIM   THAT

ἐλθὼν διασώσῃ τὸν δοῦλον αὐτοῦ. **7.4** οἱ δὲ
HAVING COME HE MIGHT CURE THE SLAVE OF HIM.   AND~THE ONES

παραγενόμενοι πρὸς τὸν Ἰησοῦν παρεκάλουν αὐτὸν
HAVING COME   TO   -   JESUS   WERE BEGGING HIM

σπουδαίως λέγοντες ὅτι Ἄξιός ἐστιν ᾧ παρέξῃ
EARNESTLY SAYING   - HE IS~WORTHY FOR WHOM YOU WILL GRANT

τοῦτο· **7.5** ἀγαπᾷ γὰρ τὸ ἔθνος ἡμῶν καὶ τὴν
THIS.   FOR~HE LOVES   THE NATION OF US AND THE

συναγωγὴν αὐτὸς ᾠκοδόμησεν ἡμῖν. **7.6** ὁ δὲ Ἰησοῦς
SYNAGOGUE   HE   BUILT   FOR US.   - AND JESUS

ἐπορεύετο σὺν αὐτοῖς. ἤδη δὲ   αὐτοῦ οὐ μακρὰν
WAS GOING WITH THEM.   NOW~BY THIS TIME HE   NOT FAR

ἀπέχοντος ἀπὸ τῆς οἰκίας ἔπεμψεν φίλους ὁ
BEING   FROM THE HOUSE, ³SENT   ⁴FRIENDS ¹THE

ἑκατοντάρχης λέγων αὐτῷ, Κύριε, μὴ σκύλλου,
²CENTURION   SAYING TO HIM, LORD, DO NOT TROUBLE [YOURSELF],

οὐ γὰρ ἱκανός εἰμι ἵνα ὑπὸ τὴν στέγην μου
FOR~NOT WORTHY AM I THAT UNDER THE ROOF OF ME

εἰσέλθῃς· **7.7** διὸ   οὐδὲ ἐμαυτὸν ἠξίωσα
YOU SHOULD ENTER. THEREFORE NOT MYSELF I CONSIDERED WORTHY

πρὸς σὲ ἐλθεῖν· ἀλλὰ εἰπὲ λόγῳ, καὶ ἰαθήτω ὁ
TO YOU TO COME. BUT SAY [THE] WORD, AND LET BE HEALED THE

παῖς μου. **7.8** καὶ γὰρ ἐγὼ ἄνθρωπός εἰμι ὑπὸ
SERVANT OF ME.   FOR~ALSO I   AM~A MAN   UNDER

ἐξουσίαν τασσόμενος ἔχων ὑπ' ἐμαυτὸν στρατιώτας,
AUTHORITY BEING PLACED, HAVING UNDER MYSELF   SOLDIERS,

καὶ λέγω τούτῳ, Πορεύθητι, καὶ πορεύεται, καὶ
AND I SAY TO THIS ONE, GO,   AND HE GOES,   AND

ἄλλῳ, Ἔρχου, καὶ ἔρχεται, καὶ τῷ   δούλῳ μου,
TO ANOTHER, COME, AND HE COMES, AND TO THE SLAVE OF ME,

Ποίησον τοῦτο, καὶ ποιεῖ. **7.9** ἀκούσας δὲ ταῦτα
DO   THIS, AND HE DOES [IT]. AND~HAVING HEARD THESE THINGS,

ὁ Ἰησοῦς ἐθαύμασεν αὐτὸν καὶ στραφεὶς τῷ
- JESUS   WAS AMAZED [AT] HIM AND HAVING TURNED TO THE

ἀκολουθοῦντι αὐτῷ ὄχλῳ εἶπεν, Λέγω ὑμῖν, οὐδὲ ἐν
²FOLLOWING   ³HIM ¹CROWD HE SAID, I SAY TO YOU°, NOT IN

τῷ Ἰσραὴλ τοσαύτην πίστιν εὗρον. **7.10** καὶ
- ISRAEL   SUCH GREAT FAITH HAVE I FOUND.   AND

ὑποστρέψαντες εἰς τὸν οἶκον οἱ   πεμφθέντες εὗρον
HAVING RETURNED TO THE HOUSE THE ONES HAVING BEEN SENT FOUND

τὸν δοῦλον ὑγιαίνοντα.
THE SLAVE   BEING IN GOOD HEALTH.

7.11 Καὶ ἐγένετο ἐν τῷ ἑξῆς   ἐπορεύθη εἰς
    AND IT CAME ABOUT ON THE NEXT DAY [THAT] HE PROCEEDED TO

πόλιν καλουμένην Ναῒν καὶ συνεπορεύοντο αὐτῷ οἱ
A CITY BEING CALLED NAIN AND WERE TRAVELING ALONG WITH HIM THE

μαθηταὶ αὐτοῦ καὶ ὄχλος πολύς. **7.12** ὡς δὲ ἤγγισεν
DISCIPLES OF HIM AND A GREAT~CROWD.   NOW~AS HE APPROACHED

τῇ πύλῃ τῆς πόλεως, καὶ ἰδοὺ ἐξεκομίζετο   τεθνηκὼς
THE GATE OF THE CITY,   - BEHOLD WAS BEING CARRIED OUT HAVING DIED

μονογενὴς υἱὸς τῇ   μητρὶ αὐτοῦ καὶ αὐτὴ ἦν χήρα,
[THE] ONLY SON TO THE MOTHER OF HIM AND SHE WAS A WIDOW,

καὶ ὄχλος τῆς πόλεως ἱκανὸς   ἦν σὺν αὐτῇ.
AND ²CROWD ³OF THE ⁴CITY ¹A CONSIDERABLE WAS WITH HER.

⁵for he loves our people, and it is he who built our synagogue for us." ⁶And Jesus went with them, but when he was not far from the house, the centurion sent friends to say to him, "Lord, do not trouble yourself, for I am not worthy to have you come under my roof; ⁷therefore I did not presume to come to you. But only speak the word, and let my servant be healed. ⁸For I also am a man set under authority, with soldiers under me; and I say to one, 'Go,' and he goes, and to another, 'Come,' and he comes, and to my slave, 'Do this,' and the slave does it." ⁹When Jesus heard this he was amazed at him, and turning to the crowd that followed him, he said, "I tell you, not even in Israel have I found such faith." ¹⁰When those who had been sent returned to the house, they found the slave in good health.

11 Soon afterwardsᶜ he went to a town called Nain, and his disciples and a large crowd went with him. ¹²As he approached the gate of the town, a man who had died was being carried out. He was his mother's only son, and she was a widow; and with her was a large crowd from the town.

ᶜ Other ancient authorities read *Next day*

13When the Lord saw her, he had compassion for her and said to her, "Do not weep." 14Then he came forward and touched the bier, and the bearers stood still. And he said, "Young man, I say to you, rise!" 15The dead man sat up and began to speak, and Jesus*d* gave him to his mother. 16Fear seized all of them; and they glorified God, saying, "A great prophet has risen among us!" and "God has looked favorably on his people!" 17This word about him spread throughout Judea and all the surrounding country.

18 The disciples of John reported all these things to him. So John summoned two of his disciples 19and sent them to the Lord to ask, "Are you the one who is to come, or are we to wait for another?" 20When the men had come to him, they said, "John the Baptist has sent us to you to ask, 'Are you the one who is to come, or are we to wait for another?'" 21Jesus*e* had just then cured many people of diseases, plagues, and evil spirits, and had given sight to many who were blind. 22And he answered them, "Go and tell John what you have seen and heard: the blind receive their sight, the lame

d Gk *he*
e Gk *He*

7.13 καὶ ἰδὼν αὐτὴν ὁ κύριος ἐσπλαγχνίσθη ἐπ᾽
AND HAVING SEEN HER, THE LORD HAD COMPASSION UPON

αὐτῇ καὶ εἶπεν αὐτῇ, Μὴ κλαῖε. **7.14** καὶ προσελθὼν
HER AND SAID TO HER, DO NOT CRY. AND HAVING APPROACHED

ἥψατο τῆς σοροῦ, οἱ δὲ βαστάζοντες ἔστησαν,
HE TOUCHED THE COFFIN, AND~THE ONES CARRYING [THE COFFIN] STOOD [STILL],

καὶ εἶπεν, Νεανίσκε, σοὶ λέγω, ἐγέρθητι. **7.15** καὶ
AND HE SAID, YOUNG MAN, TO YOU I SAY, GET UP. AND

ἀνεκάθισεν ὁ νεκρὸς καὶ ἤρξατο λαλεῖν, καὶ ἔδωκεν
SAT UP THE DEAD MAN AND HE BEGAN TO SPEAK, AND HE GAVE

αὐτὸν τῇ μητρὶ αὐτοῦ. **7.16** ἔλαβεν δὲ φόβος
HIM TO THE MOTHER OF HIM. ³SEIZED ¹AND ²FEAR

πάντας καὶ ἐδόξαζον τὸν θεὸν λέγοντες ὅτι
EVERYONE AND THEY WERE GLORIFYING - GOD SAYING,

Προφήτης μέγας ἠγέρθη ἐν ἡμῖν καὶ ὅτι
A GREAT~PROPHET WAS RAISED UP AMONG US AND -

Ἐπεσκέψατο ὁ θεὸς τὸν λαὸν αὐτοῦ. **7.17** καὶ ἐξῆλθεν
²VISITED - ¹GOD THE PEOPLE OF HIM. AND WENT OUT

ὁ λόγος οὗτος ἐν ὅλῃ τῇ Ἰουδαίᾳ περὶ αὐτοῦ καὶ
- THIS~REPORT IN ALL - JUDEA ABOUT HIM AND

πάσῃ τῇ περιχώρῳ.
IN ALL THE SURROUNDING COUNTRYSIDE.

7.18 Καὶ ἀπήγγειλαν Ἰωάννῃ οἱ μαθηταὶ αὐτοῦ περὶ
AND REPORTED TO JOHN THE DISCIPLES· OF HIM ABOUT

πάντων τούτων. καὶ προσκαλεσάμενος δύο τινὰς τῶν
ALL THESE THINGS. AND HAVING SUMMONED A CERTAIN~TWO OF THE

μαθητῶν αὐτοῦ ὁ Ἰωάννης **7.19** ἔπεμψεν πρὸς τὸν
DISCIPLES OF HIM, - JOHN SENT TO THE

κύριον λέγων, Σὺ εἶ ὁ ἐρχόμενος ἢ ἄλλον
LORD SAYING, ARE~YOU THE ONE COMING OR FOR ANOTHER

προσδοκῶμεν; **7.20** παραγενόμενοι δὲ πρὸς αὐτὸν οἱ
SHOULD WE BE LOOKING? AND~HAVING COME TO HIM THE

ἄνδρες εἶπαν, Ἰωάννης ὁ βαπτιστὴς ἀπέστειλεν ἡμᾶς
MEN SAID, JOHN THE BAPTIST SENT US

πρὸς σὲ λέγων, Σὺ εἶ ὁ ἐρχόμενος ἢ ἄλλον
TO YOU SAYING ARE~YOU THE ONE COMING OR FOR ANOTHER

προσδοκῶμεν; **7.21** ἐν ἐκείνῃ τῇ ὥρᾳ ἐθεράπευσεν
SHOULD WE BE LOOKING? IN THAT - HOUR HE HEALED

πολλοὺς ἀπὸ νόσων καὶ μαστίγων καὶ
MANY OF DISEASES AND AFFLICTIONS AND

πνευμάτων πονηρῶν καὶ τυφλοῖς πολλοῖς ἐχαρίσατο
EVIL~SPIRITS AND TO MANY~BLIND [PERSONS] HE GRANTED

βλέπειν. **7.22** καὶ ἀποκριθεὶς εἶπεν αὐτοῖς,
TO SEE. AND HAVING ANSWERED HE SAID TO THEM,

Πορευθέντες ἀπαγγείλατε Ἰωάννῃ ἃ εἴδετε καὶ
HAVING GONE REPORT TO JOHN WHAT YOU° SAW AND

ἠκούσατε· τυφλοὶ ἀναβλέπουσιν, χωλοὶ
HEARD. BLIND [PERSONS] RECEIVE SIGHT, LAME [PERSONS]

περιπατοῦσιν, λεπροὶ καθαρίζονται καὶ κωφοὶ
WALK,   LEPERS   ARE CLEANSED   AND   DEAF [PERSONS]

ἀκούουσιν, νεκροὶ ἐγείρονται, πτωχοὶ
HEAR,   DEAD [PERSONS] ARE RAISED,   POOR PEOPLE

εὐαγγελίζονται·   **7.23** καὶ μακάριός ἐστιν
HAVE THE GOOD NEWS PREACHED [TO THEM].   AND   BLESSED   IS

ὃς ἐὰν μὴ σκανδαλισθῇ ἐν ἐμοί.   **7.24** Ἀπελθόντων δὲ
WHOEVER   DOES NOT TAKE OFFENSE   AT   ME.   AND~[AS] WERE DEPARTING

τῶν ἀγγέλων Ἰωάννου ἤρξατο λέγειν πρὸς τοὺς ὄχλους
THE MESSENGERS OF JOHN,   HE BEGAN TO SAY   TO   THE   CROWDS

περὶ Ἰωάννου, Τί ἐξήλθατε εἰς τὴν ἔρημον
ABOUT   JOHN,   WHAT DID YOU° GO OUT INTO THE WILDERNESS

θεάσασθαι; κάλαμον ὑπὸ ἀνέμου σαλευόμενον;
TO SEE?   A REED   BY [THE] WIND BEING SHAKEN?

7.25 ἀλλὰ τί ἐξήλθατε ἰδεῖν; ἄνθρωπον ἐν μαλακοῖς
BUT   WHAT DID YOU° GO OUT TO SEE?   A MAN   IN   SOFT

ἱματίοις ἠμφιεσμένον; ἰδοὺ οἱ ἐν
CLOTHING   HAVING BEEN DRESSED?   BEHOLD THE ONES WITH

ἱματισμῷ ἐνδόξῳ καὶ τρυφῇ ὑπάρχοντες ἐν τοῖς
GLORIOUS~APPAREL   AND LIVING~IN LUXURY   IN   THE

βασιλείοις εἰσίν. **7.26** ἀλλὰ τί ἐξήλθατε ἰδεῖν;
PALACES   ARE.   BUT   WHAT DID YOU° GO OUT TO SEE?

προφήτην; ναί λέγω ὑμῖν, καὶ περισσότερον
A PROPHET?   YES, I SAY TO YOU°, AND MORE

προφήτου. **7.27** οὗτός ἐστιν περὶ οὗ γέγραπται,
[THAN] A PROPHET.   THIS ONE IS HE ABOUT WHOM IT HAS BEEN WRITTEN,

Ἰδοὺ ἀποστέλλω τὸν ἄγγελόν μου πρὸ
BEHOLD I SEND   THE   MESSENGER OF ME BEFORE

προσώπου σου,
YOUR~FACE,

ὃς κατασκευάσει τὴν ὁδόν σου ἔμπροσθέν
WHO WILL PREPARE   THE   WAY OF YOU IN FRONT OF

σου.
YOU.

7.28 λέγω ὑμῖν, μείζων ἐν γεννητοῖς γυναικῶν
I SAY TO YOU°, ⁶GREATER [THAN] ¹AMONG ²[THOSE] BORN ³OF WOMEN

Ἰωάννου οὐδείς ἐστιν· ὁ δὲ μικρότερος ἐν τῇ
⁷JOHN   ⁴NO ONE ⁵IS. BUT~THE ONE OF LEAST IMPORTANCE IN   THE

βασιλείᾳ τοῦ θεοῦ μείζων αὐτοῦ ἐστιν. **7.29** Καὶ
KINGDOM   -   OF GOD GREATER [THAN] HIM   IS.   AND

πᾶς ὁ λαὸς ἀκούσας καὶ οἱ τελῶναι ἐδικαίωσαν
ALL THE PEOPLE HAVING LISTENED AND THE TAX COLLECTORS JUSTIFIED

τὸν θεὸν βαπτισθέντες τὸ βάπτισμα Ἰωάννου·
-   GOD,   HAVING BEEN BAPTIZED [WITH] THE BAPTISM   OF JOHN.

7.30 οἱ δὲ Φαρισαῖοι καὶ οἱ νομικοὶ τὴν βουλὴν
BUT~THE PHARISEES   AND THE TEACHERS OF THE LAW THE PURPOSE

7:27 Mal. 3:1

walk, the lepers*f* are cleansed, the deaf hear, the dead are raised, the poor have good news brought to them. ²³And blessed is anyone who takes no offense at me."

24 When John's messengers had gone, Jesus*g* began to speak to the crowds about John:*h* "What did you go out into the wilderness to look at? A reed shaken by the wind? ²⁵What then did you go out to see? Someone*i* dressed in soft robes? Look, those who put on fine clothing and live in luxury are in royal palaces. ²⁶What then did you go out to see? A prophet? Yes, I tell you, and more than a prophet. ²⁷This is the one about whom it is written,

'See, I am sending my
    messenger ahead of
    you,
who will prepare your
    way before you.'

²⁸I tell you, among born of women no one is greater than John; yet the least in the kingdom of God is greater than he." ²⁹(And all the people who heard this, including the tax collectors, acknowledged the justice of God,*j* because they had been baptized with John's baptism. ³⁰But by refusing to be baptized by him, the Pharisees and the

f The terms *leper* and *leprosy* can refer to several diseases
g Gk *he*
h Gk *him*
i Or *Why then did you go out? To see someone*
j Or *praised God*

lawyers rejected God's purpose for themselves.) 31 "To what then will I compare the people of this generation, and what are they like? [32]They are like children sitting in the marketplace and calling to one another,

'We played the flute for you, and you did not dance;
we wailed, and you did not weep.'

[33]For John the Baptist has come eating no bread and drinking no wine, and you say, 'He has a demon'; [34]the Son of Man has come eating and drinking, and you say, 'Look, a glutton and a drunkard, a friend of tax collectors and sinners!' [35]Nevertheless, wisdom is vindicated by all her children."

36 One of the Pharisees asked Jesus[k] to eat with him, and he went into the Pharisee's house and took his place at the table. [37]And a woman in the city, who was a sinner, having learned that he was eating in the Pharisee's house, brought an alabaster jar of ointment. [38]She stood behind him at his feet, weeping, and began to bathe his feet with her tears and to dry them with her hair. Then she continued kissing his feet and anointing them with the ointment.

[k] Gk him

τοῦ θεοῦ ἠθέτησαν εἰς ἑαυτοὺς μὴ βαπτισθέντες ὑπ'
-   OF GOD   THEY SET ASIDE   FOR   THEMSELVES   NOT HAVING BEEN BAPTIZED   BY

αὐτοῦ.
HIM.

7.31 Τίνι οὖν   ὁμοιώσω   τοὺς ἀνθρώπους τῆς
THEREFORE~TO WHAT   WILL I COMPARE   THE   MEN   -

γενεᾶς ταύτης καὶ   τίνι   εἰσὶν ὅμοιοι;   **7.32** ὅμοιοί εἰσιν
OF THIS~GENERATION   AND   TO WHAT   ARE THEY   LIKE?   THEY ARE~LIKE

παιδίοις τοῖς ἐν ἀγορᾷ   καθημένοις καὶ
CHILDREN   -   IN   [THE] MARKETPLACE   SITTING   AND

προσφωνοῦσιν ἀλλήλοις ἃ   λέγει,
CALLING OUT   TO ONE ANOTHER   WHO   SAYS,

Ηὐλήσαμεν   ὑμῖν   καὶ   οὐκ ὠρχήσασθε,
WE PLAYED THE FLUTE   FOR YOU°   AND   YOU° DID NOT DANCE,

ἐθρηνήσαμεν   καὶ   οὐκ ἐκλαύσατε.
WE SANG A DIRGE   AND   YOU° DID NOT WEEP.

7.33 ἐλήλυθεν γὰρ Ἰωάννης ὁ   βαπτιστὴς μὴ ἐσθίων
FOR~HAS COME   JOHN   THE   BAPTIST   NOT EATING

ἄρτον μήτε πίνων οἶνον, καὶ λέγετε, Δαιμόνιον ἔχει.
BREAD   NOR   DRINKING   WINE,   AND   YOU° SAY,   HE HAS~A DEMON.

7.34 ἐλήλυθεν ὁ   υἱὸς τοῦ ἀνθρώπου ἐσθίων καὶ   πίνων,
HAS COME   THE   SON   -   OF MAN   EATING   AND   DRINKING,

καὶ   λέγετε, Ἰδοὺ ἄνθρωπος φάγος καὶ οἰνοπότης,
AND   YOU° SAY,   BEHOLD   A MAN [WHO IS]   A GLUTTON   AND   A DRUNKARD,

φίλος τελωνῶν   καὶ ἁμαρτωλῶν. **7.35** καὶ ἐδικαιώθη
A FRIEND   OF TAX COLLECTORS   AND   SINNERS.   AND   WAS(IS) JUSTIFIED

ἡ σοφία ἀπὸ πάντων τῶν τέκνων αὐτῆς.
-   WISDOM   BY   ALL   OF THE   CHILDREN   OF HER.

7.36 Ἠρώτα   δέ   τις   αὐτὸν τῶν Φαρισαίων ἵνα
[5]WAS ASKING   [1]NOW   [2]A CERTAIN ONE   [6]HIM   [3]OF THE   [4]PHARISEES   THAT

φάγῃ   μετ' αὐτοῦ, καὶ εἰσελθὼν εἰς τὸν οἶκον τοῦ
HE MIGHT EAT   WITH   HIM,   AND   HAVING ENTERED   INTO   THE   HOUSE   OF THE

Φαρισαίου κατεκλίθη.   **7.37** καὶ ἰδοὺ γυνὴ ἥτις
PHARISEE   HE RECLINED AT TABLE.   AND   BEHOLD   A WOMAN   WHO

ἦν ἐν τῇ πόλει ἁμαρτωλός, καὶ ἐπιγνοῦσα ὅτι
WAS   IN   THE   CITY   A SINNER,   AND   HAVING KNOWN   THAT

κατάκειται   ἐν τῇ οἰκίᾳ τοῦ Φαρισαίου, κομίσασα
HE RECLINES AT TABLE   IN   THE   HOUSE   OF THE   PHARISEE,   HAVING BROUGHT

ἀλάβαστρον μύρου **7.38** καὶ στᾶσα   ὀπίσω παρὰ
AN ALABASTER [JAR]   OF PERFUME   AND   HAVING STOOD   BEHIND   AT

τοὺς πόδας αὐτοῦ κλαίουσα τοῖς   δάκρυσιν ἤρξατο
THE   FEET   OF HIM   CRYING,   WITH THE   TEARS   SHE BEGAN

βρέχειν τοὺς πόδας αὐτοῦ καὶ ταῖς θριξὶν τῆς
TO WET   THE   FEET   OF HIM   AND   WITH THE   HAIRS   OF THE

κεφαλῆς αὐτῆς ἐξέμασσεν καὶ κατεφίλει τοὺς πόδας
HEAD   OF HER   SHE WAS WIPING   AND   WAS KISSING   THE   FEET

αὐτοῦ καὶ ἤλειφεν   τῷ   μύρῳ.
OF HIM   AND   WAS ANOINTING [THEM]   WITH THE   PERFUME.

7.39 ἰδὼν δὲ   ὁ Φαρισαῖος ὁ καλέσας αὐτὸν
BUT~HAVING SEEN [THIS] THE PHARISEE   - HAVING INVITED HIM

εἶπεν ἐν   ἑαυτῷ λέγων, Οὗτος εἰ ἦν προφήτης,
SPOKE   WITHIN HIMSELF SAYING, IF~THIS ONE WAS A PROPHET,

ἐγίνωσκεν ἂν   τίς καὶ ποταπὴ ἡ γυνὴ ἥτις ἅπτεται
HE WOULD HAVE KNOWN WHO AND WHAT SORT OF - WOMAN WHO IS TOUCHING

αὐτοῦ, ὅτι   ἁμαρτωλός ἐστιν. **7.40** καὶ ἀποκριθεὶς ὁ
HIM,   BECAUSE SHE IS~A SINNER.   AND~HAVING ANSWERED -

Ἰησοῦς εἶπεν πρὸς αὐτόν, Σίμων, ἔχω σοί τι
JESUS   SAID   TO   HIM,   SIMON, I HAVE TO YOU SOMETHING

εἰπεῖν. ὁ δέ, Διδάσκαλε, εἰπέ, φησίν. **7.41** δύο
TO SAY. AND~HE, TEACHER,   SPEAK, HE SAYS.   TWO [PERSONS]

χρεοφειλέται ἦσαν δανιστῇ τινι· ὁ εἷς ὤφειλεν
WERE~DEBTORS   TO A CERTAIN~CREDITOR; THE ONE WAS OWING

δηνάρια πεντακόσια, ὁ δὲ ἕτερος πεντήκοντα.
FIVE HUNDRED~DENARII, AND~THE OTHER   FIFTY.

7.42 μὴ ἐχόντων αὐτῶν   ἀποδοῦναι
NOT HAVING   OF THEMSELVES TO PAY,

ἀμφοτέροις ἐχαρίσατο. τίς οὖν   αὐτῶν πλεῖον
HE FORGAVE~BOTH.   THEREFORE~WHICH OF THEM 3MORE

ἀγαπήσει αὐτόν; **7.43** ἀποκριθεὶς Σίμων εἶπεν,
1WILL LOVE 2HIM?   HAVING ANSWERED SIMON   SAID,

Ὑπολαμβάνω ὅτι ᾧ   τὸ πλεῖον ἐχαρίσατο. ὁ δὲ
I SUPPOSE   - TO WHOM THE MORE HE FORGAVE.   - AND

εἶπεν αὐτῷ, Ὀρθῶς ἔκρινας. **7.44** καὶ στραφεὶς πρὸς
HE SAID TO HIM, YOU JUDGED~CORRECTLY. AND HAVING TURNED TO

τὴν γυναῖκα τῷ Σίμωνι ἔφη, Βλέπεις ταύτην τὴν
THE WOMAN   - HE SAID~TO SIMON, DO YOU SEE THIS   -

γυναῖκα; εἰσῆλθόν σου εἰς τὴν οἰκίαν, ὕδωρ μοι ἐπὶ
WOMAN?   I ENTERED   INTO~YOUR - HOUSE, WATER FOR ME ON [MY]

πόδας οὐκ ἔδωκας· αὕτη δὲ τοῖς   δάκρυσιν ἔβρεξέν
FEET   YOU DID NOT GIVE. BUT~SHE WITH THE(HER) TEARS   WET

μου τοὺς πόδας καὶ ταῖς θριξὶν αὐτῆς ἐξέμαξεν.
MY   -   FEET   AND WITH THE HAIRS OF HER WIPED [THEM].

7.45 φίλημά μοι οὐκ ἔδωκας· αὕτη δὲ ἀφ᾽ ἧς
A KISS   TO ME YOU DID NOT GIVE.   BUT~SHE, FROM [THE TIME] WHICH

εἰσῆλθον οὐ διέλιπεν καταφιλοῦσά μου τοὺς πόδας.
I ENTERED   DID NOT STOP KISSING   MY   -   FEET.

7.46 ἐλαίῳ τὴν κεφαλήν μου οὐκ ἤλειψας· αὕτη δὲ
WITH OIL THE HEAD   OF ME YOU DID NOT ANOINT. BUT~SHE

μύρῳ   ἤλειψεν τοὺς πόδας μου. **7.47** οὗ χάριν λέγω
WITH PERFUME ANOINTED THE FEET OF ME.   FOR THIS REASON, I SAY

σοι, ἀφέωνται αἱ ἁμαρτίαι αὐτῆς   αἱ πολλαί,
TO YOU, HAVE BEEN FORGIVEN THE SINS   OF HER [WHICH ARE] - MANY,

ὅτι ἠγάπησεν πολύ· ᾧ δὲ   ὀλίγον ἀφίεται,
FOR SHE LOVED   MUCH. BUT~TO WHOM LITTLE IS FORGIVEN,

ὀλίγον ἀγαπᾷ. **7.48** εἶπεν δὲ αὐτῇ, Ἀφέωνταί σου αἱ
HE LOVES~LITTLE.   AND~HE SAID TO HER, HAVE BEEN FORGIVEN YOUR -

[39]Now when the Pharisee who had invited him saw it, he said to himself, "If this man were a prophet, he would have known who and what kind of woman this is who is touching him—that she is a sinner." [40]Jesus spoke up and said to him, "Simon, I have something to say to you." "Teacher," he replied, "speak." [41]"A certain creditor had two debtors; one owed five hundred denarii,[l] and the other fifty. [42]When they could not pay, he canceled the debts for both of them. Now which of them will love him more?" [43]Simon answered, "I suppose the one for whom he canceled the greater debt." And Jesus[m] said to him, "You have judged rightly." [44]Then turning toward the woman, he said to Simon, "Do you see this woman? I entered your house; you gave me no water for my feet, but she has bathed my feet with her tears and dried them with her hair. [45]You gave me no kiss, but from the time I came in she has not stopped kissing my feet. [46]You did not anoint my head with oil, but she has anointed my feet with ointment. [47]Therefore, I tell you, her sins, which were many, have been forgiven; hence she has shown great love. But the one to whom little is forgiven, loves little." [48]Then he said to her, "Your sins are forgiven."

[l] The denarius was the usual day's wage for a laborer
[m] Gk he

49But those who were at the
table with him began to say
among themselves, "Who
is this who even forgives
sins?" 50And he said to the
woman, "Your faith has
saved you; go in peace."

ἁμαρτίαι. **7.49** καὶ   ἤρξαντο οἱ   συνανακείμενοι
SINS.   AND   BEGAN   THE ONES RECLINING WITH [HIM]

λέγειν ἐν   ἑαυτοῖς, Τίς οὗτός ἐστιν ὃς καὶ
TO SAY AMONG THEMSELVES, WHO IS~THIS   WHO EVEN

ἁμαρτίας ἀφίησιν; **7.50** εἶπεν δὲ πρὸς τὴν γυναῖκα, Ἡ
FORGIVES~SINS?   AND~HE SAID TO THE WOMAN,   THE

πίστις σου   σέσωκέν σε· πορεύου εἰς εἰρήνην.
FAITH OF YOU HAS SAVED YOU. GO   IN PEACE.

CHAPTER 8

Soon afterwards he went on
through cities and villages,
proclaiming and bringing the
good news of the kingdom
of God. The twelve were
with him, 2as well as some
women who had been cured
of evil spirits and infirmities:
Mary, called Magdalene,
from whom seven demons
had gone out, 3and Joanna,
the wife of Herod's steward
Chuza, and Susanna, and
many others, who provided
for them[n] out of their
resources.
   4 When a great crowd
gathered and people from
town after town came to
him, he said in a parable:
5"A sower went out to sow
his seed; and as he sowed,
some fell on the path and
was trampled on, and the
birds of the air ate it up.
6Some fell on the rock; and
as it grew up, it withered

[n] Other ancient authorities read him

8.1 Καὶ ἐγένετο ἐν τῷ καθεξῆς καὶ αὐτὸς
AND   IT CAME ABOUT AFTERWARDS [THAT] -   HE

διώδευεν   κατὰ πόλιν καὶ κώμην κηρύσσων καὶ
WAS TRAVELING THROUGH EVERY CITY AND VILLAGE PREACHING AND

εὐαγγελιζόμενος τὴν βασιλείαν τοῦ θεοῦ καὶ οἱ
PROCLAIMING THE GOOD NEWS [OF] THE KINGDOM - OF GOD AND THE

δώδεκα σὺν αὐτῷ, **8.2** καὶ γυναῖκές τινες αἳ
TWELVE [WERE] WITH HIM,   AND SOME~WOMEN WHO

ἦσαν τεθεραπευμέναι ἀπὸ πνευμάτων πονηρῶν καὶ
HAD BEEN HEALED   FROM EVIL~SPIRITS   AND

ἀσθενειῶν, Μαρία ἡ   καλουμένη Μαγδαληνή, ἀφ'
DISEASES, MARY THE ONE BEING CALLED MAGDALENE, FROM

ἧς δαιμόνια ἑπτὰ ἐξεληλύθει, **8.3** καὶ Ἰωάννα γυνὴ
WHOM SEVEN~DEMONS HAD GONE OUT,   AND JOANNA [THE] WIFE

Χουζᾶ ἐπιτρόπου Ἡρῴδου καὶ Σουσάννα καὶ
OF CHUZA, [THE] STEWARD OF HEROD, AND SUSANNA, AND

ἕτεραι πολλαί, αἵτινες διηκόνουν ⌜αὐτοῖς⌝ ἐκ τῶν
MANY~OTHERS, WHO   WERE PROVIDING FOR THEM FROM THE

ὑπαρχόντων αὐταῖς.
POSSESSIONS BELONGING TO THEM.

8.4 Συνιόντος δὲ ὄχλου πολλοῦ καὶ τῶν κατὰ
NOW~[WHEN] GATHERING A LARGE~CROWD AND THE ONES IN EVERY

πόλιν ἐπιπορευομένων πρὸς αὐτὸν εἶπεν διὰ
CITY MAKING THEIR WAY   TO HIM, HE SPOKE BY MEANS

παραβολῆς, **8.5** Ἐξῆλθεν ὁ   σπείρων τοῦ σπεῖραι τὸν
OF A PARABLE,   WENT OUT THE ONE SOWING - TO SOW THE

σπόρον αὐτοῦ. καὶ ἐν τῷ σπείρειν αὐτὸν ὃ μὲν
SEED   OF HIM. AND WHILE HE~SOWS,   SOME

ἔπεσεν παρὰ τὴν ὁδὸν καὶ κατεπατήθη, καὶ τὰ
FELL BESIDE THE ROAD AND IT WAS TRAMPLED UPON, AND THE

πετεινὰ τοῦ οὐρανοῦ κατέφαγεν αὐτό. **8.6** καὶ ἕτερον
BIRDS   - OF HEAVEN DEVOURED IT.   AND OTHER(S)

κατέπεσεν ἐπὶ τὴν πέτραν, καὶ φυὲν   ἐξηράνθη
FELL DOWN UPON THE ROCK,   AND HAVING GROWN UP, IT DRIED UP

8:3 text: ASV RSV NASB NIV NEB TEV NJB NRSV. var. αυτω (for him): KJV ASVmg RSVmg NRSVmg.

διὰ   τὸ μὴ ἔχειν ἰκμάδα.   **8.7** καὶ ἕτερον ἔπεσεν ἐν
BECAUSE - IT HAS NO MOISTURE.   AND OTHER(S) FELL   IN

μέσῳ   τῶν ἀκανθῶν, καὶ συμφυεῖσαι   αἱ ἄκανθαι
[THE] MIDST - OF THORNS, AND HAVING GROWN UP WITH [IT] THE THORNS

ἀπέπνιξαν αὐτό. **8.8** καὶ ἕτερον ἔπεσεν εἰς τὴν γῆν
CHOKED   IT.   AND OTHER(S) FELL   IN THE ²SOIL

τὴν ἀγαθὴν καὶ φυὲν   ἐποίησεν καρπὸν
-   ¹GOOD   AND HAVING GROWN UP IT PRODUCED FRUIT

ἑκατονταπλασίονα.   ταῦτα λέγων   ἐφώνει,   Ὁ
A HUNDREDFOLD.   SAYING~THESE THINGS, HE WAS CALLING OUT, THE ONE

ἔχων ὦτα ἀκούειν ἀκουέτω.
HAVING EARS TO HEAR   LET THAT ONE HEAR.

8.9 Ἐπηρώτων δὲ αὐτὸν οἱ μαθηταὶ αὐτοῦ τίς αὕτη
NOW~WERE QUESTIONING HIM   THE DISCIPLES OF HIM WHAT THIS

εἴη   ἡ παραβολή. **8.10** ὁ δὲ εἶπεν, Ὑμῖν
²MIGHT BE - ¹PARABLE.   - AND HE SAID, TO YOU°

δέδοται   γνῶναι τὰ μυστήρια τῆς βασιλείας τοῦ
IT HAS BEEN GRANTED TO KNOW THE MYSTERIES OF THE KINGDOM   -

θεοῦ, τοῖς δὲ λοιποῖς ἐν παραβολαῖς, ἵνα
OF GOD, BUT~TO THE OTHERS [I SPEAK] IN PARABLES,   IN ORDER THAT

βλέποντες μὴ βλέπωσιν
SEEING   THEY MAY NOT SEE

καὶ ἀκούοντες μὴ συνιῶσιν.
AND   HEARING   THEY MAY NOT UNDERSTAND.

8.11 Ἔστιν   δὲ αὕτη ἡ παραβολή· Ὁ σπόρος
³IS [THE MEANING OF] ¹NOW ²THIS THE PARABLE.   THE SEED

ἐστὶν ὁ λόγος τοῦ θεοῦ. **8.12** οἱ δὲ   παρὰ τὴν ὁδόν
IS   THE WORD   - OF GOD.   NOW~THE ONES BESIDE THE ROAD

εἰσιν οἱ   ἀκούσαντες, εἶτα ἔρχεται ὁ διάβολος καὶ
ARE   THE ONES HAVING HEARD, THEN COMES   THE DEVIL   AND

αἴρει τὸν λόγον ἀπὸ τῆς καρδίας αὐτῶν, ἵνα μὴ
TAKES AWAY THE WORD FROM THE HEART   OF THEM, LEST

πιστεύσαντες σωθῶσιν. **8.13** οἱ δὲ   ἐπὶ τῆς
HAVING BELIEVED   THEY MAY BE SAVED.   NOW~THE ONES UPON THE

πέτρας οἳ ὅταν ἀκούσωσιν μετὰ χαρᾶς δέχονται τὸν
ROCK   WHO WHEN THEY HEAR,   WITH JOY   THEY RECEIVE THE

λόγον, καὶ οὗτοι ῥίζαν οὐκ ἔχουσιν, οἳ πρὸς καιρὸν
WORD,   AND THESE DO NOT HAVE~A ROOT,   WHO FOR   A WHILE

πιστεύουσιν καὶ ἐν καιρῷ πειρασμοῦ ἀφίστανται.
BELIEVE   AND IN A TIME OF TESTING   THEY FALL AWAY.

8.14 τὸ δὲ   εἰς τὰς ἀκάνθας πεσόν,   οὗτοί εἰσιν
NOW~THE ONE IN THE THORNS   HAVING FALLEN, THESE ARE

οἱ   ἀκούσαντες, καὶ ὑπὸ μεριμνῶν καὶ πλούτου καὶ
THE ONES HAVING HEARD, AND BY [THE] ANXIETIES AND RICHES   AND

ἡδονῶν τοῦ βίου πορευόμενοι συμπνίγονται καὶ
PLEASURES - OF LIFE [WHILE] GOING ALONG THEY ARE CHOKED   AND

8:10 Isa. 6:9 LXX

for lack of moisture. ⁷Some
fell among thorns, and the
thorns grew with it and
choked it. ⁸Some fell into
good soil, and when it grew,
it produced a hundredfold."
As he said this, he called
out, "Let anyone with ears to
hear listen!"

9 Then his disciples
asked him what this parable
meant. ¹⁰He said, "To you it
has been given to know the
secrets° of the kingdom of
God; but to others I speakᵖ in
parables, so that

'looking they may not
   perceive,
and listening they may
   not understand.'

11 "Now the parable is
this: The seed is the word of
God. ¹²The ones on the path
are those who have heard;
then the devil comes and
takes away the word from
their hearts, so that they may
not believe and be saved.
¹³The ones on the rock are
those who, when they hear
the word, receive it with joy.
But these have no root; they
believe only for a while and
in a time of testing fall away.
¹⁴As for what fell among the
thorns, these are the ones
who hear; but as they go on
their way, they are choked
by the cares and riches and
pleasures of life, and their

° Or mysteries
ᵖ Gk lacks I speak

fruit does not mature. ¹⁵But as for that in the good soil, these are the ones who, when they hear the word, hold it fast in an honest and good heart, and bear fruit with patient endurance.

16 "No one after lighting a lamp hides it under a jar, or puts it under a bed, but puts it on a lampstand, so that those who enter may see the light. ¹⁷For nothing is hidden that will not be disclosed, nor is anything secret that will not become known and come to light. ¹⁸Then pay attention to how you listen; for to those who have, more will be given; and from those who do not have, even what they seem to have will be taken away."

19 Then his mother and his brothers came to him, but they could not reach him because of the crowd. ²⁰And he was told, "Your mother and your brothers are standing outside, wanting to see you." ²¹But he said to them, "My mother and my brothers are those who hear the word of God and do it."

22 One day he got into a boat with his disciples, and he said to them, "Let us go across to the other side of the lake." So they put out, ²³and while they were sailing

οὐ τελεσφοροῦσιν.   **8.15** τὸ δὲ   ἐν τῇ καλῇ γῇ, οὗτοί
DO NOT BRING FRUIT TO MATURITY.   NOW~THE ONE IN   THE   GOOD   SOIL,   THESE

εἰσιν οἵτινες ἐν καρδίᾳ καλῇ καὶ ἀγαθῇ
ARE [THOSE] WHO   WITH ⁴HEART   ¹AN HONEST ²AND ³GOOD

ἀκούσαντες τὸν λόγον κατέχουσιν καὶ καρποφοροῦσιν
HAVING HEARD,   THE   WORD   RETAIN   AND   BEAR FRUIT

ἐν ὑπομονῇ.
WITH PATIENCE.

8.16 Οὐδεὶς δὲ λύχνον ἅψας καλύπτει αὐτὸν σκεύει ἢ
AND~NO ONE   HAVING LIT~A LAMP   COVERS   IT   WITH A JAR OR

ὑποκάτω κλίνης τίθησιν, ἀλλ' ἐπὶ λυχνίας τίθησιν,
UNDER   A BED   PLACES [IT],   BUT   ON   A LAMPSTAND PLACES [IT],

ἵνα οἱ εἰσπορευόμενοι βλέπωσιν τὸ φῶς.
IN ORDER THAT THE ONES   ENTERING   MAY SEE   THE LIGHT.

8.17 οὐ γὰρ   ἐστιν κρυπτὸν ὃ   οὐ φανερὸν
FOR~NOT [ANYTHING] IS   HIDDEN   WHICH NOT EVIDENT

γενήσεται οὐδὲ   ἀπόκρυφον ὃ
WILL BECOME,   NOR [ANYTHING] SECRET   WHICH

οὐ μὴ γνωσθῇ   καὶ εἰς φανερὸν ἔλθῃ.
BY NO MEANS MAY BE MADE KNOWN AND   TO LIGHT   COME.

8.18 βλέπετε οὖν   πῶς ἀκούετε· ὃς ἂν γὰρ ἔχῃ,
THEREFORE,~BE CAREFUL HOW   YOU° LISTEN.   FOR~WHOEVER   HAS,

δοθήσεται αὐτῷ· καὶ ὃς ἂν μὴ ἔχῃ, καὶ ὃ δοκεῖ
IT WILL BE GIVEN TO HIM   AND   WHOEVER DOES NOT HAVE, EVEN WHAT HE SEEMS

ἔχειν ἀρθήσεται ἀπ' αὐτοῦ.
TO HAVE   WILL BE TAKEN   FROM HIM.

8.19 Παρεγένετο δὲ πρὸς αὐτὸν ἡ μήτηρ καὶ οἱ
AND~CAME   TO   HIM   THE MOTHER AND THE

ἀδελφοὶ αὐτοῦ καὶ οὐκ ἠδύναντο συντυχεῖν αὐτῷ
BROTHERS   OF HIM   AND   THEY WERE NOT ABLE TO JOIN   HIM

διὰ   τὸν ὄχλον. **8.20** ἀπηγγέλη δὲ αὐτῷ, Ἡ μήτηρ
BECAUSE OF THE CROWD.   AND~IT WAS ANNOUNCED TO HIM,   THE MOTHER

σου καὶ οἱ ἀδελφοί σου ἑστήκασιν ἔξω
OF YOU AND   THE BROTHERS   OF YOU HAVE BEEN STANDING OUTSIDE

ἰδεῖν θέλοντές σε. **8.21** ὁ δὲ ἀποκριθεὶς εἶπεν πρὸς
WANTING~TO SEE   YOU.   - BUT HAVING ANSWERED HE SAID   TO

αὐτούς, Μήτηρ μου καὶ ἀδελφοί μου οὗτοί εἰσιν
THEM,   [THE] MOTHER OF ME AND   BROTHERS   OF ME ARE~THESE

οἱ τὸν λόγον τοῦ θεοῦ ἀκούοντες καὶ ποιοῦντες.
THE ONES THE WORD   - OF GOD HEARING   AND   DOING.

8.22 Ἐγένετο δὲ ἐν μιᾷ τῶν ἡμερῶν καὶ αὐτὸς
NOW~IT CAME ABOUT ON ONE   OF THE DAYS [THAT]   - HE

ἐνέβη εἰς πλοῖον καὶ οἱ μαθηταὶ αὐτοῦ καὶ εἶπεν
EMBARKED INTO A BOAT   AND   THE DISCIPLES   OF HIM   AND   HE SAID

πρὸς αὐτούς, Διέλθωμεν εἰς τὸ πέραν τῆς λίμνης,
TO   THEM,   LET US GO OVER   TO   THE OTHER SIDE OF THE LAKE,

καὶ ἀνήχθησαν. **8.23** πλεόντων δὲ   αὐτῶν
AND   THEY SET OUT.   ³SAILING   ¹AND [WHILE] ²THEY,

ἀφύπνωσεν. καὶ κατέβη λαῖλαψ ἀνέμου εἰς τὴν
HE FELL ASLEEP. AND CAME DOWN A STORM OF WIND TO THE

λίμνην καὶ συνεπληροῦντο καὶ ἐκινδύνευον.
LAKE AND THEY WERE BEING SWAMPED AND WERE IN DANGER.

8.24 προσελθόντες δὲ διήγειραν αὐτὸν λέγοντες,
AND~HAVING APPROACHED, THEY WOKE HIM SAYING,

Ἐπιστάτα ἐπιστάτα, ἀπολλύμεθα. ὁ δὲ διεγερθεὶς
MASTER, MASTER, WE ARE PERISHING. - AND HAVING BEEN AWAKENED

ἐπετίμησεν τῷ ἀνέμῳ καὶ τῷ κλύδωνι τοῦ ὕδατος·
HE REBUKED THE WIND AND THE ROUGHNESS OF THE WATER.

καὶ ἐπαύσαντο καὶ ἐγένετο γαλήνη. **8.25** εἶπεν δὲ
AND THEY CEASED AND IT BECAME CALM. AND~HE SAID

αὐτοῖς, Ποῦ ἡ πίστις ὑμῶν; φοβηθέντες δὲ
TO THEM, WHERE [IS] THE FAITH OF YOU°? AND~BEING AFRAID

ἐθαύμασαν λέγοντες πρὸς ἀλλήλους, Τίς ἄρα
THEY WERE AMAZED SAYING TO ONE ANOTHER, WHO THEN

οὗτός ἐστιν ὅτι καὶ τοῖς ἀνέμοις ἐπιτάσσει καὶ τῷ
IS~THIS THAT EVEN THE WINDS HE COMMANDS AND THE

ὕδατι, καὶ ὑπακούουσιν αὐτῷ;
WATER, AND THEY OBEY HIM?

8.26 Καὶ κατέπλευσαν εἰς τὴν χώραν τῶν
AND THEY SAILED DOWN TO THE COUNTRY OF THE

⸀Γερασηνῶν,⸁ ἥτις ἐστὶν ἀντιπέρα τῆς Γαλιλαίας.
GERASENES, WHICH IS OPPOSITE - GALILEE.

8.27 ἐξελθόντι δὲ αὐτῷ ἐπὶ τὴν γῆν ὑπήντησεν
AND~HAVING GONE OUT HIM UPON THE LAND MET [HIM]

ἀνήρ τις ἐκ τῆς πόλεως ἔχων δαιμόνια καὶ
A CERTAIN~MAN FROM THE CITY HAVING DEMONS AND

χρόνῳ ἱκανῷ οὐκ ἐνεδύσατο ἱμάτιον καὶ ἐν οἰκίᾳ
FOR A CONSIDERABLE~TIME WAS NOT DRESSED [IN] CLOTHING AND IN A HOUSE

οὐκ ἔμενεν ἀλλ' ἐν τοῖς μνήμασιν. **8.28** ἰδὼν δὲ
HE WAS NOT LIVING BUT AMONG THE TOMBS. AND~HAVING SEEN

τὸν Ἰησοῦν ἀνακράξας προσέπεσεν αὐτῷ καὶ
- JESUS [AND] HAVING CRIED OUT, HE FELL DOWN BEFORE HIM AND

φωνῇ μεγάλῃ εἶπεν, Τί ἐμοὶ καὶ σοί, Ἰησοῦ υἱὲ τοῦ
IN A LOUD~VOICE SAID, WHAT TO ME AND TO YOU, JESUS SON -

θεοῦ τοῦ ὑψίστου; δέομαί σου, μή με βασανίσῃς.
OF GOD - MOST HIGH? I BEG YOU, DO NOT TORMENT~ME.

8.29 παρήγγειλεν γὰρ τῷ πνεύματι τῷ ἀκαθάρτῳ
FOR~HE GAVE ORDERS TO THE ²SPIRIT - ¹UNCLEAN

ἐξελθεῖν ἀπὸ τοῦ ἀνθρώπου. πολλοῖς γὰρ χρόνοις
TO COME OUT FROM THE MAN. FOR~MANY TIMES

συνηρπάκει αὐτὸν καὶ ἐδεσμεύετο ἁλύσεσιν καὶ
IT HAD SEIZED HIM AND HAVING BEEN BOUND WITH CHAINS AND

πέδαις φυλασσόμενος καὶ διαρρήσσων τὰ δεσμὰ
SHACKLES BEING GUARDED AND BREAKING APART THE BONDS

8:26 text [see Mark 5:1]: ASV RSV NASB NIV NEBmg TEV NJB NRSV. var. Γεργεσηνων (Gergesenes) [see Luke 8:26]: ASVmg RSVmg NIVmg NEB TEVmg NJBmg NRSVmg. var. Γαδαρηνων (Gadarenes) [see Matt. 8:28]: ASVmg RSVmg NIVmg NEBmg TEVmg NJBmg NRSVmg.

he fell asleep. A windstorm swept down on the lake, and the boat was filling with water, and they were in danger. 24 They went to him and woke him up, shouting, "Master, Master, we are perishing!" And he woke up and rebuked the wind and the raging waves; they ceased, and there was a calm. 25 He said to them, "Where is your faith?" They were afraid and amazed, and said to one another, "Who then is this, that he commands even the winds and the water, and they obey him?"

26 Then they arrived at the country of the Gerasenes,[q] which is opposite Galilee. 27 As he stepped out on land, a man of the city who had demons met him. For a long time he had worn[r] no clothes, and he did not live in a house but in the tombs. 28 When he saw Jesus, he fell down before him and shouted at the top of his voice, "What have you to do with me, Jesus, Son of the Most High God? I beg you, do not torment me"— 29 for Jesus[s] had commanded the unclean spirit to come out of the man. (For many times it had seized him; he was kept under guard and bound with chains and shackles, but he would break the bonds

q Other ancient authorities read *Gadarenes*; others, *Gergesenes*

r Other ancient authorities read *a man of the city who had had demons for a long time met him. He wore*

s Gk *he*

and be driven by the demon into the wilds.) ³⁰Jesus then asked him, "What is your name?" He said, "Legion"; for many demons had entered him. ³¹They begged him not to order them to go back into the abyss.

32 Now there on the hillside a large herd of swine was feeding; and the demons^t begged Jesus^u to let them enter these. So he gave them permission. ³³Then the demons came out of the man and entered the swine, and the herd rushed down the steep bank into the lake and was drowned.

34 When the swineherds saw what had happened, they ran off and told it in the city and in the country. ³⁵Then people came out to see what had happened, and when they came to Jesus, they found the man from whom the demons had gone sitting at the feet of Jesus, clothed and in his right mind. And they were afraid. ³⁶Those who had seen it told them how the one who had been possessed by demons had been healed. ³⁷Then all the people of the surrounding country of the Gerasenes^v asked Jesus^u to leave them; for they were seized with great fear. So he got into the boat and returned. ³⁸The man from whom the demons had gone begged him that he might be with him; but Jesus^w sent him away,

^t Gk *they*
^u Gk *him*
^v Other ancient authorities read *Gadarenes*; others, *Gergesenes*
^w Gk *he*

ἠλαύνετο ὑπὸ τοῦ δαιμονίου εἰς τὰς ἐρήμους.
HE WAS BEING DRIVEN BY THE DEMON INTO THE WILDERNESS PLACES.

8.30 ἐπηρώτησεν δὲ αὐτὸν ὁ Ἰησοῦς, Τί σοι ὄνομά
AND~QUESTIONED HIM - JESUS, WHAT TO YOU A NAME

ἐστιν; ὁ δὲ εἶπεν, Λεγιών, ὅτι εἰσῆλθεν
IS? - AND HE SAID, LEGION, BECAUSE ENTERED

δαιμόνια πολλὰ εἰς αὐτόν. **8.31** καὶ παρεκάλουν αὐτὸν
MANY~DEMONS INTO HIM. AND THEY WERE BEGGING HIM

ἵνα μὴ ἐπιτάξῃ αὐτοῖς εἰς τὴν ἄβυσσον ἀπελθεῖν.
LEST HE MIGHT COMMAND THEM INTO THE ABYSS TO DEPART.

8.32 Ἦν δὲ ἐκεῖ ἀγέλη χοίρων ἱκανῶν βοσκομένη
NOW~THERE WAS THERE A HERD OF MANY~PIGS FEEDING

ἐν τῷ ὄρει· καὶ παρεκάλεσαν αὐτὸν ἵνα ἐπιτρέψῃ
ON THE MOUNTAIN. AND THEY BEGGED HIM THAT HE MIGHT PERMIT

αὐτοῖς εἰς ἐκείνους εἰσελθεῖν· καὶ ἐπέτρεψεν αὐτοῖς.
THEM INTO THOSE TO ENTER. AND HE PERMITTED THEM.

8.33 ἐξελθόντα δὲ τὰ δαιμόνια ἀπὸ τοῦ ἀνθρώπου
AND~HAVING COME OUT THE DEMONS FROM THE MAN,

εἰσῆλθον εἰς τοὺς χοίρους, καὶ ὥρμησεν ἡ ἀγέλη κατὰ
THEY ENTERED INTO THE PIGS, AND RUSHED THE HERD DOWN

τοῦ κρημνοῦ εἰς τὴν λίμνην καὶ ἀπεπνίγη.
THE BANK INTO THE LAKE AND WERE DROWNED.

8.34 ἰδόντες δὲ οἱ βόσκοντες τὸ γεγονὸς
AND~HAVING SEEN THE ONES FEEDING THE THING HAVING HAPPENED,

ἔφυγον καὶ ἀπήγγειλαν εἰς τὴν πόλιν καὶ εἰς τοὺς
THEY FLED AND REPORTED TO THE CITY AND TO THE

ἀγρούς. **8.35** ἐξῆλθον δὲ ἰδεῖν τὸ γεγονὸς καὶ
FARMS. AND~THEY WENT OUT TO SEE THE THING HAVING HAPPENED AND

ἦλθον πρὸς τὸν Ἰησοῦν καὶ εὗρον καθήμενον τὸν
CAME TO - JESUS AND FOUND SITTING THE

ἄνθρωπον ἀφ’ οὗ τὰ δαιμόνια ἐξῆλθεν ἱματισμένον
MAN FROM WHOM THE DEMONS DEPARTED HAVING BEEN DRESSED

καὶ σωφρονοῦντα παρὰ τοὺς πόδας τοῦ Ἰησοῦ, καὶ
AND BEING OF SOUND MIND AT THE FEET - OF JESUS, AND

ἐφοβήθησαν. **8.36** ἀπήγγειλαν δὲ αὐτοῖς οἱ ἰδόντες
THEY WERE AFRAID. AND~REPORTED TO THEM THE ONES HAVING SEEN

πῶς ἐσώθη ὁ δαιμονισθείς. **8.37** καὶ ἠρώτησεν
HOW WAS HEALED THE ONE HAVING BEEN DEMON POSSESSED. AND ASKED

αὐτὸν ἅπαν τὸ πλῆθος τῆς περιχώρου τῶν
HIM ALL THE MULTITUDE OF THE SURROUNDING COUNTRY OF THE

Γερασηνῶν ἀπελθεῖν ἀπ’ αὐτῶν, ὅτι φόβῳ μεγάλῳ
GERASENES TO DEPART FROM THEM, BECAUSE WITH GREAT~FEAR

συνείχοντο· αὐτὸς δὲ ἐμβὰς εἰς πλοῖον
THEY WERE BEING SEIZED. SO~HE HAVING EMBARKED INTO A BOAT [AND]

ὑπέστρεψεν. **8.38** ἐδεῖτο δὲ αὐτοῦ ὁ ἀνὴρ ἀφ’ οὗ
RETURNED. AND~WAS BEGGING HIM THE MAN FROM WHOM

ἐξεληλύθει τὰ δαιμόνια εἶναι σὺν αὐτῷ· ἀπέλυσεν δὲ
HAD GONE OUT THE DEMONS, TO BE WITH HIM. BUT~HE SENT AWAY

αὐτὸν λέγων, **8.39** Ὑπόστρεφε εἰς τὸν οἶκόν σου καὶ
HIM   SAYING,   RETURN   TO THE HOUSE   OF YOU AND

διηγοῦ ὅσα σοι ἐποίησεν ὁ θεός. καὶ ἀπῆλθεν
TELL   WHAT FOR YOU DID   - GOD.   AND   HE WENT AWAY

καθ' ὅλην τὴν πόλιν κηρύσσων ὅσα ἐποίησεν αὐτῷ
THROUGHOUT THE~WHOLE CITY PREACHING WHAT DID   FOR HIM

ὁ Ἰησοῦς.
- JESUS.

8.40 Ἐν δὲ τῷ ὑποστρέφειν τὸν Ἰησοῦν ἀπεδέξατο
NOW~WHEN   RETURNS   -   JESUS   WELCOMED

αὐτὸν ὁ ὄχλος, ἦσαν γὰρ πάντες προσδοκῶντες αὐτόν.
HIM   THE CROWD, FOR~THEY WERE ALL   EXPECTING   HIM.

8.41 καὶ ἰδοὺ ἦλθεν ἀνὴρ ᾧ   ὄνομα
AND BEHOLD THERE CAME A MAN TO WHOM [WAS GIVEN] [THE] NAME

Ἰάϊρος καὶ οὗτος ἄρχων τῆς συναγωγῆς ὑπῆρχεν,
JAIRUS   AND THIS ONE RULER OF THE SYNAGOGUE   WAS,

καὶ πεσὼν παρὰ τοὺς πόδας [τοῦ] Ἰησοῦ
AND HAVING FALLEN AT   THE FEET   -   OF JESUS,

παρεκάλει αὐτὸν εἰσελθεῖν εἰς τὸν οἶκον αὐτοῦ,
HE WAS PLEADING [WITH] HIM TO ENTER   INTO THE HOUSE OF HIM,

8.42 ὅτι θυγάτηρ μονογενὴς ἦν αὐτῷ ὡς ἐτῶν
BECAUSE AN ONLY~DAUGHTER   WAS TO HIM ABOUT OF YEARS

δώδεκα καὶ αὐτὴ ἀπέθνησκεν.
TWELVE AND SHE WAS DYING.

Ἐν δὲ τῷ ὑπάγειν αὐτὸν οἱ ὄχλοι συνέπνιγον
NOW~WHEN HE~GOES   THE CROWDS WERE PRESSING AROUND

αὐτόν. **8.43** καὶ γυνὴ οὖσα ἐν ῥύσει αἵματος ἀπὸ
HIM.   AND A WOMAN BEING WITH A FLOW OF BLOOD FOR

ἐτῶν δώδεκα, ἥτις ⌐[ἰατροῖς προσαναλώσασα ὅλον τὸν
TWELVE~YEARS, WHO (TO PHYSICIANS HAVING SPENT   ALL   THE(HER)

βίον)⌐ οὐκ ἴσχυσεν ἀπ' οὐδενὸς θεραπευθῆναι,
PROPERTY) WAS NOT ABLE FROM ANYONE TO BE HEALED,

8.44 προσελθοῦσα ὄπισθεν ἥψατο τοῦ κρασπέδου τοῦ
HAVING APPROACHED FROM BEHIND SHE TOUCHED THE HEM   OF THE

ἱματίου αὐτοῦ καὶ παραχρῆμα ἔστη   ἡ ῥύσις τοῦ
GARMENT OF HIM AND IMMEDIATELY CAME TO AN END THE FLOW OF THE

αἵματος αὐτῆς. **8.45** καὶ εἶπεν ὁ Ἰησοῦς, Τίς ὁ
BLOOD   OF HER.   AND SAID   - JESUS,   WHO [IS] THE ONE

ἀψάμενός μου; ἀρνουμένων δὲ πάντων εἶπεν ὁ
HAVING TOUCHED ME? AND~DENYING [IT] EVERYONE, ²SAID -

Πέτρος, Ἐπιστάτα, οἱ ὄχλοι συνέχουσίν σε καὶ
¹PETER,   MASTER,   THE CROWDS SURROUND   YOU AND

ἀποθλίβουσιν. **8.46** ὁ δὲ Ἰησοῦς εἶπεν, Ἥψατό μού
ARE PRESSING AGAINST [YOU].   - BUT JESUS   SAID, ²TOUCHED ³ME

τις, ἐγὼ γὰρ ἔγνων δύναμιν ἐξεληλυθυῖαν ἀπ' ἐμοῦ.
¹SOMEONE, FOR~I KNEW   POWER   HAVING GONE OUT   FROM ME.

saying, [39]"Return to your home, and declare how much God has done for you." So he went away, proclaiming throughout the city how much Jesus had done for him.

[40] Now when Jesus returned, the crowd welcomed him, for they were all waiting for him. [41] Just then there came a man named Jairus, a leader of the synagogue. He fell at Jesus' feet and begged him to come to his house, [42] for he had an only daughter, about twelve years old, who was dying.

As he went, the crowds pressed in on him. [43] Now there was a woman who had been suffering from hemorrhages for twelve years; and though she had spent all she had on physicians,[x] no one could cure her. [44] She came up behind him and touched the fringe of his clothes, and immediately her hemorrhage stopped. [45] Then Jesus asked, "Who touched me?" When all denied it, Peter[y] said, "Master, the crowds surround you and press in on you." [46] But Jesus said, "Someone touched me; for I noticed that power had gone out from me."

[x] Other ancient authorities lack *and though she had spent all she had on physicians*

[y] Other ancient authorities add *and those who were with him*

8:43 text: KJV ASV RSVmg NASBmg NIVmg NEBmg TEV NJBmg NRSV.   omit: ASVmg RSV NASB NIV NEB TEVmg NJB NRSVmg.

⁴⁷When the woman saw that she could not remain hidden, she came trembling; and falling down before him, she declared in the presence of all the people why she had touched him, and how she had been immediately healed. ⁴⁸He said to her, "Daughter, your faith has made you well; go in peace."

49 While he was still speaking, someone came from the leader's house to say, "Your daughter is dead; do not trouble the teacher any longer." ⁵⁰When Jesus heard this, he replied, "Do not fear. Only believe, and she will be saved." ⁵¹When he came to the house, he did not allow anyone to enter with him, except Peter, John, and James, and the child's father and mother. ⁵²They were all weeping and wailing for her; but he said, "Do not weep; for she is not dead but sleeping." ⁵³And they laughed at him, knowing that she was dead. ⁵⁴But he took her by the hand and called out, "Child, get up!" ⁵⁵Her spirit returned, and she got up at once. Then he directed them to give her something to eat. ⁵⁶Her parents were astounded; but he ordered them to tell no one what had happened.

8.47 ἰδοῦσα   δὲ   ἡ   γυνὴ   ὅτι   οὐκ   ἔλαθεν
⁴HAVING SEEN ¹AND ²THE ³WOMAN THAT SHE DID NOT ESCAPE NOTICE

τρέμουσα   ἦλθεν   καὶ   προσπεσοῦσα   αὐτῷ   δι᾽   ἣν
CAME~TREMBLING   AND   HAVING FALLEN DOWN BEFORE   HIM,   FOR   WHAT

αἰτίαν   ἥψατο   αὐτοῦ   ἀπήγγειλεν   ἐνώπιον   παντὸς   τοῦ
REASON   SHE TOUCHED   HIM   SHE PROCLAIMED   BEFORE   ALL   THE

λαοῦ   καὶ   ὡς   ἰάθη   παραχρῆμα.   **8.48** ὁ   δὲ   εἶπεν
PEOPLE   AND   HOW   SHE WAS HEALED   IMMEDIATELY.   -   AND   HE SAID

αὐτῇ,   Θυγάτηρ,   ἡ   πίστις   σου   σέσωκέν   σε·   πορεύου
TO HER,   DAUGHTER,   THE   FAITH   OF YOU   HAS SAVED   YOU.   GO

εἰς   εἰρήνην.
IN   PEACE.

8.49 Ἔτι   αὐτοῦ   λαλοῦντος   ἔρχεταί   τις   παρὰ
[WHILE] STILL   HE   SPEAKING,   COMES   SOMEONE   FROM

τοῦ   ἀρχισυναγώγου   λέγων   ὅτι   Τέθνηκεν   ἡ   θυγάτηρ
THE   SYNAGOGUE RULER   SAYING   -   HAS DIED   THE   DAUGHTER

σου·   μηκέτι   σκύλλε   τὸν   διδάσκαλον.   **8.50** ὁ   δὲ
OF YOU.   NO LONGER   TROUBLE   THE   TEACHER.   -   BUT

Ἰησοῦς   ἀκούσας   ἀπεκρίθη   αὐτῷ,   Μὴ   φοβοῦ,   μόνον
JESUS   HAVING HEARD   ANSWERED   HIM,   DO NOT BE AFRAID,   ONLY

πίστευσον,   καὶ   σωθήσεται.   **8.51** ἐλθὼν δὲ   εἰς   τὴν
BELIEVE,   AND   SHE WILL BE HEALED.   AND~HAVING COME   INTO   THE

οἰκίαν   οὐκ   ἀφῆκεν   εἰσελθεῖν   τινα   σὺν   αὐτῷ   εἰ   μὴ
HOUSE   HE DID NOT PERMIT   ANYONE~TO ENTER   WITH   HIM   EXCEPT

Πέτρον   καὶ   Ἰωάννην   καὶ   Ἰάκωβον   καὶ   τὸν   πατέρα
PETER   AND   JOHN   AND   JAMES   AND   THE   FATHER

τῆς   παιδὸς   καὶ   τὴν   μητέρα.   **8.52** ἔκλαιον δὲ   πάντες
OF THE   CHILD   AND   THE   MOTHER.   AND~WERE CRYING   ALL

καὶ   ἐκόπτοντο   αὐτήν.   ὁ   δὲ   εἶπεν,   Μὴ   κλαίετε,
AND   WERE MOURNING [FOR]   HER.   -   BUT   HE SAID,   DO NOT CRY,

οὐ   γὰρ   ἀπέθανεν   ἀλλὰ   καθεύδει.   **8.53** καὶ   κατεγέλων
FOR~SHE DID NOT DIE,   BUT   IS SLEEPING.   AND   THEY WERE RIDICULING

αὐτοῦ   εἰδότες   ὅτι   ἀπέθανεν.   **8.54** αὐτὸς   δὲ   κρατήσας
HIM   HAVING KNOWN   THAT   SHE DIED.   BUT~HE   HAVING TAKEN

τῆς   χειρὸς   αὐτῆς   ἐφώνησεν   λέγων,   Ἡ   παῖς,   ἔγειρε.
THE   HAND   OF HER,   CALLED OUT,   SAYING,   -   CHILD,   GET UP.

8.55 καὶ   ἐπέστρεψεν   τὸ   πνεῦμα   αὐτῆς   καὶ   ἀνέστη
AND   RETURNED   THE   SPIRIT   OF HER   AND   SHE GOT UP

παραχρῆμα   καὶ   διέταξεν   αὐτῇ δοθῆναι   φαγεῖν.
IMMEDIATELY   AND   HE GAVE ORDERS   TO BE GIVEN~TO HER [SOMETHING]   TO EAT.

8.56 καὶ   ἐξέστησαν   οἱ   γονεῖς   αὐτῆς·   ὁ   δὲ
AND   WERE AMAZED   THE   PARENTS   OF HER.   -   BUT

παρήγγειλεν   αὐτοῖς   μηδενὶ   εἰπεῖν   τὸ   γεγονός.
HE INSTRUCTED   THEM   TO TELL~NO ONE   THE THING   HAVING HAPPENED.

9.1 Συγκαλεσάμενος δὲ τοὺς δώδεκα ἔδωκεν αὐτοῖς
AND~HAVING CALLED TOGETHER   THE   TWELVE   HE GAVE   TO THEM

δύναμιν καὶ ἐξουσίαν ἐπὶ πάντα τὰ δαιμόνια καὶ
POWER   AND   AUTHORITY   OVER   ALL   THE   DEMONS   AND

νόσους θεραπεύειν **9.2** καὶ ἀπέστειλεν αὐτοὺς κηρύσσειν
TO HEAL~DISEASES   AND   HE SENT OUT   THEM   TO PREACH

τὴν βασιλείαν τοῦ θεοῦ καὶ ἰᾶσθαι [τοὺς ἀσθενεῖς],
THE   KINGDOM   -   OF GOD   AND   TO HEAL   THE   SICK,

9.3 καὶ εἶπεν πρὸς αὐτούς, Μηδὲν αἴρετε εἰς τὴν ὁδόν,
AND   HE SAID   TO   THEM,   TAKE~NOTHING   FOR   THE   JOURNEY,

μήτε ῥάβδον μήτε πήραν μήτε ἄρτον μήτε
NEITHER   WALKING STICK   NOR   BEGGAR'S BAG   NOR   BREAD   NOR

ἀργύριον, μήτε [ἀνὰ] δύο χιτῶνας ἔχειν. **9.4** καὶ εἰς
SILVER,   NOR   EACH   TWO   SHIRTS   TO HAVE.   AND   INTO

ἣν ἂν οἰκίαν εἰσέλθητε, ἐκεῖ μένετε καὶ ἐκεῖθεν
WHATEVER   HOUSE   YOU° MAY ENTER,   REMAIN~THERE   AND   FROM THERE

ἐξέρχεσθε. **9.5** καὶ ὅσοι ἂν μὴ δέχωνται ὑμᾶς,
GO OUT.   AND   AS MANY AS   DO NOT RECEIVE   YOU°,

ἐξερχόμενοι ἀπὸ τῆς πόλεως ἐκείνης τὸν κονιορτὸν ἀπὸ
GOING OUT   FROM   -   THAT~CITY   THE   DUST   FROM

τῶν ποδῶν ὑμῶν ἀποτινάσσετε εἰς μαρτύριον ἐπ'
THE   FEET   OF YOU°   SHAKE OFF   FOR   A TESTIMONY   AGAINST

αὐτούς. **9.6** ἐξερχόμενοι δὲ διήρχοντο κατὰ τὰς
THEM.   AND~GOING OUT   THEY WERE GOING AROUND   THROUGHOUT   THE

κώμας εὐαγγελιζόμενοι καὶ θεραπεύοντες πανταχοῦ.
VILLAGES   PREACHING THE GOOD NEWS   AND   HEALING   EVERYWHERE.

9.7 Ἤκουσεν δὲ Ἡρῴδης ὁ τετραάρχης τὰ
NOW~HEARD   HEROD   THE   TETRARCH   ²THE THINGS

γινόμενα πάντα καὶ διηπόρει διὰ τὸ λέγεσθαι
³HAPPENING   ¹ALL   AND   HE WAS PERPLEXED   BECAUSE   -   IT WAS SAID

ὑπό τινων ὅτι Ἰωάννης ἠγέρθη ἐκ νεκρῶν, **9.8** ὑπό
BY   SOME   THAT   JOHN   WAS RAISED   FROM   [THE] DEAD,   BY

τινων δὲ ὅτι Ἡλίας ἐφάνη, ἄλλων δὲ ὅτι
SOME   ALSO   THAT   ELIJAH   HAD APPEARED,   BUT~OTHERS   THAT

προφήτης τις τῶν ἀρχαίων ἀνέστη. **9.9** εἶπεν δὲ
SOME~PROPHET   OF THE   ANCIENTS   AROSE.   BUT~SAID

Ἡρῴδης, Ἰωάννην ἐγὼ ἀπεκεφάλισα· τίς δέ ἐστιν
HEROD,   JOHN   I   BEHEADED.   WHO   THEN   IS

οὗτος περὶ οὗ ἀκούω τοιαῦτα; καὶ ἐζήτει ἰδεῖν
THIS   ABOUT   WHOM   I HEAR   SUCH THINGS?   AND   HE WAS SEEKING   TO SEE

αὐτόν.
HIM.

9.10 Καὶ ὑποστρέψαντες οἱ ἀπόστολοι διηγήσαντο
AND   HAVING RETURNED   THE   APOSTLES   TOLD

αὐτῷ ὅσα ἐποίησαν. καὶ παραλαβὼν αὐτοὺς
HIM   WHAT THINGS   THEY DID.   AND   HAVING TAKEN   THEM

Then Jesus[z] called the twelve together and gave them power and authority over all demons and to cure diseases, [2]and he sent them out to proclaim the kingdom of God and to heal. [3]He said to them, "Take nothing for your journey, no staff, nor bag, nor bread, nor money —not even an extra tunic. [4]Whatever house you enter, stay there, and leave from there. [5]Wherever they do not welcome you, as you are leaving that town shake the dust off your feet as a testimony against them." [6]They departed and went through the villages, bringing the good news and curing diseases everywhere.

7 Now Herod the ruler[a] heard about all that had taken place, and he was perplexed, because it was said by some that John had been raised from the dead, [8]by some that Elijah had appeared, and by others that one of the ancient prophets had arisen. [9]Herod said, "John I beheaded; but who is this about whom I hear such things?" And he tried to see him.

10 On their return the apostles told Jesus[b] all they had done. He took them

[z] Gk *he*
[a] Gk *tetrarch*
[b] Gk *him*

with him and withdrew privately to a city called Bethsaida. [11]When the crowds found out about it, they followed him; and he welcomed them, and spoke to them about the kingdom of God, and healed those who needed to be cured.

12 The day was drawing to a close, and the twelve came to him and said, "Send the crowd away, so that they may go into the surrounding villages and countryside, to lodge and get provisions; for we are here in a deserted place." [13]But he said to them, "You give them something to eat." They said, "We have no more than five loaves and two fish—unless we are to go and buy food for all these people." [14]For there were about five thousand men. And he said to his disciples, "Make them sit down in groups of about fifty each." [15]They did so and made them all sit down. [16]And taking the five loaves and the two fish, he looked up to heaven, and blessed and broke them, and gave them to the disciples to set before the crowd. [17]And all ate and were filled. What was left over was gathered up, twelve baskets of broken pieces.

18 Once when Jesus[c] was

[c] Gk he

ὑπεχώρησεν κατ᾽ ἰδίαν εἰς πόλιν καλουμένην
HE WITHDREW   PRIVATELY   TO   A CITY   BEING CALLED

Βηθσαϊδά.   **9.11** οἱ δὲ ὄχλοι γνόντες
BETHSAIDA.   BUT~THE CROWDS HAVING REALIZED [THIS]

ἠκολούθησαν αὐτῷ· καὶ ἀποδεξάμενος αὐτοὺς
FOLLOWED   HIM.   AND   HAVING WELCOMED   THEM

ἐλάλει   αὐτοῖς περὶ τῆς βασιλείας τοῦ θεοῦ, καὶ
HE WAS SPEAKING TO THEM ABOUT THE   KINGDOM   -   OF GOD, AND

τοὺς χρείαν ἔχοντας θεραπείας ἰᾶτο.   **9.12** Ἡ δὲ
THE ONES HAVING~NEED OF HEALING HE WAS HEALING.   NOW~THE

ἡμέρα ἤρξατο κλίνειν· προσελθόντες δὲ οἱ δώδεκα
DAY   BEGAN TO DECLINE.   AND~HAVING APPROACHED, THE TWELVE

εἶπαν αὐτῷ, Ἀπόλυσον τὸν ὄχλον, ἵνα   πορευθέντες
SAID   TO HIM, SEND AWAY   THE CROWD, SO THAT HAVING GONE

εἰς τὰς κύκλῳ κώμας καὶ ἀγροὺς καταλύσωσιν καὶ
INTO THE SURROUNDING VILLAGES AND FARMS, THEY MAY FIND LODGING AND

εὕρωσιν ἐπισιτισμόν, ὅτι ὧδε ἐν ἐρήμῳ τόπῳ ἐσμέν.
MAY FIND PROVISIONS,   FOR HERE IN A DESOLATE PLACE WE ARE.

9.13 εἶπεν δὲ πρὸς αὐτούς, Δότε αὐτοῖς ὑμεῖς
       AND~HE SAID TO   THEM,   GIVE TO THEM YOURSELVES [SOMETHING]

φαγεῖν. οἱ δὲ εἶπαν, Οὐκ εἰσὶν ἡμῖν πλεῖον ἢ
TO EAT.   -   BUT THEY SAID, THERE ARE NOT TO US MORE THAN

ἄρτοι πέντε καὶ ἰχθύες δύο, εἰ μήτι πορευθέντες ἡμεῖς
FIVE~LOAVES AND TWO~FISH, UNLESS HAVING GONE,   WE

ἀγοράσωμεν εἰς πάντα τὸν λαὸν τοῦτον βρώματα.
MAY BUY   FOR ALL   THE PEOPLE THIS   FOOD.

9.14 ἦσαν γὰρ ὡσεὶ ἄνδρες πεντακισχίλιοι. εἶπεν δὲ
      FOR~THERE WERE ABOUT FIVE THOUSAND~MEN.   BUT~SAID

πρὸς τοὺς μαθητὰς αὐτοῦ, Κατακλίνατε αὐτοὺς κλισίας
TO   THE DISCIPLES OF HIM, MAKE LIE DOWN   THEM [IN] GROUPS

[ὡσεὶ] ἀνὰ πεντήκοντα. **9.15** καὶ ἐποίησαν οὕτως καὶ
ABOUT   FIFTY~EACH.   AND THEY DID   SO   AND

κατέκλιναν ἅπαντας. **9.16** λαβὼν δὲ   τοὺς πέντε
ALL~RECLINED.   AND~HAVING TAKEN THE FIVE

ἄρτους καὶ τοὺς δύο ἰχθύας ἀναβλέψας εἰς τὸν οὐρανὸν
LOAVES AND THE TWO FISH [AND] HAVING LOOKED UP TO -   HEAVEN

εὐλόγησεν αὐτοὺς καὶ κατέκλασεν καὶ ἐδίδου
HE BLESSED   THEM   AND   BROKE [THEM]   AND WAS GIVING [THEM]

τοῖς μαθηταῖς παραθεῖναι τῷ ὄχλῳ. **9.17** καὶ ἔφαγον
TO THE DISCIPLES TO SET BEFORE THE CROWD.   AND THEY ATE

καὶ ἐχορτάσθησαν πάντες, καὶ ἤρθη   τὸ
AND ALL~WERE SATISFIED,   AND WAS PICKED UP THE THINGS

περισσεῦσαν αὐτοῖς κλασμάτων κόφινοι δώδεκα.
HAVING BEEN LEFT OVER BY THEM, [3]OF FRAGMENTS [2]BASKETS [1]TWELVE.

9.18 Καὶ ἐγένετο ἐν τῷ εἶναι αὐτὸν προσευχόμενον
       AND IT CAME ABOUT WHILE HE~IS   PRAYING

κατὰ μόνας συνῆσαν αὐτῷ οἱ μαθηταί, καὶ
ALONE,   WERE WITH   HIM   THE DISCIPLES,   AND

ἐπηρώτησεν αὐτοὺς λέγων, Τίνα με λέγουσιν οἱ
HE QUESTIONED   THEM   SAYING,   WHOM ⁴ME ³DECLARE   ¹[DO] THE

ὄχλοι εἶναι; **9.19** οἱ δὲ ἀποκριθέντες εἶπαν, Ἰωάννην
²CROWDS TO BE?   -   AND HAVING ANSWERED THEY SAID,   JOHN

τὸν βαπτιστήν, ἄλλοι δὲ Ἠλίαν, ἄλλοι δὲ ὅτι
THE BAPTIST,   BUT~OTHERS ELIJAH,   AND~OTHERS THAT

προφήτης τις τῶν ἀρχαίων ἀνέστη. **9.20** εἶπεν δὲ
A CERTAIN~PROPHET OF THE ANCIENTS   ROSE AGAIN.   AND~HE SAID

αὐτοῖς, Ὑμεῖς δὲ τίνα με λέγετε εἶναι; Πέτρος δὲ
TO THEM,   AND~YOU°   WHOM DO YOU° DECLARE~ME TO BE? AND~PETER

ἀποκριθεὶς εἶπεν, Τὸν Χριστὸν τοῦ θεοῦ.
HAVING ANSWERED SAID,   THE   CHRIST   -   OF GOD.

9.21 Ὁ δὲ ἐπιτιμήσας αὐτοῖς παρήγγειλεν
        -   AND HAVING WARNED   THEM   HE GAVE ORDERS

μηδενὶ λέγειν τοῦτο **9.22** εἰπὼν ὅτι Δεῖ   τὸν
TO TELL~NO ONE THIS   HAVING SAID, - IT IS NECESSARY FOR THE

υἱὸν τοῦ ἀνθρώπου πολλὰ παθεῖν καὶ ἀποδοκιμασθῆναι
SON   -   OF MAN   TO SUFFER~MUCH AND   TO BE REJECTED

ἀπὸ τῶν πρεσβυτέρων καὶ ἀρχιερέων καὶ γραμματέων
BY   THE   ELDERS   AND CHIEF PRIESTS AND   SCRIBES

καὶ ἀποκτανθῆναι καὶ τῇ τρίτῃ ἡμέρᾳ ἐγερθῆναι.
AND   TO BE KILLED   AND ON THE THIRD DAY   TO BE RAISED.

9.23 Ἔλεγεν δὲ πρὸς πάντας, Εἴ τις θέλει ὀπίσω
        AND~HE WAS SAYING TO   ALL,   IF ANYONE WISHES AFTER

μου ἔρχεσθαι, ἀρνησάσθω ἑαυτὸν καὶ ἀράτω τὸν
ME   TO COME,   LET HIM DENY   HIMSELF AND LIFT UP THE

σταυρὸν αὐτοῦ καθ᾽ ἡμέραν καὶ ἀκολουθείτω μοι.
CROSS   OF HIM DAILY   AND LET HIM FOLLOW   ME.

9.24 ὃς γὰρ ἂν θέλῃ τὴν ψυχὴν αὐτοῦ σῶσαι ἀπολέσει
        FOR~WHOEVER WISHES THE LIFE ·   OF HIM TO SAVE WILL LOSE

αὐτήν· ὃς δ᾽ ἂν ἀπολέσῃ τὴν ψυχὴν αὐτοῦ ἕνεκεν
IT.   BUT~WHOEVER LOSES   THE   LIFE   OF HIM ON ACCOUNT OF

ἐμοῦ οὗτος σώσει αὐτήν. **9.25** τί γὰρ ὠφελεῖται
ME   THIS ONE WILL SAVE IT.   FOR~WHAT PROFITS

ἄνθρωπος κερδήσας τὸν κόσμον ὅλον ἑαυτὸν δὲ
A MAN   HAVING GAINED THE WHOLE~WORLD,   BUT~HIMSELF

ἀπολέσας ἢ ζημιωθείς; **9.26** ὃς γὰρ ἂν ἐπαισχυνθῇ με
HAVING LOST OR HAVING FORFEIT?   FOR~WHOEVER IS ASHAMED   OF ME

καὶ τοὺς ἐμοὺς λόγους, τοῦτον ὁ υἱὸς τοῦ ἀνθρώπου
AND   -   MY   WORDS,   THIS ONE THE SON   -   OF MAN

ἐπαισχυνθήσεται, ὅταν ἔλθῃ ἐν τῇ δόξῃ αὐτοῦ καὶ
WILL BE ASHAMED OF,   WHEN HE COMES IN THE GLORY OF HIM AND

τοῦ πατρὸς καὶ τῶν ἁγίων ἀγγέλων. **9.27** λέγω δὲ
OF THE FATHER   AND OF THE HOLY   ANGELS.   BUT~I SAY

praying alone, with only the disciples near him, he asked them, "Who do the crowds say that I am?" 19They answered, "John the Baptist; but others, Elijah; and still others, that one of the ancient prophets has arisen." 20He said to them, "But who do you say that I am?" Peter answered, "The Messiah*d* of God."

21 He sternly ordered and commanded them not to tell anyone, 22saying, "The Son of Man must undergo great suffering, and be rejected by the elders, chief priests, and scribes, and be killed, and on the third day be raised."

23 Then he said to them all, "If any want to become my followers, let them deny themselves and take up their cross daily and follow me. 24For those who want to save their life will lose it, and those who lose their life for my sake will save it. 25What does it profit them if they gain the whole world, but lose or forfeit themselves? 26Those who are ashamed of me and of my words, of them the Son of Man will be ashamed when he comes in his glory and the glory of the Father and of the holy angels. 27But truly I tell

d Or *The Christ*

you, there are some standing here who will not taste death before they see the kingdom of God."

28 Now about eight days after these sayings Jesus*e* took with him Peter and John and James, and went up on the mountain to pray. [29]And while he was praying, the appearance of his face changed, and his clothes became dazzling white. [30]Suddenly they saw two men, Moses and Elijah, talking to him. [31]They appeared in glory and were speaking of his departure, which he was about to accomplish at Jerusalem. [32]Now Peter and his companions were weighed down with sleep; but since they had stayed awake,*f* they saw his glory and the two men who stood with him. [33]Just as they were leaving him, Peter said to Jesus, "Master, it is good for us to be here; let us make three dwellings,*g* one for you, one for Moses, and one for Elijah"—not knowing what he said. [34]While he was saying this, a cloud came and overshadowed them; and they were terrified as they entered the cloud. [35]Then from the cloud came

e Gk *he*
f Or *but when they were fully awake*
g Or *tents*

ὑμῖν ἀληθῶς, εἰσίν τινες τῶν αὐτοῦ ἑστηκότων οἳ
TO YOU° TRULY, THERE ARE SOME OF THE ONES HERE HAVING STOOD WHO

οὐ μὴ γεύσωνται θανάτου ἕως ἂν ἴδωσιν τὴν βασιλείαν
WILL BY NO MEANS TASTE DEATH UNTIL THEY SEE THE KINGDOM

τοῦ θεοῦ.
OF GOD.

9.28 Ἐγένετο δὲ μετὰ τοὺς λόγους τούτους ὡσεὶ
AND~IT CAME ABOUT AFTER - THESE~WORDS ABOUT

ἡμέραι ὀκτὼ [καὶ] παραλαβὼν Πέτρον καὶ Ἰωάννην
EIGHT~DAYS AND HAVING TAKEN PETER AND JOHN

καὶ Ἰάκωβον ἀνέβη εἰς τὸ ὄρος προσεύξασθαι.
AND JAMES HE WENT UP TO THE MOUNTAIN TO PRAY.

9.29 καὶ ἐγένετο ἐν τῷ προσεύχεσθαι αὐτὸν τὸ
AND IT CAME ABOUT [THAT] WHILE HE~PRAYS, THE

εἶδος τοῦ προσώπου αὐτοῦ ἕτερον καὶ ὁ
APPEARANCE OF THE FACE OF HIM [BECAME] DIFFERENT AND THE

ἱματισμὸς αὐτοῦ λευκὸς ἐξαστράπτων. **9.30** καὶ
CLOTHING OF HIM [BECAME] DAZZLING~WHITE. AND

ἰδοὺ ἄνδρες δύο συνελάλουν αὐτῷ, οἵτινες ἦσαν
BEHOLD TWO~MEN WERE CONVERSING WITH HIM, WHO WERE

Μωϋσῆς καὶ Ἠλίας, **9.31** οἳ ὀφθέντες ἐν δόξῃ
MOSES AND ELIJAH, WHO HAVING APPEARED IN GLORY

ἔλεγον τὴν ἔξοδον αὐτοῦ, ἣν ἤμελλεν πληροῦν ἐν
WERE SPEAKING OF THE EXODUS OF HIM, WHICH HE WAS ABOUT TO FULFILL IN

Ἰερουσαλήμ. **9.32** ὁ δὲ Πέτρος καὶ οἱ σὺν αὐτῷ
JERUSALEM. - BUT PETER AND THE ONES WITH HIM

ἦσαν βεβαρημένοι ὕπνῳ· διαγρηγορήσαντες δὲ εἶδον
HAD BEEN WEIGHED DOWN WITH SLEEP. AND~HAVING AWAKENED FULLY THEY SAW

τὴν δόξαν αὐτοῦ καὶ τοὺς δύο ἄνδρας τοὺς συνεστῶτας
THE GLORY OF HIM AND THE TWO MEN THE ONES HAVING STOOD

αὐτῷ. **9.33** καὶ ἐγένετο ἐν τῷ
WITH HIM. AND IT CAME ABOUT [THAT] WHILE

διαχωρίζεσθαι αὐτοὺς ἀπ' αὐτοῦ εἶπεν ὁ Πέτρος πρὸς
THEY~PARTED FROM HIM SAID - PETER TO

τὸν Ἰησοῦν, Ἐπιστάτα, καλόν ἐστιν ἡμᾶς ὧδε εἶναι,
- JESUS, MASTER, IT IS~GOOD FOR US TO BE~HERE,

καὶ ποιήσωμεν σκηνὰς τρεῖς, μίαν σοὶ καὶ μίαν
- LET US MAKE THREE~TENTS, ONE FOR YOU AND ONE

Μωϋσεῖ καὶ μίαν Ἠλίᾳ, μὴ εἰδὼς ὃ λέγει.
FOR MOSES AND ONE FOR ELIJAH, NOT HAVING KNOWN WHAT HE SAYS.

9.34 ταῦτα δὲ αὐτοῦ λέγοντος ἐγένετο νεφέλη
AND~[WHILE] THESE THINGS HIM SAYING, A CLOUD~CAME

καὶ ἐπεσκίαζεν αὐτούς· ἐφοβήθησαν δὲ ἐν τῷ
AND WAS OVERSHADOWING THEM. AND~THEY WERE AFRAID WHILE

εἰσελθεῖν αὐτοὺς εἰς τὴν νεφέλην. **9.35** καὶ φωνὴ
THEY~ENTERED INTO THE CLOUD. AND A VOICE

ἐγένετο ἐκ τῆς νεφέλης λέγουσα, Οὗτός ἐστιν ⌜ὁ υἱός
CAME   FROM THE CLOUD   SAYING,   THIS IS   THE SON

μου ὁ ἐκλελεγμένος,⌝ αὐτοῦ ἀκούετε. 9.36 καὶ
OF ME, THE ONE HAVING BEEN CHOSEN, LISTEN~TO HIM.   AND

ἐν τῷ γενέσθαι τὴν φωνὴν εὑρέθη Ἰησοῦς μόνος.
WHEN   BECAME [SILENT] THE VOICE, WAS FOUND JESUS ALONE.

καὶ αὐτοὶ ἐσίγησαν καὶ οὐδενὶ ἀπήγγειλαν ἐν
AND THEY WERE SILENT AND TO NO ONE REPORTED IN

ἐκείναις ταῖς ἡμέραις οὐδὲν ὧν ἑώρακαν.
THOSE   -   DAYS   ANYTHING OF WHAT THEY HAVE SEEN.

9.37 Ἐγένετο δὲ τῇ ἑξῆς ἡμέρᾳ κατελθόντων
AND~IT CAME ABOUT ON THE FOLLOWING DAY HAVING COME DOWN

αὐτῶν ἀπὸ τοῦ ὄρους συνήντησεν αὐτῷ ὄχλος πολύς.
THEM FROM THE MOUNTAIN MET   HIM   A LARGE~CROWD.

9.38 καὶ ἰδοὺ ἀνὴρ ἀπὸ τοῦ ὄχλου ἐβόησεν λέγων,
AND BEHOLD A MAN FROM THE CROWD CRIED OUT SAYING,

Διδάσκαλε, δέομαί σου ἐπιβλέψαι ἐπὶ τὸν υἱόν μου,
TEACHER, I BEG YOU TO LOOK   AT THE SON OF ME,

ὅτι μονογενής μοί ἐστιν, 9.39 καὶ ἰδοὺ πνεῦμα
FOR AN ONLY CHILD TO ME HE IS,   AND BEHOLD A SPIRIT

λαμβάνει αὐτόν καὶ ἐξαίφνης κράζει καὶ
SEIZES   HIM   AND SUDDENLY   CRIES OUT AND

σπαράσσει αὐτὸν μετὰ ἀφροῦ καὶ μόγις
THROWS INTO A CONVULSION HIM WITH FOAM [AT THE MOUTH] AND HARDLY

ἀποχωρεῖ ἀπ' αὐτοῦ συντρῖβον αὐτόν· 9.40 καὶ
DEPARTS FROM HIM [AND] IT MAULS   HIM.   AND

ἐδεήθην τῶν μαθητῶν σου ἵνα ἐκβάλωσιν αὐτό, καὶ
I BEGGED THE DISCIPLES OF YOU THAT THEY MIGHT CAST OUT IT, AND

οὐκ ἠδυνήθησαν. 9.41 ἀποκριθεὶς δὲ ὁ Ἰησοῦς εἶπεν,
THEY WERE NOT ABLE.   AND~HAVING ANSWERED - JESUS SAID,

Ὦ γενεὰ ἄπιστος καὶ διεστραμμένη, ἕως πότε
O UNBELIEVING~GENERATION AND HAVING BEEN DEPRAVED, UNTIL WHEN

ἔσομαι πρὸς ὑμᾶς καὶ ἀνέξομαι ὑμῶν; προσάγαγε
WILL I BE WITH YOU° AND WILL I PUT UP WITH YOU°? BRING

ὧδε τὸν υἱόν σου. 9.42 ἔτι δὲ προσερχομένου αὐτοῦ
HERE THE SON OF YOU.   NOW~STILL APPROACHING   HIM,

ἔρρηξεν αὐτὸν τὸ δαιμόνιον καὶ συνεσπάραξεν·
THREW DOWN HIM THE DEMON   AND CONVULSED [HIM].

ἐπετίμησεν δὲ ὁ Ἰησοῦς τῷ πνεύματι τῷ ἀκαθάρτῳ
³REBUKED ¹AND - ²JESUS ⁴THE ⁶SPIRIT - ⁵UNCLEAN

καὶ ἰάσατο τὸν παῖδα καὶ ἀπέδωκεν αὐτὸν τῷ
AND HEALED THE CHILD AND HE RETURNED HIM TO THE

πατρὶ αὐτοῦ. 9.43 ἐξεπλήσσοντο δὲ πάντες ἐπὶ τῇ
FATHER OF HIM.   AND~WERE AMAZED   ALL   AT THE

μεγαλειότητι τοῦ θεοῦ.
GREATNESS   -   OF GOD.

a voice that said, "This is my Son, my Chosen;[h] listen to him!" [36]When the voice had spoken, Jesus was found alone. And they kept silent and in those days told no one any of the things they had seen.

37 On the next day, when they had come down from the mountain, a great crowd met him. [38]Just then a man from the crowd shouted, "Teacher, I beg you to look at my son; he is my only child. [39]Suddenly a spirit seizes him, and all at once he[i] shrieks. It convulses him until he foams at the mouth; it mauls him and will scarcely leave him. [40]I begged your disciples to cast it out, but they could not." [41]Jesus answered, "You faithless and perverse generation, how much longer must I be with you and bear with you? Bring your son here." [42]While he was coming, the demon dashed him to the ground in convulsions. But Jesus rebuked the unclean spirit, healed the boy, and gave him back to his father. [43]And all were astounded at the greatness of God.

[h] Other ancient authorities read my Beloved
[i] Or it

9:35 text: ASV RSV NASB NIV NEB TEV NJB NRSV. var. ο υιος μου ο αγαπητος (my beloved Son) [see Mark 9:7; Luke 3:22] KJV ASVmg RSVmg NJBmg NRSVmg.

While everyone was amazed at all that he was doing, he said to his disciples, [44]"Let these words sink into your ears: The Son of Man is going to be betrayed into human hands." [45]But they did not understand this saying; its meaning was concealed from them, so that they could not perceive it. And they were afraid to ask him about this saying.

[46] An argument arose among them as to which one of them was the greatest. [47]But Jesus, aware of their inner thoughts, took a little child and put it by his side, [48]and said to them, "Whoever welcomes this child in my name welcomes me, and whoever welcomes me welcomes the one who sent me; for the least among all of you is the greatest."

[49] John answered, "Master, we saw someone casting out demons in your name, and we tried to stop him, because he does not follow with us." [50]But Jesus said to him, "Do not stop him; for whoever is not against you is for you."

[51] When the days drew near for him to be taken up, he set his face to go to

Πάντων δὲ θαυμαζόντων ἐπὶ πᾶσιν οἷς ἐποίει
AND~[WHILE] ALL MARVELING AT EVERYTHING WHICH HE WAS DOING
εἶπεν πρὸς τοὺς μαθητὰς αὐτοῦ, **9.44** Θέσθε ὑμεῖς εἰς
HE SAID TO THE DISCIPLES OF HIM, ESTABLISH YOU° IN
τὰ ὦτα ὑμῶν τοὺς λόγους τούτους· ὁ γὰρ υἱὸς τοῦ
THE EARS OF YOU° - THESE~WORDS. FOR~THE SON -
ἀνθρώπου μέλλει παραδίδοσθαι εἰς χεῖρας ἀνθρώπων.
OF MAN IS ABOUT TO BE DELIVERED INTO [THE] HANDS OF MEN.
9.45 οἱ δὲ ἠγνόουν τὸ ῥῆμα τοῦτο καὶ
- BUT THEY WERE NOT UNDERSTANDING - THIS~WORD AND
ἦν παρακεκαλυμμένον ἀπ' αὐτῶν ἵνα
IT HAD BEEN HIDDEN FROM THEM IN ORDER THAT
μὴ αἴσθωνται αὐτό, καὶ ἐφοβοῦντο ἐρωτῆσαι αὐτὸν
THEY MIGHT NOT UNDERSTAND IT, AND THEY WERE AFRAID TO ASK HIM
περὶ τοῦ ῥήματος τούτου.
ABOUT - THIS~WORD.
9.46 Εἰσῆλθεν δὲ διαλογισμὸς ἐν αὐτοῖς, τὸ τίς
NOW~AROSE AN ARGUMENT AMONG THEM, - WHO
ἂν εἴη μείζων αὐτῶν. **9.47** ὁ δὲ Ἰησοῦς εἰδὼς
MIGHT BE [THE] GREATEST OF THEM. - AND JESUS HAVING PERCEIVED
τὸν διαλογισμὸν τῆς καρδίας αὐτῶν, ἐπιλαβόμενος
THE THOUGHT OF THE HEART OF THEM, HAVING TAKEN
παιδίον ἔστησεν αὐτὸ παρ' ἑαυτῷ **9.48** καὶ εἶπεν
A CHILD STOOD IT(HIM) BESIDE HIMSELF AND HE SAID
αὐτοῖς, Ὃς ἐὰν δέξηται τοῦτο τὸ παιδίον ἐπὶ τῷ
TO THEM, WHOEVER RECEIVES THIS - CHILD IN THE
ὀνόματί μου, ἐμὲ δέχεται· καὶ ὃς ἂν ἐμὲ δέξηται,
NAME OF ME, RECEIVES~ME. AND WHOEVER RECEIVES~ME,
δέχεται τὸν ἀποστείλαντά με· ὁ γὰρ μικρότερος
RECEIVES THE ONE HAVING SENT ME. FOR~THE LESSER
ἐν πᾶσιν ὑμῖν ὑπάρχων οὗτός ἐστιν μέγας.
AMONG ALL OF YOU° BEING, THIS ONE IS GREAT.
9.49 Ἀποκριθεὶς δὲ Ἰωάννης εἶπεν, Ἐπιστάτα,
AND~HAVING ANSWERED JOHN SAID, MASTER,
εἴδομέν τινα ἐν τῷ ὀνόματί σου ἐκβάλλοντα
WE SAW SOMEONE IN THE NAME OF YOU CASTING OUT
δαιμόνια καὶ ἐκωλύομεν αὐτόν, ὅτι
DEMONS AND WE WERE TRYING TO STOP HIM, BECAUSE
οὐκ ἀκολουθεῖ μεθ' ἡμῶν. **9.50** εἶπεν δὲ πρὸς αὐτὸν ὁ
HE IS NOT FOLLOWING WITH US. BUT~SAID TO HIM -
Ἰησοῦς, Μὴ κωλύετε· ὃς γὰρ οὐκ ἔστιν καθ' ὑμῶν,
JESUS, DO NOT STOP [HIM]. FOR~WHO[EVER] IS NOT AGAINST YOU°,
ὑπὲρ ὑμῶν ἐστιν.
FOR YOU° IS.
9.51 Ἐγένετο δὲ ἐν τῷ συμπληροῦσθαι τὰς ἡμέρας
AND~IT CAME ABOUT WHILE APPROACHES THE DAY
τῆς ἀναλήμψεως αὐτοῦ καὶ αὐτὸς τὸ πρόσωπον
OF THE ASCENSION OF HIM AND HE THE(HIS) FACE

ἐστήρισεν   τοῦ πορεύεσθαι εἰς Ἰερουσαλήμ. **9.52** καὶ
HE RESOLUTELY SET -   TO GO   TO   JERUSALEM.   AND

ἀπέστειλεν ἀγγέλους πρὸ προσώπου αὐτοῦ. καὶ
HE SENT   MESSENGERS BEFORE [THE] FACE   OF HIM.   AND

πορευθέντες εἰσῆλθον εἰς κώμην Σαμαριτῶν ὡς
HAVING GONE   THEY ENTERED INTO A VILLAGE OF SAMARITANS IN ORDER

ἑτοιμάσαι   αὐτῷ·   **9.53** καὶ οὐκ ἐδέξαντο αὐτόν,
TO MAKE ARRANGEMENTS FOR HIM.   AND   THEY DID NOT RECEIVE HIM,

ὅτι   τὸ πρόσωπον αὐτοῦ ἦν πορευόμενον εἰς
BECAUSE THE FACE   OF HIM   WAS GOING   TO

Ἰερουσαλήμ. **9.54** ἰδόντες δὲ οἱ μαθηταὶ Ἰάκωβος καὶ
JERUSALEM.   AND~HAVING SEEN THE DISCIPLES, JAMES   AND

Ἰωάννης εἶπαν, Κύριε, θέλεις   εἴπωμεν πῦρ
JOHN   SAID,   LORD, DO YOU WANT [THAT] WE SHOULD CALL FIRE

καταβῆναι ἀπὸ τοῦ οὐρανοῦ καὶ ἀναλῶσαι αὐτούςᵀ;
TO COME DOWN FROM -   HEAVEN   -   TO CONSUME   THEM?

9.55 στραφεὶς δὲ ἐπετίμησεν αὐτοῖς.ᵀ **9.56** καὶ
AND~HAVING TURNED HE REBUKED   THEM.   AND

ἐπορεύθησαν εἰς ἑτέραν κώμην.
THEY WENT   TO ANOTHER VILLAGE.

9.57 Καὶ πορευομένων αὐτῶν ἐν τῇ ὁδῷ εἶπέν
AND   [AS] THEY WERE GOING   ON THE ROAD SAID

τις   πρὸς αὐτόν, Ἀκολουθήσω σοι ὅπου ἐὰν
A CERTAIN ONE TO HIM,   I WILL FOLLOW   YOU WHEREVER

ἀπέρχῃ. **9.58** καὶ εἶπεν αὐτῷ ὁ Ἰησοῦς, Αἱ ἀλώπεκες
YOU GO.   AND   SAID TO HIM - JESUS,   THE FOXES

φωλεοὺς ἔχουσιν καὶ τὰ πετεινὰ τοῦ οὐρανοῦ
HAVE~DENS   AND THE BIRDS   OF THE HEAVEN

κατασκηνώσεις, ὁ δὲ υἱὸς τοῦ ἀνθρώπου οὐκ ἔχει
NESTS,   BUT~THE SON -   OF MAN   DOES NOT HAVE [A PLACE]

ποῦ τὴν   κεφαλὴν κλίνῃ.   **9.59** Εἶπεν δὲ πρὸς
WHERE THE(HIS) HEAD   HE MAY LAY DOWN.   AND~HE SAID   TO

ἕτερον, Ἀκολούθει μοι. ὁ δὲ εἶπεν, [Κύριε,] ἐπίτρεψόν
ANOTHER, FOLLOW   ME. - BUT HE SAID, LORD,   ALLOW

μοι ἀπελθόντι πρῶτον θάψαι τὸν πατέρα μου.
ME   HAVING GONE,   FIRST   TO BURY THE FATHER OF ME.

9.60 εἶπεν δὲ αὐτῷ, Ἄφες τοὺς νεκροὺς θάψαι τοὺς
BUT~HE SAID TO HIM, LEAVE THE DEAD ONES TO BURY -

ἑαυτῶν νεκρούς, σὺ δὲ ἀπελθὼν διάγγελλε τὴν βασιλείαν
THEIR   DEAD ONES, BUT~YOU HAVING GONE PROCLAIM THE KINGDOM

τοῦ θεοῦ. **9.61** Εἶπεν δὲ καὶ ἕτερος, Ἀκολουθήσω σοι,
- OF GOD.   AND~SAID ALSO ANOTHER, I WILL FOLLOW   YOU,

κύριε· πρῶτον δὲ ἐπίτρεψόν μοι ἀποτάξασθαι τοῖς
LORD.   BUT~FIRST   ALLOW   ME TO SAY GOOD-BYE TO THE ONES

Jerusalem. ⁵²And he sent messengers ahead of him. On their way they entered a village of the Samaritans to make ready for him; ⁵³but they did not receive him, because his face was set toward Jerusalem. ⁵⁴When his disciples James and John saw it, they said, "Lord, do you want us to command fire to come down from heaven and consume them?"ʲ ⁵⁵But he turned and rebuked them. ⁵⁶Thenᵏ they went on to another village.

57 As they were going along the road, someone said to him, "I will follow you wherever you go." ⁵⁸And Jesus said to him, "Foxes have holes, and birds of the air have nests; but the Son of Man has nowhere to lay his head." ⁵⁹To another he said, "Follow me." But he said, "Lord, first let me go and bury my father." ⁶⁰But Jesusˡ said to him, "Let the dead bury their own dead; but as for you, go and proclaim the kingdom of God." ⁶¹Another said, "I will follow you, Lord; but let me first say farewell to those

ʲ Other ancient authorities add *as Elijah did*
ᵏ Other ancient authorities read *rebuked them, and said, "You do not know what spirit you are of, ⁵⁶for the Son of Man did not come to destroy the lives of human beings but to save them." Then*
ˡ Gk *he*

9:54 text: ASV RSV NASB NIV NEB TEV NJB NRSV. add ως και Ηλιας εποιησεν (as also Elijah did): KJV ASVmg RSVmg NIVmg NEBmg TEVmg NJBmg NRSVmg. **9:55-56** text: ASV RSV NASB NIV NEB TEV NJB NRSV. add και ειπεν, Ουκ οιδατε οιου πνευματος εστε υμεις· 56 ο γαρ υιος του ανθρωπου ουκ ηλθεν ψυχας ανθρωπων απολεσαι αλλα σωσαι (And he said, You do not know what manner of spirit you are of; for the Son of Man came not to destroy men's lives but to save them): KJV ASVmg RSVmg NASBmg NIVmg NEBmg TEVmg NJBmg NRSVmg.

at my home." ⁶²Jesus said to him, "No one who puts a hand to the plow and looks back is fit for the kingdom of God."

εἰς τὸν οἶκόν μου. **9.62** εἶπεν δὲ [πρὸς αὐτὸν] ὁ
IN   THE   HOUSE   OF ME.   BUT~SAID   TO   HIM   -

Ἰησοῦς, Οὐδεὶς ἐπιβαλὼν τὴν χεῖρα ἐπ᾽ ἄροτρον καὶ
JESUS,   NO ONE   HAVING PUT   THE(HIS) HAND   UPON [THE] PLOW   AND

βλέπων εἰς τὰ ὀπίσω εὔθετός ἐστιν τῇ βασιλείᾳ
LOOKING   TO   THE THINGS BEHIND   IS~FIT   FOR THE KINGDOM

τοῦ θεοῦ.
OF GOD.

CHAPTER 10

After this the Lord appointed seventy*ᵐ* others and sent them on ahead of him in pairs to every town and place where he himself intended to go. ²He said to them, "The harvest is plentiful, but the laborers are few; therefore ask the Lord of the harvest to send out laborers into his harvest. ³Go on your way. See, I am sending you out like lambs into the midst of wolves. ⁴Carry no purse, no bag, no sandals; and greet no one on the road. ⁵Whatever house you enter, first say, 'Peace to this house!' ⁶And if anyone is there who shares in peace, your peace will rest on that person; but if not, it will return to you. ⁷Remain in the same house, eating and drinking whatever they provide, for the laborer deserves to be paid. Do not move about from house to house.

ᵐ Other ancient authorities read *seventy-two*

10.1 Μετὰ δὲ ταῦτα ἀνέδειξεν ὁ κύριος ἑτέρους
AND~AFTER THESE THINGS, APPOINTED THE LORD   OTHERS

⌐ἑβδομήκοντα [δύο]⌐ καὶ ἀπέστειλεν αὐτοὺς
SEVENTY-TWO,   AND   HE SENT   THEM

ἀνὰ δύο [δύο] πρὸ προσώπου αὐτοῦ εἰς πᾶσαν
TWO BY TWO   BEFORE [THE] FACE OF HIM   INTO EVERY

πόλιν καὶ τόπον οὗ ἤμελλεν αὐτὸς ἔρχεσθαι.
CITY   AND   PLACE WHERE HE~WAS ABOUT   TO COME.

10.2 ἔλεγεν δὲ πρὸς αὐτούς, Ὁ μὲν θερισμὸς πολύς,
AND~HE WAS SAYING TO   THEM,   INDEED~THE HARVEST [IS] PLENTIFUL,

οἱ δὲ ἐργάται ὀλίγοι· δεήθητε οὖν τοῦ κυρίου τοῦ
BUT~THE WORKERS FEW.   THEREFORE~ASK THE LORD   OF THE

θερισμοῦ ὅπως ἐργάτας ἐκβάλῃ εἰς τὸν θερισμὸν
HARVEST THAT WORKERS HE MIGHT SEND OUT INTO THE   HARVEST

αὐτοῦ. **10.3** ὑπάγετε· ἰδοὺ ἀποστέλλω ὑμᾶς ὡς ἄρνας
OF HIM.   GO.   BEHOLD I SEND   YOU°   AS LAMBS

ἐν μέσῳ λύκων. **10.4** μὴ βαστάζετε βαλλάντιον, μὴ
IN [THE] MIDST OF WOLVES.   DO NOT CARRY   A PURSE,   NOR

πήραν, μὴ ὑποδήματα, καὶ μηδένα κατὰ τὴν ὁδὸν
A BEGGAR'S BAG, NOR SANDALS,   AND   NO ONE   ALONG   THE   WAY

ἀσπάσησθε. **10.5** εἰς ἣν δ᾽ ἂν εἰσέλθητε οἰκίαν,
GREET.   ²INTO ³WHAT ¹AND ⁴EVER HOUSE~YOU° ENTER,

πρῶτον λέγετε, Εἰρήνη τῷ οἴκῳ τούτῳ. **10.6** καὶ ἐὰν
FIRST   SAY,   PEACE   -   TO THIS~HOUSE.   AND   IF

ἐκεῖ ᾖ υἱὸς εἰρήνης, ἐπαναπαήσεται ἐπ᾽ αὐτὸν ἡ
THERE THERE IS A SON OF PEACE,   WILL REST   UPON HIM   THE

εἰρήνη ὑμῶν· εἰ δὲ μή γε, ἐφ᾽ ὑμᾶς ἀνακάμψει. **10.7** ἐν
PEACE   OF YOU°. OTHERWISE,   ON   YOU° IT WILL RETURN.   ²IN

αὐτῇ δὲ τῇ οἰκίᾳ μένετε ἐσθίοντες καὶ πίνοντες
⁴SAME ¹AND ³THE HOUSE REMAIN   EATING   AND   DRINKING

τὰ παρ᾽ αὐτῶν· ἄξιος γὰρ ὁ ἐργάτης τοῦ μισθοῦ
THE THINGS WITH THEM.   FOR~WORTHY [IS] THE WORKER   OF THE WAGE

αὐτοῦ. μὴ μεταβαίνετε ἐξ οἰκίας εἰς οἰκίαν.
OF HIM.   DO NOT MOVE   FROM HOUSE TO HOUSE.

10:1 text: ASVmg RSVmg NIV NEB TEV NJB NRSVmg. var. εβδομηκοντα (seventy) KJV ASV RSV NASB NIVmg NEBmg TEVmg NJBmg NRSV.

10.8 καὶ εἰς ἣν ἂν πόλιν εἰσέρχησθε καὶ δέχωνται
AND   INTO WHICHEVER CITY   YOU° ENTER   AND   THEY RECEIVE

ὑμᾶς, ἐσθίετε τὰ   παρατιθέμενα ὑμῖν **10.9** καὶ
YOU°,   EAT   THE THINGS BEING SET BEFORE YOU°   AND

θεραπεύετε τοὺς ἐν αὐτῇ ἀσθενεῖς καὶ λέγετε
HEAL   THE ONES IN IT [WHO ARE] SICK   AND   SAY

αὐτοῖς, Ἤγγικεν ἐφ᾽ ὑμᾶς ἡ βασιλεία τοῦ θεοῦ.
TO THEM, HAS COME NEAR TO YOU° THE KINGDOM   -   OF GOD.

10.10 εἰς ἣν δ᾽ ἂν πόλιν εἰσέλθητε καὶ
        ²INTO ³WHAT ¹AND ⁴EVER CITY YOU° ENTER   AND

μὴ δέχωνται ὑμᾶς, ἐξελθόντες εἰς τὰς πλατείας αὐτῆς
THEY DO NOT RECEIVE YOU°, HAVING GONE OUT INTO THE STREETS   OF IT

εἴπατε, **10.11** Καὶ τὸν κονιορτὸν τὸν κολληθέντα ἡμῖν
SAY,   EVEN THE DUST   -   HAVING CLUNG TO US

ἐκ τῆς πόλεως ὑμῶν εἰς τοὺς πόδας ἀπομασσόμεθα
FROM THE CITY   OF YOU° TO THE(OUR) FEET WE SHAKE OFF [AGAINST]

ὑμῖν· πλὴν τοῦτο γινώσκετε ὅτι ἤγγικεν ἡ βασιλεία
YOU°. BUT KNOW~THIS   THAT HAS COME NEAR THE KINGDOM

τοῦ θεοῦ. **10.12** λέγω ὑμῖν ὅτι Σοδόμοις ἐν τῇ
-   OF GOD.   I SAY TO YOU° THAT FOR SODOM IN -

ἡμέρᾳ ἐκείνῃ ἀνεκτότερον ἔσται ἢ τῇ πόλει ἐκείνῃ.
THAT~DAY   IT WILL BE~MORE BEARABLE THAN - WITH THAT~CITY.

10.13 Οὐαί σοι, Χοραζίν, οὐαί σοι, Βηθσαϊδά·
         WOE TO YOU, CHORAZIN, WOE TO YOU, BETHSAIDA

ὅτι εἰ ἐν Τύρῳ καὶ Σιδῶνι ἐγενήθησαν αἱ δυνάμεις
BECAUSE IF IN TYRE AND SIDON HAD OCCURRED THE MIRACLES

αἱ γενόμεναι ἐν ὑμῖν, πάλαι ἂν ἐν σάκκῳ καὶ
- HAVING HAPPENED IN YOU°, LONG AGO - IN SACKCLOTH AND

σποδῷ καθήμενοι μετενόησαν.   **10.14** πλὴν Τύρῳ
ASHES SITTING   THEY [WOULD HAVE] REPENTED.   BUT   FOR TYRE

καὶ Σιδῶνι ἀνεκτότερον ἔσται ἐν τῇ κρίσει ἢ ὑμῖν.
AND SIDON IT WILL BE~MORE BEARABLE IN THE JUDGMENT THAN FOR YOU°.

10.15 καὶ σύ, Καφαρναούμ,
        AND YOU CAPERNAUM,

μὴ   ἕως οὐρανοῦ ὑψωθήσῃ;
SURELY NOT UP TO HEAVEN WILL YOU BE EXALTED?

        ἕως τοῦ ᾅδου καταβήσῃ.
        TO   -   HADES YOU WILL COME DOWN.

10.16 Ὁ ἀκούων ὑμῶν ἐμοῦ ἀκούει, καὶ ὁ
        THE ONE LISTENING TO YOU°, LISTENS~TO ME, AND THE ONE

ἀθετῶν ὑμᾶς ἐμὲ ἀθετεῖ· ὁ δὲ ἐμὲ ἀθετῶν ἀθετεῖ
REJECTING YOU REJECTS~ME. BUT~THE ONE REJECTING~ME, REJECTS

τὸν ἀποστείλαντά με.
THE ONE HAVING SENT   ME.

10.17 Ὑπέστρεψαν δὲ οἱ ⌜ἑβδομήκοντα [δύο]⌝ μετὰ
        AND~RETURNED   THE SEVENTY-TWO   WITH

10:17 text: ASVmg RSVmg NIV NEB TEV NJB NRSVmg. var. εβδομηκοντα (seventy) KJV ASV RSV NASB
NIVmg NEBmg TEVmg NJBmg NRSV.

[8]Whenever you enter a town and its people welcome you, eat what is set before you; [9]cure the sick who are there, and say to them, 'The kingdom of God has come near to you.'[n] [10]But whenever you enter a town and they do not welcome you, go out into its streets and say, [11]'Even the dust of your town that clings to our feet, we wipe off in protest against you. Yet know this: the kingdom of God has come near.'[o] [12]I tell you, on that day it will be more tolerable for Sodom than for that town.

13 "Woe to you, Chorazin! Woe to you, Bethsaida! For if the deeds of power done in you had been done in Tyre and Sidon, they would have repented long ago, sitting in sackcloth and ashes. [14]But at the judgment it will be more tolerable for Tyre and Sidon than for you. [15]And you, Capernaum,
    will you be exalted to
        heaven?
    No, you will be
        brought down to
        Hades.

16 "Whoever listens to you listens to me, and whoever rejects you rejects me, and whoever rejects me rejects the one who sent me."

17 The seventy[p] returned

[n] Or *is at hand for you*
[o] Or *is at hand*
[p] Other ancient authorities read *seventy-two*

with joy, saying, "Lord, in your name even the demons submit to us!" [18]He said to them, "I watched Satan fall from heaven like a flash of lightning. [19]See, I have given you authority to tread on snakes and scorpions, and over all the power of the enemy; and nothing will hurt you. [20]Nevertheless, do not rejoice at this, that the spirits submit to you, but rejoice that your names are written in heaven."

21 At that same hour Jesus[q] rejoiced in the Holy Spirit[r] and said, "I thank[s] you, Father, Lord of heaven and earth, because you have hidden these things from the wise and the intelligent and have revealed them to infants; yes, Father, for such was your gracious will.[t] [22]All things have been handed over to me by my Father; and no one knows who the Son is except the Father, or who the Father is except the Son and anyone to whom the Son chooses to reveal him."

23 Then turning to the disciples, Jesus[q] said to them privately, "Blessed are the eyes that see what you see! [24]For I tell you that many prophets and kings desired to see what you see,

[q] Gk *he*
[r] Other authorities read *in the spirit*
[s] Or *praise*
[t] Or *for so it was well-pleasing in your sight*

χαρᾶς λέγοντες, Κύριε, καὶ τὰ δαιμόνια ὑποτάσσεται
JOY   SAYING,   LORD,   EVEN THE DEMONS   SUBMIT

ἡμῖν ἐν τῷ ὀνόματί σου. **10.18** εἶπεν δὲ αὐτοῖς,
TO US IN THE NAME   OF YOU.   AND~HE SAID TO THEM,

Ἐθεώρουν τὸν Σατανᾶν ὡς ἀστραπὴν ἐκ τοῦ οὐρανοῦ
I WAS SEEING - SATAN   LIKE LIGHTNING FROM - HEAVEN

πεσόντα. **10.19** ἰδοὺ δέδωκα ὑμῖν τὴν ἐξουσίαν τοῦ
HAVING FALLEN.   BEHOLD I HAVE GIVEN TO YOU° THE AUTHORITY -

πατεῖν ἐπάνω ὄφεων καὶ σκορπίων, καὶ ἐπὶ πᾶσαν
TO WALK ON SNAKES AND SCORPIONS, AND ON ALL

τὴν δύναμιν τοῦ ἐχθροῦ, καὶ οὐδὲν ὑμᾶς
THE POWER OF THE ENEMY, AND NOTHING YOU°

οὐ μὴ ἀδικήσῃ. **10.20** πλὴν ἐν τούτῳ μὴ χαίρετε ὅτι
BY ANY MEANS MAY INJURE. BUT IN THIS DO NOT REJOICE BECAUSE

τὰ πνεύματα ὑμῖν ὑποτάσσεται, χαίρετε δὲ ὅτι τὰ
THE SPIRITS SUBMIT~TO YOU°,   BUT~REJOICE THAT THE

ὀνόματα ὑμῶν ἐγγέγραπται ἐν τοῖς οὐρανοῖς.
NAMES OF YOU° HAVE BEEN RECORDED IN THE HEAVENS.

10.21 Ἐν αὐτῇ τῇ ὥρᾳ ἠγαλλιάσατο ⌐[ἐν]⌐ τῷ
IN THE~SAME HOUR HE WAS FULL OF JOY BY THE

πνεύματι τῷ ἁγίῳ⌐ καὶ εἶπεν, Ἐξομολογοῦμαί σοι,
[2]SPIRIT [1]HOLY AND HE SAID, I PRAISE   YOU,

πάτερ, κύριε τοῦ οὐρανοῦ καὶ τῆς γῆς, ὅτι ἀπέκρυψας
FATHER, LORD - OF HEAVEN AND - EARTH, THAT YOU CONCEALED

ταῦτα ἀπὸ σοφῶν καὶ συνετῶν καὶ ἀπεκάλυψας αὐτὰ
THESE THINGS FROM [THE] WISE AND INTELLIGENT AND YOU REVEALED THEM

νηπίοις· ναὶ ὁ πατήρ, ὅτι οὕτως εὐδοκία ἐγένετο
TO YOUNG CHILDREN. YES, - FATHER, FOR THUS IT WAS~WELL-PLEASING

ἔμπροσθέν σου. **10.22** Πάντα μοι παρεδόθη ὑπὸ τοῦ
BEFORE   YOU.   EVERYTHING WAS HANDED OVER~TO ME BY THE

πατρός μου, καὶ οὐδεὶς γινώσκει τίς ἐστιν ὁ υἱὸς
FATHER OF ME, AND NO ONE KNOWS   WHO IS   THE SON

εἰ μὴ ὁ πατήρ, καὶ τίς ἐστιν ὁ πατὴρ εἰ μὴ ὁ υἱὸς
EXCEPT THE FATHER, AND WHO IS THE FATHER EXCEPT THE SON

καὶ ᾧ ἐὰν βούληται ὁ υἱὸς ἀποκαλύψαι. **10.23** Καὶ
AND TO WHOMEVER WISHES THE SON TO REVEAL [HIM].   AND

στραφεὶς πρὸς τοὺς μαθητὰς κατ᾽ ἰδίαν εἶπεν,
HAVING TURNED TO THE DISCIPLES PRIVATELY HE SAID,

Μακάριοι οἱ ὀφθαλμοὶ οἱ βλέποντες ἃ βλέπετε.
BLESSED [ARE] THE EYES - SEEING WHAT YOU° SEE.

10.24 λέγω γὰρ ὑμῖν ὅτι πολλοὶ προφῆται καὶ
FOR~I SAY TO YOU° THAT MANY PROPHETS AND

βασιλεῖς ἠθέλησαν ἰδεῖν ἃ ὑμεῖς βλέπετε καὶ
KINGS WANTED TO SEE WHAT YOU° SEE AND

10:21 text: ASV RSV NASB NIV NEB TEV NJB NRSV. var. εν τω πνευματι (in the [his] spirit): KJV NEBmg TEVmg NRSVmg.

οὐκ εἶδαν,   καὶ ἀκοῦσαι ἃ   ἀκούετε καὶ
THEY DID NOT SEE [THEM],   AND   TO HEAR   WHAT YOU° HEAR   AND

οὐκ ἤκουσαν.
THEY DID NOT HEAR [THEM].

10.25 Καὶ ἰδοὺ νομικός τις ἀνέστη ἐκπειράζων αὐτὸν
AND   BEHOLD   A CERTAIN~LAWYER   STOOD UP   TESTING   HIM

λέγων, Διδάσκαλε, τί   ποιήσας ζωὴν αἰώνιον
SAYING,   TEACHER,   WHAT   HAVING DONE   3LIFE   2ETERNAL

κληρονομήσω; **10.26** ὁ δὲ εἶπεν πρὸς αὐτόν, Ἐν τῷ
1WILL I INHERIT?   -   AND   HE SAID   TO   HIM,   IN   THE

νόμῳ τί   γέγραπται;   πῶς ἀναγινώσκεις; **10.27** ὁ δὲ
LAW   WHAT   HAS BEEN WRITTEN?   HOW   DO YOU READ [IT]?   -   AND

ἀποκριθεὶς εἶπεν, Ἀγαπήσεις κύριον τὸν θεόν σου
HAVING ANSWERED   HE SAID,   YOU WILL LOVE   [THE] LORD   THE   GOD   OF YOU

ἐξ ὅλης [τῆς] καρδίας σου καὶ ἐν ὅλῃ τῇ ψυχῇ
FROM   ALL   THE   HEART   OF YOU   AND   WITH   ALL   THE   SOUL

σου καὶ ἐν ὅλῃ τῇ ἰσχύϊ σου καὶ ἐν ὅλῃ τῇ
OF YOU   AND   WITH   ALL   THE   STRENGTH   OF YOU   AND   WITH   ALL   THE

διανοίᾳ σου, καὶ τὸν πλησίον σου ὡς σεαυτόν.
MIND   OF YOU,   AND   THE   NEIGHBOR   OF YOU   AS   YOURSELF.

10.28 εἶπεν δὲ αὐτῷ, Ὀρθῶς ἀπεκρίθης· τοῦτο ποίει
AND~HE SAID   TO HIM,   YOU HAVE ANSWERED~CORRECTLY.   DO~THIS

καὶ ζήσῃ.   **10.29** ὁ δὲ θέλων δικαιῶσαι ἑαυτὸν εἶπεν
AND   YOU WILL LIVE.   -   BUT   WANTING   TO JUSTIFY   HIMSELF   HE SAID

πρὸς τὸν Ἰησοῦν, Καὶ τίς ἐστίν μου πλησίον;
TO   -   JESUS,   AND   WHO IS   MY   NEIGHBOR?

10.30 ὑπολαβὼν ὁ Ἰησοῦς εἶπεν, Ἄνθρωπός τις
HAVING REPLIED,   -   JESUS   SAID,   A CERTAIN~MAN

κατέβαινεν ἀπὸ Ἰερουσαλὴμ εἰς Ἰεριχὼ καὶ
WAS COMING DOWN   FROM   JERUSALEM   TO   JERICHO   AND

λῃσταῖς περιέπεσεν, οἳ καὶ ἐκδύσαντες αὐτὸν καὶ
HE ENCOUNTERED~ROBBERS,   WHO BOTH   HAVING STRIPPED   HIM   AND

πληγὰς ἐπιθέντες ἀπῆλθον ἀφέντες ἡμιθανῆ.
HAVING INFLICTED~BLOWS   THEY WENT AWAY   HAVING LEFT [HIM]   HALF DEAD.

10.31 κατὰ συγκυρίαν δὲ ἱερεύς τις κατέβαινεν ἐν τῇ
2BY CHANCE   1AND   A CERTAIN~PRIEST   WAS COMING DOWN   BY   -

ὁδῷ ἐκείνῃ καὶ ἰδὼν αὐτὸν ἀντιπαρῆλθεν·
THAT~WAY   AND   HAVING SEEN   HIM   HE PASSED BY ON THE OTHER SIDE.

10.32 ὁμοίως δὲ καὶ Λευίτης [γενόμενος] κατὰ τὸν
AND~LIKEWISE   ALSO   A LEVITE   HAVING HAPPENED   UPON   THE

τόπον ἐλθὼν καὶ ἰδὼν ἀντιπαρῆλθεν.
PLACE,   HAVING COME   AND   HAVING SEEN,   HE PASSED BY ON THE OTHER SIDE.

10.33 Σαμαρίτης δέ τις ὁδεύων ἦλθεν κατ’ αὐτὸν
3SAMARITAN   1BUT   2A CERTAIN   TRAVELING   CAME   UPON   HIM

καὶ ἰδὼν ἐσπλαγχνίσθη,
AND   HAVING SEEN [HIM],   HE WAS FILLED WITH COMPASSION,

10:27a Deut. 6:5   **10:27b** Lev. 19:18

but did not see it, and to hear what you hear, but did not hear it."

25 Just then a lawyer stood up to test Jesus.[u] "Teacher," he said, "what must I do to inherit eternal life?" [26]He said to him, "What is written in the law? What do you read there?" [27]He answered, "You shall love the Lord your God with all your heart, and with all your soul, and with all your strength, and with all your mind; and your neighbor as yourself." [28]And he said to him, "You have given the right answer; do this, and you will live."

29 But wanting to justify himself, he asked Jesus, "And who is my neighbor?" [30]Jesus replied, "A man was going down from Jerusalem to Jericho, and fell into the hands of robbers, who stripped him, beat him, and went away, leaving him half dead. [31]Now by chance a priest was going down that road; and when he saw him, he passed by on the other side. [32]So likewise a Levite, when he came to the place and saw him, passed by on the other side. [33]But a Samaritan while traveling came near him; and when he saw him, he was moved with pity.

[u] Gk *him*

³⁴He went to him and bandaged his wounds, having poured oil and wine on them. Then he put him on his own animal, brought him to an inn, and took care of him. ³⁵The next day he took out two denarii,ᵛ gave them to the innkeeper, and said, 'Take care of him; and when I come back, I will repay you whatever more you spend.' ³⁶Which of these three, do you think, was a neighbor to the man who fell into the hands of the robbers?" ³⁷He said, "The one who showed him mercy." Jesus said to him, "Go and do likewise."

38 Now as they went on their way, he entered a certain village, where a woman named Martha welcomed him into her home. ³⁹She had a sister named Mary, who sat at the Lord's feet and listened to what he was saying. ⁴⁰But Martha was distracted by her many tasks; so she came to him and asked, "Lord, do you not care that my sister has left me to do all the work by myself? Tell her then to help me." ⁴¹But the Lord answered her, "Martha, Martha, you are worried and distracted by many things; ⁴²there is need of only one thing.ʷ Mary has chosen the better part, which will not be taken away from her."

ᵛ The denarius was the usual day's wage for a laborer
ʷ Other ancient authorities read *few things are necessary, or only one*

10.34 καὶ προσελθὼν κατέδησεν τὰ τραύματα αὐτοῦ
AND HAVING APPROACHED HE BANDAGED THE WOUNDS OF HIM

ἐπιχέων ἔλαιον καὶ οἶνον, ἐπιβιβάσας δὲ αὐτὸν
POURING OVER [THEM] OIL AND WINE, AND~HAVING PLACED HIM

ἐπὶ τὸ ἴδιον κτῆνος ἤγαγεν αὐτὸν εἰς πανδοχεῖον
UPON THE(HIS) OWN ANIMAL, HE BROUGHT HIM TO AN INN

καὶ ἐπεμελήθη αὐτοῦ. **10.35** καὶ ἐπὶ τὴν αὔριον
AND CARED FOR HIM. AND ON THE NEXT DAY

ἐκβαλὼν ἔδωκεν δύο δηνάρια τῷ πανδοχεῖ καὶ
HAVING TAKEN OUT, HE GAVE TWO DENARII TO THE INN KEEPER AND

εἶπεν, Ἐπιμελήθητι αὐτοῦ, καὶ ὅ τι ἂν προσδαπανήσῃς
SAID, TAKE CARE OF HIM, AND WHATEVER YOU SPEND IN ADDITION

ἐγὼ ἐν τῷ ἐπανέρχεσθαί με ἀποδώσω σοι. **10.36** τίς
I, WHEN I~RETURN, WILL REPAY YOU. WHO

τούτων τῶν τριῶν πλησίον δοκεῖ σοι γεγονέναι τοῦ
OF THESE - THREE A NEIGHBOR SEEMS TO YOU TO HAVE BECOME TO THE ONE

ἐμπεσόντος εἰς τοὺς λῃστάς; **10.37** ὁ δὲ εἶπεν, Ὁ
HAVING FALLEN IN AMONG THE ROBBERS? - AND HE SAID, THE ONE

ποιήσας τὸ ἔλεος μετ' αὐτοῦ. εἶπεν δὲ αὐτῷ ὁ
HAVING SHOWN - MERCY ON HIM. AND~SAID TO HIM -

Ἰησοῦς, Πορεύου καὶ σὺ ποίει ὁμοίως.
JESUS, GO AND YOU DO LIKEWISE.

10.38 Ἐν δὲ τῷ πορεύεσθαι αὐτοὺς αὐτὸς εἰσῆλθεν εἰς
AND~WHILE THEY~WENT HE ENTERED INTO

κώμην τινά· γυνὴ δέ τις ὀνόματι Μάρθα
A CERTAIN~VILLAGE. ³WOMAN ¹AND ²A CERTAIN BY [THE] NAME MARTHA

ὑπεδέξατο αὐτόν. **10.39** καὶ τῇδε ἦν ἀδελφὴ
RECEIVED HIM. AND TO THIS [WOMAN] WAS A SISTER

καλουμένη Μαριάμ, [ἡ] καὶ παρακαθεσθεῖσα πρὸς
BEING CALLED MARY, WHO ALSO HAVING SAT DOWN BESIDE AT

τοὺς πόδας τοῦ κυρίου ἤκουεν τὸν λόγον αὐτοῦ.
THE FEET OF THE LORD WAS LISTENING TO THE WORD OF HIM.

10.40 ἡ δὲ Μάρθα περιεσπᾶτο περὶ πολλὴν
- BUT MARTHA WAS BEING DISTRACTED ABOUT MUCH

διακονίαν· ἐπιστᾶσα δὲ εἶπεν, Κύριε, οὐ μέλει
SERVICE. AND~HAVING STOOD BY SHE SAID, LORD, IS IT OF NO CONCERN

σοι ὅτι ἡ ἀδελφή μου μόνην με κατέλιπεν
TO YOU THAT THE SISTER OF ME ³ALONE ²ME ¹LEFT

διακονεῖν; εἰπὲ οὖν αὐτῇ ἵνα μοι συναντιλάβηται.
TO SERVE? SPEAK, THEN, TO HER THAT SHE MAY HELP~ME.

10.41 ἀποκριθεὶς δὲ εἶπεν αὐτῇ ὁ κύριος, Μάρθα
AND~HAVING ANSWERED SAID TO HER THE LORD, MARTHA,

Μάρθα, μεριμνᾷς καὶ θορυβάζῃ περὶ πολλά,
MARTHA, YOU ARE WORRIED AND TROUBLED ABOUT MANY THINGS,

10.42 ἑνὸς δέ ἐστιν χρεία· Μαριὰμ γὰρ τὴν ἀγαθὴν
BUT~ONE IS NECESSARY. FOR~MARY, THE GOOD

μερίδα ἐξελέξατο ἥτις οὐκ ἀφαιρεθήσεται αὐτῆς.
PART CHOSE WHICH WILL NOT BE TAKEN AWAY FROM HER.

11.1 Καὶ ἐγένετο ἐν τῷ εἶναι αὐτὸν ἐν τόπῳ τινὶ
AND   IT CAME ABOUT WHILE HE~WAS   IN   A CERTAIN~PLACE

προσευχόμενον, ὡς ἐπαύσατο, εἶπέν τις   τῶν
PRAYING,   AS HE STOPPED, SAID A CERTAIN [ONE] OF THE

μαθητῶν αὐτοῦ πρὸς αὐτόν, Κύριε, δίδαξον ἡμᾶς
DISCIPLES OF HIM TO   HIM,   LORD, TEACH   US

προσεύχεσθαι, καθὼς καὶ Ἰωάννης ἐδίδαξεν τοὺς
TO PRAY,   JUST AS ALSO JOHN   TAUGHT   THE

μαθητὰς αὐτοῦ. **11.2** εἶπεν δὲ αὐτοῖς, Ὅταν
DISCIPLES OF HIM.   AND~HE SAID TO THEM, WHEN

προσεύχησθε λέγετε,
YOU PRAY   SAY,

⌜Πάτερ,⌝ ἁγιασθήτω   τὸ ὄνομά σου·
FATHER, LET BE HELD IN REVERENCE THE NAME OF YOU.

⌜ἐλθέτω ἡ βασιλεία σου⌝·ᵀ
LET COME THE KINGDOM   OF YOU.

11.3 τὸν ἄρτον ἡμῶν τὸν ἐπιούσιον δίδου
THE ²BREAD ³OF US -   ¹DAILY   GIVE

ἡμῖν τὸ καθ᾽ ἡμέραν·
TO US -   EACH DAY.

11.4 καὶ ἄφες ἡμῖν τὰς ἁμαρτίας ἡμῶν,
AND FORGIVE US THE SINS   OF US,

καὶ γὰρ   αὐτοὶ ἀφίομεν παντὶ
FOR~INDEED [WE] OURSELVES ARE FORGIVING EVERYONE

ὀφείλοντι ἡμῖν·
BEING INDEBTED TO US.

καὶ μὴ εἰσενέγκῃς ἡμᾶς εἰς πειρασμόνᵀ.
AND MAY YOU NOT LEAD US   INTO TEMPTATION.

11.5 Καὶ εἶπεν πρὸς αὐτούς, Τίς ἐξ   ὑμῶν ἕξει
AND HE SAID TO   THEM,   WHO AMONG YOU˙ WILL HAVE

φίλον καὶ πορεύσεται πρὸς αὐτὸν μεσονυκτίου καὶ
A FRIEND AND WILL COME   TO   HIM AT MIDNIGHT   AND

εἴπῃ αὐτῷ, Φίλε, χρῆσόν μοι τρεῖς ἄρτους, **11.6** ἐπειδὴ
SAY TO HIM, FRIEND, LEND TO ME THREE LOAVES,   BECAUSE

φίλος μου παρεγένετο ἐξ   ὁδοῦ   πρός με καὶ
A FRIEND OF ME ARRIVED FROM A JOURNEY TO ME AND

οὐκ ἔχω ὃ   παραθήσω αὐτῷ· **11.7** κἀκεῖνος ἔσωθεν
I DO NOT HAVE WHAT I WILL SET BEFORE HIM.   AND THAT ONE WITHIN

ἀποκριθεὶς εἴπῃ, Μή   μοι κόπους πάρεχε· ἤδη ἡ
HAVING ANSWERED MAY SAY, [DO] NOT ²ME ³TROUBLES ¹CAUSE. ALREADY THE

He was praying in a certain place, and after he had finished, one of his disciples said to him, "Lord, teach us to pray, as John taught his disciples." ²He said to them, "When you pray, say:
Father,ˣ hallowed be
    your name.
Your kingdom come.ʸ
3 Give us each day our
    daily bread.ᶻ
4 And forgive us our
    sins,
    for we ourselves
    forgive everyone
    indebted to us.
And do not bring us to
    the time of trial."ᵃ
5 And he said to them, "Suppose one of you has a friend, and you go to him at midnight and say to him, 'Friend, lend me three loaves of bread; ⁶for a friend of mine has arrived, and I have nothing to set before him.' ⁷And he answers from within, 'Do not bother me; the door has already

ˣ Other ancient authorities read *Our Father in heaven*
ʸ A few ancient authorities read *Your Holy Spirit come upon us and cleanse us.* Other ancient authorities add *Your will be done, on earth as in heaven*
ᶻ Or *our bread for tomorrow*
ᵃ Or *us into temptation.* Other ancient authorities add *but rescue us from the evil one* (or *from evil*)

11:2a text: ASV RSV NASB NIV NEB TEV NJB NRSV. var. πατερ ημων ο εν τοις ουρανοις (our Father who is in heaven) [see Matt. 6:9] KJV ASVmg NASBmg NIVmg NEBmg NRSVmg.   **11:2b** text: all. var. ελθετω το πνευμα σου το αγιον εφ ημας και καθαρισατω ημας (your Holy Spirit come upon us and cleanse us) NIVmg NJBmg NRSVmg. var. εφ ημας ελθετω σου η βασιλεια (your kingdom come upon us): NIVmg.   **11:2c** text: ASV RSV NASB NIV NEB TEV NJB NRSV. add γενηθητω το θελημα σου ως εν ουρανω και επι της γης (your will be done on earth as in heaven): KJV ASVmg NIVmg NEBmg NRSVmg.   **11:4** text: ASV RSV NASB NIV NEB TEV NJB NRSV. add αλλα ρυσαι ημας απο του πονηρου [see Matt. 6:13] (but deliver us from evil): KJV ASVmg NASBmg NIVmg NEBmg NRSVmg.

been locked, and my children are with me in bed; I cannot get up and give you anything.' 8I tell you, even though he will not get up and give him anything because he is his friend, at least because of his persistence he will get up and give him whatever he needs.

9 "So I say to you, Ask, and it will be given you; search, and you will find; knock, and the door will be opened for you. 10For everyone who asks receives, and everyone who searches finds, and for everyone who knocks, the door will be opened. 11Is there anyone among you who, if your child asks forᵇ a fish, will give a snake instead of a fish? 12Or if the child asks for an egg, will give a scorpion? 13If you then, who are evil, know how to give good gifts to your children, how much more will the heavenly Father give the Holy Spiritᶜ to those who ask him!"

14 Now he was casting out a demon that was mute; when the demon had gone out, the one who had been mute spoke, and the crowds were amazed. 15But some of them said, "He casts out demons by Beelzebul, the ruler of the demons." 16Others, to test him, kept demanding from him a sign from heaven. 17But he knew what they were thinking and said to them, "Every kingdom divided against

ᵇ Other ancient authorities add *bread, will give a stone; or if your child asks for*
ᶜ Other ancient authorities read *the Father give the Holy Spirit from heaven*

θύρα κέκλεισται καὶ τὰ παιδία μου μετ' ἐμοῦ εἰς τὴν
DOOR   HAS BEEN SHUT   AND   THE   CHILDREN   OF ME   WITH   ME   IN   THE

κοίτην εἰσίν· οὐ δύναμαι ἀναστὰς δοῦναί σοι.
BED   ARE.   I AM NOT ABLE   HAVING ARISEN   TO GIVE   TO YOU [ANYTHING].

11.8 λέγω ὑμῖν, εἰ καὶ οὐ δώσει αὐτῷ ἀναστὰς διὰ
I SAY   TO YOU°,   EVEN~IF   HE WILL NOT GIVE   TO HIM   HAVING ARISEN   BECAUSE

τὸ εἶναι φίλον αὐτοῦ, διά γε τὴν ἀναίδειαν αὐτοῦ
-   A FRIEND~HE IS   OF HIM,   YET~BECAUSE OF   THE   PERSISTENCE   OF HIM

ἐγερθεὶς δώσει αὐτῷ ὅσων χρῄζει. **11.9** κἀγὼ
HAVING ARISEN   HE WILL GIVE   TO HIM   AS MUCH AS   HE NEEDS.   AND I

ὑμῖν λέγω, αἰτεῖτε καὶ δοθήσεται ὑμῖν, ζητεῖτε καὶ
TELL~YOU°,   ASK,   AND   IT WILL BE GIVEN   TO YOU°,   SEEK,   AND

εὑρήσετε, κρούετε καὶ ἀνοιγήσεται ὑμῖν· **11.10** πᾶς γὰρ
YOU° WILL FIND,   KNOCK   AND   IT WILL BE OPENED   TO YOU.   FOR~EVERYONE

ὁ αἰτῶν λαμβάνει καὶ ὁ ζητῶν εὑρίσκει καὶ τῷ
-   ASKING,   RECEIVES   AND   THE ONE   SEEKING,   FINDS   AND   TO THE ONE

κρούοντι ἀνοιγ[ήσ]εται. **11.11** τίνα δὲ ἐξ ὑμῶν τὸν
KNOCKING   IT WILL BE OPENED.   AND~WHAT   ²AMONG   ³YOU°   -

πατέρα αἰτήσει ὁ υἱὸς ⌐ἰχθύν, καὶ ἀντὶ ἰχθύος
¹FATHER [IS THERE]   WILL ASK   THE   SON [FOR]   A FISH,   AND   INSTEAD   OF A FISH

ὄφιν αὐτῷ ἐπιδώσει;⌐ **11.12** ἢ καὶ αἰτήσει ᾠόν,
A SNAKE   WILL GIVE~TO HIM?   OR   EVEN [IF]   HE WILL ASK   FOR AN EGG,

ἐπιδώσει αὐτῷ σκορπίον; **11.13** εἰ οὖν ὑμεῖς
WILL HE GIVE   TO HIM   A SCORPION?   IF   THEREFORE   YOU°,

πονηροὶ ὑπάρχοντες οἴδατε δόματα ἀγαθὰ διδόναι τοῖς
BEING~EVIL ONES   KNOW   GOOD~GIFTS   TO GIVE   TO THE

τέκνοις ὑμῶν, πόσῳ μᾶλλον ὁ πατὴρ [ὁ] ἐξ οὐρανοῦ
CHILDREN   OF YOU°,   HOW MUCH   MORE   THE   FATHER   -   FROM   HEAVEN

δώσει πνεῦμα ἅγιον τοῖς αἰτοῦσιν αὐτόν.
WILL GIVE   [THE] HOLY~SPIRIT   TO THE ONES ASKING   HIM.

11.14 Καὶ ἦν ἐκβάλλων δαιμόνιον [καὶ αὐτὸ ἦν]
AND   HE WAS CASTING OUT   A DEMON   AND   IT   WAS

κωφόν· ἐγένετο δὲ τοῦ δαιμονίου ἐξελθόντος
MUTE.   AND~IT CAME TO PASS [WHEN]   THE   DEMON   HAVING COME OUT

ἐλάλησεν ὁ κωφὸς καὶ ἐθαύμασαν οἱ ὄχλοι.
SPOKE   THE   MUTE   AND   WERE AMAZED   THE   CROWDS.

11.15 τινὲς δὲ ἐξ αὐτῶν εἶπον, Ἐν Βεελζεβοὺλ τῷ
BUT~SOME   OF THEM   SAID,   BY   BEELZEBUL   THE

ἄρχοντι τῶν δαιμονίων ἐκβάλλει τὰ δαιμόνια·
RULER   OF THE DEMONS   HE CASTS OUT   THE DEMONS.

11.16 ἕτεροι δὲ πειράζοντες σημεῖον ἐξ οὐρανοῦ
AND~OTHERS   TESTING [HIM],   A SIGN   FROM   HEAVEN

ἐζήτουν παρ' αὐτοῦ. **11.17** αὐτὸς δὲ εἰδὼς αὐτῶν
THEY WERE SEEKING   FROM   HIM.   BUT~HE   HAVING KNOWN   THEIR

τὰ διανοήματα εἶπεν αὐτοῖς, Πᾶσα βασιλεία ἐφ'
-   THOUGHTS   SAID   TO THEM,   EVERY   KINGDOM   AGAINST

11:11 text: ASVmg RSV NASB NIV NEB TEV NJB NRSV. add αρτον μη λιθον επιδωσει αυτω; ([if his son asks for] bread, he will not give him a stone, will he?) [see Matt. 7:9]: KJV ASV RSVmg NEBmg NJBmg NRSVmg.

ἑαυτὴν διαμερισθεῖσα ἐρημοῦται καὶ οἶκος ἐπὶ
ITSELF HAVING BEEN DIVIDED IS LAID WASTE AND A HOUSE [DIVIDED] AGAINST

οἶκον πίπτει. **11.18** εἰ δὲ καὶ ὁ Σατανᾶς ἐφ᾽ ἑαυτὸν
A HOUSE FALLS. AND~IF ALSO - SATAN AGAINST HIMSELF

διεμερίσθη, πῶς σταθήσεται ἡ βασιλεία αὐτοῦ; ὅτι
WAS DIVIDED, HOW WILL STAND THE KINGDOM OF HIM? BECAUSE

λέγετε ἐν Βεελζεβοὺλ ἐκβάλλειν με τὰ δαιμόνια.
YOU° SAY BY BEELZEBUL [THAT] I~CAST OUT THE DEMONS.

11.19 εἰ δὲ ἐγὼ ἐν Βεελζεβοὺλ ἐκβάλλω τὰ δαιμόνια, οἱ
BUT~IF I BY BEELZEBUL CAST OUT THE DEMONS, THE

υἱοὶ ὑμῶν ἐν τίνι ἐκβάλλουσιν; διὰ τοῦτο αὐτοὶ
SONS OF YOU° BY WHOM DO THEY CAST [THEM] OUT? THEREFORE THEY

ὑμῶν κριταὶ ἔσονται. **11.20** εἰ δὲ ἐν δακτύλῳ θεοῦ [ἐγὼ]
YOUR° JUDGES WILL BE. BUT~IF BY [THE] FINGER OF GOD I

ἐκβάλλω τὰ δαιμόνια, ἄρα ἔφθασεν ἐφ᾽ ὑμᾶς ἡ
CAST OUT THE DEMONS, THEN CAME UPON YOU° THE

βασιλεία τοῦ θεοῦ. **11.21** ὅταν ὁ ἰσχυρὸς
KINGDOM - OF GOD. WHEN THE STRONG ONE

καθωπλισμένος φυλάσσῃ τὴν ἑαυτοῦ αὐλήν, ἐν εἰρήνῃ
HAVING BEEN WELL EQUIPPED, GUARDS THE PALACE~OF HIMSELF IN PEACE

ἐστὶν τὰ ὑπάρχοντα αὐτοῦ· **11.22** ἐπὰν δὲ ἰσχυρότερος
IS(ARE) THE POSSESSIONS OF HIM. BUT~WHEN A STRONGER ONE

αὐτοῦ ἐπελθὼν νικήσῃ αὐτόν, τὴν πανοπλίαν αὐτοῦ
[THAN] HIM HAVING COME OVERCOMES HIM, THE ARMOR OF HIM

αἴρει ἐφ᾽ ᾗ ἐπεποίθει καὶ τὰ σκῦλα αὐτοῦ
HE TAKES, ON WHICH HE HAD DEPENDED AND THE SPOILS OF HIM

διαδίδωσιν. **11.23** ὁ μὴ ὢν μετ᾽ ἐμοῦ κατ᾽ ἐμοῦ
HE DISTRIBUTES. THE ONE NOT BEING WITH ME AGAINST ME

ἐστιν, καὶ ὁ μὴ συνάγων μετ᾽ ἐμοῦ σκορπίζει.
IS, AND THE ONE NOT GATHERING WITH ME SCATTERS.

11.24 Ὅταν τὸ ἀκάθαρτον πνεῦμα ἐξέλθῃ ἀπὸ τοῦ
WHEN THE UNCLEAN SPIRIT GOES OUT FROM THE

ἀνθρώπου, διέρχεται δι᾽ ἀνύδρων τόπων ζητοῦν
MAN IT GOES THROUGH WATERLESS PLACES SEEKING

ἀνάπαυσιν καὶ μὴ εὑρίσκον· [τότε] λέγει, Ὑποστρέψω
A RESTING PLACE AND NOT FINDING [ONE]. THEN IT SAYS, I WILL RETURN

εἰς τὸν οἶκόν μου ὅθεν ἐξῆλθον· **11.25** καὶ ἐλθὸν
TO THE HOUSE OF ME FROM WHERE I CAME OUT. AND HAVING COME

εὑρίσκει σεσαρωμένον καὶ κεκοσμημένον. **11.26** τότε
IT FINDS [IT] HAVING BEEN SWEPT AND HAVING BEEN PUT IN ORDER. THEN

πορεύεται καὶ παραλαμβάνει ἕτερα πνεύματα
IT GOES AND TAKES OTHER SPIRITS

πονηρότερα ἑαυτοῦ ἑπτὰ καὶ εἰσελθόντα κατοικεῖ
MORE EVIL THAN ITSELF, SEVEN, AND HAVING ENTERED IT DWELLS

ἐκεῖ· καὶ γίνεται τὰ ἔσχατα τοῦ ἀνθρώπου ἐκείνου
THERE. AND BECOMES THE LAST [CONDITION] - OF THAT~MAN

χείρονα τῶν πρώτων.
WORSE [THAN] THE FIRST.

itself becomes a desert, and house falls on house. [18]If Satan also is divided against himself, how will his kingdom stand? —for you say that I cast out the demons by Beelzebul. [19]Now if I cast out the demons by Beelzebul, by whom do your exorcists[d] cast them out? Therefore they will be your judges. [20]But if it is by the finger of God that I cast out the demons, then the kingdom of God has come to you. [21]When a strong man, fully armed, guards his castle, his property is safe. [22]But when one stronger than he attacks him and overpowers him, he takes away his armor in which he trusted and divides his plunder. [23]Whoever is not with me is against me, and whoever does not gather with me scatters.

24 "When the unclean spirit has gone out of a person, it wanders through waterless regions looking for a resting place, but not finding any, it says, 'I will return to my house from which I came.' [25]When it comes, it finds it swept and put in order. [26]Then it goes and brings seven other spirits more evil than itself, and they enter and live there; and the last state of that person is worse than the first."

[d] Gk sons

27 While he was saying this, a woman in the crowd raised her voice and said to him, "Blessed is the womb that bore you and the breasts that nursed you!" 28But he said, "Blessed rather are those who hear the word of God and obey it!"

29 When the crowds were increasing, he began to say, "This generation is an evil generation; it asks for a sign, but no sign will be given to it except the sign of Jonah. 30For just as Jonah became a sign to the people of Nineveh, so the Son of Man will be to this generation. 31The queen of the South will rise at the judgment with the people of this generation and condemn them, because she came from the ends of the earth to listen to the wisdom of Solomon, and see, something greater than Solomon is here! 32The people of Nineveh will rise up at the judgment with this generation and condemn it, because they repented at the proclamation of Jonah, and see, something greater than Jonah is here!

33 "No one after lighting a lamp puts it in a cellar,e but on the lampstand so that those who enter may see the light. 34Your eye is the lamp of your body.

e Other ancient authorities add or under the bushel basket

11.27 Ἐγένετο δὲ ἐν τῷ λέγειν αὐτὸν ταῦτα
AND~IT CAME ABOUT WHILE HE~SAYS THESE THINGS,

ἐπάρασά τις φωνὴν γυνὴ ἐκ τοῦ ὄχλου εἶπεν
6HAVING LIFTED UP 1A CERTAIN 7[HER] VOICE 2WOMAN 3FROM 4THE 5CROWD SAID

αὐτῷ, Μακαρία ἡ κοιλία ἡ βαστάσασά σε καὶ
TO HIM, BLESSED [IS] THE WOMB - HAVING CARRIED YOU AND

μαστοὶ οὓς ἐθήλασας. **11.28** αὐτὸς δὲ εἶπεν,
[THE] BREASTS WHICH YOU SUCKED. BUT~HE SAID,

Μενοῦν μακάριοι οἱ ἀκούοντες τὸν λόγον τοῦ
ON THE CONTRARY BLESSED [ARE] THE ONES HEARING THE WORD -

θεοῦ καὶ φυλάσσοντες.
OF GOD AND OBSERVING [IT].

11.29 Τῶν δὲ ὄχλων ἐπαθροιζομένων ἤρξατο λέγειν,
AND~[AS] THE CROWDS ARE GATHERING EVEN MORE HE BEGAN TO SAY,

Ἡ γενεὰ αὕτη γενεὰ πονηρά ἐστιν· σημεῖον ζητεῖ,
- THIS~GENERATION AN EVIL~GENERATION IS. IT IS SEEKING~A SIGN,

καὶ σημεῖον οὐ δοθήσεται αὐτῇ εἰ μὴ τὸ σημεῖον
AND A SIGN WILL NOT BE GIVEN TO IT EXCEPT THE SIGN

Ἰωνᾶ. **11.30** καθὼς γὰρ ἐγένετο Ἰωνᾶς τοῖς Νινευίταις
OF JONAH. FOR~JUST AS JONAH~BECAME TO THE NINEVITES

σημεῖον, οὕτως ἔσται καὶ ὁ υἱὸς τοῦ ἀνθρώπου τῇ
A SIGN, SO WILL BE ALSO THE SON - OF MAN -

γενεᾷ ταύτῃ. **11.31** βασίλισσα νότου ἐγερθήσεται ἐν
TO THIS~GENERATION. [THE] QUEEN OF [THE] SOUTH WILL BE RAISED AT

τῇ κρίσει μετὰ τῶν ἀνδρῶν τῆς γενεᾶς ταύτης καὶ
THE JUDGMENT WITH THE MEN - OF THIS~GENERATION AND

κατακρινεῖ αὐτούς, ὅτι ἦλθεν ἐκ τῶν περάτων τῆς
SHE WILL CONDEMN THEM, BECAUSE SHE CAME FROM THE ENDS OF THE

γῆς ἀκοῦσαι τὴν σοφίαν Σολομῶνος, καὶ ἰδοὺ
EARTH TO HEAR THE WISDOM OF SOLOMON, AND BEHOLD [ONE]

πλεῖον Σολομῶνος ὧδε. **11.32** ἄνδρες Νινευῖται
GREATER [THAN] SOLOMON [IS] HERE. MEN, NINEVITES

ἀναστήσονται ἐν τῇ κρίσει μετὰ τῆς γενεᾶς ταύτης καὶ
WILL STAND UP AT THE JUDGMENT WITH - THIS~GENERATION AND

κατακρινοῦσιν αὐτήν· ὅτι μετενόησαν εἰς τὸ
WILL CONDEMN IT. BECAUSE THEY REPENTED AT THE

κήρυγμα Ἰωνᾶ, καὶ ἰδοὺ πλεῖον Ἰωνᾶ ὧδε.
PREACHING OF JONAH, AND BEHOLD [ONE] GREATER [THAN] JONAH [IS] HERE.

11.33 Οὐδεὶς λύχνον ἅψας εἰς κρύπτην τίθησιν
NO ONE HAVING LIT~A LAMP IN A HIDDEN PLACE PUTS [IT],

⌜[οὐδὲ ὑπὸ τὸν μόδιον]⌝ ἀλλ᾽ ἐπὶ τὴν λυχνίαν,
NEITHER UNDER THE MEASURING BUCKET, BUT ON THE LAMPSTAND,

ἵνα οἱ εἰσπορευόμενοι τὸ φῶς βλέπωσιν.
IN ORDER THAT THE ONES ENTERING 2THE 3LIGHT 1MAY SEE.

11.34 ὁ λύχνος τοῦ σώματός ἐστιν ὁ ὀφθαλμός σου.
THE LAMP OF THE BODY IS THE EYE OF YOU.

11:33 text [see Matt. 5:15; Mark 4:21]: KJV ASV RSV NASB NIV NEBmg TEV NJB NRSVmg. omit: NEB TEVmg NRSV.

ὅταν ὁ ὀφθαλμός σου ἁπλοῦς ᾖ, καὶ ὅλον τὸ σῶμά
WHEN THE EYE OF YOU IS~SOUND, THEN [THE] ENTIRE - BODY

σου φωτεινόν ἐστιν· ἐπὰν δὲ πονηρὸς ᾖ, καὶ τὸ σῶμά
OF YOU IS~FULL OF LIGHT. BUT~WHEN IT IS~SICK, THEN THE BODY

σου σκοτεινόν. **11.35** σκόπει οὖν μὴ τὸ φῶς τὸ
OF YOU [IS] FULL OF DARKNESS. SEE TO IT THEN [THAT], NOT THE LIGHT -

ἐν σοὶ σκότος ἐστίν. **11.36** εἰ οὖν τὸ σῶμά σου
IN YOU IS~DARKNESS. IF THEREFORE, THE ²BODY ³OF YOU [IS]

ὅλον φωτεινόν, μὴ ἔχον μέρος τι σκοτεινόν, ἔσται
¹WHOLE FULL OF LIGHT, NOT HAVING ANY~PART DARK, IT WILL BE

φωτεινὸν ὅλον ὡς ὅταν ὁ λύχνος τῇ ἀστραπῇ
ALL~FULL OF LIGHT AS WHEN THE LAMP WITH THE LIGHT

φωτίζῃ σε.
SHINES ON YOU.

11.37 Ἐν δὲ τῷ λαλῆσαι ἐρωτᾷ αὐτὸν Φαρισαῖος
NOW~WHILE [HE] SPOKE, ASKS HIM A PHARISEE

ὅπως ἀριστήσῃ παρ' αὐτῷ· εἰσελθὼν δὲ
THAT HE MIGHT HAVE A MEAL WITH HIM. AND~HAVING ENTERED

ἀνέπεσεν. **11.38** ὁ δὲ Φαρισαῖος ἰδὼν
HE RECLINED [AT TABLE]. AND~THE PHARISEE, HAVING SEEN [THIS]

ἐθαύμασεν ὅτι οὐ πρῶτον ἐβαπτίσθη πρὸ τοῦ
WAS AMAZED THAT ²NOT ³FIRST ¹HE DID WASH BEFORE THE

ἀρίστου. **11.39** εἶπεν δὲ ὁ κύριος πρὸς αὐτόν, Νῦν
MEAL. BUT~SAID THE LORD TO HIM, NOW

ὑμεῖς οἱ Φαρισαῖοι τὸ ἔξωθεν τοῦ ποτηρίου καὶ τοῦ
YOU° - PHARISEES THE OUTSIDE OF THE CUP AND THE

πίνακος καθαρίζετε, τὸ δὲ ἔσωθεν ὑμῶν γέμει ἁρπαγῆς
DISH YOU° CLEAN, BUT~THE INSIDE OF YOU° IS FULL OF GREED

καὶ πονηρίας. **11.40** ἄφρονες, οὐχ ὁ ποιήσας τὸ
AND WICKEDNESS. FOOLS, [DID] NOT THE ONE HAVING MADE THE

ἔξωθεν καὶ τὸ ἔσωθεν ἐποίησεν; **11.41** πλὴν τὰ
OUTSIDE ALSO THE INSIDE MAKE? BUT THE THINGS

ἐνόντα δότε ἐλεημοσύνην, καὶ ἰδοὺ πάντα καθαρὰ
BEING INSIDE GIVE [AS] ALMS, AND BEHOLD EVERYTHING CLEAN

ὑμῖν ἐστιν. **11.42** ἀλλὰ οὐαὶ ὑμῖν τοῖς Φαρισαίοις,
TO YOU° IS. BUT WOE TO YOU° - PHARISEES,

ὅτι ἀποδεκατοῦτε τὸ ἡδύοσμον καὶ τὸ πήγανον καὶ
BECAUSE YOU° TITHE THE MINT AND THE RUE AND

πᾶν λάχανον καὶ παρέρχεσθε τὴν κρίσιν καὶ τὴν
EVERY HERB AND YOU° DISREGARD THE JUSTICE AND THE

ἀγάπην τοῦ θεοῦ· ταῦτα δὲ ἔδει ποιῆσαι
LOVE - OF GOD. BUT~THESE THINGS IT WAS NECESSARY TO DO

κἀκεῖνα μὴ παρεῖναι. **11.43** οὐαὶ ὑμῖν τοῖς
AND THOSE NOT TO DISREGARD. WOE TO YOU° -

Φαρισαίοις, ὅτι ἀγαπᾶτε τὴν πρωτοκαθεδρίαν ἐν
PHARISEES, BECAUSE YOU° LOVE THE PLACE OF HONOR IN

ταῖς συναγωγαῖς καὶ τοὺς ἀσπασμοὺς ἐν ταῖς
THE SYNAGOGUES AND THE GREETINGS IN THE

If your eye is healthy, your whole body is full of light; but if it is not healthy, your body is full of darkness. [35]Therefore consider whether the light in you is not darkness. [36]If then your whole body is full of light, with no part of it in darkness, it will be as full of light as when a lamp gives you light with its rays."

[37] While he was speaking, a Pharisee invited him to dine with him; so he went in and took his place at the table. [38]The Pharisee was amazed to see that he did not first wash before dinner. [39]Then the Lord said to him, "Now you Pharisees clean the outside of the cup and of the dish, but inside you are full of greed and wickedness. [40]You fools! Did not the one who made the outside make the inside also? [41]So give for alms those things that are within; and see, everything will be clean for you.

[42] "But woe to you Pharisees! For you tithe mint and rue and herbs of all kinds, and neglect justice and the love of God; it is these you ought to have practiced, without neglecting the others. [43]Woe to you Pharisees! For you love to have the seat of honor in the synagogues and to be greeted with respect in the

marketplaces. 44Woe to you! For you are like unmarked graves, and people walk over them without realizing it."

45 One of the lawyers answered him, "Teacher, when you say these things, you insult us too." 46And he said, "Woe also to you lawyers! For you load people with burdens hard to bear, and you yourselves do not lift a finger to ease them. 47Woe to you! For you build the tombs of the prophets whom your ancestors killed. 48So you are witnesses and approve of the deeds of your ancestors; for they killed them, and you build their tombs. 49Therefore also the Wisdom of God said, 'I will send them prophets and apostles, some of whom they will kill and persecute,' 50so that this generation may be charged with the blood of all the prophets shed since the foundation of the world, 51from the blood of Abel to the blood of Zechariah, who perished between the altar and the sanctuary. Yes, I tell you, it will be charged against this generation. 52Woe to you lawyers! For you have taken away the key of knowledge; you did not enter yourselves, and you hindered those who were entering."

ἀγοραῖς. **11.44** οὐαὶ ὑμῖν, ὅτι ἐστὲ ὡς τὰ
MARKETPLACES.   WOE   TO YOU°, BECAUSE YOU° ARE LIKE THE

μνημεῖα τὰ ἄδηλα, καὶ οἱ ἄνθρωποι [οἱ]
²GRAVES   -   ¹UNMARKED, AND   -   MEN,   THE ONES

περιπατοῦντες ἐπάνω οὐκ οἴδασιν.
WALKING   OVER   HAVE NOT KNOWN [IT].

11.45 Ἀποκριθεὶς δέ τις τῶν νομικῶν λέγει αὐτῷ,
       AND~HAVING ANSWERED ONE OF THE LAWYERS SAYS TO HIM,

Διδάσκαλε, ταῦτα λέγων   καὶ ἡμᾶς ὑβρίζεις. **11.46** ὁ
TEACHER,   [BY] SAYING~THESE THINGS ALSO US   YOU INSULT.

δὲ εἶπεν, Καὶ ὑμῖν τοῖς νομικοῖς οὐαί, ὅτι
BUT HE SAID, ALSO TO YOU° -   LAWYERS   WOE, BECAUSE

φορτίζετε τοὺς ἀνθρώπους φορτία δυσβάστακτα, καὶ
YOU° BURDEN -   MEN   [WITH] LOADS DIFFICULT TO CARRY, AND

αὐτοὶ ἑνὶ τῶν δακτύλων ὑμῶν οὐ προσψαύετε τοῖς
YOURSELVES [WITH] ONE OF THE FINGERS OF YOU° YOU° DO NOT TOUCH THE

φορτίοις. **11.47** οὐαὶ ὑμῖν, ὅτι οἰκοδομεῖτε τὰ
LOADS.   WOE   TO YOU°, BECAUSE YOU° BUILD   THE

μνημεῖα τῶν προφητῶν, οἱ δὲ πατέρες ὑμῶν
MEMORIALS OF THE PROPHETS, BUT~THE FATHERS OF YOU°

ἀπέκτειναν αὐτούς. **11.48** ἄρα μάρτυρές ἐστε καὶ
KILLED   THEM.   THEREFORE, WITNESSES YOU° ARE AND

συνευδοκεῖτε τοῖς ἔργοις τῶν πατέρων ὑμῶν, ὅτι
YOU° ARE IN AGREEMENT WITH THE WORKS OF THE FATHERS OF YOU°, BECAUSE

αὐτοὶ μὲν   ἀπέκτειναν αυτούς, ὑμεῖς δὲ
THEY   ON THE ONE HAND KILLED   THEM   BUT~YOU°

οἰκοδομεῖτε. **11.49** διὰ τοῦτο καὶ ἡ σοφία τοῦ θεοῦ
BUILD [THE MEMORIALS].   THEREFORE, ALSO THE WISDOM - OF GOD

εἶπεν, Ἀποστελῶ εἰς αὐτοὺς προφήτας καὶ ἀποστόλους,
SAID,   I WILL SEND TO THEM   PROPHETS   AND APOSTLES,

καὶ ἐξ αὐτῶν ἀποκτενοῦσιν καὶ διώξουσιν, **11.50** ἵνα
AND FROM THEM THEY WILL KILL AND PERSECUTE,   THAT

ἐκζητηθῇ τὸ αἷμα πάντων τῶν προφητῶν τὸ
MAY BE REQUIRED THE BLOOD OF ALL THE   PROPHETS   -

ἐκκεχυμένον ἀπὸ καταβολῆς κόσμου ἀπὸ τῆς
HAVING BEEN POURED OUT FROM [THE] CREATION OF [THE] WORLD, OF -

γενεᾶς ταύτης, **11.51** ἀπὸ αἵματος Ἄβελ ἕως αἵματος
THIS~GENERATION,   FROM [THE] BLOOD OF ABEL TO [THE] BLOOD

Ζαχαρίου τοῦ ἀπολομένου μεταξὺ τοῦ θυσιαστηρίου
OF ZECHARIAH, THE ONE HAVING PERISHED BETWEEN THE   ALTAR

καὶ τοῦ οἴκου· ναί λέγω ὑμῖν, ἐκζητηθήσεται ἀπὸ
AND THE HOUSE [OF GOD]; YES, I TELL TO YOU°, IT WILL BE REQUIRED FROM

τῆς γενεᾶς ταύτης. **11.52** οὐαὶ ὑμῖν τοῖς νομικοῖς,
-    THIS~GENERATION.   WOE   TO YOU° -   LAWYERS,

ὅτι ἤρατε τὴν κλεῖδα τῆς γνώσεως· αὐτοὶ
BECAUSE YOU° TOOK THE KEY   - OF KNOWLEDGE; YOURSELVES,

οὐκ εἰσήλθατε καὶ τοὺς εἰσερχομένους ἐκωλύσατε.
YOU° DID NOT ENTER IN AND THE ONES ENTERING IN   YOU° HINDERED.

11.53 Κἀκεῖθεν ἐξελθόντος αὐτοῦ ἤρξαντο οἱ
AND FROM THERE HE~HAVING GONE FORTH, BEGAN THE

γραμματεῖς καὶ οἱ Φαρισαῖοι δεινῶς ἐνέχειν καὶ
SCRIBES AND THE PHARISEES TO BE HOSTILE~TERRIBLY AND

ἀποστοματίζειν αὐτὸν περὶ πλειόνων, **11.54** ἐνεδρεύοντες
TO QUESTION CLOSELY HIM ABOUT MANY THINGS, PLOTTING

αὐτὸν θηρεῦσαί τι ἐκ τοῦ στόματος αὐτοῦ.
TO CATCH~HIM [IN] SOMETHING FROM THE MOUTH OF HIM.

53 When he went outside, the scribes and the Pharisees began to be very hostile toward him and to cross-examine him about many things, 54lying in wait for him, to catch him in something he might say.

CHAPTER 12

12.1 Ἐν οἷς ἐπισυναχθεισῶν τῶν μυριάδων τοῦ ὄχλου,
MEANWHILE, HAVING ASSEMBLED THE MYRIADS OF THE CROWD,

ὥστε καταπατεῖν ἀλλήλους, ἤρξατο λέγειν πρὸς τοὺς
SO AS TO TRAMPLE ON ONE ANOTHER, HE BEGAN TO SAY TO THE

μαθητὰς αὐτοῦ πρῶτον, Προσέχετε ἑαυτοῖς ἀπὸ τῆς
DISCIPLES OF HIM FIRST, PAY ATTENTION TO YOURSELVES FROM THE

ζύμης, ἥτις ἐστὶν ὑπόκρισις, τῶν Φαρισαίων.
LEAVEN, WHICH IS HYPOCRISY, OF THE PHARISEES.

12.2 οὐδὲν δὲ συγκεκαλυμμένον ἐστὶν ὃ
AND~NOTHING HAVING BEEN CONCEALED IS WHICH

οὐκ ἀποκαλυφθήσεται καὶ κρυπτὸν ὃ οὐ γνωσθήσεται.
WILL NOT BE REVEALED AND HIDDEN WHICH WILL NOT BE MADE KNOWN.

12.3 ἀνθ' ὧν ὅσα ἐν τῇ σκοτίᾳ εἴπατε ἐν τῷ φωτὶ
SO THEN, WHAT THINGS IN THE DARKNESS YOU° SAID, IN THE LIGHT

ἀκουσθήσεται, καὶ ὃ πρὸς τὸ οὖς ἐλαλήσατε ἐν τοῖς
WILL BE HEARD, AND WHAT TO THE EAR YOU° SPOKE IN THE

ταμείοις κηρυχθήσεται ἐπὶ τῶν δωμάτων.
SECRET ROOMS, WILL BE PROCLAIMED ON THE HOUSETOPS.

12.4 Λέγω δὲ ὑμῖν τοῖς φίλοις μου, μὴ φοβηθῆτε
NOW~I SAY TO YOU°, THE FRIENDS OF ME, DO NOT BE AFRAID

ἀπὸ τῶν ἀποκτεινόντων τὸ σῶμα καὶ μετὰ ταῦτα
OF THE ONES KILLING THE BODY AND AFTER THESE THINGS

μὴ ἐχόντων περισσότερόν τι ποιῆσαι. **12.5** ὑποδείξω δὲ
NOT HAVING ANYTHING~MORE TO DO. BUT~I WILL SHOW

ὑμῖν τίνα φοβηθῆτε· φοβήθητε τὸν μετὰ τὸ
YOU° SOMEONE YOU° SHOULD FEAR; FEAR THE ONE AFTER THE [BODY]

ἀποκτεῖναι ἔχοντα ἐξουσίαν ἐμβαλεῖν εἰς τὴν
KILLING HAVING AUTHORITY TO THROW INTO -

γέενναν. ναί λέγω ὑμῖν, τοῦτον φοβήθητε.
GEHENNA (HELL). YES, I SAY TO YOU°, FEAR~THIS ONE.

12.6 οὐχὶ πέντε στρουθία πωλοῦνται ἀσσαρίων δύο;
[ARE] NOT FIVE SPARROWS SOLD [FOR] TWO~ASSARION?

καὶ ἓν ἐξ αὐτῶν οὐκ ἔστιν ἐπιλελησμένον ἐνώπιον τοῦ
AND ONE OF THEM HAS NOT BEEN OVERLOOKED BEFORE -

θεοῦ. **12.7** ἀλλὰ καὶ αἱ τρίχες τῆς κεφαλῆς ὑμῶν
GOD. BUT EVEN THE HAIRS OF THE HEAD OF YOU°

Meanwhile, when the crowd gathered by the thousands, so that they trampled on one another, he began to speak first to his disciples, "Beware of the yeast of the Pharisees, that is, their hypocrisy. 2Nothing is covered up that will not be uncovered, and nothing secret that will not become known. 3Therefore whatever you have said in the dark will be heard in the light, and what you have whispered behind closed doors will be proclaimed from the housetops.

4 "I tell you, my friends, do not fear those who kill the body, and after that can do nothing more. 5But I will warn you whom to fear: fear him who, after he has killed, has authority f to cast into hell. g Yes, I tell you, fear him! 6Are not five sparrows sold for two pennies? Yet not one of them is forgotten in God's sight. 7But even the hairs of your head

f Or power
g Gk Gehenna

are all counted. Do not be afraid; you are of more value than many sparrows.

8 "And I tell you, everyone who acknowledges me before others, the Son of Man also will acknowledge before the angels of God; ⁹but whoever denies me before others will be denied before the angels of God. ¹⁰And everyone who speaks a word against the Son of Man will be forgiven; but whoever blasphemes against the Holy Spirit will not be forgiven. ¹¹When they bring you before the synagogues, the rulers, and the authorities, do not worry about how*ʰ* you are to defend yourselves or what you are to say; ¹²for the Holy Spirit will teach you at that very hour what you ought to say."

13 Someone in the crowd said to him, "Teacher, tell my brother to divide the family inheritance with me." ¹⁴But he said to him, "Friend, who set me to be a judge or arbitrator over you?" ¹⁵And he said to them, "Take care! Be on your guard against all kinds of greed; for one's life does not consist in the abundance of possessions." ¹⁶Then he told them a parable: "The land of

ʰ Other ancient authorities add or what

πᾶσαι ἠρίθμηνται.   μὴ φοβεῖσθε·   πολλῶν στρουθίων
ALL   HAVE BEEN COUNTED.   DO NOT BE AFRAID.   ²[THAN] MANY ³SPARROWS

διαφέρετε.
¹YOU° ARE WORTH MORE.

12.8 Λέγω δὲ ὑμῖν,   πᾶς   ὃς ἂν ὁμολογήσῃ ἐν ἐμοὶ
AND~I SAY   TO YOU°,   EVERYONE WHOEVER CONFESSES   -   ME

ἔμπροσθεν τῶν ἀνθρώπων, καὶ ὁ   υἱὸς τοῦ ἀνθρώπου
BEFORE   -   MEN,   ALSO THE SON   -   OF MAN

ὁμολογήσει ἐν αὐτῷ   ἔμπροσθεν τῶν ἀγγέλων τοῦ θεοῦ·
WILL CONFESS   -   HIM   BEFORE   THE ANGELS   -   OF GOD.

12.9 ὁ δὲ   ἀρνησάμενός με ἐνώπιον τῶν ἀνθρώπων
BUT~THE ONE HAVING DENIED   ME BEFORE   -   MEN

ἀπαρνηθήσεται ἐνώπιον τῶν ἀγγέλων τοῦ θεοῦ.
WILL BE DENIED   BEFORE   THE ANGELS   -   OF GOD.

12.10 καὶ   πᾶς   ὃς ἐρεῖ   λόγον εἰς   τὸν υἱὸν τοῦ
AND   EVERYONE WHO WILL SAY A WORD AGAINST THE SON   -

ἀνθρώπου, ἀφεθήσεται αὐτῷ·   τῷ δὲ   εἰς   τὸ ἅγιον
OF MAN,   IT WILL BE FORGIVEN HIM.   BUT~THE ONE AGAINST THE HOLY

πνεῦμα βλασφημήσαντι οὐκ ἀφεθήσεται.   **12.11** ὅταν δὲ
SPIRIT   HAVING BLASPHEMED   WILL NOT BE FORGIVEN.   AND~WHEN

εἰσφέρωσιν ὑμᾶς ἐπὶ   τὰς συναγωγὰς καὶ τὰς ἀρχὰς
THEY BRING IN   YOU°   BEFORE THE SYNAGOGUES   AND   THE RULERS

καὶ τὰς ἐξουσίας,   μὴ μεριμνήσητε πῶς ἢ τί
AND   THE AUTHORITIES,   DO NOT WORRY   HOW OR WHAT

ἀπολογήσησθε   ἢ τί   εἴπητε·   **12.12** τὸ γὰρ
YOU° SHOULD SPEAK IN DEFENSE   OR   WHAT   YOU° SHOULD SAY.   FOR~THE

ἅγιον πνεῦμα διδάξει ὑμᾶς ἐν αὐτῇ τῇ ὥρᾳ ἃ
HOLY   SPIRIT   WILL TEACH YOU°   IN   THE~SAME   HOUR WHAT

δεῖ   εἰπεῖν.
IT IS NECESSARY   TO SAY.

12.13 Εἶπεν δέ τις   ἐκ   τοῦ ὄχλου αὐτῷ,
AND~SAID   SOMEONE OUT OF THE   CROWD   TO HIM,

Διδάσκαλε, εἰπὲ τῷ   ἀδελφῷ μου μερίσασθαι μετ'
TEACHER,   SPEAK TO THE BROTHER   OF ME TO SHARE   WITH

ἐμοῦ τὴν κληρονομίαν.   **12.14** ὁ δὲ   εἶπεν αὐτῷ,
ME   THE INHERITANCE.   -   BUT HE SAID TO HIM,

Ἄνθρωπε, τίς με κατέστησεν κριτὴν ἢ μεριστὴν ἐφ'
MAN,   WHO APPOINTED~ME   A JUDGE   OR ARBITRATOR OVER

ὑμᾶς;   **12.15** εἶπεν δὲ πρὸς αὐτούς, Ὁρᾶτε καὶ
YOU°?   AND~HE SAID TO   THEM,   TAKE CARE AND

φυλάσσεσθε ἀπὸ πάσης πλεονεξίας, ὅτι   οὐκ ἐν τῷ
BE ON GUARD   FROM ALL   GREEDINESS,   BECAUSE ⁵NOT ⁶IN ⁷THE

περισσεύειν τινὶ   ἡ   ζωὴ αὐτοῦ ἐστιν ἐκ   τῶν
⁸ABOUND[ING]   ⁹TO ANYONE ¹THE ²LIFE ³OF HIM ⁴IS   FROM THE

ὑπαρχόντων   αὐτῷ.   **12.16** Εἶπεν δὲ παραβολὴν πρὸς
POSSESSIONS [BELONGING]   TO HIM.   AND~HE SPOKE A PARABLE   TO

αὐτοὺς λέγων, Ἀνθρώπου τινὸς   πλουσίου
THEM   SAYING,   ⁵MAN   ³OF A CERTAIN ⁴RICH

εὐφόρησεν   ἡ   χώρα. **12.17** καὶ διελογίζετο ἐν
⁶PRODUCED A GOOD CROP ¹THE ²FARM.   AND HE WAS THINKING WITHIN

ἑαυτῷ   λέγων, Τί   ποιήσω, ὅτι   οὐκ ἔχω   ποῦ
HIMSELF SAYING, WHAT SHOULD I DO, BECAUSE I DO NOT HAVE [A PLACE] WHERE

συνάξω τοὺς καρπούς μου; **12.18** καὶ εἶπεν, Τοῦτο
I WILL GATHER THE FRUITS OF ME?   AND HE SAID, THIS

ποιήσω, καθελῶ   μου τὰς ἀποθήκας καὶ
I WILL DO, I WILL TEAR DOWN MY -   BARNS   AND

μείζονας οἰκοδομήσω καὶ συνάξω   ἐκεῖ πάντα τὸν
I WILL BUILD~LARGER ONES   AND I WILL GATHER THERE   ALL   THE

σῖτον καὶ τὰ ἀγαθά μου **12.19** καὶ ἐρῶ   τῇ   ψυχῇ
GRAIN   AND THE GOODS OF ME   AND I WILL SAY TO THE SOUL

μου, Ψυχή, ἔχεις πολλὰ ἀγαθὰ κείμενα εἰς
OF ME, SOUL,   YOU HAVE MANY   GOODS STORING UP FOR

ἔτη πολλά· ἀναπαύου, φάγε, πίε,   εὐφραίνου.
MANY~YEARS. REST,   EAT,   DRINK, [AND] BE MERRY.

12.20 εἶπεν δὲ αὐτῷ ὁ θεός, Ἄφρων, ταύτῃ   τῇ
BUT~SAID TO HIM - GOD, FOOLISH [MAN], [DURING] THIS -

νυκτὶ τὴν ψυχήν σου ἀπαιτοῦσιν ἀπὸ σοῦ· ἃ δὲ
NIGHT   THE SOUL OF YOU THEY DEMAND FROM YOU. NOW~WHAT

ἡτοίμασας, τίνι   ἔσται;   **12.21** οὕτως ὁ
YOU PREPARED, TO WHOM WILL IT BE [GIVEN]?   SUCH [IS] THE ONE

θησαυρίζων ἑαυτῷ καὶ μὴ εἰς θεὸν πλουτῶν.
STORING UP FOR HIMSELF AND NOT TOWARD GOD BEING RICH.

12.22 Εἶπεν δὲ πρὸς τοὺς μαθητὰς [αὐτοῦ], Διὰ τοῦτο
AND~HE SAID TO   THE   DISCIPLES OF HIM,   THEREFORE,

λέγω ὑμῖν· μὴ μεριμνᾶτε τῇ   ψυχῇ τί φάγητε,
I SAY TO YOU°: DO NOT WORRY FOR THE(YOUR) LIFE, WHAT YOU° MAY EAT,

μηδὲ τῷ   σώματι τί   ἐνδύσησθε.
NOR   FOR THE(YOUR) BODY WHAT YOU° MAY CLOTHE YOURSELF WITH.

12.23 ἡ γὰρ ψυχὴ πλεῖόν ἐστιν τῆς τροφῆς καὶ τὸ
FOR~THE SOUL IS~MORE   [THAN] FOOD AND THE

σῶμα   τοῦ ἐνδύματος. **12.24** κατανοήσατε τοὺς
BODY [MORE] - [THAN] CLOTHING.   CONSIDER   THE

κόρακας ὅτι οὐ σπείρουσιν οὐδὲ θερίζουσιν, οἷς
RAVENS   THAT THEY DO NOT SOW   NOR   REAP,   TO WHICH

οὐκ ἔστιν ταμεῖον οὐδὲ ἀποθήκη, καὶ ὁ θεὸς τρέφει
IS NOT   A STOREROOM NOR A BARN,   AND - GOD   FEEDS

αὐτούς· πόσῳ   μᾶλλον ὑμεῖς διαφέρετε τῶν
THEM.   HOW MUCH MORE   YOU°   ARE WORTH   [THAN] THE

πετεινῶν. **12.25** τίς δὲ ἐξ ὑμῶν μεριμνῶν δύναται ἐπὶ
BIRDS.   AND~WHO OF YOU° [BY] WORRYING IS ABLE UPON

τὴν ἡλικίαν αὐτοῦ προσθεῖναι πῆχυν; **12.26** εἰ οὖν οὐδὲ
THE LIFESPAN OF HIM TO ADD   A CUBIT?   IF THEN ²NOT

ἐλάχιστον δύνασθε, τί περὶ τῶν λοιπῶν μεριμνᾶτε;
³A LITTLE THING [TO DO] ¹YOU° ARE ABLE, WHY ABOUT THE REST   DO YOU° WORRY?

12.27 κατανοήσατε τὰ κρίνα πῶς αὐξάνει· οὐ κοπιᾷ
CONSIDER   THE LILIES HOW IT GROWS.   IT DOES NOT LABOR

a rich man produced abundantly. [17]And he thought to himself, 'What should I do, for I have no place to store my crops?' [18]Then he said, 'I will do this: I will pull down my barns and build larger ones, and there I will store all my grain and my goods. [19]And I will say to my soul, Soul, you have ample goods laid up for many years; relax, eat, drink, be merry.' [20]But God said to him, 'You fool! This very night your life is being demanded of you. And the things you have prepared, whose will they be?' [21]So it is with those who store up treasures for themselves but are not rich toward God."

22 He said to his disciples, "Therefore I tell you, do not worry about your life, what you will eat, or about your body, what you will wear. [23]For life is more than food, and the body more than clothing. [24]Consider the ravens: they neither sow nor reap, they have neither storehouse nor barn, and yet God feeds them. Of how much more value are you than the birds! [25]And can any of you by worrying add a single hour to your span of life?[i] [26]If then you are not able to do so small a thing as that, why do you worry about the rest? [27]Consider the lilies, how they grow: they neither toil

[i] Or *add a cubit to your stature*

nor spin;ʲ yet I tell you, even Solomon in all his glory was not clothed like one of these. ²⁸But if God so clothes the grass of the field, which is alive today and tomorrow is thrown into the oven, how much more will he clothe you—you of little faith! ²⁹And do not keep striving for what you are to eat and what you are to drink, and do not keep worrying. ³⁰For it is the nations of the world that strive after all these things, and your Father knows that you need them. ³¹Instead, strive for hisᵏ kingdom, and these things will be given to you as well.

32 "Do not be afraid, little flock, for it is your Father's good pleasure to give you the kingdom. ³³Sell your possessions, and give alms. Make purses for yourselves that do not wear out, an unfailing treasure in heaven, where no thief comes near and no moth destroys. ³⁴For where your treasure is, there your heart will be also.

35 "Be dressed for action and have your lamps lit; ³⁶be like those who are waiting for their master to return from the wedding banquet, so that they may open the door for him as soon as he comes and knocks. ³⁷Blessed are those slaves

ʲ Other ancient authorities read
  Consider the lilies; they neither
  spin nor weave
ᵏ Other ancient authorities read God's

οὐδὲ νήθει· λέγω δὲ ὑμῖν, οὐδὲ   Σολομὼν ἐν πάσῃ
NOR   SPIN.   BUT~I SAY TO YOU°, NOT [EVEN] SOLOMON IN ALL

τῇ δόξῃ αὐτοῦ περιεβάλετο ὡς ἓν τούτων. **12.28** εἰ δὲ
THE GLORY OF HIM CLOTHED HIMSELF LIKE ONE OF THESE.   AND~IF

ἐν ἀγρῷ τὸν χόρτον ὄντα σήμερον καὶ αὔριον εἰς
IN A FIELD THE GRASS BEING TODAY AND TOMORROW INTO

κλίβανον βαλλόμενον ὁ θεὸς οὕτως ἀμφιέζει, πόσῳ
AN OVEN   BEING THROWN, - GOD THUS CLOTHES, HOW MUCH

μᾶλλον ὑμᾶς, ὀλιγόπιστοι. **12.29** καὶ ὑμεῖς
MORE   YOU°, O YOU° OF LITTLE FAITH.   AND   YOU°

μὴ ζητεῖτε τί   φάγητε καὶ τί   πίητε   καὶ
DO NOT SEEK WHAT YOU° MAY EAT AND WHAT YOU° MAY DRINK AND

μὴ μετεωρίζεσθε· **12.30** ταῦτα γὰρ πάντα τὰ ἔθνη
DO NOT BE ANXIOUS.   FOR~THESE THINGS ALL THE NATIONS

τοῦ κόσμου ἐπιζητοῦσιν, ὑμῶν δὲ ὁ πατὴρ οἶδεν   ὅτι
OF THE WORLD STRIVE FOR, BUT~YOUR° - FATHER HAS KNOWN THAT

χρῄζετε τούτων. **12.31** πλὴν ζητεῖτε τὴν βασιλείαν
YOU° NEED THESE THINGS.   BUT SEEK   THE KINGDOM

αὐτοῦ, καὶ ταῦτα   προστεθήσεται ὑμῖν.
OF HIM, AND THESE THINGS WILL BE ADDED TO YOU°.

12.32 Μὴ φοβοῦ, τὸ μικρὸν ποίμνιον, ὅτι   εὐδόκησεν
       DO NOT FEAR, - LITTLE FLOCK, BECAUSE WAS WELL PLEASED

ὁ πατὴρ ὑμῶν δοῦναι ὑμῖν τὴν βασιλείαν.
THE FATHER OF YOU° TO GIVE TO YOU° THE KINGDOM.

12.33 Πωλήσατε τὰ ὑπάρχοντα ὑμῶν καὶ δότε
       SELL   THE POSSESSIONS OF YOU° AND GIVE

ἐλεημοσύνην· ποιήσατε ἑαυτοῖς   βαλλάντια μὴ
TO CHARITY.   MAKE   FOR YOURSELVES PURSES NOT

παλαιούμενα, θησαυρὸν ἀνέκλειπτον ἐν τοῖς οὐρανοῖς,
BECOMING OLD, AN INEXHAUSTIBLE~TREASURE IN THE HEAVENS,

ὅπου κλέπτης οὐκ ἐγγίζει οὐδὲ σὴς διαφθείρει·
WHERE A THIEF DOES NOT COME NEAR NOR A MOTH DESTROYS.

12.34 ὅπου γὰρ ἔστιν ὁ θησαυρὸς ὑμῶν, ἐκεῖ καὶ ἡ
       FOR~WHERE IS THE TREASURE OF YOU°, THERE ALSO THE

καρδία ὑμῶν ἔσται.
HEART OF YOU° WILL BE.

12.35 Ἔστωσαν ὑμῶν αἱ ὀσφύες περιεζωσμέναι καὶ
       LET   YOUR - WAISTS HAVING BEEN GIRDED AND

οἱ λύχνοι καιόμενοι· **12.36** καὶ ὑμεῖς   ὅμοιοι
THE LAMPS BURNING.   AND YOU° [SHOULD BE] LIKE

ἀνθρώποις προσδεχομένοις τὸν κύριον ἑαυτῶν   πότε
MEN   WAITING FOR   THE LORD OF THEMSELVES, WHEN

ἀναλύσῃ ἐκ τῶν γάμων,   ἵνα   ἐλθόντος καὶ
HE RETURNS FROM THE WEDDING FEASTS, IN ORDER THAT HAVING COME AND

κρούσαντος εὐθέως ἀνοίξωσιν   αὐτῷ.
HAVING KNOCKED IMMEDIATELY THEY MAY OPEN [THE DOOR] FOR HIM.

12.37 μακάριοι οἱ δοῦλοι ἐκεῖνοι, οὓς ἐλθὼν ὁ
       BLESSED [ARE] - THOSE~SLAVES,   WHOM HAVING COME THE

κύριος   εὑρήσει   γρηγοροῦντας·   ἀμὴν λέγω ὑμῖν ὅτι
LORD   WILL FIND KEEPING WATCH.   TRULY I SAY TO YOU° THAT

περιζώσεται   καὶ   ἀνακλινεῖ   αὐτοὺς   καὶ   παρελθὼν
HE WILL DRESS HIMSELF AND MAKE TO RECLINE THEM AND HAVING COME BESIDE

διακονήσει αὐτοῖς.   **12.38** κἂν   ἐν   τῇ   δευτέρᾳ   κἂν   ἐν   τῇ
HE WILL SERVE THEM.   AND IF IN THE SECOND AND IF IN THE

τρίτῃ φυλακῇ ἔλθῃ   καὶ   εὕρῃ   οὕτως, μακάριοί εἰσιν
THIRD WATCH HE COMES AND HE FINDS [IT] THUS, BLESSED ARE

ἐκεῖνοι.   **12.39** τοῦτο δὲ   γινώσκετε ὅτι εἰ   ᾔδει   ὁ
THOSE.   BUT~THIS KNOW   THAT IF HAD KNOWN THE

οἰκοδεσπότης ποίᾳ ὥρᾳ ὁ   κλέπτης ἔρχεται,
MASTER OF THE HOUSE IN WHAT HOUR THE THIEF   COMES,

οὐκ ἂν ἀφῆκεν   διορυχθῆναι τὸν οἶκον αὐτοῦ.
HE WOULD NOT HAVE ALLOWED TO BE BROKEN INTO THE HOUSE OF HIM.

12.40 καὶ   ὑμεῖς γίνεσθε ἕτοιμοι, ὅτι   ᾗ   ὥρᾳ
        AND   YOU° BE   PREPARED, BECAUSE IN WHAT HOUR

οὐ δοκεῖτε   ὁ   υἱὸς τοῦ ἀνθρώπου ἔρχεται.
YOU° DO NOT THINK, THE SON -   OF MAN   COMES.

12.41 Εἶπεν δὲ   ὁ   Πέτρος, Κύριε, πρὸς ἡμᾶς τὴν
        AND~SAID -   PETER,   LORD,   TO   US   -

παραβολὴν ταύτην λέγεις   ἢ   καὶ   πρὸς πάντας;
THIS~PARABLE   DO YOU SPEAK OR ALSO TO   ALL?

12.42 καὶ   εἶπεν ὁ   κύριος, Τίς ἄρα ἐστὶν ὁ   πιστὸς
        AND   SAID THE LORD,   WHO THEN IS THE FAITHFUL [AND]

οἰκονόμος ὁ φρόνιμος, ὃν   καταστήσει ὁ   κύριος ἐπὶ
²STEWARD - ¹WISE,   WHOM WILL APPOINT THE LORD OVER

τῆς θεραπείας αὐτοῦ τοῦ διδόναι ἐν καιρῷ   [τὸ]
THE SERVANTS OF HIM - TO GIVE IN [THE] PROPER TIME THE

σιτομέτριον;   **12.43** μακάριος ὁ δοῦλος ἐκεῖνος, ὃν
FOOD ALLOWANCE?   BLESSED [IS] - THAT~SLAVE,   WHOM

ἐλθὼν   ὁ   κύριος αὐτοῦ εὑρήσει ποιοῦντα οὕτως.
HAVING COME, THE LORD OF HIM WILL FIND DOING   THUS.

12.44 ἀληθῶς λέγω ὑμῖν ὅτι ἐπὶ   πᾶσιν τοῖς
        TRULY I SAY TO YOU° THAT OVER ALL   THE

ὑπάρχουσιν αὐτοῦ καταστήσει αὐτόν.   **12.45** ἐὰν δὲ   εἴπῃ
POSSESSIONS OF HIM HE WILL APPOINT HIM.   BUT~IF SAYS

ὁ δοῦλος ἐκεῖνος ἐν τῇ καρδίᾳ αὐτοῦ, Χρονίζει ὁ
- THAT~SLAVE   IN THE HEART OF HIM, DELAYS   THE

κύριός μου ἔρχεσθαι, καὶ   ἄρξηται τύπτειν τοὺς
MASTER OF ME TO COME, AND   HE BEGINS TO BEAT THE

παῖδας   καὶ   τὰς παιδίσκας, ἐσθίειν τε   καὶ   πίνειν
MEN SERVANTS AND THE WOMEN SERVANTS, BOTH~TO EAT AND TO DRINK

καὶ   μεθύσκεσθαι, **12.46** ἥξει   ὁ   κύριος τοῦ
AND   TO BECOME DRUNK,   WILL COME THE LORD   -

δούλου ἐκείνου ἐν ἡμέρᾳ ᾗ   οὐ προσδοκᾷ καὶ ἐν
OF THAT~SLAVE   ON A DAY WHICH HE DOES NOT EXPECT AND IN

ὥρᾳ ᾗ   οὐ γινώσκει, καὶ διχοτομήσει αὐτὸν καὶ τὸ
AN HOUR WHICH HE DOES NOT KNOW, AND WILL CUT IN PIECES HIM AND THE

whom the master finds alert when he comes; truly I tell you, he will fasten his belt and have them sit down to eat, and he will come and serve them. [38]If he comes during the middle of the night, or near dawn, and finds them so, blessed are those slaves.

39 "But know this: if the owner of the house had known at what hour the thief was coming, he[l] would not have let his house be broken into. [40]You also must be ready, for the Son of Man is coming at an unexpected hour."

4.1 Peter said, "Lord, are you telling this parable for us or for everyone?" [42]And the Lord said, "Who then is the faithful and prudent manager whom his master will put in charge of his slaves, to give them their allowance of food at the proper time? [43]Blessed is that slave whom his master will find at work when he arrives. [44]Truly I tell you, he will put that one in charge of all his possessions. [45]But if that slave says to himself, 'My master is delayed in coming,' and if he begins to beat the other slaves, men and women, and to eat and drink and get drunk, [46]the master of that slave will come on a day when he does not expect him and at an hour that he does not know, and will cut him in pieces,[m]

[l] Other ancient authorities add *would have watched and*
[m] Or *cut him off*

and put him with the unfaithful. ⁴⁷That slave who knew what his master wanted, but did not prepare himself or do what was wanted, will receive a severe beating. ⁴⁸But the one who did not know and did what deserved a beating will receive a light beating. From everyone to whom much has been given, much will be required; and from the one to whom much has been entrusted, even more will be demanded.

49 "I came to bring fire to the earth, and how I wish it were already kindled! ⁵⁰I have a baptism with which to be baptized, and what stress I am under until it is completed! ⁵¹Do you think that I have come to bring peace to the earth? No, I tell you, but rather division! ⁵²From now on five in one household will be divided, three against two and two against three; ⁵³they will be divided:

father against son
  and son against father,
mother against daughter
  and daughter against mother,
mother-in-law against her daughter-in-law
  and daughter-in-law against mother-in-law."

54 He also said to the crowds, "When you see a cloud rising in the west, you immediately say,

μέρος αὐτοῦ μετὰ τῶν ἀπίστων θήσει.
PORTION OF HIM WITH THE UNBELIEVERS WILL PUT [HIM].

12.47 ἐκεῖνος δὲ ὁ δοῦλος ὁ γνοὺς τὸ θέλημα τοῦ
AND~THAT - SLAVE - HAVING KNOWN THE WILL OF THE

κυρίου αὐτοῦ καὶ μὴ ἑτοιμάσας ἢ ποιήσας πρὸς
LORD OF HIM AND NOT HAVING PREPARED OR HAVING DONE ACCORDING TO

τὸ θέλημα αὐτοῦ δαρήσεται πολλάς· **12.48** ὁ δὲ
THE WILL OF HIM WILL BE BEATEN [WITH] MANY [BLOWS]. BUT~THE ONE

μὴ γνούς, ποιήσας δὲ ἄξια πληγῶν δαρήσεται
NOT HAVING KNOWN BUT~HAVING DONE [THINGS] WORTHY OF BLOWS WILL BE BEATEN

ὀλίγας. παντὶ δὲ ᾧ ἐδόθη πολύ, πολὺ
[WITH] FEW [BLOWS]. BUT~TO EVERYONE TO WHOM MUCH~WAS GIVEN, MUCH

ζητηθήσεται παρ' αὐτοῦ, καὶ ᾧ παρέθεντο πολύ,
WILL BE REQUIRED FROM HIM, AND TO WHOM WAS ENTRUSTED MUCH,

περισσότερον αἰτήσουσιν αὐτόν.
EVEN MORE THEY WILL ASK [FROM] HIM.

12.49 Πῦρ ἦλθον βαλεῖν ἐπὶ τὴν γῆν, καὶ τί θέλω
FIRE I CAME TO THROW ON THE EARTH, AND HOW I WISH

εἰ ἤδη ἀνήφθη. **12.50** βάπτισμα δὲ ἔχω
IF ALREADY IT WAS KINDLED. AND~[THE] BAPTISM I HAVE

βαπτισθῆναι, καὶ πῶς συνέχομαι ἕως ὅτου τελεσθῇ.
TO BE BAPTIZED [WITH], AND HOW I AM DISTRESSED UNTIL IT IS COMPLETED.

12.51 δοκεῖτε ὅτι εἰρήνην παρεγενόμην δοῦναι ἐν τῇ
DO YOU° THINK THAT PEACE I CAME TO BRING ON THE

γῇ; οὐχί, λέγω ὑμῖν, ἀλλ' ἢ διαμερισμόν.
EARTH? NO, I TELL YOU°, BUT RATHER DIVISION.

12.52 ἔσονται γὰρ ἀπὸ τοῦ νῦν πέντε ἐν ἑνὶ οἴκῳ
FOR~THERE WILL BE FROM - NOW FIVE IN ONE HOUSE

διαμεμερισμένοι, τρεῖς ἐπὶ δυσὶν καὶ δύο ἐπὶ
HAVING BEEN DIVIDED, THREE AGAINST TWO AND TWO AGAINST

τρισίν,
THREE,

12.53 διαμερισθήσονται πατὴρ ἐπὶ υἱῷ
WILL BE DIVIDED FATHER AGAINST SON

καὶ υἱὸς ἐπὶ πατρί,
AND SON AGAINST FATHER,

μήτηρ ἐπὶ τὴν θυγατέρα
MOTHER AGAINST THE DAUGHTER

καὶ θυγάτηρ ἐπὶ τὴν μητέρα,
AND DAUGHTER AGAINST THE MOTHER,

πενθερὰ ἐπὶ τὴν νύμφην αὐτῆς
MOTHER-IN-LAW AGAINST THE DAUGHTER-IN-LAW OF HER

καὶ νύμφη ἐπὶ τὴν πενθεράν.
AND DAUGHTER-IN-LAW AGAINST THE MOTHER-IN-LAW.

12.54 Ἔλεγεν δὲ καὶ τοῖς ὄχλοις, Ὅταν ἴδητε [τὴν]
AND~HE WAS SAYING ALSO TO THE CROWDS, WHEN YOU° SEE THE

νεφέλην ἀνατέλλουσαν ἐπὶ δυσμῶν, εὐθέως λέγετε ὅτι
CLOUD RISING OVER [THE] WEST, IMMEDIATELY YOU° SAY -

Ὄμβρος ἔρχεται, καὶ γίνεται οὕτως· **12.55** καὶ
A RAIN STORM   IS COMING,   AND   IT HAPPENS   THUS.   AND

ὅταν   νότον   πνέοντα, λέγετε ὅτι Καύσων ἔσται,
WHEN [THERE IS] A SOUTH WIND BLOWING,   YOU° SAY -   IT WILL BE~HOT,

καὶ γίνεται. **12.56** ὑποκριταί, τὸ πρόσωπον τῆς γῆς
AND   IT HAPPENS.   HYPOCRITES,   THE APPEARANCE OF THE EARTH

καὶ τοῦ οὐρανοῦ οἴδατε   δοκιμάζειν, τὸν καιρὸν
AND THE   SKY   YOU° KNOW [HOW] TO INTERPRET,   -   6TIME

δὲ   τοῦτον πῶς   οὐκ οἴδατε   δοκιμάζειν;
2THEN [THAT] 5THIS   1HOW [IS IT] 3YOU° DO NOT KNOW [HOW] 4TO INTERPRET?

12.57 Τί δὲ καὶ ἀφ᾽ ἑαυτῶν οὐ κρίνετε   τὸ
            AND~WHY ALSO FOR YOURSELVES DO YOU° NOT JUDGE [WHAT IS] -

δίκαιον; **12.58** ὡς γὰρ ὑπάγεις μετὰ τοῦ ἀντιδίκου
RIGHT?   FOR~AS   YOU GO AWAY WITH   THE   OPPONENT

σου ἐπ᾽ ἄρχοντα, ἐν τῇ ὁδῷ δὸς ἐργασίαν
OF YOU TO A RULER,   ON THE ROAD MAKE AN EFFORT

ἀπηλλάχθαι   ἀπ᾽ αὐτοῦ, μήποτε κατασύρῃ σε πρὸς
TO RECEIVE A SETTLEMENT FROM HIM,   LEST   HE DRAG   YOU TO

τὸν κριτήν, καὶ ὁ κριτής σε παραδώσει τῷ   πράκτορι,
THE JUDGE,   AND THE JUDGE WILL HAND OVER~YOU TO THE POLICE OFFICER,

καὶ ὁ πράκτωρ σε βαλεῖ εἰς φυλακήν. **12.59** λέγω
AND THE POLICE OFFICER WILL THROW~YOU INTO JAIL.   I SAY

σοι, οὐ μὴ ἐξέλθῃς   ἐκεῖθεν, ἕως καὶ τὸ ἔσχατον
TO YOU, BY NO MEANS MAY COME OUT THAT ONE,   UNTIL EVEN THE LAST

λεπτὸν ἀποδῷς.
LEPTON   YOU PAY BACK.

'It is going to rain'; and so it happens. 55And when you see the south wind blowing, you say, 'There will be scorching heat'; and it happens. 56You hypocrites! You know how to interpret the appearance of earth and sky, but why do you not know how to interpret the present time?

57 "And why do you not judge for yourselves what is right? 58Thus, when you go with your accuser before a magistrate, on the way make an effort to settle the case,[n] or you may be dragged before the judge, and the judge hand you over to the officer, and the officer throw you in prison. 59I tell you, you will never get out until you have paid the very last penny."

[n] Gk *settle with him*

13.1 Παρῆσαν δέ   τινες ἐν αὐτῷ τῷ   καιρῷ
        NOW~THERE WERE PRESENT SOME   AT THE~SAME   TIME

ἀπαγγέλλοντες αὐτῷ περὶ τῶν Γαλιλαίων ὧν   τὸ
REPORTING   TO HIM ABOUT THE GALILEANS   WHOSE -

αἷμα Πιλᾶτος ἔμιξεν μετὰ τῶν θυσιῶν αὐτῶν.
BLOOD PILATE   MIXED   WITH   THE SACRIFICES OF THEM.

13.2 καὶ ἀποκριθεὶς εἶπεν αὐτοῖς, Δοκεῖτε ὅτι οἱ
      AND HAVING ANSWERED HE SAID TO THEM,   DO YOU° THINK THAT -

Γαλιλαῖοι οὗτοι ἁμαρτωλοὶ παρὰ πάντας τοὺς
THESE~GALILEANS   SINNERS   ABOVE   ALL   THE

Γαλιλαίους ἐγένοντο, ὅτι   ταῦτα πεπόνθασιν;
GALILEANS   WERE,   BECAUSE THEY HAVE SUFFERED~THESE THINGS?

13.3 οὐχί, λέγω ὑμῖν, ἀλλ᾽ ἐὰν μὴ μετανοῆτε
      NO,   I TELL TO YOU°, BUT UNLESS YOU° REPENT,

πάντες ὁμοίως ἀπολεῖσθε. **13.4** ἢ ἐκεῖνοι οἱ δεκαοκτὼ
LIKEWISE~ALL [OF]   YOU° WILL PERISH.   OR THOSE   -   EIGHTEEN

ἐφ᾽ οὓς ἔπεσεν ὁ πύργος ἐν τῷ Σιλωὰμ καὶ
UPON WHOM FELL   THE TOWER   IN -   SILOAM   AND

At that very time there were some present who told him about the Galileans whose blood Pilate had mingled with their sacrifices. 2He asked them, "Do you think that because these Galileans suffered in this way they were worse sinners than all other Galileans? 3No, I tell you; but unless you repent, you will all perish as they did. 4Or those eighteen who were killed when the tower of Siloam fell on them—

do you think that they were worse offenders than all the others living in Jerusalem? [5]No, I tell you; but unless you repent, you will all perish just as they did."

6 Then he told this parable: "A man had a fig tree planted in his vineyard; and he came looking for fruit on it and found none. [7]So he said to the gardener, 'See here! For three years I have come looking for fruit on this fig tree, and still I find none. Cut it down! Why should it be wasting the soil?' [8]He replied, 'Sir, let it alone for one more year, until I dig around it and put manure on it. [9]If it bears fruit next year, well and good; but if not, you can cut it down.'"

10 Now he was teaching in one of the synagogues on the sabbath. [11]And just then there appeared a woman with a spirit that had crippled her for eighteen years. She was bent over and was quite unable to stand up straight. [12]When Jesus saw her, he called her over and said, "Woman, you are set free from your ailment." [13]When he laid his hands on her, immediately she stood up straight and began praising God. [14]But the leader of the synagogue, indignant because Jesus had cured on the sabbath, kept saying to

ἀπέκτεινεν αὐτούς, δοκεῖτε ὅτι αὐτοὶ ὀφειλέται ἐγένοντο
IT KILLED THEM, DO YOU° THINK THAT THEY WERE~SINNERS

παρὰ πάντας τοὺς ἀνθρώπους τοὺς κατοικοῦντας
ABOVE ALL THE MEN - LIVING IN

Ἰερουσαλήμ; **13.5** οὐχί, λέγω ὑμῖν, ἀλλ᾽
JERUSALEM? NO, I TELL YOU°, BUT

ἐὰν μὴ μετανοῆτε πάντες ὡσαύτως ἀπολεῖσθε.
UNLESS YOU° REPENT IN THE SAME WAY~ALL [OF] YOU° WILL PERISH.

13.6 Ἔλεγεν δὲ ταύτην τὴν παραβολήν· Συκῆν
AND~HE WAS SPEAKING THIS - PARABLE. A FIG TREE

εἶχέν τις πεφυτευμένην ἐν τῷ ἀμπελῶνι αὐτοῦ,
HAD A CERTAIN MAN HAVING BEEN PLANTED IN THE VINEYARD OF HIM,

καὶ ἦλθεν ζητῶν καρπὸν ἐν αὐτῇ καὶ οὐχ εὗρεν.
AND HE CAME SEEKING FRUIT ON IT AND HE DID NOT FIND [ANY].

13.7 εἶπεν δὲ πρὸς τὸν ἀμπελουργόν, Ἰδοὺ τρία ἔτη
SO~HE SAID TO THE GARDENER, BEHOLD THREE YEARS

ἀφ᾽ οὗ ἔρχομαι ζητῶν καρπὸν ἐν τῇ συκῇ ταύτῃ καὶ
SINCE I COME SEEKING FRUIT ON - THIS~FIG TREE AND

οὐχ εὑρίσκω· ἔκκοψον [οὖν] αὐτήν, ἱνατί καὶ τὴν γῆν
I DO NOT FIND [ANY]. THEREFORE~CUT DOWN IT, WHY EVEN THE SOIL

καταργεῖ; **13.8** ὁ δὲ ἀποκριθεὶς λέγει αὐτῷ, Κύριε,
IS IT USING UP? - BUT HAVING ANSWERED HE SAYS TO HIM, LORD,

ἄφες αὐτὴν καὶ τοῦτο τὸ ἔτος, ἕως ὅτου σκάψω περὶ
LEAVE IT ALSO THIS - YEAR, UNTIL I MAY DIG AROUND

αὐτὴν καὶ βάλω κόπρια, **13.9** κἂν μὲν ποιήσῃ
IT AND MAY THROW MANURE [ON IT], AND IF INDEED IT PRODUCES

καρπὸν εἰς τὸ μέλλον· εἰ δὲ μή γε, ἐκκόψεις αὐτήν.
FRUIT IN THE FUTURE; OTHERWISE, YOU WILL CUT DOWN IT.

13.10 Ἦν δὲ διδάσκων ἐν μιᾷ τῶν συναγωγῶν ἐν τοῖς
NOW~HE WAS TEACHING IN ONE OF THE SYNAGOGUES ON THE

σάββασιν. **13.11** καὶ ἰδοὺ γυνὴ πνεῦμα ἔχουσα
SABBATHS. AND BEHOLD A WOMAN HAVING~A SPIRIT

ἀσθενείας ἔτη δεκαοκτὼ καὶ ἦν συγκύπτουσα καὶ
OF ILLNESS EIGHTEEN~YEARS AND SHE WAS BEING BENT DOUBLE AND

μὴ δυναμένη ἀνακύψαι εἰς τὸ παντελές.
NOT BEING ABLE TO STAND UPRIGHT COMPLETELY.

13.12 ἰδὼν δὲ αὐτὴν ὁ Ἰησοῦς προσεφώνησεν καὶ
AND~HAVING SEEN HER, - JESUS CALLED OUT AND

εἶπεν αὐτῇ, Γύναι, ἀπολέλυσαι τῆς ἀσθενείας
SAID TO HER, WOMAN, YOU HAVE BEEN SET FREE FROM THE ILLNESS

σου, **13.13** καὶ ἐπέθηκεν αὐτῇ τὰς χεῖρας· καὶ
OF YOU, AND HE PLACED UPON HER THE(HIS) HANDS. AND

παραχρῆμα ἀνωρθώθη καὶ ἐδόξαζεν τὸν θεόν.
IMMEDIATELY SHE WAS RESTORED AND SHE WAS GLORIFYING - GOD.

13.14 ἀποκριθεὶς δὲ ὁ ἀρχισυνάγωγος, ἀγανακτῶν ὅτι
AND~HAVING ANSWERED THE SYNAGOGUE RULER, BEING INDIGNANT THAT

τῷ σαββάτῳ ἐθεράπευσεν ὁ Ἰησοῦς, ἔλεγεν τῷ
ON THE SABBATH ²HEALED - ¹JESUS, HE WAS SAYING TO

ὄχλῳ ὅτι Ἐξ ἡμέραι εἰσὶν ἐν αἷς δεῖ
THE CROWD - SIX DAYS THERE ARE IN WHICH IT IS NECESSARY

ἐργάζεσθαι· ἐν αὐταῖς οὖν ἐρχόμενοι θεραπεύεσθε
TO WORK. ON THEM THEREFORE COMING, BE HEALED

καὶ μὴ τῇ ἡμέρᾳ τοῦ σαββάτου. **13.15** ἀπεκρίθη δὲ
AND NOT ON THE DAY OF THE SABBATH. AND~ANSWERED

αὐτῷ ὁ κύριος καὶ εἶπεν, Ὑποκριταί, ἕκαστος ὑμῶν
HIM THE LORD AND SAID, HYPOCRITES, EACH OF YOU*

τῷ σαββάτῳ οὐ λύει τὸν βοῦν αὐτοῦ ἢ τὸν ὄνον
ON THE SABBATH DOES HE NOT UNTIE THE OX OF HIM OR THE DONKEY

ἀπὸ τῆς φάτνης καὶ ἀπαγαγὼν ποτίζει;
FROM THE MANGER AND HAVING LED IT AWAY, IT DRINKS?

13.16 ταύτην δὲ θυγατέρα Ἀβραὰμ οὖσαν, ἣν
BUT~THIS ONE A DAUGHTER OF ABRAHAM BEING, WHOM

ἔδησεν ὁ Σατανᾶς ἰδοὺ δέκα καὶ ὀκτὼ ἔτη,
²BOUND - ¹SATAN BEHOLD TEN AND EIGHT YEARS,

οὐκ ἔδει λυθῆναι ἀπὸ τοῦ δεσμοῦ τούτου
WAS IT NOT NECESSARY [FOR HER] TO BE SET FREE FROM - THIS~BOND

τῇ ἡμέρᾳ τοῦ σαββάτου; **13.17** καὶ ταῦτα λέγοντος
ON THE DAY OF THE SABBATH? AND ²[BY] SAYING~THESE THINGS

αὐτοῦ κατῃσχύνοντο πάντες οἱ ἀντικείμενοι
¹HE [BY], WERE BEING PUT TO SHAME ALL THE ONES BEING OPPOSED

αὐτῷ, καὶ πᾶς ὁ ὄχλος ἔχαιρεν ἐπὶ πᾶσιν τοῖς
TO HIM, AND ALL THE CROWD WAS REJOICING OVER ALL THE

ἐνδόξοις τοῖς γινομένοις ὑπ᾽ αὐτοῦ.
GLORIOUS THINGS - BEING ACCOMPLISHED BY HIM.

13.18 Ἔλεγεν οὖν, Τίνι ὁμοία ἐστὶν ἡ
THEREFORE~HE WAS SAYING, TO WHAT COMPARISON IS THE

βασιλεία τοῦ θεοῦ καὶ τίνι ὁμοιώσω αὐτήν;
KINGDOM - OF GOD AND TO WHAT WILL I COMPARE IT?

13.19 ὁμοία ἐστὶν κόκκῳ σινάπεως, ὃν λαβὼν
IT IS~LIKE A MUSTARD~SEED, WHICH HAVING TAKEN

ἄνθρωπος ἔβαλεν εἰς κῆπον ἑαυτοῦ, καὶ ηὔξησεν καὶ
A MAN THREW INTO A GARDEN OF HIMSELF, AND IT GREW AND

ἐγένετο εἰς δένδρον, καὶ τὰ πετεινὰ τοῦ οὐρανοῦ
BECAME - A TREE, AND THE BIRDS OF THE SKY

κατεσκήνωσεν ἐν τοῖς κλάδοις αὐτοῦ.
NESTED IN THE BRANCHES OF IT.

13.20 Καὶ πάλιν εἶπεν, Τίνι ὁμοιώσω τὴν
AND AGAIN HE SAID, TO WHAT WILL I COMPARE THE

βασιλείαν τοῦ θεοῦ; **13.21** ὁμοία ἐστὶν ζύμῃ, ἣν
KINGDOM - OF GOD? IT IS~LIKE LEAVEN, WHICH

λαβοῦσα γυνὴ [ἐν]έκρυψεν εἰς ἀλεύρου σάτα τρία
A WOMAN~HAVING TAKEN, HID IN WHEAT FLOUR THREE~MEASURES

ἕως οὗ ἐζυμώθη ὅλον.
UNTIL [THE] WHOLE [BATCH]~WAS LEAVENED.

13.22 Καὶ διεπορεύετο κατὰ πόλεις καὶ κώμας
AND HE WAS TRAVELING THROUGHOUT CITIES AND VILLAGES

the crowd, "There are six days on which work ought to be done; come on those days and be cured, and not on the sabbath day." ¹⁵But the Lord answered him and said, "You hypocrites! Does not each of you on the sabbath untie his ox or his donkey from the manger, and lead it away to give it water? ¹⁶And ought not this woman, a daughter of Abraham whom Satan bound for eighteen long years, be set free from this bondage on the sabbath day?" ¹⁷When he said this, all his opponents were put to shame; and the entire crowd was rejoicing at all the wonderful things that he was doing.

18 He said therefore, "What is the kingdom of God like? And to what should I compare it? ¹⁹It is like a mustard seed that someone took and sowed in the garden; it grew and became a tree, and the birds of the air made nests in its branches."

20 And again he said, "To what should I compare the kingdom of God? ²¹It is like yeast that a woman took and mixed in with° three measures of flour until all of it was leavened."

22 Jesusᵖ went through one town and village after

° Gk *hid in*
ᵖ Gk *He*

another, teaching as he made
his way to Jerusalem.
23Someone asked him,
"Lord, will only a few be
saved?" He said to them,
24"Strive to enter through the
narrow door; for many, I tell
you, will try to enter and will
not be able. 25When once
the owner of the house has
got up and shut the door, and
you begin to stand outside
and to knock at the door,
saying, 'Lord, open to us,'
then in reply he will say to
you, 'I do not know where
you come from.' 26Then you
will begin to say, 'We ate
and drank with you, and you
taught in our streets.' 27But
he will say, 'I do not know
where you come from; go
away from me, all you
evildoers!' 28There will be
weeping and gnashing of
teeth when you see Abraham
and Isaac and Jacob and all
the prophets in the kingdom
of God, and you yourselves
thrown out. 29Then people
will come from east and
west, from north and south,
and will eat in the kingdom
of God. 30Indeed, some are
last who will be first, and
some are first who will be
last."

31 At that very hour some
Pharisees came and said to
him, "Get away from here,
for Herod wants to kill
you." 32He said to them,

διδάσκων καὶ πορείαν ποιούμενος εἰς Ἱεροσόλυμα.
TEACHING   AND   MAKING~[HIS] WAY   TO   JERUSALEM.

13.23 εἶπεν δέ τις αὐτῷ, Κύριε, εἰ ὀλίγοι οἱ
AND~SAID   SOMEONE TO HIM,   LORD,   IF   FEW [ARE]   THE ONES

σῳζόμενοι; ὁ δὲ εἶπεν πρὸς αὐτούς, **13.24** Ἀγωνίζεσθε
BEING SAVED?   -   AND HE SAID   TO   THEM,   STRIVE

εἰσελθεῖν διὰ τῆς στενῆς θύρας, ὅτι πολλοί, λέγω
TO ENTER   THROUGH THE   NARROW   DOOR,   BECAUSE MANY,   I SAY

ὑμῖν, ζητήσουσιν εἰσελθεῖν καὶ οὐκ ἰσχύσουσιν.
TO YOU°,   WILL SEEK   TO ENTER   AND   THEY WILL NOT BE ABLE TO.

13.25 ἀφ' οὗ ἂν ἐγερθῇ ὁ οἰκοδεσπότης καὶ ἀποκλείσῃ
AFTER   HAS ARISEN THE   MASTER OF THE HOUSE   AND   HE CLOSES

τὴν θύραν καὶ ἄρξησθε ἔξω ἑστάναι καὶ κρούειν τὴν
THE   DOOR   AND   YOU° BEGIN   TO STAND~OUTSIDE   AND   TO KNOCK [ON]   THE

θύραν λέγοντες, Κύριε, ἄνοιξον ἡμῖν, καὶ ἀποκριθεὶς
DOOR   SAYING,   LORD,   OPEN [UP]   FOR US,   AND   HAVING ANSWERED

ἐρεῖ ὑμῖν, Οὐκ οἶδα ὑμᾶς πόθεν ἐστέ. **13.26** τότε
HE WILL SAY TO YOU°,   I DO NOT KNOW   YOU°   FROM WHERE YOU° ARE.   THEN

ἄρξεσθε λέγειν, Ἐφάγομεν ἐνώπιόν σου καὶ ἐπίομεν,
YOU° WILL BEGIN   TO SAY,   WE ATE   BEFORE   YOU   AND   WE DRANK,

καὶ ἐν ταῖς πλατείαις ἡμῶν ἐδίδαξας· **13.27** καὶ
AND   IN   THE   STREETS   OF US   YOU TAUGHT.   AND

ἐρεῖ λέγων ὑμῖν, Οὐκ οἶδα [ὑμᾶς] πόθεν ἐστέ·
HE WILL SPEAK SAYING   TO YOU°,   I DO NOT KNOW   YOU°   FROM WHERE YOU° ARE.

ἀπόστητε ἀπ' ἐμοῦ, πάντες ἐργάται ἀδικίας.
GO AWAY   FROM   ME,   ALL   WORKERS   OF UNRIGHTEOUSNESS.

13.28 ἐκεῖ ἔσται ὁ κλαυθμὸς καὶ ὁ βρυγμὸς τῶν
THERE   WILL BE   -   WEEPING   AND   -   GNASHING   OF THE

ὀδόντων, ὅταν ὄψησθε Ἀβραὰμ καὶ Ἰσαὰκ καὶ
TEETH,   WHEN   YOU° WILL SEE   ABRAHAM   AND   ISAAC   AND

Ἰακὼβ καὶ πάντας τοὺς προφήτας ἐν τῇ βασιλείᾳ τοῦ
JACOB   AND   ALL   THE   PROPHETS   IN   THE   KINGDOM   -

θεοῦ, ὑμᾶς δὲ ἐκβαλλομένους ἔξω. **13.29** καὶ
OF GOD,   BUT~YOU°   BEING THROWN OUT   OUTSIDE.   AND

ἥξουσιν ἀπὸ ἀνατολῶν καὶ δυσμῶν καὶ ἀπὸ βορρᾶ
THEY WILL COME   FROM   EAST   AND   WEST   AND   FROM   NORTH

καὶ νότου καὶ ἀνακλιθήσονται ἐν τῇ βασιλείᾳ τοῦ
AND   SOUTH   AND   THEY WILL RECLINE AT TABLE   IN   THE   KINGDOM   -

θεοῦ. **13.30** καὶ ἰδοὺ εἰσὶν ἔσχατοι οἳ ἔσονται πρῶτοι
OF GOD.   AND   BEHOLD THERE ARE   LAST ONES   WHO WILL BE   FIRST

καὶ εἰσὶν πρῶτοι οἳ ἔσονται ἔσχατοι.
AND   THERE ARE   FIRST ONES   WHO WILL BE   LAST.

13.31 Ἐν αὐτῇ τῇ ὥρᾳ προσῆλθάν τινες Φαρισαῖοι
IN   THE~SAME   HOUR   APPROACHED   SOME   PHARISEES

λέγοντες αὐτῷ, Ἔξελθε καὶ πορεύου ἐντεῦθεν, ὅτι
SAYING   TO HIM,   DEPART   AND   GO   FROM HERE,   BECAUSE

Ἡρῴδης θέλει σε ἀποκτεῖναι. **13.32** καὶ εἶπεν αὐτοῖς,
HEROD   WANTS   TO KILL~YOU.   AND   HE SAID   TO THEM,

Πορευθέντες εἴπατε τῇ ἀλώπεκι ταύτῃ, Ἰδοὺ ἐκβάλλω
HAVING GONE   TELL   -   THIS~FOX,   BEHOLD I CAST OUT

δαιμόνια καὶ ἰάσεις ἀποτελῶ σήμερον καὶ αὔριον καὶ
DEMONS   AND I PERFORM~HEALINGS TODAY   AND TOMORROW AND

τῇ τρίτῃ τελειοῦμαι. **13.33** πλὴν δεῖ   με
ON THE THIRD [DAY] I WILL BE FINISHED.   BUT   IT IS NECESSARY FOR ME

σήμερον καὶ αὔριον καὶ τῇ ἐχομένῃ πορεύεσθαι,
TODAY   AND TOMORROW AND THE ONE FOLLOWING TO TRAVEL,

ὅτι   οὐκ ἐνδέχεται προφήτην ἀπολέσθαι ἔξω
BECAUSE IT IS NOT POSSIBLE [FOR] A PROPHET   TO DIE   OUTSIDE

Ἰερουσαλήμ. **13.34** Ἰερουσαλὴμ Ἰερουσαλήμ, ἡ
JERUSALEM.   JERUSALEM,   JERUSALEM,   THE ONE

ἀποκτείνουσα τοὺς προφήτας καὶ λιθοβολοῦσα τοὺς
KILLING   THE   PROPHETS   AND STONING   ·   THE ONES

ἀπεσταλμένους πρὸς αὐτήν, ποσάκις ἠθέλησα
HAVING BEEN SENT TO   HER,   HOW OFTEN   I WANTED

ἐπισυνάξαι τὰ τέκνα σου ὃν τρόπον   ὄρνις τὴν
TO GATHER   THE CHILDREN OF YOU IN [THE] MANNER~WHICH A HEN   -

ἑαυτῆς νοσσιὰν ὑπὸ τὰς πτέρυγας, καὶ
HER   CHICKS [GATHERS] UNDER THE(HER) WINGS,   AND

οὐκ ἠθελήσατε. **13.35** ἰδοὺ ἀφίεται ὑμῖν ὁ οἶκος
YOU° WERE NOT WILLING.   BEHOLD IS LEFT TO YOU° THE HOUSE

ὑμῶν. λέγω [δὲ] ὑμῖν, οὐ μὴ ἴδητέ   με ἕως
OF YOU°. BUT~I SAY   TO YOU°, YOU° MAY BY NO MEANS SEE ME UNTIL

[ἥξει   ὅτε] εἴπητε, Εὐλογημένος ὁ
WILL COME [THE TIME] WHEN YOU° MAY SAY, HAVING BEEN BLESSED [IS] THE ONE

ἐρχόμενος ἐν ὀνόματι κυρίου.
COMING   IN [THE] NAME OF [THE] LORD.

"Go and tell that fox for me,*q* 'Listen, I am casting out demons and performing cures today and tomorrow, and on the third day I finish my work. [33]Yet today, tomorrow, and the next day I must be on my way, because it is impossible for a prophet to be killed outside of Jerusalem.' [34]Jerusalem, Jerusalem, the city that kills the prophets and stones those who are sent to it! How often have I desired to gather your children together as a hen gathers her brood under her wings, and you were not willing! [35]See, your house is left to you. And I tell you, you will not see me until the time comes when*r* you say, 'Blessed is the one who comes in the name of the Lord.'"

q Gk lacks *for me*
r Other ancient authorities lack *the time comes when*

14.1 Καὶ ἐγένετο ἐν τῷ ἐλθεῖν αὐτὸν εἰς οἶκόν
AND IT CAME TO PASS WHILE   HE~WENT   INTO A HOUSE

τινος   τῶν ἀρχόντων [τῶν] Φαρισαίων σαββάτῳ
OF A CERTAIN ONE OF THE LEADERS   OF THE PHARISEES   ON [THE] SABBATH

φαγεῖν ἄρτον καὶ αὐτοὶ ἦσαν παρατηρούμενοι αὐτόν.
TO EAT   BREAD   AND THEY WERE WATCHING CLOSELY   HIM.

14.2 καὶ ἰδοὺ ἄνθρωπός τις ἦν ὑδρωπικὸς
AND BEHOLD A CERTAIN~MAN   WAS SUFFERING FROM DROPSY

ἔμπροσθεν αὐτοῦ. **14.3** καὶ ἀποκριθεὶς ὁ Ἰησοῦς εἶπεν
IN FRONT OF   HIM.   AND HAVING ANSWERED   - JESUS   SPOKE

πρὸς τοὺς νομικοὺς καὶ Φαρισαίους λέγων, Ἔξεστιν
TO   THE   LAWYERS   AND PHARISEES   SAYING, IS IT PERMISSIBLE

τῷ σαββάτῳ θεραπεῦσαι ἢ οὔ; **14.4** οἱ δὲ ἡσύχασαν.
ON THE SABBATH   TO HEAL   OR NOT?   -   BUT THEY WERE SILENT.

On one occasion when Jesus*s* was going to the house of a leader of the Pharisees to eat a meal on the sabbath, they were watching him closely. [2]Just then, in front of him, there was a man who had dropsy. [3]And Jesus asked the lawyers and Pharisees, "Is it lawful to cure people on the sabbath, or not?" [4]But they

s Gk *he*

13:35 Ps. 118:26

were silent. So Jesus' took him and healed him, and sent him away. ⁵Then he said to them, "If one of you has a child*ᵘ* or an ox that has fallen into a well, will you not immediately pull it out on a sabbath day?" ⁶And they could not reply to this.

7 When he noticed how the guests chose the places of honor, he told them a parable. ⁸"When you are invited by someone to a wedding banquet, do not sit down at the place of honor, in case someone more distinguished than you has been invited by your host; ⁹and the host who invited both of you may come and say to you, 'Give this person your place,' and then in disgrace you would start to take the lowest place. ¹⁰But when you are invited, go and sit down at the lowest place, so that when your host comes, he may say to you, 'Friend, move up higher'; then you will be honored in the presence of all who sit at the table with you. ¹¹For all who exalt themselves will be humbled, and those who humble themselves will be exalted."

12 He said also to the one who had invited him, "When you give a luncheon or a dinner, do not invite your friends or your brothers or your relatives or rich neighbors, in case they may invite you in return,

ᵗ Gk *he*
ᵘ Other ancient authorities read *a donkey*

καὶ ἐπιλαβόμενος ἰάσατο αὐτὸν καὶ ἀπέλυσεν.
AND HAVING TAKEN HOLD [OF HIM] HE HEALED HIM AND SENT [HIM] AWAY.

14.5 καὶ πρὸς αὐτοὺς εἶπεν, Τίνος ὑμῶν ⌐υἱὸς ἢ
AND TO THEM HE SAID, WHO OF YOU° [HAVING] A SON OR

βοῦς⌐ εἰς φρέαρ πεσεῖται, καὶ οὐκ εὐθέως ἀνασπάσει
AN OX INTO A WELL WILL FALL, AND NOT IMMEDIATELY WILL LIFT OUT

αὐτὸν ἐν ἡμέρᾳ τοῦ σαββάτου; **14.6** καὶ οὐκ ἴσχυσαν
HIM ON [THE] DAY OF THE SABBATH? AND THEY WERE NOT ABLE

ἀνταποκριθῆναι πρὸς ταῦτα.
TO MAKE A REPLY AGAINST THESE THINGS.

14.7 Ἔλεγεν δὲ πρὸς τοὺς κεκλημένους
AND~HE WAS SPEAKING TO THE ONES HAVING BEEN INVITED,

παραβολήν, ἐπέχων πῶς τὰς πρωτοκλισίας ἐξελέγοντο,
A PARABLE, NOTICING HOW THE PLACES OF HONOR THEY WERE CHOOSING,

λέγων πρὸς αὐτούς, **14.8** Ὅταν κληθῇς ὑπό τινος εἰς
SAYING TO THEM, WHEN YOU ARE INVITED BY SOMEONE TO

γάμους, μὴ κατακλιθῇς εἰς τὴν πρωτοκλισίαν,
WEDDING FESTIVITIES, YOU SHOULD NOT RECLINE AT TABLE IN THE PLACES OF HONOR,

μήποτε ἐντιμότερός σου ᾖ κεκλημένος ὑπ᾽
LEST A MORE DISTINGUISHED [PERSON] [THAN] YOU MAY HAVE BEEN INVITED BY

αὐτοῦ, **14.9** καὶ ἐλθὼν ὁ σὲ καὶ αὐτὸν καλέσας
HIM AND HAVING COME THE ONE ²YOU ³AND ⁴HE ¹HAVING INVITED

ἐρεῖ σοι, Δὸς τούτῳ τόπον, καὶ τότε ἄρξῃ
WILL SAY TO YOU, GIVE TO THIS ONE [YOUR] PLACE, AND THEN YOU WILL BEGIN

μετὰ αἰσχύνης τὸν ἔσχατον τόπον κατέχειν. **14.10** ἀλλ᾽
WITH SHAME THE LAST PLACE TO OCCUPY. BUT

ὅταν κληθῇς, πορευθεὶς ἀνάπεσε εἰς τὸν ἔσχατον
WHEN YOU ARE INVITED HAVING GONE RECLINE IN THE LAST

τόπον, ἵνα ὅταν ἔλθῃ ὁ κεκληκώς σε ἐρεῖ σοι,
PLACE, SO THAT WHEN COMES THE ONE HAVING INVITED YOU HE WILL SAY TO YOU,

Φίλε, προσανάβηθι ἀνώτερον· τότε ἔσται σοι δόξα
FRIEND, GO UP TO A HIGHER [PLACE]; THEN WILL BE TO YOU GLORY

ἐνώπιον πάντων τῶν συνανακειμένων σοι. **14.11** ὅτι
BEFORE ALL THE ONES RECLINING AT TABLE WITH YOU. BECAUSE

πᾶς ὁ ὑψῶν ἑαυτὸν ταπεινωθήσεται, καὶ ὁ
EVERYONE - EXALTING HIMSELF WILL BE HUMBLED, AND THE ONE

ταπεινῶν ἑαυτὸν ὑψωθήσεται. **14.12** Ἔλεγεν δὲ καὶ
HUMBLING HIMSELF WILL BE EXALTED. AND~HE WAS SPEAKING ALSO

τῷ κεκληκότι αὐτόν, Ὅταν ποιῇς ἄριστον ἢ
TO THE ONE HAVING INVITED HIM, WHEN YOU PREPARE A LUNCHEON OR

δεῖπνον, μὴ φώνει τοὺς φίλους σου μηδὲ τοὺς
A DINNER, DO NOT CALL THE FRIENDS OF YOU NOR THE

ἀδελφούς σου μηδὲ τοὺς συγγενεῖς σου μηδὲ
BROTHERS OF YOU NOR THE ONES RELATED TO YOU NOR

γείτονας πλουσίους, μήποτε καὶ αὐτοὶ ἀντικαλέσωσίν
RICH~NEIGHBORS, LEST ALSO THEY SHOULD INVITE IN RETURN

14:5 text: ASVmg RSV NASB NIV NEBmg TEV NJB NRSV. var. ονος η βους (a donkey or an ox): KJV ASV RSVmg NIVmg NJBmg NRSVmg.

σε καὶ γένηται ἀνταπόδομά σοι. **14.13** ἀλλ᾽
YOU AND IT BECOME REPAYMENT TO YOU. BUT

ὅταν δοχὴν ποιῇς, κάλει πτωχούς, ἀναπείρους,
WHEN YOU PREPARE~A BANQUET, INVITE [THE] POOR, [THE] CRIPPLED,

χωλούς, τυφλούς· **14.14** καὶ μακάριος ἔσῃ,
[THE] LAME, [THE] BLIND; AND YOU WILL BE~BLESSED,

ὅτι οὐκ ἔχουσιν ἀνταποδοῦναί σοι,
BECAUSE THEY DO NOT HAVE [THE MEANS] TO REPAY YOU,

ἀνταποδοθήσεται γάρ σοι ἐν τῇ ἀναστάσει τῶν
FOR~IT WILL BE REPAID TO YOU IN THE RESURRECTION OF THE

δικαίων.
RIGHTEOUS.

14.15 Ἀκούσας δέ τις τῶν συνανακειμένων
AND~HAVING HEARD ²A CERTAIN ONE ³OF THE ONES ⁴RECLINING AT TABLE WITH HIM

ταῦτα εἶπεν αὐτῷ, Μακάριος ὅστις φάγεται ἄρτον
¹THESE THINGS SAID TO HIM, BLESSED [IS HE] WHO WILL EAT BREAD

ἐν τῇ βασιλείᾳ τοῦ θεοῦ. **14.16** ὁ δὲ εἶπεν αὐτῷ,
IN THE KINGDOM - OF GOD. - AND HE SAID TO HIM,

Ἄνθρωπός τις ἐποίει δεῖπνον μέγα, καὶ ἐκάλεσεν
A CERTAIN~MAN WAS PREPARING A BIG~DINNER, AND HE INVITED

πολλούς **14.17** καὶ ἀπέστειλεν τὸν δοῦλον αὐτοῦ τῇ
MANY, AND HE SENT THE SLAVE OF HIM AT THE

ὥρᾳ τοῦ δείπνου εἰπεῖν τοῖς κεκλημένοις,
HOUR OF THE DINNER TO SAY TO THE ONES HAVING BEEN INVITED,

Ἔρχεσθε, ὅτι ἤδη ἕτοιμά ἐστιν. **14.18** καὶ ἤρξαντο
COME, BECAUSE NOW IT IS~READY. AND BEGAN

ἀπὸ μιᾶς πάντες παραιτεῖσθαι. ὁ πρῶτος εἶπεν
UNANIMOUSLY ALL TO BE EXCUSED. THE FIRST SAID

αὐτῷ, Ἀγρὸν ἠγόρασα καὶ ἔχω ἀνάγκην ἐξελθὼν
TO HIM, I BOUGHT~A FIELD AND I AM COMPELLED HAVING GONE OUT

ἰδεῖν αὐτόν· ἐρωτῶ σε, ἔχε με παρῃτημένον.
TO SEE IT. I ASK YOU, HAVE ME HAVING BEEN EXCUSED.

14.19 καὶ ἕτερος εἶπεν, Ζεύγη βοῶν ἠγόρασα πέντε
AND ANOTHER SAID, ²PAIR ³OF OXEN ⁴I BOUGHT ¹FIVE

καὶ πορεύομαι δοκιμάσαι αὐτά· ἐρωτῶ σε, ἔχε με
AND I AM GOING TO EXAMINE THEM. I ASK YOU, HAVE ME

παρῃτημένον. **14.20** καὶ ἕτερος εἶπεν, Γυναῖκα ἔγημα
HAVING BEEN EXCUSED. AND ANOTHER SAID, I MARRIED~A WOMAN

καὶ διὰ τοῦτο οὐ δύναμαι ἐλθεῖν. **14.21** καὶ
AND THEREFORE I AM NOT ABLE TO COME. AND

παραγενόμενος ὁ δοῦλος ἀπήγγειλεν τῷ κυρίῳ αὐτοῦ
HAVING ARRIVED THE SLAVE REPORTED TO THE LORD OF HIM

ταῦτα. τότε ὀργισθεὶς ὁ οἰκοδεσπότης εἶπεν τῷ
THESE THINGS. THEN HAVING BEEN ANGRY THE MASTER OF THE HOUSE SAID TO THE

δούλῳ αὐτοῦ, Ἔξελθε ταχέως εἰς τὰς πλατείας καὶ
SLAVE OF HIM, GO OUT QUICKLY INTO THE STREETS AND

ῥύμας τῆς πόλεως καὶ τοὺς πτωχοὺς καὶ ἀναπείρους
LANES OF THE CITY AND THE POOR AND [THE] CRIPPLED

and you would be repaid. [13]But when you give a banquet, invite the poor, the crippled, the lame, and the blind. [14]And you will be blessed, because they cannot repay you, for you will be repaid at the resurrection of the righteous."

15 One of the dinner guests, on hearing this, said to him, "Blessed is anyone who will eat bread in the kingdom of God!" [16]Then Jesus[v] said to him, "Someone gave a great dinner and invited many. [17]At the time for the dinner he sent his slave to say to those who had been invited, 'Come; for everything is ready now.' [18]But they all alike began to make excuses. The first said to him, 'I have bought a piece of land, and I must go out and see it; please accept my regrets.' [19]Another said, 'I have bought five yoke of oxen, and I am going to try them out; please accept my regrets.' [20]Another said, 'I have just been married, and therefore I cannot come.' [21]So the slave returned and reported this to his master. Then the owner of the house became angry and said to his slave, 'Go out at once into the streets and lanes of the town and bring in the poor,

[v] Gk *he*

the crippled, the blind, and the lame.' ²²And the slave said, 'Sir, what you ordered has been done, and there is still room.' ²³Then the master said to the slave, 'Go out into the roads and lanes, and compel people to come in, so that my house may be filled. ²⁴For I tell you,ʷ none of those who were invited will taste my dinner.' "

25 Now large crowds were traveling with him; and he turned and said to them, ²⁶"Whoever comes to me and does not hate father and mother, wife and children, brothers and sisters, yes, and even life itself, cannot be my disciple. ²⁷Whoever does not carry the cross and follow me cannot be my disciple. ²⁸For which of you, intending to build a tower, does not first sit down and estimate the cost, to see whether he has enough to complete it? ²⁹Otherwise, when he has laid a foundation and is not able to finish, all who see it will begin to ridicule him, ³⁰saying, 'This fellow began to build and was not able to finish.' ³¹Or what king, going out to wage war against another king, will not sit down first and consider whether he is able with ten thousand

ʷ The Greek word for *you* here is plural

καὶ τυφλοὺς καὶ χωλοὺς εἰσάγαγε ὧδε. **14.22** καὶ
AND [THE] BLIND AND [THE] LAME BRING [THEM] IN HERE. AND

εἶπεν ὁ δοῦλος, Κύριε, γέγονεν ὃ ἐπέταξας, καὶ
SAID THE SLAVE, LORD, HAS BEEN DONE WHAT YOU COMMANDED, AND

ἔτι τόπος ἐστίν. **14.23** καὶ εἶπεν ὁ κύριος πρὸς τὸν
STILL THERE IS~A PLACE. AND SAID THE LORD TO THE

δοῦλον, Ἔξελθε εἰς τὰς ὁδοὺς καὶ φραγμοὺς καὶ
SLAVE, GO OUT TO THE ROADWAYS AND FENCES AND

ἀνάγκασον εἰσελθεῖν, ἵνα γεμισθῇ μου ὁ οἶκος·
URGE [THEM] TO COME IN, IN ORDER THAT MAY BE FILLED MY - HOUSE.

14.24 λέγω γὰρ ὑμῖν ὅτι οὐδεὶς τῶν ἀνδρῶν ἐκείνων τῶν
FOR~I SAY TO YOU° THAT NO ONE - OF THOSE~MEN

κεκλημένων γεύσεταί μου τοῦ δείπνου.
HAVING BEEN INVITED WILL TASTE MY - DINNER.

14.25 Συνεπορεύοντο δὲ αὐτῷ ὄχλοι πολλοί, καὶ
AND~WERE ACCOMPANYING HIM A LARGE~CROWD, AND

στραφεὶς εἶπεν πρὸς αὐτούς, **14.26** Εἴ τις ἔρχεται
HAVING TURNED HE SAID TO THEM, IF SOMEONE COMES

πρός με καὶ οὐ μισεῖ τὸν πατέρα ἑαυτοῦ καὶ τὴν
TO ME AND DOES NOT HATE THE FATHER OF HIMSELF AND THE

μητέρα καὶ τὴν γυναῖκα καὶ τὰ τέκνα καὶ τοὺς
MOTHER AND THE WIFE AND THE CHILDREN AND THE

ἀδελφοὺς καὶ τὰς ἀδελφὰς ἔτι τε καὶ τὴν ψυχὴν
BROTHERS AND THE SISTERS AND~IN ADDITION ALSO THE LIFE

ἑαυτοῦ, οὐ δύναται εἶναί μου μαθητής. **14.27** ὅστις
OF HIMSELF, HE IS NOT ABLE TO BE MY DISCIPLE. WHOEVER

οὐ βαστάζει τὸν σταυρὸν ἑαυτοῦ καὶ ἔρχεται ὀπίσω
DOES NOT CARRY THE CROSS OF HIMSELF AND COMES AFTER

μου, οὐ δύναται εἶναί μου μαθητής. **14.28** τίς γὰρ ἐξ
ME, IS NOT ABLE TO BE MY DISCIPLE. FOR~WHO AMONG

ὑμῶν θέλων πύργον οἰκοδομῆσαι οὐχὶ πρῶτον
YOU° WANTING TO BUILD~A TOWER [WILL] NOT FIRST

καθίσας ψηφίζει τὴν δαπάνην, εἰ ἔχει εἰς
HAVING SAT DOWN FIGURE OUT THE COST, IF HE HAS [ENOUGH] FOR

ἀπαρτισμόν; **14.29** ἵνα μήποτε θέντος αὐτοῦ θεμέλιον
COMPLETION? LEST HAVING LAID HIS FOUNDATION

καὶ μὴ ἰσχύοντος ἐκτελέσαι πάντες οἱ θεωροῦντες
AND NOT BEING ABLE TO FINISH [IT], EVERYONE - SEEING [IT]

ἄρξωνται αὐτῷ ἐμπαίζειν **14.30** λέγοντες ὅτι Οὗτος ὁ
MAY BEGIN TO RIDICULE~HIM SAYING, THIS

ἄνθρωπος ἤρξατο οἰκοδομεῖν καὶ οὐκ ἴσχυσεν
MAN BEGAN TO BUILD AND WAS NOT ABLE

ἐκτελέσαι. **14.31** ἢ τίς βασιλεὺς πορευόμενος ἑτέρῳ
TO FINISH. OR WHAT KING GOING ²ANOTHER

βασιλεῖ συμβαλεῖν εἰς πόλεμον οὐχὶ καθίσας
³KING ¹TO ENGAGE IN BATTLE NOT HAVING SAT DOWN

πρῶτον βουλεύσεται εἰ δυνατός ἐστιν ἐν δέκα χιλιάσιν
FIRST WILL CONSIDER IF HE IS~ABLE WITH TEN THOUSAND

ὑπαντῆσαι τῷ   μετὰ εἴκοσι χιλιάδων ἐρχομένῳ ἐπ'
TO MEET   THE ONE WITH TWENTY THOUSAND HAVING COME AGAINST

αὐτόν; **14.32** εἰ δὲ μή γε, ἔτι   αὐτοῦ πόρρω ὄντος
HIM?   OTHERWISE, WHILE HE BEING~FAR AWAY

πρεσβείαν ἀποστείλας ἐρωτᾷ τὰ   πρὸς εἰρήνην.
HAVING SENT~AN AMBASSADOR HE ASKS THE [TERMS] FOR PEACE.

14.33 οὕτως οὖν πᾶς ἐξ ὑμῶν ὃς οὐκ ἀποτάσσεται
SO   THEN ·ALL OF YOU° WHO DOES NOT RENOUNCE

πᾶσιν τοῖς ἑαυτοῦ ὑπάρχουσιν οὐ δύναται εἶναί μου
ALL   -   HIS   POSSESSIONS IS NOT ABLE TO BE MY

μαθητής.
DISCIPLE.

14.34 Καλὸν οὖν   τὸ ἅλας· ἐὰν δὲ καὶ τὸ ἅλας
GOOD   THEN [IS] - SALT. BUT~IF EVEN THE SALT

μωρανθῇ,   ἐν τίνι ἀρτυθήσεται; **14.35** οὔτε εἰς
SHOULD BECOME TASTELESS, WITH WHAT WILL IT BE SEASONED?   NEITHER FOR

γῆν οὔτε εἰς κοπρίαν εὔθετόν ἐστιν, ἔξω βάλλουσιν
SOIL NOR FOR MANURE IS IT~SUITABLE; THEY THROW~OUT

αὐτό. ὁ   ἔχων ὦτα ἀκούειν ἀκουέτω.
IT. THE ONE HAVING EARS TO HEAR LET THAT ONE HEAR.

to oppose the one who comes against him with twenty thousand? [32]If he cannot, then, while the other is still far away, he sends a delegation and asks for the terms of peace. [33]So therefore, none of you can become my disciple if you do not give up all your possessions.

34 "Salt is good; but if salt has lost its taste, how can its saltiness be restored?[x] [35]It is fit neither for the soil nor for the manure pile; they throw it away. Let anyone with ears to hear listen!"

[x] Or *how can it be used for seasoning?*

15.1 Ἦσαν δὲ   αὐτῷ ἐγγίζοντες πάντες οἱ τελῶναι
NOW~THERE WERE DRAWING NEAR~TO HIM ALL   THE TAX COLLECTORS

καὶ οἱ ἁμαρτωλοὶ ἀκούειν αὐτοῦ. **15.2** καὶ διεγόγγυζον
AND THE SINNERS TO LISTEN TO HIM. AND WERE COMPLAINING

οἵ τε Φαρισαῖοι καὶ οἱ γραμματεῖς λέγοντες ὅτι
BOTH~THE PHARISEES AND THE SCRIBES SAYING, -

Οὗτος ἁμαρτωλοὺς προσδέχεται καὶ συνεσθίει αὐτοῖς.
THIS ONE WELCOMES~SINNERS AND EATS WITH THEM.

15.3 εἶπεν δὲ πρὸς αὐτοὺς τὴν παραβολὴν ταύτην λέγων,
AND~HE TOLD TO THEM - THIS~PARABLE SAYING,

15.4 Τίς ἄνθρωπος ἐξ ὑμῶν ἔχων ἑκατὸν πρόβατα καὶ
WHAT MAN OF YOU° HAVING ONE HUNDRED SHEEP AND

ἀπολέσας ἐξ αὐτῶν ἓν οὐ καταλείπει τὰ
HAVING LOST FROM THEM ONE, IS NOT LEAVING THE

ἐνενήκοντα ἐννέα ἐν τῇ ἐρήμῳ καὶ πορεύεται ἐπὶ
NINETY-NINE IN THE WILDERNESS AND GOES FOR

τὸ ἀπολωλὸς ἕως εὕρῃ αὐτό; **15.5** καὶ εὑρὼν
THE ONE HAVING BEEN LOST UNTIL HE FINDS IT? AND HAVING FOUND [IT]

ἐπιτίθησιν ἐπὶ τοὺς ὤμους αὐτοῦ χαίρων **15.6** καὶ
HE PUTS [IT] ON THE SHOULDERS OF HIM REJOICING AND

ἐλθὼν εἰς τὸν οἶκον συγκαλεῖ τοὺς φίλους καὶ
HAVING COME TO THE HOUSE HE CALLS TOGETHER - FRIENDS AND

τοὺς γείτονας λέγων αὐτοῖς, Συγχάρητέ μοι, ὅτι
-   NEIGHBORS SAYING TO THEM, REJOICE TOGETHER WITH ME, BECAUSE

Now all the tax collectors and sinners were coming near to listen to him. [2]And the Pharisees and the scribes were grumbling and saying, "This fellow welcomes sinners and eats with them."

3 So he told them this parable: [4]"Which one of you, having a hundred sheep and losing one of them, does not leave the ninety-nine in the wilderness and go after the one that is lost until he finds it? [5]When he has found it, he lays it on his shoulders and rejoices. [6]And when he comes home, he calls together his friends and neighbors, saying to them, 'Rejoice with me, for

I have found my sheep that was lost.' [7]Just so, I tell you, there will be more joy in heaven over one sinner who repents than over ninety-nine righteous persons who need no repentance.

8 "Or what woman having ten silver coins,[y] if she loses one of them, does not light a lamp, sweep the house, and search carefully until she finds it? [9]When she has found it, she calls together her friends and neighbors, saying, 'Rejoice with me, for I have found the coin that I had lost.' [10]Just so, I tell you, there is joy in the presence of the angels of God over one sinner who repents."

11 Then Jesus[z] said, "There was a man who had two sons. [12]The younger of them said to his father, 'Father, give me the share of the property that will belong to me.' So he divided his property between them. [13]A few days later the younger son gathered all he had and traveled to a distant country, and there he squandered his property in dissolute living. [14]When he had spent everything, a severe famine took place throughout that country, and he began to be in need. [15]So he went and hired himself out to one of the citizens of that country, who sent him to his fields to feed the pigs. [16]He would gladly

[y] Gk drachmas, each worth about a day's wage for a laborer
[z] Gk he

εὗρον τὸ πρόβατόν μου τὸ ἀπολωλός. **15.7** λέγω
I FOUND THE SHEEP OF ME, THE ONE HAVING BEEN LOST. I SAY

ὑμῖν ὅτι οὕτως χαρὰ ἐν τῷ οὐρανῷ ἔσται ἐπὶ ἑνὶ
TO YOU° THAT THUS JOY IN - HEAVEN THERE WILL BE OVER ONE

ἁμαρτωλῷ μετανοοῦντι ἢ ἐπὶ ἐνενήκοντα ἐννέα
SINNER REPENTING THAN OVER NINETY-NINE

δικαίοις οἵτινες οὐ χρείαν ἔχουσιν μετανοίας.
RIGHTEOUS WHO NO NEED HAVE OF REPENTANCE.

15.8 Ἢ τίς γυνὴ δραχμὰς ἔχουσα δέκα ἐὰν ἀπολέσῃ
OR WHAT WOMAN ³DRACHMAS ¹HAVING ²TEN IF SHE LOSES

δραχμὴν μίαν, οὐχὶ ἅπτει λύχνον καὶ σαροῖ τὴν
ONE~DRACHMA, [WILL] NOT LIGHT A LAMP AND SWEEP THE

οἰκίαν καὶ ζητεῖ ἐπιμελῶς ἕως οὗ εὕρῃ; **15.9** καὶ
HOUSE AND SEARCH CAREFULLY UNTIL SHE FINDS [IT]? AND

εὑροῦσα συγκαλεῖ τὰς φίλας καὶ γείτονας
HAVING FOUND [IT], SHE CALLS TOGETHER - FRIENDS AND NEIGHBORS

λέγουσα, Συγχάρητέ μοι, ὅτι εὗρον τὴν δραχμὴν
SAYING, REJOICE TOGETHER WITH ME, BECAUSE I FOUND THE DRACHMA

ἣν ἀπώλεσα. **15.10** οὕτως, λέγω ὑμῖν, γίνεται χαρὰ
WHICH I LOST. THUS, I SAY TO YOU°, THERE IS JOY

ἐνώπιον τῶν ἀγγέλων τοῦ θεοῦ ἐπὶ ἑνὶ ἁμαρτωλῷ
BEFORE THE ANGELS - OF GOD OVER ONE SINNER

μετανοοῦντι.
REPENTING.

15.11 Εἶπεν δέ, Ἄνθρωπός τις εἶχεν δύο υἱούς.
AND~HE SAID, A CERTAIN~MAN HAD TWO SONS.

15.12 καὶ εἶπεν ὁ νεώτερος αὐτῶν τῷ πατρί, Πάτερ,
AND SAID THE YOUNGER OF THEM TO THE FATHER, FATHER,

δός μοι τὸ ἐπιβάλλον μέρος τῆς οὐσίας. ὁ δὲ
GIVE TO ME THE PART~BELONGING OF THE PROPERTY. - AND

διεῖλεν αὐτοῖς τὸν βίον. **15.13** καὶ μετ' οὐ πολλὰς
HE DISTRIBUTED TO THEM THE PROPERTY. AND AFTER NOT MANY

ἡμέρας συναγαγὼν πάντα ὁ νεώτερος υἱὸς
DAYS HAVING GATHERED TOGETHER EVERYTHING THE YOUNGER SON

ἀπεδήμησεν εἰς χώραν μακρὰν καὶ ἐκεῖ διεσκόρπισεν
WENT ON A JOURNEY TO A COUNTRY FAR AWAY AND THERE HE SQUANDERED

τὴν οὐσίαν αὐτοῦ ζῶν ἀσώτως. **15.14** δαπανήσαντος δὲ
THE PROPERTY OF HIM LIVING LOOSELY. AND~HAVING SPENT

αὐτοῦ πάντα ἐγένετο λιμὸς ἰσχυρὰ κατὰ τὴν
OF HIM EVERYTHING THERE CAME A SEVERE~FAMINE THROUGHOUT -

χώραν ἐκείνην, καὶ αὐτὸς ἤρξατο ὑστερεῖσθαι.
THAT~COUNTRY, AND HE BEGAN TO GO WITHOUT.

15.15 καὶ πορευθεὶς ἐκολλήθη ἑνὶ τῶν πολιτῶν
AND HAVING GONE HE BECAME ASSOCIATED WITH ONE OF THE CITIZENS

τῆς χώρας ἐκείνης, καὶ ἔπεμψεν αὐτὸν εἰς τοὺς ἀγροὺς
- OF THAT~COUNTRY, AND HE SENT HIM INTO THE FIELDS

αὐτοῦ βόσκειν χοίρους, **15.16** καὶ ἐπεθύμει
OF HIM TO FEED PIGS, AND HE WAS LONGING

χορτασθῆναι ἐκ τῶν κερατίων ὧν ἤσθιον οἱ χοῖροι,
TO BE FED   WITH THE PODS   WHICH ³WERE EATING ¹THE ²PIGS,

καὶ οὐδεὶς ἐδίδου   αὐτῷ. **15.17** εἰς ἑαυτὸν δὲ
AND NO ONE WAS GIVING [ANYTHING] TO HIM.   ³TO ⁴HIMSELF ¹BUT

ἐλθὼν   ἔφη, Πόσοι μίσθιοι τοῦ πατρός
²HAVING COME HE SAID, HOW MANY HIRED SERVANTS OF THE FATHER

μου   περισσεύονται ἄρτων, ἐγὼ δὲ λιμῷ
OF ME [THERE ARE] HAVING LEFTOVERS OF BREAD, BUT~I WITH A FAMINE

ὧδε ἀπόλλυμαι. **15.18** ἀναστὰς πορεύσομαι πρὸς τὸν
AM PERISHING~HERE.   HAVING ARISEN I WILL GO   TO   THE

πατέρα μου καὶ ἐρῶ   αὐτῷ, Πάτερ, ἥμαρτον εἰς
FATHER OF ME AND I WILL SAY TO HIM, FATHER, I SINNED AGAINST

τὸν οὐρανὸν καὶ ἐνώπιόν σου, **15.19** οὐκέτι εἰμὶ ἄξιος
-   HEAVEN AND BEFORE YOU,   NO LONGER AM I WORTHY

κληθῆναι υἱός   σου· ποίησόν με ὡς ἕνα τῶν
TO BE CALLED [THE] SON OF YOU. MAKE ME AS ONE OF THE

μισθίων   σου. **15.20** καὶ ἀναστὰς ἦλθεν πρὸς τὸν
HIRED SERVANTS OF YOU.   AND HAVING ARISEN HE CAME TO   THE

πατέρα ἑαυτοῦ. ἔτι δὲ   αὐτοῦ μακρὰν ἀπέχοντος εἶδεν
FATHER OF HIMSELF. AND~WHILE HE [STILL] A DISTANCE BEING AWAY SAW

αὐτὸν ὁ πατὴρ αὐτοῦ καὶ ἐσπλαγχνίσθη   καὶ
HIM   THE FATHER OF HIM AND WAS FILLED WITH COMPASSION AND

δραμὼν ἐπέπεσεν ἐπὶ τὸν τράχηλον αὐτοῦ καὶ
HAVING RUN HE FELL UPON THE NECK   OF HIM AND

κατεφίλησεν αὐτόν. **15.21** εἶπεν δὲ ὁ υἱὸς αὐτῷ,
HE KISSED   HIM.   AND~SAID   THE SON TO HIM,

Πάτερ, ἥμαρτον εἰς τὸν οὐρανὸν καὶ ἐνώπιόν σου,
FATHER, I SINNED AGAINST - HEAVEN AND BEFORE YOU,

οὐκέτι εἰμὶ ἄξιος κληθῆναι υἱός   σου.ᵀ **15.22** εἶπεν δὲ
NO LONGER AM I WORTHY TO BE CALLED [THE] SON OF YOU.   BUT~SAID

ὁ πατὴρ πρὸς τοὺς δούλους αὐτοῦ, Ταχὺ ἐξενέγκατε
THE FATHER TO THE SLAVES   OF HIM, QUICK, BRING OUT

στολὴν τὴν πρώτην καὶ ἐνδύσατε αὐτόν, καὶ δότε
³ROBE ¹THE ²BEST   AND CLOTHE   HIM,   AND GIVE

δακτύλιον εἰς τὴν χεῖρα αὐτοῦ καὶ ὑποδήματα εἰς τοὺς
A RING   FOR THE HAND OF HIM AND SANDALS   FOR THE

πόδας, **15.23** καὶ φέρετε τὸν μόσχον τὸν σιτευτόν,
FEET,   AND BRING THE ²CALF   -   ¹FATTENED, [AND]

θύσατε,   καὶ φαγόντες εὐφρανθῶμεν, **15.24** ὅτι   οὗτος ὁ
SACRIFICE [IT], AND HAVING EATEN LET US BE MERRY,   BECAUSE THIS -

υἱός μου νεκρὸς ἦν καὶ ἀνέζησεν, ἦν ἀπολωλὼς καὶ
SON OF ME WAS~DEAD AND HE LIVED AGAIN, HE HAD BEEN LOST AND

εὑρέθη.   καὶ ἤρξαντο εὐφραίνεσθαι.
HE WAS FOUND. AND THEY BEGAN TO BE MERRY.

15.25 Ἦν δὲ ὁ υἱὸς αὐτοῦ ὁ πρεσβύτερος ἐν ἀγρῷ·
.   BUT~WAS THE SON OF HIM, THE OLDER,   IN [THE] FIELD.

have filled himself with[a] the pods that the pigs were eating; and no one gave him anything. [17]But when he came to himself he said, 'How many of my father's hired hands have bread enough and to spare, but here I am dying of hunger! [18]I will get up and go to my father, and I will say to him, "Father, I have sinned against heaven and before you; [19]I am no longer worthy to be called your son; treat me like one of your hired hands."' [20]So he set off and went to his father. But while he was still far off, his father saw him and was filled with compassion; he ran and put his arms around him and kissed him. [21]Then the son said to him, 'Father, I have sinned against heaven and before you; I am no longer worthy to be called your son.'[b] [22]But the father said to his slaves, 'Quickly, bring out a robe—the best one— and put it on him; put a ring on his finger and sandals on his feet. [23]And get the fatted calf and kill it, and let us eat and celebrate; [24]for this son of mine was dead and is alive again; he was lost and is found!' And they began to celebrate.

[25] "Now his elder son was in the field; and

[a] Other ancient authorities read *filled his stomach with*

[b] Other ancient authorities add *Treat me like one of your hired servants*

15:21 text: all. add ποιησον με ως ενα των μισθιων σου (make me like one of your hired men) [see Luke 15:19]: ASVmg RSVmg NIVmg NEBmg NRSVmg.

when he came and approached the house, he heard music and dancing. 26He called one of the slaves and asked what was going on. 27He replied, 'Your brother has come, and your father has killed the fatted calf, because he has got him back safe and sound.' 28Then he became angry and refused to go in. His father came out and began to plead with him. 29But he answered his father, 'Listen! For all these years I have been working like a slave for you, and I have never disobeyed your command; yet you have never given me even a young goat so that I might celebrate with my friends. 30But when this son of yours came back, who has devoured your property with prostitutes, you killed the fatted calf for him!' 31Then the father^c said to him, 'Son, you are always with me, and all that is mine is yours. 32But we had to celebrate and rejoice, because this brother of yours was dead and has come to life; he was lost and has been found.'"

καὶ ὡς ἐρχόμενος ἤγγισεν τῇ οἰκίᾳ, ἤκουσεν
AND AS COMING   HE DREW NEAR TO THE HOUSE,   HE HEARD

συμφωνίας καὶ χορῶν, 15.26 καὶ προσκαλεσάμενος ἕνα
MUSIC   AND DANCING,   AND HAVING SUMMONED   ONE

τῶν παίδων ἐπυνθάνετο τί ἂν εἴη ταῦτα. 15.27 ὁ
OF THE SERVANTS, HE WAS INQUIRING WHAT MIGHT BE THESE THINGS. -

δὲ εἶπεν αὐτῷ ὅτι Ὁ ἀδελφός σου ἥκει, καὶ
AND HE SAID TO HIM - THE BROTHER OF YOU IS PRESENT, AND

ἔθυσεν ὁ πατήρ σου τὸν μόσχον τὸν σιτευτόν, ὅτι
⁴SACRIFICED ¹THE ²FATHER ³OF YOU ⁵THE ⁷CALF - ⁶FATTENED, BECAUSE

ὑγιαίνοντα αὐτὸν ἀπέλαβεν. 15.28 ὠργίσθη δὲ καὶ
BEING IN GOOD HEALTH HE RECEIVED BACK~HIM.   AND~HE WAS ANGRY AND

οὐκ ἤθελεν εἰσελθεῖν, ὁ δὲ πατὴρ αὐτοῦ ἐξελθὼν
HE DID NOT WANT TO ENTER, BUT~THE FATHER OF HIM HAVING COME OUT

παρεκάλει αὐτόν. 15.29 ὁ δὲ ἀποκριθεὶς εἶπεν τῷ
WAS PLEADING WITH HIM.   - BUT HAVING ANSWERED HE SAID TO THE

πατρὶ αὐτοῦ, Ἰδοὺ τοσαῦτα ἔτη δουλεύω σοι καὶ
FATHER OF HIM, BEHOLD SO MANY YEARS I SERVE YOU AND

οὐδέποτε ἐντολήν σου παρῆλθον, καὶ ἐμοὶ οὐδέποτε
NEVER A COMMANDMENT OF YOU I DISOBEYED, AND NEVER~FOR ME

ἔδωκας ἔριφον ἵνα μετὰ τῶν φίλων μου εὐφρανθῶ·
DID YOU GIVE A YOUNG GOAT THAT WITH THE FRIENDS OF ME I MIGHT BE MERRY.

15.30 ὅτε δὲ ὁ υἱός σου οὗτος ὁ καταφαγών σου
     BUT~WHEN - ²SON ³OF YOU ¹THIS, THE ONE HAVING DEVOURED YOUR

τὸν βίον μετὰ πορνῶν ἦλθεν, ἔθυσας αὐτῷ τὸν
- PROPERTY WITH PROSTITUTES CAME, YOU SACRIFICED FOR HIM THE

σιτευτὸν μόσχον. 15.31 ὁ δὲ εἶπεν αὐτῷ, Τέκνον, σὺ
FATTENED CALF.   - AND HE SAID TO HIM, CHILD, YOU

πάντοτε μετ᾿ ἐμοῦ εἶ, καὶ πάντα τὰ ἐμὰ
ALWAYS   WITH ME ARE, AND EVERYTHING [WHICH IS] - MINE

σά ἐστιν· 15.32 εὐφρανθῆναι δὲ καὶ χαρῆναι
IS~YOURS.   NOW~TO BE MERRY AND TO REJOICE

ἔδει, ὅτι ὁ ἀδελφός σου οὗτος νεκρὸς ἦν καὶ
IT WAS NECESSARY, BECAUSE - ²BROTHER ³OF YOU ¹THIS WAS~DEAD AND

ἔζησεν, καὶ ἀπολωλὼς καὶ εὑρέθη.
HE LIVED, AND HAVING BEEN LOST AND WAS FOUND.

CHAPTER 16

Then Jesus^c said to the disciples, "There was a rich man who had a manager, and charges were brought to him that this man was squandering his property. 2So he summoned him and

^c Gk he

16.1 Ἔλεγεν δὲ καὶ πρὸς τοὺς μαθητάς,
     AND~HE WAS SAYING ALSO TO THE DISCIPLES,

Ἄνθρωπός τις ἦν πλούσιος ὃς εἶχεν οἰκονόμον, καὶ
A CERTAIN~MAN WAS RICH WHO HAD A STEWARD, AND

οὗτος διεβλήθη αὐτῷ ὡς διασκορπίζων τὰ
THIS WAS THE CHARGE BROUGHT AGAINST HIM: AS SQUANDERING THE

ὑπάρχοντα αὐτοῦ. 16.2 καὶ φωνήσας αὐτὸν εἶπεν
POSSESSIONS OF HIM.   AND HAVING CALLED HIM, HE SAID

αὐτῷ,   Τί   τοῦτο   ἀκούω   περὶ   σοῦ;   ἀπόδος   τὸν   λόγον
TO HIM,   WHAT [IS]   THIS   I HEAR   ABOUT   YOU?   RENDER   THE   ACCOUNT

τῆς   οἰκονομίας   σου,   οὐ   γὰρ   δύνῃ   ἔτι
OF THE   STEWARDSHIP   OF YOU,   ²NO   ¹FOR   ⁴ARE YOU ABLE   ³LONGER

οἰκονομεῖν.   **16.3** εἶπεν   δὲ   ἐν   ἑαυτῷ   ὁ   οἰκονόμος,
TO BE STEWARD.   AND~SAID   WITHIN   HIMSELF   THE   STEWARD,

Τί   ποιήσω, ὅτι   ὁ   κύριός   μου   ἀφαιρεῖται   τὴν
WHAT   MAY I DO,   BECAUSE   THE   LORD   OF ME   TAKES AWAY   THE

οἰκονομίαν   ἀπ' ἐμοῦ;   σκάπτειν   οὐκ   ἰσχύω,
STEWARDSHIP   FROM   ME?   TO DIG,   I AM NOT STRONG [ENOUGH],

ἐπαιτεῖν   αἰσχύνομαι.   **16.4** ἔγνων   τί   ποιήσω, ἵνα   ὅταν
TO BEG   I AM ASHAMED.   I KNOW   WHAT   I MAY DO,   THAT   WHEN

μετασταθῶ   ἐκ   τῆς   οἰκονομίας   δέξωνταί   με   εἰς   τοὺς
I AM REMOVED   FROM   THE   STEWARDSHIP   THEY MAY RECEIVE   ME   INTO THE

οἴκους   αὐτῶν.   **16.5** καὶ   προσκαλεσάμενος   ἕνα   ἕκαστον
HOUSES   OF THEM.   AND   HAVING SUMMONED   EACH~ONE

τῶν   χρεοφειλετῶν   τοῦ   κυρίου   ἑαυτοῦ   ἔλεγεν   τῷ
OF THE   DEBTORS   OF THE   MASTER   OF HIMSELF,   HE WAS SAYING   TO THE

πρώτῳ,   Πόσον   ὀφείλεις   τῷ   κυρίῳ   μου;   **16.6** ὁ   δὲ
FIRST,   HOW MUCH   DO YOU OWE   TO THE   LORD   OF ME?   -   AND

εἶπεν,   Ἑκατὸν   βάτους   ἐλαίου.   ὁ   δὲ   εἶπεν   αὐτῷ,
HE SAID,   ONE HUNDRED   BATHS   OF OIL.   -   AND   HE SAID   TO HIM,

Δέξαι   σου   τὰ   γράμματα   καὶ   καθίσας   ταχέως
TAKE   YOUR   -   BILLS   AND   HAVING SAT DOWN,   QUICKLY

γράψον   πεντήκοντα.   **16.7** ἔπειτα   ἑτέρῳ   εἶπεν,   Σὺ   δὲ
WRITE   FIFTY.   THEN   TO ANOTHER   HE SAID,   AND~YOU

πόσον   ὀφείλεις;   ὁ   δὲ   εἶπεν,   Ἑκατὸν   κόρους   σίτου.
HOW MUCH   DO YOU OWE?   -   AND   HE SAID,   ONE HUNDRED   MEASURES   OF WHEAT.

λέγει   αὐτῷ,   Δέξαι   σου   τὰ   γράμματα   καὶ   γράψον
HE SAYS   TO HIM,   TAKE   YOUR   -   BILLS   AND   WRITE

ὀγδοήκοντα.   **16.8** καὶ   ἐπῄνεσεν   ὁ   κύριος   τὸν
EIGHTY.   AND   ³PRAISED   ¹THE   ²LORD   ⁴THE

οἰκονόμον   τῆς   ἀδικίας   ὅτι   φρονίμως   ἐποίησεν·
⁶STEWARD   -   ⁵UNRIGHTEOUS   BECAUSE   HE ACTED~WISELY.

ὅτι   οἱ   υἱοὶ   τοῦ   αἰῶνος   τούτου   φρονιμώτεροι   ὑπὲρ   τοὺς
BECAUSE   THE   SONS   -   OF THIS~AGE   MORE WISE   THAN   THE

υἱοὺς   τοῦ   φωτὸς   εἰς   τὴν   γενεὰν   τὴν   ἑαυτῶν   εἰσιν.
SONS   OF THE LIGHT   IN   THE   GENERATION   -   OF THEMSELVES   ARE.

16.9 Καὶ   ἐγὼ   ὑμῖν   λέγω,   ἑαυτοῖς   ποιήσατε   φίλους   ἐκ
AND   I   SAY~TO YOU°,   MAKE~FOR YOURSELVES   FRIENDS   FROM

τοῦ   μαμωνᾶ   τῆς   ἀδικίας,   ἵνα   ὅταν   ἐκλίπῃ
THE   WEALTH   -   OF UNRIGHTEOUSNESS,   THAT   WHEN   IT FAILS

δέξωνται   ὑμᾶς   εἰς   τὰς   αἰωνίους   σκηνάς.
THEY MAY WELCOME   YOU°   INTO   THE   ETERNAL   TENTS.

16.10 ὁ   πιστὸς   ἐν   ἐλαχίστῳ   καὶ   ἐν   πολλῷ
THE [ONE]   FAITHFUL   IN   LITTLE,   ALSO   IN   MUCH

πιστός   ἐστιν,   καὶ   ὁ   ἐν   ἐλαχίστῳ   ἄδικος   καὶ
IS~FAITHFUL,   AND   THE [ONE BEING]   IN   LITTLE   UNRIGHTEOUS   ALSO

said to him, 'What is this that I hear about you? Give me an accounting of your management, because you cannot be my manager any longer.' ³Then the manager said to himself, 'What will I do, now that my master is taking the position away from me? I am not strong enough to dig, and I am ashamed to beg. ⁴I have decided what to do so that, when I am dismissed as manager, people may welcome me into their homes.' ⁵So, summoning his master's debtors one by one, he asked the first, 'How much do you owe my master?' ⁶He answered, 'A hundred jugs of olive oil.' He said to him, 'Take your bill, sit down quickly, and make it fifty.' ⁷Then he asked another, 'And how much do you owe?' He replied, 'A hundred containers of wheat.' He said to him, 'Take your bill and make it eighty.' ⁸And his master commended the dishonest manager because he had acted shrewdly; for the children of this age are more shrewd in dealing with their own generation than are the children of light. ⁹And I tell you, make friends for yourselves by means of dishonest wealth*d* so that when it is gone, they may welcome you into the eternal homes.*e*

10 "Whoever is faithful in a very little is faithful also in much; and whoever is dishonest in a very little

d Gk *mammon*
e Gk *tents*

is dishonest also in much. [11]If then you have not been faithful with the dishonest wealth,*f* who will entrust to you the true riches? [12]And if you have not been faithful with what belongs to another, who will give you what is your own? [13]No slave can serve two masters; for a slave will either hate the one and love the other, or be devoted to the one and despise the other. You cannot serve God and wealth.'*f*

14 The Pharisees, who were lovers of money, heard all this, and they ridiculed him. [15]So he said to them, "You are those who justify yourselves in the sight of others; but God knows your hearts; for what is prized by human beings is an abomination in the sight of God.

16 "The law and the prophets were in effect until John came; since then the good news of the kingdom of God is proclaimed, and everyone tries to enter it by force.*g* [17]But it is easier for heaven and earth to pass away, than for one stroke of a letter in the law to be dropped.

18 "Anyone who divorces his wife and marries another commits adultery, and whoever marries a woman divorced from her husband commits adultery.

19 "There was a rich man who was dressed in purple and fine linen and who feasted

f Gk *mammon*
g Or *everyone is strongly urged to enter it*

ἐν πολλῷ ἄδικός ἐστιν. **16.11** εἰ οὖν ἐν τῷ ἀδίκῳ
IN MUCH IS~UNRIGHTEOUS. IF THEN WITH - UNRIGHTEOUS

μαμωνᾷ πιστοὶ οὐκ ἐγένεσθε, τὸ ἀληθινὸν τίς ὑμῖν
WEALTH ²FAITHFUL ¹YOU° WERE NOT, - ⁶TRUE [RICHES] ³WHO ⁵TO YOU°

πιστεύσει; **16.12** καὶ εἰ ἐν τῷ ἀλλοτρίῳ
⁴WILL ENTRUST? AND IF WITH THE [THING] BELONGING TO ANOTHER

πιστοὶ οὐκ ἐγένεσθε, τὸ ὑμέτερον τίς ὑμῖν δώσει;
²FAITHFUL ¹YOU° WERE NOT, - YOUR° OWN WHO WILL GIVE~TO YOU°?

16.13 Οὐδεὶς οἰκέτης δύναται δυσὶ κυρίοις δουλεύειν·
NO SLAVE IS ABLE TWO MASTERS TO SERVE;

ἢ γὰρ τὸν ἕνα μισήσει καὶ τὸν ἕτερον ἀγαπήσει, ἢ
FOR~EITHER THE ONE HE WILL HATE AND THE OTHER HE WILL LOVE, OR

ἑνὸς ἀνθέξεται καὶ τοῦ ἑτέρου καταφρονήσει.
ONE HE WILL BE DEVOTED TO AND THE OTHER HE WILL DESPISE.

οὐ δύνασθε θεῷ δουλεύειν καὶ μαμωνᾷ.
YOU° ARE NOT ABLE TO SERVE~GOD AND WEALTH.

16.14 Ἤκουον δὲ ταῦτα πάντα οἱ Φαρισαῖοι
AND~WAS HEARING THESE THINGS ALL THE PHARISEES

φιλάργυροι ὑπάρχοντες καὶ ἐξεμυκτήριζον αὐτόν.
BEING~LOVERS OF MONEY AND THEY WERE RIDICULING HIM.

16.15 καὶ εἶπεν αὐτοῖς, Ὑμεῖς ἐστε οἱ δικαιοῦντες
AND HE SAID TO THEM, YOU ARE THE ONES JUSTIFYING

ἑαυτοὺς ἐνώπιον τῶν ἀνθρώπων, ὁ δὲ θεὸς γινώσκει τὰς
YOURSELVES BEFORE - MEN, - BUT GOD KNOWS THE

καρδίας ὑμῶν· ὅτι τὸ ἐν ἀνθρώποις
HEARTS OF YOU°. BECAUSE THE [THING] AMONG MEN

ὑψηλὸν βδέλυγμα ἐνώπιον τοῦ θεοῦ. **16.16** Ὁ
HIGHLY ESTEEMED [IS] AN ABOMINATION BEFORE - GOD. THE

νόμος καὶ οἱ προφῆται μέχρι Ἰωάννου· ἀπὸ
LAW AND THE PROPHETS [WERE PROCLAIMED] UNTIL JOHN. FROM

τότε ἡ βασιλεία τοῦ θεοῦ εὐαγγελίζεται καὶ πᾶς
THEN THE KINGDOM - OF GOD IS BEING PREACHED AND EVERYONE

εἰς αὐτὴν βιάζεται. **16.17** Εὐκοπώτερον δέ ἐστιν
INTO IT IS BEING URGENTLY INVITED. BUT~EASIER IT IS [FOR]

τὸν οὐρανὸν καὶ τὴν γῆν παρελθεῖν ἢ τοῦ νόμου
- HEAVEN AND - EARTH TO PASS AWAY THAN OF THE LAW

μίαν κεραίαν πεσεῖν. **16.18** Πᾶς ὁ ἀπολύων τὴν
ONE STROKE OF A LETTER TO DROP [OUT]. EVERYONE - DIVORCING THE

γυναῖκα αὐτοῦ καὶ γαμῶν ἑτέραν μοιχεύει, καὶ
WIFE OF HIM AND MARRYING ANOTHER COMMITS ADULTERY, AND

ὁ ἀπολελυμένην ἀπὸ ἀνδρὸς γαμῶν
THE ONE ²[THE WOMAN] HAVING BEEN DIVORCED ³BY ⁴[HER] HUSBAND, ¹MARRYING

μοιχεύει.
COMMITS ADULTERY.

16.19 Ἄνθρωπος δέ τις ἦν πλούσιος, καὶ
³MAN ¹NOW ²A CERTAIN WAS RICH, AND

ἐνεδιδύσκετο πορφύραν καὶ βύσσον εὐφραινόμενος
WAS CLOTHING HIMSELF WITH PURPLE AND LINEN, BEING MERRY

καθ᾿ ἡμέραν λαμπρῶς.   **16.20** πτωχὸς δέ τις
EVERY DAY   [EATING] SUMPTUOUSLY.   ³POOR MAN ¹AND ²A CERTAIN

ὀνόματι Λάζαρος ἐβέβλητο πρὸς τὸν πυλῶνα αὐτοῦ
BY NAME,   LAZARUS,   HAD BEEN LAID AT   THE   GATE   OF HIM

εἰλκωμένος   **16.21** καὶ ἐπιθυμῶν χορτασθῆναι
HAVING BEEN COVERED WITH SORES   AND   DESIRING   TO BE FED

ἀπὸ τῶν   πιπτόντων ἀπὸ τῆς τραπέζης τοῦ
FROM THE THINGS FALLING   FROM THE   TABLE   OF THE

πλουσίου· ἀλλὰ καὶ οἱ κύνες ἐρχόμενοι ἐπέλειχον τὰ
RICH MAN.   BUT   EVEN THE DOGS COMING   WERE LICKING THE

ἕλκη αὐτοῦ. **16.22** ἐγένετο δὲ   ἀποθανεῖν τὸν
SORES OF HIM.   AND~IT CAME TO PASS [THAT] DIED   THE

πτωχὸν καὶ ἀπενεχθῆναι αὐτὸν ὑπὸ τῶν ἀγγέλων εἰς
POOR MAN AND HE~WAS CARRIED AWAY   BY   THE ANGELS   TO

τὸν κόλπον ᾿Αβραάμ· ἀπέθανεν δὲ καὶ ὁ πλούσιος
THE BOSOM   OF ABRAHAM. AND~DIED   ALSO THE RICH MAN

καὶ ἐτάφη.   **16.23** καὶ ἐν τῷ ᾅδῃ ἐπάρας   τοὺς
AND HE WAS BURIED.   AND IN -   HADES HAVING LIFTED UP THE

ὀφθαλμοὺς αὐτοῦ, ὑπάρχων ἐν βασάνοις, ὁρᾷ
EYES   OF HIM, BEING   IN TORMENTS, HE SEES

᾿Αβραὰμ ἀπὸ μακρόθεν καὶ Λάζαρον ἐν τοῖς κόλποις
ABRAHAM FROM FAR AWAY AND LAZARUS   IN   THE   BOSOMS

αὐτοῦ. **16.24** καὶ αὐτὸς φωνήσας εἶπεν, Πάτερ
OF HIM.   AND   HE   HAVING CALLED SAID, FATHER

᾿Αβραάμ, ἐλέησόν με καὶ πέμψον Λάζαρον ἵνα
ABRAHAM, HAVE MERCY ON ME AND SEND   LAZARUS   THAT

βάψῃ τὸ ἄκρον τοῦ δακτύλου αὐτοῦ ὕδατος καὶ
HE MAY DIP THE TIP   OF THE FINGER   OF HIM [INTO] [THE] WATER AND

καταψύξῃ τὴν γλῶσσάν μου, ὅτι   ὀδυνῶμαι ἐν τῇ
MAY COOL   THE TONGUE   OF ME, BECAUSE I AM SUFFERING IN   -

φλογὶ ταύτῃ. **16.25** εἶπεν δὲ ᾿Αβραάμ, Τέκνον, μνήσθητι
THIS~FLAME.   BUT~SAID ABRAHAM, CHILD,   REMEMBER

ὅτι ἀπέλαβες τὰ ἀγαθά σου ἐν τῇ ζωῇ σου, καὶ
THAT YOU RECEIVED THE GOOD THINGS OF YOU IN THE LIFE OF YOU, AND

Λάζαρος ὁμοίως τὰ κακά· νῦν δὲ ὧδε παρακαλεῖται,
LAZARUS LIKEWISE THE BAD.   BUT~NOW HE IS COMFORTED~HERE,

σὺ δὲ ὀδυνᾶσαι. **16.26** καὶ ἐν   πᾶσι τούτοις
BUT~YOU ARE SUFFERING.   AND IN [ADDITION] TO ALL THESE THINGS

μεταξὺ ἡμῶν καὶ ὑμῶν χάσμα μέγα ἐστήρικται, ὅπως
BETWEEN US   AND YOU° A GREAT~CHASM   HAS BEEN FIXED, SO THAT

οἱ   θέλοντες διαβῆναι ἔνθεν πρὸς ὑμᾶς
THE ONES WISHING TO COME OVER FROM [HERE] TO   YOU°

μὴ δύνωνται, μηδὲ ἐκεῖθεν πρὸς ἡμᾶς διαπερῶσιν.
ARE NOT ABLE,   NEITHER FROM THERE TO   US   MAY THEY CROSS OVER.

16.27 εἶπεν δέ, ᾿Ερωτῶ σε οὖν, πάτερ, ἵνα πέμψῃς
AND~HE SAID, I ASK   YOU THEN, FATHER, THAT YOU MAY SEND

αὐτὸν εἰς τὸν οἶκον τοῦ πατρός μου, **16.28** ἔχω γὰρ
HIM   TO THE HOUSE OF THE FATHER OF ME,   FOR~I HAVE

sumptuously every day.
²⁰And at his gate lay a
poor man named Lazarus,
covered with sores, ²¹who
longed to satisfy his hunger
with what fell from the rich
man's table; even the dogs
would come and lick his
sores. ²²The poor man died
and was carried away by the
angels to be with Abraham.ʰ
The rich man also died and
was buried. ²³In Hades,
where he was being tor-
mented, he looked up and
saw Abraham far away
with Lazarus by his side.ⁱ
²⁴He called out, 'Father
Abraham, have mercy on
me, and send Lazarus to dip
the tip of his finger in water
and cool my tongue; for I am
in agony in these flames.'
²⁵But Abraham said, 'Child,
remember that during your
lifetime you received your
good things, and Lazarus in
like manner evil things; but
now he is comforted here,
and you are in agony.
²⁶Besides all this, between
you and us a great chasm has
been fixed, so that those
who might want to pass from
here to you cannot do so,
and no one can cross from
there to us.' ²⁷He said,
'Then, father, I beg you to
send him to my father's
house— ²⁸for I have

ʰ Gk to Abraham's bosom
ⁱ Gk in his bosom

five brothers—that he may warn them, so that they will not also come into this place of torment.' ²⁹Abraham replied, 'They have Moses and the prophets; they should listen to them.' ³⁰He said, 'No, father Abraham; but if someone goes to them from the dead, they will repent.' ³¹He said to him, 'If they do not listen to Moses and the prophets, neither will they be convinced even if someone rises from the dead.'"

πέντε ἀδελφούς, ὅπως διαμαρτύρηται αὐτοῖς, ἵνα μὴ
FIVE   BROTHERS,   THAT HE MAY WARN   THEM,   LEST

καὶ αὐτοὶ ἔλθωσιν εἰς τὸν τόπον τοῦτον τῆς βασάνου.
ALSO THEY MAY COME TO - THIS~PLACE   - OF TORMENT.

16.29 λέγει δὲ Ἀβραάμ, Ἔχουσι Μωϋσέα καὶ τοὺς
BUT~SAYS   ABRAHAM, THEY HAVE MOSES   AND THE

προφήτας· ἀκουσάτωσαν αὐτῶν. **16.30** ὁ δὲ εἶπεν,
PROPHETS.   LET THEM LISTEN TO THEM.   - BUT HE SAID,

Οὐχί, πάτερ Ἀβραάμ, ἀλλ᾽ ἐάν τις   ἀπὸ νεκρῶν
NO, FATHER ABRAHAM, BUT IF SOMEONE FROM [THE] DEAD

πορευθῇ πρὸς αὐτοὺς μετανοήσουσιν. **16.31** εἶπεν δὲ
SHOULD GO TO THEM THEY WILL REPENT.   BUT~HE SAID

αὐτῷ, Εἰ Μωϋσέως καὶ τῶν προφητῶν οὐκ ἀκούουσιν,
TO HIM, IF MOSES   AND THE PROPHETS THEY DO NOT LISTEN TO,

οὐδ᾽ ἐάν τις ἐκ νεκρῶν ἀναστῇ   πεισθήσονται.
NEITHER IF SOMEONE FROM [THE] DEAD SHOULD RISE AGAIN WILL THEY BE PERSUADED.

CHAPTER 17

Jesus ʲ said to his disciples, "Occasions for stumbling are bound to come, but woe to anyone by whom they come! ²It would be better for you if a millstone were hung around your neck and you were thrown into the sea than for you to cause one of these little ones to stumble. ³Be on your guard! If another disciple ᵏ sins, you must rebuke the offender, and if there is repentance, you must forgive. ⁴And if the same person sins against you seven times a day, and turns back to you seven times and says, 'I repent,' you must forgive."

5 The apostles said to the Lord, "Increase our faith!" ⁶The Lord replied, "If you had faith the size of a ˡ mustard seed, you could say

ʲ Gk He
ᵏ Gk your brother
ˡ Gk faith as a grain of

17.1 Εἶπεν δὲ πρὸς τοὺς μαθητὰς αὐτοῦ,
AND~HE SAID   TO   THE   DISCIPLES OF HIM,

Ἀνένδεκτόν ἐστιν τοῦ τὰ σκάνδαλα μὴ ἐλθεῖν, πλὴν
IT IS~IMPOSSIBLE [FOR] - THE TEMPTATIONS TO SIN NOT TO COME, BUT

οὐαὶ δι᾽ οὗ ἔρχεται· **17.2** λυσιτελεῖ αὐτῷ εἰ
WOE THROUGH WHOM IT COMES.   IT IS BETTER FOR HIM IF

λίθος μυλικὸς περίκειται περὶ τὸν τράχηλον αὐτοῦ
A MILLSTONE   IS HUNG   AROUND THE NECK   OF HIM

καὶ ἔρριπται   εἰς τὴν θάλασσαν ἢ ἵνα
AND HE HAD BEEN THROWN INTO THE SEA   THAN THAT

σκανδαλίσῃ   τῶν μικρῶν τούτων ἕνα.
HE SHOULD CAUSE TO STUMBLE - ³LITTLE ONES ²OF THESE ¹ONE.

17.3 προσέχετε ἑαυτοῖς. ἐὰν ἁμάρτῃ ὁ ἀδελφός σου
PAY ATTENTION TO YOURSELVES. IF SINS   THE BROTHER OF YOU,

ἐπιτίμησον αὐτῷ, καὶ ἐὰν μετανοήσῃ ἄφες αὐτῷ.
REBUKE   HIM, AND IF HE REPENTS FORGIVE HIM.

17.4 καὶ ἐὰν ἑπτάκις τῆς   ἡμέρας ἁμαρτήσῃ εἰς
AND IF SEVEN TIMES [DURING] THE DAY   HE SINS   AGAINST

σὲ καὶ ἑπτάκις ἐπιστρέψῃ πρὸς σὲ λέγων, Μετανοῶ,
YOU AND SEVEN TIMES HE TURNS AROUND TO YOU SAYING, I REPENT,

ἀφήσεις αὐτῷ.
YOU WILL FORGIVE HIM.

17.5 Καὶ εἶπαν οἱ ἀπόστολοι τῷ κυρίῳ, Πρόσθες
AND SAID THE APOSTLES TO THE LORD, ADD

ἡμῖν πίστιν. **17.6** εἶπεν δὲ ὁ κύριος, Εἰ ἔχετε πίστιν
TO US FAITH.   AND~SAID THE LORD, IF YOU° HAVE FAITH

ὡς κόκκον σινάπεως, ἐλέγετε ἂν   τῇ
LIKE A SEED OF MUSTARD, YOU° WOULD HAVE SAID -

συκαμίνῳ [ταύτῃ], Ἐκριζώθητι καὶ φυτεύθητι ἐν τῇ
TO THIS~MULBERRY TREE,   BE UPROOTED   AND   BE PLANTED   IN   THE

θαλάσσῃ· καὶ ὑπήκουσεν ἂν ὑμῖν.
SEA.   AND   IT WOULD HAVE OBEYED   YOU°.

17.7 Τίς δὲ ἐξ ὑμῶν δοῦλον ἔχων ἀροτριῶντα ἢ
BUT~WHO   AMONG YOU°   HAVING~A SLAVE   PLOWING   OR

ποιμαίνοντα, ὃς εἰσελθόντι ἐκ τοῦ ἀγροῦ ἐρεῖ
TENDING SHEEP,   WHO   HAVING COME IN   FROM THE   FIELD   WILL SAY

αὐτῷ, Εὐθέως παρελθὼν ἀνάπεσε, **17.8** ἀλλ᾽
TO HIM,   IMMEDIATELY   HAVING COME BESIDE,   LIE DOWN,   BUT

οὐχὶ ἐρεῖ αὐτῷ, Ἑτοίμασον τί δειπνήσω καὶ
WILL HE NOT SAY   TO HIM,   PREPARE   SOMETHING [THAT]   I MAY EAT   AND

περιζωσάμενος διακόνει μοι ἕως φάγω καὶ
HAVING WRAPPED [AN APRON] ABOUT YOURSELF   SERVE   ME   UNTIL   I EAT   AND

πίω, καὶ μετὰ ταῦτα φάγεσαι καὶ πίεσαι σύ;
DRINK,   AND   AFTER   THESE THINGS,   MAY EAT   AND   DRINK   YOU?

17.9 μὴ ἔχει χάριν τῷ δούλῳ ὅτι ἐποίησεν
[SURELY] HE DOES NOT HAVE   GRATITUDE   TO THE   SERVANT   BECAUSE   HE DID

τὰ διαταχθέντα; **17.10** οὕτως καὶ ὑμεῖς, ὅταν
THE THINGS   HAVING BEEN COMMANDED?   SO   ALSO   YOU°,   WHEN

ποιήσητε πάντα τὰ διαταχθέντα ὑμῖν, λέγετε
YOU° DO   ALL   THE THINGS   HAVING BEEN COMMANDED   YOU°,   SAY,

ὅτι Δοῦλοι ἀχρεῖοί ἐσμεν, ὃ ὠφείλομεν ποιῆσαι
-   USELESS~SLAVES   WE ARE,   WHAT   WE WERE OBLIGATED   TO DO

πεποιήκαμεν.
WE HAVE DONE.

17.11 Καὶ ἐγένετο ἐν τῷ πορεύεσθαι εἰς Ἰερουσαλὴμ
AND   IT CAME ABOUT   WHILE [HE] GOES   TO   JERUSALEM

καὶ αὐτὸς διήρχετο διὰ μέσον Σαμαρείας καὶ
AND   HE   WAS TRAVELING   THROUGH   [THE] MIDDLE   OF SAMARIA   AND

Γαλιλαίας. **17.12** καὶ εἰσερχομένου αὐτοῦ εἴς τινα
GALILEE.   AND   HE~ENTERING   INTO   A CERTAIN

κώμην ἀπήντησαν [αὐτῷ] δέκα λεπροὶ ἄνδρες, οἳ
VILLAGE   MET   HIM   TEN   LEPROUS   MEN,   WHO

ἔστησαν πόρρωθεν **17.13** καὶ αὐτοὶ ἦραν φωνὴν
STOOD   FROM A DISTANCE   AND   THEY   LIFTED UP   VOICE

λέγοντες, Ἰησοῦ ἐπιστάτα, ἐλέησον ἡμᾶς. **17.14** καὶ
SAYING,   JESUS,   MASTER,   HAVE MERCY [UPON] US.   AND

ἰδὼν εἶπεν αὐτοῖς, Πορευθέντες ἐπιδείξατε
HAVING SEEN [THIS]   HE SAID   TO THEM,   HAVING GONE   SHOW

ἑαυτοὺς τοῖς ἱερεῦσιν. καὶ ἐγένετο ἐν τῷ
YOURSELVES   TO THE PRIESTS.   AND   IT CAME ABOUT   WHILE

ὑπάγειν αὐτοὺς ἐκαθαρίσθησαν. **17.15** εἷς δὲ ἐξ αὐτῶν,
THEY~GO AWAY   THEY WERE CLEANSED.   AND~ONE   OF   THEM,

ἰδὼν ὅτι ἰάθη, ὑπέστρεψεν μετὰ φωνῆς μεγάλης
HAVING SEEN   THAT   HE WAS HEALED,   RETURNED   WITH   A LOUD~VOICE

δοξάζων τὸν θεόν, **17.16** καὶ ἔπεσεν ἐπὶ πρόσωπον
GLORIFYING   -   GOD,   AND   HE FELL   ON [HIS] FACE

to this mulberry tree, 'Be uprooted and planted in the sea,' and it would obey you.

7 "Who among you would say to your slave who has just come in from plowing or tending sheep in the field, 'Come here at once and take your place at the table'? 8 Would you not rather say to him, 'Prepare supper for me, put on your apron and serve me while I eat and drink; later you may eat and drink'? 9 Do you thank the slave for doing what was commanded? 10 So you also, when you have done all that you were ordered to do, say, 'We are worthless slaves; we have done only what we ought to have done!'"

11 On the way to Jerusalem Jesus[m] was going through the region between Samaria and Galilee. 12 As he entered a village, ten lepers[n] approached him. Keeping their distance, 13 they called out, saying, "Jesus, Master, have mercy on us!" 14 When he saw them, he said to them, "Go and show yourselves to the priests." And as they went, they were made clean. 15 Then one of them, when he saw that he was healed, turned back, praising God with a loud voice. 16 He prostrated himself

[m] Gk *he*
[n] The terms *leper* and *leprosy* can refer to several diseases

at Jesus'[o] feet and thanked him. And he was a Samaritan. [17]Then Jesus asked, "Were not ten made clean? But the other nine, where are they? [18]Was none of them found to return and give praise to God except this foreigner?" [19]Then he said to him, "Get up and go on your way; your faith has made you well."

20 Once Jesus[p] was asked by the Pharisees when the kingdom of God was coming, and he answered, "The kingdom of God is not coming with things that can be observed; [21]nor will they say, 'Look, here it is!' or 'There it is!' For, in fact, the kingdom of God is among[q] you."

22 Then he said to the disciples, "The days are coming when you will long to see one of the days of the Son of Man, and you will not see it. [23]They will say to you, 'Look there!' or 'Look here!' Do not go, do not set off in pursuit. [24]For as the lightning flashes and lights up the sky from one side to the other, so will the Son of Man be in his day.[r] [25]But first he must endure much suffering and be rejected by this generation. [26]Just as it was in the

[o] Gk *his*
[p] Gk *he*
[q] Or *within*
[r] Other ancient authorities lack *in his day*

παρὰ τοὺς πόδας αὐτοῦ εὐχαριστῶν αὐτῷ· καὶ αὐτὸς
AT THE FEET OF HIM THANKING HIM. AND HE

ἦν Σαμαρίτης. **17.17** ἀποκριθεὶς δὲ ὁ Ἰησοῦς εἶπεν,
WAS A SAMARITAN. AND~HAVING ANSWERED - JESUS SAID,

Οὐχὶ οἱ δέκα ἐκαθαρίσθησαν; οἱ δὲ ἐννέα
[WERE THERE] NOT - TEN [WHO] WERE CLEANSED? NOW~THE NINE

ποῦ; **17.18** οὐχ εὑρέθησαν ὑποστρέψαντες δοῦναι
WHERE [ARE THEY]? WERE THEY NOT FOUND HAVING RETURNED TO GIVE

δόξαν τῷ θεῷ εἰ μὴ ὁ ἀλλογενὴς οὗτος; **17.19** καὶ
GLORY - TO GOD EXCEPT - THIS~FOREIGNER? AND

εἶπεν αὐτῷ, Ἀναστὰς πορεύου· ἡ πίστις σου
HE SAID TO HIM, HAVING ARISEN, GO. THE FAITH OF YOU

σέσωκέν σε.
HAS DELIVERED YOU.

17.20 Ἐπερωτηθεὶς δὲ ὑπὸ τῶν Φαρισαίων πότε
NOW~HAVING BEEN ASKED BY THE PHARISEES WHEN

ἔρχεται ἡ βασιλεία τοῦ θεοῦ ἀπεκρίθη αὐτοῖς καὶ
COMES THE KINGDOM - OF GOD, HE QUESTIONED THEM AND

εἶπεν, Οὐκ ἔρχεται ἡ βασιλεία τοῦ θεοῦ μετὰ
SAID, ⁴IS NOT COMING ¹THE ²KINGDOM - ³OF GOD WITH

παρατηρήσεως, **17.21** οὐδὲ ἐροῦσιν, Ἰδοὺ ὧδε ἤ,
OBSERVATION, NOR WILL THEY SAY, BEHOLD HERE [IT IS], OR

Ἐκεῖ, ἰδοὺ γὰρ ἡ βασιλεία τοῦ θεοῦ ἐντὸς ὑμῶν
THERE [IT IS], FOR~BEHOLD THE KINGDOM - OF GOD INSIDE OF YOU°

ἐστιν. **17.22** Εἶπεν δὲ πρὸς τοὺς μαθητάς,
IS. AND~HE SAID TO THE DISCIPLES,

Ἐλεύσονται ἡμέραι ὅτε ἐπιθυμήσετε μίαν τῶν ἡμερῶν
DAYS~WILL COME WHEN YOU°WILL DESIRE ONE OF THE DAYS

τοῦ υἱοῦ τοῦ ἀνθρώπου ἰδεῖν καὶ οὐκ ὄψεσθε.
OF THE SON - OF MAN TO SEE AND YOU°WILL NOT SEE [IT].

17.23 καὶ ἐροῦσιν ὑμῖν, Ἰδοὺ ἐκεῖ, [ἤ,] Ἰδοὺ
AND THEY WILL SAY TO YOU°, BEHOLD THERE [IT IS], OR, BEHOLD

ὧδε· μὴ ἀπέλθητε μηδὲ διώξητε.
HERE [IT IS]. DO NOT GO OUT [AFTER THEM] NOR PURSUE [THEM].

17.24 ὥσπερ γὰρ ἡ ἀστραπὴ ἀστράπτουσα ἐκ
FOR~AS THE LIGHTNING FLASHING OUT OF

τῆς ὑπὸ τὸν οὐρανὸν εἰς τὴν ὑπ' οὐρανὸν
THE [ONE PART] UNDER THE SKY TO THE [OTHER PART] UNDER [THE] SKY

λάμπει, οὕτως ἔσται ὁ υἱὸς τοῦ ἀνθρώπου ⌜[ἐν τῇ
SHINES, THUS WILL BE THE SON - OF MAN IN THE

ἡμέρα αὐτοῦ]⌝. **17.25** πρῶτον δὲ δεῖ αὐτὸν
DAY OF HIM. BUT~FIRST IT IS NECESSARY [FOR] HIM

πολλὰ παθεῖν καὶ ἀποδοκιμασθῆναι ἀπὸ τῆς
TO SUFFER~MANY THINGS AND TO BE REJECTED BY -

γενεᾶς ταύτης. **17.26** καὶ καθὼς ἐγένετο ἐν ταῖς
THIS~GENERATION. AND JUST AS IT WAS IN THE

17:24 text: all. omit: ASVmg RSVmg NIVmg NRSVmg.

ἡμέραις Νῶε, οὕτως ἔσται καὶ ἐν ταῖς ἡμέραις τοῦ
DAYS OF NOAH, THUS WILL IT BE ALSO IN THE DAYS OF THE

υἱοῦ τοῦ ἀνθρώπου· **17.27** ἤσθιον, ἔπινον, ἐγάμουν,
SON - OF MAN. THEY WERE EATING, DRINKING, MARRYING,

ἐγαμίζοντο, ἄχρι ἧς ἡμέρας εἰσῆλθεν Νῶε εἰς
[AND] BEING GIVEN IN MARRIAGE, UNTIL WHICH DAY ENTERED NOAH INTO

τὴν κιβωτόν καὶ ἦλθεν ὁ κατακλυσμὸς καὶ ἀπώλεσεν
THE ARK AND CAME THE FLOOD AND IT DESTROYED

πάντας. **17.28** ὁμοίως καθὼς ἐγένετο ἐν ταῖς ἡμέραις
EVERYTHING. LIKEWISE, JUST AS IT WAS IN THE DAYS

Λώτ· ἤσθιον, ἔπινον, ἠγόραζον, ἐπώλουν, ἐφύτευον,
OF LOT. THEY WERE EATING, DRINKING, BUYING, SELLING, PLANTING, [AND]

ᾠκοδόμουν· **17.29** ᾗ δὲ ἡμέρᾳ ἐξῆλθεν Λὼτ ἀπὸ
BUILDING. BUT~ON WHICH DAY WENT OUT LOT FROM

Σοδόμων, ἔβρεξεν πῦρ καὶ θεῖον ἀπ᾽ οὐρανοῦ καὶ
SODOM, IT RAINED FIRE AND SULPHUR FROM HEAVEN AND

ἀπώλεσεν πάντας. **17.30** κατὰ τὰ αὐτὰ ἔσται
DESTROYED EVERYTHING. ACCORDING TO THE SAME THINGS IT WILL BE

ᾗ ἡμέρᾳ ὁ υἱὸς τοῦ ἀνθρώπου ἀποκαλύπτεται.
ON WHICH DAY THE SON - OF MAN IS REVEALED.

17.31 ἐν ἐκείνῃ τῇ ἡμέρᾳ ὃς ἔσται ἐπὶ τοῦ δώματος
ON THAT - DAY WHO WILL BE ON THE ROOF

καὶ τὰ σκεύη αὐτοῦ ἐν τῇ οἰκίᾳ, μὴ καταβάτω
AND THE PROPERTY OF HIM [WILL BE] IN THE HOUSE, LET HIM NOT COME DOWN

ἆραι αὐτά, καὶ ὁ ἐν ἀγρῷ ὁμοίως μὴ ἐπιστρεψάτω
TO TAKE THEM, AND THE ONE IN A FIELD LIKEWISE LET HIM NOT TURN BACK

εἰς τὰ ὀπίσω. **17.32** μνημονεύετε τῆς γυναικὸς Λώτ.
TO THE THINGS BEHIND. REMEMBER THE WIFE OF LOT.

17.33 ὃς ἐὰν ζητήσῃ τὴν ψυχὴν αὐτοῦ περιποιήσασθαι
WHOEVER SEEKS THE LIFE OF HIM TO PRESERVE

ἀπολέσει αὐτήν, ὃς δ᾽ ἂν ἀπολέσῃ ζωογονήσει αὐτήν.
WILL LOSE IT, BUT~WHOEVER LOSES [IT], WILL PRESERVE IT.

17.34 λέγω ὑμῖν, ταύτῃ τῇ νυκτὶ ἔσονται δύο ἐπὶ
I SAY TO YOU°, IN THIS - NIGHT THERE WILL BE TWO IN

κλίνης μιᾶς, ὁ εἷς παραλημφθήσεται καὶ ὁ ἕτερος
ONE~BED, THE ONE WILL BE TAKEN AND THE OTHER

ἀφεθήσεται· **17.35** ἔσονται δύο ἀλήθουσαι ἐπὶ τὸ
WILL BE LEFT. THERE WILL BE TWO GRINDING AT THE

αὐτό, ἡ μία παραλημφθήσεται, ἡ δὲ ἑτέρα
SAME [PLACE], THE ONE WILL BE TAKEN, BUT~THE OTHER

ἀφεθήσεται.⌐ **17.37** καὶ ἀποκριθέντες λέγουσιν αὐτῷ,
WILL BE LEFT. AND HAVING ANSWERED THEY SAY TO HIM,

Ποῦ, κύριε; ὁ δὲ εἶπεν αὐτοῖς, Ὅπου τὸ σῶμα, ἐκεῖ
WHERE, LORD? - BUT HE SAID TO THEM, WHERE THE BODY [IS], THERE

καὶ οἱ ἀετοὶ ἐπισυναχθήσονται.
ALSO THE EAGLES WILL BE GATHERED TOGETHER.

17.35 text: ASV RSV NASB NIV NEB TEV NJB NRSV. add v. 36 δυο εν αγρω· εις παραλημφθησεται και ο ετερος αφεθησεται (two men will be in the field; one will be taken and the other left) [see Matt. 24:40]: ASVmg RSVmg NASBmg NIVmg NEBmg TEVmg NJBmg NRSVmg.

---

days of Noah, so too it will be in the days of the Son of Man. [27]They were eating and drinking, and marrying and being given in marriage, until the day Noah entered the ark, and the flood came and destroyed all of them. [28]Likewise, just as it was in the days of Lot: they were eating and drinking, buying and selling, planting and building, [29]but on the day that Lot left Sodom, it rained fire and sulfur from heaven and destroyed all of them [30]—it will be like that on the day that the Son of Man is revealed. [31]On that day, anyone on the housetop who has belongings in the house must not come down to take them away; and likewise anyone in the field must not turn back. [32]Remember Lot's wife. [33]Those who try to make their life secure will lose it, but those who lose their life will keep it. [34]I tell you, on that night there will be two in one bed; one will be taken and the other left. [35]There will be two women grinding meal together; one will be taken and the other left."[s] [37]Then they asked him, "Where, Lord?" He said to them, "Where the corpse is, there the vultures will gather."

[s] Other ancient authorities add verse 36, *"Two will be in the field; one will be taken and the other left."*

CHAPTER 18

Then Jesus' told them a parable about their need to pray always and not to lose heart. [2]He said, "In a certain city there was a judge who neither feared God nor had respect for people. [3]In that city there was a widow who kept coming to him and saying, 'Grant me justice against my opponent.' [4]For a while he refused; but later he said to himself, 'Though I have no fear of God and no respect for anyone, [5]yet because this widow keeps bothering me, I will grant her justice, so that she may not wear me out by continually coming.'"[u] [6]And the Lord said, "Listen to what the unjust judge says. [7]And will not God grant justice to his chosen ones who cry to him day and night? Will he delay long in helping them? [8]I tell you, he will quickly grant justice to them. And yet, when the Son of Man comes, will he find faith on earth?"

9 He also told this parable to some who trusted in themselves that they were righteous and regarded others with contempt: [10]"Two men went up to the temple to pray, one a

[t] Gk *he*
[u] Or *so that she may not finally come and slap me in the face*

18.1 Ἔλεγεν δὲ παραβολὴν αὐτοῖς πρὸς τὸ
NOW~HE WAS SPEAKING A PARABLE TO THEM ABOUT [HOW] -

δεῖν πάντοτε προσεύχεσθαι αὐτοὺς καὶ
IT IS NECESSARY ALWAYS [FOR] THEM~TO PRAY AND

μὴ ἐγκακεῖν, **18.2** λέγων, Κριτής τις ἦν ἔν τινι πόλει
NOT TO LOSE HEART, SAYING, A CERTAIN~JUDGE WAS IN A CERTAIN CITY

τὸν θεὸν μὴ φοβούμενος καὶ ἄνθρωπον μὴ ἐντρεπόμενος.
- [2]GOD [1]NOT FEARING [3]AND [5]MAN [4]NOT RESPECTING.

18.3 χήρα δὲ ἦν ἐν τῇ πόλει ἐκείνῃ καὶ ἤρχετο
NOW~A WIDOW WAS IN - THAT~CITY AND SHE WAS COMING

πρὸς αὐτὸν λέγουσα, Ἐκδίκησόν με ἀπὸ τοῦ
TO HIM SAYING, GRANT JUSTICE TO ME AGAINST THE

ἀντιδίκου μου. **18.4** καὶ οὐκ ἤθελεν ἐπὶ χρόνον.
OPPONENT OF ME. AND HE WAS NOT WILLING FOR A TIME.

μετὰ δὲ ταῦτα εἶπεν ἐν ἑαυτῷ, Εἰ καὶ τὸν θεὸν
BUT~AFTER THESE THINGS HE SAID WITHIN HIMSELF, IF INDEED - GOD

οὐ φοβοῦμαι οὐδὲ ἄνθρωπον ἐντρέπομαι, **18.5** διά γε
I DO NOT FEAR NOR MAN DO I RESPECT, YET~BECAUSE

τὸ παρέχειν μοι κόπον τὴν χήραν ταύτην ἐκδικήσω
- CAUSES ME TROUBLE - THIS~WIDOW, I WILL GRANT JUSTICE

αὐτήν, ἵνα μὴ εἰς τέλος ἐρχομένη ὑπωπιάζῃ με.
TO HER, LEST IN [THE] END COMING SHE MAY WEAR OUT ME.

18.6 Εἶπεν δὲ ὁ κύριος, Ἀκούσατε τί ὁ κριτὴς τῆς
NOW~SAID THE LORD, LISTEN TO WHAT THE [2]JUDGE

ἀδικίας λέγει· **18.7** ὁ δὲ θεὸς οὐ μὴ ποιήσῃ
[1]UNRIGHTEOUS SAYS: - NOW [WILL NOT] GOD BY ALL MEANS BRING ABOUT

τὴν ἐκδίκησιν τῶν ἐκλεκτῶν αὐτοῦ τῶν
THE JUSTICE OF THE CHOSEN ONES OF HIM -

βοώντων αὐτῷ ἡμέρας καὶ νυκτός, καὶ μακροθυμεῖ
CRYING OUT TO HIM, DAY AND NIGHT, AND HE HAS PATIENCE

ἐπ' αὐτοῖς; **18.8** λέγω ὑμῖν ὅτι ποιήσει τὴν
WITH THEM? I SAY TO YOU° THAT HE WILL BRING ABOUT THE

ἐκδίκησιν αὐτῶν ἐν τάχει. πλὴν ὁ υἱὸς τοῦ
JUSTICE OF THEM WITH SPEED. BUT THE SON -

ἀνθρώπου ἐλθὼν ἆρα εὑρήσει τὴν πίστιν ἐπὶ τῆς
OF MAN HAVING COME, THEN WILL HE FIND - FAITH ON THE

γῆς;
EARTH?

18.9 Εἶπεν δὲ καὶ πρός τινας τοὺς πεποιθότας
AND~HE SAID ALSO TO SOME, THE ONES HAVING PUT CONFIDENCE

ἐφ' ἑαυτοῖς ὅτι εἰσὶν δίκαιοι καὶ ἐξουθενοῦντας τοὺς
IN THEMSELVES THAT THEY ARE RIGHTEOUS AND DESPISING -

λοιποὺς τὴν παραβολὴν ταύτην· **18.10** Ἄνθρωποι δύο
OTHERS, - THIS~PARABLE. TWO~MEN

ἀνέβησαν εἰς τὸ ἱερὸν προσεύξασθαι, ὁ εἷς
WENT UP TO THE TEMPLE TO PRAY, - ONE [WAS A]

Φαρισαῖος καὶ ὁ ἕτερος τελώνης. **18.11** ⌐ὁ
PHARISEE AND THE OTHER, A TAX COLLECTOR. THE

Φαρισαῖος σταθεὶς πρὸς ἑαυτὸν ταῦτα προσηύχετο,⌐
PHARISEE HAVING STOOD, TO HIMSELF WAS PRAYING~THESE THINGS,

Ὁ θεός, εὐχαριστῶ σοι ὅτι οὐκ εἰμὶ ὥσπερ οἱ λοιποὶ
- GOD, I THANK YOU THAT I AM NOT LIKE - OTHER

τῶν ἀνθρώπων, ἅρπαγες, ἄδικοι, μοιχοί, ἢ καὶ ὡς
- MEN, SWINDLERS, UNRIGHTEOUS, ADULTERERS, OR EVEN AS

οὗτος ὁ τελώνης· **18.12** νηστεύω δὶς τοῦ
THIS - TAX COLLECTOR. I FAST TWICE [DURING] THE

σαββάτου, ἀποδεκατῶ πάντα ὅσα κτῶμαι.
WEEK, I TITHE EVERYTHING AS MUCH AS I GET.

18.13 ὁ δὲ τελώνης μακρόθεν ἑστὼς οὐκ ἤθελεν οὐδὲ
BUT~THE TAX COLLECTOR HAVING STOOD~AT A DISTANCE WAS NOT WILLING EVEN

τοὺς ὀφθαλμοὺς ἐπᾶραι εἰς τὸν οὐρανόν, ἀλλ' ἔτυπτεν
THE EYES TO RAISE UP TO - HEAVEN, BUT WAS BEATING

τὸ στῆθος αὐτοῦ λέγων, Ὁ θεός, ἱλάσθητί μοι τῷ
THE CHEST OF HIM SAYING, - GOD, HAVE MERCY ON ME THE

ἁμαρτωλῷ. **18.14** λέγω ὑμῖν, κατέβη οὗτος
SINNER. I SAY TO YOU°, THIS ONE~WENT DOWN

δεδικαιωμένος εἰς τὸν οἶκον αὐτοῦ παρ' ἐκεῖνον·
HAVING BEEN JUSTIFIED TO THE HOUSE OF HIM [RATHER] THAN THAT ONE.

ὅτι πᾶς ὁ ὑψῶν ἑαυτὸν ταπεινωθήσεται, ὁ δὲ
BECAUSE EVERYONE - EXALTING HIMSELF WILL BE HUMBLED, BUT~THE ONE

ταπεινῶν ἑαυτὸν ὑψωθήσεται.
HUMBLING HIMSELF WILL BE EXALTED.

18.15 Προσέφερον δὲ αὐτῷ καὶ τὰ βρέφη ἵνα
NOW~THEY WERE BRINGING TO HIM ALSO - INFANTS THAT

αὐτῶν ἅπτηται· ἰδόντες δὲ οἱ μαθηταὶ ἐπετίμων
HE MIGHT TOUCH~THEM. BUT~HAVING SEEN [THIS], THE DISCIPLES WERE REBUKING

αὐτοῖς. **18.16** ὁ δὲ Ἰησοῦς προσεκαλέσατο αὐτὰ λέγων,
THEM. - BUT JESUS CALLED FOR THEM SAYING,

Ἄφετε τὰ παιδία ἔρχεσθαι πρός με καὶ μὴ κωλύετε
PERMIT THE CHILDREN TO COME TO ME AND DO NOT HINDER

αὐτά, τῶν γὰρ τοιούτων ἐστὶν ἡ βασιλεία τοῦ θεοῦ.
THEM, - FOR OF SUCH ONES IS THE KINGDOM - OF GOD.

18.17 ἀμὴν λέγω ὑμῖν, ὃς ἂν μὴ δέξηται τὴν
TRULY I SAY TO YOU°, WHOEVER DOES NOT WELCOME THE

βασιλείαν τοῦ θεοῦ ὡς παιδίον, οὐ μὴ εἰσέλθῃ εἰς
KINGDOM - OF GOD AS A CHILD, MAY BY NO MEANS ENTER INTO

αὐτήν.
IT.

18.18 Καὶ ἐπηρώτησέν τις αὐτὸν ἄρχων λέγων,
AND ³QUESTIONED ¹A CERTAIN ⁴HIM ²RULER SAYING,

Pharisee and the other a tax collector. ¹¹The Pharisee, standing by himself, was praying thus, 'God, I thank you that I am not like other people: thieves, rogues, adulterers, or even like this tax collector. ¹²I fast twice a week; I give a tenth of all my income.' ¹³But the tax collector, standing far off, would not even look up to heaven, but was beating his breast and saying, 'God, be merciful to me, a sinner!' ¹⁴I tell you, this man went down to his home justified rather than the other; for all who exalt themselves will be humbled, but all who humble themselves will be exalted."

15 People were bringing even infants to him that he might touch them; and when the disciples saw it, they sternly ordered them not to do it. ¹⁶But Jesus called for them and said, "Let the little children come to me, and do not stop them; for it is to such as these that the kingdom of God belongs. ¹⁷Truly I tell you, whoever does not receive the kingdom of God as a little child will never enter it."

18 A certain ruler asked

18:11 text: NEBmg TEV NRSV. var. ο Φαρισαιος σταθεις ταυτα προς εαυτον προσευξετο (the Pharisee stood and prayed these things with himself) KJV ASV RSV NASB (NIV) TEVmg NJB. var. ο Φαρισαιος σταθεις ταυτα προσευξετο (the Pharisee stood and prayed these things): NEB. var. ο Φαρισαιος σταθεις καθ εαυτον ταυτα προσευξετο (the Pharisee stood and prayed these things privately): NEBmg.

him, "Good Teacher, what must I do to inherit eternal life?" [19]Jesus said to him, "Why do you call me good? No one is good but God alone. [20]You know the commandments: 'You shall not commit adultery; You shall not murder; You shall not steal; You shall not bear false witness; Honor your father and mother.'" [21]He replied, "I have kept all these since my youth." [22]When Jesus heard this, he said to him, "There is still one thing lacking. Sell all that you own and distribute the money[v] to the poor, and you will have treasure in heaven; then come, follow me." [23]But when he heard this, he became sad; for he was very rich. [24]Jesus looked at him and said, "How hard it is for those who have wealth to enter the kingdom of God! [25]Indeed, it is easier for a camel to go through the eye of a needle than for someone who is rich to enter the kingdom of God."

[26]Those who heard it said, "Then who can be saved?" [27]He replied, "What is impossible for mortals is possible for God."

[28]Then Peter said, "Look, we have left our homes and followed you." [29]And

[v] Gk lacks the money

Διδάσκαλε ἀγαθέ, τί   ποιήσας ζωὴν αἰώνιον
GOOD~TEACHER,   WHAT HAVING DONE ETERNAL~LIFE

κληρονομήσω; **18.19** εἶπεν δὲ αὐτῷ ὁ Ἰησοῦς, Τί
WILL I INHERIT?   AND~SAID TO HIM - JESUS,   WHY

με λέγεις ἀγαθόν; οὐδεὶς ἀγαθὸς εἰ μὴ εἷς ὁ θεός.
DO YOU CALL~ME GOOD? NO ONE [IS] GOOD EXCEPT [2]ALONE - [1]GOD.

18.20 τὰς ἐντολὰς οἶδας· Μὴ μοιχεύσῃς,
        THE COMMANDMENTS YOU KNOW. DO NOT COMMIT ADULTERY,

Μὴ φονεύσῃς, Μὴ κλέψῃς, Μὴ ψευδομαρτυρήσῃς, Τίμα
DO NOT COMMIT MURDER, DO NOT STEAL, DO NOT BEAR FALSE WITNESS,   HONOR

τὸν πατέρα σου καὶ τὴν μητέρα. **18.21** ὁ δὲ εἶπεν,
THE FATHER   OF YOU AND THE MOTHER.   - AND HE SAID,

Ταῦτα πάντα ἐφύλαξα ἐκ   νεότητος.
ALL~THESE THINGS I KEPT   FROM [MY] YOUTH.

18.22 ἀκούσας δὲ ὁ Ἰησοῦς εἶπεν αὐτῷ, Ἔτι ἕν
        AND~HAVING HEARD - JESUS SAID TO HIM, STILL ONE [THING]

σοι λείπει· πάντα ὅσα ἔχεις πώλησον καὶ
FOR YOU IS LACKING. EVERYTHING, AS MUCH AS YOU HAVE, SELL   AND

διάδος πτωχοῖς, καὶ ἕξεις   θησαυρὸν ἐν [τοῖς]
DISTRIBUTE TO THE POOR, AND YOU WILL HAVE TREASURE IN THE

οὐρανοῖς, καὶ δεῦρο ἀκολούθει μοι. **18.23** ὁ δὲ
HEAVENS,   AND COME FOLLOW   ME.   - BUT

ἀκούσας ταῦτα   περίλυπος ἐγενήθη· ἦν γὰρ
HAVING HEARD THESE THINGS HE BECAME~VERY SAD.   FOR~HE WAS

πλούσιος σφόδρα.
VERY~RICH.

18.24 Ἰδὼν   δὲ αὐτὸν ὁ Ἰησοῦς [περίλυπον
        [3]HAVING SEEN [1]AND [4]HIM - [2]JESUS   [6]VERY SAD

γενόμενον] εἶπεν, Πῶς δυσκόλως οἱ   τὰ
[5]HAVING BECOME SAID, HOW WITH DIFFICULTY THE ONES -

χρήματα ἔχοντες εἰς τὴν βασιλείαν τοῦ θεοῦ
HAVING~WEALTH   INTO THE KINGDOM   - OF GOD

εἰσπορεύονται· **18.25** εὐκοπώτερον γάρ ἐστιν κάμηλον
ENTER.   FOR~EASIER   IT IS [FOR] A CAMEL

διὰ τρήματος βελόνης εἰσελθεῖν ἢ   πλούσιον εἰς
THROUGH [THE] OPENING OF A NEEDLE TO ENTER   THAN [FOR] A RICH PERSON INTO

τὴν βασιλείαν τοῦ θεοῦ εἰσελθεῖν. **18.26** εἶπαν δὲ
THE KINGDOM   OF GOD TO ENTER.   BUT~SAID

οἱ   ἀκούσαντες, Καὶ τίς δύναται σωθῆναι; **18.27** ὁ
THE ONES HAVING HEARD, AND WHO IS ABLE TO BE SAVED?   -

δὲ εἶπεν, Τὰ   ἀδύνατα παρὰ ἀνθρώποις δυνατὰ
AND HE SAID, THE THINGS IMPOSSIBLE WITH   MEN   POSSIBLE

παρὰ τῷ θεῷ ἐστιν. **18.28** Εἶπεν δὲ ὁ Πέτρος, Ἰδοὺ
WITH - GOD ARE.   AND~SAID - PETER, BEHOLD

ἡμεῖς ἀφέντες τὰ ἴδια   ἠκολουθήσαμέν σοι. **18.29** ὁ
WE   HAVING LEFT - OUR OWN FOLLOWED   YOU.   -

18:20 Exod. 20:12-16; Deut. 5:16-20

δὲ εἶπεν αὐτοῖς, Ἀμὴν λέγω ὑμῖν ὅτι οὐδείς ἐστιν
AND HE SAID TO THEM, TRULY I SAY TO YOU° THAT THERE IS~NO ONE

ὃς ἀφῆκεν οἰκίαν ἢ γυναῖκα ἢ ἀδελφοὺς ἢ γονεῖς
WHO LEFT HOUSE OR WIFE OR BROTHERS OR PARENTS

ἢ τέκνα ἕνεκεν τῆς βασιλείας τοῦ θεοῦ, **18.30** ὃς
OR CHILDREN BECAUSE OF THE KINGDOM - OF GOD, WHO

οὐχὶ μὴ [ἀπο]λάβῃ πολλαπλασίονα ἐν τῷ καιρῷ τούτῳ
WILL NOT RECEIVE MANY TIMES AS MUCH IN - THIS~TIME

καὶ ἐν τῷ αἰῶνι τῷ ἐρχομένῳ ζωὴν αἰώνιον.
AND IN THE AGE - COMING, ETERNAL~LIFE.

18.31 Παραλαβὼν δὲ τοὺς δώδεκα εἶπεν πρὸς αὐτούς,
AND~HAVING TAKEN THE TWELVE HE SAID TO THEM,

Ἰδοὺ ἀναβαίνομεν εἰς Ἰερουσαλήμ, καὶ τελεσθήσεται
BEHOLD WE ARE GOING UP TO JERUSALEM, AND WILL BE FULFILLED

πάντα τὰ γεγραμμένα διὰ τῶν προφητῶν τῷ
ALL THE THINGS HAVING BEEN WRITTEN BY THE PROPHETS ABOUT THE

υἱῷ τοῦ ἀνθρώπου· **18.32** παραδοθήσεται γὰρ τοῖς
SON - OF MAN. FOR~HE WILL BE DELIVERED UP TO THE

ἔθνεσιν καὶ ἐμπαιχθήσεται καὶ ὑβρισθήσεται καὶ
GENTILES AND HE WILL BE RIDICULED AND HE WILL BE MISTREATED AND

ἐμπτυσθήσεται **18.33** καὶ μαστιγώσαντες ἀποκτενοῦσιν
HE WILL BE SPAT UPON AND HAVING WHIPPED [HIM] THEY WILL KILL

αὐτόν, καὶ τῇ ἡμέρᾳ τῇ τρίτῃ ἀναστήσεται.
HIM, AND ON THE ²DAY - ¹THIRD HE WILL RISE AGAIN.

18.34 καὶ αὐτοὶ οὐδὲν τούτων συνῆκαν καὶ
AND THEY NONE OF THESE THINGS UNDERSTOOD AND

ἦν τὸ ῥῆμα τοῦτο κεκρυμμένον ἀπ᾽ αὐτῶν καὶ
HAD BEEN - THIS WORD HIDDEN FROM THEM, AND

οὐκ ἐγίνωσκον τὰ λεγόμενα.
THEY WERE NOT UNDERSTANDING THE THINGS BEING SAID.

18.35 Ἐγένετο δὲ ἐν τῷ ἐγγίζειν αὐτὸν εἰς Ἰεριχὼ
AND~IT CAME ABOUT WHILE HE~DREW NEAR TO JERICHO

τυφλός τις ἐκάθητο παρὰ τὴν ὁδὸν ἐπαιτῶν.
A CERTAIN~BLIND MAN WAS SITTING BESIDE THE ROAD BEGGING.

18.36 ἀκούσας δὲ ὄχλου διαπορευομένου ἐπυνθάνετο τί
AND~HAVING HEARD A CROWD TRAVELING THROUGH HE WAS ASKING WHAT

εἴη τοῦτο. **18.37** ἀπήγγειλαν δὲ αὐτῷ ὅτι Ἰησοῦς ὁ
THIS~MIGHT BE. AND~THEY REPORTED TO HIM THAT JESUS THE

Ναζωραῖος παρέρχεται. **18.38** καὶ ἐβόησεν λέγων,
NAZARENE IS GOING BY. AND HE CRIED OUT SAYING,

Ἰησοῦ υἱὲ Δαυίδ, ἐλέησόν με. **18.39** καὶ οἱ
JESUS, SON OF DAVID, HAVE MERCY ON ME. AND THE ONES

προάγοντες ἐπετίμων αὐτῷ ἵνα σιγήσῃ, αὐτὸς δὲ
GOING BEFORE [HIM] WERE REBUKING HIM THAT HE SHOULD BE SILENT, BUT~HE

πολλῷ μᾶλλον ἔκραζεν, Υἱὲ Δαυίδ, ἐλέησόν με.
MUCH MORE WAS CRYING OUT, SON OF DAVID, HAVE MERCY ON ME.

18.40 σταθεὶς δὲ ὁ Ἰησοῦς ἐκέλευσεν αὐτὸν ἀχθῆναι
AND~HAVING STOOD - JESUS COMMANDED HIM TO BE LED

he said to them, "Truly I tell you, there is no one who has left house or wife or brothers or parents or children, for the sake of the kingdom of God, ³⁰who will not get back very much more in this age, and in the age to come eternal life."

31 Then he took the twelve aside and said to them, "See, we are going up to Jerusalem, and everything that is written about the Son of Man by the prophets will be accomplished. ³²For he will be handed over to the Gentiles; and he will be mocked and insulted and spat upon. ³³After they have flogged him, they will kill him, and on the third day he will rise again." ³⁴But they understood nothing about all these things; in fact, what he said was hidden from them, and they did not grasp what was said.

35 As he approached Jericho, a blind man was sitting by the roadside begging. ³⁶When he heard a crowd going by, he asked what was happening. ³⁷They told him, "Jesus of Nazarethʷ is passing by." ³⁸Then he shouted, "Jesus, Son of David, have mercy on me!" ³⁹Those who were in front sternly ordered him to be quiet; but he shouted even more loudly, "Son of David, have mercy on me!" ⁴⁰Jesus stood still and ordered the man to be brought

to him; and when he came
near, he asked him, [41]"What
do you want me to do for
you?" He said, "Lord, let me
see again." [42]Jesus said to
him, "Receive your sight;
your faith has saved you."
[43]Immediately he regained
his sight and followed him,
glorifying God; and all the
people, when they saw it,
praised God.

πρὸς αὐτόν.   ἐγγίσαντος   δὲ   αὐτοῦ ἐπηρώτησεν αὐτόν,
TO   HIM.   3HAVING DRAWN NEAR 1AND 2HE   QUESTIONED   HIM,

18.41 Τί   σοι   θέλεις   ποιήσω;   ὁ δὲ εἶπεν, Κύριε,
WHAT FOR YOU DO YOU WISH [THAT] I MAY DO? - AND HE SAID LORD,

ἵνα   ἀναβλέψω.   **18.42** καὶ ὁ Ἰησοῦς εἶπεν αὐτῷ,
THAT I MAY REGAIN MY SIGHT.   AND - JESUS   SAID TO HIM,

Ἀνάβλεψον·   ἡ   πίστις   σου   σέσωκέν σε.   **18.43** καὶ
REGAIN YOUR SIGHT. THE FAITH OF YOU HAS HEALED YOU.   AND

παραχρῆμα ἀνέβλεψεν καὶ ἠκολούθει αὐτῷ   δοξάζων
AT ONCE   HE SAW AGAIN AND WAS FOLLOWING HIM   GLORIFYING

τὸν θεόν. καὶ πᾶς ὁ λαὸς ἰδὼν   ἔδωκεν αἶνον
-    GOD. AND ALL THE PEOPLE HAVING SEEN [THIS] GAVE   PRAISE

τῷ θεῷ.
-   TO GOD.

CHAPTER 19

He entered Jericho and was
passing through it. [2]A man
was there named Zacchaeus;
he was a chief tax collector
and was rich. [3]He was trying
to see who Jesus was, but on
account of the crowd he
could not, because he was
short in stature. [4]So he
ran ahead and climbed a
sycamore tree to see him,
because he was going to pass
that way. [5]When Jesus came
to the place, he looked up
and said to him, "Zacchaeus,
hurry and come down; for I
must stay at your house
today." [6]So he hurried down
and was happy to welcome
him. [7]All who saw it began
to grumble and said, "He
has gone to be the guest
of one who is a sinner."
[8]Zacchaeus stood there and
said to the Lord, "Look, half

19.1 Καὶ εἰσελθὼν   διήρχετο   τὴν Ἰεριχώ.
AND HAVING ENTERED HE WAS PASSING THROUGH -   JERICHO.

19.2 καὶ ἰδοὺ ἀνὴρ ὀνόματι καλούμενος Ζακχαῖος, καὶ
AND BEHOLD A MAN BY NAME BEING CALLED ZACCHAEUS,   AND

αὐτὸς ἦν ἀρχιτελώνης   καὶ αὐτὸς πλούσιος· **19.3** καὶ
HE   WAS A CHIEF TAX COLLECTOR AND HE [WAS] WEALTHY.   AND

ἐζήτει   ἰδεῖν τὸν Ἰησοῦν τίς ἐστιν καὶ οὐκ ἠδύνατο
HE WAS SEEKING TO SEE - JESUS WHO HE IS AND WAS NOT ABLE

ἀπὸ τοῦ ὄχλου, ὅτι   τῇ ἡλικίᾳ μικρὸς ἦν. **19.4** καὶ
FROM THE CROWD, BECAUSE - IN STATURE HE WAS~SHORT.   AND

προδραμὼν εἰς τὸ ἔμπροσθεν ἀνέβη   ἐπὶ
HAVING RUN AHEAD TO THE FRONT HE CLIMBED UP ONTO

συκομορέαν ἵνα ἴδῃ   αὐτόν ὅτι ἐκείνης
A SYCAMORE FIG TREE THAT HE MIGHT SEE HIM BECAUSE [BY] THAT [WAY]

ἤμελλεν διέρχεσθαι. **19.5** καὶ ὡς ἦλθεν ἐπὶ τὸν
HE WAS ABOUT TO PASS BY.   AND AS HE CAME TO THE

τόπον, ἀναβλέψας ὁ Ἰησοῦς εἶπεν πρὸς αὐτόν,
PLACE, HAVING LOOKED UP - JESUS SAID TO   HIM,

Ζακχαῖε, σπεύσας   κατάβηθι, σήμερον γὰρ ἐν τῷ οἴκῳ
ZACCHAEUS, HAVING HURRIED COME DOWN, FOR~TODAY IN THE HOUSE

σου δεῖ   με   μεῖναι. **19.6** καὶ σπεύσας
OF YOU IT IS NECESSARY FOR ME TO REMAIN.   AND HAVING HURRIED

κατέβη   καὶ ὑπεδέξατο αὐτὸν χαίρων.   **19.7** καὶ
HE CAME DOWN AND WELCOMED HIM WITH JOY.   AND

ἰδόντες πάντες διεγόγγυζον λέγοντες ὅτι Παρὰ
ALL~HAVING SEEN [THIS] WERE COMPLAINING SAYING, - WITH

ἁμαρτωλῷ ἀνδρὶ εἰσῆλθεν καταλῦσαι. **19.8** σταθεὶς δὲ
A SINFUL   MAN HE ENTERED TO REST.   AND~HAVING STOOD

Ζακχαῖος εἶπεν πρὸς τὸν κύριον, Ἰδοὺ τὰ ἡμίσιά μου
ZACCHAEUS SAID TO THE LORD, BEHOLD - HALF   OF MY

τῶν ὑπαρχόντων, κύριε, τοῖς πτωχοῖς δίδωμι, καὶ εἴ
-    POSSESSIONS,   LORD,   TO THE   POOR   I GIVE,   AND   IF

τινός   τι ἐσυκοφάντησα ἀποδίδωμι τετραπλοῦν.
[FROM] SOMEONE I DEFRAUDED~OF ANYTHING I AM PAYING BACK FOUR TIMES.

19.9 εἶπεν δὲ πρὸς αὐτὸν ὁ Ἰησοῦς ὅτι Σήμερον
AND~SAID   TO   HIM   -   JESUS,   -   TODAY

σωτηρία τῷ οἴκῳ τούτῳ ἐγένετο, καθότι καὶ αὐτὸς
SALVATION   -   TO THIS~HOUSE   CAME,   BECAUSE   ALSO   HE

υἱὸς Ἀβραάμ ἐστιν· **19.10** ἦλθεν γὰρ ὁ υἱὸς τοῦ
A SON   OF ABRAHAM   IS.   FOR~CAME   THE   SON   -

ἀνθρώπου ζητῆσαι καὶ σῶσαι τὸ ἀπολωλός.
OF MAN   TO SEEK   AND   TO SAVE   THE   LOST.

19.11 Ἀκουόντων δὲ αὐτῶν ταῦτα   προσθεὶς εἶπεν
NOW~HEARING   THEY   THESE THINGS, HAVING ADDED HE TOLD

παραβολὴν διὰ   τὸ ἐγγὺς εἶναι Ἰερουσαλὴμ αὐτὸν
A PARABLE   BECAUSE -   NEAR   TO BE   TO JERUSALEM   HIM

καὶ δοκεῖν αὐτοὺς ὅτι παραχρῆμα μέλλει ἡ βασιλεία
AND   THEY~THINK   THAT   IMMEDIATELY   IS ABOUT   THE   KINGDOM

τοῦ θεοῦ ἀναφαίνεσθαι. **19.12** εἶπεν οὖν, Ἄνθρωπός τις
-    OF GOD   TO APPEAR.   THEN~HE SAID,   A CERTAIN~MAN

εὐγενὴς ἐπορεύθη εἰς χώραν μακρὰν λαβεῖν ἑαυτῷ
OF NOBLE BIRTH TRAVELED   TO   A DISTANT~COUNTRY   TO RECEIVE   FOR HIMSELF

βασιλείαν καὶ ὑποστρέψαι. **19.13** καλέσας δὲ δέκα
A KINGDOM   AND   TO RETURN.   AND~HAVING CALLED   TEN

δούλους ἑαυτοῦ ἔδωκεν αὐτοῖς δέκα μνᾶς καὶ εἶπεν
SLAVES   OF HIMSELF   HE GAVE   TO THEM   TEN   MINAS   AND   HE SAID

πρὸς αὐτούς, Πραγματεύσασθε ἐν ᾧ ἔρχομαι. **19.14** οἱ δὲ
TO   THEM,   CONDUCT BUSINESS   WHILE I AM COMING.   BUT~THE

πολῖται αὐτοῦ ἐμίσουν αὐτὸν καὶ ἀπέστειλαν
CITIZENS   OF HIM   WERE HATING   HIM   AND   THEY SENT

πρεσβείαν ὀπίσω αὐτοῦ λέγοντες, Οὐ θέλομεν τοῦτον
AN AMBASSADOR   AFTER   HIM   SAYING,   WE DO NOT WANT   THIS ONE

βασιλεῦσαι ἐφ᾽ ἡμᾶς. **19.15** Καὶ ἐγένετο ἐν τῷ
TO RULE   OVER   US.   AND   IT CAME ABOUT   WHILE

ἐπανελθεῖν αὐτὸν λαβόντα   τὴν βασιλείαν καὶ εἶπεν
HE~RETURNED   HAVING RECEIVED   THE   KINGDOM   AND   HE SAID

φωνηθῆναι αὐτῷ τοὺς δούλους τούτους οἷς   δεδώκει
TO BE CALLED   TO HIM   -   THESE~SLAVES   TO WHOM HE HAD GIVEN

τὸ ἀργύριον, ἵνα γνοῖ   τί διεπραγματεύσαντο.
THE MONEY,   THAT HE MIGHT KNOW WHAT THEY GAINED BY TRADING.

19.16 παρεγένετο δὲ ὁ   πρῶτος λέγων, Κύριε, ἡ μνᾶ
AND~HAVING COME   THE   FIRST   SAYING,   LORD,   THE   MINA

σου δέκα προσηργάσατο μνᾶς. **19.17** καὶ εἶπεν αὐτῷ,
OF YOU TEN   MINAS~GAINED.   AND   HE SAID   TO HIM,

Εὖγε, ἀγαθὲ δοῦλε, ὅτι   ἐν ἐλαχίστῳ
EXCELLENT, GOOD   SLAVE,   BECAUSE IN   [THE] SMALLEST [THING]

πιστὸς ἐγένου, ἴσθι ἐξουσίαν ἔχων ἐπάνω δέκα
YOU WERE~FAITHFUL,   BE   HAVING~AUTHORITY   OVER   TEN

of my possessions, Lord, I will give to the poor; and if I have defrauded anyone of anything, I will pay back four times as much." [9]Then Jesus said to him, "Today salvation has come to this house, because he too is a son of Abraham. [10]For the Son of Man came to seek out and to save the lost."

,11 As they were listening to this, he went on to tell a parable, because he was near Jerusalem, and because they supposed that the kingdom of God was to appear immediately. [12]So he said, "A nobleman went to a distant country to get royal power for himself and then return. [13]He summoned ten of his slaves, and gave them ten pounds,[x] and said to them, 'Do business with these until I come back.' [14]But the citizens of his country hated him and sent a delegation after him, saying, 'We do not want this man to rule over us.' [15]When he returned, having received royal power, he ordered these slaves, to whom he had given the money, to be summoned so that he might find out what they had gained by trading. [16]The first came forward and said, 'Lord, your pound has made ten more pounds.' [17]He said to him, 'Well done, good slave! Because you have been trustworthy in a very small thing, take charge of ten

---

[x] The mina, rendered here by *pound*, was about three months' wages for a laborer

cities.' ¹⁸Then the second came, saying, 'Lord, your pound has made five pounds.' ¹⁹He said to him, 'And you, rule over five cities.' ²⁰Then the other came, saying, 'Lord, here is your pound. I wrapped it up in a piece of cloth, ²¹for I was afraid of you, because you are a harsh man; you take what you did not deposit, and reap what you did not sow.' ²²He said to him, 'I will judge you by your own words, you wicked slave! You knew, did you, that I was a harsh man, taking what I did not deposit and reaping what I did not sow? ²³Why then did you not put my money into the bank? Then when I returned, I could have collected it with interest.' ²⁴He said to the bystanders, 'Take the pound from him and give it to the one who has ten pounds.' ²⁵(And they said to him, 'Lord, he has ten pounds!') ²⁶'I tell you, to all those who have, more will be given; but from those who have nothing, even what they have will be taken away. ²⁷But as for these enemies of mine who did not want me to be king over them—bring them here and slaughter them in my presence.'"

28 After he had said this, he went on ahead, going up to Jerusalem.

29 When he had come near Bethphage and Bethany, at the place called the Mount of Olives, he sent two of the disciples,

πόλεων. **19.18** καὶ ἦλθεν ὁ δεύτερος λέγων, Ἡ μνᾶ
CITIES.   AND CAME THE SECOND SAYING, THE MINA

σου, κύριε, ἐποίησεν πέντε μνᾶς. **19.19** εἶπεν δὲ καὶ
OF YOU, LORD, MADE FIVE MINAS.   AND~HE SAID ALSO

τούτῳ, Καὶ σὺ ἐπάνω γίνου πέντε πόλεων. **19.20** καὶ
TO THIS ONE, AND YOU BE~OVER FIVE CITIES.   AND

ὁ ἕτερος ἦλθεν λέγων, Κύριε, ἰδοὺ ἡ μνᾶ σου ἦν
THE OTHER CAME SAYING, LORD, BEHOLD THE MINA OF YOU WHICH

εἶχον ἀποκειμένην ἐν σουδαρίῳ· **19.21** ἐφοβούμην γάρ
I HAD BEING PUT AWAY IN A NAPKIN.   FOR~I WAS FEARING

σε, ὅτι ἄνθρωπος αὐστηρὸς εἶ, αἴρεις ὃ
YOU, BECAUSE A MAN OF STRICTNESS YOU ARE, YOU TAKE WHAT

οὐκ ἔθηκας καὶ θερίζεις ὃ οὐκ ἔσπειρας.
YOU DID NOT DEPOSIT AND YOU REAP WHAT YOU DID NOT SOW.

19.22 λέγει αὐτῷ, Ἐκ τοῦ στόματός σου κρινῶ σε,
       HE SAYS TO HIM, FROM THE MOUTH OF YOU I WILL JUDGE YOU,

πονηρὲ δοῦλε. ᾔδεις ὅτι ἐγὼ ἄνθρωπος αὐστηρός
EVIL SLAVE. YOU HAD KNOWN THAT I A MAN OF STRICTNESS

εἰμι, αἴρων ὃ οὐκ ἔθηκα καὶ θερίζων ὃ
AM, TAKING WHAT I DID NOT DEPOSIT AND REAPING WHAT

οὐκ ἔσπειρα; **19.23** καὶ διὰ τί οὐκ ἔδωκάς μου τὸ
I DID NOT SOW?   AND WHY DID YOU NOT GIVE ME THE

ἀργύριον ἐπὶ τράπεζαν; κἀγὼ ἐλθὼν σὺν τόκῳ ἂν
MONEY ON A [BANKER'S] TABLE? AND I HAVING COME WITH INTEREST -

αὐτὸ ἔπραξα. **19.24** καὶ τοῖς παρεστῶσιν εἶπεν,
COLLECTED~IT.   AND TO THE ONES HAVING STOOD NEARBY HE SAID,

Ἄρατε ἀπ᾽ αὐτοῦ τὴν μνᾶν καὶ δότε τῷ τὰς δέκα
TAKE FROM HIM THE MINA AND GIVE [IT] TO THE ONE THE TEN

μνᾶς ἔχοντι **19.25** —καὶ εἶπαν αὐτῷ, Κύριε, ἔχει δέκα
MINAS HAVING   — AND THEY SAID TO HIM, LORD, HE HAS TEN

19.26 μνᾶς— λέγω ὑμῖν ὅτι παντὶ τῷ ἔχοντι
       MINAS— I SAY TO YOU° THAT TO EVERYONE - HAVING

δοθήσεται, ἀπὸ δὲ τοῦ μὴ ἔχοντος καὶ ὃ ἔχει
IT WILL BE GIVEN, BUT~FROM THE ONE NOT HAVING EVEN WHAT HE HAS

ἀρθήσεται. **19.27** πλὴν τοὺς ἐχθρούς μου τούτους τοὺς
WILL BE TAKEN AWAY. BUT - ENEMIES OF ME THESE THE ONES

μὴ θελήσαντάς με βασιλεῦσαι ἐπ᾽ αὐτοὺς ἀγάγετε ὧδε
NOT HAVING WANTED ME TO RULE OVER THEM BRING HERE

καὶ κατασφάξατε αὐτοὺς ἔμπροσθέν μου.
AND EXECUTE THEM BEFORE ME.

19.28 Καὶ εἰπὼν ταῦτα ἐπορεύετο ἔμπροσθεν
       AND HAVING SAID THESE THINGS HE WAS TRAVELING AHEAD

ἀναβαίνων εἰς Ἱεροσόλυμα. **19.29** Καὶ ἐγένετο ὡς
GOING UP TO JERUSALEM.   AND IT CAME ABOUT AS

ἤγγισεν εἰς Βηθφαγὴ καὶ Βηθανία[ν] πρὸς τὸ ὄρος
HE CAME NEAR TO BETHPHAGE AND BETHANY TO THE MOUNTAIN,

τὸ καλούμενον Ἐλαιῶν, ἀπέστειλεν δύο τῶν μαθητῶν
THE ONE BEING CALLED OF OLIVES, HE SENT TWO OF THE DISCIPLES

19.30 λέγων, Ὑπάγετε εἰς τὴν κατέναντι κώμην, ἐν ᾗ
SAYING,   GO   INTO THE   VILLAGE~OPPOSITE,   IN   WHICH

εἰσπορευόμενοι εὑρήσετε πῶλον δεδεμένον, ἐφ᾽ ὃν
ENTERING   YOU° WILL FIND A COLT   HAVING BEEN TIED, UPON WHICH

οὐδεὶς πώποτε ἀνθρώπων ἐκάθισεν, καὶ λύσαντες αὐτὸν
NO ONE   EVER   OF MEN   SAT,   AND   HAVING UNTIED IT

ἀγάγετε. **19.31** καὶ ἐάν τις   ὑμᾶς ἐρωτᾷ, Διὰ τί
BRING [IT HERE].   AND   IF   SOMEONE ASKS~YOU,   WHY

λύετε;   οὕτως ἐρεῖτε   ὅτι Ὁ κύριος αὐτοῦ
ARE YOU° UNTYING [IT]? THUS   YOU° WILL SAY,   -   THE LORD   OF IT

χρείαν ἔχει. **19.32** ἀπελθόντες δὲ οἱ   ἀπεσταλμένοι
HAS~NEED.   AND~HAVING DEPARTED THE ONES HAVING BEEN SENT

εὗρον καθὼς εἶπεν αὐτοῖς. **19.33** λυόντων δὲ   αὐτῶν
FOUND [IT] JUST AS HE TOLD THEM.   AND~[WHILE] UNTYING THEM

τὸν πῶλον εἶπαν οἱ κύριοι αὐτοῦ πρὸς αὐτούς, Τί
THE COLT,   SAID   THE MASTERS OF IT   TO   THEM,   WHY

λύετε   τὸν πῶλον; **19.34** οἱ δὲ εἶπαν ὅτι Ὁ κύριος
ARE YOU° UNTYING THE COLT?   -   AND THEY SAID -   THE LORD

αὐτοῦ χρείαν ἔχει. **19.35** καὶ ἤγαγον αὐτὸν πρὸς τὸν
OF IT   HAS~NEED.   AND THEY LED   IT   TO   -

Ἰησοῦν καὶ ἐπιρίψαντες αὐτῶν τὰ ἱμάτια ἐπὶ τὸν
JESUS   AND HAVING THROWN THEIR   -   GARMENTS ON   THE

πῶλον ἐπεβίβασαν τὸν Ἰησοῦν. **19.36** πορευομένου δὲ
COLT,   THEY PUT ON [IT] -   JESUS.   AND~[WHILE] GOING

αὐτοῦ ὑπεστρώννυον τὰ ἱμάτια αὐτῶν ἐν τῇ ὁδῷ.
HE,   THEY WERE SPREADING OUT THE GARMENTS OF THEM ON THE ROAD.

19.37 Ἐγγίζοντος δὲ αὐτοῦ ἤδη   πρὸς τῇ καταβάσει
AND~NEARING   HIM   ALREADY TO   THE DESCENT

τοῦ Ὄρους τῶν Ἐλαιῶν ἤρξαντο ἅπαν τὸ πλῆθος τῶν
OF THE MOUNT   -   OF OLIVES, BEGAN   ALL   THE MULTITUDE OF THE

μαθητῶν χαίροντες αἰνεῖν τὸν θεὸν φωνῇ μεγάλῃ περὶ
DISCIPLES REJOICING   TO PRAISE -   GOD   WITH A LOUD~VOICE ABOUT

πασῶν ὧν   εἶδον δυνάμεων, **19.38** λέγοντες,
ALL   ²WHICH ³THEY SAW ¹[THE] MIRACLES,   SAYING,

Εὐλογημένος ὁ   ἐρχόμενος,
HAVING BEEN BLESSED [IS] THE ONE COMING,

ὁ βασιλεὺς ἐν ὀνόματι κυρίου·
THE KING   IN [THE] NAME OF [THE] LORD;

ἐν οὐρανῷ εἰρήνη
IN   HEAVEN   PEACE

καὶ δόξα ἐν ὑψίστοις.
AND GLORY IN [THE] HIGHEST.

19.39 καὶ τινες τῶν Φαρισαίων ἀπὸ τοῦ ὄχλου εἶπαν
AND SOME OF THE PHARISEES   FROM THE CROWD SAID

πρὸς αὐτόν, Διδάσκαλε, ἐπιτίμησον τοῖς μαθηταῖς σου.
TO   HIM,   TEACHER,   REBUKE   THE DISCIPLES OF YOU.

19:38 Ps. 118:26

³⁰saying, "Go into the village ahead of you, and as you enter it you will find tied there a colt that has never been ridden. Untie it and bring it here. ³¹If anyone asks you, 'Why are you untying it?' just say this, 'The Lord needs it.'" ³²So those who were sent departed and found it as he had told them. ³³As they were untying the colt, its owners asked them, "Why are you untying the colt?" ³⁴They said, "The Lord needs it." ³⁵Then they brought it to Jesus; and after throwing their cloaks on the colt, they set Jesus on it. ³⁶As he rode along, people kept spreading their cloaks on the road. ³⁷As he was now approaching the path down from the Mount of Olives, the whole multitude of the disciples began to praise God joyfully with a loud voice for all the deeds of power that they had seen, ³⁸saying,

"Blessed is the king
who comes in the name
of the Lord!
Peace in heaven,
and glory in the highest
heaven!"

³⁹Some of the Pharisees in the crowd said to him, "Teacher, order your disciples to stop."

[40]He answered, "I tell you, if these were silent, the stones would shout out."

[41]As he came near and saw the city, he wept over it, [42]saying, "If you, even you, had only recognized on this day the things that make for peace! But now they are hidden from your eyes. [43]Indeed, the days will come upon you, when your enemies will set up ramparts around you and surround you, and hem you in on every side. [44]They will crush you to the ground, you and your children within you, and they will not leave within you one stone upon another; because you did not recognize the time of your visitation from God."[y]

[45]Then he entered the temple and began to drive out those who were selling things there; [46]and he said, "It is written,
'My house shall be a house of prayer';
but you have made it a den of robbers."

[47]Every day he was teaching in the temple. The chief priests, the scribes, and the leaders of the people kept looking for a way to kill him; [48]but they did not find anything they could do, for all the people were spellbound by what they heard.

[y] Gk lacks *from God*

19.40 καὶ ἀποκριθεὶς εἶπεν, Λέγω ὑμῖν, ἐὰν οὗτοι
AND   HAVING ANSWERED   HE SAID,   I SAY   TO YOU°,   IF   THESE

σιωπήσουσιν, οἱ λίθοι κράξουσιν.
WILL BE SILENT,   THE STONES   WILL CRY OUT.

19.41 Καὶ ὡς ἤγγισεν ἰδὼν τὴν πόλιν ἔκλαυσεν
AND   AS   HE CAME NEAR,   HAVING SEEN   THE   CITY,   HE CRIED

ἐπ᾽ αὐτήν **19.42** λέγων ὅτι Εἰ ἔγνως ἐν τῇ ἡμέρᾳ ταύτῃ
OVER   IT   SAYING   -   IF   YOU KNEW   IN   -   THIS~DAY

καὶ σὺ τὰ πρὸς εἰρήνην· νῦν δὲ ἐκρύβη ἀπὸ
EVEN   YOU   THE THINGS   [LEADING] TO   PEACE.   BUT~NOW   IT WAS HIDDEN   FROM

ὀφθαλμῶν σου. **19.43** ὅτι ἥξουσιν ἡμέραι ἐπὶ σὲ καὶ
[THE] EYES   OF YOU.   BECAUSE   WILL COME   DAYS   UPON   YOU   AND

παρεμβαλοῦσιν οἱ ἐχθροί σου χάρακά σοι καὶ
WILL CONSTRUCT   THE   ENEMIES   OF YOU   AN EMBANKMENT   AGAINST YOU   AND

περικυκλώσουσίν σε καὶ συνέξουσίν σε πάντοθεν,
THEY WILL SURROUND   YOU   AND   WILL HEM IN   YOU   FROM ALL DIRECTIONS,

19.44 καὶ ἐδαφιοῦσίν σε καὶ τὰ τέκνα σου ἐν
AND   THEY WILL DASH TO THE GROUND   YOU   AND   THE   CHILDREN   OF YOU   WITH

σοί, καὶ οὐκ ἀφήσουσιν λίθον ἐπὶ λίθον ἐν σοί,
YOU,   AND   THEY WILL NOT LEAVE   A STONE   UPON   STONE   WITHIN   YOU,

ἀνθ᾽ ὧν οὐκ ἔγνως τὸν καιρὸν τῆς ἐπισκοπῆς σου.
BECAUSE   YOU DID NOT KNOW   THE   TIME   OF THE   VISITATION   OF YOU.

19.45 Καὶ εἰσελθὼν εἰς τὸ ἱερὸν ἤρξατο ἐκβάλλειν
AND   HAVING ENTERED   INTO   THE   TEMPLE   HE BEGAN   TO THROW OUT

τοὺς πωλοῦντας **19.46** λέγων αὐτοῖς, Γέγραπται,
THE ONES   SELLING,   SAYING   TO THEM,   IT HAS BEEN WRITTEN,

Καὶ ἔσται ὁ οἶκός μου οἶκος προσευχῆς,
AND   WILL BE   THE   HOUSE   OF ME   A HOUSE   OF PRAYER,

ὑμεῖς δὲ αὐτὸν ἐποιήσατε σπήλαιον λῃστῶν.
BUT~YOU°   MADE~IT   A CAVE   OF ROBBERS.

19.47 Καὶ ἦν διδάσκων τὸ καθ᾽ ἡμέραν ἐν τῷ ἱερῷ.
AND   HE WAS TEACHING   -   DAILY   IN   THE   TEMPLE.

οἱ δὲ ἀρχιερεῖς καὶ οἱ γραμματεῖς ἐζήτουν
BUT~THE   CHIEF PRIESTS   AND   THE   SCRIBES   WERE SEEKING

αὐτὸν ἀπολέσαι καὶ οἱ πρῶτοι τοῦ λαοῦ, **19.48** καὶ
TO KILL~HIM   AND [ALSO]   THE   LEADING MEN   OF THE   PEOPLE,   AND

οὐχ εὕρισκον τὸ τί ποιήσωσιν, ὁ λαὸς γὰρ ἅπας
THEY WERE NOT FINDING   -   WHAT   THEY MIGHT DO,   [3]THE   [4]PEOPLE   [1]FOR   [2]ALL

ἐξεκρέματο αὐτοῦ ἀκούων.
HUNG UPON   HIM   LISTENING.

19:46 Isa. 56:7; Jer. 7:11

CHAPTER 20

One day, as he was teaching the people in the temple

20.1 Καὶ ἐγένετο ἐν μιᾷ τῶν ἡμερῶν
AND   IT CAME ABOUT   ON   ONE   OF THE   DAYS

διδάσκοντος αὐτοῦ τὸν λαὸν ἐν τῷ ἱερῷ καὶ
HE~TEACHING   THE   PEOPLE   IN   THE   TEMPLE   AND

εὐαγγελιζομένου   ἐπέστησαν οἱ ἀρχιερεῖς καὶ οἱ
PREACHING THE GOOD NEWS, [AND]   STOOD BY   THE CHIEF PRIESTS AND THE

γραμματεῖς σὺν τοῖς πρεσβυτέροις **20.2** καὶ εἶπαν
SCRIBES   WITH THE   ELDERS   AND THEY SPOKE

λέγοντες πρὸς αὐτόν, Εἰπὸν ἡμῖν ἐν ποίᾳ ἐξουσίᾳ
SAYING   TO   HIM,   TELL US BY WHAT AUTHORITY

ταῦτα ποιεῖς, ἢ τίς ἐστιν ὁ   δούς   σοι τὴν
YOU DO~THESE THINGS, OR WHO IS   THE ONE HAVING GIVEN TO YOU -

ἐξουσίαν ταύτην; **20.3** ἀποκριθεὶς δὲ εἶπεν πρὸς αὐτούς,
THIS~AUTHORITY?   AND~HAVING ANSWERED HE SAID TO   THEM,

Ἐρωτήσω ὑμᾶς κἀγὼ λόγον, καὶ εἴπατέ μοι· **20.4** Τὸ
WILL QUESTION YOU° I ALSO A WORD, AND YOU° TELL ME.   THE

βάπτισμα Ἰωάννου ἐξ οὐρανοῦ ἦν ἢ ἐξ ἀνθρώπων;
BAPTISM   OF JOHN FROM HEAVEN WAS IT OR FROM MEN?

20.5 οἱ δὲ συνελογίσαντο πρὸς ἑαυτοὺς λέγοντες ὅτι
      - AND THEY REASONED   TO   THEMSELVES SAYING   -

Ἐὰν εἴπωμεν, Ἐξ οὐρανοῦ, ἐρεῖ,   Διὰ τί
IF WE SAY, FROM HEAVEN, HE WILL SAY, WHY

οὐκ ἐπιστεύσατε αὐτῷ; **20.6** ἐὰν δὲ εἴπωμεν, Ἐξ
DID YOU° NOT BELIEVE HIM?   BUT~IF WE SAY,   FROM

ἀνθρώπων, ὁ λαὸς ἅπας καταλιθάσει ἡμᾶς,
MEN,   ²THE ³PEOPLE ¹ALL WILL STONE   US,

πεπεισμένος γάρ ἐστιν Ἰωάννην προφήτην εἶναι.
FOR~HAVING BEEN CONVINCED JOHN~IS   TO BE [CONSIDERED]~A PROPHET.

20.7 καὶ ἀπεκρίθησαν μὴ εἰδέναι πόθεν.
      AND THEY ANSWERED NOT TO KNOW FROM WHERE [IT CAME].

20.8 καὶ ὁ Ἰησοῦς εἶπεν αὐτοῖς, Οὐδὲ ἐγὼ λέγω
      AND - JESUS   SAID TO THEM, NEITHER I   AM TELLING

ὑμῖν ἐν ποίᾳ ἐξουσίᾳ ταῦτα ποιῶ.
YOU° BY WHAT AUTHORITY I DO~THESE THINGS.

20.9 Ἤρξατο δὲ πρὸς τὸν λαὸν λέγειν τὴν
      AND~HE BEGAN   TO   THE PEOPLE TO TELL   -

παραβολὴν ταύτην· Ἄνθρωπός [τις] ἐφύτευσεν
THIS~PARABLE.   A CERTAIN~MAN   PLANTED

ἀμπελῶνα καὶ ἐξέδετο αὐτὸν γεωργοῖς καὶ ἀπεδήμησεν
A VINEYARD AND LEASED   IT   TO FARMERS AND HE WENT AWAY [FOR]

χρόνους ἱκανούς. **20.10** καὶ καιρῷ ἀπέστειλεν πρὸς
A LONG~TIME.   AND IN SEASON HE SENT   TO

τοὺς γεωργοὺς δοῦλον ἵνα ἀπὸ τοῦ καρποῦ τοῦ
THE   FARMERS   A SLAVE THAT FROM THE FRUIT   OF THE

ἀμπελῶνος δώσουσιν αὐτῷ· οἱ δὲ γεωργοὶ
VINEYARD   THEY WILL GIVE TO HIM. BUT~THE FARMERS

ἐξαπέστειλαν αὐτὸν δείραντες κενόν. **20.11** καὶ
SENT OUT   HIM EMPTY~HAVING BEATEN [HIM].   AND

προσέθετο ἕτερον πέμψαι δοῦλον· οἱ δὲ κἀκεῖνον
HE PROCEEDED TO SEND~ANOTHER SLAVE.   - BUT HE ALSO

δείραντες καὶ ἀτιμάσαντες ἐξαπέστειλαν κενόν.
HAVING BEATEN AND HAVING DISHONORED THEY SENT OUT EMPTY.

and telling the good news, the chief priests and the scribes came with the elders [2]and said to him, "Tell us, by what authority are you doing these things? Who is it who gave you this authority?" [3]He answered them, "I will also ask you a question, and you tell me: [4]Did the baptism of John come from heaven, or was it of human origin?" [5]They discussed it with one another, saying, "If we say, 'From heaven,' he will say, 'Why did you not believe him?' [6]But if we say, 'Of human origin,' all the people will stone us; for they are convinced that John was a prophet." [7]So they answered that they did not know where it came from. [8]Then Jesus said to them, "Neither will I tell you by what authority I am doing these things."

9 He began to tell the people this parable: "A man planted a vineyard, and leased it to tenants, and went to another country for a long time. [10]When the season came, he sent a slave to the tenants in order that they might give him his share of the produce of the vineyard; but the tenants beat him and sent him away empty-handed. [11]Next he sent another slave; that one also they beat and insulted and sent away empty-handed.

12And he sent still a third; this one also they wounded and threw out. 13Then the owner of the vineyard said, 'What shall I do? I will send my beloved son; perhaps they will respect him.' 14But when the tenants saw him, they discussed it among themselves and said, 'This is the heir; let us kill him so that the inheritance may be ours.' 15So they threw him out of the vineyard and killed him. What then will the owner of the vineyard do to them? 16He will come and destroy those tenants and give the vineyard to others." When they heard this, they said, "Heaven forbid!" 17But he looked at them and said, "What then does this text mean:

'The stone that the
builders rejected
has become the
cornerstone'?ᶻ
18Everyone who falls on that stone will be broken to pieces; and it will crush anyone on whom it falls." 19When the scribes and chief priests realized that he had told this parable against them, they wanted to lay hands on him at that very hour, but they feared the people.

20 So they watched him and sent spies who

ᶻ Or *keystone*

20.12 καὶ προσέθετο τρίτον πέμψαι· οἱ δὲ καὶ
AND HE PROCEEDED A THIRD [TIME] TO SEND [SOMEONE]. - AND ALSO

τοῦτον τραυματίσαντες ἐξέβαλον. **20.13** εἶπεν δὲ ὁ
THIS ONE HAVING WOUNDED THEY THREW OUT. AND~SAID THE

κύριος τοῦ ἀμπελῶνος, Τί ποιήσω; πέμψω τὸν υἱόν
LORD OF THE VINEYARD, WHAT SHOULD I DO? I WILL SEND THE ²SON

μου τὸν ἀγαπητόν· ἴσως τοῦτον ἐντραπήσονται.
³OF ME - ¹BELOVED. PERHAPS THIS ONE THEY WILL RESPECT.

20.14 ἰδόντες δὲ αὐτὸν οἱ γεωργοὶ διελογίζοντο πρὸς
BUT~HAVING SEEN HIM THE FARMERS WERE REASONING WITH

ἀλλήλους λέγοντες, Οὗτός ἐστιν ὁ κληρονόμος·
ONE ANOTHER SAYING, THIS ONE IS THE HEIR.

ἀποκτείνωμεν αὐτόν, ἵνα ἡμῶν γένηται ἡ
LET US KILL HIM, THAT OURS MAY BECOME THE

κληρονομία. **20.15** καὶ ἐκβαλόντες αὐτὸν ἔξω τοῦ
INHERITANCE. AND HAVING DRIVEN OUT HIM OUTSIDE THE

ἀμπελῶνος ἀπέκτειναν. τί οὖν ποιήσει αὐτοῖς ὁ
VINEYARD THEY KILLED [HIM]. WHAT THEN WILL DO TO THEM THE

κύριος τοῦ ἀμπελῶνος; **20.16** ἐλεύσεται καὶ ἀπολέσει
LORD OF THE VINEYARD? HE WILL COME AND WILL DESTROY

τοὺς γεωργοὺς τούτους καὶ δώσει τὸν ἀμπελῶνα ἄλλοις.
- THESE~FARMERS AND WILL GIVE THE VINEYARD TO OTHERS.

ἀκούσαντες δὲ εἶπαν, Μὴ γένοιτο. **20.17** ὁ δὲ
AND~HAVING HEARD [THIS] THEY SAID, MAY IT NEVER BE. - BUT

ἐμβλέψας αὐτοῖς εἶπεν, Τί οὖν ἐστιν τὸ
HAVING LOOKED AT THEM HE SAID, WHAT THEN IS -

γεγραμμένον τοῦτο·
THIS~HAVING BEEN WRITTEN:

Λίθον ὃν ἀπεδοκίμασαν οἱ οἰκοδομοῦντες,
[THE] STONE WHICH REJECTED THE BUILDERS,

οὗτος ἐγενήθη εἰς κεφαλὴν γωνίας;
THIS ONE CAME TO BE FOR [THE] HEAD OF [THE] CORNER?

20.18 πᾶς ὁ πεσὼν ἐπ' ἐκεῖνον τὸν λίθον
EVERYONE HAVING FALLEN UPON THAT - STONE

συνθλασθήσεται· ἐφ' ὃν δ' ἂν πέσῃ, λικμήσει αὐτόν.
WILL BE BROKEN INTO PIECES. AND~UPON WHOMEVER IT FALLS, IT WILL CRUSH HIM.

20.19 Καὶ ἐζήτησαν οἱ γραμματεῖς καὶ οἱ ἀρχιερεῖς
AND SOUGHT THE SCRIBES AND THE CHIEF PRIESTS

ἐπιβαλεῖν ἐπ' αὐτὸν τὰς χεῖρας ἐν αὐτῇ τῇ ὥρᾳ,
TO LAY UPON HIM THE(THEIR) HANDS IN THE~SAME HOUR,

καὶ ἐφοβήθησαν τὸν λαόν, ἔγνωσαν γὰρ ὅτι πρὸς
AND THEY WERE AFRAID OF THE PEOPLE, FOR~THEY KNEW THAT AGAINST

αὐτοὺς εἶπεν τὴν παραβολὴν ταύτην.
THEM HE SPOKE - THIS~PARABLE.

20.20 Καὶ παρατηρήσαντες ἀπέστειλαν ἐγκαθέτους
AND HAVING WATCHED CAREFULLY THEY SENT SPIES

20:17 Ps. 118:22

ὑποκρινομένους ἑαυτοὺς δικαίους εἶναι, ἵνα
PRETENDING THEMSELVES TO BE~RIGHTEOUS, THAT

ἐπιλάβωνται αὐτοῦ λόγου, ὥστε παραδοῦναι αὐτὸν
THEY MIGHT CATCH [HIM IN] HIS WORD, SO AS TO DELIVER HIM

τῇ ἀρχῇ καὶ τῇ ἐξουσίᾳ τοῦ ἡγεμόνος. **20.21** καὶ
TO THE RULERS AND THE AUTHORITIES OF THE GOVERNOR. AND

ἐπηρώτησαν αὐτὸν λέγοντες, Διδάσκαλε, οἴδαμεν
THEY QUESTIONED HIM SAYING, TEACHER, WE KNOW

ὅτι ὀρθῶς λέγεις καὶ διδάσκεις καὶ οὐ λαμβάνεις
THAT YOU SPEAK~RIGHTLY AND YOU TEACH AND YOU DO NOT RECEIVE

πρόσωπον, ἀλλ᾽ ἐπ᾽ ἀληθείας τὴν ὁδὸν τοῦ θεοῦ
A FACE, BUT ON THE BASIS OF TRUTH THE WAY - OF GOD

διδάσκεις· **20.22** ἔξεστιν ἡμᾶς Καίσαρι φόρον δοῦναι
YOU TEACH. IS IT PERMISSIBLE FOR US TO CAESAR TO PAY~A TAX

ἢ οὔ; **20.23** κατανοήσας δὲ αὐτῶν τὴν πανουργίαν
OR NOT? BUT~HAVING NOTICED THEIR - CRAFTINESS

εἶπεν πρὸς αὐτούς, **20.24** Δείξατέ μοι δηνάριον· τίνος
HE SAID TO THEM, SHOW ME A DENARIUS. OF WHOM

ἔχει εἰκόνα καὶ ἐπιγραφήν; οἱ δὲ εἶπαν, Καίσαρος.
HAS IT AN IMAGE AND INSCRIPTION? - AND THEY SAID, OF CAESAR.

20.25 ὁ δὲ εἶπεν πρὸς αὐτούς, Τοίνυν ἀπόδοτε τὰ
- AND HE SAID TO THEM, THEN GIVE THE THINGS

Καίσαρος Καίσαρι καὶ τὰ τοῦ θεοῦ τῷ θεῷ.
OF CAESAR TO CAESAR AND THE THINGS - OF GOD - TO GOD.

20.26 καὶ οὐκ ἴσχυσαν ἐπιλαβέσθαι αὐτοῦ ῥήματος
AND THEY WERE NOT ABLE TO CATCH [HIM IN] HIS WORD

ἐναντίον τοῦ λαοῦ καὶ θαυμάσαντες ἐπὶ τῇ ἀποκρίσει
BEFORE THE PEOPLE AND HAVING MARVELED AT THE ANSWER

αὐτοῦ ἐσίγησαν.
OF HIM THEY WERE SILENT.

20.27 Προσελθόντες δέ τινες τῶν Σαδδουκαίων, οἱ
AND~HAVING APPROACHED SOME OF THE SADDUCEES, THE ONES

[ἀντι]λέγοντες ἀνάστασιν μὴ εἶναι, ἐπηρώτησαν
SPEAKING AGAINST [THE] RESURRECTION [SAYING IT] IS NOT TO BE, THEY QUESTIONED

αὐτὸν **20.28** λέγοντες, Διδάσκαλε, Μωϋσῆς ἔγραψεν ἡμῖν,
HIM SAYING, TEACHER, MOSES WROTE TO US,

ἐάν τινος ἀδελφὸς ἀποθάνῃ ἔχων γυναῖκα, καὶ οὗτος
IF SOMEONE'S BROTHER DIES HAVING A WIFE, AND THIS ONE

ἄτεκνος ᾖ, ἵνα λάβῃ ὁ ἀδελφὸς αὐτοῦ τὴν γυναῖκα
IS~CHILDLESS, THAT SHOULD TAKE THE BROTHER OF HIM THE WIFE

καὶ ἐξαναστήσῃ σπέρμα τῷ ἀδελφῷ αὐτοῦ.
AND HE SHOULD RAISE UP A SEED TO THE BROTHER OF HIM.

20.29 ἑπτὰ οὖν ἀδελφοὶ ἦσαν· καὶ ὁ πρῶτος
THEN~SEVEN BROTHERS THERE WERE. AND THE FIRST

λαβὼν γυναῖκα ἀπέθανεν ἄτεκνος· **20.30** καὶ ὁ
HAVING TAKEN [THE] WIFE DIED CHILDLESS. AND THE

pretended to be honest, in order to trap him by what he said, so as to hand him over to the jurisdiction and authority of the governor. [21]So they asked him, "Teacher, we know that you are right in what you say and teach, and you show deference to no one, but teach the way of God in accordance with truth. [22]Is it lawful for us to pay taxes to the emperor, or not?" [23]But he perceived their craftiness and said to them, [24]"Show me a denarius. Whose head and whose title does it bear?" They said, "The emperor's." [25]He said to them, "Then give to the emperor the things that are the emperor's, and to God the things that are God's." [26]And they were not able in the presence of the people to trap him by what he said; and being amazed by his answer, they became silent.

[27] Some Sadducees, those who say there is no resurrection, came to him [28]and asked him a question, "Teacher, Moses wrote for us that if a man's brother dies, leaving a wife but no children, the man[a] shall marry the widow and raise up children for his brother. [29]Now there were seven brothers; the first married, and died childless; [30]then the

[a] Gk *his brother*

20:28 Deut. 25:5

second ³¹and the third married her, and so in the same way all seven died childless. ³²Finally the woman also died. ³³In the resurrection, therefore, whose wife will the woman be? For the seven had married her."

34 Jesus said to them, "Those who belong to this age marry and are given in marriage; ³⁵but those who are considered worthy of a place in that age and in the resurrection from the dead neither marry nor are given in marriage. ³⁶Indeed they cannot die anymore, because they are like angels and are children of God, being children of the resurrection. ³⁷And the fact that the dead are raised Moses himself showed, in the story about the bush, where he speaks of the Lord as the God of Abraham, the God of Isaac, and the God of Jacob. ³⁸Now he is God not of the dead, but of the living; for to him all of them are alive." ³⁹Then some of the scribes answered, "Teacher, you have spoken well." ⁴⁰For they no longer dared to ask him another question.

41 Then he said to them, "How can they say that the Messiah^b is David's son? ⁴²For David himself says in the book of Psalms,

'The Lord said to my Lord,
"Sit at my right hand,

^b Or *the Christ*

δεύτερος **20.31** καὶ ὁ τρίτος ἔλαβεν αὐτήν, ὡσαύτως δὲ
SECOND   AND THE THIRD TOOK HER, AND~LIKEWISE

καὶ οἱ ἑπτὰ οὐ κατέλιπον τέκνα καὶ ἀπέθανον.
ALSO THE SEVEN DID NOT LEAVE BEHIND A CHILD AND THEY [ALL] DIED.

20.32 ὕστερον καὶ ἡ γυνὴ ἀπέθανεν. **20.33** ἡ γυνὴ οὖν
AND~FINALLY THE WOMAN DIED.   THE WOMAN THEN

ἐν τῇ ἀναστάσει τίνος αὐτῶν γίνεται γυνή; οἱ
IN THE RESURRECTION OF WHICH OF THEM DOES SHE BECOME [THE] WIFE? -

γὰρ ἑπτὰ ἔσχον αὐτὴν γυναῖκα. **20.34** καὶ εἶπεν
FOR SEVEN HAD HER [AS] WIFE.   AND SAID

αὐτοῖς ὁ Ἰησοῦς, Οἱ υἱοὶ τοῦ αἰῶνος τούτου γαμοῦσιν
TO THEM - JESUS, THE SONS - OF THIS~AGE MARRY

καὶ γαμίσκονται, **20.35** οἱ δὲ καταξιωθέντες
AND ARE GIVEN IN MARRIAGE, BUT~THE ONES HAVING BEEN CONSIDERED WORTHY

τοῦ αἰῶνος ἐκείνου τυχεῖν καὶ τῆς ἀναστάσεως
- OF THAT~AGE TO ATTAIN AND OF THE RESURRECTION

τῆς ἐκ νεκρῶν οὔτε γαμοῦσιν οὔτε γαμίζονται·
FROM~THE DEAD NEITHER MARRY NOR ARE GIVEN IN MARRIAGE.

20.36 οὐδὲ γὰρ ἀποθανεῖν ἔτι δύνανται,
FOR~NEITHER TO DIE IS IT POSSIBLE~ANY LONGER,

ἰσάγγελοι γάρ εἰσιν καὶ υἱοί εἰσιν θεοῦ τῆς
FOR~LIKE ANGELS THEY ARE AND SONS OF GOD~THEY ARE, ³OF THE

ἀναστάσεως υἱοὶ ὄντες. **20.37** ὅτι δὲ ἐγείρονται οἱ
⁴RESURRECTION ²SONS ¹BEING. BUT~THAT ARE RAISED THE

νεκροί, καὶ Μωϋσῆς ἐμήνυσεν ἐπὶ τῆς βάτου, ὡς
DEAD, EVEN MOSES REVEALED AT THE [BURNING] BUSH, AS

λέγει κύριον τὸν θεὸν Ἀβραὰμ καὶ θεὸν Ἰσαὰκ καὶ
HE CALLS [THE] LORD THE GOD OF ABRAHAM AND [THE] GOD OF ISAAC AND

θεὸν Ἰακώβ. **20.38** θεὸς δὲ οὐκ ἔστιν νεκρῶν ἀλλὰ
[THE] GOD OF JACOB. BUT~GOD IS NOT OF DEAD PERSONS BUT

ζώντων, πάντες γὰρ αὐτῷ ζῶσιν. **20.39** ἀποκριθέντες δέ
OF LIVING ONES, FOR~ALL TO HIM ARE ALIVE. AND~HAVING ANSWERED

τινες τῶν γραμματέων εἶπαν, Διδάσκαλε, καλῶς εἶπας.
SOME OF THE SCRIBES SAID, TEACHER, YOU SPOKE~WELL.

20.40 οὐκέτι γὰρ ἐτόλμων ἐπερωτᾶν αὐτὸν οὐδέν.
FOR~NO LONGER WERE THEY DARING TO QUESTION HIM ANYTHING.

20.41 Εἶπεν δὲ πρὸς αὐτούς, Πῶς λέγουσιν τὸν
AND~HE SAID TO THEM, HOW DO THEY SAY THE

Χριστὸν εἶναι Δαυὶδ υἱόν; **20.42** αὐτὸς γὰρ Δαυὶδ
CHRIST TO BE DAVID'S SON? FOR~HIMSELF DAVID

λέγει ἐν βίβλῳ ψαλμῶν,
SAYS IN [THE] BOOK OF PSALMS,

Εἶπεν κύριος τῷ κυρίῳ μου,
SAID [THE] LORD TO THE LORD OF ME,

Κάθου ἐκ δεξιῶν μου,
SIT DOWN AT [THE] RIGHT OF ME

20:37 Exod. 3:6   **20:42-43** Ps. 110:1

20.43 ἕως ἂν θῶ τοὺς ἐχθρούς σου ὑποπόδιον
UNTIL   I PUT THE ENEMIES OF YOU [AS] A FOOTSTOOL

τῶν ποδῶν σου.
OF THE FEET OF YOU.

20.44 Δαυὶδ οὖν κύριον αὐτὸν καλεῖ, καὶ πῶς αὐτοῦ
THEREFORE~DAVID, LORD CALLS~HIM, AND HOW HIS

υἱός ἐστιν;
SON IS HE?

20.45 Ἀκούοντος δὲ   παντὸς τοῦ λαοῦ εἶπεν τοῖς
⁵HEARING   ¹AND [WHILE] ²ALL   ³THE ⁴PEOPLE, HE SAID TO THE

μαθηταῖς [αὐτοῦ], **20.46** Προσέχετε ἀπὸ τῶν γραμματέων
DISCIPLES OF HIM,   BEWARE OF THE SCRIBES,

τῶν θελόντων περιπατεῖν ἐν στολαῖς καὶ φιλούντων
THE ONES WANTING TO WALK AROUND IN LONG ROBES AND LOVING

ἀσπασμοὺς ἐν ταῖς ἀγοραῖς καὶ πρωτοκαθεδρίας ἐν
FORMAL GREETINGS IN THE MARKETPLACES AND [THE] CHIEF SEATS IN

ταῖς συναγωγαῖς καὶ πρωτοκλισίας ἐν τοῖς δείπνοις,
THE SYNAGOGUES AND [THE] PLACES OF HONOR AT THE BANQUETS,

20.47 οἳ κατεσθίουσιν τὰς οἰκίας τῶν χηρῶν καὶ
WHO DEVOUR THE HOUSES OF THE WIDOWS AND

προφάσει   μακρὰ προσεύχονται· οὗτοι λήμψονται
WITH FALSE PRETENSE THEY PRAY~LENGTHY [PRAYERS]. THESE WILL RECEIVE

περισσότερον κρίμα.
GREATER   JUDGMENT.

43 until I make your
   enemies your
   footstool." '
⁴⁴David thus calls him Lord;
so how can he be his son?"
  45 In the hearing of all
the people he said to theᶜ
disciples, ⁴⁶"Beware of the
scribes, who like to walk
around in long robes, and
love to be greeted with
respect in the marketplaces,
and to have the best seats in
the synagogues and places
of honor at banquets. ⁴⁷They
devour widows' houses and
for the sake of appearance
say long prayers. They
will receive the greater
condemnation."

ᶜ Other ancient authorities read *his*

21.1 Ἀναβλέψας δὲ εἶδεν τοὺς βάλλοντας εἰς τὸ
AND~HAVING LOOKED UP HE SAW THE ONES PUTTING INTO THE

γαζοφυλάκιον τὰ δῶρα αὐτῶν πλουσίους. **21.2** εἶδεν δέ
TREASURY THE GIFTS OF THEM, [THE] WEALTHY. AND~HE SAW

τινα χήραν πενιχρὰν βάλλουσαν ἐκεῖ λεπτὰ δύο,
A CERTAIN POOR~WIDOW PUTTING [IN] THERE TWO~LEPTAS,

21.3 καὶ εἶπεν, Ἀληθῶς λέγω ὑμῖν ὅτι ἡ χήρα αὕτη ἡ
AND HE SAID, TRULY I SAY TO YOU° THAT - ³WIDOW ¹THIS -

πτωχὴ πλεῖον πάντων ἔβαλεν· **21.4** πάντες γὰρ
²POOR MORE [THAN] EVERYONE PUT [IN].   FOR~ALL

οὗτοι ἐκ τοῦ περισσεύοντος αὐτοῖς ἔβαλον εἰς τὰ
THESE FROM THE THINGS ABOUNDING TO THEM THEY PUT IN THE

δῶρα, αὕτη δὲ ἐκ τοῦ ὑστερήματος αὐτῆς πάντα
GIFTS, BUT~THIS [WIDOW] OUT OF THE NEED OF HER, ALL

τὸν βίον ὃν εἶχεν ἔβαλεν.
THE MEANS WHICH SHE HAD SHE PUT [IN].

21.5 Καὶ τινων λεγόντων περὶ τοῦ ἱεροῦ ὅτι
AND [AS] SOME [WERE] SPEAKING ABOUT THE TEMPLE THAT

λίθοις καλοῖς καὶ ἀναθήμασιν κεκόσμηται εἶπεν,
WITH BEAUTIFUL~STONES AND WITH SACRED GIFTS IT HAS BEEN DECORATED HE SAID,

He looked up and saw rich
people putting their gifts into
the treasury; ²he also saw a
poor widow put in two small
copper coins. ³He said,
"Truly I tell you, this poor
widow has put in more than
all of them; ⁴for all of them
have contributed out of their
abundance, but she out of
her poverty has put in all she
had to live on."
  5 When some were
speaking about the temple,
how it was adorned with
beautiful stones and gifts
dedicated to God, he said,

6"As for these things that you see, the days will come when not one stone will be left upon another; all will be thrown down."

7 They asked him, "Teacher, when will this be, and what will be the sign that this is about to take place?" 8And he said, "Beware that you are not led astray; for many will come in my name and say, 'I am he!'*d* and, 'The time is near!'*e* Do not go after them.

9 "When you hear of wars and insurrections, do not be terrified; for these things must take place first, but the end will not follow immediately." 10Then he said to them, "Nation will rise against nation, and kingdom against kingdom; 11there will be great earthquakes, and in various places famines and plagues; and there will be dreadful portents and great signs from heaven.

12 "But before all this occurs, they will arrest you and persecute you; they will hand you over to synagogues and prisons, and you will be brought before kings and governors because of my name. 13This will give you an opportunity to testify. 14So make up your minds not to prepare your defense in advance; 15for I will give you words*f* and a wisdom that none of your opponents will be able to

d Gk *I am*
e Or *at hand*
f Gk *a mouth*

21.6 Ταῦτα ἃ θεωρεῖτε, ἐλεύσονται ἡμέραι ἐν αἷς
THESE THINGS WHICH YOU° SEE, DAYS~WILL COME IN WHICH

οὐκ ἀφεθήσεται λίθος ἐπὶ λίθῳ ὃς οὐ καταλυθήσεται.
THERE WILL NOT BE LEFT A STONE UPON A STONE WHICH WILL NOT BE THROWN DOWN.

21.7 Ἐπηρώτησαν δὲ αὐτὸν λέγοντες, Διδάσκαλε, πότε
AND~THEY QUESTIONED HIM SAYING, TEACHER, WHEN

οὖν ταῦτα ἔσται καὶ τί τὸ σημεῖον ὅταν
THEREFORE WILL BE~THESE THINGS AND WHAT [WILL BE] THE SIGN WHEN

μέλλῃ ταῦτα γίνεσθαι; **21.8** ὁ δὲ εἶπεν, Βλέπετε
THESE THINGS~ARE ABOUT TO TAKE PLACE? - AND HE SAID, BEWARE,

μὴ πλανηθῆτε· πολλοὶ γὰρ ἐλεύσονται ἐπὶ τῷ
YOU° SHOULD NOT BE DECEIVED. FOR~MANY WILL COME IN THE

ὀνόματί μου λέγοντες, Ἐγώ εἰμι, καί, Ὁ καιρὸς
NAME OF ME SAYING, I AM [HE], AND, THE TIME

ἤγγικεν. μὴ πορευθῆτε ὀπίσω αὐτῶν. **21.9** ὅταν δὲ
HAS DRAWN NEAR. DO NOT FOLLOW AFTER THEM. BUT~WHENEVER

ἀκούσητε πολέμους καὶ ἀκαταστασίας, μὴ πτοηθῆτε·
YOU° HEAR [ABOUT] WARS AND INSURRECTIONS, DO NOT BE FRIGHTENED.

δεῖ γὰρ ταῦτα γενέσθαι πρῶτον, ἀλλ' οὐκ
FOR~IT IS NECESSARY [FOR] THESE THINGS TO OCCUR FIRST, BUT [IT IS] NOT

εὐθέως τὸ τέλος. **21.10** Τότε ἔλεγεν αὐτοῖς,
IMMEDIATELY THE END. THEN HE WAS SAYING TO THEM,

Ἐγερθήσεται ἔθνος ἐπ' ἔθνος καὶ βασιλεία ἐπὶ
WILL BE RAISED UP NATION AGAINST NATION AND KINGDOM AGAINST

βασιλείαν, **21.11** σεισμοὶ τε μεγάλοι καὶ κατὰ
KINGDOM, ³EARTHQUAKES ¹BOTH ²GREAT AND IN VARIOUS

τόπους λιμοὶ καὶ λοιμοὶ ἔσονται, φόβητρά τε καὶ ἀπ'
PLACES FAMINES AND PLAGUES THERE WILL BE, BOTH~HORRORS AND FROM

οὐρανοῦ σημεῖα μεγάλα ἔσται. **21.12** πρὸ δὲ
HEAVEN GREAT~SIGNS THERE WILL BE. BUT~BEFORE

τούτων πάντων ἐπιβαλοῦσιν ἐφ' ὑμᾶς τὰς χεῖρας αὐτῶν
ALL~THESE THINGS, THEY WILL LAY ON YOU° THE HANDS OF THEM

καὶ διώξουσιν, παραδιδόντες εἰς τὰς συναγωγὰς
AND THEY WILL PERSECUTE [YOU°], HANDING [YOU°] OVER TO THE SYNAGOGUES

καὶ φυλακάς, ἀπαγομένους ἐπὶ βασιλεῖς καὶ
AND JAILS, BEING LED AWAY TO KINGS AND

ἡγεμόνας ἕνεκεν τοῦ ὀνόματός μου· **21.13** ἀποβήσεται
GOVERNORS BECAUSE OF THE NAME OF ME. IT WILL TURN OUT

ὑμῖν εἰς μαρτύριον. **21.14** θέτε οὖν ἐν
FOR YOU° [TO BE AN OPPORTUNITY] FOR TESTIMONY. THEREFORE~KEEP IN

ταῖς καρδίαις ὑμῶν μὴ προμελετᾶν ἀπολογηθῆναι·
THE HEARTS OF YOU° NOT TO PREPARE TO DEFEND [YOURSELVES].

21.15 ἐγὼ γὰρ δώσω ὑμῖν στόμα καὶ σοφίαν ᾗ
FOR~I WILL GIVE TO YOU° A MOUTH AND WISDOM WHICH

οὐ δυνήσονται ἀντιστῆναι ἢ ἀντειπεῖν ἅπαντες οἱ
WILL NOT BE ABLE TO RESIST OR TO CONTRADICT ALL THE ONES

ἀντικείμενοι ὑμῖν. **21.16** παραδοθήσεσθε δὲ καὶ ὑπὸ
BEING OPPOSED   TO YOU°.   AND~YOU° WILL BE HANDED OVER ALSO   BY

γονέων καὶ ἀδελφῶν καὶ συγγενῶν καὶ φίλων, καὶ
PARENTS AND BROTHERS AND RELATIVES AND FRIENDS,   AND

θανατώσουσιν   ἐξ ὑμῶν, **21.17** καὶ ἔσεσθε μισούμενοι
THEY WILL PUT TO DEATH [SOME] OF YOU°,   AND   YOU° WILL BE HATED

ὑπὸ πάντων διὰ   τὸ ὄνομά μου. **21.18** καὶ θρὶξ ἐκ
BY   EVERYONE BECAUSE OF THE NAME OF ME.   AND A HAIR OF

τῆς κεφαλῆς ὑμῶν οὐ μὴ ἀπόληται. **21.19** ἐν τῇ
THE HEAD   OF YOU° MAY BY NO MEANS PERISH.   IN THE

ὑπομονῇ ὑμῶν κτήσασθε τὰς ψυχὰς ὑμῶν.
ENDURANCE OF YOU° YOU° WILL GAIN THE SOULS OF YOU°.

21.20 Ὅταν δὲ ἴδητε κυκλουμένην ὑπὸ στρατοπέδων
       BUT~WHEN YOU° SEE BEING SURROUNDED BY   ARMIES

Ἰερουσαλήμ, τότε γνῶτε ὅτι ἤγγικεν ἡ ἐρήμωσις
JERUSALEM,   THEN KNOW THAT HAS DRAWN NEAR THE DEVASTATION

αὐτῆς. **21.21** τότε οἱ   ἐν τῇ Ἰουδαίᾳ φευγέτωσαν εἰς
OF IT.   THEN THE ONES IN - JUDEA,   FLEE   TO

τὰ ὄρη   καὶ οἱ   ἐν μέσῳ αὐτῆς ἐκχωρείτωσαν
THE MOUNTAINS AND THE ONES IN [THE] MIDST OF HER LET THEM GET OUT

καὶ οἱ   ἐν ταῖς χώραις μὴ εἰσερχέσθωσαν εἰς αὐτήν,
AND THE ONES IN THE FIELDS   LET THEM NOT ENTER   INTO IT,

21.22 ὅτι   ἡμέραι ἐκδικήσεως αὗταί εἰσιν τοῦ
        BECAUSE DAYS OF VENGEANCE THESE ARE   -

πληθῆναι πάντα τὰ   γεγραμμένα. **21.23** οὐαὶ
TO BE FULFILLED ALL   THE THINGS HAVING BEEN WRITTEN.   WOE

ταῖς   ἐν γαστρὶ ἐχούσαις καὶ ταῖς   θηλαζούσαις
TO THE ONES IN [THE] WOMB HAVING [A CHILD] AND TO THE ONES NURSING

ἐν ἐκείναις ταῖς ἡμέραις· ἔσται γὰρ ἀνάγκη μεγάλη
IN THOSE   -   DAYS.   FOR~THERE WILL BE GREAT~DISTRESS

ἐπὶ τῆς γῆς καὶ ὀργὴ τῷ λαῷ τούτῳ, **21.24** καὶ
UPON THE LAND AND ANGER - [AGAINST] THIS~PEOPLE,   AND

πεσοῦνται στόματι μαχαίρης καὶ αἰχμαλωτισθήσονται
THEY WILL FALL BY [THE] EDGE OF [THE] SWORD AND THEY WILL BE LED CAPTIVE

εἰς τὰ ἔθνη πάντα, καὶ Ἰερουσαλὴμ ἔσται πατουμένη
INTO ²THE ³NATIONS ¹ALL,   AND JERUSALEM   WILL BE TRAMPLED

ὑπὸ ἐθνῶν, ἄχρι οὗ πληρωθῶσιν καιροὶ ἐθνῶν.
BY GENTILES, UNTIL ARE FULFILLED [THE] TIMES OF [THE] GENTILES.

21.25 Καὶ ἔσονται σημεῖα ἐν ἡλίῳ καὶ σελήνῃ καὶ
       AND THERE WILL BE SIGNS IN [THE] SUN AND [THE] MOON AND

ἄστροις, καὶ ἐπὶ τῆς γῆς συνοχὴ ἐθνῶν   ἐν
[THE] STARS, AND UPON THE EARTH [THE] DISMAY OF [THE] GENTILES, IN

ἀπορίᾳ   ἤχους θαλάσσης καὶ σάλου,
PERPLEXITY [AT] [THE] SOUND OF [THE] SEA AND [THE] SURF, [AND]

21.26 ἀποψυχόντων ἀνθρώπων ἀπὸ φόβου καὶ
        FAINTING   MEN   FROM FEAR AND

withstand or contradict.
[16]You will be betrayed even by parents and brothers, by relatives and friends; and they will put some of you to death. [17]You will be hated by all because of my name. [18]But not a hair of your head will perish. [19]By your endurance you will gain your souls.

20 "When you see Jerusalem surrounded by armies, then know that its desolation has come near.[g] [21]Then those in Judea must flee to the mountains, and those inside the city must leave it, and those out in the country must not enter it; [22]for these are days of vengeance, as a fulfillment of all that is written. [23]Woe to those who are pregnant and to those who are nursing infants in those days! For there will be great distress on the earth and wrath against this people; [24]they will fall by the edge of the sword and be taken away as captives among all nations; and Jerusalem will be trampled on by the Gentiles, until the times of the Gentiles are fulfilled.

25 "There will be signs in the sun, the moon, and the stars, and on the earth distress among nations confused by the roaring of the sea and the waves. [26]People will faint from fear

[g] Or *is at hand*

and foreboding of what is coming upon the world, for the powers of the heavens will be shaken. ²⁷Then they will see 'the Son of Man coming in a cloud' with power and great glory. ²⁸Now when these things begin to take place, stand up and raise your heads, because your redemption is drawing near."

29 Then he told them a parable: "Look at the fig tree and all the trees; ³⁰as soon as they sprout leaves you can see for yourselves and know that summer is already near. ³¹So also, when you see these things taking place, you know that the kingdom of God is near. ³²Truly I tell you, this generation will not pass away until all things have taken place. ³³Heaven and earth will pass away, but my words will not pass away.

34 "Be on guard so that your hearts are not weighed down with dissipation and drunkenness and the worries of this life, and that day does not catch you unexpectedly, ³⁵like a trap. For it will come upon all who live on the face of the whole earth. ³⁶Be alert at all times, praying that you may have the strength to escape all these things

προσδοκίας τῶν ἐπερχομένων τῇ οἰκουμένῃ,
EXPECTATION OF THE THINGS COMING UPON THE WORLD,

αἱ γὰρ δυνάμεις τῶν οὐρανῶν σαλευθήσονται. 21.27 καὶ
FOR~THE POWERS OF THE HEAVENS WILL BE SHAKEN. AND

τότε ὄψονται τὸν υἱὸν τοῦ ἀνθρώπου ἐρχόμενον ἐν
THEN YOU° WILL SEE THE SON - OF MAN COMING ON

νεφέλῃ μετὰ δυνάμεως καὶ δόξης πολλῆς.
A CLOUD WITH POWER AND GREAT~GLORY.

21.28 ἀρχομένων δὲ τούτων γίνεσθαι ἀνακύψατε καὶ
AND~[WHEN] BEGINNING THESE THINGS TO OCCUR, STAND ERECT AND

ἐπάρατε τὰς κεφαλὰς ὑμῶν, διότι ἐγγίζει ἡ
LIFT UP THE HEADS OF YOU°, BECAUSE DRAWS NEAR THE

ἀπολύτρωσις ὑμῶν.
REDEMPTION OF YOU°.

21.29 Καὶ εἶπεν παραβολὴν αὐτοῖς· Ἴδετε τὴν συκῆν
AND HE TOLD A PARABLE TO THEM. YOU° SEE THE FIG TREE

καὶ πάντα τὰ δένδρα· 21.30 ὅταν προβάλωσιν ἤδη,
AND ALL THE TREES. WHEN PUTS OUT [LEAVES] ALREADY,

βλέποντες ἀφ' ἑαυτῶν γινώσκετε ὅτι ἤδη ἐγγὺς τὸ
SEEING FOR YOURSELVES YOU° KNOW THAT ALREADY NEAR THE

θέρος ἐστίν· 21.31 οὕτως καὶ ὑμεῖς, ὅταν ἴδητε
SUMMER IS. THUS ALSO YOU°, WHEN YOU° SEE

ταῦτα γινόμενα, γινώσκετε ὅτι ἐγγύς ἐστιν ἡ
THESE THINGS HAPPENING, YOU° KNOW THAT NEAR IS THE

βασιλεία τοῦ θεοῦ. 21.32 ἀμὴν λέγω ὑμῖν ὅτι
KINGDOM - OF GOD. TRULY I SAY TO YOU° THAT

οὐ μὴ παρέλθῃ ἡ γενεὰ αὕτη ἕως ἂν πάντα
MAY NOT PASS AWAY - THIS~GENERATION UNTIL ALL [THESE THINGS]

γένηται. 21.33 ὁ οὐρανὸς καὶ ἡ γῆ παρελεύσονται,
MAY OCCUR. - HEAVEN AND - EARTH WILL PASS AWAY,

οἱ δὲ λόγοι μου οὐ μὴ παρελεύσονται.
BUT~THE WORDS OF ME WILL BY NO MEANS PASS AWAY.

21.34 Προσέχετε δὲ ἑαυτοῖς μήποτε βαρηθῶσιν
AND~PAY ATTENTION TO YOURSELVES LEST MAY BE BURDENED

ὑμῶν αἱ καρδίαι ἐν κραιπάλῃ καὶ μέθῃ καὶ
YOUR° - HEARTS WITH DISSIPATION AND DRUNKENNESS AND

μερίμναις βιωτικαῖς καὶ ἐπιστῇ ἐφ' ὑμᾶς αἰφνίδιος ἡ
ANXIETIES OF LIFE AND MAY COME UPON YOU° SUDDENLY -

ἡμέρα ἐκείνη 21.35 ὡς παγίς· ἐπεισελεύσεται γὰρ ἐπὶ
THAT~DAY AS A TRAP. FOR~[IT] WILL COME UPON

πάντας τοὺς καθημένους ἐπὶ πρόσωπον πάσης τῆς
ALL THE ONES SITTING ON [THE] FACE OF ALL THE

γῆς. 21.36 ἀγρυπνεῖτε δὲ ἐν παντὶ καιρῷ δεόμενοι
EARTH. BUT~BE ALERT AT EVERY TIME PRAYING

ἵνα κατισχύσητε ἐκφυγεῖν ταῦτα πάντα τὰ μέλλοντα
THAT YOU° MAY BE ABLE TO ESCAPE ALL~THESE THINGS - BEING ABOUT

21:27 Dan. 7:13

γίνεσθαι   καὶ   σταθῆναι   ἔμπροσθεν   τοῦ   υἱοῦ   τοῦ
TO HAPPEN   AND   TO STAND   BEFORE   THE   SON   -

ἀνθρώπου.
OF MAN.

21.37 Ἦν δὲ   τὰς ἡμέρας ἐν τῷ ἱερῷ
NOW~HE WAS [IN THOSE]   -   DAYS   IN   THE   TEMPLE

διδάσκων, τὰς δὲ   νύκτας ἐξερχόμενος ηὐλίζετο
TEACHING,   AND~[DURING] THE NIGHTS   GOING OUT   HE WAS SPENDING

εἰς τὸ ὄρος   τὸ   καλούμενον Ἐλαιῶν·   **21.38** καὶ πᾶς
IN   THE MOUNTAIN, THE ONE BEING CALLED   OF OLIVES.   AND   ALL

ὁ λαὸς ὤρθριζεν   πρὸς αὐτὸν ἐν τῷ ἱερῷ
THE PEOPLE WERE GETTING UP EARLY [TO COME] TO   HIM   IN   THE   TEMPLE

ἀκούειν αὐτοῦ.
TO HEAR   HIM.

that will take place, and to stand before the Son of Man."

37 Every day he was teaching in the temple, and at night he would go out and spend the night on the Mount of Olives, as it was called. [38]And all the people would get up early in the morning to listen to him in the temple.

22.1 Ἤγγιζεν δὲ   ἡ   ἑορτὴ τῶν ἀζύμων   ἡ
AND~WAS COMING NEAR THE   FEAST   -   OF UNLEAVENED BREAD, THE ONE

λεγομένη πάσχα.   **22.2** καὶ ἐζήτουν οἱ ἀρχιερεῖς
BEING CALLED   [THE] PASSOVER.   AND   WERE SEEKING THE   CHIEF PRIESTS

καὶ οἱ γραμματεῖς τὸ πῶς ἀνέλωσιν   αὐτόν,
AND   THE   SCRIBES   -   HOW   THEY MIGHT DESTROY   HIM,

ἐφοβοῦντο γὰρ   τὸν λαόν.   **22.3** Εἰσῆλθεν δὲ Σατανᾶς εἰς
FOR~THEY WERE AFRAID OF THE   PEOPLE.   AND~ENTERED   SATAN   INTO

Ἰούδαν τὸν   καλούμενον Ἰσκαριώτην, ὄντα ἐκ τοῦ
JUDAS,   THE ONE BEING CALLED   ISCARIOT,   BEING   OF   THE

ἀριθμοῦ τῶν δώδεκα·   **22.4** καὶ ἀπελθὼν   συνελάλησεν
NUMBER   OF THE TWELVE.   AND   HAVING DEPARTED HE SPOKE WITH

τοῖς ἀρχιερεῦσιν καὶ στρατηγοῖς   τὸ πῶς
THE   CHIEF PRIESTS   AND   CAPTAINS OF THE TEMPLE -   HOW

αὐτοῖς παραδῷ   αὐτόν.   **22.5** καὶ ἐχάρησαν καὶ
HE MIGHT HAND OVER~TO THEM HIM.   AND   THEY REJOICED   AND

συνέθεντο αὐτῷ ἀργύριον δοῦναι.   **22.6** καὶ
THEY AGREED   [2]HIM   [3]MONEY   [1]TO PAY.   AND

ἐξωμολόγησεν, καὶ ἐζήτει   εὐκαιρίαν τοῦ
HE CONSENTED,   AND   HE WAS SEEKING AN OPPORTUNITY -

παραδοῦναι αὐτὸν ἄτερ ὄχλου αὐτοῖς.
TO BETRAY   HIM   WITHOUT A CROWD [WITH] THEM.

22.7 Ἦλθεν δὲ ἡ ἡμέρα τῶν ἀζύμων,   [ἐν] ᾗ
NOW~CAME   THE DAY   -   OF UNLEAVENED BREAD,   IN   WHICH

ἔδει   θύεσθαι τὸ πάσχα·   **22.8** καὶ ἀπέστειλεν
IT WAS NECESSARY TO SACRIFICE THE PASSOVER LAMB.   AND   HE SENT

Πέτρον καὶ Ἰωάννην εἰπών, Πορευθέντες ἑτοιμάσατε
PETER   AND   JOHN   HAVING SAID, HAVING GONE,   PREPARE

ἡμῖν τὸ πάσχα ἵνα φάγωμεν.   **22.9** οἱ δὲ εἶπαν
FOR US   THE PASSOVER   THAT   WE MAY EAT.   -   AND   THEY SAID

Now the festival of Unleavened Bread, which is called the Passover, was near. [2]The chief priests and the scribes were looking for a way to put Jesus[h] to death, for they were afraid of the people.

3 Then Satan entered into Judas called Iscariot, who was one of the twelve; [4]he went away and conferred with the chief priests and officers of the temple police about how he might betray him to them. [5]They were greatly pleased and agreed to give him money. [6]So he consented and began to look for an opportunity to betray him to them when no crowd was present.

7 Then came the day of Unleavened Bread, on which the Passover lamb had to be sacrificed. [8]So Jesus[i] sent Peter and John, saying, "Go and prepare the Passover meal for us that we may eat it." [9]They asked

[h] Gk him
[i] Gk he

him, "Where do you want us to make preparations for it?" [10]"Listen," he said to them, "when you have entered the city, a man carrying a jar of water will meet you; follow him into the house he enters [11]and say to the owner of the house, 'The teacher asks you, "Where is the guest room, where I may eat the Passover with my disciples?" ' [12]He will show you a large room upstairs, already furnished. Make preparations for us there." [13]So they went and found everything as he had told them; and they prepared the Passover meal.

14 When the hour came, he took his place at the table, and the apostles with him. [15]He said to them, "I have eagerly desired to eat this Passover with you before I suffer; [16]for I tell you, I will not eat it[j] until it is fulfilled in the kingdom of God." [17]Then he took a cup, and after giving thanks he said, "Take this and divide it among yourselves; [18]for I tell you that from now on I will not drink of the fruit of the vine until the kingdom of God comes." [19]Then he took a loaf of bread, and when he had given thanks, he broke it and gave it to them, saying, "This is my body, which is given for you.

[j] Other ancient authorities read *never eat it again*

αὐτῷ, Ποῦ θέλεις ἑτοιμάσωμεν; **22.10** ὁ δὲ
TO HIM, WHERE DO YOU WISH [THAT] WE SHOULD PREPARE [IT]? - AND

εἶπεν αὐτοῖς, Ἰδοὺ εἰσελθόντων ὑμῶν εἰς τὴν πόλιν
HE SAID TO THEM, BEHOLD HAVING ENTERED YOU° INTO THE CITY

συναντήσει ὑμῖν ἄνθρωπος κεράμιον ὕδατος βαστάζων·
WILL MEET YOU A MAN ²A JAR ³OF WATER ¹CARRYING.

ἀκολουθήσατε αὐτῷ εἰς τὴν οἰκίαν εἰς ἣν
FOLLOW HIM INTO THE HOUSE INTO WHICH

εἰσπορεύεται **22.11** καὶ ἐρεῖτε τῷ οἰκοδεσπότῃ τῆς
HE ENTERS AND YOU° WILL SAY TO THE MASTER OF THE

οἰκίας, Λέγει σοι ὁ διδάσκαλος, Ποῦ ἐστιν τὸ
HOUSE, SAYS TO YOU THE TEACHER, WHERE IS THE

κατάλυμα ὅπου τὸ πάσχα μετὰ τῶν μαθητῶν μου
GUEST ROOM WHERE THE PASSOVER WITH THE DISCIPLES OF ME

φάγω; **22.12** κἀκεῖνος ὑμῖν δείξει ἀνάγαιον μέγα
I MAY EAT? AND THAT ONE WILL SHOW~YOU° A LARGE~UPSTAIRS ROOM

ἐστρωμένον· ἐκεῖ ἑτοιμάσατε. **22.13** ἀπελθόντες δὲ
HAVING BEEN FURNISHED. THERE PREPARE [IT]. AND~HAVING DEPARTED

εὗρον καθὼς εἰρήκει αὐτοῖς καὶ ἡτοίμασαν τὸ
THEY FOUND [THINGS] JUST AS HE HAD TOLD THEM AND THEY PREPARED THE

πάσχα.
PASSOVER.

22.14 Καὶ ὅτε ἐγένετο ἡ ὥρα, ἀνέπεσεν καὶ οἱ
AND WHEN CAME THE HOUR, HE RECLINED [AT TABLE] AND THE

ἀπόστολοι σὺν αὐτῷ. **22.15** καὶ εἶπεν πρὸς αὐτούς,
APOSTLES [WERE] WITH HIM. AND HE SAID TO THEM,

Ἐπιθυμίᾳ ἐπεθύμησα τοῦτο τὸ πάσχα φαγεῖν μεθ᾿
WITH [GREAT] DESIRE I DESIRED THIS - PASSOVER TO EAT WITH

ὑμῶν πρὸ τοῦ με παθεῖν· **22.16** λέγω γὰρ ὑμῖν ὅτι
YOU° BEFORE - ME (I) SUFFER. FOR~I SAY TO YOU° THAT

οὐ μὴ φάγω αὐτὸ ἕως ὅτου πληρωθῇ ἐν τῇ βασιλείᾳ
I MAY BY NO MEANS EAT IT UNTIL IT IS FULFILLED IN THE KINGDOM

τοῦ θεοῦ. **22.17** καὶ δεξάμενος ποτήριον εὐχαριστήσας
- OF GOD. AND HAVING TAKEN A CUP, HAVING GIVEN THANKS

εἶπεν, Λάβετε τοῦτο καὶ διαμερίσατε εἰς ἑαυτούς·
HE SAID, TAKE THIS AND SHARE [IT] AMONG YOURSELVES.

22.18 λέγω γὰρ ὑμῖν, [ὅτι] οὐ μὴ πίω ἀπὸ τοῦ νῦν
FOR~I SAY TO YOU°, THAT BY NO MEANS MAY I DRINK FROM - NOW

ἀπὸ τοῦ γενήματος τῆς ἀμπέλου ἕως οὗ ἡ βασιλεία
FROM THE FRUIT OF THE VINE UNTIL THE KINGDOM

τοῦ θεοῦ ἔλθῃ. **22.19** καὶ λαβὼν ἄρτον
- OF GOD COMES. AND HAVING TAKEN BREAD [AND]

εὐχαριστήσας ἔκλασεν καὶ ἔδωκεν αὐτοῖς λέγων,
HAVING GIVEN THANKS HE BROKE [IT] AND GAVE [IT] TO THEM SAYING,

Τοῦτό ἐστιν τὸ σῶμά μου ⌐τὸ ὑπὲρ ὑμῶν διδόμενον·
THIS IS THE BODY OF ME - FOR YOU° BEING GIVEN;

22:19b-20 text: KJV ASV RSV NASB NIV NEBmg TEV NJB NRSV. omit: ASVmg RSVmg NASBmg NEB TEVmg NRSVmg.

τοῦτο ποιεῖτε εἰς τὴν ἐμὴν ἀνάμνησιν. **22.20** καὶ τὸ
THIS DO IN - MY MEMORY. AND THE

ποτήριον ὡσαύτως μετὰ τὸ δειπνῆσαι, λέγων, Τοῦτο τὸ
CUP SIMILARLY AFTER - [THEY] ATE, SAYING, THIS -

ποτήριον ἡ καινὴ διαθήκη ἐν τῷ αἵματί μου τὸ ὑπὲρ
CUP [IS] THE NEW COVENANT IN THE BLOOD OF ME - FOR

ὑμῶν ἐκχυννόμενον.⌐ **22.21** πλὴν ἰδοὺ ἡ χεὶρ
YOU° BEING SHED. NEVERTHELESS, BEHOLD THE HAND

τοῦ παραδιδόντος με μετ᾽ ἐμοῦ ἐπὶ τῆς τραπέζη.
OF THE ONE BETRAYING ME [IS] WITH ME ON THE TABLE.

22.22 ὅτι ὁ υἱὸς μὲν τοῦ ἀνθρώπου κατὰ
BECAUSE ²THE ³SON ¹INDEED - OF MAN ACCORDING TO

τὸ ὡρισμένον πορεύεται, πλὴν οὐαὶ τῷ
THE THING HAVING BEEN DETERMINED GOES, BUT WOE -

ἀνθρώπῳ ἐκείνῳ δι᾽ οὗ παραδίδοται. **22.23** καὶ
TO THAT~MAN THROUGH WHOM HE IS BETRAYED. AND

αὐτοὶ ἤρξαντο συζητεῖν πρὸς ἑαυτοὺς τὸ τίς ἄρα
THEY BEGAN TO DISCUSS AMONG THEMSELVES - WHO THEN

εἴη ἐξ αὐτῶν ὁ τοῦτο μέλλων πράσσειν.
IT MIGHT BE OF THEM - THIS BEING ABOUT TO DO.

22.24 Ἐγένετο δὲ καὶ φιλονεικία ἐν αὐτοῖς, τὸ
AND~THERE CAME ABOUT ALSO A DISPUTE AMONG THEM, -

τίς αὐτῶν δοκεῖ εἶναι μείζων. **22.25** ὁ δὲ εἶπεν
[AS TO] WHO OF THEM SEEMS TO BE GREATER. - AND HE SAID

αὐτοῖς, Οἱ βασιλεῖς τῶν ἐθνῶν κυριεύουσιν αὐτῶν καὶ
TO THEM, THE KINGS OF THE NATIONS LORD IT OVER THEM AND

οἱ ἐξουσιάζοντες αὐτῶν εὐεργέται καλοῦνται.
THE ONES BEING IN AUTHORITY OVER THEM ARE CALLED~BENEFACTORS.

22.26 ὑμεῖς δὲ οὐχ οὕτως, ἀλλ᾽ ὁ μείζων ἐν
BUT~[WITH] YOU° [IT IS] NOT SO, BUT THE ONE BEING GREATER AMONG

ὑμῖν γινέσθω ὡς ὁ νεώτερος καὶ ὁ ἡγούμενος
YOU° LET HIM BECOME AS THE YOUNGEST AND THE ONE LEADING

ὡς ὁ διακονῶν. **22.27** τίς γὰρ μείζων, ὁ
AS THE ONE SERVING. FOR~WHO [IS] GREATER, THE ONE

ἀνακείμενος ἢ ὁ διακονῶν; οὐχὶ ὁ
RECLINING AT TABLE OR THE ONE SERVING? [IS IT] NOT THE ONE

ἀνακείμενος; ἐγὼ δὲ ἐν μέσῳ ὑμῶν εἰμι ὡς ὁ
RECLINING AT TABLE? BUT~I IN [THE] MIDST OF YOU° AM AS THE ONE

διακονῶν. **22.28** ὑμεῖς δέ ἐστε οἱ διαμεμενηκότες
SERVING. BUT~YOU° ARE THE ONES HAVING REMAINED

μετ᾽ ἐμοῦ ἐν τοῖς πειρασμοῖς μου· **22.29** κἀγὼ
WITH ME IN THE TEMPTATIONS OF ME. AND I

διατίθεμαι ὑμῖν καθὼς διέθετό μοι ὁ πατήρ μου
DECREE TO YOU° JUST AS DECREED TO ME THE FATHER OF ME

βασιλείαν, **22.30** ἵνα ἔσθητε καὶ πίνητε ἐπὶ τῆς
[THE] KINGDOM, THAT YOU° MAY EAT AND DRINK AT THE

τραπέζης μου ἐν τῇ βασιλείᾳ μου, καὶ καθήσεσθε ἐπὶ
TABLE OF ME IN THE KINGDOM OF ME, AND YOU° WILL SIT UPON

Do this in remembrance of me." [20]And he did the same with the cup after supper, saying, "This cup that is poured out for you is the new covenant in my blood.[k] [21]But see, the one who betrays me is with me, and his hand is on the table. [22]For the Son of Man is going as it has been determined, but woe to that one by whom he is betrayed!" [23]Then they began to ask one another which one of them it could be who would do this.

24 A dispute also arose among them as to which one of them was to be regarded as the greatest. [25]But he said to them, "The kings of the Gentiles lord it over them; and those in authority over them are called benefactors. [26]But not so with you; rather the greatest among you must become like the youngest, and the leader like one who serves. [27]For who is greater, the one who is at the table or the one who serves? Is it not the one at the table? But I am among you as one who serves.

28 "You are those who have stood by me in my trials; [29]and I confer on you, just as my Father has conferred on me, a kingdom, [30]so that you may eat and drink at my table in my kingdom, and you will sit on

[k] Other ancient authorities lack, in whole or in part, verses 19b-20 (which is given . . . in my blood)

thrones judging the twelve tribes of Israel.

θρόνων τὰς δώδεκα φυλὰς κρίνοντες τοῦ Ἰσραήλ.
THRONES ²THE ³TWELVE ⁴TRIBES ¹JUDGING - OF ISRAEL.

31 "Simon, Simon, listen! Satan has demanded*l* to sift all of you like wheat,

22.31 Σίμων Σίμων, ἰδοὺ ὁ Σατανᾶς ἐξητήσατο ὑμᾶς
SIMON, SIMON, BEHOLD - SATAN ASKED FOR YOU°

³²but I have prayed for you that your own faith may not fail; and you, when once you have turned back, strengthen your brothers."

τοῦ σινιάσαι ὡς τὸν σῖτον· **22.32** ἐγὼ δὲ ἐδεήθην περὶ
- TO SIFT [YOU°] LIKE - WHEAT. BUT~I PRAYED FOR

σοῦ ἵνα μὴ ἐκλίπῃ ἡ πίστις σου· καὶ σύ ποτε
YOU THAT MAY NOT FAIL THE FAITH OF YOU. AND WHEN~YOU

ἐπιστρέψας στήρισον τοὺς ἀδελφούς σου. **22.33** ὁ δὲ
HAVING RETURNED, STRENGTHEN THE BROTHERS OF YOU. - BUT

³³And he said to him, "Lord, I am ready to go with you to prison and to death!"

εἶπεν αὐτῷ, Κύριε, μετὰ σοῦ ἕτοιμός εἰμι καὶ εἰς
HE SAID TO HIM, LORD, WITH YOU I AM~PREPARED EVEN TO

³⁴Jesus*m* said, "I tell you, Peter, the cock will not crow this day, until you have denied three times that you know me."

φυλακὴν καὶ εἰς θάνατον πορεύεσθαι. **22.34** ὁ δὲ
JAIL AND TO DEATH TO GO. - BUT

εἶπεν, Λέγω σοι, Πέτρε, οὐ φωνήσει σήμερον ἀλέκτωρ
HE SAID, I TELL YOU, PETER, WILL NOT CROW TODAY A ROOSTER

ἕως τρίς με ἀπαρνήσῃ εἰδέναι.
UNTIL THREE [TIMES] ³ME ¹YOU DENY ²TO KNOW.

35 He said to them, "When I sent you out without a purse, bag, or sandals, did you lack anything?" They said, "No, not a thing." ³⁶He said to them, "But now, the one who has a purse must take it, and likewise a bag. And the one who has no sword must sell his cloak and buy one. ³⁷For I tell you, this scripture must be fulfilled in me, 'And he was counted among the lawless'; and indeed what is written about me is being fulfilled." ³⁸They said, "Lord, look, here are two swords." He replied, "It is enough."

22.35 Καὶ εἶπεν αὐτοῖς, Ὅτε ἀπέστειλα ὑμᾶς ἄτερ
AND HE SAID TO THEM, WHEN I SENT YOU° WITHOUT

βαλλαντίου καὶ πήρας καὶ ὑποδημάτων, μή τινος
A PURSE AND A BEGGAR'S BAG AND SANDALS, NOT ANYTHING

ὑστερήσατε; οἱ δὲ εἶπαν, Οὐθενός. **22.36** εἶπεν δὲ
WERE YOU° IN NEED? - AND THEY SAID, NOTHING. AND~HE SAID

αὐτοῖς, Ἀλλὰ νῦν ὁ ἔχων βαλλάντιον ἀράτω,
TO THEM, BUT NOW THE ONE HAVING A PURSE LET HIM TAKE [IT],

ὁμοίως καὶ πήραν, καὶ ὁ μὴ ἔχων πωλησάτω
LIKEWISE ALSO A BEGGAR'S BAG, AND THE ONE NOT HAVING, LET HIM SELL

τὸ ἱμάτιον αὐτοῦ καὶ ἀγορασάτω μάχαιραν.
THE GARMENT OF HIM AND LET HIM BUY A SWORD.

22.37 λέγω γὰρ ὑμῖν ὅτι τοῦτο τὸ γεγραμμένον
FOR~I SAY TO YOU°, THAT THIS - HAVING BEEN WRITTEN

δεῖ τελεσθῆναι ἐν ἐμοί, τὸ Καὶ μετὰ ἀνόμων
IT IS NECESSARY TO BE FULFILLED IN ME, - AND WITH LAWLESS PERSONS

ἐλογίσθη· καὶ γὰρ τὸ περὶ ἐμοῦ τέλος ἔχει.
HE WAS NUMBERED. FOR~EVEN THE THING CONCERNING ME HAS~AN END.

22.38 οἱ δὲ εἶπαν, Κύριε, ἰδοὺ μάχαιραι ὧδε δύο. ὁ
- AND THEY SAID, LORD, BEHOLD ³SWORDS ¹HERE [ARE] ²TWO. -

δὲ εἶπεν αὐτοῖς, Ἱκανόν ἐστιν.
AND HE SAID TO THEM, IT IS~ENOUGH.

39 He came out and went, as was his custom, to the Mount of Olives; and the disciples followed him. ⁴⁰When he reached the place, he said to

22.39 Καὶ ἐξελθὼν ἐπορεύθη κατὰ τὸ ἔθος
AND HAVING GONE OUT HE WENT ACCORDING TO THE(HIS) HABIT

εἰς τὸ Ὄρος τῶν Ἐλαιῶν, ἠκολούθησαν δὲ αὐτῷ καὶ
TO THE MOUNTAIN - OF OLIVES, AND~FOLLOWED HIM ALSO

οἱ μαθηταί. **22.40** γενόμενος δὲ ἐπὶ τοῦ τόπου εἶπεν
THE DISCIPLES. AND~HAVING COME TO THE PLACE HE SAID

l Or *has obtained permission*
m Gk *He*

22:37 Isa. 53:12

αὐτοῖς, Προσεύχεσθε μὴ εἰσελθεῖν εἰς πειρασμόν.
TO THEM,   PRAY [SO AS]   NOT TO ENTER   INTO TEMPTATION.

22.41 καὶ αὐτὸς ἀπεσπάσθη ἀπ' αὐτῶν ὡσεὶ
AND   HE   WAS WITHDRAWN   FROM THEM   ABOUT

λίθου βολὴν καὶ θεὶς τὰ γόνατα προσηύχετο
[THE] THROW~OF A STONE AND   HAVING BENT THE KNEES   HE WAS PRAYING

22.42 λέγων, Πάτερ, εἰ βούλει παρένεγκε τοῦτο τὸ
SAYING,   FATHER,   IF   YOU ARE WILLING,   TAKE AWAY   THIS   -

ποτήριον ἀπ' ἐμοῦ· πλὴν μὴ τὸ θέλημά μου ἀλλὰ
CUP   FROM ME.   NEVERTHELESS NOT THE WILL   OF ME BUT

τὸ σὸν γινέσθω. ⌜[[**22.43** ὤφθη δὲ αὐτῷ ἄγγελος ἀπ'
-   YOURS LET IT BE.   AND~APPEARED TO HIM   AN ANGEL   FROM

οὐρανοῦ ἐνισχύων αὐτόν. **22.44** καὶ γενόμενος ἐν
HEAVEN   STRENGTHENING HIM.   AND   HAVING BEEN   IN

ἀγωνίᾳ ἐκτενέστερον προσηύχετο· καὶ ἐγένετο ὁ ἱδρὼς
AGONY,   HE WAS PRAYING~MORE FERVENTLY;   AND   BECAME   THE SWEAT

αὐτοῦ ὡσεὶ θρόμβοι αἵματος καταβαίνοντες ἐπὶ τὴν
OF HIM   AS   DROPS   OF BLOOD   FALLING DOWN   UPON   THE

γῆν.]]⌝ **22.45** καὶ ἀναστὰς ἀπὸ τῆς προσευχῆς ἐλθὼν
GROUND.   AND   HAVING ARISEN FROM   -   PRAYER [AND]   HAVING COME

πρὸς τοὺς μαθητὰς εὗρεν κοιμωμένους αὐτοὺς ἀπὸ
TO   THE   DISCIPLES   HE FOUND   THEM~SLEEPING   FROM

τῆς λύπης, **22.46** καὶ εἶπεν αὐτοῖς, Τί καθεύδετε;
-   GRIEF,   AND   HE SAID   TO THEM,   WHY ARE YOU SLEEPING?

ἀναστάντες προσεύχεσθε, ἵνα μὴ εἰσέλθητε εἰς
HAVING ARISEN,   PRAY,   LEST   YOU° ENTER   INTO

πειρασμόν.
TEMPTATION.

22.47 Ἔτι αὐτοῦ λαλοῦντος ἰδοὺ ὄχλος, καὶ ὁ
YET   HIM   SPEAKING,   BEHOLD A CROWD,   AND   THE ONE

λεγόμενος Ἰούδας εἷς τῶν δώδεκα προήρχετο αὐτοὺς
BEING CALLED   JUDAS,   ONE   OF THE TWELVE,   WAS GOING BEFORE THEM

καὶ ἤγγισεν τῷ Ἰησοῦ φιλῆσαι αὐτόν. **22.48** Ἰησοῦς δὲ
AND   HE DREW NEAR -   TO JESUS TO KISS   HIM.   AND~JESUS

εἶπεν αὐτῷ, Ἰούδα, φιλήματι τὸν υἱὸν τοῦ ἀνθρώπου
SAID   TO HIM,   JUDAS,   WITH A KISS   THE SON   -   OF MAN

παραδίδως; **22.49** ἰδόντες δὲ οἱ περὶ αὐτὸν τὸ
DO YOU BETRAY?   BUT~HAVING SEEN THE ONES AROUND   HIM   THE THING

ἐσόμενον εἶπαν, Κύριε, εἰ πατάξομεν ἐν μαχαίρῃ;
GOING TO BE,   THEY SAID, LORD,   IF   WE WILL STRIKE   WITH A SWORD?

22.50 καὶ ἐπάταξεν εἷς τις ἐξ αὐτῶν τοῦ ἀρχιερέως
AND   STRUCK   A CERTAIN~ONE OF THEM   ³OF THE ⁴CHIEF PRIEST

τὸν δοῦλον καὶ ἀφεῖλεν τὸ οὖς αὐτοῦ τὸ δεξιόν.
¹THE ²SLAVE   AND   CUT OFF   THE EAR   OF HIM   THE RIGHT [ONE].

22.51 ἀποκριθεὶς δὲ ὁ Ἰησοῦς εἶπεν, Ἐᾶτε ἕως
AND~HAVING ANSWERED - JESUS   SAID,   STOP!   [NO] MORE

them, "Pray that you may not come into the time of trial."[n] [41]Then he withdrew from them about a stone's throw, knelt down, and prayed, [42]"Father, if you are willing, remove this cup from me; yet, not my will but yours be done." [[43]Then an angel from heaven appeared to him and gave him strength. [44]In his anguish he prayed more earnestly, and his sweat became like great drops of blood falling down on the ground.][o] [45]When he got up from prayer, he came to the disciples and found them sleeping because of grief, [46]and he said to them, "Why are you sleeping? Get up and pray that you may not come into the time of trial."[n]

[47] While he was still speaking, suddenly a crowd came, and the one called Judas, one of the twelve, was leading them. He approached Jesus to kiss him; [48]but Jesus said to him, "Judas, is it with a kiss that you are betraying the Son of Man?" [49]When those who were around him saw what was coming, they asked, "Lord, should we strike with the sword?" [50]Then one of them struck the slave of the high priest and cut off his right ear. [51]But Jesus said, "No more

[n] Or *into temptation*
[o] Other ancient authorities lack verses 43 and 44

22:43-44 text: KJV ASV NASB RSVmg NIV NEB TEV NJB NRSV. omit: ASVmg RSV NIVmg NEBmg TEVmg NJBmg NRSVmg. (Note: the double brackets in the Greek text indicate that this passage was a later addition to the text, which, however, was retained because of its importance in the textual tradition.)

of this!" And he touched his ear and healed him. ⁵²Then Jesus said to the chief priests, the officers of the temple police, and the elders who had come for him, "Have you come out with swords and clubs as if I were a bandit? ⁵³When I was with you day after day in the temple, you did not lay hands on me. But this is your hour, and the power of darkness!"

54 Then they seized him and led him away, bringing him into the high priest's house. But Peter was following at a distance. ⁵⁵When they had kindled a fire in the middle of the courtyard and sat down together, Peter sat among them. ⁵⁶Then a servant-girl, seeing him in the firelight, stared at him and said, "This man also was with him." ⁵⁷But he denied it, saying, "Woman, I do not know him." ⁵⁸A little later someone else, on seeing him, said, "You also are one of them." But Peter said, "Man, I am not!" ⁵⁹Then about an hour later still another kept insisting, "Surely this man also was with him; for he is a Galilean." ⁶⁰But Peter said, "Man, I do not know what you are talking about!" At that moment, while he was still speaking, the cock crowed. ⁶¹The Lord turned

τούτου· καὶ ἁψάμενος τοῦ ὠτίου ἰάσατο αὐτόν.
OF THIS! AND HAVING TOUCHED THE EAR HE HEALED HIM.

22.52 εἶπεν δὲ Ἰησοῦς πρὸς τοὺς παραγενομένους
AND~SAID JESUS TO THE ONES HAVING COME

ἐπ' αὐτὸν ἀρχιερεῖς καὶ στρατηγοὺς τοῦ ἱεροῦ
AGAINST HIM, [THE] CHIEF PRIESTS AND CAPTAINS OF THE TEMPLE

καὶ πρεσβυτέρους, Ὡς ἐπὶ λῃστὴν ἐξήλθατε μετὰ
AND [THE] ELDERS, AS AGAINST A THIEF DID YOU° COME OUT WITH

μαχαιρῶν καὶ ξύλων; **22.53** καθ' ἡμέραν ὄντος μου μεθ'
SWORDS AND CLUBS? DAILY BEING ME WITH

ὑμῶν ἐν τῷ ἱερῷ οὐκ ἐξετείνατε τὰς χεῖρας ἐπ'
YOU° IN THE TEMPLE YOU° DID NOT STRETCH OUT THE(YOUR°) HANDS AGAINST

ἐμέ, ἀλλ' αὕτη ἐστὶν ὑμῶν ἡ ὥρα καὶ ἡ ἐξουσία τοῦ
ME, BUT THIS IS YOUR° - HOUR AND THE AUTHORITY -

σκότους.
OF DARKNESS.

22.54 Συλλαβόντες δὲ αὐτὸν ἤγαγον καὶ
AND~HAVING SEIZED HIM THEY LED [HIM] AWAY AND

εἰσήγαγον εἰς τὴν οἰκίαν τοῦ ἀρχιερέως· ὁ δὲ
BROUGHT [HIM] INTO THE HOUSE OF THE CHIEF PRIEST. - AND

Πέτρος ἠκολούθει μακρόθεν. **22.55** περιαψάντων δὲ
PETER WAS FOLLOWING FROM A DISTANCE. AND~[THEY] HAVING KINDLED

πῦρ ἐν μέσῳ τῆς αὐλῆς καὶ συγκαθισάντων
A FIRE IN [THE] MIDDLE OF THE COURTYARD AND HAVING SAT DOWN TOGETHER,

ἐκάθητο ὁ Πέτρος μέσος αὐτῶν. **22.56** ἰδοῦσα δὲ
WAS SITTING - PETER [IN THE] MIDDLE OF THEM. AND~HAVING SEEN

αὐτὸν παιδίσκη τις καθήμενον πρὸς τὸ φῶς καὶ
HIM A CERTAIN~SERVANT GIRL SITTING NEAR THE LIGHT AND

ἀτενίσασα αὐτῷ εἶπεν, Καὶ οὗτος σὺν αὐτῷ ἦν.
HAVING LOOKED INTENTLY AT HIM SHE SAID, AND THIS ONE WITH HIM WAS.

22.57 ὁ δὲ ἠρνήσατο λέγων, Οὐκ οἶδα αὐτόν, γύναι.
- BUT HE DENIED [IT] SAYING, I DO NOT KNOW HIM, WOMAN.

22.58 καὶ μετὰ βραχὺ ἕτερος ἰδὼν αὐτὸν ἔφη,
AND AFTER A SHORT [WHILE] ANOTHER HAVING SEEN HIM SAID,

Καὶ σὺ ἐξ αὐτῶν εἶ. ὁ δὲ Πέτρος ἔφη, Ἄνθρωπε,
AND YOU OF THEM ARE. - BUT PETER SAID, MAN,

οὐκ εἰμί. **22.59** καὶ διαστάσης ὡσεὶ ὥρας μιᾶς
I AM NOT. AND HAVING PASSED ABOUT ONE~HOUR, [AND]

ἄλλος τις διϊσχυρίζετο λέγων, Ἐπ' ἀληθείας καὶ
A CERTAIN~OTHER WAS INSISTING SAYING, BASED ON TRUTH ALSO

οὗτος μετ' αὐτοῦ ἦν, καὶ γὰρ Γαλιλαῖός ἐστιν.
THIS ONE WITH HIM WAS, FOR~ALSO A GALILEAN HE IS.

22.60 εἶπεν δὲ ὁ Πέτρος, Ἄνθρωπε, οὐκ οἶδα ὃ
BUT~SAID - PETER, MAN, I DO NOT KNOW WHAT

λέγεις. καὶ παραχρῆμα ἔτι λαλοῦντος αὐτοῦ
YOU ARE SAYING. AND IMMEDIATELY WHILE HIM~SPEAKING,

ἐφώνησεν ἀλέκτωρ. **22.61** καὶ στραφεὶς ὁ κύριος
A ROOSTER~CROWED. AND HAVING TURNED THE LORD

ἐνέβλεψεν τῷ Πέτρῳ, καὶ ὑπεμνήσθη ὁ Πέτρος τοῦ
LOOKED AT   -   PETER,   AND   WAS REMINDED -   PETER   OF THE

ῥήματος τοῦ κυρίου ὡς εἶπεν αὐτῷ ὅτι Πρὶν
WORD   OF THE LORD   WHEN HE SAID TO HIM   -   BEFORE

ἀλέκτορα φωνῆσαι σήμερον ἀπαρνήσῃ με τρίς.
A ROOSTER   CROWS   TODAY   YOU WILL DENY ME THREE [TIMES].

22.62 καὶ ἐξελθὼν ἔξω ἔκλαυσεν πικρῶς.
       AND   HAVING GONE OUTSIDE HE CRIED   BITTERLY.

22.63 Καὶ οἱ ἄνδρες οἱ   συνέχοντες αὐτὸν
        AND   THE MEN,   THE ONES HAVING IN CUSTODY HIM

ἐνέπαιζον αὐτῷ δέροντες, **22.64** καὶ περικαλύψαντες
WERE RIDICULING HIM [AND] BEATING [HIM],   AND   HAVING BLINDFOLDED

αὐτὸν ἐπηρώτων   λέγοντες, Προφήτευσον, τίς
HIM   THEY WERE QUESTIONING [HIM] SAYING,   PROPHESY,   WHO

ἐστιν ὁ   παίσας σε; **22.65** καὶ ἕτερα πολλὰ
IS   THE ONE HAVING HIT YOU?   AND   MANY~OTHER THINGS

βλασφημοῦντες ἔλεγον   εἰς   αὐτόν.
BLASPHEMING   THEY WERE SPEAKING AGAINST HIM.

22.66 Καὶ ὡς ἐγένετο ἡμέρα, συνήχθη
        AND   WHEN IT BECAME DAY,   WERE GATHERED TOGETHER

τὸ πρεσβυτέριον τοῦ λαοῦ, ἀρχιερεῖς τε   καὶ
THE ELDERS   OF THE PEOPLE, BOTH~[THE] CHIEF PRIESTS AND

γραμματεῖς, καὶ ἀπήγαγον αὐτὸν εἰς τὸ συνέδριον
[THE] SCRIBES, AND THEY LED AWAY HIM   TO   THE COUNCIL

αὐτῶν **22.67** λέγοντες, Εἰ σὺ εἶ ὁ Χριστός, εἰπὸν ἡμῖν.
OF THEM   SAYING,   IF YOU ARE THE CHRIST,   TELL   US.

εἶπεν δὲ αὐτοῖς, Ἐὰν ὑμῖν εἴπω,   οὐ μὴ πιστεύσητε·
BUT~HE SAID TO THEM, IF   I SAY [THIS]~TO YOU°, YOU° WILL BY NO MEANS BELIEVE.

22.68 ἐὰν δὲ ἐρωτήσω,   οὐ μὴ ἀποκριθῆτε. **22.69** ἀπὸ
        AND~IF   I QUESTION [YOU°], YOU° WILL BY NO MEANS ANSWER.   2FROM

τοῦ νῦν   δὲ ἔσται ὁ υἱὸς τοῦ ἀνθρώπου καθήμενος
-   3NOW [ON] 1BUT WILL BE THE SON   -   OF MAN   SITTING

ἐκ δεξιῶν τῆς δυνάμεως τοῦ θεοῦ. **22.70** εἶπαν δὲ
AT [THE] RIGHT OF THE POWER   -   OF GOD.   AND~SAID

πάντες, Σὺ οὖν εἶ ὁ υἱὸς τοῦ θεοῦ; ὁ δὲ πρὸς
EVERYONE, THEN~YOU ARE THE SON   -   OF GOD? - AND TO

αὐτοὺς ἔφη, Ὑμεῖς λέγετε ὅτι ἐγώ εἰμι. **22.71** οἱ δὲ
THEM   HE SAID, YOU°   ARE SAYING THAT I   AM.   -   AND

εἶπαν, Τί ἔτι ἔχομεν μαρτυρίας χρείαν;   αὐτοὶ γὰρ
THEY SAID, WHY STILL DO WE HAVE NEED~OF A WITNESS?   FOR~OURSELVES

ἠκούσαμεν ἀπὸ τοῦ στόματος αὐτοῦ.
WE HEARD   FROM THE MOUTH   OF HIM.

22:69 Ps. 110:1

and looked at Peter. Then
Peter remembered the word
of the Lord, how he had said
to him, "Before the cock
crows today, you will deny
me three times." [62]And he
went out and wept bitterly.

63 Now the men who
were holding Jesus began to
mock him and beat him;
[64]they also blindfolded
him and kept asking him,
"Prophesy! Who is it that
struck you?" [65]They kept
heaping many other insults
on him.

66 When day came, the
assembly of the elders of the
people, both chief priests
and scribes, gathered
together, and they brought
him to their council. [67]They
said, "If you are the
Messiah,[p] tell us." He
replied, "If I tell you, you
will not believe; [68]and if I
question you, you will not
answer. [69]But from now on
the Son of Man will be
seated at the right hand of the
power of God." [70]All of
them asked, "Are you, then,
the Son of God?" He said to
them, "You say that I am."
[71]Then they said, "What
further testimony do we
need? We have heard it
ourselves from his own
lips!"

p Or *the Christ*

CHAPTER 23

Then the assembly rose as a body and brought Jesus[q] before Pilate. [2]They began to accuse him, saying, "We found this man perverting our nation, forbidding us to pay taxes to the emperor, and saying that he himself is the Messiah, a king."[r] [3]Then Pilate asked him, "Are you the king of the Jews?" He answered, "You say so." [4]Then Pilate said to the chief priests and the crowds, "I find no basis for an accusation against this man." [5]But they were insistent and said, "He stirs up the people by teaching throughout all Judea, from Galilee where he began even to this place."

6 When Pilate heard this, he asked whether the man was a Galilean. [7]And when he learned that he was under Herod's jurisdiction, he sent him off to Herod, who was himself in Jerusalem at that time. [8]When Herod saw Jesus, he was very glad, for he had been wanting to see him for a long time, because he had heard about him and was hoping to see him perform some sign. [9]He questioned him at some length, but Jesus[s] gave him no answer. [10]The chief priests and the scribes stood by,

[q] Gk him
[r] Or is an anointed king
[s] Gk he

23.1 Καὶ ἀναστὰν ἅπαν τὸ πλῆθος αὐτῶν ἤγαγον
AND HAVING ARISEN [THE] WHOLE - MULTITUDE OF THEM LED

αὐτὸν ἐπὶ τὸν Πιλᾶτον. **23.2** ἤρξαντο δὲ κατηγορεῖν
HIM BEFORE - PILATE. AND~THEY BEGAN TO ACCUSE

αὐτοῦ λέγοντες, Τοῦτον εὕραμεν διαστρέφοντα τὸ ἔθνος
HIM SAYING, THIS ONE WE FOUND MISLEADING THE NATION

ἡμῶν καὶ κωλύοντα φόρους Καίσαρι διδόναι καὶ
OF US AND FORBIDDING TAXES TO BE PAID~TO CAESAR AND

λέγοντα ἑαυτὸν Χριστὸν βασιλέα εἶναι. **23.3** ὁ
CALLING HIMSELF CHRIST [AND THAT HE IS] TO BE~A KING.

δὲ Πιλᾶτος ἠρώτησεν αὐτὸν λέγων, Σὺ εἶ ὁ βασιλεὺς
AND PILATE QUESTIONED HIM SAYING, ARE~YOU THE KING

τῶν Ἰουδαίων; ὁ δὲ ἀποκριθεὶς αὐτῷ ἔφη, Σὺ
OF THE JEWS? - AND HAVING ANSWERED HIM HE SAID, YOU

λέγεις. **23.4** ὁ δὲ Πιλᾶτος εἶπεν πρὸς τοὺς ἀρχιερεῖς
ARE SAYING. - AND PILATE SAID TO THE CHIEF PRIESTS

καὶ τοὺς ὄχλους, Οὐδὲν εὑρίσκω αἴτιον ἐν τῷ
AND THE CROWDS, I FIND~NO GUILT IN -

ἀνθρώπῳ τούτῳ. **23.5** οἱ δὲ ἐπίσχυον λέγοντες ὅτι
THIS~MAN. - BUT THEY WERE INSISTING SAYING, -

Ἀνασείει τὸν λαὸν διδάσκων καθ' ὅλης τῆς
HE INCITES THE PEOPLE, TEACHING THROUGHOUT ALL

Ἰουδαίας, καὶ ἀρξάμενος ἀπὸ τῆς Γαλιλαίας ἕως ὧδε.
OF JUDEA, - HAVING BEGUN FROM - GALILEE TO HERE.

23.6 Πιλᾶτος δὲ ἀκούσας ἐπηρώτησεν εἰ ὁ ἄνθρωπος
AND~PILATE HAVING HEARD QUESTIONED IF THE MAN

Γαλιλαῖός ἐστιν, **23.7** καὶ ἐπιγνοὺς ὅτι ἐκ τῆς
IS~A GALILEAN, AND HAVING LEARNED THAT OF THE

ἐξουσίας Ἡρῴδου ἐστὶν ἀνέπεμψεν αὐτὸν πρὸς
AUTHORITY OF HEROD HE IS, HE SENT HIM TO

Ἡρῴδην, ὄντα καὶ αὐτὸν ἐν Ἱεροσολύμοις ἐν ταύταις
HEROD, BEING ALSO HIM IN JERUSALEM IN THESE

ταῖς ἡμέραις. **23.8** ὁ δὲ Ἡρῴδης ἰδὼν τὸν Ἰησοῦν
- DAYS. - AND HEROD HAVING SEEN - JESUS

ἐχάρη λίαν, ἦν γὰρ ἐξ ἱκανῶν χρόνων θέλων ἰδεῖν
REJOICED GREATLY, FOR~HE WAS FOR A LONG TIME WANTING TO SEE

αὐτὸν διὰ τὸ ἀκούειν περὶ αὐτοῦ καὶ ἤλπιζέν
HIM BECAUSE - [HE] HEARS [THINGS] ABOUT HIM AND HE WAS HOPING

τι σημεῖον ἰδεῖν ὑπ' αὐτοῦ γινόμενον.
SOME SIGN TO SEE BY HIM BEING PERFORMED.

23.9 ἐπηρώτα δὲ αὐτὸν ἐν λόγοις ἱκανοῖς, αὐτὸς δὲ
AND~HE WAS QUESTIONING HIM WITH MANY~WORDS, BUT~HE

οὐδὲν ἀπεκρίνατο αὐτῷ. **23.10** εἱστήκεισαν δὲ οἱ
ANSWERED~NOTHING TO HIM. AND~HAD STOOD THE

ἀρχιερεῖς καὶ οἱ γραμματεῖς εὐτόνως κατηγοροῦντες
CHIEF PRIESTS AND THE SCRIBES   VEHEMENTLY ACCUSING

αὐτοῦ. **23.11** ἐξουθενήσας δὲ   αὐτὸν [καὶ] ὁ
HIM.   AND~HAVING TREATED WITH CONTEMPT HIM   EVEN   -

Ἡρῴδης σὺν τοῖς στρατεύμασιν αὐτοῦ καὶ
HEROD   WITH THE   TROOPS   OF HIM ALSO

ἐμπαίξας   περιβαλὼν   ἐσθῆτα λαμπρὰν
HAVING RIDICULED [HIM], HAVING CLOTHED [HIM IN] BRIGHT~CLOTHING

ἀνέπεμψεν αὐτὸν τῷ Πιλάτῳ. **23.12** ἐγένοντο δὲ φίλοι
THEY SENT BACK HIM   -   TO PILATE.   AND~BECAME   FRIENDS

ὅ τε Ἡρῴδης καὶ ὁ Πιλᾶτος ἐν αὐτῇ τῇ ἡμέρᾳ μετ'
- BOTH HEROD AND - PILATE ON THIS VERY - DAY WITH

ἀλλήλων· προϋπῆρχον γὰρ ἐν ἔχθρᾳ ὄντες πρὸς
ONE ANOTHER. FOR~THEY WERE PREVIOUSLY AT ENMITY BEING TOWARDS

αὐτούς.
THEMSELVES.

23.13 Πιλᾶτος δὲ συγκαλεσάμενος τοὺς ἀρχιερεῖς καὶ
       AND~PILATE   HAVING CALLED TOGETHER THE   CHIEF PRIESTS AND

τοὺς ἄρχοντας καὶ τὸν λαὸν **23.14** εἶπεν πρὸς αὐτούς,
THE AUTHORITIES AND THE PEOPLE   SAID TO   THEM,

Προσηνέγκατέ μοι τὸν ἄνθρωπον τοῦτον ὡς
YOU° BROUGHT TO ME - THIS~MAN   AS

ἀποστρέφοντα τὸν λαόν, καὶ ἰδοὺ ἐγὼ ἐνώπιον ὑμῶν
CAUSING TO REVOLT THE PEOPLE, AND BEHOLD I BEFORE   YOU°

ἀνακρίνας   οὐθὲν εὗρον ἐν τῷ ἀνθρώπῳ τούτῳ
HAVING EXAMINED [HIM] FOUND~NOTHING IN - THIS~MAN

αἴτιον ὧν   κατηγορεῖτε κατ' αὐτοῦ. **23.15** ἀλλ'
[OF THE] CRIME OF WHICH YOU° MAKE ACCUSATIONS AGAINST HIM.   AND

οὐδὲ   Ἡρῴδης, ἀνέπεμψεν γὰρ αὐτὸν πρὸς ἡμᾶς, καὶ
NEITHER [DID] HEROD,   FOR~HE SENT BACK HIM   TO   US,   AND

ἰδοὺ οὐδὲν ἄξιον θανάτου ἐστὶν πεπραγμένον αὐτῷ·
BEHOLD NOTHING WORTHY OF DEATH HAS BEEN DONE   BY HIM.

23.16 παιδεύσας οὖν   αὐτὸν ἀπολύσω.ᵀ
       THEREFORE,~HAVING DISCIPLINED HIM I WILL RELEASE [HIM].

23.18 ἀνέκραγον δὲ παμπληθεὶ λέγοντες, Αἶρε τοῦτον,
       BUT~THEY CRIED OUT ALL TOGETHER SAYING, TAKE AWAY THIS ONE,

ἀπόλυσον δὲ ἡμῖν τὸν Βαραββᾶν· **23.19** ὅστις ἦν διὰ
AND~RELEASE TO US - BARABBAS;   WHO WAS BECAUSE

στάσιν τινὰ   γενομένην ἐν τῇ πόλει καὶ φόνον
OF SOME~INSURRECTION HAVING OCCURRED IN THE CITY AND A MURDER

βληθεὶς ἐν τῇ φυλακῇ. **23.20** πάλιν δὲ ὁ Πιλᾶτος
THROWN INTO - JAIL.   AND~AGAIN - PILATE

προσεφώνησεν αὐτοῖς θέλων ἀπολῦσαι τὸν Ἰησοῦν.
ADDRESSED   THEM   WISHING TO RELEASE - JESUS.

vehemently accusing him.
[11]Even Herod with his
soldiers treated him with
contempt and mocked him;
then he put an elegant robe
on him, and sent him back to
Pilate. [12]That same day
Herod and Pilate became
friends with each other;
before this they had been
enemies.

13 Pilate then called
together the chief priests, the
leaders, and the people,
[14]and said to them, "You
brought me this man as one
who was perverting the
people; and here I have
examined him in your
presence and have not found
this man guilty of any of
your charges against him.
[15]Neither has Herod, for he
sent him back to us. Indeed,
he has done nothing to
deserve death. [16]I will
therefore have him flogged
and release him."ᵗ

18 Then they all shouted
out together, "Away with
this fellow! Release
Barabbas for us!" [19](This
was a man who had been put
in prison for an insurrection
that had taken place in the
city, and for murder.)
[20]Pilate, wanting to release
Jesus, addressed them again;

ᵗ Here, or after verse 19, other ancient
  authorities add verse 17, *Now he
  was obliged to release someone for
  them at the festival*

23:16 text: ASV RSV NASB NIV NEB TEV NJB NRSV. add v. 17: ASVmg RSVmg NASBmg NIVmg
NEBmg TEVmg NJBmg NRSVmg.

²¹but they kept shouting, "Crucify, crucify him!" ²²A third time he said to them, "Why, what evil has he done? I have found in him no ground for the sentence of death; I will therefore have him flogged and then release him." ²³But they kept urgently demanding with loud shouts that he should be crucified; and their voices prevailed. ²⁴So Pilate gave his verdict that their demand should be granted. ²⁵He released the man they asked for, the one who had been put in prison for insurrection and murder, and he handed Jesus over as they wished.

26 As they led him away, they seized a man, Simon of Cyrene, who was coming from the country, and they laid the cross on him, and made him carry it behind Jesus. ²⁷A great number of the people followed him, and among them were women who were beating their breasts and wailing for him. ²⁸But Jesus turned to them and said, "Daughters of Jerusalem, do not weep for me, but weep for yourselves and for your children. ²⁹For the days are surely coming when they will say, 'Blessed are the barren, and the wombs that never bore, and the breasts that never nursed.' ³⁰Then they will begin to say to the mountains,

23.21 οἱ   δὲ   ἐπεφώνουν   λέγοντες,   Σταύρου   σταύρου
-   BUT   THEY WERE CRYING OUT   SAYING   CRUCIFY [HIM],   CRUCIFY

αὐτόν.   **23.22** ὁ   δὲ   τρίτον   εἶπεν   πρὸς   αὐτούς,   Τί   γὰρ
HIM.   -   AND   A THIRD [TIME]   HE SAID   TO   THEM,   WHY,~WHAT

κακὸν   ἐποίησεν   οὗτος;   οὐδὲν   αἴτιον   θανάτου   εὗρον
EVIL   DID   THIS ONE?   NO   CRIME [WORTHY]   OF DEATH   DID I FIND

ἐν   αὐτῷ·   παιδεύσας   οὖν   αὐτὸν   ἀπολύσω.
IN   HIM.   THEREFORE,~HAVING DISCIPLINED   HIM   I WILL RELEASE [HIM].

23.23 οἱ   δὲ   ἐπέκειντο   φωναῖς   μεγάλαις   αἰτούμενοι
-   BUT   THEY INSISTED   WITH LOUD~VOICES   DEMANDING

αὐτὸν   σταυρωθῆναι,   καὶ   κατίσχυον   αἱ   φωναὶ   αὐτῶν.
HIM   TO BE CRUCIFIED,   AND   WERE PREVAILING   THE   VOICES   OF THEM.

23.24 καὶ   Πιλᾶτος   ἐπέκρινεν   γενέσθαι   τὸ   αἴτημα
AND   PILATE   DECIDED   TO BE DONE   THE   DEMAND

αὐτῶν·   **23.25** ἀπέλυσεν   δὲ   τὸν   διὰ   στάσιν
OF THEM.   AND~HE RELEASED   THE ONE   ON ACCOUNT OF   AN INSURRECTION

καὶ   φόνον   βεβλημένον   εἰς   φυλακὴν   ὃν
AND   MURDER   HAVING BEEN THROWN   INTO   A JAIL   WHOM

ἠτοῦντο,   τὸν   δὲ   Ἰησοῦν   παρέδωκεν   τῷ
THEY WERE REQUESTING,   -   BUT   JESUS   HE DELIVERED OVER   TO THE

θελήματι   αὐτῶν.
WILL   OF THEM.

23.26 Καὶ   ὡς   ἀπήγαγον   αὐτόν,   ἐπιλαβόμενοι
AND   AS   THEY LED AWAY   HIM,   HAVING SEIZED

Σίμωνά   τινα   Κυρηναῖον   ἐρχόμενον   ἀπ᾽   ἀγροῦ
A CERTAIN~SIMON,   A CYRENIAN,   COMING   FROM   [THE] COUNTRY

ἐπέθηκαν   αὐτῷ   τὸν   σταυρὸν   φέρειν   ὄπισθεν   τοῦ
THEY PUT UPON   HIM   THE   CROSS   TO CARRY   FOLLOWING   -

Ἰησοῦ.   **23.27** Ἠκολούθει   δὲ   αὐτῷ   πολὺ   πλῆθος   τοῦ
JESUS.   AND~WERE FOLLOWING   HIM   A GREAT   MULTITUDE   OF THE

λαοῦ   καὶ   γυναικῶν   αἳ   ἐκόπτοντο   καὶ   ἐθρήνουν   αὐτόν.
PEOPLE   AND   WOMEN   WHO   WERE MOURNING   AND   LAMENTING   FOR HIM.

23.28 στραφεὶς   δὲ   πρὸς   αὐτὰς   [ὁ]   Ἰησοῦς   εἶπεν,
AND~HAVING TURNED   TO   THEM   -   JESUS   SAID,

Θυγατέρες   Ἰερουσαλήμ,   μὴ   κλαίετε   ἐπ᾽   ἐμέ·   πλὴν   ἐφ᾽
DAUGHTERS   OF JERUSALEM,   DO NOT CRY   FOR   ME;   BUT   FOR

ἑαυτὰς   κλαίετε   καὶ   ἐπὶ   τὰ   τέκνα   ὑμῶν,   **23.29** ὅτι
YOURSELVES   CRY   AND   FOR   THE   CHILDREN   OF YOU°,   BECAUSE

ἰδοὺ   ἔρχονται   ἡμέραι   ἐν   αἷς   ἐροῦσιν,   Μακάριαι
BEHOLD   DAYS~ARE COMING   IN   WHICH   THEY WILL SAY,   BLESSED [ARE]

αἱ   στεῖραι   καὶ   αἱ   κοιλίαι   αἳ   οὐκ   ἐγέννησαν
THE   BARREN   AND   THE   WOMBS   WHICH   DID NOT BEAR

καὶ   μαστοὶ   οἳ   οὐκ   ἔθρεψαν.
AND   [THE] BREASTS   WHICH   DID NOT NURSE.

23.30 τότε   ἄρξονται   λέγειν   τοῖς   ὄρεσιν,
THEN   THEY WILL BEGIN   TO SAY   TO THE   MOUNTAINS,

23:30 Hos. 10:8

Πέσετε ἐφ' ἡμᾶς,
FALL   ON   US,

καὶ τοῖς βουνοῖς,
AND TO THE HILLS,

Καλύψατε ἡμᾶς·
BURY   US.

23.31 ὅτι   εἰ ἐν τῷ ὑγρῷ ξύλῳ   ταῦτα ποιοῦσιν,
BECAUSE IF WHILE A TREE [IS]~FULL OF MOISTURE THEY DO~THESE THINGS,

ἐν τῷ   ξηρῷ τί   γένηται;
WHILE [IT IS] DRY   WHAT MAY HAPPEN?

23.32 Ἤγοντο δὲ   καὶ ἕτεροι κακοῦργοι δύο σὺν
          AND~WERE BEING LED AWAY ALSO ²OTHER ³CRIMINALS ¹TWO WITH

αὐτῷ ἀναιρεθῆναι. **23.33** καὶ ὅτε ἦλθον ἐπὶ τὸν
HIM   TO BE EXECUTED.   AND WHEN THEY CAME UPON THE

τόπον τὸν καλούμενον Κρανίον, ἐκεῖ ἐσταύρωσαν αὐτὸν
PLACE -   BEING CALLED [THE] SKULL, THERE THEY CRUCIFIED HIM

καὶ τοὺς κακούργους, ὃν μὲν ἐκ δεξιῶν   ὃν δὲ ἐξ
AND THE CRIMINALS,   ONE ON [THE] RIGHT, [AND] ONE ON

ἀριστερῶν. **23.34** ⌜[[ὁ δὲ Ἰησοῦς ἔλεγεν, Πάτερ,
[THE] LEFT.   - BUT JESUS WAS SAYING, FATHER,

ἄφες αὐτοῖς, οὐ γὰρ οἴδασιν τί   ποιοῦσιν.]]⌝
FORGIVE THEM, ³NOT ¹FOR ²THEY KNOW WHAT THEY ARE DOING.

διαμεριζόμενοι δὲ τὰ ἱμάτια αὐτοῦ ἔβαλον κλήρους.
AND~DIVIDING UP THE GARMENTS OF HIM, THEY CAST LOTS.

23.35 καὶ εἱστήκει ὁ λαὸς θεωρῶν. ἐξεμυκτήριζον δὲ
          AND HAD STOOD THE PEOPLE WATCHING. AND~WERE MOCKING [HIM]

καὶ οἱ ἄρχοντες λέγοντες, Ἄλλους ἔσωσεν, σωσάτω
ALSO THE AUTHORITIES SAYING, OTHERS HE SAVED, LET HIM SAVE

ἑαυτόν, εἰ οὗτός ἐστιν ὁ Χριστὸς τοῦ θεοῦ ὁ
HIMSELF, IF THIS ONE IS THE CHRIST - OF GOD, THE

ἐκλεκτός. **23.36** ἐνέπαιξαν δὲ αὐτῷ καὶ οἱ στρατιῶται
CHOSEN [ONE].   AND~RIDICULED HIM   ALSO THE SOLDIERS

προσερχόμενοι, ὄξος προσφέροντες αὐτῷ **23.37** καὶ
APPROACHING,   OFFERING~WINE VINEGAR TO HIM   AND

λέγοντες, Εἰ σὺ εἶ ὁ βασιλεὺς τῶν Ἰουδαίων, σῶσον
SAYING,   IF YOU ARE THE KING   OF THE JEWS,   SAVE

σεαυτόν. **23.38** ἦν δὲ   καὶ ἐπιγραφὴ ἐπ' αὐτῷ, Ὁ
YOURSELF.   AND~THERE WAS ALSO AN INSCRIPTION OVER HIM, THE

βασιλεὺς τῶν Ἰουδαίων οὗτος.
KING   OF THE JEWS [IS] THIS ONE.

23.39 Εἷς δὲ τῶν κρεμασθέντων κακούργων
          AND~ONE OF THE CRIMINALS~HAVING BEEN HUNG [WITH HIM]

ἐβλασφήμει αὐτὸν λέγων, Οὐχὶ σὺ εἶ ὁ Χριστός;
WAS BLASPHEMING HIM SAYING, ³NOT ²YOU ¹ARE THE CHRIST?

σῶσον σεαυτὸν καὶ ἡμᾶς. **23.40** ἀποκριθεὶς δὲ ὁ
SAVE YOURSELF AND US.   AND~HAVING ANSWERED THE

'Fall on us'; and to the hills, 'Cover us.' 31For if they do this when the wood is green, what will happen when it is dry?"

32 Two others also, who were criminals, were led away to be put to death with him. 33When they came to the place that is called The Skull, they crucified Jesus*u* there with the criminals, one on his right and one on his left. [34Then Jesus said, "Father, forgive them; for they do not know what they are doing."]*v* And they cast lots to divide his clothing. 35And the people stood by, watching; but the leaders scoffed at him, saying, "He saved others; let him save himself if he is the Messiah*w* of God, his chosen one!" 36The soldiers also mocked him, coming up and offering him sour wine, 37and saying, "If you are the King of the Jews, save yourself!" 38There was also an inscription over him,*x* "This is the King of the Jews."

39 One of the criminals who were hanged there kept deriding*y* him and saying, "Are you not the Messiah?*w* Save yourself and us!" 40But the other rebuked

u Gk *him*
v Other ancient authorities lack the sentence *Then Jesus . . . what they are doing*
w Or *the Christ*
x Other ancient authorities add *written in Greek and Latin and Hebrew* (that is, *Aramaic*)
y Or *blaspheming*

23:34 text: all. omit: ASVmg RSVmg NASBmg NIVmg NEBmg TEVmg NJBmg NRSVmg. (Note: the double brackets in the Greek text indicate that this sentence was a later addition to the text, which, however, was retained because of its importance in the textual tradition.)

him, saying, "Do you not fear God, since you are under the same sentence of condemnation? [41]And we indeed have been condemned justly, for we are getting what we deserve for our deeds, but this man has done nothing wrong." [42]Then he said, "Jesus, remember me when you come into[z] your kingdom." [43]He replied, "Truly I tell you, today you will be with me in Paradise."

[44]It was now about noon, and darkness came over the whole land[a] until three in the afternoon, [45]while the sun's light failed;[b] and the curtain of the temple was torn in two. [46]Then Jesus, crying with a loud voice, said, "Father, into your hands I commend my spirit." Having said this, he breathed his last. [47]When the centurion saw what had taken place, he praised God and said, "Certainly this man was innocent."[c] [48]And when all the crowds who had gathered there for this spectacle saw what had taken place, they returned home, beating their breasts. [49]But all his acquaintances, including the women who had followed him from Galilee, stood at a distance, watching these things.

[50]Now there was a good and righteous man named Joseph, who,

[z] Other ancient authorities read in
[a] Or earth
[b] Or the sun was eclipsed. Other ancient authorities read the sun was darkened
[c] Or righteous

ἕτερος ἐπιτιμῶν αὐτῷ ἔφη, Οὐδὲ φοβῇ σὺ τὸν
OTHER REBUKING HIM SAID, DO YOU NOT FEAR [FOR] YOURSELF -

θεόν, ὅτι ἐν τῷ αὐτῷ κρίματι εἶ;
GOD, BECAUSE IN THE SAME [STATE OF] CONDEMNATION YOU ARE?

23.41 καὶ ἡμεῖς μὲν δικαίως, ἄξια γὰρ ὧν
AND WE INDEED JUSTLY, FOR~THINGS WORTHY OF WHICH

ἐπράξαμεν ἀπολαμβάνομεν· οὗτος δὲ οὐδὲν ἄτοπον
WE DID, WE ARE RECEIVING. BUT~THIS ONE NOTHING WRONG

ἔπραξεν. **23.42** καὶ ἔλεγεν, Ἰησοῦ, μνήσθητί μου
DID. AND HE WAS SAYING, JESUS, REMEMBER ME

ὅταν ⌜ἔλθῃς εἰς τὴν βασιλείαν σου⌝. **23.43** καὶ εἶπεν
WHEN YOU COME INTO THE KINGDOM OF YOU. AND HE SAID

αὐτῷ, Ἀμήν σοι λέγω, σήμερον μετ' ἐμοῦ ἔσῃ ἐν
TO HIM, TRULY I SAY~TO YOU, TODAY WITH ME YOU WILL BE IN

τῷ παραδείσῳ.
- PARADISE.

23.44 Καὶ ἦν ἤδη ὡσεὶ ὥρα ἕκτη καὶ σκότος
AND IT WAS ALREADY ABOUT [THE] SIXTH~HOUR AND DARKNESS

ἐγένετο ἐφ' ὅλην τὴν γῆν ἕως ὥρας ἐνάτης **23.45** τοῦ
WAS OVER [THE] WHOLE - LAND UNTIL [THE] NINTH~HOUR, THE

ἡλίου ἐκλιπόντος, ἐσχίσθη δὲ τὸ καταπέτασμα τοῦ
SUN HAVING BEEN ECLIPSED, AND~WAS TORN THE CURTAIN OF THE

ναοῦ μέσον. **23.46** καὶ φωνήσας φωνῇ μεγάλῃ ὁ
TEMPLE IN TWO. AND HAVING CRIED OUT WITH A LOUD~VOICE -

Ἰησοῦς εἶπεν, Πάτερ, εἰς χεῖράς σου παρατίθεμαι τὸ
JESUS SAID, FATHER, INTO [THE] HANDS OF YOU I ENTRUST THE

πνεῦμά μου. τοῦτο δὲ εἰπὼν ἐξέπνευσεν.
SPIRIT OF ME. AND~THIS HAVING SAID, HE BREATHED OUT [HIS LAST].

23.47 Ἰδὼν δὲ ὁ ἑκατοντάρχης τὸ γενόμενον
AND~HAVING SEEN THE CENTURION THE THING HAVING HAPPENED

ἐδόξαζεν τὸν θεὸν λέγων, Ὄντως ὁ ἄνθρωπος οὗτος
HE WAS GLORIFYING - GOD SAYING, SURELY - THIS~MAN

δίκαιος ἦν. **23.48** καὶ πάντες οἱ συμπαραγενόμενοι ὄχλοι
WAS~RIGHTEOUS. AND ALL THE CROWDS~HAVING GATHERED TOGETHER

ἐπὶ τὴν θεωρίαν ταύτην, θεωρήσαντες τὰ
AT - THIS~SPECTACLE, HAVING OBSERVED THE THINGS

γενόμενα, τύπτοντες τὰ στήθη ὑπέστρεφον.
HAVING HAPPENED, BEATING THE (THEIR) CHESTS, WERE RETURNING.

23.49 εἱστήκεισαν δὲ πάντες οἱ γνωστοὶ αὐτῷ ἀπὸ
AND~HAD STOOD ALL THE RELATIVES TO HIM FROM

μακρόθεν καὶ γυναῖκες αἱ συνακολουθοῦσαι αὐτῷ
A DISTANCE AND [THE] WOMEN, THE ONES FOLLOWING HIM

ἀπὸ τῆς Γαλιλαίας ὁρῶσαι ταῦτα.
FROM - GALILEE, SEEING THESE THINGS.

23.50 Καὶ ἰδοὺ ἀνὴρ ὀνόματι Ἰωσὴφ
AND BEHOLD A MAN BY NAME JOSEPH

23:42 text: KJV ASVmg RSV NIV NEB NJB NRSV. var. ελθης εν τη βασιλειαν σου (come in your kingdom): ASV RSVmg NASB NEBmg TEV NJBmg NRSVmg. **23:46** Ps. 31:5

βουλευτὴς ὑπάρχων   [καὶ] ἀνὴρ ἀγαθὸς καὶ δίκαιος
BEING~A MEMBER OF [THE] COUNCIL, AND A GOOD~MAN AND RIGHTEOUS

23.51 —οὗτος οὐκ ἦν συγκατατεθειμένος τῇ βουλῇ καὶ τῇ
—THIS ONE HAD NOT CONSENTED WITH   THE COUNCIL AND THE

πράξει αὐτῶν— ἀπὸ Ἀριμαθαίας πόλεως τῶν Ἰουδαίων,
ACTION OF THEM— FROM ARIMATHEA, A CITY - OF JUDEA,

ὃς προσεδέχετο τὴν βασιλείαν τοῦ θεοῦ, **23.52** οὗτος
WHO WAS WAITING FOR THE KINGDOM - OF GOD, THIS ONE

προσελθὼν τῷ Πιλάτῳ ᾐτήσατο τὸ σῶμα τοῦ Ἰησοῦ
HAVING APPROACHED - PILATE ASKED FOR THE BODY - OF JESUS

23.53 καὶ καθελὼν   ἐνετύλιξεν αὐτὸ σινδόνι
AND HAVING TAKEN DOWN [THE BODY] HE WRAPPED IT IN LINEN

καὶ ἔθηκεν αὐτὸν ἐν μνήματι λαξευτῷ οὗ οὐκ ἦν
AND PLACED IT IN A HEWN~TOMB WHERE WAS NOT

οὐδεὶς οὔπω κείμενος. **23.54** καὶ ἡμέρα ἦν
ANYONE YET LAID. AND IT WAS~[THE] DAY

παρασκευῆς καὶ σάββατον ἐπέφωσκεν.
OF PREPARATION AND [THE] SABBATH WAS DAWNING.

23.55 Κατακολουθήσασαι δὲ αἱ γυναῖκες, αἵτινες
AND~HAVING FOLLOWED AFTER, THE WOMEN WHO

ἦσαν συνεληλυθυῖαι ἐκ τῆς Γαλιλαίας αὐτῷ,
HAD COME OUT OF - GALILEE WITH HIM,

ἐθεάσαντο τὸ μνημεῖον καὶ ὡς ἐτέθη τὸ σῶμα αὐτοῦ,
SAW THE TOMB AND HOW WAS LAID THE BODY OF HIM,

23.56 ὑποστρέψασαι δὲ ἡτοίμασαν ἀρώματα καὶ μύρα.
AND~HAVING RETURNED THEY PREPARED SPICES AND OINTMENTS.

Καὶ τὸ μὲν σάββατον ἡσύχασαν κατὰ   τὴν
AND ON THE - SABBATH THEY RESTED ACCORDING TO THE

ἐντολήν.
COMMANDMENT.

though a member of the council, [51]had not agreed to their plan and action. He came from the Jewish town of Arimathea, and he was waiting expectantly for the kingdom of God. [52]This man went to Pilate and asked for the body of Jesus. [53]Then he took it down, wrapped it in a linen cloth, and laid it in a rock-hewn tomb where no one had ever been laid. [54]It was the day of Preparation, and the sabbath was beginning.[d] [55]The women who had come with him from Galilee followed, and they saw the tomb and how his body was laid. [56]Then they returned, and prepared spices and ointments.

On the sabbath they rested according to the commandment.

[d] Gk *was dawning*

24.1 τῇ δὲ μιᾷ τῶν σαββάτων ὄρθρου βαθέως
BUT~ON THE FIRST [DAY] OF THE WEEK VERY EARLY IN THE MORNING

ἐπὶ τὸ μνῆμα ἦλθον φέρουσαι ἃ
TO THE TOMB THEY CAME BRINGING WHAT

ἡτοίμασαν ἀρώματα. **24.2** εὗρον δὲ τὸν λίθον
SPICES~THEY PREPARED. BUT~THEY FOUND THE STONE

ἀποκεκυλισμένον ἀπὸ τοῦ μνημείου, **24.3** εἰσελθοῦσαι δὲ
HAVING BEEN ROLLED AWAY FROM THE TOMB, AND~HAVING ENTERED

οὐχ εὗρον τὸ σῶμα τοῦ κυρίου Ἰησοῦ. **24.4** καὶ
THEY DID NOT FIND THE BODY OF THE LORD JESUS. AND

ἐγένετο ἐν τῷ ἀπορεῖσθαι αὐτὰς περὶ τούτου καὶ
IT CAME ABOUT WHILE THEY~ARE UNCERTAIN ABOUT THIS AND

ἰδοὺ ἄνδρες δύο ἐπέστησαν αὐταῖς ἐν
BEHOLD TWO~MEN STOOD BY THEM IN

But on the first day of the week, at early dawn, they came to the tomb, taking the spices that they had prepared. [2]They found the stone rolled away from the tomb, [3]but when they went in, they did not find the body.[e] [4]While they were perplexed about this, suddenly two men in

[e] Other ancient authorities add *of the Lord Jesus*

dazzling clothes stood beside them. [5]The women[f] were terrified and bowed their faces to the ground, but the men[g] said to them, "Why do you look for the living among the dead? He is not here, but has risen.[h] [6]Remember how he told you, while he was still in Galilee, [7]that the Son of Man must be handed over to sinners, and be crucified, and on the third day rise again." [8]Then they remembered his words, [9]and returning from the tomb, they told all this to the eleven and to all the rest. [10]Now it was Mary Magdalene, Joanna, Mary the mother of James, and the other women with them who told this to the apostles. [11]But these words seemed to them an idle tale, and they did not believe them. [12]But Peter got up and ran to the tomb; stooping and looking in, he saw the linen cloths by themselves; then he went home, amazed at what had happened.[i]

13 Now on that same day two of them were going to a village called Emmaus, about seven miles[j] from Jerusalem, [14]and talking with each other about

[f] Gk *They*
[g] Gk *but they*
[h] Other ancient authorities lack *He is not here, but has risen*
[i] Other ancient authorities lack verse 12
[j] Gk *sixty stadia;* other ancient authorities read *a hundred sixty stadia*

ἐσθῆτι ἀστραπτούσῃ. **24.5** ἐμφόβων δὲ γενομένων αὐτῶν
DAZZLING~CLOTHING.   [4]AFRAID   [1]AND [3]HAVING BECOME [2]THEY

καὶ κλινουσῶν τὰ   πρόσωπα εἰς τὴν γῆν   εἶπαν
AND   BOWING   THE(THEIR) FACES   TO THE GROUND THEY SAID

πρὸς αὐτάς, Τί ζητεῖτε   τὸν   ζῶντα μετὰ τῶν
TO   THEM, WHY ARE YOU° SEEKING THE ONE LIVING AMONG THE

νεκρῶν· **24.6** οὐκ ἔστιν ὧδε, ἀλλὰ ἠγέρθη.   μνήσθητε
DEAD?   HE IS NOT HERE, BUT WAS RAISED. REMEMBER

ὡς ἐλάλησεν ὑμῖν ἔτι ὢν ἐν τῇ Γαλιλαίᾳ
HOW HE SPOKE TO YOU° WHILE BEING IN - GALILEE

24.7 λέγων τὸν υἱὸν τοῦ ἀνθρώπου ὅτι δεῖ
         SAYING   THE SON   -   OF MAN   -   IT IS NECESSARY

παραδοθῆναι εἰς χεῖρας   ἀνθρώπων ἁμαρτωλῶν καὶ
TO BE DELIVERED OVER INTO [THE] HANDS OF SINFUL~MEN   AND

σταυρωθῆναι καὶ τῇ   τρίτῃ ἡμέρᾳ ἀναστῆναι.
TO BE CRUCIFIED AND ON THE THIRD DAY   TO RISE AGAIN.

24.8 καὶ ἐμνήσθησαν τῶν ῥημάτων αὐτοῦ. **24.9** καὶ
         AND THEY REMEMBERED THE WORDS   OF HIM.   AND

ὑποστρέψασαι ἀπὸ τοῦ μνημείου ἀπήγγειλαν
HAVING RETURNED FROM THE TOMB   THEY REPORTED

ταῦτα πάντα τοῖς ἔνδεκα καὶ πᾶσιν τοῖς λοιποῖς.
ALL~THESE THINGS TO THE ELEVEN AND TO ALL THE OTHERS.

24.10 ἦσαν δὲ   ἡ Μαγδαληνὴ Μαρία καὶ Ἰωάννα καὶ
          NOW~THERE WERE - MARY~MAGDALENE   AND JOANNA AND

Μαρία ἡ   Ἰακώβου καὶ αἱ λοιπαὶ σὺν αὐταῖς.
MARY THE [MOTHER] OF JAMES AND THE OTHERS WITH THEM.

ἔλεγον   πρὸς τοὺς ἀποστόλους ταῦτα, **24.11** καὶ
THEY WERE TELLING TO THE   APOSTLES   THESE THINGS,   AND

ἐφάνησαν ἐνώπιον αὐτῶν ὡσεὶ λῆρος τὰ
APPEARED   BEFORE   THEM   AS NONSENSE -

ῥήματα ταῦτα, καὶ ἠπίστουν   αὐταῖς. **24.12** ⌐Ὁ δὲ
THESE~WORDS, AND THEY WERE DISBELIEVING THEM.   - BUT

Πέτρος ἀναστὰς ἔδραμεν ἐπὶ τὸ μνημεῖον καὶ
PETER HAVING ARISEN RAN   TO THE TOMB   AND

παρακύψας βλέπει τὰ ὀθόνια   μόνα, καὶ ἀπῆλθεν
HAVING BENT OVER HE SEES THE LINEN CLOTHS ONLY, AND HE DEPARTED

πρὸς ἑαυτὸν   θαυμάζων τὸ   γεγονός.⌐
[2]TO   [3]HIMSELF [ABOUT] [1]WONDERING THE THING HAVING HAPPENED.

24.13 Καὶ ἰδοὺ δύο ἐξ αὐτῶν ἐν αὐτῇ τῇ ἡμέρᾳ
          AND BEHOLD TWO OF THEM   ON THE~SAME   DAY

ἦσαν πορευόμενοι εἰς κώμην ἀπέχουσαν
WERE TRAVELING   TO A VILLAGE BEING DISTANT

σταδίους ἑξήκοντα ἀπὸ Ἰερουσαλήμ, ᾗ   ὄνομα
SIXTY~STADIA   FROM JERUSALEM, TO WHICH [IS] [THE] NAME

Ἐμμαοῦς, **24.14** καὶ αὐτοὶ ὡμίλουν πρὸς ἀλλήλους
EMMAUS,   AND THEY WERE SPEAKING TO ONE ANOTHER

24:12 text: KJV ASV RSVmg NASB NIV NEBmg TEV NJB. omit: ASVmg RSV NASBmg NEB TEVmg NJBmg.

περὶ   πάντων   τῶν συμβεβηκότων τούτων.   **24.15** καὶ
CONCERNING ALL   -   THESE THINGS~HAVING HAPPENED.   AND

ἐγένετο   ἐν τῷ   ὁμιλεῖν αὐτοὺς   καὶ   συζητεῖν
IT CAME ABOUT WHILE   THEY~TALKING   AND   DISCUSSING [THESE THINGS]

καὶ   αὐτὸς Ἰησοῦς ἐγγίσας   συνεπορεύετο αὐτοῖς,
ALSO   JESUS~HIMSELF HAVING COME NEAR WAS TRAVELING WITH THEM,

24.16 οἱ δὲ   ὀφθαλμοὶ αὐτῶν ἐκρατοῦντο τοῦ   μὴ
         BUT~THE EYES   OF THEM WERE HELD   -   NOT

ἐπιγνῶναι αὐτόν.   **24.17** εἶπεν δὲ   πρὸς αὐτούς, Τίνες οἱ
TO RECOGNIZE HIM.   AND~HE SAID TO   THEM,   WHAT -

λόγοι   οὗτοι οὓς ἀντιβάλλετε   πρὸς ἀλλήλους
WORDS [ARE] THESE WHICH YOU° ARE EXCHANGING WITH ONE ANOTHER

περιπατοῦντες; καὶ ἐστάθησαν σκυθρωποί.
WALKING ALONG?   AND THEY STOOD [WITH] A SAD LOOK.

24.18 ἀποκριθεὶς δὲ   εἷς ὀνόματι Κλεοπᾶς εἶπεν   πρὸς
        AND~HAVING ANSWERED ONE BY NAME CLEOPAS SAID   TO

αὐτόν, Σὺ   μόνος   παροικεῖς Ἰερουσαλὴμ καὶ
HIM, [ARE] YOU [THE] ONLY ONE VISITING JERUSALEM   AND

οὐκ ἔγνως τὰ   γενόμενα   ἐν αὐτῇ ἐν ταῖς
YOU DO NOT KNOW THE THINGS HAVING HAPPENED IN IT IN -

ἡμέραις ταύταις; **24.19** καὶ εἶπεν αὐτοῖς, Ποῖα;   οἱ
THESE~DAYS?   AND HE SAID TO THEM, WHAT THINGS? -

δὲ εἶπαν αὐτῷ, Τὰ   περὶ Ἰησοῦ τοῦ Ναζαρηνοῦ,
AND THEY SAID TO HIM, THE THINGS ABOUT JESUS THE NAZARENE,

ὃς ἐγένετο ἀνὴρ προφήτης δυνατὸς ἐν ἔργῳ καὶ λόγῳ
WHO WAS A MAN, A PROPHET POWERFUL IN DEED AND WORD

ἐναντίον τοῦ θεοῦ καὶ παντὸς τοῦ λαοῦ, **24.20** ὅπως
BEFORE - GOD AND ALL   THE PEOPLE,   HOW

τε   παρέδωκαν αὐτὸν οἱ ἀρχιερεῖς καὶ οἱ ἄρχοντες
BOTH DELIVERED OVER HIM THE CHIEF PRIESTS AND THE AUTHORITIES

ἡμῶν εἰς κρίμα   θανάτου καὶ ἐσταύρωσαν αὐτόν.
OF US TO A CONDEMNATION OF DEATH AND THEY CRUCIFIED HIM.

24.21 ἡμεῖς δὲ ἠλπίζομεν ὅτι αὐτός ἐστιν ὁ   μέλλων
        BUT~WE   WERE HOPING THAT HE IS   THE ONE ABOUT

λυτροῦσθαι τὸν Ἰσραήλ· ἀλλά γε καὶ σὺν πᾶσιν
TO REDEEM - ISRAEL.   BUT - ALSO WITH ALL

τούτοις τρίτην ταύτην ἡμέραν ἄγει ἀφ' οὗ   ταῦτα
THESE THINGS THIS,~[THE] THIRD DAY, PASSES FROM WHICH THESE THINGS

ἐγένετο. **24.22** ἀλλὰ καὶ γυναῖκές τινες ἐξ   ἡμῶν
CAME ABOUT.   BUT ALSO SOME~WOMEN   AMONG US

ἐξέστησαν ἡμᾶς, γενόμεναι ὀρθριναὶ ἐπὶ τὸ
AMAZED   US. HAVING BEEN EARLY   AT THE

μνημεῖον, **24.23** καὶ μὴ εὑροῦσαι τὸ σῶμα αὐτοῦ ἦλθον
TOMB,   AND NOT HAVING FOUND THE BODY OF HIM THEY CAME

λέγουσαι καὶ ὀπτασίαν ἀγγέλων ἑωρακέναι, οἳ
SAYING   ALSO A VISION OF ANGELS TO HAVE SEEN, WHO

λέγουσιν αὐτὸν ζῆν. **24.24** καὶ ἀπῆλθόν τινες τῶν
SAY   HIM TO LIVE.   AND DEPARTED SOME OF THE ONES

all these things that had happened. [15]While they were talking and discussing, Jesus himself came near and went with them, [16]but their eyes were kept from recognizing him. [17]And he said to them, "What are you discussing with each other while you walk along?" They stood still, looking sad.[k] [18]Then one of them, whose name was Cleopas, answered him, "Are you the only stranger in Jerusalem who does not know the things that have taken place there in these days?" [19]He asked them, "What things?" They replied, "The things about Jesus of Nazareth,[l] who was a prophet mighty in deed and word before God and all the people, [20]and how our chief priests and leaders handed him over to be condemned to death and crucified him. [21]But we had hoped that he was the one to redeem Israel.[m] Yes, and besides all this, it is now the third day since these things took place. [22]Moreover, some women of our group astounded us. They were at the tomb early this morning, [23]and when they did not find his body there, they came back and told us that they had indeed seen a vision of angels who said that he was alive. [24]Some of those who were with us went

[k] Other ancient authorities read *walk along, looking sad?*
[l] Other ancient authorities read *Jesus the Nazorean*
[m] Or *to set Israel free*

to the tomb and found it just as the women had said; but they did not see him." 25Then he said to them, "Oh, how foolish you are, and how slow of heart to believe all that the prophets have declared! 26Was it not necessary that the Messiah*n* should suffer these things and then enter into his glory?" 27Then beginning with Moses and all the prophets, he interpreted to them the things about himself in all the scriptures.

28 As they came near the village to which they were going, he walked ahead as if he were going on. 29But they urged him strongly, saying, "Stay with us, because it is almost evening and the day is now nearly over." So he went in to stay with them. 30When he was at the table with them, he took bread, blessed and broke it, and gave it to them. 31Then their eyes were opened, and they recognized him; and he vanished from their sight. 32They said to each other, "Were not our hearts burning within us*o* while he was talking to us on the road, while he was opening the scriptures to us?" 33That same hour they got up and returned to Jerusalem; and they found the eleven and their companions gathered together.

n Or *the Christ*
o Other ancient authorities lack *within us*

σὺν ἡμῖν ἐπὶ τὸ μνημεῖον, καὶ εὗρον οὕτως καθὼς
WITH US TO THE TOMB, AND THEY FOUND [IT] SO, JUST AS

καὶ αἱ γυναῖκες εἶπον, αὐτὸν δὲ οὐκ εἶδον. **24.25** καὶ
ALSO THE WOMEN SAID, BUT~HIM THEY DID NOT SEE. AND

αὐτὸς εἶπεν πρὸς αὐτούς, Ὦ ἀνόητοι καὶ βραδεῖς τῇ
HE SAID TO THEM, O FOOLISH ONES AND SLOW -

καρδίᾳ τοῦ πιστεύειν ἐπὶ πᾶσιν οἷς ἐλάλησαν οἱ
IN HEART - TO BELIEVE IN ALL WHICH SPOKE THE

προφῆται· **24.26** οὐχὶ ταῦτα ἔδει παθεῖν
PROPHETS. [WAS IT] NOT ⁵THESE THINGS ¹NECESSARY [FOR] ⁴TO SUFFER

τὸν Χριστὸν καὶ εἰσελθεῖν εἰς τὴν δόξαν αὐτοῦ;
²THE ³CHRIST AND TO ENTER INTO THE GLORY OF HIM?

24.27 καὶ ἀρξάμενος ἀπὸ Μωϋσέως καὶ ἀπὸ πάντων
AND HAVING BEGUN FROM MOSES AND FROM ALL

τῶν προφητῶν διερμήνευσεν αὐτοῖς ἐν πάσαις ταῖς
THE PROPHETS HE EXPLAINED TO THEM IN ALL THE

γραφαῖς τὰ περὶ ἑαυτοῦ.
SCRIPTURES THE THINGS CONCERNING HIMSELF.

24.28 Καὶ ἤγγισαν εἰς τὴν κώμην οὗ ἐπορεύοντο,
AND THEY DREW NEAR TO THE VILLAGE WHERE THEY WERE TRAVELING,

καὶ αὐτὸς προσεποιήσατο πορρώτερον πορεύεσθαι.
AND HE ACTED AS THOUGH TO TRAVEL~FARTHER.

24.29 καὶ παρεβιάσαντο αὐτὸν λέγοντες, Μεῖνον μεθ᾽
AND THEY STRONGLY URGED HIM SAYING, STAY WITH

ἡμῶν, ὅτι πρὸς ἑσπέραν ἐστὶν καὶ κέκλικεν ἤδη
US, BECAUSE TOWARDS EVENING IT IS AND HAS DECLINED ALREADY

ἡ ἡμέρα. καὶ εἰσῆλθεν τοῦ μεῖναι σὺν αὐτοῖς.
THE DAY. AND HE ENTERED - TO STAY WITH THEM.

24.30 καὶ ἐγένετο ἐν τῷ κατακλιθῆναι αὐτὸν μετ᾽
AND IT CAME ABOUT WHILE HE~WAS RECLINING AT TABLE WITH

αὐτῶν λαβὼν τὸν ἄρτον εὐλόγησεν καὶ κλάσας
THEM HAVING TAKEN THE BREAD HE BLESSED [IT] AND HAVING BROKEN [IT]

ἐπεδίδου αὐτοῖς· **24.31** αὐτῶν δὲ διηνοίχθησαν οἱ
HE WAS GIVING [IT] TO THEM. AND~OF THEM WERE OPENED THE

ὀφθαλμοὶ καὶ ἐπέγνωσαν αὐτόν· καὶ αὐτὸς
EYES AND THEY RECOGNIZED HIM. AND HE

ἄφαντος ἐγένετο ἀπ᾽ αὐτῶν. **24.32** καὶ εἶπαν πρὸς
BECAME~INVISIBLE FROM THEM. AND THEY SAID TO

ἀλλήλους, Οὐχὶ ἡ καρδία ἡμῶν καιομένη ἦν [ἐν
ONE ANOTHER, [WERE] NOT THE HEART[S] OF US BURNING WITHIN

ἡμῖν] ὡς ἐλάλει ἡμῖν ἐν τῇ ὁδῷ, ὡς διήνοιγεν
US AS HE WAS SPEAKING TO US ON THE ROAD, AS HE WAS OPENING

ἡμῖν τὰς γραφάς; **24.33** καὶ ἀναστάντες αὐτῇ τῇ
TO US THE SCRIPTURES? AND HAVING ARISEN THIS VERY -

ὥρᾳ ὑπέστρεψαν εἰς Ἰερουσαλὴμ καὶ εὗρον
HOUR THEY RETURNED TO JERUSALEM, AND THEY FOUND

ἠθροισμένους τοὺς ἕνδεκα καὶ τοὺς σὺν αὐτοῖς,
HAVING BEEN GATHERED TOGETHER THE ELEVEN AND THE ONES WITH THEM,

24.34 λέγοντας ὅτι ὄντως ἠγέρθη ὁ κύριος καὶ ὤφθη
SAYING THAT REALLY WAS RAISED THE LORD AND HE APPEARED

Σίμωνι. **24.35** καὶ αὐτοὶ ἐξηγοῦντο τὰ ἐν τῇ ὁδῷ
TO SIMON. AND THEY WERE EXPLAINING THE THINGS ON THE ROAD

καὶ ὡς ἐγνώσθη αὐτοῖς ἐν τῇ κλάσει τοῦ ἄρτου.
AND HOW HE WAS MADE KNOWN TO THEM IN THE BREAKING OF THE BREAD.

24.36 Ταῦτα δὲ αὐτῶν λαλούντων αὐτὸς ἔστη ἐν
AND~[WHILE] THESE THINGS THEY SPEAKING, HE STOOD IN

μέσῳ αὐτῶν ⌜καὶ λέγει αὐτοῖς, Εἰρήνη ὑμῖν.⌝
[THE] MIDST OF THEM AND HE SAYS TO THEM, PEACE TO YOU°.

24.37 πτοηθέντες δὲ καὶ ἔμφοβοι γενόμενοι
BUT~HAVING BEEN STARTLED AND HAVING BEEN~AFRAID

ἐδόκουν πνεῦμα θεωρεῖν. **24.38** καὶ εἶπεν αὐτοῖς,
THEY WERE THINKING TO SEE~A SPIRIT. AND HE SAID TO THEM,

Τί τεταραγμένοι ἐστὲ καὶ διὰ τί διαλογισμοὶ
WHY HAVE YOU° BEEN TROUBLED, AND WHY [DO] DOUBTS

ἀναβαίνουσιν ἐν τῇ καρδίᾳ ὑμῶν; **24.39** ἴδετε τὰς
ARISE IN THE HEART[S] OF YOU°? YOU° SEE THE

χεῖράς μου καὶ τοὺς πόδας μου ὅτι ἐγώ εἰμι αὐτός·
HANDS OF ME AND THE FEET OF ME THAT I AM MYSELF.

ψηλαφήσατέ με καὶ ἴδετε, ὅτι πνεῦμα σάρκα καὶ
TOUCH ME AND SEE, BECAUSE A SPIRIT FLESH AND

ὀστέα οὐκ ἔχει καθὼς ἐμὲ θεωρεῖτε ἔχοντα. **24.40** ⌜καὶ
BONES DOES NOT HAVE AS YOU° SEE~ME HAVING. AND

τοῦτο εἰπὼν ἔδειξεν αὐτοῖς τὰς χεῖρας καὶ τοὺς
THIS HAVING SAID HE SHOWED THEM THE(HIS) HANDS AND THE(HIS)

πόδας.⌝ **24.41** ἔτι δὲ ἀπιστούντων αὐτῶν ἀπὸ τῆς χαρᾶς
FEET. AND~STILL DISBELIEVING THEM FROM THE JOY

καὶ θαυμαζόντων εἶπεν αὐτοῖς, Ἔχετέ τι βρώσιμον
AND BEING AMAZED, HE SAID TO THEM, HAVE YOU° SOME FOOD

ἐνθάδε; **24.42** οἱ δὲ ἐπέδωκαν αὐτῷ ἰχθύος ὀπτοῦ
HERE? - AND THEY GAVE HIM [3]FISH [2]OF A BROILED

μέρος· **24.43** καὶ λαβὼν ἐνώπιον αὐτῶν ἔφαγεν.
[1]A PART. AND HAVING TAKEN [IT], BEFORE THEM HE ATE [IT].

24.44 Εἶπεν δὲ πρὸς αὐτούς, Οὗτοι οἱ λόγοι μου οὓς
AND~HE SAID TO THEM, THESE - WORDS OF ME WHICH

ἐλάλησα πρὸς ὑμᾶς ἔτι ὢν σὺν ὑμῖν, ὅτι δεῖ
I SPOKE TO YOU° WHILE BEING WITH YOU°, THAT IT IS NECESSARY

πληρωθῆναι πάντα τὰ γεγραμμένα ἐν τῷ νόμῳ
TO BE FULFILLED ALL THE THINGS HAVING BEEN WRITTEN IN THE LAW

Μωϋσέως καὶ τοῖς προφήταις καὶ ψαλμοῖς περὶ ἐμοῦ.
OF MOSES AND THE PROPHETS AND [THE] PSALMS ABOUT ME.

24.45 τότε διήνοιξεν αὐτῶν τὸν νοῦν τοῦ συνιέναι τὰς
THEN HE OPENED UP THEIR - MIND[S] - TO UNDERSTAND THE

γραφάς· **24.46** καὶ εἶπεν αὐτοῖς ὅτι Οὕτως
SCRIPTURES. AND HE SAID TO THEM - THUS

24:36 text: KJV ASV RSVmg NASBmg NIV NEBmg TEV NJB NRSV. omit: ASVmg RSV NASB NEB NRSVmg. **24:40** text: KJV ASV RSVmg NASBmg NIV NEBmg TEV NJB NRSV. omit: ASVmg RSV NASB NEB TEVmg NJBmg NRSVmg.

[34]They were saying, "The
Lord has risen indeed, and
he has appeared to Simon!"
[35]Then they told what had
happened on the road, and
how he had been made
known to them in the
breaking of the bread.
36 While they were
talking about this, Jesus
himself stood among them
and said to them, "Peace be
with you."[p] [37]They were
startled and terrified, and
thought that they were
seeing a ghost. [38]He said
to them, "Why are you
frightened, and why do
doubts arise in your hearts?
[39]Look at my hands and my
feet; see that it is I myself.
Touch me and see; for a
ghost does not have flesh
and bones as you see that I
have." [40]And when he had
said this, he showed them
his hands and his feet.[q]
[41]While in their joy they
were disbelieving and still
wondering, he said to them,
"Have you anything here to
eat?" [42]They gave him a
piece of broiled fish, [43]and
he took it and ate in their
presence.
44 Then he said to them,
"These are my words that I
spoke to you while I was still
with you—that everything
written about me in the law
of Moses, the prophets,
and the psalms must be
fulfilled." [45]Then he opened
their minds to understand
the scriptures, [46]and he
said to them, "Thus

[p] Other ancient authorities lack *and said to them, "Peace be with you."*
[q] Other ancient authorities lack verse 40

it is written, that the Messiah[r] is to suffer and to rise from the dead on the third day, [47]and that repentance and forgiveness of sins is to be proclaimed in his name to all nations, beginning from Jerusalem. [48]You are witnesses[s] of these things. [49]And see, I am sending upon you what my Father promised; so stay here in the city until you have been clothed with power from on high."

[50]Then he led them out as far as Bethany, and, lifting up his hands, he blessed them. [51]While he was blessing them, he withdrew from them and was carried up into heaven.[t] [52]And they worshiped him, and[u] returned to Jerusalem with great joy; [53]and they were continually in the temple blessing God.[v]

[r] Or the Christ
[s] Or nations. Beginning from Jerusalem[48] you are witnesses
[t] Other ancient authorities lack and was carried up into heaven
[u] Other ancient authorities lack worshiped him, and
[v] Other ancient authorities add Amen

γέγραπται   παθεῖν   τὸν   Χριστὸν   καὶ   ἀναστῆναι   ἐκ
IT HAS BEEN WRITTEN   TO SUFFER   THE   CHRIST   AND   TO RISE AGAIN   FROM

νεκρῶν τῇ   τρίτῃ   ἡμέρᾳ,   **24.47** καὶ   κηρυχθῆναι   ἐπὶ   τῷ
[THE] DEAD ON THE   THIRD   DAY,   AND   TO BE PREACHED   IN   THE

ὀνόματι   αὐτοῦ   μετάνοιαν   εἰς   ἄφεσιν   ἁμαρτιῶν   εἰς
NAME   OF HIM   REPENTANCE   FOR   [THE] FORGIVENESS   OF SINS   TO

πάντα   τὰ   ἔθνη.   ἀρξάμενοι   ἀπὸ   Ἰερουσαλὴμ
ALL   THE   NATIONS.   HAVING BEGUN   FROM   JERUSALEM

24.48 ὑμεῖς   μάρτυρες   τούτων.   **24.49** καὶ   [ἰδοὺ]
YOU° [ARE TO BE]   WITNESSES   OF THESE THINGS.   AND   BEHOLD

ἐγὼ ἀποστέλλω   τὴν   ἐπαγγελίαν   τοῦ   πατρός   μου   ἐφ'
I   SEND   THE   PROMISE   OF THE   FATHER   OF ME   TO

ὑμᾶς·   ὑμεῖς   δὲ   καθίσατε   ἐν   τῇ   πόλει   ἕως   οὗ
YOU°;   BUT~YOU°   SIT   IN   THE   CITY   UNTIL

ἐνδύσησθε   ἐξ   ὕψους   δύναμιν.
YOU° MAY BE CLOTHED WITH   ²FROM   ³[THE] HEIGHTS   ¹POWER.

24.50 Ἐξήγαγεν   δὲ   αὐτοὺς   [ἔξω]   ἕως   πρὸς
AND~HE LED OUT   THEM   OUTSIDE   AS FAR AS   TO

Βηθανίαν,   καὶ   ἐπάρας   τὰς   χεῖρας   αὐτοῦ   εὐλόγησεν
BETHANY,   AND   HAVING LIFTED UP   THE   HANDS   OF HIM   HE BLESSED

αὐτούς.   **24.51** καὶ   ἐγένετο   ἐν   τῷ   εὐλογεῖν   αὐτὸν
THEM.   AND   IT CAME ABOUT   WHILE   HE~BLESSES

αὐτοὺς   διέστη   ἀπ' αὐτῶν ⌐καὶ   ἀνεφέρετο   εἰς   τὸν
THEM,   HE WENT AWAY   FROM   THEM   AND   WAS BEING TAKEN UP   INTO   -

οὐρανόν.⌐   **24.52** καὶ   αὐτοὶ   ⌐προσκυνήσαντες   αὐτὸν⌐
HEAVEN.   AND   THEY   HAVING WORSHIPED   HIM

ὑπέστρεψαν   εἰς   Ἰερουσαλὴμ   μετὰ   χαρᾶς   μεγάλης
RETURNED   TO   JERUSALEM   WITH   GREAT~JOY

24.53 καὶ   ἦσαν   διὰ   παντὸς   ἐν   τῷ   ἱερῷ   εὐλογοῦντες
AND   THEY WERE   CONTINUALLY   IN   THE   TEMPLE   BLESSING

τὸν   θεόν.
-    GOD.

24:51 text: KJV ASV RSV NASBmg NIV TEV NJB NRSV. omit: ASVmg RSVmg NASB NEB TEVmg NJBmg NRSVmg.   **24:52** text: ASV RSVmg NASBmg NIV NEBmg TEV NJB NRSV. omit: ASVmg RSV NASB NEB NJBmg NRSVmg.

THE GOSPEL ACCORDING TO
JOHN

KATA   IΩANNHN
ACCORDING TO   JOHN

1.1 Ἐν ἀρχῇ   ἦν ὁ λόγος, καὶ ὁ λόγος ἦν
IN   [THE] BEGINNING WAS THE WORD,   AND   THE WORD   WAS

πρὸς τὸν θεόν, καὶ θεὸς ἦν ὁ λόγος. **1.2** οὗτος ἦν
WITH -   GOD,   AND ⁴GOD ³WAS ¹THE ²WORD.   THIS ONE WAS

ἐν ἀρχῇ   πρὸς τὸν θεόν. **1.3** πάντα δι'   αὐτοῦ
IN [THE] BEGINNING WITH - GOD.   ALL THINGS THROUGH HIM

ἐγένετο, καὶ χωρὶς αὐτοῦ ἐγένετο ⌐οὐδὲ ἕν.
CAME TO BE, AND WITHOUT HIM CAME TO BE   NOT ONE THING.

ὃ   γέγονεν **1.4** ἐν αὐτῷ ζωὴ ἦν,⌐ καὶ ἡ ζωὴ
THAT WHICH CAME INTO BEING IN HIM WAS~LIFE, AND   THE LIFE

ἦν τὸ φῶς τῶν ἀνθρώπων· **1.5** καὶ τὸ φῶς ἐν τῇ
WAS THE LIGHT - OF MEN;   AND THE LIGHT IN THE

σκοτίᾳ φαίνει, καὶ ἡ σκοτία αὐτὸ οὐ κατέλαβεν.
DARKNESS SHINES AND THE DARKNESS DID NOT GRASP~IT.

1.6 Ἐγένετο ἄνθρωπος ἀπεσταλμένος παρὰ θεοῦ,
[THERE] CAME A MAN   HAVING BEEN SENT   FROM GOD,

ὄνομα αὐτῷ Ἰωάννης· **1.7** οὗτος ἦλθεν εἰς μαρτυρίαν,
NAME TO HIM JOHN.   THIS ONE CAME FOR TESTIMONY,

ἵνα μαρτυρήσῃ περὶ τοῦ φωτός, ἵνα πάντες
THAT HE MIGHT TESTIFY ABOUT THE LIGHT, THAT ALL

πιστεύσωσιν δι'   αὐτοῦ. **1.8** οὐκ ἦν ἐκεῖνος τὸ φῶς,
MAY BELIEVE   THROUGH HIM.   THAT ONE~WAS NOT THE LIGHT,

ἀλλ'   ἵνα μαρτυρήσῃ περὶ τοῦ φωτός. **1.9** Ἦν τὸ
BUT [HE CAME] THAT HE MIGHT TESTIFY ABOUT THE LIGHT.   HE WAS THE

φῶς τὸ ἀληθινόν, ὃ   φωτίζει πάντα ἄνθρωπον,
LIGHT, THE TRUE ONE   WHICH ENLIGHTENS EVERY MAN,

ἐρχόμενον εἰς τὸν κόσμον. **1.10** ἐν τῷ κόσμῳ ἦν,
COMING   INTO THE WORLD.   IN THE WORLD HE WAS,

καὶ ὁ κόσμος δι'   αὐτοῦ ἐγένετο, καὶ ὁ κόσμος
AND THE WORLD THROUGH HIM CAME TO BE, AND THE WORLD

αὐτὸν οὐκ ἔγνω. **1.11** εἰς τὰ ἴδια ἦλθεν, καὶ οἱ ἴδιοι
DID NOT RECOGNIZE~HIM.   TO HIS OWN HE CAME, AND HIS OWN

αὐτὸν οὐ παρέλαβον. **1.12** ὅσοι δὲ   ἔλαβον αὐτόν,
DID NOT RECEIVE~HIM.   BUT~AS MANY AS RECEIVED HIM,

ἔδωκεν αὐτοῖς ἐξουσίαν τέκνα θεοῦ γενέσθαι, τοῖς
HE GAVE TO THEM [THE] RIGHT CHILDREN OF GOD TO BECOME, TO THE ONES

In the beginning was the Word, and the Word was with God, and the Word was God. ²He was in the beginning with God. ³All things came into being through him, and without him not one thing came into being. What has come into being ⁴in him was life,ᵃ and the life was the light of all people. ⁵The light shines in the darkness, and the darkness did not overcome it.

6 There was a man sent from God, whose name was John. ⁷He came as a witness to testify to the light, so that all might believe through him. ⁸He himself was not the light, but he came to testify to the light. ⁹The true light, which enlightens everyone, was coming into the world.ᵇ

10 He was in the world, and the world came into being through him; yet the world did not know him. ¹¹He came to what was his own,ᶜ and his own people did not accept him. ¹²But to all who received him, who

ᵃ Or ³through him. And without him not one thing came into being that has come into being. ⁴In him was life

ᵇ Or He was the true light that enlightens everyone coming into the world

ᶜ Or to his own home

1:3-4 text: ASVmg RSVmg NEB TEVmg NJB NRSV.   var. οὐδὲ ἕν ὃ γέγονεν. ἐν αὐτῷ ζωὴ ἦν (. . . not one thing which has come into being. In him was life . . .): KJV ASV RSV NASB NIV NEBmg TEV NJBmg NRSVmg.

believed in his name, he gave power to become children of God, [13]who were born, not of blood or of the will of the flesh or of the will of man, but of God.

14 And the Word became flesh and lived among us, and we have seen his glory, the glory as of a father's only son,[d] full of grace and truth. [15](John testified to him and cried out, "This was he of whom I said, 'He who comes after me ranks ahead of me because he was before me.'") [16]From his fullness we have all received, grace upon grace. [17]The law indeed was given through Moses; grace and truth came through Jesus Christ. [18]No one has ever seen God. It is God the only Son,[e] who is close to the Father's heart,[f] who has made him known.

19 This is the testimony given by John when the Jews sent priests and Levites from Jerusalem to ask him, "Who are you?" [20]He confessed and did not deny it, but confessed, "I am not the Messiah."[g] [21]And they asked him, "What then? Are you Elijah?" He said, "I am not." "Are you the prophet?" He answered, "No."

[d] Or the Father's only Son
[e] Other ancient authorities read It is an only Son, God, or It is the only Son
[f] Gk bosom
[g] Or the Christ

πιστεύουσιν εἰς τὸ ὄνομα αὐτοῦ, **1.13** οἳ οὐκ ἐξ
BELIEVING IN THE NAME OF HIM, THE ONES NOT OF

αἱμάτων οὐδὲ ἐκ θελήματος σαρκὸς οὐδὲ ἐκ θελήματος
BLOODS NOR OF [THE] WILL OF FLESH NOR OF [THE] WILL

ἀνδρὸς ἀλλ' ἐκ θεοῦ ἐγεννήθησαν.
OF A HUSBAND BUT OF GOD WERE BORN.

1.14 Καὶ ὁ λόγος σὰρξ ἐγένετο καὶ ἐσκήνωσεν ἐν
AND THE WORD BECAME~FLESH AND TABERNACLED AMONG

ἡμῖν, καὶ ἐθεασάμεθα τὴν δόξαν αὐτοῦ, δόξαν ὡς
US, AND WE GAZED [UPON] THE GLORY OF HIM, GLORY AS

μονογενοῦς παρὰ πατρός, πλήρης χάριτος καὶ
OF AN ONLY ONE FROM [THE] FATHER, FULL OF GRACE AND

ἀληθείας. **1.15** Ἰωάννης μαρτυρεῖ περὶ αὐτοῦ καὶ
TRUTH. JOHN TESTIFIES ABOUT HIM AND

κέκραγεν λέγων, Οὗτος ἦν ὃν εἶπον, Ὁ
HAS CRIED OUT SAYING, THIS ONE WAS HE [AS TO] WHOM I SAID, THE ONE

ὀπίσω μου ἐρχόμενος ἔμπροσθέν μου γέγονεν, ὅτι
AFTER ME COMING BEFORE ME HAS BECOME, BECAUSE

πρῶτός μου ἦν. **1.16** ὅτι ἐκ τοῦ πληρώματος αὐτοῦ
PRIOR TO ME HE WAS. BECAUSE FROM THE FULLNESS OF HIM

ἡμεῖς πάντες ἐλάβομεν καὶ χάριν ἀντὶ χάριτος·
WE ALL RECEIVED EVEN GRACE ON TOP OF GRACE.

1.17 ὅτι ὁ νόμος διὰ Μωϋσέως ἐδόθη, ἡ χάρις
BECAUSE THE LAW THROUGH MOSES WAS GIVEN, THE GRACE

καὶ ἡ ἀλήθεια διὰ Ἰησοῦ Χριστοῦ ἐγένετο.
AND THE TRUTH THROUGH JESUS CHRIST CAME.

1.18 θεὸν οὐδεὶς ἑώρακεν πώποτε· ⌜μονογενὴς θεὸς⌝
[3]GOD [1]NO ONE [2]HAS SEEN EVER; AN ONLY ONE, GOD,

ὁ ὢν εἰς τὸν κόλπον τοῦ πατρὸς ἐκεῖνος
THE ONE BEING IN THE BOSOM OF THE FATHER, THAT ONE

ἐξηγήσατο.
EXPLAINED [HIM].

1.19 Καὶ αὕτη ἐστὶν ἡ μαρτυρία τοῦ Ἰωάννου, ὅτε
AND THIS IS THE TESTIMONY - OF JOHN WHEN

ἀπέστειλαν [πρὸς αὐτὸν] οἱ Ἰουδαῖοι ἐξ Ἱεροσολύμων
SENT TO HIM THE JEWS FROM JERUSALEM

ἱερεῖς καὶ Λευίτας ἵνα ἐρωτήσωσιν αὐτόν, Σὺ τίς εἶ;
PRIESTS AND LEVITES THAT THEY MIGHT ASK HIM, [3]YOU [1]WHO [2]ARE?

1.20 καὶ ὡμολόγησεν καὶ οὐκ ἠρνήσατο, καὶ
AND HE CONFESSED AND DID NOT DENY, AND

ὡμολόγησεν ὅτι Ἐγὼ οὐκ εἰμὶ ὁ Χριστός. **1.21** καὶ
HE CONFESSED - I AM NOT THE CHRIST. AND

ἠρώτησαν αὐτόν, Τί οὖν; Σὺ Ἡλίας εἶ; καὶ λέγει,
THEY ASKED HIM, WHAT THEN? [2]YOU [3]ELIJAH [1]ARE? AND HE SAYS,

Οὐκ εἰμί. Ὁ προφήτης εἶ σύ; καὶ ἀπεκρίθη, Οὔ.
I AM NOT. THE PROPHET ARE YOU? AND HE ANSWERED, NO.

1:18 text: ASVmg RSVmg NASB NIV NEBmg TEV NJBmg (NRSV). var. ο μονογενης υιος (the only begotten Son): KJV ASV RSV NASBmg NIVmg NEB NJB NRSVmg.

1.22 εἶπαν οὖν αὐτῷ, Τίς εἶ; ἵνα ἀπόκρισιν
THEY SAID THEN TO HIM, WHO ARE YOU? THAT AN ANSWER

δῶμεν τοῖς πέμψασιν ἡμᾶς· τί λέγεις περὶ
WE MAY GIVE TO THE ONES HAVING SENT US. WHAT DO YOU SAY ABOUT

σεαυτοῦ; **1.23** ἔφη,
YOURSELF? HE SAID,

Ἐγὼ φωνὴ βοῶντος ἐν τῇ ἐρήμῳ,
I [AM] A VOICE CRYING IN THE WILDERNESS,

Εὐθύνατε τὴν ὁδὸν κυρίου,
MAKE STRAIGHT THE WAY OF [THE] LORD,

καθὼς εἶπεν Ἡσαΐας ὁ προφήτης. **1.24** Καὶ
AS SAID ISAIAH THE PROPHET. AND

ἀπεσταλμένοι ἦσαν ἐκ τῶν Φαρισαίων. **1.25** καὶ
THE ONES HAVING BEEN SENT WERE OF THE PHARISEES. AND

ἠρώτησαν αὐτὸν καὶ εἶπαν αὐτῷ, Τί οὖν βαπτίζεις εἰ
THEY ASKED HIM AND SAID TO HIM, WHY THEN DO YOU BAPTIZE IF

σὺ οὐκ εἶ ὁ Χριστὸς οὐδὲ Ἡλίας οὐδὲ ὁ προφήτης;
YOU ARE NOT THE CHRIST NOR ELIJAH NOR THE PROPHET?

1.26 ἀπεκρίθη αὐτοῖς ὁ Ἰωάννης λέγων, Ἐγὼ βαπτίζω
ANSWERED THEM - JOHN SAYING, I BAPTIZE

ἐν ὕδατι· μέσος ὑμῶν ἔστηκεν ὃν ὑμεῖς
IN WATER; AMONG YOU° HAS STOOD ONE WHOM YOU°

οὐκ οἴδατε, **1.27** ὁ ὀπίσω μου ἐρχόμενος, οὗ
DO NOT PERCEIVE, THE ONE AFTER ME COMING, OF WHOM

οὐκ εἰμὶ [ἐγὼ] ἄξιος ἵνα λύσω αὐτοῦ τὸν ἱμάντα
²AM NOT ¹I WORTHY THAT I SHOULD UNTIE OF HIM THE THONG

τοῦ ὑποδήματος. **1.28** Ταῦτα ἐν ⌐Βηθανίᾳ⌐
OF THE(HIS) SANDAL. THESE THINGS IN BETHANY

ἐγένετο πέραν τοῦ Ἰορδάνου, ὅπου ἦν ὁ Ἰωάννης
HAPPENED BEYOND THE JORDAN, WHERE WAS ²THE ONE ¹JOHN

βαπτίζων.
³BAPTIZING.

1.29 Τῇ ἐπαύριον βλέπει τὸν Ἰησοῦν ἐρχόμενον
ON THE NEXT DAY HE SEES - JESUS COMING

πρὸς αὐτὸν καὶ λέγει, Ἴδε ὁ ἀμνὸς τοῦ θεοῦ ὁ
TO HIM AND HE SAYS, LOOK, THE LAMB - OF GOD, THE ONE

αἴρων τὴν ἁμαρτίαν τοῦ κόσμου. **1.30** οὗτός ἐστιν
TAKING AWAY THE SIN OF THE WORLD. THIS ONE IS [HE]

ὑπὲρ οὗ ἐγὼ εἶπον, Ὀπίσω μου ἔρχεται ἀνὴρ ὃς
ON BEHALF OF WHOM I SAID, AFTER ME COMES A MAN WHO

ἔμπροσθέν μου γέγονεν, ὅτι πρῶτός μου ἦν.
BEFORE ME HAS BECOME, BECAUSE PRIOR TO ME HE WAS.

1.31 κἀγὼ οὐκ ᾔδειν αὐτόν, ἀλλ' ἵνα φανερωθῇ
AND I DID NOT RECOGNIZE HIM, BUT THAT HE MIGHT BE MANIFESTED

τῷ Ἰσραὴλ διὰ τοῦτο ἦλθον ἐγὼ ἐν ὕδατι βαπτίζων.
- TO ISRAEL THEREFORE CAME I ²IN ³WATER ¹BAPTIZING.

1:23 Isa. 40:3 LXX

22Then they said to him, "Who are you? Let us have an answer for those who sent us. What do you say about yourself?" 23He said,

"I am the voice of one crying out in the wilderness,
'Make straight the way of the Lord,'"

as the prophet Isaiah said.

24 Now they had been sent from the Pharisees. 25They asked him, "Why then are you baptizing if you are neither the Messiah,*h* nor Elijah, nor the prophet?" 26John answered them, "I baptize with water. Among you stands one whom you do not know, 27the one who is coming after me; I am not worthy to untie the thong of his sandal." 28This took place in Bethany across the Jordan where John was baptizing.

29 The next day he saw Jesus coming toward him and declared, "Here is the Lamb of God who takes away the sin of the world! 30This is he of whom I said, 'After me comes a man who ranks ahead of me because he was before me.' 31I myself did not know him; but I came baptizing with water for this reason, that he might be revealed to Israel."

h Or *the Christ*

32And John testified, "I saw the Spirit descending from heaven like a dove, and it remained on him. 33I myself did not know him, but the one who sent me to baptize with water said to me, 'He on whom you see the Spirit descend and remain is the one who baptizes with the Holy Spirit.' 34And I myself have seen and have testified that this is the Son of God."*i*

35 The next day John again was standing with two of his disciples, 36and as he watched Jesus walk by, he exclaimed, "Look, here is the Lamb of God!" 37The two disciples heard him say this, and they followed Jesus. 38When Jesus turned and saw them following, he said to them, "What are you looking for?" They said to him, "Rabbi" (which translated means Teacher), "where are you staying?" 39He said to them, "Come and see." They came and saw where he was staying, and they remained with him that day. It was about four o'clock in the afternoon. 40One of the two who heard John speak and followed him was Andrew, Simon Peter's brother. 41He first found his brother Simon and said to him, "We have found

i Other ancient authorities read *is God's chosen one*

1.32 Καὶ   ἐμαρτύρησεν   Ἰωάννης   λέγων   ὅτι   Τεθέαμαι   τὸ
AND   TESTIFIED   JOHN   SAYING   -   I HAVE SEEN   THE

πνεῦμα   καταβαῖνον   ὡς   περιστερὰν   ἐξ   οὐρανοῦ   καὶ
SPIRIT   DESCENDING   AS   A DOVE   OUT OF   HEAVEN   AND

ἔμεινεν   ἐπ'   αὐτόν.   **1.33** κἀγὼ   οὐκ   ᾔδειν   αὐτόν,   ἀλλ'
IT REMAINED   UPON   HIM.   AND I   DID NOT RECOGNIZE   HIM,   BUT

ὁ   πέμψας   με   βαπτίζειν   ἐν   ὕδατι   ἐκεῖνός   μοι
THE ONE   HAVING SENT   ME   TO BAPTIZE   IN   WATER   THAT ONE   TO ME

εἶπεν,   Ἐφ'   ὃν   ἂν   ἴδῃς   τὸ   πνεῦμα   καταβαῖνον   καὶ
SAID,   UPON   WHOMEVER   YOU SEE   THE   SPIRIT   DESCENDING   AND

μένον   ἐπ'   αὐτόν,   οὗτός   ἐστιν   ὁ   βαπτίζων   ἐν
REMAINING   UPON   HIM,   THIS   IS   THE ONE   BAPTIZING   IN

πνεύματι   ἁγίῳ.   **1.34** κἀγὼ   ἑώρακα   καὶ   μεμαρτύρηκα   ὅτι
[THE] HOLY~SPIRIT.   AND I   HAVE SEEN,   AND   I HAVE TESTIFIED   THAT

οὗτός   ἐστιν   ⌈ὁ   υἱὸς⌉   τοῦ   θεοῦ.
THIS ONE   IS   THE   SON   -   OF GOD.

1.35 Τῇ   ἐπαύριον   πάλιν   εἰστήκει   ὁ   Ἰωάννης   καὶ   ἐκ
ON THE   NEXT DAY   AGAIN   STOOD   -   JOHN   AND   OF

τῶν   μαθητῶν   αὐτοῦ   δύο   **1.36** καὶ   ἐμβλέψας   τῷ   Ἰησοῦ
THE   DISCIPLES   OF HIM   TWO,   AND   HAVING LOOKED AT   -   JESUS

περιπατοῦντι   λέγει,   Ἴδε   ὁ   ἀμνὸς   τοῦ   θεοῦ.   **1.37** καὶ
WALKING   HE SAYS,   LOOK,   THE   LAMB   -   OF GOD.   AND

ἤκουσαν   οἱ   δύο   μαθηταὶ   αὐτοῦ   λαλοῦντος   καὶ
4HEARD   1THE   2TWO   3DISCIPLES   HIM   SPEAKING   AND

ἠκολούθησαν   τῷ   Ἰησοῦ.   **1.38** στραφεὶς   δὲ   ὁ   Ἰησοῦς
THEY FOLLOWED   -   JESUS.   AND~HAVING TURNED   -   JESUS

καὶ   θεασάμενος   αὐτοὺς   ἀκολουθοῦντας   λέγει   αὐτοῖς,
AND   HAVING SEEN   THEM   FOLLOWING   SAYS   TO THEM,

Τί   ζητεῖτε;   οἱ   δὲ   εἶπαν   αὐτῷ,   Ῥαββί,   ὃ
WHAT   DO YOU° SEEK?   AND~THEY SAID   TO HIM,   RABBI,   WHICH

λέγεται   μεθερμηνευόμενον   Διδάσκαλε,   ποῦ   μένεις;
MEANS,   BEING TRANSLATED,   TEACHER,   WHERE   ARE YOU STAYING?

1.39 λέγει   αὐτοῖς,   Ἔρχεσθε   καὶ   ὄψεσθε.   ἦλθαν   οὖν
HE SAYS   TO THEM,   COME   AND   SEE.   THEY WENT   THEREFORE

καὶ   εἶδαν   ποῦ   μένει   καὶ   παρ'   αὐτῷ   ἔμειναν   τὴν
AND   SAW   WHERE   HE STAYS   AND   WITH   HIM   REMAINED   -

ἡμέραν   ἐκείνην·   ὥρα   ἦν   ὡς   δεκάτη.   **1.40** ⌈Ἦν
THAT~DAY.   [THE] HOUR   WAS   ABOUT   [THE] TENTH.   [IT] WAS

Ἀνδρέας   ὁ   ἀδελφὸς   Σίμωνος   Πέτρου   εἷς   ἐκ   τῶν   δύο
ANDREW,   THE   BROTHER   OF SIMON   PETER,   ONE   OF   THE   TWO

τῶν   ἀκουσάντων   παρὰ   Ἰωάννου   καὶ   ἀκολουθησάντων
-    HAVING HEARD   FROM   JOHN   AND   HAVING FOLLOWED

αὐτῷ·   **1.41** εὑρίσκει   οὗτος   ⌈πρῶτον⌉   τὸν   ἀδελφὸν   τὸν
HIM.   THIS ONE~FINDS   FIRST   -   3BROTHER   1HIS

ἴδιον   Σίμωνα   καὶ   λέγει   αὐτῷ,   Εὑρήκαμεν
2OWN   SIMON   AND   SAYS   TO HIM,   WE HAVE FOUND

1:34 text: KJV ASV RSV NASB NIV NEBmg TEV NJBmg NRSV.   var. ο εκλεκτος (the chosen One): NJB NEB.

τὸν Μεσσίαν, ὅ ἐστιν μεθερμηνευόμενον Χριστός·
THE MESSIAH, WHICH MEANS, BEING TRANSLATED, CHRIST.

1.42 ἤγαγεν αὐτὸν πρὸς τὸν Ἰησοῦν. ἐμβλέψας αὐτῷ
HE LED HIM TO - JESUS. HAVING LOOKED AT HIM

ὁ Ἰησοῦς εἶπεν, Σὺ εἶ Σίμων ὁ υἱὸς Ἰωάννου, σὺ
- JESUS SAID, YOU ARE SIMON, THE SON OF JOHN, YOU

κληθήσῃ Κηφᾶς, ὅ ἑρμηνεύεται Πέτρος.
WILL BE CALLED CEPHAS, WHICH IS TRANSLATED PETER.

1.43 Τῇ ἐπαύριον ἠθέλησεν ἐξελθεῖν εἰς τὴν
ON THE NEXT DAY HE WANTED TO GO OUT INTO -

Γαλιλαίαν καὶ εὑρίσκει Φίλιππον. καὶ λέγει αὐτῷ ὁ
GALILEE AND HE FINDS PHILIP. AND SAYS TO HIM -

Ἰησοῦς, Ἀκολούθει μοι. **1.44** ἦν δὲ ὁ Φίλιππος ἀπὸ
JESUS, FOLLOW ME. ³WAS ¹NOW - ²PHILIP FROM

Βηθσαϊδά, ἐκ τῆς πόλεως Ἀνδρέου καὶ Πέτρου.
BETHSAIDA, OF THEY CITY OF ANDREW AND PETER.

1.45 εὑρίσκει Φίλιππος τὸν Ναθαναὴλ καὶ λέγει αὐτῷ,
PHILIP~FINDS - NATHANIEL AND SAYS TO HIM,

Ὅν ἔγραψεν Μωϋσῆς ἐν τῷ νόμῳ καὶ οἱ
[HE] WHOM MOSES~WROTE [OF] IN THE LAW— AND ALSO THE

προφῆται εὑρήκαμεν, Ἰησοῦν υἱὸν τοῦ Ἰωσὴφ τὸν
PROPHETS— WE HAVE FOUND, JESUS, [THE] SON - OF JOSEPH -

ἀπὸ Ναζαρέτ. **1.46** καὶ εἶπεν αὐτῷ Ναθαναήλ, Ἐκ
FROM NAZARETH. AND SAID TO HIM NATHANIEL, OUT OF

Ναζαρὲτ δύναταί τι ἀγαθὸν εἶναι; λέγει αὐτῷ [ὁ]
NAZARETH CAN ANYTHING GOOD BE? SAYS TO HIM -

Φίλιππος, Ἔρχου καὶ ἴδε. **1.47** εἶδεν ὁ Ἰησοῦς τὸν
PHILIP, COME AND SEE. ²SAW - ¹JESUS -

Ναθαναὴλ ἐρχόμενον πρὸς αὐτὸν καὶ λέγει περὶ
NATHANIEL COMING TO HIM AND SAYS ABOUT

αὐτοῦ, Ἴδε ἀληθῶς Ἰσραηλίτης ἐν ᾧ δόλος
HIM, LOOK, A GENUINE ISRAELITE IN WHOM GUILE

οὐκ ἔστιν. **1.48** λέγει αὐτῷ Ναθαναήλ, Πόθεν
IS NOT. SAYS TO HIM NATHANIEL, HOW

με γινώσκεις; ἀπεκρίθη Ἰησοῦς καὶ εἶπεν αὐτῷ, Πρὸ
DO YOU KNOW~ME? ANSWERED JESUS AND SAID TO HIM, BEFORE

τοῦ σε Φίλιππον φωνῆσαι ὄντα ὑπὸ τὴν συκῆν εἶδόν
- ³YOU ¹PHILIP ²CALLED BEING UNDER THE FIG TREE I SAW

σε. **1.49** ἀπεκρίθη αὐτῷ Ναθαναήλ, Ῥαββί, σὺ εἶ
YOU. ANSWERED HIM NATHANIEL, RABBI, YOU ARE

ὁ υἱὸς τοῦ θεοῦ, σὺ βασιλεὺς εἶ τοῦ Ἰσραήλ.
THE SON - OF GOD, YOU ARE~KING - OF ISRAEL.

1.50 ἀπεκρίθη Ἰησοῦς καὶ εἶπεν αὐτῷ, Ὅτι εἶπόν
ANSWERED JESUS AND SAID TO HIM, BECAUSE I TOLD

σοι ὅτι εἶδόν σε ὑποκάτω τῆς συκῆς, πιστεύεις; μείζω
YOU THAT I SAW YOU UNDERNEATH THE FIG TREE, DO YOU BELIEVE? GREATER

τούτων ὄψῃ. **1.51** καὶ λέγει αὐτῷ, Ἀμὴν ἀμὴν
THINGS YOU WILL SEE. AND HE SAYS TO HIM, TRULY, TRULY,

the Messiah" (which is translated Anointed[j]). [42]He brought Simon[k] to Jesus, who looked at him and said, "You are Simon son of John. You are to be called Cephas" (which is translated Peter[l]).

43 The next day Jesus decided to go to Galilee. He found Philip and said to him, "Follow me." [44]Now Philip was from Bethsaida, the city of Andrew and Peter. [45]Philip found Nathanael and said to him, "We have found him about whom Moses in the law and also the prophets wrote, Jesus son of Joseph from Nazareth." [46]Nathanael said to him, "Can anything good come out of Nazareth?" Philip said to him, "Come and see." [47]When Jesus saw Nathanael coming toward him, he said of him, "Here is truly an Israelite in whom there is no deceit!" [48]Nathanael asked him, "Where did you get to know me?" Jesus answered, "I saw you under the fig tree before Philip called you." [49]Nathanael replied, "Rabbi, you are the Son of God! You are the King of Israel!" [50]Jesus answered, "Do you believe because I told you that I saw you under the fig tree? You will see greater things than these." [51]And he said to him, "Very truly,

[j] Or *Christ*
[k] Gk *him*
[l] From the word for *rock* in Aramaic (*kepha*) and Greek (*petra*), respectively

I tell you,[m] you will see heaven opened and the angels of God ascending and descending upon the Son of Man."

[m] Both instances of the Greek word for *you* in this verse are plural

λέγω ὑμῖν, ὄψεσθε τὸν οὐρανὸν ἀνεῳγότα καὶ
I SAY   TO YOU°, YOU° WILL SEE -   HEAVEN   HAVING BEEN OPENED AND

τοὺς ἀγγέλους τοῦ θεοῦ ἀναβαίνοντας καὶ
THE   ANGELS   - OF GOD ASCENDING   AND

καταβαίνοντας ἐπὶ τὸν υἱὸν τοῦ ἀνθρώπου.
DESCENDING   ON THE SON   -   OF MAN.

CHAPTER 2

On the third day there was a wedding in Cana of Galilee, and the mother of Jesus was there. [2]Jesus and his disciples had also been invited to the wedding. [3]When the wine gave out, the mother of Jesus said to him, "They have no wine." [4]And Jesus said to her, "Woman, what concern is that to you and to me? My hour has not yet come." [5]His mother said to the servants, "Do whatever he tells you." [6]Now standing there were six stone water jars for the Jewish rites of purification, each holding twenty or thirty gallons. [7]Jesus said to them, "Fill the jars with water." And they filled them up to the brim. [8]He said to them, "Now draw some out, and take it to the chief steward." So they took it. [9]When the steward tasted the water that had become wine, and did not know where it came from (though the servants who had drawn the water knew), the steward called the bridegroom [10]and said to him, "Everyone serves the good wine first, and then the inferior wine after the guests have become drunk.

2.1 Καὶ τῇ ἡμέρᾳ τῇ τρίτῃ γάμος ἐγένετο ἐν Κανὰ
AND ON THE [2]DAY - [1]THIRD A WEDDING THERE WAS IN CANA

τῆς Γαλιλαίας, καὶ ἦν ἡ μήτηρ τοῦ Ἰησοῦ ἐκεῖ·
-    OF GALILEE,   AND WAS THE MOTHER - OF JESUS THERE.

2.2 ἐκλήθη δὲ καὶ ὁ Ἰησοῦς καὶ οἱ μαθηταὶ αὐτοῦ εἰς
AND~WAS INVITED BOTH - JESUS   AND THE DISCIPLES OF HIM TO

τὸν γάμον. **2.3** καὶ ὑστερήσαντος οἴνου λέγει ἡ μήτηρ
THE WEDDING.   AND [WHEN] WINE~WAS LACKING SAYS THE MOTHER

τοῦ Ἰησοῦ πρὸς αὐτόν, Οἶνον οὐκ ἔχουσιν. **2.4** [καὶ]
- OF JESUS TO HIM, WINE THEY DO NOT HAVE.   AND

λέγει αὐτῇ ὁ Ἰησοῦς, Τί ἐμοὶ καὶ σοί, γύναι; οὔπω
SAYS TO HER - JESUS, WHAT TO ME AND TO YOU, WOMAN? NOT YET

ἥκει ἡ ὥρα μου. **2.5** λέγει ἡ μήτηρ αὐτοῦ τοῖς
COMES THE HOUR OF ME.   SAYS THE MOTHER OF HIM TO THE

διακόνοις, Ὅ τι ἂν λέγῃ ὑμῖν ποιήσατε. **2.6** ἦσαν δὲ
SERVANTS, WHATEVER HE TELLS YOU° DO.   NOW~THERE WERE

ἐκεῖ λίθιναι ὑδρίαι ἓξ κατὰ τὸν καθαρισμὸν τῶν
THERE [2]STONE [3]WATER JARS [1]SIX— ACCORDING TO THE PURIFICATION OF THE

Ἰουδαίων κείμεναι, χωροῦσαι ἀνὰ μετρητὰς δύο ἢ
JEWS—LYING,   HAVING ROOM EACH [FOR] MEASURES TWO OR

τρεῖς. **2.7** λέγει αὐτοῖς ὁ Ἰησοῦς, Γεμίσατε τὰς
THREE.   SAYS TO THEM - JESUS, FILL   THE

ὑδρίας ὕδατος. καὶ ἐγέμισαν αὐτὰς ἕως ἄνω.
WATER JARS WITH WATER. AND THEY FILLED THEM UP TO [THE] TOP.

2.8 καὶ λέγει αὐτοῖς, Ἀντλήσατε νῦν καὶ φέρετε τῷ
AND HE SAYS TO THEM, DRAW   NOW AND BRING   TO THE

ἀρχιτρικλίνῳ· οἱ δὲ ἤνεγκαν. **2.9** ὡς δὲ ἐγεύσατο ὁ
MASTER OF [THE] FEAST. AND~THEY BROUGHT [IT]. AND~AS TASTED THE

ἀρχιτρίκλινος τὸ ὕδωρ οἶνον γεγενημένον καὶ οὐκ ᾔδει
MASTER OF [THE] FEAST THE WATER HAVING BECOME~WINE AND DID NOT KNOW

πόθεν ἐστίν, οἱ δὲ διάκονοι ᾔδεισαν οἱ ἠντληκότες
FROM WHERE IT IS, BUT~THE SERVANTS KNEW—THE ONES HAVING DRAWN

τὸ ὕδωρ, φωνεῖ τὸν νυμφίον ὁ ἀρχιτρίκλινος **2.10** καὶ
THE WATER, [3]CALLS [4]THE [5]BRIDEGROOM [1]THE [2]MASTER OF [THE] FEAST AND

λέγει αὐτῷ, Πᾶς ἄνθρωπος πρῶτον τὸν καλὸν οἶνον
SAYS TO HIM, EVERY MAN   FIRST   THE GOOD   WINE

τίθησιν καὶ ὅταν μεθυσθῶσιν τὸν ἐλάσσω·
SETS OUT,   AND WHEN THEY HAVE BECOME DRUNK [HE SETS OUT] THE INFERIOR.

σὺ τετήρηκας τὸν καλὸν οἶνον ἕως ἄρτι. **2.11** Ταύτην
YOU HAVE KEPT   THE GOOD WINE UNTIL NOW.   ¹THIS

ἐποίησεν ἀρχὴν τῶν σημείων ὁ Ἰησοῦς ἐν Κανὰ τῆς
⁵PERFORMED ²BEGINNING - ³OF SIGNS - ⁴JESUS IN CANA -

Γαλιλαίας καὶ ἐφανέρωσεν τὴν δόξαν αὐτοῦ, καὶ
OF GALILEE AND HE MANIFESTED THE GLORY OF HIM, AND

ἐπίστευσαν εἰς αὐτὸν οἱ μαθηταὶ αὐτοῦ.
BELIEVED   IN HIM   THE DISCIPLES OF HIM.

2.12 Μετὰ τοῦτο κατέβη εἰς Καφαρναοὺμ αὐτὸς καὶ
AFTER THIS WENT DOWN TO CAPERNAUM   HE   AND

ἡ μήτηρ αὐτοῦ καὶ οἱ ἀδελφοὶ [αὐτοῦ] καὶ οἱ
THE MOTHER OF HIM AND THE BROTHERS OF HIM AND THE

μαθηταὶ αὐτοῦ καὶ ἐκεῖ ἔμειναν οὐ πολλὰς ἡμέρας.
DISCIPLES OF HIM, AND THERE THEY REMAINED NOT MANY DAYS.

2.13 Καὶ ἐγγὺς ἦν τὸ πάσχα τῶν Ἰουδαίων, καὶ
AND NEAR WAS THE PASSOVER OF THE JEWS,   AND

ἀνέβη εἰς Ἱεροσόλυμα ὁ Ἰησοῦς. **2.14** καὶ εὗρεν ἐν
WENT UP TO JERUSALEM - JESUS.   AND HE FOUND IN

τῷ ἱερῷ τοὺς πωλοῦντας βόας καὶ πρόβατα καὶ
THE TEMPLE THE ONES SELLING OXEN AND SHEEP AND

περιστερὰς καὶ τοὺς κερματιστὰς καθημένους, **2.15** καὶ
DOVES   AND THE COIN DEALERS SITTING,   AND

ποιήσας φραγέλλιον ἐκ σχοινίων πάντας ἐξέβαλεν
HAVING MADE A WHIP OUT OF ROPES HE THREW~EVERYONE

ἐκ τοῦ ἱεροῦ τά τε πρόβατα καὶ τοὺς βόας, καὶ
OUT OF THE TEMPLE, BOTH~THE SHEEP AND THE OXEN, AND

τῶν κολλυβιστῶν ἐξέχεεν τὸ κέρμα καὶ τὰς τραπέζας
OF THE MONEYCHANGERS HE POURED OUT THE COINS, AND THE TABLES

ἀνέτρεψεν, **2.16** καὶ τοῖς τὰς περιστερὰς πωλοῦσιν
HE OVERTURNED. AND TO THE ONES - SELLING~DOVES

εἶπεν, Ἄρατε ταῦτα ἐντεῦθεν, μὴ ποιεῖτε τὸν οἶκον
HE SAID, TAKE THESE THINGS FROM HERE, DO NOT MAKE THE HOUSE

τοῦ πατρός μου οἶκον ἐμπορίου. **2.17** Ἐμνήσθησαν
OF THE FATHER OF ME A HOUSE OF MERCHANDISING. REMEMBERED

οἱ μαθηταὶ αὐτοῦ ὅτι γεγραμμένον ἐστίν, Ὁ ζῆλος
THE DISCIPLES OF HIM THAT IT HAS BEEN WRITTEN, THE ZEAL

τοῦ οἴκου σου καταφάγεταί με. **2.18** ἀπεκρίθησαν
FOR THE HOUSE OF YOU WILL DEVOUR ME.   ANSWERED

οὖν οἱ Ἰουδαῖοι καὶ εἶπαν αὐτῷ, Τί σημεῖον
THEN THE JEWS AND SAID TO HIM, WHAT SIGN

δεικνύεις ἡμῖν ὅτι ταῦτα ποιεῖς; **2.19** ἀπεκρίθη
DO YOU SHOW US THAT THESE THINGS YOU DO? ANSWERED

Ἰησοῦς καὶ εἶπεν αὐτοῖς, Λύσατε τὸν ναὸν τοῦτον καὶ
JESUS AND SAID TO THEM, DESTROY - THIS~SANCTUARY AND

ἐν τρισὶν ἡμέραις ἐγερῶ αὐτόν. **2.20** εἶπαν οὖν οἱ
IN THREE DAYS I WILL RAISE IT.   SAID THEN THE

But you have kept the good wine until now." [11]Jesus did this, the first of his signs, in Cana of Galilee, and revealed his glory; and his disciples believed in him.

12 After this he went down to Capernaum with his mother, his brothers, and his disciples; and they remained there a few days.

13 The Passover of the Jews was near, and Jesus went up to Jerusalem. [14]In the temple he found people selling cattle, sheep, and doves, and the money changers seated at their tables. [15]Making a whip of cords, he drove all of them out of the temple, both the sheep and the cattle. He also poured out the coins of the money changers and over-turned their tables. [16]He told those who were selling the doves, "Take these things out of here! Stop making my Father's house a market-place!" [17]His disciples remembered that it was written, "Zeal for your house will consume me." [18]The Jews then said to him, "What sign can you show us for doing this?" [19]Jesus answered them, "Destroy this temple, and in three days I will raise it up." [20]The Jews then said,

"This temple has been under construction for forty-six years, and will you raise it up in three days?" [21]But he was speaking of the temple of his body. [22]After he was raised from the dead, his disciples remembered that he had said this; and they believed the scripture and the word that Jesus had spoken.

23 When he was in Jerusalem during the Passover festival, many believed in his name because they saw the signs that he was doing. [24]But Jesus on his part would not entrust himself to them, because he knew all people [25]and needed no one to testify about anyone; for he himself knew what was in everyone.

Ἰουδαῖοι,   Τεσσεράκοντα   καὶ   ἓξ   ἔτεσιν   οἰκοδομήθη   ὁ
JEWS,   IN FORTY   AND   SIX   YEARS   WAS BUILT   -

ναὸς οὗτος,   καὶ   σὺ   ἐν   τρισὶν   ἡμέραις   ἐγερεῖς   αὐτόν;
THIS~SANCTUARY,   AND   YOU   IN   THREE   DAYS   WILL RAISE   IT?

2.21 ἐκεῖνος   δὲ   ἔλεγεν   περὶ   τοῦ   ναοῦ   τοῦ   σώματος
BUT~THAT ONE   WAS SPEAKING   ABOUT   THE   SANCTUARY   OF THE   BODY

αὐτοῦ.   **2.22** ὅτε   οὖν   ἠγέρθη   ἐκ   νεκρῶν,
OF HIM.   THEREFORE~WHEN   HE WAS RAISED   FROM   [THE] DEAD,

ἐμνήσθησαν   οἱ   μαθηταὶ   αὐτοῦ   ὅτι   τοῦτο   ἔλεγεν,
REMEMBERED   THE   DISCIPLES   OF HIM   THAT   THIS   HE WAS SAYING,

καὶ   ἐπίστευσαν   τῇ   γραφῇ   καὶ   τῷ   λόγῳ   ὃν   εἶπεν   ὁ
AND   THEY BELIEVED   THE   SCRIPTURE   AND   THE   WORD   WHICH   SAID   -

Ἰησοῦς.
JESUS.

2.23 Ὡς   δὲ   ἦν   ἐν   τοῖς   Ἱεροσολύμοις   ἐν   τῷ
AND~WHEN   HE WAS   IN   -   JERUSALEM   DURING   THE

πάσχα   ἐν   τῇ   ἑορτῇ,   πολλοὶ   ἐπίστευσαν   εἰς   τὸ   ὄνομα
PASSOVER   AT   THE   FEAST,   MANY   BELIEVED (TRUSTED)   IN   THE   NAME

αὐτοῦ   θεωροῦντες   αὐτοῦ   τὰ   σημεῖα   ἃ   ἐποίει·
OF HIM,   SEEING   HIS   -   SIGNS   WHICH   HE WAS DOING.

2.24 αὐτὸς   δὲ   Ἰησοῦς   οὐκ   ἐπίστευεν   αὐτὸν   αὐτοῖς
[3]HIMSELF   [1]BUT   [2]JESUS   WAS NOT ENTRUSTING   HIMSELF   TO THEM

διὰ   τὸ   αὐτὸν   γινώσκειν   πάντας   **2.25** καὶ   ὅτι   οὐ
BECAUSE   -   HE   KNOWS   ALL [MEN],   AND   BECAUSE   [2]NO

χρείαν   εἶχεν   ἵνα   τις   μαρτυρήσῃ   περὶ   τοῦ   ἀνθρώπου·
[3]NEED   [1]HE HAD   THAT   ANYONE   SHOULD TESTIFY   ABOUT   -   MAN—

αὐτὸς   γὰρ   ἐγίνωσκεν   τί   ἦν   ἐν   τῷ   ἀνθρώπῳ.
FOR~HE   KNEW   WHAT   WAS IN   -   MAN.

CHAPTER 3

Now there was a Pharisee named Nicodemus, a leader of the Jews. [2]He came to Jesus[n] by night and said to him, "Rabbi, we know that you are a teacher who has come from God; for no one can do these signs that you do apart from the presence of God." [3]Jesus answered him, "Very truly,

[n] Gk *him*

3.1 Ἦν   δὲ   ἄνθρωπος   ἐκ   τῶν   Φαρισαίων,
NOW~THERE WAS   A MAN   OF   THE   PHARISEES,

Νικόδημος   ὄνομα   αὐτῷ,   ἄρχων   τῶν   Ἰουδαίων·
NICODEMUS   NAME   TO HIM,   A RULER   OF THE   JEWS.

3.2 οὗτος   ἦλθεν   πρὸς   αὐτὸν   νυκτὸς   καὶ   εἶπεν
THIS ONE   CAME   TO   HIM   DURING [THE] NIGHT   AND   SAID

αὐτῷ,   Ῥαββί,   οἴδαμεν   ὅτι   ἀπὸ   θεοῦ   ἐλήλυθας
TO HIM,   RABBI,   WE KNOW   THAT   FROM   GOD   YOU HAVE COME

διδάσκαλος·   οὐδεὶς   γὰρ   δύναται   ταῦτα   τὰ   σημεῖα
A TEACHER,   FOR~NO ONE   IS ABLE   THESE   -   SIGNS

ποιεῖν   ἃ   σὺ   ποιεῖς,   ἐὰν   μὴ   ᾖ   ὁ   θεὸς   μετ'   αὐτοῦ.
TO DO   WHICH   YOU   DO,   UNLESS   [2]IS   -   [1]GOD   WITH   HIM.

3.3 ἀπεκρίθη   Ἰησοῦς   καὶ   εἶπεν   αὐτῷ,   Ἀμὴν   ἀμὴν
ANSWERED   JESUS   AND   SAID   TO HIM,   TRULY,   TRULY

λέγω   σοι,   ἐὰν μή τις   γεννηθῇ ἄνωθεν,   οὐ δύναται
I SAY   TO YOU, UNLESS SOMEONE IS BORN   AGAIN,   HE IS NOT ABLE

ἰδεῖν   τὴν βασιλείαν τοῦ θεοῦ.   3.4 λέγει πρὸς αὐτὸν [ὁ]
TO SEE   THE KINGDOM   - OF GOD.   SAYS   TO   HIM   -

Νικόδημος, Πῶς δύναται ἄνθρωπος γεννηθῆναι γέρων ὤν;
NICODEMUS, HOW IS ABLE   A MAN   TO BE BORN   BEING~OLD?

μὴ δύναται   εἰς τὴν κοιλίαν τῆς μητρὸς αὐτοῦ
[SURELY] HE IS NOT ABLE INTO THE WOMB   OF THE MOTHER OF HIM

δεύτερον εἰσελθεῖν καὶ γεννηθῆναι; 3.5 ἀπεκρίθη
A SECOND TIME TO ENTER AND TO BE BORN?   ANSWERED

Ἰησοῦς, Ἀμὴν ἀμὴν λέγω σοι, ἐὰν μή τις   γεννηθῇ
JESUS, TRULY, TRULY I SAY TO YOU, UNLESS SOMEONE IS BORN

ἐξ ὕδατος καὶ πνεύματος, οὐ δύναται εἰσελθεῖν εἰς τὴν
OF WATER AND SPIRIT,   HE IS NOT ABLE TO ENTER INTO THE

βασιλείαν τοῦ θεοῦ. 3.6 τὸ   γεγεννημένον ἐκ τῆς
KINGDOM   - OF GOD.   THE THING HAVING BEEN BORN OF THE

σαρκὸς σάρξ ἐστιν, καὶ τὸ   γεγεννημένον ἐκ τοῦ
FLESH   IS~FLESH,   AND THE THING HAVING BEEN BORN OF THE

πνεύματος πνεῦμά ἐστιν. 3.7 μὴ θαυμάσῃς ὅτι εἶπόν
SPIRIT   IS~SPIRIT.   DO NOT MARVEL THAT I SAID

σοι, Δεῖ   ὑμᾶς γεννηθῆναι ἄνωθεν. 3.8 τὸ
TO YOU, IT IS NECESSARY [FOR] YOU° TO BE BORN AGAIN.   THE

πνεῦμα ὅπου θέλει πνεῖ καὶ τὴν φωνὴν αὐτοῦ
WIND   WHERE IT WISHES BLOWS AND THE SOUND OF IT

ἀκούεις, ἀλλ᾽ οὐκ οἶδας πόθεν ἔρχεται καὶ ποῦ
YOU HEAR, BUT YOU DO NOT KNOW WHERE IT COMES FROM AND WHERE

ὑπάγει· οὕτως ἐστὶν πᾶς ὁ γεγεννημένος ἐκ τοῦ
IT GOES AWAY; SO   IS   EVERYONE HAVING BEEN BORN OF THE

πνεύματος. 3.9 ἀπεκρίθη Νικόδημος καὶ εἶπεν αὐτῷ,
SPIRIT.   ANSWERED NICODEMUS   AND SAID TO HIM,

Πῶς δύναται ταῦτα   γενέσθαι; 3.10 ἀπεκρίθη
HOW IS IT POSSIBLE FOR THESE THINGS HAPPEN?   ANSWERED

Ἰησοῦς καὶ εἶπεν αὐτῷ, Σὺ εἶ ὁ διδάσκαλος τοῦ
JESUS   AND SAID TO HIM, YOU ARE THE TEACHER   -

Ἰσραὴλ καὶ ταῦτα   οὐ γινώσκεις; 3.11 ἀμὴν ἀμὴν
OF ISRAEL AND THESE THINGS YOU DO NOT KNOW?   TRULY, TRULY

λέγω σοι ὅτι ὃ   οἴδαμεν λαλοῦμεν καὶ ὃ
I SAY TO YOU, - THAT WHICH WE KNOW WE SPEAK AND THAT WHICH

ἑωράκαμεν μαρτυροῦμεν, καὶ τὴν μαρτυρίαν ἡμῶν
WE HAVE SEEN WE TESTIFY [ABOUT], AND THE TESTIMONY OF US

οὐ λαμβάνετε. 3.12 εἰ τὰ ἐπίγεια   εἶπον ὑμῖν καὶ
YOU° DO NOT RECEIVE.   IF THE EARTHLY THINGS I TOLD YOU° AND

οὐ πιστεύετε, πῶς ἐὰν εἴπω ὑμῖν τὰ ἐπουράνια
YOU° DO NOT BELIEVE, HOW IF I TELL YOU° THE HEAVENLY THINGS

πιστεύσετε; 3.13 καὶ οὐδεὶς ἀναβέβηκεν εἰς τὸν
WILL YOU° BELIEVE?   AND NO ONE   HAS ASCENDED   INTO -

οὐρανὸν εἰ μὴ ὁ ἐκ τοῦ οὐρανοῦ καταβάς,   ὁ
HEAVEN   EXCEPT THE ONE OUT OF - HEAVEN HAVING DESCENDED, THE

I tell you, no one can
see the kingdom of God
without being born from
above."[o] [4]Nicodemus said to
him, "How can anyone be
born after having grown
old? Can one enter a second
time into the mother's womb
and be born?" [5]Jesus
answered, "Very truly, I tell
you, no one can enter the
kingdom of God without
being born of water and
Spirit. [6]What is born of the
flesh is flesh, and what is
born of the Spirit is spirit.[p]
[7]Do not be astonished that I
said to you, 'You[q] must be
born from above.'[r] [8]The
wind[p] blows where it
chooses, and you hear the
sound of it, but you do not
know where it comes from
or where it goes. So it is with
everyone who is born of the
Spirit." [9]Nicodemus said to
him, "How can these things
be?" [10]Jesus answered him,
"Are you a teacher of Israel,
and yet you do not under-
stand these things?

11 "Very truly, I tell you,
we speak of what we know
and testify to what we have
seen; yet you[s] do not receive
our testimony. [12]If I have
told you about earthly things
and you do not believe, how
can you believe if I tell you
about heavenly things? [13]No
one has ascended into
heaven except the one who
descended from heaven, the

[o] Or born anew
[p] The same Greek word means both
wind and spirit
[q] The Greek word for you here is
plural
[r] Or anew
[s] The Greek word for you here and in
verse 12 is plural

Son of Man.[t] [14]And just as Moses lifted up the serpent in the wilderness, so must the Son of Man be lifted up, [15]that whoever believes in him may have eternal life.[u]

16 "For God so loved the world that he gave his only Son, so that everyone who believes in him may not perish but may have eternal life.

17 "Indeed, God did not send the Son into the world to condemn the world, but in order that the world might be saved through him. [18]Those who believe in him are not condemned; but those who do not believe are condemned already, because they have not believed in the name of the only Son of God. [19]And this is the judgment, that the light has come into the world, and people loved darkness rather than light because their deeds were evil. [20]For all who do evil hate the light and do not come to the light, so that their deeds may not be exposed. [21]But those who do what is true come to the light, so that it may be clearly seen that their deeds have been done in God."[u]

22 After this Jesus and his disciples went into the Judean countryside, and he spent some time there with them and baptized. [23]John

[t] Other ancient authorities add who is in heaven
[u] Some interpreters hold that the quotation concludes with verse 15

υἱὸς τοῦ ἀνθρώπου[τ]. **3.14** καὶ καθὼς Μωϋσῆς ὕψωσεν
SON - OF MAN. AND AS MOSES LIFTED UP

τὸν ὄφιν ἐν τῇ ἐρήμῳ, οὕτως ὑψωθῆναι δεῖ
THE SNAKE IN THE WILDERNESS, SO [5]TO BE LIFTED UP [1]IT IS NECESSARY [FOR]

τὸν υἱὸν τοῦ ἀνθρώπου, **3.15** ἵνα πᾶς ὁ πιστεύων ἐν
[2]THE [3]SON - [4]OF MAN, THAT EVERYONE - BELIEVING IN

αὐτῷ ἔχῃ ζωὴν αἰώνιον.
HIM MAY HAVE LIFE ETERNAL.

3.16 Οὕτως γὰρ ἠγάπησεν ὁ θεὸς τὸν κόσμον, ὥστε
FOR~THUS LOVED - GOD THE WORLD, THAT

τὸν υἱὸν τὸν μονογενῆ ἔδωκεν, ἵνα πᾶς ὁ πιστεύων
THE SON, THE UNIQUE ONE, HE GAVE, THAT EVERYONE BELIEVING

εἰς αὐτὸν μὴ ἀπόληται ἀλλ' ἔχῃ ζωὴν αἰώνιον.
IN HIM MAY NOT PERISH BUT HAVE LIFE ETERNAL.

3.17 οὐ γὰρ ἀπέστειλεν ὁ θεὸς τὸν υἱὸν εἰς τὸν κοσμον
FOR DID NOT SEND - GOD THE SON INTO THE WORLD

ἵνα κρίνῃ τὸν κόσμον, ἀλλ' ἵνα σωθῇ ὁ
THAT HE MIGHT JUDGE THE WORLD, BUT THAT MIGHT BE SAVED THE

κόσμος δι' αὐτοῦ. **3.18** ὁ πιστεύων εἰς αὐτὸν
WORLD THROUGH HIM. THE ONE BELIEVING IN HIM

οὐ κρίνεται· ὁ δὲ μὴ πιστεύων ἤδη κέκριται,
IS NOT JUDGED; BUT~THE ONE NOT BELIEVING ALREADY HAS BEEN JUDGED,

ὅτι μὴ πεπίστευκεν εἰς τὸ ὄνομα τοῦ μονογενοῦς
BECAUSE HE HAS NOT BELIEVED IN THE NAME OF THE ONLY

υἱοῦ τοῦ θεοῦ. **3.19** αὕτη δέ ἐστιν ἡ κρίσις ὅτι τὸ
SON - OF GOD. AND~THIS IS THE JUDGMENT, THAT THE

φῶς ἐλήλυθεν εἰς τὸν κόσμον καὶ ἠγάπησαν οἱ
LIGHT HAS COME INTO THE WORLD AND [2]LOVED -

ἄνθρωποι μᾶλλον τὸ σκότος ἢ τὸ φῶς· ἦν γὰρ
[1]MEN [5]RATHER [3]THE [4]DARKNESS THAN THE LIGHT; FOR~WAS(WERE)

αὐτῶν πονηρὰ τὰ ἔργα. **3.20** πᾶς γὰρ ὁ φαῦλα
[1]THEIR [3]EVIL - [2]WORKS. FOR~EVERYONE EVIL THINGS

πράσσων μισεῖ τὸ φῶς καὶ οὐκ ἔρχεται πρὸς τὸ φῶς,
PRACTISING HATES THE LIGHT AND DOES NOT COME TO THE LIGHT,

ἵνα μὴ ἐλεγχθῇ τὰ ἔργα αὐτοῦ· **3.21** ὁ δὲ ποιῶν τὴν
LEST BE EXPOSED THE WORKS OF HIM. BUT~THE ONE DOING THE

ἀλήθειαν ἔρχεται πρὸς τὸ φῶς, ἵνα φανερωθῇ αὐτοῦ
TRUTH COMES TO THE LIGHT, THAT MAY BE MANIFESTED HIS

τὰ ἔργα ὅτι ἐν θεῷ ἐστιν εἰργασμένα.
- WORKS THAT IN GOD THEY HAVE BEEN WROUGHT.

3.22 Μετὰ ταῦτα ἦλθεν ὁ Ἰησοῦς καὶ οἱ μαθηταὶ
AFTER THESE THINGS CAME - JESUS AND THE DISCIPLES

αὐτοῦ εἰς τὴν Ἰουδαίαν γῆν καὶ ἐκεῖ διέτριβεν μετ᾽
OF HIM INTO THE JUDEAN LAND, AND THERE HE WAS STAYING WITH

αὐτῶν καὶ ἐβάπτιζεν. **3.23** ἦν δὲ καὶ ὁ Ἰωάννης
THEM AND WAS BAPTIZING. AND~WAS ALSO - JOHN

3:13 text: ASVmg RSV NASB NIV NEBmg NJB NRSV. add ο ων εν τω ουρανου (the One being in heaven): KJV ASV RSVmg NIVmg NEB NRSVmg.

βαπτίζων ἐν Αἰνὼν ἐγγὺς τοῦ Σαλείμ, ὅτι
BAPTIZING IN AENON NEAR - SALIM, BECAUSE

ὕδατα πολλὰ ἦν ἐκεῖ, καὶ παρεγίνοντο καὶ
MUCH~WATER WAS THERE, AND THEY WERE COMING AND

ἐβαπτίζοντο· **3.24** οὔπω γὰρ ἦν βεβλημένος εἰς τὴν
WERE BEING BAPTIZED —FOR~NOT YET HAD BEEN THROWN INTO -

φυλακὴν ὁ Ἰωάννης. **3.25** Ἐγένετο οὖν ζήτησις ἐκ τῶν
PRISON - JOHN. THERE WAS THEN A DISCUSSION OF THE

μαθητῶν Ἰωάννου μετὰ ⌐Ἰουδαίου⌐ περὶ καθαρισμοῦ.
DISCIPLES OF JOHN WITH A JEW ABOUT PURIFICATION.

3.26 καὶ ἦλθον πρὸς τὸν Ἰωάννην καὶ εἶπαν αὐτῷ,
AND THEY CAME TO - JOHN AND SAID TO HIM,

Ῥαββί, ὃς ἦν μετὰ σοῦ πέραν τοῦ Ἰορδάνου, ᾧ
RABBI, HE WHO WAS WITH YOU BEYOND THE JORDAN, TO WHOM

σὺ μεμαρτύρηκας, ἴδε οὗτος βαπτίζει καὶ πάντες
YOU HAVE GIVEN TESTIMONY, LOOK, THIS ONE BAPTIZES AND ALL MEN

ἔρχονται πρὸς αὐτόν. **3.27** ἀπεκρίθη Ἰωάννης καὶ
ARE COMING TO HIM. ANSWERED JOHN AND

εἶπεν, Οὐ δύναται ἄνθρωπος λαμβάνειν οὐδὲ ἓν ἐὰν μὴ
SAID, A MAN~IS NOT ABLE TO RECEIVE ANYTHING UNLESS

ᾖ δεδομένον αὐτῷ ἐκ τοῦ οὐρανοῦ. **3.28** αὐτοὶ ὑμεῖς
IT HAS BEEN GIVEN TO HIM FROM - HEAVEN. YOU°~YOURSELVES°

μοι μαρτυρεῖτε ὅτι εἶπον [ὅτι] Οὐκ εἰμὶ ἐγὼ ὁ
BEAR WITNESS~TO ME THAT I SAID, - NOT AM I THE

Χριστός, ἀλλ᾽ ὅτι Ἀπεσταλμένος εἰμὶ ἔμπροσθεν
CHRIST, BUT - HAVING BEEN SENT I AM BEFORE

ἐκείνου. **3.29** ὁ ἔχων τὴν νύμφην νυμφίος ἐστίν·
THAT ONE. THE ONE HAVING THE BRIDE IS~[THE] BRIDEGROOM,

ὁ δὲ φίλος τοῦ νυμφίου ὁ ἑστηκὼς καὶ ἀκούων
BUT~THE FRIEND OF THE BRIDEGROOM, THE ONE HAVING STOOD AND HEARING

αὐτοῦ χαρᾷ χαίρει διὰ τὴν φωνὴν τοῦ νυμφίου.
HIM WITH JOY REJOICES BECAUSE OF THE VOICE OF THE BRIDEGROOM.

αὕτη οὖν ἡ χαρὰ ἡ ἐμὴ πεπλήρωται.
THEREFORE~THIS - JOY - OF MINE HAS BEEN MADE FULL.

3.30 ἐκεῖνον δεῖ αὐξάνειν, ἐμὲ δὲ ἐλαττοῦσθαι.
IT IS NECESSARY [FOR]~THAT ONE TO INCREASE, BUT~FOR ME TO DECREASE.

3.31 Ὁ ἄνωθεν ἐρχόμενος ἐπάνω πάντων ἐστίν·
THE ONE COMING~FROM ABOVE OVER ALL IS;

ὁ ὢν ἐκ τῆς γῆς ἐκ τῆς γῆς ἐστιν καὶ ἐκ τῆς
THE ONE BEING OF THE EARTH OF THE EARTH IS AND OF THE

γῆς λαλεῖ. ὁ ἐκ τοῦ οὐρανοῦ ἐρχόμενος ⌐ἐπάνω
EARTH SPEAKS. THE ONE FROM - HEAVEN COMING OVER

πάντων ἐστίν·]⌐ **3.32** ὃ ἑώρακεν καὶ ἤκουσεν
ALL IS. THAT WHICH HE HAS SEEN AND HEARD

τοῦτο μαρτυρεῖ, καὶ τὴν μαρτυρίαν αὐτοῦ οὐδεὶς
THIS HE TESTIFIES, AND THE TESTIMONY OF HIM NO ONE

also was baptizing at Aenon near Salim because water was abundant there; and people kept coming and were being baptized— [24]John, of course, had not yet been thrown into prison.

25 Now a discussion about purification arose between John's disciples and a Jew.[v] [26]They came to John and said to him, "Rabbi, the one who was with you across the Jordan, to whom you testified, here he is baptizing, and all are going to him." [27]John answered, "No one can receive anything except what has been given from heaven. [28]You yourselves are my witnesses that I said, 'I am not the Messiah,[w] but I have been sent ahead of him.' [29]He who has the bride is the bridegroom. The friend of the bridegroom, who stands and hears him, rejoices greatly at the bridegroom's voice. For this reason my joy has been fulfilled. [30]He must increase, but I must decrease."[x]

31 The one who comes from above is above all; the one who is of the earth belongs to the earth and speaks about earthly things. The one who comes from heaven is above all. [32]He testifies to what he has seen and heard, yet no one accepts his testimony.

[v] Other ancient authorities read *the Jews*
[w] Or *the Christ*
[x] Some interpreters hold that the quotation continues through verse 36

3:25 text: ASV RSV NASB NIV TEV NJB NRSV. var. Ιουδαιων (Jews): KJV NEB TEVmg NRSVmg.
3:31 text: KJV ASVmg RSV NASB NIV NEBmg TEV NRSV. omit: NEB NJB.

³³Whoever has accepted his testimony has certified^y this, that God is true. ³⁴He whom God has sent speaks the words of God, for he gives the Spirit without measure. ³⁵The Father loves the Son and has placed all things in his hands. ³⁶Whoever believes in the Son has eternal life; whoever disobeys the Son will not see life, but must endure God's wrath.

^y Gk *set a seal to*

λαμβάνει. **3.33** ὁ   λαβὼν   αὐτοῦ τὴν μαρτυρίαν
RECEIVES.   THE ONE HAVING RECEIVED HIS   -   TESTIMONY

ἐσφράγισεν ὅτι ὁ θεὸς ἀληθής ἐστιν. **3.34** ὃν γὰρ
CERTIFIED   THAT - GOD   IS~TRUE.   FOR~[HE] WHOM

ἀπέστειλεν ὁ θεὸς τὰ ῥήματα τοῦ θεοῦ λαλεῖ, οὐ γὰρ
²SENT   - ¹GOD THE WORDS   -   OF GOD SPEAKS, FOR~NOT

ἐκ μέτρου ⌐δίδωσιν τὸ πνεῦμα.⌐ **3.35** ὁ   πατὴρ ἀγαπᾷ
BY MEASURE HE GIVES THE SPIRIT.   THE FATHER LOVES

τὸν υἱόν καὶ πάντα δέδωκεν ἐν τῇ χειρὶ αὐτοῦ.
THE SON AND HAS GIVEN~ALL THINGS IN THE HAND OF HIM.

3.36 ὁ   πιστεύων εἰς τὸν υἱὸν ἔχει ζωὴν αἰώνιον·
      THE ONE BELIEVING IN THE SON HAS LIFE ETERNAL;

ὁ δὲ   ἀπειθῶν τῷ   υἱῷ   οὐκ ὄψεται ζωήν, ἀλλ᾽ ἡ
BUT~THE ONE DISOBEYING THE SON WILL NOT SEE LIFE, BUT THE

ὀργὴ τοῦ θεοῦ μένει ἐπ᾽ αὐτόν.
WRATH -   OF GOD REMAINS ON HIM.

3:34 text: ASV RSV NASB NJBmg NRSV. var. διδωσιν ο θεος το πνευμα (God gives the Spirit): KJV NIV NEB TEV NJB.

CHAPTER 4

Now when Jesus^z learned that the Pharisees had heard, "Jesus is making and baptizing more disciples than John" ²—although it was not Jesus himself but his disciples who baptized—³he left Judea and started back to Galilee. ⁴But he had to go through Samaria. ⁵So he came to a Samaritan city called Sychar, near the plot of ground that Jacob had given to his son Joseph. ⁶Jacob's well was there, and Jesus, tired out by his journey, was sitting by the well. It was about noon.

7 A Samaritan woman came to draw water,

^z Other ancient authorities read *the Lord*

4.1 Ὡς οὖν   ἔγνω ὁ ⌐Ἰησοῦς⌐ ὅτι ἤκουσαν οἱ
      THEREFORE~WHEN KNEW - JESUS   THAT HEARD   THE

Φαρισαῖοι ὅτι Ἰησοῦς πλείονας μαθητὰς ποιεῖ καὶ
PHARISEES THAT JESUS MORE   DISCIPLES MAKES AND

βαπτίζει ἢ   Ἰωάννης— **4.2** καίτοιγε Ἰησοῦς αὐτὸς
BAPTIZES THAN JOHN—   ALTHOUGH JESUS HIMSELF

οὐκ ἐβάπτιζεν ἀλλ᾽ οἱ μαθηταὶ αὐτοῦ— **4.3** ἀφῆκεν
DID NOT BAPTIZE BUT THE DISCIPLES OF HIM—   HE LEFT

τὴν Ἰουδαίαν καὶ ἀπῆλθεν πάλιν εἰς τὴν Γαλιλαίαν.
-   JUDEA   AND DEPARTED AGAIN INTO - GALILEE.

4.4 ἔδει δὲ   αὐτὸν διέρχεσθαι διὰ   τῆς
      AND~IT WAS NECESSARY [FOR] HIM TO PASS   THROUGH -

Σαμαρείας. **4.5** ἔρχεται οὖν   εἰς πόλιν τῆς
SAMARIA.   HE COMES THEREFORE INTO A CITY   -

Σαμαρείας λεγομένην Συχὰρ πλησίον τοῦ χωρίου
OF SAMARIA BEING CALLED SYCHAR NEAR   THE PARCEL

ὃ   ἔδωκεν Ἰακὼβ [τῷ] Ἰωσὴφ τῷ υἱῷ αὐτοῦ·
WHICH JACOB~GAVE   -   TO JOSEPH THE SON OF HIM.

4.6 ἦν δὲ   ἐκεῖ πηγὴ τοῦ Ἰακώβ. ὁ οὖν Ἰησοῦς
      NOW~THERE WAS THERE A WELL - OF JACOB. - THEN JESUS

κεκοπιακὼς ἐκ τῆς ὁδοιπορίας ἐκαθέζετο οὕτως ἐπὶ
HAVING BECOME WEARY FROM THE JOURNEY WAS SITTING THUS AT

τῇ πηγῇ· ὥρα ἦν ὡς   ἕκτη.
THE WELL; ⁴HOUR ¹IT WAS ²ABOUT ³[THE] SIXTH.

4.7 Ἔρχεται γυνὴ ἐκ τῆς Σαμαρείας ἀντλῆσαι ὕδωρ.
      COMES   A WOMAN OF - SAMARIA   TO DRAW   WATER.

4:1 text: NEB TEV NJB NRSV. var. κυριος (Lord): KJV ASV RSV NASB NIV NRSVmg.

λέγει αὐτῇ ὁ Ἰησοῦς, Δός μοι πεῖν· **4.8** οἱ γὰρ
SAYS TO HER - JESUS, GIVE ME TO DRINK; FOR~THE

μαθηταὶ αὐτοῦ ἀπεληλύθεισαν εἰς τὴν πόλιν ἵνα
DISCIPLES OF HIM HAD GONE AWAY INTO THE CITY THAT

τροφὰς ἀγοράσωσιν. **4.9** λέγει οὖν αὐτῷ ἡ γυνὴ
FOOD THEY MIGHT BUY. SAYS THEREFORE TO HIM THE WOMAN,

ἡ Σαμαρῖτις, Πῶς σὺ Ἰουδαῖος ὢν παρ᾽ ἐμοῦ
THE SAMARITAN, HOW [CAN] YOU BEING~A JEW FROM ME

πεῖν αἰτεῖς γυναικὸς Σαμαρίτιδος οὔσης;
TO [BE GIVEN] DRINK ASK ³WOMAN ²A SAMARITAN ¹BEING?

⌜οὐ γὰρ συγχρῶνται Ἰουδαῖοι Σαμαρίταις.⌝ **4.10** ἀπεκρίθη
(FOR DO NOT ASSOCIATE JEWS WITH SAMARITANS.) ANSWERED

Ἰησοῦς καὶ εἶπεν αὐτῇ, Εἰ ᾔδεις τὴν δωρεὰν τοῦ
JESUS AND SAID TO HER, IF YOU KNEW THE GIFT -

θεοῦ καὶ τίς ἐστιν ὁ λέγων σοι, Δός μοι πεῖν,
OF GOD AND WHO IS THE ONE SAYING TO YOU, GIVE ME TO DRINK,

σὺ ἂν ᾔτησας αὐτὸν καὶ ἔδωκεν ἄν σοι ὕδωρ ζῶν.
YOU WOULD HAVE ASKED HIM AND HE WOULD HAVE GIVEN YOU LIVING~WATER.

4.11 λέγει αὐτῷ [ἡ γυνή], Κύριε, οὔτε ἄντλημα ἔχεις
SAYS TO HIM THE WOMAN, SIR, NO BUCKET YOU HAVE

καὶ τὸ φρέαρ ἐστὶν βαθύ· πόθεν οὖν ἔχεις τὸ
AND THE WELL IS DEEP. FROM WHERE THEN DO YOU HAVE THE

ὕδωρ τὸ ζῶν; **4.12** μὴ σὺ μείζων εἶ τοῦ
²WATER - ¹LIVING? ³[SURELY] NOT ¹YOU ⁴GREATER [THAN] ²ARE THE

πατρὸς ἡμῶν Ἰακώβ, ὃς ἔδωκεν ἡμῖν τὸ φρέαρ καὶ
FATHER OF US, JACOB, WHO GAVE US THE WELL AND

αὐτὸς ἐξ αὐτοῦ ἔπιεν καὶ οἱ υἱοὶ αὐτοῦ καὶ τὰ
HIMSELF FROM IT DRANK AND THE SONS OF HIM AND THE

θρέμματα αὐτοῦ; **4.13** ἀπεκρίθη Ἰησοῦς καὶ εἶπεν
CATTLE OF HIM? ANSWERED JESUS AND SAID

αὐτῇ, Πᾶς ὁ πίνων ἐκ τοῦ ὕδατος τούτου διψήσει
TO HER, EVERYONE DRINKING FROM - THIS~WATER WILL THIRST

πάλιν· **4.14** ὃς δ᾽ ἂν πίῃ ἐκ τοῦ ὕδατος οὗ ἐγὼ
AGAIN. BUT~WHOEVER DRINKS OF THE WATER WHICH I

δώσω αὐτῷ, οὐ μὴ διψήσει εἰς τὸν αἰῶνα, ἀλλὰ τὸ
WILL GIVE TO HIM, WILL NEVER THIRST INTO THE AGE, BUT THE

ὕδωρ ὃ δώσω αὐτῷ γενήσεται ἐν αὐτῷ πηγὴ
WATER WHICH I WILL GIVE HIM WILL BECOME IN HIM A FOUNTAIN

ὕδατος ἁλλομένου εἰς ζωὴν αἰώνιον. **4.15** λέγει πρὸς
OF WATER SPRINGING UP INTO LIFE ETERNAL. SAYS TO

αὐτὸν ἡ γυνή, Κύριε, δός μοι τοῦτο τὸ ὕδωρ, ἵνα
HIM THE WOMAN, SIR, GIVE ME THIS - WATER, THAT

μὴ διψῶ μηδὲ διέρχωμαι ἐνθάδε ἀντλεῖν.
I MAY NOT THIRST NOR COME HERE TO DRAW [WATER].

4.16 Λέγει αὐτῇ, Ὕπαγε φώνησον τὸν ἄνδρα σου
HE SAYS TO HER, GO CALL THE HUSBAND OF YOU

4:9 text: all. omit: ASVmg NEBmg NJBmg NRSVmg.

and Jesus said to her, "Give me a drink." [8](His disciples had gone to the city to buy food.) [9]The Samaritan woman said to him, "How is it that you, a Jew, ask a drink of me, a woman of Samaria?" (Jews do not share things in common with Samaritans.)[a] [10]Jesus answered her, "If you knew the gift of God, and who it is that is saying to you, 'Give me a drink,' you would have asked him, and he would have given you living water." [11]The woman said to him, "Sir, you have no bucket, and the well is deep. Where do you get that living water? [12]Are you greater than our ancestor Jacob, who gave us the well, and with his sons and his flocks drank from it?" [13]Jesus said to her, "Everyone who drinks of this water will be thirsty again, [14]but those who drink of the water that I will give them will never be thirsty. The water that I will give will become in them a spring of water gushing up to eternal life." [15]The woman said to him, "Sir, give me this water, so that I may never be thirsty or have to keep coming here to draw water."

16 Jesus said to her, "Go, call your husband,

[a] Other ancient authorities lack this sentence

and come back." [17]The woman answered him, "I have no husband." Jesus said to her, "You are right in saying, 'I have no husband'; [18]for you have had five husbands, and the one you have now is not your husband. What you have said is true!" [19]The woman said to him, "Sir, I see that you are a prophet. [20]Our ancestors worshiped on this mountain, but you[b] say that the place where people must worship is in Jerusalem." [21]Jesus said to her, "Woman, believe me, the hour is coming when you will worship the Father neither on this mountain nor in Jerusalem. [22]You worship what you do not know; we worship what we know, for salvation is from the Jews. [23]But the hour is coming, and is now here, when the true worshipers will worship the Father in spirit and truth, for the Father seeks such as these to worship him. [24]God is spirit, and those who worship him must worship in spirit and truth." [25]The woman said to him, "I know that Messiah is coming" (who is called Christ). "When he comes, he will proclaim all things to us." [26]Jesus said to her, "I am he,[c] the one who is speaking to you."

27 Just then his disciples

[b] The Greek word for *you* here and in verses 21 and 22 is plural
[c] Gk *I am*

καὶ   ἐλθὲ   ἐνθάδε.   **4.17** ἀπεκρίθη   ἡ   γυνὴ   καὶ   εἶπεν
AND   COME   HERE.   ANSWERED   THE   WOMAN   AND   SAID

αὐτῷ,   Οὐκ   ἔχω   ἄνδρα.   λέγει   αὐτῇ   ὁ   Ἰησοῦς,   Καλῶς
TO HIM,   I DO NOT HAVE   A HUSBAND.   SAYS   TO HER   -   JESUS,   WELL

εἶπας   ὅτι   Ἄνδρα   οὐκ   ἔχω·   **4.18** πέντε   γὰρ   ἄνδρας
YOU SAID,   -   A HUSBAND   I DO NOT HAVE;   FOR~FIVE   HUSBANDS

ἔσχες   καὶ   νῦν   ὃν   ἔχεις   οὐκ   ἔστιν   σου   ἀνήρ·   τοῦτο
YOU HAD   AND   NOW   THE ONE   YOU HAVE   IS NOT   YOUR   HUSBAND.   THIS

ἀληθὲς   εἴρηκας.   **4.19** λέγει   αὐτῷ   ἡ   γυνή,   Κύριε,
TRULY   YOU HAVE SAID.   SAYS   TO HIM   THE   WOMAN,   SIR,

θεωρῶ ὅτι   προφήτης   εἶ σύ   **4.20** οἱ   πατέρες   ἡμῶν ἐν
I SEE   THAT   A PROPHET   YOU~ARE.   THE   FATHERS   OF US   ON

τῷ   ὄρει   τούτῳ   προσεκύνησαν·   καὶ   ὑμεῖς   λέγετε   ὅτι   ἐν
-   THIS~MOUNTAIN   WORSHIPED   AND   YOU°   SAY   THAT   IN

Ἱεροσολύμοις   ἐστὶν   ὁ   τόπος   ὅπου   προσκυνεῖν   δεῖ.
JERUSALEM   IS   THE   PLACE   WHERE   IT IS NECESSARY~TO WORSHIP.

4.21 λέγει   αὐτῇ   ὁ   Ἰησοῦς,   Πίστευέ   μοι,   γύναι,   ὅτι
SAYS   TO HER   -   JESUS,   BELIEVE   ME,   WOMAN,   THAT

ἔρχεται   ὥρα   ὅτε   οὔτε   ἐν   τῷ   ὄρει τούτῳ οὔτε   ἐν
COMES   AN HOUR   WHEN   NEITHER   ON   -   THIS~MOUNTAIN   NOR   IN

Ἱεροσολύμοις   προσκυνήσετε   τῷ   πατρί.   **4.22** ὑμεῖς
JERUSALEM   YOU° WILL WORSHIP   THE   FATHER.   YOU°

προσκυνεῖτε   ὃ   οὐκ οἴδατε·   ἡμεῖς   προσκυνοῦμεν
WORSHIP   THAT WHICH   YOU° DO NOT KNOW;   WE   WORSHIP

ὃ   οἴδαμεν,   ὅτι   ἡ   σωτηρία   ἐκ   τῶν   Ἰουδαίων
THAT WHICH   WE KNOW,   BECAUSE   -   SALVATION   FROM   THE   JEWS

ἐστίν.   **4.23** ἀλλὰ   ἔρχεται   ὥρα   καὶ   νῦν   ἐστιν,   ὅτε
IS.   BUT   IS COMING   AN HOUR   AND   NOW   IS,   WHEN

οἱ   ἀληθινοὶ   προσκυνηταὶ   προσκυνήσουσιν   τῷ   πατρὶ
THE   TRUE   WORSHIPERS   WILL WORSHIP   THE   FATHER

ἐν   πνεύματι   καὶ   ἀληθείᾳ·   καὶ   γὰρ   ὁ   πατὴρ
IN   SPIRIT   AND   TRUTH.   FOR~INDEED   THE   FATHER

τοιούτους   ζητεῖ   τοὺς   προσκυνοῦντας   αὐτόν.   **4.24** πνεῦμα
IS SEEKING~SUCH   ONES   WORSHIPING   HIM.   [2]SPIRIT

ὁ   θεός,   καὶ   τοὺς   προσκυνοῦντας   αὐτὸν   ἐν   πνεύματι
-   [1]GOD [IS],   AND   [2]THE ONES   [3]WORSHIPING   [4]HIM   [6]IN   [7]SPIRIT

καὶ   ἀληθείᾳ   δεῖ   προσκυνεῖν.   **4.25** λέγει
[8]AND   [9]TRUTH   [1]IT IS NECESSARY [FOR]   [5]TO WORSHIP.   SAYS

αὐτῷ   ἡ   γυνή,   Οἶδα   ὅτι   Μεσσίας   ἔρχεται   ὁ
TO HIM   THE   WOMAN,   I KNOW   THAT   A MESSIAH   IS COMING,   THE ONE

λεγόμενος   Χριστός·   ὅταν   ἔλθῃ   ἐκεῖνος,   ἀναγγελεῖ   ἡμῖν
BEING CALLED   CHRIST.   WHEN   COMES   THAT ONE,   HE WILL DECLARE   TO US

ἅπαντα.   **4.26** λέγει   αὐτῇ   ὁ   Ἰησοῦς,   Ἐγώ   εἰμι,   ὁ
EVERYTHING.   SAYS   TO HER   -   JESUS,   I   AM [HE],   THE ONE

λαλῶν   σοι.
SPEAKING   TO YOU.

4.27 Καὶ   ἐπὶ   τούτῳ   ἦλθαν   οἱ   μαθηταὶ   αὐτοῦ   καὶ
AND   AT   THIS [TIME]   CAME   THE   DISCIPLES   OF HIM   AND

ἐθαύμαζον   ὅτι   μετὰ   γυναικὸς   ἐλάλει·   οὐδεὶς
THEY WERE MARVELING THAT WITH   A WOMAN   HE WAS SPEAKING; NO ONE

μέντοι   εἶπεν,   Τί   ζητεῖς   ἢ   τί   λαλεῖς   μετ᾽
HOWEVER   SAID,   WHAT ARE YOU SEEKING OR WHY DO YOU SPEAK WITH

αὐτῆς;   **4.28** ἀφῆκεν   οὖν   τὴν   ὑδρίαν   αὐτῆς   ἡ   γυνὴ   καὶ
HER?   THEREFORE~LEFT   THE   WATERPOT   OF HER   THE   WOMAN   AND

ἀπῆλθεν   εἰς   τὴν   πόλιν   καὶ   λέγει   τοῖς   ἀνθρώποις,
WENT AWAY   INTO   THE   CITY   AND   SAYS   TO THE   MEN,

4.29 Δεῦτε   ἴδετε   ἄνθρωπον   ὃς   εἶπέν   μοι   πάντα
       COME   SEE   A MAN   WHO TOLD   ME   ALL THINGS

ὅσα   ἐποίησα,   μήτι   οὗτός   ἐστιν   ὁ   Χριστός;
WHATSOEVER I DID,   [SURELY] NOT   THIS ONE IS   THE   CHRIST?

4.30 ἐξῆλθον   ἐκ   τῆς   πόλεως   καὶ   ἤρχοντο   πρὸς   αὐτόν.
       THEY CAME   OUT OF   THE   CITY   AND   WERE COMING TO   HIM.

4.31 Ἐν   τῷ   μεταξὺ   ἠρώτων   αὐτὸν   οἱ   μαθηταὶ
       IN   THE   MEANWHILE WERE ASKING HIM   THE   DISCIPLES

λέγοντες,   Ῥαββί,   φάγε.   **4.32** ὁ   δὲ   εἶπεν   αὐτοῖς,   Ἐγὼ
SAYING,   RABBI,   EAT.   -   BUT~HE SAID TO THEM,   I

βρῶσιν   ἔχω   φαγεῖν   ἣν   ὑμεῖς   οὐκ   οἴδατε.
HAVE~FOOD   TO EAT   WHICH   YOU°   DO NOT KNOW [ABOUT].

4.33 ἔλεγον   οὖν   οἱ   μαθηταὶ   πρὸς   ἀλλήλους,
       WERE SAYING THEREFORE THE   DISCIPLES   TO   ONE ANOTHER,

Μή   τις   ἤνεγκεν   αὐτῷ   φαγεῖν;   **4.34** λέγει   αὐτοῖς
[SURELY] NO ONE BROUGHT   HIM   [ANYTHING] TO EAT?   SAYS   TO THEM

ὁ   Ἰησοῦς,   Ἐμὸν   βρῶμά   ἐστιν   ἵνα   ποιήσω   τὸ   θέλημα
-   JESUS,   MY   FOOD   IS   THAT   I MAY DO   THE   WILL

τοῦ   πέμψαντός   με   καὶ   τελειώσω   αὐτοῦ   τὸ   ἔργον.
OF THE ONE HAVING SENT   ME   AND   MAY COMPLETE HIS   -   WORK.

4.35 οὐχ   ὑμεῖς   λέγετε   ὅτι   Ἔτι   τετράμηνός   ἐστιν   καὶ   ὁ
       DO YOU° NOT SAY,   -   YET   FOUR MONTHS   IT IS   AND   THE

θερισμὸς   ἔρχεται;   ἰδοὺ   λέγω   ὑμῖν,   ἐπάρατε   τοὺς
HARVEST   COMES?   LOOK, I SAY TO YOU°, LIFT UP   THE

ὀφθαλμοὺς   ὑμῶν   καὶ   θεάσασθε   τὰς   χώρας   ὅτι   λευκαί
EYES   OF YOU° AND   SEE   THE   FIELDS   THAT   WHITE

εἰσιν   πρὸς   θερισμόν.   ἤδη   **4.36** ὁ   θερίζων   μισθὸν
THEY ARE FOR   HARVEST.   ALREADY   THE ONE   REAPING   WAGES

λαμβάνει   καὶ   συνάγει   καρπὸν   εἰς   ζωὴν   αἰώνιον,
RECEIVES   AND   GATHERS   FRUIT   INTO   LIFE   ETERNAL,

ἵνα   ὁ   σπείρων   ὁμοῦ   χαίρῃ   καὶ   ὁ
IN ORDER THAT ¹THE ONE ²SOWING ⁷TOGETHER ⁶MAY REJOICE ³AND ⁴THE ONE

θερίζων.   **4.37** ἐν   γὰρ   τούτῳ   ὁ   λόγος   ἐστὶν   ἀληθινὸς
⁵REAPING.   FOR~IN THIS   THE   WORD   IS   TRUE,

ὅτι   Ἄλλος   ἐστὶν   ὁ   σπείρων   καὶ   ἄλλος   ὁ
-   ANOTHER   IS   THE ONE SOWING   AND   ANOTHER THE ONE

θερίζων.   **4.38** ἐγὼ   ἀπέστειλα   ὑμᾶς   θερίζειν   ὃ
REAPING.   I   SENT   YOU°   TO REAP   THAT WHICH

οὐχ   ὑμεῖς   κεκοπιάκατε·   ἄλλοι   κεκοπιάκασιν   καὶ   ὑμεῖς
YOU° HAVE NOT LABORED [UPON].   OTHERS   HAVE LABORED   AND   YOU°

came. They were astonished
that he was speaking with a
woman, but no one said,
"What do you want?" or,
"Why are you speaking with
her?" 28Then the woman left
her water jar and went back
to the city. She said to the
people, 29"Come and see a
man who told me everything
I have ever done! He cannot
be the Messiah,*d* can he?"
30They left the city and were
on their way to him.

31 Meanwhile the
disciples were urging him,
"Rabbi, eat something."
32But he said to them, "I
have food to eat that you do
not know about." 33So the
disciples said to one another,
"Surely no one has brought
him something to eat?"
34Jesus said to them, "My
food is to do the will of him
who sent me and to complete
his work. 35Do you not say,
'Four months more, then
comes the harvest'? But I
tell you, look around you,
and see how the fields are
ripe for harvesting. 36The
reaper is already receiving*e*
wages and is gathering fruit
for eternal life, so that sower
and reaper may rejoice
together. 37For here the
saying holds true, 'One sows
and another reaps.' 38I sent
you to reap that for which
you did not labor. Others
have labored, and you

d Or *the Christ*
e Or 35. . . *the fields are already ripe
for harvesting.* 36*The reaper is
receiving*

have entered into their labor."

39 Many Samaritans from that city believed in him because of the woman's testimony, "He told me everything I have ever done." 40So when the Samaritans came to him, they asked him to stay with them; and he stayed there two days. 41And many more believed because of his word. 42They said to the woman, "It is no longer because of what you said that we believe, for we have heard for ourselves, and we know that this is truly the Savior of the world."

43 When the two days were over, he went from that place to Galilee 44(for Jesus himself had testified that a prophet has no honor in the prophet's own country). 45When he came to Galilee, the Galileans welcomed him, since they had seen all that he had done in Jerusalem at the festival; for they too had gone to the festival.

46 Then he came again to Cana in Galilee where he had changed the water into wine. Now there was a royal official whose son lay ill in Capernaum. 47When he heard that Jesus had come from Judea to Galilee, he went and begged him to come down and heal his son,

εἰς τὸν κόπον αὐτῶν εἰσεληλύθατε.
INTO THE LABOR OF THEM HAVE ENTERED.

4.39 Ἐκ δὲ τῆς πόλεως ἐκείνης πολλοὶ ἐπίστευσαν
AND~OF - THAT~CITY MANY BELIEVED

εἰς αὐτὸν τῶν Σαμαριτῶν διὰ τὸν λόγον τῆς
IN HIM OF THE SAMARITANS BECAUSE OF THE WORD OF THE

γυναικὸς μαρτυρούσης ὅτι Εἶπέν μοι πάντα ἃ
WOMAN TESTIFYING, - HE TOLD ME ALL THINGS WHICH

ἐποίησα. **4.40** ὡς οὖν ἦλθον πρὸς αὐτὸν οἱ Σαμαρῖται,
I DID. THEN~WHEN CAME TO HIM THE SAMARITANS,

ἠρώτων αὐτὸν μεῖναι παρ' αὐτοῖς· καὶ ἔμεινεν
THEY WERE ASKING HIM TO REMAIN WITH THEM, AND HE REMAINED

ἐκεῖ δύο ἡμέρας. **4.41** καὶ πολλῷ πλείους ἐπίστευσαν
THERE TWO DAYS. AND MANY~MORE BELIEVED

διὰ τὸν λόγον αὐτοῦ, **4.42** τῇ τε γυναικὶ
BECAUSE OF THE WORD OF HIM, AND~TO THE WOMAN

ἔλεγον ὅτι Οὐκέτι διὰ τὴν σὴν λαλιὰν
THEY WERE SAYING - NO LONGER BECAUSE OF - YOUR TALK

πιστεύομεν, αὐτοὶ γὰρ ἀκηκόαμεν καὶ οἴδαμεν ὅτι
DO WE BELIEVE. FOR~WE OURSELVES HAVE HEARD AND WE KNOW THAT

οὗτός ἐστιν ἀληθῶς ὁ σωτὴρ τοῦ κόσμου.
THIS ONE IS TRULY THE SAVIOR OF THE WORLD.

4.43 Μετὰ δὲ τὰς δύο ἡμέρας ἐξῆλθεν ἐκεῖθεν εἰς τὴν
AND~AFTER THE TWO DAYS HE WENT OUT FROM THERE INTO -

Γαλιλαίαν· **4.44** αὐτὸς γὰρ Ἰησοῦς ἐμαρτύρησεν ὅτι
GALILEE, ³HIMSELF ¹FOR ²JESUS TESTIFIED THAT

προφήτης ἐν τῇ ἰδίᾳ πατρίδι τιμὴν οὐκ ἔχει.
A PROPHET IN HIS OWN COUNTRY DOES NOT HAVE~HONOR.

4.45 ὅτε οὖν ἦλθεν εἰς τὴν Γαλιλαίαν, ἐδέξαντο
THEREFORE~WHEN HE CAME INTO - GALILEE, RECEIVED

αὐτὸν οἱ Γαλιλαῖοι πάντα ἑωρακότες ὅσα ἐποίησεν
HIM THE GALILEANS, ALL THINGS HAVING SEEN WHICH HE DID

ἐν Ἱεροσολύμοις ἐν τῇ ἑορτῇ, καὶ αὐτοὶ γὰρ ἦλθον
IN JERUSALEM DURING THE FEAST, ³ALSO ²THEY ¹FOR WENT

εἰς τὴν ἑορτήν.
TO THE FEAST.

4.46 Ἦλθεν οὖν πάλιν εἰς τὴν Κανὰ τῆς
HE CAME THEREFORE AGAIN INTO - CANA -

Γαλιλαίας, ὅπου ἐποίησεν τὸ ὕδωρ οἶνον. καὶ ἦν
OF GALILEE, WHERE HE MADE THE WATER WINE. AND THERE WAS

τις βασιλικὸς οὗ ὁ υἱὸς ἠσθένει ἐν Καφαρναούμ.
A CERTAIN ROYAL OFFICIAL WHOSE - SON WAS ILL IN CAPERNAUM.

4.47 οὗτος ἀκούσας ὅτι Ἰησοῦς ἥκει ἐκ τῆς Ἰουδαίας
THIS MAN, HAVING HEARD THAT JESUS COMES FROM - JUDEA

εἰς τὴν Γαλιλαίαν ἀπῆλθεν πρὸς αὐτὸν καὶ ἠρώτα
INTO - GALILEE, WENT TO HIM AND WAS ASKING

ἵνα καταβῇ καὶ ἰάσηται αὐτοῦ τὸν υἱόν,
THAT HE WOULD COME DOWN AND CURE HIS - SON,

ἤμελλεν γὰρ ἀποθνῄσκειν. **4.48** εἶπεν οὖν   ὁ Ἰησοῦς
FOR~HE WAS ABOUT   TO DIE.   SAID   THEREFORE - JESUS

πρὸς αὐτόν, Ἐὰν μὴ σημεῖα καὶ τέρατα ἴδητε,
TO HIM,   EXCEPT SIGNS AND WONDERS YOU° SEE,

οὐ μὴ πιστεύσητε. **4.49** λέγει πρὸς αὐτὸν ὁ βασιλικός,
YOU° NEVER BELIEVE.   SAYS   TO   HIM THE ROYAL OFFICIAL,

Κύριε, κατάβηθι πρὶν ἀποθανεῖν τὸ παιδίον μου.
LORD, COME DOWN BEFORE DIES   THE CHILD   OF ME.

4.50 λέγει αὐτῷ ὁ Ἰησοῦς, Πορεύου, ὁ υἱός σου ζῇ.
       SAYS TO HIM - JESUS,   GO,   THE SON OF YOU LIVES.

ἐπίστευσεν ὁ ἄνθρωπος τῷ λόγῳ ὃν εἶπεν
BELIEVED   THE MAN   THE WORD WHICH SAID

αὐτῷ ὁ Ἰησοῦς καὶ ἐπορεύετο. **4.51** ἤδη δὲ
TO HIM - JESUS AND HE WENT.   AND~ALREADY

αὐτοῦ καταβαίνοντος οἱ δοῦλοι αὐτοῦ ὑπήντησαν αὐτῷ
[WHILE] HE WAS GOING DOWN THE SLAVES OF HIM MET   HIM

λέγοντες ὅτι ὁ παῖς αὐτοῦ ζῇ. **4.52** ἐπύθετο οὖν
SAYING THAT THE CHILD OF HIM LIVES.   THEREFORE~HE INQUIRED

τὴν ὥραν παρ' αὐτῶν ἐν ᾗ   κομψότερον ἔσχεν·
THE TIME FROM THEM IN WHICH HE BECAME~BETTER.

εἶπαν οὖν αὐτῷ ὅτι Ἐχθὲς ὥραν ἑβδόμην ἀφῆκεν
THEN~THEY SAID TO HIM, - YESTERDAY [AT] [THE] SEVENTH~HOUR LEFT

αὐτὸν ὁ πυρετός. **4.53** ἔγνω οὖν ὁ πατὴρ ὅτι
HIM THE FEVER.   THEREFORE~KNEW THE FATHER THAT [IT WAS]

[ἐν] ἐκείνῃ τῇ ὥρᾳ ἐν ᾗ εἶπεν αὐτῷ ὁ Ἰησοῦς, Ὁ
IN THE SAME - HOUR IN WHICH SAID TO HIM - JESUS, THE

υἱός σου ζῇ, καὶ ἐπίστευσεν αὐτὸς καὶ ἡ οἰκία
SON OF YOU LIVES, AND HE~BELIEVED   AND ²THE ³HOUSEHOLD

αὐτοῦ ὅλη. **4.54** Τοῦτο [δὲ] πάλιν δεύτερον σημεῖον
⁴OF HIM ¹ALL.   AND~THIS   AGAIN A SECOND SIGN

ἐποίησεν ὁ Ἰησοῦς ἐλθὼν ἐκ τῆς Ἰουδαίας εἰς τὴν
DID   - JESUS HAVING COME FROM - JUDEA   INTO -

Γαλιλαίαν.
GALILEE.

for he was at the point of death. [48]Then Jesus said to him, "Unless you*f* see signs and wonders you will not believe." [49]The official said to him, "Sir, come down before my little boy dies." [50]Jesus said to him, "Go; your son will live." The man believed the word that Jesus spoke to him and started on his way. [51]As he was going down, his slaves met him and told him that his child was alive. [52]So he asked them the hour when he began to recover, and they said to him, "Yesterday at one in the afternoon the fever left him." [53]The father realized that this was the hour when Jesus had said to him, "Your son will live." So he himself believed, along with his whole household. [54]Now this was the second sign that Jesus did after coming from Judea to Galilee.

f Both instances of the Greek word for *you* in this verse are plural

5.1 Μετὰ ταῦτα ἦν ⌐ἑορτὴ⌐ τῶν Ἰουδαίων, καὶ
     AFTER THESE THINGS THERE WAS A FEAST OF THE JEWS,   AND

ἀνέβη Ἰησοῦς εἰς Ἱεροσόλυμα. **5.2** ἔστιν δὲ ἐν τοῖς
WENT UP JESUS TO JERUSALEM.   NOW~THERE IS IN -

Ἱεροσολύμοις ἐπὶ τῇ προβατικῇ κολυμβήθρα ἡ
JERUSALEM   AT THE SHEEPGATE   A POOL,   THE ONE

ἐπιλεγομένη Ἑβραϊστὶ ⌐Βηθζαθὰ⌐ πέντε στοὰς
BEING CALLED IN HEBREW BETHZATHA, FIVE   PORCHES

After this there was a festival of the Jews, and Jesus went up to Jerusalem.
2 Now in Jerusalem by the Sheep Gate there is a pool, called in Hebrew*g* Beth-zatha,*h* which has five porticoes.

g That is, *Aramaic*
h Other ancient authorities read *Bethesda*, others *Bethsaida*

5:1 text: all. var. η εορτη (the feast): ASVmg NASBmg NEBmg NJBmg.   **5:2** text: ASVmg RSV NIVmg TEV NJBmg NRSV. var. Βηθσαιδα (Bethsaida): ASVmg RSVmg NIVmg NJBmg NRSVmg. var. Βηθεσδα (Bethesda): KJV ASV RSVmg NASB NIV NEB TEVmg NJB NRSVmg.

³In these lay many invalids—blind, lame, and paralyzed.ⁱ ⁵One man was there who had been ill for thirty-eight years. ⁶When Jesus saw him lying there and knew that he had been there a long time, he said to him, "Do you want to be made well?" ⁷The sick man answered him, "Sir, I have no one to put me into the pool when the water is stirred up; and while I am making my way, someone else steps down ahead of me." ⁸Jesus said to him, "Stand up, take your mat and walk." ⁹At once the man was made well, and he took up his mat and began to walk.

Now that day was a sabbath. ¹⁰So the Jews said to the man who had been cured, "It is the sabbath; it is not lawful for you to carry your mat." ¹¹But he answered them, "The man who made me well said to me, 'Take up your mat and walk.'" ¹²They asked him, "Who is the man who said to you, 'Take it up and walk'?" ¹³Now the man who had been healed did not know

ⁱ Other ancient authorities add, wholly or in part, waiting for the stirring of the water; ⁴for an angel of the Lord went down at certain seasons into the pool, and stirred up the water; whoever stepped in first after the stirring of the water was made well from whatever disease that person had.

ἔχουσα. **5.3** ἐν ταύταις κατέκειτο πλῆθος τῶν
HAVING.   IN THESE WERE LAYING A MULTITUDE OF THE ONES

ἀσθενούντων, τυφλῶν, χωλῶν, ξηρῶνᵀ.ᵀ **5.5** ἦν δέ
BEING ILL,   BLIND, LAME, WITHERED.   AND~THERE WAS

τις   ἄνθρωπος ἐκεῖ τριάκοντα [καὶ] ὀκτὼ ἔτη
A CERTAIN MAN THERE THIRTY AND EIGHT YEARS

ἔχων   ἐν τῇ ἀσθενείᾳ αὐτοῦ· **5.6** τοῦτον ἰδὼν ὁ
HAVING [BEEN] IN - HIS~SICKNESS.   ³THIS MAN ²SEEING -

Ἰησοῦς κατακείμενον καὶ γνοὺς   ὅτι πολὺν
¹JESUS   ⁴LYING   AND HAVING KNOWN THAT MUCH

ἤδη χρόνον ἔχει,   λέγει αὐτῷ, Θέλεις
TIME~ALREADY HE HAS [BEEN THUS], SAYS TO HIM, DO YOU WANT

ὑγιὴς γενέσθαι; **5.7** ἀπεκρίθη αὐτῷ ὁ   ἀσθενῶν,
TO BECOME~HEALTHY?   ANSWERED HIM THE ONE BEING ILL,

Κύριε, ἄνθρωπον οὐκ ἔχω ἵνα ὅταν ταραχθῇ τὸ ὕδωρ
SIR, A MAN   I DO NOT HAVE THAT WHEN IS TROUBLED THE WATER

βάλῃ   με εἰς τὴν κολυμβήθραν· ἐν ᾧ δὲ ἔρχομαι ἐγώ,
HE MAY PUT ME INTO THE POOL.   BUT~WHILE I~AM COMING

ἄλλος πρὸ ἐμοῦ καταβαίνει. **5.8** λέγει αὐτῷ ὁ
ANOTHER BEFORE ME GOES DOWN.   SAYS TO HIM -

Ἰησοῦς, Ἔγειρε ἆρον τὸν κράβαττόν σου καὶ
JESUS, RISE, TAKE THE MAT   OF YOU AND

περιπάτει. **5.9** καὶ εὐθέως ἐγένετο ὑγιὴς ὁ ἄνθρωπος
WALK.   AND IMMEDIATELY BECAME HEALTHY THE MAN

καὶ ἦρεν τὸν κράβαττον αὐτοῦ καὶ περιεπάτει.
AND HE TOOK THE MAT   OF HIM AND WAS WALKING AROUND.

Ἦν δὲ σάββατον ἐν ἐκείνῃ τῇ ἡμέρᾳ. **5.10** ἔλεγον
AND~IT WAS A SABBATH ON THAT - DAY.   WERE SAYING

οὖν   οἱ Ἰουδαῖοι τῷ   τεθεραπευμένῳ,
THEREFORE THE JEWS   TO THE ONE HAVING BEEN HEALED,

Σάββατόν ἐστιν, καὶ οὐκ ἔξεστίν σοι ἆραι τὸν
IT IS~[THE] SABBATH, SO IT IS NOT LAWFUL FOR YOU TO CARRY THE

κράβαττόν σου. **5.11** ὁ δὲ   ἀπεκρίθη αὐτοῖς, Ὁ
MAT   OF YOU.   BUT~THE MAN ANSWERED THEM, THE ONE

ποιήσας με ὑγιῆ ἐκεῖνός μοι εἶπεν, Ἆρον τὸν
HAVING MADE ME HEALTHY, THAT ONE SAID~TO ME, TAKE UP THE

κράβαττόν σου καὶ περιπάτει. **5.12** ἠρώτησαν αὐτόν,
MAT   OF YOU AND WALK.   THEY ASKED HIM,

Τίς ἐστιν ὁ ἄνθρωπος ὁ εἰπών σοι, Ἆρον   καὶ
WHO IS   THE MAN   - TELLING YOU, TAKE UP [YOUR MAT] AND

περιπάτει; **5.13** ὁ δὲ   ἰαθεὶς   οὐκ ᾔδει τίς
WALK?   BUT~THE ONE HAVING BEEN HEALED DID NOT KNOW WHO

5:3 text: ASV RSV NASB NIV NEB TEV NJB NRSV. add εκδεχομενων την του υδατος κινησιν (waiting for the moving of the water): KJV ASVmg RSVmg NASBmg NIVmg NEBmg TEVmg NJBmg NRSVmg.
omit 5:4 text: ASV RSV NASB NIV NEB TEV NJB NRSV. include 5:4 (with different variations in later MSS—generally rendered as follows: "for an angel of the Lord went down at certain seasons into the pool and stirred up the water; whoever then first stepped in, after the stirring up of the water, was made well from whatever disease he was afflicted with"): KJV ASVmg RSVmg NASBmg NIVmg NEBmg TEVmg NJBmg NRSVmg.

ἐστιν, ὁ γὰρ Ἰησοῦς ἐξένευσεν ὄχλου ὄντος ἐν τῷ
IT IS, - FOR JESUS SLIPPED OUT—[THERE] BEING~A CROWD IN THE

τόπῳ. **5.14** μετὰ ταῦτα εὑρίσκει αὐτὸν ὁ Ἰησοῦς ἐν
PLACE. AFTER THESE THINGS ²FINDS ³HIM - ¹JESUS IN

τῷ ἱερῷ καὶ εἶπεν αὐτῷ, Ἴδε ὑγιὴς γέγονας,
THE TEMPLE AND SAID TO HIM, LOOK, YOU HAVE BECOME~HEALTHY,

μηκέτι ἁμάρτανε, ἵνα μὴ χεῖρόν σοί τι γένηται.
NO LONGER SIN, LEST ²WORSE ⁴TO YOU ¹SOMETHING ³HAPPENS.

5.15 ἀπῆλθεν ὁ ἄνθρωπος καὶ ἀνήγγειλεν τοῖς
WENT AWAY THE MAN AND REPORTED TO THE

Ἰουδαίοις ὅτι Ἰησοῦς ἐστιν ὁ ποιήσας αὐτὸν ὑγιή.
JEWS THAT JESUS IS THE ONE HAVING MADE HIM HEALTHY.

5.16 καὶ διὰ τοῦτο ἐδίωκον οἱ Ἰουδαῖοι τὸν
AND BECAUSE OF THIS ³PERSECUTED ¹THE ²JEWS -

Ἰησοῦν, ὅτι ταῦτα ἐποίει ἐν σαββάτῳ. **5.17** ὁ
⁴JESUS, BECAUSE THESE THINGS HE WAS DOING ON A SABBATH. -

δὲ [Ἰησοῦς] ἀπεκρίνατο αὐτοῖς, Ὁ πατήρ μου ἕως
BUT JESUS ANSWERED THEM, THE FATHER OF ME UNTIL

ἄρτι ἐργάζεται, κἀγὼ ἐργάζομαι· **5.18** διὰ τοῦτο
NOW IS WORKING, AND I AM WORKING. BECAUSE OF THIS

οὖν μᾶλλον ἐζήτουν αὐτὸν οἱ Ἰουδαῖοι
THEREFORE ⁴[ALL THE] MORE ³WERE SEEKING ⁶HIM ¹THE ²JEWS

ἀποκτεῖναι, ὅτι οὐ μόνον ἔλυεν τὸ σάββατον,
⁵TO KILL, BECAUSE NOT ONLY WAS HE BREAKING THE SABBATH,

ἀλλὰ καὶ πατέρα ἴδιον ἔλεγεν τὸν θεὸν ἴσον
BUT ALSO [HIS] OWN~FATHER HE WAS SAYING THE [VERY] GOD [TO BE] EQUAL

ἑαυτὸν ποιῶν τῷ θεῷ.
HIMSELF MAKING TO THE [VERY] GOD.

5.19 Ἀπεκρίνατο οὖν ὁ Ἰησοῦς καὶ ἔλεγεν
ANSWERED THEREFORE - JESUS AND WAS SAYING

αὐτοῖς, Ἀμὴν ἀμὴν λέγω ὑμῖν, οὐ δύναται ὁ υἱὸς
TO THEM, TRULY, TRULY I SAY TO YOU°, IS NOT ABLE THE SON

ποιεῖν ἀφ᾽ ἑαυτοῦ οὐδὲν ἐὰν μή τι βλέπῃ τὸν
TO DO FROM HIMSELF ANYTHING EXCEPT WHAT HE SEES THE

πατέρα ποιοῦντα· ἃ γὰρ ἂν ἐκεῖνος ποιῇ, ταῦτα
FATHER DOING. FOR~WHAT THINGS THAT ONE IS DOING THESE THINGS

καὶ ὁ υἱὸς ὁμοίως ποιεῖ. **5.20** ὁ γὰρ πατὴρ φιλεῖ
ALSO THE SON LIKEWISE IS DOING. FOR~THE FATHER IS FOND OF

τὸν υἱὸν καὶ πάντα δείκνυσιν αὐτῷ ἃ αὐτὸς ποιεῖ,
THE SON AND ALL THINGS HE SHOWS TO HIM WHICH HE DOES,

καὶ μείζονα τούτων δείξει αὐτῷ ἔργα, ἵνα ὑμεῖς
AND ¹GREATER ³THAN THESE ⁴HE WILL SHOW ⁵HIM ²WORKS, THAT YOU°

θαυμάζητε. **5.21** ὥσπερ γὰρ ὁ πατὴρ ἐγείρει τοὺς
MAY MARVEL. FOR~JUST AS THE FATHER RAISES THE

νεκροὺς καὶ ζῳοποιεῖ, οὕτως καὶ ὁ υἱὸς οὓς θέλει
DEAD AND MAKES [THEM] ALIVE, SO ALSO THE SON WHOM HE WILLS

ζῳοποιεῖ. **5.22** οὐδὲ γὰρ ὁ πατὴρ κρίνει οὐδένα, ἀλλὰ
MAKES ALIVE. FOR~NOT EVEN THE FATHER JUDGES ANYONE, BUT

who it was, for Jesus had disappeared in/ the crowd that was there. ¹⁴Later Jesus found him in the temple and said to him, "See, you have been made well! Do not sin any more, so that nothing worse happens to you." ¹⁵The man went away and told the Jews that it was Jesus who had made him well. ¹⁶Therefore the Jews started persecuting Jesus, because he was doing such things on the sabbath. ¹⁷But Jesus answered them, "My Father is still working, and I also am working." ¹⁸For this reason the Jews were seeking all the more to kill him, because he was not only breaking the sabbath, but was also calling God his own Father, thereby making himself equal to God.

19 Jesus said to them, "Very truly, I tell you, the Son can do nothing on his own, but only what he sees the Father doing; for whatever the Father^k does, the Son does likewise. ²⁰The Father loves the Son and shows him all that he himself is doing; and he will show him greater works than these, so that you will be astonished. ²¹Indeed, just as the Father raises the dead and gives them life, so also the Son gives life to whomever he wishes. ²²The Father judges no one but

ʲ Or had left because of
ᵏ Gk that one

has given all judgment to the Son, [23] so that all may honor the Son just as they honor the Father. Anyone who does not honor the Son does not honor the Father who sent him. [24] Very truly, I tell you, anyone who hears my word and believes him who sent me has eternal life, and does not come under judgment, but has passed from death to life.

[25] "Very truly, I tell you, the hour is coming, and is now here, when the dead will hear the voice of the Son of God, and those who hear will live. [26] For just as the Father has life in himself, so he has granted the Son also to have life in himself; [27] and he has given him authority to execute judgment, because he is the Son of Man. [28] Do not be astonished at this; for the hour is coming when all who are in their graves will hear his voice [29] and will come out—those who have done good, to the resurrection of life, and those who have done evil, to the resurrection of condemnation.

[30] "I can do nothing on my own. As I hear, I judge; and my judgment is just, because I seek to do not my own will but the will of him who sent me.

[31] "If I testify about myself, my testimony

τὴν	κρίσιν	πᾶσαν	δέδωκεν	τῷ	υἱῷ,	**5.23** ἵνα πάντες
-	ALL~JUDGMENT		HE HAS GIVEN	TO THE	SON,	THAT ALL MEN

τιμῶσι τὸν υἱὸν καθὼς τιμῶσι τὸν πατέρα. ὁ μὴ
MAY HONOR THE SON AS THEY HONOR THE FATHER. THE ONE NOT

τιμῶν τὸν υἱὸν οὐ τιμᾷ τὸν πατέρα τὸν πέμψαντα
HONORING THE SON DOES NOT HONOR THE FATHER, THE ONE HAVING SENT

αὐτόν. **5.24** Ἀμὴν ἀμὴν λέγω ὑμῖν ὅτι ὁ τὸν
HIM. TRULY, TRULY I SAY TO YOU° THAT THE ONE THE

λόγον μου ἀκούων καὶ πιστεύων τῷ πέμψαντί με
WORD OF ME HEARING AND BELIEVING THE ONE HAVING SENT ME

ἔχει ζωὴν αἰώνιον καὶ εἰς κρίσιν οὐκ ἔρχεται, ἀλλὰ
HAS LIFE ETERNAL AND INTO JUDGMENT HE DOES NOT COME, BUT

μεταβέβηκεν ἐκ τοῦ θανάτου εἰς τὴν ζωήν.
HAS BEEN TRANSFERRED OUT OF - DEATH INTO - LIFE.

5.25 ἀμὴν ἀμὴν λέγω ὑμῖν ὅτι ἔρχεται ὥρα καὶ νῦν
TRULY, TRULY I SAY TO YOU° THAT IS COMING AN HOUR AND NOW

ἔστιν ὅτε οἱ νεκροὶ ἀκούσουσιν τῆς φωνῆς τοῦ υἱοῦ
IS WHEN THE DEAD WILL HEAR THE VOICE OF THE SON

τοῦ θεοῦ καὶ οἱ ἀκούσαντες ζήσουσιν.
- OF GOD AND THE ONES HAVING HEARD WILL LIVE.

5.26 ὥσπερ γὰρ ὁ πατὴρ ἔχει ζωὴν ἐν ἑαυτῷ, οὕτως
FOR~JUST AS THE FATHER HAS LIFE IN HIMSELF, SO

καὶ τῷ υἱῷ ἔδωκεν ζωὴν ἔχειν ἐν ἑαυτῷ. **5.27** καὶ
ALSO THE SON HE GAVE LIFE TO HAVE IN HIMSELF. AND

ἐξουσίαν ἔδωκεν αὐτῷ κρίσιν ποιεῖν, ὅτι υἱὸς
AUTHORITY HE GAVE TO HIM TO MAKE~JUDGMENT, BECAUSE [THE] SON

ἀνθρώπου ἐστίν. **5.28** μὴ θαυμάζετε τοῦτο, ὅτι ἔρχεται
OF MAN HE IS. DO NOT MARVEL [AT] THIS, FOR IS COMING

ὥρα ἐν ᾗ πάντες οἱ ἐν τοῖς μνημείοις
AN HOUR IN WHICH ALL THE ONES IN THE GRAVES

ἀκούσουσιν τῆς φωνῆς αὐτοῦ **5.29** καὶ ἐκπορεύσονται,
WILL HEAR THE VOICE OF HIM AND WILL COME OUT,

οἱ τὰ ἀγαθὰ ποιήσαντες εἰς ἀνάστασιν ζωῆς,
THE ONES THE GOOD THINGS HAVING DONE TO A RESURRECTION OF LIFE,

οἱ δὲ τὰ φαῦλα πράξαντες εἰς ἀνάστασιν
BUT~THE ONES THE EVIL THINGS HAVING PRACTISED TO A RESURRECTION

κρίσεως.
OF JUDGMENT.

5.30 Οὐ δύναμαι ἐγὼ ποιεῖν ἀπ' ἐμαυτοῦ οὐδέν· καθὼς
I~AM NOT ABLE TO DO FROM MYSELF ANYTHING. AS

ἀκούω κρίνω, καὶ ἡ κρίσις ἡ ἐμὴ δικαία ἐστίν,
I HEAR I JUDGE, AND THE JUDGMENT - OF ME JUST IS,

ὅτι οὐ ζητῶ τὸ θέλημα τὸ ἐμὸν ἀλλὰ τὸ θέλημα
BECAUSE I DO NOT SEEK THE WILL - OF ME BUT THE WILL

τοῦ πέμψαντός με.
OF THE ONE HAVING SENT ME.

5.31 Ἐὰν ἐγὼ μαρτυρῶ περὶ ἐμαυτοῦ, ἡ μαρτυρία
IF I TESTIFY ABOUT MYSELF, THE TESTIMONY

μου οὐκ ἔστιν ἀληθής· **5.32** ἄλλος ἐστὶν ὁ   μαρτυρῶν
OF ME IS NOT TRUE.   ANOTHER IS   THE ONE TESTIFYING

περὶ ἐμοῦ, καὶ οἶδα ὅτι ἀληθής ἐστιν ἡ μαρτυρία
ABOUT ME, AND I KNOW THAT TRUE IS THE TESTIMONY

ἣν   μαρτυρεῖ περὶ ἐμοῦ. **5.33** ὑμεῖς ἀπεστάλκατε
WHICH HE TESTIFIES ABOUT ME.   YOU°   HAVE SENT

πρὸς Ἰωάννην, καὶ μεμαρτύρηκεν τῇ   ἀληθείᾳ·
TO   JOHN,   AND HE HAS TESTIFIED TO THE TRUTH.

5.34 ἐγὼ δὲ οὐ παρὰ ἀνθρώπου τὴν μαρτυρίαν λαμβάνω,
BUT~I NOT FROM MAN   THE TESTIMONY   RECEIVE,

ἀλλὰ ταῦτα   λέγω ἵνα ὑμεῖς σωθῆτε. **5.35** ἐκεῖνος
BUT THESE THINGS I SAY THAT YOU° MAY BE SAVED.   THAT ONE

ἦν ὁ λύχνος ὁ καιόμενος καὶ φαίνων, ὑμεῖς δὲ
WAS THE LAMP - BURNING AND SHINING, AND~YOU°

ἠθελήσατε ἀγαλλιαθῆναι πρὸς ὥραν ἐν τῷ φωτὶ αὐτοῦ.
CHOSE   TO EXULT   FOR A TIME IN THE LIGHT OF HIM.

5.36 ἐγὼ δὲ ἔχω τὴν μαρτυρίαν μείζω   τοῦ Ἰωάννου·
BUT~I HAVE - TESTIMONY GREATER [THAN] - JOHN'S.

τὰ γὰρ ἔργα ἃ   δέδωκέν μοι ὁ πατὴρ ἵνα τελειώσω
FOR~THE WORKS WHICH HAS GIVEN TO ME THE FATHER THAT I SHOULD FINISH

αὐτά, αὐτὰ τὰ ἔργα ἃ   ποιῶ μαρτυρεῖ περὶ ἐμοῦ ὅτι
THEM, THESE - WORKS WHICH I DO TESTIFY ABOUT ME THAT

ὁ πατήρ με ἀπέσταλκεν. **5.37** καὶ ὁ πέμψας με
THE FATHER HAS SENT~ME.   AND ¹THE ³HAVING SENT ⁴ME

πατὴρ ἐκεῖνος μεμαρτύρηκεν περὶ ἐμοῦ. οὔτε φωνὴν
²FATHER, THAT ONE HAS TESTIFIED ABOUT ME. NEITHER [THE] VOICE

αὐτοῦ πώποτε ἀκηκόατε οὔτε εἶδος αὐτοῦ ἑωράκατε,
OF HIM EVER HAVE YOU° HEARD NOR [THE] VISAGE OF HIM HAVE YOU° SEEN,

5.38 καὶ τὸν λόγον αὐτοῦ οὐκ ἔχετε ἐν ὑμῖν μένοντα,
AND THE WORD OF HIM YOU° DO NOT HAVE IN YOU° ABIDING,

ὅτι ὃν   ἀπέστειλεν ἐκεῖνος, τούτῳ ὑμεῖς
BECAUSE [HE] WHOM THAT ONE~SENT, THIS ONE YOU°

οὐ πιστεύετε. **5.39** ἐραυνᾶτε τὰς γραφάς, ὅτι ὑμεῖς
DO NOT BELIEVE.   YOU° SEARCH THE SCRIPTURES, BECAUSE YOU°

δοκεῖτε ἐν αὐταῖς ζωὴν αἰώνιον ἔχειν· καὶ ἐκεῖναί
THINK   IN THEM   LIFE ETERNAL TO HAVE; AND THOSE

εἰσιν αἱ   μαρτυροῦσαι περὶ ἐμοῦ· **5.40** καὶ
ARE THE ONES TESTIFYING ABOUT ME.   AND

οὐ θέλετε ἐλθεῖν πρός με ἵνα ζωὴν ἔχητε.
YOU° DO NOT WANT TO COME TO ME THAT YOU° MAY HAVE~LIFE.

5.41 Δόξαν παρὰ ἀνθρώπων οὐ λαμβάνω, **5.42** ἀλλὰ
GLORY FROM MEN   I DO NOT RECEIVE,   BUT

ἔγνωκα ὑμᾶς ὅτι τὴν ἀγάπην τοῦ θεοῦ οὐκ ἔχετε ἐν
I HAVE KNOWN YOU° THAT THE LOVE - OF GOD YOU° DO NOT HAVE IN

ἑαυτοῖς. **5.43** ἐγὼ ἐλήλυθα ἐν τῷ ὀνόματι τοῦ πατρός
YOURSELVES.   I HAVE COME IN THE NAME   OF THE FATHER

μου, καὶ οὐ λαμβάνετέ με· ἐὰν ἄλλος ἔλθῃ ἐν τῷ
OF ME, AND YOU° DO NOT RECEIVE ME. IF ANOTHER COMES IN -

is not true. ³²There is another who testifies on my behalf, and I know that his testimony to me is true. ³³You sent messengers to John, and he testified to the truth. ³⁴Not that I accept such human testimony, but I say these things so that you may be saved. ³⁵He was a burning and shining lamp, and you were willing to rejoice for a while in his light. ³⁶But I have a testimony greater than John's. The works that the Father has given me to complete, the very works that I am doing, testify on my behalf that the Father has sent me. ³⁷And the Father who sent me has himself testified on my behalf. You have never heard his voice or seen his form, ³⁸and you do not have his word abiding in you, because you do not believe him whom he has sent.

39 "You search the scriptures because you think that in them you have eternal life; and it is they that testify on my behalf. ⁴⁰Yet you refuse to come to me to have life. ⁴¹I do not accept glory from human beings. ⁴²But I know that you do not have the love of God in*l* you. ⁴³I have come in my Father's name, and you do not accept me; if another comes in

l Or *among*

his own name, you will accept him. 44How can you believe when you accept glory from one another and do not seek the glory that comes from the one who alone is God? 45Do not think that I will accuse you before the Father; your accuser is Moses, on whom you have set your hope. 46If you believed Moses, you would believe me, for he wrote about me. 47But if you do not believe what he wrote, how will you believe what I say?"

ὀνόματι τῷ ἰδίῳ, ἐκεῖνον λήμψεσθε. **5.44** πῶς
³NAME   ¹HIS   ²OWN,   THAT ONE   YOU° WILL RECEIVE.   HOW

δύνασθε ὑμεῖς πιστεῦσαι δόξαν παρὰ ἀλλήλων
ARE YOU° ABLE   TO BELIEVE,   GLORY   FROM   ONE ANOTHER

λαμβάνοντες, καὶ τὴν δόξαν τὴν παρὰ ⌐τοῦ μόνου
RECEIVING,   AND   THE   GLORY   -   FROM   THE   ONLY

θεοῦ⌐ οὐ ζητεῖτε; **5.45** μὴ δοκεῖτε ὅτι ἐγὼ κατηγορήσω
GOD   YOU° DO NOT SEEK?   DO NOT THINK   THAT   I   WILL ACCUSE

ὑμῶν πρὸς τὸν πατέρα· ἔστιν ὁ κατηγορῶν ὑμῶν
YOU°   TO   THE   FATHER;   THERE IS ONE   ACCUSING   YOU°,

Μωϋσῆς, εἰς ὃν ὑμεῖς ἠλπίκατε. **5.46** εἰ γὰρ
MOSES,   IN   WHOM   YOU°   HAVE HOPED.   FOR~IF

ἐπιστεύετε Μωϋσεῖ, ἐπιστεύετε ἂν ἐμοί·
YOU° WERE BELIEVING MOSES,   YOU° WOULD HAVE BELIEVED   ME;

περὶ γὰρ ἐμοῦ ἐκεῖνος ἔγραψεν. **5.47** εἰ δὲ τοῖς
FOR~CONCERNING ME   THAT ONE   WROTE.   BUT~IF   ¹THE

ἐκείνου γράμμασιν οὐ πιστεύετε, πῶς τοῖς ἐμοῖς
³OF THAT ONE   ²WRITINGS   YOU° DO NOT BELIEVE,   HOW   -   MY

ῥήμασιν πιστεύσετε;
WORDS   WILL YOU° BELIEVE?

5:44 text: all.   var. του μονου (the only One): ASVmg NIVmg NJBmg.

CHAPTER 6

After this Jesus went to the other side of the Sea of Galilee, also called the Sea of Tiberias.[m] 2A large crowd kept following him, because they saw the signs that he was doing for the sick. 3Jesus went up the mountain and sat down there with his disciples. 4Now the Passover, the festival of the Jews, was near. 5When he looked up and saw a large crowd coming toward him, Jesus said to Philip, "Where are we to buy bread for these people to eat?" 6He said this to test him, for he himself knew what he was going to do. 7Philip answered him, "Six months' wages[n]

[m] Gk of Galilee of Tiberias
[n] Gk Two hundred denarii; the denarius was the usual day's wage for a laborer

6.1 Μετὰ ταῦτα ἀπῆλθεν ὁ Ἰησοῦς πέραν τῆς
AFTER   THESE THINGS   DEPARTED   -   JESUS   BEYOND   THE

θαλάσσης τῆς Γαλιλαίας τῆς Τιβεριάδος.
SEA   -   OF GALILEE,   -   OF TIBERIAS.

6.2 ἠκολούθει δὲ αὐτῷ ὄχλος πολύς, ὅτι ἐθεώρουν
AND~WERE FOLLOWING HIM   A GREAT~CROWD,   BECAUSE   THEY WERE SEEING

τὰ σημεῖα ἃ ἐποίει ἐπὶ τῶν ἀσθενούντων.
THE   SIGNS   WHICH   HE WAS DOING   ON   THE ONES   BEING ILL.

6.3 ἀνῆλθεν δὲ εἰς τὸ ὄρος Ἰησοῦς καὶ ἐκεῖ ἐκάθητο
AND~WENT UP   TO   THE MOUNTAIN   JESUS   AND   THERE   HE WAS SITTING

μετὰ τῶν μαθητῶν αὐτοῦ. **6.4** ἦν δὲ ἐγγὺς τὸ πάσχα,
WITH   THE   DISCIPLES   OF HIM.   AND~WAS NEAR   THE   PASSOVER,

ἡ ἑορτὴ τῶν Ἰουδαίων. **6.5** ἐπάρας οὖν τοὺς
THE   FEAST   OF THE   JEWS.   THEREFORE~HAVING LIFTED UP   THE(HIS)

ὀφθαλμοὺς ὁ Ἰησοῦς καὶ θεασάμενος ὅτι πολὺς ὄχλος
EYES   -   JESUS   AND   HAVING SEEN   THAT   A GREAT   CROWD

ἔρχεται πρὸς αὐτὸν λέγει πρὸς Φίλιππον, Πόθεν
IS COMING   TO   HIM   HE SAYS   TO   PHILIP,   FROM WHERE

ἀγοράσωμεν ἄρτους ἵνα φάγωσιν οὗτοι; **6.6** τοῦτο δὲ
MAY WE BUY   BREAD   THAT   THESE ONES~MAY EAT?   BUT~THIS

ἔλεγεν πειράζων αὐτόν· αὐτὸς γὰρ ᾔδει τί ἔμελλεν
HE WAS SAYING   TESTING   HIM,   FOR~HE HIMSELF   KNEW   WHAT   HE WAS ABOUT

ποιεῖν. **6.7** ἀπεκρίθη αὐτῷ [ὁ] Φίλιππος, Διακοσίων
TO DO.   ANSWERED   HIM   -   PHILIP,   ²OF TWO HUNDRED

δηναρίων ἄρτοι οὐκ ἀρκοῦσιν αὐτοῖς ἵνα ἕκαστος
3DENARII 1LOAVES ARE NOT ENOUGH FOR THEM THAT EACH ONE

βραχύ [τι]   λάβῃ. **6.8** λέγει αὐτῷ εἰς ἐκ τῶν
A LITTLE SOMETHING MAY TAKE.   SAYS TO HIM ONE OF THE

μαθητῶν αὐτοῦ, Ἀνδρέας ὁ ἀδελφὸς Σίμωνος
DISCIPLES OF HIM, ANDREW THE BROTHER OF SIMON

Πέτρου, **6.9** Ἔστιν παιδάριον ὧδε ὃς ἔχει πέντε
PETER,   THERE IS A YOUNG BOY HERE WHO HAS FIVE

ἄρτους κριθίνους καὶ δύο ὀψάρια· ἀλλὰ ταῦτα τί
BARLEY~LOAVES AND TWO FISH; BUT 3THESE 1WHAT

ἐστιν εἰς τοσούτους; **6.10** εἶπεν ὁ Ἰησοῦς, Ποιήσατε
2ARE TO SO MANY?   SAID - JESUS, MAKE

τοὺς ἀνθρώπους ἀναπεσεῖν. ἦν δὲ χόρτος πολὺς ἐν
THE MEN TO RECLINE. NOW~THERE WAS MUCH~GRASS IN

τῷ τόπῳ. ἀνέπεσαν οὖν οἱ ἄνδρες τὸν ἀριθμὸν
THE PLACE. RECLINED THEREFORE THE MEN, THE NUMBER

ὡς πεντακισχίλιοι. **6.11** ἔλαβεν οὖν τοὺς ἄρτους ὁ
ABOUT FIVE THOUSAND.   THEREFORE~TOOK THE LOAVES -

Ἰησοῦς καὶ εὐχαριστήσας διέδωκεν τοῖς
JESUS AND HAVING GIVEN THANKS HE DISTRIBUTED TO THE ONES

ἀνακειμένοις ὁμοίως καὶ ἐκ τῶν ὀψαρίων ὅσον
RECLINING, LIKEWISE ALSO OF THE FISH AS MUCH AS

ἤθελον. **6.12** ὡς δὲ ἐνεπλήσθησαν, λέγει τοῖς
THEY WERE WANTING. NOW~WHEN THEY WERE FILLED, HE TELLS THE

μαθηταῖς αὐτοῦ, Συναγάγετε τὰ περισσεύσαντα
DISCIPLES OF HIM, GATHER THE LEFTOVER

κλάσματα, ἵνα μή τι ἀπόληται. **6.13** συνήγαγον οὖν
FRAGMENTS, THAT NOTHING MAY BE LOST.   THEY GATHERED THEREFORE

καὶ ἐγέμισαν δώδεκα κοφίνους κλασμάτων ἐκ τῶν
AND THEY FILLED TWELVE BASKETS OF FRAGMENTS FROM THE

πέντε ἄρτων τῶν κριθίνων ἃ ἐπερίσσευσαν τοῖς
FIVE LOAVES - OF BARLEY WHICH WERE LEFTOVER BY THE ONES

βεβρωκόσιν. **6.14** Οἱ οὖν ἄνθρωποι ἰδόντες ⌐ὃ
HAVING EATEN.   THEREFORE~THE MEN HAVING SEEN WHAT

ἐποίησεν σημεῖον⌐ ἔλεγον ὅτι Οὗτός ἐστιν ἀληθῶς ὁ
SIGN~HE DID WERE SAYING, - THIS ONE IS TRULY THE

προφήτης ὁ ἐρχόμενος εἰς τὸν κόσμον. **6.15** Ἰησοῦς
PROPHET, THE ONE COMING INTO THE WORLD.   JESUS

οὖν γνοὺς ὅτι μέλλουσιν ἔρχεσθαι καὶ ἁρπάζειν
THEREFORE HAVING KNOWN THAT THEY ARE ABOUT TO COME AND TO SEIZE

αὐτὸν ἵνα ποιήσωσιν βασιλέα, ἀνεχώρησεν πάλιν
HIM THAT THEY MIGHT MAKE [HIM] A KING, DEPARTED AGAIN

εἰς τὸ ὄρος αὐτὸς μόνος.
TO THE MOUNTAIN HIMSELF ALONE.

6.16 Ὡς δὲ ὀψία ἐγένετο κατέβησαν οἱ μαθηταὶ
AND~AS EVENING CAME WENT DOWN THE DISCIPLES

would not buy enough bread for each of them to get a little." [8]One of his disciples, Andrew, Simon Peter's brother, said to him, [9]"There is a boy here who has five barley loaves and two fish. But what are they among so many people?" [10]Jesus said, "Make the people sit down." Now there was a great deal of grass in the place; so they[o] sat down, about five thousand in all. [11]Then Jesus took the loaves, and when he had given thanks, he distributed them to those who were seated; so also the fish, as much as they wanted. [12]When they were satisfied, he told his disciples, "Gather up the fragments left over, so that nothing may be lost." [13]So they gathered them up, and from the fragments of the five barley loaves, left by those who had eaten, they filled twelve baskets. [14]When the people saw the sign that he had done, they began to say, "This is indeed the prophet who is to come into the world."

15 When Jesus realized that they were about to come and take him by force to make him king, he withdrew again to the mountain by himself.

16 When evening came, his disciples went down

[o] Gk the men

6:14 text: ASV RSV NASB NJB NRSV. var. α εποιησεν σημεια (the signs which he did): ASVmg. var. ο εποιησεν σημειον ο Ιησους (the sign which Jesus did): KJV NIV NEB TEV.

to the sea, [17]got into a boat, and started across the sea to Capernaum. It was now dark, and Jesus had not yet come to them. [18]The sea became rough because a strong wind was blowing. [19]When they had rowed about three or four miles,[p] they saw Jesus walking on the sea and coming near the boat, and they were terrified. [20]But he said to them, "It is I;[q] do not be afraid." [21]Then they wanted to take him into the boat, and immediately the boat reached the land toward which they were going.

[22] The next day the crowd that had stayed on the other side of the sea saw that there had been only one boat there. They also saw that Jesus had not got into the boat with his disciples, but that his disciples had gone away alone. [23]Then some boats from Tiberias came near the place where they had eaten the bread after the Lord had given thanks.[r] [24]So when the crowd saw that neither Jesus nor his disciples were there, they themselves got into the boats and went to Capernaum looking for Jesus.

[25] When they found him on the other side of the sea, they said to him, "Rabbi, when did you come here?" [26]Jesus answered them,

[p] Gk *about twenty-five or thirty stadia*

[q] Gk *I am*

[r] Other ancient authorities lack *after the Lord had given thanks*

αὐτοῦ ἐπὶ τὴν θάλασσαν **6.17** καὶ ἐμβάντες εἰς
OF HIM TO THE SEA, AND HAVING EMBARKED INTO

πλοῖον ἤρχοντο πέραν τῆς θαλάσσης εἰς
A BOAT THEY WERE GOING ACROSS THE SEA TO

Καφαρναούμ. καὶ σκοτία ἤδη ἐγεγόνει καὶ οὔπω
CAPERNAUM. AND DARKNESS ALREADY HAD COME AND NOT YET

ἐληλύθει πρὸς αὐτούς ὁ Ἰησοῦς, **6.18** ἥ τε θάλασσα
HAD COME TO THEM - JESUS. AND~THE SEA,

ἀνέμου μεγάλου πνέοντος διεγείρετο. **6.19** ἐληλακότες
[AS] A GREAT~WIND BLEW, WAS BEING ROUSED. HAVING ROWED

οὖν ὡς σταδίους εἴκοσι πέντε ἢ τριάκοντα
THEREFORE ABOUT [2]STADIA [1]TWENTY FIVE OR THIRTY

θεωροῦσιν τὸν Ἰησοῦν περιπατοῦντα ἐπὶ τῆς θαλάσσης
THEY SEE - JESUS WALKING ON THE SEA

καὶ ἐγγὺς τοῦ πλοίου γινόμενον, καὶ ἐφοβήθησαν.
AND NEAR THE BOAT COMING, AND THEY WERE AFRAID.

6.20 ὁ δὲ λέγει αὐτοῖς, Ἐγώ εἰμι· μὴ φοβεῖσθε.
BUT~HE SAYS TO THEM, I AM, DO NOT BE AFRAID.

6.21 ἤθελον οὖν λαβεῖν αὐτὸν εἰς τὸ πλοῖον,
THEY WERE WILLING THEREFORE TO TAKE HIM INTO THE BOAT,

καὶ εὐθέως ἐγένετο τὸ πλοῖον ἐπὶ τῆς γῆς εἰς ἣν
AND IMMEDIATELY CAME THE BOAT AT THE LAND TO WHICH

ὑπῆγον.
THEY WERE GOING.

6.22 Τῇ ἐπαύριον ὁ ὄχλος ὁ ἑστηκὼς πέραν τῆς
ON THE NEXT DAY THE CROWD - HAVING STOOD ACROSS THE

θαλάσσης εἶδον ὅτι πλοιάριον ἄλλο οὐκ ἦν ἐκεῖ εἰ μὴ
SEA SAW THAT ANOTHER~BOAT WAS NOT THERE EXCEPT

ἓν καὶ ὅτι οὐ συνεισῆλθεν τοῖς μαθηταῖς αὐτοῦ ὁ
ONE AND THAT DID NOT COME WITH THE DISCIPLES OF HIM -

Ἰησοῦς εἰς τὸ πλοῖον ἀλλὰ μόνοι οἱ μαθηταὶ αὐτοῦ
JESUS IN THE BOAT BUT ONLY THE DISCIPLES OF HIM

ἀπῆλθον· **6.23** ἄλλα ἦλθεν πλοιά[ρια] ἐκ Τιβεριάδος
DEPARTED. OTHER BOATS~CAME FROM TIBERIAS

ἐγγὺς τοῦ τόπου ὅπου ἔφαγον τὸν ἄρτον
NEAR THE PLACE WHERE THEY ATE THE BREAD

εὐχαριστήσαντος τοῦ κυρίου. **6.24** ὅτε οὖν εἶδεν ὁ
[AFTER] HAVING GIVEN THANKS THE LORD. WHEN THEREFORE SAW THE

ὄχλος ὅτι Ἰησοῦς οὐκ ἔστιν ἐκεῖ οὐδὲ οἱ μαθηταὶ
CROWD THAT JESUS IS NOT THERE NOR THE DISCIPLES

αὐτοῦ, ἐνέβησαν αὐτοὶ εἰς τὰ πλοιάρια καὶ ἦλθον εἰς
OF HIM, THEY~EMBARKED INTO THE BOATS AND CAME TO

Καφαρναοὺμ ζητοῦντες τὸν Ἰησοῦν. **6.25** καὶ εὑρόντες
CAPERNAUM SEEKING - JESUS. AND HAVING FOUND

αὐτὸν πέραν τῆς θαλάσσης εἶπον αὐτῷ, Ῥαββί, πότε
HIM ACROSS THE SEA THEY SAID TO HIM, RABBI, WHEN

ὧδε γέγονας; **6.26** ἀπεκρίθη αὐτοῖς ὁ Ἰησοῦς καὶ
DID YOU COME~HERE? ANSWERED THEM - JESUS AND

εἶπεν, Ἀμὴν ἀμὴν λέγω ὑμῖν, ζητεῖτέ   με οὐχ
SAID,   TRULY, TRULY I SAY TO YOU°, YOU° ARE SEEKING ME NOT

ὅτι εἴδετε σημεῖα, ἀλλ᾽ ὅτι ἐφάγετε ἐκ τῶν ἄρτων
BECAUSE YOU° SAW SIGNS,   BUT BECAUSE YOU° ATE OF THE LOAVES

καὶ ἐχορτάσθητε. 6.27 ἐργάζεσθε μὴ τὴν βρῶσιν τὴν
AND WERE SATISFIED.   DO NOT WORK [FOR]   THE FOOD

ἀπολλυμένην ἀλλὰ τὴν βρῶσιν τὴν μένουσαν εἰς ζωὴν
PERISHING   BUT   THE FOOD   -   REMAINING TO LIFE

αἰώνιον, ἣν ὁ υἱὸς τοῦ ἀνθρώπου ὑμῖν δώσει· τοῦτον
ETERNAL, WHICH THE SON - OF MAN   WILL GIVE~TO YOU°. ⁶THIS ONE

γὰρ ὁ πατὴρ ἐσφράγισεν ὁ θεός. 6.28 εἶπον οὖν
¹FOR ³THE ⁴FATHER ⁵CERTIFIED - ²GOD.   THEY SAID THEREFORE

πρὸς αὐτόν, Τί ποιῶμεν ἵνα ἐργαζώμεθα τὰ ἔργα τοῦ
TO   HIM,   WHAT MAY WE DO THAT WE MAY WORK THE WORKS -

θεοῦ; 6.29 ἀπεκρίθη [ὁ] Ἰησοῦς καὶ εἶπεν αὐτοῖς,
OF GOD?   ANSWERED - JESUS   AND SAID TO THEM,

Τοῦτό ἐστιν τὸ ἔργον τοῦ θεοῦ, ἵνα πιστεύητε εἰς
THIS   IS   THE WORK - OF GOD, THAT YOU° MAY BELIEVE IN

ὃν ἀπέστειλεν ἐκεῖνος. 6.30 εἶπον οὖν αὐτῷ,
[HIM] WHOM THAT ONE~SENT.   THEY SAID THEREFORE TO HIM,

Τί οὖν ποιεῖς σὺ σημεῖον, ἵνα ἴδωμεν καὶ
¹WHAT ³THEN ⁴DO YOU PERFORM ²SIGN THAT WE MAY SEE AND

πιστεύσωμέν σοι; τί ἐργάζῃ;   6.31 οἱ πατέρες
MAY BELIEVE YOU? WHAT DO YOU PERFORM?   THE FATHERS

ἡμῶν τὸ μάννα ἔφαγον ἐν τῇ ἐρήμῳ, καθὼς
OF US THE MANNA ATE IN THE WILDERNESS, AS

ἐστιν γεγραμμένον, Ἄρτον ἐκ τοῦ οὐρανοῦ ἔδωκεν
IT HAS BEEN WRITTEN, BREAD FROM - HEAVEN HE GAVE

αὐτοῖς φαγεῖν. 6.32 εἶπεν οὖν αὐτοῖς ὁ Ἰησοῦς,
THEM TO EAT.   SAID THEREFORE TO THEM - JESUS,

Ἀμὴν ἀμὴν λέγω ὑμῖν, οὐ Μωϋσῆς δέδωκεν ὑμῖν τὸν
TRULY, TRULY I SAY TO YOU°, NOT MOSES HAS GIVEN YOU° THE

ἄρτον ἐκ τοῦ οὐρανοῦ, ἀλλ᾽ ὁ πατήρ μου δίδωσιν
BREAD OUT OF - HEAVEN, BUT THE FATHER OF ME GIVES

ὑμῖν τὸν ἄρτον ἐκ τοῦ οὐρανοῦ τὸν ἀληθινόν·
YOU° - ³BREAD ⁴OUT OF - ⁵HEAVEN ¹THE ²TRUE.

6.33 ὁ γὰρ ἄρτος τοῦ θεοῦ ἐστιν ὁ   καταβαίνων ἐκ
FOR~THE BREAD - OF GOD IS THE ONE COMING DOWN OUT OF

τοῦ οὐρανοῦ καὶ ζωὴν διδοὺς τῷ κόσμῳ.
-   HEAVEN AND GIVING~LIFE TO THE WORLD.

6.34 Εἶπον οὖν πρὸς αὐτόν, Κύριε, πάντοτε δὸς
THEY SAID THEREFORE TO HIM, LORD, ALWAYS GIVE

ἡμῖν τὸν ἄρτον τοῦτον. 6.35 εἶπεν αὐτοῖς ὁ Ἰησοῦς,
US   -   THIS~BREAD.   SAID TO THEM - JESUS,

Ἐγώ εἰμι ὁ ἄρτος τῆς ζωῆς· ὁ ἐρχόμενος πρὸς
I   AM THE BREAD - OF LIFE; THE ONE COMING TO

6:31 Ps. 78:24

"Very truly, I tell you, you are looking for me, not because you saw signs, but because you ate your fill of the loaves. ²⁷Do not work for the food that perishes, but for the food that endures for eternal life, which the Son of Man will give you. For it is on him that God the Father has set his seal." ²⁸Then they said to him, "What must we do to perform the works of God?" ²⁹Jesus answered them, "This is the work of God, that you believe in him whom he has sent." ³⁰So they said to him, "What sign are you going to give us then, so that we may see it and believe you? What work are you performing? ³¹Our ancestors ate the manna in the wilderness; as it is written, 'He gave them bread from heaven to eat.'" ³²Then Jesus said to them, "Very truly, I tell you, it was not Moses who gave you the bread from heaven, but it is my Father who gives you the true bread from heaven. ³³For the bread of God is that which⁵ comes down from heaven and gives life to the world." ³⁴They said to him, "Sir, give us this bread always."

35 Jesus said to them, "I am the bread of life. Whoever comes to

⁵ Or *he who*

me will never be hungry, and whoever believes in me will never be thirsty. ³⁶But I said to you that you have seen me and yet do not believe. ³⁷Everything that the Father gives me will come to me, and anyone who comes to me I will never drive away; ³⁸for I have come down from heaven, not to do my own will, but the will of him who sent me. ³⁹And this is the will of him who sent me, that I should lose nothing of all that he has given me, but raise it up on the last day. ⁴⁰This is indeed the will of my Father, that all who see the Son and believe in him may have eternal life; and I will raise them up on the last day."

41 Then the Jews began to complain about him because he said, "I am the bread that came down from heaven." ⁴²They were saying, "Is not this Jesus, the son of Joseph, whose father and mother we know? How can he now say, 'I have come down from heaven'?" ⁴³Jesus answered them, "Do not complain among yourselves. ⁴⁴No one can come to me unless drawn by the Father who sent me; and I will raise that person up on the last day.

ἐμὲ οὐ μὴ πεινάσῃ, καὶ ὁ πιστεύων εἰς ἐμὲ
ME   NEVER HUNGERS,   AND   THE ONE BELIEVING IN   ME

οὐ μὴ διψήσει πώποτε. **6.36** ἀλλ᾽ εἶπον ὑμῖν ὅτι καὶ
WILL NEVER THIRST   AGAIN.   BUT   I TOLD YOU° THAT BOTH

ἑωράκατέ [με] καὶ οὐ πιστεύετε. **6.37** Πᾶν ὃ
YOU° HAVE SEEN ME   AND   YOU° DO NOT BELIEVE.   ALL WHICH

δίδωσίν μοι ὁ πατὴρ πρὸς ἐμὲ ἥξει, καὶ τὸν
GIVES   TO ME THE FATHER TO   ME WILL COME, AND THE ONE

ἐρχόμενον πρὸς ἐμὲ οὐ μὴ ἐκβάλω ἔξω, **6.38** ὅτι
COMING   TO   ME   I WILL NEVER THROW   OUT,   BECAUSE

καταβέβηκα ἀπὸ τοῦ οὐρανοῦ οὐχ ἵνα ποιῶ τὸ
I HAVE COME DOWN FROM -   HEAVEN   NOT THAT I MAY DO THE

θέλημα τὸ ἐμὸν ἀλλὰ τὸ θέλημα τοῦ πέμψαντός
WILL   -   OF ME BUT THE WILL OF THE ONE HAVING SENT

με. **6.39** τοῦτο δέ ἐστιν τὸ θέλημα τοῦ πέμψαντός
ME.   NOW~THIS   IS   THE   WILL   OF THE ONE HAVING SENT

με, ἵνα πᾶν ὃ δέδωκέν μοι μὴ ἀπολέσω ἐξ αὐτοῦ,
ME, THAT ALL WHICH HE HAS GIVEN ME I SHOULD NOT LOSE OF IT,

ἀλλὰ ἀναστήσω αὐτὸ [ἐν] τῇ ἐσχάτῃ ἡμέρᾳ.
BUT   I WILL RAISE UP IT   ON   THE LAST DAY.

6.40 τοῦτο γάρ ἐστιν τὸ θέλημα τοῦ πατρός μου, ἵνα
FOR~THIS   IS   THE WILL   OF THE FATHER OF ME, THAT

πᾶς ὁ θεωρῶν τὸν υἱὸν καὶ πιστεύων εἰς αὐτὸν
EVERYONE - SEEING THE SON AND BELIEVING IN HIM

ἔχῃ ζωὴν αἰώνιον, καὶ ἀναστήσω αὐτὸν ἐγὼ [ἐν] τῇ
MAY HAVE LIFE ETERNAL, AND ²WILL RAISE UP ³HIM ¹I ON THE

ἐσχάτῃ ἡμέρᾳ.
LAST   DAY.

6.41 Ἐγόγγυζον οὖν οἱ Ἰουδαῖοι περὶ αὐτοῦ ὅτι
WERE MURMURING THEREFORE THE JEWS ABOUT HIM BECAUSE

εἶπεν, Ἐγώ εἰμι ὁ ἄρτος ὁ καταβὰς ἐκ τοῦ
HE SAID, I   AM THE BREAD - HAVING COME DOWN OUT OF -

οὐρανοῦ, **6.42** καὶ ἔλεγον, Οὐχ οὗτός ἐστιν Ἰησοῦς
HEAVEN,   AND THEY WERE SAYING, ³NOT ²THIS MAN ¹IS ⁴JESUS

ὁ υἱὸς Ἰωσήφ, οὗ ἡμεῖς οἴδαμεν τὸν πατέρα καὶ
THE SON OF JOSEPH, OF WHOM WE KNOW   THE FATHER AND

τὴν μητέρα; πῶς νῦν λέγει ὅτι Ἐκ τοῦ οὐρανοῦ
THE MOTHER? HOW NOW DOES HE SAY, - OUT OF - HEAVEN

καταβέβηκα; **6.43** ἀπεκρίθη Ἰησοῦς καὶ εἶπεν αὐτοῖς,
I HAVE COME DOWN?   ANSWERED   JESUS   AND SAID TO THEM,

Μὴ γογγύζετε μετ᾽ ἀλλήλων. **6.44** οὐδεὶς δύναται ἐλθεῖν
DO NOT GRUMBLE   AMONG YOURSELVES.   NO ONE IS ABLE TO COME

πρός με ἐὰν μὴ ὁ πατὴρ ὁ πέμψας με ἑλκύσῃ
TO   ME UNLESS THE FATHER - HAVING SENT ME SHOULD DRAW

αὐτόν, κἀγὼ ἀναστήσω αὐτὸν ἐν τῇ ἐσχάτῃ ἡμέρᾳ.
HIM,   AND I WILL RAISE UP HIM   IN THE LAST   DAY.

6.45 ἔστιν γεγραμμένον ἐν τοῖς προφήταις, Καὶ
IT HAS BEEN WRITTEN   IN   THE   PROPHETS,   AND

ἔσονται πάντες διδακτοὶ θεοῦ· πᾶς ὁ ἀκούσας παρὰ
THEY SHALL BE ALL   TAUGHT ONES OF GOD. EVERYONE HAVING HEARD FROM

τοῦ πατρὸς καὶ μαθὼν ἔρχεται πρὸς ἐμέ. **6.46** οὐχ
THE FATHER   AND HAVING LEARNED COMES   TO   ME.   NOT

ὅτι τὸν πατέρα ἑώρακέν τις εἰ μὴ ὁ ὢν παρὰ
THAT ³THE ⁴FATHER ²HAS SEEN ¹ANYONE EXCEPT THE ONE BEING FROM

τοῦ θεοῦ, οὗτος ἑώρακεν τὸν πατέρα. **6.47** ἀμὴν ἀμὴν
- GOD, THIS ONE HAS SEEN THE FATHER.   TRULY, TRULY

λέγω ὑμῖν, ὁ πιστεύων ἔχει ζωὴν αἰώνιον. **6.48** ἐγώ
I SAY TO YOU°, THE ONE BELIEVING HAS LIFE ETERNAL.   I

εἰμι ὁ ἄρτος τῆς ζωῆς. **6.49** οἱ πατέρες ὑμῶν ἔφαγον
AM THE BREAD - OF LIFE.   THE FATHERS OF YOU° ATE

ἐν τῇ ἐρήμῳ τὸ μάννα καὶ ἀπέθανον· **6.50** οὗτός
IN THE WILDERNESS THE MANNA AND DIED.   THIS ONE

ἐστιν ὁ ἄρτος ὁ ἐκ τοῦ οὐρανοῦ καταβαίνων, ἵνα
IS   THE BREAD - OUT OF - HEAVEN   COMING DOWN,   THAT

τις ἐξ αὐτοῦ φάγῃ καὶ μὴ ἀποθάνῃ. **6.51** ἐγώ εἰμι
ANYONE OF IT   MAY EAT AND NOT DIE.   I   AM

ὁ ἄρτος ὁ ζῶν ὁ ἐκ τοῦ οὐρανοῦ καταβάς·
THE ²BREAD - ¹LIVING THE ONE OUT OF - HEAVEN HAVING COME DOWN.

ἐάν τις φάγῃ ἐκ τούτου τοῦ ἄρτου ζήσει εἰς τὸν
IF ANYONE EATS OF THIS - BREAD HE WILL LIVE INTO THE

αἰῶνα, καὶ ὁ ἄρτος δὲ ὃν ἐγὼ δώσω ἡ σάρξ
AGE, ²INDEED ³THE ⁴BREAD ¹AND ⁵WHICH ⁶I ⁷WILL GIVE ¹⁴THE ¹⁵FLESH

μού ἐστιν ὑπὲρ τῆς τοῦ κόσμου ζωῆς.
¹⁶OF ME ¹³IS ⁸FOR ⁹THE ¹¹OF THE ¹²WORLD ¹⁰LIFE.

6.52 Ἐμάχοντο οὖν πρὸς ἀλλήλους οἱ Ἰουδαῖοι
WERE ARGUING THEREFORE WITH ONE ANOTHER THE JEWS

λέγοντες, Πῶς δύναται οὗτος ἡμῖν δοῦναι τὴν σάρκα
SAYING,   HOW IS ABLE THIS MAN TO GIVE~US   THE FLESH

[αὐτοῦ] φαγεῖν; **6.53** εἶπεν οὖν αὐτοῖς ὁ Ἰησοῦς,
OF HIM TO EAT?   SAID THEREFORE TO THEM - JESUS,

Ἀμὴν ἀμὴν λέγω ὑμῖν, ἐὰν μὴ φάγητε τὴν σάρκα
TRULY, TRULY I SAY TO YOU°, UNLESS YOU° EAT THE FLESH

τοῦ υἱοῦ τοῦ ἀνθρώπου καὶ πίητε αὐτοῦ τὸ αἷμα,
OF THE SON - OF MAN AND DRINK HIS - BLOOD,

οὐκ ἔχετε ζωὴν ἐν ἑαυτοῖς. **6.54** ὁ τρώγων μου τὴν
YOU° DO NOT HAVE LIFE IN YOURSELVES. THE ONE FEEDING ON MY _ -

σάρκα καὶ πίνων μου τὸ αἷμα ἔχει ζωὴν αἰώνιόν,
FLESH AND DRINKING MY - BLOOD HAS LIFE ETERNAL,

κἀγὼ ἀναστήσω αὐτὸν τῇ ἐσχάτῃ ἡμέρα. **6.55** ἡ γὰρ
AND I WILL RAISE UP HIM ON THE LAST DAY.   FOR~THE

σάρξ μου ἀληθής ἐστιν βρῶσις, καὶ τὸ αἷμά μου
FLESH OF ME IS~TRUE   FOOD,   AND THE BLOOD OF ME

⁴⁵It is written in the prophets, 'And they shall all be taught by God.' Everyone who has heard and learned from the Father comes to me. ⁴⁶Not that anyone has seen the Father except the one who is from God; he has seen the Father. ⁴⁷Very truly, I tell you, whoever believes has eternal life. ⁴⁸I am the bread of life. ⁴⁹Your ancestors ate the manna in the wilderness, and they died. ⁵⁰This is the bread that comes down from heaven, so that one may eat of it and not die. ⁵¹I am the living bread that came down from heaven. Whoever eats of this bread will live forever; and the bread that I will give for the life of the world is my flesh."

52 The Jews then disputed among themselves, saying, "How can this man give us his flesh to eat?" ⁵³So Jesus said to them, "Very truly, I tell you, unless you eat the flesh of the Son of Man and drink his blood, you have no life in you. ⁵⁴Those who eat my flesh and drink my blood have eternal life, and I will raise them up on the last day; ⁵⁵for my flesh is true food and my

6:45 Isa. 54:13

blood is true drink. ⁵⁶Those who eat my flesh and drink my blood abide in me, and I in them. ⁵⁷Just as the living Father sent me, and I live because of the Father, so whoever eats me will live because of me. ⁵⁸This is the bread that came down from heaven, not like that which your ancestors ate, and they died. But the one who eats this bread will live forever." ⁵⁹He said these things while he was teaching in the synagogue at Capernaum.

60 When many of his disciples heard it, they said, "This teaching is difficult; who can accept it?" ⁶¹But Jesus, being aware that his disciples were complaining about it, said to them, "Does this offend you? ⁶²Then what if you were to see the Son of Man ascending to where he was before? ⁶³It is the spirit that gives life; the flesh is useless. The words that I have spoken to you are spirit and life. ⁶⁴But among you there are some who do not believe." For Jesus knew from the first who were the ones that did not believe, and who was the one that would betray him. ⁶⁵And he said, "For this reason I have told you that no one can come to me unless it is granted by the Father."

66 Because of this many of his disciples

ἀληθής ἐστιν πόσις. **6.56** ὁ τρώγων μου τὴν σάρκα
IS~TRUE DRINK. THE ONE FEEDING ON MY - FLESH

καὶ πίνων μου τὸ αἷμα ἐν ἐμοὶ μένει κἀγὼ ἐν αὐτῷ.
AND DRINKING MY - BLOOD IN ME ABIDES AND I IN HIM.

6.57 καθὼς ἀπέστειλέν με ὁ ζῶν πατὴρ κἀγὼ ζῶ
AS SENT ME THE LIVING FATHER AND I LIVE

διὰ τὸν πατέρα, καὶ ὁ τρώγων με κἀκεῖνος
BECAUSE OF THE FATHER, [SO] ALSO THE ONE FEEDING ON ME EVEN THAT ONE

ζήσει δι' ἐμέ. **6.58** οὗτός ἐστιν ὁ ἄρτος ὁ ἐξ
WILL LIVE BECAUSE OF ME. THIS ONE IS THE BREAD - OUT OF

οὐρανοῦ καταβάς, οὐ καθὼς ἔφαγον οἱ πατέρες καὶ
HEAVEN HAVING COME DOWN, NOT AS ATE THE FATHERS AND

ἀπέθανον· ὁ τρώγων τοῦτον τὸν ἄρτον ζήσει εἰς
DIED; THE ONE FEEDING ON THIS - BREAD WILL LIVE INTO

τὸν αἰῶνα. **6.59** Ταῦτα εἶπεν ἐν συναγωγῇ διδάσκων
THE AGE. THESE THINGS HE SAID IN A SYNAGOGUE [WHILE] TEACHING

ἐν Καφαρναούμ.
IN CAPERNAUM.

6.60 Πολλοὶ οὖν ἀκούσαντες ἐκ τῶν μαθητῶν αὐτοῦ
THEREFORE~MANY ⁵HAVING HEARD ¹OF ²THE ³DISCIPLES ⁴OF HIM

εἶπαν, Σκληρός ἐστιν ὁ λόγος οὗτος· τίς δύναται αὐτοῦ
SAID, HARD IS - THIS~WORD; WHO IS ABLE IT

ἀκούειν; **6.61** εἰδὼς δὲ ὁ Ἰησοῦς ἐν ἑαυτῷ ὅτι
TO HEAR? AND~HAVING KNOWN - JESUS IN HIMSELF THAT

γογγύζουσιν περὶ τούτου οἱ μαθηταὶ αὐτοῦ εἶπεν
ARE GRUMBLING ABOUT THIS THE DISCIPLES OF HIM HE SAID

αὐτοῖς, Τοῦτο ὑμᾶς σκανδαλίζει; **6.62** ἐὰν οὖν
TO THEM, [DOES] THIS CAUSE YOU° TO STUMBLE? [WHAT] IF THEREFORE

θεωρῆτε τὸν υἱὸν τοῦ ἀνθρώπου ἀναβαίνοντα ὅπου ἦν
YOU° SEE THE SON - OF MAN ASCENDING WHERE HE WAS

τὸ πρότερον; **6.63** τὸ πνεῦμά ἐστιν τὸ ζωοποιοῦν, ἡ
- AT FIRST? THE SPIRIT IS THE THING MAKING ALIVE; THE

σὰρξ οὐκ ὠφελεῖ οὐδέν· τὰ ῥήματα ἃ ἐγὼ λελάληκα
FLESH DOES NOT PROFIT ANYTHING. THE WORDS WHICH I HAVE SPOKEN

ὑμῖν πνεῦμά ἐστιν καὶ ζωή ἐστιν. **6.64** ἀλλ' εἰσὶν ἐξ
TO YOU° IS(ARE)~SPIRIT AND IS(ARE)~LIFE. BUT THERE ARE ²OF

ὑμῶν τινες οἳ οὐ πιστεύουσιν. ᾔδει γὰρ ἐξ ἀρχῆς
³YOU° ¹SOME WHO DO NOT BELIEVE. FOR~HAD KNOWN FROM [THE] BEGINNING

ὁ Ἰησοῦς τίνες εἰσὶν οἱ μὴ πιστεύοντες καὶ τίς
- JESUS WHO ARE THE ONES NOT BELIEVING AND WHO

ἐστιν ὁ παραδώσων αὐτόν. **6.65** καὶ ἔλεγεν, Διὰ
IS THE ONE BETRAYING HIM. AND HE WAS SAYING, BECAUSE

τοῦτο εἴρηκα ὑμῖν ὅτι οὐδεὶς δύναται ἐλθεῖν πρός με
OF THIS I HAVE TOLD YOU° THAT NO ONE IS ABLE TO COME TO ME

ἐὰν μὴ ᾖ δεδομένον αὐτῷ ἐκ τοῦ πατρός.
UNLESS IT HAS BEEN GIVEN TO HIM FROM THE FATHER.

6.66 Ἐκ τούτου πολλοὶ [ἐκ] τῶν μαθητῶν αὐτοῦ
FROM THIS [TIME] MANY OF THE DISCIPLES OF HIM

ἀπῆλθον εἰς τὰ ὀπίσω καὶ οὐκέτι μετ' αὐτοῦ
WENT   BACK   AND   NO LONGER WITH   HIM

περιεπάτουν. **6.67** εἶπεν οὖν   ὁ Ἰησοῦς τοῖς δώδεκα,
WERE WALKING.   SAID   THEREFORE - JESUS   TO THE TWELVE,

Μὴ   καὶ ὑμεῖς θέλετε ὑπάγειν; **6.68** ἀπεκρίθη
[SURELY] NOT ALSO YOU°   WANT TO GO AWAY?   ANSWERED

αὐτῷ Σίμων Πέτρος, Κύριε, πρὸς τίνα ἀπελευσόμεθα;
HIM SIMON PETER, LORD, TO WHOM WILL WE GO?

ῥήματα ζωῆς αἰωνίου ἔχεις, **6.69** καὶ ἡμεῖς
WORDS OF LIFE ETERNAL YOU HAVE,   AND   WE

πεπιστεύκαμεν καὶ ἐγνώκαμεν ὅτι σὺ εἶ ὁ ἅγιος τοῦ
HAVE BELIEVED   AND HAVE KNOWN THAT YOU ARE THE HOLY ONE -

θεοῦ. **6.70** ἀπεκρίθη αὐτοῖς ὁ Ἰησοῦς, Οὐκ ἐγὼ ὑμᾶς
OF GOD.   ANSWERED THEM   - JESUS, [DID] NOT I ²YOU°

τοὺς δώδεκα ἐξελεξάμην; καὶ ἐξ ὑμῶν εἷς
³THE ⁴TWELVE ¹CHOOSE?   AND OF YOU° ONE

διάβολός ἐστιν. **6.71** ἔλεγεν δὲ   τὸν Ἰούδαν
IS~A DEVIL.   NOW~HE WAS SPEAKING [OF] -   JUDAS

Σίμωνος Ἰσκαριώτου· οὗτος γὰρ ἔμελλεν παραδιδόναι
[SON] OF SIMON ISCARIOT.   FOR~THIS ONE WAS ABOUT   TO BETRAY

αὐτόν, εἷς ἐκ τῶν δώδεκα.
HIM,   ONE OF THE TWELVE.

turned back and no longer
went about with him. ⁶⁷So
Jesus asked the twelve, "Do
you also wish to go away?"
⁶⁸Simon Peter answered
him, "Lord, to whom can
we go? You have the words
of eternal life. ⁶⁹We have
come to believe and know
that you are the Holy One of
God."ᵗ ⁷⁰Jesus answered
them, "Did I not choose you,
the twelve? Yet one of you is
a devil." ⁷¹He was speaking
of Judas son of Simon
Iscariot,ᵘ for he, though one
of the twelve, was going to
betray him.

ᵗ Other ancient authorities read *the
  Christ, the Son of the living God*
ᵘ Other ancient authorities read *Judas
  Iscariot son of Simon;* others, *Judas
  son of Simon from Karyot* (Kerioth)

CHAPTER 7

7.1 Καὶ μετὰ ταῦτα   περιεπάτει ὁ Ἰησοῦς ἐν τῇ
     AND AFTER THESE THINGS WAS WALKING - JESUS   IN -

Γαλιλαίᾳ· οὐ γὰρ ἤθελεν ἐν τῇ Ἰουδαίᾳ περιπατεῖν,
GALILEE; FOR~HE WAS NOT WANTING IN - JUDEA   TO WALK,

ὅτι ἐζήτουν αὐτὸν οἱ Ἰουδαῖοι ἀποκτεῖναι.
BECAUSE WERE SEEKING HIM THE JEWS   TO KILL.

7.2 ἦν δὲ ἐγγὺς ἡ ἑορτὴ τῶν Ἰουδαίων ἡ
     NOW~WAS NEAR THE FEAST OF THE JEWS,   THE [FEAST OF]

σκηνοπηγία. **7.3** εἶπον οὖν πρὸς αὐτὸν οἱ ἀδελφοὶ
TABERNACLES.   SAID THEN TO   HIM   THE BROTHERS

αὐτοῦ, Μετάβηθι ἐντεῦθεν καὶ ὕπαγε εἰς τὴν Ἰουδαίαν,
OF HIM, DEPART   FROM HERE AND GO AWAY INTO -   JUDEA,

ἵνα καὶ οἱ μαθηταί σου θεωρήσουσιν σοῦ τὰ ἔργα
THAT ALSO THE DISCIPLES OF YOU WILL SEE   YOUR - WORKS

ἃ   ποιεῖς; **7.4** οὐδεὶς γὰρ τι ἐν κρυπτῷ ποιεῖ
WHICH YOU DO.   FOR~NO ONE ANYTHING IN SECRET DOES

καὶ ζητεῖ αὐτὸς ἐν παρρησίᾳ εἶναι. εἰ ταῦτα
AND SEEKS HIMSELF IN PUBLIC [VIEW] TO BE. IF THESE THINGS

ποιεῖς, φανέρωσον σεαυτὸν τῷ κόσμῳ. **7.5** οὐδὲ γὰρ
YOU DO, MANIFEST   YOURSELF TO THE WORLD.   FOR~NOT EVEN

οἱ ἀδελφοὶ αὐτοῦ ἐπίστευον εἰς αὐτόν. **7.6** λέγει
THE BROTHERS OF HIM WERE BELIEVING IN HIM.   SAYS

After this Jesus went about
in Galilee. He did not wishᵛ
to go about in Judea because
the Jews were looking for an
opportunity to kill him.
²Now the Jewish festival of
Boothsᵂ was near. ³So his
brothers said to him, "Leave
here and go to Judea so that
your disciples also may see
the works you are doing; ⁴for
no one who wantsˣ to be
widely known acts in secret.
If you do these things, show
yourself to the world." ⁵(For
not even his brothers be-
lieved in him.) ⁶Jesus said

ᵛ Other ancient authorities read *was
  not at liberty*
ᵂ Or *Tabernacles*
ˣ Other ancient authorities read
  wants it

to them, "My time has not yet come, but your time is always here. 7The world cannot hate you, but it hates me because I testify against it that its works are evil. 8Go to the festival yourselves. I am not*y* going to this festival, for my time has not yet fully come." 9After saying this, he remained in Galilee.

10 But after his brothers had gone to the festival, then he also went, not publicly but as it were*z* in secret. 11The Jews were looking for him at the festival and saying, "Where is he?" 12And there was considerable complaining about him among the crowds. While some were saying, "He is a good man," others were saying, "No, he is deceiving the crowd." 13Yet no one would speak openly about him for fear of the Jews.

14 About the middle of the festival Jesus went up into the temple and began to teach. 15The Jews were astonished at it, saying, "How does this man have such learning,*a* when he has never been taught?" 16Then Jesus answered them, "My teaching is not mine but his who sent me.

y Other ancient authorities add *yet*
z Other ancient authorities lack *as it were*
a Or *this man know his letters*

οὖν   αὐτοῖς ὁ Ἰησοῦς, Ὁ καιρὸς ὁ ἐμὸς οὔπω
THEREFORE TO THEM - JESUS, THE HOUR - OF ME NOT YET

πάρεστιν, ὁ δὲ   καιρὸς ὁ ὑμέτερος πάντοτέ ἐστιν
IS(HAS) ARRIVED, BUT~THE TIME - OF YOU° ALWAYS IS

ἕτοιμος. 7.7 οὐ δύναται ὁ   κόσμος μισεῖν ὑμᾶς, ἐμὲ δὲ
READY.   IS NOT ABLE THE WORLD TO HATE YOU°, BUT~ME

μισεῖ, ὅτι   ἐγὼ μαρτυρῶ περὶ αὐτοῦ ὅτι   τὰ ἔργα
IT HATES, BECAUSE I TESTIFY ABOUT IT BECAUSE THE WORKS

αὐτοῦ πονηρά ἐστιν. 7.8 ὑμεῖς ἀνάβητε εἰς τὴν ἑορτήν·
OF IT IS(ARE)~EVIL.   YOU° GO UP   TO THE FEAST.

⌐ἐγὼ οὐκ ἀναβαίνω⌐ εἰς τὴν ἑορτὴν ταύτην, ὅτι   ὁ
I   AM NOT GOING UP   TO - THIS~FEAST,   BECAUSE -

ἐμὸς καιρὸς οὔπω πεπλήρωται. 7.9 ταῦτα δὲ   εἰπὼν
MY   TIME NOT YET HAS BEEN FULFILLED. AND~THESE THINGS HAVING SAID,

αὐτὸς ἔμεινεν ἐν τῇ Γαλιλαίᾳ.
HE   REMAINED IN - GALILEE.

7.10 Ὡς δὲ ἀνέβησαν οἱ ἀδελφοὶ αὐτοῦ εἰς τὴν
    BUT~WHEN WENT UP THE BROTHERS OF HIM TO THE

ἑορτήν, τότε καὶ αὐτὸς ἀνέβη οὐ φανερῶς ἀλλὰ [ὡς]
FEAST, THEN ALSO HE   WENT UP NOT MANIFESTLY BUT AS

ἐν κρυπτῷ. 7.11 οἱ οὖν Ἰουδαῖοι ἐζήτουν αὐτὸν ἐν τῇ
IN SECRET.   THEN~THE JEWS WERE SEEKING HIM IN THE

ἑορτῇ καὶ ἔλεγον, Ποῦ ἐστιν ἐκεῖνος; 7.12 καὶ
FEAST AND WERE SAYING, WHERE IS THAT MAN?   AND

γογγυσμὸς περὶ αὐτοῦ ἦν   πολὺς ἐν τοῖς ὄχλοις·
MURMURING ABOUT HIM THERE WAS MUCH AMONG THE CROWDS.

οἱ μὲν ἔλεγον ὅτι Ἀγαθός ἐστιν, ἄλλοι [δὲ] ἔλεγον,
SOME WERE SAYING, - HE IS~A GOOD MAN, BUT~OTHERS WERE SAYING,

Οὔ, ἀλλὰ πλανᾷ τὸν ὄχλον. 7.13 οὐδεὶς μέντοι
NO, BUT HE DECEIVES THE CROWD.   NO ONE HOWEVER

παρρησίᾳ ἐλάλει   περὶ αὐτοῦ διὰ   τὸν φόβον τῶν
OPENLY WAS SPEAKING ABOUT HIM BECAUSE OF THE FEAR OF THE

Ἰουδαίων.
JEWS.

7.14 Ἤδη δὲ τῆς ἑορτῆς μεσούσης
    BUT~WHILE THE FEAST [WAS] BEING IN THE MIDDLE

ἀνέβη Ἰησοῦς εἰς τὸ ἱερὸν καὶ ἐδίδασκεν.
JESUS~WENT UP INTO THE TEMPLE AND WAS TEACHING.

7.15 ἐθαύμαζον οὖν   οἱ Ἰουδαῖοι λέγοντες, Πῶς οὗτος
    WERE MARVELING THEREFORE THE JEWS SAYING, HOW THIS MAN

γράμματα οἶδεν   μὴ μεμαθηκώς; 7.16 ἀπεκρίθη
LETTERS HAS KNOWN, NOT HAVING LEARNED? ANSWERED

οὖν   αὐτοῖς [ὁ] Ἰησοῦς καὶ εἶπεν, Ἡ ἐμὴ διδαχὴ
THEREFORE THEM - JESUS AND SAID, - MY TEACHING

οὐκ ἔστιν ἐμὴ ἀλλὰ τοῦ   πέμψαντός με·
IS NOT MINE BUT OF THE ONE HAVING SENT ME.

7:8 text: ASV RSV NASB NIVmg NEB TEV NJB NRSV. var. εγω ουπω αναβαινω (I am not yet going up): KJV ASVmg RSVmg NIV NEBmg NJBmg NRSVmg.

7.17 ἐάν τις   θέλῃ τὸ θέλημα αὐτοῦ ποιεῖν, γνώσεται
IF   ANYONE   WANTS   THE   WILL   OF HIM   TO DO,   HE WILL KNOW

περὶ τῆς διδαχῆς πότερον ἐκ τοῦ θεοῦ ἐστιν ἢ ἐγὼ ἀπ'
ABOUT   THE   TEACHING   WHETHER   OF -   GOD   IT IS   OR   I   FROM

ἐμαυτοῦ λαλῶ. **7.18** ὁ   ἀπ' ἑαυτοῦ λαλῶν τὴν δόξαν
MYSELF   SPEAK.   THE ONE   FROM   HIMSELF   SPEAKING -   ³GLORY

τὴν   ἰδίαν ζητεῖ· ὁ δὲ   ζητῶν τὴν δόξαν τοῦ
¹THE(HIS)   ²OWN   SEEKS;   BUT~THE ONE   SEEKING   THE   GLORY   OF THE ONE

πέμψαντος αὐτὸν οὗτος ἀληθής ἐστιν καὶ ἀδικία
HAVING SENT   HIM   THIS ONE   IS~GENUINE   AND   UNRIGHTEOUSNESS

ἐν αὐτῷ οὐκ ἔστιν. **7.19** οὐ   Μωϋσῆς δέδωκεν ὑμῖν
IN   HIM   IS NOT.   HAS NOT   MOSES   GIVEN   YOU°

τὸν νόμον; καὶ οὐδεὶς ἐξ ὑμῶν ποιεῖ τὸν νόμον. τί
THE   LAW?   AND   NONE   OF   YOU°   DOES   THE   LAW.   WHY

με ζητεῖτε   ἀποκτεῖναι; **7.20** ἀπεκρίθη ὁ ὄχλος,
ME   ARE YOU° SEEKING   TO KILL?   ANSWERED   THE CROWD,

Δαιμόνιον ἔχεις· τίς σε ζητεῖ   ἀποκτεῖναι;
YOU HAVE~A DEMON.   WHO   ³YOU   ¹IS SEEKING   ²TO KILL?

7.21 ἀπεκρίθη Ἰησοῦς καὶ εἶπεν αὐτοῖς, Ἕν ἔργον
ANSWERED   JESUS   AND   SAID   TO THEM,   ONE   WORK

ἐποίησα καὶ πάντες θαυμάζετε. **7.22** διὰ   τοῦτο
I DID   AND   EVERYONE   MARVELS.   BECAUSE OF   THIS

Μωϋσῆς δέδωκεν ὑμῖν τὴν περιτομήν— οὐχ ὅτι ἐκ τοῦ
MOSES   HAS GIVEN   YOU° -   CIRCUMCISION—   NOT   THAT   OF -

Μωϋσέως ἐστὶν ἀλλ' ἐκ τῶν πατέρων— καὶ ἐν σαββάτῳ
MOSES   IT IS   BUT   OF   THE   FATHERS—   AND   ON   A SABBATH

περιτέμνετε ἄνθρωπον. **7.23** εἰ περιτομὴν λαμβάνει
YOU° CIRCUMCISE   A MAN.   IF   CIRCUMCISION   RECEIVES

ἄνθρωπος ἐν σαββάτῳ ἵνα μὴ λυθῇ   ὁ νόμος
A MAN   ON   A SABBATH   THAT   NOT   MAY BE BROKEN   THE   LAW

Μωϋσέως, ἐμοὶ χολᾶτε ὅτι   ὅλον ἄνθρωπον ὑγιῆ
OF MOSES,   ARE YOU° ANGRY~WITH ME   BECAUSE   ³ENTIRELY   ²A MAN   ⁴HEALTHY

ἐποίησα ἐν σαββάτῳ; **7.24** μὴ κρίνετε κατ'
¹I MADE   ON   A SABBATH?   DO NOT JUDGE   ACCORDING TO

ὄψιν,   ἀλλὰ τὴν δικαίαν κρίσιν κρίνετε.
APPEARANCE,   BUT   THE   JUST   JUDGMENT   JUDGE.

7.25 Ἔλεγον οὖν   τινες ἐκ τῶν   Ἱεροσολυμιτῶν,
WERE SAYING   THEREFORE   SOME   OF   THE ONES   OF JERUSALEM,

Οὐχ οὗτός ἐστιν ὃν ζητοῦσιν   ἀποκτεῖναι; **7.26** καὶ
²NOT   ³THIS MAN   ¹IS IT   WHOM   THEY ARE SEEKING   TO KILL?   AND

ἴδε παρρησίᾳ λαλεῖ καὶ οὐδὲν αὐτῷ λέγουσιν.
LOOK   HE SPEAKS~OPENLY   AND   NOTHING   TO HIM   THEY SAY.

μήποτε ἀληθῶς ἔγνωσαν οἱ ἄρχοντες ὅτι οὗτός ἐστιν
PERHAPS   TRULY   KNEW   THE   RULERS   THAT   THIS MAN   IS

ὁ Χριστός; **7.27** ἀλλὰ τοῦτον οἴδαμεν πόθεν ἐστίν·
THE   CHRIST?   BUT   THIS MAN   WE KNOW   FROM WHERE   HE IS;

ὁ δὲ Χριστὸς ὅταν   ἔρχηται οὐδεὶς γινώσκει πόθεν
BUT~THE   CHRIST   WHENEVER   HE COMES   NO ONE   KNOWS   FROM WHERE

[17]Anyone who resolves to do the will of God will know whether the teaching is from God or whether I am speaking on my own. [18]Those who speak on their own seek their own glory; but the one who seeks the glory of him who sent him is true, and there is nothing false in him.

19 "Did not Moses give you the law? Yet none of you keeps the law. Why are you looking for an opportunity to kill me?" [20]The crowd answered, "You have a demon! Who is trying to kill you?" [21]Jesus answered them, "I performed one work, and all of you are astonished. [22]Moses gave you circumcision (it is, of course, not from Moses, but from the patriarchs), and you circumcise a man on the sabbath. [23]If a man receives circumcision on the sabbath in order that the law of Moses may not be broken, are you angry with me because I healed a man's whole body on the sabbath? [24]Do not judge by appearances, but judge with right judgment."

25 Now some of the people of Jerusalem were saying, "Is not this the man whom they are trying to kill? [26]And here he is, speaking openly, but they say nothing to him! Can it be that the authorities really know that this is the Messiah?[b] [27]Yet we know where this man is from; but when the Messiah[b] comes, no one will know

[b] Or *the Christ*

where he is from." [28]Then Jesus cried out as he was teaching in the temple, "You know me, and you know where I am from. I have not come on my own. But the one who sent me is true, and you do not know him. [29]I know him, because I am from him, and he sent me." [30]Then they tried to arrest him, but no one laid hands on him, because his hour had not yet come. [31]Yet many in the crowd believed in him and were saying, "When the Messiah[c] comes, will he do more signs than this man has done?"[d]

32 The Pharisees heard the crowd muttering such things about him, and the chief priests and Pharisees sent temple police to arrest him. [33]Jesus then said, "I will be with you a little while longer, and then I am going to him who sent me. [34]You will search for me, but you will not find me; and where I am, you cannot come." [35]The Jews said to one another, "Where does this man intend to go that we will not find him? Does he intend to go to the Dispersion among the Greeks and teach the Greeks? [36]What does he mean by saying, 'You will search for me and you will not find me' and 'Where I am, you cannot come'?"

[c] Or the Christ
[d] Other ancient authorities read is doing

ἐστίν. **7.28** ἔκραξεν οὖν ἐν τῷ ἱερῷ διδάσκων ὁ
HE IS.   CRIED OUT THEREFORE IN THE TEMPLE [WHILE] TEACHING -

Ἰησοῦς καὶ λέγων, Κἀμὲ οἴδατε καὶ οἴδατε πόθεν
JESUS AND SAYING, BOTH ME YOU° KNOW AND YOU° KNOW FROM WHERE

εἰμί· καὶ ἀπ᾽ ἐμαυτοῦ οὐκ ἐλήλυθα, ἀλλ᾽ ἔστιν
I AM. AND FROM MYSELF I HAVE NOT COME, BUT HE IS

ἀληθινὸς ὁ πέμψας με, ὃν ὑμεῖς οὐκ οἴδατε·
TRUE, THE ONE HAVING SENT ME, WHOM YOU° DO NOT KNOW.

7.29 ἐγὼ οἶδα αὐτόν, ὅτι παρ᾽ αὐτοῦ εἰμι κἀκεῖνός
I KNOW HIM, BECAUSE FROM HIM I AM AND THAT ONE

με ἀπέστειλεν. **7.30** Ἐζήτουν οὖν αὐτὸν πιάσαι,
ME SENT.   THEY WERE SEEKING THEREFORE TO ARREST~HIM,

καὶ οὐδεὶς ἐπέβαλεν ἐπ᾽ αὐτὸν τὴν χεῖρα, ὅτι
AND NO ONE LAID ON HIM THE (A) HAND, BECAUSE

οὔπω ἐληλύθει ἡ ὥρα αὐτοῦ. **7.31** Ἐκ τοῦ ὄχλου
NOT YET HAD COME THE HOUR OF HIM.   FROM THE CROWD

δὲ πολλοὶ ἐπίστευσαν εἰς αὐτὸν καὶ ἔλεγον, Ὁ
HOWEVER, MANY BELIEVED IN HIM AND WERE SAYING, THE

Χριστὸς ὅταν ἔλθῃ μὴ πλείονα σημεῖα
CHRIST WHENEVER HE COMES [SURELY] NOT MORE SIGNS

ποιήσει ὧν οὗτος ἐποίησεν;
WILL HE DO [THAN THE] THINGS WHICH THIS MAN DID?

7.32 Ἤκουσαν οἱ Φαρισαῖοι τοῦ ὄχλου γογγύζοντος
HEARD THE PHARISEES THE CROWD MURMURING

περὶ αὐτοῦ ταῦτα, καὶ ἀπέστειλαν οἱ ἀρχιερεῖς καὶ
ABOUT HIM THESE THINGS, AND SENT THE CHIEF PRIESTS AND

οἱ Φαρισαῖοι ὑπηρέτας ἵνα πιάσωσιν αὐτόν.
THE PHARISEES SERVANTS THAT THEY MIGHT ARREST HIM.

7.33 εἶπεν οὖν ὁ Ἰησοῦς, Ἔτι χρόνον μικρὸν μεθ᾽
SAID THEREFORE - JESUS, YET A LITTLE~TIME WITH

ὑμῶν εἰμι καὶ ὑπάγω πρὸς τὸν πέμψαντά με.
YOU° I AM AND I GO AWAY TO THE ONE HAVING SENT ME.

7.34 ζητήσετέ με καὶ οὐχ εὑρήσετέ [με], καὶ ὅπου
YOU° WILL SEEK ME AND NOT FIND ME, AND WHERE

εἰμὶ ἐγὼ ὑμεῖς οὐ δύνασθε ἐλθεῖν. **7.35** εἶπον οὖν
I~AM, YOU° ARE NOT ABLE TO COME.   SAID THEREFORE

οἱ Ἰουδαῖοι πρὸς ἑαυτούς, Ποῦ οὗτος μέλλει
THE JEWS TO THEMSELVES, WHERE IS THIS MAN ABOUT

πορεύεσθαι ὅτι ἡμεῖς οὐχ εὑρήσομεν αὐτόν; μὴ
TO JOURNEY THAT WE WILL NOT FIND HIM? [SURELY] NOT

εἰς τὴν διασπορὰν τῶν Ἑλλήνων μέλλει πορεύεσθαι
TO THE DISPERSION OF THE GREEKS HE IS ABOUT TO JOURNEY

καὶ διδάσκειν τοὺς Ἕλληνας; **7.36** τίς ἐστιν ὁ
AND TO TEACH THE GREEKS?   WHAT IS

λόγος οὗτος ὃν εἶπεν, Ζητήσετέ με καὶ οὐχ εὑρήσετέ
THIS~WORD WHICH HE SAID, YOU° WILL SEEK ME AND WILL NOT FIND

[με], καὶ ὅπου εἰμὶ ἐγὼ ὑμεῖς οὐ δύνασθε ἐλθεῖν;
ME, AND WHERE I AM YOU° ARE NOT ABLE TO COME?

7.37 Ἐν δὲ τῇ ἐσχάτῃ ἡμέρᾳ τῇ μεγάλῃ τῆς ἑορτῆς
NOW~ON   THE LAST   DAY,   THE GREAT [DAY] OF THE FEAST,

εἱστήκει ὁ Ἰησοῦς καὶ ἔκραξεν λέγων, Ἐάν τις
HAD STOOD - JESUS   AND   CRIED OUT SAYING, IF   ANYONE

διψᾷ ἐρχέσθω πρός με καὶ πινέτω.   **7.38** ὁ
THIRSTS LET HIM COME TO ME AND DRINK.   THE ONE

πιστεύων εἰς ἐμέ, καθὼς εἶπεν ἡ γραφή, ποταμοὶ
BELIEVING IN ME,   AS   SAID THE SCRIPTURE, ¹RIVERS

ἐκ   τῆς κοιλίας αὐτοῦ ῥεύσουσιν ὕδατος ζῶντος.
⁵OUT OF ⁶THE ⁷BELLY ⁸OF HIM ⁴WILL FLOW ³WATER ²OF LIVING.

7.39 τοῦτο δὲ εἶπεν περὶ τοῦ πνεύματος ὃ   ἔμελλον
BUT~THIS   HE SAID ABOUT THE SPIRIT   WHICH WERE ABOUT

λαμβάνειν οἱ πιστεύσαντες εἰς αὐτόν· οὔπω γὰρ ἦν
TO RECEIVE THE ONES HAVING BELIEVED IN HIM; FOR~NOT YET WAS

⌐πνεῦμα⌐, ὅτι Ἰησοῦς οὐδέπω ἐδοξάσθη.
[THE] SPIRIT, BECAUSE JESUS NOT YET WAS GLORIFIED.

7.40 Ἐκ τοῦ ὄχλου οὖν ἀκούσαντες τῶν
[SOME] OF THE CROWD THEREFORE HAVING HEARD -

λόγων τούτων ἔλεγον, Οὗτός ἐστιν ἀληθῶς ὁ
THESE~WORDS   WERE SAYING, THIS MAN IS   TRULY   THE

προφήτης· **7.41** ἄλλοι ἔλεγον, Οὗτός ἐστιν ὁ Χριστός,
PROPHET.   OTHERS WERE SAYING, THIS MAN IS THE CHRIST;

οἱ δὲ   ἔλεγον, Μὴ γὰρ ἐκ τῆς Γαλιλαίας ὁ
BUT~[SOME] MEN WERE SAYING, FOR~[SURELY] NOT FROM - GALILEE THE

Χριστὸς ἔρχεται; **7.42** οὐχ ἡ γραφὴ εἶπεν ὅτι ἐκ
CHRIST COMES?   [HAS] NOT THE SCRIPTURE SAID THAT FROM

τοῦ σπέρματος Δαυίδ καὶ ἀπὸ Βηθλέεμ τῆς κώμης
THE SEED   OF DAVID AND FROM BETHLEHEM, THE VILLAGE

ὅπου ἦν Δαυίδ ἔρχεται ὁ Χριστός; **7.43** σχίσμα οὖν
WHERE DAVID~WAS, COMES THE CHRIST?   A DIVISION THEREFORE

ἐγένετο ἐν τῷ ὄχλῳ δι᾽ αὐτόν. **7.44** τινὲς δὲ
OCCURRED AMONG THE CROWD BECAUSE OF HIM.   AND~SOME

ἤθελον ἐξ αὐτῶν πιάσαι αὐτόν, ἀλλ᾽ οὐδεὶς
³WERE WANTING ¹OF ²THEM TO ARREST HIM, BUT   NO ONE

ἐπέβαλεν ἐπ῾ αὐτὸν τὰς χεῖρας.
LAID   ON HIM THE(HIS) HANDS.

7.45 Ἦλθον οὖν οἱ ὑπηρέται πρὸς τοὺς ἀρχιερεῖς καὶ
CAME   THEN THE SERVANTS TO   THE CHIEF PRIESTS AND

Φαρισαίους, καὶ εἶπον αὐτοῖς ἐκεῖνοι, Διὰ τί
PHARISEES,   AND SAID TO THEM THOSE ONES, WHY

οὐκ ἠγάγετε αὐτόν; **7.46** ἀπεκρίθησαν οἱ ὑπηρέται,
DID YOU° NOT BRING HIM?   ANSWERED   THE SERVANTS,

Οὐδέποτε ἐλάλησεν οὕτως ἄνθρωπος. **7.47** ἀπεκρίθησαν
NEVER   SPOKE   THUS A MAN.   ANSWERED

οὖν   αὐτοῖς οἱ Φαρισαῖοι, Μὴ   καὶ ὑμεῖς
THEREFORE THEM THE PHARISEES, [SURELY] NOT ALSO YOU°

37 On the last day of the festival, the great day, while Jesus was standing there, he cried out, "Let anyone who is thirsty come to me, ³⁸and let the one who believes in me drink. As^e the scripture has said, 'Out of the believer's heart^f shall flow rivers of living water.'" ³⁹Now he said this about the Spirit, which believers in him were to receive; for as yet there was no Spirit,^g because Jesus was not yet glorified.

40 When they heard these words, some in the crowd said, "This is really the prophet." ⁴¹Others said, "This is the Messiah."^h But some asked, "Surely the Messiah^h does not come from Galilee, does he? ⁴²Has not the scripture said that the Messiah^h is descended from David and comes from Bethlehem, the village where David lived?" ⁴³So there was a division in the crowd because of him. ⁴⁴Some of them wanted to arrest him, but no one laid hands on him.

45 Then the temple police went back to the chief priests and Pharisees, who asked them, "Why did you not arrest him?" ⁴⁶The police answered, "Never has anyone spoken like this!" ⁴⁷Then the Pharisees replied, "Surely you have not been

^e Or come to me and drink. ³⁸The one who believes in me, as
^f Gk out of his belly
^g Other ancient authorities read for as yet the Spirit (others, Holy Spirit) had not been given
^h Or the Christ

7:39 text: NJB NRSV. var. πνευμα αγιον (Holy Spirit): NRSVmg. var. πνευμα δεδομενον ([the] Spirit given): ASV RSV NASB NIV NEB TEV NJB NRSVmg. var. πνευμα αγιον δεδομενον ([the] Holy Spirit given): KJV.

deceived too, have you? [48]Has any one of the authorities or of the Pharisees believed in him? [49]But this crowd, which does not know the law—they are accursed." [50]Nicodemus, who had gone to Jesus[i] before, and who was one of them, asked, [51]"Our law does not judge people without first giving them a hearing to find out what they are doing, does it?" [52]They replied, "Surely you are not also from Galilee, are you? Search and you will see that no prophet is to arise from Galilee."

[[[53]Then each of them went home,

[i] Gk *him*

πεπλάνησθε;　**7.48** μή　　　τις ἐκ τῶν ἀρχόντων
HAVE BEEN DECEIVED?　　[SURELY] NOT　ANY　OF　THE　RULERS

ἐπίστευσεν εἰς αὐτὸν ἢ ἐκ τῶν Φαρισαίων;　**7.49** ἀλλὰ
BELIEVED　IN　HIM,　OR OF THE PHARISEES?　　　　　　BUT

ὁ ὄχλος οὗτος ὁ μὴ γινώσκων τὸν νόμον
-　THIS~CROWD　-　NOT　KNOWING　　THE　LAW

ἐπάρατοί εἰσιν.　**7.50** λέγει Νικόδημος πρὸς αὐτούς,
IS~CURSED.　　　　　SAYS　NICODEMUS　TO　THEM,

ὁ　ἐλθὼν　πρὸς αὐτὸν [τὸ] πρότερον, εἰς ὢν ἐξ
THE ONE HAVING COME TO　HIM　-　EARLIER,　　BEING~ONE OF

αὐτῶν,　**7.51** Μὴ　ὁ νόμος ἡμῶν κρίνει τὸν
THEM,　　　　[SURELY] NOT THE LAW OF US JUDGES THE

ἄνθρωπον ἐὰν μὴ ἀκούσῃ πρῶτον παρ' αὐτοῦ καὶ γνῷ
MAN　　　UNLESS IT HEARS FIRST FROM HIM AND KNOWS

τί ποιεῖ;　**7.52** ἀπεκρίθησαν καὶ εἶπαν αὐτῷ,
WHAT HE DOES?　THEY ANSWERED AND SAID TO HIM,

Μὴ　καὶ σὺ ἐκ τῆς Γαλιλαίας εἶ; ἐραύνησον
[SURELY] NOT ALSO YOU FROM - GALILEE ARE? SEARCH

καὶ ἴδε ὅτι ἐκ τῆς Γαλιλαίας ⌜προφήτης⌝
AND SEE THAT FROM - GALILEE A PROPHET

οὐκ ἐγείρεται.
DOES NOT ARISE.

[[**7.53** Καὶ ἐπορεύθησαν ἕκαστος εἰς τὸν οἶκον αὐτοῦ,
AND THEY WENT EACH ONE TO THE HOUSE OF HIM,

7:52 text: all. var. ο προφητης (the prophet): NIVmg TEVmg.　**7:53—8:11** text: all (but noted in ASV NASB NIV TEV NJB NRSV as being absent in the earliest MSS). omit: ASVmg RSVmg NASBmg NIVmg NEBmg TEVmg NJBmg NRSVmg. (Note: the double brackets in the Greek text indicate that this passage was a later addition to the text, which, however, was retained because of its importance in the textual tradition.)

CHAPTER 8

[1]while Jesus went to the Mount of Olives. [2]Early in the morning he came again to the temple. All the people came to him and he sat down and began to teach them. [3]The scribes and the Pharisees brought a woman who had been caught in adultery; and making her stand before all of them, [4]they said to him, "Teacher, this woman was caught in the very act of committing adultery. [5]Now in the law Moses commanded us to stone such women. Now

8.1 Ἰησοῦς δὲ ἐπορεύθη εἰς τὸ Ὄρος τῶν Ἐλαιῶν.
BUT~JESUS WENT TO THE MOUNT - OF OLIVES.

8.2 Ὄρθρου δὲ πάλιν παρεγένετο εἰς τὸ ἱερὸν καὶ πᾶς
AND~AT DAWN AGAIN HE CAME INTO THE TEMPLE AND ALL

ὁ λαὸς ἤρχετο πρὸς αὐτόν, καὶ καθίσας ἐδίδασκεν
THE PEOPLE WERE COMING TO HIM, AND HAVING SAT HE WAS TEACHING

αὐτούς.　**8.3** ἄγουσιν δὲ οἱ γραμματεῖς καὶ οἱ
THEM.　　AND~LEAD THE SCRIBES AND THE

Φαρισαῖοι γυναῖκα ἐπὶ μοιχείᾳ κατειλημμένην καὶ
PHARISEES A WOMAN IN ADULTERY HAVING BEEN CAUGHT, AND

στήσαντες αὐτὴν ἐν μέσῳ　**8.4** λέγουσιν αὐτῷ,
HAVING STOOD HER IN [THE] MIDST THEY SAY TO HIM,

Διδάσκαλε, αὕτη ἡ γυνὴ κατείληπται ἐπ' αὐτοφώρῳ
TEACHER, THIS - WOMAN HAS BEEN CAUGHT IN THE ACT OF

μοιχευομένη·　**8.5** ἐν δὲ τῷ νόμῳ ἡμῖν Μωϋσῆς
COMMITTING ADULTERY; NOW~IN THE LAW TO US MOSES

ἐνετείλατο τὰς τοιαύτας λιθάζειν. σὺ οὖν τί
COMMANDED - TO STONE~SUCH WOMEN. YOU THEREFORE WHAT

λέγεις; **8.6** τοῦτο δὲ ἔλεγον   πειράζοντες αὐτόν, ἵνα
DO YOU SAY?   BUT~THIS THEY WERE SAYING TESTING   HIM,   THAT

ἔχωσιν   κατηγορεῖν αὐτοῦ. ὁ δὲ Ἰησοῦς
THEY MIGHT HAVE [SOMETHING] TO ACCUSE HIM.   - BUT JESUS

κάτω κύψας   τῷ   δακτύλῳ κατέγραφεν εἰς τὴν γῆν.
HAVING STOOPED~DOWN WITH HIS FINGER   WAS WRITING   IN THE GROUND.

8.7 ὡς δὲ ἐπέμενον   ἐρωτῶντες αὐτόν, ἀνέκυψεν καὶ
BUT~AS THEY WERE REMAINING QUESTIONING HIM,   HE STOOD UP AND

εἶπεν αὐτοῖς, Ὁ   ἀναμάρτητος ὑμῶν   πρῶτος ἐπ᾽
SAID TO THEM, THE ONE WITHOUT SIN   OF (AMONG) YOU° FIRST   AT

αὐτὴν βαλέτω   λίθον. **8.8** καὶ πάλιν κατακύψας
HER   LET HIM THROW A STONE.   AND AGAIN HAVING STOOPED DOWN

ἔγραφεν εἰς τὴν γῆν. **8.9** οἱ δὲ   ἀκούσαντες
HE WAS WRITING IN THE GROUND.   AND~THE ONES HAVING HEARD

ἐξήρχοντο εἷς καθ᾽ εἷς ἀρξάμενοι ἀπὸ τῶν πρεσβυτέρων
WERE DEPARTING ONE BY ONE   HAVING BEGUN FROM THE OLDER ONES,

καὶ κατελείφθη μόνος καὶ ἡ γυνὴ ἐν μέσῳ   οὖσα.
AND HE WAS LEFT ALONE AND THE WOMAN IN [THE] MIDST BEING.

8.10 ἀνακύψας δὲ ὁ Ἰησοῦς εἶπεν αὐτῇ, Γύναι, ποῦ
AND~HAVING STOOD UP - JESUS SAID TO HER, WOMAN, WHERE

εἰσιν; οὐδείς σε κατέκρινεν; **8.11** ἡ δὲ   εἶπεν,
ARE [THEY]? NO ONE   CONDEMNED~YOU?   AND~SHE SAID,

Οὐδείς, κύριε. εἶπεν δὲ ὁ Ἰησοῦς, Οὐδὲ   ἐγώ
NO ONE, LORD. AND~SAID   - JESUS,   NEITHER [DO] I

σε κατακρίνω· πορεύου, [καὶ] ἀπὸ τοῦ νῦν   μηκέτι
CONDEMN~YOU; GO,   AND   FROM THE NOW [ON] NO LONGER

ἁμάρτανε.]]⌐
SIN.

8.12 Πάλιν οὖν αὐτοῖς ἐλάλησεν ὁ Ἰησοῦς λέγων,
THEN~AGAIN TO THEM SPOKE   - JESUS   SAYING,

Ἐγώ εἰμι τὸ φῶς τοῦ κόσμου· ὁ   ἀκολουθῶν ἐμοὶ
I   AM   THE LIGHT OF THE WORLD; THE ONE FOLLOWING   ME

οὐ μὴ περιπατήσῃ ἐν τῇ σκοτίᾳ, ἀλλ᾽ ἕξει   τὸ φῶς
WILL NEVER WALK   IN THE DARKNESS, BUT WILL HAVE THE LIGHT

τῆς ζωῆς. **8.13** εἶπον οὖν   αὐτῷ οἱ Φαρισαῖοι, Σὺ
-   OF LIFE.   SAID THEREFORE TO HIM THE PHARISEES,   YOU

περὶ σεαυτοῦ μαρτυρεῖς· ἡ μαρτυρία σου οὐκ ἔστιν
ABOUT YOURSELF TESTIFY;   THE TESTIMONY OF YOU IS NOT

ἀληθής. **8.14** ἀπεκρίθη Ἰησοῦς καὶ εἶπεν αὐτοῖς, Κἂν
TRUE.   ANSWERED   JESUS   AND SAID TO THEM, EVEN IF

ἐγὼ μαρτυρῶ περὶ ἐμαυτοῦ, ἀληθής ἐστιν ἡ μαρτυρία
I   TESTIFY ABOUT MYSELF,   TRUE   IS   THE TESTIMONY

μου, ὅτι   οἶδα πόθεν   ἦλθον καὶ ποῦ ὑπάγω·
OF ME, BECAUSE I KNOW FROM WHERE I CAME AND WHERE I GO.

ὑμεῖς δὲ οὐκ οἴδατε πόθεν   ἔρχομαι ἢ ποῦ ὑπάγω.
BUT~YOU° DO NOT KNOW FROM WHERE I COME   OR WHERE I GO.

8.15 ὑμεῖς κατὰ   τὴν σάρκα κρίνετε, ἐγὼ οὐ κρίνω
YOU°   ACCORDING TO THE FLESH   JUDGE,   I   DO NOT JUDGE

what do you say?" [6]They said this to test him, so that they might have some charge to bring against him. Jesus bent down and wrote with his finger on the ground. [7]When they kept on questioning him, he straightened up and said to them, "Let anyone among you who is without sin be the first to throw a stone at her." [8]And once again he bent down and wrote on the ground.[j] [9]When they heard it, they went away, one by one, beginning with the elders; and Jesus was left alone with the woman standing before him. [10]Jesus straightened up and said to her, "Woman, where are they? Has no one condemned you?" [11]She said, "No one, sir."[k] And Jesus said, "Neither do I condemn you. Go your way, and from now on do not sin again."]][l]

12 Again Jesus spoke to them, saying, "I am the light of the world. Whoever follows me will never walk in darkness but will have the light of life." [13]Then the Pharisees said to him, "You are testifying on your own behalf; your testimony is not valid." [14]Jesus answered, "Even if I testify on my own behalf, my testimony is valid because I know where I have come from and where I am going, but you do not know where I come from or where I am going. [15]You judge by human standards;[m] I judge

[j] Other ancient authorities add *the sins of each of them*
[k] Or *Lord*
[l] The most ancient authorities lack 7.53—8.11; other authorities add the passage here or after 7.36 or after 21.25 or after Luke 21.38, with variations of text; some mark the passage as doubtful.
[m] Gk *according to the flesh*

no one. ¹⁶Yet even if I do judge, my judgment is valid; for it is not I alone who judge, but I and the Father[n] who sent me. ¹⁷In your law it is written that the testimony of two witnesses is valid. ¹⁸I testify on my own behalf, and the Father who sent me testifies on my behalf." ¹⁹Then they said to him, "Where is your Father?" Jesus answered, "You know neither me nor my Father. If you knew me, you would know my Father also." ²⁰He spoke these words while he was teaching in the treasury of the temple, but no one arrested him, because his hour had not yet come.

21 Again he said to them, "I am going away, and you will search for me, but you will die in your sin. Where I am going, you cannot come." ²²Then the Jews said, "Is he going to kill himself? Is that what he means by saying, 'Where I am going, you cannot come'?" ²³He said to them, "You are from below, I am from above; you are of this world, I am not of this world. ²⁴I told you that you would die in your sins, for you will die in your sins

[n] Other ancient authorities read he

οὐδένα. **8.16** καὶ ἐὰν κρίνω δὲ ἐγώ, ἡ κρίσις ἡ ἐμὴ
ANYONE.   ²EVEN ³IF ⁵JUDGE ¹BUT ⁴I, THE JUDGMENT - OF ME

ἀληθινή ἐστιν, ὅτι   μόνος οὐκ εἰμί, ἀλλ' ἐγὼ καὶ
IS~TRUE,   BECAUSE I AM NOT~ALONE, BUT I AND

⌐ὁ πέμψας με πατήρ⌐. **8.17** καὶ ἐν τῷ νόμῳ δὲ
THE ONE HAVING SENT ME, [THE] FATHER. ²EVEN ³IN - ⁵LAW ¹AND

τῷ ὑμετέρῳ γέγραπται ὅτι δύο ἀνθρώπων ἡ
- ⁴YOUR° IT HAS BEEN WRITTEN THAT OF TWO MEN THE

μαρτυρία ἀληθής ἐστιν. **8.18** ἐγώ εἰμι ὁ   μαρτυρῶν
TESTIMONY IS~TRUE. I AM THE ONE TESTIFYING

περὶ ἐμαυτοῦ καὶ μαρτυρεῖ περὶ ἐμοῦ ὁ   πέμψας
ABOUT MYSELF AND TESTIFIES ABOUT ME THE ONE HAVING SENT

με πατήρ. **8.19** ἔλεγον   οὖν   αὐτῷ, Ποῦ ἐστιν
ME, [THE] FATHER. THEY WERE SAYING THEREFORE TO HIM, WHERE IS

ὁ πατήρ σου; ἀπεκρίθη Ἰησοῦς, Οὔτε ἐμὲ οἴδατε
THE FATHER OF YOU? ANSWERED JESUS, NEITHER ME YOU° KNOW

οὔτε τὸν πατέρα μου· εἰ ἐμὲ ᾔδειτε, καὶ τὸν πατέρα
NOR THE FATHER OF ME; IF YOU° HAD KNOWN~ME, ALSO THE FATHER

μου ἂν ᾔδειτε. **8.20** Ταῦτα τὰ ῥήματα ἐλάλησεν
OF ME YOU° WOULD HAVE KNOWN. THESE - WORDS HE SPOKE

ἐν τῷ γαζοφυλακίῳ διδάσκων ἐν τῷ ἱερῷ· καὶ
IN THE TREASURY [WHILE] TEACHING IN THE TEMPLE; AND

οὐδεὶς ἐπίασεν αὐτόν, ὅτι   οὔπω ἐληλύθει ἡ ὥρα
NO ONE ARRESTED HIM, BECAUSE NOT YET HAD COME THE HOUR

αὐτοῦ.
OF HIM.

8.21 Εἶπεν οὖν   πάλιν αὐτοῖς, Ἐγὼ ὑπάγω καὶ
HE SAID THEREFORE AGAIN TO THEM, I GO AWAY AND

ζητήσετέ με, καὶ ἐν τῇ ἁμαρτίᾳ ὑμῶν ἀποθανεῖσθε·
YOU° WILL SEEK ME, AND IN THE SIN OF YOU° YOU° WILL DIE.

ὅπου ἐγὼ ὑπάγω ὑμεῖς οὐ δύνασθε ἐλθεῖν. **8.22** ἔλεγον
WHERE I GO AWAY YOU° ARE NOT ABLE TO COME. WERE SAYING

οὖν   οἱ Ἰουδαῖοι, Μήτι ἀποκτενεῖ ἑαυτόν, ὅτι
THEREFORE THE JEWS, [SURELY] HE WILL NOT KILL HIMSELF, BECAUSE

λέγει, Ὅπου ἐγὼ ὑπάγω ὑμεῖς οὐ δύνασθε ἐλθεῖν;
HE SAYS, WHERE I GO AWAY YOU° ARE NOT ABLE TO COME?

8.23 καὶ ἔλεγεν   αὐτοῖς, Ὑμεῖς ἐκ τῶν   κάτω
AND HE WAS SAYING TO THEM, YOU° OF THE THINGS BELOW

ἐστέ, ἐγὼ ἐκ τῶν   ἄνω εἰμί· ὑμεῖς ἐκ τούτου τοῦ
ARE, I OF THE THINGS ABOVE AM. YOU° OF THIS -

κόσμου ἐστέ, ἐγὼ οὐκ εἰμὶ ἐκ τοῦ κόσμου τούτου.
WORLD ARE, I AM NOT OF - THIS~WORLD.

8.24 εἶπον οὖν   ὑμῖν ὅτι ἀποθανεῖσθε ἐν ταῖς
I SAID THEREFORE TO YOU° THAT YOU° WILL DIE IN THE

ἁμαρτίαις ὑμῶν· ἐὰν γὰρ μὴ πιστεύσητε ὅτι ἐγώ εἰμι,
SINS OF YOU°. FOR~IF YOU° DO NOT BELIEVE THAT I AM [HE],

8:16 text: KJV ASV RSVmg NASBmg NEB TEV NRSV.   var. ο πεμψας με (the One who sent me): RSV NASB NJB NRSV.

ἀποθανεῖσθε ἐν ταῖς ἁμαρτίαις ὑμῶν. **8.25** ἔλεγον
YOU° WILL DIE   IN   THE   SINS   OF YOU°.   THEY WERE SAYING

οὖν   αὐτῷ, Σὺ τίς εἶ; εἶπεν αὐτοῖς ὁ Ἰησοῦς,
THEREFORE TO HIM, ³YOU ¹WHO ²ARE? SAID TO THEM - JESUS,

Τὴν ἀρχὴν ὅ τι καὶ λαλῶ   ὑμῖν; **8.26** πολλὰ
⁵AT ALL   ¹WHY ²EVEN ³SHOULD I SPEAK ⁴TO YOU°?   MANY THINGS

ἔχω περὶ ὑμῶν λαλεῖν καὶ κρίνειν, ἀλλ᾽ ὁ   πέμψας
I HAVE ABOUT YOU° TO SPEAK AND TO JUDGE, BUT THE ONE HAVING SENT

με ἀληθής ἐστιν, κἀγὼ ἃ ἤκουσα παρ᾽ αὐτοῦ ταῦτα
ME IS~TRUE,   AND I—WHAT I HEARD FROM HIM—THESE THINGS

λαλῶ εἰς τὸν κόσμον. **8.27** οὐκ ἔγνωσαν ὅτι τὸν
I SPEAK IN   THE WORLD.   THEY DID NOT KNOW THAT OF THE

πατέρα αὐτοῖς ἔλεγεν. **8.28** εἶπεν οὖν [αὐτοῖς] ὁ
FATHER HE WAS SPEAKING~TO THEM. SAID THEREFORE TO THEM -

Ἰησοῦς, Ὅταν ὑψώσητε τὸν υἱὸν τοῦ ἀνθρώπου, τότε
JESUS, WHEN YOU° LIFT UP THE SON - OF MAN,   THEN

γνώσεσθε ὅτι ἐγώ εἰμι, καὶ ἀπ᾽ ἐμαυτοῦ ποιῶ οὐδέν,
YOU° WILL KNOW THAT I AM [HE], AND FROM MYSELF I DO NOTHING,

ἀλλὰ καθὼς ἐδίδαξέν με ὁ πατὴρ ταῦτα   λαλῶ.
BUT   AS   TAUGHT   ME THE FATHER THESE THINGS I SPEAK.

8.29 καὶ ὁ   πέμψας με μετ᾽ ἐμοῦ ἐστιν·
AND THE ONE HAVING SENT ME WITH ME IS.

οὐκ ἀφῆκέν με μόνον, ὅτι ἐγὼ τὰ   ἀρεστὰ αὐτῷ
HE DID NOT LEAVE ME ALONE, BECAUSE I THE THINGS PLEASING TO HIM

ποιῶ πάντοτε. **8.30** Ταῦτα   αὐτοῦ λαλοῦντος πολλοὶ
DO   ALWAYS.   ³THESE THINGS ¹[AS] HE ²IS(WAS) SAYING, MANY

ἐπίστευσαν εἰς αὐτόν.
BELIEVED   IN HIM.

8.31 Ἔλεγεν οὖν   ὁ Ἰησοῦς πρὸς τοὺς
WAS SAYING THEREFORE - JESUS   TO   THE

πεπιστευκότας αὐτῷ Ἰουδαίους, Ἐὰν ὑμεῖς μείνητε
²HAVING BELIEVED ³IN HIM ¹JEWS,   IF   YOU° REMAIN

ἐν τῷ λόγῳ τῷ ἐμῷ, ἀληθῶς μαθηταί μού ἐστε
IN THE WORD - OF ME, TRULY DISCIPLES OF ME YOU° ARE

8.32 καὶ γνώσεσθε τὴν ἀλήθειαν, καὶ ἡ ἀλήθεια
AND YOU° WILL KNOW THE TRUTH,   AND THE TRUTH

ἐλευθερώσει ὑμᾶς. **8.33** ἀπεκρίθησαν πρὸς αὐτόν,
WILL FREE   YOU°.   THEY GAVE ANSWER TO   HIM,

Σπέρμα Ἀβραάμ ἐσμεν καὶ οὐδενὶ δεδουλεύκαμεν
[THE] SEED OF ABRAHAM WE ARE AND TO NO ONE HAVE BEEN ENSLAVED

πώποτε· πῶς σὺ λέγεις ὅτι Ἐλεύθεροι γενήσεσθε;
EVER.   HOW DO YOU SAY, - FREE MEN   YOU° WILL BECOME?

8.34 ἀπεκρίθη αὐτοῖς ὁ Ἰησοῦς, Ἀμὴν ἀμὴν λέγω
ANSWERED THEM - JESUS,   TRULY, TRULY I SAY

ὑμῖν ὅτι πᾶς ὁ ποιῶν τὴν ἁμαρτίαν δοῦλός ἐστιν τῆς
TO YOU° THAT EVERYONE DOING - SIN   A SLAVE IS   THE

ἁμαρτίας. **8.35** ὁ δὲ δοῦλος οὐ μένει ἐν τῇ οἰκίᾳ
OF SIN.   BUT~THE SLAVE DOES NOT REMAIN IN THE HOUSEHOLD

unless you believe that I am he."*o* 25They said to him, "Who are you?" Jesus said to them, "Why do I speak to you at all?*p* 26I have much to say about you and much to condemn; but the one who sent me is true, and I declare to the world what I have heard from him." 27They did not understand that he was speaking to them about the Father. 28So Jesus said, "When you have lifted up the Son of Man, then you will realize that I am he,*o* and that I do nothing on my own, but I speak these things as the Father instructed me. 29And the one who sent me is with me; he has not left me alone, for I always do what is pleasing to him." 30As he was saying these things, many believed in him.

31 Then Jesus said to the Jews who had believed in him, "If you continue in my word, you are truly my disciples; 32and you will know the truth, and the truth will make you free." 33They answered him, "We are descendants of Abraham and have never been slaves to anyone. What do you mean by saying, 'You will be made free'?"

34 Jesus answered them, "Very truly, I tell you, everyone who commits sin is a slave to sin. 35The slave does not have a permanent place in the household;

o Gk *I am*
p Or *What I have told you from the beginning*

the son has a place there
forever. 36So if the Son
makes you free, you will be
free indeed. 37I know that
you are descendants of
Abraham; yet you look for
an opportunity to kill me,
because there is no place in
you for my word. 38I declare
what I have seen in the
Father's presence; as for
you, you should do what
you have heard from the
Father."[q]
39 They answered him,
"Abraham is our father."
Jesus said to them, "If you
were Abraham's children,
you would be doing[r] what
Abraham did, 40but now you
are trying to kill me, a man
who has told you the truth
that I heard from God. This
is not what Abraham did.
41You are indeed doing what
your father does." They
said to him, "We are not
illegitimate children; we
have one Father, God
himself." 42Jesus said to
them, "If God were your
Father, you would love me,
for I came from God and
now I am here. I did not
come on my own, but he
sent me. 43Why do you not
understand what I say?
It is because you cannot
accept my word. 44You
are from your father the
devil, and you choose to
do your father's desires.
He was a murderer from

[q] Other ancient authorities read *you do what you have heard from your father*

[r] Other ancient authorities read *If you are Abraham's children, then do*

εἰς τὸν αἰῶνα, ὁ υἱὸς μένει εἰς τὸν αἰῶνα. **8.36** ἐὰν
INTO THE AGE. THE SON REMAINS INTO THE AGE. IF

οὖν ὁ υἱὸς ὑμᾶς ἐλευθερώσῃ, ὄντως ἐλεύθεροι
THEREFORE THE SON FREES~YOU°, REALLY FREE MEN

ἔσεσθε. **8.37** οἶδα ὅτι σπέρμα Ἀβραάμ ἐστε· ἀλλὰ
YOU° WILL BE. I KNOW THAT SEED OF ABRAHAM YOU° ARE; BUT

ζητεῖτέ με ἀποκτεῖναι, ὅτι ὁ λόγος ὁ ἐμὸς
YOU° SEEK TO KILL~ME, BECAUSE THE WORD - OF ME

οὐ χωρεῖ ἐν ὑμῖν. **8.38** ἃ ἐγὼ ἑώρακα παρὰ τῷ
HAS NO PLACE IN YOU°. THE THINGS I HAVE SEEN WITH THE

πατρὶ λαλῶ· καὶ ὑμεῖς οὖν ἃ ἠκούσατε παρὰ
FATHER I SPEAK. AND YOU° THEREFORE THE THINGS YOU° HEARD FROM

τοῦ πατρὸς ποιεῖτε.
THE(YOUR) FATHER YOU° DO.

8.39 Ἀπεκρίθησαν καὶ εἶπαν αὐτῷ, Ὁ πατὴρ ἡμῶν
THEY ANSWERED AND SAID TO HIM, THE FATHER OF US

Ἀβραάμ ἐστιν. λέγει αὐτοῖς ὁ Ἰησοῦς, Εἰ τέκνα τοῦ
IS~ABRAHAM. SAYS TO THEM - JESUS, IF CHILDREN -

Ἀβραάμ ἐστε, τὰ ἔργα τοῦ Ἀβραὰμ ⌜ἐποιεῖτε⌝·
OF ABRAHAM YOU° ARE, THE WORKS - OF ABRAHAM YOU° WOULD HAVE BEEN DOING.

8.40 νῦν δὲ ζητεῖτέ με ἀποκτεῖναι ἄνθρωπον ὃς τὴν
BUT~NOW YOU° ARE SEEKING TO KILL~ME, A MAN WHO THE

ἀλήθειαν ὑμῖν λελάληκα ἣν ἤκουσα παρὰ τοῦ θεοῦ·
TRUTH HAS TOLD~YOU°, WHICH I HEARD FROM - GOD.

τοῦτο Ἀβραὰμ οὐκ ἐποίησεν. **8.41** ὑμεῖς ποιεῖτε τὰ
THIS ABRAHAM DID NOT DO. YOU° ARE DOING THE

ἔργα τοῦ πατρὸς ὑμῶν. εἶπαν [οὖν] αὐτῷ, Ἡμεῖς
WORKS OF THE FATHER OF YOU°. SAID THEREFORE TO HIM, WE

ἐκ πορνείας οὐ γεγεννήμεθα· ἕνα πατέρα ἔχομεν τὸν
OF FORNICATION HAVE NOT BEEN BORN. ONE FATHER WE HAVE, -

θεόν. **8.42** εἶπεν αὐτοῖς ὁ Ἰησοῦς, Εἰ ὁ θεὸς πατὴρ
GOD. SAID TO THEM - JESUS, IF - GOD [THE] FATHER

ὑμῶν ἦν ἠγαπᾶτε ἂν ἐμέ, ἐγὼ γὰρ ἐκ τοῦ θεοῦ
OF YOU° WAS, YOU° WOULD HAVE LOVED ME, FOR~I FROM - GOD

ἐξῆλθον καὶ ἥκω· οὐδὲ γὰρ ἀπ' ἐμαυτοῦ ἐλήλυθα,
CAME FORTH AND I COME. FOR~NOT FROM MYSELF I HAVE COME,

ἀλλ' ἐκεῖνός με ἀπέστειλεν. **8.43** διὰ τί τὴν λαλιὰν
BUT THAT ONE SENT~ME. WHY THE SPEECH

τὴν ἐμὴν οὐ γινώσκετε; ὅτι οὐ δύνασθε ἀκούειν τὸν
- OF ME YOU° DO NOT RECOGNIZE? BECAUSE YOU° ARE NOT ABLE TO HEAR THE

λόγον τὸν ἐμόν. **8.44** ὑμεῖς ἐκ τοῦ πατρὸς τοῦ
WORD - OF ME. YOU° OF THE FATHER THE

διαβόλου ἐστὲ καὶ τὰς ἐπιθυμίας τοῦ πατρὸς ὑμῶν
DEVIL ARE AND THE DESIRES OF THE FATHER OF YOU°

θέλετε ποιεῖν. ἐκεῖνος ἀνθρωποκτόνος ἦν ἀπ'
YOU° WANT TO DO. THAT ONE WAS~A MANSLAYER FROM

8:39 text: KJV ASV RSV NIV NEB TEV NJBmg NRSV. var. ποιειτε (do—an imperative): ASVmg NASB NIVmg NEBmg TEVmg NJB NRSVmg. var. εποιειτε αν (you would have done): none.

ἀρχῆς   καὶ   ἐν   τῇ   ἀληθείᾳ   οὐκ   ἔστηκεν,   ὅτι
[THE] BEGINNING AND   IN   THE   TRUTH   HAS NOT STOOD,   BECAUSE

οὐκ ἔστιν ἀλήθεια ἐν αὐτῷ.   ὅταν λαλῇ   τὸ ψεῦδος, ἐκ
TRUTH~IS NOT   IN HIM.   WHEN HE SPEAKS THE LIE,   OF

τῶν   ἰδίων   λαλεῖ, ὅτι   ψεύστης ἐστὶν καὶ ὁ
THE(HIS) OWN THINGS HE SPEAKS, BECAUSE HE IS~A LIAR   AND   THE

πατὴρ αὐτοῦ.   8.45 ἐγὼ δὲ ὅτι   τὴν ἀλήθειαν λέγω,
FATHER   OF IT.   BUT~I BECAUSE THE TRUTH   SPEAK,

οὐ πιστεύετέ μοι.   8.46 τίς ἐξ   ὑμῶν ἐλέγχει με
YOU° DO NOT BELIEVE ME.   WHO AMONG YOU° EXPOSES   ME

περὶ   ἁμαρτίας;   εἰ ἀλήθειαν λέγω, διὰ τί ὑμεῖς
CONCERNING SIN?   IF I SPEAK~TRUTH,   WHY   YOU°

οὐ πιστεύετέ μοι;   8.47 ὁ   ὢν ἐκ τοῦ θεοῦ τὰ
DO NOT BELIEVE   ME?   THE ONE BEING FROM -   GOD   THE

ῥήματα τοῦ θεοῦ ἀκούει· διὰ τοῦτο ὑμεῖς οὐκ ἀκούετε,
WORDS   -   OF GOD HEARS.   THEREFORE YOU°   DO NOT HEAR,

ὅτι   ἐκ τοῦ θεοῦ οὐκ ἐστέ.
BECAUSE OF -   GOD   YOU° ARE NOT.

   8.48 Ἀπεκρίθησαν οἱ Ἰουδαῖοι καὶ εἶπαν αὐτῷ, Οὐ
       ANSWERED   THE JEWS   AND   SAID   TO HIM, ²NOT

καλῶς λέγομεν ἡμεῖς ὅτι Σαμαρίτης εἶ σὺ καὶ
³RIGHTLY ⁴SAY   ¹[DID] WE THAT A SAMARITAN YOU~ARE AND

δαιμόνιον ἔχεις;   8.49 ἀπεκρίθη Ἰησοῦς, Ἐγὼ
YOU HAVE~A DEMON?   ANSWERED   JESUS,   I

δαιμόνιον οὐκ ἔχω, ἀλλὰ τιμῶ τὸν πατέρα μου, καὶ
DO NOT HAVE~A DEMON,   BUT   I HONOR THE FATHER   OF ME, AND

ὑμεῖς ἀτιμάζετέ με.   8.50 ἐγὼ δὲ οὐ ζητῶ τὴν δόξαν
YOU   DISHONOR   ME.   BUT~I   DO NOT SEEK THE GLORY

μου· ἔστιν ὁ   ζητῶν καὶ κρίνων.   8.51 ἀμὴν ἀμὴν
OF ME. THERE IS THE ONE SEEKING AND JUDGING.   TRULY, TRULY

λέγω ὑμῖν, ἐάν τις   τὸν ἐμὸν λόγον τηρήσῃ, θάνατον
I SAY TO YOU°, IF ANYONE -   MY   WORD   KEEPS,   DEATH

οὐ μὴ θεωρήσῃ εἰς τὸν αἰῶνα. 8.52 εἶπον [οὖν]   αὐτῷ
HE WILL NEVER SEE   INTO THE AGE.   SAID   THEREFORE TO HIM

οἱ Ἰουδαῖοι, Νῦν ἐγνώκαμεν ὅτι δαιμόνιον ἔχεις.
THE JEWS,   NOW   WE HAVE KNOWN THAT YOU HAVE~A DEMON.

Ἀβραὰμ ἀπέθανεν καὶ οἱ προφῆται, καὶ σὺ λέγεις,
ABRAHAM   DIED   AND THE PROPHETS,   AND YOU SAY,

Ἐάν τις   τὸν λόγον μου τηρήσῃ, οὐ μὴ γεύσηται
IF ANYONE THE WORD   OF ME KEEPS,   HE WILL NEVER TASTE

θανάτου εἰς τὸν αἰῶνα. 8.53 μὴ   σὺ μείζων εἶ
DEATH   INTO THE AGE,   [SURELY] NOT YOU ARE~GREATER

τοῦ   πατρὸς ἡμῶν Ἀβραάμ, ὅστις ἀπέθανεν; καὶ οἱ
[THAN] THE FATHER   OF US, ABRAHAM,   WHO   DIED?   AND THE

προφῆται ἀπέθανον· τίνα σεαυτὸν ποιεῖς; 8.54 ἀπεκρίθη
PROPHETS   DIED;   WHOM DO YOU MAKE~YOURSELF?   ANSWERED

Ἰησοῦς, Ἐὰν ἐγὼ δοξάσω ἐμαυτόν, ἡ δόξα μου
JESUS,   IF   I   GLORIFY   MYSELF,   THE GLORY OF ME

the beginning and does not stand in the truth, because there is no truth in him. When he lies, he speaks according to his own nature, for he is a liar and the father of lies. ⁴⁵But because I tell the truth, you do not believe me. ⁴⁶Which of you convicts me of sin? If I tell the truth, why do you not believe me? ⁴⁷Whoever is from God hears the words of God. The reason you do not hear them is that you are not from God."

48 The Jews answered him, "Are we not right in saying that you are a Samaritan and have a demon?" ⁴⁹Jesus answered, "I do not have a demon; but I honor my Father, and you dishonor me. ⁵⁰Yet I do not seek my own glory; there is one who seeks it and he is the judge. ⁵¹Very truly, I tell you, whoever keeps my word will never see death." ⁵²The Jews said to him, "Now we know that you have a demon. Abraham died, and so did the prophets; yet you say, 'Whoever keeps my word will never taste death.' ⁵³Are you greater than our father Abraham, who died? The prophets also died. Who do you claim to be?" ⁵⁴Jesus answered, "If I glorify myself, my glory is

nothing. It is my Father who glorifies me, he of whom you say, 'He is our God,' [55]though you do not know him. But I know him; if I would say that I do not know him, I would be a liar like you. But I do know him and I keep his word. [56]Your ancestor Abraham rejoiced that he would see my day; he saw it and was glad." [57]Then the Jews said to him, "You are not yet fifty years old, and have you seen Abraham?"[s] [58]Jesus said to them, "Very truly, I tell you, before Abraham was, I am." [59]So they picked up stones to throw at him, but Jesus hid himself and went out of the temple.

[s] Other ancient authorities read *has Abraham seen you?*

οὐδέν ἐστιν· ἔστιν ὁ πατήρ μου ὁ δοξάζων με,
IS~NOTHING; [4]IS [1]THE [2]FATHER [3]OF ME THE ONE GLORIFYING ME,

ὃν ὑμεῖς λέγετε ὅτι θεὸς ἡμῶν ἐστιν, **8.55** καὶ
WHOM YOU° SAY THAT GOD OF US HE IS. AND

οὐκ ἐγνώκατε αὐτόν, ἐγὼ δὲ οἶδα αὐτόν. κἂν εἴπω
YOU° HAVE NOT KNOWN HIM, BUT~I HAVE KNOWN HIM. EVEN IF I SAY

ὅτι οὐκ οἶδα αὐτόν, ἔσομαι ὅμοιος ὑμῖν ψεύστης·
THAT I HAVE NOT KNOWN HIM, I WILL BE LIKE YOU°, A LIAR.

ἀλλὰ οἶδα αὐτὸν καὶ τὸν λόγον αὐτοῦ τηρῶ.
BUT I KNOW HIM AND THE WORD OF HIM I KEEP.

8.56 Ἀβραὰμ ὁ πατὴρ ὑμῶν ἠγαλλιάσατο ἵνα ἴδῃ
ABRAHAM, THE FATHER OF YOU° WAS GLAD THAT HE COULD SEE

τὴν ἡμέραν τὴν ἐμήν, καὶ εἶδεν καὶ ἐχάρη.
THE DAY - OF ME, AND HE SAW [IT] AND REJOICED.

8.57 εἶπον οὖν οἱ Ἰουδαῖοι πρὸς αὐτόν, Πεντήκοντα
SAID THEREFORE THE JEWS TO HIM, FIFTY

ἔτη οὔπω ἔχεις καὶ ⌜Ἀβραὰμ ἑώρακας⌝; **8.58** εἶπεν
YEARS NOT YET YOU POSSESS AND ABRAHAM YOU HAVE SEEN? SAID

αὐτοῖς Ἰησοῦς, Ἀμὴν ἀμὴν λέγω ὑμῖν, πρὶν Ἀβραὰμ
TO THEM JESUS, TRULY, TRULY I SAY TO YOU°, BEFORE ABRAHAM

γενέσθαι ἐγὼ εἰμί. **8.59** ἦραν οὖν λίθους ἵνα
CAME INTO BEING I AM. THEN~THEY TOOK UP STONES THAT

βάλωσιν ἐπ᾽ αὐτόν· Ἰησοῦς δὲ ἐκρύβη καὶ ἐξῆλθεν
THEY MIGHT THROW AT HIM, BUT~JESUS WAS HIDDEN AND DEPARTED

ἐκ τοῦ ἱεροῦ.
OUT OF THE TEMPLE.

8:57 text: all. var. Αβρααμ εωρακεν σε (Abraham has seen you): RSVmg NEBmg TEVmg NRSVmg.

CHAPTER 9

As he walked along, he saw a man blind from birth. [2]His disciples asked him, "Rabbi, who sinned, this man or his parents, that he was born blind?" [3]Jesus answered, "Neither this man nor his parents sinned; he was born blind so that God's works might be revealed in him. [4]We[t] must work the works of him who sent me[u] while it is day; night is coming when no one can work. [5]As long as I am in the world,

[t] Other ancient authorities read *I*
[u] Other ancient authorities read *us*

9.1 Καὶ παράγων εἶδεν ἄνθρωπον τυφλὸν ἐκ
AND PASSING ALONG HE SAW A MAN BLIND FROM

γενετῆς. **9.2** καὶ ἠρώτησαν αὐτὸν οἱ μαθηταὶ αὐτοῦ
BIRTH. AND ASKED HIM THE DISCIPLES OF HIM

λέγοντες, Ῥαββί, τίς ἥμαρτεν, οὗτος ἢ οἱ γονεῖς
SAYING, RABBI, WHO SINNED, THIS MAN OR THE PARENTS

αὐτοῦ, ἵνα τυφλὸς γεννηθῇ; **9.3** ἀπεκρίθη Ἰησοῦς,
OF HIM, THAT BLIND HE WAS BORN ANSWERED JESUS,

Οὔτε οὗτος ἥμαρτεν οὔτε οἱ γονεῖς αὐτοῦ, ἀλλ᾽
NEITHER THIS MAN SINNED NOR THE PARENTS OF HIM, BUT

ἵνα φανερωθῇ τὰ ἔργα τοῦ θεοῦ ἐν αὐτῷ.
THAT MAY BE MANIFESTED THE WORKS - OF GOD IN HIM.

9.4 ἡμᾶς δεῖ ἐργάζεσθαι τὰ ἔργα τοῦ
IT IS NECESSARY [FOR]~US TO WORK THE WORKS OF THE ONE

πέμψαντός με ἕως ἡμέρα ἐστίν· ἔρχεται νὺξ ὅτε
HAVING SENT ME WHILE IT IS~DAY. COMES NIGHT WHEN

οὐδεὶς δύναται ἐργάζεσθαι. **9.5** ὅταν ἐν τῷ κόσμῳ ὦ,
NO ONE IS ABLE TO WORK. WHEN IN THE WORLD I AM,

φῶς εἰμι τοῦ κόσμου. **9.6** ταῦτα εἰπὼν ἔπτυσεν
LIGHT I AM OF THE WORLD. THESE THINGS HAVING SAID, HE SPAT

χαμαὶ καὶ ἐποίησεν πηλὸν ἐκ τοῦ πτύσματος
ON THE GROUND AND HE MADE CLAY OUT OF THE SPITTLE,

καὶ ἐπέχρισεν αὐτοῦ τὸν πηλὸν ἐπὶ τοὺς ὀφθαλμοὺς
AND HE PUT (ANOINTED) ⁴HIS ¹THE ²CLAY ³ON - ⁵EYES,

9.7 καὶ εἶπεν αὐτῷ, Ὕπαγε νίψαι εἰς τὴν
AND SAID TO HIM, GO TO WASH IN THE

κολυμβήθραν τοῦ Σιλωάμ (ὃ ἑρμηνεύεται
POOL - OF SILOAM (WHICH IS TRANSLATED

Ἀπεσταλμένος). ἀπῆλθεν οὖν καὶ ἐνίψατο καὶ
HAVING BEEN SENT). HE WENT THEREFORE AND WASHED AND

ἦλθεν βλέπων. **9.8** Οἱ οὖν γείτονες καὶ οἱ
CAME SEEING. THEREFORE~THE NEIGHBORS AND THE ONES

θεωροῦντες αὐτὸν τὸ πρότερον ὅτι προσαίτης ἦν
SEEING HIM FORMERLY THAT A BEGGAR HE WAS

ἔλεγον, Οὐχ οὗτός ἐστιν ὁ καθήμενος καὶ
WERE SAYING, NOT IS~THIS MAN THE ONE SITTING AND

προσαιτῶν; **9.9** ἄλλοι ἔλεγον ὅτι Οὗτός ἐστιν, ἄλλοι
BEGGING? SOME WERE SAYING, - THIS IS HE; OTHERS

ἔλεγον, Οὐχί, ἀλλὰ ὅμοιος αὐτῷ ἐστιν. ἐκεῖνος
WERE SAYING, NO, BUT LIKE HIM HE IS. THAT ONE

ἔλεγεν ὅτι Ἐγώ εἰμι. **9.10** ἔλεγον οὖν
WAS SAYING, - I AM [HE]. THEY WERE SAYING THEREFORE

αὐτῷ, Πῶς [οὖν] ἠνεῴχθησάν σου οἱ ὀφθαλμοί;
TO HIM, HOW, THEN, WERE OPENED YOUR - EYES?

9.11 ἀπεκρίθη ἐκεῖνος, Ὁ ἄνθρωπος ὁ λεγόμενος
ANSWERED THAT MAN, THE MAN, THE ONE BEING CALLED

Ἰησοῦς πηλὸν ἐποίησεν καὶ ἐπέχρισέν μου τοὺς
JESUS, MADE~CLAY AND ANOINTED MY -

ὀφθαλμοὺς καὶ εἶπέν μοι ὅτι Ὕπαγε εἰς τὸν Σιλωὰμ
EYES AND SAID TO ME, - GO TO - SILOAM

καὶ νίψαι· ἀπελθὼν οὖν καὶ νιψάμενος ἀνέβλεψα.
AND WASH. HAVING GONE THEREFORE AND HAVING WASHED I SAW.

9.12 καὶ εἶπαν αὐτῷ, Ποῦ ἐστιν ἐκεῖνος; λέγει,
AND THEY SAID TO HIM, WHERE IS THAT ONE? HE SAYS,

Οὐκ οἶδα.
I DO NOT KNOW.

9.13 Ἄγουσιν αὐτὸν πρὸς τοὺς Φαρισαίους τόν ποτε
THEY LEAD HIM TO THE PHARISEES, THE ONCE

τυφλόν. **9.14** ἦν δὲ σάββατον ἐν ᾗ ἡμέρᾳ τὸν
BLIND MAN. NOW~IT WAS A SABBATH DURING WHICH DAY ³THE

πηλὸν ἐποίησεν ὁ Ἰησοῦς καὶ ἀνέῳξεν αὐτοῦ τοὺς
⁴CLAY ²MADE - ¹JESUS AND OPENED HIS -

ὀφθαλμούς. **9.15** πάλιν οὖν ἠρώτων αὐτὸν καὶ οἱ
EYES. THEN~AGAIN WERE ASKING HIM ALSO THE

Φαρισαῖοι πῶς ἀνέβλεψεν. ὁ δὲ εἶπεν αὐτοῖς, Πηλὸν
PHARISEES HOW HE SAW. AND~HE SAID TO THEM, CLAY

I am the light of the world." [6]When he had said this, he spat on the ground and made mud with the saliva and spread the mud on the man's eyes, [7]saying to him, "Go, wash in the pool of Siloam" (which means Sent). Then he went and washed and came back able to see. [8]The neighbors and those who had seen him before as a beggar began to ask, "Is this not the man who used to sit and beg?" [9]Some were saying, "It is he." Others were saying, "No, but it is someone like him." He kept saying, "I am the man." [10]But they kept asking him, "Then how were your eyes opened?" [11]He answered, "The man called Jesus made mud, spread it on my eyes, and said to me, 'Go to Siloam and wash.' Then I went and washed and received my sight." [12]They said to him, "Where is he?" He said, "I do not know."

13 They brought to the Pharisees the man who had formerly been blind. [14]Now it was a sabbath day when Jesus made the mud and opened his eyes. [15]Then the Pharisees also began to ask him how he had received his sight. He said to them, "He

put mud on my eyes. Then I washed, and now I see." [16]Some of the Pharisees said, "This man is not from God, for he does not observe the sabbath." But others said, "How can a man who is a sinner perform such signs?" And they were divided. [17]So they said again to the blind man, "What do you say about him? It was your eyes he opened." He said, "He is a prophet."

18 The Jews did not believe that he had been blind and had received his sight until they called the parents of the man who had received his sight [19]and asked them, "Is this your son, who you say was born blind? How then does he now see?" [20]His parents answered, "We know that this is our son, and that he was born blind; [21]but we do not know how it is that now he sees, nor do we know who opened his eyes. Ask him; he is of age. He will speak for himself." [22]His parents said this because they were afraid of the Jews; for the Jews had already agreed that anyone who confessed Jesus[v] to be the Messiah[w] would be put out of the synagogue. [23]Therefore his parents said, "He is of age; ask him."

[v] Gk him
[w] Or the Christ

ἐπέθηκέν μου ἐπὶ τοὺς ὀφθαλμοὺς καὶ ἐνιψάμην, καὶ
HE PLACED ON~MY - EYES, AND I WASHED, AND

βλέπω. **9.16** ἔλεγον οὖν ἐκ τῶν Φαρισαίων τινές,
I SEE. THEREFORE~WERE SAYING ²OF ³THE ⁴PHARISEES ¹SOME,

Οὐκ ἔστιν οὗτος παρὰ θεοῦ ὁ ἄνθρωπος, ὅτι τὸ
³IS NOT ¹THIS ⁴FROM ⁵GOD - ²MAN, BECAUSE THE

σάββατον οὐ τηρεῖ. ἄλλοι [δὲ] ἔλεγον, Πῶς δύναται
SABBATH HE DOES NOT KEEP. BUT~OTHERS WERE SAYING, HOW IS ABLE

ἄνθρωπος ἁμαρτωλὸς τοιαῦτα σημεῖα ποιεῖν; καὶ
A MAN [WHO IS] A SINNER SUCH SIGNS TO DO? AND

σχίσμα ἦν ἐν αὐτοῖς. **9.17** λέγουσιν οὖν τῷ
A DIVISION WAS AMONG THEM. THEY SAY THEREFORE TO THE

τυφλῷ πάλιν, Τί σὺ λέγεις περὶ αὐτοῦ, ὅτι ἠνέῳξέν
BLIND MAN AGAIN, WHAT DO YOU SAY ABOUT HIM, BECAUSE HE OPENED

σου τοὺς ὀφθαλμούς; ὁ δὲ εἶπεν ὅτι Προφήτης ἐστίν.
YOUR - EYES? - AND~HE SAID, - HE IS~A PROPHET.

9.18 Οὐκ ἐπίστευσαν οὖν οἱ Ἰουδαῖοι περὶ αὐτοῦ
DID NOT BELIEVE THEREFORE THE JEWS ABOUT HIM

ὅτι ἦν τυφλὸς καὶ ἀνέβλεψεν ἕως ὅτου ἐφώνησαν
THAT HE WAS BLIND AND SAW UNTIL THEY CALLED

τοὺς γονεῖς αὐτοῦ τοῦ ἀναβλέψαντος **9.19** καὶ
THE PARENTS OF HIM, THE ONE HAVING SEEN, AND

ἠρώτησαν αὐτοὺς λέγοντες, Οὗτός ἐστιν ὁ υἱὸς ὑμῶν,
ASKED THEM SAYING, THIS IS THE SON OF YOU°,

ὃν ὑμεῖς λέγετε ὅτι τυφλὸς ἐγεννήθη; πῶς οὖν
WHOM YOU° SAY THAT BLIND HE WAS BORN? HOW THEREFORE

βλέπει ἄρτι; **9.20** ἀπεκρίθησαν οὖν οἱ γονεῖς
DOES HE SEE NOW? ANSWERED THEREFORE THE PARENTS

αὐτοῦ καὶ εἶπαν, Οἴδαμεν ὅτι οὗτός ἐστιν ὁ υἱὸς
OF HIM AND SAID, WE KNOW THAT THIS MAN IS THE SON

ἡμῶν καὶ ὅτι τυφλὸς ἐγεννήθη· **9.21** πῶς δὲ νῦν βλέπει
OF US AND THAT HE WAS BORN~BLIND; BUT~HOW NOW HE SEES

οὐκ οἴδαμεν, ἢ τίς ἤνοιξεν αὐτοῦ τοὺς ὀφθαλμοὺς
WE DO NOT KNOW, OR WHO OPENED HIS EYES

ἡμεῖς οὐκ οἴδαμεν· αὐτὸν ἐρωτήσατε, ἡλικίαν ἔχει,
WE DO NOT KNOW. ASK~HIM, HE IS OF AGE;

αὐτὸς περὶ ἑαυτοῦ λαλήσει. **9.22** ταῦτα εἶπαν οἱ
HE ABOUT HIMSELF WILL SPEAK. THESE THINGS SAID THE

γονεῖς αὐτοῦ ὅτι ἐφοβοῦντο τοὺς Ἰουδαίους·
PARENTS OF HIM BECAUSE THEY WERE FEARING THE JEWS,

ἤδη γὰρ συνετέθειντο οἱ Ἰουδαῖοι ἵνα ἐάν τις
FOR~ALREADY HAD AGREED THE JEWS THAT IF ANYONE

αὐτὸν ὁμολογήσῃ Χριστόν, ἀποσυνάγωγος γένηται.
CONFESSED~HIM [TO BE] [THE] CHRIST, HE WOULD BE~PUT AWAY FROM [THE] SYNAGOGUE.

9.23 διὰ τοῦτο οἱ γονεῖς αὐτοῦ εἶπαν ὅτι Ἡλικίαν ἔχει,
THEREFORE THE PARENTS OF HIM SAID, - HE IS OF AGE,

αὐτὸν ἐπερωτήσατε.
ASK~HIM.

9.24 Ἐφώνησαν οὖν   τὸν ἄνθρωπον ἐκ δευτέρου ὃς
THEY CALLED   THEREFORE THE   MAN   A SECOND TIME   WHO

ἦν τυφλὸς καὶ εἶπαν αὐτῷ, Δὸς δόξαν τῷ θεῷ·
WAS BLIND   AND   SAID   TO HIM,   GIVE GLORY   -   TO GOD,

ἡμεῖς οἴδαμεν ὅτι οὗτος ὁ ἄνθρωπος ἁμαρτωλός ἐστιν.
WE   KNOW   THAT THIS   -   MAN   IS~A SINNER.

9.25 ἀπεκρίθη   οὖν   ἐκεῖνος, Εἰ ἁμαρτωλός ἐστιν
ANSWERED   THEREFORE THAT MAN,   IF   HE IS~A SINNER

οὐκ οἶδα·   ἓν   οἶδα ὅτι τυφλὸς ὢν ἄρτι βλέπω.
I DO NOT KNOW.   ONE THING I KNOW THAT BEING~BLIND NOW   I SEE.

9.26 εἶπον οὖν   αὐτῷ, Τί ἐποίησέν σοι;   πῶς
THEY SAID THEREFORE TO HIM,   WHAT DID HE DO   TO YOU?   HOW

ἤνοιξέν σου τοὺς ὀφθαλμούς; **9.27** ἀπεκρίθη αὐτοῖς,
DID HE OPEN YOUR   -   EYES?   HE ANSWERED   THEM,

Εἶπον ὑμῖν ἤδη   καὶ οὐκ ἠκούσατε· τί πάλιν
I TOLD   YOU°   ALREADY AND   YOU DID NOT LISTEN.   WHY AGAIN

θέλετε   ἀκούειν; μὴ   καὶ ὑμεῖς θέλετε αὐτοῦ
DO YOU °WANT   TO HEAR [IT]? [SURELY] NOT ALSO   YOU°   WANT   HIS

μαθηταὶ γενέσθαι; **9.28** καὶ ἐλοιδόρησαν αὐτὸν καὶ
DISCIPLES   TO BECOME?   AND   THEY REVILED   HIM   AND

εἶπον, Σὺ μαθητὴς εἶ ἐκείνου, ἡμεῖς δὲ τοῦ Μωϋσέως
SAID,   YOU ARE~A DISCIPLE OF THAT MAN, BUT~WE   -   OF MOSES

ἐσμὲν μαθηταί· **9.29** ἡμεῖς οἴδαμεν ὅτι Μωϋσεῖ
ARE   DISCIPLES.   WE   KNOW   THAT TO MOSES

λελάληκεν ὁ θεός, τοῦτον δὲ οὐκ οἴδαμεν πόθεν
HAS SPOKEN   -   GOD,   BUT~THIS MAN WE DO NOT KNOW FROM WHERE

ἐστίν. **9.30** ἀπεκρίθη ὁ ἄνθρωπος καὶ εἶπεν αὐτοῖς,
HE IS.   ANSWERED   THE MAN   AND   SAID   TO THEM,

Ἐν τούτῳ γὰρ τὸ θαυμαστόν ἐστιν, ὅτι ὑμεῖς
²IN   ³THIS ¹FOR ⁵THE ⁶THING   ⁴IS,   THAT YOU°

οὐκ οἴδατε πόθεν   ἐστίν, καὶ ἤνοιξέν μου τοὺς
DO NOT KNOW   FROM WHERE HE IS,   AND   HE OPENED   MY   -

ὀφθαλμούς. **9.31** οἴδαμεν ὅτι ἁμαρτωλῶν ὁ θεὸς
EYES.   WE KNOW   THAT SINNERS   -   GOD

οὐκ ἀκούει,   ἀλλ᾽ ἐάν τις   θεοσεβὴς ᾖ καὶ τὸ
DOES NOT LISTEN [TO], BUT   IF   ANYONE IS~GOD-FEARING AND   THE

θέλημα αὐτοῦ ποιῇ τούτου ἀκούει. **9.32** ἐκ τοῦ αἰῶνος
WILL   OF HIM DOES—THIS ONE HE HEARS.   FROM THE   AGE

οὐκ ἠκούσθη ὅτι ἠνέῳξέν τις ὀφθαλμοὺς τυφλοῦ
IT WAS NOT HEARD   THAT ANYONE~OPENED [THE] EYES   OF A BLIND MAN

γεγεννημένου· **9.33** εἰ μὴ ἦν οὗτος παρὰ θεοῦ,
HAVING BEEN BORN [THUS].   ¹IF ⁴NOT ³WAS ²THIS MAN FROM   GOD,

οὐκ ἠδύνατο   ποιεῖν οὐδέν. **9.34** ἀπεκρίθησαν καὶ
HE WOULD NOT BE ABLE TO DO   ANYTHING.   THEY ANSWERED   AND

εἶπαν αὐτῷ, Ἐν ἁμαρτίαις σὺ ἐγεννήθης ὅλος καὶ
SAID   TO HIM, IN   SINS   YOU WERE BORN   TOTALLY AND

σὺ διδάσκεις ἡμᾶς; καὶ ἐξέβαλον αὐτὸν ἔξω.
YOU TEACH   US?   AND   THEY THREW   HIM   OUT.

24 So for the second time they called the man who had been blind, and they said to him, "Give glory to God! We know that this man is a sinner." ²⁵He answered, "I do not know whether he is a sinner. One thing I do know, that though I was blind, now I see." ²⁶They said to him, "What did he do to you? How did he open your eyes?" ²⁷He answered them, "I have told you already, and you would not listen. Why do you want to hear it again? Do you also want to become his disciples?" ²⁸Then they reviled him, saying, "You are his disciple, but we are disciples of Moses. ²⁹We know that God has spoken to Moses, but as for this man, we do not know where he comes from." ³⁰The man answered, "Here is an astonishing thing! You do not know where he comes from, and yet he opened my eyes. ³¹We know that God does not listen to sinners, but he does listen to one who worships him and obeys his will. ³²Never since the world began has it been heard that anyone opened the eyes of a person born blind. ³³If this man were not from God, he could do nothing." ³⁴They answered him, "You were born entirely in sins, and are you trying to teach us?" And they drove him out.

35 Jesus heard that they had driven him out, and when he found him, he said, "Do you believe in the Son of Man?"[x] 36He answered, "And who is he, sir?[y] Tell me, so that I may believe in him." 37Jesus said to him, "You have seen him, and the one speaking with you is he." 38He said, "Lord,[y] I believe." And he worshiped him. 39Jesus said, "I came into this world for judgment so that those who do not see may see, and those who do see may become blind." 40Some of the Pharisees near him heard this and said to him, "Surely we are not blind, are we?" 41Jesus said to them, "If you were blind, you would not have sin. But now that you say, 'We see,' your sin remains.

[x] Other ancient authorities read *the Son of God*
[y] *Sir* and *Lord* translate the same Greek word

9.35 Ἤκουσεν Ἰησοῦς ὅτι ἐξέβαλον αὐτὸν ἔξω καὶ
HEARD   JESUS   THAT THEY THREW HIM   OUT AND

εὑρὼν   αὐτὸν εἶπεν, Σὺ πιστεύεις εἰς ⌐τὸν υἱὸν τοῦ
HAVING FOUND HIM   SAID, DO YOU BELIEVE IN   THE SON -

ἀνθρώπου⌐; **9.36** ἀπεκρίθη ἐκεῖνος καὶ εἶπεν, Καὶ τίς
OF MAN?   ANSWERED   THAT MAN AND SAID, AND WHO

ἐστιν, κύριε, ἵνα πιστεύσω εἰς αὐτόν; **9.37** εἶπεν αὐτῷ
IS HE, SIR, THAT I MAY BELIEVE IN HIM?   SAID TO HIM

ὁ Ἰησοῦς, Καὶ ἑώρακας αὐτὸν καὶ ὁ   λαλῶν μετὰ
- JESUS, BOTH YOU HAVE SEEN HIM AND THE ONE SPEAKING WITH

σοῦ ἐκεῖνός ἐστιν. **9.38** ὁ δὲ ἔφη, Πιστεύω κύριε· καὶ
YOU IS~THAT ONE.   - AND~HE SAID, I BELIEVE, LORD; AND

προσεκύνησεν αὐτῷ. **9.39** καὶ εἶπεν ὁ Ἰησοῦς, Εἰς
HE WORSHIPED   HIM.   AND SAID - JESUS,   FOR

κρίμα ἐγὼ εἰς τὸν κόσμον τοῦτον ἦλθον, ἵνα οἱ   μὴ
JUDGMENT I INTO - THIS~WORLD   CAME, THAT THE ONES NOT

βλέποντες βλέπωσιν καὶ οἱ βλέποντες τυφλοὶ γένωνται.
SEEING   MAY SEE   AND THE ONES SEEING MAY BECOME~BLIND.

9.40 Ἤκουσαν ἐκ   τῶν Φαρισαίων ταῦτα οἱ
[4]HEARD   [1][SOME] OF [2]THE [3]PHARISEES THESE THINGS—THE ONES

μετ' αὐτοῦ ὄντες καὶ εἶπον αὐτῷ, Μὴ   καὶ ἡμεῖς
WITH HIM BEING—AND THEY SAID TO HIM, [SURELY] NOT ALSO WE

τυφλοί ἐσμεν; **9.41** εἶπεν αὐτοῖς ὁ Ἰησοῦς, Εἰ τυφλοὶ
ARE~BLIND?   SAID TO THEM - JESUS,   IF BLIND ONES

ἦτε,   οὐκ ἂν εἴχετε ἁμαρτίαν· νῦν δὲ   λέγετε ὅτι
YOU° WERE, YOU° WOULD NOT HAVE SIN; BUT~NOW [SINCE] YOU° SAY, -

Βλέπομεν, ἡ ἁμαρτία ὑμῶν μένει.
WE SEE,   THE SIN   OF YOU° REMAINS.

9:35 text: ASVmg RSV NASB NIV NEB TEV NJB NRSV. var. τον υιον του θεου (the Son of God): KJV ASV RSVmg NEBmg NRSVmg.

CHAPTER 10

"Very truly, I tell you, anyone who does not enter the sheepfold by the gate but climbs in by another way is a thief and a bandit. 2The one who enters by the gate is the shepherd of the sheep. 3The gatekeeper opens the gate for him, and the sheep hear his voice. He calls his own sheep by name and leads them out.

10.1 Ἀμὴν ἀμὴν λέγω ὑμῖν, ὁ   μὴ εἰσερχόμενος
TRULY, TRULY I SAY TO YOU°, THE ONE NOT ENTERING

διὰ   τῆς θύρας εἰς τὴν αὐλὴν τῶν προβάτων ἀλλὰ
THROUGH THE DOOR INTO THE FOLD OF THE SHEEP   BUT

ἀναβαίνων ἀλλαχόθεν ἐκεῖνος κλέπτης ἐστὶν καὶ
GOING UP   ANOTHER WAY THAT ONE IS~A THIEF   AND

λῃστής· **10.2** ὁ δὲ   εἰσερχόμενος διὰ   τῆς θύρας
A ROBBER.   BUT~THE ONE ENTERING   THROUGH THE DOOR

ποιμήν ἐστιν τῶν προβάτων. **10.3** τούτῳ   ὁ θυρωρὸς
IS~A SHEPHERD OF THE SHEEP.   TO THIS ONE THE DOORKEEPER

ἀνοίγει, καὶ τὰ πρόβατα τῆς φωνῆς αὐτοῦ ἀκούει καὶ
OPENS,   AND THE SHEEP   THE VOICE OF HIM HEAR   AND

τὰ ἴδια πρόβατα φωνεῖ κατ' ὄνομα καὶ ἐξάγει αὐτά.
HIS~OWN SHEEP   HE CALLS BY NAME   AND LEADS OUT THEM.

10.4 ὅταν τὰ ἴδια πάντα ἐκβάλῃ, ἔμπροσθεν αὐτῶν
WHEN ²HIS OWN ¹ALL HE PUTS FORTH, BEFORE THEM

πορεύεται, καὶ τὰ πρόβατα αὐτῷ ἀκολουθεῖ, ὅτι
HE GOES, AND THE SHEEP FOLLOW~HIM, BECAUSE

οἴδασιν τὴν φωνὴν αὐτοῦ· **10.5** ἀλλοτρίῳ δὲ
THEY KNOW THE VOICE OF HIM; BUT~A STRANGER

οὐ μὴ ἀκολουθήσουσιν, ἀλλὰ φεύξονται ἀπ᾽ αὐτοῦ, ὅτι
THEY WILL NEVER FOLLOW BUT WILL FLEE FROM HIM, BECAUSE

οὐκ οἴδασιν τῶν ἀλλοτρίων τὴν φωνήν. **10.6** Ταύτην τὴν
THEY DO NOT KNOW - ³OF STRANGERS ¹THE ²VOICE. THIS -

παροιμίαν εἶπεν αὐτοῖς ὁ Ἰησοῦς, ἐκεῖνοι δὲ
SIMILITUDE ²TOLD ³THEM - ¹JESUS, BUT~THOSE MEN

οὐκ ἔγνωσαν τίνα ἦν ἃ ἐλάλει αὐτοῖς.
DID NOT UNDERSTAND WHAT THINGS THEY WERE WHICH HE WAS SPEAKING TO THEM.

10.7 Εἶπεν οὖν πάλιν ὁ Ἰησοῦς, Ἀμὴν ἀμὴν
SAID THEREFORE AGAIN - JESUS, TRULY, TRULY

λέγω ὑμῖν ὅτι ἐγώ εἰμι ἡ θύρα τῶν προβάτων.
I SAY TO YOU° THAT I AM THE DOOR OF THE SHEEP.

10.8 πάντες ὅσοι ἦλθον [πρὸ ἐμοῦ] κλέπται εἰσὶν καὶ
ALL WHO CAME BEFORE ME ARE~THIEVES AND

λῃσταί, ἀλλ᾽ οὐκ ἤκουσαν αὐτῶν τὰ πρόβατα. **10.9** ἐγώ
ROBBERS; BUT DID NOT LISTEN [TO] THEM THE SHEEP. I

εἰμι ἡ θύρα· δι᾽ ἐμοῦ ἐάν τις εἰσέλθῃ σωθήσεται
AM THE DOOR; THROUGH ME IF ANYONE ENTERS HE WILL BE SAVED

καὶ εἰσελεύσεται καὶ ἐξελεύσεται καὶ νομὴν εὑρήσει.
AND WILL GO IN AND WILL GO OUT AND WILL FIND~PASTURE.

10.10 ὁ κλέπτης οὐκ ἔρχεται εἰ μὴ ἵνα κλέψῃ
THE THIEF DOES NOT COME EXCEPT IN ORDER THAT HE MAY STEAL

καὶ θύσῃ καὶ ἀπολέσῃ· ἐγὼ ἦλθον ἵνα ζωὴν ἔχωσιν
AND KILL AND DESTROY. I CAME THAT LIFE THEY MAY HAVE

καὶ περισσὸν ἔχωσιν. **10.11** Ἐγώ εἰμι ὁ ποιμὴν ὁ
AND [THAT] MAY HAVE [IT]~ABUNDANTLY. I AM THE SHEPHERD, THE

καλός· ὁ ποιμὴν ὁ καλὸς τὴν ψυχὴν αὐτοῦ τίθησιν
GOOD ONE. THE SHEPHERD, THE GOOD ONE, THE LIFE OF HIM LAYS DOWN

ὑπὲρ τῶν προβάτων· **10.12** ὁ μισθωτὸς καὶ οὐκ ὢν
FOR THE SHEEP. THE HIRED MAN ALSO NOT BEING

ποιμήν, οὗ οὐκ ἔστιν τὰ πρόβατα ἴδια, θεωρεῖ τὸν
A SHEPHERD, OF WHOM IS(ARE) NOT THE SHEEP HIS OWN, SEES THE

λύκον ἐρχόμενον καὶ ἀφίησιν τὰ πρόβατα καὶ
WOLF COMING AND LEAVES THE SHEEP AND

φεύγει— καὶ ὁ λύκος ἁρπάζει αὐτὰ καὶ σκορπίζει—
FLEES— AND THE WOLF SEIZES THEM AND SCATTERS [THEM]—

10.13 ὅτι μισθωτὸς ἐστιν καὶ οὐ μέλει αὐτῷ περὶ
BECAUSE HE IS~A HIRED MAN AND IT DOES NOT MATTER TO HIM ABOUT

τῶν προβάτων. **10.14** Ἐγώ εἰμι ὁ ποιμὴν ὁ καλός
THE SHEEP. I AM THE SHEPHERD, THE GOOD ONE,

καὶ γινώσκω τὰ ἐμὰ καὶ γινώσκουσί με τὰ ἐμά,
AND I KNOW - MINE AND ²KNOW ³ME - ¹MINE.

[4]When he has brought out all his own, he goes ahead of them, and the sheep follow him because they know his voice. [5]They will not follow a stranger, but they will run from him because they do not know the voice of strangers." [6]Jesus used this figure of speech with them, but they did not understand what he was saying to them.

7 So again Jesus said to them, "Very truly, I tell you, I am the gate for the sheep. [8]All who came before me are thieves and bandits; but the sheep did not listen to them. [9]I am the gate. Whoever enters by me will be saved, and will come in and go out and find pasture. [10]The thief comes only to steal and kill and destroy. I came that they may have life, and have it abundantly.

11 "I am the good shepherd. The good shepherd lays down his life for the sheep. [12]The hired hand, who is not the shepherd and does not own the sheep, sees the wolf coming and leaves the sheep and runs away— and the wolf snatches them and scatters them. [13]The hired hand runs away because a hired hand does not care for the sheep. [14]I am the good shepherd. I know my own and my own know me,

15just as the Father knows me and I know the Father. And I lay down my life for the sheep. 16I have other sheep that do not belong to this fold. I must bring them also, and they will listen to my voice. So there will be one flock, one shepherd. 17For this reason the Father loves me, because I lay down my life in order to take it up again. 18No one takes[z] it from me, but I lay it down of my own accord. I have power to lay it down, and I have power to take it up again. I have received this command from my Father."

19 Again the Jews were divided because of these words. 20Many of them were saying, "He has a demon and is out of his mind. Why listen to him?" 21Others were saying, "These are not the words of one who has a demon. Can a demon open the eyes of the blind?"

22 At that time the festival of the Dedication took place in Jerusalem. It was winter, 23and Jesus was walking in the temple, in the portico of Solomon. 24So the Jews gathered around him and said to him, "How long will you keep us in suspense? If you are the Messiah,[a] tell us plainly." 25Jesus answered,

[z] Other ancient authorities read *has taken*
[a] Or *the Christ*

10.15 καθὼς γινώσκει με ὁ πατὴρ κἀγὼ γινώσκω τὸν
JUST AS   KNOWS   ME THE FATHER   AND I   KNOW   THE

πατέρα, καὶ   τὴν ψυχήν μου τίθημι ὑπὲρ τῶν
FATHER, [SO] ALSO THE LIFE OF ME I LAY DOWN FOR THE

προβάτων. **10.16** καὶ ἄλλα πρόβατα ἔχω ἃ
SHEEP.   AND OTHER SHEEP   I HAVE WHICH

οὐκ ἔστιν ἐκ τῆς αὐλῆς ταύτης· κἀκεῖνα δεῖ
ARE NOT   OF - THIS~FOLD;   THOSE ALSO IT IS NECESSARY [FOR]

με ἀγαγεῖν καὶ τῆς φωνῆς μου ἀκούσουσιν, καὶ
ME TO BRING, AND THE VOICE OF ME THEY WILL HEAR, AND

⌐γενήσονται⌐ μία ποίμνη, εἷς ποιμήν. **10.17** διὰ τοῦτό
THEY WILL BECOME ONE FLOCK, [WITH] ONE SHEPHERD.   THEREFORE

με ὁ πατὴρ ἀγαπᾷ ὅτι ἐγὼ τίθημι τὴν ψυχήν μου,
ME THE FATHER LOVES BECAUSE I LAY DOWN THE LIFE OF ME,

ἵνα πάλιν λάβω αὐτήν. **10.18** οὐδεὶς αἴρει αὐτὴν ἀπ'
THAT AGAIN I MAY TAKE IT.   NO ONE TAKES   IT   FROM

ἐμοῦ, ἀλλ' ἐγὼ τίθημι αὐτὴν ἀπ' ἐμαυτοῦ. ἐξουσίαν ἔχω
ME,   BUT I LAY DOWN IT   FROM MYSELF. I HAVE~AUTHORITY

θεῖναι αὐτήν, καὶ ἐξουσίαν ἔχω πάλιν λαβεῖν αὐτήν·
TO LAY DOWN IT, AND I HAVE~AUTHORITY AGAIN TO RECEIVE IT;

ταύτην τὴν ἐντολὴν ἔλαβον παρὰ τοῦ πατρός μου.
THIS   -   COMMAND I RECEIVED FROM THE FATHER OF ME.

10.19 Σχίσμα πάλιν ἐγένετο ἐν τοῖς Ἰουδαίοις
A DIVISION AGAIN THERE WAS AMONG THE JEWS

διὰ τοὺς λόγους τούτους. **10.20** ἔλεγον δὲ πολλοὶ
BECAUSE OF - THESE~WORDS.   AND~WERE SAYING MANY

ἐξ αὐτῶν, Δαιμόνιον ἔχει καὶ μαίνεται· τί
OF THEM, HE HAS~A DEMON AND HE IS MAD. WHY

αὐτοῦ ἀκούετε; **10.21** ἄλλοι ἔλεγον, Ταῦτα τὰ ῥήματα
DO YOU° LISTEN~TO HIM?   OTHERS SAID, THESE - WORDS

οὐκ ἔστιν δαιμονιζομένου· μὴ δαιμόνιον
ARE NOT OF ONE BEING DEMON-POSSESSED. [SURELY] NOT A DEMON

δύναται τυφλῶν ὀφθαλμοὺς ἀνοῖξαι;
IS ABLE 3OF A BLIND MAN 2EYES   1TO OPEN?

10.22 Ἐγένετο τότε τὰ ἐγκαίνια ἐν τοῖς
THERE WAS THEN THE [FEAST OF] DEDICATION AMONG THE ONES

Ἱεροσολύμοις, χειμὼν ἦν, **10.23** καὶ περιεπάτει ὁ
IN JERUSALEM. IT WAS~WINTER,   AND 2WAS WALKING AROUND -

Ἰησοῦς ἐν τῷ ἱερῷ ἐν τῇ στοᾷ τοῦ Σολομῶνος.
1JESUS IN THE TEMPLE ON THE PORCH - OF SOLOMON.

10.24 ἐκύκλωσαν οὖν αὐτὸν οἱ Ἰουδαῖοι καὶ ἔλεγον
THEN~ENCIRCLED HIM THE JEWS   AND WERE SAYING

αὐτῷ, Ἕως πότε τὴν ψυχὴν ἡμῶν αἴρεις; εἰ σὺ
TO HIM, UNTIL WHEN 2THE 3SOUL 4OF US 1HOLD [IN SUSPENSE]? IF YOU

εἶ ὁ Χριστός, εἰπὲ ἡμῖν παρρησίᾳ. **10.25** ἀπεκρίθη
ARE THE CHRIST, TELL US OPENLY.   ANSWERED

10:16 text: ASV NASB TEV. var. γενησεται (there will be): KJV ASVmg RSV NIV NEB NJB NRSV.

αὐτοῖς ὁ Ἰησοῦς, Εἶπον ὑμῖν καὶ οὐ πιστεύετε· τὰ
THEM - JESUS, I TOLD YOU° AND YOU° DO NOT BELIEVE. THE

ἔργα ἃ ἐγὼ ποιῶ ἐν τῷ ὀνόματι τοῦ πατρός μου
WORKS WHICH I DO IN THE NAME OF THE FATHER OF ME

ταῦτα μαρτυρεῖ περὶ ἐμοῦ· **10.26** ἀλλὰ ὑμεῖς
THESE TESTIFY ABOUT ME, BUT YOU°

οὐ πιστεύετε, ὅτι οὐκ ἐστὲ ἐκ τῶν προβάτων τῶν ἐμῶν.
DO NOT BELIEVE, BECAUSE YOU° ARE~NOT OF THE SHEEP - OF ME.

10.27 τὰ πρόβατα τὰ ἐμὰ τῆς φωνῆς μου ἀκούουσιν,
THE SHEEP - OF ME THE VOICE OF ME HEAR,

κἀγὼ γινώσκω αὐτά καὶ ἀκολουθοῦσίν μοι, **10.28** κἀγὼ
AND I KNOW THEM AND THEY FOLLOW ME, AND I

δίδωμι αὐτοῖς ζωὴν αἰώνιον καὶ οὐ μὴ ἀπόλωνται εἰς
GIVE TO THEM ETERNAL~LIFE AND THEY WILL NEVER PERISH INTO

τὸν αἰῶνα καὶ οὐχ ἁρπάσει τις αὐτὰ ἐκ τῆς χειρός
THE AGE, AND WILL NOT SNATCH ANYONE THEM OUT OF THE HAND

μου. **10.29** ⌜ὁ πατήρ μου ὁ δέδωκέν μοι
OF ME. ²THE ³FATHER ⁴OF ME ¹THAT WHICH HAS GIVEN ME

πάντων μεῖζόν ἐστιν,⌝ καὶ οὐδεὶς δύναται ἁρπάζειν
GREATER [THAN]~ALL IS, AND NO ONE IS ABLE TO SNATCH

ἐκ τῆς χειρὸς τοῦ πατρός. **10.30** ἐγὼ καὶ ὁ πατὴρ
OUT OF THE HAND OF THE FATHER. I AND THE FATHER

ἕν ἐσμεν.
ARE~ONE.

10.31 Ἐβάστασαν πάλιν λίθους οἱ Ἰουδαῖοι ἵνα
AGAIN~TOOK UP STONES THE JEWS THAT

λιθάσωσιν αὐτόν. **10.32** ἀπεκρίθη αὐτοῖς ὁ Ἰησοῦς,
THEY MIGHT STONE HIM. ANSWERED THEM - JESUS,

Πολλὰ ἔργα καλὰ ἔδειξα ὑμῖν ἐκ τοῦ πατρός· διὰ
MANY GOOD~WORKS I SHOWED YOU° FROM THE FATHER; BECAUSE OF

ποῖον αὐτῶν ἔργον ἐμὲ λιθάζετε; **10.33** ἀπεκρίθησαν
WHICH WORK~OF THEM DO YOU° STONE~ME? ANSWERED

αὐτῷ οἱ Ἰουδαῖοι, Περὶ καλοῦ ἔργου οὐ λιθάζομέν σε
HIM THE JEWS, FOR A GOOD WORK WE DO NOT STONE YOU

ἀλλὰ περὶ βλασφημίας, καὶ ὅτι σὺ ἄνθρωπος ὢν
BUT FOR BLASPHEMY, AND BECAUSE YOU BEING~A MAN

ποιεῖς σεαυτὸν θεόν. **10.34** ἀπεκρίθη αὐτοῖς [ὁ]
MAKE YOURSELF GOD. ANSWERED THEM -

Ἰησοῦς, Οὐκ ἔστιν γεγραμμένον ἐν τῷ νόμῳ ὑμῶν ὅτι
JESUS, HAS IT NOT BEEN WRITTEN IN THE LAW OF YOU°, -

Ἐγὼ εἶπα, Θεοί ἐστε; **10.35** εἰ ἐκείνους εἶπεν θεοὺς
I SAID, YOU° ARE~GODS? IF THOSE ONES HE CALLED GODS,

πρὸς οὓς ὁ λόγος τοῦ θεοῦ ἐγένετο, καὶ οὐ δύναται
TO WHOM THE WORD - OF GOD CAME— AND IS NOT ABLE

"I have told you, and you do not believe. The works that I do in my Father's name testify to me; ²⁶but you do not believe, because you do not belong to my sheep. ²⁷My sheep hear my voice. I know them, and they follow me. ²⁸I give them eternal life, and they will never perish. No one will snatch them out of my hand. ²⁹What my Father has given me is greater than all else, and no one can snatch it out of the Father's hand.ᵇ ³⁰The Father and I are one."

31 The Jews took up stones again to stone him. ³²Jesus replied, "I have shown you many good works from the Father. For which of these are you going to stone me?" ³³The Jews answered, "It is not for a good work that we are going to stone you, but for blasphemy, because you, though only a human being, are making yourself God." ³⁴Jesus answered, "Is it not written in your law,ᶜ 'I said, you are gods'? ³⁵If those to whom the word of God came were called 'gods'— and the scripture cannot

ᵇ Other ancient authorities read *My Father who has given them to me is greater than all, and no one can snatch them out of the Father's hand*

ᶜ Other ancient authorities read *in the law*

10:29 text: ASVmg RSVmg NASBmg NIVmg NEBmg TEV NRSV. var. ο πατηρ μου ος δεδωκεν μοι μειζων παντων εστιν (My Father who has given them to me is greater than all): KJV ASV RSV NIV NEB TEVmg NRSVmg. var. ο πατηρ μου ο δεδωκεν μοι παντων μειζων εστιν (My Father—as to that which he has given me—is greater than all): NJB. **10:34** Ps. 82:6

be annulled— ³⁶can you say that the one whom the Father has sanctified and sent into the world is blaspheming because I said, 'I am God's Son'? ³⁷If I am not doing the works of my Father, then do not believe me. ³⁸But if I do them, even though you do not believe me, believe the works, so that you may know and understand*ᵈ* that the Father is in me and I am in the Father." ³⁹Then they tried to arrest him again, but he escaped from their hands.

40 He went away again across the Jordan to the place where John had been baptizing earlier, and he remained there. ⁴¹Many came to him, and they were saying, "John performed no sign, but everything that John said about this man was true." ⁴²And many believed in him there.

ᵈ Other ancient authorities lack and understand; others read and believe

λυθῆναι ἡ γραφή, **10.36** ὃν ὁ πατὴρ ἡγίασεν
TO BE ABOLISHED THE SCRIPTURE— [OF] HIM WHOM THE FATHER SANCTIFIED

καὶ ἀπέστειλεν εἰς τὸν κόσμον ὑμεῖς λέγετε ὅτι
AND SENT INTO THE WORLD DO YOU° SAY THAT

Βλασφημεῖς, ὅτι εἶπον, Υἱὸς τοῦ θεοῦ εἰμι; **10.37** εἰ
HE BLASPHEMES, BECAUSE I SAID, SON - OF GOD I AM? IF

οὐ ποιῶ τὰ ἔργα τοῦ πατρός μου, μὴ πιστεύετέ μοι·
I DO NOT PERFORM THE WORKS OF THE FATHER OF ME, DO NOT BELIEVE ME;

10.38 εἰ δὲ ποιῶ, κἂν ἐμοὶ μὴ πιστεύητε, τοῖς ἔργοις
BUT~IF I DO, EVEN IF ME YOU° DO NOT BELIEVE, THE WORKS

πιστεύετε, ἵνα γνῶτε καὶ γινώσκητε ὅτι ἐν
BELIEVE, THAT YOU° MAY KNOW AND MAY CONTINUE TO KNOW THAT IN

ἐμοὶ ὁ πατὴρ κἀγὼ ἐν τῷ πατρί. **10.39** Ἐζήτουν
ME THE FATHER [IS] AND I IN THE FATHER. THEY WERE SEEKING

[οὖν] αὐτὸν πάλιν πιάσαι, καὶ ἐξῆλθεν ἐκ τῆς
THEREFORE HIM AGAIN TO SEIZE, AND HE WENT OUT FROM THE

χειρὸς αὐτῶν.
HAND OF THEM.

10.40 Καὶ ἀπῆλθεν πάλιν πέραν τοῦ Ἰορδάνου εἰς τὸν
AND HE WENT AWAY AGAIN ACROSS THE JORDAN TO THE

τόπον ὅπου ἦν Ἰωάννης τὸ πρῶτον βαπτίζων καὶ
PLACE WHERE JOHN~WAS AT FIRST BAPTIZING AND

ἔμεινεν ἐκεῖ. **10.41** καὶ πολλοὶ ἦλθον πρὸς αὐτὸν καὶ
HE REMAINED THERE. AND MANY CAME TO HIM AND

ἔλεγον ὅτι Ἰωάννης μὲν σημεῖον ἐποίησεν οὐδέν,
WERE SAYING, - JOHN INDEED ²SIGN ³DID ¹NO,

πάντα δὲ ὅσα εἶπεν Ἰωάννης περὶ τούτου ἀληθῆ ἦν.
BUT~EVERYTHING WHICHEVER JOHN~SAID ABOUT THIS MAN WAS~TRUE.

10.42 καὶ πολλοὶ ἐπίστευσαν εἰς αὐτὸν ἐκεῖ.
AND MANY BELIEVED IN HIM THERE.

CHAPTER 11

Now a certain man was ill, Lazarus of Bethany, the village of Mary and her sister Martha. ²Mary was the one who anointed the Lord with perfume and wiped his feet with her hair; her brother Lazarus was ill. ³So the sisters sent a message to Jesus,*ᵉ*

ᵉ Gk him

11.1 Ἦν δέ τις ἀσθενῶν, Λάζαρος ἀπὸ
NOW~THERE WAS A CERTAIN ONE BEING SICK, LAZARUS FROM

Βηθανίας, ἐκ τῆς κώμης Μαρίας καὶ Μάρθας τῆς
BETHANY, OF THE VILLAGE OF MARY AND MARTHA THE

ἀδελφῆς αὐτῆς. **11.2** ἦν δὲ Μαριὰμ ἡ ἀλείψασα
SISTER OF HER. NOW~IT WAS MARY THE ONE HAVING ANOINTED

τὸν κύριον μύρῳ καὶ ἐκμάξασα τοὺς πόδας αὐτοῦ
THE LORD WITH OINTMENT AND HAVING WIPED THE FEET OF HIM

ταῖς θριξὶν αὐτῆς, ἧς ὁ ἀδελφὸς Λάζαρος ἠσθένει.
WITH THE HAIRS OF HER, WHOSE - BROTHER LAZARUS WAS SICK.

11.3 ἀπέστειλαν οὖν αἱ ἀδελφαὶ πρὸς αὐτὸν
SENT THEREFORE THE SISTERS TO HIM

λέγουσαι, Κύριε, ἴδε ὃν   φιλεῖς   ἀσθενεῖ.
SAYING,   LORD,   LOOK, THE ONE WHOM YOU ARE FOND OF IS SICK.

11.4 ἀκούσας δὲ   ὁ Ἰησοῦς εἶπεν, Αὕτη ἡ ἀσθένεια
AND~HAVING HEARD [THIS] - JESUS   SAID,   THIS - SICKNESS

οὐκ ἔστιν πρὸς θάνατον ἀλλ' ὑπὲρ τῆς δόξης τοῦ θεοῦ,
IS~NOT   TO   DEATH   BUT FOR THE GLORY - OF GOD,

ἵνα δοξασθῇ   ὁ υἱὸς τοῦ θεοῦ δι'   αὐτῆς.
THAT MAY BE GLORIFIED THE SON - OF GOD THROUGH IT.

11.5 ἠγάπα δὲ ὁ Ἰησοῦς τὴν Μάρθαν καὶ τὴν ἀδελφὴν
NOW~LOVED - JESUS   -   MARTHA AND THE SISTER

αὐτῆς καὶ τὸν Λάζαρον. **11.6** ὡς οὖν   ἤκουσεν ὅτι
OF HER AND - LAZARUS.   WHEN THEREFORE HE HEARD THAT

ἀσθενεῖ, τότε μὲν ἔμεινεν ἐν ᾧ   ἦν   τόπῳ   δύο
HE IS SICK, THEN - HE REMAINED IN ²IN WHICH ³HE WAS ¹[THE] PLACE TWO

ἡμέρας, **11.7** ἔπειτα μετὰ τοῦτο λέγει τοῖς μαθηταῖς,
DAYS.   THEN   AFTER THIS HE SAYS TO THE DISCIPLES,

Ἄγωμεν εἰς τὴν Ἰουδαίαν πάλιν. **11.8** λέγουσιν αὐτῷ
LET US GO INTO - JUDEA   AGAIN.   SAY   TO HIM

οἱ μαθηταί, Ῥαββί, νῦν   ἐζήτουν σε λιθάσαι οἱ
THE DISCIPLES, RABBI, [JUST] NOW WERE SEEKING TO STONE~YOU THE

Ἰουδαῖοι, καὶ πάλιν ὑπάγεις ἐκεῖ; **11.9** ἀπεκρίθη
JEWS,   AND AGAIN YOU GO THERE?   ANSWERED

Ἰησοῦς, Οὐχὶ δώδεκα ὧραί εἰσιν τῆς ἡμέρας; ἐάν
JESUS,   NOT TWELVE HOURS ARE THERE OF THE DAY?   IF

τις   περιπατῇ ἐν τῇ ἡμέρᾳ, οὐ προσκόπτει, ὅτι   τὸ
ANYONE WALKS AROUND IN THE DAY, HE DOES NOT STUMBLE, BECAUSE THE

φῶς τοῦ κόσμου τούτου βλέπει· **11.10** ἐὰν δέ τις
LIGHT - OF THIS~WORLD HE SEES.   BUT~IF ANYONE

περιπατῇ ἐν τῇ νυκτί, προσκόπτει, ὅτι τὸ φῶς
WALKS AROUND DURING THE NIGHT, HE STUMBLES, BECAUSE THE LIGHT

οὐκ ἔστιν ἐν αὐτῷ. **11.11** ταῦτα   εἶπεν, καὶ μετὰ
IS NOT   IN HIM.   THESE THINGS HE SAID, AND AFTER

τοῦτο λέγει αὐτοῖς, Λάζαρος ὁ φίλος ἡμῶν
THIS HE SAYS TO THEM, LAZARUS, THE FRIEND OF US

κεκοίμηται· ἀλλὰ πορεύομαι ἵνα ἐξυπνίσω αὐτόν.
HAS FALLEN ASLEEP, BUT I AM GOING THAT I MAY AWAKEN HIM.

11.12 εἶπαν οὖν   οἱ μαθηταὶ αὐτῷ, Κύριε, εἰ
SAID THEREFORE THE DISCIPLES TO HIM, LORD, IF

κεκοίμηται   σωθήσεται. **11.13** εἰρήκει δὲ ὁ Ἰησοῦς
HE HAS FALLEN ASLEEP, HE WILL BE HEALED.   BUT~HAD SPOKEN - JESUS

περὶ τοῦ θανάτου αὐτοῦ, ἐκεῖνοι δὲ ἔδοξαν ὅτι περὶ
ABOUT THE DEATH   OF HIM, BUT~THOSE MEN SUPPOSED THAT ABOUT

τῆς κοιμήσεως τοῦ ὕπνου λέγει. **11.14** τότε οὖν
THE REST   -   OF SLEEP HE SPEAKS.   THEN THEREFORE

εἶπεν αὐτοῖς ὁ Ἰησοῦς παρρησίᾳ, Λάζαρος ἀπέθανεν,
TOLD THEM - JESUS   PLAINLY,   LAZARUS   DIED,

11.15 καὶ χαίρω δι'   ὑμᾶς ἵνα πιστεύσητε, ὅτι
AND I REJOICE BECAUSE OF YOU° THAT YOU° MAY BELIEVE, THAT

"Lord, he whom you love is ill." [4]But when Jesus heard it, he said, "This illness does not lead to death; rather it is for God's glory, so that the Son of God may be glorified through it." [5]Accordingly, though Jesus loved Martha and her sister and Lazarus, [6]after having heard that Lazarus[f] was ill, he stayed two days longer in the place where he was.

7 Then after this he said to the disciples, "Let us go to Judea again." [8]The disciples said to him, "Rabbi, the Jews were just now trying to stone you, and are you going there again?" [9]Jesus answered, "Are there not twelve hours of daylight? Those who walk during the day do not stumble, because they see the light of this world. [10]But those who walk at night stumble, because the light is not in them." [11]After saying this, he told them, "Our friend Lazarus has fallen asleep, but I am going there to awaken him." [12]The disciples said to him, "Lord, if he has fallen asleep, he will be all right." [13]Jesus, however, had been speaking about his death, but they thought that he was referring merely to sleep. [14]Then Jesus told them plainly, "Lazarus is dead. [15]For your sake I am glad I was not there, so that you may believe.

[f] Gk *he*

But let us go to him."
[16]Thomas, who was called the Twin,[g] said to his fellow disciples, "Let us also go, that we may die with him."

17 When Jesus arrived, he found that Lazarus[h] had already been in the tomb four days. [18]Now Bethany was near Jerusalem, some two miles[i] away, [19]and many of the Jews had come to Martha and Mary to console them about their brother. [20]When Martha heard that Jesus was coming, she went and met him, while Mary stayed at home. [21]Martha said to Jesus, "Lord, if you had been here, my brother would not have died. [22]But even now I know that God will give you whatever you ask of him." [23]Jesus said to her, "Your brother will rise again." [24]Martha said to him, "I know that he will rise again in the resurrection on the last day." [25]Jesus said to her, "I am the resurrection and the life.[j] Those who believe in me, even though they die, will live, [26]and everyone who lives and believes in me will never die. Do you believe this?" [27]She said to him, "Yes,

[g] Gk *Didymus*
[h] Gk *he*
[i] Gk *fifteen stadia*
[j] Other ancient authorities lack *and the life*

οὐκ ἤμην ἐκεῖ· ἀλλὰ ἄγωμεν πρὸς αὐτόν. **11.16** εἶπεν
I WAS NOT   THERE;   BUT   LET US GO   TO   HIM.   SAID

οὖν   Θωμᾶς ὁ   λεγόμενος Δίδυμος τοῖς
THEREFORE THOMAS,   THE ONE BEING CALLED   DIDYMUS,   TO THE

συμμαθηταῖς, Ἄγωμεν καὶ ἡμεῖς ἵνα ἀποθάνωμεν
FELLOW DISCIPLES,   LET US GO   ALSO   THAT~WE MAY   DIE

μετ᾽ αὐτοῦ.
WITH   HIM.

11.17 Ἐλθὼν   οὖν   ὁ Ἰησοῦς εὗρεν αὐτὸν
HAVING COME   THEREFORE   -   JESUS   FOUND   HIM

τέσσαρας ἤδη ἡμέρας ἔχοντα ἐν τῷ μνημείῳ.
ALREADY~FOUR   DAYS   HAVING [BEEN]   IN   THE   TOMB.

11.18 ἦν δὲ ἡ Βηθανία ἐγγὺς τῶν Ἱεροσολύμων ὡς
NOW~WAS   -   BETHANY   NEAR   -   JERUSALEM   ABOUT

ἀπὸ σταδίων δεκαπέντε. **11.19** πολλοὶ δὲ ἐκ τῶν
3AWAY 2STADIA 1FIFTEEN.   AND~MANY   OF   THE

Ἰουδαίων ἐληλύθεισαν πρὸς τὴν Μάρθαν καὶ Μαριὰμ
JEWS   HAD COME   TO   -   MARTHA   AND   MARY

ἵνα παραμυθήσωνται αὐτὰς περὶ τοῦ ἀδελφοῦ.
THAT   THEY MIGHT CONSOLE   THEM   ABOUT   THE(THEIR) BROTHER.

11.20 ἡ οὖν   Μάρθα ὡς ἤκουσεν ὅτι Ἰησοῦς ἔρχεται
-   THEREFORE MARTHA   WHEN SHE HEARD   THAT   JESUS   COMES

ὑπήντησεν αὐτῷ· Μαριὰμ δὲ ἐν τῷ οἴκῳ ἐκαθέζετο.
MET   HIM;   BUT~MARY   IN   THE   HOUSE   WAS SITTING.

11.21 εἶπεν οὖν   ἡ Μάρθα πρὸς τὸν Ἰησοῦν, Κύριε,
SAID   THEREFORE   -   MARTHA   TO   -   JESUS,   LORD,

εἰ ἦς   ὧδε οὐκ ἂν ἀπέθανεν ὁ ἀδελφός μου·
IF   YOU WERE   HERE   WOULD NOT HAVE DIED   THE   BROTHER   OF ME;

11.22 [ἀλλὰ] καὶ νῦν οἶδα ὅτι ὅσα ἂν αἰτήσῃ τὸν θεὸν
BUT   EVEN   NOW I KNOW THAT   WHATEVER   YOU ASK   -   GOD

δώσει σοι ὁ θεός. **11.23** λέγει αὐτῇ ὁ Ἰησοῦς,
2WILL GIVE 3YOU - 1GOD.   SAYS   TO HER   -   JESUS,

Ἀναστήσεται ὁ ἀδελφός σου. **11.24** λέγει αὐτῷ ἡ
WILL RISE AGAIN   THE   BROTHER   OF YOU.   SAYS   TO HIM   -

Μάρθα, Οἶδα ὅτι ἀναστήσεται ἐν τῇ ἀναστάσει ἐν τῇ
MARTHA,   I KNOW   THAT   HE WILL RISE   IN   THE   RESURRECTION   ON   THE

ἐσχάτῃ ἡμέρᾳ. **11.25** εἶπεν αὐτῇ ὁ Ἰησοῦς, Ἐγώ εἰμι
LAST   DAY.   SAID   TO HER   -   JESUS,   I   AM

ἡ ἀνάστασις ⌜καὶ ἡ ζωή⌝· ὁ πιστεύων εἰς ἐμὲ
THE RESURRECTION   AND   THE LIFE;   THE ONE BELIEVING   IN   ME

κἂν ἀποθάνῃ ζήσεται, **11.26** καὶ πᾶς ὁ ζῶν καὶ
EVEN IF   HE SHOULD DIE WILL LIVE,   AND   EVERYONE LIVING AND

πιστεύων εἰς ἐμὲ οὐ μὴ ἀποθάνῃ εἰς τὸν αἰῶνα·
BELIEVING   IN   ME   NEVER DIES   INTO   THE   AGE.

πιστεύεις τοῦτο; **11.27** λέγει αὐτῷ, Ναί κύριε, ἐγὼ
DO YOU BELIEVE   THIS?   SHE SAYS   TO HIM,   YES   LORD,   I

11:25 text: KJV ASV RSV NASB NIV NEB TEV NJBmg NRSV.   omit: RSVmg NEBmg NJB NRSVmg.

πεπίστευκα ὅτι σὺ εἶ ὁ Χριστὸς ὁ υἱὸς τοῦ θεοῦ
HAVE BELIEVED   THAT YOU ARE THE CHRIST,   THE SON   -   OF GOD,

ὁ   εἰς τὸν κόσμον ἐρχόμενος.
THE ONE INTO THE   WORLD   COMING.

11.28 Καὶ τοῦτο εἰποῦσα ἀπῆλθεν καὶ ἐφώνησεν
AND   THIS   HAVING SAID SHE DEPARTED AND   CALLED

Μαριὰμ τὴν ἀδελφὴν αὐτῆς λάθρα εἰποῦσα, Ὁ
MARY   THE   SISTER   OF HER   SECRETLY HAVING SAID,   THE

διδάσκαλος πάρεστιν καὶ φωνεῖ σε. **11.29** ἐκείνη δὲ
TEACHER   IS HERE   AND   CALLS   YOU.   AND~THAT WOMAN

ὡς ἤκουσεν ἠγέρθη ταχὺ καὶ ἤρχετο πρὸς αὐτόν·
WHEN SHE HEARD AROSE QUICKLY AND WAS COMING TO HIM.

11.30 οὔπω δὲ ἐληλύθει ὁ Ἰησοῦς εἰς τὴν κώμην, ἀλλή
NOW~NOT YET HAD COME - JESUS INTO THE VILLAGE, BUT

ἦν ἔτι ἐν τῷ τόπῳ ὅπου ὑπήντησεν αὐτῷ ἡ Μάρθα.
HE WAS STILL IN THE PLACE WHERE MET HIM - MARTHA.

11.31 οἱ οὖν   Ἰουδαῖοι οἱ   ὄντες μετή αὐτῆς ἐν τῇ
THEREFORE~THE JEWS, THE ONES BEING WITH HER IN THE

οἰκίᾳ καὶ παραμυθούμενοι αὐτήν, ἰδόντες τὴν Μαριὰμ
HOUSE AND CONSOLING   HER, HAVING SEEN - MARY

ὅτι ταχέως ἀνέστη καὶ ἐξῆλθεν, ἠκολούθησαν αὐτῇ
THAT QUICKLY SHE ROSE UP AND WENT OUT, FOLLOWED HER,

δόξαντες ὅτι ὑπάγει εἰς τὸ μνημεῖον ἵνα κλαύσῃ
HAVING SUPPOSED THAT SHE IS GOING TO THE TOMB THAT SHE MIGHT WEEP

ἐκεῖ. **11.32** ἡ οὖν   Μαριὰμ ὡς ἦλθεν ὅπου
THERE.   - THEREFORE MARY WHEN SHE CAME WHERE

ἦν Ἰησοῦς ἰδοῦσα αὐτὸν ἔπεσεν αὐτοῦ πρὸς τοὺς πόδας
JESUS~WAS— SEEING HIM SHE FELL AT~HIS - FEET,

λέγουσα αὐτῷ, Κύριε, εἰ ἦς   ὧδε οὐκ ἄν μου
SAYING TO HIM, LORD, IF YOU WERE HERE ³WOULD NOT ¹MY

ἀπέθανεν ὁ ἀδελφός. **11.33** Ἰησοῦς οὖν ὡς εἶδεν
⁴HAVE DIED - ²BROTHER.   THEREFORE~JESUS WHEN HE SAW

αὐτὴν κλαίουσαν καὶ τοὺς συνελθόντας αὐτῇ Ἰουδαίους
HER WEEPING AND ¹THE ³HAVING COME WITH ⁴HER ²JEWS

κλαίοντας, ἐνεβριμήσατο τῷ   πνεύματι καὶ ἐτάραξεν
WEEPING, WAS DEEPLY MOVED IN THE(HIS) SPIRIT AND WAS TROUBLED

ἑαυτὸν **11.34** καὶ εἶπεν, Ποῦ τεθείκατε αὐτόν;
IN HIMSELF   AND SAID, WHERE HAVE YOU PLACED HIM?

λέγουσιν αὐτῷ, Κύριε, ἔρχου καὶ ἴδε. **11.35** ἐδάκρυσεν
THEY SAY TO HIM, LORD, COME AND SEE.   SHED TEARS

ὁ Ἰησοῦς. **11.36** ἔλεγον οὖν   οἱ Ἰουδαῖοι, Ἴδε πῶς
- JESUS.   WERE SAYING THEREFORE THE JEWS,   SEE HOW

ἐφίλει   αὐτόν. **11.37** τινὲς δὲ ἐξ αὐτῶν εἶπαν,
FOND HE WAS OF HIM.   BUT~SOME OF THEM SAID,

Οὐκ ἐδύνατο οὗτος ὁ   ἀνοίξας τοὺς ὀφθαλμοὺς
WAS NOT ABLE THIS MAN, THE ONE HAVING OPENED THE EYES

τοῦ τυφλοῦ ποιῆσαι   ἵνα καὶ οὗτος μὴ ἀποθάνῃ;
OF THE BLIND MAN, TO BRING [IT ABOUT] THAT EVEN THIS MAN SHOULD NOT DIE?

Lord, I believe that you are the Messiah,ᵏ the Son of God, the one coming into the world."

28 When she had said this, she went back and called her sister Mary, and told her privately, "The Teacher is here and is calling for you." ²⁹And when she heard it, she got up quickly and went to him. ³⁰Now Jesus had not yet come to the village, but was still at the place where Martha had met him. ³¹The Jews who were with her in the house, consoling her, saw Mary get up quickly and go out. They followed her because they thought that she was going to the tomb to weep there. ³²When Mary came where Jesus was and saw him, she knelt at his feet and said to him, "Lord, if you had been here, my brother would not have died." ³³When Jesus saw her weeping, and the Jews who came with her also weeping, he was greatly disturbed in spirit and deeply moved. ³⁴He said, "Where have you laid him?" They said to him, "Lord, come and see." ³⁵Jesus began to weep. ³⁶So the Jews said, "See how he loved him!" ³⁷But some of them said, "Could not he who opened the eyes of the blind man have kept this man from dying?"

ᵏ Or *the Christ*

38 Then Jesus, again greatly disturbed, came to the tomb. It was a cave, and a stone was lying against it. 39Jesus said, "Take away the stone." Martha, the sister of the dead man, said to him, "Lord, already there is a stench because he has been dead four days." 40Jesus said to her, "Did I not tell you that if you believed, you would see the glory of God?" 41So they took away the stone. And Jesus looked upward and said, "Father, I thank you for having heard me. 42I knew that you always hear me, but I have said this for the sake of the crowd standing here, so that they may believe that you sent me." 43When he had said this, he cried with a loud voice, "Lazarus, come out!" 44The dead man came out, his hands and feet bound with strips of cloth, and his face wrapped in a cloth. Jesus said to them, "Unbind him, and let him go."

45 Many of the Jews therefore, who had come with Mary and had seen what Jesus did, believed in him. 46But some of them went to the Pharisees and told them what he had done. 47So the chief priests and the Pharisees called a meeting of the council, and

11.38 Ἰησοῦς οὖν πάλιν ἐμβριμώμενος ἐν ἑαυτῷ
JESUS THEREFORE AGAIN BEING DEEPLY MOVED WITHIN HIMSELF

ἔρχεται εἰς τὸ μνημεῖον· ἦν δὲ σπήλαιον καὶ λίθος
COMES TO THE TOMB. NOW~IT WAS A CAVE, AND A STONE

ἐπέκειτο ἐπ' αὐτῷ. **11.39** λέγει ὁ Ἰησοῦς, Ἄρατε
WAS LYING ACROSS IT. SAYS - JESUS, LIFT

τὸν λίθον. λέγει αὐτῷ ἡ ἀδελφὴ τοῦ
THE STONE. SAYS TO HIM THE SISTER OF THE ONE

τετελευτηκότος Μάρθα, Κύριε, ἤδη ὄζει,
HAVING DIED, [NAMELY] MARTHA, LORD, ALREADY HE SMELLS,

τεταρταῖος γάρ ἐστιν. **11.40** λέγει αὐτῇ ὁ Ἰησοῦς,
FOR~[THE] FOURTH [DAY] IT IS. SAYS TO HER - JESUS,

Οὐκ εἶπόν σοι ὅτι ἐὰν πιστεύσῃς ὄψῃ τὴν δόξαν
DID I NOT TELL YOU THAT IF YOU BELIEVED YOU WILL SEE THE GLORY

τοῦ θεοῦ; **11.41** ἦραν οὖν τὸν λίθον. ὁ δὲ Ἰησοῦς
- OF GOD? THEREFORE~THEY LIFTED THE STONE. - AND JESUS

ἦρεν τοὺς ὀφθαλμοὺς ἄνω καὶ εἶπεν, Πάτερ, εὐχαριστῶ
LIFTED THE(HIS) EYES UP AND SAID, FATHER, I THANK

σοι ὅτι ἤκουσάς μου. **11.42** ἐγὼ δὲ ᾔδειν ὅτι πάντοτέ
YOU THAT YOU HEARD ME. AND~I KNEW THAT ALWAYS

μου ἀκούεις, ἀλλὰ διὰ τὸν ὄχλον τὸν περιεστῶτα
ME YOU HEAR, BUT BECAUSE OF THE CROWD - HAVING STOOD AROUND

εἶπον, ἵνα πιστεύσωσιν ὅτι σύ με ἀπέστειλας.
I SAID [IT], THAT THEY MAY BELIEVE THAT YOU SENT~ME.

11.43 καὶ ταῦτα εἰπὼν φωνῇ μεγάλῃ ἐκραύγασεν,
AND THESE THINGS HAVING SAID, WITH GREAT~VOICE HE CRIED OUT,

Λάζαρε, δεῦρο ἔξω. **11.44** ἐξῆλθεν ὁ τεθνηκὼς
LAZARUS, COME OUT. CAME OUT THE ONE HAVING DIED

δεδεμένος τοὺς πόδας καὶ τὰς χεῖρας
HAVING BEEN BOUND THE(HIS) FEET AND THE(HIS) HANDS

κειρίαις καὶ ἡ ὄψις αὐτοῦ σουδαρίῳ
WITH GRAVE CLOTHES, AND THE FACE OF HIM WITH A FACE CLOTH

περιεδέδετο. λέγει αὐτοῖς ὁ Ἰησοῦς, Λύσατε αὐτὸν
HAD BEEN BOUND AROUND. SAYS TO THEM - JESUS, UNTIE HIM

καὶ ἄφετε αὐτὸν ὑπάγειν.
AND ALLOW HIM TO GO.

11.45 Πολλοὶ οὖν ἐκ τῶν Ἰουδαίων οἱ ἐλθόντες
MANY THEREFORE OF THE JEWS, THE ONES HAVING COME

πρὸς τὴν Μαριὰμ καὶ θεασάμενοι ἃ
TO - MARY AND HAVING SEEN THE THINGS WHICH

ἐποίησεν ἐπίστευσαν εἰς αὐτόν· **11.46** τινὲς δὲ ἐξ αὐτῶν
HE DID, BELIEVED IN HIM; BUT~SOME OF THEM

ἀπῆλθον πρὸς τοὺς Φαρισαίους καὶ εἶπαν αὐτοῖς
WENT AWAY TO THE PHARISEES AND TOLD THEM

ἃ ἐποίησεν Ἰησοῦς. **11.47** συνήγαγον οὖν
THE THINGS WHICH JESUS~DID. ASSEMBLED THEREFORE

οἱ ἀρχιερεῖς καὶ οἱ Φαρισαῖοι συνέδριον καὶ
THE CHIEF PRIESTS AND THE PHARISEES A SANHEDRIN (COUNCIL) AND

ἔλεγον, Τί ποιοῦμεν ὅτι οὗτος ὁ ἄνθρωπος
WERE SAYING, WHAT ARE WE DOING, FOR THIS - MAN

πολλὰ ποιεῖ σημεῖα; **11.48** ἐὰν ἀφῶμεν αὐτὸν οὕτως,
IS DOING~MANY SIGNS? IF WE LEAVE HIM THUS,

πάντες πιστεύσουσιν εἰς αὐτόν, καὶ ἐλεύσονται οἱ
ALL MEN WILL BELIEVE IN HIM, AND WILL COME THE

Ῥωμαῖοι καὶ ἀροῦσιν ἡμῶν καὶ τὸν τόπον καὶ τὸ
ROMANS AND WILL TAKE OF US BOTH THE [HOLY] PLACE AND THE

ἔθνος. **11.49** εἷς δέ τις ἐξ αὐτῶν Καϊάφας,
NATION. ³ONE ¹BUT ²A CERTAIN OF THEM, CAIPHAS,

ἀρχιερεὺς ὢν τοῦ ἐνιαυτοῦ ἐκείνου, εἶπεν αὐτοῖς, Ὑμεῖς
BEING~HIGH PRIEST - THAT~YEAR, SAID TO THEM, YOU°

οὐκ οἴδατε οὐδέν, **11.50** οὐδὲ λογίζεσθε ὅτι συμφέρει
DO NOT KNOW ANYTHING, NOR DO YOU° RECKON THAT IT IS BETTER

ὑμῖν ἵνα εἷς ἄνθρωπος ἀποθάνῃ ὑπὲρ τοῦ λαοῦ
FOR YOU° THAT ONE MAN SHOULD DIE ON BEHALF OF THE PEOPLE

καὶ μὴ ὅλον τὸ ἔθνος ἀπόληται. **11.51** τοῦτο δὲ·
AND NOT ALL THE NATION SHOULD PERISH. BUT~THIS

ἀφ᾽ ἑαυτοῦ οὐκ εἶπεν, ἀλλὰ ἀρχιερεὺς ὢν τοῦ
FROM HIMSELF HE DID NOT SAY, BUT BEING~HIGH PRIEST -

ἐνιαυτοῦ ἐκείνου ἐπροφήτευσεν ὅτι ἔμελλεν Ἰησοῦς
THAT~YEAR HE PROPHESIED THAT JESUS~WAS ABOUT

ἀποθνῄσκειν ὑπὲρ τοῦ ἔθνους, **11.52** καὶ οὐχ
TO DIE ON BEHALF OF THE NATION, AND NOT

ὑπὲρ τοῦ ἔθνους μόνον ἀλλ᾽ ἵνα καὶ τὰ τέκνα τοῦ
ON BEHALF OF THE NATION ONLY BUT THAT ALSO THE CHILDREN -

θεοῦ τὰ διεσκορπισμένα συναγάγῃ εἰς ἕν. **11.53** ἀπ᾽
OF GOD, THE ONES HAVING BEEN SCATTERED, HE MAY GATHER INTO ONE. FROM

ἐκείνης οὖν τῆς ἡμέρας ἐβουλεύσαντο ἵνα
THAT ²THEREFORE - ¹DAY THEY TOOK COUNSEL THAT

ἀποκτείνωσιν αὐτόν.
THEY MIGHT KILL HIM.

11.54 Ὁ οὖν Ἰησοῦς οὐκέτι παρρησίᾳ περιεπάτει
- THEREFORE JESUS NO LONGER OPENLY WAS WALKING

ἐν τοῖς Ἰουδαίοις, ἀλλὰ ἀπῆλθεν ἐκεῖθεν εἰς τὴν
AMONG THE JEWS, BUT HE WENT AWAY FROM THERE INTO THE

χώραν ἐγγὺς τῆς ἐρήμου, εἰς Ἐφραὶμ λεγομένην
COUNTRY NEAR THE WILDERNESS, INTO ³EPHRAIM ²BEING CALLED

πόλιν, κἀκεῖ ἔμεινεν μετὰ τῶν μαθητῶν.
¹A CITY, AND THERE HE REMAINED WITH THE DISCIPLES.

11.55 Ἦν δὲ ἐγγὺς τὸ πάσχα τῶν Ἰουδαίων, καὶ
NOW~WAS NEAR THE PASSOVER OF THE JEWS, AND

ἀνέβησαν πολλοὶ εἰς Ἱεροσόλυμα ἐκ τῆς χώρας πρὸ
WENT UP MANY TO JERUSALEM FROM THE COUNTRY BEFORE

τοῦ πάσχα ἵνα ἁγνίσωσιν ἑαυτούς. **11.56** ἐζήτουν
THE PASSOVER THAT THEY MIGHT PURIFY THEMSELVES. THEY WERE SEEKING

οὖν τὸν Ἰησοῦν καὶ ἔλεγον μετ᾽ ἀλλήλων ἐν
THEREFORE - JESUS AND WERE SPEAKING WITH ONE ANOTHER [WHILE] IN

said, "What are we to do? This man is performing many signs. [48]If we let him go on like this, everyone will believe in him, and the Romans will come and destroy both our holy place[l] and our nation." [49]But one of them, Caiaphas, who was high priest that year, said to them, "You know nothing at all! [50]You do not understand that it is better for you to have one man die for the people than to have the whole nation destroyed." [51]He did not say this on his own, but being high priest that year he prophesied that Jesus was about to die for the nation, [52]and not for the nation only, but to gather into one the dispersed children of God. [53]So from that day on they planned to put him to death.

54 Jesus therefore no longer walked about openly among the Jews, but went from there to a town called Ephraim in the region near the wilderness; and he remained there with the disciples.

55 Now the Passover of the Jews was near, and many went up from the country to Jerusalem before the Passover to purify themselves. [56]They were looking for Jesus and were asking one another as

[l] Or our temple; Greek our place

they stood in the temple, "What do you think? Surely he will not come to the festival, will he?" ⁵⁷Now the chief priests and the Pharisees had given orders that anyone who knew where Jesusᵐ was should let them know, so that they might arrest him.

ᵐ Gk *he*

τῷ   ἱερῷ   ἑστηκότες,   Τί   δοκεῖ   ὑμῖν;   ὅτι
THE   TEMPLE   HAVING STOOD,   WHAT   DOES [IT] APPEAR   TO YOU°?   -

οὐ μὴ ἔλθῃ   εἰς τὴν ἑορτήν;   **11.57** δεδώκεισαν δὲ οἱ
[SURELY] HE WILL NOT COME   TO   THE   FEAST?   NOW~HAD GIVEN   THE

ἀρχιερεῖς καὶ οἱ Φαρισαῖοι ἐντολὰς ἵνα ἐάν τις
CHIEF PRIESTS   AND   THE PHARISEES   COMMANDS   THAT   IF   ANYONE

γνῷ   ποῦ ἐστιν μηνύσῃ,   ὅπως πιάσωσιν   αὐτόν.
KNEW   WHERE HE IS,   HE SHOULD REVEAL [IT]   SO THAT   THEY MIGHT ARREST   HIM.

CHAPTER 12

Six days before the Passover Jesus came to Bethany, the home of Lazarus, whom he had raised from the dead. ²There they gave a dinner for him. Martha served, and Lazarus was one of those at the table with him. ³Mary took a pound of costly perfume made of pure nard, anointed Jesus' feet, and wiped themⁿ with her hair. The house was filled with the fragrance of the perfume. ⁴But Judas Iscariot, one of his disciples (the one who was about to betray him), said, ⁵"Why was this perfume not sold for three hundred denariiᵒ and the money given to the poor?" ⁶(He said this not because he cared about the poor, but because he was a thief; he kept the common purse and used to steal what was put into it.) ⁷Jesus said, "Leave her alone. She bought itᵖ so that she might keep it for the day of my burial. ⁸You always have the poor

ⁿ Gk *his feet*
ᵒ Three hundred denarii would be nearly a year's wages for a laborer
ᵖ Gk lacks *She bought it*

12.1 Ὁ οὖν Ἰησοῦς πρὸ ἓξ ἡμερῶν τοῦ πάσχα
-   THEN JESUS   ³BEFORE ¹SIX ²DAYS   THE   PASSOVER

ἦλθεν εἰς Βηθανίαν, ὅπου ἦν Λάζαρος, ὃν ἤγειρεν
CAME   INTO BETHANY,   WHERE LAZARUS~WAS,   WHOM ²RAISED

ἐκ   νεκρῶν Ἰησοῦς.   **12.2** ἐποίησαν οὖν αὐτῷ δεῖπνον
³FROM   ⁴[THE] DEAD ¹JESUS.   THEN~THEY MADE   HIM   A SUPPER

ἐκεῖ,   καὶ ἡ Μάρθα διηκόνει, ὁ δὲ Λάζαρος εἷς ἦν ἐκ
THERE,   AND - MARTHA WAS SERVING, - AND LAZARUS WAS~ONE OF

τῶν   ἀνακειμένων σὺν αὐτῷ.   **12.3** ἡ οὖν Μαριὰμ
THE ONES   RECLINING   WITH HIM.   - THEN MARY,

λαβοῦσα λίτραν μύρου νάρδου πιστικῆς πολυτίμου
HAVING TAKEN   A POUND   OF OINTMENT ³SPIKENARD ¹OF GENUINE, ²EXPENSIVE,

ἤλειψεν τοὺς πόδας τοῦ Ἰησοῦ καὶ ἐξέμαξεν ταῖς
ANOINTED   THE   FEET   - OF JESUS AND WIPED OFF   WITH THE

θριξὶν αὐτῆς τοὺς πόδας αὐτοῦ· ἡ δὲ οἰκία ἐπληρώθη
HAIRS   OF HER   THE   FEET   OF HIM;   AND~THE HOUSE   WAS FILLED

ἐκ   τῆς ὀσμῆς τοῦ μύρου.   **12.4** λέγει δὲ Ἰούδας ὁ
OF(WITH)   THE ODOR OF THE OINTMENT.   AND~SAYS   JUDAS   -

Ἰσκαριώτης εἷς [ἐκ] τῶν μαθητῶν αὐτοῦ, ὁ   μέλλων
ISCARIOT,   ONE OF THE DISCIPLES OF HIM, THE ONE BEING ABOUT

αὐτὸν παραδιδόναι,   **12.5** Διὰ τί τοῦτο   τὸ μύρον οὐκ
TO BETRAY~HIM,   WHY   [WAS] THIS - OINTMENT NOT

ἐπράθη τριακοσίων   δηναρίων καὶ ἐδόθη πτωχοῖς;
SOLD   [FOR] THREE HUNDRED DENARII   AND GIVEN   TO POOR [PEOPLE]?

12.6 εἶπεν δὲ τοῦτο οὐχ ὅτι   περὶ τῶν πτωχῶν ἔμελεν
BUT~HE SAID THIS NOT BECAUSE ABOUT THE POOR IT MATTERED

αὐτῷ, ἀλλ' ὅτι   κλέπτης ἦν καὶ τὸ γλωσσόκομον
TO HIM,   BUT   BECAUSE HE WAS~A THIEF AND THE MONEY BOX

ἔχων τὰ   βαλλόμενα ἐβάσταζεν.   **12.7** εἶπεν οὖν
HAVING ²THE THINGS ³BEING PUT [IN IT] ¹HE WAS REMOVING.   SAID   THEREFORE

ὁ Ἰησοῦς, Ἄφες αὐτήν, ἵνα εἰς τὴν ἡμέραν τοῦ
JESUS,   LET HER BE,   THAT FOR THE DAY   OF THE

ἐνταφιασμοῦ μου τηρήσῃ αὐτό·   **12.8** τοὺς πτωχοὺς γὰρ
BURIAL   OF ME SHE MAY KEEP IT.   ²THE ³POOR ¹FOR

πάντοτε ἔχετε μεθ᾽ ἑαυτῶν, ἐμὲ δὲ οὐ πάντοτε
ALWAYS YOU° HAVE WITH YOURSELVES, BUT~ME NOT ALWAYS

ἔχετε.
DO YOU° HAVE.

12.9 Ἔγνω οὖν   [ὁ] ὄχλος πολὺς ἐκ τῶν Ἰουδαίων
KNEW THEREFORE THE GREAT~CROWD OF THE JEWS

ὅτι ἐκεῖ ἐστιν καὶ ἦλθον οὐ διὰ   τὸν Ἰησοῦν
THAT THERE HE IS(WAS), AND THEY CAME NOT BECAUSE OF - JESUS

μόνον, ἀλλ᾽ ἵνα καὶ τὸν Λάζαρον ἴδωσιν ὃν
ONLY, BUT THAT ALSO - LAZARUS THEY MAY SEE WHOM

ἤγειρεν ἐκ νεκρῶν. **12.10** ἐβουλεύσαντο δὲ οἱ ἀρχιερεῖς
HE RAISED FROM [THE] DEAD. BUT~TOOK COUNSEL THE CHIEF PRIESTS

ἵνα καὶ τὸν Λάζαρον ἀποκτείνωσιν, **12.11** ὅτι   πολλοὶ
THAT ALSO - LAZARUS THEY MIGHT KILL, BECAUSE MANY

δι᾽   αὐτὸν ὑπῆγον   τῶν Ἰουδαίων καὶ
³ON ACCOUNT OF ⁴HIM ⁵WERE GOING AWAY ¹OF THE ²JEWS AND

ἐπίστευον εἰς τὸν Ἰησοῦν.
WERE BELIEVING IN - JESUS.

12.12 Τῇ ἐπαύριον ὁ ὄχλος πολὺς ὁ   ἐλθὼν εἰς
ON THE NEXT DAY THE GREAT~CROWD, THE ONE HAVING COME TO

τὴν ἑορτήν, ἀκούσαντες ὅτι ἔρχεται ὁ Ἰησοῦς εἰς
THE FEAST, HAVING HEARD THAT IS COMING - JESUS TO

Ἱεροσόλυμα **12.13** ἔλαβον τὰ βαΐα τῶν φοινίκων καὶ
JERUSALEM, TOOK THE BRANCHES OF THE PALM TREES AND

ἐξῆλθον εἰς ὑπάντησιν αὐτῷ καὶ ἐκραύγαζον,
WENT OUT TO A MEETING WITH HIM AND WERE CRYING OUT,

  Ὡσαννά·
  HOSANNA

εὐλογημένος ὁ   ἐρχόμενος ἐν ὀνόματι
HAVING BEEN BLESSED [IS] THE ONE COMING IN [THE] NAME

    κυρίου,
    OF [THE] LORD,

  [καὶ] ὁ βασιλεὺς τοῦ Ἰσραήλ.
  EVEN THE KING - OF ISRAEL,

12.14 εὑρὼν δὲ ὁ Ἰησοῦς ὀνάριον ἐκάθισεν ἐπί
AND~HAVING FOUND - JESUS A YOUNG DONKEY, HE SAT ON

αὐτό, καθὼς ἐστιν γεγραμμένον,
IT, JUST AS IT HAS BEEN WRITTEN,

12.15 Μὴ φοβοῦ, θυγάτηρ Σιών·
DO NOT FEAR, DAUGHTER OF ZION;

  ἰδοὺ ὁ βασιλεύς σου ἔρχεται,
  LOOK, THE KING OF YOU IS COMING,

  καθήμενος ἐπὶ πῶλον ὄνου.
  SITTING ON A FOAL OF A DONKEY.

12.16 ταῦτα   οὐκ ἔγνωσαν αὐτοῦ οἱ μαθηταὶ
THESE THINGS DID NOT UNDERSTAND HIS - DISCIPLES

12:13 Ps. 118:25-26 **12:15** Zech. 9:9

with you, but you do not
always have me."

9 When the great crowd
of the Jews learned that he
was there, they came not
only because of Jesus but
also to see Lazarus, whom
he had raised from the dead.
¹⁰So the chief priests
planned to put Lazarus to
death as well, ¹¹since it was
on account of him that many
of the Jews were deserting
and were believing in Jesus.

12 The next day the great
crowd that had come to the
festival heard that Jesus was
coming to Jerusalem. ¹³So
they took branches of palm
trees and went out to meet
him, shouting,
  "Hosanna!
  Blessed is the one who
    comes in the name
    of the Lord—
    the King of Israel!"
¹⁴Jesus found a young
donkey and sat on it; as it is
written:
  ¹⁵"Do not be afraid,
    daughter of Zion.
  Look, your king is
    coming,
    sitting on a donkey's
    colt!"
¹⁶His disciples did not
understand these things

at first; but when Jesus was glorified, then they remembered that these things had been written of him and had been done to him. [17]So the crowd that had been with him when he called Lazarus out of the tomb and raised him from the dead continued to testify.[q] [18]It was also because they heard that he had performed this sign that the crowd went to meet him. [19]The Pharisees then said to one another, "You see, you can do nothing. Look, the world has gone after him!"

20 Now among those who went up to worship at the festival were some Greeks. [21]They came to Philip, who was from Bethsaida in Galilee, and said to him, "Sir, we wish to see Jesus." [22]Philip went and told Andrew; then Andrew and Philip went and told Jesus. [23]Jesus answered them, "The hour has come for the Son of Man to be glorified. [24]Very truly, I tell you, unless a grain of wheat falls into the earth and dies, it remains just a single grain; but if it dies, it bears much fruit. [25]Those who love their life lose it, and those who hate their life in this world will keep it for eternal life.

[q] Other ancient authorities read *with him began to testify that he had called . . . from the dead*

τὸ πρῶτον, ἀλλ᾽ ὅτε ἐδοξάσθη Ἰησοῦς τότε ἐμνήσθησαν
AT FIRST, BUT WHEN JESUS~WAS GLORIFIED THEN THEY REMEMBERED

ὅτι ταῦτα ἦν ἐπ᾽ αὐτῷ γεγραμμένα καὶ
THAT THESE THINGS HAD BEEN [2]WITH RESPECT TO [3]HIM [1]WRITTEN AND

ταῦτα ἐποίησαν αὐτῷ. **12.17** ἐμαρτύρει οὖν ὁ
THESE THINGS THEY DID TO HIM. WERE TESTIFYING THEREFORE THE

ὄχλος ὁ ὢν μετ᾽ αὐτοῦ ὅτε τὸν Λάζαρον ἐφώνησεν
CROWD, THE ONE BEING WITH HIM WHEN - LAZARUS HE CALLED

ἐκ τοῦ μνημείου καὶ ἤγειρεν αὐτὸν ἐκ νεκρῶν.
OUT OF THE TOMB AND RAISED HIM FROM [THE] DEAD.

12.18 διὰ τοῦτο [καὶ] ὑπήντησεν αὐτῷ ὁ ὄχλος, ὅτι
THEREFORE ALSO MET HIM THE CROWD BECAUSE

ἤκουσαν τοῦτο αὐτὸν πεποιηκέναι τὸ σημεῖον.
THEY HEARD [3]THIS [1]HIM [2]TO HAVE DONE - [4]SIGN.

12.19 οἱ οὖν Φαρισαῖοι εἶπαν πρὸς ἑαυτούς,
THEREFORE~THE PHARISEES SAID TO THEMSELVES,

Θεωρεῖτε ὅτι οὐκ ὠφελεῖτε οὐδέν· ἴδε ὁ κόσμος
SEE THAT YOU° DO NOT GAIN ANYTHING. LOOK, THE WORLD

ὀπίσω αὐτοῦ ἀπῆλθεν.
AFTER HIM WENT.

12.20 Ἦσαν δὲ Ἕλληνές τινες ἐκ τῶν
NOW~THERE WERE SOME~GREEKS AMONG THE ONES

ἀναβαινόντων ἵνα προσκυνήσωσιν ἐν τῇ ἑορτῇ·
GOING UP THAT THEY MIGHT WORSHIP AT THE FEAST.

12.21 οὗτοι οὖν προσῆλθον Φιλίππῳ τῷ ἀπὸ
THESE ONES THEREFORE APPROACHED PHILIP - FROM

Βηθσαϊδὰ τῆς Γαλιλαίας καὶ ἠρώτων αὐτὸν λέγοντες,
BETHSAIDA - OF GALILEE, AND WERE ASKING HIM SAYING,

Κύριε, θέλομεν τὸν Ἰησοῦν ἰδεῖν. **12.22** ἔρχεται ὁ
SIR, WE WANT - TO SEE~JESUS. COMES -

Φίλιππος καὶ λέγει τῷ Ἀνδρέᾳ, ἔρχεται Ἀνδρέας
PHILIP AND TELLS - ANDREW, COMES ANDREW

καὶ Φίλιππος καὶ λέγουσιν τῷ Ἰησοῦ. **12.23** ὁ δὲ
AND PHILIP AND THEY TELL - JESUS. - AND

Ἰησοῦς ἀποκρίνεται αὐτοῖς λέγων, Ἐλήλυθεν ἡ ὥρα
JESUS ANSWERS THEM SAYING, HAS COME THE HOUR

ἵνα δοξασθῇ ὁ υἱὸς τοῦ ἀνθρώπου. **12.24** ἀμὴν ἀμὴν
THAT MAY BE GLORIFIED THE SON - OF MAN. TRULY, TRULY

λέγω ὑμῖν, ἐὰν μὴ ὁ κόκκος τοῦ σίτου πεσὼν εἰς
I SAY TO YOU°, UNLESS THE GRAIN - OF WHEAT HAVING FALLEN INTO

τὴν γῆν ἀποθάνῃ, αὐτὸς μόνος μένει· ἐὰν δὲ
THE GROUND DIES, IT REMAINS~ALONE; BUT~IF

ἀποθάνῃ, πολὺν καρπὸν φέρει. **12.25** ὁ φιλῶν
IT DIES, MUCH FRUIT IT BEARS. THE ONE BEING FOND OF

τὴν ψυχὴν αὐτοῦ ἀπολλύει αὐτήν, καὶ ὁ μισῶν τὴν
THE LIFE OF HIM LOSES IT, AND THE ONE HATING THE

ψυχὴν αὐτοῦ ἐν τῷ κόσμῳ τούτῳ εἰς ζωὴν αἰώνιον
LIFE OF HIM IN - THIS~WORLD INTO LIFE ETERNAL

φυλάξει αὐτήν. **12.26** ἐὰν ἐμοί τις διακονῇ,
WILL KEEP IT.   IF   ME   ANYONE SERVES,

ἐμοὶ ἀκολουθείτω, καὶ ὅπου εἰμὶ ἐγὼ ἐκεῖ καὶ ὁ
LET HIM FOLLOW~ME,   AND   WHERE I~AM   THERE ALSO THE

διάκονος ὁ ἐμὸς ἔσται· ἐάν τις ἐμοὶ διακονῇ
SERVANT   - OF ME WILL BE.   IF ANYONE SERVES~ME,

τιμήσει αὐτὸν ὁ πατήρ.
WILL HONOR HIM   THE FATHER.

12.27 Νῦν ἡ ψυχή μου τετάρακται, καὶ τί εἴπω;
        NOW THE SOUL OF ME HAS BEEN TROUBLED, AND WHAT MAY I SAY?

Πάτερ, σῶσόν με ἐκ τῆς ὥρας ταύτης; ἀλλὰ διὰ
FATHER, SAVE ME FROM - THIS~HOUR?   BUT BECAUSE OF

τοῦτο ἦλθον εἰς τὴν ὥραν ταύτην. **12.28** πάτερ, δόξασόν
THIS I CAME TO -   THIS~HOUR.   FATHER, GLORIFY

σου τὸ ὄνομα. ἦλθεν οὖν φωνὴ ἐκ τοῦ οὐρανοῦ,
YOUR - NAME. CAME THEREFORE A VOICE OUT OF - HEAVEN,

Καὶ ἐδόξασα καὶ πάλιν δοξάσω. **12.29** ὁ οὖν
BOTH I GLORIFIED [IT] AND AGAIN I WILL GLORIFY [IT].   THEREFORE~THE

ὄχλος ὁ ἑστὼς καὶ ἀκούσας ἔλεγεν βροντὴν
CROWD, THE ONE HAVING STOOD AND HAVING HEARD, WERE SAYING, THUNDER

γεγονέναι, ἄλλοι ἔλεγον, Ἄγγελος αὐτῷ λελάληκεν.
HAS HAPPENED; OTHERS WERE SAYING, AN ANGEL   HAS SPOKEN~TO HIM.

12.30 ἀπεκρίθη Ἰησοῦς καὶ εἶπεν, Οὐ δι᾽ ἐμὲ ἡ
        ANSWERED   JESUS   AND SAID,   NOT BECAUSE OF ME   -

φωνὴ αὕτη γέγονεν ἀλλὰ δι᾽ ὑμᾶς. **12.31** νῦν
THIS~VOICE   HAS COME   BUT BECAUSE OF YOU°.   NOW

κρίσις ἐστὶν τοῦ κόσμου τούτου, νῦν ὁ ἄρχων τοῦ
JUDGMENT IS   - OF THIS~WORLD,   NOW THE RULER   -

κόσμου τούτου ἐκβληθήσεται ἔξω· **12.32** κἀγὼ ἐὰν
OF THIS~WORLD   WILL BE CAST   OUT;   AND I   IF

ὑψωθῶ ἐκ τῆς γῆς, πάντας ἑλκύσω πρὸς ἐμαυτόν.
I AM LIFTED UP FROM THE EARTH, I WILL DRAW~ALL MEN TO   MYSELF.

12.33 τοῦτο δὲ ἔλεγεν σημαίνων ποίῳ θανάτῳ
        AND~THIS   HE WAS SAYING SIGNIFYING BY WHAT KIND OF DEATH

ἤμελλεν ἀποθνῄσκειν. **12.34** ἀπεκρίθη οὖν αὐτῷ ὁ
HE WAS ABOUT TO DIE.   THEN~ANSWERED   HIM THE

ὄχλος, Ἡμεῖς ἠκούσαμεν ἐκ τοῦ νόμου ὅτι ὁ
CROWD,   WE   HEARD   FROM THE LAW THAT THE

Χριστὸς μένει εἰς τὸν αἰῶνα, καὶ πῶς λέγεις σὺ ὅτι
CHRIST REMAINS INTO THE AGE,   AND HOW DO YOU SAY THAT

δεῖ ὑψωθῆναι τὸν υἱὸν τοῦ ἀνθρώπου; τίς
IT IS NECESSARY [FOR] ⁴TO BE LIFTED UP ¹THE ²SON - ³OF MAN? WHO

ἐστιν οὗτος ὁ υἱὸς τοῦ ἀνθρώπου; **12.35** εἶπεν οὖν
IS   THIS ONE, THE SON - OF MAN?   SAID THEREFORE

αὐτοῖς ὁ Ἰησοῦς, Ἔτι μικρὸν χρόνον τὸ φῶς ἐν
TO THEM - JESUS,   YET A LITTLE TIME   THE LIGHT AMONG

ὑμῖν ἐστιν. περιπατεῖτε ὡς τὸ φῶς ἔχετε, ἵνα μὴ
YOU° IS.   WALK   WHILE THE LIGHT YOU° HAVE, LEST

26Whoever serves me must follow me, and where I am, there will my servant be also. Whoever serves me, the Father will honor.

27 "Now my soul is troubled. And what should I say—'Father, save me from this hour'? No, it is for this reason that I have come to this hour. 28Father, glorify your name." Then a voice came from heaven, "I have glorified it, and I will glorify it again." 29The crowd standing there heard it and said that it was thunder. Others said, "An angel has spoken to him." 30Jesus answered, "This voice has come for your sake, not for mine. 31Now is the judgment of this world; now the ruler of this world will be driven out. 32And I, when I am lifted up from the earth, will draw all people* to myself." 33He said this to indicate the kind of death he was to die. 34The crowd answered him, "We have heard from the law that the Messiah* remains forever. How can you say that the Son of Man must be lifted up? Who is this Son of Man?" 35Jesus said to them, "The light is with you for a little longer. Walk while you have the light, so that

*ʳ Other ancient authorities read *all things*
ˢ Or the Christ

the darkness may not overtake you. If you walk in the darkness, you do not know where you are going. [36]While you have the light, believe in the light, so that you may become children of light."

After Jesus had said this, he departed and hid from them. [37]Although he had performed so many signs in their presence, they did not believe in him. [38]This was to fulfill the word spoken by the prophet Isaiah:

"Lord, who has believed
    our message,
and to whom has the
    arm of the Lord
    been revealed?"

[39]And so they could not believe, because Isaiah also said,

[40]"He has blinded their
    eyes
    and hardened their
        heart,
so that they might not
    look with their
    eyes,
and understand with
    their heart and
    turn—
and I would heal
    them."

[41]Isaiah said this because[f] he saw his glory and spoke about him. [42]Nevertheless many, even of the authorities, believed in him. But because of the Pharisees they did not confess it, for fear that they would be put out of the synagogue;

[f] Other ancient witnesses read *when*

σκοτία ὑμᾶς καταλάβῃ· καὶ ὁ περιπατῶν ἐν τῇ
DARKNESS OVERTAKES~YOU°; AND THE ONE WALKING IN THE

σκοτία οὐκ οἶδεν ποῦ ὑπάγει. **12.36** ὡς τὸ φῶς
DARKNESS DOES NOT KNOW WHERE HE IS GOING. WHILE THE LIGHT

ἔχετε, πιστεύετε εἰς τὸ φῶς, ἵνα υἱοὶ φωτὸς
YOU° HAVE, WALK IN THE LIGHT, THAT SONS OF LIGHT

γένησθε.
YOU° MAY BECOME.

Ταῦτα ἐλάλησεν Ἰησοῦς, καὶ ἀπελθὼν
THESE THINGS SPOKE JESUS, AND HAVING GONE AWAY,

ἐκρύβη ἀπ᾽ αὐτῶν. **12.37** Τοσαῦτα δὲ αὐτοῦ σημεῖα
HE WAS HIDDEN FROM THEM. THOUGH~SO MANY SIGNS~HE

πεποιηκότος ἔμπροσθεν αὐτῶν οὐκ ἐπίστευον εἰς αὐτόν,
HAVING DONE BEFORE THEM THEY WERE NOT BELIEVING IN HIM,

12.38 ἵνα ὁ λόγος Ἡσαΐου τοῦ προφήτου πληρωθῇ
THAT THE WORD OF ISAIAH THE PROPHET MAY BE FULFILLED

ὃν εἶπεν,
WHICH SAID,

Κύριε, τίς ἐπίστευσεν τῇ ἀκοῇ ἡμῶν;
LORD, WHO BELIEVED THE REPORT OF US?

καὶ ὁ βραχίων κυρίου τίνι ἀπεκαλύφθη;
AND THE ARM OF [THE] LORD TO WHOM WAS [IT] REVEALED?

12.39 διὰ τοῦτο οὐκ ἠδύναντο πιστεύειν, ὅτι πάλιν
THEREFORE THEY WERE NOT ABLE TO BELIEVE, BECAUSE AGAIN

εἶπεν Ἡσαΐας,
SAID ISAIAH,

12.40 Τετύφλωκεν αὐτῶν τοὺς ὀφθαλμοὺς
HE HAS BLINDED THEIR - EYES

καὶ ἐπώρωσεν αὐτῶν τὴν καρδίαν,
AND HARDENED THEIR - HEART,

ἵνα μὴ ἴδωσιν τοῖς ὀφθαλμοῖς
THAT THEY MIGHT NOT SEE WITH THE EYES

καὶ νοήσωσιν τῇ καρδίᾳ καὶ στραφῶσιν,
AND UNDERSTAND WITH THE HEART AND MIGHT TURN,

καὶ ἰάσομαι αὐτούς.
AND I WILL CURE THEM.

12.41 ταῦτα εἶπεν Ἡσαΐας ⌐ὅτι⌐ εἶδεν τὴν δόξαν
THESE THINGS ISAIAH~SPOKE BECAUSE HE SAW THE GLORY

αὐτοῦ, καὶ ἐλάλησεν περὶ αὐτοῦ. **12.42** ὅμως
OF HIM, AND HE SPOKE ABOUT HIM. NEVERTHELESS

μέντοι καὶ ἐκ τῶν ἀρχόντων πολλοὶ ἐπίστευσαν
HOWEVER EVEN OF THE RULERS MANY BELIEVED

εἰς αὐτόν, ἀλλὰ διὰ τοὺς Φαρισαίους
IN HIM, BUT BECAUSE OF THE PHARISEES

οὐχ ὡμολόγουν ἵνα μὴ ἀποσυνάγωγοι
THEY WERE NOT CONFESSING [HIM] LEST PUT AWAY FROM [THE] SYNAGOGUE

12:38 Isa. 53:1 LXX **12:40** Isa. 6:10 LXX **12:41** text: ASV RSV NASB NIV NEB TEV NJB NRSV. var. οτε (when): KJV NEBmg NJBmg.

γένωνται· **12.43** ἠγάπησαν γὰρ τὴν δόξαν τῶν
THEY SHOULD BECOME;   FOR~THEY LOVED   THE   GLORY   -

ἀνθρώπων μᾶλλον ἤπερ τὴν δόξαν τοῦ θεοῦ.
OF MEN   MORE   THAN   THE   GLORY   -   OF GOD.

12.44 Ἰησοῦς δὲ ἔκραξεν καὶ εἶπεν, Ὁ   πιστεύων
BUT~JESUS   CRIED OUT   AND   SAID,   THE ONE BELIEVING

εἰς ἐμὲ οὐ πιστεύει εἰς ἐμὲ ἀλλὰ εἰς τὸν   πέμψαντά
IN   ME DOES NOT BELIEVE IN   ME   BUT   IN THE ONE HAVING SENT

με, **12.45** καὶ ὁ   θεωρῶν ἐμὲ θεωρεῖ τὸν   πέμψαντά
ME,   AND THE ONE SEEING   ME   SEES THE ONE HAVING SENT

με. **12.46** ἐγὼ φῶς εἰς τὸν κόσμον ἐλήλυθα, ἵνα πᾶς ὁ
ME.   I   A LIGHT INTO THE WORLD HAVE COME,   THAT EVERYONE

πιστεύων εἰς ἐμὲ ἐν τῇ σκοτίᾳ μὴ μείνῃ.   **12.47** καὶ
BELIEVING   IN   ME   IN THE DARKNESS MAY NOT REMAIN.   AND

ἐάν τις   μου ἀκούσῃ τῶν ῥημάτων καὶ μὴ φυλάξῃ,
IF ANYONE HEARS~MY   -   WORDS   AND DOES NOT KEEP [THEM],

ἐγὼ οὐ κρίνω αὐτόν· οὐ γὰρ ἦλθον ἵνα κρίνω τὸν
I   DO NOT JUDGE HIM.   FOR~I DID NOT COME THAT I MAY JUDGE THE

κόσμον, ἀλλ' ἵνα σώσω τὸν κόσμον. **12.48** ὁ
WORLD,   BUT   THAT I MAY SAVE THE   WORLD.   THE ONE

ἀθετῶν ἐμὲ καὶ μὴ λαμβάνων τὰ ῥήματά μου ἔχει
SETTING ME ASIDE AND   NOT RECEIVING   THE   WORDS   OF ME HAS

τὸν   κρίνοντα αὐτόν· ὁ λόγος ὃν ἐλάλησα ἐκεῖνος
THE ONE JUDGING   HIM.   THE WORD WHICH I SPOKE,   THAT

κρινεῖ αὐτὸν ἐν τῇ ἐσχάτῃ ἡμέρᾳ. **12.49** ὅτι   ἐγὼ ἐξ
WILL JUDGE HIM   ON THE LAST   DAY.   BECAUSE I   OF

ἐμαυτοῦ οὐκ ἐλάλησα, ἀλλ' ὁ   πέμψας με
MYSELF   DID NOT SPEAK,   BUT   THE ONE HAVING SENT ME,

πατὴρ αὐτός μοι ἐντολὴν δέδωκεν τί   εἴπω   καὶ τί
[THE] FATHER—¹HE ³TO ME ⁴A COMMAND ²HAS GIVEN WHAT I MAY SAY AND WHAT

λαλήσω. **12.50** καὶ οἶδα ὅτι ἡ ἐντολὴ αὐτοῦ ζωὴ
I MAY SPEAK.   AND I KNOW THAT THE COMMAND OF HIM   LIFE

αἰώνιός ἐστιν. ἃ   οὖν   ἐγὼ λαλῶ, καθὼς
ETERNAL   IS.   WHAT THINGS THEREFORE I   SPEAK,   AS

εἴρηκέν μοι ὁ   πατήρ, οὕτως λαλῶ.
HAS SPOKEN TO ME THE   FATHER,   SO   I SPEAK.

43for they loved human glory more than the glory that comes from God.

44 Then Jesus cried aloud: "Whoever believes in me believes not in me but in him who sent me. 45And whoever sees me sees him who sent me. 46I have come as light into the world, so that everyone who believes in me should not remain in the darkness. 47I do not judge anyone who hears my words and does not keep them, for I came not to judge the world, but to save the world. 48The one who rejects me and does not receive my word has a judge; on the last day the word that I have spoken will serve as judge, 49for I have not spoken on my own, but the Father who sent me has himself given me a commandment about what to say and what to speak. 50And I know that his commandment is eternal life. What I speak, therefore, I speak just as the Father has told me."

CHAPTER 13

13.1 Πρὸ δὲ τῆς ἑορτῆς τοῦ πάσχα εἰδὼς   ὁ
NOW~BEFORE THE   FEAST   OF THE PASSOVER, HAVING KNOWN -

Ἰησοῦς ὅτι ἦλθεν αὐτοῦ ἡ ὥρα ἵνα μεταβῇ   ἐκ   τοῦ
JESUS   THAT CAME   HIS   - HOUR THAT HE SHOULD PASS FROM -

κόσμου τούτου πρὸς τὸν πατέρα, ἀγαπήσας τοὺς ἰδίους
THIS~WORLD   TO   THE FATHER,   HAVING LOVED   HIS OWN

τοὺς ἐν τῷ κόσμῳ εἰς τέλος ἠγάπησεν αὐτούς.
-    IN THE WORLD, TO [THE] END HE LOVED   THEM.

Now before the festival of the Passover, Jesus knew that his hour had come to depart from this world and go to the Father. Having loved his own who were in the world, he loved them to the end.

2The devil had already put it into the heart of Judas son of Simon Iscariot to betray him. And during supper 3Jesus, knowing that the Father had given all things into his hands, and that he had come from God and was going to God, 4got up from the table," took off his outer robe, and tied a towel around himself. 5Then he poured water into a basin and began to wash the disciples' feet and to wipe them with the towel that was tied around him. 6He came to Simon Peter, who said to him, "Lord, are you going to wash my feet?" 7Jesus answered, "You do not know now what I am doing, but later you will understand." 8Peter said to him, "You will never wash my feet." Jesus answered, "Unless I wash you, you have no share with me." 9Simon Peter said to him, "Lord, not my feet only but also my hands and my head!" 10Jesus said to him, "One who has bathed does not need to wash, except for the feet,v but is entirely clean. And youw are clean, though not all of you." 11For he knew who was to betray him; for this reason he said, "Not all of you are clean."

" Gk *from supper*
v Other ancient authorities lack *except for the feet*
w The Greek word for *you* here is plural

13.2 καὶ   δείπνου   γινομένου,   τοῦ   διαβόλου   ἤδη
AND   SUPPER   TAKING PLACE,   THE   DEVIL   ALREADY

βεβληκότος   εἰς   τὴν   καρδίαν   ἵνα   παραδοῖ   αὐτὸν
HAVING PUT   INTO   THE   HEART   4THAT   5HE SHOULD BETRAY   6HIM

Ἰούδας   Σίμωνος   Ἰσκαριώτου,   **13.3** εἰδὼς   ὅτι
1[OF] JUDAS   2[SON] OF SIMON   3OF ISCARIOT,   [AND JESUS] HAVING KNOWN   THAT

πάντα   ἔδωκεν   αὐτῷ   ὁ   πατὴρ   εἰς   τὰς   χεῖρας   καὶ
ALL THINGS   GAVE   HIM   THE   FATHER   INTO   THE(HIS)   HANDS   AND

ὅτι   ἀπὸ   θεοῦ   ἐξῆλθεν   καὶ   πρὸς   τὸν   θεὸν   ὑπάγει,
THAT   FROM   GOD   HE CAME FORTH   AND   TO   -   GOD   IS GOING,

13.4 ἐγείρεται   ἐκ   τοῦ   δείπνου   καὶ   τίθησιν   τὰ   ἱμάτια
HE RISES   FROM   THE   SUPPER   AND   PUTS [ASIDE]   HIS   GARMENTS

καὶ   λαβὼν   λέντιον   διέζωσεν   ἑαυτόν·   **13.5** εἶτα
AND   HAVING TAKEN   A TOWEL   HE GIRDED   HIMSELF.   THEN

βάλλει   ὕδωρ   εἰς   τὸν   νιπτῆρα   καὶ   ἤρξατο   νίπτειν   τοὺς
HE PUTS   WATER   INTO   THE   BASIN   AND   BEGAN   TO WASH   THE

πόδας   τῶν   μαθητῶν καὶ   ἐκμάσσειν   τῷ   λεντίῳ
FEET   OF THE   DISCIPLES   AND   TO WIPE [THEM]   WITH THE   TOWEL

ᾧ   ἦν   διεζωσμένος.   **13.6** ἔρχεται   οὖν   πρὸς   Σίμωνα
WITH WHICH   HE HAD GIRDED HIMSELF.   HE COMES,   THEN,   TO   SIMON

Πέτρον·   λέγει   αὐτῷ,   Κύριε,   σύ   μου   νίπτεις   τοὺς
PETER.   HE SAYS   TO HIM,   LORD,   YOU   2MY   1WASH   -

πόδας;   **13.7** ἀπεκρίθη   Ἰησοῦς   καὶ   εἶπεν   αὐτῷ,   Ὁ
3FEET?   ANSWERED   JESUS   AND   SAID   TO HIM,   WHAT

ἐγὼ   ποιῶ   σὺ   οὐκ   οἶδας   ἄρτι,   γνώσῃ   δὲ   μετὰ
I   AM DOING   YOU   DO NOT PERCEIVE   NOW,   BUT~YOU WILL UNDERSTAND   AFTER

ταῦτα.   **13.8** λέγει   αὐτῷ   Πέτρος,   Οὐ μὴ   νίψῃς
THESE THINGS.   SAYS   TO HIM   PETER,   NEVER   WILL YOU WASH

μου   τοὺς   πόδας   εἰς   τὸν   αἰῶνα.   ἀπεκρίθη   Ἰησοῦς
MY   -   FEET   INTO   THE   AGE.   JESUS~ANSWERED

αὐτῷ,   Ἐὰν   μὴ   νίψω   σε,   οὐκ   ἔχεις   μέρος   μετ᾽   ἐμοῦ.
HIM,   UNLESS   I WASH   YOU,   YOU DO NOT HAVE   A SHARE   WITH   ME.

13.9 λέγει   αὐτῷ   Σίμων   Πέτρος,   Κύριε,   μὴ   τοὺς   πόδας
SAYS   TO HIM   SIMON   PETER,   LORD,   NOT   THE   FEET

μου   μόνον   ἀλλὰ   καὶ   τὰς   χεῖρας   καὶ   τὴν   κεφαλήν.
OF ME   ONLY   BUT   ALSO   THE(MY)   HANDS   AND   THE(MY)   HEAD.

13.10 λέγει   αὐτῷ   ὁ   Ἰησοῦς,   Ὁ   λελουμένος
SAYS   TO HIM   -   JESUS,   THE ONE   HAVING BEEN BATHED

⌐οὐκ   ἔχει   χρείαν   εἰ   μὴ   τοὺς   πόδας   νίψασθαι,¬   ἀλλ᾽
DOES NOT HAVE   NEED   EXCEPT   THE(HIS)   FEET   TO WASH,   BUT

ἔστιν   καθαρὸς   ὅλος·   καὶ   ὑμεῖς   καθαροί   ἐστε,   ἀλλ᾽
IS   CLEAN   WHOLLY;   AND   YOU°   ARE~CLEAN,   BUT

οὐχὶ   πάντες.   **13.11** ᾔδει   γὰρ   τὸν   παραδιδόντα   αὐτόν·
NOT   ALL.   FOR~HE KNEW   THE ONE   BETRAYING   HIM;

διὰ   τοῦτο   εἶπεν   ὅτι   Οὐχὶ   πάντες   καθαροί   ἐστε.
THEREFORE   HE SAID,   -   NOT   ALL   ARE~CLEAN.

13:10 text: KJV ASV RSV NASB NIV NEBmg TEV NJB NRSV.   var. ουκ εχει χρειαν νιψασθαι (does not need to wash): ASVmg RSVmg NEB TEVmg NJB NRSVmg.

13.12 Ὅτε οὖν   ἔνιψεν τοὺς πόδας αὐτῶν [καὶ]
WHEN THEREFORE HE WASHED THE FEET OF THEM AND

ἔλαβεν τὰ ἱμάτια αὐτοῦ καὶ ἀνέπεσεν πάλιν, εἶπεν
TOOK THE GARMENTS OF HIM AND RECLINED AGAIN, HE SAID

αὐτοῖς, Γινώσκετε τί   πεποίηκα ὑμῖν; **13.13** ὑμεῖς
TO THEM, DO YOU° KNOW WHAT I HAVE DONE TO YOU°? YOU°

φωνεῖτέ με Ὁ διδάσκαλος καὶ Ὁ κύριος, καὶ καλῶς
CALL ME THE TEACHER AND THE LORD, AND WELL

λέγετε, εἰμὶ γάρ. **13.14** εἰ οὖν   ἐγὼ ἔνιψα ὑμῶν τοὺς
YOU° SAY, FOR~I AM. IF THEREFORE I WASHED YOUR° -

πόδας ὁ κύριος καὶ ὁ διδάσκαλος, καὶ ὑμεῖς
FEET [BEING] THE LORD AND THE TEACHER, YOU°~ALSO

ὀφείλετε ἀλλήλων νίπτειν τοὺς πόδας·
OUGHT OF ONE ANOTHER TO WASH THE FEET.

13.15 ὑπόδειγμα γὰρ ἔδωκα ὑμῖν ἵνα καθὼς ἐγὼ
FOR~AN EXAMPLE I GAVE YOU° THAT AS I

ἐποίησα ὑμῖν καὶ ὑμεῖς ποιῆτε. **13.16** ἀμὴν ἀμὴν
DID TO YOU° ALSO YOU° MAY DO. TRULY, TRULY

λέγω ὑμῖν, οὐκ ἔστιν δοῦλος μείζων   τοῦ κυρίου
I SAY TO YOU°, A SLAVE~IS NOT GREATER [THAN] THE LORD

αὐτοῦ οὐδὲ ἀπόστολος μείζων   τοῦ   πέμψαντος
OF HIM, NOR A SENT ONE GREATER [THAN] THE ONE HAVING SENT

αὐτόν. **13.17** εἰ ταῦτα   οἴδατε, μακάριοί ἐστε ἐὰν
HIM. IF THESE THINGS YOU° KNOW, YOU° ARE~BLESSED IF

ποιῆτε αὐτά. **13.18** οὐ περὶ πάντων ὑμῶν λέγω· ἐγὼ
YOU° DO THEM. NOT ABOUT ALL OF YOU° I SPEAK (I

οἶδα τίνας ἐξελεξάμην· ἀλλ᾽ ἵνα ἡ γραφὴ
KNOW WHOM I CHOSE); BUT THAT THE SCRIPTURE

πληρωθῇ, Ὁ   τρώγων μου τὸν ἄρτον ἐπῆρεν ἐπ᾽
MAY BE FULFILLED, THE ONE EATING MY - BREAD LIFTED UP AGAINST

ἐμὲ τὴν πτέρναν αὐτοῦ. **13.19** ἀπ᾽ ἄρτι   λέγω ὑμῖν
ME THE HEEL OF HIM. FROM NOW [ON] I TELL YOU°

πρὸ τοῦ γενέσθαι, ἵνα πιστεύσητε ὅταν γένηται ὅτι
BEFORE THE OCCURRENCE, THAT YOU° MAY BELIEVE WHEN IT OCCURS THAT

ἐγώ εἰμι. **13.20** ἀμὴν ἀμὴν λέγω ὑμῖν, ὁ
I AM [HE]. TRULY, TRULY I SAY TO YOU°, THE ONE

λαμβάνων ἄν τινα πέμψω ἐμὲ λαμβάνει, ὁ δὲ
RECEIVING WHOMEVER I MAY SEND RECEIVES~ME, AND~THE ONE

ἐμὲ λαμβάνων λαμβάνει τὸν   πέμψαντά με.
RECEIVING~ME RECEIVES THE ONE HAVING SENT ME.

13.21 Ταῦτα   εἰπὼν [ὁ] Ἰησοῦς ἐταράχθη τῷ
THESE THINGS HAVING SAID, - JESUS WAS TROUBLED IN THE (HIS)

πνεύματι καὶ ἐμαρτύρησεν καὶ εἶπεν, Ἀμὴν ἀμὴν
SPIRIT AND HE TESTIFIED AND SAID, TRULY, TRULY

λέγω ὑμῖν ὅτι εἷς ἐξ ὑμῶν παραδώσει με.
I SAY TO YOU° THAT ONE OF YOU° WILL BETRAY ME.

13:18 Ps. 41:9

12 After he had washed their feet, had put on his robe, and had returned to the table, he said to them, "Do you know what I have done to you? 13You call me Teacher and Lord—and you are right, for that is what I am. 14So if I, your Lord and Teacher, have washed your feet, you also ought to wash one another's feet. 15For I have set you an example, that you also should do as I have done to you. 16Very truly, I tell you, servants*x* are not greater than their master, nor are messengers greater than the one who sent them. 17If you know these things, you are blessed if you do them. 18I am not speaking of all of you; I know whom I have chosen. But it is to fulfill the scripture, 'The one who ate my bread*y* has lifted his heel against me.' 19I tell you this now, before it occurs, so that when it does occur, you may believe that I am he.*z* 20Very truly, I tell you, whoever receives one whom I send receives me; and whoever receives me receives him who sent me."

21 After saying this Jesus was troubled in spirit, and declared, "Very truly, I tell you, one of you will betray me."

x Gk *slaves*
y Other ancient authorities read *ate bread with me*
z Gk *I am*

²²The disciples looked at one another, uncertain of whom he was speaking. ²³One of his disciples—the one whom Jesus loved—was reclining next to him; ²⁴Simon Peter therefore motioned to him to ask Jesus of whom he was speaking. ²⁵So while reclining next to Jesus, he asked him, "Lord, who is it?" ²⁶Jesus answered, "It is the one to whom I give this piece of bread when I have dipped it in the dish."ᵃ So when he had dipped the piece of bread, he gave it to Judas son of Simon Iscariot.ᵇ ²⁷After he received the piece of bread,ᶜ Satan entered into him. Jesus said to him, "Do quickly what you are going to do." ²⁸Now no one at the table knew why he said this to him. ²⁹Some thought that, because Judas had the common purse, Jesus was telling him, "Buy what we need for the festival"; or, that he should give something to the poor. ³⁰So, after receiving the piece of bread, he immediately went out. And it was night.

³¹ When he had gone out, Jesus said, "Now the Son of Man has been glorified, and God has been glorified in him. ³²If God has been glorified in him,ᵈ God will also glorify him in himself

ᵃ Gk *dipped it*
ᵇ Other ancient authorities read *Judas Iscariot son of Simon*; others, *Judas son of Simon from Karyot* (Kerioth)
ᶜ Gk *After the piece of bread*
ᵈ Other ancient authorities lack *If God has been glorified in him*

13.22 ἔβλεπον εἰς ἀλλήλους οἱ μαθηταὶ ἀπορούμενοι
WERE LOOKING AT ONE ANOTHER THE DISCIPLES, BEING UNCERTAIN

περὶ τίνος λέγει. **13.23** ἦν ἀνακείμενος εἷς ἐκ τῶν
ABOUT WHOM HE SPEAKS. WAS RECLINING ONE OF THE

μαθητῶν αὐτοῦ ἐν τῷ κόλπῳ τοῦ Ἰησοῦ, ὃν ἠγάπα ὁ
DISCIPLES OF HIM ON THE BOSOM - OF JESUS, WHOM ²LOVED -

Ἰησοῦς· **13.24** νεύει οὖν τούτῳ Σίμων Πέτρος
¹JESUS. ⁴NODS ¹THEREFORE ⁵TO THIS ONE ²SIMON ³PETER

πυθέσθαι τίς ἂν εἴη περὶ οὗ λέγει.
TO ASK WHO IT MAY BE ABOUT WHOM HE SPEAKS.

13.25 ἀναπεσὼν οὖν ἐκεῖνος οὕτως ἐπὶ τὸ στῆθος
HAVING LEANED BACK, THEN, THAT ONE THUS ON THE BREAST

τοῦ Ἰησοῦ λέγει αὐτῷ, Κύριε, τίς ἐστιν;
- OF JESUS SAYS TO HIM, LORD, WHO IS [IT]?

13.26 ἀποκρίνεται [ὁ] Ἰησοῦς, Ἐκεῖνός ἐστιν ᾧ ἐγὼ
ANSWERS - JESUS, THAT ONE IT IS TO WHOM I

βάψω τὸ ψωμίον καὶ δώσω αὐτῷ. βάψας οὖν
WILL DIP THE MORSEL AND WILL GIVE TO HIM. HAVING DIPPED THEREFORE

τὸ ψωμίον [λαμβάνει καὶ] δίδωσιν Ἰούδᾳ Σίμωνος
THE MORSEL HE TAKES AND GIVES TO JUDAS [THE SON] OF SIMON

Ἰσκαριώτου. **13.27** καὶ μετὰ τὸ ψωμίον τότε εἰσῆλθεν
OF ISCARIOT. AND AFTER THE MORSEL THEN ENTERED

εἰς ἐκεῖνον ὁ Σατανᾶς. λέγει οὖν αὐτῷ ὁ Ἰησοῦς,
INTO THAT MAN - SATAN. SAYS THEREFORE TO HIM - JESUS,

Ὃ ποιεῖς ποίησον τάχιον. **13.28** τοῦτο [δὲ] οὐδεὶς
THAT WHICH YOU DO DO QUICKLY. BUT~THIS NO ONE

ἔγνω τῶν ἀνακειμένων πρὸς τί εἶπεν
KNEW OF THE ONES RECLINING FOR WHAT [PURPOSE] HE SPOKE

αὐτῷ· **13.29** τινὲς γὰρ ἐδόκουν, ἐπεὶ τὸ γλωσσόκομον
TO HIM. FOR~SOME WERE THINKING, SINCE THE MONEY BOX

εἶχεν Ἰούδας, ὅτι λέγει αὐτῷ [ὁ] Ἰησοῦς, Ἀγόρασον
HAD JUDAS, THAT SAYS TO HIM - JESUS, BUY

ὧν χρείαν ἔχομεν εἰς τὴν ἑορτήν, ἢ τοῖς
THE THINGS OF WHICH WE HAVE~NEED FOR THE FEAST, OR TO THE

πτωχοῖς ἵνα τι δῷ. **13.30** λαβὼν οὖν
POOR THAT SOMETHING HE SHOULD GIVE. HAVING TAKEN THEREFORE

τὸ ψωμίον ἐκεῖνος ἐξῆλθεν εὐθύς. ἦν δὲ νύξ.
THE MORSEL THAT MAN WENT OUT IMMEDIATELY; AND~IT WAS NIGHT.

13.31 Ὅτε οὖν ἐξῆλθεν, λέγει Ἰησοῦς, Νῦν
WHEN THEREFORE HE WENT OUT, JESUS~SAYS, NOW

ἐδοξάσθη ὁ υἱὸς τοῦ ἀνθρώπου, καὶ ὁ θεὸς
WAS (IS) GLORIFIED THE SON OF MAN, AND - GOD

ἐδοξάσθη ἐν αὐτῷ. **13.32** ⌜εἰ ὁ θεὸς ἐδοξάσθη ἐν
WAS (IS) GLORIFIED IN HIM. IF - GOD WAS (IS) GLORIFED IN

αὐτῷ⌝ καὶ ὁ θεὸς δοξάσει αὐτὸν ἐν αὐτῷ, καὶ
HIM, BOTH - GOD WILL GLORIFY HIM IN HIMSELF AND

13:32 text: all. omit: NIVmg NEBmg NJBmg.

εὐθὺς   δοξάσει   αὐτόν.   **13.33** τεκνία,   ἔτι   μικρὸν
IMMEDIATELY HE WILL GLORIFY HIM.   CHILDREN, YET   A LITTLE WHILE

μεθ᾽ ὑμῶν εἰμι· ζητήσετέ με, καὶ καθὼς εἶπον τοῖς
WITH YOU° I AM; YOU° WILL SEEK ME, AND AS   I SAID   TO THE

Ἰουδαίοις ὅτι Ὅπου ἐγὼ ὑπάγω ὑμεῖς οὐ δύνασθε
JEWS,   -   WHERE I   GO AWAY YOU°   ARE NOT ABLE

ἐλθεῖν, καὶ ὑμῖν λέγω ἄρτι. **13.34** ἐντολὴν καινὴν
TO COME, ALSO TO YOU° I SAY NOW.   A NEW~COMMAND

δίδωμι ὑμῖν, ἵνα ἀγαπᾶτε ἀλλήλους, καθὼς ἠγάπησα
I GIVE   TO YOU°, THAT YOU° LOVE ONE ANOTHER— AS   I LOVED

ὑμᾶς ἵνα καὶ ὑμεῖς ἀγαπᾶτε ἀλλήλους. **13.35** ἐν τούτῳ
YOU°   THAT ALSO YOU°   LOVE   ONE ANOTHER.   BY THIS

γνώσονται πάντες ὅτι ἐμοὶ μαθηταί ἐστε, ἐὰν
WILL KNOW   ALL MEN THAT MY   DISCIPLES YOU° ARE, IF

ἀγάπην ἔχητε ἐν ἀλλήλοις.
LOVE   YOU° HAVE AMONG ONE ANOTHER.

13.36 Λέγει αὐτῷ Σίμων Πέτρος, Κύριε, ποῦ ὑπάγεις;
         SAYS   TO HIM SIMON   PETER,   LORD,   WHERE DO YOU GO?

ἀπεκρίθη [αὐτῷ] Ἰησοῦς, Ὅπου ὑπάγω οὐ δύνασαί
ANSWERED   HIM   JESUS,   WHERE I GO   YOU ARE NOT ABLE

μοι νῦν ἀκολουθῆσαι, ἀκολουθήσεις δὲ ὕστερον.
²ME ³NOW ¹TO FOLLOW,   BUT~YOU WILL FOLLOW LATER.

13.37 λέγει αὐτῷ ὁ Πέτρος, Κύριε, διὰ τί οὐ δύναμαί
         SAYS   TO HIM - PETER,   LORD,   WHY   AM I NOT ABLE

σοι ἀκολουθῆσαι ἄρτι; τὴν ψυχήν μου ὑπὲρ σοῦ
TO FOLLOW~YOU   NOW? THE   LIFE   OF ME FOR   YOU

θήσω.   **13.38** ἀποκρίνεται Ἰησοῦς, Τὴν ψυχήν σου
I WILL LAY DOWN.   ANSWERS   JESUS,   THE   LIFE   OF YOU

ὑπὲρ ἐμοῦ θήσεις;   ἀμὴν ἀμὴν λέγω σοι,
FOR   ME   WILL YOU LAY DOWN? TRULY, TRULY I SAY TO YOU,

οὐ μὴ ἀλέκτωρ φωνήσῃ ἕως οὗ ἀρνήσῃ με τρίς.
NEVER [WILL] A COCK CROW   UNTIL   YOU DENY ME THREE TIMES.

---

and will glorify him at once. [33]Little children, I am with you only a little longer. You will look for me; and as I said to the Jews so now I say to you, 'Where I am going, you cannot come.' [34]I give you a new commandment, that you love one another. Just as I have loved you, you also should love one another. [35]By this everyone will know that you are my disciples, if you have love for one another."

36 Simon Peter said to him, "Lord, where are you going?" Jesus answered, "Where I am going, you cannot follow me now; but you will follow afterward." [37]Peter said to him, "Lord, why can I not follow you now? I will lay down my life for you." [38]Jesus answered, "Will you lay down your life for me? Very truly, I tell you, before the cock crows, you will have denied me three times.

CHAPTER 14

14.1 Μὴ ταρασσέσθω ὑμῶν ἡ καρδία· πιστεύετε εἰς
        LET NOT BE TROUBLED YOUR° -   HEART;   YOU° BELIEVE IN

τὸν θεὸν καὶ εἰς ἐμὲ πιστεύετε. **14.2** ἐν τῇ οἰκίᾳ τοῦ
-    GOD,   ALSO IN   ME   BELIEVE.   IN THE HOUSE OF THE

πατρός μου μοναὶ πολλαί εἰσιν· εἰ δὲ μή, εἶπον ἂν
FATHER   OF ME MANY~ROOMS THERE ARE; BUT~IF NOT, WOULD I HAVE TOLD

ὑμῖν ὅτι πορεύομαι ἑτοιμάσαι τόπον ὑμῖν; **14.3** καὶ
YOU°   THAT I GO   TO PREPARE   A PLACE FOR YOU°?   AND

ἐὰν πορευθῶ καὶ ἑτοιμάσω τόπον ὑμῖν, πάλιν ἔρχομαι
IF   I GO   AND PREPARE   A PLACE FOR YOU°, AGAIN I AM COMING

καὶ παραλήμψομαι ὑμᾶς πρὸς ἐμαυτόν, ἵνα ὅπου
AND WILL RECEIVE   YOU°   TO   MYSELF,   THAT WHERE

"Do not let your hearts be troubled. Believe[e] in God, believe also in me. [2]In my Father's house there are many dwelling places. If it were not so, would I have told you that I go to prepare a place for you?[f] [3]And if I go and prepare a place for you, I will come again and will take you to myself, so that where

[e] Or *You believe*
[f] Or *If it were not so, I would have told you; for I go to prepare a place for you*

I am, there you may be also.
⁴And you know the way to
the place where I am
going."ᵍ ⁵Thomas said to
him, "Lord, we do not know
where you are going. How
can we know the way?"
⁶Jesus said to him, "I am the
way, and the truth, and the
life. No one comes to the
Father except through me.
⁷If you know me, you will
knowʰ my Father also. From
now on you do know him
and have seen him."

8 Philip said to him,
"Lord, show us the Father,
and we will be satisfied."
⁹Jesus said to him, "Have I
been with you all this time,
Philip, and you still do not
know me? Whoever has
seen me has seen the Father.
How can you say, 'Show us
the Father'? ¹⁰Do you not
believe that I am in the
Father and the Father is in
me? The words that I say to
you I do not speak on my
own; but the Father who
dwells in me does his works.
¹¹Believe me that I am in the
Father and the Father is in
me; but if you do not, then
believe me because of the
works themselves. ¹²Very
truly, I tell you, the one who
believes in me will also do
the works that I do and, in
fact, will do greater works
than these, because I am
going to the Father. ¹³I will
do whatever you ask in my

ᵍ Other ancient authorities read *Where
I am going you know, and the way
you know*
ʰ Other ancient authorities read *If you
had known me, you would have
known*

εἰμὶ ἐγὼ καὶ ὑμεῖς ἦτε. **14.4** καὶ ὅπου [ἐγὼ] ὑπάγω
I~AM ALSO YOU° MAY BE.   AND WHERE I GO

οἴδατε τὴν ὁδόν. **14.5** Λέγει αὐτῷ Θωμᾶς, Κύριε,
YOU° KNOW THE WAY.   SAYS TO HIM THOMAS, LORD,

οὐκ οἴδαμεν ποῦ ὑπάγεις· πῶς δυνάμεθα τὴν ὁδὸν
WE DO NOT KNOW WHERE YOU GO; HOW ARE WE ABLE THE WAY

εἰδέναι; **14.6** λέγει αὐτῷ [ὁ] Ἰησοῦς, Ἐγώ εἰμι ἡ
TO KNOW? SAYS TO HIM - JESUS, I AM THE

ὁδὸς καὶ ἡ ἀλήθεια καὶ ἡ ζωή· οὐδεὶς ἔρχεται πρὸς
WAY AND THE TRUTH AND THE LIFE; NO ONE COMES TO

τὸν πατέρα εἰ μὴ δι' ἐμοῦ. **14.7** εἰ ⌐ἐγνώκατέ⌐ με,
THE FATHER EXCEPT THROUGH ME. IF YOU° HAVE KNOWN ME,

καὶ τὸν πατέρα μου ⌐γνώσεσθε⌐· καὶ ἀπ' ἄρτι
ALSO THE FATHER OF ME YOU° WILL KNOW; AND FROM NOW [ON]

γινώσκετε αὐτὸν καὶ ἑωράκατε αὐτόν. **14.8** λέγει αὐτῷ
YOU° KNOW HIM AND HAVE SEEN HIM. SAYS TO HIM

Φίλιππος, Κύριε, δεῖξον ἡμῖν τὸν πατέρα, καὶ ἀρκεῖ
PHILIP, LORD, SHOW US THE FATHER, AND IT IS ENOUGH

ἡμῖν. **14.9** λέγει αὐτῷ ὁ Ἰησοῦς, Τοσούτῳ χρόνῳ μεθ'
FOR US. SAYS TO HIM - JESUS, SO LONG A TIME WITH

ὑμῶν εἰμι καὶ οὐκ ἔγνωκάς με, Φίλιππε; ὁ
YOU° I AM AND YOU HAVE NOT KNOWN ME, PHILIP? THE ONE

ἑωρακὼς ἐμὲ ἑώρακεν τὸν πατέρα· πῶς σὺ λέγεις,
HAVING SEEN ME HAS SEEN THE FATHER; HOW DO YOU SAY,

Δεῖξον ἡμῖν τὸν πατέρα; **14.10** οὐ πιστεύεις ὅτι ἐγὼ ἐν
SHOW US THE FATHER?   DO YOU NOT BELIEVE THAT I [AM] IN

τῷ πατρὶ καὶ ὁ πατὴρ ἐν ἐμοί ἐστιν; τὰ ῥήματα
THE FATHER AND THE FATHER IN ME IS? THE WORDS

ἃ ἐγὼ λέγω ὑμῖν ἀπ' ἐμαυτοῦ οὐ λαλῶ, ὁ δὲ
WHICH I SPEAK TO YOU° FROM MYSELF I DO NOT SPEAK, BUT~THE

πατὴρ ἐν ἐμοὶ μένων ποιεῖ τὰ ἔργα αὐτοῦ.
FATHER IN ME ABIDING DOES THE WORKS OF HIM.

14.11 πιστεύετέ μοι ὅτι ἐγὼ ἐν τῷ πατρὶ καὶ ὁ
BELIEVE ME THAT I [AM] IN THE FATHER AND THE

πατὴρ ἐν ἐμοί· εἰ δὲ μή, διὰ τὰ ἔργα αὐτὰ
FATHER IN ME; BUT~IF NOT, BECAUSE OF THE WORKS THEMSELVES

πιστεύετε. **14.12** ἀμὴν ἀμὴν λέγω ὑμῖν, ὁ πιστεύων
BELIEVE.   TRULY, TRULY I SAY TO YOU°, THE ONE BELIEVING

εἰς ἐμὲ τὰ ἔργα ἃ ἐγὼ ποιῶ κἀκεῖνος ποιήσει καὶ
IN ME THE WORKS WHICH I DO ALSO THAT ONE WILL DO AND

μείζονα τούτων ποιήσει, ὅτι ἐγὼ πρὸς τὸν πατέρα
GREATER [THAN] THESE HE WILL DO, BECAUSE I TO THE FATHER

πορεύομαι· **14.13** καὶ ὅ τι ἂν αἰτήσητε ἐν τῷ ὀνόματί
AM GOING.   AND WHATEVER YOU° ASK IN THE NAME

14:7a text: NIVmg NEBmg TEV NJB NRSV. var. εγνωκειτε (had known): KJV ASV RSV NASB NIV NEB
TEVmg NJBmg NRSVmg. **14:7b** text: NIVmg NEBmg TEV NJB NRSV. var. εγνωκειτε αν (you would
have known) and αν ειδειτε (you would have perceived): KJV ASV RSV NASB NIV NEB TEVmg NJBmg
NRSVmg.

μου τοῦτο ποιήσω, ἵνα δοξασθῇ ὁ πατὴρ ἐν τῷ
OF ME THIS WILL I DO, THAT MAY BE GLORIFIED THE FATHER IN THE

υἱῷ· **14.14** ἐάν τι αἰτήσητέ με ἐν τῷ ὀνόματί μου
SON; IF ANYTHING YOU° ASK ME IN THE NAME OF ME

ἐγὼ ποιήσω.
I WILL DO [IT].

14.15 Ἐὰν ἀγαπᾶτέ με τὰς ἐντολὰς τὰς ἐμὰς
IF YOU° LOVE ME, THE COMMANDS - OF ME

τηρήσετε· **14.16** κἀγὼ ἐρωτήσω τὸν πατέρα καὶ ἄλλον
YOU° WILL KEEP; AND I WILL ASK THE FATHER AND ANOTHER

παράκλητον δώσει ὑμῖν, ἵνα μεθ' ὑμῶν εἰς τὸν αἰῶνα
ENCOURAGER HE WILL GIVE YOU°, THAT WITH YOU° INTO THE AGE

ᾖ, **14.17** τὸ πνεῦμα τῆς ἀληθείας, ὃ ὁ κόσμος
HE MAY BE, THE SPIRIT - OF TRUTH, WHICH THE WORLD

οὐ δύναται λαβεῖν, ὅτι οὐ θεωρεῖ αὐτὸ οὐδὲ
IS NOT ABLE TO RECEIVE, BECAUSE IT DOES NOT SEE IT(HIM) NOR

γινώσκει· ὑμεῖς γινώσκετε αὐτό, ὅτι παρ' ὑμῖν
KNOW (HIM); YOU° KNOW IT(HIM), BECAUSE WITH YOU°

μένει καὶ ἐν ὑμῖν ⌜ἔσται⌝. **14.18** οὐκ ἀφήσω ὑμᾶς
HE REMAINS AND IN YOU° HE WILL BE. I WILL NOT LEAVE YOU°

ὀρφανούς, ἔρχομαι πρὸς ὑμᾶς. **14.19** ἔτι μικρὸν καὶ
ORPHANS, I AM COMING TO YOU°. YET A LITTLE [TIME] AND

ὁ κόσμος με οὐκέτι θεωρεῖ, ὑμεῖς δὲ θεωρεῖτέ με,
THE WORLD ME NO LONGER SEES, BUT~YOU° SEE ME;

ὅτι ἐγὼ ζῶ καὶ ὑμεῖς ζήσετε. **14.20** ἐν ἐκείνῃ τῇ
BECAUSE I LIVE ALSO YOU° WILL LIVE. ON THAT -

ἡμέρᾳ γνώσεσθε ὑμεῖς ὅτι ἐγὼ ἐν τῷ πατρί μου καὶ
DAY YOU°~WILL KNOW THAT I [AM] IN THE FATHER OF ME AND

ὑμεῖς ἐν ἐμοὶ κἀγὼ ἐν ὑμῖν. **14.21** ὁ ἔχων τὰς
YOU° IN ME AND I IN YOU°. THE ONE HAVING THE

ἐντολάς μου καὶ τηρῶν αὐτὰς ἐκεῖνός ἐστιν ὁ
COMMANDS OF ME AND KEEPING THEM THAT ONE IS THE ONE

ἀγαπῶν με· ὁ δὲ ἀγαπῶν με ἀγαπηθήσεται ὑπὸ τοῦ
LOVING ME; AND~THE ONE LOVING ME WILL BE LOVED BY THE

πατρός μου, κἀγὼ ἀγαπήσω αὐτὸν καὶ ἐμφανίσω
FATHER OF ME, AND I WILL LOVE HIM AND WILL MANIFEST

αὐτῷ ἐμαυτόν. **14.22** Λέγει αὐτῷ Ἰούδας, οὐχ ὁ
MYSELF~TO HIM. SAYS TO HIM JUDAS, NOT -

Ἰσκαριώτης, Κύριε, [καὶ] τί γέγονεν ὅτι ἡμῖν
ISCARIOT, LORD, AND WHAT HAS OCCURRED THAT TO US

μέλλεις ἐμφανίζειν σεαυτὸν καὶ οὐχὶ τῷ κόσμῳ;
YOU ARE ABOUT TO MANIFEST YOURSELF AND NOT TO THE WORLD?

14.23 ἀπεκρίθη Ἰησοῦς καὶ εἶπεν αὐτῷ, Ἐάν τις
ANSWERED JESUS AND SAID TO HIM, IF ANYONE

ἀγαπᾷ με τὸν λόγον μου τηρήσει καὶ ὁ πατήρ μου
LOVES ME THE WORD OF ME HE WILL KEEP AND THE FATHER OF ME

name, so that the Father may be glorified in the Son. [14]If in my name you ask me[i] for anything, I will do it.

[15] "If you love me, you will keep[j] my commandments. [16]And I will ask the Father, and he will give you another Advocate,[k] to be with you forever. [17]This is the Spirit of truth, whom the world cannot receive, because it neither sees him nor knows him. You know him, because he abides with you, and he will be in[l] you.

[18] "I will not leave you orphaned; I am coming to you. [19]In a little while the world will no longer see me, but you will see me; because I live, you also will live. [20]On that day you will know that I am in my Father, and you in me, and I in you. [21]They who have my commandments and keep them are those who love me; and those who love me will be loved by my Father, and I will love them and reveal myself to them." [22]Judas (not Iscariot) said to him, "Lord, how is it that you will reveal yourself to us, and not to the world?" [23]Jesus answered him, "Those who love me will keep my word, and my Father

[i] Other ancient authorities lack *me*
[j] Other ancient authorities read *me, keep*
[k] Or *Helper*
[l] Or *among*

14:17 text: KJV ASV RSV NASB NIV NEBmg TEVmg NJBmg NRSV. var. εστιν (is): NIVmg NEB TEV NJB.

will love them, and we will come to them and make our home with them. ²⁴Whoever does not love me does not keep my words; and the word that you hear is not mine, but is from the Father who sent me.

25 "I have said these things to you while I am still with you. ²⁶But the Advocate,ᵐ the Holy Spirit, whom the Father will send in my name, will teach you everything, and remind you of all that I have said to you. ²⁷Peace I leave with you; my peace I give to you. I do not give to you as the world gives. Do not let your hearts be troubled, and do not let them be afraid. ²⁸You heard me say to you, 'I am going away, and I am coming to you.' If you loved me, you would rejoice that I am going to the Father, because the Father is greater than I. ²⁹And now I have told you this before it occurs, so that when it does occur, you may believe. ³⁰I will no longer talk much with you, for the ruler of this world is coming. He has no power over me; ³¹but I do as the Father has commanded me, so that the world may know that I love the Father. Rise, let us be on our way.

ᵐ Or *Helper*

ἀγαπήσει αὐτὸν καὶ πρὸς αὐτὸν ἐλευσόμεθα καὶ
WILL LOVE   HIM   AND   TO   HIM   WE WILL COME   AND

μονὴν   παρ' αὐτῷ   ποιησόμεθα.   **14.24** ὁ   μὴ
A DWELLING PLACE WITH HIM WE WILL MAKE.   THE ONE NOT

ἀγαπῶν με τοὺς λόγους μου οὐ τηρεῖ·   καὶ ὁ λόγος
LOVING   ME, THE WORDS OF ME DOES NOT KEEP. AND THE WORD

ὃν   ἀκούετε οὐκ ἔστιν ἐμὸς ἀλλὰ τοῦ   πέμψαντός με
WHICH YOU° HEAR IS NOT   MINE BUT ¹OF THE ³HAVING SENT   ⁴ME

πατρός.
²FATHER.

14.25 Ταῦτα   λελάληκα ὑμῖν παρ' ὑμῖν μένων·
THESE THINGS I HAVE TOLD   YOU° ²WITH ³YOU ¹[WHILE] ABIDING;

14.26 ὁ δὲ   παράκλητος, τὸ πνεῦμα τὸ ἅγιον ὃ
BUT~THE ENCOURAGER, THE ²SPIRIT - ¹HOLY, WHICH

πέμψει ὁ   πατὴρ ἐν τῷ   ὀνόματί μου, ἐκεῖνος
WILL SEND THE FATHER IN THE   NAME   OF ME, THAT ONE

ὑμᾶς διδάξει πάντα   καὶ ὑπομνήσει ὑμᾶς πάντα
WILL TEACH~YOU° ALL THINGS AND WILL REMIND YOU° [OF] ALL THINGS

ἃ   εἶπον ὑμῖν [ἐγώ].   **14.27** Εἰρήνην ἀφίημι ὑμῖν,
WHICH ²TOLD ³YOU° ¹I.   PEACE   I LEAVE   TO YOU°,

εἰρήνην τὴν ἐμὴν δίδωμι ὑμῖν· οὐ καθὼς ὁ   κόσμος
PEACE   - OF ME I GIVE TO YOU°; NOT AS THE WORLD

δίδωσιν ἐγὼ δίδωμι ὑμῖν.   μὴ ταρασσέσθω ὑμῶν ἡ
GIVES   I   GIVE TO YOU. LET NOT BE TROUBLED YOUR° -

καρδία μηδὲ δειλιάτω.   **14.28** ἠκούσατε ὅτι ἐγὼ
HEART   NOR LET IT BE COWARDLY.   YOU° HEARD THAT I

εἶπον ὑμῖν, Ὑπάγω καὶ ἔρχομαι πρὸς ὑμᾶς. εἰ
TOLD   YOU°, I AM GOING AND I AM COMING TO YOU.° IF

ἠγαπᾶτέ   με ἐχάρητε ἄν   ὅτι   πορεύομαι πρὸς
YOU° WERE LOVING ME YOU° WOULD HAVE REJOICED BECAUSE I GO   TO

τὸν πατέρα, ὅτι ὁ   πατὴρ μείζων   μού ἐστιν.
THE FATHER, FOR THE FATHER GREATER [THAN] ME IS.

14.29 καὶ   νῦν εἴρηκα ὑμῖν πρὶν γενέσθαι, ἵνα ὅταν
AND NOW I HAVE TOLD YOU° BEFORE IT HAPPENS, THAT WHEN

γένηται πιστεύσητε.   **14.30** οὐκέτι πολλὰ   λαλήσω μεθ'
IT HAPPENS YOU° MAY BELIEVE.   NO LONGER MANY THINGS I WILL SPEAK WITH

ὑμῶν, ἔρχεται γὰρ ὁ   τοῦ   κόσμου ἄρχων· καὶ ἐν ἐμοὶ
YOU°, FOR~IS COMING THE ²OF THE ³WORLD ¹RULER; AND IN ME

οὐκ ἔχει   οὐδέν,   **14.31** ἀλλ' ἵνα   γνῷ ὁ
HE DOES NOT HAVE ANYTHING.   BUT IN ORDER THAT MAY KNOW THE

κόσμος ὅτι ἀγαπῶ τὸν πατέρα, καὶ καθὼς ἐνετείλατό
WORLD   THAT I LOVE THE FATHER, AND AS   COMMANDED

μοι ὁ   πατήρ, οὕτως ποιῶ. Ἐγείρεσθε, ἄγωμεν
ME THE FATHER, SO I DO. ARISE,   LET US GO

ἐντεῦθεν.
FROM HERE.

15.1 Ἐγώ εἰμι ἡ ἄμπελος ἡ ἀληθινὴ καὶ ὁ πατήρ
I   AM THE VINE,   THE TRUE ONE, AND THE FATHER

μου ὁ γεωργός ἐστιν. **15.2** πᾶν κλῆμα ἐν ἐμοὶ μὴ
OF ME THE VINEDRESSER IS.   EVERY BRANCH IN ME   NOT

φέρον καρπὸν αἴρει αὐτό, καὶ πᾶν   τὸ
BEARING FRUIT HE TAKES IT,   AND EVERY [BRANCH] -

καρπὸν φέρον καθαίρει αὐτὸ ἵνα καρπὸν πλείονα
BEARING~FRUIT   HE PRUNES IT THAT MUCH~FRUIT

φέρῃ.   **15.3** ἤδη ὑμεῖς καθαροί ἐστε διὰ   τὸν
IT MAY BEAR.   ALREADY YOU° ARE~CLEAN   BECAUSE OF THE

λόγον ὃν λελάληκα ὑμῖν· **15.4** μείνατε ἐν ἐμοί, κἀγὼ
WORD WHICH I HAVE SPOKEN TO YOU°; REMAIN   IN ME, AND I

ἐν ὑμῖν. καθὼς τὸ κλῆμα οὐ δύναται καρπὸν φέρειν
IN YOU°. AS THE BRANCH IS NOT ABLE TO BEAR~FRUIT

ἀφ᾽ ἑαυτοῦ ἐὰν μὴ μένῃ ἐν τῇ ἀμπέλῳ, οὕτως οὐδὲ
FROM ITSELF UNLESS IT REMAINS ON THE VINE,   SO   NEITHER

ὑμεῖς ἐὰν μὴ ἐν ἐμοὶ μένητε.   **15.5** ἐγώ εἰμι ἡ
YOU° UNLESS IN ME YOU° REMAIN.   I AM THE

ἄμπελος, ὑμεῖς τὰ κλήματα. ὁ   μένων ἐν ἐμοὶ
VINE,   YOU° [ARE] THE BRANCHES. THE ONE REMAINING IN ME

κἀγὼ ἐν αὐτῷ οὗτος φέρει καρπὸν πολύν, ὅτι
AND I IN HIM THIS ONE BEARS MUCH~FRUIT,   BECAUSE

χωρὶς ἐμοῦ οὐ δύνασθε ποιεῖν οὐδέν. **15.6** ἐὰν μή
APART FROM ME YOU° ARE NOT ABLE TO DO ANYTHING. UNLESS

τις   μένῃ ἐν ἐμοί, ἐβλήθη ἔξω ὡς τὸ κλῆμα
SOMEONE REMAINS IN ME, HE WAS (IS) CAST OUT AS THE BRANCH

καὶ ἐξηράνθη καὶ συνάγουσιν αὐτὰ καὶ εἰς τὸ πῦρ
AND WAS (IS) DRIED UP AND THEY GATHER THEM AND INTO THE FIRE

βάλλουσιν καὶ καίεται. **15.7** ἐὰν μείνητε ἐν ἐμοὶ
THEY THROW [THEM] AND THEY ARE BURNED. IF YOU° REMAIN IN ME

καὶ τὰ ῥήματά μου ἐν ὑμῖν μείνῃ, ὃ ἐὰν θέλητε
AND THE WORDS OF ME IN YOU° REMAIN, WHATEVER YOU° WANT

αἰτήσασθε, καὶ γενήσεται ὑμῖν. **15.8** ἐν τούτῳ
ASK,   AND IT WILL BE DONE FOR YOU°.   BY THIS

ἐδοξάσθη ὁ πατήρ μου, ἵνα καρπὸν πολὺν φέρητε
WAS (IS) GLORIFIED THE FATHER OF ME, THAT MUCH~FRUIT YOU° BEAR

καὶ γένησθε ἐμοὶ μαθηταί. **15.9** καθὼς ἠγάπησέν με
AND YOU° BE TO ME DISCIPLES.   AS   LOVED   ME

ὁ πατήρ, κἀγὼ ὑμᾶς ἠγάπησα· μείνατε ἐν τῇ ἀγάπῃ
THE FATHER, SO I LOVED~YOU°;   REMAIN IN THE LOVE

τῇ ἐμῇ. **15.10** ἐὰν τὰς ἐντολάς μου τηρήσητε,
- OF ME.   IF THE COMMANDS OF ME YOU° KEEP,

μενεῖτε ἐν τῇ ἀγάπῃ μου, καθὼς ἐγὼ τὰς ἐντολὰς
YOU° WILL REMAIN IN THE LOVE OF ME, AS I THE COMMANDS

"I am the true vine, and my Father is the vinegrower. [2]He removes every branch in me that bears no fruit. Every branch that bears fruit he prunes[n] to make it bear more fruit. [3]You have already been cleansed[n] by the word that I have spoken to you. [4]Abide in me as I abide in you. Just as the branch cannot bear fruit by itself unless it abides in the vine, neither can you unless you abide in me. [5]I am the vine, you are the branches. Those who abide in me and I in them bear much fruit, because apart from me you can do nothing. [6]Whoever does not abide in me is thrown away like a branch and withers; such branches are gathered, thrown into the fire, and burned. [7]If you abide in me, and my words abide in you, ask for whatever you wish, and it will be done for you. [8]My Father is glorified by this, that you bear much fruit and become[o] my disciples. [9]As the Father has loved me, so I have loved you; abide in my love. [10]If you keep my commandments, you will abide in my love, just as I have kept my Father's

[n] The same Greek root refers to pruning and cleansing
[o] Or be

commandments and abide in his love. [11]I have said these things to you so that my joy may be in you, and that your joy may be complete.

[12]"This is my commandment, that you love one another as I have loved you. [13]No one has greater love than this, to lay down one's life for one's friends. [14]You are my friends if you do what I command you. [15]I do not call you servants[p] any longer, because the servant[q] does not know what the master is doing; but I have called you friends, because I have made known to you everything that I have heard from my Father. [16]You did not choose me but I chose you. And I appointed you to go and bear fruit, fruit that will last, so that the Father will give you whatever you ask him in my name. [17]I am giving you these commands so that you may love one another.

[18]"If the world hates you, be aware that it hated me before it hated you. [19]If you belonged to the world,[r] the world would love you as its own. Because you do not belong to the world, but I have chosen you out of the world—therefore the world hates you.

[p] Gk slaves
[q] Gk slave
[r] Gk were of the world

τοῦ   πατρός μου τετήρηκα καὶ μένω αὐτοῦ ἐν τῇ
OF THE FATHER   OF ME HAVE KEPT   AND I REMAIN IN~HIS

ἀγάπῃ.
LOVE.

15.11 Ταῦτα   λελάληκα ὑμῖν ἵνα ἡ χαρὰ ἡ ἐμὴ ἐν
THESE THINGS I HAVE SPOKEN TO YOU° THAT THE JOY   - OF ME IN

ὑμῖν   ᾖ   καὶ ἡ χαρὰ ὑμῶν πληρωθῇ.   **15.12** αὕτη
YOU°   MAY BE AND THE JOY OF YOU° MAY BE MADE FULL.   THIS

ἐστὶν ἡ ἐντολὴ ἡ ἐμή, ἵνα ἀγαπᾶτε ἀλλήλους καθὼς
IS   THE COMMAND - OF ME, THAT YOU° LOVE   ONE ANOTHER   AS

ἠγάπησα ὑμᾶς. **15.13** μείζονα ταύτης ἀγάπην
I LOVED   YOU°.   GREATER   LOVE~THAN THIS

οὐδεὶς ἔχει, ἵνα τις   τὴν ψυχὴν αὐτοῦ θῇ   ὑπὲρ
HAS~NO ONE,   THAT SOMEONE THE LIFE OF HIM HE LAY DOWN FOR

τῶν φίλων αὐτοῦ. **15.14** ὑμεῖς φίλοι μού ἐστε ἐὰν
THE FRIENDS OF HIM.   YOU°   FRIENDS OF ME ARE IF

ποιῆτε ἃ   ἐγὼ ἐντέλλομαι ὑμῖν.   **15.15** οὐκέτι
YOU° DO THE THINGS WHICH I   COMMAND   YOU°.   NO LONGER

λέγω ὑμᾶς δούλους, ὅτι   ὁ δοῦλος οὐκ οἶδεν τί
DO I CALL YOU° SLAVES,   BECAUSE THE SLAVE DOES NOT KNOW WHAT

ποιεῖ αὐτοῦ ὁ κύριος· ὑμᾶς δὲ εἴρηκα   φίλους, ὅτι
DOES HIS   - LORD;   BUT~YOU° I HAVE CALLED FRIENDS,   BECAUSE

πάντα ἃ   ἤκουσα παρὰ τοῦ πατρός μου ἐγνώρισα
ALL THINGS WHICH I HEARD FROM THE FATHER OF ME I MADE KNOWN

ὑμῖν. **15.16** οὐχ ὑμεῖς με ἐξελέξασθε, ἀλλ᾽ ἐγὼ
TO YOU°.   NOT YOU° CHOSE~ME,   BUT   I

ἐξελεξάμην ὑμᾶς καὶ ἔθηκα ὑμᾶς ἵνα ὑμεῖς ὑπάγητε
CHOSE   YOU° AND APPOINTED YOU° THAT YOU   GO

καὶ καρπὸν φέρητε καὶ ὁ καρπὸς ὑμῶν μένῃ, ἵνα
AND BEAR~FRUIT   AND THE FRUIT OF YOU° REMAINS THAT

ὅ τι ἂν αἰτήσητε τὸν πατέρα ἐν τῷ ὀνόματί μου
WHATEVER YOU° ASK   THE FATHER IN THE NAME   OF ME

δῷ   ὑμῖν. **15.17** ταῦτα   ἐντέλλομαι ὑμῖν, ἵνα
HE MAY GIVE TO YOU°.   THESE THINGS I COMMAND   YOU°,   THAT

ἀγαπᾶτε ἀλλήλους.
YOU° LOVE   ONE ANOTHER.

15.18 Εἰ ὁ κόσμος ὑμᾶς μισεῖ, γινώσκετε ὅτι ἐμὲ
IF THE WORLD HATES~YOU°,   KNOW   THAT ME

πρῶτον ὑμῶν μεμίσηκεν. **15.19** εἰ ἐκ τοῦ κόσμου
BEFORE   YOU° IT HAS HATED.   IF OF THE WORLD

ἦτε,   ὁ κόσμος ἂν   τὸ ἴδιον ἐφίλει· ὅτι δὲ   ἐκ
YOU° WERE, THE WORLD WOULD ITS OWN [HAVE] LOVED; BUT~BECAUSE FROM

τοῦ κόσμου οὐκ ἐστέ, ἀλλ᾽ ἐγὼ ἐξελεξάμην ὑμᾶς ἐκ
THE WORLD YOU° ARE NOT, BUT   I   CHOSE   YOU°   OUT OF

τοῦ κόσμου, διὰ τοῦτο μισεῖ ὑμᾶς ὁ κόσμος.
THE WORLD,   THEREFORE HATES YOU° THE WORLD.

15.20 μνημονεύετε τοῦ λόγου οὗ   ἐγὼ εἶπον ὑμῖν,
REMEMBER   THE SAYING WHICH I   TOLD   YOU,

Οὐκ ἔστιν δοῦλος μείζων   τοῦ κυρίου αὐτοῦ. εἰ ἐμὲ
A SLAVE~IS NOT   GREATER [THAN] THE LORD OF HIM. IF ME

ἐδίωξαν,   καὶ ὑμᾶς διώξουσιν·   εἰ τὸν λόγον μου
THEY PERSECUTED, ALSO YOU° THEY WILL PERSECUTE; IF THE WORD OF ME

ἐτήρησαν, καὶ τὸν ὑμέτερον τηρήσουσιν.   **15.21** ἀλλὰ
THEY KEPT,   ALSO -   YOURS°   THEY WILL KEEP.   BUT

ταῦτα πάντα ποιήσουσιν εἰς ὑμᾶς διὰ   τὸ ὄνομά
ALL~THESE THINGS THEY WILL DO TO YOU° ON ACCOUNT OF THE NAME

μου, ὅτι   οὐκ οἴδασιν τὸν πέμψαντά με.   **15.22** εἰ
OF ME, BECAUSE THEY DO NOT KNOW THE ONE HAVING SENT ME.   IF

μὴ ἦλθον καὶ ἐλάλησα αὐτοῖς, ἁμαρτίαν οὐκ εἴχοσαν·
I DID NOT COME AND SPEAK TO THEM, THEY WOULD NOT HAVE~SIN;

νῦν δὲ πρόφασιν οὐκ ἔχουσιν περὶ τῆς ἁμαρτίας αὐτῶν.
BUT~NOW A CLOAK   THEY DO NOT HAVE AROUND THE SIN   OF THEM.

15.23 ὁ   ἐμὲ μισῶν καὶ τὸν πατέρα μου μισεῖ.
            THE ONE HATING~ME ALSO THE FATHER OF ME HATES.

15.24 εἰ τὰ ἔργα μὴ ἐποίησα ἐν   αὐτοῖς ἃ
            IF THE WORKS I DID NOT DO AMONG THEM WHICH

οὐδεὶς ἄλλος ἐποίησεν, ἁμαρτίαν οὐκ εἴχοσαν· νῦν δὲ
NO OTHER MAN   DID,   THEY WOULD NOT HAVE~SIN;   BUT~NOW

καὶ ἑωράκασιν καὶ μεμισήκασιν καὶ ἐμὲ καὶ τὸν
BOTH THEY HAVE SEEN AND THEY HAVE HATED BOTH ME AND THE

πατέρα μου. **15.25** ἀλλ' ἵνα πληρωθῇ ὁ λόγος ὁ ἐν
FATHER OF ME.   BUT THAT MAY BE FULFILLED THE WORD - IN

τῷ νόμῳ αὐτῶν γεγραμμένος ὅτι Ἐμίσησάν με
THE LAW OF THEM HAVING BEEN WRITTEN, - THEY HATED ME

δωρεάν.
WITHOUT CAUSE.

15.26 Ὅταν ἔλθῃ ὁ παράκλητος ὃν ἐγὼ πέμψω
          WHEN COMES THE ENCOURAGER WHOM I WILL SEND

ὑμῖν παρὰ τοῦ πατρός, τὸ πνεῦμα τῆς ἀληθείας ὃ
TO YOU° FROM THE FATHER, THE SPIRIT - OF TRUTH, WHICH

παρὰ τοῦ πατρὸς ἐκπορεύεται, ἐκεῖνος μαρτυρήσει περὶ
FROM THE FATHER PROCEEDS,   THAT ONE WILL TESTIFY ABOUT

ἐμοῦ· **15.27** καὶ ὑμεῖς δὲ μαρτυρεῖτε, ὅτι ἀπ'
ME;   ²ALSO ³YOU° ¹AND TESTIFY,   BECAUSE FROM

ἀρχῆς   μετ' ἐμοῦ ἐστε.
[THE] BEGINNING WITH ME YOU° ARE.

15:25 Ps. 35:19; 69:4

[20]Remember the word that I said to you, 'Servants[s] are not greater than their master.' If they persecuted me, they will persecute you; if they kept my word, they will keep yours also. [21]But they will do all these things to you on account of my name, because they do not know him who sent me. [22]If I had not come and spoken to them, they would not have sin; but now they have no excuse for their sin. [23]Whoever hates me hates my Father also. [24]If I had not done among them the works that no one else did, they would not have sin. But now they have seen and hated both me and my Father. [25]It was to fulfill the word that is written in their law, 'They hated me without a cause.'

26 "When the Advocate[t] comes, whom I will send to you from the Father, the Spirit of truth who comes from the Father, he will testify on my behalf. [27]You also are to testify because you have been with me from the beginning.

[s] Gk *Slaves*
[t] Or *Helper*

CHAPTER 16

"I have said these things to you to keep you from stumbling. ²They will put you out of the synagogues. Indeed, an hour is coming when those who kill you will think that by doing so they are offering worship to God. ³And they will do this because they have not known the Father or me. ⁴But I have said these things to you so that when their hour comes you may remember that I told you about them.

"I did not say these things to you from the beginning, because I was with you. ⁵But now I am going to him who sent me; yet none of you asks me, 'Where are you going?' ⁶But because I have said these things to you, sorrow has filled your hearts. ⁷Nevertheless I tell you the truth: it is to your advantage that I go away, for if I do not go away, the Advocate[u] will not come to you; but if I go, I will send him to you. ⁸And when he comes, he will prove the world wrong about[v] sin and righteousness and judgment: ⁹about sin, because they do not believe in me; ¹⁰about righteousness, because I am going to the Father and you will see me no longer; ¹¹about judgment, because the ruler of this world has been condemned.

12 "I still have many things to say to you, but you cannot

[u] Or *Helper*
[v] Or *convict the world of*

16.1 Ταῦτα   λελάληκα ὑμῖν ἵνα   μὴ σκανδαλισθῆτε.
THESE THINGS I HAVE SPOKEN TO YOU° THAT YOU° NOT BE CAUSED TO STUMBLE.

16.2 ἀποσυναγώγους   ποιήσουσιν ὑμᾶς· ἀλλ' ἔρχεται
³AWAY FROM [THE] SYNAGOGUES ¹THEY WILL PUT ²YOU°; BUT COMES

ὥρα ἵνα πᾶς ὁ ἀποκτείνας ὑμᾶς δόξῃ
AN HOUR THAT EVERYONE HAVING KILLED YOU° MAY SUPPOSE

λατρείαν προσφέρειν τῷ θεῷ. **16.3** καὶ ταῦτα
TO OFFER~SERVICE - TO GOD. AND THESE THINGS

ποιήσουσιν ὅτι   οὐκ ἔγνωσαν τὸν πατέρα οὐδὲ ἐμέ.
THEY WILL DO BECAUSE THEY DID NOT KNOW THE FATHER NOR ME.

16.4 ἀλλὰ ταῦτα   λελάληκα ὑμῖν ἵνα ὅταν ἔλθῃ ἡ
BUT THESE THINGS I HAVE SPOKEN TO YOU° THAT WHEN COMES THE

ὥρα αὐτῶν μνημονεύητε αὐτῶν ὅτι ἐγὼ εἶπον ὑμῖν.
HOUR OF THEM YOU° MIGHT REMEMBER THEM THAT I TOLD YOU°.

Ταῦτα δὲ   ὑμῖν ἐξ ἀρχῆς   οὐκ εἶπον, ὅτι
BUT~THESE THINGS TO YOU° FROM [THE] BEGINNING I DID NOT SAY, BECAUSE

μεθ' ὑμῶν ἤμην. **16.5** νῦν δὲ ὑπάγω πρὸς τὸν
WITH YOU° I WAS. BUT~NOW I AM GOING TO THE ONE

πέμψαντά με, καὶ οὐδεὶς ἐξ ὑμῶν ἐρωτᾷ με, Ποῦ
HAVING SENT ME, AND NONE OF YOU° ASKS ME, WHERE

ὑπάγεις; **16.6** ἀλλ' ὅτι ταῦτα λελάληκα ὑμῖν ἡ
ARE YOU GOING? BUT BECAUSE I HAVE SPOKEN~THESE THINGS TO YOU° -

λύπη πεπλήρωκεν ὑμῶν τὴν καρδίαν. **16.7** ἀλλ' ἐγὼ τὴν
SORROW HAS FILLED YOUR° - HEART. BUT I THE

ἀλήθειαν λέγω ὑμῖν, συμφέρει ὑμῖν ἵνα ἐγὼ ἀπέλθω.
TRUTH TELL YOU°, IT IS BETTER FOR YOU° THAT I GO AWAY.

ἐὰν γὰρ μὴ ἀπέλθω, ὁ παράκλητος οὐκ ἐλεύσεται πρὸς
FOR~IF I DO NOT GO AWAY, THE ENCOURAGER WILL NOT COME TO

ὑμᾶς· ἐὰν δὲ πορευθῶ, πέμψω αὐτὸν πρὸς ὑμᾶς.
YOU°; BUT~IF I GO, I WILL SEND HIM TO YOU°.

16.8 καὶ ἐλθὼν ἐκεῖνος ἐλέγξει τὸν κόσμον περὶ
AND HAVING COME THAT ONE WILL EXPOSE THE WORLD CONCERNING

ἁμαρτίας καὶ περὶ δικαιοσύνης καὶ περὶ
SIN AND CONCERNING RIGHTEOUSNESS AND CONCERNING

κρίσεως· **16.9** περὶ ἁμαρτίας μέν, ὅτι
JUDGMENT. CONCERNING SIN, - BECAUSE

οὐ πιστεύουσιν εἰς ἐμέ· **16.10** περὶ δικαιοσύνης δέ,
THEY DO NOT BELIEVE IN ME; CONCERNING RIGHTEOUSNESS, -

ὅτι πρὸς τὸν πατέρα ὑπάγω καὶ οὐκέτι θεωρεῖτέ
BECAUSE TO THE FATHER I GO AND NO LONGER DO YOU° SEE

με· **16.11** περὶ δὲ κρίσεως, ὅτι ὁ ἄρχων τοῦ
ME; CONCERNING - JUDGMENT, BECAUSE THE RULER -

κόσμου τούτου κέκριται.
OF THIS~WORLD HAS BEEN JUDGED.

16.12 Ἔτι πολλὰ ἔχω ὑμῖν λέγειν, ἀλλ' οὐ δύνασθε
YET MANY THINGS I HAVE TO TELL~YOU°, BUT YOU° ARE NOT ABLE

βαστάζειν ἄρτι· **16.13** ὅταν δὲ ἔλθῃ ἐκεῖνος, τὸ
TO BEAR [THEM] NOW;   BUT~WHEN HAS COME THAT ONE, THE

πνεῦμα τῆς ἀληθείας, ὁδηγήσει ὑμᾶς ἐν τῇ
SPIRIT   -   OF TRUTH,   HE WILL GUIDE YOU°   IN -

ἀληθείᾳ πάσῃ· οὐ γὰρ λαλήσει ἀφ᾽ ἑαυτοῦ, ἀλλ᾽
EVERY~TRUTH;   FOR~NOT WILL HE SPEAK FROM HIMSELF,   BUT

ὅσα ἀκούσει λαλήσει καὶ τὰ ἐρχόμενα
WHAT THINGS HE WILL HEAR HE WILL SPEAK AND THE THINGS COMING

ἀναγγελεῖ ὑμῖν. **16.14** ἐκεῖνος ἐμὲ δοξάσει, ὅτι ἐκ
HE WILL ANNOUNCE TO YOU°.   THAT ONE WILL GLORIFY~ME, BECAUSE OF

τοῦ ἐμοῦ λήμψεται καὶ ἀναγγελεῖ ὑμῖν. **16.15** πάντα
-   MINE HE WILL RECEIVE AND WILL ANNOUNCE [IT] TO YOU°.   ALL THINGS

ὅσα ἔχει ὁ πατὴρ ἐμά ἐστιν· διὰ τοῦτο εἶπον ὅτι
WHICH ³HAS ¹THE ²FATHER ARE~MINE; THEREFORE I SAID THAT

ἐκ τοῦ ἐμοῦ λαμβάνει καὶ ἀναγγελεῖ ὑμῖν.
OF - MINE HE RECEIVES AND WILL ANNOUNCE [IT] TO YOU°.

16.16 Μικρὸν καὶ οὐκέτι θεωρεῖτέ με, καὶ πάλιν
A LITTLE [TIME] AND NO LONGER YOU° SEE ME, AND AGAIN

μικρὸν καὶ ὄψεσθέ με. **16.17** εἶπαν οὖν ἐκ
A LITTLE [TIME] AND YOU° WILL SEE ME.   SAID THEREFORE [SOME] OF

τῶν μαθητῶν αὐτοῦ πρὸς ἀλλήλους, Τί ἐστιν τοῦτο
THE DISCIPLES OF HIM TO ONE ANOTHER, WHAT IS THIS

ὃ λέγει ἡμῖν, Μικρὸν καὶ οὐ θεωρεῖτέ με, καὶ
WHICH HE SAYS TO US, A LITTLE [TIME] AND YOU° DO NOT SEE ME, AND

πάλιν μικρὸν καὶ ὄψεσθέ με; καί, Ὅτι ὑπάγω
AGAIN A LITTLE [TIME] AND YOU° WILL SEE ME? AND, BECAUSE I GO

πρὸς τὸν πατέρα; **16.18** ἔλεγον οὖν, Τί ἐστιν
TO THE FATHER?   THEY WERE SAYING THEREFORE, WHAT IS

τοῦτο [ὃ λέγει] τὸ μικρόν; οὐκ οἴδαμεν τί λαλεῖ.
THIS WHICH HE SAYS, THE LITTLE [TIME]? WE DO NOT KNOW WHAT HE SAYS.

16.19 ἔγνω [ὁ] Ἰησοῦς ὅτι ἤθελον αὐτὸν ἐρωτᾶν,
KNEW - JESUS THAT THEY WERE WANTING TO ASK~HIM,

καὶ εἶπεν αὐτοῖς, Περὶ τούτου ζητεῖτε μετ᾽ ἀλλήλων
AND HE SAID TO THEM, ABOUT THIS YOU° INQUIRE WITH ONE ANOTHER

ὅτι εἶπον, Μικρὸν καὶ οὐ θεωρεῖτέ με, καὶ πάλιν
THAT I SAID, A LITTLE [TIME] AND YOU° DO NOT SEE ME, AND AGAIN

μικρὸν καὶ ὄψεσθέ με; **16.20** ἀμὴν ἀμὴν λέγω ὑμῖν
A LITTLE [TIME] AND YOU° WILL SEE ME?   TRULY, TRULY I SAY TO YOU°

ὅτι κλαύσετε καὶ θρηνήσετε ὑμεῖς, ὁ δὲ κόσμος
THAT ²WILL WEEP ³AND ⁴WILL MOURN ¹YOU°, BUT~THE WORLD

χαρήσεται· ὑμεῖς λυπηθήσεσθε, ἀλλ᾽ ἡ λύπη ὑμῶν εἰς
WILL REJOICE. YOU° WILL BE GRIEVED, BUT THE GRIEF OF YOU° INTO

χαρὰν γενήσεται. **16.21** ἡ γυνὴ ὅταν τίκτῃ
JOY WILL BECOME.   THE WOMAN WHEN SHE GIVES BIRTH

λύπην ἔχει, ὅτι ἦλθεν ἡ ὥρα αὐτῆς· ὅταν δὲ
HAS~GRIEF, BECAUSE HAS COME THE HOUR OF HER; BUT~WHEN

γεννήσῃ τὸ παιδίον, οὐκέτι μνημονεύει τῆς θλίψεως
SHE GIVES BIRTH TO THE CHILD, NO LONGER SHE REMEMBERS THE AFFLICTION

bear them now. [13]When the Spirit of truth comes, he will guide you into all the truth; for he will not speak on his own, but will speak whatever he hears, and he will declare to you the things that are to come. [14]He will glorify me, because he will take what is mine and declare it to you. [15]All that the Father has is mine. For this reason I said that he will take what is mine and declare it to you.

16 "A little while, and you will no longer see me, and again a little while, and you will see me." [17]Then some of his disciples said to one another, "What does he mean by saying to us, 'A little while, and you will no longer see me, and again a little while, and you will see me'; and 'Because I am going to the Father'?" [18]They said, "What does he mean by this 'a little while'? We do not know what he is talking about." [19]Jesus knew that they wanted to ask him, so he said to them, "Are you discussing among yourselves what I meant when I said, 'A little while, and you will no longer see me, and again a little while, and you will see me'? [20]Very truly, I tell you, you will weep and mourn, but the world will rejoice; you will have pain, but your pain will turn into joy. [21]When a woman is in labor, she has pain, because her hour has come. But when her child is born, she no longer remembers the anguish

because of the joy of having brought a human being into the world. ²²So you have pain now; but I will see you again, and your hearts will rejoice, and no one will take your joy from you. ²³On that day you will ask nothing of me.ʷ Very truly, I tell you, if you ask anything of the Father in my name, he will give it to you.ˣ ²⁴Until now you have not asked for anything in my name. Ask and you will receive, so that your joy may be complete.

25 "I have said these things to you in figures of speech. The hour is coming when I will no longer speak to you in figures, but will tell you plainly of the Father. ²⁶On that day you will ask in my name. I do not say to you that I will ask the Father on your behalf; ²⁷for the Father himself loves you, because you have loved me and have believed that I came from God.ʸ ²⁸I came from the Father and have come into the world; again, I am leaving the world and am going to the Father."

29 His disciples said, "Yes, now you are speaking plainly, not in any figure of speech! ³⁰Now we know that you know all things, and do not need to have anyone question you; by this we

ʷ Or *will ask me no question*
ˣ Other ancient authorities read *Father, he will give it to you in my name*
ʸ Other ancient authorities read *the Father*

διὰ   τὴν   χαρὰν ὅτι ἐγεννήθη ἄνθρωπος εἰς τὸν
BECAUSE OF THE   JOY   THAT WAS BORN   A MAN(HUMAN) INTO THE

κόσμον. **16.22** καὶ ὑμεῖς οὖν   νῦν   μὲν λύπην ἔχετε·
WORLD.   AND   YOU°   THEREFORE NOW   -   HAVE~GRIEF;

πάλιν δὲ ὄψομαι ὑμᾶς, καὶ χαρήσεται ὑμῶν ἡ καρδία,
BUT~AGAIN I WILL SEE YOU°,   AND   WILL REJOICE YOUR° - HEART,

καὶ τὴν χαρὰν ὑμῶν οὐδεὶς αἴρει ἀφ' ὑμῶν. **16.23** καὶ
AND THE JOY   OF YOU° NO ONE   TAKES FROM YOU°.   AND

ἐν ἐκείνῃ τῇ ἡμέρᾳ ἐμὲ οὐκ ἐρωτήσετε οὐδέν. ἀμὴν
ON THAT   -   DAY   YOU° WILL NOT ASK~ME   ANYTHING. TRULY,

ἀμὴν λέγω ὑμῖν, ἄν τι αἰτήσητε τὸν πατέρα ⌐ἐν τῷ
TRULY I SAY TO YOU°, WHATEVER YOU° ASK THE FATHER   IN THE

ὀνόματί μου δώσει ὑμῖν.⌐ **16.24** ἕως ἄρτι
NAME   OF ME HE WILL GIVE [IT] TO YOU°.   UNTIL NOW

οὐκ ἠτήσατε οὐδὲν ἐν τῷ ὀνόματί μου· αἰτεῖτε καὶ
YOU° DID NOT ASK ANYTHING IN THE NAME   OF ME; ASK   AND

λήμψεσθε, ἵνα ἡ χαρὰ ὑμῶν ᾖ πεπληρωμένη.
YOU° WILL RECEIVE, THAT THE JOY OF YOU° MAY BE FULFILLED.

16.25 Ταῦτα ἐν παροιμίαις λελάληκα ὑμῖν· ἔρχεται
THESE THINGS IN SIMILITUDES I HAVE SPOKEN TO YOU°; COMES

ὥρα ὅτε οὐκέτι ἐν παροιμίαις λαλήσω ὑμῖν, ἀλλὰ
AN HOUR WHEN NO LONGER IN SIMILITUDES I WILL SPEAK TO YOU°, BUT

παρρησίᾳ περὶ   τοῦ πατρὸς ἀπαγγελῶ ὑμῖν.
PLAINLY   CONCERNING THE FATHER   I WILL ANNOUNCE TO YOU°.

16.26 ἐν ἐκείνῃ τῇ ἡμέρᾳ ἐν τῷ ὀνόματί μου
       ON THAT   -   DAY,   IN THE NAME   OF ME

αἰτήσεσθε, καὶ οὐ λέγω ὑμῖν ὅτι ἐγὼ ἐρωτήσω τὸν
YOU° WILL ASK, AND I DO NOT SAY TO YOU° THAT I   WILL ASK   THE

πατέρα περὶ   ὑμῶν· **16.27** αὐτὸς γὰρ ὁ πατὴρ
FATHER CONCERNING YOU°.   ⁴HIMSELF ¹FOR ²THE ³FATHER

φιλεῖ ὑμᾶς, ὅτι   ὑμεῖς ἐμὲ πεφιλήκατε καὶ
IS FOND OF OF YOU°, BECAUSE YOU° HAVE BEEN FOND OF~ME   AND

πεπιστεύκατε ὅτι ἐγὼ παρὰ [τοῦ] θεοῦ ἐξῆλθον.
HAVE BELIEVED   THAT I   FROM   -   GOD   CAME FORTH.

16.28 ἐξῆλθον παρὰ τοῦ πατρὸς καὶ ἐλήλυθα εἰς τὸν
       I CAME   FROM   THE FATHER   AND I HAVE COME INTO THE

κόσμον· πάλιν ἀφίημι τὸν κόσμον καὶ πορεύομαι
WORLD;   AGAIN I LEAVE   THE WORLD   AND GO

πρὸς τὸν πατέρα. **16.29** Λέγουσιν οἱ μαθηταὶ αὐτοῦ,
TO   THE FATHER.   SAY   THE DISCIPLES OF HIM,

Ἴδε νῦν ἐν παρρησίᾳ λαλεῖς καὶ παροιμίαν οὐδεμίαν
SEE, NOW IN PLAINNESS YOU SPEAK AND SIMILITUDES NO LONGER

λέγεις. **16.30** νῦν οἴδαμεν ὅτι οἶδας πάντα καὶ οὐ
DO YOU SPEAK.   NOW   WE KNOW   THAT YOU KNOW ALL THINGS AND NO

χρείαν ἔχεις ἵνα τίς σε ἐρωτᾷ· ἐν τούτῳ πιστεύομεν
NEED   YOU HAVE THAT ANYONE QUESTION~YOU; BY THIS WE BELIEVE

16:23 text: KJV RSV NIV NEB TEV NRSV. var. δωσει υμιν εν τω ονοματι μου (he will give [it] to you in my name): ASV NASB NEBmg TEVmg NJB NRSVmg.

ὅτι ἀπὸ θεοῦ ἐξῆλθες.   **16.31** ἀπεκρίθη αὐτοῖς
THAT FROM GOD YOU CAME FORTH.   ANSWERED   THEM

'Ιησοῦς, 'Άρτι πιστεύετε;   **16.32** ἰδοὺ ἔρχεται ὥρα καὶ
JESUS,   NOW DO YOU° BELIEVE?   LOOK, IS COMING AN HOUR AND

ἐλήλυθεν ἵνα σκορπισθῆτε ἕκαστος εἰς τὰ ἴδια κἀμὲ
HAS COME THAT YOU° ARE SCATTERED EACH ONE TO HIS OWN AND ME

μόνον ἀφῆτε· καὶ οὐκ εἰμὶ μόνος, ὅτι ὁ πατὴρ μετ'
YOU° LEAVE~ALONE; AND I AM NOT ALONE, BECAUSE THE FATHER WITH

ἐμοῦ ἐστιν. **16.33** ταῦτα λελάληκα ὑμῖν ἵνα ἐν
ME IS.   THESE THINGS I HAVE SPOKEN TO YOU° THAT IN

ἐμοὶ εἰρήνην ἔχητε· ἐν τῷ κόσμῳ θλῖψιν ἔχετε· ἀλλὰ
ME YOU° MAY HAVE~PEACE; IN THE WORLD YOU° HAVE~AFFLICTION, BUT

θαρσεῖτε, ἐγὼ νενίκηκα τὸν κόσμον.
BE CHEERFUL, I HAVE CONQUERED THE WORLD.

believe that you came from God." [31]Jesus answered them, "Do you now believe? [32]The hour is coming, indeed it has come, when you will be scattered, each one to his home, and you will leave me alone. Yet I am not alone because the Father is with me. [33]I have said this to you, so that in me you may have peace. In the world you face persecution. But take courage; I have conquered the world!"

CHAPTER 17

17.1 Ταῦτα ἐλάλησεν 'Ιησοῦς καὶ ἐπάρας τοὺς
THESE THINGS SAID JESUS, AND HAVING LIFTED UP THE

ὀφθαλμοὺς αὐτοῦ εἰς τὸν οὐρανὸν εἶπεν, Πάτερ,
EYES OF HIM TO - HEAVEN SAID, FATHER,

ἐλήλυθεν ἡ ὥρα· δόξασόν σου τὸν υἱόν, ἵνα ὁ υἱὸς
HAS COME THE HOUR; GLORIFY YOUR - SON, THAT THE SON

δοξάσῃ σέ, **17.2** καθὼς ἔδωκας αὐτῷ ἐξουσίαν πάσης
MAY GLORIFY YOU; AS YOU GAVE HIM AUTHORITY OF(OVER) ALL

σαρκός, ἵνα πᾶν ὃ δέδωκας αὐτῷ δώσῃ αὐτοῖς
FLESH, THAT [TO] ALL WHICH YOU HAVE GIVEN HIM HE MAY GIVE TO THEM

ζωὴν αἰώνιον. **17.3** αὕτη δέ ἐστιν ἡ αἰώνιος ζωὴ ἵνα
ETERNAL~LIFE. AND~THIS IS - ETERNAL LIFE, THAT

γινώσκωσιν σὲ τὸν μόνον ἀληθινὸν θεὸν καὶ ὃν
THEY MAY KNOW YOU THE ONLY TRUE GOD AND HE WHOM

ἀπέστειλας 'Ιησοῦν Χριστόν. **17.4** ἐγώ σε ἐδόξασα ἐπὶ
YOU SENT, JESUS CHRIST. I GLORIFIED~YOU ON

τῆς γῆς τὸ ἔργον τελειώσας ὃ δέδωκάς μοι ἵνα
THE EARTH, THE WORK HAVING FINISHED WHICH YOU HAVE GIVEN ME THAT

ποιήσω· **17.5** καὶ νῦν δόξασόν με σύ, πάτερ, παρὰ
I SHOULD DO. AND NOW ²GLORIFY ³ME ¹YOU, FATHER, ALONG WITH

σεαυτῷ τῇ δόξῃ ᾗ εἶχον πρὸ τοῦ τὸν κόσμον
YOURSELF WITH THE GLORY WHICH ¹I WAS HAVING ⁴BEFORE - ⁵THE ⁶WORLD

εἶναι παρὰ σοί.
⁷WAS ²WITH ³YOU.

17.6 'Εφανέρωσά σου τὸ ὄνομα τοῖς ἀνθρώποις οὓς
I MANIFESTED YOUR - NAME TO THE MEN WHOM

ἔδωκάς μοι ἐκ τοῦ κόσμου. σοὶ ἦσαν κἀμοὶ
YOU GAVE TO ME OUT OF THE WORLD. THEY WERE~YOURS AND TO ME

αὐτοὺς ἔδωκας καὶ τὸν λόγον σου τετήρηκαν. **17.7** νῦν
YOU GAVE~THEM AND THE WORD OF YOU THEY HAVE KEPT. NOW

After Jesus had spoken these words, he looked up to heaven and said, "Father, the hour has come; glorify your Son so that the Son may glorify you, [2]since you have given him authority over all people,[z] to give eternal life to all whom you have given him. [3]And this is eternal life, that they may know you, the only true God, and Jesus Christ whom you have sent. [4]I glorified you on earth by finishing the work that you gave me to do. [5]So now, Father, glorify me in your own presence with the glory that I had in your presence before the world existed.

6 "I have made your name known to those whom you gave me from the world. They were yours, and you gave them to me, and they have kept your word. [7]Now

[z] Gk *flesh*

they know that everything you have given me is from you; ⁸for the words that you gave to me I have given to them, and they have received them and know in truth that I came from you; and they have believed that you sent me. ⁹I am asking on their behalf; I am not asking on behalf of the world, but on behalf of those whom you gave me, because they are yours. ¹⁰All mine are yours, and yours are mine; and I have been glorified in them. ¹¹And now I am no longer in the world, but they are in the world, and I am coming to you. Holy Father, protect them in your name that*ᵃ* you have given me, so that they may be one, as we are one. ¹²While I was with them, I protected them in your name that*ᵃ* you have given me. I guarded them, and not one of them was lost except the one destined to be lost,*ᵇ* so that the scripture might be fulfilled. ¹³But now I am coming to you, and I speak these things in the world so that they may have my joy made complete in themselves.*ᶜ* ¹⁴I have given them your word, and the world has hated them because they do not belong to the world, just as I do not belong to the world. ¹⁵I am not asking you to take them out of the world,

ᵃ Other ancient authorities read *protect in your name those whom*
ᵇ Gk *except the son of destruction*
ᶜ Or *among themselves*

ἔγνωκαν ὅτι πάντα ὅσα δέδωκάς μοι παρὰ
THEY HAVE KNOWN THAT ALL THINGS WHATSOEVER YOU HAVE GIVEN TO ME FROM

σοῦ εἰσιν· **17.8** ὅτι τὰ ῥήματα ἃ ἔδωκάς μοι
YOU ARE; BECAUSE THE WORDS WHICH YOU GAVE ME

δέδωκα αὐτοῖς, καὶ αὐτοὶ ἔλαβον καὶ ἔγνωσαν
I HAVE GIVEN TO THEM, AND THEY RECEIVED AND KNEW

ἀληθῶς ὅτι παρὰ σοῦ ἐξῆλθον, καὶ ἐπίστευσαν ὅτι σύ
TRULY THAT FROM YOU I CAME FORTH, AND THEY BELIEVED THAT YOU

με ἀπέστειλας. **17.9** ἐγὼ περὶ αὐτῶν ἐρωτῶ, οὐ
SENT~ME. I CONCERNING THEM ASK; NOT

περὶ τοῦ κόσμου ἐρωτῶ ἀλλὰ περὶ ὧν
CONCERNING THE WORLD I ASK BUT CONCERNING THE ONES

δέδωκάς μοι, ὅτι σοί εἰσιν, **17.10** καὶ τὰ ἐμὰ
YOU HAVE GIVEN ME, BECAUSE THEY ARE~YOURS, AND ²THINGS ³OF MINE

πάντα σά ἐστιν καὶ τὰ σὰ ἐμά, καὶ
¹ALL ARE~YOURS AND THE THINGS OF YOURS MINE, AND

δεδόξασμαι ἐν αὐτοῖς. **17.11** καὶ οὐκέτι εἰμὶ ἐν τῷ
I HAVE BEEN GLORIFIED IN THEM. AND NO LONGER I AM IN THE

κόσμῳ, καὶ αὐτοὶ ἐν τῷ κόσμῳ εἰσίν, κἀγὼ πρὸς σὲ
WORLD, AND THEY IN THE WORLD ARE, AND I TO YOU

ἔρχομαι. Πάτερ ἅγιε, ⌐τήρησον αὐτοὺς ἐν τῷ ὀνόματί
AM COMING. HOLY~FATHER, KEEP THEM IN THE NAME

σου ᾧ δέδωκάς μοι,⌐ ἵνα ὦσιν ἓν καθὼς ἡμεῖς.
OF YOU WHICH YOU HAVE GIVEN ME, THAT THEY MAY BE ONE AS WE [ARE].

17.12 ὅτε ἤμην μετ' αὐτῶν ⌐ἐγὼ ἐτήρουν αὐτοὺς ἐν τῷ
WHEN I WAS WITH THEM I WAS KEEPING THEM IN THE

ὀνόματί σου ᾧ δέδωκάς μοι,⌐ καὶ ἐφύλαξα, καὶ
NAME OF YOU WHICH YOU HAVE GIVEN ME, AND I KEPT WATCH, AND

οὐδεὶς ἐξ αὐτῶν ἀπώλετο εἰ μὴ ὁ υἱὸς τῆς ἀπωλείας,
NONE OF THEM PERISHED EXCEPT THE SON - OF PERDITION,

ἵνα ἡ γραφὴ πληρωθῇ. **17.13** νῦν δὲ πρὸς σὲ
THAT THE SCRIPTURE MIGHT BE FULFILLED. AND~NOW TO YOU

ἔρχομαι καὶ ταῦτα λαλῶ ἐν τῷ κόσμῳ ἵνα ἔχωσιν
I AM COMING AND THESE THINGS I SPEAK IN THE WORLD THAT THEY MAY HAVE

τὴν χαρὰν τὴν ἐμὴν πεπληρωμένην ἐν ἑαυτοῖς.
THE JOY - OF ME HAVING BEEN FULFILLED IN THEMSELVES.

17.14 ἐγὼ δέδωκα αὐτοῖς τὸν λόγον σου καὶ ὁ
I HAVE GIVEN TO THEM THE WORD OF YOU AND THE

κόσμος ἐμίσησεν αὐτούς, ὅτι οὐκ εἰσὶν ἐκ τοῦ
WORLD HATED THEM, BECAUSE THEY ARE NOT OF THE

κόσμου καθὼς ἐγὼ οὐκ εἰμὶ ἐκ τοῦ κόσμου.
WORLD JUST AS I AM NOT OF THE WORLD.

17.15 οὐκ ἐρωτῶ ἵνα ἄρῃς αὐτοὺς ἐκ τοῦ κόσμου,
I DO NOT ASK THAT YOU TAKE THEM OUT OF THE WORLD,

17:11 text: ASV RSV NASB NEBmg TEV NJBmg NRSV. var. τηρησον αυτους εν τω ονοματι σου ους δεδωκας μοι (keep in your name those whom you have given me): KJV NEB TEVmg NJB NRSVmg.
17:12 text: ASV RSV NASB NIV NEBmg TEV NRSV. var. εγω ετηρουν αυτους εν τω ονοματι σου ους δεδωκας μοι (I was keeping in your name those whom you have given me): KJV NEB TEVmg NJB NRSVmg. var. εγω ετηρουν αυτους εν τω ονοματι σου (I was keeping them in your name): none.

ἀλλ' ἵνα τηρήσῃς αὐτοὺς ἐκ τοῦ πονηροῦ. **17.16** ἐκ
BUT   THAT YOU KEEP   THEM   FROM THE EVIL [ONE].   OF

τοῦ κόσμου οὐκ εἰσὶν καθὼς ἐγὼ οὐκ εἰμὶ ἐκ τοῦ
THE WORLD   THEY ARE NOT JUST AS I   AM NOT OF THE

κόσμου. **17.17** ἁγίασον αὐτοὺς ἐν τῇ ἀληθείᾳ·
WORLD.   SANCTIFY   THEM   IN THE TRUTH;

ὁ λόγος ὁ σὸς ἀλήθειά ἐστιν. **17.18** καθὼς
THE WORD - OF YOU IS~TRUTH.   AS

ἐμὲ ἀπέστειλας εἰς τὸν κόσμον, κἀγὼ ἀπέστειλα
YOU SENT~ME   INTO THE WORLD, [SO] ALSO I SENT

αὐτοὺς εἰς τὸν κόσμον· **17.19** καὶ ὑπὲρ αὐτῶν ἐγὼ
THEM   INTO THE WORLD;   AND FOR   THEM   I

ἁγιάζω ἐμαυτόν, ἵνα ὦσιν καὶ αὐτοὶ ἡγιασμένοι
SANCTIFY MYSELF,   THAT ³MAY HAVE BEEN ²ALSO ¹THEY SANCTIFIED

ἐν ἀληθείᾳ.
IN TRUTH.

17.20 Οὐ περὶ τούτων δὲ ἐρωτῶ μόνον, ἀλλὰ
        NOT CONCERNING THESE HOWEVER DO I ASK ONLY,   BUT

καὶ περὶ τῶν πιστευόντων διὰ τοῦ λόγου αὐτῶν
ALSO CONCERNING THE ONES BELIEVING ³BECAUSE ⁴THE ⁵WORD ⁶OF THEM

εἰς ἐμέ, **17.21** ἵνα πάντες ἐν ὦσιν, καθὼς σύ, πάτερ, ἐν
¹IN ²ME,   THAT ALL   MAY BE~ONE, AS YOU, FATHER, IN

ἐμοὶ κἀγὼ ἐν σοί, ἵνα καὶ αὐτοὶ ἐν ἡμῖν ὦσιν, ἵνα
ME [ARE] AND I IN YOU, THAT ALSO THEY IN US MAY BE, THAT

ὁ κόσμος πιστεύῃ ὅτι σύ με ἀπέστειλας. **17.22** κἀγὼ
THE WORLD MAY BELIEVE THAT YOU SENT~ME.   AND I

τὴν δόξαν ἣν δέδωκάς μοι δέδωκα αὐτοῖς, ἵνα
THE GLORY WHICH YOU HAVE GIVEN ME I HAVE GIVEN THEM, THAT

ὦσιν ἓν καθὼς ἡμεῖς ἕν· **17.23** ἐγὼ ἐν αὐτοῖς καὶ
THEY MAY BE ONE JUST AS WE [ARE] ONE.   I   IN THEM AND

σὺ ἐν ἐμοί, ἵνα ὦσιν τετελειωμένοι εἰς ἕν, ἵνα
YOU IN ME,   THAT THEY MAY BE PERFECTED INTO ONE, THAT

γινώσκῃ ὁ κόσμος ὅτι σύ με ἀπέστειλας καὶ
MAY KNOW THE WORLD THAT YOU SENT~ME   AND

ἠγάπησας αὐτοὺς καθὼς ἐμὲ ἠγάπησας. **17.24** Πάτερ,
LOVED   THEM   JUST AS YOU LOVED~ME.   FATHER,

ὃ δέδωκάς μοι, θέλω ἵνα ὅπου εἰμὶ ἐγὼ
[AS TO] THAT WHICH YOU HAVE GIVEN ME, I DESIRE THAT WHERE I~AM

κἀκεῖνοι ὦσιν μετ' ἐμοῦ, ἵνα θεωρῶσιν τὴν δόξαν τὴν
THOSE ALSO MAY BE WITH ME,   THAT THEY MAY SEE THE GLORY   -

ἐμήν, ἣν δέδωκάς μοι ὅτι ἠγάπησάς με πρὸ
OF ME WHICH YOU HAVE GIVEN ME BECAUSE YOU LOVED   ME BEFORE

καταβολῆς κόσμου. **17.25** πάτερ δίκαιε, καὶ ὁ
[THE] FOUNDATION OF [THE] WORLD.   RIGHTEOUS~FATHER, INDEED THE

κόσμος σε οὐκ ἔγνω, ἐγὼ δέ σε ἔγνων, καὶ οὗτοι
WORLD   DID NOT KNOW~YOU, BUT~I KNEW~YOU, AND THESE ONES

ἔγνωσαν ὅτι σύ με ἀπέστειλας· **17.26** καὶ ἐγνώρισα
KNEW   THAT YOU SENT~ME;   AND I MADE KNOWN

but I ask you to protect them from the evil one.[d] 16They do not belong to the world, just as I do not belong to the world. 17Sanctify them in the truth; your word is truth. 18As you have sent me into the world, so I have sent them into the world. 19And for their sakes I sanctify myself, so that they also may be sanctified in truth.

20 "I ask not only on behalf of these, but also on behalf of those who will believe in me through their word, 21that they may all be one. As you, Father, are in me and I am in you, may they also be in us,[e] so that the world may believe that you have sent me. 22The glory that you have given me I have given them, so that they may be one, as we are one, 23I in them and you in me, that they may become completely one, so that the world may know that you have sent me and have loved them even as you have loved me. 24Father, I desire that those also, whom you have given me, may be with me where I am, to see my glory, which you have given me because you loved me before the foundation of the world.

25 "Righteous Father, the world does not know you, but I know you; and these know that you have sent me. 26I made your name known

d Or *from evil*
e Other ancient authorities read *be one in us*

to them, and I will make it known, so that the love with which you have loved me may be in them, and I in them."

αὐτοῖς τὸ ὄνομά σου καὶ γνωρίσω, ἵνα ἦ
TO THEM   THE   NAME   OF YOU   AND   WILL MAKE [IT] KNOWN,   THAT   THE

ἀγάπη ἦν ἠγάπησάς με ἐν αὐτοῖς ἦ κἀγὼ ἐν
LOVE   [WITH] WHICH   YOU LOVED   ME   IN   THEM   MAY BE   AND I   IN

αὐτοῖς.
THEM.

CHAPTER 18

After Jesus had spoken these words, he went out with his disciples across the Kidron valley to a place where there was a garden, which he and his disciples entered. [2]Now Judas, who betrayed him, also knew the place, because Jesus often met there with his disciples. [3]So Judas brought a detachment of soldiers together with police from the chief priests and the Pharisees, and they came there with lanterns and torches and weapons. [4]Then Jesus, knowing all that was to happen to him, came forward and asked them, "Whom are you looking for?" [5]They answered, "Jesus of Nazareth."[f] Jesus replied, "I am he."[g] Judas, who betrayed him, was standing with them. [6]When Jesus[h] said to them, "I am he,"[g] they stepped back and fell to the ground. [7]Again he asked them, "Whom are you looking for?" And they said, "Jesus of Nazareth."[f] [8]Jesus answered, "I told you that I am he.[g] So if you are looking for me, let these men go." [9]This was to fulfill

[f] Gk the Nazorean
[g] Gk I am
[h] Gk he

18.1 Ταῦτα εἰπὼν Ἰησοῦς ἐξῆλθεν σὺν τοῖς
THESE THINGS   HAVING SAID   JESUS   WENT OUT   WITH   THE

μαθηταῖς αὐτοῦ πέραν τοῦ χειμάρρου τοῦ Κεδρὼν ὅπου
DISCIPLES   OF HIM   ACROSS   THE   [2]RAVINE,   -   [1]KIDRON,   WHERE

ἦν κῆπος, εἰς ὃν εἰσῆλθεν αὐτὸς καὶ οἱ μαθηταὶ
THERE WAS   A GARDEN,   INTO   WHICH   HE~ENTERED   AND   THE   DISCIPLES

αὐτοῦ. **18.2** ᾔδει δὲ καὶ Ἰούδας ὁ παραδιδοὺς αὐτὸν
OF HIM.   NOW~KNEW   ALSO   JUDAS,   THE ONE   BETRAYING   HIM

τὸν τόπον, ὅτι πολλάκις συνήχθη Ἰησοῦς ἐκεῖ μετὰ
THE   PLACE,   BECAUSE   OFTEN   JESUS~GATHERED   THERE   WITH

τῶν μαθητῶν αὐτοῦ. **18.3** ὁ οὖν Ἰούδας λαβὼν τὴν
THE   DISCIPLES   OF HIM.   -   THEN   JUDAS,   HAVING TAKEN   THE

σπεῖραν καὶ ἐκ τῶν ἀρχιερέων καὶ ἐκ τῶν
BAND OF SOLDIERS   AND   [2]OF   [3]THE   [4]CHIEF PRIESTS   [5]AND   [6]OF   [7]THE

Φαρισαίων ὑπηρέτας ἔρχεται ἐκεῖ μετὰ φανῶν καὶ
[8]PHARISEES   [1]SERVANTS,   COMES   THERE   WITH   LANTERNS   AND

λαμπάδων καὶ ὅπλων. **18.4** Ἰησοῦς οὖν εἰδὼς
LAMPS   AND   WEAPONS.   JESUS   THEREFORE   HAVING KNOWN

πάντα τὰ ἐρχόμενα ἐπ' αὐτὸν ἐξῆλθεν καὶ λέγει
EVERYTHING   COMING   UPON   HIM,   WENT OUT   AND   SAYS

αὐτοῖς, Τίνα ζητεῖτε; **18.5** ἀπεκρίθησαν αὐτῷ,
TO THEM,   WHOM   DO YOU° SEEK?   THEY ANSWERED   HIM,

Ἰησοῦν τὸν Ναζωραῖον. λέγει αὐτοῖς, Ἐγώ εἰμι.
JESUS   THE   NAZARENE.   HE SAYS   TO THEM,   I   AM [HE].

εἰστήκει δὲ καὶ Ἰούδας ὁ παραδιδοὺς αὐτὸν μετ'
NOW~HAD STOOD   ALSO   JUDAS,   THE ONE   BETRAYING   HIM,   WITH

αὐτῶν. **18.6** ὡς οὖν εἶπεν αὐτοῖς, Ἐγώ εἰμι,
THEM.   WHEN   THEREFORE   HE TOLD   THEM,   I   AM [HE],

ἀπῆλθον εἰς τὰ ὀπίσω καὶ ἔπεσαν χαμαί.
THEY WITHDREW   BACKWARD   AND   FELL   TO [THE] GROUND.

18.7 πάλιν οὖν ἐπηρώτησεν αὐτούς, Τίνα ζητεῖτε;
AGAIN   THEREFORE   HE QUESTIONED   THEM,   WHOM   DO YOU° SEEK?

οἱ δὲ εἶπαν, Ἰησοῦν τὸν Ναζωραῖον. **18.8** ἀπεκρίθη
AND~THEY SAID,   JESUS   THE   NAZARENE.   ANSWERED

Ἰησοῦς, Εἶπον ὑμῖν ὅτι ἐγώ εἰμι· εἰ οὖν
JESUS,   I TOLD   YOU°   THAT I   AM [HE];   IF   THEREFORE

ἐμὲ ζητεῖτε, ἄφετε τούτους ὑπάγειν· **18.9** ἵνα πληρωθῇ
YOU° SEEK~ME,   LET   THESE MEN   GO AWAY;   THAT   MAY BE FULFILLED

ὁ λόγος ὃν εἶπεν ὅτι Οὓς δέδωκάς μοι
THE WORD WHICH SAID, - [THOSE] WHOM YOU HAVE GIVEN ME

οὐκ ἀπώλεσα ἐξ αὐτῶν οὐδένα. **18.10** Σίμων οὖν Πέτρος
I DID NOT LOSE OF THEM ANYONE. THEN~SIMON PETER

ἔχων μάχαιραν εἵλκυσεν αὐτὴν καὶ ἔπαισεν τὸν τοῦ
HAVING A SWORD DREW IT AND STRUCK THE ²OF THE

ἀρχιερέως δοῦλον καὶ ἀπέκοψεν αὐτοῦ τὸ ὠτάριον τὸ
³HIGH PRIEST ¹SLAVE ⁴AND ⁵CUT OFF ⁶HIS - ⁸EAR -

δεξιόν· ἦν δὲ ὄνομα τῷ δούλῳ Μάλχος. **18.11** εἶπεν
⁷RIGHT; AND~WAS [THE] NAME TO THE SLAVE MALCHUS. SAID

οὖν ὁ Ἰησοῦς τῷ Πέτρῳ, Βάλε τὴν μάχαιραν εἰς
THEREFORE - JESUS - TO PETER, PUT THE SWORD INTO

τὴν θήκην· τὸ ποτήριον ὃ δέδωκέν μοι ὁ πατὴρ
THE SHEATH; THE CUP WHICH HAS GIVEN ME THE FATHER

οὐ μὴ πίω αὐτό;
SHOULD I NEVER DRINK IT?

18.12 Ἡ οὖν σπεῖρα καὶ ὁ χιλίαρχος καὶ
THEN~THE BAND OF SOLDIERS AND THE COMMANDER OF THE COHORT AND

οἱ ὑπηρέται τῶν Ἰουδαίων συνέλαβον τὸν Ἰησοῦν
THE SERVANTS OF THE JEWS TOOK - JESUS

καὶ ἔδησαν αὐτὸν **18.13** καὶ ἤγαγον πρὸς Ἄνναν
AND BOUND HIM AND LED [HIM] TO ANNAS

πρῶτον· ἦν γὰρ πενθερὸς τοῦ Καϊάφα, ὃς ἦν
FIRST; FOR~HE WAS [THE] FATHER-IN-LAW - OF CAIAPHAS, WHO WAS

ἀρχιερεὺς τοῦ ἐνιαυτοῦ ἐκείνου· **18.14** ἦν δὲ
HIGH PRIEST - THAT~YEAR. NOW~IT WAS

Καϊάφας ὁ συμβουλεύσας τοῖς Ἰουδαίοις ὅτι
CAIAPHAS, THE ONE HAVING GIVEN COUNSEL TO THE JEWS THAT

συμφέρει ἕνα ἄνθρωπον ἀποθανεῖν ὑπὲρ τοῦ λαοῦ.
IT IS BETTER [FOR] ONE MAN TO DIE FOR THE PEOPLE.

18.15 Ἠκολούθει δὲ τῷ Ἰησοῦ Σίμων Πέτρος καὶ
⁷WERE FOLLOWING ¹NOW - ⁸JESUS ²SIMON ³PETER ⁴AND

ἄλλος μαθητής. ὁ δὲ μαθητὴς ἐκεῖνος ἦν γνωστὸς
⁵ANOTHER ⁶DISCIPLE. - AND THAT~DISCIPLE WAS KNOWN

τῷ ἀρχιερεῖ καὶ συνεισῆλθεν τῷ Ἰησοῦ εἰς τὴν
TO THE HIGH PRIEST AND HE ENTERED WITH - JESUS INTO THE

αὐλὴν τοῦ ἀρχιερέως, **18.16** ὁ δὲ Πέτρος εἱστήκει πρὸς
COURT OF THE HIGH PRIEST, - BUT PETER HAD STOOD AT

τῇ θύρᾳ ἔξω. ἐξῆλθεν οὖν ὁ μαθητὴς ὁ ἄλλος
THE DOOR OUTSIDE. WENT OUT THEREFORE THE ²DISCIPLE - ¹OTHER,

ὁ γνωστὸς τοῦ ἀρχιερέως καὶ εἶπεν τῇ θυρωρῷ
THE ONE KNOWN TO THE HIGH PRIEST, AND SPOKE TO THE DOORKEEPER

καὶ εἰσήγαγεν τὸν Πέτρον. **18.17** λέγει οὖν τῷ
AND BROUGHT IN - PETER. SAYS THEREFORE -

Πέτρῳ ἡ παιδίσκη ἡ θυρωρός, Μὴ καὶ σὺ ἐκ
TO PETER THE MAID, THE DOORKEEPER, [SURELY] NOT ALSO YOU OF

τῶν μαθητῶν εἶ τοῦ ἀνθρώπου τούτου; λέγει ἐκεῖνος,
THE DISCIPLES ARE - OF THIS~MAN? SAYS THAT ONE,

the word that he had spoken, "I did not lose a single one of those whom you gave me." ¹⁰Then Simon Peter, who had a sword, drew it, struck the high priest's slave, and cut off his right ear. The slave's name was Malchus. ¹¹Jesus said to Peter, "Put your sword back into its sheath. Am I not to drink the cup that the Father has given me?"

12 So the soldiers, their officer, and the Jewish police arrested Jesus and bound him. ¹³First they took him to Annas, who was the father-in-law of Caiaphas, the high priest that year. ¹⁴Caiaphas was the one who had advised the Jews that it was better to have one person die for the people.

15 Simon Peter and another disciple followed Jesus. Since that disciple was known to the high priest, he went with Jesus into the courtyard of the high priest, ¹⁶but Peter was standing outside at the gate. So the other disciple, who was known to the high priest, went out, spoke to the woman who guarded the gate, and brought Peter in. ¹⁷The woman said to Peter, "You are not also one of this man's disciples, are you?"

He said, "I am not." [18]Now the slaves and the police had made a charcoal fire because it was cold, and they were standing around it and warming themselves. Peter also was standing with them and warming himself.

19 Then the high priest questioned Jesus about his disciples and about his teaching. [20]Jesus answered, "I have spoken openly to the world; I have always taught in synagogues and in the temple, where all the Jews come together. I have said nothing in secret. [21]Why do you ask me? Ask those who heard what I said to them; they know what I said." [22]When he had said this, one of the police standing nearby struck Jesus on the face, saying, "Is that how you answer the high priest?" [23]Jesus answered, "If I have spoken wrongly, testify to the wrong. But if I have spoken rightly, why do you strike me?" [24]Then Annas sent him bound to Caiaphas the high priest.

25 Now Simon Peter was standing and warming himself. They asked him, "You are not also one of his disciples, are you?" He denied it and said, "I am not." [26]One of the slaves of the high priest, a relative of the man whose ear Peter had cut off, asked, "Did I not see you in the garden with him?"

Οὐκ εἰμί.   **18.18** εἰστήκεισαν δὲ οἱ δοῦλοι καὶ οἱ
I AM NOT.   AND~HAD STOOD   THE SLAVES   AND   THE

ὑπηρέται ἀνθρακιὰν πεποιηκότες, ὅτι ψῦχος ἦν, καὶ
SERVANTS—   A FIRE   HAVING BEEN MADE, FOR   IT WAS~COLD, AND

ἐθερμαίνοντο·   ἦν δὲ καὶ ὁ Πέτρος μετή αὐτῶν
THEY WERE WARMING THEMSELVES; AND~WAS ALSO - PETER   WITH   THEM

ἑστὼς καὶ θερμαινόμενος.
HAVING STOOD AND   WARMING HIMSELF.

18.19 Ὁ οὖν ἀρχιερεὺς ἠρώτησεν τὸν Ἰησοῦν περὶ τῶν
THEN~THE HIGH PRIEST QUESTIONED - JESUS ABOUT THE

μαθητῶν αὐτοῦ καὶ περὶ τῆς διδαχῆς αὐτοῦ.
DISCIPLES OF HIM AND ABOUT THE TEACHING OF HIM.

18.20 ἀπεκρίθη αὐτῷ Ἰησοῦς, Ἐγὼ παρρησίᾳ λελάληκα
ANSWERED   HIM   JESUS, I   IN PUBLIC [VIEW] HAVE SPOKEN

τῷ κόσμῳ, ἐγὼ πάντοτε ἐδίδαξα ἐν συναγωγῇ καὶ ἐν
TO THE WORLD; I ALWAYS   TAUGHT IN A SYNAGOGUE AND IN

τῷ ἱερῷ, ὅπου πάντες οἱ Ἰουδαῖοι συνέρχονται, καὶ
THE TEMPLE, WHERE ALL THE JEWS   COME TOGETHER, AND

ἐν κρυπτῷ ἐλάλησα οὐδέν.   **18.21** τί με ἐρωτᾷς;
IN SECRET I SPOKE NOTHING.   WHY DO YOU QUESTION~ME?

ἐρώτησον τοὺς ἀκηκοότας τί ἐλάλησα αὐτοῖς· ἴδε
QUESTION THE ONES HAVING HEARD WHAT I SPOKE TO THEM. LOOK,

οὗτοι οἴδασιν ἃ εἶπον ἐγώ.   **18.22** ταῦτα δὲ
THESE ONES KNOW   WHAT THINGS I~SAID.   BUT~THESE THINGS

αὐτοῦ εἰπόντος εἷς παρεστηκὼς τῶν ὑπηρετῶν ἔδωκεν
HE   HAVING SAID, ONE [3]HAVING STOOD NEARBY [1]OF THE [2]SERVANTS GAVE

ῥάπισμα τῷ Ἰησοῦ εἰπών, Οὕτως ἀποκρίνῃ τῷ
A BLOW - TO JESUS, HAVING SAID, THUS DO YOU ANSWER THE

ἀρχιερεῖ;   **18.23** ἀπεκρίθη αὐτῷ Ἰησοῦς, Εἰ
HIGH PRIEST?   ANSWERED   HIM   JESUS, IF

κακῶς ἐλάλησα, μαρτύρησον περὶ τοῦ κακοῦ· εἰ δὲ
I SPOKE~BADLY   TESTIFY   ABOUT THE BAD; BUT~IF

καλῶς, τί με δέρεις;   **18.24** ἀπέστειλεν οὖν αὐτὸν ὁ
GOOD, WHY DO YOU BEAT~ME?   [3]SENT   [1]THEN [4]HIM -

Ἄννας δεδεμένον πρὸς Καϊάφαν τὸν ἀρχιερέα.
[2]ANNAS, HAVING BEEN BOUND, TO   CAIAPHAS THE HIGH PRIEST.

18.25 Ἦν δὲ Σίμων Πέτρος ἑστὼς καὶ
NOW~WAS SIMON PETER HAVING STOOD AND

θερμαινόμενος. εἶπον οὖν αὐτῷ, Μὴ καὶ σὺ
WARMING HIMSELF. THEY SAID THEREFORE TO HIM, [SURELY] NOT ALSO YOU

ἐκ τῶν μαθητῶν αὐτοῦ εἶ; ἠρνήσατο ἐκεῖνος καὶ
OF THE DISCIPLES OF HIM ARE? ANSWERED THAT ONE AND

εἶπεν, Οὐκ εἰμί.   **18.26** λέγει εἷς ἐκ τῶν δούλων τοῦ
SAID, I AM NOT.   SAYS ONE OF THE SLAVES OF THE

ἀρχιερέως, συγγενὴς ὢν οὗ ἀπέκοψεν Πέτρος
HIGH PRIEST, BEING~A RELATIVE [OF HIM] OF WHOM PETER~CUT OFF

τὸ ὠτίον, Οὐκ ἐγώ σε εἶδον ἐν τῷ κήπῳ μετ' αὐτοῦ;
THE(HIS) EAR, DID I NOT SEE~YOU IN THE GARDEN WITH HIM?

18.27 πάλιν οὖν   ἠρνήσατο Πέτρος, καὶ εὐθέως
AGAIN THEREFORE DENIED   PETER,   AND   IMMEDIATELY

ἀλέκτωρ ἐφώνησεν.
A COCK   CROWED.

18.28 Ἄγουσιν οὖν   τὸν Ἰησοῦν ἀπὸ τοῦ Καϊάφα
THEY LED THEREFORE -   JESUS   FROM -   CAIAPHAS

εἰς τὸ πραιτώριον· ἦν δὲ πρωΐ· καὶ αὐτοὶ
TO THE PRAETORIUM;   AND~IT WAS EARLY;   AND THEY

οὐκ εἰσῆλθον εἰς τὸ πραιτώριον, ἵνα μὴ μιανθῶσιν
DID NOT ENTER   INTO THE PRAETORIUM,   LEST   THEY SHOULD BE DEFILED

ἀλλὰ φάγωσιν τὸ πάσχα. **18.29** ἐξῆλθεν οὖν   ὁ
BUT MIGHT EAT THE PASSOVER.   WENT FORTH THEREFORE -

Πιλᾶτος ἔξω πρὸς αὐτοὺς καὶ φησίν, Τίνα
PILATE   OUTSIDE TO   THEM   AND SAYS,   WHAT

κατηγορίαν φέρετε [κατὰ] τοῦ ἀνθρώπου τούτου;
ACCUSATION   DO YOU° BRING AGAINST -   THIS~MAN?

18.30 ἀπεκρίθησαν καὶ εἶπαν αὐτῷ, Εἰ μὴ ἦν οὗτος
THEY ANSWERED   AND SAID TO HIM,   UNLESS THIS MAN~WAS

κακὸν ποιῶν, οὐκ ἄν σοι παρεδώκαμεν αὐτόν.
DOING~EVIL,   WOULD NOT WE HAVE DELIVERED~TO YOU   HIM.

18.31 εἶπεν οὖν   αὐτοῖς ὁ Πιλᾶτος, Λάβετε αὐτὸν
SAID THEREFORE TO THEM - PILATE,   ²TAKE   ³HIM

ὑμεῖς καὶ κατὰ τὸν νόμον ὑμῶν κρίνατε αὐτόν.
¹YOU° AND ACCORDING TO THE LAW   OF YOU° JUDGE   HIM.

εἶπον αὐτῷ οἱ Ἰουδαῖοι, Ἡμῖν οὐκ ἔξεστιν
SAID TO HIM THE JEWS,   FOR US IT IS NOT LAWFUL

ἀποκτεῖναι οὐδένα· **18.32** ἵνα ὁ λόγος τοῦ Ἰησοῦ
TO KILL   ANYONE—   THAT THE WORD -   OF JESUS

πληρωθῇ ὃν εἶπεν σημαίνων ποίῳ θανάτῳ ἤμελλεν
MAY BE FULFILLED WHICH HE SAID SIGNIFYING BY WHAT DEATH HE WAS ABOUT

ἀποθνῄσκειν. **18.33** Εἰσῆλθεν οὖν πάλιν εἰς τὸ
TO DIE.   THEREFORE~ENTERED AGAIN INTO THE

πραιτώριον ὁ Πιλᾶτος καὶ ἐφώνησεν τὸν Ἰησοῦν καὶ
PRAETORIUM - PILATE   AND CALLED -   JESUS AND

εἶπεν αὐτῷ, Σὺ εἶ ὁ βασιλεὺς τῶν Ἰουδαίων;
SAID TO HIM, YOU ARE THE KING   OF THE THE JEWS?

18.34 ἀπεκρίθη Ἰησοῦς, Ἀπὸ σεαυτοῦ σὺ τοῦτο λέγεις
ANSWERED JESUS, FROM YOURSELF YOU SAY~THIS

ἢ ἄλλοι εἶπόν σοι περὶ ἐμοῦ; **18.35** ἀπεκρίθη ὁ
OR OTHERS TOLD YOU ABOUT ME?   ANSWERED -

Πιλᾶτος, Μήτι ἐγὼ Ἰουδαῖός εἰμι; τὸ ἔθνος τὸ σὸν
PILATE, [SURELY] NOT I AM~A JEW?   THE NATION - OF YOU

καὶ οἱ ἀρχιερεῖς παρέδωκάν σε ἐμοί· τί ἐποίησας;
AND THE HIGH PRIEST DELIVERED YOU TO ME. WHAT DID YOU DO?

18.36 ἀπεκρίθη Ἰησοῦς, Ἡ βασιλεία ἡ ἐμὴ οὐκ ἔστιν
ANSWERED JESUS, THE KINGDOM - OF ME IS NOT

ἐκ τοῦ κόσμου τούτου· εἰ ἐκ τοῦ κόσμου τούτου ἦν ἡ
OF - THIS~WORLD;   IF OF - THIS~WORLD   WAS THE

[27]Again Peter denied it, and at that moment the cock crowed.

28 Then they took Jesus from Caiaphas to Pilate's headquarters.[i] It was early in the morning. They themselves did not enter the headquarters,[i] so as to avoid ritual defilement and to be able to eat the Passover. [29]So Pilate went out to them and said, "What accusation do you bring against this man?" [30]They answered, "If this man were not a criminal, we would not have handed him over to you." [31]Pilate said to them, "Take him yourselves and judge him according to your law." The Jews replied, "We are not permitted to put anyone to death." [32](This was to fulfill what Jesus had said when he indicated the kind of death he was to die.)

33 Then Pilate entered the headquarters[i] again, summoned Jesus, and asked him, "Are you the King of the Jews?" [34]Jesus answered, "Do you ask this on your own, or did others tell you about me?" [35]Pilate replied, "I am not a Jew, am I? Your own nation and the chief priests have handed you over to me. What have you done?" [36]Jesus answered, "My kingdom is not from this world. If my kingdom were from this world,

[i] Gk *the praetorium*

my followers would be fighting to keep me from being handed over to the Jews. But as it is, my kingdom is not from here." [37]Pilate asked him, "So you are a king?" Jesus answered, "You say that I am a king. For this I was born, and for this I came into the world, to testify to the truth. Everyone who belongs to the truth listens to my voice." [38]Pilate asked him, "What is truth?"

After he had said this, he went out to the Jews again and told them, "I find no case against him. [39]But you have a custom that I release someone for you at the Passover. Do you want me to release for you the King of the Jews?" [40]They shouted in reply, "Not this man, but Barabbas!" Now Barabbas was a bandit.

βασιλεία ἡ ἐμή, οἱ ὑπηρέται οἱ ἐμοὶ ἠγωνίζοντο [ἄν],
KINGDOM   - OF ME, THE SERVANTS   - OF ME WOULD HAVE FOUGHT,

ἵνα μὴ παραδοθῶ   τοῖς Ἰουδαίοις· νῦν δὲ ἡ
THAT I SHOULD NOT BE DELIVERED TO THE JEWS;   BUT~NOW THE

βασιλεία ἡ ἐμὴ οὐκ ἔστιν ἐντεῦθεν. **18.37** εἶπεν οὖν
KINGDOM   - OF ME IS NOT   FROM HERE.   SAID THEREFORE

αὐτῷ ὁ Πιλᾶτος, Οὐκοῦν βασιλεὺς εἶ σύ; ἀπεκρίθη ὁ
TO HIM - PILATE,   SO   A KING   ARE YOU? ANSWERED -

Ἰησοῦς, Σὺ λέγεις ὅτι βασιλεύς εἰμι. ἐγὼ εἰς τοῦτο
JESUS, YOU SAY THAT I AM~A KING.   I   FOR THIS

γεγέννημαι καὶ εἰς τοῦτο ἐλήλυθα εἰς τὸν κόσμον, ἵνα
HAVE BEEN BORN AND FOR THIS HAVE COME INTO THE WORLD, THAT

μαρτυρήσω τῇ ἀληθείᾳ· πᾶς ὁ ὢν ἐκ τῆς ἀληθείας
I MIGHT TESTIFY TO THE TRUTH; EVERYONE BEING OF THE TRUTH

ἀκούει μου τῆς φωνῆς. **18.38** λέγει αὐτῷ ὁ Πιλᾶτος,
HEARS MY - VOICE.   SAYS TO HIM - PILATE,

Τί ἐστιν ἀλήθεια;
WHAT IS TRUTH?

Καὶ τοῦτο εἰπὼν   πάλιν ἐξῆλθεν πρὸς τοὺς
AND THIS HAVING SAID, AGAIN HE WENT OUT TO THE

Ἰουδαίους καὶ λέγει αὐτοῖς, Ἐγὼ οὐδεμίαν εὑρίσκω ἐν
JEWS   AND SAYS TO THEM, I   FIND~NOT ANY   ²IN

αὐτῷ αἰτίαν. **18.39** ἔστιν δὲ συνήθεια ὑμῖν ἵνα ἕνα
³HIM ¹FAULT.   BUT~THERE IS A CUSTOM FOR YOU° THAT ONE

ἀπολύσω ὑμῖν ἐν τῷ πάσχα· βούλεσθε οὖν
I MAY RELEASE TO YOU° DURING THE PASSOVER. DO YOU° WANT THEREFORE

ἀπολύσω ὑμῖν τὸν βασιλέα τῶν Ἰουδαίων;
[THAT] I RELEASE TO YOU° THE KING OF THE JEWS?

18.40 ἐκραύγασαν οὖν   πάλιν λέγοντες, Μὴ τοῦτον
        THEY CRIED OUT THEREFORE AGAIN SAYING,   NOT THIS MAN

ἀλλὰ τὸν Βαραββᾶν. ἦν δὲ ὁ Βαραββᾶς
BUT - BARABBAS.   ³WAS ¹NOW - ²BARABBAS

λῃστής.
⁴A REVOLUTIONARY.

CHAPTER 19

Then Pilate took Jesus and had him flogged. [2]And the soldiers wove a crown of thorns and put it on his head, and they dressed him in a purple robe. [3]They kept coming up to him, saying, "Hail,

19.1 Τότε οὖν   ἔλαβεν ὁ Πιλᾶτος τὸν Ἰησοῦν καὶ
        THEN THEREFORE ²TOOK - ¹PILATE   - ³JESUS AND

ἐμαστίγωσεν. **19.2** καὶ οἱ στρατιῶται πλέξαντες
SCOURGED [HIM].   AND THE SOLDIERS   HAVING WOVEN

στέφανον ἐξ ἀκανθῶν ἐπέθηκαν αὐτοῦ τῇ κεφαλῇ,
A WREATH OUT OF THORNS PUT [IT] ON HIS - HEAD,

καὶ ἱμάτιον πορφυροῦν περιέβαλον αὐτὸν **19.3** καὶ
AND A PURPLE~GARMENT THREW AROUND HIM,   AND

ἤρχοντο   πρὸς αὐτὸν καὶ ἔλεγον, Χαῖρε ὁ
THEY WERE COMING TO HIM   AND WERE SAYING, HAIL, THE

βασιλεὺς τῶν Ἰουδαίων· καὶ ἐδίδοσαν αὐτῷ
KING   OF THE JEWS;   AND THEY WERE GIVING HIM

ῥαπίσματα. **19.4** Καὶ ἐξῆλθεν πάλιν ἔξω ὁ Πιλᾶτος
BLOWS.   AND WENT FORTH AGAIN OUTSIDE - PILATE

καὶ λέγει αὐτοῖς, Ἴδε ἄγω ὑμῖν αὐτὸν ἔξω, ἵνα
AND SAYS TO THEM, LOOK, I BRING ³TO YOU° ¹HIM ²OUT, THAT

γνῶτε   ὅτι οὐδεμίαν αἰτίαν εὑρίσκω ἐν αὐτῷ.
YOU° MAY KNOW THAT NOT ANY FAULT I FIND IN HIM.

19.5 ἐξῆλθεν οὖν   ὁ Ἰησοῦς ἔξω,   φορῶν τὸν
      CAME FORTH THEREFORE - JESUS OUTSIDE, WEARING THE

ἀκάνθινον στέφανον καὶ τὸ πορφυροῦν ἱμάτιον. καὶ
THORNY   WREATH   AND THE PURPLE   GARMENT. AND

λέγει αὐτοῖς, Ἰδοὺ ὁ ἄνθρωπος. **19.6** ὅτε οὖν
HE SAYS TO THEM, SEE THE MAN.   WHEN THEREFORE

εἶδον αὐτὸν οἱ ἀρχιερεῖς καὶ οἱ ὑπηρέται ἐκραύγασαν
SAW   HIM THE CHIEF PRIESTS AND THE SERVANTS THEY CRIED OUT

λέγοντες, Σταύρωσον σταύρωσον. λέγει αὐτοῖς ὁ
SAYING,   CRUCIFY,   CRUCIFY.   SAYS TO THEM -

Πιλᾶτος, Λάβετε αὐτὸν ὑμεῖς καὶ σταυρώσατε· ἐγὼ γὰρ
PILATE, ²TAKE ³HIM ¹YOU° AND YOU° CRUCIFY FOR~I

οὐχ εὑρίσκω ἐν αὐτῷ αἰτίαν. **19.7** ἀπεκρίθησαν αὐτῷ
DO NOT FIND IN HIM FAULT,   ANSWERED   HIM

οἱ Ἰουδαῖοι, Ἡμεῖς νόμον ἔχομεν καὶ κατὰ   τὸν
THE JEWS,   WE   HAVE~A LAW   AND ACCORDING TO THE

νόμον ὀφείλει ἀποθανεῖν, ὅτι   υἱὸν   θεοῦ
LAW   HE OUGHT TO DIE,   BECAUSE [THE] SON OF GOD

ἑαυτὸν ἐποίησεν.
HE MADE~HIMSELF.

19.8 Ὅτε οὖν   ἤκουσεν ὁ Πιλᾶτος τοῦτον τὸν
       WHEN THEREFORE HEARD - PILATE   THIS   -

λόγον, μᾶλλον ἐφοβήθη, **19.9** καὶ εἰσῆλθεν εἰς τὸ
WORD,   HE WAS AFRAID~[EVEN] MORE, AND HE ENTERED INTO THE

πραιτώριον πάλιν καὶ λέγει τῷ Ἰησοῦ, Πόθεν   εἶ σύ;
PRAETORIUM AGAIN AND SAYS - TO JESUS, FROM WHERE ARE YOU?

ὁ δὲ Ἰησοῦς ἀπόκρισιν οὐκ ἔδωκεν αὐτῷ. **19.10** λέγει
- BUT JESUS AN ANSWER DID NOT GIVE HIM.   SAYS

οὖν   αὐτῷ ὁ Πιλᾶτος, Ἐμοὶ   σὺ λαλεῖς;
THEREFORE TO HIM - PILATE, TO ME   YOU DO NOT SPEAK?

οὐκ οἶδας ὅτι ἐξουσίαν ἔχω ἀπολῦσαί σε καὶ
DO YOU NOT KNOW THAT I HAVE~AUTHORITY TO FREE YOU AND

ἐξουσίαν ἔχω σταυρῶσαί σε; **19.11** ἀπεκρίθη [αὐτῷ]
I HAVE~AUTHORITY TO CRUCIFY YOU?   ANSWERED   HIM

Ἰησοῦς, Οὐκ εἶχες ἐξουσίαν κατ' ἐμοῦ οὐδεμίαν
JESUS,   YOU DO NOT HAVE AUTHORITY AGAINST ME AT ALL

εἰ μὴ ἦν δεδομένον σοι ἄνωθεν· διὰ τοῦτο ὁ
EXCEPT IT HAD BEEN GIVEN TO YOU FROM ABOVE; THEREFORE, THE ONE

παραδούς μέ σοι μείζονα ἁμαρτίαν ἔχει. **19.12** ἐκ
HAVING DELIVERED ME TO YOU GREATER SIN   HAS.   FROM

King of the Jews!" and
striking him on the face.
[4]Pilate went out again and
said to them, "Look, I am
bringing him out to you to let
you know that I find no case
against him." [5]So Jesus
came out, wearing the crown
of thorns and the purple
robe. Pilate said to them,
"Here is the man!" [6]When
the chief priests and the
police saw him, they
shouted, "Crucify him!
Crucify him!" Pilate said to
them, "Take him yourselves
and crucify him; I find no
case against him." [7]The
Jews answered him, "We
have a law, and according to
that law he ought to die
because he has claimed to be
the Son of God."

[8] Now when Pilate heard
this, he was more afraid than
ever. [9]He entered his headquarters[j] again and asked
Jesus, "Where are you
from?" But Jesus gave him
no answer. [10]Pilate therefore
said to him, "Do you refuse
to speak to me? Do you not
know that I have power to
release you, and power to
crucify you?" [11]Jesus
answered him, "You would
have no power over me
unless it had been given you
from above; therefore the
one who handed me over to
you is guilty of a greater
sin." [12]From then on

[j] Gk the praetorium

Pilate tried to release him, but the Jews cried out, "If you release this man, you are no friend of the emperor. Everyone who claims to be a king sets himself against the emperor."

13 When Pilate heard these words, he brought Jesus outside and sat[k] on the judge's bench at a place called The Stone Pavement, or in Hebrew[l] Gabbatha. [14]Now it was the day of Preparation for the Passover; and it was about noon. He said to the Jews, "Here is your King!" [15]They cried out, "Away with him! Away with him! Crucify him!" Pilate asked them, "Shall I crucify your King?" The chief priests answered, "We have no king but the emperor." [16]Then he handed him over to them to be crucified.

So they took Jesus; [17]and carrying the cross by himself, he went out to what is called The Place of the Skull, which in Hebrew[l] is called Golgotha. [18]There they crucified him, and with him two others, one on either side, with Jesus between him. [19]Pilate also had an inscription written and put on the cross. It read, "Jesus of Nazareth,[m] the King of the Jews." [20]Many of the Jews read this inscription, because the

[k] Or seated him
[l] That is, Aramaic
[m] Gk the Nazorean

τούτου   ὁ Πιλᾶτος   ἐζήτει   ἀπολῦσαι αὐτόν· οἱ δὲ
THIS [INCIDENT] - PILATE BEGAN SEEKING TO FREE HIM; BUT~THE

Ἰουδαῖοι   ἐκραύγασαν λέγοντες, Ἐὰν τοῦτον ἀπολύσῃς,
JEWS CRIED OUT SAYING, IF THIS MAN YOU FREE,

οὐκ εἶ   φίλος τοῦ Καίσαρος· πᾶς ὁ βασιλέα
YOU ARE NOT A FRIEND - OF CAESAR; EVERYONE A KING

ἑαυτὸν ποιῶν ἀντιλέγει τῷ Καίσαρι.
MAKING~HIMSELF SPEAKS AGAINST - CAESAR.

19.13 Ὁ οὖν   Πιλᾶτος ἀκούσας τῶν λόγων τούτων
- THEREFORE PILATE HAVING HEARD - , THESE~WORDS

ἤγαγεν ἔξω τὸν Ἰησοῦν καὶ ἐκάθισεν ἐπὶ βήματος εἰς
LED OUT - JESUS AND HE SAT UPON A TRIBUNAL IN

τόπον λεγόμενον Λιθόστρωτον, Ἑβραϊστὶ δὲ   Γαββαθα.
A PLACE BEING CALLED [THE] PAVEMENT, BUT~IN HEBREW, GABBATHA.

19.14 ἦν δὲ   παρασκευὴ   τοῦ πάσχα, ὥρα ἦν
NOW~IT WAS [THE] PREPARATION [DAY] OF THE PASSOVER, [4]HOUR [1]IT WAS

ὡς ἕκτη.   καὶ λέγει τοῖς Ἰουδαίοις, Ἴδε ὁ
[2]ABOUT [3][THE] SIXTH. AND HE SAYS TO THE JEWS, BEHOLD THE

βασιλεὺς ὑμῶν. **19.15** ἐκραύγασαν οὖν   ἐκεῖνοι, Ἆρον
KING OF YOU°. CRIED OUT THEREFORE THESE ONES, AWAY,

ἆρον, σταύρωσον αὐτόν. λέγει αὐτοῖς ὁ Πιλᾶτος, Τὸν
AWAY, CRUCIFY HIM. SAYS TO THEM - PILATE, THE

βασιλέα ὑμῶν σταυρώσω; ἀπεκρίθησαν οἱ ἀρχιερεῖς,
KING OF YOU° SHALL I CRUCIFY? ANSWERED THE HIGH PRIEST,

Οὐκ ἔχομεν βασιλέα εἰ μὴ Καίσαρα. **19.16** τότε οὖν
WE DO NOT HAVE A KING EXCEPT CAESAR. THEN THEREFORE

παρέδωκεν αὐτὸν αὐτοῖς ἵνα σταυρωθῇ.
HE DELIVERED HIM TO THEM THAT HE SHOULD BE CRUCIFIED.

Παρέλαβον οὖν   τὸν Ἰησοῦν, **19.17** καὶ βαστάζων
THEY TOOK THEREFORE - JESUS, AND CARRYING

ἑαυτῷ τὸν σταυρὸν ἐξῆλθεν εἰς τὸν   λεγόμενον
BY HIMSELF THE CROSS HE WENT OUT TO THE [PLACE] BEING CALLED

Κρανίου Τόπον, ὃ   λέγεται Ἑβραϊστὶ   Γολγοθᾶ,
[THE] PLACE~OF [THE] SKULL, WHICH IS CALLED IN HEBREW GOLGOTHA,

19.18 ὅπου αὐτὸν ἐσταύρωσαν καὶ μετ' αὐτοῦ
WHERE HIM THEY CRUCIFIED AND WITH HIM

ἄλλους δύο ἐντεῦθεν καὶ ἐντεῦθεν, μέσον δὲ   τὸν
TWO~OTHERS ON THIS SIDE AND ON THAT, AND~IN [THE] MIDDLE -

Ἰησοῦν. **19.19** ἔγραψεν δὲ καὶ τίτλον ὁ Πιλᾶτος καὶ
JESUS. AND~WROTE ALSO A TITLE - PILATE AND

ἔθηκεν ἐπὶ τοῦ σταυροῦ· ἦν δὲ γεγραμμένον, Ἰησοῦς
PLACED [IT] UPON THE CROSS; AND~IT HAD BEEN WRITTEN, JESUS

ὁ Ναζωραῖος ὁ βασιλεὺς τῶν Ἰουδαίων.
THE NAZARENE THE KING OF THE JEWS.

19.20 τοῦτον οὖν   τὸν τίτλον πολλοὶ ἀνέγνωσαν τῶν
[1]THIS [3]THEREFORE - [2]TITLE [4]MANY [7]READ [5]OF THE

Ἰουδαίων, ὅτι   ἐγγὺς ἦν ὁ τόπος τῆς πόλεως ὅπου
[6]JEWS, BECAUSE NEAR WAS THE PLACE THE CITY WHERE

ἐσταυρώθη ὁ Ἰησοῦς· καὶ ἦν γεγραμμένον Ἑβραϊστί,
WAS CRUCIFIED   -   JESUS;   AND   IT HAD BEEN WRITTEN   IN HEBREW,

Ῥωμαϊστί, Ἑλληνιστί. **19.21** ἔλεγον οὖν τῷ
IN LATIN,   [AND] IN GREEK.   WERE SAYING THEREFORE   -

Πιλάτῳ οἱ ἀρχιερεῖς τῶν Ἰουδαίων, Μὴ γράφε, Ὁ
TO PILATE   THE   CHIEF PRIESTS   OF THE   JEWS,   DO NOT WRITE,   THE

βασιλεὺς τῶν Ἰουδαίων, ἀλλ᾽ ὅτι ἐκεῖνος εἶπεν,
KING   OF THE   JEWS,   BUT   THAT   THAT ONE   SAID,

Βασιλεύς εἰμι τῶν Ἰουδαίων. **19.22** ἀπεκρίθη ὁ
KING   I AM   OF THE   JEWS.   ANSWERED   -

Πιλᾶτος, Ὁ γέγραφα, γέγραφα.
PILATE,   WHAT   I HAVE WRITTEN,   I HAVE WRITTEN.

19.23 Οἱ οὖν στρατιῶται, ὅτε ἐσταύρωσαν τὸν
THEREFORE~THE SOLDIERS   WHEN   THEY CRUCIFIED   -

Ἰησοῦν, ἔλαβον τὰ ἱμάτια αὐτοῦ καὶ ἐποίησαν
JESUS,   TOOK   THE   GARMENTS   OF HIM   AND   MADE

τέσσαρα μέρη, ἑκάστῳ στρατιώτῃ μέρος, καὶ τὸν
FOUR   PARTS,   TO EACH   SOLDIER   A PART,   AND   THE

χιτῶνα. ἦν δὲ ὁ χιτὼν ἄραφος, ἐκ τῶν ἄνωθεν
TUNIC.   NOW~WAS   THE   TUNIC   SEAMLESS,   FROM   THE   TOP

ὑφαντὸς δι᾽ ὅλου. **19.24** εἶπαν οὖν πρὸς
WOVEN   THROUGH [THE] WHOLE.   THEY SAID THEREFORE TO

ἀλλήλους, Μὴ σχίσωμεν αὐτόν, ἀλλὰ λάχωμεν περὶ
ONE ANOTHER,   LET US NOT SPLIT   IT,   BUT   LET US CAST LOTS   FOR

αὐτοῦ τίνος ἔσται· ἵνα ἡ γραφὴ πληρωθῇ [ἡ
IT   OF WHOSE IT WILL BE;   THAT   THE   SCRIPTURE   MIGHT BE FULFILLED   THE ONE

λέγουσα],
SAYING,

Διεμερίσαντο τὰ ἱμάτιά μου ἑαυτοῖς
THEY DIVIDED   THE   GARMENTS   OF ME   FOR THEMSELVES

καὶ ἐπὶ τὸν ἱματισμόν μου ἔβαλον κλῆρον.
AND   FOR   THE   CLOTHING   OF ME   THEY THREW   LOTS.

Οἱ μὲν οὖν στρατιῶται ταῦτα ἐποίησαν.
²THE   -   ¹THEREFORE ³SOLDIERS   DID~THESE THINGS.

19.25 εἱστήκεισαν δὲ παρὰ τῷ σταυρῷ τοῦ Ἰησοῦ ἡ
BUT~THERE HAD STOOD   BESIDE   THE   CROSS   -   OF JESUS   THE

μήτηρ αὐτοῦ καὶ ἡ ἀδελφὴ τῆς μητρὸς αὐτοῦ, Μαρία
MOTHER   OF HIM   AND   THE   SISTER   OF THE   MOTHER   OF HIM,   MARY

ἡ τοῦ Κλωπᾶ καὶ Μαρία ἡ Μαγδαληνή.
THE [WIFE]   -   OF CLOPAS,   AND   MARY   -   MAGDALENE.

19.26 Ἰησοῦς οὖν ἰδὼν τὴν μητέρα καὶ τὸν
JESUS   THEREFORE HAVING SEEN THE(HIS) MOTHER   AND   THE

μαθητὴν παρεστῶτα ὃν ἠγάπα, λέγει τῇ μητρί,
DISCIPLE   HAVING STOOD BY WHOM HE WAS LOVING,   SAYS   TO THE(HIS) MOTHER,

Γύναι, ἴδε ὁ υἱός σου. **19.27** εἶτα λέγει τῷ
WOMAN,   BEHOLD THE SON   OF YOU.   THEN   HE SAYS   TO THE

place where Jesus was crucified was near the city; and it was written in Hebrew,[n] in Latin, and in Greek. 21Then the chief priests of the Jews said to Pilate, "Do not write, 'The King of the Jews,' but, 'This man said, I am King of the Jews.'" 22Pilate answered, "What I have written I have written." 23When the soldiers had crucified Jesus, they took his clothes and divided them into four parts, one for each soldier. They also took his tunic; now the tunic was seamless, woven in one piece from the top. 24So they said to one another, "Let us not tear it, but cast lots for it to see who will get it." This was to fulfill what the scripture says,

"They divided my
    clothes among
        themselves,
    and for my clothing
        they cast lots."

25And that is what the soldiers did.

Meanwhile, standing near the cross of Jesus were his mother, and his mother's sister, Mary the wife of Clopas, and Mary Magdalene. 26When Jesus saw his mother and the disciple whom he loved standing beside her, he said to his mother, "Woman, here is your son." 27Then he said to the

[n] That is, *Aramaic*

19:24 Ps. 22:18

disciple, "Here is your mother." And from that hour the disciple took her into his own home.

28 After this, when Jesus knew that all was now finished, he said (in order to fulfill the scripture), "I am thirsty." 29A jar full of sour wine was standing there. So they put a sponge full of the wine on a branch of hyssop and held it to his mouth. 30When Jesus had received the wine, he said, "It is finished." Then he bowed his head and gave up his spirit.

31 Since it was the day of Preparation, the Jews did not want the bodies left on the cross during the sabbath, especially because that sabbath was a day of great solemnity. So they asked Pilate to have the legs of the crucified men broken and the bodies removed. 32Then the soldiers came and broke the legs of the first and of the other who had been crucified with him. 33But when they came to Jesus and saw that he was already dead, they did not break his legs. 34Instead, one of the soldiers pierced his side with a spear, and at once blood and water came out. 35(He who saw this has testified so that you also may believe. His testimony is true, and he knows° that he tells the truth.) 36These things

° Or *there is one who knows*

μαθητῇ, Ἴδε ἡ μήτηρ σου. καὶ ἀπ᾽ ἐκείνης τῆς
DISCIPLE,   BEHOLD THE MOTHER OF YOU. AND FROM THAT   -

ὥρας ἔλαβεν ὁ μαθητὴς αὐτὴν εἰς τὰ ἴδια.
HOUR   ³TOOK ¹THE ²DISCIPLE ⁴HER INTO THE(HIS) OWN [CARE].

19.28 Μετὰ τοῦτο εἰδὼς ὁ Ἰησοῦς ὅτι ἤδη
AFTER THIS, HAVING KNOWN - JESUS THAT ALREADY

πάντα τετέλεσται, ἵνα τελειωθῇ ἡ γραφή, λέγει,
EVERYTHING HAS BEEN COMPLETED, THAT MAY BE FULFILLED THE SCRIPTURE, HE SAYS,

Διψῶ. **19.29** σκεῦος ἔκειτο ὄξους μεστόν· σπόγγον οὖν
I THIRST.   A VESSEL WAS SET FULL~OF VINEGAR; THEN~A SPONGE

μεστὸν τοῦ ὄξους ὑσσώπῳ περιθέντες
FULL   -   OF VINEGAR HAVING BEEN WRAPPED AROUND~A HYSSOP BRANCH

προσήνεγκαν αὐτοῦ τῷ στόματι. **19.30** ὅτε οὖν
THEY BROUGHT [IT TO] HIS - MOUTH.   WHEN THEREFORE

ἔλαβεν τὸ ὄξος [ὁ] Ἰησοῦς εἶπεν, Τετέλεσται,
²RECEIVED ³THE ⁴VINEGAR - ¹JESUS, HE SAID, IT HAS BEEN ACCOMPLISHED,

καὶ κλίνας τὴν κεφαλὴν παρέδωκεν τὸ πνεῦμα.
AND HAVING BOWED THE(HIS) HEAD HE GAVE UP THE(HIS) SPIRIT.

19.31 Οἱ οὖν Ἰουδαῖοι, ἐπεὶ παρασκευὴ ἦν,
THEREFORE~THE JEWS, SINCE IT WAS~[THE] PREPARATION [DAY],

ἵνα μὴ μείνῃ ἐπὶ τοῦ σταυροῦ τὰ σώματα ἐν τῷ
THAT MAY NOT STAY UPON THE CROSS THE BODIES DURING THE

σαββάτῳ, ἦν γὰρ μεγάλη ἡ ἡμέρα ἐκείνου τοῦ
SABBATH, FOR~WAS GREAT THE DAY OF THAT

σαββάτου, ἠρώτησαν τὸν Πιλᾶτον ἵνα κατεαγῶσιν αὐτῶν
SABBATH, THEY ASKED - PILATE THAT MIGHT BE BROKEN THEIR

τὰ σκέλη καὶ ἀρθῶσιν. **19.32** ἦλθον οὖν οἱ στρατιῶται
- LEGS AND TAKEN AWAY.   THEREFORE~CAME THE SOLDIERS

καὶ τοῦ μὲν πρώτου κατέαξαν τὰ σκέλη καὶ τοῦ
AND OF THE - FIRST MAN BROKE THE LEGS AND OF THE

ἄλλου τοῦ συσταυρωθέντος αὐτῷ· **19.33** ἐπὶ δὲ τὸν
OTHER - HAVING BEEN CRUCIFIED WITH HIM; BUT~UPON -

Ἰησοῦν ἐλθόντες ὡς εἶδον ἤδη αὐτὸν τεθνηκότα,
HAVING COME [TO]~JESUS, WHEN THEY SAW [THAT] ALREADY HE HAS DIED,

οὐ κατέαξαν αὐτοῦ τὰ σκέλη, **19.34** ἀλλ᾽ εἷς τῶν
THEY DID NOT BREAK HIS - LEGS, BUT ONE OF THE

στρατιωτῶν λόγχῃ αὐτοῦ τὴν πλευρὰν ἔνυξεν, καὶ
SOLDIERS WITH A SPEAR ²HIS - ³SIDE ¹PIERCED, AND

ἐξῆλθεν εὐθὺς αἷμα καὶ ὕδωρ. **19.35** καὶ ὁ
IMMEDIATELY~OUT CAME BLOOD AND WATER. AND THE ONE

ἑωρακὼς μεμαρτύρηκεν, καὶ ἀληθινὴ αὐτοῦ ἐστιν ἡ
HAVING SEEN [THIS] HAS TESTIFIED, AND TRUE IS~HIS -

μαρτυρία, καὶ ἐκεῖνος οἶδεν ὅτι ἀληθῆ λέγει, ἵνα
TESTIMONY, AND THAT ONE KNOWS THAT TRULY HE SPEAKS, THAT

καὶ ὑμεῖς πιστεύ[σ]ητε. **19.36** ἐγένετο γὰρ ταῦτα
ALSO YOU* MAY BELIEVE.   FOR~HAPPENED THESE THINGS

19:28 Ps. 69:21 **19:36** Exod. 12:46; Num. 9:12

ἵνα ἡ γραφὴ πληρωθῇ,   Ὀστοῦν οὐ συντριβήσεται
THAT THE SCRIPTURE MIGHT BE FULFILLED, A BONE   SHALL NOT BE BROKEN

αὐτοῦ. **19.37** καὶ πάλιν ἑτέρα   γραφὴ λέγει, Ὄψονται
OF HIM.   AND AGAIN A DIFFERENT SCRIPTURE SAYS, THEY WILL LOOK

εἰς ὃν   ἐξεκέντησαν.
AT [HIM] WHOM THEY PIERCED.

19.38 Μετὰ δὲ ταῦτα   ἠρώτησεν τὸν Πιλᾶτον Ἰωσὴφ
NOW~AFTER THESE THINGS 14ASKED   -   15PILATE   1JOSEPH

[ὁ] ἀπὸ Ἀριμαθαίας, ὢν   μαθητὴς τοῦ Ἰησοῦ
-   2FROM 3ARIMATHEA,   4BEING 5A DISCIPLE -   6OF JESUS

κεκρυμμένος δὲ διὰ   τὸν φόβον τῶν Ἰουδαίων,
8SECRETLY   7BUT 9BECAUSE OF 10THE 11FEAR 12OF THE 13JEWS,

ἵνα ἄρῃ   τὸ σῶμα τοῦ Ἰησοῦ· καὶ ἐπέτρεψεν ὁ
THAT HE MIGHT TAKE THE BODY - OF JESUS; AND ALLOWED [IT] -

Πιλᾶτος. ἦλθεν οὖν   καὶ ἦρεν τὸ σῶμα αὐτοῦ.
PILATE.   HE CAME THEREFORE AND TOOK THE BODY OF HIM.

19.39 ἦλθεν δὲ καὶ Νικόδημος, ὁ   ἐλθὼν   πρὸς
AND~CAME ALSO NICODEMUS,   THE ONE HAVING COME TO

αὐτὸν νυκτὸς   τὸ πρῶτον, φέρων μίγμα σμύρνης
HIM   DURING [THE] NIGHT - [AT] FIRST, BEARING A MIXTURE OF MYRRH

καὶ ἀλόης ὡς λίτρας ἑκατόν. **19.40** ἔλαβον οὖν   τὸ
AND ALOES ABOUT ONE HUNDRED~POUNDS.   THEY TOOK THEREFORE THE

σῶμα τοῦ Ἰησοῦ καὶ ἔδησαν αὐτὸ ὀθονίοις   μετὰ τῶν
BODY   -   OF JESUS AND BOUND   IT   IN LINEN CLOTHS WITH -

ἀρωμάτων, καθὼς ἔθος ἐστὶν τοῖς Ἰουδαίοις
SPICES,   AS   IS~[THE] CUSTOM WITH THE JEWS

ἐνταφιάζειν. **19.41** ἦν δὲ   ἐν τῷ τόπῳ ὅπου
TO BURY.   NOW~THERE WAS IN THE PLACE WHERE

ἐσταυρώθη κῆπος, καὶ ἐν τῷ κήπῳ μνημεῖον καινὸν
HE WAS CRUCIFIED A GARDEN, AND IN THE GARDEN A NEW~TOMB

ἐν ᾧ   οὐδέπω οὐδεὶς ἦν τεθειμένος· **19.42** ἐκεῖ
IN WHICH NEVER YET ANYONE HAD BEEN PLACED.   THERE

οὖν   διὰ   τὴν παρασκευὴν τῶν Ἰουδαίων, ὅτι
THEREFORE, BECAUSE OF THE PREPARATION OF THE JEWS,   BECAUSE

ἐγγὺς ἦν τὸ μνημεῖον, ἔθηκαν τὸν Ἰησοῦν.
NEAR   WAS THE TOMB,   THEY PLACED - JESUS.

19:37 Zech. 12:10

occurred so that the scripture might be fulfilled, "None of his bones shall be broken." [37]And again another passage of scripture says, "They will look on the one whom they have pierced."

38 After these things, Joseph of Arimathea, who was a disciple of Jesus, though a secret one because of his fear of the Jews, asked Pilate to let him take away the body of Jesus. Pilate gave him permission; so he came and removed his body. [39]Nicodemus, who had at first come to Jesus by night, also came, bringing a mixture of myrrh and aloes, weighing about a hundred pounds. [40]They took the body of Jesus and wrapped it with the spices in linen cloths, according to the burial custom of the Jews. [41]Now there was a garden in the place where he was crucified, and in the garden there was a new tomb in which no one had ever been laid. [42]And so, because it was the Jewish day of Preparation, and the tomb was nearby, they laid Jesus there.

CHAPTER 20

20.1 Τῇ δὲ μιᾷ   τῶν σαββάτων Μαρία ἡ
NOW~ON THE FIRST [DAY] OF THE WEEK   MARY -

Μαγδαληνὴ ἔρχεται πρωῒ σκοτίας ἔτι οὔσης εἰς τὸ
MAGDALENE   COMES EARLY, 3DARK 2STILL 1IT BEING, TO THE

μνημεῖον καὶ βλέπει τὸν λίθον ἠρμένον   ἐκ τοῦ
TOMB   AND SEES   THE STONE HAVING BEEN TAKEN FROM THE

μνημείου. **20.2** τρέχει οὖν   καὶ ἔρχεται πρὸς
TOMB.   SHE RUNS THEREFORE AND COMES   TO

Early on the first day of the week, while it was still dark, Mary Magdalene came to the tomb and saw that the stone had been removed from the tomb. [2]So she ran and went to

Simon Peter and the other disciple, the one whom Jesus loved, and said to them, "They have taken the Lord out of the tomb, and we do not know where they have laid him." ³Then Peter and the other disciple set out and went toward the tomb. ⁴The two were running together, but the other disciple outran Peter and reached the tomb first. ⁵He bent down to look in and saw the linen wrappings lying there, but he did not go in. ⁶Then Simon Peter came, following him, and went into the tomb. He saw the linen wrappings lying there, ⁷and the cloth that had been on Jesus' head, not lying with the linen wrappings but rolled up in a place by itself. ⁸Then the other disciple, who reached the tomb first, also went in, and he saw and believed; ⁹for as yet they did not understand the scripture, that he must rise from the dead. ¹⁰Then the disciples returned to their homes.

11 But Mary stood weeping outside the tomb. As she wept, she bent over to look*ᵖ* into the tomb; ¹²and she saw two angels in white, sitting where the body of Jesus had been lying, one at the head and the other at the feet. ¹³They said to her, "Woman, why are you weeping?" She said

ᵖ Gk lacks *to look*

Σίμωνα Πέτρον καὶ πρὸς τὸν ἄλλον μαθητὴν ὃν
SIMON PETER AND TO THE OTHER DISCIPLE WHOM

ἐφίλει ὁ Ἰησοῦς καὶ λέγει αὐτοῖς, Ἦραν τὸν
²WAS BEING FOND OF - ¹JESUS AND SAYS TO THEM, THEY TOOK THE

κύριον ἐκ τοῦ μνημείου, καὶ οὐκ οἴδαμεν ποῦ
LORD FROM THE TOMB, AND WE DO NOT KNOW WHERE

ἔθηκαν αὐτόν. **20.3** Ἐξῆλθεν οὖν ὁ Πέτρος καὶ ὁ
THEY PLACED HIM. WENT FORTH THEREFORE - PETER AND THE

ἄλλος μαθητής, καὶ ἤρχοντο εἰς τὸ μνημεῖον.
OTHER DISCIPLE, AND THEY WERE COMING TO THE TOMB.

20.4 ἔτρεχον δὲ οἱ δύο ὁμοῦ· καὶ ὁ ἄλλος μαθητὴς
AND~WERE RUNNING THE TWO TOGETHER; AND THE OTHER DISCIPLE

προέδραμεν τάχιον τοῦ Πέτρου καὶ ἦλθεν πρῶτος εἰς
RAN AHEAD FASTER [THAN] - PETER AND CAME FIRST TO

τὸ μνημεῖον, **20.5** καὶ παρακύψας βλέπει κείμενα
THE TOMB, AND HAVING STOOPED DOWN HE SEES LYING

τὰ ὀθόνια, οὐ μέντοι εἰσῆλθεν. **20.6** ἔρχεται οὖν καὶ
THE LINEN CLOTHS, ²NOT ³HOWEVER ¹HE ENTERED. THEN~COMES ALSO

Σίμων Πέτρος ἀκολουθῶν αὐτῷ καὶ εἰσῆλθεν εἰς τὸ
SIMON PETER FOLLOWING HIM AND HE ENTERED INTO THE

μνημεῖον, καὶ θεωρεῖ τὰ ὀθόνια κείμενα, **20.7** καὶ
TOMB, AND HE SEES THE LINEN CLOTHS LYING, AND

τὸ σουδάριον, ὃ ἦν ἐπὶ τῆς κεφαλῆς αὐτοῦ, οὐ
THE FACE CLOTH, WHICH WAS UPON THE HEAD OF HIM, NOT

μετὰ τῶν ὀθονίων κείμενον ἀλλὰ χωρὶς ἐντετυλιγμένον
WITH THE LINEN CLOTHS LYING BUT APART, HAVING BEEN FOLDED UP

εἰς ἕνα τόπον. **20.8** τότε οὖν εἰσῆλθεν καὶ ὁ ἄλλος
IN ONE PLACE. THEN THEREFORE ENTERED ALSO THE OTHER

μαθητὴς ὁ ἐλθὼν πρῶτος εἰς τὸ μνημεῖον καὶ
DISCIPLE, THE ONE HAVING COME FIRST TO THE TOMB, AND

εἶδεν καὶ ἐπίστευσεν· **20.9** οὐδέπω γὰρ ᾔδεισαν τὴν
HE SAW AND BELIEVED, FOR NOT YET THEY KNEW THE

γραφὴν ὅτι δεῖ αὐτὸν ἐκ νεκρῶν ἀναστῆναι.
SCRIPTURE THAT IT IS NECESSARY [FOR] HIM FROM [THE] DEAD TO RISE UP.

20.10 ἀπῆλθον οὖν πάλιν πρὸς αὐτοὺς οἱ μαθηταί.
THEN~WENT AWAY AGAIN TO THEIR [OWN PLACES] THE DISCIPLES.

20.11 Μαρία δὲ εἱστήκει πρὸς τῷ μνημείῳ ἔξω
NOW~MARY HAD STOOD AT THE TOMB OUTSIDE

κλαίουσα. ὡς οὖν ἔκλαιεν, παρέκυψεν εἰς τὸ
WEEPING. THEN~AS SHE WAS WEEPING, SHE STOOPED INTO THE

μνημεῖον **20.12** καὶ θεωρεῖ δύο ἀγγέλους ἐν λευκοῖς
TOMB AND SEES TWO ANGELS IN WHITE

καθεζομένους, ἕνα πρὸς τῇ κεφαλῇ καὶ ἕνα πρὸς τοῖς
SITTING, ONE AT THE HEAD AND ONE AT THE

ποσίν, ὅπου ἔκειτο τὸ σῶμα τοῦ Ἰησοῦ. **20.13** καὶ
FEET, WHERE WAS LYING THE BODY - OF JESUS. AND

λέγουσιν αὐτῇ ἐκεῖνοι, Γύναι, τί κλαίεις; λέγει
SAY TO HER THOSE ONES, WOMAN, WHY DO YOU WEEP? SHE SAYS

αὐτοῖς ὅτι Ἦραν τὸν κύριόν μου, καὶ οὐκ οἶδα ποῦ
TO THEM,   -   THEY TOOK THE LORD   OF ME, AND I DO NOT KNOW WHERE

ἔθηκαν αὐτόν. **20.14** ταῦτα   εἰποῦσα ἐστράφη
THEY PLACED HIM.   THESE THINGS HAVING SAID SHE TURNED

εἰς τὰ ὀπίσω, καὶ θεωρεῖ τὸν Ἰησοῦν ἑστῶτα   καὶ
BACK AROUND, AND SHE SEES   -   JESUS   HAVING STOOD, AND

οὐκ ᾔδει ὅτι Ἰησοῦς ἐστιν. **20.15** λέγει αὐτῇ Ἰησοῦς,
DID NOT KNOW THAT IT IS(WAS)~JESUS.   SAYS   TO HER JESUS,

Γύναι, τί κλαίεις; τίνα ζητεῖς; ἐκείνη δοκοῦσα ὅτι
WOMAN, WHY DO YOU WEEP? WHOM DO YOU SEEK? THAT ONE SUPPOSING THAT

ὁ κηπουρός ἐστιν λέγει αὐτῷ, Κύριε, εἰ σὺ
THE GARDENER   HE IS (WAS) SAYS TO HIM, SIR,   IF YOU

ἐβάστασας αὐτόν, εἰπέ μοι ποῦ ἔθηκας αὐτόν, κἀγὼ
CARRIED AWAY   HIM,   TELL ME WHERE YOU PLACED HIM,   AND I

αὐτὸν ἀρῶ. **20.16** λέγει αὐτῇ Ἰησοῦς, Μαριάμ.
WILL TAKE~HIM.   SAYS TO HER JESUS,   MARY.

στραφεῖσα ἐκείνη λέγει αὐτῷ Ἑβραϊστί, Ῥαββουνι
HAVING TURNED THAT WOMAN SAYS TO HIM IN HEBREW,   RABBI,

(ὃ λέγεται Διδάσκαλε). **20.17** λέγει αὐτῇ Ἰησοῦς,
(WHICH MEANS TEACHER).   SAYS TO HER JESUS,

Μή μου ἅπτου, οὔπω γὰρ ἀναβέβηκα πρὸς τὸν πατέρα·
STOP TOUCHING ME,   FOR NOT YET I HAVE ASCENDED   TO   THE   FATHER;

πορεύου δὲ πρὸς τοὺς ἀδελφούς μου καὶ εἰπὲ αὐτοῖς,
BUT~GO   TO   THE   BROTHERS   OF ME AND TELL THEM,

Ἀναβαίνω πρὸς τὸν πατέρα μου καὶ πατέρα ὑμῶν
I ASCEND   TO   THE FATHER   OF ME AND FATHER OF YOU°

καὶ θεόν μου καὶ θεὸν ὑμῶν. **20.18** ἔρχεται Μαριὰμ ἡ
AND GOD OF ME AND GOD OF YOU°.   COMES   MARY   -

Μαγδαληνὴ ἀγγέλλουσα τοῖς μαθηταῖς ὅτι Ἑώρακα
MAGDALENE   ANNOUNCING   TO THE DISCIPLES,   -   I HAVE SEEN

τὸν κύριον, καὶ ταῦτα   εἶπεν αὐτῇ.
THE LORD,   AND THESE THINGS HE SAID TO HER.

20.19 Οὔσης οὖν   ὀψίας   τῇ ἡμέρᾳ ἐκείνῃ τῇ μιᾷ
       BEING THEREFORE EARLY EVENING - THAT~DAY,   THE FIRST

σαββάτων καὶ τῶν θυρῶν κεκλεισμένων ὅπου ἦσαν οἱ
OF THE WEEK,   AND   THE DOORS HAVING BEEN SHUT WHERE WERE THE

μαθηταὶ διὰ   τὸν φόβον τῶν Ἰουδαίων, ἦλθεν ὁ
DISCIPLES BECAUSE OF THE FEAR OF THE JEWS,   CAME   -

Ἰησοῦς καὶ ἔστη εἰς τὸ μέσον καὶ λέγει αὐτοῖς,
JESUS   AND STOOD IN THE MIDST AND SAYS TO THEM,

Εἰρήνη ὑμῖν. **20.20** καὶ τοῦτο εἰπὼν ἔδειξεν τὰς
PEACE   TO YOU°.   AND HAVING SAID~THIS HE SHOWED THE(HIS)

χεῖρας καὶ τὴν πλευρὰν αὐτοῖς. ἐχάρησαν οὖν
HANDS   AND THE(HIS) SIDE   TO THEM.   REJOICED   THEREFORE

οἱ μαθηταὶ ἰδόντες   τὸν κύριον. **20.21** εἶπεν οὖν
THE DISCIPLES [AT] HAVING SEEN THE LORD.   SAID THEREFORE

αὐτοῖς [ὁ Ἰησοῦς] πάλιν, Εἰρήνη ὑμῖν· καθὼς
TO THEM   -   JESUS   AGAIN,   PEACE   TO YOU°.   AS

to them, "They have taken away my Lord, and I do not know where they have laid him." [14]When she had said this, she turned around and saw Jesus standing there, but she did not know that it was Jesus. [15]Jesus said to her, "Woman, why are you weeping? Whom are you looking for?" Supposing him to be the gardener, she said to him, "Sir, if you have carried him away, tell me where you have laid him, and I will take him away." [16]Jesus said to her, "Mary!" She turned and said to him in Hebrew,*q* "Rabbouni!" (which means Teacher). [17]Jesus said to her, "Do not hold on to me, because I have not yet ascended to the Father. But go to my brothers and say to them, 'I am ascending to my Father and your Father, to my God and your God.'" [18]Mary Magdalene went and announced to the disciples, "I have seen the Lord"; and she told them that he had said these things to her.

19 When it was evening on that day, the first day of the week, and the doors of the house where the disciples had met were locked for fear of the Jews, Jesus came and stood among them and said, "Peace be with you." [20]After he said this, he showed them his hands and his side. Then the disciples rejoiced when they saw the Lord. [21]Jesus said to them again, "Peace be with you.

q That is, *Aramaic*

As the Father has sent me, so I send you." 22When he had said this, he breathed on them and said to them, "Receive the Holy Spirit. 23If you forgive the sins of any, they are forgiven them; if you retain the sins of any, they are retained."

24 But Thomas (who was called the Twin[r]), one of the twelve, was not with them when Jesus came. 25So the other disciples told him, "We have seen the Lord." But he said to them, "Unless I see the mark of the nails in his hands, and put my finger in the mark of the nails and my hand in his side, I will not believe."

26 A week later his disciples were again in the house, and Thomas was with them. Although the doors were shut, Jesus came and stood among them and said, "Peace be with you." 27Then he said to Thomas, "Put your finger here and see my hands. Reach out your hand and put it in my side. Do not doubt but believe." 28Thomas answered him, "My Lord and my God!" 29Jesus said to him, "Have you believed because you have seen me? Blessed are those who have not seen and yet have come to believe."

30 Now Jesus did many

[r] Gk *Didymus*

ἀπέσταλκέν με ὁ πατήρ, κἀγὼ πέμπω ὑμᾶς.
HAS SENT ME THE FATHER, [SO] ALSO I SEND YOU°.

20.22 καὶ τοῦτο εἰπὼν ἐνεφύσησεν καὶ λέγει αὐτοῖς,
AND HAVING SAID~THIS HE BREATHED ON [THEM] AND SAYS TO THEM,

Λάβετε πνεῦμα ἅγιον· **20.23** ἄν τινων ἀφῆτε τὰς
RECEIVE [THE] HOLY~SPIRIT OF WHOMEVER YOU° FORGIVE THE

ἁμαρτίας ἀφέωνται αὐτοῖς, ἄν τινων κρατῆτε
SINS THEY HAVE BEEN FORGIVEN TO THEM; OF WHOMEVER YOU° HOLD

κεκράτηνται.
THEY HAVE BEEN HELD.

20.24 Θωμᾶς δὲ εἷς ἐκ τῶν δώδεκα, ὁ λεγόμενος
BUT~THOMAS, ONE OF THE TWELVE, THE ONE BEING CALLED

Δίδυμος, οὐκ ἦν μετ' αὐτῶν ὅτε ἦλθεν Ἰησοῦς.
DIDYMUS, WAS NOT WITH THEM WHEN CAME JESUS.

20.25 ἔλεγον οὖν αὐτῷ οἱ ἄλλοι μαθηταί,
THEREFORE~WERE SAYING TO HIM THE OTHER DISCIPLES,

Ἑωράκαμεν τὸν κύριον. ὁ δὲ εἶπεν αὐτοῖς, Ἐὰν μὴ
WE HAVE SEEN THE LORD. BUT~HE SAID TO THEM, UNLESS

ἴδω ἐν ταῖς χερσὶν αὐτοῦ τὸν τύπον τῶν ἥλων καὶ
I SEE IN THE HANDS OF HIM THE MARK OF THE NAILS AND

βάλω τὸν δάκτυλόν μου εἰς τὸν τύπον τῶν ἥλων καὶ
I PUT THE FINGER OF ME INTO THE PLACE OF THE NAILS AND

βάλω μου τὴν χεῖρα εἰς τὴν πλευρὰν αὐτοῦ,
I PUT MY - HAND INTO THE SIDE OF HIM,

οὐ μὴ πιστεύσω. **20.26** Καὶ μεθ' ἡμέρας ὀκτὼ πάλιν
I WILL NEVER BELIEVE. AND AFTER EIGHT~DAYS AGAIN

ἦσαν ἔσω οἱ μαθηταὶ αὐτοῦ καὶ Θωμᾶς μετ' αὐτῶν.
WERE INSIDE THE DISCIPLES OF HIM AND THOMAS WITH THEM.

ἔρχεται ὁ Ἰησοῦς τῶν θυρῶν κεκλεισμένων καὶ ἔστη
COMES - JESUS— THE DOORS HAVING BEEN SHUT— AND STOOD

εἰς τὸ μέσον καὶ εἶπεν, Εἰρήνη ὑμῖν. **20.27** εἶτα
IN THE MIDST AND SAID, PEACE TO YOU°. THEN

λέγει τῷ Θωμᾷ, Φέρε τὸν δάκτυλόν σου ὧδε καὶ ἴδε
HE SAYS - TO THOMAS, BRING THE FINGER OF YOU HERE AND SEE

τὰς χεῖράς μου καὶ φέρε τὴν χεῖρά σου καὶ βάλε
THE HANDS OF ME, AND BRING THE HAND OF YOU AND PUT [IT]

εἰς τὴν πλευράν μου, καὶ μὴ γίνου ἄπιστος ἀλλὰ
INTO THE SIDE OF ME, AND DO NOT BECOME FAITHLESS BUT

πιστός. **20.28** ἀπεκρίθη Θωμᾶς καὶ εἶπεν αὐτῷ, Ὁ
FAITHFUL. ANSWERED THOMAS AND SAID TO HIM, THE

κύριός μου καὶ ὁ θεός μου. **20.29** λέγει αὐτῷ ὁ
LORD OF ME AND THE GOD OF ME. SAYS TO HIM -

Ἰησοῦς, Ὅτι ἑώρακάς με πεπίστευκας; μακάριοι
JESUS, BECAUSE YOU HAVE SEEN ME HAVE YOU BELIEVED? BLESSED [ARE]

οἱ μὴ ἰδόντες καὶ πιστεύσαντες.
THE ONES NOT HAVING SEEN AND HAVING BELIEVED.

20.30 Πολλὰ μὲν οὖν καὶ ἄλλα σημεῖα ἐποίησεν
MANY - THEREFORE [3]ALSO [1]OTHER [2]SIGNS DID

ὁ Ἰησοῦς ἐνώπιον τῶν μαθητῶν [αὐτοῦ], ἃ
\- JESUS   BEFORE   THE   DISCIPLES   OF HIM,   WHICH

οὐκ ἔστιν γεγραμμένα ἐν τῷ βιβλίῳ τούτῳ·
HAVE NOT BEEN WRITTEN   IN -   THIS~BOOK.

20.31 ταῦτα δὲ   γέγραπται ἵνα ⌜πιστεύ[σ]ητε⌝ ὅτι
BUT~THESE THINGS HAVE BEEN WRITTEN THAT YOU° MIGHT BELIEVE   THAT

Ἰησοῦς ἐστιν ὁ Χριστὸς ὁ υἱὸς τοῦ θεοῦ, καὶ ἵνα
JESUS   IS   THE CHRIST,   THE SON   OF   GOD,   AND   THAT

πιστεύοντες ζωὴν ἔχητε ἐν τῷ ὀνόματι αὐτοῦ.
BELIEVING,   YOU° MAY HAVE~LIFE IN THE   NAME   OF HIM.

20:31 text: KJV ASV RSV NASB NIV TEV NJB NRSV. var. πιστευητε (you may continue to believe): NIVmg
NEB TEVmg NRSVmg.

---

other signs in the presence of
his disciples, which are not
written in this book. [31]But
these are written so that you
may come to believe[s] that
Jesus is the Messiah,[t] the
Son of God, and that
through believing you may
have life in his name.

[s] Other ancient authorities read *may
continue to believe*
[t] Or *the Christ*

21.1 Μετὰ ταῦτα ἐφανέρωσεν ἑαυτὸν πάλιν ὁ
AFTER   THESE THINGS MANIFESTED HIMSELF   AGAIN -

Ἰησοῦς τοῖς μαθηταῖς ἐπὶ τῆς θαλάσσης τῆς
JESUS   TO THE DISCIPLES   AT   THE   SEA

Τιβεριάδος· ἐφανέρωσεν δὲ οὕτως. **21.2** ἦσαν ὁμοῦ
OF TIBERIAS; NOW~HE WAS MANIFESTED THUS.   THERE WERE TOGETHER

Σίμων Πέτρος καὶ Θωμᾶς ὁ   λεγόμενος Δίδυμος
SIMON PETER   AND THOMAS THE ONE BEING CALLED DIDYMUS

καὶ Ναθαναὴλ ὁ   ἀπὸ Κανὰ τῆς Γαλιλαίας καὶ
AND NATHANAEL THE ONE FROM CANA -   OF GALILEE   AND

οἱ   τοῦ Ζεβεδαίου καὶ ἄλλοι ἐκ τῶν μαθητῶν αὐτοῦ
THE [SONS] - OF ZEBEDEE   AND OTHERS OF THE DISCIPLES OF HIM

δύο. **21.3** λέγει αὐτοῖς Σίμων Πέτρος, Ὑπάγω ἁλιεύειν.
TWO.   SAYS   TO THEM SIMON PETER,   I AM GOING TO FISH.

λέγουσιν αὐτῷ, Ἐρχόμεθα καὶ ἡμεῖς σὺν σοί.
THEY SAY TO HIM, ³ARE COMING ²ALSO ¹WE WITH YOU.

ἐξῆλθον καὶ ἐνέβησαν εἰς τὸ πλοῖον, καὶ ἐν
THEY WENT FORTH AND EMBARKED INTO THE BOAT,   AND DURING

ἐκείνῃ τῇ νυκτὶ ἐπίασαν οὐδέν. **21.4** πρωΐας δὲ
THAT   -   NIGHT THEY CAUGHT NOTHING.   NOW~EARLY MORNING

ἤδη γενομένης ἔστη Ἰησοῦς εἰς τὸν αἰγιαλόν, οὐ
ALREADY HAVING COME, STOOD JESUS   ON THE SHORE;   NOT

μέντοι ᾔδεισαν οἱ μαθηταὶ ὅτι Ἰησοῦς ἐστιν.
HOWEVER HAD REALIZED THE DISCIPLES THAT IT IS(WAS)~JESUS.

21.5 λέγει οὖν   αὐτοῖς [ὁ] Ἰησοῦς, Παιδία, μή
SAYS THEREFORE TO THEM -   JESUS,   CHILDREN, [SURELY] NOT

τι προσφάγιον ἔχετε; ἀπεκρίθησαν αὐτῷ, Οὔ.
ANY FISH   YOU° HAVE? THEY ANSWERED HIM,   NO.

21.6 ὁ δὲ εἶπεν αὐτοῖς, Βάλετε εἰς τὰ δεξιὰ μέρη τοῦ
AND~HE SAID TO THEM, THROW   TO THE RIGHT SIDE OF THE

πλοίου τὸ δίκτυον, καὶ εὑρήσετε.   ἔβαλον
BOAT   THE NET,   AND YOU° WILL FIND [FISH]. THEY THREW [IT]

After these things Jesus
showed himself again to the
disciples by the Sea of
Tiberias; and he showed
himself in this way.
[2]Gathered there together
were Simon Peter, Thomas
called the Twin,[u] Nathanael
of Cana in Galilee, the sons
of Zebedee, and two others
of his disciples. [3]Simon
Peter said to them, "I am
going fishing." They said to
him, "We will go with you."
They went out and got into
the boat, but that night they
caught nothing.
    4 Just after daybreak,
Jesus stood on the beach; but
the disciples did not know
that it was Jesus. [5]Jesus said
to them, "Children, you
have no fish, have you?"
They answered him, "No."
[6]He said to them, "Cast the
net to the right side of the
boat, and you will find
some." So they cast it,

[u] Gk *Didymus*

and now they were not able to haul it in because there were so many fish. ⁷That disciple whom Jesus loved said to Peter, "It is the Lord!" When Simon Peter heard that it was the Lord, he put on some clothes, for he was naked, and jumped into the sea. ⁸But the other disciples came in the boat, dragging the net full of fish, for they were not far from the land, only about a hundred yards[v] off.

9 When they had gone ashore, they saw a charcoal fire there, with fish on it, and bread. ¹⁰Jesus said to them, "Bring some of the fish that you have just caught." ¹¹So Simon Peter went aboard and hauled the net ashore, full of large fish, a hundred fifty-three of them; and though there were so many, the net was not torn. ¹²Jesus said to them, "Come and have breakfast." Now none of the disciples dared to ask him, "Who are you?" because they knew it was the Lord. ¹³Jesus came and took the bread and gave it to them, and did the same with the fish. ¹⁴This was now the third time that Jesus appeared to the disciples after he was raised from the dead.

15 When they had finished breakfast, Jesus said to Simon Peter,

[v] Gk *two hundred cubits*

οὖν,   καὶ οὐκέτι αὐτὸ ἑλκύσαι ἴσχυον
THEREFORE, AND NO LONGER ³IT ²TO DRAW ¹WERE THEY STRONG [ENOUGH]

ἀπὸ τοῦ πλήθους τῶν ἰχθύων. 21.7 λέγει οὖν   ὁ
FROM THE MULTITUDE OF THE FISH.   SAYS   THEREFORE -

μαθητὴς ἐκεῖνος ὃν ἠγάπα ὁ Ἰησοῦς τῷ Πέτρῳ, Ὁ
THAT~DISCIPLE   WHOM ²WAS LOVING - ¹JESUS - TO PETER, THE

κύριός ἐστιν. Σίμων οὖν Πέτρος ἀκούσας ὅτι ὁ
LORD   IT IS.   THEREFORE~SIMON PETER, HAVING HEARD THAT THE

κύριός ἐστιν τὸν ἐπενδύτην διεζώσατο, ἦν γὰρ
LORD   IT IS,   THE OUTER GARMENT TIED AROUND HIMSELF, FOR~HE WAS

γυμνός, καὶ ἔβαλεν ἑαυτὸν εἰς τὴν θάλασσαν,
UNCLOTHED, AND THREW   HIMSELF   INTO THE SEA.

21.8 οἱ δὲ ἄλλοι μαθηταὶ τῷ πλοιαρίῳ ἦλθον, οὐ
BUT~THE OTHER DISCIPLES IN THE BOAT CAME,   ³NOT

γὰρ ἦσαν μακρὰν ἀπὸ τῆς γῆς ἀλλὰ ὡς ἀπὸ
¹FOR ²THEY WERE FAR   FROM THE LAND BUT   ABOUT FROM

πηχῶν διακοσίων, σύροντες τὸ δίκτυον τῶν ἰχθύων.
TWO HUNDRED~CUBITS, DRAGGING THE NET   OF THE FISH.

21.9 ὡς οὖν   ἀπέβησαν εἰς τὴν γῆν βλέπουσιν
WHEN THEREFORE THEY DISEMBARKED ONTO THE LAND THEY SEE

ἀνθρακιὰν κειμένην καὶ ὀψάριον ἐπικείμενον καὶ
A CHARCOAL FIRE LYING   AND FISH   LYING UPON [IT]   AND

ἄρτον. **21.10** λέγει αὐτοῖς ὁ Ἰησοῦς, Ἐνέγκατε ἀπὸ
BREAD.   SAYS   TO THEM - JESUS,   BRING   FROM

τῶν ὀψαρίων ὧν ἐπιάσατε νῦν. **21.11** ἀνέβη οὖν
THE FISH   WHICH YOU° CAUGHT NOW.   WENT UP THEREFORE

Σίμων Πέτρος καὶ εἵλκυσεν τὸ δίκτυον εἰς τὴν γῆν
SIMON   PETER   AND DRAGGED   THE NET   ONTO THE LAND

μεστὸν ἰχθύων μεγάλων ἑκατὸν   πεντήκοντα τριῶν·
FULL OF LARGE~FISH,   A HUNDRED [AND] FIFTY   THREE;

καὶ   τοσούτων ὄντων οὐκ ἐσχίσθη τὸ δίκτυον.
AND [THOUGH] BEING~SO MANY   DID NOT SPLIT THE NET.

21.12 λέγει αὐτοῖς ὁ Ἰησοῦς, Δεῦτε ἀριστήσατε.
SAYS   TO THEM - JESUS,   COME   EAT BREAKFAST.

οὐδεὶς δὲ ἐτόλμα τῶν μαθητῶν ἐξετάσαι αὐτόν, Σὺ
NOW~NOT ONE ³WAS DARING ¹OF THE ²DISCIPLES TO ASK   HIM, ³YOU

τίς εἶ; εἰδότες ὅτι ὁ κύριός ἐστιν. **21.13** ἔρχεται
¹WHO ²ARE? HAVING KNOWN THAT THE LORD   IT IS.   COMES

Ἰησοῦς καὶ λαμβάνει τὸν ἄρτον καὶ δίδωσιν αὐτοῖς,
JESUS   AND TAKES   THE BREAD AND GIVES   TO THEM,

καὶ τὸ ὀψάριον ὁμοίως. **21.14** τοῦτο   ἤδη τρίτον
AND THE FISH   LIKEWISE.   THIS [WAS] NOW [THE] THIRD [TIME]

ἐφανερώθη Ἰησοῦς τοῖς μαθηταῖς ἐγερθεὶς   ἐκ
JESUS~WAS MANIFESTED TO THE DISCIPLES HAVING BEEN RAISED FROM

νεκρῶν.
[THE] DEAD.

21.15 Ὅτε οὖν ἠρίστησαν λέγει τῷ Σίμωνι Πέτρῳ ὁ
THEN~WHEN THEY ATE   SAYS   - TO SIMON   PETER -

Ἰησοῦς, Σίμων Ἰωάννου, ἀγαπᾷς με πλέον τούτων;
JESUS, SIMON [SON] OF JOHN, DO YOU LOVE ME MORE [THAN] THESE ONES?

λέγει αὐτῷ, Ναὶ κύριε, σὺ οἶδας ὅτι φιλῶ σε.
HE SAYS TO HIM, YES, LORD, YOU KNOW THAT I AM FOND OF YOU.

λέγει αὐτῷ, Βόσκε τὰ ἀρνία μου. **21.16** λέγει αὐτῷ
HE SAYS TO HIM, FEED THE LAMBS OF ME. SAYS TO HIM

πάλιν δεύτερον, Σίμων Ἰωάννου, ἀγαπᾷς με; λέγει
AGAIN A SECOND [TIME], SIMON [SON] OF JOHN, DO YOU LOVE ME? HE SAYS

αὐτῷ, Ναὶ κύριε, σὺ οἶδας ὅτι φιλῶ σε. λέγει
TO HIM, YES, LORD, YOU KNOW THAT I AM FOND OF YOU. HE SAYS

αὐτῷ, Ποίμαινε τὰ πρόβατά μου. **21.17** λέγει αὐτῷ τὸ
TO HIM, SHEPHERD THE SHEEP OF ME. HE SAYS TO HIM THE

τρίτον, Σίμων Ἰωάννου, φιλεῖς με; ἐλυπήθη ὁ
THIRD [TIME], SIMON [SON] OF JOHN, ARE YOU FOND OF ME? WAS GRIEVED -

Πέτρος ὅτι εἶπεν αὐτῷ τὸ τρίτον, Φιλεῖς με;
PETER BECAUSE HE SAID TO HIM THE THIRD [TIME], ARE YOU FOND OF ME?

καὶ λέγει αὐτῷ, Κύριε, πάντα σὺ οἶδας, σὺ γινώσκεις
AND HE SAYS TO HIM, LORD, ALL THINGS YOU KNOW, YOU KNOW

ὅτι φιλῶ σε. λέγει αὐτῷ [ὁ Ἰησοῦς], Βόσκε τὰ
THAT I AM FOND OF YOU. SAYS TO HIM - JESUS, FEED THE

πρόβατά μου. **21.18** ἀμὴν ἀμὴν λέγω σοι, ὅτε ἦς
SHEEP OF ME. TRULY, TRULY I SAY TO YOU, WHEN YOU WERE

νεώτερος, ἐζώννυες σεαυτὸν καὶ περιεπάτεις ὅπου
YOUNG, YOU WERE GIRDING YOURSELF AND WERE WALKING WHERE

ἤθελες· ὅταν δὲ γηράσῃς, ἐκτενεῖς τὰς χεῖράς σου,
YOU WANTED; BUT~WHEN YOU GROW OLD, YOU WILL EXTEND THE HANDS OF YOU,

καὶ ἄλλος σε ζώσει καὶ οἴσει ὅπου οὐ θέλεις.
AND ANOTHER WILL GIRD~YOU AND CARRY [YOU] WHERE YOU-DO NOT WISH [TO GO].

21.19 τοῦτο δὲ εἶπεν σημαίνων ποίῳ θανάτῳ δοξάσει
AND~THIS HE SAID SIGNIFYING [BY] WHAT DEATH HE WILL GLORIFY

τὸν θεόν. καὶ τοῦτο εἰπὼν λέγει αὐτῷ, Ἀκολούθει μοι.
- GOD. AND HAVING SAID~THIS, HE SAYS TO HIM, FOLLOW ME.

21.20 Ἐπιστραφεὶς ὁ Πέτρος βλέπει τὸν μαθητὴν
HAVING TURNED - PETER SEES THE DISCIPLE

ὃν ἠγάπα ὁ Ἰησοῦς ἀκολουθοῦντα, ὃς καὶ
WHOM ²WAS LOVING - ¹JESUS FOLLOWING, WHO ALSO

ἀνέπεσεν ἐν τῷ δείπνῳ ἐπὶ τὸ στῆθος αὐτοῦ καὶ
RECLINED DURING THE SUPPER UPON THE BREAST OF HIM AND

εἶπεν, Κύριε, τίς ἐστιν ὁ παραδιδούς σε;
SAID, LORD, WHO IS THE ONE BETRAYING YOU?

21.21 τοῦτον οὖν ἰδὼν ὁ Πέτρος λέγει τῷ Ἰησοῦ,
⁴THIS ONE ¹THEN ³HAVING SEEN - ²PETER SAYS - TO JESUS,

Κύριε, οὗτος δὲ τί; **21.22** λέγει αὐτῷ ὁ
LORD, ³THIS MAN ¹AND ²WHAT [ABOUT]? SAYS TO HIM -

Ἰησοῦς, Ἐὰν αὐτὸν θέλω μένειν ἕως ἔρχομαι,
JESUS, IF I WANT~HIM TO REMAIN UNTIL I COME,

τί πρὸς σέ; σύ μοι ἀκολούθει. **21.23** ἐξῆλθεν
WHAT [IS THAT] TO YOU? YOU FOLLOW~ME. WENT OUT

"Simon son of John, do you love me more than these?" He said to him, "Yes, Lord; you know that I love you." Jesus said to him, "Feed my lambs." [16]A second time he said to him, "Simon son of John, do you love me?" He said to him, "Yes, Lord; you know that I love you." Jesus said to him, "Tend my sheep." [17]He said to him the third time, "Simon son of John, do you love me?" Peter felt hurt because he said to him the third time, "Do you love me?" And he said to him, "Lord, you know everything; you know that I love you." Jesus said to him, "Feed my sheep. [18]Very truly, I tell you, when you were younger, you used to fasten your own belt and to go wherever you wished. But when you grow old, you will stretch out your hands, and someone else will fasten a belt around you and take you where you do not wish to go." [19](He said this to indicate the kind of death by which he would glorify God.) After this he said to him, "Follow me."

[20] Peter turned and saw the disciple whom Jesus loved following them; he was the one who had reclined next to Jesus at the supper and had said, "Lord, who is it that is going to betray you?" [21]When Peter saw him, he said to Jesus, "Lord, what about him?" [22]Jesus said to him, "If it is my will that he remain until I come, what is that to you? Follow me!" [23]So the rumor

spread in the community[w] that this disciple would not die. Yet Jesus did not say to him that he would not die, but, "If it is my will that he remain until I come, what is that to you?"[x]

24 This is the disciple who is testifying to these things and has written them, and we know that his testimony is true. [25]But there are also many other things that Jesus did; if every one of them were written down, I suppose that the world itself could not contain the books that would be written.

[w] Gk *among the brothers*
[x] Other ancient authorities lack *what is that to you*

οὖν οὗτος ὁ λόγος εἰς τοὺς ἀδελφοὺς ὅτι ὁ
THEREFORE THIS ONE - SAYING TO THE BROTHERS THAT -

μαθητὴς ἐκεῖνος οὐκ ἀποθνῄσκει· οὐκ εἶπεν δὲ αὐτῷ ὁ
THAT~DISCIPLE WOULD NOT DIE. BUT~DID NOT TELL HIM -

Ἰησοῦς ὅτι οὐκ ἀποθνῄσκει ἀλλ', Ἐὰν αὐτὸν θέλω
JESUS THAT HE WOULD NOT DIE BUT, IF I WANT~HIM

μένειν ἕως ἔρχομαι[, τί πρὸς σέ];
TO REMAIN UNTIL I COME, WHAT [IS THAT] TO YOU?

21.24 Οὗτός ἐστιν ὁ μαθητὴς ὁ μαρτυρῶν περὶ
THIS IS THE DISCIPLE, THE ONE TESTIFYING ABOUT

τούτων καὶ ὁ γράψας ταῦτα, καὶ οἴδαμεν
THESE THINGS AND THE ONE HAVING WRITTEN THESE THINGS, AND WE KNOW

ὅτι ἀληθὴς αὐτοῦ ἡ μαρτυρία ἐστίν.
THAT TRUE HIS - TESTIMONY IS.

21.25 Ἔστιν δὲ καὶ ἄλλα πολλὰ ἃ ἐποίησεν ὁ
AND~THERE IS(ARE) ALSO MANY~OTHER THINGS WHICH DID -

Ἰησοῦς, ἅτινα ἐὰν γράφηται καθ' ἕν, οὐδ' αὐτὸν
JESUS, WHICH IF THEY ARE WRITTEN ONE BY ONE, [5]NOT [4]ITSELF

οἶμαι τὸν κόσμον χωρῆσαι τὰ γραφόμενα βιβλία.
[1]I THINK [2]THE [3]WORLD [6]TO HAVE ROOM FOR THE BOOKS~BEING WRITTEN.

THE
ACTS
OF THE APOSTLES

ΠΡΑΞΕΙΣ ΑΠΟΣΤΟΛΩΝ
ACTS   OF [THE] APOSTLES

1.1 Τὸν μὲν πρῶτον λόγον ἐποιησάμην περὶ πάντων,
THE - FIRST WORD I MADE ABOUT EVERYTHING,

ὦ Θεόφιλε, ὧν ἤρξατο ὁ Ἰησοῦς ποιεῖν τε καὶ
O THEOPHILUS, WHICH BEGAN - JESUS BOTH~TO DO AND

διδάσκειν, **1.2** ἄχρι ἧς ἡμέρας ἐντειλάμενος τοῖς
TO TEACH, UNTIL [THE] DAY HAVING GIVEN ORDERS TO THE

ἀποστόλοις διὰ πνεύματος ἁγίου οὓς ἐξελέξατο
APOSTLES THROUGH [THE] HOLY~SPIRIT WHOM HE CHOSE,

ἀνελήμφθη· **1.3** οἷς καὶ παρέστησεν ἑαυτὸν ζῶντα
HE WAS TAKEN UP. TO WHOM ALSO HE PRESENTED HIMSELF LIVING,

μετὰ τὸ παθεῖν αὐτὸν ἐν πολλοῖς τεκμηρίοις, δι'
AFTER - HE~DIED, BY MANY PROOFS, DURING

ἡμερῶν τεσσεράκοντα ὀπτανόμενος αὐτοῖς καὶ λέγων
FORTY~DAYS APPEARING TO THEM AND SAYING

τὰ περὶ τῆς βασιλείας τοῦ θεοῦ· **1.4** καὶ
THINGS CONCERNING THE KINGDOM - OF GOD. AND

συναλιζόμενος παρήγγειλεν αὐτοῖς ἀπὸ Ἰεροσολύμων
[WHILE] EATING TOGETHER HE GAVE INSTRUCTIONS TO THEM FROM JERUSALEM

μὴ χωρίζεσθαι ἀλλὰ περιμένειν τὴν ἐπαγγελίαν τοῦ
NOT TO DEPART, BUT TO WAIT FOR THE PROMISE OF THE

πατρὸς ἣν ἠκούσατέ μου, **1.5** ὅτι Ἰωάννης
FATHER WHICH YOU° HEARD FROM ME, BECAUSE JOHN

μὲν ἐβάπτισεν ὕδατι, ὑμεῖς δὲ ἐν πνεύματι
ON THE ONE HAND BAPTIZED WITH WATER, BUT~YOU° ²IN ⁴SPIRIT

βαπτισθήσεσθε ἁγίῳ οὐ μετὰ πολλὰς ταύτας ἡμέρας.
¹WILL BE BAPTIZED ³[THE] HOLY NOT AFTER THESE~MANY DAYS.

1.6 Οἱ μὲν οὖν συνελθόντες ἠρώτων αὐτὸν
²THE ONES - ¹THEN HAVING COME TOGETHER WERE QUESTIONING HIM

λέγοντες, Κύριε, εἰ ἐν τῷ χρόνῳ τούτῳ ἀποκαθιστάνεις
SAYING, LORD, IF IN - THIS~TIME YOU ARE RESTORING

τὴν βασιλείαν τῷ Ἰσραήλ; **1.7** εἶπεν δὲ πρὸς αὐτούς,
THE KINGDOM - TO ISRAEL? BUT~HE SAID TO THEM,

Οὐχ ὑμῶν ἐστιν γνῶναι χρόνους ἢ καιροὺς οὓς ὁ
NOT FOR YOU° IS IT TO KNOW TIMES OR SEASONS WHICH THE

πατὴρ ἔθετο ἐν τῇ ἰδίᾳ ἐξουσίᾳ, **1.8** ἀλλὰ λήμψεσθε
FATHER HAS SET BY - HIS OWN AUTHORITY, BUT YOU° WILL RECEIVE

δύναμιν ἐπελθόντος τοῦ ἁγίου πνεύματος ἐφ' ὑμᾶς καὶ
POWER HAVING COME THE HOLY SPIRIT UPON YOU° AND

In the first book, Theophilus, I wrote about all that Jesus did and taught from the beginning [2]until the day when he was taken up to heaven, after giving instructions through the Holy Spirit to the apostles whom he had chosen. [3]After his suffering he presented himself alive to them by many convincing proofs, appearing to them during forty days and speaking about the kingdom of God. [4]While staying[a] with them, he ordered them not to leave Jerusalem, but to wait there for the promise of the Father. "This," he said, "is what you have heard from me; [5]for John baptized with water, but you will be baptized with[b] the Holy Spirit not many days from now."

[6] So when they had come together, they asked him, "Lord, is this the time when you will restore the kingdom to Israel?" [7]He replied, "It is not for you to know the times or periods that the Father has set by his own authority. [8]But you will receive power when the Holy Spirit has come upon you; and

[a] Or *eating*
[b] Or *by*

you will be my witnesses in Jerusalem, in all Judea and Samaria, and to the ends of the earth." [9]When he had said this, as they were watching, he was lifted up, and a cloud took him out of their sight. [10]While he was going and they were gazing up toward heaven, suddenly two men in white robes stood by them. [11]They said, "Men of Galilee, why do you stand looking up toward heaven? This Jesus, who has been taken up from you into heaven, will come in the same way as you saw him go into heaven."

12 Then they returned to Jerusalem from the mount called Olivet, which is near Jerusalem, a sabbath day's journey away. [13]When they had entered the city, they went to the room upstairs where they were staying, Peter, and John, and James, and Andrew, Philip and Thomas, Bartholomew and Matthew, James son of Alphaeus, and Simon the Zealot, and Judas son of[c] James. [14]All these were constantly devoting themselves to prayer, together with certain women, including Mary the mother of Jesus, as well as his brothers.

15 In those days Peter stood up among

[c] Or the brother of

ἔσεσθέ   μου   μάρτυρες   ἔν   τε   Ἰερουσαλὴμ   καὶ   [ἐν]
YOU° WILL BE   MY   WITNESSES   IN   BOTH   JERUSALEM   AND   IN

πάσῃ   τῇ   Ἰουδαίᾳ   καὶ   Σαμαρείᾳ   καὶ   ἕως   ἐσχάτου
ALL   -   JUDEA   AND   SAMARIA   AND   AS FAR AS   [THE] END

τῆς   γῆς.   1.9 καὶ   ταῦτα   εἰπὼν   βλεπόντων αὐτῶν
OF THE   EARTH.   AND   THESE THINGS   HAVING SAID,   [WHILE] THEY~[WERE] LOOKING

ἐπήρθη   καὶ   νεφέλη   ὑπέλαβεν   αὐτὸν   ἀπὸ   τῶν
HE WAS TAKEN UP,   AND   A CLOUD   TOOK UP   HIM   FROM   THE

ὀφθαλμῶν   αὐτῶν.   1.10 καὶ   ὡς   ἀτενίζοντες   ἦσαν   εἰς   τὸν
EYES   OF THEM.   AND   AS   THEY WERE LOOKING INTENTLY   INTO   -

οὐρανὸν   πορευομένου   αὐτοῦ,   καὶ   ἰδοὺ   ἄνδρες   δύο
HEAVEN   HE~GOING,   AND   BEHOLD   TWO~MEN

παρειστήκεισαν   αὐτοῖς   ἐν   ἐσθήσεσι   λευκαῖς,   1.11 οἳ
HAD BEEN PRESENT   WITH THEM   IN   WHITE~CLOTHING,   WHO

καὶ   εἶπαν,   Ἄνδρες   Γαλιλαῖοι,   τί   ἐστήκατε
ALSO   SAID,   MEN   OF GALILEE,   WHY   HAVE YOU° STOOD

[ἐμ]βλέποντες   εἰς   τὸν   οὐρανόν;   οὗτος   ὁ   Ἰησοῦς   ὁ
LOOKING   INTO   -   HEAVEN?   THIS   -   JESUS,   THE ONE

ἀναλημφθεὶς   ἀφ᾽   ὑμῶν   εἰς   τὸν   οὐρανὸν   οὕτως
HAVING BEEN TAKEN UP   FROM   YOU°   INTO   -   HEAVEN,   THUS

ἐλεύσεται   ὃν   τρόπον   ἐθεάσασθε   αὐτὸν   πορευόμενον
WILL COME   IN WHICH   MANNER   YOU° SAW   HIM   GOING

εἰς   τὸν   οὐρανόν.
INTO   -   HEAVEN.

1.12 Τότε   ὑπέστρεψαν   εἰς   Ἰερουσαλὴμ   ἀπὸ   ὄρους
THEN   THEY RETURNED   TO   JERUSALEM   FROM   [THE] MOUNTAIN

τοῦ   καλουμένου   Ἐλαιῶνος,   ὃ   ἐστιν   ἐγγὺς
-    BEING CALLED   OF OLIVES,   WHICH   IS   NEAR

Ἰερουσαλὴμ   σαββάτου   ἔχον   ὁδόν.   1.13 καὶ
JERUSALEM   ³OF A SABBATH   ¹BEING SITUATED   ²A JOURNEY.   AND

ὅτε   εἰσῆλθον,   εἰς   τὸ   ὑπερῷον   ἀνέβησαν   οὗ
WHEN   THEY ENTERED,   INTO   THE   UPSTAIRS   THEY WENT UP   WHERE

ἦσαν   καταμένοντες,   ὅ   τε   Πέτρος   καὶ   Ἰωάννης   καὶ
THEY WERE STAYING,   -   BOTH   PETER   AND   JOHN   AND

Ἰάκωβος   καὶ   Ἀνδρέας,   Φίλιππος   καὶ   Θωμᾶς,
JAMES   AND   ANDREW,   PHILIP   AND   THOMAS,

Βαρθολομαῖος   καὶ   Μαθθαῖος,   Ἰάκωβος   Ἀλφαίου
BARTHOLOMEW   AND   MATTHEW,   JAMES   [THE SON] OF ALPHAEUS

καὶ   Σίμων   ὁ   Ζηλωτὴς   καὶ   Ἰούδας   Ἰακώβου.
AND   SIMON   THE   ZEALOT   AND   JUDAS   [THE SON OF] JAMES.

1.14 οὗτοι   πάντες   ἦσαν   προσκαρτεροῦντες   ὁμοθυμαδὸν   τῇ
THESE   ALL   WERE DEVOTING THEMSELVES   WITH ONE MIND   -

προσευχῇ   σὺν   γυναιξὶν   καὶ   Μαριὰμ   τῇ   μητρὶ   τοῦ
TO PRAYER   WITH   [THE] WOMEN   AND   MARY   THE   MOTHER   -

Ἰησοῦ   καὶ   τοῖς   ἀδελφοῖς   αὐτοῦ.
OF JESUS   AND   THE   BROTHERS   OF HIM.

1.15 Καὶ   ἐν   ταῖς   ἡμέραις   ταύταις   ἀναστὰς   Πέτρος   ἐν
AND   IN   -   THESE~DAYS   HAVING ARISEN   PETER   IN

μέσῳ τῶν ἀδελφῶν εἶπεν· ἦν τε ὄχλος
[THE] MIDST OF THE BROTHERS SAID: AND~WAS [THE] CROWD

ὀνομάτων ἐπὶ τὸ αὐτὸ ὡσεὶ ἑκατὸν εἴκοσι·
OF NAMES (PERSONS) AT THE SAME [PLACE] ABOUT A HUNDRED [AND] TWENTY.

1.16 Ἄνδρες ἀδελφοί, ἔδει πληρωθῆναι τὴν
MEN, BROTHERS, IT WAS NECESSARY TO BE FULFILLED THE

γραφὴν ἣν προεῖπεν τὸ πνεῦμα τὸ ἅγιον διὰ
SCRIPTURE WHICH FORETOLD THE ²SPIRIT - ¹HOLY THROUGH

στόματος Δαυὶδ περὶ Ἰούδα τοῦ γενομένου ὁδηγοῦ
[THE] MOUTH OF DAVID CONCERNING JUDAS, THE ONE HAVING BECOME A GUIDE

τοῖς συλλαβοῦσιν Ἰησοῦν, **1.17** ὅτι κατηριθμημένος ἦν
TO THE ONES HAVING SEIZED JESUS, FOR HE HAD BEEN NUMBERED

ἐν καὶ ἔλαχεν τὸν κλῆρον τῆς
AMONG AND HE RECEIVED THE PORTION -

διακονίας ταύτης. **1.18** Οὗτος μὲν οὖν ἐκτήσατο
OF THIS~MINISTRY. ²THIS ONE - ¹THEREFORE ACQUIRED

χωρίον ἐκ μισθοῦ τῆς ἀδικίας καὶ
A FIELD OUT OF [THE] REWARD - OF UNRIGHTEOUSNESS AND

πρηνὴς γενόμενος ἐλάκησεν μέσος καὶ ἐξεχύθη
HAVING FALLEN~HEADLONG HE BURST OPEN [IN] [THE] MIDDLE AND WAS POURED OUT

πάντα τὰ σπλάγχνα αὐτοῦ· **1.19** καὶ γνωστὸν ἐγένετο
ALL THE INWARD PARTS OF HIM. AND IT BECAME~KNOWN

πᾶσι τοῖς κατοικοῦσιν Ἰερουσαλήμ, ὥστε κληθῆναι τὸ
TO ALL THE ONES INHABITING JERUSALEM, SO AS TO BE CALLED -

χωρίον ἐκεῖνο τῇ ἰδίᾳ διαλέκτῳ αὐτῶν Ἀκελδαμάχ,
THAT~FIELD IN THEIR OWN LANGUAGE OF THEM, AKELDAMA,

τοῦτ᾽ ἔστιν Χωρίον Αἵματος. **1.20** Γέγραπται γὰρ ἐν
THAT IS, FIELD OF BLOOD. FOR~IT HAS BEEN WRITTEN IN

βίβλῳ ψαλμῶν,
[THE] BOOK OF PSALMS,

Γενηθήτω ἡ ἔπαυλις αὐτοῦ ἔρημος
LET BECOME THE RESIDENCE OF HIM DESOLATE

καὶ μὴ ἔστω ὁ κατοικῶν ἐν αὐτῇ,
AND LET NOT BE THE ONE DWELLING IN IT,

καί,
AND,

Τὴν ἐπισκοπὴν αὐτοῦ λαβέτω ἕτερος.
THE OFFICE OF HIM LET RECEIVE ANOTHER.

1.21 δεῖ οὖν τῶν συνελθόντων ἡμῖν
IT IS NECESSARY THEREFORE [THAT] THE ²HAVING ACCOMPANIED ³US

ἀνδρῶν ἐν παντὶ χρόνῳ ᾧ εἰσῆλθεν καὶ ἐξῆλθεν
¹MEN DURING ALL [THE] TIME IN WHICH WENT IN AND WENT OUT

ἐφ᾽ ἡμᾶς ὁ κύριος Ἰησοῦς, **1.22** ἀρξάμενος ἀπὸ τοῦ
AMONG US THE LORD JESUS, HAVING BEGUN FROM THE

βαπτίσματος Ἰωάννου ἕως τῆς ἡμέρας ἧς ἀνελήμφθη
BAPTISM OF JOHN UNTIL THE DAY WHEN HE WAS TAKEN UP

1:20a Ps. 69:25 **1:20b** Ps. 109:8

the believers*d* (together the crowd numbered about one hundred twenty persons) and said, [16]"Friends,*e* the scripture had to be fulfilled, which the Holy Spirit through David foretold concerning Judas, who became a guide for those who arrested Jesus— [17]for he was numbered among us and was allotted his share in this ministry." [18](Now this man acquired a field with the reward of his wickedness; and falling headlong,*f* he burst open in the middle and all his bowels gushed out. [19]This became known to all the residents of Jerusalem, so that the field was called in their language Hakeldama, that is, Field of Blood.) [20]"For it is written in the book of Psalms,

'Let his homestead
    become desolate,
and let there be no one
    to live in it';

and

'Let another take his
    position of
    overseer.'

[21]So one of the men who have accompanied us during all the time that the Lord Jesus went in and out among us, [22]beginning from the baptism of John until the day when he was taken up

d Gk *brothers*
e Gk *Men, brothers*
f Or *swelling up*

from us—one of these must become a witness with us to his resurrection." 23So they proposed two, Joseph called Barsabbas, who was also known as Justus, and Matthias. 24Then they prayed and said, "Lord, you know everyone's heart. Show us which one of these two you have chosen 25to take the place *g* in this ministry and apostleship from which Judas turned aside to go to his own place." 26And they cast lots for them, and the lot fell on Matthias; and he was added to the eleven apostles.

g Other ancient authorities read *the share*

ἀφ' ἡμῶν, μάρτυρα τῆς ἀναστάσεως αὐτοῦ σὺν ἡμῖν
FROM US, A WITNESS OF THE RESURRECTION OF HIM WITH US

γενέσθαι ἕνα τούτων. **1.23** καὶ ἔστησαν δύο,
TO BECOME ONE OF THESE. AND THEY PUT FORWARD TWO [MEN],

Ἰωσὴφ τὸν καλούμενον Βαρσαββᾶν ὃς ἐπεκλήθη
JOSEPH THE ONE BEING CALLED BARSABBAS, WHO WAS ALSO CALLED

Ἰοῦστος, καὶ Μαθθίαν. **1.24** καὶ προσευξάμενοι εἶπαν,
JUSTUS, AND MATTHIAS. AND HAVING PRAYED THEY SAID,

Σὺ κύριε καρδιογνῶστα πάντων, ἀνάδειξον ὃν
YOU, LORD, KNOWER OF [THE] HEARTS OF ALL, REVEAL WHOM

ἐξελέξω ἐκ τούτων τῶν δύο ἕνα **1.25** λαβεῖν τὸν τόπον
YOU CHOSE OF THESE - TWO, ONE TO TAKE THE PLACE

τῆς διακονίας ταύτης καὶ ἀποστολῆς, ἀφ' ἧς παρέβη
- OF THIS~MINISTRY AND APOSTLESHIP, FROM WHICH TURNED ASIDE

Ἰούδας πορευθῆναι εἰς τὸν τόπον τὸν ἴδιον. **1.26** καὶ
JUDAS TO GO TO - ²PLACE - ¹HIS OWN. AND

ἔδωκαν κλήρους αὐτοῖς καὶ ἔπεσεν ὁ κλῆρος ἐπὶ
THEY CAST LOTS FOR THEM AND FELL THE LOT TO

Μαθθίαν καὶ συγκατεψηφίσθη μετὰ τῶν ἕνδεκα
MATTHIAS AND HE WAS NUMBERED WITH THE ELEVEN

ἀποστόλων.
APOSTLES.

CHAPTER 2

When the day of Pentecost had come, they were all together in one place. 2And suddenly from heaven there came a sound like the rush of a violent wind, and it filled the entire house where they were sitting. 3Divided tongues, as of fire, appeared among them, and a tongue rested on each of them. 4All of them were filled with the Holy Spirit and began to speak in other languages, as the Spirit gave them ability.
5 Now there were devout Jews from every nation under

2.1 Καὶ ἐν τῷ συμπληροῦσθαι τὴν ἡμέραν τῆς
AND WHEN IS FULFILLED THE DAY -

πεντηκοστῆς ἦσαν πάντες ὁμοῦ ἐπὶ τὸ αὐτό.
OF PENTECOST THEY WERE ALL TOGETHER AT THE SAME [PLACE].

2.2 καὶ ἐγένετο ἄφνω ἐκ τοῦ οὐρανοῦ ἦχος ὥσπερ
AND THERE WAS SUDDENLY FROM - HEAVEN A SOUND LIKE

φερομένης πνοῆς βιαίας καὶ ἐπλήρωσεν ὅλον τὸν
[THE] RUSHING OF A VIOLENT~WIND AND IT FILLED [THE] WHOLE -

οἶκον οὗ ἦσαν καθήμενοι **2.3** καὶ ὤφθησαν αὐτοῖς
HOUSE WHERE THEY WERE SITTING. AND APPEARED TO THEM

διαμεριζόμεναι γλῶσσαι ὡσεὶ πυρὸς καὶ ἐκάθισεν ἐφ'
TONGUES~BEING DIVIDED AS FIRE AND IT SAT ON

ἕνα ἕκαστον αὐτῶν, **2.4** καὶ ἐπλήσθησαν πάντες
EACH~ONE OF THEM, AND ALL~WERE FILLED

πνεύματος ἁγίου καὶ ἤρξαντο λαλεῖν ἑτέραις γλώσσαις
WITH [THE] HOLY~SPIRIT AND THEY BEGAN TO SPEAK IN OTHER LANGUAGES

καθὼς τὸ πνεῦμα ἐδίδου ἀποφθέγγεσθαι αὐτοῖς.
AS THE SPIRIT WAS GIVING [THE ABILITY] TO SPEAK TO THEM.

2.5 Ἦσαν δὲ εἰς Ἰερουσαλὴμ κατοικοῦντες Ἰουδαῖοι,
NOW~THERE WERE IN JERUSALEM JEWS~LIVING,

ἄνδρες εὐλαβεῖς ἀπὸ παντὸς ἔθνους τῶν ὑπὸ τὸν
DEVOUT~MEN FROM ALL [THE] NATIONS - UNDER -

οὐρανόν. **2.6** γενομένης δὲ τῆς φωνῆς ταύτης συνῆλθεν
HEAVEN.   AND~HAVING HAPPENED -   THIS~SOUND,   ASSEMBLED

τὸ πλῆθος καὶ συνεχύθη, ὅτι ἤκουον
THE MULTITUDE AND IT WAS CONFUSED, BECAUSE THEY WERE HEARING

εἷς ἕκαστος τῇ ἰδίᾳ διαλέκτῳ λαλούντων αὐτῶν.
EACH~ONE   -   IN HIS OWN LANGUAGE THEM~SPEAKING.

2.7 ἐξίσταντο δὲ καὶ ἐθαύμαζον λέγοντες, Οὐχ ἰδοὺ
AND~THEY WERE AMAZED AND WERE MARVELING SAYING,   ³NOT ¹BEHOLD,

ἅπαντες οὗτοί εἰσιν οἱ λαλοῦντες Γαλιλαῖοι; **2.8** καὶ
⁴ALL   ⁵THESE ²ARE - SPEAKING   GALILEANS?   AND

πῶς ἡμεῖς ἀκούομεν ἕκαστος τῇ ἰδίᾳ διαλέκτῳ ἡμῶν
HOW ARE HEARING~WE   EACH   - IN HIS OWN LANGUAGE OF US

ἐν ᾗ ἐγεννήθημεν; **2.9** Πάρθοι καὶ Μῆδοι καὶ
IN WHICH WE WERE BORN?   PARTHIANS AND MEDES AND

Ἐλαμῖται καὶ οἱ κατοικοῦντες τὴν Μεσοποταμίαν,
ELAMITES, AND THE ONES LIVING IN   -   MESOPOTAMIA,

Ἰουδαίαν τε καὶ Καππαδοκίαν, Πόντον καὶ τὴν
BOTH~JUDEA AND CAPPADOCIA,   PONTUS AND -

Ἀσίαν, **2.10** Φρυγίαν τε καὶ Παμφυλίαν, Αἴγυπτον
ASIA,   BOTH~PHRYGIA AND PAMPHYLIA,   EGYPT

καὶ τὰ μέρη τῆς Λιβύης τῆς κατὰ Κυρήνην, καὶ
AND THE REGIONS - OF LIBYA -   TOWARD CYRENE,   AND

οἱ ἐπιδημοῦντες Ῥωμαῖοι, **2.11** Ἰουδαῖοί τε καὶ
THE VISITING   ROMANS,   BOTH~JEWS   AND

προσήλυτοι, Κρῆτες καὶ Ἄραβες, ἀκούομεν
PROSELYTES, CRETANS AND ARABS,   WE HEAR

λαλούντων αὐτῶν ταῖς ἡμετέραις γλώσσαις τὰ μεγαλεῖα
THEM~SPEAKING   -   IN OTHER   LANGUAGES THE MIGHTY ACTS

τοῦ θεοῦ. **2.12** ἐξίσταντο δὲ πάντες καὶ διηπόρουν,
-   OF GOD.   AND WERE AMAZED ALL   AND WERE PERPLEXED,

ἄλλος πρὸς ἄλλον λέγοντες, Τί θέλει τοῦτο εἶναι;
ONE TO ANOTHER   SAYING,   WHAT CAN THIS MEAN?

2.13 ἕτεροι δὲ διαχλευάζοντες ἔλεγον ὅτι Γλεύκους
BUT~OTHERS MOCKING   WERE SAYING - OF SWEET WINE

μεμεστωμένοι εἰσίν.
THEY HAVE BEEN FILLED.

2.14 Σταθεὶς δὲ ὁ Πέτρος σὺν τοῖς ἕνδεκα ἐπῆρεν
AND~HAVING STOOD - PETER   WITH THE   ELEVEN, HE LIFTED UP

τὴν φωνὴν αὐτοῦ καὶ ἀπεφθέγξατο αὐτοῖς, Ἄνδρες
THE VOICE   OF HIM AND HE DECLARED   TO THEM, MEN,

Ἰουδαῖοι καὶ οἱ κατοικοῦντες Ἰερουσαλὴμ πάντες,
JEWS,   AND THE ONES INHABITING   JERUSALEM   ALL,

τοῦτο ὑμῖν γνωστὸν ἔστω καὶ ἐνωτίσασθε τὰ ῥήματά
THIS TO YOU° LET IT BE~KNOWN AND GIVE EAR   TO THE WORDS

μου. **2.15** οὐ γὰρ ὡς ὑμεῖς ὑπολαμβάνετε οὗτοι
OF ME.   FOR~NOT AS YOU° SUPPOSE   THESE ONES

μεθύουσιν, ἔστιν γὰρ ὥρα τρίτη τῆς ἡμέρας,
ARE DRUNK,   FOR~IT IS [THE] THIRD~HOUR OF THE DAY,

heaven living in Jerusalem. ⁶And at this sound the crowd gathered and was bewildered, because each one heard them speaking in the native language of each. ⁷Amazed and astonished, they asked, "Are not all these who are speaking Galileans? ⁸And how is it that we hear, each of us, in our own native language? ⁹Parthians, Medes, Elamites, and residents of Mesopotamia, Judea and Cappadocia, Pontus and Asia, ¹⁰Phrygia and Pamphylia, Egypt and the parts of Libya belonging to Cyrene, and visitors from Rome, both Jews and proselytes, ¹¹Cretans and Arabs—in our own languages we hear them speaking about God's deeds of power." ¹²All were amazed and perplexed, saying to one another, "What does this mean?" ¹³But others sneered and said, "They are filled with new wine."

14 But Peter, standing with the eleven, raised his voice and addressed them, "Men of Judea and all who live in Jerusalem, let this be known to you, and listen to what I say. ¹⁵Indeed, these are not drunk, as you suppose, for it is only nine o'clock in the morning.

¹⁶No, this is what was
spoken through the prophet
Joel:

¹⁷ 'In the last days it will be,
God declares,
that I will pour out
my Spirit upon
all flesh,
and your sons and your
daughters shall
prophesy,
and your young men
shall see visions,
and your old men shall
dream dreams.
¹⁸ Even upon my slaves,
both men and
women,
in those days I will pour
out my Spirit;
and they shall
prophesy.
¹⁹ And I will show portents
in the heaven above
and signs on the
earth below,
blood, and fire, and
smoky mist.
²⁰ The sun shall be turned
to darkness
and the moon to blood,
before the coming of
the Lord's great and
glorious day.

2.16 ἀλλὰ τοῦτό ἐστιν τὸ εἰρημένον διὰ τοῦ
BUT THIS IS THE THING HAVING BEEN SPOKEN BY THE

προφήτου Ἰωήλ,
PROPHET JOEL,

2.17 Καὶ ἔσται ἐν ταῖς ἐσχάταις ἡμέραις, λέγει ὁ
AND IT WILL BE IN THE LAST DAYS, SAYS -

θεός,
GOD,

ἐκχεῶ ἀπὸ τοῦ πνεύματός μου ἐπὶ πᾶσαν
I WILL POUR OUT FROM THE SPIRIT OF ME ON ALL

σάρκα,
FLESH,

καὶ προφητεύσουσιν οἱ υἱοὶ ὑμῶν
AND WILL PROPHESY THE SONS OF YOU°

καὶ αἱ θυγατέρες ὑμῶν
AND THE DAUGHTERS OF YOU°

καὶ οἱ νεανίσκοι ὑμῶν ὁράσεις ὄψονται
AND THE YOUNG MEN OF YOU° WILL SEE~VISIONS

καὶ οἱ πρεσβύτεροι ὑμῶν
AND THE ELDERS OF YOU°

ἐνυπνίοις ἐνυπνιασθήσονται·
WILL DREAM~DREAMS.

2.18 καί γε ἐπὶ τοὺς δούλους μου καὶ ἐπὶ τὰς
AND - UPON THE MALE SLAVES OF ME AND UPON THE

δούλας μου
FEMALE SLAVES OF ME

ἐν ταῖς ἡμέραις ἐκείναις ἐκχεῶ ἀπὸ
IN - THOSE~DAYS I WILL POUR OUT FROM

τοῦ πνεύματός μου,
THE SPIRIT OF ME,

καὶ προφητεύσουσιν.
AND THEY WILL PROPHESY.

2.19 καὶ δώσω τέρατα ἐν τῷ οὐρανῷ ἄνω
AND I WILL GIVE WONDERS IN THE HEAVEN ABOVE

καὶ σημεῖα ἐπὶ τῆς γῆς κάτω,
AND SIGNS ON THE EARTH BELOW,

αἷμα καὶ πῦρ καὶ ἀτμίδα καπνοῦ
BLOOD AND FIRE AND A VAPOR OF SMOKE.

2.20 ὁ ἥλιος μεταστραφήσεται εἰς σκότος
THE SUN WILL BE TRANSFORMED INTO DARKNESS

καὶ ἡ σελήνη εἰς αἷμα,
AND THE MOON INTO BLOOD,

πρὶν ἐλθεῖν ἡμέραν κυρίου τὴν
BEFORE TO COME ⁵DAY ⁶OF [THE] LORD ¹THE

μεγάλην καὶ ἐπιφανῆ.
²GREAT ³AND ⁴GLORIOUS.

2:17-21 Joel 2:28-32 LXX

2.21 καὶ ἔσται πᾶς ὃς ἂν ἐπικαλέσηται τὸ
AND IT WILL BE [THAT] EVERYONE WHOEVER CALLS UPON THE

ὄνομα κυρίου σωθήσεται.
NAME OF [THE] LORD WILL BE SAVED.

2.22 Ἄνδρες Ἰσραηλῖται, ἀκούσατε τοὺς
MEN, ISRAELITES, LISTEN -

λόγους τούτους· Ἰησοῦν τὸν Ναζωραῖον, ἄνδρα
TO THESE~WORDS: JESUS THE NAZARENE, A MAN

ἀποδεδειγμένον ἀπὸ τοῦ θεοῦ εἰς ὑμᾶς δυνάμεσι καὶ
HAVING BEEN ATTESTED BY - GOD TO YOU° WITH MIRACLES AND

τέρασι καὶ σημείοις οἷς ἐποίησεν δι᾽ αὐτοῦ ὁ
WONDERS AND SIGNS WHICH 2DID 3THROUGH 4HIM -

θεὸς ἐν μέσῳ ὑμῶν καθὼς αὐτοὶ οἴδατε, **2.23** τοῦτον
1GOD IN [THE] MIDST OF YOU° JUST AS YOURSELVES YOU° KNOW, THIS ONE

τῇ ὡρισμένῃ βουλῇ καὶ προγνώσει τοῦ θεοῦ
BY THE HAVING BEEN DETERMINED PURPOSE AND FOREKNOWLEDGE - OF GOD [WAS]

ἔκδοτον διὰ χειρὸς ἀνόμων προσπήξαντες
DELIVERED UP BY [THE] HAND OF LAWLESS MEN, HAVING NAILED [HIM TO THE CROSS]

ἀνείλατε, **2.24** ὃν ὁ θεὸς ἀνέστησεν λύσας τὰς
YOU° KILLED [HIM], WHOM - GOD RAISED HAVING DESTROYED THE

ὠδῖνας τοῦ θανάτου, καθότι οὐκ ἦν δυνατὸν
BIRTH PAINS - OF DEATH, BECAUSE IT WAS NOT POSSIBLE [FOR]

κρατεῖσθαι αὐτὸν ὑπ᾽ αὐτοῦ. **2.25** Δαυὶδ γὰρ λέγει εἰς
HIM~TO BE HELD BY IT. FOR~DAVID SAYS OF

αὐτόν,
HIM,

Προορώμην τὸν κύριον ἐνώπιόν μου διὰ παντός,
I WAS FORESEEING THE LORD BEFORE ME ALWAYS,

ὅτι ἐκ δεξιῶν μού ἐστιν ἵνα μὴ σαλευθῶ.
BECAUSE ON [THE] RIGHT OF ME HE IS THAT I MAY NOT BE SHAKEN.

2.26 διὰ τοῦτο ηὐφράνθη ἡ καρδία μου καὶ
THEREFORE, WAS CHEERED UP THE HEART OF ME AND

ἠγαλλιάσατο ἡ γλῶσσά μου,
EXULTED THE TONGUE OF ME,

ἔτι δὲ καὶ ἡ σάρξ μου κατασκηνώσει
AND~IN ADDITION ALSO THE BODY OF ME WILL LIVE

ἐπ᾽ ἐλπίδι,
IN HOPE,

2.27 ὅτι οὐκ ἐγκαταλείψεις τὴν ψυχήν μου εἰς
BECAUSE YOU WILL NOT ABANDON THE SOUL OF ME TO

ᾅδην
DESTRUCTION

οὐδὲ δώσεις τὸν ὅσιόν σου
NOR WILL YOU GIVE THE HOLY ONE OF YOU

ἰδεῖν διαφθοράν.
TO SEE CORRUPTION.

21 Then everyone who calls on the name of the Lord shall be saved.'
22 "You that are Israelites,[h] listen to what I have to say: Jesus of Nazareth,[i] a man attested to you by God with deeds of power, wonders, and signs that God did through him among you, as you yourselves know— 23this man, handed over to you according to the definite plan and foreknowledge of God, you crucified and killed by the hands of those outside the law. 24But God raised him up, having freed him from death,[j] because it was impossible for him to be held in its power. 25For David says concerning him,
'I saw the Lord always before me,
for he is at my right hand so that I will not be shaken;
26therefore my heart was glad, and my tongue rejoiced;
moreover my flesh will live in hope.
27For you will not abandon my soul to Hades, or let your Holy One experience corruption.

[h] Gk Men, Israelites
[i] Gk the Nazorean
[j] Gk the pains of death

2:25-28 Ps. 16:8-11 LXX

28 You have made known to
me the ways of life;
you will make me full
of gladness with
your presence.'
29 "Fellow Israelites,[k] I
may say to you confidently
of our ancestor David that he
both died and was buried,
and his tomb is with us to
this day. 30Since he was a
prophet, he knew that God
had sworn with an oath to
him that he would put one of
his descendants on his
throne. 31Foreseeing this,
David[l] spoke of the resurrection of the Messiah,[m]
saying,
'He was not abandoned
to Hades,
nor did his flesh
experience
corruption.'
32This Jesus God raised up,
and of that all of us are
witnesses. 33Being therefore
exalted at[n] the right hand of
God, and having received
from the Father the promise
of the Holy Spirit, he has
poured out this that you both
see and hear. 34For David
did not ascend into the
heavens, but he himself
says,
'The Lord said to my
Lord,
"Sit at my right hand,
35   until I make your
enemies your
footstool."'

[k] Gk Men, brothers
[l] Gk he
[m] Or the Christ
[n] Or by

2.28 ἐγνώρισάς μοι ὁδοὺς ζωῆς,
YOU MADE KNOWN TO ME [THE] WAYS OF LIFE,

πληρώσεις με εὐφροσύνης μετὰ τοῦ προσώπου
YOU WILL FILL ME WITH JOY WITH THE PRESENCE

σου.
OF YOU.

2.29 Ἄνδρες ἀδελφοί, ἐξὸν εἰπεῖν μετὰ
MEN, BROTHERS, IT IS PERMITTED TO SPEAK WITH

παρρησίας πρὸς ὑμᾶς περὶ τοῦ πατριάρχου Δαυὶδ ὅτι
CONFIDENCE TO YOU° ABOUT THE PATRIARCH DAVID THAT

καὶ ἐτελεύτησεν καὶ ἐτάφη, καὶ τὸ μνῆμα αὐτοῦ
ALSO HE DIED AND WAS BURIED, AND THE TOMB OF HIM

ἔστιν ἐν ἡμῖν ἄχρι τῆς ἡμέρας ταύτης.
IS WITH US UNTIL - THIS~DAY.

2.30 προφήτης οὖν ὑπάρχων, καὶ εἰδὼς ὅτι ὅρκῳ
THEREFORE~A PROPHET BEING, AND HAVING KNOWN THAT WITH AN OATH

ὤμοσεν αὐτῷ ὁ θεὸς ἐκ καρποῦ τῆς ὀσφύος αὐτοῦ
SWORE TO HIM - GOD FROM [THE] FRUIT OF THE LOINS OF HIM

καθίσαι ἐπὶ τὸν θρόνον αὐτοῦ, **2.31** προϊδὼν
TO SIT UPON THE THRONE OF HIM, HAVING FORESEEN [IT]

ἐλάλησεν περὶ τῆς ἀναστάσεως τοῦ Χριστοῦ ὅτι
HE SPOKE ABOUT THE RESURRECTION - OF CHRIST -

οὔτε ἐγκατελείφθη εἰς ᾅδην
NEITHER WAS HE ABANDONED TO DESTRUCTION

οὔτε ἡ σὰρξ αὐτοῦ εἶδεν διαφθοράν.
NOR THE BODY OF HIM SAW CORRUPTION.

2.32 τοῦτον τὸν Ἰησοῦν ἀνέστησεν ὁ θεός, οὗ
THIS - JESUS ²RAISED - ¹GOD, OF WHICH

πάντες ἡμεῖς ἐσμεν μάρτυρες· **2.33** τῇ δεξιᾷ οὖν τοῦ
WE~ALL ARE WITNESSES. TO THE RIGHT THEN -

θεοῦ ὑψωθείς, τήν τε ἐπαγγελίαν τοῦ πνεύματος
OF GOD HAVING BEEN EXALTED, AND~THE PROMISE OF THE ²SPIRIT

τοῦ ἁγίου λαβὼν παρὰ τοῦ πατρός, ἐξέχεεν τοῦτο
- ¹HOLY HAVING RECEIVED FROM THE FATHER, HE POURED OUT THIS

ὃ ὑμεῖς [καὶ] βλέπετε καὶ ἀκούετε. **2.34** οὐ γὰρ
WHICH YOU° ALSO SEE AND HEAR. FOR~NOT

Δαυὶδ ἀνέβη εἰς τοὺς οὐρανούς, λέγει δὲ αὐτός,
DAVID ASCENDED INTO THE HEAVENS, BUT~SAYS HE,

Εἶπεν [ὁ] κύριος τῷ κυρίῳ μου,
SAID THE LORD TO THE LORD OF ME,

Κάθου ἐκ δεξιῶν μου,
SIT DOWN AT [THE] RIGHT OF ME,

2.35 ἕως ἂν θῶ τοὺς ἐχθρούς σου ὑποπόδιον
UNTIL I MAKE THE ENEMIES OF YOU A FOOTSTOOL

τῶν ποδῶν σου.
OF THE FEET OF YOU.

2:30 Ps. 132:11   **2:31** Ps. 16:10   **2:34-35** Ps. 110:1

2.36 ἀσφαλῶς οὖν   γινωσκέτω πᾶς οἶκος   Ἰσραὴλ
THEREFORE~ASSUREDLY LET KNOW   ALL   [THE] HOUSE OF ISRAEL

ὅτι καὶ κύριον αὐτὸν καὶ Χριστὸν ἐποίησεν ὁ θεός,
THAT ⁴BOTH ⁵LORD ³HIM ⁶AND ⁷CHRIST ²MADE   - ¹GOD,

τοῦτον τὸν Ἰησοῦν ὃν ὑμεῖς ἐσταυρώσατε.
THIS   -   JESUS WHOM YOU° CRUCIFIED.

2.37 Ἀκούσαντες δὲ κατενύγησαν τὴν καρδίαν
AND~HAVING HEARD [THIS] THEY WERE PIERCED IN THE HEART

εἶπόν τε   πρὸς τὸν Πέτρον καὶ τοὺς λοιποὺς
AND~THEY SAID TO -   PETER   AND THE OTHER

ἀποστόλους, Τί   ποιήσωμεν, ἄνδρες ἀδελφοί;
APOSTLES,   WHAT SHOULD WE DO, MEN,   BROTHERS?

2.38 Πέτρος δὲ   πρὸς αὐτούς, Μετανοήσατε, [φησίν,] καὶ
AND~PETER [SAID] TO THEM,   REPENT,   HE SAYS,   AND

βαπτισθήτω ἕκαστος ὑμῶν ἐπὶ τῷ ὀνόματι Ἰησοῦ
LET BE BAPTIZED EACH OF YOU° IN THE NAME   OF JESUS

Χριστοῦ εἰς ἄφεσιν   τῶν ἁμαρτιῶν ὑμῶν καὶ
CHRIST FOR [THE] FORGIVENESS OF THE SINS   OF YOU° AND

λήμψεσθε   τὴν δωρεὰν τοῦ ἁγίου πνεύματος.
YOU° WILL RECEIVE THE GIFT   OF THE HOLY SPIRIT.

2.39 ὑμῖν γάρ ἐστιν ἡ ἐπαγγελία καὶ τοῖς τέκνοις
FOR~TO YOU° IS THE PROMISE   AND TO THE CHILDREN

ὑμῶν καὶ πᾶσιν τοῖς εἰς μακρὰν, ὅσους ἂν
OF YOU° AND TO ALL THE ONES AT A DISTANCE, AS MANY AS

προσκαλέσηται κύριος ὁ θεὸς ἡμῶν. **2.40** ἑτέροις τε
MAY CALL TO   [THE] LORD THE GOD OF US.   AND~WITH OTHER

λόγοις πλείοσιν διεμαρτύρατο καὶ παρεκάλει αὐτοὺς
WORDS MANY   HE TESTIFIED   AND WAS APPEALING TO THEM

λέγων, Σώθητε ἀπὸ τῆς γενεᾶς τῆς σκολιᾶς ταύτης.
SAYING, BE SAVED FROM - ³GENERATION - ²CROOKED ¹THIS.

2.41 οἱ   μὲν οὖν ἀποδεξάμενοι τὸν λόγον αὐτοῦ
THE ONES -   THEN HAVING WELCOMED THE WORD OF HIM

ἐβαπτίσθησαν καὶ προσετέθησαν ἐν τῇ ἡμέρᾳ ἐκείνῃ
WERE BAPTIZED AND THERE WERE ADDED IN - THAT~DAY

ψυχαὶ ὡσεὶ τρισχίλιαι. **2.42** ἦσαν δὲ προσκαρτεροῦντες
SOULS ABOUT THREE THOUSAND.   AND~THEY WERE DEVOTING [THEMSELVES]

τῇ   διδαχῇ τῶν ἀποστόλων καὶ τῇ κοινωνίᾳ, τῇ
TO THE TEACHING OF THE APOSTLES AND TO THE FELLOWSHIP, THE

κλάσει τοῦ ἄρτου καὶ ταῖς προσευχαῖς.
BREAKING - OF BREAD, AND - TO PRAYERS.

2.43 Ἐγίνετο δὲ   πάσῃ ψυχῇ φόβος, πολλά τε τέρατα
AND~WAS OCCURRING IN EVERY SOUL AWE, AND~MANY WONDERS

καὶ σημεῖα διὰ   τῶν ἀποστόλων ἐγίνετο.
AND SIGNS THROUGH THE APOSTLES WERE BEING PERFORMED.

2.44 πάντες δὲ οἱ   πιστεύοντες ἦσαν ἐπὶ τὸ αὐτὸ
AND~ALL THE ONES BELIEVING WERE AT THE SAME [PLACE]

καὶ εἶχον   ἅπαντα κοινά **2.45** καὶ τὰ κτήματα
AND THEY WERE HAVING ALL THINGS IN COMMON, AND THE PROPERTIES

36Therefore let the entire house of Israel know with certainty that God has made him both Lord and Messiah,ᵒ this Jesus whom you crucified."

37 Now when they heard this, they were cut to the heart and said to Peter and to the other apostles, "Brothers,ᵖ what should we do?" 38Peter said to them, "Repent, and be baptized every one of you in the name of Jesus Christ so that your sins may be forgiven; and you will receive the gift of the Holy Spirit. 39For the promise is for you, for your children, and for all who are far away, everyone whom the Lord our God calls to him." 40And he testified with many other arguments and exhorted them, saying, "Save yourselves from this corrupt generation." 41So those who welcomed his message were baptized, and that day about three thousand persons were added. 42They devoted themselves to the apostles' teaching and fellowship, to the breaking of bread and the prayers.

43 Awe came upon everyone, because many wonders and signs were being done by the apostles. 44All who believed were together and had all things in common; 45they would sell

ᵒ Or Christ
ᵖ Gk Men, brothers

their possessions and goods and distribute the proceeds*q* to all, as any had need. [46]Day by day, as they spent much time together in the temple, they broke bread at home*r* and ate their food with glad and generous*s* hearts, [47]praising God and having the goodwill of all the people. And day by day the Lord added to their number those who were being saved.

q Gk *them*
r Or *from house to house*
s Or *sincere*

καὶ   τὰς   ὑπάρξεις   ἐπίπρασκον   καὶ   διεμέριζον
AND   THE   POSSESSIONS   THEY WERE SELLING   AND   WERE DISTRIBUTING

αὐτὰ   πᾶσιν   καθότι ἄν τις   χρείαν εἶχεν·
THESE THINGS   TO EVERYONE   AS   SOMEONE   HAD~NEED.

2.46 καθ᾿ ἡμέραν τε προσκαρτεροῦντες ὁμοθυμαδὸν
AND~DAY BY DAY   DEVOTING [THEMSELVES]   WITH ONE MIND

ἐν τῷ   ἱερῷ,   κλῶντές τε κατ᾿ οἶκον   ἄρτον,
IN   THE   TEMPLE,   AND~BREAKING   [2]FROM HOUSE TO HOUSE   [1]BREAD,

μετελάμβανον τροφῆς ἐν ἀγαλλιάσει καὶ ἀφελότητι
THEY WERE SHARING   FOOD   WITH   EXULTATION   AND   SIMPLICITY

καρδίας **2.47** αἰνοῦντες τὸν θεὸν καὶ ἔχοντες χάριν
OF HEART,   PRAISING   -   GOD   AND   HAVING   FAVOR

πρὸς ὅλον τὸν λαόν. ὁ δὲ   κύριος προσετίθει τοὺς
WITH   ALL   THE   PEOPLE.   AND~THE LORD   WAS ADDING   TO THE ONES

σῳζομένους καθ᾿ ἡμέραν ἐπὶ τὸ αὐτό.
BEING SAVED   DAY BY DAY   IN   THE   SAME [PLACE].

CHAPTER 3

One day Peter and John were going up to the temple at the hour of prayer, at three o'clock in the afternoon. [2]And a man lame from birth was being carried in. People would lay him daily at the gate of the temple called the Beautiful Gate so that he could ask for alms from those entering the temple. [3]When he saw Peter and John about to go into the temple, he asked them for alms. [4]Peter looked intently at him, as did John, and said, "Look at us." [5]And he fixed his attention on them, expecting to receive something from them. [6]But Peter said, "I have no silver or gold, but what I have I give you; in the name of Jesus Christ of Nazareth,*t* stand up and

t Gk *the Nazorean*

3.1 Πέτρος δὲ καὶ Ἰωάννης ἀνέβαινον εἰς τὸ ἱερὸν
NOW~PETER   AND   JOHN   WERE GOING UP   TO   THE TEMPLE

ἐπὶ τὴν ὥραν τῆς προσευχῆς τὴν ἐνάτην. **3.2** καί
AT   THE   HOUR   -   OF PRAYER   THE   NINTH.   AND

τις   ἀνὴρ χωλὸς ἐκ κοιλίας μητρὸς   αὐτοῦ
A CERTAIN MAN   LAME   FROM [THE] WOMB OF [THE] MOTHER   OF HIM

ὑπάρχων ἐβαστάζετο,   ὃν   ἐτίθουν   καθ᾿ ἡμέραν
BEING,   WAS BEING CARRIED,   WHOM   THEY WERE PUTTING   DAY BY DAY

πρὸς τὴν θύραν τοῦ ἱεροῦ τὴν λεγομένην Ὡραίαν
AT   THE   DOOR   OF THE TEMPLE,   THE ONE   BEING CALLED   BEAUTIFUL

τοῦ αἰτεῖν ἐλεημοσύνην παρὰ τῶν   εἰσπορευομένων
-   TO BEG   ALMS   FROM   THE ONES   ENTERING

εἰς τὸ ἱερόν· **3.3** ὃς ἰδὼν   Πέτρον καὶ Ἰωάννην
INTO THE TEMPLE;   WHO HAVING SEEN PETER   AND   JOHN

μέλλοντας εἰσιέναι εἰς τὸ ἱερόν, ἠρώτα
BEING ABOUT   TO ENTER   INTO THE TEMPLE,   WAS BEGGING

ἐλεημοσύνην λαβεῖν. **3.4** ἀτενίσας δὲ Πέτρος εἰς αὐτὸν
TO RECEIVE~ALMS.   BUT~HAVING GAZED   PETER   AT   HIM

σὺν τῷ Ἰωάννῃ εἶπεν, Βλέψον εἰς ἡμᾶς. **3.5** ὁ δὲ
WITH   -   JOHN   HE SAID,   LOOK   AT US.   -   AND

ἐπεῖχεν   αὐτοῖς προσδοκῶν τι   παρ᾿ αὐτῶν
HE WAS PAYING ATTENTION   TO THEM   EXPECTING   SOMETHING FROM   THEM

λαβεῖν. **3.6** εἶπεν δὲ Πέτρος, Ἀργύριον καὶ χρυσίον
TO RECEIVE.   AND~SAID   PETER,   SILVER   AND   GOLD

οὐχ ὑπάρχει μοι, ὃ δὲ   ἔχω τοῦτό σοι δίδωμι·   ἐν τῷ
IS NOT POSSESSED   BY ME, BUT~WHAT I HAVE, THIS   I GIVE~TO YOU: IN   THE

ὀνόματι Ἰησοῦ Χριστοῦ τοῦ Ναζωραίου [ἔγειρε καὶ]
NAME   OF JESUS   CHRIST,   THE   NAZARENE   GET UP   AND

περιπάτει. **3.7** καὶ πιάσας αὐτὸν τῆς δεξιᾶς χειρὸς
WALK.   AND   HAVING GRASPED   HIM   BY THE   RIGHT   HAND

ἤγειρεν αὐτόν· παραχρῆμα δὲ ἐστερεώθησαν αἱ
HE RAISED UP HIM.   AND~IMMEDIATELY   WERE STRENGTHENED   THE

βάσεις αὐτοῦ καὶ τὰ σφυδρά, **3.8** καὶ ἐξαλλόμενος
FEET   OF HIM   AND   THE   ANKLES,   AND   LEAPING UP

ἔστη καὶ περιεπάτει καὶ εἰσῆλθεν σὺν αὐτοῖς εἰς
HE STOOD AND   WAS WALKING AROUND   AND   HE ENTERED   WITH   THEM   INTO

τὸ ἱερὸν περιπατῶν καὶ ἀλλόμενος καὶ αἰνῶν τὸν
THE TEMPLE   WALKING   AND   LEAPING   AND   PRAISING -

θεόν. **3.9** καὶ εἶδεν πᾶς ὁ λαὸς αὐτὸν περιπατοῦντα
GOD.   AND   SAW   ALL   THE PEOPLE   HIM   WALKING

καὶ αἰνοῦντα τὸν θεόν· **3.10** ἐπεγίνωσκον δὲ αὐτὸν ὅτι
AND   PRAISING   -   GOD.   AND~THEY RECOGNIZED   HIM   THAT

αὐτὸς ἦν ὁ πρὸς τὴν ἐλεημοσύνην καθήμενος ἐπὶ
HE   WAS THE ONE FOR   -   ALMS   SITTING   AT

τῇ Ὡραίᾳ Πύλῃ τοῦ ἱεροῦ καὶ ἐπλήσθησαν θάμβους
THE BEAUTIFUL   GATE   OF THE TEMPLE   AND   THEY WERE FILLED   WITH WONDER

καὶ ἐκστάσεως ἐπὶ τῷ συμβεβηκότι αὐτῷ.
AND   AMAZEMENT   AT   THE THING HAVING HAPPENED   TO HIM.

3.11 Κρατοῦντος δὲ αὐτοῦ τὸν Πέτρον καὶ τὸν
NOW~[WHILE] HOLDING   HIM,   -   PETER   AND   -

Ἰωάννην συνέδραμεν πᾶς ὁ λαὸς πρὸς αὐτοὺς ἐπὶ
JOHN   RAN TOGETHER   ALL   THE PEOPLE TO   THEM   AT

τῇ στοᾷ τῇ καλουμένῃ Σολομῶντος ἔκθαμβοι.
THE PORTICO   THE ONE BEING CALLED   OF SOLOMON,   UTTERLY ASTONISHED.

3.12 ἰδὼν δὲ ὁ Πέτρος ἀπεκρίνατο πρὸς τὸν
AND~HAVING SEEN [THIS] - PETER   ANSWERED   TO   THE

λαόν, Ἄνδρες Ἰσραηλῖται, τί θαυμάζετε ἐπὶ τούτῳ
PEOPLE, MEN,   ISRAELITES,   WHY ARE YOU° MARVELING   AT   THIS

ἢ ἡμῖν τί ἀτενίζετε ὡς ἰδίᾳ δυνάμει ἢ εὐσεβείᾳ
OR AT US WHY ARE YOU° GAZING AS [IF] BY OUR OWN POWER   OR GODLINESS

πεποιηκόσιν τοῦ περιπατεῖν αὐτόν; **3.13** ὁ θεὸς
HAVING MADE   -   HIM~TO WALK?   THE GOD

Ἀβραὰμ καὶ [ὁ θεὸς] Ἰσαὰκ καὶ [ὁ θεὸς] Ἰακώβ, ὁ
OF ABRAHAM AND   THE GOD   OF ISAAC   AND   THE GOD   OF JACOB, THE

θεὸς τῶν πατέρων ἡμῶν, ἐδόξασεν τὸν παῖδα αὐτοῦ
GOD   OF THE FATHERS   OF US,   GLORIFIED   THE SERVANT   OF HIM

Ἰησοῦν ὃν ὑμεῖς μὲν παρεδώκατε καὶ ἠρνήσασθε
JESUS,   WHOM YOU°   -   DELIVERED OVER   AND   DENIED

κατὰ πρόσωπον Πιλάτου, κρίναντος ἐκείνου
IN THE PRESENCE   OF PILATE,   HAVING DECIDED THAT [OTHER] ONE

ἀπολύειν· **3.14** ὑμεῖς δὲ τὸν ἅγιον καὶ δίκαιον
TO RELEASE.   BUT~YOU°   THE HOLY   AND   RIGHTEOUS ONE

ἠρνήσασθε καὶ ᾐτήσασθε ἄνδρα φονέα χαρισθῆναι
DENIED,   AND   YOU° REQUESTED A MAN,   A MURDERER TO BE GRANTED

3:13 Exod. 3:6, 15

walk." [7] And he took him by the right hand and raised him up; and immediately his feet and ankles were made strong. [8] Jumping up, he stood and began to walk, and he entered the temple with them, walking and leaping and praising God. [9] All the people saw him walking and praising God, [10] and they recognized him as the one who used to sit and ask for alms at the Beautiful Gate of the temple; and they were filled with wonder and amazement at what had happened to him.

11 While he clung to Peter and John, all the people ran together to them in the portico called Solomon's Portico, utterly astonished. [12] When Peter saw it, he addressed the people, "You Israelites,[u] why do you wonder at this, or why do you stare at us, as though by our own power or piety we had made him walk? [13] The God of Abraham, the God of Isaac, and the God of Jacob, the God of our ancestors has glorified his servant[v] Jesus, whom you handed over and rejected in the presence of Pilate, though he had decided to release him. [14] But you rejected the Holy and Righteous One and asked to have a murderer

[u] Gk *Men, Israelites*
[v] Or *child*

given to you, [15]and you killed the Author of life, whom God raised from the dead. To this we are witnesses. [16]And by faith in his name, his name itself has made this man strong, whom you see and know; and the faith that is through Jesus[w] has given him this perfect health in the presence of all of you.

[17] "And now, friends,[x] I know that you acted in ignorance, as did also your rulers. [18]In this way God fulfilled what he had foretold through all the prophets, that his Messiah[y] would suffer. [19]Repent therefore, and turn to God so that your sins may be wiped out, [20]so that times of refreshing may come from the presence of the Lord, and that he may send the Messiah[z] appointed for you, that is, Jesus, [21]who must remain in heaven until the time of universal restoration that God announced long ago through his holy prophets. [22]Moses said, 'The Lord your God will raise up for you from your own people[x] a prophet like me. You must listen to whatever he tells you. [23]And it will be that everyone who does not listen to that prophet will be utterly rooted out of the people.'

[w] Gk *him*
[x] Gk *brothers*
[y] Or *his Christ*
[z] Or *the Christ*

ὑμῖν, **3.15** τὸν δὲ ἀρχηγὸν τῆς ζωῆς ἀπεκτείνατε ὃν ὁ
TO YOU°,   BUT~THE AUTHOR   -   OF LIFE YOU° KILLED,   WHOM -

θεὸς ἤγειρεν ἐκ νεκρῶν, οὗ ἡμεῖς μάρτυρές ἐσμεν.
GOD RAISED FROM [THE] DEAD, OF WHICH WE   ARE~WITNESSES.

3.16 καὶ ἐπὶ   τῇ πίστει τοῦ ὀνόματος αὐτοῦ
        AND ON THE BASIS OF THE FAITH IN THE NAME   OF HIM,

τοῦτον ὃν θεωρεῖτε καὶ οἴδατε, ἐστερέωσεν τὸ ὄνομα
THIS ONE WHOM YOU° SEE   AND KNOW,   ⁴MADE STRONG ¹THE ²NAME

αὐτοῦ, καὶ ἡ πίστις ἡ δι' αὐτοῦ ἔδωκεν αὐτῷ τὴν
³OF HIM, AND THE FAITH - THROUGH HIM GAVE   TO HIM -

ὁλοκληρίαν ταύτην ἀπέναντι πάντων ὑμῶν. **3.17** καὶ
THIS~WHOLENESS   BEFORE   ALL   OF YOU°.   AND

νῦν, ἀδελφοί, οἶδα ὅτι κατὰ   ἄγνοιαν ἐπράξατε
NOW, BROTHERS, I KNOW THAT ACCORDING TO IGNORANCE YOU° ACTED,

ὥσπερ καὶ οἱ ἄρχοντες ὑμῶν· **3.18** ὁ δὲ θεός,
AS   ALSO THE AUTHORITIES OF YOU°.   - BUT GOD,

ἃ   προκατήγγειλεν διὰ στόματος πάντων
THE THINGS WHICH HE ANNOUNCED BEFOREHAND THROUGH [THE] MOUTH   OF ALL

τῶν προφητῶν παθεῖν τὸν Χριστὸν αὐτοῦ, ἐπλήρωσεν
THE PROPHETS [THAT] TO SUFFER THE CHRIST   OF HIM   HE FULFILLED

οὕτως. **3.19** μετανοήσατε οὖν καὶ ἐπιστρέψατε εἰς
THUS.   THEREFORE,~REPENT   AND TURN   IN ORDER THAT

τὸ ἐξαλειφθῆναι ὑμῶν τὰς ἁμαρτίας, **3.20** ὅπως ἂν
- TO BE REMOVED   OF YOU° THE SINS,   IN ORDER THAT

ἔλθωσιν καιροὶ ἀναψύξεως ἀπὸ προσώπου τοῦ κυρίου
MAY COME TIMES OF REST   FROM [THE] PRESENCE OF THE LORD

καὶ ἀποστείλῃ τὸν προκεχειρισμένον ὑμῖν
AND HE MAY SEND THE ONE HAVING BEEN PROCLAIMED BEFOREHAND TO YOU°,

Χριστὸν Ἰησοῦν, **3.21** ὃν δεῖ οὐρανὸν μὲν
[THE] CHRIST, JESUS,   WHOM IT IS NECESSARY FOR HEAVEN -

δέξασθαι ἄχρι χρόνων ἀποκαταστάσεως πάντων ὧν
TO RECEIVE UNTIL [THE] TIMES OF RESTORATION   OF ALL THINGS OF WHICH

ἐλάλησεν ὁ θεὸς διὰ στόματος τῶν ἁγίων ἀπ'
SPOKE   - GOD THROUGH [THE] MOUTH OF THE HOLY ²FROM

αἰῶνος αὐτοῦ προφητῶν. **3.22** Μωϋσῆς μὲν εἶπεν ὅτι
³[THE] AGE ⁴OF HIM ¹PROPHETS.   MOSES   INDEED SAID -

Προφήτην ὑμῖν ἀναστήσει κύριος ὁ θεὸς ὑμῶν ἐκ
A PROPHET FOR YOU° WILL RAISE UP [THE] LORD THE GOD OF YOU° FROM

τῶν ἀδελφῶν ὑμῶν ὡς ἐμέ· αὐτοῦ ἀκούσεσθε κατὰ
THE BROTHERS OF YOU° LIKE ME.   YOU° WILL LISTEN~TO HIM ACCORDING TO

ἐκ πάντα ὅσα ἂν λαλήσῃ πρὸς ὑμᾶς.
- EVERYTHING WHATEVER HE MAY SPEAK TO   YOU°.

3.23 ἔσται δὲ πᾶσα ψυχὴ ἥτις ἐὰν μὴ ἀκούσῃ τοῦ
       AND~IT WILL BE [THAT] EVERY SOUL WHOEVER DOES NOT LISTEN TO -

προφήτου ἐκείνου ἐξολεθρευθήσεται ἐκ τοῦ λαοῦ.
THAT~PROPHET   WILL BE UTTERLY DESTROYED FROM THE PEOPLE.

3:22 Deut. 18:15-16   **3:23a** Deut. 18:19   **3:23b** Lev. 23:29

3.24 καὶ   πάντες   δὲ   οἱ   προφῆται   ἀπὸ   Σαμουὴλ   καὶ   τῶν
AND   ALSO~ALL   THE   PROPHETS   FROM   SAMUEL   AND   THE

καθεξῆς   ὅσοι   ἐλάλησαν   καὶ   κατήγγειλαν   τὰς
SUCCESSORS [OF HIM],   AS MANY AS   SPOKE   ALSO   ANNOUNCED   -

ἡμέρας ταύτας.   **3.25** ὑμεῖς   ἐστε   οἱ   υἱοὶ   τῶν   προφητῶν
THIS~DAY.   YOU°   ARE   THE   SONS   OF THE   PROPHETS

καὶ   τῆς   διαθήκης   ἧς   διέθετο   ὁ   θεὸς   πρὸς   τοὺς
AND   OF THE   COVENANT   WHICH   DECREED   -   GOD   TO   THE

πατέρας   ὑμῶν   λέγων   πρὸς   Ἀβραάμ,   Καὶ   ἐν   τῷ
FATHERS   OF YOU°   SAYING   TO   ABRAHAM,   AND   IN   THE

σπέρματί   σου   [ἐν]ευλογηθήσονται   πᾶσαι   αἱ   πατριαὶ
SEED   OF YOU   WILL BE BLESSED   ALL   THE   FAMILIES

τῆς   γῆς.   **3.26** ὑμῖν   πρῶτον   ἀναστήσας   ὁ   θεὸς   τὸν
OF THE EARTH.   TO YOU°   FIRST   ²HAVING RAISED   -   ¹GOD   THE

παῖδα   αὐτοῦ   ἀπέστειλεν   αὐτὸν   εὐλογοῦντα   ὑμᾶς   ἐν
SERVANT   OF HIM   HE SENT   HIM   BLESSING   YOU°   BY

τῷ   ἀποστρέφειν   ἕκαστον   ἀπὸ   τῶν   πονηριῶν   ὑμῶν.
THE   TURNING AWAY   EACH [ONE]   FROM   THE   WICKED [WAYS]   OF YOU°.

3:25 Gen. 22:18; 26:4

24 And all the prophets, as many as have spoken, from Samuel and those after him, also predicted these days. 25You are the descendants of the prophets and of the covenant that God gave to your ancestors, saying to Abraham, 'And in your descendants all the families of the earth shall be blessed.' 26When God raised up his servant,ᵃ he sent him first to you, to bless you by turning each of you from your wicked ways."

ᵃ Or child

4.1 Λαλούντων   δὲ   αὐτῶν   πρὸς   τὸν   λαὸν   ἐπέστησαν
NOW~ [WHILE] ²WERE SPEAKING ¹THEY   TO   THE   PEOPLE,   APPROACHED

αὐτοῖς   οἱ   ἱερεῖς   καὶ   ὁ   στρατηγὸς   τοῦ   ἱεροῦ   καὶ
THEM   THE   PRIESTS   AND   THE   CAPTAIN   OF THE   TEMPLE   AND

οἱ   Σαδδουκαῖοι,   **4.2** διαπονούμενοι   διὰ   τὸ
THE   SADDUCEES,   BEING GREATLY ANNOYED   BECAUSE   -

διδάσκειν   αὐτοὺς   τὸν   λαὸν   καὶ   καταγγέλλειν   ἐν   τῷ
THEY~TEACH   THE   PEOPLE   AND   ANNOUNCE   BY   -

Ἰησοῦ   τὴν   ἀνάστασιν   τὴν   ἐκ   νεκρῶν,   **4.3** καὶ
JESUS   THE   RESURRECTION   -   FROM   [THE] DEAD,   AND

ἐπέβαλον   αὐτοῖς   τὰς   χεῖρας   καὶ   ἔθεντο   εἰς
THEY LAID ON   THEM   THE(THEIR)   HANDS   AND   PUT [THEM]   IN

τήρησιν   εἰς   τὴν   αὔριον·   ἦν   γὰρ   ἑσπέρα   ἤδη.
JAIL   INTO   THE   NEXT DAY.   FOR~IT WAS   EVENING   ALREADY.

4.4 πολλοὶ   δὲ   τῶν   ἀκουσάντων   τὸν   λόγον
AND~MANY   OF THE ONES   HAVING LISTENED TO   THE   WORD

ἐπίστευσαν   καὶ   ἐγενήθη   [ὁ]   ἀριθμὸς   τῶν   ἀνδρῶν
BELIEVED,   AND   BECAME   THE   NUMBER   OF THE   MEN

[ὡς]   χιλιάδες   πέντε.
ABOUT   FIVE~THOUSAND.

4.5 Ἐγένετο   δὲ   ἐπὶ   τὴν   αὔριον   συναχθῆναι   αὐτῶν
AND~IT CAME ABOUT   ON   THE   NEXT DAY   TO BE ASSEMBLED   OF THEM

τοὺς   ἄρχοντας   καὶ   τοὺς   πρεσβυτέρους   καὶ   τοὺς
THE   RULERS   AND   THE   ELDERS   AND   THE

γραμματεῖς   ἐν   Ἰερουσαλήμ,   **4.6** καὶ   Ἄννας   ὁ
SCRIBES   IN   JERUSALEM,   AND   ANNAS   THE

While Peter and Johnᵇ were speaking to the people, the priests, the captain of the temple, and the Sadducees came to them, 2much annoyed because they were teaching the people and proclaiming that in Jesus there is the resurrection of the dead. 3So they arrested them and put them in custody until the next day, for it was already evening. 4But many of those who heard the word believed; and they numbered about five thousand.

5 The next day their rulers, elders, and scribes assembled in Jerusalem, 6with Annas the high

ᵇ Gk *While they*

priest, Caiaphas, John,*c* and Alexander, and all who were of the high-priestly family. [7]When they had made the prisoners*d* stand in their midst, they inquired, "By what power or by what name did you do this?" [8]Then Peter, filled with the Holy Spirit, said to them, "Rulers of the people and elders, [9]if we are questioned today because of a good deed done to someone who was sick and are asked how this man has been healed, [10]let it be known to all of you, and to all the people of Israel, that this man is standing before you in good health by the name of Jesus Christ of Nazareth,*e* whom you crucified, whom God raised from the dead. [11]This Jesus*f* is

'the stone that was rejected by you, the builders; it has become the cornerstone.'*g*

[12]There is salvation in no one else, for there is no other name under heaven given among mortals by which we must be saved."

13 Now when they saw the boldness of Peter and John and realized that they were uneducated and ordinary men, they were amazed and recognized them as companions of Jesus. [14]When they saw the

c Other ancient authorities read *Jonathan*
d Gk *them*
e Gk *the Nazorean*
f Gk *This*
g Or *keystone*

ἀρχιερεὺς καὶ Καϊάφας καὶ Ἰωάννης καὶ
HIGH PRIEST AND CAIAPHAS AND JOHN AND

Ἀλέξανδρος καὶ ὅσοι ἦσαν ἐκ γένους ἀρχιερατικοῦ,
ALEXANDER AND AS MANY AS WERE OF HIGH-PRIESTLY~DESCENT,

4.7 καὶ στήσαντες αὐτοὺς ἐν τῷ μέσῳ ἐπυνθάνοντο,
AND HAVING PLACED THEM IN THE MIDST THEY WERE INQUIRING,

Ἐν ποίᾳ δυνάμει ἢ ἐν ποίῳ ὀνόματι ἐποιήσατε τοῦτο
BY WHAT POWER OR BY WHAT NAME DID THIS

ὑμεῖς; **4.8** τότε Πέτρος πλησθεὶς πνεύματος ἁγίου
YOU°? THEN PETER HAVING BEEN FILLED WITH [THE] HOLY~SPIRIT

εἶπεν πρὸς αὐτούς, Ἄρχοντες τοῦ λαοῦ καὶ
SAID TO THEM, RULERS OF THE PEOPLE AND

πρεσβύτεροι, **4.9** εἰ ἡμεῖς σήμερον ἀνακρινόμεθα
ELDERS, IF WE TODAY ARE BEING EXAMINED

ἐπὶ εὐεργεσίᾳ ἀνθρώπου ἀσθενοῦς ἐν
ON ACCOUNT OF [THE] KINDNESS [SHOWN TO] A HANDICAPPED~MAN, BY

τίνι οὗτος σέσωται, **4.10** γνωστὸν ἔστω πᾶσιν
WHAT [MEANS] THIS ONE HAS BEEN HEALED, LET IT BE~KNOWN TO ALL

ὑμῖν καὶ παντὶ τῷ λαῷ Ἰσραὴλ ὅτι ἐν τῷ ὀνόματι
YOU° AND TO ALL THE PEOPLE OF ISRAEL THAT IN THE NAME

Ἰησοῦ Χριστοῦ τοῦ Ναζωραίου ὃν ὑμεῖς ἐσταυρώσατε,
OF JESUS CHRIST THE NAZARENE WHOM YOU° CRUCIFIED,

ὃν ὁ θεὸς ἤγειρεν ἐκ νεκρῶν, ἐν τούτῳ οὗτος
WHOM - GOD RAISED FROM [THE] DEAD, BY THIS [NAME] THIS ONE

παρέστηκεν ἐνώπιον ὑμῶν ὑγιής. **4.11** οὗτός ἐστιν
HAS STOOD BEFORE YOU° HEALTHY. THIS IS

ὁ λίθος, ὁ ἐξουθενηθεὶς ὑφ' ὑμῶν τῶν οἰκοδόμων,
THE STONE, - HAVING BEEN REJECTED BY YOU° THE [ONES] BUILDING,

ὁ γενόμενος εἰς κεφαλὴν γωνίας.
THE ONE HAVING BECOME - [THE] HEAD OF [THE] CORNER.

4.12 καὶ οὐκ ἔστιν ἐν ἄλλῳ οὐδενὶ ἡ σωτηρία, οὐδὲ
AND THERE IS NOT IN ANY~OTHER, - SALVATION, [3]NO

γὰρ ὄνομά ἐστιν ἕτερον ὑπὸ τὸν οὐρανὸν τὸ
[1]FOR [5]NAME [2]THERE IS [4]OTHER UNDER - HEAVEN -

δεδομένον ἐν ἀνθρώποις ἐν ᾧ δεῖ
HAVING BEEN GIVEN AMONG MEN BY WHICH IT IS NECESSARY

σωθῆναι ἡμᾶς. **4.13** Θεωροῦντες δὲ τὴν τοῦ
FOR YOU°~TO BE SAVED. AND~OBSERVING THE -

Πέτρου παρρησίαν καὶ Ἰωάννου καὶ καταλαβόμενοι
CONFIDENCE~OF PETER AND JOHN AND HAVING PERCEIVED

ὅτι ἄνθρωποι ἀγράμματοί εἰσιν καὶ ἰδιῶται,
THAT UNEDUCATED~MEN THEY ARE AND UNTRAINED,

ἐθαύμαζον ἐπεγίνωσκόν τε αὐτοὺς ὅτι σὺν τῷ
THEY WERE MARVELING AND~WERE RECOGNIZING THEM THAT WITH -

Ἰησοῦ ἦσαν, **4.14** τόν τε ἄνθρωπον βλέποντες σὺν
JESUS THEY WERE, [3]THE [1]AND [4]MAN [2]SEEING WITH

4:11 Ps. 118:22

αὐτοῖς ἑστῶτα τὸν τεθεραπευμένον οὐδὲν εἶχον
THEM   HAVING STOOD,   THE ONE HAVING BEEN HEALED,   THEY HAD~NOTHING

ἀντειπεῖν. **4.15** κελεύσαντες δὲ αὐτοὺς ἔξω τοῦ
TO SAY IN REPLY.   AND~HAVING COMMANDED THEM   OUTSIDE THE

συνεδρίου ἀπελθεῖν συνέβαλλον πρὸς ἀλλήλους
COUNCIL   TO DEPART,   THEY WERE CONFERRING WITH   ONE ANOTHER

4.16 λέγοντες, Τί ποιήσωμεν τοῖς ἀνθρώποις τούτοις;
SAYING   WHAT SHOULD WE DO   -   WITH THESE~MEN?

ὅτι μὲν γὰρ γνωστὸν σημεῖον γέγονεν δι᾽ αὐτῶν
FOR THAT INDEED   A REMARKABLE SIGN   HAS OCCURRED THROUGH THEM,

πᾶσιν τοῖς κατοικοῦσιν Ἰερουσαλὴμ φανερὸν καὶ
TO ALL   THE ONES INHABITING   JERUSALEM [IS]   CLEAR   AND

οὐ δυνάμεθα ἀρνεῖσθαι· **4.17** ἀλλ᾽ ἵνα μὴ ἐπὶ πλεῖον
WE ARE NOT ABLE   TO DENY [IT].   BUT   LEST   FURTHER

διανεμηθῇ εἰς τὸν λαὸν ἀπειλησώμεθα αὐτοῖς
IT MAY BE SPREAD TO THE PEOPLE, WE MAY WARN THEM

μηκέτι λαλεῖν ἐπὶ τῷ ὀνόματι τούτῳ μηδενὶ ἀνθρώπων.
TO SPEAK~NO LONGER IN - THIS~NAME TO ANY MEN.

4.18 καὶ καλέσαντες αὐτοὺς παρήγγειλαν τὸ καθόλου
AND HAVING CALLED THEM, THEY GAVE ORDERS - [2]AT ALL

μὴ φθέγγεσθαι μηδὲ διδάσκειν ἐπὶ τῷ ὀνόματι τοῦ
[1]NOT TO SPEAK NOR TO TEACH IN THE NAME -

Ἰησοῦ. **4.19** ὁ δὲ Πέτρος καὶ Ἰωάννης ἀποκριθέντες
OF JESUS. - BUT PETER AND JOHN HAVING ANSWERED

εἶπον πρὸς αὐτούς, Εἰ δίκαιόν ἐστιν ἐνώπιον τοῦ
SAID TO THEM, IF IT IS~RIGHT BEFORE -

θεοῦ ὑμῶν ἀκούειν μᾶλλον ἢ τοῦ θεοῦ, κρίνατε·
GOD TO LISTEN~TO YOU° RATHER THAN - GOD, YOU° DECIDE.

4.20 οὐ δυνάμεθα γὰρ ἡμεῖς ἃ εἴδαμεν καὶ
[3]ARE NOT ABLE [1]FOR [2]WE WHAT WE SAW AND

ἠκούσαμεν μὴ λαλεῖν. **4.21** οἱ δὲ προσαπειλησάμενοι
HEARD NOT TO SPEAK. - AND HAVING THREATENED [THEM] FURTHER,

ἀπέλυσαν αὐτούς, μηδὲν εὑρίσκοντες τὸ πῶς
THEY RELEASED THEM, FINDING~NOTHING - HOW

κολάσωνται αὐτούς, διὰ τὸν λαόν, ὅτι πάντες
THEY MIGHT PUNISH THEM, BECAUSE OF THE PEOPLE, BECAUSE ALL

ἐδόξαζον τὸν θεὸν ἐπὶ τῷ γεγονότι·
WERE GLORIFYING - GOD ON ACCOUNT OF THE THING HAVING HAPPENED.

4.22 ἐτῶν γὰρ ἦν πλειόνων τεσσεράκοντα ὁ ἄνθρωπος
FOR~OF YEARS WAS MORE [THAN] FORTY THE MAN

ἐφ᾽ ὃν γεγόνει τὸ σημεῖον τοῦτο τῆς ἰάσεως.
UPON WHOM HAD HAPPENED - THIS~SIGN - OF HEALING.

4.23 Ἀπολυθέντες δὲ ἦλθον πρὸς τοὺς ἰδίους
AND~[AFTER] HAVING BEEN RELEASED THEY CAME TO THEIR OWN [PEOPLE]

καὶ ἀπήγγειλαν ὅσα πρὸς αὐτοὺς οἱ ἀρχιερεῖς καὶ
AND REPORTED WHAT THINGS TO THEM THE CHIEF PRIESTS AND

οἱ πρεσβύτεροι εἶπαν. **4.24** οἱ δὲ ἀκούσαντες
THE ELDERS SAID. - AND~HAVING HEARD,

man who had been cured standing beside them, they had nothing to say in opposition. [15]So they ordered them to leave the council while they discussed the matter with one another. [16]They said, "What will we do with them? For it is obvious to all who live in Jerusalem that a notable sign has been done through them; we cannot deny it. [17]But to keep it from spreading further among the people, let us warn them to speak no more to anyone in this name." [18]So they called them and ordered them not to speak or teach at all in the name of Jesus. [19]But Peter and John answered them, "Whether it is right in God's sight to listen to you rather than to God, you must judge; [20]for we cannot keep from speaking about what we have seen and heard." [21]After threatening them again, they let them go, finding no way to punish them because of the people, for all of them praised God for what had happened. [22]For the man on whom this sign of healing had been performed was more than forty years old.

23 After they were released, they went to their friends[h] and reported what the chief priests and the elders had said to them. [24]When they heard it,

[h] Gk *their own*

they raised their voices together to God and said, "Sovereign Lord, who made the heaven and the earth, the sea, and everything in them, 25it is you who said by the Holy Spirit through our ancestor David, your servant:[i]

'Why did the Gentiles rage,
  and the peoples imagine vain things?
26 The kings of the earth took their stand,
  and the rulers have gathered together against the Lord and against his Messiah.'[j]

27For in this city, in fact, both Herod and Pontius Pilate, with the Gentiles and the peoples of Israel, gathered together against your holy servant[i] Jesus, whom you anointed, 28to do whatever your hand and your plan had predestined to take place. 29And now, Lord, look at their threats, and grant to your servants[k] to speak your word with all boldness, 30while you stretch out your hand to heal, and signs and wonders are performed through the name of your holy servant[i] Jesus." 31When they had prayed, the place in which they were gathered together was shaken; and they were all filled with the

[i] Or *child*
[j] Or *his Christ*
[k] Gk *slaves*

ὁμοθυμαδὸν ἦραν φωνὴν πρὸς τὸν θεὸν καὶ εἶπαν,
WITH ONE MIND   THEY LIFTED   [THEIR] VOICE   TO   -   GOD   AND   SAID,

Δέσποτα, σὺ ὁ ποιήσας τὸν οὐρανὸν καὶ τὴν γῆν
MASTER,   YOU   THE ONE   HAVING MADE   THE   HEAVEN   AND   THE   EARTH

καὶ τὴν θάλασσαν καὶ πάντα τὰ ἐν αὐτοῖς,
AND   THE   SEA   AND   ALL   THE THINGS   IN   THEM,

4.25 ὁ τοῦ πατρὸς ἡμῶν διὰ ⌜πνεύματος ἁγίου⌝
THE ONE   7THE   8FATHER   9OF US   2THROUGH   4SPIRIT   3[THE] HOLY

στόματος Δαυὶδ παιδός σου εἰπών,
5BY [THE] MOUTH   6OF DAVID   10[THE] SERVANT   11OF YOU   1HAVING SPOKEN,

  Ἱνατί ἐφρύαξαν ἔθνη
  WHY   RAGED   [THE] NATIONS

    καὶ λαοὶ ἐμελέτησαν κενά;
    AND   [THE] PEOPLE   IMAGINED   EMPTY THINGS?

4.26 παρέστησαν οἱ βασιλεῖς τῆς γῆς
TOOK THEIR STAND   THE   KINGS   OF THE   EARTH

    καὶ οἱ ἄρχοντες συνήχθησαν ἐπὶ τὸ αὐτὸ
    AND   THE   RULERS   ASSEMBLED   TOGETHER

      κατὰ τοῦ κυρίου καὶ κατὰ τοῦ Χριστοῦ
      AGAINST   THE   LORD   AND   AGAINST   THE   CHRIST

αὐτοῦ.
OF HIM.

4.27 συνήχθησαν γὰρ ἐπ' ἀληθείας ἐν τῇ πόλει ταύτῃ
FOR~WERE ASSEMBLED   IN   TRUTH   IN   -   THIS~CITY

ἐπὶ τὸν ἅγιον παῖδά σου Ἰησοῦν ὃν ἔχρισας,
AGAINST   THE   HOLY   SERVANT   OF YOU,   JESUS,   WHOM   YOU ANOINTED,

Ἡρῴδης τε καὶ Πόντιος Πιλᾶτος σὺν ἔθνεσιν καὶ
BOTH~HEROD   AND   PONTIUS   PILATE   WITH   [THE] GENTILES   AND

λαοῖς Ἰσραήλ, **4.28** ποιῆσαι ὅσα ἡ χείρ σου καὶ
[THE] PEOPLE   OF ISRAEL,   TO DO   WHATEVER   THE   HAND   OF YOU   AND

ἡ βουλή [σου] προώρισεν γενέσθαι. **4.29** καὶ τὰ νῦν,
THE   WILL   OF YOU   PREDESTINED   TO OCCUR.   AND   -   NOW,

κύριε, ἔπιδε ἐπὶ τὰς ἀπειλὰς αὐτῶν καὶ δὸς τοῖς
LORD,   LOOK   UPON   THE   THREATS   OF THEM   AND   GIVE   TO THE

δούλοις σου μετὰ παρρησίας πάσης λαλεῖν τὸν λόγον
SLAVES   OF YOU   WITH   ALL~BOLDNESS   TO SPEAK   THE   WORD

σου, **4.30** ἐν τῷ τὴν χεῖρά [σου] ἐκτείνειν σε εἰς ἴασιν
OF YOU,   WHILE   -   YOUR~HAND   YOU~STRETCH OUT   FOR   HEALING

καὶ σημεῖα καὶ τέρατα γίνεσθαι διὰ τοῦ
AND   SIGNS   AND   WONDERS   TO OCCUR   THROUGH   THE

ὀνόματος τοῦ ἁγίου παιδός σου Ἰησοῦ. **4.31** καὶ
NAME   OF THE   HOLY   SERVANT   OF YOU,   JESUS.   AND

δεηθέντων αὐτῶν ἐσαλεύθη ὁ τόπος ἐν ᾧ
[AFTER] THEY~HAVING PRAYED   WAS SHAKEN   THE   PLACE   IN   WHICH

ἦσαν συνηγμένοι, καὶ ἐπλήσθησαν ἅπαντες τοῦ
THEY HAD ASSEMBLED,   AND   EVERYONE~WAS FILLED   WITH THE

4:25 text: ASV RSV NASB NIV NEB TEV NJB NRSV. omit: KJV NEBmg.   **4:25-26** Ps. 2:1-2 LXX

ἁγίου πνεύματος καὶ ἐλάλουν   τὸν λόγον τοῦ θεοῦ
HOLY   SPIRIT   AND THEY WERE SPEAKING THE   WORD   -   OF GOD

μετὰ παρρησίας.
WITH   BOLDNESS.

4.32 Τοῦ δὲ   πλήθους τῶν   πιστευσάντων ἦν
         NOW~THE   NUMBER   OF THE ONES HAVING BELIEVED   WERE

καρδία καὶ ψυχὴ μία, καὶ οὐδὲ εἷς τι τῶν
²HEART   ³AND ⁴SOUL ¹ONE [IN], AND   NOT   ONE ANY OF THE

ὑπαρχόντων   αὐτῷ ἔλεγεν   ἴδιον εἶναι ἀλλ' ἦν
POSSESSIONS [BELONGING] TO HIM WAS SAYING [THAT] IT WAS~HIS OWN, BUT   WAS

αὐτοῖς ἅπαντα κοινά.   **4.33** καὶ δυνάμει μεγάλη
TO THEM EVERYTHING [IN] COMMON.   AND   WITH GREAT~POWER

ἀπεδίδουν τὸ μαρτύριον οἱ ἀπόστολοι τῆς ἀναστάσεως
WERE GIVING   -   TESTIMONY   THE APOSTLES   OF THE RESURRECTION

τοῦ κυρίου Ἰησοῦ, χάρις τε μεγάλη ἦν ἐπὶ
OF THE LORD   JESUS,   ³GRACE ¹AND ²GREAT   WAS UPON

πάντας αὐτούς. **4.34** οὐδὲ γὰρ ἐνδεής τις ἦν ἐν
THEM~ALL.   FOR~NOT   NEEDY   WAS~ANYONE AMONG

αὐτοῖς· ὅσοι γὰρ κτήτορες χωρίων ἢ οἰκιῶν ὑπῆρχον,
THEM;   FOR~AS MANY AS OWNERS   OF LANDS   OR HOUSES   WERE,

πωλοῦντες ἔφερον   τὰς τιμὰς τῶν
SELLING [THEM], THEY WERE BRINGING THE   PROCEEDS OF THE THINGS

πιπρασκομένων **4.35** καὶ ἐτίθουν   παρὰ τοὺς πόδας
BEING SOLD   AND WERE PLACING [THEM] AT   THE   FEET

τῶν ἀποστόλων, διεδίδετο δὲ   ἑκάστῳ καθότι ἄν
OF THE APOSTLES,   AND~THEY WERE DISTRIBUTING TO EACH [ONE] AS

τις χρείαν εἶχεν. **4.36** Ἰωσὴφ δὲ ὁ   ἐπικληθεὶς
ANYONE WAS HAVING~NEED.   AND~JOSEPH,   THE ONE HAVING BEEN NAMED

Βαρναβᾶς ἀπὸ τῶν ἀποστόλων, ὅ
BARNABAS   BY   THE   APOSTLES,   WHICH

ἐστιν μεθερμηνευόμενον υἱὸς παρακλήσεως, Λευίτης,
BEING TRANSLATED MEANS   SON   OF ENCOURAGEMENT,   A LEVITE,

Κύπριος τῷ γένει, **4.37** ὑπάρχοντος αὐτῷ ἀγροῦ
OF CYPRUS   BY   NATIONALITY,   BELONGING   TO HIM   A FIELD,

πωλήσας ἤνεγκεν τὸ χρῆμα καὶ ἔθηκεν πρὸς τοὺς
HAVING SOLD [IT] HE BROUGHT THE MONEY   AND LAID [IT]   AT   THE

πόδας τῶν ἀποστόλων.
FEET   OF THE APOSTLES.

5.1 Ἀνὴρ δέ τις   Ἀνανίας ὀνόματι σὺν Σαπφίρῃ
       ³MAN ¹AND ²A CERTAIN ANANIAS   BY NAME   WITH SAPPHIRA

τῇ γυναικὶ αὐτοῦ ἐπώλησεν κτῆμα **5.2** καὶ ἐνοσφίσατο
THE WIFE   OF HIM   SOLD   PROPERTY   AND   HE MISAPPROPRIATED

ἀπὸ τῆς τιμῆς, συνειδυίης καὶ τῆς γυναικός, καὶ
FROM THE PRICE,   HAVING KNOWN   ALSO THE   WIFE,   AND

Holy Spirit and spoke the word of God with boldness. 32 Now the whole group of those who believed were of one heart and soul, and no one claimed private ownership of any possessions, but everything they owned was held in common. [33]With great power the apostles gave their testimony to the resurrection of the Lord Jesus, and great grace was upon them all. [34]There was not a needy person among them, for as many as owned lands or houses sold them and brought the proceeds of what was sold. [35]They laid it at the apostles' feet, and it was distributed to each as any had need. [36]There was a Levite, a native of Cyprus, Joseph, to whom the apostles gave the name Barnabas (which means "son of encouragement"). [37]He sold a field that belonged to him, then brought the money, and laid it at the apostles' feet.

But a man named Ananias, with the consent of his wife Sapphira, sold a piece of property; [2]with his wife's knowledge, he kept back some of the proceeds, and brought only a part and laid it at the apostles' feet. [3]"Ananias," Peter asked, "why has Satan filled your heart to lie to the Holy Spirit and to keep back part of the proceeds of the land? [4]While it remained unsold, did it not remain your own? And after it was sold, were not the proceeds at your disposal? How is it that you have contrived this deed in your heart? You did not lie to us[l] but to God!" [5]Now when Ananias heard these words, he fell down and died. And great fear seized all who heard of it. [6]The young men came and wrapped up his body,[m] then carried him out and buried him.

7 After an interval of about three hours his wife came in, not knowing what had happened. [8]Peter said to her, "Tell me whether you and your husband sold the land for such and such a price." And she said, "Yes, that was the price." [9]Then Peter said to her, "How is it that you have agreed together to put the Spirit of the Lord to the test? Look, the feet of those who have buried your husband are at the door, and they will carry you out." [10]Immediately she fell down at his feet and died. When the young men came in they found her dead, so they carried her out and buried her beside her husband. [11]And great fear seized the whole

[l] Gk *to men*
[m] Meaning of Gk uncertain

ἐνέγκας   μέρος τι   παρὰ τοὺς πόδας τῶν ἀποστόλων
HAVING BROUGHT A CERTAIN~PART AT   THE   FEET   OF THE APOSTLES

ἔθηκεν.   5.3 εἶπεν δὲ ὁ Πέτρος, Ἀνανία, διὰ τί
HE LAID [IT].   BUT~SAID - PETER,   ANANIAS,   WHY

ἐπλήρωσεν ὁ Σατανᾶς τὴν καρδίαν σου,
FILLED   - SATAN   THE HEART   OF YOU, [THAT]

ψεύσασθαί σε τὸ   πνεῦμα τὸ ἅγιον καὶ νοσφίσασθαι
YOU~LIED   TO THE ²SPIRIT - ¹HOLY AND MISAPPROPRIATED

ἀπὸ τῆς τιμῆς τοῦ χωρίου; 5.4 οὐχὶ μένον   σοι
FROM THE PRICE OF THE LAND?   NOT [WHILE] REMAINING WITH YOU

ἔμενεν   καὶ πραθὲν   ἐν τῇ σῇ ἐξουσίᾳ ὑπῆρχεν;
IT WAS REMAINING AND HAVING BEEN SOLD IN - YOUR AUTHORITY IT WAS?

τί ὅτι ἔθου ἐν τῇ καρδίᾳ σου τὸ πρᾶγμα τοῦτο;
WHY   WAS PUT IN THE HEART   OF YOU - THIS~DEED?

οὐκ ἐψεύσω ἀνθρώποις ἀλλὰ τῷ θεῷ. 5.5 ἀκούων δὲ ὁ
YOU DID NOT LIE TO MEN   BUT   - TO GOD.   AND~HEARING   -

Ἀνανίας τοὺς λόγους τούτους πεσὼν   ἐξέψυξεν,
ANANIAS   -   THESE~WORDS   HAVING FALLEN DOWN, HE DIED,

καὶ ἐγένετο φόβος μέγας ἐπὶ πάντας τοὺς ἀκούοντας.
AND THERE CAME GREAT~FEAR   UPON ALL   THE ONES LISTENING.

5.6 ἀναστάντες δὲ οἱ νεώτεροι συνέστειλαν αὐτὸν καὶ
AND~HAVING ARISEN, THE YOUNG MEN WRAPPED UP   HIM   AND

ἐξενέγκαντες   ἔθαψαν.
HAVING CARRIED [HIM] OUT THEY BURIED [HIM].

5.7 Ἐγένετο δὲ ὡς   ὡρῶν τριῶν διάστημα καὶ ἡ
AND~THERE WAS ²ABOUT ⁴HOURS ³THREE ¹AN INTERVAL OF AND THE

γυνὴ αὐτοῦ μὴ εἰδυῖα τὸ   γεγονὸς   εἰσῆλθεν.
WIFE OF HIM NOT HAVING KNOWN THE THING HAVING HAPPENED, ENTERED.

5.8 ἀπεκρίθη δὲ   πρὸς αὐτὴν Πέτρος, Εἰπέ μοι, εἰ
AND~HAVING ANSWERED TO   HER   PETER [SAID], TELL ME, IF

τοσούτου τὸ χωρίον ἀπέδοσθε; ἡ δὲ εἶπεν, Ναί,
FOR SO MUCH THE LAND YOU SOLD? - AND SHE SAID, YES,

τοσούτου. 5.9 ὁ δὲ Πέτρος πρὸς αὐτήν, Τί ὅτι
FOR SO MUCH.   - AND PETER   TO   HER,   WHY

συνεφωνήθη ὑμῖν πειράσαι τὸ πνεῦμα κυρίου; ἰδοὺ
WAS IT AGREED BY YOU° TO TEST THE SPIRIT OF [THE] LORD? BEHOLD

οἱ πόδες τῶν   θαψάντων τὸν ἄνδρα σου ἐπὶ τῇ
THE FEET OF THE ONES HAVING BURIED THE HUSBAND OF YOU [ARE] AT THE

θύρᾳ καὶ ἐξοίσουσίν σε. 5.10 ἔπεσεν δὲ παραχρῆμα
DOOR AND THEY WILL CARRY OUT YOU. AND~SHE FELL   IMMEDIATELY

πρὸς τοὺς πόδας αὐτοῦ καὶ ἐξέψυξεν· εἰσελθόντες δὲ
AT   THE   FEET OF HIM AND DIED.   AND~HAVING ENTERED

οἱ νεανίσκοι εὗρον   αὐτὴν νεκρὰν καὶ
THE YOUNG MEN THEY FOUND HER   DEAD   AND

ἐξενέγκαντες   ἔθαψαν πρὸς τὸν ἄνδρα αὐτῆς,
HAVING CARRIED [HER] OUT, THEY BURIED [HER] WITH THE HUSBAND OF HER,

5.11 καὶ ἐγένετο φόβος μέγας ἐφ' ὅλην   τὴν
AND THERE CAME GREAT~FEAR   UPON [THE] WHOLE -

ἐκκλησίαν   καὶ   ἐπὶ   πάντας   τοὺς   ἀκούοντας   ταῦτα.
CHURCH   AND   UPON   ALL   THE ONES   HEARING   THESE THINGS.

5.12 Διὰ   δὲ   τῶν   χειρῶν   τῶν   ἀποστόλων   ἐγίνετο
NOW~BY   THE   HANDS   OF THE   APOSTLES   WERE BEING PERFORMED

σημεῖα   καὶ   τέρατα   πολλὰ   ἐν   τῷ   λαῷ.   καὶ   ἦσαν
²SIGNS   ³AND   ⁴WONDERS   ¹MANY   AMONG THE   PEOPLE.   AND   WERE

ὁμοθυμαδὸν   ἅπαντες   ἐν   τῇ   Στοᾷ   Σολομῶντος,
WITH ONE MIND   EVERYONE   IN   THE   PORTICO   OF SOLOMON,

5.13 τῶν   δὲ   λοιπῶν   οὐδεὶς   ἐτόλμα   κολλᾶσθαι   αὐτοῖς,
BUT~OF THE   REST   NO ONE   WAS DARING   TO ASSOCIATE   WITH THEM,

ἀλλ᾽   ἐμεγάλυνεν   αὐτοὺς   ὁ   λαός.   **5.14** μᾶλλον   δὲ
BUT   WERE EXALTING   THEM   THE   PEOPLE.   AND~MORE

προσετίθεντο   πιστεύοντες   τῷ   κυρίῳ,   πλήθη   ἀνδρῶν   τε
WERE BEING ADDED   [ONES] BELIEVING   IN THE   LORD,   MULTITUDES   OF BOTH~MEN

καὶ   γυναικῶν,   **5.15** ὥστε   καὶ   εἰς   τὰς   πλατείας   ἐκφέρειν
AND   WOMEN,   SO AS   EVEN   INTO   THE   STREETS   TO CARRY OUT

τοὺς   ἀσθενεῖς   καὶ   τιθέναι   ἐπὶ   κλιναρίων   καὶ
THE   SICK   AND   TO PUT [THEM]   ON   BEDS   AND

κραβάττων,   ἵνα   ἐρχομένου   Πέτρου   κἂν   ἡ   σκιὰ
MATS,   THAT   COMING,   ⁴OF PETER   ¹AT LEAST   ²THE   ³SHADOW

ἐπισκιάσῃ   τινὶ   αὐτῶν.   **5.16** συνήρχετο   δὲ   καὶ   τὸ
MIGHT FALL UPON   SOME   OF THEM.   AND~WAS ASSEMBLING   ALSO   THE

πλῆθος   τῶν   πέριξ   πόλεων   Ἰερουσαλὴμ   φέροντες
MULTITUDE   OF THE   CITIES~SURROUNDING   JERUSALEM   CARRYING

ἀσθενεῖς   καὶ   ὀχλουμένους   ὑπὸ
[THE] SICK   AND [THE ONES]   BEING TORMENTED   BY

πνευμάτων   ἀκαθάρτων,   οἵτινες   ἐθεραπεύοντο   ἅπαντες.
UNCLEAN~SPIRITS,   WHO   ALL~WERE BEING HEALED.

5.17 Ἀναστὰς   δὲ   ὁ   ἀρχιερεὺς   καὶ   πάντες   οἱ   σὺν
AND~HAVING ARISEN   THE   HIGH PRIEST   AND   ALL   THE ONES   WITH

αὐτῷ,   ἡ   οὖσα   αἵρεσις   τῶν   Σαδδουκαίων,   ἐπλήσθησαν
HIM,   (BEING~THE   SECT   OF THE   SADDUCEES),   THEY WERE FILLED

ζήλου   **5.18** καὶ   ἐπέβαλον   τὰς   χεῖρας   ἐπὶ   τοὺς
WITH JEALOUSY   AND   LAID   THE (THEIR)   HANDS   UPON   THE

ἀποστόλους   καὶ   ἔθεντο   αὐτοὺς   ἐν   τηρήσει   δημοσίᾳ.
APOSTLES   AND   PUT   THEM   IN   [THE] PUBLIC~JAIL.

5.19 ἄγγελος   δὲ   κυρίου   διὰ   νυκτὸς   ἀνοίξας   τὰς
AND~AN ANGEL   OF [THE] LORD   DURING   [THE] NIGHT   HAVING OPENED   THE

θύρας   τῆς   φυλακῆς   ἐξαγαγών   τε   αὐτοὺς   εἶπεν,
DOORS   OF THE   JAIL   AND~HAVING LED OUT   THEM   SAID,

5.20 Πορεύεσθε   καὶ   σταθέντες   λαλεῖτε   ἐν   τῷ   ἱερῷ
GO   AND   HAVING STOOD,   SPEAK   IN   THE   TEMPLE

τῷ   λαῷ   πάντα   τὰ   ῥήματα   τῆς   ζωῆς   ταύτης.
TO THE   PEOPLE   ALL   THE   WORDS   -   OF THIS~LIFE.

5.21 ἀκούσαντες   δὲ   εἰσῆλθον   ὑπὸ   τὸν   ὄρθρον   εἰς   τὸ
AND~HAVING HEARD   THEY ENTERED   ABOUT   -   DAYBREAK   INTO   THE

ἱερὸν   καὶ   ἐδίδασκον.   Παραγενόμενος   δὲ   ὁ   ἀρχιερεὺς
TEMPLE   AND   WERE TEACHING.   AND~HAVING COME   THE   HIGH PRIEST

church and all who heard of these things.

12 Now many signs and wonders were done among the people through the apostles. And they were all together in Solomon's Portico. [13]None of the rest dared to join them, but the people held them in high esteem. [14]Yet more than ever believers were added to the Lord, great numbers of both men and women, [15]so that they even carried out the sick into the streets, and laid them on cots and mats, in order that Peter's shadow might fall on some of them as he came by. [16]A great number of people would also gather from the towns around Jerusalem, bringing the sick and those tormented by unclean spirits, and they were all cured.

17 Then the high priest took action; he and all who were with him (that is, the sect of the Sadducees), being filled with jealousy, [18]arrested the apostles and put them in the public prison. [19]But during the night an angel of the Lord opened the prison doors, brought them out, and said, [20]"Go, stand in the temple and tell the people the whole message about this life." [21]When they heard this, they entered the temple at daybreak and went on with their teaching.

When the high priest and those with him arrived,

they called together the council and the whole body of the elders of Israel, and sent to the prison to have them brought. [22]But when the temple police went there, they did not find them in the prison; so they returned and reported, [23]"We found the prison securely locked and the guards standing at the doors, but when we opened them, we found no one inside." [24]Now when the captain of the temple and the chief priests heard these words, they were perplexed about them, wondering what might be going on. [25]Then someone arrived and announced, "Look, the men whom you put in prison are standing in the temple and teaching the people!" [26]Then the captain went with the temple police and brought them, but without violence, for they were afraid of being stoned by the people.

[27] When they had brought them, they had them stand before the council. The high priest questioned them, [28]saying, "We gave you strict orders not to teach in this name,[n] yet here you have filled Jerusalem with your teaching and you are determined to bring this man's blood on us." [29]But Peter and the

[n] Other ancient authorities read *Did we not give you strict orders not to teach in this name?*

καὶ οἱ σὺν αὐτῷ συνεκάλεσαν τὸ συνέδριον καὶ
AND THE ONES WITH HIM, THEY CALLED TOGETHER THE COUNCIL AND

πᾶσαν τὴν γερουσίαν τῶν υἱῶν Ἰσραὴλ καὶ
ALL THE ASSEMBLY OF ELDERS OF THE SONS OF ISRAEL AND

ἀπέστειλαν εἰς τὸ δεσμωτήριον ἀχθῆναι αὐτούς.
THEY SENT TO THE JAIL [FOR THE PRISONERS] TO BE BROUGHT TO THEM.

5.22 οἱ δὲ παραγενόμενοι ὑπηρέται οὐχ εὗρον αὐτοὺς ἐν
BUT~THE SERVANTS~HAVING COME DID NOT FIND THEM IN

τῇ φυλακῇ· ἀναστρέψαντες δὲ ἀπήγγειλαν
THE JAIL. AND~HAVING RETURNED THEY REPORTED [THESE THINGS]

5.23 λέγοντες ὅτι Τὸ δεσμωτήριον εὕρομεν κεκλεισμένον
SAYING, - THE JAIL WE FOUND HAVING BEEN CLOSED

ἐν πάσῃ ἀσφαλείᾳ καὶ τοὺς φύλακας ἑστῶτας ἐπὶ
WITH ALL SECURITY AND THE GUARDS HAVING STOOD AT

τῶν θυρῶν, ἀνοίξαντες δὲ ἔσω οὐδένα εὕρομεν.
THE DOORS, BUT~HAVING OPENED [IT], INSIDE WE FOUND~NO ONE.

5.24 ὡς δὲ ἤκουσαν τοὺς λόγους τούτους ὅ τε
AND~WHEN THEY HEARD - THESE~WORDS BOTH~THE

στρατηγὸς τοῦ ἱεροῦ καὶ οἱ ἀρχιερεῖς, διηπόρουν
CAPTAIN OF THE TEMPLE AND THE CHIEF PRIESTS, WERE PERPLEXED

περὶ αὐτῶν τί ἂν γένοιτο τοῦτο.
ABOUT THEM, WHAT THIS~MIGHT COME TO BE.

5.25 παραγενόμενος δέ τις ἀπήγγειλεν αὐτοῖς ὅτι
AND~HAVING COME SOMEONE REPORTED TO THEM, -

Ἰδοὺ οἱ ἄνδρες οὓς ἔθεσθε ἐν τῇ φυλακῇ εἰσὶν ἐν
BEHOLD THE MEN WHOM YOU° PUT IN THE JAIL ARE IN

τῷ ἱερῷ ἑστῶτες καὶ διδάσκοντες τὸν λαόν.
THE TEMPLE HAVING STOOD AND TEACHING THE PEOPLE.

5.26 τότε ἀπελθὼν ὁ στρατηγὸς σὺν τοῖς
THEN HAVING DEPARTED, THE CAPTAIN [OF THE TEMPLE] WITH THE

ὑπηρέταις ἦγεν αὐτούς οὐ μετὰ βίας,
SERVANTS WERE LEADING THEM NOT WITH FORCE,

ἐφοβοῦντο γὰρ τὸν λαὸν μὴ λιθασθῶσιν.
FOR~THEY FEARED THE PEOPLE LEST THEY SHOULD BE STONED.

5.27 Ἀγαγόντες δὲ αὐτοὺς ἔστησαν ἐν τῷ συνεδρίῳ.
AND~HAVING BROUGHT THEM, THEY STOOD IN THE COUNCIL.

καὶ ἐπηρώτησεν αὐτοὺς ὁ ἀρχιερεὺς **5.28** λέγων,
AND QUESTIONED THEM THE HIGH PRIEST SAYING,

[Οὐ] παραγγελίᾳ παρηγγείλαμεν ὑμῖν μὴ
[DID WE] NOT WITH A STRICT COMMAND CHARGE YOU° NOT

διδάσκειν ἐπὶ τῷ ὀνόματι τούτῳ, καὶ ἰδοὺ
TO TEACH IN - THIS~NAME, AND BEHOLD

πεπληρώκατε τὴν Ἰερουσαλὴμ τῆς διδαχῆς ὑμῶν καὶ
YOU HAVE FILLED - JERUSALEM WITH THE TEACHING OF YOU° AND

βούλεσθε ἐπαγαγεῖν ἐφ᾽ ἡμᾶς τὸ αἷμα τοῦ
ARE DETERMINED TO BRING UPON US THE BLOOD -

ἀνθρώπου τούτου. **5.29** ἀποκριθεὶς δὲ Πέτρος καὶ οἱ
OF THIS~MAN. AND~HAVING ANSWERED, PETER AND THE

ἀπόστολοι εἶπαν, Πειθαρχεῖν δεῖ θεῷ μᾶλλον ἢ
APOSTLES   SAID,   IT IS NECESSARY~TO OBEY GOD   RATHER   THAN

ἀνθρώποις. **5.30** ὁ θεὸς τῶν πατέρων ἡμῶν ἤγειρεν
MEN.   THE GOD OF THE FATHERS OF US RAISED

Ἰησοῦν ὃν ὑμεῖς διεχειρίσασθε κρεμάσαντες ἐπὶ
JESUS WHOM YOU°   KILLED   HAVING HUNG   ON

ξύλου· **5.31** τοῦτον ὁ θεὸς ἀρχηγὸν καὶ σωτῆρα ὕψωσεν
A TREE.   THIS ONE, - GOD [AS] A PRINCE AND SAVIOR EXALTED

τῇ δεξιᾷ αὐτοῦ [τοῦ] δοῦναι μετάνοιαν τῷ Ἰσραὴλ
TO THE RIGHT OF HIM [-] TO GRANT REPENTANCE - TO ISRAEL

καὶ ἄφεσιν ἁμαρτιῶν. **5.32** καὶ ἡμεῖς ἐσμεν μάρτυρες
AND FORGIVENESS OF SINS.   AND WE   ARE   WITNESSES

τῶν ῥημάτων τούτων καὶ τὸ πνεῦμα τὸ ἅγιον ὃ
- OF THESE~MATTERS AND THE ²SPIRIT - ¹HOLY ³WHICH

ἔδωκεν ὁ θεὸς τοῖς πειθαρχοῦσιν αὐτῷ.
⁵GAVE   - ⁴GOD TO THE ONES OBEYING   HIM.

5.33 Οἱ δὲ ἀκούσαντες διεπρίοντο καὶ ἐβούλοντο
AND~THE ONES HAVING HEARD WERE INFURIATED AND WERE DECIDING

ἀνελεῖν αὐτούς. **5.34** ἀναστὰς δέ τις ἐν τῷ
TO DO AWAY WITH THEM.   BUT~HAVING ARISEN A CERTAIN ²IN ³THE

συνεδρίῳ Φαρισαῖος ὀνόματι Γαμαλιήλ, νομοδιδάσκαλος
⁴COUNCIL   ¹PHARISEE   BY NAME GAMALIEL,   A TEACHER OF THE LAW,

τίμιος παντὶ τῷ λαῷ, ἐκέλευσεν ἔξω βραχὺ
RESPECTED BY ALL THE PEOPLE, COMMANDED OUTSIDE [FOR] A LITTLE [WHILE]

τοὺς ἀνθρώπους ποιῆσαι **5.35** εἶπέν τε πρὸς αὐτούς,
THE   MEN   TO PUT   AND~SAID   TO   THEM,

Ἄνδρες Ἰσραηλῖται, προσέχετε ἑαυτοῖς ἐπὶ τοῖς
MEN,   ISRAELITES, PAY ATTENTION TO YOURSELVES WITH -

ἀνθρώποις τούτοις τί μέλλετε πράσσειν. **5.36** πρὸ γὰρ
THESE~MEN   WHAT YOU° ARE ABOUT TO DO.   FOR~BEFORE

τούτων τῶν ἡμερῶν ἀνέστη Θευδᾶς λέγων εἶναί τινα
THESE   -   DAYS   AROSE THEUDAS SAYING TO BE SOMEONE

ἑαυτόν, ᾧ προσεκλίθη ἀνδρῶν ἀριθμὸς ὡς
HIMSELF, TO WHOM WERE ASSOCIATED A NUMBER~OF MEN, ABOUT

τετρακοσίων· ὃς ἀνῃρέθη, καὶ πάντες ὅσοι
FOUR HUNDRED; WHO WAS DONE AWAY WITH, AND ALL   AS MANY AS

ἐπείθοντο αὐτῷ διελύθησαν καὶ ἐγένοντο εἰς οὐδέν.
WERE OBEYING HIM WERE DISPERSED AND IT CAME TO NOTHING.

5.37 μετὰ τοῦτον ἀνέστη Ἰούδας ὁ Γαλιλαῖος ἐν ταῖς
AFTER THIS   AROSE JUDAS THE GALILEAN   IN THE

ἡμέραις τῆς ἀπογραφῆς καὶ ἀπέστησεν λαὸν
DAYS   OF THE CENSUS   AND MISLED   [THE] PEOPLE

ὀπίσω αὐτοῦ· κἀκεῖνος ἀπώλετο καὶ πάντες
[TO] FOLLOW AFTER HIM. AND THAT ONE PERISHED AND ALL

ὅσοι ἐπείθοντο αὐτῷ διεσκορπίσθησαν. **5.38** καὶ τὰ
AS MANY AS WERE OBEYING HIM WERE SCATTERED.   AND -

νῦν λέγω ὑμῖν, ἀπόστητε ἀπὸ τῶν ἀνθρώπων τούτων
NOW I SAY TO YOU°, STAY AWAY FROM - THESE~MEN

apostles answered, "We must obey God rather than any human authority.ᵒ ³⁰The God of our ancestors raised up Jesus, whom you had killed by hanging him on a tree. ³¹God exalted him at his right hand as Leader and Savior that he might give repentance to Israel and forgiveness of sins. ³²And we are witnesses to these things, and so is the Holy Spirit whom God has given to those who obey him."

33 When they heard this, they were enraged and wanted to kill them. ³⁴But a Pharisee in the council named Gamaliel, a teacher of the law, respected by all the people, stood up and ordered the men to be put outside for a short time. ³⁵Then he said to them, "Fellow Israelites,ᵖ consider carefully what you propose to do to these men. ³⁶For some time ago Theudas rose up, claiming to be somebody, and a number of men, about four hundred, joined him; but he was killed, and all who followed him were dispersed and disappeared. ³⁷After him Judas the Galilean rose up at the time of the census and got people to follow him; he also perished, and all who followed him were scattered. ³⁸So in the present case, I tell you, keep away from these men

ᵒ Gk than men
ᵖ Gk Men, Israelites

and let them alone; because if this plan or this under- taking is of human origin, it will fail; ³⁹but if it is of God, you will not be able to overthrow them—in that case you may even be found fighting against God!"

They were convinced by him, ⁴⁰and when they had called in the apostles, they had them flogged. Then they ordered them not to speak in the name of Jesus, and let them go. ⁴¹As they left the council, they rejoiced that they were considered worthy to suffer dishonor for the sake of the name. ⁴²And every day in the temple and at home^q they did not cease to teach and proclaim Jesus as the Messiah.^r

^q Or *from house to house*
^r Or *the Christ*

καὶ ἄφετε αὐτούς· ὅτι ἐὰν ᾖ ἐξ ἀνθρώπων ἡ
AND LEAVE THEM [ALONE]. BECAUSE IF IT IS OF MEN -

βουλὴ αὕτη ἢ τὸ ἔργον τοῦτο, καταλυθήσεται, **5.39** εἰ δὲ
THIS~PLAN OR - THIS~MATTER, IT WILL BE OVERTHROWN, BUT~IF

ἐκ θεοῦ ἐστιν, οὐ δυνήσεσθε καταλῦσαι αὐτούς μήποτε
FROM GOD IT IS, YOU° ARE NOT ABLE TO OVERTHROW THEM LEST

καὶ θεομάχοι εὑρεθῆτε. ἐπείσθησαν δὲ αὐτῷ
ALSO YOU° MAY BE FOUND~OPPOSING GOD. AND~THEY WERE PERSUADED BY HIM

5.40 καὶ προσκαλεσάμενοι τοὺς ἀποστόλους δείραντες
AND HAVING CALLED TOGETHER THE APOSTLES, [AND] HAVING BEAT [THEM]

παρήγγειλαν μὴ λαλεῖν ἐπὶ τῷ ὀνόματι τοῦ Ἰησοῦ
THEY WARNED [THEM] NOT TO SPEAK IN THE NAME - OF JESUS

καὶ ἀπέλυσαν. **5.41** Οἱ μὲν οὖν ἐπορεύοντο
AND THEY RELEASED [THEM]. - - THEREFORE THEY WERE GOING

χαίροντες ἀπὸ προσώπου τοῦ συνεδρίου, ὅτι
REJOICING FROM [THE] PRESENCE OF THE COUNCIL THAT

κατηξιώθησαν ὑπὲρ τοῦ ὀνόματος ἀτιμασθῆναι,
THEY WERE CONSIDERED WORTHY FOR THE NAME TO SUFFER SHAME,

5.42 πᾶσάν τε ἡμέραν ἐν τῷ ἱερῷ καὶ κατ' οἶκον
AND~EVERY DAY IN THE TEMPLE AND FROM HOUSE TO HOUSE

οὐκ ἐπαύοντο διδάσκοντες καὶ εὐαγγελιζόμενοι τὸν
THEY DID NOT STOP TEACHING AND PREACHING -

Χριστὸν Ἰησοῦν.
CHRIST JESUS.

CHAPTER 6

Now during those days, when the disciples were increasing in number, the Hellenists complained against the Hebrews because their widows were being neglected in the daily distribution of food. ²And the twelve called together the whole community of the disciples and said, "It is not right that we should neglect the word of God in order to wait on tables.^{s 3}Therefore, friends,^t select from among yourselves seven men of good standing, full of the Spirit and of wisdom, whom we may appoint to this task, ⁴while we, for our part, will devote ourselves to prayer

⁵ Or *keep accounts*
^t Gk *brothers*

6.1 Ἐν δὲ ταῖς ἡμέραις ταύταις πληθυνόντων τῶν
NOW~IN - THESE~DAYS OF BEING INCREASED THE

μαθητῶν ἐγένετο γογγυσμὸς τῶν Ἑλληνιστῶν πρὸς
DISCIPLES, THERE WAS A COMPLAINT BY THE HELLENISTS AGAINST

τοὺς Ἑβραίους, ὅτι παρεθεωροῦντο ἐν τῇ διακονίᾳ τῇ
THE HEBREWS, THAT WERE BEING OVERLOOKED IN THE ²SUPPORT -

καθημερινῇ αἱ χῆραι αὐτῶν. **6.2** προσκαλεσάμενοι δὲ
¹DAILY THE WIDOWS OF THEM. ⁴HAVING CALLED TOGETHER ¹AND

οἱ δώδεκα τὸ πλῆθος τῶν μαθητῶν εἶπαν, Οὐκ ἀρεστόν
²THE ³TWELVE THE MULTITUDE OF THE DISCIPLES SAID, NOT DESIRABLE

ἐστιν ἡμᾶς καταλείψαντας τὸν λόγον τοῦ θεοῦ
IS IT FOR US HAVING NEGLECTED THE WORD - OF GOD

διακονεῖν τραπέζαις. **6.3** ἐπισκέψασθε δέ, ἀδελφοί,
TO SERVE TABLES. BUT~SELECT, BROTHERS,

ἄνδρας ἐξ ὑμῶν μαρτυρουμένους ἑπτά, πλήρεις
MEN AMONG YOU° SEVEN~BEING WELL SPOKEN OF, FULL

πνεύματος καὶ σοφίας, οὓς καταστήσομεν ἐπὶ τῆς
OF [THE] SPIRIT AND WISDOM, WHOM WE WILL APPOINT OVER -

χρείας ταύτης, **6.4** ἡμεῖς δὲ τῇ προσευχῇ καὶ τῇ
THIS~DUTY, BUT~WE - TO PRAYER AND TO THE

διακονίᾳ   τοῦ   λόγου   προσκαρτερήσομεν.   **6.5** καὶ   ἤρεσεν
SERVICE   OF THE   WORD   WILL BE DEVOTED.   AND   [3]PLEASED

ὁ   λόγος   ἐνώπιον   παντὸς   τοῦ   πλήθους   καὶ   ἐξελέξαντο
[1]THE   [2]WORD   BEFORE   ALL   THE   MULTITUDE   AND   THEY CHOSE

Στέφανον,   ἄνδρα   πλήρης   πίστεως   καὶ   πνεύματος ἁγίου,
STEPHEN,   A MAN   FULL   OF FAITH   AND   [THE] HOLY~SPIRIT,

καὶ   Φίλιππον   καὶ   Πρόχορον   καὶ   Νικάνορα   καὶ
AND   PHILIP   AND   PROCHORUS   AND   NICANOR   AND

Τίμωνα   καὶ   Παρμενᾶν   καὶ   Νικόλαον   προσήλυτον
TIMON   AND   PARMENAS,   AND   NICOLAS   A PROSELYTE

Ἀντιοχέα,   **6.6** οὓς   ἔστησαν   ἐνώπιον   τῶν ἀποστόλων,
OF ANTIOCH,   WHOM   THEY PLACED   BEFORE   THE   APOSTLES,

καὶ   προσευξάμενοι   ἐπέθηκαν   αὐτοῖς   τὰς   χεῖρας.
AND   HAVING PRAYED   THEY LAID UPON   THEM   THE(THEIR)   HANDS.

6.7 Καὶ   ὁ   λόγος   τοῦ   θεοῦ   ηὔξανεν   καὶ
AND   THE   WORD   -   OF GOD   WAS INCREASING   AND

ἐπληθύνετο   ὁ   ἀριθμὸς   τῶν   μαθητῶν ἐν   Ἰερουσαλὴμ
WAS BEING MULTIPLIED   THE   NUMBER   OF THE   DISCIPLES   IN   JERUSALEM

σφόδρα,   πολύς τε   ὄχλος   τῶν   ἱερέων   ὑπήκουον   τῇ
GREATLY,   AND~A GREAT   CROWD   OF THE   PRIESTS   WERE OBEYING   THE

πίστει.
FAITH.

6.8 Στέφανος   δὲ   πλήρης   χάριτος   καὶ   δυνάμεως
AND~STEPHEN,   FULL   OF GRACE   AND   POWER

ἐποίει   τέρατα   καὶ   σημεῖα μεγάλα   ἐν   τῷ   λαῷ.
WAS PERFORMING   WONDERS   AND   GREAT~SIGNS   AMONG   THE   PEOPLE.

6.9 ἀνέστησαν δέ   τινες   τῶν   ἐκ   τῆς   συναγωγῆς
BUT~HAVING ARISEN   SOME   OF THE ONES   FROM   THE   SYNAGOGUE,

τῆς   λεγομένης   Λιβερτίνων   καὶ   Κυρηναίων   καὶ
-   BEING CALLED   FREEDMEN   AND   CYRENIANS   AND

Ἀλεξανδρέων   καὶ   τῶν   ἀπὸ   Κιλικίας   καὶ   Ἀσίας
ALEXANDRIANS   AND   THE ONES   FROM   CILICIA   AND   ASIA

συζητοῦντες   τῷ   Στεφάνῳ,   **6.10** καὶ   οὐκ ἴσχυον
DEBATING   -   WITH STEPHEN,   AND   THEY WERE NOT ABLE

ἀντιστῆναι   τῇ   σοφίᾳ   καὶ   τῷ   πνεύματι   ᾧ
TO CONTRADICT   THE   WISDOM   AND   THE   SPIRIT   WITH WHICH

ἐλάλει.   **6.11** τότε   ὑπέβαλον   ἄνδρας   λέγοντας
HE WAS SPEAKING.   THEN   THEY SECRETLY INSTIGATED   MEN   SAYING

ὅτι Ἀκηκόαμεν   αὐτοῦ   λαλοῦντος   ῥήματα   βλάσφημα
-   WE HAVE HEARD   HIM   SPEAKING   BLASPHEMOUS~WORDS

εἰς   Μωϋσῆν   καὶ   τὸν   θεόν.   **6.12** συνεκίνησάν τε   τὸν
AGAINST   MOSES   AND   -   GOD.   AND~THEY AROUSED   THE

λαὸν   καὶ   τοὺς   πρεσβυτέρους   καὶ   τοὺς   γραμματεῖς   καὶ
PEOPLE   AND   THE   ELDERS   AND   THE   SCRIBES,   AND

ἐπιστάντες   συνήρπασαν   αὐτὸν   καὶ   ἤγαγον
THEY CAME UPON [HIM AND]   THEY SEIZED   HIM   AND   THEY BROUGHT [HIM]

εἰς   τὸ   συνέδριον,   **6.13** ἔστησάν τε   μάρτυρας   ψευδεῖς
TO   THE   COUNCIL,   AND~THEY SET UP   FALSE~WITNESSES

and to serving the word." [5]What they said pleased the whole community, and they chose Stephen, a man full of faith and the Holy Spirit, together with Philip, Prochorus, Nicanor, Timon, Parmenas, and Nicolaus, a proselyte of Antioch. [6]They had these men stand before the apostles, who prayed and laid their hands on them.

7 The word of God continued to spread; the number of the disciples increased greatly in Jerusalem, and a great many of the priests became obedient to the faith.

8 Stephen, full of grace and power, did great wonders and signs among the people. [9]Then some of those who belonged to the synagogue of the Freedmen (as it was called), Cyrenians, Alexandrians, and others of those from Cilicia and Asia, stood up and argued with Stephen. [10]But they could not withstand the wisdom and the Spirit[u] with which he spoke. [11]Then they secretly instigated some men to say, "We have heard him speak blasphemous words against Moses and God." [12]They stirred up the people as well as the elders and the scribes; then they suddenly confronted him, seized him, and brought him before the council. [13]They set up false

[u] Or *spirit*

witnesses who said, "This man never stops saying things against this holy place and the law; [14]for we have heard him say that this Jesus of Nazareth[v] will destroy this place and will change the customs that Moses handed on to us." [15]And all who sat in the council looked intently at him, and they saw that his face was like the face of an angel.

[v] Gk *the Nazorean*

λέγοντας, Ὁ ἄνθρωπος οὗτος οὐ παύεται λαλῶν ῥήματα
SAYING, - THIS~MAN IS NOT STOPPING SPEAKING WORDS

κατὰ τοῦ τόπου τοῦ ἁγίου [τούτου] καὶ τοῦ νόμου·
AGAINST - ³PLACE ²HOLY ¹THIS AND THE LAW.

6.14 ἀκηκόαμεν γὰρ αὐτοῦ λέγοντος ὅτι Ἰησοῦς ὁ
FOR~WE HAVE HEARD HIM SAYING THAT ²JESUS ³THE

Ναζωραῖος οὗτος καταλύσει τὸν τόπον τοῦτον καὶ
⁴NAZARENE ¹THIS WILL DESTROY - THIS~PLACE AND

ἀλλάξει τὰ ἔθη ἃ παρέδωκεν ἡμῖν Μωϋσῆς.
WILL CHANGE THE CUSTOMS WHICH HANDED DOWN TO US MOSES.

6.15 καὶ ἀτενίσαντες εἰς αὐτὸν πάντες οἱ
AND HAVING LOOKED INTENTLY AT HIM ALL THE ONES

καθεζόμενοι ἐν τῷ συνεδρίῳ εἶδον τὸ πρόσωπον αὐτοῦ
SITTING IN THE COUNCIL SAW THE FACE OF HIM

ὡσεὶ πρόσωπον ἀγγέλου.
LIKE [THE] FACE OF AN ANGEL.

CHAPTER 7

Then the high priest asked him, "Are these things so?" [2]And Stephen replied:
"Brothers[w] and fathers, listen to me. The God of glory appeared to our ancestor Abraham when he was in Mesopotamia, before he lived in Haran, [3]and said to him, 'Leave your country and your relatives and go to the land that I will show you.' [4]Then he left the country of the Chaldeans and settled in Haran. After his father died, God had him move from there to this country in which you are now living. [5]He did not give him any of it as a heritage, not even a foot's length, but promised to give it to him as his possession and to his descendants after

[w] Gk *Men, brothers*

7.1 Εἶπεν δὲ ὁ ἀρχιερεύς, Εἰ ταῦτα οὕτως ἔχει;
AND~SAID THE HIGH PRIEST, IF THESE THINGS THUS IT IS?

7.2 ὁ δὲ ἔφη, Ἄνδρες ἀδελφοὶ καὶ πατέρες, ἀκούσατε.
- AND HE SAID, MEN, BROTHERS AND FATHERS, LISTEN.

Ὁ θεὸς τῆς δόξης ὤφθη τῷ πατρὶ ἡμῶν Ἀβραὰμ
THE GOD - OF GLORY APPEARED TO THE FATHER OF US ABRAHAM

ὄντι ἐν τῇ Μεσοποταμίᾳ πρὶν ἢ κατοικῆσαι αὐτὸν
[WHILE] BEING IN - MESOPOTAMIA BEFORE HE~LIVED

ἐν Χαρρὰν **7.3** καὶ εἶπεν πρὸς αὐτόν, Ἔξελθε ἐκ τῆς
IN HARAN AND HE SAID TO HIM, DEPART FROM THE

γῆς σου καὶ [ἐκ] τῆς συγγενείας σου, καὶ δεῦρο εἰς
LAND OF YOU AND FROM THE RELATIVES OF YOU, AND COME TO

τὴν γῆν ἣν ἄν σοι δείξω. **7.4** τότε ἐξελθὼν ἐκ
THE LAND WHICHEVER I MAY SHOW~YOU. THEN HAVING DEPARTED FROM

γῆς Χαλδαίων κατῴκησεν ἐν Χαρράν. κἀκεῖθεν
[THE] LAND OF [THE] CHALDEANS HE SETTLED IN HARAN. AND FROM THERE

μετὰ τὸ ἀποθανεῖν τὸν πατέρα αὐτοῦ μετῴκισεν αὐτὸν
AFTER THE DEATH [OF] THE FATHER OF HIM, HE RESETTLED HIM

εἰς τὴν γῆν ταύτην εἰς ἣν ὑμεῖς νῦν κατοικεῖτε,
IN - THIS~LAND IN WHICH WE NOW ARE LIVING,

7.5 καὶ οὐκ ἔδωκεν αὐτῷ κληρονομίαν ἐν αὐτῇ οὐδὲ
AND HE DID NOT GIVE TO HIM AN INHERITANCE IN IT NOR

βῆμα ποδὸς καὶ ἐπηγγείλατο δοῦναι αὐτῷ εἰς
[THE] STEP OF A FOOT AND HE PROMISED TO GIVE TO HIM FOR

κατάσχεσιν αὐτὴν καὶ τῷ σπέρματι αὐτοῦ μετ'
A POSSESSION IT AND TO THE SEED OF HIM AFTER

7:3 Gen. 12:1 **7:5** Gen. 17:8; 48:4

αὐτόν, οὐκ ὄντος αὐτῷ τέκνου. **7.6** ἐλάλησεν δὲ οὕτως
HIM,   NOT   BEING TO HIM A CHILD.   AND~SPOKE   THUS

ὁ θεὸς ὅτι ἔσται τὸ σπέρμα αὐτοῦ πάροικον ἐν
- GOD, THAT WILL BE THE SEED OF HIM A STRANGER IN

γῇ ἀλλοτρίᾳ καὶ δουλώσουσιν αὐτὸ καὶ
ANOTHER'S~LAND AND THEY WILL ENSLAVE IT(THEM) AND

κακώσουσιν   ἔτη τετρακόσια· **7.7** καὶ τὸ ἔθνος
THEY WILL MISTREAT [THEM] FOUR HUNDRED~YEARS.   AND THE NATION

ᾧ ἐὰν   δουλεύσουσιν   κρινῶ ἐγώ, ὁ θεὸς εἶπεν, καὶ
IN WHICHEVER THEY WILL SERVE AS SLAVES I~WILL JUDGE, - GOD SAID, AND

μετὰ ταῦτα   ἐξελεύσονται καὶ λατρεύσουσίν μοι ἐν
AFTER THESE THINGS THEY WILL COME OUT AND WILL SERVE ME IN

τῷ τόπῳ τούτῳ. **7.8** καὶ ἔδωκεν αὐτῷ διαθήκην
- THIS~PLACE.   AND HE GAVE TO HIM A COVENANT

περιτομῆς· καὶ οὕτως ἐγέννησεν   τὸν Ἰσαὰκ
OF CIRCUMCISION. AND THUS HE BECAME [THE] FATHER OF - ISAAC

καὶ περιέτεμεν αὐτὸν τῇ ἡμέρᾳ τῇ ὀγδόῃ, καὶ
AND CIRCUMCISED HIM ON THE ²DAY - ¹EIGHTH, AND

Ἰσαὰκ   τὸν Ἰακώβ, καὶ Ἰακὼβ τοὺς δώδεκα
ISAAC [BECAME THE FATHER OF] - JACOB, AND JACOB, [OF] THE TWELVE

πατριάρχας.
PATRIARCHS.

7.9 Καὶ οἱ πατριάρχαι ζηλώσαντες   τὸν Ἰωσὴφ
AND THE PATRIARCHS HAVING BEEN JEALOUS OF - JOSEPH

ἀπέδοντο εἰς Αἴγυπτον. καὶ ἦν ὁ θεὸς μετ' αὐτοῦ
SOLD [HIM] INTO EGYPT. AND ²WAS - ¹GOD WITH HIM,

7.10 καὶ ἐξείλατο αὐτὸν ἐκ πασῶν τῶν θλίψεων αὐτοῦ
AND HE DELIVERED HIM FROM ALL THE TRIBULATIONS OF HIM

καὶ ἔδωκεν αὐτῷ χάριν καὶ σοφίαν ἐναντίον Φαραὼ
AND GAVE TO HIM GRACE AND WISDOM BEFORE PHARAOH,

βασιλέως Αἰγύπτου καὶ κατέστησεν αὐτὸν ἡγούμενον
KING   OF EGYPT,   AND HE APPOINTED HIM [THE ONE] RULING

ἐπ' Αἴγυπτον καὶ [ἐφ'] ὅλον τὸν οἶκον αὐτοῦ.
OVER EGYPT AND OVER THE~WHOLE HOUSE OF HIM.

7.11 ἦλθεν δὲ λιμὸς ἐφ' ὅλην τὴν Αἴγυπτον καὶ
NOW~CAME A FAMINE OVER ALL - EGYPT   AND

Χανάαν καὶ θλῖψις μεγάλη, καὶ οὐχ ηὕρισκον
CANAAN AND GREAT~TRIBULATION, AND WERE NOT FINDING

χορτάσματα οἱ πατέρες ἡμῶν. **7.12** ἀκούσας δὲ Ἰακὼβ
FOOD   THE FATHERS OF US.   AND~HAVING HEARD JACOB,

ὄντα σιτία εἰς Αἴγυπτον ἐξαπέστειλεν τοὺς πατέρας
WHEAT~BEING IN EGYPT, HE SENT OUT   THE FATHERS

ἡμῶν πρῶτον. **7.13** καὶ ἐν τῷ δευτέρῳ ἀνεγνωρίσθη
OF US FIRST.   AND ON THE SECOND [VISIT] WAS MADE KNOWN AGAIN

Ἰωσὴφ τοῖς ἀδελφοῖς αὐτοῦ καὶ φανερὸν ἐγένετο τῷ
JOSEPH TO THE BROTHERS OF HIM AND BECAME~MANIFEST -

him, even though he had no child. ⁶And God spoke in these terms, that his descendants would be resident aliens in a country belonging to others, who would enslave them and mistreat them during four hundred years. ⁷'But I will judge the nation that they serve,' said God, 'and after that they shall come out and worship me in this place.' ⁸Then he gave him the covenant of circumcision. And so Abraham ˣ became the father of Isaac and circumcised him on the eighth day; and Isaac became the father of Jacob, and Jacob of the twelve patriarchs.

9 "The patriarchs, jealous of Joseph, sold him into Egypt; but God was with him, ¹⁰and rescued him from all his afflictions, and enabled him to win favor and to show wisdom when he stood before Pharaoh, king of Egypt, who appointed him ruler over Egypt and over all his household. ¹¹Now there came a famine throughout Egypt and Canaan, and great suffering, and our ancestors could find no food. ¹²But when Jacob heard that there was grain in Egypt, he sent our ancestors there on their first visit. ¹³On the second visit Joseph made himself known to his brothers,

ˣ Gk *he*

7:6-7 Gen. 15:13-14   **7:7** Exod. 3:12

and Joseph's family became known to Pharaoh. [14]Then Joseph sent and invited his father Jacob and all his relatives to come to him, seventy-five in all; [15]so Jacob went down to Egypt. He himself died there as well as our ancestors, [16]and their bodies[y] were brought back to Shechem and laid in the tomb that Abraham had bought for a sum of silver from the sons of Hamor in Shechem.

17 "But as the time drew near for the fulfillment of the promise that God had made to Abraham, our people in Egypt increased and multiplied [18]until another king who had not known Joseph ruled over Egypt. [19]He dealt craftily with our race and forced our ancestors to abandon their infants so that they would die. [20]At this time Moses was born, and he was beautiful before God. For three months he was brought up in his father's house; [21]and when he was abandoned, Pharaoh's daughter adopted him and brought him up as her own son. [22]So Moses was instructed in all the wisdom of the Egyptians and was powerful in his words and deeds.

23 "When he was forty

[y] Gk *they*

Φαραὼ τὸ γένος [τοῦ] Ἰωσήφ. **7.14** ἀποστείλας δὲ
TO PHARAOH   THE   FAMILY   -   OF JOSEPH.   AND~HAVING SENT,

Ἰωσὴφ μετεκαλέσατο Ἰακὼβ τὸν πατέρα αὐτοῦ καὶ
JOSEPH   SUMMONED   JACOB,   THE   FATHER   OF HIM,   AND

πᾶσαν τὴν συγγένειαν ἐν ψυχαῖς ἑβδομήκοντα πέντε.
ALL   THE   RELATIVES,   IN   SOULS   SEVENTY-FIVE.

7.15 καὶ κατέβη Ἰακὼβ εἰς Αἴγυπτον καὶ
AND   CAME DOWN   JACOB   TO   EGYPT   AND

ἐτελεύτησεν αὐτὸς καὶ οἱ πατέρες ἡμῶν, **7.16** καὶ
HE~DIED   AND   THE   FATHERS   OF US,   AND

μετετέθησαν εἰς Συχὲμ καὶ ἐτέθησαν ἐν τῷ
THEY WERE BROUGHT BACK   TO   SHECHEM   AND   WERE PLACED   IN   THE

μνήματι ᾧ ὠνήσατο Ἀβραὰμ τιμῆς ἀργυρίου παρὰ
TOMB   WHICH   ABRAHAM~BOUGHT   FOR A SUM   OF SILVER   FROM

τῶν υἱῶν Ἐμμὼρ ἐν Συχέμ.
THE   SONS   OF HAMOR   IN   SHECHEM.

7.17 Καθὼς δὲ ἤγγιζεν ὁ χρόνος τῆς ἐπαγγελίας
NOW~AS   WAS DRAWING NEAR   THE   TIME   OF THE   PROMISE

ἧς ὡμολόγησεν ὁ θεὸς τῷ Ἀβραάμ, ηὔξησεν ὁ
WHICH   PROMISED   -   GOD   -   TO ABRAHAM,   [3]GREW   [1]THE

λαὸς καὶ ἐπληθύνθη ἐν Αἰγύπτῳ **7.18** ἄχρι οὗ ἀνέστη
[2]PEOPLE   AND   WERE MULTIPLIED   IN   EGYPT   UNTIL   AROSE

βασιλεὺς ἕτερος [ἐπ᾽ Αἴγυπτον] ὃς οὐκ ᾔδει τὸν
ANOTHER~KING   OVER   EGYPT   WHO   HAD NOT KNOWN   -

Ἰωσήφ. **7.19** οὗτος κατασοφισάμενος τὸ γένος ἡμῶν
JOSEPH.   THIS ONE   HAVING TAKEN ADVANTAGE OF   THE   NATION   OF US

ἐκάκωσεν τοὺς πατέρας [ἡμῶν] τοῦ ποιεῖν τὰ βρέφη
MISTREATED   THE   FATHERS   OF US   -   TO MAKE   THE   INFANTS

ἔκθετα αὐτῶν εἰς τὸ μὴ ζῳογονεῖσθαι. **7.20** ἐν ᾧ
OF THEM~EXPOSED   IN ORDER   -   NOT   TO KEEP [THEM] ALIVE.   IN   WHICH

καιρῷ ἐγεννήθη Μωϋσῆς καὶ ἦν ἀστεῖος τῷ θεῷ·
TIME   WAS BORN   MOSES,   AND   HE WAS   WELL-PLEASING   -   TO GOD;

ὃς ἀνετράφη μῆνας τρεῖς ἐν τῷ οἴκῳ τοῦ
WHO   WAS NURTURED [FOR]   THREE~MONTHS   IN   THE   HOUSE   OF THE(HIS)

πατρός, **7.21** ἐκτεθέντος δὲ αὐτοῦ ἀνείλατο αὐτὸν ἡ
FATHER,   AND~HAVING BEEN EXPOSED   HIM,   TOOK UP   HIM   THE

θυγάτηρ Φαραὼ καὶ ἀνεθρέψατο αὐτὸν ἑαυτῇ εἰς
DAUGHTER   OF PHARAOH   AND   SHE RAISED   HIM   FOR HERSELF   AS

υἱόν. **7.22** καὶ ἐπαιδεύθη Μωϋσῆς [ἐν] πάσῃ σοφίᾳ
A SON.   AND   MOSES~WAS INSTRUCTED   IN   ALL   [THE] WISDOM

Αἰγυπτίων, ἦν δὲ δυνατὸς ἐν λόγοις καὶ ἔργοις
OF [THE] EGYPTIANS,   AND~HE WAS   POWERFUL   IN   WORDS   AND   DEEDS

αὐτοῦ.
OF HIM.

7.23 Ὡς δὲ ἐπληροῦτο αὐτῷ τεσσερακονταετὴς χρόνος,
BUT~WHEN   WAS FULFILLED   IN HIM   FORTY YEARS   TIME,

7:18 Exod. 1:8

ἀνέβη ἐπὶ τὴν καρδίαν αὐτοῦ ἐπισκέψασθαι τοὺς
AROSE UPON THE HEART OF HIM TO VISIT THE

ἀδελφοὺς αὐτοῦ τοὺς υἱοὺς Ἰσραήλ. **7.24** καὶ ἰδών
BROTHERS OF HIM, THE SONS OF ISRAEL. AND HAVING SEEN

τινα ἀδικούμενον ἠμύνατο καὶ ἐποίησεν
SOMEONE BEING TREATED UNJUSTLY, HE RETALIATED AND BROUGHT

ἐκδίκησιν τῷ καταπονουμένῳ πατάξας τὸν
JUSTICE FOR THE ONE BEING OPPRESSED, HAVING STRUCK DOWN THE

Αἰγύπτιον. **7.25** ἐνόμιζεν δὲ συνιέναι τοὺς ἀδελφοὺς
EGYPTIAN. NOW~HE WAS THINKING ⁴TO UNDERSTAND ¹THE ²BROTHERS

[αὐτοῦ] ὅτι ὁ θεὸς διὰ χειρὸς αὐτοῦ δίδωσιν σωτηρίαν
³OF HIM THAT - GOD BY [THE] HAND OF HIM IS GIVING SALVATION

αὐτοῖς· οἱ δὲ οὐ συνῆκαν. **7.26** τῇ τε ἐπιούσῃ
TO THEM. - BUT THEY DID NOT UNDERSTAND. AND~ON THE NEXT

ἡμέρᾳ ὤφθη αὐτοῖς μαχομένοις καὶ
DAY HE APPEARED TO THEM [AS THEY WERE] FIGHTING AND

συνήλλασσεν αὐτοὺς εἰς εἰρήνην εἰπών, Ἄνδρες,
WAS RECONCILING THEM TO PEACE HAVING SAID, MEN,

ἀδελφοί ἐστε· ἱνατί ἀδικεῖτε ἀλλήλους;
YOU°ARE~BROTHERS. WHY ARE YOU° INJURING ONE ANOTHER?

7.27 ὁ δὲ ἀδικῶν τὸν πλησίον ἀπώσατο αὐτὸν
BUT~THE ONE INJURING THE(HIS) NEIGHBOR PUSHED ASIDE HIM

εἰπών, Τίς σε κατέστησεν ἄρχοντα καὶ δικαστὴν ἐφ'
HAVING SAID, WHO APPOINTED~YOU RULER AND JUDGE OVER

ἡμῶν; **7.28** μὴ ἀνελεῖν με σὺ θέλεις ὃν τρόπον
US? ²[DO] NOT ⁴TO KILL ⁵ME ¹YOU ³WISH IN THE SAME MANNER AS

ἀνεῖλες ἐχθὲς τὸν Αἰγύπτιον; **7.29** ἔφυγεν δὲ Μωϋσῆς
YOU KILLED YESTERDAY THE EGYPTIAN? AND~FLED MOSES

ἐν τῷ λόγῳ τούτῳ καὶ ἐγένετο πάροικος ἐν γῇ
AT - THIS~WORD AND BECAME A STRANGER IN [THE] LAND

Μαδιάμ, οὗ ἐγέννησεν υἱοὺς δύο.
OF MIDIAN, WHERE HE BECAME [THE] FATHER OF TWO~SONS.

7.30 Καὶ πληρωθέντων ἐτῶν τεσσεράκοντα ὤφθη
AND HAVING BEEN FULFILLED FORTY~YEARS, APPEARED

αὐτῷ ἐν τῇ ἐρήμῳ τοῦ ὄρους Σινᾶ ἄγγελος ἐν
TO HIM IN THE DESERT OF THE MOUNTAIN SINAI, AN ANGEL IN

φλογὶ πυρὸς βάτου. **7.31** ὁ δὲ Μωϋσῆς ἰδών
[THE] FLAME OF A THORN BUSH~OF FIRE. - AND MOSES HAVING SEEN [THIS]

ἐθαύμαζεν τὸ ὅραμα, προσερχομένου δὲ αὐτοῦ
WAS AMAZED AT THE VISION, AND~APPROACHING IT

κατανοῆσαι ἐγένετο φωνὴ κυρίου, **7.32** Ἐγὼ ὁ
TO LOOK [MORE] CLOSELY, CAME [THE] VOICE OF [THE] LORD, I [AM] THE

θεὸς τῶν πατέρων σου, ὁ θεὸς Ἀβραὰμ καὶ Ἰσαὰκ
GOD OF THE FATHERS OF YOU, THE GOD OF ABRAHAM AND ISAAC

καὶ Ἰακώβ. ἔντρομος δὲ γενόμενος Μωϋσῆς
AND JACOB. BUT~TREMBLING HAVING BECOME MOSES

7:27-28 Exod. 2:14   **7:30** Exod. 3:2   **7:32** Exod. 3:6

years old, it came into his heart to visit his relatives, the Israelites.ᶻ ²⁴When he saw one of them being wronged, he defended the oppressed man and avenged him by striking down the Egyptian. ²⁵He supposed that his kinsfolk would understand that God through him was rescuing them, but they did not understand. ²⁶The next day he came to some of them as they were quarreling and tried to reconcile them, saying, 'Men, you are brothers; why do you wrong each other?' ²⁷But the man who was wronging his neighbor pushed Mosesᵃ aside, saying, 'Who made you a ruler and a judge over us? ²⁸Do you want to kill me as you killed the Egyptian yesterday?' ²⁹When he heard this, Moses fled and became a resident alien in the land of Midian. There he became the father of two sons.

30 "Now when forty years had passed, an angel appeared to him in the wilderness of Mount Sinai, in the flame of a burning bush. ³¹When Moses saw it, he was amazed at the sight; and as he approached to look, there came the voice of the Lord: ³²'I am the God of your ancestors, the God of Abraham, Isaac, and Jacob.' Moses began to tremble

ᶻ Gk *his brothers, the sons of Israel*
ᵃ Gk *him*

and did not dare to look. 33Then the Lord said to him, 'Take off the sandals from your feet, for the place where you are standing is holy ground. 34I have surely seen the mistreatment of my people who are in Egypt and have heard their groaning, and I have come down to rescue them. Come now, I will send you to Egypt.'

35 "It was this Moses whom they rejected when they said, 'Who made you a ruler and a judge?' and whom God now sent as both ruler and liberator through the angel who appeared to him in the bush. 36He led them out, having performed wonders and signs in Egypt, at the Red Sea, and in the wilderness for forty years. 37This is the Moses who said to the Israelites, 'God will raise up a prophet for you from your own people[b] as he raised me up.' 38He is the one who was in the congregation in the wilderness with the angel who spoke to him at Mount Sinai, and with our ancestors; and he received living oracles to give to us. 39Our ancestors were unwilling to obey him; instead, they pushed him aside, and in their hearts they turned back to Egypt, 40saying to Aaron, 'Make gods for us who will lead the

[b] Gk *your brothers*

οὐκ ἐτόλμα κατανοῆσαι. **7.33** εἶπεν δὲ αὐτῷ ὁ κύριος,
HE WAS NOT DARING TO LOOK. AND~SAID TO HIM THE LORD,

Λῦσον τὸ ὑπόδημα τῶν ποδῶν σου, ὁ γὰρ τόπος ἐφ'
UNTIE THE SANDAL OF THE FEET OF YOU, FOR~THE PLACE ON

ᾧ ἕστηκας γῆ ἁγία ἐστίν. **7.34** ἰδὼν εἶδον
WHICH YOU HAVE STOOD ³GROUND ²HOLY ¹IS. HAVING SEEN, I SAW

τὴν κάκωσιν τοῦ λαοῦ μου τοῦ ἐν Αἰγύπτῳ καὶ τοῦ
THE MISTREATMENT OF THE PEOPLE OF ME - IN EGYPT AND THE

στεναγμοῦ αὐτῶν ἤκουσα, καὶ κατέβην ἐξελέσθαι
GROANING OF THEM I HEARD, AND I CAME DOWN TO DELIVER

αὐτούς· καὶ νῦν δεῦρο ἀποστείλω σε εἰς Αἴγυπτον.
THEM. AND NOW COME, [THAT] I MAY SEND YOU TO EGYPT.

7.35 Τοῦτον τὸν Μωϋσῆν, ὃν ἠρνήσαντο εἰπόντες, Τίς
THIS - MOSES, WHOM THEY DENIED HAVING SAID, WHO

σε κατέστησεν ἄρχοντα καὶ δικαστήν; τοῦτον ὁ θεὸς
APPOINTED~YOU RULER AND JUDGE? THIS ONE - GOD

[καὶ] ἄρχοντα καὶ λυτρωτὴν ἀπέσταλκεν σὺν χειρὶ
BOTH A RULER AND REDEEMER HAS SENT WITH [THE] HAND

ἀγγέλου τοῦ ὀφθέντος αὐτῷ ἐν τῇ βάτῳ.
OF [THE] ANGEL - HAVING APPEARED TO HIM IN THE THORN BUSH.

7.36 οὗτος ἐξήγαγεν αὐτοὺς ποιήσας τέρατα καὶ σημεῖα
THIS ONE LED OUT THEM HAVING DONE WONDERS AND SIGNS

ἐν γῇ Αἰγύπτῳ καὶ ἐν Ἐρυθρᾷ Θαλάσσῃ καὶ ἐν
IN [THE] LAND [OF] EGYPT AND IN [THE] RED SEA AND IN

τῇ ἐρήμῳ ἔτη τεσσεράκοντα. **7.37** οὗτός ἐστιν ὁ
THE DESERT FORTY~YEARS. THIS IS THE

Μωϋσῆς ὁ εἴπας τοῖς υἱοῖς Ἰσραήλ, Προφήτην
MOSES THE ONE HAVING SAID TO THE SONS OF ISRAEL, ⁴A PROPHET

ὑμῖν ἀναστήσει ὁ θεὸς ἐκ τῶν ἀδελφῶν ὑμῶν ὡς
³FOR YOU° ²WILL RAISE UP - ¹GOD FROM THE BROTHERS OF YOU° LIKE

ἐμέ. **7.38** οὗτός ἐστιν ὁ γενόμενος ἐν τῇ ἐκκλησίᾳ
ME. THIS IS THE ONE HAVING BEEN IN THE ASSEMBLY

ἐν τῇ ἐρήμῳ μετὰ τοῦ ἀγγέλου τοῦ λαλοῦντος αὐτῷ ἐν
IN THE DESERT WITH THE ANGEL - SPEAKING TO HIM AT

τῷ ὄρει Σινᾶ καὶ τῶν πατέρων ἡμῶν, ὃς ἐδέξατο
THE MOUNTAIN OF SINAI AND THE FATHERS OF US, WHO RECEIVED

λόγια ζῶντα δοῦναι ἡμῖν, **7.39** ᾧ οὐκ ἠθέλησαν
LIVING~WORDS TO GIVE TO US, TO WHOM DID NOT WANT

ὑπήκοοι γενέσθαι οἱ πατέρες ἡμῶν, ἀλλὰ
TO BECOME~OBEDIENT THE FATHERS OF US, BUT

ἀπώσαντο καὶ ἐστράφησαν ἐν ταῖς καρδίαις
THEY PUSHED [HIM] ASIDE AND TURNED AWAY IN THE HEARTS

αὐτῶν εἰς Αἴγυπτον **7.40** εἰπόντες τῷ Ἀαρών, Ποίησον
OF THEM TO EGYPT, HAVING SAID - TO AARON, MAKE

ἡμῖν θεοὺς οἳ προπορεύσονται ἡμῶν· ὁ γὰρ
FOR US GODS WHO WILL GO ON BEFORE US. - FOR

7:33 Exod. 3:5   **7:34** Exod. 3:7-8, 10   **7:35** Exod. 2:14   **7:37** Deut. 18:15   **7:40** Exod. 32:1, 23

Μωϋσῆς οὗτος, ὃς ἐξήγαγεν ἡμᾶς ἐκ γῆς Αἰγύπτου,
THIS~MOSES,   WHO LED OUT   US   FROM [THE] LAND OF EGYPT,

οὐκ οἴδαμεν τί ἐγένετο αὐτῷ. **7.41** καὶ
WE DO NOT KNOW WHAT HAPPENED TO HIM.   AND

ἐμοσχοποίησαν ἐν ταῖς ἡμέραις ἐκείναις καὶ
THEY MADE A CALF   IN   -   THOSE~DAYS   AND

ἀνήγαγον θυσίαν τῷ εἰδώλῳ καὶ εὐφραίνοντο ἐν
BROUGHT   AN OFFERING TO THE IDOL   AND WERE TAKING DELIGHT IN

τοῖς ἔργοις τῶν χειρῶν αὐτῶν. **7.42** ἔστρεψεν δὲ ὁ θεὸς
THE WORKS   OF THE HANDS OF THEM.   BUT~TURNED AWAY -   GOD

καὶ παρέδωκεν αὐτοὺς λατρεύειν τῇ στρατιᾷ τοῦ
AND HANDED OVER   THEM   TO SERVE   THE ARMY   -

οὐρανοῦ καθὼς γέγραπται ἐν βίβλῳ τῶν προφητῶν,
OF HEAVEN JUST AS IT HAS BEEN WRITTEN IN [THE] BOOK OF THE PROPHETS,

Μὴ σφάγια καὶ θυσίας προσηνέγκατέ μοι
NOT SACRIFICES AND OFFERINGS DID YOU° BRING   TO ME

ἔτη τεσσεράκοντα ἐν τῇ ἐρήμῳ, οἶκος
FORTY~YEARS   IN   THE DESERT, HOUSE

Ἰσραήλ;
OF ISRAEL, [DID YOU°]?

7.43 καὶ ἀνελάβετε τὴν σκηνὴν τοῦ Μόλοχ
AND YOU° TOOK UP   THE TENT   -   OF MOLOCH

καὶ τὸ ἄστρον τοῦ θεοῦ [ὑμῶν] Ῥαιφάν,
AND THE STAR   OF THE GOD OF YOU° REPHAN,

τοὺς τύπους οὓς ἐποιήσατε προσκυνεῖν
THE   IMAGES WHICH YOU° MADE   TO WORSHIP

αὐτοῖς,
THEM,

καὶ μετοικιῶ ὑμᾶς ἐπέκεινα Βαβυλῶνος.
AND I WILL DEPORT YOU° BEYOND   BABYLON.

7.44 Ἡ σκηνὴ τοῦ μαρτυρίου ἦν τοῖς πατράσιν ἡμῶν
THE TENT   -   OF WITNESS WAS TO THE FATHERS   OF US

ἐν τῇ ἐρήμῳ καθὼς διετάξατο ὁ λαλῶν τῷ Μωϋσῇ
IN THE DESERT JUST AS COMMANDED THE ONE SPEAKING - TO MOSES

ποιῆσαι αὐτὴν κατὰ τὸν τύπον ὃν ἑωράκει·
TO MAKE   IT   ACCORDING TO THE PATTERN WHICH HE HAD SEEN;

7.45 ἣν καὶ εἰσήγαγον διαδεξάμενοι οἱ πατέρες
WHICH ALSO THEY BROUGHT IN, HAVING RECEIVED [IT] IN TURN THE FATHERS

ἡμῶν μετὰ Ἰησοῦ ἐν τῇ κατασχέσει τῶν
OF US WITH JOSHUA IN - TAKING POSSESSION [OF THE LAND] OF THE

ἐθνῶν, ὧν ἐξῶσεν ὁ θεὸς ἀπὸ προσώπου τῶν πατέρων
GENTILES, WHOM ²DROVE OUT - ¹GOD FROM [THE] PRESENCE OF THE FATHERS

ἡμῶν ἕως τῶν ἡμερῶν Δαυίδ, **7.46** ὃς εὗρεν χάριν
OF US UNTIL THE DAYS   OF DAVID,   WHO FOUND GRACE

ἐνώπιον τοῦ θεοῦ καὶ ᾐτήσατο εὑρεῖν σκήνωμα
BEFORE   -   GOD AND HE ASKED   TO FIND   A DWELLING PLACE

7:42-43 Amos 5:25-27 LXX

way for us; as for this Moses who led us out from the land of Egypt, we do not know what has happened to him.' [41]At that time they made a calf, offered a sacrifice to the idol, and reveled in the works of their hands. [42]But God turned away from them and handed them over to worship the host of heaven, as it is written in the book of the prophets:

'Did you offer to me
    slain victims and
    sacrifices
forty years in the
    wilderness, O
    house of Israel?
[43]No; you took along the
    tent of Moloch,
and the star of your god
    Rephan,
    the images that you
    made to worship;
so I will remove you
    beyond Babylon.'

[44]"Our ancestors had the tent of testimony in the wilderness, as God[c] directed when he spoke to Moses, ordering him to make it according to the pattern he had seen. [45]Our ancestors in turn brought it in with Joshua when they dispossessed the nations that God drove out before our ancestors. And it was there until the time of David, [46]who found favor with God and asked that he might find a dwelling place

[c] Gk *he*

for the house of Jacob.[d]
[47]But it was Solomon who built a house for him. [48]Yet the Most High does not dwell in houses made with human hands;[e] as the prophet says,

[49] 'Heaven is my throne,
and the earth is my footstool.
What kind of house will you build for me,
says the Lord,
or what is the place of my rest?
[50]Did not my hand make all these things?'

51 "You stiff-necked people, uncircumcised in heart and ears, you are forever opposing the Holy Spirit, just as your ancestors used to do. [52]Which of the prophets did your ancestors not persecute? They killed those who foretold the coming of the Righteous One, and now you have become his betrayers and murderers. [53]You are the ones that received the law as ordained by angels, and yet you have not kept it."

54 When they heard these things, they became enraged and ground their teeth at Stephen.[f] [55]But filled with the Holy Spirit, he gazed into heaven and saw the glory of God and Jesus standing at the right hand of God. [56]"Look," he said, "I see the heavens opened and the Son

[d] Other ancient authorities read for the God of Jacob
[e] Gk with hands
[f] Gk him

⌐τῷ   οἴκῳ   Ἰακώβ.⌐ **7.47** Σολομῶν δὲ οἰκοδόμησεν
FOR THE HOUSE OF JACOB.   AND~SOLOMON   BUILT

αὐτῷ   οἶκον.   **7.48** ἀλλ'   οὐχ ὁ   ὕψιστος ἐν
FOR HIM A HOUSE.   BUT   ⁴NOT ¹THE ²MOST HIGH ⁵IN

χειροποιήτοις   κατοικεῖ, καθὼς ὁ προφήτης
⁶[A PLACE] MADE BY HUMAN HANDS ³DWELLS, JUST AS THE PROPHET

λέγει,
SAYS,

7.49 Ὁ οὐρανός μοι θρόνος,
-        HEAVEN [IS] MY THRONE,

    ἡ δὲ   γῆ   ὑποπόδιον τῶν ποδῶν μου·
    AND~THE EARTH [IS THE] FOOTSTOOL OF THE FEET OF ME.

    ποῖον   οἶκον οἰκοδομήσετέ μοι, λέγει κύριος,
    WHAT KIND OF HOUSE WILL YOU° BUILD FOR ME, SAYS [THE] LORD,

    ἢ τίς τόπος τῆς καταπαύσεώς μου;
    OR WHAT PLACE -   OF REST [IS THERE] FOR ME?

7.50 οὐχὶ ἡ χείρ μου ἐποίησεν ταῦτα πάντα;
         [DID] NOT THE HAND OF ME MAKE   ALL~THESE THINGS?

7.51 Σκληροτράχηλοι καὶ ἀπερίτμητοι καρδίαις
         [YOU°] STIFF-NECKED [PEOPLE] AND UNCIRCUMCISED OF HEART

καὶ τοῖς ὠσίν, ὑμεῖς ἀεὶ τῷ πνεύματι τῷ ἁγίῳ
AND -   EARS, YOU° ALWAYS ²THE ⁴SPIRIT - ³HOLY

ἀντιπίπτετε ὡς οἱ πατέρες ὑμῶν καὶ ὑμεῖς.
¹RESIST, LIKE THE FATHERS OF YOU° [SO] ALSO [ARE] YOU°.

7.52 τίνα τῶν προφητῶν οὐκ ἐδίωξαν οἱ πατέρες ὑμῶν;
         WHICH OF THE PROPHETS DID ⁴NOT PERSECUTE ¹THE ²FATHERS ³OF YOU°?

καὶ ἀπέκτειναν τοὺς προκαταγγείλαντας περὶ τῆς
AND THEY KILLED THE ONES HAVING ANNOUNCED BEFOREHAND ABOUT THE

ἐλεύσεως τοῦ δικαίου, οὗ νῦν ὑμεῖς προδόται
COMING   OF THE RIGHTEOUS [ONE], OF WHOM NOW YOU° BETRAYERS

καὶ φονεῖς ἐγένεσθε, **7.53** οἵτινες ἐλάβετε τὸν νόμον
AND MURDERERS BECAME,   WHO   RECEIVED THE LAW

εἰς διαταγὰς ἀγγέλων καὶ οὐκ ἐφυλάξατε.
BY DIRECTIONS OF ANGELS AND YOU° DID NOT KEEP [IT].

7.54 Ἀκούοντες δὲ ταῦτα   διεπρίοντο   ταῖς
         AND~HEARING THESE THINGS THEY WERE INFURIATED IN THE

καρδίαις αὐτῶν καὶ ἔβρυχον τοὺς ὀδόντας ἐπ'
HEARTS OF THEM AND THEY WERE GRINDING THE(THEIR) TEETH AT

αὐτόν. **7.55** ὑπάρχων δὲ πλήρης πνεύματος ἁγίου
HIM.   BUT~BEING FULL   OF [THE] HOLY~SPIRIT, [AND]

ἀτενίσας εἰς τὸν οὐρανὸν εἶδεν δόξαν θεοῦ καὶ
HAVING GAZED INTO - HEAVEN, HE SAW [THE] GLORY OF GOD AND

Ἰησοῦν ἑστῶτα ἐκ δεξιῶν τοῦ θεοῦ. **7.56** καὶ εἶπεν,
JESUS HAVING STOOD AT [THE] RIGHT - OF GOD.   AND HE SAID,

Ἰδοὺ θεωρῶ τοὺς οὐρανοὺς διηνοιγμένους καὶ τὸν υἱὸν
BEHOLD I SEE THE HEAVENS   HAVING BEEN OPENED AND THE SON

7:46 text: NASBmg NIVmg NJB TEVmg NRSV. var. τω θεω Ιακωβ (the God of Jacob) [see Ps. 132:5]: KJV
ASV RSV NASB NIV NJBmg TEV NRSVmg.   **7:49-50** Isa. 66:1-2

τοῦ   ἀνθρώπου   ἐκ   δεξιῶν   ἑστῶτα   τοῦ   θεοῦ.
\-   OF MAN   ²AT   ³[THE] RIGHT   ¹HAVING STOOD   -   OF GOD.

7.57 κράξαντες   δὲ   φωνῇ   μεγάλῃ   συνέσχον   τὰ   ὦτα   αὐτῶν
      AND~HAVING CRIED OUT   WITH A LOUD~VOICE   THEY SHUT   THE   EARS   OF THEM

καὶ   ὥρμησαν   ὁμοθυμαδὸν   ἐπ᾽   αὐτὸν   **7.58** καὶ
AND   THEY RUSHED DOWN   WITH ONE IMPULSE   UPON   HIM   AND

ἐκβαλόντες   ἔξω   τῆς   πόλεως   ἐλιθοβόλουν.   καὶ
HAVING DRIVEN [HIM] OUT   OUTSIDE   THE   CITY,   THEY WERE STONING [HIM].   AND

οἱ   μάρτυρες   ἀπέθεντο   τὰ   ἱμάτια   αὐτῶν   παρὰ   τοὺς
THE   WITNESSES   TOOK OFF   THE   GARMENTS   OF THEM   AT   THE

πόδας   νεανίου   καλουμένου   Σαύλου,   **7.59** καὶ
FEET   OF A YOUNG MAN   BEING CALLED   SAUL,   AND

ἐλιθοβόλουν   τὸν   Στέφανον   ἐπικαλούμενον   καὶ
THEY WERE STONING   -   STEPHEN, [AND HE]   CALLING UPON [GOD]   AND

λέγοντα,   Κύριε   Ἰησοῦ,   δέξαι   τὸ   πνεῦμά   μου.
SAYING,   LORD   JESUS,   RECEIVE   THE   SPIRIT   OF ME.

7.60 θεὶς   δὲ   τὰ   γόνατα   ἔκραξεν   φωνῇ   μεγάλῃ,
      AND~HAVING FALLEN ON   THE   KNEES,   HE CRIED OUT   IN A LOUD~VOICE,

Κύριε,   μὴ   στήσῃς   αὐτοῖς   ταύτην   τὴν   ἁμαρτίαν.
LORD,   MAY YOU NOT PLACE   [AGAINST] THEM   THIS   -   SIN.

καὶ   τοῦτο   εἰπὼν   ἐκοιμήθη.
AND   THIS   HAVING SAID,   HE FELL ASLEEP.

of Man standing at the right hand of God!" [57]But they covered their ears, and with a loud shout all rushed together against him. [58]Then they dragged him out of the city and began to stone him; and the witnesses laid their coats at the feet of a young man named Saul. [59]While they were stoning Stephen, he prayed, "Lord Jesus, receive my spirit." [60]Then he knelt down and cried out in a loud voice, "Lord, do not hold this sin against them." When he had said this, he died.[g]

[g] Gk *fell asleep*

CHAPTER 8

8.1 Σαῦλος   δὲ   ἦν   συνευδοκῶν τῇ   ἀναιρέσει   αὐτοῦ.
    AND~SAUL   WAS GIVING APPROVAL   TO THE   MURDER   OF HIM.

Ἐγένετο   δὲ   ἐν   ἐκείνῃ   τῇ   ἡμέρᾳ   διωγμὸς   μέγας
AND~THERE CAME ABOUT   IN   THAT   -   DAY   A GREAT~PERSECUTION

ἐπὶ   τὴν   ἐκκλησίαν   τὴν   ἐν   Ἱεροσολύμοις,   πάντες   δὲ
AGAINST   THE   CHURCH   -   IN   JERUSALEM,   AND~EVERYONE

διεσπάρησαν   κατὰ   τὰς   χώρας   τῆς   Ἰουδαίας   καὶ
WAS SCATTERED   THROUGHOUT   THE   REGIONS   -   OF JUDEA   AND

Σαμαρείας   πλὴν   τῶν   ἀποστόλων.   **8.2** συνεκόμισαν
SAMARIA   EXCEPT   THE   APOSTLES.   ⁴BURIED

δὲ   τὸν   Στέφανον   ἄνδρες   εὐλαβεῖς   καὶ   ἐποίησαν
¹AND   -   ⁵STEPHEN   ³MEN   ²DEVOUT   AND   THEY MADE

κοπετὸν   μέγαν   ἐπ᾽   αὐτῷ.   **8.3** Σαῦλος   δὲ   ἐλυμαίνετο
LOUD~LAMENTATION   OVER   HIM.   BUT~SAUL   WAS DESTROYING

τὴν   ἐκκλησίαν   κατὰ   τοὺς   οἴκους   εἰσπορευόμενος,   σύρων
THE   CHURCH   ²HOUSE BY HOUSE   ¹ENTERING   DRAGGING

τε   ἄνδρας   καὶ   γυναῖκας   παρεδίδου   εἰς   φυλακήν.
BOTH   MEN   AND   WOMEN,   HE WAS DELIVERING [THEM]   TO   JAIL.

8.4 Οἱ   μὲν   οὖν   διασπαρέντες   διῆλθον
    THE ONES   -   THEREFORE   HAVING BEEN SCATTERED,   WENT ABOUT

εὐαγγελιζόμενοι   τὸν   λόγον.   **8.5** Φίλιππος   δὲ
PREACHING   THE   WORD.   NOW~PHILIP

And Saul approved of their killing him.

That day a severe persecution began against the church in Jerusalem, and all except the apostles were scattered throughout the countryside of Judea and Samaria. [2]Devout men buried Stephen and made loud lamentation over him. [3]But Saul was ravaging the church by entering house after house; dragging off both men and women, he committed them to prison.

[4] Now those who were scattered went from place to place, proclaiming the word. [5]Philip

went down to the city[h] of Samaria and proclaimed the Messiah[i] to them. [6]The crowds with one accord listened eagerly to what was said by Philip, hearing and seeing the signs that he did, [7]for unclean spirits, crying with loud shrieks, came out of many who were possessed; and many others who were paralyzed or lame were cured. [8]So there was great joy in that city.

9 Now a certain man named Simon had previously practiced magic in the city and amazed the people of Samaria, saying that he was someone great. [10]All of them, from the least to the greatest, listened to him eagerly, saying, "This man is the power of God that is called Great." [11]And they listened eagerly to him because for a long time he had amazed them with his magic. [12]But when they believed Philip, who was proclaiming the good news about the kingdom of God and the name of Jesus Christ, they were baptized, both men and women. [13]Even Simon himself believed. After being baptized, he stayed constantly with Philip and was amazed when he saw the signs and great miracles that took place.

14 Now when the apostles at Jerusalem heard that Samaria had accepted the word of God, they sent Peter and John to them.

[h] Other ancient authorities read a city
[i] Or the Christ

κατελθὼν εἰς [τὴν] πόλιν τῆς Σαμαρείας ἐκήρυσσεν
HAVING GONE DOWN TO THE CITY - OF SAMARIA WAS PREACHING

αὐτοῖς τὸν Χριστόν. **8.6** προσεῖχον δὲ οἱ ὄχλοι
TO THEM THE CHRIST. AND~WERE PAYING ATTENTION THE CROWDS

τοῖς λεγομένοις ὑπὸ τοῦ Φιλίππου ὁμοθυμαδὸν
TO THE THINGS BEING SAID BY - PHILIP WITH ONE ACCORD

ἐν τῷ ἀκούειν αὐτοὺς καὶ βλέπειν τὰ σημεῖα
WHILE THEY~HEAR [HIM] AND SEE THE SIGNS

ἃ ἐποίει. **8.7** πολλοὶ γὰρ τῶν ἐχόντων
WHICH HE WAS DOING. FOR~MANY OF THE ONES HAVING

πνεύματα ἀκάθαρτα βοῶντα φωνῇ μεγάλῃ ἐξήρχοντο,
UNCLEAN~SPIRITS, CRYING OUT WITH A LOUD~VOICE, WERE COMING OUT,

πολλοὶ δὲ παραλελυμένοι καὶ χωλοὶ ἐθεραπεύθησαν·
AND~MANY HAVING BEEN PARALYZED AND LAME [ONES] WERE HEALED.

8.8 ἐγένετο δὲ πολλὴ χαρὰ ἐν τῇ πόλει ἐκείνῃ.
AND~THERE WAS GREAT JOY IN - THAT~CITY.

8.9 Ἀνὴρ δέ τις ὀνόματι Σίμων προὐπῆρχεν ἐν
[3]MAN [1]NOW [2]A CERTAIN BY NAME SIMON WAS PREVIOUSLY IN

τῇ πόλει μαγεύων καὶ ἐξιστάνων τὸ ἔθνος τῆς
THE CITY PRACTICING MAGIC AND ASTONISHING THE PEOPLE -

Σαμαρείας, λέγων εἶναί τινα ἑαυτὸν μέγαν, **8.10** ᾧ
OF SAMARIA, SAYING TO BE HIMSELF~SOMEONE GREAT, TO WHOM

προσεῖχον πάντες ἀπὸ μικροῦ ἕως μεγάλου
WERE PAYING ATTENTION EVERYONE FROM [THE] SMALL TO [THE] GREAT

λέγοντες, Οὗτός ἐστιν ἡ δύναμις τοῦ θεοῦ ἡ
SAYING, THIS IS THE POWER OF GOD -

καλουμένη Μεγάλη. **8.11** προσεῖχον δὲ αὐτῷ
BEING CALLED GREAT. AND~THEY WERE PAYING ATTENTION TO HIM

διὰ τὸ ἱκανῷ χρόνῳ ταῖς μαγείαις ἐξεστακέναι
BECAUSE [HE] - FOR A LONG TIME BY THE MAGIC TRICKS TO HAVE ASTONISHED

αὐτούς. **8.12** ὅτε δὲ ἐπίστευσαν τῷ Φιλίππῳ
THEM. BUT~WHEN THEY BELIEVED - PHILIP

εὐαγγελιζομένῳ περὶ τῆς βασιλείας τοῦ θεοῦ καὶ τοῦ
PREACHING ABOUT THE KINGDOM - OF GOD AND THE

ὀνόματος Ἰησοῦ Χριστοῦ, ἐβαπτίζοντο ἄνδρες τε καὶ
NAME OF JESUS CHRIST, WERE BEING BAPTIZED BOTH~MEN AND

γυναῖκες. **8.13** ὁ δὲ Σίμων καὶ αὐτὸς ἐπίστευσεν καὶ
WOMEN. - AND SIMON HIMSELF~ALSO BELIEVED AND

βαπτισθεὶς ἦν προσκαρτερῶν τῷ Φιλίππῳ, θεωρῶν τε
HAVING BEEN BAPTIZED HE WAS FOLLOWING - PHILIP, AND~SEEING

σημεῖα καὶ δυνάμεις μεγάλας γινομένας ἐξίστατο.
SIGNS AND GREAT~MIRACLES BEING DONE, HE WAS AMAZED.

8.14 Ἀκούσαντες δὲ οἱ ἐν Ἱεροσολύμοις ἀπόστολοι
AND~HAVING HEARD THE [2]IN [3]JERUSALEM [1]APOSTLES

ὅτι δέδεκται ἡ Σαμάρεια τὸν λόγον τοῦ θεοῦ,
THAT [2]HAS ACCEPTED - [1]SAMARIA THE WORD - OF GOD,

ἀπέστειλαν πρὸς αὐτοὺς Πέτρον καὶ Ἰωάννην,
THEY SENT TO THEM PETER AND JOHN,

8.15 οἵτινες καταβάντες προσηύξαντο περὶ αὐτῶν ὅπως
WHO   HAVING COME DOWN,   PRAYED   FOR   THEM   THAT

λάβωσιν πνεῦμα ἅγιον· **8.16** οὐδέπω γὰρ
THEY MIGHT RECEIVE   [THE] HOLY~SPIRIT.   FOR~NOT YET

ἦν ἐπ’ οὐδενὶ αὐτῶν ἐπιπεπτωκός, μόνον δὲ
HAD HE UPON ANYONE OF THEM FALLEN,   BUT~ONLY

βεβαπτισμένοι ὑπῆρχον εἰς τὸ ὄνομα τοῦ κυρίου
THEY HAD BEEN BAPTIZED   IN THE NAME OF THE LORD

Ἰησοῦ. **8.17** τότε ἐπετίθεσαν τὰς χεῖρας ἐπ’ αὐτοὺς
JESUS.   THEN THEY WERE LAYING THE(THEIR) HANDS UPON THEM

καὶ ἐλάμβανον πνεῦμα ἅγιον. **8.18** ἰδὼν δὲ ὁ
AND THEY WERE RECEIVING [THE] HOLY~SPIRIT.   AND~HAVING SEEN -

Σίμων ὅτι διὰ τῆς ἐπιθέσεως τῶν χειρῶν τῶν
SIMON THAT THROUGH THE LAYING ON OF THE HANDS OF THE

ἀποστόλων δίδοται ⌜τὸ πνεῦμα,⌝ προσήνεγκεν αὐτοῖς
APOSTLES IS GIVEN THE SPIRIT, HE BROUGHT TO THEM

χρήματα **8.19** λέγων, Δότε κἀμοὶ τὴν ἐξουσίαν ταύτην
MONEY   SAYING, GIVE ME ALSO - THIS~AUTHORITY

ἵνα ᾧ ἐὰν ἐπιθῶ τὰς χεῖρας λαμβάνῃ
THAT WHOMEVER I MAY LAY THE(MY) HANDS HE MAY RECEIVE

πνεῦμα ἅγιον. **8.20** Πέτρος δὲ εἶπεν πρὸς αὐτόν, Τὸ
[THE] HOLY~SPIRIT.   BUT~PETER SAID TO HIM, THE

ἀργύριόν σου σὺν σοὶ εἴη εἰς ἀπώλειαν ὅτι τὴν
SILVER OF YOU WITH YOU MAY IT BE TO DESTRUCTION BECAUSE THE

δωρεὰν τοῦ θεοῦ ἐνόμισας διὰ χρημάτων κτᾶσθαι·
GIFT - OF GOD YOU THOUGHT BY MONEY TO ACQUIRE.

8.21 οὐκ ἔστιν σοι μερὶς οὐδὲ κλῆρος ἐν τῷ
THERE IS NOT TO YOU A PART NOR SHARE IN -

λόγῳ τούτῳ, ἡ γὰρ καρδία σου οὐκ ἔστιν εὐθεῖα ἔναντι
THIS~MATTER, FOR~THE HEART OF YOU IS NOT UPRIGHT BEFORE

τοῦ θεοῦ. **8.22** μετανόησον οὖν ἀπὸ τῆς κακίας σου
- GOD.   THEREFORE~REPENT OF - ²WICKEDNESS ³OF YOU

ταύτης καὶ δεήθητι τοῦ κυρίου, εἰ ἄρα ἀφεθήσεταί
¹THIS AND PRAY TO THE LORD IF PERHAPS WILL BE FORGIVEN

σοι ἡ ἐπίνοια τῆς καρδίας σου, **8.23** εἰς γὰρ
YOU THE INTENT OF THE HEART OF YOU,   FOR~IN

χολὴν πικρίας καὶ σύνδεσμον ἀδικίας ὁρῶ σε
BITTER~GALL AND [THE] BOND OF UNRIGHTEOUSNESS I SEE YOU

ὄντα. **8.24** ἀποκριθεὶς δὲ ὁ Σίμων εἶπεν, Δεήθητε ὑμεῖς
BEING.   AND~HAVING ANSWERED - SIMON SAID, YOU°~PRAY

ὑπὲρ ἐμοῦ πρὸς τὸν κύριον ὅπως μηδὲν ἐπέλθῃ ἐπ’
FOR ME TO THE LORD THAT NOTHING MAY COME UPON

ἐμὲ ὧν εἰρήκατε.
ME OF WHICH YOU° HAVE SPOKEN.

8.25 Οἱ μὲν οὖν διαμαρτυράμενοι καὶ λαλήσαντες
THE ONES - THEN HAVING TESTIFIED AND SPOKEN

¹⁵The two went down and prayed for them that they might receive the Holy Spirit ¹⁶(for as yet the Spirit had not come[j] upon any of them; they had only been baptized in the name of the Lord Jesus). ¹⁷Then Peter and John[k] laid their hands on them, and they received the Holy Spirit. ¹⁸Now when Simon saw that the Spirit was given through the laying on of the apostles' hands, he offered them money, ¹⁹saying, "Give me also this power so that anyone on whom I lay my hands may receive the Holy Spirit." ²⁰But Peter said to him, "May your silver perish with you, because you thought you could obtain God's gift with money! ²¹You have no part or share in this, for your heart is not right before God. ²²Repent therefore of this wickedness of yours, and pray to the Lord that, if possible, the intent of your heart may be forgiven you. ²³For I see that you are in the gall of bitterness and the chains of wickedness." ²⁴Simon answered, "Pray for me to the Lord, that nothing of what you[l] have said may happen to me."

25 Now after Peter and John[m] had testified and

j Gk *fallen*
k Gk *they*
l The Greek word for *you* and the verb *pray* are plural
m Gk *after they*

8:18 text: ASVmg RSV NASB NIV NEB TEV NJB NRSV. var. πνευμα το αγιον (the Holy Spirit): KJV ASV.

spoken the word of the Lord, they returned to Jerusalem, proclaiming the good news to many villages of the Samaritans.

26 Then an angel of the Lord said to Philip, "Get up and go toward the south[n] to the road that goes down from Jerusalem to Gaza." (This is a wilderness road.) [27]So he got up and went. Now there was an Ethiopian eunuch, a court official of the Candace, queen of the Ethiopians, in charge of her entire treasury. He had come to Jerusalem to worship [28]and was returning home; seated in his chariot, he was reading the prophet Isaiah. [29]Then the Spirit said to Philip, "Go over to this chariot and join it." [30]So Philip ran up to it and heard him reading the prophet Isaiah. He asked, "Do you understand what you are reading?" [31]He replied, "How can I, unless someone guides me?" And he invited Philip to get in and sit beside him. [32]Now the passage of the scripture that he was reading was this:

"Like a sheep he was led
to the slaughter,
and like a lamb silent
before its shearer,

[n] Or *go at noon*

τὸν λόγον τοῦ κυρίου ὑπέστρεφον εἰς Ἰεροσόλυμα,
THE WORD OF THE LORD WERE RETURNING TO JERUSALEM,

πολλάς τε κώμας τῶν Σαμαριτῶν εὐηγγελίζοντο.
AND~TO MANY VILLAGES OF THE SAMARITANS WERE PREACHING THE GOOD NEWS.

8.26 Ἄγγελος δὲ κυρίου ἐλάλησεν πρὸς Φίλιππον
AND~AN ANGEL OF [THE] LORD SPOKE TO PHILIP

λέγων, Ἀνάστηθι καὶ πορεύου κατὰ μεσημβρίαν ἐπὶ
SAYING, GET UP AND GO TOWARD [THE] SOUTH ON

τὴν ὁδὸν τὴν καταβαίνουσαν ἀπὸ Ἰερουσαλὴμ εἰς
THE ROAD - GOING DOWN FROM JERUSALEM TO

Γάζαν, αὕτη ἐστὶν ἔρημος. **8.27** καὶ ἀναστὰς
GAZA, THIS IS DESERT. AND HAVING ARISEN,

ἐπορεύθη. καὶ ἰδοὺ ἀνὴρ Αἰθίοψ εὐνοῦχος δυνάστης
HE WENT. AND BEHOLD AN ETHIOPIAN~MAN, A EUNUCH, A COURT OFFICIAL

Κανδάκης βασιλίσσης Αἰθιόπων, ὃς ἦν ἐπὶ πάσης
OF CANDACE, QUEEN OF [THE] ETHIOPIANS, WHO WAS OVER ALL

τῆς γάζης αὐτῆς, ὃς ἐληλύθει προσκυνήσων εἰς
THE TREASURY OF HER, WHO HAD COME WORSHIPING TO

Ἰερουσαλήμ, **8.28** ἦν τε ὑποστρέφων καὶ καθήμενος
JERUSALEM, AND~HE WAS RETURNING AND SITTING

ἐπὶ τοῦ ἅρματος αὐτοῦ καὶ ἀνεγίνωσκεν τὸν
IN THE CHARIOT OF HIM AND HE WAS READING THE

προφήτην Ἠσαΐαν. **8.29** εἶπεν δὲ τὸ πνεῦμα τῷ
PROPHET ISAIAH. AND~SAID THE SPIRIT -

Φιλίππῳ, Πρόσελθε καὶ κολλήθητι τῷ ἅρματι τούτῳ.
TO PHILIP, APPROACH AND JOIN - THIS~CHARIOT.

8.30 προσδραμὼν δὲ ὁ Φίλιππος ἤκουσεν αὐτοῦ
AND~HAVING RUN - PHILIP HEARD HIM

ἀναγινώσκοντος Ἠσαΐαν τὸν προφήτην καὶ εἶπεν,
READING ISAIAH THE PROPHET AND HE SAID,

Ἆρά γε γινώσκεις ἃ ἀναγινώσκεις; **8.31** ὁ δὲ
THEN DO YOU UNDERSTAND WHAT YOU ARE READING? - AND

εἶπεν, Πῶς γὰρ ἂν δυναίμην ἐὰν μή τις ὁδηγήσει
HE SAID, HOW THEN MIGHT I BE ABLE UNLESS SOMEONE WILL GUIDE

με; παρεκάλεσέν τε τὸν Φίλιππον ἀναβάντα καθίσαι
ME? AND~HE INVITED - PHILIP HAVING COME UP TO SIT

σὺν αὐτῷ. **8.32** ἡ δὲ περιοχὴ τῆς γραφῆς ἦν
WITH HIM. NOW~THE PASSAGE OF THE SCRIPTURE WHICH

ἀνεγίνωσκεν ἦν αὕτη·
HE WAS READING WAS THIS:

Ὡς πρόβατον ἐπὶ σφαγὴν ἤχθη
AS A SHEEP TO [THE] SLAUGHTER HE WAS LED

καὶ ὡς ἀμνὸς ἐναντίον τοῦ κείραντος
AND AS A LAMB BEFORE THE ONE HAVING SHEARED

αὐτὸν ἄφωνος,
IT [IS] SILENT,

8:32-33 Isa. 53:7-8 LXX

οὕτως οὐκ ἀνοίγει τὸ στόμα αὐτοῦ.
SO HE DOES NOT OPEN THE MOUTH OF HIM.

so he does not open
his mouth.

8.33 Ἐν τῇ ταπεινώσει [αὐτοῦ] ἡ κρίσις αὐτοῦ
IN THE HUMILIATION OF HIM, THE JUDGMENT OF HIM

ἤρθη·
WAS TAKEN AWAY.

τὴν γενεὰν αὐτοῦ τίς διηγήσεται;
THE DESCENDANTS OF HIM WHO WILL TELL?

ὅτι αἴρεται ἀπὸ τῆς γῆς ἡ ζωὴ
BECAUSE IS TAKEN AWAY FROM THE EARTH THE LIFE

αὐτοῦ.
OF HIM.

33 In his humiliation justice
was denied him.
Who can describe his
generation?
For his life is taken
away from the
earth."

8.34 Ἀποκριθεὶς δὲ ὁ εὐνοῦχος τῷ Φιλίππῳ εἶπεν,
AND~HAVING ANSWERED, THE EUNUCH - TO PHILIP SAID,

Δέομαί σου, περὶ τίνος ὁ προφήτης λέγει τοῦτο;
I ASK YOU, ABOUT WHOM THE PROPHET SAYS THIS?

περὶ ἑαυτοῦ ἢ περὶ ἑτέρου τινός; **8.35** ἀνοίξας δὲ ὁ
ABOUT HIMSELF OR ABOUT SOME~OTHER [PERSON]? AND~HAVING OPENED, -

Φίλιππος τὸ στόμα αὐτοῦ καὶ ἀρξάμενος ἀπὸ τῆς
PHILIP, THE MOUTH OF HIM AND HAVING BEGUN FROM -

γραφῆς ταύτης εὐηγγελίσατο αὐτῷ τὸν Ἰησοῦν.
THIS~SCRIPTURE, HE PREACHED TO HIM - JESUS.

8.36 ὡς δὲ ἐπορεύοντο κατὰ τὴν ὁδόν, ἦλθον ἐπί τι
NOW~AS THEY WERE GOING ALONG THE ROAD, THEY CAME UPON SOME

ὕδωρ, καὶ φησιν ὁ εὐνοῦχος, Ἰδοὺ ὕδωρ, τί κωλύει
WATER, AND SAYS THE EUNUCH, BEHOLD, WATER. WHAT PREVENTS

με βαπτισθῆναι; **8.38** καὶ ἐκέλευσεν στῆναι τὸ ἅρμα
ME TO BE BAPTIZED? AND HE COMMANDED TO STAND THE CHARIOT,

καὶ κατέβησαν ἀμφότεροι εἰς τὸ ὕδωρ, ὅ τε
AND WENT DOWN BOTH INTO THE WATER, - BOTH

Φίλιππος καὶ ὁ εὐνοῦχος, καὶ ἐβάπτισεν αὐτόν.
PHILIP AND THE EUNUCH, AND HE BAPTIZED HIM.

8.39 ὅτε δὲ ἀνέβησαν ἐκ τοῦ ὕδατος, πνεῦμα κυρίου
AND~WHEN THEY CAME UP FROM THE WATER, [THE] SPIRIT OF [THE] LORD

ἥρπασεν τὸν Φίλιππον καὶ οὐκ εἶδεν αὐτὸν οὐκέτι ὁ
TOOK AWAY - PHILIP AND DID NOT SEE HIM ANY LONGER THE

εὐνοῦχος, ἐπορεύετο γὰρ τὴν ὁδὸν αὐτοῦ χαίρων.
EUNUCH. FOR~HE WAS GOING THE WAY OF HIM REJOICING.

8.40 Φίλιππος δὲ εὑρέθη εἰς Ἄζωτον· καὶ διερχόμενος
BUT~PHILIP WAS FOUND IN AZOTUS. AND PASSING THROUGH

εὐηγγελίζετο τὰς πόλεις πάσας ἕως τοῦ
HE WAS PREACHING THE GOOD NEWS ²THE ³CITIES ¹TO ALL UNTIL -

ἐλθεῖν αὐτὸν εἰς Καισάρειαν.
HE~CAME TO CAESAREA.

34The eunuch asked Philip,
"About whom, may I ask
you, does the prophet say
this, about himself or about
someone else?" 35Then
Philip began to speak, and
starting with this scripture,
he proclaimed to him the
good news about Jesus.
36As they were going along
the road, they came to
some water; and the eunuch
said, "Look, here is water!
What is to prevent me from
being baptized?"ᵒ 38He
commanded the chariot to
stop, and both of them,
Philip and the eunuch, went
down into the water, and
Philipᵖ baptized him.
39When they came up out of
the water, the Spirit of the
Lord snatched Philip away;
the eunuch saw him no
more, and went on his way
rejoicing. 40But Philip found
himself at Azotus, and as he
was passing through the
region, he proclaimed the
good news to all the towns
until he came to Caesarea.

ᵒ Other ancient authorities add all or
most of verse 37, *And Philip said,
"If you believe with all your heart,
you may." And he replied, "I
believe that Jesus Christ is the Son
of God."*
ᵖ Gk *he*

8:36 text: ASV RSV NASB NIV NEB TEV NJB NRSV. add v. 37 ειπε δε ο Φιλιππος, Ει πιστευεις εξ ολης της
καρδιας, εξεστιν· αποκριθεις δε ειπε, Πιστευω τον υιον του θεου ειναι τον Ιησουν Χριστουν (And Philip said,
"If you believe with all your heart, you can." And he answered him, "I believe Jesus Christ is the Son of
God."): KJV ASVmg RSVmg NASBmg NIVmg NEBmg TEVmg NJBmg NRSVmg.

CHAPTER 9

Meanwhile Saul, still breathing threats and murder against the disciples of the Lord, went to the high priest ²and asked him for letters to the synagogues at Damascus, so that if he found any who belonged to the Way, men or women, he might bring them bound to Jerusalem. ³Now as he was going along and approaching Damascus, suddenly a light from heaven flashed around him. ⁴He fell to the ground and heard a voice saying to him, "Saul, Saul, why do you persecute me?" ⁵He asked, "Who are you, Lord?" The reply came, "I am Jesus, whom you are persecuting. ⁶But get up and enter the city, and you will be told what you are to do." ⁷The men who were traveling with him stood speechless because they heard the voice but saw no one. ⁸Saul got up from the ground, and though his eyes were open, he could see nothing; so they led him by the hand and brought him into Damascus. ⁹For three days he was without sight, and neither ate nor drank.

10 Now there was a disciple in Damascus named Ananias. The Lord said to him in a vision, "Ananias." He answered, "Here I am, Lord." ¹¹The

9.1 Ὁ δὲ Σαῦλος ἔτι ἐμπνέων ἀπειλῆς καὶ φόνου
\- NOW SAUL, STILL BREATHING A THREAT EVEN OF MURDER

εἰς τοὺς μαθητὰς τοῦ κυρίου, προσελθὼν τῷ
TO THE DISCIPLES OF THE LORD, HAVING APPROACHED THE

ἀρχιερεῖ **9.2** ἠτήσατο παρ᾽ αὐτοῦ ἐπιστολὰς εἰς
HIGH PRIEST, HE REQUESTED FROM HIM LETTERS TO

Δαμασκὸν πρὸς τὰς συναγωγάς, ὅπως ἐάν τινας
DAMASCUS TO THE SYNAGOGUES, THAT IF SOMEONE

εὕρῃ τῆς ὁδοῦ ὄντας, ἄνδρας τε καὶ γυναῖκας,
HE SHOULD FIND OF THE WAY BEING, BOTH~MEN AND WOMEN,

δεδεμένους ἀγάγῃ εἰς Ἰερουσαλήμ. **9.3** ἐν δὲ τῷ
HAVING BEEN BOUND HE MAY LEAD [THEM] TO JERUSALEM. NOW~AS [HE]

πορεύεσθαι ἐγένετο αὐτὸν ἐγγίζειν τῇ Δαμασκῷ,
GOES, IT CAME ABOUT [THAT] HE COMES NEAR - DAMASCUS,

ἐξαίφνης τε αὐτὸν περιήστραψεν φῶς ἐκ τοῦ οὐρανοῦ
AND~SUDDENLY SHONE AROUND~HIM A LIGHT FROM - HEAVEN

9.4 καὶ πεσὼν ἐπὶ τὴν γῆν ἤκουσεν φωνὴν
AND HAVING FALLEN ON THE GROUND HE HEARD A VOICE

λέγουσαν αὐτῷ, Σαοὺλ Σαούλ, τί με διώκεις;
SAYING TO HIM, SAUL, SAUL, WHY ARE YOU PERSECUTING~ME?

9.5 εἶπεν δέ, Τίς εἶ, κύριε; ὁ δέ, Ἐγώ εἰμι
AND~HE SAID, WHO ARE YOU, LORD? - AND [HE SAID], I AM

Ἰησοῦς ὃν σὺ διώκεις· **9.6** ἀλλὰ ἀνάστηθι καὶ
JESUS WHOM YOU ARE PERSECUTING. BUT GET UP AND

εἴσελθε εἰς τὴν πόλιν καὶ λαληθήσεταί σοι ὅ τι
ENTER INTO THE CITY, AND IT WILL BE TOLD TO YOU WHAT

σε δεῖ ποιεῖν. **9.7** οἱ δὲ ἄνδρες οἱ συνοδεύοντες
IT IS NECESSARY~FOR YOU TO DO. AND~THE MEN - TRAVELING WITH

αὐτῷ εἱστήκεισαν ἐνεοί, ἀκούοντες μὲν τῆς φωνῆς
HIM HAD STOOD SPEECHLESS, HEARING - THE VOICE

μηδένα δὲ θεωροῦντες. **9.8** ἠγέρθη δὲ Σαῦλος ἀπὸ
BUT~NO ONE SEEING. AND~WAS RAISED SAUL FROM

τῆς γῆς, ἀνεῳγμένων δὲ τῶν ὀφθαλμῶν αὐτοῦ
THE GROUND, AND~HAVING BEEN OPENED THE EYES OF HIM

οὐδὲν ἔβλεπεν· χειραγωγοῦντες δὲ αὐτὸν εἰσήγαγον εἰς
HE WAS SEEING~NOTHING. AND~BEING LED BY THE HAND, THEY BROUGHT~HIM INTO

Δαμασκόν. **9.9** καὶ ἦν ἡμέρας τρεῖς μὴ βλέπων καὶ
DAMASCUS. AND HE WAS THREE~DAYS NOT SEEING, AND

οὐκ ἔφαγεν οὐδὲ ἔπιεν.
DID NOT EAT NOR DRINK.

9.10 Ἦν δέ τις μαθητὴς ἐν Δαμασκῷ ὀνόματι
NOW~THERE WAS A CERTAIN DISCIPLE IN DAMASCUS BY NAME

Ἀνανίας, καὶ εἶπεν πρὸς αὐτὸν ἐν ὁράματι ὁ κύριος,
ANANIAS, AND SPOKE TO HIM IN A VISION THE LORD,

Ἀνανία. ὁ δὲ εἶπεν, Ἰδοὺ ἐγώ, κύριε. **9.11** ὁ δὲ
ANANIAS. - AND HE SAID, BEHOLD, I [AM HERE], LORD. AND~THE

κύριος πρὸς αὐτόν, Ἀναστὰς πορεύθητι ἐπὶ τὴν ῥύμην
LORD [SAID] TO HIM, HAVING ARISEN, GO TO THE STREET

τὴν καλουμένην Εὐθεῖαν καὶ ζήτησον ἐν οἰκίᾳ
- BEING CALLED STRAIGHT AND SEEK IN [THE] HOUSE

Ἰούδα Σαῦλον ὀνόματι Ταρσέα· ἰδοὺ γὰρ
OF JUDAS ³SAUL ²BY NAME ¹[A MAN] FROM TARSUS. FOR~BEHOLD

προσεύχεται 9.12 καὶ εἶδεν ἄνδρα [ἐν ὁράματι]
HE IS PRAYING AND HE SAW A MAN IN A VISION

Ἀνανίαν ὀνόματι εἰσελθόντα καὶ ἐπιθέντα αὐτῷ
ANANIAS BY NAME HAVING ENTERED AND HAVING PLACED UPON HIM

[τὰς] χεῖρας ὅπως ἀναβλέψῃ. 9.13 ἀπεκρίθη δὲ
THE(HIS) HANDS THAT HE MAY SEE AGAIN. AND~ANSWERED

Ἀνανίας, Κύριε, ἤκουσα ἀπὸ πολλῶν περὶ τοῦ
ANANIAS, LORD, I HEARD FROM MANY ABOUT -

ἀνδρὸς τούτου ὅσα κακὰ τοῖς ἁγίοις σου
THIS~MAN HOW MANY EVIL THINGS TO THE SAINTS OF YOU

ἐποίησεν ἐν Ἰερουσαλήμ· 9.14 καὶ ὧδε ἔχει ἐξουσίαν
HE DID IN JERUSALEM. AND HERE HE HAS AUTHORITY

παρὰ τῶν ἀρχιερέων δῆσαι πάντας τοὺς
FROM THE CHIEF PRIESTS TO BIND ALL THE ONES

ἐπικαλουμένους τὸ ὄνομά σου. 9.15 εἶπεν δὲ πρὸς
CALLING UPON THE NAME OF YOU. BUT~SAID TO

αὐτὸν ὁ κύριος, Πορεύου, ὅτι σκεῦος ἐκλογῆς ἐστίν
HIM THE LORD, GO, FOR A CHOSEN~INSTRUMENT IS

μοι οὗτος τοῦ βαστάσαι τὸ ὄνομά μου ἐνώπιον
TO ME THIS ONE - TO CARRY THE NAME OF ME BEFORE

ἐθνῶν τε καὶ βασιλέων υἱῶν τε Ἰσραήλ·
BOTH~GENTILES AND KINGS AND~[THE] SONS OF ISRAEL.

9.16 ἐγὼ γὰρ ὑποδείξω αὐτῷ ὅσα δεῖ αὐτὸν
FOR~I WILL SHOW TO HIM HOW MUCH IT IS NECESSARY FOR HIM

ὑπὲρ τοῦ ὀνόματός μου παθεῖν. 9.17 Ἀπῆλθεν δὲ
ON BEHALF OF THE NAME OF ME TO SUFFER. AND~DEPARTED

Ἀνανίας καὶ εἰσῆλθεν εἰς τὴν οἰκίαν καὶ ἐπιθεὶς
ANANIAS AND ENTERED INTO THE HOUSE AND HAVING PLACED

ἐπ᾽ αὐτὸν τὰς χεῖρας εἶπεν, Σαοὺλ ἀδελφέ, ὁ κύριος
UPON HIM THE(HIS) HANDS, HE SAID, BROTHER~SAUL, THE LORD

ἀπέσταλκέν με, Ἰησοῦς ὁ ὀφθείς σοι ἐν τῇ
HAS SENT ME, JESUS, THE ONE HAVING APPEARED TO YOU ON THE

ὁδῷ ᾗ ἤρχου, ὅπως ἀναβλέψῃς καὶ πλησθῇς
ROAD BY WHICH YOU WERE COMING, THAT YOU MAY SEE AGAIN AND MAY BE FILLED

πνεύματος ἁγίου. 9.18 καὶ εὐθέως ἀπέπεσαν
WITH [THE] HOLY~SPIRIT. AND IMMEDIATELY FELL

αὐτοῦ ἀπὸ τῶν ὀφθαλμῶν ὡς λεπίδες,
FROM~HIS - EYES [SOMETHING] LIKE SCALES,

ἀνέβλεψέν τε καὶ ἀναστὰς ἐβαπτίσθη 9.19 καὶ
AND~HE SAW AGAIN AND HAVING ARISEN HE WAS BAPTIZED AND

λαβὼν τροφὴν ἐνίσχυσεν.
HAVING RECEIVED FOOD, HE REGAINED STRENGTH.

Lord said to him, "Get up and go to the street called Straight, and at the house of Judas look for a man of Tarsus named Saul. At this moment he is praying, [12]and he has seen in a vision[q] a man named Ananias come in and lay his hands on him so that he might regain his sight." [13]But Ananias answered, "Lord, I have heard from many about this man, how much evil he has done to your saints in Jerusalem; [14]and here he has authority from the chief priests to bind all who invoke your name." [15]But the Lord said to him, "Go, for he is an instrument whom I have chosen to bring my name before Gentiles and kings and before the people of Israel; [16]I myself will show him how much he must suffer for the sake of my name." [17]So Ananias went and entered the house. He laid his hands on Saul[r] and said, "Brother Saul, the Lord Jesus, who appeared to you on your way here, has sent me so that you may regain your sight and be filled with the Holy Spirit." [18]And immediately something like scales fell from his eyes, and his sight was restored. Then he got up and was baptized, [19]and after taking some food, he regained his strength.

[q] Other ancient authorities lack in a vision
[r] Gk him

For several days he was with the disciples in Damascus, 20and immediately he began to proclaim Jesus in the synagogues, saying, "He is the Son of God." 21All who heard him were amazed and said, "Is not this the man who made havoc in Jerusalem among those who invoked this name? And has he not come here for the purpose of bringing them bound before the chief priests?" 22Saul became increasingly more powerful and confounded the Jews who lived in Damascus by proving that Jesus*s* was the Messiah.*t*

23 After some time had passed, the Jews plotted to kill him, 24but their plot became known to Saul. They were watching the gates day and night so that they might kill him; 25but his disciples took him by night and let him down through an opening in the wall,*u* lowering him in a basket.

26 When he had come to Jerusalem, he attempted to join the disciples; and they were all afraid of him, for they did not believe that he was a disciple. 27But Barnabas took him, brought him to the apostles, and described for them how on the road he had seen the Lord, who had spoken to

s Gk that this
t Or the Christ
u Gk through the wall

Ἐγένετο δὲ μετὰ τῶν ἐν Δαμασκῷ μαθητῶν
NOW~HE WAS   WITH   THE ²IN ³DAMASCUS ¹DISCIPLES

ἡμέρας τινὰς 9.20 καὶ εὐθέως ἐν ταῖς συναγωγαῖς
SOME~DAYS,   AND IMMEDIATELY IN THE SYNAGOGUES

ἐκήρυσσεν τὸν Ἰησοῦν ὅτι οὗτός ἐστιν ὁ υἱὸς τοῦ
HE WAS PREACHING - JESUS, THAT THIS ONE IS THE SON -

θεοῦ. 9.21 ἐξίσταντο δὲ πάντες οἱ ἀκούοντες καὶ
OF GOD.   AND~WERE ASTONISHED ALL THE ONES LISTENING AND

ἔλεγον, Οὐχ οὗτός ἐστιν ὁ πορθήσας εἰς
THEY WERE SAYING, ²NOT ³THIS ONE ¹IS THE ONE HAVING DESTROYED IN

Ἰερουσαλὴμ τοὺς ἐπικαλουμένους τὸ ὄνομα τοῦτο, καὶ
JERUSALEM THE ONES CALLING UPON - THIS~NAME,   AND

ὧδε εἰς τοῦτο ἐληλύθει ἵνα δεδεμένους αὐτοὺς
HERE FOR THIS [REASON] HE HAD COME THAT HAVING BOUND THEM

ἀγάγῃ ἐπὶ τοὺς ἀρχιερεῖς; 9.22 Σαῦλος δὲ
HE MIGHT LEAD [THEM] TO THE CHIEF PRIESTS?   BUT~SAUL

μᾶλλον ἐνεδυναμοῦτο καὶ συνέχυννεν [τοὺς]
[EVEN] MORE WAS BEING STRENGTHENED AND WAS CONFOUNDING THE

Ἰουδαίους τοὺς κατοικοῦντας ἐν Δαμασκῷ
JEWS,   THE ONES DWELLING   IN DAMASCUS,

συμβιβάζων ὅτι οὗτός ἐστιν ὁ Χριστός.
DEMONSTRATING THAT THIS ONE IS THE CHRIST.

9.23 Ὡς δὲ ἐπληροῦντο ἡμέραι ἱκαναί,
BUT~WHEN WERE FULFILLED MANY~DAYS,

συνεβουλεύσαντο οἱ Ἰουδαῖοι ἀνελεῖν αὐτόν·
PLOTTED   THE JEWS   TO KILL HIM.

9.24 ἐγνώσθη δὲ τῷ Σαύλῳ ἡ ἐπιβουλὴ αὐτῶν.
BUT~WAS MADE KNOWN - TO SAUL THE PLOT OF THEM.

παρετηροῦντο δὲ καὶ τὰς πύλας ἡμέρας τε καὶ νυκτὸς
AND~THEY WERE WATCHING ALSO THE GATES BOTH~DAY AND NIGHT

ὅπως αὐτὸν ἀνέλωσιν· 9.25 λαβόντες δὲ οἱ μαθηταὶ
THAT HIM THEY MIGHT KILL. ⁴HAVING TAKEN ¹BUT ²THE ³DISCIPLES

αὐτοῦ νυκτὸς διὰ τοῦ τείχους καθῆκαν αὐτὸν
HIM   DURING [THE] NIGHT THROUGH THE WALL THEY LET DOWN HIM

χαλάσαντες ἐν σπυρίδι.
HAVING LOWERED [HIM] IN A BASKET.

9.26 Παραγενόμενος δὲ εἰς Ἰερουσαλὴμ ἐπείραζεν
AND~HAVING ARRIVED IN JERUSALEM HE WAS TRYING

κολλᾶσθαι τοῖς μαθηταῖς, καὶ πάντες ἐφοβοῦντο
TO BE ASSOCIATED WITH THE DISCIPLES, AND ALL WERE AFRAID

αὐτὸν μὴ πιστεύοντες ὅτι ἐστὶν μαθητής.
OF HIM NOT BELIEVING THAT HE IS A DISCIPLE.

9.27 Βαρναβᾶς δὲ ἐπιλαβόμενος αὐτὸν ἤγαγεν πρὸς
BUT~BARNABAS HAVING TAKEN HOLD OF HIM BROUGHT [HIM] TO

τοὺς ἀποστόλους καὶ διηγήσατο αὐτοῖς πῶς ἐν τῇ
THE APOSTLES AND TOLD   THEM HOW ON THE

ὁδῷ εἶδεν τὸν κύριον καὶ ὅτι ἐλάλησεν αὐτῷ καὶ
ROAD HE SAW THE LORD AND THAT HE SPOKE TO HIM, AND

πῶς ἐν   Δαμασκῷ   ἐπαρρησιάσατο   ἐν τῷ   ὀνόματι τοῦ
HOW IN DAMASCUS   HE SPOKE BOLDLY   IN THE NAME   -

Ἰησοῦ.   **9.28** καὶ ἦν   μετ' αὐτῶν εἰσπορευόμενος καὶ
OF JESUS.   AND HE WAS WITH THEM   ENTERING   AND

ἐκπορευόμενος εἰς Ἰερουσαλήμ, παρρησιαζόμενος ἐν
EXITING   IN   JERUSALEM,   SPEAKING BOLDLY   IN

τῷ   ὀνόματι τοῦ κυρίου,   **9.29** ἐλάλει τε   καὶ
THE NAME   OF THE LORD,   AND~HE WAS SPEAKING AND

συνεζήτει πρὸς τοὺς Ἑλληνιστάς, οἱ δὲ ἐπεχείρουν
DEBATING   WITH   THE   HELLENISTS,   -   AND THEY WERE ATTEMPTING

ἀνελεῖν αὐτόν. **9.30** ἐπιγνόντες δὲ   οἱ ἀδελφοὶ
TO KILL   HIM.   BUT~HAVING LEARNED [OF THIS], THE BROTHERS

κατήγαγον αὐτὸν εἰς Καισάρειαν καὶ ἐξαπέστειλαν
BROUGHT DOWN HIM   TO   CAESAREA   AND SENT OUT

αὐτὸν εἰς Ταρσόν.
HIM   TO   TARSUS.

9.31 Ἡ μὲν οὖν ἐκκλησία καθ'   ὅλης τῆς
  ²THE -   ¹THEN CHURCH   THROUGHOUT ALL   -

Ἰουδαίας καὶ Γαλιλαίας καὶ Σαμαρείας εἶχεν εἰρήνην
OF JUDEA   AND GALILEE   AND SAMARIA   HAD   PEACE,

οἰκοδομουμένη καὶ πορευομένη τῷ   φόβῳ τοῦ   κυρίου
BEING BUILT UP   AND GOING [ON]   IN THE FEAR OF THE LORD

καὶ τῇ παρακλήσει τοῦ ἁγίου πνεύματος
AND IN THE COMFORT   OF THE HOLY   SPIRIT

ἐπληθύνετο.
IT WAS INCREASING.

9.32 Ἐγένετο δὲ   Πέτρον διερχόμενον διὰ
NOW~IT CAME ABOUT [THAT] PETER   PASSING   THROUGH

πάντων κατελθεῖν καὶ   πρὸς τοὺς ἁγίους τοὺς
ALL [AREAS] TO COME DOWN ALSO TO   THE   SAINTS, THE ONES

κατοικοῦντας Λύδδα. **9.33** εὗρεν δὲ ἐκεῖ ἄνθρωπόν τινα
DWELLING   IN LYDDA.   AND~HE FOUND THERE A CERTAIN~MAN

ὀνόματι Αἰνέαν ἐξ ἐτῶν ὀκτὼ κατακείμενον ἐπὶ
BY NAME   AENEAS, OF YEARS EIGHT LAYING   ON

κραβάττου, ὃς ἦν παραλελυμένος. **9.34** καὶ εἶπεν
A MAT,   WHO HAD BEEN PARALYZED.   AND SAID

αὐτῷ ὁ Πέτρος, Αἰνέα, ἰαταί σε Ἰησοῦς Χριστός·
TO HIM - PETER, AENEAS, HEALS YOU JESUS   CHRIST.

ἀνάστηθι καὶ στρῶσον σεαυτῷ.   καὶ εὐθέως
GET UP   AND MAKE YOUR BED FOR YOURSELF. AND IMMEDIATELY

ἀνέστη. **9.35** καὶ εἶδαν αὐτὸν πάντες οἱ
HE GOT UP.   AND SAW   HIM   ALL   THE ONES

κατοικοῦντες Λύδδα καὶ τὸν Σαρῶνα, οἵτινες
DWELLING   IN LYDDA AND   -   SHARON,   WHO

ἐπέστρεψαν ἐπὶ τὸν κύριον.
TURNED   TO   THE   LORD.

9.36 Ἐν Ἰόππῃ δέ τις ἦν   μαθήτρια ὀνόματι
  ²IN ³JOPPA ¹NOW THERE WAS~A CERTAIN DISCIPLE   BY NAME

him, and how in Damascus he had spoken boldly in the name of Jesus. ²⁸So he went in and out among them in Jerusalem, speaking boldly in the name of the Lord. ²⁹He spoke and argued with the Hellenists; but they were attempting to kill him. ³⁰When the believers[v] learned of it, they brought him down to Caesarea and sent him off to Tarsus.

31 Meanwhile the church throughout Judea, Galilee, and Samaria had peace and was built up. Living in the fear of the Lord and in the comfort of the Holy Spirit, it increased in numbers.

32 Now as Peter went here and there among all the believers,[w] he came down also to the saints living in Lydda. ³³There he found a man named Aeneas, who had been bedridden for eight years, for he was paralyzed. ³⁴Peter said to him, "Aeneas, Jesus Christ heals you; get up and make your bed!" And immediately he got up. ³⁵And all the residents of Lydda and Sharon saw him and turned to the Lord.

36 Now in Joppa there was a disciple whose name

ᵛ Gk *brothers*
ʷ Gk *all of them*

was Tabitha, which in Greek is Dorcas.ˣ She was devoted to good works and acts of charity. ³⁷At that time she became ill and died. When they had washed her, they laid her in a room upstairs. ³⁸Since Lydda was near Joppa, the disciples, who heard that Peter was there, sent two men to him with the request, "Please come to us without delay." ³⁹So Peter got up and went with them; and when he arrived, they took him to the room upstairs. All the widows stood beside him, weeping and showing tunics and other clothing that Dorcas had made while she was with them. ⁴⁰Peter put all of them outside, and then he knelt down and prayed. He turned to the body and said, "Tabitha, get up." Then she opened her eyes, and seeing Peter, she sat up. ⁴¹He gave her his hand and helped her up. Then calling the saints and widows, he showed her to be alive. ⁴²This became known throughout Joppa, and many believed in the Lord. ⁴³Meanwhile he stayed in Joppa for some time with a certain Simon, a tanner.

ˣ The name Tabitha in Aramaic and the name Dorcas in Greek mean *a gazelle*

Ταβιθά, ἡ διερμηνευομένη λέγεται Δορκάς· αὕτη
TABITHA, WHICH BEING TRANSLATED MEANS, DORCAS. THIS ONE

ἦν πλήρης ἔργων ἀγαθῶν καὶ ἐλεημοσυνῶν ὧν
WAS FULL OF GOOD~WORKS AND OF ALMS[GIVING] WHICH

ἐποίει. **9.37** ἐγένετο δὲ ἐν ταῖς ἡμέραις ἐκείναις
SHE WAS DOING. AND~IT CAME ABOUT IN - THOSE~DAYS

ἀσθενήσασαν αὐτὴν ἀποθανεῖν· λούσαντες δὲ
HAVING BECOME SICK THIS ONE DIED. AND~HAVING WASHED [HER]

ἔθηκαν [αὐτὴν] ἐν ὑπερῴῳ. **9.38** ἐγγὺς δὲ οὔσης
THEY PUT THIS ONE IN [THE] UPPER STORY. AND~NEAR BEING

Λύδδας τῇ Ἰόππῃ οἱ μαθηταὶ ἀκούσαντες ὅτι Πέτρος
LYDDA - TO JOPPA, THE DISCIPLES HAVING HEARD THAT PETER

ἐστὶν ἐν αὐτῇ ἀπέστειλαν δύο ἄνδρας πρὸς αὐτὸν
IS IN IT, THEY SENT TWO MEN TO HIM

παρακαλοῦντες, Μὴ ὀκνήσῃς διελθεῖν ἕως ἡμῶν.
SUMMONING [HIM], [THAT] HE MAY NOT HESITATE TO COME TO US.

9.39 ἀναστὰς δὲ Πέτρος συνῆλθεν αὐτοῖς· ὃν
AND~HAVING ARISEN PETER WENT WITH THEM; WHOM

παραγενόμενον ἀνήγαγον εἰς τὸ ὑπερῷον καὶ
HAVING ARRIVED THEY BROUGHT UP INTO THE UPPER STORY AND

παρέστησαν αὐτῷ πᾶσαι αἱ χῆραι κλαίουσαι καὶ
STOOD BESIDE HIM ALL THE WIDOWS CRYING AND

ἐπιδεικνύμεναι χιτῶνας καὶ ἱμάτια ὅσα ἐποίει
SHOWING [THE] SHIRTS AND GARMENTS AS MANY AS ²WAS MAKING

μετ' αὐτῶν οὖσα ἡ Δορκάς. **9.40** ἐκβαλὼν δὲ ἔξω
⁴WITH ⁵THEM ³[WHILE] BEING - ¹DORCAS. AND~HAVING PUT OUT OUTSIDE

πάντας ὁ Πέτρος καὶ θεὶς τὰ γόνατα
EVERYONE - PETER, AND HAVING FALLEN ON THE(HIS) KNEES,

προσηύξατο καὶ ἐπιστρέψας πρὸς τὸ σῶμα εἶπεν,
HE PRAYED AND HAVING TURNED TO THE BODY HE SAID,

Ταβιθά, ἀνάστηθι. ἡ δὲ ἤνοιξεν τοὺς ὀφθαλμοὺς
TABITHA, GET UP. - AND SHE OPENED THE EYES

αὐτῆς, καὶ ἰδοῦσα τὸν Πέτρον ἀνεκάθισεν.
OF HER, AND HAVING SEEN - PETER SHE SAT UP.

9.41 δοὺς δὲ αὐτῇ χεῖρα ἀνέστησεν αὐτήν·
AND~HAVING GIVEN TO HER [HIS] HAND HE RAISED UP HER.

φωνήσας δὲ τοὺς ἁγίους καὶ τὰς χήρας παρέστησεν
AND~HAVING CALLED THE SAINTS AND THE WIDOWS HE PRESENTED

αὐτὴν ζῶσαν. **9.42** γνωστὸν δὲ ἐγένετο καθ' ὅλης
HER LIVING. ³KNOWN ¹AND ²IT BECAME THROUGHOUT ALL

τῆς Ἰόππης καὶ ἐπίστευσαν πολλοὶ ἐπὶ τὸν κύριον.
- JOPPA, AND MANY~BELIEVED ON THE LORD.

9.43 Ἐγένετο δὲ ἡμέρας ἱκανὰς μεῖναι ἐν Ἰόππῃ
AND~IT CAME ABOUT MANY~DAYS [HE] REMAINED IN JOPPA

παρά τινι Σίμωνι βυρσεῖ.
WITH A CERTAIN SIMON, A TANNER.

10.1 Ἀνὴρ δέ τις ἐν Καισαρείᾳ ὀνόματι
³MAN ¹NOW ²A CERTAIN IN CAESAREA BY NAME

Κορνήλιος, ἑκατοντάρχης ἐκ σπείρης τῆς καλουμένης
CORNELIUS, A CENTURION FROM [THE] COHORT - BEING CALLED

Ἰταλικῆς, **10.2** εὐσεβὴς καὶ φοβούμενος τὸν θεὸν σὺν
[THE] ITALIAN, DEVOUT AND FEARING - GOD WITH

παντὶ τῷ οἴκῳ αὐτοῦ, ποιῶν ἐλεημοσύνας πολλὰς
ALL THE HOUSE OF HIM, PRACTICING MUCH~CHARITABLE GIVING

τῷ λαῷ καὶ δεόμενος τοῦ θεοῦ διὰ παντός, **10.3** εἶδεν
TO THE PEOPLE AND PRAYING - TO GOD ALWAYS, HE SAW

ἐν ὁράματι φανερῶς ὡσεὶ περὶ ὥραν ἐνάτην τῆς
IN A VISION CLEARLY ABOUT AROUND [THE] NINTH~HOUR OF THE

ἡμέρας ἄγγελον τοῦ θεοῦ εἰσελθόντα πρὸς αὐτὸν καὶ
DAY AN ANGEL - OF GOD HAVING COME TO HIM AND

εἰπόντα αὐτῷ, Κορνήλιε. **10.4** ὁ δὲ ἀτενίσας
HAVING SAID TO HIM, CORNELIUS. - AND HAVING LOOKED INTENTLY

αὐτῷ καὶ ἔμφοβος γενόμενος εἶπεν, Τί ἐστιν,
AT HIM AND HAVING BECOME~AFRAID HE SAID, WHAT IS IT,

κύριε; εἶπεν δὲ αὐτῷ, Αἱ προσευχαί σου καὶ αἱ
LORD? AND~HE SAID TO HIM, THE PRAYERS OF YOU AND THE

ἐλεημοσύναι σου ἀνέβησαν εἰς μνημόσυνον
CHARITABLE GIVING OF YOU WENT UP FOR A MEMORIAL OFFERING

ἔμπροσθεν τοῦ θεοῦ. **10.5** καὶ νῦν πέμψον ἄνδρας εἰς
BEFORE - GOD. AND NOW SEND [SOME] MEN TO

Ἰόππην καὶ μετάπεμψαι Σίμωνά τινα ὃς ἐπικαλεῖται
JOPPA AND SEND FOR A CERTAIN~SIMON WHO IS [ALSO] CALLED

Πέτρος· **10.6** οὗτος ξενίζεται παρά τινι Σίμωνι
PETER. THIS ONE IS STAYING WITH A CERTAIN SIMON,

βυρσεῖ, ᾧ ἐστιν οἰκία παρὰ θάλασσαν. **10.7** ὡς δὲ
A TANNER, TO WHOM IS A HOUSE BY [THE] SEA. AND~AS

ἀπῆλθεν ὁ ἄγγελος ὁ λαλῶν αὐτῷ, φωνήσας δύο
DEPARTED THE ANGEL, THE ONE SPEAKING TO HIM, HAVING CALLED TWO

τῶν οἰκετῶν καὶ στρατιώτην εὐσεβῆ τῶν
- HOUSEHOLD SERVANTS AND A DEVOUT~SOLDIER OF THE ONES

προσκαρτερούντων αὐτῷ **10.8** καὶ ἐξηγησάμενος ἅπαντα
WAITING UPON HIM AND HAVING EXPLAINED EVERYTHING

αὐτοῖς ἀπέστειλεν αὐτοὺς εἰς τὴν Ἰόππην.
TO THEM, HE SENT THEM TO - JOPPA.

10.9 Τῇ δὲ ἐπαύριον, ὁδοιπορούντων ἐκείνων καὶ
NOW~ON THE NEXT DAY, [AS] THOSE ONES~TRAVELING AND

τῇ πόλει ἐγγιζόντων, ἀνέβη Πέτρος ἐπὶ τὸ δῶμα
TO THE CITY DRAWING NEAR, WENT UP PETER ONTO THE ROOF

προσεύξασθαι περὶ ὥραν ἕκτην. **10.10** ἐγένετο δὲ
TO PRAY AROUND [THE] SIXTH~HOUR. AND~HE BECAME

πρόσπεινος καὶ ἤθελεν γεύσασθαι.
HUNGRY AND WAS WANTING TO PARTAKE [OF A MEAL].

In Caesarea there was a man named Cornelius, a centurion of the Italian Cohort, as it was called. ²He was a devout man who feared God with all his household; he gave alms generously to the people and prayed constantly to God. ³One afternoon at about three o'clock he had a vision in which he clearly saw an angel of God coming in and saying to him, "Cornelius." ⁴He stared at him in terror and said, "What is it, Lord?" He answered, "Your prayers and your alms have ascended as a memorial before God. ⁵Now send men to Joppa for a certain Simon who is called Peter; ⁶he is lodging with Simon, a tanner, whose house is by the seaside." ⁷When the angel who spoke to him had left, he called two of his slaves and a devout soldier from the ranks of those who served him, ⁸and after telling them everything, he sent them to Joppa.

9 About noon the next day, as they were on their journey and approaching the city, Peter went up on the roof to pray. ¹⁰He became hungry and wanted something to eat;

and while it was being prepared, he fell into a trance. [11]He saw the heaven opened and something like a large sheet coming down, being lowered to the ground by its four corners. [12]In it were all kinds of four-footed creatures and reptiles and birds of the air. [13]Then he heard a voice saying, "Get up, Peter; kill and eat." [14]But Peter said, "By no means, Lord; for I have never eaten anything that is profane or unclean." [15]The voice said to him again, a second time, "What God has made clean, you must not call profane." [16]This happened three times, and the thing was suddenly taken up to heaven.

17 Now while Peter was greatly puzzled about what to make of the vision that he had seen, suddenly the men sent by Cornelius appeared. They were asking for Simon's house and were standing by the gate. [18]They called out to ask whether Simon, who was called Peter, was staying there. [19]While Peter was still thinking about the vision, the Spirit said to him, "Look, three[y] men are searching for you. [20]Now get up, go down, and go with them without hesitation; for I have sent them."

[y] One ancient authority reads two; others lack the word

παρασκευαζόντων δὲ αὐτῶν ἐγένετο ἐπ᾽ αὐτὸν
AND~[WHILE] MAKING PREPARATIONS THEY WERE, THERE CAME OVER HIM

ἔκστασις **10.11** καὶ θεωρεῖ τὸν οὐρανὸν ἀνεῳγμένον
A TRANCE AND HE SEES - HEAVEN HAVING BEEN OPENED

καὶ καταβαῖνον σκεῦός τι ὡς ὀθόνην μεγάλην
AND COMING DOWN A CERTAIN~OBJECT LIKE A LARGE~LINEN CLOTH

τέσσαρσιν ἀρχαῖς καθιέμενον ἐπὶ τῆς γῆς, **10.12** ἐν
BY FOUR CORNERS BEING LET DOWN UPON THE GROUND, IN

ᾧ ὑπῆρχεν πάντα τὰ τετράποδα καὶ ἑρπετὰ τῆς
WHICH WERE ALL THE FOUR-FOOTED ANIMALS AND REPTILES OF THE

γῆς καὶ πετεινὰ τοῦ οὐρανοῦ. **10.13** καὶ ἐγένετο
EARTH AND BIRDS OF THE HEAVEN. AND THERE CAME

φωνὴ πρὸς αὐτόν, Ἀναστάς, Πέτρε, θῦσον καὶ φάγε.
A VOICE TO HIM, HAVING ARISEN, PETER, KILL AND EAT.

10.14 ὁ δὲ Πέτρος εἶπεν, Μηδαμῶς, κύριε, ὅτι
- BUT PETER SAID, BY NO MEANS, LORD, BECAUSE

οὐδέποτε ἔφαγον πᾶν κοινὸν καὶ ἀκάθαρτον.
NEVER DID I EAT ALL THINGS COMMON AND UNCLEAN.

10.15 καὶ φωνὴ πάλιν ἐκ δευτέρου πρὸς αὐτόν,
AND [THE] VOICE AGAIN FOR A SECOND [TIME CAME] TO HIM,

Ἃ ὁ θεὸς ἐκαθάρισεν, σὺ μὴ κοίνου.
WHAT - GOD MADE CLEAN, YOU DO NOT DECLARE UNCLEAN.

10.16 τοῦτο δὲ ἐγένετο ἐπὶ τρὶς καὶ εὐθὺς
AND~THIS HAPPENED ON THREE [OCCASIONS] AND IMMEDIATELY

ἀνελήμφθη τὸ σκεῦος εἰς τὸν οὐρανόν.
WAS TAKEN UP THE OBJECT INTO - HEAVEN.

10.17 Ὡς δὲ ἐν ἑαυτῷ διηπόρει ὁ Πέτρος τί
NOW~AS WITHIN HIMSELF WAS PERPLEXED - PETER WHAT

ἂν εἴη τὸ ὅραμα ὃ εἶδεν, ἰδοὺ οἱ ἄνδρες οἱ
MIGHT BE THE VISION WHICH HE SAW, BEHOLD THE MEN -

ἀπεσταλμένοι ὑπὸ τοῦ Κορνηλίου διερωτήσαντες τὴν
HAVING BEEN SENT BY - CORNELIUS HAVING FOUND BY INQUIRING THE

οἰκίαν τοῦ Σίμωνος ἐπέστησαν ἐπὶ τὸν πυλῶνα,
HOUSE - OF SIMON, THEY STOOD AT THE GATE,

10.18 καὶ φωνήσαντες ἐπυνθάνοντο εἰ Σίμων ὁ
AND HAVING CALLED THEY WERE ASKING IF SIMON, THE ONE

ἐπικαλούμενος Πέτρος ἐνθάδε ξενίζεται. **10.19** τοῦ δὲ
BEING CALLED PETER IS STAYING~HERE. - NOW [AS]

Πέτρου διενθυμουμένου περὶ τοῦ ὁράματος εἶπεν
PETER, REFLECTING ON THE VISION, SAID

[αὐτῷ] τὸ πνεῦμα, Ἰδοὺ ἄνδρες ⌜τρεῖς⌝ ζητοῦντές σε,
TO HIM THE SPIRIT, BEHOLD, MEN [ARE] THREE LOOKING FOR YOU,

10.20 ἀλλὰ ἀναστὰς κατάβηθι καὶ πορεύου σὺν αὐτοῖς
BUT HAVING ARISEN GO DOWN AND GO WITH THEM

μηδὲν διακρινόμενος ὅτι ἐγὼ ἀπέσταλκα αὐτούς.
WITHOUT HESITATING BECAUSE I HAVE SENT THEM.

10:19 text: KJV ASV RSV NASB NIV NEBmg NJBmg NRSV. var. δυο (two): NASBmg NIVmg NEBmg NRSVmg. var. τινες (some) NEB TEVmg NJB. omit: NIVmg NRSVmg.

10.21 καταβὰς δὲ Πέτρος πρὸς τοὺς ἄνδρας εἶπεν,
AND~HAVING COME DOWN PETER TO THE MEN HE SAID,

Ἰδοὺ ἐγώ εἰμι ὃν ζητεῖτε· τίς ἡ αἰτία δι᾽
BEHOLD I AM WHOM YOU° ARE SEEKING. WHAT [IS] THE REASON FOR

ἣν πάρεστε; **10.22** οἱ δὲ εἶπαν, Κορνήλιος
WHICH YOU° ARE PRESENT? - AND THEY SAID, CORNELIUS,

ἑκατοντάρχης, ἀνὴρ δίκαιος καὶ φοβούμενος τὸν θεόν,
A CENTURION, A RIGHTEOUS~MAN AND FEARING - GOD,

μαρτυρούμενός τε ὑπὸ ὅλου τοῦ ἔθνους τῶν Ἰουδαίων,
AND~BEING WELL SPOKEN OF BY ALL THE NATION OF THE JEWS,

ἐχρηματίσθη ὑπὸ ἀγγέλου ἁγίου μεταπέμψασθαί σε
WAS DIRECTED BY A HOLY~ANGEL TO SUMMON YOU

εἰς τὸν οἶκον αὐτοῦ καὶ ἀκοῦσαι ῥήματα παρὰ σοῦ.
TO THE HOUSE OF HIM AND TO HEAR WORDS FROM YOU.

10.23 εἰσκαλεσάμενος οὖν αὐτοὺς ἐξένισεν.
THEREFORE~HAVING INVITED IN THEM, HE RECEIVED [THEM] AS GUESTS.

Τῇ δὲ ἐπαύριον ἀναστὰς ἐξῆλθεν σὺν αὐτοῖς καὶ
AND~ON THE NEXT DAY, HAVING ARISEN HE WENT OUT WITH THEM, AND

τινες τῶν ἀδελφῶν τῶν ἀπὸ Ἰόππης συνῆλθον
SOME OF THE BROTHERS OF THE ONES FROM JOPPA ACCOMPANIED

αὐτῷ. **10.24** τῇ δὲ ἐπαύριον εἰσῆλθεν εἰς τὴν
HIM. AND~ON THE NEXT DAY HE ENTERED INTO -

Καισάρειαν. ὁ δὲ Κορνήλιος ἦν προσδοκῶν αὐτοὺς
CAESAREA. - AND CORNELIUS WAS EXPECTING THEM,

συγκαλεσάμενος τοὺς συγγενεῖς αὐτοῦ καὶ τοὺς
HAVING CALLED TOGETHER THE RELATIVES OF HIM AND THE

ἀναγκαίους φίλους. **10.25** ὡς δὲ ἐγένετο τοῦ
CLOSE FRIENDS. NOW~WHEN IT CAME ABOUT [THAT] -

εἰσελθεῖν τὸν Πέτρον, συναντήσας αὐτῷ ὁ Κορνήλιος
ENTERED - PETER, HAVING MET HIM - CORNELIUS

πεσὼν ἐπὶ τοὺς πόδας προσεκύνησεν. **10.26** ὁ δὲ
HAVING FALLEN AT THE (HIS) FEET WORSHIPED [HIM]. - BUT

Πέτρος ἤγειρεν αὐτὸν λέγων, Ἀνάστηθι· καὶ ἐγὼ
PETER RAISED UP HIM SAYING, STAND UP. I~ALSO

αὐτὸς ἄνθρωπός εἰμι. **10.27** καὶ συνομιλῶν αὐτῷ
MYSELF AM~A MAN. AND TALKING WITH HIM

εἰσῆλθεν καὶ εὑρίσκει συνεληλυθότας πολλούς,
HE ENTERED AND FINDS MANY~HAVING ASSEMBLED,

10.28 ἔφη τε πρὸς αὐτούς, Ὑμεῖς ἐπίστασθε ὡς
AND~HE SAID TO THEM, YOU° KNOW THAT

ἀθέμιτόν ἐστιν ἀνδρὶ Ἰουδαίῳ κολλᾶσθαι ἢ
IT IS~UNLAWFUL FOR A JEWISH~MAN TO ASSOCIATE WITH OR

προσέρχεσθαι ἀλλοφύλῳ· κἀμοὶ ὁ θεὸς ἔδειξεν μηδένα
TO APPROACH A FOREIGNER. AND TO ME - GOD SHOWED NO ONE

κοινὸν ἢ ἀκάθαρτον λέγειν ἄνθρωπον· **10.29** διὸ
COMMON OR UNCLEAN TO CALL A MAN. THEREFORE

καὶ ἀναντιρρήτως ἦλθον μεταπεμφθείς.
ALSO RAISING NO OBJECTIONS I CAME HAVING BEEN SUMMONED.

[21]So Peter went down to the men and said, "I am the one you are looking for; what is the reason for your coming?" [22]They answered, "Cornelius, a centurion, an upright and God-fearing man, who is well spoken of by the whole Jewish nation, was directed by a holy angel to send for you to come to his house and to hear what you have to say." [23]So Peter[z] invited them in and gave them lodging.

The next day he got up and went with them, and some of the believers[a] from Joppa accompanied him. [24]The following day they came to Caesarea. Cornelius was expecting them and had called together his relatives and close friends. [25]On Peter's arrival Cornelius met him, and falling at his feet, worshiped him. [26]But Peter made him get up, saying, "Stand up; I am only a mortal." [27]And as he talked with him, he went in and found that many had assembled; [28]and he said to them, "You yourselves know that it is unlawful for a Jew to associate with or to visit a Gentile; but God has shown me that I should not call anyone profane or unclean. [29]So when I was sent for, I came without objection.

[z] Gk *he*
[a] Gk *brothers*

Now may I ask why you sent for me?"

30 Cornelius replied, "Four days ago at this very hour, at three o'clock, I was praying in my house when suddenly a man in dazzling clothes stood before me. [31]He said, 'Cornelius, your prayer has been heard and your alms have been remembered before God. [32]Send therefore to Joppa and ask for Simon, who is called Peter; he is staying in the home of Simon, a tanner, by the sea.' [33]Therefore I sent for you immediately, and you have been kind enough to come. So now all of us are here in the presence of God to listen to all that the Lord has commanded you to say."

34 Then Peter began to speak to them: "I truly understand that God shows no partiality, [35]but in every nation anyone who fears him and does what is right is acceptable to him. [36]You know the message he sent to the people of Israel, preaching peace by Jesus Christ—he is Lord of all. [37]That message spread throughout Judea, beginning in Galilee after the baptism that John announced: [38]how God anointed Jesus of

πυνθάνομαι οὖν τίνι λόγῳ μετεπέμψασθέ με;
THEREFORE~I ASK   FOR WHAT REASON YOU° SUMMONED   ME?

10.30 καὶ ὁ Κορνήλιος ἔφη, Ἀπὸ τετάρτης ἡμέρας
AND - CORNELIUS   SAID,   FROM [THE] FOURTH DAY

μέχρι ταύτης τῆς ὥρας ἤμην τὴν ἐνάτην
UNTIL THIS   -   ⁴HOUR ¹I WAS ²AT THE ³NINTH

προσευχόμενος ἐν τῷ οἴκῳ μου, καὶ ἰδοὺ ἀνὴρ ἔστη
PRAYING   IN THE HOUSE OF ME, AND BEHOLD A MAN STOOD

ἐνώπιόν μου ἐν ἐσθῆτι λαμπρᾷ **10.31** καὶ φησίν,
BEFORE   ME IN SHINING~CLOTHING   AND HE SAYS,

Κορνήλιε, εἰσηκούσθη σου ἡ προσευχὴ καὶ αἱ
CORNELIUS, WAS HEARD   YOUR - PRAYER   AND THE

ἐλεημοσύναι σου ἐμνήσθησαν ἐνώπιον τοῦ θεοῦ.
CHARITABLE GIVING OF YOU ARE REMEMBERED BEFORE - GOD.

10.32 πέμψον οὖν εἰς Ἰόππην καὶ μετακάλεσαι Σίμωνα
THEREFORE,~SEND TO JOPPA AND SUMMON   SIMON

ὃς ἐπικαλεῖται Πέτρος, οὗτος ξενίζεται ἐν οἰκίᾳ
WHO IS CALLED   PETER, THIS ONE IS STAYING IN [THE] HOUSE

Σίμωνος βυρσέως παρὰ θάλασσαν. **10.33** ἐξαυτῆς οὖν
OF SIMON, [THE] TANNER, BY [THE] SEA.   THEREFORE~AT ONCE

ἔπεμψα πρὸς σέ, σύ τε καλῶς ἐποίησας παραγενόμενος.
I SENT   FOR YOU, AND~YOU DID~WELL   HAVING COME.

νῦν οὖν πάντες ἡμεῖς ἐνώπιον τοῦ θεοῦ πάρεσμεν
THEREFORE~NOW ALL   WE   BEFORE   - GOD   ARE PRESENT

ἀκοῦσαι πάντα τὰ προστεταγμένα σοι ὑπὸ τοῦ
TO HEAR ALL THE THINGS HAVING BEEN COMMANDED TO YOU BY THE

κυρίου.
LORD.

10.34 Ἀνοίξας δὲ Πέτρος τὸ στόμα εἶπεν,
AND~²HAVING OPENED ¹PETER THE(HIS) MOUTH, HE SAID,

Ἐπ' ἀληθείας καταλαμβάνομαι ὅτι οὐκ ἔστιν
TRULY,   I UNDERSTAND   THAT ²IS NOT

προσωπολήμπτης ὁ θεός, **10.35** ἀλλ' ἐν παντὶ ἔθνει
³ONE TO SHOW PARTIALITY - ¹GOD,   BUT IN EVERY NATION

ὁ φοβούμενος αὐτὸν καὶ ἐργαζόμενος δικαιοσύνην
THE ONE FEARING HIM   AND WORKING   RIGHTEOUSNESS

δεκτὸς αὐτῷ ἐστιν. **10.36** τὸν λόγον [ὃν] ἀπέστειλεν
ACCEPTABLE TO HIM IS.   THE WORD WHICH HE SENT

τοῖς υἱοῖς Ἰσραὴλ εὐαγγελιζόμενος εἰρήνην διὰ
TO THE SONS OF ISRAEL PREACHING   PEACE THROUGH

Ἰησοῦ Χριστοῦ, οὗτός ἐστιν πάντων κύριος, **10.37** ὑμεῖς
JESUS   CHRIST, THIS ONE IS LORD~OF ALL,   YOU°

οἴδατε τὸ γενόμενον ῥῆμα καθ' ὅλης τῆς Ἰουδαίας,
KNOW   THE THING~HAVING HAPPENED THROUGHOUT ALL - JUDEA,

ἀρξάμενος ἀπὸ τῆς Γαλιλαίας μετὰ τὸ βάπτισμα ὃ
HAVING BEGUN FROM - GALILEE   AFTER THE BAPTISM WHICH

ἐκήρυξεν Ἰωάννης, **10.38** Ἰησοῦν τὸν ἀπὸ Ναζαρέθ,
JOHN~PREACHED,   JESUS,   THE ONE FROM NAZARETH,

ὡς   ἔχρισεν   αὐτὸν   ὁ θεὸς   πνεύματι ἁγίῳ καὶ   δυνάμει,
HOW ²ANOINTED ³HIM - ¹GOD WITH [THE] HOLY~SPIRIT AND WITH POWER,

ὃς   διῆλθεν   εὐεργετῶν καὶ   ἰώμενος πάντας τοὺς
WHO WENT ABOUT DOING GOOD AND HEALING ALL   THE ONES

καταδυναστευομένους ὑπὸ   τοῦ διαβόλου, ὅτι   ὁ θεὸς
BEING OPPRESSED   BY   THE DEVIL,   BECAUSE - GOD

ἦν μετ' αὐτοῦ. **10.39** καὶ   ἡμεῖς μάρτυρες πάντων   ὧν
WAS WITH HIM.   AND   WE [ARE] WITNESSES OF ALL THINGS WHICH

ἐποίησεν ἔν τε τῇ χώρᾳ τῶν Ἰουδαίων καὶ [ἐν]
HE DID   BOTH~IN THE COUNTRY OF THE JEWS AND IN

Ἰερουσαλήμ.   ὃν   καὶ   ἀνεῖλαν κρεμάσαντες ἐπὶ
JERUSALEM;   WHOM ALSO THEY KILLED HAVING HUNG [HIM] ON

ξύλου, **10.40** τοῦτον ὁ θεὸς ἤγειρεν [ἐν] τῇ τρίτῃ ἡμέρᾳ
A TREE,   THIS ONE - GOD RAISED UP ON   THE THIRD DAY

καὶ ἔδωκεν αὐτὸν ἐμφανῆ γενέσθαι, **10.41** οὐ παντὶ τῷ
AND GRANTED TO HIM TO BE~VISIBLE,   NOT TO ALL THE

λαῷ, ἀλλὰ μάρτυσιν τοῖς προκεχειροτονημένοις ὑπὸ
PEOPLE BUT TO WITNESSES - HAVING BEEN CHOSEN BEFOREHAND BY

τοῦ θεοῦ, ἡμῖν, οἵτινες συνεφάγομεν καὶ συνεπίομεν
- GOD, TO US, WHO ATE TOGETHER AND DRANK TOGETHER

αὐτῷ μετὰ τὸ ἀναστῆναι αὐτὸν ἐκ νεκρῶν· **10.42** καὶ
WITH HIM AFTER - HE~ROSE AGAIN FROM [THE] DEAD.   AND

παρήγγειλεν ἡμῖν κηρύξαι τῷ λαῷ καὶ
HE COMMANDED US TO PREACH TO THE PEOPLE AND

διαμαρτύρασθαι ὅτι οὗτός ἐστιν ὁ ὡρισμένος
TO TESTIFY   THAT THIS ONE IS THE ONE HAVING BEEN APPOINTED

ὑπὸ τοῦ θεοῦ κριτὴς ζώντων καὶ νεκρῶν.
BY - GOD [AS] JUDGE OF [THE] LIVING AND [THE] DEAD.

10.43 τούτῳ πάντες οἱ προφῆται μαρτυροῦσιν ἄφεσιν
       TO THIS ONE ALL THE PROPHETS BEAR WITNESS, FORGIVENESS

ἁμαρτιῶν λαβεῖν διὰ τοῦ ὀνόματος αὐτοῦ πάντα τὸν
OF SINS   TO RECEIVE THROUGH THE NAME OF HIM EVERYONE -

πιστεύοντα εἰς αὐτόν.
BELIEVING IN HIM.

10.44 Ἔτι λαλοῦντος τοῦ Πέτρου τὰ ῥήματα ταῦτα
       [WHILE] STILL SPEAKING - PETER - THESE~WORDS

ἐπέπεσεν τὸ πνεῦμα τὸ ἅγιον ἐπὶ πάντας τοὺς
⁴FELL   ¹THE ³SPIRIT - ²HOLY UPON ALL THE ONES

ἀκούοντας τὸν λόγον. **10.45** καὶ ἐξέστησαν οἱ ἐκ
HEARING   THE WORD.   AND WERE AMAZED THE ²OF

περιτομῆς πιστοὶ ὅσοι συνῆλθαν τῷ Πέτρῳ, ὅτι
³[THE] CIRCUMCISION ¹FAITHFUL AS MANY AS ACCOMPANIED - PETER, THAT

καὶ ἐπὶ τὰ ἔθνη ἡ δωρεὰ τοῦ ἁγίου πνεύματος
ALSO UPON THE GENTILES THE GIFT OF THE HOLY SPIRIT

ἐκκέχυται· **10.46** ἤκουον γὰρ αὐτῶν λαλούντων
HAS BEEN POURED OUT. FOR~THEY WERE HEARING THEM SPEAKING

γλώσσαις καὶ μεγαλυνόντων τὸν θεόν. τότε ἀπεκρίθη
IN TONGUES AND EXALTING - GOD. THEN ANSWERED

Nazareth with the Holy Spirit and with power; how he went about doing good and healing all who were oppressed by the devil, for God was with him. ³⁹We are witnesses to all that he did both in Judea and in Jerusalem. They put him to death by hanging him on a tree; ⁴⁰but God raised him on the third day and allowed him to appear, ⁴¹not to all the people but to us who were chosen by God as witnesses, and who ate and drank with him after he rose from the dead. ⁴²He commanded us to preach to the people and to testify that he is the one ordained by God as judge of the living and the dead. ⁴³All the prophets testify about him that everyone who believes in him receives forgiveness of sins through his name."

44 While Peter was still speaking, the Holy Spirit fell upon all who heard the word. ⁴⁵The circumcised believers who had come with Peter were astounded that the gift of the Holy Spirit had been poured out even on the Gentiles, ⁴⁶for they heard them speaking in tongues and extolling God.

Then Peter said, [47]"Can anyone withhold the water for baptizing these people who have received the Holy Spirit just as we have?" [48]So he ordered them to be baptized in the name of Jesus Christ. Then they invited him to stay for several days.

Πέτρος, **10.47** Μήτι τὸ ὕδωρ δύναται κωλῦσαί τις
PETER, [SURELY] NOT ⁴THE ⁵WATER ¹IS ABLE ³TO REFUSE ²ANYONE

τοῦ μὴ βαπτισθῆναι τούτους, οἵτινες τὸ πνεῦμα τὸ
- NOT TO BE BAPTIZED THESE, WHO THE ²SPIRIT -

ἅγιον ἔλαβον ὡς καὶ ἡμεῖς; **10.48** προσέταξεν δὲ
¹HOLY RECEIVED AS ALSO WE? AND~HE COMMANDED

αὐτοὺς ἐν τῷ ὀνόματι Ἰησοῦ Χριστοῦ βαπτισθῆναι.
THEM IN THE NAME OF JESUS CHRIST TO BE BAPTIZED.

τότε ἠρώτησαν αὐτὸν ἐπιμεῖναι ἡμέρας τινάς.
THEN THEY ASKED HIM TO REMAIN SOME~DAYS.

CHAPTER 11

Now the apostles and the believers[b] who were in Judea heard that the Gentiles had also accepted the word of God. ²So when Peter went up to Jerusalem, the circumcised believers[c] criticized him, ³saying, "Why did you go to uncircumcised men and eat with them?" ⁴Then Peter began to explain it to them, step by step, saying, ⁵"I was in the city of Joppa praying, and in a trance I saw a vision. There was something like a large sheet coming down from heaven, being lowered by its four corners; and it came close to me. ⁶As I looked at it closely I saw four-footed animals, beasts of prey, reptiles, and birds of the air. ⁷I also heard a voice saying to me, 'Get up, Peter; kill and eat.' ⁸But I replied, 'By no means, Lord; for nothing profane or unclean has ever

[b] Gk brothers
[c] Gk lacks believers

11.1 Ἤκουσαν δὲ οἱ ἀπόστολοι καὶ οἱ ἀδελφοὶ
AND~HEARD THE APOSTLES AND THE BROTHERS

οἱ ὄντες κατὰ τὴν Ἰουδαίαν ὅτι καὶ τὰ ἔθνη
THE ONES BEING THROUGHOUT - JUDEA THAT ALSO THE GENTILES

ἐδέξαντο τὸν λόγον τοῦ θεοῦ. **11.2** ὅτε δὲ ἀνέβη
RECEIVED THE WORD - OF GOD. BUT~WHEN WENT UP

Πέτρος εἰς Ἰερουσαλήμ, διεκρίνοντο πρὸς αὐτὸν οἱ
PETER TO JERUSALEM, WERE TAKING ISSUE WITH HIM THE ONES

ἐκ περιτομῆς **11.3** λέγοντες ὅτι Εἰσῆλθες πρὸς
OF [THE] CIRCUMCISION SAYING, - YOU ENTERED TO [A HOUSE]

ἄνδρας ἀκροβυστίαν ἔχοντας καὶ συνέφαγες αὐτοῖς.
³MEN ²UNCIRCUMCISED ¹HAVING AND YOU ATE WITH THEM.

11.4 ἀρξάμενος δὲ Πέτρος ἐξετίθετο αὐτοῖς καθεξῆς
AND~HAVING BEGUN, PETER WAS EXPLAINING TO THEM IN ORDER

λέγων, **11.5** Ἐγὼ ἤμην ἐν πόλει Ἰόππῃ προσευχόμενος
SAYING, I WAS IN [THE] CITY OF JOPPA PRAYING

καὶ εἶδον ἐν ἐκστάσει ὅραμα, καταβαῖνον σκεῦός τι
AND I SAW IN A TRANCE A VISION, COMING DOWN A CERTAIN~OBJECT

ὡς ὀθόνην μεγάλην τέσσαρσιν ἀρχαῖς καθιεμένην ἐκ
LIKE A LARGE~LINEN CLOTH BY FOUR CORNERS BEING LET DOWN FROM

τοῦ οὐρανοῦ, καὶ ἦλθεν ἄχρι ἐμοῦ. **11.6** εἰς ἣν
- HEAVEN, AND IT CAME UP TO ME. INTO WHICH

ἀτενίσας κατενόουν καὶ εἶδον τὰ τετράποδα τῆς
HAVING GAZED I WAS OBSERVING AND I SAW - FOUR-FOOTED ANIMALS OF THE

γῆς καὶ τὰ θηρία καὶ τὰ ἑρπετὰ καὶ τὰ πετεινὰ
EARTH AND - BEASTS AND - REPTILES AND - BIRDS

τοῦ οὐρανοῦ. **11.7** ἤκουσα δὲ καὶ φωνῆς λεγούσης μοι,
OF THE HEAVEN. AND~I HEARD ALSO A VOICE SAYING TO ME,

Ἀναστάς, Πέτρε, θῦσον καὶ φάγε. **11.8** εἶπον δέ,
HAVING ARISEN, PETER, KILL AND EAT. BUT~I SAID,

Μηδαμῶς, κύριε, ὅτι κοινὸν ἢ ἀκάθαρτον οὐδέποτε
BY NO MEANS, LORD, BECAUSE COMMON OR UNCLEAN [THINGS] NEVER

εἰσῆλθεν εἰς τὸ στόμα μου. **11.9** ἀπεκρίθη δὲ φωνὴ
ENTERED INTO THE STOMACH OF ME.   AND~ANSWERED [THE] VOICE

ἐκ δευτέρου ἐκ τοῦ οὐρανοῦ, ῞Α ὁ θεὸς ἐκαθάρισεν,
FOR A SECOND [TIME] FROM - HEAVEN, WHAT - GOD MADE CLEAN

σὺ μὴ κοίνου. **11.10** τοῦτο δὲ ἐγένετο ἐπὶ
YOU DO NOT DECLARE UNCLEAN.   AND~THIS HAPPENED ON

τρίς, καὶ ἀνεσπάσθη πάλιν ἅπαντα εἰς τὸν
THREE [OCCASIONS], AND WAS PULLED UP AGAIN EVERYTHING INTO -

οὐρανόν. **11.11** καὶ ἰδοὺ ἐξαυτῆς τρεῖς ἄνδρες
HEAVEN.   AND BEHOLD AT ONCE THREE MEN

ἐπέστησαν ἐπὶ τὴν οἰκίαν ἐν ᾗ ⌐ἦμεν,⌐
STOOD AT THE HOUSE IN WHICH I WAS,

ἀπεσταλμένοι ἀπὸ Καισαρείας πρός με. **11.12** εἶπεν δὲ
HAVING BEEN SENT FROM CAESAREA TO ME.   AND~SAID

τὸ πνεῦμά μοι συνελθεῖν αὐτοῖς μηδὲν διακρίναντα.
THE SPIRIT TO ME TO ACCOMPANY THEM WITHOUT MAKING A DISTINCTION.

ἦλθον δὲ σὺν ἐμοὶ καὶ οἱ ἓξ ἀδελφοὶ οὗτοι καὶ
AND~CAME WITH ME ALSO - ²SIX ³BROTHERS ¹THESE AND

εἰσήλθομεν εἰς τὸν οἶκον τοῦ ἀνδρός.
WE ENTERED INTO THE HOUSE OF THE MAN.

11.13 ἀπήγγειλεν δὲ ἡμῖν πῶς εἶδεν [τὸν] ἄγγελον ἐν
AND~HE REPORTED TO US HOW HE SAW THE ANGEL IN

τῷ οἴκῳ αὐτοῦ σταθέντα καὶ εἰπόντα, ᾿Απόστειλον εἰς
THE HOUSE OF HIM HAVING STOOD AND HAVING SAID, SEND TO

᾿Ιόππην καὶ μετάπεμψαι Σίμωνα τὸν ἐπικαλούμενον
JOPPA AND SUMMON SIMON, THE ONE BEING CALLED

Πέτρον, **11.14** ὃς λαλήσει ῥήματα πρὸς σὲ ἐν οἷς
PETER,   WHO WILL SPEAK WORDS TO YOU BY WHICH

σωθήσῃ σὺ καὶ πᾶς ὁ οἶκός σου. **11.15** ἐν δὲ τῷ
WILL BE SAVED YOU AND ALL THE HOUSE OF YOU.   AND~AS

ἄρξασθαί με λαλεῖν ἐπέπεσεν τὸ πνεῦμα τὸ ἅγιον
I~BEGAN TO SPEAK FELL THE ²SPIRIT - ¹HOLY

ἐπ᾿ αὐτοὺς ὥσπερ καὶ ἐφ᾿ ἡμᾶς ἐν ἀρχῇ.
UPON THEM JUST AS ALSO UPON US IN [THE] BEGINNING.

11.16 ἐμνήσθην δὲ τοῦ ῥήματος τοῦ κυρίου ὡς
AND~I REMEMBERED THE WORD OF THE LORD HOW

ἔλεγεν, ᾿Ιωάννης μὲν ἐβάπτισεν ὕδατι, ὑμεῖς δὲ
HE WAS SAYING, JOHN - BAPTIZED WITH WATER, BUT~YOU°

βαπτισθήσεσθε ἐν πνεύματι ἁγίῳ. **11.17** εἰ οὖν τὴν
WILL BE BAPTIZED WITH [THE] HOLY~SPIRIT.   IF THEN THE

ἴσην δωρεὰν ἔδωκεν αὐτοῖς ὁ θεὸς ὡς καὶ ἡμῖν
SAME GIFT ²GAVE ³TO THEM - ¹GOD AS ALSO TO US

πιστεύσασιν ἐπὶ τὸν κύριον ᾿Ιησοῦν Χριστόν, ἐγὼ τίς
HAVING BELIEVED ON THE LORD JESUS CHRIST, ³I [TO BE] ¹WHO

ἤμην δυνατὸς κωλῦσαι τὸν θεόν; **11.18** ἀκούσαντες δὲ
²WAS ABLE TO HINDER - GOD?   AND~HAVING HEARD

11:11 text: ASV RSV NASB NEBmg TEVmg NEB NRSV.   var. ημην (I was): KJV NEB NIV TEV.

entered my mouth.' [9]But a second time the voice answered from heaven, 'What God has made clean, you must not call profane.' [10]This happened three times; then everything was pulled up again to heaven. [11]At that very moment three men, sent to me from Caesarea, arrived at the house where we were. [12]The Spirit told me to go with them and not to make a distinction between them and us.[d] These six brothers also accompanied me, and we entered the man's house. [13]He told us how he had seen the angel standing in his house and saying, 'Send to Joppa and bring Simon, who is called Peter; [14]he will give you a message by which you and your entire household will be saved.' [15]And as I began to speak, the Holy Spirit fell upon them just as it had upon us at the beginning. [16]And I remembered the word of the Lord, how he had said, 'John baptized with water, but you will be baptized with the Holy Spirit.' [17]If then God gave them the same gift that he gave us when we believed in the Lord Jesus Christ, who was I that I could hinder God?" [18]When they heard

[d] Or *not to hesitate*

this, they were silenced. And they praised God, saying, "Then God has given even to the Gentiles the repentance that leads to life."

19 Now those who were scattered because of the persecution that took place over Stephen traveled as far as Phoenicia, Cyprus, and Antioch, and they spoke the word to no one except Jews. [20]But among them were some men of Cyprus and Cyrene who, on coming to Antioch, spoke to the Hellenists[e] also, proclaiming the Lord Jesus. [21]The hand of the Lord was with them, and a great number became believers and turned to the Lord. [22]News of this came to the ears of the church in Jerusalem, and they sent Barnabas to Antioch. [23]When he came and saw the grace of God, he rejoiced, and he exhorted them all to remain faithful to the Lord with steadfast devotion; [24]for he was a good man, full of the Holy Spirit and of faith. And a great many people were brought to the Lord. [25]Then Barnabas went to Tarsus to look for Saul, [26]and when he had found him, he brought him to Antioch. So it was that for an entire year they met with[f] the church and

[e] Other ancient authorities read Greeks
[f] Or were guests of

ταῦτα   ἡσύχασαν   καὶ   ἐδόξασαν   τὸν   θεὸν
THESE THINGS   THEY REMAINED SILENT   AND   GLORIFIED   -   GOD

λέγοντες,   Ἄρα   καὶ   τοῖς   ἔθνεσιν   ὁ   θεὸς   τὴν   μετάνοιαν
SAYING,   THEN   ALSO   TO THE   GENTILES   -   GOD   -   [2]REPENTANCE

εἰς   ζωὴν   ἔδωκεν.
[3]TO   [4]LIFE   [1]GAVE.

11.19 Οἱ   μὲν   οὖν   διασπαρέντες   ἀπὸ   τῆς   θλίψεως
THE ONES   -   THEN,   HAVING BEEN SCATTERED   FROM   THE   TRIBULATION

τῆς   γενομένης   ἐπὶ   Στεφάνῳ   διῆλθον   ἕως   Φοινίκης
OF THE THING   HAVING HAPPENED   TO   STEPHEN,   CAME   TO   PHOENICIA

καὶ   Κύπρου   καὶ   Ἀντιοχείας   μηδενὶ   λαλοῦντες   τὸν
AND   CYPRUS   AND   ANTIOCH,   TO NO ONE   SPEAKING   THE

λόγον   εἰ   μὴ   μόνον   Ἰουδαίοις.   **11.20** ἦσαν   δέ   τινες   ἐξ
WORD   EXCEPT   ONLY   TO JEWS.   AND~THERE WERE   SOME   OF

αὐτῶν   ἄνδρες   Κύπριοι   καὶ   Κυρηναῖοι,   οἵτινες   ἐλθόντες
THEM   MEN   OF CYPRUS   AND   CYRENE,   WHO   HAVING COME

εἰς   Ἀντιόχειαν   ἐλάλουν   καὶ   πρὸς   τοὺς   Ἑλληνιστὰς
TO   ANTIOCH   WERE SPEAKING   ALSO   TO   THE   GREEKS

εὐαγγελιζόμενοι   τὸν   κύριον   Ἰησοῦν.   **11.21** καὶ   ἦν
PREACHING   THE   LORD   JESUS.   AND   WAS

χεὶρ   κυρίου   μετ'   αὐτῶν,   πολύς   τε   ἀριθμὸς   ὁ
[THE] HAND   OF [THE] LORD   WITH   THEM,   AND~A LARGE   NUMBER   -

πιστεύσας   ἐπέστρεψεν   ἐπὶ   τὸν   κύριον.   **11.22** ἠκούσθη   δὲ
HAVING BELIEVED   TURNED   TO   THE   LORD.   AND~WAS HEARD

ὁ   λόγος   εἰς   τὰ   ὦτα   τῆς   ἐκκλησίας   τῆς   οὔσης   ἐν
THE   REPORT   IN   THE   EARS   OF THE   CHURCH,   THE ONE   BEING   IN

Ἰερουσαλὴμ   περὶ   αὐτῶν   καὶ   ἐξαπέστειλαν   Βαρναβᾶν
JERUSALEM,   ABOUT   THEM   AND   THEY SENT OUT   BARNABAS

[διελθεῖν]   ἕως   Ἀντιοχείας.   **11.23** ὃς   παραγενόμενος
TO GO   TO   ANTIOCH;   WHO   HAVING COME

καὶ   ἰδὼν   τὴν   χάριν   [τὴν]   τοῦ   θεοῦ,   ἐχάρη   καὶ
AND   HAVING SEEN   THE   GRACE   -   OF GOD,   REJOICED   AND

παρεκάλει   πάντας   τῇ   προθέσει   τῆς   καρδίας
WAS ENCOURAGING   EVERYONE   -   [2]DEVOTED   -   [3]OF HEART

προσμένειν   τῷ   κυρίῳ,   **11.24** ὅτι   ἦν   ἀνὴρ   ἀγαθὸς
[1]TO REMAIN   TO THE   LORD,   BECAUSE   HE WAS   A GOOD~MAN

καὶ   πλήρης   πνεύματος   ἁγίου   καὶ   πίστεως.   καὶ
AND   FULL   OF [THE] HOLY~SPIRIT   AND   FAITH.   AND

προσετέθη   ὄχλος   ἱκανὸς   τῷ   κυρίῳ.   **11.25** ἐξῆλθεν   δὲ
WAS ADDED   A LARGE~CROWD   TO THE   LORD.   AND~HE LEFT

εἰς   Ταρσὸν   ἀναζητῆσαι   Σαῦλον,   **11.26** καὶ   εὑρὼν
FOR   TARSUS   TO LOOK   FOR SAUL,   AND   HAVING FOUND [HIM]

ἤγαγεν   εἰς   Ἀντιόχειαν.   ἐγένετο   δὲ   αὐτοῖς   καὶ
HE BROUGHT [HIM]   TO   ANTIOCH.   AND~IT CAME ABOUT   FOR THEM   ALSO

ἐνιαυτὸν   ὅλον   συναχθῆναι   ἐν   τῇ   ἐκκλησίᾳ   καὶ   διδάξαι
AN ENTIRE~YEAR   TO BE ASSEMBLED   IN   THE   CHURCH   AND   TO TEACH

ὄχλον ἱκανόν, χρηματίσαι τε πρώτως ἐν Ἀντιοχείᾳ
A LARGE~CROWD,   AND~TO CALL   FIRST   IN   ANTIOCH

τοὺς μαθητὰς Χριστιανούς.
THE   DISCIPLES   CHRISTIANS.

11.27 Ἐν ταύταις δὲ ταῖς ἡμέραις κατῆλθον
    ²IN   ³THESE   ¹NOW -   DAYS   CAME DOWN

ἀπὸ Ἱεροσολύμων προφῆται εἰς Ἀντιόχειαν.
FROM   JERUSALEM   PROPHETS   TO   ANTIOCH.

11.28 ἀναστὰς δὲ εἷς ἐξ αὐτῶν ὀνόματι Ἅγαβος
    AND~HAVING ARISEN ONE   OF   THEM   BY NAME   AGABUS

ἐσήμανεν διὰ τοῦ πνεύματος λιμὸν μεγάλην μέλλειν
INDICATED   THROUGH THE   SPIRIT   A GREAT~FAMINE   TO BE ABOUT

ἔσεσθαι ἐφ' ὅλην τὴν οἰκουμένην, ἥτις ἐγένετο
TO BE   ON   ALL   THE   INHABITED EARTH,   WHICH   OCCURRED

ἐπὶ Κλαυδίου. **11.29** τῶν δὲ μαθητῶν, καθὼς
DURING [THE TIME] OF CLAUDIUS.   NOW~OF THE   DISCIPLES,   AS

εὐπορεῖτό τις ὥρισαν ἕκαστος αὐτῶν εἰς διακονίαν
ANY~HAVING MEANS   DETERMINED   EACH   OF THEM   FOR   SUPPORT

πέμψαι τοῖς κατοικοῦσιν ἐν τῇ Ἰουδαίᾳ ἀδελφοῖς·
TO SEND   TO THE   ²DWELLING   ³IN -   ⁴JUDEA   ¹BROTHERS;

11.30 ὃ καὶ ἐποίησαν ἀποστείλαντες πρὸς τοὺς
    WHICH   ALSO   THEY DID   HAVING SENT   TO   THE

πρεσβυτέρους διὰ χειρὸς Βαρναβᾶ καὶ Σαύλου.
ELDERS   BY   [THE] HAND   OF BARNABAS   AND   SAUL.

taught a great many people, and it was in Antioch that the disciples were first called "Christians."

27 At that time prophets came down from Jerusalem to Antioch. ²⁸One of them named Agabus stood up and predicted by the Spirit that there would be a severe famine over all the world; and this took place during the reign of Claudius. ²⁹The disciples determined that according to their ability, each would send relief to the believers[g] living in Judea; ³⁰this they did, sending it to the elders by Barnabas and Saul.

CHAPTER 12

12.1 Κατ' ἐκεῖνον δὲ τὸν καιρὸν ἐπέβαλεν Ἡρῴδης
    ²DURING ³THAT   ¹NOW -   TIME   ⁴LAID ON   ¹HEROD

ὁ βασιλεὺς τὰς χεῖρας κακῶσαί τινας τῶν ἀπὸ
²THE ³KING   THE(HIS) HANDS   TO HARM   SOME   OF THE ONES FROM

τῆς ἐκκλησίας. **12.2** ἀνεῖλεν δὲ Ἰάκωβον τὸν ἀδελφὸν
THE   CHURCH.   AND~HE KILLED   JAMES   THE   BROTHER

Ἰωάννου μαχαίρῃ. **12.3** ἰδὼν δὲ ὅτι ἀρεστόν ἐστιν
OF JOHN   WITH A SWORD.   AND~HAVING SEEN THAT   IT IS~PLEASING

τοῖς Ἰουδαίοις, προσέθετο συλλαβεῖν καὶ
TO THE   JEWS,   HE PROCEEDED   TO ARREST   ALSO

Πέτρον,—ἦσαν δὲ [αἱ] ἡμέραι τῶν
PETER,—AND~[THESE THINGS] WERE [DURING]   THE   DAYS   OF THE

ἀζύμων— **12.4** ὃν καὶ πιάσας ἔθετο εἰς
UNLEAVENED [BREAD]—   WHOM   ALSO   HAVING SEIZED   HE PUT   IN

φυλακήν, παραδοὺς τέσσαρσιν τετραδίοις
JAIL,   HAVING HANDED [HIM] OVER   TO FOUR   SQUADS OF FOUR

στρατιωτῶν φυλάσσειν αὐτόν, βουλόμενος μετὰ τὸ
SOLDIERS   TO GUARD   HIM,   INTENDING   AFTER   THE

About that time King Herod laid violent hands upon some who belonged to the church. ²He had James, the brother of John, killed with the sword. ³After he saw that it pleased the Jews, he proceeded to arrest Peter also. (This was during the festival of Unleavened Bread.) ⁴When he had seized him, he put him in prison and handed him over to four squads of soldiers to guard him, intending

g Gk *brothers*

to bring him out to the people after the Passover. [5]While Peter was kept in prison, the church prayed fervently to God for him.

6 The very night before Herod was going to bring him out, Peter, bound with two chains, was sleeping between two soldiers, while guards in front of the door were keeping watch over the prison. [7]Suddenly an angel of the Lord appeared and a light shone in the cell. He tapped Peter on the side and woke him, saying, "Get up quickly." And the chains fell off his wrists. [8]The angel said to him, "Fasten your belt and put on your sandals." He did so. Then he said to him, "Wrap your cloak around you and follow me." [9]Peter[h] went out and followed him; he did not realize that what was happening with the angel's help was real; he thought he was seeing a vision. [10]After they had passed the first and the second guard, they came before the iron gate leading into the city. It opened for them of its own accord, and they went outside and walked along a lane, when suddenly the angel left him. [11]Then Peter came to himself and said, "Now I am

[h] Gk He

πάσχα ἀναγαγεῖν αὐτὸν τῷ λαῷ. **12.5** ὁ μὲν
PASSOVER   TO BRING   HIM [BEFORE] THE   PEOPLE.   - -

οὖν   Πέτρος ἐτηρεῖτο ἐν τῇ φυλακῇ· προσευχὴ δὲ
THEREFORE PETER   WAS BEING KEPT IN   THE JAIL.   BUT~PRAYER

ἦν ἐκτενῶς γινομένη ὑπὸ τῆς ἐκκλησίας πρὸς τὸν θεὸν
WAS EARNESTLY BEING MADE   BY   THE   CHURCH   TO   -   GOD

περὶ αὐτοῦ.
FOR HIM.

12.6 Ὅτε δὲ ἤμελλεν προαγαγεῖν αὐτὸν ὁ Ἡρῴδης, τῇ
BUT~WHEN [2]WAS ABOUT [3]TO LEAD OUT [4]HIM - [1]HEROD,   -

νυκτὶ ἐκείνῃ ἦν ὁ Πέτρος κοιμώμενος μεταξὺ δύο
IN THAT~NIGHT WAS - PETER   SLEEPING   BETWEEN TWO

στρατιωτῶν δεδεμένος ἁλύσεσιν δυσίν φύλακές τε πρὸ
SOLDIERS   HAVING BEEN BOUND WITH TWO~CHAINS,   AND~GUARDS BEFORE

τῆς θύρας ἐτήρουν   τὴν φυλακήν. **12.7** καὶ ἰδοὺ
THE DOOR WERE KEEPING WATCH OVER THE JAIL.   AND BEHOLD

ἄγγελος κυρίου ἐπέστη καὶ φῶς ἔλαμψεν ἐν τῷ
AN ANGEL OF [THE] LORD APPROACHED AND LIGHT SHONE   IN THE

οἰκήματι· πατάξας δὲ τὴν πλευρὰν τοῦ Πέτρου
ROOM.   AND~HAVING STRUCK THE SIDE   -   OF PETER

ἤγειρεν αὐτὸν λέγων, Ἀνάστα ἐν τάχει. καὶ
HE RAISED UP HIM SAYING, GET UP   WITH QUICKNESS. AND

ἐξέπεσαν αὐτοῦ αἱ ἁλύσεις ἐκ τῶν χειρῶν.
FELL OFF   OF HIM THE CHAINS   FROM THE(HIS) HANDS.

12.8 εἶπεν δὲ ὁ ἄγγελος πρὸς αὐτόν, Ζῶσαι καὶ
AND~SAID THE ANGEL   TO   HIM, PUT YOUR BELT ON AND

ὑπόδησαι τὰ σανδάλιά σου. ἐποίησεν δὲ οὕτως. καὶ
TIE   THE SANDALS   OF YOU. AND~HE DID   SO.   AND

λέγει αὐτῷ, Περιβαλοῦ τὸ ἱμάτιόν σου καὶ ἀκολούθει
HE SAYS TO HIM, PUT ON   THE GARMENT OF YOU AND FOLLOW

μοι. **12.9** καὶ ἐξελθὼν ἠκολούθει καὶ
ME.   AND HAVING GONE OUT, HE WAS FOLLOWING [HIM] AND

οὐκ ᾔδει ὅτι ἀληθές ἐστιν τὸ γινόμενον διὰ
HE HAD NOT KNOWN THAT REAL   IS   THE THING HAPPENING THROUGH

τοῦ ἀγγέλου· ἐδόκει δὲ ὅραμα βλέπειν.
THE ANGEL.   BUT~HE WAS THINKING TO SEE~A VISION.

12.10 διελθόντες δὲ πρώτην φυλακὴν καὶ δευτέραν
AND~HAVING GONE THROUGH [THE] FIRST GUARD   AND [THE] SECOND

ἦλθαν ἐπὶ τὴν πύλην τὴν σιδηρᾶν τὴν φέρουσαν εἰς
THEY CAME UPON THE [2]GATE - [1]IRON -   LEADING   TO

τὴν πόλιν, ἥτις αὐτομάτη ἠνοίγη αὐτοῖς καὶ
THE CITY,   WHICH BY ITSELF WAS OPENED TO THEM AND

ἐξελθόντες προῆλθον ῥύμην μίαν, καὶ εὐθέως
HAVING GONE OUT THEY WENT ALONG ONE~STREET   AND IMMEDIATELY

ἀπέστη ὁ ἄγγελος ἀπ᾽ αὐτοῦ. **12.11** καὶ ὁ Πέτρος ἐν
WENT AWAY THE ANGEL   FROM HIM.   AND - PETER   TO

ἑαυτῷ γενόμενος εἶπεν, Νῦν οἶδα ἀληθῶς ὅτι
HIMSELF HAVING COME   SAID,   NOW I KNOW TRULY   THAT

ἐξαπέστειλεν [ὁ] κύριος τὸν ἄγγελον αὐτοῦ καὶ
³SENT OUT   ¹THE   ²LORD   THE   ANGEL   OF HIM   AND

ἐξείλατό με ἐκ χειρὸς Ἡρῴδου καὶ πάσης τῆς
DELIVERED   ME   FROM [THE] HAND   OF HEROD   AND   FROM ALL   THE

προσδοκίας τοῦ λαοῦ τῶν Ἰουδαίων.
EXPECTATION   OF THE   PEOPLE   OF THE   JEWS.

12.12 συνιδών τε   ἦλθεν ἐπὶ τὴν οἰκίαν τῆς
AND~HAVING REALIZED [THIS]   HE CAME   UPON   THE   HOUSE   -

Μαρίας τῆς μητρὸς Ἰωάννου τοῦ ἐπικαλουμένου
OF MARY,   THE   MOTHER   OF JOHN,   THE ONE   BEING CALLED

Μάρκου, οὗ ἦσαν ἱκανοὶ συνηθροισμένοι καὶ
MARK,   WHERE   THERE WERE   MANY   HAVING BEEN ASSEMBLED   AND

προσευχόμενοι. **12.13** κρούσαντος δὲ αὐτοῦ τὴν θύραν
PRAYING.   AND~HAVING KNOCKED   HE [ON]   THE   DOOR

τοῦ πυλῶνος προσῆλθεν παιδίσκη ὑπακοῦσαι ὀνόματι
OF THE   GATE,   APPROACHED   A SERVANT GIRL   TO LISTEN   BY NAME

Ῥόδη, **12.14** καὶ ἐπιγνοῦσα   τὴν φωνὴν τοῦ Πέτρου
RHODA,   AND   HAVING RECOGNIZED   THE   VOICE   -   OF PETER,

ἀπὸ τῆς χαρᾶς οὐκ ἤνοιξεν τὸν πυλῶνα, εἰσδραμοῦσα δὲ
FROM   -   JOY   SHE DID NOT OPEN   THE   GATE,   BUT~HAVING RUN INSIDE,

ἀπήγγειλεν ἑστάναι τὸν Πέτρον πρὸ τοῦ πυλῶνος.
SHE REPORTED [THAT]   ²HAS STOOD   -   ¹PETER   AT   THE   GATE.

12.15 οἱ δὲ   πρὸς αὐτὴν εἶπαν, Μαίνῃ.
BUT~THE ONES [THERE]   TO   HER   SAID,   YOU ARE OUT OF YOUR MIND.

ἡ δὲ διϊσχυρίζετο οὕτως ἔχειν. οἱ δὲ ἔλεγον, Ὁ
-   BUT   SHE KEPT INSISTING [IT]   TO BE~SO.   -   BUT   THEY WERE SAYING,   ²THE

ἄγγελός ἐστιν αὐτοῦ. **12.16** ὁ δὲ Πέτρος ἐπέμενεν
³ANGEL   ¹IT IS   ⁴OF HIM.   -   BUT   PETER   WAS CONTINUING

κρούων· ἀνοίξαντες δὲ   εἶδαν αὐτὸν καὶ
KNOCKING.   AND~HAVING OPENED [THE GATE]   THEY SAW   HIM   AND

ἐξέστησαν. **12.17** κατασείσας δὲ αὐτοῖς τῇ
WERE AMAZED.   AND~HAVING MOTIONED   TO THEM   WITH THE(HIS)

χειρὶ σιγᾶν διηγήσατο [αὐτοῖς] πῶς ὁ κύριος
HAND   TO BE SILENT,   HE TOLD   THEM   HOW   THE   LORD

αὐτὸν ἐξήγαγεν ἐκ τῆς φυλακῆς εἶπέν τε,
LED OUT~HIM   FROM   THE   JAIL   AND~SAID,

Ἀπαγγείλατε Ἰακώβῳ καὶ τοῖς ἀδελφοῖς ταῦτα.
REPORT   TO JAMES   AND   TO THE   BROTHERS   THESE THINGS.

καὶ ἐξελθὼν ἐπορεύθη εἰς ἕτερον τόπον.
AND   HAVING GONE OUT,   HE WENT   TO   ANOTHER   PLACE.

12.18 Γενομένης δὲ ἡμέρας ἦν   τάραχος οὐκ
NOW~HAVING BECOME   DAY,   THERE WAS   COMMOTION   NOT

ὀλίγος ἐν τοῖς στρατιώταις τί ἄρα ὁ
A LITTLE   AMONG   THE   SOLDIERS   WHAT   THEN   -

Πέτρος ἐγένετο. **12.19** Ἡρῴδης δὲ ἐπιζητήσας αὐτὸν
BECAME~OF PETER.   NOW~HEROD   HAVING SOUGHT AFTER   HIM

καὶ μὴ εὑρών, ἀνακρίνας τοὺς φύλακας
AND   NOT HAVING FOUND [THEM],   HAVING QUESTIONED   THE   GUARDS,

sure that the Lord has sent his angel and rescued me from the hands of Herod and from all that the Jewish people were expecting."

12 As soon as he realized this, he went to the house of Mary, the mother of John whose other name was Mark, where many had gathered and were praying. [13]When he knocked at the outer gate, a maid named Rhoda came to answer. [14]On recognizing Peter's voice, she was so overjoyed that, instead of opening the gate, she ran in and announced that Peter was standing at the gate. [15]They said to her, "You are out of your mind!" But she insisted that it was so. They said, "It is his angel." [16]Meanwhile Peter continued knocking; and when they opened the gate, they saw him and were amazed. [17]He motioned to them with his hand to be silent, and described for them how the Lord had brought him out of the prison. And he added, "Tell this to James and to the believers."[i] Then he left and went to another place.

18 When morning came, there was no small commotion among the soldiers over what had become of Peter. [19]When Herod had searched for him and could not find him, he examined the guards

[i] Gk brothers

and ordered them to be put to death. Then he went down from Judea to Caesarea and stayed there.

20 Now Herod[j] was angry with the people of Tyre and Sidon. So they came to him in a body; and after winning over Blastus, the king's chamberlain, they asked for a reconciliation, because their country depended on the king's country for food. [21]On an appointed day Herod put on his royal robes, took his seat on the platform, and delivered a public address to them. [22]The people kept shouting, "The voice of a god, and not of a mortal!" [23]And immediately, because he had not given the glory to God, an angel of the Lord struck him down, and he was eaten by worms and died.

24 But the word of God continued to advance and gain adherents. [25]Then after completing their mission Barnabas and Saul returned to[k] Jerusalem and brought with them John, whose other name was Mark.

[j] Gk he
[k] Other ancient authorities read from

ἐκέλευσεν   ἀπαχθῆναι, καὶ κατελθὼν   ἀπὸ τῆς
COMMANDED [THEM] TO BE LED AWAY, AND HAVING COME DOWN FROM -

Ἰουδαίας εἰς Καισάρειαν διέτριβεν.
JUDEA   TO   CAESAREA,   HE WAS STAYING [THERE].

12.20 Ἦν δὲ θυμομαχῶν Τυρίοις   καὶ Σιδωνίοις·
NOW~HE WAS VERY ANGRY WITH [THE] TYRIANS AND [THE] SIDONIANS.

ὁμοθυμαδὸν δὲ παρῆσαν   πρὸς αὐτὸν καὶ πείσαντες
AND~WITH ONE MIND THEY WERE COMING TO HIM   AND HAVING WON OVER

Βλάστον, τὸν ἐπὶ τοῦ κοιτῶνος τοῦ βασιλέως,
BLASTUS,   THE ONE OVER THE BEDROOM OF THE KING,

ἠτοῦντο   εἰρήνην διὰ τὸ τρέφεσθαι αὐτῶν τὴν
THEY WERE REQUESTING PEACE BECAUSE TO BE FED   THEIR   -

χώραν ἀπὸ τῆς βασιλικῆς. **12.21** τακτῇ δὲ   ἡμέρᾳ
COUNTRY BY THE ROYAL [COUNTRY].   NOW~ON THE APPOINTED DAY,

ὁ Ἡρῴδης, ἐνδυσάμενος   ἐσθῆτα βασιλικὴν [καὶ]
- HEROD,   HAVING CLOTHED HIMSELF WITH ROYAL~CLOTHING AND

καθίσας   ἐπὶ τοῦ βήματος ἐδημηγόρει
HAVING SAT DOWN ON THE JUDGMENT SEAT, WAS DELIVERING A PUBLIC ADDRESS

πρὸς αὐτούς, **12.22** ὁ δὲ   δῆμος ἐπεφώνει, Θεοῦ φωνὴ
TO THEM,   AND~THE CROWD WAS CRYING OUT, [THE] VOICE~OF GOD

καὶ οὐκ ἀνθρώπου. **12.23** παραχρῆμα δὲ ἐπάταξεν αὐτὸν
AND NOT OF MAN.   AND~IMMEDIATELY   STRUCK   HIM

ἄγγελος κυρίου   ἀνθ' ὧν οὐκ ἔδωκεν τὴν δόξαν τῷ
AN ANGEL OF [THE] LORD BECAUSE HE DID NOT GIVE THE GLORY -

θεῷ, καὶ γενόμενος σκωληκόβρωτος ἐξέψυξεν.
TO GOD, AND HAVING BECOME EATEN WITH WORMS HE DIED.

12.24 Ὁ δὲ λόγος τοῦ θεοῦ ηὔξανεν καὶ ἐπληθύνετο.
AND~THE WORD -   OF GOD WAS GROWING AND WAS INCREASING.

12.25 Βαρναβᾶς δὲ καὶ Σαῦλος ⌐ὑπέστρεψαν εἰς
AND~BARNABAS AND SAUL   RETURNED   TO

Ἰερουσαλὴμ⌐ πληρώσαντες τὴν   διακονίαν,
JERUSALEM,   HAVING COMPLETED THE [RAISING OF] SUPPORT,

συμπαραλαβόντες Ἰωάννην τὸν   ἐπικληθέντα Μᾶρκον.
HAVING TAKEN ALONG JOHN,   THE ONE HAVING BEEN CALLED MARK.

12:25 text: ASVmg RSVmg NASBmg NIVmg NEBmg TEVmg NJB (which translates this portion, "Barnabas and Saul completed their task at Jerusalem and came back") NRSV. var. ὑπεστετρεψαν εξ [or απο in some MSS] Ιερουσαλημ (they returned from Jerusalem): KJV ASV RSV NASB NIV NEB NJBmg NRSVmg.

CHAPTER 13

Now in the church at Antioch there were prophets and teachers: Barnabas, Simeon who was called Niger, Lucius of Cyrene, Manaen a member of the court of Herod the ruler,[l]

[l] Gk tetrarch

13.1 Ἦσαν δὲ ἐν Ἀντιοχείᾳ κατὰ τὴν οὖσαν
NOW~THERE WERE IN ANTIOCH   AMONG THE EXISTING

ἐκκλησίαν προφῆται καὶ διδάσκαλοι ὅ τε Βαρναβᾶς
CHURCH,   PROPHETS AND TEACHERS,   - BOTH BARNABAS

καὶ Συμεὼν ὁ   καλούμενος Νίγερ καὶ Λούκιος ὁ
AND SIMEON, THE ONE BEING CALLED NIGER AND LUCIUS   THE

Κυρηναῖος, Μαναήν τε Ἡρῴδου τοῦ τετραάρχου
CYRENIAN,   AND~MANAEN, OF HEROD THE TETRARCH

σύντροφος   καὶ   Σαῦλος.   **13.2** λειτουργούντων δὲ αὐτῶν
[THE] FOSTER BROTHER, AND   SAUL.   AND~MINISTERING   THEY

τῷ   κυρίῳ καὶ νηστευόντων εἶπεν τὸ πνεῦμα τὸ ἅγιον,
TO THE LORD   AND   FASTING,   SAID   THE ²SPIRIT   -   ¹HOLY,

Ἀφορίσατε   δή   μοι   τὸν Βαρναβᾶν καὶ Σαῦλον εἰς
SET APART   THEN FOR ME -   BARNABAS   AND   SAUL   TO

τὸ   ἔργον ὃ   προσκέκλημαι αὐτούς.   **13.3** τότε
THE WORK [FOR] WHICH I HAVE CALLED   THEM.   THEN

νηστεύσαντες καὶ προσευξάμενοι καὶ ἐπιθέντες τὰς
HAVING FASTED   AND   HAVING PRAYED   AND   HAVING LAID   THE(THEIR)

χεῖρας   αὐτοῖς ἀπέλυσαν.
HANDS [UPON] THEM   THEY SENT [THEM] AWAY.

13.4 Αὐτοὶ μὲν οὖν ἐκπεμφθέντες ὑπὸ τοῦ ἁγίου
        THEY   -   THEN HAVING BEEN SENT OUT   BY   THE   HOLY

πνεύματος κατῆλθον εἰς Σελεύκειαν, ἐκεῖθέν τε
SPIRIT   WENT DOWN   TO   SELEUCIA,   AND~FROM THERE

ἀπέπλευσαν εἰς Κύπρον **13.5** καὶ γενόμενοι ἐν
THEY SAILED AWAY   TO   CYPRUS,   AND   HAVING BEEN   IN

Σαλαμῖνι κατήγγελλον   τὸν λόγον τοῦ θεοῦ ἐν ταῖς
SALAMIS,   THEY WERE PROCLAIMING THE WORD   -   OF GOD IN   THE

συναγωγαῖς τῶν Ἰουδαίων. εἶχον δὲ καὶ Ἰωάννην
SYNAGOGUES   OF THE JEWS.   AND~THEY HAD ALSO   JOHN [MARK]

ὑπηρέτην.   **13.6** διελθόντες δὲ   ὅλην   τὴν
[AS] AN ASSISTANT.   AND~HAVING PASSED THROUGH [THE] WHOLE -

νῆσον   ἄχρι Πάφου εὗρον ἄνδρα τινὰ μάγον
ISLAND   AS FAR AS PAPHOS THEY FOUND A CERTAIN~MAN   A MAGICIAN,

ψευδοπροφήτην Ἰουδαῖον ᾧ   ὄνομα Βαριησοῦ
A JEWISH~FALSE PROPHET   TO WHOM [WAS] [THE] NAME BAR-JESUS

13.7 ὃς ἦν σὺν τῷ ἀνθυπάτῳ Σεργίῳ Παύλῳ,
      WHO WAS WITH THE PROCONSUL,   SERGIUS   PAULUS,

ἀνδρὶ συνετῷ. οὗτος προσκαλεσάμενος Βαρναβᾶν καὶ
AN INTELLIGENT~MAN. THIS ONE HAVING SUMMONED   BARNABAS   AND

Σαῦλον ἐπεζήτησεν ἀκοῦσαι τὸν λόγον τοῦ θεοῦ.
SAUL   SOUGHT   TO HEAR   THE WORD   -   OF GOD.

13.8 ἀνθίστατο δὲ αὐτοῖς Ἐλύμας ὁ   μάγος, οὕτως γὰρ
       BUT~WAS OPPOSING THEM   ELYMAS,   THE MAGICIAN, FOR~THUS

μεθερμηνεύεται τὸ ὄνομα αὐτοῦ, ζητῶν διαστρέψαι τὸν
IS TRANSLATED   THE NAME   OF HIM,   SEEKING TO TURN AWAY   THE

ἀνθύπατον ἀπὸ τῆς πίστεως.   **13.9** Σαῦλος δέ, ὁ
PROCONSUL   FROM THE   FAITH.   BUT~SAUL,   THE ONE

καὶ   Παῦλος, πλησθεὶς   πνεύματος ἁγίου
ALSO [CALLED] PAUL,   HAVING BEEN FILLED WITH [THE] HOLY~SPIRIT,

ἀτενίσας εἰς αὐτὸν **13.10** εἶπεν, Ὦ   πλήρης παντὸς
HAVING GAZED   AT   HIM,   SAID,   O [MAN] FULL   OF ALL

δόλου καὶ πάσης ῥαδιουργίας, υἱὲ διαβόλου, ἐχθρὲ
DECEIT   AND   ALL   FRAUD,   SON OF [THE] DEVIL, ENEMY

πάσης δικαιοσύνης, οὐ παύσῃ   διαστρέφων τὰς ὁδοὺς
OF ALL   RIGHTEOUSNESS, WILL YOU NOT STOP MAKING CROOKED THE   ²PATHS

and Saul. ²While they were worshiping the Lord and fasting, the Holy Spirit said, "Set apart for me Barnabas and Saul for the work to which I have called them." ³Then after fasting and praying they laid their hands on them and sent them off.

4 So, being sent out by the Holy Spirit, they went down to Seleucia; and from there they sailed to Cyprus. ⁵When they arrived at Salamis, they proclaimed the word of God in the synagogues of the Jews. And they had John also to assist them. ⁶When they had gone through the whole island as far as Paphos, they met a certain magician, a Jewish false prophet, named Bar-Jesus. ⁷He was with the proconsul, Sergius Paulus, an intelligent man, who summoned Barnabas and Saul and wanted to hear the word of God. ⁸But the magician Elymas (for that is the translation of his name) opposed them and tried to turn the proconsul away from the faith. ⁹But Saul, also known as Paul, filled with the Holy Spirit, looked intently at him ¹⁰and said, "You son of the devil, you enemy of all righteousness, full of all deceit and villainy, will you not stop making crooked the straight paths

of the Lord? [11]And now listen—the hand of the Lord is against you, and you will be blind for a while, unable to see the sun." Immediately mist and darkness came over him, and he went about groping for someone to lead him by the hand. [12]When the proconsul saw what had happened, he believed, for he was astonished at the teaching about the Lord.

13 Then Paul and his companions set sail from Paphos and came to Perga in Pamphylia. John, however, left them and returned to Jerusalem; [14]but they went on from Perga and came to Antioch in Pisidia. And on the sabbath day they went into the synagogue and sat down. [15]After the reading of the law and the prophets, the officials of the synagogue sent them a message, saying, "Brothers, if you have any word of exhortation for the people, give it." [16]So Paul stood up and with a gesture began to speak: "You Israelites,[m] and others who fear God, listen. [17]The God of this people Israel chose our ancestors and made the people great during their stay in the land of Egypt, and with uplifted arm he led them out of it.

[m] Gk Men, Israelites

[τοῦ] κυρίου τὰς εὐθείας; **13.11** καὶ νῦν ἰδοὺ χεὶρ
³OF THE ⁴LORD - ¹STRAIGHT?   AND   NOW BEHOLD [THE] HAND

κυρίου ἐπὶ σὲ καὶ ἔσῃ τυφλὸς μὴ βλέπων
OF [THE] LORD [IS] ON YOU AND YOU WILL BE BLIND NOT SEEING

τὸν ἥλιον ἄχρι καιροῦ. παραχρῆμά τε ἔπεσεν ἐπ'
THE SUN FOR A WHILE. AND~IMMEDIATELY FELL   ON

αὐτὸν ἀχλὺς καὶ σκότος καὶ περιάγων ἐζήτει
HIM MISTINESS AND DARKNESS AND GOING ABOUT, HE WAS SEEKING

χειραγωγούς. **13.12** τότε ἰδὼν ὁ ἀνθύπατος τὸ
LEADERS [TO GUIDE HIM].   THEN ³HAVING SEEN ¹THE ²PROCONSUL THE THING

γεγονὸς ἐπίστευσεν ἐκπλησσόμενος ἐπὶ τῇ διδαχῇ
HAVING HAPPENED, HE BELIEVED, BEING AMAZED   AT THE TEACHING

τοῦ κυρίου.
OF THE LORD.

13.13 Ἀναχθέντες δὲ ἀπὸ τῆς Πάφου οἱ περὶ
NOW~HAVING PUT OUT TO SEA FROM - PAPHOS THE ONES AROUND

Παῦλον ἦλθον εἰς Πέργην τῆς Παμφυλίας,
PAUL   CAME   TO PERGA   -   OF PAMPHYLIA.

Ἰωάννης δὲ ἀποχωρήσας ἀπ' αὐτῶν ὑπέστρεψεν εἰς
BUT~JOHN [MARK] HAVING GONE AWAY FROM THEM, RETURNED TO

Ἱεροσόλυμα. **13.14** αὐτοὶ δὲ διελθόντες ἀπὸ τῆς Πέργης
JERUSALEM.   BUT~THEY HAVING GONE ON FROM - PERGA

παρεγένοντο εἰς Ἀντιόχειαν τὴν Πισιδίαν, καὶ
CAME   TO   ANTIOCH [IN]   -   PISIDIA,   AND

[εἰσ]ελθόντες εἰς τὴν συναγωγὴν τῇ ἡμέρᾳ τῶν
HAVING ENTERED INTO THE SYNAGOGUE ON THE DAY OF THE

σαββάτων ἐκάθισαν. **13.15** μετὰ δὲ τὴν ἀνάγνωσιν
SABBATHS, THEY SAT DOWN. AND~AFTER THE READING

τοῦ νόμου καὶ τῶν προφητῶν ἀπέστειλαν οἱ
OF THE LAW AND THE PROPHETS,   SENT   THE

ἀρχισυνάγωγοι πρὸς αὐτοὺς λέγοντες, Ἄνδρες
RULERS OF THE SYNAGOGUE TO THEM SAYING,   MEN,

ἀδελφοί, εἴ τίς ἐστιν ἐν ὑμῖν λόγος παρακλήσεως
BROTHERS, IF THERE IS~ANY ³AMONG ⁴YOU° ¹WORD ²OF ENCOURAGEMENT

πρὸς τὸν λαόν, λέγετε. **13.16** ἀναστὰς δὲ Παῦλος καὶ
TO THE PEOPLE, SAY [IT].   AND~HAVING ARISEN PAUL AND

κατασείσας τῇ χειρὶ εἶπεν·
HAVING MOTIONED WITH THE(HIS) HAND HE SAID:

Ἄνδρες Ἰσραηλῖται καὶ οἱ φοβούμενοι τὸν θεόν,
MEN,   ISRAELITES AND THE ONES FEARING - GOD,

ἀκούσατε. **13.17** ὁ θεὸς τοῦ λαοῦ τούτου Ἰσραὴλ
LISTEN.   THE GOD - OF THIS~PEOPLE ISRAEL

ἐξελέξατο τοὺς πατέρας ἡμῶν καὶ τὸν λαὸν ὕψωσεν
CHOSE   THE FATHERS OF US, AND THE PEOPLE HE MADE GREAT

ἐν τῇ παροικίᾳ ἐν γῇ Αἰγύπτου καὶ μετὰ
IN THE(THEIR) SOJOURN IN [THE] LAND OF EGYPT AND WITH

βραχίονος ὑψηλοῦ ἐξήγαγεν αὐτοὺς ἐξ αὐτῆς,
AN UPLIFTED~ARM HE LED OUT THEM OUT OF IT,

13.18 καὶ   ὡς   τεσσερακονταετῆ χρόνον ⌜ἐτροποφόρησεν⌝
AND   ABOUT FORTY YEARS   TIME   HE PUT UP WITH

αὐτοὺς ἐν τῇ ἐρήμῳ **13.19** καὶ καθελὼν   ἔθνη ἑπτὰ
THEM   IN THE DESERT,   AND HAVING DESTROYED SEVEN~NATIONS

ἐν γῇ   Χανάαν κατεκληρονόμησεν τὴν γῆν αὐτῶν
IN [THE] LAND OF CANAAN, HE GAVE AS AN INHERITANCE THE LAND OF THEM

13.20 ὡς   ἔτεσιν τετρακοσίοις καὶ πεντήκοντα. καὶ
ABOUT ⁴YEARS ¹FOUR HUNDRED   ²AND ³FIFTY.   AND

μετὰ ταῦτα   ἔδωκεν κριτὰς ἕως Σαμουὴλ [τοῦ]
AFTER THESE THINGS HE GAVE JUDGES UNTIL SAMUEL   THE

προφήτου. **13.21** κἀκεῖθεν ἠτήσαντο βασιλέα καὶ
PROPHET.   AND THEN THEY ASKED FOR A KING   AND

ἔδωκεν αὐτοῖς ὁ θεὸς τὸν Σαοὺλ υἱὸν Κίς,   ἄνδρα
²GAVE ³TO THEM ¹GOD -   SAUL,   [THE] SON OF KISH, A MAN

ἐκ φυλῆς Βενιαμίν, ἔτη τεσσεράκοντα, **13.22** καὶ
FROM [THE] TRIBE OF BENJAMIN, FORTY~YEARS,   AND

μεταστήσας   αὐτὸν ἤγειρεν τὸν Δαυὶδ αὐτοῖς εἰς
[AFTER] HAVING REMOVED HIM,   HE RAISED UP -   DAVID   TO THEM FOR

βασιλέα ᾧ   καὶ εἶπεν μαρτυρήσας,   Εὗρον
A KING TO WHOM ALSO HE SAID HAVING SPOKEN FAVORABLY, I FOUND

Δαυὶδ τὸν   τοῦ Ἰεσσαί, ἄνδρα κατὰ   τὴν
DAVID THE [SON] - OF JESSE, A MAN IN ACCORDANCE WITH THE

καρδίαν μου, ὃς ποιήσει πάντα τὰ θελήματά μου.
HEART OF ME, WHO WILL DO ALL   THE WILL   OF ME.

13.23 τούτου ὁ θεὸς ἀπὸ τοῦ σπέρματος κατ'
⁴OF THIS ONE, - ⁵GOD, ¹FROM ²THE ³SEED   ACCORDING TO

ἐπαγγελίαν ἤγαγεν τῷ Ἰσραὴλ σωτῆρα Ἰησοῦν,
[THE] PROMISE, BROUGHT - TO ISRAEL A SAVIOR, JESUS,

13.24 προκηρύξαντος   Ἰωάννου πρὸ προσώπου τῆς
HAVING PREVIOUSLY PROCLAIMED JOHN   BEFORE [THE] PRESENCE OF THE

εἰσόδου αὐτοῦ βάπτισμα μετανοίας παντὶ τῷ λαῷ
ENTRANCE OF HIM, A BAPTISM OF REPENTANCE TO ALL THE PEOPLE

Ἰσραήλ. **13.25** ὡς δὲ ἐπλήρου   Ἰωάννης τὸν δρόμον,
OF ISRAEL.   NOW~WHEN WAS COMPLETING JOHN   THE COURSE,

ἔλεγεν, Τί ἐμὲ ὑπονοεῖτε εἶναι; οὐκ εἰμὶ ἐγώ·
HE WAS SAYING, WHAT DO YOU° SUPPOSE~ME TO BE? ²AM NOT [HE] ¹I.

ἀλλ' ἰδοὺ ἔρχεται μετ' ἐμὲ οὗ   οὐκ εἰμὶ ἄξιος τὸ
BUT BEHOLD HE COMES AFTER ME OF WHOM I AM NOT WORTHY THE

ὑπόδημα τῶν ποδῶν λῦσαι.
SANDAL   OF THE FEET TO UNTIE.

13.26 Ἄνδρες ἀδελφοί, υἱοὶ γένους   Ἀβραὰμ καὶ
MEN,   BROTHERS, SONS OF [THE] FAMILY OF ABRAHAM AND

οἱ ἐν ὑμῖν φοβούμενοι τὸν θεόν, ἡμῖν ὁ λόγος
THE ONES AMONG YOU° FEARING - GOD, TO US THE WORD

τῆς σωτηρίας ταύτης ἐξαπεστάλη. **13.27** οἱ γὰρ
- OF THIS~SALVATION WAS SENT OUT.   FOR~THE ONES

18For about forty years he put up with[n] them in the wilderness. 19After he had destroyed seven nations in the land of Canaan, he gave them their land as an inheritance 20for about four hundred fifty years. After that he gave them judges until the time of the prophet Samuel. 21Then they asked for a king; and God gave them Saul son of Kish, a man of the tribe of Benjamin, who reigned for forty years. 22When he had removed him, he made David their king. In his testimony about him he said, 'I have found David, son of Jesse, to be a man after my heart, who will carry out all my wishes.' 23Of this man's posterity God has brought to Israel a Savior, Jesus, as he promised; 24before his coming John had already proclaimed a baptism of repentance to all the people of Israel. 25And as John was finishing his work, he said, 'What do you suppose that I am? I am not he. No, but one is coming after me; I am not worthy to untie the thong of the sandals[o] on his feet.'

26 "My brothers, you descendants of Abraham's family, and others who fear God, to us[p] the message of this salvation has been sent. 27Because the residents

[n] Other ancient authorities read *cared for*

[o] Gk *untie the sandals*

[p] Other ancient authorities read *you*

13:18 text: KJV ASVmg NASB RSV NIV NEB NJBmg NRSV. var. ετροφοφορησεν (cared for) [see Deut. 1:31]: ASV NASBmg RSVmg NIVmg NEBmg NJB NRSVmg.   **13:22a** Ps. 89:20   **13:22b** 1 Sam. 13:14

of Jerusalem and their
leaders did not recognize
him or understand the words
of the prophets that are read
every sabbath, they fulfilled
those words by condemning
him. 28Even though they
found no cause for a
sentence of death, they
asked Pilate to have him
killed. 29When they had
carried out everything that
was written about him, they
took him down from the tree
and laid him in a tomb.
30But God raised him from
the dead; 31and for many
days he appeared to those
who came up with him from
Galilee to Jerusalem, and
they are now his witnesses to
the people. 32And we bring
you the good news that what
God promised to our an-
cestors 33he has fulfilled for
us, their children, by raising
Jesus; as also it is written in
the second psalm,
    'You are my Son;
        today I have begotten
        you.'
34As to his raising him from
the dead, no more to return
to corruption, he has spoken
in this way,
    'I will give you the holy
        promises made to
        David.'
35Therefore he has also said
in another psalm,

κατοικοῦντες ἐν Ἰερουσαλὴμ καὶ οἱ ἄρχοντες αὐτῶν
DWELLING   IN   JERUSALEM   AND THE RULERS   OF THEM

τοῦτον ἀγνοήσαντες καὶ τὰς φωνὰς τῶν προφητῶν τὰς
NOT HAVING KNOWN~THIS ONE AND   THE VOICES OF THE PROPHETS   -

κατὰ πᾶν σάββατον ἀναγινωσκομένας κρίναντες
EVERY   SABBATH   BEING READ,   HAVING JUDGED,

ἐπλήρωσαν,   13.28 καὶ μηδεμίαν αἰτίαν θανάτου
THEY FULFILLED [THESE WORDS], AND WITHOUT A REASON FOR DEATH

εὑρόντες ἠτήσαντο Πιλᾶτον ἀναιρεθῆναι αὐτόν.
HAVING FOUND, THEY ASKED PILATE [THAT] HE~BE DONE AWAY WITH.

13.29 ὡς δὲ ἐτέλεσαν πάντα τὰ περὶ αὐτοῦ
AND~WHEN THEY FINISHED ALL THE THINGS ABOUT HIM

γεγραμμένα, καθελόντες ἀπὸ τοῦ ξύλου ἔθηκαν
HAVING BEEN WRITTEN, HAVING TAKEN [HIM] DOWN FROM THE TREE, THEY PUT [HIM]

εἰς μνημεῖον. 13.30 ὁ δὲ θεὸς ἤγειρεν αὐτὸν ἐκ
INTO A TOMB.   - BUT GOD RAISED UP HIM FROM

νεκρῶν, 13.31 ὃς ὤφθη ἐπὶ ἡμέρας πλείους τοῖς
[THE] DEAD,   WHO WAS SEEN OVER MANY~DAYS   TO THE ONES

συναναβᾶσιν αὐτῷ ἀπὸ τῆς Γαλιλαίας εἰς
HAVING COME UP WITH HIM FROM -   GALILEE   TO

Ἰερουσαλήμ, οἵτινες [νῦν] εἰσιν μάρτυρες αὐτοῦ πρὸς
JERUSALEM,   WHO   NOW ARE WITNESSES OF HIM TO

τὸν λαόν. 13.32 καὶ ἡμεῖς ὑμᾶς εὐαγγελιζόμεθα τὴν
THE PEOPLE.   AND   WE   ARE PREACHING~TO YOU°   THE

πρὸς τοὺς πατέρας ἐπαγγελίαν γενομένην, 13.33 ὅτι
3TO   4THE 5FATHERS   1PROMISE   2HAVING COME,   THAT

ταύτην ὁ θεὸς ἐκπεπλήρωκεν τοῖς τέκνοις [αὐτῶν]
THESE THINGS - GOD HAS FULFILLED   TO THE CHILDREN OF THEM,

ἡμῖν ἀναστήσας Ἰησοῦν ὡς καὶ ἐν ⌜τῷ ψαλμῷ
TO US, HAVING RAISED JESUS,   AS ALSO IN THE 2PSALM

γέγραπται τῷ δευτέρῳ,⌝
3IT HAS BEEN WRITTEN - 1SECOND,

    Υἱός μου εἶ σύ,
    [THE] SON OF ME YOU~ARE,

    ἐγὼ σήμερον γεγέννηκά σε.
    TODAY~I   HAVE BECOME A FATHER TO YOU.

13.34 ὅτι δὲ ἀνέστησεν αὐτὸν ἐκ νεκρῶν μηκέτι
AND~THAT HE RAISED   HIM FROM [THE] DEAD NO LONGER

μέλλοντα ὑποστρέφειν εἰς διαφθοράν, οὕτως εἴρηκεν
BEING ABOUT   TO RETURN   TO DECAY,   THUS   HE HAS SAID

ὅτι
-

    Δώσω ὑμῖν τὰ ὅσια Δαυὶδ τὰ πιστά.
    I WILL GIVE TO YOU° THE 2DECREES 3OF DAVID - 1TRUSTWORTHY.

13.35 διότι καὶ ἐν ἑτέρῳ λέγει,
THEREFORE ALSO IN ANOTHER [PSALM] HE SAYS,

13.33a text: KJV ASV RSV NASB NIV NEB TEV NJBmg NRSV. var. τω πρωτω ψαλμω γεγραπται (in the
first psalm it is written): NEBmg NJBmg. var. τοις ψαλμοις γεγραπται (in the psalms): NJB.
13.33b Ps. 2:7 **13.34** Isa. 55:3 LXX **13.35** Ps. 16:10 LXX

Οὐ δώσεις τὸν ὅσιόν σου ἰδεῖν διαφθοράν.
YOU WILL NOT PERMIT THE HOLY ONE OF YOU TO EXPERIENCE DECAY.

13.36 Δαυὶδ μὲν γὰρ ἰδίᾳ γενεᾷ ὑπηρετήσας τῇ
²DAVID - ¹FOR, IN HIS OWN GENERATION HAVING SERVED BY THE

τοῦ θεοῦ βουλῇ ἐκοιμήθη καὶ προσετέθη πρὸς τοὺς
- WILL~OF GOD, FELL ASLEEP AND HE WAS GATHERED TO THE

πατέρας αὐτοῦ καὶ εἶδεν διαφθοράν· **13.37** ὃν δὲ
FATHERS OF HIM AND HE EXPERIENCED DECAY. BUT~WHOM

ὁ θεὸς ἤγειρεν, οὐκ εἶδεν διαφθοράν. **13.38** γνωστὸν
- GOD RAISED, DID NOT EXPERIENCE DECAY. ³KNOWN

οὖν ἔστω ὑμῖν, ἄνδρες ἀδελφοί, ὅτι διὰ τούτου
¹THEREFORE ²LET IT BE TO YOU°, MEN, BROTHERS, THAT THROUGH THIS ONE

ὑμῖν ἄφεσις ἁμαρτιῶν καταγγέλλεται[, καὶ] ἀπὸ
TO YOU° FORGIVENESS OF SINS IS PROCLAIMED, AND FROM

πάντων ὧν οὐκ ἠδυνήθητε ἐν νόμῳ Μωϋσέως
ALL THINGS OF WHICH YOU° WERE NOT ABLE BY [THE] LAW OF MOSES

δικαιωθῆναι, **13.39** ἐν τούτῳ πᾶς ὁ πιστεύων
TO BE JUSTIFIED, BY THIS ONE EVERYONE - BELIEVING

δικαιοῦται. **13.40** βλέπετε οὖν μὴ ἐπέλθῃ
IS JUSTIFIED. BE CAREFUL THEN [THAT] MAY NOT COME UPON [YOU°]

τὸ εἰρημένον ἐν τοῖς προφήταις,
THE THING HAVING BEEN SPOKEN BY THE PROPHETS,

13.41 Ἴδετε, οἱ καταφρονηταί,
LOOK, - SCOFFERS,

καὶ θαυμάσατε καὶ ἀφανίσθητε,
AND MARVEL AND PERISH,

ὅτι ἔργον ἐργάζομαι ἐγὼ ἐν ταῖς ἡμέραις ὑμῶν,
BECAUSE A WORK I~AM WORKING IN THE DAYS OF YOU°,

ἔργον ὃ οὐ μὴ πιστεύσητε ἐάν
A WORK WHICH YOU° MAY BY NO MEANS BELIEVE IF

τις ἐκδιηγῆται ὑμῖν.
SOMEONE SHOULD TELL YOU°.

13.42 Ἐξιόντων δὲ αὐτῶν παρεκάλουν εἰς τὸ μεταξὺ
AND~GOING OUT THEM, THEY WERE BEGGING FOR THE NEXT

σάββατον λαληθῆναι αὐτοῖς τὰ ῥήματα ταῦτα.
SABBATH TO BE SPOKEN TO THEM - THESE~WORDS.

13.43 λυθείσης δὲ τῆς συναγωγῆς ἠκολούθησαν
AND~HAVING BROKEN UP THE GATHERING, ⁸FOLLOWED

πολλοὶ τῶν Ἰουδαίων καὶ τῶν σεβομένων
¹MANY ²OF THE ³JEWS ⁴AND ⁵OF THE ⁶WORSHIPING

προσηλύτων τῷ Παύλῳ καὶ τῷ Βαρναβᾷ, οἵτινες
⁷PROSELYTES PAUL AND - BARNABAS, WHO

προσλαλοῦντες αὐτοῖς ἔπειθον αὐτοὺς προσμένειν
SPEAKING TO THEM, WERE CONVINCING THEM TO REMAIN

τῇ χάριτι τοῦ θεοῦ.
IN THE GRACE - OF GOD.

13:41 Hab. 1:5 LXX

'You will not let your Holy One experience corruption.' ³⁶For David, after he had served the purpose of God in his own generation, died,�q was laid beside his ancestors, and experienced corruption; ³⁷but he whom God raised up experienced no corruption. ³⁸Let it be known to you therefore, my brothers, that through this man forgiveness of sins is proclaimed to you; ³⁹by this Jesusʳ everyone who believes is set free from all those sinsˢ from which you could not be freed by the law of Moses. ⁴⁰Beware, therefore, that what the prophets said does not happen to you:

⁴¹ 'Look, you scoffers!
Be amazed and perish,
for in your days I am
doing a work,
a work that you will
never believe, even
if someone tells
you.'"

⁴² As Paul and Barnabasʳ were going out, the people urged them to speak about these things again the next sabbath. ⁴³When the meeting of the synagogue broke up, many Jews and devout converts to Judaism followed Paul and Barnabas, who spoke to them and urged them to continue in the grace of God.

q Gk fell asleep
r Gk this
s Gk all
t Gk they

44 The next sabbath almost the whole city gathered to hear the word of the Lord.ᵘ ⁴⁵But when the Jews saw the crowds, they were filled with jealousy; and blaspheming, they contradicted what was spoken by Paul. ⁴⁶Then both Paul and Barnabas spoke out boldly, saying, "It was necessary that the word of God should be spoken first to you. Since you reject it and judge yourselves to be unworthy of eternal life, we are now turning to the Gentiles. ⁴⁷For so the Lord has commanded us, saying,
'I have set you to be a
    light for the
    Gentiles,
so that you may bring
    salvation to the ends
    of the earth.' "
48 When the Gentiles heard this, they were glad and praised the word of the Lord; and as many as had been destined for eternal life became believers. ⁴⁹Thus the word of the Lord spread throughout the region. ⁵⁰But the Jews incited the devout women of high standing and the leading men of the city, and stirred up persecution against Paul and Barnabas, and drove them out of their region. ⁵¹So they shook the

ᵘ Other ancient authorities read *God*

13.44 Τῷ δὲ ἐρχομένῳ σαββάτῳ σχεδὸν πᾶσα ἡ
NOW~ON THE COMING SABBATH NEARLY ALL THE

πόλις συνήχθη ἀκοῦσαι τὸν λόγον τοῦ κυρίου.
CITY WAS ASSEMBLED TO HEAR THE WORD OF THE LORD.

13.45 ἰδόντες δὲ οἱ Ἰουδαῖοι τοὺς ὄχλους
⁴HAVING SEEN ¹AND ²THE ³JEWS THE CROWD,

ἐπλήσθησαν ζήλου καὶ ἀντέλεγον τοῖς
THEY WERE FILLED WITH JEALOUSY AND WERE CONTRADICTING THE THINGS

ὑπὸ Παύλου λαλουμένοις βλασφημοῦντες.
BY PAUL BEING SPOKEN, BLASPHEMING.

13.46 παρρησιασάμενοί τε ὁ Παῦλος καὶ ὁ Βαρναβᾶς
AND~HAVING SPOKEN BOLDLY - PAUL AND - BARNABAS

εἶπαν, Ὑμῖν ἦν ἀναγκαῖον πρῶτον λαληθῆναι τὸν
SAID, TO YOU° IT WAS NECESSARY FIRST TO BE SPOKEN THE

λόγον τοῦ θεοῦ· ἐπειδὴ ἀπωθεῖσθε αὐτὸν καὶ οὐκ
WORD - OF GOD. SINCE YOU° REJECT IT AND NOT

ἀξίους κρίνετε ἑαυτοὺς τῆς αἰωνίου ζωῆς, ἰδοὺ
WORTHY DO YOU° JUDGE YOURSELVES - OF ETERNAL LIFE, BEHOLD

στρεφόμεθα εἰς τὰ ἔθνη. **13.47** οὕτως γὰρ ἐντέταλται
WE ARE TURNING TO THE GENTILES. FOR~THUS HAS COMMANDED

ἡμῖν ὁ κύριος,
US THE LORD,

Τέθεικά σε εἰς φῶς ἐθνῶν
I HAVE APPOINTED YOU FOR A LIGHT TO [THE] GENTILES [THAT]

τοῦ εἶναί σε εἰς σωτηρίαν ἕως ἐσχάτου τῆς
- YOU~BE FOR SALVATION UNTO [THE] END OF THE

γῆς.
EARTH.

13.48 ἀκούοντα δὲ τὰ ἔθνη ἔχαιρον καὶ ἐδόξαζον
NOW~HEARING [THIS], THE GENTILES WERE REJOICING AND WERE GLORIFYING

⌜τὸν λόγον τοῦ κυρίου⌝ καὶ ἐπίστευσαν ὅσοι
THE WORD OF THE LORD AND AS MANY AS~BELIEVED

ἦσαν τεταγμένοι εἰς ζωὴν αἰώνιον· **13.49** διεφέρετο δὲ
HAD BEEN APPOINTED TO ETERNAL~LIFE. AND~WAS SPREADING

ὁ λόγος τοῦ κυρίου δι' ὅλης τῆς χώρας.
THE WORD OF THE LORD THROUGH [THE] ENTIRE - REGION.

13.50 οἱ δὲ Ἰουδαῖοι παρώτρυναν τὰς σεβομένας
BUT~THE JEWS AROUSED THE ²WORSHIPING

γυναῖκας τὰς εὐσχήμονας καὶ τοὺς πρώτους τῆς
³WOMEN - ¹PROMINENT AND THE LEADING [MEN] OF THE

πόλεως καὶ ἐπήγειραν διωγμὸν ἐπὶ τὸν Παῦλον καὶ
CITY AND THEY INSTIGATED A PERSECUTION AGAINST - PAUL AND

Βαρναβᾶν καὶ ἐξέβαλον αὐτοὺς ἀπὸ τῶν ὁρίων
BARNABAS AND THEY DROVE OUT THEM FROM THE BOUNDARIES

αὐτῶν. **13.51** οἱ δὲ ἐκτιναξάμενοι τὸν κονιορτὸν τῶν
OF THEM. - AND HAVING SHAKEN OFF THE DUST OF THE

13:47 Isa. 49:6 **13:48** text: KJV ASVmg NASB NIV NEB TEV NJB NRSV. var. τον λογον του θεου (the word of God): ASV RSV NJBmg.

ποδῶν ἐπ᾽   αὐτοὺς ἦλθον εἰς Ἰκόνιον, **13.52** οἵ τε
FEET   AGAINST   THEM THEY CAME TO ICONIUM,   AND~THE

μαθηταὶ ἐπληροῦντο   χαρᾶς καὶ πνεύματος ἁγίου.
DISCIPLES WERE BEING FILLED WITH JOY   AND   [THE] HOLY~SPIRIT.

dust off their feet in protest
against them, and went to
Iconium. [52]And the disciples
were filled with joy and with
the Holy Spirit.

CHAPTER 14

14.1 Ἐγένετο δὲ ἐν Ἰκονίῳ   κατὰ τὸ αὐτὸ εἰσελθεῖν
NOW~IT CAME ABOUT IN ICONIUM [THAT] [3]TOGETHER   [2]ENTERED

αὐτοὺς εἰς τὴν συναγωγὴν τῶν Ἰουδαίων καὶ λαλῆσαι
[1]THEY INTO THE SYNAGOGUE OF THE JEWS   AND TO SPEAK

οὕτως ὥστε πιστεῦσαι Ἰουδαίων τε καὶ Ἑλλήνων πολὺ
THUS SO THAT TO BELIEVE   BOTH~JEWS   AND GREEKS   A GREAT

πλῆθος. **14.2** οἱ δὲ ἀπειθήσαντες Ἰουδαῖοι ἐπήγειραν
MULTITUDE.   AND~THE JEWS~HAVING DISOBEYED,   AROUSED

καὶ ἐκάκωσαν τὰς ψυχὰς τῶν ἐθνῶν κατὰ τῶν
AND MADE ANGRY THE SOULS OF THE GENTILES AGAINST THE

ἀδελφῶν. **14.3** ἱκανὸν μὲν οὖν   χρόνον διέτριψαν
BROTHERS.   [3]A LONG -   [1]THEREFORE [4]TIME [2]THEY SPENT

παρρησιαζόμενοι ἐπὶ τῷ κυρίῳ τῷ μαρτυροῦντι [ἐπὶ]
SPEAKING BOLDLY   FOR THE LORD,   - WITNESSING   TO

τῷ λόγῳ τῆς χάριτος αὐτοῦ, διδόντι σημεῖα καὶ
THE WORD OF THE GRACE OF HIM, [AND] GRANTING SIGNS AND

τέρατα γίνεσθαι διὰ τῶν χειρῶν αὐτῶν. **14.4** ἐσχίσθη δὲ
WONDERS TO HAPPEN BY THE HANDS OF THEM.   AND~WAS DIVIDED

τὸ πλῆθος τῆς   πόλεως, καὶ οἱ μὲν ἦσαν σὺν τοῖς
THE MULTITUDE OF THE CITY,   AND SOME WERE WITH THE

Ἰουδαίοις, οἱ δὲ   σὺν τοῖς ἀποστόλοις. **14.5** ὡς δὲ
JEWS,   BUT~OTHERS WITH THE APOSTLES.   AND~WHEN

ἐγένετο ὁρμὴ   τῶν ἐθνῶν τε   καὶ Ἰουδαίων σὺν
CAME   AN ATTEMPT [2]THE [3]GENTILES [1][BY] BOTH AND [THE] JEWS WITH

τοῖς ἄρχουσιν αὐτῶν ὑβρίσαι καὶ λιθοβολῆσαι αὐτούς,
THE RULERS   OF THEM TO MISTREAT AND TO STONE   THEM,

14.6 συνιδόντες   κατέφυγον εἰς τὰς πόλεις
    HAVING BECOME AWARE [OF THIS] THEY FLED   TO THE CITIES

τῆς Λυκαονίας Λύστραν καὶ Δέρβην καὶ τὴν
 - OF LYCAONIA, LYSTRA,   AND DERBE AND THE

περίχωρον,   **14.7** κἀκεῖ εὐαγγελιζόμενοι ἦσαν.
SURROUNDING COUNTRYSIDE, AND THERE THEY WERE PREACHING THE GOOD NEWS.

14.8 Καί τις   ἀνὴρ ἀδύνατος   ἐν Λύστροις τοῖς
    AND A CERTAIN MAN [3]WITHOUT STRENGTH [1]IN [2]LYSTRA IN THE (HIS)

ποσὶν ἐκάθητο, χωλὸς ἐκ κοιλίας μητρὸς αὐτοῦ
FEET WAS SITTING, LAME FROM [THE] WOMB OF [THE] MOTHER OF HIM,

ὃς οὐδέποτε περιεπάτησεν. **14.9** οὗτος ἤκουσεν τοῦ
WHO NEVER   WALKED.   THIS ONE HEARD   -

The same thing occurred in
Iconium, where Paul and
Barnabas[v] went into the
Jewish synagogue and
spoke in such a way that
a great number of both
Jews and Greeks became
believers. [2]But the un-
believing Jews stirred up
the Gentiles and poisoned
their minds against the
brothers. [3]So they remained
for a long time, speaking
boldly for the Lord, who
testified to the word of his
grace by granting signs and
wonders to be done through
them. [4]But the residents of
the city were divided; some
sided with the Jews, and
some with the apostles.
[5]And when an attempt was
made by both Gentiles and
Jews, with their rulers, to
mistreat them and to stone
them, [6]the apostles[v] learned
of it and fled to Lystra and
Derbe, cities of Lycaonia,
and to the surrounding
country; [7]and there they
continued proclaiming the
good news.

8 In Lystra there was
a man sitting who could
not use his feet and had
never walked, for he
had been crippled from
birth. [9]He listened to

[v] Gk *they*

Paul as he was speaking. And Paul, looking at him intently and seeing that he had faith to be healed, ¹⁰said in a loud voice, "Stand upright on your feet." And the manʷ sprang up and began to walk. ¹¹When the crowds saw what Paul had done, they shouted in the Lycaonian language, "The gods have come down to us in human form!" ¹²Barnabas they called Zeus, and Paul they called Hermes, because he was the chief speaker. ¹³The priest of Zeus, whose temple was just outside the city,ˣ brought oxen and garlands to the gates; he and the crowds wanted to offer sacrifice. ¹⁴When the apostles Barnabas and Paul heard of it, they tore their clothes and rushed out into the crowd, shouting, ¹⁵"Friends,ʸ why are you doing this? We are mortals just like you, and we bring you good news, that you should turn from these worthless things to the living God, who made the heaven and the earth and the sea and all that is in them. ¹⁶In past generations he allowed all the nations to follow their own ways; ¹⁷yet he has not left himself without a witness in doing good— giving you rains from heaven and fruitful seasons, and filling you with food and your hearts with joy."

ʷ Gk *he*
ˣ Or *The priest of Zeus-Outside-the-City*
ʸ Gk *Men*

Παύλου λαλοῦντος· ὃς ἀτενίσας αὐτῷ καὶ ἰδὼν
PAUL SPEAKING; WHO HAVING GAZED AT HIM AND HAVING SEEN

ὅτι ἔχει πίστιν τοῦ σωθῆναι, **14.10** εἶπεν
THAT HE HAS FAITH - TO BE RESTORED TO HEALTH, HE SAID

μεγάλῃ φωνῇ, Ἀνάστηθι ἐπὶ τοὺς πόδας σου ὀρθός.
IN A LOUD VOICE, STAND UP ON THE FEET OF YOU UPRIGHT.

καὶ ἥλατο καὶ περιεπάτει. **14.11** οἵ τε ὄχλοι
AND HE JUMPED UP AND WAS WALKING AROUND. AND~THE CROWDS

ἰδόντες ὃ ἐποίησεν Παῦλος ἐπῆραν τὴν φωνὴν αὐτῶν
HAVING SEEN WHAT PAUL~DID RAISED UP THE VOICE OF THEM

Λυκαονιστὶ λέγοντες, Οἱ θεοὶ ὁμοιωθέντες
IN THE LYCAONIAN [DIALECT] SAYING, THE GODS, HAVING BEEN MADE LIKE

ἀνθρώποις κατέβησαν πρὸς ἡμᾶς, **14.12** ἐκάλουν τε
MEN, CAME DOWN TO US, AND~THEY WERE CALLING

τὸν Βαρναβᾶν Δία, τὸν δὲ Παῦλον Ἑρμῆν, ἐπειδὴ
- BARNABAS, ZEUS, - AND PAUL, HERMES, SINCE

αὐτὸς ἦν ὁ ἡγούμενος τοῦ λόγου. **14.13** ὅ τε ἱερεὺς
HE WAS THE ONE LEADING THE SPEECH. AND~THE PRIEST

τοῦ Διὸς τοῦ ὄντος πρὸ τῆς πόλεως ταύρους καὶ
- OF ZEUS - BEING OUTSIDE THE CITY, BULLS AND

στέμματα ἐπὶ τοὺς πυλῶνας ἐνέγκας σὺν τοῖς
FLOWER WREATHS TO THE GATES HAVING BROUGHT, WITH THE

ὄχλοις ἤθελεν θύειν. **14.14** ἀκούσαντες δὲ οἱ
CROWDS WAS WANTING TO OFFER A SACRIFICE. BUT~HAVING HEARD [THIS], THE

ἀπόστολοι Βαρναβᾶς καὶ Παῦλος διαρρήξαντες τὰ
APOSTLES, BARNABAS AND PAUL, HAVING TORN THE

ἱμάτια αὐτῶν ἐξεπήδησαν εἰς τὸν ὄχλον κράζοντες
GARMENTS OF THEM, RUSHED OUT INTO THE CROWD CRYING OUT

14.15 καὶ λέγοντες, Ἄνδρες, τί ταῦτα ποιεῖτε;
AND SAYING, MEN, WHY ARE YOU° DOING~THESE THINGS?

καὶ ἡμεῖς ὁμοιοπαθεῖς ἐσμεν ὑμῖν ἄνθρωποι
WE~ALSO ³OF THE SAME NATURE [AS] ¹ARE ⁴YOU° ²MEN

εὐαγγελιζόμενοι ὑμᾶς ἀπὸ τούτων τῶν ματαίων
PREACHING TO YOU° FROM THESE - WORTHLESS [THINGS]

ἐπιστρέφειν ἐπὶ θεὸν ζῶντα, ὃς ἐποίησεν τὸν οὐρανὸν
TO TURN TO [THE] LIVING~GOD, WHO MADE THE HEAVEN

καὶ τὴν γῆν καὶ τὴν θάλασσαν καὶ πάντα τὰ ἐν
AND THE EARTH AND THE SEA AND ALL THE THINGS IN

αὐτοῖς· **14.16** ὃς ἐν ταῖς παρῳχημέναις γενεαῖς εἴασεν
THEM; WHO IN THE GENERATIONS~HAVING PASSED BY ALLOWED

πάντα τὰ ἔθνη πορεύεσθαι ταῖς ὁδοῖς αὐτῶν·
ALL THE NATIONS TO GO THE WAYS OF THEM.

14.17 καίτοι οὐκ ἀμάρτυρον αὐτὸν ἀφῆκεν ἀγαθουργῶν,
AND YET NOT WITHOUT WITNESS DID HE LEAVE~HIMSELF DOING GOOD,

οὐρανόθεν ὑμῖν ὑετοὺς διδοὺς καὶ καιροὺς καρποφόρους,
FROM HEAVEN TO YOU° GIVING~RAINS AND SEASONS OF BEARING FRUIT,

ἐμπιπλῶν τροφῆς καὶ εὐφροσύνης τὰς καρδίας ὑμῶν.
FILLING WITH FOOD AND WITH JOY THE HEARTS OF YOU°.

14.18 καὶ   ταῦτα   λέγοντες μόλις   κατέπαυσαν τοὺς
AND   THESE THINGS SAYING,   WITH DIFFICULTY THEY RESTRAINED THE

ὄχλους τοῦ μὴ θύειν   αὐτοῖς.
CROWDS   -   NOT TO OFFER SACRIFICE TO THEM.

14.19 Ἐπῆλθαν δὲ ἀπὸ Ἀντιοχείας καὶ Ἰκονίου
AND~CAME   FROM ANTIOCH   AND ICONIUM

Ἰουδαῖοι καὶ πείσαντες τοὺς ὄχλους καὶ λιθάσαντες
JEWS,   AND HAVING WON OVER THE CROWDS AND HAVING STONED

τὸν Παῦλον ἔσυρον   ἔξω   τῆς πόλεως
 -    PAUL,   THEY WERE DRAGGING [HIM] OUTSIDE THE CITY,

νομίζοντες αὐτὸν τεθνηκέναι. **14.20** κυκλωσάντων
THINKING   HIM   TO HAVE DIED.   ⁴HAVING SURROUNDED

δὲ   τῶν μαθητῶν αὐτὸν ἀναστὰς εἰσῆλθεν εἰς τὴν
¹AND [AFTER] ²THE ³DISCIPLES HIM,   HAVING ARISEN, HE ENTERED INTO THE

πόλιν. καὶ τῇ ἐπαύριον ἐξῆλθεν σὺν τῷ Βαρναβᾷ
CITY.   AND ON THE NEXT DAY HE WENT OUT WITH - BARNABAS

εἰς Δέρβην.
TO   DERBE.

14.21 Εὐαγγελισάμενοί τε   τὴν πόλιν ἐκείνην καὶ
AND~HAVING PREACHED THE GOOD NEWS [IN] -   THAT~CITY   AND

μαθητεύσαντες ἱκανοὺς ὑπέστρεψαν εἰς τὴν Λύστραν
HAVING MADE DISCIPLES MANY,   THEY RETURNED TO - LYSTRA

καὶ εἰς Ἰκόνιον καὶ εἰς Ἀντιόχειαν **14.22** ἐπιστηρίζοντες
AND TO ICONIUM AND TO ANTIOCH,   STRENGTHENING

τὰς ψυχὰς τῶν μαθητῶν, παρακαλοῦντες ἐμμένειν τῇ
THE SOULS OF THE DISCIPLES, ENCOURAGING [THEM] TO REMAIN IN THE

πίστει καὶ ὅτι διὰ   πολλῶν θλίψεων δεῖ
FAITH AND THAT THROUGH MANY   TRIBULATIONS IT IS NECESSARY

ἡμᾶς εἰσελθεῖν εἰς τὴν βασιλείαν τοῦ θεοῦ.
[FOR] US TO ENTER   INTO THE KINGDOM   -   OF GOD.

14.23 χειροτονήσαντες δὲ αὐτοῖς κατ' ἐκκλησίαν
AND~HAVING ELECTED   FOR THEM IN EVERY CHURCH

πρεσβυτέρους, προσευξάμενοι μετὰ νηστειῶν παρέθεντο
ELDERS,   HAVING PRAYED   WITH FASTINGS, THEY COMMENDED

αὐτοὺς τῷ κυρίῳ εἰς ὃν πεπιστεύκεισαν. **14.24** καὶ
THEM   TO THE LORD IN WHOM THEY HAD BELIEVED.   AND

διελθόντες   τὴν Πισιδίαν ἦλθον εἰς τὴν Παμφυλίαν
HAVING GONE THROUGH - PISIDIA, THEY CAME TO - PAMPHYLIA

14.25 καὶ λαλήσαντες ἐν Πέργῃ τὸν λόγον κατέβησαν
AND HAVING SPOKEN IN PERGA THE WORD, THEY WENT DOWN

εἰς Ἀττάλειαν **14.26** κἀκεῖθεν ἀπέπλευσαν εἰς
TO   ATTALIA   AND FROM THERE THEY SAILED AWAY TO

Ἀντιόχειαν, ὅθεν   ἦσαν παραδεδομένοι τῇ   χάριτι
ANTIOCH,   FROM WHICH THEY HAD BEEN COMMENDED TO THE GRACE

τοῦ θεοῦ εἰς τὸ ἔργον ὃ   ἐπλήρωσαν.
 -    OF GOD TO THE WORK WHICH THEY FINISHED.

14.27 παραγενόμενοι δὲ καὶ συναγαγόντες τὴν
AND~HAVING COME   AND HAVING ASSEMBLED THE

[18]Even with these words, they scarcely restrained the crowds from offering sacrifice to them.

19 But Jews came there from Antioch and Iconium and won over the crowds. Then they stoned Paul and dragged him out of the city, supposing that he was dead. [20]But when the disciples surrounded him, he got up and went into the city. The next day he went on with Barnabas to Derbe.

21 After they had proclaimed the good news to that city and had made many disciples, they returned to Lystra, then on to Iconium and Antioch. [22]There they strengthened the souls of the disciples and encouraged them to continue in the faith, saying, "It is through many persecutions that we must enter the kingdom of God." [23]And after they had appointed elders for them in each church, with prayer and fasting they entrusted them to the Lord in whom they had come to believe.

24 Then they passed through Pisidia and came to Pamphylia. [25]When they had spoken the word in Perga, they went down to Attalia. [26]From there they sailed back to Antioch, where they had been commended to the grace of God for the work[z] that they had completed. [27]When they arrived, they called the

[z] Or *committed in the grace of God to the work*

church together and related all that God had done with them, and how he had opened a door of faith for the Gentiles. 28And they stayed there with the disciples for some time.

ἐκκλησίαν   ἀνήγγελλον   ὅσα   ἐποίησεν ὁ θεὸς μετ'
CHURCH   THEY WERE REPORTING WHAT THINGS DID   - GOD WITH

αὐτῶν καὶ ὅτι ἤνοιξεν τοῖς ἔθνεσιν θύραν πίστεως.
THEM AND THAT HE OPENED FOR THE GENTILES A DOOR OF FAITH.

14.28 διέτριβον δὲ   · χρόνον οὐκ ὀλίγον σὺν τοῖς
AND~THEY WERE SPENDING TIME   NOT A LITTLE WITH THE

μαθηταῖς.
DISCIPLES.

CHAPTER 15

Then certain individuals came down from Judea and were teaching the brothers, "Unless you are circumcised according to the custom of Moses, you cannot be saved." 2And after Paul and Barnabas had no small dissension and debate with them, Paul and Barnabas and some of the others were appointed to go up to Jerusalem to discuss this question with the apostles and the elders. 3So they were sent on their way by the church, and as they passed through both Phoenicia and Samaria, they reported the conversion of the Gentiles, and brought great joy to all the believers.[a] 4When they came to Jerusalem, they were welcomed by the church and the apostles and the elders, and they reported all that God had done with them. 5But some believers who belonged to the sect of the Pharisees stood up and said, "It is necessary for them to be circumcised

[a] Gk brothers

15.1 Καὶ   τινες κατελθόντες ἀπὸ τῆς Ἰουδαίας
AND   SOME   HAVING COME DOWN FROM - JUDEA

ἐδίδασκον τοὺς ἀδελφοὺς ὅτι Ἐὰν μὴ περιτμηθῆτε
WERE TEACHING THE BROTHERS IF YOU° ARE NOT CIRCUMCISED

τῷ ἔθει τῷ Μωϋσέως, οὐ δύνασθε σωθῆναι.
BY THE CUSTOM - OF MOSES, YOU° ARE NOT ABLE TO BE SAVED.

15.2 γενομένης δὲ   στάσεως καὶ ζητήσεως οὐκ
NOW~HAVING HAPPENED A DISPUTE AND A DEBATE [OF] NO

ὀλίγης '   τῷ Παύλῳ καὶ τῷ Βαρναβᾷ πρὸς αὐτούς,
LITTLE [PROPORTION] - BY PAUL AND - BARNABAS WITH THEM,

ἔταξαν   ἀναβαίνειν Παῦλον καὶ Βαρναβᾶν καὶ
THEY APPOINTED TO GO UP PAUL AND BARNABAS AND

τινας ἄλλους ἐξ αὐτῶν πρὸς τοὺς ἀποστόλους καὶ
SOME OTHERS FROM THEM TO THE APOSTLES AND

πρεσβυτέρους εἰς Ἰερουσαλὴμ περὶ   τοῦ
ELDERS   IN JERUSALEM CONCERNING -

ζητήματος τούτου. **15.3** Οἱ μὲν οὖν προπεμφθέντες
THIS~ISSUE.   THEN HAVING BEEN SENT ON THEIR WAY

ὑπὸ τῆς ἐκκλησίας διήρχοντο   τήν τε Φοινίκην
BY THE CHURCH, THEY WERE PASSING THROUGH - BOTH PHOENICIA

καὶ Σαμάρειαν ἐκδιηγούμενοι τὴν ἐπιστροφὴν τῶν
AND SAMARIA   TELLING IN DETAIL THE CONVERSION OF THE

ἐθνῶν καὶ ἐποίουν   χαρὰν μεγάλην πᾶσιν τοῖς
GENTILES AND THEY WERE BRINGING GREAT~JOY TO ALL THE

ἀδελφοῖς. **15.4** παραγενόμενοι δὲ εἰς Ἰερουσαλὴμ
BROTHERS.   AND~HAVING COME TO JERUSALEM,

παρεδέχθησαν ἀπὸ τῆς ἐκκλησίας καὶ τῶν ἀποστόλων
THEY WERE RECEIVED BY THE CHURCH AND THE APOSTLES

καὶ τῶν πρεσβυτέρων, ἀνήγγειλάν τε ὅσα   ὁ θεὸς
AND THE ELDERS,   AND~THEY REPORTED WHAT THINGS - GOD

ἐποίησεν μετ' αὐτῶν. **15.5** ἐξανέστησαν δέ τινες
DID WITH THEM.   BUT~ROSE UP SOME

τῶν   ἀπὸ τῆς αἱρέσεως τῶν Φαρισαίων
OF THE ONES FROM THE SECT OF THE PHARISEES

πεπιστευκότες λέγοντες ὅτι δεῖ   περιτέμνειν
HAVING BELIEVED SAYING THAT IT IS NECESSARY TO CIRCUMCISE

αὐτοὺς παραγγέλλειν τε τηρεῖν τὸν νόμον Μωϋσέως.
THEM   AND~TO COMMAND [THEM]   TO KEEP   THE   LAW   OF MOSES.

15.6 Συνήχθησάν τε   οἱ ἀπόστολοι καὶ οἱ
AND~WERE GATHERED TOGETHER   THE   APOSTLES   AND   THE

πρεσβύτεροι ἰδεῖν περὶ τοῦ λόγου τούτου.
ELDERS   TO SEE   ABOUT   -   THIS~MATTER.

15.7 πολλῆς δὲ ζητήσεως γενομένης ἀναστὰς Πέτρος
AND [AFTER]~MUCH   DISCUSSION   HAVING TAKEN PLACE,   HAVING ARISEN,   PETER

εἶπεν πρὸς αὐτούς, Ἄνδρες ἀδελφοί, ὑμεῖς ἐπίστασθε
SAID   TO   THEM,   MEN,   BROTHERS,   YOU°   KNOW

ὅτι ἀφ' ἡμερῶν ἀρχαίων ἐν ὑμῖν ἐξελέξατο ὁ θεὸς
THAT FROM DAYS   OF OLD   AMONG YOU°   ²CHOSE   -   ¹GOD

διὰ   τοῦ στόματός μου ἀκοῦσαι τὰ ἔθνη τὸν λόγον
THROUGH THE   MOUTH   OF ME TO HEAR   THE   GENTILES THE   WORD

τοῦ εὐαγγελίου καὶ πιστεῦσαι. **15.8** καὶ ὁ
OF THE GOOD NEWS   AND   TO BELIEVE.   AND   THE

καρδιογνώστης θεὸς ἐμαρτύρησεν αὐτοῖς δοὺς
KNOWER OF HEARTS,   GOD,   BORE WITNESS   TO THEM   HAVING GIVEN

τὸ   πνεῦμα τὸ ἅγιον καθὼς καὶ ἡμῖν **15.9** καὶ
THE   ²SPIRIT   -   ¹HOLY   JUST AS ALSO TO US,   AND

οὐθὲν διέκρινεν   μεταξὺ ἡμῶν τε καὶ αὐτῶν τῇ πίστει
HE DIFFERENTIATED~NOTHING BETWEEN   BOTH~US   AND   THEM,   -   BY FAITH

καθαρίσας τὰς καρδίας αὐτῶν. **15.10** νῦν οὖν   τί
HAVING CLEANSED   THE   HEARTS   OF THEM.   THEREFORE~NOW WHY

πειράζετε τὸν θεὸν ἐπιθεῖναι ζυγὸν ἐπὶ τὸν τράχηλον
ARE YOU° TESTING   -   GOD   TO LAY   A YOKE   UPON   THE   NECK

τῶν μαθητῶν ὃν   οὔτε οἱ πατέρες ἡμῶν οὔτε ἡμεῖς
OF THE DISCIPLES   WHICH NEITHER THE FATHERS   OF US   NOR   WE

ἰσχύσαμεν βαστάσαι; **15.11** ἀλλὰ διὰ τῆς χάριτος τοῦ
WERE ABLE   TO BEAR?   BUT   BY   THE   GRACE   OF THE

κυρίου Ἰησοῦ πιστεύομεν σωθῆναι καθ' ὃν τρόπον
LORD   JESUS   WE BELIEVE   TO BE SAVED   IN THE SAME WAY AS

κἀκεῖνοι.
THOSE ALSO.

15.12 Ἐσίγησεν δὲ πᾶν τὸ πλῆθος καὶ ἤκουον
AND~WAS SILENT   ALL   THE   MULTITUDE, AND   THEY WERE LISTENING

Βαρναβᾶ καὶ Παύλου ἐξηγουμένων ὅσα ἐποίησεν ὁ
TO BARNABAS   AND   PAUL   DESCRIBING   WHAT   ⁵DID   -

θεὸς σημεῖα καὶ τέρατα ἐν   τοῖς ἔθνεσιν δι'
⁴GOD ¹SIGNS   ²AND ³WONDERS AMONG THE   GENTILES   THROUGH

αὐτῶν. **15.13** Μετὰ δὲ   τὸ   σιγῆσαι αὐτοὺς
THEM.   AND~AFTER   -   THEY~KEPT SILENT,

ἀπεκρίθη Ἰάκωβος λέγων, Ἄνδρες ἀδελφοί, ἀκούσατέ
JAMES~ANSWERED,   SAYING,   MEN,   BROTHERS,   LISTEN

μου. **15.14** Συμεὼν ἐξηγήσατο καθὼς πρῶτον ὁ θεὸς
TO ME.   SIMON   EXPLAINED   HOW   ²FIRST   -   ¹GOD

ἐπεσκέψατο λαβεῖν ἐξ ἐθνῶν   λαὸν τῷ ὀνόματι
CONCERNED HIMSELF TO RECEIVE   FROM [THE] GENTILES, A PEOPLE FOR THE NAME

and ordered to keep the law of Moses."

6 The apostles and the elders met together to consider this matter. [7] After there had been much debate, Peter stood up and said to them, "My brothers,[b] you know that in the early days God made a choice among you, that I should be the one through whom the Gentiles would hear the message of the good news and become believers. [8] And God, who knows the human heart, testified to them by giving them the Holy Spirit, just as he did to us; [9] and in cleansing their hearts by faith he has made no distinction between them and us. [10] Now therefore why are you putting God to the test by placing on the neck of the disciples a yoke that neither our ancestors nor we have been able to bear? [11] On the contrary, we believe that we will be saved through the grace of the Lord Jesus, just as they will."

12 The whole assembly kept silence, and listened to Barnabas and Paul as they told of all the signs and wonders that God had done through them among the Gentiles. [13] After they finished speaking, James replied, "My brothers,[b] listen to me. [14] Simeon has related how God first looked favorably on the Gentiles, to take from among them a people for his name.

[b] Gk *Men, brothers*

15This agrees with the words of the prophets, as it is written,

16'After this I will return, and I will rebuild the dwelling of David, which has fallen; from its ruins I will rebuild it, and I will set it up,

17 so that all other peoples may seek the Lord— even all the Gentiles over whom my name has been called. Thus says the Lord, who has been making these things

18 known from long ago.'c

19Therefore I have reached the decision that we should not trouble those Gentiles who are turning to God, 20but we should write to them to abstain only from things polluted by idols and from fornication and from whatever has been strangledd and from blood. 21For in every city, for generations past, Moses has had those who proclaim him, for he has been read aloud every sabbath in the synagogues."

22 Then the apostles and

c Other ancient authorities read things. 18Known to God from of old are all his works.'
d Other ancient authorities lack and from whatever has been strangled

αὐτοῦ. **15.15** καὶ   τούτῳ   συμφωνοῦσιν οἱ λόγοι τῶν
OF HIM.   AND   WITH THIS IS IN AGREEMENT THE WORDS OF THE

προφητῶν καθὼς γέγραπται,
PROPHETS,   JUST AS   IT HAS BEEN WRITTEN,

15.16 Μετὰ ταῦτα   ἀναστρέψω
        AFTER THESE THINGS I WILL RETURN

καὶ ἀνοικοδομήσω τὴν σκηνὴν Δαυὶδ τὴν
AND   I WILL REBUILD   THE TENT OF DAVID THE ONE

πεπτωκυῖαν
HAVING FALLEN

καὶ τὰ   κατεσκαμμένα αὐτῆς
AND THE THINGS HAVING BEEN TORN DOWN OF IT

ἀνοικοδομήσω
I WILL REBUILD

καὶ ἀνορθώσω αὐτήν,
AND I WILL RESTORE IT,

15.17 ὅπως ἂν ἐκζητήσωσιν οἱ   κατάλοιποι τῶν
         SO THAT 4MIGHT SEEK OUT 1THE ONES 2REMAINING -

ἀνθρώπων τὸν κύριον
3OF MEN, THE LORD

καὶ πάντα τὰ ἔθνη ἐφ' οὓς ἐπικέκληται
AND ALL   THE GENTILES, UPON WHOM HAS BEEN INVOKED

τὸ ὄνομά μου ἐπ' αὐτούς,
THE NAME OF ME OVER THEM,

λέγει κύριος ποιῶν ταῦτα
SAYS [THE] LORD DOING THESE THINGS

15.18 γνωστὰ ἀπ' αἰῶνος.
         KNOWN FROM [THE] AGES.

15.19 διὸ   ἐγὼ κρίνω μὴ παρενοχλεῖν τοῖς   ἀπὸ
         THEREFORE, I DECIDE NOT TO TROUBLE THE ONES FROM

τῶν ἐθνῶν ἐπιστρέφουσιν ἐπὶ τὸν θεόν, **15.20** ἀλλὰ
THE GENTILES TURNING   TO - GOD,   BUT

ἐπιστεῖλαι αὐτοῖς τοῦ ἀπέχεσθαι τῶν ἀλισγημάτων
TO WRITE   TO THEM - TO KEEP AWAY FROM THE POLLUTION

τῶν εἰδώλων καὶ τῆς πορνείας   καὶ τοῦ
-   OF IDOLS AND - OF SEXUAL IMMORALITY AND OF THE THING

πνικτοῦ καὶ τοῦ αἵματος. **15.21** Μωϋσῆς γὰρ ἐκ
STRANGLED AND - OF BLOOD.   FOR~MOSES,   FROM

γενεῶν ἀρχαίων κατὰ πόλιν τοὺς   κηρύσσοντας αὐτὸν
ANCIENT~GENERATIONS IN EVERY CITY 2THE ONES 3PREACHING   4HIM

ἔχει ἐν ταῖς συναγωγαῖς κατὰ πᾶν σάββατον
1HAS IN THE SYNAGOGUES ON EVERY   SABBATH

ἀναγινωσκόμενος.
BEING READ.

15.22 Τότε ἔδοξε   τοῖς ἀποστόλοις καὶ τοῖς
         THEN IT SEEMED [GOOD] TO THE APOSTLES   AND THE

15:16-17 Amos 9:11-12

πρεσβυτέροις σὺν ὅλῃ   τῇ ἐκκλησίᾳ ἐκλεξαμένους
ELDERS   WITH [THE] ENTIRE - CHURCH,   HAVING CHOSEN

ἄνδρας ἐξ αὐτῶν πέμψαι εἰς ᾽Αντιόχειαν σὺν τῷ
MEN   FROM THEM TO SEND TO ANTIOCH   WITH -

Παύλῳ καὶ Βαρναβᾷ, ᾽Ιούδαν τὸν καλούμενον
PAUL   AND BARNABAS, JUDAS,   THE ONE BEING CALLED

Βαρσαββᾶν καὶ Σιλᾶν, ἄνδρας ἡγουμένους ἐν   τοῖς
BARSABBAS AND SILAS, LEADING~MEN   AMONG THE

ἀδελφοῖς, 15.23 γράψαντες διὰ χειρὸς αὐτῶν, Οἱ
BROTHERS,   HAVING WRITTEN WITH [THE] HAND OF THEM, THE

ἀπόστολοι καὶ οἱ πρεσβύτεροι ἀδελφοὶ τοῖς κατὰ
APOSTLES   AND THE ELDERS,   BROTHERS, TO THE ²THROUGHOUT

τὴν ᾽Αντιόχειαν καὶ Συρίαν καὶ Κιλικίαν ἀδελφοῖς
-   ³ANTIOCH   ⁴AND ⁵SYRIA ⁶AND ⁷CILICIA ¹BROTHERS,

τοῖς ἐξ ἐθνῶν χαίρειν.   15.24 ᾽Επειδὴ ἠκούσαμεν
THE ONES OF [THE] GENTILES, GREETINGS.   SINCE   WE HEARD

ὅτι τινὲς ἐξ ἡμῶν [ἐξελθόντες] ἐτάραξαν ὑμᾶς λόγοις
THAT SOME FROM US HAVING COME OUT COMMANDED YOU° WITH WORDS,

ἀνασκευάζοντες τὰς ψυχὰς ὑμῶν οἷς   οὐ διεστειλάμεθα,
UNSETTLING   THE SOULS   OF YOU° TO WHOM WE DID NOT GIVE ORDERS,

15.25 ἔδοξεν   ἡμῖν γενομένοις ὁμοθυμαδὸν
      IT SEEMED [GOOD] TO US HAVING BECOME OF ONE MIND

ἐκλεξαμένοις ἄνδρας πέμψαι πρὸς ὑμᾶς σὺν τοῖς
HAVING CHOSEN MEN   TO SEND TO   YOU° WITH THE

ἀγαπητοῖς ἡμῶν Βαρναβᾷ καὶ Παύλῳ, 15.26 ἀνθρώποις
BELOVED   OF US, BARNABAS AND PAUL,   MEN

παραδεδωκόσι τὰς ψυχὰς αὐτῶν ὑπὲρ τοῦ ὀνόματος τοῦ
HAVING HANDED OVER THE LIVES OF THEM FOR THE NAME   OF THE

κυρίου ἡμῶν ᾽Ιησοῦ Χριστοῦ. 15.27 ἀπεστάλκαμεν οὖν
LORD   OF US, JESUS CHRIST.   THEREFORE~WE HAVE SENT

᾽Ιούδαν καὶ Σιλᾶν καὶ αὐτοὺς διὰ λόγου
JUDAS   AND SILAS AND THEY,   BY WORD [OF MOUTH]

ἀπαγγέλλοντας τὰ αὐτά.   15.28 ἔδοξεν γὰρ   τῷ
REPORTING   THE SAME THINGS.   FOR~IT SEEMED [GOOD] TO THE

πνεύματι τῷ ἁγίῳ καὶ ἡμῖν μηδὲν πλέον ἐπιτίθεσθαι
²SPIRIT   - ¹HOLY AND TO US NO   MORE   ²TO LAY UPON

ὑμῖν βάρος πλὴν τούτων τῶν ἐπάναγκες,
³YOU° ¹BURDEN EXCEPT THESE, THE NECESSARY THINGS,

15.29 ἀπέχεσθαι εἰδωλοθύτων καὶ αἵματος καὶ
      TO KEEP AWAY FROM MEAT SACRIFICED TO IDOLS AND BLOOD   AND

πνικτῶν   καὶ πορνείας,   ἐξ ὧν διατηροῦντες
STRANGLED THINGS AND SEXUAL IMMORALITY, FROM WHICH KEEPING

ἑαυτοὺς εὖ πράξετε.   ῎Ερρωσθε.
YOURSELVES YOU° WILL DO~WELL. GOOD-BYE.

15.30 Οἱ μὲν οὖν   ἀπολυθέντες   κατῆλθον εἰς
      - -   -   THEREFORE HAVING BEEN DISMISSED, THEY WENT DOWN TO

᾽Αντιόχειαν, καὶ συναγαγόντες   τὸ πλῆθος ἐπέδωκαν
ANTIOCH,   AND HAVING GATHERED TOGETHER THE MULTITUDE THEY DELIVERED

the elders, with the consent of the whole church, decided to choose men from among their members*e* and to send them to Antioch with Paul and Barnabas. They sent Judas called Barsabbas, and Silas, leaders among the brothers, 23with the following letter: "The brothers, both the apostles and the elders, to the believers*f* of Gentile origin in Antioch and Syria and Cilicia, greetings. 24Since we have heard that certain persons who have gone out from us, though with no instructions from us, have said things to disturb you and have unsettled your minds,*g* 25we have decided unanimously to choose representatives*h* and send them to you, along with our beloved Barnabas and Paul, 26who have risked their lives for the sake of our Lord Jesus Christ. 27We have therefore sent Judas and Silas, who themselves will tell you the same things by word of mouth. 28For it has seemed good to the Holy Spirit and to us to impose on you no further burden than these essentials: 29that you abstain from what has been sacrificed to idols and from blood and from what is strangled*i* and from fornication. If you keep yourselves from these, you will do well. Farewell."

30 So they were sent off and went down to Antioch. When they gathered the congregation together, they

e Gk *from among them*
f Gk *brothers*
g Other ancient authorities add *saying, 'You must be circumcised and keep the law,'*
h Gk *men*
i Other ancient authorities lack *and from what is strangled*

delivered the letter. [31]When its members[j] read it, they rejoiced at the exhortation. [32]Judas and Silas, who were themselves prophets, said much to encourage and strengthen the believers.[k] [33]After they had been there for some time, they were sent off in peace by the believers[k] to those who had sent them.[l] [35]But Paul and Barnabas remained in Antioch, and there, with many others, they taught and proclaimed the word of the Lord.

36 After some days Paul said to Barnabas, "Come, let us return and visit the believers[k] in every city where we proclaimed the word of the Lord and see how they are doing." [37]Barnabas wanted to take with them John called Mark. [38]But Paul decided not to take with them one who had deserted them in Pamphylia and had not accompanied them in the work. [39]The disagreement became so sharp that they parted company; Barnabas took Mark with him and sailed away to Cyprus. [40]But Paul chose Silas and set out, the believers[k] commending him to the grace of the Lord. [41]He went through

[j] Gk When they
[k] Gk brothers
[l] Other ancient authorities add verse 34, But it seemed good to Silas to remain there.

τὴν ἐπιστολήν. **15.31** ἀναγνόντες δὲ ἐχάρησαν ἐπὶ τῇ
THE LETTER.   AND~HAVING READ [IT],   THEY REJOICED   AT   THE

παρακλήσει. **15.32** Ἰούδας τε καὶ Σιλᾶς καὶ αὐτοὶ
EXHORTATION.   BOTH~JUDAS   AND   SILAS,   ALSO   THEMSELVES

προφῆται ὄντες διὰ λόγου πολλοῦ παρεκάλεσαν τοὺς
BEING~PROPHETS,   WITH   MANY~WORDS   COMFORTED   THE

ἀδελφοὺς καὶ ἐπεστήριξαν, **15.33** ποιήσαντες δὲ χρόνον
BROTHERS   AND   STRENGTHENED [THEM],   AND~HAVING SPENT   TIME,

ἀπελύθησαν μετ᾽ εἰρήνης ἀπὸ τῶν ἀδελφῶν πρὸς τοὺς
THEY WERE DISMISSED   WITH   PEACE   FROM   THE BROTHERS   TO   THE ONES

ἀποστείλαντας αὐτούς.⸆ **15.35** Παῦλος δὲ καὶ Βαρναβᾶς
HAVING SENT   THEM.   AND~PAUL   AND   BARNABAS

διέτριβον ἐν Ἀντιοχείᾳ διδάσκοντες καὶ
WERE STAYING   IN   ANTIOCH   TEACHING   AND

εὐαγγελιζόμενοι μετὰ καὶ ἑτέρων πολλῶν τὸν λόγον
PREACHING   WITH   ALSO   MANY~OTHERS   THE   WORD

τοῦ κυρίου.
OF THE   LORD.

15.36 Μετὰ δέ τινας ἡμέρας εἶπεν πρὸς Βαρναβᾶν
AND~AFTER   SOME   DAYS,   SAID   TO   BARNABAS

Παῦλος, Ἐπιστρέψαντες δὴ ἐπισκεψώμεθα τοὺς
PAUL,   HAVING RETURNED   THEN   LET US VISIT   THE

ἀδελφοὺς κατὰ πόλιν πᾶσαν ἐν αἷς κατηγγείλαμεν
BROTHERS   THROUGHOUT   EVERY~CITY   IN   WHICH   WE PROCLAIMED

τὸν λόγον τοῦ κυρίου πῶς ἔχουσιν.
THE   WORD   OF THE   LORD [TO SEE]   HOW   THEY ARE.

15.37 Βαρναβᾶς δὲ ἐβούλετο συμπαραλαβεῖν καὶ τὸν
AND~BARNABAS   WAS DECIDING   TO TAKE ALONG   ALSO   -

Ἰωάννην τὸν καλούμενον Μᾶρκον· **15.38** Παῦλος δὲ
JOHN,   THE ONE   BEING CALLED   MARK.   BUT~PAUL

ἠξίου, τὸν ἀποστάντα ἀπ᾽ αὐτῶν ἀπὸ Παμφυλίας
WAS INSISTING,   THE ONE   HAVING WITHDRAWN   FROM   THEM   FROM   PAMPHYLIA

καὶ μὴ συνελθόντα αὐτοῖς εἰς τὸ ἔργον μὴ
AND   NOT   HAVING GONE WITH   THEM   TO   THE WORK   NOT

συμπαραλαμβάνειν τοῦτον. **15.39** ἐγένετο δὲ
TO TAKE ALONG   THIS ONE.   AND~THERE WAS

παροξυσμὸς ὥστε ἀποχωρισθῆναι αὐτοὺς ἀπ᾽
A SHARP DISAGREEMENT   SO THAT   THEY~WERE SEPARATED   FROM

ἀλλήλων, τόν τε Βαρναβᾶν παραλαβόντα τὸν Μᾶρκον
ONE ANOTHER,   -   AND   BARNABAS   HAVING TAKEN   -   MARK,

ἐκπλεῦσαι εἰς Κύπρον, **15.40** Παῦλος δὲ ἐπιλεξάμενος
TO SAIL AWAY   TO   CYPRUS,   AND~PAUL   HAVING CHOSEN

Σιλᾶν ἐξῆλθεν παραδοθεὶς τῇ χάριτι τοῦ κυρίου
SILAS   DEPARTED,   HAVING BEEN COMMENDED   TO THE   GRACE   OF THE   LORD

ὑπὸ τῶν ἀδελφῶν. **15.41** διήρχετο δὲ τὴν
BY   THE   BROTHERS.   AND~THEY WERE TRAVELING THROUGH   -

15:33 text: ASV RSV NASB NIV NEB TEV NJB NRSV.   add v. 34 εδοξε δε τω Σιλα επιμειναι αυτου (But it seemed good to Silas to remain there): KJV ASVmg RSVmg NASBmg NIVmg NEBmg TEVmg NJBmg NRSVmg.

Συρίαν καὶ [τὴν] Κιλικίαν ἐπιστηρίζων τὰς
SYRIA AND - CILICIA STRENGTHENING THE

ἐκκλησίας.
CHURCHES.

16.1 Κατήντησεν δὲ [καὶ] εἰς Δέρβην καὶ εἰς
AND~HE ARRIVED ALSO IN DERBE AND IN

Λύστραν. καὶ ἰδοὺ μαθητής τις ἦν ἐκεῖ ὀνόματι
LYSTRA. AND BEHOLD A CERTAIN~DISCIPLE WAS THERE BY NAME

Τιμόθεος, υἱὸς γυναικὸς Ἰουδαίας πιστῆς,
TIMOTHY, [THE] SON 3WOMAN 2JEWISH 1OF A FAITHFUL,

πατρὸς δὲ Ἕλληνος, **16.2** ὃς ἐμαρτυρεῖτο ὑπὸ
BUT~[WHOSE] FATHER [WAS] GREEK, WHO WAS WELL SPOKEN OF BY

τῶν ἐν Λύστροις καὶ Ἰκονίῳ ἀδελφῶν. **16.3** τοῦτον
THE 2IN 3LYSTRA 4AND 5ICONIUM 1BROTHERS. 3THIS ONE

ἠθέλησεν ὁ Παῦλος σὺν αὐτῷ ἐξελθεῖν, καὶ
2WANTED - 1PAUL WITH HIM TO GO OUT, AND

λαβὼν περιέτεμεν αὐτὸν διὰ τοὺς Ἰουδαίους
HAVING TAKEN [HIM], HE CIRCUMCISED HIM BECAUSE OF THE JEWS

τοὺς ὄντας ἐν τοῖς τόποις ἐκείνοις· ᾔδεισαν γὰρ
- BEING IN - THOSE~PLACES. FOR~HAD KNOWN

ἅπαντες ὅτι Ἕλλην ὁ πατὴρ αὐτοῦ ὑπῆρχεν.
EVERYONE THAT GREEK THE FATHER OF HIM WAS.

16.4 ὡς δὲ διεπορεύοντο τὰς πόλεις, παρεδίδοσαν
AND~AS THEY WERE TRAVELING THROUGH THE CITIES, THEY WERE PASSING ON

αὐτοῖς φυλάσσειν τὰ δόγματα τὰ κεκριμένα ὑπὸ
TO THEM TO KEEP THE COMMANDMENTS - HAVING BEEN DECIDED BY

τῶν ἀποστόλων καὶ πρεσβυτέρων τῶν ἐν Ἱεροσολύμοις.
THE APOSTLES AND ELDERS - IN JERUSALEM.

16.5 αἱ μὲν οὖν ἐκκλησίαι ἐστερεοῦντο τῇ πίστει καὶ
THE - CHURCHES~THEREFORE WERE GROWING IN THE FAITH AND

ἐπερίσσευον τῷ ἀριθμῷ καθ᾽ ἡμέραν.
WERE INCREASING - IN NUMBER DAILY.

16.6 Διῆλθον δὲ τὴν Φρυγίαν καὶ Γαλατικὴν
AND~THEY TRAVELED THROUGH THE PHRYGIAN AND GALATIAN

χώραν κωλυθέντες ὑπὸ τοῦ ἁγίου πνεύματος
COUNTRY HAVING BEEN PREVENTED BY THE HOLY SPIRIT

λαλῆσαι τὸν λόγον ἐν τῇ Ἀσίᾳ· **16.7** ἐλθόντες δὲ
TO SPEAK THE WORD IN - ASIA. AND~HAVING COME

κατὰ τὴν Μυσίαν ἐπείραζον εἰς τὴν Βιθυνίαν
TO - MYSIA, THEY WERE TRYING TOWARD - BITHYNIA

πορευθῆναι, καὶ οὐκ εἴασεν αὐτοὺς τὸ πνεῦμα Ἰησοῦ·
TO GO, AND DID NOT PERMIT THEM THE SPIRIT OF JESUS.

16.8 παρελθόντες δὲ τὴν Μυσίαν κατέβησαν εἰς
AND~HAVING PASSED THROUGH - MYSIA THEY CAME DOWN TO

Paul[m] went on also to Derbe and to Lystra, where there was a disciple named Timothy, the son of a Jewish woman who was a believer; but his father was a Greek. [2]He was well spoken of by the believers[n] in Lystra and Iconium. [3]Paul wanted Timothy to accompany him; and he took him and had him circumcised because of the Jews who were in those places, for they all knew that his father was a Greek. [4]As they went from town to town, they delivered to them for observance the decisions that had been reached by the apostles and elders who were in Jerusalem. [5]So the churches were strengthened in the faith and increased in numbers daily.

6 They went through the region of Phrygia and Galatia, having been forbidden by the Holy Spirit to speak the word in Asia. [7]When they had come opposite Mysia, they attempted to go into Bithynia, but the Spirit of Jesus did not allow them; [8]so, passing by Mysia, they went down to

[m] Gk *He*
[n] Gk *brothers*

ACTS 16:9

Troas. ⁹During the night Paul had a vision: there stood a man of Macedonia pleading with him and saying, "Come over to Macedonia and help us." ¹⁰When he had seen the vision, we immediately tried to cross over to Macedonia, being convinced that God had called us to proclaim the good news to them.

11 We set sail from Troas and took a straight course to Samothrace, the following day to Neapolis, ¹²and from there to Philippi, which is a leading city of the district^o of Macedonia and a Roman colony. We remained in this city for some days. ¹³On the sabbath day we went outside the gate by the river, where we supposed there was a place of prayer; and we sat down and spoke to the women who had gathered there. ¹⁴A certain woman named Lydia, a worshiper of God, was listening to us; she was from the city of Thyatira and a dealer in purple cloth. The Lord opened her heart to listen eagerly to what was said by Paul. ¹⁵When she and her household were baptized, she urged us, saying, "If you have judged me to be faithful to the Lord, come and stay at my home." And she prevailed upon us.

16 One day, as we were

^o Other authorities read *a city of the first district*

Τρῳάδα. 16.9 καὶ ὅραμα διὰ [τῆς] νυκτὸς τῷ
TROAS. AND A VISION DURING THE NIGHT -

Παύλῳ ὤφθη, ἀνὴρ Μακεδών τις ἦν ἑστὼς καὶ
APPEARED~TO PAUL, ³MAN ²MACEDONIAN ¹A CERTAIN HAD BEEN STANDING AND

παρακαλῶν αὐτὸν καὶ λέγων, Διαβὰς εἰς
[WAS] BEGGING HIM AND SAYING, HAVING COME OVER TO

Μακεδονίαν βοήθησον ἡμῖν. **16.10** ὡς δὲ τὸ ὅραμα
MACEDONIA, HELP US. AND~WHEN THE VISION

εἶδεν, εὐθέως ἐζητήσαμεν ἐξελθεῖν εἰς Μακεδονίαν
HE SAW, IMMEDIATELY HE SOUGHT TO GO OUT TO MACEDONIA

συμβιβάζοντες ὅτι προσκέκληται ἡμᾶς ὁ θεὸς
CONCLUDING THAT ²HAS CALLED ³US - ¹GOD

εὐαγγελίσασθαι αὐτούς.
TO PREACH THE GOOD NEWS TO THEM.

16.11 Ἀναχθέντες δὲ ἀπὸ Τρῳάδος εὐθυδρομήσαμεν εἰς
AND~HAVING SET SAIL FROM TROAS, WE RAN A STRAIGHT COURSE TO

Σαμοθρᾴκην, τῇ δὲ ἐπιούσῃ εἰς Νέαν Πόλιν
SAMOTHRACE, AND~ON THE NEXT DAY TO NEAPOLIS

16.12 κἀκεῖθεν εἰς Φιλίππους, ἥτις ἐστὶν πρώτη[ς]
AND FROM THERE TO PHILIPPI, WHICH IS A PROMINENT

μερίδος τῆς Μακεδονίας πόλις, κολωνία. ἦμεν δὲ
²OF [THE] DISTRICT - ³OF MACEDONIA ¹CITY, A COLONY. AND~WE WERE

ἐν ταύτῃ τῇ πόλει διατρίβοντες ἡμέρας τινάς.
IN THIS - CITY STAYING SOME~DAYS.

16.13 τῇ τε ἡμέρᾳ τῶν σαββάτων ἐξήλθομεν ἔξω
AND~ON THE DAY OF THE SABBATHS WE WENT OUT OUTSIDE

τῆς πύλης παρὰ ποταμὸν οὗ ἐνομίζομεν
THE GATE BESIDE A RIVER WHERE WE WERE SUPPOSING

προσευχὴν εἶναι, καὶ καθίσαντες ἐλαλοῦμεν ταῖς
TO BE~[A PLACE] OF PRAYER, AND HAVING SAT DOWN, WE WERE SPEAKING WITH THE

συνελθούσαις γυναιξίν. **16.14** καί τις γυνὴ ὀνόματι
WOMEN~HAVING ASSEMBLED. AND A CERTAIN WOMAN, BY NAME

Λυδία, πορφυρόπωλις πόλεως Θυατείρων σεβομένη
LYDIA, A DEALER IN PURPLE CLOTH OF [THE] CITY OF THYATIRA, WORSHIPING

τὸν θεόν, ἤκουεν, ἧς ὁ κύριος διήνοιξεν τὴν
- GOD, WAS LISTENING, OF WHOM THE LORD OPENED THE

καρδίαν προσέχειν τοῖς λαλουμένοις ὑπὸ τοῦ
HEART TO PAY ATTENTION TO THE THINGS BEING SPOKEN BY -

Παύλου. **16.15** ὡς δὲ ἐβαπτίσθη καὶ ὁ οἶκος αὐτῆς,
PAUL. AND~WHEN SHE WAS BAPTIZED AND THE HOUSE OF HER,

παρεκάλεσεν λέγουσα, Εἰ κεκρίκατέ με πιστὴν τῷ
SHE BEGGED [US] SAYING, IF YOU° HAVE JUDGED ME FAITHFUL TO THE

κυρίῳ εἶναι, εἰσελθόντες εἰς τὸν οἶκόν μου μένετε·
LORD TO BE, HAVING ENTERED INTO THE HOUSE OF ME STAY.

καὶ παρεβιάσατο ἡμᾶς.
AND SHE PREVAILED UPON US.

16.16 Ἐγένετο δὲ πορευομένων ἡμῶν εἰς τὴν
AND~IT CAME ABOUT [WHEN] WE~GOING TO THE

προσευχὴν   παιδίσκην τινὰ   ἔχουσαν   πνεῦμα
PLACE OF PRAYER [THAT] A CERTAIN~SLAVE GIRL   HAVING   A SPIRIT

πύθωνα   ὑπαντῆσαι   ἡμῖν,   ἥτις
OF [THE] PYTHON [CAME OUT] TO MEET   US,   WHO

ἐργασίαν πολλὴν   παρεῖχεν   τοῖς κυρίοις αὐτῆς
MUCH~PROFIT   WAS BRINGING TO THE MASTERS OF HER [BY]

μαντευομένη.   **16.17** αὕτη   κατακολουθοῦσα τῷ   Παύλῳ
PROPHESYING.   THIS ONE, FOLLOWING   -   PAUL

καὶ ἡμῖν ἔκραζεν   λέγουσα, Οὗτοι οἱ ἄνθρωποι
AND US,   WAS CRYING OUT SAYING,   THESE - MEN

δοῦλοι τοῦ   θεοῦ τοῦ ὑψίστου εἰσίν,   οἵτινες
SLAVES OF THE GOD,   -   MOST HIGH ARE,   WHO

καταγγέλλουσιν ὑμῖν ὁδὸν   σωτηρίας.   **16.18** τοῦτο δὲ
ARE PROCLAIMING TO YOU° [THE] WAY OF SALVATION.   AND~THIS

ἐποίει   ἐπὶ πολλὰς ἡμέρας. διαπονηθεὶς δὲ
SHE WAS DOING FOR MANY DAYS.   BUT~HAVING BECOME ANNOYED

Παῦλος καὶ ἐπιστρέψας τῷ   πνεύματι εἶπεν,
-PAUL   AND HAVING TURNED, TO THE SPIRIT   HE SAID,

Παραγγέλλω σοι ἐν ὀνόματι Ἰησοῦ Χριστοῦ ἐξελθεῖν
I COMMAND   YOU IN [THE] NAME OF JESUS CHRIST TO COME OUT

ἀπ᾽ αὐτῆς·   καὶ ἐξῆλθεν αὐτῇ τῇ ὥρᾳ.   **16.19** ἰδόντες δὲ
FROM HER.   AND IT CAME OUT IN THE~SAME HOUR.   AND~HAVING SEEN

οἱ κύριοι αὐτῆς ὅτι ἐξῆλθεν ἡ ἐλπὶς τῆς ἐργασίας
THE MASTERS OF HER THAT WENT OUT THE HOPE OF THE PROFIT

αὐτῶν, ἐπιλαβόμενοι τὸν Παῦλον καὶ τὸν Σιλᾶν
OF THEM, HAVING SEIZED   -   PAUL   AND - SILAS,

εἵλκυσαν   εἰς τὴν ἀγορὰν ἐπὶ τοὺς ἄρχοντας
THEY DRAGGED [THEM] INTO THE MARKETPLACE BEFORE THE AUTHORITIES

16.20 καὶ   προσαγαγόντες αὐτοὺς τοῖς στρατηγοῖς
    AND HAVING BROUGHT   THEM TO THE CHIEF MAGISTRATES

εἶπαν, Οὗτοι οἱ   ἄνθρωποι ἐκταράσσουσιν ἡμῶν τὴν
THEY SAID, THESE - MEN   ARE DISTURBING   OUR -

πόλιν, Ἰουδαῖοι ὑπάρχοντες,   **16.21** καὶ   καταγγέλλουσιν
CITY,   BEING~JEWS,   AND   THEY ARE PROCLAIMING

ἔθη   ἃ   οὐκ ἔξεστιν ἡμῖν παραδέχεσθαι οὐδὲ
CUSTOMS WHICH IT IS NOT PERMITTED FOR US TO ACCEPT   NOR

ποιεῖν Ῥωμαίοις οὖσιν.   **16.22** καὶ συνεπέστη   ὁ   ὄχλος
TO DO, BEING~ROMANS.   AND ROSE UP TOGETHER THE CROWD

κατ᾽ αὐτῶν καὶ οἱ στρατηγοὶ   περιρήξαντες αὐτῶν
AGAINST THEM AND THE CHIEF MAGISTRATES HAVING TORN OFF THEIR

τὰ ἱμάτια ἐκέλευον   ῥαβδίζειν,   **16.23** πολλάς τε
- GARMENTS, WERE COMMANDING TO BEAT [THEM],   ⁴MANY ¹AND

ἐπιθέντες   αὐτοῖς πληγὰς ἔβαλον   εἰς φυλακὴν
²HAVING INFLICTED UPON ³THEM BLOWS, THEY THREW [THEM] INTO JAIL

παραγγείλαντες τῷ δεσμοφύλακι ἀσφαλῶς τηρεῖν
HAVING ORDERED   THE JAILER   TO GUARD~SECURELY

αὐτούς.   **16.24** ὃς   παραγγελίαν τοιαύτην λαβὼν
THEM.   WHO, SUCH~AN ORDER   HAVING RECEIVED

going to the place of prayer, we met a slave-girl who had a spirit of divination and brought her owners a great deal of money by fortune-telling. [17]While she followed Paul and us, she would cry out, "These men are slaves of the Most High God, who proclaim to you*p* a way of salvation." [18]She kept doing this for many days. But Paul, very much annoyed, turned and said to the spirit, "I order you in the name of Jesus Christ to come out of her." And it came out that very hour.

[19] But when her owners saw that their hope of making money was gone, they seized Paul and Silas and dragged them into the marketplace before the authorities. [20]When they had brought them before the magistrates, they said, "These men are disturbing our city; they are Jews [21]and are advocating customs that are not lawful for us as Romans to adopt or observe." [22]The crowd joined in attacking them, and the magistrates had them stripped of their clothing and ordered them to be beaten with rods. [23]After they had given them a severe flogging, they threw them into prison and ordered the jailer to keep them securely. [24]Following these instructions,

p Other ancient authorities read *to us*

he put them in the innermost cell and fastened their feet in the stocks.

25 About midnight Paul and Silas were praying and singing hymns to God, and the prisoners were listening to them. [26]Suddenly there was an earthquake, so violent that the foundations of the prison were shaken; and immediately all the doors were opened and everyone's chains were unfastened. [27]When the jailer woke up and saw the prison doors wide open, he drew his sword and was about to kill himself, since he supposed that the prisoners had escaped. [28]But Paul shouted in a loud voice, "Do not harm yourself, for we are all here." [29]The jailer[q] called for lights, and rushing in, he fell down trembling before Paul and Silas. [30]Then he brought them outside and said, "Sirs, what must I do to be saved?" [31]They answered, "Believe on the Lord Jesus, and you will be saved, you and your household." [32]They spoke the word of the Lord[r] to him and to all who were in his house. [33]At the same hour of the night he took them and washed their wounds; then he and his entire family were baptized without delay. [34]He brought them up into the

[q] Gk *He*
[r] Other ancient authorities read *word of God*

ἔβαλεν αὐτοὺς εἰς τὴν ἐσωτέραν φυλακὴν καὶ τοὺς
THREW THEM INTO THE INNER JAIL AND THE

πόδας ἠσφαλίσατο αὐτῶν εἰς τὸ ξύλον.
FEET OF THEM~HE FASTENED IN THE STOCK.

16.25 Κατὰ δὲ τὸ μεσονύκτιον Παῦλος καὶ Σιλᾶς
AND~ABOUT - MIDNIGHT PAUL AND SILAS [WERE]

προσευχόμενοι ὕμνουν τὸν θεόν, ἐπηκροῶντο δὲ
PRAYING [AND] WERE SINGING HYMNS - TO GOD, AND~WERE LISTENING TO

αὐτῶν οἱ δέσμιοι. **16.26** ἄφνω δὲ σεισμὸς ἐγένετο
THEM THE PRISONERS. AND~SUDDENLY [3]EARTHQUAKE [1]THERE CAME

μέγας ὥστε σαλευθῆναι τὰ θεμέλια τοῦ δεσμωτηρίου·
[2]A GREAT SO AS TO BE SHAKEN THE FOUNDATIONS OF THE JAIL.

ἠνεῴχθησαν δὲ παραχρῆμα αἱ θύραι πᾶσαι καὶ
AND~WERE OPENED IMMEDIATELY [2]THE [3]DOORS [1]ALL AND

πάντων τὰ δεσμὰ ἀνέθη. **16.27** ἔξυπνος δὲ
OF EVERYONE THE CHAINS WERE UNFASTENED. AND~AWAKE

γενόμενος ὁ δεσμοφύλαξ καὶ ἰδὼν ἀνεῳγμένας τὰς
HAVING BECOME THE JAILER AND HAVING SEEN HAVING BEEN OPENED THE

θύρας τῆς φυλακῆς, σπασάμενος [τὴν] μάχαιραν
DOORS OF THE JAIL, HAVING DRAWN THE SWORD

ἤμελλεν ἑαυτὸν ἀναιρεῖν νομίζων ἐκπεφευγέναι τοὺς
HE WAS ABOUT TO KILL~HIMSELF THINKING TO HAVE RUN AWAY THE

δεσμίους. **16.28** ἐφώνησεν δὲ μεγάλη φωνῇ [ὁ] Παῦλος
PRISONERS. BUT~SHOUTED WITH A LOUD VOICE - PAUL

λέγων, Μηδὲν πράξῃς σεαυτῷ κακόν, ἅπαντες γάρ
SAYING, [2]NOTHING [OF] [1]DO [4]TO YOURSELF [3]HARM, [7]ALL [5]FOR

ἐσμεν ἐνθάδε. **16.29** αἰτήσας δὲ φῶτα εἰσεπήδησεν
[6]WE ARE HERE. AND~HAVING ASKED FOR LIGHTS, HE RUSHED IN

καὶ ἔντρομος γενόμενος προσέπεσεν τῷ Παύλῳ καὶ
AND TREMBLING HAVING BECOME, HE FELL DOWN BEFORE - PAUL AND

[τῷ] Σιλᾷ **16.30** καὶ προαγαγὼν αὐτοὺς ἔξω ἔφη,
- SILAS AND HAVING LED THEM OUTSIDE HE SAID,

Κύριοι, τί με δεῖ ποιεῖν ἵνα σωθῶ;
SIRS, WHAT IS IT NECESSARY~FOR ME TO DO THAT I MAY BE SAVED?

16.31 οἱ δὲ εἶπαν, Πίστευσον ἐπὶ τὸν κύριον Ἰησοῦν
- AND THEY SAID, BELIEVE ON THE LORD JESUS

καὶ σωθήσῃ σὺ καὶ ὁ οἶκός σου. **16.32** καὶ
AND YOU~WILL BE SAVED AND THE HOUSE OF YOU. AND

ἐλάλησαν αὐτῷ τὸν λόγον τοῦ κυρίου σὺν πᾶσιν
THEY SPOKE TO HIM THE WORD OF THE LORD WITH ALL

τοῖς ἐν τῇ οἰκίᾳ αὐτοῦ. **16.33** καὶ παραλαβὼν αὐτοὺς
THE ONES IN THE HOUSE OF HIM. AND HAVING TAKEN THEM

ἐν ἐκείνῃ τῇ ὥρᾳ τῆς νυκτὸς ἔλουσεν ἀπὸ τῶν πληγῶν,
IN THAT - HOUR OF THE NIGHT, HE WASHED FROM THE WOUNDS,

καὶ ἐβαπτίσθη αὐτὸς καὶ οἱ αὐτοῦ πάντες
AND HE~WAS BAPTIZED AND THE ONES OF HIM ALL

παραχρῆμα, **16.34** ἀναγαγών τε αὐτοὺς εἰς τὸν οἶκον
AT ONCE, AND~HAVING LED THEM TO THE HOUSE

παρέθηκεν   τράπεζαν   καὶ   ἠγαλλιάσατο
HE SET BEFORE [THEM]   A TABLE,   AND   HE WAS OVERJOYED

πανοικεὶ   πεπιστευκὼς   τῷ   θεῷ.
WITH THE WHOLE HOUSEHOLD   HAVING BELIEVED   -   IN GOD.

16.35 Ἡμέρας δὲ γενομένης ἀπέστειλαν οἱ στρατηγοὶ
AND~DAY   HAVING BECOME,   SENT   THE MAGISTRATES

τοὺς   ῥαβδούχους   λέγοντες,   Ἀπόλυσον   τοὺς
THE   POLICEMEN   SAYING,   RELEASE

ἀνθρώπους ἐκείνους. **16.36** ἀπήγγειλεν δὲ ὁ δεσμοφύλαξ
THOSE~MEN.   AND~REPORTED   THE JAILER

τοὺς   λόγους [τούτους]   πρὸς τὸν Παῦλον ὅτι
-       THESE~WORDS   TO   -   PAUL,

Ἀπέσταλκαν οἱ στρατηγοὶ ἵνα ἀπολυθῆτε·   νῦν
HAVE SENT   THE MAGISTRATES THAT YOU°MAY BE RELEASED. NOW

οὖν   ἐξελθόντες πορεύεσθε ἐν εἰρήνῃ. **16.37** ὁ δὲ
THEREFORE HAVING GONE OUT, GO   IN   PEACE.   -   BUT

Παῦλος ἔφη πρὸς αὐτούς, Δείραντες ἡμᾶς δημοσίᾳ
PAUL   SAID   TO   THEM,   HAVING BEATEN US   IN PUBLIC

ἀκατακρίτους, ἀνθρώπους Ῥωμαίους ὑπάρχοντας,
UNCONDEMNED,   ROMAN~MEN   BEING,

ἔβαλαν   εἰς φυλακήν, καὶ νῦν λάθρᾳ ἡμᾶς
THEY THREW [US] INTO JAIL,   AND NOW SECRETLY US

ἐκβάλλουσιν;   οὐ γάρ, ἀλλὰ ἐλθόντες αὐτοὶ
THEY ARE SENDING OUT? NO INDEED, BUT HAVING COME THEMSELVES

ἡμᾶς ἐξαγαγέτωσαν. **16.38** ἀπήγγειλαν δὲ τοῖς
LET THEM LEAD OUT~US.   AND~REPORTED   TO THE

στρατηγοῖς οἱ ῥαβδοῦχοι τὰ ῥήματα ταῦτα.
MAGISTRATES   THE POLICEMEN   -   THESE~WORDS.

ἐφοβήθησαν δὲ ἀκούσαντες ὅτι Ῥωμαῖοί εἰσιν,
AND~THEY WERE AFRAID HAVING HEARD   THAT THEY ARE~ROMANS,

16.39 καὶ ἐλθόντες παρεκάλεσαν αὐτοὺς καὶ
AND   HAVING COME, THEY BEGGED   THEM   AND

ἐξαγαγόντες   ἠρώτων   ἀπελθεῖν ἀπὸ τῆς
HAVING BROUGHT [THEM] OUT, THEY WERE ASKING [THEM] TO DEPART FROM THE

πόλεως. **16.40** ἐξελθόντες δὲ ἀπὸ τῆς φυλακῆς εἰσῆλθον
CITY.   AND~HAVING COME OUT FROM THE JAIL   THEY CAME

πρὸς τὴν Λυδίαν καὶ ἰδόντες   παρεκάλεσαν τοὺς
TO   -   LYDIA   AND HAVING SEEN [THEM], THEY ENCOURAGED THE

ἀδελφοὺς καὶ ἐξῆλθαν.
BROTHERS   AND   WENT OUT.

house and set food before them; and he and his entire household rejoiced that he had become a believer in God.

35 When morning came, the magistrates sent the police, saying, "Let those men go." [36]And the jailer reported the message to Paul, saying, "The magistrates sent word to let you go; therefore come out now and go in peace." [37]But Paul replied, "They have beaten us in public, uncondemned, men who are Roman citizens, and have thrown us into prison; and now are they going to discharge us in secret? Certainly not! Let them come and take us out themselves." [38]The police reported these words to the magistrates, and they were afraid when they heard that they were Roman citizens; [39]so they came and apologized to them. And they took them out and asked them to leave the city. [40]After leaving the prison they went to Lydia's home; and when they had seen and encouraged the brothers and sisters[s] there, they departed.

[s] Gk *brothers*

17.1 Διοδεύσαντες δὲ   τὴν Ἀμφίπολιν καὶ τὴν
NOW~HAVING PASSED THROUGH -   AMPHIPOLIS   AND   -

Ἀπολλωνίαν ἦλθον εἰς Θεσσαλονίκην ὅπου ἦν
APOLLONIA,   THEY CAME TO THESSALONICA,   WHERE THERE WAS

After Paul and Silas[r] had passed through Amphipolis and Apollonia, they came to Thessalonica, where there

[r] Gk *they*

was a synagogue of the Jews. ²And Paul went in, as was his custom, and on three sabbath days argued with them from the scriptures, ³explaining and proving that it was necessary for the Messiah*ᵘ* to suffer and to rise from the dead, and saying, "This is the Messiah,*ᵘ* Jesus whom I am proclaiming to you." ⁴Some of them were persuaded and joined Paul and Silas, as did a great many of the devout Greeks and not a few of the leading women. ⁵But the Jews became jealous, and with the help of some ruffians in the marketplaces they formed a mob and set the city in an uproar. While they were searching for Paul and Silas to bring them out to the assembly, they attacked Jason's house. ⁶When they could not find them, they dragged Jason and some believers*ᵛ* before the city authorities,*ʷ* shouting, "These people who have been turning the world upside down have come here also, ⁷and Jason has entertained them as guests. They are all acting contrary to the decrees of the emperor, saying that there is another king named Jesus." ⁸The people and the city officials were disturbed when they heard this, ⁹and after they had taken bail from Jason and the others, they let them go.

10 That very night the believers*ᵛ* sent

ᵘ Or the Christ
ᵛ Gk brothers
ʷ Gk politarchs

συναγωγὴ τῶν Ἰουδαίων. **17.2** κατὰ δὲ τὸ εἰωθὸς
A SYNAGOGUE   OF THE   JEWS.   AND~ACCORDING TO   THE   CUSTOM

τῷ Παύλῳ εἰσῆλθεν πρὸς αὐτοὺς καὶ ἐπὶ
-    WITH PAUL,   HE CAME   TO   THEM   AND   ON

σάββατα τρία διελέξατο αὐτοῖς ἀπὸ τῶν γραφῶν,
THREE~SABBATHS   HE PREACHED   TO THEM   FROM   THE   SCRIPTURES,

17.3 διανοί~·~ν καὶ παρατιθέμενος ὅτι τὸν Χριστὸν
EXPLAINING   AND   DEMONSTRATING   THAT ²THE ³CHRIST

ἔδει παθεῖν καὶ ἀναστῆναι ἐκ νεκρῶν καὶ
¹IT WAS NECESSARY [FOR]   TO SUFFER   AND   TO RISE   FROM   [THE] DEAD   AND

ὅτι οὗτός ἐστιν ὁ Χριστὸς [ὁ] Ἰησοῦς ὃν ἐγὼ
THAT   THIS ONE   IS   THE   CHRIST,   -   JESUS,   WHOM   I

καταγγέλλω ὑμῖν. **17.4** καί τινες ἐξ αὐτῶν ἐπείσθησαν
AM PROCLAIMING   TO YOU°.   AND   SOME   OF   THEM   WERE PERSUADED

καὶ προσεκληρώθησαν τῷ Παύλῳ καὶ τῷ Σιλᾷ,
AND   WERE JOINED   -   TO PAUL   AND   -   SILAS,

τῶν τε σεβομένων Ἑλλήνων πλῆθος πολύ, γυναικῶν
BOTH~OF THE   WORSHIPING   GREEKS   A GREAT~MULTITUDE,   ⁴WOMEN

τε τῶν πρώτων οὐκ ὀλίγαι. **17.5** Ζηλώσαντες δὲ
¹AND ²OF THE ³PROMINENT   NOT   A FEW.   AND~HAVING BECOME JEALOUS,

οἱ Ἰουδαῖοι καὶ προσλαβόμενοι τῶν ἀγοραίων
THE   JEWS   AND   HAVING TAKEN   OF THE   PEOPLE OF THE MARKET

ἄνδρας τινὰς πονηροὺς καὶ ὀχλοποιήσαντες
³MEN ¹SOME ²EVIL   AND   HAVING FORMED A MOB,

ἐθορύβουν τὴν πόλιν καὶ ἐπιστάντες τῇ
THEY WERE THROWING INTO AN UPROAR   THE   CITY   AND   HAVING STOOD BESIDE   THE

οἰκίᾳ Ἰάσονος ἐζήτουν αὐτοὺς προαγαγεῖν εἰς τὸν
HOUSE   OF JASON   THEY WERE SEEKING   TO BRING~THEM   TO   THE

δῆμον· **17.6** μὴ εὑρόντες δὲ αὐτοὺς ἔσυρον
CROWD.   ²NOT HAVING FOUND ¹BUT   THEM,   THEY WERE DRAGGING

Ἰάσονα καί τινας ἀδελφοὺς ἐπὶ τοὺς πολιτάρχας
JASON   AND   SOME   BROTHERS   TO   THE   CITY AUTHORITIES

βοῶντες ὅτι Οἱ τὴν οἰκουμένην ἀναστατώσαντες οὗτοι
SHOUTING   -   - ³THE ⁴WORLD   ²HAVING TROUBLED   ¹THESE ONES

καὶ ἐνθάδε πάρεισιν, **17.7** οὓς ὑποδέδεκται Ἰάσων·
AND   HERE   ARE PRESENT,   WHOM   JASON~HAS RECEIVED.

καὶ οὗτοι πάντες ἀπέναντι τῶν δογμάτων Καίσαρος
AND   ALL~THESE ONES   AGAINST   THE   DECREES   OF CAESAR

πράσσουσι βασιλέα ἕτερον λέγοντες εἶναι Ἰησοῦν.
ARE ACTING   ANOTHER~KING   SAYING   TO BE   JESUS.

17.8 ἐτάραξαν δὲ τὸν ὄχλον καὶ τοὺς πολιτάρχας
AND~THEY STIRRED UP   THE   CROWD,   AND   THE   CITY AUTHORITIES

ἀκούοντας ταῦτα, **17.9** καὶ λαβόντες τὸ ἱκανὸν παρὰ
HEARING   THESE THINGS,   AND   HAVING TAKEN   THE   BOND MONEY   FROM

τοῦ Ἰάσονος καὶ τῶν λοιπῶν ἀπέλυσαν αὐτούς.
-   JASON   AND   THE   REST,   THEY RELEASED   THEM.

17.10 Οἱ δὲ ἀδελφοὶ εὐθέως διὰ νυκτὸς ἐξέπεμψαν
AND~THE   BROTHERS   IMMEDIATELY   DURING   [THE] NIGHT   SENT OUT

τόν τε   Παῦλον καὶ τὸν Σιλᾶν εἰς Βέροιαν, οἵτινες
- BOTH PAUL   AND - SILAS TO BEREA,   WHO

παραγενόμενοι εἰς τὴν συναγωγὴν τῶν Ἰουδαίων
HAVING ARRIVED,   INTO THE SYNAGOGUE OF THE JEWS

ἀπῄεσαν. **17.11** οὗτοι δὲ ἦσαν εὐγενέστεροι   τῶν
WERE GOING.   BUT~THESE WERE MORE NOBLE-MINDED [THAN] THE ONES

ἐν Θεσσαλονίκῃ, οἵτινες ἐδέξαντο τὸν λόγον μετὰ
IN THESSALONICA,   WHO   RECEIVED   THE WORD WITH

πάσης προθυμίας καθ᾽ ἡμέραν ἀνακρίνοντες τὰς
ALL   READINESS,   DAILY   EXAMINING   THE

γραφὰς εἰ ἔχοι ταῦτα   οὕτως. **17.12** πολλοὶ μὲν
SCRIPTURES IF THESE THINGS~MIGHT BE SO.   MANY   -

οὖν   ἐξ αὐτῶν ἐπίστευσαν καὶ τῶν Ἑλληνίδων
THEREFORE OF THEM BELIEVED   AND OF THE ²GREEK

γυναικῶν τῶν εὐσχημόνων καὶ ἀνδρῶν οὐκ ὀλίγοι.
³WOMEN   - ¹PROMINENT   AND MEN   NOT A FEW [BELIEVED].

17.13 Ὡς δὲ ἔγνωσαν οἱ ἀπὸ τῆς Θεσσαλονίκης
BUT~WHEN ⁵REALIZED ¹THE ³FROM - ⁴THESSALONICA

Ἰουδαῖοι ὅτι καὶ ἐν τῇ Βεροίᾳ κατηγγέλη ὑπὸ τοῦ
²JEWS   THAT ALSO IN - BEREA WAS PROCLAIMED BY   -

Παύλου ὁ λόγος τοῦ θεοῦ, ἦλθον κἀκεῖ σαλεύοντες
PAUL   THE WORD - OF GOD, THEY CAME THERE ALSO AGITATING

καὶ ταράσσοντες τοὺς ὄχλους. **17.14** εὐθέως δὲ   τότε
AND STIRRING UP   THE CROWDS.   AND~IMMEDIATELY THEN

τὸν Παῦλον ἐξαπέστειλαν οἱ ἀδελφοὶ πορεύεσθαι
- ⁴PAUL   ³SENT AWAY   ¹THE ²BROTHERS TO GO

ἕως ἐπὶ τὴν θάλασσαν, ὑπέμεινάν τε ὅ τε   Σιλᾶς
AS FAR AS TO THE SEA,   AND~REMAINED - BOTH SILAS

καὶ ὁ Τιμόθεος ἐκεῖ. **17.15** οἱ δὲ   καθιστάνοντες τὸν
AND - TIMOTHY THERE.   NOW~THE ONES ESCORTING

Παῦλον ἤγαγον ἕως   Ἀθηνῶν, καὶ λαβόντες
PAUL   BROUGHT [HIM] AS FAR AS ATHENS,   AND HAVING RECEIVED

ἐντολὴν πρὸς τὸν Σιλᾶν καὶ τὸν Τιμόθεον ἵνα ὡς
A COMMAND TO - SILAS AND - TIMOTHY   THAT AS

τάχιστα   ἔλθωσιν πρὸς αὐτὸν ἐξῄεσαν.
QUICKLY [AS POSSIBLE] THEY MAY COME TO HIM,   THEY WERE DEPARTING.

17.16 Ἐν δὲ ταῖς Ἀθήναις ἐκδεχομένου αὐτοὺς τοῦ
AND~IN - ATHENS   AWAITING   THEM,   -

Παύλου παρωξύνετο τὸ πνεῦμα αὐτοῦ ἐν   αὐτῷ
PAUL, WAS BEING AROUSED THE SPIRIT OF HIM WITHIN HIM

θεωροῦντος κατείδωλον οὖσαν τὴν πόλιν.
OBSERVING [THAT] FULL OF IDOLS BEING THE CITY.

17.17 διελέγετο   μὲν οὖν   ἐν τῇ συναγωγῇ τοῖς
HE WAS ARGUING   -   THEREFORE IN THE SYNAGOGUE WITH THE

Ἰουδαίοις καὶ τοῖς   σεβομένοις καὶ ἐν τῇ
JEWS   AND WITH THE ONES WORSHIPING AND IN THE

ἀγορᾷ   κατὰ πᾶσαν ἡμέραν πρὸς τοὺς
MARKETPLACE EVERY   DAY   TO THE ONES

Paul and Silas off to Beroea; and when they arrived, they went to the Jewish synagogue. [11]These Jews were more receptive than those in Thessalonica, for they welcomed the message very eagerly and examined the scriptures every day to see whether these things were so. [12]Many of them therefore believed, including not a few Greek women and men of high standing. [13]But when the Jews of Thessalonica learned that the word of God had been proclaimed by Paul in Beroea as well, they came there too, to stir up and incite the crowds. [14]Then the believers[x] immediately sent Paul away to the coast, but Silas and Timothy remained behind. [15]Those who conducted Paul brought him as far as Athens; and after receiving instructions to have Silas and Timothy join him as soon as possible, they left him.

16 While Paul was waiting for them in Athens, he was deeply distressed to see that the city was full of idols. [17]So he argued in the synagogue with the Jews and the devout persons, and also in the marketplace[y] every day with those

[x] Gk *brothers*
[y] Or *civic center;* Gk *agora*

who happened to be there.
[18]Also some Epicurean and
Stoic philosophers debated
with him. Some said, "What
does this babbler want to
say?" Others said, "He
seems to be a proclaimer of
foreign divinities." (This
was because he was telling
the good news about Jesus
and the resurrection.) [19]So
they took him and brought
him to the Areopagus and
asked him, "May we know
what this new teaching is
that you are presenting? [20]It
sounds rather strange to us,
so we would like to know
what it means." [21]Now all
the Athenians and the
foreigners living there would
spend their time in nothing
but telling or hearing
something new.

[22] Then Paul stood in
front of the Areopagus and
said, "Athenians, I see how
extremely religious you are
in every way. [23]For as I went
through the city and looked
carefully at the objects of
your worship, I found
among them an altar with
the inscription, 'To an
unknown god.' What
therefore you worship as
unknown, this I proclaim
to you. [24]The God who
made the world and every-
thing in it, he who is Lord of
heaven and earth, does not
live in shrines made by
human hands, [25]nor is

παρατυγχάνοντας. **17.18** τινὲς δὲ καὶ τῶν Ἐπικουρείων
HAPPENING TO BE THERE.   AND~SOME   ALSO OF THE EPICUREANS

καὶ Στοϊκῶν φιλοσόφων συνέβαλλον αὐτῷ, καί τινες
AND STOIC   PHILOSOPHERS   WERE CONVERSING WITH HIM, AND SOME

ἔλεγον, Τί ἂν θέλοι ὁ σπερμολόγος οὗτος λέγειν;
WERE SAYING, WHAT MIGHT WISH - THIS~BABBLER   TO SAY?

οἱ δέ, Ξένων δαιμονίων δοκεῖ καταγγελεὺς εἶναι,
AND~OTHERS [SAID], OF STRANGE DEITIES HE SEEMS TO BE~A PROCLAIMER,

ὅτι τὸν Ἰησοῦν καὶ τὴν ἀνάστασιν εὐηγγελίζετο.
BECAUSE - JESUS   AND THE RESURRECTION HE WAS PREACHING.

17.19 ἐπιλαβόμενοί τε αὐτοῦ ἐπὶ τὸν Ἄρειον Πάγον
AND~HAVING TAKEN HOLD OF HIM TO THE AREOPAGUS

ἤγαγον λέγοντες, Δυνάμεθα γνῶναι τίς ἡ
THEY BROUGHT [HIM] SAYING,   ARE WE ABLE TO KNOW WHAT -

καινὴ αὕτη ἡ ὑπὸ σοῦ λαλουμένη διδαχή;
THIS~NEW - 3BY 4YOU [IS] 2BEING SPOKEN 1TEACHING?

17.20 ξενίζοντα γάρ τινα εἰσφέρεις εἰς τὰς ἀκοὰς
3SURPRISING [THINGS] 1FOR 2SOME YOU BRING TO THE HEARING

ἡμῶν· βουλόμεθα οὖν γνῶναι τίνα θέλει ταῦτα εἶναι.
OF US. THEREFORE~WE DESIRE TO KNOW WHAT WISHES THESE THINGS TO MEAN.

17.21 Ἀθηναῖοι δὲ πάντες καὶ οἱ ἐπιδημοῦντες ξένοι
3ATHENIANS 1NOW 2ALL AND THE STRANGERS~VISITING

εἰς οὐδὲν ἕτερον ηὐκαίρουν ἢ λέγειν τι
FOR NOTHING DIFFERENT WERE FINDING OPPORTUNITY THAN TO SAY SOMETHING

ἢ ἀκούειν τι καινότερον.
OR TO HEAR SOMETHING NEWER.

17.22 Σταθεὶς δὲ [ὁ] Παῦλος ἐν μέσῳ τοῦ
AND~HAVING STOOD - PAUL IN [THE] MIDDLE OF THE

Ἀρείου Πάγου ἔφη, Ἄνδρες Ἀθηναῖοι, κατὰ
AREOPAGUS   HE SAID, MEN,   ATHENIANS,   WITH RESPECT TO

πάντα ὡς δεισιδαιμονεστέρους ὑμᾶς θεωρῶ.
EVERYTHING HOW VERY RELIGIOUS   I OBSERVE~YOU° [TO BE].

17.23 διερχόμενος γὰρ καὶ ἀναθεωρῶν τὰ
FOR~PASSING THROUGH AND LOOKING CAREFULLY AT THE

σεβάσματα ὑμῶν εὗρον καὶ βωμὸν ἐν ᾧ
OBJECTS OF WORSHIP OF YOU°, I FOUND ALSO AN ALTAR ON WHICH

ἐπεγέγραπτο, Ἀγνώστῳ θεῷ. ὃ οὖν ἀγνοοῦντες
HAD BEEN INSCRIBED, TO [THE] UNKNOWN GOD. THEREFORE~WHAT NOT KNOWING

εὐσεβεῖτε, τοῦτο ἐγὼ καταγγέλλω ὑμῖν. **17.24** ὁ θεὸς
YOU° WORSHIP, THIS I PROCLAIM TO YOU°.   - GOD,

ὁ ποιήσας τὸν κόσμον καὶ πάντα τὰ ἐν αὐτῷ,
THE ONE HAVING MADE THE WORLD AND ALL THE THINGS IN IT,

οὗτος οὐρανοῦ καὶ γῆς ὑπάρχων κύριος οὐκ ἐν
THIS ONE OF HEAVEN AND EARTH BEING LORD NOT IN

χειροποιήτοις ναοῖς κατοικεῖ **17.25** οὐδὲ ὑπὸ
TEMPLES~MADE BY HUMAN HANDS DWELLS   NOR BY

χειρῶν ἀνθρωπίνων θεραπεύεται προσδεόμενός τινος,
HUMAN~HANDS   IS SERVED [AS IF]   BEING IN NEED   OF SOMETHING,

αὐτὸς διδοὺς πᾶσι ζωὴν καὶ πνοὴν καὶ τὰ πάντα·
HE   GIVING   TO ALL   LIFE   AND BREATH AND ALL~THESE THINGS.

17.26 ἐποίησέν τε ἐξ ἑνὸς πᾶν ἔθνος ἀνθρώπων
AND~HE MADE   FROM ONE EVERY NATION OF MEN

κατοικεῖν ἐπὶ παντὸς προσώπου τῆς γῆς, ὁρίσας
TO DWELL   ON   ALL   [THE] FACE   OF THE EARTH, HAVING SET

προστεταγμένους καιροὺς καὶ τὰς ὁροθεσίας τῆς
[THE] HAVING BEEN DETERMINED SEASONS AND THE FIXED BOUNDARIES OF THE

κατοικίας αὐτῶν **17.27** ζητεῖν τὸν θεόν, εἰ ἄρα γε
HABITATIONS OF THEM   TO SEEK   -   GOD,   IF PERHAPS

ψηλαφήσειαν αὐτὸν καὶ εὕροιεν, καί γε οὐ μακρὰν
THEY MIGHT GROPE   FOR HIM   AND MIGHT FIND [HIM], THOUGH   NOT FAR

ἀπὸ ἑνὸς ἑκάστου ἡμῶν ὑπάρχοντα.
FROM EACH~ONE   OF US   BEING.

17.28 Ἐν αὐτῷ γὰρ ζῶμεν καὶ κινούμεθα καὶ ἐσμέν,
       2IN 3HIM 1FOR WE LIVE AND MOVE   AND ARE,

ὡς καὶ τινες τῶν καθ᾽ ὑμᾶς ποιητῶν εἰρήκασιν,
AS ALSO SOME OF THE 2AMONG 3YOU° 1POETS   HAVE SAID,

Τοῦ γὰρ καὶ γένος ἐσμέν.
FOR~OF HIM   ALSO   WE ARE~OFFSPRING.

17.29 γένος οὖν ὑπάρχοντες τοῦ θεοῦ
       3OFFSPRING 1THEREFORE 2BEING   -   OF GOD,

οὐκ ὀφείλομεν νομίζειν χρυσῷ ἢ ἀργύρῳ ἢ λίθῳ,
WE OUGHT NOT   TO THINK   WITH GOLD OR SILVER OR STONE,

χαράγματι τέχνης καὶ ἐνθυμήσεως ἀνθρώπου, τὸ
AN IMAGE FORMED BY [THE] SKILL AND THOUGHT   OF MAN,   THE

θεῖον εἶναι ὅμοιον. **17.30** τοὺς μὲν οὖν χρόνους τῆς
DIVINE TO BE LIKE.   SO~THE   TIMES~THEN   -

ἀγνοίας ὑπεριδὼν ὁ θεός, τὰ νῦν παραγγέλλει τοῖς
OF IGNORANCE 2HAVING OVERLOOKED - 1GOD, - NOW HE PROCLAIMS   -

ἀνθρώποις πάντας πανταχοῦ μετανοεῖν, **17.31** καθότι
TO ALL~MEN   EVERYWHERE   TO REPENT,   BECAUSE

ἔστησεν ἡμέραν ἐν ᾗ μέλλει κρίνειν τὴν
HE SET   A DAY   IN WHICH HE IS ABOUT TO JUDGE   THE

οἰκουμένην ἐν δικαιοσύνῃ, ἐν ἀνδρὶ ᾧ ὥρισεν,
WORLD   IN RIGHTEOUSNESS BY A MAN   WHOM HE APPOINTED,

πίστιν παρασχὼν πᾶσιν ἀναστήσας αὐτὸν ἐκ νεκρῶν.
HAVING FURNISHED~PROOF TO ALL [BY] HAVING RAISED HIM   FROM [THE] DEAD.

17.32 Ἀκούσαντες δὲ ἀνάστασιν νεκρῶν οἱ μὲν
       AND~HAVING HEARD [OF] [THE] RESURRECTION OF [THE] DEAD SOME

ἐχλεύαζον, οἱ δὲ εἶπαν, Ἀκουσόμεθά σου περὶ
WERE MOCKING [HIM], BUT~OTHERS SAID,   WE WILL LISTEN TO   YOU   ABOUT

τούτου καὶ πάλιν. **17.33** οὕτως ὁ Παῦλος ἐξῆλθεν ἐκ
THIS   ALSO   AGAIN.   THUS   - PAUL   WENT OUT FROM

he served by human hands, as though he needed anything, since he himself gives to all mortals life and breath and all things. 26From one ancestor[z] he made all nations to inhabit the whole earth, and he allotted the times of their existence and the boundaries of the places where they would live, 27so that they would search for God[a] and perhaps grope for him and find him—though indeed he is not far from each one of us. 28For 'In him we live and move and have our being'; as even some of your own poets have said,

'For we too are his offspring.'

29Since we are God's offspring, we ought not to think that the deity is like gold, or silver, or stone, an image formed by the art and imagination of mortals. 30While God has overlooked the times of human ignorance, now he commands all people everywhere to repent, 31because he has fixed a day on which he will have the world judged in righteousness by a man whom he has appointed, and of this he has given assurance to all by raising him from the dead."

32 When they heard of the resurrection of the dead, some scoffed; but others said, "We will hear you again about this." 33At that point Paul left

[z] Gk *From one;* other ancient authorities read *From one blood*
[a] Other ancient authorities read *the Lord*

them. [34]But some of them
joined him and became
believers, including
Dionysius the Areopagite
and a woman named
Damaris, and others with
them.

μέσου   αὐτῶν.   **17.34** τινὲς δὲ   ἄνδρες   κολληθέντες
[THE] MIDST   OF THEM.   AND~SOME   MEN   HAVING BEEN JOINED

αὐτῷ   ἐπίστευσαν,   ἐν   οἷς   καὶ   Διονύσιος ὁ
TO HIM   BELIEVED,   AMONG   WHOM [ARE]   BOTH   DIONYSIUS,   THE

Ἀρεοπαγίτης   καὶ   γυνὴ   ὀνόματι   Δάμαρις καὶ   ἕτεροι
AREOPAGITE,   AND   A WOMAN   BY NAME   DAMARIS   AND   OTHERS

σὺν   αὐτοῖς.
WITH   THEM.

CHAPTER 18

After this Paul[b] left Athens
and went to Corinth. [2]There
he found a Jew named
Aquila, a native of Pontus,
who had recently come from
Italy with his wife Priscilla,
because Claudius had
ordered all Jews to leave
Rome. Paul[c] went to see
them, [3]and, because he was
of the same trade, he stayed
with them, and they worked
together—by trade they
were tentmakers. [4]Every
sabbath he would argue in
the synagogue and would
try to convince Jews and
Greeks.
   5 When Silas and
Timothy arrived from
Macedonia, Paul was oc-
cupied with proclaiming the
word,[d] testifying to the Jews
that the Messiah[e] was Jesus.
[6]When they opposed and
reviled him, in protest he
shook the dust from his
clothes[f] and said to them,
"Your blood be on your own
heads! I am innocent. From
now on I will go to the
Gentiles." [7]Then he left the
synagogue[g] and went to the

[b] Gk he
[c] Gk He
[d] Gk with the word
[e] Or the Christ
[f] Gk reviled him, he shook out his
    clothes
[g] Gk left there

18.1 Μετὰ   ταῦτα   χωρισθεὶς   ἐκ   τῶν   Ἀθηνῶν ἦλθεν
AFTER   THESE THINGS,   HAVING LEFT   FROM   -   ATHENS,   HE CAME

εἰς   Κόρινθον.   **18.2** καὶ   εὑρών   τινα   Ἰουδαῖον   ὀνόματι
TO   CORINTH.   AND   HAVING FOUND   SOME   JEWS   BY NAME

Ἀκύλαν,   Ποντικὸν τῷ   γένει   προσφάτως   ἐληλυθότα
AQUILA,   OF PONTUS   -   BY BIRTH,   RECENTLY   HAVING COME

ἀπὸ   τῆς   Ἰταλίας   καὶ   Πρίσκιλλαν   γυναῖκα   αὐτοῦ,
FROM   -   ITALY   AND   PRISCILLA   [THE] WIFE   OF HIM

διὰ   τὸ   διατεταχέναι   Κλαύδιον   χωρίζεσθαι
BECAUSE OF   THE THING   TO HAVE COMMANDED   CLAUDIUS [THAT]   TO LEAVE

πάντας   τοὺς   Ἰουδαίους   ἀπὸ   τῆς   Ῥώμης,   προσῆλθεν
ALL   THE   JEWS   FROM   -   ROME,   HE APPROACHED

αὐτοῖς   **18.3** καὶ   διὰ   τὸ ὁμότεχνον   εἶναι   ἔμενεν
THEM,   AND   BECAUSE OF   THE SAME TRADE   TO BE,   HE WAS STAYING

παρ᾽   αὐτοῖς,   καὶ   ἠργάζετο·   ἦσαν γὰρ σκηνοποιοὶ   τῇ
WITH   THEM   AND   HE WAS WORKING;   FOR~THEY WERE TENTMAKERS   -

τέχνῃ.   **18.4** διελέγετο δὲ   ἐν   τῇ   συναγωγῇ   κατὰ   πᾶν
BY TRADE.   AND~HE WAS DEBATING   IN   THE   SYNAGOGUE   EVERY

σάββατον   ἔπειθέν τε   Ἰουδαίους   καὶ   Ἕλληνας.
SABBATH,   AND~HE WAS CONVINCING   JEWS   AND   GREEKS.

18.5 Ὡς   δὲ   κατῆλθον   ἀπὸ   τῆς   Μακεδονίας   ὅ τε
NOW~WHEN   CAME DOWN   FROM   -   MACEDONIA   -   BOTH

Σιλᾶς   καὶ   ὁ   Τιμόθεος,   συνείχετο   τῷ   λόγῳ ὁ   Παῦλος
SILAS   AND   -   TIMOTHY,   WAS OCCUPIED WITH   THE   WORD   -   PAUL,

διαμαρτυρόμενος   τοῖς   Ἰουδαίοις   εἶναι   τὸν   Χριστὸν
TESTIFYING   TO THE   JEWS   TO BE   THE   CHRIST,

Ἰησοῦν.   **18.6** ἀντιτασσομένων   δὲ   αὐτῶν   καὶ
JESUS.   [3]OPPOSING   [1]BUT   [2][WHEN] THEY   AND

βλασφημούντων   ἐκτιναξάμενος   τὰ   ἱμάτια   εἶπεν   πρὸς
BLASPHEMING,   HAVING SHAKEN OUT   THE   GARMENTS,   HE SAID   TO

αὐτούς,   Τὸ   αἷμα   ὑμῶν   ἐπὶ   τὴν   κεφαλὴν   ὑμῶν·
THEM,   THE   BLOOD   OF YOU˚ [BE]   UPON   THE   HEAD   OF YOU˚;

καθαρὸς   ἐγώ.   ἀπὸ   τοῦ   νῦν   εἰς   τὰ   ἔθνη   πορεύσομαι.
I [AM]~CLEAN.   FROM   -   NOW [ON]   TO   THE   GENTILES   I WILL GO.

18.7 καὶ   μεταβὰς   ἐκεῖθεν   εἰσῆλθεν   εἰς   οἰκίαν
AND   HAVING PASSED OVER   FROM THERE,   HE ENTERED   INTO   [THE] HOUSE

τινὸς   ὀνόματι Τιτίου Ἰούστου σεβομένου τὸν
OF A CERTAIN MAN   BY NAME   TITIUS   JUSTUS,   WORSHIPING -

θεόν,   οὗ   ἡ οἰκία ἦν συνομοροῦσα τῇ συναγωγῇ.
GOD,   WHOSE - HOUSE WAS BORDERING ON   THE SYNAGOGUE.

18.8 Κρίσπος δὲ ὁ ἀρχισυνάγωγος ἐπίστευσεν τῷ
AND~CRISPUS,   THE SYNAGOGUE LEADER,   BELIEVED   IN THE

κυρίῳ σὺν ὅλῳ   τῷ οἴκῳ αὐτοῦ, καὶ πολλοὶ τῶν
LORD WITH [THE] ENTIRE - HOUSE OF HIM,   AND   MANY   OF THE

Κορινθίων ἀκούοντες ἐπίστευον καὶ ἐβαπτίζοντο.
CORINTHIANS HEARING   WERE BELIEVING AND   WERE BEING BAPTIZED.

18.9 εἶπεν δὲ ὁ κύριος ἐν νυκτὶ δι᾽ ὁράματος τῷ
AND~SAID THE LORD IN [THE] NIGHT THROUGH A VISION -

Παύλῳ, Μὴ φοβοῦ, ἀλλὰ λάλει καὶ μὴ σιωπήσῃς,
TO PAUL, DO NOT FEAR,   BUT   SPEAK   AND   DO NOT KEEP SILENT,

18.10 διότι ἐγώ εἰμι μετὰ σοῦ καὶ οὐδεὶς ἐπιθήσεταί
FOR   I   AM   WITH YOU AND NO ONE   WILL ATTACK

σοι τοῦ κακῶσαί σε, διότι λαός ἐστί μοι πολὺς ἐν τῇ
YOU - TO HARM YOU, FOR ⁴PEOPLE ¹IT IS ²TO ME ³MANY IN -

πόλει ταύτῃ. **18.11** Ἐκάθισεν δὲ ἐνιαυτὸν καὶ μῆνας ἓξ
THIS~CITY.   AND~HE SAT   A YEAR   AND   SIX~MONTHS

διδάσκων ἐν αὐτοῖς τὸν λόγον τοῦ θεοῦ.
TEACHING AMONG THEM   THE WORD   OF GOD.

18.12 Γαλλίωνος δὲ ἀνθυπάτου ὄντος τῆς Ἀχαΐας,
AND~GALLIO,   BEING~PROCONSUL - OF ACHAIA,

κατεπέστησαν ὁμοθυμαδὸν οἱ Ἰουδαῖοι τῷ Παύλῳ καὶ
ROSE UP   WITH ONE ACCORD THE JEWS [AGAINST] - PAUL   AND

ἤγαγον αὐτὸν ἐπὶ τὸ βῆμα **18.13** λέγοντες ὅτι
THEY BROUGHT HIM BEFORE THE JUDGMENT SEAT   SAYING, -

Παρὰ τὸν νόμον ἀναπείθει οὗτος τοὺς ἀνθρώπους
AGAINST THE LAW   THIS ONE~PERSUADES -   MEN

σέβεσθαι τὸν θεόν. **18.14** μέλλοντος δὲ τοῦ Παύλου
TO WORSHIP - GOD.   ³BEING ABOUT ¹AND - ²PAUL

ἀνοίγειν τὸ στόμα εἶπεν ὁ Γαλλίων πρὸς τοὺς
TO OPEN THE MOUTH, SPOKE - GALLIO TO   THE

Ἰουδαίους, Εἰ μὲν ἦν ἀδίκημά τι ἢ
JEWS,   IF - IT WAS SOME~WRONG   OR

ῥᾳδιούργημα πονηρόν, ὦ Ἰουδαῖοι, κατὰ λόγον
EVIL~CRIME,   O JEWS,   REASONABLY

ἂν ἀνεσχόμην ὑμῶν, **18.15** εἰ δὲ ζητήματά ἐστιν περὶ
I MIGHT PUT UP WITH YOU°.   BUT~IF IT IS~QUESTIONS ABOUT

λόγου καὶ ὀνομάτων καὶ νόμου τοῦ καθ᾽ ὑμᾶς,
A WORD AND   NAMES   AND ²LAW - ¹YOUR,

ὄψεσθε αὐτοί· κριτὴς ἐγὼ τούτων
YOU° WILL SEE [TO IT FOR] YOURSELVES. I~A JUDGE   OF THESE THINGS

οὐ βούλομαι εἶναι. **18.16** καὶ ἀπήλασεν αὐτοὺς ἀπὸ
DO NOT INTEND TO BE.   AND HE DROVE AWAY THEM FROM

τοῦ βήματος. **18.17** ἐπιλαβόμενοι δὲ πάντες Σωσθένην
THE JUDGMENT SEAT. ³HAVING SEIZED ¹BUT ²EVERYONE SOSTHENES,

---

house of a man named Titius[h] Justus, a worshiper of God; his house was next door to the synagogue. [8]Crispus, the official of the synagogue, became a believer in the Lord, together with all his household; and many of the Corinthians who heard Paul became believers and were baptized. [9]One night the Lord said to Paul in a vision, "Do not be afraid, but speak and do not be silent; [10]for I am with you, and no one will lay a hand on you to harm you, for there are many in this city who are my people." [11]He stayed there a year and six months, teaching the word of God among them.

12 But when Gallio was proconsul of Achaia, the Jews made a united attack on Paul and brought him before the tribunal. [13]They said, "This man is persuading people to worship God in ways that are contrary to the law." [14]Just as Paul was about to speak, Gallio said to the Jews, "If it were a matter of crime or serious villainy, I would be justified in accepting the complaint of you Jews; [15]but since it is a matter of questions about words and names and your own law, see to it yourselves; I do not wish to be a judge of these matters." [16]And he dismissed them from the tribunal. [17]Then all of them[i] seized Sosthenes,

[h] Other ancient authorities read *Titus*
[i] Other ancient authorities read *all the Greeks*

the official of the synagogue, and beat him in front of the tribunal. But Gallio paid no attention to any of these things.

18 After staying there for a considerable time, Paul said farewell to the believers[j] and sailed for Syria, accompanied by Priscilla and Aquila. At Cenchreae he had his hair cut, for he was under a vow. [19]When they reached Ephesus, he left them there, but first he himself went into the synagogue and had a discussion with the Jews. [20]When they asked him to stay longer, he declined; [21]but on taking leave of them, he said, "I[k] will return to you, if God wills." Then he set sail from Ephesus.

22 When he had landed at Caesarea, he went up to Jerusalem[l] and greeted the church, and then went down to Antioch. [23]After spending some time there he departed and went from place to place through the region of Galatia[m] and Phrygia, strengthening all the disciples.

24 Now there came to Ephesus a Jew named Apollos, a native of Alexandria. He was an eloquent man, well-versed in the scriptures. [25]He had been instructed in the Way of the Lord; and he spoke with burning enthusiasm and taught accurately the things

[j] Gk brothers
[k] Other ancient authorities read I must
  at all costs keep the approaching
  festival in Jerusalem, but I
[l] Gk went up
[m] Gk the Galatian region

τὸν ἀρχισυνάγωγον ἔτυπτον ἔμπροσθεν τοῦ
THE SYNAGOGUE LEADER, THEY WERE BEATING [HIM] BEFORE THE

βήματος· καὶ οὐδὲν τούτων τῷ Γαλλίωνι
JUDGMENT SEAT. AND NONE OF THESE THINGS - TO GALLIO

ἔμελεν.
WAS A CONCERN.

18.18 Ὁ δὲ Παῦλος ἔτι προσμείνας ἡμέρας ἱκανὰς
- BUT PAUL STILL HAVING REMAINED A NUMBER~OF DAYS,

τοῖς ἀδελφοῖς ἀποταξάμενος ἐξέπλει εἰς τὴν
TO THE BROTHERS HAVING SAID GOOD-BYE, HE WAS SAILING AWAY TO -

Συρίαν, καὶ σὺν αὐτῷ Πρίσκιλλα καὶ Ἀκύλας,
SYRIA, AND WITH HIM PRISCILLA AND AQUILA,

κειράμενος ἐν Κεγχρεαῖς τὴν κεφαλήν, εἶχεν γὰρ
HAVING SHAVED IN CENCHREA THE(HIS) HEAD, FOR~HE HAD [TAKEN]

εὐχήν. **18.19** κατήντησαν δὲ εἰς Ἔφεσον, κἀκείνους
A VOW. AND~THEY ARRIVED IN EPHESUS, AND THOSE

κατέλιπεν αὐτοῦ, αὐτὸς δὲ εἰσελθὼν εἰς τὴν
HE LEFT THERE, BUT~HE HAVING ENTERED INTO THE

συναγωγὴν διελέξατο τοῖς Ἰουδαίοις. **18.20** ἐρωτώντων
SYNAGOGUE DEBATED WITH THE JEWS. [3]ASKING [HIM]

δὲ αὐτῶν ἐπὶ πλείονα χρόνον μεῖναι
[1]AND [2][WHEN] THEY FOR A LONGER TIME TO STAY,

οὐκ ἐπένευσεν, **18.21** ἀλλὰ ἀποταξάμενος καὶ εἰπών,
HE DID NOT GIVE HIS CONSENT, BUT HAVING SAID GOOD-BYE AND HAVING SAID,

Πάλιν ἀνακάμψω πρὸς ὑμᾶς τοῦ θεοῦ θέλοντος,
I WILL RETURN~AGAIN TO YOU° - GOD WILLING,

ἀνήχθη ἀπὸ τῆς Ἐφέσου, **18.22** καὶ κατελθὼν
HE SET SAIL FROM - EPHESUS, AND HAVING COME DOWN

εἰς Καισάρειαν, ἀναβὰς καὶ ἀσπασάμενος τὴν
TO CAESAREA, AND~HAVING GONE UP [AND] HAVING GREETED THE

ἐκκλησίαν κατέβη εἰς Ἀντιόχειαν. **18.23** καὶ ποιήσας
CHURCH, HE WENT DOWN TO ANTIOCH, AND HAVING SPENT

χρόνον τινὰ ἐξῆλθεν διερχόμενος καθεξῆς τὴν
SOME~TIME HE WENT OUT, PASSING THROUGH IN ORDER THE

Γαλατικὴν χώραν καὶ Φρυγίαν, ἐπιστηρίζων πάντας
GALATIAN COUNTRY AND PHRYGIA, STRENGTHENING ALL

τοὺς μαθητάς.
THE DISCIPLES.

18.24 Ἰουδαῖος δέ τις Ἀπολλῶς ὀνόματι,
[3]JEW [1]NOW [2]A CERTAIN, APOLLOS BY NAME,

Ἀλεξανδρεὺς τῷ γένει, ἀνὴρ λόγιος, κατήντησεν εἰς
AN ALEXANDRIAN - BY BIRTH, A LEARNED~MAN, ARRIVED IN

Ἔφεσον, δυνατὸς ὢν ἐν ταῖς γραφαῖς. **18.25** οὗτος
EPHESUS, BEING~STRONG IN THE SCRIPTURES. THIS ONE

ἦν κατηχημένος τὴν ὁδὸν τοῦ κυρίου καὶ ζέων τῷ
HAD BEEN TAUGHT THE WAY OF THE LORD AND BURNING -

πνεύματι ἐλάλει καὶ ἐδίδασκεν ἀκριβῶς τὰ
IN SPIRIT HE WAS SPEAKING AND TEACHING ACCURATELY THE THINGS

περὶ   τοῦ   Ἰησοῦ,   ἐπιστάμενος   μόνον   τὸ   βάπτισμα
ABOUT   -   JESUS,   BEING ACQUAINTED WITH   ONLY   THE   BAPTISM

Ἰωάννου·   **18.26** οὗτός τε   ἤρξατο   παρρησιάζεσθαι   ἐν
OF JOHN.   AND~THIS ONE BEGAN   TO SPEAK BOLDLY   IN

τῇ   συναγωγῇ.   ἀκούσαντες δὲ   αὐτοῦ   Πρίσκιλλα   καὶ
THE   SYNAGOGUE.   AND~HAVING HEARD   HIM   PRISCILLA   AND

Ἀκύλας   προσελάβοντο   αὐτὸν   καὶ   ἀκριβέστερον
AQUILA   TOOK   HIM   AND   MORE ACCURATELY

αὐτῷ ἐξέθεντο   τὴν   ὁδὸν   [τοῦ   θεοῦ].   **18.27** βουλομένου δὲ
EXPLAINED~TO HIM   THE   WAY   -   OF GOD.   AND~DESIRING

αὐτοῦ   διελθεῖν   εἰς   τὴν   Ἀχαΐαν,   προτρεψάμενοι   οἱ
HE   TO GO   TO   -   ACHAIA,   HAVING BEEN ENCOURAGED,   THE

ἀδελφοὶ   ἔγραψαν   τοῖς   μαθηταῖς   ἀποδέξασθαι   αὐτόν,
BROTHERS   WROTE   TO THE   DISCIPLES   TO WELCOME   HIM,

ὃς   παραγενόμενος   συνεβάλετο   πολὺ   τοῖς
WHO   HAVING COME   HE HELPED   GREATLY   THE ONES

πεπιστευκόσιν   διὰ   τῆς   χάριτος·   **18.28** εὐτόνως   γὰρ
HAVING BELIEVED   THROUGH   -   GRACE.   FOR~POWERFULLY

τοῖς   Ἰουδαίοις   διακατηλέγχετο   δημοσίᾳ   ἐπιδεικνὺς
²THE   ³JEWS   ¹HE WAS REFUTING   IN PUBLIC,   SHOWING

διὰ   τῶν   γραφῶν   εἶναι   τὸν   Χριστὸν   Ἰησοῦν.
THROUGH   THE   SCRIPTURES   TO BE   THE   CHRIST,   JESUS.

concerning Jesus, though he knew only the baptism of John. [26]He began to speak boldly in the synagogue; but when Priscilla and Aquila heard him, they took him aside and explained the Way of God to him more accurately. [27]And when he wished to cross over to Achaia, the believers[n] encouraged him and wrote to the disciples to welcome him. On his arrival he greatly helped those who through grace had become believers, [28]for he powerfully refuted the Jews in public, showing by the scriptures that the Messiah[o] is Jesus.

[n] Gk brothers
[o] Or the Christ

19.1 Ἐγένετο δὲ   ἐν τῷ   τὸν   Ἀπολλῶ εἶναι   ἐν   Κορίνθῳ
AND~IT CAME ABOUT   WHILE   -   APOLLOS   WAS   IN   CORINTH,

Παῦλον   διελθόντα   τὰ   ἀνωτερικὰ   μέρη
PAUL   HAVING TRAVELED THROUGH   THE   UPPER   REGIONS,

[κατ]ελθεῖν   εἰς   Ἔφεσον   καὶ   εὑρεῖν   τινας   μαθητὰς
TO COME DOWN   TO   EPHESUS   AND   TO FIND   SOME   DISCIPLES,

19.2 εἶπέν τε   πρὸς   αὐτούς,   Εἰ   πνεῦμα ἅγιον   ἐλάβετε
AND~HE SAID   TO   THEM,   IF   [THE] HOLY~SPIRIT   YOU° RECEIVED

πιστεύσαντες;   οἱ δὲ   πρὸς   αὐτόν,   Ἀλλ'   οὐδ'   εἰ
HAVING BELIEVED?   BUT~THEY   [SAID] TO   HIM,   ¹BUT   ³NOT   ⁴IF

πνεῦμα   ἅγιον   ἔστιν   ἠκούσαμεν.   **19.3** εἶπέν τε,   Εἰς
⁷SPIRIT   ⁶A HOLY   ⁵THERE IS   ²WE HEARD.   AND~HE SAID,   INTO

τί   οὖν   ἐβαπτίσθητε;   οἱ δὲ   εἶπαν,   Εἰς τὸ
WHAT   THEN   WERE YOU° BAPTIZED?   -   AND   THEY SAID,   INTO   THE

Ἰωάννου   βάπτισμα.   **19.4** εἶπεν δὲ   Παῦλος,   Ἰωάννης
BAPTISM~OF JOHN.   AND~SAID   PAUL,   JOHN

ἐβάπτισεν   βάπτισμα   μετανοίας   τῷ   λαῷ   λέγων   εἰς
BAPTIZED [WITH]   A BAPTISM   OF REPENTANCE,   TO THE   PEOPLE   SAYING,   IN

τὸν   ἐρχόμενον   μετ'   αὐτὸν   ἵνα   πιστεύσωσιν,   τοῦτ'
THE ONE   COMING   AFTER   HIM   THAT   THEY SHOULD BELIEVE,   THIS

ἔστιν   εἰς   τὸν   Ἰησοῦν.   **19.5** ἀκούσαντες δὲ
MEANS   IN   -   JESUS.   AND~HAVING HEARD [THIS]

While Apollos was in Corinth, Paul passed through the interior regions and came to Ephesus, where he found some disciples. [2]He said to them, "Did you receive the Holy Spirit when you became believers?" They replied, "No, we have not even heard that there is a Holy Spirit." [3]Then he said, "Into what then were you baptized?" They answered, "Into John's baptism." [4]Paul said, "John baptized with the baptism of repentance, telling the people to believe in the one who was to come after him, that is, in Jesus." [5]On hearing this, they were baptized in the name of the Lord Jesus. ⁶When Paul had laid his hands on them, the Holy Spirit came upon them, and they spoke in tongues and prophesied— ⁷altogether there were about twelve of them.

8 He entered the synagogue and for three months spoke out boldly, and argued persuasively about the kingdom of God. ⁹When some stubbornly refused to believe and spoke evil of the Way before the congregation, he left them, taking the disciples with him, and argued daily in the lecture hall of Tyrannus.ᵖ ¹⁰This continued for two years, so that all the residents of Asia, both Jews and Greeks, heard the word of the Lord.

11 God did extraordinary miracles through Paul, ¹²so that when the handkerchiefs or aprons that had touched his skin were brought to the sick, their diseases left them, and the evil spirits came out of them. ¹³Then some itinerant Jewish exorcists tried to use the name of the Lord Jesus over those who had evil spirits, saying, "I adjure you by the Jesus whom Paul

ᵖ Other ancient authorities read *of a certain Tyrannus, from eleven o'clock in the morning to four in the afternoon*

ἐβαπτίσθησαν εἰς τὸ ὄνομα τοῦ κυρίου Ἰησοῦ,
THEY WERE BAPTIZED IN THE NAME OF THE LORD JESUS,

19.6 καὶ ἐπιθέντος   αὐτοῖς τοῦ Παύλου [τὰς] χεῖρας
AND ²HAVING PLACED UPON ³THEM - ¹PAUL THE(HIS) HANDS,

ἦλθε τὸ πνεῦμα τὸ ἅγιον ἐπ᾽ αὐτούς, ἐλάλουν τε
CAME THE ²SPIRIT - ¹HOLY UPON THEM, AND~THEY WERE SPEAKING

γλώσσαις καὶ ἐπροφήτευον. **19.7** ἦσαν δὲ οἱ πάντες
TONGUES AND WERE PROPHESYING. AND~WERE ALL~THE

ἄνδρες ὡσεὶ δώδεκα.
MEN ABOUT TWELVE.

19.8 Εἰσελθὼν δὲ εἰς τὴν συναγωγὴν ἐπαρρησιάζετο
AND~HAVING ENTERED INTO THE SYNAGOGUE HE WAS SPEAKING BOLDLY

ἐπὶ μῆνας τρεῖς διαλεγόμενος καὶ πείθων
OVER THREE~MONTHS DEBATING AND PERSUADING

[τὰ] περὶ   τῆς βασιλείας τοῦ θεοῦ. **19.9** ὡς δέ
CONCERNING~THE THINGS OF THE KINGDOM - OF GOD. BUT~WHEN

τινες ἐσκληρύνοντο καὶ ἠπείθουν κακολογοῦντες τὴν
SOME WERE BEING HARDENED AND WERE DISOBEYING SPEAKING EVIL OF THE

ὁδὸν ἐνώπιον τοῦ πλήθους, ἀποστὰς ἀπ᾽ αὐτῶν
WAY BEFORE THE MULTITUDE, HAVING WITHDRAWN FROM THEM,

ἀφώρισεν τοὺς μαθητὰς καθ᾽ ἡμέραν διαλεγόμενος ἐν
HE TOOK THE DISCIPLES, DAILY DEBATING IN

τῇ σχολῇ Τυράννου. **19.10** τοῦτο δὲ ἐγένετο ἐπὶ
THE SCHOOL OF TYRANNUS. AND~THIS HAPPENED OVER

ἔτη δύο, ὥστε πάντας τοὺς κατοικοῦντας τὴν Ἀσίαν
TWO~YEARS, SO THAT ALL THE ONES INHABITING - ASIA

ἀκοῦσαι τὸν λόγον τοῦ κυρίου, Ἰουδαίους τε καὶ
TO HEAR THE WORD OF THE LORD, BOTH~JEWS AND

Ἕλληνας.
GREEKS.

19.11 Δυνάμεις τε οὐ τὰς τυχούσας ὁ θεὸς
AND~MIRACLES NOT THE ONES HAVING COMMONLY OCCURRED - GOD

ἐποίει διὰ τῶν χειρῶν Παύλου, **19.12** ὥστε καὶ ἐπὶ
PERFORMED BY THE HANDS OF PAUL, SO THAT ALSO UPON

τοὺς ἀσθενοῦντας ἀποφέρεσθαι ἀπὸ τοῦ χρωτὸς αὐτοῦ
THE ONES BEING SICK TO BE TAKEN AWAY FROM THE SKIN OF HIM

σουδάρια ἢ σιμικίνθια καὶ ἀπαλλάσσεσθαι ἀπ᾽ αὐτῶν
HANDKERCHIEFS OR APRONS AND TO BE TAKEN AWAY FROM THEM

τὰς νόσους, τά τε πνεύματα τὰ πονηρὰ ἐκπορεύεσθαι.
THE DISEASES, AND~THE ²SPIRITS - ¹EVIL TO GO OUT.

19.13 ἐπεχείρησαν δέ τινες καὶ τῶν περιερχομένων
AND~ATTEMPTED ALSO~SOME OF THE ONES GOING AROUND,

Ἰουδαίων ἐξορκιστῶν ὀνομάζειν ἐπὶ τοὺς ἔχοντας τὰ
JEWISH EXORCISTS, TO NAME OVER THE ONES HAVING -

πνεύματα τὰ πονηρὰ τὸ ὄνομα τοῦ κυρίου Ἰησοῦ
²SPIRITS - ¹EVIL THE NAME OF THE LORD JESUS

λέγοντες, Ὁρκίζω ὑμᾶς τὸν Ἰησοῦν ὃν Παῦλος
SAYING, I COMMAND YOU° [BY] THE JESUS WHOM PAUL

κηρύσσει. **19.14** ἦσαν δέ τινος Σκευᾶ Ἰουδαίου
PREACHES.   AND~THERE WERE OF A CERTAIN SCEVA,   A JEWISH

ἀρχιερέως ἑπτὰ υἱοὶ τοῦτο ποιοῦντες.
CHIEF PRIEST,   SEVEN   SONS   DOING~THIS.

19.15 ἀποκριθὲν δὲ τὸ πνεῦμα τὸ πονηρὸν εἶπεν
       AND~HAVING ANSWERED THE ²SPIRIT   -   ¹EVIL   SAID

αὐτοῖς, Τὸν [μὲν] Ἰησοῦν γινώσκω καὶ τὸν Παῦλον
TO THEM,   -   -   I KNOW~JESUS   AND [WITH]   -   PAUL

ἐπίσταμαι ὑμεῖς δὲ τίνες ἐστέ; **19.16** καὶ ἐφαλόμενος
I AM ACQUAINTED,   BUT~YOU°,   WHO   ARE YOU°?   AND   ⁹HAVING LEAPED

ὁ ἄνθρωπος ἐπ' αὐτοὺς ἐν ᾧ ἦν τὸ πνεῦμα τὸ
¹THE ²MAN   ¹⁰UPON ¹¹THEM ³IN ⁴WHOM ⁵WAS ⁶THE ⁸SPIRIT   -

πονηρόν, κατακυριεύσας ἀμφοτέρων ἴσχυσεν κατ'
⁷EVIL,   HAVING SUBDUED   ALL,   HE OVERPOWERED AGAINST

αὐτῶν ὥστε γυμνοὺς καὶ τετραυματισμένους ἐκφυγεῖν
THEM   SO THAT NAKED   AND   HAVING BEEN WOUNDED   TO FLEE

ἐκ τοῦ οἴκου ἐκείνου. **19.17** τοῦτο δὲ ἐγένετο γνωστὸν
FROM   -   THAT~HOUSE.   AND~THIS   BECAME   KNOWN

πᾶσιν Ἰουδαίοις τε καὶ Ἕλλησιν τοῖς κατοικοῦσιν
TO ALL   [THE] JEWS   AND ALSO [THE] GREEKS   -   INHABITING

τὴν Ἔφεσον καὶ ἐπέπεσεν φόβος ἐπὶ πάντας αὐτούς
-   EPHESUS,   AND   FEAR~FELL   UPON ALL   OF THEM

καὶ ἐμεγαλύνετο τὸ ὄνομα τοῦ κυρίου Ἰησοῦ.
AND   THEY WERE EXALTING THE NAME   OF THE LORD   JESUS.

19.18 πολλοί τε τῶν πεπιστευκότων ἤρχοντο
       AND~MANY   OF THE ONES HAVING BELIEVED   WERE COMING

ἐξομολογούμενοι καὶ ἀναγγέλλοντες τὰς πράξεις αὐτῶν.
CONFESSING   AND   DISCLOSING   THE   ACTIONS   OF THEM.

19.19 ἱκανοὶ δὲ τῶν τὰ περίεργα πραξάντων
       AND~A NUMBER   OF THE ONES   -   HAVING PRACTICED~MAGIC,

συνενέγκαντες τὰς βίβλους κατέκαιον ἐνώπιον
HAVING BROUGHT TOGETHER THE   BOOKS,   WERE BURNING [THEM] BEFORE

πάντων, καὶ συνεψήφισαν τὰς τιμὰς αὐτῶν καὶ
EVERYONE.   AND   THEY ADDED UP   THE   PRICE   OF THEM AND

εὗρον ἀργυρίου μυριάδας πέντε. **19.20** Οὕτως
THEY FOUND [IT TO BE] OF SILVER   FIFTY~THOUSAND [PIECES].   SO

κατὰ κράτος τοῦ κυρίου ὁ λόγος ηὔξανεν καὶ
POWERFULLY   ³OF THE ⁴LORD ¹THE ²WORD   WAS GROWING AND

ἴσχυεν.
WAS BECOMING STRONG.

19.21 Ὡς δὲ ἐπληρώθη ταῦτα, ἔθετο ὁ Παῦλος ἐν
       AND~WHEN WERE FULFILLED THESE THINGS, RESOLVED   -   PAUL   IN

τῷ πνεύματι διελθὼν τὴν Μακεδονίαν καὶ
THE(HIS) SPIRIT,   HAVING TRAVELED THROUGH   -   MACEDONIA   AND

Ἀχαΐαν πορεύεσθαι εἰς Ἱεροσόλυμα εἰπὼν ὅτι Μετὰ
ACHAIA   TO GO   TO   JERUSALEM   HAVING SAID   AFTER

τὸ γενέσθαι με ἐκεῖ δεῖ με καὶ Ῥώμην ἰδεῖν.
-   I~AM   THERE,   IT IS NECESSARY FOR ME ALSO   TO SEE~ROME.

proclaims." ¹⁴Seven sons of a Jewish high priest named Sceva were doing this. ¹⁵But the evil spirit said to them in reply, "Jesus I know, and Paul I know; but who are you?" ¹⁶Then the man with the evil spirit leaped on them, mastered them all, and so overpowered them that they fled out of the house naked and wounded. ¹⁷When this became known to all residents of Ephesus, both Jews and Greeks, everyone was awestruck; and the name of the Lord Jesus was praised. ¹⁸Also many of those who became believers confessed and disclosed their practices. ¹⁹A number of those who practiced magic collected their books and burned them publicly; when the value of these books*q* was calculated, it was found to come to fifty thousand silver coins. ²⁰So the word of the Lord grew mightily and prevailed.

21 Now after these things had been accomplished, Paul resolved in the Spirit to go through Macedonia and Achaia, and then to go on to Jerusalem. He said, "After I have gone there, I must also see Rome."

q Gk *them*

²²So he sent two of his helpers, Timothy and Erastus, to Macedonia, while he himself stayed for some time longer in Asia.

23 About that time no little disturbance broke out concerning the Way. ²⁴A man named Demetrius, a silversmith who made silver shrines of Artemis, brought no little business to the artisans. ²⁵These he gathered together, with the workers of the same trade, and said, "Men, you know that we get our wealth from this business. ²⁶You also see and hear that not only in Ephesus but in almost the whole of Asia this Paul has persuaded and drawn away a considerable number of people by saying that gods made with hands are not gods. ²⁷And there is danger not only that this trade of ours may come into disrepute but also that the temple of the great goddess Artemis will be scorned, and she will be deprived of her majesty that brought all Asia and the world to worship her."

28 When they heard this, they were enraged and shouted, "Great is Artemis of the Ephesians!" ²⁹The city was filled with the confusion; and peopleʳ rushed together to the theater, dragging with them Gaius and Aristarchus, Macedonians

ʳ Gk they

19.22 ἀποστείλας δὲ εἰς τὴν Μακεδονίαν δύο τῶν
AND~HAVING SENT TO - MACEDONIA TWO OF THE ONES

διακονούντων αὐτῷ, Τιμόθεον καὶ Ἔραστον, αὐτὸς
SERVING WITH HIM, TIMOTHY AND ERASTUS, HE

ἐπέσχεν χρόνον εἰς τὴν Ἀσίαν.
STAYED A WHILE IN - ASIA.

19.23 Ἐγένετο δὲ κατὰ τὸν καιρὸν ἐκεῖνον τάραχος
NOW~THERE WAS DURING - THAT~TIME ³DISTURBANCE

οὐκ ὀλίγος περὶ τῆς ὁδοῦ. **19.24** Δημήτριος γάρ
¹NO ²SMALL CONCERNING THE WAY. ⁴DEMETRIUS ¹FOR

τις ὀνόματι, ἀργυροκόπος, ποιῶν ναοὺς ἀργυροῦς
²A CERTAIN ONE ³BY NAME, A SILVERSMITH, MAKING SILVER~SHRINES

Ἀρτέμιδος παρείχετο τοῖς τεχνίταις οὐκ ὀλίγην
OF ARTEMIS, WAS PROVIDING FOR THE CRAFTSMEN NO SMALL

ἐργασίαν, **19.25** οὓς συναθροίσας καὶ τοὺς περὶ
PROFIT, WHOM HAVING ASSEMBLED ALSO THE ²OCCUPIED WITH

τὰ τοιαῦτα ἐργάτας εἶπεν, Ἄνδρες, ἐπίστασθε ὅτι
- ³SUCH THINGS ¹WORKMEN HE SAID, MEN, YOU° KNOW THAT

ἐκ ταύτης τῆς ἐργασίας ἡ εὐπορία ἡμῖν ἐστιν
FROM THIS - TRADE - PROSPERITY TO US IS,

19.26 καὶ θεωρεῖτε καὶ ἀκούετε ὅτι οὐ μόνον Ἐφέσου
AND YOU° SEE AND HEAR THAT NOT ONLY OF EPHESUS

ἀλλὰ σχεδὸν πάσης τῆς Ἀσίας ὁ Παῦλος οὗτος
BUT [IN] ALMOST ALL - OF ASIA - THIS~PAUL

πείσας μετέστησεν ἱκανὸν ὄχλον λέγων ὅτι
HAVING PERSUADED [SOME], TURNED AWAY A LARGE CROWD SAYING THAT

οὐκ εἰσὶν θεοὶ οἱ διὰ χειρῶν γινόμενοι. **19.27** οὐ
ARE NOT GODS THE THINGS WITH HANDS BEING MADE. ³NOT

μόνον δὲ τοῦτο κινδυνεύει ἡμῖν τὸ μέρος εἰς
⁴ONLY ¹AND ²THIS IS A DANGER TO US THE PART INTO

ἀπελεγμὸν ἐλθεῖν ἀλλὰ καὶ τὸ τῆς μεγάλης θεᾶς
DISREPUTE TO COME, BUT ALSO THE ²OF THE ³GREAT ⁴GODDESS

Ἀρτέμιδος ἱερὸν εἰς οὐθὲν λογισθῆναι, μέλλειν τε καὶ
⁵ARTEMIS ¹TEMPLE AS NOTHING TO BE CONSIDERED, AND~TO BE ABOUT ALSO

καθαιρεῖσθαι τῆς μεγαλειότητος αὐτῆς ἣν ὅλη ἡ
TO SUFFER [THE] LOSS OF THE MAJESTY OF HER WHICH ALL -

Ἀσία καὶ ἡ οἰκουμένη σέβεται.
ASIA AND THE WORLD WORSHIP.

19.28 Ἀκούσαντες δὲ καὶ γενόμενοι πλήρεις θυμοῦ
AND~HAVING LISTENED AND HAVING BECOME FULL OF ANGER

ἔκραζον λέγοντες, Μεγάλη ἡ Ἄρτεμις
THEY WERE CRYING OUT SAYING, GREAT [IS] - ARTEMIS

Ἐφεσίων. **19.29** καὶ ἐπλήσθη ἡ πόλις τῆς
OF [THE] EPHESIANS. AND WAS FILLED THE CITY -

συγχύσεως, ὥρμησάν τε ὁμοθυμαδὸν εἰς τὸ θέατρον
WITH CONFUSION, AND~THEY RUSHED WITH ONE IMPULSE INTO THE THEATER,

συναρπάσαντες Γάϊον καὶ Ἀρίσταρχον Μακεδόνας,
HAVING SEIZED GAIUS AND ARISTARCHUS, MACEDONIANS,

συνεκδήμους Παύλου. **19.30** Παύλου δὲ βουλομένου
TRAVELING COMPANIONS OF PAUL. AND~PAUL DESIRING

εἰσελθεῖν εἰς τὸν δῆμον οὐκ εἴων αὐτὸν οἱ
TO ENTER INTO THE ASSEMBLY, WERE NOT ALLOWING HIM THE

μαθηταί· **19.31** τινὲς δὲ καὶ τῶν Ἀσιαρχῶν, ὄντες
DISCIPLES. AND~SOME ALSO OF THE ASIARCHS, BEING

αὐτῷ φίλοι, πέμψαντες πρὸς αὐτὸν παρεκάλουν μὴ
TO HIM FRIENDS, HAVING SENT TO HIM, WERE BEGGING [HIM] NOT

δοῦναι ἑαυτὸν εἰς τὸ θέατρον. **19.32** ἄλλοι μὲν οὖν
TO GIVE HIMSELF TO THE THEATER. OTHERS THEN

ἄλλο τι ἔκραζον· ἦν γὰρ ἡ ἐκκλησία
SOMETHING~DIFFERENT WERE CRYING OUT. FOR~HAD THE ASSEMBLY

συγκεχυμένη καὶ οἱ πλείους οὐκ ᾔδεισαν τίνος ἕνεκα
BEEN CONFUSED AND THE MAJORITY HAD NOT KNOWN WHY

συνεληλύθεισαν. **19.33** ἐκ δὲ τοῦ ὄχλου συνεβίβασαν
THEY HAD ASSEMBLED. AND~FROM THE CROWD THEY PROMPTED

Ἀλέξανδρον, προβαλόντων αὐτὸν τῶν Ἰουδαίων· ὁ
ALEXANDER, ³HAVING BROUGHT FORWARD ⁴HIM ¹THE ²JEWS. -

δὲ Ἀλέξανδρος κατασείσας τὴν χεῖρα ἤθελεν
AND ALEXANDER, HAVING WAVED THE(HIS) HAND WAS WANTING

ἀπολογεῖσθαι τῷ δήμῳ. **19.34** ἐπιγνόντες δὲ ὅτι
TO DEFEND HIMSELF TO THE ASSEMBLY. BUT~HAVING KNOWN THAT

Ἰουδαῖός ἐστιν, φωνὴ ἐγένετο μία ἐκ πάντων ὡς ἐπὶ
HE IS~A JEW, ³VOICE ¹THERE WAS ²ONE FROM EVERYONE FOR~ABOUT

ὥρας δύο κραζόντων, Μεγάλη ἡ Ἄρτεμις Ἐφεσίων.
TWO~HOURS CRYING OUT, GREAT [IS] - ARTEMIS OF [THE] EPHESIANS.

19.35 καταστείλας δὲ ὁ γραμματεὺς τὸν ὄχλον
⁴HAVING RESTRAINED ¹AND ²THE ³TOWN CLERK THE CROWD

φησίν, Ἄνδρες Ἐφέσιοι, τίς γάρ ἐστιν ἀνθρώπων ὃς
SAYS, MEN, EPHESIANS, WHO INDEED IS THERE OF MEN WHO

οὐ γινώσκει τὴν Ἐφεσίων πόλιν νεωκόρον οὖσαν
DOES NOT KNOW THE EPHESIAN CITY [AS] BEING~[THE] GUARDIAN OF THE TEMPLE

τῆς μεγάλης Ἀρτέμιδος καὶ τοῦ διοπετοῦς;
OF THE GREAT ARTEMIS AND OF THE [IMAGE] FALLEN FROM HEAVEN?

19.36 ἀναντιρρήτων οὖν ὄντων τούτων δέον ἐστὶν
UNDENIABLE, THEREFORE BEING THESE THINGS, IT IS~NECESSARY

ὑμᾶς κατεσταλμένους ὑπάρχειν καὶ μηδὲν προπετὲς
FOR YOU° HAVING BECOME CALM TO BE, AND NOTHING RECKLESS

πράσσειν. **19.37** ἠγάγετε γὰρ τοὺς ἄνδρας τούτους οὔτε
TO DO. FOR~YOU° BROUGHT - THESE~MEN [HERE] NEITHER

ἱεροσύλους οὔτε βλασφημοῦντας τὴν θεὸν ἡμῶν. **19.38** εἰ
TEMPLE ROBBERS NOR BLASPHEMING THE GOD OF US. IF

μὲν οὖν Δημήτριος καὶ οἱ σὺν αὐτῷ τεχνῖται
- THEREFORE DEMETRIUS AND THE ²WITH ³HIM ¹CRAFTSMEN

ἔχουσι πρός τινα λόγον, ἀγοραῖοι ἄγονται καὶ
HAVE AGAINST ANYONE A COMPLAINT, COURTS ARE IN SESSION AND

ἀνθύπατοί εἰσιν, ἐγκαλείτωσαν ἀλλήλοις.
THERE ARE~PROCONSULS, LET THEM BRING CHARGES AGAINST ONE ANOTHER.

who were Paul's travel companions. ³⁰Paul wished to go into the crowd, but the disciples would not let him; ³¹even some officials of the province of Asia,ˢ who were friendly to him, sent him a message urging him not to venture into the theater. ³²Meanwhile, some were shouting one thing, some another; for the assembly was in confusion, and most of them did not know why they had come together. ³³Some of the crowd gave instructions to Alexander, whom the Jews had pushed forward. And Alexander motioned for silence and tried to make a defense before the people. ³⁴But when they recognized that he was a Jew, for about two hours all of them shouted in unison, "Great is Artemis of the Ephesians!" ³⁵But when the town clerk had quieted the crowd, he said, "Citizens of Ephesus, who is there that does not know that the city of the Ephesians is the temple keeper of the great Artemis and of the statue that fell from heaven?ᵗ ³⁶Since these things cannot be denied, you ought to be quiet and do nothing rash. ³⁷You have brought these men here who are neither temple robbers nor blasphemers of ourᵘ goddess. ³⁸If therefore Demetrius and the artisans with him have a complaint against anyone, the courts are open, and there are proconsuls; let them bring charges there against one another.

ˢ Gk *some of the Asiarchs*
ᵗ Meaning of Gk uncertain
ᵘ Other ancient authorities read *your*

[39]If there is anything further[v] you want to know, it must be settled in the regular assembly. [40]For we are in danger of being charged with rioting today, since there is no cause that we can give to justify this commotion." [41]When he had said this, he dismissed the assembly.

[v] Other ancient authorities read *about other matters*

19.39 εἰ δέ τι περαιτέρω ἐπιζητεῖτε, ἐν τῇ ἐννόμῳ
AND~IF ANYTHING FURTHER YOU° SEEK, IN THE LAWFUL

ἐκκλησίᾳ ἐπιλυθήσεται. **19.40** καὶ γὰρ κινδυνεύομεν
ASSEMBLY IT WILL BE SETTLED. FOR~INDEED WE ARE IN DANGER

ἐγκαλεῖσθαι στάσεως περὶ τῆς σήμερον, μηδενὸς
TO BE CHARGED WITH AN UPRISING CONCERNING - TODAY, NOTHING

αἰτίου ὑπάρχοντος περὶ οὗ [οὐ] δυνησόμεθα
OF A REASON BEING ABOUT WHICH WE WILL NOT BE ABLE

ἀποδοῦναι λόγον περὶ τῆς συστροφῆς ταύτης. καὶ
TO RENDER AN ACCOUNT CONCERNING - THIS~COMMOTION. AND

ταῦτα εἰπὼν ἀπέλυσεν τὴν ἐκκλησίαν.
THESE THINGS HAVING SAID, HE DISMISSED THE ASSEMBLY.

CHAPTER 20

After the uproar had ceased, Paul sent for the disciples; and after encouraging them and saying farewell, he left for Macedonia. [2]When he had gone through those regions and had given the believers[w] much encouragement, he came to Greece, [3]where he stayed for three months. He was about to set sail for Syria when a plot was made against him by the Jews, and so he decided to return through Macedonia. [4]He was accompanied by Sopater son of Pyrrhus from Beroea, by Aristarchus and Secundus from Thessalonica, by Gaius from Derbe, and by Timothy, as well as by Tychicus and Trophimus from Asia. [5]They went ahead and were waiting for us in Troas; [6]but we sailed from Philippi after the days of Unleavened Bread, and in five days we joined them in

[w] Gk *given them*

20.1 Μετὰ δὲ τὸ παύσασθαι τὸν θόρυβον
AND~AFTER - HAD ENDED THE UPROAR

μεταπεμψάμενος ὁ Παῦλος τοὺς μαθητὰς καὶ
[2]HAVING SUMMONED - [1]PAUL THE DISCIPLES AND

παρακαλέσας, ἀσπασάμενος ἐξῆλθεν πορεύεσθαι
HAVING EXHORTED [THEM], [AND] HAVING SAID GOOD-BYE, HE DEPARTED TO GO

εἰς Μακεδονίαν. **20.2** διελθὼν δὲ τὰ
TO MACEDONIA. AND~HAVING TRAVELED THROUGH -

μέρη ἐκεῖνα καὶ παρακαλέσας αὐτοὺς λόγῳ πολλῷ
THOSE~REGIONS AND HAVING EXHORTED THEM WITH MANY~WORD[S],

ἦλθεν εἰς τὴν Ἑλλάδα **20.3** ποιήσας τε μῆνας τρεῖς·
HE CAME TO - GREECE AND~HAVING SPENT THREE~MONTHS [THERE],

γενομένης ἐπιβουλῆς αὐτῷ ὑπὸ τῶν Ἰουδαίων
HAVING BECOME A PLOT AGAINST HIM BY THE JEWS

μέλλοντι ἀνάγεσθαι εἰς τὴν Συρίαν, ἐγένετο γνώμης
BEING ABOUT TO SET SAIL FOR - SYRIA, HE WAS OF A MIND

τοῦ ὑποστρέφειν διὰ Μακεδονίας.
- TO RETURN THROUGH MACEDONIA.

20.4 συνείπετο δὲ αὐτῷ Σώπατρος Πύρρου
AND~WERE ACCOMPANYING HIM, SOPATER [THE SON] OF PYRRHUS,

Βεροιαῖος, Θεσσαλονικέων δὲ Ἀρίσταρχος καὶ
[THE] BEREAN, AND~OF [THE] THESSALONIANS, ARISTARCHUS AND

Σεκοῦνδος, καὶ Γάϊος Δερβαῖος καὶ Τιμόθεος,
SECUNDUS, AND GAIUS, OF DERBE AND TIMOTHY,

Ἀσιανοὶ δὲ Τύχικος καὶ Τρόφιμος. **20.5** οὗτοι δὲ
AND~[THE] ASIANS, TYCHICUS AND TROPHIMUS. AND~THESE

προελθόντες ἔμενον ἡμᾶς ἐν Τρῳάδι, **20.6** ἡμεῖς δὲ
HAVING GONE AHEAD WERE WAITING FOR US IN TROAS, AND~WE

ἐξεπλεύσαμεν μετὰ τὰς ἡμέρας τῶν ἀζύμων
SAILED AWAY AFTER THE DAYS OF THE UNLEAVENED BREAD [FEAST]

ἀπὸ Φιλίππων καὶ ἤλθομεν πρὸς αὐτοὺς εἰς τὴν
FROM PHILIPPI, AND WE CAME TO THEM IN -

Τρῳάδα ἄχρι ἡμερῶν πέντε, ὅπου διετρίψαμεν
TROAS   WITHIN   FIVE~DAYS,   WHERE   WE STAYED

ἡμέρας ἑπτά.
SEVEN~DAYS.

20.7 Ἐν δὲ τῇ μιᾷ τῶν σαββάτων συνηγμένων
AND~ON - ONE OF THE SABBATHS   HAVING BEEN ASSEMBLED

ἡμῶν κλάσαι ἄρτον, ὁ Παῦλος διελέγετο αὐτοῖς
US   TO BREAK BREAD,   - PAUL   WAS LECTURING THEM

μέλλων ἐξιέναι τῇ ἐπαύριον, παρέτεινέν τε τὸν λόγον
BEING ABOUT TO DEPART ON THE NEXT DAY, AND~WAS EXTENDING THE MESSAGE

μέχρι μεσονυκτίου. **20.8** ἦσαν δὲ λαμπάδες ἱκαναὶ
UNTIL MIDNIGHT.   AND~THERE WERE A NUMBER OF~LAMPS

ἐν τῷ ὑπερῴῳ οὗ ἦμεν συνηγμένοι.
IN THE UPPER STORY WHERE WE HAD ASSEMBLED.

20.9 καθεζόμενος δέ τις νεανίας ὀνόματι Εὔτυχος
AND~SITTING   A CERTAIN YOUNG MAN BY NAME EUTYCHUS

ἐπὶ τῆς θυρίδος, καταφερόμενος ὕπνῳ βαθεῖ
ON THE WINDOW [SILL], BEING OVERCOME BY A DEEP~SLEEP,

διαλεγομένου τοῦ Παύλου ἐπὶ πλεῖον, κατενεχθεὶς
LECTURING   -   PAUL   FOR A LONG [TIME], HAVING BEEN OVERCOME

ἀπὸ τοῦ ὕπνου ἔπεσεν ἀπὸ τοῦ τριστέγου κάτω καὶ
FROM - SLEEP HE FELL FROM THE THIRD STORY DOWNWARDS AND

ἤρθη νεκρός. **20.10** καταβὰς δὲ ὁ Παῦλος
WAS PICKED UP DEAD.   AND~HAVING COME DOWN - PAUL

ἐπέπεσεν αὐτῷ καὶ συμπεριλαβὼν εἶπεν,
FELL UPON HIM AND HAVING EMBRACED [HIM] HE SAID,

Μὴ θορυβεῖσθε, ἡ γὰρ ψυχὴ αὐτοῦ ἐν αὐτῷ ἐστιν.
DO NOT BE TROUBLED, FOR~THE LIFE OF HIM IN HIM IS.

20.11 ἀναβὰς δὲ καὶ κλάσας τὸν ἄρτον καὶ
AND~HAVING GONE UP AND HAVING BROKEN THE BREAD AND

γευσάμενος ἐφ᾽ ἱκανόν τε ὁμιλήσας ἄχρι
HAVING PARTAKEN [OF IT], ²FOR ³A CONSIDERABLE [TIME] ¹AND HAVING SPOKEN UNTIL

αὐγῆς, οὕτως ἐξῆλθεν. **20.12** ἤγαγον δὲ τὸν παῖδα
DAWN, THUS HE DEPARTED.   AND~THEY LED AWAY THE YOUNG MAN

ζῶντα καὶ παρεκλήθησαν οὐ μετρίως.
LIVING AND THEY WERE COMFORTED NOT MODERATELY.

20.13 Ἡμεῖς δὲ προελθόντες ἐπὶ τὸ πλοῖον
AND~WE   HAVING GONE AHEAD TO THE BOAT

ἀνήχθημεν ἐπὶ τὴν Ἆσσον ἐκεῖθεν μέλλοντες
SET SAIL   FOR - ASSOS, FROM THERE INTENDING

ἀναλαμβάνειν τὸν Παῦλον· οὕτως γὰρ
TO TAKE ALONG - PAUL.   FOR~THUS

διατεταγμένος ἦν μέλλων αὐτὸς πεζεύειν.
HE HAD ARRANGED IT INTENDING HIMSELF TO TRAVEL BY LAND.

20.14 ὡς δὲ συνέβαλλεν ἡμῖν εἰς τὴν Ἆσσον,
AND~WHEN HE WAS MEETING US IN - ASSOS,

ἀναλαβόντες αὐτὸν ἤλθομεν εἰς Μιτυλήνην,
HAVING TAKEN ALONG HIM WE CAME TO MITYLENE,

Troas, where we stayed for seven days.

7 On the first day of the week, when we met to break bread, Paul was holding a discussion with them; since he intended to leave the next day, he continued speaking until midnight. [8]There were many lamps in the room upstairs where we were meeting. [9]A young man named Eutychus, who was sitting in the window, began to sink off into a deep sleep while Paul talked still longer. Overcome by sleep, he fell to the ground three floors below and was picked up dead. [10]But Paul went down, and bending over him took him in his arms, and said, "Do not be alarmed, for his life is in him." [11]Then Paul went upstairs, and after he had broken bread and eaten, he continued to converse with them until dawn; then he left. [12]Meanwhile they had taken the boy away alive and were not a little comforted.

13 We went ahead to the ship and set sail for Assos, intending to take Paul on board there; for he had made this arrangement, intending to go by land himself. [14]When he met us in Assos, we took him on board and went to Mitylene.

¹⁵We sailed from there, and on the following day we arrived opposite Chios. The next day we touched at Samos, and* the day after that we came to Miletus. ¹⁶For Paul had decided to sail past Ephesus, so that he might not have to spend time in Asia; he was eager to be in Jerusalem, if possible, on the day of Pentecost.

17 From Miletus he sent a message to Ephesus, asking the elders of the church to meet him. ¹⁸When they came to him, he said to them:

"You yourselves know how I lived among you the entire time from the first day that I set foot in Asia, ¹⁹serving the Lord with all humility and with tears, enduring the trials that came to me through the plots of the Jews. ²⁰I did not shrink from doing anything helpful, proclaiming the message to you and teaching you publicly and from house to house, ²¹as I testified to both Jews and Greeks about repentance toward God and faith toward our Lord Jesus. ²²And now, as a captive to the Spirit,ʸ I am on my way to Jerusalem, not knowing what will happen to me there, ²³except that the Holy Spirit testifies to me in every

*ˣ Other ancient authorities add *after remaining at Trogyllium*
ʸ Or *And now, bound in the spirit*

20.15 κἀκεῖθεν ἀποπλεύσαντες τῇ ἐπιούσῃ
AND FROM THERE   HAVING SAILED AWAY   ON THE   NEXT [DAY]

κατηντήσαμεν ἄντικρυς Χίου, τῇ δὲ ἑτέρᾳ
WE ARRIVED   OPPOSITE   CHIOS,   AND~ON THE NEXT [DAY]

παρεβάλομεν εἰς Σάμον, τῇ δὲ ἐχομένῃ ἤλθομεν
WE CROSSED OVER   TO   SAMOS,   AND~ON THE FOLLOWING [DAY] WE CAME

εἰς Μίλητον. **20.16** κεκρίκει γὰρ ὁ Παῦλος
TO   MILETUS.   FOR~HAD DECIDED   -   PAUL

παραπλεῦσαι τὴν Ἔφεσον, ὅπως μὴ γένηται αὐτῷ
TO SAIL PAST   -   EPHESUS,   SO AS   IT WOULD NOT BE   TO HIM

χρονοτριβῆσαι ἐν τῇ Ἀσίᾳ· ἔσπευδεν γὰρ εἰ δυνατὸν
TO SPEND TIME   IN - ASIA.   FOR~HE WAS HURRYING IF POSSIBLE

εἴη αὐτῷ τὴν ἡμέραν τῆς πεντηκοστῆς γενέσθαι εἰς
IT MIGHT BE TO HIM THE DAY   -   OF PENTECOST   TO COME   IN

Ἱεροσόλυμα.
JERUSALEM.

20.17 Ἀπὸ δὲ τῆς Μιλήτου πέμψας εἰς Ἔφεσον
          AND~FROM -   MILETUS,   HAVING SENT TO EPHESUS,

μετεκαλέσατο τοὺς πρεσβυτέρους τῆς ἐκκλησίας.
HE SUMMONED   THE   ELDERS   OF THE CHURCH.

20.18 ὡς δὲ παρεγένοντο πρὸς αὐτὸν εἶπεν αὐτοῖς,
          AND~WHEN THEY CAME   TO   HIM   HE SAID TO THEM,

Ὑμεῖς ἐπίστασθε, ἀπὸ πρώτης ἡμέρας ἀφ' ἧς
YOU°   KNOW,   FROM [THE] FIRST DAY   FROM WHICH

ἐπέβην εἰς τὴν Ἀσίαν, πῶς μεθ' ὑμῶν τὸν πάντα
I SET FOOT IN - ASIA,   HOW WITH YOU°   THE ENTIRE

χρόνον ἐγενόμην, **20.19** δουλεύων τῷ κυρίῳ μετὰ πάσης
TIME   I WAS,   SERVING   THE LORD WITH   ALL

ταπεινοφροσύνης καὶ δακρύων καὶ πειρασμῶν τῶν
HUMILITY   AND TEARS   AND   TRIALS,   -

συμβάντων μοι ἐν ταῖς ἐπιβουλαῖς τῶν Ἰουδαίων,
HAVING HAPPENED TO ME BY THE   PLOTS   OF THE JEWS,

20.20 ὡς οὐδὲν ὑπεστειλάμην τῶν συμφερόντων τοῦ
          HOW I KEPT BACK~NOTHING   OF THE THINGS BEING PROFITABLE   -

μὴ ἀναγγεῖλαι ὑμῖν καὶ διδάξαι ὑμᾶς δημοσίᾳ καὶ
NOT TO DISCLOSE TO YOU° AND TO TEACH YOU°   IN PUBLIC AND

κατ' οἴκους, **20.21** διαμαρτυρόμενος Ἰουδαίοις τε καὶ
FROM HOUSE TO HOUSE,   TESTIFYING   BOTH~TO JEWS   AND

Ἕλλησιν τὴν εἰς θεὸν μετάνοιαν καὶ πίστιν εἰς τὸν
GREEKS   - TOWARD GOD REPENTANCE AND FAITH IN THE

κύριον ἡμῶν Ἰησοῦν. **20.22** καὶ νῦν ἰδοὺ δεδεμένος ἐγὼ
LORD   OF US JESUS.   AND NOW BEHOLD I,~HAVING BEEN BOUND

τῷ πνεύματι πορεύομαι εἰς Ἰερουσαλὴμ τὰ ἐν
BY THE SPIRIT   AM GOING   TO JERUSALEM   ³THE THINGS ⁴IN

αὐτῇ συναντήσοντά μοι μὴ εἰδώς, **20.23** πλὴν ὅτι
⁵IT ⁶GOING TO HAPPEN ⁷TO ME ¹NOT ²HAVING KNOWN,   ⁸EXCEPT ⁹THAT

τὸ πνεῦμα τὸ ἅγιον κατὰ πόλιν διαμαρτύρεταί μοι
¹⁰THE ¹²SPIRIT - ¹¹HOLY IN EVERY CITY   TESTIFIES   TO ME

λέγον ὅτι δεσμὰ καὶ θλίψεις με μένουσιν. **20.24** ἀλλ᾽
SAYING THAT BONDS AND TRIBULATIONS ARE WAITING~FOR ME. BUT

οὐδενὸς λόγου ποιοῦμαι τὴν ψυχὴν τιμίαν ἐμαυτῷ
OF NO ACCOUNT DO I MAKE THE(MY) LIFE VALUABLE TO MYSELF

ὡς τελειῶσαι τὸν δρόμον μου καὶ τὴν διακονίαν ἣν
SO AS TO FINISH THE COURSE OF ME AND THE MINISTRY WHICH

ἔλαβον παρὰ τοῦ κυρίου Ἰησοῦ, διαμαρτύρασθαι τὸ
I RECEIVED FROM THE LORD JESUS, TO BEAR WITNESS TO THE

εὐαγγέλιον τῆς χάριτος τοῦ θεοῦ.
GOOD NEWS OF THE GRACE - OF GOD.

20.25 Καὶ νῦν ἰδοὺ ἐγὼ οἶδα ὅτι οὐκέτι ὄψεσθε τὸ
AND NOW BEHOLD I KNOW THAT NO LONGER WILL YOU° SEE THE

πρόσωπόν μου ὑμεῖς πάντες ἐν οἷς διῆλθον
FACE OF ME, ALL~OF YOU° AMONG WHOM I WENT ABOUT

κηρύσσων τὴν βασιλείαν. **20.26** διότι μαρτύρομαι
PREACHING THE KINGDOM. THEREFORE I TESTIFY

ὑμῖν ἐν τῇ σήμερον ἡμέρᾳ ὅτι καθαρός εἰμι ἀπὸ
TO YOU° ON [THIS VERY] - DAY~TODAY THAT I AM~INNOCENT OF

τοῦ αἵματος πάντων· **20.27** οὐ γὰρ ὑπεστειλάμην τοῦ
THE BLOOD OF ALL. FOR~I DID NOT SHRINK BACK FROM -

μὴ ἀναγγεῖλαι πᾶσαν τὴν βουλὴν τοῦ θεοῦ ὑμῖν.
NOT TO DISCLOSE ALL THE WILL - OF GOD TO YOU°.

20.28 προσέχετε ἑαυτοῖς καὶ παντὶ τῷ ποιμνίῳ, ἐν
PAY ATTENTION TO YOURSELVES AND TO ALL THE FLOCK, IN

ᾧ ὑμᾶς τὸ πνεῦμα τὸ ἅγιον ἔθετο ἐπισκόπους
WHICH YOU° THE ²SPIRIT - ¹HOLY PLACED [AS] OVERSEERS,

ποιμαίνειν ⌜τὴν ἐκκλησίαν τοῦ θεοῦ,⌝ ἣν
TO SHEPHERD THE CHURCH - OF GOD, WHICH

περιεποιήσατο διὰ τοῦ αἵματος τοῦ ἰδίου. **20.29** ἐγὼ
HE PURCHASED WITH - ²BLOOD - ¹HIS OWN. I

οἶδα ὅτι εἰσελεύσονται μετὰ τὴν ἄφιξίν μου
KNOW THAT WILL COME IN AFTER THE DEPARTURE OF ME

λύκοι βαρεῖς εἰς ὑμᾶς μὴ φειδόμενοι τοῦ ποιμνίου,
SAVAGE~WOLVES AMONG YOU° NOT SPARING THE FLOCK,

20.30 καὶ ἐξ ὑμῶν αὐτῶν ἀναστήσονται ἄνδρες
AND FROM YOU° YOURSELVES WILL RISE UP MEN

λαλοῦντες διεστραμμένα τοῦ ἀποσπᾶν τοὺς μαθητὰς
SPEAKING [THINGS] HAVING BEEN PERVERTED - TO DRAW AWAY THE DISCIPLES

ὀπίσω αὐτῶν. **20.31** διὸ γρηγορεῖτε μνημονεύοντες
AFTER THEM. THEREFORE, BE ALERT, HAVING REMEMBERED

ὅτι τριετίαν νύκτα καὶ ἡμέραν οὐκ ἐπαυσάμην μετὰ
THAT THREE YEARS, NIGHT AND DAY, I DID NOT STOP WITH

δακρύων νουθετῶν ἕνα ἕκαστον. **20.32** καὶ τὰ νῦν
TEARS ADMONISHING EACH~ONE [OF YOU°]. AND - NOW

παρατίθεμαι ὑμᾶς τῷ θεῷ καὶ τῷ λόγῳ τῆς
I COMMEND YOU° - TO GOD AND TO THE WORD OF THE

city that imprisonment and persecutions are waiting for me. [24]But I do not count my life of any value to myself, if only I may finish my course and the ministry that I received from the Lord Jesus, to testify to the good news of God's grace.

[25] "And now I know that none of you, among whom I have gone about proclaiming the kingdom, will ever see my face again. [26]Therefore I declare to you this day that I am not responsible for the blood of any of you, [27]for I did not shrink from declaring to you the whole purpose of God. [28]Keep watch over yourselves and over all the flock, of which the Holy Spirit has made you overseers, to shepherd the church of God[z] that he obtained with the blood of his own Son.[a] [29]I know that after I have gone, savage wolves will come in among you, not sparing the flock. [30]Some even from your own group will come distorting the truth in order to entice the disciples to follow them. [31]Therefore be alert, remembering that for three years I did not cease night or day to warn everyone with tears. [32]And now I commend you to God and to the message of

---

[z] Other ancient authorities read *of the Lord*

[a] Or *with his own blood*; Gk *with the blood of his Own*

20:28 text: KJV ASVmg RSV NASB NIV NEBmg TEV NJB NRSV. var. την εκκλησιαν του κυριου (the church of the Lord): ASV RSVmg NASBmg NIVmg NEB TEVmg NJBmg NRSVmg.

his grace, a message that is able to build you up and to give you the inheritance among all who are sanctified. [33]I coveted no one's silver or gold or clothing. [34]You know for yourselves that I worked with my own hands to support myself and my companions. [35]In all this I have given you an example that by such work we must support the weak, remembering the words of the Lord Jesus, for he himself said, 'It is more blessed to give than to receive.'"

36 When he had finished speaking, he knelt down with them all and prayed. [37]There was much weeping among them all; they embraced Paul and kissed him, [38]grieving especially because of what he had said, that they would not see him again. Then they brought him to the ship.

χάριτος αὐτοῦ, τῷ δυναμένῳ οἰκοδομῆσαι καὶ δοῦναι
GRACE OF HIM, - BEING ABLE TO BUILD AND TO GIVE

τὴν κληρονομίαν ἐν τοῖς ἡγιασμένοις πᾶσιν.
THE INHERITANCE AMONG ²THE ONES ³HAVING BEEN SANCTIFIED ¹ALL.

20.33 ἀργυρίου ἢ χρυσίου ἢ ἱματισμοῦ οὐδενὸς
SILVER OR GOLD OR [THE] CLOTHING OF NO ONE

ἐπεθύμησα· **20.34** αὐτοὶ γινώσκετε ὅτι ταῖς χρείαις
DID I LONG FOR. YOURSELVES YOU° KNOW THAT FOR THE NEEDS

μου καὶ τοῖς οὖσιν μετ' ἐμοῦ ὑπηρέτησαν αἱ
OF ME AND THE ONES BEING WITH ME, SERVED -

χεῖρες αὗται. **20.35** πάντα ὑπέδειξα ὑμῖν ὅτι οὕτως
THESE~HANDS. EVERYTHING I SHOWED TO YOU° THAT THUS

κοπιῶντας δεῖ ἀντιλαμβάνεσθαι τῶν ἀσθενούντων,
WORKING HARD IT IS NECESSARY TO HELP THE WEAK,

μνημονεύειν τε τῶν λόγων τοῦ κυρίου Ἰησοῦ ὅτι
AND~TO REMEMBER THE WORDS OF THE LORD JESUS THAT

αὐτὸς εἶπεν, Μακάριόν ἐστιν μᾶλλον διδόναι ἢ
HE SAID~HIMSELF, BLESSED IT IS MORE TO GIVE THAN

λαμβάνειν.
TO RECEIVE.

20.36 Καὶ ταῦτα εἰπὼν θεὶς τὰ γόνατα αὐτοῦ
AND THESE THINGS HAVING SAID, HAVING BENT THE KNEES OF HIM,

σὺν πᾶσιν αὐτοῖς προσηύξατο. **20.37** ἱκανὸς δὲ
WITH THEM~ALL HE PRAYED. AND~MUCH

κλαυθμὸς ἐγένετο πάντων καὶ ἐπιπεσόντες ἐπὶ τὸν
CRYING THERE WAS OF EVERYONE AND HAVING FALLEN UPON THE

τράχηλον τοῦ Παύλου κατεφίλουν αὐτόν,
NECK - OF PAUL, THEY WERE KISSING HIM,

20.38 ὀδυνώμενοι μάλιστα ἐπὶ τῷ λόγῳ ᾧ εἰρήκει
GRIEVING ABOVE ALL AT THE WORD IN WHICH HE HAD SAID

ὅτι οὐκέτι μέλλουσιν τὸ πρόσωπον αὐτοῦ θεωρεῖν.
THAT NO LONGER THEY WERE ABOUT THE FACE OF HIM TO SEE.

προέπεμπον δὲ αὐτὸν εἰς τὸ πλοῖον.
AND~THEY WERE ACCOMPANYING HIM TO THE BOAT.

CHAPTER 21

When we had parted from them and set sail, we came by a straight course to Cos, and the next day to Rhodes, and from there to Patara.[b] [2]When we found a ship bound for Phoenicia, we went on board and set sail.

[b] Other ancient authorities add *and Myra*

21.1 Ὡς δὲ ἐγένετο ἀναχθῆναι ἡμᾶς
AND~WHEN IT CAME ABOUT [THAT] WE~SET SAIL,

ἀποσπασθέντας ἀπ' αὐτῶν, εὐθυδρομήσαντες ἤλθομεν
HAVING PARTED FROM THEM, HAVING RUN A STRAIGHT COURSE, WE CAME

εἰς τὴν Κῶ, τῇ δὲ ἑξῆς εἰς τὴν Ῥόδον κἀκεῖθεν
TO - COS, AND~ON THE NEXT [DAY] TO - RHODES AND FROM THERE

εἰς Πάταρα, **21.2** καὶ εὑρόντες πλοῖον διαπερῶν εἰς
TO PATARA. AND HAVING FOUND A BOAT CROSSING OVER TO

Φοινίκην ἐπιβάντες ἀνήχθημεν.
PHOENICIA, HAVING EMBARKED WE SET SAIL.

21.3 ἀναφάναντες δὲ   τὴν Κύπρον καὶ   καταλιπόντες
AND~HAVING COME WITHIN SIGHT -   OF CYPRUS AND   HAVING LEFT BEHIND

αὐτὴν εὐώνυμον ἐπλέομεν εἰς Συρίαν καὶ   κατήλθομεν
IT   ON THE LEFT   WE WERE SAILING TO   SYRIA   AND   WE ARRIVED

εἰς Τύρον·   ἐκεῖσε γὰρ τὸ πλοῖον ἦν ἀποφορτιζόμενον
IN   TYRE.   FOR~THERE   THE BOAT   WAS UNLOADING

τὸν γόμον. **21.4** ἀνευρόντες δὲ   τοὺς μαθητὰς
THE CARGO.   AND~[AFTER] HAVING SEARCHED FOR THE DISCIPLES,

ἐπεμείναμεν αὐτοῦ ἡμέρας ἑπτά, οἵτινες τῷ
WE STAYED   THERE   SEVEN~DAYS,   WHO

Παύλῳ ἔλεγον διὰ τοῦ πνεύματος μὴ ἐπιβαίνειν εἰς
WERE TELLING~PAUL BY THE SPIRIT   NOT TO GO UP   TO

Ἱεροσόλυμα. **21.5** ὅτε δὲ ἐγένετο   ἡμᾶς ἐξαρτίσαι τὰς
JERUSALEM.   BUT~WHEN IT CAME ABOUT TO BE FINISHED~FOR US THE

ἡμέρας, ἐξελθόντες ἐπορευόμεθα προπεμπόντων ἡμᾶς
DAYS,   HAVING GONE OUT, WE WERE GOING,   ACCOMPANYING   US

πάντων σὺν γυναιξὶ καὶ τέκνοις ἕως ἔξω τῆς
EVERYONE WITH WIVES   AND CHILDREN AS FAR AS OUTSIDE THE

πόλεως, καὶ θέντες τὰ γόνατα ἐπὶ τὸν αἰγιαλὸν
CITY,   AND HAVING BENT THE KNEES   ON THE BEACH,

προσευξάμενοι **21.6** ἀπησπασάμεθα ἀλλήλους καὶ
HAVING PRAYED   WE SAID GOOD-BYE   TO ONE ANOTHER AND

ἀνέβημεν εἰς τὸ πλοῖον, ἐκεῖνοι δὲ ὑπέστρεψαν εἰς τὰ
WE EMBARKED INTO THE BOAT,   AND~THOSE ONES RETURNED   TO   -

ἴδια.
THEIR OWN [HOMES].

21.7 Ἡμεῖς δὲ τὸν πλοῦν διανύσαντες ἀπὸ Τύρου
AND~WE,   THE VOYAGE HAVING COMPLETED FROM TYRE,

κατηντήσαμεν εἰς Πτολεμαΐδα καὶ ἀσπασάμενοι τοὺς
ARRIVED   IN PTOLEMAIS   AND HAVING GREETED   THE

ἀδελφοὺς ἐμείναμεν ἡμέραν μίαν παρ' αὐτοῖς.
BROTHERS   WE STAYED   ONE~DAY   WITH THEM.

21.8 τῇ δὲ   ἐπαύριον ἐξελθόντες ἤλθομεν εἰς
AND~ON THE NEXT DAY,   HAVING GONE OUT, WE CAME   TO

Καισάρειαν καὶ εἰσελθόντες εἰς τὸν οἶκον Φιλίππου
CAESAREA   AND HAVING ENTERED INTO THE HOUSE OF PHILIP,

τοῦ εὐαγγελιστοῦ, ὄντος ἐκ τῶν ἑπτά, ἐμείναμεν παρ'
THE EVANGELIST,   BEING [ONE] OF THE SEVEN, WE STAYED   WITH

αὐτῷ. **21.9** τούτῳ δὲ ἦσαν   θυγατέρες τέσσαρες
HIM.   AND~TO THIS ONE THERE WERE FOUR~DAUGHTERS,

παρθένοι προφητεύουσαι. **21.10** ἐπιμενόντων δὲ
VIRGINS,   PROPHESYING.   AND~REMAINING

ἡμέρας πλείους κατῆλθέν τις   ἀπὸ τῆς Ἰουδαίας
MANY~DAYS   CAME DOWN A CERTAIN ONE FROM THE JEWS,

προφήτης ὀνόματι Ἄγαβος, **21.11** καὶ ἐλθὼν   πρὸς
A PROPHET   BY NAME   AGABUS,   AND HAVING COME TO

ἡμᾶς καὶ ἄρας   τὴν ζώνην τοῦ Παύλου, δήσας
US   AND HAVING TAKEN THE BELT   -   OF PAUL,   HAVING BOUND

[3]We came in sight of Cyprus; and leaving it on our left, we sailed to Syria and landed at Tyre, because the ship was to unload its cargo there. [4]We looked up the disciples and stayed there for seven days. Through the Spirit they told Paul not to go on to Jerusalem. [5]When our days there were ended, we left and proceeded on our journey; and all of them, with wives and children, escorted us outside the city. There we knelt down on the beach and prayed [6]and said farewell to one another. Then we went on board the ship, and they returned home.

7 When we had finished[c] the voyage from Tyre, we arrived at Ptolemais; and we greeted the believers[d] and stayed with them for one day. [8]The next day we left and came to Caesarea; and we went into the house of Philip the evangelist, one of the seven, and stayed with him. [9]He had four unmarried daughters[e] who had the gift of prophecy. [10]While we were staying there for several days, a prophet named Agabus came down from Judea. [11]He came to us and took Paul's belt, bound

[c] Or *continued*
[d] Gk *brothers*
[e] Gk *four daughters, virgins*

his own feet and hands with it, and said, "Thus says the Holy Spirit, 'This is the way the Jews in Jerusalem will bind the man who owns this belt and will hand him over to the Gentiles.'" [12]When we heard this, we and the people there urged him not to go up to Jerusalem. [13]Then Paul answered, "What are you doing, weeping and breaking my heart? For I am ready not only to be bound but even to die in Jerusalem for the name of the Lord Jesus." [14]Since he would not be persuaded, we remained silent except to say, "The Lord's will be done."

15 After these days we got ready and started to go up to Jerusalem. [16]Some of the disciples from Caesarea also came along and brought us to the house of Mnason of Cyprus, an early disciple, with whom we were to stay.

17 When we arrived in Jerusalem, the brothers welcomed us warmly. [18]The next day Paul went with us to visit James; and all the elders were present. [19]After greeting them, he related one by one the things that God had done among the Gentiles through his ministry. [20]When they heard it, they praised

ἑαυτοῦ τοὺς πόδας καὶ τὰς χεῖρας εἶπεν, Τάδε
OF HIMSELF THE FEET AND THE HANDS HE SAID, THESE THINGS

λέγει τὸ πνεῦμα τὸ ἅγιον, Τὸν ἄνδρα οὗ ἐστιν ἡ
SAYS THE ²SPIRIT - ¹HOLY, THE MAN OF WHOM IS -

ζώνη αὕτη, οὕτως δήσουσιν ἐν Ἰερουσαλὴμ οἱ Ἰουδαῖοι
THIS~BELT, THUS WILL BIND IN JERUSALEM THE JEWS

καὶ παραδώσουσιν εἰς χεῖρας ἐθνῶν. **21.12** ὡς δὲ
AND WILL DELIVER [HIM] INTO [THE] HANDS OF [THE] GENTILES. AND~WHEN

ἠκούσαμεν ταῦτα, παρεκαλοῦμεν ἡμεῖς τε καὶ οἱ
WE HEARD THESE THINGS, WE WERE BEGGING [HIM] BOTH~WE AND THE

ἐντόπιοι τοῦ μὴ ἀναβαίνειν αὐτὸν εἰς Ἰερουσαλήμ.
LOCAL RESIDENTS - NOT TO GO UP HIM TO JERUSALEM.

21.13 τότε ἀπεκρίθη ὁ Παῦλος, Τί ποιεῖτε κλαίοντες
THEN ANSWERED - PAUL, WHAT ARE YOU° DOING WEEPING

καὶ συνθρύπτοντές μου τὴν καρδίαν; ἐγὼ γὰρ οὐ
AND BREAKING MY - HEART? FOR~I NOT

μόνον δεθῆναι ἀλλὰ καὶ ἀποθανεῖν εἰς Ἰερουσαλὴμ
ONLY TO BE BOUND BUT ALSO TO DIE IN JERUSALEM

ἑτοίμως ἔχω ὑπὲρ τοῦ ὀνόματος τοῦ κυρίου Ἰησοῦ.
AM~PREPARED FOR THE NAME OF THE LORD JESUS.

21.14 μὴ πειθομένου δὲ αὐτοῦ ἡσυχάσαμεν εἰπόντες,
²NOT ³PERSUADING ¹AND HIM, WE REMAINED SILENT HAVING SAID,

Τοῦ κυρίου τὸ θέλημα γινέσθω.
⁴OF THE ⁵LORD ²THE ³WILL ¹LET BE [DONE].

21.15 Μετὰ δὲ τὰς ἡμέρας ταύτας ἐπισκευασάμενοι
AND~AFTER - THESE~DAYS HAVING MADE PREPARATIONS,

ἀνεβαίνομεν εἰς Ἰεροσόλυμα· **21.16** συνῆλθον δὲ
WE WERE GOING UP TO JERUSALEM. AND~TRAVELED

καὶ τῶν μαθητῶν ἀπὸ Καισαρείας σὺν ἡμῖν,
ALSO [SOME] OF THE DISCIPLES FROM CAESAREA WITH US,

ἄγοντες παρ' ᾧ ξενισθῶμεν Μνάσωνί τινι Κυπρίῳ,
BRINGING [ONE] WITH WHOM WE MIGHT STAY, MNASON, A CERTAIN A CYPRIAN,

ἀρχαίῳ μαθητῇ.
A DISCIPLE~OF LONG STANDING.

21.17 Γενομένων δὲ ἡμῶν εἰς Ἰεροσόλυμα ἀσμένως
AND~HAVING COME US TO JERUSALEM, GLADLY

ἀπεδέξαντο ἡμᾶς οἱ ἀδελφοί. **21.18** τῇ δὲ ἐπιούσῃ
WELCOMED US THE BROTHERS. AND~ON THE FOLLOWING [DAY]

εἰσῄει ὁ Παῦλος σὺν ἡμῖν πρὸς Ἰάκωβον, πάντες τε
WAS GOING IN - PAUL WITH US TO JAMES, AND~ALL

παρεγένοντο οἱ πρεσβύτεροι. **21.19** καὶ ἀσπασάμενος
³CAME ¹THE ²ELDERS. AND HAVING GREETED

αὐτοὺς ἐξηγεῖτο καθ' ἓν ἕκαστον, ὧν
THEM HE WAS EXPLAINING ONE BY ONE, OF WHAT [THINGS]

ἐποίησεν ὁ θεὸς ἐν τοῖς ἔθνεσιν διὰ τῆς
DID - GOD AMONG THE GENTILES THROUGH THE

διακονίας αὐτοῦ. **21.20** οἱ δὲ ἀκούσαντες ἐδόξαζον
MINISTRY OF HIM. AND~THE ONES HAVING HEARD WERE GLORIFYING

τὸν θεὸν εἰπόν τε αὐτῷ, Θεωρεῖς, ἀδελφέ, πόσαι
- GOD   AND~THEY SAID TO HIM, YOU SEE,   BROTHER, HOW MANY

μυριάδες εἰσὶν ἐν τοῖς Ἰουδαίοις τῶν πεπιστευκότων
THOUSANDS THERE ARE AMONG THE JEWS   -   HAVING BELIEVED

καὶ πάντες ζηλωταὶ τοῦ νόμου ὑπάρχουσιν·
AND   ALL   ZEALOTS OF THE LAW   ARE.

21.21 κατηχήθησαν δὲ περὶ σοῦ ὅτι
AND~THEY WERE INFORMED ABOUT YOU THAT

ἀποστασίαν διδάσκεις ἀπὸ Μωϋσέως τοὺς   κατὰ
YOU TEACH~APOSTASY   FROM MOSES   4THE ONES [LIVING] 5AMONG

τὰ ἔθνη πάντας Ἰουδαίους λέγων μὴ περιτέμνειν
6THE 7GENTILES 2ALL   3JEWS, 1TELLING 8NOT 9TO CIRCUMCISE

αὐτοὺς τὰ   τέκνα μηδὲ τοῖς ἔθεσιν περιπατεῖν.
10THEM, THE(THEIR) CHILDREN, NOR IN THE CUSTOMS TO WALK.

21.22 τί   οὖν ἐστιν;   πάντως ἀκούσονται ὅτι
WHAT THEN IS TO BE [DONE]? CERTAINLY THEY WILL HEAR THAT

ἐλήλυθας. **21.23** τοῦτο οὖν   ποίησον ὅ
YOU HAVE COME.   3THIS 1THEREFORE 2DO   WHICH

σοι λέγομεν·   εἰσὶν ἡμῖν ἄνδρες τέσσαρες
WE TELL~YOU.   THERE ARE WITH US FOUR~MEN

εὐχὴν ἔχοντες ἐφ' ἑαυτῶν. **21.24** τούτους παραλαβὼν
HAVING~A VOW UPON THEMSELVES.   HAVING TAKEN~THESE

ἁγνίσθητι σὺν αὐτοῖς καὶ δαπάνησον ἐπ' αὐτοῖς ἵνα
PURIFY YOURSELF WITH THEM AND SPEND [MONEY] ON THEM THAT

ξυρήσονται τὴν   κεφαλήν, καὶ γνώσονται πάντες ὅτι
THEY WILL SHAVE THE(THEIR) HEAD(S), AND EVERYONE~WILL KNOW THAT

ὧν   κατήχηνται   περὶ σοῦ οὐδέν ἐστιν ἀλλὰ
OF WHICH THEY HAVE BEEN INFORMED ABOUT YOU THERE IS~NOTHING BUT

στοιχεῖς   καὶ αὐτὸς   φυλάσσων τὸν νόμον.
YOU ARE IN AGREEMENT ALSO YOURSELF [WITH] KEEPING THE LAW.

21.25 περὶ δὲ   τῶν πεπιστευκότων ἐθνῶν ἡμεῖς
AND~CONCERNING THE GENTILES~HAVING BELIEVED, WE

ἐπεστείλαμεν κρίναντες   φυλάσσεσθαι αὐτοὺς τό τε
WROTE,   HAVING DECIDED [THAT] THEY~AVOID   BOTH~THE

εἰδωλόθυτον καὶ αἷμα καὶ πνικτὸν   καὶ
MEAT OFFERED TO IDOLS AND BLOOD AND STRANGLED [THINGS] AND

πορνείαν. **21.26** τότε ὁ Παῦλος παραλαβὼν τοὺς
SEXUAL IMMORALITY.   THEN - PAUL   HAVING TAKEN   THE

ἄνδρας τῇ   ἐχομένῃ ἡμέρᾳ σὺν αὐτοῖς ἁγνισθεὶς,
MEN   ON THE FOLLOWING DAY, WITH THEM HAVING BEEN PURIFIED

εἰσῄει   εἰς τὸ ἱερόν διαγγέλλων τὴν ἐκπλήρωσιν
HE WAS ENTERING INTO THE TEMPLE GIVING NOTICE OF THE COMPLETION

τῶν ἡμερῶν τοῦ ἁγνισμοῦ ἕως οὗ προσηνέχθη ὑπὲρ
OF THE DAYS OF THE PURIFICATION UNTIL WAS OFFERED FOR

ἑνὸς ἑκάστου αὐτῶν ἡ προσφορά.
EACH~ONE   OF THEM THE OFFERING.

21.27 Ὡς δὲ ἔμελλον αἱ ἑπτὰ ἡμέραι συντελεῖσθαι,
NOW~WHEN WERE ABOUT THE SEVEN DAYS TO BE COMPLETED,

God. Then they said to him, "You see, brother, how many thousands of believers there are among the Jews, and they are all zealous for the law. [21]They have been told about you that you teach all the Jews living among the Gentiles to forsake Moses, and that you tell them not to circumcise their children or observe the customs. [22]What then is to be done? They will certainly hear that you have come. [23]So do what we tell you. We have four men who are under a vow. [24]Join these men, go through the rite of purification with them, and pay for the shaving of their heads. Thus all will know that there is nothing in what they have been told about you, but that you yourself observe and guard the law. [25]But as for the Gentiles who have become believers, we have sent a letter with our judgment that they should abstain from what has been sacrificed to idols and from blood and from what is strangled[f] and from fornication." [26]Then Paul took the men, and the next day, having purified himself, he entered the temple with them, making public the completion of the days of purification when the sacrifice would be made for each of them.

27 When the seven days were almost completed,

f Other ancient authorities lack *and from what is strangled*

the Jews from Asia, who had seen him in the temple, stirred up the whole crowd. They seized him, [28]shouting, "Fellow Israelites, help! This is the man who is teaching everyone everywhere against our people, our law, and this place; more than that, he has actually brought Greeks into the temple and has defiled this holy place." [29]For they had previously seen Trophimus the Ephesian with him in the city, and they supposed that Paul had brought him into the temple. [30]Then all the city was aroused, and the people rushed together. They seized Paul and dragged him out of the temple, and immediately the doors were shut. [31]While they were trying to kill him, word came to the tribune of the cohort that all Jerusalem was in an uproar. [32]Immediately he took soldiers and centurions and ran down to them. When they saw the tribune and the soldiers, they stopped beating Paul. [33]Then the tribune came, arrested him, and ordered him to be bound with two chains; he inquired who he was and what he had done. [34]Some in the crowd shouted one thing, some another; and as he could not learn the facts because of the uproar,

οἱ   ἀπὸ   τῆς   ᾿Ασίας   ᾿Ιουδαῖοι   θεασάμενοι   αὐτὸν   ἐν   τῷ
[1]THE [3]FROM - [4]ASIA [2]JEWS HAVING SEEN HIM IN THE

ἱερῷ   συνέχεον   πάντα   τὸν   ὄχλον   καὶ   ἐπέβαλον   ἐπ᾽
TEMPLE WERE STIRRING UP ALL THE CROWD AND THEY LAID ON

αὐτὸν   τὰς   χεῖρας   21.28 κράζοντες,   ῎Ανδρες
HIM THE(THEIR) HANDS   CRYING OUT, MEN,

᾿Ισραηλῖται,   βοηθεῖτε·   οὗτός   ἐστιν   ὁ   ἄνθρωπος   ὁ
ISRAELITES, HELP [US]! THIS ONE IS THE MAN -

κατὰ   τοῦ   λαοῦ   καὶ   τοῦ   νόμου   καὶ   τοῦ   τόπου   τούτου
AGAINST THE PEOPLE AND THE LAW AND - THIS~PLACE,

πάντας   πανταχῇ   διδάσκων,   ἔτι   τε   καὶ
EVERYONE EVERYWHERE TEACHING, AND~IN ADDITION ALSO

῞Ελληνας   εἰσήγαγεν   εἰς   τὸ   ἱερὸν   καὶ   κεκοίνωκεν   τὸν
HE BROUGHT~GREEKS INTO THE TEMPLE AND HAS DEFILED -

ἅγιον   τόπον   τοῦτον.   21.29 ἦσαν   γὰρ   προεωρακότες
[2]HOLY [3]PLACE [1]THIS.   FOR~THEY HAD PREVIOUSLY SEEN

Τρόφιμον   τὸν   ᾿Εφέσιον   ἐν   τῇ   πόλει   σὺν   αὐτῷ,   ὃν
TROPHIMUS, THE EPHESIAN IN THE CITY WITH HIM, WHOM

ἐνόμιζον   ὅτι   εἰς   τὸ   ἱερὸν   εἰσήγαγεν   ὁ   Παῦλος.
THEY WERE SUPPOSING THAT INTO THE TEMPLE [2]BROUGHT - [1]PAUL.

21.30 ἐκινήθη   τε   ἡ   πόλις   ὅλη   καὶ   ἐγένετο
AND~WAS AROUSED THE WHOLE~CITY AND THERE WAS

συνδρομὴ   τοῦ   λαοῦ,   καὶ   ἐπιλαβόμενοι   τοῦ   Παύλου
A RUNNING TOGETHER OF THE PEOPLE, AND HAVING SEIZED - PAUL

εἷλκον   αὐτὸν   ἔξω   τοῦ   ἱεροῦ   καὶ   εὐθέως
THEY WERE DRAGGING HIM OUTSIDE THE TEMPLE AND IMMEDIATELY

ἐκλείσθησαν   αἱ   θύραι.   21.31 ζητούντων   τε
WERE SHUT THE DOORS.   AND~[WHILE] SEEKING

αὐτὸν   ἀποκτεῖναι   ἀνέβη   φάσις   τῷ   χιλιάρχῳ   τῆς
TO KILL~HIM   A REPORT~WENT UP TO THE COMMANDER OF THE

σπείρης   ὅτι   ὅλη   συγχύννεται   ᾿Ιερουσαλήμ.   21.32 ὃς
COHORT THAT ALL JERUSALEM~IS IN CONFUSION;   WHO

ἐξαυτῆς   παραλαβὼν   στρατιώτας   καὶ   ἑκατοντάρχας
AT ONCE HAVING TAKEN SOLDIERS AND CENTURIONS,

κατέδραμεν   ἐπ᾽   αὐτούς,   οἱ   δὲ   ἰδόντες   τὸν   χιλίαρχον
RAN DOWN TO THEM, - AND HAVING SEEN THE COMMANDER

καὶ   τοὺς   στρατιώτας   ἐπαύσαντο   τύπτοντες   τὸν   Παῦλον.
AND THE SOLDIERS, THEY STOPPED BEATING - PAUL.

21.33 τότε   ἐγγίσας   ὁ   χιλίαρχος   ἐπελάβετο   αὐτοῦ
THEN HAVING COME NEAR THE COMMANDER TOOK HOLD OF HIM

καὶ   ἐκέλευσεν   δεθῆναι   ἁλύσεσι   δυσί,   καὶ   ἐπυνθάνετο
AND ORDERED [HIM] TO BE BOUND WITH TWO~CHAINS, AND HE WAS INQUIRING

τίς   εἴη   καὶ   τί   ἐστιν   πεποιηκώς.   21.34 ἄλλοι   δὲ
WHO HE MIGHT BE AND WHAT HE HAS DONE.   AND~OTHERS

ἄλλο   τι   ἐπεφώνουν   ἐν   τῷ   ὄχλῳ.   μὴ   δυναμένου
SOMETHING~DIFFERENT WERE SHOUTING IN THE CROWD. [3]NOT [4]BEING ABLE

δὲ   αὐτοῦ   γνῶναι   τὸ   ἀσφαλὲς   διὰ   τὸν   θόρυβον
[1]AND [2]HE TO KNOW - SOMETHING DEFINITE BECAUSE OF THE NOISE,

ἐκέλευσεν ἄγεσθαι αὐτὸν εἰς τὴν παρεμβολήν.
ORDERED   HIM~TO BE BROUGHT   INTO THE   BARRACKS.

21.35 ὅτε δὲ ἐγένετο ἐπὶ τοὺς ἀναβαθμούς,
        AND~WHEN HE WAS ON   THE   STEPS,

συνέβη   βαστάζεσθαι αὐτὸν ὑπὸ τῶν στρατιωτῶν
IT CAME ABOUT [THAT] HE~IS CARRIED   BY   THE   SOLDIERS

διὰ   τὴν βίαν τοῦ ὄχλου, **21.36** ἠκολούθει γὰρ τὸ
BECAUSE OF THE VIOLENCE OF THE CROWD,   FOR~WERE FOLLOWING THE

πλῆθος τοῦ   λαοῦ κράζοντες, Αἶρε   αὐτόν.
MULTITUDE OF THE PEOPLE CRYING OUT,   TAKE AWAY HIM!

21.37 Μέλλων τε εἰσάγεσθαι εἰς τὴν παρεμβολὴν ὁ
        AND~BEING ABOUT TO BE BROUGHT   INTO THE   BARRACKS   -

Παῦλος λέγει τῷ χιλιάρχῳ, Εἰ ἔξεστίν   μοι εἰπεῖν
PAUL   SAYS TO THE COMMANDER, IF IT IS PERMISSIBLE FOR ME TO SAY

τι   πρὸς σέ; ὁ δὲ ἔφη, Ἑλληνιστὶ γινώσκεις;
SOMETHING TO   YOU? - AND HE SAID, DO YOU KNOW~GREEK?

21.38 οὐκ ἄρα σὺ εἶ ὁ Αἰγύπτιος ὁ πρὸ τούτων τῶν
        ⁴NOT ¹THEN ²YOU ³ARE THE EGYPTIAN - BEFORE THESE   -

ἡμερῶν ἀναστατώσας καὶ ἐξαγαγὼν εἰς τὴν ἔρημον
DAYS   HAVING RAISED A REVOLT AND   HAVING LED OUT INTO THE DESERT

τοὺς τετρακισχιλίους ἄνδρας τῶν σικαρίων;
THE   FOUR THOUSAND   MEN   OF THE ASSASSINS?

21.39 εἶπεν δὲ ὁ Παῦλος, Ἐγὼ ἄνθρωπος μέν εἰμι
        AND~SAID - PAUL,   I   A MAN   -   AM

Ἰουδαῖος, Ταρσεὺς τῆς Κιλικίας, οὐκ ἀσήμου
A JEW, [FROM] TARSUS   -   OF CILICIA,   NOT ²OF AN INSIGNIFICANT

πόλεως πολίτης· δέομαι δέ σου, ἐπίτρεψόν μοι
³CITY,   ¹A CITIZEN. AND~I ASK   YOU, ALLOW   ME

λαλῆσαι πρὸς τὸν λαόν. **21.40** ἐπιτρέψαντος δὲ αὐτοῦ
TO SPEAK   TO   THE PEOPLE.   ³HAVING PERMITTED [IT] ¹AND ²HE,

ὁ Παῦλος ἑστὼς ἐπὶ τῶν ἀναβαθμῶν κατέσεισεν
- PAUL   HAVING STOOD ON THE STEPS   MOTIONED

τῇ   χειρὶ τῷ λαῷ. πολλῆς δὲ σιγῆς γενομένης
WITH THE(HIS) HAND TO THE PEOPLE. AND~A GREAT SILENCE HAVING COME,

προσεφώνησεν τῇ Ἑβραΐδι διαλέκτῳ λέγων,
HE ADDRESSED [THEM] IN THE HEBREW   LANGUAGE SAYING,

he ordered him to be brought into the barracks. [35]When Paul[g] came to the steps, the violence of the mob was so great that he had to be carried by the soldiers. [36]The crowd that followed kept shouting, "Away with him!"

37 Just as Paul was about to be brought into the barracks, he said to the tribune, "May I say something to you?" The tribune[h] replied, "Do you know Greek? [38]Then you are not the Egyptian who recently stirred up a revolt and led the four thousand assassins out into the wilderness?" [39]Paul replied, "I am a Jew, from Tarsus in Cilicia, a citizen of an important city; I beg you, let me speak to the people." [40]When he had given him permission, Paul stood on the steps and motioned to the people for silence; and when there was a great hush, he addressed them in the Hebrew[i] language, saying:

[g] Gk *he*
[h] Gk *He*

CHAPTER 22

22.1 Ἄνδρες ἀδελφοὶ καὶ πατέρες, ἀκούσατέ μου τῆς
       MEN,   BROTHERS, AND   FATHERS,   LISTEN   TO MY   -

πρὸς ὑμᾶς νυνὶ ἀπολογίας. **22.2** ἀκούσαντες δὲ ὅτι τῇ
²TO   ³YOU⁵ ⁴NOW ¹DEFENSE.   AND~HAVING HEARD   THAT IN THE

Ἑβραΐδι διαλέκτῳ προσεφώνει αὐτοῖς, μᾶλλον παρέσχον
HEBREW   LANGUAGE HE WAS ADDRESSING THEM   THEY BECAME~EVEN MORE

ἡσυχίαν. καὶ φησίν, **22.3** Ἐγώ εἰμι ἀνὴρ Ἰουδαῖος,
QUIET.   AND HE SAYS,   I   AM   A JEWISH~MAN,

"Brothers and fathers, listen to the defense that I now make before you."

2 When they heard him addressing them in Hebrew,[i] they became even more quiet. Then he said:

3 "I am a Jew, born

[i] That is, *Aramaic*

in Tarsus in Cilicia, but brought up in this city at the feet of Gamaliel, educated strictly according to our ancestral law, being zealous for God, just as all of you are today. [4]I persecuted this Way up to the point of death by binding both men and women and putting them in prison, [5]as the high priest and the whole council of elders can testify about me. From them I also received letters to the brothers in Damascus, and I went there in order to bind those who were there and to bring them back to Jerusalem for punishment.

6 "While I was on my way and approaching Damascus, about noon a great light from heaven suddenly shone about me. [7]I fell to the ground and heard a voice saying to me, 'Saul, Saul, why are you persecuting me?' [8]I answered, 'Who are you, Lord?' Then he said to me, 'I am Jesus of Nazareth/ whom you are persecuting.' [9]Now those who were with me saw the light but did not hear the voice of the one who was speaking to me. [10]I asked, 'What am I to do, Lord?' The Lord said to me, 'Get up and go to Damascus; there you will be told everything that has been assigned to you

[j] Gk the Nazorean

γεγεννημένος   ἐν   Ταρσῷ   τῆς   Κιλικίας,
HAVING BEEN BORN   IN   TARSUS   -   OF CILICIA,

ἀνατεθραμμένος δὲ   ἐν   τῇ   πόλει ταύτῃ,   παρὰ   τοὺς   πόδας
BUT~HAVING BEEN BROUGHT UP   IN   -   THIS~CITY   AT   THE   FEET

Γαμαλιὴλ   πεπαιδευμένος   κατὰ   ἀκρίβειαν   τοῦ
OF GAMALIEL   HAVING BEEN EDUCATED   ACCORDING TO   [THE] STRICTNESS   OF THE

πατρῴου νόμου,   ζηλωτὴς ὑπάρχων   τοῦ   θεοῦ   καθὼς
LAW~OF OUR FATHERS,   BEING~ZEALOUS   -   FOR GOD   JUST AS

πάντες ὑμεῖς   ἐστε   σήμερον·   22.4 ὃς   ταύτην τὴν ὁδὸν
ALL   YOU°   ARE   TODAY;   WHO   THIS   -   WAY

ἐδίωξα   ἄχρι   θανάτου   δεσμεύων   καὶ   παραδιδοὺς   εἰς
PERSECUTED   [EVEN] TO   DEATH,   BINDING   AND   DELIVERING   TO

φυλακὰς   ἄνδρας τε   καὶ   γυναῖκας,   22.5 ὡς καὶ   ὁ
JAIL   BOTH~MEN   AND   WOMEN,   EVEN~AS   THE

ἀρχιερεὺς   μαρτυρεῖ   μοι   καὶ   πᾶν   τὸ   πρεσβυτέριον,
HIGH PRIEST   TESTIFIES   TO ME   AND   ALL   THE   COUNCIL OF ELDERS,

παρ᾽   ὧν   καὶ   ἐπιστολὰς   δεξάμενος   πρὸς   τοὺς
FROM   WHOM   ALSO   LETTERS   HAVING RECEIVED   TO   THE

ἀδελφοὺς   εἰς   Δαμασκὸν   ἐπορευόμην,   ἄξων   καὶ
BROTHERS   IN   DAMASCUS   I WAS GOING,   LEADING AWAY   ALSO

τοὺς   ἐκεῖσε ὄντας   δεδεμένους   εἰς   Ἰερουσαλὴμ ἵνα
THE ONES   BEING~THERE   HAVING BEEN BOUND   TO   JERUSALEM   THAT

τιμωρηθῶσιν.
THEY MIGHT BE PUNISHED.

22.6 Ἐγένετο δέ   μοι   πορευομένῳ καὶ   ἐγγίζοντι   τῇ
AND~IT HAPPENED   TO ME   [WHILE] TRAVELING AND   DRAWING NEAR   -

Δαμασκῷ   περὶ   μεσημβρίαν   ἐξαίφνης   ἐκ   τοῦ
TO DAMASCUS   ABOUT   MIDDAY,   SUDDENLY   FROM   -

οὐρανοῦ   περιαστράψαι φῶς ἱκανὸν   περὶ   ἐμέ,
HEAVEN   TO SHINE   A VERY BRIGHT~LIGHT   AROUND   ME,

22.7 ἔπεσά τε   εἰς   τὸ   ἔδαφος   καὶ   ἤκουσα φωνῆς
AND~I FELL   TO   THE   GROUND   AND   I HEARD   A VOICE

λεγούσης   μοι,   Σαοὺλ   Σαούλ,   τί   με διώκεις;
SAYING   TO ME,   SAUL,   SAUL,   WHY   ARE YOU PERSECUTING~ME?

22.8 ἐγὼ δὲ ἀπεκρίθην,   Τίς   εἶ,   κύριε;   εἶπέν τε   πρός
AND~I   ANSWERED,   WHO   ARE YOU,   LORD?   AND~HE SAID   TO

με,   Ἐγώ εἰμι   Ἰησοῦς   ὁ   Ναζωραῖος,   ὃν   σὺ
ME,   I   AM   JESUS,   THE   NAZARENE,   WHOM   YOU

διώκεις.   22.9 οἱ δὲ   σὺν ἐμοὶ ὄντες   τὸ   μὲν   φῶς
ARE PERSECUTING.   AND~THE ONES WITH   ME   BEING,   THE   -   LIGHT

ἐθεάσαντο   τὴν δὲ   φωνὴν   οὐκ ἤκουσαν   τοῦ   λαλοῦντός
SAW,   BUT~THE   VOICE   THEY DID NOT HEAR   -   SPEAKING

μοι.   22.10 εἶπον δέ,   Τί   ποιήσω, κύριε;   ὁ δὲ   κύριος
TO ME.   AND~I SAID,   WHAT   MAY I DO,   LORD?   AND~THE   LORD

εἶπεν   πρός   με,   Ἀναστὰς   πορεύου   εἰς   Δαμασκὸν κἀκεῖ
SAID   TO   ME,   HAVING ARISEN,   GO   INTO   DAMASCUS   AND THERE

σοι   λαληθήσεται περὶ   πάντων   ὧν   τέτακταί   σοι
TO YOU   IT WILL BE TOLD   ABOUT   EVERYTHING   WHICH   HAS BEEN APPOINTED   FOR YOU

ποιῆσαι. **22.11** ὡς δὲ   οὐκ ἐνέβλεπον ἀπὸ τῆς δόξης
TO DO.   AND~BECAUSE I WAS NOT SEEING   FROM THE GLORY

τοῦ φωτὸς ἐκείνου, χειραγωγούμενος ὑπὸ τῶν
-      OF THAT~LIGHT, BEING LED BY THE HAND   BY   THE ONES

συνόντων μοι ἦλθον εἰς Δαμασκόν.
BEING WITH ME, I CAME INTO DAMASCUS.

22.12 Ἀνανίας δέ τις,   ἀνὴρ εὐλαβὴς κατὰ
³ANANIAS   ¹AND ²A CERTAIN, A DEVOUT~MAN   ACCORDING TO

τὸν νόμον, μαρτυρούμενος ὑπὸ πάντων τῶν
THE LAW,   BEING WELL-SPOKEN OF BY ALL   THE

κατοικούντων Ἰουδαίων, **22.13** ἐλθὼν   πρός με καὶ
JEWS~LIVING [THERE],   HAVING COME TO ME AND

ἐπιστὰς   εἶπέν μοι, Σαοὺλ ἀδελφέ, ἀνάβλεψον.
HAVING STOOD BY, HE SAID TO ME, BROTHER~SAUL, RECEIVE YOUR SIGHT.

κἀγὼ αὐτῇ τῇ ὥρᾳ ἀνέβλεψα εἰς αὐτόν. **22.14** ὁ δὲ
AND I THIS - HOUR LOOKED UP AT HIM.   - AND

εἶπεν, Ὁ θεὸς τῶν πατέρων ἡμῶν προεχειρίσατό σε
HE SAID, THE GOD OF THE FATHERS OF US APPOINTED   YOU

γνῶναι τὸ θέλημα αὐτοῦ καὶ ἰδεῖν τὸν δίκαιον καὶ
TO KNOW THE WILL OF HIM AND TO SEE THE RIGHTEOUS ONE AND

ἀκοῦσαι φωνὴν ἐκ τοῦ στόματος αὐτοῦ, **22.15** ὅτι
TO HEAR A CALL FROM THE MOUTH OF HIM,   BECAUSE

ἔσῃ   μάρτυς αὐτῷ πρὸς πάντας ἀνθρώπους ὧν
YOU WILL BE A WITNESS TO HIM TO ALL   MEN   OF WHAT

ἑώρακας καὶ ἤκουσας. **22.16** καὶ νῦν τί
YOU HAVE SEEN AND HEARD.   AND NOW WHAT

μέλλεις;   ἀναστὰς βάπτισαι καὶ ἀπόλουσαι τὰς
DO YOU INTEND [TO DO]? HAVING ARISEN, BE BAPTIZED AND WASH AWAY THE

ἁμαρτίας σου ἐπικαλεσάμενος τὸ ὄνομα αὐτοῦ.
SINS   OF YOU, HAVING CALLED UPON THE NAME OF HIM.

22.17 Ἐγένετο δέ μοι ὑποστρέψαντι εἰς Ἰερουσαλὴμ
AND~IT HAPPENED TO ME HAVING RETURNED TO JERUSALEM

καὶ προσευχομένου μου ἐν τῷ ἱερῷ   γενέσθαι με
AND [AS] I [WAS]~PRAYING IN THE TEMPLE [THAT] I~CAME TO BE

ἐν ἐκστάσει **22.18** καὶ ἰδεῖν αὐτὸν λέγοντά μοι,
IN A TRANCE,   AND TO SEE HIM SAYING   TO ME,

Σπεῦσον καὶ ἔξελθε ἐν τάχει ἐξ Ἰερουσαλήμ, διότι
HURRY   AND GET OUT QUICKLY FROM JERUSALEM,   BECAUSE

οὐ παραδέξονταί σου μαρτυρίαν περὶ   ἐμοῦ.
THEY WILL NOT RECEIVE YOUR TESTIMONY CONCERNING ME.

22.19 κἀγὼ εἶπον, Κύριε, αὐτοὶ ἐπίστανται ὅτι ἐγὼ
AND I SAID, LORD, THEY KNOW~THEMSELVES THAT I

ἤμην φυλακίζων καὶ δέρων κατὰ   τὰς συναγωγὰς
WAS IMPRISONING AND BEATING THROUGHOUT THE SYNAGOGUES

τοὺς πιστεύοντας ἐπὶ σέ, **22.20** καὶ ὅτε ἐξεχύννετο
THE ONES BELIEVING ON YOU,   AND WHEN WAS BEING POURED OUT

τὸ αἷμα Στεφάνου τοῦ μάρτυρός σου, καὶ αὐτὸς
THE BLOOD OF STEPHEN, THE WITNESS OF YOU, ALSO MYSELF

to do.' [11]Since I could not see because of the brightness of that light, those who were with me took my hand and led me to Damascus.

[12]"A certain Ananias, who was a devout man according to the law and well spoken of by all the Jews living there, [13]came to me; and standing beside me, he said, 'Brother Saul, regain your sight!' In that very hour I regained my sight and saw him. [14]Then he said, 'The God of our ancestors has chosen you to know his will, to see the Righteous One and to hear his own voice; [15]for you will be his witness to all the world of what you have seen and heard. [16]And now why do you delay? Get up, be baptized, and have your sins washed away, calling on his name.'

[17]"After I had returned to Jerusalem and while I was praying in the temple, I fell into a trance [18]and saw Jesus[k] saying to me, 'Hurry and get out of Jerusalem quickly, because they will not accept your testimony about me.' [19]And I said, 'Lord, they themselves know that in every synagogue I imprisoned and beat those who believed in you. [20]And while the blood of your witness Stephen was shed, I myself

[k] Gk *him*

was standing by, approving and keeping the coats of those who killed him.' ²¹Then he said to me, 'Go, for I will send you far away to the Gentiles.'"

22 Up to this point they listened to him, but then they shouted, "Away with such a fellow from the earth! For he should not be allowed to live." ²³And while they were shouting, throwing off their cloaks, and tossing dust into the air, ²⁴the tribune directed that he was to be brought into the barracks, and ordered him to be examined by flogging, to find out the reason for this outcry against him. ²⁵But when they had tied him up with thongs,ˡ Paul said to the centurion who was standing by, "Is it legal for you to flog a Roman citizen who is uncondemned?" ²⁶When the centurion heard that, he went to the tribune and said to him, "What are you about to do? This man is a Roman citizen." ²⁷The tribune came and asked Paul,ᵐ "Tell me, are you a Roman citizen?" And he said, "Yes." ²⁸The tribune answered, "It cost me a large sum of money to get my citizenship." Paul said, "But I was born a citizen." ²⁹Immediately those who were about to examine him drew back

ˡ Or up for the lashes
ᵐ Gk him

ἤμην ἐφεστὼς καὶ συνευδοκῶν καὶ φυλάσσων τὰ
I HAD BEEN STANDING [BY] AND AGREEING AND PROTECTING THE

ἱμάτια τῶν ἀναιρούντων αὐτόν. **22.21** καὶ εἶπεν
GARMENTS OF THE ONES KILLING HIM. AND HE SAID

πρός με, Πορεύου, ὅτι ἐγὼ εἰς ἔθνη μακρὰν
TO ME, GO, BECAUSE I TO [THE] GENTILES FAR AWAY

ἐξαποστελῶ σε.
I WILL SEND OUT YOU.

22.22 Ἤκουον δὲ αὐτοῦ ἄχρι τούτου τοῦ λόγου
AND~THEY WERE LISTENING TO HIM UP TO THIS - WORD

καὶ ἐπῆραν τὴν φωνὴν αὐτῶν λέγοντες, Αἶρε ἀπὸ
AND THEY LIFTED UP THE VOICE OF THEM SAYING, TAKE AWAY FROM

τῆς γῆς τὸν τοιοῦτον, οὐ γὰρ καθῆκεν αὐτὸν ζῆν.
THE EARTH - SUCH A ONE, FOR~IT WAS NOT FITTING FOR HIM TO LIVE.

22.23 κραυγαζόντων τε αὐτῶν καὶ ῥιπτούντων τὰ
AND~CRYING OUT THEY AND THROWING OFF THE(THEIR)

ἱμάτια καὶ κονιορτὸν βαλλόντων εἰς τὸν ἀέρα,
GARMENTS AND THROWING~DUST INTO THE AIR,

22.24 ἐκέλευσεν ὁ χιλίαρχος εἰσάγεσθαι αὐτὸν εἰς τὴν
³ORDERED ¹THE ²COMMANDER ⁵TO BE BROUGHT ⁴HIM INTO THE

παρεμβολήν, εἴπας μάστιξιν ἀνετάζεσθαι αὐτὸν ἵνα
BARRACKS, HAVING SAID WITH WHIPS TO BE EXAMINED HIM THAT

ἐπιγνῷ δι' ἣν αἰτίαν οὕτως ἐπεφώνουν αὐτῷ.
HE MAY KNOW FOR WHAT REASON THEY WERE SHOUTING~THUS TO HIM.

22.25 ὡς δὲ προέτειναν αὐτὸν τοῖς ἱμᾶσιν, εἶπεν
AND~WHEN THEY STRETCHED OUT HIM WITH THE STRAPS, SAID

πρὸς τὸν ἑστῶτα ἑκατόνταρχον ὁ Παῦλος, Εἰ ἄνθρωπον
TO THE CENTURION~HAVING STOOD [BY] - PAUL, IF A MAN [IS]

Ῥωμαῖον καὶ ἀκατάκριτον ἔξεστιν ὑμῖν μαστίζειν;
A ROMAN AND UNCONDEMNED, IT IS LAWFUL FOR YOU° TO WHIP [HIM]?

22.26 ἀκούσας δὲ ὁ ἑκατοντάρχης προσελθὼν τῷ
AND~HAVING HEARD [THIS], THE CENTURION HAVING APPROACHED THE

χιλιάρχῳ ἀπήγγειλεν λέγων, Τί μέλλεις ποιεῖν;
COMMANDER, REPORTED SAYING, WHAT ARE YOU ABOUT TO DO?

ὁ γὰρ ἄνθρωπος οὗτος Ῥωμαῖός ἐστιν.
- FOR THIS~MAN IS~A ROMAN.

22.27 προσελθὼν δὲ ὁ χιλίαρχος εἶπεν αὐτῷ, Λέγε
AND~HAVING APPROACHED THE COMMANDER SAID TO HIM, TELL

μοι, σὺ Ῥωμαῖος εἶ; ὁ δὲ ἔφη, Ναί.
ME, ²YOU ³A ROMAN ¹ARE? - AND HE SAID, YES.

22.28 ἀπεκρίθη δὲ ὁ χιλίαρχος, Ἐγὼ πολλοῦ
AND~ANSWERED THE COMMANDER, I [WITH] A LARGE

κεφαλαίου τὴν πολιτείαν ταύτην ἐκτησάμην. ὁ δὲ
SUM OF MONEY - THIS~CITIZENSHIP ACQUIRED. - AND

Παῦλος ἔφη, Ἐγὼ δὲ καὶ γεγέννημαι.
PAUL SAID, BUT~I INDEED HAVE BEEN BORN [A CITIZEN].

22.29 εὐθέως οὖν ἀπέστησαν ἀπ' αὐτοῦ οἱ
IMMEDIATELY THEN WITHDREW FROM HIM THE ONES

μέλλοντες αὐτὸν ἀνετάζειν, καὶ ὁ χιλίαρχος δὲ
BEING ABOUT   TO EXAMINE~HIM,   ALSO THE COMMANDER,   AND

ἐφοβήθη ἐπιγνοὺς ὅτι Ῥωμαῖός ἐστιν καὶ ὅτι αὐτὸν
HE WAS AFRAID HAVING LEARNED THAT HE IS~A ROMAN   AND   THAT HIM

ἦν δεδεκώς.
HE HAD BOUND.

22.30 Τῇ δὲ ἐπαύριον βουλόμενος γνῶναι τὸ
         AND~ON THE NEXT DAY   DESIRING   TO KNOW   -

ἀσφαλές, τὸ τί κατηγορεῖται ὑπὸ τῶν Ἰουδαίων,
SOMETHING DEFINITE, - WHY HE IS ACCUSED   BY   THE   JEWS,

ἔλυσεν αὐτὸν καὶ ἐκέλευσεν συνελθεῖν τοὺς ἀρχιερεῖς
HE RELEASED HIM   AND   ORDERED   TO BE ASSEMBLED THE   CHIEF PRIESTS

καὶ πᾶν τὸ συνέδριον, καὶ καταγαγὼν τὸν Παῦλον
AND ALL THE   COUNCIL,   AND HAVING BROUGHT DOWN -   PAUL,

ἔστησεν εἰς αὐτούς.
HE SET [HIM] BEFORE THEM.

from him; and the tribune also was afraid, for he realized that Paul was a Roman citizen and that he had bound him.

30 Since he wanted to find out what Paul[n] was being accused of by the Jews, the next day he released him and ordered the chief priests and the entire council to meet. He brought Paul down and had him stand before them.

[n] Gk *he*

23.1 ἀτενίσας δὲ ὁ Παῦλος τῷ συνεδρίῳ εἶπεν,
        AND~HAVING GAZED   -   PAUL   AT THE COUNCIL,   HE SAID,

Ἄνδρες ἀδελφοί, ἐγὼ πάσῃ συνειδήσει ἀγαθῇ
MEN,   BROTHERS,   I   IN ALL   GOOD~CONSCIENCE

πεπολίτευμαι τῷ θεῷ ἄχρι ταύτης τῆς ἡμέρας.
I HAVE LIVED [BEFORE] -   GOD UNTIL THIS   -   DAY.

23.2 ὁ δὲ ἀρχιερεὺς Ἀνανίας ἐπέταξεν τοῖς
        AND~THE HIGH PRIEST   ANANIAS   ORDERED   THE ONES

παρεστῶσιν αὐτῷ τύπτειν αὐτοῦ τὸ στόμα. **23.3** τότε ὁ
HAVING STOOD [BY] HIM   TO STRIKE   HIS   -   MOUTH.   THEN -

Παῦλος πρὸς αὐτὸν εἶπεν, Τύπτειν σε μέλλει ὁ
PAUL   TO   HIM   SAID, [3]TO STRIKE [4]YOU, [YOU] [2]IS ABOUT -

θεός, τοῖχε κεκονιαμένε· καὶ σὺ κάθῃ κρίνων με
[1]GOD, WALL HAVING BEEN WHITEWASHED. AND YOU SIT JUDGING ME

κατὰ τὸν νόμον καὶ παρανομῶν κελεύεις με
ACCORDING TO THE LAW   AND VIOLATING THE LAW DO YOU COMMAND ME

τύπτεσθαι; **23.4** οἱ δὲ παρεστῶτες εἶπαν, Τὸν
TO BE HIT?   AND~THE ONES HAVING STOOD [BY] SAID,   THE

ἀρχιερέα τοῦ θεοῦ λοιδορεῖς; **23.5** ἔφη τε ὁ Παῦλος,
HIGH PRIEST   -   OF GOD DO YOU REVILE?   AND~SAID -   PAUL,

Οὐκ ᾔδειν, ἀδελφοί, ὅτι ἐστὶν ἀρχιερεύς·
I HAD NOT KNOWN, BROTHERS,   THAT HE IS [THE] HIGH PRIEST.

γέγραπται γὰρ ὅτι Ἄρχοντα τοῦ λαοῦ σου
FOR~IT HAS BEEN WRITTEN, - A RULER   OF THE PEOPLE OF YOU

οὐκ ἐρεῖς κακῶς.
YOU WILL NOT SPEAK EVIL [OF].

While Paul was looking intently at the council he said, "Brothers,[o] up to this day I have lived my life with a clear conscience before God." [2]Then the high priest Ananias ordered those standing near him to strike him on the mouth. [3]At this Paul said to him, "God will strike you, you whitewashed wall! Are you sitting there to judge me according to the law, and yet in violation of the law you order me to be struck?" [4]Those standing nearby said, "Do you dare to insult God's high priest?" [5]And Paul said, "I did not realize, brothers, that he was high priest; for it is written, 'You shall not speak evil of a leader of your people.'"

[o] Gk *Men, brothers*

23:5 Exod. 22:28

6 When Paul noticed that some were Sadducees and others were Pharisees, he called out in the council, "Brothers, I am a Pharisee, a son of Pharisees. I am on trial concerning the hope of the resurrection*p* of the dead." 7When he said this, a dissension began between the Pharisees and the Sadducees, and the assembly was divided. 8(The Sadducees say that there is no resurrection, or angel, or spirit; but the Pharisees acknowledge all three.) 9Then a great clamor arose, and certain scribes of the Pharisees' group stood up and contended, "We find nothing wrong with this man. What if a spirit or an angel has spoken to him?" 10When the dissension became violent, the tribune, fearing that they would tear Paul to pieces, ordered the soldiers to go down, take him by force, and bring him into the barracks.

11 That night the Lord stood near him and said, "Keep up your courage! For just as you have testified for me in Jerusalem, so you must bear witness also in Rome."

12 In the morning the Jews joined in a conspiracy and bound themselves by an

p Gk *concerning hope and resurrection*

23.6 Γνοὺς δὲ ὁ Παῦλος ὅτι τὸ ἓν μέρος ἐστὶν
AND~HAVING KNOWN - PAUL THAT - ONE PARTY IS

Σαδδουκαίων τὸ δὲ ἕτερον Φαρισαίων ἔκραζεν ἐν
OF SADDUCEES AND~THE OTHER OF PHARISEES, HE WAS CRYING OUT IN

τῷ συνεδρίῳ, Ἄνδρες ἀδελφοί, ἐγὼ Φαρισαῖός εἰμι,
THE COUNCIL, MEN, BROTHERS, I AM~A PHARISEE,

υἱὸς Φαρισαίων, περὶ ἐλπίδος καὶ ἀναστάσεως
[THE] SON OF PHARISEES; CONCERNING [THE] HOPE AND [THE] RESURRECTION

νεκρῶν [ἐγὼ] κρίνομαι. **23.7** τοῦτο δὲ αὐτοῦ εἰπόντος
OF [THE] DEAD I AM BEING JUDGED. NOW~THIS HE HAVING SAID,

ἐγένετο στάσις τῶν Φαρισαίων καὶ Σαδδουκαίων
THERE CAME ABOUT A DISPUTE OF THE PHARISEES AND SADDUCEES

καὶ ἐσχίσθη τὸ πλῆθος. **23.8** Σαδδουκαῖοι μὲν γὰρ
AND WAS DIVIDED THE MULTITUDE. 2SADDUCEES - 1FOR

λέγουσιν μὴ εἶναι ἀνάστασιν μήτε ἄγγελον μήτε
SAY NOT TO BE A RESURRECTION NOR AN ANGEL NOR

πνεῦμα, Φαρισαῖοι δὲ ὁμολογοῦσιν τὰ ἀμφότερα.
A SPIRIT, BUT~PHARISEES ACKNOWLEDGE ALL~THESE THINGS.

23.9 ἐγένετο δὲ κραυγὴ μεγάλη, καὶ ἀναστάντες τινὲς
AND~THERE WAS A LOUD~CRY, AND HAVING ARISEN SOME

τῶν γραμματέων τοῦ μέρους τῶν Φαρισαίων
OF THE SCRIBES OF THE PARTIES OF THE PHARISEES,

διεμάχοντο λέγοντες, Οὐδὲν κακὸν εὑρίσκομεν ἐν
WERE ARGUING VIGOROUSLY SAYING, NOTHING EVIL DO WE FIND IN

τῷ ἀνθρώπῳ τούτῳ· εἰ δὲ πνεῦμα ἐλάλησεν αὐτῷ
- THIS~MAN. AND~[WHAT] IF A SPIRIT SPOKE TO HIM

ἢ ἄγγελος; **23.10** Πολλῆς δὲ γινομένης στάσεως
OR AN ANGEL? 3MUCH 1AND 2COMING ABOUT 4DISSENSION,

φοβηθεὶς ὁ χιλίαρχος μὴ διασπασθῇ ὁ Παῦλος
HAVING BEEN AFRAID THE COMMANDER LEST MAY BE TORN TO PIECES - PAUL

ὑπ' αὐτῶν ἐκέλευσεν τὸ στράτευμα καταβὰν
BY THEM, HE ORDERED THE TROOPS HAVING GONE DOWN

ἁρπάσαι αὐτὸν ἐκ μέσου αὐτῶν ἄγειν τε εἰς τὴν
TO TAKE AWAY HIM FROM [THE] MIDST OF THEM AND~TO BRING [HIM] INTO THE

παρεμβολήν.
BARRACKS.

23.11 Τῇ δὲ ἐπιούσῃ νυκτὶ ἐπιστὰς αὐτῷ ὁ
AND~ON THE FOLLOWING NIGHT HAVING STOOD [BY] HIM THE

κύριος εἶπεν, Θάρσει· ὡς γὰρ διεμαρτύρω
LORD SAID, BE COURAGEOUS. FOR~AS YOU TESTIFIED

τὰ περὶ ἐμοῦ εἰς Ἰερουσαλήμ, οὕτω σε δεῖ
ABOUT~THE THINGS OF ME IN JERUSALEM, THUS IT IS NECESSARY~FOR YOU

καὶ εἰς Ῥώμην μαρτυρῆσαι.
ALSO IN ROME TO TESTIFY.

23.12 Γενομένης δὲ ἡμέρας ποιήσαντες συστροφὴν οἱ
NOW~HAVING BECOME DAY, HAVING FORMED A CONSPIRACY THE

Ἰουδαῖοι ἀνεθεμάτισαν ἑαυτοὺς λέγοντες μήτε
JEWS, THEY BOUND WITH AN OATH THEMSELVES SAYING NEITHER

φαγεῖν μήτε πιεῖν ἕως οὗ ἀποκτείνωσιν τὸν Παῦλον.
TO EAT   NOR   DRINK UNTIL   THEY MAY KILL   -   PAUL.

23.13 ἦσαν δὲ   πλείους τεσσεράκοντα οἱ   ταύτην
NOW~THERE WERE MORE [THAN] FORTY   THE ONES THIS

τὴν συνωμοσίαν ποιησάμενοι, **23.14** οἵτινες
-    PLOT   HAVING FORMED,   WHO

προσελθόντες τοῖς ἀρχιερεῦσιν καὶ τοῖς πρεσβυτέροις
HAVING APPROACHED THE CHIEF PRIESTS AND THE ELDERS

εἶπαν, Ἀναθέματι ἀνεθεματίσαμεν ἑαυτοὺς μηδενὸς
SAID, WITH AN OATH WE BOUND   OURSELVES, OF NOTHING

γεύσασθαι ἕως οὗ ἀποκτείνωμεν τὸν Παῦλον. **23.15** νῦν
TO TASTE   UNTIL   WE MAY KILL   -   PAUL.   NOW

οὖν   ὑμεῖς ἐμφανίσατε τῷ χιλιάρχῳ σὺν τῷ
THEREFORE YOU° NOTIFY   THE COMMANDER WITH THE

συνεδρίῳ ὅπως καταγάγῃ   αὐτὸν εἰς ὑμᾶς ὡς
COUNCIL   SO THAT HE MAY BRING DOWN HIM   TO YOU°, AS

μέλλοντας διαγινώσκειν ἀκριβέστερον τὰ   περὶ
INTENDING TO DETERMINE MORE ACCURATELY THE THINGS CONCERNING

αὐτοῦ· ἡμεῖς δὲ πρὸ τοῦ ἐγγίσαι αὐτὸν ἕτοιμοί ἐσμεν
HIM.   AND~WE   BEFORE - HE~DRAWS NEAR ARE~READY

τοῦ ἀνελεῖν αὐτόν. **23.16** Ἀκούσας δὲ ὁ υἱὸς τῆς
-   TO KILL   HIM.   NOW~HAVING HEARD THE SON OF THE

ἀδελφῆς Παύλου τὴν ἐνέδραν, παραγενόμενος καὶ
SISTER OF PAUL   THE AMBUSH, HAVING COME   AND

εἰσελθὼν εἰς τὴν παρεμβολὴν ἀπήγγειλεν τῷ Παύλῳ.
HAVING ENTERED INTO THE BARRACKS   HE REPORTED [THIS] - TO PAUL.

23.17 προσκαλεσάμενος δὲ ὁ Παῦλος ἕνα τῶν
³HAVING SUMMONED   ¹AND - ²PAUL   ONE OF THE

ἑκατονταρχῶν ἔφη, Τὸν νεανίαν τοῦτον ἀπάγαγε πρὸς
CENTURIONS   SAID, - THIS~YOUNG MAN   BRING   TO

τὸν χιλίαρχον, ἔχει γὰρ ἀπαγγεῖλαί τι αὐτῷ. **23.18** ὁ
THE COMMANDER, FOR~HE HAS SOMETHING~TO REPORT TO HIM.   -

μὲν οὖν   παραλαβὼν αὐτὸν ἤγαγεν   πρὸς τὸν
-   THEREFORE HAVING TAKEN HIM, HE BROUGHT [HIM] TO THE

χιλίαρχον καὶ φησίν, Ὁ δέσμιος Παῦλος
COMMANDER AND HE SAYS, THE PRISONER PAUL

προσκαλεσάμενός με ἠρώτησεν τοῦτον τὸν νεανίσκον
HAVING SUMMONED   ME ASKED [ME] THIS   -   YOUNG MAN

ἀγαγεῖν πρὸς σέ ἔχοντά τι   λαλῆσαί σοι.
TO BRING TO YOU, HAVING SOMETHING TO SAY TO YOU.

23.19 ἐπιλαβόμενος δὲ τῆς   χειρὸς αὐτοῦ ὁ χιλίαρχος
AND~HAVING GRASPED   THE(HIS) HAND OF HIM, THE COMMANDER,

καὶ ἀναχωρήσας κατ᾽ ἰδίαν ἐπυνθάνετο, Τί ἐστιν ὃ
AND HAVING WITHDRAWN PRIVATELY HE WAS INQUIRING, WHAT IS IT WHICH

ἔχεις ἀπαγγεῖλαί μοι; **23.20** εἶπεν δὲ ὅτι Οἱ
YOU HAVE TO REPORT   TO ME?   AND~HE SAID, - THE

Ἰουδαῖοι συνέθεντο τοῦ ἐρωτῆσαί σε ὅπως αὔριον τὸν
JEWS   AGREED   -   TO ASK   YOU SO THAT TOMORROW -

oath neither to eat nor drink until they had killed Paul. [13]There were more than forty who joined in this conspiracy. [14]They went to the chief priests and elders and said, "We have strictly bound ourselves by an oath to taste no food until we have killed Paul. [15]Now then, you and the council must notify the tribune to bring him down to you, on the pretext that you want to make a more thorough examination of his case. And we are ready to do away with him before he arrives."

16 Now the son of Paul's sister heard about the ambush; so he went and gained entrance to the barracks and told Paul. [17]Paul called one of the centurions and said, "Take this young man to the tribune, for he has something to report to him." [18]So he took him, brought him to the tribune, and said, "The prisoner Paul called me and asked me to bring this young man to you; he has something to tell you." [19]The tribune took him by the hand, drew him aside privately, and asked, "What is it that you have to report to me?" [20]He answered, "The Jews have agreed to ask you

to bring Paul down to the council tomorrow, as though they were going to inquire more thoroughly into his case. ²¹But do not be persuaded by them, for more than forty of their men are lying in ambush for him. They have bound themselves by an oath neither to eat nor drink until they kill him. They are ready now and are waiting for your consent." ²²So the tribune dismissed the young man, ordering him, "Tell no one that you have informed me of this."

23 Then he summoned two of the centurions and said, "Get ready to leave by nine o'clock tonight for Caesarea with two hundred soldiers, seventy horsemen, and two hundred spearmen. ²⁴Also provide mounts for Paul to ride, and take him safely to Felix the governor." ²⁵He wrote a letter to this effect:

26 "Claudius Lysias to his Excellency the governor Felix, greetings. ²⁷This man was seized by the Jews and was about to be killed by them, but when I had learned that he was a Roman citizen, I came with the guard and rescued him. ²⁸Since I wanted to know the charge for which they accused him, I had him brought to their council.

Παῦλον   καταγάγῃς   εἰς τὸ συνέδριον ὡς μέλλον
PAUL   MAY BE BROUGHT DOWN TO THE COUNCIL AS INTENDING

τι   ἀκριβέστερον πυνθάνεσθαι περὶ   αὐτοῦ.
SOMETHING MORE ACCURATE TO INQUIRE   CONCERNING HIM.

23.21 σὺ οὖν   μὴ πεισθῇς   αὐτοῖς·
        THEREFORE~YOU   SHOULD NOT BE PERSUADED BY THEM.

ἐνεδρεύουσιν γὰρ   αὐτὸν ἐξ αὐτῶν ἄνδρες πλείους
FOR~THEY ARE LYING IN WAIT FOR HIM,   OF THEM   MEN   MORE [THAN]

τεσσεράκοντα, οἵτινες ἀνεθεμάτισαν ἑαυτοὺς μήτε
FORTY,   WHO   TOOK AN OATH UPON THEMSELVES NEITHER

φαγεῖν μήτε πιεῖν ἕως οὗ ἀνέλωσιν αὐτόν, καὶ νῦν
TO EAT   NOR   TO DRINK UNTIL   THEY MAY KILL HIM,   AND   NOW

εἰσιν ἕτοιμοι προσδεχόμενοι τὴν ἀπὸ σοῦ ἐπαγγελίαν.
THEY ARE READY,   ANTICIPATING   THE ²FROM ³YOU ¹PROMISE.

23.22 ὁ μὲν οὖν   χιλίαρχος ἀπέλυσε τὸν νεανίσκον
        ²THE -   ¹THEREFORE COMMANDER DISMISSED THE YOUNG MAN

παραγγείλας μηδενὶ ἐκλαλῆσαι ὅτι ταῦτα ἐνεφάνισας
HAVING GIVEN ORDERS TO TELL~NO ONE   THAT YOU REPORTED~THESE THINGS

πρός με.
TO   ME.

23.23 Καὶ προσκαλεσάμενος δύο [τινὰς] τῶν
        AND   HAVING SUMMONED   A CERTAIN~TWO   OF THE

ἑκατονταρχῶν εἶπεν, Ἑτοιμάσατε στρατιώτας διακοσίους,
CENTURIONS   HE SAID, PREPARE   TWO HUNDRED~SOLDIERS,

ὅπως πορευθῶσιν ἕως Καισαρείας, καὶ
SO THAT THEY MAY GO   TO   CAESAREA,   AND

ἱππεῖς ἑβδομήκοντα καὶ δεξιολάβους διακοσίους ἀπὸ
SEVENTY~HORSEMEN   AND TWO HUNDRED~BOWMEN   FROM

τρίτης ὥρας τῆς νυκτός, **23.24** κτήνη τε παραστῆσαι
[THE] THIRD HOUR OF THE NIGHT,   AND~ANIMALS TO STAND BY

ἵνα ἐπιβιβάσαντες τὸν Παῦλον διασώσωσι   πρὸς
THAT HAVING PUT ON   -   PAUL,   THEY MAY BRING [HIM] SAFELY TO

Φήλικα τὸν ἡγεμόνα, **23.25** γράψας   ἐπιστολὴν
FELIX,   THE GOVERNOR,   HAVING WRITTEN A LETTER

ἔχουσαν τὸν τύπον τοῦτον· **23.26** Κλαύδιος Λυσίας τῷ
HAVING   -   THIS~FORM: CLAUDIUS   LYSIAS, TO THE

κρατίστῳ ἡγεμόνι Φήλικι χαίρειν. **23.27** Τὸν
MOST EXCELLENT GOVERNOR, FELIX,   GREETINGS.   -

ἄνδρα τοῦτον συλλημφθέντα ὑπὸ τῶν Ἰουδαίων καὶ
THIS~MAN   HAVING BEEN SEIZED BY   THE   JEWS   AND

μέλλοντα ἀναιρεῖσθαι ὑπ' αὐτῶν ἐπιστὰς   σὺν τῷ
BEING ABOUT TO BE KILLED   BY   THEM,   HAVING APPROACHED WITH THE

στρατεύματι ἐξειλάμην μαθὼν   ὅτι Ῥωμαῖός ἐστιν.
SOLDIERS,   I DELIVERED [HIM] HAVING LEARNED THAT HE IS~A ROMAN.

23.28 βουλόμενός τε ἐπιγνῶναι τὴν αἰτίαν δι' ἣν
        AND~DESIRING   TO KNOW   THE CAUSE   FOR WHICH

ἐνεκάλουν   αὐτῷ, κατήγαγον   εἰς τὸ συνέδριον
THEY WERE ACCUSING HIM,   I BROUGHT [HIM] DOWN TO THE COUNCIL

αὐτῶν **23.29** ὃν   εὗρον ἐγκαλούμενον περὶ ζητημάτων
OF THEM,   WHOM I FOUND BEING ACCUSED   ABOUT ISSUES

τοῦ νόμου αὐτῶν, μηδὲν δὲ ἄξιον θανάτου ἢ δεσμῶν
OF THE LAW   OF THEM, AND~NOTHING WORTHY OF DEATH OR OF BONDS

ἔχοντα ἔγκλημα. **23.30** μηνυθείσης δέ   μοι ἐπιβουλῆς
HAVING A CHARGE.   AND~HAVING BEEN REVEALED TO ME A PLOT

εἰς   τὸν ἄνδρα ἔσεσθαι ἐξαυτῆς ἔπεμψα πρὸς σέ
AGAINST THE MAN   TO BE,   IMMEDIATELY I SENT [HIM] TO   YOU,

παραγγείλας καὶ τοῖς κατηγόροις λέγειν [τὰ]
HAVING GIVEN ORDERS ALSO TO THE ACCUSERS   TO SPEAK THESE THINGS

πρὸς αὐτὸν ἐπὶ σοῦ.
AGAINST HIM   TO YOU.

23.31 Οἱ μὲν οὖν στρατιῶται κατὰ   τὸ
        THE -   SOLDIERS~THEREFORE ACCORDING TO THE THING

διατεταγμένον   αὐτοῖς ἀναλαβόντες τὸν Παῦλον
HAVING BEEN COMMANDED THEM,   HAVING TAKEN ALONG -   PAUL,

ἤγαγον διὰ νυκτὸς εἰς τὴν Ἀντιπατρίδα,
BROUGHT [HIM] DURING [THE] NIGHT TO -   ANTIPATRIS,

23.32 τῇ δὲ   ἐπαύριον ἐάσαντες τοὺς ἱππεῖς
        AND~ON THE NEXT DAY, HAVING ALLOWED THE   HORSEMEN

ἀπέρχεσθαι σὺν αὐτῷ ὑπέστρεψαν εἰς τὴν
TO DEPART   WITH HIM,   THEY RETURNED TO THE

παρεμβολήν· **23.33** οἵτινες εἰσελθόντες εἰς τὴν
BARRACKS;   WHO   HAVING ENTERED INTO -

Καισάρειαν καὶ ἀναδόντες τὴν ἐπιστολὴν τῷ ἡγεμόνι
CAESAREA   AND HAVING DELIVERED THE LETTER   TO THE GOVERNOR,

παρέστησαν καὶ τὸν Παῦλον αὐτῷ.   **23.34** ἀναγνοὺς δὲ
THEY PRESENTED ALSO - PAUL   TO HIM.   AND~HAVING READ

καὶ ἐπερωτήσας ἐκ ποίας ἐπαρχείας ἐστὶν, καὶ
AND HAVING ASKED FROM WHAT PROVINCE   HE IS, AND

πυθόμενος ὅτι   ἀπὸ Κιλικίας, **23.35** Διακούσομαί
HAVING LEARNED THAT [HE WAS] FROM CILICIA,   I WILL GIVE A HEARING

σου, ἔφη, ὅταν καὶ οἱ κατήγοροί σου παραγένωνται·
TO YOU, HE SAID, WHEN ALSO THE ACCUSERS OF YOU ARRIVE;

κελεύσας   ἐν τῷ πραιτωρίῳ τοῦ Ἡρῴδου
HAVING COMMANDED IN THE PRAETORIUM - OF HEROD

φυλάσσεσθαι αὐτόν.
TO BE GUARDED   HIM.

CHAPTER 24

24.1 Μετὰ δὲ πέντε ἡμέρας κατέβη ὁ ἀρχιερεὺς
        AND~AFTER FIVE DAYS CAME DOWN THE HIGH PRIEST

Ἀνανίας μετὰ πρεσβυτέρων τινῶν καὶ ῥήτορος
ANANIAS WITH SOME~ELDERS   AND AN ORATOR

Τερτύλλου τινός, οἵτινες ἐνεφάνισαν τῷ
A CERTAIN~TERTULLUS, WHO EXPLAINED   TO THE

[29]I found that he was accused concerning questions of their law, but was charged with nothing deserving death or imprisonment. [30]When I was informed that there would be a plot against the man, I sent him to you at once, ordering his accusers also to state before you what they have against him.*q*"

31 So the soldiers, according to their instructions, took Paul and brought him during the night to Antipatris. [32]The next day they let the horsemen go on with him, while they returned to the barracks. [33]When they came to Caesarea and delivered the letter to the governor, they presented Paul also before him. [34]On reading the letter, he asked what province he belonged to, and when he learned that he was from Cilicia, [35]he said, "I will give you a hearing when your accusers arrive." Then he ordered that he be kept under guard in Herod's headquarters.*r*

q Other ancient authorities add *Farewell*
r Gk *praetorium*

Five days later the high priest Ananias came down with some elders and an attorney, a certain Tertullus, and they reported their case against Paul to the governor. ²When Paul⁵ had been summoned, Tertullus began to accuse him, saying:

"Your Excellency,ᵗ because of you we have long enjoyed peace, and reforms have been made for this people because of your foresight. ³We welcome this in every way and everywhere with utmost gratitude. ⁴But, to detain you no further, I beg you to hear us briefly with your customary graciousness. ⁵We have, in fact, found this man a pestilent fellow, an agitator among all the Jews throughout the world, and a ringleader of the sect of the Nazarenes.ᵘ ⁶He even tried to profane the temple, and so we seized him.ᵛ ⁸By examining him yourself you will be able to learn from him concerning everything of which we accuse him."

9 The Jews also joined in the charge by asserting that all this was true.

10 When the governor motioned to him to speak, Paul replied:

"I cheerfully make my defense, knowing that for many years you have been a judge over this nation. ¹¹As you can find out, it is not more than twelve days since

⁵ Gk he
ᵗ Gk lacks Your Excellency
ᵘ Gk Nazoreans
ᵛ Other ancient authorities add and we would have judged him according to our law. ⁷But the chief captain Lysias came and with great violence took him out of our hands, ⁸commanding his accusers to come before you.

ἡγεμόνι κατὰ τοῦ Παύλου. **24.2** κληθέντος δὲ
GOVERNOR [THE CHARGES] AGAINST - PAUL. AND~HAVING CALLED

αὐτοῦ ἤρξατο κατηγορεῖν ὁ Τέρτυλλος λέγων, Πολλῆς
HIM, ²BEGAN ³TO ACCUSE [HIM] - ¹TERTULLUS, SAYING, MUCH

εἰρήνης τυγχάνοντες διὰ σοῦ καὶ διορθωμάτων
PEACE HAVING ATTAINED THROUGH YOU AND REFORMS

γινομένων τῷ ἔθνει τούτῳ διὰ τῆς σῆς προνοίας,
COMING - TO THIS~NATION BY - YOUR FORESIGHT,

24.3 πάντῃ τε καὶ πανταχοῦ ἀποδεχόμεθα,
BOTH~IN EVERY WAY AND EVERYWHERE WE ACKNOWLEDGE [THIS],

κράτιστε Φῆλιξ, μετὰ πάσης εὐχαριστίας.
MOST EXCELLENT FELIX, WITH ALL GRATITUDE.

24.4 ἵνα δὲ μὴ ἐπὶ πλεῖόν σε ἐγκόπτω, παρακαλῶ
BUT~IN ORDER THAT NOT ANY LONGER I MAY DETAIN~YOU, I BEG

ἀκοῦσαί σε ἡμῶν συντόμως τῇ σῇ ἐπιεικείᾳ.
YOU~TO HEAR US BRIEFLY - IN YOUR KINDNESS.

24.5 εὑρόντες γὰρ τὸν ἄνδρα τοῦτον λοιμὸν καὶ
FOR~HAVING FOUND - THIS~MAN TROUBLESOME AND

κινοῦντα στάσεις πᾶσιν τοῖς Ἰουδαίοις τοῖς κατὰ
INCITING RIOTS [AMONG] ALL THE JEWS - THROUGHOUT

τὴν οἰκουμένην πρωτοστάτην τε τῆς τῶν Ναζωραίων
THE WORLD, AND~A LEADER OF THE ²OF THE ³NAZARENES

αἱρέσεως, **24.6** ὃς καὶ τὸ ἱερὸν ἐπείρασεν βεβηλῶσαι
¹SECT, WHO ALSO THE TEMPLE TRIED TO DESECRATE

ὃν καὶ ἐκρατήσαμεν,ᵀ **24.8** παρ' οὗ δυνήσῃ
WHOM ALSO WE APPREHENDED, FROM WHOM YOU WILL BE ABLE

αὐτὸς ἀνακρίνας περὶ πάντων τούτων
YOURSELF HAVING EXAMINED [HIM] CONCERNING ALL THESE THINGS

ἐπιγνῶναι ὧν ἡμεῖς κατηγοροῦμεν αὐτοῦ.
TO FIND OUT OF WHAT WE ACCUSE HIM.

24.9 συνεπέθεντο δὲ καὶ οἱ Ἰουδαῖοι φάσκοντες
AND~JOINED IN THE ATTACK ALSO THE JEWS SAYING

ταῦτα οὕτως ἔχειν.
THESE THINGS TO BE~SO.

24.10 Ἀπεκρίθη τε ὁ Παῦλος νεύσαντος αὐτῷ τοῦ
AND~ANSWERED - PAUL, HAVING NODDED TO HIM THE

ἡγεμόνος λέγειν, Ἐκ πολλῶν ἐτῶν ὄντα σε κριτὴν
GOVERNOR TO SPEAK, [THAT] FOR MANY YEARS YOU~BEING A JUDGE

τῷ ἔθνει τούτῳ ἐπιστάμενος εὐθύμως τὰ περὶ
- TO THIS NATION KNOWING, CHEERFULLY THE THINGS CONCERNING

ἐμαυτοῦ ἀπολογοῦμαι, **24.11** δυναμένου σου ἐπιγνῶναι
ME I MAKE MY DEFENSE, YOU~BEING ABLE TO LEARN

ὅτι οὐ πλείους εἰσίν μοι ἡμέραι δώδεκα ἀφ' ἧς
THAT NOT MORE [THAN] ³THERE ARE ⁴TO ME ²DAYS ¹TWELVE FROM WHICH

24:6 text: ASV RSV NASB NIV NEB TEV NJB NRSV. add vv. 6b-8a; and we would have judged him according to our law. 7 But the chief captain Lysias came and with great violence took him out of our hands, 8 commanding his accusers to come before you—KJV ASVmg RSVmg NASBmg NIVmg NEBmg TEVmg NJBmg NRSVmg.

ἀνέβην προσκυνήσων εἰς Ἱερουσαλήμ. **24.12** καὶ οὔτε
I WENT UP   WORSHIPING   TO   JERUSALEM.   AND   NEITHER

ἐν τῷ ἱερῷ εὗρόν με πρός τινα διαλεγόμενον ἢ
IN   THE   TEMPLE   DID THEY FIND   ME   WITH   ANYONE   CONVERSING   OR

ἐπίστασιν ποιοῦντα ὄχλου οὔτε ἐν ταῖς συναγωγαῖς
STIRRING UP   MAKING   [THE] CROWD   NOR   IN   THE   SYNAGOGUES

οὔτε κατὰ τὴν πόλιν, **24.13** οὐδὲ παραστῆσαι δύνανταί
NOR   THROUGHOUT   THE   CITY,   NOR   ARE THEY ABLE~TO PROVE

σοι περὶ ὧν νυνὶ κατηγοροῦσίν μου.
TO YOU   CONCERNING   [THE THINGS] OF WHICH   NOW   THEY ARE ACCUSING   ME.

24.14 ὁμολογῶ δὲ τοῦτό σοι ὅτι κατὰ τὴν ὁδὸν ἣν
BUT~I CONFESS   THIS   TO YOU   THAT   ACCORDING TO THE   WAY   WHICH

λέγουσιν αἵρεσιν, οὕτως λατρεύω τῷ πατρῴῳ θεῷ,
THEY CALL   A SECT,   THUS   I SERVE   THE   ANCESTRAL   GOD,

πιστεύων πᾶσι τοῖς κατὰ τὸν νόμον καὶ τοῖς
BELIEVING   IN ALL   THE THINGS   ACCORDING TO   THE   LAW   AND   THE THINGS

ἐν τοῖς προφήταις γεγραμμένοις, **24.15** ἐλπίδα ἔχων
IN   THE   PROPHETS   HAVING BEEN WRITTEN,   HAVING~HOPE

εἰς τὸν θεόν ἣν καὶ αὐτοὶ οὗτοι προσδέχονται,
TOWARD   -   GOD,   WHICH   ALSO   THESE ONES~THEMSELVES ANTICIPATE,

ἀνάστασιν μέλλειν ἔσεσθαι δικαίων τε καὶ
A RESURRECTION   TO BE ABOUT   TO BE   OF BOTH~[THE] RIGHTEOUS   AND

ἀδίκων. **24.16** ἐν τούτῳ καὶ αὐτὸς ἀσκῶ
[THE] UNRIGHTEOUS.   BY   THIS   ALSO   MYSELF   I DO MY BEST

ἀπρόσκοπον συνείδησιν ἔχειν πρὸς τὸν θεὸν καὶ τοὺς
²A BLAMELESS   ³CONSCIENCE   ¹TO HAVE   TOWARD   -   GOD   AND   -

ἀνθρώπους διὰ παντός. **24.17** δι᾽ ἐτῶν δὲ πλειόνων
MEN   ALWAYS.   ²AFTER   ⁴YEARS   ¹NOW   ³MANY

ἐλεημοσύνας ποιήσων εἰς τὸ ἔθνος μου παρεγενόμην
BRINGING~ALMS   TO   THE   NATION   OF ME   I CAME

καὶ προσφοράς, **24.18** ἐν αἷς εὗρόν με
AND [MADE]   SACRIFICES,   IN   WHICH   THEY FOUND   ME

ἡγνισμένον ἐν τῷ ἱερῷ οὐ μετὰ ὄχλου οὐδὲ μετὰ
HAVING BEEN PURIFIED   IN   THE   TEMPLE,   NOT   WITH   A CROWD   NOR   WITH

θορύβου, **24.19** τινὲς δὲ ἀπὸ τῆς Ἀσίας Ἰουδαῖοι, οὓς
AN UPROAR,   BUT~SOME   ²FROM   -   ³ASIA   ¹JEWS,   WHO

ἔδει ἐπὶ σοῦ παρεῖναι καὶ κατηγορεῖν εἰ
IT WAS NECESSARY   BEFORE   YOU   TO BE PRESENT   AND   TO MAKE ACCUSATION   IF

τι ἔχοιεν πρὸς ἐμέ. **24.20** ἢ αὐτοὶ οὗτοι
SOMETHING   THEY MIGHT HAVE   AGAINST   ME.   OR   THESE~THEMSELVES,

εἰπάτωσαν τί εὗρον ἀδίκημα στάντος μου ἐπὶ
LET THEM SAY   WHAT   CRIME~THEY FOUND   [WHEN] HAVING STOOD   ME   BEFORE

τοῦ συνεδρίου, **24.21** ἢ περὶ μιᾶς ταύτης φωνῆς
THE   COUNCIL,   UNLESS   ABOUT   THIS~ONE   DECLARATION

ἧς ἐκέκραξα ἐν αὐτοῖς ἑστὼς ὅτι Περὶ
WHICH   I CRIED OUT   AMONG   THEM   HAVING STOOD,   -   CONCERNING

ἀναστάσεως νεκρῶν ἐγὼ κρίνομαι σήμερον ἐφ᾽ ὑμῶν.°
[THE] RESURRECTION   OF [THE] DEAD   I   AM BEING JUDGED   TODAY   BY   YOU.

I went up to worship in Jerusalem. [12]They did not find me disputing with anyone in the temple or stirring up a crowd either in the synagogues or throughout the city. [13]Neither can they prove to you the charge that they now bring against me. [14]But this I admit to you, that according to the Way, which they call a sect, I worship the God of our ancestors, believing everything laid down according to the law or written in the prophets. [15]I have a hope in God—a hope that they themselves also accept—that there will be a resurrection of both[w] the righteous and the unrighteous. [16]Therefore I do my best always to have a clear conscience toward God and all people. [17]Now after some years I came to bring alms to my nation and to offer sacrifices. [18]While I was doing this, they found me in the temple, completing the rite of purification, without any crowd or disturbance. [19]But there were some Jews from Asia—they ought to be here before you to make an accusation, if they have anything against me. [20]Or let these men here tell what crime they had found when I stood before the council, [21]unless it was this one sentence that I called out while standing before them, 'It is about the resurrection ot the dead that I am on trial before you today.'"

[w] Other ancient authorities read *of the dead, both of*

22 But Felix, who was rather well informed about the Way, adjourned the hearing with the comment, "When Lysias the tribune comes down, I will decide your case." ²³Then he ordered the centurion to keep him in custody, but to let him have some liberty and not to prevent any of his friends from taking care of his needs.

24 Some days later when Felix came with his wife Drusilla, who was Jewish, he sent for Paul and heard him speak concerning faith in Christ Jesus. ²⁵And as he discussed justice, self-control, and the coming judgment, Felix became frightened and said, "Go away for the present; when I have an opportunity, I will send for you." ²⁶At the same time he hoped that money would be given him by Paul, and for that reason he used to send for him very often and converse with him.

27 After two years had passed, Felix was succeeded by Porcius Festus; and since he wanted to grant the Jews a favor, Felix left Paul in prison.

24.22 Ἀνεβάλετο   δὲ   αὐτοὺς   ὁ   Φῆλιξ,
³ADJOURNED   ¹AND   ⁴THEM   -   ²FELIX,

ἀκριβέστερον εἰδὼς   τὰ   περὶ τῆς ὁδοῦ εἴπας,
HAVING KNOWN~MORE ACCURATELY THE THINGS ABOUT THE WAY, HAVING SAID,

Ὅταν Λυσίας ὁ   χιλίαρχος   καταβῇ,   διαγνώσομαι
WHEN LYSIAS, THE COMMANDER, COMES DOWN, I WILL DECIDE

τὰ   καθ'   ὑμᾶς·   **24.23** διαταξάμενος τῷ
THE THINGS RELATING TO YOU°.   HAVING GIVEN ORDERS TO THE

ἑκατοντάρχῃ τηρεῖσθαι αὐτὸν ἔχειν τε   ἄνεσιν καὶ
CENTURION TO GUARD HIM AND~TO HAVE [SOME] FREEDOM AND

μηδένα κωλύειν τῶν ἰδίων αὐτοῦ ὑπηρετεῖν αὐτῷ.
TO PREVENT~NO ONE - OF HIS~OWN TO SERVE HIM.

24.24 Μετὰ δὲ   ἡμέρας τινὰς παραγενόμενος ὁ Φῆλιξ
AND~AFTER SOME~DAYS, HAVING ARRIVED - FELIX

σὺν Δρουσίλλῃ τῇ ἰδίᾳ γυναικὶ οὔσῃ Ἰουδαίᾳ
WITH DRUSILLA, HIS OWN WIFE, BEING A JEWESS,

μετεπέμψατο τὸν Παῦλον καὶ ἤκουσεν αὐτοῦ περὶ
HE SUMMONED - PAUL AND HE LISTENED TO HIM CONCERNING

τῆς εἰς Χριστὸν Ἰησοῦν πίστεως.   **24.25** διαλεγομένου
- ²IN ³CHRIST ⁴JESUS ¹FAITH.   ³CONVERSING

δὲ αὐτοῦ περὶ δικαιοσύνης καὶ ἐγκρατείας καὶ τοῦ
¹AND ²HE ABOUT RIGHTEOUSNESS AND SELF-CONTROL AND OF THE

κρίματος τοῦ μέλλοντος, ἔμφοβος γενόμενος ὁ Φῆλιξ
²JUDGMENT - ¹COMING, HAVING BECOME~AFRAID - FELIX

ἀπεκρίθη, Τὸ νῦν ἔχον   πορεύου, καιρὸν δὲ
ANSWERED, - FOR THE PRESENT, GO, ³TIME ¹AND

μεταλαβὼν μετακαλέσομαί σε,   **24.26** ἅμα   καὶ
²HAVING FOUND, I WILL SEND FOR YOU, AT THE SAME TIME ALSO

ἐλπίζων ὅτι χρήματα δοθήσεται αὐτῷ ὑπὸ τοῦ
HOPING THAT MONEY WILL BE GIVEN TO HIM BY -

Παῦλου· διὸ   καὶ πυκνότερον αὐτὸν μεταπεμπόμενος
PAUL. THEREFORE ALSO MORE FREQUENTLY SENDING FOR~HIM

ὡμίλει   αὐτῷ.
HE WAS CONVERSING WITH HIM.

24.27 Διετίας δὲ   πληρωθείσης ἔλαβεν διάδοχον ὁ
AND~TWO YEARS HAVING PASSED ²RECEIVED ³A SUCCESSOR -

Φῆλιξ Πόρκιον Φῆστον, θέλων τε χάριτα καταθέσθαι
¹FELIX, PORCIUS FESTUS, AND~WANTING TO GRANT~A FAVOR

τοῖς Ἰουδαίοις ὁ Φῆλιξ κατέλιπε τὸν Παῦλον
TO THE JEWS, - FELIX LEFT - PAUL

δεδεμένον.
HAVING BEEN BOUND.

25.1 Φῆστος οὖν ἐπιβὰς τῇ ἐπαρχείᾳ μετὰ τρεῖς
THEREFORE~FESTUS HAVING ARRIVED IN THE PROVINCE, AFTER THREE

ἡμέρας ἀνέβη εἰς Ἱεροσόλυμα ἀπὸ Καισαρείας,
DAYS, HE WENT UP TO JERUSALEM FROM CAESAREA,

25.2 ἐνεφάνισάν τε αὐτῷ οἱ ἀρχιερεῖς καὶ οἱ πρῶτοι
AND~EXPLAINED TO HIM THE CHIEF PRIESTS AND THE LEADING MEN

τῶν Ἰουδαίων κατὰ τοῦ Παύλου καὶ παρεκάλουν
OF THE JEWS [THE CHARGES] AGAINST - PAUL AND THEY WERE BEGGING

αὐτὸν **25.3** αἰτούμενοι χάριν κατ' αὐτοῦ ὅπως
HIM ASKING A FAVOR OF HIM SO THAT

μεταπέμψηται αὐτὸν εἰς Ἱερουσαλήμ, ἐνέδραν ποιοῦντες
HE MIGHT SUMMON HIM TO JERUSALEM, [WHILE] FORMING~A PLOT

ἀνελεῖν αὐτὸν κατὰ τὴν ὁδόν. **25.4** ὁ μὲν οὖν
TO KILL HIM ALONG THE WAY. - - THEREFORE

Φῆστος ἀπεκρίθη τηρεῖσθαι τὸν Παῦλον εἰς
FESTUS ANSWERED TO BE KEPT - PAUL IN

Καισάρειαν, ἑαυτὸν δὲ μέλλειν ἐν τάχει ἐκπορεύεσθαι·
CAESAREA, AND~[HE] HIMSELF TO INTEND QUICKLY TO GO OUT [THERE].

25.5 Οἱ οὖν ἐν ὑμῖν, φησίν, δυνατοὶ
- THEREFORE, AMONG YOU°, HE SAYS, [THE] PROMINENT MEN

συγκαταβάντες εἴ τί ἐστιν ἐν τῷ ἀνδρὶ
HAVING COME DOWN WITH [ME] IF ANYTHING IS ²WITH ³THE ⁴MAN

ἄτοπον κατηγορείτωσαν αὐτοῦ.
¹WRONG LET THEM BRING CHARGES AGAINST HIM.

25.6 Διατρίψας δὲ ἐν αὐτοῖς ἡμέρας οὐ πλείους ὀκτὼ
AND~HAVING STAYED WITH THEM DAYS NO MORE [THAN] EIGHT

ἢ δέκα, καταβὰς εἰς Καισάρειαν, τῇ ἐπαύριον
OR TEN, HAVING COME DOWN TO CAESAREA, ON THE NEXT DAY

καθίσας ἐπὶ τοῦ βήματος ἐκέλευσεν τὸν Παῦλον
HAVING SAT ON THE JUDGMENT SEAT, HE ORDERED - PAUL

ἀχθῆναι. **25.7** παραγενομένου δὲ αὐτοῦ
TO BE BROUGHT. ³HAVING ARRIVED, ¹AND [AFTER] ²HE,

περιέστησαν αὐτὸν οἱ ἀπὸ Ἱεροσολύμων
⁹STOOD AROUND ¹⁰HIM ⁴THE ⁷FROM ⁸JERUSALEM

καταβεβηκότες Ἰουδαῖοι πολλὰ καὶ βαρέα αἰτιώματα
⁶HAVING COME DOWN ⁵JEWS, MANY AND SERIOUS CHARGES

καταφέροντες ἃ οὐκ ἴσχυον ἀποδεῖξαι, **25.8** τοῦ
BRINGING AGAINST [HIM] WHICH THEY WERE NOT ABLE TO PROVE,

Παύλου ἀπολογουμένου ὅτι Οὔτε εἰς τὸν νόμον
PAUL DEFENDING HIMSELF [SAYING], - NEITHER AGAINST THE LAW

τῶν Ἰουδαίων οὔτε εἰς τὸ ἱερὸν οὔτε εἰς
OF THE JEWS, NOR AGAINST THE TEMPLE, NOR AGAINST

Καίσαρά τι ἥμαρτον. **25.9** ὁ Φῆστος δὲ θέλων
CAESAR HAVE I SINNED [AGAINST]~ANYTHING. - AND~FESTUS WANTING

τοῖς Ἰουδαίοις χάριν καταθέσθαι ἀποκριθεὶς τῷ
FOR THE JEWS TO GRANT~A FAVOR, HAVING ANSWERED -

Three days after Festus had arrived in the province, he went up from Caesarea to Jerusalem ²where the chief priests and the leaders of the Jews gave him a report against Paul. They appealed to him ³and requested, as a favor to them against Paul,ˣ to have him transferred to Jerusalem. They were, in fact, planning an ambush to kill him along the way. ⁴Festus replied that Paul was being kept at Caesarea, and that he himself intended to go there shortly. ⁵"So," he said, "let those of you who have the authority come down with me, and if there is anything wrong about the man, let them accuse him."

6 After he had stayed among them not more than eight or ten days, he went down to Caesarea; the next day he took his seat on the tribunal and ordered Paul to be brought. ⁷When he arrived, the Jews who had gone down from Jerusalem surrounded him, bringing many serious charges against him, which they could not prove. ⁸Paul said in his defense, "I have in no way committed an offense against the law of the Jews, or against the temple, or against the emperor." ⁹But Festus, wishing to do the Jews a favor, asked

ˣ Gk *him*

Paul, "Do you wish to go up to Jerusalem and be tried there before me on these charges?" [10]Paul said, "I am appealing to the emperor's tribunal; this is where I should be tried. I have done no wrong to the Jews, as you very well know. [11]Now if I am in the wrong and have committed something for which I deserve to die, I am not trying to escape death; but if there is nothing to their charges against me, no one can turn me over to them. I appeal to the emperor." [12]Then Festus, after he had conferred with his council, replied, "You have appealed to the emperor; to the emperor you will go."

[13] After several days had passed, King Agrippa and Bernice arrived at Caesarea to welcome Festus. [14]Since they were staying there several days, Festus laid Paul's case before the king, saying, "There is a man here who was left in prison by Felix. [15]When I was in Jerusalem, the chief priests and the elders of the Jews informed me about him and asked for a sentence against him. [16]I told them that it was not the custom of the Romans to hand over anyone before the accused had met the accusers face to face

Παύλῳ εἶπεν, Θέλεις εἰς Ἱεροσόλυμα ἀναβὰς ἐκεῖ
PAUL, SAID, DO YOU WANT TO JERUSALEM HAVING GONE UP THERE

περὶ τούτων κριθῆναι ἐπ' ἐμοῦ; **25.10** εἶπεν δὲ ὁ
CONCERNING THESE THINGS TO BE JUDGED BY ME? AND~SAID -

Παῦλος, Ἐπὶ τοῦ βήματος Καίσαρός ἐστώς εἰμι, οὗ
PAUL, BEFORE THE JUDGMENT SEAT OF CAESAR I HAVE STOOD, WHERE

με δεῖ κρίνεσθαι. Ἰουδαίους οὐδὲν ἠδίκησα
IT IS NECESSARY~FOR ME TO BE JUDGED. ³JEWS ²NO ¹I WRONGED

ὡς καὶ σὺ κάλλιον ἐπιγινώσκεις. **25.11** εἰ μὲν οὖν
AS ALSO YOU VERY WELL KNOW. IF - THEN

ἀδικῶ καὶ ἄξιον θανάτου πέπραχά τι,
I DO WRONG AND WORTHY OF DEATH I HAVE DONE ANYTHING,

οὐ παραιτοῦμαι τὸ ἀποθανεῖν· εἰ δὲ οὐδέν ἐστιν
I DO NOT REFUSE - TO DIE. BUT~IF THERE IS~NOTHING

ὧν οὗτοι κατηγοροῦσίν μου, οὐδείς με
OF [THE THINGS] WHICH THESE ONES ACCUSE ME, NO ONE ³ME

δύναται αὐτοῖς χαρίσασθαι· Καίσαρα ἐπικαλοῦμαι.
¹IS ABLE ⁴TO THEM ²TO HAND OVER. I APPEAL~TO CAESAR.

25.12 τότε ὁ Φῆστος συλλαλήσας μετὰ τοῦ συμβουλίου
THEN - FESTUS HAVING TALKED WITH THE COUNCIL

ἀπεκρίθη, Καίσαρα ἐπικέκλησαι, ἐπὶ Καίσαρα
ANSWERED, TO CAESAR YOU HAVE APPEALED, TO CAESAR

πορεύσῃ.
YOU WILL GO.

25.13 Ἡμερῶν δὲ διαγενομένων τινῶν Ἀγρίππας
³DAYS ¹NOW [AFTER] ⁴HAVING PASSED ²SOME, AGRIPPA,

ὁ βασιλεὺς καὶ Βερνίκη κατήντησαν εἰς Καισάρειαν
THE KING, AND BERNICE ARRIVED IN CAESAREA

ἀσπασάμενοι τὸν Φῆστον. **25.14** ὡς δὲ πλείους
HAVING PAID THEIR RESPECTS - TO FESTUS. AND~WHILE MANY

ἡμέρας διέτριβον ἐκεῖ, ὁ Φῆστος τῷ βασιλεῖ
DAYS THEY WERE SPENDING THERE, - FESTUS TO THE KING

ἀνέθετο τὰ κατὰ τὸν Παῦλον λέγων,
LAID OUT THE THINGS WITH RESPECT TO - PAUL SAYING,

Ἀνήρ τίς ἐστιν καταλελειμμένος ὑπὸ Φήλικος δέσμιος,
A CERTAIN~MAN HAS BEEN LEFT BEHIND BY FELIX, A PRISONER,

25.15 περὶ οὗ γενομένου μου εἰς Ἱεροσόλυμα
ABOUT WHOM, I~HAVING GONE TO JERUSALEM,

ἐνεφάνισαν οἱ ἀρχιερεῖς καὶ οἱ πρεσβύτεροι τῶν
MADE KNOWN THE CHIEF PRIESTS AND THE ELDERS OF THE

Ἰουδαίων αἰτούμενοι κατ' αὐτοῦ καταδίκην.
JEWS REQUESTING AGAINST HIM A SENTENCE OF CONDEMNATION.

25.16 πρὸς οὓς ἀπεκρίθην ὅτι οὐκ ἔστιν ἔθος
TO WHOM I ANSWERED THAT IT IS NOT A CUSTOM -

Ῥωμαίοις χαρίζεσθαί τινα ἄνθρωπον πρὶν ἢ ὁ
WITH ROMANS TO HAND OVER ANY MAN, BEFORE THE ONE

κατηγορούμενος κατὰ πρόσωπον ἔχοι τοὺς
BEING ACCUSED FACE TO FACE SHOULD HAVE THE

κατηγόρους τόπον τε   ἀπολογίας λάβοι
ACCUSERS   AND~AN OPPORTUNITY [FOR] A DEFENSE   MIGHT RECEIVE

περὶ   τοῦ ἐγκλήματος. **25.17** συνελθόντων οὖν
CONCERNING THE ACCUSATION.   ³HAVING ASSEMBLED ¹THEREFORE

[αὐτῶν] ἐνθάδε ἀναβολὴν μηδεμίαν ποιησάμενος τῇ
²THEY   HERE,   NO DELAY   HAVING MADE,   ON THE

ἑξῆς   καθίσας ἐπὶ τοῦ βήματος ἐκέλευσα
NEXT [DAY] HAVING SAT DOWN ON THE JUDGMENT SEAT I ORDERED

ἀχθῆναι τὸν ἄνδρα· **25.18** περὶ οὗ   σταθέντες   οἱ
TO BE BROUGHT THE MAN.   ABOUT WHOM, HAVING BEEN STANDING, THE

κατήγοροι οὐδεμίαν αἰτίαν ἔφερον   ὧν   ἐγὼ
ACCUSERS   ²NO   ³CHARGE ¹WERE BRINGING ⁴OF WHICH ⁶I

ὑπενόουν   πονηρῶν, **25.19** ζητήματα δέ τινα περὶ τῆς
⁷WAS SUSPECTING ⁵EVIL THINGS,   ¹⁰ISSUES   ⁸BUT ⁹CERTAIN ABOUT -

ἰδίας δεισιδαιμονίας εἶχον πρὸς αὐτὸν καὶ περί
THEIR OWN RELIGION   THEY HAD AGAINST HIM   AND ABOUT

τινος Ἰησοῦ τεθνηκότος ὃν   ἔφασκεν ὁ Παῦλος ζῆν.
A CERTAIN JESUS HAVING DIED,   WHOM WAS SAYING -   PAUL   TO LIVE.

25.20 ἀπορούμενος δὲ ἐγὼ τὴν περὶ
       ³BEING UNCERTAIN ¹BUT ²I   -   ABOUT

τούτων ζήτησιν   ἔλεγον εἰ βούλοιτο πορεύεσθαι
[THE] INVESTIGATION~OF THESE THINGS, WAS SAYING IF HE MIGHT WISH TO GO

εἰς Ἱεροσόλυμα κἀκεῖ κρίνεσθαι περὶ   τούτων.
TO   JERUSALEM   AND THERE TO BE JUDGED CONCERNING THESE THINGS.

25.21 τοῦ δὲ Παύλου ἐπικαλεσαμένου τηρηθῆναι αὐτὸν
       -    BUT PAUL   HAVING APPEALED [THAT]   HE~BE KEPT

εἰς τὴν τοῦ Σεβαστοῦ διάγνωσιν, ἐκέλευσα
FOR THE ²OF THE ³EMPEROR   ¹DECISION,   I ORDERED

τηρεῖσθαι αὐτὸν ἕως οὗ ἀναπέμψω αὐτὸν πρὸς
HIM~TO BE KEPT   UNTIL   I MAY SEND   HIM   TO

Καίσαρα. **25.22** Ἀγρίππας δὲ πρὸς τὸν Φῆστον,
CAESAR.   AND~AGRIPPA [SAID] TO   -   FESTUS,

Ἐβουλόμην καὶ αὐτὸς τοῦ ἀνθρώπου ἀκοῦσαι. Αὔριον,
I WAS DESIRING ALSO MYSELF ²THE ³MAN   ¹TO HEAR.   TOMORROW,

φησίν, ἀκούσῃ αὐτοῦ.
HE SAYS,   YOU WILL HEAR HIM.

25.23 Τῇ οὖν ἐπαύριον ἐλθόντος τοῦ Ἀγρίππα καὶ
       THEN~ON THE NEXT DAY,   HAVING COME   -   AGRIPPA   AND

τῆς Βερνίκης μετὰ πολλῆς φαντασίας καὶ εἰσελθόντων
-    BERNICE   WITH   GREAT   PAGEANTRY   AND   HAVING ENTERED

εἰς τὸ ἀκροατήριον σύν τε χιλιάρχοις καὶ ἀνδράσιν
INTO THE AUDITORIUM   WITH BOTH COMMANDERS   AND ³MEN

τοῖς κατ᾽ ἐξοχὴν τῆς πόλεως καὶ κελεύσαντος τοῦ
¹THE ²PROMINENT   OF THE CITY   AND   HAVING GIVEN ORDERS -

Φήστου ἤχθη   ὁ Παῦλος. **25.24** καὶ φησιν ὁ Φῆστος,
FESTUS, WAS BROUGHT - PAUL.   AND SAYS   - FESTUS,

Ἀγρίππα βασιλεῦ καὶ πάντες οἱ συμπαρόντες   ἡμῖν
KING~AGRIPPA   AND ALL   THE ²BEING PRESENT TOGETHER ³WITH US

and had been given an
opportunity to make a
defense against the charge.
[17]So when they met here, I
lost no time, but on the next
day took my seat on the
tribunal and ordered the man
to be brought. [18]When the
accusers stood up, they did
not charge him with any of
the crimes[y] that I was
expecting. [19]Instead they
had certain points of
disagreement with him
about their own religion and
about a certain Jesus, who
had died, but whom Paul
asserted to be alive. [20]Since I
was at a loss how to investi-
gate these questions, I asked
whether he wished to go to
Jerusalem and be tried there
on these charges.[z] [21]But
when Paul had appealed to
be kept in custody for the
decision of his Imperial
Majesty, I ordered him to be
held until I could send him to
the emperor." [22]Agrippa
said to Festus, "I would like
to hear the man myself."
"Tomorrow," he said, "you
will hear him."

   23 So on the next day
Agrippa and Bernice came
with great pomp, and they
entered the audience hall
with the military tribunes
and the prominent men of
the city. Then Festus gave
the order and Paul was
brought in. [24]And Festus
said, "King Agrippa and
all here present with us,

[y] Other ancient authorities read *with
    anything*
[z] Gk *on them*

you see this man about whom the whole Jewish community petitioned me, both in Jerusalem and here, shouting that he ought not to live any longer. 25But I found that he had done nothing deserving death; and when he appealed to his Imperial Majesty, I decided to send him. 26But I have nothing definite to write to our sovereign about him. Therefore I have brought him before all of you, and especially before you, King Agrippa, so that, after we have examined him, I may have something to write— 27for it seems to me unreasonable to send a prisoner without indicating the charges against him."

ἄνδρες, θεωρεῖτε τοῦτον περὶ οὗ ἅπαν τὸ πλῆθος
1MEN,   YOU° SEE   THIS ONE ABOUT WHOM ALL   THE MULTITUDE

τῶν Ἰουδαίων ἐνέτυχόν μοι ἔν τε Ἱεροσολύμοις καὶ
OF THE JEWS   APPEALED   TO ME IN BOTH JERUSALEM   AND

ἐνθάδε βοῶντες   μὴ δεῖν   αὐτὸν ζῆν μηκέτι.
HERE   CRYING OUT [THAT] IT IS NOT FITTING FOR HIM TO LIVE ANY LONGER.

25.25 ἐγὼ δὲ κατελαβόμην μηδὲν ἄξιον αὐτὸν θανάτου
        BUT~I FOUND   3NOTHING 4WORTHY 1HIM 5OF DEATH

πεπραχέναι, αὐτοῦ δὲ τούτου ἐπικαλεσαμένου τὸν
2TO HAVE DONE, BUT~HIMSELF THIS ONE HAVING APPEALED TO THE

Σεβαστὸν ἔκρινα πέμπειν. **25.26** περὶ οὗ   ἀσφαλές τι
EMPEROR, I DECIDED TO SEND [HIM].   ABOUT WHOM SOMETHING~DEFINITE

γράψαι τῷ   κυρίῳ οὐκ ἔχω, διὸ   προήγαγον αὐτὸν
TO WRITE TO THE LORD I DO NOT HAVE, THEREFORE I BROUGHT FORWARD HIM

ἐφ' ὑμῶν καὶ μάλιστα ἐπὶ σοῦ, βασιλεῦ Ἀγρίππα,
BEFORE YOU° AND ABOVE ALL BEFORE YOU, KING   AGRIPPA,

ὅπως τῆς ἀνακρίσεως γενομένης σχῶ τί
SO THAT THE INVESTIGATION HAVING HAPPENED, I MAY HAVE SOMETHING

γράψω· **25.27** ἄλογον γάρ μοι δοκεῖ πέμποντα δέσμιον
I MAY WRITE.   FOR~UNREASONABLE IT SEEMS~TO ME SENDING   A PRISONER

μὴ καὶ τὰς κατ' αὐτοῦ αἰτίας σημᾶναι.
NOT ALSO THE 2AGAINST 3HIM 1CHARGES TO REPORT.

CHAPTER 26

Agrippa said to Paul, "You have permission to speak for yourself." Then Paul stretched out his hand and began to defend himself:

2 "I consider myself fortunate that it is before you, King Agrippa, I am to make my defense today against all the accusations of the Jews, 3because you are especially familiar with all the customs and controversies of the Jews; therefore I beg of you to listen to me patiently.

4 "All the Jews know my way of life from my youth, a life spent from the beginning among my own people and in Jerusalem.

26.1 Ἀγρίππας δὲ πρὸς τὸν Παῦλον ἔφη,
     AND~AGRIPPA   TO   -   PAUL   SAID,

Ἐπιτρέπεταί σοι περὶ σεαυτοῦ λέγειν. τότε ὁ
IT IS PERMITTED FOR YOU CONCERNING YOURSELF TO SPEAK. THEN -

Παῦλος ἐκτείνας   τὴν χεῖρα ἀπελογεῖτο,
PAUL   HAVING STRETCHED OUT THE(HIS) HAND, WAS MAKING HIS DEFENSE,

26.2 Περὶ πάντων ὧν   ἐγκαλοῦμαι ὑπὸ Ἰουδαίων,
    CONCERNING EVERYTHING OF WHICH I AM BEING ACCUSED BY [THE] JEWS,

βασιλεῦ Ἀγρίππα, ἥγημαι   ἐμαυτὸν μακάριον ἐπὶ
KING   AGRIPPA, I HAVE CONSIDERED MYSELF FORTUNATE BEFORE

σοῦ μέλλων σήμερον ἀπολογεῖσθαι **26.3** μάλιστα
YOU INTENDING TODAY TO MAKE MY DEFENSE,   MOST OF ALL

γνώστην ὄντα σε πάντων τῶν κατὰ Ἰουδαίους ἐθῶν
3AN EXPERT 2BEING 1YOU 4OF ALL - 9OF 10[THE] JEWS 6CUSTOMS

τε καὶ ζητημάτων, διὸ   δέομαι μακροθύμως
5BOTH 7AND 8ISSUES,   THEREFORE, I BEG [YOU] PATIENTLY

ἀκοῦσαί μου. **26.4** Τὴν μὲν οὖν βίωσίν μου [τὴν]
TO LISTEN TO ME.   SO~THE   MANNER OF LIFE~THEN OF ME -

ἐκ   νεότητος τὴν ἀπ' ἀρχῆς   γενομένην ἐν τῷ
FROM [MY] YOUTH   FROM [THE] BEGINNING HAVING BEEN IN THE

ἔθνει μου ἔν τε Ἱεροσολύμοις ἴσασι πάντες [οἱ]
NATION OF ME AND~IN JERUSALEM   HAVE KNOWN ALL   THE

Ἰουδαῖοι   **26.5** προγινώσκοντές με ἄνωθεν,   ἐὰν
JEWS,   PREVIOUSLY KNOWING   ME   FOR A LONG TIME, IF

θέλωσι   μαρτυρεῖν, ὅτι κατὰ   τὴν ἀκριβεστάτην
THEY ARE WILLING TO TESTIFY,   THAT ACCORDING TO THE   MOST STRICT

αἵρεσιν τῆς ἡμετέρας θρησκείας ἔζησα Φαρισαῖος.
SECT   -   OF OUR   RELIGION   I LIVED [AS] A PHARISEE.

26.6 καὶ   νῦν ἐπ᾽ ἐλπίδι τῆς εἰς τοὺς πατέρας ἡμῶν
AND   NOW   ON [THE] HOPE OF THE ²TO ³THE ⁴FATHERS ⁵OF US

ἐπαγγελίας γενομένης ὑπὸ τοῦ θεοῦ ἕστηκα
¹PROMISE   HAVING BEEN MADE BY   -   GOD,   I HAVE STOOD

κρινόμενος, **26.7** εἰς ἣν   τὸ δωδεκάφυλον ἡμῶν ἐν
BEING JUDGED,   TO WHICH THE TWELVE TRIBES   OF US WITH

ἐκτενείᾳ νύκτα καὶ ἡμέραν λατρεῦον ἐλπίζει
EARNESTNESS NIGHT AND   DAY   WORSHIPING,   HOPES

καταντῆσαι, περὶ ἧς   ἐλπίδος ἐγκαλοῦμαι ὑπὸ
TO ATTAIN,   ABOUT WHICH HOPE   I AM BEING ACCUSED BY

Ἰουδαίων, βασιλεῦ. **26.8** τί ἄπιστον κρίνεται   παρ᾽
[THE] JEWS,   [O] KING.   WHY IS IT CONSIDERED~UNBELIEVABLE BY

ὑμῖν εἰ ὁ θεὸς νεκροὺς ἐγείρει;   **26.9** ἐγὼ μὲν οὖν
YOU° IF - GOD RAISES~[THE] DEAD?   I   -   THEREFORE

ἔδοξα ἐμαυτῷ πρὸς τὸ ὄνομα Ἰησοῦ τοῦ Ναζωραίου
THOUGHT TO MYSELF AGAINST THE NAME   OF JESUS, THE   NAZARENE,

δεῖν   πολλὰ ἐναντία πρᾶξαι, **26.10** ὃ   καὶ
IT IS NECESSARY MANY HOSTILE THINGS TO DO,   WHICH ALSO

ἐποίησα ἐν Ἱεροσολύμοις, καὶ πολλούς τε τῶν ἁγίων
I DID   IN   JERUSALEM,   AND MANY   - OF THE SAINTS

ἐγὼ ἐν φυλακαῖς κατέκλεισα τὴν παρὰ τῶν ἀρχιερέων
I   IN JAILS   LOCKED UP,   - ²FROM ³THE ⁴CHIEF PRIESTS

ἐξουσίαν λαβὼν   ἀναιρουμένων τε αὐτῶν κατήνεγκα
⁵AUTHORITY ¹HAVING RECEIVED ⁸BEING KILLED,   ⁶AND ⁷THEY I CAST

ψῆφον. **26.11** καὶ κατὰ   πάσας τὰς συναγωγὰς
A VOTE.   AND THROUGHOUT ALL   THE SYNAGOGUES,

πολλάκις τιμωρῶν αὐτοὺς ἠνάγκαζον βλασφημεῖν
OFTEN   PUNISHING THEM, I WAS FORCING [THEM] TO BLASPHEME

περισσῶς τε ἐμμαινόμενος αὐτοῖς ἐδίωκον   ἕως
AND~EVEN MORE BEING ENRAGED   AT THEM, I WAS PERSECUTING AS FAR AS

καὶ εἰς τὰς ἔξω πόλεις.
EVEN TO THE CITIES~OUTSIDE.

26.12 Ἐν οἷς   πορευόμενος εἰς τὴν Δαμασκὸν μετ᾽
IN WHICH TRAVELING   TO   -   DAMASCUS   WITH

ἐξουσίας καὶ ἐπιτροπῆς τῆς τῶν ἀρχιερέων
AUTHORITY AND PERMISSION   - OF THE CHIEF PRIESTS, [AT]

26.13 ἡμέρας μέσης κατὰ τὴν ὁδὸν εἶδον, βασιλεῦ,
MID~DAY   ALONG THE WAY I SAW, [O] KING,

οὐρανόθεν ὑπὲρ τὴν λαμπρότητα τοῦ ἡλίου
FROM HEAVEN, BEYOND THE BRILLIANCE   OF THE SUN,

περιλάμψαν με φῶς καὶ τοὺς   σὺν ἐμοὶ
HAVING SHONE AROUND ME A LIGHT AND THE ONES WITH ME

[5]They have known for a long time, if they are willing to testify, that I have belonged to the strictest sect of our religion and lived as a Pharisee. [6]And now I stand here on trial on account of my hope in the promise made by God to our ancestors, [7]a promise that our twelve tribes hope to attain, as they earnestly worship day and night. It is for this hope, your Excellency,[a] that I am accused by Jews! [8]Why is it thought incredible by any of you that God raises the dead?

9 "Indeed, I myself was convinced that I ought to do many things against the name of Jesus of Nazareth.[b] [10]And that is what I did in Jerusalem; with authority received from the chief priests, I not only locked up many of the saints in prison, but I also cast my vote against them when they were being condemned to death. [11]By punishing them often in all the synagogues I tried to force them to blaspheme; and since I was so furiously enraged at them, I pursued them even to foreign cities.

12 "With this in mind, I was traveling to Damascus with the authority and commission of the chief priests, [13]when at midday along the road, your Excellency,[a] I saw a light from heaven, brighter than the sun, shining around me

[a] Gk O king
[b] Gk the Nazorean

and my companions.
[14]When we had all fallen to the ground, I heard a voice saying to me in the Hebrew[c] language, 'Saul, Saul, why are you persecuting me? It hurts you to kick against the goads.' [15]I asked, 'Who are you, Lord?' The Lord answered, 'I am Jesus whom you are persecuting. [16]But get up and stand on your feet; for I have appeared to you for this purpose, to appoint you to serve and testify to the things in which you have seen me[d] and to those in which I will appear to you. [17]I will rescue you from your people and from the Gentiles—to whom I am sending you [18]to open their eyes so that they may turn from darkness to light and from the power of Satan to God, so that they may receive forgiveness of sins and a place among those who are sanctified by faith in me.'

[19] "After that, King Agrippa, I was not disobedient to the heavenly vision, [20]but declared first to those in Damascus, then in Jerusalem and throughout the countryside of Judea, and also to the Gentiles, that they should repent and turn to God and do deeds consistent with repentance. [21]For this reason the Jews seized me in the temple and tried to kill me. [22]To this day I have had help

[c] That is, Aramaic
[d] Other ancient authorities read the things that you have seen

πορευομένους. **26.14** πάντων τε καταπεσόντων ἡμῶν εἰς
TRAVELING.   AND~ALL   OF US~HAVING FALLEN DOWN   TO

τὴν γῆν ἤκουσα φωνὴν λέγουσαν πρός με τῇ
THE GROUND, I HEARD A VOICE SAYING TO ME IN THE

Ἑβραΐδι διαλέκτῳ, Σαοὺλ Σαούλ, τί με διώκεις;
HEBREW LANGUAGE, SAUL, SAUL, WHY ARE YOU PERSECUTING~ME?

σκληρόν σοι πρὸς κέντρα λακτίζειν. **26.15** ἐγὼ δὲ
[IT IS] HARD FOR YOU AGAINST [THE] PROD TO KICK.   AND~I

εἶπα, Τίς εἶ, κύριε; ὁ δὲ κύριος εἶπεν, Ἐγώ εἰμι
SAID, WHO ARE YOU, LORD? AND~THE LORD SAID, I AM

Ἰησοῦς ὃν σὺ διώκεις. **26.16** ἀλλὰ ἀνάστηθι καὶ
JESUS WHOM YOU ARE PERSECUTING. BUT GET UP AND

στῆθι ἐπὶ τοὺς πόδας σου· εἰς τοῦτο γὰρ ὤφθην
STAND ON THE FEET OF YOU. FOR THIS [PURPOSE] THEN, I APPEARED

σοι, προχειρίσασθαί σε ὑπηρέτην καὶ μάρτυρα
TO YOU, TO APPOINT YOU A SERVANT AND WITNESS

ὧν τε εἰδές ⸀[με]⸀ ὧν τε ὀφθήσομαί
BOTH~OF [THINGS IN] WHICH YOU SAW ME AND~THE [THINGS IN] WHICH I WILL APPEAR

σοι, **26.17** ἐξαιρούμενός σε ἐκ τοῦ λαοῦ καὶ ἐκ τῶν
TO YOU, DELIVERING YOU FROM THE PEOPLE AND FROM THE

ἐθνῶν εἰς οὓς ἐγὼ ἀποστέλλω σε **26.18** ἀνοῖξαι
GENTILES, TO WHOM I AM SENDING YOU, TO OPEN

ὀφθαλμοὺς αὐτῶν, τοῦ ἐπιστρέψαι ἀπὸ σκότους εἰς
[THE] EYES OF THEM, - TO TURN [THEM] FROM [THE] DARKNESS TO

φῶς καὶ τῆς ἐξουσίας τοῦ Σατανᾶ ἐπὶ τὸν θεόν,
[THE] LIGHT AND THE AUTHORITY - OF SATAN TO - GOD, [THAT]

τοῦ λαβεῖν αὐτοὺς ἄφεσιν ἁμαρτιῶν καὶ κλῆρον ἐν
- THEY~RECEIVE FORGIVENESS OF SINS AND A SHARE AMONG

τοῖς ἡγιασμένοις πίστει τῇ εἰς ἐμέ.
THE ONES HAVING BEEN SANCTIFIED BY FAITH - IN ME.

26.19 Ὅθεν, βασιλεῦ Ἀγρίππα, οὐκ ἐγενόμην
FROM WHICH, KING AGRIPPA, I WAS NOT

ἀπειθὴς τῇ οὐρανίῳ ὀπτασίᾳ **26.20** ἀλλὰ τοῖς ἐν
DISOBEDIENT TO THE HEAVENLY VISION, BUT TO THE ONES IN

Δαμασκῷ πρῶτόν τε καὶ Ἱεροσολύμοις, πᾶσάν τε τὴν
DAMASCUS FIRST AND ALSO IN JERUSALEM, AND~ALL THE

χώραν τῆς Ἰουδαίας καὶ τοῖς ἔθνεσιν ἀπήγγελλον
REGION - OF JUDEA AND TO THE GENTILES I WAS ANNOUNCING

μετανοεῖν καὶ ἐπιστρέφειν ἐπὶ τὸν θεόν, ἄξια τῆς
TO REPENT AND TO TURN TO - GOD, [3]WORTHY -

μετανοίας ἔργα πράσσοντας. **26.21** ἕνεκα τούτων με
[4]OF REPENTANCE [2]WORKS [1]DOING. BECAUSE OF THESE THINGS [3]ME

Ἰουδαῖοι συλλαβόμενοι [ὄντα] ἐν τῷ ἱερῷ ἐπειρῶντο
[1][THE] JEWS [2]HAVING SEIZED BEING IN THE TEMPLE WERE TRYING

διαχειρίσασθαι. **26.22** ἐπικουρίας οὖν τυχὼν τῆς
TO KILL [ME]. HELP, THEN, HAVING OBTAINED -

26:16 text: ASV NASBmg RSV NIV NEB TEV NJB NRSV. omit KJV NASB TEVmg NRSVmg.

ἀπὸ τοῦ θεοῦ ἄχρι τῆς ἡμέρας ταύτης ἕστηκα
FROM - GOD, UP TO - THIS~DAY I HAVE STOOD

μαρτυρόμενος μικρῷ τε καὶ μεγάλῳ οὐδὲν ἐκτὸς λέγων
WITNESSING BOTH~TO SMALL AND GREAT ²NOTHING ³EXCEPT ¹SAYING

ὧν τε οἱ προφῆται ἐλάλησαν μελλόντων
WHAT THINGS BOTH THE PROPHETS SAID BEING ABOUT

γίνεσθαι καὶ Μωϋσῆς, 26.23 εἰ παθητὸς ὁ
TO HAPPEN AND MOSES, IF SUBJECT TO SUFFERING THE

Χριστός, εἰ πρῶτος ἐξ ἀναστάσεως νεκρῶν φῶς
CHRIST, IF FIRST BY A RESURRECTION OF [THE] DEAD A LIGHT

μέλλει καταγγέλλειν τῷ τε λαῷ καὶ τοῖς ἔθνεσιν.
IS ABOUT TO ANNOUNCE BOTH~TO THE PEOPLE AND TO THE GENTILES.

26.24 Ταῦτα δὲ αὐτοῦ ἀπολογουμένου ὁ Φῆστος
AND~THESE THINGS, HE, SAYING IN HIS DEFENSE, - FESTUS

μεγάλῃ τῇ φωνῇ φησιν, Μαίνῃ, Παῦλε· τὰ πολλά
IN A LOUD - VOICE SAYS, YOU ARE INSANE, PAUL. THE GREATNESS OF

σε γράμματα εἰς μανίαν περιτρέπει. 26.25 ὁ δὲ
YOUR LEARNING TO INSANITY IS TURNING [YOU]. - BUT

Παῦλος, Οὐ μαίνομαι, φησίν, κράτιστε Φῆστε, ἀλλὰ
PAUL, I AM NOT INSANE, HE SAYS, MOST EXCELLENT FESTUS, BUT

ἀληθείας καὶ σωφροσύνης ῥήματα ἀποφθέγγομαι.
TRUE AND REASONABLE WORDS I AM SPEAKING.

26.26 ἐπίσταται γὰρ περὶ τούτων ὁ βασιλεύς πρὸς
FOR~KNOWS ABOUT THESE MATTERS THE KING TO

ὃν καὶ παρρησιαζόμενος λαλῶ, λανθάνειν γὰρ αὐτὸν
WHOM ALSO SPEAKING FREELY I SPEAK, FOR~TO ESCAPE NOTICE [OF] HIM

[τι] τούτων οὐ πείθομαι οὐθέν· οὐ γάρ ἐστιν
SOMETHING OF THESE THINGS I AM NOT PERSUADED AT ALL. ⁴NOT ¹FOR ³HAS

ἐν γωνίᾳ πεπραγμένον τοῦτο. 26.27 πιστεύεις, βασιλεῦ
⁶IN ⁷A CORNER ⁵BEEN DONE ²THIS. DO YOU BELIEVE, KING

Ἀγρίππα, τοῖς προφήταις; οἶδα ὅτι πιστεύεις. 26.28 ὁ
AGRIPPA, IN THE PROPHETS? I KNOW THAT YOU BELIEVE. -

δὲ Ἀγρίππας πρὸς τὸν Παῦλον, Ἐν ὀλίγῳ
AND AGRIPPA [SAID] TO - PAUL, IN A LITTLE [WHILE]

με πείθεις Χριστιανὸν ποιῆσαι. 26.29 ὁ δὲ Παῦλος,
YOU ARE PERSUADING~ME, TO MAKE [ME]~A CHRISTIAN. - BUT PAUL,

Εὐξαίμην ἂν τῷ θεῷ καὶ ἐν ὀλίγῳ καὶ ἐν
I WOULD PRAY - TO GOD [THAT] BOTH IN A LITTLE [WHILE] AND IN

μεγάλῳ οὐ μόνον σὲ ἀλλὰ καὶ πάντας τοὺς
A GREAT [WHILE] NOT ONLY YOU, BUT ALSO ALL THE ONES

ἀκούοντάς μου σήμερον γενέσθαι τοιούτους ὁποῖος καὶ
LISTENING TO ME TODAY, [THAT] SUCH ONES~BECOME OF WHAT SORT ALSO

ἐγώ εἰμι παρεκτὸς τῶν δεσμῶν τούτων.
I AM APART FROM - THESE~CHAINS.

26.30 Ἀνέστη τε ὁ βασιλεὺς καὶ ὁ ἡγεμὼν ἥ
AROSE BOTH THE KING AND THE GOVERNOR -

τε Βερνίκη καὶ οἱ συγκαθήμενοι αὐτοῖς,
AND BERNICE AND THE ONES SITTING WITH THEM,

from God, and so I stand here, testifying to both small and great, saying nothing but what the prophets and Moses said would take place: ²³that the Messiah[e] must suffer, and that, by being the first to rise from the dead, he would proclaim light both to our people and to the Gentiles."

24 While he was making this defense, Festus exclaimed, "You are out of your mind, Paul! Too much learning is driving you insane!" ²⁵But Paul said, "I am not out of my mind, most excellent Festus, but I am speaking the sober truth. ²⁶Indeed the king knows about these things, and to him I speak freely; for I am certain that none of these things has escaped his notice, for this was not done in a corner. ²⁷King Agrippa, do you believe the prophets? I know that you believe." ²⁸Agrippa said to Paul, "Are you so quickly persuading me to become a Christian?"[f] ²⁹Paul replied, "Whether quickly or not, I pray to God that not only you but also all who are listening to me today might become such as I am—except for these chains."

30 Then the king got up, and with him the governor and Bernice and those who had been seated with them;

[e] Or the Christ
[f] Or Quickly you will persuade me to play the Christian

31and as they were leaving, they said to one another, "This man is doing nothing to deserve death or imprisonment." 32Agrippa said to Festus, "This man could have been set free if he had not appealed to the emperor."

26.31 καὶ ἀναχωρήσαντες ἐλάλουν πρὸς ἀλλήλους
AND   HAVING WITHDRAWN, THEY WERE SPEAKING TO   ONE ANOTHER

λέγοντες ὅτι Οὐδὲν θανάτου ἢ δεσμῶν ἄξιον [τι]
SAYING   -   4NOT [DO] 7OF DEATH 8OR 9CHAINS 6WORTHY 5ANYTHING

πράσσει ὁ ἄνθρωπος οὗτος. **26.32** Ἀγρίππας δὲ τῷ
3DOES   - 2MAN   1THIS.   AND~AGRIPPA   -

Φήστῳ ἔφη, Ἀπολελύσθαι ἐδύνατο ὁ ἄνθρωπος οὗτος
TO FESTUS SAID, 4TO HAVE BEEN RELEASED 3WAS ABLE - 2MAN   1THIS

εἰ μὴ ἐπεκέκλητο Καίσαρα.
IF   HE HAD NOT APPEALED TO CAESAR.

CHAPTER 27

When it was decided that we were to sail for Italy, they transferred Paul and some other prisoners to a centurion of the Augustan Cohort, named Julius. 2Embarking on a ship of Adramyttium that was about to set sail to the ports along the coast of Asia, we put to sea, accompanied by Aristarchus, a Macedonian from Thessalonica. 3The next day we put in at Sidon; and Julius treated Paul kindly, and allowed him to go to his friends to be cared for. 4Putting out to sea from there, we sailed under the lee of Cyprus, because the winds were against us. 5After we had sailed across the sea that is off Cilicia and Pamphylia, we came to Myra in Lycia. 6There the centurion found an Alexandrian ship bound for Italy and put us on board. 7We sailed slowly for a

27.1 Ὡς δὲ ἐκρίθη   τοῦ ἀποπλεῖν ἡμᾶς εἰς τὴν
AND~WHEN IT WAS DECIDED [THAT] - WE~SET SAIL   TO -

Ἰταλίαν, παρεδίδουν τόν τε Παῦλον καί τινας
ITALY,   THEY WERE HANDING OVER - BOTH PAUL AND SOME

ἑτέρους δεσμώτας ἑκατοντάρχῃ ὀνόματι Ἰουλίῳ
OTHER   PRISONERS TO A CENTURION BY NAME JULIUS

σπείρης Σεβαστῆς.   **27.2** ἐπιβάντες δὲ
OF [THE] IMPERIAL~COHORT.   AND~HAVING EMBARKED

πλοίῳ Ἀδραμυττηνῷ μέλλοντι πλεῖν εἰς τοὺς
IN AN ADRAMYTTIUM~SHIP BEING ABOUT TO SAIL TO -

κατὰ   τὴν Ἀσίαν τόπους ἀνήχθημεν ὄντος σὺν
2ALONG [THE COAST OF] - 3ASIA 1PLACES WE SET SAIL, BEING WITH

ἡμῖν Ἀριστάρχου Μακεδόνος Θεσσαλονικέως. **27.3** τῇ
US   ARISTARCHUS A MACEDONIAN OF THESSALONICA.

τε ἑτέρᾳ   κατήχθημεν εἰς Σιδῶνα, φιλανθρώπως
AND ON ANOTHER [DAY] WE PUT IN AT A HARBOR IN SIDON, 4KINDLY

τε ὁ Ἰούλιος τῷ Παύλῳ χρησάμενος ἐπέτρεψεν πρὸς
1AND - 2JULIUS - 5PAUL 3HAVING TREATED PERMITTED [HIM] TO

τοὺς φίλους πορευθέντι ἐπιμελείας τυχεῖν.
THE FRIENDS HAVING GONE TO OBTAIN~CARE.

27.4 κἀκεῖθεν ἀναχθέντες ὑπεπλεύσαμεν τὴν
AND FROM THERE HAVING PUT OUT TO SEA, WE SAILED TO ONE SIDE OF -

Κύπρον διὰ τὸ τοὺς ἀνέμους εἶναι ἐναντίους,
CYPRUS BECAUSE - THE WINDS TO BE CONTRARY,

27.5 τό τε πέλαγος τὸ κατὰ   τὴν Κιλικίαν καὶ
AND~THE OPEN SEA - ALONG [THE COAST OF] - CILICIA AND

Παμφυλίαν διαπλεύσαντες κατήλθομεν εἰς Μύρα τῆς
PAMPHYLIA HAVING SAILED THROUGH, WE CAME DOWN TO MYRA -

Λυκίας. **27.6** κἀκεῖ εὑρὼν   ὁ ἑκατοντάρχης
OF LYCIA. AND THERE 3HAVING FOUND 1THE 2CENTURION

πλοῖον Ἀλεξανδρῖνον πλέον εἰς τὴν Ἰταλίαν
AN ALEXANDRIAN~SHIP   SAILING TO - ITALY,

ἐνεβίβασεν ἡμᾶς εἰς αὐτό. **27.7** ἐν ἱκαναῖς δὲ
HE PUT ON BOARD US IN IT.   2IN 3MANY 1BUT

ἡμέραις βραδυπλοοῦντες καὶ μόλις   γενόμενοι
DAYS   SAILING SLOWLY   AND   WITH DIFFICULTY HAVING COME

κατὰ   τὴν Κνίδον, μὴ προσεῶντος   ἡμᾶς
ALONG [THE COAST OF] -   CNIDUS, ³NOT ⁴PERMITTING TO GO FARTHER ⁵US

τοῦ ἀνέμου ὑπεπλεύσαμεν τὴν Κρήτην κατὰ
¹THE ²WIND,   WE SAILED TO ONE SIDE OF - CRETE   ACROSS FROM

Σαλμώνην, 27.8 μόλις τε   παραλεγόμενοι αὐτὴν
SALMONE,   AND~WITH DIFFICULTY SAILING PAST   IT

ἤλθομεν εἰς τόπον τινὰ καλούμενον Καλοὺς Λιμένας
WE CAME   TO A CERTAIN~PLACE BEING CALLED FAIR   HAVENS,

ᾧ ἐγγὺς   πόλις ἦν Λασαία.
NEAR~TO WHICH WAS~[THE] CITY LASEA.

27.9 Ἱκανοῦ δὲ   χρόνου διαγενομένου καὶ ὄντος ἤδη
AND~CONSIDERABLE TIME   HAVING PASSED   AND BEING ALREADY

ἐπισφαλοῦς τοῦ πλοὸς διὰ   τὸ καὶ τὴν νηστείαν
UNSAFE [FOR]   - A VOYAGE BECAUSE OF - ALSO THE FAST

ἤδη   παρεληλυθέναι παρῄνει   ὁ Παῦλος
ALREADY TO HAVE GONE BY,   WAS RECOMMENDING - PAUL

27.10 λέγων αὐτοῖς, Ἄνδρες, θεωρῶ ὅτι μετὰ ὕβρεως
SAYING TO THEM, MEN,   I SEE THAT WITH HARDSHIP

καὶ πολλῆς ζημίας οὐ μόνου τοῦ φορτίου καὶ τοῦ
AND MUCH LOSS,   NOT ONLY OF THE CARGO AND THE

πλοίου ἀλλὰ καὶ τῶν ψυχῶν ἡμῶν μέλλειν ἔσεσθαι τὸν
SHIP,   BUT ALSO THE LIVES OF US ARE ABOUT TO BE   THE

πλοῦν. 27.11 ὁ δὲ ἑκατοντάρχης τῷ κυβερνήτῃ καὶ
VOYAGE.   BUT~THE CENTURION   BY THE PILOT   AND

τῷ ναυκλήρῳ μᾶλλον ἐπείθετο ἢ τοῖς   ὑπὸ Παύλου
THE OWNER   WAS PERSUADED~RATHER THAN THE THINGS BY PAUL

λεγομένοις. 27.12 ἀνευθέτου δὲ   τοῦ λιμένος
BEING SPOKEN.   BUT~UNFAVORABLY SITUATED THE PORT

ὑπάρχοντος πρὸς παραχειμασίαν οἱ πλείονες ἔθεντο
BEING   FOR SPENDING THE WINTER, THE MAJORITY MADE

βουλὴν ἀναχθῆναι ἐκεῖθεν, εἴ πως   δύναιντο
A DECISION TO SET SAIL   FROM THERE, IF SOMEHOW THEY MIGHT BE ABLE

καταντήσαντες εἰς Φοίνικα παραχειμάσαι λιμένα τῆς
HAVING ARRIVED IN PHOENIX   TO SPEND THE WINTER [IN] A HARBOR -

Κρήτης βλέποντα κατὰ λίβα   καὶ κατὰ
OF CRETE FACING   TOWARD [THE] SOUTHWEST AND TOWARD

χῶρον.
[THE] NORTHWEST.

27.13 Ὑποπνεύσαντος δὲ νότου   δόξαντες τῆς
AND~HAVING BLOWN GENTLY A SOUTH WIND, HAVING THOUGHT THE

προθέσεως   κεκρατηκέναι, ἄραντες
PURPOSE   TO HAVE ATTAINED, HAVING RAISED [ANCHOR]

ἆσσον παρελέγοντο τὴν Κρήτην. 27.14 μετ᾽ οὐ
THEY WERE SAILING PAST~CLOSE BY - CRETE.   ²AFTER ³NOT

πολὺ δὲ ἔβαλεν κατ᾽ αὐτῆς ἄνεμος τυφωνικὸς
⁴MUCH [TIME] ¹BUT RUSHED DOWN AGAINST IT   A HURRICANE [FORCE]~WIND,

number of days and arrived with difficulty off Cnidus, and as the wind was against us, we sailed under the lee of Crete off Salmone. [8]Sailing past it with difficulty, we came to a place called Fair Havens, near the city of Lasea.

9 Since much time had been lost and sailing was now dangerous, because even the Fast had already gone by, Paul advised them, [10]saying, "Sirs, I can see that the voyage will be with danger and much heavy loss, not only of the cargo and the ship, but also of our lives." [11]But the centurion paid more attention to the pilot and to the owner of the ship than to what Paul said. [12]Since the harbor was not suitable for spending the winter, the majority was in favor of putting to sea from there, on the chance that somehow they could reach Phoenix, where they could spend the winter. It was a harbor of Crete, facing southwest and northwest.

13 When a moderate south wind began to blow, they thought they could achieve their purpose; so they weighed anchor and began to sail past Crete, close to the shore. [14]But soon a violent wind,

called the northeaster, rushed down from Crete.[g] [15]Since the ship was caught and could not be turned head-on into the wind, we gave way to it and were driven. [16]By running under the lee of a small island called Cauda[h] we were scarcely able to get the ship's boat under control. [17]After hoisting it up they took measures[i] to undergird the ship; then, fearing that they would run on the Syrtis, they lowered the sea anchor and so were driven. [18]We were being pounded by the storm so violently that on the next day they began to throw the cargo overboard, [19]and on the third day with their own hands they threw the ship's tackle overboard. [20]When neither sun nor stars appeared for many days, and no small tempest raged, all hope of our being saved was at last abandoned.

[21] Since they had been without food for a long time, Paul then stood up among them and said, "Men, you should have listened to me and not have set sail from Crete and thereby avoided this damage and loss. [22]I urge you now to keep up your courage, for there will be no loss of life among you, but only of the ship. [23]For last night there stood by me an angel of the God to whom I belong and whom I worship,

[g] Gk it
[h] Other ancient authorities read Clauda
[i] Gk helps

ὁ καλούμενος Εὐρακύλων·
THE ONE BEING CALLED, [THE] NORTHEASTER;

27.15 συναρπασθέντος δὲ
AND~HAVING BEEN CAUGHT [IN IT],

τοῦ πλοίου καὶ μὴ δυναμένου ἀντοφθαλμεῖν τῷ ἀνέμῳ
THE SHIP, AND NOT BEING ABLE TO DIRECTLY FACE THE WIND,

ἐπιδόντες ἐφερόμεθα.
HAVING GIVEN UP, WE ALLOWED OURSELVES TO DRIFT ALONG.

27.16 νησίον δέ
[4]LITTLE ISLAND [1]AND

τι ὑποδραμόντες καλούμενον Καῦδα ἰσχύσαμεν
[3]A CERTAIN [2]HAVING RUN TO ONE SIDE OF BEING CALLED CAUDA, WE WERE ABLE

μόλις περικρατεῖς γενέσθαι τῆς σκάφης,
WITH DIFFICULTY TO GET~UNDER CONTROL THE LIFEBOAT,

27.17 ἣν
WHICH

ἄραντες βοηθείαις ἐχρῶντο ὑποζωννύντες τὸ
HAVING LIFTED [IT] UP, THEY WERE USING~SUPPORTS, PASSING [THEM] UNDERNEATH THE

πλοῖον, φοβούμενοί τε μὴ εἰς τὴν Σύρτιν
SHIP, AND~FEARING LEST ON [THE SHALLOWS OF] - SYRTIS

ἐκπέσωσιν, χαλάσαντες τὸ σκεῦος, οὕτως
THEY MIGHT RUN AGROUND, HAVING LET DOWN THE EQUIPMENT, THUS

ἐφέροντο.
THEY WERE BEING DRIVEN ALONG.

27.18 σφοδρῶς δὲ χειμαζομένων
[4]VIOLENTLY [1]AND [3]BEING TOSSED

ἡμῶν τῇ ἑξῆς ἐκβολὴν ἐποιοῦντο
[2]WE ON THE NEXT [DAY] THEY WERE THROWING THE CARGO OVERBOARD,

27.19 καὶ
AND

τῇ τρίτῃ αὐτόχειρες τὴν σκευὴν τοῦ πλοίου
ON THE THIRD [DAY], WITH THEIR OWN HANDS, THE EQUIPMENT OF THE BOAT

ἔρριψαν.
THEY THREW OUT.

27.20 μήτε δὲ ἡλίου μήτε ἄστρων
AND~NEITHER SUN NOR STARS

ἐπιφαινόντων ἐπὶ πλείονας ἡμέρας, χειμῶνός τε οὐκ
APPEARING OVER MANY DAYS AND~STORMY WEATHER NOT

ὀλίγου ἐπικειμένου, λοιπὸν περιῃρεῖτο ἐλπὶς πᾶσα
A LITTLE ASSAILING [US], FINALLY WAS BEING ABANDONED ALL~HOPE [FOR]

τοῦ σῴζεσθαι ἡμᾶς.
- US~TO BE SAVED.

27.21 Πολλῆς τε ἀσιτίας ὑπαρχούσης τότε
AND~[AFTER] MUCH LOSS OF APPETITE HAVING, THEN

σταθεὶς ὁ Παῦλος ἐν μέσῳ αὐτῶν εἶπεν,
HAVING STOOD UP - PAUL IN [THE] MIDST OF THEM SAID,

Ἔδει μέν, ὦ ἄνδρες, πειθαρχήσαντάς μοι μὴ
IT WAS NECESSARY, - O MEN, HAVING OBEYED ME NOT

ἀνάγεσθαι ἀπὸ τῆς Κρήτης κερδῆσαί τε τὴν
TO PUT OUT TO SEA FROM - CRETE AND~TO SPARE YOURSELVES -

ὕβριν ταύτην καὶ τὴν ζημίαν.
THIS~HARDSHIP AND - LOSS.

27.22 καὶ τὰ νῦν
AND - NOW

παραινῶ ὑμᾶς εὐθυμεῖν· ἀποβολὴ γὰρ ψυχῆς
I ADVISE YOU° TO BE COURAGEOUS; [4]LOSS [1]FOR [5]OF LIFE

οὐδεμία ἔσται ἐξ ὑμῶν πλὴν τοῦ πλοίου.
[3]NO [2]THERE WILL BE OF YOU° EXCEPT THE SHIP.

27.23 παρέστη γάρ μοι ταύτῃ τῇ νυκτὶ τοῦ θεοῦ,
FOR~STOOD BY ME [DURING] THIS - NIGHT, OF THE GOD

οὗ εἰμι [ἐγὼ] ᾧ καὶ λατρεύω, ἄγγελος
OF WHOM I~AM, WHOM ALSO I SERVE, AN ANGEL

27.24 λέγων, Μὴ φοβοῦ, Παῦλε, Καίσαρί σε
SAYING, DO NOT BE AFRAID, PAUL, ⁴CAESAR ²YOU

δεῖ παραστῆναι, καὶ ἰδοὺ κεχάρισταί σοι ὁ
¹IT IS NECESSARY FOR ³TO STAND BEFORE, ⁵AND ⁶BEHOLD ⁸HAS GIVEN ⁹TO YOU -

θεὸς πάντας τοὺς πλέοντας μετὰ σοῦ. **27.25** διὸ
⁷GOD ALL THE ONES SAILING WITH YOU. THEREFORE

εὐθυμεῖτε, ἄνδρες· πιστεύω γὰρ τῷ θεῷ ὅτι
BE CHEERFUL, MEN. FOR~I BELIEVE - GOD THAT

οὕτως ἔσται καθ᾽ ὃν τρόπον λελάληταί μοι. **27.26** εἰς
IT WILL BE~SO IN EVERY WAY IN WHICH IT HAS BEEN SPOKEN TO ME. ²ONTO

νῆσον δέ τινα δεῖ ἡμᾶς ἐκπεσεῖν.
⁴ISLAND ¹BUT ³A CERTAIN IT IS NECESSARY FOR US TO RUN AGROUND.

27.27 Ὡς δὲ τεσσαρεσκαιδεκάτη νὺξ ἐγένετο
NOW~WHEN [THE] FOURTEENTH NIGHT CAME

διαφερομένων ἡμῶν ἐν τῷ Ἀδρίᾳ, κατὰ μέσον τῆς
[WHILE] WE~BEING DRIVEN ABOUT IN THE ADRIATIC SEA, TOWARD [THE] MIDDLE OF THE

νυκτὸς ὑπενόουν οἱ ναῦται προσάγειν τινὰ αὐτοῖς
NIGHT, WERE SUPPOSING THE SAILORS TO BE APPROACHING ²SOME ¹TO THEM

χώραν. **27.28** καὶ βολίσαντες εὗρον
³LAND. AND HAVING TAKEN SOUNDINGS THEY FOUND

ὀργυιὰς εἴκοσι, βραχὺ δὲ διαστήσαντες καὶ πάλιν
TWENTY~FATHOMS, AND~A LITTLE [FARTHER] HAVING SAILED AND AGAIN

βολίσαντες εὗρον ὀργυιὰς δεκαπέντε·
HAVING TAKEN SOUNDINGS THEY FOUND FIFTEEN~FATHOMS.

27.29 φοβούμενοί τε μή που κατὰ τραχεῖς τόπους
AND~FEARING LEST SOMEHOW AGAINST [THE] ROUGH PLACES

ἐκπέσωμεν, ἐκ πρύμνης ῥίψαντες ἀγκύρας τέσσαρας
WE MIGHT RUN AGROUND, OFF [THE] STERN HAVING THROWN FOUR~ANCHORS,

ηὔχοντο ἡμέραν γενέσθαι. **27.30** τῶν δὲ ναυτῶν
THEY WERE PRAYING [FOR IT] TO BECOME~DAY. NOW~THE SAILORS

ζητούντων φυγεῖν ἐκ τοῦ πλοίου καὶ χαλασάντων τὴν
SEEKING TO FLEE FROM THE SHIP AND HAVING LET DOWN THE

σκάφην εἰς τὴν θάλασσαν προφάσει ὡς ἐκ
LIFEBOAT INTO THE SEA PRETENDING AS THOUGH FROM

πρῴρης ἀγκύρας μελλόντων ἐκτείνειν, **27.31** εἶπεν ὁ
[THE] BOW ANCHORS INTENDING TO CAST OUT, SAID -

Παῦλος τῷ ἑκατοντάρχῃ καὶ τοῖς στρατιώταις,
PAUL TO THE CENTURION AND TO THE SOLDIERS,

Ἐὰν μὴ οὗτοι μείνωσιν ἐν τῷ πλοίῳ, ὑμεῖς σωθῆναι
UNLESS THESE REMAIN IN THE BOAT, YOU° ²TO BE SAVED

οὐ δύνασθε. **27.32** τότε ἀπέκοψαν οἱ στρατιῶται τὰ
¹ARE NOT ABLE. THEN ³CUT OFF ¹THE ²SOLDIERS THE

σχοινία τῆς σκάφης καὶ εἴασαν αὐτὴν ἐκπεσεῖν.
ROPES OF THE LIFEBOAT AND LET IT FALL AWAY.

27.33 Ἄχρι δὲ οὗ ἡμέρα ἤμελλεν γίνεσθαι,
NOW~UNTIL DAY WAS ABOUT TO COME,

παρεκάλει ὁ Παῦλος ἅπαντας μεταλαβεῖν τροφῆς
²WAS ENCOURAGING - ¹PAUL EVERYONE TO TAKE FOOD

²⁴and he said, 'Do not be afraid, Paul; you must stand before the emperor; and indeed, God has granted safety to all those who are sailing with you.' ²⁵So keep up your courage, men, for I have faith in God that it will be exactly as I have been told. ²⁶But we will have to run aground on some island."

27 When the fourteenth night had come, as we were drifting across the sea of Adria, about midnight the sailors suspected that they were nearing land. ²⁸So they took soundings and found twenty fathoms; a little farther on they took soundings again and found fifteen fathoms. ²⁹Fearing that we might run on the rocks, they let down four anchors from the stern and prayed for day to come. ³⁰But when the sailors tried to escape from the ship and had lowered the boat into the sea, on the pretext of putting out anchors from the bow, ³¹Paul said to the centurion and the soldiers, "Unless these men stay in the ship, you cannot be saved." ³²Then the soldiers cut away the ropes of the boat and set it adrift.

33 Just before daybreak, Paul urged all of them to take some food,

saying, "Today is the fourteenth day that you have
been in suspense and
remaining without food,
having eaten nothing.
³⁴Therefore I urge you to
take some food, for it will
help you survive; for none of
you will lose a hair from
your heads." ³⁵After he had
said this, he took bread; and
giving thanks to God in the
presence of all, he broke it
and began to eat. ³⁶Then all
of them were encouraged
and took food for them-
selves. ³⁷(We were in all
two hundred seventy-six*ʲ*
persons in the ship.) ³⁸After
they had satisfied their
hunger, they lightened the
ship by throwing the wheat
into the sea.

39 In the morning they
did not recognize the land,
but they noticed a bay with
a beach, on which they
planned to run the ship
ashore, if they could. ⁴⁰So
they cast off the anchors and
left them in the sea. At the
same time they loosened the
ropes that tied the steering-
oars; then hoisting the
foresail to the wind, they
made for the beach. ⁴¹But
striking a reef,*ᵏ* they ran the
ship aground; the bow stuck
and remained immovable,
but the stern was being
broken up by the force
of the waves. ⁴²The

ʲ Other ancient authorities read
seventy-six; others, *about seventy-
six*
ᵏ Gk *place of two seas*

λέγων, Τεσσαρεσκαιδεκάτην σήμερον ἡμέραν
SAYING,   TODAY [IS]~[THE] FOURTEENTH   DAY

προσδοκῶντες   ἄσιτοι   διατελεῖτε
WAITING   WITHOUT EATING   YOU° ARE CONTINUING,

μηθὲν προσλαβόμενοι. **27.34** διὸ   παρακαλῶ ὑμᾶς
HAVING TAKEN~NOTHING.   THEREFORE, I ENCOURAGE   YOU°

μεταλαβεῖν τροφῆς· τοῦτο γὰρ πρὸς τῆς ὑμετέρας
TO TAKE   FOOD;   THIS THEN ²FOR -   ³YOUR°

σωτηρίας ὑπάρχει, οὐδενὸς γὰρ ὑμῶν θρὶξ ἀπὸ τῆς
⁴DELIVERANCE ¹IS,   FOR~OF NO ONE OF YOU° A HAIR FROM THE

κεφαλῆς ἀπολεῖται. **27.35** εἴπας δὲ ταῦτα   καὶ
HEAD   WILL BE LOST.   AND~HAVING SAID THESE THINGS, AND

λαβὼν   ἄρτον εὐχαρίστησεν τῷ θεῷ ἐνώπιον πάντων
HAVING TAKEN BREAD, HE GAVE THANKS - TO GOD BEFORE   ALL

καὶ κλάσας   ἤρξατο ἐσθίειν. **27.36** εὔθυμοι δὲ
AND HAVING BROKEN [IT] HE BEGAN TO EAT.   ⁴ENCOURAGED ¹AND

γενόμενοι πάντες καὶ αὐτοὶ προσελάβοντο τροφῆς.
³HAVING BECOME ²EVERYONE, THEY~ALSO TOOK   FOOD.

27.37 ἤμεθα δὲ αἱ πᾶσαι ψυχαὶ ἐν τῷ πλοίῳ
       NOW~WERE ALL~THE   SOULS IN THE SHIP

διακόσιαι ἑβδομήκοντα ἕξ. **27.38** κορεσθέντες δὲ   τροφῆς
TWO HUNDRED AND SEVENTY-SIX.   AND~HAVING EATEN ENOUGH FOOD,

ἐκούφιζον   τὸ πλοῖον ἐκβαλλόμενοι τὸν σῖτον εἰς
THEY WERE LIGHTENING THE SHIP [BY] THROWING OVERBOARD THE WHEAT INTO

τὴν θάλασσαν.
THE   SEA.

27.39 Ὅτε δὲ ἡμέρα ἐγένετο,   τὴν γῆν
       AND~WHEN IT BECAME~DAY,   THE LAND

οὐκ ἐπεγίνωσκον, κόλπον δέ τινα   κατενόουν
THEY WERE NOT RECOGNIZING, ³BAY ¹BUT ²A CERTAIN THEY WERE NOTICING

ἔχοντα αἰγιαλὸν εἰς ὃν ἐβουλεύοντο εἰ δύναιντο
HAVING A SHORE ONTO WHICH THEY WERE DESIRING IF THEY MIGHT BE ABLE

ἐξῶσαι   τὸ πλοῖον. **27.40** καὶ τὰς ἀγκύρας
TO RUN AGROUND THE SHIP.   AND THE ANCHORS

περιελόντες εἴων   εἰς τὴν θάλασσαν, ἅμα
HAVING CAST OFF THEY WERE LEAVING IN THE SEA,   AT THE SAME TIME

ἀνέντες   τὰς ζευκτηρίας τῶν πηδαλίων καὶ
HAVING LOOSENED THE ROPES   OF THE RUDDERS   AND

ἐπάραντες τὸν ἀρτέμωνα τῇ   πνεούσῃ κατεῖχον
HAVING RAISED THE SAIL   TO THE BREEZE, THEY WERE STEERING

εἰς   τὸν αἰγιαλόν. **27.41** περιπεσόντες δὲ εἰς τόπον
TOWARD THE SHORE.   BUT~HAVING FALLEN   INTO A PLACE

διθάλασσον ἐπέκειλαν τὴν ναῦν καὶ ἡ μὲν πρῷρα
BETWEEN TWO SEAS, THEY RAN AGROUND THE SHIP AND WHILE~THE BOW

ἐρείσασα ἔμεινεν ἀσάλευτος, ἡ δὲ πρύμνα
HAVING STUCK REMAINED IMMOVABLE, THE - STERN

ἐλύετο   ὑπὸ τῆς βίας [τῶν κυμάτων]. **27.42** τῶν
WAS BEING DESTROYED BY THE FORCE OF THE WAVES.   ³OF THE

δὲ στρατιωτῶν βουλὴ ἐγένετο ἵνα τοὺς δεσμώτας
¹NOW ⁴SOLDIERS ²[THE] PLAN WAS THAT THE PRISONERS

ἀποκτείνωσιν, μή τις ἐκκολυμβήσας διαφύγη.
THEY SHOULD KILL, LEST ANYONE HAVING SWUM AWAY SHOULD ESCAPE.

27.43 ὁ δὲ ἑκατοντάρχης βουλόμενος διασῶσαι τὸν
BUT~THE CENTURION DESIRING TO SAVE -

Παῦλον ἐκώλυσεν αὐτοὺς τοῦ βουλήματος,
PAUL, KEPT THEM [FROM CARRYING OUT] THE PLAN,

ἐκέλευσέν τε τοὺς δυναμένους κολυμβᾶν
AND~HE ORDERED THE ONES BEING ABLE TO SWIM

ἀπορίψαντας πρώτους ἐπὶ τὴν γῆν ἐξιέναι
HAVING THROWN THEMSELVES [OVERBOARD] FIRST, UPON THE LAND TO GO OUT

27.44 καὶ τοὺς λοιποὺς οὓς μὲν ἐπὶ σανίσιν, οὓς δὲ
AND THE REST, SOME ON BOARDS, OTHERS

ἐπί τινων τῶν ἀπὸ τοῦ πλοίου. καὶ οὕτως
ON SOME OF THE THINGS FROM THE SHIP. AND SO

ἐγένετο πάντας διασωθῆναι ἐπὶ τὴν γῆν.
IT CAME ABOUT EVERYONE TO BE BROUGHT SAFELY ONTO THE LAND.

soldiers' plan was to kill the prisoners, so that none might swim away and escape; [43]but the centurion, wishing to save Paul, kept them from carrying out their plan. He ordered those who could swim to jump overboard first and make for the land, [44]and the rest to follow, some on planks and others on pieces of the ship. And so it was that all were brought safely to land.

28.1 Καὶ διασωθέντες τότε ἐπέγνωμεν ὅτι
AND HAVING BEEN BROUGHT SAFELY THROUGH, THEN WE FOUND OUT THAT

Μελίτη ἡ νῆσος καλεῖται. **28.2** οἵ τε βάρβαροι
MALTA, THE ISLAND IS CALLED. AND~THE FOREIGNERS

παρεῖχον οὐ τὴν τυχοῦσαν φιλανθρωπίαν ἡμῖν,
WERE SHOWING NOT THE ORDINARY KINDNESS TO US,

ἅψαντες γὰρ πυρὰν προσελάβοντο πάντας ἡμᾶς διὰ
FOR~HAVING LIT A FIRE THEY WELCOMED US~ALL BECAUSE OF

τὸν ὑετὸν τὸν ἐφεστῶτα καὶ διὰ τὸ ψῦχος.
THE RAIN - HAVING SET IN AND BECAUSE OF THE COLD.

28.3 συστρέψαντος δὲ τοῦ Παύλου φρυγάνων τι
AND~HAVING GATHERED - PAUL ³OF STICKS ¹A CERTAIN

πλῆθος καὶ ἐπιθέντος ἐπὶ τὴν πυράν, ἔχιδνα ἀπὸ
²NUMBER AND HAVING PLACED [THEM] ON THE FIRE, A VIPER FROM

τῆς θέρμης ἐξελθοῦσα καθῆψεν τῆς χειρὸς αὐτοῦ.
THE HEAT HAVING COME OUT FASTENED ONTO THE HAND OF HIM.

28.4 ὡς δὲ εἶδον οἱ βάρβαροι κρεμάμενον τὸ θηρίον
AND~WHEN SAW THE FOREIGNERS ³HANGING ¹THE ²CREATURE

ἐκ τῆς χειρὸς αὐτοῦ, πρὸς ἀλλήλους ἔλεγον,
FROM THE HAND OF HIM, TO ONE ANOTHER THEY WERE SAYING,

Πάντως φονεύς ἐστιν ὁ ἄνθρωπος οὗτος ὃν
SURELY IS~A MURDERER - THIS~MAN WHOM

διασωθέντα ἐκ τῆς θαλάσσης ἡ δίκη ζῆν
HAVING BEEN BROUGHT SAFELY FROM THE SEA, - JUSTICE ²TO LIVE

οὐκ εἴασεν. **28.5** ὁ μὲν οὖν ἀποτινάξας τὸ θηρίον εἰς
¹DID NOT ALLOW. - - THEN HAVING SHAKEN OFF THE CREATURE INTO

After we had reached safety, we then learned that the island was called Malta. [2]The natives showed us unusual kindness. Since it had begun to rain and was cold, they kindled a fire and welcomed all of us around it. [3]Paul had gathered a bundle of brushwood and was putting it on the fire, when a viper, driven out by the heat, fastened itself on his hand. [4]When the natives saw the creature hanging from his hand, they said to one another, "This man must be a murderer; though he has escaped from the sea, justice has not allowed him to live." [5]He, however, shook off the creature into the fire and suffered no harm. [6]They were expecting him to swell up or drop dead, but after they had waited a long time and saw that nothing unusual had happened to him, they changed their minds and began to say that he was a god.

7 Now in the neighborhood of that place were lands belonging to the leading man of the island, named Publius, who received us and entertained us hospitably for three days. [8]It so happened that the father of Publius lay sick in bed with fever and dysentery. Paul visited him and cured him by praying and puting his hands on him. [9]After this happened, the rest of the people on the island who had diseases also came and were cured. [10]They bestowed many honors on us, and when we were about to sail, they put on board all the provisions we needed.

11 Three months later we set sail on a ship that had wintered at the island, an Alexandrian ship with the Twin Brothers as its figurehead. [12]We put in at Syracuse and stayed there for three days; [13]then we weighed anchor and came to Rhegium. After one day there a south wind sprang up, and on the second day we came to Puteoli. [14]There we found believers[l] and

[l] Gk brothers

τὸ πῦρ ἔπαθεν οὐδὲν κακόν, **28.6** οἱ δὲ προσεδόκων
THE FIRE, HE SUFFERED NO ILL [EFFECTS], - BUT THEY WERE EXPECTING

αὐτὸν μέλλειν πίμπρασθαι ἢ καταπίπτειν ἄφνω
HIM TO BE ABOUT TO SWELL UP OR TO FALL DOWN SUDDENLY

νεκρόν. ἐπὶ πολὺ δὲ αὐτῶν προσδοκώντων καὶ
DEAD. ²FOR ³A LONG [TIME] ¹BUT THEY EXPECTING AND

θεωρούντων μηδὲν ἄτοπον εἰς αὐτὸν γινόμενον
OBSERVING NOTHING UNUSUAL TO HIM HAPPENING,

μεταβαλόμενοι ἔλεγον αὐτὸν εἶναι θεόν.
HAVING CHANGED THEIR MINDS THEY WERE SAYING HIM TO BE A GOD.

28.7 Ἐν δὲ τοῖς περὶ τὸν τόπον ἐκεῖνον
NOW~IN THE [NEIGHBORHOODS] AROUND - THAT~PLACE

ὑπῆρχεν χωρία τῷ πρώτῳ τῆς νήσου ὀνόματι
WERE LANDS [BELONGING] TO THE LEADING MAN OF THE ISLAND BY NAME

Ποπλίῳ, ὃς ἀναδεξάμενος ἡμᾶς τρεῖς ἡμέρας
PUBLIUS, WHO HAVING WELCOMED US, THREE DAYS

φιλοφρόνως ἐξένισεν. **28.8** ἐγένετο δὲ τὸν
HOSPITABLY HE ENTERTAINED [US]. AND~IT CAME ABOUT [THAT] THE

πατέρα τοῦ Ποπλίου πυρετοῖς καὶ δυσεντερίῳ
FATHER - OF PUBLIUS ²WITH FEVERS ³AND ⁴DYSENTERY

συνεχόμενον κατακεῖσθαι, πρὸς ὃν ὁ Παῦλος
¹SUFFERING TO BE LYING DOWN, TO WHOM - PAUL,

εἰσελθὼν καὶ προσευξάμενος ἐπιθεὶς τὰς χεῖρας
HAVING APPROACHED AND HAVING PRAYED, HAVING LAID THE(HIS) HANDS [ON]

αὐτῷ ἰάσατο αὐτόν. **28.9** τούτου δὲ γενομένου καὶ οἱ
HIM, HE HEALED HIM. AND~THIS HAVING HAPPENED ALSO THE

λοιποὶ οἱ ἐν τῇ νήσῳ ἔχοντες ἀσθενείας προσήρχοντο
REST - ON THE ISLAND HAVING ILLNESSES WERE APPROACHING [HIM]

καὶ ἐθεραπεύοντο, **28.10** οἳ καὶ πολλαῖς τιμαῖς
AND WERE BEING HEALED, WHO ALSO WITH MANY HONORS

ἐτίμησαν ἡμᾶς καὶ ἀναγομένοις ἐπέθεντο τὰ
THEY HONORED US AND [WHILE] BEING PUT OUT TO SEA, THEY GAVE [US] THE THINGS

πρὸς τὰς χρείας.
FOR THE NEEDS [OF US].

28.11 Μετὰ δὲ τρεῖς μῆνας ἀνήχθημεν ἐν πλοίῳ
AND~AFTER THREE MONTHS WE SET SAIL IN A SHIP,

παρακεχειμακότι ἐν τῇ νήσῳ, Ἀλεξανδρίνῳ, παρασήμῳ
HAVING SPENT THE WINTER ON THE ISLAND, AN ALEXANDRIAN [SHIP], MARKED

Διοσκούροις. **28.12** καὶ καταχθέντες εἰς
BY THE INSIGNIA OF THE TWIN BROTHERS. AND HAVING PUT IN AT

Συρακούσας ἐπεμείναμεν ἡμέρας τρεῖς, **28.13** ὅθεν
SYRACUSE, WE STAYED THREE~DAYS, FROM WHICH

περιελόντες κατηντήσαμεν εἰς Ῥήγιον. καὶ μετὰ
HAVING GONE AROUND WE ARRIVED AT RHEGIUM. AND AFTER

μίαν ἡμέραν ἐπιγενομένου νότου δευτεραῖοι
ONE DAY, HAVING COME UP A SOUTHWEST WIND ON [THE] SECOND DAY,

ἤλθομεν εἰς Ποτιόλους, **28.14** οὗ εὑρόντες ἀδελφοὺς
WE CAME TO PUTEOLI, WHERE HAVING FOUND BROTHERS,

παρεκλήθημεν παρ' αὐτοῖς ἐπιμεῖναι ἡμέρας ἑπτά·
WE WERE INVITED   BY   THEM   TO STAY   SEVEN~DAYS;

καὶ οὕτως εἰς τὴν Ῥώμην ἤλθαμεν. **28.15** κἀκεῖθεν οἱ
AND THUS   TO -   ROME   WE CAME.   AND FROM THERE THE

ἀδελφοὶ ἀκούσαντες τὰ   περὶ ἡμῶν ἦλθαν εἰς
BROTHERS HAVING HEARD THE THINGS ABOUT US   CAME   TO

ἀπάντησιν ἡμῖν ἄχρι   Ἀππίου Φόρου καὶ Τριῶν
A MEETING WITH US AS FAR AS [THE] FORUM~OF APPIUS AND [THE] THREE

Ταβερνῶν, οὓς ἰδὼν   ὁ Παῦλος εὐχαριστήσας τῷ
TAVERNS,   WHOM ²HAVING SEEN - ¹PAUL, [AND] HAVING GIVEN THANKS -

θεῷ ἔλαβε θάρσος.
TO GOD HE TOOK COURAGE.

28.16 Ὅτε δὲ εἰσήλθομεν εἰς Ῥώμην, ἐπετράπη   τῷ
       NOW~WHEN WE ENTERED INTO ROME,   IT WAS PERMITTED -

Παύλῳ μένειν καθ' ἑαυτὸν σὺν τῷ φυλάσσοντι αὐτὸν
TO PAUL TO REMAIN BY HIMSELF WITH THE ²GUARDING ³HIM

στρατιώτῃ.
¹SOLDIER.

28.17 Ἐγένετο δὲ   μετὰ   ἡμέρας   τρεῖς
       AND~IT CAME ABOUT AFTER THREE~DAYS [THAT]

συγκαλέσασθαι αὐτὸν τοὺς   ὄντας   τῶν
HE~CALLED TOGETHER   THE ONES BEING   -

Ἰουδαίων πρώτους· συνελθόντων δὲ αὐτῶν ἔλεγεν
PROMINENT~JEWS.   ³HAVING ASSEMBLED ¹AND ²THEY, HE WAS SAYING

πρὸς αὐτούς, Ἐγώ, ἄνδρες ἀδελφοί, οὐδὲν ἐναντίον
TO   THEM,   I,   MEN,   BROTHERS, NOTHING OPPOSED

ποιήσας τῷ λαῷ ἢ τοῖς ἔθεσι τοῖς πατρῴοις
HAVING DONE TO THE PEOPLE OR TO THE ²CUSTOMS - ¹ANCESTRAL,

δέσμιος ἐξ Ἱεροσολύμων παρεδόθην εἰς τὰς χεῖρας
A PRISONER FROM JERUSALEM, I WAS DELIVERED INTO THE HANDS

τῶν Ῥωμαίων, **28.18** οἵτινες ἀνακρίναντές με
OF THE ROMANS,   WHO,   HAVING EXAMINED ME,

ἐβούλοντο ἀπολῦσαι διὰ τὸ μηδεμίαν αἰτίαν
WERE DESIRING TO RELEASE [ME] BECAUSE - NO   REASON [FOR]

θανάτου ὑπάρχειν ἐν ἐμοί. **28.19** ἀντιλεγόντων δὲ
DEATH   TO BE [FOUND] IN ME.   BUT~[WHEN] SPEAKING AGAINST [THIS]

τῶν Ἰουδαίων ἠναγκάσθην ἐπικαλέσασθαι Καίσαρα
THE JEWS,   I WAS FORCED TO APPEAL   TO CAESAR,

οὐχ ὡς τοῦ ἔθνους μου ἔχων τι   κατηγορεῖν.
NOT AS [IF] THE NATION OF ME HAVING ANYTHING TO ACCUSE [ME].

28.20 διὰ   ταύτην οὖν   τὴν αἰτίαν παρεκάλεσα
       ON ACCOUNT OF THIS ²THEREFORE - ¹REASON I SUMMONED

ὑμᾶς ἰδεῖν   καὶ προσλαλῆσαι, ἕνεκεν γὰρ τῆς
YOU° TO SEE [YOU°] AND TO SPEAK WITH [YOU°], FOR THE SAKE, THEN, OF THE

ἐλπίδος τοῦ Ἰσραὴλ τὴν ἄλυσιν ταύτην περίκειμαι.
HOPE   - OF ISRAEL, - THIS~CHAIN   I AM WEARING.

28.21 οἱ δὲ πρὸς αὐτὸν εἶπαν, Ἡμεῖς οὔτε γράμματα
       - AND TO HIM   THEY SAID, WE   NEITHER LETTERS

were invited to stay with them for seven days. And so we came to Rome. [15]The believers[m] from there, when they heard of us, came as far as the Forum of Appius and Three Taverns to meet us. On seeing them, Paul thanked God and took courage.

16 When we came into Rome, Paul was allowed to live by himself, with the soldier who was guarding him.

17 Three days later he called together the local leaders of the Jews. When they had assembled, he said to them, "Brothers, though I had done nothing against our people or the customs of our ancestors, yet I was arrested in Jerusalem and handed over to the Romans. [18]When they had examined me, the Romans[n] wanted to release me, because there was no reason for the death penalty in my case. [19]But when the Jews objected, I was compelled to appeal to the emperor—even though I had no charge to bring against my nation. [20]For this reason therefore I have asked to see you and speak with you,[o] since it is for the sake of the hope of Israel that I am bound with this chain." [21]They replied, "We have received no letters

[m] Gk brothers
[n] Gk they
[o] Or I have asked you to see me and speak with me

from Judea about you, and none of the brothers coming here has reported or spoken anything evil about you. ²²But we would like to hear from you what you think, for with regard to this sect we know that everywhere it is spoken against."

23 After they had set a day to meet with him, they came to him at his lodgings in great numbers. From morning until evening he explained the matter to them, testifying to the kingdom of God and trying to convince them about Jesus both from the law of Moses and from the prophets. ²⁴Some were convinced by what he had said, while others refused to believe. ²⁵So they disagreed with each other; and as they were leaving, Paul made one further statement: "The Holy Spirit was right in saying to your ancestors through the prophet Isaiah,

²⁶ 'Go to this people and say,
   You will indeed listen,
      but never
         understand,
      and you will indeed
         look, but never
         perceive.
²⁷ For this people's heart
      has grown dull,
   and their ears are hard
      of hearing,
   and they have shut
      their eyes;
   so that they might not
      look with their eyes,

περὶ σοῦ ἐδεξάμεθα ἀπὸ τῆς Ἰουδαίας οὔτε
ABOUT YOU RECEIVED FROM - JUDEA NOR

παραγενόμενός τις τῶν ἀδελφῶν ἀπήγγειλεν ἢ
HAVING ARRIVED, [HAS] ANYONE OF THE BROTHERS REPORTED OR

ἐλάλησέν τι   περὶ σοῦ πονηρόν. 28.22 ἀξιοῦμεν δὲ
SPOKEN ANYTHING ²ABOUT ³YOU ¹EVIL.   BUT~WE DESIRE

παρὰ σοῦ ἀκοῦσαι ἃ   φρονεῖς, περὶ μὲν γὰρ τῆς
FROM YOU TO HEAR WHAT YOU THINK, ²ABOUT - ¹FOR -

αἱρέσεως ταύτης γνωστὸν ἡμῖν ἐστιν ὅτι πανταχοῦ
⁴SECT ³THIS ⁶KNOWN ⁷TO US ⁵IT IS THAT EVERYWHERE

ἀντιλέγεται.
IT IS SPOKEN AGAINST.

28.23 Ταξάμενοι δὲ αὐτῷ ἡμέραν ἦλθον πρὸς αὐτὸν
      AND~HAVING SET FOR HIM A DAY, CAME TO HIM

εἰς τὴν ξενίαν πλείονες οἷς ἐξετίθετο
IN THE GUEST ROOM MANY,   TO WHOM HE WAS EXPLAINING,

διαμαρτυρόμενος τὴν βασιλείαν τοῦ θεοῦ πείθων τε
TESTIFYING ABOUT THE KINGDOM - OF GOD, AND~PERSUADING

αὐτοὺς περὶ τοῦ Ἰησοῦ ἀπό τε τοῦ νόμου Μωϋσέως
THEM ABOUT - JESUS FROM BOTH THE LAW OF MOSES

καὶ τῶν προφητῶν, ἀπὸ πρωῒ ἕως ἑσπέρας. 28.24 καὶ
AND THE PROPHETS, FROM MORNING UNTIL EVENING.   AND

οἱ μὲν ἐπείθοντο   τοῖς   λεγομένοις, οἱ δὲ
SOME WERE BEING PERSUADED BY THE THINGS BEING SAID, OTHERS

ἠπίστουν· 28.25 ἀσύμφωνοι δὲ ὄντες πρὸς ἀλλήλους
WERE NOT BELIEVING. AND~AT VARIANCE BEING TOWARD ONE ANOTHER,

ἀπελύοντο   εἰπόντος τοῦ Παύλου ῥῆμα ἓν, ὅτι Καλῶς
THEY WERE DISMISSED, ²HAVING SAID - ¹PAUL ONE~WORD, - RIGHTLY

τὸ πνεῦμα τὸ ἅγιον ἐλάλησεν διὰ   Ἠσαΐου τοῦ
THE ²SPIRIT - ¹HOLY SPOKE THROUGH ISAIAH THE

προφήτου πρὸς τοὺς πατέρας ὑμῶν 28.26 λέγων,
PROPHET TO THE FATHERS OF YOU°   SAYING

   Πορεύθητι πρὸς τὸν λαὸν τοῦτον καὶ εἰπόν,
   GO   TO   - THIS~PEOPLE AND SAY,

   Ἀκοῇ ἀκούσετε καὶ   οὐ μὴ συνῆτε
   IN HEARING YOU° WILL HEAR AND [YET] BY NO MEANS UNDERSTAND,

   καὶ βλέποντες βλέψετε καὶ   οὐ μὴ ἴδητε·
   AND SEEING, YOU° WILL SEE AND [YET] BY NO MEANS PERCEIVE.

28.27 ἐπαχύνθη γὰρ ἡ καρδία τοῦ λαοῦ τούτου
   FOR~HAS BECOME DULL THE HEART - OF THIS~PEOPLE

      καὶ τοῖς   ὠσὶν βαρέως   ἤκουσαν
      AND WITH THE(THEIR) EARS WITH DIFFICULTY THEY HEAR

      καὶ τοὺς ὀφθαλμοὺς αὐτῶν ἐκάμμυσαν·
      AND THE EYES   OF THEM THEY CLOSED;

      μήποτε ἴδωσιν τοῖς   ὀφθαλμοῖς
      OTHERWISE THEY MAY SEE WITH THE(THEIR) EYES

28:26-27 Isa. 6:9-10 LXX

καὶ τοῖς ὠσὶν ἀκούσωσιν
AND WITH THE(THEIR) EARS MAY HEAR

καὶ τῇ καρδίᾳ συνῶσιν καὶ
AND WITH THE(THEIR) HEART THEY MAY UNDERSTAND AND

ἐπιστρέψωσιν,
THEY MAY TURN,

καὶ ἰάσομαι αὐτούς.
AND I WILL HEAL THEM.

28.28 γνωστὸν οὖν ἔστω ὑμῖν ὅτι τοῖς ἔθνεσιν
[3]KNOWN [1]THEREFORE [2]LET IT BE TO YOU° THAT TO THE GENTILES

ἀπεστάλη τοῦτο τὸ σωτήριον τοῦ θεοῦ· αὐτοὶ καὶ
WAS SENT THIS - SALVATION - OF GOD. AND~THEY

ἀκούσονται.⊤
WILL LISTEN.

28.30 Ἐνέμεινεν δὲ διετίαν ὅλην ἐν ἰδίῳ μισθώματι
AND~HE REMAINED AN ENTIRE~TWO YEARS IN HIS OWN RENTED HOUSE

καὶ ἀπεδέχετο πάντας τοὺς εἰσπορευομένους πρὸς
AND WAS WELCOMING ALL THE ONES COMING TO

αὐτόν, **28.31** κηρύσσων τὴν βασιλείαν τοῦ θεοῦ καὶ
HIM, PREACHING THE KINGDOM - OF GOD AND

διδάσκων τὰ περὶ τοῦ κυρίου Ἰησοῦ Χριστοῦ
TEACHING THE THINGS CONCERNING THE LORD JESUS CHRIST

μετὰ πάσης παρρησίας ἀκωλύτως.
WITH ALL OPENNESS WITHOUT HINDRANCE.

28:28 text: ASV RSV NASB NIV NEB TEV NJB NRSV. add v. 29 και ταυτα αυτου ειποντος απηλθον οι Ιουδαιοι, πολλην εχοντες εν εαυτοις συζητησιν (And after he said these things, the Jews went away, arguing greatly among themselves): KJV ASVmg RSVmg NASBmg NIVmg NEBmg TEVmg NJBmg NRSVmg.

and listen with their
ears,
and understand with their
heart and turn—
and I would heal them.'
28Let it be known to you then
that this salvation of God has
been sent to the Gentiles;
they will listen."[p]
30 He lived there two
whole years at his own
expense[q] and welcomed all
who came to him,
31proclaiming the kingdom
of God and teaching about
the Lord Jesus Christ with all
boldness and without
hindrance.

[p] Other ancient authorities add verse 29, *And when he had said these words, the Jews departed, arguing vigorously among themselves*

[q] Or *in his own hired dwelling*

THE LETTER OF PAUL TO THE
ROMANS

ΠΡΟΣ ΡΩΜΑΙΟΥΣ
TO   [THE] ROMANS

1.1 Παῦλος δοῦλος Χριστοῦ Ἰησοῦ, κλητὸς ἀπόστολος
PAUL,   A SLAVE   OF CHRIST JESUS,   A CALLED APOSTLE

ἀφωρισμένος εἰς εὐαγγέλιον θεοῦ, **1.2** ὃ
HAVING BEEN SET APART FOR [THE] GOSPEL OF GOD, WHICH

προεπηγγείλατο διὰ τῶν προφητῶν αὐτοῦ ἐν γραφαῖς
HE PROMISED BEFORE THROUGH THE PROPHETS OF HIM IN SCRIPTURES

ἁγίαις **1.3** περὶ τοῦ υἱοῦ αὐτοῦ τοῦ γενομένου ἐκ
HOLY   CONCERNING THE SON OF HIM - HAVING COME FROM

σπέρματος Δαυὶδ κατὰ σάρκα, **1.4** τοῦ
[THE] SEED OF DAVID ACCORDING TO FLESH, -

ὁρισθέντος υἱοῦ θεοῦ ἐν δυνάμει κατὰ πνεῦμα
HAVING BEEN DESIGNATED SON OF GOD IN POWER ACCORDING TO A SPIRIT

ἁγιωσύνης ἐξ ἀναστάσεως νεκρῶν, Ἰησοῦ Χριστοῦ τοῦ
OF HOLINESS BY A RESURRECTION OF DEAD ONES, JESUS CHRIST THE

κυρίου ἡμῶν, **1.5** δι’ οὗ ἐλάβομεν χάριν καὶ
LORD OF US, THROUGH WHOM WE RECEIVED GRACE AND

ἀποστολὴν εἰς ὑπακοὴν πίστεως ἐν πᾶσιν τοῖς
APOSTLESHIP FOR OBEDIENCE OF FAITH AMONG ALL THE

ἔθνεσιν ὑπὲρ τοῦ ὀνόματος αὐτοῦ, **1.6** ἐν οἷς ἐστε
NATIONS ON BEHALF OF THE NAME OF HIM, AMONG WHOM ARE

καὶ ὑμεῖς κλητοὶ Ἰησοῦ Χριστοῦ, **1.7** πᾶσιν τοῖς
ALSO YOU° CALLED ONES OF JESUS CHRIST, TO ALL THE ONES

οὖσιν ἐν Ῥώμῃ ἀγαπητοῖς θεοῦ, κλητοῖς ἁγίοις, χάρις
BEING IN ROME, LOVED ONES OF GOD, CALLED ONES, SAINTS, GRACE

ὑμῖν καὶ εἰρήνη ἀπὸ θεοῦ πατρὸς ἡμῶν καὶ κυρίου
TO YOU° AND PEACE FROM GOD [THE] FATHER OF US AND LORD

Ἰησοῦ Χριστοῦ.
JESUS CHRIST.

1.8 Πρῶτον μὲν εὐχαριστῶ τῷ θεῷ μου διὰ Ἰησοῦ
FIRST, - I THANK THE GOD OF ME THROUGH JESUS

Χριστοῦ περὶ πάντων ὑμῶν ὅτι ἡ πίστις ὑμῶν
CHRIST CONCERNING ALL OF YOU° BECAUSE THE FAITH OF YOU°

καταγγέλλεται ἐν ὅλῳ τῷ κόσμῳ. **1.9** μάρτυς γάρ μού
IS BEING PROCLAIMED IN ALL THE WORLD. ⁵WITNESS ¹FOR ⁴MY

ἐστιν ὁ θεός, ᾧ λατρεύω ἐν τῷ πνεύματί μου ἐν
³IS - ²GOD, WHOM I SERVE IN THE SPIRIT OF ME IN

τῷ εὐαγγελίῳ τοῦ υἱοῦ αὐτοῦ, ὡς ἀδιαλείπτως
THE GOSPEL OF THE SON OF HIM, HOW UNCEASINGLY

Paul, a servant[a] of Jesus Christ, called to be an apostle, set apart for the gospel of God, [2]which he promised beforehand through his prophets in the holy scriptures, [3]the gospel concerning his Son, who was descended from David according to the flesh [4]and was declared to be Son of God with power according to the spirit[b] of holiness by resurrection from the dead, Jesus Christ our Lord, [5]through whom we have received grace and apostleship to bring about the obedience of faith among all the Gentiles for the sake of his name, [6]including yourselves who are called to belong to Jesus Christ,

7 To all God's beloved in Rome, who are called to be saints:

Grace to you and peace from God our Father and the Lord Jesus Christ.

8 First, I thank my God through Jesus Christ for all of you, because your faith is proclaimed throughout the world. [9]For God, whom I serve with my spirit by announcing the gospel[c] of his Son, is my witness that without ceasing

[a] Gk *slave*
[b] Or *Spirit*
[c] Gk *my spirit in the gospel*

I remember you always in my prayers, [10]asking that by God's will I may somehow at last succeed in coming to you. [11]For I am longing to see you so that I may share with you some spiritual gift to strengthen you— [12]or rather so that we may be mutually encouraged by each other's faith, both yours and mine. [13]I want you to know, brothers and sisters,[d] that I have often intended to come to you (but thus far have been prevented), in order that I may reap some harvest among you as I have among the rest of the Gentiles. [14]I am a debtor both to Greeks and to barbarians, both to the wise and to the foolish [15]— hence my eagerness to proclaim the gospel to you also who are in Rome.

[16] For I am not ashamed of the gospel; it is the power of God for salvation to everyone who has faith, to the Jew first and also to the Greek. [17]For in it the righteousness of God is revealed through faith for faith; as it is written, "The one who is righteous will live by faith."[e]

[18] For the wrath of God is revealed from heaven against all ungodliness and wickedness of those who by their wickedness suppress the truth.

[d] Gk brothers
[e] Or The one who is righteous through faith will live

μνείαν ὑμῶν ποιοῦμαι **1.10** πάντοτε ἐπὶ τῶν προσευχῶν
MENTION OF YOU° I MAKE   ALWAYS AT THE PRAYERS

μου δεόμενος εἴ πως ἤδη ποτὲ εὐοδωθήσομαι
OF ME REQUESTING IF SOMEHOW NOW AT SOME TIME I WILL MAKE MY WAY

ἐν τῷ θελήματι τοῦ θεοῦ ἐλθεῖν πρὸς ὑμᾶς.
BY THE WILL - OF GOD TO COME TO YOU°.

1.11 ἐπιποθῶ γὰρ ἰδεῖν ὑμᾶς, ἵνα τι μεταδῶ χάρισμα
FOR~I LONG TO SEE YOU°, THAT [2]SOME [1]I MAY IMPART [4]GIFT

ὑμῖν πνευματικὸν εἰς τὸ στηριχθῆναι ὑμᾶς, **1.12** τοῦτο
[5]TO YOU° [3]SPIRITUAL TO THE [END] YOU°~MAY BE ESTABLISHED, THAT

δέ ἐστιν συμπαρακληθῆναι ἐν ὑμῖν διὰ τῆς
- IS TO BE ENCOURAGED TOGETHER [WHILE] AMONG YOU° THROUGH [1]THE

ἐν ἀλλήλοις πίστεως ὑμῶν τε καὶ ἐμοῦ. **1.13** οὐ
[3]IN [4]ONE ANOTHER [2]FAITH [6]YOURS° [5]BOTH [7]AND [8]MINE. [3]NOT

θέλω δὲ ὑμᾶς ἀγνοεῖν, ἀδελφοί, ὅτι πολλάκις
[2]I WISH [1]NOW YOU° TO BE UNAWARE, BROTHERS, THAT OFTEN

προεθέμην ἐλθεῖν πρὸς ὑμᾶς, καὶ ἐκωλύθην ἄχρι τοῦ
I PLANNED TO COME TO YOU°, AND WAS HINDERED UNTIL THE

δεῦρο, ἵνα τινὰ καρπὸν σχῶ καὶ ἐν ὑμῖν καθὼς
PRESENT, THAT SOME FRUIT I MAY HAVE ALSO AMONG YOU° EVEN AS

καὶ ἐν τοῖς λοιποῖς ἔθνεσιν. **1.14** Ἕλλησίν τε καὶ
ALSO AMONG THE REMAINING NATIONS. ' BOTH~TO GREEKS AND

βαρβάροις, σοφοῖς τε καὶ ἀνοήτοις ὀφειλέτης εἰμί,
TO FOREIGNERS, BOTH~TO WISE AND TO UNINTELLIGENT I AM~A DEBTOR,

1.15 οὕτως τὸ κατ' ἐμὲ πρόθυμον καὶ ὑμῖν τοῖς
SO AS FAR AS DEPENDS ON ME [I AM] EAGER [2]ALSO [3]TO YOU° [4]THE ONES

ἐν Ῥώμῃ εὐαγγελίσασθαι.
[5]IN [6]ROME [1]TO PREACH.

1.16 Οὐ γὰρ ἐπαισχύνομαι τὸ εὐαγγέλιον, δύναμις γὰρ
FOR~NOT I AM ASHAMED OF THE GOOD NEWS, FOR~[THE] POWER

θεοῦ ᾿στιν εἰς σωτηρίαν παντὶ τῷ πιστεύοντι,
OF GOD IT IS UNTO SALVATION TO EVERYONE BELIEVING,

Ἰουδαίῳ τε πρῶτον καὶ Ἕλληνι. **1.17** δικαιοσύνη γὰρ
BOTH~TO JEW FIRST AND TO GREEK. FOR~[THE] RIGHTEOUSNESS

θεοῦ ἐν αὐτῷ ἀποκαλύπτεται ἐκ πίστεως εἰς πίστιν,
OF GOD IN IT IS REVEALED FROM FAITH TO FAITH,

καθὼς γέγραπται, Ὁ δὲ δίκαιος ἐκ πίστεως
AS IT HAS BEEN WRITTEN, BUT~THE RIGHTEOUS MAN BY FAITH

ζήσεται.
WILL LIVE.

1.18 Ἀποκαλύπτεται γὰρ ὀργὴ θεοῦ ἀπ' οὐρανοῦ
[4]IS REVEALED [1]FOR [3]WRATH [2]GOD'S FROM HEAVEN

ἐπὶ πᾶσαν ἀσέβειαν καὶ ἀδικίαν ἀνθρώπων τῶν
AGAINST ALL UNGODLINESS AND UNRIGHTEOUSNESS OF MEN -

τὴν ἀλήθειαν ἐν ἀδικίᾳ κατεχόντων,
[2]THE [3]TRUTH [4]IN [5]UNRIGHTEOUSNESS [1]REPRESSING,

1:17 Hab. 2:4

1.19 διότι   τὸ   γνωστὸν   τοῦ θεοῦ   φανερόν ἐστιν
BECAUSE   THAT WHICH [MAY BE] KNOWN   -   OF(ABOUT) GOD   IS~MANIFEST

ἐν   αὐτοῖς· ὁ θεὸς γὰρ αὐτοῖς ἐφανέρωσεν.
AMONG   THEM;   -   ²GOD ¹FOR   ⁴TO THEM ³MANIFESTED [IT].

1.20 τὰ γὰρ ἀόρατα   αὐτοῦ ἀπὸ κτίσεως κόσμου   τοῖς
FOR~THE   INVISIBLE THINGS OF HIM ²FROM ⁴CREATION ³[THE] WORLD'S ⁶BY THE

ποιήμασιν νοούμενα   καθορᾶται, ἥ τε   ἀΐδιος αὐτοῦ
⁷THINGS MADE ⁵BEING UNDERSTOOD ¹ARE CLEARLY SEEN, -   BOTH HIS~EVERLASTING

δύναμις   καὶ   θειότης,   εἰς τὸ εἶναι αὐτοὺς
POWER   AND   DIVINITY,   FOR   -   THEM~TO BE

ἀναπολογήτους, **1.21** διότι   γνόντες   τὸν θεὸν οὐχ ὡς
WITHOUT EXCUSE,   BECAUSE HAVING KNOWN -   GOD ²NOT ³AS

θεὸν ἐδόξασαν   ἢ   ηὐχαρίστησαν, ἀλλ᾽
⁴GOD   ¹THEY GLORIFIED [HIM] NOR THANKED [HIM],   BUT

ἐματαιώθησαν ἐν τοῖς διαλογισμοῖς αὐτῶν καὶ
BECAME VAIN   IN   THE REASONINGS   OF THEM AND

ἐσκοτίσθη ἡ ἀσύνετος αὐτῶν καρδία. **1.22** φάσκοντες
⁴WAS DARKENED - ²SENSELESS ¹THEIR ³HEART.   PROFESSING

εἶναι σοφοὶ ἐμωράνθησαν **1.23** καὶ ἤλλαξαν τὴν δόξαν
TO BE WISE THEY BECAME FOOLISH,   AND CHANGED   THE GLORY

τοῦ ἀφθάρτου θεοῦ ἐν ὁμοιώματι εἰκόνος φθαρτοῦ
OF THE INCORRUPTIBLE GOD IN[TO] A LIKENESS OF AN IMAGE OF CORRUPTIBLE

ἀνθρώπου καὶ πετεινῶν καὶ τετραπόδων καὶ ἑρπετῶν.
MAN   AND   BIRDS   AND QUADRUPEDS   AND REPTILES.

1.24 Διὸ   παρέδωκεν αὐτοὺς ὁ θεὸς ἐν ταῖς
THEREFORE ²GAVE OVER ³THEM   - ¹GOD IN THE

ἐπιθυμίαις τῶν καρδιῶν αὐτῶν εἰς ἀκαθαρσίαν τοῦ
LUSTS   OF THE HEARTS OF THEM TO IMPURITY   -

ἀτιμάζεσθαι τὰ σώματα αὐτῶν ἐν αὐτοῖς·
TO BE DISHONORED THE BODIES OF THEM AMONG THEMSELVES;

1.25 οἵτινες μετήλλαξαν τὴν ἀλήθειαν τοῦ θεοῦ ἐν τῷ
WHO   CHANGED   THE TRUTH   OF GOD IN[TO] THE

ψεύδει καὶ ἐσεβάσθησαν καὶ ἐλάτρευσαν τῇ κτίσει
LIE   AND WORSHIPED   AND SERVED   THE CREATURE

παρὰ τὸν κτίσαντα, ὅς ἐστιν εὐλογητὸς εἰς τοὺς
RATHER THAN THE ONE HAVING CREATED, WHO IS BLESSED   INTO THE

αἰῶνας, ἀμήν. **1.26** διὰ τοῦτο   παρέδωκεν αὐτοὺς ὁ θεὸς
AGES,   AMEN.   BECAUSE OF THIS ²GAVE OVER ³THEM   - ¹GOD

εἰς πάθη ἀτιμίας, αἵ τε γὰρ θήλειαι αὐτῶν
TO PASSIONS OF DISHONOR, ³THE ²EVEN ¹FOR FEMALES   OF THEM

μετήλλαξαν τὴν φυσικὴν χρῆσιν εἰς τὴν παρὰ   φύσιν,
CHANGED   THE NATURAL FUNCTION INTO THAT CONTRARY TO NATURE,

1.27 ὁμοίως τε καὶ οἱ ἄρσενες ἀφέντες τὴν φυσικὴν
AND~LIKEWISE ALSO THE MALES   HAVING LEFT THE NATURAL

χρῆσιν τῆς θηλείας ἐξεκαύθησαν ἐν τῇ ὀρέξει αὐτῶν
FUNCTION OF THE FEMALE BURNED   IN THE CRAVING OF THEM

εἰς ἀλλήλους, ἄρσενες ἐν ἄρσεσιν τὴν ἀσχημοσύνην
TOWARD ONE ANOTHER, MALES   WITH MALES ²THE ³INDECENT [ACT]

¹⁹For what can be known about God is plain to them, because God has shown it to them. ²⁰Ever since the creation of the world his eternal power and divine nature, invisible though they are, have been understood and seen through the things he has made. So they are without excuse; ²¹for though they knew God, they did not honor him as God or give thanks to him, but they became futile in their thinking, and their senseless minds were darkened. ²²Claiming to be wise, they became fools; ²³and they exchanged the glory of the immortal God for images resembling a mortal human being or birds or four-footed animals or reptiles.

24 Therefore God gave them up in the lusts of their hearts to impurity, to the degrading of their bodies among themselves, ²⁵because they exchanged the truth about God for a lie and worshiped and served the creature rather than the Creator, who is blessed forever! Amen.

26 For this reason God gave them up to degrading passions. Their women exchanged natural intercourse for unnatural, ²⁷and in the same way also the men, giving up natural intercourse with women, were consumed with passion for one another. Men committed shameless acts with men

and received in their own persons the due penalty for their error.

28 And since they did not see fit to acknowledge God, God gave them up to a debased mind and to things that should not be done. [29]They were filled with every kind of wickedness, evil, covetousness, malice. Full of envy, murder, strife, deceit, craftiness, they are gossips, [30]slanderers, God-haters,[f] insolent, haughty, boastful, inventors of evil, rebellious toward parents, [31]foolish, faithless, heartless, ruthless. [32]They know God's decree, that those who practice such things deserve to die—yet they not only do them but even applaud others who practice them.

[f] Or God-hated

κατεργαζόμενοι καὶ τὴν ἀντιμισθίαν ἣν ἔδει
[1]PERFORMING   AND   [4]THE [5]RETRIBUTION   [6]WHICH [7][WAS THEIR] DUE

τῆς   πλάνης αὐτῶν ἐν ἑαυτοῖς ἀπολαμβάνοντες.
[8][BECAUSE] OF THE [9]ERROR   [10]OF THEM [2]IN [3]THEMSELVES [1]RECEIVING BACK.

1.28 καὶ καθὼς οὐκ ἐδοκίμασαν τὸν θεὸν ἔχειν ἐν
AND   AS   THEY DID NOT APPROVE   -   TO HOLD~GOD IN

ἐπιγνώσει, παρέδωκεν αὐτοὺς ὁ θεὸς εἰς ἀδόκιμον
[THEIR] KNOWLEDGE, [2]GAVE OVER [3]THEM - [1]GOD TO A DISAPPROVED

νοῦν, ποιεῖν τὰ   μὴ καθήκοντα, **1.29** πεπληρωμένους
MIND, TO DO THE THINGS NOT BEING PROPER,   HAVING BEEN FILLED

πάσῃ ἀδικίᾳ   πονηρίᾳ πλεονεξίᾳ κακίᾳ, μεστοὺς
WITH ALL UNRIGHTEOUSNESS, WICKEDNESS, GREEDINESS, EVIL,   FULL

φθόνου φόνου ἔριδος δόλου κακοηθείας, ψιθυριστὰς
OF ENVY, MURDER, STRIFE, DECEIT, MALICE,   WHISPERERS,

1.30 καταλάλους θεοστυγεῖς ὑβριστὰς ὑπερηφάνους
BACKBITERS,   GOD-HATERS, INSOLENT,   ARROGANT

ἀλαζόνας, ἐφευρετὰς κακῶν, γονεῦσιν ἀπειθεῖς,
BOASTERS,   INVENTORS OF BAD THINGS, TO PARENTS DISOBEDIENT,

1.31 ἀσυνέτους ἀσυνθέτους ἀστόργους ἀνελεήμονας·
SENSELESS,   FAITHLESS,   UNAFFECTIONATE, MERCILESS;

1.32 οἵτινες τὸ δικαίωμα   τοῦ θεοῦ ἐπιγνόντες ὅτι
WHO   [2]THE [3]JUST REQUIREMENTS -   [4]OF GOD [1]KNOWING THAT

οἱ   τὰ τοιαῦτα πράσσοντες ἄξιοι θανάτου εἰσίν, οὐ
THE ONES - SUCH THINGS PRACTISING WORTHY OF DEATH ARE,   NOT

μόνον αὐτὰ ποιοῦσιν ἀλλὰ καὶ συνευδοκοῦσιν τοῖς
ONLY   DO~THEM   BUT ALSO APPROVE OF   THE ONES

πράσσουσιν.
PRACTISING [THEM].

CHAPTER 2

Therefore you have no excuse, whoever you are, when you judge others; for in passing judgment on another you condemn yourself, because you, the judge, are doing the very same things. [2]You say,[g] "We know that God's judgment on those who do such things is in accordance with truth." [3]Do you imagine, whoever you are, that when you judge those who do such things and yet do them yourself, you will escape the judgment of God? [4]Or do you despise the riches

[g] Gk lacks You say

2.1 Διὸ   ἀναπολόγητος εἶ,   ὦ ἄνθρωπε πᾶς ὁ
WHEREFORE INEXCUSABLE   YOU ARE, O MAN   EVERYONE

κρίνων· ἐν ᾧ γὰρ κρίνεις τὸν ἕτερον, σεαυτὸν
JUDGING; [2]IN [3]WHAT [1]FOR YOU JUDGE THE OTHER,   YOURSELF

κατακρίνεις, τὰ γὰρ αὐτὰ   πράσσεις ὁ   κρίνων.
YOU CONDEMN; FOR~THE SAME THINGS YOU PRACTISE, THE ONE JUDGING.

2.2 οἴδαμεν δὲ ὅτι τὸ κρίμα τοῦ θεοῦ ἐστιν κατὰ
BUT~WE KNOW   THAT THE JUDGMENT -   OF GOD IS   ACCORDING TO

ἀλήθειαν ἐπὶ τοὺς τὰ τοιαῦτα πράσσοντας.
TRUTH   UPON THE ONES - SUCH THINGS PRACTISING.

2.3 λογίζῃ δὲ   τοῦτο, ὦ ἄνθρωπε ὁ   κρίνων τοὺς
AND~DO YOU RECKON THIS, O MAN,   THE ONE JUDGING THE ONES

τὰ τοιαῦτα πράσσοντας καὶ ποιῶν αὐτά, ὅτι σὺ
- SUCH THINGS PRACTISING   AND DOING THEM, THAT YOU

ἐκφεύξῃ τὸ κρίμα   τοῦ θεοῦ; **2.4** ἢ τοῦ πλούτου τῆς
WILL ESCAPE THE JUDGMENT -   OF GOD?   OR THE RICHES   OF THE

χρηστότητος αὐτοῦ καὶ τῆς ἀνοχῆς καὶ τῆς
KINDNESS   OF HIM AND THE FORBEARANCE AND THE

μακροθυμίας καταφρονεῖς, ἀγνοῶν ὅτι τὸ χρηστὸν
LONGSUFFERING DO YOU SCORN,   NOT REALIZING THAT THE KINDNESS

τοῦ θεοῦ εἰς μετάνοιάν σε ἄγει; 2.5 κατὰ δὲ
-    OF GOD ³TO ⁴REPENTANCE ²YOU ¹LEADS?   BUT~ACCORDING TO

τὴν σκληρότητά σου καὶ ἀμετανόητον καρδίαν
THE HARDNESS   OF YOU AND UNREPENTANT   HEART

θησαυρίζεις σεαυτῷ ὀργὴν ἐν ἡμέρᾳ ὀργῆς καὶ
YOU STORE UP FOR YOURSELF WRATH IN A DAY OF WRATH AND

ἀποκαλύψεως δικαιοκρισίας τοῦ θεοῦ 2.6 ὃς
REVELATION   OF [THE] RIGHTEOUS JUDGMENT - OF GOD, WHO

ἀποδώσει ἑκάστῳ κατὰ τὰ ἔργα αὐτοῦ·
WILL RECOMPENSE TO EACH MAN ACCORDING TO THE WORKS OF HIM;

2.7 τοῖς μὲν καθ' ὑπομονὴν ἔργου ἀγαθοῦ δόξαν
TO THE ONES ON ONE HAND BY ENDURANCE ²WORK ¹OF(IN) GOOD ⁴GLORY

καὶ τιμὴν καὶ ἀφθαρσίαν ζητοῦσιν ζωὴν αἰώνιον,
⁵AND ⁶HONOR ⁷AND ⁸INCORRUPTIBILITY ³SEEKING, LIFE ETERNAL,

2.8 τοῖς δὲ ἐξ ἐριθείας καὶ ἀπειθοῦσι τῇ
TO THE ONES ON THE OTHER HAND [BEING] SELFISH AND DISOBEYING THE

ἀληθείᾳ πειθομένοις δὲ τῇ ἀδικίᾳ ὀργὴ καὶ
TRUTH   BUT~BEING OBEDIENT - TO UNRIGHTEOUSNESS, WRATH AND

θυμός. 2.9 θλῖψις καὶ στενοχωρία ἐπὶ πᾶσαν ψυχὴν
ANGER.   AFFLICTION AND DISTRESS ON EVERY SOUL

ἀνθρώπου τοῦ κατεργαζομένου τὸ κακόν, Ἰουδαίου τε
OF MAN - WORKING   THE EVIL, BOTH~OF JEW

πρῶτον καὶ Ἕλληνος· 2.10 δόξα δὲ καὶ τιμὴ καὶ
FIRST   AND OF GREEK;   BUT~GLORY AND HONOR AND

εἰρήνη παντὶ τῷ ἐργαζομένῳ τὸ ἀγαθόν, Ἰουδαίῳ τε
PEACE TO EVERYONE - WORKING   THE GOOD, BOTH~TO JEW

πρῶτον καὶ Ἕλληνι· 2.11 οὐ γάρ ἐστιν
FIRST   AND TO GREEK;   ³NOT ¹FOR ²[THERE] IS

προσωπολημψία παρὰ τῷ θεῷ. 2.12 ὅσοι γὰρ
RESPECT OF PERSONS WITH - GOD.   FOR~AS MANY AS

ἀνόμως ἥμαρτον, ἀνόμως καὶ ἀπολοῦνται, καὶ
WITHOUT LAW SINNED, WITHOUT LAW ALSO WILL PERISH, AND

ὅσοι ἐν νόμῳ ἥμαρτον, διὰ νόμου κριθήσονται·
AS MANY AS IN(UNDER) LAW SINNED, BY LAW WILL BE JUDGED;

2.13 οὐ γὰρ οἱ ἀκροαταὶ νόμου δίκαιοι παρὰ [τῷ]
   FOR~NOT THE HEARERS OF LAW [ARE] JUST WITH

θεῷ, ἀλλ' οἱ ποιηταὶ νόμου δικαιωθήσονται.
GOD, BUT THE DOERS OF LAW WILL BE JUSTIFIED.

2.14 ὅταν γὰρ ἔθνη τὰ μὴ νόμον ἔχοντα φύσει τὰ
   FOR~WHEN GENTILES - NOT HAVING~[THE] LAW BY NATURE THE THINGS

τοῦ νόμου ποιῶσιν, οὗτοι νόμον μὴ ἔχοντες ἑαυτοῖς
OF THE LAW PRACTISE, THESE A LAW NOT HAVING TO THEMSELVES

εἰσιν νόμος· 2.15 οἵτινες ἐνδείκνυνται τὸ ἔργον τοῦ
ARE A LAW;   WHO DEMONSTRATE   THE WORK OF THE

of his kindness and
forbearance and patience?
Do you not realize that
God's kindness is meant to
lead you to repentance? [5]But
by your hard and impenitent
heart you are storing up
wrath for yourself on the day
of wrath, when God's
righteous judgment will be
revealed. [6]For he will repay
according to each one's
deeds: [7]to those who by
patiently doing good seek
for glory and honor and
immortality, he will give
eternal life; [8]while for those
who are self-seeking and
who obey not the truth but
wickedness, there will be
wrath and fury. [9]There will
be anguish and distress for
everyone who does evil, the
Jew first and also the Greek,
[10]but glory and honor and
peace for everyone who does
good, the Jew first and also
the Greek. [11]For God shows
no partiality.

[12]All who have sinned
apart from the law will also
perish apart from the law,
and all who have sinned
under the law will be judged
by the law. [13]For it is not the
hearers of the law who are
righteous in God's sight, but
the doers of the law who
will be justified. [14]When
Gentiles, who do not possess
the law, do instinctively
what the law requires, these,
though not having the law,
are a law to themselves.
[15]They show that what
the law requires is

written on their hearts, to which their own conscience also bears witness; and their conflicting thoughts will accuse or perhaps excuse them [16]on the day when, according to my gospel, God, through Jesus Christ, will judge the secret thoughts of all.

[17] But if you call yourself a Jew and rely on the law and boast of your relation to God [18]and know his will and determine what is best because you are instructed in the law, [19]and if you are sure that you are a guide to the blind, a light to those who are in darkness, [20]a corrector of the foolish, a teacher of children, having in the law the embodiment of knowledge and truth, [21]you, then, that teach others, will you not teach yourself? While you preach against stealing, do you steal? [22]You that forbid adultery, do you commit adultery? You that abhor idols, do you rob temples? [23]You that boast in the law, do you dishonor God by breaking the law? [24]For, as it is written, "The name of God is blasphemed among the Gentiles because of you."

[25] Circumcision indeed is of value if you obey the law; but if you break the law, your circumcision has become uncircumcision. [26]So, if those who are

νόμου γραπτὸν ἐν ταῖς καρδίαις αὐτῶν,
LAW   WRITTEN   IN   THE   HEARTS   OF THEM,

συμμαρτυρούσης αὐτῶν τῆς συνειδήσεως καὶ μεταξὺ
[3]BEARING JOINT-WITNESS [1]THEIR - [2]CONSCIENCE AND [7]BETWEEN

ἀλλήλων τῶν λογισμῶν κατηγορούντων ἢ καὶ
[8]ONE ANOTHER [1]THEIR [2]THOUGHTS [3]ACCUSING   [4]OR [5]EVEN

ἀπολογουμένων, 2.16 ἐν ἡμέρᾳ ὅτε κρίνει ὁ θεὸς τὰ
[6]DEFENDING,   IN A DAY WHEN [2]JUDGES - [1]GOD THE

κρυπτὰ τῶν ἀνθρώπων κατὰ τὸ εὐαγγέλιόν μου
HIDDEN THINGS - OF MEN, ACCORDING TO THE GOSPEL   OF ME,

διὰ Χριστοῦ Ἰησοῦ.
THROUGH CHRIST JESUS.

2.17 Εἰ δὲ σὺ Ἰουδαῖος ἐπονομάζῃ καὶ ἐπαναπαύῃ
     BUT~IF YOU A JEW   ARE CALLED   AND RELY UPON

νόμῳ καὶ καυχᾶσαι ἐν θεῷ 2.18 καὶ γινώσκεις
[THE] LAW AND BOAST   IN GOD   AND   KNOW

τὸ θέλημα καὶ δοκιμάζεις τὰ διαφέροντα
THE WILL   AND APPROVE   THE THINGS EXCELLING

κατηχούμενος ἐκ τοῦ νόμου, 2.19 πέποιθάς τε
BEING INSTRUCTED FROM THE LAW,   AND~HAVING CONFIDENCE

σεαυτὸν ὁδηγὸν εἶναι τυφλῶν, φῶς τῶν ἐν σκότει,
YOURSELF A GUIDE TO BE OF BLIND ONES, A LIGHT OF THE ONES IN DARKNESS,

2.20 παιδευτὴν ἀφρόνων, διδάσκαλον νηπίων, ἔχοντα
     AN INSTRUCTOR OF FOOLISH ONES, A TEACHER OF BABES, HAVING

τὴν μόρφωσιν τῆς γνώσεως καὶ τῆς ἀληθείας ἐν τῷ
THE EMBODIMENT - OF KNOWLEDGE AND OF THE TRUTH IN THE

νόμῳ· 2.21 ὁ οὖν διδάσκων ἕτερον σεαυτὸν
LAW—   THEREFORE~THE ONE TEACHING ANOTHER YOURSELF

οὐ διδάσκεις; ὁ κηρύσσων μὴ κλέπτειν κλέπτεις;
DO YOU NOT TEACH? THE ONE PROCLAIMING NOT TO STEAL DO YOU STEAL?

2.22 ὁ λέγων μὴ μοιχεύειν μοιχεύεις;
     THE ONE SAYING NOT TO COMMIT ADULTERY DO YOU COMMIT ADULTERY?

ὁ βδελυσσόμενος τὰ εἴδωλα ἱεροσυλεῖς;
THE ONE ABHORRING   THE IDOLS DO YOU PLUNDER TEMPLES?

2.23 ὃς ἐν νόμῳ καυχᾶσαι, διὰ τῆς παραβάσεως
     WHO IN [THE] LAW BOAST, THROUGH - TRANSGRESSION

τοῦ νόμου τὸν θεὸν ἀτιμάζεις· 2.24 τὸ γὰρ ὄνομα τοῦ
OF THE LAW - DISHONOR~GOD.   FOR~THE NAME   -

θεοῦ δι' ὑμᾶς βλασφημεῖται ἐν τοῖς ἔθνεσιν,
OF GOD BECAUSE OF YOU° IS BLASPHEMED AMONG THE NATIONS,

καθὼς γέγραπται. 2.25 περιτομὴ μὲν γὰρ ὠφελεῖ ἐὰν
AS   IT HAS BEEN WRITTEN. [3]CIRCUMCISION [2]INDEED [1]FOR PROFITS IF

νόμον πράσσῃς· ἐὰν δὲ παραβάτης νόμου ᾖς, ἡ
[THE] LAW YOU PRACTISE; BUT~IF A TRANSGRESSOR OF LAW YOU ARE, THE

περιτομή σου ἀκροβυστία γέγονεν. 2.26 ἐὰν οὖν ἡ
CIRCUMCISION OF YOU UNCIRCUMCISION HAS BECOME. IF THEREFORE THE

2:24 Isa. 52:5 LXX

ἀκροβυστία τὰ δικαιώματα τοῦ νόμου φυλάσσῃ,
UNCIRCUMCISION THE JUST REQUIREMENTS OF THE LAW KEEPS,

οὐχ ἡ ἀκροβυστία αὐτοῦ εἰς περιτομὴν
[WILL] NOT THE UNCIRCUMCISION OF HIM FOR CIRCUMCISION

λογισθήσεται; **2.27** καὶ κρινεῖ ἡ ἐκ φύσεως
BE ACCOUNTED? AND 8WILL JUDGE 1THE 3BY 4NATURE

ἀκροβυστία τὸν νόμον τελοῦσα σὲ τὸν διὰ γράμματος
2CIRCUMCISION 6THE 7LAW 5KEEPING 9YOU 10THE 13BY 14LETTER

καὶ περιτομῆς παραβάτην νόμου. **2.28** οὐ γὰρ ὁ
15AND 16UNCIRCUMCISION 11TRANSGRESSOR 12OF LAW. FOR~NOT 2THE

ἐν τῷ φανερῷ Ἰουδαῖός ἐστιν οὐδὲ ἡ ἐν τῷ φανερῷ
4OUTWARDLY 3JEW 1HE IS NOR 1THE 3OUTWARDLY

ἐν σαρκὶ περιτομή, **2.29** ἀλλ᾽ ὁ ἐν τῷ κρυπτῷ
4IN 5FLESH 2CIRCUMCISION, BUT 1THE 3INWARDLY

Ἰουδαῖος, καὶ περιτομὴ καρδίας ἐν πνεύματι οὐ
2JEW [IS], AND CIRCUMCISION [IS] OF HEART IN SPIRIT NOT

γράμματι, οὗ ὁ ἔπαινος οὐκ ἐξ ἀνθρώπων ἀλλ᾽
LETTER, WHOSE - PRAISE [IS] NOT FROM MEN BUT

ἐκ τοῦ θεοῦ.
FROM - GOD.

uncircumcised keep the requirements of the law, will not their uncircumcision be regarded as circumcision? 27Then those who are physically uncircumcised but keep the law will condemn you that have the written code and circumcision but break the law. 28For a person is not a Jew who is one outwardly, nor is true circumcision something external and physical. 29Rather, a person is a Jew who is one inwardly, and real circumcision is a matter of the heart—it is spiritual and not literal. Such a person receives praise not from others but from God.

3.1 Τί οὖν τὸ περισσὸν τοῦ Ἰουδαίου ἢ τίς ἡ
WHAT THEN [IS] THE ADVANTAGE OF THE JEW, OR WHAT THE

ὠφέλεια τῆς περιτομῆς; **3.2** πολὺ κατὰ πάντα
PROFIT - OF CIRCUMCISION? MUCH ACCORDING TO EVERY

τρόπον. πρῶτον μὲν [γὰρ] ὅτι ἐπιστεύθησαν τὰ
WAY. 2FIRST 3INDEED 1FOR THAT THEY WERE ENTRUSTED [WITH] THE

λόγια τοῦ θεοῦ. **3.3** τί γάρ; εἰ ἠπίστησάν τινες,
ORACLES - OF GOD. FOR WHAT? IF SOME~DISBELIEVED,

μὴ ἡ ἀπιστία αὐτῶν τὴν πίστιν τοῦ θεοῦ
[SURELY] NOT THE UNBELIEF OF THEM THE FAITH(FULNESS) - OF GOD

καταργήσει; **3.4** μὴ γένοιτο· γινέσθω δὲ ὁ θεὸς
WILL NULLIFY? MAY IT NEVER BE; 2LET 4BE 1BUT - 3GOD

ἀληθής, πᾶς δὲ ἄνθρωπος ψεύστης, καθὼς γέγραπται,
5TRUE, AND~EVERY MAN A LIAR, AS IT HAS BEEN WRITTEN,

Ὅπως ἂν δικαιωθῇς ἐν τοῖς λόγοις σου
SO AS - YOU MAY BE JUSTIFIED IN THE SAYINGS OF YOU

καὶ νικήσεις ἐν τῷ κρίνεσθαί σε.
AND WILL BE VICTOR IN THE JUDGMENT OF YOU.

3.5 εἰ δὲ ἡ ἀδικία ἡμῶν θεοῦ δικαιοσύνην
BUT~IF THE UNRIGHTEOUSNESS OF US 3OF GOD 2[THE] RIGHTEOUSNESS

Then what advantage has the Jew? Or what is the value of circumcision? 2Much, in every way. For in the first place the Jews*h* were entrusted with the oracles of God. 3What if some were unfaithful? Will their faithlessness nullify the faithfulness of God? 4By no means! Although everyone is a liar, let God be proved true, as it is written,
"So that you may be justified in your words,
and prevail in your judging."*i*
5But if our injustice serves to confirm the justice of God,

h Gk they
i Gk when you are being judged

3:4 Ps. 51:4 LXX

what should we say? That God is unjust to inflict wrath on us? (I speak in a human way.) [6]By no means! For then how could God judge the world? [7]But if through my falsehood God's truthfulness abounds to his glory, why am I still being condemned as a sinner? [8]And why not say (as some people slander us by saying that we say), "Let us do evil so that good may come"? Their condemnation is deserved!

9 What then? Are we any better off?[j] No, not at all; for we have already charged that all, both Jews and Greeks, are under the power of sin, [10]as it is written:
"There is no one who is righteous, not even one;
[11]   there is no one who has understanding, there is no one who seeks God.
[12] All have turned aside, together they have become worthless; there is no one who shows kindness, there is not even one."
[13] "Their throats are opened graves; they use their tongues to deceive."
"The venom of vipers is under their lips."
[14]   "Their mouths are full of cursing and bitterness."
[15] "Their feet are swift to shed blood;

[j] Or at any disadvantage?

συνίστησιν, τί ἐροῦμεν; μὴ ἄδικος ὁ θεὸς
[1]COMMENDS,   WHAT WILL WE SAY? [5][IS SURELY] NOT [6]UNRIGHTEOUS - [1]GOD

ὁ ἐπιφέρων τὴν ὀργήν; κατὰ ἄνθρωπον λέγω.
[2]THE ONE [3]INFLICTING - [4]WRATH? ACCORDING TO MAN   I SPEAK.

3.6 μὴ γένοιτο· ἐπεὶ πῶς κρινεῖ ὁ θεὸς τὸν κόσμον;
MAY IT NOT BE;   OTHERWISE HOW WILL JUDGE - GOD THE WORLD?

3.7 εἰ δὲ ἡ ἀλήθεια τοῦ θεοῦ ἐν τῷ ἐμῷ ψεύσματι
BUT~IF THE TRUTH - OF GOD BY - MY LIE

ἐπερίσσευσεν εἰς τὴν δόξαν αὐτοῦ, τί ἔτι κἀγὼ
ABOUNDED   TO THE GLORY OF HIM, WHY STILL ALSO

ὡς ἁμαρτωλὸς κρίνομαι; **3.8** καὶ μὴ καθὼς
AS A SINNER AM I JUDGED?   AND NOT AS

βλασφημούμεθα καὶ καθὼς φασίν τινες ἡμᾶς λέγειν
WE ARE SLANDEROUSLY CHARGED AND AS SOME~AFFIRM US TO SAY,

ὅτι Ποιήσωμεν τὰ κακά, ἵνα ἔλθῃ τὰ ἀγαθά;
- LET US PRACTISE - BAD THINGS, THAT MAY COME - GOOD THINGS.

ὧν τὸ κρίμα ἔνδικόν ἐστιν.
WHOSE - JUDGMENT IS~DESERVED.

3.9 Τί οὖν; προεχόμεθα; οὐ πάντως·
WHAT THEN? DO WE EXCEL? NOT AT ALL;

προῃτιασάμεθα γὰρ Ἰουδαίους τε καὶ Ἕλληνας πάντας
FOR~WE HAVE BEFORE CHARGED BOTH~JEWS AND GREEKS ALL

ὑφ' ἁμαρτίαν εἶναι, **3.10** καθὼς γέγραπται ὅτι
UNDER SIN   TO BE,   AS IT HAS BEEN WRITTEN, -

Οὐκ ἔστιν δίκαιος οὐδὲ εἷς,
THERE IS~NOT A RIGHTEOUS MAN NOT ONE,

3.11   οὐκ ἔστιν ὁ συνίων,
THERE IS~NOT THE ONE UNDERSTANDING,

οὐκ ἔστιν ὁ ἐκζητῶν τὸν θεόν.
THERE IS~NOT THE ONE SEEKING - GOD.

3.12 πάντες ἐξέκλιναν ἅμα ἠχρεώθησαν·
ALL   TURNED AWAY, TOGETHER THEY BECAME USELESS;

οὐκ ἔστιν ὁ ποιῶν χρηστότητα,
THERE IS~NOT THE ONE DOING GOOD,

[οὐκ ἔστιν] ἕως ἑνός.
THERE IS~NOT SO MUCH AS ONE.

3.13 τάφος ἀνεῳγμένος ὁ λάρυγξ αὐτῶν,
A GRAVE HAVING BEEN OPENED [IS] THE THROAT OF THEM,

ταῖς γλώσσαις αὐτῶν ἐδολιοῦσαν,
WITH THE TONGUES OF THEM THEY WERE WORKING DECEIT,

ἰὸς ἀσπίδων ὑπὸ τὰ χείλη αὐτῶν·
POISON OF ASPS [IS] UNDER THE LIPS OF THEM;

3.14 ὧν τὸ στόμα ἀρᾶς καὶ πικρίας γέμει,
WHOSE - MOUTH [2]OF CURSING [3]AND [4]BITTERNESS [1]IS FULL,

3.15 ὀξεῖς οἱ πόδες αὐτῶν ἐκχέαι αἷμα,
SWIFT [ARE] THE FEET OF THEM TO SHED BLOOD,

3:10-12 Ps. 14:1-3 (= 53:1-3)   **3:13a** Ps. 5:9 LXX   **3:13b** Ps. 140:3 LXX   **3:14** Ps. 10:7 LXX
3:15-17 Isa. 59:7-8

3.16 σύντριμμα καὶ ταλαιπωρία ἐν ταῖς ὁδοῖς
RUIN   AND   MISERY   [ARE] IN THE PATHS

αὐτῶν,
OF THEM,

3.17 καὶ ὁδὸν εἰρήνης οὐκ ἔγνωσαν.
AND [THE] WAY OF PEACE THEY DID NOT KNOW.

3.18 οὐκ ἔστιν φόβος θεοῦ
THERE IS~NOT A FEAR OF GOD

ἀπέναντι τῶν ὀφθαλμῶν αὐτῶν.
BEFORE   THE EYES   OF THEM.

3.19 Οἴδαμεν δὲ ὅτι ὅσα ὁ νόμος λέγει τοῖς
BUT~WE KNOW THAT WHATEVER THE LAW SAYS TO THE ONES

ἐν τῷ νόμῳ λαλεῖ, ἵνα πᾶν στόμα φραγῇ καὶ
IN(UNDER) THE LAW IT SPEAKS, THAT EVERY MOUTH MAY BE STOPPED AND

ὑπόδικος γένηται πᾶς ὁ κόσμος τῷ θεῷ·
⁵UNDER JUDGMENT ⁴MAY COME ¹ALL ²THE ³WORLD - ⁶BY GOD;

3.20 διότι ἐξ ἔργων νόμου οὐ δικαιωθήσεται πᾶσα
BECAUSE BY WORKS OF LAW NOT WILL BE JUSTIFIED ALL

σὰρξ ἐνώπιον αὐτοῦ, διὰ γὰρ νόμου ἐπίγνωσις
FLESH BEFORE HIM, FOR~THROUGH LAW [IS] FULL RECOGNITION

ἁμαρτίας.
OF SIN.

3.21 Νυνὶ δὲ χωρὶς νόμου δικαιοσύνη θεοῦ
BUT~NOW APART FROM LAW A RIGHTEOUSNESS OF GOD

πεφανέρωται μαρτυρουμένη ὑπὸ τοῦ νόμου καὶ τῶν
HAS BEEN MANIFESTED, BEING ATTESTED TO BY THE LAW AND THE

προφητῶν, **3.22** δικαιοσύνη δὲ θεοῦ διὰ πίστεως
PROPHETS, A RIGHTEOUSNESS - OF GOD THROUGH FAITH

Ἰησοῦ Χριστοῦ εἰς πάντας τοὺς πιστεύοντας. οὐ
OF(IN) JESUS CHRIST TO ALL THE ONES BELIEVING. ³NO

γάρ ἐστιν διαστολή, **3.23** πάντες γὰρ ἥμαρτον καὶ
¹FOR ²THERE IS ⁴DISTINCTION, FOR~ALL SINNED AND

ὑστεροῦνται τῆς δόξης τοῦ θεοῦ **3.24** δικαιούμενοι
COME SHORT OF THE GLORY - OF GOD, BEING JUSTIFIED

δωρεὰν τῇ αὐτοῦ χάριτι διὰ τῆς ἀπολυτρώσεως τῆς
FREELY - BY HIS GRACE THROUGH THE REDEMPTION -

ἐν Χριστῷ Ἰησοῦ· **3.25** ὃν προέθετο ὁ θεὸς
IN CHRIST JESUS; WHOM ²DISPLAYED - ¹GOD

ἱλαστήριον διὰ [τῆς] πίστεως ἐν τῷ αὐτοῦ αἵματι
[AS] A PROPITIATION THROUGH - FAITH IN - HIS BLOOD

εἰς ἔνδειξιν τῆς δικαιοσύνης αὐτοῦ διὰ τὴν
FOR A DISPLAY OF THE RIGHTEOUSNESS OF HIM BECAUSE OF THE

πάρεσιν τῶν προγεγονότων ἁμαρτημάτων **3.26** ἐν
PASSING BY OF THE ²HAVING PREVIOUSLY OCCURRED ¹SINS IN

τῇ ἀνοχῇ τοῦ θεοῦ, πρὸς τὴν ἔνδειξιν τῆς
THE FORBEARANCE - OF GOD, FOR THE DISPLAY OF THE

16 ruin and misery are in
their paths,
17 and the way of peace
they have not
known."
18 "There is no fear of
God before their
eyes."
19 Now we know that
whatever the law says, it
speaks to those who are
under the law, so that every
mouth may be silenced, and
the whole world may be held
accountable to God. 20For
"no human being will be
justified in his sight" by
deeds prescribed by the law,
for through the law comes
the knowledge of sin.
21 But now, apart from
law, the righteousness of
God has been disclosed, and
is attested by the law and the
prophets, 22the righteousness of God through faith in
Jesus Christ[k] for all who believe. For there is no distinction, 23since all have sinned
and fall short of the glory of
God; 24they are now justified
by his grace as a gift, through
the redemption that is in
Christ Jesus, 25whom God
put forward as a sacrifice of
atonement[l] by his blood,
effective through faith. He
did this to show his righteousness, because in his divine
forbearance he had passed
over the sins previously
committed; 26it was to prove

[k] Or through the faith of Jesus Christ
[l] Or a place of atonement

3:18 Ps. 36:1

at the present time that he himself is righteous and that he justifies the one who has faith in Jesus.[m]

27 Then what becomes of boasting? It is excluded. By what law? By that of works? No, but by the law of faith. [28]For we hold that a person is justified by faith apart from works prescribed by the law. [29]Or is God the God of Jews only? Is he not the God of Gentiles also? Yes, of Gentiles also, [30]since God is one; and he will justify the circumcised on the ground of faith and the uncircumcised through that same faith. [31]Do we then overthrow the law by this faith? By no means! On the contrary, we uphold the law.

[m] Or *who has the faith of Jesus*

δικαιοσύνης αὐτοῦ ἐν τῷ νῦν καιρῷ, εἰς τὸ
RIGHTEOUSNESS OF HIM IN THE PRESENT TIME, FOR -

εἶναι αὐτὸν δίκαιον καὶ δικαιοῦντα τὸν ἐκ πίστεως
HIM~TO BE JUST AND JUSTIFYING THE ONE OF FAITH

Ἰησοῦ.
OF(IN) JESUS.

3.27 Ποῦ οὖν ἡ καύχησις; ἐξεκλείσθη. διὰ
WHERE THEREFORE [IS] THE BOASTING? IT WAS EXCLUDED. THROUGH

ποίου νόμου; τῶν ἔργων; οὐχί, ἀλλὰ διὰ νόμου
WHAT PRINCIPLE? - OF WORKS? NO, BUT THROUGH A PRINCIPLE

πίστεως. **3.28** λογιζόμεθα γὰρ δικαιοῦσθαι πίστει
OF FAITH. FOR~WE CONSIDER ²TO BE JUSTIFIED ³BY FAITH

ἄνθρωπον χωρὶς ἔργων νόμου. **3.29** ἢ Ἰουδαίων
¹A MAN APART FROM WORKS OF LAW. OR OF JEWS

ὁ θεὸς μόνον; οὐχὶ καὶ ἐθνῶν; ναὶ καὶ
[IS HE] THE GOD ONLY? NOT ALSO OF GENTILES? YES ALSO

ἐθνῶν, **3.30** εἴπερ εἷς ὁ θεός ὃς δικαιώσει
OF GENTILES, SINCE ONE - GOD [THERE IS] WHO WILL JUSTIFY

περιτομὴν ἐκ πίστεως καὶ ἀκροβυστίαν διὰ τῆς
[THE] CIRCUMCISION BY FAITH AND UNCIRCUMCISION THROUGH -

πίστεως. **3.31** νόμον οὖν καταργοῦμεν διὰ τῆς
FAITH. ³[THE] LAW ¹THEREFORE ²DO WE ANNUL THROUGH -

πίστεως; μὴ γένοιτο· ἀλλὰ νόμον ἱστάνομεν
FAITH? MAY IT NOT BE. RATHER [THE] LAW WE CONFIRM.

CHAPTER 4

What then are we to say was gained by[n] Abraham, our ancestor according to the flesh? [2]For if Abraham was justified by works, he has something to boast about, but not before God. [3]For what does the scripture say? "Abraham believed God, and it was reckoned to him as righteousness." [4]Now to one who works, wages are not reckoned as a gift but as something due. [5]But to one who without works trusts him who justifies the ungodly, such faith is reckoned as righteousness.

[n] Other ancient authorities read *say about*

4.1 Τί οὖν ⌜ἐροῦμεν εὑρηκέναι Ἀβραὰμ τὸν
WHAT THEN WILL WE SAY ⁷TO HAVE DISCOVERED ¹ABRAHAM ²THE

προπάτορα ἡμῶν⌝ κατὰ σάρκα; **4.2** εἰ γὰρ Ἀβραὰμ
³FOREFATHER ⁴OF US ⁵ACCORDING TO ⁶FLESH? FOR~IF ABRAHAM

ἐξ ἔργων ἐδικαιώθη, ἔχει καύχημα, ἀλλ' οὐ πρὸς θεόν.
BY WORKS WAS JUSTIFIED, HE HAS A BOAST, BUT NOT TOWARD GOD.

4.3 τί γὰρ ἡ γραφὴ λέγει; Ἐπίστευσεν δὲ Ἀβραὰμ
FOR~WHAT ²THE ³SCRIPTURE ¹SAYS? ³BELIEVED ¹AND ²ABRAHAM

τῷ θεῷ καὶ ἐλογίσθη αὐτῷ εἰς δικαιοσύνην.
- GOD, AND IT WAS ACCOUNTED TO HIM FOR RIGHTEOUSNESS.

4.4 τῷ δὲ ἐργαζομένῳ ὁ μισθὸς οὐ λογίζεται
NOW~TO THE ONE WORKING THE REWARD NOT IS ACCOUNTED

κατὰ χάριν ἀλλὰ κατὰ ὀφείλημα, **4.5** τῷ δὲ
ACCORDING TO GRACE BUT ACCORDING TO DEBT, BUT~TO THE ONE

μὴ ἐργαζομένῳ πιστεύοντι δὲ ἐπὶ τὸν δικαιοῦντα τὸν
NOT WORKING BUT~BELIEVING ON THE ONE JUSTIFYING THE

ἀσεβῆ λογίζεται ἡ πίστις αὐτοῦ εἰς δικαιοσύνην·
UNGODLY IS ACCOUNTED THE FAITH OF HIM FOR RIGHTEOUSNESS;

4:3 Gen. 15:6

4.6 καθάπερ καὶ Δαυὶδ λέγει τὸν μακαρισμὸν τοῦ
EVEN AS   ALSO   DAVID   SPEAKS OF THE BLESSEDNESS   OF THE

ἀνθρώπου ᾧ   ὁ θεὸς λογίζεται δικαιοσύνην χωρὶς
MAN   TO WHOM - GOD   ACCOUNTS   RIGHTEOUSNESS   APART FROM

ἔργων,
WORKS,

4.7 Μακάριοι   ὧν   ἀφέθησαν αἱ ἀνομίαι
[THEY ARE] BLESSED OF WHOM WERE FORGIVEN THE LAWLESS DEEDS

        καὶ ὧν   ἐπεκαλύφθησαν αἱ ἁμαρτίαι·
        AND OF WHOM WERE COVERED OVER   THE SINS.

4.8 μακάριος ἀνὴρ οὗ   οὐ μὴ λογίσηται κύριος
BLESSED   [IS] A MAN OF WHOM NEVER   [THE] LORD~WOULD ACCOUNT

        ἁμαρτίαν.
        SIN.

4.9 ὁ μακαρισμὸς οὖν   οὗτος ἐπὶ τὴν περιτομὴν ἢ
-   ²BLESSEDNESS   ³THEREFORE ¹[IS] THIS UPON THE CIRCUMCISION OR

καὶ ἐπὶ τὴν ἀκροβυστίαν; λέγομεν γάρ, Ἐλογίσθη
ALSO UPON THE UNCIRCUMCISION?   FOR~WE SAY,   ³WAS ACCOUNTED

τῷ Ἀβραὰμ ἡ   πίστις εἰς δικαιοσύνην. **4.10** πῶς
-   ⁴TO ABRAHAM ¹THE(HIS) ²FAITH ⁵FOR ⁶RIGHTEOUSNESS.   HOW

οὖν ἐλογίσθη;   ἐν περιτομῇ ὄντι ἢ ἐν ἀκροβυστίᾳ;
THEN WAS IT ACCOUNTED? IN CIRCUMCISION BEING OR IN UNCIRCUMCISION?

οὐκ ἐν περιτομῇ ἀλλ᾽ ἐν ἀκροβυστίᾳ· **4.11** καὶ
NOT IN CIRCUMCISION BUT IN UNCIRCUMCISION   AND

σημεῖον ἔλαβεν περιτομῆς σφραγίδα τῆς
²A SIGN   ¹HE RECEIVED ³OF CIRCUMCISION, A SEAL   OF THE

δικαιοσύνης τῆς   πίστεως τῆς ἐν   τῇ ἀκροβυστίᾳ,
RIGHTEOUSNESS OF THE(HIS) FAITH -   [WHILE] IN -   UNCIRCUMCISION,

εἰς τὸ εἶναι αὐτὸν πατέρα πάντων τῶν   πιστευόντων
FOR -   HIM~TO BE A FATHER OF ALL   THE ONES BELIEVING

δι᾽   ἀκροβυστίας, εἰς τὸ λογισθῆναι [καὶ] αὐτοῖς
THROUGH UNCIRCUMCISION, FOR - ³TO BE ACCOUNTED ⁴ALSO ⁵TO THEM

[τὴν] δικαιοσύνην, **4.12** καὶ πατέρα περιτομῆς τοῖς
¹THE ²RIGHTEOUSNESS,   AND A FATHER OF CIRCUMCISION TO THE ONES

οὐκ ἐκ περιτομῆς μόνον ἀλλὰ καὶ τοῖς   στοιχοῦσιν
NOT OF CIRCUMCISION ONLY BUT ALSO TO THE ONES KEEPING IN STEP

τοῖς ἴχνεσιν τῆς ἐν   ἀκροβυστίᾳ πίστεως τοῦ
WITH THE STEPS ¹OF THE ⁷[WHILE] IN ⁸UNCIRCUMCISION ²FAITH ³OF THE

πατρὸς ἡμῶν Ἀβραάμ.
⁴FATHER ⁵OF US ⁶ABRAHAM.

    4.13 Οὐ γὰρ διὰ   νόμου ἡ   ἐπαγγελία τῷ
        FOR~NOT THROUGH LAW [WAS] THE PROMISE   -

Ἀβραὰμ ἢ τῷ σπέρματι αὐτοῦ, τὸ κληρονόμον
TO ABRAHAM OR TO THE SEED OF HIM, THAT ³HEIR

αὐτὸν εἶναι κόσμου,   ἀλλὰ διὰ   δικαιοσύνης
¹HE   ²SHOULD BE ⁴OF [THE] WORLD, BUT THROUGH A RIGHTEOUSNESS

4:7-8 Ps. 32:1-2   **4:9** Gen. 15:6

[6]So also David speaks of the blessedness of those to whom God reckons righteousness apart from works:

[7] "Blessed are those
    whose iniquities are
    forgiven,
  and whose sins are
    covered;
[8] blessed is the one against
    whom the Lord will
    not reckon sin."

9 Is this blessedness, then, pronounced only on the circumcised, or also on the uncircumcised? We say, "Faith was reckoned to Abraham as righteousness." [10]How then was it reckoned to him? Was it before or after he had been circumcised? It was not after, but before he was circumcised. [11]He received the sign of circumcision as a seal of the righteousness that he had by faith while he was still uncircumcised. The purpose was to make him the ancestor of all who believe without being circumcised and who thus have righteousness reckoned to them, [12]and likewise the ancestor of the circumcised who are not only circumcised but who also follow the example of the faith that our ancestor Abraham had before he was circumcised.

13 For the promise that he would inherit the world did not come to Abraham or to his descendants through the law but through the righteousness

of faith. ¹⁴If it is the adherents of the law who are to be the heirs, faith is null and the promise is void. ¹⁵For the law brings wrath; but where there is no law, neither is there violation.

16 For this reason it depends on faith, in order that the promise may rest on grace and be guaranteed to all his descendants, not only to the adherents of the law but also to those who share the faith of Abraham (for he is the father of all of us, ¹⁷as it is written, "I have made you the father of many nations")—in the presence of the God in whom he believed, who gives life to the dead and calls into existence the things that do not exist. ¹⁸Hoping against hope, he believed that he would become "the father of many nations," according to what was said, "So numerous shall your descendants be." ¹⁹He did not weaken in faith when he considered his own body, which was already*o* as good as dead (for he was about a hundred years old), or when he considered the barrenness of Sarah's womb. ²⁰No distrust made him waver concerning the promise of God, but he grew strong in his faith as he gave glory to God, ²¹being fully convinced that God was able to do what he had promised. ²²Therefore his faith*p* "was reckoned to him as righteousness." ²³Now the words, "it was reckoned to him," were written not for his sake alone,

o Other ancient authorities lack *already*
p Gk *Therefore it*

πίστεως. **4.14** εἰ γὰρ οἱ ἐκ νόμου κληρονόμοι,
OF FAITH.   FOR~IF ¹THE ³[ARE] OF ⁴LAW   ²HEIRS,

κεκένωται ἡ πίστις καὶ κατήργηται ἡ ἐπαγγελία·
²HAS BEEN MADE VOID - ¹FAITH ³AND ⁶HAS BEEN NULLIFIED ⁴THE ⁵PROMISE;

4.15 ὁ γὰρ νόμος ὀργὴν κατεργάζεται· οὗ δὲ οὐκ ἔστιν
FOR~THE LAW WORKS~WRATH   BUT~WHERE THERE IS~NOT

νόμος οὐδὲ παράβασις.   **4.16** διὰ τοῦτο ἐκ
A LAW, NEITHER [IS THERE] TRANSGRESSION.   [IT IS] THEREFORE OF

πίστεως, ἵνα κατὰ χάριν, εἰς τὸ εἶναι
FAITH,   THAT ACCORDING TO GRACE [IT MAY BE], FOR - ³TO BE

βεβαίαν τὴν ἐπαγγελίαν παντὶ τῷ σπέρματι, οὐ
⁴SURE ¹THE ²PROMISE   TO ALL THE SEED,   NOT

τῷ ἐκ τοῦ νόμου μόνον ἀλλὰ καὶ τῷ ἐκ
TO THE [SEED] OF THE LAW ONLY BUT ALSO TO THE [SEED] OF

πίστεως Ἀβραάμ, ὅς ἐστιν πατὴρ πάντων ἡμῶν,
[THE] FAITH OF ABRAHAM, WHO IS FATHER OF US~ALL,

4.17 καθὼς γέγραπται ὅτι Πατέρα πολλῶν ἐθνῶν
AS   IT HAS BEEN WRITTEN, - A FATHER OF MANY NATIONS

τέθεικά σε, κατέναντι οὗ ἐπίστευσεν θεοῦ τοῦ
I HAVE APPOINTED YOU, BEFORE ²WHOM ³HE BELIEVED ¹GOD THE ONE

ζῳοποιοῦντος τοὺς νεκροὺς καὶ καλοῦντος τὰ μὴ
MAKING ALIVE   THE DEAD ONES AND CALLING THE THINGS NOT

ὄντα ὡς ὄντα· **4.18** ὃς παρ' ἐλπίδα ἐπ' ἐλπίδι
BEING AS BEING;   WHO BEYOND HOPE ON HOPE

ἐπίστευσεν εἰς τὸ γενέσθαι αὐτὸν πατέρα πολλῶν ἐθνῶν
BELIEVED   THAT - HE~SHOULD BECOME A FATHER OF MANY NATIONS

κατὰ τὸ εἰρημένον, Οὕτως ἔσται τὸ σπέρμα
ACCORDING TO THE THING HAVING BEEN SPOKEN, SO WILL BE THE SEED

σου, **4.19** καὶ μὴ ἀσθενήσας τῇ πίστει ⌜κατενόησεν⌝
OF YOU,   AND NOT HAVING WEAKENED - IN FAITH HE CONSIDERED

τὸ ἑαυτοῦ σῶμα [ἤδη] νενεκρωμένον, ἑκατονταετής
- HIS OWN BODY ALREADY HAVING BEEN DEAD, ³ONE HUNDRED YEARS [OLD]

που ὑπάρχων, καὶ τὴν νέκρωσιν τῆς μήτρας Σάρρας·
²ABOUT ¹BEING, AND THE DEADNESS OF THE WOMB OF SARAH;

4.20 εἰς δὲ τὴν ἐπαγγελίαν τοῦ θεοῦ οὐ διεκρίθη τῇ
BUT~AT THE PROMISE   - OF GOD HE DID NOT WAVER -

ἀπιστίᾳ ἀλλ' ἐνεδυναμώθη τῇ πίστει, δοὺς δόξαν τῷ
IN UNBELIEF, BUT WAS EMPOWERED - BY FAITH, GIVING GLORY -

θεῷ **4.21** καὶ πληροφορηθεὶς ὅτι ὃ ἐπήγγελται
TO GOD   AND HAVING BEEN FULLY PERSUADED THAT WHAT HE HAS PROMISED

δυνατός ἐστιν καὶ ποιῆσαι. **4.22** διὸ [καὶ]
HE IS~ABLE   ALSO TO DO.   WHEREFORE ALSO

ἐλογίσθη αὐτῷ εἰς δικαιοσύνην. **4.23** Οὐκ ἐγράφη
IT WAS ACCOUNTED TO HIM FOR RIGHTEOUSNESS.   ³NOT ²IT WAS WRITTEN

δὲ δι' αὐτὸν μόνον ὅτι ἐλογίσθη αὐτῷ
¹NOW BECAUSE OF HIM ONLY THAT IT WAS ACCOUNTED TO HIM

4:17 Gen. 17:5   **4:18a** Gen. 17:5   **4:18b** Gen. 15:5   **4:22** Gen. 15:6

4.24 ἀλλὰ καὶ δι' ἡμᾶς, οἷς μέλλει λογίζεσθαι,
BUT   ALSO BECAUSE OF US,   TO WHOM IT IS ABOUT TO BE ACCOUNTED,

τοῖς   πιστεύουσιν ἐπὶ τὸν ἐγείραντα Ἰησοῦν τὸν
TO THE ONES BELIEVING   ON THE ONE HAVING RAISED JESUS   THE

κύριον ἡμῶν ἐκ νεκρῶν, **4.25** ὃς παρεδόθη
LORD   OF US FROM THE DEAD ONES,   WHO WAS GIVEN OVER [TO DEATH]

διὰ   τὰ παραπτώματα ἡμῶν καὶ ἠγέρθη διὰ   τὴν
BECAUSE OF THE TRESPASSES   OF US AND WAS RAISED BECAUSE OF THE

δικαίωσιν ἡμῶν.
JUSTIFICATION OF US.

24but for ours also. It will be reckoned to us who believe in him who raised Jesus our Lord from the dead, 25who was handed over to death for our trespasses and was raised for our justification.

5.1 Δικαιωθέντες οὖν   ἐκ πίστεως ⌜εἰρήνην
HAVING BEEN JUSTIFIED THEREFORE BY FAITH   PEACE

ἔχομεν⌝ πρὸς τὸν θεὸν διὰ   τοῦ κυρίου ἡμῶν Ἰησοῦ
WE HAVE TOWARD -   GOD THROUGH THE LORD OF US JESUS

Χριστοῦ **5.2** δι'   οὗ καὶ τὴν προσαγωγὴν ἐσχήκαμεν
CHRIST   THROUGH WHOM ALSO THE ACCESS   WE HAVE HAD

[τῇ πίστει] εἰς τὴν χάριν ταύτην ἐν ᾗ   ἑστήκαμεν
- BY FAITH INTO - THIS~GRACE IN WHICH WE STAND

καὶ καυχώμεθα ἐπ' ἐλπίδι τῆς δόξης τοῦ θεοῦ.
AND BOAST   ON HOPE OF THE GLORY - OF GOD.

5.3 οὐ μόνον δέ, ἀλλὰ καὶ καυχώμεθα ἐν ταῖς
    2NOT 3ONLY (SO) 1AND, BUT ALSO WE BOAST   IN -

θλίψεσιν, εἰδότες ὅτι ἡ θλῖψις ὑπομονὴν κατεργάζεται,
TRIBULATIONS, KNOWING THAT - TRIBULATION ENDURANCE PRODUCES,

5.4 ἡ δὲ ὑπομονὴ δοκιμήν, ἡ δὲ δοκιμὴ   ἐλπίδα.
    - AND ENDURANCE APPROVEDNESS, - AND APPROVEDNESS HOPE.

5.5 ἡ δὲ ἐλπὶς οὐ καταισχύνει, ὅτι ἡ ἀγάπη τοῦ
    - AND HOPE DOES NOT PUT TO SHAME, BECAUSE THE LOVE -

θεοῦ ἐκκέχυται   ἐν ταῖς καρδίαις ἡμῶν διὰ
OF GOD HAS BEEN POURED OUT IN THE HEARTS   OF US THROUGH

πνεύματος ἁγίου τοῦ δοθέντος   ἡμῖν. **5.6** ἔτι γὰρ
2SPIRIT   1[THE] HOLY - HAVING BEEN GIVEN TO US.   - FOR

Χριστὸς ὄντων ἡμῶν ἀσθενῶν ἔτι κατὰ καιρὸν ὑπὲρ
CHRIST, [WHEN] WE~WERE STILL~WEAK, IN DUE TIME ON BEHALF OF

ἀσεβῶν ἀπέθανεν. **5.7** μόλις γὰρ ὑπὲρ   δικαίου
UNGODLY ONES DIED.   FOR~SCARCELY ON BEHALF OF A RIGHTEOUS MAN

τις   ἀποθανεῖται· ὑπὲρ γὰρ τοῦ ἀγαθοῦ τάχα
ANYONE WILL DIE;   FOR~ON BEHALF OF THE GOOD MAN PERHAPS

τις καὶ τολμᾷ ἀποθανεῖν· **5.8** συνίστησιν δὲ τὴν
SOMEONE EVEN DARES TO DIE;   3DEMONSTRATES 1BUT -

ἑαυτοῦ ἀγάπην εἰς ἡμᾶς ὁ θεὸς, ὅτι ἔτι ἁμαρτωλῶν
4HIS OWN 5LOVE   6TO 7US - 2GOD, THAT 3STILL 4SINNERS

Therefore, since we are justified by faith, weq have peace with God through our Lord Jesus Christ, 2through whom we have obtained accessr to this grace in which we stand; and wes boast in our hope of sharing the glory of God. 3And not only that, but wes also boast in our sufferings, knowing that suffering produces endurance, 4and endurance produces character, and character produces hope, 5and hope does not disappoint us, because God's love has been poured into our hearts through the Holy Spirit that has been given to us.

6 For while we were still weak, at the right time Christ died for the ungodly. 7Indeed, rarely will anyone die for a righteous person—though perhaps for a good person someone might actually dare to die. 8But God proves his love for us in that while we still were sinners

q Other ancient authorities read let us
r Other ancient authorities add by faith
s Or let us

5:1 text: KJV ASV RSV NASB NIV NEBmg TEV NJB NRSV. var. ειρηνην εχωμεν (let us have peace): ASVmg RSVmg NASBmg NIVmg NEB TEVmg NJBmg NRSVmg.

Christ died for us. ⁹Much more surely then, now that we have been justified by his blood, will we be saved through him from the wrath of God.ᶠ ¹⁰For if while we were enemies, we were reconciled to God through the death of his Son, much more surely, having been reconciled, will we be saved by his life. ¹¹But more than that, we even boast in God through our Lord Jesus Christ, through whom we have now received reconciliation.

12 Therefore, just as sin came into the world through one man, and death came through sin, and so death spread to all because all have sinned— ¹³sin was indeed in the world before the law, but sin is not reckoned when there is no law. ¹⁴Yet death exercised dominion from Adam to Moses, even over those whose sins were not like the transgression of Adam, who is a type of the one who was to come.

15 But the free gift is not like the trespass. For if the many died through the one man's trespass, much more surely have the grace of God and the free gift in the grace of the one man, Jesus Christ, abounded for the many. ¹⁶And the free gift is not like the effect of the one man's sin.

ᶠ Gk the wrath

ὄντων ἡμῶν Χριστὸς ὑπὲρ   ἡμῶν ἀπέθανεν.
²BEING   ¹WE CHRIST ON BEHALF OF US   DIED.

5.9 πολλῷ   οὖν μᾶλλον δικαιωθέντες   νῦν ἐν τῷ
BY MUCH THEN RATHER HAVING BEEN JUSTIFIED NOW IN(BY) THE

αἵματι αὐτοῦ σωθησόμεθα δι'   αὐτοῦ ἀπὸ τῆς ὀργῆς.
BLOOD   OF HIM WE WILL BE SAVED THROUGH HIM   FROM THE WRATH.

5.10 εἰ γὰρ ἐχθροὶ ὄντες κατηλλάγημεν   τῷ θεῷ
FOR IF ENEMIES BEING WE WERE RECONCILED -   TO GOD

διὰ   τοῦ θανάτου τοῦ υἱοῦ αὐτοῦ, πολλῷ μᾶλλον
THROUGH THE DEATH OF THE SON OF HIM, BY MUCH RATHER

καταλλαγέντες σωθησόμεθα ἐν   τῇ ζωῇ αὐτοῦ·
HAVING BEEN RECONCILED WE WILL BE SAVED IN(BY) THE LIFE OF HIM.

5.11 οὐ μόνον δέ, ἀλλὰ καὶ καυχώμενοι ἐν τῷ θεῷ
²NOT ³ONLY [SO] ¹AND, BUT   ALSO BOASTING IN -   GOD

διὰ   τοῦ κυρίου ἡμῶν Ἰησοῦ Χριστοῦ δι'   οὗ νῦν
THROUGH THE LORD OF US JESUS CHRIST THROUGH WHOM NOW

τὴν καταλλαγὴν ἐλάβομεν.
THE RECONCILIATION WE RECEIVED.

5.12 Διὰ τοῦτο ὥσπερ δι'   ἑνὸς ἀνθρώπου ἡ ἁμαρτία
THEREFORE AS THROUGH ONE MAN   - SIN

εἰς τὸν κόσμον εἰσῆλθεν καὶ διὰ   τῆς ἁμαρτίας ὁ
INTO THE WORLD ENTERED AND THROUGH - SIN -

θάνατος, καὶ οὕτως εἰς πάντας ἀνθρώπους ὁ θάνατος
DEATH, SO~ALSO TO ALL MEN - DEATH

διῆλθεν, ἐφ' ᾧ   πάντες ἥμαρτον· **5.13** ἄχρι γὰρ νόμου
CAME, INASMUCH AS ALL SINNED; FOR~UNTIL LAW

ἁμαρτία ἦν ἐν κόσμῳ, ἁμαρτία δὲ οὐκ ἐλλογεῖται
SIN WAS IN [THE] WORLD, BUT~SIN IS NOT ACCOUNTED

μὴ ὄντος   νόμου, **5.14** ἀλλὰ ἐβασίλευσεν ὁ θάνατος
[WHEN THERE] IS NOT A LAW, BUT ²REIGNED - ¹DEATH

ἀπὸ Ἀδὰμ μέχρι Μωϋσέως καὶ ἐπὶ τοὺς μὴ
FROM ADAM UNTIL MOSES EVEN OVER THE ONES NOT

ἁμαρτήσαντας ἐπὶ τῷ ὁμοιώματι τῆς παραβάσεως
HAVING SINNED ON(IN) THE LIKENESS OF THE TRANSGRESSION

Ἀδάμ ὅς ἐστιν τύπος τοῦ μέλλοντος.
OF ADAM WHO IS A TYPE OF THE ONE COMING.

5.15 Ἀλλ' οὐχ ὡς τὸ παράπτωμα, οὕτως καὶ τὸ
BUT NOT AS THE TRESPASS, SO ALSO THE

χάρισμα· εἰ γὰρ τῷ τοῦ ἑνὸς παραπτώματι οἱ
GIFT; FOR~IF ¹BY THE ³OF THE ⁴ONE MAN ²TRESPASS THE

πολλοὶ ἀπέθανον, πολλῷ μᾶλλον ἡ χάρις τοῦ θεοῦ
MANY DIED, BY MUCH RATHER THE GRACE - OF GOD

καὶ ἡ δωρεὰ ἐν χάριτι τῇ τοῦ ἑνὸς ἀνθρώπου Ἰησοῦ
AND THE GIFT IN GRACE - OF THE ONE MAN JESUS

Χριστοῦ εἰς τοὺς πολλοὺς ἐπερίσσευσεν. **5.16** καὶ οὐχ
CHRIST TO THE MANY ABOUNDED. AND NOT

ὡς δι'   ἑνὸς ἁμαρτήσαντος τὸ δώρημα· τὸ
AS THROUGH ONE MAN HAVING SINNED [IS] THE GIFT; ³THE

μὲν   γὰρ κρίμα ἐξ   ἑνὸς   εἰς
²ON ONE HAND ¹FOR   JUDGMENT [WAS] FROM ONE [TRESPASS] [RESULTING] IN

κατάκριμα, τὸ δὲ   χάρισμα ἐκ   πολλῶν
JUDGMENT,   ON THE OTHER~THE GIFT   [FOLLOWS] FROM MANY

παραπτωμάτων εἰς   δικαίωμα.   5.17 εἰ γὰρ τῷ
TRESPASSES   [RESULTING] IN JUSTIFICATION.   FOR~IF   ¹BY THE

τοῦ ἑνὸς   παραπτώματι ὁ θάνατος ἐβασίλευσεν διὰ
³OF THE ⁴ONE MAN ²TRESPASS   -   DEATH   REIGNED   THROUGH

τοῦ ἑνός,   πολλῷ   μᾶλλον οἱ   τὴν περισσείαν τῆς
THE   ONE MAN, BY MUCH   RATHER   ¹THE ONES ³THE   ⁴ABUNDANCE   ⁵OF THE

χάριτος καὶ τῆς   δωρεᾶς τῆς δικαιοσύνης λαμβάνοντες
⁶GRACE   ⁷AND   ⁸OF THE ⁹GIFT   -   ¹⁰OF RIGHTEOUSNESS ²RECEIVING

ἐν ζωῇ βασιλεύσουσιν διὰ   τοῦ ἑνὸς   Ἰησοῦ Χριστοῦ.
IN LIFE WILL REIGN   THROUGH THE ONE MAN JESUS   CHRIST.

5.18 Ἄρα οὖν ὡς δι'   ἑνὸς παραπτώματος εἰς
SO   THEN AS THROUGH ONE   TRESPASS   ³FOR

πάντας ἀνθρώπους εἰς   κατάκριμα, οὕτως καὶ
⁴ALL   ⁵MEN   ¹[RESULTING] IN ²JUDGMENT,   SO   ALSO

δι'   ἑνὸς δικαιώματος εἰς πάντας ἀνθρώπους εἰς
THROUGH ONE   RIGHTEOUS ACT   ⁴TO   ⁵ALL   ⁶MEN   ¹[RESULTING] IN

δικαίωσιν ζωῆς·   5.19 ὥσπερ γὰρ διὰ   τῆς παρακοῆς
²JUSTIFICATION   ³OF(FOR) LIFE.   FOR~AS   THROUGH THE DISOBEDIENCE

τοῦ ἑνὸς ἀνθρώπου ἁμαρτωλοὶ κατεστάθησαν οἱ
OF THE ONE   MAN   ⁴SINNERS   ³WERE MADE   ¹THE

πολλοί, οὕτως καὶ διὰ   τῆς ὑπακοῆς τοῦ ἑνὸς
²MANY,   SO   ALSO THROUGH THE OBEDIENCE OF THE ONE MAN

δίκαιοι κατασταθήσονται οἱ   πολλοί.   5.20 νόμος δὲ
⁴RIGHTEOUS ³WILL BE MADE   ¹THE ²MANY.   BUT~[THE] LAW

παρεισῆλθεν, ἵνα πλεονάσῃ τὸ παράπτωμα·   οὗ δὲ
ENTERED   THAT SHOULD INCREASE THE TRESPASS;   BUT~WHERE

ἐπλεόνασεν ἡ ἁμαρτία, ὑπερεπερίσσευσεν ἡ χάρις,
INCREASED   - SIN,   MORE INCREASED   - GRACE,

5.21 ἵνα ὥσπερ ἐβασίλευσεν ἡ ἁμαρτία ἐν τῷ θανάτῳ,
THAT JUST AS ²REIGNED   - ¹SIN   IN   - DEATH,

οὕτως καὶ ἡ χάρις βασιλεύσῃ διὰ   δικαιοσύνης
SO   ALSO - GRACE MAY REIGN   THROUGH RIGHTEOUSNESS

εἰς   ζωὴν αἰώνιον διὰ   Ἰησοῦ Χριστοῦ τοῦ
[RESULTING] IN LIFE ETERNAL THROUGH JESUS   CHRIST   THE

κυρίου ἡμῶν.
LORD   OF US.

For the judgment following one trespass brought condemnation, but the free gift following many trespasses brings justification. [17]If, because of the one man's trespass, death exercised dominion through that one, much more surely will those who receive the abundance of grace and the free gift of righteousness exercise dominion in life through the one man, Jesus Christ.

18 Therefore just as one man's trespass led to condemnation for all, so one man's act of righteousness leads to justification and life for all. [19]For just as by the one man's disobedience the many were made sinners, so by the one man's obedience the many will be made righteous. [20]But law came in, with the result that the trespass multiplied; but where sin increased, grace abounded all the more, [21]so that, just as sin exercised dominion in death, so grace might also exercise dominion through justification[u] leading to eternal life through Jesus Christ our Lord.

[u] Or righteousness

CHAPTER 6

6.1 Τί   οὖν ἐροῦμεν; ἐπιμένωμεν τῇ ἁμαρτίᾳ, ἵνα
WHAT THEN WILL WE SAY? SHOULD WE CONTINUE - IN SIN,   THAT

ἡ χάρις πλεονάσῃ; 6.2 μὴ γένοιτο. οἵτινες ἀπεθάνομεν
- GRACE MAY INCREASE?   MAY IT NEVER BE. ²WHO   ¹WE ³DIED

What then are we to say? Should we continue in sin in order that grace may abound? [2]By no means! How can we who died to sin go on living in it? ³Do you not know that all of us who have been baptized into Christ Jesus were baptized into his death? ⁴Therefore we have been buried with him by baptism into death, so that, just as Christ was raised from the dead by the glory of the Father, so we too might walk in newness of life.

5 For if we have been united with him in a death like his, we will certainly be united with him in a resurrection like his. ⁶We know that our old self was crucified with him so that the body of sin might be destroyed, and we might no longer be enslaved to sin. ⁷For whoever has died is freed from sin. ⁸But if we have died with Christ, we believe that we will also live with him. ⁹We know that Christ, being raised from the dead, will never die again; death no longer has dominion over him. ¹⁰The death he died, he died to sin, once for all; but the life he lives, he lives to God. ¹¹So you also must consider yourselves dead to sin and alive to God in Christ Jesus.

12 Therefore, do not let sin exercise dominion in your mortal bodies, to make you obey their passions. ¹³No longer present your members to sin as instruments^v of wickedness, but present yourselves

^{v} Or *weapons*

τῇ ἁμαρτίᾳ, πῶς ἔτι ζήσομεν ἐν αὐτῇ; **6.3** ἢ
\- TO SIN, HOW STILL WILL WE LIVE IN IT? OR

ἀγνοεῖτε ὅτι, ὅσοι ἐβαπτίσθημεν εἰς Χριστὸν
ARE YOU° IGNORANT THAT AS MANY AS WERE BAPTIZED INTO CHRIST

Ἰησοῦν, εἰς τὸν θάνατον αὐτοῦ ἐβαπτίσθημεν;
JESUS, INTO THE DEATH OF HIM WERE BAPTIZED?

6.4 συνετάφημεν οὖν αὐτῷ διὰ τοῦ βαπτίσματος
THEREFORE~WE WERE BURIED WITH HIM THROUGH - BAPTISM

εἰς τὸν θάνατον, ἵνα ὥσπερ ἠγέρθη Χριστὸς ἐκ νεκρῶν
INTO - DEATH, THAT JUST AS WAS RAISED CHRIST FROM DEAD ONES

διὰ τῆς δόξης τοῦ πατρός, οὕτως καὶ ἡμεῖς ἐν
THROUGH THE GLORY OF THE FATHER, SO ALSO WE IN

καινότητι ζωῆς περιπατήσωμεν. **6.5** εἰ γὰρ
NEWNESS OF LIFE MAY WALK. FOR~IF

σύμφυτοι γεγόναμεν τῷ ὁμοιώματι τοῦ θανάτου αὐτοῦ,
WE HAVE~GROWN TOGETHER IN THE LIKENESS OF THE DEATH OF HIM,

ἀλλὰ καὶ τῆς ἀναστάσεως ἐσόμεθα· **6.6** τοῦτο
YET(SO) ALSO ²OF THE(HIS) ³RESURRECTION ¹WE SHALL BE; THIS

γινώσκοντες ὅτι ὁ παλαιὸς ἡμῶν ἄνθρωπος
KNOWING THAT ²OLD ¹OUR ³HUMANITY

συνεσταυρώθη, ἵνα καταργηθῇ τὸ σῶμα τῆς
WAS CRUCIFIED WITH [HIM], THAT MAY BE MADE INEFFECTIVE THE BODY -

ἁμαρτίας, τοῦ μηκέτι δουλεύειν ἡμᾶς τῇ ἁμαρτίᾳ·
OF SIN, [THAT] NO LONGER ¹[SHOULD] ³SERVE ²WE - SIN;

6.7 ὁ γὰρ ἀποθανὼν δεδικαίωται ἀπὸ τῆς ἁμαρτίας.
FOR~THE ONE HAVING DIED HAS BEEN JUSTIFIED FROM - SIN.

6.8 εἰ δὲ ἀπεθάνομεν σὺν Χριστῷ, πιστεύομεν ὅτι καὶ
BUT~IF WE DIED WITH CHRIST, WE BELIEVE THAT ALSO

συζήσομεν αὐτῷ, **6.9** εἰδότες ὅτι Χριστὸς ἐγερθεὶς
WE WILL LIVE WITH HIM, KNOWING THAT CHRIST HAVING BEEN RAISED

ἐκ νεκρῶν οὐκέτι ἀποθνῄσκει, θάνατος αὐτοῦ οὐκέτι
FROM DEAD ONES NO MORE DIES, ¹DEATH ⁴HIM ²NO MORE

κυριεύει. **6.10** ὃ γὰρ ἀπέθανεν, τῇ ἁμαρτίᾳ ἀπέθανεν
³LORDS IT OVER. FOR~IN THAT HE DIED, - TO SIN HE DIED

ἐφάπαξ· ὃ δὲ ζῇ, ζῇ τῷ θεῷ. **6.11** οὕτως καὶ
ONCE; BUT~IN THAT HE LIVES, HE LIVES - TO GOD. SO ALSO

ὑμεῖς λογίζεσθε ἑαυτοὺς [εἶναι] νεκροὺς μὲν τῇ
YOU° ACCOUNT YOURSELVES TO BE DEAD ONES INDEED -

ἁμαρτίᾳ ζῶντας δὲ τῷ θεῷ ἐν Χριστῷ Ἰησοῦ.
TO SIN BUT~LIVING - TO GOD IN CHRIST JESUS.

6.12 Μὴ οὖν βασιλευέτω ἡ ἁμαρτία ἐν τῷ θνητῷ
³NOT ¹THEREFORE ²LET ⁵REIGN - ⁴SIN ⁶IN - ⁸MORTAL

ὑμῶν σώματι εἰς τὸ ὑπακούειν ταῖς ἐπιθυμίαις αὐτοῦ,
⁷YOUR° ⁹BODY SO AS - TO OBEY THE LUSTS OF IT,

6.13 μηδὲ παριστάνετε τὰ μέλη ὑμῶν ὅπλα
NEITHER PRESENT THE MEMBERS OF YOU° [AS] TOOLS

ἀδικίας τῇ ἁμαρτίᾳ, ἀλλὰ παραστήσατε ἑαυτοὺς
OF UNRIGHTEOUSNESS - TO SIN, BUT PRESENT YOURSELVES

τῷ   θεῷ   ὡσεὶ   ἐκ   νεκρῶν ζῶντας καὶ   τὰ   μέλη
-    TO GOD AS   OUT FROM DEAD ONES LIVING AND   THE MEMBERS

ὑμῶν ὅπλα   δικαιοσύνης τῷ   θεῷ.   **6.14** ἁμαρτία γὰρ
OF YOU° TOOLS OF RIGHTEOUSNESS -   TO GOD.   FOR~SIN

ὑμῶν οὐ κυριεύσει·   οὐ   γάρ   ἐστε   ὑπὸ   νόμον   ἀλλὰ
²YOU° ¹WILL NOT LORD IT OVER; ³NOT ¹FOR   ²YOU° ARE UNDER LAW   BUT

ὑπὸ   χάριν.
UNDER GRACE.

6.15 Τί   οὖν;   ἁμαρτήσωμεν, ὅτι   οὐκ ἐσμὲν ὑπὸ
       WHAT THEN?   MAY WE SIN,   BECAUSE WE ARE~NOT UNDER

νόμον ἀλλὰ ὑπὸ   χάριν;   μὴ γένοιτο.   **6.16** οὐκ οἴδατε
LAW   BUT   UNDER GRACE?   MAY IT NEVER BE.   DO YOU° NOT KNOW

ὅτι ᾧ   παριστάνετε ἑαυτοὺς δούλους εἰς ὑπακοήν,
THAT TO WHOM YOU° PRESENT   YOURSELVES SLAVES   FOR OBEDIENCE,

δοῦλοί   ἐστε   ᾧ   ὑπακούετε, ἤτοι   ἁμαρτίας
[HIS] SLAVES YOU° ARE WHOM YOU° OBEY,   WHETHER OF SIN

εἰς   θάνατον ἢ ὑπακοῆς εἰς   δικαιοσύνην;
[RESULTING] IN DEATH   OR OF OBEDIENCE [RESULTING] IN RIGHTEOUSNESS?

6.17 χάρις δὲ   τῷ   θεῷ   ὅτι ἦτε   δοῦλοι τῆς
       BUT~THANKS [BE] -   TO GOD THAT YOU° USED TO BE SLAVES   -

ἁμαρτίας ὑπηκούσατε δὲ ἐκ   καρδίας εἰς ὃν
OF SIN   BUT~YOU° OBEYED   FROM [THE] HEART ³TO ⁴WHICH

παρεδόθητε   τύπον   διδαχῆς, **6.18** ἐλευθερωθέντες δὲ
⁵YOU° WERE COMMITTED ¹[THE] PATTERN ²OF TEACHING,   AND~HAVING BEEN FREED

ἀπὸ   τῆς ἁμαρτίας ἐδουλώθητε   τῇ δικαιοσύνῃ.
FROM   -   SIN   YOU° WERE ENSLAVED -   TO RIGHTEOUSNESS.

6.19 ἀνθρώπινον λέγω   διὰ   τὴν ἀσθένειαν τῆς
       HUMANLY   I SPEAK BECAUSE OF THE WEAKNESS   OF THE

σαρκὸς ὑμῶν. ὥσπερ γὰρ παρεστήσατε τὰ   μέλη ὑμῶν
FLESH   OF YOU°. FOR~JUST AS   YOU° PRESENTED THE   MEMBERS OF YOU°

δοῦλα τῇ ἀκαθαρσίᾳ καὶ τῇ ἀνομίᾳ   εἰς   τὴν
SLAVES - TO IMPURITY   AND - TO LAWLESSNESS [RESULTING] IN   -

ἀνομίαν, οὕτως νῦν παραστήσατε τὰ   μέλη ὑμῶν δοῦλα
LAWLESSNESS, SO   NOW   PRESENT   THE   MEMBERS OF YOU° SLAVES

τῇ δικαιοσύνῃ εἰς   ἁγιασμόν. **6.20** ὅτε γὰρ δοῦλοι
- TO RIGHTEOUSNESS [RESULTING] IN SANCTIFICATION.   FOR~WHEN SLAVES

ἦτε   τῆς ἁμαρτίας, ἐλεύθεροι ἦτε   τῇ δικαιοσύνῃ.
YOU° WERE -   OF SIN,   FREE ONES   YOU° WERE - TO RIGHTEOUSNESS.

6.21 τίνα οὖν   καρπὸν εἴχετε τότε; ἐφ' οἷς   νῦν
       THEREFORE~WHAT FRUIT   HAD YOU° THEN? OVER WHICH THINGS NOW

ἐπαισχύνεσθε, τὸ γὰρ τέλος ἐκείνων   θάνατος.
YOU° ARE ASHAMED,   FOR~THE   RESULT OF THOSE THINGS [IS] DEATH.

6.22 νυνὶ δέ ἐλευθερωθέντες ἀπὸ   τῆς ἁμαρτίας
       BUT~NOW HAVING BEEN FREED   FROM   -   SIN

δουλωθέντες δὲ   τῷ   θεῷ   ἔχετε   τὸν καρπὸν ὑμῶν
AND~HAVING BEEN ENSLAVED -   TO GOD YOU° HAVE THE   FRUIT   OF YOU°

εἰς   ἁγιασμόν, τὸ δὲ τέλος ζωὴν αἰώνιον.
[RESULTING] IN SANCTIFICATION, AND~THE RESULT LIFE   ETERNAL.

to God as those who have
been brought from death to
life, and present your members to God as instruments[w]
of righteousness. [14]For sin
will have no dominion over
you, since you are not under
law but under grace.

15 What then? Should we
sin because we are not under
law but under grace? By no
means! [16]Do you not know
that if you present yourselves
to anyone as obedient slaves,
you are slaves of the one
whom you obey, either of
sin, which leads to death, or
of obedience, which leads to
righteousness? [17]But thanks
be to God that you, having
once been slaves of sin, have
become obedient from the
heart to the form of teaching
to which you were entrusted,
[18]and that you, having been
set free from sin, have
become slaves of righteousness. [19]I am speaking in
human terms because of
your natural limitations.[x] For
just as you once presented
your members as slaves to
impurity and to greater and
greater iniquity, so now
present your members as
slaves to righteousness for
sanctification.

20 When you were slaves
of sin, you were free in
regard to righteousness. [21]So
what advantage did you then
get from the things of which
you now are ashamed? The
end of those things is death.
[22]But now that you have been
freed from sin and enslaved
to God, the advantage you
get is sanctification. The
end is eternal life.

[w] Or *weapons*
[x] Gk *the weakness of your flesh*

23For the wages of sin is death, but the free gift of God is eternal life in Christ Jesus our Lord.

6.23 τὰ γὰρ ὀψώνια τῆς ἁμαρτίας θάνατος, τὸ δὲ
FOR~THE   WAGES   -   OF SIN   [IS] DEATH,   BUT~THE

χάρισμα τοῦ θεοῦ ζωὴ αἰώνιος ἐν Χριστῷ Ἰησοῦ τῷ
FREE GIFT   -   OF GOD [IS] LIFE ETERNAL   IN   CHRIST   JESUS   THE

κυρίῳ ἡμῶν.
LORD   OF US.

CHAPTER 7

Do you not know, brothers and sisters[y] —for I am speaking to those who know the law—that the law is binding on a person only during that person's lifetime? 2Thus a married woman is bound by the law to her husband as long as he lives; but if her husband dies, she is discharged from the law concerning the husband. 3Accordingly, she will be called an adulteress if she lives with another man while her husband is alive. But if her husband dies, she is free from that law, and if she marries another man, she is not an adulteress.

4 In the same way, my friends,[y] you have died to the law through the body of Christ, so that you may belong to another, to him who has been raised from the dead in order that we may bear fruit for God. 5While we were living in the flesh, our sinful passions, aroused by the law, were at work in our members to bear fruit for death. 6But now we are discharged from the law, dead to that which held us captive, so that we are slaves not under the old written code but in the new life of the Spirit.

[y] Gk brothers

7.1 Ἢ ἀγνοεῖτε, ἀδελφοί, γινώσκουσιν γὰρ νόμον
OR   ARE YOU° IGNORANT, BROTHERS,   FOR~TO ONES KNOWING   [THE] LAW

λαλῶ, ὅτι ὁ νόμος κυριεύει τοῦ ἀνθρώπου ἐφ᾽ ὅσον
I SPEAK, THAT THE LAW   LORDS IT OVER THE   PERSON   OVER SUCH

χρόνον ζῇ; **7.2** ἡ γὰρ ὕπανδρος γυνὴ τῷ ζῶντι
TIME   [AS] HE LIVES?   FOR~THE WOMAN~MARRIED   TO THE LIVING

ἀνδρὶ δέδεται νόμῳ· ἐὰν δὲ ἀποθάνη ὁ ἀνήρ,
HUSBAND HAS BEEN BOUND BY LAW; BUT~IF   DIES   THE HUSBAND,

κατήργηται ἀπὸ τοῦ νόμου τοῦ ἀνδρός. **7.3** ἄρα οὖν
SHE HAS BEEN RELEASED FROM THE LAW   OF THE HUSBAND.   SO   THEN

ζῶντος τοῦ ἀνδρὸς μοιχαλὶς χρηματίσει ἐὰν
¹[WHILE]⁴LIVES ²THE ³HUSBAND AN ADULTERESS SHE WILL BE CALLED   IF

γένηται ἀνδρὶ ἑτέρῳ· ἐὰν δὲ ἀποθάνη ὁ
SHE BECOMES JOINED TO A DIFFERENT~HUSBAND; BUT~IF   ³DIES   ¹THE

ἀνήρ, ἐλευθέρα ἐστὶν ἀπὸ τοῦ νόμου, τοῦ μὴ εἶναι
²HUSBAND, FREE   SHE IS   FROM THE LAW,   -   NOT IS

αὐτὴν μοιχαλίδα γενομένην ἀνδρὶ ἑτέρῳ. **7.4** ὥστε,
SHE   AN ADULTERESS HAVING BEEN JOINED TO A DIFFERENT~HUSBAND.   SO THAT,

ἀδελφοί μου, καὶ ὑμεῖς ἐθανατώθητε τῷ νόμῳ διὰ
BROTHERS OF ME, ALSO YOU°   WERE PUT TO DEATH   TO THE LAW   THROUGH

τοῦ σώματος τοῦ Χριστοῦ, εἰς τὸ γενέσθαι ὑμᾶς
THE BODY   -   OF CHRIST, ¹FOR - ³TO BE JOINED ²YOU°

ἑτέρῳ, τῷ ἐκ νεκρῶν ἐγερθέντι, ἵνα
⁴TO A DIFFERENT ONE, TO THE ONE FROM DEAD ONES HAVING BEEN RAISED,   THAT

καρποφορήσωμεν τῷ θεῷ. **7.5** ὅτε γὰρ ἦμεν ἐν τῇ
WE MAY BEAR FRUIT   -   TO GOD.   FOR~WHEN WE WERE IN THE

σαρκί, τὰ παθήματα τῶν ἁμαρτιῶν τὰ διὰ τοῦ νόμου
FLESH, THE PASSIONS   -   OF SINS   -   THROUGH THE LAW

ἐνηργεῖτο ἐν τοῖς μέλεσιν ἡμῶν, εἰς τὸ καρποφορῆσαι
WERE WORKING IN THE MEMBERS   OF US, SO AS - TO BEAR FRUIT

τῷ θανάτῳ· **7.6** νυνὶ δὲ κατηργήθημεν ἀπὸ τοῦ νόμου
- TO DEATH;   BUT~NOW WE WERE RELEASED FROM THE LAW

ἀποθανόντες ἐν ᾧ κατειχόμεθα, ὥστε δουλεύειν
HAVING DIED   [TO THAT] IN WHICH WE WERE BEING HELD, SO AS TO SERVE

ἡμᾶς ἐν καινότητι πνεύματος καὶ οὐ παλαιότητι
-   IN NEWNESS   OF SPIRIT   AND NOT IN OLDNESS

γράμματος.
OF LETTER.

7.7 Τί οὖν ἐροῦμεν; ὁ νόμος ἁμαρτία;
WHAT THEN WILL WE SAY? [IS] THE LAW SIN?

μὴ γένοιτο· ἀλλὰ τὴν ἁμαρτίαν οὐκ ἔγνων εἰ μὴ
MAY IT NEVER BE. BUT - SIN I DID NOT KNOW EXCEPT

διὰ νόμου· τήν τε γὰρ ἐπιθυμίαν οὐκ ᾔδειν εἰ μὴ
THROUGH LAW; FOR~ALSO LUST I WAS NOT KNOWING EXCEPT

ὁ νόμος ἔλεγεν, Οὐκ ἐπιθυμήσεις. **7.8** ἀφορμὴν δὲ
THE LAW WAS SAYING, NOT YOU SHALL LUST. ⁴OPPORTUNITY ¹BUT

λαβοῦσα ἡ ἁμαρτία διὰ τῆς ἐντολῆς κατειργάσατο
³HAVING TAKEN - ²SIN THROUGH THE COMMANDMENT PRODUCED

ἐν ἐμοὶ πᾶσαν ἐπιθυμίαν· χωρὶς γὰρ νόμου
IN ME EVERY [KIND OF] LUST; FOR~WITHOUT LAW

ἁμαρτία νεκρά. **7.9** ἐγὼ δὲ ἔζων χωρὶς νόμου ποτέ,
SIN [IS] DEAD. AND~I WAS LIVING WITHOUT LAW ONCE,

ἐλθούσης δὲ τῆς ἐντολῆς ἡ ἁμαρτία ἀνέζησεν,
⁴HAVING COME ¹BUT ²THE ³COMMANDMENT - SIN REVIVED,

7.10 ἐγὼ δὲ ἀπέθανον καὶ εὑρέθη μοι ἡ
AND~I DIED, AND [IT] WAS DISCOVERED BY ME [THAT] THE

ἐντολὴ ἡ εἰς ζωήν, αὕτη εἰς θάνατον· **7.11** ἡ γὰρ
COMMANDMENT - FOR LIFE THIS [WAS]FOR DEATH. - FOR

ἁμαρτία ἀφορμὴν λαβοῦσα διὰ τῆς ἐντολῆς
SIN OPPORTUNITY TAKING THROUGH THE COMMANDMENT

ἐξηπάτησέν με καὶ δι᾽ αὐτῆς ἀπέκτεινεν. **7.12** ὥστε
DECEIVED ME AND THROUGH IT KILLED [ME]. SO

ὁ μὲν νόμος ἅγιος καὶ ἡ ἐντολὴ ἁγία καὶ
THE - LAW [IS] HOLY AND THE COMMANDMENT HOLY AND

δικαία καὶ ἀγαθή.
JUST AND GOOD.

7.13 Τὸ οὖν ἀγαθὸν ἐμοὶ ἐγένετο θάνατος;
THEN~THE GOOD TO ME BECAME DEATH?

μὴ γένοιτο· ἀλλὰ ἡ ἁμαρτία, ἵνα φανῇ
MAY IT NEVER BE. BUT - SIN, THAT IT MAY BE SHOWN [AS]

ἁμαρτία, διὰ τοῦ ἀγαθοῦ μοι κατεργαζομένη
SIN, THROUGH THE GOOD ³TO ME ¹WORKING

θάνατον, ἵνα γένηται καθ᾽ ὑπερβολὴν ἁμαρτωλὸς ἡ
²DEATH, THAT ⁵MIGHT BECOME ⁶EXCEEDINGLY ⁷SINFUL -

ἁμαρτία διὰ τῆς ἐντολῆς. **7.14** οἴδαμεν γὰρ ὅτι
¹SIN ²THROUGH ³THE ⁴COMMANDMENT. FOR~WE KNOW THAT

ὁ νόμος πνευματικός ἐστιν, ἐγὼ δὲ σάρκινός εἰμι
THE LAW SPIRITUAL IS, BUT~I AM~CARNAL

πεπραμένος ὑπὸ τὴν ἁμαρτίαν. **7.15** ὃ γὰρ
HAVING BEEN SOLD UNDER - SIN. FOR~WHAT

κατεργάζομαι οὐ γινώσκω· οὐ γὰρ ὃ θέλω τοῦτο
I WORK I DO NOT KNOW; FOR~NOT WHAT I WANT THIS

πράσσω, ἀλλ᾽ ὃ μισῶ τοῦτο ποιῶ. **7.16** εἰ δὲ ὃ
I DO, BUT WHAT I HATE THIS I DO. NOW~IF WHAT

7 What then should we say? That the law is sin? By no means! Yet, if it had not been for the law, I would not have known sin. I would not have known what it is to covet if the law had not said, "You shall not covet." ⁸But sin, seizing an opportunity in the commandment, produced in me all kinds of covetousness. Apart from the law sin lies dead. ⁹I was once alive apart from the law, but when the commandment came, sin revived ¹⁰and I died, and the very commandment that promised life proved to be death to me. ¹¹For sin, seizing an opportunity in the commandment, deceived me and through it killed me. ¹²So the law is holy, and the commandment is holy and just and good.

13 Did what is good, then, bring death to me? By no means! It was sin, working death in me through what is good, in order that sin might be shown to be sin, and through the commandment might become sinful beyond measure.

14 For we know that the law is spiritual; but I am of the flesh, sold into slavery under sin.ᶻ ¹⁵I do not understand my own actions. For I do not do what I want, but I do the very thing I hate. ¹⁶Now if

ᶻ Gk sold under sin

I do what I do not want, I agree that the law is good. ¹⁷But in fact it is no longer I that do it, but sin that dwells within me. ¹⁸For I know that nothing good dwells within me, that is, in my flesh. I can will what is right, but I cannot do it. ¹⁹For I do not do the good I want, but the evil I do not want is what I do. ²⁰Now if I do what I do not want, it is no longer I that do it, but sin that dwells within me.

21 So I find it to be a law that when I want to do what is good, evil lies close at hand. ²²For I delight in the law of God in my inmost self, ²³but I see in my members another law at war with the law of my mind, making me captive to the law of sin that dwells in my members. ²⁴Wretched man that I am! Who will rescue me from this body of death? ²⁵Thanks be to God through Jesus Christ our Lord!

So then, with my mind I am a slave to the law of God, but with my flesh I am a slave to the law of sin.

οὐ θέλω τοῦτο ποιῶ, σύμφημι τῷ νόμῳ ὅτι καλός.
I DO NOT WANT THIS I DO, I AGREE WITH THE LAW THAT [IT IS] GOOD.

7.17 νυνὶ δὲ οὐκέτι ἐγὼ κατεργάζομαι αὐτὸ ἀλλὰ ἡ
BUT~NOW NO LONGER I WORK IT BUT ¹THE

οἰκοῦσα ἐν ἐμοὶ ἁμαρτία. **7.18** οἶδα γὰρ ὅτι οὐκ οἰκεῖ
³DWELLING ⁴IN ⁵ME ²SIN. FOR~I KNOW THAT NOT DWELLS

ἐν ἐμοί, τοῦτ᾽ ἔστιν ἐν τῇ σαρκί μου, ἀγαθόν· τὸ
IN ME, THAT IS IN THE FLESH OF ME, [ANYTHING] GOOD; -

γὰρ θέλειν παράκειταί μοι, τὸ δὲ κατεργάζεσθαι τὸ
FOR TO WILL IS PRESENT WITH ME, - BUT TO WORK THE

καλὸν οὔ· **7.19** οὐ γὰρ ὃ θέλω ποιῶ ἀγαθόν,
GOOD [IS] NOT. FOR~[I DO] NOT [DO] ¹THE ³I WANT ⁴TO DO ²GOOD,

ἀλλὰ ὃ οὐ θέλω κακὸν τοῦτο πράσσω. **7.20** εἰ δὲ
BUT WHAT I DO NOT WANT [TO DO] THIS~EVIL I PRACTISE. BUT~IF

ὃ οὐ θέλω [ἐγὼ] τοῦτο ποιῶ, οὐκέτι ἐγὼ
WHAT I DO NOT WANT ²I ¹THIS ³DO, NO LONGER I

κατεργάζομαι αὐτὸ ἀλλὰ ἡ οἰκοῦσα ἐν ἐμοὶ
WORK IT BUT ¹THE ³DWELLING ⁴IN ⁵ME

ἁμαρτία. **7.21** Εὑρίσκω ἄρα τὸν νόμον, τῷ θέλοντι
²SIN. I FIND THEN THE PRINCIPLE, ²THE ONE ³WANTING

ἐμοὶ ποιεῖν τὸ καλὸν, ὅτι ἐμοὶ τὸ κακὸν παράκειται·
¹TO ME TO DO THE GOOD, THAT TO ME THE EVIL IS PRESENT.

7.22 συνήδομαι γὰρ τῷ νόμῳ τοῦ θεοῦ κατὰ τὸν
FOR~I DELIGHT IN THE LAW - OF GOD WITH RESPECT TO THE

ἔσω ἄνθρωπον, **7.23** βλέπω δὲ ἕτερον νόμον ἐν τοῖς
INNER MAN, BUT~I SEE A DIFFERENT LAW IN THE

μέλεσίν μου ἀντιστρατευόμενον τῷ νόμῳ τοῦ νοός μου
MEMBERS OF ME WARRING AGAINST THE LAW OF THE MIND OF ME

καὶ αἰχμαλωτίζοντά με ἐν τῷ νόμῳ τῆς ἁμαρτίας τῷ
AND CAPTURING ME BY THE LAW - OF SIN -

ὄντι ἐν τοῖς μέλεσίν μου. **7.24** ταλαίπωρος ἐγὼ
BEING IN THE MEMBERS OF ME. ¹MISERABLE ³I AM

ἄνθρωπος· τίς με ῥύσεται ἐκ τοῦ σώματος τοῦ
²MAN; WHO WILL RESCUE~ME FROM THE BODY OF

θανάτου τούτου; **7.25** χάρις δὲ τῷ θεῷ διὰ Ἰησοῦ
THIS~DEATH? BUT~THANKS - TO GOD THROUGH JESUS

Χριστοῦ τοῦ κυρίου ἡμῶν. ἄρα οὖν αὐτὸς ἐγὼ τῷ
CHRIST THE LORD OF US. SO THEN I~MYSELF ²WITH THE

μὲν νοῒ δουλεύω νόμῳ θεοῦ τῇ δὲ
¹ON ONE HAND ³MIND SERVE [THE] LAW OF GOD ²WITH THE ¹ON THE OTHER

σαρκὶ νόμῳ ἁμαρτίας.
³FLESH [THE] LAW OF SIN.

8.1 Οὐδὲν ἄρα νῦν κατάκριμα τοῖς ἐν
3NO   2THEN   1[THERE IS] NOW   4CONDEMNATION   TO THE ONES   IN

Χριστῷ Ἰησοῦ· **8.2** ὁ γὰρ νόμος τοῦ πνεύματος τῆς
CHRIST   JESUS.   FOR~THE   LAW   OF THE   SPIRIT   -

ζωῆς ἐν Χριστῷ Ἰησοῦ ἠλευθέρωσέν ⌜σε⌝ ἀπὸ τοῦ
OF LIFE   IN   CHRIST   JESUS   FREED   YOU   FROM   THE

νόμου τῆς ἁμαρτίας καὶ τοῦ θανάτου.
LAW   -   OF SIN   AND   -   OF DEATH.

8.3 τὸ γὰρ ἀδύνατον τοῦ νόμου ἐν ᾧ ἠσθένει
FOR~WHAT WAS IMPOSSIBLE [FOR]   THE   LAW [TO DO],   IN   THAT   IT WAS WEAK[ENED]

διὰ τῆς σαρκός, ὁ θεὸς τὸν ἑαυτοῦ υἱὸν πέμψας
BY   THE   FLESH,   -   GOD [DID]   -   2HIS OWN   3SON   1[BY] HAVING SENT

ἐν ὁμοιώματι σαρκὸς ἁμαρτίας καὶ περὶ ἁμαρτίας
IN   [THE] LIKENESS   OF FLESH   OF SIN,   AND   CONCERNING   SIN

κατέκρινεν τὴν ἁμαρτίαν ἐν τῇ σαρκί, **8.4** ἵνα τὸ
HE CONDEMNED   -   SIN   IN   THE   FLESH,   THAT   THE

δικαίωμα τοῦ νόμου πληρωθῇ ἐν ἡμῖν τοῖς
RIGHTEOUS REQUIREMENTS   OF THE   LAW   MAY BE FULFILLED   IN   US   THE ONES

μὴ κατὰ σάρκα περιπατοῦσιν ἀλλὰ κατὰ
NOT   ACCORDING TO   FLESH   WALKING   BUT   ACCORDING TO

πνεῦμα. **8.5** οἱ γὰρ κατὰ σάρκα ὄντες τὰ
SPIRIT.   FOR~THE ONES   ACCORDING TO   FLESH   BEING   THE THINGS

τῆς σαρκὸς φρονοῦσιν, οἱ δὲ κατὰ πνεῦμα
OF THE   FLESH   THINK [ABOUT],   BUT~THE ONES   ACCORDING TO   SPIRIT

τὰ τοῦ πνεύματος. **8.6** τὸ γὰρ φρόνημα
THE THINGS   OF THE   SPIRIT.   FOR~THE   MIND

τῆς σαρκὸς θάνατος, τὸ δὲ φρόνημα
OF (BELONGING TO) THE   FLESH   [IS] DEATH,   BUT~THE   MIND

τοῦ πνεύματος ζωὴ καὶ εἰρήνη· **8.7** διότι
OF (BELONGING TO) THE   SPIRIT   [IS] LIFE   AND   PEACE.   BECAUSE

τὸ φρόνημα τῆς σαρκὸς ἔχθρα εἰς θεόν,
THE   MIND   OF (BELONGING TO) THE   FLESH   [IS] ENMITY   AGAINST   GOD,

τῷ γὰρ νόμῳ τοῦ θεοῦ οὐχ ὑποτάσσεται, οὐδὲ γὰρ
FOR~TO THE   LAW   -   OF GOD   IT IS NOT SUBJECT,   FOR~NEITHER

δύναται· **8.8** οἱ δὲ ἐν σαρκὶ ὄντες θεῷ ἀρέσαι οὐ
CAN IT BE.   AND~THE ONES   IN   [THE] FLESH   BEING   5GOD   4TO PLEASE   2NOT

δύνανται. **8.9** ὑμεῖς δὲ οὐκ ἐστὲ ἐν σαρκὶ ἀλλὰ ἐν
1ARE 3ABLE.   BUT~YOU°   ARE~NOT   IN   [THE] FLESH   BUT   IN

πνεύματι, εἴπερ πνεῦμα θεοῦ οἰκεῖ ἐν ὑμῖν. εἰ δέ
S(S)PIRIT,   SINCE   [THE] SPIRIT   OF GOD   DWELLS   IN   YOU°.   BUT~IF

τις πνεῦμα Χριστοῦ οὐκ ἔχει, οὗτος οὐκ ἔστιν αὐτοῦ.
ANYONE   [THE] SPIRIT   OF CHRIST   DOES NOT HAVE,   THIS ONE   IS~NOT   OF HIM.

There is therefore now no condemnation for those who are in Christ Jesus. [2]For the law of the Spirit[a] of life in Christ Jesus has set you[b] free from the law of sin and of death. [3]For God has done what the law, weakened by the flesh, could not do: by sending his own Son in the likeness of sinful flesh, and to deal with sin,[c] he condemned sin in the flesh, [4]so that the just requirement of the law might be fulfilled in us, who walk not according to the flesh but according to the Spirit.[a] [5]For those who live according to the flesh set their minds on the things of the flesh, but those who live according to the Spirit[a] set their minds on the things of the Spirit.[a] [6]To set the mind on the flesh is death, but to set the mind on the Spirit[a] is life and peace. [7]For this reason the mind that is set on the flesh is hostile to God; it does not submit to God's law—indeed it cannot, [8]and those who are in the flesh cannot please God.

9 But you are not in the flesh; you are in the Spirit,[a] since the Spirit of God dwells in you. Anyone who does not have the Spirit of Christ does not belong to him.

[a] Or *spirit*
[b] Here the Greek word *you* is singular number; other ancient authorities read *me* or *us*
[c] Or *and as a sin offering*

8:1 text: ASV RSV NASB NIV NEB TEV NJB NRSV.   add μη κατα σαρκα περιπατουσιν αλλα κατα πνευμα ([to those] not walking according to flesh but according to Spirit): KJV NIVmg.   **8:2** text: NASB NEB TEVmg NJB NRSV.   var. με (me): KJV ASV RSV NASBmg NIV TEV NJBmg NRSVmg.   var. ημας (us): TEVmg NJBmg NRSVmg.

10But if Christ is in you, though the body is dead because of sin, the Spirit[d] is life because of righteousness. 11If the Spirit of him who raised Jesus from the dead dwells in you, he who raised Christ[e] from the dead will give life to your mortal bodies also through[f] his Spirit that dwells in you.

12 So then, brothers and sisters,[g] we are debtors, not to the flesh, to live according to the flesh— 13for if you live according to the flesh, you will die; but if by the Spirit you put to death the deeds of the body, you will live. 14For all who are led by the Spirit of God are children of God. 15For you did not receive a spirit of slavery to fall back into fear, but you have received a spirit of adoption. When we cry, "Abba![h] Father!" 16it is that very Spirit bearing witness[i] with our spirit that we are children of God, 17and if children, then heirs, heirs of God and joint heirs with Christ—if, in fact, we suffer with him so that we may also be glorified with him.

18 I consider that the sufferings of this present time are not worth comparing with the glory about to be revealed to us. 19For the creation waits with eager longing for the revealing of the children of God; 20for the creation was subjected to futility,

d Or *spirit*
e Other ancient authorities read *the Christ* or *Christ Jesus* or *Jesus Christ*
f Other ancient authorities read *on account of*
g Gk *brothers*
h Aramaic for *Father*
i Or 15*a spirit of adoption, by which we cry, "Abba! Father!"* 16*The Spirit itself bears witness*

8.10 εἰ δὲ Χριστὸς ἐν ὑμῖν, τὸ μὲν σῶμα νεκρὸν
AND~IF CHRIST [IS] IN YOU°, 2THE 1ON ONE HAND 3BODY [IS] DEAD

διὰ ἁμαρτίαν τὸ δὲ πνεῦμα ζωὴ διὰ
BECAUSE OF SIN 2THE 1ON THE OTHER 3SPIRIT [IS] LIFE BECAUSE OF

δικαιοσύνην. **8.11** εἰ δὲ τὸ πνεῦμα τοῦ ἐγείραντος
RIGHTEOUSNESS. AND~IF THE SPIRIT OF THE ONE HAVING RAISED

τὸν Ἰησοῦν ἐκ νεκρῶν οἰκεῖ ἐν ὑμῖν, ὁ ἐγείρας
- JESUS FROM DEAD ONES DWELLS IN YOU°, THE ONE HAVING RAISED

Χριστὸν ἐκ νεκρῶν ζῳοποιήσει καὶ τὰ θνητὰ σώματα
CHRIST FROM DEAD ONES WILL MAKE ALIVE ALSO THE MORTAL BODIES

ὑμῶν διὰ τοῦ ἐνοικοῦντος αὐτοῦ πνεύματος ἐν ὑμῖν.
OF YOU° THROUGH - 2INDWELLING 1HIS 3SPIRIT IN YOU°.

8.12 Ἄρα οὖν, ἀδελφοί, ὀφειλέται ἐσμὲν οὐ τῇ
SO THEN, BROTHERS, DEBTORS WE ARE NOT TO THE

σαρκὶ τοῦ κατὰ σάρκα ζῆν, **8.13** εἰ γὰρ κατὰ
FLESH - ACCORDING TO FLESH TO LIVE. FOR~IF ACCORDING TO

σάρκα ζῆτε, μέλλετε ἀποθνῄσκειν· εἰ δὲ πνεύματι
FLESH YOU° LIVE, YOU° ARE DESTINED TO DIE; BUT~IF BY [THE] SPIRIT

τὰς πράξεις τοῦ σώματος θανατοῦτε, ζήσεσθε.
THE PRACTISES OF THE BODY YOU° PUT TO DEATH, YOU° WILL LIVE.

8.14 ὅσοι γὰρ πνεύματι θεοῦ ἄγονται, οὗτοι υἱοὶ θεοῦ
FOR~AS MANY AS BY [THE] SPIRIT OF GOD ARE LED, THESE SONS OF GOD

εἰσιν. **8.15** οὐ γὰρ ἐλάβετε πνεῦμα δουλείας πάλιν εἰς
ARE. FOR~NOT YOU° RECEIVED A SPIRIT OF SLAVERY AGAIN TO

φόβον ἀλλὰ ἐλάβετε πνεῦμα υἱοθεσίας ἐν ᾧ
FEAR BUT YOU° RECEIVED A SPIRIT OF SONSHIP IN(BY) WHICH

κράζομεν, Ἀββα ὁ πατήρ. **8.16** αὐτὸ τὸ πνεῦμα
WE CRY, ABBA - FATHER. 3ITSELF 1THE 2SPIRIT

συμμαρτυρεῖ τῷ πνεύματι ἡμῶν ὅτι ἐσμὲν τέκνα θεοῦ.
WITNESSES WITH THE SPIRIT OF US THAT WE ARE CHILDREN OF GOD.

8.17 εἰ δὲ τέκνα, καὶ κληρονόμοι· κληρονόμοι μὲν
AND~IF CHILDREN, ALSO HEIRS; HEIRS ON ONE HAND

θεοῦ, συγκληρονόμοι δὲ Χριστοῦ, εἴπερ
OF GOD, CO-HEIRS ON THE OTHER OF CHRIST, IF INDEED

συμπάσχομεν ἵνα καὶ συνδοξασθῶμεν.
WE SUFFER WITH [HIM] THAT ALSO WE MAY BE GLORIFIED WITH [HIM].

8.18 Λογίζομαι γὰρ ὅτι οὐκ ἄξια τὰ παθήματα
FOR~I RECKON THAT 6[ARE] NOT 7WORTHY 1THE 2SUFFERINGS

τοῦ νῦν καιροῦ πρὸς τὴν μέλλουσαν δόξαν
3OF THE 4PRESENT 5TIME [TO BE COMPARED] WITH THE COMING GLORY

ἀποκαλυφθῆναι εἰς ἡμᾶς. **8.19** ἡ γὰρ ἀποκαραδοκία
TO BE REVEALED TO(IN) US. FOR~THE ANXIOUS EXPECTATION

τῆς κτίσεως τὴν ἀποκάλυψιν τῶν υἱῶν τοῦ θεοῦ
OF THE CREATION 2THE 3UNVEILING 4OF THE 5SONS - 6OF GOD

ἀπεκδέχεται. **8.20** τῇ γὰρ ματαιότητι ἡ κτίσις
1IS EAGERLY EXPECTING. - FOR TO VANITY THE CREATION

ὑπετάγη, οὐχ ἑκοῦσα ἀλλὰ διὰ τὸν
WAS SUBJECTED, NOT WILLING[LY], BUT BECAUSE OF THE ONE

ὑποτάξαντα, ⌐ἐφ᾽ ἐλπίδι **8.21** ὅτι⌐ καὶ αὐτὴ ἡ
HAVING SUBJECTED [IT], IN HOPE THAT EVEN ³ITSELF ¹THE

κτίσις ἐλευθερωθήσεται ἀπὸ τῆς δουλείας τῆς φθορᾶς
²CREATION WILL BE FREED FROM THE SLAVERY - OF CORRUPTION

εἰς τὴν ἐλευθερίαν τῆς δόξης τῶν τέκνων τοῦ θεοῦ.
INTO THE FREEDOM OF THE GLORY OF THE CHILDREN - OF GOD.

8.22 οἴδαμεν γὰρ ὅτι πᾶσα ἡ κτίσις συστενάζει καὶ
FOR~WE KNOW THAT ALL THE CREATION GROANS TOGETHER AND

συνωδίνει ἄχρι τοῦ νῦν· **8.23** οὐ μόνον δέ,
TRAVAILS IN PAIN TOGETHER UNTIL - NOW; ²NOT ³ONLY [SO] ¹AND,

ἀλλὰ καὶ αὐτοὶ τὴν ἀπαρχὴν τοῦ πνεύματος
BUT ALSO OURSELVES ²THE ³FIRSTFRUITS ⁴OF THE ⁵SPIRIT

ἔχοντες, ἡμεῖς καὶ αὐτοὶ ἐν ἑαυτοῖς στενάζομεν
¹HAVING, WE ALSO OURSELVES IN OURSELVES GROAN

υἱοθεσίαν ἀπεκδεχόμενοι, τὴν ἀπολύτρωσιν τοῦ
EAGERLY EXPECTING~SONSHIP, THE REDEMPTION OF THE

σώματος ἡμῶν. **8.24** τῇ γὰρ ἐλπίδι ἐσώθημεν·
BODY OF US. FOR~WITH THIS HOPE WE WERE SAVED;

ἐλπὶς δὲ βλεπομένη οὐκ ἔστιν ἐλπίς· ὁ γὰρ
BUT~HOPE BEING SEEN IS~NOT HOPE; FOR~WHAT

βλέπει τίς ἐλπίζει; **8.25** εἰ δὲ ὃ οὐ βλέπομεν
ANYONE~SEES WHY DOES HE HOPE [FOR IT]? BUT~IF WHAT WE DO NOT SEE

ἐλπίζομεν, δι᾽ ὑπομονῆς ἀπεκδεχόμεθα.
WE HOPE [FOR], THROUGH PATIENCE WE EAGERLY EXPECT [IT].

8.26 Ὡσαύτως δὲ καὶ τὸ πνεῦμα συναντιλαμβάνεται
AND~IN LIKE MANNER ALSO THE SPIRIT JOINS IN TO HELP

τῇ ἀσθενείᾳ ἡμῶν· τὸ γὰρ τί προσευξώμεθα καθὸ
THE WEAKNESS OF US; - FOR WHAT WE SHOULD PRAY AS

δεῖ οὐκ οἴδαμεν, ἀλλὰ αὐτὸ τὸ πνεῦμα
IS NECESSARY WE DO NOT KNOW, BUT ³ITSELF ¹THE ²SPIRIT

ὑπερεντυγχάνει στεναγμοῖς ἀλαλήτοις· **8.27** ὁ δὲ
INTERCEDES ON [OUR] BEHALF WITH GROANINGS UNEXPRESSED; BUT~THE ONE

ἐραυνῶν τὰς καρδίας οἶδεν τί τὸ φρόνημα τοῦ
SEARCHING THE HEARTS KNOWS WHAT [IS] THE MIND OF THE

πνεύματος, ὅτι κατὰ θεὸν ἐντυγχάνει ὑπὲρ
SPIRIT, BECAUSE ACCORDING TO GOD HE INTERCEDES ON BEHALF OF

ἁγίων. **8.28** οἴδαμεν δὲ ὅτι τοῖς ἀγαπῶσιν τὸν θεὸν
SAINTS. AND~WE KNOW THAT TO THE ONES LOVING - GOD

⌐πάντα συνεργεῖ⌐ εἰς ἀγαθόν, τοῖς κατὰ
ALL THINGS HE WORKS TOGETHER FOR GOOD, TO THE ONES ³ACCORDING TO

πρόθεσιν κλητοῖς οὖσιν. **8.29** ὅτι οὓς προέγνω, καὶ
⁴[HIS] PURPOSE ²CALLED ¹BEING. BECAUSE WHOM HE FOREKNEW, ALSO

8:28 text: KJV ASV RSVmg NASBmg NEB TEVmg NJBmg NRSV. var. παντα συνεργει ο θεος (God works all things): ASVmg RSV NASB NIV NEBmg TEV NJB NRSVmg.

---

not of its own will but by the will of the one who subjected it, in hope [21]that the creation itself will be set free from its bondage to decay and will obtain the freedom of the glory of the children of God. [22]We know that the whole creation has been groaning in labor pains until now; [23]and not only the creation, but we ourselves, who have the first fruits of the Spirit, groan inwardly while we wait for adoption, the redemption of our bodies. [24]For in[j] hope we were saved. Now hope that is seen is not hope. For who hopes[k] for what is seen? [25]But if we hope for what we do not see, we wait for it with patience.

[26]Likewise the Spirit helps us in our weakness; for we do not know how to pray as we ought, but that very Spirit intercedes[l] with sighs too deep for words. [27]And God,[m] who searches the heart, knows what is the mind of the Spirit, because the Spirit[n] intercedes for the saints according to the will of God.[o]

[28]We know that all things work together for good[p] for those who love God, who are called according to his purpose. [29]For those whom he foreknew he also

[j] Or by
[k] Other ancient authorities read awaits
[l] Other ancient authorities add for us
[m] Gk the one
[n] Gk he or it
[o] Gk according to God
[p] Other ancient authorities read God makes all things work together for good, or in all things God works for good

predestined to be conformed to the image of his Son, in order that he might be the firstborn within a large family.*q* 30And those whom he predestined he also called; and those whom he called he also justified; and those whom he justified he also glorified.

31 What then are we to say about these things? If God is for us, who is against us? 32He who did not withhold his own Son, but gave him up for all of us, will he not with him also give us everything else? 33Who will bring any charge against God's elect? It is God who justifies. 34Who is to condemn? It is Christ Jesus, who died, yes, who was raised, who is at the right hand of God, who indeed intercedes for us.*r* 35Who will separate us from the love of Christ? Will hardship, or distress, or persecution, or famine, or nakedness, or peril, or sword? 36As it is written,

"For your sake we are being killed all day long;
we are accounted as sheep to be slaughtered."

37No, in all these things we are more than conquerors through him who loved us. 38For I am convinced that neither death, nor life, nor angels, nor rulers, nor things present, nor things to come, nor powers, 39nor height,

q Gk among many brothers
r Or Is it Christ Jesus . . . for us?

προώρισεν   συμμόρφους τῆς εἰκόνος τοῦ υἱοῦ αὐτοῦ,
HE PREDESTINED [TO BE] CONFORMED TO THE IMAGE OF THE SON OF HIM,

εἰς τὸ εἶναι αὐτὸν πρωτότοκον ἐν   πολλοῖς ἀδελφοῖς·
FOR - HIM~TO BE   FIRSTBORN   AMONG MANY   BROTHERS;

8.30 οὓς δὲ   προώρισεν, τούτους καὶ ἐκάλεσεν·   καὶ οὓς
AND~WHOM HE PREDESTINED, THESE ALSO HE CALLED;   AND WHOM

ἐκάλεσεν, τούτους καὶ ἐδικαίωσεν·   οὓς δὲ ἐδικαίωσεν,
HE CALLED,   THESE ALSO HE JUSTIFIED;   AND~WHOM HE JUSTIFIED,

τούτους καὶ ἐδόξασεν.
THESE ALSO HE GLORIFIED.

8.31 Τί   οὖν ἐροῦμεν πρὸς ταῦτα;   εἰ ὁ θεὸς ὑπὲρ
WHAT THEN WILL WE SAY TO   THESE THINGS? IF - GOD [IS] FOR

ἡμῶν, τίς καθ᾽ ἡμῶν; **8.32** ὅς γε τοῦ ἰδίου υἱοῦ
US,   WHO AGAINST US?   WHO INDEED HIS OWN   SON

οὐκ ἐφείσατο   ἀλλὰ ὑπὲρ   ἡμῶν πάντων
DID NOT SPARE   BUT   ON BEHALF OF US   ALL

παρέδωκεν αὐτόν, πῶς οὐχὶ καὶ σὺν αὐτῷ τὰ πάντα
GAVE HIM UP,   HOW NOT ALSO WITH HIM   - ALL THINGS

ἡμῖν χαρίσεται; **8.33** τίς ἐγκαλέσει   κατὰ ἐκλεκτῶν
TO US WILL HE FREELY GIVE?   WHO WILL BRING A CHARGE AGAINST CHOSEN ONES

θεοῦ;   θεὸς ὁ   δικαιῶν· **8.34** τίς   ὁ
OF GOD? GOD [IS] THE ONE JUSTIFYING.   WHO [IS] THE ONE

κατακρινῶν; Χριστὸς [Ἰησοῦς] ὁ   ἀποθανών,
CONDEMNING? CHRIST   JESUS   [IS] THE ONE HAVING DIED,

μᾶλλον δὲ ἐγερθείς,   ὃς καί ἐστιν ἐν δεξιᾷ
BUT~RATHER   HAVING BEEN RAISED, WHO ALSO IS   AT [THE] RIGHT [HAND]

τοῦ θεοῦ, ὃς καὶ ἐντυγχάνει ὑπὲρ   ἡμῶν. **8.35** τίς
-   OF GOD, WHO ALSO INTERCEDES ON BEHALF OF US.   WHO

ἡμᾶς χωρίσει ἀπὸ τῆς ἀγάπης τοῦ Χριστοῦ; θλῖψις ἢ
WILL SEPARATE~US FROM THE LOVE   -   OF CHRIST? TRIBULATION OR

στενοχωρία ἢ διωγμὸς ἢ λιμὸς ἢ γυμνότης ἢ
DISTRESS   OR PERSECUTION OR FAMINE OR NAKEDNESS   OR

κίνδυνος ἢ μάχαιρα; **8.36** καθὼς γέγραπται ὅτι
PERIL   OR SWORD?   AS   IT HAS BEEN WRITTEN, -

Ἕνεκεν σοῦ θανατούμεθα   ὅλην τὴν ἡμέραν,
FOR THE SAKE OF YOU WE ARE BEING PUT TO DEATH ALL   THE   DAY,

ἐλογίσθημεν ὡς πρόβατα σφαγῆς.
WE WERE CONSIDERED AS   SHEEP   OF(FOR) SLAUGHTER.

8.37 ἀλλ᾽ ἐν τούτοις πᾶσιν ὑπερνικῶμεν διὰ   τοῦ
BUT   IN ALL~THESE THINGS WE MORE THAN CONQUER THROUGH THE ONE

ἀγαπήσαντος ἡμᾶς. **8.38** πέπεισμαι γὰρ ὅτι οὔτε
HAVING LOVED   US.   FOR~I HAVE BEEN PERSUADED THAT NEITHER

θάνατος οὔτε ζωὴ οὔτε ἄγγελοι οὔτε ἀρχαὶ οὔτε
DEATH   NOR LIFE NOR ANGELS   NOR RULERS NOR

ἐνεστῶτα οὔτε μέλλοντα οὔτε δυνάμεις **8.39** οὔτε ὕψωμα
THINGS PRESENT NOR THINGS COMING NOR POWERS   NOR   HEIGHT

8:36 Ps. 44:22

οὔτε βάθος οὔτε τις κτίσις ἑτέρα δυνήσεται ἡμᾶς
NOR DEPTH NOR ANY OTHER~CREATURE WILL BE ABLE US

χωρίσαι ἀπὸ τῆς ἀγάπης τοῦ θεοῦ τῆς ἐν Χριστῷ
TO SEPARATE FROM THE LOVE - OF GOD - IN CHRIST

Ἰησοῦ τῷ κυρίῳ ἡμῶν.
JESUS THE LORD OF US.

nor depth, nor anything else in all creation, will be able to separate us from the love of God in Christ Jesus our Lord.

CHAPTER 9

9.1 Ἀλήθειαν λέγω ἐν Χριστῷ, οὐ ψεύδομαι,
TRUTH I SPEAK IN CHRIST, I DO NOT LIE,

συμμαρτυρούσης μοι τῆς συνειδήσεώς μου ἐν πνεύματι
WITNESSING WITH ME THE CONSCIENCE OF ME IN ²SPIRIT

ἁγίῳ, **9.2** ὅτι λύπη μοί ἐστιν μεγάλη καὶ
¹[THE] HOLY, THAT ³GRIEF ⁴TO ME ¹[THERE] IS ²GREAT AND

ἀδιάλειπτος ὀδύνη τῇ καρδίᾳ μου. **9.3** ηὐχόμην γὰρ
UNCEASING PAIN IN THE HEART OF ME. FOR~I WAS PRAYING

ἀνάθεμα εἶναι αὐτὸς ἐγὼ ἀπὸ τοῦ Χριστοῦ
³A CURSE ²TO BE ¹MYSELF [SEPARATED] FROM - CHRIST

ὑπὲρ τῶν ἀδελφῶν μου τῶν συγγενῶν μου κατὰ
ON BEHALF OF THE BROTHERS OF ME THE KINSMEN OF ME ACCORDING TO

σάρκα, **9.4** οἵτινές εἰσιν Ἰσραηλῖται, ὧν ἡ
FLESH, WHO ARE ISRAELITES, OF WHOM THE

υἱοθεσία καὶ ἡ δόξα καὶ αἱ διαθῆκαι καὶ ἡ
SONSHIP AND THE GLORY AND THE COVENANTS AND THE

νομοθεσία καὶ ἡ λατρεία καὶ αἱ ἐπαγγελίαι,
RECEIVING OF [THE] LAW AND THE [TEMPLE] SERVICE AND THE PROMISES,

9.5 ὧν οἱ πατέρες καὶ ἐξ ὧν ὁ Χριστὸς τὸ
OF WHOM THE FATHERS AND OUT OF WHOM THE CHRIST -

κατὰ σάρκα, ὁ ὢν ἐπὶ πάντων θεὸς εὐλογητὸς
ACCORDING TO FLESH, THE ONE BEING ²OVER ³ALL ¹GOD BLESSED

εἰς τοὺς αἰῶνας, ἀμήν.
INTO THE AGES, AMEN.

9.6 Οὐχ οἶον δὲ ὅτι ἐκπέπτωκεν ὁ λόγος τοῦ θεοῦ.
NOT HOWEVER THAT HAS FAILED THE WORD - OF GOD.

οὐ γὰρ πάντες οἱ ἐξ Ἰσραὴλ οὗτοι Ἰσραήλ·
FOR~NOT ALL THE ONES OF ISRAEL - [ARE] ISRAEL;

9.7 οὐδ' ὅτι εἰσὶν σπέρμα Ἀβραὰμ πάντες τέκνα,
NEITHER BECAUSE THEY ARE SEED OF ABRAHAM [ARE THEY] ALL CHILDREN,

ἀλλ', Ἐν Ἰσαὰκ κληθήσεταί σοι σπέρμα. **9.8** τοῦτ'
BUT, IN ISAAC ¹WILL ⁴BE CALLED ²YOUR ³SEED. THIS(THAT)

ἔστιν, οὐ τὰ τέκνα τῆς σαρκὸς ταῦτα τέκνα τοῦ
IS, NOT THE CHILDREN OF THE FLESH - [ARE] CHILDREN -

θεοῦ ἀλλὰ τὰ τέκνα τῆς ἐπαγγελίας λογίζεται εἰς
OF GOD BUT THE CHILDREN OF THE PROMISE ARE CONSIDERED FOR

I am speaking the truth in Christ—I am not lying; my conscience confirms it by the Holy Spirit— ²I have great sorrow and unceasing anguish in my heart. ³For I could wish that I myself were accursed and cut off from Christ for the sake of my own people,⁵ my kindred according to the flesh. ⁴They are Israelites, and to them belong the adoption, the glory, the covenants, the giving of the law, the worship, and the promises; ⁵to them belong the patriarchs, and from them, according to the flesh, comes the Messiah,ᵗ who is over all, God blessed forever.ᵘ Amen.

6 It is not as though the word of God had failed. For not all Israelites truly belong to Israel, ⁷and not all of Abraham's children are his true descendants; but "It is through Isaac that descendants shall be named for you." ⁸This means that it is not the children of the flesh who are the children of God, but the children of the promise are counted as

⁵ Gk *my brothers*
ᵗ Or *the Christ*
ᵘ Or *Messiah, who is God over all, blessed forever;* or *Messiah. May he who is God over all be blessed forever*

9:7 Gen. 21:12

descendants. [9]For this is what the promise said, "About this time I will return and Sarah shall have a son." [10]Nor is that all; something similar happened to Rebecca when she had conceived children by one husband, our ancestor Isaac. [11]Even before they had been born or had done anything good or bad (so that God's purpose of election might continue, [12]not by works but by his call) she was told, "The elder shall serve the younger." [13]As it is written,

"I have loved Jacob,
but I have hated Esau."

14 What then are we to say? Is there injustice on God's part? By no means! [15]For he says to Moses,

"I will have mercy on whom I have mercy,
and I will have compassion on whom I have compassion."

[16]So it depends not on human will or exertion, but on God who shows mercy. [17]For the scripture says to Pharaoh, "I have raised you up for the very purpose of showing my power in you, so that my name may be proclaimed in all the earth." [18]So then he has mercy on whomever he chooses, and he hardens the heart of whomever he chooses.

19 You will say to me then, "Why then does he still find fault? For who can resist his will?" [20]But who indeed are you, a human being,

σπέρμα. **9.9** ἐπαγγελίας γὰρ ὁ λόγος οὗτος, Κατὰ
A SEED.   [5]OF PROMISE   [1]FOR   [3]THE   [4]WORD   [2]THIS [IS],   ACCORDING TO

τὸν καιρὸν τοῦτον ἐλεύσομαι καὶ ἔσται τῇ Σάρρᾳ
-   THIS~TIME   I WILL COME   AND   THERE WILL BE   -   TO SARAH

υἱός. **9.10** οὐ μόνον δέ, ἀλλὰ καὶ Ῥεβέκκα ἐξ ἑνὸς
A SON.   [2]NOT   [3]ONLY [SO]   [1]AND, BUT   ALSO   REBECCA   [2]OF   [3]ONE MAN

κοίτην ἔχουσα, Ἰσαὰκ τοῦ πατρὸς ἡμῶν·
[1]CONCEIVING,   ISAAC   THE   FATHER   OF US;

9.11 μήπω γὰρ γεννηθέντων μηδὲ πραξάντων τι
FOR~NOT YET   HAVING BEEN BORN   NOR   PRACTISING   ANYTHING

ἀγαθὸν ἢ φαῦλον, ἵνα ἡ κατ' ἐκλογὴν πρόθεσις
GOOD   OR BAD,   THAT   [1]THE   [5]ACCORDING TO   [6]SELECTION   [2]PURPOSE

τοῦ θεοῦ μένῃ, **9.12** οὐκ ἐξ ἔργων ἀλλ' ἐκ τοῦ
-   [3]OF GOD   [4]MIGHT REMAIN,   NOT   OF WORKS   BUT   OF   THE ONE

καλοῦντος, ἐρρέθη αὐτῇ ὅτι Ὁ μείζων δουλεύσει τῷ
CALLING,   IT WAS SAID   TO HER,   -   THE GREATER ONE   WILL SERVE   THE

ἐλάσσονι, **9.13** καθὼς γέγραπται,
LESSER ONE;   EVEN AS   IT HAS BEEN WRITTEN,

Τὸν Ἰακὼβ ἠγάπησα,
-   JACOB   I LOVED,

τὸν δὲ Ἠσαῦ ἐμίσησα.
-   BUT ESAU   I HATED.

9.14 Τί οὖν ἐροῦμεν; μὴ ἀδικία παρὰ
WHAT   THEN   WILL WE SAY?   [SURELY THERE IS] NOT   UNRIGHTEOUSNESS   WITH

τῷ θεῷ; μὴ γένοιτο. **9.15** τῷ Μωϋσεῖ γὰρ λέγει,
-   GOD?   MAY IT NEVER BE.   -   FOR~TO MOSES   HE SAYS,

Ἐλεήσω ὃν ἂν ἐλεῶ
I WILL HAVE MERCY ON   WHOMEVER   I HAVE MERCY,

καὶ οἰκτιρήσω ὃν ἂν οἰκτίρω.
AND   I WILL HAVE COMPASSION ON   WHOMEVER   I HAVE COMPASSION.

9.16 ἄρα οὖν οὐ τοῦ θέλοντος οὐδὲ τοῦ
SO   THEN   [IT IS] NOT   OF THE ONE DESIRING   NOR   OF THE ONE

τρέχοντος ἀλλὰ τοῦ ἐλεῶντος θεοῦ. **9.17** λέγει γὰρ
RUNNING   BUT   OF THE ONE HAVING MERCY,   GOD.   FOR~SAYS

ἡ γραφὴ τῷ Φαραὼ ὅτι Εἰς αὐτὸ τοῦτο ἐξήγειρά σε
THE SCRIPTURE   -   TO PHARAOH,   -   FOR   THIS VERY THING   I RAISED UP   YOU,

ὅπως ἐνδείξωμαι ἐν σοὶ τὴν δύναμίν μου καὶ ὅπως
SO THAT   I MAY DEMONSTRATE   IN YOU   THE POWER   OF ME   AND   SO AS

διαγγελῇ τὸ ὄνομά μου ἐν πάσῃ τῇ γῇ. **9.18** ἄρα
MAY BE DECLARED   THE NAME   OF ME   IN   ALL   THE EARTH.   SO

οὖν ὃν θέλει ἐλεεῖ, ὃν δὲ θέλει σκληρύνει.
THEN   [ON] WHOM   HE WILLS   HE HAS MERCY,   AND~WHOM   HE WILLS   HE HARDENS.

9.19 Ἐρεῖς μοι οὖν, Τί [οὖν] ἔτι μέμφεται; τῷ
YOU SAY   TO ME   THEREFORE,   WHY   THEN   STILL   HE FINDS FAULT?   -

γὰρ βουλήματι αὐτοῦ τίς ἀνθέστηκεν; **9.20** ὦ ἄνθρωπε,
FOR   [4]INTENTION   [3]HIS   [1]WHO   [2]HAS RESISTED?   O MAN,

9:9 Gen. 18:10, 14   **9:12** Gen. 25:23   **9:13** Mal. 1:2-3   **9:15** Exod. 33:19   **9:17** Exod. 9:16 LXX

μενοῦνγε σὺ τίς εἶ ὁ   ἀνταποκρινόμενος τῷ θεῷ;
RATHER   ³YOU ¹WHO ²ARE THE ONE REPLYING AGAINST   -   GOD?

μὴ   ἐρεῖ   τὸ πλάσμα τῷ   πλάσαντι, Τί
[SURELY] NOT WILL SAY THE THING FORMED   TO THE ONE HAVING FORMED [IT], WHY

με ἐποίησας οὕτως; 9.21 ἢ οὐκ ἔχει ἐξουσίαν ὁ
DID YOU MAKE~ME SO?   OR HAS~NOT ³[THE] RIGHT ¹THE

κεραμεὺς τοῦ   πηλοῦ ἐκ   τοῦ αὐτοῦ φυράματος
²POTTER   OF(OVER) THE CLAY OUT OF THE SAME   LUMP

ποιῆσαι ὃ μὲν εἰς τιμὴν   σκεῦος ὃ δὲ   εἰς
TO MAKE ¹THIS ³FOR ⁴HONOR[ABLE USE] ²VESSEL AND~THAT FOR

ἀτιμίαν;   9.22 εἰ δὲ   θέλων ὁ θεὸς ἐνδείξασθαι
DISHONOR[ABLE USE]?   BUT~[WHAT] IF ²WANTING - ¹GOD   TO DEMONSTRATE

τὴν ὀργὴν καὶ γνωρίσαι τὸ δυνατὸν αὐτοῦ ἤνεγκεν
THE(HIS) WRATH AND TO MAKE KNOWN THE POWER OF HIM ENDURED

ἐν πολλῇ μακροθυμίᾳ σκεύη ὀργῆς κατηρτισμένα εἰς
WITH MUCH LONGSUFFERING VESSELS OF WRATH HAVING BEEN PREPARED FOR

ἀπώλειαν, 9.23 καὶ ἵνα γνωρίσῃ   τὸν πλοῦτον τῆς
DESTRUCTION,   SO   THAT HE MIGHT MAKE KNOWN THE RICHES OF THE

δόξης αὐτοῦ ἐπὶ σκεύη ἐλέους ἃ   προητοίμασεν εἰς
GLORY OF HIM ON VESSELS OF MERCY WHICH HE PREPARED BEFOREHAND FOR

δόξαν; 9.24 οὓς   καὶ ἐκάλεσεν ἡμᾶς οὐ μόνον
GLORY?   [AMONG] WHOM ALSO HE CALLED US,   NOT ONLY

ἐξ Ἰουδαίων ἀλλὰ καὶ ἐξ ἐθνῶν, 9.25 ὡς καὶ ἐν
FROM JEWS   BUT ALSO FROM GENTILES,   AS ALSO IN

τῷ Ὡσηὲ λέγει,
-   HOSEA HE SAYS,

    Καλέσω τὸν οὐ λαόν μου λαόν μου
    I WILL CALL THE ²NOT ¹PEOPLE ³OF ME A PEOPLE OF ME

    καὶ τὴν   οὐκ ἠγαπημένην
    AND THE ONE NOT HAVING BEEN LOVED

    ἠγαπημένην·
    HAVING BEEN LOVED(BELOVED).

9.26 καὶ ἔσται ἐν τῷ τόπῳ οὗ   ἐρρέθη αὐτοῖς,
    AND IT WILL BE IN THE PLACE WHERE IT WAS SAID TO THEM,

    Οὐ λαός μου ὑμεῖς,
    NOT A PEOPLE OF ME YOU° ARE,

    ἐκεῖ κληθήσονται υἱοὶ θεοῦ ζῶντος.
    THERE THEY WILL BE CALLED SONS OF A LIVING~GOD.

9.27 Ἠσαΐας δὲ κράζει ὑπὲρ   τοῦ Ἰσραήλ, Ἐὰν ᾖ
    AND~ISAIAH   CRIES ON BEHALF OF - ISRAEL,   IF   BE

ὁ ἀριθμὸς τῶν υἱῶν Ἰσραὴλ ὡς ἡ ἄμμος τῆς
THE NUMBER OF THE SONS OF ISRAEL AS THE SAND OF THE

θαλάσσης, τὸ ὑπόλειμμα σωθήσεται· 9.28 λόγον γὰρ
SEA,   THE REMNANT   WILL BE SAVED;   ⁴[THE] WORD ¹FOR

συντελῶν καὶ συντέμνων ποιήσει κύριος ἐπὶ τῆς
⁵FINISHING [IT] ⁶AND ⁷CUTTING [IT] SHORT ³WILL EXECUTE ²[THE] LORD ON THE

9:25 Hos. 2:23   **9:26** Hos. 1:10   **9:27-28** Isa. 10:22-23 LXX

to argue with God? Will what is molded say to the one who molds it, "Why have you made me like this?" 21Has the potter no right over the clay, to make out of the same lump one object for special use and another for ordinary use? 22What if God, desiring to show his wrath and to make known his power, has endured with much patience the objects of wrath that are made for destruction; 23and what if he has done so in order to make known the riches of his glory for the objects of mercy, which he has prepared beforehand for glory— 24including us whom he has called, not from the Jews only but also from the Gentiles? 25As indeed he says in Hosea,

"Those who were not my
    people I will call
    'my people,'
and her who was not
    beloved I will call
    'beloved.'"
26"And in the very place
    where it was said to
    them, 'You are not
    my people,'
there they shall be
    called children of
    the living God."

27 And Isaiah cries concerning Israel, "Though the number of the children of Israel were like the sand of the sea, only a remnant of them will be saved; 28for the Lord will execute his sentence on the

earth quickly and decisively."[v 29]And as Isaiah predicted,

"If the Lord of hosts had not left survivors[w] to us, we would have fared like Sodom and been made like Gomorrah."

30 What then are we to say? Gentiles, who did not strive for righteousness, have attained it, that is, righteousness through faith; [31]but Israel, who did strive for the righteousness that is based on the law, did not succeed in fulfilling that law. [32]Why not? Because they did not strive for it on the basis of faith, but as if it were based on works. They have stumbled over the stumbling stone, [33]as it is written,

"See, I am laying in Zion a stone that will make people stumble, a rock that will make them fall, and whoever believes in him[x] will not be put to shame."

[v] Other ancient authorities read *for he will finish his work and cut it short in righteousness, because the Lord will make the sentence shortened on the earth*

[w] Or *descendants*; Gk *seed*

[x] Or *trusts in it*

γῆς. **9.29** καὶ καθὼς προείρηκεν Ἡσαΐας,
EARTH.   AND   AS   ISAIAH~HAS SAID BEFORE,

Εἰ μὴ κύριος Σαβαὼθ   ἐγκατέλιπεν ἡμῖν
EXCEPT, [THE] LORD OF SABAOTH(HOSTS) LEFT   TO US

σπέρμα,
A SEED,

ὡς Σόδομα ἂν ἐγενήθημεν
AS   SODOM   WE WOULD HAVE BECOME

καὶ ὡς Γόμορρα ἂν ὡμοιώθημεν.
AND   AS   GOMORRAH   WE WOULD HAVE BEEN MADE LIKE.

9.30 Τί   οὖν ἐροῦμεν; ὅτι ἔθνη   τὰ μὴ διώκοντα
WHAT THEN WILL WE SAY? THAT GENTILES -   NOT PURSUING

δικαιοσύνην κατέλαβεν δικαιοσύνην, δικαιοσύνην δὲ τὴν
RIGHTEOUSNESS ATTAINED   RIGHTEOUSNESS,   AND~A RIGHTEOUSNESS   -

ἐκ πίστεως, **9.31** Ἰσραὴλ δὲ διώκων νόμον δικαιοσύνης
BY   FAITH?   BUT~ISRAEL   PURSUING A LAW   OF RIGHTEOUSNESS

εἰς νόμον οὐκ ἔφθασεν. **9.32** διὰ τί; ὅτι   οὐκ
TO(AT) [THAT] LAW DID NOT ARRIVE.   WHY?   BECAUSE [IT WAS] NOT

ἐκ πίστεως ἀλλ᾽ ὡς ἐξ ἔργων· προσέκοψαν τῷ λίθῳ
BY   FAITH   BUT   AS BY WORKS;   THEY STUMBLED   AT THE STONE

τοῦ προσκόμματος, **9.33** καθὼς γέγραπται,
-      OF STUMBLING,   AS   IT HAS BEEN WRITTEN,

Ἰδοὺ τίθημι ἐν Σιὼν λίθον προσκόμματος
BEHOLD I PLACE   IN   ZION   A STONE   OF STUMBLING

καὶ πέτραν σκανδάλου,
AND   A ROCK   OF OFFENSE,

καὶ ὁ   πιστεύων ἐπ᾽ αὐτῷ
AND   THE ONE BELIEVING   ON   HIM

οὐ καταισχυνθήσεται.
WILL NOT BE PUT TO SHAME.

9:29 Isa. 1:9 LXX   **9:33** Isa. 8:14; 28:16 LXX

CHAPTER 10

Brothers and sisters,[y] my heart's desire and prayer to God for them is that they may be saved. [2]I can testify that they have a zeal for God, but it is not enlightened. [3]For, being ignorant of the righteousness that comes from God, and seeking to establish their own, they have not submitted to God's righteousness. [4]For Christ is the end of the law

[y] Gk *Brothers*

10.1 Ἀδελφοί, ἡ μὲν εὐδοκία   τῆς ἐμῆς καρδίας
BROTHERS,   THE   -   GOOD PLEASURE   -   OF MY   HEART

καὶ ἡ δέησις   πρὸς τὸν θεὸν ὑπὲρ   αὐτῶν εἰς
AND   THE SUPPLICATION TO   -   GOD   ON BEHALF OF THEM   [IS] FOR

σωτηρίαν. **10.2** μαρτυρῶ γὰρ αὐτοῖς ὅτι ζῆλον
SALVATION.   FOR~I BEAR WITNESS TO THEM   THAT A ZEAL

θεοῦ   ἔχουσιν ἀλλ᾽ οὐ κατ᾽   ἐπίγνωσιν·
OF(FOR) GOD THEY HAVE, BUT   NOT ACCORDING TO KNOWLEDGE;

10.3 ἀγνοοῦντες γὰρ τὴν τοῦ θεοῦ δικαιοσύνην καὶ τὴν
FOR~BEING IGNORANT OF THE   -   RIGHTEOUSNESS~OF GOD   AND THE[IR]

ἰδίαν [δικαιοσύνην] ζητοῦντες στῆσαι, τῇ δικαιοσύνῃ
OWN   RIGHTEOUSNESS   SEEKING   TO ESTABLISH, TO THE RIGHTEOUSNESS

τοῦ θεοῦ οὐχ ὑπετάγησαν· **10.4** τέλος γὰρ νόμου
-    OF GOD THEY DID NOT SUBMIT;   [3]END [1]FOR [4]OF LAW

Χριστὸς εἰς δικαιοσύνην παντὶ τῷ πιστεύοντι.
²CHRIST [IS] [RESULTING] IN RIGHTEOUSNESS TO EVERYONE BELIEVING.

10.5 Μωϋσῆς γὰρ γράφει τὴν δικαιοσύνην τὴν ἐκ [τοῦ]
FOR~MOSES WRITES [OF] THE RIGHTEOUSNESS - OF THE

νόμου ὅτι ὁ ποιήσας αὐτὰ ἄνθρωπος ζήσεται ἐν
LAW THAT ¹THE ³HAVING DONE ⁴THESE THINGS ²MAN WILL LIVE IN(BY)

αὐτοῖς. **10.6** ἡ δὲ ἐκ πίστεως δικαιοσύνη οὕτως λέγει,
THEM. BUT~THE ²OF ³FAITH ¹RIGHTEOUSNESS THUS SPEAKS,

Μὴ εἴπῃς ἐν τῇ καρδίᾳ σου, Τίς ἀναβήσεται εἰς τὸν
DO NOT SAY IN THE HEART OF YOU, WHO WILL ASCEND INTO -

οὐρανόν; τοῦτ' ἔστιν Χριστὸν καταγαγεῖν· **10.7** ἤ,
HEAVEN? THIS(THAT) IS CHRIST TO BRING DOWN; OR,

Τίς καταβήσεται εἰς τὴν ἄβυσσον; τοῦτ' ἔστιν
WHO WILL DESCEND INTO THE ABYSS? THIS(THAT) IS

Χριστὸν ἐκ νεκρῶν ἀναγαγεῖν. **10.8** ἀλλὰ τί
²CHRIST ³FROM ⁴DEAD ONES ¹TO BRING UP. BUT WHAT

λέγει;
DOES [IT] SAY?

Ἐγγύς σου τὸ ῥῆμά ἐστιν
NEAR YOU THE WORD IS

ἐν τῷ στόματί σου καὶ ἐν τῇ καρδίᾳ
IN THE MOUTH OF YOU AND IN THE HEART

σου,
OF YOU,

τοῦτ' ἔστιν τὸ ῥῆμα τῆς πίστεως ὃ κηρύσσομεν.
THIS(THAT) IS THE WORD - OF FAITH WHICH WE PREACH.

10.9 ὅτι ἐὰν ὁμολογήσῃς ἐν τῷ στόματί σου κύριον
BECAUSE IF YOU CONFESS WITH THE MOUTH OF YOU LORD

Ἰησοῦν καὶ πιστεύσῃς ἐν τῇ καρδίᾳ σου ὅτι ὁ θεὸς
JESUS AND YOU BELIEVE IN THE HEART OF YOU THAT - GOD

αὐτὸν ἤγειρεν ἐκ νεκρῶν, σωθήσῃ· **10.10** καρδίᾳ γὰρ
RAISED~HIM FROM DEAD ONES, YOU WILL BE SAVED. FOR~WITH [THE] HEART

πιστεύεται εἰς δικαιοσύνην, στόματι δὲ
ONE BELIEVES [RESULTING] IN RIGHTEOUSNESS, AND~WITH [THE] MOUTH

ὁμολογεῖται εἰς σωτηρίαν. **10.11** λέγει γὰρ ἡ
ONE CONFESSES [RESULTING] IN SALVATION. FOR~SAYS THE

γραφή, Πᾶς ὁ πιστεύων ἐπ' αὐτῷ οὐ καταισχυνθήσεται.
SCRIPTURE, EVERYONE BELIEVING ON HIM WILL NOT BE PUT TO SHAME.

10.12 οὐ γάρ ἐστιν διαστολὴ Ἰουδαίου τε καὶ Ἕλληνος,
³NO ¹FOR ²[THERE] IS DIFFERENCE BETWEEN JEW AND GREEK,

ὁ γὰρ αὐτὸς κύριος πάντων, πλουτῶν εἰς πάντας τοὺς
FOR~THE SAME LORD OF ALL, [IS] BEING RICH TO ALL THE ONES

ἐπικαλουμένους αὐτόν· **10.13** πᾶς γὰρ ὃς ἂν
CALLING ON HIM; FOR~EVERYONE WHOEVER

ἐπικαλέσηται τὸ ὄνομα κυρίου σωθήσεται.
CALLS ON THE LORD'S~NAME WILL BE SAVED.

so that there may be righteousness for everyone
who believes.
5 Moses writes
concerning the righ-
teousness that comes
from the law, that "the
person who does these
things will live by them."
⁶But the righteousness that
comes from faith says, "Do
not say in your heart, 'Who
will ascend into heaven?' "
(that is, to bring Christ
down) ⁷"or 'Who will
descend into the abyss?' "
(that is, to bring Christ up
from the dead). ⁸But what
does it say?
"The word is near you,
on your lips and in your
heart"
(that is, the word of faith that
we proclaim); ⁹becauseᶻ if
you confess with your lips
that Jesus is Lord and believe
in your heart that God raised
him from the dead, you will
be saved. ¹⁰For one believes
with the heart and so is
justified, and one confesses
with the mouth and so is
saved. ¹¹The scripture says,
"No one who believes in him
will be put to shame." ¹²For
there is no distinction
between Jew and Greek; the
same Lord is Lord of all and
is generous to all who call
on him. ¹³For, "Everyone
who calls on the name of
the Lord shall be saved."

ᶻ Or namely, that

10:5 Lev. 18:5 **10:6** Deut. 9:4 **10:6-8** Deut. 30:12-14 **10:11** Isa. 28:16 LXX **10:13** Joel 2:32

14 But how are they to call on one in whom they have not believed? And how are they to believe in one of whom they have never heard? And how are they to hear without someone to proclaim him? 15And how are they to proclaim him unless they are sent? As it is written, "How beautiful are the feet of those who bring good news!" 16But not all have obeyed the good news;[a] for Isaiah says, "Lord, who has believed our message?" 17So faith comes from what is heard, and what is heard comes through the word of Christ.[b]

18 But I ask, have they not heard? Indeed they have; for

"Their voice has gone
    out to all the earth,
and their words to the
    ends of the world."

19Again I ask, did Israel not understand? First Moses says,

"I will make you jealous
    of those who are not
    a nation;
with a foolish nation I
    will make you
    angry."

20Then Isaiah is so bold as to say,

"I have been found by
    those who did not
    seek me;
I have shown myself to
    those who did not
    ask for me."

[a] Or gospel
[b] Or about Christ; other ancient authorities read of God

10.14 Πῶς οὖν ἐπικαλέσωνται εἰς ὃν
HOW THEN MAY THEY CALL ON [ONE] IN WHOM

οὐκ ἐπίστευσαν; πῶς δὲ πιστεύσωσιν οὗ
THEY DID NOT BELIEVE? AND~HOW MAY THEY BELIEVE [HIM] OF WHOM

οὐκ ἤκουσαν; πῶς δὲ ἀκούσωσιν χωρὶς κηρύσσοντος;
THEY DID NOT HEAR? AND~HOW MAY THEY HEAR WITHOUT ONE PREACHING?

10.15 πῶς δὲ κηρύξωσιν ἐὰν μὴ ἀποσταλῶσιν; καθὼς
AND~HOW MAY THEY PREACH IF THEY ARE NOT SENT? AS

γέγραπται, Ὡς ὡραῖοι οἱ πόδες τῶν
IT HAS BEEN WRITTEN, HOW BEAUTIFUL THE FEET OF THE ONES

εὐαγγελιζομένων [τὰ] ἀγαθά. **10.16** Ἀλλ᾽ οὐ
PROCLAIMING GOOD NEWS - [OF] GOOD THINGS. BUT NOT

πάντες ὑπήκουσαν τῷ εὐαγγελίῳ. Ἡσαΐας γὰρ λέγει,
ALL OBEYED THE GOOD NEWS. FOR~ISAIAH SAYS,

Κύριε, τίς ἐπίστευσεν τῇ ἀκοῇ ἡμῶν; **10.17** ἄρα ἡ
LORD, WHO BELIEVED THE REPORT OF US? THEN -

πίστις ἐξ ἀκοῆς, ἡ δὲ ἀκοὴ διὰ ῥήματος
FAITH [COMES] FROM HEARING, - AND HEARING THROUGH [THE] WORD

⌜Χριστοῦ.⌝ **10.18** ἀλλὰ λέγω, μὴ οὐκ ἤκουσαν;
OF CHRIST. BUT I SAY, - DID THEY NOT HEAR?

μενοῦνγε,
INDEED [THEY DID],

Εἰς πᾶσαν τὴν γῆν ἐξῆλθεν ὁ φθόγγος αὐτῶν
INTO ALL THE EARTH WENT OUT THE VOICE OF THEM

καὶ εἰς τὰ πέρατα τῆς οἰκουμένης
AND TO THE ENDS OF THE INHABITED WORLD

τὰ ῥήματα αὐτῶν.
THE WORDS OF THEM.

10.19 ἀλλὰ λέγω, μὴ Ἰσραὴλ οὐκ ἔγνω; πρῶτος
BUT I SAY, - [DID] ISRAEL NOT KNOW? FIRST

Μωϋσῆς λέγει,
MOSES SAYS,

Ἐγὼ παραζηλώσω ὑμᾶς ἐπ᾽ οὐκ ἔθνει,
I WILL PROVOKE TO JEALOUSY YOU° BY [ONE] NOT A NATION,

ἐπ᾽ ἔθνει ἀσυνέτῳ παροργιῶ ὑμᾶς.
BY A NATION WITHOUT UNDERSTANDING I WILL ANGER YOU°.

10.20 Ἡσαΐας δὲ ἀποτολμᾷ καὶ λέγει,
BUT~ISAIAH IS VERY BOLD AND SAYS,

Εὑρέθην [ἐν] τοῖς ἐμὲ μὴ ζητοῦσιν,
I WAS FOUND BY THE ONES ³ME ¹NOT ²SEEKING,

ἐμφανὴς ἐγενόμην τοῖς ἐμὲ μὴ
I BECAME~MANIFEST TO THE ONES ³ME ¹NOT

ἐπερωτῶσιν.
²ASKING FOR.

10:15 Isa. 52:7   **10:16** Isa. 53:1 LXX   **10:17** text: ASV RSV NASB NIV NEB TEV NJB NRSV. var. θεου
(of God): KJV NJBmg NRSVmg.   **10:18** Ps. 19:4 LXX   **10:19** Deut. 32:21   **10:20** Isa. 65:1 LXX

10.21 πρὸς δὲ τὸν Ἰσραὴλ λέγει, Ὅλην τὴν ἡμέραν
BUT~TO - ISRAEL HE SAYS, ALL THE DAY

ἐξεπέτασα τὰς χεῖράς μου πρὸς λαὸν ἀπειθοῦντα καὶ
I REACHED OUT THE HANDS OF ME TOWARD A PEOPLE DISOBEYING AND

ἀντιλέγοντα.
OPPOSING.

10:21 Isa. 65:2 LXX

[21]But of Israel he says, "All day long I have held out my hands to a disobedient and contrary people."

11.1 Λέγω οὖν, μὴ   ἀπώσατο ὁ θεὸς τὸν λαὸν
I SAY THEN, [2][SURELY DID] NOT [3]PUT AWAY - [1]GOD THE PEOPLE

αὐτοῦ; μὴ γένοιτο· καὶ γὰρ ἐγὼ Ἰσραηλίτης εἰμί,
OF HIM? MAY IT NEVER BE; FOR~ALSO I AN ISRAELITE AM,

ἐκ σπέρματος Ἀβραάμ, φυλῆς Βενιαμίν.
FROM [THE] SEED OF ABRAHAM, OF [THE] TRIBE OF BENJAMIN.

11.2 οὐκ ἀπώσατο ὁ θεὸς τὸν λαὸν αὐτοῦ ὃν προέγνω.
[2]DID NOT PUT AWAY - [1]GOD THE PEOPLE OF HIM WHOM HE FOREKNEW.

ἢ οὐκ οἴδατε ἐν   Ἠλίᾳ τί λέγει ἡ γραφή, ὡς
OR DO YOU° NOT KNOW IN(ABOUT) ELIJAH WHAT SAYS THE SCRIPTURE, HOW

ἐντυγχάνει τῷ θεῷ κατὰ τοῦ Ἰσραήλ; **11.3** Κύριε, τοὺς
HE PLEADS WITH - GOD AGAINST - ISRAEL? LORD, THE

προφήτας σου ἀπέκτειναν, τὰ θυσιαστήριά σου
PROPHETS OF YOU THEY KILLED, THE ALTARS OF(FOR) YOU

κατέσκαψαν, κἀγὼ ὑπελείφθην μόνος καὶ ζητοῦσιν
THEY DUG DOWN, AND I WAS LEFT BEHIND ALONE AND THEY SEEK

τὴν ψυχήν μου. **11.4** ἀλλὰ τί λέγει αὐτῷ ὁ
THE LIFE OF ME. BUT WHAT SAYS TO HIM THE

χρηματισμός; Κατέλιπον ἐμαυτῷ ἑπτακισχιλίους
DIVINE ANSWER? I RESERVED FOR MYSELF SEVEN THOUSAND

ἄνδρας, οἵτινες οὐκ ἔκαμψαν γόνυ τῇ Βάαλ.
MEN, WHO DID NOT BOW A KNEE - TO BAAL.

11.5 οὕτως οὖν καὶ ἐν τῷ νῦν καιρῷ λεῖμμα
SO THEN ALSO IN THE PRESENT TIME A REMNANT

κατ' ἐκλογὴν χάριτος γέγονεν· **11.6** εἰ δὲ
ACCORDING TO A SELECTION OF GRACE HAS COME INTO BEING. BUT~IF

χάριτι, οὐκέτι ἐξ ἔργων, ἐπεὶ ἡ χάρις οὐκέτι γίνεται
BY GRACE, NO MORE OF WORKS, SINCE - GRACE NO MORE BECOMES

χάρις.ᵀ **11.7** τί οὖν; ὃ ἐπιζητεῖ Ἰσραήλ, τοῦτο
GRACE. WHAT THEN? WHAT ISRAEL~IS SEEKING THIS

οὐκ ἐπέτυχεν, ἡ δὲ ἐκλογὴ ἐπέτυχεν· οἱ δὲ λοιποὶ
IT DID NOT OBTAIN, BUT~THE ELECT OBTAINED [IT]. AND~THE REST

I ask, then, has God rejected his people? By no means! I myself am an Israelite, a descendant of Abraham, a member of the tribe of Benjamin. [2]God has not rejected his people whom he foreknew. Do you not know what the scripture says of Elijah, how he pleads with God against Israel? [3]"Lord, they have killed your prophets, they have demolished your altars; I alone am left, and they are seeking my life." [4]But what is the divine reply to him? "I have kept for myself seven thousand who have not bowed the knee to Baal." [5]So too at the present time there is a remnant, chosen by grace. [6]But if it is by grace, it is no longer on the basis of works, otherwise grace would no longer be grace.ᶜ

7 What then? Israel failed to obtain what it was seeking. The elect obtained it, but the rest were

ᶜ Other ancient authorities add *But if it is by works, it is no longer on the basis of grace, otherwise work would no longer be work*

11:3 1 Kings 19:10, 14 **11:4** 1 Kings 19:18 **11:6** text: ASV RSV NASB NIV NEB TEV NJB NRSV. add ει δε εξ εργων, ουκετι εστι χαρις, επει το εργον ουκετι εστιν εργον (but it by works, it is no longer grace; otherwise, work would no longer be work): KJV NIVmg NRSVmg.

hardened, [8]as it is written,
"God gave them a
    sluggish spirit,
eyes that would not see
and ears that would not
    hear,
down to this very day."
[9]And David says,
"Let their table become a
    snare and a trap,
a stumbling block and a
    retribution for them;
[10]let their eyes be darkened
    so that they cannot
    see,
and keep their backs
    forever bent."
11 So I ask, have they
stumbled so as to fall? By no
means! But through their
stumbling[d] salvation has
come to the Gentiles, so as
to make Israel[e] jealous.
[12]Now if their stumbling[d]
means riches for the world,
and if their defeat means
riches for Gentiles, how
much more will their full
inclusion mean!
13 Now I am speaking to
you Gentiles. Inasmuch then
as I am an apostle of the
Gentiles, I glorify my
ministry [14]in order to make
my own people[f] jealous,
and thus save some of
them. [15]For if their

[d] Gk *transgression*
[e] Gk *them*
[f] Gk *my flesh*

ἐπωρώθησαν, **11.8** καθὼς γέγραπται,
WERE HARDENED,   AS   IT HAS BEEN WRITTEN,

Ἔδωκεν αὐτοῖς ὁ θεὸς πνεῦμα κατανύξεως,
[2]GAVE   [3]TO THEM   -   [1]GOD   A SPIRIT   OF DEEP SLEEP,

ὀφθαλμοὺς τοῦ μὴ βλέπειν
EYES   -   NOT   TO SEE

καὶ ὦτα τοῦ μὴ ἀκούειν,
AND   EARS   -   NOT   TO HEAR,

ἕως τῆς σήμερον ἡμέρας.
UNTIL   THIS VERY   DAY.

11.9 καὶ Δαυὶδ λέγει,
AND   DAVID   SAYS,

Γενηθήτω ἡ τράπεζα αὐτῶν εἰς παγίδα καὶ εἰς
LET BECOME   THE TABLE   OF THEM   FOR   A SNARE   AND   FOR

θήραν
A NET

καὶ εἰς σκάνδαλον καὶ εἰς ἀνταπόδομα
AND   FOR   A TRAP   AND   FOR   A RETRIBUTION

αὐτοῖς,
TO THEM,

11.10 σκοτισθήτωσαν οἱ ὀφθαλμοὶ αὐτῶν τοῦ μὴ
LET BE DARKENED   THE EYES   OF THEM   -   NOT

βλέπειν
TO SEE

καὶ τὸν νῶτον αὐτῶν διὰ παντὸς σύγκαμψον.
AND   THE   BACK   OF THEM   CONTINUALLY   LET BEND.

11.11 Λέγω οὖν, μὴ ἔπταισαν ἵνα πέσωσιν;
I SAY   THEN,   [SURELY] THEY DID NOT STUMBLE THAT   THEY MIGHT FALL?

μὴ γένοιτο· ἀλλὰ τῷ αὐτῶν παραπτώματι ἡ σωτηρία
MAY IT NEVER BE.   BUT   BY   THEIR   TRESPASS   THE SALVATION

τοῖς ἔθνεσιν εἰς τὸ παραζηλῶσαι αὐτούς.
[CAME] TO THE   GENTILES,   SO AS TO   PROVOKE TO JEALOUSY   THEM.

11.12 εἰ δὲ τὸ παράπτωμα αὐτῶν πλοῦτος κόσμου
NOW~IF   THE TRESPASS   OF THEM   [MEANS] RICHES   OF(FOR) [THE] WORLD

καὶ τὸ ἥττημα αὐτῶν πλοῦτος ἐθνῶν, πόσῳ
AND   THE   FAILURE   OF THEM   [MEANS] RICHES   OF(FOR) [THE] GENTILES,   BY HOW MUCH

μᾶλλον τὸ πλήρωμα αὐτῶν.
MORE   THE FULLNESS   OF THEM.

11.13 Ὑμῖν δὲ λέγω τοῖς ἔθνεσιν· ἐφ' ὅσον μὲν
NOW~TO YOU°   I SPEAK,   THE   GENTILES;   [2]INASMUCH AS   -

οὖν εἰμι ἐγὼ ἐθνῶν ἀπόστολος, τὴν διακονίαν
[1]THEREFORE   [4]AM   [3]I   [6]OF [THE] GENTILES   [5]AN APOSTLE,   THE   MININSTRY

μου δοξάζω, **11.14** εἴ πως παραζηλώσω μου
OF ME   I GLORIFY,   IF   SOMEHOW   I MAY PROVOKE TO JEALOUSY   [THOSE OF] MY

τὴν σάρκα καὶ σώσω τινὰς ἐξ αὐτῶν. **11.15** εἰ γὰρ ἡ
-   FLESH   AND   MAY SAVE   SOME   OF   THEM.   FOR~IF   THE

11:8 Deut. 29:4; Isa. 29:10   **11:9-10** Ps. 69:22-23 LXX

ἀποβολὴ αὐτῶν καταλλαγὴ
CASTING AWAY OF THEM [BRINGS THE] RECONCILIATION

κόσμου, τίς
OF [THE] WORLD, WHAT [WILL MEAN]

ἡ πρόσλημψις εἰ μὴ ζωὴ ἐκ
THE[IR] ACCEPTANCE IF NOT LIFE FROM

νεκρῶν; **11.16** εἰ δὲ ἡ
DEAD ONES? NOW~IF THE

ἀπαρχὴ ἁγία, καὶ τὸ φύραμα· καὶ εἰ ἡ ῥίζα ἁγία,
FIRSTFRUIT [IS] HOLY, ALSO THE LUMP; AND IF THE ROOT [IS] HOLY,

καὶ οἱ κλάδοι.
ALSO THE BRANCHES.

11.17 Εἰ δέ τινες τῶν κλάδων ἐξεκλάσθησαν, σὺ δὲ
BUT~IF SOME OF THE BRANCHES WERE BROKEN OFF, AND~YOU

ἀγριέλαιος ὢν ἐνεκεντρίσθης ἐν αὐτοῖς καὶ
BEING~A WILD OLIVE TREE WERE GRAFTED IN AMONG THEM AND

συγκοινωνὸς ⌐τῆς ῥίζης τῆς πιότητος⌐ τῆς ἐλαίας
A PARTAKER OF THE ROOT OF THE FATNESS OF THE OLIVE TREE

ἐγένου, **11.18** μὴ κατακαυχῶ τῶν κλάδων· εἰ δὲ
BECAME, DO NOT BOAST OF THE BRANCHES; BUT~IF

κατακαυχᾶσαι οὐ σὺ τὴν ῥίζαν βαστάζεις ἀλλὰ ἡ
YOU BOAST, NOT YOU ²THE ³ROOT ¹BEAR BUT THE

ῥίζα σέ. **11.19** ἐρεῖς οὖν, Ἐξεκλάσθησαν κλάδοι
ROOT YOU. YOU WILL SAY THEN, WERE BROKEN OFF BRANCHES

ἵνα ἐγὼ ἐγκεντρισθῶ. **11.20** καλῶς· τῇ ἀπιστίᾳ
THAT I MIGHT BE GRAFTED IN. [YOU SAY] WELL; FOR UNBELIEF

ἐξεκλάσθησαν, σὺ δὲ τῇ πίστει ἕστηκας. μὴ ὑψηλὰ
THEY WERE BROKEN OFF, BUT~YOU - BY FAITH HAVE STOOD. ²NOT ³HIGH THINGS

φρόνει ἀλλὰ φοβοῦ· **11.21** εἰ γὰρ ὁ θεὸς τῶν κατὰ
¹MIND BUT FEAR; FOR~IF - GOD ²THE ⁴ACCORDING TO

φύσιν κλάδων οὐκ ἐφείσατο, [μή πως] οὐδὲ σοῦ
⁵NATURE ³BRANCHES ¹DID NOT SPARE, PERHAPS NEITHER YOU

φείσεται. **11.22** ἴδε οὖν χρηστότητα καὶ ἀποτομίαν
WILL HE SPARE. SEE THEN [THE] KINDNESS AND SEVERITY

θεοῦ· ἐπὶ μὲν τοὺς πεσόντας ἀποτομία, ἐπὶ δὲ σὲ
OF GOD; ON - THE ONES HAVING FALLEN SEVERITY, BUT~ON YOU

χρηστότης θεοῦ, ἐὰν ἐπιμένῃς τῇ χρηστότητι,
[THE] KINDNESS OF GOD, IF YOU CONTINUE IN THE(HIS) KINDNESS,

ἐπεὶ καὶ σὺ ἐκκοπήσῃ. **11.23** κἀκεῖνοι δέ, ἐὰν
SINCE [OTHERWISE] ALSO YOU WILL BE CUT OFF. AND~THOSE ONES ALSO, IF

μὴ ἐπιμένωσιν τῇ ἀπιστίᾳ, ἐγκεντρισθήσονται· δυνατὸς
THEY DO NOT CONTINUE - IN UNBELIEF, WILL BE GRAFTED IN; ⁴ABLE

γάρ ἐστιν ὁ θεὸς πάλιν ἐγκεντρίσαι αὐτούς.
¹FOR ³IS - ²GOD AGAIN TO ENGRAFT THEM.

11.24 εἰ γὰρ σὺ ἐκ τῆς κατὰ φύσιν ἐξεκόπης
FOR~IF YOU ²FROM ³THE ⁵ACCORDING TO ⁶NATURE ¹WERE CUT

ἀγριελαίου καὶ παρὰ φύσιν ἐνεκεντρίσθης εἰς
⁴OLIVE TREE AND AGAINST NATURE WERE ENGRAFTED INTO

καλλιέλαιον, πόσῳ μᾶλλον οὗτοι οἱ κατὰ
A CULTIVATED OLIVE TREE, BY HOW MUCH MORE THESE ONES - ACCORDING TO

φύσιν ἐγκεντρισθήσονται τῇ ἰδίᾳ ἐλαίᾳ.
NATURE WILL BE GRAFTED INTO THE[IR] OWN OLIVE TREE.

rejection is the reconciliation of the world, what will their acceptance be but life from the dead! [16]If the part of the dough offered as first fruits is holy, then the whole batch is holy; and if the root is holy, then the branches also are holy.

[17] But if some of the branches were broken off, and you, a wild olive shoot, were grafted in their place to share the rich root[g] of the olive tree, [18]do not boast over the branches. If you do boast, remember that it is not you that support the root, but the root that supports you. [19]You will say, "Branches were broken off so that I might be grafted in." [20]That is true. They were broken off because of their unbelief, but you stand only through faith. So do not become proud, but stand in awe. [21]For if God did not spare the natural branches, perhaps he will not spare you.[h] [22]Note then the kindness and the severity of God: severity toward those who have fallen, but God's kindness toward you, provided you continue in his kindness; otherwise you also will be cut off. [23]And even those of Israel,[i] if they do not persist in unbelief, will be grafted in, for God has the power to graft them in again. [24]For if you have been cut from what is by nature a wild olive tree and grafted, contrary to nature, into a cultivated olive tree, how much more will these natural branches be grafted back into their own olive tree.

[g] Other ancient authorities read *the richness*
[h] Other ancient authorities read *neither will he spare you*
[i] Gk lacks *of Israel*

25 So that you may not claim to be wiser than you are, brothers and sisters,[j] I want you to understand this mystery: a hardening has come upon part of Israel, until the full number of the Gentiles has come in. [26]And so all Israel will be saved; as it is written,

"Out of Zion will come
    the Deliverer;
he will banish
    ungodliness from
    Jacob."
[27]"And this is my covenant
    with them,
when I take away their
    sins."

[28]As regards the gospel they are enemies of God[k] for your sake; but as regards election they are beloved, for the sake of their ancestors; [29]for the gifts and the calling of God are irrevocable. [30]Just as you were once disobedient to God but have now received mercy because of their disobedience, [31]so they have now been disobedient in order that, by the mercy shown to you, they too may now[l] receive mercy. [32]For God has imprisoned all in disobedience so that he may be merciful to all.

33 O the depth of the riches and wisdom and knowledge of God! How unsearchable are his judgments and how inscrutable his ways!
[34]"For who has known the mind of the Lord?
    Or who has been his counselor?"

[j] Gk *brothers*
[k] Gk lacks *of God*
[l] Other ancient authorities lack *now*

11.25 Οὐ γὰρ θέλω ὑμᾶς ἀγνοεῖν, ἀδελφοί, τὸ
FOR~I DO NOT WANT   YOU°   TO BE IGNORANT   BROTHERS,   -

μυστήριον τοῦτο, ἵνα μὴ ἦτε [παρ'] ἑαυτοῖς φρόνιμοι,
[OF] THIS~MYSTERY,   LEST   YOU° BE IN   YOURSELVES   WISE,

ὅτι πώρωσις ἀπὸ μέρους τῷ Ἰσραὴλ γέγονεν ἄχρις οὗ
THAT HARDNESS   IN PART   -   TO ISRAEL   HAS HAPPENED   UNTIL

τὸ πλήρωμα τῶν ἐθνῶν εἰσέλθη **11.26** καὶ οὕτως πᾶς
THE FULLNESS   OF THE GENTILES   COMES IN,   AND   SO   ALL

Ἰσραὴλ σωθήσεται, καθὼς γέγραπται,
ISRAEL   WILL BE SAVED;   AS   IT HAS BEEN WRITTEN,

Ἥξει ἐκ Σιὼν ὁ ῥυόμενος,
3WILL COME 4OUT OF 5ZION 1THE ONE 2DELIVERING,

ἀποστρέψει ἀσεβείας ἀπὸ Ἰακώβ.
HE WILL TURN AWAY   UNGODLINESS   FROM   JACOB.

11.27 καὶ αὕτη αὐτοῖς ἡ παρ' ἐμοῦ διαθήκη,
AND   THIS   5TO THEM 1[IS] THE 3FROM 4ME 2COVENANT,

ὅταν ἀφέλωμαι τὰς ἁμαρτίας αὐτῶν.
WHEN   I TAKE AWAY   THE   SINS   OF THEM.

11.28 κατὰ μὲν τὸ εὐαγγέλιον ἐχθροὶ δι'
ACCORDING TO   -   THE   GOOD NEWS   [THEY ARE] ENEMIES   BECAUSE OF

ὑμᾶς, κατὰ δὲ τὴν ἐκλογὴν ἀγαπητοὶ διὰ
YOU°,   BUT~ACCORDING TO THE   ELECTION   [THEY ARE] BELOVED   BECAUSE OF

τοὺς πατέρας· **11.29** ἀμεταμέλητα γὰρ τὰ χαρίσματα
THE   FATHERS;   FOR~[ARE] IRREVOCABLE   THE   FREE GIFTS

καὶ ἡ κλῆσις τοῦ θεοῦ. **11.30** ὥσπερ γὰρ ὑμεῖς ποτε
AND   THE CALLING   -   OF GOD.   FOR~JUST AS   YOU°   ONCE

ἠπειθήσατε τῷ θεῷ, νῦν δὲ ἠλεήθητε τῇ
DISOBEYED   -   GOD,   BUT~NOW   YOU° RECEIVED MERCY   1BY THE

τούτων ἀπειθείᾳ, **11.31** οὕτως καὶ οὗτοι νῦν
3OF THESE ONES 2DISOBEDIENCE,   SO   ALSO   THESE ONES   NOW

ἠπείθησαν τῷ ὑμετέρῳ ἐλέει, ἵνα καὶ αὐτοὶ
WERE DISOBEDIENT   -   TO [WHAT WAS] FOR YOU°   MERCY,   THAT   ALSO   THEY

⌐[νῦν]⌐ ἐλεηθῶσιν. **11.32** συνέκλεισεν γὰρ ὁ θεὸς τοὺς
NOW   MAY RECEIVE MERCY.   3CONSIGNED   1FOR   -   2GOD   -

πάντας εἰς ἀπείθειαν, ἵνα τοὺς πάντας ἐλεήσῃ.
ALL   IN   DISOBEDIENCE,   THAT   -   TO ALL   HE MAY SHOW MERCY.

11.33 Ὦ βάθος πλούτου καὶ σοφίας καὶ
O   [THE] DEPTH   OF [THE] RICHES   AND   OF [THE] WISDOM   AND

γνώσεως θεοῦ· ὡς ἀνεξεραύνητα τὰ κρίματα αὐτοῦ
KNOWLEDGE   OF GOD;   HOW   UNSEARCHABLE   THE   JUDGMENTS   OF HIM

καὶ ἀνεξιχνίαστοι αἱ ὁδοὶ αὐτοῦ.
AND   UNTRACEABLE   THE   WAYS   OF HIM.

11.34 Τίς γὰρ ἔγνω νοῦν κυρίου;
FOR~WHO   KNEW   [THE] MIND   OF [THE] LORD?

ἢ τίς σύμβουλος αὐτοῦ ἐγένετο;
OR   WHO   A COUNSELLOR   OF HIM   BECAME?

11:26-27a Isa. 59:20-21 LXX   **11:27b** Isa. 27:9 LXX   **11:31** text: ASV NASB NIV TEV NEB NRSV. omit: KJV RSV TEVmg NJB NRSVmg.   **11:34** Isa. 40:13 LXX

11.35 ἢ τίς προέδωκεν αὐτῷ,
OR   WHO   PREVIOUSLY GAVE   TO HIM,

καὶ ἀνταποδοθήσεται αὐτῷ;
AND   IT WILL BE REPAID   TO HIM?

11.36 ὅτι ἐξ αὐτοῦ καὶ δι᾽ αὐτοῦ καὶ εἰς
BECAUSE   FROM HIM   AND   THROUGH HIM   AND   TO

αὐτὸν τὰ πάντα· αὐτῷ ἡ δόξα εἰς τοὺς αἰῶνας,
HIM   -   [ARE] ALL THINGS;   TO HIM   [BE] THE   GLORY   INTO   THE   AGES,

ἀμήν.
AMEN.

11:35 Job 41:11

35 "Or who has given a gift to him,
   to receive a gift in return?"
36 For from him and through him and to him are all things. To him be the glory forever. Amen.

12.1 Παρακαλῶ οὖν ὑμᾶς, ἀδελφοί, διὰ τῶν
THEREFORE~I URGE   YOU°,   BROTHERS,   THROUGH THE

οἰκτιρμῶν τοῦ θεοῦ παραστῆσαι τὰ σώματα ὑμῶν
COMPASSIONS   -   OF GOD   TO PRESENT   THE   BODIES   OF YOU°

θυσίαν ζῶσαν ἁγίαν εὐάρεστον τῷ θεῷ, τὴν
A SACRIFICE LIVING,   HOLY,   WELL-PLEASING   -   TO GOD,   [WHICH IS] THE

λογικὴν λατρείαν ὑμῶν· **12.2** καὶ μὴ συσχηματίζεσθε
SPIRITUAL   SERVICE   OF YOU°;   AND   DO NOT BE CONFORMED

τῷ αἰῶνι τούτῳ, ἀλλὰ μεταμορφοῦσθε τῇ ἀνακαινώσει
-   TO THIS~AGE,   BUT   BE TRANSFORMED   BY THE   RENEWING

τοῦ νοὸς εἰς τὸ δοκιμάζειν ὑμᾶς τί τὸ θέλημα
OF THE(YOUR)   MIND   FOR   -   YOU°~TO PROVE   WHAT   [IS] THE   WILL

τοῦ θεοῦ, τὸ ἀγαθὸν καὶ εὐάρεστον καὶ τέλειον.
-   OF GOD,   THE   GOOD   AND   WELL-PLEASING   AND   PERFECT [WILL].

12.3 Λέγω γὰρ διὰ τῆς χάριτος τῆς δοθείσης μοι
FOR~I SAY   THROUGH   THE   GRACE   -   HAVING BEEN GIVEN   TO ME

παντὶ τῷ ὄντι ἐν ὑμῖν μὴ ὑπερφρονεῖν παρ᾽ ὃ
TO EVERYONE   BEING   AMONG YOU°,   NOT   TO THINK MORE HIGHLY   BEYOND   WHAT

δεῖ φρονεῖν ἀλλὰ φρονεῖν εἰς τὸ σωφρονεῖν,
IS NECESSARY   TO THINK   BUT   TO THINK   SO AS   -   TO BE SOBER-MINDED,

ἑκάστῳ ὡς ὁ θεὸς ἐμέρισεν μέτρον πίστεως.
⁴TO EACH   ¹AS   -   ²GOD   ³APPORTIONED   A MEASURE   OF FAITH.

12.4 καθάπερ γὰρ ἐν ἑνὶ σώματι πολλὰ μέλη ἔχομεν,
FOR~AS   IN   ONE   BODY   MANY   MEMBERS   WE HAVE,

τὰ δὲ μέλη πάντα οὐ τὴν αὐτὴν ἔχει πρᾶξιν,
³THE   ¹AND   ⁴MEMBERS   ²ALL   ⁶NOT   ⁷THE   ⁸SAME   ⁵HAVE   ⁹ACTION,

12.5 οὕτως οἱ πολλοὶ ἓν σῶμά ἐσμεν ἐν Χριστῷ,
SO   [WE] THE   MANY   ONE BODY   ARE   IN   CHRIST,

τὸ δὲ καθ᾽ εἷς ἀλλήλων μέλη. **12.6** ἔχοντες δὲ
-   AND   EACH   ONE   MEMBERS~OF ONE ANOTHER.   AND~HAVING

χαρίσματα κατὰ τὴν χάριν τὴν δοθεῖσαν ἡμῖν
GIFTS   ²ACCORDING TO   ³THE   ⁴GRACE   -   ⁵HAVING BEEN GIVEN   ⁶TO US

διάφορα, εἴτε προφητείαν κατὰ τὴν ἀναλογίαν
¹DIFFERING,   WHETHER PROPHECY   ACCORDING TO THE   PROPORTION

I appeal to you therefore, brothers and sisters,ᵐ by the mercies of God, to present your bodies as a living sacrifice, holy and acceptable to God, which is your spiritualⁿ worship. 2 Do not be conformed to this world,ᵒ but be transformed by the renewing of your minds, so that you may discern what is the will of God—what is good and acceptable and perfect.ᵖ

3 For by the grace given to me I say to everyone among you not to think of yourself more highly than you ought to think, but to think with sober judgment, each according to the measure of faith that God has assigned. 4 For as in one body we have many members, and not all the members have the same function, 5 so we, who are many, are one body in Christ, and individually we are members one of another. 6 We have gifts that differ according to the grace given to us: prophecy, in proportion

ᵐ Gk *brothers*
ⁿ Or *reasonable*
ᵒ Gk *age*
ᵖ Or *what is the good and acceptable and perfect will of God*

to faith; [7]ministry, in ministering; the teacher, in teaching; [8]the exhorter, in exhortation; the giver, in generosity; the leader, in diligence; the compassionate, in cheerfulness.

9 Let love be genuine; hate what is evil, hold fast to what is good; [10]love one another with mutual affection; outdo one another in showing honor. [11]Do not lag in zeal, be ardent in spirit, serve the Lord.[q] [12]Rejoice in hope, be patient in suffering, persevere in prayer. [13]Contribute to the needs of the saints; extend hospitality to strangers.

14 Bless those who persecute you; bless and do not curse them. [15]Rejoice with those who rejoice, weep with those who weep. [16]Live in harmony with one another; do not be haughty, but associate with the lowly;[r] do not claim to be wiser than you are. [17]Do not repay anyone evil for evil, but take thought for what is noble in the sight of all. [18]If it is possible, so far as it depends on you, live peaceably with all. [19]Beloved, never avenge yourselves, but leave room

[q] Other ancient authorities read *serve the opportune time*
[r] Or *give yourselves to humble tasks*

τῆς πίστεως, **12.7** εἴτε διακονίαν ἐν τῇ διακονίᾳ, εἴτε
OF THE FAITH, OR MINISTRY IN THE MINISTRY, OR

ὁ διδάσκων ἐν τῇ διδασκαλίᾳ, **12.8** εἴτε ὁ
THE ONE TEACHING IN THE TEACHING, OR THE ONE

παρακαλῶν ἐν τῇ παρακλήσει· ὁ μεταδιδοὺς ἐν
ENCOURAGING IN THE ENCOURAGEMENT; THE ONE CONTRIBUTING WITH

ἁπλότητι, ὁ προϊστάμενος ἐν σπουδῇ, ὁ
GENEROSITY, THE ONE GOVERNING IN DILIGENCE, THE ONE

ἐλεῶν ἐν ἱλαρότητι.
SHOWING MERCY IN CHEERFULNESS.

12.9 Ἡ ἀγάπη ἀνυπόκριτος. ἀποστυγοῦντες τὸ
- [LET] LOVE [BE] UNHYPOCRITICAL. ABHORRING THE

πονηρόν, κολλώμενοι τῷ ἀγαθῷ, **12.10** τῇ φιλαδελφίᾳ
EVIL, CLINGING TO THE GOOD, - WITH BROTHERLY LOVE

εἰς ἀλλήλους φιλόστοργοι, τῇ τιμῇ ἀλλήλους
TO ONE ANOTHER LOVING DEARLY, - IN HONOR ONE ANOTHER

προηγούμενοι, **12.11** τῇ σπουδῇ μὴ ὀκνηροί, τῷ
PREFERRING, - IN ZEAL NOT LAZY, -

πνεύματι ζέοντες, τῷ κυρίῳ δουλεύοντες, **12.12** τῇ
IN SPIRIT BURNING, THE LORD SERVING, -

ἐλπίδι χαίροντες, τῇ θλίψει ὑπομένοντες, τῇ
IN HOPE REJOICING, - IN TRIBULATION ENDURING, -

προσευχῇ προσκαρτεροῦντες, **12.13** ταῖς χρείαις τῶν
IN PRAYER PERSEVERING, TO THE NEEDS OF THE

ἁγίων κοινωνοῦντες, τὴν φιλοξενίαν διώκοντες.
SAINTS CONTRIBUTING, - HOSPITALITY SEEKING.

12.14 εὐλογεῖτε τοὺς διώκοντας [ὑμᾶς], εὐλογεῖτε καὶ
BLESS THE ONES PERSECUTING YOU°, BLESS AND

μὴ καταρᾶσθε. **12.15** χαίρειν μετὰ χαιρόντων, κλαίειν
DO NOT CURSE. REJOICE WITH REJOICING ONES, WEEP

μετὰ κλαιόντων. **12.16** τὸ αὐτὸ εἰς ἀλλήλους
WITH WEEPING ONES. THE SAME THING TOWARD ONE ANOTHER

φρονοῦντες, μὴ τὰ ὑψηλὰ φρονοῦντες ἀλλὰ τοῖς
THINKING, NOT THE HIGH THINGS THINKING BUT [2]TO THE

ταπεινοῖς συναπαγόμενοι. μὴ γίνεσθε φρόνιμοι
[3]HUMBLE THINGS(ONES) [1]BEING WILLING TO GO. DO NOT BECOME WISE

παρ᾽ ἑαυτοῖς. **12.17** μηδενὶ κακὸν ἀντὶ κακοῦ
WITH YOURSELVES. TO NO ONE EVIL FOR EVIL

ἀποδιδόντες, προνοούμενοι καλὰ ἐνώπιον πάντων
RETURNING, TAKING FORETHOUGHT [FOR] GOOD THINGS BEFORE ALL

ἀνθρώπων· **12.18** εἰ δυνατὸν τὸ ἐξ ὑμῶν, μετὰ
MEN; IF POSSIBLE AS FAR AS IT DEPENDS ON YOU°, WITH

πάντων ἀνθρώπων εἰρηνεύοντες· **12.19** μὴ
ALL MEN LIVING IN PEACE; NOT

ἑαυτοὺς ἐκδικοῦντες, ἀγαπητοί, ἀλλὰ δότε τόπον
AVENGING~YOURSELVES, BELOVED, BUT GIVE PLACE

12:19 Deut. 32:35

τῇ   ὀργῇ, γέγραπται γάρ, Ἐμοὶ ἐκδίκησις, ἐγὼ
TO THE(HIS) WRATH, FOR~IT HAS BEEN WRITTEN, VENGEANCE~[IS] MINE,   I

ἀνταποδώσω, λέγει κύριος. **12.20** ἀλλὰ ἐὰν πεινᾷ ὁ
WILL REPAY,   SAYS [THE] LORD.   BUT IF HUNGERS THE

ἐχθρός σου, ψώμιζε αὐτόν· ἐὰν διψᾷ, πότιζε αὐτόν·
ENEMY OF YOU, FEED HIM;   IF HE THIRSTS GIVE HIM A DRINK;

τοῦτο γὰρ ποιῶν ἄνθρακας πυρὸς σωρεύσεις ἐπὶ τὴν
FOR~THIS DOING COALS OF FIRE YOU WILL HEAP UPON THE

κεφαλὴν αὐτοῦ. **12.21** μὴ νικῶ   ὑπὸ τοῦ κακοῦ ἀλλὰ
HEAD OF HIM.   BE NOT CONQUERED BY THE EVIL BUT

νίκα ἐν τῷ ἀγαθῷ τὸ κακόν.
CONQUER ³WITH ⁴THE ⁵GOOD ¹THE ²EVIL.

12:20 Prov. 25:21, 22 LXX

for the wrath of God;⁵ for it is written, "Vengeance is mine, I will repay, says the Lord." ²⁰No, "if your enemies are hungry, feed them; if they are thirsty, give them something to drink; for by doing this you will heap burning coals on their heads." ²¹Do not be overcome by evil, but overcome evil with good.

⁵ Gk *the wrath*

CHAPTER 13

13.1 Πᾶσα ψυχὴ ἐξουσίαις ὑπερεχούσαις ὑποτασσέσθω.
    ²EVERY ³PERSON ⁶AUTHORITIES ⁵TO SUPERIOR ¹LET ⁴BE SUBJECT.

οὐ γὰρ ἔστιν ἐξουσία εἰ μὴ ὑπὸ θεοῦ, αἱ δὲ οὖσαι
³NOT ¹FOR ²THERE IS AUTHORITY EXCEPT BY GOD, AND~THE EXISTING ONES

ὑπὸ θεοῦ τεταγμέναι εἰσίν· **13.2** ὥστε ὁ
BY GOD HAVE BEEN APPOINTED;   THEREFORE THE ONE

ἀντιτασσόμενος τῇ ἐξουσίᾳ τῇ τοῦ θεοῦ διαταγῇ
OPPOSING   THE AUTHORITY ²THE - ⁴OF GOD ³ORDINANCE

ἀνθέστηκεν, οἱ δὲ   ἀνθεστηκότες ἑαυτοῖς κρίμα
¹HAS OPPOSED, AND~THE ONES HAVING OPPOSED TO THEMSELVES JUDGMENT

λήμψονται. **13.3** οἱ γὰρ ἄρχοντες οὐκ εἰσὶν φόβος τῷ
WILL RECEIVE.   FOR~THE RULERS ARE~NOT A TERROR TO THE

ἀγαθῷ ἔργῳ ἀλλὰ τῷ κακῷ. θέλεις δὲ μὴ
GOOD WORK BUT TO THE EVIL. AND~DO YOU WANT NOT

φοβεῖσθαι τὴν ἐξουσίαν· τὸ ἀγαθὸν ποίει, καὶ
TO FEAR THE AUTHORITY; THE GOOD DO, AND

ἕξεις   ἔπαινον ἐξ αὐτῆς· **13.4** θεοῦ γὰρ διάκονός
YOU WILL HAVE PRAISE FROM IT;   ⁴OF GOD ¹FOR ³A SERVANT

ἐστιν σοὶ εἰς τὸ ἀγαθόν. ἐὰν δὲ τὸ κακὸν ποιῇς,
²HE IS TO YOU FOR THE GOOD. BUT~IF - EVIL YOU DO,

φοβοῦ· οὐ γὰρ εἰκῇ τὴν μάχαιραν φορεῖ· θεοῦ
FEAR; FOR~NOT IN VAIN THE SWORD HE BEARS; ⁴OF GOD

γὰρ διάκονός ἐστιν ἔκδικος εἰς ὀργὴν τῷ   τὸ
¹FOR ³A SERVANT ²HE IS, AN AVENGER FOR WRATH TO THE ONE -

κακὸν πράσσοντι. **13.5** διὸ   ἀνάγκη ὑποτάσσεσθαι,
PRACTISING~EVIL.   THEREFORE IT IS NECESSARY TO BE SUBJECT,

οὐ μόνον διὰ   τὴν ὀργὴν ἀλλὰ καὶ διὰ   τὴν
NOT ONLY BECAUSE OF - WRATH BUT ALSO BECAUSE OF -

συνείδησιν. **13.6** διὰ   τοῦτο γὰρ καὶ φόρους
CONSCIENCE.   ²BECAUSE OF ³THIS ¹FOR ALSO TAXES

τελεῖτε· λειτουργοὶ γὰρ θεοῦ εἰσιν εἰς αὐτὸ τοῦτο
YOU° PAY; FOR~PUBLIC SERVANTS OF GOD THEY ARE FOR THIS VERY THING

Let every person be subject to the governing authorities; for there is no authority except from God, and those authorities that exist have been instituted by God. ²Therefore whoever resists authority resists what God has appointed, and those who resist will incur judgment. ³For rulers are not a terror to good conduct, but to bad. Do you wish to have no fear of the authority? Then do what is good, and you will receive its approval; ⁴for it is God's servant for your good. But if you do what is wrong, you should be afraid, for the authority' does not bear the sword in vain! It is the servant of God to execute wrath on the wrongdoer. ⁵Therefore one must be subject, not only because of wrath but also because of conscience. ⁶For the same reason you also pay taxes, for the authorities are God's servants,

ᵗ Gk *it*

busy with this very thing.
⁷Pay to all what is due
them—taxes to whom taxes
are due, revenue to whom
revenue is due, respect to
whom respect is due, honor
to whom honor is due.

8 Owe no one anything,
except to love one another;
for the one who loves
another has fulfilled the law.
⁹The commandments, "You
shall not commit adultery;
You shall not murder; You
shall not steal; You shall not
covet"; and any other commandment, are summed up
in this word, "Love your
neighbor as yourself."
¹⁰Love does no wrong to a
neighbor; therefore, love is
the fulfilling of the law.

11 Besides this, you know
what time it is, how it is now
the moment for you to wake
from sleep. For salvation is
nearer to us now than when
we became believers; ¹²the
night is far gone, the day is
near. Let us then lay aside
the works of darkness and
put on the armor of light;
¹³let us live honorably as in
the day, not in reveling and
drunkenness, not in de-
bauchery and licentiousness,
not in quarreling and
jealousy. ¹⁴Instead, put on
the Lord Jesus Christ, and
make no provision for the
flesh, to gratify its desires.

προσκαρτεροῦντες. **13.7** ἀπόδοτε πᾶσιν τὰς ὀφειλάς,
ATTENDING CONTINUALLY.   GIVE   TO ALL MEN THE[IR] DUES,

τῷ   τὸν   φόρον τὸν   φόρον, τῷ   τὸ τέλος
TO THE ONE [REQUIRING] THE TAX   [GIVE] THE TAX,   TO THE ONE THE REVENUE

τὸ τέλος, τῷ   τὸν φόβον τὸν φόβον, τῷ   τὴν
THE REVENUE, TO THE ONE THE FEAR   THE FEAR, TO THE ONE THE

τιμὴν τὴν τιμήν.
HONOR   THE HONOR.

13.8 Μηδενὶ μηδὲν ὀφείλετε εἰ μὴ τὸ ἀλλήλους
TO NO ONE ANYTHING OWE,   EXCEPT -   ONE ANOTHER

ἀγαπᾶν· ὁ γὰρ   ἀγαπῶν τὸν ἕτερον νόμον
TO LOVE; FOR~THE ONE LOVING   THE OTHER   [THE] LAW

πεπλήρωκεν. **13.9** τὸ γὰρ Οὐ μοιχεύσεις,
HAS FULFILLED.   -   FOR   YOU SHALL NOT COMMIT ADULTERY,

Οὐ φονεύσεις, Οὐ κλέψεις,   Οὐκ ἐπιθυμήσεις, καὶ
YOU SHALL NOT MURDER, YOU SHALL NOT STEAL, YOU SHALL NOT COVET,   AND

εἴ τις   ἑτέρα ἐντολή,   ἐν τῷ λόγῳ τούτῳ
IF [THERE IS] ANY OTHER   COMMANDMENT, IN -   THIS~WORD

ἀνακεφαλαιοῦται [ἐν τῷ] Ἀγαπήσεις τὸν πλησίον
IT IS SUMMED UP,   IN THIS,   YOU SHALL LOVE THE NEIGHBOR

σου ὡς σεαυτόν. **13.10** ἡ ἀγάπη τῷ   πλησίον κακὸν
OF YOU AS YOURSELF.   -   LOVE   TO THE NEIGHBOR EVIL

οὐκ ἐργάζεται· πλήρωμα   οὖν   νόμου ἡ ἀγάπη.
DOES NOT WORK;   ³[IS] A FULFILLMENT ¹THEREFORE ⁴OF [THE] LAW - ²LOVE.

13.11 Καὶ τοῦτο εἰδότες τὸν καιρόν, ὅτι ὥρα
AND THIS, KNOWING THE TIME,   THAT [THE] HOUR

ἤδη   ὑμᾶς ἐξ ὕπνου ἐγερθῆναι, νῦν γὰρ ἐγγύτερον
ALREADY [IS] FOR YOU° OUT OF SLEEP TO BE AWAKENED, FOR~NOW [IS] NEARER

ἡμῶν ἡ σωτηρία ἢ   ὅτε ἐπιστεύσαμεν. **13.12** ἡ νὺξ
OUR - SALVATION THAN WHEN WE BELIEVED.   THE NIGHT

προέκοψεν ἡ δὲ ἡμέρα ἤγγικεν.   ἀποθώμεθα οὖν
[HAS] ADVANCED AND~THE DAY HAS DRAWN NEAR. LET US PUT AWAY THEREFORE

τὰ ἔργα τοῦ σκότους, ἐνδυσώμεθα [δὲ] τὰ ὅπλα τοῦ
THE WORKS -   OF DARKNESS, AND~LET US PUT ON   THE WEAPONS OF THE

φωτός. **13.13** ὡς ἐν ἡμέρα εὐσχημόνως περιπατήσωμεν,
LIGHT.   AS IN [THE] DAY DECENTLY   LET US WALK,

μὴ κώμοις καὶ μέθαις, μὴ κοίταις   καὶ
NOT IN ORGIES AND DRUNKENNESS, NOT IN SEXUAL IMMORALITY AND

ἀσελγείαις, μὴ ἔριδι καὶ ζήλῳ, **13.14** ἀλλὰ ἐνδύσασθε
DEBAUCHERY,   NOT IN STRIFE AND JEALOUSY,   BUT   PUT ON

τὸν κύριον Ἰησοῦν Χριστὸν καὶ τῆς   σαρκὸς
THE LORD   JESUS   CHRIST   AND ³[CONCERNING] THE ⁴FLESH

πρόνοιαν μὴ ποιεῖσθε εἰς   ἐπιθυμίας.
²FORETHOUGHT ¹DO NOT GIVE   ⁵FOR [FULFILLING] ⁶[ITS] LUSTS.

13:9a Exod. 20:13-15, 17; Deut. 5:17-19, 21   **13:9b** Lev. 19:18

14.1 Τὸν δὲ   ἀσθενοῦντα   τῇ   πίστει
NOW~THE ONE   BEING WEAK   IN THE   FAITH

προσλαμβάνεσθε, μὴ εἰς   διακρίσεις διαλογισμῶν.
RECEIVE,   NOT [WITH A VIEW] TO PASSING   JUDGMENT.

14.2 ὃς   μὲν   πιστεύει φαγεῖν πάντα,   ὁ δὲ
ONE MAN   INDEED   BELIEVES   TO EAT   ALL THINGS, BUT~THE ONE

ἀσθενῶν λάχανα ἐσθίει.   **14.3** ὁ   ἐσθίων τὸν   μὴ
BEING WEAK   VEGETABLES   EATS.   ³THE ONE ⁴EATING   ⁶THE ONE ⁷NOT

ἐσθίοντα μὴ ἐξουθενείτω, ὁ δὲ   μὴ ἐσθίων τὸν
⁸EATING   ²NOT ¹LET ⁶DESPISE,   AND~THE ONE NOT   EATING   ²THE ONE

ἐσθίοντα μὴ κρινέτω, ὁ θεὸς γὰρ αὐτὸν προσελάβετο.
³EATING   ¹LET HIM NOT JUDGE, - FOR~GOD   RECEIVED~HIM.

14.4 σὺ   τίς εἶ ὁ   κρίνων ἀλλότριον
³YOU ¹WHO ²ARE ⁴THE ONE ⁵JUDGING   ⁷[BELONGING] TO ANOTHER

οἰκέτην;   τῷ ἰδίῳ κυρίῳ στήκει ἢ πίπτει·
⁶ A HOUSEHOLD SERVANT?   TO HIS OWN   LORD   HE STANDS OR FALLS;

σταθήσεται δέ, δυνατεῖ γὰρ ὁ   κύριος στῆσαι αὐτόν.
BUT~HE WILL BE UPHELD, ⁴IS ABLE   ¹FOR ²THE ³LORD   TO MAKE HIM STAND.

14.5 ὃς   μὲν [γὰρ] κρίνει ἡμέραν παρ' ἡμέραν,
²ONE MAN -   ¹FOR   ESTEEMS   A DAY   ABOVE   A DAY,

ὃς δὲ   κρίνει πᾶσαν ἡμέραν· ἕκαστος ἐν τῷ ἰδίῳ
BUT~ANOTHER ESTEEMS   EVERY   DAY;   EACH MAN   IN   HIS   OWN

νοῒ πληροφορείσθω.   **14.6** ὁ   φρονῶν τὴν ἡμέραν
MIND LET HIM BE CONVINCED.   THE ONE REGARDING THE   DAY

κυρίῳ   φρονεῖ· καὶ ὁ   ἐσθίων κυρίῳ   ἐσθίει,
TO [THE] LORD REGARDS [IT]. AND   THE ONE EATING   TO [THE] LORD HE EATS,

εὐχαριστεῖ γὰρ τῷ θεῷ· καὶ ὁ   μὴ ἐσθίων
FOR~HE GIVES THANKS -   TO GOD; AND   THE ONE NOT EATING

κυρίῳ   οὐκ ἐσθίει καὶ εὐχαριστεῖ τῷ θεῷ.
TO [THE] LORD HE DOES NOT EAT AND   GIVES THANKS -   TO GOD.

14.7 οὐδεὶς γὰρ ἡμῶν ἑαυτῷ   ζῇ καὶ οὐδεὶς ἑαυτῷ
FOR~NO ONE   OF US TO HIMSELF LIVES AND   NO ONE   TO HIMSELF

ἀποθνήσκει·   **14.8** ἐάν τε γὰρ ζῶμεν, τῷ   κυρίῳ ζῶμεν,
DIES;   FOR~WHETHER   WE LIVE, TO THE LORD   WE LIVE,

ἐάν τε ἀποθνήσκωμεν, τῷ   κυρίῳ ἀποθνήσκομεν.
OR IF   WE DIE,   TO THE LORD   WE DIE.

ἐάν τε οὖν   ζῶμεν ἐάν τε ἀποθνήσκωμεν, τοῦ κυρίου
WHETHER   THEREFORE WE LIVE OR IF   WE DIE,   THE   LORD'S

ἐσμέν.   **14.9** εἰς τοῦτο γὰρ Χριστὸς ἀπέθανεν καὶ
WE ARE.   ⁶FOR ⁷THIS ¹FOR ²CHRIST   ³DIED   ⁴AND

ἔζησεν, ἵνα καὶ νεκρῶν   καὶ ζώντων   κυριεύσῃ.
⁵LIVED,   THAT BOTH OF DEAD ONES AND   OF LIVING ONES HE MIGHT BE LORD.

14.10 σὺ δὲ τί   κρίνεις τὸν ἀδελφόν σου;   ἢ καὶ
⁴YOU ¹AND ²WHY ³DO ⁵JUDGE THE   BROTHER   OF YOU? OR ²INDEED

Welcome those who are weak in faith,ᵘ but not for the purpose of quarreling over opinions. ²Some believe in eating anything, while the weak eat only vegetables. ³Those who eat must not despise those who abstain, and those who abstain must not pass judgment on those who eat; for God has welcomed them. ⁴Who are you to pass judgment on servants of another? It is before their own lord that they stand or fall. And they will be upheld, for the Lordᵛ is able to make them stand.

5 Some judge one day to be better than another, while others judge all days to be alike. Let all be fully convinced in their own minds. ⁶Those who observe the day, observe it in honor of the Lord. Also those who eat, eat in honor of the Lord, since they give thanks to God; while those who abstain, abstain in honor of the Lord and give thanks to God.

7 We do not live to ourselves, and we do not die to ourselves. ⁸If we live, we live to the Lord, and if we die, we die to the Lord; so then, whether we live or whether we die, we are the Lord's. ⁹For to this end Christ died and lived again, so that he might be Lord of both the dead and the living.

10 Why do you pass judgment on your brother or sister?ʷ Or you,

ᵘ Or *conviction*
ᵛ Other ancient authorities read *for God*
ʷ Gk *brother*

why do you despise your brother or sister?[x] For we will all stand before the judgment seat of God.[y] [11]For it is written,

"As I live, says the Lord, every knee shall bow to me, and every tongue shall give praise to[z] God."

[12]So then, each of us will be accountable to God.[a]

13 Let us therefore no longer pass judgment on one another, but resolve instead never to put a stumbling block or hindrance in the way of another.[b] [14]I know and am persuaded in the Lord Jesus that nothing is unclean in itself; but it is unclean for anyone who thinks it unclean. [15]If your brother or sister[x] is being injured by what you eat, you are no longer walking in love. Do not let what you eat cause the ruin of one for whom Christ died. [16]So do not let your good be spoken of as evil. [17]For the kingdom of God is not food and drink but righteousness and peace and joy in the Holy Spirit. [18]The one who thus serves Christ is acceptable to God and has human approval. [19]Let us then pursue what makes for peace and for mutual upbuilding. [20]Do not, for the sake of food,

[x] Gk *brother*
[y] Other ancient authorities read *of Christ*
[z] Or *confess*
[a] Other ancient authorities lack *to God*
[b] Gk *of a brother*

σὺ τί ἐξουθενεῖς τὸν ἀδελφόν σου; πάντες γὰρ
[4]YOU [1]WHY [3]DESPISE THE BROTHER OF YOU? FOR~ALL

παραστησόμεθα τῷ βήματι τοῦ θεοῦ,
WE WILL STAND BEFORE THE JUDGMENT SEAT - OF GOD,

14.11 γέγραπται γάρ,
FOR~IT HAS BEEN WRITTEN,

Ζῶ ἐγώ, λέγει κύριος, ὅτι ἐμοὶ κάμψει πᾶν γόνυ
LIVE I, SAYS [THE] LORD, THAT TO ME WILL BEND EVERY KNEE

καὶ πᾶσα γλῶσσα ἐξομολογήσεται τῷ θεῷ.
AND EVERY TONGUE WILL CONFESS - TO GOD.

14.12 ἄρα [οὖν] ἕκαστος ἡμῶν περὶ ἑαυτοῦ λόγον
SO THEN EACH ONE OF US CONCERNING HIMSELF ACCOUNT

δώσει [τῷ θεῷ].
WILL GIVE - TO GOD.

14.13 Μηκέτι οὖν ἀλλήλους κρίνωμεν· ἀλλὰ
[4]NO LONGER [1]THEREFORE [3]ONE ANOTHER [2]LET US JUDGE; BUT

τοῦτο κρίνατε μᾶλλον, τὸ μὴ τιθέναι πρόσκομμα τῷ
JUDGE~THIS RATHER, - NOT TO PUT A STUMBLING BLOCK TO ONE'S

ἀδελφῷ ἢ σκάνδαλον. **14.14** οἶδα καὶ πέπεισμαι
BROTHER OR A TRAP. I KNOW AND HAVE BEEN PERSUADED

ἐν κυρίῳ Ἰησοῦ ὅτι οὐδὲν κοινὸν δι᾽ ἑαυτοῦ,
IN [THE] LORD JESUS THAT NOTHING [IS] COMMON THROUGH(IN) ITSELF,

εἰ μὴ τῷ λογιζομένῳ τι κοινὸν εἶναι, ἐκείνῳ
EXCEPT TO THE ONE COUNTING ANYTHING COMMON TO BE, TO THAT MAN

κοινόν. **14.15** εἰ γὰρ διὰ βρῶμα ὁ ἀδελφός σου
[IT IS] COMMON. FOR~IF BECAUSE OF FOOD THE BROTHER OF YOU

λυπεῖται, οὐκέτι κατὰ ἀγάπην περιπατεῖς· μὴ
IS GRIEVED, NO LONGER ACCORDING TO LOVE YOU WALK; NOT

τῷ βρώματί σου ἐκεῖνον ἀπόλλυε ὑπὲρ οὗ
BY THE FOOD OF YOU THAT MAN RUIN ON BEHALF OF WHOM

Χριστὸς ἀπέθανεν. **14.16** μὴ βλασφημείσθω οὖν
CHRIST DIED. LET NOT BE SPOKEN AGAINST THEREFORE

ὑμῶν τὸ ἀγαθόν. **14.17** οὐ γὰρ ἐστιν ἡ βασιλεία τοῦ
YOUR° - GOOD. FOR~NOT IS THE KINGDOM -

θεοῦ βρῶσις καὶ πόσις ἀλλὰ δικαιοσύνη καὶ εἰρήνη
OF GOD EATING AND DRINKING BUT RIGHTEOUSNESS AND PEACE

καὶ χαρὰ ἐν πνεύματι ἁγίῳ· **14.18** ὁ γὰρ ἐν τούτῳ
AND JOY IN [THE] SPIRIT HOLY; FOR~THE ONE IN THIS

δουλεύων τῷ Χριστῷ εὐάρεστος τῷ θεῷ καὶ
SERVING - CHRIST [IS] WELL-PLEASING - TO GOD AND

δόκιμος τοῖς ἀνθρώποις. **14.19** ἄρα οὖν τὰ τῆς
APPROVED - BY MEN. SO THEN THE THINGS -

εἰρήνης διώκωμεν καὶ τὰ τῆς οἰκοδομῆς τῆς εἰς
OF PEACE LET US PURSUE AND THE THINGS - OF BUILDING UP - FOR

ἀλλήλους. **14.20** μὴ ἕνεκεν βρώματος κατάλυε τὸ
ONE ANOTHER. NOT FOR THE SAKE OF FOOD DESTROY THE

14:11a Isa. 49:18 **14:11b** Isa. 45:23 LXX

ἔργον τοῦ θεοῦ. πάντα μὲν καθαρά, ἀλλὰ κακὸν τῷ
WORK - OF GOD. ALL THINGS INDEED [ARE] CLEAN, BUT EVIL TO THE

ἀνθρώπῳ τῷ διὰ προσκόμματος ἐσθίοντι. 14.21 καλὸν
MAN [WHO] - ¹BY ³[CAUSES] STUMBLING ²EATING. [IT IS] GOOD

τὸ μὴ φαγεῖν κρέα μηδὲ πιεῖν οἶνον μηδὲ ἐν
- NOT TO EAT FLESH NOR TO DRINK WINE NOR [ANYTHING] BY

ᾧ ὁ ἀδελφός σου προσκόπτει. 14.22 σὺ πίστιν
WHICH THE BROTHER OF YOU STUMBLES. ³YOU ¹[THE] FAITH

[ἣν] ἔχεις κατὰ σεαυτὸν ἔχε ἐνώπιον τοῦ θεοῦ.
²WHICH ⁴HAVE ⁶BY ⁷YOURSELF ⁵HAVE BEFORE - GOD.

μακάριος ὁ μὴ κρίνων ἑαυτὸν ἐν ᾧ δοκιμάζει·
BLESSED THE ONE NOT JUDGING HIMSELF IN (FOR) WHAT HE APPROVES;

14.23 ὁ δὲ διακρινόμενος ἐὰν φάγῃ κατακέκριται,
BUT~THE ONE BEING DOUBTFUL ²IF ³HE EATS ¹HAS BEEN CONDEMNED

ὅτι οὐκ ἐκ πίστεως· πᾶν δὲ ὃ οὐκ ἐκ
BECAUSE [IT IS] NOT OUT OF FAITH; AND~ALL WHICH [IS] NOT OUT OF

πίστεως ἁμαρτία ἐστίν.ᵀ⁻
FAITH IS~SIN.

14:23 After this verse, a few MSS add the verses found in Rom. 16:25-27 (see note there). Some translations note this: ASVmg RSVmg NEBmg NRSVmg.

destroy the work of God. Everything is indeed clean, but it is wrong for you to make others fall by what you eat; ²¹it is good not to eat meat or drink wine or do anything that makes your brother or sister *c* stumble.*d* ²²The faith that you have, have as your own conviction before God. Blessed are those who have no reason to condemn themselves because of what they approve. ²³But those who have doubts are condemned if they eat, because they do not act from faith;*e* for whatever does not proceed from faith*e* is sin.*f*

c Gk *brother*
d Other ancient authorities add *or be upset or be weakened*
e Or *conviction*
f Other authorities, some ancient, add here 16.25-27

CHAPTER 15

15.1 Ὀφείλομεν δὲ ἡμεῖς οἱ δυνατοὶ τὰ
⁵OUGHT ¹NOW ²WE ³THE ⁴STRONG ⁷THE

ἀσθενήματα τῶν ἀδυνάτων βαστάζειν καὶ μὴ
⁸WEAKNESSES ⁹OF THE ONES ¹⁰NOT STRONG ⁶TO BEAR, AND NOT

ἑαυτοῖς ἀρέσκειν. 15.2 ἕκαστος ἡμῶν τῷ πλησίον
OURSELVES TO PLEASE. EACH ONE OF US THE (HIS) NEIGHBOR

ἀρεσκέτω εἰς τὸ ἀγαθὸν πρὸς οἰκοδομήν·
LET HIM PLEASE FOR - GOOD WITH A VIEW TO BUILDING UP;

15.3 καὶ γὰρ ὁ Χριστὸς οὐχ ἑαυτῷ ἤρεσεν, ἀλλὰ καθὼς
FOR~EVEN - CHRIST NOT HIMSELF PLEASED; BUT AS

γέγραπται, Οἱ ὀνειδισμοὶ τῶν ὀνειδιζόντων σε
IT HAS BEEN WRITTEN, THE REPROACHES OF THE ONES REPROACHING YOU

ἐπέπεσαν ἐπ' ἐμέ. 15.4 ὅσα γὰρ προεγράφη, εἰς
FELL ON ME. FOR~WHATEVER THINGS WERE WRITTEN BEFORE, FOR

τὴν ἡμετέραν διδασκαλίαν ἐγράφη, ἵνα διὰ τῆς
- OUR TEACHING WERE WRITTEN, THAT THROUGH -

ὑπομονῆς καὶ διὰ τῆς παρακλήσεως τῶν γραφῶν τὴν
ENDURANCE AND THROUGH THE ENCOURAGEMENT OF THE SCRIPTURES -

ἐλπίδα ἔχωμεν. 15.5 ὁ δὲ θεὸς τῆς ὑπομονῆς καὶ τῆς
HOPE WE MAY HAVE. NOW~THE GOD - OF ENDURANCE AND -

παρακλήσεως δῴη ὑμῖν τὸ αὐτὸ φρονεῖν ἐν
ENCOURAGEMENT GIVE TO YOU° ²THE SAME THING ¹TO THINK AMONG

We who are strong ought to put up with the failings of the weak, and not to please ourselves. ²Each of us must please our neighbor for the good purpose of building up the neighbor. ³For Christ did not please himself; but, as it is written, "The insults of those who insult you have fallen on me." ⁴For whatever was written in former days was written for our instruction, so that by steadfastness and by the encouragement of the scriptures we might have hope. ⁵May the God of steadfastness and encouragement grant you to live in harmony with

15:3 Ps. 69:9

one another, in accordance with Christ Jesus, ⁶so that together you may with one voice glorify the God and Father of our Lord Jesus Christ.

7 Welcome one another, therefore, just as Christ has welcomed you, for the glory of God. ⁸For I tell you that Christ has become a servant of the circumcised on behalf of the truth of God in order that he might confirm the promises given to the patriarchs, ⁹and in order that the Gentiles might glorify God for his mercy. As it is written,

"Therefore I will confessᵍ you among the Gentiles, and sing praises to your name";

¹⁰and again he says,
"Rejoice, O Gentiles, with his people";

¹¹and again,
"Praise the Lord, all you Gentiles, and let all the peoples praise him";

¹²and again Isaiah says,
"The root of Jesse shall come, the one who rises to rule the Gentiles; in him the Gentiles shall hope."

¹³May the God of hope fill you with all joy and peace in believing, so that you

ᵍ Or *thank*

ἀλλήλοις κατὰ   Χριστὸν Ἰησοῦν, **15.6** ἵνα
ONE ANOTHER ACCORDING TO CHRIST   JESUS,   THAT

ὁμοθυμαδὸν   ἐν   ἑνὶ   στόματι δοξάζητε   τὸν θεὸν
WITH ONE ACCORD [AND] WITH ONE MOUTH   YOU° MAY GLORIFY THE GOD

καὶ πατέρα   τοῦ   κυρίου ἡμῶν Ἰησοῦ Χριστοῦ.
AND FATHER OF THE LORD OF US JESUS   CHRIST.

15.7 Διὸ   προσλαμβάνεσθε ἀλλήλους, καθὼς καὶ
       WHEREFORE RECEIVE   ONE ANOTHER, AS   ALSO

ὁ Χριστὸς προσελάβετο ὑμᾶς εἰς δόξαν   τοῦ θεοῦ.
- CHRIST   RECEIVED   YOU° TO [THE] GLORY - OF GOD.

15.8 λέγω γὰρ   Χριστὸν   διάκονον γεγενῆσθαι
        FOR~I SAY CHRIST   TO HAVE BECOME~A SERVANT

περιτομῆς   ὑπὲρ   ἀληθείας   θεοῦ, εἰς τὸ
OF [THE] CIRCUMCISION ON BEHALF OF [THE] TRUTH[FULNESS] OF GOD, SO AS TO -

βεβαιῶσαι τὰς ἐπαγγελίας τῶν   πατέρων, **15.9** τὰ δὲ
CONFIRM   THE PROMISES   OF(TO) THE FATHERS,   AND THE

ἔθνη ὑπὲρ ἐλέους   δοξάσαι τὸν θεόν, καθὼς
GENTILES ³FOR ⁴[HIS] MERCY ¹TO GLORIFY -   ²GOD,   AS

γέγραπται,
IT HAS BEEN WRITTEN,

Διὰ τοῦτο ἐξομολογήσομαί σοι ἐν ἔθνεσιν
THEREFORE I WILL GIVE PRAISE   TO YOU AMONG GENTILES

καὶ τῷ ὀνοματί σου ψαλῶ.
AND TO THE NAME OF YOU I WILL SING PRAISE.

15.10 καὶ πάλιν λέγει,
         AND AGAIN   HE SAYS,

Εὐφράνθητε, ἔθνη, μετὰ τοῦ λαοῦ αὐτοῦ.
REJOICE,   GENTILES, WITH THE PEOPLE OF HIM.

15.11 καὶ πάλιν,
         AND AGAIN,

Αἰνεῖτε, πάντα τὰ ἔθνη, τὸν κύριον
PRAISE,   ALL   THE GENTILES, THE LORD,

καὶ ἐπαινεσάτωσαν αὐτὸν πάντες οἱ λαοί.
AND LET PRAISE   HIM   ALL   THE PEOPLES.

15.12 καὶ πάλιν Ἠσαΐας λέγει,
         AND AGAIN ISAIAH SAYS,

Ἔσται ἡ ῥίζα τοῦ Ἰεσσαί
THERE WILL BE THE ROOT - OF JESSE

καὶ ὁ   ἀνιστάμενος ἄρχειν ἐθνῶν,
EVEN THE ONE RISING UP   TO RULE GENTILES,

ἐπ᾿ αὐτῷ ἔθνη ἐλπιοῦσιν.
ON HIM GENTILES WILL HOPE.

15.13 ὁ δὲ   θεὸς τῆς ἐλπίδος πληρώσαι ὑμᾶς
         NOW [MAY]~THE GOD - OF HOPE   FILL   YOU°

πάσης χαρᾶς καὶ εἰρήνης ἐν τῷ πιστεύειν, εἰς τὸ
WITH ALL JOY   AND PEACE   IN - BELIEVING,   FOR -

15:9 Ps. 18:49 (= 2 Sam. 22:50) **15:10** Deut. 32:43 **15:11** Ps. 117:1 **15:12** Isa. 11:10 LXX

περισσεύειν ὑμᾶς ἐν τῇ ἐλπίδι ἐν δυνάμει πνεύματος
YOU°~TO ABOUND   IN - HOPE   BY [THE] POWER OF [THE] SPIRIT

ἁγίου.
HOLY.

15.14 Πέπεισμαι δέ,   ἀδελφοί μου, καὶ αὐτὸς ἐγὼ
AND~I HAVE BEEN PERSUADED, BROTHERS OF ME, EVEN I~[MY]SELF

περὶ   ὑμῶν ὅτι καὶ αὐτοὶ   μεστοί ἐστε   ἀγαθωσύνης,
CONCERNING YOU° THAT ALSO YOURSELVES ARE~FULL   OF GOODNESS,

πεπληρωμένοι πάσης [τῆς] γνώσεως, δυνάμενοι καὶ
HAVING BEEN FILLED WITH ALL - KNOWLEDGE, BEING ABLE ALSO

ἀλλήλους νουθετεῖν. **15.15** τολμηρότερον δὲ ἔγραψα
ONE ANOTHER TO ADMONISH.   BUT~BOLDLY   I WROTE

ὑμῖν ἀπὸ μέρους ὡς ἐπαναμιμνῄσκων ὑμᾶς διὰ
TO YOU° IN PART   AS   REMINDING   YOU° ON ACCOUNT OF

τὴν χάριν τὴν δοθεῖσάν   μοι ὑπὸ τοῦ θεοῦ **15.16** εἰς
THE GRACE - HAVING BEEN GIVEN TO ME FROM - GOD   FOR

τὸ εἶναί με λειτουργὸν Χριστοῦ Ἰησοῦ εἰς τὰ ἔθνη,
- ME~TO BE A SERVANT OF CHRIST JESUS TO THE GENTILES,

ἱερουργοῦντα   τὸ εὐαγγέλιον τοῦ θεοῦ, ἵνα
ADMINISTERING IN SACRED SERVICE THE GOOD NEWS - OF GOD, THAT

γένηται ἡ   προσφορὰ τῶν ἐθνῶν εὐπρόσδεκτος,
⁵MAY BE ¹THE ²OFFERING ³OF THE ⁴GENTILES ⁶ACCEPTABLE,

ἡγιασμένη   ἐν πνεύματι ἁγίῳ. **15.17** ἔχω οὖν
HAVING BEEN SANCTIFIED BY [THE] SPIRIT HOLY.   I HAVE THEREFORE

[τὴν] καύχησιν ἐν Χριστῷ Ἰησοῦ τὰ   πρὸς
THE(MY) BOASTING IN CHRIST JESUS [AS TO] THE THINGS PERTAINING TO

τὸν θεόν· **15.18** οὐ γὰρ τολμήσω τι   λαλεῖν
- GOD;   FOR~NOT I WILL DARE ANYTHING TO SPEAK

ὧν   οὐ κατειργάσατο Χριστὸς δι’   ἐμοῦ εἰς
OF THE THINGS WHICH ²DID NOT WORK OUT ¹CHRIST THROUGH ME FOR

ὑπακοὴν ἐθνῶν, λόγῳ καὶ ἔργῳ, **15.19** ἐν δυνάμει
OBEDIENCE OF GENTILES, IN WORD AND WORK,   BY POWER

σημείων καὶ τεράτων, ἐν δυνάμει ⌐πνεύματος [θεοῦ]⌐·
OF SIGNS AND WONDERS, BY POWER OF [THE] SPIRIT OF GOD;

ὥστε με ἀπὸ Ἰερουσαλὴμ καὶ κύκλῳ μέχρι τοῦ
SO AS FOR ME, FROM JERUSALEM   AND AROUND UNTO -

Ἰλλυρικοῦ πεπληρωκέναι τὸ εὐαγγέλιον τοῦ Χριστοῦ,
ILLYRICUM, I HAVE FULLY PROCLAIMED THE GOOD NEWS - OF CHRIST,

15.20 οὕτως δὲ φιλοτιμούμενον εὐαγγελίζεσθαι οὐχ ὅπου
AND~SO   ASPIRING   TO PREACH THE GOOD NEWS NOT WHERE

ὠνομάσθη Χριστός, ἵνα μὴ ἐπ’ ἀλλότριον θεμέλιον
CHRIST~WAS NAMED,   THAT NOT ON ANOTHER'S FOUNDATION

οἰκοδομῶ, **15.21** ἀλλὰ καθὼς γέγραπται,
I MIGHT BUILD,   BUT   AS   IT HAS BEEN WRITTEN,

Οἷς   οὐκ ἀνηγγέλη περὶ   αὐτοῦ ὄψονται,
[THE ONES] TO WHOM IT WAS NOT ANNOUNCED CONCERNING HIM WILL SEE,

may abound in hope by the power of the Holy Spirit.

14 I myself feel confident about you, my brothers and sisters,[h] that you yourselves are full of goodness, filled with all knowledge, and able to instruct one another. [15]Nevertheless on some points I have written to you rather boldly by way of reminder, because of the grace given me by God [16]to be a minister of Christ Jesus to the Gentiles in the priestly service of the gospel of God, so that the offering of the Gentiles may be acceptable, sanctified by the Holy Spirit. [17]In Christ Jesus, then, I have reason to boast of my work for God. [18]For I will not venture to speak of anything except what Christ has accomplished[i] through me to win obedience from the Gentiles, by word and deed, [19]by the power of signs and wonders, by the power of the Spirit of God,[j] so that from Jerusalem and as far around as Illyricum I have fully proclaimed the good news[k] of Christ. [20]Thus I make it my ambition to proclaim the good news,[k] not where Christ has already been named, so that I do not build on someone else's foundation, [21]but as it is written,

"Those who have never been told of him shall see,

[h] Gk brothers
[i] Gk speak of those things that Christ has not accomplished
[j] Other ancient authorities read of the Spirit or of the Holy Spirit
[k] Or gospel

15:19 text: KJV ASVmg TEV NJB NRSV. var. πνευματος ([the] Spirit): ASVmg NASB NIV NRSVmg. var. πνευματος αγιου ([the] Holy Spirit): ASV RSV NEB NRSVmg. **15:21** Isa. 52:15 LXX and those who have never heard of him shall understand."

22 This is the reason that I have so often been hindered from coming to you. 23But now, with no further place for me in these regions, I desire, as I have for many years, to come to you 24when I go to Spain. For I do hope to see you on my journey and to be sent on by you, once I have enjoyed your company for a little while. 25At present, however, I am going to Jerusalem in a ministry to the saints; 26for Macedonia and Achaia have been pleased to share their resources with the poor among the saints at Jerusalem. 27They were pleased to do this, and indeed they owe it to them; for if the Gentiles have come to share in their spiritual blessings, they ought also to be of service to them in material things. 28So, when I have completed this, and have delivered to them what has been collected,*l* I will set out by way of you to Spain; 29and I know that when I come to you, I will come in the fullness of the blessing*m* of Christ.

30 I appeal to you, brothers and sisters,*n* by our Lord Jesus Christ and by the love of the Spirit, to join me in earnest prayer to God on my behalf, 31that I may be

l Gk *have sealed to them this fruit*
m Other ancient authorities add *of the gospel*
n Gk *brothers*

καὶ   οἳ   οὐκ ἀκηκόασιν συνήσουσιν.
AND   THE ONES [WHO] HAVE NOT HEARD   WILL UNDERSTAND.

15.22 Διὸ   καὶ ἐνεκοπτόμην τὰ πολλὰ τοῦ ἐλθεῖν
THEREFORE ALSO I WAS BEING HINDERED GREATLY   -   TO COME

πρὸς ὑμᾶς· **15.23** νυνὶ δὲ μηκέτι τόπον ἔχων ἐν τοῖς
TO   YOU°;   BUT~NOW NO LONGER HAVING~A PLACE IN   -

κλίμασι τούτοις, ἐπιποθίαν δὲ ἔχων τοῦ ἐλθεῖν πρὸς
THESE~REGIONS,   ³A DESIRE ¹BUT ²HAVING -   TO COME TO

ὑμᾶς ἀπὸ πολλῶν ἐτῶν, **15.24** ὡς ἂν πορεύωμαι εἰς τὴν
YOU° FOR SEVERAL YEARS,   WHENEVER I TAKE A JOURNEY TO -

Σπανίαν·   ἐλπίζω γὰρ διαπορευόμενος θεάσασθαι
SPAIN;   FOR~I AM HOPING WHILE TRAVELING THROUGH TO SEE

ὑμᾶς καὶ ὑφ' ὑμῶν προπεμφθῆναι ἐκεῖ   ἐὰν ὑμῶν
YOU° AND BY YOU° TO BE SENT ONWARD [FROM] THERE IF [WITH] YOU°

πρῶτον ἀπὸ μέρους ἐμπλησθῶ. **15.25** νυνὶ δὲ πορεύομαι
FIRST   IN PART   I MAY BE FILLED.   BUT~NOW I AM GOING

εἰς Ἰερουσαλὴμ διακονῶν τοῖς ἁγίοις.   **15.26** εὐδόκησαν
TO   JERUSALEM   MINISTERING TO THE SAINTS.   ⁵WERE PLEASED

γὰρ Μακεδονία καὶ Ἀχαΐα κοινωνίαν τινὰ
¹FOR ²MACEDONIA ● ³AND ⁴ACHAIA ⁸CONTRIBUTION ⁷SOME

ποιήσασθαι εἰς τοὺς πτωχοὺς τῶν ἁγίων τῶν ἐν
⁶TO MAKE   FOR THE POOR   OF THE SAINTS   - IN

Ἰερουσαλήμ. **15.27** εὐδόκησαν γὰρ καὶ ὀφειλέται εἰσὶν
JERUSALEM.   FOR~THEY WERE PLEASED AND DEBTORS   THEY ARE

αὐτῶν· εἰ γὰρ τοῖς πνευματικοῖς αὐτῶν ἐκοινώνησαν
OF THEM; FOR~IF IN THE SPIRITUAL THINGS OF THEM ³SHARED

τὰ ἔθνη, ὀφείλουσιν καὶ ἐν τοῖς σαρκικοῖς
¹THE ²GENTILES, THEY OUGHT ALSO IN THE MATERIAL THINGS

λειτουργῆσαι αὐτοῖς. **15.28** τοῦτο οὖν   ἐπιτελέσας
TO GIVE SERVICE TO THEM.   THIS   THEREFORE HAVING COMPLETED

καὶ σφραγισάμενος αὐτοῖς τὸν καρπὸν τοῦτον,
AND HAVING SEALED   TO THEM -   THIS~FRUIT,

ἀπελεύσομαι δι' ὑμῶν εἰς Σπανίαν· **15.29** οἶδα δὲ
I WILL GO   THROUGH YOU° TO SPAIN.   AND~I KNOW

ὅτι ἐρχόμενος πρὸς ὑμᾶς ἐν πληρώματι εὐλογίας
THAT COMING   TO   YOU° ²IN ³[THE] FULLNESS ⁴OF [THE] BLESSING

Χριστοῦ ἐλεύσομαι.
⁵ OF CHRIST ¹I WILL COME.

15.30 Παρακαλῶ δὲ ὑμᾶς[, ἀδελφοί,] διὰ   τοῦ κυρίου
NOW~I URGE   YOU°,   BROTHERS, THROUGH THE LORD

ἡμῶν Ἰησοῦ Χριστοῦ καὶ διὰ   τῆς ἀγάπης τοῦ
OF US JESUS CHRIST AND THROUGH THE LOVE   OF THE

πνεύματος συναγωνίσασθαί μοι ἐν ταῖς   προσευχαῖς
SPIRIT   TO STRIVE TOGETHER WITH ME IN THE(YOUR) PRAYERS

ὑπὲρ   ἐμοῦ πρὸς τὸν θεόν, **15.31** ἵνα ῥυσθῶ   ἀπὸ
ON BEHALF OF ME BEFORE -   GOD,   THAT I MAY BE RESCUED FROM

τῶν   ἀπειθούντων ἐν τῇ Ἰουδαίᾳ καὶ ἡ διακονία
THE ONES DISOBEYING   IN   -   JUDEA   AND THE SERVICE

μου ἡ εἰς Ἰερουσαλὴμ εὐπρόσδεκτος τοῖς ἁγίοις
OF ME - FOR JERUSALEM   ²ACCEPTABLE   ³TO THE ⁴SAINTS

γένηται, 15.32 ἵνα ἐν χαρᾷ ἐλθὼν   πρὸς ὑμᾶς διὰ
¹MAY BE,   THAT IN JOY HAVING COME TO   YOU° THROUGH

θελήματος θεοῦ συναναπαύσωμαι ὑμῖν. 15.33 ὁ δὲ
[THE] WILL   OF GOD I MAY REST WITH   YOU°.   NOW~THE

θεὸς τῆς εἰρήνης μετὰ πάντων ὑμῶν, ἀμήν.ᵀ
GOD   -   OF PEACE [BE] WITH YOU°~ALL,   AMEN.

15:33 At the end of this verse, one early MS (P46) adds the verses found in Rom. 16:25-27 (see note there).   This is noted in NEBmg NRSVmg.

rescued from the unbelievers in Judea, and that my ministry⁰ to Jerusalem may be acceptable to the saints, ³²so that by God's will I may come to you with joy and be refreshed in your company. ³³The God of peace be with all of you.ᵖ Amen.

⁰ Other ancient authorities read *my bringing of a gift*
ᵖ One ancient authority adds 16.25-27 here

16.1 Συνίστημι δὲ ὑμῖν Φοίβην τὴν ἀδελφὴν ἡμῶν,
         NOW~I COMMEND TO YOU° PHOEBE   THE SISTER   OF US,

οὖσαν [καὶ] διάκονον τῆς ἐκκλησίας τῆς ἐν
BEING ALSO A DEACON   OF THE CHURCH   -   IN

Κεγχρεαῖς, 16.2 ἵνα αὐτὴν προσδέξησθε ἐν κυρίῳ
CENCHREA,   THAT YOU° MAY RECEIVE~HER   IN [THE] LORD

ἀξίως τῶν ἁγίων καὶ παραστῆτε αὐτῇ ἐν ᾧ ἂν   ὑμῶν
AS BEFITS THE SAINTS AND MAY STAND BY HER IN ¹WHATEVER ⁴OF YOU°

χρῄζῃ   πράγματι· καὶ γὰρ αὐτὴ προστάτις πολλῶν
³SHE MAY NEED ²MATTER;   FOR~INDEED SHE   A HELPER   OF MANY

ἐγενήθη καὶ ἐμοῦ αὐτοῦ.
BECAME   AND OF MYSELF.

16.3 Ἀσπάσασθε Πρίσκαν καὶ Ἀκύλαν τοὺς
          GREET   PRISCA   AND AQUILA   THE

συνεργούς μου ἐν Χριστῷ Ἰησοῦ, 16.4 οἵτινες ὑπὲρ
CO-WORKERS OF ME IN CHRIST   JESUS,   WHO   ON BEHALF OF

τῆς ψυχῆς μου τὸν ἑαυτῶν τράχηλον ὑπέθηκαν, οἷς
THE LIFE OF ME - THEIR OWN NECK(S)   RISKED,   TO WHOM

οὐκ ἐγὼ μόνος εὐχαριστῶ ἀλλὰ καὶ πᾶσαι αἱ
NOT   I   ONLY GIVE THANKS BUT ALSO ALL   THE

ἐκκλησίαι τῶν ἐθνῶν, 16.5 καὶ   τὴν κατ᾽ οἶκον
CHURCHES   OF THE GENTILES, AND [GREET] ¹THE ³IN   ⁴HOUSE

αὐτῶν ἐκκλησίαν.   ἀσπάσασθε Ἐπαίνετον τὸν
⁵OF THEM ²CHURCH(ASSEMBLY). GREET   EPAENETUS   THE

ἀγαπητόν μου, ὅς ἐστιν ἀπαρχὴ τῆς Ἀσίας εἰς
BELOVED   OF ME, WHO IS FIRSTFRUIT   -   OF ASIA FOR

Χριστόν. 16.6 ἀσπάσασθε Μαρίαν, ἥτις πολλὰ
CHRIST.   GREET   MARY,   WHO   GREATLY

ἐκοπίασεν εἰς ὑμᾶς. 16.7 ἀσπάσασθε Ἀνδρόνικον καὶ
LABORED   FOR YOU°.   GREET   ANDRONICUS   AND

I commend to you our sister Phoebe, a deacon⁹ of the church at Cenchreae, ²so that you may welcome her in the Lord as is fitting for the saints, and help her in whatever she may require from you, for she has been a benefactor of many and of myself as well.

3 Greet Prisca and Aquila, who work with me in Christ Jesus, ⁴and who risked their necks for my life, to whom not only I give thanks, but also all the churches of the Gentiles. ⁵Greet also the church in their house. Greet my beloved Epaenetus, who was the first convertʳ in Asia for Christ. ⁶Greet Mary, who has worked very hard among you. ⁷Greet Andronicus and

⁹ Or *minister*
ʳ Gk *first fruits*

Junia,[s] my relatives[t] who were in prison with me; they are prominent among the apostles, and they were in Christ before I was. [8]Greet Ampliatus, my beloved in the Lord. [9]Greet Urbanus, our co-worker in Christ, and my beloved Stachys. [10]Greet Apelles, who is approved in Christ. Greet those who belong to the family of Aristobulus. [11]Greet my relative[u] Herodion. Greet those in the Lord who belong to the family of Narcissus. [12]Greet those workers in the Lord, Tryphaena and Tryphosa. Greet the beloved Persis, who has worked hard in the Lord. [13]Greet Rufus, chosen in the Lord; and greet his mother—a mother to me also. [14]Greet Asyncritus, Phlegon, Hermes, Patrobas, Hermas, and the brothers and sisters[v] who are with them. [15]Greet Philologus, Julia, Nereus and his sister, and Olympas, and all the saints who are with them. [16]Greet one another with a holy kiss. All the churches of Christ greet you.

17 I urge you, brothers and sisters,[v] to keep an eye

[s] Or *Junias;* other ancient authorities read *Julia*
[t] Or *compatriots*
[u] Or *compatriot*
[v] Gk *brothers*

⌐Ἰουνιᾶν⌐ τοὺς συγγενεῖς μου καὶ συναιχμαλώτους μου,
JUNIAS   THE   KINSMEN   OF ME AND   FELLOW-PRISONERS   OF ME,

οἵτινές εἰσιν ἐπίσημοι ἐν τοῖς ἀποστόλοις, οἳ καὶ
WHO   ARE   NOTABLE   AMONG THE   APOSTLES,   WHO ALSO

πρὸ ἐμοῦ γέγοναν ἐν Χριστῷ.   **16.8** ἀσπάσασθε
BEFORE ME   HAVE BEEN   IN   CHRIST.   GREET

Ἀμπλιᾶτον τὸν ἀγαπητόν μου ἐν κυρίῳ.
AMPLIATUS   THE   BELOVED   OF ME   IN   [THE] LORD.

16.9 ἀσπάσασθε Οὐρβανὸν τὸν συνεργὸν ἡμῶν ἐν
GREET   URBANUS   THE   CO-WORKER   OF US   IN

Χριστῷ καὶ Στάχυν τὸν ἀγαπητόν μου.
CHRIST   AND   STACHYS   THE   BELOVED   OF ME.

16.10 ἀσπάσασθε Ἀπελλῆν τὸν δόκιμον ἐν Χριστῷ.
GREET   APELLES   THE   APPROVED ONE   IN   CHRIST.

ἀσπάσασθε τοὺς ἐκ τῶν   Ἀριστοβούλου.
GREET   THE ONES OF   THE [HOUSEHOLD]   OF ARISTOBULUS.

16.11 ἀσπάσασθε Ἡρῳδίωνα τὸν συγγενῆ μου.
GREET   HERODION   THE   KINSMAN   OF ME.

ἀσπάσασθε τοὺς ἐκ τῶν   Ναρκίσσου τοὺς
GREET   THE ONES OF   THE [HOUSEHOLD]   OF NARCISSUS   THE ONES

ὄντας ἐν κυρίῳ.   **16.12** ἀσπάσασθε Τρύφαιναν καὶ
BEING   IN   [THE] LORD.   GREET   TRYPHAENA   AND

Τρυφῶσαν τὰς κοπιώσας ἐν κυρίῳ.   ἀσπάσασθε
TRYPHOSA   THE ONES LABORING   IN   [THE] LORD.   GREET

Περσίδα τὴν ἀγαπητήν, ἥτις πολλὰ ἐκοπίασεν ἐν
PERSIS   THE   BELOVED,   WHO   GREATLY   LABORED   IN

κυρίῳ.   **16.13** ἀσπάσασθε Ῥοῦφον τὸν ἐκλεκτὸν
[THE] LORD.   GREET   RUFUS   THE   CHOSEN ONE

ἐν κυρίῳ καὶ τὴν μητέρα αὐτοῦ καὶ ἐμοῦ.
IN   [THE] LORD AND   THE   MOTHER   OF HIM   AND   OF ME.

16.14 ἀσπάσασθε Ἀσύγκριτον, Φλέγοντα, Ἑρμῆν,
GREET   ASYNCRITUS,   PHLEGON,   HERMES,

Πατροβᾶν, Ἑρμᾶν, καὶ τοὺς σὺν αὐτοῖς ἀδελφούς.
PATROBAS,   HERMAS,   AND   THE   [2]WITH [3]THEM   [1]BROTHERS.

16.15 ἀσπάσασθε Φιλόλογον καὶ ⌐Ἰουλίαν,⌐ Νηρέα καὶ
GREET   PHILOLOGUS   AND   JULIA,   NEREUS   AND

τὴν ἀδελφὴν αὐτοῦ, καὶ Ὀλυμπᾶν καὶ τοὺς σὺν
THE   SISTER   OF HIM,   AND   OLYMPAS,   AND   [2]THE   [4]WITH

αὐτοῖς πάντας ἁγίους.   **16.16** Ἀσπάσασθε ἀλλήλους ἐν
[5]THEM   [1]ALL   [3]SAINTS.   GREET   ONE ANOTHER   WITH

φιλήματι ἁγίῳ. Ἀσπάζονται ὑμᾶς αἱ ἐκκλησίαι
A HOLY~KISS.   GREET   [6]YOU°   [2]THE [3]CHURCHES

πᾶσαι τοῦ Χριστοῦ.
[1]ALL   -   [4]OF CHRIST.

16.17 Παρακαλῶ δὲ ὑμᾶς, ἀδελφοί, σκοπεῖν τοὺς
NOW~I URGE   YOU°,   BROTHERS,   TO WATCH   [1]THE ONES

τὰς διχοστασίας καὶ τὰ σκάνδαλα παρὰ τὴν διδαχὴν
3THE 4DIVISIONS 5AND 6THE 7OBSTACLES 8AGAINST 9THE 10TEACHING

ἣν ὑμεῖς ἐμάθετε ποιοῦντας, καὶ ἐκκλίνετε ἀπ᾽
11WHICH 12YOU° 13LEARNED 2MAKING, AND TURN AWAY FROM

αὐτῶν· **16.18** οἱ γὰρ τοιοῦτοι τῷ κυρίῳ ἡμῶν Χριστῷ
THEM; - FOR SUCH MEN 2THE 3LORD 4OF US, 5CHRIST

οὐ δουλεύουσιν ἀλλὰ τῇ ἑαυτῶν κοιλίᾳ, καὶ διὰ τῆς
1DO NOT SERVE BUT THEIR OWN BELLY, AND THROUGH -

χρηστολογίας καὶ εὐλογίας ἐξαπατῶσιν τὰς καρδίας
SMOOTH SPEECH AND PRAISE DECEIVE THE HEARTS

τῶν ἀκάκων. **16.19** ἡ γὰρ ὑμῶν ὑπακοὴ εἰς
OF THE SIMPLE. - FOR [NEWS] OF YOUR° OBEDIENCE TO

πάντας ἀφίκετο· ἐφ᾽ ὑμῖν οὖν χαίρω, θέλω δὲ
ALL MEN REACHED; CONCERNING YOU° THEREFORE I REJOICE, BUT~I WANT

ὑμᾶς σοφοὺς εἶναι εἰς τὸ ἀγαθόν, ἀκεραίους δὲ εἰς τὸ
YOU° WISE TO BE TO THE GOOD, AND~PURE TO THE

κακόν. **16.20** ὁ δὲ θεὸς τῆς εἰρήνης συντρίψει τὸν
EVIL. NOW~THE GOD - OF PEACE WILL CRUSH -

Σατανᾶν ὑπὸ τοὺς πόδας ὑμῶν ἐν τάχει. ⌐ἡ χάρις
SATAN UNDER THE FEET OF YOU° SOON. THE GRACE

τοῦ κυρίου ἡμῶν Ἰησοῦ μεθ᾽ ὑμῶν.⌐
OF THE LORD OF US JESUS [BE] WITH YOU°.

16.21 Ἀσπάζεται ὑμᾶς Τιμόθεος ὁ συνεργός μου
5GREETS 6YOU° 1TIMOTHY 2THE 3CO-WORKER 4OF ME,

καὶ Λούκιος καὶ Ἰάσων καὶ Σωσίπατρος οἱ συγγενεῖς
AND LUCIUS AND JASON AND SOSIPATER THE KINSMEN

μου. **16.22** ἀσπάζομαι ὑμᾶς ἐγὼ Τέρτιος ὁ
OF ME. 7GREET 8YOU° 1I 2TERTIUS 3THE ONE

γράψας τὴν ἐπιστολὴν ἐν κυρίῳ. **16.23** ἀσπάζεται
4HAVING WRITTEN 5THE 6EPISTLE 7IN 8[THE] LORD. 9GREETS

ὑμᾶς Γάϊος ὁ ξένος μου καὶ ὅλης τῆς ἐκκλησίας.
10YOU° 1GAIUS 2THE 3HOST 4OF ME 5AND 6ALL 7THE 8CHURCH.

ἀσπάζεται ὑμᾶς Ἔραστος ὁ οἰκονόμος τῆς πόλεως
6GREETS 7YOU° 1ERASTUS 2THE 3TREASURER 4OF THE 5CITY

καὶ Κούαρτος ὁ ἀδελφός.⌐
AND QUARTUS THE BROTHER.

⌐**[16.25** Τῷ δὲ δυναμένῳ ὑμᾶς στηρίξαι κατὰ
NOW~TO THE ONE BEING ABLE TO ESTABLISH~YOU° ACCORDING TO

τὸ εὐαγγέλιόν μου καὶ τὸ κήρυγμα Ἰησοῦ Χριστοῦ,
THE GOOD NEWS OF ME AND THE PROCLAMATION OF JESUS CHRIST,

κατὰ ἀποκάλυψιν μυστηρίου χρόνοις αἰωνίοις
ACCORDING [THE] REVELATION OF [THE] MYSTERY IN TIMES ETERNAL

on those who cause dissensions and offenses, in opposition to the teaching that you have learned; avoid them. [18]For such people do not serve our Lord Christ, but their own appetites,[w] and by smooth talk and flattery they deceive the hearts of the simple-minded. [19]For while your obedience is known to all, so that I rejoice over you, I want you to be wise in what is good and guileless in what is evil. [20]The God of peace will shortly crush Satan under your feet. The grace of our Lord Jesus Christ be with you.[x]

[21] Timothy, my co-worker, greets you; so do Lucius and Jason and Sosipater, my relatives.[y]

[22] I Tertius, the writer of this letter, greet you in the Lord.[z]

[23] Gaius, who is host to me and to the whole church, greets you. Erastus, the city treasurer, and our brother Quartus, greet you.[a]

[25] Now to God[b] who is able to strengthen you according to my gospel and the proclamation of Jesus Christ, according to the revelation of the mystery

w Gk *their own belly*
x Other ancient authorities lack this sentence
y Or *compatriots*
z Or *I Tertius, writing this letter in the Lord, greet you*
a Other ancient authorities add verse 24, *The grace of our Lord Jesus Christ be with all of you. Amen.*
b Gk *the one*

16:23 text: ASV RSV NASB NIV NEB TEV NJB NRSV. add v. 24 η χαρις του κυριου ημων Ιησου Χριστου μετα παντων υμων. αμην. (The grace of our Lord Jesus Christ [be] with you° all. Amen.): KJV ASVmg RSVmg NASBmg NIVmg NEBmg TEVmg NJBmg NRSVmg. **16:25-27** Some MSS insert this portion (called the doxology) at the end of Rom. 14:33 and one MS has it after Rom. 15:33. All the translations keep Rom. 16:25-27 at the very end of the book (as here in the Greek text), and some translations note the various positions of the doxology--see ASVmg NEBmg TEVmg NRSVmg.

that was kept secret for long ages ²⁶but is now disclosed, and through the prophetic writings is made known to all the Gentiles, according to the command of the eternal God, to bring about the obedience of faith— ²⁷to the only wise God, through Jesus Christ, to whomᶜ be the glory forever! Amen.ᵈ

ᶜ Other ancient authorities lack *to whom*. The verse then reads, *to the only wise God be the glory through Jesus Christ forever. Amen.*

ᵈ Other ancient authorities lack 16.25-27 or include it after 14.23 or 15.33; others put verse 24 after verse 27

σεσιγημένου,   **16.26** φανερωθέντος   δὲ   νῦν   διά τε
HAVING BEEN KEPT SECRET,   ³MANIFESTED   ¹BUT ²NOW AND~THROUGH

γραφῶν προφητικῶν κατ᾽   ἐπιταγὴν τοῦ   αἰωνίου
PROPHETIC~SCRIPTURES   ACCORDING TO A COMMAND   OF THE   ETERNAL

θεοῦ εἰς ὑπακοὴν πίστεως εἰς πάντα τὰ ἔθνη
GOD   ⁶FOR ⁷OBEDIENCE   ⁸OF FAITH   ²TO   ³ALL   ⁴THE ⁵GENTILES

γνωρισθέντος,   **16.27** μόνῳ σοφῷ   θεῷ,   διὰ   Ἰησοῦ
¹HAVING BEEN MADE KNOWN,   ²ONLY ³WISE   ¹TO GOD, THROUGH JESUS

Χριστοῦ, ᾧ   ἡ   δόξα εἰς τοὺς αἰῶνας, ἀμήν.]⌐
CHRIST,   TO WHOM [BE] THE GLORY INTO THE   AGES,   AMEN.

THE FIRST LETTER OF PAUL TO THE
CORINTHIANS

ΠΡΟΣ ΚΟΡΙΝΘΙΟΥΣ Α
TO   [THE] CORINTHIANS   1

1.1 Παῦλος κλητὸς ἀπόστολος Χριστοῦ Ἰησοῦ διὰ
PAUL   A CALLED   APOSTLE   OF CHRIST   JESUS   THROUGH

θελήματος θεοῦ καὶ Σωσθένης ὁ ἀδελφὸς **1.2** τῇ
[THE] WILL   OF GOD   AND   SOSTHENES   THE   BROTHER   TO THE

ἐκκλησίᾳ τοῦ θεοῦ τῇ οὔσῃ ἐν Κορίνθῳ,
CHURCH   -   OF GOD   -   EXISTING   IN   CORINTH,

ἡγιασμένοις ἐν Χριστῷ Ἰησοῦ, κλητοῖς ἁγίοις,
TO ONES HAVING BEEN SANCTIFIED   IN   CHRIST   JESUS,   [THE] CALLED   SAINTS,

σὺν πᾶσιν τοῖς ἐπικαλουμένοις τὸ ὄνομα τοῦ κυρίου
WITH   ALL   THE ONES   CALLING ON   THE   NAME   OF THE   LORD

ἡμῶν Ἰησοῦ Χριστοῦ ἐν παντὶ τόπῳ, αὐτῶν καὶ ἡμῶν·
OF US   JESUS   CHRIST   IN   EVERY   PLACE,   THEIRS   AND   OURS;

1.3 χάρις ὑμῖν καὶ εἰρήνη ἀπὸ θεοῦ πατρὸς ἡμῶν καὶ
GRACE   TO YOU°   AND   PEACE   FROM   GOD   [THE] FATHER   OF US   AND

κυρίου Ἰησοῦ Χριστοῦ.
LORD   JESUS   CHRIST.

1.4 Εὐχαριστῶ τῷ θεῷ μου πάντοτε περὶ ὑμῶν
I GIVE THANKS   TO THE   GOD   OF ME   ALWAYS   CONCERNING   YOU°

ἐπὶ τῇ χάριτι τοῦ θεοῦ τῇ δοθείσῃ ὑμῖν ἐν
FOR   THE   GRACE   -   OF GOD   -   HAVING BEEN GIVEN   TO YOU°   IN

Χριστῷ Ἰησοῦ, **1.5** ὅτι ἐν παντὶ ἐπλουτίσθητε ἐν
CHRIST   JESUS,   THAT   IN   EVERYTHING   YOU WERE ENRICHED   IN

αὐτῷ, ἐν παντὶ λόγῳ καὶ πάσῃ γνώσει, **1.6** καθὼς
HIM,   IN   ALL   EXPRESSION,   AND   ALL   KNOWLEDGE,   EVEN AS

τὸ μαρτύριον τοῦ Χριστοῦ ἐβεβαιώθη ἐν ὑμῖν, **1.7** ὥστε
THE   TESTIMONY   -   OF CHRIST   WAS CONFIRMED   IN   YOU°,   SO THAT

ὑμᾶς μὴ ὑστερεῖσθαι ἐν μηδενὶ χαρίσματι,
YOU°   ARE NOT LACKING   IN   ANY   GIFT,

ἀπεκδεχομένους τὴν ἀποκάλυψιν τοῦ κυρίου ἡμῶν
AWAITING   THE   REVELATION   OF THE   LORD   OF US

Ἰησοῦ Χριστοῦ· **1.8** ὃς καὶ βεβαιώσει ὑμᾶς ἕως
JESUS   CHRIST;   WHO   ALSO   WILL CONFIRM(STRENGTHEN)   YOU°   TO

τέλους ἀνεγκλήτους ἐν τῇ ἡμέρᾳ τοῦ κυρίου ἡμῶν
[THE] END,   UNREPROVABLE   IN   THE   DAY   OF THE   LORD   OF US

Ἰησοῦ [Χριστοῦ]. **1.9** πιστὸς ὁ θεός, δι' οὗ
JESUS   CHRIST.   FAITHFUL [IS]   -   GOD   THROUGH   WHOM

Paul, called to be an apostle of Christ Jesus by the will of God, and our brother Sosthenes,

2 To the church of God that is in Corinth, to those who are sanctified in Christ Jesus, called to be saints, together with all those who in every place call on the name of our Lord Jesus Christ, both their Lord[a] and ours:

3 Grace to you and peace from God our Father and the Lord Jesus Christ.

4 I give thanks to my[b] God always for you because of the grace of God that has been given you in Christ Jesus, 5for in every way you have been enriched in him, in speech and knowledge of every kind— 6just as the testimony of[c] Christ has been strengthened among you— 7so that you are not lacking in any spiritual gift as you wait for the revealing of our Lord Jesus Christ. 8He will also strengthen you to the end, so that you may be blameless on the day of our Lord Jesus Christ. 9God is faithful; by him

[a] Gk *theirs*
[b] Other ancient authorities lack *my*
[c] Or *to*

you were called into the fellowship of his Son, Jesus Christ our Lord.

10 Now I appeal to you, brothers and sisters,*d* by the name of our Lord Jesus Christ, that all of you be in agreement and that there be no divisions among you, but that you be united in the same mind and the same purpose. [11]For it has been reported to me by Chloe's people that there are quarrels among you, my brothers and sisters.*e* [12]What I mean is that each of you says, "I belong to Paul," or "I belong to Apollos," or "I belong to Cephas," or "I belong to Christ." [13]Has Christ been divided? Was Paul crucified for you? Or were you baptized in the name of Paul? [14]I thank God*f* that I baptized none of you except Crispus and Gaius, [15]so that no one can say that you were baptized in my name. [16](I did baptize also the household of Stephanas; beyond that, I do not know whether I baptized anyone else.) [17]For Christ did not send me to baptize but to proclaim the gospel, and not with eloquent wisdom, so that the cross of Christ might not be emptied of its power.

18 For the message about the cross is foolishness to those who are perishing, but to us who are being saved it is the power of God. [19]For it is written,

d Gk brothers
e Gk my brothers
f Other ancient authorities read I am thankful

ἐκλήθητε   εἰς κοινωνίαν τοῦ υἱοῦ αὐτοῦ Ἰησοῦ
YOU° WERE CALLED INTO [THE] FELLOWSHIP OF THE SON OF HIM JESUS

Χριστοῦ τοῦ κυρίου ἡμῶν.
CHRIST THE LORD OF US.

1.10 Παρακαλῶ δὲ ὑμᾶς, ἀδελφοί, διὰ   τοῦ ὀνόματος
NOW~I EXHORT YOU°, BROTHERS, THROUGH THE NAME

τοῦ κυρίου ἡμῶν Ἰησοῦ Χριστοῦ, ἵνα τὸ αὐτὸ
OF THE LORD OF US JESUS CHRIST, THAT THE SAME THING

λέγητε πάντες καὶ μὴ ᾖ ἐν ὑμῖν σχίσματα,
YOU° ALL SPEAK AND NOT BE AMONG YOU° DIVISIONS,

ἦτε δὲ   κατηρτισμένοι ἐν τῷ αὐτῷ νοῒ καὶ ἐν
BUT~YOU° MAY BE UNITED IN THE SAME MIND AND IN

τῇ αὐτῇ γνώμῃ. **1.11** ἐδηλώθη γάρ   μοι περὶ ὑμῶν,
THE SAME THOUGHT. FOR~IT WAS MADE CLEAR TO ME ABOUT YOU°,

ἀδελφοί μου, ὑπὸ τῶν Χλόης ὅτι ἔριδες ἐν ὑμῖν
BROTHERS OF ME, BY THE ONES OF CHLOE THAT STRIFES AMONG YOU°

εἰσιν. **1.12** λέγω δὲ τοῦτο ὅτι ἕκαστος ὑμῶν λέγει,
THERE ARE. NOW~I SAY THIS, BECAUSE EACH OF YOU° SAYS,

Ἐγὼ μέν εἰμι Παύλου, Ἐγὼ δὲ Ἀπολλῶ, Ἐγὼ δὲ Κηφᾶ,
I — AM OF PAUL, BUT~I OF APOLLOS, BUT~I OF CEPHAS,

Ἐγὼ δὲ Χριστοῦ. **1.13** μεμέρισται ὁ Χριστός;   μὴ
BUT~I OF CHRIST; HAS BEEN DIVIDED - CHRIST? [SURELY] NOT

Παῦλος ἐσταυρώθη ὑπὲρ ὑμῶν, ἢ εἰς τὸ ὄνομα Παύλου
PAUL WAS CRUCIFIED FOR YOU°, OR IN THE NAME OF PAUL

ἐβαπτίσθητε; **1.14** εὐχαριστῶ [τῷ θεῷ] ὅτι οὐδένα
WERE YOU° BAPTIZED? I THANK - GOD THAT NOT ONE

ὑμῶν ἐβάπτισα εἰ μὴ Κρίσπον καὶ Γάϊον, **1.15** ἵνα μή
OF YOU° I BAPTIZED EXCEPT CRISPUS AND GAIUS, LEST

τις εἴπῃ   ὅτι εἰς τὸ ἐμὸν ὄνομα ἐβαπτίσθητε.
ANYONE SHOULD SAY THAT IN - MY NAME YOU° WERE BAPTIZED.

1.16 ἐβάπτισα δὲ καὶ τὸν Στεφανᾶ οἶκον,   λοιπὸν
NOW~I BAPTIZED ALSO - STEPHANAS' HOUSEHOLD, [AS TO] THE REST

οὐκ οἶδα εἴ τινα ἄλλον ἐβάπτισα. **1.17** οὐ   γὰρ
I DO NOT KNOW IF ANY OTHER I BAPTIZED. ⁵NOT ¹FOR

ἀπέστειλέν με Χριστὸς βαπτίζειν ἀλλὰ
³SENT ⁴ME ²CHRIST ⁶TO BAPTIZE BUT

εὐαγγελίζεσθαι, οὐκ ἐν σοφίᾳ λόγου, ἵνα μὴ
TO PREACH THE GOOD NEWS, NOT BY WISDOM OF SPEECH, LEST

κενωθῇ   ὁ σταυρὸς τοῦ Χριστοῦ.
⁴BE EMPTIED [OF ITS POWER] ¹THE ²CROSS - ³OF CHRIST.

1.18 Ὁ λόγος γὰρ ὁ τοῦ σταυροῦ τοῖς   μὲν
²THE ³MESSAGE ¹FOR - OF THE CROSS TO THE ONES -

ἀπολλυμένοις μωρία ἐστίν, τοῖς δὲ σῳζομένοις ἡμῖν
PERISHING IS~SENSELESS, - BUT TO US~BEING SAVED

δύναμις θεοῦ ἐστιν. **1.19** γέγραπται γάρ,
[THE] POWER OF GOD IT IS. FOR~IT HAS BEEN WRITTEN,

1:19 Isa. 29:14 LXX

Ἀπολῶ τὴν σοφίαν τῶν σοφῶν
I WILL DESTROY THE WISDOM OF THE WISE ONES

καὶ τὴν σύνεσιν τῶν συνετῶν ἀθετήσω.
AND THE UNDERSTANDING OF THE INTELLIGENT I WILL SET ASIDE.

1.20 ποῦ σοφός; ποῦ γραμματεύς; ποῦ
WHERE [IS THE] WISE MAN? WHERE [IS THE] SCRIBE? WHERE

συζητητὴς τοῦ αἰῶνος τούτου; οὐχὶ ἐμώρανεν ὁ θεὸς
[IS THE] DEBATER - OF THIS~AGE? [DID] NOT ²MAKE FOOLISH - ¹GOD

τὴν σοφίαν τοῦ κόσμου; **1.21** ἐπειδὴ γὰρ ἐν τῇ σοφίᾳ
THE WISDOM OF THE WORLD? FOR~SINCE BY THE WISDOM

τοῦ θεοῦ οὐκ ἔγνω ὁ κόσμος διὰ τῆς σοφίας τὸν
- OF GOD ⁶DID NOT KNOW ¹THE ²WORLD ³THROUGH ⁴THE(ITS) ⁵WISDOM -

θεόν, εὐδόκησεν ὁ θεὸς διὰ τῆς μωρίας τοῦ
⁷GOD, WAS PLEASED - GOD THROUGH THE FOOLISHNESS OF THE

κηρύγματος σῶσαι τοὺς πιστεύοντας· **1.22** ἐπειδὴ
PROCLAMATION TO SAVE THE ONES BELIEVING; SINCE

καὶ Ἰουδαῖοι σημεῖα αἰτοῦσιν καὶ Ἕλληνες
INDEED JEWS ASK~SIGNS AND GREEKS

σοφίαν ζητοῦσιν, **1.23** ἡμεῖς δὲ κηρύσσομεν Χριστὸν
SEEK~WISDOM, BUT~WE PROCLAIM CHRIST

ἐσταυρωμένον, Ἰουδαίοις μὲν σκάνδαλον, ἔθνεσιν δὲ
HAVING BEEN CRUCIFIED, TO JEWS - AN OFFENSE, TO GENTILES -

μωρίαν, **1.24** αὐτοῖς δὲ τοῖς κλητοῖς, Ἰουδαίοις τε καὶ
FOOLISHNESS, BUT~TO THEM THE CALLED ONES, BOTH~TO JEWS AND

Ἕλλησιν, Χριστὸν θεοῦ δύναμιν καὶ θεοῦ σοφίαν·
TO GREEKS, CHRIST, GOD'S POWER AND GOD'S WISDOM.

1.25 ὅτι τὸ μωρὸν τοῦ θεοῦ σοφώτερον τῶν
BECAUSE THE FOOLISH[NESS] - OF GOD WISER

ἀνθρώπων ἐστὶν καὶ τὸ ἀσθενὲς τοῦ θεοῦ ἰσχυρότερον
THAN MEN IS AND THE WEAK[NESS] - OF GOD [IS] STRONGER

τῶν ἀνθρώπων.
- THAN MEN.

1.26 Βλέπετε γὰρ τὴν κλῆσιν ὑμῶν, ἀδελφοί, ὅτι οὐ
FOR~YOU° SEE THE CALLING OF YOU°, BROTHERS, THAT NOT

πολλοὶ σοφοὶ κατὰ σάρκα, οὐ πολλοὶ δυνατοί,
MANY WISE MEN ACCORDING TO FLESH, NOT MANY POWERFUL MEN,

οὐ πολλοὶ εὐγενεῖς· **1.27** ἀλλὰ τὰ μωρὰ τοῦ
NOT MANY WELL-BORN; BUT THE FOOLISH THINGS(ONES) OF THE

κόσμου ἐξελέξατο ὁ θεός, ἵνα καταισχύνῃ τοὺς σοφούς,
WORLD ²CHOSE- - ¹GOD, THAT HE MIGHT SHAME THE WISE MEN,

καὶ τὰ ἀσθενῆ τοῦ κόσμου ἐξελέξατο ὁ θεός, ἵνα
AND THE WEAK THINGS(ONES) OF THE WORLD ²CHOSE - ¹GOD, THAT

καταισχύνῃ τὰ ἰσχυρά, **1.28** καὶ τὰ ἀγενῆ τοῦ
HE MIGHT SHAME THE STRONG THINGS(ONES), AND THE LOW-BORN OF THE

κόσμου καὶ τὰ ἐξουθενημένα ἐξελέξατο ὁ θεός,
WORLD AND THE THINGS(ONES) HAVING BEEN DESPISED ²CHOSE - ¹GOD,

τὰ μὴ ὄντα, ἵνα τὰ ὄντα καταργήσῃ,
THE THINGS(ONES) NOT BEING, THAT THE THINGS(ONES) BEING HE MIGHT NULLIFY,

---

"I will destroy the
wisdom of the wise,
and the discernment of
the discerning I will
thwart."

²⁰Where is the one who is
wise? Where is the scribe?
Where is the debater of this
age? Has not God made
foolish the wisdom of the
world? ²¹For since, in the
wisdom of God, the world
did not know God through
wisdom, God decided,
through the foolishness of
our proclamation, to save
those who believe. ²²For
Jews demand signs and
Greeks desire wisdom,
²³but we proclaim Christ
crucified, a stumbling block
to Jews and foolishness to
Gentiles, ²⁴but to those who
are the called, both Jews and
Greeks, Christ the power of
God and the wisdom of
God. ²⁵For God's
foolishness is wiser than
human wisdom, and God's
weakness is stronger than
human strength.

26 Consider your own
call, brothers and sisters:ᵍ
not many of you were wise
by human standards,ʰ not
many were powerful, not
many were of noble birth.
²⁷But God chose what is
foolish in the world to shame
the wise; God chose what
is weak in the world to
shame the strong; ²⁸God
chose what is low and de-
spised in the world, things
that are not, to reduce to
nothing things that are,

ᵍ Gk *brothers*
ʰ Gk *according to the flesh*

²⁹so that no one' might boast in the presence of God. ³⁰He is the source of your life in Christ Jesus, who became for us wisdom from God, and righteousness and sanctification and redemption, ³¹in order that, as it is written, "Let the one who boasts, boast in' the Lord."

i Gk *no flesh*
j Or *of*

1.29 ὅπως μὴ καυχήσηται πᾶσα σὰρξ ἐνώπιον τοῦ θεοῦ.
SO THAT   NOT   MAY BOAST   ANY   FLESH   BEFORE   -   GOD.

1.30 ἐξ αὐτοῦ δὲ ὑμεῖς ἐστε ἐν Χριστῷ Ἰησοῦ, ὃς
²OF ³HIM   ¹BUT   YOU°   ARE   IN   CHRIST   JESUS,   WHO

ἐγενήθη σοφία ἡμῖν ἀπὸ θεοῦ, δικαιοσύνη τε καὶ
BECAME   WISDOM   TO US   FROM   GOD,   BOTH~RIGHTEOUSNESS   AND

ἁγιασμὸς καὶ ἀπολύτρωσις, **1.31** ἵνα καθὼς
SANCTIFICATION   AND   REDEMPTION,   THAT   ACCORDING AS

γέγραπται, Ὁ καυχώμενος ἐν κυρίῳ καυχάσθω.
IT HAS BEEN WRITTEN,   THE ONE   BOASTING   ²IN   ³[THE] LORD   ¹LET HIM BOAST.

1:31 Jer. 9:24

CHAPTER 2

When I came to you, brothers and sisters,*k* I did not come proclaiming the mystery*l* of God to you in lofty words or wisdom. ²For I decided to know nothing among you except Jesus Christ, and him crucified. ³And I came to you in weakness and in fear and in much trembling. ⁴My speech and my proclamation were not with plausible words of wisdom,*m* but with a demonstration of the Spirit and of power, ⁵so that your faith might rest not on human wisdom but on the power of God.

6 Yet among the mature we do speak wisdom, though it is not a wisdom of this age or of the rulers of this age, who are doomed to perish. ⁷But we speak God's wisdom, secret and hidden, which God decreed before the ages for our glory. ⁸None of the rulers

k Gk *brothers*
l Other ancient authorities read *testimony*
m Other ancient authorities read *the persuasiveness of wisdom*

2.1 Κἀγὼ ἐλθὼν πρὸς ὑμᾶς, ἀδελφοί, ἦλθον οὐ
AND I   HAVING COME   TO   YOU°,   BROTHERS,   CAME   NOT

καθ' ὑπεροχὴν λόγου ἢ σοφίας καταγγέλλων
ACCORDING TO   EXCELLENCE   OF SPEECH   OR   OF WISDOM   ANNOUNCING

ὑμῖν τὸ ⌐μυστήριον¬ τοῦ θεοῦ. **2.2** οὐ γὰρ ἔκρινά
TO YOU°   THE   MYSTERY   -   OF GOD.   ³NOT   ¹FOR   ²I DECIDED

τι εἰδέναι ἐν ὑμῖν εἰ μὴ Ἰησοῦν Χριστὸν καὶ
⁵ANYTHING   ⁴TO KNOW   AMONG   YOU°   EXCEPT   JESUS   CHRIST   AND

τοῦτον ἐσταυρωμένον. **2.3** κἀγὼ ἐν ἀσθενείᾳ καὶ ἐν
THIS ONE   HAVING BEEN CRUCIFIED.   AND I   IN   WEAKNESS   AND   IN

φόβῳ καὶ ἐν τρόμῳ πολλῷ ἐγενόμην πρὸς ὑμᾶς,
FEAR   AND   IN   MUCH~TREMBLING   WAS   WITH   YOU°,

2.4 καὶ ὁ λόγος μου καὶ τὸ κήρυγμά μου οὐκ ἐν
AND   THE   SPEECH   OF ME   AND   THE   PROCLAMATION   OF ME   [WAS] NOT   IN

πειθοῖ[ς] σοφίας [λόγοις] ἀλλ' ἐν ἀποδείξει πνεύματος
PERSUASIVE   WORDS~OF WISDOM   BUT   IN   DEMONSTRATION   OF [THE] SPIRIT

καὶ δυνάμεως, **2.5** ἵνα ἡ πίστις ὑμῶν μὴ ᾖ ἐν
AND   POWER,   THAT   THE   FAITH   OF YOU°   MAY NOT BE   IN

σοφίᾳ ἀνθρώπων ἀλλ' ἐν δυνάμει θεοῦ.
[THE] WISDOM   OF MEN   BUT   IN   [THE] POWER   OF GOD.

2.6 Σοφίαν δὲ λαλοῦμεν ἐν τοῖς τελείοις,
BUT~WISDOM   WE SPEAK   AMONG   THE   MATURE,

σοφίαν δὲ οὐ τοῦ αἰῶνος τούτου οὐδὲ τῶν ἀρχόντων
YET~A WISDOM   NOT   -   OF THIS~AGE   NEITHER   OF THE   RULERS

τοῦ αἰῶνος τούτου τῶν καταργουμένων· **2.7** ἀλλὰ
-   OF THIS~AGE,   THE ONES   BEING BROUGHT TO NOTHING;   BUT

λαλοῦμεν θεοῦ σοφίαν ἐν μυστηρίῳ τὴν
WE SPEAK   GOD'S   WISDOM   IN   A MYSTERY   -

ἀποκεκρυμμένην, ἣν προώρισεν ὁ θεὸς πρὸ τῶν
HAVING BEEN HIDDEN,   WHICH   ²PREDESTINED   -   ¹GOD   BEFORE   THE

αἰώνων εἰς δόξαν ἡμῶν, **2.8** ἣν οὐδεὶς τῶν ἀρχόντων
AGES   FOR   [THE] GLORY   OF US;   WHICH   NOT ONE   OF THE   RULERS

2:1 text: ASVmg RSVmg NASBmg NIVmg NEBmg TEV NJB NRSV.   var. μαρτυριον (testimony): KJV ASV RSV NASB NIV NEB TEVmg NJBmg NRSVmg.

τοῦ αἰῶνος τούτου ἔγνωκεν· εἰ γὰρ ἔγνωσαν, οὐκ ἄν
-   OF THIS~AGE   HAS KNOWN,   FOR~IF THEY KNEW, NOT WOULD

τὸν κύριον τῆς δόξης ἐσταύρωσαν.   2.9 ἀλλὰ καθὼς
THE LORD   -   OF GLORY THEY CRUCIFIED.   BUT   EVEN AS

γέγραπται,
IT HAS BEEN WRITTEN,

"Α   ὀφθαλμὸς οὐκ εἶδεν καὶ οὗς οὐκ ἤκουσεν
THINGS WHICH EYE   DID NOT SEE AND EAR DID NOT HEAR

καὶ ἐπὶ καρδίαν ἀνθρώπου οὐκ ἀνέβη,
AND ON(IN) HEART   OF MAN   DID NOT COME UP,

ἃ   ἡτοίμασεν ὁ θεὸς τοῖς   ἀγαπῶσιν
THE THINGS ²PREPARED   - ¹GOD FOR THE ONES LOVING

αὐτόν.
HIM.

2.10 ἡμῖν δὲ ἀπεκάλυψεν ὁ θεὸς διὰ   τοῦ
BUT~TO US ²REVEALED [THEM] - ¹GOD THROUGH THE

πνεύματος· τὸ γὰρ πνεῦμα πάντα ἐραυνᾷ, καὶ τὰ
SPIRIT;   FOR~THE SPIRIT ALL THINGS SEARCHES, EVEN THE

βάθη   τοῦ θεοῦ.   **2.11** τίς γὰρ οἶδεν ἀνθρώπων τὰ
DEEP THINGS - OF GOD.   FOR~WHO OF MEN~KNOWS   THE THINGS

τοῦ ἀνθρώπου εἰ μὴ τὸ πνεῦμα τοῦ ἀνθρώπου τὸ ἐν
-   OF A MAN   EXCEPT THE SPIRIT   -   OF MAN   -   IN

αὐτῷ; οὕτως καὶ τὰ   τοῦ θεοῦ οὐδεὶς ἔγνωκεν
HIM?   SO   ALSO THE THINGS -   OF GOD NO ONE HAS KNOWN

εἰ μὴ τὸ πνεῦμα τοῦ θεοῦ.   **2.12** ἡμεῖς δὲ οὐ τὸ πνεῦμα
EXCEPT THE SPIRIT   -   OF GOD.   NOW~WE°   NOT THE SPIRIT

τοῦ κόσμου ἐλάβομεν ἀλλὰ τὸ πνεῦμα τὸ ἐκ τοῦ
OF THE WORLD   RECEIVED   BUT   THE SPIRIT   - FROM -

θεοῦ, ἵνα εἰδῶμεν τὰ   ὑπὸ τοῦ θεοῦ χαρισθέντα
GOD,   THAT WE MAY KNOW THE THINGS BY - GOD HAVING BEEN FREELY GIVEN

ἡμῖν· **2.13** ἃ   καὶ λαλοῦμεν οὐκ ἐν διδακτοῖς
TO US;   WHICH THINGS ALSO WE SPEAK NOT IN ²TAUGHT

ἀνθρωπίνης σοφίας λόγοις ἀλλ᾽ ἐν διδακτοῖς
³BY HUMAN   ⁴WISDOM ¹WORDS BUT IN [WORDS] TAUGHT

πνεύματος, πνευματικοῖς πνευματικὰ συγκρίνοντες.
BY [THE] SPIRIT, ³WITH SPIRITUAL THINGS ²SPIRITUAL THINGS ¹MATCHING.

2.14 ψυχικὸς δὲ ἄνθρωπος οὐ δέχεται τὰ   τοῦ
BUT~A NATURAL MAN   DOES NOT RECEIVE THE THINGS OF THE

πνεύματος τοῦ θεοῦ· μωρία γὰρ αὐτῷ ἐστιν· καὶ
SPIRIT   -   OF GOD, FOR~FOOLISHNESS TO HIM THEY ARE, AND

οὐ δύναται γνῶναι,   ὅτι   πνευματικῶς ἀνακρίνεται.
HE IS NOT ABLE TO KNOW [THEM], BECAUSE THEY ARE DISCERNED~SPIRITUALLY;

2.15 ὁ δὲ   πνευματικὸς ἀνακρίνει [τὰ] πάντα, αὐτὸς δὲ
NOW~THE SPIRITUAL MAN DISCERNS   -   ALL THINGS, BUT~HE

ὑπ᾽ οὐδενὸς ἀνακρίνεται.
BY   NO ONE   IS DISCERNED.

2:9 Isa. 64:4

---

of this age understood this;
for if they had, they would
not have crucified the Lord
of glory. [9]But, as it is
written,

"What no eye has seen,
    nor ear heard,
    nor the human heart
        conceived,
    what God has prepared
        for those who love
        him"—

[10]these things God has
revealed to us through the
Spirit; for the Spirit searches
everything, even the depths
of God. [11]For what human
being knows what is truly
human except the human
spirit that is within? So also
no one comprehends what is
truly God's except the Spirit
of God. [12]Now we have
received not the spirit of the
world, but the Spirit that is
from God, so that we may
understand the gifts
bestowed on us by God.
[13]And we speak of these
things in words not taught by
human wisdom but taught
by the Spirit, interpreting
spiritual things to those who
are spiritual.[n]

14 Those who are
unspiritual[o] do not receive
the gifts of God's Spirit, for
they are foolishness to them,
and they are unable to understand them because they
are spiritually discerned.
[15]Those who are spiritual
discern all things, and they
are themselves subject to no
one else's scrutiny.

[n] Or interpreting spiritual things in
     spiritual language, or comparing
     spiritual things with spiritual
[o] Or natural

16 "For who has known the mind of the Lord so as to instruct him?" But we have the mind of Christ.

2.16 τίς γὰρ ἔγνω νοῦν κυρίου,
FOR~WHO KNEW [THE] MIND OF [THE] LORD,

ὃς συμβιβάσει αὐτόν;
WHO WILL INSTRUCT HIM?

ἡμεῖς δὲ νοῦν Χριστοῦ ἔχομεν.
BUT~WE [THE] MIND OF CHRIST HAVE.

2:16 Isa. 40:13 LXX

CHAPTER 3

And so, brothers and sisters,ᵖ I could not speak to you as spiritual people, but rather as people of the flesh, as infants in Christ. ²I fed you with milk, not solid food, for you were not ready for solid food. Even now you are still not ready, ³for you are still of the flesh. For as long as there is jealousy and quarreling among you, are you not of the flesh, and behaving according to human inclinations? ⁴For when one says, "I belong to Paul," and another, "I belong to Apollos," are you not merely human?

5 What then is Apollos? What is Paul? Servants through whom you came to believe, as the Lord assigned to each. ⁶I planted, Apollos watered, but God gave the growth. ⁷So neither the one who plants nor the one who waters is anything, but only God who gives the growth. ⁸The one who plants and the one who waters have a common purpose, and each will receive wages according to the labor of each. ⁹For we are God's servants, working together; you are God's field, God's building.

10 According to the grace of God given to me, like a skilled master builder I laid a foundation, and someone

ᵖ Gk brothers

3.1 Κἀγώ, ἀδελφοί, οὐκ ἠδυνήθην λαλῆσαι ὑμῖν ὡς
AND I, BROTHERS, WAS NOT ABLE TO SPEAK TO YOU° AS

πνευματικοῖς ἀλλ᾽ ὡς σαρκίνοις, ὡς νηπίοις ἐν
TO SPIRITUAL MEN BUT AS TO CARNAL MEN, AS TO INFANTS IN

Χριστῷ. **3.2** γάλα ὑμᾶς ἐπότισα, οὐ βρῶμα· οὔπω γὰρ
CHRIST. MILK I GAVE YOU° TO DRINK, NOT SOLID FOOD, ²NOT YET ¹FOR

ἐδύνασθε. ἀλλ᾽ οὐδὲ ἔτι νῦν δύνασθε,
³YOU° WERE ABLE [TO RECEIVE IT]. BUT NEITHER YET NOW ARE YOU° ABLE,

3.3 ἔτι γὰρ σαρκικοί ἐστε. ὅπου γὰρ ἐν ὑμῖν
FOR~STILL CARNAL YOU° ARE. FOR~SINCE AMONG YOU°

ζῆλος καὶ ἔρις, οὐχὶ σαρκικοί ἐστε καὶ
[THERE IS] JEALOUSY AND STRIFE, ²NOT ³CARNAL ¹ARE YOU° AND

κατὰ ἄνθρωπον περιπατεῖτε; **3.4** ὅταν γὰρ λέγῃ
ACCORDING TO A HUMAN [STANDARD] WALK? FOR~WHENEVER SAYS

τις, Ἐγὼ μέν εἰμι Παύλου, ἕτερος δέ, Ἐγὼ Ἀπολλῶ,
ANYONE, I - AM OF PAUL, BUT~ANOTHER, I OF APOLLOS,

οὐκ ἄνθρωποί ἐστε; **3.5** τί οὖν ἐστιν Ἀπολλῶς; τί
²NOT ³MEN ¹ARE YOU°? WHAT THEN IS APOLLOS? AND

δέ ἐστιν Παῦλος; διάκονοι δι᾽ ὧν ἐπιστεύσατε,
WHAT IS PAUL? MINISTERS THROUGH WHOM YOU° BELIEVED,

καὶ ἑκάστῳ ὡς ὁ κύριος ἔδωκεν. **3.6** ἐγὼ ἐφύτευσα,
EVEN AS~TO EACH ONE THE LORD GAVE. I PLANTED,

Ἀπολλῶς ἐπότισεν, ἀλλὰ ὁ θεὸς ηὔξανεν· **3.7** ὥστε
APOLLOS WATERED, BUT - GOD WAS GIVING GROWTH; SO THAT

οὔτε ὁ φυτεύων ἐστίν τι οὔτε ὁ ποτίζων
NEITHER THE ONE PLANTING IS ANYTHING NOR THE ONE WATERING

ἀλλ᾽ ὁ αὐξάνων θεός. **3.8** ὁ φυτεύων δὲ καὶ
BUT THE ONE GIVING GROWTH, GOD. ²THE ONE ³PLANTING ¹NOW AND

ὁ ποτίζων ἕν εἰσιν, ἕκαστος δὲ τὸν ἴδιον μισθὸν
THE ONE WATERING ARE~ONE, AND~EACH ONE THE(HIS) OWN REWARD

λήμψεται κατὰ τὸν ἴδιον κόπον· **3.9** θεοῦ γάρ
WILL RECEIVE ACCORDING TO HIS OWN LABOR; FOR~OF GOD

ἐσμεν συνεργοί, θεοῦ γεώργιον, θεοῦ οἰκοδομή ἐστε.
WE ARE CO-WORKERS, GOD'S FARM, GOD'S BUILDING YOU° ARE.

3.10 Κατὰ τὴν χάριν τοῦ θεοῦ τὴν δοθεῖσάν μοι
ACCORDING TO THE GRACE - OF GOD - HAVING BEEN GIVEN TO ME

ὡς σοφὸς ἀρχιτέκτων θεμέλιον ἔθηκα, ἄλλος δὲ
AS A WISE BUILDER, A FOUNDATION I LAID, AND~ANOTHER

ἐποικοδομεῖ. ἕκαστος δὲ βλεπέτω πῶς ἐποικοδομεῖ.
BUILDS ON [IT].   BUT~EACH ONE   LET HIM BEWARE HOW HE BUILDS ON [IT].

3.11 θεμέλιον γὰρ ἄλλον οὐδεὶς δύναται θεῖναι παρὰ
³FOUNDATION   ¹FOR ²OTHER NO ONE IS ABLE TO LAY BESIDE

τὸν κείμενον, ὅς ἐστιν Ἰησοῦς Χριστός. **3.12** εἰ δέ
THE ONE BEING LAID, WHO IS JESUS CHRIST, BUT~IF

τις ἐποικοδομεῖ ἐπὶ τὸν θεμέλιον χρυσόν, ἄργυρον,
ANYONE BUILDS ON THE FOUNDATION GOLD, SILVER,

λίθους τιμίους, ξύλα, χόρτον, καλάμην, **3.13** ἑκάστου τὸ
PRECIOUS~STONES, WOOD, HAY, STUBBLE, OF EACH ONE THE

ἔργον φανερὸν γενήσεται, ἡ γὰρ ἡμέρα δηλώσει,
WORK WILL BECOME~MANIFEST, FOR~THE DAY WILL MAKE [IT] CLEAR,

ὅτι ἐν πυρὶ ἀποκαλύπτεται· καὶ ἑκάστου τὸ ἔργον
BECAUSE BY FIRE IT IS REVEALED; AND OF EACH ONE THE WORK

ὁποῖόν ἐστιν τὸ πῦρ [αὐτὸ] δοκιμάσει. **3.14** εἴ τινος
OF WHAT KIND IT IS THE FIRE ITSELF WILL TEST. IF ANYONE'S

τὸ ἔργον μενεῖ ὃ ἐποικοδόμησεν, μισθὸν λήμψεται·
- WORK WILL REMAIN WHICH HE BUILT ON [IT], A REWARD HE WILL RECEIVE;

3.15 εἴ τινος τὸ ἔργον κατακαήσεται, ζημιωθήσεται,
IF ANYONE'S - WORK WILL BE CONSUMED, HE WILL SUFFER LOSS,

αὐτὸς δὲ σωθήσεται, οὕτως δὲ ὡς διὰ πυρός.
³HIMSELF ¹BUT ²WILL BE SAVED, YET~SO AS THROUGH FIRE.

3.16 οὐκ οἴδατε ὅτι ναὸς θεοῦ ἐστε καὶ τὸ
DO YOU° NOT KNOW THAT A SANCTUARY OF GOD YOU° ARE AND THE

πνεῦμα τοῦ θεοῦ οἰκεῖ ἐν ὑμῖν; **3.17** εἴ τις τὸν
SPIRIT - OF GOD DWELLS IN YOU°? IF ANYONE THE

ναὸν τοῦ θεοῦ φθείρει, φθερεῖ τοῦτον ὁ θεός·
SANCTUARY - OF GOD ATTEMPTS TO DESTROY, ²WILL DESTROY ³THIS MAN - ¹GOD;

ὁ γὰρ ναὸς τοῦ θεοῦ ἅγιός ἐστιν, οἵτινές ἐστε
FOR~THE SANCTUARY - OF GOD HOLY IS, WHO(WHICH) ARE

ὑμεῖς.
YOU°.

3.18 Μηδεὶς ἑαυτὸν ἐξαπατάτω· εἴ τις δοκεῖ
NO ONE HIMSELF LET DECEIVE; IF ANYONE SUPPOSES

σοφὸς εἶναι ἐν ὑμῖν ἐν τῷ αἰῶνι τούτῳ, μωρὸς
TO BE~WISE AMONG YOU° IN - THIS~AGE, FOOLISH

γενέσθω, ἵνα γένηται σοφός. **3.19** ἡ γὰρ σοφία τοῦ
LET HIM BECOME, THAT HE MAY BECOME WISE. FOR~THE WISDOM -

κόσμου τούτου μωρία παρὰ τῷ θεῷ ἐστιν.
OF THIS~WORLD ²FOOLISHNESS ³WITH - ⁴GOD ¹IS.

γέγραπται γάρ,
FOR~IT HAS BEEN WRITTEN,

Ὁ δρασσόμενος τοὺς σοφοὺς ἐν τῇ
[HE IS] THE ONE CATCHING THE WISE IN THE

πανουργίᾳ αὐτῶν·
CRAFTINESS OF THEM.

else is building on it. Each builder must choose with care how to build on it. [11]For no one can lay any foundation other than the one that has been laid; that foundation is Jesus Christ. [12]Now if anyone builds on the foundation with gold, silver, precious stones, wood, hay, straw— [13]the work of each builder will become visible, for the Day will disclose it, because it will be revealed with fire, and the fire will test what sort of work each has done. [14]If what has been built on the foundation survives, the builder will receive a reward. [15]If the work is burned up, the builder will suffer loss; the builder will be saved, but only as through fire.

16 Do you not know that you are God's temple and that God's Spirit dwells in you?[q] [17]If anyone destroys God's temple, God will destroy that person. For God's temple is holy, and you are that temple.

18 Do not deceive yourselves. If you think that you are wise in this age, you should become fools so that you may become wise. [19]For the wisdom of this world is foolishness with God. For it is written,

"He catches the wise in
their craftiness,"

[q] In verses 16 and 17 the Greek word for *you* is plural

²⁰and again,
    "The Lord knows the
        thoughts of the
        wise,
    that they are futile."
²¹So let no one boast about
human leaders. For all
things are yours, ²²whether
Paul or Apollos or Cephas or
the world or life or death or
the present or the future—
all belong to you, ²³and you
belong to Christ, and Christ
belongs to God.

3.20 καὶ πάλιν,
AND   AGAIN,

Κύριος γινώσκει τοὺς διαλογισμοὺς τῶν σοφῶν
[THE] LORD KNOWS   THE   REASONINGS   OF THE WISE

ὅτι εἰσὶν μάταιοι.
THAT THEY ARE VAIN.

3.21 ὥστε μηδεὶς καυχάσθω ἐν ἀνθρώποις· πάντα γὰρ
SO   LET NO ONE BOAST   IN   MEN;   FOR~ALL THINGS

ὑμῶν ἐστιν, **3.22** εἴτε   Παῦλος εἴτε Ἀπολλῶς εἴτε
YOURS° ARE,   WHETHER PAUL   OR   APOLLOS   OR

Κηφᾶς, εἴτε κόσμος εἴτε ζωὴ εἴτε θάνατος, εἴτε
CEPHAS,   OR [THE] WORLD OR LIFE OR DEATH,   OR

ἐνεστῶτα εἴτε μέλλοντα· πάντα ὑμῶν,
THINGS PRESENT OR THINGS COMING;   ALL THINGS [ARE] YOURS°,

3.23 ὑμεῖς δὲ   Χριστοῦ, Χριστὸς δὲ θεοῦ.
AND~YOU°   [ARE] CHRIST'S, AND~CHRIST   [IS] GOD'S.

3:20 Ps. 94:11

CHAPTER 4

Think of us in this way, as
servants of Christ and
stewards of God's mys-
teries. ²Moreover, it is
required of stewards that
they be found trustworthy.
³But with me it is a very
small thing that I should be
judged by you or by any
human court. I do not even
judge myself. ⁴I am not
aware of anything against
myself, but I am not thereby
acquitted. It is the Lord who
judges me. ⁵Therefore do
not pronounce judgment
before the time, before the
Lord comes, who will bring
to light the things now
hidden in darkness and will
disclose the purposes of the
heart. Then each one will
receive commendation from
God.

6 I have applied all this to
Apollos and myself for your
benefit, brothers and sisters,ʳ

ʳ Gk *brothers*

4.1 Οὕτως ἡμᾶς λογιζέσθω ἄνθρωπος ὡς ὑπηρέτας
SO   ⁴US   ¹LET ³ACCOUNT ²A MAN   AS   ATTENDANTS

Χριστοῦ καὶ οἰκονόμους μυστηρίων θεοῦ. **4.2** ὧδε λοιπὸν
OF CHRIST AND STEWARDS OF MYSTERIES OF GOD.   FURTHERMORE,

ζητεῖται ἐν τοῖς οἰκονόμοις, ἵνα πιστός τις εὑρεθῇ.
IT IS SOUGHT IN   -   STEWARDS   THAT ³FAITHFUL ¹ONE ²BE FOUND.

4.3 ἐμοὶ δὲ εἰς ἐλάχιστόν   ἐστιν, ἵνα ὑφ' ὑμῶν
³ME   ¹BUT ²TO ⁵A VERY SMALL THING ⁴IT IS   THAT BY   YOU°

ἀνακριθῶ ἢ ὑπὸ ἀνθρωπίνης ἡμέρας·   ἀλλ' οὐδὲ
I AM JUDGED OR BY   A HUMAN   DAY [OF JUDGMENT]; BUT   NOT

ἐμαυτὸν ἀνακρίνω. **4.4** οὐδὲν   γὰρ ἐμαυτῷ
MYSELF   I JUDGE.   ³[OF] NOTHING ¹FOR ⁴AGAINST MYSELF

σύνοιδα,   ἀλλ' οὐκ ἐν τούτῳ δεδικαίωμαι, ὁ δὲ
²I AM CONSCIOUS, BUT   NOT IN THIS   HAVE I BEEN JUSTIFIED, BUT~THE ONE

ἀνακρίνων με κύριός ἐστιν. **4.5** ὥστε μὴ πρὸ καιροῦ
JUDGING   ME IS~LORD.   SO AS NOT BEFORE [THE] TIME

τι   κρίνετε ἕως ἂν ἔλθῃ ὁ κύριος, ὃς καὶ
ANYTHING JUDGE   UNTIL COMES THE LORD,   WHO BOTH

φωτίσει   τὰ κρυπτὰ   τοῦ σκότους καὶ φανερώσει
WILL BRING TO LIGHT THE HIDDEN THINGS OF THE DARKNESS AND   MANIFEST

τὰς βουλὰς τῶν καρδιῶν· καὶ τότε ὁ ἔπαινος
THE   MOTIVES OF THE HEARTS;   AND THEN THE PRAISE

γενήσεται ἑκάστῳ ἀπὸ τοῦ θεοῦ.
WILL BE   TO EACH ONE FROM   -   GOD.

4.6 Ταῦτα δέ,   ἀδελφοί, μετεσχημάτισα
NOW~THESE THINGS, BROTHERS,   I MADE INTO A FIGURE [OF SPEECH]

εἰς   ἐμαυτὸν καὶ Ἀπολλῶν δι' ὑμᾶς, ἵνα
WITH RESPECT TO MYSELF   AND   APOLLOS   FOR YOU°,   THAT

ἐν	ἡμῖν	μάθητε	τὸ	Μὴ	ὑπὲρ	ἃ
BY(THROUGH)	US	YOU° MAY LEARN	-	NOT	[TO GO] BEYOND	WHAT THINGS

γέγραπται,	ἵνα	μὴ	εἷς	ὑπὲρ	τοῦ	ἑνὸς	φυσιοῦσθε
HAVE BEEN WRITTEN,	LEST		²ONE	³FOR	⁴THE	⁵ONE	¹YOU° ARE PUFFED UP

κατὰ	τοῦ	ἑτέρου.	**4.7** τίς γὰρ	σε	διακρίνει;	τί	δὲ
AGAINST	THE	OTHER.	FOR~WHO		DISTINGUISHES~YOU?	AND~WHAT

ἔχεις	ὃ	οὐκ ἔλαβες;	εἰ δὲ	καὶ	ἔλαβες,
DO YOU° HAVE	WHICH	YOU° DID NOT RECEIVE?	AND~IF	INDEED	YOU° RECEIVED [IT],

τί	καυχᾶσαι	ὡς	μὴ	λαβών;	**4.8** ἤδη
WHY	DO YOU° BOAST	AS	NOT	HAVING RECEIVED [IT]?	ALREADY

κεκορεσμένοι ἐστέ,	ἤδη	ἐπλουτήσατε,	χωρὶς	ἡμῶν
YOU° HAVE BEEN SATIATED,	ALREADY	YOU° BECAME RICH,	WITHOUT	US

ἐβασιλεύσατε·	καὶ	ὄφελόν	γε	ἐβασιλεύσατε,	ἵνα
YOU° BECAME KINGS;	AND	I WOULD [THAT]	REALLY	YOU° BECAME KINGS	THAT

καὶ	ἡμεῖς	ὑμῖν	συμβασιλεύσωμεν.	**4.9** δοκῶ γάρ, ὁ
ALSO	WE		MIGHT BECOME KINGS WITH~YOU°.	FOR~I THINK -

θεὸς	ἡμᾶς	τοὺς	ἀποστόλους	ἐσχάτους	ἀπέδειξεν	ὡς
GOD	²US	³THE	⁴APOSTLES	⁵LAST	¹SHOWED FORTH	AS

ἐπιθανατίους,	ὅτι	θέατρον	ἐγενήθημεν	τῷ	κόσμῳ
CONDEMNED TO DEATH,	BECAUSE	A SPECTACLE	WE BECAME	TO THE	WORLD

καὶ	ἀγγέλοις	καὶ	ἀνθρώποις.	**4.10** ἡμεῖς	μωροὶ	διὰ
BOTH	TO ANGELS	AND	TO MEN.	WE [ARE]	FOOLS	BECAUSE OF

Χριστόν,	ὑμεῖς δὲ	φρόνιμοι	ἐν	Χριστῷ·	ἡμεῖς
CHRIST,	BUT~YOU° ARE	WISE	IN	CHRIST;	WE

ἀσθενεῖς,	ὑμεῖς δὲ	ἰσχυροί·	ὑμεῖς	ἔνδοξοι,	ἡμεῖς δὲ
[ARE] WEAK,	BUT~YOU°	STRONG;	YOU°	[ARE] HONORABLE,	BUT~WE

ἄτιμοι.	**4.11** ἄχρι	τῆς	ἄρτι	ὥρας καὶ	πεινῶμεν	καὶ
DISHONORABLE.	UNTIL	THE	PRESENT	HOUR ²BOTH	¹WE ³HUNGER	AND

διψῶμεν καὶ	γυμνιτεύομεν	καὶ	κολαφιζόμεθα	καὶ
THIRST AND	ARE NAKED	AND	ARE BEATEN	AND

ἀστατοῦμεν	**4.12** καὶ	κοπιῶμεν	ἐργαζόμενοι	ταῖς	ἰδίαις
ARE UNSETTLED	AND	WE LABOR	WORKING [WITH]	THE(OUR)	OWN

χερσίν·	λοιδορούμενοι	εὐλογοῦμεν,	διωκόμενοι
HANDS;	BEING REVILED	WE BLESS,	BEING PERSECUTED

ἀνεχόμεθα,	**4.13** δυσφημούμενοι	παρακαλοῦμεν·	ὡς
WE BEAR [IT],	BEING DEFAMED	WE IMPLORE;	AS

περικαθάρματα	τοῦ	κόσμου	ἐγενήθημεν,
OFFSCOURINGS	OF THE	WORLD	WE BECAME,

πάντων	περίψημα	ἕως	ἄρτι.
[THE] REFUSE~OF ALL THINGS		UNTIL	NOW.

4.14 Οὐκ	ἐντρέπων	ὑμᾶς	γράφω	ταῦτα	ἀλλ᾽	ὡς
NOT	SHAMING	YOU°	I WRITE	THESE THINGS	BUT	AS

τέκνα	μου	ἀγαπητὰ	νουθετῶ[ν].	**4.15** ἐὰν γὰρ	μυρίους
³CHILDREN	⁴OF ME	²BELOVED	¹ADMONISHING.	FOR~THOUGH	TEN THOUSAND

παιδαγωγοὺς	ἔχητε	ἐν	Χριστῷ	ἀλλ᾽	οὐ	πολλοὺς
GUIDES	YOU° HAVE	IN	CHRIST	BUT	NOT	MANY

πατέρας·	ἐν γὰρ	Χριστῷ	Ἰησοῦ	διὰ	τοῦ	εὐαγγελίου
FATHERS;	FOR~IN	CHRIST	JESUS	THROUGH	THE	GOOD NEWS

so that you may learn through us the meaning of the saying, "Nothing beyond what is written," so that none of you will be puffed up in favor of one against another. [7]For who sees anything different in you?[5] What do you have that you did not receive? And if you received it, why do you boast as if it were not a gift?

8 Already you have all you want! Already you have become rich! Quite apart from us you have become kings! Indeed, I wish that you had become kings, so that we might be kings with you! [9]For I think that God has exhibited us apostles as last of all, as though sentenced to death, because we have become a spectacle to the world, to angels and to mortals. [10]We are fools for the sake of Christ, but you are wise in Christ. We are weak, but you are strong. You are held in honor, but we in disrepute. [11]To the present hour we are hungry and thirsty, we are poorly clothed and beaten and homeless, [12]and we grow weary from the work of our own hands. When reviled, we bless; when persecuted, we endure; [13]when slandered, we speak kindly. We have become like the rubbish of the world, the dregs of all things, to this very day.

14 I am not writing this to make you ashamed, but to admonish you as my beloved children. [15]For though you might have ten thousand guardians in Christ, you do not have many fathers. Indeed, in Christ Jesus

[5] Or *Who makes you different from another?*

I became your father through the gospel. ¹⁶I appeal to you, then, be imitators of me. ¹⁷For this reason I sent* you Timothy, who is my beloved and faithful child in the Lord, to remind you of my ways in Christ Jesus, as I teach them everywhere in every church. ¹⁸But some of you, thinking that I am not coming to you, have become arrogant. ¹⁹But I will come to you soon, if the Lord wills, and I will find out not the talk of these arrogant people but their power. ²⁰For the kingdom of God depends not on talk but on power. ²¹What would you prefer? Am I to come to you with a stick, or with love in a spirit of gentleness?

Or am sending

ἐγὼ ὑμᾶς ἐγέννησα. **4.16** παρακαλῶ οὖν ὑμᾶς, μιμηταί
I   BEGOT~YOU°.   THEREFORE~I ENCOURAGE YOU°,   IMITATORS

μου γίνεσθε. **4.17** διὰ   τοῦτο ἔπεμψα ὑμῖν
OF ME BECOME.   BECAUSE OF THIS   I SENT   TO YOU°

Τιμόθεον, ὅς ἐστίν μου τέκνον ἀγαπητὸν καὶ
TIMOTHY,   WHO IS   MY CHILD BELOVED   AND

πιστὸν ἐν κυρίῳ, ὃς ὑμᾶς ἀναμνήσει τὰς   ὁδούς
TRUSTWORTHY IN [THE] LORD, WHO WILL REMIND~YOU° [OF] THE WAYS

μου τὰς ἐν Χριστῷ ['Ἰησοῦ], καθὼς πανταχοῦ ἐν πάσῃ
OF ME -   IN CHRIST   JESUS,   EVEN AS EVERYWHERE IN EVERY

ἐκκλησίᾳ διδάσκω. **4.18** ὡς μὴ ἐρχομένου δέ μου
CHURCH   I TEACH.   ²AS TO ⁴NOT ⁵COMING   ¹NOW ³MY

πρὸς ὑμᾶς ἐφυσιώθησάν τινες· **4.19** ἐλεύσομαι δὲ
TO   YOU° SOME~WERE PUFFED UP;   BUT~I WILL COME

ταχέως πρὸς ὑμᾶς ἐὰν ὁ κύριος θελήσῃ, καὶ γνώσομαι
SHORTLY TO   YOU°, IF THE LORD   WILLS,   AND I WILL FIND OUT

οὐ τὸν λόγον τῶν   πεφυσιωμένων ἀλλὰ τὴν
NOT THE SPEECH OF THE ONES HAVING BEEN PUFFED UP BUT   THE

δύναμιν· **4.20** οὐ γὰρ ἐν λόγῳ ἡ   βασιλεία τοῦ θεοῦ
POWER;   FOR~NOT IN SPEECH [IS] THE KINGDOM   -   OF GOD

ἀλλ' ἐν δυνάμει. **4.21** τί θέλετε;   ἐν ῥάβδῳ
BUT   IN POWER.   WHAT DO YOU° WANT? WITH A ROD

ἔλθω   πρὸς ὑμᾶς ἢ ἐν ἀγάπῃ πνεύματί τε
SHOULD I COME TO   YOU° OR IN LOVE   AND~A SPIRIT

πραΰτητος;
OF MEEKNESS?

CHAPTER 5

It is actually reported that there is sexual immorality among you, and of a kind that is not found even among pagans; for a man is living with his father's wife. ²And you are arrogant! Should you not rather have mourned, so that he who has done this would have been removed from among you?

3 For though absent in body, I am present in spirit; and as if present I have already pronounced judgment ⁴in the name of the Lord Jesus on the man who has done such a thing.ᵘ When you are assembled,

ᵘ Or *on the man who has done such a thing in the name of the Lord Jesus*

5.1 Ὅλως ἀκούεται ἐν   ὑμῖν πορνεία, καὶ τοιαύτη
ACTUALLY ²IS REPORTED ³AMONG ⁴YOU° ¹FORNICATION, AND SUCH

πορνεία ἥτις οὐδὲ ἐν τοῖς ἔθνεσιν, ὥστε γυναῖκά
FORNICATION WHICH [IS] NOT EVEN AMONG THE GENTILES, SO THAT ³WIFE

τινα τοῦ πατρὸς ἔχειν. **5.2** καὶ ὑμεῖς
¹ONE ⁴OF THE ⁵FATHER ²TO HAVE.   AND YOU°

πεφυσιωμένοι ἐστὲ καὶ οὐχὶ μᾶλλον ἐπενθήσατε, ἵνα
HAVE BEEN PUFFED UP AND NOT RATHER   GRIEVED,   THAT

ἀρθῇ   ἐκ μέσου ὑμῶν ὁ   τὸ ἔργον τοῦτο
SHOULD BE TAKEN FROM [THE] MIDST OF YOU° THE ONE - THIS~DEED

πράξας; **5.3** ἐγὼ μὲν γάρ, ἀπὼν   τῷ   σώματι
HAVING DONE?   ³I ²INDEED ¹FOR, BEING ABSENT IN THE(MY) BODY

παρὼν δὲ   τῷ   πνεύματι, ἤδη κέκρικα ὡς
BUT~BEING PRESENT IN THE(MY) SPIRIT, ALREADY HAVE I JUDGED, AS

παρὼν   τὸν οὕτως τοῦτο κατεργασάμενον· **5.4** ἐν τῷ
BEING PRESENT, THE ONE SO   HAVING DONE~THIS THING.   IN THE

ὀνόματι τοῦ κυρίου [ἡμῶν] 'Ἰησοῦ συναχθέντων
NAME   OF THE LORD OF US   JESUS HAVING BEEN GATHERED TOGETHER

ὑμῶν καὶ τοῦ ἐμοῦ πνεύματος σὺν τῇ δυνάμει τοῦ
YOU° AND - MY SPIRIT WITH THE POWER OF THE

κυρίου ἡμῶν Ἰησοῦ, **5.5** παραδοῦναι τὸν τοιοῦτον τῷ
LORD OF US JESUS, TO HAND OVER SUCH A PERSON -

Σατανᾷ εἰς ὄλεθρον τῆς σαρκός, ἵνα τὸ πνεῦμα
TO SATAN FOR DESTRUCTION OF THE FLESH, THAT THE(HIS) SPIRIT

σωθῇ ἐν τῇ ἡμέρᾳ τοῦ κυρίουᵀ. **5.6** Οὐ καλὸν τὸ
MAY BE SAVED IN THE DAY OF THE LORD. NOT GOOD [IS] THE

καύχημα ὑμῶν. οὐκ οἴδατε ὅτι μικρὰ ζύμη ὅλον τὸ
BOAST OF YOU°. DO YOU° NOT KNOW THAT A LITTLE LEAVEN ALL THE

φύραμα ζυμοῖ; **5.7** ἐκκαθάρατε τὴν παλαιὰν ζύμην, ἵνα
MIXTURE LEAVENS? PURGE OUT THE OLD LEAVEN, THAT

ἦτε νέον φύραμα, καθώς ἐστε ἄζυμοι·
YOU° MAY BE A NEW MIXTURE, AS YOU° ARE [REALLY] UNLEAVENED;

καὶ γὰρ τὸ πάσχα ἡμῶν ἐτύθη Χριστός.
FOR~INDEED THE PASSOVER [LAMB] OF US WAS SACRIFICED, CHRIST.

5.8 ὥστε ἑορτάζωμεν μὴ ἐν ζύμῃ παλαιᾷ μηδὲ ἐν
SO LET US KEEP THE FEAST NOT WITH OLD~LEAVEN NOR WITH

ζύμῃ κακίας καὶ πονηρίας ἀλλ᾽ ἐν ἀζύμοις
LEAVEN OF MALICE AND EVIL BUT WITH UNLEAVENED [BREAD]

εἰλικρινείας καὶ ἀληθείας.
OF PURITY AND TRUTH.

5.9 Ἔγραψα ὑμῖν ἐν τῇ ἐπιστολῇ μὴ
I WROTE TO YOU° IN THE EPISTLE NOT

συναναμίγνυσθαι πόρνοις, **5.10** οὐ
TO MIX WITH FORNICATORS, NOT [MEANING]

πάντως τοῖς πόρνοις τοῦ κόσμου τούτου ἢ
COMPLETE [DISSOCIATION FROM] THE FORNICATORS OF THIS~WORLD OR

τοῖς πλεονέκταις καὶ ἅρπαξιν ἢ εἰδωλολάτραις, ἐπεὶ
THE GREEDY AND SWINDLERS OR IDOLATERS, SINCE

ὠφείλετε ἄρα ἐκ τοῦ κόσμου ἐξελθεῖν. **5.11** νῦν δὲ
¹YOU° WOULD HAVE ³THEN ⁴FROM ⁵THE ⁶WORLD ²TO GO OUT. BUT~NOW

ἔγραψα ὑμῖν μὴ συναναμίγνυσθαι ἐάν τις ἀδελφὸς
I WROTE TO YOU° NOT TO MIX WITH ³IF ¹ANY ²BROTHER

ὀνομαζόμενος ᾖ πόρνος ἢ πλεονέκτης ἢ εἰδωλολάτρης
HE IS BEING CALLED A FORNICATOR OR A GREEDY MAN OR AN IDOLATER

ἢ λοίδορος ἢ μέθυσος ἢ ἅρπαξ, τῷ τοιούτῳ μηδὲ
OR A REVILER OR A DRUNKARD OR A SWINDLER, WITH SUCH A MAN NOT

συνεσθίειν. **5.12** τί γὰρ μοι τοὺς ἔξω κρίνειν;
TO EAT. FOR~WHAT [IS IT] TO ME ²THE ONES ³OUTSIDE ¹TO JUDGE?

οὐχὶ τοὺς ἔσω ὑμεῖς κρίνετε; **5.13** τοὺς δὲ ἔξω ὁ
³NOT ⁴THE ONES ⁵WITHIN ²YOU° ¹JUDGE? BUT~THE ONES OUTSIDE -

θεὸς κρινεῖ. ἐξάρατε τὸν πονηρὸν ἐξ ὑμῶν αὐτῶν.
GOD JUDGES. REMOVE THE EVIL MAN FROM [AMONG] YOURSELVES.

and my spirit is present with the power of our Lord Jesus, [5]you are to hand this man over to Satan for the destruction of the flesh, so that his spirit may be saved in the day of the Lord.ᵛ

6 Your boasting is not a good thing. Do you not know that a little yeast leavens the whole batch of dough? [7]Clean out the old yeast so that you may be a new batch, as you really are unleavened. For our paschal lamb, Christ, has been sacrificed. [8]Therefore, let us celebrate the festival, not with the old yeast, the yeast of malice and evil, but with the unleavened bread of sincerity and truth.

9 I wrote to you in my letter not to associate with sexually immoral persons— [10]not at all meaning the immoral of this world, or the greedy and robbers, or idolaters, since you would then need to go out of the world. [11]But now I am writing to you not to associate with anyone who bears the name of brother or sisterʷ who is sexually immoral or greedy, or is an idolater, reviler, drunkard, or robber. Do not even eat with such a one. [12]For what have I to do with judging those outside? Is it not those who are inside that you are to judge? [13]God will judge those outside. "Drive out the wicked person from among you."

ᵛ Other ancient authorities add *Jesus*
ʷ Gk *brother*

5:5 text: ASVmg RSVmg NASBmg NIV NEB TEV NJB NRSV. add Iησου (Jesus): KJV ASV RSV NASB NRSVmg. **5:13** Deut. 17:7 LXX

CHAPTER 6

When any of you has a grievance against another, do you dare to take it to court before the unrighteous, instead of taking it before the saints? [2]Do you not know that the saints will judge the world? And if the world is to be judged by you, are you incompetent to try trivial cases? [3]Do you not know that we are to judge angels— to say nothing of ordinary matters? [4]If you have ordinary cases, then, do you appoint as judges those who have no standing in the church? [5]I say this to your shame. Can it be that there is no one among you wise enough to decide between one believer[x] and another, [6]but a believer[x] goes to court against a believer[x] —and before unbelievers at that?

7 In fact, to have lawsuits at all with one another is already a defeat for you. Why not rather be wronged? Why not rather be defrauded? [8]But you yourselves wrong and defraud—and believers[y] at that.

9 Do you not know that wrongdoers will not inherit the kingdom of God? Do not be deceived! Fornicators, idolators, adulterers, male prostitutes, sodomites, [10]thieves, the greedy, drunkards, revilers, robbers— none of these will inherit the kingdom of God. [11]And this is what some of you used to be. But you were washed, you were sanctified,

[x] Gk brother
[y] Gk brothers

6.1 Τολμᾷ τις ὑμῶν πρᾶγμα ἔχων πρὸς τὸν ἕτερον
DARES ANYONE OF YOU° HAVING~A DISPUTE WITH THE OTHER

κρίνεσθαι ἐπὶ τῶν ἀδίκων καὶ οὐχὶ ἐπὶ τῶν ἁγίων;
TO BE JUDGED BEFORE THE UNRIGHTEOUS AND NOT BEFORE THE SAINTS?

6.2 ἢ οὐκ οἴδατε ὅτι οἱ ἅγιοι τὸν κόσμον κρινοῦσιν;
OR DO YOU° NOT KNOW THAT THE SAINTS THE WORLD WILL JUDGE?

καὶ εἰ ἐν ὑμῖν κρίνεται ὁ κόσμος, ἀνάξιοί ἐστε
AND IF ⁴BY ⁵YOU° ³IS JUDGED ¹THE ²WORLD, ARE YOU°~INCOMPETENT

κριτηρίων ἐλαχίστων; **6.3** οὐκ οἴδατε ὅτι
JUDGES [OF THE] SMALLEST MATTERS? DO YOU° NOT KNOW THAT

ἀγγέλους κρινοῦμεν, μήτιγε βιωτικά;
ANGELS WE WILL JUDGE, NOT TO MENTION [THE] THINGS OF THIS LIFE?

6.4 βιωτικὰ μὲν οὖν κριτήρια ἐὰν ἔχητε,
⁵[CONCERNING] THINGS OF THIS LIFE - ²THEN ⁴A CASE ¹IF ³YOU° HAVE,

τοὺς ἐξουθενημένους ἐν τῇ ἐκκλησίᾳ, τούτους
- ³BEING LITTLE ESTEEMED ⁴BY ⁵THE ⁶CHURCH ²SUCH ONES

καθίζετε; **6.5** πρὸς ἐντροπὴν ὑμῖν λέγω.
¹[HOW] COULD YOU° APPOINT [AS JUDGES]? TO YOUR°~SHAME I SPEAK.

οὕτως οὐκ ἔνι ἐν ὑμῖν οὐδεὶς σοφός, ὃς δυνήσεται
THUS IS THERE NOT AMONG YOU° NOT EVEN ONE WISE MAN WHO WILL BE ABLE

διακρῖναι ἀνὰ μέσον τοῦ ἀδελφοῦ αὐτοῦ; **6.6** ἀλλὰ
TO MAKE JUDGMENT BETWEEN THE BROTHER[S] OF HIM? BUT

ἀδελφὸς μετὰ ἀδελφοῦ κρίνεται καὶ τοῦτο ἐπὶ
BROTHER WITH BROTHER IS JUDGED AND THIS BEFORE

ἀπίστων; **6.7** ἤδη μὲν [οὖν] ὅλως ἥττημα ὑμῖν
UNBELIEVERS? ALREADY - THEREFORE ²ALTOGETHER ³A DEFEAT ⁴FOR YOU°

ἐστιν ὅτι κρίματα ἔχετε μεθ᾽ ἑαυτῶν. διὰ τί οὐχὶ
¹IT IS THAT YOU° HAVE~LAWSUITS WITH ONE ANOTHER. WHY NOT

μᾶλλον ἀδικεῖσθε; διὰ τί οὐχὶ μᾶλλον ἀποστερεῖσθε;
RATHER BE WRONGED? WHY NOT RATHER BE CHEATED?

6.8 ἀλλὰ ὑμεῖς ἀδικεῖτε καὶ ἀποστερεῖτε, καὶ τοῦτο
BUT YOU° DO WRONG AND CHEAT, AND THIS

ἀδελφούς. **6.9** ἢ οὐκ οἴδατε ὅτι ἄδικοι
[TO YOUR°] BROTHERS. OR DO YOU° NOT KNOW THAT [THE] UNRIGHTEOUS ONES

θεοῦ βασιλείαν οὐ κληρονομήσουσιν; μὴ πλανᾶσθε·
²GOD'S ³KINGDOM ¹WILL NOT INHERIT? BE NOT.DECEIVED;

οὔτε πόρνοι οὔτε εἰδωλολάτραι οὔτε μοιχοὶ οὔτε
NEITHER FORNICATORS NOR IDOLATERS NOR ADULTERERS NOR

μαλακοὶ οὔτε ἀρσενοκοῖται **6.10** οὔτε κλέπται οὔτε
EFFEMINATE NOR HOMOSEXUALS NOR THIEVES NOR

πλεονέκται, οὐ μέθυσοι, οὐ λοίδοροι, οὐχ ἅρπαγες
GREEDY ONES NOR DRUNKARDS NOR REVILERS NOR SWINDLERS

βασιλείαν θεοῦ κληρονομήσουσιν. **6.11** καὶ ταῦτά
[THE] KINGDOM OF GOD WILL INHERIT. AND THESE THINGS

τινες ἦτε· ἀλλὰ ἀπελούσασθε, ἀλλὰ ἡγιάσθητε,
SOME [OF YOU°] WERE; BUT YOU° WERE WASHED, BUT YOU° WERE SANCTIFIED,

ἀλλὰ ἐδικαιώθητε ἐν τῷ ὀνόματι τοῦ κυρίου Ἰησοῦ
BUT YOU° WERE JUSTIFIED IN THE NAME OF THE LORD JESUS

Χριστοῦ καὶ ἐν τῷ πνεύματι τοῦ θεοῦ ἡμῶν.
CHRIST AND IN THE SPIRIT OF THE GOD OF US.

6.12 Πάντα μοι ἔξεστιν ἀλλ' οὐ πάντα συμφέρει·
ALL THINGS TO ME [ARE] LAWFUL BUT NOT ALL THINGS BENEFICIAL.

πάντα μοι ἔξεστιν ἀλλ' οὐκ ἐγὼ ἐξουσιασθήσομαι
ALL THINGS TO ME [ARE] LAWFUL BUT ³NOT ¹I ²WILL ⁴BE MASTERED

ὑπό τινος. **6.13** τὰ βρώματα τῇ κοιλίᾳ καὶ ἡ
BY ANYTHING. - FOODS FOR THE STOMACH AND THE

κοιλία τοῖς βρώμασιν, ὁ δὲ θεὸς καὶ ταύτην καὶ
STOMACH - FOR FOODS, - BUT GOD BOTH THIS AND

ταῦτα καταργήσει. τὸ δὲ σῶμα οὐ τῇ πορνείᾳ
THESE WILL DESTROY. BUT~THE BODY [IS] NOT - FOR FORNICATION

ἀλλὰ τῷ κυρίῳ, καὶ ὁ κύριος τῷ σώματι· **6.14** ὁ
BUT FOR THE LORD, AND THE LORD FOR THE BODY. -

δὲ θεὸς καὶ τὸν κύριον ἤγειρεν καὶ ἡμᾶς ἐξεγερεῖ
AND GOD BOTH THE LORD RAISED UP AND ALSO US WILL RAISE UP

διὰ τῆς δυνάμεως αὐτοῦ. **6.15** οὐκ οἴδατε ὅτι τὰ
THROUGH THE POWER OF HIM. DO YOU° NOT KNOW THAT THE

σώματα ὑμῶν μέλη Χριστοῦ ἐστιν; ἄρας οὖν τὰ
BODIES OF YOU° MEMBERS OF CHRIST ARE? HAVING TAKEN THEN THE

μέλη τοῦ Χριστοῦ ποιήσω πόρνης μέλη;
MEMBERS - OF CHRIST SHOULD I MAKE [THEM] MEMBERS~OF A PROSTITUTE?

μὴ γένοιτο. **6.16** [ἢ] οὐκ οἴδατε ὅτι ὁ κολλώμενος
MAY IT NEVER BE. OR DO YOU° NOT KNOW THAT THE ONE JOINING HIMSELF

τῇ πόρνῃ ἓν σῶμά ἐστιν; Ἔσονται γάρ, φησίν, οἱ
- TO A PROSTITUTE ONE BODY IS? ⁸WILL BE ¹FOR ²IT SAYS ³THE

δύο εἰς σάρκα μίαν. **6.17** ὁ δὲ κολλώμενος τῷ
⁴TWO ⁵INTO ⁷FLESH ⁶ONE. BUT~THE ONE JOINING HIMSELF TO THE

κυρίῳ ἓν πνεῦμά ἐστιν. **6.18** φεύγετε τὴν πορνείαν.
LORD ONE SPIRIT IS. FLEE - FORNICATION.

πᾶν ἁμάρτημα ὃ ἐὰν ποιήσῃ ἄνθρωπος ἐκτὸς τοῦ
EVERY SIN WHICHEVER A MAN~MAY DO, OUTSIDE THE

σώματός ἐστιν· ὁ δὲ πορνεύων εἰς τὸ ἴδιον σῶμα
BODY IS; BUT~THE ONE FORNICATING AGAINST THE(HIS) OWN BODY

ἁμαρτάνει. **6.19** ἢ οὐκ οἴδατε ὅτι τὸ σῶμα ὑμῶν
SINS. OR DO YOU° NOT KNOW THAT THE BODY OF YOU°

ναὸς τοῦ ἐν ὑμῖν ἁγίου πνεύματός ἐστιν οὗ
²A SANCTUARY ³OF THE ⁶IN ⁷YOU° ⁴HOLY ⁵SPIRIT ¹IS, WHOM

ἔχετε ἀπὸ θεοῦ, καὶ οὐκ ἐστὲ ἑαυτῶν;
YOU° HAVE FROM GOD, AND YOU° ARE~NOT YOUR° OWN?

6.20 ἠγοράσθητε γὰρ τιμῆς· δοξάσατε δὴ τὸν θεὸν ἐν
FOR~YOU° WERE BOUGHT WITH A PRICE; GLORIFY THEN - GOD IN

τῷ σώματι ὑμῶν.
THE BODY OF YOU°.

6:16 Gen. 2:24

you were justified in the name of the Lord Jesus Christ and in the Spirit of our God.

12 "All things are lawful for me," but not all things are beneficial. "All things are lawful for me," but I will not be dominated by anything. 13"Food is meant for the stomach and the stomach for food,"ᶻ and God will destroy both one and the other. The body is meant not for fornication but for the Lord, and the Lord for the body. 14And God raised the Lord and will also raise us by his power. 15Do you not know that your bodies are members of Christ? Should I therefore take the members of Christ and make them members of a prostitute? Never! 16Do you not know that whoever is united to a prostitute becomes one body with her? For it is said, "The two shall be one flesh." 17But anyone united to the Lord becomes one spirit with him. 18Shun fornication! Every sin that a person commits is outside the body; but the fornicator sins against the body itself. 19Or do you not know that your body is a templeᵃ of the Holy Spirit within you, which you have from God, and that you are not your own? 20For you were bought with a price; therefore glorify God in your body.

ᶻ The quotation may extend to the word *other*
ᵃ Or *sanctuary*

CHAPTER 7

Now concerning the matters about which you wrote: "It is well for a man not to touch a woman." ²But because of cases of sexual immorality, each man should have his own wife and each woman her own husband. ³The husband should give to his wife her conjugal rights, and likewise the wife to her husband. ⁴For the wife does not have authority over her own body, but the husband does; likewise the husband does not have authority over his own body, but the wife does. ⁵Do not deprive one another except perhaps by agreement for a set time, to devote yourselves to prayer, and then come together again, so that Satan may not tempt you because of your lack of self-control. ⁶This I say by way of concession, not of command. ⁷I wish that all were as I myself am. But each has a particular gift from God, one having one kind and another a different kind.

8 To the unmarried and the widows I say that it is well for them to remain unmarried as I am. ⁹But if they are not practicing self-control, they should marry. For it is better to marry than to be aflame with passion.

10 To the married I give this command—not I but the Lord—that the wife should not separate from her husband ¹¹(but if she does separate, let her remain unmarried or else be reconciled to her husband),

7.1 Περὶ δὲ ὧν ἐγράψατε, καλὸν ἀνθρώπῳ
NOW~CONCERNING THINGS OF WHICH YOU° WROTE, [IT IS] GOOD FOR A MAN

γυναικὸς μὴ ἅπτεσθαι· **7.2** διὰ δὲ τὰς πορνείας
³A WOMAN ¹NOT ²TO TOUCH; BUT~BECAUSE OF THE ACTS OF FORNICATION

ἕκαστος τὴν ἑαυτοῦ γυναῖκα ἐχέτω καὶ ἑκάστη
EACH MAN - ²HIS OWN ³WIFE ¹LET HIM HAVE AND EACH WOMAN

τὸν ἴδιον ἄνδρα ἐχέτω. **7.3** τῇ γυναικὶ ὁ ἀνὴρ
THE(HER) OWN HUSBAND LET HER HAVE. TO THE WIFE ²THE ³HUSBAND

τὴν ὀφειλὴν ἀποδιδότω, ὁμοίως δὲ καὶ ἡ γυνὴ τῷ
⁵THE ⁶DEBT ¹LET ⁴RENDER, AND~LIKEWISE ALSO THE WIFE TO THE

ἀνδρί. **7.4** ἡ γυνὴ τοῦ ἰδίου σώματος
HUSBAND. THE WIFE [OVER] THE(HER) OWN BODY

οὐκ ἐξουσιάζει ἀλλὰ ὁ ἀνήρ, ὁμοίως δὲ καὶ ὁ
DOES NOT HAVE AUTHORITY BUT THE HUSBAND, LIKEWISE - ALSO THE

ἀνὴρ τοῦ ἰδίου σώματος οὐκ ἐξουσιάζει ἀλλὰ ἡ
HUSBAND OF THE(HIS) OWN BODY DOES NOT HAVE AUTHORITY BUT THE

γυνή. **7.5** μὴ ἀποστερεῖτε ἀλλήλους, εἰ μήτι ἂν ἐκ
WIFE [DOES]. DO NOT DEPRIVE EACH OTHER, UNLESS BY

συμφώνου πρὸς καιρόν, ἵνα σχολάσητε τῇ
AGREEMENT FOR A TIME, THAT YOU° MAY DEVOTE [YOURSELVES] -

προσευχῇ καὶ πάλιν ἐπὶ τὸ αὐτὸ ἦτε, ἵνα μὴ
TO PRAYER AND ³AGAIN ²TOGETHER ¹YOU° MAY BE, LEST

πειράζῃ ὑμᾶς ὁ Σατανᾶς διὰ τὴν ἀκρασίαν
²TEMPT ³YOU° - ¹SATAN BECAUSE OF THE LACK OF SELF-CONTROL

ὑμῶν. **7.6** τοῦτο δὲ λέγω κατὰ συγγνώμην οὐ
OF YOU°. BUT~THIS I SAY ACCORDING TO CONCESSION, NOT

κατ' ἐπιταγήν. **7.7** θέλω δὲ πάντας ἀνθρώπους
ACCORDING TO COMMAND. BUT~I WISH ALL MEN

εἶναι ὡς καὶ ἐμαυτόν· ἀλλὰ ἕκαστος ἴδιον ἔχει
TO BE AS EVEN MYSELF; BUT EACH MAN HAS~HIS OWN

χάρισμα ἐκ θεοῦ, ὁ μὲν οὕτως, ὁ δὲ οὕτως.
GIFT FROM GOD, ONE - THIS, AND~ANOTHER THAT.

7.8 Λέγω δὲ τοῖς ἀγάμοις καὶ ταῖς χήραις, καλὸν
BUT~I SAY TO THE UNMARRIED MEN AND TO THE WIDOWS, [IT IS] GOOD

αὐτοῖς ἐὰν μείνωσιν ὡς κἀγώ· **7.9** εἰ δὲ
FOR THEM IF THEY REMAIN AS I ALSO; BUT~IF

οὐκ ἐγκρατεύονται, γαμησάτωσαν, κρεῖττον γάρ ἐστιν
THEY DO NOT HAVE SELF-CONTROL, LET THEM MARRY, FOR~BETTER IT IS

γαμῆσαι ἢ πυροῦσθαι. **7.10** τοῖς δὲ
TO MARRY THAN TO BE CONSUMED WITH PASSION. BUT~TO THE ONES

γεγαμηκόσιν παραγγέλλω, οὐκ ἐγὼ ἀλλὰ ὁ κύριος,
HAVING MARRIED I CHARGE, NOT I BUT THE LORD,

γυναῖκα ἀπὸ ἀνδρὸς μὴ χωρισθῆναι, **7.11** — ἐὰν δὲ
A WIFE FROM [HER] HUSBAND NOT TO BE SEPARATED — BUT~IF

καὶ χωρισθῇ, μενέτω ἄγαμος ἢ τῷ ἀνδρὶ
INDEED SHE IS SEPARATED, LET HER REMAIN UNMARRIED OR TO THE HUSBAND

καταλλαγήτω, — καὶ ἄνδρα γυναῖκα μὴ ἀφιέναι.
BE RECONCILED, — AND A HUSBAND [HIS] WIFE NOT TO LEAVE.

7.12 Τοῖς δὲ λοιποῖς λέγω ἐγώ οὐχ ὁ κύριος· εἴ τις
BUT~TO THE REST SAY I, NOT THE LORD: IF ANY

ἀδελφὸς γυναῖκα ἔχει ἄπιστον καὶ αὕτη συνευδοκεῖ
BROTHER ³WIFE ¹HAS ²AN UNBELIEVING AND SHE IS WILLING

οἰκεῖν μετ᾽ αὐτοῦ, μὴ ἀφιέτω αὐτήν· **7.13** καὶ γυνὴ εἴ
TO LIVE WITH HIM, LET HIM NOT LEAVE HER; AND IF~A WIFE

τις ἔχει ἄνδρα ἄπιστον καὶ οὗτος συνευδοκεῖ οἰκεῖν
- HAS AN UNBELIEVING~HUSBAND, AND THIS MAN IS WILLING TO DWELL

μετ᾽ αὐτῆς, μὴ ἀφιέτω τὸν ἄνδρα. **7.14** ἡγίασται
WITH HER, LET HER NOT LEAVE THE(HER) HUSBAND. ⁵HAS BEEN SANCTIFIED

γὰρ ὁ ἀνὴρ ὁ ἄπιστος ἐν τῇ γυναικὶ καὶ
¹FOR ²THE ⁴HUSBAND - ³UNBELIEVING BY THE WIFE AND

ἡγίασται ἡ γυνὴ ἡ ἄπιστος ἐν τῷ ἀδελφῷ·
⁴HAS BEEN SANCTIFIED ¹THE ³WIFE - ²UNBELIEVING BY THE BROTHER;

ἐπεὶ ἄρα τὰ τέκνα ὑμῶν ἀκάθαρτά ἐστιν, νῦν δὲ
OTHERWISE THE CHILDREN OF YOU° IMPURE ARE, BUT~NOW

ἅγιά ἐστιν. **7.15** εἰ δὲ ὁ ἄπιστος χωρίζεται,
THEY ARE~HOLY. BUT~IF THE UNBELIEVING ONE SEPARATES HIMSELF(HERSELF),

χωριζέσθω· οὐ δεδούλωται ὁ ἀδελφὸς ἢ ἡ
LET HIM(HER) SEPARATE; ⁶HAS NOT BEEN ENSLAVED ¹THE ²BROTHER ³OR ⁴THE

ἀδελφὴ ἐν τοῖς τοιούτοις· ἐν δὲ εἰρήνῃ κέκληκεν
⁵SISTER IN SUCH MATTERS; BUT~IN PEACE ²HAS CALLED

⌜ὑμᾶς⌝ ὁ θεός. **7.16** τί γὰρ οἶδας, γύναι, εἰ
³YOU° - ¹GOD. FOR~WHAT(HOW) DO YOU KNOW, WIFE, IF

τὸν ἄνδρα σώσεις; ἢ τί οἶδας, ἄνερ, εἰ
THE(YOUR) HUSBAND YOU WILL SAVE? OR WHAT(HOW) DO YOU KNOW, HUSBAND, IF

τὴν γυναῖκα σώσεις;
THE(YOUR) WIFE YOU WILL SAVE?

7.17 Εἰ μὴ ἑκάστῳ ὡς ἐμέρισεν ὁ κύριος, ἕκαστον
ONLY ⁵TO EACH ONE ¹AS ⁴ASSIGNED ²THE ³LORD, ⁴EACH ONE

ὡς κέκληκεν ὁ θεός, οὕτως περιπατείτω. καὶ οὕτως
¹AS ³HAS CALLED - ²GOD, SO LET HIM WALK. AND SO

ἐν ταῖς ἐκκλησίαις πάσαις διατάσσομαι.
IN ²THE ³CHURCHES ¹ALL I ORDER.

7.18 περιτετμημένος τις ἐκλήθη, μὴ ἐπισπάσθω·
[IF] HAVING BEEN CIRCUMCISED ANYONE WAS CALLED, LET HIM NOT CONCEAL [IT].

ἐν ἀκροβυστίᾳ κέκληταί τις, μὴ περιτεμνέσθω.
IN UNCIRCUMCISION HAS ANYONE BEEN CALLED; LET HIM NOT BE CIRCUMCISED.

7.19 ἡ περιτομὴ οὐδέν ἐστιν καὶ ἡ ἀκροβυστία οὐδέν
- CIRCUMCISION NOTHING IS AND - UNCIRCUMCISION NOTHING

ἐστιν, ἀλλὰ τήρησις ἐντολῶν θεοῦ. **7.20** ἕκαστος
IS, BUT KEEPING [THE] COMMANDMENTS OF GOD. EACH ONE

ἐν τῇ κλήσει ᾗ ἐκλήθη, ἐν ταύτῃ μενέτω.
IN THE CALLING IN WHICH HE WAS CALLED, IN THIS LET HIM REMAIN.

7:15 text: ASVmg NASBmg RSVmg TEV NJB NRSV. var. ημας (us) KJV ASV RSV NASB NIV NJBmg NRSVmg.

---

and that the husband should not divorce his wife.

12 To the rest I say—I and not the Lord—that if any believer[b] has a wife who is an unbeliever, and she consents to live with him, he should not divorce her. [13]And if any woman has a husband who is an unbeliever, and he consents to live with her, she should not divorce him. [14]For the unbelieving husband is made holy through his wife, and the unbelieving wife is made holy through her husband. Otherwise, your children would be unclean, but as it is, they are holy. [15]But if the unbelieving partner separates, let it be so; in such a case the brother or sister is not bound. It is to peace that God has called you.[c] [16]Wife, for all you know, you might save your husband. Husband, for all you know, you might save your wife.

17 However that may be, let each of you lead the life that the Lord has assigned, to which God called you. This is my rule in all the churches. [18]Was anyone at the time of his call already circumcised? Let him not seek to remove the marks of circumcision. Was anyone at the time of his call uncircumcised? Let him not seek circumcision. [19]Circumcision is nothing, and uncircumcision is nothing; but obeying the commandments of God is everything. [20]Let each of you remain in the condition in which you were called.

b Gk brother
c Other ancient authorities read us

21 Were you a slave when called? Do not be concerned about it. Even if you can gain your freedom, make use of your present condition now more than ever.*d* 22For whoever was called in the Lord as a slave is a freed person belonging to the Lord, just as whoever was free when called is a slave of Christ. 23You were bought with a price; do not become slaves of human masters. 24In whatever condition you were called, brothers and sisters,*e* there remain with God.

25 Now concerning virgins, I have no command of the Lord, but I give my opinion as one who by the Lord's mercy is trustworthy. 26I think that, in view of the impending*f* crisis, it is well for you to remain as you are. 27Are you bound to a wife? Do not seek to be free. Are you free from a wife? Do not seek a wife. 28But if you marry, you do not sin, and if a virgin marries, she does not sin. Yet those who marry will experience distress in this life,*g* and I would spare you that. 29I mean, brothers and sisters,*e* the appointed time has grown short; from now on, let even those who have wives be as though they had none, 30and those who mourn as though they were not mourning, and those who rejoice as though they were not rejoicing, and those who buy as though they had no possessions, 31and those who deal with the world as though they had no dealings with it.

d Or *avail yourself of the opportunity*
e Gk *brothers*
f Or *present*
g Gk *in the flesh*

7.21 δοῦλος ἐκλήθης, μή σοι μελέτω· ἀλλ᾽ εἰ
[WHILE] A SLAVE WERE YOU CALLED, NOT TO YOU LET IT MATTER; BUT IF

καὶ δύνασαι ἐλεύθερος γενέσθαι, μᾶλλον χρῆσαι.
INDEED YOU ARE ABLE TO BECOME~FREE, RATHER MAKE USE [OF IT].

7.22 ὁ γὰρ ἐν κυρίῳ κληθεὶς δοῦλος
FOR~THE ONE IN [THE] LORD HAVING BEEN CALLED [WHILE] A SLAVE

ἀπελεύθερος κυρίου ἐστίν, ὁμοίως ὁ
A FREEDMAN OF [THE] LORD IS, LIKEWISE THE ONE

ἐλεύθερος κληθεὶς δοῦλός ἐστιν Χριστοῦ.
HAVING BEEN CALLED~[WHILE] A FREEDMAN A SLAVE IS OF CHRIST.

7.23 τιμῆς ἠγοράσθητε· μὴ γίνεσθε δοῦλοι ἀνθρώπων.
WITH A PRICE YOU° WERE BOUGHT; DO NOT BECOME SLAVES OF MEN.

7.24 ἕκαστος ἐν ᾧ ἐκλήθη, ἀδελφοί, ἐν τούτῳ
EACH ONE IN WHAT [POSITION] HE WAS CALLED, BROTHERS, IN THIS

μενέτω παρὰ θεῷ.
LET HIM REMAIN WITH GOD.

7.25 Περὶ δὲ τῶν παρθένων ἐπιταγὴν κυρίου
NOW~CONCERNING THE VIRGINS, A COMMANDMENT OF [THE] LORD

οὐκ ἔχω, γνώμην δὲ δίδωμι ὡς ἠλεημένος
I DO NOT HAVE, BUT~AN OPINION I GIVE AS [HAVING BEEN SHOWN] MERCY

ὑπὸ κυρίου πιστὸς εἶναι. **7.26** Νομίζω οὖν τοῦτο
BY [THE] LORD TO BE~FAITHFUL. I CONSIDER THEN THIS

καλὸν ὑπάρχειν διὰ τὴν ἐνεστῶσαν ἀνάγκην, ὅτι
TO BE~GOOD BECAUSE OF THE PRESENT NECESSITY, THAT

καλὸν ἀνθρώπῳ τὸ οὕτως εἶναι. **7.27** δέδεσαι
[IT IS] GOOD FOR A MAN - SO TO BE. [IF] YOU HAVE BEEN BOUND

γυναικί, μὴ ζήτει λύσιν· λέλυσαι ἀπὸ
TO A WIFE, DO NOT SEEK SEPARATION; [IF] YOU HAVE BEEN FREED FROM

γυναικός, μὴ ζήτει γυναῖκα. **7.28** ἐὰν δὲ καὶ γαμήσῃς,
A WIFE, DO NOT SEEK A WIFE. BUT~IF INDEED YOU MARRY,

οὐχ ἥμαρτες, καὶ ἐὰν γήμῃ ἡ παρθένος,
YOU DID NOT SIN; AND IF ³MARRIES ¹THE ²VIRGIN,

οὐχ ἥμαρτεν· θλῖψιν δὲ τῇ σαρκὶ ἕξουσιν οἱ τοιοῦτοι,
SHE DID NOT SIN. BUT~AFFLICTION IN THE FLESH ²WILL HAVE - ¹SUCH ONES,

ἐγὼ δὲ ὑμῶν φείδομαι. **7.29** τοῦτο δέ φημι, ἀδελφοί, ὁ
BUT~I AM TRYING TO SPARE~YOU°. BUT~THIS I SAY, BROTHERS, THE

καιρὸς συνεσταλμένος ἐστίν· τὸ λοιπὸν, ἵνα καὶ
TIME HAS BEEN SHORTENED; FROM NOW ON, THAT BOTH

οἱ ἔχοντες γυναῖκας ὡς μὴ ἔχοντες ὦσιν **7.30** καὶ
THE ONES HAVING WIVES AS NOT HAVING MAY BE, AND

οἱ κλαίοντες ὡς μὴ κλαίοντες καὶ οἱ
THE ONES WEEPING AS NOT WEEPING AND THE ONES

χαίροντες ὡς μὴ χαίροντες καὶ οἱ ἀγοράζοντες
REJOICING AS NOT REJOICING AND THE ONES BUYING

ὡς μὴ κατέχοντες, **7.31** καὶ οἱ χρώμενοι τὸν
AS NOT POSSESSING, AND THE ONES USING THE

κόσμον ὡς μὴ καταχρώμενοι· παράγει γὰρ τὸ
WORLD AS NOT FULLY USING [IT]; FOR~IS PASSING AWAY THE

σχῆμα   τοῦ κόσμου τούτου.   **7.32** θέλω δὲ ὑμᾶς
PRESENT FORM   -   OF THIS~WORLD.   BUT~I DESIRE YOU°

ἀμερίμνους εἶναι.   ὁ ἄγαμος   μεριμνᾷ τὰ   τοῦ
TO BE~FREE FROM CARE.   THE UNMARRIED MAN CARES FOR   THE THINGS OF THE

κυρίου,   πῶς   ἀρέσῃ   τῷ   κυρίῳ·   **7.33** ὁ δὲ
LORD,   HOW   HE MAY PLEASE THE   LORD;   BUT~THE ONE

γαμήσας μεριμνᾷ τὰ   τοῦ κόσμου, πῶς ἀρέσῃ
HAVING MARRIED CARES FOR THE THINGS OF THE WORLD,   HOW HE MAY PLEASE

τῇ   γυναικί, **7.34** καὶ μεμέρισται.   καὶ ἡ γυνὴ ἡ
THE(HIS) WIFE,   AND HE HAS BEEN DISTRACTED. BOTH THE ²WOMAN -

ἄγαμος καὶ ἡ παρθένος μεριμνᾷ τὰ   τοῦ κυρίου,
¹UNMARRIED AND THE VIRGIN   CARE FOR   THE THINGS OF THE LORD,

ἵνα ᾖ   ἁγία καὶ τῷ σώματι καὶ τῷ πνεύματι·
THAT SHE MAY BE HOLY BOTH IN THE BODY AND IN THE SPIRIT;

ἡ δὲ   γαμήσασα μεριμνᾷ τὰ   τοῦ κόσμου, πῶς
BUT~THE WOMAN HAVING MARRIED CARES FOR THE THINGS OF THE WORLD,   HOW

ἀρέσῃ   τῷ   ἀνδρί.   **7.35** τοῦτο δὲ πρὸς τὸ
SHE MAY PLEASE THE(HER) HUSBAND.   NOW~THIS FOR   -

ὑμῶν αὐτῶν σύμφορον λέγω,   οὐχ ἵνα βρόχον
YOUR° OWN   PROFIT   I SPEAK, NOT THAT A NOOSE

ὑμῖν ἐπιβάλω ἀλλὰ   πρὸς   τὸ   εὔσχημον
I MAY PUT ON~YOU° BUT [I SPEAK] WITH RESPECT TO WHAT [IS] PROPER

καὶ εὐπάρεδρον τῷ   κυρίῳ ἀπερισπάστως.
AND CONSTANT SERVICE TO THE LORD IN AN UNDISTRACTED WAY.

7.36 Εἰ δέ τις   ἀσχημονεῖν ἐπὶ   τὴν παρθένον
     BUT~IF ANYONE ²TO BEHAVE IMPROPERLY ³TOWARD ⁴THE ⁵VIRGIN

αὐτοῦ νομίζει, ἐὰν ᾖ   ὑπέρακμος καὶ οὕτως
⁶OF HIM ¹THINKS, IF SHE IS PAST HER PRIME, AND THUS

ὀφείλει γίνεσθαι, ὃ   θέλει   ποιείτω, οὐχ ἁμαρτάνει,
IT HAS TO BE,   WHAT HE DESIRES LET HIM DO, HE DOES NOT SIN,

γαμείτωσαν. **7.37** ὃς δὲ ἕστηκεν ἐν τῇ καρδίᾳ αὐτοῦ
LET THEM MARRY.   BUT~HE WHO HAS STOOD IN THE HEART OF HIM

ἑδραῖος μὴ ἔχων ἀνάγκην, ἐξουσίαν δὲ ἔχει περὶ
FIRM,   NOT HAVING [THE] NEED, BUT~MASTERY HAS CONCERNING

τοῦ ἰδίου θελήματος καὶ τοῦτο κέκρικεν ἐν τῇ ἰδίᾳ
HIS OWN DESIRE,   AND THIS HE HAS DECIDED IN HIS OWN

καρδίᾳ, τηρεῖν τὴν ἑαυτοῦ παρθένον, καλῶς ποιήσει.
HEART,   TO KEEP [HER], HIS OWN WOMAN, A VIRGIN, HE DOES~WELL.

7.38 ὥστε καὶ ὁ   γαμίζων τὴν ἑαυτοῦ παρθένον
     SO THEN BOTH THE ONE MARRYING HIS OWN   VIRGIN

καλῶς ποιεῖ καὶ ὁ   μὴ γαμίζων κρεῖσσον ποιήσει.
DOES~WELL   AND THE ONE NOT MARRYING WILL DO~BETTER.

7.39 Γυνὴ δέδεται   ἐφ' ὅσον χρόνον ζῇ ὁ ἀνὴρ
     A WIFE HAS BEEN BOUND FOR SO LONG A TIME AS LIVES THE HUSBAND

αὐτῆς· ἐὰν δὲ κοιμηθῇ ὁ   ἀνήρ, ἐλευθέρα ἐστὶν
OF HER; BUT~IF ³SHOULD SLEEP ¹THE(HER) ²HUSBAND, FREE   SHE IS

ᾧ   θέλει   γαμηθῆναι, μόνον ἐν κυρίῳ.
²TO WHOM ³SHE DESIRES ¹TO BE MARRIED, ONLY IN [THE] LORD.

For the present form of this world is passing away.

32 I want you to be free from anxieties. The unmarried man is anxious about the affairs of the Lord, how to please the Lord; [33]but the married man is anxious about the affairs of the world, how to please his wife, [34]and his interests are divided. And the unmarried woman and the virgin are anxious about the affairs of the Lord, so that they may be holy in body and spirit; but the married woman is anxious about the affairs of the world, how to please her husband. [35]I say this for your own benefit, not to put any restraint upon you, but to promote good order and unhindered devotion to the Lord.

36 If anyone thinks that he is not behaving properly toward his fiancée,[h] if his passions are strong, and so it has to be, let him marry as he wishes; it is no sin. Let them marry. [37]But if someone stands firm in his resolve, being under no necessity but having his own desire under control, and has determined in his own mind to keep her as his fiancée,[h] he will do well. [38]So then, he who marries his fiancée[h] does well; and he who refrains from marriage will do better.

39 A wife is bound as long as her husband lives. But if the husband dies,[i] she is free to marry anyone she wishes, only in the Lord.

[h] Gk *virgin*
[i] Gk *falls asleep*

⁴⁰But in my judgment she is more blessed if she remains as she is. And I think that I too have the Spirit of God.

7.40 μακαριωτέρα δέ ἐστιν ἐὰν οὕτως μείνῃ, κατὰ
BUT~MORE BLESSED   SHE IS   IF   SO   SHE REMAINS,   ACCORDING TO

τὴν ἐμὴν γνώμην· δοκῶ δὲ κἀγὼ πνεῦμα θεοῦ
-   MY   OPINION;   AND~I CONSIDER [MYSELF]   ALSO   ²[THE] SPIRIT ³OF GOD

ἔχειν.
¹TO HAVE.

CHAPTER 8

Now concerning food sacrificed to idols: we know that "all of us possess knowledge." Knowledge puffs up, but love builds up. ²Anyone who claims to know something does not yet have the necessary knowledge; ³but anyone who loves God is known by him.

4 Hence, as to the eating of food offered to idols, we know that "no idol in the world really exists," and that "there is no God but one." ⁵Indeed, even though there may be so-called gods in heaven or on earth—as in fact there are many gods and many lords— ⁶yet for us there is one God, the Father, from whom are all things and for whom we exist, and one Lord, Jesus Christ, through whom are all things and through whom we exist.

7 It is not everyone, however, who has this knowledge. Since some have become so accustomed to idols until now, they still think of the food they eat as food offered to an idol; and their conscience, being weak, is defiled. ⁸"Food will not bring us close to God."ʲ We are no worse off if we do not eat, and no better off if

ʲ The quotation may extend to the end of the verse

8.1 Περὶ δὲ τῶν εἰδωλοθύτων, οἴδαμεν ὅτι πάντες
NOW~CONCERNING THE IDOLATROUS SACRIFICES,   WE KNOW   THAT   ²ALL

γνῶσιν ἔχομεν. ἡ γνῶσις φυσιοῖ, ἡ δὲ ἀγάπη
⁴KNOWLEDGE ¹WE ³HAVE.   -   KNOWLEDGE   PUFFS UP,   -   BUT   LOVE

οἰκοδομεῖ· **8.2** εἴ τις δοκεῖ ἐγνωκέναι τι, οὔπω
BUILDS UP;   IF   ANYONE   THINKS   TO HAVE KNOWN   ANYTHING,   NOT YET

ἔγνω καθὼς δεῖ γνῶναι· **8.3** εἰ δέ τις ἀγαπᾷ
HE KNEW AS   IT IS NECESSARY   TO KNOW;   BUT~IF   ANYONE   LOVES

τὸν θεόν, οὗτος ἔγνωσται ὑπ' αὐτοῦ. **8.4** Περὶ τῆς
-   GOD,   THIS ONE   HAS BEEN KNOWN   BY   HIM.   CONCERNING THE

βρώσεως οὖν τῶν εἰδωλοθύτων, οἴδαμεν ὅτι
EATING   THEREFORE OF THE IDOLATROUS SACRIFICES,   WE KNOW   THAT

οὐδὲν εἴδωλον ἐν κόσμῳ καὶ ὅτι οὐδεὶς θεὸς εἰ μὴ
AN IDOL~[IS] NOTHING   IN [THE] WORLD,   AND THAT [THERE IS] NO GOD EXCEPT

εἷς. **8.5** καὶ γὰρ εἴπερ εἰσὶν λεγόμενοι θεοὶ εἴτε ἐν
ONE.   FOR~EVEN   IF   THERE ARE   ONES BEING CALLED GODS   EITHER IN

οὐρανῷ εἴτε ἐπὶ γῆς, ὥσπερ εἰσὶν θεοὶ πολλοὶ καὶ
HEAVEN   OR   ON   EARTH,   EVEN AS   THERE ARE GODS   MANY   AND

κύριοι πολλοί, **8.6** ἀλλ' ἡμῖν εἷς θεὸς ὁ πατήρ
LORDS   MANY,   YET   TO US   [THERE IS] ONE GOD   THE FATHER

ἐξ οὗ τὰ πάντα καὶ ἡμεῖς εἰς αὐτόν, καὶ εἷς
OF WHOM - [ARE] ALL THINGS AND WE IN HIM,   AND ONE

κύριος Ἰησοῦς Χριστός δι' οὗ τὰ πάντα καὶ
LORD   JESUS   CHRIST   THROUGH WHOM - [ARE] ALL THINGS AND

ἡμεῖς δι' αὐτοῦ.
WE   THROUGH HIM.

8.7 Ἀλλ' οὐκ ἐν πᾶσιν ἡ γνῶσις· τινὲς δὲ
BUT   [THERE IS] NOT IN   ALL MEN THE(THIS) KNOWLEDGE;   BUT~SOME

τῇ συνηθείᾳ ἕως ἄρτι τοῦ εἰδώλου ὡς
-   [BEING] ACCUSTOMED UNTIL NOW   TO THE   IDOL   ²AS

εἰδωλόθυτον ἐσθίουσιν, καὶ ἡ συνείδησις αὐτῶν
³AN IDOLATROUS SACRIFICE ¹EAT [FOOD],   AND   THE CONSCIENCE   OF THEM

ἀσθενὴς οὖσα μολύνεται. **8.8** βρῶμα δὲ ἡμᾶς
BEING~WEAK   IS DEFILED.   BUT~FOOD   ²US

οὐ παραστήσει τῷ θεῷ· οὔτε ἐὰν μὴ φάγωμεν
¹WILL NOT COMMEND   -   TO GOD;   NEITHER IF   WE DO NOT EAT

ὑστερούμεθα, οὔτε ἐὰν φάγωμεν περισσεύομεν.
ARE WE LACKING,   NOR   IF   WE EAT   ARE WE BETTER.

8.9 βλέπετε δὲ μή πως   ἡ ἐξουσία ὑμῶν αὕτη
BUT~BEWARE   LEST SOMEHOW - ²RIGHT   ³OF YOU° ¹THIS

πρόσκομμα γένηται τοῖς ἀσθενέσιν. **8.10** ἐὰν γάρ
A STUMBLING BLOCK BECOMES TO THE WEAK ONES.   FOR~IF

τις   ἴδη σὲ τὸν ἔχοντα γνῶσιν ἐν εἰδωλείῳ
ANYONE SEES YOU, THE ONE HAVING KNOWLEDGE, IN AN IDOL'S TEMPLE

κατακείμενον, οὐχὶ ἡ συνείδησις αὐτοῦ ἀσθενοῦς
RECLINING(EATING), ²NOT ³THE ⁴CONSCIENCE ⁵OF HIM ⁷WEAK

ὄντος οἰκοδομηθήσεται εἰς τὸ τὰ εἰδωλόθυτα
⁶BEING ¹WILL ⁸BE BOLSTERED   ⁹SO AS ¹¹THE ¹²IDOLATROUS SACRIFICES

ἐσθίειν; **8.11** ἀπόλλυται γὰρ ὁ   ἀσθενῶν ἐν τῇ σῇ
¹⁰TO EAT?   ⁴IS BEING DESTROYED ¹FOR ²THE ONE ³BEING WEAK BY - YOUR

γνώσει, ὁ ἀδελφὸς δι'   ὃν Χριστὸς ἀπέθανεν.
KNOWLEDGE, THE BROTHER FOR THE SAKE OF WHOM CHRIST DIED.

8.12 οὕτως δὲ ἁμαρτάνοντες εἰς   τοὺς ἀδελφοὺς καὶ
AND~THUS SINNING   AGAINST THE BROTHERS   AND

τύπτοντες αὐτῶν τὴν συνείδησιν ἀσθενοῦσαν εἰς
WOUNDING THEIR -   CONSCIENCE BEING WEAK,   AGAINST

Χριστὸν ἁμαρτάνετε. **8.13** διόπερ εἰ βρῶμα σκανδαλίζει
CHRIST   YOU° SIN.   THEREFORE IF FOOD CAUSES TO STUMBLE

τὸν ἀδελφόν μου, οὐ μὴ φάγω κρέα εἰς τὸν αἰῶνα,
THE BROTHER OF ME, NEVER SHOULD I EAT MEAT INTO THE AGE,

ἵνα μὴ τὸν ἀδελφόν μου σκανδαλίσω.
LEST THE BROTHER OF ME I CAUSE TO STUMBLE.

we do. ⁹But take care that this liberty of yours does not somehow become a stumbling block to the weak. ¹⁰For if others see you, who possess knowledge, eating in the temple of an idol, might they not, since their conscience is weak, be encouraged to the point of eating food sacrificed to idols? ¹¹So by your knowledge those weak believers for whom Christ died are destroyed.ᵏ ¹²But when you thus sin against members of your family,ˡ and wound their conscience when it is weak, you sin against Christ. ¹³Therefore, if food is a cause of their falling,ᵐ I will never eat meat, so that I may not cause one of themⁿ to fall.

ᵏ Gk *the weak brother . . . is destroyed*
ˡ Gk *against the brothers*
ᵐ Gk *my brother's falling*
ⁿ Gk *cause my brother*

CHAPTER 9

9.1 Οὐκ εἰμὶ ἐλεύθερος; οὐκ εἰμὶ ἀπόστολος; οὐχὶ
AM I~NOT FREE?   AM I~NOT AN APOSTLE?   NOT

Ἰησοῦν τὸν κύριον ἡμῶν ἑόρακα; οὐ τὸ ἔργον μου
JESUS   THE LORD   OF US HAVE I SEEN? NOT THE WORK OF ME

ὑμεῖς ἐστε ἐν κυρίῳ; **9.2** εἰ ἄλλοις οὐκ εἰμὶ
YOU° ARE IN [THE] LORD?   IF TO OTHERS I AM~NOT

ἀπόστολος, ἀλλά γε ὑμῖν εἰμι· ἡ γὰρ σφραγίς μου
AN APOSTLE, YET INDEED TO YOU° I AM; FOR~THE SEAL OF MY

τῆς ἀποστολῆς ὑμεῖς ἐστε ἐν κυρίῳ.
-   APOSTLESHIP YOU° ARE IN [THE] LORD.

9.3 Ἡ ἐμὴ ἀπολογία τοῖς   ἐμὲ ἀνακρίνουσίν ἐστιν
-   MY DEFENSE TO THE ONES EXAMINING~ME   IS

αὕτη. **9.4** μὴ οὐκ ἔχομεν ἐξουσίαν φαγεῖν καὶ πεῖν;
THIS.   -   NOT HAVE I [THE] RIGHT TO EAT AND TO DRINK?

9.5 μὴ οὐκ ἔχομεν ἐξουσίαν ἀδελφὴν γυναῖκα περιάγειν
-   NOT HAVE I [THE] RIGHT A SISTER A WIFE   TO TAKE ALONG

ὡς καὶ οἱ λοιποὶ ἀπόστολοι καὶ οἱ ἀδελφοὶ τοῦ
AS EVEN THE REST OF THE APOSTLES AND THE BROTHERS OF THE

κυρίου καὶ Κηφᾶς; **9.6** ἢ μόνος ἐγὼ καὶ Βαρναβᾶς
LORD   AND CEPHAS?   OR ONLY I   AND BARNABAS,

Am I not free? Am I not an apostle? Have I not seen Jesus our Lord? Are you not my work in the Lord? ²If I am not an apostle to others, at least I am to you; for you are the seal of my apostleship in the Lord.

3 This is my defense to those who would examine me. ⁴Do we not have the right to our food and drink? ⁵Do we not have the right to be accompanied by a believing wife,ᵒ as do the other apostles and the brothers of the Lord and Cephas? ⁶Or is it only Barnabas and I who

ᵒ Gk *a sister as wife*

have no right to refrain from working for a living? 7Who at any time pays the expenses for doing military service? Who plants a vineyard and does not eat any of its fruit? Or who tends a flock and does not get any of its milk?

8 Do I say this on human authority? Does not the law also say the same? 9For it is written in the law of Moses, "You shall not muzzle an ox while it is treading out the grain." Is it for oxen that God is concerned? 10Or does he not speak entirely for our sake? It was indeed written for our sake, for whoever plows should plow in hope and whoever threshes should thresh in hope of a share in the crop. 11If we have sown spiritual good among you, is it too much if we reap your material benefits? 12If others share this rightful claim on you, do not we still more?

Nevertheless, we have not made use of this right, but we endure anything rather than put an obstacle in the way of the gospel of Christ. 13Do you not know that those who are employed in the temple service get their food from the temple, and those who serve at the altar share in what is sacrificed on the altar? 14In the same way, the Lord commanded that those who proclaim the gospel should get their living by the gospel.

15 But I have made no use

οὐκ ἔχομεν ἐξουσίαν μὴ ἐργάζεσθαι; **9.7** τίς
HAVE WE~NOT [THE] RIGHT NOT TO WORK? WHO

στρατεύεται ἰδίοις ὀψωνίοις ποτέ; τίς φυτεύει
SERVES AS A SOLDIER BY HIS OWN WAGES AT ANY TIME? WHO PLANTS

ἀμπελῶνα καὶ τὸν καρπὸν αὐτοῦ οὐκ ἐσθίει; ἢ τίς
A VINEYARD AND THE FRUIT OF IT DOES NOT EAT? OR WHO

ποιμαίνει ποίμνην καὶ ἐκ τοῦ γάλακτος τῆς ποίμνης
SHEPHERDS A FLOCK AND OF THE MILK OF THE FLOCK

οὐκ ἐσθίει; **9.8** Μὴ κατὰ ἄνθρωπον
DOES NOT EAT? [SURELY] NOT ACCORDING TO A HUMAN [PERSPECTIVE]

ταῦτα λαλῶ ἢ καὶ ὁ νόμος ταῦτα οὐ λέγει;
THESE THINGS I SPEAK, OR ALSO THESE THINGS THE LAW SAYS~NOT?

9.9 ἐν γὰρ τῷ Μωϋσέως νόμῳ γέγραπται,
FOR~IN THE LAW~OF MOSES IT HAS BEEN WRITTEN,

Οὐ κημώσεις βοῦν ἀλοῶντα. μὴ τῶν βοῶν
YOU SHALL NOT MUZZLE AN OX TREADING [GRAIN]. [SURELY IT IS] NOT THE OXEN

μέλει τῷ θεῷ **9.10** ἢ δι' ἡμᾶς
[THAT] MATTER - TO GOD, RATHER ²BECAUSE OF ³US

πάντως λέγει; δι' ἡμᾶς γὰρ ἐγράφη
¹[IS IT NOT] ALTOGETHER HE SAYS [THIS]? ²BECAUSE OF ³US ¹FOR IT WAS WRITTEN

ὅτι ὀφείλει ἐπ' ἐλπίδι ὁ ἀροτριῶν ἀροτριᾶν καὶ
THAT ³OUGHT ⁵ON(IN) ⁶HOPE ¹THE ONE ²PLOUGHING ⁴TO PLOW, AND

ὁ ἀλοῶν ἐπ' ἐλπίδι τοῦ μετέχειν. **9.11** εἰ ἡμεῖς
THE ONE THRESHING ON(WITH) HOPE - TO PARTAKE. IF WE

ὑμῖν τὰ πνευματικὰ ἐσπείραμεν, μέγα εἰ ἡμεῖς
TO YOU° THE SPIRITUAL THINGS SOWED, [IS IT] A GREAT THING IF WE

ὑμῶν τὰ σαρκικὰ θερίσομεν; **9.12** εἰ ἄλλοι τῆς
YOUR° - MATERIAL THINGS WILL REAP? IF OTHERS -

ὑμῶν ἐξουσίας μετέχουσιν, οὐ μᾶλλον ἡμεῖς;
[OVER] YOU° [THIS] RIGHT HAVE, NOT RATHER WE?

Ἀλλ' οὐκ ἐχρησάμεθα τῇ ἐξουσίᾳ ταύτῃ, ἀλλὰ
BUT WE DID NOT MAKE USE OF - THIS~RIGHT, BUT

πάντα στέγομεν, ἵνα μή τινα ἐγκοπὴν δῶμεν τῷ
ALL THINGS WE ENDURE, LEST ANY HINDRANCE WE SHOULD GIVE TO THE

εὐαγγελίῳ τοῦ Χριστοῦ. **9.13** οὐκ οἴδατε ὅτι οἱ τὰ
GOSPEL - OF CHRIST. DO YOU° NOT KNOW THAT THE ONES ²THE

ἱερὰ ἐργαζόμενοι [τὰ] ἐκ τοῦ ἱεροῦ ἐσθίουσιν,
³TEMPLE SERVICES ¹PERFORMING THE THINGS OF THE TEMPLE EATS,

οἱ τῷ θυσιαστηρίῳ παρεδρεύοντες τῷ θυσιαστηρίῳ
THE ONES ²THE ³ALTAR ¹ATTENDING WITH THE ALTAR

συμμερίζονται; **9.14** οὕτως καὶ ὁ κύριος διέταξεν
HAVE [THEIR] SHARE? SO ALSO THE LORD APPOINTED

τοῖς τὸ εὐαγγέλιον καταγγέλλουσιν ἐκ τοῦ
THE ONES ²THE ³GOSPEL ¹PROCLAIMING FROM THE

εὐαγγελίου ζῆν. **9.15** ἐγὼ δὲ οὐ κέχρημαι
GOSPEL TO GET [THEIR] LIVING. BUT~I HAVE NOT USED

9:9 Deut. 25:4

οὐδενὶ τούτων.
ANY OF THESE THINGS.

οὐκ ἔγραψα δὲ ταῦτα, ἵνα οὕτως
I DID NOT WRITE - THESE THINGS THAT THUS

γένηται ἐν ἐμοί· καλὸν γάρ μοι μᾶλλον ἀποθανεῖν
IT MIGHT BE WITH ME; FOR~[IT IS] BETTER FOR ME RATHER TO DIE

ἤ—τὸ καύχημά μου οὐδεὶς κενώσει.
THAN—[THAT] THE BOAST OF ME NO ONE WILL MAKE VOID.

9.16 ἐὰν γὰρ εὐαγγελίζωμαι, οὐκ ἔστιν μοι καύχημα·
FOR~IF I PREACH THE GOOD NEWS THERE IS~NOT FOR ME A BOAST;

ἀνάγκη γάρ μοι ἐπίκειται· οὐαὶ γάρ μοί ἐστιν ἐὰν
FOR~NECESSITY IS LAID ON~ME; FOR~WOE TO ME IS IF

μὴ εὐαγγελίσωμαι. **9.17** εἰ γὰρ ἑκὼν τοῦτο πράσσω,
I DO NOT PREACH THE GOOD NEWS. FOR~IF WILLINGLY I DO~THIS,

μισθὸν ἔχω· εἰ δὲ ἄκων, οἰκονομίαν
A REWARD I HAVE; BUT~IF UNWILLINGLY, A STEWARDSHIP

πεπίστευμαι· **9.18** τίς οὖν μού ἐστιν ὁ μισθός;
I HAVE BEEN ENTRUSTED [WITH]. WHAT THEN IS~MY - REWARD?

ἵνα εὐαγγελιζόμενος ἀδάπανον θήσω τὸ
THAT [IN] PREACHING THE GOOD NEWS ⁴WITHOUT CHARGE ¹I MAY MAKE ²THE

εὐαγγέλιον εἰς τὸ μὴ καταχρήσασθαι τῇ ἐξουσίᾳ μου
³GOOD NEWS SO AS NOT TO MAKE FULL USE - OF MY~RIGHT

ἐν τῷ εὐαγγελίῳ.
IN THE GOSPEL.

9.19 Ἐλεύθερος γὰρ ὢν ἐκ πάντων πᾶσιν
³FREE ¹FOR ²BEING FROM ALL MEN, TO ALL MEN

ἐμαυτὸν ἐδούλωσα, ἵνα τοὺς πλείονας κερδήσω·
I ENSLAVED~MYSELF, THAT THE MORE I MIGHT GAIN;

9.20 καὶ ἐγενόμην τοῖς Ἰουδαίοις ὡς Ἰουδαῖος, ἵνα
AND I BECAME TO THE JEWS AS A JEW, THAT

Ἰουδαίους κερδήσω· τοῖς ὑπὸ νόμον ὡς ὑπὸ
JEWS I MIGHT GAIN; TO THE ONES UNDER LAW AS UNDER

νόμον, μὴ ὢν αὐτὸς ὑπὸ νόμον, ἵνα τοὺς ὑπὸ
LAW, NOT BEING MYSELF UNDER LAW, THAT THE ONES UNDER

νόμον κερδήσω· **9.21** τοῖς ἀνόμοις ὡς ἄνομος, μὴ
LAW I MIGHT GAIN; TO THE ONES WITHOUT LAW AS WITHOUT LAW, NOT

ὢν ἄνομος θεοῦ ἀλλ᾽ ἔννομος Χριστοῦ, ἵνα κερδάνω
BEING WITHOUT GOD'S LAW BUT WITHIN CHRIST'S LAW, THAT I MAY GAIN

τοὺς ἀνόμους· **9.22** ἐγενόμην τοῖς ἀσθενέσιν ἀσθενής,
THE ONES WITHOUT LAW; I BECAME ²TO THE ³WEAK ONES ¹WEAK,

ἵνα τοὺς ἀσθενεῖς κερδήσω· τοῖς πᾶσιν γέγονα
THAT THE WEAK ONES I MIGHT GAIN; - TO ALL MEN I HAVE BECOME

πάντα, ἵνα πάντως τινὰς σώσω. **9.23** πάντα δὲ ποιῶ
ALL THINGS, THAT BY ALL MEANS I MIGHT SAVE~SOME. AND~ALL THINGS I DO

διὰ τὸ εὐαγγέλιον, ἵνα συγκοινωνὸς αὐτοῦ
BECAUSE OF THE GOSPEL, THAT A FELLOW-PARTAKER OF IT

γένωμαι.
I MAY BECOME.

9.24 Οὐκ οἴδατε ὅτι οἱ ἐν σταδίῳ τρέχοντες
DO YOU° NOT KNOW THAT THE ONES ²IN ³A RACECOURSE ¹RUNNING

---

of any of these rights, nor am I writing this so that they may be applied in my case. Indeed, I would rather die than that—no one will deprive me of my ground for boasting! ¹⁶If I proclaim the gospel, this gives me no ground for boasting, for an obligation is laid on me, and woe to me if I do not proclaim the gospel! ¹⁷For if I do this of my own will, I have a reward; but if not of my own will, I am entrusted with a commission. ¹⁸What then is my reward? Just this: that in my proclamation I may make the gospel free of charge, so as not to make full use of my rights in the gospel.

19 For though I am free with respect to all, I have made myself a slave to all, so that I might win more of them. ²⁰To the Jews I became as a Jew, in order to win Jews. To those under the law I became as one under the law (though I myself am not under the law) so that I might win those under the law. ²¹To those outside the law I became as one outside law (though I am not free from God's law but am under Christ's law) so that I might win those outside the law. ²²To the weak I became weak, so that I might win the weak. I have become all things to all people, that I might by all means save some. ²³I do it all for the sake of the gospel, so that I may share in its blessings.

24 Do you not know that in a race the runners

all compete, but only one receives the prize? Run in such a way that you may win it. ²⁵Athletes exercise self-control in all things; they do it to receive a perishable wreath, but we an imperishable one. ²⁶So I do not run aimlessly, nor do I box as though beating the air; ²⁷but I punish my body and enslave it, so that after proclaiming to others I myself should not be disqualified.

πάντες μὲν τρέχουσιν, εἰς δὲ λαμβάνει τὸ βραβεῖον;
ALL INDEED RUN, BUT~ONE RECEIVES THE PRIZE?

οὕτως τρέχετε ἵνα καταλάβητε. **9.25** πᾶς δὲ ὁ
SO RUN THAT YOU MAY OBTAIN [IT]. AND EVERYONE

ἀγωνιζόμενος πάντα ἐγκρατεύεται, ἐκεῖνοι μὲν
COMPETING [IN THE GAMES] [IN] ALL THINGS EXERCISES SELF-CONTROL, THOSE ONES -

οὖν ἵνα φθαρτὸν στέφανον λάβωσιν, ἡμεῖς δὲ
THEREFORE THAT ²A PERISHABLE ³WREATH ¹THEY MAY RECEIVE, BUT~WE

ἄφθαρτον. **9.26** ἐγὼ τοίνυν οὕτως τρέχω ὡς οὐκ
AN IMPERISHABLE. I THEREFORE SO RUN AS NOT

ἀδήλως, οὕτως πυκτεύω ὡς οὐκ ἀέρα δέρων·
[WITH] UNCERTAINTY, SO I BOX AS NOT BEATING~[THE] AIR;

9.27 ἀλλὰ ὑπωπιάζω μου τὸ σῶμα καὶ δουλαγωγῶ,
BUT I TREAT ROUGHLY MY - BODY AND MAKE IT [MY] SLAVE,

μή πως ἄλλοις κηρύξας αὐτὸς ἀδόκιμος γένωμαι.
LEST TO OTHERS HAVING PREACHED ²MYSELF ⁴DISQUALIFIED ¹I ³MAY BECOME.

CHAPTER 10

I do not want you to be unaware, brothers and sisters,ᵖ that our ancestors were all under the cloud, and all passed through the sea, ²and all were baptized into Moses in the cloud and in the sea, ³and all ate the same spiritual food, ⁴and all drank the same spiritual drink. For they drank from the spiritual rock that followed them, and the rock was Christ. ⁵Nevertheless, God was not pleased with most of them, and they were struck down in the wilderness.

6 Now these things occurred as examples for us, so that we might not desire evil as they did. ⁷Do not become idolaters as some

ᵖ Gk brothers

10.1 Οὐ θέλω γὰρ ὑμᾶς ἀγνοεῖν, ἀδελφοί, ὅτι οἱ
²I DO NOT WANT ¹FOR YOU° TO BE IGNORANT, BROTHERS, THAT THE

πατέρες ἡμῶν πάντες ὑπὸ τὴν νεφέλην ἦσαν καὶ
FATHERS OF US ALL UNDER THE CLOUD WERE AND

πάντες διὰ τῆς θαλάσσης διῆλθον **10.2** καὶ πάντες
ALL THROUGH THE SEA PASSED AND ALL

εἰς τὸν Μωϋσῆν ἐβαπτίσθησαν ἐν τῇ νεφέλῃ καὶ ἐν
INTO - MOSES WERE BAPTIZED IN THE CLOUD AND IN

τῇ θαλάσσῃ **10.3** καὶ πάντες τὸ αὐτὸ πνευματικὸν
THE SEA AND ALL THE SAME SPIRITUAL

βρῶμα ἔφαγον **10.4** καὶ πάντες τὸ αὐτὸ πνευματικὸν
FOOD ATE AND ALL ²THE ³SAME ⁴SPIRITUAL

ἔπιον πόμα· ἔπινον γὰρ ἐκ πνευματικῆς
¹DRANK ⁵DRINK; FOR~THEY WERE DRINKING FROM A SPIRITUAL

ἀκολουθούσης πέτρας, ἡ πέτρα δὲ ἦν ὁ Χριστός.
ROCK~FOLLOWING [THEM]. ²THE ³ROCK ¹AND WAS - CHRIST.

10.5 ἀλλ' οὐκ ἐν τοῖς πλείοσιν αὐτῶν εὐδόκησεν ὁ
BUT NOT WITH THE MAJORITY OF THEM ¹WAS ³PLEASED -

θεός, κατεστρώθησαν γὰρ ἐν τῇ ἐρήμῳ.
²GOD, FOR~THEY WERE STREWN ABOUT IN THE WILDERNESS.

10.6 ταῦτα δὲ τύποι ἡμῶν ἐγενήθησαν, εἰς τὸ
NOW~THESE THINGS ²[AS] EXAMPLES ³OF(FOR) US ¹OCCURRED, FOR -

μὴ εἶναι ἡμᾶς ἐπιθυμητὰς κακῶν, καθὼς κἀκεῖνοι
²NOT ³TO BE ¹US ONES DESIRING AFTER EVIL THINGS, AS ALSO THOSE ONES

ἐπεθύμησαν. **10.7** μηδὲ εἰδωλολάτραι γίνεσθε
DESIRED. NEITHER IDOLATERS SHOULD YOU° BECOME,

10:7 Exod. 32:6

καθὼς τινες αὐτῶν, ὥσπερ γέγραπται,   Ἐκάθισεν ὁ
AS   SOME   OF THEM, AS   IT HAS BEEN WRITTEN, SAT DOWN   THE

λαὸς φαγεῖν καὶ πεῖν καὶ ἀνέστησαν παίζειν.
PEOPLE TO EAT AND TO DRINK AND STOOD UP   TO PLAY.

10.8 μηδὲ πορνεύωμεν,   καθὼς τινες αὐτῶν
        NEITHER LET US COMMIT FORNICATION AS   SOME OF THEM

ἐπόρνευσαν   καὶ ἔπεσαν μιᾷ ἡμέρᾳ εἴκοσι τρεῖς
COMMITTED FORNICATION AND FELL   IN ONE DAY   TWENTY-THREE

χιλιάδες. **10.9** μηδὲ ἐκπειράζωμεν τὸν ⌐Χριστόν⌐,
THOUSAND.   NEITHER LET US TEMPT   -   CHRIST,

καθὼς τινες αὐτῶν ἐπείρασαν καὶ ὑπὸ τῶν ὄφεων
AS   SOME OF THEM TEMPTED   AND BY THE SERPENTS

ἀπώλλυντο.   **10.10** μηδὲ γογγύζετε, καθάπερ τινὲς
WERE BEING DESTROYED.   NEITHER MURMUR,   EVEN AS   SOME

αὐτῶν ἐγόγγυσαν καὶ ἀπώλοντο   ὑπὸ τοῦ ὀλοθρευτοῦ.
OF THEM MURMURED, AND THEY WERE DESTROYED BY THE DESTROYER.

10.11 ταῦτα δὲ   τυπικῶς συνέβαινεν ἐκείνοις,
         NOW~THESE THINGS AS EXAMPLES HAPPENED   TO THOSE ONES,

ἐγράφη δὲ   πρὸς νουθεσίαν ἡμῶν, εἰς οὓς τὰ τέλη
BUT~IT WAS WRITTEN FOR ADMONITION OF US, TO WHOM THE ENDS

τῶν αἰώνων κατήντηκεν. **10.12** ὥστε ὁ   δοκῶν
OF THE AGES HAVE COME.   SO THEN THE ONE ASSUMING

ἑστάναι βλεπέτω μὴ πέσῃ.   **10.13** πειρασμὸς ὑμᾶς
TO HAVE STOOD TAKE HEED LEST HE SHOULD FALL.   A TEMPTATION ²YOU°

οὐκ εἴληφεν εἰ μὴ ἀνθρώπινος· πιστὸς δὲ ὁ θεός,
¹HAS NOT TAKEN EXCEPT [THAT WHICH IS] HUMAN; BUT~FAITHFUL - [IS] GOD,

ὃς οὐκ ἐάσει ὑμᾶς πειρασθῆναι ὑπὲρ ὃ   δύνασθε
WHO WILL NOT LET YOU° TO BE TEMPTED BEYOND WHAT YOU° ARE ABLE

ἀλλὰ ποιήσει σὺν τῷ πειρασμῷ καὶ τὴν ἔκβασιν τοῦ
BUT WILL MAKE WITH THE TEMPTATION ALSO THE WAY OUT   -

δύνασθαι   ὑπενεγκεῖν.
[FOR YOU°] TO BE ABLE TO ENDURE.

10.14 Διόπερ, ἀγαπητοί μου, φεύγετε ἀπὸ τῆς
         THEREFORE, BELOVED OF ME, FLEE   FROM   -

εἰδωλολατρίας. **10.15** ὡς   φρονίμοις   λέγω·
IDOLATRY.   AS   TO THOUGHTFUL MEN I SPEAK;

κρίνατε ὑμεῖς ὃ   φημι. **10.16** τὸ ποτήριον τῆς
YOU°~JUDGE WHAT I SAY.   THE CUP   -

εὐλογίας ὃ   εὐλογοῦμεν, οὐχὶ κοινωνία ἐστὶν τοῦ
OF BLESSING WHICH WE BLESS,   ²NOT ³A SHARING ¹IS IT OF THE

αἵματος τοῦ Χριστοῦ; τὸν ἄρτον ὃν κλῶμεν, οὐχὶ
BLOOD   -   OF CHRIST? THE BREAD WHICH WE BREAK, ²NOT

κοινωνία τοῦ σώματος τοῦ Χριστοῦ ἐστιν; **10.17** ὅτι
³A SHARING ⁴OF THE ⁵BODY   - ⁶OF CHRIST ¹IS IT?   BECAUSE

εἷς ἄρτος, ἓν σῶμα οἱ πολλοί ἐσμεν, οἱ γὰρ
ONE BREAD, ONE BODY [WE] THE MANY ARE,   - FOR

10:9 text: KJV ASVmg RSVmg NEBmg TEVmg NJBmg NRSV. var. κυριον (Lord): ASV RSV NASB NIV
NEB TEV NJB NRSVmg.

---

of them did; as it is written,
"The people sat down to eat
and drink, and they rose up
to play." [8]We must not
indulge in sexual immorality
as some of them did, and
twenty-three thousand fell in
a single day. [9]We must not
put Christ[q] to the test, as
some of them did, and were
destroyed by serpents.
[10]And do not complain as
some of them did, and were
destroyed by the destroyer.
[11]These things happened to
them to serve as an example,
and they were written down
to instruct us, on whom the
ends of the ages have come.
[12]So if you think you are
standing, watch out that you
do not fall. [13]No testing has
overtaken you that is not
common to everyone. God
is faithful, and he will not let
you be tested beyond your
strength, but with the testing
he will also provide the way
out so that you may be able
to endure it.

14 Therefore, my dear
friends,[r] flee from the
worship of idols. [15]I speak as
to sensible people; judge for
yourselves what I say. [16]The
cup of blessing that we bless,
is it not a sharing in the blood
of Christ? The bread that we
break, is it not a sharing in
the body of Christ? [17]Because
there is one bread, we who
are many are one body, for

[q] Other ancient authorities read *the
Lord*
[r] Gk *my beloved*

we all partake of the one bread. [18]Consider the people of Israel;[s] are not those who eat the sacrifices partners in the altar? [19]What do I imply then? That food sacrificed to idols is anything, or that an idol is anything? [20]No, I imply that what pagans sacrifice, they sacrifice to demons and not to God. I do not want you to be partners with demons. [21]You cannot drink the cup of the Lord and the cup of demons. You cannot partake of the table of the Lord and the table of demons. [22]Or are we provoking the Lord to jealousy? Are we stronger than he?

23 "All things are lawful," but not all things are beneficial. "All things are lawful," but not all things build up. [24]Do not seek your own advantage, but that of the other. [25]Eat whatever is sold in the meat market without raising any question on the ground of conscience, [26]for "the earth and its fullness are the Lord's." [27]If an unbeliever invites you to a meal and you are disposed to go, eat whatever is set before you without raising any question on the ground of conscience. [28]But if someone says to you, "This has been offered in sacrifice," then do not eat it, out of consideration for the one who informed you, and for the sake of conscience— [29]I mean the other's conscience,

[s] Gk Israel according to the flesh

πάντες ἐκ τοῦ ἑνὸς ἄρτου μετέχομεν. **10.18** βλέπετε
ALL   OF   THE ONE   BREAD WE PARTAKE.   LOOK AT

τὸν Ἰσραὴλ κατὰ σάρκα· οὐχ οἱ ἐσθίοντες
-   ISRAEL ACCORDING TO [THE] FLESH; [2]NOT [3]THE ONES [4]EATING

τὰς θυσίας κοινωνοὶ τοῦ θυσιαστηρίου εἰσίν;
[5]THE [6]SACRIFICES [7]PARTAKERS [8]OF THE [8]ALTAR   [1]ARE?

10.19 τί οὖν φημι; ὅτι εἰδωλόθυτόν τί ἐστιν ἢ
      WHAT THEN AM I SAYING? THAT AN IDOLATROUS SACRIFICE IS~ANYTHING OR

ὅτι εἴδωλόν τί ἐστιν; **10.20** ἀλλ' ὅτι ἃ
THAT AN IDOL IS~ANYTHING?   BUT   THAT THE THINGS WHICH

θύουσιν, δαιμονίοις καὶ οὐ θεῷ [θύουσιν]· οὐ θέλω
THEY SACRIFICE, TO DEMONS AND NOT TO GOD THEY SACRIFICE; I DO NOT WANT

δὲ ὑμᾶς κοινωνοὺς τῶν δαιμονίων γίνεσθαι.
- YOU° SHARERS   OF THE DEMONS   TO BECOME.

10.21 οὐ δύνασθε ποτήριον κυρίου πίνειν καὶ ποτήριον
      YOU° ARE NOT ABLE [THE] CUP OF [THE] LORD TO DRINK AND [THE] CUP

δαιμονίων, οὐ δύνασθε τραπέζης κυρίου μετέχειν καὶ
OF DEMONS, YOU° ARE NOT ABLE [THE] LORD'S~TABLE TO PARTAKE [OF] AND

τραπέζης δαιμονίων. **10.22** ἢ παραζηλοῦμεν τὸν κύριον;
A TABLE OF DEMONS.   OR DO WE MAKE JEALOUS THE LORD?

μὴ ἰσχυρότεροι αὐτοῦ ἐσμεν;
[SURELY] NOT STRONGER THAN HE ARE WE?

10.23 Πάντα ἔξεστιν ἀλλ' οὐ πάντα συμφέρει·
      ALL THINGS [ARE] LAWFUL BUT NOT ALL THINGS [ARE] BENEFICIAL;

πάντα ἔξεστιν ἀλλ' οὐ πάντα οἰκοδομεῖ.
ALL THINGS [ARE] LAWFUL BUT NOT ALL THINGS EDIFY.

10.24 μηδεὶς τὸ ἑαυτοῦ ζητείτω ἀλλὰ τὸ
      [2]NO ONE [4]HIS OWN THING(GOOD) [1]LET [3]SEEK BUT THE THING(GOOD)

τοῦ ἑτέρου. **10.25** Πᾶν τὸ ἐν μακέλλῳ πωλούμενον
OF THE OTHER.   EVERYTHING [2]IN [3]A MEAT MARKET [1]BEING SOLD

ἐσθίετε μηδὲν ἀνακρίνοντες διὰ τὴν συνείδησιν·
EAT   WITHOUT RAISING QUESTIONS BECAUSE OF - CONSCIENCE;

10.26 τοῦ κυρίου γὰρ ἡ γῆ καὶ τὸ πλήρωμα
      [2]OF THE [3]LORD [1]FOR [IS] THE EARTH AND THE FULLNESS

αὐτῆς. **10.27** εἰ τις καλεῖ ὑμᾶς τῶν ἀπίστων καὶ
OF IT.   IF ANYONE [3]INVITES [4]YOU° [1]OF THE [2]UNBELIEVERS AND

θέλετε πορεύεσθαι, πᾶν τὸ παρατιθέμενον ὑμῖν ἐσθίετε
YOU° WANT TO GO,   EVERYTHING BEING SET BEFORE YOU° EAT

μηδὲν ἀνακρίνοντες διὰ τὴν συνείδησιν.
WITHOUT RAISING QUESTIONS BECAUSE OF - CONSCIENCE.

10.28 ἐὰν δέ τις ὑμῖν εἴπῃ, Τοῦτο ἱερόθυτόν ἐστιν,
      BUT~IF ANYONE SHOULD SAY~TO YOU°, THIS IS~OFFERED IN SACRIFICE,

μὴ ἐσθίετε δι' ἐκεῖνον τὸν μηνύσαντα καὶ τὴν
DO NOT EAT BECAUSE OF THAT MAN - HAVING REVEALED [IT] AND -

συνείδησιν· **10.29** συνείδησιν δὲ λέγω οὐχὶ τὴν
[BECAUSE OF] CONSCIENCE;   [5]CONSCIENCE [1]BUT [2]I SAY [3]NOT [4]THE

10:26 Ps. 24:1

ἑαυτοῦ ἀλλὰ τὴν   τοῦ ἑτέρου. ἱνατί γὰρ ἡ
OF HIMSELF BUT THE [CONSCIENCE] OF THE OTHER MAN. FOR~WHY THE

ἐλευθερία μου κρίνεται ὑπὸ ἄλλης συνειδήσεως;
FREEDOM OF ME IS JUDGED BY ANOTHER'S CONSCIENCE?

10.30 εἰ ἐγὼ χάριτι   μετέχω, τί βλασφημοῦμαι
IF I WITH THANKSGIVING PARTAKE, WHY AM I BLAMED

ὑπὲρ οὗ ἐγὼ εὐχαριστῶ; **10.31** εἴτε οὖν ἐσθίετε
FOR WHAT I GIVE THANKS [FOR]? WHETHER THEREFORE YOU° EAT

εἴτε πίνετε εἴτε τι   ποιεῖτε, πάντα εἰς δόξαν
OR YOU° DRINK OR WHAT[EVER] YOU° DO, ALL THINGS TO [THE] GLORY

θεοῦ ποιεῖτε. **10.32** ἀπρόσκοποι καὶ Ἰουδαίοις γίνεσθε
OF GOD DO. ²WITHOUT OFFENSE ³BOTH ⁴TO JEWS ¹BE

καὶ Ἕλλησιν καὶ τῇ ἐκκλησίᾳ τοῦ θεοῦ, **10.33** καθὼς
AND TO GREEKS AND TO THE CHURCH - OF GOD, EVEN AS

κἀγὼ πάντα πᾶσιν ἀρέσκω μὴ ζητῶν τὸ ἐμαυτοῦ
I ALSO [IN] ALL THINGS ALL MEN PLEASE, NOT SEEKING - MY OWN

σύμφορον ἀλλὰ τὸ τῶν πολλῶν, ἵνα σωθῶσιν.
ADVANTAGE BUT THAT OF THE MANY, THAT THEY MAY BE SAVED.

not your own. For why should my liberty be subject to the judgment of someone else's conscience? ³⁰If I partake with thankfulness, why should I be denounced because of that for which I give thanks?

31 So, whether you eat or drink, or whatever you do, do everything for the glory of God. ³²Give no offense to Jews or to Greeks or to the church of God, ³³just as I try to please everyone in everything I do, not seeking my own advantage, but that of many, so that they may be saved.

11.1 μιμηταί μου γίνεσθε καθὼς κἀγὼ Χριστοῦ.
IMITATORS OF ME BECOME AS I ALSO [AM] OF CHRIST.

11.2 Ἐπαινῶ δὲ ὑμᾶς ὅτι πάντα μου μέμνησθε
NOW~I PRAISE YOU° THAT [IN] ALL THINGS YOU° HAVE REMEMBERED~ME

καί, καθὼς παρέδωκα ὑμῖν, τὰς παραδόσεις
AND, JUST AS I HANDED [THEM] OVER TO YOU°, THE TRADITIONS

κατέχετε. **11.3** θέλω δὲ ὑμᾶς εἰδέναι ὅτι παντὸς
YOU° HOLD FAST. BUT~I WANT YOU° TO KNOW THAT OF EVERY

ἀνδρὸς ἡ κεφαλὴ ὁ Χριστός ἐστιν, κεφαλὴ δὲ γυναικὸς
MAN THE HEAD - CHRIST IS, AND~[THE] HEAD OF A WOMAN

ὁ ἀνήρ, κεφαλὴ δὲ τοῦ Χριστοῦ ὁ θεός. **11.4** πᾶς
[IS] THE MAN, AND~[THE] HEAD - OF CHRIST - [IS] GOD. EVERY

ἀνὴρ προσευχόμενος ἢ προφητεύων κατὰ κεφαλῆς
MAN PRAYING OR PROPHESYING ²DOWN OVER ³[HIS] HEAD

ἔχων κατaισχύνει τὴν κεφαλὴν αὐτοῦ.
¹HAVING [ANYTHING] SHAMES THE HEAD OF HIM.

11.5 πᾶσα δὲ γυνὴ προσευχομένη ἢ προφητεύουσα
BUT~EVERY WOMAN PRAYING OR PROPHESYING

ἀκατακαλύπτῳ τῇ κεφαλῇ καταισχύνει τὴν
³UNCOVERED ¹WITH THE(HER) ²HEAD SHAMES THE

κεφαλὴν αὐτῆς· ἓν γάρ ἐστιν καὶ τὸ αὐτὸ τῇ
HEAD OF HER; ³ONE ¹FOR ²IT IS AND THE SAME -

ἐξυρημένη. **11.6** εἰ γὰρ οὐ κατακαλύπτεται γυνή,
WITH HAVING BEEN SHAVED. FOR~IF ²IS NOT COVERED ¹A WOMAN,

καὶ κειράσθω· εἰ δὲ αἰσχρὸν γυναικὶ τὸ
ALSO LET HER BE SHORN; BUT~SINCE [IT IS] SHAMEFUL FOR A WOMAN -

Be imitators of me, as I am of Christ.

2 I commend you because you remember me in every-thing and maintain the traditions just as I handed them on to you. ³But I want you to understand that Christ is the head of every man, and the husband^t is the head of his wife,^u and God is the head of Christ. ⁴Any man who prays or prophesies with something on his head disgraces his head, ⁵but any woman who prays or prophesies with her head unveiled disgraces her head—it is one and the same thing as having her head shaved. ⁶For if a woman will not veil herself, then she should cut off her hair; but if it is disgraceful for a woman

^t The same Greek word means *man* or *husband*
^u Or *head of the woman*

to have her hair cut off or to be shaved, she should wear a veil. [7]For a man ought not to have his head veiled, since he is the image and reflection[v] of God; but woman is the reflection[v] of man. [8]Indeed, man was not made from woman, but woman from man. [9]Neither was man created for the sake of woman, but woman for the sake of man. [10]For this reason a woman ought to have a symbol of[w] authority on her head,[x] because of the angels. [11]Nevertheless, in the Lord woman is not independent of man or man independent of woman. [12]For just as woman came from man, so man comes through woman; but all things come from God. [13]Judge for yourselves: is it proper for a woman to pray to God with her head, unveiled? [14]Does not nature itself teach you that if a man wears long hair, it is degrading to him, [15]but if a woman has long hair, it is her glory? For her hair is given to her for a covering. [16]But if anyone is disposed to be contentious—we have no such custom, nor do the churches of God.

17 Now in the following instructions I do not commend you, because when you come together it is not for the better but for the worse. [18]For, to begin with, when you come together as a church, I hear that there are divisions among you; and to

[v] Or *glory*
[w] Gk lacks *a symbol of*
[x] Or *have freedom of choice regarding her head*

κείρασθαι ἢ ξυρᾶσθαι, κατακαλυπτέσθω. **11.7** ἀνὴρ
TO BE SHORN   OR   TO BE SHAVED,   LET HER BE COVERED.   ²A MAN

μὲν γὰρ οὐκ ὀφείλει κατακαλύπτεσθαι τὴν κεφαλὴν
³INDEED ¹FOR OUGHT~NOT   TO BE COVERED ON   THE   HEAD,

εἰκὼν καὶ δόξα θεοῦ ὑπάρχων· ἡ γυνὴ δὲ
²[THE] IMAGE ³AND ⁴GLORY ⁵OF GOD ¹BEING;   ²THE ³WOMAN ¹BUT

δόξα ἀνδρός ἐστιν. **11.8** οὐ γάρ ἐστιν ἀνὴρ ἐκ
[THE] GLORY OF A MAN IS.   FOR~NOT IS   MAN   OF

γυναικός ἀλλὰ γυνὴ ἐξ ἀνδρός· **11.9** καὶ γὰρ οὐκ
WOMAN   BUT   WOMAN OF MAN;   FOR~ALSO NOT

ἐκτίσθη ἀνὴρ διὰ τὴν γυναῖκα ἀλλὰ γυνὴ διὰ
WAS CREATED MAN BECAUSE OF THE WOMAN,   BUT   WOMAN BECAUSE OF

τὸν ἄνδρα. **11.10** διὰ τοῦτο ὀφείλει ἡ γυνὴ
THE MAN.   BECAUSE OF THIS OUGHT   THE WOMAN

ἐξουσίαν ἔχειν ἐπὶ τῆς κεφαλῆς διὰ τοὺς
AUTHORITY TO HAVE ON THE HEAD   BECAUSE OF THE

ἀγγέλους. **11.11** πλὴν οὔτε γυνὴ χωρὶς ἀνδρὸς οὔτε
ANGELS.   HOWEVER NEITHER [IS] WOMAN WITHOUT MAN   OR

ἀνὴρ χωρὶς γυναικὸς ἐν κυρίῳ· **11.12** ὥσπερ γὰρ ἡ
MAN WITHOUT WOMAN IN [THE] LORD.   FOR~JUST AS   THE

γυνὴ ἐκ τοῦ ἀνδρός, οὕτως καὶ ὁ ἀνὴρ διὰ τῆς
WOMAN [IS] OF THE MAN,   SO   ALSO [IS] THE MAN THROUGH THE

γυναικός· τὰ δὲ πάντα ἐκ τοῦ θεοῦ. **11.13** ἐν
WOMAN;   BUT ALL THINGS [ARE] OF - GOD.   AMONG

ὑμῖν αὐτοῖς κρίνατε· πρέπον ἐστὶν γυναῖκα
YOURSELVES   JUDGE;   IS IT FITTING   [FOR] A WOMAN

ἀκατακάλυπτον τῷ θεῷ προσεύχεσθαι; **11.14** οὐδὲ ἡ
³UNCOVERED   - ²TO GOD ¹TO PRAY?   [DOES] NOT -

φύσις αὐτὴ διδάσκει ὑμᾶς ὅτι ἀνὴρ μὲν ἐὰν
NATURE HERSELF TEACH YOU° THAT ²A MAN - ¹IF

κομᾷ ἀτιμία αὐτῷ ἐστιν, **11.15** γυνὴ δὲ ἐὰν
WEARS LONG HAIR A DISHONOR TO HIM IT IS,   ³A WOMAN ¹BUT ²IF

κομᾷ δόξα αὐτῇ ἐστιν; ὅτι ἡ κόμη ἀντὶ
WEARS LONG HAIR A GLORY TO HER IT IS?   BECAUSE THE LONG HAIR INSTEAD OF

περιβολαίου δέδοται [αὐτῇ]. **11.16** Εἰ δέ τις δοκεῖ
A COVERING   HAS BEEN GIVEN TO HER.   BUT~IF ANYONE THINKS

φιλόνεικος εἶναι, ἡμεῖς τοιαύτην συνήθειαν οὐκ ἔχομεν
TO BE~CONTENTIOUS,   WE   SUCH   A CUSTOM   DO NOT HAVE,

οὐδὲ αἱ ἐκκλησίαι τοῦ θεοῦ.
NEITHER THE CHURCHES - OF GOD.

11.17 Τοῦτο δὲ παραγγέλλων οὐκ ἐπαινῶ ὅτι
³THIS ⁵[THAT FOLLOWS] ¹BUT ²IN GIVING ⁴CHARGE I GIVE NOT PRAISE BECAUSE

οὐκ εἰς τὸ κρεῖσσον ἀλλὰ εἰς τὸ ἧσσον συνέρχεσθε.
NOT FOR THE BETTER   BUT   FOR THE WORSE YOU° COME TOGETHER.

11.18 πρῶτον μὲν γὰρ συνερχομένων ὑμῶν ἐν ἐκκλησίᾳ
²FIRST ³INDEED ¹FOR WHEN YOU° COME TOGETHER IN AN ASSEMBLY

ἀκούω σχίσματα ἐν ὑμῖν ὑπάρχειν καὶ μέρος τι
I HEAR DIVISIONS AMONG YOU° TO EXIST AND PARTLY

πιστεύω. **11.19** δεῖ γὰρ καὶ αἰρέσεις ἐν ὑμῖν
I BELIEVE [IT].　　　FOR~IT IS NECESSARY ALSO [FOR] SECTS AMONG YOU°

εἶναι, ἵνα [καὶ] οἱ δόκιμοι φανεροὶ γένωνται ἐν
TO BE,　THAT　ALSO　THE APPROVED ONES MANIFEST　MAY BECOME　AMONG

ὑμῖν. **11.20** Συνερχομένων οὖν ὑμῶν ἐπὶ τὸ αὐτὸ
YOU°.　　　　²COMING TOGETHER　³THEREFORE ¹YOUR°　INTO ONE PLACE

οὐκ ἔστιν κυριακὸν δεῖπνον φαγεῖν· **11.21** ἕκαστος γὰρ
IS IT~NOT　[THE] LORD'S　SUPPER　[YOU] EAT;　　　FOR~EACH ONE

τὸ ἴδιον δεῖπνον προλαμβάνει ἐν τῷ φαγεῖν, καὶ ὃς
HIS OWN　SUPPER　TAKES FIRST　IN　-　EATING,　AND　ONE

μὲν πεινᾷ ὃς δὲ μεθύει. **11.22** μὴ γὰρ οἰκίας
-　HUNGERS　AND~ONE IS DRUNK.　-　FOR　²HOUSES

οὐκ ἔχετε εἰς τὸ ἐσθίειν καὶ πίνειν; ἢ τῆς
¹DO YOU° NOT HAVE IN WHICH TO EAT AND TO DRINK? OR THE

ἐκκλησίας τοῦ θεοῦ καταφρονεῖτε, καὶ καταισχύνετε
CHURCH　-　OF GOD DO YOU° DESPISE AND DO YOU° SHAME

τοὺς μὴ ἔχοντας; τί εἴπω ὑμῖν; ἐπαινέσω
THE ONES NOT HAVING? WHAT SHOULD I SAY TO YOU°? WILL I PRAISE

ὑμᾶς; ἐν τούτῳ οὐκ ἐπαινῶ.
YOU°? IN THIS I DO NOT PRAISE [YOU].

11.23 Ἐγὼ γὰρ παρέλαβον ἀπὸ τοῦ κυρίου, ὃ
FOR~I　RECEIVED　FROM THE LORD THAT WHICH

καὶ παρέδωκα ὑμῖν, ὅτι ὁ κύριος Ἰησοῦς ἐν τῇ
ALSO I PASSED ON TO YOU°, THAT THE LORD JESUS IN THE

νυκτὶ ᾗ παρεδίδετο ἔλαβεν ἄρτον **11.24** καὶ
NIGHT IN WHICH HE WAS BEING BETRAYED TOOK BREAD AND

εὐχαριστήσας ἔκλασεν καὶ εἶπεν, Τοῦτό μού ἐστιν τὸ
HAVING GIVEN THANKS HE BROKE [IT] AND SAID, THIS IS~MY -

σῶμα τὸ ὑπὲρ ὑμῶν· τοῦτο ποιεῖτε εἰς τὴν ἐμὴν
BODY - ON BEHALF OF YOU°; THIS DO IN - MY

ἀνάμνησιν. **11.25** ὡσαύτως καὶ τὸ ποτήριον μετὰ τὸ
REMEMBRANCE.　IN LIKE MANNER ALSO THE CUP AFTER THE

δειπνῆσαι λέγων, Τοῦτο τὸ ποτήριον ἡ καινὴ διαθήκη
EATING OF SUPPER SAYING, THIS - CUP THE NEW COVENANT

ἐστὶν ἐν τῷ ἐμῷ αἵματι· τοῦτο ποιεῖτε, ὁσάκις ἐὰν
IS IN - MY BLOOD; THIS DO AS OFTEN AS

πίνητε, εἰς τὴν ἐμὴν ἀνάμνησιν. **11.26** ὁσάκις γὰρ ἐὰν
YOU° DRINK IN - MY REMEMBRANCE.　FOR~AS OFTEN AS

ἐσθίητε τὸν ἄρτον τοῦτον καὶ τὸ ποτήριον πίνητε, τὸν
YOU° EAT - THIS~BREAD AND THE CUP DRINK, THE

θάνατον τοῦ κυρίου καταγγέλλετε ἄχρις οὗ ἔλθῃ.
DEATH OF THE LORD YOU° PROCLAIM UNTIL HE COMES.

11.27 Ὥστε ὃς ἂν ἐσθίῃ τὸν ἄρτον ἢ πίνῃ τὸ
SO WHOEVER EATS THE BREAD OR DRINKS THE

ποτήριον τοῦ κυρίου ἀναξίως, ἔνοχος ἔσται τοῦ
CUP OF THE LORD UNWORTHILY, GUILTY WILL BE OF THE

σώματος καὶ τοῦ αἵματος τοῦ κυρίου.
BODY AND OF THE BLOOD - OF [THE] LORD.

some extent I believe it. [19]Indeed, there have to be factions among you, for only so will it become clear who among you are genuine. [20]When you come together, it is not really to eat the Lord's supper. [21]For when the time comes to eat, each of you goes ahead with your own supper, and one goes hungry and another becomes drunk. [22]What! Do you not have homes to eat and drink in? Or do you show contempt for the church of God and humiliate those who have nothing? What should I say to you? Should I commend you? In this matter I do not commend you!

23 For I received from the Lord what I also handed on to you, that the Lord Jesus on the night when he was betrayed took a loaf of bread, [24]and when he had given thanks, he broke it and said, "This is my body that is for[y] you. Do this in remembrance of me." [25]In the same way he took the cup also, after supper, saying, "This cup is the new covenant in my blood. Do this, as often as you drink it, in remembrance of me." [26]For as often as you eat this bread and drink the cup, you proclaim the Lord's death until he comes.

27 Whoever, therefore, eats the bread or drinks the cup of the Lord in an unworthy manner will be answerable for the body and blood of the Lord.

[y] Other ancient authorities read *is broken for*

²⁸Examine yourselves, and only then eat of the bread and drink of the cup. ²⁹For all who eat and drink[z] without discerning the body,[a] eat and drink judgment against themselves. ³⁰For this reason many of you are weak and ill, and some have died.[b] ³¹But if we judged ourselves, we would not be judged. ³²But when we are judged by the Lord, we are disciplined[c] so that we may not be condemned along with the world.

33 So then, my brothers and sisters,[d] when you come together to eat, wait for one another. ³⁴If you are hungry, eat at home, so that when you come together, it will not be for your condemnation. About the other things I will give instructions when I come.

[z] Other ancient authorities add *in an unworthy manner,*
[a] Other ancient authorities read *the Lord's body*
[b] Gk *fallen asleep*
[c] Or *When we are judged, we are being disciplined by the Lord*
[d] Gk *brothers*

11.28 δοκιμαζέτω δὲ ἄνθρωπος ἑαυτόν καὶ οὕτως ἐκ
   ²LET ⁴EXAMINE ¹BUT ³A MAN   ⁵HIMSELF AND SO OF

τοῦ ἄρτου ἐσθιέτω καὶ ἐκ τοῦ ποτηρίου πινέτω·
THE BREAD LET HIM EAT AND OF THE CUP LET HIM DRINK;

11.29 ὁ γὰρ ἐσθίων καὶ πίνων κρίμα ἑαυτῷ ἐσθίει
   FOR~THE ONE EATING AND DRINKING ⁴JUDGMENT ⁵TO HIMSELF ¹EATS

καὶ πίνει μὴ διακρίνων τὸ σῶμα. **11.30** διὰ
²AND ³DRINKS [WHEN] NOT DISCERNING THE BODY.   BECAUSE OF

τοῦτο ἐν ὑμῖν πολλοὶ ἀσθενεῖς καὶ ἄρρωστοι καὶ
THIS AMONG YOU° MANY [ARE] WEAK AND SICK AND

κοιμῶνται ἱκανοί. **11.31** εἰ δὲ ἑαυτοὺς διεκρίνομεν,
A NUMBER~ARE ASLEEP.   BUT~IF WE WERE JUDGING~OURSELVES,

οὐκ ἂν ἐκρινόμεθα· **11.32** κρινόμενοι δὲ ὑπὸ [τοῦ]
WE WOULD NOT BE JUDGED;   BUT~BEING JUDGED BY THE

κυρίου παιδευόμεθα, ἵνα μὴ σὺν τῷ κόσμῳ
LORD WE ARE BEING DISCIPLINED, THAT NOT WITH THE WORLD

κατακριθῶμεν. **11.33** ὥστε, ἀδελφοί μου,
WOULD WE BE CONDEMNED.   SO THEN BROTHERS OF ME,

συνερχόμενοι εἰς τὸ φαγεῖν ἀλλήλους ἐκδέχεσθε.
[WHEN] COMING TOGETHER - - TO EAT WAIT FOR~ONE ANOTHER.

11.34 εἴ τις πεινᾷ, ἐν οἴκῳ ἐσθιέτω, ἵνα μὴ εἰς
   IF ANYONE HUNGERS, IN [HIS] HOME LET HIM EAT, LEST FOR

κρίμα συνέρχησθε. Τὰ δὲ λοιπὰ ὡς ἂν ἔλθω
JUDGMENT YOU° COME TOGETHER. AND~THE REMAINING MATTERS WHENEVER I COME

διατάξομαι.
I WILL SET IN ORDER.

CHAPTER 12

Now concerning spiritual gifts,[e] brothers and sisters,[d] I do not want you to be uninformed. ²You know that when you were pagans, you were enticed and led astray to idols that could not speak. ³Therefore I want you to understand that no one speaking by the Spirit of God ever says "Let Jesus be cursed!" and no one can say "Jesus is Lord" except by the Holy Spirit.

4 Now there are varieties of gifts, but the same Spirit; ⁵and there are varieties of services, but the same

[e] Or *spiritual persons*

12.1 Περὶ δὲ τῶν πνευματικῶν, ἀδελφοί, οὐ θέλω
   NOW~CONCERNING - SPIRITUAL THINGS, BROTHERS, I DO NOT WANT

ὑμᾶς ἀγνοεῖν. **12.2** Οἴδατε ὅτι ὅτε ἔθνη ἦτε πρὸς
YOU° TO BE IGNORANT.   YOU° KNOW THAT WHEN YOU° WERE~GENTILES ³TO

τὰ εἴδωλα τὰ ἄφωνα ὡς ἂν ἤγεσθε
⁴THE ⁶IDOLS - ⁵MUTE ¹WHENEVER ²YOU° WERE BEING LED

ἀπαγόμενοι. **12.3** διὸ γνωρίζω ὑμῖν ὅτι
[YOU° WERE] BEING CARRIED AWAY.   WHEREFORE I MAKE KNOWN TO YOU° THAT

οὐδεὶς ἐν πνεύματι θεοῦ λαλῶν λέγει, Ἀνάθεμα
NO ONE ²BY ³THE] SPIRIT ⁴OF GOD ¹SPEAKING SAYS, A CURSE

Ἰησοῦς, καὶ οὐδεὶς δύναται εἰπεῖν, Κύριος Ἰησοῦς,
[IS] JESUS, AND NO ONE IS ABLE TO SAY, LORD JESUS,

εἰ μὴ ἐν πνεύματι ἁγίῳ.
EXCEPT BY [THE] HOLY~SPIRIT.

12.4 Διαιρέσεις δὲ χαρισμάτων εἰσίν, τὸ δὲ αὐτὸ
   DIFFERENT [KINDS] - OF GIFTS THERE ARE, BUT~THE SAME

πνεῦμα· **12.5** καὶ διαιρέσεις διακονιῶν εἰσιν, καὶ ὁ
SPIRIT;   AND DIFFERENT [KINDS] OF MINISTRIES THERE ARE, AND THE

αὐτὸς κύριος· **12.6** καὶ διαιρέσεις ἐνεργημάτων εἰσίν,
SAME LORD; AND DIFFERENT [KINDS] OF OPERATIONS THERE ARE,

ὁ δὲ αὐτὸς θεὸς ὁ ἐνεργῶν τὰ πάντα ἐν πᾶσιν.
BUT~THE SAME GOD - WORKING - ALL THINGS IN ALL.

12.7 ἑκάστῳ δὲ δίδοται ἡ φανέρωσις τοῦ πνεύματος
BUT~TO EACH IS GIVEN THE MANIFESTATION OF THE SPIRIT

πρὸς τὸ συμφέρον. **12.8** ᾧ μὲν γὰρ διὰ τοῦ
FOR - PROFIT. ²TO ONE - ¹FOR THROUGH THE

πνεύματος δίδοται λόγος σοφίας, ἄλλῳ δὲ λόγος
SPIRIT IS GIVEN A WORD OF WISDOM, AND~TO ANOTHER, A WORD

γνώσεως κατὰ τὸ αὐτὸ πνεῦμα, **12.9** ἑτέρῳ πίστις
OF KNOWLEGE ACCORDING TO THE SAME SPIRIT, TO ANOTHER FAITH

ἐν τῷ αὐτῷ πνεύματι, ἄλλῳ δὲ χαρίσματα ἰαμάτων
BY THE SAME SPIRIT, AND~TO ANOTHER GIFTS OF HEALINGS

ἐν τῷ ἑνὶ πνεύματι, **12.10** ἄλλῳ δὲ ἐνεργήματα
BY THE ONE SPIRIT, AND~TO ANOTHER [THE] WORKINGS

δυνάμεων, ἄλλῳ [δὲ] προφητεία, ἄλλῳ [δὲ]
OF [MIRACULOUS] POWERS, AND~TO ANOTHER PROPHECY, AND~TO ANOTHER

διακρίσεις πνευμάτων, ἑτέρῳ γένη γλωσσῶν,
DISCERNINGS OF SPIRITS, TO ANOTHER KINDS OF TONGUES,

ἄλλῳ δὲ ἑρμηνεία γλωσσῶν· **12.11** πάντα δὲ ταῦτα
AND~TO ANOTHER INTERPRETATION OF TONGUES; ALL - THESE THINGS

ἐνεργεῖ τὸ ἓν καὶ τὸ αὐτὸ πνεῦμα διαιροῦν ἰδίᾳ
WORKS THE ONE AND THE SAME SPIRIT, DISTRIBUTING INDIVIDUALLY

ἑκάστῳ καθὼς βούλεται.
TO EACH ONE AS HE DETERMINES.

12.12 Καθάπερ γὰρ τὸ σῶμα ἕν ἐστιν καὶ μέλη πολλὰ
FOR~EVEN AS THE BODY IS~ONE AND MANY~MEMBERS

ἔχει, πάντα δὲ τὰ μέλη τοῦ σώματος πολλὰ ὄντα
HAS, ALL - THE MEMBERS OF THE BODY BEING~MANY

ἕν ἐστιν σῶμα, οὕτως καὶ ὁ Χριστός· **12.13** καὶ γὰρ ἐν
ARE~ONE BODY, SO ALSO - CHRIST; FOR~ALSO IN

ἑνὶ πνεύματι ἡμεῖς πάντες εἰς ἓν σῶμα ἐβαπτίσθημεν,
ONE SPIRIT WE ALL INTO ONE BODY WERE BAPTIZED,

εἴτε Ἰουδαῖοι εἴτε Ἕλληνες εἴτε δοῦλοι εἴτε
WHETHER JEWS OR GREEKS, WHETHER SLAVES OR

ἐλεύθεροι, καὶ πάντες ἓν πνεῦμα ἐποτίσθημεν.
FREE MEN, AND ALL ONE SPIRIT WE WERE GIVEN TO DRINK.

12.14 καὶ γὰρ τὸ σῶμα οὐκ ἔστιν ἓν μέλος ἀλλὰ
FOR~ALSO THE BODY IS~NOT ONE MEMBER BUT

πολλά. **12.15** ἐὰν εἴπῃ ὁ πούς, Ὅτι οὐκ εἰμὶ χείρ,
MANY. IF SAYS THE FOOT, BECAUSE I AM~NOT A HAND,

οὐκ εἰμὶ ἐκ τοῦ σώματος, οὐ παρὰ τοῦτο
NOT AM I OF THE BODY, NOT FOR THIS [REASON]

οὐκ ἔστιν ἐκ τοῦ σώματος; **12.16** καὶ ἐὰν εἴπῃ τὸ
[WOULD IT] CEASE TO BE OF THE BODY. AND IF SAYS THE

οὖς, Ὅτι οὐκ εἰμὶ ὀφθαλμός, οὐκ εἰμὶ ἐκ τοῦ
EAR, BECAUSE I AM~NOT AN EYE, NOT AM I OF THE

Lord; ⁶and there are varieties of activities, but it is the same God who activates all of them in everyone. ⁷To each is given the manifestation of the Spirit for the common good. ⁸To one is given through the Spirit the utterance of wisdom, and to another the utterance of knowledge according to the same Spirit, ⁹to another faith by the same Spirit, to another gifts of healing by the one Spirit, ¹⁰to another the working of miracles, to another prophecy, to another the discernment of spirits, to another various kinds of tongues, to another the interpretation of tongues. ¹¹All these are activated by one and the same Spirit, who allots to each one individually just as the Spirit chooses.

12 For just as the body is one and has many members, and all the members of the body, though many, are one body, so it is with Christ. ¹³For in the one Spirit we were all baptized into one body—Jews or Greeks, slaves or free—and we were all made to drink of one Spirit.

14 Indeed, the body does not consist of one member but of many. ¹⁵If the foot would say, "Because I am not a hand, I do not belong to the body," that would not make it any less a part of the body. ¹⁶And if the ear would say, "Because I am not an eye, I do not belong to the

body," that would not make it any less a part of the body. [17]If the whole body were an eye, where would the hearing be? If the whole body were hearing, where would the sense of smell be? [18]But as it is, God arranged the members in the body, each one of them, as he chose. [19]If all were a single member, where would the body be? [20]As it is, there are many members, yet one body. [21]The eye cannot say to the hand, "I have no need of you," nor again the head to the feet, "I have no need of you." [22]On the contrary, the members of the body that seem to be weaker are indispensable, [23]and those members of the body that we think less honorable we clothe with greater honor, and our less respectable members are treated with greater respect; [24]whereas our more respectable members do not need this. But God has so arranged the body, giving the greater honor to the inferior member, [25]that there may be no dissension within the body, but the members may have the same care for one another. [26]If one member suffers, all suffer together with it; if one member is honored, all rejoice together with it.

[27] Now you are the body of Christ and individually members of it. [28]And God has appointed in the

σώματος, οὐ παρὰ τοῦτο οὐκ ἔστιν ἐκ τοῦ
BODY,   NOT FOR   THIS [REASON] [WOULD IT] CEASE TO BE OF THE

σώματος; **12.17** εἰ ὅλον τὸ σῶμα ὀφθαλμός, ποῦ
BODY?   IF ALL   THE BODY [WAS] AN EYE,   WHERE

ἡ   ἀκοή; εἰ ὅλον ἀκοή, ποῦ ἡ
[WOULD BE] THE HEARING? IF ALL   HEARING, WHERE [WOULD BE] THE

ὄσφρησις; **12.18** νυνὶ δὲ ὁ θεὸς ἔθετο τὰ μέλη,
SMELLING?   BUT~NOW - GOD SET   THE MEMBERS,

ἓν ἕκαστον αὐτῶν ἐν τῷ σώματι καθὼς ἠθέλησεν.
EACH~ONE   OF THEM IN THE BODY   AS   HE WANTED.

12.19 εἰ δὲ ἦν τὰ πάντα ἓν μέλος, ποῦ τὸ
          AND~IF ²WERE - ¹ALL   ONE MEMBER, WHERE [WOULD BE] THE

σῶμα; **12.20** νῦν δὲ πολλὰ μὲν μέλη, ἓν δὲ σῶμα.
BODY?   BUT~NOW MANY   -   MEMBERS, BUT~ONE BODY.

12.21 οὐ δύναται δὲ ὁ ὀφθαλμὸς εἰπεῖν τῇ χειρί,
          ⁴IS NOT ABLE ¹AND ²THE ³EYE   TO SAY TO THE HAND,

Χρείαν σου οὐκ ἔχω, ἢ πάλιν ἡ κεφαλὴ τοῖς ποσίν,
NEED   OF YOU I DO NOT HAVE, OR AGAIN THE HEAD TO THE FEET,

Χρείαν ὑμῶν οὐκ ἔχω· **12.22** ἀλλὰ πολλῷ μᾶλλον τὰ
NEED   OF YOU° I DO NOT HAVE;   BUT   MUCH   RATHER ¹THE

δοκοῦντα μέλη τοῦ σώματος ἀσθενέστερα ὑπάρχειν
⁵APPEARING ²MEMBERS ³OF THE ⁴BODY   ⁷WEAKER   ⁶TO BE

ἀναγκαῖά ἐστιν, **12.23** καὶ ἃ δοκοῦμεν ἀτιμότερα
⁹NECESSARY ⁸ARE,   AND ¹THOSE ⁴[WHICH] WE THINK ⁶DISHONORABLE

εἶναι τοῦ σώματος τούτοις τιμὴν περισσοτέραν
⁵TO BE ²OF THE ³BODY   ON THESE HONOR MORE ABUNDANT

περιτίθεμεν, καὶ τὰ ἀσχήμονα ἡμῶν
WE CLOTHE,   AND THE SHAMEFUL PARTS OF US

εὐσχημοσύνην περισσοτέραν ἔχει, **12.24** τὰ δὲ
GREATER~PROMINENCE   HAVE,   BUT~THE

εὐσχήμονα ἡμῶν οὐ χρείαν ἔχει. ἀλλὰ ὁ θεὸς
COMELY [MEMBERS] OF US ²NO ³NEED ¹HAVE. BUT   - GOD

συνεκέρασεν τὸ σῶμα τῷ ὑστερουμένῳ
COMBINED [THE MEMBERS OF] THE BODY, TO THE LACKING [MEMBER]

περισσοτέραν δοὺς τιμήν, **12.25** ἵνα μὴ ᾖ σχίσμα ἐν
GIVING~MORE ABUNDANT HONOR,   LEST THERE BE DIVISION IN

τῷ σώματι ἀλλὰ τὸ αὐτὸ ὑπὲρ ἀλλήλων μεριμνῶσιν
THE BODY,   BUT ⁴THE ⁵SAME ⁶FOR ⁷ONE ANOTHER ³SHOULD CARE

τὰ μέλη. **12.26** καὶ εἴτε πάσχει ἓν μέλος,
¹THE ²MEMBERS.   AND WHETHER ³SUFFERS ¹ONE ²MEMBER,

συμπάσχει πάντα τὰ μέλη· εἴτε δοξάζεται [ἓν] μέλος,
SUFFERS WITH [IT] ALL THE MEMBERS; OR ³IS HONORED ¹ONE ²MEMBER,

συγχαίρει πάντα τὰ μέλη.
REJOICES WITH [IT] ALL THE MEMBERS.

12.27 Ὑμεῖς δέ ἐστε σῶμα Χριστοῦ καὶ μέλη
          NOW~YOU° ARE CHRIST'S~BODY AND MEMBERS

ἐκ μέρους. **12.28** καὶ οὓς μὲν ἔθετο ὁ θεὸς ἐν τῇ
IN PART.   AND ³SOME - ²PLACED - ¹GOD IN THE

ἐκκλησίᾳ πρῶτον ἀποστόλους, δεύτερον προφήτας,
CHURCH FIRST APOSTLES, SECOND PROPHETS,

τρίτον διδασκάλους, ἔπειτα δυνάμεις,
THIRD TEACHERS, THEN [THOSE HAVING] WORKS [OF MIRACLES],

ἔπειτα χαρίσματα ἰαμάτων, ἀντιλήμψεις, κυβερνήσεις,
THEN GIFTS OF HEALING, HELPFUL DEEDS, ADMINISTRATIONS,

γένη γλωσσῶν. **12.29** μὴ   πάντες ἀπόστολοι;
KINDS OF TONGUES. [SURELY] NOT ALL APOSTLES [ARE]?

μὴ   πάντες προφῆται; μὴ   πάντες διδάσκαλοι;
[SURELY] NOT ALL PROPHETS [ARE]? [SURELY] NOT ALL TEACHERS [ARE]?

μὴ   πάντες δυνάμεις;   **12.30** μὴ   πάντες
[SURELY] NOT ALL WORKERS [OF MIRACLES ARE]? [SURELY] NOT ALL

χαρίσματα ἔχουσιν ἰαμάτων; μὴ   πάντες
HAVE~GIFTS OF HEALING? [SURELY] NOT ALL

γλώσσαις λαλοῦσιν; μὴ   πάντες διερμηνεύουσιν;
SPEAK~IN TONGUES? [SURELY] NOT ALL INTERPRET?

12.31 ζηλοῦτε δὲ   τὰ χαρίσματα τὰ μείζονα.
BUT~YOU° EARNESTLY DESIRE THE ²GIFTS - ¹GREATER.

Καὶ ἔτι καθ' ὑπερβολὴν ὁδὸν ὑμῖν δείκνυμι.
AND YET ⁴BEYOND COMPARISON ³A WAY ²TO YOU° ¹I SHOW.

church first apostles, second prophets, third teachers; then deeds of power, then gifts of healing, forms of assistance, forms of leadership, various kinds of tongues. ²⁹Are all apostles? Are all prophets? Are all teachers? Do all work miracles? ³⁰Do all possess gifts of healing? Do all speak in tongues? Do all interpret? ³¹But strive for the greater gifts. And I will show you a still more excellent way.

CHAPTER 13

13.1 Ἐὰν ταῖς γλώσσαις τῶν ἀνθρώπων λαλῶ καὶ τῶν
IF IN THE TONGUES - OF MEN I SPEAK AND -

ἀγγέλων, ἀγάπην δὲ μὴ ἔχω, γέγονα χαλκὸς ἠχῶν
OF ANGELS, BUT~LOVE I DO NOT HAVE, I HAVE BECOME A SOUNDING~BRASS (GONG)

ἢ κύμβαλον ἀλαλάζον. **13.2** καὶ ἐὰν ἔχω προφητείαν
OR CLANGING~CYMBAL. AND IF I HAVE PROPHECY

καὶ εἰδῶ τὰ μυστήρια πάντα καὶ πᾶσαν τὴν γνῶσιν
AND KNOW ²THE ³MYSTERIES ¹ALL AND ALL THE KNOWLEDGE

καὶ ἐὰν ἔχω πᾶσαν τὴν πίστιν ὥστε ὄρη μεθιστάναι,
,AND IF I HAVE ALL THE FAITH SO AS TO REMOVE~MOUNTAINS,

ἀγάπην δὲ μὴ ἔχω, οὐθέν εἰμι. **13.3** κἂν ψωμίσω
BUT~LOVE I DO NOT HAVE, NOTHING I AM. AND IF I GIVE AWAY

πάντα τὰ ὑπάρχοντά μου καὶ ἐὰν παραδῶ τὸ σῶμά
ALL THE POSSESSIONS OF ME AND IF I GIVE OVER THE BODY

μου ἵνα ⌜καυχήσωμαι,⌝ ἀγάπην δὲ μὴ ἔχω, οὐδὲν
OF ME THAT I MAY BOAST, BUT~LOVE I DO NOT HAVE, NOTHING

ὠφελοῦμαι.
I HAVE GAINED.

13.4 Ἡ ἀγάπη μακροθυμεῖ, χρηστεύεται ἡ ἀγάπη,
- LOVE SUFFERS LONG, ²IS KIND - ¹LOVE,

οὐ ζηλοῖ, [ἡ ἀγάπη] οὐ περπερεύεται, οὐ φυσιοῦται,
IS NOT JEALOUS, - LOVE DOES NOT BRAG, IS NOT PUFFED UP,

If I speak in the tongues of mortals and of angels, but do not have love, I am a noisy gong or a clanging cymbal. ²And if I have prophetic powers, and understand all mysteries and all knowledge, and if I have all faith, so as to remove mountains, but do not have love, I am nothing. ³If I give away all my possessions, and if I hand over my body so that I may boast, ⸠but do not have love, I gain nothing.

4 Love is patient; love is kind; love is not envious or boastful or arrogant

⸠ Other ancient authorities read *body to be burned*

13:3 text: ASVmg RSVmg NASBmg NIVmg NEBmg TEVmg NJBmg NRSV. var. καυθησομαι (I will be burned): KJV ASV RSV NASB NIV NEB TEV NJB NRSVmg.

⁵or rude. It does not insist on its own way; it is not irritable or resentful; ⁶it does not rejoice in wrongdoing, but rejoices in the truth. ⁷It bears all things, believes all things, hopes all things, endures all things.

8 Love never ends. But as for prophecies, they will come to an end; as for tongues, they will cease; as for knowledge, it will come to an end. ⁹For we know only in part, and we prophesy only in part; ¹⁰but when the complete comes, the partial will come to an end. ¹¹When I was a child, I spoke like a child, I thought like a child, I reasoned like a child; when I became an adult, I put an end to childish ways. ¹²For now we see in a mirror, dimly,ᵍ but then we will see face to face. Now I know only in part; then I will know fully, even as I have been fully known. ¹³And now faith, hope, and love abide, these three; and the greatest of these is love.

ᵍ Gk in a riddle

13.5 οὐκ ἀσχημονεῖ, οὐ ζητεῖ τὰ ἑαυτῆς,
DOES NOT BEHAVE DISGRACEFULLY, DOES NOT SEEK THE THINGS OF ITSELF,

οὐ παροξύνεται, οὐ λογίζεται τὸ κακόν,
IS NOT PROVOKED, DOES NOT KEEP RECORD - OF WRONG[S],

13.6 οὐ χαίρει ἐπὶ τῇ ἀδικίᾳ, συγχαίρει δὲ τῇ
DOES NOT REJOICE OVER - UNRIGHTEOUSNESS, BUT~REJOICES WITH THE

ἀληθείᾳ· **13.7** πάντα στέγει, πάντα πιστεύει, πάντα
TRUTH; ALL THINGS COVERS, ALL THINGS BELIEVES, ALL THINGS

ἐλπίζει, πάντα ὑπομένει.
HOPES, ALL THINGS ENDURES.

13.8 Ἡ ἀγάπη οὐδέποτε πίπτει· εἴτε δὲ
- LOVE NEVER FAILS; BUT~WHETHER

προφητεῖαι, καταργηθήσονται· εἴτε γλῶσσαι,
PROPHECIES, THEY WILL BE ABOLISHED; OR TONGUES,

παύσονται· εἴτε γνῶσις, καταργηθήσεται. **13.9** ἐκ μέρους
THEY WILL CEASE, OR KNOWLEDGE, IT WILL BE ABOLISHED. ²IN PART

γὰρ γινώσκομεν καὶ ἐκ μέρους προφητεύομεν·
¹FOR WE KNOW AND IN PART WE PROPHESY;

13.10 ὅταν δὲ ἔλθῃ τὸ τέλειον, τὸ ἐκ μέρους
BUT~WHEN COMES THE COMPLETION, THE THING IN PART

καταργηθήσεται. **13.11** ὅτε ἤμην νήπιος, ἐλάλουν ὡς
WILL BE ABOLISHED. WHEN I WAS A CHILD, I USED TO SPEAK LIKE

νήπιος, ἐφρόνουν ὡς νήπιος, ἐλογιζόμην ὡς νήπιος·
A CHILD, I USED TO THINK LIKE A CHILD, I USED TO REASON LIKE A CHILD;

ὅτε γέγονα ἀνήρ, κατήργηκα τὰ τοῦ
WHEN I HAVE(HAD) BECOME A MAN, I HAVE(HAD) ABOLISHED THE THINGS OF THE

νηπίου. **13.12** βλέπομεν γὰρ ἄρτι δι' ἐσόπτρου
CHILD. FOR~WE SEE STILL THROUGH A MIRROR

ἐν αἰνίγματι, τότε δὲ πρόσωπον πρὸς πρόσωπον· ἄρτι
INDISTINCTLY, BUT~THEN FACE TO FACE; YET

γινώσκω ἐκ μέρους, τότε δὲ ἐπιγνώσομαι καθὼς καὶ
I KNOW IN PART, BUT~THEN I WILL FULLY KNOW EVEN AS ALSO

ἐπεγνώσθην. **13.13** νυνὶ δὲ μένει πίστις, ἐλπίς, ἀγάπη,
I WAS FULLY KNOWN, BUT~NOW REMAINS FAITH, HOPE, LOVE,

τὰ τρία ταῦτα· μείζων δὲ τούτων ἡ ἀγάπη.
- THESE~THREE; AND~[THE] GREATEST OF THESE - [IS] LOVE.

CHAPTER 14

Pursue love and strive for the spiritual gifts, and especially that you may prophesy. ²For those who speak in a tongue do not speak to other people but to God; for nobody understands them, since they are speaking mysteries in the Spirit. ³On the other hand,

14.1 Διώκετε τὴν ἀγάπην, ζηλοῦτε δὲ τὰ πνευματικά,
PURSUE - LOVE, AND~EAGERLY DESIRE THE SPIRITUAL THINGS,

μᾶλλον δὲ ἵνα προφητεύητε. **14.2** ὁ γὰρ λαλῶν
BUT~RATHER THAT YOU° MAY PROPHESY. FOR~THE ONE SPEAKING

γλώσσῃ οὐκ ἀνθρώποις λαλεῖ ἀλλὰ θεῷ· οὐδεὶς γὰρ
IN A TONGUE NOT TO MEN SPEAKS BUT TO GOD; FOR~NO ONE

ἀκούει, πνεύματι δὲ λαλεῖ μυστήρια· **14.3** ὁ δὲ
HEARS, BUT~IN SPIRIT HE SPEAKS MYSTERIES; BUT~THE ONE

προφητεύων   ἀνθρώποις   λαλεῖ   οἰκοδομὴν   καὶ
PROPHESYING   TO MEN   SPEAKS   [FOR] EDIFICATION   AND

παράκλησιν   καὶ   παραμυθίαν.   **14.4** ὁ   λαλῶν γλώσσῃ
ENCOURAGEMENT   AND   CONSOLATION.   THE ONE   SPEAKING   IN A TONGUE

ἑαυτὸν οἰκοδομεῖ·   ὁ δὲ   προφητεύων ἐκκλησίαν
EDIFIES~HIMSELF;   BUT~THE ONE   PROPHESYING   AN ASSEMBLY

οἰκοδομεῖ.   **14.5** θέλω δὲ   πάντας ὑμᾶς λαλεῖν γλώσσαις,
EDIFIES.   NOW~I DESIRE   ALL [OF]   YOU°   TO SPEAK   IN TONGUES,

μᾶλλον δὲ ἵνα   προφητεύητε·   μείζων δὲ ὁ
BUT~RATHER   THAT   YOU° MAY PROPHESY;   NOW~GREATER   [IS] THE ONE

προφητεύων ἢ   ὁ   λαλῶν γλώσσαις ἐκτὸς εἰ μὴ
PROPHESYING   THAN   THE ONE   SPEAKING   IN TONGUES   -   UNLESS

διερμηνεύῃ, ἵνα ἡ   ἐκκλησία   οἰκοδομὴν λάβῃ.
HE INTERPRETS,   THAT   THE   CHURCH   EDIFICATION   MAY RECEIVE.

14.6 Νῦν δέ, ἀδελφοί, ἐὰν ἔλθω πρὸς ὑμᾶς γλώσσαις
BUT~NOW,   BROTHERS,   IF   I COME   TO   YOU°   IN TONGUES

λαλῶν, τί   ὑμᾶς ὠφελήσω ἐὰν μὴ ὑμῖν λαλήσω ἢ   ἐν
SPEAKING,   WHAT   WILL I BENEFIT~YOU°,   EXCEPT   I SPEAK~TO YOU°   EITHER   WITH

ἀποκαλύψει ἢ ἐν γνώσει ἢ ἐν   προφητείᾳ ἢ [ἐν]
A REVELATION   OR WITH   KNOWLEDGE   OR WITH   A PROPHECY   OR WITH

διδαχῇ;   **14.7** ὅμως   τὰ   ἄψυχα   φωνὴν διδόντα, εἴτε
A TEACHING?   EVEN   -   LIFELESS THINGS   GIVING~A SOUND,   WHETHER

αὐλὸς εἴτε   κιθάρα, ἐὰν διαστολὴν τοῖς   φθόγγοις
FLUTE   OR   HARP,   IF   A DISTINCTION   IN THE   NOTES

μὴ δῷ,   πῶς γνωσθήσεται τὸ   αὐλούμενον   ἢ
THEY DO NOT GIVE,   HOW   WILL IT BE KNOWN   WHAT   IS BEING PLAYED [ON THE FLUTE]   OR

τὸ   κιθαριζόμενον;   **14.8** καὶ γὰρ   ἐὰν ἄδηλον σάλπιγξ
WHAT   IS BEING HARPED?   FOR~INDEED   IF   [3]AN UNCLEAR   [1]A TRUMPET

φωνὴν δῷ,   τίς παρασκευάσεται εἰς   πόλεμον;
[4]CALL   [2]GIVES, WHO   WILL PREPARE HIMSELF   FOR   BATTLE?

14.9 οὕτως καὶ ὑμεῖς διὰ τῆς   γλώσσης ἐὰν μὴ
SO   ALSO   [2]YOU°   [3]BY   [4]THE(YOUR)   [5]TONGUE   [1]UNLESS

εὔσημον   λόγον δῶτε, πῶς γνωσθήσεται τὸ
AN INTELLIGIBLE   MESSAGE   GIVE,   HOW   WILL IT BE KNOWN   THE THING

λαλούμενον;   ἔσεσθε γὰρ   εἰς   ἀέρα   λαλοῦντες.
BEING SAID?   FOR~YOU° WILL BE   [2]INTO   [3][THE] AIR   [1]SPEAKING.

14.10 τοσαῦτα εἰ τύχοι γένη φωνῶν   εἰσιν ἐν κόσμῳ
SO MANY,   IT MAY BE,   KINDS   OF LANGUAGES   THERE ARE   IN   [THE] WORLD,

καὶ οὐδὲν ἄφωνον·   **14.11** ἐὰν   οὖν   μὴ εἰδῶ τὴν
AND   NOT ONE   [IS] MEANINGLESS;   IF   THEREFORE   I DO NOT KNOW   THE

δύναμιν τῆς   φωνῆς, ἔσομαι τῷ   λαλοῦντι βάρβαρος
MEANING   OF THE   VOICE,   I WILL BE   TO THE ONE   SPEAKING   A FOREIGNER

καὶ ὁ   λαλῶν ἐν ἐμοὶ βάρβαρος.   **14.12** οὕτως καὶ
AND   THE ONE   SPEAKING   WITH   ME   A FOREIGNER.   SO   ALSO

ὑμεῖς, ἐπεὶ ζηλωταί ἐστε   πνευμάτων,   πρὸς τὴν
YOU°,   SINCE   ZEALOTS   YOU° ARE   OF SPIRITUAL THINGS,   FOR   THE

οἰκοδομὴν τῆς   ἐκκλησίας ζητεῖτε ἵνα περισσεύητε.
EDIFICATION   OF THE   CHURCH   BE ZEALOUS   THAT   YOU° MAY ABOUND.

those who prophesy speak to other people for their upbuilding and encouragement and consolation. [4]Those who speak in a tongue build up themselves, but those who prophesy build up the church. [5]Now I would like all of you to speak in tongues, but even more to prophesy. One who prophesies is greater than one who speaks in tongues, unless someone interprets, so that the church may be built up.

6 Now, brothers and sisters,[h] if I come to you speaking in tongues, how will I benefit you unless I speak to you in some revelation or knowledge or prophecy or teaching? [7]It is the same way with lifeless instruments that produce sound, such as the flute or the harp. If they do not give distinct notes, how will anyone know what is being played? [8]And if the bugle gives an indistinct sound, who will get ready for battle? [9]So with yourselves; if in a tongue you utter speech that is not intelligible, how will anyone know what is being said? For you will be speaking into the air. [10]There are doubtless many different kinds of sounds in the world, and nothing is without sound. [11]If then I do not know the meaning of a sound, I will be a foreigner to the speaker and the speaker a foreigner to me. [12]So with yourselves; since you are eager for spiritual gifts, strive to excel in them for building up the church.

[h] Gk brothers

13 Therefore, one who speaks in a tongue should pray for the power to interpret. ¹⁴For if I pray in a tongue, my spirit prays but my mind is unproductive. ¹⁵What should I do then? I will pray with the spirit, but I will pray with the mind also; I will sing praise with the spirit, but I will sing praise with the mind also. ¹⁶Otherwise, if you say a blessing with the spirit, how can anyone in the position of an outsider say the "Amen" to your thanksgiving, since the outsider does not know what you are saying? ¹⁷For you may give thanks well enough, but the other person is not built up. ¹⁸I thank God that I speak in tongues more than all of you; ¹⁹nevertheless, in church I would rather speak five words with my mind, in order to instruct others also, than ten thousand words in a tongue.

20 Brothers and sisters,ⁱ do not be children in your thinking; rather, be infants in evil, but in thinking be adults. ²¹In the law it is written,

"By people of strange tongues
and by the lips of foreigners
I will speak to this people;
yet even then they will not listen to me,"
says the Lord.
²²Tongues, then, are a sign

ⁱ Gk brothers

14.13 διὸ ὁ λαλῶν γλώσσῃ προσευχέσθω ἵνα
THEREFORE THE ONE SPEAKING IN A TONGUE LET HIM PRAY THAT

διερμηνεύῃ. **14.14** ἐὰν [γὰρ] προσεύχωμαι γλώσσῃ, τὸ
HE MAY INTERPRET. FOR~IF I PRAY IN A TONGUE, THE

πνεῦμά μου προσεύχεται, ὁ δὲ νοῦς μου
SPIRIT OF ME PRAYS, BUT~THE MIND OF ME

ἄκαρπός ἐστιν. **14.15** τί οὖν ἐστιν; προσεύξομαι
IS~UNFRUITFUL. WHAT THEN IS [THIS]? I WILL PRAY

τῷ πνεύματι, προσεύξομαι δὲ καὶ τῷ νοΐ·
WITH THE(MY) SPIRIT, AND~I WILL PRAY ALSO WITH THE(MY) MIND;

ψαλῶ τῷ πνεύματι, ψαλῶ δὲ καὶ τῷ νοΐ.
I WILL SING WITH THE(MY) SPIRIT, AND~I WILL SING ALSO WITH THE(MY) MIND.

14.16 ἐπεὶ ἐὰν εὐλογῇς [ἐν] πνεύματι, ὁ
OTHERWISE IF YOU PRAISE IN [YOUR] SPIRIT, ³THE ONE

ἀναπληρῶν τὸν τόπον τοῦ ἰδιώτου πῶς ἐρεῖ τὸ
⁴OCCUPYING ⁵THE ⁶PLACE ⁷OF THE ⁸UNINSTRUCTED ¹HOW ²WILL ⁹SAY THE

Ἀμήν ἐπὶ τῇ σῇ εὐχαριστίᾳ; ἐπειδὴ τί λέγεις
AMEN AT - YOUR GIVING OF THANKS? SINCE WHAT YOU SAY

οὐκ οἶδεν· **14.17** σὺ μὲν γὰρ καλῶς εὐχαριστεῖς ἀλλ᾽
HE DOES NOT KNOW; ²YOU ³INDEED ¹FOR ⁵WELL ⁴GIVE THANKS BUT

ὁ ἕτερος οὐκ οἰκοδομεῖται. **14.18** εὐχαριστῶ τῷ θεῷ,
THE OTHER MAN IS NOT BEING EDIFIED. I THANK - GOD,

πάντων ὑμῶν μᾶλλον γλώσσαις λαλῶ· **14.19** ἀλλὰ ἐν
⁴ALL ⁵OF YOU³ ³MORE THAN ²IN TONGUES ¹I SPEAK; BUT IN

ἐκκλησίᾳ θέλω πέντε λόγους τῷ νοΐ μου λαλῆσαι,
AN ASSEMBLY I WANT ²FIVE ³WORDS ⁴WITH THE ⁵MIND ⁶OF ME ¹TO SPEAK,

ἵνα καὶ ἄλλους κατηχήσω, ἢ μυρίους
THAT ALSO OTHERS I MAY INSTRUCT, [RATHER] THAN [SPEAK] TEN THOUSAND

λόγους ἐν γλώσσῃ.
WORDS IN A TONGUE.

14.20 Ἀδελφοί, μὴ παιδία γίνεσθε ταῖς φρεσίν
BROTHERS, ²NOT ³CHILDREN ¹BE IN THE(YOUR³) MINDS,

ἀλλὰ τῇ κακίᾳ νηπιάζετε, ταῖς δὲ φρεσὶν
BUT - [AS] TO MALICE BE CHILDLIKE, AND~IN THE(YOUR³) UNDERSTANDING

τέλειοι γίνεσθε. **14.21** ἐν τῷ νόμῳ γέγραπται ὅτι
BECOME~MATURE. IN THE LAW IT HAS BEEN WRITTEN -

Ἐν ἑτερογλώσσοις
IN OTHER TONGUES

καὶ ἐν χείλεσιν ἑτέρων
AND WITH LIPS OF OTHERS

λαλήσω τῷ λαῷ τούτῳ
I WILL SPEAK - TO THIS~PEOPLE

καὶ οὐδ᾽ οὕτως εἰσακούσονταί μου,
¹EVEN ³NOT ²SO WILL THEY HEAR ME,

λέγει κύριος. **14.22** ὥστε αἱ γλῶσσαι εἰς σημεῖόν
SAYS [THE] LORD. SO THEN THE TONGUES FOR A SIGN

14:21 Isa. 28:11-12

εἰσιν οὐ τοῖς   πιστεύουσιν ἀλλὰ τοῖς ἀπίστοις, ἡ
ARE,   NOT TO THE ONES BELIEVING   BUT   TO THE UNBELIEVERS,   -

δὲ προφητεία οὐ   τοῖς ἀπίστοις ἀλλὰ τοῖς
BUT PROPHECY [IS] NOT TO THE UNBELIEVERS BUT TO THE ONES

πιστεύουσιν. **14.23** Ἐὰν οὖν   συνέλθη ἡ   ἐκκλησία
BELIEVING.   IF   THEREFORE ⁴COMES ¹THE ³CHURCH

ὅλη ἐπὶ τὸ αὐτὸ καὶ πάντες λαλῶσιν γλώσσαις,
²WHOLE TOGETHER   AND ALL   SPEAK   IN TONGUES,

εἰσέλθωσιν δὲ ἰδιῶται   ἢ ἄπιστοι, οὐκ ἐροῦσιν ὅτι
AND~ENTERS   UNLEARNED ONES OR UNBELIEVERS, WILL THEY NOT SAY THAT

μαίνεσθε;   **14.24** ἐὰν δὲ πάντες προφητεύωσιν,
YOU° ARE OUT OF YOUR MINDS?   BUT~IF   ALL   PROPHESY,

εἰσέλθη δέ τις ἄπιστος ἢ ἰδιώτης,   ἐλέγχεται ὑπὸ
AND~ENTER SOME UNBELIEVER OR UNLEARNED ONE, HE IS CONVICTED BY

πάντων, ἀνακρίνεται ὑπὸ πάντων, **14.25** τὰ κρυπτὰ
ALL,   HE IS JUDGED   BY   ALL,   THE HIDDEN THINGS

τῆς καρδίας αὐτοῦ φανερὰ γίνεται, καὶ οὕτως
OF THE HEART OF HIM BECOME~MANIFEST, AND SO

πεσὼν ἐπὶ πρόσωπον προσκυνήσει τῷ θεῷ
HAVING FALLEN ON [HIS] FACE   HE WILL WORSHIP -   GOD,

ἀπαγγέλλων ὅτι Ὄντως ὁ θεὸς ἐν ὑμῖν ἐστιν.
DECLARING,   - ³REALLY - ¹GOD ⁴AMONG ⁵YOU° ²IS.

14.26 Τί   οὖν ἐστιν, ἀδελφοί; ὅταν συνέρχησθε,
        WHAT(HOW) THEN IS IT,   BROTHERS? WHEN YOU° COME TOGETHER,

ἕκαστος ψαλμὸν ἔχει, διδαχὴν ἔχει, ἀποκάλυψιν ἔχει,
EACH ONE A PSALM HAS, A TEACHING HAS, A REVELATION   HAS,

γλῶσσαν ἔχει, ἑρμηνείαν   ἔχει· πάντα   πρὸς
A TONGUE HAS, AN INTERPRETATION HAS; ²ALL THINGS ⁴FOR

οἰκοδομὴν γινέσθω. **14.27** εἴτε γλώσσῃ τις λαλεῖ,
⁵EDIFICATION ¹LET ³BE.   IF   IN A TONGUE ANYONE SPEAKS,

κατὰ δύο ἢ τὸ πλεῖστον τρεῖς καὶ ἀνὰ μέρος, καὶ
BY   TWO OR THE MOST   THREE, AND IN TURN,   AND

εἷς διερμηνευέτω· **14.28** ἐὰν δὲ μὴ ᾖ   διερμηνευτής,
LET ONE INTERPRET;   BUT~IF THERE IS~NOT AN INTERPRETER,

σιγάτω   ἐν ἐκκλησίᾳ, ἑαυτῷ δὲ λαλείτω καὶ τῷ
LET HIM BE SILENT IN AN ASSEMBLY, AND~TO HIMSELF LET HIM SPEAK AND -

θεῷ.   **14.29** προφῆται δὲ δύο ἢ τρεῖς λαλείτωσαν
TO GOD.   AND~PROPHETS TWO OR THREE LET THEM SPEAK

καὶ οἱ ἄλλοι διακρινέτωσαν· **14.30** ἐὰν δὲ
AND THE OTHERS LET DISCERN;   BUT~IF

ἄλλῳ ἀποκαλυφθῇ   καθημένῳ, ὁ πρῶτος σιγάτω.
[SOMETHING] IS REVEALED~TO ANOTHER SITTING [BY], THE FIRST LET BE SILENT.

14.31 δύνασθε γὰρ καθ᾽ ἕνα πάντες προφητεύειν, ἵνα
        ¹FOR~YOU° ARE ³ABLE ⁴ONE BY ONE ²ALL ⁵TO PROPHESY,   THAT

πάντες μανθάνωσιν καὶ πάντες παρακαλῶνται.
ALL   MAY LEARN   AND ALL   MAY BE ENCOURAGED.

14.32 καὶ πνεύματα προφητῶν προφήταις ὑποτάσσεται,
        AND [THE] SPIRITS OF PROPHETS TO PROPHETS ARE SUBJECT,

not for believers but for unbelievers, while prophecy is not for unbelievers but for believers. 23If, therefore, the whole church comes together and all speak in tongues, and outsiders or unbelievers enter, will they not say that you are out of your mind? 24But if all prophesy, an unbeliever or outsider who enters is reproved by all and called to account by all. 25After the secrets of the unbeliever's heart are disclosed, that person will bow down before God and worship him, declaring, "God is really among you."

26 What should be done then, my friends?ʲ When you come together, each one has a hymn, a lesson, a revelation, a tongue, or an interpretation. Let all things be done for building up. 27If anyone speaks in a tongue, let there be only two or at most three, and each in turn; and let one interpret. 28But if there is no one to interpret, let them be silent in church and speak to themselves and to God. 29Let two or three prophets speak, and let the others weigh what is said. 30If a revelation is made to someone else sitting nearby, let the first person be silent. 31For you can all prophesy one by one, so that all may learn and all be encouraged. 32And the spirits of prophets are subject to the prophets,

ʲ Gk brothers

³³for God is a God not of disorder but of peace.

(As in all the churches of the saints, ³⁴women should be silent in the churches. For they are not permitted to speak, but should be subordinate, as the law also says. ³⁵If there is anything they desire to know, let them ask their husbands at home. For it is shameful for a woman to speak in church.ᵏ ³⁶Or did the word of God originate with you? Or are you the only ones it has reached?)

37 Anyone who claims to be a prophet, or to have spiritual powers, must acknowledge that what I am writing to you is a command of the Lord. ³⁸Anyone who does not recognize this is not to be recognized. ³⁹So, my friends,ˡ be eager to prophesy, and do not forbid speaking in tongues; ⁴⁰but all things should be done decently and in order.

ᵏ Other ancient authorities put verses 34-35 after verse 40
ˡ Gk my brothers

14.33 οὐ γάρ ἐστιν ἀκαταστασίας ὁ θεὸς ἀλλὰ εἰρήνης.
³NOT ¹FOR ²HE IS ⁶OF CONFUSION ⁴THE ⁵GOD ⁷BUT ⁸OF PEACE.

'Ὡς ἐν πάσαις ταῖς ἐκκλησίαις τῶν ἁγίων
AS IN ALL THE CHURCHES OF THE SAINTS,

14.34 αἱ γυναῖκες ἐν ταῖς ἐκκλησίαις σιγάτωσαν·
²THE ³WOMEN ⁴IN ⁵THE ⁶ASSEMBLIES ¹LET ⁷BE SILENT;

οὐ γάρ ἐπιτρέπεται αὐταῖς λαλεῖν, ἀλλὰ
³NOT ¹FOR ²IT IS ⁴PERMITTED TO THEM TO SPEAK, BUT

ὑποτασσέσθωσαν, καθὼς καὶ ὁ νόμος λέγει.
LET THEM BE SUBMISSIVE, AS ALSO THE LAW SAYS.

14.35 εἰ δέ τι μαθεῖν θέλουσιν, ἐν οἴκῳ τοὺς
AND~IF ³ANYTHING ²TO LEARN ¹THEY DESIRE, IN [THE] HOME ²THE[IR]

ἰδίους ἄνδρας ἐπερωτάτωσαν· αἰσχρὸν γάρ ἐστιν
³OWN ⁴HUSBANDS ¹LET THEM ASK. FOR~A SHAME IT IS

γυναικὶ λαλεῖν ἐν ἐκκλησίᾳ. **14.36** ἢ ἀφ' ὑμῶν ὁ
FOR A WOMAN TO SPEAK IN AN ASSEMBLY. OR FROM YOU° THE

λόγος τοῦ θεοῦ ἐξῆλθεν, ἢ εἰς ὑμᾶς μόνους
WORD - OF GOD WENT FORTH, OR TO YOU° ONLY

κατήντησεν;
DID IT REACH?

14.37 Εἴ τις δοκεῖ προφήτης εἶναι ἢ πνευματικός,
IF ANYONE THINKS TO BE~A PROPHET OR A SPIRITUAL MAN,

ἐπιγινωσκέτω ἃ γράφω ὑμῖν ὅτι κυρίου ἐστὶν
LET HIM FULLY KNOW THE THINGS I WRITE TO YOU° THAT OF [THE] LORD THEY ARE

ἐντολή· **14.38** εἰ δέ τις ἀγνοεῖ,
A COMMANDMENT; BUT~IF ANYONE DOES NOT RECOGNIZE [THIS],

⌐ἀγνοεῖται.⌐ **14.39** ὥστε, ἀδελφοί [μου], ζηλοῦτε τὸ
HE IS NOT RECOGNIZED. SO THEN, BROTHERS OF ME, EARNESTLY DESIRE -

προφητεύειν, καὶ τὸ λαλεῖν μὴ κωλύετε γλώσσαις·
TO PROPHESY, AND - ²TO SPEAK ¹DO NOT FORBID IN TONGUES;

14.40 πάντα δὲ εὐσχημόνως καὶ κατὰ τάξιν
³ALL THINGS ¹BUT ⁵DECENTLY ⁶AND ⁷ACCORDING TO ⁸ORDER

γινέσθω.
²LET ⁴BE DONE.

14:38 text: ASVmg RSV NASB NIV NEB TEV NJB. var. αγνοειτω (let him be ignorant): KJV ASV NASBmg NIVmg NEBmg NJBmg.

CHAPTER 15

Now I would remind you, brothers and sisters,ᵐ of the good newsⁿ that I proclaimed to you, which you in turn received, in which also you stand, ²through which also you are being saved, if you hold firmly to the message that I proclaimed to you—

ᵐ Gk brothers
ⁿ Or gospel

15.1 Γνωρίζω δὲ ὑμῖν, ἀδελφοί, τὸ εὐαγγέλιον ὃ
NOW~I MAKE KNOWN TO YOU°, BROTHERS, THE GOOD NEWS WHICH

εὐηγγελισάμην ὑμῖν, ὃ καὶ παρελάβετε, ἐν ᾧ
I PREACHED TO YOU°, WHICH ALSO YOU° RECEIVED, IN WHICH

καὶ ἑστήκατε, **15.2** δι' οὗ καὶ σῴζεσθε, τίνι
ALSO YOU° HAVE STOOD, THROUGH WHICH ALSO YOU° ARE SAVED, WITH WHAT

λόγῳ εὐηγγελισάμην ὑμῖν εἰ κατέχετε, ἐκτὸς
WORD I PREACHED TO YOU° IF(PROVIDED) YOU° HOLD [IT] FAST, -

εἰ μὴ εἰκῇ ἐπιστεύσατε. **15.3** παρέδωκα γὰρ ὑμῖν ἐν
UNLESS IN VAIN YOU° BELIEVED. FOR~I HANDED ON TO YOU° AMONG

πρώτοις, ὃ καὶ παρέλαβον, ὅτι Χριστὸς
THE FIRST THINGS, THAT WHICH ALSO I RECEIVED, THAT CHRIST

ἀπέθανεν ὑπὲρ τῶν ἁμαρτιῶν ἡμῶν κατὰ τὰς
DIED FOR THE SINS OF US ACCORDING TO THE

γραφὰς **15.4** καὶ ὅτι ἐτάφη καὶ ὅτι ἐγήγερται τῇ
SCRIPTURES, AND THAT HE WAS BURIED AND THAT HE WAS RAISED ON THE

ἡμέρᾳ τῇ τρίτῃ κατὰ τὰς γραφὰς **15.5** καὶ ὅτι
²DAY - ¹THIRD ACCORDING TO THE SCRIPTURES AND THAT

ὤφθη Κηφᾷ εἶτα τοῖς δώδεκα· **15.6** ἔπειτα ὤφθη
HE WAS SEEN BY CEPHAS THEN BY THE TWELVE; AFTERWARD HE WAS SEEN

ἐπάνω πεντακοσίοις ἀδελφοῖς ἐφάπαξ, ἐξ ὧν οἱ
[BY] OVER FIVE HUNDRED BROTHERS AT ONE TIME, OF WHOM THE

πλείονες μένουσιν ἕως ἄρτι, τινὲς δὲ ἐκοιμήθησαν·
MAJORITY REMAIN UNTIL NOW, BUT~SOME FELL ASLEEP;

15.7 ἔπειτα ὤφθη Ἰακώβῳ, εἶτα τοῖς ἀποστόλοις
AFTERWARD HE WAS SEEN BY JAMES, THEN BY THE APOSTLES

πᾶσιν· **15.8** ἔσχατον δὲ πάντων ὡσπερεὶ τῷ
ALL; AND~LAST OF ALL EVEN AS IF TO ONE

ἐκτρώματι ὤφθη κἀμοί. **15.9** Ἐγὼ γάρ εἰμι ὁ
UNTIMELY BORN HE WAS SEEN BY ME ALSO. FOR~I AM THE

ἐλάχιστος τῶν ἀποστόλων ὃς οὐκ εἰμὶ ἱκανὸς
LEAST OF THE APOSTLES, WHO IS NOT QUALIFIED

καλεῖσθαι ἀπόστολος, διότι ἐδίωξα τὴν ἐκκλησίαν
TO BE CALLED AN APOSTLE, BECAUSE I PERSECUTED THE CHURCH

τοῦ θεοῦ· **15.10** χάριτι δὲ θεοῦ εἰμι ὅ εἰμι, καὶ
- OF GOD; BUT~BY [THE] GRACE OF GOD I AM WHAT I AM, AND

ἡ χάρις αὐτοῦ ἡ εἰς ἐμὲ οὐ κενὴ ἐγενήθη, ἀλλὰ
THE GRACE OF HIM - TO ME NOT IN VAIN WAS, BUT

περισσότερον αὐτῶν πάντων ἐκοπίασα, οὐκ ἐγὼ δὲ
²MORE ABUNDANTLY ³THAN THEM ⁴ALL ¹I LABORED, ²NOT ³I ¹YET

ἀλλὰ ἡ χάρις τοῦ θεοῦ [ἡ] σὺν ἐμοί. **15.11** εἴτε
BUT THE GRACE - OF GOD - WITH ME. WHETHER

οὖν ἐγὼ εἴτε ἐκεῖνοι, οὕτως κηρύσσομεν καὶ οὕτως
THEREFORE I OR THOSE ONES, SO WE PREACH AND SO

ἐπιστεύσατε.
YOU° BELIEVED.

15.12 Εἰ δὲ Χριστὸς κηρύσσεται ὅτι ἐκ νεκρῶν
AND~IF CHRIST IS BEING PREACHED THAT FROM [THE] DEAD

ἐγήγερται, πῶς λέγουσιν ἐν ὑμῖν τινες ὅτι
HE HAS BEEN RAISED, HOW SAY ²AMONG ³YOU° ¹SOME THAT

ἀνάστασις νεκρῶν οὐκ ἔστιν; **15.13** εἰ δὲ ἀνάστασις
A RESURRECTION OF DEAD PERSONS THERE IS~NOT? AND~IF A RESURRECTION

νεκρῶν οὐκ ἔστιν, οὐδὲ Χριστὸς ἐγήγερται·
OF DEAD PERSONS THERE IS~NOT, NEITHER CHRIST HAS BEEN RAISED;

15.14 εἰ δὲ Χριστὸς οὐκ ἐγήγερται, κενὸν ἄρα [καὶ] τὸ
AND~IF CHRIST HAS NOT BEEN RAISED, IN VAIN THEN ALSO [IS] THE

unless you have come to believe in vain.

3 For I handed on to you as of first importance what I in turn had received: that Christ died for our sins in accordance with the scriptures, [4]and that he was buried, and that he was raised on the third day in accordance with the scriptures, [5]and that he appeared to Cephas, then to the twelve. [6]Then he appeared to more than five hundred brothers and sisters[o] at one time, most of whom are still alive, though some have died.[p] [7]Then he appeared to James, then to all the apostles. [8]Last of all, as to one untimely born, he appeared also to me. [9]For I am the least of the apostles, unfit to be called an apostle, because I persecuted the church of God. [10]But by the grace of God I am what I am, and his grace toward me has not been in vain. On the contrary, I worked harder than any of them—though it was not I, but the grace of God that is with me. [11]Whether then it was I or they, so we proclaim and so you have come to believe.

12 Now if Christ is proclaimed as raised from the dead, how can some of you say there is no resurrection of the dead? [13]If there is no resurrection of the dead, then Christ has not been raised; [14]and if Christ has not been raised, then our proclamation has been in vain

[o] Gk *brothers*
[p] Gk *fallen asleep*

and your faith has been in vain. ¹⁵We are even found to be misrepresenting God, because we testified of God that he raised Christ— whom he did not raise if it is true that the dead are not raised. ¹⁶For if the dead are not raised, then Christ has not been raised. ¹⁷If Christ has not been raised, your faith is futile and you are still in your sins. ¹⁸Then those also who have died*q* in Christ have perished. ¹⁹If for this life only we have hoped in Christ, we are of all people most to be pitied.

20 But in fact Christ has been raised from the dead, the first fruits of those who have died.*q* ²¹For since death came through a human being, the resurrection of the dead has also come through a human being; ²²for as all die in Adam, so all will be made alive in Christ. ²³But each in his own order: Christ the first fruits, then at his coming those who belong to Christ. ²⁴Then comes the end,*r* when he hands over the kingdom to God the Father, after he has destroyed every ruler and every authority and power. ²⁵For he must reign until he has put all his enemies under his feet. ²⁶The last enemy to be

q Gk *fallen asleep*
r Or *Then come the rest*

κήρυγμα ἡμῶν, κενὴ καὶ ἡ πίστις ὑμῶν·
PREACHING OF US, IN VAIN ALSO THE FAITH OF YOU°;

15.15 εὑρισκόμεθα δὲ καὶ ψευδομάρτυρες τοῦ θεοῦ, ὅτι
AND~WE ARE FOUND ALSO FALSE WITNESSES - OF GOD, BECAUSE

ἐμαρτυρήσαμεν κατὰ τοῦ θεοῦ ὅτι ἤγειρεν τὸν Χριστόν,
WE WITNESSED AS TO - GOD THAT HE RAISED - CHRIST,

ὃν οὐκ ἤγειρεν εἴπερ ἄρα νεκροὶ οὐκ ἐγείρονται.
WHOM HE DID NOT RAISE IF THEN DEAD PERSONS ARE NOT RAISED.

15.16 εἰ γὰρ νεκροὶ οὐκ ἐγείρονται, οὐδὲ Χριστὸς
FOR~IF DEAD PERSONS ARE NOT RAISED, NEITHER CHRIST

ἐγήγερται· **15.17** εἰ δὲ Χριστὸς οὐκ ἐγήγερται, ματαία
HAS BEEN RAISED; AND~IF CHRIST HAS NOT BEEN RAISED, FUTILE [IS]

ἡ πίστις ὑμῶν, ἔτι ἐστὲ ἐν ταῖς ἁμαρτίαις ὑμῶν,
THE FAITH OF YOU°, YOU° ARE~STILL IN THE SINS OF YOU°,

15.18 ἄρα καὶ οἱ κοιμηθέντες ἐν Χριστῷ
THEN ALSO THE ONES HAVING FALLEN ASLEEP IN CHRIST

ἀπώλοντο. **15.19** εἰ ἐν τῇ ζωῇ ταύτῃ ἐν Χριστῷ
PERISHED. IF IN - THIS~LIFE ³IN ⁴CHRIST

ἠλπικότες ἐσμὲν μόνον, ἐλεεινότεροι πάντων ἀνθρώπων
²WE HAVE HOPED ¹ONLY, ²TO BE PITIED MORE ³THAN ALL ⁴MEN

ἐσμέν.
¹WE ARE

15.20 Νυνὶ δὲ Χριστὸς ἐγήγερται ἐκ νεκρῶν
BUT~NOW CHRIST HAS BEEN RAISED FROM [THE] DEAD,

ἀπαρχὴ τῶν κεκοιμημένων. **15.21** ἐπειδὴ γὰρ
[THE] FIRSTFRUITS OF THE ONES HAVING FALLEN ASLEEP. FOR~SINCE

δι' ἀνθρώπου θάνατος, καὶ δι' ἀνθρώπου
THROUGH A MAN [CAME] DEATH, ALSO THROUGH A MAN

ἀνάστασις νεκρῶν. **15.22** ὥσπερ γὰρ ἐν τῷ
[CAME] A RESURRECTION OF DEAD PERSONS. FOR~AS IN -

Ἀδὰμ πάντες ἀποθνήσκουσιν, οὕτως καὶ ἐν τῷ
ADAM ALL DIE, SO ALSO IN -

Χριστῷ πάντες ζῳοποιηθήσονται. **15.23** ἕκαστος δὲ ἐν
CHRIST ALL WILL BE MADE ALIVE. BUT~EACH ONE IN

τῷ ἰδίῳ τάγματι· ἀπαρχὴ Χριστός, ἔπειτα οἱ
THE(HIS) OWN ORDER; [THE] FIRSTFRUITS, CHRIST, AFTERWARD THE ONES

τοῦ Χριστοῦ ἐν τῇ παρουσίᾳ αὐτοῦ, **15.24** εἶτα τὸ
- OF CHRIST IN THE COMING OF HIM, THEN THE

τέλος, ὅταν παραδιδῷ τὴν βασιλείαν τῷ θεῷ καὶ
END, WHEN HE GIVES OVER THE KINGDOM - TO GOD EVEN

πατρί, ὅταν καταργήσῃ πᾶσαν ἀρχὴν καὶ πᾶσαν
[THE] FATHER, WHEN HE ABOLISHES ALL RULE AND ALL

ἐξουσίαν καὶ δύναμιν. **15.25** δεῖ γὰρ αὐτὸν
AUTHORITY AND POWER. FOR~IT IS NECESSARY [FOR] HIM

βασιλεύειν ἄχρι οὗ θῇ πάντας τοὺς ἐχθροὺς ὑπὸ
TO REIGN UNTIL HE PUTS ALL THE(HIS) ENEMIES UNDER

τοὺς πόδας αὐτοῦ. **15.26** ἔσχατος ἐχθρὸς καταργεῖται ὁ
THE FEET OF HIM. [THE] LAST ENEMY BEING ABOLISHED -

θάνατος· **15.27** πάντα γὰρ ὑπέταξεν ὑπὸ τοὺς πόδας
[IS] DEATH;   FOR~ALL THINGS HE SUBJECTED UNDER THE FEET

αὐτοῦ. ὅταν δὲ εἴπῃ ὅτι πάντα ὑποτέτακται, δῆλον
OF HIM. BUT~WHEN HE SAYS THAT ALL THINGS HAVE BEEN SUBJECTED, [IT IS] CLEAR

ὅτι ἐκτὸς   τοῦ   ὑποτάξαντος αὐτῷ τὰ πάντα.
THAT [HE IS] EXCEPTED, THE ONE HAVING SUBJECTED TO HIM - ALL THINGS.

15.28 ὅταν δὲ ὑποταγῇ   αὐτῷ   τὰ πάντα, τότε [καὶ]
        BUT~WHEN ARE SUBJECTED TO HIM - ALL THINGS, THEN ALSO

αὐτὸς ὁ υἱὸς ὑποταγήσεται τῷ   ὑποτάξαντι αὐτῷ
³HIMSELF ¹THE ²SON WILL BE SUBJECTED TO THE ONE HAVING SUBJECTED TO HIM

τὰ πάντα, ἵνα ᾖ   ὁ θεὸς [τὰ] πάντα ἐν πᾶσιν.
- ALL THINGS, THAT ²MAY BE - ¹GOD - ALL THINGS IN ALL.

15.29 Ἐπεὶ   τί   ποιήσουσιν οἱ   βαπτιζόμενοι
        OTHERWISE WHAT WILL THEY DO, THE ONES BEING BAPTIZED

ὑπὲρ   τῶν νεκρῶν; εἰ ὅλως νεκροὶ   οὐκ ἐγείρονται,
ON BEHALF OF THE DEAD? IF REALLY DEAD PERSONS ARE NOT RAISED,

τί καὶ βαπτίζονται ὑπὲρ   αὐτῶν; **15.30** τί καὶ
WHY INDEED ARE THEY BAPTIZED ON BEHALF OF THEM?   WHY ALSO

ἡμεῖς κινδυνεύομεν πᾶσαν ὥραν; **15.31** καθ' ἡμέραν
ARE WE IN DANGER EVERY HOUR?   DAILY

ἀποθνῄσκω, νὴ   τὴν ὑμετέραν καύχησιν, [ἀδελφοί,]
I DIE,   I SWEAR BY - YOUR°   BOASTING,   BROTHERS,

ἣν ἔχω ἐν Χριστῷ Ἰησοῦ τῷ κυρίῳ ἡμῶν. **15.32** εἰ
WHICH I HAVE IN CHRIST JESUS THE LORD OF US.   IF

κατὰ ἄνθρωπον ἐθηριομάχησα   ἐν Ἐφέσῳ, τί   μοι
AS A MERE MAN I FOUGHT WITH WILD BEASTS IN EPHESUS, WHAT [IS] ³TO ME

τὸ ὄφελος; εἰ νεκροὶ   οὐκ ἐγείρονται,
¹THE ²BENEFIT? IF DEAD PERSONS ARE NOT RAISED,

    Φάγωμεν καὶ πίωμεν,
    LET US EAT AND LET US DRINK,

        αὔριον γὰρ ἀποθνῄσκομεν.
        FOR~TOMORROW WE DIE.

15.33 μὴ πλανᾶσθε·
        DO NOT BE DECEIVED;

    Φθείρουσιν ἤθη   χρηστὰ ὁμιλίαι   κακαί.
    ³CORRUPT   ⁵MORALS ⁴GOOD   ²COMPANIONSHIPS ¹BAD.

15.34 ἐκνήψατε   δικαίως   καὶ μὴ ἁμαρτάνετε,
        COME TO YOUR° SENSES, [LIVE] RIGHTEOUSLY, AND STOP SINNING,

ἀγνωσίαν γὰρ θεοῦ τινες ἔχουσιν, πρὸς ἐντροπὴν ὑμῖν
⁴AN IGNORANCE ¹FOR ⁵OF GOD ²SOME ³HAVE,   TO YOUR°~SHAME

λαλῶ.
I SPEAK [THIS].

15.35 Ἀλλὰ ἐρεῖ τις,   Πῶς ἐγείρονται οἱ νεκροί;
        BUT SOMEONE~WILL SAY, HOW ARE RAISED THE DEAD?

ποίῳ δὲ   σώματι ἔρχονται; **15.36** ἄφρων,   σὺ ὃ
AND~WITH WHAT KIND OF BODY DO THEY COME?   FOOLISH MAN, WHAT~YOU

15:27 Ps. 8:6 **15:32** Isa. 22:13

destroyed is death. [27]For
"God[s] has put all things in
subjection under his feet."
But when it says, "All things
are put in subjection," it is
plain that this does not
include the one who put all
things in subjection under
him. [28]When all things are
subjected to him, then the
Son himself will also be
subjected to the one who put
all things in subjection under
him, so that God may be all
in all.

29 Otherwise, what will
those people do who receive
baptism on behalf of the
dead? If the dead are not
raised at all, why are people
baptized on their behalf?

30 And why are we
putting ourselves in danger
every hour? [31]I die every
day! That is as certain,
brothers and sisters,[t] as my
boasting of you—a boast
that I make in Christ Jesus
our Lord. [32]If with merely
human hopes I fought with
wild animals at Ephesus,
what would I have gained by
it? If the dead are not raised,
    "Let us eat and drink,
    for tomorrow we die."
[33]Do not be deceived:
    "Bad company ruins
    good morals."
[34]Come to a sober and right
mind, and sin no more; for
some people have no
knowledge of God. I say this
to your shame.

35 But someone will ask,
"How are the dead raised?
With what kind of body do
they come?" [36]Fool! What

[s] Gk *he*
[t] Gk *brothers*

you sow does not come to life unless it dies. ³⁷And as for what you sow, you do not sow the body that is to be, but a bare seed, perhaps of wheat or of some other grain. ³⁸But God gives it a body as he has chosen, and to each kind of seed its own body. ³⁹Not all flesh is alike, but there is one flesh for human beings, another for animals, another for birds, and another for fish. ⁴⁰There are both heavenly bodies and earthly bodies, but the glory of the heavenly is one thing, and that of the earthly is another. ⁴¹There is one glory of the sun, and another glory of the moon, and another glory of the stars; indeed, star differs from star in glory.

42 So it is with the resurrection of the dead. What is sown is perishable, what is raised is imperishable. ⁴³It is sown in dishonor, it is raised in glory. It is sown in weakness, it is raised in power. ⁴⁴It is sown a physical body, it is raised a spiritual body. If there is a physical body, there is also a spiritual body. ⁴⁵Thus it is written, "The first man, Adam, became a living being"; the last Adam became a life-giving spirit. ⁴⁶But it is not the spiritual that is first, but the physical, and then the

σπείρεις, οὐ ζῳοποιεῖται ἐὰν μὴ ἀποθάνῃ· **15.37** καὶ
SOW,   IS NOT MADE ALIVE   UNLESS IT DIES;   AND

ὃ σπείρεις, οὐ τὸ σῶμα τὸ γενησόμενον σπείρεις
WHAT YOU SOW, ²NOT ³THE ⁴BODY - ⁵GOING TO BECOME ¹YOU SOW

ἀλλὰ γυμνὸν κόκκον εἰ τύχοι σίτου ἤ τινος τῶν
BUT   A BARE GRAIN PERHAPS OF WHEAT OR SOME OF THE

λοιπῶν· **15.38** ὁ δὲ θεὸς δίδωσιν αὐτῷ σῶμα καθὼς
OTHER [GRAINS];   - BUT GOD GIVES   TO IT A BODY AS

ἠθέλησεν, καὶ ἑκάστῳ τῶν σπερμάτων ἴδιον σῶμα.
HE WANTED,   AND TO EACH OF THE SEEDS   [ITS] OWN BODY.

15.39 οὐ πᾶσα σὰρξ ἡ   αὐτὴ σάρξ ἀλλὰ ἄλλη
         NOT ALL FLESH [IS] THE SAME FLESH BUT [THERE IS] ANOTHER

μὲν ἀνθρώπων, ἄλλη δὲ σὰρξ κτηνῶν, ἄλλη δὲ σὰρξ
 -    OF MEN,   AND~ANOTHER FLESH OF ANIMALS, AND~ANOTHER FLESH

πτηνῶν, ἄλλη δὲ ἰχθύων. **15.40** καὶ σώματα
OF BIRDS, AND~ANOTHER OF FISHES.   AND [THERE ARE] BODIES

ἐπουράνια, καὶ σώματα ἐπίγεια· ἀλλὰ ἑτέρα μὲν
HEAVENLY,   AND BODIES EARTHLY;   BUT   DIFFERENT -

ἡ τῶν ἐπουρανίων δόξα, ἑτέρα δὲ ἡ   τῶν
[IS] THE ²OF THE ³HEAVENLY ¹GLORY, AND~DIFFERENT THE [GLORY] OF THE

ἐπιγείων. **15.41** ἄλλη   δόξα ἡλίου, καὶ ἄλλη
EARTHLY.   [THERE IS] ANOTHER GLORY OF [THE] SUN, AND ANOTHER

δόξα σελήνης, καὶ ἄλλη δόξα ἀστέρων· ἀστὴρ γὰρ
GLORY OF [THE] MOON, AND ANOTHER GLORY OF [THE] STARS; FOR~STAR

ἀστέρος διαφέρει ἐν δόξῃ.
FROM STAR DIFFERS   IN GLORY.

15.42 Οὕτως καὶ ἡ ἀνάστασις τῶν νεκρῶν.
         SO   ALSO [IS] THE RESURRECTION OF THE DEAD.

σπείρεται ἐν φθορᾷ, ἐγείρεται ἐν ἀφθαρσίᾳ·
IT IS SOWN   -   [AS] PERISHABLE, IT IS RAISED WITH IMPERISHABILITY;

15.43 σπείρεται ἐν ἀτιμίᾳ, ἐγείρεται ἐν δόξῃ·
          IT IS SOWN IN DISHONOR, IT IS RAISED IN GLORY;

σπείρεται ἐν ἀσθενείᾳ, ἐγείρεται ἐν δυνάμει·
IT IS SOWN IN WEAKNESS,   IT IS RAISED IN POWER;

15.44 σπείρεται σῶμα ψυχικόν, ἐγείρεται
          IT IS SOWN A NATURAL~BODY,   IT IS RAISED

σῶμα πνευματικόν. εἰ ἔστιν σῶμα ψυχικόν, ἔστιν καὶ
A SPIRITUAL~BODY.   IF THERE IS A NATURAL~BODY, THERE IS ALSO

πνευματικόν. **15.45** οὕτως καὶ γέγραπται, Ἐγένετο ὁ
A SPIRITUAL ONE.   SO   ALSO IT HAS BEEN WRITTEN, ⁵BECAME ¹THE

πρῶτος ἄνθρωπος Ἀδὰμ εἰς ψυχὴν ζῶσαν, ὁ ἔσχατος
²FIRST ³MAN   ⁴ADAM - ⁷SOUL ⁶A LIVING, THE LAST

Ἀδὰμ εἰς πνεῦμα ζῳοποιοῦν. **15.46** ἀλλ' οὐ πρῶτον
ADAM   - [BECAME] A LIFE-GIVING~SPIRIT.   BUT NOT FIRST

τὸ πνευματικὸν ἀλλὰ τὸ ψυχικόν, ἔπειτα τὸ
[IS] THE SPIRITUAL [BODY] BUT THE NATURAL, AFTERWARD THE

15:45 Gen. 2:7

πνευματικόν. **15.47** ὁ πρῶτος ἄνθρωπος ἐκ γῆς
SPIRITUAL.　　　　　　　THE　FIRST　MAN　　[IS] OUT OF　EARTH,

χοϊκός, ὁ δεύτερος ἄνθρωπος ἐξ οὐρανοῦ.
MADE OF DUST,　THE　SECOND　MAN　　　[IS] OUT OF　HEAVEN.

15.48 οἷος ὁ χοϊκός, τοιοῦτοι καὶ οἱ χοϊκοί, καὶ
AS　　THE　MAN OF DUST,　SUCH　　ALSO　[ARE] THE　MEN OF DUST,　AND

οἷος ὁ ἐπουράνιος, τοιοῦτοι καὶ οἱ ἐπουράνιοι·
AS　THE　HEAVENLY MAN　SUCH　　ALSO　[ARE] THE　HEAVENLY ONES;

15.49 καὶ καθὼς ἐφορέσαμεν τὴν εἰκόνα τοῦ χοϊκοῦ,
AND　AS　WE BORE　THE　IMAGE　OF THE　MAN OF DUST,

⌜φορέσομεν⌝ καὶ τὴν εἰκόνα τοῦ ἐπουρανίου.
WE WILL BEAR　ALSO　THE　IMAGE　OF THE　HEAVENLY MAN.

15.50 Τοῦτο δέ φημι, ἀδελφοί, ὅτι σὰρξ καὶ αἷμα
NOW~THIS　I SAY,　BROTHERS,　THAT FLESH　AND　BLOOD

βασιλείαν θεοῦ κληρονομῆσαι οὐ δύναται οὐδὲ ἡ
3[THE] KINGDOM　4OF GOD　2TO INHERIT　1ARE NOT ABLE,　NEITHER　THE

φθορὰ τὴν ἀφθαρσίαν κληρονομεῖ. **15.51** ἰδοὺ
PERISHABLE　2THE　3IMPERISHABLE　1INHERITS.　　BEHOLD

μυστήριον ὑμῖν λέγω· πάντες οὐ κοιμηθησόμεθα,
A MYSTERY　TO YOU· I SPEAK;　ALL　WE WILL NOT SLEEP,

πάντες δὲ ἀλλαγησόμεθα, **15.52** ἐν ἀτόμῳ, ἐν ῥιπῇ
BUT~ALL　WE WILL BE CHANGED,　IN　A MOMENT, IN　A WINK

ὀφθαλμοῦ, ἐν τῇ ἐσχάτῃ σάλπιγγι· σαλπίσει γάρ
OF AN EYE,　IN(AT)　THE LAST　TRUMPET;　FOR~A TRUMPET WILL SOUND,

καὶ οἱ νεκροὶ ἐγερθήσονται ἄφθαρτοι καὶ ἡμεῖς
AND　THE　DEAD　WILL BE RAISED　IMPERISHABLE,　AND　WE

ἀλλαγησόμεθα. **15.53** δεῖ γὰρ τὸ
WILL BE CHANGED.　FOR~IT IS NECESSARY [FOR]　-

φθαρτὸν τοῦτο ἐνδύσασθαι ἀφθαρσίαν καὶ τὸ
THIS~PERISHABLE [NATURE] TO PUT ON　[THE] IMPERISHABLE　AND　-

θνητὸν τοῦτο ἐνδύσασθαι ἀθανασίαν. **15.54** ⌜ὅταν δὲ τὸ
THIS~MORTAL [NATURE] TO PUT ON　[THE] IMMORTAL.　BUT~WHEN　-

φθαρτὸν τοῦτο ἐνδύσηται ἀφθαρσίαν καὶ τὸ
THIS~PERISHABLE [NATURE]　PUTS ON　[THE] IMPERISHABLE　AND　-

θνητὸν τοῦτο ἐνδύσηται ἀθανασίαν,⌝ τότε γενήσεται
THIS~MORTAL [NATURE]　PUTS ON　[THE] IMMORTAL,　THEN　WILL COME TO PASS

ὁ λόγος ὁ γεγραμμένος,
THE WORD　-　HAVING BEEN WRITTEN,

Κατεπόθη ὁ θάνατος εἰς νῖκος.
2WAS SWALLOWED UP　-　1DEATH　IN　VICTORY.

15.55 ποῦ σου, θάνατε, τὸ νῖκος;
WHERE　OF YOU,　[O] DEATH,　[IS] THE　VICTORY?

ποῦ σου, θάνατε, τὸ κέντρον;
WHERE　OF YOU,　[O] DEATH,　[IS] THE　STING?

spiritual. [47]The first man was from the earth, a man of dust; the second man is[u] from heaven. [48]As was the man of dust, so are those who are of the dust; and as is the man of heaven, so are those who are of heaven. [49]Just as we have borne the image of the man of dust, we will[v] also bear the image of the man of heaven.

50 What I am saying, brothers and sisters,[w] is this: flesh and blood cannot inherit the kingdom of God, nor does the perishable inherit the imperishable. [51]Listen, I will tell you a mystery! We will not all die,[x] but we will all be changed, [52]in a moment, in the twinkling of an eye, at the last trumpet. For the trumpet will sound, and the dead will be raised imperishable, and we will be changed. [53]For this perishable body must put on imperishability, and this mortal body must put on immortality. [54]When this perishable body puts on imperishability, and this mortal body puts on immortality, then the saying that is written will be fulfilled:

"Death has been swallowed up in victory."
[55]"Where, O death, is your victory?
Where, O death, is your sting?"

[u] Other ancient authorities add *the Lord*
[v] Other ancient authorities read *let us*
[w] Gk *brothers*
[x] Gk *fall asleep*

15:49 text: all. var. φορεσωμεν (let us bear): ASVmg RSVmg NASBmg NIVmg TEVmg NJBmg NRSVmg.
15:54a text: KJV ASV RSV NASB NIV NEBmg NRSV. var. οταν δε το θνητον τουτο ενδυσηται την αθανασιαν (now when this mortal [body] has been clothed with immortality): ASVmg NEB TEV NJBmg.
15:54b Isa. 25:8　**15:55** Hos. 13:14 LXX

⁵⁶The sting of death is sin, and the power of sin is the law. ⁵⁷But thanks be to God, who gives us the victory through our Lord Jesus Christ.

58 Therefore, my beloved,ʸ be steadfast, immovable, always excelling in the work of the Lord, because you know that in the Lord your labor is not in vain.

ʸ Gk *beloved brothers*

15.56 τὸ δὲ κέντρον τοῦ θανάτου ἡ ἁμαρτία, ἡ δὲ
NOW~THE STING - OF DEATH - [IS] SIN, AND~THE

δύναμις τῆς ἁμαρτίας ὁ νόμος· **15.57** τῷ δὲ
POWER - OF SIN [IS] THE LAW; - BUT

θεῷ χάρις τῷ διδόντι ἡμῖν τὸ νῖκος διὰ τοῦ
THANKS [BE]~TO GOD, THE ONE GIVING US THE VICTORY THROUGH THE

κυρίου ἡμῶν Ἰησοῦ Χριστοῦ. **15.58** Ὥστε, ἀδελφοί μου
LORD OF US JESUS CHRIST. SO THEN, BROTHERS OF ME

ἀγαπητοί, ἑδραῖοι γίνεσθε, ἀμετακίνητοι, περισσεύοντες
BELOVED, BE~STEADFAST ONES, IMMOVABLE ONES, ABOUNDING

ἐν τῷ ἔργῳ τοῦ κυρίου πάντοτε, εἰδότες ὅτι ὁ κόπος
IN THE WORK OF THE LORD ALWAYS, KNOWING THAT THE LABOR

ὑμῶν οὐκ ἔστιν κενὸς ἐν κυρίῳ.
OF YOU° IS~NOT IN VAIN IN [THE] LORD.

CHAPTER 16

Now concerning the collection for the saints: you should follow the directions I gave to the churches of Galatia. ²On the first day of every week, each of you is to put aside and save whatever extra you earn, so that collections need not be taken when I come. ³And when I arrive, I will send any whom you approve with letters to take your gift to Jerusalem. ⁴If it seems advisable that I should go also, they will accompany me.

5 I will visit you after passing through Macedonia—for I intend to pass through Macedonia— ⁶and perhaps I will stay with you or even spend the winter, so that you may send me on my way, wherever I go. ⁷I do not want to see you now just in passing,

16.1 Περὶ δὲ τῆς λογείας τῆς εἰς τοὺς ἁγίους
NOW~CONCERNING THE COLLECTION - FOR THE SAINTS,

ὥσπερ διέταξα ταῖς ἐκκλησίαις τῆς Γαλατίας, οὕτως
AS I DIRECTED THE CHURCHES - OF GALATIA, SO

καὶ ὑμεῖς ποιήσατε. **16.2** κατὰ μίαν σαββάτου
ALSO DO~YOU°. EVERY FIRST [DAY] OF A WEEK

ἕκαστος ὑμῶν παρ' ἑαυτῷ τιθέτω θησαυρίζων
EACH OF YOU° BY HIMSELF (AT HOME) SET [SOMETHING] ASIDE, STORING UP

ὅ τι ἐὰν εὐοδῶται, ἵνα μὴ ὅταν ἔλθω τότε
WHATEVER HE MAY HAVE PROSPERED IN, LEST WHEN I COME

λογεῖαι γίνωνται. **16.3** ὅταν δὲ παραγένωμαι, οὓς ἐὰν
THERE SHOULD BE~COLLECTIONS. AND~WHEN I ARRIVE, WHOMEVER

δοκιμάσητε, δι' ἐπιστολῶν τούτους πέμψω ἀπενεγκεῖν
YOU° APPROVE, WITH LETTERS THESE ONES I WILL SEND TO CARRY

τὴν χάριν ὑμῶν εἰς Ἰερουσαλήμ· **16.4** ἐὰν δὲ
THE GIFT OF YOU° TO JERUSALEM; AND~IF

ἄξιον ᾖ τοῦ κἀμὲ πορεύεσθαι, σὺν ἐμοὶ
IT IS~FITTING [FOR] - ME ALSO TO GO, WITH ME

πορεύσονται.
THEY WILL GO.

16.5 Ἐλεύσομαι δὲ πρὸς ὑμᾶς ὅταν
AND~I WILL COME TO YOU° WHENEVER

Μακεδονίαν διέλθω· Μακεδονίαν γὰρ διέρχομαι,
I PASS THROUGH~MACEDONIA; FOR~MACEDONIA I AM PASSING THROUGH,

16.6 πρὸς ὑμᾶς δὲ τυχὸν παραμενῶ ἢ καὶ
²WITH ³YOU° ¹AND POSSIBLY I WILL STAY OR EVEN

παραχειμάσω, ἵνα ὑμεῖς με προπέμψητε οὗ ἐὰν
SPEND THE WINTER, THAT YOU° MAY SEND ME FORWARD WHEREVER

πορεύωμαι. **16.7** οὐ θέλω γὰρ ὑμᾶς ἄρτι ἐν παρόδῳ
I MAY GO. ²I DO NOT WANT ¹FOR ⁴YOU° ⁵NOW ⁶IN ⁷PASSING

ἰδεῖν, ἐλπίζω γὰρ χρόνον τινὰ ἐπιμεῖναι πρὸς ὑμᾶς
[3]TO SEE,   [FOR~I HOPE]   [3]TIME [2]SOME [1]TO REMAIN   WITH   YOU°

ἐὰν ὁ κύριος ἐπιτρέψῃ. **16.8** ἐπιμενῶ δὲ ἐν Ἐφέσῳ ἕως
IF   THE LORD   PERMITS.   BUT~I WILL REMAIN IN   EPHESUS   UNTIL

τῆς πεντηκοστῆς· **16.9** θύρα γὰρ μοι ἀνέῳγεν μεγάλη
-    PENTECOST;   [5]DOOR [1]FOR [7]TO ME [6]HAS OPENED [2]A GREAT

καὶ ἐνεργής, καὶ ἀντικείμενοι πολλοί.
[3]AND [4]EFFECTIVE, AND [THERE ARE] MANY~OPPOSING ONES.

16.10 Ἐὰν δὲ ἔλθῃ Τιμόθεος, βλέπετε, ἵνα ἀφόβως
       NOW~IF TIMOTHY~COMES, SEE THAT WITHOUT FEAR

γένηται πρὸς ὑμᾶς· τὸ γὰρ ἔργον κυρίου ἐργάζεται
HE MAY BE WITH YOU; FOR~THE WORK OF [THE] LORD HE WORKS

ὡς κἀγώ· **16.11** μή τις οὖν αὐτὸν ἐξουθενήσῃ.
AS I ALSO;   [LET] NOT ANYONE THEREFORE DESPISE~HIM.

προπέμψατε δὲ αὐτὸν ἐν εἰρήνῃ, ἵνα ἔλθῃ πρός
[2]SEND[4]FORWARD [1]BUT [3]HIM IN PEACE, THAT HE MAY COME TO

με· ἐκδέχομαι γὰρ αὐτὸν μετὰ τῶν ἀδελφῶν.
ME; FOR~I AM WAITING [FOR] HIM WITH THE BROTHERS.

16.12 Περὶ δὲ Ἀπολλῶ τοῦ ἀδελφοῦ, πολλὰ
       NOW~CONCERNING APOLLOS THE BROTHER, [3]GREATLY

παρεκάλεσα αὐτόν, ἵνα ἔλθῃ πρὸς ὑμᾶς μετὰ
[1]I URGED [2]HIM, THAT HE WOULD COME TO YOU° WITH

τῶν ἀδελφῶν· καὶ πάντως οὐκ ἦν θέλημα ἵνα
THE BROTHERS; AND ALTOGETHER IT WAS~NOT [HIS] DESIRE THAT

νῦν ἔλθῃ· ἐλεύσεται δὲ ὅταν εὐκαιρήσῃ.
HE SHOULD COME~NOW;   BUT~HE WILL COME WHENEVER HE HAS AN OPPORTUNITY.

16.13 Γρηγορεῖτε, στήκετε ἐν τῇ πίστει, ἀνδρίζεσθε,
       WATCH,   STAND FIRM IN THE FAITH, BE MEN,

κραταιοῦσθε. **16.14** πάντα ὑμῶν ἐν ἀγάπῃ γινέσθω.
BE STRONG.   [2]ALL [4]THINGS [3]YOUR° [5]IN [6]LOVE [1]LET BE DONE.

16.15 Παρακαλῶ δὲ ὑμᾶς, ἀδελφοί· οἴδατε τὴν οἰκίαν
       NOW~I URGE YOU°, BROTHERS—YOU° KNOW THE HOUSEHOLD

Στεφανᾶ, ὅτι ἐστὶν ἀπαρχὴ τῆς Ἀχαΐας καὶ
OF STEPHANAS, THAT IT IS [THE] FIRSTFRUITS - OF ACHAIA AND

εἰς διακονίαν τοῖς ἁγίοις ἔταξαν ἑαυτούς·
[THAT] [3]INTO [4]A MINISTRY [5]FOR THE [6]SAINTS [1]THEY PUT [2]THEMSELVES—

16.16 ἵνα καὶ ὑμεῖς ὑποτάσσησθε τοῖς τοιούτοις καὶ
       THAT ALSO YOU° MAY BE SUBMISSIVE - TO SUCH ONES AND

παντὶ τῷ συνεργοῦντι καὶ κοπιῶντι. **16.17** χαίρω δὲ
TO EVERYONE JOINING IN THE WORK AND LABORING.   NOW~I REJOICE

ἐπὶ τῇ παρουσίᾳ Στεφανᾶ καὶ Φορτουνάτου καὶ
AT THE COMING OF STEPHANAS AND OF FORTUNATUS AND

Ἀχαϊκοῦ, ὅτι τὸ ὑμέτερον ὑστέρημα οὗτοι
OF ACHAICUS, BECAUSE - YOUR° DEFICIENCY(ABSENCE) THESE MEN

ἀνεπλήρωσαν· **16.18** ἀνέπαυσαν γὰρ τὸ ἐμὸν πνεῦμα
FILLED UP;   FOR~THEY REFRESHED - MY SPIRIT

καὶ τὸ ὑμῶν. ἐπιγινώσκετε οὖν τοὺς τοιούτους.
AND - YOURS°. GIVE RECOGNITION THEREFORE - TO SUCH MEN.

for I hope to spend some time with you, if the Lord permits. [8]But I will stay in Ephesus until Pentecost, [9]for a wide door for effective work has opened to me, and there are many adversaries.

10 If Timothy comes, see that he has nothing to fear among you, for he is doing the work of the Lord just as I am; [11]therefore let no one despise him. Send him on his way in peace, so that he may come to me; for I am expecting him with the brothers.

12 Now concerning our brother Apollos, I strongly urged him to visit you with the other brothers, but he was not at all willing[z] to come now. He will come when he has the opportunity.

13 Keep alert, stand firm in your faith, be courageous, be strong. [14]Let all that you do be done in love.

15 Now, brothers and sisters,[a] you know that members of the household of Stephanas were the first converts in Achaia, and they have devoted themselves to the service of the saints; [16]I urge you to put yourselves at the service of such people, and of everyone who works and toils with them. [17]I rejoice at the coming of Stephanas and Fortunatus and Achaicus, because they have made up for your absence; [18]for they refreshed my spirit as well as yours. So give recognition to such persons.

[z] Or *it was not at all God's will for him*
[a] Gk *brothers*

19 The churches of Asia send greetings. Aquila and Prisca, together with the church in their house, greet you warmly in the Lord. [20]All the brothers and sisters[b] send greetings. Greet one another with a holy kiss.

21 I, Paul, write this greeting with my own hand. [22]Let anyone be accursed who has no love for the Lord. Our Lord, come![c] [23]The grace of the Lord Jesus be with you. [24]My love be with all of you in Christ Jesus.[d]

[b] Gk brothers
[c] Gk Marana tha. These Aramaic words can also be read Maran atha, meaning Our Lord has come
[d] Other ancient authorities add Amen

16.19 Ἀσπάζονται ὑμᾶς αἱ ἐκκλησίαι τῆς Ἀσίας.
⁴GREET   ⁵YOU°   ¹THE ²CHURCHES   -   ³OF ASIA.

ἀσπάζεται ὑμᾶς ἐν κυρίῳ πολλὰ Ἀκύλας καὶ
⁴GREET   ⁵YOU°   ⁷IN ⁸[THE] LORD ⁶HEARTILY ¹AQUILA ²AND

Πρίσκα σὺν τῇ κατ᾽ οἶκον αὐτῶν ἐκκλησίᾳ.
³PRISCA   ⁹WITH ¹⁰THE ¹²IN [THE] HOUSE ¹³OF THEM ¹¹CHURCH [MEETING].

16.20 ἀσπάζονται ὑμᾶς οἱ ἀδελφοὶ πάντες.
⁴GREET   ⁵YOU°   ²THE ³BROTHERS   ¹ALL.

Ἀσπάσασθε ἀλλήλους ἐν φιλήματι ἁγίῳ.
GREET   ONE ANOTHER WITH A HOLY~KISS.

16.21 Ὁ ἀσπασμὸς τῇ ἐμῇ χειρὶ Παύλου.
      THE   GREETING   -   WITH MY OWN HAND—PAUL'S.

16.22 εἴ τις οὐ φιλεῖ τὸν κύριον, ἤτω ἀνάθεμα.
      IF ANYONE DOES NOT LOVE THE LORD, LET HIM BE A CURSE.

Μαρανα θα. **16.23** ἡ χάρις τοῦ κυρίου Ἰησοῦ
MARANA(OUR LORD) THA(COME). THE GRACE OF THE LORD JESUS

μεθ᾽ ὑμῶν. **16.24** ἡ ἀγάπη μου μετὰ πάντων ὑμῶν ἐν
[BE] WITH YOU°.   THE LOVE OF ME [BE] WITH YOU°~ALL   IN

Χριστῷ Ἰησοῦ.
CHRIST   JESUS.

THE SECOND LETTER OF PAUL TO THE
CORINTHIANS

ΠΡΟΣ ΚΟΡΙΝΘΙΟΥΣ Β
TO   [THE] CORINTHIANS   2

1.1 Παῦλος ἀπόστολος Χριστοῦ Ἰησοῦ διὰ
PAUL   AN APOSTLE   OF CHRIST   JESUS   THROUGH

θελήματος θεοῦ καὶ Τιμόθεος ὁ ἀδελφὸς τῇ
[THE] WILL   OF GOD AND   TIMOTHY   THE BROTHER,   TO THE

ἐκκλησίᾳ τοῦ θεοῦ τῇ οὔσῃ ἐν Κορίνθῳ σὺν τοῖς
CHURCH   -   OF GOD - BEING IN   CORINTH   WITH ²THE

ἁγίοις πᾶσιν τοῖς οὖσιν ἐν ὅλῃ τῇ Ἀχαΐᾳ, **1.2** χάρις
³SAINTS ¹ALL   -   BEING   IN ALL   -   ACHAIA,   GRACE

ὑμῖν καὶ εἰρήνη ἀπὸ θεοῦ πατρὸς ἡμῶν καὶ κυρίου
TO YOU° AND PEACE   FROM GOD [THE] FATHER OF US   AND   LORD

Ἰησοῦ Χριστοῦ.
JESUS CHRIST.

1.3 Εὐλογητὸς ὁ θεὸς καὶ πατὴρ τοῦ κυρίου ἡμῶν
BLESSED [BE] THE GOD AND FATHER OF THE LORD   OF US

Ἰησοῦ Χριστοῦ, ὁ πατὴρ τῶν οἰκτιρμῶν καὶ θεὸς
JESUS CHRIST, THE FATHER - OF COMPASSIONS AND   GOD

πάσης παρακλήσεως, **1.4** ὁ παρακαλῶν ἡμᾶς
OF ALL   ENCOURAGEMENT,   THE ONE ENCOURAGING   US

ἐπὶ πάσῃ τῇ θλίψει ἡμῶν εἰς τὸ δύνασθαι ἡμᾶς
WITH RESPECT TO ALL THE AFFLICTION OF US SO AS - TO ENABLE   US

παρακαλεῖν τοὺς ἐν πάσῃ θλίψει διὰ τῆς
TO ENCOURAGE THE ONES [BEING] IN EVERY(ANY) AFFLICTION THROUGH THE

παρακλήσεως ἧς παρακαλούμεθα αὐτοὶ ὑπὸ τοῦ
ENCOURAGEMENT BY WHICH WE OURSELVES ARE ENCOURAGED   BY   -

θεοῦ. **1.5** ὅτι καθὼς περισσεύει τὰ παθήματα τοῦ
GOD.   BECAUSE AS   ⁴ABOUND   ¹THE ²SUFFERINGS   -

Χριστοῦ εἰς ἡμᾶς, οὕτως διὰ τοῦ Χριστοῦ περισσεύει
³OF CHRIST TO US,   SO   THROUGH - CHRIST   ABOUNDS

καὶ ἡ παράκλησις ἡμῶν. **1.6** εἴτε δὲ θλιβόμεθα,
ALSO THE ENCOURAGEMENT OF(TO) US.   NOW~WHETHER WE ARE BEING AFFLICTED,

ὑπὲρ τῆς ὑμῶν παρακλήσεως καὶ σωτηρίας· εἴτε
[IT IS] FOR -   YOUR° ENCOURAGEMENT   AND   SALVATION;   OR IF

παρακαλούμεθα, ὑπὲρ τῆς ὑμῶν παρακλήσεως τῆς
WE ARE BEING ENCOURAGED, [IT IS] FOR -   YOUR° ENCOURAGEMENT   -

ἐνεργουμένης ἐν ὑπομονῇ τῶν αὐτῶν παθημάτων
PRODUCING   IN [YOU°] AN ENDURANCE OF THE SAME   SUFFERINGS

ὧν καὶ ἡμεῖς πάσχομεν. **1.7** καὶ ἡ ἐλπὶς ἡμῶν
WHICH ALSO WE   SUFFER.   AND THE HOPE OF US

Paul, an apostle of Christ Jesus by the will of God, and Timothy our brother,

To the church of God that is in Corinth, including all the saints throughout Achaia:

2 Grace to you and peace from God our Father and the Lord Jesus Christ.

3 Blessed be the God and Father of our Lord Jesus Christ, the Father of mercies and the God of all consolation, 4who consoles us in all our affliction, so that we may be able to console those who are in any affliction with the consolation with which we ourselves are consoled by God. 5For just as the sufferings of Christ are abundant for us, so also our consolation is abundant through Christ. 6If we are being afflicted, it is for your consolation and salvation; if we are being consoled, it is for your consolation, which you experience when you patiently endure the same sufferings that we are also suffering. 7Our hope

for you is unshaken; for we know that as you share in our sufferings, so also you share in our consolation.

8 We do not want you to be unaware, brothers and sisters,[a] of the affliction we experienced in Asia; for we were so utterly, unbearably crushed that we despaired of life itself. [9]Indeed, we felt that we had received the sentence of death so that we would rely not on ourselves but on God who raises the dead. [10]He who rescued us from so deadly a peril will continue to rescue us; on him we have set our hope that he will rescue us again, [11]as you also join in helping us by your prayers, so that many will give thanks on our[b] behalf for the blessing granted us through the prayers of many.

12 Indeed, this is our boast, the testimony of our conscience: we have behaved in the world with frankness[c] and godly sincerity, not by earthly wisdom but by the grace of God—and all the more toward you. [13]For we write you nothing other than what you can read and also understand; I hope you will understand until the end— [14]as you have already understood us in part—

[a] Gk brothers
[b] Other ancient authorities read your
[c] Other ancient authorities read holiness

βεβαία ὑπὲρ ὑμῶν εἰδότες ὅτι ὡς κοινωνοί ἐστε τῶν
[IS] FIRM [1]FOR [2]YOU°, KNOWING THAT AS SHARERS YOU° ARE OF THE

παθημάτων, οὕτως καὶ τῆς παρακλήσεως.
SUFFERINGS, SO ALSO OF THE ENCOURAGEMENT.

1.8 Οὐ γὰρ θέλομεν ὑμᾶς ἀγνοεῖν, ἀδελφοί, ὑπὲρ
FOR~NOT WE WANT YOU° TO BE IGNORANT, BROTHERS, AS TO

τῆς θλίψεως ἡμῶν τῆς γενομένης ἐν τῇ Ἀσίᾳ, ὅτι
THE AFFLICTION OF US - HAVING HAPPENED IN - ASIA, THAT

καθ' ὑπερβολὴν ὑπὲρ δύναμιν ἐβαρήθημεν ὥστε
EXCESSIVELY BEYOND [OUR] POWER WE WERE BURDENED CAUSING

ἐξαπορηθῆναι ἡμᾶς καὶ τοῦ ζῆν· **1.9** ἀλλὰ αὐτοὶ
US~TO DESPAIR EVEN - TO LIVE. BUT [WE] OURSELVES

ἐν ἑαυτοῖς τὸ ἀπόκριμα τοῦ θανάτου ἐσχήκαμεν, ἵνα
IN OURSELVES THE SENTENCE - OF DEATH HAVE HAD, THAT

μὴ πεποιθότες ὦμεν ἐφ' ἑαυτοῖς ἀλλ' ἐπὶ τῷ θεῷ
[2]NOT [3]HAVE TRUST [1]WE SHOULD ON OURSELVES BUT ON - GOD,

τῷ ἐγείροντι τοὺς νεκρούς· **1.10** ὃς ἐκ τηλικούτου
THE ONE RAISING THE DEAD; WHO OUT OF SO GREAT

θανάτου ἐρρύσατο ἡμᾶς καὶ ῥύσεται, εἰς ὃν
A DEATH DELIVERED US AND WILL DELIVER, IN WHOM

ἠλπίκαμεν [ὅτι] καὶ ἔτι ῥύσεται, **1.11** συνυπουργούντων
WE HAVE HOPED THAT ALSO YET HE WILL DELIVER, [3]LABORING TOGETHER

καὶ ὑμῶν ὑπὲρ ἡμῶν τῇ δεήσει, ἵνα ἐκ πολλῶν
[2]ALSO [1]YOU° FOR US - BY SUPPLICATION, THAT [4]BY [5]MANY

προσώπων τὸ εἰς ἡμᾶς χάρισμα διὰ πολλῶν
[6]PERSONS [7][FOR] THE [9]TO [10]US [8]GIFT [11]THROUGH [12]MANY

εὐχαριστηθῇ ὑπὲρ ἡμῶν.
[1]THANKS MAY BE GIVEN [2]FOR [3]US.

1.12 Ἡ γὰρ καύχησις ἡμῶν αὕτη ἐστίν, τὸ μαρτύριον
FOR~THE BOASTING OF US IS~THIS, THE TESTIMONY

τῆς συνειδήσεως ἡμῶν, ὅτι ἐν ⌜ἁπλότητι⌝ καὶ
OF THE CONSCIENCE OF US, BECAUSE IN SIMPLICITY AND

εἰλικρινείᾳ τοῦ θεοῦ, [καὶ] οὐκ ἐν σοφίᾳ σαρκικῇ
SINCERITY - OF GOD, AND NOT IN WISDOM FLESHLY

ἀλλ' ἐν χάριτι θεοῦ, ἀνεστράφημεν ἐν τῷ κόσμῳ,
BUT IN [THE] GRACE OF GOD, WE CONDUCTED [OURSELVES] IN THE WORLD,

περισσοτέρως δὲ πρὸς ὑμᾶς. **1.13** οὐ γὰρ ἄλλα
AND~MORE ESPECIALLY TOWARD YOU°. [3]NOT [1]FOR [4]OTHER THINGS

γράφομεν ὑμῖν ἀλλ' ἢ ἃ ἀναγινώσκετε ἢ καὶ
[2]WE WRITE TO YOU° - THAN WHAT YOU° READ OR ALSO

ἐπιγινώσκετε· ἐλπίζω δὲ ὅτι ἕως τέλους ἐπιγνώσεσθε,
KNOW; AND~I HOPE THAT TO [THE] END YOU° WILL KNOW FULLY,

1.14 καθὼς καὶ ἐπέγνωτε ἡμᾶς ἀπὸ μέρους, ὅτι
AS ALSO YOU° KNEW US IN PART, BECAUSE

1:12 text: KJV NEBmg TEV NJBmg NRSV. var. αγιοτητι (holiness): ASV RSV NASB NIV NEB TEVmg NJB NRSVmg.

καύχημα ὑμῶν ἐσμεν καθάπερ καὶ ὑμεῖς ἡμῶν ἐν τῇ
³BOAST   ²YOUR° ¹WE ARE EVEN AS ALSO YOU°   OURS IN THE

ἡμέρᾳ τοῦ κυρίου [ἡμῶν] Ἰησοῦ.
DAY   OF THE LORD OF US   JESUS.

1.15 Καὶ ταύτῃ τῇ πεποιθήσει ἐβουλόμην πρότερον
          AND WITH THIS - CONFIDENCE I PLANNED PREVIOUSLY

πρὸς ὑμᾶς ἐλθεῖν, ἵνα δευτέραν χάριν σχῆτε,
²TO   ³YOU° ¹TO COME, THAT A SECOND FAVOR YOU° MIGHT HAVE,

1.16 καὶ δι' ὑμῶν διελθεῖν εἰς Μακεδονίαν
         AND THROUGH YOU° TO PASS THROUGH INTO MACEDONIA

καὶ πάλιν ἀπὸ Μακεδονίας ἐλθεῖν πρὸς ὑμᾶς
AND AGAIN FROM MACEDONIA   TO COME   TO   YOU°

καὶ ὑφ' ὑμῶν προπεμφθῆναι εἰς τὴν Ἰουδαίαν.
AND BY YOU° TO BE SENT ON   TO -   JUDEA.

1.17 τοῦτο οὖν βουλόμενος μήτι ἄρα τῇ
         THIS THEREFORE PLANNING [SURELY] NOT THEN -

ἐλαφρίᾳ ἐχρησάμην; ἢ ἃ βουλεύομαι,
DID I ACT WITH~FICKLENESS? OR THE THINGS WHICH I PLAN,

κατὰ σάρκα βουλεύομαι, ἵνα ᾖ παρ' ἐμοὶ
ACCORDING TO [THE] FLESH DO I PLAN, THAT THERE MAY BE WITH ME

τὸ Ναὶ ναὶ καὶ τὸ Οὒ οὔ; **1.18** πιστὸς δὲ ὁ θεὸς ὅτι
THE YES YES AND THE NO NO?   BUT~FAITHFUL - [IS] GOD THAT

ὁ λόγος ἡμῶν ὁ πρὸς ὑμᾶς οὐκ ἔστιν Ναὶ καὶ Οὔ.
THE WORD OF US - TO YOU° IS~NOT YES AND NO.

1.19 ὁ τοῦ θεοῦ γὰρ υἱὸς Ἰησοῦς Χριστὸς ὁ ἐν
         ²THE - ⁴OF GOD ¹FOR ³SON, JESUS CHRIST, ¹THE ONE ³AMONG

ὑμῖν δι' ἡμῶν κηρυχθείς, δι' ἐμοῦ καὶ
⁴YOU° ⁵BY ⁶US ²HAVING BEEN PREACHED, THROUGH ME AND

Σιλουανοῦ καὶ Τιμοθέου, οὐκ ἐγένετο Ναὶ καὶ Οὒ
SILVANUS   AND TIMOTHY,   WAS~NOT   YES AND NO

ἀλλὰ Ναὶ ἐν αὐτῷ γέγονεν. **1.20** ὅσαι γὰρ
BUT   ²YES ³IN ⁴HIM ¹IT HAS [ALWAYS] BEEN.   FOR~AS MANY

ἐπαγγελίαι θεοῦ, ἐν αὐτῷ τὸ Ναί· διὸ
PROMISES   OF GOD [THERE ARE], IN HIM [IS] THE YES; WHEREFORE

καὶ δι' αὐτοῦ τὸ Ἀμὴν τῷ θεῷ πρὸς δόξαν δι'
ALSO THROUGH HIM THE AMEN - ³TO GOD ¹FOR ²GLORY THROUGH

ἡμῶν. **1.21** ὁ δὲ βεβαιῶν ἡμᾶς σὺν ὑμῖν εἰς
US.   BUT~THE ONE ESTABLISHING US WITH YOU° IN

Χριστὸν καὶ χρίσας ἡμᾶς θεός, **1.22** ὁ καὶ
CHRIST   AND HAVING ANOINTED US [IS] GOD, THE ONE ALSO

σφραγισάμενος ἡμᾶς καὶ δοὺς τὸν ἀρραβῶνα τοῦ
HAVING SEALED   US AND HAVING GIVEN THE EARNEST OF THE

πνεύματος ἐν ταῖς καρδίαις ἡμῶν.
SPIRIT   IN THE HEARTS   OF US.

1.23 Ἐγὼ δὲ μάρτυρα τὸν θεὸν ἐπικαλοῦμαι ἐπὶ τὴν
         NOW~I ⁴[AS] A WITNESS - ³GOD ¹CALL   ²UPON -

that on the day of the Lord Jesus we are your boast even as you are our boast.

15 Since I was sure of this, I wanted to come to you first, so that you might have a double favor;[d] 16I wanted to visit you on my way to Macedonia, and to come back to you from Macedonia and have you send me on to Judea. 17Was I vacillating when I wanted to do this? Do I make my plans according to ordinary human standards,[e] ready to say "Yes, yes" and "No, no" at the same time? 18As surely as God is faithful, our word to you has not been "Yes and No." 19For the Son of God, Jesus Christ, whom we proclaimed among you, Silvanus and Timothy and I, was not "Yes and No"; but in him it is always "Yes." 20For in him every one of God's promises is a "Yes." For this reason it is through him that we say the "Amen," to the glory of God. 21But it is God who establishes us with you in Christ and has anointed us, 22by putting his seal on us and giving us his Spirit in our hearts as a first installment.

23 But I call on God as

[d] Other ancient authorities read *pleasure*
[e] Gk *according to the flesh*

witness against me: it was to spare you that I did not come again to Corinth. 24I do not mean to imply that we lord it over your faith; rather, we are workers with you for your joy, because you stand firm in the faith.

ἐμὴν ψυχήν, ὅτι φειδόμενος ὑμῶν οὐκέτι ἦλθον εἰς
TO MY   SOUL,   THAT SPARING   YOU°   NO LONGER I CAME   TO

Κόρινθον. **1.24** οὐχ ὅτι κυριεύομεν ὑμῶν τῆς πίστεως
CORINTH.   NOT THAT WE LORD IT OVER YOUR°   -   FAITH

ἀλλὰ συνεργοί ἐσμεν τῆς   χαρᾶς ὑμῶν· τῇ γὰρ
BUT   CO-WORKERS WE ARE OF(FOR) THE JOY   OF YOU°;   -   FOR

πίστει ἑστήκατε.
BY FAITH   YOU° HAVE STOOD.

CHAPTER 2

So I made up my mind not to make you another painful visit. 2For if I cause you pain, who is there to make me glad but the one whom I have pained? 3And I wrote as I did, so that when I came, I might not suffer pain from those who should have made me rejoice; for I am confident about all of you, that my joy would be the joy of all of you. 4For I wrote you out of much distress and anguish of heart and with many tears, not to cause you pain, but to let you know the abundant love that I have for you.

5 But if anyone has caused pain, he has caused it not to me, but to some extent— not to exaggerate it—to all of you. 6This punishment by the majority is enough for such a person; 7so now instead you should forgive and console him, so that he may not be overwhelmed by excessive sorrow. 8So I urge

2.1 ἔκρινα γὰρ ἐμαυτῷ τοῦτο τὸ μὴ πάλιν ἐν λύπῃ
FOR~I DECIDED   THIS~IN MYSELF   -   NOT AGAIN   IN   GRIEF

πρὸς ὑμᾶς ἐλθεῖν. **2.2** εἰ γὰρ ἐγὼ λυπῶ ὑμᾶς, καὶ τίς
²TO ³YOU° ¹TO COME.   FOR~IF   I   GRIEVE YOU°,   THEN WHO

ὁ   εὐφραίνων με εἰ μὴ ὁ   λυπούμενος ἐξ ἐμοῦ;
[IS] THE ONE CHEERING ME EXCEPT THE ONE BEING GRIEVED   BY ME?

2.3 καὶ ἔγραψα τοῦτο αὐτό, ἵνα μὴ ἐλθὼν λύπην
AND I WROTE THIS   VERY THING, LEST HAVING COME, GRIEF

σχῶ   ἀφ' ὧν   ἔδει   με χαίρειν,
I SHOULD HAVE FROM [THOSE] OF WHOM IT WAS NEEDFUL [FOR] ME TO HAVE JOY,

πεποιθὼς   ἐπὶ πάντας ὑμᾶς ὅτι ἡ ἐμὴ χαρὰ πάντων
HAVING CONFIDENCE IN   YOU°~ALL   THAT - MY JOY ³ALL

ὑμῶν ἐστιν. **2.4** ἐκ γὰρ πολλῆς θλίψεως καὶ συνοχῆς
²OF YOU° ¹IS [THAT].   FOR~OUT OF MUCH   AFFLICTION   AND DISTRESS

καρδίας ἔγραψα ὑμῖν διὰ πολλῶν δακρύων, οὐχ ἵνα
OF HEART I WROTE TO YOU° WITH MANY   TEARS,   NOT THAT

λυπηθῆτε   ἀλλὰ τὴν ἀγάπην ἵνα γνῶτε   ἣν
YOU° SHOULD BE GRIEVED BUT ³THE ⁴LOVE ¹THAT ²YOU° MAY KNOW WHICH

ἔχω περισσοτέρως εἰς ὑμᾶς.
I HAVE MORE ABUNDANTLY   FOR YOU°.

2.5 Εἰ δέ τις   λελύπηκεν, οὐκ ἐμὲ λελύπηκεν, ἀλλὰ
NOW~IF ANYONE HAS CAUSED GRIEF, NOT ME HE HAS GRIEVED, BUT

ἀπὸ μέρους, ἵνα μὴ ἐπιβαρῶ,   πάντας ὑμᾶς.
IN PART,   LEST   I BE TOO SEVERE [ON] YOU°~ALL.

2.6 ἱκανὸν τῷ τοιούτῳ ἡ ἐπιτιμία αὕτη ἡ ὑπὸ τῶν
SUFFICIENT - TO SUCH A MAN - [WAS] THIS~PUNISHMENT - BY THE

πλειόνων, **2.7** ὥστε τοὐναντίον μᾶλλον ὑμᾶς
MAJORITY,   SO THAT ON THE CONTRARY   RATHER   YOU°

χαρίσασθαι καὶ παρακαλέσαι, μή πως τῇ περισσοτέρᾳ
[OUGHT] TO FORGIVE AND ENCOURAGE [HIM], LEST   -   WITH MORE ABUNDANT

λύπῃ καταποθῇ   ὁ τοιοῦτος. **2.8** διὸ   παρακαλῶ
GRIEF ²MAY BE SWALLOWED UP - ¹SUCH A ONE.   THEREFORE I URGE

ὑμᾶς κυρῶσαι εἰς αὐτὸν ἀγάπην·   **2.9** εἰς τοῦτο   γὰρ
YOU°   TO CONFIRM TO   HIM   [YOUR°] LOVE;   ²TO   ³THIS [END]   ¹FOR

καὶ ἔγραψα, ἵνα γνῶ   τὴν δοκιμὴν ὑμῶν, εἰ εἰς
ALSO   I WROTE,   THAT   I MAY KNOW THE   PROOF   OF YOU°,   IF   IN

πάντα ὑπήκοοί ἐστε.   **2.10** ᾧ δὲ   τι   χαρίζεσθε,
ALL THINGS   YOU° ARE~OBEDIENT.   NOW~TO WHOM   ANYTHING   YOU° FORGIVE,

κἀγώ·   καὶ γὰρ ἐγὼ ὃ   κεχάρισμαι, εἴ τι
I ALSO;   FOR~INDEED   ²I   ¹WHAT   ³HAVE FORGIVEN,   IF   ANYTHING

κεχάρισμαι, δι   ὑμᾶς ἐν προσώπῳ Χριστοῦ,
I HAVE FORGIVEN,   [IT IS] BECAUSE OF   YOU°,   IN   [THE] PERSON   OF CHRIST,

2.11 ἵνα μὴ πλεονεκτηθῶμεν ὑπὸ τοῦ Σατανᾶ·   οὐ γὰρ
LEST   WE SHOULD BE OUTSMARTED   BY   -   SATAN;   FOR~NOT

αὐτοῦ τὰ νοήματα ἀγνοοῦμεν.
OF HIS   -   DESIGNS   ARE WE IGNORANT.

2.12 Ἐλθὼν δὲ   εἰς τὴν Τρῳάδα εἰς τὸ εὐαγγέλιον
BUT~HAVING COME TO   -   TROAS   FOR THE   GOSPEL

τοῦ Χριστοῦ καὶ θύρας μοι ἀνεῳγμένης ἐν κυρίῳ,
-   OF CHRIST   AND   A DOOR   TO ME HAVING BEEN OPENED   BY   [THE] LORD,

2.13 οὐκ ἔσχηκα   ἄνεσιν   τῷ   πνεύματί   μου   τῷ
I DID NOT HAVE   REST (PEACE)   IN THE   SPIRIT   OF ME   -

μὴ εὑρεῖν με   Τίτον τὸν ἀδελφόν μου, ἀλλὰ
[WHEN] I WAS NOT ABLE TO FIND   TITUS,   THE   BROTHER   OF ME,   BUT

ἀποταξάμενος αὐτοῖς ἐξῆλθον εἰς Μακεδονίαν.
HAVING SAID FAREWELL   TO THEM   I DEPARTED   INTO   MACEDONIA.

2.14 Τῷ   δὲ θεῷ χάρις τῷ   πάντοτε
BUT THANKS~TO GOD,   THE ONE   ALWAYS

θριαμβεύοντι ἡμᾶς ἐν τῷ   Χριστῷ   καὶ τὴν ὀσμὴν τῆς
LEADING US IN TRIUMPH   IN   -   CHRIST   AND   THE   FRAGRANCE OF THE

γνώσεως αὐτοῦ φανεροῦντι δι'   ἡμῶν ἐν παντὶ τόπῳ·
KNOWLEDGE   OF HIM   MANIFESTING   THROUGH   US   IN   EVERY   PLACE;

2.15 ὅτι   Χριστοῦ εὐωδία ἐσμὲν τῷ θεῷ ἐν   τοῖς
BECAUSE   OF CHRIST   AN AROMA   WE ARE   -   TO GOD   AMONG   THE ONES

σῳζομένοις καὶ ἐν   τοῖς   ἀπολλυμένοις,
BEING SAVED   AND   AMONG   THE ONES   PERISHING,

2.16 οἷς   μὲν ὀσμὴ   ἐκ θανάτου εἰς θάνατον,
TO THE [LATTER] ONES   -   A FRAGRANCE   OF   DEATH   UNTO DEATH,

οἷς δὲ   ὀσμὴ ἐκ ζωῆς εἰς ζωήν. καὶ
BUT~TO THE [FORMER] ONES A FRAGRANCE OF   LIFE   UNTO LIFE.   AND

πρὸς   ταῦτα   τίς ἱκανός;   **2.17** οὐ   γὰρ
WITH RESPECT TO   [DOING] THESE THINGS,   WHO   [IS] COMPETENT?   ³NOT   ¹FOR

ἐσμεν ὡς οἱ πολλοὶ καπηλεύοντες τὸν λόγον τοῦ
²WE ARE   AS   THE MANY,   PEDDLING   THE   WORD   -

θεοῦ, ἀλλ' ὡς ἐξ εἰλικρινείας, ἀλλ' ὡς ἐκ θεοῦ
OF GOD, BUT   AS   FROM SINCERITY,   BUT   AS   FROM   GOD,

κατέναντι θεοῦ ἐν Χριστῷ λαλοῦμεν.
BEFORE   GOD,   IN   CHRIST   WE SPEAK.

you to reaffirm your love for him. [9]I wrote for this reason: to test you and to know whether you are obedient in everything. [10]Anyone whom you forgive, I also forgive. What I have forgiven, if I have forgiven anything, has been for your sake in the presence of Christ. [11]And we do this so that we may not be outwitted by Satan; for we are not ignorant of his designs.

12 When I came to Troas to proclaim the good news of Christ, a door was opened for me in the Lord; [13]but my mind could not rest because I did not find my brother Titus there. So I said farewell to them and went on to Macedonia.

14 But thanks be to God, who in Christ always leads us in triumphal procession, and through us spreads in every place the fragrance that comes from knowing him. [15]For we are the aroma of Christ to God among those who are being saved and among those who are perishing; [16]to the one a fragrance from death to death, to the other a fragrance from life to life. Who is sufficient for these things? [17]For we are not peddlers of God's word like so many,[f] but in Christ we speak as persons of sincerity, as persons sent from God and standing in his presence.

[f] Other ancient authorities read *like the others*

CHAPTER 3

Are we beginning to commend ourselves again? Surely we do not need, as some do, letters of recommendation to you or from you, do we? [2] You yourselves are our letter, written on our[g] hearts, to be known and read by all; [3] and you show that you are a letter of Christ, prepared by us, written not with ink but with the Spirit of the living God, not on tablets of stone but on tablets of human hearts.

[4] Such is the confidence that we have through Christ toward God. [5] Not that we are competent of ourselves to claim anything as coming from us; our competence is from God, [6] who has made us competent to be ministers of a new covenant, not of letter but of spirit; for the letter kills, but the Spirit gives life.

[7] Now if the ministry of death, chiseled in letters on stone tablets,[h] came in glory so that the people of Israel could not gaze at Moses' face because of the glory of his face, a glory now set aside, [8] how much more will the ministry of the Spirit come in glory? [9] For if

[g] Other ancient authorities read *your*
[h] Gk *on stones*

3.1 Ἀρχόμεθα πάλιν ἑαυτοὺς συνιστάνειν; ἢ
DO WE BEGIN   AGAIN   OURSELVES   TO COMMEND?   OR

μὴ χρῄζομεν ὥς τινες συστατικῶν ἐπιστολῶν πρὸς
[SURELY] WE DO NOT NEED, AS SOME [DO], COMMENDATORY LETTERS   TO

ὑμᾶς ἢ ἐξ ὑμῶν; **3.2** ἡ ἐπιστολὴ ἡμῶν ὑμεῖς ἐστε,
YOU° OR FROM YOU°?   THE LETTER   OF US   YOU°   ARE,

ἐγγεγραμμένη ἐν ταῖς καρδίαις ⌜ἡμῶν,⌝ γινωσκομένη
HAVING BEEN WRITTEN IN THE HEARTS OF US,   BEING KNOWN

καὶ ἀναγινωσκομένη ὑπὸ πάντων ἀνθρώπων,
AND BEING READ   BY ALL   MEN,

3.3 φανερούμενοι ὅτι ἐστὲ ἐπιστολὴ Χριστοῦ
BEING MANIFESTED THAT YOU° ARE A LETTER OF(FROM) CHRIST

διακονηθεῖσα ὑφ' ἡμῶν, ἐγγεγραμμένη οὐ μέλανι
HAVING BEEN CARED FOR BY US,   HAVING BEEN WRITTEN NOT WITH INK

ἀλλὰ πνεύματι θεοῦ ζῶντος, οὐκ ἐν πλαξὶν λιθίναις
BUT   WITH [THE] SPIRIT OF A LIVING~GOD, NOT IN(ON) TABLETS OF STONE

ἀλλ' ἐν πλαξὶν καρδίαις σαρκίναις.
BUT IN(ON) TABLETS [WHICH ARE] HEARTS OF FLESH.

3.4 Πεποίθησιν δὲ τοιαύτην ἔχομεν διὰ τοῦ
³CONFIDENCE ¹AND ²SUCH WE HAVE THROUGH -

Χριστοῦ πρὸς τὸν θεόν. **3.5** οὐχ ὅτι ἀφ' ἑαυτῶν
CHRIST TOWARD - GOD.   NOT THAT FROM OURSELVES

ἱκανοί ἐσμεν λογίσασθαί τι ὡς ἐξ ἑαυτῶν, ἀλλ'
WE ARE~COMPETENT TO CONSIDER ANYTHING AS OF OURSELVES, BUT

ἡ ἱκανότης ἡμῶν ἐκ τοῦ θεοῦ, **3.6** ὃς καὶ
THE COMPETENCE OF US [IS] FROM - GOD,   WHO ALSO

ἱκάνωσεν ἡμᾶς διακόνους καινῆς διαθήκης, οὐ
MADE US COMPETENT [AS] MINISTERS OF A NEW COVENANT,   NOT

γράμματος ἀλλὰ πνεύματος· τὸ γὰρ γράμμα
OF LETTER BUT OF SPIRIT; FOR~THE LETTER

ἀποκτέννει, τὸ δὲ πνεῦμα ζωοποιεῖ.
KILLS,   BUT~THE SPIRIT GIVES LIFE.

3.7 Εἰ δὲ ἡ διακονία τοῦ θανάτου ἐν γράμμασιν
NOW~IF THE MINISTRY - OF DEATH IN LETTERS

ἐντετυπωμένη λίθοις ἐγενήθη ἐν δόξῃ, ὥστε
HAVING BEEN ENGRAVED IN STONES CAME WITH GLORY, SO THAT

μὴ δύνασθαι ἀτενίσαι τοὺς υἱοὺς Ἰσραὴλ εἰς τὸ
⁴ARE(WERE) NOT ABLE ⁵TO GAZE ¹THE ²SONS ³OF ISRAEL INTO THE

πρόσωπον Μωϋσέως διὰ τὴν δόξαν τοῦ προσώπου
FACE   OF MOSES BECAUSE OF THE GLORY OF THE FACE

αὐτοῦ τὴν καταργουμένην, **3.8** πῶς οὐχὶ μᾶλλον ἡ
OF HIM, THE [GLORY] [WHICH] IS FADING,   HOW ²NOT ³RATHER ⁴THE

διακονία τοῦ πνεύματος ἔσται ἐν δόξῃ; **3.9** εἰ γὰρ τῇ
⁵MINISTRY ⁶OF THE ⁷SPIRIT ¹WILL ⁸BE IN GLORY?   FOR~IF THE

3:2 text: KJV ASV RSVmg NASB NIV NEB TEV NJB NRSV. var. υμων (your°): RSV NJBmg NRSVmg.

διακονία τῆς κατακρίσεως δόξα, πολλῷ μᾶλλον
MINISTRY   -   OF CONDEMNATION   [IS] GLORY,   MUCH   RATHER

περισσεύει ἡ διακονία τῆς δικαιοσύνης δόξῃ.
ABOUNDS   THE   MINISTRY   -   OF RIGHTEOUSNESS IN GLORY.

3.10 καὶ γὰρ οὐ δεδόξασται τὸ δεδοξασμένον ἐν
FOR~INDEED ³HAS NOT BEEN GLORIFIED ¹THE THING ²HAVING BEEN GLORIFIED IN

τούτῳ τῷ μέρει εἵνεκεν τῆς ὑπερβαλλούσης δόξης.
THIS   -   RESPECT, ON ACCOUNT OF THE   SURPASSING   GLORY.

3.11 εἰ γὰρ τὸ καταργούμενον διὰ δόξης,
FOR~IF THE THING [WHICH] [NOW] IS FADING AWAY [CAME] WITH GLORY,

πολλῷ μᾶλλον τὸ μένον ἐν δόξῃ.
MUCH   MORE   THE THING REMAINING [IS] IN GLORY.

3.12 Ἔχοντες οὖν τοιαύτην ἐλπίδα πολλῇ
HAVING   THEREFORE SUCH   HOPE,   WITH MUCH

παρρησίᾳ χρώμεθα **3.13** καὶ οὐ καθάπερ Μωϋσῆς
BOLDNESS WE ACT,   AND [ARE] NOT AS   MOSES

ἐτίθει κάλυμμα ἐπὶ τὸ πρόσωπον αὐτοῦ πρὸς τὸ
[WHO] WAS PUTTING A VEIL OVER THE FACE   OF HIM   SO THAT

μὴ ἀτενίσαι τοὺς υἱοὺς Ἰσραὴλ εἰς τὸ τέλος τοῦ
⁴[WERE] NOT ABLE TO SEE ¹THE ²SONS ³OF ISRAEL -   THE END   OF THE THING

καταργουμένου. **3.14** ἀλλὰ ἐπωρώθη τὰ νοήματα
FADING AWAY.   BUT   WERE HARDENED THE THOUGHTS(MINDS)

αὐτῶν. ἄχρι γὰρ τῆς σήμερον ἡμέρας τὸ αὐτὸ κάλυμμα
OF THEM. FOR~UNTIL THE PRESENT   DAY   THE SAME   VEIL

ἐπὶ τῇ ἀναγνώσει τῆς παλαιᾶς διαθήκης μένει, μὴ
²AT ³THE ⁴READING ⁵OF THE ⁶OLD   ⁷COVENANT ¹REMAINS, NOT

ἀνακαλυπτόμενον ὅτι ἐν Χριστῷ καταργεῖται·
BEING UNVEILED,   BECAUSE IN CHRIST   IT IS BEING ABOLISHED.

3.15 ἀλλ' ἕως σήμερον ἡνίκα ἂν ἀναγινώσκηται Μωϋσῆς,
BUT   UNTIL TODAY   WHENEVER   MOSES~IS BEING READ,

κάλυμμα ἐπὶ τὴν καρδίαν αὐτῶν κεῖται·
A VEIL   ON   THE HEART   OF THEM LIES;

3.16 ἡνίκα δὲ ἐὰν ἐπιστρέψῃ πρὸς κύριον, περιαιρεῖται
BUT WHENEVER   ONE TURNS   TO   [THE] LORD, ³IS TAKEN AWAY

τὸ κάλυμμα. **3.17** ὁ δὲ κύριος τὸ πνεῦμά ἐστιν·
¹THE ²VEIL.   NOW~THE LORD ²THE ³SPIRIT ¹IS;

οὗ δὲ τὸ πνεῦμα κυρίου, ἐλευθερία.
AND~WHERE THE SPIRIT   OF [THE] LORD [IS], [THERE IS] FREEDOM.

3.18 ἡμεῖς δὲ πάντες ἀνακεκαλυμμένῳ προσώπῳ τὴν
NOW~WE   ALL,   WITH A FACE~HAVING BEEN UNVEILED,   THE

δόξαν κυρίου κατοπτριζόμενοι τὴν αὐτὴν εἰκόνα
GLORY OF [THE] LORD SEEING REFLECTED IN A MIRROR, ²[INTO] THE ³SAME ⁴IMAGE

μεταμορφούμεθα ἀπὸ δόξης εἰς δόξαν καθάπερ ἀπὸ
¹ARE BEING TRANSFORMED FROM GLORY TO GLORY, EVEN AS FROM

κυρίου πνεύματος.
[THE] LORD, [THE] SPIRIT.

there was glory in the ministry of condemnation, much more does the ministry of justification abound in glory! [10]Indeed, what once had glory has lost its glory because of the greater glory; [11]for if what was set aside came through glory, much more has the permanent come in glory!

12 Since, then, we have such a hope, we act with great boldness, [13]not like Moses, who put a veil over his face to keep the people of Israel from gazing at the end of the glory that[i] was being set aside. [14]But their minds were hardened. Indeed, to this very day, when they hear the reading of the old covenant, that same veil is still there, since only in Christ is it set aside. [15]Indeed, to this very day whenever Moses is read, a veil lies over their minds; [16]but when one turns to the Lord, the veil is removed. [17]Now the Lord is the Spirit, and where the Spirit of the Lord is, there is freedom. [18]And all of us, with unveiled faces, seeing the glory of the Lord as though reflected in a mirror, are being transformed into the same image from one degree of glory to another; for this comes from the Lord, the Spirit.

_____
[i] Gk *of what*

CHAPTER 4

Therefore, since it is by God's mercy that we are engaged in this ministry, we do not lose heart. ²We have renounced the shameful things that one hides; we refuse to practice cunning or to falsify God's word; but by the open statement of the truth we commend ourselves to the conscience of everyone in the sight of God. ³And even if our gospel is veiled, it is veiled to those who are perishing. ⁴In their case the god of this world has blinded the minds of the unbelievers, to keep them from seeing the light of the gospel of the glory of Christ, who is the image of God. ⁵For we do not proclaim ourselves; we proclaim Jesus Christ as Lord and ourselves as your slaves for Jesus' sake. ⁶For it is the God who said, "Let light shine out of darkness," who has shone in our hearts to give the light of the knowledge of the glory of God in the face of Jesus Christ.

7 But we have this treasure in clay jars, so that it may be made clear that this extraordinary power belongs to God and does not come from us. ⁸We are afflicted in every way, but not crushed; perplexed, but not driven to despair; ⁹persecuted, but not forsaken; struck down, but

4.1 Διὰ τοῦτο, ἔχοντες τὴν διακονίαν ταύτην καθὼς
THEREFORE, HAVING - THIS~MINISTRY AS

ἠλεήθημεν, οὐκ ἐγκακοῦμεν **4.2** ἀλλὰ ἀπειπάμεθα τὰ
WE RECEIVED MERCY, WE DO NOT LOSE HEART, BUT WE RENOUNCED THE

κρυπτὰ τῆς αἰσχύνης, μὴ περιπατοῦντες ἐν
HIDDEN THINGS - OF SHAME, NOT GOING ABOUT WITH

πανουργίᾳ μηδὲ δολοῦντες τὸν λόγον τοῦ θεοῦ ἀλλὰ
CUNNING NOR FALSIFYING THE WORD - OF GOD BUT

τῇ φανερώσει τῆς ἀληθείας συνιστάνοντες ἑαυτοὺς
BY THE MANIFESTATION OF THE TRUTH PRESENTING OURSELVES

πρὸς πᾶσαν συνείδησιν ἀνθρώπων ἐνώπιον τοῦ θεοῦ.
TO EVERY CONSCIENCE OF MEN BEFORE - GOD.

4.3 εἰ δὲ καὶ ἔστιν κεκαλυμμένον τὸ εὐαγγέλιον ἡμῶν,
BUT~IF INDEED HAS BEEN HIDDEN THE GOOD NEWS OF US,

ἐν τοῖς ἀπολλυμένοις ἐστὶν κεκαλυμμένον, **4.4** ἐν
AMONG THE ONES PERISHING IT HAS BEEN HIDDEN, IN

οἷς ὁ θεὸς τοῦ αἰῶνος τούτου ἐτύφλωσεν τὰ
WHOSE [CASE] THE GOD - OF THIS~AGE BLINDED THE

νοήματα τῶν ἀπίστων εἰς τὸ μὴ αὐγάσαι τὸν
THOUGHTS(MINDS) OF THE ONES UNBELIEVING SO AS - NOT TO SHINE FORTH THE

φωτισμὸν τοῦ εὐαγγελίου τῆς δόξης τοῦ Χριστοῦ, ὅς
ILLUMINATION OF THE GOOD NEWS OF THE GLORY - OF CHRIST, WHO

ἐστιν εἰκὼν τοῦ θεοῦ. **4.5** οὐ γὰρ ἑαυτοὺς κηρύσσομεν
IS [THE] IMAGE - OF GOD. FOR~NOT OURSELVES WE PREACH

ἀλλὰ Ἰησοῦν Χριστὸν κύριον, ἑαυτοὺς δὲ δούλους ὑμῶν
BUT JESUS CHRIST [THE] LORD, AND~OURSELVES SLAVES OF YOU°

διὰ Ἰησοῦν. **4.6** ὅτι ὁ θεὸς ὁ εἰπών, Ἐκ
BECAUSE OF JESUS. BECAUSE - GOD, THE ONE HAVING SPOKEN, OUT OF

σκότους φῶς λάμψει, ὃς ἔλαμψεν ἐν ταῖς καρδίαις
DARKNESS LIGHT WILL SHINE, [IS] HE WHO SHONE IN THE HEARTS

ἡμῶν πρὸς φωτισμὸν τῆς γνώσεως τῆς δόξης τοῦ θεοῦ
OF US FOR AN ILLUMINATION OF THE KNOWLEDGE OF THE GLORY - OF GOD

ἐν προσώπῳ [Ἰησοῦ] Χριστοῦ.
IN [THE] FACE OF JESUS CHRIST.

4.7 Ἔχομεν δὲ τὸν θησαυρὸν τοῦτον ἐν ὀστρακίνοις
NOW~WE HAVE - THIS~TREASURE IN EARTHEN

σκεύεσιν, ἵνα ἡ ὑπερβολὴ τῆς δυνάμεως ᾖ τοῦ
VESSELS, THAT THE EXCELLENCE OF THE POWER MAY BE -

θεοῦ καὶ μὴ ἐξ ἡμῶν· **4.8** ἐν παντὶ θλιβόμενοι
OF GOD AND NOT OF US; BY EVERY [SIDE] BEING OPPRESSED

ἀλλ' οὐ στενοχωρούμενοι, ἀπορούμενοι ἀλλ' οὐκ
BUT NOT BEING CRUSHED, BEING PERPLEXED BUT NOT

ἐξαπορούμενοι, **4.9** διωκόμενοι ἀλλ' οὐκ
DESPAIRING, BEING PERSECUTED BUT NOT

ἐγκαταλειπόμενοι, καταβαλλόμενοι ἀλλ' οὐκ
BEING FORSAKEN, BEING CAST DOWN BUT NOT

ἀπολλύμενοι, **4.10** πάντοτε τὴν νέκρωσιν τοῦ Ἰησοῦ ἐν
BEING DESTRQYED,   ALWAYS   THE   DYING   -   OF JESUS   IN

τῷ   σώματι περιφέροντες, ἵνα καὶ ἡ ζωὴ τοῦ Ἰησοῦ
THE(MY) BODY   BEARING ABOUT,   THAT ALSO THE LIFE - OF JESUS

ἐν τῷ σώματι ἡμῶν φανερωθῇ.   **4.11** ἀεὶ γὰρ ἡμεῖς
IN THE BODY   OF US   MIGHT BE MANIFESTED.   FOR~ALWAYS WE,

οἱ   ζῶντες, εἰς θάνατον παραδιδόμεθα διὰ
THE ONES LIVING,   TO DEATH   ARE BEING GIVEN OVER BECAUSE OF

Ἰησοῦν, ἵνα καὶ ἡ ζωὴ τοῦ Ἰησοῦ φανερωθῇ ἐν τῇ
JESUS,   THAT ALSO THE LIFE - OF JESUS MAY BE MANIFESTED IN THE

θνητῇ σαρκὶ ἡμῶν. **4.12** ὥστε ὁ θάνατος ἐν ἡμῖν
MORTAL FLESH OF US.   SO THEN - DEATH   IN US

ἐνεργεῖται, ἡ δὲ ζωὴ ἐν ὑμῖν. **4.13** ἔχοντες δὲ τὸ αὐτὸ
WORKS,   - BUT LIFE IN YOU°.   AND~HAVING   THE SAME

πνεῦμα τῆς πίστεως κατὰ   τὸ   γεγραμμένον,
SPIRIT   - OF FAITH ACCORDING TO THE THING HAVING BEEN WRITTEN,

Ἐπίστευσα, διὸ   ἐλάλησα, καὶ ἡμεῖς πιστεύομεν,
I BELIEVED, THEREFORE I SPOKE, BOTH WE   BELIEVE,

διὸ καὶ   λαλοῦμεν, **4.14** εἰδότες ὅτι ὁ   ἐγείρας τὸν
AND~THEREFORE WE SPEAK,   KNOWING THAT THE ONE HAVING RAISED THE

κύριον Ἰησοῦν καὶ ἡμᾶς σὺν Ἰησοῦ ἐγερεῖ καὶ
LORD   JESUS   ALSO ²US ³WITH ⁴JESUS ¹WILL RAISE AND

παραστήσει σὺν ὑμῖν. **4.15** τὰ γὰρ πάντα δι'
WILL PRESENT [US] WITH YOU°.   - FOR ALL THINGS [ARE] BECAUSE OF

ὑμᾶς, ἵνα ἡ χάρις πλεονάσασα διὰ τῶν πλειόνων
YOU°, THAT THE GRACE, HAVING INCREASED THROUGH THE MANY,

τὴν εὐχαριστίαν περισσεύσῃ εἰς τὴν δόξαν τοῦ θεοῦ.
²THE ³THANKSGIVING ¹MAY INCREASE TO THE GLORY - OF GOD.

4.16 Διὸ   οὐκ ἐγκακοῦμεν, ἀλλ' εἰ καὶ ὁ ἔξω ἡμῶν
       THEREFORE WE DO NOT LOSE HEART, BUT IF INDEED - OUR~OUTWARD

ἄνθρωπος διαφθείρεται, ἀλλ' ὁ ἔσω ἡμῶν
MAN   IS BEING DECAYED, YET - OUR~INWARD [MAN]

ἀνακαινοῦται ἡμέρα καὶ ἡμέρα. **4.17** τὸ γὰρ παραυτίκα
IS BEING RENEWED DAY BY DAY.   FOR~THE PRESENT

ἐλαφρὸν τῆς θλίψεως ἡμῶν καθ' ὑπερβολὴν εἰς
LIGHTNESS OF THE AFFLICTION OF US FROM EXCESS   UNTO

ὑπερβολὴν αἰώνιον βάρος δόξης κατεργάζεται ἡμῖν,
[MORE] EXCESS ³AN ETERNAL ⁴WEIGHT ⁵OF GLORY ¹WORKS OUT   ²FOR US,

4.18 μὴ   σκοπούντων ἡμῶν τὰ   βλεπόμενα
      [WHILE] ²NOT ³LOOKING AT ¹WE [ARE] THE THINGS BEING SEEN

ἀλλὰ τὰ   μὴ βλεπόμενα· τὰ γὰρ   βλεπόμενα
BUT THE THINGS NOT BEING SEEN; FOR~THE THINGS BEING SEEN

πρόσκαιρα, τὰ δὲ μὴ βλεπόμενα αἰώνια.
[ARE] TEMPORARY, BUT~THE THINGS NOT BEING SEEN [ARE] ETERNAL.

4:13 Ps. 116:10 LXX

not destroyed; [10]always carrying in the body the death of Jesus, so that the life of Jesus may also be made visible in our bodies. [11]For while we live, we are always being given up to death for Jesus' sake, so that the life of Jesus may be made visible in our mortal flesh. [12]So death is at work in us, but life in you.

13 But just as we have the same spirit of faith that is in accordance with scripture— "I believed, and so I spoke"—we also believe, and so we speak, [14]because we know that the one who raised the Lord Jesus will raise us also with Jesus, and will bring us with you into his presence. [15]Yes, everything is for your sake, so that grace, as it extends to more and more people, may increase thanksgiving, to the glory of God.

16 So we do not lose heart. Even though our outer nature is wasting away, our inner nature is being renewed day by day. [17]For this slight momentary affliction is preparing us for an eternal weight of glory beyond all measure, [18]because we look not at what can be seen but at what cannot be seen; for what can be seen is temporary, but what cannot be seen is eternal.

CHAPTER 5

For we know that if the earthly tent we live in is destroyed, we have a building from God, a house not made with hands, eternal in the heavens. [2]For in this tent we groan, longing to be clothed with our heavenly dwelling— [3]if indeed, when we have taken it off[j] we will not be found naked. [4]For while we are still in this tent, we groan under our burden, because we wish not to be unclothed but to be further clothed, so that what is mortal may be swallowed up by life. [5]He who has prepared us for this very thing is God, who has given us the Spirit as a guarantee.

6 So we are always confident; even though we know that while we are at home in the body we are away from the Lord— [7]for we walk by faith, not by sight. [8]Yes, we do have confidence, and we would rather be away from the body and at home with the Lord. [9]So whether we are at home or away, we make it our aim to please him. [10]For all of us must appear before the judgment seat of Christ, so that each may receive recompense for what has been done in the body, whether good or evil.

11 Therefore, knowing the fear of the Lord,

[j] Other ancient authorities read put it on

5.1 Οἴδαμεν γὰρ ὅτι ἐὰν ἡ ἐπίγειος ἡμῶν οἰκία
FOR~WE KNOW   THAT IF   -   OUR~EARTHLY   HOUSE

τοῦ   σκήνους καταλυθῇ, οἰκοδομὴν ἐκ   θεοῦ ἔχομεν,
OF THE(OUR) TABERNACLE IS DESTROYED, A BUILDING FROM GOD   WE HAVE,

οἰκίαν ἀχειροποίητον αἰώνιον ἐν τοῖς οὐρανοῖς.
A HOUSE NOT MADE WITH HANDS ETERNAL IN THE HEAVENS.

5.2 καὶ γὰρ ἐν τούτῳ στενάζομεν τὸ οἰκητήριον ἡμῶν τὸ
FOR~INDEED IN THIS WE GROAN,   [3]THE [4]DWELLING   [5]OF US -

ἐξ οὐρανοῦ ἐπενδύσασθαι ἐπιποθοῦντες, **5.3** εἴ γε καὶ
[6]FROM [7]HEAVEN [2]TO BE CLOTHED WITH [1]LONGING,   IF - INDEED

ἐκδυσάμενοι οὐ γυμνοὶ εὑρεθησόμεθα. **5.4** καὶ γὰρ
HAVING BEEN UNCLOTHED NOT NAKED WE WILL BE FOUND.   FOR~INDEED

οἱ ὄντες ἐν τῷ σκήνει στενάζομεν βαρούμενοι,
[2]THE ONES [3]BEING [4]IN [5]THE [6]TABERNACLE [1]WE [7]GROAN, BEING BURDENED,

ἐφ' ᾧ οὐ θέλομεν ἐκδύσασθαι ἀλλ' ἐπενδύσασθαι,
INASMUCH AS WE DO NOT WANT TO BE UNCLOTHED BUT TO BE CLOTHED,

ἵνα καταποθῇ τὸ θνητὸν ὑπὸ τῆς ζωῆς.
THAT [3]MAY BE SWALLOWED UP [1]THE [2]MORTAL BY THE LIFE.

5.5 ὁ δὲ κατεργασάμενος ἡμᾶς εἰς αὐτὸ τοῦτο θεός,
NOW~THE ONE HAVING MADE   US   FOR THIS VERY THING [IS] GOD,

ὁ δοὺς ἡμῖν τὸν ἀρραβῶνα τοῦ πνεύματος.
THE ONE HAVING GIVEN TO US THE EARNEST   OF THE SPIRIT.

5.6 Θαρροῦντες οὖν   πάντοτε καὶ εἰδότες ὅτι
BEING CONFIDENT THEREFORE ALWAYS   AND KNOWING THAT

ἐνδημοῦντες ἐν τῷ σώματι ἐκδημοῦμεν ἀπὸ
BEING AT HOME IN THE BODY WE ARE AWAY FROM HOME [WHEN] AWAY FROM

τοῦ κυρίου· **5.7** διὰ πίστεως γὰρ περιπατοῦμεν, οὐ διὰ
THE LORD;   [2]BY [3]FAITH [1]FOR WE WALK,   NOT BY

εἴδους· **5.8** θαρροῦμεν δὲ καὶ εὐδοκοῦμεν μᾶλλον
SIGHT;   WE ARE CONFIDENT THEN AND ARE PLEASED RATHER

ἐκδημῆσαι ἐκ τοῦ σώματος καὶ ἐνδημῆσαι πρὸς
TO LEAVE HOME OUT FROM THE(OUR) BODY AND TO BE AT HOME WITH

τὸν κύριον. **5.9** διὸ καὶ φιλοτιμούμεθα, εἴτε
THE LORD.   THEREFORE ALSO WE ARE ASPIRING,   WHETHER

ἐνδημοῦντες εἴτε ἐκδημοῦντες, εὐάρεστοι αὐτῷ εἶναι.
BEING AT HOME OR BEING AWAY FROM HOME, WELLPLEASING TO HIM TO BE.

5.10 τοὺς γὰρ πάντας ἡμᾶς φανερωθῆναι δεῖ
-      FOR [3]ALL [OF] [2]US [4]TO BE REVEALED [1]IT IS NECESSARY [FOR]

ἔμπροσθεν τοῦ βήματος τοῦ Χριστοῦ, ἵνα
BEFORE   THE JUDGMENT SEAT - OF CHRIST,   THAT

κομίσηται ἕκαστος τὰ διὰ τοῦ σώματος
EACH ONE~MAY BE RECOMPENSED [FOR] THE THINGS [DONE] THROUGH THE BODY

πρὸς ἃ ἔπραξεν, εἴτε ἀγαθὸν εἴτε φαῦλον.
ACCORDING TO WHAT THINGS HE PRACTISED, WHETHER GOOD OR BAD.

5.11 Εἰδότες οὖν τὸν φόβον τοῦ κυρίου
KNOWING THEREFORE THE FEAR OF THE LORD

ἀνθρώπους πείθομεν, θεῷ δὲ πεφανερώμεθα·
WE PERSUADE~MEN,   AND~TO GOD WE HAVE BEEN MADE MANIFEST;

ἐλπίζω δὲ καὶ ἐν ταῖς συνειδήσεσιν ὑμῶν
AND~I HOPE ALSO IN THE CONSCIENCES OF YOU°

πεφανερῶσθαι.   **5.12** οὐ πάλιν ἑαυτοὺς συνιστάνομεν
TO HAVE BEEN MADE MANIFEST.   NOT AGAIN   WE COMMEND~OURSELVES

ὑμῖν ἀλλὰ ἀφορμὴν διδόντες ὑμῖν καυχήματος ὑπὲρ
TO YOU° BUT AN OPPORTUNITY GIVING TO YOU° OF(FOR) A BOAST ON BEHALF

ἡμῶν, ἵνα ἔχητε   πρὸς τοὺς ἐν προσώπῳ
OF US, THAT YOU° MAY HAVE [SUCH] TOWARD THE ONES IN APPEARANCE

καυχωμένους καὶ μὴ ἐν καρδίᾳ.   **5.13** εἴτε γὰρ
BOASTING   AND NOT IN HEART.   FOR~WHETHER

ἐξέστημεν,   θεῷ·   εἴτε σωφρονοῦμεν,
WE WERE BESIDE OURSELVES, [IT WAS] TO GOD; OR WE WERE IN OUR RIGHT MIND,

ὑμῖν.   **5.14** ἡ γὰρ ἀγάπη τοῦ Χριστοῦ συνέχει
[IT WAS] FOR YOU°. FOR~THE LOVE   -   OF CHRIST   CONTROLS

ἡμᾶς, κρίναντας τοῦτο, ὅτι εἷς ὑπὲρ   πάντων
US,   HAVING JUDGED THIS, THAT ONE ON BEHALF OF ALL

ἀπέθανεν, ἄρα οἱ πάντες ἀπέθανον· **5.15** καὶ ὑπὲρ
DIED,   THEN - ALL   DIED;   AND ON BEHALF OF

πάντων ἀπέθανεν, ἵνα οἱ   ζῶντες μηκέτι ἑαυτοῖς
OF ALL HE DIED,   THAT THE ONES LIVING NO LONGER TO THEMSELVES

ζῶσιν ἀλλὰ τῷ   ὑπὲρ αὐτῶν ἀποθανόντι καὶ
MAY LIVE BUT TO THE ONE ON BEHALF OF THEM HAVING DIED   AND

ἐγερθέντι.
HAVING BEEN RAISED.

5.16 Ὥστε ἡμεῖς ἀπὸ τοῦ νῦν   οὐδένα οἴδαμεν
       SO THAT WE   FROM - NOW [ON] KNOW~NO ONE

κατὰ σάρκα· εἰ καὶ ἐγνώκαμεν κατὰ   σάρκα
ACCORDING TO FLESH; IF INDEED WE HAVE KNOWN ²ACCORDING TO ³FLESH

Χριστόν, ἀλλὰ νῦν οὐκέτι γινώσκομεν. **5.17** ὥστε εἴ
¹CHRIST, BUT NOW NO LONGER WE KNOW [HIM THUS].   SO THAT IF

τις ἐν Χριστῷ, καινὴ κτίσις· τὰ ἀρχαῖα
ANYONE [IS] IN CHRIST, [HE IS] A NEW CREATION; THE OLD THINGS

παρῆλθεν, ἰδοὺ γέγονεν καινά. **5.18** τὰ δὲ πάντα
PASSED AWAY, BEHOLD HE HAS BECOME NEW.   - AND ALL THINGS

ἐκ   τοῦ θεοῦ τοῦ καταλλάξαντος ἡμᾶς ἑαυτῷ διὰ
[ARE] OF - GOD THE ONE HAVING RECONCILED US TO HIMSELF THROUGH

Χριστοῦ καὶ δόντος ἡμῖν τὴν διακονίαν τῆς
CHRIST   AND HAVING GIVEN TO US THE MINISTRY

καταλλαγῆς, **5.19** ὡς ὅτι θεὸς ἦν ἐν Χριστῷ κόσμον
OF RECONCILIATION, THAT IS [THAT] GOD WAS IN CHRIST, [THE] WORLD

καταλλάσσων ἑαυτῷ, μὴ λογιζόμενος αὐτοῖς τὰ
RECONCILING   TO HIMSELF, NOT RECKONING TO THEM THE

παραπτώματα αὐτῶν καὶ θέμενος ἐν ἡμῖν τὸν λόγον
TRESPASSES   OF THEM AND HAVING PUT IN US THE MESSAGE

τῆς καταλλαγῆς. **5.20** ὑπὲρ   Χριστοῦ οὖν
-    OF RECONCILIATION.   ON BEHALF OF CHRIST THEREFORE

we try to persuade others; but we ourselves are well known to God, and I hope that we are also well known to your consciences. [12]We are not commending ourselves to you again, but giving you an opportunity to boast about us, so that you may be able to answer those who boast in outward appearance and not in the heart. [13]For if we are beside ourselves, it is for God; if we are in our right mind, it is for you. [14]For the love of Christ urges us on, because we are convinced that one has died for all; therefore all have died. [15]And he died for all, so that those who live might live no longer for themselves, but for him who died and was raised for them.

16 From now on, therefore, we regard no one from a human point of view;[k] even though we once knew Christ from a human point of view,[k] we know him no longer in that way. [17]So if anyone is in Christ, there is a new creation: everything old has passed away; see, everything has become new! [18]All this is from God, who reconciled us to himself through Christ, and has given us the ministry of reconciliation; [19]that is, in Christ God was reconciling the world to himself,[l] not counting their trespasses against them, and entrusting the message of reconciliation to us. [20]So we are ambassadors for Christ,

[k] Gk *according to the flesh*
[l] Or *God was in Christ reconciling the world to himself*

since God is making his appeal through us; we entreat you on behalf of Christ, be reconciled to God. ²¹For our sake he made him to be sin who knew no sin, so that in him we might become the righteousness of God.

πρεσβεύομεν ὡς τοῦ θεοῦ παρακαλοῦντος δι᾽ ἡμῶν·
WE ARE AMBASSADORS AS [IF] - GOD [WERE] ENTREATING THROUGH US;

δεόμεθα ὑπὲρ Χριστοῦ, καταλλάγητε τῷ θεῷ.
WE ASK ON BEHALF OF CHRIST, BE RECONCILED - TO GOD.

5.21 τὸν μὴ γνόντα ἁμαρτίαν ὑπὲρ ἡμῶν
THE ONE NOT KNOWING SIN ³ON BEHALF OF ⁴US

ἁμαρτίαν ἐποίησεν, ἵνα ἡμεῖς γενώμεθα δικαιοσύνη
²SIN ¹HE MADE, THAT WE MIGHT BECOME [THE] RIGHTEOUSNESS

θεοῦ ἐν αὐτῷ.
OF GOD IN HIM.

CHAPTER 6

As we work together with him,ᵐ we urge you also not to accept the grace of God in vain. ²For he says,
"At an acceptable time I
have listened to
you,
and on a day of
salvation I have
helped you."
See, now is the acceptable time; see, now is the day of salvation! ³We are putting no obstacle in anyone's way, so that no fault may be found with our ministry, ⁴but as servants of God we have commended ourselves in every way: through great endurance, in afflictions, hardships, calamities, ⁵beatings, imprisonments, riots, labors, sleepless nights, hunger; ⁶by purity, knowledge, patience, kindness, holiness of spirit, genuine love, ⁷truthful speech, and the power of God; with the

ᵐ Gk As we work together

6.1 Συνεργοῦντες δὲ καὶ παρακαλοῦμεν
[AS] ONES WORKING TOGETHER WITH [HIM], - ALSO WE URGE

μὴ εἰς κενὸν τὴν χάριν τοῦ θεοῦ δέξασθαι ὑμᾶς·
²NOT ⁷IN ⁸VAIN ⁴THE ⁵GRACE - ⁶OF GOD ³TO RECEIVE ¹YOU;

6.2 λέγει γάρ,
FOR~HE SAYS,

Καιρῷ δεκτῷ ἐπήκουσά σου
IN A TIME ACCEPTABLE I HEARD YOU

καὶ ἐν ἡμέρᾳ σωτηρίας ἐβοήθησά σοι.
AND IN A DAY OF SALVATION I HELPED YOU.

ἰδοὺ νῦν καιρὸς εὐπρόσδεκτος, ἰδοὺ νῦν ἡμέρα
BEHOLD NOW [IS] A TIME ACCEPTABLE, BEHOLD NOW [IS] A DAY

σωτηρίας· **6.3** μηδεμίαν ἐν μηδενὶ διδόντες
OF SALVATION; NOT IN ANYTHING GIVING

προσκοπήν, ἵνα μὴ μωμηθῇ ἡ διακονία, **6.4** ἀλλ᾽
A CAUSE FOR STUMBLING, LEST ³BE BLAMED ¹THE ²MINISTRY, BUT

ἐν παντὶ συνίσταντες ἑαυτοὺς ὡς θεοῦ διάκονοι,
IN EVERYTHING PRESENTING OURSELVES AS GOD'S SERVANTS,

ἐν ὑπομονῇ πολλῇ, ἐν θλίψεσιν, ἐν ἀνάγκαις, ἐν
IN MUCH~ENDURANCE IN AFFLICTIONS, IN HARDSHIPS, IN

στενοχωρίαις, **6.5** ἐν πληγαῖς, ἐν φυλακαῖς, ἐν
DISTRESSES, IN BEATINGS, IN IMPRISONMENTS, IN

ἀκαταστασίαις, ἐν κόποις, ἐν ἀγρυπνίαις, ἐν
RIOTS, IN LABORS, IN WATCHINGS, IN

νηστείαις, **6.6** ἐν ἁγνότητι, ἐν γνώσει, ἐν μακροθυμίᾳ,
FASTINGS, IN PURITY, IN KNOWLEDGE, IN LONGSUFFERING,

ἐν χρηστότητι, ἐν πνεύματι ἁγίῳ, ἐν ἀγάπῃ ἀνυποκρίτῳ,
IN KINDNESS, IN [THE] HOLY~SPIRIT, IN LOVE UNHYPOCRITICAL,

6.7 ἐν λόγῳ ἀληθείας, ἐν δυνάμει θεοῦ· διὰ τῶν
IN [THE] WORD OF TRUTH, IN [THE] POWER OF GOD; THROUGH THE

6:2 Isa. 49:8

ὅπλων τῆς δικαιοσύνης τῶν δεξιῶν καὶ ἀριστερῶν,
WEAPONS -   OF RIGHTEOUSNESS OF THE RIGHT [HAND] AND   OF [THE] LEFT,

6.8 διὰ   δόξης καὶ ἀτιμίας, διὰ   δυσφημίας καὶ
THROUGH HONOR AND DISHONOR, THROUGH ILL REPUTE   AND

εὐφημίας· ὡς πλάνοι καὶ   ἀληθεῖς, **6.9** ὡς
GOOD REPUTE;   AS   DECEIVERS AND [YET] TRUE,   AS

ἀγνοούμενοι καὶ   ἐπιγινωσκόμενοι, ὡς ἀποθνῄσκοντες
BEING UNKNOWN AND [YET] BEING WELL-KNOWN,   AS   DYING

καὶ ἰδοὺ ζῶμεν, ὡς   παιδευόμενοι καὶ μὴ
AND BEHOLD WE LIVE, AS   BEING PUNISHED   AND NOT

θανατούμενοι, **6.10** ὡς λυπούμενοι ἀεὶ δὲ   χαίροντες,
BEING PUT TO DEATH,   AS   BEING GRIEVED   BUT~ALWAYS REJOICING,

ὡς πτωχοὶ πολλοὺς δὲ πλουτίζοντες, ὡς
AS   POOR   ³MANY   ¹BUT ²ENRICHING,   AS

μηδὲν ἔχοντες καὶ   πάντα κατέχοντες.
HAVING~NOTHING AND [YET] ALL THINGS POSSESSING.

6.11 Τὸ στόμα ἡμῶν ἀνέῳγεν πρὸς ὑμᾶς, Κορίνθιοι, ἡ
THE MOUTH OF US HAS OPENED TO   YOU°, CORINTHIANS, THE

καρδία ἡμῶν πεπλάτυνται· **6.12** οὐ στενοχωρεῖσθε ἐν
HEART OF US HAS BEEN ENLARGED;   YOU° ARE NOT BEING RESTRICTED BY

ἡμῖν, στενοχωρεῖσθε δὲ ἐν τοῖς σπλάγχνοις ὑμῶν·
US,   BUT~YOU° ARE RESTRICTED IN THE BOWELS(AFFECTIONS) OF YOU°;

6.13 τὴν δὲ αὐτὴν   ἀντιμισθίαν, ὡς τέκνοις λέγω,
NOW~IN THE SAME [KIND OF] EXCHANGE,   AS TO CHILDREN I SPEAK,

πλατύνθητε καὶ ὑμεῖς.
BE ENLARGED   ALSO YOU°.

6.14 Μὴ γίνεσθε ἑτεροζυγοῦντες ἀπίστοις· τίς γὰρ
DO NOT BECOME UNEQUALLY YOKED   WITH UNBELIEVERS; FOR~WHAT

μετοχὴ δικαιοσύνη   καὶ ἀνομίᾳ ἢ τίς κοινωνία
PARTNERSHIP [HAVE] RIGHTEOUSNESS AND LAWLESSNESS OR WHAT FELLOWSHIP

φωτὶ πρὸς σκότος; **6.15** τίς δὲ συμφώνησις Χριστοῦ
[HAS] LIGHT WITH DARKNESS?   AND~WHAT HARMONY   OF CHRIST

πρὸς Βελιάρ, ἢ τίς μερὶς πιστῷ   μετὰ ἀπίστου;
WITH BELIAR, OR WHAT PART [HAS] A BELIEVER WITH AN UNBELIEVER?

6.16 τίς δὲ συγκατάθεσις ναῷ   θεοῦ μετὰ εἰδώλων;
AND~WHAT AGREEMENT [HAS] A SANCTUARY OF GOD WITH IDOLS?

ἡμεῖς γὰρ ναὸς   θεοῦ ἐσμεν ζῶντος, καθὼς εἶπεν ὁ
FOR~WE   ²A SANCTUARY ⁴GOD ¹ARE ³OF A LIVING, AS   SAID   -

θεὸς ὅτι
GOD, -

Ἐνοικήσω ἐν αὐτοῖς καὶ ἐμπεριπατήσω
I WILL DWELL IN THEM   AND I WILL WALK AMONG [THEM],

καὶ ἔσομαι αὐτῶν θεός
AND I WILL BE THEIR   GOD

καὶ αὐτοὶ ἔσονταί μου λαός.
AND THEY   WILL BE   MY PEOPLE.

6:16 Lev. 26:12; Ezek. 37:27

weapons of righteousness for the right hand and for the left; [8]in honor and dishonor, in ill repute and good repute. We are treated as impostors, and yet are true; [9]as unknown, and yet are well known; as dying, and see— we are alive; as punished, and yet not killed; [10]as sorrowful, yet always rejoicing; as poor, yet making many rich; as having nothing, and yet possessing everything.

11 We have spoken frankly to you Corinthians; our heart is wide open to you. [12]There is no restriction in our affections, but only in yours. [13]In return—I speak as to children—open wide your hearts also.

14 Do not be mismatched with unbelievers. For what partnership is there between righteousness and lawlessness? Or what fellowship is there between light and darkness? [15]What agreement does Christ have with Beliar? Or what does a believer share with an unbeliever? [16]What agreement has the temple of God with idols? For we[n] are the temple of the living God; as God said,

"I will live in them and
   walk among them,
and I will be their God,
and they shall be my
people.

[n] Other ancient authorities read *you*

¹⁷Therefore come out from them,
and be separate from them, says the Lord,
and touch nothing unclean;
then I will welcome you,
¹⁸and I will be your father, and you shall be my sons and daughters, says the Lord Almighty."

6.17 διὸ ἐξέλθατε ἐκ μέσου αὐτῶν
THEREFORE COME OUT FROM [THE] MIDST OF THEM

καὶ ἀφορίσθητε, λέγει κύριος,
AND BE SEPARATED, SAYS [THE] LORD,

καὶ ἀκαθάρτου μὴ ἅπτεσθε·
AND AN UNCLEAN THING DO NOT TOUCH;

κἀγὼ εἰσδέξομαι ὑμᾶς
AND I WILL RECEIVE YOU°

6.18 καὶ ἔσομαι ὑμῖν εἰς πατέρα
AND I WILL BE TO YOU° - A FATHER

καὶ ὑμεῖς ἔσεσθέ μοι εἰς υἱοὺς καὶ
AND YOU° WILL BE TO ME - SONS AND

θυγατέρας,
DAUGHTERS,

λέγει κύριος παντοκράτωρ.
SAYS [THE] LORD [THE] ALMIGHTY.

6:17a Isa. 52:11   **6:17b** Ezek. 20:34   **6:18** 2 Sam. 7:8, 14

CHAPTER 7

Since we have these promises, beloved, let us cleanse ourselves from every defilement of body and of spirit, making holiness perfect in the fear of God.
2 Make room in your hearts° for us; we have wronged no one, we have corrupted no one, we have taken advantage of no one. ³I do not say this to condemn you, for I said before that you are in our hearts, to die together and to live together. ⁴I often boast about you; I have great pride in you; I am filled with consolation; I am overjoyed in all our affliction.
5 For even when we came into Macedonia,

°Gk lacks in your hearts

7.1 ταύτας οὖν ἔχοντες τὰς ἐπαγγελίας, ἀγαπητοί,
³THESE ¹THEREFORE ²HAVING - ⁴PROMISES, BELOVED,

καθαρίσωμεν ἑαυτοὺς ἀπὸ παντὸς μολυσμοῦ σαρκὸς
LET US CLEANSE OURSELVES FROM EVERY DEFILEMENT OF FLESH

καὶ πνεύματος, ἐπιτελοῦντες ἁγιωσύνην ἐν φόβῳ
AND SPIRIT, PERFECTING HOLINESS IN [THE] FEAR

θεοῦ.
OF GOD.

7.2 Χωρήσατε ἡμᾶς· οὐδένα ἠδικήσαμεν, οὐδένα
MAKE ROOM FOR US; NO ONE WE WRONGED, NO ONE

ἐφθείραμεν, οὐδένα ἐπλεονεκτήσαμεν. **7.3** πρὸς
WE RUINED, NO ONE WE EXPLOITED. AS TO

κατάκρισιν οὐ λέγω· προείρηκα γὰρ ὅτι ἐν ταῖς
CONDEMNATION I DO NOT SPEAK; FOR~I HAVE SAID BEFORE THAT IN THE

καρδίαις ἡμῶν ἐστε εἰς τὸ συναποθανεῖν καὶ
HEARTS OF US YOU° ARE SO AS - TO DIE WITH [YOU°] AND

συζῆν. **7.4** πολλή μοι παρρησία πρὸς ὑμᾶς,
TO LIVE WITH [YOU°]. I HAVE MUCH BOLDNESS TOWARD YOU°,

πολλή μοι καύχησις ὑπὲρ ὑμῶν· πεπλήρωμαι τῇ
I HAVE MUCH BOASTING ON BEHALF OF YOU°; I HAVE BEEN FILLED -

παρακλήσει, ὑπερπερισσεύομαι τῇ χαρᾷ ἐπὶ πάσῃ τῇ
WITH ENCOURAGEMENT, I AM FILLED TO OVERFLOWING - WITH JOY AT ALL THE

θλίψει ἡμῶν.
AFFLICTION OF US.

7.5 Καὶ γὰρ ἐλθόντων ἡμῶν εἰς Μακεδονίαν οὐδεμίαν
FOR~INDEED [WHEN] WE HAD COME INTO MACEDONIA, ⁵NO

ἔσχηκεν ἄνεσιν ἡ σαρξ ἡμῶν ἀλλ᾽ ἐν παντὶ
⁴HAD   ⁶REST ¹THE ²BODY ³OF US, BUT IN EVERY [WAY]

θλιβόμενοι· ἔξωθεν μάχαι, ἔσωθεν φόβοι. **7.6** ἀλλ᾽
BEING AFFLICTED; OUTSIDE [WERE] BATTLES, INSIDE, FEARS.   ¹BUT

ὁ   παρακαλῶν τοὺς ταπεινοὺς παρεκάλεσεν ἡμᾶς ὁ
³THE ONE ⁴ENCOURAGING ⁵THE ⁶LOWLY ⁷ENCOURAGED ⁸US   -

θεὸς ἐν τῇ παρουσίᾳ Τίτου, **7.7** οὐ μόνον δὲ ἐν τῇ
²GOD BY THE COMING OF TITUS, ²NOT ³ONLY ¹AND BY THE

παρουσίᾳ αὐτοῦ ἀλλὰ καὶ ἐν τῇ παρακλήσει ᾗ
COMING   OF HIM BUT ALSO BY THE ENCOURAGEMENT BY WHICH

παρεκλήθη ἐφ᾽ ὑμῖν, ἀναγγέλλων ἡμῖν τὴν ὑμῶν
HE WAS ENCOURAGED OVER YOU°, REPORTING TO US - YOUR°

ἐπιπόθησιν, τὸν ὑμῶν ὀδυρμόν, τὸν ὑμῶν ζῆλον ὑπὲρ
LONGING, - YOUR° MOURNING, - YOUR° ZEAL FOR

ἐμοῦ ὥστε με   μᾶλλον χαρῆναι. **7.8** ὅτι εἰ καὶ
ME SO THAT [IT CAUSED] ME TO REJOICE~MORE. BECAUSE IF INDEED

ἐλύπησα ὑμᾶς ἐν τῇ ἐπιστολῇ, οὐ μεταμέλομαι· εἰ
I GRIEVED YOU° BY THE LETTER I DO NOT REGRET [IT]; IF

καὶ μετεμελόμην, βλέπω [γὰρ] ὅτι ἡ ἐπιστολὴ ἐκείνη
INDEED I WAS REGRETTING [IT], FOR~I SEE THAT - THAT~LETTER,

εἰ καὶ πρὸς ὥραν ἐλύπησεν ὑμᾶς, **7.9** νῦν χαίρω, οὐχ
IF EVEN FOR AN HOUR, GRIEVED YOU,   NOW I REJOICE, NOT

ὅτι ἐλυπήθητε ἀλλ᾽ ὅτι ἐλυπήθητε εἰς μετάνοιαν·
THAT YOU° WERE GRIEVED BUT THAT YOU° WERE GRIEVED TO REPENTANCE;

ἐλυπήθητε γὰρ κατὰ   θεόν, ἵνα ἐν μηδενὶ
FOR~YOU° WERE GRIEVED ACCORDING TO GOD, THAT IN NOTHING

ζημιωθῆτε   ἐξ ἡμῶν. **7.10** ἡ γὰρ κατὰ   θεὸν
YOU° MIGHT SUFFER LOSS BY US. ²THE ¹FOR ⁴ACCORDING TO ⁵GOD

λύπη μετάνοιαν εἰς σωτηρίαν ἀμεταμέλητον ἐργάζεται·
³GRIEF ⁷REPENTANCE ⁸TO ⁹SALVATION ¹⁰NOT TO BE REGRETTED ⁶WORKS;

ἡ δὲ τοῦ κόσμου λύπη θάνατον κατεργάζεται.
²THE ¹BUT ⁴OF THE ⁵WORLD ³GRIEF ⁷DEATH ⁶WORKS OUT.

7.11 ἰδοὺ γὰρ αὐτὸ τοῦτο τὸ κατὰ   θεὸν λυπηθῆναι
FOR~BEHOLD THIS SAME THING, - ²ACCORDING TO ³GOD ¹TO BE GRIEVED,

πόσην κατειργάσατο ὑμῖν σπουδήν, ἀλλὰ ἀπολογίαν,
¹WHAT ³IT PRODUCED ⁴IN YOU° ²DILIGENCE, BUT [WHAT] DEFENSE,

ἀλλὰ ἀγανάκτησιν, ἀλλὰ φόβον, ἀλλὰ ἐπιπόθησιν,
BUT [WHAT] INDIGNATION, BUT [WHAT] FEAR, BUT [WHAT] LONGING,

ἀλλὰ ζῆλον, ἀλλὰ ἐκδίκησιν. ἐν παντὶ
BUT [WHAT] ZEAL, BUT [WHAT] VENGEANCE. IN EVERYTHING

συνεστήσατε ἑαυτοὺς ἁγνοὺς εἶναι τῷ πράγματι.
YOU° PRESENTED YOURSELVES TO BE~PURE IN THE MATTER.

7.12 ἄρα εἰ καὶ ἔγραψα ὑμῖν, οὐχ ἕνεκεν τοῦ
THEN IF INDEED I WROTE TO YOU°, [IT WAS] NOT FOR THE SAKE OF THE ONE

ἀδικήσαντος οὐδὲ ἕνεκεν τοῦ ἀδικηθέντος ἀλλ᾽
HAVING DONE WRONG NOR FOR THE SAKE OF THE ONE HAVING BEEN WRONGED, BUT

ἕνεκεν   τοῦ φανερωθῆναι τὴν σπουδὴν ὑμῶν τὴν
FOR THE SAKE OF - BEING MADE MANIFEST ⁵THE ⁶ZEAL ⁷OF YOU° -

our bodies had no rest, but we were afflicted in every way—disputes without and fears within. ⁶But God, who consoles the downcast, consoled us by the arrival of Titus, ⁷and not only by his coming, but also by the consolation with which he was consoled about you, as he told us of your longing, your mourning, your zeal for me, so that I rejoiced still more. ⁸For even if I made you sorry with my letter, I do not regret it (though I did regret it, for I see that I grieved you with that letter, though only briefly). ⁹Now I rejoice, not because you were grieved, but because your grief led to repentance; for you felt a godly grief, so that you were not harmed in any way by us. ¹⁰For godly grief produces a repentance that leads to salvation and brings no regret, but worldly grief produces death. ¹¹For see what earnestness this godly grief has produced in you, what eagerness to clear yourselves, what indignation, what alarm, what longing, what zeal, what punishment! At every point you have proved yourselves guiltless in the matter. ¹²So although I wrote to you, it was not on account of the one who did the wrong, nor on account of the one who was wronged, but in order that your zeal for us might be made known to you before God. [13]In this we find comfort.

In addition to our own consolation, we rejoiced still more at the joy of Titus, because his mind has been set at rest by all of you. [14]For if I have been somewhat boastful about you to him, I was not disgraced; but just as everything we said to you was true, so our boasting to Titus has proved true as well. [15]And his heart goes out all the more to you, as he remembers the obedience of all of you, and how you welcomed him with fear and trembling. [16]I rejoice, because I have complete confidence in you.

ὑπὲρ ἡμῶν πρὸς ὑμᾶς ἐνώπιον τοῦ θεοῦ. **7.13** διὰ τοῦτο
[8]FOR [9]US [1]TO [2]YOU° [3]BEFORE - [4]GOD. THEREFORE

παρακεκλήμεθα.
WE HAVE BEEN ENCOURAGED.

Ἐπὶ δὲ τῇ παρακλήσει ἡμῶν περισσοτέρως μᾶλλον
BUT~AS TO THE ENCOURAGEMENT OF US EXCEEDINGLY MORE

ἐχάρημεν ἐπὶ τῇ χαρᾷ Τίτου, ὅτι ἀναπέπαυται τὸ
WE REJOICED AT THE JOY OF TITUS, BECAUSE [4]HAS BEEN SET AT REST [1]THE

πνεῦμα αὐτοῦ ἀπὸ πάντων ὑμῶν· **7.14** ὅτι εἴ τι
[2]SPIRIT [3]OF HIM FROM(BY) YOU°~ALL; BECAUSE IF ANYTHING

αὐτῷ ὑπὲρ ὑμῶν κεκαύχημαι, οὐ κατῃσχύνθην, ἀλλ' ὡς
TO HIM ABOUT YOU° I HAVE BOASTED, I WAS NOT PUT TO SHAME BUT AS

πάντα ἐν ἀληθείᾳ ἐλαλήσαμεν ὑμῖν, οὕτως καὶ ἡ
ALL THINGS IN TRUTH WE SPOKE TO YOU°, SO ALSO THE

καύχησις ἡμῶν ἡ ἐπὶ Τίτου ἀλήθεια ἐγενήθη. **7.15** καὶ
BOASTING OF US - AS TO TITUS BECAME~TRUTH. AND

τὰ σπλάγχνα αὐτοῦ περισσοτέρως εἰς ὑμᾶς ἐστιν
THE BOWELS(AFFECTIONS) OF HIM MORE ABUNDANTLY TOWARD YOU° ARE,

ἀναμιμνῃσκομένου τὴν πάντων ὑμῶν ὑπακοήν, ὡς
REMEMBERING [1]THE [4]ALL [3]OF YOU° [2]OBEDIENCE, AS

μετὰ φόβου καὶ τρόμου ἐδέξασθε αὐτόν. **7.16** χαίρω
WITH FEAR AND TREMBLING YOU° RECEIVED HIM. I REJOICE

ὅτι ἐν παντὶ θαρρῶ ἐν ὑμῖν.
THAT IN EVERYTHING I HAVE CONFIDENCE IN YOU°.

CHAPTER 8

We want you to know, brothers and sisters,[p] about the grace of God that has been granted to the churches of Macedonia; [2]for during a severe ordeal of affliction, their abundant joy and their extreme poverty have overflowed in a wealth of generosity on their part. [3]For, as I can testify, they voluntarily gave according to their means, and even beyond their means, [4]begging us earnestly for the privilege[q] of sharing in this ministry to the saints— [5]and this, not merely as we expected; they gave themselves first to the Lord

[p] Gk *brothers*
[q] Gk *grace*

8.1 Γνωρίζομεν δὲ ὑμῖν, ἀδελφοί, τὴν χάριν τοῦ θεοῦ
NOW~WE MAKE KNOWN TO YOU°, BROTHERS, THE GRACE - OF GOD

τὴν δεδομένην ἐν ταῖς ἐκκλησίαις τῆς Μακεδονίας,
- HAVING BEEN GIVEN AMONG THE CHURCHES - OF MACEDONIA,

8.2 ὅτι ἐν πολλῇ δοκιμῇ θλίψεως ἡ περισσεία τῆς
THAT BY A GREAT TEST OF AFFLICTION THE ABUNDANCE OF THE

χαρᾶς αὐτῶν καὶ ἡ κατὰ βάθους πτωχεία αὐτῶν
JOY OF THEM AND THE EXTREME DEPTH OF [THE] POVERTY OF THEM

ἐπερίσσευσεν εἰς τὸ πλοῦτος τῆς ἁπλότητος αὐτῶν·
ABOUNDED TO THE RICHES OF THE GENEROSITY OF THEM;

8.3 ὅτι κατὰ δύναμιν, μαρτυρῶ, καὶ παρὰ δύναμιν,
THAT ACCORDING TO [THEIR] ABILITY, I TESTIFY, AND BEYOND [THEIR] ABILITY,

αὐθαίρετοι **8.4** μετὰ πολλῆς παρακλήσεως δεόμενοι
OF THEIR OWN ACCORD WITH MUCH APPEAL REQUESTING

ἡμῶν τὴν χάριν καὶ τὴν κοινωνίαν
OF US [TO RECEIVE] THE FAVOR AND [TO PARTICIPATE IN] THE CONTRIBUTION

τῆς διακονίας τῆς εἰς τοὺς ἁγίους, **8.5** καὶ οὐ καθὼς
OF THE MINISTRY - TO THE SAINTS, AND NOT AS

ἠλπίσαμεν ἀλλ' ἑαυτοὺς ἔδωκαν πρῶτον τῷ κυρίῳ
WE HOPED BUT THEMSELVES THEY GAVE FIRST TO THE LORD

καὶ ἡμῖν διὰ   θελήματος θεοῦ **8.6** εἰς   τὸ
AND TO US THROUGH [THE] WILL OF GOD SO THAT -

παρακαλέσαι ἡμᾶς Τίτον, ἵνα καθὼς προενήρξατο
[IT WAS NECESSARY FOR] US~TO ASK TITUS, THAT AS   HE BEGAN BEFORE

οὕτως καὶ ἐπιτελέσῃ   εἰς   ὑμᾶς καὶ τὴν
SO   ALSO HE SHOULD COMPLETE AMONG YOU° ALSO -

χάριν ταύτην. **8.7** ἀλλ᾽ ὥσπερ ἐν παντὶ περισσεύετε,
THIS~[ACT OF] GRACE. BUT JUST AS IN EVERYTHING YOU° ABOUND,

πίστει καὶ λόγῳ καὶ γνώσει καὶ πάσῃ σπουδῇ καὶ
IN FAITH AND IN WORD AND IN KNOWLEDGE AND IN ALL DILIGENCE AND

τῇ ἐξ ⌐ἡμῶν ἐν ὑμῖν ἀγάπῃ⌐, ἵνα   καὶ ἐν ταύτῃ
IN THE ²FROM ³US - ⁴TO YOU° ¹LOVE, [SEE] THAT ALSO IN THIS

τῇ χάριτι περισσεύητε.
- GRACE YOU° ABOUND.

8.8 Οὐ κατ᾽   ἐπιταγὴν λέγω ἀλλὰ διὰ   τῆς
NOT ACCORDING TO A COMMAND I SPEAK, BUT THROUGH ¹THE

ἑτέρων σπουδῆς καὶ τὸ τῆς ὑμετέρας ἀγάπης γνήσιον
³OF OTHERS ²DILIGENCE AND ¹THE - ³OF YOUR° ⁴LOVE ²GENUINENESS

δοκιμάζων· **8.9** γινώσκετε γὰρ τὴν χάριν τοῦ κυρίου
⁵TESTING;   FOR~YOU° KNOW THE GRACE OF THE LORD

ἡμῶν Ἰησοῦ Χριστοῦ, ὅτι δι᾽   ὑμᾶς ἐπτώχευσεν
OF US JESUS CHRIST, THAT BECAUSE OF YOU° HE BECAME POOR

πλούσιος ὤν, ἵνα ὑμεῖς τῇ   ἐκείνου πτωχείᾳ
[THOUGH] BEING~RICH, THAT YOU° BY THE POVERTY~OF THAT ONE

πλουτήσητε. **8.10** καὶ γνώμην ἐν τούτῳ δίδωμι·
MAY BECOME RICH.   AND AN OPINION IN THIS I GIVE;

τοῦτο γὰρ ὑμῖν συμφέρει, οἵτινες οὐ μόνον τὸ
FOR~THIS FOR YOU° IS PROFITABLE, WHO NOT ONLY THE

ποιῆσαι ἀλλὰ καὶ τὸ θέλειν προενήρξασθε ἀπὸ
DOING   BUT ALSO THE WILLING YOU° PREVIOUSLY BEGAN FROM

πέρυσι· **8.11** νυνὶ δὲ καὶ τὸ ποιῆσαι ἐπιτελέσατε,
LAST YEAR;   BUT~NOW ALSO ²THE ³DOING ¹COMPLETE,

ὅπως καθάπερ ἡ   προθυμία τοῦ   θέλειν,
SO JUST AS [THERE WAS] THE EAGERNESS OF(FOR) THE WILLINGNESS,

οὕτως καὶ τὸ ἐπιτελέσαι ἐκ τοῦ ἔχειν. **8.12** εἰ γὰρ
SO   ALSO THE COMPLETING OF WHAT [YOU°] HAVE.   FOR~IF

ἡ   προθυμία πρόκειται,   καθὸ   ἐὰν   ἔχῃ
THE EAGERNESS IS ALREADY PRESENT, ACCORDING TO WHATEVER ONE MAY HAVE

εὐπρόσδεκτος, οὐ καθὸ   οὐκ ἔχει. **8.13** οὐ γὰρ
[IT IS] ACCEPTABLE, NOT ACCORDING TO [WHAT] ONE DOES NOT HAVE. FOR~NOT

ἵνα ἄλλοις ἄνεσις, ὑμῖν   θλῖψις, ἀλλ᾽ ἐξ
THAT TO OTHERS [THERE BE] RELIEF, [AND] TO YOU° DISTRESS, BUT BY

ἰσότητος· **8.14** ἐν τῷ νῦν καιρῷ τὸ ὑμῶν
EQUALITY;   DURING THE PRESENT TIME - YOUR°

περίσσευμα εἰς τὸ ἐκείνων ὑστέρημα, ἵνα καὶ τὸ
ABUNDANCE FOR - THOSE ONES' LACK, THAT ALSO -

and, by the will of God, to us, ⁶so that we might urge Titus that, as he had already made a beginning, so he should also complete this generous undertaking[r] among you. ⁷Now as you excel in everything—in faith, in speech, in knowledge, in utmost eagerness, and in our love for you[s]—so we want you to excel also in this generous undertaking.[r]

8 I do not say this as a command, but I am testing the genuineness of your love against the earnestness of others. ⁹For you know the generous act[t] of our Lord Jesus Christ, that though he was rich, yet for your sakes he became poor, so that by his poverty you might become rich. ¹⁰And in this matter I am giving my advice: it is appropriate for you who began last year not only to do something but even to desire to do something— ¹¹now finish doing it, so that your eagerness may be matched by completing it according to your means. ¹²For if the eagerness is there, the gift is acceptable according to what one has— not according to what one does not have. ¹³I do not mean that there should be relief for others and pressure on you, but it is a question of a fair balance between ¹⁴your present abundance and their need, so that

r Gk this grace
s Other ancient authorities read your love for us
t Gk the grace

8:7 text: NASB NIVmg NEBmg NRSV. var. υμων εν ημιν αγαπη (your° love for us): KJV ASV RSV NASBmg NIV TEV NEB NJB NRSVmg.

their abundance may be for your need, in order that there may be a fair balance. [15]As it is written,

"The one who had much did not have too much,

and the one who had little did not have too little."

16 But thanks be to God who put in the heart of Titus the same eagerness for you that I myself have. [17]For he not only accepted our appeal, but since he is more eager than ever, he is going to you of his own accord. [18]With him we are sending the brother who is famous among all the churches for his proclaiming the good news;[u] [19]and not only that, but he has also been appointed by the churches to travel with us while we are administering this generous undertaking[v] for the glory of the Lord himself[w] and to show our goodwill. [20]We intend that no one should blame us about this generous gift that we are administering, [21]for we intend to do what is right not only in the Lord's sight but also in the sight of others. [22]And with them we are sending our brother whom we have often tested and found eager in many matters, but who is now more eager than ever because of his great confidence in you. [23]As for Titus, he is my partner and co-worker in your service;

[u] Or the gospel
[v] Gk this grace
[w] Other ancient authorities lack himself

ἐκείνων περίσσευμα γένηται εἰς τὸ ὑμῶν ὑστέρημα,
THOSE ONES' ABUNDANCE   MAY BE   FOR - YOUR°   LACK,

ὅπως γένηται ἰσότης, **8.15** καθὼς γέγραπται,
SO   THERE MAY BE EQUALITY,   AS   IT HAS BEEN WRITTEN,

Ὁ   τὸ πολὺ οὐκ ἐπλεόνασεν,
THE ONE [THAT GATHERED] THE MUCH DID NOT ABOUND,

καὶ ὁ   τὸ ὀλίγον
AND   THE ONE [THAT GATHERED] THE LITTLE

οὐκ ἠλαττόνησεν.
DID NOT ABOUND.

8.16 Χάρις δὲ τῷ θεῷ τῷ δόντι τὴν αὐτὴν
BUT~THANKS [BE] - TO GOD, THE ONE HAVING GIVEN THE SAME

σπουδὴν ὑπὲρ ὑμῶν ἐν τῇ καρδίᾳ Τίτου, **8.17** ὅτι τὴν
DILIGENCE FOR YOU° IN THE HEART OF TITUS,   BECAUSE THE

μὲν παράκλησιν ἐδέξατο, σπουδαιότερος δὲ ὑπάρχων
- ENCOURAGMENT HE RECEIVED, [3]MORE DILIGENT [1]AND [2]BEING

αὐθαίρετος ἐξῆλθεν πρὸς ὑμᾶς. **8.18** συνεπέμψαμεν δὲ
OF HIS OWN ACCORD HE WENT FORTH TO YOU°.   AND~WE SENT

μετ᾽ αὐτοῦ τὸν ἀδελφὸν οὗ ὁ ἔπαινος ἐν τῷ
WITH HIM   THE BROTHER WHOSE - PRAISE IN THE

εὐαγγελίῳ διὰ   πασῶν τῶν ἐκκλησιῶν, **8.19** οὐ
GOSPEL   [IS] THROUGH[OUT] ALL THE CHURCHES,   [2]NOT

μόνον δὲ, ἀλλὰ καὶ χειροτονηθεὶς ὑπὸ τῶν
[3]ONLY [THIS] [1]AND BUT ALSO HAVING BEEN HANDPICKED BY THE

ἐκκλησιῶν συνέκδημος ἡμῶν σὺν τῇ χάριτι ταύτῃ
CHURCHES   [AS] A TRAVELING COMPANION OF US WITH - THIS~[GRACIOUS] GIFT

τῇ διακονουμένῃ ὑφ᾽ ἡμῶν πρὸς τὴν [αὐτοῦ] τοῦ
- BEING ADMINISTERED BY US TO [1]THE [5]HIMSELF [3]OF THE

κυρίου δόξαν καὶ προθυμίαν ἡμῶν,
[4]LORD [2]GLORY AND [A TESTIMONY OF THE] EAGERNESS OF YOU°,

8.20 στελλόμενοι τοῦτο, μή τις ἡμᾶς μωμήσηται ἐν
AVOIDING   THIS,   LEST ANYONE SHOULD BLAME~US IN

τῇ ἁδρότητι ταύτῃ τῇ διακονουμένῃ ὑφ᾽ ἡμῶν·
- THIS~ABUNDANCE - BEING ADMINISTERED BY US;

8.21 προνοοῦμεν γὰρ καλὰ οὐ μόνον ἐνώπιον κυρίου
FOR~WE HAVE REGARD FOR GOOD THINGS NOT ONLY BEFORE [THE] LORD

ἀλλὰ καὶ ἐνώπιον ἀνθρώπων. **8.22** συνεπέμψαμεν δὲ
BUT ALSO BEFORE MEN.   AND~WE SENT WITH

αὐτοῖς τὸν ἀδελφὸν ἡμῶν ὃν ἐδοκιμάσαμεν ἐν
THEM   THE BROTHER OF US WHOM WE APPROVED IN

πολλοῖς πολλάκις σπουδαῖον ὄντα, νυνὶ δὲ πολὺ
MANY THINGS MANY TIMES BEING~DILIGENT,   AND~NOW [BEING] MUCH

σπουδαιότερον πεποιθήσει πολλῇ τῇ εἰς ὑμᾶς.
MORE DILIGENT   BY [HIS] GREAT~CONFIDENCE - IN YOU°.

8.23 εἴτε ὑπὲρ Τίτου, κοινωνὸς ἐμὸς καὶ εἰς ὑμᾶς
WHETHER AS REGARDS TITUS, [HE IS] MY~PARTNER AND FOR YOU°

8:15 Exod. 16:18

συνεργός· εἴτε ἀδελφοὶ ἡμῶν, ἀπόστολοι ἐκκλησιῶν,
A CO-WORKER; OR BROTHERS OF US, [THEY ARE] APOSTLES OF CHURCHES,

δόξα Χριστοῦ. **8.24** τὴν οὖν ἔνδειξιν τῆς ἀγάπης
[THE] GLORY OF CHRIST. THEREFORE~THE DEMONSTRATION OF THE LOVE

ὑμῶν καὶ ἡμῶν καυχήσεως ὑπὲρ ὑμῶν εἰς
OF YOU° AND OUR BOASTING ABOUT YOU° TO

αὐτοὺς ἐνδεικνύμενοι εἰς πρόσωπον τῶν ἐκκλησιῶν.
THEM—[BE] DISPLAYING [THESE] IN [THE] PRESENCE OF THE CHURCHES.

as for our brothers, they are messengers[x] of the churches, the glory of Christ. [24]Therefore openly before the churches, show them the proof of your love and of our reason for boasting about you.

[x] Gk *apostles*

9.1 Περὶ μὲν γὰρ τῆς διακονίας τῆς εἰς τοὺς
²CONCERNING - ¹FOR THE SERVICE - FOR THE

ἁγίους περισσόν μοί ἐστιν τὸ γράφειν ὑμῖν·
SAINTS ²SUPERFLUOUS ³FOR ME ¹IT IS - TO WRITE TO YOU°;

9.2 οἶδα γὰρ τὴν προθυμίαν ὑμῶν ἣν ὑπὲρ ὑμῶν
FOR~I KNOW THE EAGERNESS OF YOU° WHICH ON BEHALF OF YOU°

καυχῶμαι Μακεδόσιν, ὅτι Ἀχαΐα παρεσκεύασται ἀπὸ
I BOAST TO MACEDONIANS, THAT ACHAIA HAS BEEN PREPARED SINCE

πέρυσι, καὶ τὸ ὑμῶν ζῆλος ἠρέθισεν τοὺς πλείονας.
LAST YEAR, AND - YOUR° ZEAL STIRRED UP THE MANY.

9.3 ἔπεμψα δὲ τοὺς ἀδελφούς, ἵνα μὴ τὸ καύχημα ἡμῶν
AND~I SENT THE BROTHERS, LEST THE BOAST OF US

τὸ ὑπὲρ ὑμῶν κενωθῇ ἐν τῷ μέρει τούτῳ, ἵνα
- ON BEHALF OF YOU° SHOULD BE MADE EMPTY IN - THIS~RESPECT, THAT

καθὼς ἔλεγον παρεσκευασμένοι ἦτε, **9.4** μή πως ἐὰν
AS I WAS SAYING YOU° HAVE BEEN PREPARED, LEST PERHAPS IF

ἔλθωσιν σὺν ἐμοὶ Μακεδόνες καὶ εὕρωσιν ὑμᾶς
²SHOULD COME ³WITH ⁴ME ¹MACEDONIANS AND THEY FIND YOU°

ἀπαρασκευάστους καταισχυνθῶμεν ἡμεῖς, ἵνα
UNPREPARED WE~SHOULD BE ASHAMED, (THAT

μὴ λέγω ὑμεῖς, ἐν τῇ ὑποστάσει ταύτῃ.
WE SHOULD NOT SAY YOU°), IN - THIS~CONFIDENCE.

9.5 ἀναγκαῖον οὖν ἡγησάμην παρακαλέσαι τοὺς
³NECESSARY ¹THEREFORE ²I CONSIDERED [IT] TO ENCOURAGE THE

ἀδελφούς, ἵνα προέλθωσιν εἰς ὑμᾶς καὶ
BROTHERS, THAT THEY SHOULD GO BEFORE TO YOU° AND

προκαταρτίσωσιν τὴν προεπηγγελμένην εὐλογίαν
HAVING ARRANGED BEFOREHAND ¹THE ³HAVING BEEN PREVIOUSLY PROMISED ²BLESSING(GIFT)

ὑμῶν, ταύτην ἑτοίμην εἶναι οὕτως ὡς εὐλογίαν καὶ
BY YOU°, THIS [GIFT] TO BE~READY SO AS [TO BE] A BLESSING AND

μὴ ὡς πλεονεξίαν.
NOT AS AN EXACTION.

9.6 Τοῦτο δέ, ὁ σπείρων φειδομένως φειδομένως
AND~THIS, THE ONE SOWING SPARINGLY SPARINGLY

Now it is not necessary for me to write you about the ministry to the saints, [2]for I know your eagerness, which is the subject of my boasting about you to the people of Macedonia, saying that Achaia has been ready since last year; and your zeal has stirred up most of them. [3]But I am sending the brothers in order that our boasting about you may not prove to have been empty in this case, so that you may be ready, as I said you would be; [4]otherwise, if some Macedonians come with me and find that you are not ready, we would be humiliated—to say nothing of you—in this undertaking.[y] [5]So I thought it necessary to urge the brothers to go on ahead to you, and arrange in advance for this bountiful gift that you have promised, so that it may be ready as a voluntary gift and not as an extortion.

6 The point is this: the one who sows sparingly will also reap sparingly,

[y] Other ancient authorities add *of boasting*

and the one who sows bountifully will also reap bountifully. [7]Each of you must give as you have made up your mind, not reluctantly or under compulsion, for God loves a cheerful giver. [8]And God is able to provide you with every blessing in abundance, so that by always having enough of everything, you may share abundantly in every good work. [9]As it is written,

"He scatters abroad, he gives to the poor; his righteousness[z] endures forever."

[10]He who supplies seed to the sower and bread for food will supply and multiply your seed for sowing and increase the harvest of your righteousness.[z] [11]You will be enriched in every way for your great generosity, which will produce thanksgiving to God through us; [12]for the rendering of this ministry not only supplies the needs of the saints but also overflows with many thanksgivings to God. [13]Through the testing of this ministry you glorify God by your obedience to the confession of the gospel of Christ and by the generosity of your sharing with them and with all others, [14]while

[z] Or *benevolence*

καὶ θερίσει, καὶ ὁ σπείρων ἐπ᾽ εὐλογίαις ἐπ᾽
ALSO WILL REAP, AND THE ONE SOWING FOR A BLESSING(BOUNTY) -

εὐλογίαις καὶ θερίσει. **9.7** ἕκαστος καθὼς
A BLESSING(BOUNTY) ALSO WILL REAP. EACH ONE AS

προῄρηται τῇ καρδίᾳ, μὴ ἐκ λύπης ἢ
HE HAS DECIDED PREVIOUSLY IN THE(HIS) HEART, NOT OUT OF GRIEF NOR

ἐξ ἀνάγκης· ἱλαρὸν γὰρ δότην ἀγαπᾷ ὁ θεός.
OUT OF NECESSITY; FOR~A CHEERFUL GIVER [2]LOVES - [1]GOD.

9.8 δυνατεῖ δὲ ὁ θεὸς πᾶσαν χάριν περισσεῦσαι εἰς
[3]IS ABLE [1]AND - [2]GOD [5]ALL [6]GRACE [4]TO CAUSE TO ABOUND [7]TO

ὑμᾶς, ἵνα ἐν παντὶ πάντοτε πᾶσαν αὐτάρκειαν
[8]YOU°, THAT IN EVERYTHING ALWAYS [2]ALL [3]SUFFICIENCY

ἔχοντες περισσεύητε εἰς πᾶν ἔργον ἀγαθόν, **9.9** καθὼς
[1]HAVING YOU° MAY ABOUND TO EVERY GOOD~WORK, AS

γέγραπται,
IT HAS BEEN WRITTEN,

Ἐσκόρπισεν, ἔδωκεν τοῖς πένησιν,
HE SCATTERED, HE GAVE TO THE POOR,

ἡ δικαιοσύνη αὐτοῦ μένει εἰς τὸν αἰῶνα.
THE RIGHTEOUSNESS OF HIM REMAINS TO THE AGE.

9.10 ὁ δὲ ἐπιχορηγῶν σπόρον τῷ σπείροντι καὶ
NOW~THE ONE SUPPLYING SEED TO THE ONE SOWING BOTH

ἄρτον εἰς βρῶσιν χορηγήσει καὶ πληθυνεῖ τὸν σπόρον
[2]BREAD [3]FOR [4]FOOD [1]WILL SUPPLY AND WILL MULTIPLY THE SEED

ὑμῶν καὶ αὐξήσει τὰ γενήματα τῆς δικαιοσύνης
OF YOU° AND WILL INCREASE THE FRUITS OF THE RIGHTEOUSNESS

ὑμῶν· **9.11** ἐν παντὶ πλουτιζόμενοι εἰς πᾶσαν
OF YOU°; IN EVERYTHING BEING ENRICHED TO ALL

ἁπλότητα, ἥτις κατεργάζεται δι᾽ ἡμῶν εὐχαριστίαν
GENEROSITY, WHICH PRODUCES THROUGH US THANKSGIVING

τῷ θεῷ· **9.12** ὅτι ἡ διακονία τῆς
- TO GOD; BECAUSE THE MINISTRY -

λειτουργίας ταύτης οὐ μόνον ἐστὶν προσαναπληροῦσα
OF THIS~SERVICE NOT ONLY IS FILLING UP

τὰ ὑστερήματα τῶν ἁγίων, ἀλλὰ καὶ
THE THINGS LACKING OF THE SAINTS, BUT [IS] ALSO

περισσεύουσα διὰ πολλῶν εὐχαριστιῶν τῷ θεῷ·
ABOUNDING THROUGH MANY THANKSGIVINGS - TO GOD;

9.13 διὰ τῆς δοκιμῆς τῆς διακονίας ταύτης δοξάζοντες
THROUGH THE PROOF - OF THIS~MINISTRY GLORIFYING

τὸν θεὸν ἐπὶ τῇ ὑποταγῇ τῆς ὁμολογίας
- GOD ON [THE BASIS OF] THE(YOUR°) SUBMISSION OF(TO) THE CONFESSION

ὑμῶν εἰς τὸ εὐαγγέλιον τοῦ Χριστοῦ καὶ ἁπλότητι
OF YOU° TO THE GOSPEL - OF CHRIST AND [ON THE] GENEROSITY

τῆς κοινωνίας εἰς αὐτοὺς καὶ εἰς πάντας, **9.14** καὶ
OF THE CONTRIBUTION TO THEM AND TO ALL MEN, AND [ALSO]

9:9 Ps. 112:9

αὐτῶν δεήσει   ὑπὲρ ὑμῶν ἐπιποθούντων   ὑμᾶς
THEIR   SUPPLICATION FOR   YOU°, HAVING GREAT AFFECTION FOR YOU°

διὰ   τὴν ὑπερβάλλουσαν χάριν τοῦ θεοῦ ἐφ᾽ ὑμῖν.
BECAUSE OF THE SURPASSING   GRACE - OF GOD UPON YOU°.

9.15 χάρις τῷ θεῷ   ἐπὶ τῇ ἀνεκδιηγήτῳ αὐτοῦ δωρεᾷ.
THANKS - [BE] TO GOD FOR - HIS~INDESCRIBABLE   GIFT.

they long for you and pray for you because of the surpassing grace of God that he has given you. [15]Thanks be to God for his indescribable gift!

10.1 Αὐτὸς δὲ ἐγὼ Παῦλος παρακαλῶ ὑμᾶς διὰ   τῆς
³MYSELF ¹NOW ²I PAUL APPEAL   TO YOU° THROUGH THE

πραΰτητος καὶ ἐπιεικείας τοῦ Χριστοῦ, ὃς κατὰ
HUMILITY   AND GENTLENESS - OF CHRIST, WHO ACCORDING TO

πρόσωπον μὲν ταπεινὸς ἐν   ὑμῖν, ἀπὼν δὲ   θαρρῶ
APPEARANCE - [AM] LOWLY AMONG YOU°, BUT~BEING ABSENT AM BOLD

εἰς ὑμᾶς· **10.2** δέομαι δὲ τὸ μὴ παρὼν   θαρρῆσαι
TOWARD YOU°;   NOW~I REQUEST - NOT BEING PRESENT TO BE BOLD

τῇ πεποιθήσει ᾗ λογίζομαι τολμῆσαι ἐπί
IN THE CONFIDENCE WHICH I CONSIDER TO BE DARING TOWARD

τινας   τοὺς λογιζομένους ἡμᾶς ὡς κατὰ   σάρκα
SOME PEOPLE, THE ONES CONSIDERING   US   AS ²ACCORDING TO ³FLESH

περιπατοῦντας. **10.3** ἐν   σαρκὶ γὰρ περιπατοῦντες
¹WALKING.   ²[THOUGH] IN ³FLESH ¹FOR ⁴WALKING,

οὐ κατὰ   σάρκα στρατευόμεθα, **10.4** τὰ γὰρ ὅπλα
NOT ACCORDING TO FLESH WE WAR,   FOR~THE WEAPONS

τῆς στρατείας ἡμῶν οὐ   σαρκικὰ ἀλλὰ δυνατὰ τῷ
OF THE WARFARE   OF US [ARE] NOT FLESHLY   BUT   POWERFUL -

θεῷ   πρὸς καθαίρεσιν ὀχυρωμάτων,
THROUGH GOD TO [THE] OVERTHROW OF STRONGHOLDS,

λογισμοὺς καθαιροῦντες   **10.5** καὶ   πᾶν ὕψωμα
OVERTHROWING~REASONINGS   AND   EVERY HIGH THING

ἐπαιρόμενον κατὰ τῆς γνώσεως τοῦ θεοῦ, καὶ
RISING UP   AGAINST THE KNOWLEDGE - OF GOD, AND

αἰχμαλωτίζοντες πᾶν νόημα εἰς τὴν ὑπακοὴν τοῦ
LEADING CAPTIVE   EVERY THOUGHT INTO THE OBEDIENCE -

Χριστοῦ, **10.6** καὶ ἐν ἑτοίμῳ ἔχοντες ἐκδικῆσαι πᾶσαν
OF CHRIST,   AND - HAVING~A READINESS TO AVENGE   ALL

παρακοήν, ὅταν   πληρωθῇ ὑμῶν ἡ ὑπακοή.
DISOBEDIENCE, WHENEVER IS FULFILLED YOUR° - OBEDIENCE.

10.7 Τὰ   κατὰ   πρόσωπον βλέπετε. εἴ τις
       THE THINGS ACCORDING TO APPEARANCE YOU° LOOK [AT]. IF ANYONE

πέποιθεν ἑαυτῷ Χριστοῦ εἶναι, τοῦτο λογιζέσθω
HAS PERSUADED HIMSELF OF CHRIST TO BE, THIS LET HIM CONSIDER

πάλιν ἐφ᾽ ἑαυτοῦ, ὅτι καθὼς αὐτὸς Χριστοῦ, οὕτως καὶ
AGAIN AS TO HIMSELF, THAT AS HE [IS] OF CHRIST, SO   ALSO

ἡμεῖς. **10.8** ἐὰν [τε] γὰρ περισσότερόν τι καυχήσωμαι
WE [ARE].   ³IF ²EVEN ¹FOR MORE ABUNDANTLY I SHOULD BOAST~SOMETHING

I myself, Paul, appeal to you by the meekness and gentleness of Christ—I who am humble when face to face with you, but bold toward you when I am away!— [2]I ask that when I am present I need not show boldness by daring to oppose those who think we are acting according to human standards.[a] [3]Indeed, we live as human beings,[b] but we do not wage war according to human standards;[a] [4]for the weapons of our warfare are not merely human,[c] but they have divine power to destroy strongholds. We destroy arguments [5]and every proud obstacle raised up against the knowledge of God, and we take every thought captive to obey Christ. [6]We are ready to punish every disobedience when your obedience is complete.

[7] Look at what is before your eyes. If you are confident that you belong to Christ, remind yourself of this, that just as you belong to Christ, so also do we. [8]Now, even if I boast a little too much

[a] Gk *according to the flesh*
[b] Gk *in the flesh*
[c] Gk *fleshly*

of our authority, which the Lord gave for building you up and not for tearing you down, I will not be ashamed of it. [9]I do not want to seem as though I am trying to frighten you with my letters. [10]For they say, "His letters are weighty and strong, but his bodily presence is weak, and his speech contemptible." [11]Let such people understand that what we say by letter when absent, we will also do when present.

12 We do not dare to classify or compare ourselves with some of those who commend themselves. But when they measure themselves by one another, and compare themselves with one another, they do not show good sense. [13]We, however, will not boast beyond limits, but will keep within the field that God has assigned to us, to reach out even as far as you. [14]For we were not overstepping our limits when we reached you; we were the first to come all the way to you with the good news[d] of Christ. [15]We do not boast beyond limits, that is, in the labors of others; but our hope is that, as your faith increases, our sphere of action among you may be greatly enlarged, [16]so that we may proclaim the good news[d] in lands beyond you, without boasting of work already done in someone else's sphere of action.

[d] Or the gospel

περὶ τῆς ἐξουσίας ἡμῶν ἧς ἔδωκεν ὁ κύριος εἰς
ABOUT THE AUTHORITY OF US, WHICH ³GAVE ¹THE ²LORD FOR

οἰκοδομὴν καὶ οὐκ εἰς καθαίρεσιν ὑμῶν,
BUILDING UP AND NOT FOR [THE] OVERTHROW OF YOU°,

οὐκ αἰσχυνθήσομαι. **10.9**ἵνα μὴ δόξω ὡς ἂν ἐκφοβεῖν
I WILL NOT BE PUT TO SHAME, THAT I MAY NOT SEEM AS IF TO FRIGHTEN

ὑμᾶς διὰ τῶν ἐπιστολῶν· **10.10**ὅτι, Αἱ
YOU° THROUGH THE(MY) LETTERS; BECAUSE, THE(HIS)

ἐπιστολαὶ μέν, φησίν, βαρεῖαι καὶ ἰσχυραί, ἡ δὲ
EPISTLES INDEED, HE SAYS, [ARE] WEIGHTY AND STRONG, BUT~THE

παρουσία τοῦ σώματος ἀσθενὴς καὶ ὁ λόγος
PRESENCE OF THE(HIS) BODY [IS] WEAK AND THE(HIS) SPEECH

ἐξουθενημένος. **10.11**τοῦτο λογιζέσθω ὁ τοιοῦτος, ὅτι
[IS] BEING DESPISED. THIS ¹LET ³CONSIDER ²SUCH A ONE, THAT

οἷοί ἐσμεν τῷ λόγῳ δι' ἐπιστολῶν ἀπόντες,
SUCH AS WE ARE - IN WORD THROUGH LETTERS BEING ABSENT,

τοιοῦτοι καὶ παρόντες τῷ ἔργῳ.
SUCH ONES ALSO [WE ARE] BEING PRESENT - IN DEED.

10.12Οὐ γὰρ τολμῶμεν ἐγκρῖναι ἢ συγκρῖναι ἑαυτούς
³NOT ¹FOR ²DARE WE TO CLASSIFY OR TO COMPARE OURSELVES

τισιν τῶν ἑαυτοὺς συνιστανόντων, ἀλλὰ αὐτοὶ
WITH SOME OF THE ONES COMMENDING~THEMSELVES, BUT THEY

ἐν ἑαυτοῖς ἑαυτοὺς μετροῦντες καὶ συγκρίνοντες
AMONG THEMSELVES MEASURING~THEMSELVES AND COMPARING

ἑαυτοὺς ἑαυτοῖς οὐ συνιᾶσιν. **10.13**ἡμεῖς δὲ οὐκ εἰς
THEMSELVES WITH THEMSELVES DO NOT UNDERSTAND. BUT~WE NOT TO

τὰ ἄμετρα καυχησόμεθα ἀλλὰ κατὰ τὸ
THE THINGS BEYOND MEASURE WILL BOAST BUT ACCORDING TO THE

μέτρον τοῦ κανόνος οὗ ἐμέρισεν ἡμῖν ὁ θεὸς
MEASURE OF THE SPHERE WHICH ³APPORTIONED ⁴TO US - ¹GOD

μέτρου, ἐφικέσθαι ἄχρι καὶ ὑμῶν. **10.14**οὐ γὰρ ὡς
²[BY A] MEASURE, TO REACH AS FAR AS EVEN YOU°. FOR~NOT AS

μὴ ἐφικνούμενοι εἰς ὑμᾶς ὑπερεκτείνομεν ἑαυτούς,
NOT REACHING TO YOU° DO WE OVEREXTEND OURSELVES,

ἄχρι γὰρ καὶ ὑμῶν ἐφθάσαμεν ἐν τῷ εὐαγγελίῳ τοῦ
FOR~AS FAR AS EVEN YOU° WE CAME WITH THE GOSPEL -

Χριστοῦ, **10.15**οὐκ εἰς τὰ ἄμετρα καυχώμενοι
OF CHRIST, NOT ²IN ³THE THINGS ⁴BEYOND MEASURE ¹BOASTING

ἐν ἀλλοτρίοις κόποις, ἐλπίδα δὲ ἔχοντες αὐξανομένης
IN OTHERS' LABORS, ³HOPE ¹BUT ²HAVING, [WHILE IS] GROWING

τῆς πίστεως ὑμῶν ἐν ὑμῖν μεγαλυνθῆναι κατὰ
THE FAITH OF YOU°, AMONG YOU° TO BE ENLARGED ACCORDING TO

τὸν κανόνα ἡμῶν εἰς περισσείαν **10.16**εἰς
THE SPHERE OF US [RESULTING] IN ABUNDANCE, TO

τὰ ὑπερέκεινα ὑμῶν εὐαγγελίσασθαι, οὐκ ἐν
THE [REGIONS] BEYOND YOU° TO PREACH GOOD NEWS, ¹NOT ³IN

ἀλλοτρίῳ κανόνι εἰς τὰ ἕτοιμα καυχήσασθαι.
⁴ANOTHER'S ⁵SPHERE ⁶AS TO ⁷THINGS ⁸ALREADY DONE ²TO BOAST.

10.17 Ὁ δὲ   καυχώμενος ἐν κυρίῳ   καυχάσθω·
BUT~THE ONE BOASTING,   IN   [THE] LORD LET HIM BOAST;

10.18 οὐ γὰρ ὁ   ἑαυτὸν συνιστάνων, ἐκεῖνός ἐστιν
FOR~NOT THE ONE HIMSELF COMMENDING,   THAT ONE   IS

δόκιμος, ἀλλὰ ὃν ὁ κύριος συνίστησιν.
APPROVED,   BUT   WHOM THE LORD COMMENDS.

10:17 Jer. 9:24

11.1 Ὄφελον   ἀνείχεσθέ   μου μικρόν τι
I WOULD [THAT] YOU° WERE BEARING WITH ME   IN A LITTLE BIT

ἀφροσύνης·   ἀλλὰ καὶ   ἀνέχεσθέ   μου.
OF FOOLISHNESS; BUT   INDEED YOU° DO BEAR WITH ME.

11.2 ζηλῶ γὰρ ὑμᾶς θεοῦ ζήλῳ,   ἡρμοσάμην γὰρ
FOR~I AM JEALOUS FOR YOU° WITH A JEALOUSY~OF GOD, FOR~I BETROTHED

ὑμᾶς ἑνὶ ἀνδρὶ παρθένον ἁγνὴν παραστῆσαι τῷ
YOU°   TO ONE HUSBAND, ³VIRGIN   ²A PURE   ¹TO PRESENT [YOU°] -

Χριστῷ· **11.3** φοβοῦμαι δὲ μή πως, ὡς ὁ ὄφις
TO CHRIST;   BUT~I FEAR LEST SOMEHOW, AS THE SERPENT

ἐξηπάτησεν Εὕαν ἐν τῇ πανουργίᾳ αὐτοῦ,
DECEIVED   EVE BY THE CUNNING   OF HIM,

φθαρῇ   τὰ νοήματα ὑμῶν ἀπὸ τῆς ἀπλότητος
⁴SHOULD BE LED ASTRAY ¹THE ²THOUGHTS ³OF YOU° FROM THE SIMPLICITY

⌜[καὶ τῆς ἀγνότητος]⌝ τῆς εἰς τὸν Χριστόν. **11.4** εἰ
AND THE PURITY   - IN - CHRIST.   ²IF

μὲν γὰρ ὁ   ἐρχόμενος ἄλλον Ἰησοῦν κηρύσσει ὃν
³INDEED ¹FOR THE ONE COMING ²ANOTHER ³JESUS ¹PREACHES WHOM

οὐκ ἐκηρύξαμεν, ἢ πνεῦμα ἕτερον λαμβάνετε ὃ
WE DID NOT PREACH, OR A DIFFERENT~SPIRIT YOU° RECEIVE WHICH

οὐκ ἐλάβετε, ἢ εὐαγγέλιον ἕτερον ὃ   οὐκ ἐδέξασθε,
YOU° DID NOT RECEIVE, OR A DIFFERENT~GOSPEL WHICH YOU° DID NOT RECEIVE,

καλῶς ἀνέχεσθε.   **11.5** λογίζομαι γὰρ μηδὲν
YOU° PUT UP WITH [THAT]~WELL [ENOUGH]. FOR~I CONSIDER   NOTHING

ὑστερηκέναι τῶν ὑπερλίαν ἀποστόλων.   **11.6** εἰ δὲ καὶ
TO HAVE COME BEHIND THE "SUPER-APOSTLES."   BUT~IF INDEED

ἰδιώτης   τῷ λόγῳ, ἀλλ᾽ οὐ τῇ γνώσει, ἀλλ᾽ ἐν
[I AM] UNSKILLED - IN SPEECH, YET NOT - IN KNOWLEDGE, BUT   IN

παντὶ φανερώσαντες ἐν πᾶσιν εἰς ὑμᾶς.
EVERY [WAY] HAVING MANIFESTED [THIS] IN ALL THINGS TO YOU°.

11.7 Ἢ ἁμαρτίαν ἐποίησα ἐμαυτὸν ταπεινῶν ἵνα
OR A SIN   DID I COMMIT [BY] HUMBLING~MYSELF THAT

ὑμεῖς . ὑψωθῆτε,   ὅτι   δωρεὰν τὸ τοῦ
YOU°   MIGHT BE EXALTED, BECAUSE GRATUITOUSLY THE -

θεοῦ εὐαγγέλιον εὐηγγελισάμην ὑμῖν; **11.8** ἄλλας
GOOD NEWS~OF GOD I PROCLAIMED   TO YOU°?   OTHER

11:3 text: ASV RSV NASB NIV NEBmg (TEV) NJB NRSV. omit: KJV NEB NJB.

¹⁷"Let the one who boasts, boast in the Lord." ¹⁸For it is not those who commend themselves that are approved, but those whom the Lord commends.

I wish you would bear with me in a little foolishness. Do bear with me! ²I feel a divine jealousy for you, for I promised you in marriage to one husband, to present you as a chaste virgin to Christ. ³But I am afraid that as the serpent deceived Eve by its cunning, your thoughts will be led astray from a sincere and pure[e] devotion to Christ. ⁴For if someone comes and proclaims another Jesus than the one we proclaimed, or if you receive a different spirit from the one you received, or a different gospel from the one you accepted, you submit to it readily enough. ⁵I think that I am not in the least inferior to these super-apostles. ⁶I may be untrained in speech, but not in knowledge; certainly in every way and in all things we have made this evident to you.

7 Did I commit a sin by humbling myself so that you might be exalted, because I proclaimed God's good news[f] to you free of charge? ⁸I robbed other

[e] Other ancient authorities lack *and pure*
[f] Gk *the gospel of God*

churches by accepting support from them in order to serve you. ⁹And when I was with you and was in need, I did not burden anyone, for my needs were supplied by the friends⁸ who came from Macedonia. So I refrained and will continue to refrain from burdening you in any way. ¹⁰As the truth of Christ is in me, this boast of mine will not be silenced in the regions of Achaia. ¹¹And why? Because I do not love you? God knows I do!

12 And what I do I will also continue to do, in order to deny an opportunity to those who want an opportunity to be recognized as our equals in what they boast about. ¹³For such boasters are false apostles, deceitful workers, disguising themselves as apostles of Christ. ¹⁴And no wonder! Even Satan disguises himself as an angel of light. ¹⁵So it is not strange if his ministers also disguise themselves as ministers of righteousness. Their end will match their deeds.

16 I repeat, let no one think that I am a fool; but if you do, then accept me as a fool, so that I too may boast a little. ¹⁷What I am saying in regard to this boastful confidence, I am saying not with the Lord's authority,

⁸ Gk brothers

ἐκκλησίας ἐσύλησα λαβὼν ὀψώνιον πρὸς τὴν ὑμῶν
CHURCHES I ROBBED HAVING TAKEN WAGES FOR ¹THE ³OF(TO) YOU°

διακονίαν, **11.9** καὶ παρὼν πρὸς ὑμᾶς καὶ
²SERVICE, AND BEING PRESENT WITH YOU° AND

ὑστερηθεὶς οὐ κατενάρκησα οὐθενός· τὸ γὰρ
HAVING BEEN LACKING I DID NOT BURDEN ANYONE; FOR~THE

ὑστέρημά μου προσανεπλήρωσαν οἱ ἀδελφοὶ ἐλθόντες
LACK OF ME MADE UP THE BROTHERS HAVING COME

ἀπὸ Μακεδονίας, καὶ ἐν παντὶ ἀβαρῆ ἐμαυτὸν
FROM MACEDONIA, AND IN EVERY [WAY] ³UNBURDENSOME ²MYSELF

ὑμῖν ἐτήρησα καὶ τηρήσω. **11.10** ἔστιν ἀλήθεια
⁴TO YOU° ¹I KEPT AND I WILL KEEP. ³IS ¹[THE] TRUTH

Χριστοῦ ἐν ἐμοὶ ὅτι ἡ καύχησις αὕτη οὐ φραγήσεται
²OF CHRIST IN ME THAT - THIS~BOASTING WILL NOT BE SILENCED

εἰς ἐμὲ ἐν τοῖς κλίμασιν τῆς Ἀχαΐας. **11.11** διὰ τί;
IN ME IN THE REGIONS - OF ACHAIA. WHY?

ὅτι οὐκ ἀγαπῶ ὑμᾶς; ὁ θεὸς οἶδεν.
BECAUSE I DO NOT LOVE YOU°? - GOD KNOWS.

11.12 Ὃ δὲ ποιῶ, καὶ ποιήσω, ἵνα ἐκκόψω τὴν
BUT~WHAT I DO, ALSO I WILL DO, THAT I MAY CUT OFF THE

ἀφορμὴν τῶν θελόντων ἀφορμήν, ἵνα ἐν ᾧ
OPPORTUNITY OF THE ONES WANTING AN OPPORTUNITY, ⁴THAT ¹IN ²WHICH

καυχῶνται εὑρεθῶσιν καθὼς καὶ ἡμεῖς. **11.13** οἱ
³THEY [COULD] BOAST ⁵THEY MAY BE FOUND AS ALSO WE [ARE].

γὰρ τοιοῦτοι ψευδαπόστολοι, ἐργάται δόλιοι,
FOR SUCH ONES [ARE] FALSE APOSTLES, DECEITFUL~WORKERS,

μετασχηματιζόμενοι εἰς ἀποστόλους Χριστοῦ. **11.14** καὶ
TRANSFORMING THEMSELVES INTO APOSTLES OF CHRIST. AND

οὐ θαῦμα· αὐτὸς γὰρ ὁ Σατανᾶς μετασχηματίζεται
NO WONDER; ³HIMSELF ¹FOR - ²SATAN TRANSFORMS HIMSELF

εἰς ἄγγελον φωτός. **11.15** οὐ μέγα οὖν εἰ καὶ
INTO AN ANGEL OF LIGHT. [IT IS] NO GREAT THING THEREFORE IF ALSO

οἱ διάκονοι αὐτοῦ μετασχηματίζονται ὡς διάκονοι
THE MINISTERS OF HIM TRANSFORM THEMSELVES AS MINISTERS

δικαιοσύνης· ὧν τὸ τέλος ἔσται κατὰ τὰ ἔργα
OF RIGHTEOUSNESS; WHOSE - END WILL BE ACCORDING TO THE WORKS

αὐτῶν.
OF THEM.

11.16 Πάλιν λέγω, μή τίς με δόξῃ ἄφρονα εἶναι·
AGAIN I SAY, NOT ANYONE SHOULD THINK~ME FOOLISH TO BE;

εἰ δὲ μή γε, κἂν ὡς ἄφρονα δέξασθέ με, ἵνα κἀγὼ
BUT~IF OTHERWISE, EVEN IF AS FOOLISH, RECEIVE ME, THAT I ALSO

μικρόν τι καυχήσωμαι. **11.17** ὃ λαλῶ, οὐ κατὰ
A LITTLE BIT MAY BOAST. WHAT I SPEAK, NOT ACCORDING TO

κύριον λαλῶ ἀλλ' ὡς ἐν ἀφροσύνῃ, ἐν ταύτῃ τῇ
[THE] LORD I SPEAK BUT AS IN FOOLISHNESS, IN THIS -

ὑποστάσει τῆς καυχήσεως. **11.18** ἐπεὶ πολλοὶ καυχῶνται
CONFIDENCE - OF BOASTING. SINCE MANY BOAST

κατὰ σάρκα, κἀγὼ καυχήσομαι. **11.19** ἡδέως γὰρ
ACCORDING TO FLESH, I ALSO WILL BOAST. FOR~GLADLY

ἀνέχεσθε τῶν ἀφρόνων φρόνιμοι ὄντες·
¹YOU° ⁴PUT UP WITH ⁵THE ⁶FOOLS ³INTELLIGENT ²BEING;

11.20 ἀνέχεσθε γὰρ εἴ τις ὑμᾶς καταδουλοῖ, εἴ τις
FOR~YOU° PUT UP WITH [IT] IF ANYONE BRINGS YOU° INTO BONDAGE, IF ANYONE

κατεσθίει, εἴ τις λαμβάνει, εἴ τις ἐπαίρεται, εἴ
DEVOURS [YOU°], IF ANYONE TAKES [FROM YOU°], IF ANYONE EXALTS HIMSELF, IF

τις εἰς πρόσωπον ὑμᾶς δέρει. **11.21** κατὰ ἀτιμίαν
ANYONE ³IN ⁴[THE] FACE ¹HITS ²YOU°. TO [MY] SHAME

λέγω, ὡς ὅτι ἡμεῖς ἠσθενήκαμεν. ἐν ᾧ δ᾿ ἄν τις
I SPEAK, THAT [IN THIS] WE HAVE BEEN WEAK. BUT IN WHATEVER [WAY] ANYONE

τολμᾷ, ἐν ἀφροσύνῃ λέγω, τολμῶ κἀγώ.
MAY BE DARING, IN FOOLISHNESS I SPEAK, I ALSO~AM DARING.

11.22 Ἑβραῖοί εἰσιν; κἀγώ. Ἰσραηλῖταί εἰσιν;
HEBREWS ARE THEY? I ALSO. ISRAELITES ARE THEY?

κἀγώ. σπέρμα Ἀβραάμ εἰσιν; κἀγώ. **11.23** διάκονοι
I ALSO. SEED OF ABRAHAM ARE THEY? I ALSO. MINISTERS

Χριστοῦ εἰσιν; παραφρονῶν λαλῶ, ὑπὲρ ἐγώ· ἐν
OF CHRIST ARE THEY? [AS] BEING OUT OF [MY] MIND I SPEAK, I~MORE; IN

κόποις περισσοτέρως, ἐν φυλακαῖς περισσοτέρως, ἐν
LABORS MORE ABUNDANTLY, IN IMPRISONMENTS MORE FREQUENTLY, IN

πληγαῖς ὑπερβαλλόντως, ἐν θανάτοις πολλάκις.
BEATINGS FAR MORE, IN DEATHS OFTEN.

11.24 ὑπὸ Ἰουδαίων πεντάκις τεσσεράκοντα παρὰ μίαν
BY JEWS FIVE TIMES FORTY [LASHES] LESS ONE

ἔλαβον, **11.25** τρὶς ἐραβδίσθην, ἅπαξ ἐλιθάσθην,
I RECEIVED, THREE TIMES I WAS BEATEN WITH RODS ONE TIME I WAS STONED,

τρὶς ἐναυάγησα, νυχθήμερον ἐν τῷ βυθῷ
THREE TIMES I WAS SHIPWRECKED, A NIGHT AND A DAY IN THE DEEP

πεποίηκα· **11.26** ὁδοιπορίαις πολλάκις, κινδύνοις
I HAVE BEEN; IN JOURNEYS OFTEN, IN DANGERS

ποταμῶν, κινδύνοις λῃστῶν, κινδύνοις ἐκ γένους,
OF RIVERS, IN DANGERS OF ROBBERS, IN DANGERS FROM [MY OWN] RACE,

κινδύνοις ἐξ ἐθνῶν, κινδύνοις ἐν πόλει, κινδύνοις ἐν
IN DANGERS FROM GENTILES, IN DANGERS IN [THE] CITY, IN DANGERS IN

ἐρημίᾳ, κινδύνοις ἐν θαλάσσῃ, κινδύνοις ἐν
[THE] WILDERNESS, IN DANGERS IN [THE] SEA, IN DANGERS AMONG

ψευδαδέλφοις, **11.27** κόπῳ καὶ μόχθῳ, ἐν ἀγρυπνίαις
FALSE BROTHERS, IN LABOR AND TOIL, IN WATCHINGS

πολλάκις, ἐν λιμῷ καὶ δίψει, ἐν νηστείαις πολλάκις,
OFTEN, IN FAMINE AND THIRST, IN FASTINGS OFTEN,

ἐν ψύχει καὶ γυμνότητι· **11.28** χωρὶς τῶν παρεκτὸς
IN COLD AND NAKEDNESS; BESIDE THE THINGS [FROM] WITHOUT

but as a fool; [18]since many boast according to human standards,[h] I will also boast. [19]For you gladly put up with fools, being wise yourselves! [20]For you put up with it when someone makes slaves of you, or preys upon you, or takes advantage of you, or puts on airs, or gives you a slap in the face. [21]To my shame, I must say, we were too weak for that!

But whatever anyone dares to boast of—I am speaking as a fool—I also dare to boast of that. [22]Are they Hebrews? So am I. Are they Israelites? So am I. Are they descendants of Abraham? So am I. [23]Are they ministers of Christ? I am talking like a madman—I am a better one: with far greater labors, far more imprisonments, with countless floggings, and often near death. [24]Five times I have received from the Jews the forty lashes minus one. [25]Three times I was beaten with rods. Once I received a stoning. Three times I was shipwrecked; for a night and a day I was adrift at sea; [26]on frequent journeys, in danger from rivers, danger from bandits, danger from my own people, danger from Gentiles, danger in the city, danger in the wilderness, danger at sea, danger from false brothers and sisters;[i] [27]in toil and hardship, through many a sleepless night, hungry and thirsty, often without food, cold and naked. [28]And, besides other things,

[h] Gk *according to the flesh*
[i] Gk *brothers*

I am under daily pressure because of my anxiety for all the churches. 29Who is weak, and I am not weak? Who is made to stumble, and I am not indignant?

30 If I must boast, I will boast of the things that show my weakness. 31The God and Father of the Lord Jesus (blessed be he forever!) knows that I do not lie. 32In Damascus, the governor*ʲ* under King Aretas guarded the city of Damascus in order to*ᵏ* seize me, 33but I was let down in a basket through a window in the wall,*ˡ* and escaped from his hands.

ʲ Gk *ethnarch*
ᵏ Other ancient authorities read *and wanted to*
ˡ Gk *through the wall*

ἡ ἐπίστασίς μοι ἡ καθ' ἡμέραν, ἡ μέριμνα πασῶν
THE PRESSURE TO ME - DAY BY DAY, THE CARE OF ALL

τῶν ἐκκλησιῶν. **11.29** τίς ἀσθενεῖ καὶ οὐκ ἀσθενῶ; τίς
THE CHURCHES. WHO IS WEAK AND I AM NOT WEAK? WHO

σκανδαλίζεται καὶ οὐκ ἐγὼ πυροῦμαι;
IS CAUSED TO SIN AND ³NOT ¹I ²DO ⁴BURN?

11.30 Εἰ καυχᾶσθαι δεῖ, τὰ τῆς ἀσθενείας μου
IF IT IS NECESSARY~TO BOAST, THE THINGS OF THE WEAKNESS OF ME

καυχήσομαι. **11.31** ὁ θεὸς καὶ πατὴρ τοῦ κυρίου
I WILL BOAST. THE GOD AND FATHER OF THE LORD

Ἰησοῦ οἶδεν, ὁ ὢν εὐλογητὸς εἰς τοὺς αἰῶνας, ὅτι
JESUS KNOWS, THE ONE BEING BLESSED INTO THE AGES, THAT

οὐ ψεύδομαι. **11.32** ἐν Δαμασκῷ ὁ ἐθνάρχης Ἀρέτα
I AM NOT LYING. IN DAMASCUS THE ETHNARCH OF ARETAS

τοῦ βασιλέως ἐφρούρει τὴν πόλιν Δαμασκηνῶν πιάσαι
THE KING WAS GUARDING THE CITY OF [THE] DAMASCENES TO ARREST

με, **11.33** καὶ διὰ θυρίδος ἐν σαργάνῃ ἐχαλάσθην
ME, AND THROUGH A WINDOW IN A BASKET I WAS LET DOWN

διὰ τοῦ τείχους καὶ ἐξέφυγον τὰς χεῖρας αὐτοῦ.
THROUGH THE WALL AND ESCAPED THE HANDS OF HIM.

CHAPTER 12

It is necessary to boast; nothing is to be gained by it, but I will go on to visions and revelations of the Lord. 2I know a person in Christ who fourteen years ago was caught up to the third heaven—whether in the body or out of the body I do not know; God knows. 3And I know that such a person— whether in the body or out of the body I do not know; God knows— 4was caught up into Paradise and heard things that are not to be told, that no mortal is permitted to repeat. 5On behalf of such a one I will boast, but on my own behalf I will not boast, except of my weaknesses.

12.1 Καυχᾶσθαι δεῖ, οὐ συμφέρον μέν,
IT IS NECESSARY [FOR ME]~TO BOAST, ²NOT ³PROFITABLE ¹THOUGH,

ἐλεύσομαι δὲ εἰς ὀπτασίας καὶ ἀποκαλύψεις
BUT~I WILL COME TO VISIONS AND REVELATIONS

κυρίου. **12.2** οἶδα ἄνθρωπον ἐν Χριστῷ πρὸ
OF [THE] LORD. I KNOW A MAN IN CHRIST BEFORE

ἐτῶν δεκατεσσάρων, εἴτε ἐν σώματι οὐκ οἶδα, εἴτε
FOURTEEN~YEARS, WHETHER IN [THE] BODY I DO NOT KNOW, OR

ἐκτὸς τοῦ σώματος οὐκ οἶδα, ὁ θεὸς οἶδεν,
OUT OF THE BODY I DO NOT KNOW, - GOD KNOWS,

ἁρπαγέντα τὸν τοιοῦτον ἕως τρίτου οὐρανοῦ.
²HAVING BEEN CAUGHT AWAY - ¹SUCH A ONE TO [THE] THIRD HEAVEN.

12.3 καὶ οἶδα τὸν τοιοῦτον ἄνθρωπον, εἴτε ἐν σώματι
AND· I KNOW - SUCH A MAN, WHETHER IN [THE] BODY

εἴτε χωρὶς τοῦ σώματος οὐκ οἶδα, ὁ θεὸς οἶδεν,
OR OUTSIDE THE BODY I DO NOT KNOW, - GOD KNOWS,

12.4 ὅτι ἡρπάγη εἰς τὸν παράδεισον καὶ ἤκουσεν
THAT HE WAS CAUGHT AWAY INTO - PARADISE AND HEARD

ἄρρητα ῥήματα ἃ οὐκ ἐξὸν ἀνθρώπῳ λαλῆσαι.
INEXPRESSIBLE WORDS WHICH IT IS NOT PERMITTED FOR MAN TO SPEAK.

12.5 ὑπὲρ τοῦ τοιούτου καυχήσομαι, ὑπὲρ δὲ
ON BEHALF OF - SUCH A ONE I WILL BOAST, BUT~ON BEHALF OF

ἐμαυτοῦ οὐ καυχήσομαι εἰ μὴ ἐν ταῖς ἀσθενείαις.
MYSELF I WILL NOT BOAST EXCEPT IN THE(MY) WEAKNESSES.

12.6 ἐὰν γὰρ θελήσω καυχήσασθαι, οὐκ ἔσομαι ἄφρων,
FOR~IF   I DESIRE   TO BOAST,   I WILL NOT BE   FOOLISH,

ἀλήθειαν γὰρ ἐρῶ·   φείδομαι δέ, μή τις   εἰς ἐμὲ
FOR~TRUTH   I WILL SPEAK;   BUT~I SPARE [YOU*],   LEST ANYONE TO   ME

λογίσηται ὑπὲρ ὃ βλέπει με ἢ ἀκούει [τι] ἐξ
GIVES CREDIT   BEYOND WHAT   HE SEES [IN]   ME   OR HEARS   SOMETHING OF

ἐμοῦ **12.7** καὶ   τῇ ὑπερβολῇ τῶν   ἀποκαλύψεων.
ME—   ESPECIALLY BY THE EXCESS   OF THE(MY)   REVELATIONS.

διὸ   ἵνα μὴ ὑπεραίρωμαι,   ἐδόθη   μοι σκόλοψ
THEREFORE LEST   I SHOULD BE TOO EXALTED,   THERE WAS GIVEN   TO ME   A THORN

τῇ σαρκί, ἄγγελος Σατανᾶ, ἵνα με κολαφίζῃ, ἵνα μὴ
IN THE FLESH,   A MESSENGER OF SATAN,   THAT   HE MIGHT BEAT~ME,   LEST

ὑπεραίρωμαι.   **12.8** ὑπὲρ τούτου τρὶς   τὸν κύριον
I SHOULD BE TOO EXALTED.   AS TO   THIS   THREE TIMES   THE   LORD

παρεκάλεσα ἵνα ἀποστῇ   ἀπ' ἐμοῦ.   **12.9** καὶ εἴρηκέν
I CALLED UPON   THAT   IT MIGHT DEPART   FROM ME.   AND   HE HAS SAID

μοι, Ἀρκεῖ   σοι ἡ χάρις μου, ἡ γὰρ   δύναμις
TO ME,   ³IS SUFFICIENT   ⁴FOR YOU -   ²GRACE ¹MY,   FOR~THE(MY) POWER

ἐν ἀσθενείᾳ τελεῖται. ἥδιστα οὖν   μᾶλλον
IN   WEAKNESS   IS PERFECTED.   MOST GLADLY THEREFORE   RATHER

καυχήσομαι ἐν ταῖς ἀσθενείαις μου, ἵνα ἐπισκηνώσῃ
I WILL BOAST   IN   THE   WEAKNESSES   OF ME, THAT   ⁴MIGHT BE A SHELTER

ἐπ' ἐμὲ ἡ δύναμις τοῦ Χριστοῦ.   **12.10** διὸ
⁵OVER ⁶ME ¹THE ²POWER -   ³OF CHRIST.   WHEREFORE

εὐδοκῶ ἐν ἀσθενείαις, ἐν ὕβρεσιν, ἐν ἀνάγκαις, ἐν
I TAKE PLEASURE IN   WEAKNESSES,   IN   INSULTS,   IN   HARDSHIPS,   IN

διωγμοῖς καὶ στενοχωρίαις, ὑπὲρ   Χριστοῦ·
PERSECUTIONS   AND   DISTRESSES   ON BEHALF OF   CHRIST;

ὅταν γὰρ ἀσθενῶ, τότε δυνατός εἰμι.
FOR~WHENEVER I AM WEAK,   THEN   I AM~POWERFUL.

12.11 Γέγονα   ἄφρων, ὑμεῖς με ἠναγκάσατε. ἐγὼ γὰρ
I HAVE BECOME FOOLISH,   YOU*   COMPELLED~ME.   FOR~I

ὤφειλον ὑφ' ὑμῶν συνίστασθαι·   οὐδὲν γὰρ ὑστέρησα
OUGHT   BY   YOU*   TO BE COMMENDED;   FOR~[IN] NOTHING   I WAS BEHIND

τῶν ὑπερλίαν ἀποστόλων   εἰ καὶ   οὐδέν εἰμι.
THE   "SUPER-APOSTLES,"   EVEN~IF   I AM~NOTHING.

12.12 τὰ μὲν σημεῖα τοῦ   ἀποστόλου κατειργάσθη ἐν
INDEED~THE SIGNS   OF THE APOSTLE   WERE PERFORMED   AMONG

ὑμῖν ἐν πάσῃ ὑπομονῇ, σημείοις τε καὶ τέρασιν καὶ
YOU*   IN   ALL   ENDURANCE,   BOTH~BY SIGNS   AND   WONDERS   AND

δυνάμεσιν.   **12.13** τί γὰρ ἐστιν ὃ   ἡσσώθητε ὑπὲρ
WORKS OF POWER.   FOR~WHAT IS IT   THAT   YOU* WERE LESS THAN

τὰς λοιπὰς ἐκκλησίας, εἰ μὴ ὅτι αὐτὸς ἐγὼ
THE   REST [OF THE] CHURCHES,   EXCEPT THAT   I~MYSELF

οὐ κατενάρκησα ὑμῶν; χαρίσασθέ μοι τὴν
WAS NOT A BURDEN   [ON] YOU*?   FORGIVE   ME   -

ἀδικίαν ταύτην.   **12.14** Ἰδοὺ   τρίτον τοῦτο
THIS~WRONG.   BEHOLD   THIS [IS]~[THE] THIRD [TIME]

⁶But if I wish to boast, I will not be a fool, for I will be speaking the truth. But I refrain from it, so that no one may think better of me than what is seen in me or heard from me, ⁷even considering the exceptional character of the revelations. Therefore, to keep*m* me from being too elated, a thorn was given me in the flesh, a messenger of Satan to torment me, to keep me from being too elated.*n* ⁸Three times I appealed to the Lord about this, that it would leave me, ⁹but he said to me, "My grace is sufficient for you, for power*o* is made perfect in weakness." So, I will boast all the more gladly of my weaknesses, so that the power of Christ may dwell in me. ¹⁰Therefore I am content with weaknesses, insults, hardships, persecutions, and calamities for the sake of Christ; for whenever I am weak, then I am strong.

11 I have been a fool! You forced me to it. Indeed you should have been the ones commending me, for I am not at all inferior to these super-apostles, even though I am nothing. ¹²The signs of a true apostle were performed among you with utmost patience, signs and wonders and mighty works. ¹³How have you been worse off than the other churches, except that I myself did not burden you? Forgive me this wrong!

14 Here I am, ready to come to you this third time.

m Other ancient authorities read *To keep*
n Other ancient authorities lack *to keep me from being too elated*
o Other ancient authorities read *my power*

And I will not be a burden, because I do not want what is yours but you; for children ought not to lay up for their parents, but parents for their children. ¹⁵I will most gladly spend and be spent for you. If I love you more, am I to be loved less? ¹⁶Let it be assumed that I did not burden you. Nevertheless (you say) since I was crafty, I took you in by deceit. ¹⁷Did I take advantage of you through any of those whom I sent to you? ¹⁸I urged Titus to go, and sent the brother with him. Titus did not take advantage of you, did he? Did we not conduct ourselves with the same spirit? Did we not take the same steps?

19 Have you been thinking all along that we have been defending ourselves before you? We are speaking in Christ before God. Everything we do, beloved, is for the sake of building you up. ²⁰For I fear that when I come, I may find you not as I wish, and that you may find me not as you wish; I fear that there may perhaps be quarreling, jealousy, anger, selfishness, slander, gossip, conceit, and disorder. ²¹I fear that when I come again, my God may humble me before you, and that I may have to mourn over many who previously sinned and have not repented of the impurity, sexual immorality, and licentiousness that they have practiced.

ἑτοίμως ἔχω ἐλθεῖν πρὸς ὑμᾶς, καὶ οὐ καταναρκήσω·
I AM READY TO COME TO YOU°, AND I WILL NOT BE A BURDEN;

οὐ γὰρ ζητῶ τὰ ὑμῶν ἀλλὰ ὑμᾶς. οὐ γὰρ
³NOT ¹FOR ²I SEEK THE THINGS OF YOU° BUT YOU°. ⁵NOT ¹FOR

ὀφείλει τὰ τέκνα τοῖς γονεῦσιν θησαυρίζειν ἀλλὰ
⁴OUGHT ²THE ³CHILDREN FOR THE PARENTS TO TREASURE(SAVE) UP BUT

οἱ γονεῖς τοῖς τέκνοις. **12.15** ἐγὼ δὲ ἥδιστα
THE PARENTS FOR THE CHILDREN. BUT~I MOST GLADLY

δαπανήσω καὶ ἐκδαπανηθήσομαι ὑπὲρ τῶν ψυχῶν ὑμῶν.
WILL SPEND AND WILL BE UTTERLY SPENT FOR THE SOULS OF YOU°.

εἰ περισσοτέρως ὑμᾶς ἀγαπῶ[ν], ἧσσον ἀγαπῶμαι;
IF MORE ABUNDANTLY I LOVE~YOU°, AM I [TO BE] LOVED~LESS?

12.16 ἔστω δέ, ἐγὼ οὐ κατεβάρησα ὑμᾶς· ἀλλὰ
BUT~LET IT BE, I DID NOT BURDEN YOU°; BUT

ὑπάρχων πανοῦργος δόλῳ ὑμᾶς ἔλαβον.
BEING CRAFTY, WITH DECEIT I TOOK~YOU°.

12.17 μή τινα ὧν ἀπέσταλκα πρὸς ὑμᾶς, δι᾽
[SURELY] NOT ANY OF WHOM I HAVE SENT TO YOU°, THROUGH

αὐτοῦ ἐπλεονέκτησα ὑμᾶς; **12.18** παρεκάλεσα Τίτον
HIM DID I EXPLOIT YOU°? I URGED TITUS [TO GO]

καὶ συναπέστειλα τὸν ἀδελφόν· μήτι ἐπλεονέκτησεν
AND I SENT WITH [HIM] THE BROTHER; ¹[SURELY] ³DID NOT EXPLOIT

ὑμᾶς Τίτος; οὐ τῷ αὐτῷ πνεύματι περιεπατήσαμεν;
⁴YOU° ²TITUS? ²NOT ³BY THE ⁴SAME ⁵SPIRIT ¹WALKED WE?

οὐ τοῖς αὐτοῖς ἴχνεσιν;
NOT IN THE SAME STEPS?

12.19 Πάλαι δοκεῖτε ὅτι ὑμῖν ἀπολογούμεθα.
ALL ALONG ARE YOU° THINKING THAT TO YOU° WE ARE MAKING A DEFENSE.

κατέναντι θεοῦ ἐν Χριστῷ λαλοῦμεν· τὰ δὲ πάντα,
BEFORE GOD IN CHRIST WE SPEAK; - BUT ALL THINGS,

ἀγαπητοί, ὑπὲρ τῆς ὑμῶν οἰκοδομῆς.
BELOVED, [ARE] FOR - YOUR° EDIFICATION.

12.20 φοβοῦμαι γὰρ μή πως ἐλθὼν οὐχ οἵους θέλω
FOR~I FEAR LEST PERHAPS HAVING COME NOT SUCH AS I WISH

εὕρω ὑμᾶς κἀγὼ εὑρεθῶ ὑμῖν οἷον οὐ θέλετε· μή
I MAY FIND YOU° AND I MAY BE FOUND BY YOU° SUCH AS YOU° DO NOT WISH; LEST

πως ἔρις, ζῆλος, θυμοί, ἐριθεῖαι, καταλαλιαί,
PERHAPS [THERE BE] STRIFE, JEALOUSY, ANGER, FACTIONS, SLANDER,

ψιθυρισμοί, φυσιώσεις, ἀκαταστασίαι· **12.21** μὴ πάλιν
GOSSIP, CONCEIT, COMMOTIONS; LEST AGAIN

ἐλθόντος μου ταπεινώσῃ με ὁ θεός μου πρὸς ὑμᾶς
HAVING COME - ⁴MAY MAKE ME HUMBLE ¹THE ²GOD ³OF ME BEFORE YOU°

καὶ πενθήσω πολλοὺς τῶν προημαρτηκότων καὶ
AND I SHOULD MOURN MANY OF THE ONES HAVING SINNED BEFORE AND

μὴ μετανοησάντων ἐπὶ τῇ ἀκαθαρσίᾳ καὶ πορνείᾳ
NOT HAVING REPENTED OVER THE UNCLEANNESS AND FORNICATION

καὶ ἀσελγείᾳ ᾗ ἔπραξαν.
AND DEBAUCHERY WHICH THEY PRACTISED.

13.1 Τρίτον τοῦτο   ἔρχομαι πρὸς ὑμᾶς·   ἐπὶ
THIS [IS]~[THE] THIRD TIME   I AM COMING TO   YOU°;   ON(BY)

στόματος δύο   μαρτύρων καὶ   τριῶν σταθήσεται   πᾶν
[THE] MOUTH OF TWO WITNESSES AND OF THREE WILL BE ESTABLISHED EVERY

ῥῆμα. **13.2** προείρηκα καὶ   προλέγω,   ὡς παρὼν   τὸ
WORD.   I HAVE FORETOLD AND I SAY BEFOREHAND, AS BEING PRESENT THE

δεύτερον καὶ   ἀπὼν   νῦν, τοῖς   προημαρτηκόσιν
SECOND [TIME] AND BEING ABSENT NOW, TO THE ONES HAVING SINNED PREVIOUSLY

καὶ τοῖς λοιποῖς πᾶσιν, ὅτι ἐὰν ἔλθω εἰς τὸ πάλιν
AND ¹TO ³THE ⁴REST   ²ALL,   THAT IF I COME -   -   AGAIN

οὐ φείσομαι, **13.3** ἐπεὶ δοκιμὴν ζητεῖτε τοῦ ἐν ἐμοὶ
I WILL NOT SPARE,   SINCE YOU° SEEK~A PROOF   - IN ME

λαλοῦντος Χριστοῦ, ὃς εἰς ὑμᾶς οὐκ ἀσθενεῖ ἀλλὰ
OF CHRIST~SPEAKING, WHO TOWARD YOU° IS NOT WEAK   BUT

δυνατεῖ ἐν ὑμῖν. **13.4** καὶ γὰρ ἐσταυρώθη ἐξ
IS POWERFUL IN YOU°.   FOR~INDEED HE WAS CRUCIFIED OUT OF(IN)

ἀσθενείας, ἀλλὰ ζῇ   ἐκ δυνάμεως θεοῦ. καὶ γὰρ
WEAKNESS,   BUT HE LIVES BY [THE] POWER OF GOD. FOR~INDEED

ἡμεῖς ἀσθενοῦμεν ἐν αὐτῷ, ἀλλὰ ζήσομεν σὺν αὐτῷ
WE   ARE WEAK   IN HIM, BUT WE WILL LIVE WITH HIM

ἐκ δυνάμεως θεοῦ εἰς ὑμᾶς.
BY [THE] POWER OF GOD TOWARD YOU°.

13.5 Ἑαυτοὺς πειράζετε εἰ ἐστὲ ἐν τῇ πίστει,
TEST~YOURSELVES   IF YOU° ARE IN THE FAITH,

ἑαυτοὺς δοκιμάζετε· ἢ οὐκ ἐπιγινώσκετε ἑαυτοὺς ὅτι
PROVE~YOURSELVES;   OR DO YOU° NOT REALIZE YOURSELVES THAT

Ἰησοῦς Χριστὸς ἐν ὑμῖν; εἰ μήτι ἀδόκιμοί ἐστε.
JESUS   CHRIST [IS] IN YOU°? UNLESS YOU° ARE~UNAPPROVED.

13.6 ἐλπίζω δὲ ὅτι γνώσεσθε ὅτι ἡμεῖς οὐκ ἐσμὲν
BUT~I HOPE   THAT YOU° WILL KNOW THAT WE   ARE~NOT

ἀδόκιμοι. **13.7** εὐχόμεθα δὲ   πρὸς τὸν   θεὸν
UNAPPROVED.   NOW~WE PRAY   TO   -   GOD

μὴ ποιῆσαι ὑμᾶς κακὸν μηδέν, οὐχ ἵνα ἡμεῖς
[THAT] YOU° DO NOT DO ANY~EVIL,   NOT THAT WE

δόκιμοι φανῶμεν, ἀλλ' ἵνα ὑμεῖς τὸ καλὸν ποιῆτε,
MAY APPEAR~APPROVED, BUT THAT YOU° THE GOOD MAY DO,

ἡμεῖς δὲ ὡς ἀδόκιμοι ὦμεν. **13.8** οὐ γὰρ δυνάμεθά
AND~WE AS UNAPPROVED MAY BE.   ³NOT ¹FOR ²WE ARE⁴ABLE [TO DO]

τι   κατὰ τῆς ἀληθείας ἀλλὰ ὑπὲρ τῆς ἀληθείας.
ANYTHING AGAINST THE TRUTH   BUT FOR THE TRUTH.

13.9 χαίρομεν γὰρ ὅταν ἡμεῖς ἀσθενῶμεν, ὑμεῖς δὲ
FOR~WE REJOICE WHEN WE   ARE WEAK,   AND~YOU°

δυνατοὶ ἦτε·   τοῦτο καὶ εὐχόμεθα, τὴν ὑμῶν
ARE~STRONG;   THIS ALSO WE PRAY,   - YOUR°

13:1 Deut. 19:15

This is the third time I am coming to you. "Any charge must be sustained by the evidence of two or three witnesses." [2]I warned those who sinned previously and all the others, and I warn them now while absent, as I did when present on my second visit, that if I come again, I will not be lenient— [3]since you desire proof that Christ is speaking in me. He is not weak in dealing with you, but is powerful in you. [4]For he was crucified in weakness, but lives by the power of God. For we are weak in him,[p] but in dealing with you we will live with him by the power of God.

5 Examine yourselves to see whether you are living in the faith. Test yourselves. Do you not realize that Jesus Christ is in you?—unless, indeed, you fail to meet the test! [6]I hope you will find out that we have not failed. [7]But we pray to God that you may not do anything wrong—not that we may appear to have met the test, but that you may do what is right, though we may seem to have failed. [8]For we cannot do anything against the truth, but only for the truth. [9]For we rejoice when we are weak and you are strong. This is what we pray for, that you

[p] Other ancient authorities read *with him*

may become perfect. [10]So I write these things while I am away from you, so that when I come, I may not have to be severe in using the authority that the Lord has given me for building up and not for tearing down.

11 Finally, brothers and sisters,[q] farewell.[r] Put things in order, listen to my appeal,[s] agree with one another, live in peace; and the God of love and peace will be with you. [12]Greet one another with a holy kiss. All the saints greet you.

13 The grace of the Lord Jesus Christ, the love of God, and the communion of[t] the Holy Spirit be with all of you.

[q] Gk *brothers*
[r] Or *rejoice*
[s] Or *encourage one another*
[t] Or *and the sharing in*

κατάρτισιν.
PERFECTION(RESTORATION).

13.10 διὰ τοῦτο ταῦτα ἀπὼν
THEREFORE [2]THESE THINGS [3]BEING ABSENT

γράφω, ἵνα παρὼν μὴ ἀποτόμως χρήσωμαι
[1]I WRITE, THAT BEING PRESENT NOT WITH SEVERITY I MAY TREAT [YOU°]

κατὰ τὴν ἐξουσίαν ἣν ὁ κύριος ἔδωκέν μοι εἰς
ACCORDING TO THE AUTHORITY WHICH THE LORD GAVE ME FOR

οἰκοδομὴν καὶ οὐκ εἰς καθαίρεσιν.
EDIFICATION AND NOT FOR DESTRUCTION.

13.11 Λοιπόν, ἀδελφοί, χαίρετε, καταρτίζεσθε,
FOR THE REST, BROTHERS, REJOICE, BE RESTORED,

παρακαλεῖσθε, τὸ αὐτὸ φρονεῖτε, εἰρηνεύετε, καὶ
BE ENCOURAGED, [2]THE [3]SAME THING [1]THINK, BE AT PEACE, AND

ὁ θεὸς τῆς ἀγάπης καὶ εἰρήνης ἔσται μεθ' ὑμῶν.
THE GOD - OF LOVE AND PEACE WILL BE WITH YOU°.

13.12 ἀσπάσασθε ἀλλήλους ἐν ἁγίῳ φιλήματι.
GREET ONE ANOTHER WITH A HOLY KISS.

ἀσπάζονται ὑμᾶς οἱ ἅγιοι πάντες.
[4]GREET [5]YOU° [2]THE [3]SAINTS [1]ALL.

13.13 Ἡ χάρις τοῦ κυρίου Ἰησοῦ Χριστοῦ καὶ ἡ
THE GRACE OF THE LORD JESUS CHRIST AND THE

ἀγάπη τοῦ θεοῦ καὶ ἡ κοινωνία τοῦ ἁγίου
LOVE - OF GOD AND THE FELLOWSHIP OF THE HOLY

πνεύματος μετὰ πάντων ὑμῶν.
SPIRIT [BE] WITH YOU°~ALL.

THE LETTER OF PAUL TO THE
GALATIANS

ΠΡΟΣ ΓΑΛΑΤΑΣ
TO   [THE] GALATIANS

1.1 Παῦλος ἀπόστολος οὐκ ἀπ᾽ ἀνθρώπων οὐδὲ δι᾽
PAUL   AN APOSTLE,   NOT   FROM   MEN   NOR   THROUGH

ἀνθρώπου ἀλλὰ διὰ   Ἰησοῦ Χριστοῦ καὶ θεοῦ
MAN   BUT THROUGH JESUS CHRIST AND GOD

πατρὸς τοῦ ἐγείραντος αὐτὸν ἐκ νεκρῶν, **1.2** καὶ οἱ
[THE] FATHER, THE ONE HAVING RAISED HIM FROM [THE] DEAD, AND ²THE

σὺν ἐμοὶ πάντες ἀδελφοί ταῖς ἐκκλησίαις τῆς
⁴WITH ⁵ME ¹ALL ²BROTHERS TO THE CHURCHES   -

Γαλατίας, **1.3** χάρις ὑμῖν καὶ εἰρήνη ἀπὸ θεοῦ πατρὸς
OF GALATIA,   GRACE TO YOU° AND PEACE FROM GOD [THE] FATHER

ἡμῶν καὶ κυρίου Ἰησοῦ Χριστοῦ **1.4** τοῦ δόντος
OF US AND [THE] LORD JESUS CHRIST,   THE ONE HAVING GIVEN

ἑαυτὸν ὑπὲρ τῶν ἁμαρτιῶν ἡμῶν, ὅπως ἐξέληται
HIMSELF ON BEHALF OF THE SINS OF US, SO THAT HE MIGHT RESCUE

ἡμᾶς ἐκ τοῦ αἰῶνος τοῦ ἐνεστῶτος πονηροῦ κατὰ
US OUT OF THE ³AGE -   ¹PRESENT - ²EVIL   ACCORDING TO

τὸ θέλημα τοῦ θεοῦ καὶ πατρὸς ἡμῶν, **1.5** ᾧ   ἡ
THE WILL - OF GOD, EVEN [THE] FATHER OF US, TO WHOM [BE] THE

δόξα εἰς τοὺς αἰῶνας τῶν αἰώνων, ἀμήν.
GLORY INTO THE AGES   OF THE AGES, AMEN.

1.6 Θαυμάζω ὅτι οὕτως ταχέως μετατίθεσθε ἀπὸ
I MARVEL   THAT SO   QUICKLY YOU° ARE BEING TURNED FROM

τοῦ καλέσαντος ὑμᾶς ἐν χάριτι ⌜[Χριστοῦ]⌝ εἰς
THE ONE HAVING CALLED YOU° IN (BY) [THE] GRACE OF CHRIST TO

ἕτερον εὐαγγέλιον, **1.7** ὃ οὐκ ἔστιν ἄλλο, εἰ μή
A DIFFERENT GOSPEL,   WHICH IS~NOT ANOTHER, EXCEPT

τινές εἰσιν οἱ ταράσσοντες ὑμᾶς καὶ θέλοντες
THERE ARE~SOME - TROUBLING   YOU° AND [ARE] DESIRING

μεταστρέψαι τὸ εὐαγγέλιον τοῦ Χριστοῦ. **1.8** ἀλλὰ καὶ
TO PERVERT THE GOSPEL   - OF CHRIST.   BUT   EVEN

ἐὰν ἡμεῖς ἢ ἄγγελος ἐξ οὐρανοῦ εὐαγγελίζηται
IF WE   OR AN ANGEL FROM HEAVEN SHOULD PREACH A GOSPEL

[ὑμῖν] παρ᾽ ὃ   εὐηγγελισάμεθα ὑμῖν,
TO YOU° BESIDES THAT WHICH WE PREACHED   TO YOU°,

ἀνάθεμα ἔστω. **1.9** ὡς προειρήκαμεν καὶ ἄρτι πάλιν
LET HIM BE~A CURSE. AS WE HAVE PREVIOUSLY SAID, AND NOW AGAIN

Paul an apostle—sent neither by human commission nor from human authorities, but through Jesus Christ and God the Father, who raised him from the dead— ²and all the members of God's family[a] who are with me,

To the churches of Galatia:

3 Grace to you and peace from God our Father and the Lord Jesus Christ, ⁴who gave himself for our sins to set us free from the present evil age, according to the will of our God and Father, ⁵to whom be the glory forever and ever. Amen.

6 I am astonished that you are so quickly deserting the one who called you in the grace of Christ and are turning to a different gospel— ⁷not that there is another gospel, but there are some who are confusing you and want to pervert the gospel of Christ. ⁸But even if we or an angel[b] from heaven should proclaim to you a gospel contrary to what we proclaimed to you, let that one be accursed! ⁹As we have said before, so now

[a] Gk all the brothers
[b] Or a messenger

1:6 text: KJV ASV RSV NASB NIV NEBmg TEV NJB NRSV. omit: NEB TEVmg.

I repeat, if anyone proclaims to you a gospel contrary to what you received, let that one be accursed!

10 Am I now seeking human approval, or God's approval? Or am I trying to please people? If I were still pleasing people, I would not be a servant[c] of Christ.

11 For I want you to know, brothers and sisters,[d] that the gospel that was proclaimed by me is not of human origin; [12]for I did not receive it from a human source, nor was I taught it, but I received it through a revelation of Jesus Christ.

13 You have heard, no doubt, of my earlier life in Judaism. I was violently persecuting the church of God and was trying to destroy it. [14]I advanced in Judaism beyond many among my people of the same age, for I was far more zealous for the traditions of my ancestors. [15]But when God, who had set me apart before I was born and called me through his grace, was pleased [16]to reveal his Son to me,[e] so that I might proclaim him among the Gentiles, I did not confer with any human being, [17]nor did I go up to Jerusalem to those who were already apostles before me, but I went away at once into Arabia, and afterwards I returned to Damascus.

[c] Gk slave
[d] Gk brothers
[e] Gk in me

λέγω, εἴ τις ὑμᾶς εὐαγγελίζεται παρ' ὃ
I SAY,   IF   ANYONE   PREACHES A GOSPEL~TO YOU°   BESIDES   THAT WHICH

παρελάβετε, ἀνάθεμα ἔστω.
YOU° RECEIVED,   LET HIM BE~A CURSE.

1.10 Ἄρτι γὰρ ἀνθρώπους πείθω ἢ τὸν θεόν;
FOR~NOW   ²MEN   ¹AM I TRYING TO CONVINCE   OR   -   GOD?

ἢ ζητῶ ἀνθρώποις ἀρέσκειν; εἰ ἔτι ἀνθρώποις
OR   AM I SEEKING   TO PLEASE~MEN?   IF   STILL   MEN

ἤρεσκον, Χριστοῦ δοῦλος οὐκ ἂν ἤμην.
I WERE PLEASING,   CHRIST'S   SLAVE   I WOULD NOT HAVE BEEN.

1.11 Γνωρίζω γὰρ ὑμῖν, ἀδελφοί, τὸ εὐαγγέλιον τὸ
FOR~I MAKE KNOWN   TO YOU°,   BROTHERS,   THE   GOSPEL   -

εὐαγγελισθὲν ὑπ' ἐμοῦ ὅτι οὐκ ἔστιν κατὰ
HAVING BEEN PREACHED   BY   ME,   THAT   IT IS~NOT   ACCORDING TO

ἄνθρωπον· **1.12** οὐδὲ γὰρ ἐγὼ παρὰ ἀνθρώπου
MAN;   FOR~NEITHER   I   FROM   MAN

παρέλαβον αὐτὸ οὔτε ἐδιδάχθην ἀλλὰ δι'
RECEIVED   IT   NOR   WAS I TAUGHT [IT]   BUT   THROUGH

ἀποκαλύψεως Ἰησοῦ Χριστοῦ.
A REVELATION   OF JESUS   CHRIST.

1.13 Ἠκούσατε γὰρ τὴν ἐμὴν ἀναστροφήν ποτε ἐν τῷ
FOR~YOU° HEARD [OF]   -   MY   MANNER OF LIFE   ONCE   IN   -

Ἰουδαϊσμῷ, ὅτι καθ' ὑπερβολὴν ἐδίωκον τὴν
JUDAISM,   -   EXCESSIVELY   I WAS PERSECUTING   THE

ἐκκλησίαν τοῦ θεοῦ καὶ ἐπόρθουν αὐτήν, **1.14** καὶ
CHURCH   -   OF GOD   AND   WAS RAVAGING   IT,   AND

προέκοπτον ἐν τῷ Ἰουδαϊσμῷ ὑπὲρ πολλοὺς
I WAS ADVANCING   IN   -   JUDAISM   BEYOND   MANY

συνηλικιώτας ἐν τῷ γένει μου, περισσοτέρως
CONTEMPORARIES   IN   THE   NATION   OF ME,   MORE ABUNDANTLY

ζηλωτὴς ὑπάρχων τῶν πατρικῶν μου παραδόσεων.
BEING~A ZEALOT   -   ²ANCESTRAL   ¹OF MY   ³TRADITIONS.

1.15 ὅτε δὲ εὐδόκησεν [ὁ θεὸς] ὁ ἀφορίσας με ἐκ
BUT~WHEN   ²WAS PLEASED   -   ¹GOD,   THE ONE HAVING SEPARATED   ME   FROM

κοιλίας μητρός μου καὶ καλέσας διὰ τῆς
[THE] WOMB   OF [THE] MOTHER   OF ME   AND   HAVING CALLED [ME]   THROUGH THE

χάριτος αὐτοῦ **1.16** ἀποκαλύψαι τὸν υἱὸν αὐτοῦ ἐν ἐμοὶ,
GRACE   OF HIM,   TO REVEAL   THE   SON   OF HIM   IN   ME,

ἵνα εὐαγγελίζωμαι αὐτὸν ἐν τοῖς ἔθνεσιν, εὐθέως
THAT   I MIGHT PREACH   HIM   AMONG THE   GENTILES,   IMMEDIATELY

οὐ προσανεθέμην σαρκὶ καὶ αἵματι **1.17** οὐδὲ ἀνῆλθον
I DID NOT CONSULT   WITH FLESH AND   BLOOD   NOR   DID I GO UP

εἰς Ἱεροσόλυμα πρὸς τοὺς πρὸ ἐμοῦ ἀποστόλους,
TO   JERUSALEM   TO   ¹THE   ³BEFORE   ⁴ME   ²APOSTLES,

ἀλλὰ ἀπῆλθον εἰς Ἀραβίαν καὶ πάλιν ὑπέστρεψα εἰς
BUT   I WENT AWAY   INTO ARABIA   AND   AGAIN   I RETURNED   TO

Δαμασκόν.
DAMASCUS.

1.18 Ἔπειτα μετὰ ἔτη τρία ἀνῆλθον εἰς Ἱεροσόλυμα
THEN AFTER THREE~YEARS I WENT UP TO JERUSALEM

ἱστορῆσαι Κηφᾶν καὶ ἐπέμεινα πρὸς αὐτὸν
TO GET ACQUAINTED WITH CEPHAS AND I STAYED WITH HIM

ἡμέρας δεκαπέντε, **1.19** ἕτερον δὲ τῶν ἀποστόλων
FIFTEEN~DAYS, BUT~OTHER OF THE APOSTLES

οὐκ εἶδον εἰ μὴ Ἰάκωβον τὸν ἀδελφὸν τοῦ κυρίου.
I DID NOT SEE EXCEPT JAMES THE BROTHER OF THE LORD.

1.20 ἃ δὲ γράφω ὑμῖν, ἰδοὺ ἐνώπιον τοῦ θεοῦ
NOW~WHAT THINGS I WRITE TO YOU°, BEHOLD BEFORE - GOD

ὅτι οὐ ψεύδομαι. **1.21** ἔπειτα ἦλθον εἰς τὰ κλίματα τῆς
- I DO NOT LIE. THEN I WENT INTO THE REGIONS -

Συρίας καὶ τῆς Κιλικίας· **1.22** ἤμην δὲ ἀγνοούμενος
OF SYRIA AND - OF CILICIA; BUT~I WAS UNKNOWN

τῷ προσώπῳ ταῖς ἐκκλησίαις τῆς Ἰουδαίας ταῖς ἐν
- IN PERSON BY THE CHURCHES - OF JUDEA - IN

Χριστῷ. **1.23** μόνον δὲ ἀκούοντες ἦσαν ὅτι Ὁ
CHRIST. BUT~ONLY THEY WERE HEARING, - THE ONE

διώκων ἡμᾶς ποτε νῦν εὐαγγελίζεται τὴν πίστιν ἥν
PERSECUTING US ONCE NOW IS PREACHING THE FAITH WHICH

ποτε ἐπόρθει, **1.24** καὶ ἐδόξαζον ἐν ἐμοὶ τὸν
ONCE HE WAS RAVAGING, AND THEY WERE GLORIFYING ²IN ³ME -

θεόν.
¹GOD.

18 Then after three years I did go up to Jerusalem to visit Cephas and stayed with him fifteen days; ¹⁹but I did not see any other apostle except James the Lord's brother. ²⁰In what I am writing to you, before God, I do not lie! ²¹Then I went into the regions of Syria and Cilicia, ²²and I was still unknown by sight to the churches of Judea that are in Christ; ²³they only heard it said, "The one who formerly was persecuting us is now proclaiming the faith he once tried to destroy." ²⁴And they glorified God because of me.

CHAPTER 2

2.1 Ἔπειτα διὰ δεκατεσσάρων ἐτῶν πάλιν ἀνέβην εἰς
THEN AFTER FOURTEEN YEARS AGAIN I WENT UP TO

Ἱεροσόλυμα μετὰ Βαρναβᾶ συμπαραλαβὼν καὶ Τίτον·
JERUSALEM WITH BARNABAS, HAVING TAKEN WITH [ME] ALSO TITUS;

2.2 ἀνέβην δὲ κατὰ ἀποκάλυψιν· καὶ ἀνεθέμην
YET~I WENT UP ACCORDING TO A REVELATION; AND I LAID BEFORE

αὐτοῖς τὸ εὐαγγέλιον ὃ κηρύσσω ἐν τοῖς ἔθνεσιν,
THEM THE GOSPEL WHICH I PROCLAIM AMONG THE GENTILES,

κατ' ἰδίαν δὲ τοῖς δοκοῦσιν, μή πως εἰς
²PRIVATELY ¹BUT TO THE ONES SEEMING [TO BE SOMETHING,] LEST SOMEHOW IN

κενὸν τρέχω ἢ ἔδραμον. **2.3** ἀλλ' οὐδὲ Τίτος ὁ
VAIN I SHOULD RUN OR DID RUN. BUT NOT TITUS, THE ONE

σὺν ἐμοί, Ἕλλην ὤν, ἠναγκάσθη περιτμηθῆναι·
WITH ME, A GREEK BEING, WAS COMPELLED TO BE CIRCUMCISED;

2.4 διὰ δὲ τοὺς παρεισάκτους ψευδαδέλφους, οἵτινες
BUT~BECAUSE OF ¹THE ³SECRETLY BROUGHT IN ²FALSE BROTHERS, WHO

παρεισῆλθον κατασκοπῆσαι τὴν ἐλευθερίαν ἡμῶν ἣν
CREPT IN TO SPY OUT THE FREEDOM OF US WHICH

ἔχομεν ἐν Χριστῷ Ἰησοῦ, ἵνα ἡμᾶς καταδουλώσουσιν,
WE HAVE IN CHRIST JESUS, THAT THEY MIGHT ENSLAVE~US,

Then after fourteen years I went up again to Jerusalem with Barnabas, taking Titus along with me. ²I went up in response to a revelation. Then I laid before them (though only in a private meeting with the acknowledged leaders) the gospel that I proclaim among the Gentiles, in order to make sure that I was not running, or had not run, in vain. ³But even Titus, who was with me, was not compelled to be circumcised, though he was a Greek. ⁴But because of false believersᶠ secretly brought in, who slipped in to spy on the freedom we have in Christ Jesus, so that they might enslave us—

ᶠ Gk *false brothers*

[5]we did not submit to them even for a moment, so that the truth of the gospel might always remain with you. [6]And from those who were supposed to be acknowledged leaders (what they actually were makes no difference to me; God shows no partiality)—those leaders contributed nothing to me. [7]On the contrary, when they saw that I had been entrusted with the gospel for the uncircumcised, just as Peter had been entrusted with the gospel for the circumcised [8](for he who worked through Peter making him an apostle to the circumcised also worked through me in sending me to the Gentiles), [9]and when James and Cephas and John, who were acknowledged pillars, recognized the grace that had been given to me, they gave to Barnabas and me the right hand of fellowship, agreeing that we should go to the Gentiles and they to the circumcised. [10]They asked only one thing, that we remember the poor, which was actually what I was[g] eager to do.

11 But when Cephas came to Antioch, I opposed him to his face, because he stood self-condemned; [12]for until certain people came from James, he used to eat with the Gentiles. But after they came, he drew back and kept himself separate for fear of the circumcision faction. [13]And the other Jews joined him in this hypocrisy, so that even Barnabas was led astray by their hypocrisy. [14]But when

[g] Or *had been*

2.5 οἷς οὐδὲ πρὸς ὥραν εἴξαμεν τῇ ὑποταγῇ, ἵνα ἡ
TO WHOM NOT FOR AN HOUR DID WE YIELD - IN SUBJECTION, THAT THE

ἀλήθεια τοῦ εὐαγγελίου διαμείνῃ πρὸς ὑμᾶς.
TRUTH OF THE GOSPEL MIGHT CONTINUE WITH YOU°.

2.6 ἀπὸ δὲ τῶν δοκούντων εἶναί τι,— ὁποῖοί
BUT~FROM THE ONES SEEMING TO BE SOMETHING,— OF WHAT KIND

ποτε ἦσαν οὐδέν μοι διαφέρει· πρόσωπον [ὁ] θεὸς
THEY WERE~ONCE [2]NOTHING [3]TO ME [1]MATTERS; [1][THE] FACE - [3]GOD

ἀνθρώπου οὐ λαμβάνει — ἐμοὶ γὰρ οἱ
[2]OF A PERSON DOES NOT ACCEPT — FOR~TO ME THE ONES

δοκοῦντες οὐδὲν προσανέθεντο, **2.7** ἀλλὰ
SEEMING [TO BE SOMETHING] NOTHING ADDED, BUT

τοὐναντίον ἰδόντες ὅτι πεπίστευμαι τὸ
ON THE CONTRARY HAVING SEEN THAT I HAVE BEEN ENTRUSTED [WITH] THE

εὐαγγέλιον τῆς ἀκροβυστίας καθὼς Πέτρος τῆς
GOSPEL OF(FOR) THE UNCIRCUMCISION AS PETER OF(FOR) THE

περιτομῆς, **2.8** ὁ γὰρ ἐνεργήσας Πέτρῳ εἰς ἀποστολὴν
CIRCUMCISION, FOR~THE ONE HAVING WORKED IN PETER FOR AN APOSTLESHIP

τῆς περιτομῆς ἐνήργησεν καὶ ἐμοὶ εἰς τὰ ἔθνη,
OF THE CIRCUMCISION WORKED ALSO IN ME FOR THE GENTILES,

2.9 καὶ γνόντες τὴν χάριν τὴν δοθεῖσάν μοι,
AND REALIZING THE GRACE - HAVING BEEN GIVEN TO ME,

Ἰάκωβος καὶ Κηφᾶς καὶ Ἰωάννης, οἱ δοκοῦντες
JAMES AND CEPHAS AND JOHN, THE ONES SEEMING

στῦλοι εἶναι, δεξιὰς ἔδωκαν ἐμοὶ καὶ Βαρναβᾷ
TO BE~PILLARS, [1][THE] RIGHT HANDS [3]GAVE [4]TO ME [5]AND [6]BARNABAS

κοινωνίας, ἵνα ἡμεῖς εἰς τὰ ἔθνη, αὐτοὶ δὲ εἰς τὴν
[2]OF FELLOWSHIP, THAT WE [SHOULD BE] FOR THE GENTILES, BUT~THEY FOR THE

περιτομήν· **2.10** μόνον τῶν πτωχῶν ἵνα μνημονεύωμεν,
CIRCUMCISION; ONLY [3]THE [4]POOR [1]THAT [2]WE SHOULD REMEMBER,

ὃ καὶ ἐσπούδασα αὐτὸ τοῦτο ποιῆσαι.
WHICH ALSO I WAS EAGER THIS VERY THING TO DO.

2.11 Ὅτε δὲ ἦλθεν Κηφᾶς εἰς Ἀντιόχειαν,
BUT~WHEN CEPHAS~CAME TO ANTIOCH,

κατὰ πρόσωπον αὐτῷ ἀντέστην, ὅτι
TO [HIS] FACE I STOOD AGAINST~HIM, BECAUSE

κατεγνωσμένος ἦν. **2.12** πρὸ τοῦ γὰρ ἐλθεῖν τινας
HE HAD BEEN CONDEMNED. [2]BEFORE - [1]FOR [4]CAME [3]CERTAIN ONES

ἀπὸ Ἰακώβου μετὰ τῶν ἐθνῶν συνήσθιεν· ὅτε δὲ
[5]FROM [6]JAMES, WITH THE GENTILES HE WAS EATING; BUT~WHEN

ἦλθον, ὑπέστελλεν καὶ ἀφώριζεν ἑαυτὸν φοβούμενος
THEY CAME, HE WAS DRAWING BACK AND WAS SEPARATING HIMSELF FEARING

τοὺς ἐκ περιτομῆς. **2.13** καὶ συνυπεκρίθησαν αὐτῷ
THE ONES OF [THE] CIRCUMCISION. AND JOINED IN PRETENSE WITH HIM

[καὶ] οἱ λοιποὶ Ἰουδαῖοι, ὥστε καὶ Βαρναβᾶς
ALSO THE REST OF [THE] JEWS, SO THAT ALSO BARNABAS

συναπήχθη αὐτῶν τῇ ὑποκρίσει. **2.14** ἀλλ' ὅτε
WAS CARRIED AWAY WITH THEIR - HYPOCRISY. BUT WHEN

εἶδον ὅτι οὐκ ὀρθοποδοῦσιν πρὸς τὴν ἀλήθειαν
I SAW   THAT THEY DID NOT WALK CORRECTLY WITH RESPECT TO THE TRUTH

τοῦ εὐαγγελίου, εἶπον τῷ Κηφᾷ ἔμπροσθεν πάντων,
OF THE GOSPEL,   I SAID - TO CEPHAS BEFORE   ALL,

Εἰ σὺ Ἰουδαῖος ὑπάρχων ἐθνικῶς καὶ οὐχὶ Ἰουδαϊκῶς
IF YOU BEING~A JEW   AS A GENTILE AND NOT AS A JEW

ζῆς, πῶς τὰ ἔθνη ἀναγκάζεις Ἰουδαΐζειν;
LIVE, HOW ²THE ³GENTILES ¹DO YOU COMPEL TO LIVE AS JEWS?

2.15 Ἡμεῖς φύσει Ἰουδαῖοι καὶ οὐκ ἐξ ἐθνῶν
          WE   BY NATURE JEWS   AND NOT ²OF ³[THE] GENTILES

ἁμαρτωλοί· **2.16** εἰδότες [δὲ] ὅτι οὐ δικαιοῦται
¹SINNERS,   KNOWING   -   THAT ²IS NOT JUSTIFIED

ἄνθρωπος ἐξ ἔργων νόμου ἐὰν μὴ διὰ πίστεως
¹A MAN   BY WORKS OF LAW BUT   THROUGH FAITH

Ἰησοῦ Χριστοῦ, καὶ ἡμεῖς εἰς Χριστὸν Ἰησοῦν
OF(IN) JESUS CHRIST,   AND WE   IN CHRIST   JESUS

ἐπιστεύσαμεν, ἵνα δικαιωθῶμεν ἐκ πίστεως Χριστοῦ
BELIEVED,   THAT WE MIGHT BE JUSTIFIED BY FAITH   OF(IN) CHRIST

καὶ οὐκ ἐξ ἔργων νόμου, ὅτι ἐξ ἔργων νόμου
AND NOT BY WORKS OF LAW, THAT BY WORKS OF LAW

οὐ δικαιωθήσεται πᾶσα σάρξ. **2.17** εἰ δὲ ζητοῦντες
WILL NOT BE JUSTIFIED   ALL(ANY) FLESH.   NOW~IF SEEKING

δικαιωθῆναι ἐν Χριστῷ εὑρέθημεν καὶ αὐτοὶ
TO BE JUSTIFIED   IN CHRIST   WE WERE FOUND ALSO [OUR]SELVES

ἁμαρτωλοί, ἄρα Χριστὸς ἁμαρτίας διάκονος;
SINNERS [TO BE], THEN [IS] CHRIST A MINISTER~OF SIN?

μὴ γένοιτο. **2.18** εἰ γὰρ ἃ κατέλυσα ταῦτα πάλιν
MAY IT NEVER BE.   FOR~IF WHAT I DESTROYED THESE THINGS AGAIN

οἰκοδομῶ, παραβάτην ἐμαυτὸν συνιστάνω. **2.19** ἐγὼ γὰρ
I BUILD,   A TRANSGRESSOR I DEMONSTRATE~MYSELF [TO BE].   FOR~I

διὰ νόμου νόμῳ ἀπέθανον, ἵνα θεῷ ζήσω. Χριστῷ
THROUGH LAW TO LAW DIED,   THAT TO GOD I MAY LIVE. WITH CHRIST

συνεσταύρωμαι· **2.20** ζῶ δὲ οὐκέτι ἐγώ, ζῇ δὲ ἐν
I HAVE BEEN CRUCIFIED;   BUT~I AM LIVING NO LONGER [AS] I, ³LIVES ¹BUT ⁴IN

ἐμοὶ Χριστός· ὁ δὲ νῦν ζῶ ἐν σαρκί, ἐν
⁵ME   ²CHRIST;   AND~THAT WHICH NOW I LIVE IN [THE] FLESH, IN(BY)

πίστει ζῶ τῇ τοῦ υἱοῦ τοῦ θεοῦ τοῦ ἀγαπήσαντός
FAITH   I LIVE, THAT OF THE SON   -   OF GOD, THE ONE HAVING LOVED

με καὶ παραδόντος ἑαυτὸν ὑπὲρ ἐμοῦ.
ME AND HAVING GIVEN HIMSELF OVER   ON BEHALF OF ME.

2.21 οὐκ ἀθετῶ τὴν χάριν τοῦ θεοῦ· εἰ γὰρ διὰ
          I DO NOT SET ASIDE THE GRACE   - OF GOD; FOR~IF THROUGH

νόμου δικαιοσύνη, ἄρα Χριστὸς δωρεὰν ἀπέθανεν.
LAW   RIGHTEOUSNESS [IS], THEN CHRIST   DIED~FOR NOTHING.

I saw that they were not acting consistently with the truth of the gospel, I said to Cephas before them all, "If you, though a Jew, live like a Gentile and not like a Jew, how can you compel the Gentiles to live like Jews?"[h]

15 We ourselves are Jews by birth and not Gentile sinners; [16]yet we know that a person is justified[i] not by the works of the law but through faith in Jesus Christ.[j] And we have come to believe in Christ Jesus, so that we might be justified by faith in Christ,[k] and not by doing the works of the law, because no one will be justified by the works of the law. [17]But if, in our effort to be justified in Christ, we ourselves have been found to be sinners, is Christ then a servant of sin? Certainly not! [18]But if I build up again the very things that I once tore down, then I demonstrate that I am a transgressor. [19]For through the law I died to the law, so that I might live to God. I have been crucified with Christ; [20]and it is no longer I who live, but it is Christ who lives in me. And the life I now live in the flesh I live by faith in the Son of God,[l] who loved me and gave himself for me. [21]I do not nullify the grace of God; for if justification[m] comes through the law, then Christ died for nothing.

[h] Some interpreters hold that the quotation extends into the following paragraph
[i] Or *reckoned as righteous;* and so elsewhere
[j] Or *the faith of Jesus Christ*
[k] Or *the faith of Christ*
[l] Or *by the faith of the Son of God*
[m] Or *righteousness*

CHAPTER 3

You foolish Galatians! Who has bewitched you? It was before your eyes that Jesus Christ was publicly exhibited as crucified? [2]The only thing I want to learn from you is this: Did you receive the Spirit by doing the works of the law or by believing what you heard? [3]Are you so foolish? Having started with the Spirit, are you now ending with the flesh? [4]Did you experience so much for nothing?—if it really was for nothing. [5]Well then, does God[n] supply you with the Spirit and work miracles among you by your doing the works of the law, or by your believing what you heard?

6 Just as Abraham "believed God, and it was reckoned to him as righteousness," [7]so, you see, those who believe are the descendants of Abraham. [8]And the scripture, foreseeing that God would justify the Gentiles by faith, declared the gospel beforehand to Abraham, saying, "All the Gentiles shall be blessed in you." [9]For this reason, those who believe are blessed with Abraham who believed.

10 For all who rely on the works of the law are under a curse; for it is written, "Cursed is everyone who does not observe and obey all the things written in the book of the law." [11]Now it is evident that no one is justified before God by the law; for

[n] Gk he

3.1 Ὦ ἀνόητοι Γαλάται, τίς ὑμᾶς ἐβάσκανεν,
O SENSELESS GALATIANS, WHO BEWITCHED~YOU°,

οἷς κατ' ὀφθαλμοὺς Ἰησοῦς Χριστὸς προεγράφη
BEFORE~WHOSE EYES JESUS CHRIST WAS OPENLY PORTRAYED

ἐσταυρωμένος; **3.2** τοῦτο μόνον θέλω μαθεῖν ἀφ'
[AS] HAVING BEEN CRUCIFIED? THIS ONLY I WANT TO LEARN FROM

ὑμῶν· ἐξ ἔργων νόμου τὸ πνεῦμα ἐλάβετε ἢ ἐξ
YOU°; BY WORKS OF LAW THE SPIRIT YOU° RECEIVED OR BY

ἀκοῆς πίστεως; **3.3** οὕτως ἀνόητοί ἐστε,
[THE] HEARING OF(WITH) FAITH? SO SENSELESS YOU° ARE;

ἐναρξάμενοι πνεύματι νῦν σαρκὶ ἐπιτελεῖσθε;
HAVING BEGUN IN [THE] SPIRIT NOW IN [THE] FLESH ARE YOU° BEING PERFECTED?

3.4 τοσαῦτα ἐπάθετε εἰκῆ; εἴ γε καὶ εἰκῆ.
SO MANY THINGS DID YOU° SUFFER IN VAIN? IF REALLY INDEED IN VAIN.

3.5 ὁ οὖν ἐπιχορηγῶν ὑμῖν τὸ πνεῦμα καὶ
THE ONE, THEREFORE, SUPPLYING TO YOU° THE SPIRIT AND

ἐνεργῶν δυνάμεις ἐν ὑμῖν, ἐξ ἔργων νόμου ἢ ἐξ
PRODUCING WORKS OF POWER AMONG YOU°, [IS IT] BY WORKS OF LAW OR BY

ἀκοῆς πίστεως; **3.6** καθὼς Ἀβραὰμ ἐπίστευσεν τῷ
[THE] HEARING OF(WITH) FAITH? AS ABRAHAM BELIEVED -

θεῷ, καὶ ἐλογίσθη αὐτῷ εἰς δικαιοσύνην.
GOD, AND IT WAS ACCOUNTED TO HIM FOR RIGHTEOUSNESS.

3.7 Γινώσκετε ἄρα ὅτι οἱ ἐκ πίστεως, οὗτοι υἱοί
KNOW THEN THAT THE ONES OF FAITH, THESE ONES SONS

εἰσιν Ἀβραάμ. **3.8** προϊδοῦσα δὲ ἡ γραφὴ ὅτι
ARE OF ABRAHAM. [4]HAVING FORESEEN [1]AND [2]THE [3]SCRIPTURE THAT

ἐκ πίστεως δικαιοῖ τὰ ἔθνη ὁ θεός,
BY FAITH [2]WOULD JUSTIFY [3]THE [4]NATIONS - [1]GOD,

προευηγγελίσατο τῷ Ἀβραὰμ ὅτι
PREACHED THE GOOD NEWS BEFORE - TO ABRAHAM, -

Ἐνευλογηθήσονται ἐν σοὶ πάντα τὰ ἔθνη· **3.9** ὥστε
WILL BE BLESSED IN YOU ALL THE NATIONS; SO

οἱ ἐκ πίστεως εὐλογοῦνται σὺν τῷ πιστῷ
THE ONES OF FAITH ARE BLESSED WITH THE BELIEVING

Ἀβραάμ. **3.10** ὅσοι γὰρ ἐξ ἔργων νόμου εἰσὶν, ὑπὸ
ABRAHAM. FOR~AS MANY AS [2]OF [3]WORKS [4]OF LAW [1]ARE, UNDER

κατάραν εἰσίν· γέγραπται γὰρ ὅτι Ἐπικατάρατος
A CURSE ARE; FOR~IT HAS BEEN WRITTEN, - CURSED [IS]

πᾶς ὃς οὐκ ἐμμένει πᾶσιν τοῖς γεγραμμένοις ἐν
EVERYONE WHO DOES NOT ABIDE BY ALL THE THINGS HAVING BEEN WRITTEN IN

τῷ βιβλίῳ τοῦ νόμου τοῦ ποιῆσαι αὐτά. **3.11** ὅτι δὲ
THE BOOK OF THE LAW - TO DO THEM. NOW~THAT

ἐν νόμῳ οὐδεὶς δικαιοῦται παρὰ τῷ θεῷ δῆλον, ὅτι
BY LAW NO ONE IS BEING JUSTIFIED BEFORE - GOD [IS] CLEAR, BECAUSE,

3:6 Gen. 15:6 **3:8** Gen. 12:3; 18:18 **3:10** Deut. 27:26 LXX **3:11** Hab. 2:4

Ὁ δίκαιος ἐκ πίστεως ζήσεται· **3.12** ὁ δὲ νόμος
THE JUST BY FAITH WILL LIVE; BUT~THE LAW

οὐκ ἔστιν ἐκ πίστεως, ἀλλ᾽ Ὁ ποιήσας αὐτὰ
IS~NOT OF FAITH, BUT, THE ONE HAVING DONE THESE THINGS

ζήσεται ἐν αὐτοῖς. **3.13** Χριστὸς ἡμᾶς ἐξηγόρασεν ἐκ
WILL LIVE IN THEM. CHRIST REDEEMED~US FROM

τῆς κατάρας τοῦ νόμου γενόμενος ὑπὲρ ἡμῶν
THE CURSE OF THE LAW, HAVING BECOME ²ON BEHALF OF ³US

κατάρα, ὅτι γέγραπται, Ἐπικατάρατος πᾶς ὁ
¹A CURSE, BECAUSE IT HAS BEEN WRITTEN, CURSED [IS] EVERYONE

κρεμάμενος ἐπὶ ξύλου, **3.14** ἵνα εἰς τὰ ἔθνη ἡ
HAVING HUNG ON A TREE, THAT TO THE NATIONS THE

εὐλογία τοῦ Ἀβραὰμ γένηται ἐν Χριστῷ Ἰησοῦ, ἵνα
BLESSING - OF ABRAHAM MIGHT COME IN(BY) CHRIST JESUS, THAT

τὴν ἐπαγγελίαν τοῦ πνεύματος λάβωμεν διὰ τῆς
THE PROMISE OF THE SPIRIT WE MIGHT RECEIVE THROUGH -

πίστεως.
FAITH.

3.15 Ἀδελφοί, κατὰ ἄνθρωπον λέγω· ὅμως
BROTHERS, ACCORDING TO MAN I SPEAK; EVEN

ἀνθρώπου κεκυρωμένην διαθήκην οὐδεὶς ἀθετεῖ ἢ
³BY MAN ²HAVING BEEN CONFIRMED ¹A COVENANT NO ONE SETS ASIDE OR

ἐπιδιατάσσεται. **3.16** τῷ δὲ Ἀβραὰμ ἐρρέθησαν αἱ
ADDS TO [IT]. - NOW TO ABRAHAM WERE SPOKEN THE

ἐπαγγελίαι καὶ τῷ σπέρματι αὐτοῦ. οὐ λέγει, Καὶ
PROMISES AND TO THE SEED OF HIM. HE DOES NOT SAY, AND

τοῖς σπέρμασιν, ὡς ἐπὶ πολλῶν ἀλλ᾽ ὡς ἐφ᾽
TO THE SEEDS, AS CONCERNING MANY, BUT AS CONCERNING

ἑνός, Καὶ τῷ σπέρματί σου, ὅς ἐστιν Χριστός.
ONE, AND TO THE SEED OF YOU, WHO IS CHRIST.

3.17 τοῦτο δὲ λέγω· διαθήκην προκεκυρωμένην
AND~THIS I SAY: A COVENANT HAVING BEEN PREVIOUSLY CONFIRMED

ὑπὸ τοῦ θεοῦ ὁ μετὰ τετρακόσια καὶ τριάκοντα ἔτη
BY - GOD ¹THE ⁴AFTER ⁵FOUR HUNDRED ⁶AND ⁷THIRTY ⁸YEARS

γεγονὼς νόμος οὐκ ἀκυροῖ εἰς τὸ καταργῆσαι
³HAVING COME INTO BEING ²LAW DOES NOT ANNUL SO AS - TO ABOLISH

τὴν ἐπαγγελίαν. **3.18** εἰ γὰρ ἐκ νόμου ἡ
THE PROMISE. FOR~IF BY LAW [IS] THE

κληρονομία, οὐκέτι ἐξ ἐπαγγελίας· τῷ δὲ
INHERITANCE, [IT IS] NO LONGER BY PROMISE; - BUT

Ἀβραὰμ δι᾽ ἐπαγγελίας κεχάρισται ὁ θεός. **3.19** Τί
TO ABRAHAM ³BY ⁴PROMISE ²HAS GIVEN [IT] - ¹GOD. WHY

οὖν ὁ νόμος; τῶν παραβάσεων χάριν προσετέθη,
THEN THE LAW? ²THE ³TRANSGRESSIONS ¹FOR THE SAKE OF IT WAS ADDED,

ἄχρις οὗ ἔλθῃ τὸ σπέρμα ᾧ ἐπήγγελται,
UNTIL - SHOULD COME THE SEED TO WHOM IT HAS BEEN PROMISED,

3:12 Lev. 18:5 **3:13** Deut. 21:23 **3:16** Gen. 12:7

"The one who is righteous will live by faith."[o] 12But the law does not rest on faith; on the contrary, "Whoever does the works of the law[p] will live by them." 13Christ redeemed us from the curse of the law by becoming a curse for us—for it is written, "Cursed is everyone who hangs on a tree"— 14in order that in Christ Jesus the blessing of Abraham might come to the Gentiles, so that we might receive the promise of the Spirit through faith.

15 Brothers and sisters,[q] I give an example from daily life: once a person's will[r] has been ratified, no one adds to it or annuls it. 16Now the promises were made to Abraham and to his off-spring;[s] it does not say, "And to offsprings,"[t] as of many; but it says, "And to your offspring,"[s] that is, to one person, who is Christ. 17My point is this: the law, which came four hundred thirty years later, does not annul a covenant previously ratified by God, so as to nullify the promise. 18For if the inheritance comes from the law, it no longer comes from the promise; but God granted it to Abraham through the promise.

19 Why then the law? It was added because of transgressions, until the off-spring[s] would come to whom the promise had been made;

[o] Or The one who is righteous through faith will live
[p] Gk does them
[q] Gk Brothers
[r] Or covenant (as in verse 17)
[s] Gk seed
[t] Gk seeds

and it was ordained through angels by a mediator. 20Now a mediator involves more than one party; but God is one.

21 Is the law then opposed to the promises of God? Certainly not! For if a law had been given that could make alive, then righteousness would indeed come through the law. 22But the scripture has imprisoned all things under the power of sin, so that what was promised through faith in Jesus Christ*u* might be given to those who believe.

23 Now before faith came, we were imprisoned and guarded under the law until faith would be revealed. 24Therefore the law was our disciplinarian until Christ came, so that we might be justified by faith. 25But now that faith has come, we are no longer subject to a disciplinarian, 26for in Christ Jesus you are all children of God through faith. 27As many of you as were baptized into Christ have clothed yourselves with Christ. 28There is no longer Jew or Greek, there is no longer slave or free, there is no longer male and female; for all of you are one in Christ Jesus. 29And if you belong to Christ, then you are Abraham's offspring,*v* heirs according to the promise.

u Or *through the faith of Jesus Christ*
v Gk *seed*

διαταγεὶς   δι'   ἀγγέλων ἐν χειρὶ   μεσίτου.
HAVING BEEN ORDAINED   THROUGH   ANGELS   BY [THE] HAND OF A MEDIATOR.

3.20 ὁ δὲ   μεσίτης ἑνὸς οὐκ ἔστιν, ὁ δὲ θεὸς
       NOW~THE MEDIATOR   3OF ONE 2NOT   1IS,   -   BUT GOD

εἷς ἐστιν.
IS~ONE.

3.21 Ὁ   οὖν νόμος κατὰ τῶν ἐπαγγελιῶν [τοῦ θεοῦ];
       [IS] THE LAW~THEREFORE AGAINST THE   PROMISES   -   OF GOD?

μὴ γένοιτο.   εἰ γὰρ   ἐδόθη νόμος ὁ δυνάμενος
MAY IT NEVER BE.   FOR~IF   A LAW~WAS GIVEN   -   BEING ABLE

ζωοποιῆσαι, ὄντως ἐκ νόμου ἂν ἦν   ἡ δικαιοσύνη·
TO GIVE LIFE, REALLY   BY   LAW   WOULD HAVE BEEN   -   RIGHTEOUSNESS;

3.22 ἀλλὰ συνέκλεισεν ἡ   γραφὴ τὰ πάντα ὑπὸ
       BUT   3CONSIGNED   1THE 2SCRIPTURE -   ALL THINGS UNDER

ἁμαρτίαν, ἵνα ἡ ἐπαγγελία ἐκ πίστεως Ἰησοῦ
SIN,   THAT THE PROMISE   BY FAITH   OF(IN) JESUS

Χριστοῦ δοθῇ   τοῖς   πιστεύουσιν.
CHRIST   MIGHT BE GIVEN TO THE ONES BELIEVING.

3.23 Πρὸ τοῦ δὲ ἐλθεῖν τὴν πίστιν ὑπὸ νόμον
       2BEFORE   -   1BUT 5CAME   3THE   4FAITH,   UNDER LAW

ἐφρουρούμεθα συγκλειόμενοι εἰς τὴν μέλλουσαν πίστιν
WE WERE BEING KEPT,   BEING CONFINED   AS TO THE   FAITH~BEING ABOUT

ἀποκαλυφθῆναι, **3.24** ὥστε ὁ νόμος παιδαγωγὸς ἡμῶν
TO BE REVEALED;   SO THAT THE LAW   3GUARDIAN   2OUR

γέγονεν εἰς   Χριστόν, ἵνα ἐκ πίστεως
1HAS BEEN TO [LEAD US TO] CHRIST,   THAT BY   FAITH

δικαιωθῶμεν· **3.25** ἐλθούσης δὲ τῆς πίστεως οὐκέτι
WE MIGHT BE JUSTIFIED;   3HAVING COME 1BUT -   2FAITH,   5NO LONGER

ὑπὸ παιδαγωγόν ἐσμεν.
6UNDER 7A GUARDIAN   4WE ARE.

3.26 Πάντες γὰρ υἱοὶ θεοῦ ἐστε διὰ   τῆς πίστεως
       FOR~ALL   SONS OF GOD YOU° ARE THROUGH   -   FAITH

ἐν Χριστῷ Ἰησοῦ· **3.27** ὅσοι γὰρ εἰς Χριστὸν
IN CHRIST   JESUS;   FOR~AS MANY AS INTO CHRIST

ἐβαπτίσθητε, Χριστὸν ἐνεδύσασθε. **3.28** οὐκ ἔνι
WERE BAPTIZED,   PUT ON~CHRIST.   THERE IS~NOT

Ἰουδαῖος οὐδὲ Ἕλλην, οὐκ ἔνι δοῦλος οὐδὲ ἐλεύθερος,
JEW   NOR   GREEK,   THERE IS~NOT SLAVE   NOR   FREE,

οὐκ ἔνι ἄρσεν καὶ θῆλυ· πάντες γὰρ ὑμεῖς εἷς ἐστε
THERE IS~NOT MALE   AND FEMALE;   FOR~ALL   YOU°   ARE~ONE MAN

ἐν Χριστῷ Ἰησοῦ. **3.29** εἰ δὲ ὑμεῖς Χριστοῦ, ἄρα τοῦ
IN CHRIST   JESUS.   AND~IF YOU° [ARE] CHRIST'S, THEN -

Ἀβραὰμ σπέρμα ἐστέ, κατ'   ἐπαγγελίαν
OF ABRAHAM'S SEED   YOU° ARE, 2ACCORDING TO 3PROMISE

κληρονόμοι.
1HEIRS.

4.1 Λέγω δέ, ἐφ' ὅσον   χρόνον ὁ   κληρονόμος
NOW~I SAY,   FOR [HOWEVER] MUCH TIME   [AS] THE HEIR

νήπιός ἐστιν, οὐδὲν διαφέρει δούλου   κύριος
IS~AN INFANT, HE DIFFERS~NOTHING FROM A SLAVE, [THOUGH] ²LORD(OWNER)

πάντων ὤν, **4.2** ἀλλὰ ὑπὸ ἐπιτρόπους ἐστὶν καὶ
³OF ALL   ¹BEING,   BUT ²UNDER ³GUARDIANS   ¹IS   AND

οἰκονόμους ἄχρι τῆς προθεσμίας   τοῦ πατρός.
STEWARDS   UNTIL THE TIME PREVIOUSLY APPOINTED BY THE FATHER.

4.3 οὕτως καὶ ἡμεῖς, ὅτε ἦμεν νήπιοι, ὑπὸ τὰ
SO   ALSO WE,   WHEN WE WERE INFANTS, ²UNDER ³THE

στοιχεῖα   τοῦ κόσμου ἤμεθα δεδουλωμένοι·
⁴FUNDAMENTAL PRINCIPLES ⁵OF THE ⁶WORLD ¹WE HAD BEEN ENSLAVED;

4.4 ὅτε δὲ ἦλθεν τὸ πλήρωμα τοῦ χρόνου, ἐξαπέστειλεν
BUT~WHEN CAME THE FULLNESS OF THE TIME,   ²SENT FORTH

ὁ θεὸς τὸν υἱὸν αὐτοῦ, γενόμενον ἐκ γυναικός,
- ¹GOD THE SON OF HIM, HAVING COME FROM A WOMAN,

γενόμενον ὑπὸ νόμον, **4.5** ἵνα τοὺς ὑπὸ νόμον
HAVING COME UNDER LAW,   THAT THE ONES UNDER LAW

ἐξαγοράσῃ, ἵνα τὴν υἱοθεσίαν ἀπολάβωμεν.
HE MIGHT REDEEM, THAT ²THE ³SONSHIP ¹WE MIGHT RECEIVE.

4.6 Ὅτι δὲ ἐστε υἱοί, ἐξαπέστειλεν ὁ θεὸς τὸ
AND~BECAUSE YOU° ARE SONS, ²SENT FORTH   - ¹GOD THE

πνεῦμα τοῦ υἱοῦ αὐτοῦ εἰς τὰς καρδίας ἡμῶν κρᾶζον,
SPIRIT OF THE SON OF HIM INTO THE HEARTS OF US CRYING,

Αββα ὁ πατήρ. **4.7** ὥστε οὐκέτι εἶ δοῦλος ἀλλὰ
ABBA - FATHER.   SO   NO LONGER ARE YOU A SLAVE BUT

υἱός· εἰ δὲ υἱὸς, καὶ κληρονόμος διὰ θεοῦ.
A SON; AND~IF A SON, ALSO AN HEIR   THROUGH GOD.

4.8 Ἀλλὰ τότε μὲν οὐκ εἰδότες θεὸν ἐδουλεύσατε
BUT THEN INDEED NOT KNOWING GOD YOU° SERVED AS SLAVES

τοῖς φύσει μὴ οὖσιν θεοῖς· **4.9** νῦν δὲ γνόντες
THE ONES BY NATURE NOT BEING GODS;   BUT~NOW HAVING KNOWN

θεόν, μᾶλλον δὲ γνωσθέντες ὑπὸ θεοῦ, πῶς
GOD, YET~RATHER HAVING BEEN KNOWN BY GOD, HOW

ἐπιστρέφετε πάλιν ἐπὶ τὰ ἀσθενῆ καὶ πτωχὰ
DO YOU° TURN AGAIN TO THE WEAK AND IMPOVERISHED

στοιχεῖα   οἷς πάλιν ἄνωθεν δουλεύειν
FUNDAMENTAL PRINCIPLES, TO WHICH AGAIN ³ANEW ²TO SERVE AS SLAVES

θέλετε; **4.10** ἡμέρας παρατηρεῖσθε καὶ μῆνας καὶ
¹YOU° WANT?   YOU° OBSERVE~DAYS   AND MONTHS AND

καιροὺς καὶ ἐνιαυτούς, **4.11** φοβοῦμαι ὑμᾶς μή πως
SEASONS AND YEARS;   I FEAR FOR YOU° LEST SOMEHOW

εἰκῇ κεκοπίακα εἰς ὑμᾶς.
IN VAIN I HAVE LABORED FOR YOU°.

4.12 Γίνεσθε ὡς ἐγώ, ὅτι κἀγὼ ὡς ὑμεῖς,
BECOME AS I [AM], BECAUSE I ALSO [BECAME] AS YOU° [ARE],

My point is this: heirs, as long as they are minors, are no better than slaves, though they are the owners of all the property; ²but they remain under guardians and trustees until the date set by the father. ³So with us; while we were minors, we were enslaved to the elemental spirits[w] of the world. ⁴But when the fullness of time had come, God sent his Son, born of a woman, born under the law, ⁵in order to redeem those who were under the law, so that we might receive adoption as children. ⁶And because you are children, God has sent the Spirit of his Son into our[x] hearts, crying, "Abba![y] Father!" ⁷So you are no longer a slave but a child, and if a child then also an heir, through God.[z]

8 Formerly, when you did not know God, you were enslaved to beings that by nature are not gods. ⁹Now, however, that you have come to know God, or rather to be known by God, how can you turn back again to the weak and beggarly elemental spirits?[a] How can you want to be enslaved to them again? ¹⁰You are observing special days, and months, and seasons, and years. ¹¹I am afraid that my work for you may have been wasted.

12 Friends,[b] I beg you, become as I am, for I also have become as you are.

w Or *the rudiments*
x Other ancient authorities read *your*
y Aramaic for *Father*
z Other ancient authorities read *an heir of God through Christ*
a Or *beggarly rudiments*
b Gk *Brothers*

You have done me no wrong. [13]You know that it was because of a physical infirmity that I first announced the gospel to you; [14]though my condition put you to the test, you did not scorn or despise me, but welcomed me as an angel of God, as Christ Jesus. [15]What has become of the goodwill you felt? For I testify that, had it been possible, you would have torn out your eyes and given them to me. [16]Have I now become your enemy by telling you the truth? [17]They make much of you, but for no good purpose; they want to exclude you, so that you may make much of them. [18]It is good to be made much of for a good purpose at all times, and not only when I am present with you. [19]My little children, for whom I am again in the pain of childbirth until Christ is formed in you, [20]I wish I were present with you now and could change my tone, for I am perplexed about you.

21 Tell me, you who desire to be subject to the law, will you not listen to the law? [22]For it is written that Abraham had two sons, one by a slave woman and the other by a free woman. [23]One, the child of the slave, was born according to the flesh; the other, the child of the free woman, was born through the promise. [24]Now this is an allegory: these women are two covenants. One woman, in fact, is Hagar, from Mount Sinai,

ἀδελφοί,   δέομαι   ὑμῶν.   οὐδέν   με ἠδικήσατε·
BROTHERS,   I BEG   OF YOU°. [IN] NOTHING YOU° INJURED~ME;

4.13 οἴδατε δὲ   ὅτι δι᾽   ἀσθένειαν τῆς σαρκὸς
AND~YOU° KNOW   THAT THROUGH WEAKNESS   OF THE FLESH

εὐηγγελισάμην   ὑμῖν   τὸ πρότερον, **4.14** καὶ τὸν
I PREACHED THE GOOD NEWS TO YOU°   AT THE FIRST,   AND   THE

πειρασμὸν ὑμῶν ἐν τῇ σαρκί μου οὐκ ἐξουθενήσατε
TRIAL   OF YOU° IN THE FLESH OF ME NOT   YOU° DESPISED

οὐδὲ ἐξεπτύσατε, ἀλλὰ ὡς ἄγγελον θεοῦ ἐδέξασθέ με,
NOR   LOATHED,   BUT   AS AN ANGEL OF GOD YOU° RECEIVED ME,

ὡς   Χριστὸν Ἰησοῦν. **4.15** ποῦ οὖν ὁ   μακαρισμὸς
AS   CHRIST   JESUS.   WHERE THEN [IS] THE BLESSEDNESS

ὑμῶν; μαρτυρῶ γὰρ ὑμῖν ὅτι εἰ δυνατὸν τοὺς
OF YOU°? FOR~I TESTIFY TO YOU° THAT IF POSSIBLE   THE

ὀφθαλμοὺς ὑμῶν ἐξορύξαντες ἐδώκατέ   μοι.
EYES   OF YOU° HAVING TORN OUT YOU° [WOULD] HAVE GIVEN [THEM] TO ME.

4.16 ὥστε ἐχθρὸς ὑμῶν γέγονα   ἀληθεύων ὑμῖν;
SO THAT AN ENEMY OF YOU° HAVE I BECOME SPEAKING TRUTH TO YOU°?

4.17 ζηλοῦσιν   ὑμᾶς οὐ καλῶς, ἀλλὰ ἐκκλεῖσαι ὑμᾶς
THEY ARE ZEALOUS OF YOU°   NOT WELL,   BUT   ²TO EXCLUDE ³YOU°

θέλουσιν, ἵνα αὐτοὺς ζηλοῦτε·   **4.18** καλὸν δὲ
¹THEY DESIRE, THAT YOU° MAY BE ZEALOUS OF~THEM;   BUT~[IT IS] GOOD

ζηλοῦσθαι ἐν καλῷ   πάντοτε καὶ μὴ μόνον ἐν τῷ
TO BE ZEALOUS IN A GOOD THING ALWAYS   AND NOT ONLY   DURING

παρεῖναί με πρὸς ὑμᾶς. **4.19** τέκνα μου, οὓς   πάλιν
MY PRESENCE   WITH YOU°.   CHILDREN OF ME, FOR WHOM AGAIN

ὠδίνω   μέχρις οὗ μορφωθῇ Χριστὸς ἐν ὑμῖν·
I SUFFER BIRTH PAINS UNTIL   CHRIST~IS FORMED   IN   YOU°;

4.20 ἤθελον δὲ   παρεῖναι πρὸς ὑμᾶς ἄρτι καὶ
NOW~I WAS DESIRING TO BE PRESENT WITH YOU°   JUST NOW AND

ἀλλάξαι τὴν φωνήν μου, ὅτι   ἀπορούμαι ἐν   ὑμῖν.
TO CHANGE THE TONE OF ME, BECAUSE I AM PERPLEXED IN (ABOUT) YOU°.

4.21 Λέγετέ μοι, οἱ   ὑπὸ νόμον θέλοντες εἶναι,
TELL   ME,   THE ONES ³UNDER ⁴LAW ¹DESIRING   ²TO BE,

τὸν νόμον οὐκ ἀκούετε; **4.22** γέγραπται γὰρ ὅτι
THE LAW   DO YOU° NOT HEAR?   FOR~IT HAS BEEN WRITTEN, -

Ἀβραὰμ δύο υἱοὺς ἔσχεν, ἕνα ἐκ τῆς παιδίσκης καὶ
ABRAHAM   TWO SONS   HAD,   ONE OF THE MAIDSERVANT AND

ἕνα ἐκ τῆς ἐλευθέρας. **4.23** ἀλλ᾽ ὁ   μὲν ἐκ τῆς
ONE OF THE FREE WOMAN.   BUT THE ONE - OF THE

παιδίσκης κατὰ   σάρκα γεγέννηται, ὁ δὲ   ἐκ τῆς
MAIDSERVANT ACCORDING TO FLESH HAS BEEN BORN, AND~THE ONE OF THE

ἐλευθέρας δι᾽   ἐπαγγελίας. **4.24** ἅτινά
FREE WOMAN THROUGH [THE] PROMISE.   WHICH THINGS

ἐστιν ἀλληγορούμενα· αὗται γάρ εἰσιν δύο διαθῆκαι,
ARE ALLEGORIZED;   FOR~THESE ARE   TWO COVENANTS,

μία μὲν ἀπὸ ὄρους Σινᾶ εἰς δουλείαν γεννῶσα, ἥτις
ONE   - FROM MOUNT SINAI, ²TO ³SLAVERY   ¹BRINGING FORTH, WHO

ἐστὶν Ἁγάρ.   **4.25** τὸ   δὲ   ⌐Ἁγὰρ   Σινᾶ   ὄρος   ἐστὶν   ἐν
IS   HAGAR.   ⁴THE ¹NOW ²HAGAR ⁶SINAI ⁵MOUNT ³IS   IN

τῇ Ἀραβίᾳ⌐·   συστοιχεῖ   δὲ   τῇ   νῦν   Ἱερουσαλήμ,
-   ARABIA;   AND~CORRESPONDS TO THE NOW(PRESENT) JERUSALEM,

δουλεύει   γὰρ   μετὰ   τῶν   τέκνων   αὐτῆς.   **4.26** ἡ δὲ   ἄνω
FOR~SHE IS IN SLAVERY WITH   THE   CHILDREN OF HER.   BUT~THE ABOVE

Ἱερουσαλὴμ   ἐλευθέρα   ἐστίν,   ἥτις   ἐστὶν   μήτηρ   ἡμῶν·
JERUSALEM   IS~FREE,   WHO   IS   [THE] MOTHER OF US;

4.27 γέγραπται   γάρ,
FOR~IT HAS BEEN WRITTEN,

    Εὐφράνθητι,   στεῖρα   ἡ   οὐ   τίκτουσα,
    REJOICE,   [O] BARREN, THE ONE NOT GIVING BIRTH,

      ῥῆξον   καὶ   βόησον,   ἡ   οὐκ   ὠδίνουσα·
      BREAK FORTH AND   SHOUT,   THE ONE NOT   SUFFERING BIRTH PAINS;

  ὅτι   πολλὰ   τὰ   τέκνα   τῆς   ἐρήμου   μᾶλλον   ἢ
  BECAUSE MANY   [ARE] THE CHILDREN OF THE DESOLATE   RATHER   THAN

        τῆς   ἐχούσης   τὸν   ἄνδρα.
        THE ONE HAVING   THE   HUSBAND.

4.28 ὑμεῖς   δέ,   ἀδελφοί,   κατὰ   Ἰσαὰκ   ἐπαγγελίας
BUT~YOU°,   BROTHERS,   ACCORDING TO   ISAAC,   ³OF PROMISE

τέκνα   ἐστέ.   **4.29** ἀλλ᾽   ὥσπερ   τότε   ὁ   κατὰ
²CHILDREN ¹ARE.   BUT   AS   THEN   THE ONE ACCORDING TO

σάρκα   γεννηθεὶς   ἐδίωκεν   τὸν   κατὰ
FLESH   HAVING BEEN BORN WAS PERSECUTING THE ONE [BORN] ACCORDING TO

πνεῦμα,   οὕτως   καὶ   νῦν.   **4.30** ἀλλὰ   τί   λέγει   ἡ
SPIRIT,   SO   ALSO   NOW.   BUT   WHAT SAYS   THE

γραφή;   Ἔκβαλε   τὴν   παιδίσκην   καὶ   τὸν   υἱὸν   αὐτῆς·
SCRIPTURE? CAST OUT   THE   MAIDSERVANT   AND   THE   SON   OF HER;

οὐ   γὰρ   μὴ   κληρονομήσει   ὁ   υἱὸς   τῆς   παιδίσκης   μετὰ
FOR NEVER   WILL ⁵INHERIT   ¹THE ²SON ³OF THE ⁴MAIDSERVANT   WITH

τοῦ   υἱοῦ   τῆς   ἐλευθέρας.   **4.31** διό,   ἀδελφοί,
THE   SON   OF THE FREE WOMAN.   THEREFORE, BROTHERS,

οὐκ   ἐσμὲν   παιδίσκης   τέκνα   ἀλλὰ   τῆς   ἐλευθέρας.
WE ARE~NOT   CHILDREN~OF A MAIDSERVANT BUT   OF THE FREEWOMAN.

4:25 text: KJV ASV RSV NASB NIV TEV NJBmg NRSV.   var. γαρ Σινα ορος εστιν εν τη Αραβια (for Sinai is
a mountain in Arabia): ASVmg RSVmg TEVmg NEB NJB NRSVmg.   **4:27** Isa. 54:1   **4:30** Gen. 21:10

5.1 τῇ   ἐλευθερίᾳ   ἡμᾶς   Χριστὸς   ἠλευθέρωσεν·
FOR THE(THIS) FREEDOM   ³US   ¹CHRIST   ²FREED;

στήκετε   οὖν   καὶ   μὴ   πάλιν   ζυγῷ   δουλείας
STAND FAST THEREFORE AND   NOT   AGAIN   BY A YOKE OF SLAVERY

ἐνέχεσθε.
BE HELD.

5.2 Ἴδε   ἐγὼ   Παῦλος   λέγω   ὑμῖν   ὅτι   ἐὰν
BEHOLD I   PAUL   SAY   TO YOU° THAT   IF

περιτέμνησθε,   Χριστὸς   ὑμᾶς   οὐδὲν   ὠφελήσει.
YOU° ARE CIRCUMCISED, CHRIST   ²YOU°   ³NOTHING ¹WILL PROFIT.

---

bearing children for slavery.
²⁵Now Hagar is Mount Sinai
in Arabia[c] and corresponds
to the present Jerusalem, for
she is in slavery with her
children. ²⁶But the other
woman corresponds to the
Jerusalem above; she is free,
and she is our mother. ²⁷For
it is written,
  "Rejoice, you childless
    one, you who bear
    no children,
  burst into song and
    shout, you who
    endure no
    birth pangs;
  for the children of the
    desolate woman are
    more numerous
  than the children of the
    one who is
    married."
²⁸Now you,[d] my friends,[e]
are children of the promise,
like Isaac. ²⁹But just as at
that time the child who was
born according to the flesh
persecuted the child who
was born according to the
Spirit, so it is now also.
³⁰But what does the scripture
say? "Drive out the slave
and her child; for the child of
the slave will not share the
inheritance with the child of
the free woman." ³¹So then,
friends,[e] we are children, not
of the slave but of the free
woman.

[c] Other ancient authorities read *For
  Sinai is a mountain in Arabia*
[d] Other ancient authorities read *we*
[e] Gk *brothers*

For freedom Christ has set
us free. Stand firm, therefore, and do not submit
again to a yoke of slavery.
  2 Listen! I, Paul, am telling you that if you let yourselves be circumcised, Christ
will be of no benefit to you.

³Once again I testify to every man who lets himself be circumcised that he is obliged to obey the entire law. ⁴You who want to be justified by the law have cut yourselves off from Christ; you have fallen away from grace. ⁵For through the Spirit, by faith, we eagerly wait for the hope of righteousness. ⁶For in Christ Jesus neither circumcision nor uncircumcision counts for anything; the only thing that counts is faith working[f] through love.

7 You were running well; who prevented you from obeying the truth? ⁸Such persuasion does not come from the one who calls you. ⁹A little yeast leavens the whole batch of dough. ¹⁰I am confident about you in the Lord that you will not think otherwise. But whoever it is that is confusing you will pay the penalty. ¹¹But my friends,[g] why am I still being persecuted if I am still preaching circumcision? In that case the offense of the cross has been removed. ¹²I wish those who unsettle you would castrate themselves!

13 For you were called to freedom, brothers and sisters;[g] only do not use your freedom as an opportunity for self-indulgence,[h] but through love become slaves to one another. ¹⁴For the whole law is summed up in a single commandment, "You shall love your neighbor as yourself."

[f] Or made effective
[g] Gk brothers
[h] Gk the flesh

5.3 μαρτύρομαι δὲ πάλιν παντὶ ἀνθρώπῳ περιτεμνομένῳ
AND~I TESTIFY AGAIN TO EVERY MAN BEING CIRCUMCISED

ὅτι ὀφειλέτης ἐστὶν ὅλον τὸν νόμον ποιῆσαι.
THAT HE IS~A DEBTOR ³WHOLE ²THE ⁴LAW ¹TO DO.

5.4 κατηργήθητε ἀπὸ Χριστοῦ, οἵτινες ἐν νόμῳ
YOU° WERE ESTRANGED FROM CHRIST, WHOEVER BY LAW

δικαιοῦσθε, τῆς χάριτος ἐξεπέσατε. **5.5** ἡμεῖς γὰρ
ARE BEING JUSTIFIED, - YOU° FELL FROM~GRACE. FOR~WE

πνεύματι ἐκ πίστεως ἐλπίδα δικαιοσύνης
BY [THE] SPIRIT BY FAITH [THE] HOPE OF RIGHTEOUSNESS

ἀπεκδεχόμεθα. **5.6** ἐν γὰρ Χριστῷ Ἰησοῦ οὔτε
EAGERLY AWAIT. FOR~IN CHRIST JESUS NEITHER

περιτομή τι ἰσχύει οὔτε ἀκροβυστία ἀλλὰ πίστις
CIRCUMCISION IS OF ANY FORCE NOR UNCIRCUMCISION, BUT FAITH

δι᾽ ἀγάπης ἐνεργουμένη.
THROUGH LOVE WORKING.

5.7 Ἐτρέχετε καλῶς· τίς ὑμᾶς ἐνέκοψεν [τῇ]
YOU° WERE RUNNING WELL; WHO HINDERED~YOU° ³BY THE

ἀληθείᾳ μὴ πείθεσθαι; **5.8** ἡ πεισμονὴ οὐκ ἐκ
⁴TRUTH ¹NOT ²TO BE PERSUADED? THE(THIS) PERSUASION [IS] NOT OF

τοῦ καλοῦντος ὑμᾶς. **5.9** μικρὰ ζύμη ὅλον τὸ φύραμα
THE ONE CALLING YOU°. A LITTLE LEAVEN ALL THE LUMP

ζυμοῖ. **5.10** ἐγὼ πέποιθα εἰς ὑμᾶς ἐν κυρίῳ ὅτι
LEAVENS. I HAVE CONFIDENCE IN YOU° IN [THE] LORD THAT

οὐδὲν ἄλλο φρονήσετε· ὁ δὲ ταράσσων ὑμᾶς
²NOTHING ³OTHER ¹YOU° WILL THINK; BUT~THE ONE TROUBLING YOU°

βαστάσει τὸ κρίμα, ὅστις ἐὰν ᾖ. **5.11** ἐγὼ δέ,
WILL BEAR THE JUDGMENT, WHOEVER HE MAY BE. BUT~I,

ἀδελφοί, εἰ περιτομὴν ἔτι κηρύσσω, τί ἔτι
BROTHERS, IF CIRCUMCISION STILL I PROCLAIM, WHY STILL

διώκομαι; ἄρα κατήργηται τὸ σκάνδαλον τοῦ
AM I BEING PERSECUTED? THEN HAS BEEN ABOLISHED THE STUMBLING BLOCK OF THE

σταυροῦ. **5.12** ὄφελον καὶ ἀποκόψονται οἱ
CROSS. I WOULD [THAT] EVEN ⁴WILL EMASCULATE THEMSELVES ¹THE ONES

ἀναστατοῦντες ὑμᾶς.
²TROUBLING ³YOU°.

5.13 Ὑμεῖς γὰρ ἐπ᾽ ἐλευθερίᾳ ἐκλήθητε, ἀδελφοί·
FOR~YOU° FOR FREEDOM WERE CALLED, BROTHERS;

μόνον μὴ τὴν ἐλευθερίαν εἰς ἀφορμὴν τῇ σαρκί,
ONLY [USE] NOT THE FREEDOM FOR A PRETEXT FOR THE FLESH,

ἀλλὰ διὰ τῆς ἀγάπης δουλεύετε ἀλλήλοις.
BUT THROUGH - LOVE SERVE AS SLAVES ONE ANOTHER.

5.14 ὁ γὰρ πᾶς νόμος ἐν ἑνὶ λόγῳ πεπλήρωται,
FOR~THE ENTIRE LAW IN ONE WORD(STATEMENT) HAS BEEN SUMMED UP

ἐν τῷ Ἀγαπήσεις τὸν πλησίον σου ὡς σεαυτόν.
IN THE [WORD], LOVE THE NEIGHBOR OF YOU AS YOURSELF.

5:14 Lev. 19:18

5.15 εἰ δὲ ἀλλήλους δάκνετε καὶ κατεσθίετε, βλέπετε
BUT~IF   ONE ANOTHER   YOU° BITE   AND   DEVOUR,   BEWARE

μὴ ὑπ' ἀλλήλων ἀναλωθῆτε.
LEST BY   ONE ANOTHER   YOU° ARE DESTROYED.

5.16 Λέγω δέ, πνεύματι περιπατεῖτε καὶ ἐπιθυμίαν
BUT~I SAY,   BY [THE] SPIRIT WALK   AND   [THE] LUST

σαρκὸς οὐ μὴ τελέσητε. **5.17** ἡ γὰρ σάρξ
OF [THE] FLESH BY NO MEANS COULD YOU° PERFORM.   FOR~THE   FLESH

ἐπιθυμεῖ κατὰ τοῦ πνεύματος, τὸ δὲ πνεῦμα κατὰ τῆς
LUSTS   AGAINST THE   SPIRIT,   AND~THE SPIRIT   AGAINST THE

σαρκός, ταῦτα γὰρ ἀλλήλοις ἀντίκειται, ἵνα μὴ
FLESH,   FOR~THESE THINGS OPPOSE~EACH OTHER,   SO THAT NOT

ἃ ἐὰν θέλητε ταῦτα ποιῆτε. **5.18** εἰ δὲ πνεύματι
WHATEVER YOU° DESIRE [CAN] THESE THINGS YOU° DO.   BUT~IF   BY [THE] SPIRIT

ἄγεσθε, οὐκ ἐστὲ ὑπὸ νόμον. **5.19** φανερὰ δέ ἐστιν
YOU° ARE LED, YOU° ARE~NOT UNDER LAW.   ³MANIFEST ¹NOW ²ARE

τὰ ἔργα τῆς σαρκός, ἅτινά ἐστιν πορνεία, ἀκαθαρσία,
THE WORKS OF THE FLESH,   WHICH   ARE   FORNICATION, IMPURITY,

ἀσέλγεια, **5.20** εἰδωλολατρία, φαρμακεία, ἔχθραι, ἔρις,
LICENTIOUSNESS,   IDOLATRY,   SORCERY,   ENMITIES, STRIFE,

ζῆλος, θυμοί, ἐριθεῖαι, διχοστασίαι, αἱρέσεις,
JEALOUSY, ANGER, SELFISHNESS, DIVISIONS,   SECTS,

5.21 φθόνοι, μέθαι, κῶμοι καὶ τὰ ὅμοια τούτοις,
ENVYINGS, DRUNKENNESSES, CAROUSINGS AND THINGS LIKE   THESE,

ἃ προλέγω ὑμῖν καθὼς προεῖπον ὅτι οἱ
[OF] WHICH I TELL ²BEFOREHAND ¹YOU°   AS   I SAID BEFORE   THAT THE ONES

τὰ τοιαῦτα πράσσοντες βασιλείαν θεοῦ
-    SUCH THINGS PRACTISING   [THE] KINGDOM   OF GOD

οὐ κληρονομήσουσιν.
WILL NOT INHERIT.

5.22 Ὁ δὲ καρπὸς τοῦ πνεύματός ἐστιν ἀγάπη χαρά
BUT~THE FRUIT OF THE SPIRIT   IS   LOVE,   JOY,

εἰρήνη, μακροθυμία χρηστότης ἀγαθωσύνη, πίστις
PEACE,   LONGSUFFERING, KINDNESS,   GOODNESS,   FAITH,

5.23 πραΰτης ἐγκράτεια· κατὰ τῶν τοιούτων οὐκ ἔστιν
MEEKNESS,   SELF-CONTROL;   AGAINST -   SUCH THINGS THERE IS~NOT

νόμος. **5.24** οἱ δὲ τοῦ Χριστοῦ [Ἰησοῦ] τὴν σάρκα
A LAW.   BUT~THE ONES -   OF CHRIST   JESUS   ²THE ³FLESH

ἐσταύρωσαν σὺν τοῖς παθήμασιν καὶ ταῖς ἐπιθυμίαις.
¹CRUCIFIED   WITH THE(ITS) PASSIONS   AND THE(ITS) LUSTS.

5.25 εἰ ζῶμεν πνεύματι, πνεύματι καὶ στοιχῶμεν.
IF   WE LIVE   BY [THE] SPIRIT, ⁴WITH [THE] SPIRIT ²ALSO ¹WE SHOULD ³BE IN LINE.

5.26 μὴ γινώμεθα κενόδοξοι, ἀλλήλους προκαλούμενοι,
LET US NOT BECOME   CONCEITED,   PROVOKING~ONE ANOTHER,

ἀλλήλοις φθονοῦντες.
ENVYING~ONE ANOTHER.

¹⁵If, however, you bite and devour one another, take care that you are not consumed by one another.

16 Live by the Spirit, I say, and do not gratify the desires of the flesh. ¹⁷For what the flesh desires is opposed to the Spirit, and what the Spirit desires is opposed to the flesh; for these are opposed to each other, to prevent you from doing what you want. ¹⁸But if you are led by the Spirit, you are not subject to the law. ¹⁹Now the works of the flesh are obvious: fornication, impurity, licentiousness, ²⁰idolatry, sorcery, enmities, strife, jealousy, anger, quarrels, dissensions, factions, ²¹envy,[i] drunkenness, carousing, and things like these. I am warning you, as I warned you before: those who do such things will not inherit the kingdom of God.

22 By contrast, the fruit of the Spirit is love, joy, peace, patience, kindness, generosity, faithfulness, ²³gentleness, and self-control. There is no law against such things. ²⁴And those who belong to Christ Jesus have crucified the flesh with its passions and desires. ²⁵If we live by the Spirit, let us also be guided by the Spirit. ²⁶Let us not become conceited, competing against one another, envying one another.

[i] Other ancient authorities add *murder*

CHAPTER 6

My friends,[j] if anyone is detected in a transgression, you who have received the Spirit should restore such a one in a spirit of gentleness. Take care that you yourselves are not tempted. [2]Bear one another's burdens, and in this way you will fulfill[k] the law of Christ. [3]For if those who are nothing think they are something, they deceive themselves. [4]All must test their own work; then that work, rather than their neighbor's work, will become a cause for pride. [5]For all must carry their own loads.

6 Those who are taught the word must share in all good things with their teacher.

7 Do not be deceived; God is not mocked, for you reap whatever you sow. [8]If you sow to your own flesh, you will reap corruption from the flesh; but if you sow to the Spirit, you will reap eternal life from the Spirit. [9]So let us not grow weary in doing what is right, for we will reap at harvest time, if we do not give up. [10]So then, whenever we have an opportunity, let us work for the good of all, and especially for those of the family of faith.

11 See what large letters I make when I am writing in my own hand! [12]It is those who want to make a good showing in the flesh that try to compel you to be circumcised—

[j] Gk *Brothers*
[k] Other ancient authorities read *in this way fulfill*

6.1 Ἀδελφοί, ἐὰν καὶ προλημφθῇ ἄνθρωπος ἔν τινι
BROTHERS, IF INDEED A MAN~IS OVERTAKEN IN SOME

παραπτώματι, ὑμεῖς οἱ πνευματικοὶ καταρτίζετε τὸν
TRANSGRESSION, YOU° THE SPIRITUAL ONES RESTORE -

τοιοῦτον ἐν πνεύματι πραΰτητος, σκοπῶν σεαυτὸν μὴ
SUCH A ONE IN A SPIRIT OF MEEKNESS, WATCHING OUT FOR YOURSELF LEST

καὶ σὺ πειρασθῇς. **6.2** Ἀλλήλων τὰ βάρη βαστάζετε
ALSO YOU BE TEMPTED. ONE ANOTHER'S - BURDENS BEAR

καὶ οὕτως ἀναπληρώσετε τὸν νόμον τοῦ Χριστοῦ.
AND THUS YOU° WILL FULFILL THE LAW - OF CHRIST.

6.3 εἰ γὰρ δοκεῖ τις εἶναί τι μηδὲν ὤν,
FOR~IF ANYONE~THINKS TO BE SOMETHING, BEING~NOTHING,

φρεναπατᾷ ἑαυτόν. **6.4** τὸ δὲ ἔργον ἑαυτοῦ δοκιμαζέτω
HE DECEIVES HIMSELF. BUT~THE WORK OF HIMSELF [1]LET [3]PROVE

ἕκαστος, καὶ τότε εἰς ἑαυτὸν μόνον τὸ καύχημα
[2]EACH MAN, AND THEN IN HIMSELF ALONE THE BOAST

ἕξει καὶ οὐκ εἰς τὸν ἕτερον· **6.5** ἕκαστος γὰρ
HE WILL HAVE AND NOT IN THE OTHER MAN; FOR~EACH MAN

τὸ ἴδιον φορτίον βαστάσει. **6.6** Κοινωνείτω δὲ ὁ
HIS OWN LOAD WILL BEAR. [2]LET [7]SHARE [1]AND [3]THE ONE

κατηχούμενος τὸν λόγον τῷ κατηχοῦντι ἐν πᾶσιν
[4]BEING INSTRUCTED [IN] [5]THE [6]WORD WITH THE ONE INSTRUCTING IN ALL

ἀγαθοῖς. **6.7** Μὴ πλανᾶσθε, θεὸς οὐ μυκτηρίζεται.
GOOD THINGS. DO NOT BE LED ASTRAY; GOD IS NOT MOCKED.

ὃ γὰρ ἐὰν σπείρῃ ἄνθρωπος, τοῦτο καὶ θερίσει·
FOR WHATEVER A MAN~SOWS, THIS ALSO HE WILL REAP;

6.8 ὅτι ὁ σπείρων εἰς τὴν σάρκα ἑαυτοῦ ἐκ τῆς
BECAUSE THE ONE SOWING TO THE FLESH OF HIMSELF OF THE

σαρκὸς θερίσει φθοράν, ὁ δὲ σπείρων εἰς τὸ
FLESH WILL REAP CORRUPTION, BUT~THE ONE SOWING TO THE

πνεῦμα ἐκ τοῦ πνεύματος θερίσει ζωὴν αἰώνιον. **6.9** τὸ
SPIRIT, OF THE SPIRIT WILL REAP LIFE ETERNAL.

δὲ καλὸν ποιοῦντες μὴ ἐγκακῶμεν, καιρῷ γὰρ ἰδίῳ
NOW [IN] WELL DOING LET US NOT BECOME WEARY, [3]TIME [1]FOR [2]IN ITS OWN

θερίσομεν μὴ ἐκλυόμενοι. **6.10** ἄρα οὖν ὡς
WE WILL REAP, NOT FAINTING. THEREFORE~THEN AS

καιρὸν ἔχομεν, ἐργαζώμεθα τὸ ἀγαθὸν πρὸς πάντας,
WE HAVE~OPPORTUNITY, WE SHOULD WORK THE GOOD TOWARDS ALL,

μάλιστα δὲ πρὸς τοὺς οἰκείους τῆς πίστεως.
AND~ESPECIALLY TOWARDS THE HOUSEHOLD - OF FAITH.

6.11 Ἴδετε πηλίκοις ὑμῖν γράμμασιν ἔγραψα τῇ
SEE WITH WHAT LARGE LETTERS~TO YOU° I WROTE -

ἐμῇ χειρί. **6.12** ὅσοι θέλουσιν εὐπροσωπῆσαι
WITH MY OWN HAND. AS MANY AS DESIRE TO MAKE A GOOD SHOWING

ἐν σαρκί, οὗτοι ἀναγκάζουσιν ὑμᾶς περιτέμνεσθαι,
IN [THE] FLESH, THESE COMPEL YOU° TO BE CIRCUMCISED,

μόνον ἵνα τῷ   σταυρῷ τοῦ Χριστοῦ μὴ διώκωνται.
ONLY   THAT ²FOR THE ³CROSS   -   ⁴OF CHRIST ¹THEY BE NOT PERSECUTED.

6.13 οὐδὲ γὰρ οἱ   περιτεμνόμενοι αὐτοὶ   νόμον
FOR~NEITHER THE ONES BEING CIRCUMCISED ³THEMSELVES ²[THE] LAW

φυλάσσουσιν ἀλλὰ θέλουσιν ὑμᾶς περιτέμνεσθαι, ἵνα
¹KEEP   BUT   THEY DESIRE YOU° TO BE CIRCUMCISED, THAT

ἐν τῇ ὑμετέρᾳ σαρκὶ καυχήσωνται. **6.14** ἐμοὶ δὲ
IN - YOUR°   FLESH THEY MAY BOAST.   BUT~TO ME

μὴ γένοιτο καυχᾶσθαι εἰ μὴ ἐν τῷ   σταυρῷ τοῦ
MAY IT NOT BE TO BOAST   EXCEPT IN THE CROSS   OF THE

κυρίου ἡμῶν Ἰησοῦ Χριστοῦ, δι᾽   οὗ ἐμοὶ κόσμος
LORD   OF US JESUS CHRIST, THROUGH WHOM TO ME [THE] WORLD

ἐσταύρωται κἀγὼ κόσμῳ. **6.15** οὔτε γὰρ περιτομή
HAS BEEN CRUCIFIED AND I TO THE WORLD.   FOR~NEITHER CIRCUMCISION

τί ἐστιν οὔτε ἀκροβυστία ἀλλὰ καινὴ κτίσις. **6.16** καὶ
IS~ANYTHING NOR UNCIRCUMCISION BUT A NEW CREATION.   AND

ὅσοι   τῷ κανόνι τούτῳ στοιχήσουσιν, εἰρήνη ἐπ᾽
AS MANY AS - ³RULE ²WITH THIS ¹WILL KEEP IN LINE, PEACE UPON

αὐτοὺς καὶ ἔλεος καὶ ἐπὶ τὸν Ἰσραὴλ τοῦ θεοῦ.
THEM   AND MERCY, EVEN UPON THE ISRAEL - OF GOD.

6.17 Τοῦ λοιποῦ κόπους μοι μηδεὶς παρεχέτω·
FOR THE REST, ⁴TROUBLES ⁵TO ME ²NO ONE ¹LET ³GIVE;

ἐγὼ γὰρ τὰ στίγματα τοῦ Ἰησοῦ ἐν τῷ   σώματί μου
FOR~I   THE MARKS   - OF JESUS IN THE BODY OF ME

βαστάζω.
BEAR.

6.18 Ἡ χάρις τοῦ κυρίου ἡμῶν Ἰησοῦ Χριστοῦ μετὰ
THE GRACE OF THE LORD OF US JESUS CHRIST [BE] WITH

τοῦ πνεύματος ὑμῶν, ἀδελφοί· ἀμήν.
THE SPIRIT   OF YOU°, BROTHERS; AMEN.

only that they may not be persecuted for the cross of Christ. [13]Even the circumcised do not themselves obey the law, but they want you to be circumcised so that they may boast about your flesh. [14]May I never boast of anything except the cross of our Lord Jesus Christ, by which[l] the world has been crucified to me, and I to the world. [15]For[m] neither circumcision nor uncircumcision is anything; but a new creation is everything! [16]As for those who will follow this rule—peace be upon them, and mercy, and upon the Israel of God.

[17] From now on, let no one make trouble for me; for I carry the marks of Jesus branded on my body.

[18] May the grace of our Lord Jesus Christ be with your spirit, brothers and sisters.[n] Amen.

[l] Or *through whom*
[m] Other ancient authorities add *in Christ Jesus*
[n] Gk *brothers*

THE LETTER OF PAUL TO THE
EPHESIANS

ΠΡΟΣ ΕΦΕΣΙΟΥΣ
TO   [THE] EPHESIANS

1.1 Παῦλος ἀπόστολος Χριστοῦ Ἰησοῦ διὰ
PAUL   AN APOSTLE   OF CHRIST   JESUS   THROUGH

θελήματος θεοῦ τοῖς ἁγίοις τοῖς οὖσιν ⌜[ἐν Ἐφέσῳ]⌝
[THE] WILL   OF GOD   TO THE   SAINTS   -   BEING   IN   EPHESUS

καὶ πιστοῖς ἐν Χριστῷ Ἰησοῦ, **1.2** χάρις ὑμῖν καὶ
AND   BELIEVERS   IN   CHRIST   JESUS,   GRACE   TO YOU°   AND

εἰρήνη ἀπὸ θεοῦ πατρὸς ἡμῶν καὶ κυρίου Ἰησοῦ
PEACE   FROM   GOD   [THE] FATHER   OF US   AND   LORD   JESUS

Χριστοῦ.
CHRIST.

1.3 Εὐλογητὸς ὁ θεὸς καὶ πατὴρ τοῦ κυρίου ἡμῶν
     BLESSED [BE]   THE GOD   AND   FATHER   OF THE LORD   OF US,

Ἰησοῦ Χριστοῦ, ὁ   εὐλογήσας ἡμᾶς ἐν πάσῃ
JESUS   CHRIST,   THE ONE   HAVING BLESSED   US   WITH   EVERY

εὐλογίᾳ πνευματικῇ ἐν τοῖς ἐπουρανίοις ἐν Χριστῷ,
SPIRITUAL ~ BLESSING   IN   THE   HEAVENLIES   IN   CHRIST,

1.4 καθὼς ἐξελέξατο ἡμᾶς ἐν αὐτῷ πρὸ καταβολῆς
     EVEN AS   HE CHOSE   US   IN   HIM   BEFORE   [THE] FOUNDATION

κόσμου εἶναι ἡμᾶς ἁγίους καὶ ἀμώμους κατενώπιον
OF [THE] WORLD   [FOR] US ~ TO BE   HOLY   AND   BLAMELESS   IN [THE] SIGHT

αὐτοῦ ἐν ἀγάπῃ, **1.5** προορίσας ἡμᾶς εἰς υἱοθεσίαν
OF HIM,   IN   LOVE   HAVING PREDESTINED   US   TO   SONSHIP

διὰ   Ἰησοῦ Χριστοῦ εἰς αὐτόν, κατὰ   τὴν
THROUGH   JESUS   CHRIST   TO   HIM[SELF],   ACCORDING TO   THE

εὐδοκίαν τοῦ θελήματος αὐτοῦ, **1.6** εἰς ἔπαινον
GOOD PLEASURE   OF THE   WILL   OF HIM,   TO   [THE] PRAISE

δόξης   τῆς χάριτος αὐτοῦ ἧς   ἐχαρίτωσεν ἡμᾶς
OF [THE] GLORY   OF THE   GRACE   OF HIM   [BY] WHICH   HE FAVORED   US

ἐν τῷ ἠγαπημένῳ. **1.7** ἐν ᾧ   ἔχομεν τὴν ἀπολύτρωσιν
IN   THE   BELOVED ONE;   IN   WHOM   WE HAVE   -   REDEMPTION

διὰ   τοῦ αἵματος αὐτοῦ, τὴν ἄφεσιν τῶν
THROUGH   THE   BLOOD   OF HIM,   THE   FORGIVENESS   -

παραπτωμάτων, κατὰ   τὸ πλοῦτος τῆς χάριτος
OF TRESPASSES,   ACCORDING TO   THE   WEALTH   OF THE   GRACE

αὐτοῦ **1.8** ἧς ἐπερίσσευσεν εἰς ἡμᾶς, ἐν πάσῃ σοφίᾳ
OF HIM,   WHICH   HE LAVISHED   IN(ON)   US,   IN   ALL   WISDOM

καὶ φρονήσει, **1.9** γνωρίσας   ἡμῖν τὸ μυστήριον τοῦ
AND   UNDERSTANDING,   HAVING MADE KNOWN   TO US   THE   MYSTERY   OF THE

Paul, an apostle of Christ Jesus by the will of God,

To the saints who are in Ephesus and are faithful[a] in Christ Jesus:

2 Grace to you and peace from God our Father and the Lord Jesus Christ.

3 Blessed be the God and Father of our Lord Jesus Christ, who has blessed us in Christ with every spiritual blessing in the heavenly places, [4]just as he chose us in Christ[b] before the foundation of the world to be holy and blameless before him in love. [5]He destined us for adoption as his children through Jesus Christ, according to the good pleasure of his will, [6]to the praise of his glorious grace that he freely bestowed on us in the Beloved. [7]In him we have redemption through his blood, the forgiveness of our trespasses, according to the riches of his grace [8]that he lavished on us. With all wisdom and insight [9]he has made known to us the mystery of

[a] Other ancient authorities lack *in Ephesus*, reading *saints who are also faithful*
[b] Gk *in him*

his will, according to his good pleasure that he set forth in Christ, [10]as a plan for the fullness of time, to gather up all things in him, things in heaven and things on earth. [11]In Christ we have also obtained an inheritance,[c] having been destined according to the purpose of him who accomplishes all things according to his counsel and will, [12]so that we, who were the first to set our hope on Christ, might live for the praise of his glory. [13]In him you also, when you had heard the word of truth, the gospel of your salvation, and had believed in him, were marked with the seal of the promised Holy Spirit; [14]this[d] is the pledge of our inheritance toward redemption as God's own people, to the praise of his glory.

15 I have heard of your faith in the Lord Jesus and your love[e] toward all the saints, and for this reason [16]I do not cease to give thanks for you as I remember you in my prayers. [17]I pray that the God of our Lord Jesus Christ, the Father of glory, may give you a spirit of wisdom and revelation as you come to know him, [18]so that, with the eyes of your heart enlightened, you may know what is the hope

[c] Or *been made a heritage*
[d] Other ancient authorities read *who*
[e] Other ancient authorities lack *and your love*

θελήματος αὐτοῦ, κατὰ τὴν εὐδοκίαν αὐτοῦ ἣν
WILL   OF HIM,   ACCORDING TO THE   GOOD PLEASURE OF HIM   WHICH

προέθετο ἐν αὐτῷ **1.10** εἰς οἰκονομίαν τοῦ
HE PURPOSED IN HIM   FOR A STEWARDSHIP   OF(BELONGING TO) THE

πληρώματος τῶν καιρῶν, ἀνακεφαλαιώσασθαι τὰ πάντα
FULLNESS   OF THE TIMES,   TO SUM UP   -   ALL THINGS

ἐν τῷ Χριστῷ, τὰ ἐπὶ τοῖς οὐρανοῖς καὶ τὰ
IN - CHRIST,   THE THINGS ON(IN) THE   HEAVENS   AND THE THINGS

ἐπὶ τῆς γῆς ἐν αὐτῷ. **1.11** ἐν ᾧ καὶ
ON THE EARTH, IN HIM;   IN WHOM ALSO

ἐκληρώθημεν προορισθέντες κατὰ πρόθεσιν
WE WERE MADE AN INHERITANCE, HAVING BEEN PREDESTINED ACCORDING TO [THE] PLAN

τοῦ τὰ πάντα ἐνεργοῦντος κατὰ τὴν βουλὴν τοῦ
OF THE ONE -   WORKING~ALL THINGS   ACCORDING TO THE   COUNSEL   OF THE

θελήματος αὐτοῦ **1.12** εἰς τὸ εἶναι ἡμᾶς εἰς ἔπαινον
WILL   OF HIM,   FOR -   US~TO BE   TO [THE] PRAISE

δόξης αὐτοῦ τοὺς προηλπικότας ἐν τῷ Χριστῷ.
OF [THE] GLORY OF HIM, THE ONES HAVING PREVIOUSLY HOPED IN - CHRIST;

1.13 ἐν ᾧ καὶ ὑμεῖς ἀκούσαντες τὸν λόγον τῆς
IN WHOM ALSO YOU°, HAVING HEARD   THE MESSAGE OF THE

ἀληθείας, τὸ εὐαγγέλιον τῆς σωτηρίας ὑμῶν, ἐν ᾧ
TRUTH,   THE GOOD NEWS   OF THE SALVATION OF YOU°, IN WHOM

καὶ πιστεύσαντες ἐσφραγίσθητε τῷ πνεύματι τῆς
ALSO HAVING BELIEVED   YOU° WERE SEALED WITH [THE] [THE] SPIRIT -

ἐπαγγελίας τῷ ἁγίῳ, **1.14** ὅ ἐστιν ἀρραβὼν τῆς
[THE] OF PROMISE - [THE] HOLY,   WHICH IS   AN EARNEST OF THE

κληρονομίας ἡμῶν, εἰς ἀπολύτρωσιν τῆς
INHERITANCE   OF US, TO(UNTIL) [THE] REDEMPTION OF THE

περιποιήσεως, εἰς ἔπαινον τῆς δόξης αὐτοῦ.
POSSESSION,   TO [THE] PRAISE OF THE GLORY OF HIM.

1.15 Διὰ τοῦτο κἀγὼ ἀκούσας τὴν καθ' ὑμᾶς
THEREFORE I ALSO HAVING HEARD [OF] [THE] [THE] AMONG [THE] YOU°

πίστιν ἐν τῷ κυρίῳ Ἰησοῦ καὶ τὴν ἀγάπην τὴν εἰς
[THE] FAITH IN THE LORD   JESUS AND THE LOVE   -   TO

πάντας τοὺς ἁγίους **1.16** οὐ παύομαι εὐχαριστῶν ὑπὲρ
ALL   THE SAINTS,   DO NOT CEASE   GIVING THANKS   FOR

ὑμῶν μνείαν ποιούμενος ἐπὶ τῶν προσευχῶν μου,
YOU° MAKING~MENTION [OF YOU°] AT(IN) THE PRAYERS   OF ME,

1.17 ἵνα ὁ θεὸς τοῦ κυρίου ἡμῶν Ἰησοῦ Χριστοῦ, ὁ
THAT THE GOD OF THE LORD   OF US JESUS   CHRIST,   THE

πατὴρ τῆς δόξης, δώῃ ὑμῖν πνεῦμα σοφίας καὶ
FATHER - OF GLORY, MAY GIVE TO YOU° A SPIRIT OF WISDOM AND

ἀποκαλύψεως ἐν ἐπιγνώσει αὐτοῦ,
REVELATION   IN   A FULLER KNOWLEDGE OF HIM,

1.18 πεφωτισμένους τοὺς ὀφθαλμοὺς τῆς καρδίας
HAVING BEEN ENLIGHTENED THE   EYES   OF THE HEART

[ὑμῶν] εἰς τὸ εἰδέναι ὑμᾶς τίς ἐστιν ἡ ἐλπὶς τῆς
OF YOU° FOR -   YOU°~TO KNOW WHAT IS   THE HOPE OF THE

κλήσεως αὐτοῦ, τίς ὁ   πλοῦτος τῆς δόξης τῆς
CALLING   OF HIM,   WHAT [IS]THE WEALTH   OF THE GLORY   OF THE

κληρονομίας αὐτοῦ ἐν τοῖς ἁγίοις, **1.19** καὶ τί   τὸ
INHERITANCE   OF HIM IN   THE   SAINTS,   AND WHAT [IS] THE

ὑπερβάλλον μέγεθος τῆς δυνάμεως αὐτοῦ εἰς ἡμᾶς
SURPASSING   GREATNESS OF THE POWER   OF HIM TO US

τοὺς   πιστεύοντας κατὰ   τὴν ἐνέργειαν τοῦ κράτους
THE ONES BELIEVING   ACCORDING TO THE WORKING   OF THE MIGHT

τῆς ἰσχύος αὐτοῦ. **1.20** ἣν   ἐνήργησεν ἐν τῷ Χριστῷ
OF THE STRENGTH OF HIM,   WHICH HE EXERTED IN   -   CHRIST

ἐγείρας αὐτὸν ἐκ νεκρῶν καὶ καθίσας   ἐν
HAVING RAISED HIM FROM [THE] DEAD AND HAVING SEATED [HIM] IN(ON)

δεξιᾷ   αὐτοῦ ἐν τοῖς ἐπουρανίοις **1.21** ὑπεράνω πάσης
[THE] RIGHT OF HIM IN THE HEAVENLIES   FAR ABOVE ALL

ἀρχῆς καὶ ἐξουσίας καὶ δυνάμεως καὶ κυριότητος καὶ
RULE AND AUTHORITY AND POWER   AND LORDSHIP   AND

παντὸς ὀνόματος ὀνομαζομένου, οὐ μόνον ἐν τῷ
EVERY   NAME   BEING NAMED,   NOT ONLY IN -

αἰῶνι τούτῳ ἀλλὰ καὶ ἐν τῷ μέλλοντι· **1.22** καὶ
THIS~AGE   BUT   ALSO IN THE COMING ONE;   AND

πάντα ὑπέταξεν   ὑπὸ τοὺς πόδας αὐτοῦ καὶ
HE SUBORDINATED~ALL THINGS UNDER THE FEET OF HIM AND

αὐτὸν ἔδωκεν κεφαλὴν ὑπὲρ πάντα τῇ   ἐκκλησίᾳ,
GAVE~HIM   [AS] HEAD OVER ALL THINGS TO THE CHURCH,

1.23 ἥτις ἐστὶν τὸ σῶμα αὐτοῦ, τὸ πλήρωμα τοῦ   τὰ
WHICH IS   THE BODY OF HIM, THE FULLNESS   OF THE ONE -

πάντα ἐν πᾶσιν πληρουμένου.
²ALL   ³WITH ⁴ALL   ¹FILLING.

to which he has called you,
what are the riches of his
glorious inheritance among
the saints, [19]and what is the
immeasurable greatness of
his power for us who
believe, according to the
working of his great power.
[20]God[f] put this power to
work in Christ when he
raised him from the dead
and seated him at his right
hand in the heavenly places,
[21]far above all rule and
authority and power and
dominion, and above every
name that is named, not only
in this age but also in the age
to come. [22]And he has put
all things under his feet and
has made him the head over
all things for the church,
[23]which is his body, the
fullness of him who fills all
in all.

f Gk *He*

2.1 Καὶ ὑμᾶς ὄντας νεκροὺς τοῖς παραπτώμασιν καὶ
AND   YOU° BEING DEAD   IN THE TRESPASSES   AND

ταῖς ἁμαρτίαις ὑμῶν, **2.2** ἐν αἷς   ποτε περιεπατήσατε
THE SINS   OF YOU°,   IN WHICH ONCE YOU° WALKED

κατὰ   τὸν αἰῶνα τοῦ κόσμου τούτου, κατὰ   τὸν
ACCORDING TO THE AGE   - OF THIS~WORLD, ACCORDING TO THE

ἄρχοντα τῆς ἐξουσίας τοῦ ἀέρος, τοῦ πνεύματος τοῦ
RULER   OF THE AUTHORITY OF THE AIR, THE SPIRIT   -

νῦν ἐνεργοῦντος ἐν τοῖς υἱοῖς τῆς ἀπειθείας· **2.3** ἐν
NOW WORKING   IN THE SONS -   OF DISOBEDIENCE;   AMONG

οἷς καὶ ἡμεῖς πάντες ἀνεστράφημέν ποτε ἐν ταῖς
WHOM ALSO WE   ALL   CONDUCTED OURSELVES ONCE IN THE

ἐπιθυμίαις τῆς σαρκὸς ἡμῶν ποιοῦντες τὰ θελήματα
LUSTS   OF THE FLESH OF US, PERFORMING THE DESIRES

τῆς σαρκὸς καὶ τῶν διανοιῶν, καὶ ἤμεθα τέκνα φύσει
OF THE FLESH AND OF THE THOUGHTS, AND WE WERE BY NATURE~CHILDREN

You were dead through the
trespasses and sins [2]in which
you once lived, following
the course of this world,
following the ruler of the
power of the air, the spirit
that is now at work among
those who are disobedient.
[3]All of us once lived among
them in the passions of our
flesh, following the desires
of flesh and senses, and we
were by nature children

of wrath, like everyone else. [4]But God, who is rich in mercy, out of the great love with which he loved us [5]even when we were dead through our trespasses, made us alive together with Christ[g]—by grace you have been saved— [6]and raised us up with him and seated us with him in the heavenly places in Christ Jesus, [7]so that in the ages to come he might show the immeasurable riches of his grace in kindness toward us in Christ Jesus. [8]For by grace you have been saved through faith, and this is not your own doing; it is the gift of God— [9]not the result of works, so that no one may boast. [10]For we are what he has made us, created in Christ Jesus for good works, which God prepared beforehand to be our way of life.

11 So then, remember that at one time you Gentiles by birth,[h] called "the uncircumcision" by those who are called "the circumcision"—a physical circumcision made in the flesh by human hands— [12]remember that you were at that time without Christ, being aliens from the commonwealth of Israel, and strangers to the covenants of promise, having no hope and without God in the world. [13]But now in Christ Jesus you who once were far off have been brought near by the blood of Christ.

[g] Other ancient authorities read *in Christ*
[h] Gk *in the flesh*

ὀργῆς ὡς καὶ οἱ λοιποί· **2.4** ὁ δὲ θεὸς πλούσιος ὢν
OF WRATH AS ALSO THE REST; - BUT GOD BEING~RICH

ἐν ἐλέει, διὰ τὴν πολλὴν ἀγάπην αὐτοῦ ἣν
IN MERCY, BECAUSE OF THE GREAT LOVE OF HIM [WITH] WHICH

ἠγάπησεν ἡμᾶς, **2.5** καὶ ὄντας ἡμᾶς νεκροὺς τοῖς
HE LOVED US, EVEN [WHEN] WE~WERE DEAD IN THE

παραπτώμασιν συνεζωοποίησεν τῷ Χριστῷ, — χάριτί
TRESPASSES, HE MADE [US] ALIVE WITH - CHRIST, — BY GRACE

ἐστε σεσῳσμένοι — **2.6** καὶ συνήγειρεν καὶ
YOU° HAVE BEEN SAVED — AND HE RAISED [US] WITH [HIM] AND

συνεκάθισεν ἐν τοῖς ἐπουρανίοις ἐν Χριστῷ Ἰησοῦ,
SEATED US WITH [HIM] IN THE HEAVENLIES IN CHRIST JESUS,

2.7 ἵνα ἐνδείξηται ἐν τοῖς αἰῶσιν τοῖς ἐπερχομένοις τὸ
THAT HE MIGHT DISPLAY IN THE [2]AGES - [1]COMING THE

ὑπερβάλλον πλοῦτος τῆς χάριτος αὐτοῦ ἐν χρηστότητι
SURPASSING WEALTH OF THE GRACE OF HIM IN [HIS] KINDNESS

ἐφ' ἡμᾶς ἐν Χριστῷ Ἰησοῦ. **2.8** τῇ γὰρ χάριτί
TOWARDS US IN CHRIST JESUS. - FOR BY GRACE

ἐστε σεσῳσμένοι διὰ πίστεως· καὶ τοῦτο οὐκ ἐξ
YOU° HAVE BEEN SAVED THROUGH FAITH; AND THIS NOT OF

ὑμῶν, θεοῦ τὸ δῶρον· **2.9** οὐκ ἐξ ἔργων, ἵνα μὴ
YOUR[SELVES], [IT IS] GOD'S - GIFT; NOT OF WORKS, LEST

τις καυχήσηται. **2.10** αὐτοῦ γάρ ἐσμεν ποίημα,
ANYONE SHOULD BOAST. [3]HIS [1]FOR [2]WE ARE [4]MASTERPIECE,

κτισθέντες ἐν Χριστῷ Ἰησοῦ ἐπὶ ἔργοις ἀγαθοῖς
HAVING BEEN CREATED IN CHRIST JESUS FOR GOOD~WORKS

οἷς προητοίμασεν ὁ θεός, ἵνα ἐν αὐτοῖς
WHICH [2]PREVIOUSLY PREPARED - [1]GOD, THAT IN THEM

περιπατήσωμεν.
WE SHOULD WALK.

2.11 Διὸ μνημονεύετε ὅτι ποτὲ ὑμεῖς τὰ ἔθνη
THEREFORE REMEMBER THAT ONCE YOU°, THE GENTILES

ἐν σαρκί, οἱ λεγόμενοι ἀκροβυστία ὑπὸ τῆς
IN [THE] FLESH, THE ONES BEING CALLED UNCIRCUMCISION BY THE

λεγομένης περιτομῆς ἐν σαρκὶ χειροποιήτου, **2.12** ὅτι
[ONES] BEING CALLED CIRCUMCISION [2]IN [3][THE] FLESH [1][DONE] BY HAND, THAT

ἦτε τῷ καιρῷ ἐκείνῳ χωρὶς Χριστοῦ,
YOU° WERE - AT THAT~TIME WITHOUT CHRIST,

ἀπηλλοτριωμένοι τῆς πολιτείας τοῦ Ἰσραὴλ καὶ
HAVING BEEN ALIENATED FROM THE CITIZENSHIP - OF ISRAEL AND

ξένοι τῶν διαθηκῶν τῆς ἐπαγγελίας, ἐλπίδα μὴ
STRANGERS OF THE COVENANTS OF THE PROMISE, [3]HOPE [1]NOT

ἔχοντες καὶ ἄθεοι ἐν τῷ κόσμῳ. **2.13** νυνὶ δὲ ἐν
[2]HAVING AND WITHOUT GOD IN THE WORLD. BUT~NOW IN

Χριστῷ Ἰησοῦ ὑμεῖς οἱ ποτε ὄντες μακρὰν
CHRIST JESUS YOU°, THE ONES ONCE BEING FAR OFF

ἐγενήθητε ἐγγὺς ἐν τῷ αἵματι τοῦ Χριστοῦ.
HAVE BEEN BROUGHT NEAR BY THE BLOOD - OF CHRIST.

2.14 Αὐτὸς γάρ ἐστιν ἡ εἰρήνη ἡμῶν, ὁ ποιήσας
FOR~HE　　IS　　THE PEACE　OF US,　THE ONE　HAVING MADE

τὰ ἀμφότερα ἓν καὶ τὸ μεσότοιχον τοῦ φραγμοῦ
THE TWO　　ONE AND　²THE ³MIDDLE WALL　　⁴OF THE ⁵PARTITION

λύσας, τὴν ἔχθραν ἐν τῇ σαρκὶ αὐτοῦ, **2.15** τὸν
¹HAVING BROKEN,　THE HOSTILITY　IN　THE FLESH　OF HIM,　　THE

νόμον τῶν ἐντολῶν ἐν δόγμασιν καταργήσας, ἵνα
LAW　OF THE COMMANDMENTS IN　ORDINANCES　HAVING ANNULED,　THAT

τοὺς δύο κτίσῃ ἐν αὐτῷ εἰς ἕνα καινὸν ἄνθρωπον
²THE　³TWO ¹HE MIGHT CREATE IN　HIMSELF INTO ONE　NEW　MAN,

ποιῶν εἰρήνην **2.16** καὶ ἀποκαταλλάξῃ τοὺς ἀμφοτέρους
MAKING PEACE,　　AND　HE MIGHT RECONCILE　THE　TWO

ἐν ἑνὶ σώματι τῷ θεῷ διὰ τοῦ σταυροῦ,
IN　ONE　BODY　-　TO GOD THROUGH　THE　CROSS,

ἀποκτείνας τὴν ἔχθραν ἐν αὐτῷ. **2.17** καὶ ἐλθὼν
HAVING KILLED　THE　HOSTILITY　BY IT.　　AND　HAVING COME

εὐηγγελίσατο εἰρήνην ὑμῖν τοῖς μακρὰν καὶ εἰρήνην
HE PREACHED　　PEACE　TO YOU°, THE ONES FAR OFF,　AND　PEACE

τοῖς ἐγγύς· **2.18** ὅτι δι' αὐτοῦ ἔχομεν τὴν
TO THE ONES NEAR;　　BECAUSE THROUGH HIM　¹WE ³HAVE　⁴THE

προσαγωγὴν οἱ ἀμφότεροι ἐν ἑνὶ πνεύματι πρὸς τὸν
⁵ACCESS　　-　²BOTH　　IN(BY) ONE　SPIRIT　TO　THE

πατέρα. **2.19** ἄρα οὖν οὐκέτι ἐστὲ ξένοι καὶ
FATHER.　　THEREFORE~THEN NO LONGER ARE YOU° STRANGERS AND

πάροικοι ἀλλὰ ἐστὲ συμπολῖται τῶν ἁγίων καὶ
ALIENS　　BUT　YOU° ARE FELLOW CITIZENS　OF THE SAINTS　AND

οἰκεῖοι τοῦ θεοῦ, **2.20** ἐποικοδομηθέντες ἐπὶ
MEMBERS OF [THE] HOUSEHOLD　-　OF GOD,　HAVING BEEN BUILT　UPON

τῷ θεμελίῳ τῶν ἀποστόλων καὶ προφητῶν, ὄντος
THE　FOUNDATION OF THE APOSTLES　AND　PROPHETS,　⁴BEING

ἀκρογωνιαίου αὐτοῦ Χριστοῦ Ἰησοῦ, **2.21** ἐν ᾧ πᾶσα
⁵[THE] CORNERSTONE　³HIM[SELF] ¹CHRIST　²JESUS,　IN　WHOM ALL

οἰκοδομὴ συναρμολογουμένη αὔξει εἰς ναὸν ἅγιον ἐν
[THE] BUILDING BEING FITLY JOINED TOGETHER　GROWS INTO A HOLY~SANCTUARY IN

κυρίῳ, **2.22** ἐν ᾧ καὶ ὑμεῖς συνοικοδομεῖσθε εἰς
[THE] LORD,　IN　WHOM ALSO　YOU°　ARE BEING BUILT TOGETHER　INTO

κατοικητήριον τοῦ θεοῦ ἐν πνεύματι.
A DWELLING PLACE　-　OF GOD IN　SPIRIT.

14For he is our peace; in his flesh he has made both groups into one and has broken down the dividing wall, that is, the hostility between us. 15He has abolished the law with its commandments and ordinances, that he might create in himself one new humanity in place of the two, thus making peace, 16and might reconcile both groups to God in one body[i] through the cross, thus putting to death that hostility through it.[j] 17So he came and proclaimed peace to you who were far off and peace to those who were near; 18for through him both of us have access in one Spirit to the Father. 19So then you are no longer strangers and aliens, but you are citizens with the saints and also members of the household of God, 20built upon the foundation of the apostles and prophets, with Christ Jesus himself as the cornerstone.[k] 21In him the whole structure is joined together and grows into a holy temple in the Lord; 22in whom you also are built together spiritually[l] into a dwelling place for God.

[i] Or reconcile both of us in one body for God
[j] Or in him, or in himself
[k] Or keystone
[l] Gk in the Spirit

3.1 Τούτου χάριν ἐγὼ Παῦλος ὁ δέσμιος τοῦ Χριστοῦ
FOR THIS CAUSE　I　PAUL　THE PRISONER　-　OF CHRIST

[Ἰησοῦ] ὑπὲρ ὑμῶν τῶν ἐθνῶν — **3.2** εἴ γε ἠκούσατε
JESUS　FOR　YOU°　-　GENTILES —　IF INDEED YOU° HEARD [OF]

τὴν οἰκονομίαν τῆς χάριτος τοῦ θεοῦ τῆς δοθείσης
THE　STEWARDSHIP　OF THE GRACE　-　OF GOD -　HAVING BEEN GIVEN

This is the reason that I Paul am a prisoner for[m] Christ Jesus for the sake of you Gentiles— 2for surely you have already heard of the commission of God's grace that was given

[m] Or of

me for you, [3]and how the mystery was made known to me by revelation, as I wrote above in a few words, [4]a reading of which will enable you to perceive my understanding of the mystery of Christ. [5]In former generations this mystery[n] was not made known to humankind, as it has now been revealed to his holy apostles and prophets by the Spirit: [6]that is, the Gentiles have become fellow heirs, members of the same body, and sharers in the promise in Christ Jesus through the gospel.

[7] Of this gospel I have become a servant according to the gift of God's grace that was given me by the working of his power. [8]Although I am the very least of all the saints, this grace was given to me to bring to the Gentiles the news of the boundless riches of Christ, [9]and to make everyone see[o] what is the plan of the mystery hidden for ages in[p] God who created all things; [10]so that through the church the wisdom of God in its rich variety might now be made known to the rulers and authorities in the heavenly places. [11]This was in accordance with the eternal purpose that he has carried out in Christ Jesus our Lord, [12]in whom we have access to God in boldness and confidence through faith in him.[q]

[n] Gk it
[o] Other ancient authorities read *to bring to light*
[p] Or *by*
[q] Or *the faith of him*

μοι εἰς ὑμᾶς, **3.3** [ὅτι] κατὰ   ἀποκάλυψιν ἐγνωρίσθη
TO ME FOR YOU°,   THAT ACCORDING TO REVELATION   [3]WAS MADE KNOWN

μοι τὸ μυστήριον, καθὼς προέγραψα ἐν ὀλίγῳ, **3.4** πρὸς
[4]TO ME [1]THE [2]MYSTERY,   AS I WROTE BEFORE IN BRIEF,   AS TO

ὃ   δύνασθε ἀναγινώσκοντες νοῆσαι   τὴν σύνεσίν
WHICH [2]YOU° ARE ABLE [1][BY] READING   TO UNDERSTAND THE INSIGHT

μου ἐν τῷ μυστηρίῳ τοῦ Χριστοῦ, **3.5** ὃ   ἑτέραις
OF ME IN THE MYSTERY   - OF CHRIST,   WHICH IN OTHER

γενεαῖς οὐκ ἐγνωρίσθη τοῖς υἱοῖς τῶν ἀνθρώπων ὡς
GENERATIONS WAS NOT MADE KNOWN TO THE SONS - OF MEN   AS

νῦν ἀπεκαλύφθη τοῖς ἁγίοις ἀποστόλοις αὐτοῦ καὶ
NOW IT WAS(IS) REVEALED TO THE HOLY APOSTLES OF HIM AND

προφήταις ἐν   πνεύματι, **3.6** εἶναι   τὰ ἔθνη
PROPHETS IN(BY) [THE] SPIRIT,   [THAT] [3][ARE] TO BE [1]THE [2]GENTILES

συγκληρονόμα καὶ σύσσωμα καὶ συμμέτοχα τῆς
JOINT-HEIRS   AND A JOINT-BODY AND JOINT-PARTAKERS OF THE

ἐπαγγελίας ἐν Χριστῷ Ἰησοῦ διὰ   τοῦ εὐαγγελίου,
PROMISE   IN CHRIST JESUS THROUGH THE GOOD NEWS,

3.7 οὗ   ἐγενήθην διάκονος κατὰ   τὴν δωρεὰν τῆς
OF WHICH I BECAME A MINISTER ACCORDING TO THE GIFT OF THE

χάριτος τοῦ θεοῦ τῆς δοθείσης   μοι κατὰ   τὴν
GRACE   - OF GOD - HAVING BEEN GIVEN TO ME ACCORDING TO THE

ἐνέργειαν τῆς δυνάμεως αὐτοῦ. **3.8** ἐμοὶ τῷ
WORKING   OF THE POWER OF HIM.   TO ME THE

ἐλαχιστοτέρῳ πάντων ἁγίων ἐδόθη ἡ χάρις αὕτη, τοῖς
LESS THAN THE LEAST OF ALL SAINTS WAS GIVEN - THIS~GRACE,   [2]TO THE

ἔθνεσιν εὐαγγελίσασθαι τὸ ἀνεξιχνίαστον πλοῦτος τοῦ
[3]GENTILES [1]TO PREACH   THE UNSEARCHABLE   WEALTH -

Χριστοῦ **3.9** καὶ ⌐φωτίσαι [πάντας]⌐ τίς   ἡ
OF CHRIST   AND TO ENLIGHTEN ALL MEN   [AS TO] WHAT [IS] THE

οἰκονομία τοῦ μυστηρίου τοῦ ἀποκεκρυμμένου ἀπὸ τῶν
STEWARDSHIP OF THE MYSTERY - HAVING BEEN HIDDEN FROM THE

αἰώνων ἐν τῷ θεῷ τῷ τὰ πάντα κτίσαντι, **3.10** ἵνα
AGES IN - GOD, THE ONE - HAVING CREATED~ALL THINGS,   THAT

γνωρισθῇ νῦν ταῖς ἀρχαῖς καὶ ταῖς ἐξουσίαις
MIGHT BE MADE KNOWN NOW TO THE RULERS AND THE AUTHORITIES

ἐν τοῖς ἐπουρανίοις διὰ   τῆς ἐκκλησίας ἡ
IN THE HEAVENLIES THROUGH THE CHURCH   THE

πολυποίκιλος σοφία τοῦ θεοῦ, **3.11** κατὰ   πρόθεσιν
MANY-FACETED WISDOM - OF GOD,   ACCORDING TO [THE] PLAN

τῶν αἰώνων ἣν ἐποίησεν ἐν τῷ Χριστῷ Ἰησοῦ τῷ
OF THE AGES WHICH HE MADE IN - CHRIST JESUS THE

κυρίῳ ἡμῶν, **3.12** ἐν ᾧ ἔχομεν τὴν παρρησίαν καὶ
LORD OF US,   IN WHOM WE HAVE - BOLDNESS AND

προσαγωγὴν ἐν πεποιθήσει διὰ   τῆς πίστεως αὐτοῦ.
ACCESS   IN CONFIDENCE THROUGH THE FAITH OF(IN) HIM.

3:9 text: KJV ASV RSV NIV TEV NRSV. var. φωτισαι (to bring to light): ASVmg NASB NEB NJB.

3.13 διὸ   αἰτοῦμαι μὴ ἐγκακεῖν ἐν   ταῖς
THEREFORE I ASK [YOU°] NOT TO DESPAIR AT(CONCERNING) THE

θλίψεσίν μου ὑπὲρ ὑμῶν, ἥτις ἐστὶν δόξα ὑμῶν.
AFFLICTIONS OF ME FOR YOU°, WHICH IS [FOR] YOUR°~GLORY.

3.14 Τούτου χάριν κάμπτω τὰ γόνατά μου πρὸς τὸν
FOR THIS CAUSE I BEND THE KNEES OF ME TO THE

πατέρα, **3.15** ἐξ   οὗ πᾶσα πατριὰ ἐν οὐρανοῖς καὶ
FATHER,   FROM WHOM EVERY FAMILY IN [THE] HEAVENS AND

ἐπὶ γῆς ὀνομάζεται, **3.16** ἵνα δῷ   ὑμῖν κατὰ
ON EARTH IS NAMED,   THAT HE MAY GRANT YOU° ACCORDING TO

τὸ πλοῦτος τῆς δόξης αὐτοῦ δυνάμει κραταιωθῆναι
THE WEALTH   OF THE GLORY OF HIM TO BECOME MIGHTILY EMPOWERED

διὰ   τοῦ πνεύματος αὐτοῦ εἰς τὸν ἔσω ἄνθρωπον,
THROUGH THE SPIRIT   OF HIM IN THE INNER MAN,

3.17 κατοικῆσαι   τὸν Χριστὸν διὰ   τῆς πίστεως ἐν
[FOR] ²TO MAKE [HIS] HOME   ¹CHRIST THROUGH -   FAITH IN

ταῖς καρδίαις ὑμῶν, ἐν ἀγάπη ἐρριζωμένοι καὶ
THE HEARTS   OF YOU°, IN LOVE HAVING BEEN ROOTED AND

τεθεμελιωμένοι,   **3.18** ἵνα   ἐξισχύσητε
HAVING BEEN FOUNDED,   THAT YOU° MIGHT BE EXTRA-STRONG

καταλαβέσθαι σὺν   πᾶσιν τοῖς ἁγίοις τί τὸ
TO GRASP   TOGETHER WITH ALL THE SAINTS WHAT [IS] THE

πλάτος καὶ μῆκος καὶ ὕψος καὶ βάθος,
BREADTH AND LENGTH AND HEIGHT AND DEPTH [OF HIS LOVE],

3.19 γνῶναί τε τὴν ὑπερβάλλουσαν τῆς γνώσεως ἀγάπην
AND~TO KNOW ¹THE ⁴SURPASSING   - ⁵KNOWLEDGE ²LOVE

τοῦ Χριστοῦ, ἵνα πληρωθῆτε εἰς πᾶν τὸ πλήρωμα τοῦ
- ³OF CHRIST, THAT YOU° MAY BE FILLED TO ALL THE FULLNESS -

θεοῦ.
OF GOD.

3.20 Τῷ δὲ   δυναμένῳ ὑπὲρ πάντα ποιῆσαι
NOW~TO THE ONE BEING ABLE BEYOND ALL THINGS TO DO

ὑπερεκπερισσοῦ ὧν   αἰτούμεθα ἢ νοοῦμεν
SUPERABUNDANTLY [ABOVE] [THE THINGS] WHICH WE ASK OR THINK

κατὰ   τὴν δύναμιν τὴν ἐνεργουμένην ἐν ἡμῖν,
ACCORDING TO THE POWER - WORKING IN US,

3.21 αὐτῷ ἡ   δόξα ἐν τῇ ἐκκλησίᾳ καὶ ἐν Χριστῷ
TO HIM [BE] THE GLORY IN THE CHURCH AND IN CHRIST

Ἰησοῦ εἰς πάσας τὰς γενεὰς τοῦ αἰῶνος τῶν αἰώνων,
JESUS TO ALL THE GENERATIONS OF THE AGE OF THE AGES,

ἀμήν.
AMEN.

[13]I pray therefore that you[r] may not lose heart over my sufferings for you; they are your glory.

14 For this reason I bow my knees before the Father,[s] [15]from whom every family[t] in heaven and on earth takes its name. [16]I pray that, according to the riches of his glory, he may grant that you may be strengthened in your inner being with power through his Spirit, [17]and that Christ may dwell in your hearts through faith, as you are being rooted and grounded in love. [18]I pray that you may have the power to comprehend, with all the saints, what is the breadth and length and height and depth, [19]and to know the love of Christ that surpasses knowledge, so that you may be filled with all the fullness of God.

20 Now to him who by the power at work within us is able to accomplish abundantly far more than all we can ask or imagine, [21]to him be glory in the church and in Christ Jesus to all generations, forever and ever. Amen.

[r] Or I
[s] Other ancient authorities add of our Lord Jesus Christ
[t] Gk fatherhood

CHAPTER 4

I therefore, the prisoner in the Lord, beg you to lead a life worthy of the calling to which you have been called, ²with all humility and gentleness, with patience, bearing with one another in love, ³making every effort to maintain the unity of the Spirit in the bond of peace. ⁴There is one body and one Spirit, just as you were called to the one hope of your calling, ⁵one Lord, one faith, one baptism, ⁶one God and Father of all, who is above all and through all and in all.

7 But each of us was given grace according to the measure of Christ's gift. ⁸Therefore it is said,

"When he ascended on high he made captivity itself a captive;

he gave gifts to his people."

⁹(When it says, "He ascended," what does it mean but that he had also descended[u] into the lower parts of the earth? ¹⁰He who descended is the same one who ascended far above all the heavens, so that he might fill all things.) ¹¹The gifts he gave were that some would be apostles, some prophets, some evangelists, some pastors and teachers, ¹²to equip the saints for

[u] Other ancient authorities add first

4.1 Παρακαλῶ οὖν ὑμᾶς ἐγὼ ὁ δέσμιος ἐν κυρίῳ
THEREFORE~I ENCOURAGE YOU°, I THE PRISONER IN [THE] LORD,

ἀξίως περιπατῆσαι τῆς κλήσεως ἧς ἐκλήθητε,
TO WALK~WORTHY OF THE CALLING BY WHICH YOU° WERE CALLED,

4.2 μετὰ πάσης ταπεινοφροσύνης καὶ πραΰτητος, μετὰ
WITH ALL HUMILITY OF MIND AND MEEKNESS, WITH

μακροθυμίας, ἀνεχόμενοι ἀλλήλων ἐν ἀγάπῃ,
LONGSUFFERING, FORBEARING ONE ANOTHER IN LOVE,

4.3 σπουδάζοντες τηρεῖν τὴν ἑνότητα τοῦ πνεύματος ἐν
BEING EAGER TO KEEP THE ONENESS OF THE SPIRIT IN

τῷ συνδέσμῳ τῆς εἰρήνης· **4.4** ἓν σῶμα καὶ ἓν
THE UNITING BOND - OF PEACE; [AS THERE IS] ONE BODY AND ONE

πνεῦμα, καθὼς καὶ ἐκλήθητε ἐν μιᾷ ἐλπίδι τῆς
SPIRIT, AS ALSO YOU° WERE CALLED IN(WITH) ONE HOPE OF THE

κλήσεως ὑμῶν· **4.5** εἷς κύριος, μία πίστις, ἓν
CALLING OF YOU°; ONE LORD, ONE FAITH, ONE

βάπτισμα, **4.6** εἷς θεὸς καὶ πατὴρ πάντων, ὁ ἐπὶ
BAPTISM, ONE GOD AND FATHER OF ALL, THE ONE OVER

πάντων καὶ διὰ πάντων καὶ ἐν πᾶσιν.
ALL AND THROUGH ALL AND IN ALL.

4.7 Ἑνὶ δὲ ἑκάστῳ ἡμῶν ἐδόθη ἡ χάρις κατὰ τὸ
³ONE ¹BUT ²TO EACH ⁴OF US WAS GIVEN - GRACE ACCORDING TO THE

μέτρον τῆς δωρεᾶς τοῦ Χριστοῦ. **4.8** διὸ λέγει,
MEASURE OF THE GIFT - OF CHRIST. WHEREFORE IT SAYS,

Ἀναβὰς εἰς ὕψος ᾐχμαλώτευσεν
HAVING ASCENDED TO [THE] HEIGHT HE LED CAPTIVE

αἰχμαλωσίαν,
CAPTIVITY,

ἔδωκεν δόματα τοῖς ἀνθρώποις.
HE GAVE GIFTS - TO MEN.

4.9 τὸ δὲ Ἀνέβη τί ἐστιν, εἰ μὴ ὅτι καὶ
NOW~[AS TO] THE "HE ASCENDED" WHAT IS [IT] EXCEPT THAT ALSO

κατέβη εἰς τὰ κατώτερα [μέρη] τῆς γῆς; **4.10** ὁ
HE DESCENDED INTO THE LOWER PARTS OF THE EARTH? THE ONE

καταβὰς αὐτός ἐστιν καὶ ὁ ἀναβὰς ὑπεράνω
HAVING DESCENDED IS~HIMSELF ALSO THE ONE HAVING ASCENDED FAR ABOVE

πάντων τῶν οὐρανῶν, ἵνα πληρώσῃ τὰ πάντα. **4.11** καὶ
ALL THE HEAVENS, THAT HE MIGHT FILL - ALL THINGS. AND

αὐτὸς ἔδωκεν τοὺς μὲν ἀποστόλους, τοὺς δὲ προφήτας,
HE GAVE SOME - APOSTLES, AND~SOME PROPHETS,

τοὺς δὲ εὐαγγελιστάς, τοὺς δὲ ποιμένας καὶ
AND~SOME EVANGELISTS, AND~SOME SHEPHERDS AND

διδασκάλους, **4.12** πρὸς τὸν καταρτισμὸν τῶν ἁγίων εἰς
TEACHERS, FOR THE EQUIPPING OF THE SAINTS TO

4:8 Ps. 68:18

ἔργον διακονίας, εἰς οἰκοδομὴν τοῦ σώματος τοῦ
[THE] WORK OF MINISTRY, TO [THE] BUILDING UP OF THE BODY -

Χριστοῦ, **4.13** μέχρι καταντήσωμεν οἱ πάντες εἰς τὴν
OF CHRIST, UNTIL ¹WE ³ARRIVE - ²ALL ⁴AT THE

ἑνότητα τῆς πίστεως καὶ τῆς ἐπιγνώσεως τοῦ υἱοῦ
UNITY OF THE FAITH AND [AT] THE FULLER KNOWLEDGE OF THE SON

τοῦ θεοῦ, εἰς ἄνδρα τέλειον, εἰς μέτρον
- OF GOD, AT A MAN OF COMPLETE MATURITY, AT [THE] MEASURE

ἡλικίας τοῦ πληρώματος τοῦ Χριστοῦ, **4.14** ἵνα
OF [THE] STATURE OF THE FULLNESS - OF CHRIST, THAT

μηκέτι ὦμεν νήπιοι, κλυδωνιζόμενοι καὶ
NO LONGER WE SHOULD BE INFANTS, TOSSED BY WAVES AND

περιφερόμενοι παντὶ ἀνέμῳ τῆς διδασκαλίας ἐν τῇ
CARRIED AROUND BY EVERY WIND - OF TEACHING, BY THE

κυβείᾳ τῶν ἀνθρώπων, ἐν πανουργίᾳ πρὸς τὴν
CUNNING - OF MEN, WITH CRAFTINESS [LEADING] TO THE

μεθοδείαν τῆς πλάνης, **4.15** ἀληθεύοντες δὲ ἐν ἀγάπῃ
SCHEMING - OF DECEPTION, BUT~HOLDING TO TRUTH IN LOVE

αὐξήσωμεν εἰς αὐτὸν τὰ πάντα, ὅς ἐστιν ἡ κεφαλή,
LET US GROW UP INTO HIM [IN] ALL THINGS, WHO IS THE HEAD,

Χριστός, **4.16** ἐξ οὗ πᾶν τὸ σῶμα
CHRIST, OUT FROM WHOM ALL THE BODY

συναρμολογούμενον καὶ συμβιβαζόμενον διὰ πάσης
BEING FITLY JOINED TOGETHER AND BEING UNITED THROUGH EVERY

ἁφῆς τῆς ἐπιχορηγίας κατ᾽ ἐνέργειαν ἐν μέτρῳ
JOINT OF THE SUPPLY, ACCORDING TO [THE] WORKING IN [THE] MEASURE

ἑνὸς ἑκάστου μέρους τὴν αὔξησιν τοῦ σώματος
OF EACH~SINGLE PART ²THE ³GROWTH ⁴OF THE ⁵BODY

ποιεῖται εἰς οἰκοδομὴν ἑαυτοῦ ἐν ἀγάπῃ.
¹MAKES UNTO [THE] BUILDING UP OF ITSELF IN LOVE.

4.17 Τοῦτο οὖν λέγω καὶ μαρτύρομαι ἐν κυρίῳ,
THIS THEREFORE I SAY AND TESTIFY IN [THE] LORD,

μηκέτι ὑμᾶς περιπατεῖν, καθὼς καὶ τὰ ἔθνη
NO LONGER [ARE] YOU° TO WALK(LIVE) AS ALSO THE GENTILES

περιπατεῖ ἐν ματαιότητι τοῦ νοὸς αὐτῶν,
WALK(LIVE) IN [THE] FUTILITY OF THE MINDS OF THEM,

4.18 ἐσκοτωμένοι τῇ διανοίᾳ ὄντες,
²DARKENED ³IN THE[IR] ⁴UNDERSTANDING ¹BEING,

ἀπηλλοτριωμένοι τῆς ζωῆς τοῦ θεοῦ διὰ τὴν
HAVING BEEN ALIENATED FROM THE LIFE OF GOD BECAUSE OF THE

ἄγνοιαν τὴν οὖσαν ἐν αὐτοῖς, διὰ τὴν πώρωσιν
IGNORANCE - EXISTING IN THEM, BECAUSE OF THE HARDNESS

τῆς καρδίας αὐτῶν, **4.19** οἵτινες ἀπηλγηκότες
OF THE HEARTS OF THEM, WHO HAVING PUT AWAY REMORSE

ἑαυτοὺς παρέδωκαν τῇ ἀσελγείᾳ εἰς ἐργασίαν
GAVE~THEMSELVES - TO LEWDNESS FOR [THE] PRACTISE

ἀκαθαρσίας πάσης ἐν πλεονεξίᾳ. **4.20** ὑμεῖς δὲ
OF EVERY [KIND OF]~IMPURITY WITH GREEDINESS. BUT~YOU°

the work of ministry, for building up the body of Christ, [13]until all of us come to the unity of the faith and of the knowledge of the Son of God, to maturity, to the measure of the full stature of Christ. [14]We must no longer be children, tossed to and fro and blown about by every wind of doctrine, by people's trickery, by their craftiness in deceitful scheming. [15]But speaking the truth in love, we must grow up in every way into him who is the head, into Christ, [16]from whom the whole body, joined and knit together by every ligament with which it is equipped, as each part is working properly, promotes the body's growth in building itself up in love.

17 Now this I affirm and insist on in the Lord: you must no longer live as the Gentiles live, in the futility of their minds. [18]They are darkened in their understanding, alienated from the life of God because of their ignorance and hardness of heart. [19]They have lost all sensitivity and have abandoned themselves to licentiousness, greedy to practice every kind of impurity. [20]That is not

the way you learned Christ! [21]For surely you have heard about him and were taught in him, as truth is in Jesus. [22]You were taught to put away your former way of life, your old self, corrupt and deluded by its lusts, [23]and to be renewed in the spirit of your minds, [24]and to clothe yourselves with the new self, created according to the likeness of God in true righteousness and holiness.

25 So then, putting away falsehood, let all of us speak the truth to our neighbors, for we are members of one another. [26]Be angry but do not sin; do not let the sun go down on your anger, [27]and do not make room for the devil. [28]Thieves must give up stealing; rather let them labor and work honestly with their own hands, so as to have something to share with the needy. [29]Let no evil talk come out of your mouths, but only what is useful for building up,[v] as there is need, so that your words may give grace to those who hear. [30]And do not grieve the Holy Spirit of God, with which you were marked with a seal for the day of redemption. [31]Put away from you all bitterness and wrath and anger

[v] Other ancient authorities read *building up faith*

οὐχ οὕτως ἐμάθετε τὸν Χριστόν, **4.21** εἴ γε
DID NOT SO LEARN — CHRIST, IF INDEED

αὐτὸν ἠκούσατε καὶ ἐν αὐτῷ ἐδιδάχθητε, καθώς
YOU° HEARD~HIM AND [2]IN [3]HIM [1]WERE TAUGHT AS

ἐστιν ἀλήθεια ἐν τῷ Ἰησοῦ, **4.22** ἀποθέσθαι ὑμᾶς
TRUTH~IS IN — JESUS, [FOR] YOU°~TO PUT OFF

κατὰ τὴν προτέραν ἀναστροφὴν τὸν παλαιὸν
AS CONCERNING THE (YOUR°) FORMER MANNER OF LIFE THE OLD

ἄνθρωπον τὸν φθειρόμενον κατὰ τὰς ἐπιθυμίας
MAN, THE ONE BEING CORRUPTED ACCORDING TO THE LUSTS

τῆς ἀπάτης, **4.23** ἀνανεοῦσθαι δὲ τῷ πνεύματι
— OF DECEIT, AND~TO BE RENEWED BY THE SPIRIT

τοῦ νοὸς ὑμῶν **4.24** καὶ ἐνδύσασθαι τὸν καινὸν
[CONTROLING] THE MIND OF YOU°, AND TO PUT ON THE NEW

ἄνθρωπον τὸν κατὰ θεὸν κτισθέντα ἐν
MAN, THE ONE [2]ACCORDING TO [3]GOD [1]HAVING BEEN CREATED IN

δικαιοσύνῃ καὶ ὁσιότητι τῆς ἀληθείας.
RIGHTEOUSNESS AND SANCTITY OF THE TRUTH.

4.25 Διὸ ἀποθέμενοι τὸ ψεῦδος λαλεῖτε ἀλήθειαν
WHEREFORE HAVING PUT OFF — FALSEHOOD LET US SPEAK TRUTH

ἕκαστος μετὰ τοῦ πλησίον αὐτοῦ, ὅτι ἐσμὲν
EACH ONE WITH THE NEIGHBOR OF HIM, BECAUSE WE ARE

ἀλλήλων μέλη. **4.26** ὀργίζεσθε καὶ μὴ ἁμαρτάνετε·
MEMBERS~ONE OF ANOTHER. BE ANGRY AND DO NOT SIN;

ὁ ἥλιος μὴ ἐπιδυέτω ἐπὶ [τῷ] παροργισμῷ ὑμῶν,
[3]THE [4]SUN [2]NOT [1]LET [5]SET ON THE ANGER OF YOU°,

4.27 μηδὲ δίδοτε τόπον τῷ διαβόλῳ. **4.28** ὁ
NEITHER GIVE PLACE TO THE DEVIL. THE ONE

κλέπτων μηκέτι κλεπτέτω, μᾶλλον δὲ κοπιάτω
STEALING NO LONGER LET HIM STEAL, BUT~RATHER LET HIM LABOR

ἐργαζόμενος ταῖς [ἰδίαις] χερσὶν τὸ ἀγαθόν, ἵνα
WORKING WITH HIS OWN HANDS [AT] SOMETHING GOOD, THAT

ἔχῃ μεταδιδόναι τῷ χρείαν ἔχοντι.
HE MAY HAVE [SOMETHING] TO SHARE WITH THE ONE HAVING~NEED.

4.29 πᾶς λόγος σαπρὸς ἐκ τοῦ στόματος ὑμῶν
EVERY (ANY) CORRUPT~WORD FROM THE MOUTH OF YOU°

μὴ ἐκπορευέσθω, ἀλλὰ εἴ τις ἀγαθὸς πρὸς
SHOULD NOT PROCEED, BUT IF ANY GOOD [WORD] [LET IT BE] FOR

οἰκοδομὴν τῆς χρείας, ἵνα δῷ χάριν
EDIFICATION [IN ACCORDANCE WITH] THE NEED, THAT IT MAY GIVE GRACE

τοῖς ἀκούουσιν. **4.30** καὶ μὴ λυπεῖτε τὸ πνεῦμα τὸ
TO THE ONES HEARING. AND DO NOT GRIEVE . THE [2]SPIRIT —

ἅγιον τοῦ θεοῦ, ἐν ᾧ ἐσφραγίσθητε εἰς ἡμέραν
[1]HOLY — OF GOD, BY WHOM YOU° WERE SEALED FOR [THE] DAY

ἀπολυτρώσεως. **4.31** πᾶσα πικρία καὶ θυμὸς καὶ ὀργὴ
OF REDEMPTION. [LET] ALL BITTERNESS AND ANGER AND WRATH

4:25 Zech. 8:16   **4:26** Ps. 4:4 LXX

καὶ κραυγὴ καὶ βλασφημία ἀρθήτω ἀφ᾽ ὑμῶν σὺν
AND CLAMOR AND SLANDER BE REMOVED FROM YOU° WITH

πάσῃ κακίᾳ. **4.32** γίνεσθε [δὲ] εἰς ἀλλήλους χρηστοί,
ALL EVIL. AND~BE ²TO ³ONE ANOTHER ¹KIND,

εὔσπλαγχνοι, χαριζόμενοι ἑαυτοῖς, καθὼς καὶ ὁ θεὸς
TENDERHEARTED, FORGIVING EACH OTHER, AS ALSO - GOD

ἐν Χριστῷ ἐχαρίσατο ὑμῖν.
IN(BY) CHRIST FORGAVE YOU°.

and wrangling and slander, together with all malice, ³²and be kind to one another, tenderhearted, forgiving one another, as God in Christ has forgiven you.ʷ

ʷ Other ancient authorities read *us*

5.1 γίνεσθε οὖν μιμηταὶ τοῦ θεοῦ ὡς τέκνα ἀγαπητὰ
BE THEREFORE IMITATORS - OF GOD AS BELOVED~CHILDREN

5.2 καὶ περιπατεῖτε ἐν ἀγάπῃ, καθὼς καὶ ὁ Χριστὸς
AND WALK IN LOVE, AS ALSO - CHRIST

ἠγάπησεν ἡμᾶς καὶ παρέδωκεν ἑαυτὸν ὑπὲρ ἡμῶν
LOVED US AND GAVE UP HIMSELF ON BEHALF OF US

προσφορὰν καὶ θυσίαν τῷ θεῷ εἰς ὀσμὴν
[AS] AN OFFERING AND SACRIFICE - TO GOD FOR A FRAGRANCE

εὐωδίας. **5.3** πορνεία δὲ καὶ ἀκαθαρσία πᾶσα ἢ
OF SWEET SMELL. BUT~FORNICATION AND ALL~IMPURITY OR

πλεονεξία μηδὲ ὀνομαζέσθω ἐν ὑμῖν, καθὼς
GREEDINESS LET IT NOT BE NAMED AMONG YOU°, AS

πρέπει ἁγίοις, **5.4** καὶ αἰσχρότης καὶ μωρολογία ἢ
IS PROPER [FOR] SAINTS, ALSO INDECENCY AND FOOLISH TALKING OR

εὐτραπελία, ἃ οὐκ ἀνῆκεν, ἀλλὰ μᾶλλον εὐχαριστία.
COARSE JESTING, WHICH ARE NOT FITTING, BUT RATHER THANKSGIVING.

5.5 τοῦτο γὰρ ἴστε γινώσκοντες, ὅτι πᾶς πόρνος ἢ
FOR~THIS YOU° KNOW [BY] RECOGNIZING THAT EVERY FORNICATOR OR

ἀκάθαρτος ἢ πλεονέκτης, ὅ ἐστιν εἰδωλολάτρης,
IMPURE PERSON OR COVETOUS PERSON, THAT IS, AN IDOLATER,

οὐκ ἔχει κληρονομίαν ἐν τῇ βασιλείᾳ τοῦ Χριστοῦ
DOES NOT HAVE AN INHERITANCE IN THE KINGDOM - OF CHRIST

καὶ θεοῦ.
AND OF GOD.

5.6 Μηδεὶς ὑμᾶς ἀπατάτω κενοῖς λόγοις· διὰ
²NO ONE ⁴YOU° ¹LET ³DECEIVE WITH EMPTY WORDS; ²BECAUSE OF

ταῦτα γὰρ ἔρχεται ἡ ὀργὴ τοῦ θεοῦ ἐπὶ τοὺς υἱοὺς
³THESE THINGS ¹FOR COMES THE WRATH - OF GOD UPON THE SONS

τῆς ἀπειθείας. **5.7** μὴ οὖν γίνεσθε συμμέτοχοι
- OF DISOBEDIENCE. ³NOT ¹THEREFORE ²BE JOINT-PARTAKERS

αὐτῶν· **5.8** ἦτε γὰρ ποτε σκότος, νῦν δὲ φῶς ἐν
WITH THEM; FOR~YOU° WERE ONCE DARKNESS, BUT~NOW LIGHT IN

κυρίῳ· ὡς τέκνα φωτὸς περιπατεῖτε **5.9** — ὁ γὰρ
[THE] LORD; AS CHILDREN OF LIGHT WALK — FOR~THE

¹Therefore be imitators of God, as beloved children, ²and live in love, as Christ loved usˣ and gave himself up for us, a fragrant offering and sacrifice to God.

3 But fornication and impurity of any kind, or greed, must not even be mentioned among you, as is proper among saints. ⁴Entirely out of place is obscene, silly, and vulgar talk; but instead, let there be thanksgiving. ⁵Be sure of this, that no fornicator or impure person, or one who is greedy (that is, an idolater), has any inheritance in the kingdom of Christ and of God.

6 Let no one deceive you with empty words, for because of these things the wrath of God comes on those who are disobedient. ⁷Therefore do not be associated with them. ⁸For once you were darkness, but now in the Lord you are light. Live as children of light— ⁹for the

ˣ Other ancient authorities read *you*

fruit of the light is found in all that is good and right and true. ¹⁰Try to find out what is pleasing to the Lord. ¹¹Take no part in the unfruitful works of darkness, but instead expose them. ¹²For it is shameful even to mention what ʰsuch people do secretly; ¹³but everything exposed by the light becomes visible, ¹⁴for everything that becomes visible is light. Therefore it says,

"Sleeper, awake!
Rise from the dead,
and Christ will shine on you."

15 Be careful then how you live, not as unwise people but as wise, ¹⁶making the most of the time, because the days are evil. ¹⁷So do not be foolish, but understand what the will of the Lord is. ¹⁸Do not get drunk with wine, for that is debauchery; but be filled with the Spirit, ¹⁹as you sing psalms and hymns and spiritual songs among yourselves, singing and making melody to the Lord in your hearts, ²⁰giving thanks to God the Father at all times and for everything in the name of our Lord Jesus Christ.

21 Be subject to one another out of reverence for Christ.

καρπὸς τοῦ φωτὸς ἐν πάσῃ ἀγαθωσύνῃ καὶ
FRUIT   OF THE LIGHT [IS] IN ALL   GOODNESS   AND

δικαιοσύνῃ καὶ ἀληθείᾳ — 5.10 δοκιμάζοντες τί ἐστιν
RIGHTEOUSNESS AND TRUTH   —   PROVING   WHAT IS

εὐάρεστον τῷ κυρίῳ, 5.11 καὶ μὴ συγκοινωνεῖτε τοῖς
WELL-PLEASING TO THE LORD, AND DO NOT PARTICIPATE IN THE

ἔργοις τοῖς ἀκάρποις τοῦ σκότους, μᾶλλον δὲ καὶ
²WORKS - ¹UNFRUITFUL - OF DARKNESS, BUT~RATHER EVEN

ἐλέγχετε. 5.12 τὰ γὰρ κρυφῇ γινόμενα ὑπ' αὐτῶν
EXPOSE [THEM]. FOR~[AS TO] THE THINGS IN SECRET BEING DONE BY THEM

αἰσχρόν ἐστιν καὶ λέγειν, 5.13 τὰ δὲ πάντα
IT IS~SHAMEFUL EVEN TO SPEAK [OF THEM], - BUT EVERYTHING

ἐλεγχόμενα ὑπὸ τοῦ φωτὸς φανεροῦται,
BEING EXPOSED BY THE LIGHT BECOMES VISIBLE,

5.14 πᾶν γὰρ τὸ φανερούμενον φῶς ἐστιν. διὸ
FOR~EVERY(ANY)THING - BECOMING VISIBLE IS~LIGHT. THEREFORE

λέγει,
IT SAYS,

Ἔγειρε, ὁ καθεύδων,
ARISE, THE ONE SLEEPING,

καὶ ἀνάστα ἐκ τῶν νεκρῶν,
AND RISE UP FROM THE DEAD,

καὶ ἐπιφαύσει σοι ὁ Χριστός.
AND ²WILL SHINE ON ³YOU - ¹CHRIST.

5.15 Βλέπετε οὖν ἀκριβῶς πῶς περιπατεῖτε μὴ ὡς
SEE THEREFORE HOW~CAREFULLY YOU° WALK NOT AS

ἄσοφοι ἀλλ' ὡς σοφοί, 5.16 ἐξαγοραζόμενοι τὸν
UNWISE BUT AS WISE, REDEEMING THE

καιρόν, ὅτι αἱ ἡμέραι πονηραί εἰσιν. 5.17 διὰ τοῦτο
TIME, BECAUSE THE DAYS ARE~EVIL. THEREFORE

μὴ γίνεσθε ἄφρονες, ἀλλὰ συνίετε τί τὸ θέλημα
DO NOT BE FOOLISH, BUT UNDERSTAND WHAT THE WILL

τοῦ κυρίου. 5.18 καὶ μὴ μεθύσκεσθε οἴνῳ, ἐν ᾧ
OF THE LORD [IS]. AND DO NOT BECOME DRUNK WITH WINE, IN WHICH

ἐστιν ἀσωτία, ἀλλὰ πληροῦσθε ἐν πνεύματι,
IS DISSIPATION, BUT BE FILLED IN(BY) [THE] SPIRIT,

5.19 λαλοῦντες ἑαυτοῖς [ἐν] ψαλμοῖς καὶ ὕμνοις καὶ
SPEAKING TO ONE ANOTHER IN PSALMS AND HYMNS AND

ᾠδαῖς πνευματικαῖς, ᾄδοντες καὶ ψάλλοντες τῇ καρδίᾳ
SPIRITUAL~SONGS, SINGING AND MAKING MELODY IN THE HEART(S)

ὑμῶν τῷ κυρίῳ, 5.20 εὐχαριστοῦντες πάντοτε ὑπὲρ
OF YOU° TO THE LORD, GIVING THANKS ALWAYS FOR

πάντων ἐν ὀνόματι τοῦ κυρίου ἡμῶν Ἰησοῦ Χριστοῦ
ALL THINGS IN [THE] NAME OF THE LORD OF US JESUS CHRIST

τῷ θεῷ καὶ πατρί.
- TO GOD EVEN [THE] FATHER;

5.21 Ὑποτασσόμενοι ἀλλήλοις ἐν φόβῳ Χριστοῦ,
BEING SUBMISSIVE TO ONE ANOTHER IN [THE] FEAR OF CHRIST,

5.22 αἱ γυναῖκες τοῖς ἰδίοις ἀνδράσιν ὡς τῷ κυρίῳ,
THE WIVES   TO THEIR OWN HUSBANDS   AS   TO THE LORD,

5.23 ὅτι ἀνήρ ἐστιν κεφαλὴ τῆς γυναικὸς ὡς καὶ
BECAUSE A HUSBAND IS   HEAD   OF THE WIFE   AS ALSO

ὁ Χριστὸς κεφαλὴ τῆς ἐκκλησίας, αὐτὸς σωτὴρ
- CHRIST   [IS] HEAD OF THE CHURCH,   [BEING] HIMSELF [THE] SAVIOR

τοῦ σώματος·   **5.24** ἀλλὰ ὡς ἡ ἐκκλησία
OF THE BODY.   BUT   AS THE CHURCH

ὑποτάσσεται τῷ Χριστῷ, οὕτως καὶ αἱ γυναῖκες
IS SUBMISSIVE - TO CHRIST, SO   ALSO THE WIVES

τοῖς ἀνδράσιν ἐν παντί.   **5.25** Οἱ ἄνδρες, ἀγαπᾶτε
TO THE(IR) HUSBANDS IN EVERYTHING. THE HUSBANDS, LOVE

τὰς γυναῖκας, καθὼς καὶ ὁ Χριστὸς ἠγάπησεν τὴν
THE(YOUR*) WIVES, AS   ALSO - CHRIST   LOVED   THE

ἐκκλησίαν καὶ ἑαυτὸν παρέδωκεν ὑπὲρ αὐτῆς,
CHURCH   AND GAVE UP~HIMSELF ON BEHALF OF HER,

5.26 ἵνα αὐτὴν ἁγιάσῃ καθαρίσας τῷ λουτρῷ τοῦ
THAT HE MIGHT SANCTIFY~HER HAVING CLEANSED [HER] BY THE WASHING OF THE

ὕδατος ἐν ῥήματι, **5.27** ἵνα παραστήσῃ αὐτὸς ἑαυτῷ
WATER IN [THE] WORD,   THAT HE~MIGHT PRESENT   ³TO HIMSELF

ἔνδοξον τὴν ἐκκλησίαν, μὴ ἔχουσαν σπίλον ἢ ῥυτίδα
¹A GLORIOUS - ²CHURCH,   NOT HAVING   SPOT OR WRINKLE

ἤ τι τῶν τοιούτων, ἀλλ' ἵνα ᾖ ἁγία καὶ
OR ANY - SUCH THINGS, BUT THAT SHE MAY BE HOLY AND

ἄμωμος.   **5.28** οὕτως ὀφείλουσιν [καὶ] οἱ ἄνδρες
BLEMISHLESS.   SO   OUGHT   ALSO THE HUSBANDS

ἀγαπᾶν τὰς ἑαυτῶν γυναῖκας ὡς τὰ ἑαυτῶν σώματα.
TO LOVE - THEIR OWN WIVES(WIFE) AS - THEIR OWN BODIES(BODY).

ὁ ἀγαπῶν τὴν ἑαυτοῦ γυναῖκα ἑαυτὸν ἀγαπᾷ.
THE ONE LOVING - HIS OWN WIFE LOVES~HIMSELF.

5.29 οὐδεὶς γάρ ποτε τὴν ἑαυτοῦ σάρκα ἐμίσησεν ἀλλὰ
FOR~NO ONE   EVER - HIS OWN FLESH HATED   BUT

ἐκτρέφει καὶ θάλπει αὐτήν, καθὼς καὶ ὁ Χριστὸς τὴν
NOURISHES AND CHERISHES IT, AS   ALSO - CHRIST [TO] THE

ἐκκλησίαν, **5.30** ὅτι μέλη ἐσμὲν τοῦ σώματος αὐτοῦ.
CHURCH,   BECAUSE WE ARE~MEMBERS OF THE BODY OF HIM.

5.31 ἀντὶ τούτου καταλείψει ἄνθρωπος [τὸν] πατέρα
BECAUSE OF THIS A MAN~WILL LEAVE   THE(HIS) FATHER

καὶ [τὴν] μητέρα καὶ προσκολληθήσεται πρὸς τὴν
AND THE(HIS) MOTHER AND WILL BE JOINED   TO   THE

γυναῖκα αὐτοῦ, καὶ ἔσονται οἱ δύο εἰς σάρκα μίαν.
WIFE   OF HIM, AND ³WILL BE ¹THE ²TWO - ONE~FLESH.

5.32 τὸ μυστήριον τοῦτο μέγα ἐστίν· ἐγὼ δὲ λέγω εἰς
- THIS~MYSTERY   IS~GREAT;   BUT~I SPEAK AS TO

Χριστὸν καὶ εἰς τὴν ἐκκλησίαν. **5.33** πλὴν καὶ
CHRIST   AND AS TO THE CHURCH.   NEVERTHELESS ALSO

5:31 Gen. 2:24

22 Wives, be subject to your husbands as you are to the Lord. 23For the husband is the head of the wife just as Christ is the head of the church, the body of which he is the Savior. 24Just as the church is subject to Christ, so also wives ought to be, in everything, to their husbands.

25 Husbands, love your wives, just as Christ loved the church and gave himself up for her, 26in order to make her holy by cleansing her with the washing of water by the word, 27so as to present the church to himself in splendor, without a spot or wrinkle or anything of the kind—yes, so that she may be holy and without blemish. 28In the same way, husbands should love their wives as they do their own bodies. He who loves his wife loves himself. 29For no one ever hates his own body, but he nourishes and tenderly cares for it, just as Christ does for the church, 30because we are members of his body.y 31"For this reason a man will leave his father and mother and be joined to his wife, and the two will become one flesh." 32This is a great mystery, and I am applying it to Christ and the church. 33Each of you, however,

y Other ancient authorities add *of his flesh and of his bones*

should love his wife as himself, and a wife should respect her husband.

ὑμεῖς οἱ καθ' ἕνα, ἕκαστος τὴν ἑαυτοῦ γυναῖκα οὕτως
YOU°,   ONE BY ONE,   ³EACH   -   ⁴HIS OWN   ⁵WIFE   ¹SO

ἀγαπάτω ὡς ἑαυτόν, ἡ δὲ γυνὴ ἵνα φοβῆται τὸν
²LET ⁶LOVE   ⁷AS   ⁸HIMSELF,   AND~THE WIFE   THAT   SHE RESPECTS   THE(HER)

ἄνδρα.
HUSBAND

CHAPTER 6

Children, obey your parents in the Lord,ᶻ for this is right. ²"Honor your father and mother"—this is the first commandment with a promise: ³"so that it may be well with you and you may live long on the earth."

4 And, fathers, do not provoke your children to anger, but bring them up in the discipline and instruction of the Lord.

5 Slaves, obey your earthly masters with fear and trembling, in singleness of heart, as you obey Christ; ⁶not only while being watched, and in order to please them, but as slaves of Christ, doing the will of God from the heart. ⁷Render service with enthusiasm, as to the Lord and not to men and women, ⁸knowing that whatever good we do, we will receive the same again from the Lord, whether we are slaves or free.

9 And, masters, do the same to them. Stop threatening them, for you know that

ᶻ Other ancient authorities lack *in the Lord*

6.1 Τὰ τέκνα, ὑπακούετε τοῖς γονεῦσιν ὑμῶν [ἐν
THE   CHILDREN,   OBEY   THE   PARENTS   OF YOU°   IN

κυρίῳ]· τοῦτο γάρ ἐστιν δίκαιον. **6.2** τίμα τὸν πατέρα
[THE] LORD;   FOR~THIS   IS   RIGHT.   HONOR   THE   FATHER

σου καὶ τὴν μητέρα, ἥτις ἐστὶν ἐντολὴ πρώτη
OF YOU   AND   THE(YOUR) MOTHER,   WHICH IS   [THE] FIRST~COMMANDMENT

ἐν ἐπαγγελίᾳ, **6.3** ἵνα εὖ σοι γένηται καὶ ἔσῃ
WITH   A PROMISE,   THAT   ²WELL   ³WITH YOU   ¹IT MAY BE   AND   YOU WILL BE

μακροχρόνιος ἐπὶ τῆς γῆς. **6.4** Καὶ οἱ πατέρες,
A LONG TIME   ON   THE   EARTH.   AND   THE   FATHERS,

μὴ παροργίζετε τὰ τέκνα ὑμῶν ἀλλὰ ἐκτρέφετε αὐτὰ
DO NOT MAKE ANGRY   THE   CHILDREN OF YOU°   BUT   NURTURE   THEM

ἐν παιδείᾳ καὶ νουθεσίᾳ κυρίου.
IN   [THE] TRAINING   AND   ADMONITION   OF [THE] LORD.

6.5 Οἱ δοῦλοι, ὑπακούετε τοῖς κατὰ σάρκα
THE   SLAVES,   OBEY   ¹THE(YOUR°)   ³ACCORDING TO   ⁴FLESH

κυρίοις μετὰ φόβου καὶ τρόμου ἐν ἁπλότητι τῆς
²MASTERS   WITH   FEAR   AND   TREMBLING   IN   SINGLENESS   OF THE

καρδίας ὑμῶν ὡς τῷ Χριστῷ, **6.6** μὴ κατ'
HEART   OF YOU°   AS   -   TO CHRIST,   NOT   BY WAY OF

ὀφθαλμοδουλίαν ὡς ἀνθρωπάρεσκοι ἀλλ' ὡς δοῦλοι
EYE-SERVICE   AS   MEN-PLEASERS   BUT   AS   SLAVES

Χριστοῦ ποιοῦντες τὸ θέλημα τοῦ θεοῦ ἐκ ψυχῆς,
OF CHRIST   DOING   THE   WILL   -   OF GOD   FROM   [THE] SOUL,

6.7 μετ' εὐνοίας δουλεύοντες ὡς τῷ κυρίῳ καὶ οὐκ
WITH   GOOD WILL   DOING SERVICE   AS   TO THE   LORD   AND   NOT

ἀνθρώποις, **6.8** εἰδότες ὅτι ἕκαστος ἐάν τι
TO MEN,   KNOWING   THAT   EACH MAN   WHATEVER

ποιήσῃ ἀγαθόν, τοῦτο κομίσεται παρὰ κυρίου εἴτε
GOOD THING~HE DOES,   THIS   HE WILL RECEIVE   FROM   [THE] LORD   WHETHER

δοῦλος εἴτε ἐλεύθερος. **6.9** Καὶ οἱ κύριοι, τὰ αὐτὰ
A SLAVE   OR   A FREEMAN.   AND   THE   MASTERS,   THE SAME THINGS

ποιεῖτε πρὸς αὐτούς, ἀνιέντες τὴν ἀπειλήν, εἰδότες ὅτι
DO   TOWARDS THEM,   FORBEARING   -   THREATENING,   KNOWING   THAT

6:2-3 Exod. 20:12; Deut. 5:16

καὶ αὐτῶν καὶ ὑμῶν ὁ κύριός ἐστιν ἐν οὐρανοῖς καὶ
BOTH THEIR AND YOUR° - LORD IS IN [THE] HEAVENS AND

προσωπολημψία οὐκ ἔστιν παρ᾽ αὐτῷ.
RESPECT OF PERSONS THERE IS~NOT WITH HIM.

6.10 Τοῦ λοιποῦ, ἐνδυναμοῦσθε ἐν κυρίῳ καὶ ἐν
[FOR] THE REST, BE CONTINUALLY EMPOWERED IN [THE] LORD AND IN

τῷ κράτει τῆς ἰσχύος αὐτοῦ. **6.11** ἐνδύσασθε τὴν
THE MIGHT OF THE STRENGTH OF HIM. PUT ON THE

πανοπλίαν τοῦ θεοῦ πρὸς τὸ δύνασθαι ὑμᾶς στῆναι
WHOLE ARMOR - OF GOD FOR - YOU°~TO BE ABLE TO STAND

πρὸς τὰς μεθοδείας τοῦ διαβόλου· **6.12** ὅτι οὐκ
AGAINST THE SCHEMES OF THE DEVIL; ¹BECAUSE ⁵NOT

ἔστιν ἡμῖν ἡ πάλη πρὸς αἷμα καὶ σάρκα ἀλλὰ
⁴IS ⁶TO US ²THE ³WRESTLING AGAINST BLOOD AND FLESH, BUT

πρὸς τὰς ἀρχάς, πρὸς τὰς ἐξουσίας, πρὸς τοὺς
AGAINST THE RULERS, AGAINST THE AUTHORITIES, AGAINST THE

κοσμοκράτορας τοῦ σκότους τούτου, πρὸς τὰ πνευματικὰ
WORLD POWERS - OF THIS~DARKNESS, AGAINST THE SPIRITUAL FORCES

τῆς πονηρίας ἐν τοῖς ἐπουρανίοις. **6.13** διὰ τοῦτο
- OF EVIL IN THE HEAVENLIES. THEREFORE

ἀναλάβετε τὴν πανοπλίαν τοῦ θεοῦ, ἵνα δυνηθῆτε
TAKE UP THE WHOLE ARMOR - OF GOD, THAT YOU° MAY BE ABLE

ἀντιστῆναι ἐν τῇ ἡμέρᾳ τῇ πονηρᾷ καὶ
TO WITHSTAND IN THE ²DAY - ¹EVIL AND

ἅπαντα κατεργασάμενοι στῆναι. **6.14** στῆτε οὖν
HAVING DONE~ALL TO STAND. STAND THEREFORE

περιζωσάμενοι τὴν ὀσφὺν ὑμῶν ἐν ἀληθείᾳ καὶ
HAVING GIRDED THE WAIST OF YOU° WITH TRUTH AND

ἐνδυσάμενοι τὸν θώρακα τῆς δικαιοσύνης **6.15** καὶ
HAVING PUT ON THE BREASTPLATE - OF RIGHTEOUSNESS AND

ὑποδησάμενοι τοὺς πόδας ἐν ἑτοιμασίᾳ τοῦ
HAVING PUT SHOES ON THE (YOUR°) FEET WITH [THE] FIRM FOOTING OF THE

εὐαγγελίου τῆς εἰρήνης, **6.16** ἐν πᾶσιν
GOOD NEWS - OF PEACE, WITH ALL [THESE] THINGS

ἀναλαβόντες τὸν θυρεὸν τῆς πίστεως, ἐν ᾧ
HAVING TAKEN UP THE SHIELD - OF FAITH, BY WHICH

δυνήσεσθε πάντα τὰ βέλη τοῦ πονηροῦ [τὰ]
YOU° WILL BE ABLE ²ALL ³THE ⁵DARTS ⁶OF THE ⁷EVIL ONE -

πεπυρωμένα σβέσαι· **6.17** καὶ τὴν περικεφαλαίαν τοῦ
⁴FLAMING ¹TO QUENCH; AND ²THE ³HELMET -

σωτηρίου δέξασθε καὶ τὴν μάχαιραν τοῦ πνεύματος,
⁴OF SALVATION ¹TAKE AND THE SWORD OF THE SPIRIT,

ὁ ἐστιν ῥῆμα θεοῦ. **6.18** διὰ πάσης προσευχῆς
WHICH IS [THE] WORD OF GOD, BY MEANS OF ALL PRAYER

καὶ δεήσεως προσευχόμενοι ἐν παντὶ καιρῷ ἐν
AND PETITION PRAYING AT EVERY TIME IN

πνεύματι, καὶ εἰς αὐτὸ ἀγρυπνοῦντες ἐν πάσῃ
SPIRIT, AND TO THIS VERY THING KEEPING WATCH WITH ALL

both of you have the same Master in heaven, and with him there is no partiality.

10 Finally, be strong in the Lord and in the strength of his power. ¹¹Put on the whole armor of God, so that you may be able to stand against the wiles of the devil. ¹²For our*ᵃ* struggle is not against enemies of blood and flesh, but against the rulers, against the authorities, against the cosmic powers of this present darkness, against the spiritual forces of evil in the heavenly places. ¹³Therefore take up the whole armor of God, so that you may be able to withstand on that evil day, and having done everything, to stand firm. ¹⁴Stand therefore, and fasten the belt of truth around your waist, and put on the breastplate of righteousness. ¹⁵As shoes for your feet put on whatever will make you ready to proclaim the gospel of peace. ¹⁶With all of these,*ᵇ* take the shield of faith, with which you will be able to quench all the flaming arrows of the evil one. ¹⁷Take the helmet of salvation, and the sword of the Spirit, which is the word of God.

18 Pray in the Spirit at all times in every prayer and supplication. To that end keep alert and always

ᵃ Other ancient authorities read *your*
ᵇ Or *In all circumstances*

persevere in supplication for all the saints. [19]Pray also for me, so that when I speak, a message may be given to me to make known with boldness the mystery of the gospel,[c] [20]for which I am an ambassador in chains. Pray that I may declare it boldly, as I must speak.

21 So that you also may know how I am and what I am doing, Tychicus will tell you everything. He is a dear brother and a faithful minister in the Lord. [22]I am sending him to you for this very purpose, to let you know how we are, and to encourage your hearts.

23 Peace be to the whole community,[d] and love with faith, from God the Father and the Lord Jesus Christ. [24]Grace be with all who have an undying love for our Lord Jesus Christ.[e]

[c] Other ancient authorities lack *of the gospel*
[d] Gk *to the brothers*
[e] Other ancient authorities add *Amen*

προσκαρτερήσει καὶ δεήσει περὶ πάντων τῶν ἁγίων
PERSEVERANCE   AND   PETITION CONCERNING ALL   THE SAINTS

6.19 καὶ ὑπὲρ ἐμοῦ, ἵνα μοι δοθῇ λόγος ἐν
AND FOR ME, THAT TO ME MAY BE GIVEN UTTERANCE IN

ἀνοίξει τοῦ στόματός μου, ἐν παρρησίᾳ γνωρίσαι
OPENING THE   MOUTH   OF ME, IN BOLDNESS TO MAKE KNOWN

τὸ μυστήριον τοῦ εὐαγγελίου, **6.20** ὑπὲρ οὗ
THE MYSTERY OF THE GOSPEL,   ON BEHALF OF WHICH

πρεσβεύω ἐν ἁλύσει, ἵνα ἐν αὐτῷ παρρησιάσωμαι
I AM AN AMBASSADOR IN CHAIN[S], THAT IN IT I MAY BE BOLD

ὡς δεῖ με λαλῆσαι.
AS IT IS NECESSARY [FOR] ME TO SPEAK.

6.21 Ἵνα δὲ εἰδῆτε καὶ ὑμεῖς τὰ κατ' ἐμέ, τί
NOW~THAT [3]MAY KNOW [2]ALSO [1]YOU° THE THINGS ABOUT ME, WHAT

πράσσω, πάντα γνωρίσει ὑμῖν Τυχικὸς ὁ
I AM DOING, ALL THINGS [10]WILL MAKE KNOWN [11]TO YOU° [1]TYCHICUS [2]THE

ἀγαπητὸς ἀδελφὸς καὶ πιστὸς διάκονος ἐν κυρίῳ,
[3]BELOVED [4]BROTHER [5]AND [6]FAITHFUL [7]MINISTER [8]IN [9][THE] LORD,

6.22 ὃν ἔπεμψα πρὸς ὑμᾶς εἰς αὐτὸ τοῦτο, ἵνα
WHOM I SENT TO YOU° FOR THIS VERY THING, THAT

γνῶτε τὰ περὶ ἡμῶν καὶ παρακαλέσῃ τὰς
YOU° MAY KNOW THE THINGS CONCERNING US AND HE MAY ENCOURAGE THE

καρδίας ὑμῶν.
HEARTS OF YOU°.

6.23 Εἰρήνη τοῖς ἀδελφοῖς καὶ ἀγάπη μετὰ πίστεως
PEACE TO THE BROTHERS AND LOVE WITH FAITH

ἀπὸ θεοῦ πατρὸς καὶ κυρίου Ἰησοῦ Χριστοῦ. **6.24** ἡ
FROM GOD [THE] FATHER AND LORD JESUS CHRIST.   -

χάρις μετὰ πάντων τῶν ἀγαπώντων τὸν κύριον ἡμῶν
GRACE [BE] WITH ALL THE ONES LOVING THE LORD OF US

Ἰησοῦν Χριστὸν ἐν ἀφθαρσίᾳ.
JESUS CHRIST WITH AN INCORRUPTIBLE [LOVE].

THE LETTER OF PAUL TO THE
PHILIPPIANS

ΠΡΟΣ ΦΙΛΙΠΠΗΣΙΟΥΣ
TO   [THE] PHILIPPIANS

1.1 Παῦλος καὶ Τιμόθεος δοῦλοι Χριστοῦ Ἰησοῦ
PAUL   AND   TIMOTHY,   SLAVES   OF CHRIST   JESUS,

πᾶσιν τοῖς ἁγίοις ἐν Χριστῷ Ἰησοῦ τοῖς οὖσιν ἐν
TO ALL   THE   SAINTS   IN   CHRIST   JESUS   -   BEING   IN

Φιλίπποις σὺν ἐπισκόποις καὶ διακόνοις, **1.2** χάρις
PHILIPPI   WITH   [THE] OVERSEERS   AND   DEACONS,   GRACE

ὑμῖν καὶ εἰρήνη ἀπὸ θεοῦ πατρὸς ἡμῶν καὶ κυρίου
TO YOU°   AND   PEACE   FROM   GOD   [THE] FATHER   OF US   AND   LORD

Ἰησοῦ Χριστοῦ.
JESUS   CHRIST.

1.3 Εὐχαριστῶ τῷ θεῷ μου ἐπὶ πάσῃ τῇ μνείᾳ
I THANK   THE   GOD   OF ME   AT   EVERY   -   REMEMBRANCE

ὑμῶν **1.4** πάντοτε ἐν πάσῃ δεήσει μου ὑπὲρ
OF YOU°,   ALWAYS   IN   EVERY   SUPPLICATION   OF ME   ON BEHALF OF

πάντων ὑμῶν, μετὰ χαρᾶς τὴν δέησιν ποιούμενος,
YOU°~ALL,   WITH   JOY   [2]THE   [3]SUPPLICATION   [1]MAKING,

1.5 ἐπὶ τῇ κοινωνίᾳ ὑμῶν εἰς τὸ εὐαγγέλιον ἀπὸ τῆς
IN VIEW OF   THE   PARTICIPATION   OF YOU°   IN   THE   GOSPEL   FROM   THE

πρώτης ἡμέρας ἄχρι τοῦ νῦν, **1.6** πεποιθὼς
FIRST   DAY   UNTIL   -   NOW,   HAVING BECOME CONFIDENT OF

αὐτὸ τοῦτο, ὅτι ὁ ἐναρξάμενος ἐν ὑμῖν
THIS VERY THING,   THAT   THE ONE   HAVING BEGUN   IN   YOU°

ἔργον ἀγαθὸν ἐπιτελέσει ἄχρι ἡμέρας Χριστοῦ Ἰησοῦ·
A GOOD~WORK   WILL COMPLETE [IT]   UNTIL   [THE] DAY   OF CHRIST   JESUS;

1.7 καθώς ἐστιν δίκαιον ἐμοὶ τοῦτο φρονεῖν ὑπὲρ
EVEN AS   IT IS   RIGHT   FOR ME   TO THINK~THIS   ON BEHALF OF

πάντων ὑμῶν διὰ τὸ ἔχειν με ἐν τῇ καρδίᾳ
YOU°~ALL   BECAUSE   -   [2]HAVE   [3]ME   [4]IN   [5]THE(YOUR°)   [6]HEART

ὑμᾶς, ἔν τε τοῖς δεσμοῖς μου καὶ ἐν τῇ ἀπολογίᾳ
[1]YOU°,   BOTH~IN THE   BONDS   OF ME   AND   IN   THE   DEFENSE

καὶ βεβαιώσει τοῦ εὐαγγελίου συγκοινωνούς μου τῆς
AND   VINDICATION   OF THE   GOOD NEWS   [4]PARTAKERS   [5]OF MY   THE

χάριτος πάντας ὑμᾶς ὄντας. **1.8** μάρτυς γάρ μου ὁ
[6]GRACE   [2]ALL   [1]YOU°   [3]BEING.   [3]WITNESS   [1]FOR   [2]MY   -

θεός ὡς ἐπιποθῶ πάντας ὑμᾶς ἐν σπλάγχνοις
[IS] GOD   HOW   I YEARN FOR   YOU°~ALL   IN   [THE] BOWELS(AFFECTIONS)

Χριστοῦ Ἰησοῦ. **1.9** καὶ τοῦτο προσεύχομαι, ἵνα ἡ
OF CHRIST   JESUS.   AND   THIS   I PRAY,   THAT   THE

Paul and Timothy, servants[a] of Christ Jesus,

To all the saints in Christ Jesus who are in Philippi, with the bishops[b] and deacons:[c]

2 Grace to you and peace from God our Father and the Lord Jesus Christ.

3 I thank my God every time I remember you, [4]constantly praying with joy in every one of my prayers for all of you, [5]because of your sharing in the gospel from the first day until now. [6]I am confident of this, that the one who began a good work among you will bring it to completion by the day of Jesus Christ. [7]It is right for me to think this way about all of you, because you hold me in your heart,[d] for all of you share in God's grace[e] with me, both in my imprisonment and in the defense and confirmation of the gospel. [8]For God is my witness, how I long for all of you with the compassion of Christ Jesus. [9]And this is my prayer,

[a] Gk *slaves*
[b] Or *overseers*
[c] Or *overseers and helpers*
[d] Or *because I hold you in my heart*
[e] Gk *in grace*

that your love may overflow more and more with knowledge and full insight [10]to help you to determine what is best, so that in the day of Christ you may be pure and blameless, [11]having produced the harvest of righteousness that comes through Jesus Christ for the glory and praise of God.

12 I want you to know, beloved,*f* that what has happened to me has actually helped to spread the gospel, [13]so that it has become known throughout the whole imperial guard*g* and to everyone else that my imprisonment is for Christ; [14]and most of the brothers and sisters,*f* having been made confident in the Lord by my imprisonment, dare to speak the word*h* with greater boldness and without fear.

15 Some proclaim Christ from envy and rivalry, but others from goodwill. [16]These proclaim Christ out of love, knowing that I have been put here for the defense of the gospel; [17]the others proclaim Christ out of selfish ambition, not sincerely but intending to increase my suffering in my imprisonment. [18]What does it matter? Just this, that Christ is proclaimed in every way, whether out of false motives or true; and in that I rejoice. Yes, and I will continue to rejoice, [19]for I know that

f Gk *brothers*
g Gk *whole praetorium*
h Other ancient authorities read *word of God*

ἀγάπη ὑμῶν ἔτι μᾶλλον καὶ μᾶλλον περισσεύῃ ἐν
LOVE   OF YOU° YET   MORE   AND   MORE   MAY INCREASE IN

ἐπιγνώσει καὶ πάσῃ αἰσθήσει **1.10** εἰς τὸ
DEEPER KNOWLEDGE AND ALL PERCEPTION, FOR -

δοκιμάζειν ὑμᾶς τὰ διαφέροντα, ἵνα ἦτε
YOU°~TO APPROVE THE THINGS BEING SUPERIOR, THAT YOU° MAY BE

εἰλικρινεῖς καὶ ἀπρόσκοποι εἰς ἡμέραν Χριστοῦ,
PURE   AND   BLAMELESS   IN   [THE] DAY OF CHRIST,

1.11 πεπληρωμένοι καρπὸν δικαιοσύνης τὸν διὰ
HAVING BEEN FILLED [WITH] [THE] FRUIT OF RIGHTEOUSNESS - THROUGH

Ἰησοῦ Χριστοῦ εἰς δόξαν καὶ ἔπαινον θεοῦ.
JESUS   CHRIST   TO [THE] GLORY AND PRAISE OF GOD.

1.12 Γινώσκειν δὲ ὑμᾶς βούλομαι, ἀδελφοί, ὅτι
⁴TO KNOW   ¹NOW ³YOU° ²I WANT,   BROTHERS, THAT

τὰ κατ’ ἐμὲ μᾶλλον εἰς προκοπὴν τοῦ
THE THINGS CONCERNING ME ²EVEN MORE ³TO ⁴AN ADVANCEMENT ⁵OF THE

εὐαγγελίου ἐλήλυθεν, **1.13** ὥστε τοὺς δεσμούς μου
⁶GOOD NEWS ¹HAVE COME,   SO THAT THE BONDS OF ME

φανεροὺς ἐν Χριστῷ γενέσθαι ἐν ὅλῳ τῷ πραιτωρίῳ
²MANIFEST ³IN ⁴CHRIST ¹TO HAVE BECOME IN ALL THE PRAETORIUM

καὶ τοῖς λοιποῖς πᾶσιν, **1.14** καὶ τοὺς πλείονας τῶν
AND TO ²THE ³REST ¹ALL,   AND - MOST OF THE

ἀδελφῶν ἐν κυρίῳ πεποιθότας τοῖς
BROTHERS IN [THE] LORD HAVING BECOME CONFIDENT [WITH RESPECT] TO THE

δεσμοῖς μου περισσοτέρως τολμᾶν ἀφόβως τὸν
BONDS   OF ME [ARE] MORE READILY [WILLING] TO DARE ⁴FEARLESSLY ²THE

λόγον λαλεῖν.
³WORD ¹TO SPEAK.

1.15 Τινὲς μὲν καὶ διὰ φθόνον καὶ ἔριν,
SOME   INDEED EVEN BECAUSE OF ENVY AND STRIFE,

τινὲς δὲ καὶ δι’ εὐδοκίαν τὸν
BUT~SOME INDEED BECAUSE OF GOOD INTENTION -

Χριστὸν κηρύσσουσιν· **1.16** οἱ μὲν ἐξ ἀγάπης,
PROCLAIM~CHRIST;   [THESE] ONES - OUT OF LOVE,

εἰδότες ὅτι εἰς ἀπολογίαν τοῦ εὐαγγελίου κεῖμαι,
KNOWING THAT FOR A DEFENSE OF THE GOOD NEWS I AM APPOINTED,

1.17 οἱ δὲ ἐξ ἐριθείας τὸν
BUT~[THOSE OTHER] ONES OUT OF RIVALRY -

Χριστὸν καταγγέλλουσιν, οὐχ ἁγνῶς, οἰόμενοι
PREACH~CHRIST,   NOT PURELY, SUPPOSING

θλῖψιν ἐγείρειν τοῖς δεσμοῖς μου. **1.18** τί γάρ;
TO RAISE(STIR) UP~TROUBLE [AS I AM] IN THE BONDS OF ME. WHAT THEN?

πλὴν ὅτι παντὶ τρόπῳ, εἴτε προφάσει εἴτε ἀληθείᾳ,
ONLY THAT IN EVERY WAY, WHETHER IN PRETENSE OR IN TRUTH,

Χριστὸς καταγγέλλεται, καὶ ἐν τούτῳ χαίρω. ἀλλὰ
CHRIST   IS PREACHED,   AND IN THIS I REJOICE. AND

καὶ χαρήσομαι, **1.19** οἶδα γὰρ ὅτι τοῦτό μοι
IN ADDITION I WILL REJOICE,   FOR~I KNOW THAT THIS FOR ME

ἀποβήσεται εἰς σωτηρίαν   διὰ   τῆς ὑμῶν δεήσεως
WILL TURN OUT FOR [MY] DELIVERANCE THROUGH - YOUR° PRAYERS

καὶ ἐπιχορηγίας   τοῦ πνεύματος Ἰησοῦ Χριστοῦ
AND [THE] BOUNTIFUL SUPPLY OF THE SPIRIT   OF JESUS   CHRIST

1.20 κατὰ   τὴν ἀποκαραδοκίαν καὶ ἐλπίδα μου, ὅτι
ACCORDING TO THE EARNEST EXPECTATION AND HOPE OF ME, THAT

ἐν οὐδενὶ αἰσχυνθήσομαι ἀλλ' ἐν πάσῃ παρρησίᾳ ὡς
IN NOTHING I WILL BE PUT TO SHAME BUT WITH ALL COURAGE AS

πάντοτε καὶ νῦν μεγαλυνθήσεται Χριστὸς ἐν τῷ
ALWAYS   EVEN NOW CHRIST~WILL BE MAGNIFIED   IN THE

σώματί μου, εἴτε διὰ ζωῆς εἴτε διὰ θανάτου.
BODY   OF ME, WHETHER THROUGH LIFE OR THROUGH DEATH.

1.21 ἐμοὶ γὰρ τὸ ζῆν   Χριστὸς καὶ τὸ ἀποθανεῖν
FOR~TO ME   - TO LIVE(LIVING) [IS] CHRIST AND - TO DIE(DYING)

κέρδος. **1.22** εἰ δὲ   τὸ ζῆν ἐν σαρκί, τοῦτό μοι
[IS] GAIN.   BUT~IF [IT MEANS] - TO LIVE IN [THE] FLESH, THIS FOR ME

καρπὸς ἔργου, καὶ τί αἱρήσομαι οὐ γνωρίζω.
[IS] FRUIT OF LABOR, AND WHAT I WILL CHOOSE I DO NOT KNOW.

1.23 συνέχομαι δὲ ἐκ τῶν δύο,   τὴν ἐπιθυμίαν
NOW~I AM HARD-PRESSED FROM - TWO [SIDES], ²THE ³DESIRE

ἔχων εἰς τὸ ἀναλῦσαι καὶ σὺν Χριστῷ εἶναι,
¹HAVING - - TO DEPART AND ²WITH ³CHRIST ¹TO BE,

πολλῷ [γὰρ] μᾶλλον κρεῖσσον· **1.24** τὸ δὲ ἐπιμένειν
FOR~MUCH   MUCH BETTER [THIS IS];   - BUT TO REMAIN

[ἐν] τῇ σαρκὶ ἀναγκαιότερον δὶ   ὑμᾶς. **1.25** καὶ
IN THE FLESH [IS] MORE NECESSARY FOR THE SAKE OF YOU°.   AND

τοῦτο πεποιθὼς   οἶδα ὅτι μενῶ   καὶ
THIS HAVING BEEN PERSUADED OF I KNOW THAT I WILL REMAIN AND

παραμενῶ πᾶσιν ὑμῖν εἰς τὴν ὑμῶν προκοπὴν καὶ
WILL CONTINUE WITH YOU°~ALL FOR - YOUR° PROGRESS AND

χαρὰν τῆς πίστεως, **1.26** ἵνα τὸ καύχημα ὑμῶν
JOY OF THE FAITH,   THAT THE BOAST OF YOU°

περισσεύῃ ἐν Χριστῷ Ἰησοῦ ἐν ἐμοὶ διὰ τῆς ἐμῆς
MAY INCREASE IN CHRIST JESUS IN ME THROUGH - MY

παρουσίας πάλιν πρὸς ὑμᾶς.
PRESENCE AGAIN WITH YOU°.

1.27 Μόνον ἀξίως τοῦ εὐαγγελίου τοῦ Χριστοῦ
ONLY WORTHILY OF THE GOOD NEWS - OF CHRIST

πολιτεύεσθε,   ἵνα εἴτε ἐλθὼν καὶ ἰδὼν
CONDUCT [YOUR°] CITIZENSHIP, THAT WHETHER HAVING COME AND HAVING SEEN

ὑμᾶς εἴτε ἀπὼν ἀκούω τὰ περὶ ὑμῶν, ὅτι
YOU° OR BEING ABSENT I MAY HEAR [OF] THE THINGS CONCERNING YOU°, THAT

στήκετε   ἐν ἑνὶ πνεύματι, μιᾷ ψυχῇ συναθλοῦντες
YOU° ARE STANDING IN ONE SPIRIT, WITH ONE SOUL CONTENDING

τῇ πίστει τοῦ εὐαγγελίου **1.28** καὶ μὴ πτυρόμενοι
FOR THE FAITH OF THE GOOD NEWS   AND NOT BEING FRIGHTENED

ἐν μηδενὶ ὑπὸ τῶν ἀντικειμένων, ἥτις ἐστὶν
IN ANYTHING BY THE ONES OPPOSING,   WHICH IS

through your prayers and the help of the Spirit of Jesus Christ this will turn out for my deliverance. [20]It is my eager expectation and hope that I will not be put to shame in any way, but that by my speaking with all boldness, Christ will be exalted now as always in my body, whether by life or by death. [21]For to me, living is Christ and dying is gain. [22]If I am to live in the flesh, that means fruitful labor for me; and I do not know which I prefer. [23]I am hard pressed between the two: my desire is to depart and be with Christ, for that is far better; [24]but to remain in the flesh is more necessary for you. [25]Since I am convinced of this, I know that I will remain and continue with all of you for your progress and joy in faith, [26]so that I may share abundantly in your boasting in Christ Jesus when I come to you again.

[27]Only, live your life in a manner worthy of the gospel of Christ, so that, whether I come and see you or am absent and hear about you, I will know that you are standing firm in one spirit, striving side by side with one mind for the faith of the gospel, [28]and are in no way intimidated by your opponents. For them this is

evidence of their destruction, but of your salvation.
And this is God's doing.
²⁹For he has graciously
granted you the privilege not
only of believing in Christ,
but of suffering for him as
well— ³⁰since you are
having the same struggle
that you saw I had and now
hear that I still have.

αὐτοῖς ἔνδειξις ἀπωλείας,   ὑμῶν δὲ σωτηρίας, καὶ
A PROOF~TO THEM   OF [THEIR] DESTRUCTION, BUT~OF YOUR° SALVATION,   AND

τοῦτο ἀπὸ θεοῦ·   **1.29** ὅτι   ὑμῖν ἐχαρίσθη τὸ ὑπὲρ
THIS   FROM GOD;   BECAUSE TO YOU° IT WAS GIVEN   -   ON BEHALF

Χριστοῦ, οὐ μόνον τὸ εἰς αὐτὸν πιστεύειν ἀλλὰ καὶ τὸ
OF CHRIST, NOT ONLY   - ²IN ³HIM ¹TO BELIEVE   BUT ALSO -

ὑπὲρ   αὐτοῦ πάσχειν, **1.30** τὸν αὐτὸν ἀγῶνα ἔχοντες,
ON BEHALF OF HIM   TO SUFFER,   THE SAME STRUGGLE HAVING,

οἷον εἴδετε ἐν ἐμοὶ καὶ νῦν ἀκούετε ἐν ἐμοί.
WHICH YOU° SAW IN ME   AND NOW HEAR [TO BE] IN   ME.

CHAPTER 2

If then there is any encouragement in Christ, any consolation from love, any
sharing in the Spirit, any
compassion and sympathy,
²make my joy complete: be
of the same mind, having the
same love, being in full
accord and of one mind. ³Do
nothing from selfish ambition or conceit, but in humility regard others as better
than yourselves. ⁴Let each of
you look not to your own
interests, but to the interests
of others. ⁵Let the same
mind be in you that was^i in
Christ Jesus,

6 who, though he was in
    the form of God,
    did not regard equality
    with God
    as something to be
    exploited,
7 but emptied himself,
    taking the form of a
    slave,
    being born in human
    likeness.
    And being found in
    human form,
8   he humbled himself
    and became obedient to
    the point of death—
    even death on a cross.
9 Therefore God also
    highly exalted him
    and gave him the

^i Or *that you have*

2.1 Εἴ   τις οὖν   παράκλησις ἐν Χριστῷ, εἰ
        ²IF [THERE IS] ³ANY ¹THEREFORE ⁴ENCOURAGEMENT IN   CHRIST,   IF

τι παραμύθιον ἀγάπης, εἴ τις κοινωνία πνεύματος, εἴ
ANY CONSOLATION OF LOVE, IF ANY FELLOWSHIP OF [THE] SPIRIT, IF

τις σπλάγχνα καὶ οἰκτιρμοί, **2.2** πληρώσατέ μου τὴν
ANY BOWELS(AFFECTION) AND COMPASSIONS,   ¹MAKE ⁴COMPLETE ²MY   -

χαρὰν ἵνα τὸ αὐτὸ   φρονῆτε, τὴν αὐτὴν ἀγάπην
³JOY   THAT THE SAME THING YOU° THINK, THE SAME   LOVE

ἔχοντες, σύμψυχοι,   τὸ ἓν   φρονοῦντες,
HAVING, [AS] ONES JOINED IN SOUL, THE ONE THING THINKING,

2.3 μηδὲν   κατ'   ἐριθείαν μηδὲ κατὰ
     [DOING] NOTHING ACCORDING TO RIVALRY NEITHER ACCORDING TO

κενοδοξίαν ἀλλὰ τῇ ταπεινοφροσύνῃ ἀλλήλους ἡγούμενοι
EMPTY CONCEIT BUT - IN HUMILITY,   ONE ANOTHER~ESTEEMING

ὑπερέχοντας ἑαυτῶν, **2.4** μὴ τὰ   ἑαυτῶν   ἕκαστος
ABOVE   THEMSELVES,   ¹NOT ⁴THE THINGS ⁵OF THEMSELVES ²EVERY PERSON

σκοποῦντες ἀλλὰ [καὶ] τὰ   ἑτέρων ἕκαστοι.
³LOOKING AT, BUT ²ALSO ³[AT] THE THINGS ⁴OF OTHERS ¹EACH PERSON.

2.5 τοῦτο φρονεῖτε ἐν ὑμῖν ὃ   καὶ   ἐν Χριστῷ
    [LET] THIS THINK[ING BE] IN YOU° WHICH [WAS] ALSO IN   CHRIST

Ἰησοῦ, **2.6** ὃς ἐν μορφῇ θεοῦ ὑπάρχων οὐχ
JESUS,   WHO IN [THE] FORM OF GOD EXISTING   ²NOT

ἁρπαγμὸν   ἡγήσατο τὸ εἶναι ἴσα θεῷ, **2.7** ἀλλὰ
⁷A THING TO BE GRASPED ¹DID ³REGARD - ⁴TO BE ⁵EQUAL ⁶WITH GOD,   BUT

ἑαυτὸν ἐκένωσεν μορφὴν δούλου λαβών, ἐν ὁμοιώματι
HE POURED OUT~HIMSELF, [THE] FORM OF A SLAVE TAKING, ²IN ³[THE] LIKENESS

ἀνθρώπων γενόμενος· καὶ σχήματι εὑρεθεὶς   ὡς
⁴OF MEN   ¹HAVING BEEN BORN; AND   HAVING BEEN FOUND~IN APPEARANCE AS

ἄνθρωπος **2.8** ἐταπείνωσεν ἑαυτὸν γενόμενος ὑπήκοος
A MAN,   HE HUMBLED   HIMSELF HAVING BECOME OBEDIENT

μέχρι θανάτου, θανάτου δὲ σταυροῦ. **2.9** διὸ   καὶ
UNTO DEATH,   AND [THAT]~A DEATH OF(BY) A CROSS.   WHEREFORE ALSO

ὁ θεὸς αὐτὸν ὑπερύψωσεν καὶ ἐχαρίσατο αὐτῷ τὸ
- GOD EXALTED~HIM   AND GAVE   TO HIM THE

ὄνομα τὸ ὑπὲρ πᾶν ὄνομα, **2.10** ἵνα ἐν τῷ ὀνόματι
NAME   -   ABOVE EVERY NAME,   THAT IN(AT) THE NAME

Ἰησοῦ πᾶν γόνυ κάμψῃ ἐπουρανίων καὶ ἐπιγείων
OF JESUS EVERY KNEE SHOULD BEND, OF [BEINGS] IN HEAVEN AND ON EARTH

καὶ καταχθονίων **2.11** καὶ πᾶσα γλῶσσα
AND   UNDER THE EARTH,   AND   EVERY TONGUE

ἐξομολογήσηται ὅτι κύριος Ἰησοῦς Χριστὸς εἰς δόξαν
SHOULD CONFESS,   -   [THE] LORD [IS] JESUS CHRIST TO [THE] GLORY

θεοῦ πατρός.
OF GOD [THE] FATHER.

   2.12 Ὥστε, ἀγαπητοί μου, καθὼς πάντοτε ὑπηκούσατε,
   THEREFORE, MY~BELOVED,   AS   ALWAYS   YOU° OBEYED,

μὴ ὡς ἐν τῇ παρουσίᾳ μου μόνον ἀλλὰ νῦν πολλῷ
NOT AS IN THE PRESENCE OF ME ONLY   BUT   NOW MUCH

μᾶλλον ἐν τῇ ἀπουσίᾳ μου, μετὰ φόβου καὶ τρόμου
MORE   IN THE ABSENCE OF ME, WITH FEAR   AND TREMBLING

τὴν ἑαυτῶν σωτηρίαν κατεργάζεσθε· **2.13** θεὸς γάρ
-    YOUR° OWN SALVATION   WORK OUT.   FOR~GOD

ἐστιν ὁ ἐνεργῶν ἐν ὑμῖν καὶ τὸ θέλειν καὶ τὸ
IS   THE ONE WORKING IN YOU° BOTH -   TO WILL AND -

ἐνεργεῖν ὑπὲρ τῆς εὐδοκίας. **2.14** πάντα ποιεῖτε
TO WORK   ON BEHALF OF THE(HIS) GOOD PLEASURE. ALL THINGS DO

χωρὶς γογγυσμῶν καὶ διαλογισμῶν, **2.15** ἵνα γένησθε
WITHOUT GRUMBLINGS AND ARGUMENTS,   THAT YOU° MAY BE

ἄμεμπτοι καὶ ἀκέραιοι, τέκνα θεοῦ ἄμωμα
BLAMELESS AND PURE,   ²CHILDREN ³OF GOD ¹WITHOUT BLEMISH

μέσον γενεᾶς σκολιᾶς καὶ διεστραμμένης, ἐν
IN [THE] MIDST OF A GENERATION CROOKED AND HAVING BEEN PERVERTED, AMONG

οἷς φαίνεσθε ὡς φωστῆρες ἐν κόσμῳ, **2.16** λόγον
WHOM YOU° SHINE AS LUMINARIES IN [THE] WORLD,   [THE] WORD

ζωῆς ἐπέχοντες, εἰς καύχημα ἐμοὶ εἰς ἡμέραν Χριστοῦ,
OF LIFE HOLDING [FORTH], FOR A BOAST TO ME IN [THE] DAY OF CHRIST,

ὅτι οὐκ εἰς κενὸν ἔδραμον οὐδὲ εἰς κενὸν ἐκοπίασα.
THAT NOT IN VAIN I RAN   NOR IN VAIN   LABORED.

2.17 ἀλλὰ εἰ καὶ σπένδομαι   ἐπὶ τῇ θυσίᾳ
BUT   IF INDEED I AM POURED OUT [AS A DRINK OFFERING] UPON THE SACRIFICE

καὶ λειτουργίᾳ τῆς πίστεως ὑμῶν, χαίρω καὶ
AND PRIESTLY SERVICE OF THE FAITH OF YOU°, I REJOICE AND

συγχαίρω πᾶσιν ὑμῖν· **2.18** τὸ δὲ αὐτὸ καὶ
REJOICE TOGETHER WITH YOU°~ALL;   AND~[IN] THE SAME [WAY] ALSO

ὑμεῖς χαίρετε καὶ συγχαίρετέ μοι.
YOU°   REJOICE   AND REJOICE TOGETHER WITH ME.

2.19 Ἐλπίζω δὲ ἐν κυρίῳ Ἰησοῦ Τιμόθεον ταχέως
I HOPE   -   IN [THE] LORD JESUS ³TIMOTHY ¹SOON

πέμψαι ὑμῖν, ἵνα κἀγὼ εὐψυχῶ γνοὺς τὰ
²TO SEND TO YOU°, THAT I ALSO MAY BE CHEERED UP KNOWING THE THINGS

περὶ ὑμῶν. **2.20** οὐδένα γὰρ ἔχω ἰσόψυχον, ὅστις
CONCERNING YOU°.   FOR~NO ONE I HAVE LIKEMINDED,   WHO

name
that is above every
  name,
10 so that at the name of
  Jesus
every knee should
  bend,
in heaven and on earth
  and under the earth,
11 and every tongue should
  confess
that Jesus Christ is
  Lord,
to the glory of God the
  Father.
12 Therefore, my
beloved, just as you have
always obeyed me, not only
in my presence, but much
more now in my absence,
work out your own salvation
with fear and trembling;
13 for it is God who is at work
in you, enabling you both to
will and to work for his good
pleasure.
14 Do all things without
murmuring and arguing,
15 so that you may be
blameless and innocent,
children of God without
blemish in the midst of a
crooked and perverse
generation, in which you
shine like stars in the world.
16 It is by your holding fast to
the word of life that I can
boast on the day of Christ
that I did not run in vain or
labor in vain. 17 But even if I
am being poured out as a
libation over the sacrifice
and the offering of your
faith, I am glad and rejoice
with all of you— 18 and in
the same way you also must
be glad and rejoice with me.
19 I hope in the Lord
Jesus to send Timothy to
you soon, so that I may be
cheered by news of you. 20 I
have no one like him who

will be genuinely concerned for your welfare. 21All of them are seeking their own interests, not those of Jesus Christ. 22But Timothy's[j] worth you know, how like a son with a father he has served with me in the work of the gospel. 23I hope therefore to send him as soon as I see how things go with me; 24and I trust in the Lord that I will also come soon.

25 Still, I think it necessary to send to you Epaphroditus—my brother and co-worker and fellow soldier, your messenger[k] and minister to my need; 26for he has been longing for[l] all of you, and has been distressed because you heard that he was ill. 27He was indeed so ill that he nearly died. But God had mercy on him, and not only on him but on me also, so that I would not have one sorrow after another. 28I am the more eager to send him, therefore, in order that you may rejoice at seeing him again, and that I may be less anxious. 29Welcome him then in the Lord with all joy, and honor such people, 30because he came close to death for the work of Christ,[m] risking his life to make up for those services that you could not give me.

[j] Gk his
[k] Gk apostle
[l] Other ancient authorities read longing to see
[m] Other ancient authorities read of the Lord

γνησίως τὰ περὶ ὑμῶν μεριμνήσει· **2.21** οἱ
GENUINELY 2THE THINGS 3CONCERNING 4YOU° 1WILL CARE FOR; -

πάντες γὰρ τὰ ἑαυτῶν ζητοῦσιν, οὐ τὰ
FOR~ALL THE THINGS OF THEMSELVES SEEK, NOT THE THINGS

Ἰησοῦ Χριστοῦ. **2.22** τὴν δὲ δοκιμὴν αὐτοῦ γινώσκετε,
OF JESUS CHRIST; BUT~THE PROVEN WORTH OF HIM YOU° KNOW,

ὅτι ὡς πατρὶ τέκνον σὺν ἐμοὶ ἐδούλευσεν εἰς τὸ
BECAUSE AS A CHILD~WITH A FATHER 2WITH 3ME 1HE SERVED IN THE

εὐαγγέλιον. **2.23** τοῦτον μὲν οὖν ἐλπίζω πέμψαι
GOSPEL. THIS ONE - THEREFORE I HOPE TO SEND

ὡς ἂν ἀφίδω τὰ περὶ ἐμὲ ἐξαυτῆς·
2WHENEVER 3I SEE 4[HOW] THE THINGS 5CONCERNING 6ME [WILL GO] 1IMMEDIATELY;

2.24 πέποιθα δὲ ἐν κυρίῳ ὅτι καὶ αὐτὸς ταχέως
BUT~I HAVE CONFIDENCE IN [THE] LORD THAT INDEED 2MYSELF 4QUICKLY

ἐλεύσομαι.
1I 3WILL COME.

2.25 Ἀναγκαῖον δὲ ἡγησάμην Ἐπαφρόδιτον τὸν
3NECESSARY 1BUT 2I CONSIDERED [IT] 7EPAPHRODITUS 8THE

ἀδελφὸν καὶ συνεργὸν καὶ συστρατιώτην μου, ὑμῶν δὲ
9BROTHER 10AND 11CO-WORKER 12AND 13FELLOW-SOLDIER 14OF ME, 15BUT~YOUR°

ἀπόστολον καὶ λειτουργὸν τῆς χρείας μου, πέμψαι
16APOSTLE 17AND 18PRIESTLY MINISTER 19OF THE 20NEED 21OF ME, 4TO SEND

πρὸς ὑμᾶς, **2.26** ἐπειδὴ ἐπιποθῶν ἦν πάντας ὑμᾶς
5TO 6YOU°, SINCE HE WAS~YEARNING AFTER YOU°~ALL

καὶ ἀδημονῶν, διότι ἠκούσατε ὅτι ἠσθένησεν.
AND [WAS] BEING HOMESICK, BECAUSE YOU° HEARD THAT HE WAS SICK.

2.27 καὶ γὰρ ἠσθένησεν παραπλήσιον θανάτῳ· ἀλλὰ ὁ
FOR~INDEED HE WAS SICK COMING NEAR TO DEATH; BUT -

θεὸς ἠλέησεν αὐτόν, οὐκ αὐτὸν δὲ μόνον ἀλλὰ
GOD HAD MERCY [ON] HIM, 2NOT 3[ON] HIM 1AND ONLY BUT

καὶ ἐμέ, ἵνα μὴ λύπην ἐπὶ λύπην σχῶ.
ALSO [ON] ME, LEST SORROW UPON SORROW I SHOULD HAVE.

2.28 σπουδαιοτέρως οὖν ἔπεμψα αὐτόν, ἵνα ἰδόντες
MORE EAGERLY THEREFORE I SENT HIM, THAT HAVING SEEN

αὐτὸν πάλιν χαρῆτε κἀγὼ ἀλυπότερος ὦ.
HIM AGAIN YOU° MAY REJOICE AND I MAY BE~LESS SORROWFUL.

2.29 προσδέχεσθε οὖν αὐτὸν ἐν κυρίῳ μετὰ πάσης
THEREFORE~RECEIVE HIM IN [THE] LORD WITH ALL

χαρᾶς καὶ τοὺς τοιούτους ἐντίμους ἔχετε, **2.30** ὅτι
JOY AND - 2SUCH ONES 3IN ESTEEM 1HOLD, BECAUSE

διὰ τὸ ἔργον Χριστοῦ μέχρι θανάτου ἤγγισεν
ON ACCOUNT OF THE WORK OF CHRIST 2TO 3DEATH 1HE CAME NEAR

παραβολευσάμενος τῇ ψυχῇ, ἵνα ἀναπληρώσῃ τὸ
HAVING RISKED THE (HIS) LIFE, THAT HE MIGHT FILL UP -

ὑμῶν ὑστέρημα τῆς πρός με λειτουργίας.
YOUR° DEFICIENCY - 2TO 3ME 1OF SERVICE.

3.1 Τὸ   λοιπόν, ἀδελφοί μου, χαίρετε ἐν κυρίῳ.
[AS TO] THE REST,   BROTHERS   OF ME, REJOICE IN [THE] LORD.

τὰ αὐτὰ   γράφειν ὑμῖν ἐμοὶ μὲν οὐκ ὀκνηρόν,
²THE ³SAME THINGS ¹TO WRITE TO YOU˚ FOR ME - [IS] NOT TROUBLESOME,

ὑμῖν δὲ   ἀσφαλές.
BUT~FOR YOU˚ [IS] A SAFEGUARD.

3.2 Βλέπετε   τοὺς κύνας, βλέπετε   τοὺς κακοὺς
WATCH OUT [FOR] THE DOGS, WATCH OUT [FOR] THE EVIL

ἐργάτας, βλέπετε   τὴν κατατομήν. **3.3** ἡμεῖς γάρ
WORKERS, WATCH OUT [FOR] THE MUTILATORS.   FOR~WE

ἐσμεν ἡ περιτομή, ⌐οἱ   πνεύματι θεοῦ λατρεύοντες⌐
ARE   THE CIRCUMCISION, THE ONES BY [THE] SPIRIT OF GOD WORSHIPING

καὶ καυχώμενοι ἐν Χριστῷ Ἰησοῦ καὶ οὐκ ἐν σαρκὶ
AND BOASTING   IN CHRIST JESUS AND NOT ²IN ³[THE] FLESH

πεποιθότες, **3.4** καίπερ ἐγὼ ἔχων   πεποίθησιν
¹HAVING CONFIDENCE, EVEN THOUGH I [COULD BE] HAVING CONFIDENCE

καὶ ἐν σαρκί. εἴ τις δοκεῖ ἄλλος   πεποιθέναι ἐν
ALSO IN [THE] FLESH; IF ¹ANY ³THINKS ²OTHER PERSON TO HAVE CONFIDENCE IN

σαρκί, ἐγὼ μᾶλλον· **3.5** περιτομῇ   ὀκταήμερος, ἐκ
[THE] FLESH, I   MORE;   AS TO CIRCUMCISION [ON THE] EIGHTH DAY, OF

γένους Ἰσραήλ, φυλῆς Βενιαμίν, Ἑβραῖος ἐξ
[THE] RACE OF ISRAEL, [THE] TRIBE OF BENJAMIN, A HEBREW OF

Ἑβραίων, κατὰ   νόμον Φαρισαῖος, **3.6** κατὰ
HEBREWS, ACCORDING TO [THE] LAW A PHARISEE,   ACCORDING TO

ζῆλος διώκων τὴν ἐκκλησίαν, κατὰ   δικαιοσύνην
ZEAL PERSECUTING THE CHURCH, ACCORDING TO RIGHTEOUSNESS

τὴν ἐν νόμῳ γενόμενος ἄμεμπτος. **3.7** [ἀλλὰ] ἅτινα
- IN [THE] LAW, HAVING BECOME BLAMELESS.   BUT WHAT THINGS

ἦν μοι κέρδη, ταῦτα ἥγημαι   διὰ   τὸν
WERE GAINS~TO ME, THESE I HAVE CONSIDERED ²ON ACCOUNT OF -

Χριστὸν ζημίαν. **3.8** ἀλλὰ μενοῦνγε καὶ ἡγοῦμαι
³CHRIST ¹LOSS.   BUT EVEN~MORE SO   I CONSIDER

πάντα ζημίαν εἶναι διὰ   τὸ ὑπερέχον τῆς
ALL THINGS TO BE~LOSS ON ACCOUNT OF THE EXCELLENCY OF THE

γνώσεως Χριστοῦ Ἰησοῦ τοῦ κυρίου μου, δι   ὃν
KNOWLEDGE OF CHRIST JESUS THE LORD OF ME, ON ACCOUNT OF WHOM

τὰ πάντα ἐζημιώθην, καὶ ἡγοῦμαι σκύβαλα, ἵνα
- ALL THINGS I SUFFERED LOSS, AND I CONSIDER [THEM] REFUSE, THAT

Χριστὸν κερδήσω **3.9** καὶ εὑρεθῶ ἐν αὐτῷ, μὴ ἔχων
I MAY GAIN~CHRIST   AND BE FOUND IN HIM, NOT HAVING

ἐμὴν δικαιοσύνην τὴν ἐκ νόμου ἀλλὰ τὴν
MY OWN RIGHTEOUSNESS THE ONE OF [THE] LAW BUT THE [RIGHTEOUSNESS]

διὰ   πίστεως Χριστοῦ, τὴν ἐκ θεοῦ δικαιοσύνην
THROUGH FAITH OF(IN) CHRIST, ¹THE ³OF ⁴GOD ²RIGHTEOUSNESS

Finally, my brothers and sisters,[n] rejoice[o] in the Lord.

To write the same things to you is not troublesome to me, and for you it is a safeguard.

2 Beware of the dogs, beware of the evil workers, beware of those who mutilate the flesh![p] 3For it is we who are the circumcision, who worship in the Spirit of God[q] and boast in Christ Jesus and have no confidence in the flesh— 4even though I, too, have reason for confidence in the flesh.

If anyone else has reason to be confident in the flesh, I have more: 5circumcised on the eighth day, a member of the people of Israel, of the tribe of Benjamin, a Hebrew born of Hebrews; as to the law, a Pharisee; 6as to zeal, a persecutor of the church; as to righteousness under the law, blameless.

7 Yet whatever gains I had, these I have come to regard as loss because of Christ. 8More than that, I regard everything as loss because of the surpassing value of knowing Christ Jesus my Lord. For his sake I have suffered the loss of all things, and I regard them as rubbish, in order that I may gain Christ 9and be found in him, not having a righteousness of my own that comes from the law, but one that comes through faith in Christ,[r] the righteousness from God

[n] Gk *my brothers*
[o] Or *farewell*
[p] Gk *the mutilation*
[q] Other ancient authorities read *worship God in spirit*
[r] Or *through the faith of Christ*

3:3 text: ASV RSVmg NIV NEBmg TEV NJB NRSV. var. οι πνευματι θεω λατρευοντες (the ones worshiping God in spirit): KJV RSV NEBmg NJB NRSVmg. var. οι πνευματι λατρευοντες (the ones worshiping in spirit): none.

based on faith. ¹⁰I want to know Christ⁵ and the power of his resurrection and the sharing of his sufferings by becoming like him in his death, ¹¹if somehow I may attain the resurrection from the dead.

12 Not that I have already obtained this or have already reached the goal;ᵗ but I press on to make it my own, because Christ Jesus has made me his own. ¹³Beloved,ᵘ I do not consider that I have made it my own;ᵛ but this one thing I do: forgetting what lies behind and straining forward to what lies ahead, ¹⁴I press on toward the goal for the prize of the heavenlyʷ call of God in Christ Jesus. ¹⁵Let those of us then who are mature be of the same mind; and if you think differently about anything, this too God will reveal to you. ¹⁶Only let us hold fast to what we have attained.

17 Brothers and sisters,ᵘ join in imitating me, and observe those who live according to the example you have in us. ¹⁸For many live as enemies of the cross of Christ; I have often told you of them, and now I tell you even with tears. ¹⁹Their end is destruction; their god is the belly; and their glory is in their shame; their minds are set on earthly things. ²⁰But our citizenshipˣ is in

ˢ Gk *him*
ᵗ Or *have already been made perfect*
ᵘ Gk *Brothers*
ᵛ Other ancient authorities read *my own yet*
ʷ Gk *upward*
ˣ Or *commonwealth*

ἐπὶ τῇ πίστει, **3.10** τοῦ γνῶναι αὐτὸν καὶ τὴν
[BASED] UPON - FAITH, - TO KNOW HIM AND THE

δύναμιν τῆς ἀναστάσεως αὐτοῦ καὶ [τὴν] κοινωνίαν
POWER OF THE RESURRECTION OF HIM AND THE FELLOWSHIP

[τῶν] παθημάτων αὐτοῦ, συμμορφιζόμενος τῷ θανάτῳ
OF THE SUFFERINGS OF HIM BEING CONFORMED TO THE DEATH

αὐτοῦ, **3.11** εἴ πως καταντήσω εἰς τὴν ἐξανάστασιν
OF HIM, IF SOMEHOW I MAY ATTAIN TO THE RESURRECTION

τὴν ἐκ νεκρῶν.
- FROM [THE] DEAD.

3.12 Οὐχ ὅτι ἤδη ἔλαβον ἢ ἤδη τετελείωμαι,
NOT THAT ALREADY I OBTAINED OR ALREADY HAVE BEEN PERFECTED,

διώκω δὲ εἰ καὶ καταλάβω, ἐφ' ᾧ καὶ
BUT~I PURSUE IF INDEED I MAY LAY HOLD OF THAT FOR WHICH ALSO

κατελήμφθην ὑπὸ Χριστοῦ ['Ιησοῦ]. **3.13** ἀδελφοί, ἐγὼ
I WAS LAID HOLD OF BY CHRIST JESUS. BROTHERS, ¹I

ἐμαυτὸν οὐ λογίζομαι κατειληφέναι· ἓν δέ, τὰ
³MYSELF ²DO NOT CONSIDER TO HAVE LAID HOLD; BUT~ONE THING, ²THE THINGS

μὲν ὀπίσω ἐπιλανθανόμενος τοῖς δὲ ἔμπροσθεν
- ³BEHIND ¹FORGETTING ⁶TO THE THINGS ⁴AND ⁷BEFORE

ἐπεκτεινόμενος, **3.14** κατὰ σκοπὸν διώκω εἰς τὸ
⁵STRETCHING FORWARD, ACCORDING TO [THE] GOAL I PURSUE FOR THE

βραβεῖον τῆς ἄνω κλήσεως τοῦ θεοῦ ἐν Χριστῷ
PRIZE OF THE HIGH CALLING - OF GOD IN CHRIST

'Ιησοῦ. **3.15** Ὅσοι οὖν τέλειοι,
JESUS. THEREFORE~AS MANY AS [WOULD BE] PERFECT,

τοῦτο φρονῶμεν· καὶ εἴ τι ἑτέρως φρονεῖτε, καὶ
LET US THINK~THIS; AND IF ANYTHING DIFFERENT YOU° THINK, EVEN

τοῦτο ὁ θεὸς ὑμῖν ἀποκαλύψει· **3.16** πλὴν εἰς ὃ
THIS - GOD WILL REVEAL~TO YOU°; NEVERTHELESS TO WHAT

ἐφθάσαμεν, τῷ αὐτῷ στοιχεῖν.
WE ATTAINED, BY THE SAME [RULE] [WE ARE] TO FOLLOW.

3.17 Συμμιμηταί μου γίνεσθε, ἀδελφοί, καὶ
²IMITATORS TOGETHER ³OF ME ¹BE, BROTHERS, AND

σκοπεῖτε τοὺς οὕτω περιπατοῦντας καθὼς ἔχετε
NOTICE THE ONES THUS WALKING AS YOU° HAVE

τύπον ἡμᾶς. **3.18** πολλοὶ γὰρ περιπατοῦσιν οὓς
US~[AS] AN EXAMPLE. FOR~MANY WALK [OF] WHOM

πολλάκις ἔλεγον ὑμῖν, νῦν δὲ καὶ κλαίων λέγω,
OFTEN I WAS TELLING YOU°, AND~NOW ALSO WEEPING I SAY,

τοὺς ἐχθροὺς τοῦ σταυροῦ τοῦ Χριστοῦ, **3.19** ὧν
[THEY ARE] THE ENEMIES OF THE CROSS - OF CHRIST, WHOSE

τὸ τέλος ἀπώλεια, ὧν ὁ θεὸς ἡ κοιλία καὶ
- END [IS] DESTRUCTION, WHOSE - GOD [IS] THE[IR] BELLY AND

ἡ δόξα ἐν τῇ αἰσχύνῃ αὐτῶν, οἱ τὰ
THE[IR] GLORY IN THE SHAME OF THEM, THE ONES -

ἐπίγεια φρονοῦντες. **3.20** ἡμῶν γὰρ τὸ πολίτευμα ἐν
THINKING~EARTHLY THINGS. FOR~OUR - CITIZENSHIP IN

οὐρανοῖς ὑπάρχει, ἐξ οὗ καὶ σωτῆρα ἀπεκδεχόμεθα
[THE] HEAVENS EXISTS,   FROM WHERE ALSO WE EAGERLY AWAIT~A SAVIOR,

κύριον Ἰησοῦν Χριστόν, **3.21** ὃς μετασχηματίσει τὸ
[THE] LORD JESUS CHRIST,   WHO WILL TRANSFIGURE THE

σῶμα τῆς ταπεινώσεως ἡμῶν σύμμορφον τῷ σώματι
BODY OF THE HUMILIATION OF US [INTO] CONFORMITY WITH THE BODY

τῆς δόξης αὐτοῦ κατὰ τὴν ἐνέργειαν τοῦ δύνασθαι
OF THE GLORY OF HIM ACCORDING TO THE WORKING OF THE POWER

αὐτὸν καὶ ὑποτάξαι αὐτῷ τὰ πάντα.
OF HIM EVEN TO SUBJECT TO HIM[SELF] - ALL THINGS.

heaven, and it is from there that we are expecting a Savior, the Lord Jesus Christ. ²¹He will transform the body of our humiliation[y] that it may be conformed to the body of his glory,[z] by the power that also enables him to make all things subject to himself.

[y] Or *our humble bodies*
[z] Or *his glorious body*

4.1 Ὥστε, ἀδελφοί μου ἀγαπητοὶ καὶ ἐπιπόθητοι,
SO THEN, BROTHERS OF ME, BELOVED AND LONGED FOR,

χαρὰ καὶ στέφανός μου, οὕτως στήκετε ἐν κυρίῳ,
[THE] JOY AND CROWN OF ME, SO STAND [FIRM] IN [THE] LORD,

ἀγαπητοί.
BELOVED.

4.2 Εὐοδίαν παρακαλῶ καὶ Συντύχην παρακαλῶ τὸ
I APPEAL TO~EUODIA AND I APPEAL TO~SYNTYCHE ²THE

αὐτὸ φρονεῖν ἐν κυρίῳ. **4.3** ναὶ ἐρωτῶ καὶ σέ,
³SAME THING ¹TO THINK IN [THE] LORD. YES I ASK ALSO YOU,

γνήσιε σύζυγε, συλλαμβάνου αὐταῖς, αἵτινες ἐν τῷ
TRUE YOKE-FELLOW, ASSIST THEM, WHO IN THE

εὐαγγελίῳ συνήθλησάν μοι μετὰ καὶ Κλήμεντος καὶ
GOSPEL CONTENDED ALONGSIDE ME WITH BOTH CLEMENT AND

τῶν λοιπῶν συνεργῶν μου, ὧν τὰ ὀνόματα ἐν
THE REST OF [THE] CO-WORKERS OF ME, WHOSE - NAMES [ARE] IN

βίβλῳ ζωῆς. **4.4** Χαίρετε ἐν κυρίῳ πάντοτε· πάλιν
[THE] BOOK OF LIFE. REJOICE IN [THE] LORD ALWAYS; AGAIN

ἐρῶ, χαίρετε. **4.5** τὸ ἐπιεικὲς ὑμῶν γνωσθήτω
I WILL SAY, REJOICE. THE REASONABLENESS OF YOU° LET IT BE KNOWN

πᾶσιν ἀνθρώποις. ὁ κύριος ἐγγύς. **4.6** μηδὲν
TO ALL MEN. THE LORD [IS] NEAR. [IN] NOTHING

μεριμνᾶτε, ἀλλ' ἐν παντὶ τῇ προσευχῇ καὶ τῇ δεήσει
BE ANXIOUS, BUT IN EVERYTHING - BY PRAYER AND - BY PETITION

μετὰ εὐχαριστίας τὰ αἰτήματα ὑμῶν γνωριζέσθω πρὸς
WITH THANKSGIVING THE REQUESTS OF YOU° LET BE MADE KNOWN TO

τὸν θεόν. **4.7** καὶ ἡ εἰρήνη τοῦ θεοῦ ἡ ὑπερέχουσα
- GOD. AND THE PEACE - OF GOD - SURPASSING

πάντα νοῦν φρουρήσει τὰς καρδίας ὑμῶν καὶ τὰ
ALL UNDERSTANDING WILL GUARD THE HEARTS OF YOU° AND THE

νοήματα ὑμῶν ἐν Χριστῷ Ἰησοῦ.
THOUGHTS OF YOU° IN CHRIST JESUS.

4.8 Τὸ λοιπόν, ἀδελφοί, ὅσα ἐστὶν ἀληθῆ,
[AS TO] THE REST, BROTHERS, WHATEVER THINGS ARE TRUE,

¹Therefore, my brothers and sisters,[a] whom I love and long for, my joy and crown, stand firm in the Lord in this way, my beloved.

2 I urge Euodia and I urge Syntyche to be of the same mind in the Lord. ³Yes, and I ask you also, my loyal companion,[b] help these women, for they have struggled beside me in the work of the gospel, together with Clement and the rest of my co-workers, whose names are in the book of life.

4 Rejoice[c] in the Lord always; again I will say, Rejoice.[c] ⁵Let your gentleness be known to everyone. The Lord is near. ⁶Do not worry about anything, but in everything by prayer and supplication with thanksgiving let your requests be made known to God. ⁷And the peace of God, which surpasses all understanding, will guard your hearts and your minds in Christ Jesus.

8 Finally, beloved,[d] whatever is true,

[a] Gk *my brothers*
[b] Or *loyal Syzygus*
[c] Or *Farewell*
[d] Gk *brothers*

whatever is honorable, whatever is just, whatever is pure, whatever is pleasing, whatever is commendable, if there is any excellence and if there is anything worthy of praise, think about[e] these things. [9]Keep on doing the things that you have learned and received and heard and seen in me, and the God of peace will be with you.

[10] I rejoice[f] in the Lord greatly that now at last you have revived your concern for me; indeed, you were concerned for me, but had no opportunity to show it.[g] [11]Not that I am referring to being in need; for I have learned to be content with whatever I have. [12]I know what it is to have little, and I know what it is to have plenty. In any and all circumstances I have learned the secret of being well-fed and of going hungry, of having plenty and of being in need. [13]I can do all things through him who strengthens me. [14]In any case, it was kind of you to share my distress.

[15] You Philippians indeed know that in the early days of the gospel, when I left Macedonia, no church shared with me in the matter of giving and receiving, except you alone. [16]For even when I was in Thessalonica, you sent me help for my needs more than once. [17]Not that I seek the gift, but I seek the profit that accumulates to your account. [18]I have been paid in full and have more

[e] Gk take account of
[f] Gk I rejoiced
[g] Gk lacks to show it

ὅσα σεμνά, ὅσα δίκαια, ὅσα ἁγνά, ὅσα
WHATEVER HONORABLE, WHATEVER RIGHTEOUS, WHATEVER PURE, WHATEVER

προσφιλῆ, ὅσα εὔφημα, εἴ τις ἀρετὴ καὶ εἴ τις
LOVELY, WHATEVER WELL-SPOKEN OF, IF ANY VIRTUE AND IF ANY

ἔπαινος, ταῦτα λογίζεσθε· **4.9** ἃ καὶ ἐμάθετε
PRAISE, THESE THINGS TAKE ACCOUNT OF; WHICH THINGS BOTH YOU° LEARNED

καὶ παρελάβετε καὶ ἠκούσατε καὶ εἴδετε ἐν ἐμοί,
AND YOU° RECEIVED AND YOU° HEARD AND YOU° SAW IN ME,

ταῦτα πράσσετε· καὶ ὁ θεὸς τῆς εἰρήνης ἔσται μεθ'
THESE PRACTISE; AND THE GOD - OF PEACE WILL BE WITH

ὑμῶν.
YOU°.

4.10 Ἐχάρην δὲ ἐν κυρίῳ μεγάλως ὅτι ἤδη ποτὲ
I REJOICED - IN [THE] LORD GREATLY THAT NOW AT LAST

ἀνεθάλετε τὸ ὑπὲρ ἐμοῦ φρονεῖν, ἐφ' ᾧ καὶ
YOU° BLOSSOMED ANEW - ²OF ³ME ¹[SO AS] TO THINK, AS TO WHOM INDEED

ἐφρονεῖτε, ἠκαιρεῖσθε δέ. **4.11** οὐχ ὅτι καθ'
YOU° WERE THINKING, BUT~WERE LACKING OPPORTUNITY. NOT THAT ²ACCORDING TO

ὑστέρησιν λέγω, ἐγὼ γὰρ ἔμαθον ἐν οἷς
³LACK ¹I SPEAK, FOR~I LEARNED IN WHATEVER [CIRCUMSTANCES]

εἰμι αὐτάρκης εἶναι. **4.12** οἶδα καὶ ταπεινοῦσθαι,
I AM TO BE~CONTENT. I KNOW BOTH TO BE HUMBLED,

οἶδα καὶ περισσεύειν· ἐν παντὶ καὶ ἐν πᾶσιν
AND~I KNOW [HOW] TO ABOUND; IN EVERYTHING AND IN ALL THINGS

μεμύημαι, καὶ χορτάζεσθαι καὶ πεινᾶν καὶ
I HAVE LEARNED [THE] SECRET, BOTH TO BE FILLED AND TO HUNGER, BOTH

περισσεύειν καὶ ὑστερεῖσθαι· **4.13** πάντα ἰσχύω ἐν
TO ABOUND AND TO HAVE LACK; I CAN DO~ALL THINGS IN

τῷ ἐνδυναμοῦντί με. **4.14** πλὴν καλῶς ἐποιήσατε
THE ONE EMPOWERING ME. NEVERTHELESS YOU° DID~WELL

συγκοινωνήσαντές μου τῇ θλίψει.
[IN] HAVING BECOME PARTNERS WITH [ME] OF MY - AFFLICTION.

4.15 Οἴδατε δὲ καὶ ὑμεῖς, Φιλιππήσιοι, ὅτι ἐν
³KNOW ¹AND ⁴ALSO ²YOU°, PHILIPPIANS, THAT IN

ἀρχῇ τοῦ εὐαγγελίου, ὅτε ἐξῆλθον ἀπὸ
[THE] BEGINNING OF THE GOSPEL, WHEN I WENT OUT FROM

Μακεδονίας, οὐδεμία μοι ἐκκλησία ἐκοινώνησεν εἰς
MACEDONIA, NOT ONE ³ME ¹CHURCH ²SHARED WITH IN

λόγον δόσεως καὶ λήμψεως εἰ μὴ ὑμεῖς μόνοι,
AN ACCOUNTING OF EXPENDITURES AND RECEIPTS EXCEPT YOU° ONLY,

4.16 ὅτι καὶ ἐν Θεσσαλονίκῃ καὶ ἅπαξ καὶ δὶς εἰς
BECAUSE INDEED IN THESSALONICA BOTH ONCE AND TWICE TO

τὴν χρείαν μοι ἐπέμψατε. **4.17** οὐχ ὅτι ἐπιζητῶ τὸ
THE NEED OF ME YOU° SENT. NOT THAT I SEEK THE

δόμα, ἀλλὰ ἐπιζητῶ τὸν καρπὸν τὸν πλεονάζοντα εἰς
GIFT, BUT I SEEK THE FRUIT - INCREASING TO

λόγον ὑμῶν. **4.18** ἀπέχω δὲ πάντα καὶ περισσεύω·
[THE] ACCOUNT OF YOU°. BUT~I HAVE ALL THINGS AND I ABOUND;

πεπλήρωμαι δεξάμενος παρὰ Ἐπαφροδίτου τὰ
I HAVE BEEN FILLED   HAVING RECEIVED FROM   EPAPHRODITUS   THE THINGS

παρ' ὑμῶν, ὀσμὴν εὐωδίας, θυσίαν δεκτήν,
FROM YOU°, A FRAGRANT~ODOR,   AN ACCEPTABLE~SACRIFICE,

εὐάρεστον τῷ θεῷ.   4.19 ὁ δὲ   θεός μου πληρώσει
WELL-PLEASING -   TO GOD.   AND~THE GOD OF ME WILL FILL

πᾶσαν χρείαν ὑμῶν κατὰ   τὸ πλοῦτος αὐτοῦ ἐν
EVERY   NEED   OF YOU° ACCORDING TO THE WEALTH   OF HIM   IN

δόξῃ ἐν Χριστῷ Ἰησοῦ.   4.20 τῷ δὲ   θεῷ καὶ πατρὶ
GLORY IN   CHRIST   JESUS.   NOW~TO THE GOD AND   FATHER

ἡμῶν ἡ   δόξα εἰς τοὺς αἰῶνας τῶν αἰώνων, ἀμήν.
OF US [BE] THE GLORY INTO THE   AGES OF THE AGES,   AMEN.

4.21 Ἀσπάσασθε πάντα ἅγιον ἐν Χριστῷ Ἰησοῦ.
GREET   EVERY SAINT IN CHRIST   JESUS;

ἀσπάζονται ὑμᾶς οἱ σὺν ἐμοὶ ἀδελφοί.
⁵GREET   ⁶YOU° ¹THE ³WITH ⁴ME   ²BROTHERS.

4.22 ἀσπάζονται ὑμᾶς πάντες οἱ ἅγιοι, μάλιστα δὲ
⁴GREET   ⁵YOU° ¹ALL ²THE ³SAINTS, AND~ESPECIALLY

οἱ ἐκ τῆς Καίσαρος οἰκίας.   4.23 ἡ χάρις τοῦ
THE ONES OF -   CAESAR'S   HOUSEHOLD.   THE GRACE OF THE

κυρίου Ἰησοῦ Χριστοῦ μετὰ τοῦ πνεύματος ὑμῶν.
LORD   JESUS   CHRIST [BE] WITH THE SPIRIT   OF YOU°.

than enough; I am fully satisfied, now that I have received from Epaphroditus the gifts you sent, a fragrant offering, a sacrifice acceptable and pleasing to God. ¹⁹And my God will fully satisfy every need of yours according to his riches in glory in Christ Jesus. ²⁰To our God and Father be glory forever and ever. Amen.

21 Greet every saint in Christ Jesus. The friends[h] who are with me greet you. ²²All the saints greet you, especially those of the emperor's household.

23 The grace of the Lord Jesus Christ be with your spirit.[i]

[h] Gk brothers
[i] Other ancient authorities add Amen

THE LETTER OF PAUL TO THE
COLOSSIANS

ΠΡΟΣ ΚΟΛΟΣΣΑΕΙΣ
TO   [THE] COLOSSIANS

1.1 Παῦλος ἀπόστολος Χριστοῦ Ἰησοῦ διὰ
PAUL   AN APOSTLE   OF CHRIST   JESUS   THROUGH

θελήματος θεοῦ καὶ Τιμόθεος ὁ ἀδελφὸς **1.2** τοῖς ἐν
[THE] WILL   OF GOD   AND   TIMOTHY   THE BROTHER,   TO THE   ²IN

Κολοσσαῖς ἁγίοις καὶ πιστοῖς ἀδελφοῖς ἐν Χριστῷ,
³COLOSSAE   ¹SAINTS   AND   FAITHFUL   BROTHERS   IN   CHRIST,

χάρις ὑμῖν καὶ εἰρήνη ἀπὸ θεοῦ πατρὸς ἡμῶν.
GRACE   TO YOU°   AND   PEACE   FROM   GOD   [THE] FATHER   OF US.

1.3 Εὐχαριστοῦμεν τῷ θεῷ πατρὶ τοῦ κυρίου ἡμῶν
WE GIVE THANKS   -   TO GOD   [THE] FATHER   OF THE   LORD   OF US

Ἰησοῦ Χριστοῦ πάντοτε περὶ ὑμῶν προσευχόμενοι,
JESUS   CHRIST,   ²ALWAYS   ³CONCERNING   ⁴YOU°   ¹PRAYING,

1.4 ἀκούσαντες τὴν πίστιν ὑμῶν ἐν Χριστῷ Ἰησοῦ καὶ
HAVING HEARD [OF]   THE   FAITH   OF YOU°   IN   CHRIST   JESUS   AND

τὴν ἀγάπην ἣν ἔχετε εἰς πάντας τοὺς ἁγίους
THE   LOVE   WHICH   YOU° HAVE   TO   ALL   THE   SAINTS

1.5 διὰ τὴν ἐλπίδα τὴν ἀποκειμένην ὑμῖν ἐν
ON ACCOUNT OF   THE   HOPE   -   BEING LAID UP   FOR YOU°   IN

τοῖς οὐρανοῖς, ἣν προηκούσατε ἐν τῷ λόγῳ τῆς
THE   HEAVENS,   WHICH   YOU° HEARD BEFORE   IN   THE   WORD   OF THE

ἀληθείας τοῦ εὐαγγελίου **1.6** τοῦ παρόντος εἰς ὑμᾶς,
TRUTH   OF THE   GOOD NEWS   -   COMING   TO   YOU°,

καθὼς καὶ ἐν παντὶ τῷ κόσμῳ ἐστὶν καρποφορούμενον
AS   ALSO   IN   ALL   THE   WORLD   IT IS BEARING FRUIT

καὶ αὐξανόμενον καθὼς καὶ ἐν ὑμῖν, ἀφ' ἧς ἡμέρας
AND   GROWING,   AS   ALSO   IN   YOU°,   FROM   [THE] DAY~IN WHICH

ἠκούσατε καὶ ἐπέγνωτε τὴν χάριν τοῦ θεοῦ ἐν
YOU° HEARD [IT]   AND   KNEW   THE   GRACE   -   OF GOD   IN

ἀληθείᾳ· **1.7** καθὼς ἐμάθετε ἀπὸ Ἐπαφρᾶ τοῦ
REALITY;   AS   YOU° LEARNED   FROM   EPAPHRAS   THE

ἀγαπητοῦ συνδούλου ἡμῶν, ὅς ἐστιν πιστὸς ὑπὲρ
BELOVED   FELLOW SLAVE   OF US,   WHO   IS   A FAITHFUL   ³FOR

⌐ὑμῶν⌐ διάκονος τοῦ Χριστοῦ, **1.8** ὁ καὶ δηλώσας ἡμῖν
⁴YOU°   ¹MINISTER   -   ²OF CHRIST,   WHO ALSO   REVEALED   TO US

τὴν ὑμῶν ἀγάπην ἐν πνεύματι.
-    YOUR°   LOVE   IN   [THE] SPIRIT.

1.9 Διὰ τοῦτο καὶ ἡμεῖς, ἀφ' ἧς ἡμέρας ἠκούσαμεν,
THEREFORE   WE~ALSO,   FROM   [THE] DAY~WHICH   WE HEARD,

Paul, an apostle of Christ Jesus by the will of God, and Timothy our brother,

2 To the saints and faithful brothers and sisters[a] in Christ in Colossae:

Grace to you and peace from God our Father.

3 In our prayers for you we always thank God, the Father of our Lord Jesus Christ, [4]for we have heard of your faith in Christ Jesus and of the love that you have for all the saints, [5]because of the hope laid up for you in heaven. You have heard of this hope before in the word of the truth, the gospel [6]that has come to you. Just as it is bearing fruit and growing in the whole world, so it has been bearing fruit among yourselves from the day you heard it and truly comprehended the grace of God. [7]This you learned from Epaphras, our beloved fellow servant.[b] He is a faithful minister of Christ on your[c] behalf, [8]and he has made known to us your love in the Spirit.

9 For this reason, since the day we heard it,

[a] Gk *brothers*
[b] Gk *slave*
[c] Other ancient authorities read *our*

1:7 text: KJV ASVmg RSVmg NASBmg NIVmg NEBmg TEVmg NJBmg NRSV. var. ημων (us): ASV RSV NASB NIV NEB TEV NJB NRSVmg.

we have not ceased praying for you and asking that you may be filled with the knowledge of God's[d] will in all spiritual wisdom and understanding, [10]so that you may lead lives worthy of the Lord, fully pleasing to him, as you bear fruit in every good work and as you grow in the knowledge of God. [11]May you be made strong with all the strength that comes from his glorious power, and may you be prepared to endure everything with patience, while joyfully [12]giving thanks to the Father, who has enabled[e] you[f] to share in the inheritance of the saints in the light. [13]He has rescued us from the power of darkness and transferred us into the kingdom of his beloved Son, [14]in whom we have redemption, the forgiveness of sins.[g]

15 He is the image of the invisible God, the firstborn of all creation; [16]for in[h] him all things in heaven and on earth were created, things visible and invisible, whether thrones or dominions or rulers or powers—all things have been created through him and for him. [17]He himself is before all things, and in[h] him all things hold together. [18]He is the head of the body, the church; he is the beginning, the firstborn from the dead, so that he might come to have first place in everything. [19]For in him

[d] Gk his
[e] Other ancient authorities read called
[f] Other ancient authorities read us
[g] Other ancient authorities add through his blood
[h] Or by

οὐ παυόμεθα ὑπὲρ ὑμῶν προσευχόμενοι καὶ αἰτούμενοι,
DO NOT CEASE   ²FOR   ³YOU°   ¹PRAYING   AND   ASKING

ἵνα πληρωθῆτε τὴν ἐπίγνωσιν τοῦ θελήματος
THAT   YOU° MAY BE FILLED [WITH] THE   KNOWLEDGE   OF THE   WILL

αὐτοῦ ἐν πάσῃ σοφίᾳ καὶ συνέσει πνευματικῇ,
OF HIM   IN   ALL   WISDOM   AND   SPIRITUAL~UNDERSTANDING,

1.10 περιπατῆσαι ἀξίως τοῦ κυρίου εἰς πᾶσαν
TO WALK   WORTHY   OF THE   LORD   IN   EVERY [WAY]

ἀρεσκείαν, ἐν παντὶ ἔργῳ ἀγαθῷ καρποφοροῦντες καὶ
PLEASING [TO HIM], IN   EVERY   GOOD~WORK   BEARING FRUIT   AND

αὐξανόμενοι τῇ ἐπιγνώσει τοῦ θεοῦ, 1.11 ἐν πάσῃ
GROWING   IN THE   KNOWLEDGE   -   OF GOD,   WITH ALL

δυνάμει δυναμούμενοι κατὰ τὸ κράτος τῆς δόξης
POWER   BEING EMPOWERED   ACCORDING TO THE   MIGHT   OF THE   GLORY

αὐτοῦ εἰς πᾶσαν ὑπομονὴν καὶ μακροθυμίαν. μετὰ
OF HIM   FOR ALL   ENDURANCE   AND   LONG-SUFFERING;   WITH

χαρᾶς 1.12 εὐχαριστοῦν τῷ πατρὶ τῷ ἱκανώσαντι
JOY   GIVING THANKS   TO THE   FATHER,   THE ONE HAVING QUALIFIED

ὑμᾶς εἰς τὴν μερίδα τοῦ κλήρου τῶν ἁγίων ἐν τῷ
YOU°   FOR THE   SHARE   OF THE   ALLOTMENT   OF THE SAINTS   IN   THE

φωτί· 1.13 ὃς ἐρρύσατο ἡμᾶς ἐκ τῆς ἐξουσίας τοῦ
LIGHT;   WHO   RESCUED   US   FROM THE   AUTHORITY   -

σκότους καὶ μετέστησεν εἰς τὴν βασιλείαν τοῦ υἱοῦ
OF DARKNESS AND   TRANSFERRED [US]   INTO THE   KINGDOM   OF THE SON

τῆς ἀγάπης αὐτοῦ, 1.14 ἐν ᾧ ἔχομεν τὴν
-   OF HIS~LOVE,   IN   WHOM   WE HAVE   THE

ἀπολύτρωσιν, τὴν ἄφεσιν τῶν ἁμαρτιῶν· 1.15 ὅς ἐστιν
REDEMPTION,   THE   FORGIVENESS   -   OF SINS;   WHO IS

εἰκὼν τοῦ θεοῦ τοῦ ἀοράτου, πρωτότοκος πάσης
[THE] IMAGE OF THE ²GOD   -   ¹INVISIBLE,   [THE] FIRSTBORN   OF ALL

κτίσεως, 1.16 ὅτι ἐν αὐτῷ ἐκτίσθη τὰ πάντα ἐν
CREATION,   BECAUSE IN   HIM   WERE CREATED   -   ALL THINGS IN

τοῖς οὐρανοῖς καὶ ἐπὶ τῆς γῆς, τὰ ὁρατὰ καὶ τὰ
THE   HEAVENS   AND   ON   THE   EARTH, THE VISIBLE THINGS AND   THE

ἀόρατα, εἴτε θρόνοι εἴτε κυριότητες εἴτε ἀρχαὶ
INVISIBLE THINGS, WHETHER THRONES OR   LORDSHIPS   WHETHER RULERS

εἴτε ἐξουσίαι· τὰ πάντα δι' αὐτοῦ καὶ εἰς αὐτὸν
OR   AUTHORITIES;   -   ALL THINGS THROUGH HIM   AND   FOR HIM

ἔκτισται· 1.17 καὶ αὐτός ἐστιν πρὸ πάντων καὶ τὰ
HAVE BEEN CREATED;   AND   HE   IS   BEFORE ALL THINGS AND   -

πάντα ἐν αὐτῷ συνέστηκεν, 1.18 καὶ αὐτός ἐστιν
ALL THINGS IN   HIM   HAVE BEEN HELD TOGETHER   AND   HE   IS

ἡ κεφαλὴ τοῦ σώματος τῆς ἐκκλησίας· ὅς ἐστιν
THE HEAD   OF THE BODY,   THE   CHURCH;   WHO IS

ἀρχή, πρωτότοκος ἐκ τῶν νεκρῶν, ἵνα γένηται ἐν
[ITS] BEGINNING, [THE] FIRSTBORN   FROM THE   DEAD,   THAT ²MIGHT BE ⁴IN

πᾶσιν αὐτὸς πρωτεύων, 1.19 ὅτι ἐν αὐτῷ
⁵EVERYTHING ¹HE   ³HOLDING THE FIRST PLACE,   BECAUSE IN   HIM

εὐδόκησεν πᾶν τὸ πλήρωμα κατοικῆσαι **1.20** καὶ δι᾽
⁴WAS PLEASED ¹ALL ²THE ³FULLNESS ⁵TO DWELL AND THROUGH

αὐτοῦ ἀποκαταλλάξαι τὰ πάντα εἰς αὐτόν,
HIM TO RECONCILE - ALL THINGS TO HIM[SELF],

εἰρηνοποιήσας διὰ τοῦ αἵματος τοῦ σταυροῦ αὐτοῦ,
HAVING MADE PEACE THROUGH THE BLOOD OF THE CROSS OF HIM,

[δι᾽ αὐτοῦ] εἴτε τὰ ἐπὶ τῆς γῆς εἴτε τὰ
THROUGH HIM, WHETHER THE THINGS ON THE EARTH OR THE THINGS

ἐν τοῖς οὐρανοῖς.
IN THE HEAVENS.

1.21 Καὶ ὑμᾶς ποτε ὄντας ἀπηλλοτριωμένους καὶ
AND YOU° ONCE HAVING BEEN ALIENATED AND

ἐχθροὺς τῇ διανοίᾳ ἐν τοῖς ἔργοις τοῖς πονηροῖς,
ENEMIES IN THE MIND BY - ²WORKS - ¹EVIL,

1.22 νυνὶ δὲ ἀποκατήλλαξεν ἐν τῷ σώματι τῆς σαρκὸς
YET~NOW HE RECONCILED IN THE BODY OF THE FLESH

αὐτοῦ διὰ τοῦ θανάτου παραστῆσαι ὑμᾶς ἁγίους
OF HIM THROUGH THE(HIS) DEATH TO PRESENT YOU° HOLY

καὶ ἀμώμους καὶ ἀνεγκλήτους κατενώπιον αὐτοῦ,
AND BLAMELESS AND WITHOUT REPROACH BEFORE HIM,

1.23 εἴ γε ἐπιμένετε τῇ πίστει τεθεμελιωμένοι καὶ
IF INDEED YOU° REMAIN IN THE FAITH HAVING BEEN FOUNDED AND

ἑδραῖοι καὶ μὴ μετακινούμενοι ἀπὸ τῆς ἐλπίδος τοῦ
ESTABLISHED AND NOT MOVING AWAY FROM THE HOPE OF THE

εὐαγγελίου οὗ ἠκούσατε, τοῦ κηρυχθέντος ἐν
GOOD NEWS WHICH YOU° HEARD, - [IT] HAVING BEEN PROCLAIMED IN

πάσῃ κτίσει τῇ ὑπὸ τὸν οὐρανόν, οὗ ἐγενόμην ἐγὼ
ALL CREATION - UNDER THE HEAVEN, OF WHICH ³BECAME ¹I

Παῦλος διάκονος.
²PAUL ⁴A MINISTER.

1.24 Νῦν χαίρω ἐν τοῖς παθήμασιν ὑπὲρ ὑμῶν καὶ
NOW I REJOICE IN THE(MY) SUFFERINGS ON BEHALF OF YOU° AND

ἀνταναπληρῶ τὰ ὑστερήματα τῶν θλίψεων τοῦ
I FILL UP THE THINGS LACKING OF THE AFFLICTIONS -

Χριστοῦ ἐν τῇ σαρκί μου ὑπὲρ τοῦ σώματος αὐτοῦ,
OF CHRIST IN THE FLESH OF ME ON BEHALF OF THE BODY OF HIM,

ὅ ἐστιν ἡ ἐκκλησία, **1.25** ἧς ἐγενόμην ἐγὼ
WHICH IS THE CHURCH, OF WHICH I~BECAME

διάκονος κατὰ τὴν οἰκονομίαν τοῦ θεοῦ τὴν
A MINISTER ACCORDING TO THE STEWARDSHIP - OF GOD -

δοθεῖσάν μοι εἰς ὑμᾶς πληρῶσαι τὸν λόγον τοῦ
HAVING BEEN GIVEN TO ME FOR YOU°, TO COMPLETE THE WORD(MESSAGE) -

θεοῦ, **1.26** τὸ μυστήριον τὸ ἀποκεκρυμμένον ἀπὸ τῶν
OF GOD, THE MYSTERY - HAVING BEEN HIDDEN FROM THE

αἰώνων καὶ ἀπὸ τῶν γενεῶν — νῦν δὲ ἐφανερώθη
AGES AND FROM THE GENERATIONS — BUT~NOW WAS MADE MANIFEST

τοῖς ἁγίοις αὐτοῦ, **1.27** οἷς ἠθέλησεν ὁ θεὸς
TO THE SAINTS OF HIM, TO WHOM ²WANTED - ¹GOD

all the fullness of God was pleased to dwell, ²⁰and through him God was pleased to reconcile to himself all things, whether on earth or in heaven, by making peace through the blood of his cross.

21 And you who were once estranged and hostile in mind, doing evil deeds, ²²he has now reconciled[i] in his fleshly body[j] through death, so as to present you holy and blameless and irreproachable before him— ²³provided that you continue securely established and steadfast in the faith, without shifting from the hope promised by the gospel that you heard, which has been proclaimed to every creature under heaven. I, Paul, became a servant of this gospel.

24 I am now rejoicing in my sufferings for your sake, and in my flesh I am completing what is lacking in Christ's afflictions for the sake of his body, that is, the church. ²⁵I became its servant according to God's commission that was given to me for you, to make the word of God fully known, ²⁶the mystery that has been hidden throughout the ages and generations but has now been revealed to his saints. ²⁷To them God chose

[i] Other ancient authorities read *you have now been reconciled*
[j] Gk *in the body of his flesh*

to make known how great among the Gentiles are the riches of the glory of this mystery, which is Christ in you, the hope of glory. ²⁸It is he whom we proclaim, warning everyone and teaching everyone in all wisdom, so that we may present everyone mature in Christ. ²⁹For this I toil and struggle with all the energy that he powerfully inspires within me.

γνωρίσαι   τί   τὸ   πλοῦτος   τῆς   δόξης   τοῦ
TO MAKE KNOWN   WHAT [IS]   THE   WEALTH   OF THE   GLORY   -

μυστηρίου τούτου ἐν   τοῖς ἔθνεσιν, ὅ   ἐστιν Χριστὸς
OF THIS~MYSTERY   AMONG THE   GENTILES,   WHICH IS   CHRIST

ἐν ὑμῖν, ἡ   ἐλπὶς   τῆς δόξης· 1.28 ὃν   ἡμεῖς
IN YOU°,   THE   HOPE   -   OF GLORY;   WHOM   WE

καταγγέλλομεν νουθετοῦντες πάντα ἄνθρωπον καὶ
ANNOUNCE,   WARNING   EVERY   MAN   AND

διδάσκοντες πάντα ἄνθρωπον ἐν πάσῃ σοφίᾳ, ἵνα
TEACHING   EVERY   MAN   IN ALL   WISDOM,   THAT

παραστήσωμεν πάντα ἄνθρωπον τέλειον ἐν Χριστῷ·
WE MAY PRESENT   EVERY   MAN   MATURE   IN CHRIST;

1.29 εἰς ὃ   καὶ κοπιῶ ἀγωνιζόμενος κατὰ   τὴν
        FOR WHICH ALSO I LABOR,   STRIVING   ACCORDING TO THE

ἐνέργειαν αὐτοῦ τὴν ἐνεργουμένην ἐν ἐμοὶ ἐν
WORKING   OF HIM   -   WORKING   IN ME   WITH

δυνάμει.
POWER.

CHAPTER 2

For I want you to know how much I am struggling for you, and for those in Laodicea, and for all who have not seen me face to face. ²I want their hearts to be encouraged and united in love, so that they may have all the riches of assured understanding and have the knowledge of God's mystery, that is, Christ himself,ᵏ ³in whom are hidden all the treasures of wisdom and knowledge. ⁴I am saying this so that no one may deceive you with plausible arguments. ⁵For though I am absent in body, yet I am with you in spirit, and I rejoice to see your

ᵏ Other ancient authorities read of the mystery of God, both of the Father and of Christ

2.1 Θέλω γὰρ ὑμᾶς εἰδέναι ἡλίκον ἀγῶνα ἔχω ὑπὲρ
      FOR~I WANT   YOU°   TO KNOW HOW GREAT A STRUGGLE I HAVE FOR

ὑμῶν καὶ τῶν   ἐν Λαοδικείᾳ καὶ ὅσοι   οὐχ ἑόρακαν
YOU°   AND THE ONES IN   LAODICEA   AND AS MANY AS HAVE NOT SEEN

τὸ πρόσωπόν μου ἐν σαρκί, 2.2 ἵνα παρακληθῶσιν αἱ
THE FACE   OF ME IN [THE] FLESH,   THAT MAY BE ENCOURAGED THE

καρδίαι αὐτῶν συμβιβασθέντες ἐν ἀγάπῃ καὶ εἰς
HEARTS   OF THEM, HAVING BEEN UNITED TOGETHER IN LOVE   AND   IN

πᾶν πλοῦτος τῆς πληροφορίας τῆς συνέσεως,
ALL WEALTH   OF THE FULL ASSURANCE   -   OF UNDERSTANDING,

εἰς   ἐπίγνωσιν ⌜τοῦ μυστηρίου τοῦ θεοῦ,
[RESULTING] IN [THE] KNOWLEDGE OF THE MYSTERY   -   OF GOD,

Χριστοῦ,⌝ 2.3 ἐν ᾧ   εἰσιν πάντες οἱ θησαυροὶ τῆς
[NAMELY] CHRIST,   IN WHOM ARE   ALL   THE ²TREASURES   -

σοφίας καὶ γνώσεως ἀπόκρυφοι. 2.4 Τοῦτο λέγω, ἵνα
³OF WISDOM ⁴AND ⁵KNOWLEDGE ¹HIDDEN.   THIS   I SAY   SO THAT

μηδεὶς ὑμᾶς παραλογίζηται ἐν πιθανολογίᾳ.
NO ONE   MAY DELUDE~YOU°   WITH PERSUASIVE SPEECH.

2.5 εἰ γὰρ καὶ τῇ σαρκὶ ἄπειμι, ἀλλὰ τῷ πνεύματι
      FOR~IF INDEED IN THE FLESH I AM ABSENT, BUT IN THE SPIRIT

σὺν ὑμῖν εἰμι, χαίρων καὶ βλέπων ὑμῶν τὴν τάξιν
²WITH ³YOU° ¹I AM, REJOICING AND SEEING YOUR°   -   ORDER

2:2 text: ASV RSV NASB NIV NEB TEV NRSV. var. του μυστηριου του θεου ο εστιν Χριστος (the mystery of God which is Christ): ASVmg. var. του μυστηριου του θεου πατρος του Χριστου (the mystery of God [the] Father, Christ--or, the mystery of God, [the] Father of Christ): TEVmg NJBmg. var. του μυστηριου του θεου και πατρος και του Χριστου (the mystery of God and of [the] Father] and of Christ): KJV NIVmg TEVmg NJBmg NRSVmg. var. του μυστηριου του θεου (the mystery of God): TEVmg NJB. του μυστηριου του Χριστου (the mystery of Christ): NJBmg.

καὶ τὸ στερέωμα τῆς εἰς Χριστὸν πίστεως ὑμῶν.
AND THE FIRMNESS - ³IN ⁴CHRIST ²FAITH ¹OF YOUR°.

2.6 Ὡς οὖν παρελάβετε τὸν Χριστὸν Ἰησοῦν τὸν
AS THEREFORE YOU° RECEIVED - CHRIST JESUS THE

κύριον, ἐν αὐτῷ περιπατεῖτε, **2.7** ἐρριζωμένοι καὶ
LORD, IN HIM WALK, HAVING BEEN ROOTED AND

ἐποικοδομούμενοι ἐν αὐτῷ καὶ βεβαιούμενοι τῇ
BEING BUILT UP IN HIM AND BEING FIRMLY FOUNDED IN THE

πίστει καθὼς ἐδιδάχθητε, περισσεύοντες ἐν εὐχαριστίᾳ.
FAITH AS YOU° WERE TAUGHT, ABOUNDING IN THANKSGIVING.

2.8 βλέπετε μή τις ὑμᾶς ἔσται ὁ συλαγωγῶν
BEWARE LEST ²ANYONE [OF] ³YOU° ¹THERE BE - BEING TAKEN CAPTIVE

διὰ τῆς φιλοσοφίας καὶ κενῆς ἀπάτης κατὰ τὴν
THROUGH - PHILOSOPHY AND EMPTY DECEIT ACCORDING TO THE

παράδοσιν τῶν ἀνθρώπων, κατὰ τὰ στοιχεῖα
TRADITION - OF MEN, ACCORDING TO THE ELEMENTARY PRINCIPLES

τοῦ κόσμου καὶ οὐ κατὰ Χριστόν· **2.9** ὅτι ἐν
OF THE WORLD AND NOT ACCORDING TO CHRIST; BECAUSE IN

αὐτῷ κατοικεῖ πᾶν τὸ πλήρωμα τῆς θεότητος
HIM DWELLS ALL THE FULLNESS OF THE GODHEAD

σωματικῶς, **2.10** καὶ ἐστὲ ἐν αὐτῷ πεπληρωμένοι, ὅς
BODILY, AND YOU° ARE ²IN ³HIM ¹HAVING BEEN MADE FULL, WHO

ἐστιν ἡ κεφαλὴ πάσης ἀρχῆς καὶ ἐξουσίας. **2.11** ἐν
IS THE HEAD OF ALL RULE AND AUTHORITY. IN

ᾧ καὶ περιετμήθητε περιτομῇ ἀχειροποιήτῳ ἐν
WHOM ALSO YOU° WERE CIRCUMCISED WITH A CIRCUMCISION NOT MADE WITH HANDS IN

τῇ ἀπεκδύσει τοῦ σώματος τῆς σαρκός, ἐν τῇ
THE PUTTING OFF OF THE BODY OF THE FLESH, IN THE

περιτομῇ τοῦ Χριστοῦ, **2.12** συνταφέντες αὐτῷ ἐν
CIRCUMCISION - OF CHRIST, HAVING BEEN BURIED TOGETHER WITH HIM IN

τῷ βαπτισμῷ, ἐν ᾧ καὶ συνηγέρθητε διὰ
THE(HIS) BAPTISM, WITH WHOM ALSO YOU° WERE RAISED TOGETHER THROUGH

τῆς πίστεως τῆς ἐνεργείας τοῦ θεοῦ τοῦ
THE(YOUR°) FAITH OF(IN) THE WORKING - OF GOD -

ἐγείραντος αὐτὸν ἐκ νεκρῶν· **2.13** καὶ ὑμᾶς
HAVING RAISED HIM FROM [THE] DEAD; AND YOU°

νεκροὺς ὄντας [ἐν] τοῖς παραπτώμασιν καὶ τῇ
BEING~DEAD IN THE TRESPASSES AND THE

ἀκροβυστίᾳ τῆς σαρκὸς ὑμῶν, συνεζωοποίησεν ὑμᾶς
UNCIRCUMCISION OF THE FLESH OF YOU°, HE MADE ALIVE TOGETHER YOU°

σὺν αὐτῷ, χαρισάμενος ἡμῖν πάντα τὰ παραπτώματα.
WITH HIM, HAVING FORGIVEN US ALL THE TRESPASSES;

2.14 ἐξαλείψας τὸ καθ᾽ ἡμῶν χειρόγραφον τοῖς
HAVING WIPED OUT ¹THE ⁵AGAINST ⁶US ²HANDWRITING ³IN THE

δόγμασιν ὃ ἦν ὑπεναντίον ἡμῖν, καὶ αὐτὸ ἦρκεν
⁴ORDINANCES, WHICH WAS CONTRARY TO US, AND HE HAS TAKEN~IT

ἐκ τοῦ μέσου προσηλώσας αὐτὸ τῷ σταυρῷ·
OUT OF THE MIDST(WAY) [BY] HAVING NAILED IT TO THE CROSS;

---

morale and the firmness of your faith in Christ.

6 As you therefore have received Christ Jesus the Lord, continue to live your lives*l* in him, [7]rooted and built up in him and established in the faith, just as you were taught, abounding in thanksgiving.

8 See to it that no one takes you captive through philosophy and empty deceit, according to human tradition, according to the elemental spirits of the universe,*m* and not according to Christ. [9]For in him the whole fullness of deity dwells bodily, [10]and you have come to fullness in him, who is the head of every ruler and authority. [11]In him also you were circumcised with a spiritual circumcision,*n* by putting off the body of the flesh in the circumcision of Christ; [12]when you were buried with him in baptism, you were also raised with him through faith in the power of God, who raised him from the dead. [13]And when you were dead in trespasses and the uncircumcision of your flesh, God*o* made you*p* alive together with him, when he forgave us all our trespasses, [14]erasing the record that stood against us with its legal demands. He set this aside, nailing it to the cross.

l Gk *to walk*
m Or *the rudiments of the world*
n Gk *a circumcision made without hands*
o Gk *he*
p Other ancient authorities read *made us*; others, *made*

15 He disarmed[q] the rulers and authorities and made a public example of them, triumphing over them in it.

16 Therefore do not let anyone condemn you in matters of food and drink or of observing festivals, new moons, or sabbaths. 17 These are only a shadow of what is to come, but the substance belongs to Christ. 18 Do not let anyone disqualify you, insisting on self-abasement and worship of angels, dwelling[r] on visions,[s] puffed up without cause by a human way of thinking,[t] 19 and not holding fast to the head, from whom the whole body, nourished and held together by its ligaments and sinews, grows with a growth that is from God.

20 If with Christ you died to the elemental spirits of the universe,[u] why do you live as if you still belonged to the world? Why do you submit to regulations, 21 "Do not handle, Do not taste, Do not touch"? 22 All these regulations refer to things that perish with use; they are simply human commands and teachings. 23 These have indeed an appearance of wisdom in promoting self-imposed piety, humility, and severe treatment of the body, but they are of no value in checking self-indulgence.[v]

[q] Or *divested himself of*
[r] Other ancient authorities read *not dwelling*
[s] Meaning of Gk uncertain
[t] Gk *by the mind of his flesh*
[u] Or *the rudiments of the world*
[v] Or *are of no value, serving only to indulge the flesh*

2.15 ἀπεκδυσάμενος τὰς ἀρχὰς καὶ τὰς ἐξουσίας
HAVING DISARMED THE RULERS AND THE AUTHORITIES

ἐδειγμάτισεν ἐν παρρησίᾳ, θριαμβεύσας αὐτοὺς
HE MADE A SHOW [OF THEM] IN PUBLIC, HAVING TRIUMPHED [OVER] THEM

ἐν αὐτῷ.
IN (BY) IT.

2.16 Μὴ οὖν τις ὑμᾶς κρινέτω ἐν βρώσει καὶ
THEREFORE~[LET] NOT ANYONE JUDGE~YOU° IN EATING AND

ἐν πόσει ἢ ἐν μέρει ἑορτῆς ἢ νεομηνίας ἢ
IN DRINKING OR IN RESPECT TO A FEAST OR A NEW MOON OR

σαββάτων· **2.17** ἅ ἐστιν σκιὰ τῶν μελλόντων, τὸ δὲ
SABBATHS; WHICH IS(ARE) A SHADOW OF THE COMING THINGS, BUT~THE

σῶμα τοῦ Χριστοῦ. **2.18** μηδεὶς ὑμᾶς καταβραβευέτω
REALITY - [IS] OF CHRIST. [LET] NO ONE DEPRIVE YOU° OF THE PRIZE

θέλων ἐν ταπεινοφροσύνῃ καὶ θρησκείᾳ τῶν
[BY] DELIGHTING IN HUMILITY AND VENERATION OF THE

ἀγγέλων, ⸀ἃ ἑόρακεν⸀ ἐμβατεύων,
ANGELS, ²THINGS WHICH ³HE HAS SEEN ¹DELVING INTO,

εἰκῇ φυσιούμενος ὑπὸ τοῦ νοὸς τῆς σαρκὸς αὐτοῦ,
BEING VAINLY PUFFED UP BY THE MIND OF THE FLESH OF HIM,

2.19 καὶ οὐ κρατῶν τὴν κεφαλήν, ἐξ οὗ πᾶν τὸ
AND NOT HOLDING THE HEAD, OUT FROM WHOM ALL THE

σῶμα διὰ τῶν ἁφῶν καὶ συνδέσμων ἐπιχορηγούμενον
BODY THROUGH THE JOINTS AND LIGAMENTS BEING FULLY SUPPLIED

καὶ συμβιβαζόμενον αὔξει τὴν αὔξησιν τοῦ θεοῦ.
AND BEING UNITED TOGETHER GROWS WITH THE GROWTH - OF GOD.

2.20 Εἰ ἀπεθάνετε σὺν Χριστῷ ἀπὸ τῶν
SINCE YOU° DIED WITH CHRIST FROM THE

στοιχείων τοῦ κόσμου, τί ὡς ζῶντες ἐν
ELEMENTARY PRINCIPLES OF THE WORLD, WHY AS [THOUGH] LIVING IN

κόσμῳ δογματίζεσθε; **2.21** Μὴ ἅψῃ μηδὲ
[THE] WORLD DO YOU° SUBJECT YOURSELVES TO ORDINANCES? DO NOT TOUCH NOR

γεύσῃ μηδὲ θίγῃς, **2.22** ἅ ἐστιν πάντα εἰς
TASTE NOR HANDLE, WHICH THINGS ARE ALL [DESTINED] TO

φθορὰν τῇ ἀποχρήσει, κατὰ τὰ ἐντάλματα καὶ
DETERIORATION - WITH USE, ACCORDING TO THE COMMANDMENTS AND

διδασκαλίας τῶν ἀνθρώπων, **2.23** ἅτινά ἐστιν
TEACHINGS - OF MEN, WHICH THINGS ARE

λόγον μὲν ἔχοντα σοφίας ἐν ἐθελοθρησκίᾳ καὶ
²AN APPEARANCE - ¹HAVING OF WISDOM IN SELF-IMPOSED RELIGION AND

ταπεινοφροσύνῃ [καὶ] ἀφειδίᾳ σώματος, οὐκ ἐν
HUMILITY AND SEVERE TREATMENT OF [THE] BODY, NOT IN(OF)

τιμῇ τινι πρὸς πλησμονὴν τῆς σαρκός.
ANY~VALUE AGAINST [THE] INDULGENCE OF THE FLESH.

2:18 text: ASV RSV NASB NIV NEB TEV NJB NRSV. var. α μη εορακεν (things which he has not seen): KJV ASVmg NJBmg.

3.1 Εἰ οὖν συνηγέρθητε τῷ Χριστῷ, τὰ ἄνω
IF THEREFORE YOU° WERE RAISED WITH - CHRIST, THE THINGS ABOVE

ζητεῖτε, οὗ ὁ Χριστός ἐστιν ἐν δεξιᾷ τοῦ
SEEK, WHERE - CHRIST ¹IS ³IN(AT) ⁴[THE] RIGHT [HAND] -

θεοῦ καθήμενος· **3.2** τὰ ἄνω φρονεῖτε, μὴ τὰ
⁵OF GOD ²SITTING; ²THE THINGS ³ABOVE ¹THINK [ABOUT], NOT THE THINGS

ἐπὶ τῆς γῆς. **3.3** ἀπεθάνετε γάρ καὶ ἡ ζωὴ ὑμῶν
ON THE EARTH. FOR~YOU° DIED AND THE LIFE OF YOU°

κέκρυπται σὺν τῷ Χριστῷ ἐν τῷ θεῷ· **3.4** ὅταν ὁ
HAS BEEN HIDDEN WITH - CHRIST IN - GOD; WHEN -

Χριστὸς φανερωθῇ, ἡ ζωὴ ⌜ὑμῶν⌝, τότε καὶ ὑμεῖς σὺν
CHRIST IS MANIFESTED, THE LIFE OF YOU°, THEN ALSO YOU° WITH

αὐτῷ φανερωθήσεσθε ἐν δόξῃ.
HIM WILL BE MANIFESTED IN GLORY.

3.5 Νεκρώσατε οὖν τὰ μέλη τὰ ἐπὶ τῆς γῆς,
THEREFORE~PUT TO DEATH THE(YOUR°) MEMBERS - ON THE EARTH,

πορνείαν ἀκαθαρσίαν πάθος ἐπιθυμίαν κακήν, καὶ τὴν
FORNICATION, UNCLEANNESS, PASSION, EVIL~DESIRE, AND -

πλεονεξίαν, ἥτις ἐστὶν εἰδωλολατρία, **3.6** δι᾽
COVETOUSNESS, WHICH IS IDOLATRY, BECAUSE OF

ἃ ἔρχεται ἡ ὀργὴ τοῦ θεοῦ ⌜[ἐπὶ τοὺς υἱοὺς
WHICH THINGS COMES THE WRATH - OF GOD ON THE SONS

τῆς ἀπειθείας].⌝ **3.7** ἐν οἷς καὶ ὑμεῖς
- OF DISOBEDIENCE; AMONG WHOM ALSO YOU°

περιεπατήσατέ ποτε, ὅτε ἐζῆτε ἐν τούτοις·
WALKED ONCE, WHEN YOU° WERE LIVING IN THESE THINGS;

3.8 νυνὶ δὲ ἀπόθεσθε καὶ ὑμεῖς τὰ πάντα, ὀργήν,
BUT~NOW ³PUT AWAY ²ALSO ¹YOU° ALL~THE[SE] THINGS, WRATH,

θυμόν, κακίαν, βλασφημίαν, αἰσχρολογίαν ἐκ τοῦ
ANGER, MALICE, BLASPHEMY, INDECENT LANGUAGE FROM THE

στόματος ὑμῶν· **3.9** μὴ ψεύδεσθε εἰς ἀλλήλους,
MOUTH OF YOU°; DO NOT LIE TO ONE ANOTHER,

ἀπεκδυσάμενοι τὸν παλαιὸν ἄνθρωπον σὺν ταῖς
HAVING PUT OFF THE OLD MAN WITH THE

πράξεσιν αὐτοῦ **3.10** καὶ ἐνδυσάμενοι τὸν νέον τὸν
PRACTISES OF HIM AND HAVING PUT ON THE NEW [MAN], THE ONE

ἀνακαινούμενον εἰς ἐπίγνωσιν κατ᾽ εἰκόνα
BEING RENEWED IN KNOWLEDGE IN ACCORDANCE WITH [THE] IMAGE

τοῦ κτίσαντος αὐτόν, **3.11** ὅπου οὐκ ἔνι Ἕλλην καὶ
OF THE ONE HAVING CREATED HIM, WHERE THERE IS NOT GREEK AND

Ἰουδαῖος, περιτομὴ καὶ ἀκροβυστία, βάρβαρος, Σκύθης,
JEW, CIRCUMCISION AND UNCIRCUMCISION, BARBARIAN, SCYTHIAN,

So if you have been raised with Christ, seek the things that are above, where Christ is, seated at the right hand of God. ²Set your minds on things that are above, not on things that are on earth, ³for you have died, and your life is hidden with Christ in God. ⁴When Christ who is your[w] life is revealed, then you also will be revealed with him in glory.

5 Put to death, therefore, whatever in you is earthly: fornication, impurity, passion, evil desire, and greed (which is idolatry). ⁶On account of these the wrath of God is coming on those who are disobedient.[x] ⁷These are the ways you also once followed, when you were living that life.[y] ⁸But now you must get rid of all such things—anger, wrath, malice, slander, and abusive[z] language from your mouth. ⁹Do not lie to one another, seeing that you have stripped off the old self with its practices ¹⁰and have clothed yourselves with the new self, which is being renewed in knowledge according to the image of its creator. ¹¹In that renewal[a] there is no longer Greek and Jew, circumcised and uncircumcised, barbarian,

[w] Other authorities read *our*
[x] Other ancient authorities lack *on those who are disobedient* (Gk *the children of disobedience*)
[y] Or *living among such people*
[z] Or *filthy*
[a] Gk *its creator*, ¹¹*where*

3:4 text: ASVmg NIV TEV NJB NRSV. var. ημων (of us): KJV ASV RSV NASB NEB NJBmg NRSVmg.
3:6 text: KJV ASV RSVmg NASBmg NIVmg TEV NJB NRSV. omit: ASVmg RSV NASB NIV NEB TEVmg NJBmg NRSVmg.

Scythian, slave and free; but Christ is all and in all!

12 As God's chosen ones, holy and beloved, clothe yourselves with compassion, kindness, humility, meekness, and patience. [13]Bear with one another and, if anyone has a complaint against another, forgive each other; just as the Lord[b] has forgiven you, so you also must forgive. [14]Above all, clothe yourselves with love, which binds everything together in perfect harmony. [15]And let the peace of Christ rule in your hearts, to which indeed you were called in the one body. And be thankful. [16]Let the word of Christ[c] dwell in you richly; teach and admonish one another in all wisdom; and with gratitude in your hearts sing psalms, hymns, and spiritual songs to God.[d] [17]And whatever you do, in word or deed, do everything in the name of the Lord Jesus, giving thanks to God the Father through him.

18 Wives, be subject to your husbands, as is fitting in the Lord. [19]Husbands, love your wives and never treat them harshly.

20 Children, obey your parents in everything, for this is your acceptable duty in the Lord.

[b] Other ancient authorities read *just as Christ*
[c] Other ancient authorities read *of God*, or *of the Lord*
[d] Other ancient authorities read *to the Lord*

δοῦλος, ἐλεύθερος, ἀλλὰ [τὰ] πάντα καὶ ἐν πᾶσιν
SLAVE,   FREEMAN,   BUT   -   ²ALL THINGS ³AND ⁴IN ⁵ALL

Χριστός.
¹CHRIST [IS].

3.12 Ἐνδύσασθε οὖν,   ὡς   ἐκλεκτοὶ τοῦ θεοῦ ἅγιοι
PUT ON   THEREFORE, AS CHOSEN ONES -   OF GOD, HOLY

καὶ ἠγαπημένοι, σπλάγχνα οἰκτιρμοῦ χρηστότητα
AND BELOVED,   BOWELS(FEELINGS) OF COMPASSION, KINDNESS,

ταπεινοφροσύνην πραΰτητα μακροθυμίαν,
HUMILITY,   MEEKNESS, LONG-SUFFERING,

3.13 ἀνεχόμενοι ἀλλήλων καὶ χαριζόμενοι ἑαυτοῖς ἐάν
FORBEARING   ONE ANOTHER AND FORGIVING   EACH OTHER IF

τις   πρός τινα ἔχῃ μομφήν· καθὼς καὶ ὁ κύριος
ANYONE AGAINST ANYONE MAY HAVE A COMPLAINT; AS ALSO THE LORD

ἐχαρίσατο ὑμῖν, οὕτως καὶ ὑμεῖς· **3.14** ἐπὶ πᾶσιν
FORGAVE   YOU,° SO   ALSO YOU° [SHOULD DO].   ²TO ³ALL

δὲ τούτοις τὴν τῆς ἀγάπην, ὃ   ἐστιν σύνδεσμος τῆς
¹AND ⁴THESE THINGS - [ADD] LOVE, WHICH IS A BOND   -

τελειότητος. **3.15** καὶ ἡ εἰρήνη τοῦ Χριστοῦ βραβευέτω
OF PERFECTION.   AND ²THE ³PEACE -   ⁴OF CHRIST ¹LET ⁵ARBITRATE

ἐν ταῖς καρδίαις ὑμῶν, εἰς ἣν   καὶ ἐκλήθητε
IN THE HEARTS   OF YOU°, TO WHICH [PEACE] ALSO YOU° WERE CALLED

ἐν ἑνὶ σώματι· καὶ εὐχάριστοι γίνεσθε. **3.16** ὁ   λόγος
IN ONE BODY;   AND BE~THANKFUL.   ²THE ³WORD

τοῦ Χριστοῦ ἐνοικείτω ἐν ὑμῖν πλουσίως, ἐν πάσῃ
-   ⁴OF CHRIST ¹LET ⁵DWELL IN YOU° RICHLY,   IN ALL

σοφίᾳ διδάσκοντες καὶ νουθετοῦντες ἑαυτούς, ψαλμοῖς
WISDOM TEACHING   AND ADMONISHING ONE ANOTHER, WITH PSALMS,

ὕμνοις ᾠδαῖς πνευματικαῖς ἐν [τῇ] χάριτι ᾄδοντες ἐν
HYMNS, SPIRITUAL~SONGS   ²WITH ³GRACE ¹SINGING IN

ταῖς καρδίαις ὑμῶν τῷ θεῷ· **3.17** καὶ πᾶν ὅ τι ἐὰν
THE HEARTS   OF YOU° - TO GOD;   AND EVERYTHING WHATEVER

ποιῆτε ἐν λόγῳ ἢ ἐν ἔργῳ, πάντα ἐν ὀνόματι
YOU° DO IN WORD OR IN WORK, [DO] ALL THINGS IN [THE] NAME

κυρίου Ἰησοῦ, εὐχαριστοῦντες τῷ θεῷ πατρὶ δι'
OF [THE] LORD JESUS, GIVING THANKS - TO GOD [THE] FATHER THROUGH

αὐτοῦ.
HIM.

3.18 Αἱ γυναῖκες, ὑποτάσσεσθε τοῖς   ἀνδράσιν ὡς
THE WIVES,   SUBJECT YOURSELVES TO THE(YOUR°) HUSBANDS AS

ἀνῆκεν ἐν κυρίῳ. **3.19** Οἱ ἄνδρες, ἀγαπᾶτε τὰς
IS PROPER IN [THE] LORD. THE HUSBANDS, LOVE   THE(YOUR°)

γυναῖκας καὶ μὴ πικραίνεσθε πρὸς αὐτάς.
WIVES   AND DO NOT BE BITTER AGAINST THEM.

3.20 Τὰ τέκνα, ὑπακούετε τοῖς   γονεῦσιν κατὰ
THE CHILDREN, OBEY THE(YOUR°) PARENTS IN

πάντα, τοῦτο γὰρ εὐάρεστόν ἐστιν ἐν κυρίῳ.
ALL THINGS, FOR~THIS IS~WELL-PLEASING IN [THE] LORD.

3.21 Οἱ πατέρες, μὴ ἐρεθίζετε τὰ τέκνα ὑμῶν, ἵνα μὴ
THE FATHERS, DO NOT PROVOKE THE CHILDREN OF YOU°, LEST

ἀθυμῶσιν.
THEY BE DISHEARTENED.

3.22 Οἱ δοῦλοι, ὑπακούετε κατὰ πάντα τοῖς
THE SLAVES, OBEY IN ALL THINGS ¹THE(YOUR°)

κατὰ σάρκα κυρίοις, μὴ ἐν ὀφθαλμοδουλίᾳ ὡς
³ACCORDING TO ⁴FLESH ²MASTERS, NOT WITH EYESERVICE AS

ἀνθρωπάρεσκοι, ἀλλ' ἐν ἁπλότητι καρδίας φοβούμενοι
MEN-PLEASERS, BUT IN SINGLENESS OF HEART, FEARING

τὸν κύριον. **3.23** ὃ ἐὰν ποιῆτε, ἐκ ψυχῆς ἐργάζεσθε
THE LORD. WHATEVER YOU° DO, FROM [THE] SOUL WORK

ὡς τῷ κυρίῳ καὶ οὐκ ἀνθρώποις, **3.24** εἰδότες ὅτι
AS TO THE LORD AND NOT TO MEN, KNOWING THAT

ἀπὸ κυρίου ἀπολήμψεσθε τὴν ἀνταπόδοσιν τῆς
FROM [THE] LORD YOU° WILL RECEIVE THE RECOMPENSE OF THE

κληρονομίας. τῷ κυρίῳ Χριστῷ δουλεύετε·
INHERITANCE. ²THE ³LORD ⁴CHRIST ¹YOU° SERVE;

3.25 ὁ γὰρ ἀδικῶν κομίσεται ὃ ἠδίκησεν, καὶ
FOR~THE ONE DOING WRONG WILL BE REPAID [FOR] WHAT HE DID WRONG, AND

οὐκ ἔστιν προσωπολημψία.
THERE IS~NO RESPECT OF PERSONS.

21Fathers, do not provoke your children, or they may lose heart. 22Slaves, obey your earthly masters*e* in everything, not only while being watched and in order to please them, but wholeheartedly, fearing the Lord.*e* 23Whatever your task, put yourselves into it, as done for the Lord and not for your masters,*f* 24since you know that from the Lord you will receive the inheritance as your reward; you serve*g* the Lord Christ. 25For the wrongdoer will be paid back for whatever wrong has been done, and there is no partiality.

e In Greek the same word is used for master and Lord
f Gk not for men
g Or you are slaves of, or be slaves of

CHAPTER 4

4.1 Οἱ κύριοι, τὸ δίκαιον καὶ τὴν ἰσότητα
THE MASTERS, THAT WHICH [IS] JUST AND - EQUAL

τοῖς δούλοις παρέχεσθε, εἰδότες ὅτι καὶ ὑμεῖς
²TO THE(YOUR°) ³SLAVES ¹GIVE, KNOWING THAT ALSO YOU°

ἔχετε κύριον ἐν οὐρανῷ.
HAVE A LORD(MASTER) IN HEAVEN.

4.2 Τῇ προσευχῇ προσκαρτερεῖτε, γρηγοροῦντες ἐν
- IN PRAYER PERSEVERE, KEEPING WATCH IN

αὐτῇ ἐν εὐχαριστίᾳ, **4.3** προσευχόμενοι ἅμα καὶ
IT WITH THANKSGIVING, PRAYING TOGETHER ALSO

περὶ ἡμῶν, ἵνα ὁ θεὸς ἀνοίξῃ ἡμῖν θύραν τοῦ
CONCERNING US, THAT - GOD MAY OPEN FOR US A DOOR OF(FOR) THE

λόγου λαλῆσαι τὸ μυστήριον τοῦ Χριστοῦ, δι'
MESSAGE, TO SPEAK THE MYSTERY - OF CHRIST, ON ACCOUNT OF

ὃ καὶ δέδεμαι, **4.4** ἵνα φανερώσω αὐτὸ ὡς
WHICH ALSO I HAVE BEEN BOUND, THAT I MAY MANIFEST IT AS

δεῖ με λαλῆσαι. **4.5** Ἐν σοφίᾳ περιπατεῖτε
IT IS NECESSARY [FOR] ME TO SPEAK. IN WISDOM WALK

πρὸς τοὺς ἔξω τὸν καιρὸν ἐξαγοραζόμενοι. **4.6** ὁ
TOWARD THE ONES OUTSIDE, ²THE ³TIME ¹REDEEMING. THE

λόγος ὑμῶν πάντοτε ἐν χάριτι, ἅλατι
SPEECH OF YOU° [MAY IT BE] ALWAYS WITH GRACE, WITH SALT

1Masters, treat your slaves justly and fairly, for you know that you also have a Master in heaven.

2 Devote yourselves to prayer, keeping alert in it with thanksgiving. 3At the same time pray for us as well that God will open to us a door for the word, that we may declare the mystery of Christ, for which I am in prison, 4so that I may reveal it clearly, as I should.

5 Conduct yourselves wisely toward outsiders, making the most of the time.*h* 6Let your speech always be gracious, seasoned with salt,

h Or opportunity

so that you may know how you ought to answer everyone.

7 Tychicus will tell you all the news about me; he is a beloved brother, a faithful minister, and a fellow servant[i] in the Lord. [8]I have sent him to you for this very purpose, so that you may know how we are[j] and that he may encourage your hearts; [9]he is coming with Onesimus, the faithful and beloved brother, who is one of you. They will tell you about everything here.

10 Aristarchus my fellow prisoner greets you, as does Mark the cousin of Barnabas, concerning whom you have received instructions— if he comes to you, welcome him. [11]And Jesus who is called Justus greets you. These are the only ones of the circumcision among my co-workers for the kingdom of God, and they have been a comfort to me. [12]Epaphras, who is one of you, a servant[i] of Christ Jesus, greets you. He is always wrestling in his prayers on your behalf, so that you may stand mature and fully assured in everything that God wills. [13]For I testify for him that he has worked hard for you and for those in Laodicea and in Hierapolis. [14]Luke, the beloved physician, and Demas greet you. [15]Give my greetings to the brothers and sisters[k] in Laodicea, and to Nympha and the church

[i] Gk slave
[j] Other authorities read that I may know how you are
[k] Gk brothers

ἠρτυμένος, εἰδέναι πῶς δεῖ ὑμᾶς ἑνὶ ἑκάστῳ
HAVING BEEN SEASONED, TO KNOW HOW IT IS NECESSARY [FOR] YOU° ³ONE ²EACH

ἀποκρίνεσθαι.
¹TO ANSWER.

4.7 Τὰ κατ᾽ ἐμὲ πάντα γνωρίσει ὑμῖν Τυχικὸς
²THE THINGS ³ABOUT ⁴ME ¹ALL ⁶WILL MAKE KNOWN ⁷TO YOU° ⁵TYCHICUS,

ὁ ἀγαπητὸς ἀδελφὸς καὶ πιστὸς διάκονος καὶ
THE BELOVED BROTHER AND FAITHFUL MINISTER AND

σύνδουλος ἐν κυρίῳ, **4.8** ὃν ἔπεμψα πρὸς ὑμᾶς εἰς
FELLOW-SLAVE IN [THE] LORD, WHOM I SENT TO YOU° FOR

αὐτὸ τοῦτο, ἵνα γνῶτε τὰ περὶ ἡμῶν καὶ
THIS~VERY THING THAT YOU° MIGHT KNOW THE THINGS CONCERNING US AND

παρακαλέσῃ τὰς καρδίας ὑμῶν, **4.9** σὺν Ὀνησίμῳ τῷ
HE MIGHT ENCOURAGE THE HEARTS OF YOU°, WITH ONESIMUS, THE

πιστῷ καὶ ἀγαπητῷ ἀδελφῷ, ὅς ἐστιν ἐξ ὑμῶν·
FAITHFUL AND BELOVED BROTHER, WHO IS OF YOU°;

πάντα ὑμῖν γνωρίσουσιν τὰ ὧδε.
¹ALL ⁵TO YOU° ⁴THEY WILL MAKE KNOWN ²THE THINGS ³HERE.

4.10 Ἀσπάζεται ὑμᾶς Ἀρίσταρχος ὁ συναιχμάλωτός
²GREETS ³YOU° ¹ARISTARCHUS, THE FELLOW-PRISONER

μου καὶ Μᾶρκος ὁ ἀνεψιὸς Βαρναβᾶ (περὶ οὗ
OF ME, AND MARK THE COUSIN OF BARNABAS CONCERNING WHOM

ἐλάβετε ἐντολάς, ἐὰν ἔλθῃ πρὸς ὑμᾶς, δέξασθε
YOU° RECEIVED COMMANDS, IF HE SHOULD COME TO YOU°, RECEIVE

αὐτόν) **4.11** καὶ Ἰησοῦς ὁ λεγόμενος Ἰοῦστος, οἱ
HIM) AND JESUS THE ONE BEING CALLED JUSTUS, THE ONES

ὄντες ἐκ περιτομῆς, οὗτοι μόνοι συνεργοὶ εἰς
BEING OF [THE] CIRCUMCISION, THESE ONLY [ARE MY] CO-WORKERS IN

τὴν βασιλείαν τοῦ θεοῦ, οἵτινες ἐγενήθησάν μοι
THE KINGDOM - OF GOD, WHO BECAME TO ME

παρηγορία. **4.12** ἀσπάζεται ὑμᾶς Ἐπαφρᾶς ὁ ἐξ
AN ENCOURAGEMENT. ²GREETS ³YOU° ¹EPAPHRAS, THE ONE [BEING]

ὑμῶν, δοῦλος Χριστοῦ [Ἰησοῦ], πάντοτε ἀγωνιζόμενος
OF YOU°, A SLAVE OF CHRIST JESUS, ALWAYS STRIVING

ὑπὲρ ὑμῶν ἐν ταῖς προσευχαῖς, ἵνα σταθῆτε
FOR YOU° IN THE (HIS) PRAYERS, THAT YOU° MIGHT STAND

τέλειοι καὶ πεπληροφορημένοι ἐν παντὶ θελήματι τοῦ
MATURE AND HAVING BEEN FULLY ASSURED IN ALL [THE] WILL -

θεοῦ. **4.13** μαρτυρῶ γὰρ αὐτῷ ὅτι ἔχει πολὺν πόνον
OF GOD. FOR~I TESTIFY FOR HIM THAT HE HAS MUCH LABOR

ὑπὲρ ὑμῶν καὶ τῶν ἐν Λαοδικείᾳ καὶ τῶν ἐν
FOR YOU° AND THE ONES IN LAODICEA AND THE ONES IN

Ἱεραπόλει. **4.14** ἀσπάζεται ὑμᾶς Λουκᾶς ὁ ἰατρὸς ὁ
HIERAPOLIS. ²GREETS ³YOU° ¹LUKE, THE PHYSICIAN -

ἀγαπητὸς καὶ Δημᾶς. **4.15** Ἀσπάσασθε τοὺς ἐν
BELOVED, AND DEMAS. GREET THE ²IN

Λαοδικείᾳ ἀδελφοὺς καὶ Νύμφαν καὶ τὴν κατ᾽ οἶκον
³LAODICEA ¹BROTHERS AND NYMPHA AND ¹THE ³AT ⁴HOUSE

αὐτῆς ἐκκλησίαν.   **4.16** καὶ ὅταν   ἀναγνωσθῇ παρ'
⁵HER   ²CHURCH.   AND   WHENEVER IS READ   BEFORE

ὑμῖν ἡ   ἐπιστολή, ποιήσατε ἵνα καὶ ἐν τῇ
YOU° THE(THIS) EPISTLE,   MAKE [SURE] THAT ALSO IN THE

Λαοδικέων ἐκκλησίᾳ   ἀναγνωσθῇ, καὶ τὴν
CHURCH~OF [THE] LAODICEANS IT IS READ,   AND   ⁵THE [EPISTLE]

ἐκ   Λαοδικείας ἵνα   καὶ ὑμεῖς ἀναγνῶτε.
⁶OF (BELONGING TO) ⁷LAODECIA ¹THAT ²ALSO ³YOU° ⁴SHOULD READ [IT].

4.17 καὶ εἴπατε Ἀρχίππῳ, Βλέπε   τὴν διακονίαν
      AND   SAY TO   ARCHIPPUS, GIVE ATTENTION TO THE MINISTRY

ἣν   παρέλαβες ἐν κυρίῳ, ἵνα αὐτὴν πληροῖς.
WHICH YOU RECEIVED IN [THE] LORD, THAT YOU FULFILL~IT.

4.18 Ὁ ἀσπασμὸς τῇ ἐμῇ χειρὶ Παύλου.   μνημονεύετέ
      THE GREETING   -   BY MY HAND, PAUL'S.   REMEMBER

μου τῶν δεσμῶν. ἡ χάρις μεθ' ὑμῶν.
MY   -   BONDS.   - GRACE [BE] WITH YOU°.

in her house. ¹⁶And when this letter has been read among you, have it read also in the church of the Laodiceans; and see that you read also the letter from Laodicea. ¹⁷And say to Archippus, "See that you complete the task that you have received in the Lord."

18 I, Paul, write this greeting with my own hand. Remember my chains. Grace be with you.[l]

[l] Other ancient authorities add *Amen*

THE FIRST LETTER OF PAUL TO THE
THESSALONIANS

ΠΡΟΣ ΘΕΣΣΑΛΟΝΙΚΕΙΣ Α
TO   [THE] THESSALONIANS   1

1.1 Παῦλος καὶ Σιλουανὸς καὶ Τιμόθεος τῇ
PAUL   AND   SILVANUS   AND   TIMOTHY   TO THE

ἐκκλησίᾳ Θεσσαλονικέων ἐν θεῷ πατρὶ καὶ κυρίῳ
CHURCH   OF [THE] THESSALONIANS IN   GOD [THE] FATHER AND [THE] LORD

Ἰησοῦ Χριστῷ, χάρις ὑμῖν καὶ εἰρήνη.
JESUS   CHRIST,   GRACE TO YOU° AND   PEACE.

1.2 Εὐχαριστοῦμεν τῷ θεῷ πάντοτε περὶ πάντων
WE GIVE THANKS   -   TO GOD ALWAYS CONCERNING ALL

ὑμῶν μνείαν ποιούμενοι ἐπὶ τῶν προσευχῶν ἡμῶν,
OF YOU°, MAKING~MENTION AT(DURING) THE PRAYERS   OF US,

ἀδιαλείπτως **1.3** μνημονεύοντες ὑμῶν τοῦ ἔργου τῆς
UNCEASINGLY   REMEMBERING   YOUR° -   WORK   -

πίστεως καὶ τοῦ κόπου τῆς ἀγάπης καὶ τῆς ὑπομονῆς
OF FAITH AND   - LABOR   - OF LOVE AND   -   ENDURANCE

τῆς ἐλπίδος τοῦ κυρίου ἡμῶν Ἰησοῦ Χριστοῦ
-   OF HOPE OF(IN) THE LORD OF US JESUS   CHRIST

ἔμπροσθεν τοῦ θεοῦ καὶ πατρὸς ἡμῶν, **1.4** εἰδότες,
BEFORE   THE GOD AND FATHER OF US,   KNOWING,

ἀδελφοὶ ἠγαπημένοι ὑπὸ [τοῦ] θεοῦ, τὴν ἐκλογὴν ὑμῶν,
BROTHERS BELOVED   BY   -   GOD, THE ELECTION OF YOU°,

1.5 ὅτι τὸ εὐαγγέλιον ἡμῶν οὐκ ἐγενήθη εἰς ὑμᾶς
BECAUSE THE GOOD NEWS   OF US DID NOT COME TO YOU°

ἐν λόγῳ μόνον ἀλλὰ καὶ ἐν δυνάμει καὶ ἐν
IN WORD ONLY   BUT ALSO IN POWER   AND IN

πνεύματι ἁγίῳ καὶ [ἐν] πληροφορίᾳ πολλῇ, καθὼς
[THE] HOLY~SPIRIT AND IN MUCH~ASSURANCE,   EVEN AS

οἴδατε οἷοι ἐγενήθημεν [ἐν] ὑμῖν δι᾽
YOU° KNOW WHAT KIND [OF MEN] WE WERE AMONG YOU° BECAUSE OF

ὑμᾶς. **1.6** καὶ ὑμεῖς μιμηταὶ ἡμῶν ἐγενήθητε καὶ τοῦ
YOU°.   AND YOU° ²IMITATORS ³OF US ¹BECAME   AND OF THE

κυρίου, δεξάμενοι τὸν λόγον ἐν θλίψει πολλῇ μετὰ
LORD,   HAVING RECEIVED THE WORD IN MUCH~AFFLICTION WITH

χαρᾶς πνεύματος ἁγίου, **1.7** ὥστε γενέσθαι ὑμᾶς τύπον
JOY   OF [THE] HOLY~SPIRIT,   SO THAT YOU°~CAME TO BE AN EXAMPLE

πᾶσιν τοῖς πιστεύουσιν ἐν τῇ Μακεδονίᾳ καὶ ἐν τῇ
TO ALL THE ONES BELIEVING IN - MACEDONIA   AND IN -

Ἀχαΐᾳ. **1.8** ἀφ᾽ ὑμῶν γὰρ ἐξήχηται ὁ λόγος τοῦ
ACHAIA.   ²FROM ³YOU° ¹FOR HAS SOUNDED OUT THE WORD OF THE

CHAPTER 1

Paul, Silvanus, and Timothy,

To the church of the Thessalonians in God the Father and the Lord Jesus Christ:

Grace to you and peace.

2 We always give thanks to God for all of you and mention you in our prayers, constantly [3]remembering before our God and Father your work of faith and labor of love and steadfastness of hope in our Lord Jesus Christ. [4]For we know, brothers and sisters[a] beloved by God, that he has chosen you, [5]because our message of the gospel came to you not in word only, but also in power and in the Holy Spirit and with full conviction; just as you know what kind of persons we proved to be among you for your sake. [6]And you became imitators of us and of the Lord, for in spite of persecution you received the word with joy inspired by the Holy Spirit, [7]so that you became an example to all the believers in Macedonia and in Achaia. [8]For the word of the Lord has sounded forth from you

[a] Gk brothers

not only in Macedonia and Achaia, but in every place your faith in God has become known, so that we have no need to speak about it. ⁹For the people of those regions[b] report about us what kind of welcome we had among you, and how you turned to God from idols, to serve a living and true God, ¹⁰and to wait for his Son from heaven, whom he raised from the dead—Jesus, who rescues us from the wrath that is coming.

[b] Gk *For they*

κυρίου	οὐ	μόνον	ἐν	τῇ	Μακεδονίᾳ	καὶ	[ἐν	τῇ]	’Αχαΐᾳ,
LORD	NOT	ONLY	IN	-	MACEDONIA	AND	IN	-	ACHAIA,

ἀλλ’	ἐν	παντὶ	τόπῳ	ἡ	πίστις	ὑμῶν	ἡ	πρὸς	τὸν	θεὸν
BUT	IN	EVERY	PLACE	THE	FAITH	OF YOU°	-	TOWARD	-	GOD

ἐξελήλυθεν,	ὥστε	μὴ	χρείαν	ἔχειν	ἡμᾶς	λαλεῖν	τι.
HAS GONE OUT,	SO THAT	²NO	³NEED	¹WE~HAVE		TO SPEAK	ANYTHING.

1.9 αὐτοὶ γὰρ περὶ ἡμῶν ἀπαγγέλλουσιν ὁποίαν

FOR~THEY THEMSELVES ²CONCERNING ³US ¹REPORT WHAT SORT OF

εἴσοδον	ἔσχομεν	πρὸς	ὑμᾶς,	καὶ	πῶς	ἐπεστρέψατε
WELCOME	WE HAD	WITH	YOU°,	AND	HOW	YOU° TURNED

πρὸς	τὸν	θεὸν	ἀπὸ	τῶν	εἰδώλων	δουλεύειν	θεῷ	ζῶντι
TO	-	GOD	FROM	THE	IDOLS	TO SERVE	A GOD	LIVING

καὶ	ἀληθινῷ	**1.10** καὶ	ἀναμένειν	τὸν	υἱὸν	αὐτοῦ	ἐκ
AND	TRUE	AND	TO WAIT [FOR]	THE	SON	OF HIM	FROM

τῶν	οὐρανῶν,	ὃν	ἤγειρεν	ἐκ	[τῶν]	νεκρῶν,	’Ιησοῦν
THE	HEAVENS,	WHOM	HE RAISED	FROM	THE	DEAD,	JESUS,

τὸν	ῥυόμενον	ἡμᾶς	ἐκ	τῆς	ὀργῆς	τῆς	ἐρχομένης.
THE ONE	DELIVERING	US	FROM	THE	²WRATH	-	¹COMING.

CHAPTER 2

You yourselves know, brothers and sisters,[c] that our coming to you was not in vain, ²but though we had already suffered and been shamefully mistreated at Philippi, as you know, we had courage in our God to declare to you the gospel of God in spite of great opposition. ³For our appeal does not spring from deceit or impure motives or trickery, ⁴but just as we have been approved by God to be entrusted with the message of the gospel, even so we speak, not to please mortals, but to please God who tests our hearts. ⁵As you know and as God is our witness, we never came with words of flattery

[c] Gk *brothers*

2.1 Αὐτοὶ γὰρ οἴδατε, ἀδελφοί, τὴν εἴσοδον ἡμῶν

³YOURSELVES ¹FOR ²YOU° KNOW, BROTHERS, THE VISIT OF US

τὴν	πρὸς	ὑμᾶς	ὅτι	οὐ	κενὴ	γέγονεν,	**2.2** ἀλλὰ
-	TO	YOU°	THAT	²NOT	⁴IN VAIN	¹IT HAS ³BEEN,	BUT

προπαθόντες	καὶ	ὑβρισθέντες,	καθὼς	οἴδατε,	ἐν
HAVING SUFFERED PREVIOUSLY	AND	HAVING BEEN MISTREATED,	AS	YOU° KNOW,	IN

Φιλίπποις	ἐπαρρησιασάμεθα	ἐν	τῷ	θεῷ	ἡμῶν	λαλῆσαι
PHILIPPI	WE TOOK COURAGE	IN	THE	GOD	OF US	TO SPEAK

πρὸς	ὑμᾶς	τὸ	εὐαγγέλιον	τοῦ	θεοῦ	ἐν	πολλῷ
TO	YOU°	THE	GOOD NEWS	-	OF GOD	IN(WITH)	GREAT

ἀγῶνι.	**2.3** ἡ	γὰρ	παράκλησις	ἡμῶν	οὐκ	ἐκ	πλάνης
CONFLICT.	FOR~THE		EXHORTATION	OF US	[WAS] NOT	OF	DECEPTION

οὐδὲ	ἐξ	ἀκαθαρσίας	οὐδὲ	ἐν	δόλῳ,	**2.4** ἀλλὰ	καθὼς
NOR	OF	IMPURITY	NOR	IN	GUILE,	BUT	EVEN AS

δεδοκιμάσμεθα	ὑπὸ	τοῦ	θεοῦ	πιστευθῆναι
WE HAVE BEEN APPROVED	BY	-	GOD	TO BE ENTRUSTED [WITH]

τὸ	εὐαγγέλιον,	οὕτως	λαλοῦμεν,	οὐχ	ὡς
THE	GOOD NEWS,	SO	WE SPEAK,	NOT	AS

ἀνθρώποις	ἀρέσκοντες	ἀλλὰ	θεῷ	τῷ	δοκιμάζοντι	τὰς
PLEASING~MEN,		BUT	GOD,	THE ONE	EXAMINING	THE

καρδίας	ἡμῶν.	**2.5** οὔτε	γὰρ	ποτε	ἐν	λόγῳ	κολακείας
HEARTS	OF US.	FOR~NEITHER		THEN	WITH	A WORD	OF FLATTERY

ἐγενήθημεν, καθὼς οἴδατε, οὔτε ἐν προφάσει
WERE WE [FOUND],   AS   YOU° KNOW, NOR WITH A MOTIVE

πλεονεξίας, θεὸς μάρτυς, **2.6** οὔτε ζητοῦντες ἐξ
OF (FOR) GREED, GOD [IS] WITNESS,   NOR   SEEKING   OF

ἀνθρώπων δόξαν οὔτε ἀφ᾽ ὑμῶν οὔτε ἀπ᾽ ἄλλων,
MEN   GLORY, NEITHER FROM YOU° NOR FROM OTHERS,

2.7 δυνάμενοι ἐν βάρει εἶναι ὡς Χριστοῦ ἀπόστολοι.
BEING ABLE   TO BE~WITH WEIGHT (WEIGHTY) AS APOSTLES~OF CHRIST.

ἀλλὰ ἐγενήθημεν ⌜νήπιοι⌝ ἐν μέσῳ ὑμῶν, ὡς ἐὰν
BUT   WE BECAME   BABES   IN [THE] MIDST OF YOU°; AS IF

τροφὸς θάλπῃ τὰ ἑαυτῆς τέκνα, **2.8** οὕτως
A NURSING MOTHER WOULD CHERISH - HER OWN CHILDREN— ²SO

ὀμειρόμενοι ὑμῶν εὐδοκοῦμεν μεταδοῦναι ὑμῖν
¹BEING ³AFFECTIONATELY DESIROUS OF YOU° WE WERE PLEASED TO IMPART TO YOU°

οὐ μόνον τὸ εὐαγγέλιον τοῦ θεοῦ ἀλλὰ καὶ τὰς
NOT ONLY THE GOOD NEWS   -   OF GOD BUT ALSO -

ἑαυτῶν ψυχάς, διότι ἀγαπητοὶ ἡμῖν ἐγενήθητε.
OUR OWN SOULS, BECAUSE ²BELOVED ³TO US ¹YOU° BECAME.

2.9 μνημονεύετε γάρ, ἀδελφοί, τὸν κόπον ἡμῶν καὶ τὸν
FOR~YOU° REMEMBER, BROTHERS,   THE LABOR   OF US AND THE

μόχθον· νυκτὸς καὶ ἡμέρας ἐργαζόμενοι πρὸς τὸ μὴ
HARDSHIP; NIGHT AND DAY   WORKING   SO AS - NOT

ἐπιβαρῆσαί τινα ὑμῶν ἐκηρύξαμεν εἰς ὑμᾶς τὸ
TO BE A BURDEN ON ANY ONE OF YOU°, WE PROCLAIMED TO YOU° THE

εὐαγγέλιον τοῦ θεοῦ. **2.10** ὑμεῖς μάρτυρες καὶ ὁ θεός,
GOOD NEWS   -   OF GOD.   YOU°   [ARE] WITNESSES AND - GOD,

ὡς ὁσίως καὶ δικαίως καὶ ἀμέμπτως ὑμῖν τοῖς
HOW DEVOUTLY AND RIGHTEOUSLY AND BLAMELESSLY ²WITH YOU° ³THE ONES

πιστεύουσιν ἐγενήθημεν, **2.11** καθάπερ οἴδατε, ὡς
⁴BELIEVING ¹WE WERE,   EVEN AS YOU° KNOW, HOW

ἕνα ἕκαστον ὑμῶν ὡς πατὴρ τέκνα ἑαυτοῦ
[TO] EACH~ONE OF YOU° [WE WERE] AS A FATHER [WITH] HIS OWN~CHILDREN,

2.12 παρακαλοῦντες ὑμᾶς καὶ παραμυθούμενοι καὶ
EXHORTING   YOU° AND ENCOURAGING   AND

μαρτυρόμενοι εἰς τὸ περιπατεῖν ὑμᾶς ἀξίως τοῦ θεοῦ
TESTIFYING   FOR - YOU°~TO WALK   WORTHILY - OF GOD,

τοῦ καλοῦντος ὑμᾶς εἰς τὴν ἑαυτοῦ βασιλείαν καὶ
THE ONE CALLING YOU° INTO - HIS OWN KINGDOM   AND

δόξαν.
GLORY.

2.13 Καὶ διὰ τοῦτο καὶ ἡμεῖς εὐχαριστοῦμεν τῷ
AND BECAUSE OF THIS WE~ALSO GIVE THANKS   -

θεῷ ἀδιαλείπτως, ὅτι παραλαβόντες λόγον ἀκοῆς
TO GOD UNCEASINGLY, THAT HAVING RECEIVED [THE] WORD OF [THE] REPORT

παρ᾽ ἡμῶν τοῦ θεοῦ ἐδέξασθε οὐ λόγον ἀνθρώπων
FROM US,   - OF GOD YOU° RECEIVED [IT] NOT [AS] A WORD OF MEN

2:7 text: ASVmg RSVmg NASBmg TEVmg NRSVmg. var. ηπιοι (gentle): all.

or with a pretext for greed; [6]nor did we seek praise from mortals, whether from you or from others, [7]though we might have made demands as apostles of Christ. But we were gentle[d] among you, like a nurse tenderly caring for her own children. [8]So deeply do we care for you that we are determined to share with you not only the gospel of God but also our own selves, because you have become very dear to us.

9 You remember our labor and toil, brothers and sisters;[e] we worked night and day, so that we might not burden any of you while we proclaimed to you the gospel of God. [10]You are witnesses, and God also, how pure, upright, and blameless our conduct was toward you believers. [11]As you know, we dealt with each one of you like a father with his children, [12]urging and encouraging you and pleading that you lead a life worthy of God, who calls you into his own kingdom and glory.

13 We also constantly give thanks to God for this, that when you received the word of God that you heard from us, you accepted it not as a human word

[d] Other ancient authorities read *infants*
[e] Gk *brothers*

but as what it really is, God's word, which is also at work in you believers. [14]For you, brothers and sisters,[f] became imitators of the churches of God in Christ Jesus that are in Judea, for you suffered the same things from your own compatriots as they did from the Jews, [15]who killed both the Lord Jesus and the prophets,[g] and drove us out; they displease God and oppose everyone [16]by hindering us from speaking to the Gentiles so that they may be saved. Thus they have constantly been filling up the measure of their sins; but God's wrath has overtaken them at last.[h]

17 As for us, brothers and sisters,[f] when, for a short time, we were made orphans by being separated from you—in person, not in heart—we longed with great eagerness to see you face to face. [18]For we wanted to come to you—certainly I, Paul, wanted to again and again—but Satan blocked our way. [19]For what is our hope or joy or crown of boasting before our Lord Jesus at his coming? Is it not you? [20]Yes, you are our glory and joy!

[f] Gk brothers
[g] Other ancient authorities read their own prophets
[h] Or completely or forever

ἀλλὰ καθώς ἐστιν ἀληθῶς λόγον θεοῦ, ὃς καὶ
BUT   AS   IT IS   TRULY [THE] WORD OF GOD, WHICH ALSO

ἐνεργεῖται ἐν ὑμῖν τοῖς πιστεύουσιν. **2.14**ὑμεῖς γὰρ
WORKS   IN   YOU°, THE ONES BELIEVING.   FOR~YOU°

μιμηταὶ ἐγενήθητε, ἀδελφοί, τῶν ἐκκλησιῶν τοῦ θεοῦ
BECAME~IMITATORS,   BROTHERS, OF THE CHURCHES - OF GOD

τῶν οὐσῶν ἐν τῇ Ἰουδαίᾳ ἐν Χριστῷ Ἰησοῦ, ὅτι τὰ
- BEING IN - JUDEA IN CHRIST JESUS, BECAUSE THE

αὐτὰ ἐπάθετε καὶ ὑμεῖς ὑπὸ τῶν ἰδίων
SAME THINGS ³SUFFERED ²ALSO ¹YOU° BY THE(YOUR°) OWN

συμφυλετῶν καθὼς καὶ αὐτοὶ ὑπὸ τῶν Ἰουδαίων,
FELLOW-COUNTRYMEN AS ALSO THEY   BY THE JEWS,

2.15τῶν καὶ τὸν κύριον ἀποκτεινάντων Ἰησοῦν καὶ
     THE ONES BOTH ¹THE ²LORD ⁴HAVING KILLED ³JESUS AND

τοὺς προφήτας καὶ ἡμᾶς ἐκδιωξάντων καὶ θεῷ
THE PROPHETS AND HAVING SEVERELY PERSECUTED~US AND ³GOD

μὴ ἀρεσκόντων καὶ πᾶσιν ἀνθρώποις ἐναντίων,
¹NOT ²PLEASING   AND TO ALL   MEN   CONTRARY,

2.16κωλυόντων ἡμᾶς τοῖς ἔθνεσιν λαλῆσαι ἵνα
     FORBIDDING US   ²TO THE ³GENTILES ¹TO SPEAK THAT

σωθῶσιν, εἰς τὸ ἀναπληρῶσαι αὐτῶν τὰς ἁμαρτίας
THEY MIGHT BE SAVED, SO AS - TO FILL UP THEIR - SINS

πάντοτε. ἔφθασεν δὲ ἐπ' αὐτοὺς ἡ ὀργὴ εἰς τέλος.
ALWAYS.   ⁴CAME ¹BUT ⁵ON ⁶THEM ²THE ³WRATH TO [THE] END.

2.17Ἡμεῖς δέ, ἀδελφοί, ἀπορφανισθέντες ἀφ' ὑμῶν
     BUT~WE,   BROTHERS, HAVING BEEN SEPARATED FROM YOU°

πρὸς καιρὸν ὥρας, προσώπῳ οὐ καρδίᾳ,
FOR   A TIME [EVEN] AN HOUR, IN PRESENCE NOT IN HEART,

περισσοτέρως ἐσπουδάσαμεν τὸ πρόσωπον ὑμῶν ἰδεῖν
MORE ABUNDANTLY WE WERE EAGER ²THE ³FACE ⁴OF YOU° ¹TO SEE

ἐν πολλῇ ἐπιθυμίᾳ. **2.18**διότι ἠθελήσαμεν ἐλθεῖν
WITH MUCH DESIRE.   THEREFORE WE WANTED TO COME

πρὸς ὑμᾶς, ἐγὼ μὲν Παῦλος καὶ ἅπαξ καὶ δίς,
TO YOU°, INDEED~I PAUL BOTH ONCE AND TWICE(AGAIN),

καὶ ἐνέκοψεν ἡμᾶς ὁ Σατανᾶς. **2.19**τίς γὰρ ἡμῶν
AND ²HINDERED ³US - ¹SATAN.   FOR~WHAT [IS] OUR

ἐλπὶς ἢ χαρὰ ἢ στέφανος καυχήσεως — ἢ οὐχὶ καὶ
HOPE OR JOY OR CROWN   OF BOASTING — - [IS IT] NOT EVEN

ὑμεῖς — ἔμπροσθεν τοῦ κυρίου ἡμῶν Ἰησοῦ ἐν τῇ
YOU° — BEFORE   THE LORD OF US, JESUS, IN(AT) -

αὐτοῦ παρουσίᾳ; **2.20**ὑμεῖς γὰρ ἐστε ἡ δόξα ἡμῶν
HIS   COMING?   FOR~YOU° ARE THE GLORY OF US

καὶ ἡ χαρά.
AND THE JOY.

3.1 Διὸ   μηκέτι στέγοντες εὐδοκήσαμεν
WHEREFORE NO LONGER ENDURING,   WE WERE PLEASED

καταλειφθῆναι ἐν ᾿Αθήναις μόνοι **3.2** καὶ ἐπέμψαμεν
TO BE LEFT   IN   ATHENS   ALONE,   AND   WE SENT

Τιμόθεον, τὸν ἀδελφὸν ἡμῶν καὶ ⌐συνεργὸν τοῦ θεοῦ⌐
TIMOTHY,   THE BROTHER OF US AND CO-WORKER - OF GOD

ἐν τῷ εὐαγγελίῳ τοῦ Χριστοῦ, εἰς τὸ στηρίξαι ὑμᾶς
IN THE GOSPEL   - OF CHRIST, SO AS - TO ESTABLISH YOU°

καὶ παρακαλέσαι ὑπὲρ τῆς πίστεως ὑμῶν **3.3** τὸ
AND TO ENCOURAGE [YOU°] FOR THE FAITH OF YOU° -

μηδένα σαίνεσθαι ἐν ταῖς θλίψεσιν ταύταις. αὐτοὶ
[FOR] NO ONE TO BE SHAKEN BY -   THESE~AFFLICTIONS.   ³YOURSELVES

γὰρ οἴδατε ὅτι εἰς τοῦτο κείμεθα·   **3.4** καὶ γὰρ ὅτε
¹FOR ²YOU° KNOW THAT TO THIS WE ARE APPOINTED; FOR~EVEN WHEN

πρὸς ὑμᾶς ἦμεν, προελέγομεν ὑμῖν ὅτι μέλλομεν
WITH   YOU° WE WERE, WE WERE SAYING BEFORE TO YOU° THAT WE ARE ABOUT

θλίβεσθαι, καθὼς καὶ ἐγένετο καὶ οἴδατε.
TO BE AFFLICTED, EVEN AS ALSO IT HAPPENED AND YOU° KNOW.

3.5 διὰ τοῦτο κἀγὼ μηκέτι στέγων ἔπεμψα εἰς τὸ
THEREFORE I ALSO NO LONGER BEARING [IT] SENT [TIMOTHY] SO AS -

γνῶναι τὴν πίστιν ὑμῶν, μή πως ἐπείρασεν ὑμᾶς ὁ
TO KNOW THE FAITH OF YOU°, LEST SOMEHOW ³TEMPTED   ⁴YOU° ¹THE

πειράζων καὶ εἰς κενὸν γένηται ὁ κόπος ἡμῶν.
²TEMPTING ONE AND IN VAIN BECAME THE LABOR OF US.

3.6 ῎Αρτι δὲ ἐλθόντος Τιμοθέου πρὸς ἡμᾶς ἀφ᾿ ὑμῶν
BUT~NOW TIMOTHY~HAVING COME TO US FROM YOU°

καὶ εὐαγγελισαμένου ἡμῖν τὴν πίστιν καὶ τὴν
AND HAVING BROUGHT GOOD NEWS TO US [OF] THE FAITH AND THE

ἀγάπην ὑμῶν καὶ ὅτι ἔχετε μνείαν ἡμῶν ἀγαθὴν
LOVE   OF YOU° AND THAT YOU° HAVE ²REMEMBRANCE ³OF US ¹GOOD

πάντοτε, ἐπιποθοῦντες ἡμᾶς ἰδεῖν καθάπερ καὶ ἡμεῖς
ALWAYS,   LONGING   TO SEE~US EVEN AS ALSO WE

ὑμᾶς, **3.7** διὰ τοῦτο παρεκλήθημεν, ἀδελφοί, ἐφ᾿ ὑμῖν
YOU°;   THEREFORE WE WERE ENCOURAGED, BROTHERS, AS TO YOU°,

ἐπὶ πάσῃ τῇ ἀνάγκῃ καὶ θλίψει ἡμῶν διὰ τῆς ὑμῶν
FOR ALL THE DISTRESS AND AFFLICTION OF US, THROUGH - YOUR°

πίστεως, **3.8** ὅτι νῦν ζῶμεν ἐὰν ὑμεῖς στήκετε ἐν
FAITH,   BECAUSE NOW WE LIVE IF YOU° STAND FIRM IN

κυρίῳ. **3.9** τίνα γὰρ εὐχαριστίαν δυνάμεθα τῷ
[THE] LORD. FOR~WHAT THANKS   ARE WE ABLE -

θεῷ ἀνταποδοῦναι περὶ ὑμῶν ἐπὶ πάσῃ τῇ χαρᾷ
TO RETURN~TO GOD CONCERNING YOU° FOR ALL THE JOY

3:2 text: ASV NASB NIV NEB (TEV) NJB NRSV. var. συνεργον (co-worker): NIVmg NEBmg. var.
διακονον του θεου (servant of God): ASV RSV NIVmg. NJB. var. διακονον του θεου και συνεργον ημων
(servant of God and our co-worker): KJV NJBmg.

Therefore when we could bear it no longer, we decided to be left alone in Athens; [2]and we sent Timothy, our brother and co-worker for God in proclaiming[i] the gospel of Christ, to strengthen and encourage you for the sake of your faith, [3]so that no one would be shaken by these persecutions. Indeed, you yourselves know that this is what we are destined for. [4]In fact, when we were with you, we told you beforehand that we were to suffer persecution; so it turned out, as you know. [5]For this reason, when I could bear it no longer, I sent to find out about your faith; I was afraid that somehow the tempter had tempted you and that our labor had been in vain.

6 But Timothy has just now come to us from you, and has brought us the good news of your faith and love. He has told us also that you always remember us kindly and long to see us—just as we long to see you. [7]For this reason, brothers and sisters,[j] during all our distress and persecution we have been encouraged about you through your faith. [8]For we now live, if you continue to stand firm in the Lord. [9]How can we thank God enough for you in return for all the

[i] Gk lacks *proclaiming*
[j] Gk *brothers*

joy that we feel before our God because of you? ¹⁰Night and day we pray most earnestly that we may see you face to face and restore whatever is lacking in your faith.

11 Now may our God and Father himself and our Lord Jesus direct our way to you. ¹²And may the Lord make you increase and abound in love for one another and for all, just as we abound in love for you. ¹³And may he so strengthen your hearts in holiness that you may be blameless before our God and Father at the coming of our Lord Jesus with all his saints.

ᾗ   χαίρομεν δι᾽   ὑμᾶς ἔμπροσθεν τοῦ θεοῦ
[WITH] WHICH WE REJOICE BECAUSE OF YOU° BEFORE   THE GOD

ἡμῶν, 3.10 νυκτὸς καὶ ἡμέρας ὑπερεκπερισσοῦ δεόμενοι
OF US,   NIGHT   AND DAY   EXCEEDINGLY   ASKING [GOD]

εἰς   τὸ ἰδεῖν ὑμῶν τὸ πρόσωπον καὶ καταρτίσαι τὰ
SO AS -   TO SEE YOUR° -   FACE   AND TO SUPPLY   THE

ὑστερήματα τῆς πίστεως ὑμῶν;
SHORTCOMINGS OF THE FAITH   OF YOU°?

3.11 Αὐτὸς δὲ   ὁ θεὸς καὶ πατὴρ ἡμῶν καὶ ὁ
   ³HIMSELF ¹NOW - ²GOD EVEN [THE] FATHER OF US AND THE

κύριος ἡμῶν Ἰησοῦς κατευθύναι τὴν ὁδὸν ἡμῶν πρὸς
LORD   OF US, JESUS,   MAY HE DIRECT THE WAY   OF US TO

ὑμᾶς· 3.12 ὑμᾶς δὲ   ὁ κύριος πλεονάσαι   καὶ
YOU°;   ⁶YOU° ¹AND ³THE ⁴LORD ²MAY ⁵CAUSE ⁷TO INCREASE AND

περισσεύσαι τῇ ἀγάπῃ εἰς ἀλλήλους καὶ εἰς πάντας
TO ABOUND   -   IN LOVE TO   ONE ANOTHER AND TO   ALL

καθάπερ καὶ ἡμεῖς εἰς ὑμᾶς, 3.13 εἰς τὸ στηρίξαι
EVEN AS   ALSO WE [DO] TO   YOU°,   SO AS -   TO ESTABLISH

ὑμῶν τὰς καρδίας ἀμέμπτους ἐν ἁγιωσύνῃ ἔμπροσθεν
YOUR° -   HEARTS   BLAMELESS   IN HOLINESS   BEFORE

τοῦ θεοῦ καὶ πατρὸς ἡμῶν ἐν τῇ παρουσίᾳ τοῦ
THE GOD AND FATHER   OF US IN(AT) THE COMING   OF THE

κυρίου ἡμῶν Ἰησοῦ μετὰ πάντων τῶν ἁγίων αὐτοῦ,
LORD   OF US, JESUS, WITH   ALL   THE SAINTS   OF HIM,

[ἀμήν].
AMEN.

CHAPTER 4

Finally, brothers and sisters,^k we ask and urge you in the Lord Jesus that, as you learned from us how you ought to live and to please God (as, in fact, you are doing), you should do so more and more. ²For you know what instructions we gave you through the Lord Jesus. ³For this is the will of God, your sanctification: that you abstain from fornication; ⁴that each one of you know

^k Gk *brothers*

4.1 Λοιπὸν οὖν,   ἀδελφοί, ἐρωτῶμεν ὑμᾶς καὶ
   FOR THE REST THEREFORE, BROTHERS,   WE ASK   YOU° AND

παρακαλοῦμεν ἐν κυρίῳ Ἰησοῦ, ἵνα καθὼς παρελάβετε
WE ENCOURAGE   IN [THE] LORD JESUS, THAT AS   YOU° RECEIVED

παρ᾽ ἡμῶν τὸ πῶς δεῖ   ὑμᾶς περιπατεῖν
FROM   US   -   HOW IT IS NECESSARY [FOR] YOU° TO WALK

καὶ ἀρέσκειν θεῷ, καθὼς καὶ περιπατεῖτε, ἵνα
AND TO PLEASE   GOD,   AS   INDEED YOU° DO WALK,   THAT

περισσεύητε μᾶλλον. 4.2 οἴδατε γὰρ τίνας παραγγελίας
YOU° ABOUND   MORE.   FOR~YOU° KNOW WHAT ORDERS

ἐδώκαμεν ὑμῖν διὰ   τοῦ κυρίου Ἰησοῦ. 4.3 τοῦτο γάρ
WE GAVE   TO YOU° THROUGH THE LORD   JESUS.   FOR~THIS

ἐστιν θέλημα τοῦ θεοῦ, ὁ ἁγιασμὸς ὑμῶν,
IS   [THE] WILL -   OF GOD, THE SANCTIFICATION OF YOU°,

ἀπέχεσθαι ὑμᾶς ἀπὸ τῆς πορνείας, 4.4 εἰδέναι ἕκαστον
[FOR] YOU°~TO ABSTAIN FROM -   FORNICATION,   ³TO KNOW ¹EACH ONE

ὑμῶν τὸ ἑαυτοῦ σκεῦος κτᾶσθαι ἐν ἁγιασμῷ καὶ
²OF YOU° - ⁵HIS OWN ⁶VESSEL ⁴[HOW] TO CONTROL IN SANCTIFICATION AND

τιμῇ, **4.5** μὴ ἐν πάθει ἐπιθυμίας καθάπερ καὶ τὰ ἔθνη
HONOR, NOT IN PASSION OF LUST EVEN AS ALSO THE GENTILES

τὰ μὴ εἰδότα τὸν θεόν, **4.6** τὸ μὴ ὑπερβαίνειν καὶ
- NOT KNOWING - GOD, - NOT TO OVERSTEP AND

πλεονεκτεῖν ἐν τῷ πράγματι τὸν ἀδελφὸν αὐτοῦ,
TO WRONG IN THE(THIS) MATTER THE BROTHER OF HIM,

διότι ἔκδικος κύριος περὶ πάντων τούτων, καθὼς
BECAUSE AN AVENGER [IS THE] LORD CONCERNING ALL THESE THINGS, EVEN AS

καὶ προείπαμεν ὑμῖν καὶ διεμαρτυράμεθα. **4.7** οὐ
ALSO WE SAID BEFORE TO YOU° AND WE FULLY TESTIFIED. ⁴NOT

γὰρ ἐκάλεσεν ἡμᾶς ὁ θεὸς ἐπὶ ἀκαθαρσίᾳ ἀλλ᾽ ἐν
¹FOR ³DID ⁵CALL ⁶US - ²GOD TO IMPURITY BUT IN

ἁγιασμῷ. **4.8** τοιγαροῦν ὁ ἀθετῶν οὐκ ἄνθρωπον
SANCTIFICATION. THEREFORE THE ONE REJECTING [THIS] ²NOT ³MAN

ἀθετεῖ ἀλλὰ τὸν θεὸν τὸν [καὶ] διδόντα τὸ πνεῦμα
¹REJECTS BUT - GOD, THE ONE ALSO GIVING - ³SPIRIT

αὐτοῦ τὸ ἅγιον εἰς ὑμᾶς.
¹HIS - ²HOLY TO YOU°.

4.9 Περὶ δὲ τῆς φιλαδελφίας οὐ χρείαν ἔχετε
NOW~CONCERNING - BROTHERLY LOVE ²NO ³NEED ¹YOU° HAVE

γράφειν ὑμῖν, αὐτοὶ γὰρ ὑμεῖς θεοδίδακτοί ἐστε
[FOR ME] TO WRITE TO YOU°, ³YOURSELVES ¹FOR ²YOU° ⁵TAUGHT OF GOD ⁴ARE

εἰς τὸ ἀγαπᾶν ἀλλήλους, **4.10** καὶ γὰρ ποιεῖτε αὐτὸ εἰς
- - TO LOVE ONE ANOTHER, FOR~INDEED YOU° DO IT TO

πάντας τοὺς ἀδελφοὺς [τοὺς] ἐν ὅλη τῇ Μακεδονίᾳ.
ALL THE BROTHERS - IN THE~WHOLE OF MACEDONIA.

παρακαλοῦμεν δὲ ὑμᾶς, ἀδελφοί, περισσεύειν μᾶλλον
BUT~WE ENCOURAGE YOU°, BROTHERS, TO ABOUND MORE

4.11 καὶ φιλοτιμεῖσθαι ἡσυχάζειν καὶ πράσσειν τὰ
AND TO ASPIRE TO LIVE QUIETLY AND TO DO(MIND) THE(YOUR)

ἴδια καὶ ἐργάζεσθαι ταῖς [ἰδίαις] χερσὶν ὑμῶν,
OWN THINGS AND TO WORK - ¹WITH ³OWN ⁴HANDS ²YOUR°,

καθὼς ὑμῖν παρηγγείλαμεν, **4.12** ἵνα περιπατῆτε
EVEN AS WE CHARGED~YOU°, THAT YOU° MAY WALK

εὐσχημόνως πρὸς τοὺς ἔξω καὶ μηδενὸς χρείαν
PROPERLY TOWARD THE ONES OUTSIDE AND ³OF NOTHING ²NEED

ἔχητε.
¹YOU° MAY HAVE.

4.13 Οὐ θέλομεν δὲ ὑμᾶς ἀγνοεῖν, ἀδελφοί,
²WE DO NOT WANT ¹NOW YOU° TO BE IGNORANT, BROTHERS,

περὶ τῶν κοιμωμένων, ἵνα μὴ λυπῆσθε καθὼς
CONCERNING THE ONES SLEEPING, LEST YOU° BE SORROWFUL AS

καὶ οἱ λοιποὶ οἱ μὴ ἔχοντες ἐλπίδα. **4.14** εἰ γὰρ
ALSO THE REST - NOT HAVING HOPE. FOR~IF

πιστεύομεν ὅτι Ἰησοῦς ἀπέθανεν καὶ ἀνέστη, οὕτως
WE BELIEVE THAT JESUS DIED AND ROSE, SO

how to control your own body[l] in holiness and honor, [5]not with lustful passion, like the Gentiles who do not know God; [6]that no one wrong or exploit a brother or sister[m] in this matter, because the Lord is an avenger in all these things, just as we have already told you beforehand and solemnly warned you. [7]For God did not call us to impurity but in holiness. [8]Therefore whoever rejects this rejects not human authority but God, who also gives his Holy Spirit to you.

9 Now concerning love of the brothers and sisters,[n] you do not need to have anyone write to you, for you yourselves have been taught by God to love one another; [10]and indeed you do love all the brothers and sisters[n] throughout Macedonia. But we urge you, beloved,[n] to do so more and more, [11]to aspire to live quietly, to mind your own affairs, and to work with your hands, as we directed you, [12]so that you may behave properly toward outsiders and be dependent on no one.

13 But we do not want you to be uninformed, brothers and sisters,[n] about those who have died,[o] so that you may not grieve as others do who have no hope. [14]For since we believe that Jesus died and rose again,

[l] Or *how to take a wife for himself*
[m] Gk *brother*
[n] Gk *brothers*
[o] Gk *fallen asleep*

even so, through Jesus, God
will bring with him those
who have died.*p* 15For this
we declare to you by the
word of the Lord, that we
who are alive, who are left
until the coming of the Lord,
will by no means precede
those who have died.*p* 16For
the Lord himself, with a cry
of command, with the archangel's call and with the
sound of God's trumpet,
will descend from heaven,
and the dead in Christ will
rise first. 17Then we who are
alive, who are left, will be
caught up in the clouds
together with them to meet
the Lord in the air; and so
we will be with the Lord
forever. 18Therefore en-
courage one another with
these words.

p Gk *fallen asleep*

καὶ ὁ θεὸς τοὺς κοιμηθέντας διὰ τοῦ Ἰησοῦ
ALSO - ³GOD ⁷THE ONES ⁸HAVING FALLEN ASLEEP ¹THROUGH - ²JESUS

ἄξει σὺν αὐτῷ.
⁴WILL BRING ⁵WITH ⁶HIM.

4.15 Τοῦτο γὰρ ὑμῖν λέγομεν ἐν λόγῳ κυρίου,
FOR~THIS TO YOU° WE SAY BY A WORD OF(FROM) [THE] LORD,

ὅτι ἡμεῖς οἱ ζῶντες οἱ περιλειπόμενοι εἰς τὴν
THAT WE THE ONES LIVING, THE ONES REMAINING TO THE

παρουσίαν τοῦ κυρίου οὐ μὴ φθάσωμεν τοὺς
COMING OF THE LORD, IN NO WAY MAY PRECEDE THE ONES

κοιμηθέντας· **4.16** ὅτι αὐτὸς ὁ κύριος ἐν
HAVING FALLEN ASLEEP; BECAUSE ³HIMSELF ¹THE ²LORD WITH

κελεύσματι, ἐν φωνῇ ἀρχαγγέλου καὶ ἐν σάλπιγγι
A CRY OF COMMAND, WITH A VOICE OF AN ARCHANGEL AND WITH A TRUMPET

θεοῦ, καταβήσεται ἀπ᾽ οὐρανοῦ καὶ οἱ νεκροὶ ἐν
OF GOD, WILL DESCEND FROM HEAVEN AND THE DEAD IN

Χριστῷ ἀναστήσονται πρῶτον, **4.17** ἔπειτα ἡμεῖς οἱ
CHRIST WILL RISE FIRST, THEN WE, THE ONES

ζῶντες, οἱ περιλειπόμενοι ἅμα σὺν αὐτοῖς
LIVING, THE ONES REMAINING, TOGETHER WITH THEM

ἁρπαγησόμεθα ἐν νεφέλαις εἰς ἀπάντησιν τοῦ
WILL BE CAUGHT UP IN CLOUDS TO A MEETING OF(WITH) THE

κυρίου εἰς ἀέρα· καὶ οὕτως πάντοτε σὺν κυρίῳ
LORD IN [THE] AIR; AND SO ALWAYS WITH [THE] LORD

ἐσόμεθα. **4.18** Ὥστε παρακαλεῖτε ἀλλήλους ἐν τοῖς
WE WILL BE. SO THEN, ENCOURAGE ONE ANOTHER WITH -

λόγοις τούτοις.
THESE~WORDS.

CHAPTER 5

Now concerning the times
and the seasons, brothers
and sisters,*q* you do not need
to have anything written to
you. 2For you yourselves
know very well that the day
of the Lord will come like a
thief in the night. 3When
they say, "There is peace and
security," then sudden
destruction will come upon
them, as labor pains come
upon a pregnant woman,
and there will be no escape!
4But you, beloved,*q* are not
in darkness, for that day to
surprise you like a thief;

q Gk *brothers*

5.1 Περὶ δὲ τῶν χρόνων καὶ τῶν καιρῶν, ἀδελφοί,
BUT~CONCERNING THE TIMES AND THE SEASONS, BROTHERS,

οὐ χρείαν ἔχετε ὑμῖν γράφεσθαι, **5.2** αὐτοὶ γὰρ
²NO ³NEED ¹YOU° HAVE FOR YOU° TO BE WRITTEN [TO], ³YOURSELVES ¹FOR

ἀκριβῶς οἴδατε ὅτι ἡμέρα κυρίου ὡς κλέπτης ἐν
⁵ACCURATELY ²YOU° ⁴KNOW THAT [THE] DAY OF [THE] LORD AS A THIEF IN

νυκτὶ οὕτως ἔρχεται. **5.3** ὅταν λέγωσιν, Εἰρήνη καὶ
[THE] NIGHT SO COMES. WHENEVER THEY SAY, PEACE AND

ἀσφάλεια, τότε αἰφνίδιος αὐτοῖς ἐφίσταται ὄλεθρος
SECURITY, THEN SUDDEN ³THEM ²COMES UPON ¹DESTRUCTION

ὥσπερ ἡ ὠδὶν τῇ ἐν γαστρὶ ἐχούσῃ, καὶ
AS THE BIRTH PAIN TO THE ONE ²IN ³[HER] WOMB ¹HAVING [A CHILD], AND

οὐ μὴ ἐκφύγωσιν. **5.4** ὑμεῖς δέ, ἀδελφοί, οὐκ ἐστὲ ἐν
THEY CAN CERTAINLY NOT ESCAPE. BUT~YOU°, BROTHERS, ARE~NOT IN

σκότει, ἵνα ἡ ἡμέρα ὑμᾶς ὡς κλέπτης καταλάβῃ·
DARKNESS, THAT THE DAY ²YOU° ³AS ⁴A THIEF ¹SHOULD OVERTAKE;

5.5 πάντες γὰρ ὑμεῖς υἱοὶ φωτός ἐστε καὶ υἱοὶ
FOR~ALL　　　YOU°　SONS　OF LIGHT　ARE　AND　SONS

ἡμέρας. οὐκ ἐσμὲν νυκτὸς οὐδὲ σκότους· **5.6** ἄρα οὖν
OF DAY.　WE ARE~NOT　OF NIGHT　OR　OF DARKNESS;　　THEREFORE,

μὴ καθεύδωμεν ὡς οἱ λοιποὶ ἀλλὰ γρηγορῶμεν καὶ
LET US NOT SLEEP　AS　THE REST　BUT　LET US KEEP AWAKE AND

νήφωμεν. **5.7** οἱ γὰρ καθεύδοντες νυκτὸς καθεύδουσιν
BE SOBER.　FOR~THE ONES SLEEPING　SLEEP~BY NIGHT,

καὶ οἱ μεθυσκόμενοι νυκτὸς μεθύουσιν· **5.8** ἡμεῖς δὲ
AND　THE ONES BEING DRUNK　ARE DRUNK~BY NIGHT;　　BUT~WE

ἡμέρας ὄντες νήφωμεν ἐνδυσάμενοι θώρακα
BEING~OF [THE] DAY,　LET US BE SOBER,　HAVING CLOTHED OURSELVES WITH　A BREASTPLATE

πίστεως καὶ ἀγάπης καὶ περικεφαλαίαν ἐλπίδα
OF FAITH　AND　LOVE　AND　[AS] A HELMET　　[THE] HOPE

σωτηρίας· **5.9** ὅτι οὐκ ἔθετο ἡμᾶς ὁ θεὸς εἰς ὀργὴν
OF SALVATION;　BECAUSE ²DID NOT APPOINT ³US ‑ ¹GOD TO WRATH

ἀλλὰ εἰς περιποίησιν σωτηρίας διὰ τοῦ κυρίου ἡμῶν
BUT　TO　[THE] ATTAINMENT　OF SALVATION　THROUGH THE LORD　OF US,

Ἰησοῦ Χριστοῦ **5.10** τοῦ ἀποθανόντος ὑπὲρ ἡμῶν,
JESUS　CHRIST,　THE ONE HAVING DIED　ON BEHALF OF　US,

ἵνα εἴτε γρηγορῶμεν εἴτε καθεύδωμεν ἅμα σὺν
THAT WHETHER WE ARE AWAKE　OR　WE ARE SLEEPING ²TOGETHER ³WITH

αὐτῷ ζήσωμεν. **5.11** Διὸ παρακαλεῖτε ἀλλήλους καὶ
⁴HIM ¹WE MAY LIVE.　THEREFORE ENCOURAGE　ONE ANOTHER　AND

οἰκοδομεῖτε εἰς τὸν ἕνα, καθὼς καὶ ποιεῖτε.
BUILD UP　ONE　THE　[OTHER] ONE, AS　ALSO　YOU° DO.

5.12 Ἐρωτῶμεν δὲ ὑμᾶς, ἀδελφοί, εἰδέναι τοὺς
NOW~WE ASK　　YOU°,　BROTHERS,　TO KNOW　THE ONES

κοπιῶντας ἐν ὑμῖν καὶ προϊσταμένους ὑμῶν ἐν
LABORING　AMONG YOU°　AND　EXERCISING LEADERSHIP　[OVER] YOU°　IN

κυρίῳ καὶ νουθετοῦντας ὑμᾶς **5.13** καὶ ἡγεῖσθαι αὐτοὺς
[THE] LORD AND　ADMONISHING　YOU°　　AND　TO ESTEEM　THEM

ὑπερεκπερισσοῦ ἐν ἀγάπῃ διὰ τὸ ἔργον αὐτῶν.
MOST EXCEEDINGLY　IN　LOVE　BECAUSE THE WORK　OF THEM.

εἰρηνεύετε ἐν ἑαυτοῖς. **5.14** παρακαλοῦμεν δὲ ὑμᾶς,
BE AT PEACE　AMONG YOURSELVES.　AND~WE ENCOURAGE　　YOU°,

ἀδελφοί, νουθετεῖτε τοὺς ἀτάκτους, παραμυθεῖσθε τοὺς
BROTHERS,　ADMONISH　THE　IDLE ONES,　CONSOLE　　THE

ὀλιγοψύχους, ἀντέχεσθε τῶν ἀσθενῶν, μακροθυμεῖτε
FAINT-HEARTED,　UPHOLD　THE ONES BEING WEAK,　BE LONGSUFFERING

πρὸς πάντας. **5.15** ὁρᾶτε μή τις κακὸν ἀντὶ
TOWARDS ALL.　SEE [THAT] NOT ANYONE EVIL　INSTEAD OF (FOR)

κακοῦ τινι ἀποδῷ, ἀλλὰ πάντοτε τὸ ἀγαθὸν διώκετε
EVIL　RENDER~TO ANYONE, BUT　ALWAYS　²THE ³GOOD ¹PURSUE

[καὶ] εἰς ἀλλήλους καὶ εἰς πάντας.
BOTH　FOR ONE ANOTHER AND　FOR ALL.

5.16 Πάντοτε χαίρετε, **5.17** ἀδιαλείπτως προσεύχεσθε,
ALWAYS　REJOICE,　UNCEASINGLY　PRAY,

⁵for you are all children of light and children of the day; we are not of the night or of darkness. ⁶So then let us not fall asleep as others do, but let us keep awake and be sober; ⁷for those who sleep sleep at night, and those who are drunk get drunk at night. ⁸But since we belong to the day, let us be sober, and put on the breastplate of faith and love, and for a helmet the hope of salvation. ⁹For God has destined us not for wrath but for obtaining salvation through our Lord Jesus Christ, ¹⁰who died for us, so that whether we are awake or asleep we may live with him. ¹¹Therefore encourage one another and build up each other, as indeed you are doing.

12 But we appeal to you, brothers and sisters,ʳ to respect those who labor among you, and have charge of you in the Lord and admonish you; ¹³esteem them very highly in love because of their work. Be at peace among yourselves. ¹⁴And we urge you, beloved,ʳ to admonish the idlers, encourage the fainthearted, help the weak, be patient with all of them. ¹⁵See that none of you repays evil for evil, but always seek to do good to one another and to all. ¹⁶Rejoice always, ¹⁷pray without ceasing,

ʳ Gk brothers

¹⁸give thanks in all circumstances; for this is the will of God in Christ Jesus for you. ¹⁹Do not quench the Spirit. ²⁰Do not despise the words of prophets,^s ²¹but test everything; hold fast to what is good; ²²abstain from every form of evil.

23 May the God of peace himself sanctify you entirely; and may your spirit and soul and body be kept sound^t and blameless at the coming of our Lord Jesus Christ. ²⁴The one who calls you is faithful, and he will do this.

25 Beloved,^u pray for us. 26 Greet all the brothers and sisters^v with a holy kiss. ²⁷I solemnly command you by the Lord that this letter be read to all of them.^w

28 The grace of our Lord Jesus Christ be with you.^x

^s Gk *despise prophecies*
^t Or *complete*
^u Gk *Brothers*
^v Gk *brothers*
^w Gk *to all the brothers*
^x Other ancient authorities add *Amen*

5.18 ἐν παντὶ εὐχαριστεῖτε· τοῦτο γὰρ θέλημα
IN   EVERYTHING   GIVE THANKS;   FOR~THIS [IS]   [THE] WILL

θεοῦ   ἐν   Χριστῷ   Ἰησοῦ   εἰς   ὑμᾶς.   **5.19** τὸ   πνεῦμα
OF GOD   IN   CHRIST   JESUS   FOR   YOU°.   THE   SPIRIT

μὴ σβέννυτε,   **5.20** προφητείας   μὴ ἐξουθενεῖτε,
DO NOT QUENCH,   PROPHECIES   DO NOT REJECT,

5.21 πάντα   δὲ   δοκιμάζετε, τὸ καλὸν κατέχετε, **5.22** ἀπὸ
³ALL THINGS ¹BUT ²TEST,   THE GOOD   HOLD FAST,   FROM

παντὸς εἴδους πονηροῦ ἀπέχεσθε.
EVERY   FORM   OF EVIL   ABSTAIN.

5.23 Αὐτὸς δὲ ὁ θεὸς τῆς εἰρήνης ἁγιάσαι ὑμᾶς
⁵HIMSELF ¹NOW ²THE ³GOD - ⁴OF PEACE MAY HE SANCTIFY YOU°

ὁλοτελεῖς, καὶ ὁλόκληρον ὑμῶν τὸ πνεῦμα καὶ ἡ ψυχὴ
WHOLLY,   AND   YOUR°~WHOLE   -   SPIRIT   AND   - SOUL

καὶ τὸ σῶμα ἀμέμπτως ἐν τῇ παρουσίᾳ τοῦ κυρίου
AND - BODY ²BLAMELESS ³IN(AT) ⁴THE ⁵COMING ⁶OF THE ⁷LORD

ἡμῶν Ἰησοῦ Χριστοῦ τηρηθείη.   **5.24** πιστὸς
⁸OF US ⁹JESUS ¹⁰CHRIST ¹MAY THEY BE PRESERVED.   FAITHFUL

ὁ   καλῶν ὑμᾶς, ὃς καὶ ποιήσει.
[IS] THE ONE CALLING YOU°,   WHO ALSO WILL DO [IT].

5.25 Ἀδελφοί, προσεύχεσθε [καὶ] περὶ ἡμῶν.
BROTHERS,   PRAY   ALSO CONCERNING US.

5.26 Ἀσπάσασθε τοὺς ἀδελφοὺς πάντας ἐν
GREET   ²THE ³BROTHERS ¹ALL   WITH

φιλήματι ἁγίῳ. **5.27** Ἐνορκίζω ὑμᾶς τὸν κύριον
A HOLY~KISS.   I ADJURE YOU° [BY] THE LORD

ἀναγνωσθῆναι τὴν ἐπιστολὴν πᾶσιν τοῖς
³[HAS] TO BE READ ¹[THAT] THE(THIS) ²LETTER TO ALL THE

ἀδελφοῖς.
BROTHERS.

5.28 Ἡ χάρις τοῦ κυρίου ἡμῶν Ἰησοῦ Χριστοῦ
THE GRACE OF THE LORD OF US, JESUS CHRIST,

μεθ᾽ ὑμῶν.
[BE] WITH YOU°.

THE SECOND LETTER OF PAUL TO THE
THESSALONIANS

ΠΡΟΣ ΘΕΣΣΑΛΟΝΙΚΕΙΣ Β
TO   [THE] THESSALONIANS   2

1.1 Παῦλος καὶ Σιλουανὸς καὶ Τιμόθεος τῇ
PAUL   AND   SILVANUS   AND   TIMOTHY   TO THE

ἐκκλησίᾳ Θεσσαλονικέων ἐν θεῷ πατρὶ ἡμῶν καὶ
CHURCH   OF [THE] THESSALONIANS   IN   GOD   [THE] FATHER   OF US   AND

κυρίῳ Ἰησοῦ Χριστῷ, **1.2** χάρις ὑμῖν καὶ εἰρήνη ἀπὸ
LORD   JESUS   CHRIST,   GRACE   TO YOU°   AND   PEACE   FROM

θεοῦ πατρὸς [ἡμῶν] καὶ κυρίου Ἰησοῦ Χριστοῦ.
GOD   [THE] FATHER   OF US   AND   LORD   JESUS   CHRIST.

1.3 Εὐχαριστεῖν ὀφείλομεν τῷ θεῷ πάντοτε περὶ
WE OUGHT~TO THANK   -   GOD   ALWAYS   CONCERNING

ὑμῶν, ἀδελφοί, καθὼς ἄξιόν ἐστιν, ὅτι ὑπεραυξάνει
YOU°,   BROTHERS,   EVEN AS   IT IS~FITTING,   BECAUSE   [4]GROWS ABUNDANTLY

ἡ πίστις ὑμῶν καὶ πλεονάζει ἡ ἀγάπη
[1]THE   [2]FAITH   [3]OF YOU°   AND   INCREASES   THE   LOVE

ἑνὸς ἑκάστου πάντων ὑμῶν εἰς ἀλλήλους, **1.4** ὥστε
OF EACH~ONE   OF YOU°~ALL   TO   ONE ANOTHER,   SO THAT

αὐτοὺς ἡμᾶς ἐν ὑμῖν ἐγκαυχᾶσθαι ἐν ταῖς
WE~OURSELVES   [2]IN   [3]YOU°   [1][HAVE] TO BOAST   IN(AMONG)   THE

ἐκκλησίαις τοῦ θεοῦ ὑπὲρ τῆς ὑπομονῆς ὑμῶν καὶ
CHURCHES   -   OF GOD   FOR   THE   ENDURANCE   OF YOU°   AND

πίστεως ἐν πᾶσιν τοῖς διωγμοῖς ὑμῶν καὶ ταῖς
FAITH   IN   ALL   THE   PERSECUTIONS   OF YOU°   AND   THE

θλίψεσιν αἷς ἀνέχεσθε, **1.5** ἔνδειγμα τῆς
TRIBULATIONS   WHICH   YOU° ARE ENDURING,   AN EVIDENT INDICATION   OF THE

δικαίας κρίσεως τοῦ θεοῦ εἰς τὸ καταξιωθῆναι ὑμᾶς
RIGHTEOUS   JUDGMENT   -   OF GOD,   FOR   -   YOU°~TO BE COUNTED WORTHY

τῆς βασιλείας τοῦ θεοῦ, ὑπὲρ ἧς καὶ πάσχετε,
OF THE   KINGDOM   -   OF GOD,   ON BEHALF OF   WHICH   ALSO   YOU° SUFFER,

1.6 εἴπερ δίκαιον παρὰ θεῷ ἀνταποδοῦναι τοῖς
IF INDEED   [IT IS] A JUST THING   WITH   GOD   TO RECOMPENSE   [2]TO THE ONES

θλίβουσιν ὑμᾶς θλῖψιν **1.7** καὶ ὑμῖν τοῖς
[3]OPPRESSING   [4]YOU°   [1]TRIBULATION   AND   TO YOU°,   THE ONES

θλιβομένοις ἄνεσιν μεθ' ἡμῶν, ἐν τῇ ἀποκαλύψει τοῦ
BEING OPPRESSED,   REST   WITH   US   IN(AT) THE   REVELATION   OF THE

κυρίου Ἰησοῦ ἀπ' οὐρανοῦ μετ' ἀγγέλων δυνάμεως
LORD   JESUS   FROM   HEAVEN   WITH   ANGELS   OF POWER

αὐτοῦ **1.8** ἐν πυρὶ φλογός, διδόντος ἐκδίκησιν τοῖς
OF HIM   IN   FLAMING~FIRE   GIVING   PUNISHMENT   TO THE ONES

Paul, Silvanus, and Timothy,
To the church of the Thessalonians in God our Father and the Lord Jesus Christ:

2 Grace to you and peace from God our[a] Father and the Lord Jesus Christ.

3 We must always give thanks to God for you, brothers and sisters,[b] as is right, because your faith is growing abundantly, and the love of everyone of you for one another is increasing. [4]Therefore we ourselves boast of you among the churches of God for your steadfastness and faith during all your persecutions and the afflictions that you are enduring.

5 This is evidence of the righteous judgment of God, and is intended to make you worthy of the kingdom of God, for which you are also suffering. [6]For it is indeed just of God to repay with affliction those who afflict you, [7]and to give relief to the afflicted as well as to us, when the Lord Jesus is revealed from heaven with his mighty angels [8]in flaming fire, inflicting vengeance on those

[a] Other ancient authorities read the
[b] Gk brothers

who do not know God and on those who do not obey the gospel of our Lord Jesus. [9]These will suffer the punishment of eternal destruction, separated from the presence of the Lord and from the glory of his might, [10]when he comes to be glorified by his saints and to be marveled at on that day among all who have believed, because our testimony to you was believed. [11]To this end we always pray for you, asking that our God will make you worthy of his call and will fulfill by his power every good resolve and work of faith, [12]so that the name of our Lord Jesus may be glorified in you, and you in him, according to the grace of our God and the Lord Jesus Christ.

μὴ εἰδόσιν θεὸν καὶ τοῖς   μὴ ὑπακούουσιν τῷ
NOT KNOWING GOD AND TO THE ONES NOT OBEYING   THE

εὐαγγελίῳ τοῦ κυρίου ἡμῶν Ἰησοῦ, 1.9 οἵτινες
GOOD NEWS OF THE LORD OF US, JESUS,   [THESE] ONES

δίκην τίσουσιν ὄλεθρον αἰώνιον ἀπὸ   προσώπου τοῦ
WILL PAY~A PENALTY, ETERNAL~DESTRUCTION [AWAY] FROM [THE] PRESENCE OF THE

κυρίου καὶ ἀπὸ τῆς δόξης τῆς ἰσχύος αὐτοῦ, 1.10 ὅταν
LORD AND FROM THE GLORY OF THE STRENGTH OF HIM,   WHEN

ἔλθῃ ἐνδοξασθῆναι ἐν τοῖς ἁγίοις αὐτοῦ καὶ
HE COMES TO BE GLORIFIED IN THE SAINTS OF HIM AND

θαυμασθῆναι ἐν πᾶσιν τοῖς πιστεύσασιν, ὅτι
TO BE MARVELED [AT] IN ALL THE ONES HAVING BELIEVED, BECAUSE

ἐπιστεύθη τὸ μαρτύριον ἡμῶν ἐφ᾽ ὑμᾶς, ἐν τῇ
[6]WAS BELIEVED [1]THE [2]TESTIMONY [3]OF US [4]TO [5]YOU° IN -

ἡμέρᾳ ἐκείνῃ. 1.11 εἰς ὃ   καὶ προσευχόμεθα πάντοτε
THAT~DAY.   FOR WHICH ALSO WE PRAY ALWAYS

περὶ ὑμῶν, ἵνα ὑμᾶς ἀξιώσῃ   τῆς κλήσεως ὁ
CONCERNING YOU°, THAT [5]YOU° [4]MAY COUNT [6]WORTHY [7]OF THE [8]CALLING [1]THE

θεὸς ἡμῶν καὶ πληρώσῃ πᾶσαν εὐδοκίαν ἀγαθωσύνης
[2]GOD [3]OF US AND MAY FULFILL EVERY DESIRE FOR GOODNESS

καὶ ἔργον πίστεως ἐν δυνάμει, 1.12 ὅπως ἐνδοξασθῇ
AND WORK OF FAITH IN POWER,   SO THAT MAY BE GLORIFIED

τὸ ὄνομα τοῦ κυρίου ἡμῶν Ἰησοῦ ἐν ὑμῖν, καὶ ὑμεῖς
THE NAME OF THE LORD OF US, JESUS, IN YOU°, AND YOU°

ἐν αὐτῷ, κατὰ   τὴν χάριν τοῦ θεοῦ ἡμῶν καὶ
IN HIM, ACCORDING TO THE GRACE OF THE GOD OF US AND

κυρίου Ἰησοῦ Χριστοῦ.
LORD JESUS CHRIST.

CHAPTER 2

As to the coming of our Lord Jesus Christ and our being gathered together to him, we beg you, brothers and sisters,[c] [2]not to be quickly shaken in mind or alarmed, either by spirit or by word or by letter, as though from us, to the effect that the day of the Lord is already here. [3]Let no one deceive you in any way; for that day will not come unless the rebellion comes first

[c] Gk brothers

2.1 Ἐρωτῶμεν δὲ ὑμᾶς, ἀδελφοί, ὑπὲρ   τῆς
NOW~WE ASK YOU°, BROTHERS, WITH REGARD TO THE

παρουσίας τοῦ κυρίου ἡμῶν Ἰησοῦ Χριστοῦ καὶ ἡμῶν
COMING OT THE LORD OF US, JESUS CHRIST, AND OUR

ἐπισυναγωγῆς ἐπ᾽ αὐτὸν 2.2 εἰς τὸ μὴ ταχέως
GATHERING TOGETHER TO HIM, [1]FOR - [3]NOT [5]QUICKLY

σαλευθῆναι ὑμᾶς ἀπὸ τοῦ   νοὸς μηδὲ θροεῖσθαι,
[4]TO BE SHAKEN [2]YOU° FROM THE(YOUR°) MIND NOR TO BE ALARMED,

μήτε διὰ πνεύματος μήτε διὰ λόγου μήτε δι᾽ ἐπιστολῆς
NEITHER BY A SPIRIT NOR BY A WORD NOR BY A LETTER

ὡς δι᾽ ἡμῶν, ὡς ὅτι ἐνέστηκεν ἡ ἡμέρα τοῦ
AS [IF] BY US, AS [IF] THAT [5]HAS COME [1]THE [2]DAY [3]OF THE

κυρίου· 2.3 μή τις ὑμᾶς ἐξαπατήσῃ κατὰ μηδένα
[4]LORD. [LET] NOT ANYONE DECEIVE~YOU° BY(IN) ANY

τρόπον. ὅτι ἐὰν μὴ ἔλθῃ ἡ ἀποστασία πρῶτον
WAY; BECAUSE UNLESS COMES THE APOSTASY(REBELLION) FIRST

καὶ ἀποκαλυφθῇ ⌜ὁ ἄνθρωπος τῆς ἀνομίας,⌝ ὁ
AND   4BE REVEALED   1THE   2MAN   -   3OF LAWLESSNESS,   THE

υἱὸς τῆς ἀπωλείας, **2.4** ὁ   ἀντικείμενος   καὶ
SON   -   OF DESTRUCTION,   THE ONE SETTING HIMSELF AGAINST   AND

ὑπεραιρόμενος ἐπὶ πάντα λεγόμενον θεὸν ἢ
EXALTING HIMSELF   ABOVE   ALL   BEING CALLED   GOD   OR

σέβασμα,   ὥστε αὐτὸν εἰς τὸν ναὸν τοῦ θεοῦ
AN OBJECT OF VENERATION,   SO AS   [FOR] HIM   IN   THE   TEMPLE   -   OF GOD

καθίσαι ἀποδεικνύντα ἑαυτὸν ὅτι ἔστιν θεός.
TO SIT,   PRESENTING   HIMSELF   THAT   HE IS   GOD.

2.5 Οὐ μνημονεύετε ὅτι ἔτι   ὢν   πρὸς ὑμᾶς ταῦτα
DO YOU° NOT REMEMBER   THAT [WHILE] YET BEING WITH   YOU°   3THESE THINGS

ἔλεγον ὑμῖν; **2.6** καὶ νῦν τὸ   κατέχον   οἴδατε
1I WAS TELLING 2YOU°?   AND   NOW   THE ONE HOLDING [HIM] BACK   YOU° KNOW

εἰς τὸ ἀποκαλυφθῆναι αὐτὸν ἐν τῷ ἑαυτοῦ καιρῷ.
FOR   -   HIM~TO BE REVEALED   IN   -   HIS OWN   TIME.

2.7 τὸ γὰρ μυστήριον ἤδη   ἐνεργεῖται τῆς ἀνομίας·
FOR~THE   MYSTERY   2ALREADY   3IS WORKING   -   1OF LAWLESSNESS;

μόνον ὁ   κατέχων   ἄρτι   ἕως ἐκ   μέσου
ONLY   [THERE IS] ONE   HOLDING [IT] BACK   JUST NOW   UNTIL   OUT OF   [THE] MIDST(WAY)

γένηται. **2.8** καὶ τότε ἀποκαλυφθήσεται ὁ   ἄνομος,
HE IS GONE.   AND   THEN   WILL BE REVEALED   THE   LAWLESS ONE,

ὃν ὁ κύριος [Ἰησοῦς] ἀνελεῖ   τῷ   πνεύματι τοῦ
WHOM THE LORD   JESUS   WILL CONSUME BY THE BREATH   OF THE

στόματος αὐτοῦ καὶ καταργήσει τῇ   ἐπιφανείᾳ τῆς
MOUTH   OF HIM   AND   WILL DESTROY   BY THE APPEARANCE   OF THE

παρουσίας αὐτοῦ, **2.9** οὗ   ἐστιν ἡ παρουσία κατ'
COMING   OF HIM;   WHOSE 2IS   -   1COMING   ACCORDING TO

ἐνέργειαν τοῦ Σατανᾶ ἐν πάσῃ δυνάμει καὶ σημείοις
[THE] WORKING   -   OF SATAN   WITH ALL   POWER   AND   SIGNS

καὶ τέρασιν ψεύδους **2.10** καὶ ἐν   πάσῃ ἀπάτῃ
AND   WONDERS   OF FALSEHOOD   AND   WITH EVERY   DECEPTION

ἀδικίας   τοῖς   ἀπολλυμένοις, ἀνθ' ὧν τὴν
OF UNRIGHTEOUSNESS   FOR THE ONES   BEING DESTROYED,   BECAUSE   THE

ἀγάπην τῆς ἀληθείας οὐκ ἐδέξαντο εἰς τὸ
LOVE   OF THE   TRUTH   THEY DID NOT ACCEPT   FOR   -

σωθῆναι αὐτούς. **2.11** καὶ διὰ τοῦτο πέμπει αὐτοῖς ὁ
THEM~TO BE SAVED.   AND   THEREFORE   2SENDS   3TO THEM   -

θεὸς ἐνέργειαν πλάνης εἰς τὸ πιστεῦσαι αὐτοὺς τῷ
1GOD   A POWERFUL~DELUSION   FOR   -   THEM~TO BELIEVE   THE

ψεύδει, **2.12** ἵνα κριθῶσιν πάντες οἱ   μὴ
FALSEHOOD,   THAT   MAY BE JUDGED   ALL   THE ONES NOT

πιστεύσαντες τῇ ἀληθείᾳ ἀλλὰ εὐδοκήσαντες τῇ
HAVING BELIEVED   THE   TRUTH   BUT   HAVING HAD PLEASURE   -

ἀδικίᾳ.
IN UNRIGHTEOUSNESS.

and the lawless one[d] is revealed, the one destined for destruction.[e] [4]He opposes and exalts himself above every so-called god or object of worship, so that he takes his seat in the temple of God, declaring himself to be God. [5]Do you not remember that I told you these things when I was still with you? [6]And you know what is now restraining him, so that he may be revealed when his time comes. [7]For the mystery of lawlessness is already at work, but only until the one who now restrains it is removed. [8]And then the lawless one will be revealed, whom the Lord Jesus[f] will destroy[g] with the breath of his mouth, annihilating him by the manifestation of his coming. [9]The coming of the lawless one is apparent in the working of Satan, who uses all power, signs, lying wonders, [10]and every kind of wicked deception for those who are perishing, because they refused to love the truth and so be saved. [11]For this reason God sends them a powerful delusion, leading them to believe what is false, [12]so that all who have not believed the truth but took pleasure in unrighteousness will be condemned.

[d] Gk *the man of lawlessness;* other ancient authorities read *the man of sin*
[e] Gk *the son of destruction*
[f] Other ancient authorities lack *Jesus*
[g] Other ancient authorities read *consume*

2:3 text: ASVmg RSV NASB (NEB TEV NJB) NRSV. var. ο ανθρωπος της αμαρτιας (the man of sin): KJV ASV RSVmg NASBmg NRSVmg.

13 But we must always give thanks to God for you, brothers and sisters[h] beloved by the Lord, because God chose you as the first fruits[i] for salvation through sanctification by the Spirit and through belief in the truth. [14]For this purpose he called you through our proclamation of the good news,[j] so that you may obtain the glory of our Lord Jesus Christ. [15]So then, brothers and sisters,[h] stand firm and hold fast to the traditions that you were taught by us, either by word of mouth or by our letter.

16 Now may our Lord Jesus Christ himself and God our Father, who loved us and through grace gave us eternal comfort and good hope, [17]comfort your hearts and strengthen them in every good work and word.

[h] Gk *brothers*

2.13 Ἡμεῖς	δὲ	ὀφείλομεν	εὐχαριστεῖν	τῷ	θεῷ
BUT~WE		OUGHT	TO THANK	-	GOD

πάντοτε	περὶ	ὑμῶν,	ἀδελφοὶ	ἠγαπημένοι	ὑπὸ
ALWAYS	CONCERNING	YOU°,	BROTHERS	HAVING BEEN LOVED	BY

κυρίου, ὅτι εἴλατο ὑμᾶς ὁ θεὸς ⌜ἀπαρχὴν⌝ εἰς
[THE] LORD, BECAUSE ²CHOSE ³YOU° - ¹GOD [AS] FIRSTFRUITS FOR

σωτηρίαν ἐν ἁγιασμῷ πνεύματος καὶ πίστει
SALVATION IN(BY) SANCTIFICATION OF [THE] SPIRIT AND BELIEF

ἀληθείας, **2.14** εἰς ὃ [καὶ] ἐκάλεσεν ὑμᾶς διὰ τοῦ
OF [THE] TRUTH, TO WHICH ALSO HE CALLED YOU° THROUGH THE

εὐαγγελίου ἡμῶν εἰς περιποίησιν δόξης τοῦ κυρίου
GOOD NEWS OF US, TO [THE] OBTAINING OF [THE] GLORY OF THE LORD

ἡμῶν Ἰησοῦ Χριστοῦ. **2.15** ἄρα οὖν, ἀδελφοί, στήκετε,
OF US, JESUS CHRIST. SO THEN, BROTHERS, STAND FIRM

καὶ κρατεῖτε τὰς παραδόσεις ἃς ἐδιδάχθητε εἴτε διὰ
AND HOLD THE TRADITIONS WHICH YOU° WERE TAUGHT EITHER BY

λόγου εἴτε δι' ἐπιστολῆς ἡμῶν. **2.16** Αὐτὸς δὲ ὁ
WORD OR BY A LETTER OF(FROM) US. ⁴HIMSELF ¹NOW ²THE

κύριος ἡμῶν Ἰησοῦς Χριστὸς καὶ [ὁ] θεὸς ὁ πατὴρ
³LORD OF US, JESUS CHRIST, AND - GOD THE FATHER

ἡμῶν ὁ ἀγαπήσας ἡμᾶς καὶ δοὺς
OF US, THE ONE HAVING LOVED US AND HAVING GIVEN

παράκλησιν αἰωνίαν καὶ ἐλπίδα ἀγαθὴν ἐν χάριτι,
ETERNAL~ENCOURAGEMENT AND GOOD~HOPE IN(BY) GRACE,

2.17 παρακαλέσαι ὑμῶν τὰς καρδίας καὶ στηρίξαι
MAY HE ENCOURAGE YOUR° - HEARTS AND MAY HE ESTABLISH [YOU°]

ἐν παντὶ ἔργῳ καὶ λόγῳ ἀγαθῷ.
IN EVERY ²WORK ³AND ⁴WORD ¹GOOD.

2:13 text: ASVmg RSVmg NASBmg NIVmg NEBmg TEV NJBmg NRSV. var. απ αρξης (from [the] beginning): KJV ASV RSV NASB NIV NEB TEVmg NJB NRSVmg.

CHAPTER 3

Finally, brothers and sisters,[h] pray for us, so that the word of the Lord may spread rapidly and be glorified everywhere, just as it is among you, ²and that we may be rescued from wicked and evil people; for not all have faith. ³But the Lord is faithful; he will strengthen you and guard you from the evil one.[k] ⁴And we have confidence in the Lord concerning you, that

[h] Gk *brothers*
[i] Other ancient authorities read *from the beginning*
[j] Or *through our gospel*
[k] Or *from evil*

3.1 Τὸ λοιπὸν προσεύχεσθε ἀδελφοί, περὶ ἡμῶν,
FOR THE REST PRAY, BROTHERS, CONCERNING US,

ἵνα ὁ λόγος τοῦ κυρίου τρέχῃ καὶ δοξάζηται καθὼς
THAT THE WORD OF THE LORD MAY RUN AND MAY BE GLORIFIED EVEN AS

καὶ πρὸς ὑμᾶς, **3.2** καὶ ἵνα ῥυσθῶμεν ἀπὸ τῶν
ALSO WITH YOU°, AND THAT WE MAY BE DELIVERED FROM -

ἀτόπων καὶ πονηρῶν ἀνθρώπων· οὐ γὰρ
WICKED AND EVIL MEN; ⁴[IS] NOT ¹FOR

πάντων ἡ πίστις. **3.3** πιστὸς δέ ἐστιν ὁ
⁵[THE POSSESSION] OF ALL ²THE ³FAITH. BUT~FAITHFUL IS THE

κύριος, ὃς στηρίξει ὑμᾶς καὶ φυλάξει ἀπὸ τοῦ
LORD, WHO WILL ESTABLISH YOU° AND WILL GUARD [YOU°] FROM THE

πονηροῦ. **3.4** πεποίθαμεν δὲ ἐν κυρίῳ ἐφ' ὑμᾶς, ὅτι
EVIL ONE. AND~WE HAVE CONFIDENCE IN [THE] LORD AS TO YOU°, THAT

ἃ   παραγγέλλομεν [καὶ] ποιεῖτε καὶ ποιήσετε.
WHAT THINGS WE CHARGE   BOTH YOU° DO AND WILL DO.

3.5 Ὁ δὲ κύριος κατευθύναι ὑμῶν τὰς καρδίας εἰς τὴν
³THE ¹NOW ⁴LORD ²MAY ⁵DIRECT YOUR° -   HEARTS INTO THE

ἀγάπην τοῦ θεοῦ καὶ εἰς τὴν ὑπομονὴν τοῦ Χριστοῦ.
LOVE - OF GOD AND INTO THE PERSEVERANCE - OF CHRIST.

3.6 Παραγγέλλομεν δὲ ὑμῖν, ἀδελφοί, ἐν ὀνόματι
NOW~WE CHARGE   YOU°, BROTHERS, IN [THE] NAME

τοῦ κυρίου [ἡμῶν] Ἰησοῦ Χριστοῦ στέλλεσθαι ὑμᾶς
OF THE LORD OF US, JESUS CHRIST, YOU°~[OUGHT] TO KEEP AWAY

ἀπὸ παντὸς ἀδελφοῦ ἀτάκτως περιπατοῦντος καὶ μὴ
FROM EVERY BROTHER WALKING~IDLY   AND NOT

κατὰ   τὴν παράδοσιν ἣν παρελάβοσαν παρ' ἡμῶν.
ACCORDING TO THE TRADITION WHICH YOU° RECEIVED FROM US.

3.7 αὐτοὶ γὰρ οἴδατε πῶς δεῖ   μιμεῖσθαι ἡμᾶς,
³YOURSELVES ¹FOR ²YOU° ³KNOW HOW IT IS NECESSARY TO IMITATE US,

ὅτι   οὐκ ἠτακτήσαμεν ἐν   ὑμῖν **3.8** οὐδὲ δωρεὰν
BECAUSE WE WERE NOT IDLE AMONG YOU°, NOT AS A GIFT

ἄρτον ἐφάγομεν παρά τινος, ἀλλ' ἐν κόπῳ καὶ μόχθῳ
DID WE EAT~BREAD FROM ANYONE, BUT IN LABOR AND HARDSHIP

νυκτὸς καὶ ἡμέρας ἐργαζόμενοι πρὸς τὸ μὴ
BY NIGHT AND BY DAY WORKING   SO AS - NOT

ἐπιβαρῆσαί   τινα ὑμῶν· **3.9** οὐχ ὅτι οὐκ ἔχομεν
TO BE BURDENSOME [TO] ANYONE OF YOU°; NOT THAT WE DO NOT HAVE

ἐξουσίαν, ἀλλ' ἵνα ἑαυτοὺς τύπον   δῶμεν   ὑμῖν
AUTHORITY, BUT THAT ²OURSELVES ³[AS] A PATTERN ¹WE MIGHT GIVE FOR YOU°

εἰς τὸ μιμεῖσθαι ἡμᾶς. **3.10** καὶ γὰρ ὅτε ἦμεν πρὸς
- - TO IMITATE US.   FOR~EVEN WHEN WE WERE WITH

ὑμᾶς, τοῦτο παρηγγέλλομεν ὑμῖν, ὅτι εἴ τις
YOU°, THIS WE CHARGED   YOU°, THAT IF ANYONE

οὐ θέλει ἐργάζεσθαι μηδὲ ἐσθιέτω. **3.11** ἀκούομεν γάρ
DOES NOT WANT TO WORK NEITHER LET HIM EAT. FOR~WE HEAR [OF]

τινας περιπατοῦντας ἐν   ὑμῖν ἀτάκτως μηδὲν
SOME WALKING   AMONG YOU° IDLE,   NOT AT ALL

ἐργαζομένους ἀλλὰ περιεργαζομένους· **3.12** τοῖς δὲ
WORKING   BUT BEING BUSYBODIES.   -   NOW

τοιούτοις παραγγέλλομεν καὶ παρακαλοῦμεν ἐν
TO SUCH ONES WE WERE CHARGING AND WE EXHORT   IN(BY)

κυρίῳ Ἰησοῦ Χριστῷ, ἵνα μετὰ ἡσυχίας ἐργαζόμενοι
[THE] LORD JESUS CHRIST, THAT ²WITH ³QUIETNESS ¹WORKING

τὸν ἑαυτῶν ἄρτον ἐσθίωσιν. **3.13** Ὑμεῖς δέ, ἀδελφοί,
- THEIR OWN BREAD THEY MAY EAT. BUT~YOU°, BROTHERS,

μὴ ἐγκακήσητε καλοποιοῦντες. **3.14** εἰ δέ τις
DO NOT LOSE HEART [IN] DOING GOOD.   AND~IF ANYONE

οὐχ ὑπακούει τῷ λόγῳ ἡμῶν διὰ τῆς ἐπιστολῆς,
DOES NOT OBEY THE WORD OF US THROUGH THE(THIS) LETTER,

τοῦτον σημειοῦσθε μὴ συναναμίγνυσθαι αὐτῷ, ἵνα
THIS MAN MARK,   NOT TO ASSOCIATE WITH HIM, THAT

you are doing and will go on doing the things that we command. ⁵May the Lord direct your hearts to the love of God and to the steadfastness of Christ.

6 Now we command you, beloved,ˡ in the name of our Lord Jesus Christ, to keep away from believers who areᵐ living in idleness and not according to the tradition that theyⁿ received from us. ⁷For you yourselves know how you ought to imitate us; we were not idle when we were with you, ⁸and we did not eat anyone's bread without paying for it; but with toil and labor we worked night and day, so that we might not burden any of you. ⁹This was not because we do not have that right, but in order to give you an example to imitate. ¹⁰For even when we were with you, we gave you this command: Anyone unwilling to work should not eat. ¹¹For we hear that some of you are living in idleness, mere busybodies, not doing any work. ¹²Now such persons we command and exhort in the Lord Jesus Christ to do their work quietly and to earn their own living. ¹³Brothers and sisters,ᵒ do not be weary in doing what is right.

14 Take note of those who do not obey what we say in this letter; have nothing to do with them, so that

ˡ Gk brothers
ᵐ Gk from every brother who is
ⁿ Other ancient authorities read you
ᵒ Gk Brothers

they may be ashamed. 15Do
not regard them as enemies,
but warn them as believers.[p]
16 Now may the Lord
of peace himself give you
peace at all times in all ways.
The Lord be with all of you.
17 I, Paul, write this
greeting with my own hand.
This is the mark in every
letter of mine; it is the way I
write. 18The grace of our
Lord Jesus Christ be with all
of you.[q]

[p] Gk *a brother*
[q] Other ancient authorities add *Amen*

ἐντραπῇ· HE MAY BE PUT TO SHAME; **3.15** καὶ AND [YET] μὴ 2NOT ὡς 4AS ἐχθρὸν 5AN ENEMY ἡγεῖσθε, 1DO 3CONSIDER [HIM], ἀλλὰ BUT νουθετεῖτε ADMONISH [HIM] ὡς AS ἀδελφόν. A BROTHER.

3.16 Αὐτὸς 5HIMSELF δὲ 1NOW ὁ 2THE κύριος 3LORD τῆς - εἰρήνης 4OF PEACE δῴη MAY HE GIVE ὑμῖν TO YOU° τὴν - εἰρήνην PEACE διὰ παντὸς CONTINUALLY ἐν IN παντὶ EVERY τρόπῳ. WAY. ὁ THE κύριος LORD μετὰ [BE] WITH πάντων ὑμῶν. YOU°~ALL.

3.17 Ὁ THE ἀσπασμὸς GREETING τῇ - ἐμῇ χειρὶ BY MY HAND, Παύλου, PAUL'S, ὅ WHICH ἐστιν IS σημεῖον A SIGN ἐν IN πάσῃ EVERY ἐπιστολῇ· LETTER; οὕτως THUS γράφω. I WRITE. **3.18** ἡ THE χάρις GRACE τοῦ OF THE κυρίου LORD ἡμῶν OF US, Ἰησοῦ JESUS Χριστοῦ CHRIST, μετὰ [BE] WITH πάντων ὑμῶν. YOU°~ALL.

THE FIRST LETTER OF PAUL TO
TIMOTHY

ΠΡΟΣ ΤΙΜΟΘΕΟΝ Α
TO   TIMOTHY   1

1.1 Παῦλος ἀπόστολος Χριστοῦ Ἰησοῦ κατ'
PAUL   AN APOSTLE   OF CHRIST   JESUS   ACCORDING TO

ἐπιταγὴν θεοῦ σωτῆρος ἡμῶν καὶ Χριστοῦ Ἰησοῦ τῆς
A COMMAND OF GOD [THE] SAVIOR OF US AND CHRIST   JESUS   THE

ἐλπίδος ἡμῶν **1.2** Τιμοθέῳ γνησίῳ τέκνῳ ἐν πίστει,
HOPE   OF US   TO TIMOTHY A TRUE-BORN CHILD IN(BY) FAITH,

χάρις ἔλεος εἰρήνη ἀπὸ θεοῦ πατρὸς καὶ Χριστοῦ
GRACE, MERCY, PEACE   FROM GOD [THE] FATHER AND CHRIST

Ἰησοῦ τοῦ κυρίου ἡμῶν.
JESUS   THE LORD   OF US.

1.3 Καθὼς παρεκάλεσά σε προσμεῖναι ἐν Ἐφέσῳ
EVEN AS   I URGED   YOU TO REMAIN   IN EPHESUS,

πορευόμενος εἰς Μακεδονίαν, ἵνα παραγγείλῃς
[WHILE I WAS] GOING INTO MACEDONIA,   THAT YOU MAY CHARGE

τισὶν μὴ ἑτεροδιδασκαλεῖν **1.4** μηδὲ προσέχειν
CERTAIN ONES NOT TO TEACH DIFFERENTLY   NOR   TO PAY ATTENTION

μύθοις καὶ γενεαλογίαις ἀπεράντοις, αἵτινες
TO MYTHS AND ENDLESS~GENEALOGIES,   WHICH

ἐκζητήσεις παρέχουσιν μᾶλλον ἢ οἰκονομίαν θεοῦ τὴν
CAUSE~USELESS SPECULATIONS,   RATHER THAN A STEWARDSHIP OF GOD -

ἐν πίστει. **1.5** τὸ δὲ τέλος τῆς παραγγελίας ἐστὶν
IN FAITH.   BUT~THE END(AIM) OF THE CHARGE   IS

ἀγάπη ἐκ καθαρᾶς καρδίας καὶ συνειδήσεως ἀγαθῆς
LOVE OUT OF A PURE   HEART   AND   A GOOD~CONSCIENCE

καὶ πίστεως ἀνυποκρίτου, **1.6** ὧν τινες
AND FAITH   WITHOUT HYPOCRISY,   FROM WHICH THINGS SOME

ἀστοχήσαντες ἐξετράπησαν εἰς ματαιολογίαν
HAVING MISSED THE MARK TURNED ASIDE   TO   VAIN TALKING,

1.7 θέλοντες εἶναι νομοδιδάσκαλοι, μὴ νοοῦντες
WANTING   TO BE   TEACHERS OF [THE] LAW, NOT UNDERSTANDING

μήτε ἃ λέγουσιν μήτε περὶ τίνων
EITHER WHAT THINGS THEY SAY NOR CONCERNING WHAT THINGS

διαβεβαιοῦνται.
THEY CONFIDENTLY AFFIRM.

1.8 Οἴδαμεν δὲ ὅτι καλὸς ὁ νόμος, ἐάν τις αὐτῷ
BUT~WE KNOW   THAT GOOD   [IS] THE LAW, IF   ANYONE ²IT

νομίμως χρῆται, **1.9** εἰδὼς τοῦτο, ὅτι δικαίῳ
³LAWFULLY ¹USES,   KNOWING THIS,   THAT FOR A RIGHTEOUS ONE

Paul, an apostle of Christ Jesus by the command of God our Savior and of Christ Jesus our hope,

2 To Timothy, my loyal child in the faith:

Grace, mercy, and peace from God the Father and Christ Jesus our Lord.

3 I urge you, as I did when I was on my way to Macedonia, to remain in Ephesus so that you may instruct certain people not to teach any different doctrine, [4]and not to occupy themselves with myths and endless genealogies that promote speculations rather than the divine training[a] that is known by faith. [5]But the aim of such instruction is love that comes from a pure heart, a good conscience, and sincere faith. [6]Some people have deviated from these and turned to meaningless talk, [7]desiring to be teachers of the law, without understanding either what they are saying or the things about which they make assertions.

8 Now we know that the law is good, if one uses it legitimately. [9]This means understanding that the law is laid down not for the innocent

[a] Or *plan*

but for the lawless and disobedient, for the godless and sinful, for the unholy and profane, for those who kill their father or mother, for murderers, [10]fornicators, sodomites, slave traders, liars, perjurers, and whatever else is contrary to the sound teaching [11]that conforms to the glorious gospel of the blessed God, which he entrusted to me.

12 I am grateful to Christ Jesus our Lord, who has strengthened me, because he judged me faithful and appointed me to his service, [13]even though I was formerly a blasphemer, a persecutor, and a man of violence. But I received mercy because I had acted ignorantly in unbelief, [14]and the grace of our Lord overflowed for me with the faith and love that are in Christ Jesus. [15]The saying is sure and worthy of full acceptance, that Christ Jesus came into the world to save sinners—of whom I am the foremost. [16]But for that very reason I received mercy, so that in me, as the foremost, Jesus Christ might display the utmost patience, making me an example to those who would come to believe in him for eternal life. [17]To the King of the ages, immortal, invisible, the only God, be honor and glory forever and ever.[b] Amen.

[b] Gk to the ages of the ages

νόμος οὐ κεῖται, ἀνόμοις δὲ καὶ ἀνυποτάκτοις,
LAW DOES NOT EXIST, BUT~FOR [THE] LAWLESS AND REBELLIOUS,

ἀσεβέσι καὶ ἁμαρτωλοῖς, ἀνοσίοις καὶ βεβήλοις,
UNGODLY AND SINNERS, UNHOLY AND PROFANE,

πατρολῴαις καὶ μητρολῴαις, ἀνδροφόνοις **1.10** πόρνοις
PATRICIDES AND MATRICIDES, MURDERERS, FORNICATORS,

ἀρσενοκοίταις ἀνδραποδισταῖς ψεύσταις ἐπιόρκοις, καὶ
HOMOSEXUALS, SLAVE DEALERS, LIARS, PERJURERS, AND

εἴ τι ἕτερον τῇ ὑγιαινούσῃ διδασκαλίᾳ ἀντίκειται
IF ANY OTHER THING ²THE ³HEALTHY ⁴TEACHING ¹[WHICH] OPPOSES,

1.11 κατὰ τὸ εὐαγγέλιον τῆς δόξης τοῦ μακαρίου
ACCORDING TO THE GOOD NEWS OF THE GLORY OF THE BLESSED

θεοῦ, ὃ ἐπιστεύθην ἐγώ.
GOD, [WITH] WHICH I~WAS ENTRUSTED.

1.12 Χάριν ἔχω τῷ ἐνδυναμώσαντί με Χριστῷ
GRATITUDE I HAVE TO THE ONE HAVING EMPOWERED ME, CHRIST

Ἰησοῦ τῷ κυρίῳ ἡμῶν, ὅτι πιστόν με ἡγήσατο
JESUS THE LORD OF US, BECAUSE ³FAITHFUL ²ME ¹HE CONSIDERED

θέμενος εἰς διακονίαν **1.13** τὸ πρότερον ὄντα
HAVING PUT [ME] INTO [HIS] SERVICE, - PREVIOUSLY BEING

βλάσφημον καὶ διώκτην καὶ ὑβριστήν, ἀλλὰ
A BLASPHEMER AND PERSECUTOR AND AN INSOLENT MAN, BUT

ἠλεήθην, ὅτι ἀγνοῶν ἐποίησα ἐν ἀπιστίᾳ·
I RECEIVED MERCY, BECAUSE BEING IGNORANT I DID [IT] IN UNBELIEF;

1.14 ὑπερεπλεόνασεν δὲ ἡ χάρις τοῦ κυρίου ἡμῶν
AND~SUPERABOUNDED THE GRACE OF THE LORD OF US

μετὰ πίστεως καὶ ἀγάπης τῆς ἐν Χριστῷ Ἰησοῦ.
WITH FAITH AND LOVE - IN CHRIST JESUS.

1.15 πιστὸς ὁ λόγος καὶ πάσης ἀποδοχῆς ἄξιος,
FAITHFUL [IS] THE WORD AND ²OF ALL ³ACCEPTANCE ¹WORTHY,

ὅτι Χριστὸς Ἰησοῦς ἦλθεν εἰς τὸν κόσμον
THAT CHRIST JESUS CAME INTO THE WORLD

ἁμαρτωλοὺς σῶσαι, ὧν πρῶτός εἰμι ἐγώ.
TO SAVE~SINNERS, OF WHOM [THE] FOREMOST AM I.

1.16 ἀλλὰ διὰ τοῦτο ἠλεήθην, ἵνα ἐν ἐμοὶ
BUT BECAUSE OF THIS I RECEIVED MERCY, THAT IN ME,

πρώτῳ ἐνδείξηται Χριστὸς Ἰησοῦς τὴν ἅπασαν
[THE] FOREMOST, ³MIGHT DISPLAY ¹CHRIST ²JESUS - ALL

μακροθυμίαν πρὸς ὑποτύπωσιν τῶν μελλόντων
LONGSUFFERING FOR A MODEL OF THE ONES BEING ABOUT

πιστεύειν ἐπ᾽ αὐτῷ εἰς ζωὴν αἰώνιον.
TO BELIEVE ON HIM [RESULTING] IN LIFE ETERNAL.

1.17 τῷ δὲ βασιλεῖ τῶν αἰώνων, ἀφθάρτῳ ἀοράτῳ
NOW~TO THE KING OF THE AGES, INCORRUPTIBLE, INVISIBLE,

μόνῳ θεῷ, τιμὴ καὶ δόξα εἰς τοὺς αἰῶνας τῶν
[THE] ONLY GOD, [BE] HONOR AND GLORY INTO THE AGES OF THE

αἰώνων, ἀμήν.
AGES, AMEN.

1.18 Ταύτην τὴν παραγγελίαν παρατίθεμαί σοι,
THIS   -   CHARGE   I COMMIT   TO YOU,

τέκνον Τιμόθεε, κατὰ τὰς προαγούσας ἐπὶ σὲ
CHILD   TIMOTHY,   ACCORDING TO ¹THE ³BEING MADE PREVIOUSLY ⁴ABOUT ⁵YOU

προφητείας, ἵνα στρατεύῃ ἐν αὐταῖς τὴν καλὴν
²PROPHECIES,   THAT   YOU MIGHT WAR   BY   THEM   THE   GOOD

στρατείαν **1.19** ἔχων πίστιν καὶ ἀγαθὴν συνείδησιν,
WARFARE,   HOLDING FAITH   AND   A GOOD   CONSCIENCE,

ἣν τινες ἀπωσάμενοι περὶ τὴν πίστιν ἐναυάγησαν,
WHICH   SOME,   HAVING PUT AWAY,   ²AS TO   ³THE[IR] ⁴FAITH   ¹CAUSED A SHIPWRECK,

1.20 ὧν ἐστιν Ὑμέναιος καὶ Ἀλέξανδρος, οὓς
OF WHOM   ARE   HYMENAEUS   AND   ALEXANDER,   WHOM

παρέδωκα τῷ Σατανᾷ, ἵνα παιδευθῶσιν μὴ
I DELIVERED   -   TO SATAN,   THAT   THEY MIGHT BE TAUGHT   NOT

βλασφημεῖν.
TO BLASPHEME.

18 I am giving you these instructions, Timothy, my child, in accordance with the prophecies made earlier about you, so that by following them you may fight the good fight, ¹⁹having faith and a good conscience. By rejecting conscience, certain persons have suffered shipwreck in the faith; ²⁰among them are Hymenaeus and Alexander, whom I have turned over to Satan, so that they may learn not to blaspheme.

CHAPTER 2

2.1 Παρακαλῶ οὖν πρῶτον πάντων ποιεῖσθαι
I URGE,   THEREFORE, FIRST   OF ALL   TO BE MADE

δεήσεις προσευχὰς ἐντεύξεις εὐχαριστίας ὑπὲρ
SUPPLICATIONS,   PRAYERS,   INTERCESSIONS, THANKSGIVINGS   ON BEHALF OF

πάντων ἀνθρώπων, **2.2** ὑπὲρ βασιλέων καὶ πάντων
ALL   MEN,   ON BEHALF OF KINGS   AND   OF ALL

τῶν ἐν ὑπεροχῇ ὄντων, ἵνα ἤρεμον καὶ ἡσύχιον βίον
THE ONES ²IN ³AUTHORITY ¹BEING,   THAT   A TRANQUIL AND   QUIET   LIFE

διάγωμεν ἐν πάσῃ εὐσεβείᾳ καὶ σεμνότητι. **2.3** τοῦτο
WE MAY LEAD   IN   ALL   PIETY   AND   REVERENCE.   THIS

καλὸν καὶ ἀπόδεκτον ἐνώπιον τοῦ σωτῆρος ἡμῶν θεοῦ,
[IS] GOOD AND   ACCEPTABLE   BEFORE   THE   SAVIOR   OF US,   GOD,

2.4 ὃς πάντας ἀνθρώπους θέλει σωθῆναι καὶ εἰς
WHO ²ALL   ³MEN   ¹WANTS TO BE SAVED AND   ²TO

ἐπίγνωσιν ἀληθείας ἐλθεῖν. **2.5** εἷς γὰρ θεός, εἷς
³A KNOWLEDGE   ⁴OF [THE] TRUTH ¹TO COME.   ²ONE ¹FOR [THERE IS] ³GOD,   ONE

καὶ μεσίτης θεοῦ καὶ ἀνθρώπων, ἄνθρωπος Χριστὸς
ALSO   MEDIATOR OF GOD AND   OF MEN,   A MAN   CHRIST

Ἰησοῦς, **2.6** ὁ δοὺς ἑαυτὸν ἀντίλυτρον ὑπὲρ
JESUS,   THE ONE HAVING GIVEN HIMSELF   A RANSOM   ON BEHALF OF

πάντων, τὸ μαρτύριον καιροῖς ἰδίοις. **2.7** εἰς
ALL,   THE   TESTIMONY   IN ITS OWN~TIMES;   FOR

ὃ ἐτέθην ἐγὼ κῆρυξ καὶ ἀπόστολος, ἀλήθειαν
WHICH [TESTIMONY] I~WAS APPOINTED A HERALD AND   AN APOSTLE,   [THE] TRUTH

λέγω οὐ ψεύδομαι, διδάσκαλος ἐθνῶν ἐν πίστει καὶ
I SPEAK, I DO NOT LIE,   A TEACHER   OF GENTILES IN   FAITH   AND

ἀληθείᾳ.
TRUTH.

First of all, then, I urge that supplications, prayers, intercessions, and thanksgivings be made for everyone, ²for kings and all who are in high positions, so that we may lead a quiet and peaceable life in all godliness and dignity. ³This is right and is acceptable in the sight of God our Savior, ⁴who desires everyone to be saved and to come to the knowledge of the truth. ⁵For
   there is one God;
    there is also one
      mediator between
      God and
      humankind,
    Christ Jesus, himself
    human,
6 who gave himself a
    ransom for all
—this was attested at the right time. ⁷For this I was appointed a herald and an apostle (I am telling the truth,ᶜ I am not lying), a teacher of the Gentiles in faith and truth.

ᶜ Other ancient authorities add *in Christ*

8 I desire, then, that in every place the men should pray, lifting up holy hands without anger or argument; [9]also that the women should dress themselves modestly and decently in suitable clothing, not with their hair braided, or with gold, pearls, or expensive clothes, [10]but with good works, as is proper for women who profess reverence for God. [11]Let a woman[d] learn in silence with full submission. [12]I permit no woman[e] to teach or to have authority over a man;[e] she is to keep silent. [13]For Adam was formed first, then Eve; [14]and Adam was not deceived, but the woman was deceived and became a transgressor. [15]Yet she will be saved through childbearing, provided they continue in faith and love and holiness, with modesty.

[d] Or *wife*
[e] Or *her husband*

2.8 Βούλομαι οὖν προσεύχεσθαι τοὺς ἄνδρας ἐν
I WANT   THEREFORE [3]TO PRAY   [1]THE [2]MEN   IN

παντὶ τόπῳ   ἐπαίροντας ὁσίους χεῖρας χωρὶς
EVERY PLACE [OF MEETING] LIFTING UP HOLY HANDS WITHOUT

ὀργῆς καὶ διαλογισμοῦ. **2.9** ὡσαύτως [καὶ] γυναῖκας
ANGER AND DOUBT.   SIMILARLY ALSO WOMEN

ἐν καταστολῇ κοσμίῳ μετὰ αἰδοῦς καὶ σωφροσύνης
IN MODEST~APPEARANCE, [3]WITH [4]DECENCY [5]AND [6]PROPRIETY

κοσμεῖν ἑαυτάς, μὴ ἐν πλέγμασιν καὶ χρυσίῳ ἢ
[1]TO ADORN [2]THEMSELVES, NOT WITH BRAIDED HAIR AND GOLD OR

μαργαρίταις ἢ ἱματισμῷ πολυτελεῖ, **2.10** ἀλλ᾽ ὃ
PEARLS   OR COSTLY~CLOTHING,   BUT WHAT

πρέπει γυναιξὶν ἐπαγγελλομέναις θεοσέβειαν, δι᾽
IS PROPER FOR WOMEN PROFESSING   GODLY REVERENCE, BY MEANS OF

ἔργων ἀγαθῶν. **2.11** γυνὴ ἐν ἡσυχίᾳ μανθανέτω
GOOD~WORKS.   [2]A WOMAN [4]IN [5]SILENCE [1]LET [3]LEARN

ἐν πάσῃ ὑποταγῇ· **2.12** διδάσκειν δὲ γυναικὶ
IN ALL SUBJECTION.   [3]TO TEACH - [2]A WOMAN

οὐκ ἐπιτρέπω οὐδὲ αὐθεντεῖν ἀνδρός, ἀλλ᾽ εἶναι
[1]I DO NOT ALLOW NOR TO HAVE AUTHORITY OF(OVER) A MAN, BUT TO BE

ἐν ἡσυχίᾳ. **2.13** Ἀδὰμ γὰρ πρῶτος ἐπλάσθη, εἶτα Εὔα.
IN SILENCE. FOR~ADAM FIRST WAS FORMED, THEN EVE.

2.14 καὶ Ἀδὰμ οὐκ ἠπατήθη, ἡ δὲ γυνὴ ἐξαπατηθεῖσα
AND ADAM WAS NOT DECEIVED, BUT~THE WOMAN HAVING BEEN DECEIVED

ἐν παραβάσει γέγονεν· **2.15** σωθήσεται δὲ διὰ
[2]IN [3]TRANSGRESSION [1]HAS COME TO BE; BUT~SHE WILL BE SAVED THROUGH

τῆς τεκνογονίας, ἐὰν μείνωσιν ἐν πίστει καὶ ἀγάπῃ
THE(HER) CHILDBEARING, IF THEY REMAIN IN FAITH AND LOVE

καὶ ἁγιασμῷ μετὰ σωφροσύνης.
AND HOLINESS WITH PROPRIETY.

CHAPTER 3

The saying is sure:[f] whoever aspires to the office of bishop[g] desires a noble task. [2]Now a bishop[h] must be above reproach, married only once,[i] temperate, sensible, respectable, hospitable, an apt teacher, [3]not a drunkard, not violent but gentle, not quarrelsome, and not a lover of money. [4]He must manage his own household well,

[f] Some interpreters place these words at the end of the previous paragraph. Other ancient authorities read *The saying is commonly accepted*
[g] Or *overseer*
[h] Or *an overseer*
[i] Gk *the husband of one wife*

3.1 Πιστὸς ὁ λόγος.
TRUSTWORTHY [IS] THE WORD.

Εἴ τις ἐπισκοπῆς ὀρέγεται, καλοῦ ἔργου ἐπιθυμεῖ.
IF ANYONE ASPIRES TO~[BEING] AN OVERSEER, A GOOD WORK HE DESIRES.

3.2 δεῖ οὖν τὸν ἐπίσκοπον
IT IS NECESSARY THEREFORE [FOR] THE OVERSEER

ἀνεπίλημπτον εἶναι, μιᾶς γυναικὸς ἄνδρα, νηφάλιον
TO BE~WITHOUT REPROACH, [2]OF ONE [3]WIFE [1]A HUSBAND, TEMPERATE,

σώφρονα κόσμιον φιλόξενον διδακτικόν, **3.3** μὴ
SENSIBLE, RESPECTABLE, HOSPITABLE, SKILLFUL IN TEACHING, NOT

πάροινον μὴ πλήκτην, ἀλλὰ ἐπιεικῆ ἄμαχον
GIVEN TO MUCH WINE, NOT VIOLENT, BUT FORBEARING, NOT QUARRELSOME,

ἀφιλάργυρον, **3.4** τοῦ ἰδίου οἴκου καλῶς
NOT A LOVER OF MONEY, [3]THE(HIS) [4]OWN [5]HOUSEHOLD [2]WELL

προϊστάμενον,　τέκνα ἔχοντα　ἐν ὑποταγῇ,　μετὰ πάσης
¹MANAGING,　HAVING~[HIS] CHILDREN　IN　SUBJECTION,　WITH　ALL

σεμνότητος　3.5 εἰ δέ　τις　τοῦ　ἰδίου　οἴκου
RESPECT,　(NOW~IF　ANYONE　THE(HIS)　OWN　HOUSEHOLD

προστῆναι　οὐκ οἶδεν,　πῶς　ἐκκλησίας　θεοῦ
²TO MANAGE　¹DOES NOT KNOW,　HOW　²A CHURCH　³OF GOD

ἐπιμελήσεται;),　3.6 μὴ νεόφυτον,　ἵνα μὴ
¹WILL HE CARE FOR?),　NOT A NEW CONVERT,　LEST

τυφωθεὶς　εἰς　κρίμα　ἐμπέσῃ　τοῦ　διαβόλου.
HAVING BECOME CONCEITED　²INTO　³[THE] JUDGMENT　¹HE MIGHT FALL　OF THE　DEVIL.

3.7 δεῖ δὲ　καὶ　μαρτυρίαν καλὴν ἔχειν ἀπὸ τῶν
NOW~IT IS NECESSARY　ALSO　A GOOD~TESTIMONY　TO HAVE　FROM　THE ONES

ἔξωθεν, ἵνα μὴ εἰς ὀνειδισμὸν ἐμπέσῃ καὶ παγίδα
OUTSIDE,　LEST　²INTO ³REPROACH　¹HE MIGHT FALL　AND　A TRAP

τοῦ διαβόλου.
OF THE DEVIL.

3.8 Διακόνους ὡσαύτως σεμνούς,　μὴ διλόγους,
DEACONS　SIMILARLY　[MUST BE] RESPECTABLE,　NOT DOUBLE-TONGUED,

μὴ οἴνῳ πολλῷ προσέχοντας, μὴ αἰσχροκερδεῖς,
NOT ³WINE ²IN MUCH ¹INDULGING,　NOT FOND OF DISHONEST GAIN,

3.9 ἔχοντας τὸ μυστήριον τῆς πίστεως ἐν καθαρᾷ
KEEPING　THE MYSTERY　OF THE FAITH　WITH A CLEAN

συνειδήσει. 3.10 καὶ οὗτοι δὲ δοκιμαζέσθωσαν
CONSCIENCE.　³ALSO ²THESE ONES ¹AND LET [THEM] BE TESTED

πρῶτον, εἶτα διακονείτωσαν ἀνέγκλητοι ὄντες.
FIRST,　THEN LET THEM SERVE [AS DEACONS],　BEING~UNREPROVABLE.

3.11 γυναῖκας ὡσαύτως σεμνάς,　μὴ
WOMEN [DEACONESSES] SIMILARLY [MUST BE] RESPECTABLE, NOT

διαβόλους, νηφαλίους, πιστὰς ἐν πᾶσιν. 3.12 διάκονοι
SLANDERERS,　TEMPERATE,　FAITHFUL IN ALL THINGS.　²DEACONS

ἔστωσαν μιᾶς γυναικὸς ἄνδρες,　τέκνων
¹LET ³BE ⁵OF ONE ⁶WIFE ⁴HUSBANDS,　[THEIR] CHILDREN

καλῶς προϊστάμενοι καὶ τῶν ἰδίων οἴκων.
MANAGING~WELL　AND THE[IR] OWN HOUSEHOLD.

3.13 οἱ γὰρ καλῶς διακονήσαντες βαθμὸν ἑαυτοῖς
FOR~THE ONES HAVING SERVED~WELL　⁴STANDING ²FOR THEMSELVES

καλὸν περιποιοῦνται καὶ πολλὴν παρρησίαν ἐν πίστει
³A GOOD ¹ACQUIRE AND MUCH CONFIDENCE IN FAITH

τῇ ἐν Χριστῷ Ἰησοῦ.
- IN CHRIST JESUS.

3.14 Ταῦτά σοι γράφω ἐλπίζων ἐλθεῖν πρὸς σὲ
THESE THINGS TO YOU I WRITE HOPING TO COME TO YOU

ἐν τάχει· 3.15 ἐὰν δὲ βραδύνω, ἵνα εἰδῇς πῶς
QUICKLY;　BUT~IF I DELAY, THAT YOU MAY KNOW HOW

δεῖ ἐν οἴκῳ θεοῦ ἀναστρέφεσθαι, ἥτις ἐστὶν
[ONE] OUGHT ²IN ³[THE] HOUSE ⁴OF GOD ¹TO CONDUCT ONESELF, WHICH IS

ἐκκλησία θεοῦ ζῶντος, στῦλος καὶ ἑδραίωμα τῆς
[THE] CHURCH OF A LIVING~GOD,　[THE] PILLAR AND FOUNDATION OF THE

keeping his children submissive and respectful in every way— ⁵for if someone does not know how to manage his own household, how can he take care of God's church? ⁶He must not be a recent convert, or he may be puffed up with conceit and fall into the condemnation of the devil. ⁷Moreover, he must be well thought of by outsiders, so that he may not fall into disgrace and the snare of the devil.

8 Deacons likewise must be serious, not double-tongued, not indulging in much wine, not greedy for money; ⁹they must hold fast to the mystery of the faith with a clear conscience. ¹⁰And let them first be tested; then, if they prove themselves blameless, let them serve as deacons. ¹¹Women/ likewise must be serious, not slanderers, but temperate, faithful in all things. ¹²Let deacons be married only once,ᵏ and let them manage their children and their households well; ¹³for those who serve well as deacons gain a good standing for themselves and great boldness in the faith that is in Christ Jesus.

14 I hope to come to you soon, but I am writing these instructions to you so that, ¹⁵if I am delayed, you may know how one ought to behave in the household of God, which is the church of the living God, the pillar and bulwark of the

ʲ Or Their wives, or Women deacons
ᵏ Gk be husbands of one wife

truth. [16]Without any doubt, the mystery of our religion is great:

He[l] was revealed in flesh,
vindicated[m] in spirit,[n]
seen by angels,
proclaimed among Gentiles,
believed in throughout the world,
taken up in glory.

[l] Gk Who; other ancient authorities read God; others, Which
[m] Or justified
[n] Or by the Spirit

ἀληθείας. **3.16** καὶ ὁμολογουμένως μέγα ἐστὶν τὸ τῆς
TRUTH.   AND   CONFESSEDLY   GREAT   IS   THE -

εὐσεβείας μυστήριον·
MYSTERY ~ OF GODLINESS:

⌜Ὃς⌝ ἐφανερώθη ἐν σαρκί,
WHO   WAS MANIFESTED IN FLESH,

ἐδικαιώθη ἐν πνεύματι,
WAS VINDICATED IN(BY) [THE] SPIRIT,

ὤφθη ἀγγέλοις,
WAS SEEN BY ANGELS,

ἐκηρύχθη ἐν ἔθνεσιν,
WAS PROCLAIMED AMONG GENTILES,

ἐπιστεύθη ἐν κόσμῳ,
WAS BELIEVED [ON] IN   [THE] WORLD,

ἀνελήμφθη ἐν δόξῃ.
WAS TAKEN UP   IN   GLORY.

3:16 text: ASV RSV NASB NIV NEB TEV NJB NRSV. var. θεος (God): KJV ASVmg RSVmg NASBmg NRSVmg. var. ὅ (which) ASVmg RSVmg (NJBmg) NRSVmg.

CHAPTER 4

Now the Spirit expressly says that in later[o] times some will renounce the faith by paying attention to deceitful spirits and teachings of demons, [2]through the hypocrisy of liars whose consciences are seared with a hot iron. [3]They forbid marriage and demand abstinence from foods, which God created to be received with thanksgiving by those who believe and know the truth. [4]For everything created by God is good, and nothing is to be rejected, provided it is received with thanksgiving; [5]for it is sanctified by God's word and by prayer.

6 If you put these instructions before the brothers and sisters,[p] you will be a good servant[q] of Christ Jesus, nourished on the words of the faith and of the sound teaching that

[o] Or the last
[p] Gk brothers
[q] Or deacon

4.1 Τὸ δὲ πνεῦμα ῥητῶς λέγει ὅτι ἐν ὑστέροις
NOW ~ THE SPIRIT   EXPRESSLY SAYS   THAT IN LATTER

καιροῖς ἀποστήσονταί τινες τῆς πίστεως προσέχοντες
TIMES   SOME ~ WILL DEPART FROM   THE FAITH,   GIVING HEED TO

πνεύμασιν πλάνοις καὶ διδασκαλίαις δαιμονίων, **4.2** ἐν
DECEITFUL ~ SPIRITS   AND   TEACHINGS   OF DEMONS,   IN

ὑποκρίσει ψευδολόγων, κεκαυστηριασμένων τὴν ἰδίαν
HYPOCRISY   OF ONES SPEAKING LIES, HAVING BEEN SEARED [IN]   THE[IR] OWN

συνείδησιν, **4.3** κωλυόντων γαμεῖν, ἀπέχεσθαι
CONSCIENCE,   FORBIDDING   TO MARRY, [COMMANDING] TO ABSTAIN FROM

βρωμάτων, ἃ ὁ θεὸς ἔκτισεν εἰς μετάλημψιν μετὰ
FOODS,   WHICH - GOD CREATED   FOR PARTAKING   WITH

εὐχαριστίας τοῖς πιστοῖς καὶ ἐπεγνωκόσι τὴν
THANKSGIVING   BY THE BELIEVERS AND   ONES HAVING KNOWN THE

ἀλήθειαν. **4.4** ὅτι πᾶν κτίσμα θεοῦ καλὸν καὶ οὐδὲν
TRUTH.   BECAUSE EVERY CREATURE OF GOD [IS] GOOD AND NOTHING

ἀπόβλητον μετὰ εὐχαριστίας λαμβανόμενον·
[IS TO BE] REJECTED [2]WITH [3]THANKSGIVING   [1]BEING RECEIVED.

4.5 ἁγιάζεται γὰρ διὰ λόγου θεοῦ καὶ ἐντεύξεως.
FOR ~ IT IS BEING SANCTIFIED THROUGH [THE] WORD OF GOD AND   INTERCESSION.

4.6 Ταῦτα ὑποτιθέμενος τοῖς ἀδελφοῖς καλὸς ἔσῃ
[BY] SUGGESTING ~ THESE THINGS   TO THE BROTHERS   YOU WILL BE ~ A GOOD

διάκονος Χριστοῦ Ἰησοῦ, ἐντρεφόμενος τοῖς λόγοις
SERVANT   OF CHRIST   JESUS,   BEING NOURISHED   WITH THE WORDS

τῆς πίστεως καὶ τῆς καλῆς διδασκαλίας ᾗ
OF THE FAITH   AND OF THE GOOD   TEACHING   WHICH

παρηκολούθηκας· **4.7** τοὺς δὲ βεβήλους καὶ γραώδεις
YOU HAVE FOLLOWED;   BUT~THE PROFANE AND OLD WIVES'

μύθους παραιτοῦ. γύμναζε δὲ σεαυτὸν πρὸς εὐσέβειαν·
TALES REFUSE. AND~TRAIN YOURSELF FOR GODLINESS;

4.8 ἡ γὰρ σωματικὴ γυμνασία πρὸς ὀλίγον ἐστὶν
- FOR BODILY TRAINING FOR A LITTLE IS

ὠφέλιμος, ἡ δὲ εὐσέβεια πρὸς πάντα ὠφέλιμός ἐστιν
PROFITABLE, - BUT GODLINESS FOR ALL THINGS IS~PROFITABLE,

ἐπαγγελίαν ἔχουσα ζωῆς τῆς νῦν καὶ τῆς
HAVING~PROMISE ³LIFE ¹OF THE ²NOW(PRESENT) AND OF THE

μελλούσης. **4.9** πιστὸς ὁ λόγος καὶ πάσης
COMING ONE. TRUSTWORTHY [IS] THE WORD AND ²OF ALL

ἀποδοχῆς ἄξιος· **4.10** εἰς τοῦτο γὰρ κοπιῶμεν καὶ
³ACCEPTANCE ¹WORTHY; ²TO ³THIS [END] ¹FOR WE LABOR AND

⌐ἀγωνιζόμεθα,⌐ ὅτι ἠλπίκαμεν ἐπὶ θεῷ ζῶντι, ὅς
STRIVE, BECAUSE WE HAVE PUT [OUR] HOPE ON A LIVING~GOD, WHO

ἐστιν σωτὴρ πάντων ἀνθρώπων μάλιστα πιστῶν.
IS A SAVIOR OF ALL MEN, ESPECIALLY OF BELIEVERS.

4.11 Παράγγελλε ταῦτα καὶ δίδασκε. **4.12** μηδείς
COMMAND THESE THINGS AND TEACH. ²NO ONE

σου τῆς νεότητος καταφρονείτω, ἀλλὰ τύπος γίνου
⁴YOUR - ⁵YOUTH ¹LET ³DESPISE, BUT BECOME~AN EXAMPLE

τῶν πιστῶν ἐν λόγῳ, ἐν ἀναστροφῇ, ἐν ἀγάπῃ, ἐν
OF(FOR) THE BELIEVERS IN SPEECH, IN CONDUCT, IN LOVE, IN

πίστει, ἐν ἁγνείᾳ. **4.13** ἕως ἔρχομαι πρόσεχε τῇ
FAITH, IN PURITY. UNTIL I COME ATTEND TO THE

ἀναγνώσει, τῇ παρακλήσει, τῇ διδασκαλίᾳ.
[PUBLIC] READING [OF SCRIPTURE], TO THE EXHORTATION, TO THE TEACHING.

4.14 μὴ ἀμέλει τοῦ ἐν σοὶ χαρίσματος, ὃ ἐδόθη
DO NOT NEGLECT THE ²IN ³YOU ¹GIFT, WHICH WAS GIVEN

σοι διὰ προφητείας μετὰ ἐπιθέσεως τῶν χειρῶν
TO YOU BY MEANS OF PROPHECY WITH [THE] LAYING ON OF THE HANDS

τοῦ πρεσβυτερίου. **4.15** ταῦτα μελέτα, ἐν τούτοις
OF THE COUNCIL OF ELDERS. THESE THINGS PRACTISE, IN THESE THINGS

ἴσθι, ἵνα σου ἡ προκοπὴ φανερὰ ᾖ πᾶσιν.
BE [INVOLVED], THAT YOUR - PROGRESS MAY BE~MANIFEST TO ALL.

4.16 ἔπεχε σεαυτῷ καὶ τῇ διδασκαλίᾳ, ἐπίμενε
WATCH YOURSELF AND THE(YOUR) TEACHING, PERSEVERE

αὐτοῖς· τοῦτο γὰρ ποιῶν καὶ σεαυτὸν σώσεις καὶ
IN THEM. FOR~THIS DOING BOTH YOURSELF YOU WILL SAVE AND

τοὺς ἀκούοντάς σου.
THE ONES HEARING YOU.

4:10 text: ASV RSV NASB NIV NEB TEV NJB NRSV. var. ονειδιζομεθα (suffer reproach): KJV RSVmg NEBmg TEVmg NRSVmg.

you have followed. [7]Have nothing to do with profane myths and old wives' tales. Train yourself in godliness, [8]for, while physical training is of some value, godliness is valuable in every way, holding promise for both the present life and the life to come. [9]The saying is sure and worthy of full acceptance. [10]For to this end we toil and struggle,[r] because we have our hope set on the living God, who is the Savior of all people, especially of those who believe.

11 These are the things you must insist on and teach. [12]Let no one despise your youth, but set the believers an example in speech and conduct, in love, in faith, in purity. [13]Until I arrive, give attention to the public reading of scripture,[s] to exhorting, to teaching. [14]Do not neglect the gift that is in you, which was given to you through prophecy with the laying on of hands by the council of elders.[t] [15]Put these things into practice, devote yourself to them, so that all may see your progress. [16]Pay close attention to yourself and to your teaching; continue in these things, for in doing this you will save both yourself and your hearers.

[r] Other ancient authorities read *suffer reproach*
[s] Gk *to the reading*
[t] Gk *by the presbytery*

CHAPTER 5

Do not speak harshly to an older man,[u] but speak to him as to a father, to younger men as brothers, [2]to older women as mothers, to younger women as sisters— with absolute purity.

3 Honor widows who are really widows. [4]If a widow has children or grand-children, they should first learn their religious duty to their own family and make some repayment to their parents; for this is pleasing in God's sight. [5]The real widow, left alone, has set her hope on God and continues in supplications and prayers night and day; [6]but the widow[v] who lives for pleasure is dead even while she lives. [7]Give these commands as well, so that they may be above reproach. [8]And whoever does not provide for relatives, and especially for family members, has denied the faith and is worse than an unbeliever.

9 Let a widow be put on the list if she is not less than sixty years old and has been married only once;[w] [10]she must be well attested for her good works, as one who has brought up children, shown hospitality, washed the saints' feet, helped the afflicted, and devoted herself to doing good in every way. [11]But refuse to put younger widows on the list; for when their sensual desires alienate them from Christ, they want to marry, [12]and so they incur condemnation for having violated their first pledge. [13]Besides

[u] Or *an elder*, or *a presbyter*
[v] Gk *she*
[w] Gk *the wife of one husband*

5.1 Πρεσβυτέρῳ μὴ ἐπιπλήξῃς ἀλλὰ παρακάλει ὡς
AN ELDERLY MAN   DO NOT REBUKE   BUT   ENTREAT   AS

πατέρα, νεωτέρους ὡς ἀδελφούς, **5.2** πρεσβυτέρας ὡς
A FATHER,   YOUNGER MEN   AS   BROTHERS,   ELDERLY WOMEN   AS

μητέρας, νεωτέρας ὡς ἀδελφὰς ἐν πάσῃ ἁγνείᾳ.
MOTHERS,   YOUNGER WOMEN   AS   SISTERS   IN   ALL   PURITY.

5.3 Χήρας τίμα τὰς ὄντως χήρας. **5.4** εἰ δέ τις
HONOR~WIDOWS   -   [THAT ARE] REALLY   WIDOWS.   BUT~IF   ANY

χήρα τέκνα ἢ ἔκγονα ἔχει, μανθανέτωσαν
WIDOW   [2]CHILDREN   [3]OR   [4]GRANDCHILDREN   [1]HAS,   LET THEM LEARN

πρῶτον τὸν ἴδιον οἶκον εὐσεβεῖν καὶ
FIRST   [2]THE[IR]   [3]OWN   [4]HOUSEHOLD   [1]TO SHOW PIETY [TO]   AND

ἀμοιβὰς ἀποδιδόναι τοῖς προγόνοις· τοῦτο γάρ ἐστιν
TO RENDER~RECOMPENSE   TO THE   PARENTS.   FOR~THIS   IS

ἀπόδεκτον ἐνώπιον τοῦ θεοῦ. **5.5** ἡ δὲ ὄντως χήρα
ACCEPTABLE   IN THE SIGHT   -   OF GOD.   NOW~THE   REALLY(TRUE)   WIDOW,

καὶ μεμονωμένη ἤλπικεν ἐπὶ θεὸν καὶ
EVEN   THE ONE HAVING BECOME SINGLE(ALONE)   HAS SET [HER] HOPE   ON   GOD   AND

προσμένει ταῖς δεήσεσιν καὶ ταῖς προσευχαῖς
CONTINUES   IN THE(HER) SUPPLICATIONS   AND   THE(HER) PRAYERS

νυκτὸς καὶ ἡμέρας, **5.6** ἡ δὲ σπαταλῶσα
NIGHT   AND   DAY,   BUT~THE ONE   LIVING IN PLEASURE

ζῶσα τέθνηκεν. **5.7** καὶ ταῦτα παράγγελλε, ἵνα
HAS DIED~[WHILE] LIVING.   AND   THESE THINGS   CHARGE,   THAT

ἀνεπίλημπτοι ὦσιν. **5.8** εἰ δέ τις τῶν ἰδίων
THEY MAY BE~IRREPROACHABLE.   BUT~IF   ANYONE   [2]THE(HIS)   [3]OWN [RELATIVES]

καὶ μάλιστα οἰκείων οὐ προνοεῖ, τὴν
[4]AND   [5]ESPECIALLY   [6][HIS] HOUSEHOLD MEMBERS   [1]DOES NOT PROVIDE FOR,   [2]THE

πίστιν ἤρνηται καὶ ἔστιν ἀπίστου χείρων.
[3]FAITH   [1]HE HAS DENIED   AND   IS   WORSE [THAN]~AN UNBELIEVER.

5.9 Χήρα καταλεγέσθω μὴ ἔλαττον ἐτῶν ἐξήκοντα
LET A WIDOW BE PUT ON [THE] LIST   NOT   LESS [THAN]   SIXTY~YEARS

γεγονυῖα, ἑνὸς ἀνδρὸς γυνή, **5.10** ἐν ἔργοις καλοῖς
HAVING LIVED,   [2]OF ONE   [3]MAN   [1]A WIFE,   [2]BY   [3]GOOD~DEEDS

μαρτυρουμένη, εἰ ἐτεκνοτρόφησεν, εἰ ἐξενοδόχησεν, εἰ
[1]BEING ATTESTED TO,   IF   SHE BROUGHT UP CHILDREN,   IF   SHE SHOWED HOSPITALITY,   IF

ἁγίων πόδας ἔνιψεν, εἰ θλιβομένοις ἐπήρκεσεν,
SAINTS'   FEET   SHE WASHED,   IF   TO ONES BEING OPPRESSED   SHE GAVE ASSISTANCE,

εἰ παντὶ ἔργῳ ἀγαθῷ ἐπηκολούθησεν. **5.11** νεωτέρας δὲ
IF   TO EVERY   GOOD~WORK   SHE DEVOTED [HERSELF].   BUT~YOUNGER

χήρας παραιτοῦ· ὅταν γὰρ καταστρηνιάσωσιν τοῦ
WIDOWS   REFUSE;   FOR~WHEN   THEY HAVE SEXUAL DESIRES IN DISREGARD   -

Χριστοῦ, γαμεῖν θέλουσιν **5.12** ἔχουσαι κρίμα ὅτι
OF CHRIST,   THEY WANT~TO MARRY,   HAVING   JUDGMENT   BECAUSE

τὴν πρώτην πίστιν ἠθέτησαν· **5.13** ἅμα δὲ καὶ
[2]THE[IR]   [3]FIRST   [4]PLEDGE   [1]THEY VIOLATED;   AND~AT THE SAME TIME   ALSO

ἀργαὶ μανθάνουσιν περιερχόμεναι τὰς οἰκίας, οὐ
THEY LEARN [TO BE]~IDLE   GOING AROUND TO   THE HOUSES, ²NOT

μόνον δὲ ἀργαὶ ἀλλὰ καὶ φλύαροι καὶ περίεργοι,
³ONLY ¹AND IDLE BUT ALSO GOSSIPS AND BUSYBODIES,

λαλοῦσαι τὰ   μὴ δέοντα. 5.14 βούλομαι οὖν
SPEAKING THE THINGS THEY OUGHT NOT.   I COUNSEL   THEREFORE

νεωτέρας   γαμεῖν, τεκνογονεῖν, οἰκοδεσποτεῖν,
YOUNGER [WIDOWS] TO MARRY, TO BEAR CHILDREN, TO RULE THE HOUSE,

μηδεμίαν ἀφορμὴν διδόναι τῷ   ἀντικειμένῳ
²NO   ³OCCASION ¹TO GIVE TO THE ADVERSARY

λοιδορίας χάριν· 5.15 ἤδη γὰρ τινες ἐξετράπησαν
FOR THE SAKE OF~REPROACH;   FOR~ALREADY SOME TURNED ASIDE

ὀπίσω τοῦ Σατανᾶ. 5.16 εἴ τις πιστὴ   ἔχει χήρας,
AFTER - SATAN.   IF ANY BELIEVING WOMAN HAS WIDOWS,

ἐπαρκείτω αὐταῖς καὶ μὴ βαρείσθω ἡ ἐκκλησία,
LET HER ASSIST THEM AND NOT LET BE BURDENED THE CHURCH,

ἵνα ταῖς ὄντως   χήραις ἐπαρκέσῃ.
THAT ²THE ONES ³[WHO ARE] REALLY ⁴WIDOWS ¹IT MAY ASSIST.

5.17 Οἱ καλῶς προεστῶτες πρεσβύτεροι διπλῆς τιμῆς
     ²THE ⁵WELL ⁴HAVING RULED ³ELDERS   ⁷OF DOUBLE ⁸HONOR

ἀξιούσθωσαν,   μάλιστα οἱ   κοπιῶντες ἐν
¹LET ⁶BE CONSIDERED WORTHY, ESPECIALLY THE ONES LABORING IN

λόγῳ   καὶ διδασκαλίᾳ. 5.18 λέγει γὰρ ἡ γραφή,
WORD(PREACHING) AND TEACHING.   FOR~SAYS THE SCRIPTURE,

Βοῦν ἀλοῶντα   οὐ φιμώσεις, καί, Ἄξιος ὁ
AN OX TREADING OUT GRAIN YOU SHALL NOT MUZZLE, AND, WORTHY [IS] THE

ἐργάτης τοῦ μισθοῦ αὐτοῦ. 5.19 κατὰ πρεσβυτέρου
WORKMAN OF THE WAGE[S] OF HIM.   AGAINST AN ELDER

κατηγορίαν μὴ παραδέχου, ἐκτὸς εἰ μὴ ἐπὶ
AN ACCUSATION DO NOT RECEIVE, - UNLESS ON [THE TESTIMONY OF]

δύο ἢ τριῶν μαρτύρων. 5.20 τοὺς   ἁμαρτάνοντας
TWO OR THREE WITNESSES.   THE ONES SINNING

ἐνώπιον πάντων ἔλεγχε, ἵνα καὶ οἱ λοιποὶ
²BEFORE ³ALL ¹EXPOSE, THAT ALSO THE REST

φόβον ἔχωσιν. 5.21 Διαμαρτύρομαι ἐνώπιον τοῦ θεοῦ
MAY HAVE~FEAR.   I EARNESTLY TESTIFY BEFORE - GOD

καὶ Χριστοῦ Ἰησοῦ καὶ τῶν ἐκλεκτῶν ἀγγέλων, ἵνα
AND CHRIST JESUS AND THE CHOSEN ANGELS, THAT

ταῦτα   φυλάξῃς χωρὶς προκρίματος,
THESE THINGS(COMMANDS) YOU KEEP, WITHOUT DISCRIMINATION,

μηδὲν ποιῶν κατὰ   πρόσκλισιν. 5.22 Χεῖρας ταχέως
DOING~NOTHING ACCORDING TO PARTIALITY.   ²HANDS ³QUICKLY

μηδενὶ ἐπιτίθει μηδὲ κοινώνει ἁμαρτίαις ἀλλοτρίαις·
⁵NO ONE ¹LAY ⁴ON, NOR PARTICIPATE IN SINS OF OTHERS;

σεαυτὸν ἁγνὸν τήρει. 5.23 Μηκέτι ὑδροπότει, ἀλλὰ
²YOURSELF ³PURE ¹KEEP.   NO LONGER DRINK WATER [ONLY], BUT

5:18 Deut. 25:4; Luke 10:7

that, they learn to be idle,
gadding about from house
to house; and they are not
merely idle, but also gossips
and busybodies, saying
what they should not say.
[14]So I would have younger
widows marry, bear chil-
dren, and manage their
households, so as to give the
adversary no occasion to
revile us. [15]For some have
already turned away to
follow Satan. [16]If any believing woman[x] has relatives
who are really widows, let
her assist them; let the
church not be burdened, so
that it can assist those who
are real widows.

17 Let the elders who rule
well be considered worthy of
double honor,[y] especially
those who labor in preaching
and teaching; [18]for the
scripture says, "You shall not
muzzle an ox while it is
treading out the grain," and,
"The laborer deserves to be
paid." [19]Never accept any
accusation against an elder
except on the evidence of
two or three witnesses. [20]As
for those who persist in sin,
rebuke them in the presence
of all, so that the rest also
may stand in fear. [21]In the
presence of God and of
Christ Jesus and of the elect
angels, I warn you to keep
these instructions without
prejudice, doing nothing on
the basis of partiality. [22]Do
not ordain[z] anyone hastily,
and do not participate in the
sins of others; keep yourself
pure.

23 No longer drink only

[x] Other ancient authorities read
   believing man or woman; others,
   believing man
[y] Or *compensation*
[z] Gk *Do not lay hands on*

water, but take a little wine for the sake of your stomach and your frequent ailments.

24 The sins of some people are conspicuous and precede them to judgment, while the sins of others follow them there. 25So also good works are conspicuous; and even when they are not, they cannot remain hidden.

οἴνῳ ὀλίγῳ χρῶ διὰ   τὸν   στόμαχον καὶ τὰς
A LITTLE~WINE   USE   BECAUSE OF   THE(YOUR)   STOMACH   AND   -

πυκνάς σου ἀσθενείας.
YOUR~FREQUENT   ILLNESSES.

5.24 Τινῶν ἀνθρώπων αἱ ἁμαρτίαι πρόδηλοί εἰσιν
     ³OF SOME ⁴MEN   ¹THE ²SINS   ARE~EVIDENT,

προάγουσαι εἰς κρίσιν, τισὶν δὲ καὶ ἐπακολουθοῦσιν·
GOING BEFORE [THEM] TO   JUDGMENT,   BUT~SOME   INDEED   FOLLOW AFTER;

5.25 ὡσαύτως καὶ τὰ ἔργα τὰ καλὰ πρόδηλα, καὶ
     LIKEWISE   ALSO   THE ²DEEDS   -   ¹GOOD   [ARE] EVIDENT,   AND

τὰ   ἄλλως ἔχοντα κρυβῆναι οὐ δύνανται.
THE ONES   BEING~OTHERWISE   ²TO BE HIDDEN   ¹ARE NOT ABLE.

CHAPTER 6

Let all who are under the yoke of slavery regard their masters as worthy of all honor, so that the name of God and the teaching may not be blasphemed. ²Those who have believing masters must not be disrespectful to them on the ground that they are members of the church;*a* rather they must serve them all the more, since those who benefit by their service are believers and beloved.*b*

Teach and urge these duties. ³Whoever teaches otherwise and does not agree with the sound words of our Lord Jesus Christ and the teaching that is in accordance with godliness, ⁴is conceited, understanding nothing, and has a morbid craving for controversy and for disputes about words. From these come envy, dissension, slander, base suspicions, ⁵and wrangling among those who are depraved in mind and bereft of the truth, imagining

a Gk *are brothers*
b Or *since they are believers and beloved, who devote themselves to good deeds*

6.1 Ὅσοι εἰσὶν ὑπὸ ζυγὸν δοῦλοι, τοὺς ἰδίους
     AS MANY AS   ARE   UNDER   A YOKE   [AS] SLAVES,   ²THE[IR]   ³OWN

δεσπότας πάσης τιμῆς ἀξίους ἡγείσθωσαν, ἵνα μὴ τὸ
⁴MASTERS   ⁶OF ALL   ⁷HONOR   ⁵WORTHY   ¹LET THEM CONSIDER,   LEST   THE

ὄνομα τοῦ θεοῦ καὶ ἡ διδασκαλία βλασφημῆται.
NAME   -   OF GOD   AND   THE   TEACHING   BE BLASPHEMED.

6.2 οἱ δὲ   πιστοὺς ἔχοντες δεσπότας
     AND~THE ONES   ²BELIEVING   ¹HAVING   ³MASTERS

μὴ καταφρονείτωσαν, ὅτι ἀδελφοί εἰσιν, ἀλλὰ
LET THEM NOT DISRESPECT [THEM],   BECAUSE   BROTHERS   THEY ARE,   BUT

μᾶλλον δουλευέτωσαν, ὅτι πιστοί εἰσιν καὶ
ALL THE MORE   LET THEM SERVE [THEM],   BECAUSE   BELIEVERS   THEY ARE   AND

ἀγαπητοὶ οἱ   τῆς   εὐεργεσίας ἀντιλαμβανόμενοι.
BELOVED,   THE ONES   ²FROM THE[IR]   ³GOOD SERVICE   ¹RECEIVING HELP.

Ταῦτα   δίδασκε καὶ παρακάλει. **6.3** εἴ τις
THESE THINGS   TEACH   AND   ENCOURAGE.   IF   ANYONE

ἑτεροδιδασκαλεῖ   καὶ μὴ προσέρχεται ὑγιαίνουσιν
TEACHES DIFFERENT DOCTRINE   AND   DOES NOT AGREE WITH   [THE] HEALTHY

λόγοις τοῖς τοῦ κυρίου ἡμῶν Ἰησοῦ Χριστοῦ καὶ τῇ
WORDS   -   OF THE   LORD   OF US,   JESUS   CHRIST,   AND   ¹TO THE

κατ’   εὐσέβειαν διδασκαλίᾳ, **6.4** τετύφωται,
³ACCORDING TO   ⁴GODLINESS   ²TEACHING,   HE HAS BECOME CONCEITED,

μηδὲν ἐπιστάμενος, ἀλλὰ νοσῶν   περὶ
HAVING UNDERSTOOD~NOTHING,   BUT   HAVING A MORBID CRAVING   FOR

ζητήσεις καὶ λογομαχίας, ἐξ ὧν γίνεται φθόνος
CONTROVERSIES   AND   DISPUTES OVER WORDS,   OUT OF   WHICH   COMES   ENVY,

ἔρις βλασφημίαι, ὑπόνοιαι πονηραί, **6.5** διαπαρατριβαὶ
STRIFE,   EVIL SPEAKINGS,   EVIL~SUSPICIONS,   CONSTANT FRICTION

διεφθαρμένων ἀνθρώπων τὸν   νοῦν καὶ
OF(BETWEEN) MEN~HAVING BEEN CORRUPTED   [AS TO] THE[IR]   MIND[S]   AND

ἀπεστερημένων τῆς ἀληθείας, νομιζόντων πορισμὸν
HAVING BECOME BEREFT   OF THE   TRUTH,   THINKING   ³GAIN

εἶναι τὴν εὐσέβειαν. **6.6** ἔστιν δὲ πορισμὸς μέγας
²TO BE   -   ¹GODLINESS.   ⁵IS   ¹BUT   ⁷GAIN   ⁶GREAT

ἡ εὐσέβεια μετὰ αὐταρκείας· **6.7** οὐδὲν γὰρ
-   ²GODLINESS   ³WITH   ⁴CONTENTMENT;   FOR~NOTHING

εἰσηνέγκαμεν εἰς τὸν κόσμον, ὅτι οὐδὲ ἐξενεγκεῖν
WE BROUGHT   INTO THE WORLD,   -   NEITHER ²TO CARRY OUT

τι δυνάμεθα· **6.8** ἔχοντες δὲ διατροφὰς καὶ
³ANYTHING ¹ARE WE ABLE.   BUT~HAVING   SUSTENANCE   AND

σκεπάσματα, τούτοις ἀρκεσθησόμεθα. **6.9** οἱ δὲ
COVERING,   WITH THESE THINGS WE WILL BE SATISFIED.   BUT~THE ONES

βουλόμενοι πλουτεῖν ἐμπίπτουσιν εἰς πειρασμὸν καὶ
DESIRING   TO BE RICH   FALL   INTO TEMPTATION   AND

παγίδα καὶ ἐπιθυμίας πολλὰς ἀνοήτους καὶ βλαβεράς,
A TRAP AND ⁵LUSTS   ¹MANY   ²FOOLISH   ³AND ⁴HARMFUL,

αἵτινες βυθίζουσιν τοὺς ἀνθρώπους εἰς ὄλεθρον καὶ
WHICH   PLUNGE   -   MEN   INTO RUIN   AND

ἀπώλειαν. **6.10** ῥίζα γὰρ πάντων τῶν κακῶν ἐστιν ἡ
DESTRUCTION.   FOR~A ROOT OF ALL   -   EVILS   IS   THE

φιλαργυρία, ἧς τινες ὀρεγόμενοι ἀπεπλανήθησαν /
LOVE OF MONEY, OF WHICH SOME   CRAVING   WERE LED AWAY

ἀπὸ τῆς πίστεως καὶ ἑαυτοὺς περιέπειραν
FROM THE FAITH   AND   PIERCED~THEMSELVES

ὀδύναις πολλαῖς.
WITH MANY~SORROWS.

6.11 Σὺ δέ, ὦ ἄνθρωπε θεοῦ, ταῦτα φεῦγε· δίωκε δὲ
BUT~YOU, O MAN   OF GOD, FLEE~THESE THINGS; BUT~PURSUE

δικαιοσύνην εὐσέβειαν πίστιν, ἀγάπην ὑπομονὴν
RIGHTEOUSNESS, GODLINESS, FAITH,   LOVE,   ENDURANCE,

πραϋπαθίαν. **6.12** ἀγωνίζου τὸν καλὸν ἀγῶνα τῆς
MEEKNESS.   FIGHT   THE GOOD   FIGHT OF THE

πίστεως, ἐπιλαβοῦ τῆς αἰωνίου ζωῆς, εἰς ἣν
FAITH,   LAY HOLD   OF THE ETERNAL LIFE, TO WHICH

ἐκλήθης καὶ ὡμολόγησας τὴν καλὴν ὁμολογίαν
YOU WERE CALLED AND CONFESSED   THE GOOD   CONFESSION

ἐνώπιον πολλῶν μαρτύρων. **6.13** παραγγέλλω [σοι]
BEFORE   MANY   WITNESSES.   I CHARGE   YOU

ἐνώπιον τοῦ θεοῦ τοῦ ζῳογονοῦντος τὰ πάντα καὶ
BEFORE   -   GOD THE ONE GIVING LIFE TO - ALL THINGS AND

Χριστοῦ Ἰησοῦ τοῦ μαρτυρήσαντος ἐπὶ Ποντίου
CHRIST   JESUS THE ONE HAVING TESTIFIED BEFORE PONTIUS

Πιλάτου τὴν καλὴν ὁμολογίαν, **6.14** τηρῆσαί σε τὴν
PILATE   THE GOOD CONFESSION,   TO KEEP   -   THE

ἐντολὴν ἄσπιλον ἀνεπίλημπτον μέχρι τῆς
COMMANDMENT SPOTLESS, IRREPROACHABLE,   UNTIL THE

ἐπιφανείας τοῦ κυρίου ἡμῶν Ἰησοῦ Χριστοῦ, **6.15** ἣν
APPEARING   OF THE LORD OF US, JESUS   CHRIST,   WHICH

καιροῖς ἰδίοις δείξει ὁ μακάριος καὶ μόνος
IN ITS OWN~TIMES ⁶WILL SHOW ¹THE ²BLESSED   ³AND ⁴ONLY

that godliness is a means of gain.ᶜ ⁶Of course, there is great gain in godliness combined with contentment; ⁷for we brought nothing into the world, so thatᵈ we can take nothing out of it; ⁸but if we have food and clothing, we will be content with these. ⁹But those who want to be rich fall into temptation and are trapped by many senseless and harmful desires that plunge people into ruin and destruction. ¹⁰For the love of money is a root of all kinds of evil, and in their eagerness to be rich some have wandered away from the faith and pierced themselves with many pains.

11 But as for you, man of God, shun all this; pursue righteousness, godliness, faith, love, endurance, gentleness. ¹²Fight the good fight of the faith; take hold of the eternal life, to which you were called and for which you madeᵉ the good confession in the presence of many witnesses. ¹³In the presence of God, who gives life to all things, and of Christ Jesus, who in his testimony before Pontius Pilate made the good confession, I charge you ¹⁴to keep the commandment without spot or blame until the manifestation of our Lord Jesus Christ, ¹⁵which he will bring about at the right time—he who is the blessed and only

ᶜ Other ancient authorities add
    Withdraw yourself from such
    people
ᵈ Other ancient authorities read
    world—it is certain that
ᵉ Gk *confessed*

Sovereign, the King of kings and Lord of lords. [16]It is he alone who has immortality and dwells in unapproachable light, whom no one has ever seen or can see; to him be honor and eternal dominion. Amen.

17 As for those who in the present age are rich, command them not to be haughty, or to set their hopes on the uncertainty of riches, but rather on God who richly provides us with everything for our enjoyment. [18]They are to do good, to be rich in good works, generous, and ready to share, [19]thus storing up for themselves the treasure of a good foundation for the future, so that they may take hold of the life that really is life.

20 Timothy, guard what has been entrusted to you. Avoid the profane chatter and contradictions of what is falsely called knowledge; [21]by professing it some have missed the mark as regards the faith.

Grace be with you.[f]

[f] The Greek word for *you* here is plural; in other ancient authorities it is singular. Other ancient authorities add *Amen*

δυνάστης, ὁ βασιλεὺς τῶν βασιλευόντων καὶ
[5]SOVEREIGN, THE KING OF THE ONES REIGNING AS KINGS AND

κύριος τῶν κυριευόντων, **6.16** ὁ μόνος ἔχων
LORD OF THE ONES RULING AS LORDS, THE ONLY ONE HAVING

ἀθανασίαν, φῶς οἰκῶν ἀπρόσιτον, ὃν εἶδεν οὐδεὶς
IMMORTALITY DWELLING~[IN] LIGHT UNAPPROACHABLE, WHOM [3]SAW [1]NO ONE

ἀνθρώπων οὐδὲ ἰδεῖν δύναται· ᾧ τιμὴ καὶ
[2]OF(AMONG) MEN NEITHER IS ABLE~TO SEE; TO WHOM [BE] HONOR AND

κράτος αἰώνιον, ἀμήν.
POWER ETERNAL, AMEN.

6.17 Τοῖς πλουσίοις ἐν τῷ νῦν αἰῶνι παράγγελλε
TO THE RICH IN THE PRESENT AGE CHARGE,

μὴ ὑψηλοφρονεῖν μηδὲ ἠλπικέναι ἐπὶ
NOT TO BE HIGH-MINDED NEITHER TO HAVE HOPE ON(IN)

πλούτου ἀδηλότητι ἀλλ᾽ ἐπὶ θεῷ τῷ παρέχοντι ἡμῖν
[THE] UNCERTAINTY~OF RICHES BUT ON(IN) GOD, THE ONE GRANTING TO US

πάντα πλουσίως εἰς ἀπόλαυσιν, **6.18** ἀγαθοεργεῖν,
ALL THINGS RICHLY FOR ENJOYMENT, TO DO GOOD,

πλουτεῖν ἐν ἔργοις καλοῖς, εὐμεταδότους εἶναι,
TO BE RICH IN GOOD~WORKS, TO BE~GENEROUS,

κοινωνικούς, **6.19** ἀποθησαυρίζοντας ἑαυτοῖς
ONES WILLING TO SHARE, TREASURING UP FOR THEMSELVES

θεμέλιον καλὸν εἰς τὸ μέλλον, ἵνα ἐπιλάβωνται τῆς
A GOOD~FOUNDATION FOR THE FUTURE, THAT THEY MAY LAY HOLD OF THE

ὄντως ζωῆς.
REAL LIFE.

6.20 Ὦ Τιμόθεε, τὴν παραθήκην φύλαξον
O TIMOTHY, [2]THE [3]DEPOSIT ENTRUSTED [TO YOU] [1]GUARD,

ἐκτρεπόμενος τὰς βεβήλους κενοφωνίας καὶ ἀντιθέσεις
TURNING AWAY FROM THE PROFANE, EMPTY UTTERANCES AND OPPOSITIONS

τῆς ψευδωνύμου γνώσεως, **6.21** ἣν τινες
OF THE FALSELY NAMED "KNOWLEDGE," WHICH SOME

ἐπαγγελλόμενοι περὶ τὴν πίστιν ἠστόχησαν.
PROFESSING CONCERNING THE FAITH MISSED [THE] MARK.

Ἡ χάρις μεθ᾽ ὑμῶν.
- GRACE [BE] WITH YOU°.

THE SECOND LETTER OF PAUL TO
TIMOTHY

ΠΡΟΣ ΤΙΜΟΘΕΟΝ Β
TO   TIMOTHY   2

1.1 Παῦλος ἀπόστολος Χριστοῦ Ἰησοῦ διὰ θελήματος
PAUL   AN APOSTLE   OF CHRIST   JESUS   BY   [THE] WILL

θεοῦ κατ'   ἐπαγγελίαν ζωῆς τῆς ἐν Χριστῷ Ἰησοῦ
OF GOD ACCORDING TO [THE] PROMISE   OF LIFE - IN CHRIST   JESUS,

1.2 Τιμοθέῳ ἀγαπητῷ τέκνῳ, χάρις ἔλεος εἰρήνη ἀπὸ
TO TIMOTHY, [MY] BELOVED   CHILD,   GRACE,   MERCY,   PEACE   FROM

θεοῦ πατρὸς καὶ Χριστοῦ Ἰησοῦ τοῦ κυρίου ἡμῶν.
GOD [THE] FATHER AND   CHRIST   JESUS   THE   LORD   OF US.

1.3 Χάριν ἔχω τῷ θεῷ, ᾧ λατρεύω ἀπὸ προγόνων
I HAVE~GRATITUDE - TO GOD, WHOM I SERVE   FROM [MY] FOREFATHERS

ἐν καθαρᾷ συνειδήσει, ὡς ἀδιάλειπτον ἔχω τὴν
IN A CLEAN   CONSCIENCE,   AS UNCEASINGLY   I HAVE ¹THE

περὶ σοῦ μνείαν ἐν ταῖς δεήσεσίν μου νυκτὸς
³CONCERNING ⁴YOU ²REMEMBRANCE IN THE   PRAYERS   OF ME NIGHT

καὶ ἡμέρας, **1.4** ἐπιποθῶν σε ἰδεῖν, μεμνημένος σου τῶν
AND DAY,   LONGING   TO SEE~YOU, HAVING REMEMBERED YOUR -

δακρύων, ἵνα χαρᾶς πληρωθῶ, **1.5** ὑπόμνησιν λαβὼν
TEARS,   THAT WITH JOY I MAY BE FILLED,   HAVING TAKEN~REMEMBRANCE

τῆς ἐν σοὶ ἀνυποκρίτου πίστεως, ἥτις ἐνῴκησεν
¹OF THE ⁴IN ⁵YOU ²GENUINE   ³FAITH,   WHICH DWELT

πρῶτον ἐν τῇ μάμμῃ σου Λωΐδι καὶ τῇ μητρὶ
FIRST   IN THE GRANDMOTHER OF YOU, LOIS,   AND IN THE MOTHER

σου Εὐνίκῃ, πέπεισμαι δὲ ὅτι καὶ ἐν σοί.
OF YOU, EUNICE, AND~I HAVE BEEN PERSUADED THAT [IT DWELLS] ALSO IN   YOU.

1.6 δι' ἣν αἰτίαν ἀναμιμνῄσκω σε ἀναζωπυρεῖν τὸ
FOR WHICH CAUSE   I REMIND   YOU TO REKINDLE THE

χάρισμα τοῦ θεοῦ, ὅ ἐστιν ἐν σοὶ διὰ τῆς
GIFT   -   OF GOD, WHICH IS   IN   YOU THROUGH THE

ἐπιθέσεως τῶν χειρῶν μου. **1.7** οὐ γὰρ ἔδωκεν ἡμῖν ὁ
LAYING ON   OF THE HANDS OF ME.   ³NOT ¹FOR ⁴GAVE ⁵TO US -

θεὸς πνεῦμα δειλίας ἀλλὰ δυνάμεως καὶ ἀγάπης
²GOD A SPIRIT OF COWARDICE, BUT OF POWER   AND OF LOVE

καὶ σωφρονισμοῦ. **1.8** μὴ οὖν ἐπαισχυνθῇς τὸ
AND OF SELF-DISCIPLINE. [DO] NOT THEREFORE BE ASHAMED OF   THE

μαρτύριον τοῦ κυρίου ἡμῶν μηδὲ ἐμὲ τὸν δέσμιον
TESTIMONY OF THE LORD OF US NOR [OF] ME, THE PRISONER

αὐτοῦ, ἀλλὰ συγκακοπάθησον τῷ εὐαγγελίῳ
OF HIM, BUT   SUFFER TOGETHER WITH [ME] FOR THE GOSPEL

Paul, an apostle of Christ Jesus by the will of God, for the sake of the promise of life that is in Christ Jesus,

2 To Timothy, my beloved child:

Grace, mercy, and peace from God the Father and Christ Jesus our Lord.

3 I am grateful to God—whom I worship with a clear conscience, as my ancestors did—when I remember you constantly in my prayers night and day. ⁴Recalling your tears, I long to see you so that I may be filled with joy. ⁵I am reminded of your sincere faith, a faith that lived first in your grandmother Lois and your mother Eunice and now, I am sure, lives in you. ⁶For this reason I remind you to rekindle the gift of God that is within you through the laying on of my hands; ⁷for God did not give us a spirit of cowardice, but rather a spirit of power and of love and of self-discipline.

8 Do not be ashamed, then, of the testimony about our Lord or of me his prisoner, but join with me in suffering for the gospel,

relying on the power of God, [9] who saved us and called us with a holy calling, not according to our works but according to his own purpose and grace. This grace was given to us in Christ Jesus before the ages began, [10] but it has now been revealed through the appearing of our Savior Christ Jesus, who abolished death and brought life and immortality to light through the gospel. [11] For this gospel I was appointed a herald and an apostle and a teacher,[a] [12] and for this reason I suffer as I do. But I am not ashamed, for I know the one in whom I have put my trust, and I am sure that he is able to guard until that day what I have entrusted to him.[b] [13] Hold to the standard of sound teaching that you have heard from me, in the faith and love that are in Christ Jesus. [14] Guard the good treasure entrusted to you, with the help of the Holy Spirit living in us.

[15] You are aware that all who are in Asia have turned away from me, including Phygelus and Hermogenes. [16] May the Lord grant mercy to the household of Onesiphorus, because he often refreshed me and was not ashamed of my chain; [17] when he arrived in Rome, he eagerly[c] searched for me and found me [18]—may the Lord

[a] Other ancient authorities add *of the Gentiles*
[b] Or *what has been entrusted to me*
[c] Or *promptly*

κατὰ δύναμιν θεοῦ, **1.9** τοῦ σώσαντος ἡμᾶς καὶ
ACCORDING TO [THE] POWER OF GOD, THE ONE HAVING SAVED US AND

καλέσαντος κλήσει ἁγίᾳ, οὐ κατὰ τὰ ἔργα ἡμῶν
HAVING CALLED [US] WITH A HOLY~CALLING, NOT ACCORDING TO THE WORKS OF US

ἀλλὰ κατὰ ἰδίαν πρόθεσιν καὶ χάριν, τὴν
BUT ACCORDING TO HIS OWN PURPOSE AND GRACE, -

δοθεῖσαν ἡμῖν ἐν Χριστῷ Ἰησοῦ πρὸ χρόνων
HAVING BEEN GIVEN TO US IN CHRIST JESUS BEFORE TIME

αἰωνίων, **1.10** φανερωθεῖσαν δὲ νῦν διὰ τῆς
ETERNAL, BUT~HAVING BEEN MANIFESTED NOW THROUGH THE

ἐπιφανείας τοῦ σωτῆρος ἡμῶν Χριστοῦ Ἰησοῦ,
APPEARING OF THE SAVIOR OF US, CHRIST JESUS,

καταργήσαντος μὲν τὸν θάνατον
ON THE ONE HAND~HAVING NULLIFIED - DEATH,

φωτίσαντος δὲ ζωὴν καὶ ἀφθαρσίαν διὰ
ON THE OTHER~HAVING BROUGHT TO LIGHT LIFE AND INCORRUPTIBILITY THROUGH

τοῦ εὐαγγελίου **1.11** εἰς ὃ ἐτέθην ἐγὼ κῆρυξ καὶ
THE GOOD NEWS, FOR WHICH I~WAS APPOINTED A HERALD AND

ἀπόστολος καὶ διδάσκαλος, **1.12** δι' ἣν αἰτίαν καὶ
AN APOSTLE AND A TEACHER, FOR WHICH CAUSE ALSO

ταῦτα πάσχω· ἀλλ' οὐκ ἐπαισχύνομαι, οἶδα γὰρ
THESE THINGS I SUFFER; BUT I AM NOT ASHAMED, FOR~I KNOW

ᾧ πεπίστευκα καὶ πέπεισμαι ὅτι δυνατός ἐστιν
WHOM I HAVE BELIEVED AND I HAVE BEEN PERSUADED THAT HE IS~ABLE

τὴν παραθήκην μου φυλάξαι εἰς ἐκείνην τὴν
[2]THE [3]DEPOSIT [ENTRUSTED TO HIM] [4]OF(BY) ME [1]TO GUARD FOR - THAT

ἡμέραν. **1.13** ὑποτύπωσιν ἔχε ὑγιαινόντων λόγων ὧν
DAY. FOLLOW~[THE] PATTERN OF HEALTHY WORDS WHICH

παρ' ἐμοῦ ἤκουσας ἐν πίστει καὶ ἀγάπῃ τῇ ἐν
FROM ME YOU HEARD IN FAITH AND LOVE - IN

Χριστῷ Ἰησοῦ· **1.14** τὴν καλὴν παραθήκην
CHRIST JESUS. THE GOOD DEPOSIT ENTRUSTED [TO YOU]

φύλαξον διὰ πνεύματος ἁγίου τοῦ ἐνοικοῦντος ἐν
GUARD THROUGH [THE] HOLY~SPIRIT - DWELLING IN

ἡμῖν.
US.

1.15 Οἶδας τοῦτο, ὅτι ἀπεστράφησάν με πάντες οἱ
THIS~YOU KNOW, THAT TURNED AWAY FROM ME ALL THE ONES

ἐν τῇ Ἀσίᾳ, ὧν ἐστιν Φύγελος καὶ Ἑρμογένης.
IN - ASIA, OF WHOM IS (ARE) PHYGELUS AND HERMOGENES.

1.16 δῴη ἔλεος ὁ κύριος τῷ Ὀνησιφόρου οἴκῳ,
[1]MAY [4]GRANT [5]MERCY [2]THE [3]LORD - TO ONESIPHORUS' HOUSEHOLD,

ὅτι πολλάκις με ἀνέψυξεν καὶ τὴν ἅλυσίν μου
BECAUSE OFTEN HE REFRESHED~ME AND THE CHAIN[S] OF ME

οὐκ ἐπαισχύνθη, **1.17** ἀλλὰ γενόμενος ἐν Ῥώμῃ
WAS NOT ASHAMED OF, BUT HAVING BEEN IN ROME,

σπουδαίως ἐζήτησέν με καὶ εὗρεν· **1.18** δῴη
DILIGENTLY HE SOUGHT ME AND FOUND [ME]; [1]MAY [4]GRANT

αὐτῷ   ὁ   κύριος   εὑρεῖν   ἔλεος   παρὰ   κυρίου   ἐν   ἐκείνῃ
⁵TO HIM ²THE ³LORD TO FIND MERCY FROM [THE] LORD IN THAT

τῇ ἡμέρᾳ.   καὶ   ὅσα   ἐν   Ἐφέσῳ   διηκόνησεν,
- DAY. AND [IN] HOW MANY WAYS [WHILE] IN EPHESUS HE SERVED,

βέλτιον   σὺ   γινώσκεις.
[AS] VERY WELL YOU KNOW.

grant that he will find mercy from the Lord on that day! And you know very well how much service he rendered in Ephesus.

2.1 Σὺ   οὖν,   τέκνον   μου,   ἐνδυναμοῦ   ἐν   τῇ   χάριτι
YOU, THEREFORE, CHILD OF ME, BE EMPOWERED IN THE GRACE

τῇ ἐν Χριστῷ Ἰησοῦ, **2.2** καὶ   ἃ   ἤκουσας   παρ᾽
- IN CHRIST JESUS, AND WHAT THINGS YOU HEARD FROM

ἐμοῦ   διὰ   πολλῶν μαρτύρων,   ταῦτα   παράθου
ME THROUGH MANY WITNESSES, THESE THINGS COMMIT

πιστοῖς   ἀνθρώποις,   οἵτινες   ἱκανοὶ ἔσονται   καὶ
TO TRUSTWORTHY MEN, WHO WILL BE~QUALIFIED ALSO

ἑτέρους διδάξαι.   **2.3** συγκακοπάθησον   ὡς   καλὸς
TO TEACH~OTHERS. TAKE [YOUR] PART IN SUFFERING AS A GOOD

στρατιώτης Χριστοῦ Ἰησοῦ.   **2.4** οὐδεὶς   στρατευόμενος
SOLDIER OF CHRIST JESUS. NO ONE SERVING AS A SOLDIER

ἐμπλέκεται   ταῖς   τοῦ   βίου πραγματείαις,   ἵνα   τῷ
IS ENTANGLED WITH THE - AFFAIRS OF~[CIVILIAN] LIFE, THAT ²THE ONE

στρατολογήσαντι   ἀρέσῃ.   **2.5** ἐὰν   δὲ   καὶ
³HAVING ENLISTED [HIM] HE MAY PLEASE. AND~IF ALSO

ἀθλῇ τις,   οὐ στεφανοῦται   ἐὰν μὴ
ANYONE~COMPETES [AS AN ATHLETE], HE IS NOT CROWNED UNLESS

νομίμως ἀθλήσῃ.   **2.6** τὸν   κοπιῶντα γεωργὸν
HE COMPETES~ACCORDING TO THE RULES. ²THE ³LABORING ⁴FARMER

δεῖ   πρῶτον   τῶν   καρπῶν μεταλαμβάνειν.
¹IT IS NECESSARY [FOR] ⁵[TO BE THE] FIRST ⁷OF THE ⁸FRUITS ⁶TO PARTAKE.

2.7 νόει   ὃ   λέγω·   δώσει   γάρ   σοι   ὁ   κύριος
CONSIDER WHAT I SAY; ⁴WILL GIVE ¹FOR ⁵TO YOU ²THE ³LORD

σύνεσιν   ἐν   πᾶσιν.
UNDERSTANDING IN ALL THINGS.

2.8 Μνημόνευε   Ἰησοῦν   Χριστὸν   ἐγηγερμένον   ἐκ
REMEMBER JESUS CHRIST HAVING BEEN RAISED FROM

νεκρῶν,   ἐκ σπέρματος   Δαυίδ,   κατὰ   τὸ   εὐαγγέλιόν
[THE] DEAD, OF [THE] SEED OF DAVID, ACCORDING TO THE GOSPEL

μου,   **2.9** ἐν   ᾧ   κακοπαθῶ μέχρι   δεσμῶν
OF ME, IN(FOR) WHICH I SUFFER EVEN TO THE POINT OF BONDS(IMPRISONMENT)

ὡς   κακοῦργος,   ἀλλὰ   ὁ   λόγος   τοῦ   θεοῦ   οὐ δέδεται·
AS AN EVILDOER, BUT THE WORD - OF GOD HAS NOT BEEN BOUND;

2.10 διὰ   τοῦτο   πάντα   ὑπομένω   διὰ   τοὺς   ἐκλεκτούς,
THEREFORE ALL THINGS I ENDURE BECAUSE OF THE CHOSEN ONES,

ἵνα   καὶ   αὐτοὶ   σωτηρίας τύχωσιν   τῆς   ἐν   Χριστῷ
THAT ALSO THEY MAY OBTAIN~[THE] SALVATION - IN CHRIST

You then, my child, be strong in the grace that is in Christ Jesus; ²and what you have heard from me through many witnesses entrust to faithful people who will be able to teach others as well. ³Share in suffering like a good soldier of Christ Jesus. ⁴No one serving in the army gets entangled in everyday affairs; the soldier's aim is to please the enlisting officer. ⁵And in the case of an athlete, no one is crowned without competing according to the rules. ⁶It is the farmer who does the work who ought to have the first share of the crops. ⁷Think over what I say, for the Lord will give you understanding in all things.

8 Remember Jesus Christ, raised from the dead, a descendant of David—that is my gospel, ⁹for which I suffer hardship, even to the point of being chained like a criminal. But the word of God is not chained. ¹⁰Therefore I endure everything for the sake of the elect, so that they may also obtain the salvation that is in Christ

Jesus, with eternal glory. [11]The saying is sure:

> If we have died with
> him, we will also
> live with him;
> [12]if we endure, we will
> also reign with him;
> if we deny him, he will
> also deny us;
> [13]if we are faithless, he
> remains faithful—
> for he cannot deny
> himself.

14 Remind them of this, and warn them before God[d] that they are to avoid wrangling over words, which does no good but only ruins those who are listening. [15]Do your best to present yourself to God as one approved by him, a worker who has no need to be ashamed, rightly explaining the word of truth. [16]Avoid profane chatter, for it will lead people into more and more impiety, [17]and their talk will spread like gangrene. Among them are Hymenaeus and Philetus, [18]who have swerved from the truth by claiming that the resurrection has already taken place. They are upsetting the faith of some. [19]But God's firm foundation stands, bearing this inscription: "The Lord knows those who are his," and, "Let everyone who calls on the name of the Lord turn away from wickedness."

20 In a large house there are utensils not only of gold and silver but also of wood

[d] Other ancient authorities read the Lord

Ἰησοῦ μετὰ δόξης αἰωνίου. **2.11** πιστὸς ὁ λόγος·
JESUS   WITH   GLORY   ETERNAL.   TRUSTWORTHY [IS] THE   WORD:

εἰ γὰρ συναπεθάνομεν, καὶ συζήσομεν·
FOR~IF   WE DIED WITH [HIM],   ALSO   WE WILL LIVE WITH [HIM];

2.12 εἰ ὑπομένομεν, καὶ συμβασιλεύσομεν·
IF   WE ENDURE,   ALSO   WE WILL REIGN WITH [HIM];

εἰ ἀρνησόμεθα, κἀκεῖνος ἀρνήσεται ἡμᾶς·
IF   WE WILL DENY [HIM],   THAT ONE ALSO   WILL DENY   US;

2.13 εἰ ἀπιστοῦμεν, ἐκεῖνος πιστὸς μένει,
IF   WE ARE UNFAITHFUL,   THAT ONE   REMAINS~FAITHFUL,

ἀρνήσασθαι γὰρ ἑαυτὸν οὐ δύναται.
[3]TO DENY   [1]FOR   [4]HIMSELF   [2]HE IS NOT ABLE.

2.14 Ταῦτα ὑπομίμνησκε διαμαρτυρόμενος ἐνώπιον
THESE THINGS REMIND [THEM OF],   EARNESTLY TESTIFYING   BEFORE

⌜τοῦ θεοῦ⌝ μὴ λογομαχεῖν, ἐπ' οὐδὲν
-   GOD   NOT   TO BE ENGAGED IN DISPUTES OVER WORDS,   [2]FOR   [3]NOTHING

χρήσιμον, ἐπὶ καταστροφῇ τῶν ἀκουόντων.
[1]PROFITABLE,   TO   [THE] RUIN   OF THE ONES   HEARING.

2.15 σπούδασον σεαυτὸν δόκιμον παραστῆσαι τῷ θεῷ,
BE DILIGENT   [2]YOURSELF   [3]APPROVED   [1]TO PRESENT   -   [4]TO GOD,

ἐργάτην ἀνεπαίσχυντον, ὀρθοτομοῦντα τὸν λόγον
A WORKMAN   UNASHAMED,   [1]KEEPING [5][ON] A STRAIGHT COURSE   [2]THE   [3]MESSAGE

τῆς ἀληθείας. **2.16** τὰς δὲ βεβήλους κενοφωνίας
-   [4]OF TRUTH.   -   BUT   PROFANE,   EMPTY UTTERANCES

περιΐστασο· ἐπὶ πλεῖον γὰρ προκόψουσιν ἀσεβείας
AVOID;   [3]TO   [4]MORE   [1]FOR   [2]THEY WILL ADVANCE   [5]UNGODLINESS

2.17 καὶ ὁ λόγος αὐτῶν ὡς γάγγραινα
AND   THE   WORD   OF THEM   AS   GANGRENE

νομὴν ἕξει. ὧν ἐστιν Ὑμέναιος καὶ
WILL HAVE~A SPREADING [EFFECT];   OF WHOM   IS (ARE)   HYMENAEUS   AND

Φίλητος, **2.18** οἵτινες περὶ τὴν ἀλήθειαν ἠστόχησαν,
PHILETUS,   WHO   CONCERNING   THE   TRUTH   MISSED [THE] MARK,

λέγοντες [τὴν] ἀνάστασιν ἤδη γεγονέναι, καὶ
SAYING   THE   RESURRECTION   ALREADY   TO HAVE HAPPENED,   AND

ἀνατρέπουσιν τήν τινων πίστιν. **2.19** ὁ μέντοι
THEY ARE OVERTHROWING   THE   FAITH~OF SOME.   -   NEVERTHELESS

στερεὸς θεμέλιος τοῦ θεοῦ ἕστηκεν, ἔχων τὴν
[2]SOLID   [3]FOUNDATION   -   [1]GOD'S   HAS STOOD FIRM,   HAVING   -

σφραγῖδα ταύτην· Ἔγνω κύριος τοὺς ὄντας αὐτοῦ,
THIS~SEAL: [THE] LORD~KNOWS   THE ONES BEING   HIS,

καί, Ἀποστήτω ἀπὸ ἀδικίας πᾶς ὁ ὀνομάζων τὸ
AND,   LET DEPART   FROM   UNRIGHTEOUSNESS EVERYONE NAMING   THE

ὄνομα κυρίου. **2.20** Ἐν μεγάλῃ δὲ οἰκίᾳ οὐκ ἔστιν
NAME   OF [THE] LORD.   [2]IN   [3]A GREAT   [1]BUT   HOUSE   THERE ARE~NOT

μόνον σκεύη χρυσᾶ καὶ ἀργυρᾶ ἀλλὰ καὶ ξύλινα καὶ
ONLY   VESSELS   GOLDEN   AND   SILVER   BUT   ALSO   WOODEN   AND

2:14 text: ASVmg RSVmg NASB NIV NEB TEV NJB NRSV.   var. του κυριος (the Lord): KJV ASV RSV NJBmg NRSVmg.   **2:19** Num. 16:5

ὀστράκινα, καὶ ἃ μὲν εἰς τιμὴν ἃ δὲ εἰς
EARTHEN,   AND   SOME -   FOR HONOR[ABLE USE] BUT~OTHERS FOR

ἀτιμίαν· **2.21** ἐὰν οὖν τις ἐκκαθάρῃ ἑαυτὸν
DISHONOR[ABLE USE];   IF THEREFORE ANYONE CLEANSES   HIMSELF

ἀπὸ τούτων, ἔσται σκεῦος εἰς τιμήν,
FROM THESE THINGS, HE WILL BE A VESSEL FOR HONOR[ABLE USE],

ἡγιασμένον, εὔχρηστον τῷ δεσπότῃ, εἰς πᾶν
HAVING BEEN SANCTIFIED, USEFUL   TO THE MASTER,   FOR EVERY

ἔργον ἀγαθὸν ἡτοιμασμένον. **2.22** τὰς δὲ νεωτερικὰς
GOOD~WORK   HAVING BEEN PREPARED.   -   BUT YOUTHFUL

ἐπιθυμίας φεῦγε, δίωκε δὲ δικαιοσύνην πίστιν ἀγάπην
LUSTS   FLEE,   AND~PURSUE RIGHTEOUSNESS, FAITH,   LOVE,

εἰρήνην μετὰ τῶν ἐπικαλουμένων τὸν κύριον ἐκ
PEACE,   WITH THE ONES CALLING ON   THE LORD OUT FROM

καθαρᾶς καρδίας. **2.23** τὰς δὲ μωρὰς καὶ ἀπαιδεύτους
A CLEAN   HEART.   -   BUT FOOLISH AND IGNORANT

ζητήσεις παραιτοῦ, εἰδὼς ὅτι γεννῶσιν μάχας·
SPECULATIONS REFUSE,   KNOWING THAT THEY PRODUCE FIGHTS;

2.24 δοῦλον δὲ κυρίου οὐ δεῖ μάχεσθαι ἀλλὰ
      AND~A SLAVE OF [THE] LORD OUGHT~NOT TO FIGHT   BUT

ἤπιον εἶναι πρὸς πάντας, διδακτικόν, ἀνεξίκακον,
[OUGHT] TO BE~GENTLE TO   ALL,   SKILLED IN TEACHING, PATIENT,

2.25 ἐν πραΰτητι παιδεύοντα τοὺς ἀντιδιατιθεμένους,
      IN MEEKNESS   INSTRUCTING   THE ONES OPPOSING,

μήποτε δώῃ αὐτοῖς ὁ θεὸς μετάνοιαν εἰς
IF PERHAPS ²MAY GRANT ³THEM - ¹GOD REPENTANCE [RESULTING] IN

ἐπίγνωσιν ἀληθείας **2.26** καὶ ἀνανήψωσιν
ACKNOWLEDGMENT OF [THE] TRUTH,   AND THEY MAY COME TO [THEIR] SENSES

ἐκ τῆς τοῦ διαβόλου παγίδος, ἐζωγρημένοι ὑπ'
[AWAY] FROM ¹THE ³OF THE ⁴DEVIL   ²TRAP,   HAVING BEEN CAPTURED BY

αὐτοῦ εἰς τὸ ἐκείνου θέλημα.
HIM   FOR(IN) -   THAT ONE'S   WILL.

and clay, some for special use, some for ordinary. ²¹All who cleanse themselves of the things I have mentioned[e] will become special utensils, dedicated and useful to the owner of the house, ready for every good work. ²²Shun youthful passions and pursue righteousness, faith, love, and peace, along with those who call on the Lord from a pure heart. ²³Have nothing to do with stupid and senseless controversies; you know that they breed quarrels. ²⁴And the Lord's servant[f] must not be quarrelsome but kindly to everyone, an apt teacher, patient, ²⁵correcting opponents with gentleness. God may perhaps grant that they will repent and come to know the truth, ²⁶and that they may escape from the snare of the devil, having been held captive by him to do his will.[g]

[e] Gk *of these things*
[f] Gk *slave*
[g] Or *by him, to do his* (that is, God's) *will*

3.1 Τοῦτο δὲ γίνωσκε, ὅτι ἐν ἐσχάταις ἡμέραις
      BUT~THIS   KNOW,   THAT IN [THE] LAST   DAYS

ἐνστήσονται καιροὶ χαλεποί· **3.2** ἔσονται γὰρ οἱ
³WILL BE IMMINENT ²TIMES ¹HARD;   ³WILL BE ¹FOR -

ἄνθρωποι φίλαυτοι φιλάργυροι ἀλαζόνες ὑπερήφανοι
²MEN   LOVERS OF SELF, LOVERS OF MONEY, BOASTERS, PROUD,

βλάσφημοι, γονεῦσιν ἀπειθεῖς, ἀχάριστοι ἀνόσιοι
SPEAKERS OF EVIL, DISOBEDIENT TO~PARENTS, UNGRATEFUL, IRREVERENT,

3.3 ἄστοργοι ἄσπονδοι διάβολοι ἀκρατεῖς
      UNLOVING, IRRECONCILABLE, SLANDEROUS, WITHOUT SELF-CONTROL,

ἀνήμεροι ἀφιλάγαθοι **3.4** προδόται προπετεῖς
SAVAGE,   NOT LOVERS OF GOOD,   TREACHEROUS, RECKLESS,

You must understand this, that in the last days distressing times will come. ²For people will be lovers of themselves, lovers of money, boasters, arrogant, abusive, disobedient to their parents, ungrateful, unholy, ³inhuman, implacable, slanderers, profligates, brutes, haters of good, ⁴treacherous, reckless, swollen with conceit, lovers of pleasure rather than lovers of God, [5]holding to the outward form of godliness but denying its power. Avoid them! [6]For among them are those who make their way into households and captivate silly women, overwhelmed by their sins and swayed by all kinds of desires, [7]who are always being instructed and can never arrive at a knowledge of the truth. [8]As Jannes and Jambres opposed Moses, so these people, of corrupt mind and counterfeit faith, also oppose the truth. [9]But they will not make much progress, because, as in the case of those two men,[h] their folly will become plain to everyone.

10 Now you have observed my teaching, my conduct, my aim in life, my faith, my patience, my love, my steadfastness, [11]my persecutions, and my suffering the things that happened to me in Antioch, Iconium, and Lystra. What persecutions I endured! Yet the Lord rescued me from all of them. [12]Indeed, all who want to live a godly life in Christ Jesus will be persecuted. [13]But wicked people and impostors will go from bad to worse, deceiving others and being deceived. [14]But as for you, continue in what you have learned and firmly believed, knowing from whom you learned it, [15]and how from

[h] Gk lacks *two men*

τετυφωμένοι, φιλήδονοι μᾶλλον ἢ φιλόθεοι,
HAVING BECOME CONCEITED, LOVERS OF PLEASURE RATHER THAN LOVERS OF GOD,

3.5 ἔχοντες μόρφωσιν εὐσεβείας τὴν δὲ δύναμιν αὐτῆς
HAVING A FORM OF GODLINESS BUT~THE POWER OF IT

ἠρνημένοι· καὶ τούτους ἀποτρέπου. **3.6** ἐκ τούτων
HAVING DENIED; AND THESE ONES TURN AWAY FROM. [2]OF [3]THESE

γάρ εἰσιν οἱ ἐνδύνοντες εἰς τὰς οἰκίας καὶ
[1]FOR ARE THE ONES ENTERING INTO - HOMES AND

αἰχμαλωτίζοντες γυναικάρια σεσωρευμένα ἁμαρτίαις,
CAPTURING WEAK-WILLED WOMEN HAVING BEEN LADEN WITH SINS,

ἀγόμενα ἐπιθυμίαις ποικίλαις, **3.7** πάντοτε μανθάνοντα
BEING LED AWAY BY VARIOUS~LUSTS, ALWAYS LEARNING

καὶ μηδέποτε εἰς ἐπίγνωσιν ἀληθείας
AND NEVER TO A KNOWLEDGE OF TRUTH

ἐλθεῖν δυνάμενα. **3.8** ὃν τρόπον δὲ Ἰάννης καὶ
BEING ABLE~TO COME. [2]IN THE WAY [1]NOW JANNES AND

Ἰαμβρῆς ἀντέστησαν Μωϋσεῖ, οὕτως καὶ οὗτοι
JAMBRES OPPOSED MOSES, SO ALSO THESE ONES

ἀνθίστανται τῇ ἀληθείᾳ, ἄνθρωποι κατεφθαρμένοι
OPPOSE THE TRUTH, MEN HAVING BEEN CORRUPTED

τὸν νοῦν, ἀδόκιμοι περὶ τὴν πίστιν. **3.9** ἀλλ᾽
[IN] THE[IR] MIND, FAILURES WITH RESPECT TO THE FAITH; BUT

οὐ προκόψουσιν ἐπὶ πλεῖον· ἡ γὰρ ἄνοια αὐτῶν
THEY WILL NOT ADVANCE FARTHER; FOR~THE FOLLY OF THEM

ἔκδηλος ἔσται πᾶσιν, ὡς καὶ ἡ ἐκείνων ἐγένετο.
WILL BE~PLAIN TO ALL, AS ALSO THE [FOLLY] OF THOSE MEN BECAME.

3.10 Σὺ δὲ παρηκολούθησάς μου τῇ διδασκαλίᾳ, τῇ
BUT~YOU CLOSELY FOLLOWED MY - TEACHING, -

ἀγωγῇ, τῇ προθέσει, τῇ πίστει, τῇ μακροθυμίᾳ, τῇ
WAY OF LIFE, - PURPOSE, - FAITH, - LONGSUFFERING, -

ἀγάπῃ, τῇ ὑπομονῇ, **3.11** τοῖς διωγμοῖς, τοῖς
LOVE, - ENDURANCE, - PERSECUTIONS, -

παθήμασιν, οἷά μοι ἐγένετο ἐν Ἀντιοχείᾳ, ἐν Ἰκονίῳ,
SUFFERINGS, WHICH HAPPENED~TO ME IN ANTIOCH, IN ICONIUM,

ἐν Λύστροις, οἵους διωγμοὺς ὑπήνεγκα καὶ ἐκ
IN LYSTRA, WHAT KIND OF PERSECUTIONS I ENDURED, AND OUT OF

πάντων με ἐρρύσατο ὁ κύριος. **3.12** καὶ πάντες δὲ
ALL [4]ME [3]RESCUED [1]THE [2]LORD. [2]ALSO [3]ALL [1]AND

οἱ θέλοντες εὐσεβῶς ζῆν ἐν Χριστῷ Ἰησοῦ
THE ONES WANTING TO LIVE~GODLY IN CHRIST JESUS

διωχθήσονται. **3.13** πονηροὶ δὲ ἄνθρωποι καὶ γόητες
WILL BE PERSECUTED. BUT~EVIL MEN AND IMPOSTORS

προκόψουσιν ἐπὶ τὸ χεῖρον πλανῶντες καὶ πλανώμενοι.
WILL ADVANCE TO THE WORST, MISLEADING AND BEING MISLED.

3.14 σὺ δὲ μένε ἐν οἷς ἔμαθες καὶ ἐπιστώθης,
BUT~YOU REMAIN IN WHAT THINGS YOU LEARNED AND WERE CONVINCED OF,

εἰδὼς παρὰ τίνων ἔμαθες, **3.15** καὶ ὅτι ἀπὸ
KNOWING FROM WHOM° YOU LEARNED, AND THAT FROM

βρέφους   [τὰ] ἱερὰ γράμματα οἶδας,   τὰ
AN INFANT(INFANCY) THE HOLY SCRIPTURES YOU KNEW, THE ONES

δυνάμενά σε σοφίσαι εἰς   σωτηρίαν διὰ
BEING ABLE TO MAKE YOU WISE [WITH A VIEW] TO SALVATION THROUGH

πίστεως τῆς ἐν Χριστῷ Ἰησοῦ. **3.16** πᾶσα γραφὴ
FAITH   -   IN CHRIST JESUS.   ALL   SCRIPTURE

θεόπνευστος καὶ ὠφέλιμος πρὸς διδασκαλίαν, πρὸς
[IS] GOD-BREATHED AND USEFUL FOR TEACHING,   FOR

ἐλεγμόν, πρὸς ἐπανόρθωσιν, πρὸς παιδείαν τὴν ἐν
REPROOF, FOR CORRECTION,   FOR TRAINING   -   IN

δικαιοσύνῃ, **3.17** ἵνα ἄρτιος ᾖ   ὁ   τοῦ θεοῦ
RIGHTEOUSNESS, THAT ⁵PROFICIENT ⁴MAY BE ¹THE - ³OF GOD

ἄνθρωπος, πρὸς πᾶν ἔργον ἀγαθὸν ἐξηρτισμένος.
²MAN,   FOR EVERY GOOD~WORK HAVING BEEN EQUIPPED.

childhood you have known the sacred writings that are able to instruct you for salvation through faith in Christ Jesus. [16]All scripture is inspired by God and is[i] useful for teaching, for reproof, for correction, and for training in righteousness, [17]so that everyone who belongs to God may be proficient, equipped for every good work.

[i] Or *Every scripture inspired by God is also*

CHAPTER 4

4.1 Διαμαρτύρομαι ἐνώπιον τοῦ θεοῦ καὶ Χριστοῦ
I SOLEMNLY CHARGE [YOU] BEFORE - GOD AND CHRIST

Ἰησοῦ τοῦ   μέλλοντος κρίνειν ζῶντας καὶ νεκρούς,
JESUS, THE ONE BEING ABOUT TO JUDGE [THE] LIVING AND DEAD,

καὶ τὴν ἐπιφάνειαν αὐτοῦ καὶ τὴν βασιλείαν αὐτοῦ·
AND [BY] THE APPEARING OF HIM AND THE KINGDOM OF HIM:

4.2 κήρυξον τὸν λόγον, ἐπίστηθι εὐκαίρως ἀκαίρως,
PREACH THE WORD, BE READY IN SEASON, OUT OF SEASON,

ἔλεγξον, ἐπιτίμησον, παρακάλεσον, ἐν   πάσῃ
EXPOSE,   REBUKE,   ENCOURAGE,   WITH ALL

μακροθυμίᾳ καὶ διδαχῇ. **4.3** ἔσται γὰρ καιρὸς ὅτε τῆς
LONGSUFFERING AND TEACHING. FOR~THERE WILL BE A TIME WHEN -

ὑγιαινούσης διδασκαλίας οὐκ ἀνέξονται ἀλλὰ κατὰ
HEALTHY TEACHING THEY WILL NOT BEAR BUT ACCORDING TO

τὰς ἰδίας ἐπιθυμίας ἑαυτοῖς   ἐπισωρεύσουσιν
THE - LUSTS OF THEMSELVES WILL ACCUMULATE

διδασκάλους κνηθόμενοι τὴν ἀκοὴν **4.4** καὶ ἀπὸ μὲν
TEACHERS   TICKLING   THE EAR,   AND FROM -

τῆς ἀληθείας τὴν ἀκοὴν ἀποστρέψουσιν, ἐπὶ δὲ τοὺς
THE TRUTH   THE[IR] EAR THEY WILL TURN AWAY, AND~TO -

μύθους ἐκτραπήσονται. **4.5** σὺ δὲ νήφε   ἐν
MYTHS WILL BE TURNED ASIDE. BUT~YOU BE'SELF-CONTROLLED IN

πᾶσιν, κακοπάθησον, ἔργον ποίησον εὐαγγελιστοῦ, τὴν
ALL THINGS, SUFFER HARDSHIP, DO~[THE] WORK OF AN EVANGELIST, THE

διακονίαν σου πληροφόρησον.
MINISTRY OF YOU FULLY CARRY OUT.

4.6 Ἐγὼ γὰρ ἤδη   σπένδομαι,   καὶ ὁ καιρὸς τῆς
FOR~I ALREADY AM BEING POURED OUT, AND THE TIME OF THE

ἀναλύσεώς μου ἐφέστηκεν. **4.7** τὸν καλὸν ἀγῶνα
DEPARTURE OF ME HAS COME.   THE GOOD FIGHT

In the presence of God and of Christ Jesus, who is to judge the living and the dead, and in view of his appearing and his kingdom, I solemnly urge you: [2]proclaim the message; be persistent whether the time is favorable or unfavorable; convince, rebuke, and encourage, with the utmost patience in teaching. [3]For the time is coming when people will not put up with sound doctrine, but having itching ears, they will accumulate for themselves teachers to suit their own desires, [4]and will turn away from listening to the truth and wander away to myths. [5]As for you, always be sober, endure suffering, do the work of an evangelist, carry out your ministry fully.

6 As for me, I am already being poured out as a libation, and the time of my departure has come. [7]I have fought the good fight,

I have finished the race, I have kept the faith. ⁸From now on there is reserved for me the crown of righteousness, which the Lord, the righteous judge, will give me on that day, and not only to me but also to all who have longed for his appearing.

9 Do your best to come to me soon, ¹⁰for Demas, in love with this present world, has deserted me and gone to Thessalonica; Crescens has gone to Galatia,ʲ Titus to Dalmatia. ¹¹Only Luke is with me. Get Mark and bring him with you, for he is useful in my ministry. ¹²I have sent Tychicus to Ephesus. ¹³When you come, bring the cloak that I left with Carpus at Troas, also the books, and above all the parchments. ¹⁴Alexander the coppersmith did me great harm; the Lord will pay him back for his deeds. ¹⁵You also must beware of him, for he strongly opposed our message.

16 At my first defense no one came to my support, but all deserted me. May it not be counted against them! ¹⁷But the Lord stood by me and gave me strength, so that through me the message might be fully proclaimed and all the Gentiles might hear it. So I was rescued from the lion's mouth. ¹⁸The Lord will rescue me

ʲ Other ancient authorities read *Gaul*

ἠγώνισμαι, τὸν δρόμον τετέλεκα, τὴν πίστιν τετήρηκα·
I HAVE FOUGHT, THE COURSE I HAVE FINISHED, THE FAITH I HAVE KEPT;

4.8 λοιπὸν ἀπόκειταί μοι ὁ τῆς δικαιοσύνης
HENCEFORTH, THERE IS LAID UP FOR ME ¹THE - ³OF RIGHTEOUSNESS

στέφανος, ὃν ἀποδώσει μοι ὁ κύριος ἐν ἐκείνῃ τῇ
²CROWN(WREATH), WHICH ³WILL GIVE ⁴TO ME ¹THE ²LORD IN THAT -

ἡμέρᾳ, ὁ δίκαιος κριτής, οὐ μόνον δὲ ἐμοὶ ἀλλὰ
DAY, THE RIGHTEOUS JUDGE, ²NOT ³ONLY ¹AND TO ME BUT

καὶ πᾶσι τοῖς ἠγαπηκόσι τὴν ἐπιφάνειαν αὐτοῦ.
ALSO TO ALL THE ONES HAVING LOVED THE APPEARING OF HIM.

4.9 Σπούδασον ἐλθεῖν πρός με ταχέως·
BE DILIGENT TO COME TO ME QUICKLY;

4.10 Δημᾶς γάρ με ἐγκατέλιπεν ἀγαπήσας τὸν νῦν
FOR~DEMAS FORSOOK~ME, HAVING LOVED THE NOW(PRESENT)

αἰῶνα καὶ ἐπορεύθη εἰς Θεσσαλονίκην, Κρήσκης εἰς
AGE AND WENT TO THESSALONICA, CRESCENS TO

Γαλατίαν, Τίτος εἰς Δαλματίαν· **4.11** Λουκᾶς
GALATIA, TITUS TO DALMATIA; LUKE

ἐστιν μόνος μετ' ἐμοῦ. Μᾶρκον ἀναλαβὼν ἄγε μετὰ
ALONE~IS WITH ME. HAVING TAKEN~MARK, BRING WITH

σεαυτοῦ, ἔστιν γάρ μοι εὔχρηστος εἰς διακονίαν.
YOURSELF, FOR~HE IS USEFUL~TO ME FOR SERVICE.

4.12 Τυχικὸν δὲ ἀπέστειλα εἰς Ἔφεσον. **4.13** τὸν
NOW~TYCHICUS I SENT TO EPHESUS. THE

φαιλόνην ὃν ἀπέλιπον ἐν Τρῳάδι παρὰ Κάρπῳ
CLOAK WHICH I LEFT BEHIND IN TROAS WITH CARPUS

ἐρχόμενος φέρε, καὶ τὰ βιβλία μάλιστα τὰς
[WHEN] COMING BRING, AND THE SCROLLS, ESPECIALLY THE

μεμβράνας. **4.14** Ἀλέξανδρος ὁ χαλκεὺς πολλά μοι
PARCHMENTS. ALEXANDER THE COPPERSMITH ²MANY ⁴TO ME

κακὰ ἐνεδείξατο· ἀποδώσει αὐτῷ ὁ κύριος
³EVIL THINGS ¹DID; ³WILL REPAY ⁴HIM ¹THE ²LORD

κατὰ τὰ ἔργα αὐτοῦ· **4.15** ὃν καὶ σὺ φυλάσσου,
ACCORDING TO THE WORKS OF HIM; WHOM ALSO YOU WATCH [OUT FOR],

λίαν γὰρ ἀντέστη τοῖς ἡμετέροις λόγοις.
FOR~GREATLY HE OPPOSED - OUR WORDS.

4.16 Ἐν τῇ πρώτῃ μου ἀπολογίᾳ οὐδείς
IN(AT) - MY~FIRST DEFENSE NO ONE

μοι παρεγένετο, ἀλλὰ πάντες με ἐγκατέλιπον· μὴ
CAME TO BE~WITH ME BUT ALL FORSOOK~ME; NOT

αὐτοῖς λογισθείη· **4.17** ὁ δὲ κύριός μοι παρέστη
AGAINST THEM MAY IT BE COUNTED; BUT~THE LORD STOOD WITH~ME

καὶ ἐνεδυνάμωσέν με, ἵνα δι' ἐμοῦ τὸ κήρυγμα
AND EMPOWERED ME, THAT THROUGH ME THE PROCLAMATION

πληροφορηθῇ καὶ ἀκούσωσιν πάντα τὰ ἔθνη, καὶ
MIGHT BE FULLY MADE, AND ⁴MIGHT HEAR [IT] ¹ALL ²THE ³GENTILES, AND

ἐρρύσθην ἐκ στόματος λέοντος. **4.18** ῥύσεταί με ὁ
I WAS RESCUED OUT OF A LION'S~MOUTH. ³WILL RESCUE ⁴ME ¹THE

κύριος ἀπὸ παντὸς ἔργου πονηροῦ καὶ σώσει
²LORD   FROM EVERY   EVIL~WORK   AND WILL BRING [ME] SAFELY

εἰς τὴν βασιλείαν αὐτοῦ τὴν ἐπουράνιον· ᾧ   ἡ
INTO THE ³KINGDOM   ¹HIS -   ²HEAVENLY;   TO WHOM [BE] THE

δόξα εἰς τοὺς αἰῶνας τῶν αἰώνων, ἀμήν.
GLORY INTO THE AGES OF THE AGES,   AMEN.

4.19 Ἄσπασαι Πρίσκαν καὶ Ἀκύλαν καὶ τὸν
          GREET   PRISCA   AND AQUILA AND -

Ὀνησιφόρου οἶκον. **4.20** Ἔραστος ἔμεινεν ἐν Κορίνθῳ,
ONESIPHORUS' HOUSEHOLD.   ERASTUS   REMAINED IN CORINTH,

Τρόφιμον δὲ ἀπέλιπον ἐν Μιλήτῳ ἀσθενοῦντα.
BUT~TROPHIMUS I LEFT BEHIND IN MILETUS AILING.

4.21 Σπούδασον πρὸ χειμῶνος ἐλθεῖν. Ἀσπάζεταί σε
          MAKE HASTE BEFORE WINTER TO COME. GREETS   YOU

Εὔβουλος καὶ Πούδης καὶ Λίνος καὶ Κλαυδία καὶ οἱ
EUBULUS   AND PUDENS AND LINUS AND CLAUDIA AND ²THE

ἀδελφοὶ πάντες. **4.22** Ὁ κύριος μετὰ τοῦ πνεύματός
³BROTHERS ¹ALL.   THE LORD [BE] WITH THE SPIRIT

σου. ἡ χάρις μεθ᾽ ὑμῶν.
OF YOU. - GRACE [BE] WITH YOU°.

from every evil attack and save me for his heavenly kingdom. To him be the glory forever and ever. Amen.

19 Greet Prisca and Aquila, and the household of Onesiphorus. [20]Erastus remained in Corinth; Trophimus I left ill in Miletus. [21]Do your best to come before winter. Eubulus sends greetings to you, as do Pudens and Linus and Claudia and all the brothers and sisters.[k]

22 The Lord be with your spirit. Grace be with you.[l]

[k] Gk *all the brothers*
[l] The Greek word for *you* here is plural. Other ancient authorities add *Amen*

THE LETTER OF PAUL TO
TITUS

ΠΡΟΣ ΤΙΤΟΝ
TO   TITUS

1.1 Παῦλος δοῦλος θεοῦ, ἀπόστολος δὲ Ἰησοῦ Χριστοῦ
PAUL   A SLAVE   OF GOD, AND~AN APOSTLE   OF JESUS   CHRIST

κατὰ   πίστιν ἐκλεκτῶν   θεοῦ καὶ ἐπίγνωσιν
ACCORDING TO [THE] FAITH OF [THE] CHOSEN ONES OF GOD AND   KNOWLEDGE

ἀληθείας τῆς κατ'   εὐσέβειαν **1.2** ἐπ'   ἐλπίδι
OF TRUTH   -   ACCORDING TO GODLINESS,   [BASED] ON A HOPE

ζωῆς αἰωνίου, ἣν   ἐπηγγείλατο ὁ   ἀψευδὴς θεὸς πρὸ
OF LIFE ETERNAL, WHICH ⁴PROMISED   ¹THE ²TRUTHFUL ³GOD BEFORE

χρόνων αἰωνίων, **1.3** ἐφανέρωσεν δὲ καιροῖς ἰδίοις τὸν
[THE] AGES~OF TIME,   BUT~MANIFESTED   IN ITS OWN~TIMES   THE

λόγον αὐτοῦ ἐν κηρύγματι, ὃ   ἐπιστεύθην ἐγὼ
WORD   OF HIM IN(BY) PROCLAMATION, WHICH I~WAS ENTRUSTED WITH

κατ'   ἐπιταγὴν τοῦ σωτῆρος ἡμῶν θεοῦ, **1.4** Τίτῳ
ACCORDING TO [THE] COMMAND OF THE SAVIOR OF US, GOD,   TO TITUS,

γνησίῳ τέκνῳ κατὰ   κοινὴν   πίστιν, χάρις καὶ
[MY] TRUE CHILD ACCORDING TO A COMMON(SHARED) FAITH, GRACE AND

εἰρήνη ἀπὸ θεοῦ πατρὸς καὶ Χριστοῦ Ἰησοῦ τοῦ
PEACE FROM GOD [THE] FATHER AND CHRIST   JESUS THE

σωτῆρος ἡμῶν.
SAVIOR   OF US.

1.5 Τούτου χάριν ἀπέλιπόν σε ἐν Κρήτῃ, ἵνα τὰ
[FOR] THIS CAUSE I LEFT   YOU IN CRETE, THAT THE THINGS

λείποντα ἐπιδιορθώσῃ   καὶ καταστήσῃς κατὰ πόλιν
LACKING YOU SHOULD SET RIGHT AND SHOULD APPOINT IN EVERY CITY

πρεσβυτέρους, ὡς ἐγώ σοι διεταξάμην, **1.6** εἴ τίς
ELDERS,   AS I   ORDERED~YOU,   IF ANYONE

ἐστιν ἀνέγκλητος, μιᾶς γυναικὸς ἀνήρ, τέκνα ἔχων
IS   BLAMELESS,   ²OF ONE ³WIFE ¹A HUSBAND, ³CHILDREN ¹HAVING

πιστά, μὴ ἐν   κατηγορίᾳ ἀσωτίας ἢ ἀνυπότακτα.
²BELIEVING NOT IN(UNDER) ACCUSATION OF DEBAUCHERY OR INSUBORDINATION.

1.7 δεῖ γὰρ   τὸν ἐπίσκοπον ἀνέγκλητον εἶναι
FOR~IT IS NECESSARY [FOR] THE OVERSEER   TO BE~BLAMELESS

ὡς θεοῦ οἰκονόμον, μὴ αὐθάδη, μὴ ὀργίλον,   μὴ
AS GOD'S STEWARD,   NOT ARROGANT, NOT QUICK-TEMPERED, NOT

πάροινον,   μὴ πλήκτην, μὴ αἰσχροκερδῆ, **1.8** ἀλλὰ
GIVEN TO MUCH WINE, NOT VIOLENT, NOT FOND OF DISHONEST GAIN, BUT

φιλόξενον φιλάγαθον σώφρονα δίκαιον ὅσιον ἐγκρατῆ,
HOSPITABLE, A LOVER OF GOOD, SENSIBLE, JUST, HOLY, SELF-CONTROLED,

Paul, a servant[a] of God and an apostle of Jesus Christ, for the sake of the faith of God's elect and the knowledge of the truth that is in accordance with godliness, [2]in the hope of eternal life that God, who never lies, promised before the ages began — [3]in due time he revealed his word through the proclamation with which I have been entrusted by the command of God our Savior,

4 To Titus, my loyal child in the faith we share:

Grace[b] and peace from God the Father and Christ Jesus our Savior.

5 I left you behind in Crete for this reason, so that you should put in order what remained to be done, and should appoint elders in every town, as I directed you: [6]someone who is blameless, married only once,[c] whose children are believers, not accused of debauchery and not rebellious. [7]For a bishop,[d] as God's steward, must be blameless; he must not be arrogant or quick-tempered or addicted to wine or violent or greedy for gain; [8]but he must be hospitable, a lover of goodness, prudent, upright, devout, and self-controlled.

---

[a] Gk slave
[b] Other ancient authorities read Grace, mercy,
[c] Gk husband of one wife
[d] Or an overseer

⁹He must have a firm grasp of the word that is trustworthy in accordance with the teaching, so that he may be able both to preach with sound doctrine and to refute those who contradict it.

10 There are also many rebellious people, idle talkers and deceivers, especially those of the circumcision; ¹¹they must be silenced, since they are upsetting whole families by teaching for sordid gain what it is not right to teach. ¹²It was one of them, their very own prophet, who said,

"Cretans are always liars, vicious brutes, lazy gluttons."

¹³That testimony is true. For this reason rebuke them sharply, so that they may become sound in the faith, ¹⁴not paying attention to Jewish myths or to commandments of those who reject the truth. ¹⁵To the pure all things are pure, but to the corrupt and unbelieving nothing is pure. Their very minds and consciences are corrupted. ¹⁶They profess to know God, but they deny him by their actions. They are detestable, disobedient, unfit for any good work.

1.9 ἀντεχόμενον τοῦ κατὰ τὴν διδαχὴν πιστοῦ
HOLDING TO   THE   ³ACCORDING TO ⁴THE ⁵TEACHING ¹FAITHFUL

λόγου, ἵνα δυνατὸς ᾖ καὶ παρακαλεῖν ἐν τῇ
²WORD,   THAT HE MAY BE~ABLE ALSO TO ENCOURAGE BY THE

διδασκαλίᾳ τῇ ὑγιαινούσῃ καὶ τοὺς ἀντιλέγοντας
²TEACHING   -   ¹HEALTHY   AND ²THE ONES ³OPPOSING

ἐλέγχειν.
¹TO EXPOSE.

1.10 Εἰσὶν γὰρ πολλοὶ [καὶ] ἀνυπότακτοι,
FOR~THERE ARE MANY INDEED OPPOSING ONES,

ματαιολόγοι καὶ φρεναπάται, μάλιστα οἱ ἐκ τῆς
IDLE TALKERS AND DECEIVERS,   ESPECIALLY THE ONES OF THE

περιτομῆς, **1.11** οὓς δεῖ ἐπιστομίζειν, οἵτινες
CIRCUMCISION,   WHOM IT IS NECESSARY TO STOP THE MOUTHS OF, WHO

ὅλους οἴκους ἀνατρέπουσιν διδάσκοντες ἃ
ENTIRE HOUSEHOLDS OVERTURN,   TEACHING   WHAT

μὴ δεῖ αἰσχροῦ κέρδους χάριν. **1.12** εἶπέν
[THEY OUGHT~NOT, ²DISHONEST ³GAIN ¹FOR [THE] SAKE OF.   SAID

τις ἐξ αὐτῶν ἴδιος αὐτῶν προφήτης,
A CERTAIN ONE OF THEM, ³OWN ²OF THEIR ¹A PROPHET,

Κρῆτες ἀεὶ ψεῦσται, κακὰ θηρία,
CRETANS [ARE] ALWAYS LIARS,   WICKED BEASTS,

γαστέρες ἀργαί.
LAZY~GLUTTONS.

1.13 ἡ μαρτυρία αὕτη ἐστὶν ἀληθής. δι᾽ ἣν αἰτίαν
-   THIS~TESTIMONY IS TRUE.   FOR WHICH CAUSE

ἔλεγχε αὐτοὺς ἀποτόμως, ἵνα ὑγιαίνωσιν ἐν τῇ
REPROVE THEM   SEVERELY,   THAT THEY MAY BE HEALTHY IN THE

πίστει, **1.14** μὴ προσέχοντες Ἰουδαϊκοῖς μύθοις καὶ
FAITH,   NOT PAYING ATTENTION TO JEWISH   MYTHS AND

ἐντολαῖς ἀνθρώπων ἀποστρεφομένων τὴν ἀλήθειαν.
COMMANDMENTS OF MEN   TURNING AWAY FROM   THE TRUTH.

1.15 πάντα καθαρὰ τοῖς καθαροῖς· τοῖς δὲ
ALL THINGS [ARE] PURE TO THE PURE;   BUT~TO THE ONES

μεμιαμμένοις καὶ ἀπίστοις οὐδὲν καθαρόν, ἀλλὰ
HAVING BEEN DEFILED AND UNBELIEVING ONES NOTHING [IS] PURE, BUT

μεμίανται αὐτῶν καὶ ὁ νοῦς καὶ ἡ συνείδησις.
HAS BEEN DEFILED BOTH~THEIR - MIND AND THE[IR] CONSCIENCE.

1.16 θεὸν ὁμολογοῦσιν εἰδέναι, τοῖς δὲ ἔργοις
³GOD ¹THEY PROFESS ²TO KNOW, BUT~BY THE[IR] WORKS

ἀρνοῦνται, βδελυκτοὶ ὄντες καὶ ἀπειθεῖς καὶ πρὸς
THEY DENY [HIM], BEING~DETESTABLE AND DISOBEDIENT AND AS TO

πᾶν ἔργον ἀγαθὸν ἀδόκιμοι.
EVERY GOOD~WORK   UNFIT.

2.1 Σὺ δὲ λάλει ἃ   πρέπει   τῇ ὑγιαινούσῃ
BUT~YOU, SPEAK THE THINGS WHICH ARE SUITABLE -   TO HEALTHY

διδασκαλίᾳ. **2.2** πρεσβύτας νηφαλίους εἶναι, σεμνούς,
TEACHING.   AGED MEN [NEED] TO BE~TEMPERATE, RESPECTABLE,

σώφρονας, ὑγιαίνοντας τῇ   πίστει, τῇ ἀγάπῃ, τῇ
SENSIBLE, BEING HEALTHY IN THE FAITH, - IN LOVE, -

ὑπομονῇ· **2.3** πρεσβύτιδας ὡσαύτως ἐν καταστήματι
IN ENDURANCE; AGED WOMEN SIMILARLY IN BEHAVIOR

ἱεροπρεπεῖς, μὴ διαβόλους μὴ οἴνῳ   πολλῷ
AS BEFITS HOLINESS, NOT SLANDERERS NOR 2TO 4WINE 3MUCH

δεδουλωμένας, καλοδιδασκάλους, **2.4** ἵνα σωφρονίζωσιν
1HAVING BEEN ENSLAVED, TEACHERS OF GOOD, THAT THEY MAY ENCOURAGE

τὰς νέας   φιλάνδρους εἶναι,   φιλοτέκνους
THE YOUNG WOMEN TO BE~LOVERS OF [THEIR] HUSBANDS, LOVERS OF [THEIR] CHILDREN,

2.5 σώφρονας ἁγνὰς οἰκουργοὺς ἀγαθάς, ὑποτασσομένας
SENSIBLE, PURE, WORKERS AT HOME, GOOD, BEING SUBJECT

τοῖς ἰδίοις ἀνδράσιν, ἵνα μὴ ὁ λόγος τοῦ θεοῦ
TO THE[IR] OWN HUSBANDS, LEST THE WORD - OF GOD

βλασφημῆται. **2.6** τοὺς νεωτέρους ὡσαύτως παρακάλει
BE EVIL SPOKEN OF. THE YOUNGER MEN SIMILARLY EXHORT

σωφρονεῖν **2.7** περὶ πάντα, σεαυτὸν παρεχόμενος τύπον
TO BE SENSIBLE ABOUT ALL THINGS, SHOWING~YOURSELF A MODEL

καλῶν ἔργων, ἐν τῇ διδασκαλίᾳ ἀφθορίαν, σεμνότητα,
OF GOOD WORKS, IN THE TEACHING [SHOW] INTEGRITY, SERIOUSNESS,

2.8 λόγον ὑγιῆ ἀκατάγνωστον, ἵνα ὁ   ἐξ
HEALTHY~SPEECH BEYOND REPROACH, THAT THE ONE OF

ἐναντίας   ἐντραπῇ μηδὲν ἔχων λέγειν περὶ ἡμῶν
[THE] OPPOSING [SIDE] MAY BE SHAMED 2NOTHING 1HAVING 4TO SAY 5ABOUT 6US

φαῦλον. **2.9** δούλους ἰδίοις δεσπόταις ὑποτάσσεσθαι
3BAD.   SLAVES TO THE[IR] OWN MASTERS [NEED] TO BE SUBJECT

ἐν πᾶσιν, εὐαρέστους εἶναι, μὴ ἀντιλέγοντας, **2.10** μὴ
IN EVERYTHING, TO BE~WELL-PLEASING, NOT TALKING BACK, NOT

νοσφιζομένους, ἀλλὰ πᾶσαν πίστιν ἐνδεικνυμένους
PILFERING, BUT 2ALL 4FIDELITY 1DEMONSTRATING

ἀγαθήν, ἵνα τὴν διδασκαλίαν τὴν τοῦ   σωτῆρος ἡμῶν
2GOOD, THAT 4THE 5TEACHING - 6OF THE 7SAVIOR 8OF US,

θεοῦ κοσμῶσιν ἐν πᾶσιν.
9GOD, 1THEY MAY ADORN 2IN 3ALL THINGS.

2.11 Ἐπεφάνη γὰρ ἡ   χάρις τοῦ θεοῦ
5APPEARED 1FOR 2THE 3GRACE - 4OF GOD

σωτήριος   πᾶσιν ἀνθρώποις **2.12** παιδεύουσα
6[THAT WHICH BRINGS] SALVATION TO ALL MEN, INSTRUCTING

ἡμᾶς, ἵνα ἀρνησάμενοι τὴν ἀσέβειαν καὶ τὰς
US, THAT HAVING DENIED - UNGODLINESS AND -

κοσμικὰς ἐπιθυμίας σωφρόνως καὶ δικαίως καὶ
WORLDLY DESIRES, 2SENSIBLY 3AND 4RIGHTEOUSLY 5AND

But as for you, teach what is consistent with sound doctrine. [2]Tell the older men to be temperate, serious, prudent, and sound in faith, in love, and in endurance.

3 Likewise, tell the older women to be reverent in behavior, not to be slanderers or slaves to drink; they are to teach what is good, [4]so that they may encourage the young women to love their husbands, to love their children, [5]to be self-controlled, chaste, good managers of the household, kind, being submissive to their husbands, so that the word of God may not be discredited.

6 Likewise, urge the younger men to be self-controlled. [7]Show yourself in all respects a model of good works, and in your teaching show integrity, gravity, [8]and sound speech that cannot be censured; then any opponent will be put to shame, having nothing evil to say of us.

9 Tell slaves to be submissive to their masters and to give satisfaction in every respect; they are not to talk back, [10]not to pilfer, but to show complete and perfect fidelity, so that in everything they may be an ornament to the doctrine of God our Savior.

11 For the grace of God has appeared, bringing salvation to all,[e] [12]training us to renounce impiety and worldly passions, and in the present age to live lives that are self-controlled, upright,

[e] Or *has appeared to all, bringing salvation*

and godly, [13]while we wait for the blessed hope and the manifestation of the glory of our great God and Savior,[f] Jesus Christ. [14]He it is who gave himself for us that he might redeem us from all iniquity and purify for himself a people of his own who are zealous for good deeds.

15 Declare these things; exhort and reprove with all authority.[g] Let no one look down on you.

[f] Or *of the great God and our Savior*
[g] Gk *commandment*

εὐσεβῶς ζήσωμεν ἐν τῷ νῦν αἰῶνι,
[6]GODLY [1]WE SHOULD LIVE IN THE NOW(PRESENT) AGE,

2.13 προσδεχόμενοι τὴν μακαρίαν ἐλπίδα καὶ
AWAITING THE BLESSED HOPE AND

ἐπιφάνειαν τῆς δόξης τοῦ μεγάλου θεοῦ καὶ σωτῆρος
APPEARING OF THE GLORY OF THE GREAT GOD AND SAVIOR

ἡμῶν Ἰησοῦ Χριστοῦ, **2.14** ὃς ἔδωκεν ἑαυτὸν ὑπὲρ
OF US, JESUS CHRIST, WHO GAVE HIMSELF ON BEHALF OF

ἡμῶν ἵνα λυτρώσηται ἡμᾶς ἀπὸ πάσης ἀνομίας καὶ
US THAT HE MIGHT REDEEM US FROM ALL LAWLESSNESS AND

καθαρίσῃ ἑαυτῷ λαὸν περιούσιον, ζηλωτὴν
MIGHT CLEANSE(PURIFY) FOR HIMSELF A PEOPLE [AS HIS] POSSESSION, ZEALOUS

καλῶν ἔργων. **2.15** Ταῦτα λάλει καὶ παρακάλει καὶ
OF GOOD WORKS. THESE THINGS SPEAK, AND ENCOURAGE AND

ἔλεγχε μετὰ πάσης ἐπιταγῆς· μηδείς σου
REPROVE WITH EVERY COMMAND; [2]NO ONE [4]YOU

περιφρονείτω.
[1]LET [3]DISREGARD.

CHAPTER 3

Remind them to be subject to rulers and authorities, to be obedient, to be ready for every good work, [2]to speak evil of no one, to avoid quarreling, to be gentle, and to show every courtesy to everyone. [3]For we ourselves were once foolish, disobedient, led astray, slaves to various passions and pleasures, passing our days in malice and envy, despicable, hating one another. [4]But when the goodness and loving-kindness of God our Savior appeared, [5]he saved us, not because of any works of righteousness that we had done, but according to his mercy, through the water[h] of rebirth and renewal by the Holy Spirit.

[h] Gk *washing*

3.1 Ὑπομίμνησκε αὐτοὺς ἀρχαῖς ἐξουσίαις
REMIND THEM [2]TO RULERS, [3]TO AUTHORITIES,

ὑποτάσσεσθαι, πειθαρχεῖν, πρὸς πᾶν ἔργον ἀγαθὸν
[1]TO BE SUBJECT, TO BE OBEDIENT, [3]FOR [4]EVERY [6]WORK [5]GOOD

ἑτοίμους εἶναι, **3.2** μηδένα βλασφημεῖν,
[2]READY [1]TO BE, NO ONE TO SPEAK EVIL OF,

ἀμάχους εἶναι, ἐπιεικεῖς, πᾶσαν ἐνδεικνυμένους
TO BE~NOT QUARRELSOME, GENTLE, DISPLAYING~ALL

πραΰτητα πρὸς πάντας ἀνθρώπους. **3.3** Ἦμεν γάρ ποτε
MEEKNESS TO ALL MEN. [3]WERE [1]FOR [5]ONCE

καὶ ἡμεῖς ἀνόητοι, ἀπειθεῖς, πλανώμενοι, δουλεύοντες
[4]ALSO [2]WE FOOLISH, DISOBEDIENT, BEING LED ASTRAY, BEING SLAVES

ἐπιθυμίαις καὶ ἡδοναῖς ποικίλαις, ἐν κακίᾳ καὶ
[2]LUSTS [3]AND [4]PLEASURES [1]TO VARIOUS, IN MALICE AND

φθόνῳ διάγοντες, στυγητοί, μισοῦντες ἀλλήλους.
ENVY SPENDING [OUR] LIVES, HATED, HATING ONE ANOTHER.

3.4 ὅτε δὲ ἡ χρηστότης καὶ ἡ φιλανθρωπία ἐπεφάνη
BUT~WHEN THE KINDNESS AND THE LOVE TO MAN [3]APPEARED

τοῦ σωτῆρος ἡμῶν θεοῦ, **3.5** οὐκ ἐξ ἔργων τῶν ἐν
- [1]OF OUR~SAVIOR [2]GOD, NOT BY WORKS - [4]IN

δικαιοσύνῃ ἃ ἐποιήσαμεν ἡμεῖς ἀλλὰ κατὰ τὸ
[5]RIGHTEOUSNESS [1]WHICH [3]DID [2]WE BUT ACCORDING TO -

αὐτοῦ ἔλεος ἔσωσεν ἡμᾶς διὰ λουτροῦ
HIS MERCY HE SAVED US THROUGH [THE] WASHING

παλιγγενεσίας καὶ ἀνακαινώσεως πνεύματος ἁγίου,
OF REGENERATION AND RENEWING OF [THE] HOLY~SPIRIT,

3.6 οὗ   ἐξέχεεν   ἐφ' ἡμᾶς πλουσίως διὰ   Ἰησοῦ
WHICH HE POURED OUT ON   US   RICHLY   THROUGH JESUS

Χριστοῦ τοῦ σωτῆρος ἡμῶν, **3.7** ἵνα δικαιωθέντες τῇ
CHRIST, THE SAVIOR   OF US,   THAT HAVING BEEN JUSTIFIED -

ἐκείνου χάριτι κληρονόμοι γενηθῶμεν κατ'   ἐλπίδα
BY THAT ONE'S GRACE, WE MIGHT BECOME~HEIRS   ACCORDING TO [THE] HOPE

ζωῆς αἰωνίου.
OF LIFE ETERNAL.

3.8 Πιστὸς   ὁ   λόγος· καὶ   περὶ   τούτων
TRUSTWORTHY [IS] THE WORD;   AND CONCERNING THESE THINGS

βούλομαί σε διαβεβαιοῦσθαι, ἵνα φροντίζωσιν καλῶν
I COUNSEL YOU TO STRONGLY AFFIRM [THEM], THAT ⁴MAY TAKE THOUGHT ⁶GOOD

ἔργων προΐστασθαι οἱ   πεπιστευκότες θεῷ·
⁷WORKS ⁵TO BE INVOLVED WITH ¹THE ONES ²HAVING BELIEVED ³GOD;

ταῦτά   ἐστιν καλὰ καὶ ὠφέλιμα τοῖς ἀνθρώποις.
THESE THINGS ARE GOOD AND PROFITABLE -   TO MEN.

3.9 μωρὰς δὲ ζητήσεις καὶ γενεαλογίας καὶ ἔρεις
BUT~FOOLISH CONTROVERSIES AND GENEALOGIES AND QUARRELS

καὶ μάχας νομικὰς περιΐστασο· εἰσὶν γὰρ
AND FIGHTS [ABOUT THE] LAW AVOID;   FOR~THEY ARE

ἀνωφελεῖς καὶ μάταιοι. **3.10** αἱρετικὸν ἄνθρωπον μετὰ
UNPROFITABLE AND FUTILE.   A DIVISIVE   MAN   AFTER

μίαν καὶ δευτέραν νουθεσίαν παραιτοῦ, **3.11** εἰδὼς ὅτι
ONE AND A SECOND WARNING   AVOID,   KNOWING THAT

ἐξέστραπται ὁ τοιοῦτος καὶ ἁμαρτάνει ὢν
²HAS BEEN PERVERTED - ¹SUCH A MAN AND SINS,   BEING

αὐτοκατάκριτος.
SELF-CONDEMNED.

3.12 Ὅταν πέμψω Ἀρτεμᾶν πρὸς σὲ ἢ Τύχικον,
WHEN I WILL SEND ARTEMAS TO   YOU OR TYCHICUS,

σπούδασον ἐλθεῖν πρός με εἰς Νικόπολιν, ἐκεῖ γὰρ
MAKE HASTE TO COME TO ME IN NICOPOLIS, FOR~THERE

κέκρικα παραχειμάσαι. **3.13** Ζηνᾶν τὸν νομικὸν καὶ
I HAVE DECIDED TO SPEND [THE] WINTER. ZENAS THE LAWYER AND

Ἀπολλῶν σπουδαίως πρόπεμψον, ἵνα μηδὲν
APOLLOS EAGERLY   SEND FORTH, THAT NOTHING

αὐτοῖς λείπῃ. **3.14** μανθανέτωσαν δὲ καὶ οἱ
MAY BE LACKING~FOR THEM. ²LET ⁴LEARN ¹AND ⁵ALSO -

ἡμέτεροι καλῶν ἔργων προΐστασθαι εἰς   τὰς
³OUR OWN [PEOPLE] ⁷GOOD ⁸WORKS ⁶TO BE CONCERNED ABOUT FOR [SUPPLYING] THE

ἀναγκαίας χρείας, ἵνα μὴ ὦσιν ἄκαρποι.
PRESSING NEEDS, THAT THEY MAY NOT BE UNFRUITFUL(UNPRODUCTIVE).

3.15 Ἀσπάζονταί σε οἱ   μετ' ἐμοῦ πάντες.
⁵GREET   ⁶YOU ²THE ONES ³WITH ⁴ME ¹ALL.

Ἄσπασαι τοὺς φιλοῦντας ἡμᾶς ἐν πίστει. ἡ χάρις
GREET   THE ONES LOVING   US IN [THE] FAITH. - GRACE

μετὰ πάντων ὑμῶν.
[BE] WITH YOU°~ALL.

⁶This Spirit he poured out on us richly through Jesus Christ our Savior, ⁷so that, having been justified by his grace, we might become heirs according to the hope of eternal life. ⁸The saying is sure.

I desire that you insist on these things, so that those who have come to believe in God may be careful to devote themselves to good works; these things are excellent and profitable to everyone. ⁹But avoid stupid controversies, genealogies, dissensions, and quarrels about the law, for they are unprofitable and worthless. ¹⁰After a first and second admonition, have nothing more to do with anyone who causes divisions, ¹¹since you know that such a person is perverted and sinful, being self-condemned.

12 When I send Artemas to you, or Tychicus, do your best to come to me at Nicopolis, for I have decided to spend the winter there. ¹³Make every effort to send Zenas the lawyer and Apollos on their way, and see that they lack nothing. ¹⁴And let people learn to devote themselves to good works in order to meet urgent needs, so that they may not be unproductive.

15 All who are with me send greetings to you. Greet those who love us in the faith.

Grace be with all of you.ⁱ

ⁱ Other ancient authorities add *Amen*

THE LETTER OF PAUL TO
PHILEMON

ΠΡΟΣ ΦΙΛΗΜΟΝΑ
TO   PHILEMON

1.1 Παῦλος δέσμιος Χριστοῦ Ἰησοῦ καὶ Τιμόθεος ὁ
PAUL   A PRISONER   OF CHRIST   JESUS   AND   TIMOTHY   THE

ἀδελφὸς Φιλήμονι τῷ ἀγαπητῷ καὶ συνεργῷ ἡμῶν
BROTHER TO PHILEMON THE BELOVED ONE AND CO-WORKER OF US

1.2 καὶ Ἀπφίᾳ τῇ ἀδελφῇ καὶ Ἀρχίππῳ τῷ
AND   APPHIA   THE SISTER   AND   ARCHIPPUS   THE

συστρατιώτῃ ἡμῶν καὶ τῇ κατ᾽ οἶκόν σου ἐκκλησίᾳ,
FELLOW SOLDIER OF US AND TO THE ²IN ⁴HOUSE ³YOUR ¹CHURCH,

1.3 χάρις ὑμῖν καὶ εἰρήνη ἀπὸ θεοῦ πατρὸς ἡμῶν καὶ
GRACE TO YOU° AND PEACE FROM GOD [THE] FATHER OF US   AND

κυρίου Ἰησοῦ Χριστοῦ.
LORD   JESUS   CHRIST.

1.4 Εὐχαριστῶ τῷ θεῷ μου πάντοτε μνείαν σου
I GIVE THANKS TO THE GOD OF ME ALWAYS ²MENTION ³OF YOU

ποιούμενος ἐπὶ τῶν προσευχῶν μου, **1.5** ἀκούων σου τὴν
¹MAKING   AT(IN) THE   PRAYERS   OF ME,   HEARING OF YOUR -

ἀγάπην καὶ τὴν πίστιν, ἣν ἔχεις πρὸς τὸν κύριον
LOVE   AND - FAITH   WHICH YOU HAVE FOR THE LORD

Ἰησοῦν καὶ εἰς πάντας τοὺς ἁγίους, **1.6** ὅπως ἡ
JESUS   AND FOR ALL   THE SAINTS,   SO THAT THE

κοινωνία τῆς πίστεώς σου ἐνεργὴς γένηται ἐν
SHARING OF THE FAITH OF YOU MAY BECOME~EFFECTIVE IN

ἐπιγνώσει παντὸς ἀγαθοῦ τοῦ ἐν ἡμῖν εἰς
[THE] ACKNOWLEDGMENT OF ALL [THE] GOOD - IN US FOR

Χριστόν. **1.7** χαρὰν γὰρ πολλὴν ἔσχον καὶ παράκλησιν
CHRIST.   ³JOY   ¹FOR ²MUCH I HAD AND ENCOURAGEMENT

ἐπὶ τῇ ἀγάπῃ σου, ὅτι τὰ σπλάγχνα τῶν
WITH RESPECT TO THE LOVE OF YOU, BECAUSE THE INWARD PARTS (HEARTS) OF THE

ἁγίων ἀναπέπαυται διὰ σοῦ, ἀδελφέ.
SAINTS   HAVE BEEN REFRESHED THROUGH YOU,   BROTHER.

1.8 Διὸ πολλὴν ἐν Χριστῷ παρρησίαν ἔχων
THEREFORE, ¹MUCH ⁴IN ⁵CHRIST ²BOLDNESS ³HAVING,

ἐπιτάσσειν σοι τὸ ἀνῆκον **1.9** διὰ τὴν
TO ORDER   YOU [TO DO] WHAT [IS] REQUIRED, BECAUSE OF THE(OUR)

ἀγάπην μᾶλλον παρακαλῶ, τοιοῦτος ὢν ὡς Παῦλος
LOVE   RATHER I MAKE AN APPEAL, BEING~SUCH A ONE AS PAUL

πρεσβύτης νυνὶ δὲ καὶ δέσμιος Χριστοῦ Ἰησοῦ·
AN OLD MAN BUT~NOW ALSO A PRISONER OF CHRIST   JESUS;

1 Paul, a prisoner of Christ Jesus, and Timothy our brother,[a] To Philemon our dear friend and co-worker, ²to Apphia our sister,[b] to Archippus our fellow soldier, and to the church in your house:

3 Grace to you and peace from God our Father and the Lord Jesus Christ.

4 When I remember you[c] in my prayers, I always thank my God ⁵because I hear of your love for all the saints and your faith toward the Lord Jesus. ⁶I pray that the sharing of your faith may become effective when you perceive all the good that we[d] may do for Christ. ⁷I have indeed received much joy and encouragement from your love, because the hearts of the saints have been refreshed through you, my brother.

8 For this reason, though I am bold enough in Christ to command you to your duty, ⁹yet I would rather appeal to you on the basis of love—and I, Paul, do this as an old man, and now also as a prisoner of Christ Jesus.[e]

[a] Gk *the brother*
[b] Gk *the sister*
[c] From verse 4 through verse 21, *you* is singular
[d] Other ancient authorities read *you* (plural)
[e] Or *as an ambassador of Christ Jesus, and now also his prisoner*

¹⁰I am appealing to you for my child, Onesimus, whose father I have become during my imprisonment. ¹¹Formerly he was useless to you, but now he is indeed useful*ᶠ* both to you and to me. ¹²I am sending him, that is, my own heart, back to you. ¹³I wanted to keep him with me, so that he might be of service to me in your place during my imprisonment for the gospel; ¹⁴but I preferred to do nothing without your consent, in order that your good deed might be voluntary and not something forced. ¹⁵Perhaps this is the reason he was separated from you for a while, so that you might have him back forever, ¹⁶no longer as a slave but more than a slave, a beloved brother—especially to me but how much more to you, both in the flesh and in the Lord.

17 So if you consider me your partner, welcome him as you would welcome me. ¹⁸If he has wronged you in any way, or owes you anything, charge that to my account. ¹⁹I, Paul, am writing this with my own hand: I will repay it. I say nothing about your owing me even your own self. ²⁰Yes, brother, let me have this benefit from you in the Lord! Refresh my heart in Christ. ²¹Confident of your obedience, I am writing to you, knowing that you will do even more than I say.

22 One thing more—

ᶠ The name Onesimus means *useful* or (compare verse 20) *beneficial*

1.10 παρακαλῶ σε περὶ τοῦ ἐμοῦ τέκνου, ὃν
I APPEAL TO YOU CONCERNING - MY CHILD, WHOM

ἐγέννησα ἐν τοῖς δεσμοῖς, Ὀνήσιμον, **1.11** τόν
I GAVE BIRTH TO [WHILE] IN THE(MY) BONDS, ONESIMUS, THE ONE

ποτέ σοι ἄχρηστον νυνὶ δὲ [καὶ] σοὶ καὶ ἐμοὶ
ONCE USELESS~TO YOU BUT~NOW BOTH TO YOU AND TO ME

εὔχρηστον, **1.12** ὃν ἀνέπεμψά σοι, αὐτόν, τοῦτ᾽
USEFUL, WHOM I SENT BACK TO YOU, HIM, THIS(THAT)

ἔστιν τὰ ἐμὰ σπλάγχνα· **1.13** ὃν ἐγὼ ἐβουλόμην
IS, - MY INWARD PARTS(HEART); WHOM I WAS DESIRING

πρὸς ἐμαυτὸν κατέχειν, ἵνα ὑπὲρ σοῦ μοι διακονῇ
²WITH ³MYSELF ¹TO KEEP, THAT ON BEHALF OF YOU HE MIGHT SERVE~ME

ἐν τοῖς δεσμοῖς τοῦ εὐαγγελίου, **1.14** χωρὶς δὲ
[WHILE] IN THE BONDS OF(FOR) THE GOSPEL, BUT~WITHOUT

τῆς σῆς γνώμης οὐδὲν ἠθέλησα ποιῆσαι, ἵνα μὴ ὡς
- YOUR CONSENT ³NOTHING ¹I WANTED ²TO DO, THAT NOT AS

κατὰ ἀνάγκην τὸ ἀγαθόν σου ᾖ ἀλλὰ κατὰ
OF NECESSITY - ³GOOD[NESS] ²YOUR ¹MIGHT BE BUT ACCORDING TO

ἑκούσιον. **1.15** τάχα γὰρ διὰ τοῦτο ἐχωρίσθη
[YOUR] WILLINGNESS. FOR~PERHAPS BECAUSE OF THIS HE WAS SEPARATED

πρὸς ὥραν, ἵνα αἰώνιον αὐτὸν ἀπέχῃς, **1.16** οὐκέτι ὡς
FOR AN HOUR, THAT ETERNALLY YOU MIGHT HAVE~HIM, NO LONGER AS

δοῦλον ἀλλ᾽ ὑπὲρ δοῦλον, ἀδελφὸν ἀγαπητόν,
A SLAVE BUT MORE THAN A SLAVE, A BROTHER BELOVED,

μάλιστα ἐμοί, πόσῳ δὲ μᾶλλον σοὶ καὶ ἐν σαρκὶ
ESPECIALLY TO ME, AND~HOW MUCH MORE TO YOU BOTH IN [THE] FLESH

καὶ ἐν κυρίῳ.
AND IN [THE] LORD.

1.17 Εἰ οὖν με ἔχεις κοινωνόν, προσλαβοῦ αὐτὸν ὡς
IF THEN YOU HOLD~ME [AS] A PARTNER, RECEIVE HIM AS

ἐμέ. **1.18** εἰ δέ τι ἠδίκησέν σε ἢ ὀφείλει, τοῦτο
ME. BUT~IF [IN] ANYTHING HE WRONGED YOU OR OWES [YOU], THIS

ἐμοὶ ἐλλόγα. **1.19** ἐγὼ Παῦλος ἔγραψα τῇ ἐμῇ χειρί,
PUT TO MY ACCOUNT. I PAUL WROTE - WITH MY HAND,

ἐγὼ ἀποτίσω· ἵνα μὴ λέγω σοι ὅτι καὶ σεαυτόν
I WILL REPAY; NOT~THAT I [COULD] SAY TO YOU THAT EVEN YOURSELF

μοι προσοφείλεις. **1.20** ναὶ ἀδελφέ, ἐγώ σου
YOU ALSO OWE~TO ME. YES, BROTHER, ²I ⁴OF(FROM) YOU

ὀναίμην ἐν κυρίῳ· ἀνάπαυσόν μου τὰ σπλάγχνα
¹MAY ³HAVE PROFIT IN [THE] LORD; REFRESH MY - INWARD PARTS (HEART)

ἐν Χριστῷ.
IN CHRIST.

1.21 Πεποιθὼς τῇ ὑπακοῇ σου ἔγραψά σοι, εἰδὼς
HAVING CONFIDENCE IN THE OBEDIENCE OF YOU I WROTE TO YOU, KNOWING

ὅτι καὶ ὑπὲρ ἃ λέγω ποιήσεις. **1.22** ἅμα δὲ
THAT EVEN ABOVE WHAT I SAY YOU WILL DO. YET~AT THE SAME TIME

καὶ ἑτοίμαζέ μοι ξενίαν· ἐλπίζω γὰρ ὅτι διὰ τῶν
ALSO PREPARE FOR ME LODGING; FOR~I HOPE THAT THROUGH THE

προσευχῶν ὑμῶν χαρισθήσομαι ὑμῖν.
PRAYERS OF YOU° TO BE RESTORED TO YOU°.

1.23 Ἀσπάζεταί σε Ἐπαφρᾶς ὁ συναιχμάλωτός
⁸GREETS ⁹YOU ¹EPAPHRAS ²THE ³FELLOW PRISONER

μου ἐν Χριστῷ Ἰησοῦ, **1.24** Μᾶρκος, Ἀρίσταρχος,
⁴OF ME ⁵IN ⁶CHRIST ⁷JESUS, [AND] MARK, ARISTARCHUS,

Δημᾶς, Λουκᾶς, οἱ συνεργοί μου. **1.25** Ἡ χάρις τοῦ
DEMAS, LUKE, THE CO-WORKERS OF ME. THE GRACE OF THE

κυρίου Ἰησοῦ Χριστοῦ μετὰ τοῦ πνεύματος ὑμῶν.
LORD JESUS CHRIST [BE] WITH THE SPIRIT OF YOU°.

prepare a guest room for me, for I am hoping through your prayers to be restored to you.

23 Epaphras, my fellow prisoner in Christ Jesus, sends greetings to you,[g] 24and so do Mark, Aristarchus, Demas, and Luke, my fellow workers.

25 The grace of the Lord Jesus Christ be with your spirit.[h]

[g] Here *you* is singular
[h] Other ancient authorities add *Amen*

THE LETTER TO THE
HEBREWS

ΠΡΟΣ ΕΒΡΑΙΟΥΣ
TO   [THE] HEBREWS

1.1 Πολυμερῶς καὶ πολυτρόπως πάλαι ὁ θεὸς
IN MANY WAYS   AND   IN VARIOUS WAYS, LONG AGO - GOD

λαλήσας τοῖς πατράσιν ἐν τοῖς προφήταις **1.2** ἐπ'
HAVING SPOKEN TO THE FATHERS   BY THE   PROPHETS   AT

ἐσχάτου τῶν ἡμερῶν τούτων ἐλάλησεν ἡμῖν ἐν υἱῷ,
[THE] END -   OF THESE~DAYS,   HE SPOKE   TO US BY [THE] SON,

ὃν ἔθηκεν κληρονόμον πάντων, δι' οὗ καὶ
WHOM HE APPOINTED HEIR   OF ALL THINGS, THROUGH WHOM ALSO

ἐποίησεν τοὺς αἰῶνας· **1.3** ὃς ὢν ἀπαύγασμα τῆς
HE MADE   THE   AGES;   WHO, BEING [THE] RADIANCE OF THE

δόξης καὶ χαρακτὴρ τῆς ὑποστάσεως αὐτοῦ,
GLORY AND [THE] REPRESENTATION OF THE ESSENCE   OF HIM,

φέρων τε τὰ πάντα τῷ ῥήματι τῆς δυνάμεως αὐτοῦ,
AND~SUSTAINING -   EVERYTHING BY THE WORD OF THE POWER   OF HIM,

καθαρισμὸν τῶν ἁμαρτιῶν ποιησάμενος ἐκάθισεν ἐν
²A PURIFICATION - ³OF SINS   ¹HAVING MADE,   HE SAT DOWN AT

δεξιᾷ τῆς μεγαλωσύνης ἐν ὑψηλοῖς, **1.4** τοσούτῳ
[THE] RIGHT [HAND] OF THE MAJESTY   ON HIGH,   BY SO MUCH

κρείττων γενόμενος τῶν ἀγγέλων ὅσῳ
BETTER   HAVING BECOME [THAN] THE ANGELS,   BY SO MUCH

διαφορώτερον παρ' αὐτοὺς κεκληρονόμηκεν ὄνομα.
MORE EXCELLENT THAN THEM,   HE HAS INHERITED   A NAME.

1.5 Τίνι γὰρ εἶπέν ποτε τῶν ἀγγέλων,
FOR~TO WHICH ³DID HE SAY ⁴EVER ¹OF THE ²ANGELS,

Υἱός μου εἶ σύ,
[THE] SON OF ME YOU~ARE,

ἐγὼ σήμερον γεγέννηκά σε;
I   TODAY   HAVE BECOME A FATHER [TO] YOU?

καὶ πάλιν,
AND AGAIN,

Ἐγὼ ἔσομαι αὐτῷ εἰς πατέρα,
I   WILL BE TO HIM - A FATHER,

καὶ αὐτὸς ἔσται μοι εἰς υἱόν;
AND HE   WILL BE TO ME - A SON?

1.6 ὅταν δὲ πάλιν εἰσαγάγῃ τὸν πρωτότοκον εἰς τὴν
³WHEN ¹AND ²AGAIN HE BRINGS THE FIRST-BORN   INTO THE

οἰκουμένην, λέγει,
WORLD,   HE SAYS,

Long ago God spoke to our ancestors in many and various ways by the prophets, [2]but in these last days he has spoken to us by a Son,[a] whom he appointed heir of all things, through whom he also created the worlds. [3]He is the reflection of God's glory and the exact imprint of God's very being, and he sustains[b] all things by his powerful word. When he had made purification for sins, he sat down at the right hand of the Majesty on high, [4]having become as much superior to angels as the name he has inherited is more excellent than theirs.

5 For to which of the angels did God ever say,

"You are my Son;
   today I have begotten
     you"?

Or again,

"I will be his Father,
   and he will be my
     Son"?

[6]And again, when he brings the firstborn into the world, he says,

[a] Or *the Son*
[b] Or *bears along*

"Let all God's angels
worship him."

Καὶ προσκυνησάτωσαν αὐτῷ πάντες ἄγγελοι
AND   LET WORSHIP   HIM   ALL   [THE] ANGELS

θεοῦ.
OF GOD.

[7]Of the angels he says,
"He makes his angels
winds,
and his servants flames
of fire."

1.7 καὶ πρὸς μὲν τοὺς ἀγγέλους λέγει,
AND   TO   -   THE   ANGELS   HE SAYS,

'Ο ποιῶν τοὺς ἀγγέλους αὐτοῦ πνεύματα
THE ONE MAKING THE ANGELS   OF HIM   WINDS

καὶ τοὺς λειτουργοὺς αὐτοῦ πυρὸς φλόγα,
AND   THE   SERVANTS   OF HIM   A FLAME~OF FIRE,

[8]But of the Son he says,
"Your throne, O God, is[c]
forever and ever,
and the righteous
scepter is the
scepter of your[d]
kingdom.

1.8 πρὸς δὲ τὸν υἱόν,
AND~TO   THE   SON,

'Ο θρόνος σου ὁ θεός   εἰς τὸν αἰῶνα τοῦ
THE THRONE   OF YOU - [O] GOD [IS] TO THE   AGE   OF THE

αἰῶνος,
AGE,

καὶ ἡ ῥάβδος τῆς εὐθύτητος ῥάβδος
AND THE SCEPTER   OF THE RIGHTEOUS [IS] [THE] SCEPTER

τῆς βασιλείας ⌐σου.⌐
OF THE KINGDOM   OF YOU.

[9] You have loved
righteousness and
hated wickedness;
therefore God, your
God, has anointed
you
with the oil of gladness
beyond your
companions."

1.9 ἠγάπησας δικαιοσύνην καὶ ἐμίσησας ἀνομίαν·
YOU LOVED   RIGHTEOUSNESS   AND   HATED   LAWLESSNESS.

διὰ   τοῦτο ἔχρισέν σε ὁ θεός ὁ θεός σου
ON ACCOUNT OF THIS   [5]ANOINTED [6]YOU - [1]GOD, [2]THE [3]GOD [4]OF YOU,

ἔλαιον ἀγαλλιάσεως παρὰ τοὺς μετόχους
WITH [THE] OIL OF GLADNESS   MORE THAN   THE   COMPANIONS

, σου.
OF YOU.

[10]And,
"In the beginning, Lord,
you founded the
earth,
and the heavens are the
work of your hands;

1.10 καί,
AND,

Σὺ κατ' ἀρχάς, κύριε, τὴν γῆν ἐθεμελίωσας,
YOU, IN THE BEGINNING, LORD, [2]OF THE [3]EARTH [1]LAID THE FOUNDATION,

καὶ ἔργα   τῶν χειρῶν σού εἰσιν οἱ
AND [THE] WORKS OF THE HANDS   OF YOU   ARE   THE

οὐρανοί·
HEAVENS.

[11]they will perish, but you
remain;
they will all wear out
like clothing;

1.11 αὐτοὶ ἀπολοῦνται, σὺ δὲ διαμένεις,
THEY   WILL PERISH,   BUT~YOU   REMAIN,

καὶ πάντες ὡς ἱμάτιον παλαιωθήσονται,
AND   ALL   AS   A GARMENT   WILL GROW OLD,

[12]like a cloak you will roll
them up,
and like clothing[e] they
will be changed.
But you are the same,

1.12 καὶ ὡσεὶ περιβόλαιον ἑλίξεις   αὐτούς,
AND   AS   A COAT   YOU WILL ROLL UP   THEM,

ὡς ἱμάτιον καὶ ἀλλαγήσονται·
AS   A GARMENT ALSO THEY WILL BE CHANGED.

σὺ δὲ ὁ αὐτὸς εἶ
BUT~YOU [2]THE [3]SAME [1]ARE

[c] Or *God is your throne*
[d] Other ancient authorities read *his*
[e] Other ancient authorities lack *like
clothing*

1:7 Ps. 104:4 LXX   **1:8** text: KJV ASV RSV NASBmg NIV TEV NJBmg NRSV. var. αυτου (of him) ASVmg
RSVmg NASB NEB TEVmg NJB NRSVmg.   **1:8-9** Ps. 45:6-7   **1:10-12** Ps. 102:25-27 LXX

καὶ τὰ ἔτη σου οὐκ ἐκλείψουσιν.
AND THE YEARS OF YOU WILL NOT COME TO AN END.

1.13 πρὸς τίνα δὲ τῶν ἀγγέλων εἴρηκέν ποτε,
²TO ³WHICH ¹AND OF THE ANGELS HAS HE SAID EVER,

Κάθου ἐκ δεξιῶν μου,
SIT AT [THE] RIGHT [HAND] OF ME,

ἕως ἂν θῶ τοὺς ἐχθρούς σου ὑποπόδιον
UNTIL I PUT THE ENEMIES OF YOU [AS] A FOOTSTOOL

τῶν ποδῶν σου;
OF THE FEET OF YOU?

1.14 οὐχὶ πάντες εἰσὶν λειτουργικὰ πνεύματα εἰς
²NOT ³ALL ¹ARE MINISTERING SPIRITS FOR

διακονίαν ἀποστελλόμενα διὰ τοὺς μέλλοντας
SERVICE BEING SENT OUT ON ACCOUNT OF THE ONES BEING ABOUT

κληρονομεῖν σωτηρίαν;
TO INHERIT SALVATION?

1:13 Ps. 110:1

and your years will
never end."
¹³But to which of the angels
has he ever said,
"Sit at my right hand
until I make your
enemies a footstool
for your feet"?
¹⁴Are not all angels[f] spirits
in the divine service, sent to
serve for the sake of those
who are to inherit salvation?

[f] Gk *all of them*

2.1 Διὰ τοῦτο δεῖ περισσοτέρως
ON ACCOUNT OF THIS ¹IT IS NECESSARY [FOR] ⁴FAR MORE

προσέχειν ἡμᾶς τοῖς ἀκουσθεῖσιν, μήποτε
³TO PAY ATTENTION ²US TO THE THINGS HAVING BEEN HEARD, LEST

παραρυῶμεν. **2.2** εἰ γὰρ ὁ δι᾽ ἀγγέλων
WE MAY DRIFT AWAY. FOR~IF THE ³THROUGH ⁴ANGELS

λαληθεὶς λόγος ἐγένετο βέβαιος καὶ πᾶσα
²HAVING BEEN SPOKEN ¹WORD BECAME FIRMLY ESTABLISHED AND EVERY

παράβασις καὶ παρακοὴ ἔλαβεν ἔνδικον
TRANSGRESSION AND DISOBEDIENCE RECEIVED A JUST

μισθαποδοσίαν, **2.3** πῶς ἡμεῖς ἐκφευξόμεθα
PENALTY, HOW WILL WE~ESCAPE,

τηλικαύτης ἀμελήσαντες σωτηρίας, ἥτις ἀρχὴν
HAVING NEGLECTED~SO IMPORTANT A SALVATION, WHICH AT FIRST

λαβοῦσα λαλεῖσθαι διὰ τοῦ κυρίου ὑπὸ
HAVING RECEIVED TO BE SPOKEN THROUGH THE LORD BY

τῶν ἀκουσάντων εἰς ἡμᾶς ἐβεβαιώθη,
THE ONES HAVING HEARD ²TO ³US ¹[IT] WAS CONFIRMED,

2.4 συνεπιμαρτυροῦντος τοῦ θεοῦ σημείοις τε καὶ
²TESTIFYING - ¹GOD [WITH] BOTH~SIGNS AND

τέρασιν καὶ ποικίλαις δυνάμεσιν καὶ πνεύματος ἁγίου
WONDERS AND VARIOUS MIRACLES AND OF [THE] HOLY~SPIRIT, [WITH]

μερισμοῖς κατὰ τὴν αὐτοῦ θέλησιν;
DISTRIBUTIONS ACCORDING TO - HIS WILL?

2.5 Οὐ γὰρ ἀγγέλοις ὑπέταξεν τὴν οἰκουμένην τὴν
FOR~NOT TO ANGELS DID HE SUBJECT THE ³WORLD, ¹THE

Therefore we must pay
greater attention to what we
have heard, so that we do not
drift away from it. ²For if the
message declared through
angels was valid, and every
transgression or disobedience received a just penalty,
³how can we escape if we
neglect so great a salvation?
It was declared at first
through the Lord, and it was
attested to us by those who
heard him, ⁴while God
added his testimony by signs
and wonders and various
miracles, and by gifts of the
Holy Spirit, distributed
according to his will.
5 Now God[g] did not
subject the coming world,

[g] Gk *he*

about which we are speaking, to angels. [6]But someone has testified somewhere,

"What are human beings that you are mindful of them,[h] or mortals, that you care for them?[i]

[7] You have made them for a little while lower[j] than the angels; you have crowned them with glory and honor,[k]

[8] subjecting all things under their feet."

Now in subjecting all things to them, God[l] left nothing outside their control. As it is, we do not yet see everything in subjection to them, [9]but we do see Jesus, who for a little while was made lower[m] than the angels, now crowned with glory and honor because of the suffering of death, so that by the grace of God[n] he might taste death for everyone.

[10] It was fitting that God,[l] for whom and through whom all things exist, in bringing many children to glory, should make the pioneer of their salvation perfect through sufferings. [11]For the one who sanctifies and those who are sanctified all have one Father.[o] For this reason Jesus[l] is not ashamed to call them brothers and sisters,[p] [12]saying,

"I will proclaim your name to my brothers and sisters,[p]

[h] Gk *What is man that you are mindful of him?*
[i] Gk *or the son of man that you care for him?* In the Hebrew of Psalm 8:4-6 both *man* and *son of man* refer to all humankind
[j] Or *them only a little lower*
[k] Other ancient authorities add *and set them over the works of your hands*
[l] Gk *he*
[m] Or *who was made a little lower*
[n] Other ancient authorities read *apart from God*
[o] Gk *are all of one*
[p] Gk *brothers*

μέλλουσαν, περὶ ἧς λαλοῦμεν. **2.6** διεμαρτύρατο δέ
[2]COMING, ABOUT WHICH WE ARE SPEAKING. AND~TESTIFIED

πού τις λέγων,
SOMEONE~SOMEWHERE SAYING,

Τί ἐστιν ἄνθρωπος ὅτι μιμνῄσκῃ αὐτοῦ,
WHAT IS MAN THAT YOU REMEMBER HIM,

ἢ υἱὸς ἀνθρώπου ὅτι ἐπισκέπτῃ
OR [THE] SON OF A MAN THAT YOU ARE CONCERNED ABOUT

αὐτόν;
HIM?

2.7 ἠλάττωσας αὐτὸν βραχύ τι παρ' ἀγγέλους,
YOU MADE HIM LOWER FOR A SHORT TIME THAN ANGELS,

δόξῃ καὶ τιμῇ ἐστεφάνωσας αὐτόν,[τ]
WITH GLORY AND HONOR YOU CROWNED HIM,

2.8 πάντα ὑπέταξας ὑποκάτω τῶν ποδῶν αὐτοῦ.
YOU SUBJECTED~EVERYTHING UNDER THE FEET OF HIM.

ἐν τῷ γὰρ ὑποτάξαι [αὐτῷ] τὰ πάντα
[2]WHILE [HE] [1]FOR SUBJECTED TO HIM - ALL THINGS,

οὐδὲν ἀφῆκεν αὐτῷ ἀνυπότακτον. νῦν δὲ οὔπω ὁρῶμεν
HE LEFT~NOTHING UNSUBJECTED~TO HIM. BUT~NOW NOT YET DO WE SEE

αὐτῷ τὰ πάντα ὑποτεταγμένα· **2.9** τὸν δὲ βραχύ τι
TO HIM - ALL THINGS HAVING BEEN SUBJECTED. - BUT FOR A SHORT TIME

παρ' ἀγγέλους ἠλαττωμένον βλέπομεν Ἰησοῦν
[2]THAN [3]ANGELS [1]HAVING BEEN MADE LOWER, WE SEE JESUS

διὰ τὸ πάθημα τοῦ θανάτου δόξῃ καὶ τιμῇ
BECAUSE OF THE SUFFERING - OF DEATH, WITH GLORY AND HONOR

ἐστεφανωμένον, ὅπως χάριτι θεοῦ ὑπὲρ
HAVING BEEN CROWNED, IN ORDER THAT BY [THE] GRACE OF GOD ON BEHALF OF

παντὸς γεύσηται θανάτου.
ALL HE MIGHT TASTE DEATH.

2.10 Ἔπρεπεν γὰρ αὐτῷ, δι' ὃν τὰ πάντα
FOR~IT WAS FITTING FOR HIM, ON ACCOUNT OF WHOM [ARE] - ALL THINGS

καὶ δι' οὗ τὰ πάντα, πολλοὺς υἱοὺς εἰς δόξαν
AND THROUGH WHOM [ARE] - ALL THINGS, MANY SONS TO GLORY

ἀγαγόντα τὸν ἀρχηγὸν τῆς σωτηρίας αὐτῶν διὰ
HAVING LED, THE FOUNDER OF THE SALVATION OF THEM THROUGH

παθημάτων τελειῶσαι. **2.11** ὅ τε γὰρ ἁγιάζων καὶ
SUFFERINGS TO PERFECT. [3]THE ONE [2]BOTH [1]FOR SANCTIFYING AND

οἱ ἁγιαζόμενοι ἐξ ἑνὸς πάντες· δι' ἣν
THE ONES BEING SANCTIFIED FROM ONE ALL [ARE]; ON ACCOUNT OF WHICH

αἰτίαν οὐκ ἐπαισχύνεται ἀδελφοὺς αὐτοὺς καλεῖν
REASON HE IS NOT ASHAMED BROTHERS TO CALL~THEM

2.12 λέγων,
SAYING,

Ἀπαγγελῶ τὸ ὄνομά σου τοῖς ἀδελφοῖς μου,
I WILL PROCLAIM THE NAME OF YOU TO THE BROTHERS OF ME,

2:6-8 Ps. 8:4-6 LXX. **2:7** text ASVmg RSV NASBmg NIV NEB TEV NJB NRSV. add καὶ κατεστησας αυτον επι τα εργα των χειρων σου (and set him over the works of your hands) [see Ps. 8:6 LXX]: KJV ASV RSVmg NASB TEVmg NRSVmg. **2:12** Ps. 22:22

ἐν μέσῳ   ἐκκλησίας   ὑμνήσω   σε,
IN [THE] MIDST OF [THE] CONGREGATION I WILL SING HYMNS TO YOU,

2.13 καὶ πάλιν,
AND AGAIN,

Ἐγὼ ἔσομαι πεποιθὼς ἐπ᾽ αὐτῷ,
I WILL PUT MY CONFIDENCE IN HIM,

καὶ πάλιν,
AND AGAIN,

Ἰδοὺ ἐγὼ καὶ τὰ παιδία ἅ   μοι ἔδωκεν ὁ θεός.
BEHOLD I AND THE CHILDREN WHICH ³TO ME ²GAVE - ¹GOD.

2.14 ἐπεὶ οὖν   τὰ παιδία κεκοινώνηκεν αἵματος καὶ
THEREFORE~SINCE THE CHILDREN HAVE SHARED IN [THE] BLOOD AND

σαρκός, καὶ αὐτὸς παραπλησίως μετέσχεν τῶν αὐτῶν,
FLESH, AND HE ∕ LIKEWISE SHARED IN THE SAME THINGS,

ἵνα διὰ   τοῦ θανάτου καταργήσῃ τὸν   τὸ
THAT THROUGH - DEATH HE MIGHT DESTROY THE ONE -

κράτος ἔχοντα τοῦ θανάτου, τοῦτ᾽ ἔστιν τὸν διάβολον,
HAVING~POWER OVER - DEATH, THAT IS THE DEVIL,

2.15 καὶ ἀπαλλάξῃ τούτους, ὅσοι   φόβῳ θανάτου διὰ
AND HE MIGHT FREE THESE, AS MANY AS BY FEAR OF DEATH THROUGH

παντὸς τοῦ ζῆν ἔνοχοι ἦσαν   δουλείας. **2.16** οὐ γὰρ
ALL [THEIR] - LIVING WERE BEING~SUBJECT TO SLAVERY. ³NOT ¹FOR

δήπου ἀγγέλων ἐπιλαμβάνεται ἀλλὰ σπέρματος
²SURELY OF ANGELS HE TAKES INTEREST, BUT OF [THE] SEED

Ἀβραὰμ ἐπιλαμβάνεται. **2.17** ὅθεν   ὤφειλεν
OF ABRAHAM HE TAKES INTEREST. FOR WHICH REASON HE WAS OBLIGATED

κατὰ πάντα   τοῖς   ἀδελφοῖς ὁμοιωθῆναι, ἵνα
IN EVERY RESPECT ²THE ³BROTHERS ¹TO BECOME LIKE, THAT

ἐλεήμων γένηται   καὶ   πιστὸς ἀρχιερεὺς τὰ
HE MIGHT BECOME~A MERCIFUL AND FAITHFUL HIGH PRIEST [IN] THE THINGS

πρὸς   τὸν θεὸν εἰς   τὸ ἱλάσκεσθαι   τὰς
[PERTAINING] TO - GOD, IN ORDER - TO MAKE ATONEMENT FOR THE

ἁμαρτίας τοῦ λαοῦ. **2.18** ἐν ᾧ   γὰρ πέπονθεν   αὐτὸς
SINS OF THE PEOPLE. ²BECAUSE ¹FOR HE HAS SUFFERED, HIMSELF

πειρασθείς, δύναται τοῖς   πειραζομένοις βοηθῆσαι.
HAVING BEEN TESTED, HE IS ABLE THE ONES BEING TESTED TO HELP.

2:13a Isa. 8:17 LXX **2:13b** Isa. 8:18

in the midst of the congregation I will praise you."

¹³And again,

"I will put my trust in him."

And again,

"Here am I and the children whom God has given me."

14 Since, therefore, the children share flesh and blood, he himself likewise shared the same things, so that through death he might destroy the one who has the power of death, that is, the devil, ¹⁵and free those who all their lives were held in slavery by the fear of death. ¹⁶For it is clear that he did not come to help angels, but the descendants of Abraham. ¹⁷Therefore he had to become like his brothers and sisters[q] in every respect, so that he might be a merciful and faithful high priest in the service of God, to make a sacrifice of atonement for the sins of the people. ¹⁸Because he himself was tested by what he suffered, he is able to help those who are being tested.

[q] Gk *brothers*

3.1 Ὅθεν,   ἀδελφοὶ ἅγιοι, κλήσεως ἐπουρανίου
FOR WHICH REASON, HOLY~BROTHERS, ³CALLING ²A HEAVENLY

μέτοχοι, κατανοήσατε τὸν ἀπόστολον καὶ ἀρχιερέα
¹PARTNERS [IN], CONSIDER CAREFULLY THE APOSTLE AND HIGH PRIEST

τῆς ὁμολογίας ἡμῶν Ἰησοῦν, **3.2** πιστὸν ὄντα τῷ
OF THE CONFESSION OF US, JESUS, BEING~FAITHFUL TO THE ONE

Therefore, brothers and sisters,[q] holy partners in a heavenly calling, consider that Jesus, the apostle and high priest of our confession, ²was faithful to the one

[q] Gk *brothers*

who appointed him, just as Moses also "was faithful in all' God's⁵ house." ³Yet Jesus' is worthy of more glory than Moses, just as the builder of a house has more honor than the house itself. ⁴(For every house is built by someone, but the builder of all things is God.) ⁵Now Moses was faithful in all God's⁵ house as a servant, to testify to the things that would be spoken later. ⁶Christ, however, was faithful over God's⁵ house as a son, and we are his house if we hold firm" the confidence and the pride that belong to hope.

7 Therefore, as the Holy Spirit says,

"Today, if you hear his voice,
⁸ do not harden your hearts as in the rebellion, as on the day of testing in the wilderness,
⁹ where your ancestors put me to the test, though they had seen my works
¹⁰ for forty years.
Therefore I was angry with that generation, and I said, 'They always go astray in their hearts,

' Other ancient authorities lack *all*
⁵ Gk *his*
' Gk *this one*
" Other ancient authorities add *to the end*

ποιήσαντι αὐτὸν ὡς καὶ Μωϋσῆς ⌐ἐν [ὅλῳ]
HAVING APPOINTED HIM, AS ALSO MOSES [WAS FAITHFUL] IN [THE] WHOLE

τῷ οἴκῳ αὐτοῦ.⌐ 3.3 πλείονος γὰρ οὗτος δόξης παρὰ
- HOUSE OF HIM. ³OF GREATER ¹FOR ²THIS ONE GLORY THAN

Μωϋσῆν ἠξίωται, καθ᾽ ὅσον πλείονα τιμὴν
MOSES HAS BEEN CONSIDERED WORTHY, BECAUSE MORE HONOR

ἔχει τοῦ οἴκου ὁ κατασκευάσας αὐτόν·
HAS ⁴THE ⁵HOUSE [ITSELF] ¹THE ONE ²HAVING BUILT ³IT [THAN].

3.4 πᾶς γὰρ οἶκος κατασκευάζεται ὑπό τινος, ὁ δὲ
FOR~EVERY HOUSE IS BUILT BY SOMEONE, BUT~THE ONE

πάντα κατασκευάσας θεός. 3.5 καὶ Μωϋσῆς μὲν πιστὸς
HAVING BUILT~EVERYTHING [IS] GOD. AND MOSES [WAS] - FAITHFUL

ἐν ὅλῳ τῷ οἴκῳ αὐτοῦ ὡς θεράπων εἰς μαρτύριον
IN [THE] WHOLE - HOUSE OF HIM AS A SERVANT FOR A TESTIMONY

τῶν λαληθησομένων, 3.6 Χριστὸς δὲ ὡς υἱὸς
OF THE THINGS [WHICH] WILL BE SPOKEN, BUT~CHRIST AS A SON

ἐπὶ τὸν οἶκον αὐτοῦ· οὗ οἶκός ἐσμεν ἡμεῖς,
OVER THE HOUSE OF HIM [WAS FAITHFUL]; WHOSE HOUSE WE~ARE,

ἐάν[περ] τὴν παρρησίαν καὶ τὸ καύχημα τῆς ἐλπίδος
IF INDEED THE CONFIDENCE AND THE BOAST OF THE HOPE

⌐κατάσχωμεν.⌐
WE MAY KEEP HOLD OF.

3.7 Διό, καθὼς λέγει τὸ πνεῦμα τὸ ἅγιον,
THEREFORE, JUST AS SAYS THE ²SPIRIT - ¹HOLY,

Σήμερον ἐὰν τῆς φωνῆς αὐτοῦ ἀκούσητε,
TODAY, IF THE VOICE OF HIM YOU HEAR,

3.8 μὴ σκληρύνητε τὰς καρδίας ὑμῶν ὡς ἐν τῷ
DO NOT HARDEN THE HEARTS OF YOU° AS IN THE

παραπικρασμῷ
REBELLION

κατὰ τὴν ἡμέραν τοῦ πειρασμοῦ ἐν
IN ACCORDANCE WITH THE DAY OF THE TESTING IN

τῇ ἐρήμῳ,
THE DESERT,

3.9 οὗ ἐπείρασαν οἱ πατέρες ὑμῶν ἐν δοκιμασίᾳ
WHERE ⁴TESTED ¹THE ²FATHERS ³OF YOU° WITH TESTING

καὶ εἶδον τὰ ἔργα μου 3.10 τεσσεράκοντα
AND THEY SAW THE WORKS OF ME [FOR] FORTY

ἔτη·
YEARS;

διὸ προσώχθισα τῇ γενεᾷ ταύτῃ
THEREFORE, I WAS ANGRY - WITH THIS~GENERATION

καὶ εἶπον, Ἀεὶ πλανῶνται τῇ καρδίᾳ,
AND I SAID, ALWAYS THEY ARE GOING ASTRAY IN THE[IR] HEART,

3:2 text [see Num. 12:7 LXX]: KJV ASV RSVmg NASB NIV TEV NJB NRSV. var. εν τω οικω αυτου (in his house): RSV NEB NRSVmg. **3:6** text: RSV NIV NEB TEV NJB NRSV. var. μεχρι τελους βεβαιαν κατασχωμεν (if we hold fast firm until [the] end) [see Heb. 3:14]: KJV ASV RSVmg NASB NJBmg NRSVmg. **3:7-11** Ps. 95:7-11

αὐτοὶ δὲ   οὐκ ἔγνωσαν   τὰς ὁδούς μου,
AND~THEY   DID NOT KNOW   THE   WAYS   OF ME,

3.11 ὡς   ὤμοσα ἐν   τῇ ὀργῇ μου·
AS   I SWORE   IN   THE   ANGER   OF ME:

Εἰ εἰσελεύσονται εἰς τὴν κατάπαυσίν μου.
THEY WILL NOT ENTER   INTO THE   REST   OF ME.

3.12 Βλέπετε,   ἀδελφοί,   μήποτε ἔσται   ἔν τινι   ὑμῶν
BEWARE,   BROTHERS,   LEST   THERE WILL BE IN   ANYONE   OF YOU°

καρδία πονηρὰ   ἀπιστίας ἐν τῷ   ἀποστῆναι ἀπὸ
AN EVIL~HEART   OF UNBELIEF   IN   THE   WITHDRAWING   FROM

θεοῦ ζῶντος,   **3.13** ἀλλὰ   παρακαλεῖτε   ἑαυτοὺς
[THE] LIVING~GOD,   BUT   ENCOURAGE   YOURSELVES

καθ᾽ ἑκάστην ἡμέραν, ἄχρις οὗ τὸ Σήμερον καλεῖται,
EACH AND EVERY DAY,   AS LONG AS   -   IT IS CALLED~TODAY,

ἵνα μὴ σκληρυνθῇ τις ἐξ ὑμῶν ἀπάτῃ   τῆς
THAT   MAY NOT BE HARDENED   SOME OF YOU°   BY [THE] DECEITFULNESS   -

ἁμαρτίας—   **3.14** μέτοχοι γὰρ τοῦ Χριστοῦ γεγόναμεν,
OF SIN—   ³PARTNERS   ¹FOR   -   ⁴OF CHRIST   ²WE HAVE BECOME,

ἐάνπερ τὴν ἀρχὴν τῆς ὑποστάσεως μέχρι τέλους
IF INDEED   THE   BEGINNING OF THE   CONVICTION   UNTIL   [THE] END

βεβαίαν κατάσχωμεν—   **3.15** ἐν τῷ   λέγεσθαι,
WE MAY HOLD~FIRM—   WHILE   BEING SAID,

Σήμερον ἐὰν τῆς φωνῆς αὐτοῦ ἀκούσητε,
TODAY,   IF   THE VOICE   OF HIM   YOU° MAY HEAR,

Μὴ σκληρύνητε τὰς καρδίας ὑμῶν ὡς ἐν τῷ
DO NOT HARDEN   THE   HEARTS   OF YOU° AS   IN   THE

παραπικρασμῷ.
REBELLION.

3.16 τίνες γὰρ   ἀκούσαντες παρεπίκραναν;   ἀλλ᾽ οὐ
FOR~WHO   HAVING HEARD,   REBELLED?   SURELY NOT

πάντες οἱ   ἐξελθόντες ἐξ   Αἰγύπτου διὰ   Μωϋσέως;
ALL   THE ONES   HAVING GONE OUT FROM   EGYPT   THROUGH   MOSES?

3.17 τίσιν δὲ   προσώχθισεν τεσσεράκοντα ἔτη;   οὐχὶ
AND~WITH WHOM   WAS HE ANGRY   FORTY   YEARS?   [WAS IT] NOT

τοῖς   ἁμαρτήσασιν, ὧν   τὰ κῶλα ἔπεσεν ἐν τῇ
WITH THE ONES   HAVING SINNED,   WHOSE   -   BODIES FELL   IN   THE

ἐρήμῳ;   **3.18** τίσιν δὲ   ὤμοσεν μὴ εἰσελεύσεσθαι εἰς τὴν
DESERT?   AND~TO WHOM   DID HE SWEAR   NOT TO ENTER   INTO THE

κατάπαυσιν αὐτοῦ εἰ μὴ τοῖς   ἀπειθήσασιν;   **3.19** καὶ
REST   OF HIM,   EXCEPT   THE ONES   HAVING DISOBEYED?   AND

βλέπομεν ὅτι οὐκ ἠδυνήθησαν εἰσελθεῖν δι᾽
WE SEE   THAT   THEY WERE NOT ABLE   TO ENTER   BECAUSE OF

ἀπιστίαν.
UNBELIEF.

3:15 Ps. 95:7-8 LXX

and they have not
  known my ways.'
¹¹ As in my anger I swore,
  'They will not enter my
  rest.'"
¹²Take care, brothers and
sisters,ᵛ that none of you
may have an evil, unbe-
lieving heart that turns away
from the living God. ¹³But
exhort one another every
day, as long as it is called
"today," so that none of you
may be hardened by the
deceitfulness of sin. ¹⁴For
we have become partners of
Christ, if only we hold our
first confidence firm to the
end. ¹⁵As it is said,
  "Today, if you hear his
  voice,
  do not harden your hearts
  as in the rebellion."
¹⁶Now who were they who
heard and yet were rebel-
lious? Was it not all those
who left Egypt under the
leadership of Moses? ¹⁷But
with whom was he angry
forty years? Was it not those
who sinned, whose bodies
fell in the wilderness? ¹⁸And
to whom did he swear that
they would not enter his rest,
if not to those who were
disobedient? ¹⁹So we see
that they were unable to
enter because of unbelief.

ᵛ Gk *brothers*

CHAPTER 4

Therefore, while the promise of entering his rest is still open, let us take care that none of you should seem to have failed to reach it. ²For indeed the good news came to us just as to them; but the message they heard did not benefit them, because they were not united by faith with those who listened.ʷ ³For we who have believed enter that rest, just as Godˣ has said,

"As in my anger I swore, 'They shall not enter my rest,'"

though his works were finished at the foundation of the world. ⁴For in one place it speaks about the seventh day as follows, "And God rested on the seventh day from all his works." ⁵And again in this place it says, "They shall not enter my rest." ⁶Since therefore it remains open for some to enter it, and those who formerly received the good news failed to enter because of disobedience, ⁷again he sets a certain day—"today"—saying through David much later, in the words already quoted,

ʷ Other ancient authorities read *it did not meet with faith in those who listened*
ˣ Gk *he*

4.1 Φοβηθῶμεν οὖν, μήποτε καταλειπομένης
LET US FEAR   THEREFORE,   LEST,   [WHILE] BEING LEFT OPEN

ἐπαγγελίας εἰσελθεῖν εἰς τὴν κατάπαυσιν αὐτοῦ δοκῇ
A PROMISE   TO ENTER   INTO THE   REST   OF HIM,   ⁴MAY SEEM

τις ἐξ ὑμῶν ὑστερηκέναι. **4.2** καὶ γάρ
¹ANYONE ²OF ³YOU°   TO HAVE FALLEN SHORT.   FOR~SURELY

ἐσμεν εὐηγγελισμένοι καθάπερ κἀκεῖνοι· ἀλλ'
WE HAVE HAD THE GOOD NEWS PREACHED [TO US]   JUST AS   THEY ALSO.   BUT

οὐκ ὠφέλησεν ⌈ὁ λόγος τῆς ἀκοῆς ἐκείνους μὴ
⁴DID NOT BENEFIT   ¹THE ²WORD - ³OF PREACHING THOSE ONES NOT

συγκεκερασμένους τῇ πίστει τοῖς
HAVING BEEN UNITED - BY FAITH WITH THE ONES

ἀκούσασιν.⌉ **4.3** εἰσερχόμεθα γὰρ εἰς [τὴν]
HAVING HEARD [THE MESSAGE].   FOR~WE ENTER   INTO THE

κατάπαυσιν οἱ πιστεύσαντες, καθὼς εἴρηκεν,
REST,   THE ONES HAVING BELIEVED,   JUST AS   HE HAS SAID,

Ὡς ὤμοσα ἐν τῇ ὀργῇ μου,
AS   I VOWED   IN   THE ANGER OF ME,

Εἰ εἰσελεύσονται εἰς τὴν κατάπαυσίν μου,
THEY WILL NOT ENTER   INTO THE   REST   OF ME,

καίτοι τῶν ἔργων ἀπὸ καταβολῆς κόσμου
ALTHOUGH THE WORKS   FROM [THE] FOUNDATION OF [THE] WORLD

γενηθέντων. **4.4** εἴρηκεν γάρ που περὶ τῆς
HAVING COME INTO BEING.   FOR~HE HAS SAID SOMEWHERE CONCERNING THE

ἑβδόμης οὕτως, Καὶ κατέπαυσεν ὁ θεὸς ἐν τῇ ἡμέρᾳ
SEVENTH [DAY] THUS,   AND RESTED - GOD ON THE ²DAY

τῇ ἑβδόμῃ ἀπὸ πάντων τῶν ἔργων αὐτοῦ, **4.5** καὶ ἐν
- ¹SEVENTH FROM ALL   OF THE WORKS   OF HIM,   AND IN

τούτῳ πάλιν, Εἰ εἰσελεύσονται εἰς τὴν κατάπαυσίν
THIS PLACE AGAIN,   THEY WILL NOT ENTER   INTO THE   REST

μου. **4.6** ἐπεὶ οὖν ἀπολείπεται τινὰς εἰσελθεῖν
OF ME.   THEREFORE~SINCE IT IS RESERVED   FOR SOME TO ENTER

εἰς αὐτήν, καὶ οἱ πρότερον
INTO IT,   AND THE ONES AT AN EARLIER TIME

εὐαγγελισθέντες οὐκ εἰσῆλθον δι'
HAVING HAD THE GOOD NEWS PREACHED [TO THEM] DID NOT ENTER   BECAUSE OF

ἀπείθειαν, **4.7** πάλιν τινὰ ὁρίζει ἡμέραν, Σήμερον,
DISOBEDIENCE,   AGAIN ON A CERTAIN DAY~HE DETERMINES,   TODAY,

ἐν Δαυὶδ λέγων μετὰ τοσοῦτον χρόνον, καθὼς
IN [A PSALM OF] DAVID SAYING AFTER SO MUCH TIME,   JUST AS

προείρηται,
IT HAS BEEN SAID BEFORE,

4:2 text: ASVmg RSVmg NASBmg NIVmg NJB NRSV. var. ο λογος της ακοης εκεινους μη συγκεκερασμενος τη πιστει τοις ακουσασιν (those who heard the word did not combine it with faith): KJV RSV NASB NIV NEB TEV NJBmg NRSVmg. **4:3, 5** Ps. 95:11 **4:4** Gen. 2:2 **4:7** Ps. 95:7-8 LXX

Σήμερον ἐὰν τῆς φωνῆς αὐτοῦ ἀκούσητε,
TODAY,   IF   THE VOICE OF HIM YOU° MAY HEAR,

μὴ σκληρύνητε τὰς καρδίας ὑμῶν.
DO NOT HARDEN   THE HEARTS   OF YOU°.

4.8 εἰ γὰρ αὐτοὺς Ἰησοῦς κατέπαυσεν,   οὐκ ἂν
FOR~IF ³THEM ¹JOSHUA ²BROUGHT TO A PLACE OF REST, ⁵NOT -

περὶ ἄλλης ἐλάλει   μετὰ ταῦτα ἡμέρας.
⁶ABOUT ⁷ANOTHER ⁴HE WOULD HAVE SPOKEN ⁹AFTER ¹⁰THESE ⁸DAY.

4.9 ἄρα   ἀπολείπεται σαββατισμὸς τῷ λαῷ τοῦ
THEREFORE, THERE REMAINS A SABBATH REST FOR THE PEOPLE -

θεοῦ. **4.10** ὁ γὰρ εἰσελθὼν εἰς τὴν κατάπαυσιν αὐτοῦ
OF GOD.   FOR~THE ONE HAVING ENTERED INTO THE REST   OF HIM

καὶ αὐτὸς κατέπαυσεν ἀπὸ τῶν ἔργων αὐτοῦ ὥσπερ
ALSO HIMSELF RESTED   FROM THE WORKS OF HIM, JUST AS

ἀπὸ τῶν ἰδίων   ὁ θεός. **4.11** σπουδάσωμεν οὖν
FROM - HIS OWN [WORKS] - GOD [RESTED]. THEREFORE~LET US BE DILIGENT

εἰσελθεῖν εἰς ἐκείνην τὴν κατάπαυσιν, ἵνα μὴ ἐν τῷ
TO ENTER INTO THAT   -   REST,   LEST   BY THE

αὐτῷ τις   ὑποδείγματι πέσῃ τῆς ἀπειθείας.
SAME ³SOMEONE ¹EXAMPLE ⁴MAY FALL - ²OF DISOBEDIENCE.

4.12 Ζῶν γὰρ ὁ λόγος τοῦ θεοῦ καὶ ἐνεργὴς καὶ
FOR~LIVING [IS] THE WORD - OF GOD AND EFFECTIVE AND

τομώτερος ὑπὲρ πᾶσαν μάχαιραν δίστομον καὶ
SHARPER   THAN EVERY DOUBLED-EDGED~SWORD AND

διϊκνούμενος ἄχρι μερισμοῦ ψυχῆς καὶ πνεύματος,
PENETRATING AS FAR AS [THE] DIVISION OF SOUL AND SPIRIT,

ἁρμῶν τε καὶ μυελῶν, καὶ κριτικὸς ἐνθυμήσεων καὶ
BOTH~OF JOINTS AND MARROW, AND ABLE TO DISCERN [THE] THOUGHTS AND

ἐννοιῶν καρδίας· **4.13** καὶ οὐκ ἔστιν κτίσις ἀφανὴς
INSIGHTS OF [THE] HEART.   AND THERE IS NOT A CREATURE HIDDEN

ἐνώπιον αὐτοῦ, πάντα δὲ   γυμνὰ καὶ τετραχηλισμένα
FROM BEFORE HIM, BUT~ALL THINGS [ARE] BARE AND HAVING BEEN EXPOSED

τοῖς ὀφθαλμοῖς αὐτοῦ, πρὸς ὃν ἡμῖν ὁ λόγος.
TO THE EYES   OF HIM, TO WHOM OUR - ACCOUNT [IS GIVEN].

4.14 Ἔχοντες οὖν   ἀρχιερέα μέγαν διεληλυθότα
THEREFORE~[SINCE] HAVING A GREAT~HIGH PRIEST HAVING GONE THROUGH

τοὺς οὐρανούς, Ἰησοῦν τὸν υἱὸν τοῦ θεοῦ, κρατῶμεν
THE HEAVENS, JESUS, THE SON - OF GOD, LET US HOLD FIRMLY

τῆς ὁμολογίας. **4.15** οὐ γὰρ ἔχομεν ἀρχιερέα μὴ
TO THE CONFESSION.   FOR~WE DO NOT HAVE A HIGH PRIEST NOT

δυνάμενον συμπαθῆσαι ταῖς ἀσθενείαις ἡμῶν,
BEING ABLE TO SYMPATHIZE WITH THE WEAKNESSES OF US,

πεπειρασμένον δὲ κατὰ πάντα καθ᾽ ὁμοιότητα χωρὶς
BUT~HAVING BEEN TEMPTED IN EVERY WAY IN SIMILAR FASHION [YET] WITHOUT

"Today, if you hear his
  voice,
do not harden your
  hearts."
[8]For if Joshua had given
them rest, God[y] would not
speak later about another
day. [9]So then, a sabbath rest
still remains for the people of
God; [10]for those who enter
God's rest also cease from
their labors as God did from
his. [11]Let us therefore make
every effort to enter that
rest, so that no one may fall
through such disobedience
as theirs.
  [12]Indeed, the word of
God is living and active,
sharper than any two-edged
sword, piercing until it
divides soul from spirit,
joints from marrow; it is able
to judge the thoughts and
intentions of the heart.
[13]And before him no
creature is hidden, but all are
naked and laid bare to the
eyes of the one to whom we
must render an account.
  [14]Since, then, we have a
great high priest who has
passed through the heavens,
Jesus, the Son of God, let us
hold fast to our confession.
[15]For we do not have a high
priest who is unable to
sympathize with our weak-
nesses, but we have one who
in every respect has been
tested[z] as we are, yet without

[y] Gk *he*
[z] Or *tempted*

sin. [16]Let us therefore approach the throne of grace with boldness, so that we may receive mercy and find grace to help in time of need.

ἀμαρτίας. 4.16 προσερχώμεθα οὖν μετὰ παρρησίας
SIN. THEREFORE~LET US APPROACH WITH BOLDNESS

τῷ θρόνῳ τῆς χάριτος, ἵνα λάβωμεν ἔλεος καὶ
TO THE THRONE - OF GRACE, THAT WE MAY RECEIVE MERCY AND

χάριν εὕρωμεν εἰς εὔκαιρον βοήθειαν.
MAY FIND~GRACE FOR TIMELY HELP.

CHAPTER 5

Every high priest chosen from among mortals is put in charge of things pertaining to God on their behalf, to offer gifts and sacrifices for sins. [2]He is able to deal gently with the ignorant and wayward, since he himself is subject to weakness; [3]and because of this he must offer sacrifice for his own sins as well as for those of the people. [4]And one does not presume to take this honor, but takes it only when called by God, just as Aaron was.

5 So also Christ did not glorify himself in becoming a high priest, but was appointed by the one who said to him,

"You are my Son,
today I have begotten
you";

[6]as he says also in another place,

"You are a priest forever,
according to the order
of Melchizedek."

7 In the days of his flesh, Jesus[a] offered up prayers

[a] Gk *he*

5.1 Πᾶς γὰρ ἀρχιερεὺς ἐξ ἀνθρώπων λαμβανόμενος
FOR~EVERY HIGH PRIEST OF MEN BEING CHOSEN

ὑπὲρ ἀνθρώπων καθίσταται τὰ πρὸς τὸν θεόν,
IN BEHALF OF MEN IS APPOINTED TO THE THINGS TOWARD - GOD,

ἵνα προσφέρῃ δῶρά τε καὶ θυσίας ὑπὲρ ἀμαρτιῶν,
THAT HE MAY OFFER BOTH~GIFTS AND SACRIFICES FOR SINS,

5.2 μετριοπαθεῖν δυνάμενος τοῖς ἀγνοοῦσιν καὶ
BEING ABLE~TO DEAL GENTLY WITH THE ONES BEING IGNORANT AND

πλανωμένοις, ἐπεὶ καὶ αὐτὸς περίκειται ἀσθένειαν
BEING MISLED, SINCE ALSO HE IS SURROUNDED BY WEAKNESS

5.3 καὶ δι' αὐτὴν ὀφείλει, καθὼς περὶ τοῦ
AND BECAUSE OF IT HE IS OBLIGATED, AS CONCERNING THE

λαοῦ, οὕτως καὶ περὶ αὐτοῦ προσφέρειν περὶ
PEOPLE, THUS ALSO CONCERNING HIMSELF TO OFFER [SACRIFICES] FOR

ἀμαρτιῶν. **5.4** καὶ οὐχ ἑαυτῷ τις λαμβάνει τὴν
SINS. AND NOT ANYONE~FOR HIMSELF TAKES THE

τιμὴν ἀλλὰ καλούμενος ὑπὸ τοῦ θεοῦ καθώσπερ καὶ
HONOR BUT BEING CALLED BY - GOD JUST AS ALSO

Ἀαρών.
AARON.

5.5 Οὕτως καὶ ὁ Χριστὸς οὐχ ἑαυτὸν ἐδόξασεν
SO ALSO - CHRIST DID NOT GLORIFY~HIMSELF

γενηθῆναι ἀρχιερέα ἀλλ' ὁ λαλήσας πρὸς αὐτόν,
TO BECOME HIGH PRIEST BUT THE ONE HAVING SAID TO HIM,

Υἱός μου εἶ σύ,
[THE] SON OF ME YOU~ARE,

ἐγὼ σήμερον γεγέννηκά σε·
TODAY~I HAVE BECOME A FATHER TO YOU;

5.6 καθὼς καὶ ἐν ἑτέρῳ λέγει,
AS ALSO IN ANOTHER [PLACE] HE SAYS,

Σὺ ἱερεὺς εἰς τὸν αἰῶνα
YOU [ARE] A PRIEST FOREVER

κατὰ τὴν τάξιν Μελχισέδεκ,
ACCORDING TO THE ORDER OF MELCHIZEDEK,

5.7 ὃς ἐν ταῖς ἡμέραις τῆς σαρκὸς αὐτοῦ δεήσεις τε
WHO IN THE DAYS OF THE FLESH OF HIM BOTH~PRAYERS

5:5 Ps. 2:7 **5:6** Ps. 110:4

καὶ ἱκετηρίας πρὸς τὸν δυνάμενον σῴζειν αὐτὸν
AND PLEADINGS   TO   THE ONE BEING ABLE   TO SAVE   HIM

ἐκ θανάτου μετὰ κραυγῆς ἰσχυρᾶς καὶ δακρύων
FROM DEATH   WITH A LOUD~CRY   AND   TEARS

προσενέγκας καὶ εἰσακουσθεὶς ἀπὸ τῆς εὐλαβείας,
HAVING OFFERED AND HAVING BEEN HEARD BECAUSE OF THE PIETY [OF HIM],

5.8 καίπερ ὢν υἱός, ἔμαθεν ἀφ' ὧν ἔπαθεν
    ALTHOUGH BEING A SON, HE LEARNED ²FROM [THE THINGS] ³WHICH ⁴HE SUFFERED

τὴν ὑπακοήν, **5.9** καὶ τελειωθεὶς ἐγένετο πᾶσιν
-    ¹OBEDIENCE,   AND HAVING BEEN MADE PERFECT, HE BECAME TO ALL

τοῖς ὑπακούουσιν αὐτῷ αἴτιος σωτηρίας αἰωνίου,
THE ONES OBEYING   HIM [THE] SOURCE OF ETERNAL~SALVATION,

5.10 προσαγορευθεὶς ὑπὸ τοῦ θεοῦ ἀρχιερεὺς κατὰ
     HAVING BEEN CALLED   BY   -   GOD [AS] HIGH PRIEST   ACCORDING TO

τὴν τάξιν Μελχισέδεκ.
THE ORDER OF MELCHIZEDEK.

5.11 Περὶ οὗ πολὺς ἡμῖν ὁ λόγος καὶ
     ABOUT WHOM MUCH TO US [IS] THE WORD   AND [IT IS]

δυσερμήνευτος λέγειν, ἐπεὶ νωθροὶ γεγόνατε ταῖς
HARD   TO EXPLAIN, SINCE YOU° HAVE BECOME~HARD   -

ἀκοαῖς. **5.12** καὶ γὰρ ὀφείλοντες εἶναι διδάσκαλοι
OF HEARING.   FOR~INDEED BEING OBLIGATED TO BE   TEACHERS

διὰ τὸν χρόνον, πάλιν χρείαν ἔχετε τοῦ
ON ACCOUNT OF THE TIME,   AGAIN YOU° HAVE~NEED [FOR] -

διδάσκειν ὑμᾶς τινὰ τὰ στοιχεῖα τῆς ἀρχῆς τῶν
²TO TEACH   ³YOU° ¹SOMEONE THE FUNDAMENTALS OF THE BEGINNING OF THE

λογίων τοῦ θεοῦ καὶ γεγόνατε χρείαν ἔχοντες
ORACLES   -   OF GOD AND YOU° HAVE BECOME [ONES] HAVING~NEED

γάλακτος [καὶ] οὐ στερεᾶς τροφῆς. **5.13** πᾶς γὰρ ὁ
OF MILK   AND NOT SOLID   FOOD.   FOR~EVERY[ONE] -

μετέχων γάλακτος ἄπειρος λόγου δικαιοσύνης,
PARTAKING OF MILK [IS] UNACQUAINTED WITH [THE] WORD OF RIGHTEOUSNESS,

νήπιος γάρ ἐστιν· **5.14** τελείων δέ ἐστιν
³AN INFANT ¹FOR ²HE IS.   BUT~[FOR THE] MATURE ONES IS

ἡ στερεὰ τροφή, τῶν διὰ τὴν ἕξιν τὰ
THE SOLID   FOOD, THE ONES BECAUSE OF - PRACTICE, ²THE

αἰσθητήρια γεγυμνασμένα ἐχόντων πρὸς διάκρισιν
³FACULTIES OF PERCEPTION ⁴HAVING BEEN TRAINED ¹HAVING FOR DISTINGUISHING

καλοῦ τε καὶ κακοῦ.
BOTH~GOOD AND EVIL.

and supplications, with loud cries and tears, to the one who was able to save him from death, and he was heard because of his reverent submission. [8]Although he was a Son, he learned obedience through what he suffered; [9]and having been made perfect, he became the source of eternal salvation for all who obey him, [10]having been designated by God a high priest according to the order of Melchizedek.

11 About this[b] we have much to say that is hard to explain, since you have become dull in understanding. [12]For though by this time you ought to be teachers, you need someone to teach you again the basic elements of the oracles of God. You need milk, not solid food; [13]for everyone who lives on milk, being still an infant, is unskilled in the word of righteousness. [14]But solid food is for the mature, for those whose faculties have been trained by practice to distinguish good from evil.

[b] Or him

6.1 Διὸ ἀφέντες τὸν τῆς ἀρχῆς τοῦ Χριστοῦ
    THEREFORE HAVING LEFT THE ²OF THE ³ELEMENTAL [THINGS] - ⁴OF CHRIST

λόγον ἐπὶ τὴν τελειότητα φερώμεθα, μὴ πάλιν
¹TEACHING TOWARD -   MATURITY   LET US BE MOVED ON, NOT AGAIN

Therefore let us go on toward perfection,[c] leaving behind the basic teaching about Christ, and not laying

[c] Or toward maturity

again the foundation: repentance from dead works and faith toward God, ²instruction about baptisms, laying on of hands, resurrection of the dead, and eternal judgment. ³And we will do*d* this, if God permits. ⁴For it is impossible to restore again to repentance those who have once been enlightened, and have tasted the heavenly gift, and have shared in the Holy Spirit, ⁵and have tasted the goodness of the word of God and the powers of the age to come, ⁶and then have fallen away, since on their own they are crucifying again the Son of God and are holding him up to contempt. ⁷Ground that drinks up the rain falling on it repeatedly, and that produces a crop useful to those for whom it is cultivated, receives a blessing from God. ⁸But if it produces thorns and thistles, it is worthless and on the verge of being cursed; its end is to be burned over.

9 Even though we speak in this way, beloved, we are confident of better things in your case, things that belong to salvation. ¹⁰For God is not unjust; he will not overlook your work and the love that you showed for his sake*e* in serving the saints, as you still do. ¹¹And we want each one of you to show the same diligence so as

d Other ancient authorities read *let us do*

e Gk *for his name*

θεμέλιον καταβαλλόμενοι μετανοίας ἀπὸ νεκρῶν ἔργων
LAYING~A FOUNDATION   OF REPENTANCE FROM DEAD WORKS

καὶ πίστεως ἐπὶ θεόν, **6.2** βαπτισμῶν διδαχῆς
AND FAITH TOWARD GOD,   OF TEACHING~OF RITUAL WASHINGS

ἐπιθέσεώς τε χειρῶν, ἀναστάσεώς τε νεκρῶν καὶ
AND~OF [THE] LAYING ON OF HANDS, AND~OF [THE] RESURRECTION FROM [THE] DEAD AND

κρίματος αἰωνίου. **6.3** καὶ τοῦτο ποιήσομεν, ἐάνπερ
OF ETERNAL~JUDGMENT.   AND WE WILL DO~THIS,   IF INDEED

ἐπιτρέπῃ ὁ θεός. **6.4** Ἀδύνατον γὰρ τοὺς ἅπαξ
²MAY PERMIT - ¹GOD.   FOR~[IT IS] IMPOSSIBLE FOR THE ONES ONCE

φωτισθέντας, γευσαμένους τε τῆς δωρεᾶς τῆς
HAVING BEEN ENLIGHTENED, BOTH~HAVING TASTED OF THE ²GIFT -

ἐπουρανίου καὶ μετόχους γενηθέντας πνεύματος ἁγίου
¹HEAVENLY AND HAVING BECOME~PARTNERS OF [THE] HOLY~SPIRIT

6.5 καὶ καλὸν γευσαμένους θεοῦ ῥῆμα δυνάμεις τε
AND HAVING TASTED~[THE] GOOD WORD~OF GOD AND~[THE] POWERS

μέλλοντος αἰῶνος **6.6** καὶ παραπεσόντας,
OF THE COMING AGE   AND   HAVING FALLEN AWAY,

πάλιν ἀνακαινίζειν εἰς μετάνοιαν, ἀνασταυροῦντας
TO RENEW~AGAIN   TO REPENTANCE,   CRUCIFYING

ἑαυτοῖς τὸν υἱὸν τοῦ θεοῦ καὶ παραδειγματίζοντας.
TO THEMSELVES THE SON - OF GOD AND HOLDING [HIM] UP TO CONTEMPT.

6.7 γῆ γὰρ ἡ πιοῦσα τὸν ἐπ᾽ αὐτῆς ἐρχόμενον
FOR~[THE] EARTH, - HAVING DRUNK THE ⁴UPON ⁵IT ³COMING

πολλάκις ὑετόν καὶ τίκτουσα βοτάνην εὔθετον
²OFTEN ¹RAIN AND BRINGING FORTH PLANT[S] SUITABLE

ἐκείνοις δι᾽ οὓς καὶ γεωργεῖται, μεταλαμβάνει
FOR THOSE FOR WHOM ALSO IT IS CULTIVATED, RECEIVES

εὐλογίας ἀπὸ τοῦ θεοῦ· **6.8** ἐκφέρουσα δὲ ἀκάνθας
A BLESSING FROM - GOD.   BUT~[IF IT IS] PRODUCING THORNS

καὶ τριβόλους, ἀδόκιμος καὶ κατάρας ἐγγύς, ἧς τὸ
AND THISTLES, [IT IS] WORTHLESS AND NEAR~[TO BEING] CURSED, WHOSE -

τέλος εἰς καῦσιν.
END [IS] FOR BURNING.

6.9 Πεπείσμεθα δὲ περὶ ὑμῶν, ἀγαπητοί, τὰ
BUT~WE HAVE BEEN CONVINCED ABOUT YOU°, BELOVED ONES, [OF] -

κρείσσονα καὶ ἐχόμενα σωτηρίας, εἰ καὶ οὕτως
BETTER [THINGS] AND [OF THINGS] BELONGING TO SALVATION, IF INDEED THUS

λαλοῦμεν. **6.10** οὐ γὰρ ἄδικος ὁ θεὸς ἐπιλαθέσθαι
WE MAY SPEAK. ³NOT ¹FOR ⁴UNJUST - ²GOD [IS] TO FORGET

τοῦ ἔργου ὑμῶν καὶ τῆς ἀγάπης ἧς ἐνεδείξασθε
THE WORK OF YOU° AND THE LOVE WHICH YOU° DEMONSTRATED

εἰς τὸ ὄνομα αὐτοῦ, διακονήσαντες τοῖς ἁγίοις
TOWARD THE NAME OF HIM, HAVING SERVED THE SAINTS

καὶ διακονοῦντες. **6.11** ἐπιθυμοῦμεν δὲ ἕκαστον
AND [STILL] SERVING [THEM].   AND~WE DESIRE EACH

ὑμῶν τὴν αὐτὴν ἐνδείκνυσθαι σπουδὴν πρὸς τὴν
OF YOU° [WITH] THE SAME EAGERNESS~TO DEMONSTRATE TOWARD THE

πληροφορίαν τῆς ἐλπίδος ἄχρι τέλους, 6.12 ἵνα μὴ
FULL ASSURANCE   OF THE HOPE   UNTIL [THE] END,   THAT NOT

νωθροὶ γένησθε,   μιμηταὶ δὲ τῶν   διὰ   πίστεως
LAZY   YOU° MAY BECOME, BUT~IMITATORS OF THE ONES THROUGH FAITH

καὶ μακροθυμίας κληρονομούντων τὰς ἐπαγγελίας.
AND PATIENCE   INHERITING   THE PROMISES.

6.13 Τῷ γὰρ Ἀβραὰμ ἐπαγγειλάμενος ὁ θεός, ἐπεὶ
     -    FOR TO ABRAHAM ²HAVING PROMISED   - ¹GOD,   ³SINCE

κατ' οὐδενὸς εἶχεν μείζονος ὁμόσαι, ὤμοσεν   καθ'
⁵BY ⁶NO ONE ⁴HE HAD GREATER TO SWEAR, HE TOOK AN OATH BY

ἑαυτοῦ 6.14 λέγων, Εἰ μὴν εὐλογῶν εὐλογήσω σε καὶ
HIMSELF   SAYING, SURELY BLESSING, I WILL BLESS YOU AND

πληθύνων πληθυνῶ σε· 6.15 καὶ οὕτως μακροθυμήσας
MULTIPLYING I WILL MULTIPLY YOU.   AND THUS HAVING WAITED PATIENTLY,

ἐπέτυχεν τῆς ἐπαγγελίας. 6.16 ἄνθρωποι γὰρ κατὰ τοῦ
HE OBTAINED   THE PROMISE.   FOR~MEN   BY   THE

μείζονος   ὀμνύουσιν, καὶ πάσης αὐτοῖς ἀντιλογίας
GREATER [PERSON] SWEAR,   AND ⁷OF EVERY ³FOR THEM ⁸DISPUTE

πέρας   εἰς βεβαίωσιν ὁ ὅρκος· 6.17 ἐν ᾧ
⁶OF [THE] END ⁴FOR ⁵[THE] CONFIRMATION ¹THE ²OATH [IS].   BY WHICH

περισσότερον βουλόμενος ὁ θεὸς ἐπιδεῖξαι τοῖς
EVEN MORE   ²WANTING   - ¹GOD TO SHOW   . TO THE

κληρονόμοις τῆς ἐπαγγελίας τὸ ἀμετάθετον τῆς
HEIRS   OF THE PROMISE,   THE UNCHANGEABLENESS OF THE

βουλῆς αὐτοῦ ἐμεσίτευσεν ὅρκῳ, 6.18 ἵνα διὰ δύο
DECISION OF HIM, GUARANTEED [IT] WITH AN OATH,   THAT BY TWO

πραγμάτων ἀμεταθέτων, ἐν οἷς   ἀδύνατον
UNCHANGEABLE~THINGS,   IN WHICH [IT IS] IMPOSSIBLE FOR

ψεύσασθαι [τὸν] θεόν, ἰσχυρὰν παράκλησιν ἔχωμεν
²TO LIE   -   ¹GOD, STRONG ENCOURAGEMENT WE MAY HAVE,

οἱ   καταφυγόντες κρατῆσαι τῆς προκειμένης ἐλπίδος·
THE ONES HAVING FLED   TO TAKE HOLD OF THE HOPE~LAYING BEFORE [US];

6.19 ἣν ὡς ἄγκυραν ἔχομεν τῆς ψυχῆς ἀσφαλῆ τε
     WHICH ²AS ³AN ANCHOR ¹WE HAVE OF THE SOUL,   BOTH~SECURE

καὶ βεβαίαν καὶ εἰσερχομένην εἰς τὸ ἐσώτερον τοῦ
AND RELIABLE AND ENTERING   INTO THE INSIDE   OF THE

καταπετάσματος, 6.20 ὅπου πρόδρομος ὑπὲρ   ἡμῶν
CURTAIN,   WHERE A FORERUNNER ON BEHALF OF US

εἰσῆλθεν Ἰησοῦς, κατὰ   τὴν τάξιν Μελχισέδεκ
ENTERED,   JESUS, ACCORDING TO THE ORDER OF MELCHIZEDEK,

ἀρχιερεὺς γενόμενος εἰς τὸν αἰῶνα.
HAVING BECOME~A HIGH PRIEST   FOREVER.

6:13-14 Gen. 22:16-17

to realize the full assurance of hope to the very end, ¹²so that you may not become sluggish, but imitators of those who through faith and patience inherit the promises.

13 When God made a promise to Abraham, because he had no one greater by whom to swear, he swore by himself, ¹⁴saying, "I will surely bless you and multiply you." ¹⁵And thus Abraham,ᶠ having patiently endured, obtained the promise. ¹⁶Human beings, of course, swear by someone greater than themselves, and an oath given as confirmation puts an end to all dispute. ¹⁷In the same way, when God desired to show even more clearly to the heirs of the promise the unchangeable character of his purpose, he guaranteed it by an oath, ¹⁸so that through two unchangeable things, in which it is impossible that God would prove false, we who have taken refuge might be strongly encouraged to seize the hope set before us. ¹⁹We have this hope, a sure and steadfast anchor of the soul, a hope that enters the inner shrine behind the curtain, ²⁰where Jesus, a forerunner on our behalf, has entered, having become a high priest forever according to the order of Melchizedek.

ᶠ Gk *he*

CHAPTER 7

This "King Melchizedek of Salem, priest of the Most High God, met Abraham as he was returning from defeating the kings and blessed him"; ²and to him Abraham apportioned "one-tenth of everything." His name, in the first place, means "king of righteousness"; next he is also king of Salem, that is, "king of peace." ³Without father, without mother, without genealogy, having neither beginning of days nor end of life, but resembling the Son of God, he remains a priest forever.

4 See how great he is! Even[g] Abraham the patriarch gave him a tenth of the spoils. ⁵And those descendants of Levi who receive the priestly office have a commandment in the law to collect tithes[h] from the people, that is, from their kindred,[i] though these also are descended from Abraham. ⁶But this man, who does not belong to their ancestry, collected tithes[h] from Abraham and blessed him who had received the promises. ⁷It is beyond dispute that the inferior is blessed by the superior. ⁸In the one case, tithes are received by those who are mortal; in the other, by one of whom it is testified that he lives.

[g] Other ancient authorities lack *Even*
[h] Or *a tenth*
[i] Gk *brothers*

7.1 Οὗτος γὰρ ὁ Μελχισέδεκ, βασιλεὺς Σαλήμ, ἱερεὺς
FOR~THIS   -   MELCHIZEDEK,   KING   OF SALEM,   PRIEST

τοῦ θεοῦ τοῦ ὑψίστου, ὁ   συναντήσας Ἀβραὰμ
OF THE GOD   -   MOST HIGH,   THE ONE HAVING MET   ABRAHAM

ὑποστρέφοντι ἀπὸ τῆς κοπῆς τῶν βασιλέων καὶ
RETURNING   FROM THE SLAUGHTER OF THE KINGS   AND

εὐλογήσας αὐτόν, **7.2** ᾧ   καὶ δεκάτην ἀπὸ πάντων
HAVING BLESSED HIM,   WITH WHOM ALSO A TENTH OF   EVERYTHING

ἐμέρισεν Ἀβραάμ, πρῶτον μὲν ἑρμηνευόμενος βασιλεὺς
ABRAHAM~DIVIDED,   FIRST,   -   BEING TRANSLATED   KING

δικαιοσύνης ἔπειτα δὲ καὶ βασιλεὺς Σαλήμ, ὅ   ἐστιν
OF RIGHTEOUSNESS, AND~THEN ALSO KING   OF SALEM, WHICH MEANS

βασιλεὺς εἰρήνης, **7.3** ἀπάτωρ ἀμήτωρ ἀγενεαλόγητος,
KING   OF PEACE, [BEING]   FATHERLESS, MOTHERLESS, WITHOUT GENEALOGY,

μήτε ἀρχὴν ἡμερῶν μήτε ζωῆς τέλος ἔχων,
NEITHER A BEGINNING OF DAYS, NOR END~OF LIFE   HAVING,

ἀφωμοιωμένος δὲ τῷ υἱῷ τοῦ θεοῦ, μένει ἱερεὺς
BUT~HAVING BEEN MADE LIKE THE SON - OF GOD, HE REMAINS A PRIEST

εἰς τὸ διηνεκές.
PERPETUALLY.

7.4 Θεωρεῖτε δὲ πηλίκος οὗτος,   ᾧ   [καὶ]
NOW~CONSIDER   HOW GREAT THIS ONE [WAS] TO WHOM ALSO

δεκάτην Ἀβραὰμ ἔδωκεν ἐκ τῶν ἀκροθινίων ὁ
A TENTH   ABRAHAM ³GAVE ⁴FROM ⁵THE ⁶BOOTY   ¹THE

πατριάρχης. **7.5** καὶ οἱ   μὲν ἐκ τῶν υἱῶν Λευὶ τὴν
²PATRIARCH.   AND THE ONES - OF THE SONS OF LEVI, ²THE

ἱερατείαν λαμβάνοντες ἐντολὴν ἔχουσιν ἀποδεκατοῦν
³PRIESTLY OFFICE ¹HAVING RECEIVED HAVE~A COMMAND TO COLLECT THE TITHE FROM

τὸν λαὸν κατὰ   τὸν νόμον, τοῦτ' ἔστιν τοὺς
THE PEOPLE ACCORDING TO THE LAW,   THAT IS TO SAY, THE

ἀδελφοὺς αὐτῶν, καίπερ ἐξεληλυθότας ἐκ τῆς ὀσφύος
BROTHERS   OF THEM, ALTHOUGH HAVING COME OUT FROM THE LOIN

Ἀβραάμ· **7.6** ὁ δὲ   μὴ γενεαλογούμενος ἐξ αὐτῶν
OF ABRAHAM.   BUT~THE ONE NOT TRACING HIS DESCENT   FROM THEM,

δεδεκάτωκεν   Ἀβραὰμ καὶ τὸν ἔχοντα τὰς
HAS RECEIVED TITHES FROM ABRAHAM AND THE ONE HAVING THE

ἐπαγγελίας εὐλόγηκεν. **7.7** χωρὶς δὲ   πάσης
PROMISES,   HE HAS BLESSED.   AND~APART FROM ALL

ἀντιλογίας τὸ ἔλαττον ὑπὸ τοῦ κρείττονος εὐλογεῖται.
DISPUTE,   THE INFERIOR BY THE SUPERIOR   IS BLESSED.

7.8 καὶ ὧδε μὲν δεκάτας ἀποθνήσκοντες ἄνθρωποι
AND HERE, - TITHES,   DYING   MEN

λαμβάνουσιν, ἐκεῖ δὲ   μαρτυρούμενος ὅτι ζῇ.
RECEIVE,   BUT~THERE, [ONE] TESTIFYING   THAT HE LIVES.

7:1-2 Gen. 14:17-20

7.9 καὶ ὡς ἔπος εἰπεῖν, δι'   Ἀβραὰμ καὶ Λευὶ ὁ
AND   SO TO SPEAK,   THROUGH ABRAHAM, EVEN LEVI, THE ONE

δεκάτας λαμβάνων δεδεκάτωται· **7.10** ἔτι γὰρ ἐν τῇ
RECEIVING~TITHES,   HAS PAID TITHES.   FOR~YET IN THE

ὀσφύϊ τοῦ   πατρὸς ἦν ὅτε συνήντησεν αὐτῷ
LOIN   OF THE(HIS) FATHER HE WAS WHEN ²MET   ³HIM

Μελχισέδεκ.
¹MELCHIZEDEK.

7.11 Εἰ μὲν οὖν τελείωσις διὰ   τῆς Λευιτικῆς
IF   -   THEN PERFECTION THROUGH THE LEVITICAL

ἱερωσύνης ἦν, ὁ λαὸς γὰρ ἐπ'   αὐτῆς
PRIESTHOOD WAS, ²THE ³PEOPLE ¹FOR ON THE BASIS OF IT

νενομοθέτηται, τίς ἔτι   χρεία κατὰ   τὴν τάξιν
HAVE RECEIVED LAWS, WHAT FURTHER NEED ACCORDING TO THE ORDER

Μελχισέδεκ ἕτερον   ἀνίστασθαι ἱερέα καὶ οὐ
OF MELCHIZEDEK [FOR] ANOTHER PRIEST~TO ARISE   AND NOT

κατὰ   τὴν τάξιν Ἀαρὼν λέγεσθαι;
ACCORDING TO THE ORDER OF AARON TO BE NAMED?

7.12 μετατιθεμένης γὰρ τῆς ἱερωσύνης ἐξ ἀνάγκης καὶ
FOR~[WHEN] BEING CHANGED THE PRIESTLY OFFICE, OF NECESSITY ALSO

νόμου μετάθεσις γίνεται. **7.13** ἐφ'   ὃν   γὰρ
A CHANGE~OF LAW   OCCURS.   ²ABOUT ³WHOM ¹FOR

λέγεται ταῦτα, φυλῆς ἑτέρας μετέσχηκεν, ἀφ' ἧς
THESE THINGS~ARE SAID, TO A DIFFERENT~TRIBE HE HAS BELONGED, FROM WHICH

οὐδεὶς   προσέσχηκεν τῷ   θυσιαστηρίῳ·
NO ONE   HAS OFFICIATED AT THE ALTAR.

7.14 πρόδηλον γὰρ ὅτι ἐξ   Ἰούδα ἀνατέταλκεν ὁ
FOR~[IT IS] OBVIOUS   THAT FROM JUDAH HAS DESCENDED THE

κύριος ἡμῶν, εἰς ἣν φυλὴν περὶ   ἱερέων οὐδὲν
LORD   OF US, ABOUT WHICH TRIBE CONCERNING PRIESTS ³NOTHING

Μωϋσῆς ἐλάλησεν. **7.15** καὶ περισσότερον ἔτι
¹MOSES ²SAID.   AND EVEN~MUCH MORE

κατάδηλόν ἐστιν, εἰ κατὰ   τὴν ὁμοιότητα
EVIDENT   IT IS, IF ACCORDING TO THE LIKENESS

Μελχισέδεκ ἀνίσταται ἱερεὺς ἕτερος, **7.16** ὃς οὐ
OF MELCHIZEDEK ARISES   ANOTHER~PRIEST,   WHO NOT

κατὰ   νόμον ἐντολῆς σαρκίνης γέγονεν ἀλλὰ
ACCORDING TO [THE] LAW OF A FLESHLY~COMMAND HAS BECOME, BUT

κατὰ   δύναμιν ζωῆς ἀκαταλύτου.
ACCORDING TO [THE] POWER OF AN INDESTRUCTIBLE~LIFE.

7.17 μαρτυρεῖται γὰρ ὅτι
FOR~IT IS TESTIFIED [OF HIM] -

        Σὺ   ἱερεὺς εἰς τὸν αἰῶνα
        YOU [ARE] A PRIEST FOREVER

        κατὰ   τὴν τάξιν Μελχισέδεκ.
        ACCORDING TO THE ORDER OF MELCHIZEDEK.

7:17 Ps. 110:4

⁹One might even say that Levi himself, who receives tithes, paid tithes through Abraham, ¹⁰for he was still in the loins of his ancestor when Melchizedek met him.

11 Now if perfection had been attainable through the levitical priesthood—for the people received the law under this priesthood—what further need would there have been to speak of another priest arising according to the order of Melchizedek, rather than one according to the order of Aaron? ¹²For when there is a change in the priesthood, there is necessarily a change in the law as well. ¹³Now the one of whom these things are spoken belonged to another tribe, from which no one has ever served at the altar. ¹⁴For it is evident that our Lord was descended from Judah, and in connection with that tribe Moses said nothing about priests.

15 It is even more obvious when another priest arises, resembling Melchizedek, ¹⁶one who has become a priest, not through a legal requirement concerning physical descent, but through the power of an indestructible life. ¹⁷For it is attested of him,

"You are a priest forever, according to the order of Melchizedek."

18There is, on the one hand, the abrogation of an earlier commandment because it was weak and ineffectual 19(for the law made nothing perfect); there is, on the other hand, the introduction of a better hope, through which we approach God.

20 This was confirmed with an oath; for others who became priests took their office without an oath, 21but this one became a priest with an oath, because of the one who said to him,

"The Lord has sworn
and will not change his
mind,
'You are a priest
forever'"—

22accordingly Jesus has also become the guarantee of a better covenant.

23 Furthermore, the former priests were many in number, because they were prevented by death from continuing in office; 24but he holds his priesthood permanently, because he continues forever. 25Consequently he is able for all time to savej those who approach God through him, since he always lives to make intercession for them.

26 For it was fitting that we should have such a high priest, holy, blameless, undefiled, separated from sinners, and exalted above the heavens. 27Unlike the otherk high priests, he has no need

j Or able to save completely
k Gk lacks other

7.18 ἀθέτησις   μὲν   γὰρ   γίνεται   προαγούσης   ἐντολῆς
3AN ANNULMENT -   1FOR   2THERE IS   OF [THE] PRECEDING COMMANDMENT

διὰ   τὸ   αὐτῆς   ἀσθενὲς   καὶ   ἀνωφελές—   **7.19** οὐδὲν
BECAUSE OF -   ITS   WEAKNESS   AND   USELESSNESS—   5NOTHING

γὰρ   ἐτελείωσεν   ὁ   νόμος—ἐπεισαγωγὴ   δὲ   κρείττονος
1FOR   4PERFECTED   2THE   3LAW—BUT~[THE] INTRODUCTION   OF A BETTER

ἐλπίδος   δι’   ἧς   ἐγγίζομεν   τῷ   θεῷ.
HOPE   THROUGH WHICH WE DRAW NEAR -   TO GOD.

7.20 Καὶ   καθ’ ὅσον   οὐ   χωρὶς   ὀρκωμοσίας·   οἱ
AND   IN AS MUCH AS [IT WAS] NOT WITHOUT AN OATH.   2THE ONES

μὲν   γὰρ   χωρὶς   ὀρκωμοσίας   εἰσὶν   ἱερεῖς   γεγονότες,
-     1FOR   WITHOUT AN OATH   ARE   HAVING BECOME~PRIESTS,

7.21 ὁ   δὲ   μετὰ   ὀρκωμοσίας   διὰ   τοῦ   λέγοντος
BUT~THE ONE WITH   AN OATH   THROUGH THE ONE SAYING

πρὸς   αὐτόν,
TO   HIM,

Ὤμοσεν κύριος
[THE] LORD~VOWED,

καὶ   οὐ μεταμεληθήσεται,
AND   HE WILL NOT CHANGE HIS MIND,

Σὺ   ἱερεὺς   εἰς τὸν αἰῶνα.
YOU [ARE] A PRIEST FOREVER.

7.22 κατὰ   τοσοῦτο [καὶ] κρείττονος διαθήκης
ACCORDING TO SUCH [A VOW] ALSO   A BETTER   COVENANT

γέγονεν ἔγγυος   Ἰησοῦς.   **7.23** καὶ οἱ μὲν πλείονές
2HAS BECOME 3A GUARANTEE 1JESUS.   AND THE -   MANY

εἰσιν γεγονότες ἱερεῖς διὰ   τὸ θανάτῳ κωλύεσθαι
HAVE BECOME   PRIESTS BECAUSE -   TO BE HINDERED~BY DEATH

παραμένειν·   **7.24** ὁ δὲ διὰ   τὸ μένειν αὐτὸν
TO CONTINUE.   -   BUT BECAUSE -   HE~CONTINUES

εἰς τὸν αἰῶνα ἀπαράβατον ἔχει τὴν ἱερωσύνην·
FOREVER,   HE HAS~AN UNCHANGEABLE -   PRIESTHOOD.

7.25 ὅθεν   καὶ σῴζειν εἰς τὸ παντελὲς δύναται τοὺς
FROM WHICH ALSO 2TO SAVE 3COMPLETELY   1HE IS ABLE THE ONES

προσερχομένους δι’   αὐτοῦ τῷ θεῷ, πάντοτε ζῶν εἰς
COMING   THROUGH HIM   -   TO GOD, ALWAYS LIVING FOR

τὸ   ἐντυγχάνειν ὑπὲρ αὐτῶν.
THE [PURPOSE OF] PLEADING   FOR   THEM.

7.26 Τοιοῦτος γὰρ   ἡμῖν καὶ   ἔπρεπεν ἀρχιερεύς,
FOR~SUCH   4FOR US 3INDEED 2WAS SUITABLE 1A HIGH PRIEST,

ὅσιος ἄκακος ἀμίαντος, κεχωρισμένος ἀπὸ τῶν
HOLY, INNOCENT, UNDEFILED, HAVING BEEN SEPARATED FROM   -

ἁμαρτωλῶν καὶ ὑψηλότερος τῶν οὐρανῶν γενόμενος,
SINNERS   AND HIGHER [THAN] THE HEAVENS HAVING BECOME,

7.27 ὃς οὐκ ἔχει καθ’ ἡμέραν ἀνάγκην, ὥσπερ οἱ
WHO DOES NOT HAVE DAILY   NEED,   AS   THE [OTHER]

7:21 Ps. 110:4

ἀρχιερεῖς,   πρότερον   ὑπὲρ   τῶν   ἰδίων   ἁμαρτιῶν
HIGH PRIESTS,   FIRST   FOR   HIS OWN   SINS

θυσίας ἀναφέρειν   ἔπειτα   τῶν   τοῦ   λαοῦ·
TO OFFER UP~A SACRIFICE, [AND]   THEN   FOR THE [SINS]   OF THE   PEOPLE.

τοῦτο γὰρ   ἐποίησεν   ἐφάπαξ   ἑαυτὸν ἀνενέγκας.   **7.28** ὁ
FOR~THIS ONE   DID [THIS]   ONCE   HAVING OFFERED UP~HIMSELF.   ²THE

νόμος γὰρ   ἀνθρώπους καθίστησιν   ἀρχιερεῖς   ἔχοντας
³LAW   ¹FOR   APPOINTS~MEN [AS]   HIGH PRIESTS,   HAVING

ἀσθένειαν, ὁ   λόγος δὲ   τῆς   ὀρκωμοσίας   τῆς   μετὰ
WEAKNESS[ES], ²THE ³WORD, ¹BUT OF THE   OATH   -   AFTER

τὸν νόμον   υἱὸν   εἰς τὸν αἰῶνα τετελειωμένον.
THE   LAW [APPOINTS] [THE] SON ²FOREVER   ¹HAVING BEEN MADE PERFECT.

to offer sacrifices day after day, first for his own sins, and then for those of the people; this he did once for all when he offered himself. ²⁸For the law appoints as high priests those who are subject to weakness, but the word of the oath, which came later than the law, appoints a Son who has been made perfect forever.

8.1 Κεφάλαιον δὲ   ἐπὶ   τοῖς   λεγομένοις,
NOW~[THE] MAIN POINT OF   THE THINGS   BEING SAID [IS THIS],

τοιοῦτον ἔχομεν   ἀρχιερέα,   ὃς   ἐκάθισεν   ἐν   δεξιᾷ
WE HAVE~SUCH   A HIGH PRIEST,   WHO SAT DOWN   AT [THE] RIGHT [HAND]

τοῦ   θρόνου τῆς   μεγαλωσύνης ἐν   τοῖς   οὐρανοῖς,
OF THE   THRONE OF THE MAJESTY   IN   THE   HEAVENS,

8.2 τῶν   ἁγίων   λειτουργὸς καὶ   τῆς   σκηνῆς   τῆς
²OF THE ³HOLY THINGS ¹A SERVANT   ⁴AND ⁵OF THE   ⁷TABERNACLE -

ἀληθινῆς, ἣν   ἔπηξεν ὁ   κύριος,   οὐκ   ἄνθρωπος.
⁶TRUE,   ⁸WHICH ¹¹SET UP ⁹THE ¹⁰LORD,   NOT   MAN.

8.3 πᾶς γὰρ   ἀρχιερεὺς εἰς   τὸ προσφέρειν   δῶρά τε καὶ
FOR~EVERY   HIGH PRIEST IN ORDER -   TO OFFER   BOTH~GIFTS AND

θυσίας καθίσταται·   ὅθεν   ἀναγκαῖον   ἔχειν
SACRIFICES IS APPOINTED.   FROM WHICH [IT WAS] NECESSARY FOR   ²TO HAVE

τι   καὶ   τοῦτον ὃ   προσενέγκῃ.   **8.4** εἰ   μὲν   οὖν
³SOMETHING ⁴ALSO ¹THIS ONE WHICH HE MIGHT OFFER.   IF   -   THEREFORE

ἦν   ἐπὶ γῆς,   οὐδ' ἂν ἦν ἱερεύς, ὄντων   τῶν
HE WERE ON   EARTH, HE WOULD NOT BE A PRIEST, BEING   THE ONES

προσφερόντων κατὰ   νόμον τὰ   δῶρα·   **8.5** οἵτινες
OFFERING   ACCORDING TO [THE] LAW THE   GIFTS;   WHO

ὑποδείγματι καὶ   σκιᾷ   λατρεύουσιν τῶν   ἐπουρανίων,
A COPY   AND   A SHADOW THEY SERVE   OF THE   HEAVENLY THINGS,

καθὼς κεχρημάτισται Μωϋσῆς μέλλων ἐπιτελεῖν   τὴν
JUST AS   MOSES~HAS BEEN WARNED,   BEING ABOUT TO COMPLETE   THE

σκηνήν, Ὅρα γὰρ φησίν,   ποιήσεις   πάντα κατὰ
TABERNACLE, FOR~SEE [TO IT], HE SAYS, [THAT] YOU WILL MAKE [IT] ACCORDING TO~ALL

τὸν τύπον τὸν δειχθέντα   σοι ἐν τῷ   ὄρει·
THE PATTERN -   HAVING BEEN SHOWN TO YOU ON THE   MOUNTAIN.

8.6 νυν[ὶ] δὲ   διαφορωτέρας τέτυχεν   λειτουργίας,
BUT~NOW   HE HAS ATTAINED TO~A MORE EXCELLENT SERVICE,

Now the main point in what we are saying is this: we have such a high priest, one who is seated at the right hand of the throne of the Majesty in the heavens, ²a minister in the sanctuary and the true tent/ that the Lord, and not any mortal, has set up. ³For every high priest is appointed to offer gifts and sacrifices; hence it is necessary for this priest also to have something to offer. ⁴Now if he were on earth, he would not be a priest at all, since there are priests who offer gifts according to the law. ⁵They offer worship in a sanctuary that is a sketch and shadow of the heavenly one; for Moses, when he was about to erect the tent,/ was warned, "See that you make everything according to the pattern that was shown you on the mountain." ⁶But Jesus™ has now obtained a more excellent ministry,

/ Or tabernacle
™ Gk he

8:5 Exod. 25:40

and to that degree he is the mediator of a better covenant, which has been enacted through better promises. ⁷For if that first covenant had been faultless, there would have been no need to look for a second one.

8 God[n] finds fault with them when he says:

"The days are surely
    coming, says the
    Lord,
when I will establish a
    new covenant with
    the house of Israel
    and with the house of
    Judah;
⁹ not like the covenant that
    I made with their
    ancestors,
on the day when I took
    them by the hand to
    lead them out of the
    land of Egypt;
for they did not continue
    in my covenant,
    and so I had no concern
    for them, says the
    Lord.
¹⁰This is the covenant that I
    will make with the
    house of Israel
after those days, says
    the Lord:
I will put my laws in their
    minds,
    and write them on their
    hearts,
and I will be their God,
    and they shall be my
    people.

[n] Gk He

ὅσῳ   καὶ   κρείττονός ἐστιν διαθήκης μεσίτης, ἥτις
IN AS MUCH AS ALSO   OF A BETTER   HE IS COVENANT~   [THE] MEDIATOR, WHICH

ἐπὶ   κρείττοσιν ἐπαγγελίαις νενομοθέτηται.
UPON   BETTER   PROMISES   HAS BEEN ENACTED.

8.7 Εἰ γὰρ ἡ πρώτη ἐκείνη ἦν ἄμεμπτος, οὐκ ἂν
FOR~IF   -   THAT~FIRST [COVENANT] WAS FAULTLESS,   ²NOT   -

δευτέρας ἐζητεῖτο   τόπος.   **8.8** μεμφόμενος γὰρ
⁴A SECOND ¹WOULD HAVE BEEN SOUGHT ³A PLACE [FOR].   FOR~FINDING FAULT [WITH]

αὐτοὺς λέγει,
THEM   HE SAYS,

    Ἰδοὺ ἡμέραι ἔρχονται, λέγει κύριος,
    BEHOLD, DAYS   ARE COMING,   SAYS [THE] LORD,

        καὶ συντελέσω ἐπὶ τὸν οἶκον Ἰσραὴλ
        AND I WILL ESTABLISH WITH THE HOUSE   OF ISRAEL

        καὶ ἐπὶ τὸν οἶκον Ἰούδα διαθήκην καινήν,
        AND WITH THE HOUSE   OF JUDAH A NEW~COVENANT,

8.9 οὐ κατὰ   τὴν διαθήκην, ἣν ἐποίησα τοῖς
NOT ACCORDING TO THE COVENANT   WHICH I MADE   WITH THE

            πατράσιν αὐτῶν
            FATHERS   OF THEM

        ἐν ἡμέρᾳ ἐπιλαβομένου μου τῆς χειρὸς
        ON [THE] DAY HAVING TAKEN   ME (I) THE   HAND

            αὐτῶν
            OF THEM

            ἐξαγαγεῖν αὐτοὺς ἐκ γῆς   Αἰγύπτου,
            TO LEAD OUT   THEM   FROM [THE] LAND OF EGYPT,

ὅτι αὐτοὶ οὐκ ἐνέμειναν ἐν τῇ διαθήκῃ μου,
BECAUSE THEY DID NOT CONTINUE IN THE COVENANT   OF ME,

    κἀγὼ ἠμέλησα   αὐτῶν, λέγει κύριος·
    AND I WAS UNCONCERNED ABOUT THEM, SAYS [THE] LORD.

8.10 ὅτι αὕτη ἡ διαθήκη, ἣν διαθήσομαι τῷ
BECAUSE THIS [IS] THE COVENANT   WHICH I WILL MAKE WITH THE

            οἴκῳ Ἰσραὴλ
            HOUSE OF ISRAEL

    μετὰ τὰς ἡμέρας ἐκείνας, λέγει κύριος·
    AFTER   -   THOSE~DAYS,   SAYS [THE] LORD;

διδοὺς νόμους μου εἰς τὴν διάνοιαν αὐτῶν
PUTTING [THE] LAWS OF ME INTO THE MIND   OF THEM,

    καὶ ἐπὶ καρδίας αὐτῶν ἐπιγράψω αὐτούς,
    AND UPON [THE] HEARTS OF THEM I WILL WRITE THEM,

καὶ ἔσομαι αὐτοῖς εἰς θεὸν,
AND I WILL BE TO THEM   - GOD,

    καὶ αὐτοὶ ἔσονταί μοι εἰς λαόν·
    AND THEY   WILL BE   TO ME - A PEOPLE;

8:8-12 Jer. 31:31-34

8.11 καὶ οὐ μὴ διδάξωσιν   ἕκαστος τὸν πολίτην
AND   BY NO MEANS MAY THEY TEACH EACH ONE THE FELLOW CITIZEN

αὐτοῦ
OF HIM

καὶ ἕκαστος τὸν ἀδελφὸν αὐτοῦ λέγων,
AND   EACH ONE   THE   BROTHER   OF HIM   SAYING,

Γνῶθι τὸν κύριον,
KNOW   THE   LORD,

ὅτι   πάντες εἰδήσουσίν με
BECAUSE ALL   WILL KNOW   ME

ἀπὸ μικροῦ ἕως μεγάλου αὐτῶν,
FROM [THE] SMALL TO [THE] GREAT OF THEM,

8.12 ὅτι   ἵλεως ἔσομαι ταῖς ἀδικίαις αὐτῶν
BECAUSE I WILL BE~MERCIFUL WITH THE WRONGDOINGS OF THEM

καὶ τῶν ἁμαρτιῶν αὐτῶν οὐ μὴ μνησθῶ
AND OF THE SINS   OF THEM BY NO MEANS MAY I REMEMBER

ἔτι.
ANY LONGER.

8.13 ἐν τῷ λέγειν Καινὴν πεπαλαίωκεν τὴν πρώτην·
WHEN   HE SAYS,   NEW,   HE HAS MADE OBSOLETE THE FIRST.

τὸ δὲ   παλαιούμενον καὶ γηράσκον ἐγγὺς
AND~THE THING BEING MADE OBSOLETE AND GROWING OLD [IS] CLOSE

ἀφανισμοῦ.
TO DESTRUCTION.

[11] And they shall not teach
one another
or say to each other,
'Know the Lord,'
for they shall all know
me,
from the least of them
to the greatest.
[12] For I will be merciful
toward their
iniquities,
and I will remember
their sins no more."
[13] In speaking of "a new
covenant," he has made the
first one obsolete. And what
is obsolete and growing old
will soon disappear.

CHAPTER 9

9.1 Εἶχε μὲν οὖν   [καὶ] ἡ πρώτη   δικαιώματα
[5]HAD   -   [1]THEREFORE [2]ALSO [3]THE [4]FIRST [COVENANT] REGULATIONS

λατρείας τό τε ἅγιον κοσμικόν. **9.2** σκηνὴ γὰρ
OF SERVICE AND~THE EARTHLY~SANCTUARY.   FOR~[THE] TENT

κατεσκευάσθη ἡ πρώτη ἐν ᾗ   ἥ τε λυχνία
WAS FURNISHED, [THAT IS] THE FIRST, IN WHICH [WERE] BOTH~THE LAMPSTAND

καὶ ἡ τράπεζα καὶ ἡ πρόθεσις τῶν ἄρτων, ἥτις
AND THE TABLE   AND THE SETTING OUT OF THE BREAD, WHICH

λέγεται Ἅγια·   **9.3** μετὰ δὲ τὸ δεύτερον
IS CALLED, [THE] HOLY PLACE.   AND~BEHIND THE SECOND

καταπέτασμα σκηνὴ ἡ λεγομένη Ἅγια Ἁγίων,
CURTAIN [WAS]   [THE] TENT - BEING CALLED, [THE] HOLY OF HOLIES,

9.4 χρυσοῦν ἔχουσα θυμιατήριον καὶ τὴν κιβωτὸν τῆς
HAVING~A GOLDEN   ALTAR OF INCENSE AND THE ARK   OF THE

διαθήκης περικεκαλυμμένην πάντοθεν χρυσίῳ, ἐν
COVENANT   HAVING BEEN COVERED   ON ALL SIDES WITH GOLD, IN

ᾗ   στάμνος χρυσῆ ἔχουσα τὸ μάννα καὶ ἡ
WHICH [WAS] A GOLDEN~JAR HAVING   THE MANNA AND THE

Now even the first covenant
had regulations for worship
and an earthly sanctuary.
[2] For a tent[o] was constructed,
the first one, in which were
the lampstand, the table, and
the bread of the Presence;[p]
this is called the Holy Place.
[3] Behind the second curtain
was a tent[o] called the Holy of
Holies. [4] In it stood the golden altar of incense and the
ark of the covenant overlaid
on all sides with gold, in
which there were a golden
urn holding the manna, and

[o] Or *tabernacle*
[p] Gk *the presentation of the loaves*

Aaron's rod that budded, and the tablets of the covenant; [5]above it were the cherubim of glory overshadowing the mercy seat.[q] Of these things we cannot speak now in detail.

6 Such preparations having been made, the priests go continually into the first tent[r] to carry out their ritual duties; [7]but only the high priest goes into the second, and he but once a year, and not without taking the blood that he offers for himself and for the sins committed unintentionally by the people. [8]By this the Holy Spirit indicates that the way into the sanctuary has not yet been disclosed as long as the first tent[r] is still standing. [9]This is a symbol[s] of the present time, during which gifts and sacrifices are offered that cannot perfect the conscience of the worshiper, [10]but deal only with food and drink and various baptisms, regulations for the body imposed until the time comes to set things right.

11 But when Christ came as a high priest of the good things that have come,[t] then through the greater and perfect[u] tent[r] (not made with hands, that is, not of this creation), [12]he entered once for all into the Holy Place, not with the blood of goats

[q] Or the place of atonement
[r] Or tabernacle
[s] Gk parable
[t] Other ancient authorities read good
   things to come
[u] Gk more perfect

ῥάβδος Ἀαρὼν   ἡ βλαστήσασα καὶ αἱ πλάκες τῆς
ROD   OF AARON [WHICH] - HAVING SPROUTED AND THE TABLETS   OF THE

διαθήκης, 9.5 ὑπεράνω δὲ αὐτῆς Χερουβὶν δόξης
COVENANT,   AND~ABOVE   IT   [THE] CHERUBIM OF GLORY

κατασκιάζοντα τὸ ἱλαστήριον·   περὶ ὧν
OVERSHADOWING   THE PLACE OF PROPITIATION; ABOUT WHICH THINGS

οὐκ ἔστιν   νῦν λέγειν κατὰ μέρος.
IT IS NOT [POSSIBLE] TO SPEAK~NOW   PART BY PART (IN DETAIL).

9.6 Τούτων δὲ   οὕτως κατεσκευασμένων εἰς μὲν τὴν
BUT~THESE THINGS THUS   HAVING BEEN PREPARED,   INTO -   THE

πρώτην σκηνὴν διὰ παντὸς εἰσίασιν οἱ ἱερεῖς τὰς
FIRST   TENT   ALWAYS   ENTER   THE PRIESTS, [2]THE

λατρείας ἐπιτελοῦντες, 9.7 εἰς δὲ τὴν δευτέραν ἅπαξ
[3]DIVINE SERVICES [1]PERFORMING,   BUT~INTO THE SECOND [TENT] ONCE

τοῦ ἐνιαυτοῦ   μόνος ὁ ἀρχιερεύς, οὐ χωρὶς αἵματος
- A YEAR [ENTERS] [3]ALONE [1]THE [2]HIGH PRIEST, NOT WITHOUT BLOOD

ὃ   προσφέρει ὑπὲρ ἑαυτοῦ καὶ τῶν τοῦ λαοῦ
WHICH HE OFFERS   FOR   HIMSELF AND [FOR] THE [2]OF THE [3]PEOPLE

ἀγνοημάτων, 9.8 τοῦτο δηλοῦντος   τοῦ πνεύματος τοῦ
[1]SINS OF IGNORANCE,   [BECAUSE] MAKING THIS CLEAR, THE   [2]SPIRIT   -

ἁγίου, μήπω πεφανερῶσθαι τὴν τῶν ἁγίων   ὁδὸν
[1]HOLY,   NOT YET TO HAVE BEEN REVEALED THE [2]THE [3]HOLY [PLACES] [1]WAY [INTO],

ἔτι τῆς πρώτης σκηνῆς ἐχούσης στάσιν, 9.9 ἥτις
YET THE FIRST   TABERNACLE HAVING   EXISTENCE,   WHICH [IS]

παραβολὴ εἰς τὸν καιρὸν τὸν ἐνεστηκότα,   καθ᾽
A PARABLE   FOR THE TIME   -   HAVING BECOME PRESENT, ACCORDING TO

ἣν δῶρά τε καὶ θυσίαι προσφέρονται μὴ δυνάμεναι
WHICH BOTH~GIFTS AND SACRIFICES ARE BEING OFFERED NOT BEING ABLE

κατὰ   συνείδησιν τελειῶσαι τὸν λατρεύοντα,
WITH RESPECT TO [THE] CONSCIENCE TO PERFECT THE ONE SERVING,

9.10 μόνον ἐπὶ βρώμασιν καὶ πόμασιν καὶ διαφόροις
ONLY   WITH FOODS   AND DRINKS   AND DIFFERENT

βαπτισμοῖς, δικαιώματα σαρκὸς μέχρι καιροῦ
WASHINGS,   HUMAN~REGULATIONS   UNTIL [THE] TIME

διορθώσεως ἐπικείμενα.
OF [THE] NEW ORDER BEING IMPOSED.

9.11 Χριστὸς δὲ παραγενόμενος ἀρχιερεὺς τῶν
NOW~CHRIST   HAVING BECOME   HIGH PRIEST   OF THE

⌐γενομένων ἀγαθῶν⌐ διὰ   τῆς μείζονος καὶ
GOOD THINGS~HAVING COME ABOUT THROUGH THE GREATER   AND

τελειοτέρας σκηνῆς οὐ χειροποιήτου, τοῦτ᾽ ἔστιν οὐ
MORE PERFECT   TABERNACLE NOT MADE BY HUMAN HANDS, THAT IS,   NOT

ταύτης τῆς κτίσεως, 9.12 οὐδὲ δι᾽   αἵματος τράγων
OF THIS -   CREATION,   NEITHER THROUGH [THE] BLOOD OF GOATS

9:11 text: ASVmg RSV NIV NASBmg NEB TEV NJBmg NRSV. var. μελλοντων αγαθων (good things
being about to come): KJV ASV RSVmg NASB NIVmg NEBmg TEVmg NJB NRSVmg.

καὶ μόσχων διὰ δὲ τοῦ ἰδίου αἵματος εἰσῆλθεν
AND OF BULLS BUT~THROUGH HIS OWN BLOOD HE ENTERED

ἐφάπαξ εἰς τὰ ἅγια αἰωνίαν λύτρωσιν εὑράμενος.
ONLY ONCE INTO THE [HOLY OF] HOLIES, ETERNAL REDEMPTION HAVING SECURED.

9.13 εἰ γὰρ τὸ αἷμα τράγων καὶ ταύρων καὶ σποδὸς
FOR~IF THE BLOOD OF GOATS AND BULLS AND [THE] ASH[ES]

δαμάλεως ῥαντίζουσα τοὺς κεκοινωμένους ἁγιάζει
OF A HEIFER SPRINKLING, ²THE ONES ³HAVING BEEN DEFILED ¹SANCTIFIES

πρὸς τὴν τῆς σαρκὸς καθαρότητα, **9.14** πόσῳ
⁴FOR ⁵THE ⁷OF THE ⁸FLESH ⁶PURITY, BY HOW MUCH

μᾶλλον τὸ αἷμα τοῦ Χριστοῦ, ὃς διὰ
MORE THE BLOOD - OF CHRIST, WHO THROUGH

πνεύματος αἰωνίου ἑαυτὸν προσήνεγκεν ἄμωμον τῷ
[THE] ETERNAL~SPIRIT OFFERED~HIMSELF BLAMELESS -

θεῷ, καθαριεῖ τὴν συνείδησιν ἡμῶν ἀπὸ νεκρῶν ἔργων
TO GOD, WILL PURIFY THE CONSCIENCE OF US FROM DEAD WORKS

εἰς τὸ λατρεύειν θεῷ ζῶντι.
IN ORDER - TO SERVE [THE] LIVING~GOD.

9.15 Καὶ διὰ τοῦτο διαθήκης καινῆς μεσίτης ἐστίν,
AND FOR THIS REASON OF A NEW~COVENANT HE IS~[THE] MEDIATOR,

ὅπως θανάτου γενομένου εἰς ἀπολύτρωσιν τῶν ἐπὶ
IN ORDER THAT DEATH HAVING HAPPENED FOR [THE] REDEMPTION OF THE ²UNDER

τῇ πρώτῃ διαθήκῃ παραβάσεων τὴν ἐπαγγελίαν
³THE ⁴FIRST ⁵COVENANT, ¹TRANSGRESSIONS ⁹THE ¹⁰PROMISE

λάβωσιν οἱ κεκλημένοι τῆς αἰωνίου
⁸MIGHT RECEIVE ⁶THE ONES ⁷HAVING BEEN CALLED OF THE ETERNAL

κληρονομίας. **9.16** ὅπου γὰρ διαθήκη,
INHERITANCE. FOR~WHERE [THERE IS] A COVENANT,

θάνατον ἀνάγκη φέρεσθαι τοῦ διαθεμένου·
IT IS NECESSARY FOR~DEATH TO BE OFFERED OF THE ONE HAVING MADE A COVENANT.

9.17 διαθήκη γὰρ ἐπὶ νεκροῖς βεβαία, ἐπεὶ
FOR~A COVENANT OVER DEAD BODIES [IS] RATIFIED, BECAUSE

μήποτε ἰσχύει ὅτε ζῇ ὁ διαθέμενος.
IT NEVER IS VALID WHEN LIVES THE ONE HAVING MADE A COVENANT.

9.18 ὅθεν οὐδὲ ἡ πρώτη χωρὶς αἵματος
FROM WHICH NOT THE FIRST [COVENANT] WITHOUT BLOOD

ἐγκεκαίνισται· **9.19** λαληθείσης γὰρ πάσης ἐντολῆς
HAS BEEN INAUGURATED. FOR~HAVING BEEN SPOKEN EVERY COMMAND

κατὰ τὸν νόμον ὑπὸ Μωϋσέως παντὶ τῷ λαῷ,
ACCORDING TO THE LAW BY MOSES TO ALL THE PEOPLE,

λαβὼν τὸ αἷμα τῶν μόσχων [καὶ τῶν τράγων] μετὰ
HAVING TAKEN THE BLOOD - OF BULLS AND - GOATS WITH

ὕδατος καὶ ἐρίου κοκκίνου καὶ ὑσσώπου αὐτό τε τὸ
WATER AND SCARLET~WOOL AND HYSSOP, ⁴ITSELF ¹BOTH ²THE

9:20 Exod. 24:8

and calves, but with his own blood, thus obtaining eternal redemption. ¹³For if the blood of goats and bulls, with the sprinkling of the ashes of a heifer, sanctifies those who have been defiled so that their flesh is purified, ¹⁴how much more will the blood of Christ, who through the eternal Spirit[v] offered himself without blemish to God, purify our[w] conscience from dead works to worship the living God!

15 For this reason he is the mediator of a new covenant, so that those who are called may receive the promised eternal inheritance, because a death has occurred that redeems them from the transgressions under the first covenant.[x] ¹⁶Where a will[x] is involved, the death of the one who made it must be established. ¹⁷For a will[x] takes effect only at death, since it is not in force as long as the one who made it is alive. ¹⁸Hence not even the first covenant was inaugurated without blood. ¹⁹For when every commandment had been told to all the people by Moses in accordance with the law, he took the blood of calves and goats,[y] with water and scarlet wool and hyssop, and sprinkled both the scroll itself

[v] Other ancient authorities read Holy Spirit
[w] Other ancient authorities read your
[x] The Greek word used here means both *covenant* and *will*
[y] Other ancient authorities lack *and goats*

and all the people, [20]saying, "This is the blood of the covenant that God has ordained for you." [21]And in the same way he sprinkled with the blood both the tent[z] and all the vessels used in worship. [22]Indeed, under the law almost everything is purified with blood, and without the shedding of blood there is no forgiveness of sins.

23 Thus it was necessary for the sketches of the heavenly things to be purified with these rites, but the heavenly things themselves need better sacrifices than these. [24]For Christ did not enter a sanctuary made by human hands, a mere copy of the true one, but he entered into heaven itself, now to appear in the presence of God on our behalf. [25]Nor was it to offer himself again and again, as the high priest enters the Holy Place year after year with blood that is not his own; [26]for then he would have had to suffer again and again since the foundation of the world. But as it is, he has appeared once for all at the end of the age to remove sin by the sacrifice of himself. [27]And just as it is appointed for mortals to die once, and after that the judgment, [28]so Christ, having been offered once

[z] Or *tabernacle*

βιβλίον καὶ πάντα τὸν λαὸν ἐράντισεν **9.20** λέγων,
[3]BOOK AND ALL THE PEOPLE HE SPRINKLED SAYING,

Τοῦτο τὸ αἷμα τῆς διαθήκης ἧς ἐνετείλατο πρὸς
THIS [IS] THE BLOOD OF THE COVENANT WHICH [2]COMMANDED [3]TO

ὑμᾶς ὁ θεός. **9.21** καὶ τὴν σκηνὴν δὲ καὶ πάντα τὰ
[4]YOU° - [1]GOD. AND THE TABERNACLE AND ALSO ALL THE

σκεύη τῆς λειτουργίας τῷ αἵματι ὁμοίως
UTENSILS OF THE DIVINE SERVICE WITH THE BLOOD IN THE SAME WAY

ἐράντισεν. **9.22** καὶ σχεδὸν ἐν αἵματι πάντα
HE SPRINKLED. AND INDEED [IT IS] BY BLOOD [THAT] EVERYTHING

καθαρίζεται κατὰ τὸν νόμον καὶ χωρὶς
IS PURIFIED ACCORDING TO THE LAW AND WITHOUT

αἱματεκχυσίας οὐ γίνεται ἄφεσις.
[THE] SHEDDING OF BLOOD THERE IS NO FORGIVENESS.

9.23 Ἀνάγκη οὖν τὰ μὲν ὑποδείγματα
THEREFORE~IT IS NECESSARY [THAT] THE - PATTERNS

τῶν ἐν τοῖς οὐρανοῖς τούτοις καθαρίζεσθαι,
OF THE THINGS IN THE HEAVENS BE PURIFIED~WITH THESE THINGS,

αὐτὰ δὲ τὰ ἐπουράνια κρείττοσιν
[4]THEMSELVES [1]BUT [2]THE [3]HEAVENLY THINGS [MUST BE PURIFIED] WITH BETTER

θυσίαις παρὰ ταύτας. **9.24** οὐ γὰρ εἰς χειροποίητα
SACRIFICES THAN THESE. FOR~NOT INTO [2]MADE BY HUMAN HANDS

εἰσῆλθεν ἅγια Χριστός, ἀντίτυπα τῶν
[3]ENTERED [1][THE HOLY OF] HOLIES CHRIST, [WHICH ARE] COPIES OF THE

ἀληθινῶν, ἀλλ᾽ εἰς αὐτὸν τὸν οὐρανόν, νῦν
TRUE THINGS, BUT INTO [2]ITSELF - [1]HEAVEN, NOW

ἐμφανισθῆναι τῷ προσώπῳ τοῦ θεοῦ ὑπὲρ ἡμῶν·
TO APPEAR BEFORE THE FACE - OF GOD FOR US.

9.25 οὐδ᾽ ἵνα πολλάκις προσφέρῃ ἑαυτόν, ὥσπερ ὁ
NOT IN ORDER THAT FREQUENTLY HE MAY OFFER HIMSELF, LIKE THE

ἀρχιερεὺς εἰσέρχεται εἰς τὰ ἅγια κατ᾽ ἐνιαυτὸν
HIGH PRIEST [WHO] ENTERS INTO THE [HOLY OF] HOLIES YEAR BY YEAR

ἐν αἵματι ἀλλοτρίῳ, **9.26** ἐπεὶ ἔδει αὐτὸν
WITH BLOOD [BELONGING] TO ANOTHER, SINCE IT WAS NECESSARY FOR HIM

πολλάκις παθεῖν ἀπὸ καταβολῆς κόσμου· νυνὶ δὲ
FREQUENTLY TO SUFFER FROM [THE] CREATION OF [THE] WORLD. BUT~NOW

ἅπαξ ἐπὶ συντελείᾳ τῶν αἰώνων εἰς ἀθέτησιν [τῆς]
ONCE AT [THE] END OF THE AGES FOR [THE] REMOVAL -

ἁμαρτίας διὰ τῆς θυσίας αὐτοῦ πεφανέρωται.
OF SINS THROUGH THE SACRIFICE OF HIMSELF HE HAS APPEARED.

9.27 καὶ καθ᾽ ὅσον ἀπόκειται τοῖς ἀνθρώποις
AND IN AS MUCH AS IT IS DESTINED - FOR MEN

ἅπαξ ἀποθανεῖν, μετὰ δὲ τοῦτο κρίσις, **9.28** οὕτως
TO DIE~ONCE, AND~AFTER THIS [COMES] JUDGMENT, SO

καὶ ὁ Χριστὸς ἅπαξ προσενεχθεὶς εἰς τὸ
ALSO - CHRIST HAVING BEEN OFFERED UP~ONCE IN ORDER -

πολλῶν ἀνενεγκεῖν ἁμαρτίας, ἐκ δευτέρου χωρὶς
TO CARRY AWAY~OF MANY   [THE] SINS,   FOR A SECOND [TIME] WITHOUT

ἁμαρτίας ὀφθήσεται τοῖς   αὐτὸν ἀπεκδεχομένοις εἰς
SIN   HE WILL APPEAR TO THE ONES AWAITING~HIM   FOR

σωτηρίαν.
SALVATION.

to bear the sins of many, will appear a second time, not to deal with sin, but to save those who are eagerly waiting for him.

10.1 Σκιὰν   γὰρ   ἔχων   ὁ   νόμος   τῶν
⁵A SHADOW ¹FOR ⁴BEING ²THE ³LAW OF THE

μελλόντων ἀγαθῶν, οὐκ   αὐτὴν   τὴν   εἰκόνα τῶν
GOOD THINGS~COMING, NOT [THE] VERY -   IMAGE OF THE

πραγμάτων, κατ᾽ ἐνιαυτὸν ταῖς   αὐταῖς θυσίαις ἃς
THINGS,   YEAR BY YEAR WITH THE SAME SACRIFICES WHICH

προσφέρουσιν εἰς τὸ διηνεκὲς οὐδέποτε δύναται
THEY OFFER   CONTINUOUSLY   NEVER   IS ABLE

τοὺς   προσερχομένους τελειῶσαι· **10.2** ἐπεὶ
²THE ONES ³APPROACHING   ¹TO PERFECT.   FOR OTHERWISE

οὐκ ἂν ἐπαύσαντο προσφερόμεναι διὰ   τὸ μηδεμίαν
WOULD THEY NOT HAVE STOPPED BEING OFFERED   BECAUSE -   ³NOT

ἔχειν ἔτι   συνείδησιν ἁμαρτιῶν τοὺς   λατρεύοντας
⁴TO HAVE ⁵STILL ⁶CONSCIOUSNESS ⁷OF SINS ¹THE ONES ²WORSHIPING

ἅπαξ κεκαθαρισμένους; **10.3** ἀλλ᾽ ἐν αὐταῖς
HAVING BEEN CLEANSED~ONCE?   BUT   BY THEM [IS]

ἀνάμνησις   ἁμαρτιῶν κατ᾽ ἐνιαυτόν·
[THE] REMEMBRANCE OF SINS   YEAR BY YEAR.

10.4 ἀδύνατον γὰρ αἷμα   ταύρων καὶ τράγων
FOR~IT IS IMPOSSIBLE FOR [THE] BLOOD OF BULLS AND OF GOATS

ἀφαιρεῖν ἁμαρτίας.
TO TAKE AWAY   SINS.

10.5 Διὸ   εἰσερχόμενος εἰς τὸν κόσμον λέγει,
THEREFORE ENTERING   INTO THE WORLD HE SAYS,

Θυσίαν καὶ   προσφορὰν οὐκ ἠθέλησας,
SACRIFICE AND OFFERING   YOU DID NOT DESIRE,

σῶμα δὲ κατηρτίσω μοι·
BUT~A BODY YOU PREPARED FOR ME.

10.6 ὁλοκαυτώματα καὶ   περὶ ἁμαρτίας
WHOLE BURNT OFFERINGS AND [OFFERINGS] FOR SIN

οὐκ εὐδόκησας.
YOU DID NOT TAKE PLEASURE IN.

10.7 τότε εἶπον,
THEN I SAID,

Ἰδοὺ ἥκω,
BEHOLD I HAVE COME,

Since the law has only a shadow of the good things to come and not the true form of these realities, it[a] can never, by the same sacrifices that are continually offered year after year, make perfect those who approach. [2]Otherwise, would they not have ceased being offered, since the worshipers, cleansed once for all, would no longer have any consciousness of sin? [3]But in these sacrifices there is a reminder of sin year after year. [4]For it is impossible for the blood of bulls and goats to take away sins. [5]Consequently, when Christ[b] came into the world, he said,

"Sacrifices and offerings
    you have not
    desired,
but a body you have
    prepared for me;
⁶ in burnt offerings and sin
    offerings
    you have taken no
    pleasure.
⁷ Then I said, 'See, God, I
    have come

[a] Other ancient authorities read *they*
[b] Gk *he*

10:5-7 Ps. 40:6-8

to do your will, O God'
(in the scroll of the
book^c it is written of
me)."
⁸When he said above, "You
have neither desired nor
taken pleasure in sacrifices
and offerings and burnt
offerings and sin offerings"
(these are offered according
to the law), ⁹then he added,
"See, I have come to do your
will." He abolishes the first
in order to establish the
second. ¹⁰And it is by God's
will^d that we have been
sanctified through the
offering of the body of Jesus
Christ once for all.

11 And every priest
stands day after day at his
service, offering again and
again the same sacrifices
that can never take away
sins. ¹²But when Christ^e had
offered for all time a single
sacrifice for sins, "he sat
down at the right hand of
God," ¹³and since then has
been waiting "until his
enemies would be made a
footstool for his feet." ¹⁴For
by a single offering he has
perfected for all time those
who are sanctified. ¹⁵And
the Holy Spirit also testifies
to us, for after saying,
¹⁶"This is the covenant that
I will make with
them

^c Meaning of Gk uncertain
^d Gk *by that will*
^e Gk *this one*

ἐν κεφαλίδι βιβλίου γέγραπται
IN [THE] ROLL OF A BOOK IT HAS BEEN WRITTEN

περὶ ἐμοῦ,
CONCERNING ME,

τοῦ ποιῆσαι ὁ θεὸς τὸ θέλημά σου.
- TO DO - [O] GOD THE WILL OF YOU.

10.8 ἀνώτερον λέγων ὅτι Θυσίας καὶ προσφορὰς καὶ
[AFTER] SAYING~ABOVE THAT SACRIFICES AND OFFERINGS AND

ὁλοκαυτώματα καὶ περὶ ἁμαρτίας οὐκ ἠθέλησας
WHOLE BURNT OFFERINGS AND [OFFERINGS] FOR SIN, YOU DID NOT DESIRE

οὐδὲ εὐδόκησας, αἵτινες κατὰ νόμον
NOR DID YOU TAKE PLEASURE IN, WHICH ACCORDING TO [THE] LAW

προσφέρονται, **10.9** τότε εἴρηκεν, Ἰδοὺ ἥκω τοῦ ποιῆσαι
ARE OFFERED, THEN HE HAS SAID, BEHOLD I COME - TO DO

τὸ θέλημά σου. ἀναιρεῖ τὸ πρῶτον ἵνα τὸ δεύτερον
THE WILL OF YOU. HE TAKES AWAY THE FIRST THAT THE SECOND

στήσῃ, **10.10** ἐν ᾧ θελήματι ἡγιασμένοι ἐσμὲν
HE MAY ESTABLISH, BY \ WHOSE WILL WE HAVE BEEN SANCTIFIED

διὰ τῆς προσφορᾶς τοῦ σώματος Ἰησοῦ Χριστοῦ
THROUGH THE OFFERING OF THE BODY OF JESUS CHRIST

ἐφάπαξ.
ONCE AND FOR ALL.

10.11 Καὶ πᾶς μὲν ἱερεὺς ἕστηκεν καθ' ἡμέραν
AND EVERY - PRIEST HAS STOOD DAY BY DAY

λειτουργῶν καὶ τὰς αὐτὰς πολλάκις προσφέρων θυσίας,
SERVING AND ²THE ³SAME ⁵FREQUENTLY ¹OFFERING ⁴SACRIFICES,

αἵτινες οὐδέποτε δύνανται περιελεῖν ἁμαρτίας,
WHICH NEVER ARE ABLE TO TAKE AWAY SINS,

10.12 οὗτος δὲ μίαν ὑπὲρ ἁμαρτιῶν προσενέγκας θυσίαν
BUT~THIS ONE ²ONE ⁴FOR ⁵SINS ¹HAVING OFFERED ³SACRIFICE

εἰς τὸ διηνεκὲς ἐκάθισεν ἐν δεξιᾷ τοῦ θεοῦ,
⁷FOREVER ⁶SAT DOWN AT [THE] RIGHT [HAND] - OF GOD,

10.13 τὸ λοιπὸν ἐκδεχόμενος ἕως τεθῶσιν οἱ ἐχθροὶ
FROM THIS TIME FORWARD WAITING UNTIL ARE PUT THE ENEMIES

αὐτοῦ ὑποπόδιον τῶν ποδῶν αὐτοῦ. **10.14** μιᾷ γὰρ
OF HIM A FOOTSTOOL OF THE FEET OF HIM. FOR~BY ONE

προσφορᾷ τετελείωκεν εἰς τὸ διηνεκὲς τοὺς
OFFERING HE HAS PERFECTED FOREVER THE ONES

ἁγιαζομένους.
BEING SANCTIFIED.

10.15 Μαρτυρεῖ δὲ ἡμῖν καὶ τὸ πνεῦμα τὸ ἅγιον·
AND~BEARS WITNESS TO US ALSO THE ²SPIRIT - ¹HOLY;

μετὰ γὰρ τὸ εἰρηκέναι,
FOR~AFTER [THIS] - HE HAS SAID,

10.16 Αὕτη ἡ διαθήκη ἣν διαθήσομαι πρὸς αὐτοὺς
THIS [IS] THE COVENANT WHICH I WILL MAKE WITH THEM

10:16-17 Jer. 31:33-34

μετὰ τὰς ἡμέρας ἐκείνας, λέγει κύριος·
AFTER   -   THOSE~DAYS,   SAYS   [THE] LORD;

διδοὺς νόμους μου ἐπὶ καρδίας αὐτῶν
PUTTING   [THE] LAWS OF ME ON   [THE] HEARTS OF THEM

καὶ ἐπὶ τὴν διάνοιαν αὐτῶν ἐπιγράψω
AND UPON THE   MIND   OF THEM I WILL INSCRIBE

αὐτούς,
THEM,

10.17 καὶ τῶν ἁμαρτιῶν αὐτῶν καὶ τῶν ἀνομιῶν αὐτῶν
AND OF THE SINS   OF THEM AND   THE LAWLESSNESSES OF THEM

οὐ μὴ μνησθήσομαι ἔτι.
I WILL BY NO MEANS REMEMBER   ANY LONGER.

10.18 ὅπου δὲ   ἄφεσις τούτων,   οὐκέτι
NOW~WHERE [THERE IS] FORGIVENESS OF THESE THINGS, [THERE IS] NO LONGER

προσφορὰ περὶ ἁμαρτίας.
AN OFFERING   FOR   SIN.

10.19 Ἔχοντες οὖν,   ἀδελφοί, παρρησίαν εἰς τὴν
HAVING   THEREFORE, BROTHERS, BOLDNESS   FOR -

εἴσοδον τῶν ἁγίων ἐν τῷ αἵματι Ἰησοῦ,
ENTERING [THE HOLY] -   OF HOLIES BY THE BLOOD   OF JESUS,

10.20 ἣν ἐνεκαίνισεν ἡμῖν ὁδὸν πρόσφατον καὶ ζῶσαν
WHICH HE OPENED   FOR US A NEW~WAY   AND   LIVING

διὰ τοῦ καταπετάσματος, τοῦτ' ἔστιν τῆς σαρκὸς
THROUGH THE   CURTAIN,   THAT IS TO SAY,   THE FLESH

αὐτοῦ, **10.21** καὶ   ἱερέα μέγαν ἐπὶ τὸν οἶκον
OF HIM,   AND [SINCE WE HAVE] A GREAT~PRIEST OVER THE HOUSE

τοῦ θεοῦ, **10.22** προσερχώμεθα μετὰ ἀληθινῆς καρδίας
-   OF GOD,   LET US APPROACH [GOD] WITH   A TRUE   HEART

ἐν πληροφορίᾳ πίστεως ῥεραντισμένοι τὰς καρδίας
WITH FULL CONFIDENCE   OF FAITH   HAVING BEEN SPRINKLED THE HEARTS

ἀπὸ συνειδήσεως πονηρᾶς καὶ λελουσμένοι τὸ σῶμα
FROM A CONSCIENCE   OF EVIL   AND   HAVING BEEN WASHED THE BODY

ὕδατι καθαρῷ· **10.23** κατέχωμεν τὴν ὁμολογίαν
WITH PURE~WATER.   LET US HOLD FIRMLY THE   CONFESSION

τῆς ἐλπίδος ἀκλινῆ,   πιστὸς γὰρ ὁ
OF THE HOPE   WITHOUT WAVERING, FOR~TRUSTWORTHY [IS] THE ONE

ἐπαγγειλάμενος, **10.24** καὶ κατανοῶμεν ἀλλήλους
HAVING PROMISED,   AND LET US CONSIDER ³ONE ANOTHER [TO]

εἰς παροξυσμὸν ἀγάπης καὶ καλῶν ἔργων,
¹FOR ²STIRRING UP   LOVE   AND GOOD   WORKS,

10.25 μὴ ἐγκαταλείποντες τὴν ἐπισυναγωγὴν ἑαυτῶν,
NOT ABANDONING   THE   GATHERING TOGETHER OF OURSELVES,

καθὼς ἔθος τισίν, ἀλλὰ παρακαλοῦντες,   καὶ
AS [IT IS] [THE] HABIT [OF] SOME, BUT   ENCOURAGING [ONE ANOTHER], AND

τοσούτῳ μᾶλλον ὅσῳ βλέπετε ἐγγίζουσαν τὴν ἡμέραν.
BY SO MUCH MORE   AS YOU° SEE APPROACHING   THE   DAY.

10.26 Ἑκουσίως γὰρ ἁμαρτανόντων ἡμῶν μετὰ τὸ
FOR~[WHEN] INTENTIONALLY SINNING   AFTER~WE   -

after those days, says
   the Lord:
I will put my laws in their
   hearts,
and I will write them on
   their minds,"
[17]he also adds,
   "I will remember[f] their
   sins and their
   lawless deeds no
   more."
[18]Where there is forgiveness
of these, there is no longer
any offering for sin.

19 Therefore, my
friends,[g] since we have
confidence to enter the
sanctuary by the blood of
Jesus, [20]by the new and
living way that he opened for
us through the curtain (that
is, through his flesh), [21]and
since we have a great priest
over the house of God, [22]let
us approach with a true heart
in full assurance of faith,
with our hearts sprinkled
clean from an evil con-
science and our bodies
washed with pure water.
[23]Let us hold fast to the
confession of our hope
without wavering, for he
who has promised is faithful.
[24]And let us consider how to
provoke one another to love
and good deeds, [25]not
neglecting to meet together,
as is the habit of some, but
encouraging one another,
and all the more as you see
the Day approaching.
   26 For if we willfully
persist in sin after having

[f] Gk on their minds and I will
   remember
[g] Gk Therefore, brothers

received the knowledge of the truth, there is no longer remains a sacrifice for sins, [27]but a fearful prospect of judgment, and a fury of fire that will consume the adversaries. [28]Anyone who has violated the law of Moses dies without mercy "on the testimony of two or three witnesses." [29]How much worse punishment do you think will be deserved by those who have spurned the Son of God, profaned the blood of the covenant by which they were sanctified, and outraged the Spirit of grace? [30]For we know the one who said, "Vengeance is mine, I will repay." And again, "The Lord will judge his people." [31]It is a fearful thing to fall into the hands of the living God.

32 But recall those earlier days when, after you had been enlightened, you endured a hard struggle with sufferings, [33]sometimes being publicly exposed to abuse and persecution, and sometimes being partners with those so treated. [34]For you had compassion for those who were in prison, and you cheerfully accepted the plundering of your possessions,

λαβεῖν τὴν ἐπίγνωσιν τῆς ἀληθείας, οὐκέτι περὶ
RECEIVED THE FULL KNOWLDEGE OF THE TRUTH, NO LONGER FOR

ἁμαρτιῶν ἀπολείπεται θυσία, **10.27** φοβερὰ δέ τις
SINS THERE REMAINS A SACRIFICE, ³TERRIBLE ¹BUT ²SOME

ἐκδοχὴ κρίσεως καὶ πυρὸς ζῆλος ἐσθίειν μέλλοντος
EXPECTATION OF JUDGMENT AND OF A BLAZING~FIRE BEING ABOUT~TO CONSUME

τοὺς ὑπεναντίους. **10.28** ἀθετήσας τις νόμον
THE ONES OPPOSED. ANYONE~HAVING DECLARED INVALID [THE] LAW

Μωϋσέως χωρὶς οἰκτιρμῶν ἐπὶ δυσὶν ἢ τρισὶν
OF MOSES, WITHOUT MERCY UPON [THE WORD OF] TWO OR THREE

μάρτυσιν ἀποθνήσκει· **10.29** πόσῳ δοκεῖτε
WITNESSES DIES. BY HOW MUCH ³DO YOU° THINK

χείρονος ἀξιωθήσεται τιμωρίας ὁ τὸν υἱὸν
¹WORSE ⁴WILL BE CONSIDERED WORTHY ²PUNISHMENT ⁵THE ONE ⁷THE ⁸SON

τοῦ θεοῦ καταπατήσας καὶ τὸ αἷμα τῆς διαθήκης
- ⁹OF GOD ⁶HAVING TRAMPLED ON AND THE BLOOD OF THE COVENANT

κοινὸν ἡγησάμενος, ἐν ᾧ ἡγιάσθη, καὶ τὸ
HAVING CONSIDERED~A COMMON THING, BY WHICH HE WAS SANCTIFIED AND THE

πνεῦμα τῆς χάριτος ἐνυβρίσας; **10.30** οἴδαμεν γὰρ
SPIRIT - OF GRACE HAVING INSULTED? FOR~WE KNOW

τὸν εἰπόντα,
THE ONE HAVING SAID,

Ἐμοὶ ἐκδίκησις, ἐγὼ ἀνταποδώσω.
TO ME [IS] VENGEANCE, I WILL REPAY.

καὶ πάλιν,
AND AGAIN,

Κρινεῖ κύριος τὸν λαὸν αὐτοῦ.
[THE] LORD~WILL JUDGE THE PEOPLE OF HIM.

10.31 φοβερὸν τὸ ἐμπεσεῖν εἰς χεῖρας
[IT IS] A FEARFUL THING - TO FALL INTO [THE] HANDS

θεοῦ ζῶντος.
OF [THE] LIVING~GOD.

10.32 Ἀναμιμνῄσκεσθε δὲ τὰς πρότερον ἡμέρας,
BUT~REMEMBER THE EARLIER DAYS,

ἐν αἷς φωτισθέντες πολλὴν ἄθλησιν
IN WHICH HAVING BEEN ENLIGHTENED A GREAT STRUGGLE

ὑπεμείνατε παθημάτων, **10.33** τοῦτο μὲν ὀνειδισμοῖς τε
OF SUFFERING~YOU° ENDURED, SOMETIMES BOTH~TO INSULTS

καὶ θλίψεσιν θεατριζόμενοι, τοῦτο δὲ κοινωνοὶ
AND TO PERSECUTIONS BEING MADE A PUBLIC SPECTACLE, OTHER TIMES ²PARTNERS

τῶν οὕτως ἀναστρεφομένων γενηθέντες.
³OF THE ONES ⁵THUS ⁴HAVING LIVED ¹HAVING BECOME.

10.34 καὶ γὰρ τοῖς δεσμίοις συνεπαθήσατε καὶ τὴν
FOR~INDEED - WITH PRISONERS YOU° SYMPATHIZED AND THE

ἁρπαγὴν τῶν ὑπαρχόντων ὑμῶν μετὰ χαρᾶς
SEIZING OF THE POSSESSIONS OF YOU° WITH JOY

10:30 Deut. 32:35-36

προσεδέξασθε γινώσκοντες ἔχειν ἑαυτοὺς κρείττονα
YOU° WELCOMED   KNOWING   TO HAVE FOR YOURSELVES A BETTER

ὕπαρξιν καὶ μένουσαν.   **10.35** μὴ ἀποβάλητε οὖν τὴν
POSSESSION AND AN ENDURING [ONE].   DO NOT THROW AWAY   THEN,   THE

παρρησίαν ὑμῶν, ἥτις ἔχει μεγάλην μισθαποδοσίαν.
CONFIDENCE   OF YOU° WHICH HAS   GREAT   REWARD.

10.36 ὑπομονῆς γὰρ ἔχετε χρείαν ἵνα τὸ θέλημα τοῦ
        ⁴OF ENDURANCE ¹FOR ²YOU° HAVE ³NEED   THAT THE WILL   -

θεοῦ ποιήσαντες κομίσησθε τὴν ἐπαγγελίαν.
OF GOD HAVING DONE,   YOU° MAY RECEIVE THE   PROMISE.

10.37 ἔτι γὰρ μικρὸν ὅσον ὅσον,
        FOR~YET   IN A VERY LITTLE WHILE,

    ὁ   ἐρχόμενος ἥξει   καὶ οὐ χρονίσει·
    THE ONE COMING   WILL COME AND   WILL NOT DELAY;

10.38 ὁ δὲ δίκαιός μου ἐκ πίστεως ζήσεται,
        AND~THE RIGHTEOUS ONE OF ME BY FAITH   WILL LIVE,

καὶ ἐὰν ὑποστείληται,
AND IF HE DRAWS BACK,

        οὐκ εὐδοκεῖ ἡ ψυχή μου ἐν αὐτῷ.
        IS NOT PLEASED   THE SOUL OF ME WITH HIM.

10.39 ἡμεῖς δὲ οὐκ ἐσμὲν ὑποστολῆς   εἰς
        BUT~WE   ARE NOT   OF [THOSE] SHRINKING BACK TOWARD

ἀπώλειαν ἀλλὰ πίστεως εἰς   περιποίησιν ψυχῆς.
DESTRUCTION BUT   OF FAITH TOWARD [THE] PRESERVING OF [THE] SOUL.

10:37-38 Hab. 2:3-4 LXX

knowing that you yourselves possessed something better and more lasting. ³⁵Do not, therefore, abandon that confidence of yours; it brings a great reward. ³⁶For you need endurance, so that when you have done the will of God, you may receive what was promised. ³⁷For yet

"in a very little while,
    the one who is coming
    will come and will
    not delay;
³⁸ but my righteous one will
    live by faith.
My soul takes no
    pleasure in anyone
    who shrinks back."
³⁹But we are not among those who shrink back and so are lost, but among those who have faith and so are saved.

11.1 Ἔστιν δὲ πίστις ἐλπιζομένων ὑπόστασις,
        ³IS   ¹NOW ²FAITH   [THE] ASSURANCE~[OF THINGS] BEING HOPED FOR,

πραγμάτων ἔλεγχος οὐ βλεπομένων. **11.2** ἐν ταύτῃ γὰρ
[THE] CONVICTION~OF THINGS   NOT HAVING SEEN.   ²BY ³THIS   ¹FOR

ἐμαρτυρήθησαν οἱ πρεσβύτεροι.
WERE GIVEN APPROVAL THE ELDERS.

11.3 Πίστει νοοῦμεν κατηρτίσθαι τοὺς αἰῶνας
        BY FAITH WE UNDERSTAND TO HAVE BEEN CREATED THE   WORLDS

ῥήματι θεοῦ, εἰς τὸ μὴ ἐκ φαινομένων τὸ
BY [THE] WORD OF GOD, SO AS NOT FROM VISIBLE [THINGS] THE THING[S]

βλεπόμενον γεγονέναι.
SEEING   TO HAVE COME TO BE.

11.4 Πίστει πλείονα θυσίαν ῎Αβελ παρὰ Κάϊν
        BY FAITH ⁴A GREATER ⁵SACRIFICE ¹ABEL ⁶THAN ⁷CAIN

προσήνεγκεν τῷ θεῷ, δι᾽ ἧς ἐμαρτυρήθη εἶναι
²OFFERED   -   ³TO GOD, BY WHICH HE WAS COMMENDED TO BE

δίκαιος, μαρτυροῦντος ἐπὶ τοῖς δώροις αὐτοῦ τοῦ θεοῦ,
RIGHTEOUS, ²BEARING WITNESS ³TO ⁴THE ⁵GIFTS ⁶OF HIM -   ¹GOD,

Now faith is the assurance of things hoped for, the conviction of things not seen. ²Indeed, by faith[h] our ancestors received approval. ³By faith we understand that the worlds were prepared by the word of God, so that what is seen was made from things that are not visible.[i]

4 By faith Abel offered to God a more acceptable[j] sacrifice than Cain's. Through this he received approval as righteous, God himself giving approval to

[h] Gk *by this*
[i] Or *was not made out of visible things*
[j] Gk *greater*

his gifts; he died, but through his faith[k] he still speaks. [5]By faith Enoch was taken so that he did not experience death; and "he was not found, because God had taken him." For it was attested before he was taken away that "he had pleased God." [6]And without faith it is impossible to please God, for whoever would approach him must believe that he exists and that he rewards those who seek him. [7]By faith Noah, warned by God about events as yet unseen, respected the warning and built an ark to save his household; by this he condemned the world and became an heir to the righteousness that is in accordance with faith.

8 By faith Abraham obeyed when he was called to set out for a place that he was to receive as an inheritance; and he set out, not knowing where he was going. [9]By faith he stayed for a time in the land he had been promised, as in a foreign land, living in tents, as did Isaac and Jacob, who were heirs with him of the same promise. [10]For he looked forward to the city that has foundations, whose architect and builder is God. [11]By faith he received power of procreation, even though he was too old—and Sarah herself was barren—because he considered him faithful who had promised.[l]

[k] Gk *through it*
[l] Or *By faith Sarah herself, though barren, received power to conceive, even when she was too old, because she considered him faithful who had promised.*

καὶ δι' αὐτῆς ἀποθανὼν ἔτι λαλεῖ.   **11.5** Πίστει Ἐνὼχ
AND BY IT, HAVING DIED, YET HE SPEAKS.   BY FAITH ENOCH

μετετέθη τοῦ μὴ ἰδεῖν θάνατον, καὶ οὐχ ηὑρίσκετο
WAS TAKEN UP - NOT TO SEE DEATH, AND HE WAS NOT FOUND

διότι μετέθηκεν αὐτὸν ὁ θεός. πρὸ γὰρ τῆς
BECAUSE [2]TOOK UP [3]HIM - [1]GOD. FOR~BEFORE [HE WAS] -

μεταθέσεως μεμαρτύρηται εὐαρεστηκέναι τῷ θεῷ·
TAKEN UP, HE HAS RECEIVED TESTIMONY TO HAVE BEEN PLEASING - TO GOD.

11.6 χωρὶς δὲ πίστεως ἀδύνατον εὐαρεστῆσαι·
AND~WITHOUT FAITH IT IS IMPOSSIBLE TO PLEASE [HIM].

πιστεῦσαι γὰρ δεῖ τὸν προσερχόμενον τῷ
[5]TO BELIEVE [1]FOR [2]IT IS NECESSARY FOR [3]THE ONE [4]APPROACHING -

θεῷ ὅτι ἔστιν καὶ τοῖς ἐκζητοῦσιν αὐτὸν
[6]IN GOD, THAT HE IS AND TO THE ONES SEEKING HIM

μισθαποδότης γίνεται.   **11.7** Πίστει χρηματισθεὶς Νῶε
HE BECOMES~[THE] REWARDER.   BY FAITH NOAH~HAVING BEEN WARNED

περὶ τῶν μηδέπω βλεπομένων, εὐλαβηθεὶς
NOAH ABOUT THE THINGS NOT YET BEING SEEN, HAVING BEEN REVERENT,

κατεσκεύασεν κιβωτὸν εἰς σωτηρίαν τοῦ οἴκου αὐτοῦ
HE BUILT [THE] ARK FOR [THE] SALVATION OF THE HOUSE OF HIM

δι' ἧς κατέκρινεν τὸν κόσμον, καὶ τῆς κατὰ
BY WHICH HE CONDEMNED THE WORLD, AND [3]OF THE [5]ACCORDING TO

πίστιν δικαιοσύνης ἐγένετο κληρονόμος.
[6]FAITH [4]RIGHTEOUSNESS [1]HE BECAME [2]HEIR.

11.8 Πίστει καλούμενος Ἀβραὰμ ὑπήκουσεν ἐξελθεῖν
BY FAITH ABRAHAM~BEING CALLED, OBEYED TO GO OUT

εἰς τόπον ὃν ἤμελλεν λαμβάνειν εἰς κληρονομίαν,
TO A PLACE WHICH HE WAS ABOUT TO RECEIVE FOR AN INHERITANCE,

καὶ ἐξῆλθεν μὴ ἐπιστάμενος ποῦ ἔρχεται.   **11.9** Πίστει
AND HE WENT OUT NOT KNOWING WHERE HE IS GOING.   BY FAITH

παρῴκησεν εἰς γῆν τῆς ἐπαγγελίας ὡς ἀλλοτρίαν
HE MIGRATED TO [THE] LAND OF THE PROMISE AS [IN] A STRANGE [LAND],

ἐν σκηναῖς κατοικήσας μετὰ Ἰσαὰκ καὶ Ἰακὼβ τῶν
IN TENTS HAVING LIVED WITH ISAAC AND JACOB, THE

συγκληρονόμων τῆς ἐπαγγελίας τῆς αὐτῆς·
FELLOW-HEIRS OF THE [2]PROMISE - [1]SAME.

11.10 ἐξεδέχετο γὰρ τὴν τοὺς θεμελίους ἔχουσαν
FOR~HE WAS LOOKING FORWARD TO THE - [3]FOUNDATIONS [2]HAVING

πόλιν ἧς τεχνίτης καὶ δημιουργὸς ὁ θεός.
[1]CITY OF WHICH [THE] DESIGNER AND MAKER [IS] - GOD.

11.11 ⌜Πίστει καὶ αὐτὴ Σάρρα στεῖρα δύναμιν
BY FAITH ALSO SARAH~HERSELF, A BARREN [WOMAN], [2]ABILITY

εἰς καταβολὴν σπέρματος ἔλαβεν⌝ καὶ
[3]TO [4]ESTABLISH [5]A POSTERITY [1]RECEIVED EVEN

παρὰ καιρὸν ἡλικίας, ἐπεὶ πιστὸν ἡγήσατο τὸν
BEYOND NORMAL AGE, SINCE SHE CONSIDERED~FAITHFUL THE ONE

11:5 Gen. 5:24 LXX   **11:11** text: NIV TEV NRSV.   var. πιστει και αυτη Σαρρα δυναμιν εις καταβολην σπερματος ελαβεν (by faith even Sarah herself received power to conceive [from] a seed): KJV ASV NASB RSV NIVmg NEB TEVmg NJB NRSVmg.

ἐπαγγειλάμενον· **11.12** διὸ   καὶ ἀφ’ ἑνὸς
HAVING PROMISED.   THEREFORE ALSO FROM ONE [PERSON]

ἐγεννήθησαν, καὶ ταῦτα νενεκρωμένου,   καθὼς
WERE BORN [MANY],   AND   THESE   HAVING BEEN AS GOOD AS DEAD, AS [NUMEROUS AS]

τὰ ἄστρα τοῦ οὐρανοῦ τῷ πλήθει καὶ ὡς ἡ ἄμμος ἡ
THE STARS   -   OF HEAVEN -   IN NUMBER AND AS   THE ²SAND   -

παρὰ τὸ χεῖλος τῆς θαλάσσης ἡ ἀναρίθμητος.
³ALONG ⁴THE ⁵SHORE ⁶OF THE ⁷SEA   -   ¹INNUMERABLE.

11.13 Κατὰ   πίστιν ἀπέθανον οὗτοι πάντες, μὴ
          ACCORDING TO FAITH ³DIED   ¹THESE ²ALL,   NOT

λαβόντες τὰς ἐπαγγελίας ἀλλὰ πόρρωθεν
HAVING RECEIVED THE PROMISES   BUT   FROM A DISTANCE

αὐτὰς ἰδόντες καὶ ἀσπασάμενοι   καὶ ὁμολογήσαντες
HAVING SEEN~THESE AND   HAVING WELCOMED [THEM] AND   HAVING CONFESSED

ὅτι ξένοι καὶ παρεπίδημοί εἰσιν ἐπὶ τῆς γῆς.
THAT STRANGERS AND   EXILES   THEY ARE ON   THE EARTH.

11.14 οἱ γὰρ   τοιαῦτα λέγοντες ἐμφανίζουσιν ὅτι
          FOR~THE ONES SAYING~SUCH THINGS   MAKE IT CLEAR   THAT

πατρίδα ἐπιζητοῦσιν.   **11.15** καὶ   εἰ   μὲν
THEY ARE SEARCHING FOR~A COUNTRY.   AND   IF   -

ἐκείνης ἐμνημόνευον   ἀφ’ ἧς   ἐξέβησαν,
THEY WERE REMEMBERING~THAT [COUNTRY] FROM WHICH THEY CAME OUT,

εἶχον ἂν   καιρὸν ἀνακάμψαι· **11.16** νῦν δὲ
THEY WOULD HAVE HAD AN OPPORTUNITY TO RETURN.   BUT~NOW

κρείττονος ὀρέγονται, τοῦτ’ ἔστιν ἐπουρανίου. διὸ
THEY STRIVE FOR~A BETTER [COUNTRY], THAT IS TO SAY A HEAVENLY [ONE]. THEREFORE

οὐκ ἐπαισχύνεται αὐτοὺς ὁ θεὸς θεὸς ἐπικαλεῖσθαι
²IS NOT ASHAMED   ³OF THEM - ¹GOD TO BE CALLED~[THE] GOD

αὐτῶν· ἡτοίμασεν γὰρ αὐτοῖς πόλιν.
OF THEM.   FOR~HE PREPARED   FOR THEM A CITY.

11.17 Πίστει προσενήνοχεν Ἀβραὰμ τὸν Ἰσαὰκ
          BY FAITH ABRAHAM~HAS OFFERED   -   ISAAC,

πειραζόμενος καὶ   τὸν μονογενῆ προσέφερεν, ὁ
BEING TESTED   AND [HIS] -   ONLY [SON] HE WAS OFFERING, THE ONE

τὰς ἐπαγγελίας ἀναδεξάμενος, **11.18** πρὸς ὃν ἐλαλήθη
THE PROMISES   HAVING RECEIVED,   ABOUT WHOM IT WAS SAID,

ὅτι Ἐν Ἰσαὰκ κληθήσεταί σοι σπέρμα,
-   IN   ISAAC   WILL BE CALLED YOUR SEED,

11.19 λογισάμενος ὅτι καὶ ἐκ νεκρῶν ἐγείρειν
          HAVING CONSIDERED THAT ³ALSO ⁴FROM ⁵[THE] DEAD ⁶TO RAISE UP

δυνατὸς ὁ θεός, ὅθεν   αὐτὸν καὶ ἐν παραβολῇ
²ABLE   - ¹GOD [IS], FROM WHICH HE   ALSO SYMBOLICALLY

ἐκομίσατο.   **11.20** Πίστει καὶ περὶ
RECEIVED [HIM] BACK [FROM THE DEAD].   BY FAITH ALSO CONCERNING [THE THINGS]

μελλόντων εὐλόγησεν Ἰσαὰκ τὸν Ἰακὼβ
ABOUT TO BE, ISAAC~BLESSED   -   JACOB

11:18 Gen. 21:12

[12]Therefore from one person, and this one as good as dead, descendants were born, "as many as the stars of heaven and as the innumerable grains of sand by the seashore."

13 All of these died in faith without having received the promises, but from a distance they saw and greeted them. They confessed that they were strangers and foreigners on the earth, [14]for people who speak in this way make it clear that they are seeking a homeland. [15]If they had been thinking of the land that they had left behind, they would have had opportunity to return. [16]But as it is, they desire a better country, that is, a heavenly one. Therefore God is not ashamed to be called their God; indeed, he has prepared a city for them.

17 By faith Abraham, when put to the test, offered up Isaac. He who had received the promises was ready to offer up his only son, [18]of whom he had been told, "It is through Isaac that descendants shall be named for you." [19]He considered the fact that God is able even to raise someone from the dead—and figuratively speaking, he did receive him back. [20]By faith Isaac invoked blessings for the future on Jacob

and Esau. ²¹By faith Jacob, when dying, blessed each of the sons of Joseph, "bowing in worship over the top of his staff." ²²By faith Joseph, at the end of his life, made mention of the exodus of the Israelites and gave instructions about his burial.^m

23 By faith Moses was hidden by his parents for three months after his birth, because they saw that the child was beautiful; and they were not afraid of the king's edict.ⁿ ²⁴By faith Moses, when he was grown up, refused to be called a son of Pharaoh's daughter, ²⁵choosing rather to share ill-treatment with the people of God than to enjoy the fleeting pleasures of sin. ²⁶He considered abuse suffered for the Christ^o to be greater wealth than the treasures of Egypt, for he was looking ahead to the reward. ²⁷By faith he left Egypt, unafraid of the king's anger; for he persevered as though^p he saw him who is invisible. ²⁸By faith he kept the Passover and the sprinkling of blood, so that the destroyer of the firstborn would not touch the firstborn of Israel.^q

29 By faith the people passed through the Red Sea as if it were dry land, but when the Egyptians attempted to do so they were drowned.

^m Gk his bones
ⁿ Other ancient authorities add By faith Moses, when he was grown up, killed the Egyptian, because he observed the humiliation of his people (Gk brothers)
^o Or the Messiah
^p Or because
^q Gk would not touch them

καὶ τὸν Ἠσαῦ. **11.21** Πίστει Ἰακὼβ ἀποθνῄσκων
AND - ESAU. BY FAITH JACOB [WHILE] DYING

ἕκαστον τῶν υἱῶν Ἰωσὴφ εὐλόγησεν καὶ προσεκύνησεν
EACH OF THE SONS OF JOSEPH BLESSED AND HE WORSHIPED

ἐπὶ τὸ ἄκρον τῆς ῥάβδου αὐτοῦ. **11.22** Πίστει Ἰωσὴφ
ON THE TOP OF THE STAFF OF HIM. BY FAITH JOSEPH

τελευτῶν περὶ τῆς ἐξόδου τῶν υἱῶν Ἰσραὴλ
[WHILE] DYING, CONCERNING THE EXODUS OF THE SONS OF ISRAEL

ἐμνημόνευσεν καὶ περὶ τῶν ὀστέων αὐτοῦ
MADE MENTION AND CONCERNING THE BONES OF HIM

ἐνετείλατο.
HE GAVE ORDERS.

11.23 Πίστει Μωϋσῆς γεννηθεὶς ἐκρύβη τρίμηνον
BY FAITH MOSES HAVING BEEN BORN WAS HIDDEN THREE MONTHS

ὑπὸ τῶν πατέρων αὐτοῦ, διότι εἶδον ἀστεῖον τὸ
BY THE PARENTS OF HIM, BECAUSE THEY SAW [THAT] ³BEAUTIFUL ¹THE

παιδίον καὶ οὐκ ἐφοβήθησαν τὸ διάταγμα τοῦ
²CHILD [WAS] AND THEY WERE NOT AFRAID OF THE DECREE OF THE

βασιλέως. **11.24** Πίστει Μωϋσῆς μέγας γενόμενος
KING. BY FAITH MOSES HAVING BECOME~FULL GROWN

ἠρνήσατο λέγεσθαι υἱὸς θυγατρὸς Φαραώ,
REFUSED TO BE CALLED [THE] SON OF [THE] DAUGHTER OF PHARAOH,

11.25 μᾶλλον ἑλόμενος συγκακουχεῖσθαι τῷ λαῷ τοῦ
RATHER HAVING CHOSEN TO BE MISTREATED WITH THE PEOPLE -

θεοῦ ἢ πρόσκαιρον ἔχειν ἁμαρτίας ἀπόλαυσιν,
OF GOD THAN TEMPORARILY TO HAVE [THE] ENJOYMENT~OF SIN,

11.26 μείζονα πλοῦτον ἡγησάμενος τῶν
GREATER WEALTH HAVING CONSIDERED [THAN] THE

Αἰγύπτου θησαυρῶν τὸν ὀνειδισμὸν τοῦ Χριστοῦ·
TREASURES~OF EGYPT THE REPROACH - OF CHRIST.

ἀπέβλεπεν γὰρ εἰς τὴν μισθαποδοσίαν. **11.27** Πίστει
FOR~HE WAS PAYING ATTENTION TO THE REWARD. BY FAITH

κατέλιπεν Αἴγυπτον μὴ φοβηθεὶς τὸν θυμὸν τοῦ
HE LEFT EGYPT NOT HAVING FEARED THE ANGER OF THE

βασιλέως· τὸν γὰρ ἀόρατον ὡς ὁρῶν ἐκαρτέρησεν.
KING; FOR~THE ONE UNSEEN AS SEEING HE PERSEVERED.

11.28 Πίστει πεποίηκεν τὸ πάσχα καὶ τὴν πρόσχυσιν
BY FAITH HE HAS INSTITUTED THE PASSOVER AND THE POURING OUT

τοῦ αἵματος, ἵνα μὴ ὁ ὀλοθρεύων τὰ πρωτότοκα
OF THE BLOOD, LEST THE ONE DESTROYING THE FIRSTBORN CHILDREN

θίγῃ αὐτῶν. **11.29** Πίστει διέβησαν τὴν
HE MIGHT TOUCH THEM. BY FAITH THEY WENT THROUGH THE

Ἐρυθρὰν Θάλασσαν ὡς διὰ ξηρᾶς γῆς, ἧς
RED SEA AS THROUGH DRY LAND, OF WHICH

πεῖραν λαβόντες οἱ Αἰγύπτιοι κατεπόθησαν.
AN ATTEMPT HAVING MADE THE EGYPTIANS WERE DROWNED.

11:21 Gen. 47:31 LXX

11.30 Πίστει τὰ τείχη Ἰεριχὼ ἔπεσαν κυκλωθέντα
BY FAITH   THE   WALLS   OF JERICHO FELL   HAVING BEEN ENCIRCLED

ἐπὶ ἑπτὰ ἡμέρας. **11.31** Πίστει Ῥαὰβ ἡ πόρνη
FOR   SEVEN DAYS.   BY FAITH   RAHAB,   THE PROSTITUTE,

οὐ συναπώλετο τοῖς ἀπειθήσασιν δεξαμένη τοὺς
DID NOT PERISH WITH   THE ONES HAVING DISOBEYED, HAVING WELCOMED THE

κατασκόπους μετ᾽ εἰρήνης.
SPIES   WITH   PEACE.

11.32 Καὶ τί ἔτι λέγω;   ἐπιλείψει με γὰρ
AND   WHAT MORE SHOULD I SAY? ³WILL FAIL ⁴ME ¹FOR

διηγούμενον ὁ χρόνος περὶ Γεδεών, Βαράκ, Σαμψών,
⁵TELLING   - ²TIME   ABOUT GIDEON, BARAK,   SAMSON,

Ἰεφθάε, Δαυίδ τε καὶ Σαμουὴλ καὶ τῶν προφητῶν,
JEPHTHAH, BOTH~DAVID AND SAMUEL   AND   THE PROPHETS,

11.33 οἳ διὰ πίστεως κατηγωνίσαντο βασιλείας,
WHO BY   FAITH   CONQUERED   KINGS,

εἰργάσαντο δικαιοσύνην, ἐπέτυχον ἐπαγγελιῶν, ἔφραξαν
WORKED   RIGHTEOUSNESS, ATTAINED   PROMISES,   SHUT

στόματα λεόντων, **11.34** ἔσβεσαν δύναμιν πυρός,
[THE] MOUTHS OF LIONS,   QUENCHED   [THE] POWER OF FIRE,

ἔφυγον στόματα μαχαίρης, ἐδυναμώθησαν ἀπὸ
ESCAPED FROM [THE] EDGES OF [THE] SWORD, WERE MADE STRONG FROM

ἀσθενείας, ἐγενήθησαν ἰσχυροὶ ἐν πολέμῳ, παρεμβολὰς
WEAKNESS,   BECAME   STRONG   IN   WAR,   ARMIES

ἔκλιναν ἀλλοτρίων.   **11.35** ἔλαβον γυναῖκες ἐξ
OF FOREIGNERS~THEY TURNED BACK.   WOMEN~RECEIVED,   BY

ἀναστάσεως τοὺς νεκροὺς αὐτῶν· ἄλλοι δὲ
RESURRECTION,   THE   DEAD   OF THEM. BUT~OTHERS

ἐτυμπανίσθησαν οὐ προσδεξάμενοι τὴν ἀπολύτρωσιν,
WERE TORTURED TO DEATH,   NOT HAVING RECEIVED   -   DELIVERANCE,

ἵνα κρείττονος ἀναστάσεως τύχωσιν· **11.36** ἕτεροι δὲ
THAT A BETTER   RESURRECTION THEY MIGHT ATTAIN TO.   AND~OTHERS

ἐμπαιγμῶν καὶ μαστίγων πεῖραν ἔλαβον, ἔτι δὲ
OF MOCKINGS AND WHIPPINGS   RECEIVED~TESTING,   AND~STILL [OTHERS]

δεσμῶν   καὶ φυλακῆς· **11.37** ἐλιθάσθησαν,
OF IMPRISONMENTS AND OF JAILS.   THEY WERE STONED,

⌐ἐπρίσθησαν,⌐ ἐν φόνῳ μαχαίρης ἀπέθανον,
SAWN IN TWO,   BY   MURDER OF [THE] SWORD THEY DIED,

περιῆλθον ἐν μηλωταῖς, ἐν αἰγείοις δέρμασιν,
THEY WENT AROUND IN SHEEPSKINS, IN   GOAT   SKINS,

ὑστερούμενοι, θλιβόμενοι, κακουχούμενοι, **11.38** ὧν
BEING IN NEED,   BEING OPPRESSED, BEING MISTREATED,   OF WHOM

οὐκ ἦν ἄξιος ὁ κόσμος, ἐπὶ ἐρημίαις πλανώμενοι καὶ
WAS NOT WORTHY THE WORLD,   IN   DESERTS   WANDERING   AND

ὄρεσιν καὶ σπηλαίοις καὶ ταῖς ὀπαῖς τῆς γῆς.
IN MOUNTAINS AND IN CAVES   AND IN THE HOLES   OF THE GROUND.

³⁰By faith the walls of Jericho fell after they had been encircled for seven days. ³¹By faith Rahab the prostitute did not perish with those who were disobedient,ʳ because she had received the spies in peace.

32 And what more should I say? For time would fail me to tell of Gideon, Barak, Samson, Jephthah, of David and Samuel and the prophets —³³who through faith conquered kingdoms, administered justice, obtained promises, shut the mouths of lions, ³⁴quenched raging fire, escaped the edge of the sword, won strength out of weakness, became mighty in war, put foreign armies to flight. ³⁵Women received their dead by resurrection. Others were tortured, refusing to accept release, in order to obtain a better resurrection. ³⁶Others suffered mocking and flogging, and even chains and imprisonment. ³⁷They were stoned to death, they were sawn in two,ˢ they were killed by the sword; they went about in skins of sheep and goats, destitute, persecuted, tormented— ³⁸of whom the world was not worthy. They wandered in deserts and mountains, and in caves and holes in the ground.

ʳ Or *unbelieving*
ˢ Other ancient authorities add *they were tempted*

11:37 text: RSV NASBmg NIV NEB TEV NJB NRSV. add επειρασθησαν (they were tested) either before or after επρισθησαν (they were sawn in two): KJV ASV RSVmg NASB NIVmg NEBmg NJBmg NRSVmg.

39 Yet all these, though they were commended for their faith, did not receive what was promised, [40]since God had provided something better so that they would not, apart from us, be made perfect.

11.39 Καὶ   οὗτοι πάντες   μαρτυρηθέντες   διὰ   τῆς
AND   ALL~THESE   HAVING BEEN COMMENDED THROUGH   -

πίστεως   οὐκ ἐκομίσαντο   τὴν ἐπαγγελίαν,   **11.40** τοῦ
FAITH   DID NOT RECEIVE   THE   PROMISE,   -

θεοῦ περὶ   ἡμῶν κρεῖττόν τι   προβλεψαμένου, ἵνα μὴ
GOD   FOR   US   SOMETHING~BETTER HAVING FORESEEN,   LEST

χωρὶς   ἡμῶν τελειωθῶσιν.
WITHOUT US   THEY MIGHT BE MADE PERFECT.

CHAPTER 12

Therefore, since we are surrounded by so great a cloud of witnesses, let us also lay aside every weight and the sin that clings so closely,[*] and let us run with perseverance the race that is set before us, [2]looking to Jesus the pioneer and perfecter of our faith, who for the sake of[u] the joy that was set before him endured the cross, disregarding its shame, and has taken his seat at the right hand of the throne of God.

3 Consider him who endured such hostility against himself from sinners,[v] so that you may not grow weary or lose heart. [4]In your struggle against sin you have not yet resisted to the point of shedding your blood. [5]And you have forgotten the exhortation that addresses you as children—

"My child, do not regard
  lightly the
  discipline of the
  Lord,
 or lose heart when you
  are punished by
  him;
[6] for the Lord disciplines
  those whom he
  loves,

[*] Other ancient authorities read *sin that easily distracts*
[u] Or *who instead of*
[v] Other ancient authorities read *such hostility from sinners against themselves*

12.1 Τοιγαροῦν   καὶ ἡμεῖς   τοσοῦτον ἔχοντες
SO THEREFORE,   WE~ALSO   HAVING~SUCH

περικείμενον   ἡμῖν νέφος   μαρτύρων,   ὄγκον ἀποθέμενοι
[3]SURROUNDING   [4]US   [1]A CLOUD [2]OF WITNESSES,   [7]WEIGHT [5]HAVING LAID ASIDE

πάντα καὶ   τὴν εὐπερίστατον   ἁμαρτίαν,   δι᾽ ὑπομονῆς
[6]EVERY   AND   -   EASILY ENSNARING   SIN,   WITH ENDURANCE

τρέχωμεν   τὸν προκείμενον   ἡμῖν ἀγῶνα **12.2** ἀφορῶντες
LET US RUN   THE [2]LAYING BEFORE   [3]US [1]RACE   [4]FIXING OUR GAZE

εἰς   τὸν τῆς   πίστεως   ἀρχηγὸν καὶ   τελειωτὴν Ἰησοῦν,
[5]ON [7]THE [11]OF THE [12]FAITH [8]FOUNDER [9]AND [10]PERFECTER   [6]JESUS,

ὃς ἀντὶ   τῆς προκειμένης αὐτῷ   χαρᾶς ὑπέμεινεν
WHO BECAUSE OF THE BEING SET BEFORE HIM   JOY,   HE ENDURED

σταυρὸν αἰσχύνης καταφρονήσας ἐν δεξιᾷ   τε
[THE] CROSS HAVING DESPISED~[THE] SHAME   [2]AT [3][THE] RIGHT [HAND] [1]AND

τοῦ   θρόνου τοῦ θεοῦ κεκάθικεν.   **12.3** ἀναλογίσασθε γὰρ
OF THE THRONE   -   OF GOD HE HAS SAT DOWN.   FOR~CONSIDER

τὸν   τοιαύτην ὑπομεμενηκότα ὑπὸ τῶν ἁμαρτωλῶν εἰς
THE ONE HAVING ENDURED~SUCH   [2]BY   -   [3]SINNERS   [4]AGAINST

ἑαυτὸν ἀντιλογίαν, ἵνα   μὴ κάμητε   ταῖς ψυχαῖς
[5]HIMSELF [1]OPPOSITION,   THAT YOU° MAY NOT BE WEARY IN THE SOULS

ὑμῶν ἐκλυόμενοι.
OF YOU°, LOSING HEART.

12.4 Οὔπω   μέχρις   αἵματος ἀντικατέστητε πρὸς τὴν
NOT YET   TO THE POINT OF BLOOD   HAVE YOU° RESISTED [2]AGAINST -

ἁμαρτίαν ἀνταγωνιζόμενοι.   **12.5** καὶ   ἐκλέλησθε   τῆς
[3]SIN   [1][WHILE] STRUGGLING.   AND   HAVE YOU° FORGOTTEN THE

παρακλήσεως, ἥτις ὑμῖν ὡς   υἱοῖς διαλέγεται,
ENCOURAGEMENT,   WHICH TO YOU° AS   SONS   HE SPEAKS,

Υἱέ   μου, μὴ ὀλιγώρει   παιδείας   κυρίου
SON   OF ME, DO NOT THINK LIGHTLY OF [THE] DISCIPLINE OF [THE] LORD

μηδὲ ἐκλύου ὑπ᾽ αὐτοῦ ἐλεγχόμενος·
DO NOT LOSE HEART [2]BY [3]HIM   [1]BEING REBUKED;

12.6 ὃν γὰρ ἀγαπᾷ κύριος παιδεύει,
FOR~WHOM [THE] LORD~LOVES   HE DISCIPLINES,

12:5-6 Prov. 3:11-12 LXX

μαστιγοῖ δὲ πάντα υἱὸν ὃν παραδέχεται.
AND~HE PUNISHES EVERY SON WHOM HE RECEIVES.

12.7 εἰς παιδείαν ὑπομένετε, ὡς υἱοῖς ὑμῖν
FOR DISCIPLINE YOU° ENDURE, AS SONS ³YOU°

προσφέρεται ὁ θεός. τίς γὰρ υἱὸς ὃν
²DEALS WITH - ¹GOD. FOR~WHAT SON [IS THERE] WHOM

οὐ παιδεύει πατήρ; **12.8** εἰ δὲ χωρίς ἐστε παιδείας
²DOES NOT DISCIPLINE ¹[THE] FATHER? BUT~IF YOU° ARE~WITHOUT DISCIPLINE,

ἧς μέτοχοι γεγόνασιν πάντες, ἄρα νόθοι καὶ οὐχ
OF WHICH PARTAKERS ALL~HAVE BECOME, THEN ILLEGITIMATE AND NOT

υἱοί ἐστε. **12.9** εἶτα τοὺς μὲν τῆς σαρκὸς ἡμῶν
SONS YOU° ARE. FURTHERMORE, ²THE - ⁴OF THE ⁵FLESH ⁶OF US [AS]

πατέρας εἴχομεν παιδευτὰς καὶ ἐνετρεπόμεθα· οὐ
³FATHERS ¹WE HAD, TEACHERS AND WE WERE RESPECTING [THEM]. ³NOT

πολὺ [δὲ] μᾶλλον ὑποταγησόμεθα τῷ πατρὶ τῶν
⁴MUCH ¹AND ⁵MORE ²WILL WE SUBJECT OURSELVES TO THE FATHER

πνευμάτων καὶ ζήσομεν; **12.10** οἱ μὲν γὰρ πρὸς
OF SPIRITS AND WE WILL LIVE? ²THEY - ¹FOR FOR

ὀλίγας ἡμέρας κατὰ τὸ δοκοῦν αὐτοῖς
A FEW DAYS ACCORDING TO THE THING SEEMING GOOD TO THEM

ἐπαίδευον, ὁ δὲ ἐπὶ τὸ συμφέρον εἰς τὸ
WERE DISCIPLINING [US], BUT~HE FOR THE THING BENEFITING [US] IN ORDER -

μεταλαβεῖν τῆς ἁγιότητος αὐτοῦ. **12.11** πᾶσα δὲ
TO SHARE IN THE HOLINESS OF HIM. BUT~ALL

παιδεία πρὸς μὲν τὸ παρὸν οὐ δοκεῖ χαρᾶς εἶναι
DISCIPLINE FOR - THE PRESENT DOES NOT SEEM TO BE~PLEASANT

ἀλλὰ λύπης, ὕστερον δὲ καρπὸν εἰρηνικὸν τοῖς δι᾽
BUT PAINFUL, BUT~LATER ³FRUIT ²[THE] PEACEFUL ⁵TO THE ONES ⁷BY

αὐτῆς γεγυμνασμένοις ἀποδίδωσιν δικαιοσύνης.
⁸IT ⁶HAVING BEEN TRAINED ¹IT PAYS BACK ⁴OF RIGHTEOUSNESS.

12.12 Διὸ τὰς παρειμένας χεῖρας καὶ τὰ
THEREFORE, THE HANDS~HAVING BECOME WEAK AND THE

παραλελυμένα γόνατα ἀνορθώσατε, **12.13** καὶ
KNEES~HAVING BECOME FEEBLE, RESTORE, AND

τροχιὰς ὀρθὰς ποιεῖτε τοῖς ποσὶν ὑμῶν, ἵνα μὴ τὸ
STRAIGHT~PATHS MAKE FOR THE FEET OF YOU°, LEST THE

χωλὸν ἐκτραπῇ, ἰαθῇ δὲ μᾶλλον.
LAME MAY BE TURNED ASIDE, ³MAY BE HEALED ¹BUT ²RATHER.

12.14 Εἰρήνην διώκετε μετὰ πάντων καὶ τὸν
PURSUE~PEACE WITH EVERYONE, AND [PURSUE] -

ἁγιασμόν, οὗ χωρὶς οὐδεὶς ὄψεται τὸν κύριον,
HOLINESS, WITHOUT~WHICH NO ONE WILL SEE THE LORD,

12.15 ἐπισκοποῦντες μή τις ὑστερῶν ἀπὸ τῆς χάριτος
SEEING TO IT LEST ANYONE FALLING FROM THE GRACE

τοῦ θεοῦ, μή τις ῥίζα πικρίας ἄνω φύουσα
- OF GOD, LEST SOME ROOT OF BITTERNESS SPROUTING~UP

ἐνοχλῇ καὶ δι᾽ αὐτῆς μιανθῶσιν πολλοί, **12.16** μή
MAY TROUBLE [YOU°] AND BY IT MANY~BE DEFILED, LEST

and chastises every child whom he accepts."

⁷Endure trials for the sake of discipline. God is treating you as children; for what child is there whom a parent does not discipline? ⁸If you do not have that discipline in which all children share, then you are illegitimate and not his children. ⁹Moreover, we had human parents to discipline us, and we respected them. Should we not be even more willing to be subject to the Father of spirits and live? ¹⁰For they disciplined us for a short time as seemed best to them, but he disciplines us for our good, in order that we may share his holiness. ¹¹Now, discipline always seems painful rather than pleasant at the time, but later it yields the peaceful fruit of righteousness to those who have been trained by it.

12 Therefore lift your drooping hands and strengthen your weak knees, ¹³and make straight paths for your feet, so that what is lame may not be put out of joint, but rather be healed.

14 Pursue peace with everyone, and the holiness without which no one will see the Lord. ¹⁵See to it that no one fails to obtain the grace of God; that no root of bitterness springs up and causes trouble, and through it many become defiled. ¹⁶See to it that no one

becomes like Esau, an immoral and godless person, who sold his birthright for a single meal. [17]You know that later, when he wanted to inherit the blessing, he was rejected, for he found no chance to repent,[w] even though he sought the blessing[x] with tears.

18 You have not come to something[y] that can be touched, a blazing fire, and darkness, and gloom, and a tempest, [19]and the sound of a trumpet, and a voice whose words made the hearers beg that not another word be spoken to them. [20](For they could not endure the order that was given, "If even an animal touches the mountain, it shall be stoned to death." [21]Indeed, so terrifying was the sight that Moses said, "I tremble with fear.") [22]But you have come to Mount Zion and to the city of the living God, the heavenly Jerusalem, and to innumerable angels in festal gathering, [23]and to the assembly[z] of the firstborn who are enrolled in heaven, and to God the judge of all, and to the spirits of the righteous made perfect, [24]and to Jesus, the mediator of a new covenant, and to the sprinkled blood that speaks a better word than the blood of Abel.

25 See that you do not refuse the one who is speaking;

[w] Or *no chance to change his father's mind*
[x] Gk *it*
[y] Other ancient authorities read *a mountain*
[z] Or *angels, and to the festal gathering* [23]*and assembly*

τις πόρνος ἢ βέβηλος ὡς Ἠσαῦ, ὃς
SOME SEXUALLY IMMORAL OR IRRELIGIOUS [PERSON] LIKE ESAU, WHO

ἀντὶ βρώσεως μιᾶς ἀπέδετο τὰ πρωτοτόκια
IN EXCHANGE FOR ONE~MEAL SOLD THE BIRTHRIGHT

ἑαυτοῦ. **12.17** ἴστε γὰρ ὅτι καὶ μετέπειτα θέλων
OF HIMSELF. FOR~YOU° KNOW THAT ALSO AFTERWARDS WANTING

κληρονομῆσαι τὴν εὐλογίαν ἀπεδοκιμάσθη, μετανοίας
TO INHERIT THE BLESSING, HE WAS REJECTED, [3]OF REPENTANCE

γὰρ τόπον οὐχ εὗρεν καίπερ μετὰ δακρύων ἐκζητήσας
[1]FOR [2]A PLACE HE DID NOT FIND, ALTHOUGH WITH TEARS HAVING SOUGHT

αὐτήν.
IT.

12.18 Οὐ γὰρ προσεληλύθατε ψηλαφωμένῳ καὶ
FOR~YOU° HAVE NOT COME TO [A MOUNTAIN] BEING TOUCHED AND

κεκαυμένῳ πυρὶ καὶ γνόφῳ καὶ ζόφῳ καὶ θυέλλῃ
TO A FIRE~HAVING BEEN BLAZING AND TO DARKNESS AND TO GLOOM AND TO A STORM

12.19 καὶ σάλπιγγος ἤχῳ καὶ φωνῇ ῥημάτων,
AND TO [THE] NOISE~OF A TRUMPET AND TO [THE] SOUND OF WORDS,

ἧς οἱ ἀκούσαντες παρῃτήσαντο μὴ προστεθῆναι
WHICH THE ONES HAVING HEARD BEGGED NOT TO BE ADDED

αὐτοῖς λόγον, **12.20** οὐκ ἔφερον γὰρ τὸ
TO THEM A WORD, FOR~THEY WERE NOT ENDURING THE THING

διαστελλόμενον, Κἂν θηρίον θίγῃ τοῦ ὄρους,
BEING COMMANDED, EVEN IF AN ANIMAL SHOULD TOUCH THE MOUNTAIN,

λιθοβοληθήσεται· **12.21** καί, οὕτω φοβερὸν ἦν τὸ
IT WILL BE STONED [TO DEATH]. AND, SO FEARFUL WAS THE THING

φανταζόμενον, Μωϋσῆς εἶπεν, Ἔκφοβός εἰμι καὶ
APPEARING, MOSES SAID, I AM~TERRIFIED AND

ἔντρομος. **12.22** ἀλλὰ προσεληλύθατε Σιὼν ὄρει καὶ
TREMBLING. BUT YOU° HAVE COME TO MOUNT~ZION AND

πόλει θεοῦ ζῶντος, Ἰερουσαλὴμ ἐπουρανίῳ, καὶ
TO [THE] CITY OF [THE] LIVING~GOD, TO [THE] HEAVENLY~JERUSALEM, AND

μυριάσιν ἀγγέλων, πανηγύρει **12.23** καὶ ἐκκλησίᾳ
TO MYRIADS OF ANGELS, TO A FESTAL GATHERING AND TO [THE] CHURCH

πρωτοτόκων ἀπογεγραμμένων ἐν οὐρανοῖς καὶ
OF [THE] FIRSTBORN ONES HAVING BEEN REGISTERED IN [THE] HEAVENS AND

κριτῇ θεῷ πάντων καὶ πνεύμασι δικαίων
TO [THE] JUDGE, [THE] GOD OF ALL AND TO [THE] SPIRITS OF [THE] UPRIGHT

τετελειωμένων **12.24** καὶ διαθήκης νέας μεσίτῃ
HAVING BEEN PERFECTED AND [4]COVENANT [3]OF [THE] NEW [2][THE] MEDIATOR

Ἰησοῦ καὶ αἵματι ῥαντισμοῦ κρεῖττον λαλοῦντι
[1]TO JESUS, AND TO [THE] BLOOD OF SPRINKLING SPEAKING~BETTER

παρὰ τὸν Ἄβελ.
THAN - ABEL.

12.25 Βλέπετε μὴ παραιτήσησθε τὸν λαλοῦντα·
SEE TO IT [THAT] YOU° MAY NOT REJECT THE ONE SPEAKING;

12:20 Exod. 19:12-13 **12:21** Deut. 9:19

εἰ γὰρ ἐκεῖνοι οὐκ ἐξέφυγον ἐπὶ γῆς παραιτησάμενοι
FOR~IF   THOSE ONES   DID NOT ESCAPE,   ⁴ON   ⁵EARTH   ¹HAVING REJECTED

τὸν χρηματίζοντα, πολὺ μᾶλλον ἡμεῖς οἱ
²THE ONE ³WARNING [THEM],   [HOW] MUCH MORE   WE,   THE ONES

τὸν ἀπ᾽ οὐρανῶν ἀποστρεφόμενοι, **12.26** οὗ ἡ
THE [WARNING] FROM [THE] HEAVENS TURNING AWAY FROM,   WHOSE -

φωνὴ τὴν γῆν ἐσάλευσεν τότε, νῦν δὲ ἐπήγγελται
VOICE   ²THE ³EARTH ¹SHOOK   THEN,   BUT~NOW   HE HAS PROMISED

λέγων, Ἔτι ἅπαξ ἐγὼ σείσω οὐ μόνον τὴν γῆν ἀλλὰ
SAYING,   ONCE~AGAIN   I   WILL SHAKE NOT ONLY - EARTH BUT

καὶ τὸν οὐρανόν. **12.27** τὸ δὲ,   Ἔτι ἅπαξ δηλοῖ
ALSO - HEAVEN.   NOW~THE [PHRASE],   ONCE~AGAIN   MAKES CLEAR

[τὴν] τῶν σαλευομένων μετάθεσιν ὡς,
THE   ²OF THE THINGS ³BEING SHAKEN   ¹REMOVAL   AS

πεποιημένων, ἵνα μείνῃ τὰ μὴ σαλευόμενα.
OF [THINGS] HAVING BEEN MADE,   THAT   MAY REMAIN THE THINGS NOT   BEING SHAKEN.

12.28 Διὸ βασιλείαν ἀσάλευτον παραλαμβάνοντες
THEREFORE,   AN UNSHAKEABLE~KINGDOM   RECEIVING

ἔχωμεν χάριν, δι᾽ ἧς λατρεύωμεν εὐαρέστως
LET US HOLD ON TO GRACE,   THROUGH   WHICH   LET US WORSHIP   ²IN AN ACCEPTABLE WAY

τῷ θεῷ μετὰ εὐλαβείας καὶ δέους· **12.29** καὶ γὰρ ὁ
-   ¹GOD   WITH   REVERENCE   AND   AWE.   FOR~INDEED   THE

θεὸς ἡμῶν πῦρ καταναλίσκον.
GOD   OF US [IS]   A CONSUMING~FIRE.

12:26 Hag. 2:6 LXX

for if they did not escape when they refused the one who warned them on earth, how much less will we escape if we reject the one who warns from heaven! ²⁶At that time his voice shook the earth; but now he has promised, "Yet once more I will shake not only the earth but also the heaven." ²⁷This phrase, "Yet once more," indicates the removal of what is shaken—that is, created things—so that what cannot be shaken may remain. ²⁸Therefore, since we are receiving a kingdom that cannot be shaken, let us give thanks, by which we offer to God an acceptable worship with reverence and awe; ²⁹for indeed our God is a consuming fire.

13.1 Ἡ φιλαδελφία μενέτω. **13.2** τῆς φιλοξενίας
-   LET CONTINUE~BROTHERLY LOVE.   -   ²HOSPITALITY

μὴ ἐπιλανθάνεσθε, διὰ ταύτης γὰρ ἔλαθόν τινες
¹DO NOT NEGLECT,   ⁴BY   ⁵THIS   ³FOR   SOME~WITHOUT KNOWING IT

ξενίσαντες ἀγγέλους. **13.3** μιμνῄσκεσθε τῶν δεσμίων
HAVING ENTERTAINED ANGELS.   REMEMBER   THE PRISONERS

ὡς συνδεδεμένοι, τῶν κακουχουμένων ὡς
AS [IF]   HAVING BEEN IMPRISONED WITH [THEM, AND] THE ONES BEING MISTREATED   AS

καὶ αὐτοὶ ὄντες ἐν σώματι. **13.4** Τίμιος ὁ
ALSO   YOURSELVES   BEING   IN   [THE] BODY.   ²[BE] RESPECTED -

γάμος ἐν πᾶσιν καὶ ἡ κοίτη ἀμίαντος,
¹[LET] MARRIAGE BY   ALL   AND [LET]   THE   MARRIAGE BED [BE]   UNDEFILED,

πόρνους γὰρ καὶ μοιχοὺς κρινεῖ ὁ θεός.
FOR~[THE] SEXUALLY IMMORAL AND   ADULTERERS ²WILL JUDGE - ¹GOD.

13.5 Ἀφιλάργυρος ὁ τρόπος, ἀρκούμενοι
³NOT GREEDY   ¹[LET BE] THE   ²MANNER OF LIFE,   BEING CONTENT

τοῖς παροῦσιν. αὐτὸς γὰρ εἴρηκεν, Οὐ μὴ
WITH THE THINGS HAVING.   FOR~HE   HAS SAID,   BY NO MEANS

13:5 Deut. 31:6, 8

Let mutual love continue. ²Do not neglect to show hospitality to strangers, for by doing that some have entertained angels without knowing it. ³Remember those who are in prison, as though you were in prison with them; those who are being tortured, as though you yourselves were being tortured.[a] ⁴Let marriage be held in honor by all, and let the marriage bed be kept undefiled; for God will judge fornicators and adulterers. ⁵Keep your lives free from the love of money, and be content with what you have; for he has said, "I will never

[a] Gk *were in the body*

leave you or forsake you."
6So we can say with
confidence,

"The Lord is my helper;
I will not be afraid.
What can anyone do to
me?"

7 Remember your
leaders, those who spoke
the word of God to you;
consider the outcome of
their way of life, and imitate
their faith. 8Jesus Christ is
the same yesterday and
today and forever. 9Do not
be carried away by all kinds
of strange teachings; for it is
well for the heart to be
strengthened by grace, not
by regulations about food,b
which have not benefited
those who observe them.
10We have an altar from
which those who officiate in
the tentc have no right to eat.
11For the bodies of those
animals whose blood is
brought into the sanctuary by
the high priest as a sacrifice
for sin are burned outside the
camp. 12Therefore Jesus
also suffered outside the city
gate in order to sanctify the
people by his own blood.
13Let us then go to him outside the camp and bear the
abuse he endured. 14For here
we have no lasting city, but

b Gk not by foods
c Or tabernacle

σε ἀνῶ   οὐδ᾽ οὐ μή   σε ἐγκαταλίπω,   13.6 ὥστε
MAY I ABANDON~YOU, NOR   BY ANY MEANS MAY I FORSAKE~YOU,   SO THAT

θαρροῦντας ἡμᾶς λέγειν,
US~BEING CONFIDENT   TO SAY,

Κύριος   ἐμοὶ βοηθός,
[THE] LORD [IS] MY   HELPER,

[καὶ] οὐ φοβηθήσομαι,
AND   I WILL NOT BE AFRAID,

τί   ποιήσει μοι ἄνθρωπος;
WHAT   WILL DO   TO ME A MAN?

13.7 Μνημονεύετε τῶν   ἡγουμένων ὑμῶν, οἵτινες
     REMEMBER   THE ONES LEADING   YOU°,   WHO

ἐλάλησαν ὑμῖν   τὸν λόγον τοῦ θεοῦ, ὧν
SPOKE   TO YOU° THE   WORD   -   OF GOD, OF WHOM

ἀναθεωροῦντες τὴν ἔκβασιν τῆς   ἀναστροφῆς
CONSIDERING   THE   OUTCOME OF THE(THEIR) WAY OF LIFE,

μιμεῖσθε τὴν   πίστιν.   13.8 Ἰησοῦς Χριστὸς ἐχθὲς
IMITATE   THE(THEIR) FAITH.   JESUS   CHRIST [IS] ³YESTERDAY

καὶ σήμερον ὁ   αὐτός καὶ εἰς τοὺς αἰῶνας.
⁴AND ⁵TODAY   ¹THE ²SAME   AND   FOREVER.

13.9 διδαχαῖς ποικίλαις καὶ ξέναις μὴ παραφέρεσθε·
     ⁵TEACHINGS ²BY VARIOUS ³AND ⁴STRANGE ¹DO NOT BE CARRIED AWAY.

καλὸν γὰρ   χάριτι βεβαιοῦσθαι τὴν καρδίαν, οὐ
FOR~[IT IS] GOOD [FOR] ⁴BY GRACE ³TO BE STRENGTHENED ¹THE ²HEART,   NOT

βρώμασιν ἐν οἷς   οὐκ ὠφελήθησαν οἱ   περιπατοῦντες.
WITH FOODS, BY WHICH WERE NOT HELPED   THE ONES WALKING.

13.10 ἔχομεν θυσιαστήριον ἐξ   οὗ   φαγεῖν οὐκ ἔχουσιν
      WE HAVE AN ALTAR   FROM WHICH TO EAT [THAT] DO NOT HAVE

ἐξουσίαν   οἱ   τῇ   σκηνῇ   λατρεύοντες.
AUTHORITY   THE ONES IN THE TABERNACLE SERVING.

13.11 ὧν γὰρ   εἰσφέρεται ζῴων   τὸ αἷμα περὶ
      FOR~OF WHICH THINGS IS BROUGHT IN ³OF ANIMALS ¹THE ²BLOOD CONCERNING

ἁμαρτίας εἰς   τὰ ἅγια διὰ τοῦ ἀρχιερέως,
SIN   INTO [THE HOLY OF] - HOLIES BY   THE HIGH PRIEST,

τούτων τὰ σώματα κατακαίεται ἔξω τῆς παρεμβολῆς.
OF THESE, THE BODIES   ARE BURNED   OUTSIDE OF THE CAMP.

13.12 διὸ   καὶ Ἰησοῦς, ἵνα ἁγιάσῃ   διὰ
      THEREFORE ALSO JESUS,   THAT HE MIGHT SANCTIFY THROUGH

τοῦ ἰδίου αἵματος τὸν λαόν, ἔξω τῆς πύλης ἔπαθεν.
HIS OWN   BLOOD   THE PEOPLE, ²OUTSIDE ³THE ⁴GATE   ¹SUFFERED.

13.13 τοίνυν ἐξερχώμεθα πρὸς αὐτὸν ἔξω   τῆς
      SO THEN   LET US GO OUT   TO   HIM   OUTSIDE THE

παρεμβολῆς τὸν ὀνειδισμὸν αὐτοῦ φέροντες·
CAMP,   THE REPROACH   OF HIM BEARING.

13.14 οὐ γὰρ ἔχομεν ὧδε μένουσαν πόλιν ἀλλὰ τὴν
      FOR~WE DO NOT HAVE HERE A LASTING CITY   BUT   THE ONE

13:6 Ps. 118:6 LXX

μέλλουσαν ἐπιζητοῦμεν. **13.15** δι᾽   αὐτοῦ [οὖν]
COMING   WE ARE SEEKING.   THROUGH HIM   THEREFORE,

ἀναφέρωμεν θυσίαν αἰνέσεως διὰ παντὸς τῷ θεῷ,
LET US OFFER UP   A SACRIFICE OF PRAISE   ALWAYS   -   TO GOD,

τοῦτ᾽ ἔστιν καρπὸν χειλέων ὁμολογούντων τῷ ὀνόματι
THAT IS TO SAY, [THE] FRUIT OF LIPS CONFESSING   THE   NAME

αὐτοῦ. **13.16** τῆς δὲ εὐποιΐας καὶ κοινωνίας
OF HIM.   BUT~OF THE DOING OF GOOD AND SHARING

μὴ ἐπιλανθάνεσθε· τοιαύταις γὰρ θυσίαις εὐαρεστεῖται
DO NOT NEGLECT;   FOR~WITH SUCH   SACRIFICES ²IS PLEASED

ὁ θεός.
- ¹GOD.

13.17 Πείθεσθε τοῖς   ἡγουμένοις ὑμῶν καὶ ὑπείκετε,
         OBEY   THE ONES LEADING   YOU°   AND   SUBMIT [TO THEM],

αὐτοὶ γὰρ ἀγρυπνοῦσιν ὑπὲρ   τῶν ψυχῶν ὑμῶν ὡς
FOR~THEY   ARE KEEPING WATCH ON BEHALF OF THE SOULS   OF YOU° AS [ONES]

λόγον ἀποδώσοντες, ἵνα μετὰ χαρᾶς τοῦτο ποιῶσιν καὶ
RENDERING~AN ACCOUNT, THAT WITH JOY   THEY MAY DO~THIS   AND

μὴ στενάζοντες·   ἀλυσιτελὲς γὰρ ὑμῖν   τοῦτο.
NOT GROANING;   ³UNPROFITABLE ¹FOR ⁴FOR YOU° ²THIS [WOULD BE].

13.18 Προσεύχεσθε περὶ ἡμῶν· πειθόμεθα γὰρ ὅτι
         PRAY   FOR   US;   FOR~WE ARE PERSUADED THAT

καλὴν συνείδησιν ἔχομεν, ἐν πᾶσιν καλῶς θέλοντες
A GOOD CONSCIENCE WE HAVE,   IN EVERYTHING WISHING~COMMENDABLY

ἀναστρέφεσθαι. **13.19** περισσοτέρως δὲ   παρακαλῶ
TO CONDUCT [OURSELVES].   AND~EVEN MORE   I URGE [YOU°]

τοῦτο ποιῆσαι, ἵνα τάχιον   ἀποκατασταθῶ ὑμῖν.
TO DO~THIS,   THAT MORE QUICKLY I MAY BE RESTORED   TO YOU°.

13.20 Ὁ δὲ θεὸς τῆς εἰρήνης, ὁ   ἀναγαγὼν   ἐκ
         NOW~THE GOD   -   OF PEACE,   THE ONE HAVING BROUGHT UP FROM

νεκρῶν τὸν ποιμένα τῶν προβάτων τὸν μέγαν ἐν
[THE] DEAD THE ²SHEPHERD ³OF THE ⁴SHEEP   -   ¹GREAT   BY

αἵματι διαθήκης αἰωνίου, τὸν κύριον ἡμῶν Ἰησοῦν,
[THE] BLOOD OF [THE] ETERNAL~COVENANT, THE LORD OF US, JESUS,

13.21 καταρτίσαι ὑμᾶς ἐν παντὶ ἀγαθῷ εἰς   τὸ
         MAY HE EQUIP   YOU° WITH EVERY GOOD THING IN ORDER -

ποιῆσαι τὸ θέλημα αὐτοῦ, ποιῶν ἐν ᾽ἡμῖν᾽ τὸ
TO DO   THE WILL   OF HIM, DOING IN   US   THE THING

εὐάρεστον ἐνώπιον αὐτοῦ διὰ   Ἰησοῦ Χριστοῦ,
WELL-PLEASING BEFORE HIM   THROUGH JESUS   CHRIST,

ᾧ   ἡ δόξα εἰς τοὺς αἰῶνας [τῶν αἰώνων], ἀμήν.
TO WHOM [BE] THE GLORY INTO THE   AGES   OF THE AGES,   AMEN.

13.22 Παρακαλῶ δὲ ὑμᾶς, ἀδελφοί, ἀνέχεσθε τοῦ
         NOW~I URGE   YOU°,   BROTHERS, BEAR WITH   THE

λόγου τῆς παρακλήσεως, καὶ γὰρ διὰ   βραχέων
WORD   -   OF EXHORTATION, FOR~INDEED BY MEANS OF FEW [WORDS]

---

we are looking for the city that is to come. ¹⁵Through him, then, let us continually offer a sacrifice of praise to God, that is, the fruit of lips that confess his name. ¹⁶Do not neglect to do good and to share what you have, for such sacrifices are pleasing to God.

17 Obey your leaders and submit to them, for they are keeping watch over your souls and will give an account. Let them do this with joy and not with sighing—for that would be harmful to you.

18 Pray for us; we are sure that we have a clear conscience, desiring to act honorably in all things. ¹⁹I urge you all the more to do this, so that I may be restored to you very soon.

20 Now may the God of peace, who brought back from the dead our Lord Jesus, the great shepherd of the sheep, by the blood of the eternal covenant, ²¹make you complete in everything good so that you may do his will, working among us*d* that which is pleasing in his sight, through Jesus Christ, to whom be the glory forever and ever. Amen.

22 I appeal to you, brothers and sisters,*e* bear with my word of exhortation, for I have written

d Other ancient authorities read *you*
e Gk *brothers*

13:21 text: ASV RSVmg NASB NIV NEB TEV NJB NRSV. var. υμιν (you°): KJV ASVmg RSV NRSVmg.

to you briefly. ²³I want you
to know that our brother
Timothy has been set free;
and if he comes in time, he
will be with me when I see
you. ²⁴Greet all your leaders
and all the saints. Those
from Italy send you greetings.
²⁵Grace be with all of you.ᶠ

ᶠ Other ancient authorities add *Amen*

ἐπέστειλα ὑμῖν. **13.23** Γινώσκετε τὸν ἀδελφὸν ἡμῶν
I WROTE   TO YOU°.   KNOW [THAT]   THE   BROTHER   OF US,

Τιμόθεον ἀπολελυμένον μεθ' οὗ   ἐὰν τάχιον ἔρχηται
TIMOTHY,   HAVING BEEN RELEASED, WITH WHOM IF HE COMES~QUICKLY,

ὄψομαι ὑμᾶς.
I WILL SEE   YOU°.

13.24 Ἀσπάσασθε πάντας τοὺς   ἡγουμένους ὑμῶν καὶ
            GREET   ALL   THE ONES LEADING   YOU° AND

πάντας τοὺς ἁγίους. ἀσπάζονται ὑμᾶς οἱ   ἀπὸ τῆς
ALL   THE SAINTS.   ⁴GREET   ⁵YOU° ¹THE ONES ²FROM -

Ἰταλίας. **13.25** ἡ χάρις μετὰ πάντων ὑμῶν.
³ITALY.   -   GRACE [BE] WITH ALL   OF YOU°.

THE LETTER OF
JAMES

ΙΑΚΩΒΟΥ
OF JAMES

1.1 Ἰάκωβος θεοῦ καὶ κυρίου Ἰησοῦ Χριστοῦ
JAMES   2OF GOD   3AND   4OF [THE] LORD   5JESUS   6CHRIST

δοῦλος ταῖς δώδεκα φυλαῖς ταῖς ἐν τῇ διασπορᾷ
1A SLAVE,   TO THE   TWELVE   TRIBES   -   IN   THE   DISPERSION,

χαίρειν.
GRACE.

1.2 Πᾶσαν χαρὰν ἡγήσασθε, ἀδελφοί μου, ὅταν
ALL   JOY   CONSIDER [IT],   BROTHERS   OF ME,   WHENEVER

πειρασμοῖς περιπέσητε ποικίλοις,
3TRIALS   1YOU FALL   2INTO VARIOUS,

1.3 γινώσκοντες ὅτι τὸ δοκίμιον ὑμῶν τῆς πίστεως
KNOWING   THAT THE TESTING   OF YOUR°   -   FAITH

κατεργάζεται ὑπομονήν. **1.4** ἡ δὲ ὑπομονὴ ἔργον
WORKS   ENDURANCE.   -   AND   2ENDURANCE   5WORK

τέλειον ἐχέτω, ἵνα ἦτε τέλειοι καὶ ὁλόκληροι
4[ITS] COMPLETE   1LET 3HAVE,   THAT   YOU° MAY BE   MATURE   AND   COMPLETE,

ἐν μηδενὶ λειπόμενοι. **1.5** Εἰ δέ τις ὑμῶν λείπεται
IN   NOTHING   LACKING.   BUT~IF ANYONE OF YOU° IS LACKING

σοφίας, αἰτείτω παρὰ τοῦ διδόντος θεοῦ πᾶσιν
WISDOM,   LET HIM ASK   FROM   2THE ONE 3GIVING   1GOD   TO ALL

ἁπλῶς καὶ μὴ ὀνειδίζοντος καὶ δοθήσεται
GENEROUSLY AND   NOT(WITHOUT) REPROACHING,   AND   IT WILL BE GIVEN

αὐτῷ. **1.6** αἰτείτω δὲ ἐν πίστει μηδὲν διακρινόμενος·
TO HIM.   BUT~LET HIM ASK IN   FAITH,   NOTHING   DOUBTING;

ὁ γὰρ διακρινόμενος ἔοικεν κλύδωνι θαλάσσης
FOR~THE ONE DOUBTING   IS LIKE   A WAVE   OF [THE] SEA

ἀνεμιζομένῳ καὶ ῥιπιζομένῳ. **1.7** μὴ γὰρ οἰέσθω ὁ
BEING BLOWN BY THE WIND   AND   BEING TOSSED.   3NOT   1FOR   2LET 6THINK   -

ἄνθρωπος ἐκεῖνος ὅτι λήμψεταί τι παρὰ τοῦ
5MAN   4THAT   THAT HE WILL RECEIVE ANYTHING FROM   THE

κυρίου, **1.8** ἀνὴρ δίψυχος, ἀκατάστατος ἐν πάσαις
LORD,   [HE IS] A MAN DOUBLE-MINDED, UNSTABLE   IN   ALL

ταῖς ὁδοῖς αὐτοῦ.
THE   WAYS   OF HIM.

1.9 Καυχάσθω δὲ ὁ ἀδελφὸς ὁ ταπεινὸς ἐν τῷ
2LET 6BOAST   1BUT   3THE   5BROTHER   -   4LOWLY   IN   THE

ὕψει αὐτοῦ, **1.10** ὁ δὲ πλούσιος ἐν τῇ ταπεινώσει
EXALTATION OF HIM,   AND~THE RICH ONE   IN   THE   HUMILIATION

James, a servant[a] of God and of the Lord Jesus Christ,

To the twelve tribes in the Dispersion:

Greetings.

2 My brothers and sisters,[b] whenever you face trials of any kind, consider it nothing but joy, 3because you know that the testing of your faith produces endurance; 4and let endurance have its full effect, so that you may be mature and complete, lacking in nothing.

5 If any of you is lacking in wisdom, ask God, who gives to all generously and ungrudgingly, and it will be given you. 6But ask in faith, never doubting, for the one who doubts is like a wave of the sea, driven and tossed by the wind; 7, 8for the doubter, being double-minded and unstable in every way, must not expect to receive anything from the Lord.

9 Let the believer[c] who is lowly boast in being raised up, 10and the rich in being

[a] Gk slave
[b] Gk brothers
[c] Gk brother

brought low, because the rich will disappear like a flower in the field. ¹¹For the sun rises with its scorching heat and withers the field; its flower falls, and its beauty perishes. It is the same way with the rich; in the midst of a busy life, they will wither away.

12 Blessed is anyone who endures temptation. Such a one has stood the test and will receive the crown of life that the Lord*d* has promised to those who love him. ¹³No one, when tempted, should say, "I am being tempted by God"; for God cannot be tempted by evil and he himself tempts no one. ¹⁴But one is tempted by one's own desire, being lured and enticed by it; ¹⁵then, when that desire has conceived, it gives birth to sin, and that sin, when it is fully grown, gives birth to death. ¹⁶Do not be deceived, my beloved.*e*

17 Every generous act of giving, with every perfect gift, is from above, coming down from the Father of lights, with whom there is no variation or shadow due to change.*f* ¹⁸In fulfillment of his own purpose he gave us birth by the word of truth, so that we would become a kind of first fruits of his creatures.

19 You must understand this, my beloved:*e* let everyone be quick to listen, slow to speak, slow to anger; ²⁰for your anger

d Gk *he;* other ancient authorities read *God*
e Gk *my beloved brothers*
f Other ancient authorities read *variation due to a shadow of turning*

αὐτοῦ, ὅτι ὡς ἄνθος χόρτου παρελεύσεται.
OF HIM, BECAUSE LIKE A FLOWER OF [THE] GRASS HE WILL PASS AWAY.

1.11 ἀνέτειλεν γὰρ ὁ ἥλιος σὺν τῷ καύσωνι καὶ
⁴ROSE ¹FOR ²THE ³SUN WITH THE BURNING HEAT AND

ἐξήρανεν τὸν χόρτον καὶ τὸ ἄνθος αὐτοῦ ἐξέπεσεν καὶ
DRIED THE GRASS AND THE FLOWER OF IT FELL AND

ἡ εὐπρέπεια τοῦ προσώπου αὐτοῦ ἀπώλετο· οὕτως
THE BEAUTY OF THE APPEARANCE OF IT PERISHED; THUS

καὶ ὁ πλούσιος ἐν ταῖς πορείαις αὐτοῦ μαρανθήσεται.
ALSO THE RICH MAN IN THE GOINGS OF HIM WILL FADE AWAY.

1.12 Μακάριος ἀνὴρ ὃς ὑπομένει πειρασμόν, ὅτι
BLESSED [IS THE] MAN WHO ENDURES TRIAL[S], BECAUSE

δόκιμος γενόμενος λήμψεται τὸν στέφανον τῆς ζωῆς
HAVING BECOME~APPROVED HE WILL RECEIVE THE CROWN - OF LIFE

ὃν ἐπηγγείλατο τοῖς ἀγαπῶσιν αὐτόν. **1.13** μηδεὶς
WHICH HE PROMISED TO THE ONES LOVING HIM. ²NO ONE

πειραζόμενος λεγέτω ὅτι Ἀπὸ θεοῦ πειράζομαι· ὁ γὰρ
³BEING TEMPTED ¹LET ⁴SAY, - FROM GOD I AM BEING TEMPTED; - FOR

θεὸς ἀπείραστός ἐστιν κακῶν, πειράζει δὲ αὐτὸς
GOD IS~NOT TEMPTED OF(BY) EVIL THINGS, ²HE ⁴TEMPTS ¹AND ³HIMSELF

οὐδένα. **1.14** ἕκαστος δὲ πειράζεται ὑπὸ τῆς ἰδίας
NO ONE. BUT~EACH ONE IS TEMPTED BY THE(HIS) OWN

ἐπιθυμίας ἐξελκόμενος καὶ δελεαζόμενος· **1.15** εἶτα ἡ
DESIRE, BEING DRAWN AWAY AND BEING ALLURED; THEN THE

ἐπιθυμία συλλαβοῦσα τίκτει ἁμαρτίαν, ἡ δὲ
DESIRE HAVING CONCEIVED GIVES BIRTH TO SIN, AND~THE

ἁμαρτία ἀποτελεσθεῖσα ἀποκύει θάνατον.
SIN HAVING COME TO FULL GROWTH BRINGS FORTH DEATH.

1.16 Μὴ πλανᾶσθε, ἀδελφοί μου ἀγαπητοί. **1.17** πᾶσα
DO NOT BE DECEIVED, ³BROTHERS ¹MY ²BELOVED. EVERY

δόσις ἀγαθὴ καὶ πᾶν δώρημα τέλειον ἄνωθέν ἐστιν
GOOD~ENDOWMENT AND EVERY PERFECT~GIFT IS~FROM ABOVE,

καταβαῖνον ἀπὸ τοῦ πατρὸς τῶν φώτων, παρ' ᾧ
COMING DOWN FROM THE FATHER - OF LIGHTS, WITH WHOM

οὐκ ἔνι παραλλαγὴ ⌜ἢ τροπῆς ἀποσκίασμα.⌝
THERE IS~NO VARIATION OR SHADOW~OF TURNING.

1.18 βουληθεὶς ἀπεκύησεν ἡμᾶς λόγῳ ἀληθείας εἰς
HAVING WILLED [IT], HE GAVE BIRTH [TO] US BY [THE] WORD OF TRUTH FOR

τὸ εἶναι ἡμᾶς ἀπαρχήν τινα τῶν αὐτοῦ κτισμάτων.
- US~TO BE A SORT OF~FIRSTFRUIT - OF HIS CREATURES.

1.19 Ἴστε, ἀδελφοί μου ἀγαπητοί· ἔστω δὲ πᾶς
KNOW [THIS], ³BROTHERS ¹MY ²BELOVED; NOW~LET ³BE ¹EVERY

ἄνθρωπος ταχὺς εἰς τὸ ἀκοῦσαι, βραδὺς εἰς τὸ
²MAN QUICK - TO HEAR, SLOW

λαλῆσαι, βραδὺς εἰς ὀργήν· **1.20** ὀργὴ γὰρ ἀνδρὸς
TO SPEAK, SLOW TO ANGER; FOR~[THE] ANGER OF MAN

1:17 text: KJV ASV RSV NASB NEBmg TEV NRSV. var. η τροπης αποσκιασματος ([which consists in] the turning of a shadow): RSVmg NIV NEB NJB NRSVmg.

δικαιοσύνην θεοῦ οὐκ ἐργάζεται. **1.21** διὸ
²[THE] RIGHTEOUSNESS ³OF GOD ¹DOES NOT ACHIEVE.   THEREFORE

ἀποθέμενοι πᾶσαν ῥυπαρίαν καὶ περισσείαν κακίας
HAVING PUT AWAY ALL FILTHINESS AND [WHAT] REMAINS OF WICKEDNESS,

ἐν πραΰτητι, δέξασθε τὸν ἔμφυτον λόγον τὸν
IN MEEKNESS RECEIVE THE IMPLANTED WORD -

δυναμενον σῶσαι τὰς ψυχὰς ὑμῶν.
BEING ABLE TO SAVE THE SOULS OF YOU°.

1.22 Γίνεσθε δὲ ποιηταὶ λόγου καὶ μὴ μόνον
NOW~BE DOERS OF [THE] WORD AND NOT ONLY

ἀκροαταὶ παραλογιζόμενοι ἑαυτούς. **1.23** ὅτι εἴ τις
HEARERS DECEIVING YOURSELVES. BECAUSE IF ANYONE

ἀκροατὴς λόγου ἐστὶν καὶ οὐ ποιητής, οὗτος ἔοικεν
²A HEARER ³OF [THE] WORD ¹IS AND NOT A DOER, THIS ONE IS LIKE

ἀνδρὶ κατανοοῦντι τὸ πρόσωπον τῆς γενέσεως αὐτοῦ ἐν
A MAN OBSERVING - ³FACE - ²NATURAL ¹HIS IN

ἐσόπτρῳ· **1.24** κατενόησεν γὰρ ἑαυτὸν καὶ ἀπελήλυθεν
A MIRROR; FOR~HE OBSERVED HIMSELF AND HAS GONE AWAY

καὶ εὐθέως ἐπελάθετο ὁποῖος ἦν. **1.25** ὁ δὲ
AND IMMEDIATELY FORGOT ¹WHAT ³LIKE ²HE WAS. BUT~THE ONE

παρακύψας εἰς νόμον τέλειον τὸν τῆς ἐλευθερίας καὶ
HAVING LOOKED INTO [THE] PERFECT~LAW, THE ONE - OF FREEDOM, AND

παραμείνας, οὐκ ἀκροατὴς ἐπιλησμονῆς γενόμενος
HAVING REMAINED [THERE], NOT A FORGETFUL~HEARER HAVING BECOME

ἀλλὰ ποιητὴς ἔργου, οὗτος μακάριος ἐν τῇ ποιήσει
BUT A DOER OF [THE] WORK, THIS ONE ²BLESSED ³IN ⁴THE ⁵DOING

αὐτοῦ ἔσται.
⁶OF HIM ¹WILL BE.

1.26 Εἴ τις δοκεῖ θρησκὸς εἶναι μὴ
IF ANYONE CONSIDERS [HIMSELF] TO BE~RELIGIOUS, NOT

χαλιναγωγῶν γλῶσσαν αὐτοῦ ἀλλὰ ἀπατῶν καρδίαν
BRIDLING [THE] TONGUE OF HIM BUT DECEIVING [THE] HEART

αὐτοῦ, τούτου μάταιος ἡ θρησκεία. **1.27** θρησκεία
OF HIM, THIS ONE'S ²[IS] WORTHLESS - ¹RELIGION. RELIGION

καθαρὰ καὶ ἀμίαντος παρὰ τῷ θεῷ καὶ πατρὶ
PURE AND UNDEFILED BEFORE - GOD EVEN [THE] FATHER

αὕτη ἐστίν, ἐπισκέπτεσθαι ὀρφανοὺς καὶ χήρας ἐν τῇ
IS~THIS: TO VISIT ORPHANS AND WIDOWS IN THE

θλίψει αὐτῶν, ἄσπιλον ἑαυτὸν τηρεῖν ἀπὸ τοῦ κόσμου.
AFFLICTION OF THEM, ³UNSPOTTED ²ONESELF ¹TO KEEP FROM THE WORLD.

CHAPTER 2

2.1 Ἀδελφοί μου, μὴ ἐν προσωπολημψίαις ἔχετε τὴν
BROTHERS OF ME, NOT IN(WITH) PARTIALITY HAVE THE

πίστιν τοῦ κυρίου ἡμῶν Ἰησοῦ Χριστοῦ τῆς δόξης.
FAITH OF THE LORD OF US, JESUS CHRIST, - [THE LORD] OF GLORY.

does not produce God's righteousness. 21Therefore rid yourselves of all sordidness and rank growth of wickedness, and welcome with meekness the implanted word that has the power to save your souls.

22 But be doers of the word, and not merely hearers who deceive themselves. 23For if any are hearers of the word and not doers, they are like those who look at themselvesᵍ in a mirror; 24for they look at themselves and, on going away, immediately forget what they were like. 25But those who look into the perfect law, the law of liberty, and persevere, being not hearers who forget but doers who act—they will be blessed in their doing.

26 If any think they are religious, and do not bridle their tongues but deceive their hearts, their religion is worthless. 27Religion that is pure and undefiled before God, the Father, is this: to care for orphans and widows in their distress, and to keep oneself unstained by the world.

ᵍ Gk *at the face of his birth*

My brothers and sisters,ʰ do you with your acts of favoritism really believe in our glorious Lord Jesus Christ?ⁱ

ʰ Gk *My brothers*
ⁱ Or *hold the faith of our glorious Lord Jesus Christ without acts of favoritism*

²For if a person with gold rings and in fine clothes comes into your assembly, and if a poor person in dirty clothes also comes in, ³and if you take notice of the one wearing the fine clothes and say, "Have a seat here, please," while to the one who is poor you say, "Stand there," or, "Sit at my feet,"ʲ ⁴have you not made distinctions among yourselves, and become judges with evil thoughts? ⁵Listen, my beloved brothers and sisters.ᵏ Has not God chosen the poor in the world to be rich in faith and to be heirs of the kingdom that he has promised to those who love him? ⁶But you have dishonored the poor. Is it not the rich who oppress you? Is it not they who drag you into court? ⁷Is it not they who blaspheme the excellent name that was invoked over you?

8 You do well if you really fulfill the royal law according to the scripture, "You shall love your neighbor as yourself." ⁹But if you show partiality, you commit sin and are convicted by the law as transgressors. ¹⁰For whoever keeps the whole law but fails in one point has become accountable for all of it. ¹¹For the one who said, "You shall not commit adultery," also said, "You shall not murder." Now if you do not commit adultery

ʲ Gk *Sit under my footstool*
ᵏ Gk *brothers*

2.2 ἐὰν γὰρ   εἰσέλθη   εἰς   συναγωγὴν ὑμῶν
FOR~IF   [THERE] ENTERS INTO [THE] SYNAGOGUE OF YOU°

ἀνὴρ   χρυσοδακτύλιος   ἐν   ἐσθῆτι λαμπρᾷ,
A MAN   WITH GOLD RINGS ON [HIS] FINGERS IN   SPLENDID~CLOTHING,

εἰσέλθη δὲ   καὶ   πτωχὸς ἐν   ῥυπαρᾷ ἐσθῆτι,
AND~[THERE] ENTERS ALSO A POOR MAN IN SHABBY   CLOTHING,

2.3 ἐπιβλέψητε δὲ ἐπὶ τὸν   φοροῦντα τὴν ἐσθῆτα τὴν
AND~YOU° LOOK   ON   THE ONE WEARING THE ²CLOTHING -

λαμπρὰν καὶ εἴπητε, Σὺ κάθου ὧδε καλῶς,   καὶ
¹SPLENDID AND SAY,   YOU SIT HERE WELL[-SITUATED], AND

τῷ   πτωχῷ εἴπητε, Σὺ στῆθι ἐκεῖ ἢ κάθου ὑπὸ τὸ
TO THE POOR MAN YOU SAY°, YOU STAND THERE OR SIT UNDER THE

ὑποπόδιόν μου, **2.4** οὐ διεκρίθητε   ἐν   ἑαυτοῖς
FOOTSTOOL OF ME,   DID YOU° NOT MAKE DISTINCTIONS AMONG YOURSELVES

καὶ ἐγένεσθε κριταὶ διαλογισμῶν πονηρῶν;
AND BECAME   JUDGES OF(WITH) EVIL~THOUGHTS?

2.5 Ἀκούσατε, ἀδελφοί μου ἀγαπητοί·   οὐχ   ὁ θεὸς
LISTEN,   ³BROTHERS ¹MY ²BELOVED;   [DID] NOT - GOD

ἐξελέξατο τοὺς πτωχοὺς τῷ κόσμῳ πλουσίους ἐν
CHOOSE   THE POOR ONES OF THE WORLD [TO BE] RICH IN

πίστει καὶ κληρονόμους τῆς βασιλείας ἧς
FAITH AND HEIRS   OF THE KINGDOM   WHICH

ἐπηγγείλατο τοῖς   ἀγαπῶσιν αὐτόν; **2.6** ὑμεῖς δὲ
HE PROMISED TO THE ONES LOVING   HIM?   BUT~YOU°

ἠτιμάσατε τὸν πτωχόν. οὐχ οἱ πλούσιοι
DISHONORED THE POOR MAN. [DO] NOT THE RICH ONES

καταδυναστεύουσιν ὑμῶν καὶ αὐτοὶ ἕλκουσιν ὑμᾶς εἰς
OPPRESS   YOU° AND THEY DRAG   YOU° INTO

κριτήρια; **2.7** οὐκ αὐτοὶ βλασφημοῦσιν τὸ καλὸν
LAWCOURTS?   [DO] NOT THEY BLASPHEME   THE GOOD

ὄνομα τὸ ἐπικληθὲν   ἐφ᾽ ὑμᾶς; **2.8** εἰ μέντοι νόμον
NAME - HAVING BEEN NAMED UPON YOU°?   IF INDEED ³LAW

τελεῖτε   βασιλικὸν κατὰ   τὴν γραφήν, Ἀγαπήσεις
¹YOU PERFORM ²[THE] ROYAL ACCORDING TO THE SCRIPTURE, YOU SHALL LOVE

τὸν πλησίον σου ὡς σεαυτόν, καλῶς ποιεῖτε· **2.9** εἰ δὲ
THE NEIGHBOR OF YOU AS YOURSELF, YOU° DO~WELL;   BUT~IF

προσωπολημπτεῖτε, ἁμαρτίαν ἐργάζεσθε ἐλεγχόμενοι
YOU° SHOW PARTIALITY YOU° COMMIT~SIN,   BEING EXPOSED

ὑπὸ τοῦ νόμου ὡς παραβάται. **2.10** ὅστις γὰρ ὅλον τὸν
BY THE LAW   AS TRANSGRESSORS.   FOR~WHOEVER ²ALL ³THE

νόμον τηρήσῃ πταίσῃ δὲ ἐν ἑνί, γέγονεν
⁴LAW ¹KEEPS BUT~STUMBLES IN ONE [POINT], HE HAS BECOME

πάντων ἔνοχος. **2.11** ὁ γὰρ εἰπών, Μὴ μοιχεύσῃς,
GUILTY~OF ALL.   FOR~THE ONE HAVING SAID, DO NOT COMMIT ADULTERY,

εἶπεν καί, Μὴ φονεύσῃς· εἰ δὲ οὐ μοιχεύεις
SAID ALSO, DO NOT MURDER; NOW~IF YOU DO NOT COMMIT ADULTERY

2:8 Lev. 19:18   **2:11** Exod. 20:13-14; Deut. 5:17-18

φονεύεις δέ, γέγονας   παραβάτης νόμου.   **2.12** οὕτως
BUT~YOU MURDER, YOU HAVE BECOME A TRANSGRESSOR OF [THE] LAW.   SO

λαλεῖτε καὶ οὕτως ποιεῖτε ὡς διὰ   νόμου
SPEAK   AND   SO   DO   AS   THROUGH(BY) [THE] LAW

ἐλευθερίας μέλλοντες κρίνεσθαι.   **2.13** ἡ γὰρ κρίσις
OF FREEDOM   BEING ABOUT TO BE JUDGED.   FOR~THE   JUDGMENT

ἀνέλεος   τῷ   μὴ ποιήσαντι ἔλεος·
[WILL BE] MERCILESS TO THE ONE NOT HAVING SHOWN MERCY;

κατακαυχᾶται ἔλεος κρίσεως.
MERCY~TRIUMPHS OVER   JUDGMENT.

2.14 Τί τὸ   ὄφελος, ἀδελφοί μου, ἐὰν πίστιν λέγῃ
        WHAT [IS] THE PROFIT,   BROTHERS OF ME, IF ⁴FAITH ²SAYS

τις   ἔχειν ἔργα δὲ μὴ ἔχῃ;   μὴ   δύναται ἡ
¹ANYONE ³TO HAVE BUT~WORKS DOES NOT HAVE? [SURELY] NOT IS ABLE THE

πίστις σῶσαι αὐτόν; **2.15** ἐὰν ἀδελφὸς ἢ ἀδελφὴ
FAITH   TO SAVE HIM?   IF   A BROTHER OR SISTER

γυμνοὶ ὑπάρχωσιν καὶ λειπόμενοι τῆς ἐφημέρου τροφῆς
IS LIVING~UNCLOTHED AND LACKING   -   DAILY   FOOD,

2.16 εἴπῃ δέ τις αὐτοῖς ἐξ ὑμῶν, Ὑπάγετε ἐν εἰρήνῃ,
       AND~SAYS ¹ANYONE ⁴TO THEM ²OF ³YOU°, GO   IN PEACE,

θερμαίνεσθε καὶ χορτάζεσθε, μὴ δῶτε δὲ αὐτοῖς τὰ
BE WARMED   AND FED,   ²YOU° DO NOT GIVE ¹BUT TO THEM   THE

ἐπιτήδεια τοῦ   σώματος, τί τὸ   ὄφελος; **2.17** οὕτως
NEEDFUL THINGS [FOR] THE BODY,   WHAT [IS] THE PROFIT?   SO

καὶ ἡ πίστις, ἐὰν μὴ ἔχῃ   ἔργα, νεκρά ἐστιν καθ'
ALSO - FAITH,   IF IT DOES NOT HAVE WORKS, IS~DEAD   BY

ἑαυτήν.
ITSELF.

2.18 Ἀλλ' ἐρεῖ τις,   Σὺ πίστιν ἔχεις, κἀγὼ
        BUT   SOMEONE~WILL SAY, YOU HAVE~FAITH,   AND I

ἔργα ἔχω· δεῖξόν μοι τὴν πίστιν σου χωρὶς τῶν
HAVE~WORKS; SHOW   ME THE FAITH OF YOU WITHOUT THE

ἔργων, κἀγώ σοι δείξω ἐκ τῶν ἔργων μου τὴν
WORKS,   AND I WILL SHOW~YOU FROM THE WORKS OF ME THE(MY)

πίστιν. **2.19** σὺ πιστεύεις ὅτι εἷς ἐστιν ὁ θεός,
FAITH.   YOU BELIEVE   THAT ³ONE ²IS - ¹GOD,

καλῶς ποιεῖς· καὶ τὰ δαιμόνια πιστεύουσιν καὶ
YOU DO~WELL.   EVEN THE DEMONS   BELIEVE   AND

φρίσσουσιν. **2.20** θέλεις δὲ   γνῶναι, ὦ ἄνθρωπε κενέ,
SHUDDER.   BUT~ARE YOU WILLING TO KNOW, O HOLLOW~MAN,

ὅτι ἡ πίστις χωρὶς τῶν ἔργων ⌜ἀργή⌝ ἐστιν;
THAT - FAITH WITHOUT - WORKS IS~UNPRODUCTIVE?

2.21 Ἀβραὰμ ὁ πατὴρ ἡμῶν οὐκ ἐξ   ἔργων
        ABRAHAM, THE FATHER OF US ²NOT ⁴FROM(BY) ⁵WORKS

ἐδικαιώθη ἀνενέγκας Ἰσαὰκ τὸν υἱὸν αὐτοῦ ἐπὶ τὸ
¹WAS HE ³JUSTIFIED, HAVING OFFERED UP ISAAC THE SON OF HIM UPON THE

2:20 text: ASV RSV NASB NIV NEB TEV NJB NRSV. var. νεκρα (dead): KJV NIVmg TEVmg.

but if you murder, you have become a transgressor of the law. ¹²So speak and so act as those who are to be judged by the law of liberty. ¹³For judgment will be without mercy to anyone who has shown no mercy; mercy triumphs over judgment.

14 What good is it, my brothers and sisters,ⁱ if you say you have faith but do not have works? Can faith save you? ¹⁵If a brother or sister is naked and lacks daily food, ¹⁶and one of you says to them, "Go in peace; keep warm and eat your fill," and yet you do not supply their bodily needs, what is the good of that? ¹⁷So faith by itself, if it has no works, is dead.

18 But someone will say, "You have faith and I have works." Show me your faith apart from your works, and I by my works will show you my faith. ¹⁹You believe that God is one; you do well. Even the demons believe— and shudder. ²⁰Do you want to be shown, you senseless person, that faith apart from works is barren? ²¹Was not our ancestor Abraham justified by works when he offered his son Isaac on the

ⁱ Gk brothers

altar? ²²You see that faith was active along with his works, and faith was brought to completion by the works. ²³Thus the scripture was fulfilled that says, "Abraham believed God, and it was reckoned to him as righteousness," and he was called the friend of God. ²⁴You see that a person is justified by works and not by faith alone. ²⁵Likewise, was not Rahab the prostitute also justified by works when she welcomed the messengers and sent them out by another road? ²⁶For just as the body without the spirit is dead, so faith without works is also dead.

θυσιαστήριον;   **2.22** βλέπεις ὅτι ἡ πίστις συνήργει τοῖς
ALTAR?   YOU SEE   THAT - FAITH   WAS WORKING WITH THE

ἔργοις αὐτοῦ καὶ ἐκ   τῶν ἔργων ἡ πίστις
WORKS   OF HIM AND FROM(BY) THE WORKS   THE FAITH

ἐτελειώθη,   **2.23** καὶ ἐπληρώθη ἡ γραφὴ ἡ λέγουσα,
WAS MADE COMPLETE,   AND WAS FULFILLED THE SCRIPTURE - SAYING,

Ἐπίστευσεν δὲ Ἀβραὰμ τῷ θεῷ, καὶ ἐλογίσθη
³BELIEVED   ¹AND ²ABRAHAM - GOD, AND IT WAS ACCOUNTED

αὐτῷ εἰς δικαιοσύνην καὶ φίλος θεοῦ ἐκλήθη.
TO HIM FOR RIGHTEOUSNESS, AND A FRIEND OF GOD HE WAS CALLED.

2.24 ὁρᾶτε ὅτι ἐξ   ἔργων δικαιοῦται ἄνθρωπος καὶ
       YOU SEE THAT FROM(BY) WORKS A MAN~IS JUSTIFIED   AND

οὐκ ἐκ   πίστεως μόνον. **2.25** ὁμοίως δὲ καὶ Ῥαὰβ
NOT FROM(BY) FAITH ALONE.   AND~LIKEWISE ALSO ³RAHAB

ἡ πόρνη οὐκ ἐξ   ἔργων ἐδικαιώθη ὑποδεξαμένη
⁴THE ⁵PROSTITUTE ²NOT ⁷FROM(BY) ⁸WORKS ¹WAS ⁶JUSTIFIED, HAVING RECEIVED

τοὺς ἀγγέλους καὶ ἑτέρα   ὁδῷ ἐκβαλοῦσα;
THE   MESSENGERS AND BY A DIFFERENT WAY HAVING SENT [THEM] OUT?

2.26 ὥσπερ γὰρ τὸ σῶμα χωρὶς πνεύματος νεκρόν ἐστιν,
        FOR~JUST AS THE BODY WITHOUT SPIRIT(BREATH) IS~DEAD,

οὕτως καὶ ἡ πίστις χωρὶς ἔργων νεκρά ἐστιν.
SO   ALSO - FAITH WITHOUT WORKS IS~DEAD.

2:23 Gen. 15:6

CHAPTER 3

Not many of you should become teachers, my brothers and sisters,ᵐ for you know that we who teach will be judged with greater strictness. ²For all of us make many mistakes. Anyone who makes no mistakes in speaking is perfect, able to keep the whole body in check with a bridle. ³If we put bits into the mouths of horses to make them obey us, we guide their whole bodies. ⁴Or look at ships: though they are so large that it takes strong winds to drive them, yet they are guided by a very small rudder wherever the

ᵐ Gk brothers

3.1 Μὴ πολλοὶ διδάσκαλοι γίνεσθε, ἀδελφοί μου,
      ²NOT ³MANY ⁴TEACHERS ¹BE,   BROTHERS   OF ME,

εἰδότες ὅτι μεῖζον κρίμα λημψόμεθα. **3.2** πολλὰ γὰρ
KNOWING THAT GREATER JUDGMENT WE WILL RECEIVE. FOR~[IN] MANY [WAYS]

πταίομεν ἅπαντες. εἴ τις ἐν λόγῳ οὐ πταίει, οὗτος
¹WE ³STUMBLE ²ALL.   IF ANYONE IN SPEECH DOES NOT STUMBLE, THIS ONE

τέλειος ἀνὴρ δυνατὸς χαλιναγωγῆσαι καὶ ὅλον τὸ
[IS] A PERFECT MAN ABLE TO BRIDLE   ALSO THE~WHOLE

σῶμα. **3.3** εἰ δὲ τῶν ἵππων τοὺς χαλινοὺς εἰς τὰ
BODY.   AND~IF - HORSES' -   BITS   ²INTO ³THE[IR]

στόματα βάλλομεν εἰς τὸ πείθεσθαι αὐτοὺς ἡμῖν, καὶ
⁴MOUTHS ¹WE PUT SO AS - ¹TO MAKE ³OBEY ²THEM US, AND

ὅλον τὸ σῶμα αὐτῶν μετάγομεν. **3.4** ἰδοὺ καὶ τὰ πλοῖα
THE~WHOLE BODY OF THEM WE DIRECT.   BEHOLD ALSO THE SHIPS

τηλικαῦτα ὄντα καὶ ὑπὸ ἀνέμων σκληρῶν ἐλαυνόμενα,
BEING~SO GREAT AND BY HARD~WINDS   BEING DRIVEN,

μετάγεται ὑπὸ ἐλαχίστου πηδαλίου ὅπου ἡ ὁρμὴ
IS(ARE) GUIDED . BY A VERY SMALL RUDDER WHEREVER THE IMPULSE

τοῦ   εὐθύνοντος βούλεται, **3.5** οὕτως καὶ ἡ   γλῶσσα
OF THE ONE STEERING   DECIDES,   SO   ALSO THE TONGUE

μικρὸν μέλος ἐστὶν καὶ μεγάλα αὐχεῖ.
A SMALL MEMBER IS   AND BOASTS~GREAT THINGS.

'Ιδοὺ ἡλίκον πῦρ ἡλίκην ὕλην ἀνάπτει· **3.6** καὶ ἡ
BEHOLD A SMALL FIRE [2]HOW GREAT [3]A FOREST [1]BURNS;   AND THE

γλῶσσα πῦρ·   ὁ   κόσμος τῆς ἀδικίας   ἡ
TONGUE [IS] A FIRE; [4]THE [5]SUM TOTAL - [6]OF UNRIGHTEOUSNESS [1]THE

γλῶσσα καθίσταται ἐν τοῖς μέλεσιν   ἡμῶν, ἡ
[2]TONGUE [3]BECOMES AMONG THE [PHYSICAL] MEMBERS OF US,   -

σπιλοῦσα ὅλον τὸ σῶμα καὶ φλογίζουσα τὸν τροχὸν
STAINING   THE~WHOLE BODY AND SETTING ON FIRE THE COURSE(WHEEL)

τῆς γενέσεως καὶ φλογιζομένη ὑπὸ τῆς γεέννης.
-    OF LIFE   AND BEING SET ON FIRE BY   -   GEHENNA.

3.7 πᾶσα γὰρ φύσις θηρίων τε καὶ πετεινῶν, ἑρπετῶν τε
FOR~EVERY   SPECIES BOTH~OF BEASTS AND BIRDS,   BOTH~OF REPTILES

καὶ ἐναλίων δαμάζεται καὶ δεδάμασται τῇ φύσει
AND SEA CREATURES IS TAMED AND HAS BEEN TAMED - [3]SPECIES

τῇ   ἀνθρωπίνῃ, **3.8** τὴν δὲ γλῶσσαν οὐδεὶς δαμάσαι
[1]BY THE [2]HUMAN,   BUT~THE TONGUE   [1]NO ONE [3]IS ABLE

δύναται ἀνθρώπων, ἀκατάστατον κακόν, μεστὴ
[4]TO TAME [2]OF MEN,   AN UNCONTROLLABLE EVIL,   FULL

ἰοῦ θανατηφόρου. **3.9** ἐν αὐτῇ εὐλογοῦμεν τὸν κύριον
OF DEATH-BRINGING~POISON. WITH THIS WE BLESS   THE LORD

καὶ πατέρα καὶ ἐν αὐτῇ καταρώμεθα τοὺς ἀνθρώπους
AND FATHER AND WITH THIS WE CURSE   THE   MEN

τοὺς καθ'   ὁμοίωσιν θεοῦ γεγονότας, **3.10** ἐκ
-    [2]ACCORDING TO [3][THE] LIKENESS [4]OF GOD [1]HAVING BEEN MADE; OUT OF

τοῦ αὐτοῦ στόματος ἐξέρχεται εὐλογία καὶ κατάρα.
THE SAME MOUTH   COMES FORTH BLESSING AND CURSING.

οὐ χρή,   ἀδελφοί μου, ταῦτα   οὕτως γίνεσθαι.
IT IS NOT NECESSARY, BROTHERS OF ME, THESE THINGS SO   TO BE.

3.11 μήτι   ἡ πηγὴ ἐκ τῆς αὐτῆς ὀπῆς βρύει   τὸ
[SURELY] NOT THE FOUNTAIN OUT OF THE SAME OPENING POURS FORTH THE

γλυκὺ καὶ τὸ πικρόν; **3.12** μὴ δύναται,   ἀδελφοί μου,
SWEET AND THE BITTER?   [1][SURELY] [3]IS NOT ABLE, [6]BROTHERS [7]OF ME,

συκῆ ἐλαίας ποιῆσαι ἢ ἄμπελος σῦκα; οὔτε ἀλυκὸν
[2]A FIG TREE [5]OLIVES [4]TO PRODUCE OR A VINE FIGS? NEITHER [1]SALT

γλυκὺ ποιῆσαι ὕδωρ.
[4]SWEET [3]TO MAKE [2]WATER.

3.13 Τίς σοφὸς καὶ ἐπιστήμων ἐν ὑμῖν; δειξάτω
WHO [IS] WISE AND UNDERSTANDING AMONG YOU°? LET HIM SHOW [IT]

ἐκ τῆς   καλῆς ἀναστροφῆς τὰ ἔργα αὐτοῦ ἐν
BY THE(HIS) GOOD CONDUCT   THE WORKS OF HIM IN(WITH)

πραΰτητι σοφίας. **3.14** εἰ δὲ ζῆλον πικρὸν ἔχετε καὶ
MEEKNESS OF WISDOM.   BUT~IF BITTER~JEALOUSY YOU° HAVE AND

will of the pilot directs. [5]So also the tongue is a small member, yet it boasts of great exploits.

How great a forest is set ablaze by a small fire! [6]And the tongue is a fire. The tongue is placed among our members as a world of iniquity; it stains the whole body, sets on fire the cycle of nature,[n] and is itself set on fire by hell.[o] [7]For every species of beast and bird, of reptile and sea creature, can be tamed and has been tamed by the human species, [8]but no one can tame the tongue—a restless evil, full of deadly poison. [9]With it we bless the Lord and Father, and with it we curse those who are made in the likeness of God. [10]From the same mouth come blessing and cursing. My brothers and sisters,[p] this ought not to be so. [11]Does a spring pour forth from the same opening both fresh and brackish water? [12]Can a fig tree, my brothers and sisters,[q] yield olives, or a grapevine figs? No more can salt water yield fresh.

13 Who is wise and understanding among you? Show by your good life that your works are done with gentleness born of wisdom. [14]But if you have bitter envy

[n] Or *wheel of birth*
[o] Gk *Gehenna*
[p] Gk *My brothers*
[q] Gk *my brothers*

and selfish ambition in your hearts, do not be boastful and false to the truth. [15]Such wisdom does not come down from above, but is earthly, unspiritual, devilish. [16]For where there is envy and selfish ambition, there will also be disorder and wickedness of every kind. [17]But the wisdom from above is first pure, then peaceable, gentle, willing to yield, full of mercy and good fruits, without a trace of partiality or hypocrisy. [18]And a harvest of righteousness is sown in peace for[r] those who make peace.

[r] Or *by*

ἐριθείαν ἐν τῇ καρδίᾳ ὑμῶν, μὴ κατακαυχᾶσθε καὶ
SELFISHNESS   IN   THE   HEART   OF YOU°,   DO NOT BOAST   AND

ψεύδεσθε κατὰ τῆς ἀληθείας. **3.15** οὐκ ἔστιν αὕτη ἡ
LIE   AGAINST THE   TRUTH.   ³NOT ²IS   ¹THIS THE

σοφία ἄνωθεν κατερχομένη ἀλλὰ ἐπίγειος, ψυχική,
WISDOM COMING DOWN~FROM ABOVE   BUT   [IS] EARTHLY,   NATURAL,

δαιμονιώδης. **3.16** ὅπου γὰρ ζῆλος καὶ ἐριθεία,
DEMONIC.   FOR~WHERE JEALOUSY AND SELFISHNESS [ARE],

ἐκεῖ ἀκαταστασία καὶ πᾶν φαῦλον πρᾶγμα.
THERE [IS] DISORDER   AND EVERY EVIL   PRACTICE.

3.17 ἡ δὲ ἄνωθεν σοφία πρῶτον μὲν ἁγνή ἐστιν, ἔπειτα
      BUT~THE WISDOM~FROM ABOVE ²FIRST   -   ³PURE ¹IS,   THEN

εἰρηνική, ἐπιεικής εὐπειθής, μεστὴ ἐλέους καὶ
PEACE-LOVING, CONSIDERATE, YIELDING, FULL OF MERCY AND

καρπῶν ἀγαθῶν, ἀδιάκριτος, ἀνυπόκριτος.
GOOD~FRUITS,   IMPARTIAL,   UNHYPOCRITICAL.

3.18 καρπὸς δὲ δικαιοσύνης ἐν εἰρήνῃ σπείρεται τοῖς
AND~[THE] FRUIT OF RIGHTEOUSNESS IN PEACE   IS SOWN   BY THE ONES

ποιοῦσιν εἰρήνην.
MAKING   PEACE.

CHAPTER 4

Those conflicts and disputes among you, where do they come from? Do they not come from your cravings that are at war within you? [2]You want something and do not have it; so you commit murder. And you covet[s] something and cannot obtain it; so you engage in disputes and conflicts. You do not have, because you do not ask. [3]You ask and do not receive, because you ask wrongly, in order to spend what you get on your pleasures. [4]Adulterers! Do you not know that friendship with the world is enmity with God? Therefore whoever wishes to be a friend of the world becomes an enemy of God. [5]Or do you suppose that it is for nothing that the scripture says, "God[t] yearns jealously for the spirit that he has made to dwell

[s] Or *you murder and you covet*
[t] Gk *He*

4.1 Πόθεν πόλεμοι καὶ πόθεν μάχαι ἐν ὑμῖν;
FROM WHERE [COME] WARS AND FROM WHERE [COME] FIGHTS AMONG YOU°?

οὐκ ἐντεῦθεν, ἐκ τῶν ἡδονῶν ὑμῶν τῶν στρατευομένων
[IS IT] NOT FROM HERE—FROM THE PLEASURES OF YOU° -   WARRING

ἐν τοῖς μέλεσιν ὑμῶν; **4.2** ἐπιθυμεῖτε καὶ οὐκ ἔχετε,
IN THE MEMBERS   OF YOU°?   YOU° DESIRE   AND YOU° DO NOT HAVE,

φονεύετε καὶ ζηλοῦτε καὶ οὐ δύνασθε ἐπιτυχεῖν,
YOU° KILL   AND YOU° ENVY AND YOU° ARE NOT ABLE TO OBTAIN,

μάχεσθε καὶ πολεμεῖτε, οὐκ ἔχετε διὰ τὸ
YOU° FIGHT AND YOU° WAR,   YOU° DO NOT HAVE BECAUSE -

μὴ αἰτεῖσθαι ὑμᾶς, **4.3** αἰτεῖτε καὶ οὐ λαμβάνετε διότι
²FAIL TO ASK   ¹YOU°,   YOU ASK° AND YOU° DO NOT RECEIVE BECAUSE

κακῶς αἰτεῖσθε, ἵνα ἐν ταῖς ἡδοναῖς ὑμῶν
YOU° ASK~BADLY(WRONGLY), THAT ON THE   PLEASURES   OF YOU°

δαπανήσητε. **4.4** μοιχαλίδες, οὐκ οἴδατε ὅτι ἡ φιλία
YOU MAY SPEND [IT].   ADULTERESSES,   DO YOU° NOT KNOW THAT THE FRIENDSHIP

τοῦ κόσμου ἔχθρα τοῦ θεοῦ ἐστιν; ὃς ἐὰν οὖν
OF THE WORLD   ENMITY - [WITH] GOD IS?   WHOEVER   THEREFORE

βουληθῇ φίλος εἶναι τοῦ κόσμου, ἐχθρὸς τοῦ θεοῦ
CHOOSES TO BE~A FRIEND OF THE WORLD, ²AN ENEMY -   ³OF GOD

καθίσταται. **4.5** ἢ δοκεῖτε ὅτι κενῶς ἡ γραφὴ λέγει,
¹IS MADE.   OR DO YOU° THINK THAT IN VAIN THE SCRIPTURE SAYS,

Πρὸς φθόνον ἐπιποθεῖ τὸ πνεῦμα ὃ κατῴκισεν
⁸WITH ⁹JEALOUSY ⁷DESIRES [US] ¹THE ²SPIRIT ³WHICH ⁴HE CAUSED TO DWELL

ἐν ἡμῖν, **4.6** μείζονα δὲ δίδωσιν χάριν; διὸ λέγει,
⁵IN ⁶US[?] ³GREATER ¹BUT ²HE GIVES ⁴GRACE[.] THEREFORE IT SAYS,

Ὁ θεὸς ὑπερηφάνοις ἀντιτάσσεται,
- GOD OPPOSES~PROUD MEN,

ταπεινοῖς δὲ δίδωσιν χάριν.
BUT~TO HUMBLE MEN HE GIVES GRACE.

4.7 ὑποτάγητε οὖν τῷ θεῷ, ἀντίστητε δὲ τῷ
BE SUBJECT THEREFORE - TO GOD, BUT~OPPOSE THE

διαβόλῳ καὶ φεύξεται ἀφ᾽ ὑμῶν, **4.8** ἐγγίσατε τῷ θεῷ
DEVIL AND HE WILL FLEE FROM YOU°; DRAW NEAR - TO GOD

καὶ ἐγγιεῖ ὑμῖν. καθαρίσατε χεῖρας,
AND HE WILL DRAW NEAR TO YOU°. CLEANSE [YOUR°] HANDS,

ἁμαρτωλοί, καὶ ἁγνίσατε καρδίας, δίψυχοι.
SINNERS, AND SANCTIFY [YOUR°] HEARTS, DOUBLE-MINDED ONES.

4.9 ταλαιπωρήσατε καὶ πενθήσατε καὶ κλαύσατε. ὁ
LAMENT AND MOURN AND WEEP. THE

γέλως ὑμῶν εἰς πένθος μετατραπήτω καὶ ἡ χαρὰ εἰς
LAUGHTER OF YOU° ²INTO ³MOURNING ¹LET IT BE CHANGED AND THE JOY INTO

κατήφειαν. **4.10** ταπεινώθητε ἐνώπιον κυρίου καὶ
GLOOM. BE HUMBLED BEFORE [THE] LORD AND

ὑψώσει ὑμᾶς.
HE WILL EXALT YOU°.

4.11 Μὴ καταλαλεῖτε ἀλλήλων, ἀδελφοί. ὁ
DO NOT SPEAK AGAINST ONE ANOTHER, BROTHERS. THE ONE

καταλαλῶν ἀδελφοῦ ἢ κρίνων τὸν ἀδελφὸν αὐτοῦ
SPEAKING AGAINST A BROTHER OR JUDGING THE BROTHER OF HIM

καταλαλεῖ νόμου καὶ κρίνει νόμον· εἰ δὲ νόμον
SPEAKS AGAINST [THE] LAW AND JUDGES [THE] LAW; NOW~IF [THE] LAW

κρίνεις, οὐκ εἶ ποιητὴς νόμου ἀλλὰ κριτής. **4.12** εἷς
YOU JUDGE, YOU ARE~NOT A DOER OF [THE] LAW BUT A JUDGE. ONE

ἐστιν [ὁ] νομοθέτης καὶ κριτὴς ὁ δυνάμενος σῶσαι
IS THE LAWGIVER AND JUDGE, THE ONE BEING ABLE TO SAVE

καὶ ἀπολέσαι· σὺ δὲ τίς εἶ ὁ κρίνων τὸν
AND TO DESTROY; ⁴YOU ¹BUT ²WHO ³ARE, THE ONE JUDGING THE (YOUR)

πλησίον;
NEIGHBOR?

4.13 Ἄγε νῦν οἱ λέγοντες, Σήμερον ἢ αὔριον
COME NOW, THE ONES SAYING, TODAY OR TOMORROW

πορευσόμεθα εἰς τήνδε τὴν πόλιν καὶ ποιήσομεν
WE WILL GO INTO THIS OR THAT CITY AND WE WILL DO [BUSINESS]

ἐκεῖ ἐνιαυτὸν καὶ ἐμπορευσόμεθα καὶ κερδήσομεν·
THERE A YEAR AND WILL MERCHANDIZE AND WILL MAKE A PROFIT;

4.14 οἵτινες οὐκ ἐπίστασθε τὸ τῆς αὔριον ποία
YOU° WHO DO NOT KNOW WHAT - TOMORROW [WILL BE] [OR] WHAT

ἡ ζωὴ ὑμῶν· ἀτμὶς γάρ ἐστε ἡ πρὸς ὀλίγον
THE LIFE OF YOU° [WILL BE]; FOR~A MIST YOU° ARE - FOR A LITTLE WHILE

4:6 Prov. 3:34 LXX

in us"? ⁶But he gives all the more grace; therefore it says,

"God opposes the proud,
but gives grace to the humble."

⁷Submit yourselves therefore to God. Resist the devil, and he will flee from you. ⁸Draw near to God, and he will draw near to you. Cleanse your hands, you sinners, and purify your hearts, you double-minded. ⁹Lament and mourn and weep. Let your laughter be turned into mourning and your joy into dejection. ¹⁰Humble yourselves before the Lord, and he will exalt you.

11 Do not speak evil against one another, brothers and sisters.ᵘ Whoever speaks evil against another or judges another, speaks evil against the law and judges the law; but if you judge the law, you are not a doer of the law but a judge. ¹²There is one lawgiver and judge who is able to save and to destroy. So who, then, are you to judge your neighbor?

13 Come now, you who say, "Today or tomorrow we will go to such and such a town and spend a year there, doing business and making money." ¹⁴Yet you do not even know what tomorrow will bring. What is your life? For you are a mist that appears for a little while

ᵘ Gk *brothers*

and then vanishes. [15]Instead you ought to say, "If the Lord wishes, we will live and do this or that." [16]As it is, you boast in your arrogance; all such boasting is evil. [17]Anyone, then, who knows the right thing to do and fails to do it, commits sin.

φαινομένη, ἔπειτα καὶ ἀφανιζομένη. **4.15** ἀντὶ
APPEARING,   THEN   INDEED DISAPPEARING.   INSTEAD OF [THIS]

τοῦ λέγειν ὑμᾶς, Ἐὰν ὁ κύριος θελήσῃ καὶ ζήσομεν
-    YOU° [OUGHT]~TO SAY, IF   THE LORD   WILLS   AND   WE WILL LIVE

καὶ ποιήσομεν τοῦτο ἢ ἐκεῖνο. **4.16** νῦν δὲ καυχᾶσθε
ALSO WE WILL DO   THIS OR THAT.   BUT~NOW YOU° BOAST

ἐν ταῖς ἀλαζονείαις ὑμῶν· πᾶσα καύχησις τοιαύτη
IN THE   PRETENSIONS   OF YOU°. ALL   SUCH~BOASTING

πονηρά ἐστιν. **4.17** εἰδότι   οὖν   καλὸν ποιεῖν
IS~EVIL.   TO [THE] ONE KNOWING THEREFORE TO DO~GOOD

καὶ μὴ ποιοῦντι, ἁμαρτία αὐτῷ ἐστιν.
AND NOT DOING [IT],   3SIN   1TO HIM 2IT IS.

CHAPTER 5

Come now, you rich people, weep and wail for the miseries that are coming to you. [2]Your riches have rotted, and your clothes are moth-eaten. [3]Your gold and silver have rusted, and their rust will be evidence against you, and it will eat your flesh like fire. You have laid up treasure[v] for the last days. [4]Listen! The wages of the laborers who mowed your fields, which you kept back by fraud, cry out, and the cries of the harvesters have reached the ears of the Lord of hosts. [5]You have lived on the earth in luxury and in pleasure; you have fattened your hearts in a day of slaughter. [6]You have condemned and murdered the righteous one, who does not resist you.

7 Be patient, therefore, beloved,[w] until the coming of the Lord. The farmer waits for the

[v] Or will eat your flesh, since you
    have stored up fire
[w] Gk brothers

5.1 Ἄγε νῦν οἱ πλούσιοι, κλαύσατε ὀλολύζοντες ἐπὶ
COME NOW THE RICH MEN,   WEEP,   HOWLING   OVER

ταῖς ταλαιπωρίαις ὑμῶν ταῖς ἐπερχομέναις. **5.2** ὁ
THE   MISERIES   OF YOU° -   COMING UPON [YOU°].   THE

πλοῦτος ὑμῶν σέσηπεν καὶ τὰ ἱμάτια ὑμῶν
WEALTH   OF YOU° HAS ROTTED AND THE CLOTHES OF YOU°

σητόβρωτα γέγονεν, **5.3** ὁ χρυσὸς ὑμῶν καὶ ὁ ἄργυρος
HAVE BECOME~MOTH-EATEN,   THE GOLD   OF YOU° AND THE SILVER

κατίωται   καὶ ὁ ἰὸς   αὐτῶν εἰς μαρτύριον ὑμῖν
HAS BEEN CORRODED AND THE CORROSION OF THEM 2FOR 3A TESTIMONY 4TO YOU°

ἔσται καὶ φάγεται τὰς σάρκας ὑμῶν ὡς πῦρ.
1WILL BE AND WILL EAT   THE FLESH OF YOU° AS   FIRE.

ἐθησαυρίσατε ἐν ἐσχάταις ἡμέραις. **5.4** ἰδοὺ ὁ
YOU° STORED UP TREASURE IN [THE] LAST   DAYS.   BEHOLD, THE

μισθὸς τῶν   ἐργατῶν τῶν ἀμησάντων τὰς χώρας ὑμῶν
PAY   OF(FOR) THE WORKMEN -   HAVING MOWED THE FIELDS OF YOU°

ὁ   ἀπεστερημένος ἀφ' ὑμῶν κράζει, καὶ αἱ βοαὶ
WHICH (PAY) HAVING BEEN WITHHELD BY   YOU° CRIES [OUT], AND THE CRIES

τῶν   θερισάντων εἰς τὰ ὦτα κυρίου   Σαβαὼθ
OF THE ONES HAVING REAPED 2INTO 3THE 4EARS 5OF [THE] LORD 6OF HOSTS

εἰσελήλυθασιν. **5.5** ἐτρυφήσατε   ἐπὶ τῆς γῆς καὶ
1HAVE ENTERED.   YOU° LIVED IN INDULGENCE UPON THE EARTH AND

ἐσπαταλήσατε, ἐθρέψατε τὰς καρδίας ὑμῶν ἐν ἡμέρᾳ
LIVED LUXURIOUSLY,   YOU° NOURISHED THE HEARTS   OF YOU° [AS] IN A DAY

σφαγῆς, **5.6** κατεδικάσατε, ἐφονεύσατε τὸν δίκαιον,
OF SLAUGHTER,   YOU° CONDEMNED,   YOU° KILLED   THE RIGHTEOUS MAN,

οὐκ ἀντιτάσσεται ὑμῖν.
HE DOES NOT RESIST   YOU°.

5.7 Μακροθυμήσατε οὖν,   ἀδελφοί, ἕως τῆς
BE PATIENT   THEREFORE, BROTHERS, UNTIL THE

παρουσίας τοῦ κυρίου. ἰδοὺ ὁ γεωργὸς ἐκδέχεται
COMING   OF THE LORD.   BEHOLD THE FARMER   AWAITS

τὸν τίμιον καρπὸν τῆς γῆς μακροθυμῶν ἐπ’ αὐτῷ
THE PRECIOUS FRUIT OF THE EARTH, BEING PATIENT FOR IT

ἕως λάβῃ πρόϊμον καὶ ὄψιμον. **5.8** μακροθυμήσατε
UNTIL IT RECEIVES [THE] EARLY AND LATTER [RAIN]. ¹BE ⁴PATIENT

καὶ ὑμεῖς, στηρίξατε τὰς καρδίας ὑμῶν, ὅτι ἡ
³ALSO ²YOU°, ESTABLISH THE HEARTS OF YOU°, BECAUSE THE

παρουσία τοῦ κυρίου ἤγγικεν. **5.9** μὴ στενάζετε,
COMING OF THE LORD HAS DRAWN NEAR. DO NOT MURMUR,

ἀδελφοί, κατ’ ἀλλήλων ἵνα μὴ κριθῆτε· ἰδοὺ ὁ
BROTHERS, AGAINST ONE ANOTHER LEST YOU° BE JUDGED; BEHOLD, THE

κριτὴς πρὸ τῶν θυρῶν ἔστηκεν. **5.10** ὑπόδειγμα λάβετε,
JUDGE BEFORE THE DOORS HAS STOOD. TAKE~[AS] AN EXAMPLE,

ἀδελφοί, τῆς κακοπαθίας καὶ τῆς μακροθυμίας τοὺς
BROTHERS, - OF SUFFERING EVIL AND - OF PATIENCE, THE

προφήτας οἳ ἐλάλησαν ἐν τῷ ὀνόματι κυρίου.
PROPHETS, WHO SPOKE IN THE NAME OF [THE] LORD.

5.11 ἰδοὺ μακαρίζομεν τοὺς ὑπομείναντας· τὴν
BEHOLD, WE CALL BLESSED THE ONES HAVING ENDURED; THE

ὑπομονὴν Ἰὼβ ἠκούσατε καὶ τὸ τέλος κυρίου
ENDURANCE OF JOB YOU° HEARD [OF] AND THE END RESULT FROM [THE] LORD

εἴδετε, ὅτι πολύσπλαγχνός ἐστιν ὁ κύριος καὶ
YOU° SAW, THAT FULL OF TENDER COMPASSION IS THE LORD AND

οἰκτίρμων.
MERCIFUL.

5.12 Πρὸ πάντων δέ, ἀδελφοί μου, μὴ ὀμνύετε
²BEFORE ³ALL THINGS ¹BUT, BROTHERS OF ME, DO NOT SWEAR,

μήτε τὸν οὐρανὸν μήτε τὴν γῆν μήτε ἄλλον τινὰ
NEITHER [BY] THE HEAVEN NOR THE EARTH NOR ANY~OTHER

ὅρκον· ἤτω δὲ ὑμῶν τὸ Ναὶ ναὶ καὶ τὸ   Οὒ οὔ,
OATH; BUT~LET BE YOUR° - YES YES AND THE (YOUR°) NO NO,

ἵνα μὴ ὑπὸ κρίσιν πέσητε.
LEST UNDER JUDGMENT YOU° FALL.

5.13 Κακοπαθεῖ   τις   ἐν   ὑμῖν, προσευχέσθω·
⁴IS SUFFERING MISFORTUNE ¹[IF] ANYONE ²AMONG ³YOU, LET HIM PRAY;

εὐθυμεῖ τις, ψαλλέτω· **5.14** ἀσθενεῖ τις   ἐν
[IF] ANYONE~IS HAPPY, LET HIM SING PRAISE; ⁴IS SICK ¹[IF] ANYONE ²AMONG

ὑμῖν, προσκαλεσάσθω τοὺς πρεσβυτέρους τῆς
³YOU°, LET HIM CALL THE ELDERS OF THE

ἐκκλησίας καὶ προσευξάσθωσαν ἐπ’ αὐτὸν ἀλείψαντες
CHURCH, AND LET THEM PRAY OVER HIM, HAVING ANOINTED

[αὐτὸν] ἐλαίῳ ἐν τῷ ὀνόματι τοῦ κυρίου. **5.15** καὶ ἡ
HIM WITH OIL IN THE NAME OF THE LORD. AND THE

εὐχὴ τῆς πίστεως σώσει τὸν κάμνοντα καὶ ἐγερεῖ
PRAYER - OF FAITH WILL DELIVER THE SICK ONE AND ³WILL RAISE ⁵UP

αὐτὸν ὁ κύριος· κἂν ἁμαρτίας ᾖ πεποιηκώς,
⁴HIM ¹THE ²LORD; AND IF ²SINS ¹HE MAY HAVE BEEN COMMITTING,

ἀφεθήσεται αὐτῷ. **5.16** ἐξομολογεῖσθε οὖν ἀλλήλοις
IT WILL BE FORGIVEN TO HIM. CONFESS, THEREFORE, TO ONE ANOTHER

precious crop from the earth, being patient with it until it receives the early and the late rains. [8]You also must be patient. Strengthen your hearts, for the coming of the Lord is near.[x] [9]Beloved,[y] do not grumble against one another, so that you may not be judged. See, the Judge is standing at the doors! [10]As an example of suffering and patience, beloved,[z] take the prophets who spoke in the name of the Lord. [11]Indeed we call blessed those who showed endurance. You have heard of the endurance of Job, and you have seen the purpose of the Lord, how the Lord is compassionate and merciful.

12 Above all, my beloved,[z] do not swear, either by heaven or by earth or by any other oath, but let your "Yes" be yes and your "No" be no, so that you may not fall under condemnation.

13 Are any among you suffering? They should pray. Are any cheerful? They should sing songs of praise. [14]Are any among you sick? They should call for the elders of the church and have them pray over them, anointing them with oil in the name of the Lord. [15]The prayer of faith will save the sick, and the Lord will raise them up; and anyone who has committed sins will be forgiven. [16]Therefore confess your sins to one

[x] Or is at hand
[y] Gk Brothers
[z] Gk brothers

another, and pray for one another, so that you may be healed. The prayer of the righteous is powerful and effective. [17]Elijah was a human being like us, and he prayed fervently that it might not rain, and for three years and six months it did not rain on the earth. [18]Then he prayed again, and the heaven gave rain and the earth yielded its harvest.

19 My brothers and sisters,[a] if anyone among you wanders from the truth and is brought back by another, [20]you should know that whoever brings back a sinner from wandering will save the sinner's[b] soul from death and will cover a multitude of sins.

[a] Gk *My brothers*
[b] Gk *his*

τὰς   ἁμαρτίας καὶ   εὔχεσθε ὑπὲρ   ἀλλήλων   ὅπως
THE(YOUR*) SINS   AND   PRAY   ON BEHALF OF ONE ANOTHER SO THAT

ἰαθῆτε.   πολὺ   ἰσχύει δέησις   δικαίου
YOU* MAY BE CURED. 4[HAS] GREAT 5POWER 1[THE] PETITION 2OF A RIGHTEOUS MAN

ἐνεργουμένη.   **5.17** Ἡλίας ἄνθρωπος ἦν   ὁμοιοπαθὴς
3BEING EFFECTIVE.   ELIJAH   WAS~A MAN   OF LIKE NATURE

ἡμῖν, καὶ   προσευχῇ   προσηύξατο τοῦ μὴ βρέξαι, καὶ
TO US, AND   WITH PRAYER HE PRAYED [FOR IT] -   NOT TO RAIN,   AND

οὐκ ἔβρεξεν ἐπὶ τῆς γῆς ἐνιαυτοὺς τρεῖς καὶ μῆνας ἕξ·
IT DID NOT RAIN UPON THE EARTH THREE~YEARS   AND   SIX~MONTHS;

5.18 καὶ   πάλιν   προσηύξατο, καὶ ὁ   οὐρανὸς
        AND   AGAIN   HE PRAYED,   AND THE HEAVEN

ὑετὸν ἔδωκεν καὶ ἡ γῆ ἐβλάστησεν τὸν καρπὸν
GAVE~RAIN   AND THE EARTH CAUSED TO SPROUT THE FRUIT

αὐτῆς.
OF IT.

5.19 Ἀδελφοί   μου, ἐάν τις   ἐν   ὑμῖν πλανηθῇ
         BROTHERS   OF ME, IF ANYONE AMONG YOU* WANDERS

ἀπὸ τῆς ἀληθείας καὶ ἐπιστρέψῃ τις   αὐτόν,
FROM THE TRUTH   AND 2TURNS 4BACK 1SOMEONE 3HIM,

5.20 γινωσκέτω ὅτι ὁ   ἐπιστρέψας   ἁμαρτωλὸν ἐκ
        LET HIM KNOW THAT THE ONE HAVING TURNED BACK A SINNER   FROM

πλάνης   ὁδοῦ   αὐτοῦ σώσει ψυχὴν αὐτοῦ ἐκ
[THE] WANDERING OF [THE] WAY OF HIM WILL SAVE [THE] SOUL OF HIM FROM

θανάτου καὶ καλύψει πλῆθος ἁμαρτιῶν.
DEATH   AND   WILL COVER A MULTITUDE OF SINS.

THE FIRST LETTER OF
PETER

ΠΕΤΡΟΥ Α
OF PETER   1

1.1 Πέτρος ἀπόστολος Ἰησοῦ Χριστοῦ ἐκλεκτοῖς
PETER   AN APOSTLE   OF JESUS   CHRIST   TO [THE] CHOSEN

παρεπιδήμοις διασπορᾶς Πόντου, Γαλατίας,
EXILES   OF [THE] DISPERSION OF PONTUS,   OF GALATIA,

Καππαδοκίας, Ἀσίας καὶ Βιθυνίας, **1.2** κατὰ
OF CAPPADOCIA,   OF ASIA,   AND   OF BITHYNIA,   ACCORDING TO

πρόγνωσιν θεοῦ πατρός ἐν ἁγιασμῷ πνεύματος
[THE] FOREKNOWLEDGE OF GOD [THE] FATHER IN(BY) SANCTIFICATION OF [THE] SPIRIT

εἰς ὑπακοὴν καὶ ῥαντισμὸν αἵματος Ἰησοῦ
[RESULTING] IN OBEDIENCE   AND   SPRINKLING   OF [THE] BLOOD OF JESUS

Χριστοῦ, χάρις ὑμῖν καὶ εἰρήνη πληθυνθείη.
CHRIST,   GRACE   TO YOU° AND   PEACE   MAY IT BE MULTIPLIED.

1.3 Εὐλογητὸς ὁ θεὸς καὶ πατὴρ τοῦ κυρίου ἡμῶν
BLESSED [BE]   THE GOD   AND FATHER OF THE LORD   OF US,

Ἰησοῦ Χριστοῦ, ὁ κατὰ τὸ πολὺ αὐτοῦ ἔλεος
JESUS   CHRIST,   THE ONE ACCORDING TO - HIS~GREAT   MERCY

ἀναγεννήσας ἡμᾶς εἰς ἐλπίδα ζῶσαν δι' ἀναστάσεως
HAVING REGENERATED US   TO   A LIVING~HOPE   THROUGH [THE] RESURRECTION

Ἰησοῦ Χριστοῦ ἐκ νεκρῶν, **1.4** εἰς κληρονομίαν
OF JESUS   CHRIST   FROM [THE] DEAD,   TO   AN INHERITANCE

ἄφθαρτον καὶ ἀμίαντον καὶ ἀμάραντον, τετηρημένην
IMPERISHABLE AND UNDEFILED   AND   UNFADING,   HAVING BEEN KEPT

ἐν οὐρανοῖς εἰς ὑμᾶς **1.5** τοὺς ἐν δυνάμει θεοῦ
IN [THE] HEAVENS FOR YOU°,   THE ONES IN(BY) [THE] POWER OF GOD

φρουρουμένους διὰ πίστεως εἰς σωτηρίαν ἑτοίμην
BEING GUARDED   THROUGH FAITH   FOR   A SALVATION   READY

ἀποκαλυφθῆναι ἐν καιρῷ ἐσχάτῳ. **1.6** ἐν ᾧ
TO BE REVEALED   IN   [THE] LAST~TIME.   IN   WHICH(THIS)

ἀγαλλιᾶσθε, ὀλίγον ἄρτι εἰ δέον [ἐστὶν]
YOU° GREATLY REJOICE, FOR A LITTLE WHILE NOW   IF   IT IS~NECESSARY

λυπηθέντες ἐν ποικίλοις πειρασμοῖς, **1.7** ἵνα τὸ
HAVING BEEN GRIEVED BY   VARIOUS   TRIALS,   THAT   THE

δοκίμιον ὑμῶν τῆς πίστεως πολυτιμότερον χρυσίου τοῦ
GENUINENESS OF YOUR° -   FAITH,   MUCH MORE VALUABLE [THAN] ²GOLD -

ἀπολλυμένου διὰ πυρὸς δὲ δοκιμαζομένου, εὑρεθῇ εἰς
¹PERISHING,   ³BY ⁴FIRE ¹YET ²BEING TESTED,   MAY BE FOUND TO

ἔπαινον καὶ δόξαν καὶ τιμὴν ἐν ἀποκαλύψει Ἰησοῦ
PRAISE   AND GLORY   AND HONOR IN(AT) [THE] REVELATION OF JESUS

Peter, an apostle of Jesus Christ,

To the exiles of the Dispersion in Pontus, Galatia, Cappadocia, Asia, and Bithynia, ²who have been chosen and destined by God the Father and sanctified by the Spirit to be obedient to Jesus Christ and to be sprinkled with his blood:

May grace and peace be yours in abundance.

3 Blessed be the God and Father of our Lord Jesus Christ! By his great mercy he has given us a new birth into a living hope through the resurrection of Jesus Christ from the dead, ⁴and into an inheritance that is imperishable, undefiled, and unfading, kept in heaven for you, ⁵who are being protected by the power of God through faith for a salvation ready to be revealed in the last time. ⁶In this you rejoice,ᵃ even if now for a little while you have had to suffer various trials, ⁷so that the genuineness of your faith—being more precious than gold that, though perishable, is tested by fire—may be found to result in praise and glory and honor when Jesus Christ is

ᵃ Or *Rejoice in this*

revealed. [8]Although you have not seen[b] him, you love him; and even though you do not see him now, you believe in him and rejoice with an indescribable and glorious joy, [9]for you are receiving the outcome of your faith, the salvation of your souls.

10 Concerning this salvation, the prophets who prophesied of the grace that was to be yours made careful search and inquiry, [11]inquiring about the person or time that the Spirit of Christ within them indicated when it testified in advance to the sufferings destined for Christ and the subsequent glory. [12]It was revealed to them that they were serving not themselves but you, in regard to the things that have now been announced to you through those who brought you good news by the Holy Spirit sent from heaven— things into which angels long to look!

13 Therefore prepare your minds for action;[c] discipline yourselves; set all your hope on the grace that Jesus Christ will bring you when he is revealed. [14]Like obedient children, do not be conformed to the desires that you formerly had in ignorance. [15]Instead, as he who called you is holy, be holy yourselves in all your conduct; [16]for it is written, "You shall be holy, for I am holy."

[b] Other ancient authorities read known
[c] Gk gird up the loins of your mind

Χριστοῦ· **1.8** ὃν οὐκ ἰδόντες ἀγαπᾶτε, εἰς ὃν ἄρτι
CHRIST; WHOM NOT HAVING SEEN YOU° LOVE, IN WHOM NOW

μὴ ὁρῶντες πιστεύοντες δὲ ἀγαλλιᾶσθε χαρᾷ ἀνεκλαλήτῳ
NOT SEEING BUT~BELIEVING YOU° REJOICE WITH JOY INEXPRESSIBLE

καὶ δεδοξασμένη **1.9** κομιζόμενοι τὸ τέλος τῆς
AND HAVING BEEN GLORIFIED, OBTAINING THE OUTCOME OF THE

πίστεως [ὑμῶν] σωτηρίαν ψυχῶν.
FAITH OF YOU°, [THE] SALVATION OF [YOUR°] SOULS.

1.10 Περὶ ἧς σωτηρίας ἐξεζήτησαν καὶ
CONCERNING WHICH SALVATION [8]SOUGHT OUT [9]AND

ἐξηραύνησαν προφῆται οἱ περὶ τῆς εἰς ὑμᾶς
[10]INQUIRED [1]PROPHETS - [3]CONCERNING [4]THE [6]FOR [7]YOU°

χάριτος προφητεύσαντες, **1.11** ἐραυνῶντες εἰς τίνα ἢ
[5]GRACE [2]HAVING PROPHESIED, SEARCHING FOR WHAT OR

ποῖον καιρὸν ἐδήλου τὸ ἐν αὐτοῖς πνεῦμα
WHAT KIND OF TIME(OCCASION) [6]WAS MAKING CLEAR [1]THE [4]IN [5]THEM [2]SPIRIT

Χριστοῦ προμαρτυρόμενον τὰ εἰς Χριστὸν παθήματα
[3]OF CHRIST, TESTIFYING BEFOREHAND [1]THE [3]FOR [4]CHRIST [2]SUFFERINGS

καὶ τὰς μετὰ ταῦτα δόξας. **1.12** οἷς ἀπεκαλύφθη ὅτι
AND THE [2]AFTER [1]THESE [3]GLORIES. TO WHOM IT WAS REVEALED THAT

οὐχ ἑαυτοῖς ὑμῖν δὲ διηκόνουν αὐτά, ἃ νῦν
NOT TO THEMSELVES BUT~TO YOU° THEY WERE MINISTERING THESE THINGS, WHICH NOW

ἀνηγγέλη ὑμῖν διὰ τῶν εὐαγγελισαμένων
WERE ANNOUNCED TO YOU° THROUGH THE ONES HAVING PREACHED THE GOSPEL [TO]

ὑμᾶς [ἐν] πνεύματι ἁγίῳ ἀποσταλέντι ἀπ᾽ οὐρανοῦ, εἰς
YOU° IN(BY) [THE] HOLY~SPIRIT, HAVING BEEN SENT FROM HEAVEN, INTO

ἃ ἐπιθυμοῦσιν ἄγγελοι παρακύψαι.
WHICH THINGS ANGELS~LONG TO LOOK.

1.13 Διὸ ἀναζωσάμενοι τὰς ὀσφύας τῆς διανοίας
THEREFORE HAVING GIRDED UP THE LOINS OF THE MIND

ὑμῶν νήφοντες τελείως ἐλπίσατε ἐπὶ τὴν
OF YOU°, BEING SELF-CONTROLED, HOPE~COMPLETELY ON [1]THE

φερομένην ὑμῖν χάριν ἐν ἀποκαλύψει Ἰησοῦ
[3]BEING BROUGHT [4]TO YOU° [2]GRACE IN(AT) [THE] REVELATION OF JESUS

Χριστοῦ. **1.14** ὡς τέκνα ὑπακοῆς μὴ συσχηματιζόμενοι
CHRIST. AS CHILDREN OF OBEDIENCE, NOT CONFORMING YOURSELVES

ταῖς πρότερον ἐν τῇ ἀγνοίᾳ ὑμῶν ἐπιθυμίαις
[1]TO THE [4]FORMER - - [5]IGNORANCE [3]OF YOUR° [2]PASSIONS,

1.15 ἀλλὰ κατὰ τὸν καλέσαντα ὑμᾶς ἅγιον καὶ
BUT ACCORDING TO [1]THE [3]HAVING CALLED [4]YOU° [2]HOLY ONE [SO] ALSO

αὐτοὶ ἅγιοι ἐν πάσῃ ἀναστροφῇ γενήθητε, **1.16** διότι
YOURSELVES [2]HOLY [3]IN [4]ALL [5]CONDUCT [1]BECOME, BECAUSE

γέγραπται [ὅτι] Ἅγιοι ἔσεσθε, ὅτι ἐγὼ
IT HAS BEEN WRITTEN, - HOLY YOU° WILL BE, BECAUSE I

ἅγιός [εἰμι].
AM~HOLY.

1:16 Lev. 19:2

1.17 Καὶ　εἰ　πατέρα ἐπικαλεῖσθε　τὸν
AND　　IF　　YOU° CALL UPON~[AS] FATHER　　THE ONE

ἀπροσωπολήμπτως κρίνοντα κατὰ　　τὸ ἑκάστου
IMPARTIALLY　　　　　　JUDGING　ACCORDING TO　-　EACH ONE'S

ἔργον, ἐν　φόβῳ τὸν　　τῆς παροικίας ὑμῶν　χρόνον
WORK,　²WITH ³FEAR ⁴[DURING] THE　-　⁷EXILE　　⁶OF YOUR° ⁵TIME

ἀναστράφητε,　**1.18** εἰδότες ὅτι οὐ φθαρτοῖς,
¹CONDUCT [YOURSELVES],　　　KNOWING THAT NOT WITH PERISHABLE THINGS,

ἀργυρίῳ ἢ χρυσίῳ, ἐλυτρώθητε　ἐκ　τῆς ματαίας ὑμῶν
[AS] SILVER OR GOLD,　　YOU° WERE REDEEMED FROM　-　　YOUR°~VAIN

ἀναστροφῆς πατροπαραδότου　　　**1.19** ἀλλὰ　τιμίῳ
MANNER OF LIFE　HANDED DOWN FROM [YOUR°] FATHERS,　　BUT　WITH PRECIOUS

αἵματι ὡς　ἀμνοῦ ἀμώμου καὶ ἀσπίλου Χριστοῦ,
BLOOD　AS　OF A LAMB UNBLEMISHED AND　UNSPOTTED,　[THE BLOOD] OF CHRIST,

1.20 προεγνωσμένου μὲν　πρὸ　καταβολῆς κόσμου
HAVING BEEN FOREKNOWN　-　　BEFORE [THE] FOUNDATION OF [THE] WORLD

φανερωθέντος δὲ　ἐπ᾽ ἐσχάτου τῶν χρόνων δι᾽ ὑμᾶς
YET~HAVING BEEN MANIFESTED IN　[THE] LAST OF THE TIMES　FOR YOU°,

1.21 τοὺς δι᾽　　αὐτοῦ πιστοὺς εἰς θεὸν τὸν　ἐγείραντα
¹THE ³THROUGH ⁴HIM　²BELIEVERS IN　GOD,　THE ONE HAVING RAISED

αὐτὸν ἐκ　νεκρῶν καὶ δόξαν αὐτῷ δόντα,　ὥστε τὴν
HIM　FROM [THE] DEAD AND　GLORY HAVING GIVEN~TO HIM, FOR　THE

πίστιν ὑμῶν καὶ ἐλπίδα εἶναι εἰς θεόν.
FAITH　OF YOU° AND　HOPE　TO BE　IN　GOD.

1.22 Τὰς ψυχὰς ὑμῶν ἡγνικότες ἐν τῇ ὑπακοῇ τῆς
²THE ³SOULS ⁴OF YOU° ¹HAVING PURIFIED BY　-　OBEDIENCE TO THE

ἀληθείας εἰς　　φιλαδελφίαν ἀνυπόκριτον, ἐκ
TRUTH　　[RESULTING] IN UNHYPOCRITICAL~BROTHERLY LOVE,　　FROM

⌜[καθαρᾶς]⌝ καρδίας ἀλλήλους ἀγαπήσατε ἐκτενῶς
A PURE　　　HEART　LOVE~ONE ANOTHER　　　FERVENTLY,

1.23 ἀναγεγεννημένοι οὐκ ἐκ　σπορᾶς φθαρτῆς ἀλλὰ
HAVING BEEN REGENERATED　NOT FROM PERISHABLE~SEED　BUT

ἀφθάρτου διὰ　λόγου ζῶντος θεοῦ καὶ μένοντος.
IMPERISHABLE THROUGH ⁴WORD ¹[THE] LIVING ⁵OF GOD ²AND ³REMAINING.

1.24 διότι
BECAUSE

πᾶσα σὰρξ ὡς　χόρτος
ALL　　FLESH [IS] AS GRASS

καὶ πᾶσα δόξα　αὐτῆς ὡς　ἄνθος　χόρτου·
AND　ALL　[THE] GLORY OF IT　AS　[THE] FLOWER OF GRASS;

ἐξηράνθη ὁ　χόρτος
WAS DRIED UP THE GRASS

καὶ τὸ ἄνθος ἐξέπεσεν·
AND THE FLOWER FELL OFF;

1.25 τὸ δὲ ῥῆμα κυρίου　μένει εἰς τὸν αἰῶνα.
BUT~THE WORD OF [THE] LORD REMAINS INTO THE　AGE.

17 If you invoke as Father the one who judges all people impartially according to their deeds, live in reverent fear during the time of your exile. ¹⁸You know that you were ransomed from the futile ways inherited from your ancestors, not with perishable things like silver or gold, ¹⁹but with the precious blood of Christ, like that of a lamb without defect or blemish. ²⁰He was destined before the foundation of the world, but was revealed at the end of the ages for your sake. ²¹Through him you have come to trust in God, who raised him from the dead and gave him glory, so that your faith and hope are set on God.

22 Now that you have purified your souls by your obedience to the truth[d] so that you have genuine mutual love, love one another deeply[e] from the heart.[f] ²³You have been born anew, not of perishable but of imperishable seed, through the living and enduring word of God.[g] ²⁴For

"All flesh is like grass
　and all its glory like the
　　flower of grass.
The grass withers,
　and the flower falls,
²⁵but the word of the Lord
　endures forever."

[d] Other ancient authorities add *through the Spirit*
[e] Or *constantly*
[f] Other ancient authorities read *a pure heart*
[g] Or *through the word of the living and enduring God*

1:22 text: KJV ASVmg NASBmg NIVmg TEVmg NJBmg NRSVmg.　omit: ASV RSV NASB NIV NEB TEV NJB NRSV.　**1:24-25** Isa. 40:6-8

That word is the good news
that was announced to you.

τοῦτο δέ ἐστιν τὸ ῥῆμα τὸ εὐαγγελισθὲν
AND~THIS   IS   THE WORD   -   HAVING BEEN PROCLAIMED AS GOOD NEWS

εἰς ὑμᾶς.
TO   YOUᵖ.

CHAPTER 2

Rid yourselves, therefore, of all malice, and all guile, insincerity, envy, and all slander. ²Like newborn infants, long for the pure, spiritual milk, so that by it you may grow into salvation—³if indeed you have tasted that the Lord is good.

4 Come to him, a living stone, though rejected by mortals yet chosen and precious in God's sight, and ⁵like living stones, let yourselves be built[h] into a spiritual house, to be a holy priesthood, to offer spiritual sacrifices acceptable to God through Jesus Christ. ⁶For it stands in scripture:

"See, I am laying in Zion a stone,
a cornerstone chosen and precious;
and whoever believes in him[i] will not be put to shame."

⁷To you then who believe, he is precious; but for those who do not believe,

"The stone that the builders rejected has become the very head of the corner,"

[h] Or you yourselves are being built
[i] Or it

2.1 Ἀποθέμενοι οὖν   πᾶσαν κακίαν καὶ πάντα
HAVING PUT AWAY,   THEREFORE, ALL   MALICE   AND   ALL

δόλον καὶ ὑποκρίσεις καὶ φθόνους καὶ πάσας
GUILE AND HYPOCRISIES AND ENVIES   AND ALL

καταλαλιάς, **2.2** ὡς ἀρτιγέννητα βρέφη τὸ λογικὸν
EVIL SPEAKINGS,   AS   NEWBORN   BABES ²THE ⁴SPIRITUAL

ἄδολον γάλα ἐπιποθήσατε, ἵνα ἐν αὐτῷ αὐξηθῆτε εἰς
³PURE   ⁵MILK ¹DESIRE,   THAT BY IT   YOUᵖ MAY GROW INTO

σωτηρίαν, **2.3** εἰ ἐγεύσασθε ὅτι χρηστὸς ὁ κύριος.
SALVATION,   IF YOUᵖ TASTED THAT ³[IS] GOOD ¹THE ²LORD.

2.4 πρὸς ὃν   προσερχόμενοι λίθον ζῶντα ὑπὸ ἀνθρώπων
TO   WHOM COMING,   A LIVING~STONE, BY   MEN

μὲν ἀποδεδοκιμασμένον παρὰ δὲ θεῷ ἐκλεκτὸν
-    HAVING BEEN REJECTED   BUT~WITH GOD CHOSEN,

ἔντιμον, **2.5** καὶ αὐτοὶ ὡς λίθοι ζῶντες οἰκοδομεῖσθε
PRECIOUS,   YOURSELVES~ALSO AS LIVING~STONES ARE BEING BUILT UP

οἶκος πνευματικὸς εἰς ἱεράτευμα ἅγιον ἀνενέγκαι
A SPIRITUAL~HOUSE   FOR A HOLY~PRIESTHOOD TO OFFER UP

πνευματικὰς θυσίας εὐπροσδέκτους [τῷ] θεῷ διὰ
SPIRITUAL   SACRIFICES ACCEPTABLE   -   TO GOD THROUGH

Ἰησοῦ Χριστοῦ. **2.6** διότι περιέχει ἐν γραφῇ,
JESUS CHRIST;   BECAUSE IT STANDS IN SCRIPTURE,

Ἰδοὺ τίθημι ἐν Σιὼν λίθον ἀκρογωνιαῖον
BEHOLD I PLACE IN ZION A CORNER~STONE,

ἐκλεκτὸν ἔντιμον
CHOSEN,   PRECIOUS

καὶ ὁ πιστεύων ἐπ᾽ αὐτῷ οὐ μὴ καταισχυνθῇ.
AND THE ONE BELIEVING ON   HIM NEVER WILL BE ASHAMED.

2.7 ὑμῖν οὖν ἡ τιμὴ τοῖς πιστεύουσιν,
TO YOUᵖ THEREFORE ³[IS] THE ⁴PRECIOUSNESS ¹THE ONES ²BELIEVING,

ἀπιστοῦσιν δὲ
BUT~TO THE UNBELIEVING ONES,

λίθος ὃν ἀπεδοκίμασαν οἱ οἰκοδομοῦντες,
A STONE WHICH ³REJECTED   ¹THE ONES ²BUILDING,

οὗτος ἐγενήθη εἰς κεφαλὴν γωνίας
THIS ONE BECAME   -   HEAD   OF [THE] CORNER

2:6 Isa. 28:16 LXX   **2:7** Ps. 118:22

2.8 καὶ
AND

λίθος   προσκόμματος
A STONE   OF(FOR) STUMBLING [OVER]

καὶ   πέτρα   σκανδάλου·
AND   A ROCK   OF(FOR) FALL[ING OVER];

οἳ   προσκόπτουσιν   τῷ   λόγῳ   ἀπειθοῦντες   εἰς   ὃ
WHO   STUMBLE   AT THE   WORD,   BEING DISOBEDIENT,   TO   WHICH

καὶ   ἐτέθησαν.
ALSO   THEY WERE APPOINTED.

2.9 Ὑμεῖς   δὲ   γένος   ἐκλεκτόν,   βασίλειον   ἱεράτευμα,
BUT~YOU°   [ARE] A CHOSEN~RACE,   A KINGLY   PRIESTHOOD,

ἔθνος   ἅγιον,   λαὸς   εἰς   περιποίησιν,   ὅπως   τὰς   ἀρετὰς
A HOLY~NATION,   A PEOPLE   FOR   [GOD'S] POSSESSION,   SO THAT   ²THE   ³VIRTUES

ἐξαγγείλητε   τοῦ   ἐκ   σκότους   ὑμᾶς   καλέσαντος   εἰς
¹YOU° MAY EXPRESS   ⁴OF THE ONE   ⁷OUT OF   ⁸DARKNESS   ⁶YOU°   ⁵HAVING CALLED   INTO

τὸ   θαυμαστὸν   αὐτοῦ   φῶς·
-    HIS~MARVELOUS   LIGHT.

2.10 οἵ   ποτε   οὐ   λαὸς
WHO   ONCE   [WERE] NOT   A PEOPLE

νῦν   δὲ   λαὸς   θεοῦ,
BUT~NOW   [ARE] A PEOPLE   OF GOD,

οἱ   οὐκ   ἠλεημένοι
THE ONES   HAVING NOT RECEIVED MERCY,

νῦν   δὲ   ἐλεηθέντες.
BUT~NOW   HAVING RECEIVED MERCY.

2.11 Ἀγαπητοί,   παρακαλῶ   ὡς   παροίκους   καὶ
BELOVED,   I ENCOURAGE [YOU°]   AS   ALIENS   AND

παρεπιδήμους   ἀπέχεσθαι   τῶν   σαρκικῶν   ἐπιθυμιῶν
EXILES   TO ABSTAIN FROM   -   FLESHLY   LUSTS

αἵτινες   στρατεύονται   κατὰ   τῆς   ψυχῆς·   **2.12** τὴν
WHICH   WAR   AGAINST   THE   SOUL;   ²THE

ἀναστροφὴν   ὑμῶν   ἐν   τοῖς   ἔθνεσιν   ἔχοντες   καλήν,
³CONDUCT   ⁴OF YOU°   ⁶AMONG   ⁷THE   ⁸GENTILES   ¹HAVING   ⁵GOOD,

ἵνα,   ἐν   ᾧ   καταλαλοῦσιν   ὑμῶν   ὡς   κακοποιῶν   ἐκ
THAT,   WHEREIN   THEY SPEAK AGAINST   YOU°   AS   EVILDOERS,   BY

τῶν   καλῶν   ἔργων   ἐποπτεύοντες   δοξάσωσιν   τὸν   θεὸν
THE(YOUR°)   GOOD   WORKS   OBSERVING   THEY MAY GLORIFY   -   GOD

ἐν   ἡμέρᾳ   ἐπισκοπῆς.
IN   [THE] DAY   OF VISITATION.

2.13 Ὑποτάγητε   πάσῃ   ἀνθρωπίνῃ   κτίσει   διὰ   τὸν
SUBMIT   TO EVERY   HUMAN   INSTITUTION   BECAUSE OF   THE

κύριον,   εἴτε   βασιλεῖ   ὡς   ὑπερέχοντι,   **2.14** εἴτε
LORD,   WHETHER   TO A KING   AS   BEING IN AUTHORITY,   OR

ἡγεμόσιν   ὡς   δι᾽   αὐτοῦ   πεμπομένοις   εἰς   ἐκδίκησιν
TO GOVERNORS   AS   BY   HIM   BEING SENT   FOR   VENGEANCE

2:8 Isa. 8:14   **2:9a** Isa. 43:20 LXX   **2:9b** Exod. 19:6 LXX   **2:9c** Isa. 43:21 LXX

[8]and
"A stone that makes them stumble, and a rock that makes them fall." They stumble because they disobey the word, as they were destined to do.

9 But you are a chosen race, a royal priesthood, a holy nation, God's own people,[j] in order that you may proclaim the mighty acts of him who called you out of darkness into his marvelous light. [10]Once you were not a people, but now you are God's people; once you had not received mercy, but now you have received mercy.

11 Beloved, I urge you as aliens and exiles to abstain from the desires of the flesh that wage war against the soul. [12]Conduct yourselves honorably among the Gentiles, so that, though they malign you as evildoers, they may see your honorable deeds and glorify God when he comes to judge.[k] 13 For the Lord's sake accept the authority of every human institution,[l] whether of the emperor as supreme, [14]or of governors, as sent by him to punish

[j] Gk a people for his possession
[k] Gk God on the day of visitation
[l] Or every institution ordained for human beings

those who do wrong and to praise those who do right. ¹⁵For it is God's will that by doing right you should silence the ignorance of the foolish. ¹⁶As servants*m* of God, live as free people, yet do not use your freedom as a pretext for evil. ¹⁷Honor everyone. Love the family of believers.*n* Fear God. Honor the emperor.

18 Slaves, accept the authority of your masters with all deference, not only those who are kind and gentle but also those who are harsh. ¹⁹For it is a credit to you if, being aware of God, you endure pain while suffering unjustly. ²⁰If you endure when you are beaten for doing wrong, what credit is that? But if you endure when you do right and suffer for it, you have God's approval. ²¹For to this you have been called, because Christ also suffered for you, leaving you an example, so that you should follow in his steps.

²² "He committed no sin, and no deceit was found in his mouth."

²³When he was abused, he did not return abuse; when he suffered, he did not threaten; but he entrusted himself to the one who judges justly. ²⁴He himself bore our sins in his

m Gk *slaves*
n Gk *Love the brotherhood*

κακοποιῶν ἔπαινον δὲ ἀγαθοποιῶν· **2.15** ὅτι οὕτως
[ON] EVILDOERS   BUT~PRAISE   OF ONES DOING GOOD;   BECAUSE SO

ἐστὶν τὸ θέλημα τοῦ θεοῦ ἀγαθοποιοῦντας φιμοῦν τὴν
IS   THE WILL   -   OF GOD, [BY] DOING GOOD   TO SILENCE ¹THE

τῶν ἀφρόνων ἀνθρώπων ἀγνωσίαν, **2.16** ὡς ἐλεύθεροι
-    ³OF SENSELESS ⁴MEN   ²IGNORANCE,   AS   FREE

καὶ μὴ ὡς ἐπικάλυμμα ἔχοντες τῆς κακίας τὴν
AND   NOT ⁴AS   ⁵A CLOAK   ¹HAVING   -   ⁶OF EVIL   ²THE

ἐλευθερίαν ἀλλ᾽ ὡς θεοῦ δοῦλοι. **2.17** πάντας τιμήσατε,
³FREEDOM,   BUT   AS   GOD'S SLAVES.   HONOR~ALL MEN,

τὴν ἀδελφότητα ἀγαπᾶτε, τὸν θεὸν φοβεῖσθε, τὸν
²THE ³BROTHERHOOD ¹LOVE,   -   FEAR~GOD,   ²THE

βασιλέα τιμᾶτε.
³KING   ¹HONOR.

2.18 Οἱ οἰκέται ὑποτασσόμενοι ἐν παντὶ φόβῳ
-    HOUSEHOLD SLAVES, [BE] SUBMITTING YOURSELVES IN ALL   FEAR

τοῖς δεσπόταις, οὐ μόνον τοῖς ἀγαθοῖς καὶ
TO THE(YOUR°) MASTERS,   NOT ONLY   TO THE GOOD ONES AND

ἐπιεικέσιν ἀλλὰ καὶ τοῖς σκολιοῖς. **2.19** τοῦτο γὰρ
GENTLE   BUT   ALSO TO THE HARSH ONES.   FOR~THIS

χάρις εἰ διὰ συνείδησιν θεοῦ ὑποφέρει τις
[IS] COMMENDABLE—IF BECAUSE OF A CONSCIOUSNESS OF GOD ANYONE~BEARS UP UNDER

λύπας πάσχων ἀδίκως. **2.20** ποῖον γὰρ κλέος εἰ
PAIN   [WHILE] SUFFERING UNJUSTLY.   FOR~WHAT   MERIT [IS IT] IF

ἁμαρτάνοντες καὶ κολαφιζόμενοι ὑπομενεῖτε; ἀλλ᾽ εἰ
SINNING   AND   BEING BEATEN   YOU° ENDURE?   BUT   IF

ἀγαθοποιοῦντες καὶ πάσχοντες ὑπομενεῖτε, τοῦτο
DOING GOOD   AND   SUFFERING   YOU° ENDURE,   THIS

χάρις παρὰ θεῷ. **2.21** εἰς τοῦτο γὰρ
[IS] COMMENDABLE   WITH(BEFORE) GOD.   ²TO   ³THIS   ¹FOR

ἐκλήθητε, ὅτι καὶ Χριστὸς ⌜ἔπαθεν⌝ ὑπὲρ ὑμῶν
YOU° WERE CALLED, BECAUSE ALSO CHRIST   SUFFERED   ON BEHALF OF YOU°,

ὑμῖν ὑπολιμπάνων ὑπογραμμὸν ἵνα ἐπακολουθήσητε
TO YOU° LEAVING   A PATTERN   THAT YOU° SHOULD FOLLOW

τοῖς ἴχνεσιν αὐτοῦ,
IN THE STEPS   OF HIM,

2.22 ὃς ἁμαρτίαν οὐκ ἐποίησεν
WHO ²SIN   ¹DID NOT COMMIT

οὐδὲ εὑρέθη δόλος ἐν τῷ στόματι αὐτοῦ,
NOR   WAS FOUND GUILE IN THE MOUTH   OF HIM,

2.23 ὃς λοιδορούμενος οὐκ ἀντελοιδόρει πάσχων
WHO BEING REVILED   DID NOT RETALIATE,   SUFFERING

οὐκ ἠπείλει, παρεδίδου δὲ τῷ κρίνοντι δικαίως·
HE DID NOT THREATEN, BUT~HANDED HIMSELF OVER TO THE ONE JUDGING RIGHTEOUSLY;

2.24 ὃς τὰς ἁμαρτίας ἡμῶν αὐτὸς ἀνήνεγκεν ἐν τῷ
¹WHO ⁴THE ⁵SINS   ⁶OF US ²HIMSELF ³BORE   IN THE

2:21 text: all. var. απεθανεν (died): NEBmg NJBmg.   **2:22** Isa. 53:9

σώματι αὐτοῦ ἐπὶ τὸ ξύλον, ἵνα ταῖς ἁμαρτίαις
BODY   OF HIM ON THE TREE,   THAT ²TO THE(OUR) ³SINS

ἀπογενόμενοι τῇ δικαιοσύνῃ ζήσωμεν, οὗ τῷ
¹HAVING DIED   -   WE MIGHT LIVE~TO RIGHTEOUSNESS; BY WHOSE -

μώλωπι ἰάθητε.   **2.25** ἦτε γὰρ ὡς πρόβατα
WOUND   YOU° WERE HEALED.   FOR~YOU° WERE AS SHEEP

πλανώμενοι, ἀλλὰ ἐπεστράφητε νῦν ἐπὶ τὸν ποιμένα
BEING LED ASTRAY, BUT   YOU° RETURNED NOW TO THE SHEPHERD

καὶ ἐπίσκοπον τῶν ψυχῶν ὑμῶν.
AND OVERSEER   OF THE SOULS OF YOU°.

body on the cross,° so that, free from sins, we might live for righteousness; by his wounds^p you have been healed. ²⁵For you were going astray like sheep, but now you have returned to the shepherd and guardian of your souls.

° Or *carried up our sins in his body to the tree*
^p Gk *bruise*

3.1 Ὁμοίως [αἱ] γυναῖκες, ὑποτασσόμεναι τοῖς ἰδίοις
   LIKEWISE THE WIVES,   BEING SUBMISSIVE   TO [THEIR] OWN

ἀνδράσιν, ἵνα καὶ εἴ τινες ἀπειθοῦσιν τῷ λόγῳ,
HUSBANDS, THAT EVEN IF ANY MEN ARE DISOBEDIENT TO THE WORD(MESSAGE),

διὰ τῆς τῶν γυναικῶν ἀναστροφῆς ἄνευ λόγου
THROUGH THE - WIVES'   CONDUCT   WITHOUT [THE] WORD

κερδηθήσονται, **3.2** ἐποπτεύσαντες τὴν ἐν φόβῳ ἁγνὴν
THEY WILL BE GAINED,   HAVING OBSERVED ¹THE ⁵IN ⁶FEAR ²PURE

ἀναστροφὴν ὑμῶν. **3.3** ὧν   ἔστω οὐχ ὁ
³CONDUCT   ⁴OF YOU°;   [CONCERNING] WHOSE° ²LET IT NOT BE ³THE

ἔξωθεν ἐμπλοκῆς τριχῶν καὶ περιθέσεως χρυσίων ἢ
⁴OUTWARD ⁵BRAIDING ⁶OF HAIRS ⁷AND ⁸PUTTING ON ⁹OF GOLD ¹⁰OR

ἐνδύσεως ἱματίων κόσμος **3.4** ἀλλ' ὁ κρυπτὸς τῆς
¹¹WEARING ¹²OF GARMENTS ¹ADORNMENT, BUT THE HIDDEN ²OF THE

καρδίας ἄνθρωπος ἐν τῷ ἀφθάρτῳ   τοῦ
³HEART ¹SELF IN(BY) THE INCORRUPTIBLE [ADORNING] OF THE

πραέως καὶ ἡσυχίου πνεύματος, ὅ ἐστιν ἐνώπιον τοῦ
HUMBLE AND QUIET   SPIRIT,   WHICH IS   BEFORE   -

θεοῦ πολυτελές. **3.5** οὕτως γὰρ ποτε καὶ αἱ ἅγιαι
GOD OF GREAT WORTH.   FOR~SO   FORMERLY ALSO THE HOLY

γυναῖκες αἱ ἐλπίζουσαι εἰς θεὸν ἐκόσμουν ἑαυτὰς
WOMEN, THE ONES HOPING IN GOD, WERE ADORNING THEMSELVES,

ὑποτασσόμεναι τοῖς ἰδίοις ἀνδράσιν, **3.6** ὡς Σάρρα
SUBMITTING THEMSELVES TO THE[IR] OWN HUSBANDS,   AS SARAH

ὑπήκουσεν τῷ Ἀβραὰμ κύριον αὐτὸν καλοῦσα, ἧς
OBEYED   - ABRAHAM, ³LORD ²HIM ¹CALLING, OF WHOM

ἐγενήθητε τέκνα ἀγαθοποιοῦσαι καὶ μὴ φοβούμεναι
YOU° BECAME CHILDREN DOING GOOD   AND NOT FEARING

μηδεμίαν πτόησιν.
ANY   INTIMIDATION.

3.7 Οἱ ἄνδρες ὁμοίως, συνοικοῦντες κατὰ γνῶσιν
   THE HUSBANDS LIKEWISE, DWELLING WITH [THEM] ACCORDING TO KNOWLEDGE

ὡς ἀσθενεστέρῳ σκεύει τῷ γυναικείῳ, ἀπονέμοντες
AS WITH A WEAKER VESSEL—THE FEMALE,   SHOWING [THEM]

Wives, in the same way, accept the authority of your husbands, so that, even if some of them do not obey the word, they may be won over without a word by their wives' conduct, ²when they see the purity and reverence of your lives. ³Do not adorn yourselves outwardly by braiding your hair, and by wearing gold ornaments or fine clothing; ⁴rather, let your adornment be the inner self with the lasting beauty of a gentle and quiet spirit, which is very precious in God's sight. ⁵It was in this way long ago that the holy women who hoped in God used to adorn themselves by accepting the authority of their husbands. ⁶Thus Sarah obeyed Abraham and called him lord. You have become her daughters as long as you do what is good and never let fears alarm you.

7 Husbands, in the same way, show consideration for your wives in your life together,

paying honor to the woman as the weaker sex,[q] since they too are also heirs of the gracious gift of life—so that nothing may hinder your prayers.

8 Finally, all of you, have unity of spirit, sympathy, love for one another, a tender heart, and a humble mind. [9]Do not repay evil for evil or abuse for abuse; but, on the contrary, repay with a blessing. It is for this that you were called—that you might inherit a blessing. [10]For

"Those who desire life and desire to see good days, let them keep their tongues from evil and their lips from speaking deceit;

[11] let them turn away from evil and do good; let them seek peace and pursue it.

[12] For the eyes of the Lord are on the righteous, and his ears are open to their prayer. But the face of the Lord is against those who do evil."

13 Now who will harm you if you are eager to do what is good? [14]But even if you do suffer for doing what is right, you are blessed. Do not fear what they fear,[r] and do not be intimidated, [15]but in your hearts sanctify Christ as Lord. Always be ready to make your defense to anyone who demands from you an accounting for the hope that is in you; [16]yet do it with

[q] Gk *vessel*
[r] Gk *their fear*

τιμὴν ὡς καὶ συγκληρονόμοις χάριτος ζωῆς εἰς τὸ
HONOR AS ALSO [BEING] CO-HEIRS OF [THE] GRACE OF LIFE, SO AS -

μὴ ἐγκόπτεσθαι τὰς προσευχὰς ὑμῶν.
NOT TO BE HINDERED THE PRAYERS OF YOU°.

3.8 Τὸ δὲ τέλος πάντες ὁμόφρονες, συμπαθεῖς,
NOW~THE SUMMARY, ALL [BE] OF ONE MIND, SYMPATHETIC,

φιλάδελφοι, εὔσπλαγχνοι, ταπεινόφρονες, **3.9** μὴ
LOVING [THE] BROTHERS, TENDERHEARTED, HUMBLE-MINDED, NOT

ἀποδιδόντες κακὸν ἀντὶ κακοῦ ἢ λοιδορίαν ἀντὶ
RENDERING EVIL FOR EVIL OR ABUSE FOR

λοιδορίας, τοὐναντίον δὲ εὐλογοῦντες ὅτι εἰς τοῦτο
ABUSE, BUT~ON THE CONTRARY BLESSING, BECAUSE TO THIS

ἐκλήθητε ἵνα εὐλογίαν κληρονομήσητε.
YOU° WERE CALLED THAT YOU° MAY INHERIT~BLESSING.

3.10 ὁ γὰρ θέλων ζωὴν ἀγαπᾶν
FOR~THE ONE WANTING TO LOVE~LIFE

καὶ ἰδεῖν ἡμέρας ἀγαθὰς
AND TO SEE GOOD~DAYS

παυσάτω τὴν γλῶσσαν ἀπὸ κακοῦ
LET HIM STOP THE(HIS) TONGUE FROM [SPEAKING] EVIL

καὶ χείλη τοῦ μὴ λαλῆσαι δόλον,
AND [HIS] LIPS - NOT TO SPEAK DECEIT,

3.11 ἐκκλινάτω δὲ ἀπὸ κακοῦ καὶ ποιησάτω ἀγαθόν,
AND~LET HIM TURN AWAY FROM EVIL AND LET HIM DO GOOD,

ζητησάτω εἰρήνην καὶ διωξάτω αὐτήν·
LET HIM SEEK PEACE AND PURSUE IT;

3.12 ὅτι ὀφθαλμοὶ κυρίου ἐπὶ δικαίους
BECAUSE [THE] EYES OF [THE] LORD [ARE] ON [THE] RIGHTEOUS ONES

καὶ ὦτα αὐτοῦ εἰς δέησιν αὐτῶν,
AND [THE] EARS OF HIM [ARE OPEN] TO [THE] PRAYERS OF THEM,

πρόσωπον δὲ κυρίου ἐπὶ ποιοῦντας κακά.
BUT~[THE] FACE OF [THE] LORD [IS] AGAINST ONES DOING EVIL(HARM).

3.13 Καὶ τίς ὁ κακώσων ὑμᾶς ἐὰν τοῦ ἀγαθοῦ
AND WHO [IS] THE ONE HARMING YOU° IF [2]OF THE [3]GOOD

ζηλωταὶ γένησθε; **3.14** ἀλλ' εἰ καὶ πάσχοιτε
[1]YOU° BECOME~ZEALOTS? BUT IF INDEED YOU° SHOULD SUFFER

διὰ δικαιοσύνην, μακάριοι. τὸν δὲ φόβον αὐτῶν
BECAUSE OF RIGHTEOUSNESS, [YOU° ARE] BLESSED. BUT~THE FEAR(TERROR) OF THEM

μὴ φοβηθῆτε μηδὲ ταραχθῆτε, **3.15** κύριον δὲ τὸν
DO NOT FEAR, NEITHER BE TROUBLED, [4][AS] LORD [1]BUT -

Χριστὸν ἁγιάσατε ἐν ταῖς καρδίαις ὑμῶν, ἕτοιμοι
[3]CHRIST [2]REVERENCE IN THE HEARTS OF YOU°, PREPARED

ἀεὶ πρὸς ἀπολογίαν παντὶ τῷ αἰτοῦντι ὑμᾶς
ALWAYS FOR A DEFENSE TO EVERYONE - ASKING YOU°

λόγον περὶ τῆς ἐν ὑμῖν ἐλπίδος, **3.16** ἀλλὰ μετὰ
A WORD CONCERNING [1]THE [3]IN [4]YOU° [2]HOPE, BUT WITH

3:10-12 Ps. 34:12-16

πραΰτητος καὶ φόβου, συνείδησιν ἔχοντες ἀγαθήν,
MEEKNESS   AND   FEAR,   ³CONSCIENCE ¹HAVING   ²A GOOD,

ἵνα ἐν ᾧ καταλαλεῖσθε καταισχυνθῶσιν οἱ
THAT WHEREAS YOU° ARE SPOKEN AGAINST ³MAY BE HUMILIATED ¹THE ONES

ἐπηρεάζοντες ὑμῶν τὴν ἀγαθὴν ἐν Χριστῷ
²MISTREATING [YOU°] ⁴[BY] YOUR°   -   ⁵GOOD   ⁷IN ⁸CHRIST

ἀναστροφήν. 3.17 κρεῖττον γὰρ ἀγαθοποιοῦντας, εἰ
⁶CONDUCT.   FOR~[IT IS] BETTER [FOR] DOING GOOD,   IF

θέλοι τὸ θέλημα τοῦ θεοῦ, πάσχειν ἢ
[SO] WILLS THE WILL   - OF GOD, TO SUFFER THAN

κακοποιοῦντας. 3.18 ὅτι καὶ Χριστὸς ἅπαξ περὶ
[FOR] DOING WRONG.   BECAUSE INDEED CHRIST ONCE FOR

ἁμαρτιῶν ⌐ἔπαθεν⌐, δίκαιος ὑπὲρ ἀδίκων,
SINS   SUFFERED,   A RIGHTEOUS MAN ON BEHALF OF UNRIGHTEOUS MEN,

ἵνα ὑμᾶς προσαγάγῃ τῷ θεῷ θανατωθεὶς μὲν
THAT HE MIGHT BRING~YOU° - TO GOD, HAVING BEEN PUT TO DEATH -

σαρκὶ ζωοποιηθεὶς δὲ πνεύματι· 3.19 ἐν ᾧ καὶ
IN [THE] FLESH YET~HAVING BEEN MADE ALIVE IN SPIRIT;   IN(BY) WHICH ALSO

τοῖς ἐν φυλακῇ πνεύμασιν πορευθεὶς ἐκήρυξεν,
³TO THE ⁵IN ⁶PRISON ⁴SPIRITS   ¹HAVING GONE ²HE MADE A PROCLAMATION,

3.20 ἀπειθήσασίν ποτε ὅτε ἀπεξεδέχετο ἡ τοῦ
TO ONES HAVING DISOBEYED [BACK] THEN WHEN ⁴WAS WAITING ¹THE -

θεοῦ μακροθυμία ἐν ἡμέραις Νῶε κατασκευαζομένης
³OF GOD ²LONGSUFFERING IN [THE] DAYS OF NOAH [WHILE WAS] BEING PREPARED

κιβωτοῦ εἰς ἣν ὀλίγοι, τοῦτ' ἔστιν ὀκτὼ ψυχαί,
[THE] ARK IN WHICH A FEW, THIS(THAT) IS, EIGHT SOULS(PEOPLE),

διεσώθησαν δι' ὕδατος. 3.21 ὃ καὶ ὑμᾶς
WERE SAVED THROUGH WATER;   ¹WHICH ³ALSO ⁶YOU°

ἀντίτυπον νῦν σῴζει βάπτισμα, οὐ σαρκὸς
²FULFILLMENT OF [THE] TYPE ⁴NOW ⁵SAVES ⁷[EVEN] BAPTISM, NOT ³OF(FROM) [THE] BODY

ἀπόθεσις ῥύπου ἀλλὰ συνειδήσεως ἀγαθῆς ἐπερώτημα
¹A REMOVAL ²OF DIRT BUT ³CONSCIENCE ²OF A GOOD ¹[THE] PLEDGE

εἰς θεόν, δι' ἀναστάσεως Ἰησοῦ Χριστοῦ, 3.22 ὅς
TOWARD GOD, THROUGH [THE] RESURRECTION OF JESUS CHRIST,   WHO

ἔστιν ἐν δεξιᾷ [τοῦ] θεοῦ πορευθεὶς εἰς οὐρανὸν
IS AT [THE] RIGHT [HAND] - OF GOD, HAVING GONE INTO HEAVEN,

ὑποταγέντων αὐτῷ ἀγγέλων καὶ ἐξουσιῶν καὶ
⁶HAVING BEEN SUBJECTED ⁷TO HIM ¹ANGELS ²AND ³AUTHORITIES ⁴AND

δυνάμεων.
⁵POWERS.

gentleness and reverence.[s] Keep your conscience clear, so that, when you are maligned, those who abuse you for your good conduct in Christ may be put to shame. [17]For it is better to suffer for doing good, if suffering should be God's will, than to suffer for doing evil. [18]For Christ also suffered[f] for sins once for all, the righteous for the unrighteous, in order to bring you[u] to God. He was put to death in the flesh, but made alive in the spirit, [19]in which also he went and made a proclamation to the spirits in prison, [20]who in former times did not obey, when God waited patiently in the days of Noah, during the building of the ark, in which a few, that is, eight persons, were saved through water. [21]And baptism, which this prefigured, now saves you—not as a removal of dirt from the body, but as an appeal to God for[v] a good conscience, through the resurrection of Jesus Christ, [22]who has gone into heaven and is at the right hand of God, with angels, authorities, and powers made subject to him.

[s] Or respect
[f] Other ancient authorities read died
[u] Other ancient authorities read us
[v] Or a pledge to God from

3:18 text: KJV ASV RSVmg NEBmg TEVmg NRSV. var. απεθανεν (died): ASVmg RSV NASB NIV NEB TEV NJB NRSVmg.

CHAPTER 4

Since therefore Christ suffered in the flesh,[w] arm yourselves also with the same intention (for whoever has suffered in the flesh has finished with sin), [2]so as to live for the rest of your earthly life[x] no longer by human desires but by the will of God. [3]You have already spent enough time in doing what the Gentiles like to do, living in licentiousness, passions, drunkenness, revels, carousing, and lawless idolatry. [4]They are surprised that you no longer join them in the same excesses of dissipation, and so they blaspheme.[y] [5]But they will have to give an accounting to him who stands ready to judge the living and the dead. [6]For this is the reason the gospel was proclaimed even to the dead, so that, though they had been judged in the flesh as everyone is judged, they might live in the spirit as God does.

[7] The end of all things is near;[z] therefore be serious and discipline yourselves for the sake of your prayers. [8]Above all, maintain constant love for one another, for love covers a multitude of sins. [9]Be hospitable to one another without complaining. [10]Like good stewards of the manifold grace of God, serve one another with whatever gift each of you has received. [11]Whoever

[w] Other ancient authorities add *for us;* others, *for you*
[x] Gk *rest of the time in the flesh*
[y] Or *they malign you*
[z] Or *is at hand*

4.1 Χριστοῦ οὖν παθόντος σαρκὶ καὶ ὑμεῖς τὴν
THEREFORE~CHRIST HAVING SUFFERED IN [THE] FLESH ALSO YOU° [2]THE

αὐτὴν ἔννοιαν ὁπλίσασθε, ὅτι ὁ
[3]SAME [4][WAY OF] THINKING [1]ARM YOURSELVES [WITH], BECAUSE THE ONE

παθὼν σαρκὶ πέπαυται ἁμαρτίας **4.2** εἰς τὸ
HAVING SUFFERED IN [THE] FLESH HAS CEASED FROM SIN, SO AS -

μηκέτι ἀνθρώπων ἐπιθυμίαις ἀλλὰ θελήματι θεοῦ τὸν
[1]NO LONGER [9]OF MEN [8]IN [THE] LUSTS [10]BUT [11]IN [THE] WILL [12]OF GOD [3]THE

ἐπίλοιπον ἐν σαρκὶ βιῶσαι χρόνον. **4.3** ἀρκετὸς γὰρ
[4]REMAINING [6]IN [7][THE] FLESH [2]TO LIVE [5]TIME. FOR~[IS] SUFFICIENT

ὁ παρεληλυθὼς χρόνος τὸ βούλημα τῶν ἐθνῶν
THE TIME~HAVING GONE BY [2][IN] THE [3]DESIRE[S] [4]OF THE [5]GENTILES

κατειργάσθαι πεπορευμένους ἐν ἀσελγείαις,
[1]TO HAVE PARTICIPATED, HAVING PROCEEDED IN LICENTIOUSNESS,

ἐπιθυμίαις, οἰνοφλυγίαις, κώμοις, πότοις καὶ
LUSTS, DRUNKENNESS, ORGIES, DRINKING [PARTIES] AND

ἀθεμίτοις εἰδωλολατρίαις. **4.4** ἐν ᾧ ξενίζονται
UNLAWFUL IDOLATRY. WHEREIN THEY THINK IT STRANGE

μὴ συντρεχόντων ὑμῶν εἰς τὴν αὐτὴν τῆς
[2][ARE] NOT RUNNING WITH [THEM] [1]YOU° INTO THE SAME -

ἀσωτίας ἀνάχυσιν βλασφημοῦντες, **4.5** οἳ ἀποδώσουσιν
FLOOD~OF DISSIPATION, BLASPHEMING, WHO WILL GIVE

λόγον τῷ ἑτοίμως ἔχοντι κρῖναι ζῶντας
AN ACCOUNT TO THE ONE BEING~READY TO JUDGE [THE] LIVING

καὶ νεκρούς. **4.6** εἰς τοῦτο γὰρ καὶ
AND [THE] DEAD. [2]TO [3]THIS [END] [1]FOR INDEED

νεκροῖς εὐηγγελίσθη, ἵνα κριθῶσι μὲν
WAS [THE] GOOD NEWS PREACHED~TO [THE] DEAD, THAT THEY MIGHT BE JUDGED INDEED

κατὰ ἀνθρώπους σαρκὶ ζῶσι δὲ κατὰ θεὸν
AS MEN IN [THE] FLESH(BODY) BUT~LIVE AS GOD [DOES]

πνεύματι.
IN SPIRIT.

4.7 Πάντων δὲ τὸ τέλος ἤγγικεν. σωφρονήσατε
[4]OF ALL THINGS [1]NOW [2]THE [3]END [5]HAS DRAWN NEAR. BE SOBER-MINDED

οὖν καὶ νήψατε εἰς προσευχάς· **4.8** πρὸ
THEREFORE AND BE SELF-CONTROLLED IN [YOUR°] PRAYERS; BEFORE

πάντων τὴν εἰς ἑαυτοὺς ἀγάπην ἐκτενῆ ἔχοντες,
ALL THINGS - [4]AMONG [5]YOURSELVES [3]LOVE [2]FERVENT [1]HAVING,

ὅτι ἀγάπη καλύπτει πλῆθος ἁμαρτιῶν. **4.9** φιλόξενοι
BECAUSE LOVE COVERS A MULTITUDE OF SINS. [BE] HOSPITABLE

εἰς ἀλλήλους ἄνευ γογγυσμοῦ, **4.10** ἕκαστος καθὼς
TO ONE ANOTHER WITHOUT COMPLAINT, EACH ONE ACCORDING AS

ἔλαβεν χάρισμα εἰς ἑαυτοὺς αὐτὸ διακονοῦντες ὡς
HE RECEIVED A GIFT [3]TO [4]EACH OTHER [2]IT [1]MINISTERING AS

καλοὶ οἰκονόμοι ποικίλης χάριτος θεοῦ. **4.11** εἴ τις
GOOD STEWARDS OF [THE] VARIED GRACE OF GOD. IF ANYONE

λαλεῖ,   ὡς   λόγια   θεοῦ· εἴ τις   διακονεῖ,
SPEAKS, AS THOUGH [IT WERE THE] ORACLES OF GOD; IF ANYONE MINISTERS,

ὡς ἐξ ἰσχύος ἧς χορηγεῖ ὁ θεός, ἵνα ἐν πᾶσιν
AS BY STRENGTH WHICH ²SUPPLIES - ¹GOD, THAT IN ALL THINGS

δοξάζηται ὁ θεὸς διὰ Ἰησοῦ Χριστοῦ, ᾧ ἐστιν
²MAY BE GLORIFIED - ¹GOD THROUGH JESUS CHRIST, TO WHOM IS

ἡ δόξα καὶ τὸ κράτος εἰς τοὺς αἰῶνας τῶν αἰώνων,
THE GLORY AND THE DOMINION INTO THE AGES OF THE AGES,

ἀμήν.
AMEN.

4.12 Ἀγαπητοί, μὴ ξενίζεσθε   τῇ ἐν ὑμῖν
BELOVED, DO NOT BE SURPRISED [AT] ¹THE ³AMONG ⁴YOU°

πυρώσει πρὸς πειρασμὸν ὑμῖν γινομένῃ ὡς
²FIERY [TRIAL] - ⁶[AS] A TEST ⁷FOR YOU° ⁵COMING, AS

ξένου ὑμῖν συμβαίνοντος, **4.13** ἀλλὰ καθὸ
A STRANGE THING HAPPENING~TO YOU°, BUT IN SO FAR AS

κοινωνεῖτε τοῖς τοῦ Χριστοῦ παθήμασιν χαίρετε, ἵνα
YOU° SHARE IN THE - SUFFERINGS~OF CHRIST, REJOICE, THAT

καὶ ἐν τῇ ἀποκαλύψει τῆς δόξης αὐτοῦ χαρῆτε
ALSO IN THE REVELATION OF THE GLORY OF HIM YOU° MAY REJOICE,

ἀγαλλιώμενοι. **4.14** εἰ ὀνειδίζεσθε   ἐν ὀνόματι
BEING GLAD. IF YOU° ARE REPROACHED IN(FOR) [THE] NAME

Χριστοῦ, μακάριοι,   ὅτι   τὸ   τῆς δόξηςᵀ καὶ
OF CHRIST, [YOU° ARE] BLESSED ONES, BECAUSE THE [SPIRIT] - OF GLORY AND

τὸ τοῦ θεοῦ πνεῦμα ἐφ' ὑμᾶς ἀναπαύεται. **4.15** μὴ
¹THE - ³OF GOD ²SPIRIT UPON YOU° RESTS. ³NOT

γάρ τις ὑμῶν πασχέτω ὡς φονεὺς ἢ κλέπτης ἢ
¹FOR ⁴ANY ⁵OF YOU° ²LET ⁶SUFFER AS A MURDERER OR A THIEF OR

κακοποιὸς ἢ ὡς ἀλλοτριεπίσκοπος· **4.16** εἰ δὲ ὡς
AN EVILDOER OR AS A MEDDLER; BUT~IF AS

Χριστιανός, μὴ αἰσχυνέσθω, δοξαζέτω δὲ τὸν θεὸν ἐν
A CHRISTIAN, LET HIM NOT BE ASHAMED, BUT~LET HIM GLORIFY - GOD IN(BY)

τῷ ὀνόματι τούτῳ. **4.17** ὅτι   [ὁ] καιρὸς   τοῦ
- THIS~NAME. BECAUSE THE TIME [HAS COME] -

ἄρξασθαι τὸ κρίμα ἀπὸ τοῦ οἴκου τοῦ θεοῦ· εἰ δὲ
TO BEGIN THE JUDGMENT FROM THE HOUSE - OF GOD; AND~IF

πρῶτον ἀφ' ἡμῶν, τί τὸ τέλος τῶν
FIRSTLY FROM US, WHAT [WILL BE] THE END OF THE ONES

ἀπειθούντων τῷ τοῦ θεοῦ εὐαγγελίῳ;
DISOBEYING THE - GOOD NEWS~OF GOD?

4.18 καὶ εἰ ὁ δίκαιος   μόλις   σῴζεται,
AND IF THE RIGHTEOUS MAN WITH DIFFICULTY IS SAVED,

ὁ ἀσεβὴς καὶ ἁμαρτωλὸς ποῦ φανεῖται;
³THE ⁴UNGODLY ⁵AND ⁶SINNER ¹WHERE ²WILL ⁷APPEAR?

4.19 ὥστε καὶ οἱ πάσχοντες κατὰ τὸ
THEREFORE INDEED THE ONES SUFFERING ACCORDING TO THE

speaks must do so as one speaking the very words of God; whoever serves must do so with the strength that God supplies, so that God may be glorified in all things through Jesus Christ. To him belong the glory and the power forever and ever. Amen.

12 Beloved, do not be surprised at the fiery ordeal that is taking place among you to test you, as though something strange were happening to you. 13But rejoice insofar as you are sharing Christ's sufferings, so that you may also be glad and shout for joy when his glory is revealed. 14If you are reviled for the name of Christ, you are blessed, because the spirit of glory,ᵃ which is the Spirit of God, is resting on you.ᵇ 15But let none of you suffer as a murderer, a thief, a criminal, or even as a mischief maker. 16Yet if any of you suffers as a Christian, do not consider it a disgrace, but glorify God because you bear this name. 17For the time has come for judgment to begin with the household of God; if it begins with us, what will be the end for those who do not obey the gospel of God? 18And

> "If it is hard for the
>   righteous to be
>   saved,
> what will become of
>   the ungodly and the
>   sinners?"

19Therefore, let those suffering in accordance with

ᵃ Other ancient authorities add *and of power*
ᵇ Other ancient authorities add *On their part he is blasphemed, but on your part he is glorified*

4:14 text: all. add καὶ δυναμεως (and of power): RSVmg NJBmg NRSVmg.   **4:18** Prov. 11:31 LXX

God's will entrust themselves to a faithful Creator, while continuing to do good.

θέλημα τοῦ θεοῦ πιστῷ κτίστῃ παρατιθέσθωσαν
WILL - OF GOD, ³TO A TRUSTWORTHY ⁴CREATOR ¹LET THEM COMMIT

τὰς ψυχὰς αὐτῶν ἐν ἀγαθοποιΐᾳ.
- ²THEIR~SOULS IN DOING GOOD.

CHAPTER 5

Now as an elder myself and a witness of the sufferings of Christ, as well as one who shares in the glory to be revealed, I exhort the elders among you ²to tend the flock of God that is in your charge, exercising the oversight,ᶜ not under compulsion but willingly, as God would have you do itᵈ—not for sordid gain but eagerly. ³Do not lord it over those in your charge, but be examples to the flock. ⁴And when the chief shepherd appears, you will win the crown of glory that never fades away. ⁵In the same way, you who are younger must accept the authority of the elders.ᵉ And all of you must clothe yourselves with humility in your dealings with one another, for

"God opposes the proud, but gives grace to the humble."

6 Humble yourselves therefore under the mighty hand of God, so that he may exalt you in due time. ⁷Cast

ᶜ Other ancient authorities lack exercising the oversight
ᵈ Other ancient authorities lack as God would have you do it
ᵉ Or of those who are older

5.1 Πρεσβυτέρους οὖν ἐν ὑμῖν παρακαλῶ ὁ
THEREFORE~ELDERS AMONG YOU° I ENCOURAGE, THE

συμπρεσβύτερος καὶ μάρτυς τῶν τοῦ
CO-ELDER AND WITNESS OF THE -

Χριστοῦ παθημάτων, ὁ καὶ τῆς μελλούσης
SUFFERINGS~OF CHRIST, ¹THE ³ALSO ⁴OF THE ⁶ABOUT

ἀποκαλύπτεσθαι δόξης κοινωνός· **5.2** ποιμάνατε τὸ
⁷TO BE REVEALED ⁵GLORY ²PARTAKER; SHEPHERD ¹THE

ἐν ὑμῖν ποίμνιον τοῦ θεοῦ ⌐[ἐπισκοποῦντες]⌐ μὴ
⁴AMONG ⁵YOU° ²FLOCK - ³OF GOD, SERVING AS OVERSEERS NOT

ἀναγκαστῶς ἀλλὰ ἑκουσίως ⌐κατὰ θεόν,⌐ μηδὲ
BY COMPULSION BUT WILLINGLY ACCORDING TO GOD, NOT

αἰσχροκερδῶς ἀλλὰ προθύμως, **5.3** μηδ᾽ ὡς
[FROM] FONDNESS FOR DISHONEST GAIN BUT EAGERLY, NOT AS

κατακυριεύοντες τῶν κλήρων ἀλλὰ
LORDING IT OVER THE ONES ALLOTTED(ASSIGNED) [TO YOUR° CARE] BUT

τύποι γινόμενοι τοῦ ποιμνίου· **5.4** καὶ φανερωθέντος
BEING~EXAMPLES OF THE FLOCK; AND ³HAVING BEEN REVEALED

τοῦ ἀρχιποίμενος κομιεῖσθε τὸν ἀμαράντινον τῆς
¹[AFTER] THE ²CHIEF SHEPHERD, YOU° WILL RECEIVE THE UNFADING -

δόξης στέφανον.
CROWN~OF GLORY.

5.5 Ὁμοίως, νεώτεροι, ὑποτάγητε πρεσβυτέροις·
LIKEWISE, YOUNGER MEN, BE SUBMISSIVE TO ELDERS;

πάντες δὲ ἀλλήλοις τὴν ταπεινοφροσύνην
AND~ALL ³TO[WARD] ONE ANOTHER - ²HUMILITY

ἐγκομβώσασθε, ὅτι
¹CLOTHE YOURSELVES WITH, BECAUSE

[Ὁ] θεὸς ὑπερηφάνοις ἀντιτάσσεται,
- GOD OPPOSES~PROUD MEN,

ταπεινοῖς δὲ δίδωσιν χάριν.
BUT~TO HUMBLE MEN HE GIVES GRACE.

5.6 Ταπεινώθητε οὖν ὑπὸ τὴν κραταιὰν χεῖρα τοῦ
BE HUMBLED THEREFORE UNDER THE MIGHTY HAND -

θεοῦ, ἵνα ὑμᾶς ὑψώσῃ ἐν καιρῷ, **5.7** πᾶσαν τὴν
OF GOD, THAT YOU° MAY BE EXALTED IN [DUE] TIME, ALL THE

5:2a text: KJV ASV RSVmg NIV NJB NRSV. omit: ASVmg RSV NASB NEB TEV NJBmg NRSVmg.
5:2b text: ASV RSVmg NASB NIV NEB TEV NJB NRSV. omit: KJV ASVmg RSV NJBmg NRSVmg.
5:5 Prov. 3:34 LXX

μέριμναν ὑμῶν ἐπιρίψαντες ἐπ' αὐτόν, ὅτι
ANXIETY   OF YOU° HAVING CAST   UPON HIM,   BECAUSE

αὐτῷ μέλει περὶ ὑμῶν.
IT MATTERS~TO HIM CONCERNING YOU°.

5.8 Νήψατε, γρηγορήσατε. ὁ ἀντίδικος ὑμῶν
BE SOBER,   WATCH.   THE ADVERSARY OF YOU°,

διάβολος ὡς λέων ὠρυόμενος περιπατεῖ ζητῶν [τινα]
[THE] DEVIL, AS A LION ROARING   WALKS AROUND SEEKING WHOM

καταπιεῖν· **5.9** ᾧ ἀντίστητε στερεοὶ τῇ πίστει·
TO DEVOUR;   WHOM OPPOSE   FIRM   IN THE FAITH,

εἰδότες τὰ αὐτὰ τῶν παθημάτων τῇ ἐν [τῷ] κόσμῳ
KNOWING THE SAME - SUFFERINGS   - ⁴IN ⁵THE ⁶WORLD

ὑμῶν ἀδελφότητι ἐπιτελεῖσθαι. **5.10** Ὁ δὲ θεὸς πάσης
²YOUR° ³BROTHERHOOD ¹TO BE LAID UPON.   NOW~THE GOD OF ALL

χάριτος, ὁ καλέσας ὑμᾶς εἰς τὴν αἰώνιον αὐτοῦ
GRACE,   THE ONE HAVING CALLED YOU° INTO - HIS~ETERNAL

δόξαν ἐν Χριστῷ ['Ιησοῦ], ὀλίγον παθόντας
GLORY IN CHRIST JESUS,   A LITTLE WHILE [AFTER] HAVING SUFFERED,

αὐτὸς καταρτίσει, στηρίξει, σθενώσει, θεμελιώσει.
HE HIMSELF WILL RESTORE, CONFIRM, STRENGTHEN, [AND] ESTABLISH [YOU°].

5.11 αὐτῷ τὸ κράτος εἰς τοὺς αἰῶνας, ἀμήν.
TO HIM [IS] THE DOMINION INTO THE AGES,   AMEN.

5.12 Διὰ Σιλουανοῦ ὑμῖν τοῦ πιστοῦ ἀδελφοῦ, ὡς
THROUGH SILVANUS ⁴TO YOU° ¹THE ²FAITHFUL ³BROTHER, AS

λογίζομαι, δι' ὀλίγων ἔγραψα παρακαλῶν καὶ
I CONSIDER, BRIEFLY   I WROTE ENCOURAGING [YOU°] AND

ἐπιμαρτυρῶν ταύτην εἶναι ἀληθῆ χάριν τοῦ θεοῦ εἰς
TESTIFYING THIS   TO BE [THE] TRUE GRACE - OF GOD IN

ἣν στῆτε. **5.13** Ἀσπάζεται ὑμᾶς ἡ ἐν Βαβυλῶνι
WHICH YOU° STAND. ⁵GREETS   ⁶YOU° ¹SHE ²IN ³BABYLON

συνεκλεκτὴ καὶ Μᾶρκος ὁ υἱός μου. **5.14** ἀσπάσασθε
⁴A CO-CHOSEN ONE, ALSO MARK THE SON OF ME.   GREET

ἀλλήλους ἐν φιλήματι ἀγάπης. εἰρήνη ὑμῖν πᾶσιν
ONE ANOTHER WITH A KISS OF LOVE. PEACE TO YOU° ALL,

τοῖς ἐν Χριστῷ.
THE ONES IN CHRIST.

all your anxiety on him, because he cares for you. [8]Discipline yourselves, keep alert.*f* Like a roaring lion your adversary the devil prowls around, looking for someone to devour. [9]Resist him, steadfast in your faith, for you know that your brothers and sisters*g* in all the world are undergoing the same kinds of suffering. [10]And after you have suffered for a little while, the God of all grace, who has called you to his eternal glory in Christ, will himself restore, support, strengthen, and establish you. [11]To him be the power forever and ever. Amen.

12 Through Silvanus, whom I consider a faithful brother, I have written this short letter to encourage you and to testify that this is the true grace of God. Stand fast in it. [13]Your sister church*h* in Babylon, chosen together with you, sends you greetings; and so does my son Mark. [14]Greet one another with a kiss of love.

Peace to all of you who are in Christ.*i*

f Or *be vigilant*
g Gk *your brotherhood*
h Gk *She who is*
i Other ancient authorities add *Amen*

THE SECOND LETTER OF
PETER

ΠΕΤΡΟΥ Β
OF PETER   2

1.1 Συμεὼν Πέτρος δοῦλος καὶ ἀπόστολος Ἰησοῦ
SIMON   PETER   A SLAVE   AND   APOSTLE   OF JESUS

Χριστοῦ τοῖς   ἰσότιμον   ἡμῖν λαχοῦσιν   πίστιν
CHRIST   TO THE ONES ³EQUALLY PRECIOUS ²WITH US ¹HAVING OBTAINED ⁴FAITH

ἐν   δικαιοσύνῃ   τοῦ θεοῦ ἡμῶν καὶ   σωτῆρος   Ἰησοῦ
IN(BY) [THE] RIGHTEOUSNESS - OF~OUR GOD AND SAVIOR, JESUS

Χριστοῦ, **1.2** χάρις ὑμῖν καὶ εἰρήνη πληθυνθείη   ἐν
CHRIST,   GRACE TO YOU° AND PEACE—MAY [THEY] BE MULTIPLIED BY

ἐπιγνώσει τοῦ θεοῦ καὶ Ἰησοῦ τοῦ κυρίου ἡμῶν.
[THE] KNOWLEDGE - OF GOD AND JESUS THE LORD OF US.

1.3 Ὡς πάντα ἡμῖν τῆς   θείας δυνάμεως αὐτοῦ τὰ
AS   ALL THINGS ⁶TO US ⁷[BY] THE DIVINE ⁸POWER ⁹OF HIM -

πρὸς ζωὴν καὶ εὐσέβειαν δεδωρημένης   διὰ   τῆς
¹FOR ²LIFE ³AND ⁴GODLINESS ⁵HAVING(HAVE) BEEN GIVEN THROUGH THE

ἐπιγνώσεως τοῦ   καλέσαντος ἡμᾶς ⌐ἰδίᾳ⌐ δόξῃ καὶ
KNOWLEDGE OF THE ONE HAVING CALLED US TO HIS OWN GLORY AND

ἀρετῇ, **1.4** δι᾽   ὧν   τὰ τίμια καὶ μέγιστα ἡμῖν
VIRTUE,   THROUGH WHICH THINGS ³THE ⁴PRECIOUS ⁵AND ⁶GREAT ²TO US

ἐπαγγέλματα δεδώρηται, ἵνα διὰ   τούτων γένησθε
⁷PROMISES   ¹HE HAS GIVEN, THAT THROUGH THESE YOU° MAY BECOME

θείας   κοινωνοὶ φύσεως ἀποφυγόντες τῆς ἐν τῷ
²OF [THE] DIVINE] ¹SHARERS ³NATURE, HAVING ESCAPED ¹THE ³IN ⁴THE

κόσμῳ ἐν ἐπιθυμίᾳ φθορᾶς.   **1.5** καὶ αὐτὸ τοῦτο   δὲ
⁵WORLD ⁶BY ⁷LUST ²CORRUPTION.   ALSO FOR THIS VERY REASON -

σπουδὴν πᾶσαν παρεισενέγκαντες ἐπιχορηγήσατε ἐν
³DILIGENCE ²ALL ¹HAVING APPLIED   SUPPLY   IN(BY)

τῇ πίστει ὑμῶν τὴν ἀρετήν, ἐν δὲ   τῇ ἀρετῇ τὴν
THE FAITH OF YOU° - VIRTUE, AND~IN(BY) THE VIRTUE -

γνῶσιν, **1.6** ἐν δὲ   τῇ γνώσει τὴν ἐγκράτειαν, ἐν δὲ
KNOWLEDGE, AND~IN(BY) THE KNOWLEDGE - SELF-CONTROL, AND~IN(BY)

τῇ ἐγκρατείᾳ τὴν ὑπομονήν, ἐν δὲ   τῇ ὑπομονῇ τὴν
THE SELF-CONTROL - ENDURANCE, AND~IN(BY) THE ENDURANCE -

εὐσέβειαν, **1.7** ἐν δὲ   τῇ εὐσεβείᾳ τὴν φιλαδελφίαν,
GODLINESS,   AND~IN(BY) THE GODLINESS - BROTHERLY LOVE,

ἐν δὲ   τῇ φιλαδελφίᾳ τὴν ἀγάπην. **1.8** ταῦτα γὰρ
AND~IN(BY) THE BROTHERLY LOVE - LOVE.   FOR~THESE THINGS

ὑμῖν ὑπάρχοντα καὶ πλεονάζοντα οὐκ ἀργοὺς   οὐδὲ
BEING~IN YOU°   AND ABOUNDING ²NOT ³UNPRODUCTIVE ³NOR

1:3 text: all. var. δια (through): ASVmg TEVmg NRSVmg.

Simeon[a] Peter, a servant[b] and apostle of Jesus Christ,

To those who have received a faith as precious as ours through the righteousness of our God and Savior Jesus Christ:[c]

2 May grace and peace be yours in abundance in the knowledge of God and of Jesus our Lord.

3 His divine power has given us everything needed for life and godliness, through the knowledge of him who called us by[d] his own glory and goodness. [4]Thus he has given us, through these things, his precious and very great promises, so that through them you may escape from the corruption that is in the world because of lust, and may become participants of the divine nature. [5]For this very reason, you must make every effort to support your faith with goodness, and goodness with knowledge, [6]and knowledge with self-control, and self-control with endurance, and endurance with godliness, [7]and godliness with mutual[e] affection, and mutual[e] affection with love. [8]For if these things are yours and are increasing among you, they keep you from being

[a] Other ancient authorities read *Simon*
[b] Gk *slave*
[c] Or *of our God and the Savior Jesus Christ*
[d] Other ancient authorities read *through*
[e] Gk *brotherly*

ineffective and unfruitful in the knowledge of our Lord Jesus Christ. ⁹For anyone who lacks these things is nearsighted and blind, and is forgetful of the cleansing of past sins. ¹⁰Therefore, brothers and sisters,ᶠ be all the more eager to confirm your call and election, for if you do this, you will never stumble. ¹¹For in this way, entry into the eternal kingdom of our Lord and Savior Jesus Christ will be richly provided for you.

12 Therefore I intend to keep on reminding you of these things, though you know them already and are established in the truth that has come to you. ¹³I think it right, as long as I am in this body,ᵍ to refresh your memory, ¹⁴since I know that my deathʰ will come soon, as indeed our Lord Jesus Christ has made clear to me. ¹⁵And I will make every effort so that after my departure you may be able at any time to recall these things.

16 For we did not follow cleverly devised myths when we made known to you the power and coming of our Lord Jesus Christ, but we had been eyewitnesses of his majesty. ¹⁷For he received honor and glory

ᶠ Gk brothers
ᵍ Gk tent
ʰ Gk the putting off of my tent

ἀκάρπους καθίστησιν εἰς τὴν τοῦ κυρίου ἡμῶν Ἰησοῦ
⁴UNFRUITFUL ¹MAKES [YOU°] IN ¹THE ³OF THE ⁴LORD ⁵OF US ⁶JESUS

Χριστοῦ ἐπίγνωσιν· **1.9** ᾧ γὰρ μὴ πάρεστιν
⁷CHRIST ²KNOWLEDGE; FOR~WITH WHOM ARE NOT PRESENT

ταῦτα, τυφλός ἐστιν μυωπάζων, λήθην λαβὼν τοῦ
THESE THINGS, HE IS~BLIND, BEING SHORTSIGHTED, HAVING~FORGOTTEN THE

καθαρισμοῦ τῶν πάλαι αὐτοῦ ἁμαρτιῶν. **1.10** διὸ
CLEANSING - OF HIS~OLD(PAST) SINS. THEREFORE

μᾶλλον, ἀδελφοί, σπουδάσατε βεβαίαν ὑμῶν τὴν
RATHER, BROTHERS, BE DILIGENT ⁶SURE ²YOUR° -

κλῆσιν καὶ ἐκλογὴν ποιεῖσθαι· ταῦτα γὰρ ποιοῦντες
³CALLING ⁴AND ⁵ELECTION ¹TO MAKE; FOR~THESE THINGS DOING

οὐ μὴ πταίσητέ ποτε. **1.11** οὕτως γὰρ πλουσίως
NEVER ONCE~WILL YOU° STUMBLE(FALL). FOR~SO ³RICHLY

ἐπιχορηγηθήσεται ὑμῖν ἡ εἴσοδος εἰς τὴν αἰώνιον
¹WILL BE PROVIDED ²FOR YOU° THE ENTRANCE INTO THE ETERNAL

βασιλείαν τοῦ κυρίου ἡμῶν καὶ σωτῆρος Ἰησοῦ
KINGDOM OF THE LORD OF US AND SAVIOR, JESUS

Χριστοῦ.
CHRIST.

1.12 Διὸ μελλήσω ἀεὶ ὑμᾶς ὑπομιμνῄσκειν
THEREFORE I WILL INTEND ALWAYS TO REMIND~YOU°

περὶ τούτων καίπερ εἰδότας καὶ
CONCERNING THESE THINGS—EVEN THOUGH KNOWING [THEM] AND

ἐστηριγμένους ἐν τῇ παρούσῃ ἀληθείᾳ. **1.13** δίκαιον
HAVING BEEN ESTABLISHED IN THE PRESENT TRUTH. ³RIGHT

δὲ ἡγοῦμαι, ἐφ᾽ ὅσον εἰμὶ ἐν τούτῳ τῷ σκηνώματι,
¹BUT ²I CONSIDER [IT], AS LONG AS I AM IN THIS - TABERNACLE,

διεγείρειν ὑμᾶς ἐν ὑπομνήσει, **1.14** εἰδὼς ὅτι ταχινή
TO AROUSE YOU° WITH A REMINDER, KNOWING THAT SOON

ἐστιν ἡ ἀπόθεσις τοῦ σκηνώματός μου καθὼς καὶ
IS THE PUTTING OFF OF THE TABERNACLE OF ME AS EVEN

ὁ κύριος ἡμῶν Ἰησοῦς Χριστὸς ἐδήλωσέν μοι,
THE LORD OF US, JESUS CHRIST, MADE CLEAR TO ME;

1.15 σπουδάσω δὲ καὶ ἑκάστοτε ἔχειν ὑμᾶς μετὰ τὴν
AND~I AM EAGER ALSO ⁴ALWAYS ³TO HAVE ²YOU° ⁸AFTER -

ἐμὴν ἔξοδον τὴν τούτων μνήμην ποιεῖσθαι.
⁹MY ¹⁰EXODUS(DEPARTURE) ⁵THE ⁷OF THESE THINGS ⁶MEMORY ¹TO CAUSE.

1.16 Οὐ γὰρ σεσοφισμένοις μύθοις
FOR~NOT ³HAVING BEEN CLEVERLY CRAFTED ²FABLES

ἐξακολουθήσαντες ἐγνωρίσαμεν ὑμῖν τὴν τοῦ κυρίου
¹HAVING FOLLOWED, WE MADE KNOWN TO YOU° ¹THE ⁵OF THE ⁶LORD

ἡμῶν Ἰησοῦ Χριστοῦ δύναμιν καὶ παρουσίαν ἀλλ᾽
⁷OF US ⁸JESUS ⁹CHRIST ²POWER ³AND ⁴COMING BUT

ἐπόπται γενηθέντες τῆς ἐκείνου μεγαλειότητος.
HAVING BEEN~EYEWITNESSES - OF THAT ONE'S MAJESTY.

1.17 λαβὼν γὰρ παρὰ θεοῦ πατρὸς τιμὴν καὶ δόξαν
FOR~HAVING RECEIVED FROM GOD [THE] FATHER HONOR AND GLORY,

φωνῆς ἐνεχθείσης   αὐτῷ   τοιᾶσδε ὑπὸ τῆς
²A VOICE ³HAVING BEEN BROUGHT ⁴TO HIM ¹SUCH BY THE

μεγαλοπρεποῦς δόξης, Ὁ υἱός μου ὁ ἀγαπητός μου
MAGNIFICENT   ·GLORY, THE SON OF ME, THE BELOVED OF ME

οὗτός ἐστιν, εἰς ὃν ἐγὼ εὐδόκησα, 1.18 καὶ ταύτην
THIS ONE IS,   IN WHOM I   WAS WELL PLEASED,   AND THIS

τὴν φωνὴν ἡμεῖς ἠκούσαμεν ἐξ   οὐρανοῦ
-   VOICE WE   HEARD   ²OUT OF ³HEAVEN

ἐνεχθεῖσαν   σὺν αὐτῷ ὄντες ἐν τῷ ἁγίῳ ὄρει.
¹HAVING BEEN BROUGHT ⁵WITH ⁶HIM ⁴BEING IN(ON) THE HOLY MOUNTAIN.

1.19 καὶ ἔχομεν βεβαιότερον τὸν προφητικὸν λόγον,
AND WE HAVE ⁴[MADE] MORE SURE ¹THE ²PROPHETIC   ³WORD,

ᾧ   καλῶς ποιεῖτε προσέχοντες   ὡς λύχνῳ
TO WHICH YOU° DO~WELL [IN] PAYING ATTENTION [TO IT] AS TO A LAMP

φαίνοντι ἐν αὐχμηρῷ τόπῳ, ἕως οὗ ἡμέρα διαυγάσῃ
SHINING IN A DARK   PLACE, UNTIL DAY DAWNS

καὶ φωσφόρος ἀνατείλῃ ἐν ταῖς καρδίαις ὑμῶν,
AND [THE] MORNING STAR RISES IN THE HEARTS OF YOU°,

1.20 τοῦτο πρῶτον γινώσκοντες ὅτι πᾶσα προφητεία
THIS KNOWING~FIRST   THAT EVERY PROPHECY

γραφῆς ἰδίας ἐπιλύσεως οὐ γίνεται· 1.21 οὐ γὰρ
OF SCRIPTURE ²OF ONE'S OWN ³INTERPRETATION ¹IS~NOT; FOR~NOT

θελήματι ἀνθρώπου ἠνέχθη προφητεία ποτέ, ἀλλὰ
BY [THE] WILL OF MAN WAS BROUGHT A PROPHECY AT ANY TIME, BUT

⌜ὑπὸ πνεύματος ἁγίου φερόμενοι ἐλάλησαν ἀπὸ
³BY ⁴[THE] HOLY~SPIRIT ²BEING CARRIED [ALONG] ⁵SPOKE ⁶FROM

θεοῦ ἄνθρωποι.⌝
⁷GOD ¹MEN.

1:21 text: ASV RSV NASB NIV NEB TEV NJB NRSV. var. υπο πνευματος αγιου φερομενοι ελαλησαν αγιοι
θεου (carried along by the Holy Spirit holy men of God spoke): KJV RSVmg NRSVmg.

from God the Father when that voice was conveyed to him by the Majestic Glory, saying, "This is my Son, my Beloved,[i] with whom I am well pleased." [18]We ourselves heard this voice come from heaven, while we were with him on the holy mountain.

19 So we have the prophetic message more fully confirmed. You will do well to be attentive to this as to a lamp shining in a dark place, until the day dawns and the morning star rises in your hearts. [20]First of all you must understand this, that no prophecy of scripture is a matter of one's own interpretation, [21]because no prophecy ever came by human will, but men and women moved by the Holy Spirit spoke from God.[j]

[i] Other ancient authorities read my beloved Son
[j] Other ancient authorities read but moved by the Holy Spirit saints of God spoke

CHAPTER 2

2.1 Ἐγένοντο δὲ καὶ ψευδοπροφῆται ἐν τῷ λαῷ,
BUT~THERE WERE ALSO FALSE PROPHETS AMONG THE PEOPLE,

ὡς καὶ ἐν ὑμῖν ἔσονται ψευδοδιδάσκαλοι, οἵτινες
AS ALSO AMONG YOU° THERE WILL BE FALSE TEACHERS, WHO

παρεισάξουσιν αἱρέσεις ἀπωλείας   καὶ τὸν
WILL SECRETLY BRING IN HERESIES OF(PRODUCING) DESTRUCTION, EVEN ²THE

ἀγοράσαντα αὐτοὺς δεσπότην ἀρνούμενοι. ἐπάγοντες
⁴HAVING BOUGHT ⁵THEM ³MASTER ¹DENYING, BRINGING UPON

ἑαυτοῖς ταχινὴν ἀπώλειαν, 2.2 καὶ πολλοὶ
THEMSELVES SWIFT DESTRUCTION; AND MANY

ἐξακολουθήσουσιν αὐτῶν ταῖς ἀσελγείαις δι᾽ οὓς
WILL FOLLOW THEIR - LICENTIOUSNESS, BECAUSE OF WHOM

ἡ ὁδὸς τῆς ἀληθείας βλασφημηθήσεται, 2.3 καὶ ἐν
THE WAY OF THE TRUTH WILL BE EVIL SPOKEN OF, AND IN(BY)

But false prophets also arose among the people, just as there will be false teachers among you, who will secretly bring in destructive opinions. They will even deny the Master who bought them—bringing swift destruction on themselves. [2]Even so, many will follow their licentious ways, and because of these teachers[k] the way of truth will be maligned. [3]And in their

[k] Gk because of them

greed they will exploit you with deceptive words. Their condemnation, pronounced against them long ago, has not been idle, and their destruction is not asleep.

4 For if God did not spare the angels when they sinned, but cast them into hell[l] and committed them to chains[m] of deepest darkness to be kept until the judgment; [5]and if he did not spare the ancient world, even though he saved Noah, a herald of righteousness, with seven others, when he brought a flood on a world of the ungodly; [6]and if by turning the cities of Sodom and Gomorrah to ashes he condemned them to extinction[n] and made them an example of what is coming to the ungodly;[o] [7]and if he rescued Lot, a righteous man greatly distressed by the licentiousness of the lawless [8](for that righteous man, living among them day after day, was tormented in his righteous soul by their lawless deeds that he saw and heard), [9]then the Lord knows how to rescue the godly from trial, and to keep the unrighteous under punishment until the day of judgment [10]—especially those who indulge their flesh in depraved lust, and who despise authority.

Bold and willful, they are not afraid to slander the glorious ones,[p] [11]whereas angels, though greater in

[l] Gk Tartaros
[m] Other ancient authorities read pits
[n] Other ancient authorities lack to extinction
[o] Other ancient authorities read an example to those who were to be ungodly
[p] Or angels; Gk glories

πλεονεξία πλαστοῖς λόγοις ὑμᾶς ἐμπορεύσονται, οἷς
COVETOUSNESS WITH MADE-UP WORDS THEY WILL EXPLOIT~YOU°, FOR WHOM

τὸ κρίμα ἔκπαλαι οὐκ ἀργεῖ καὶ ἡ ἀπώλεια αὐτῶν
THE JUDGMENT OF OLD IS NOT IDLE AND THE DESTRUCTION OF THEM

οὐ νυστάζει.
DOES NOT SLUMBER.

2.4 Εἰ γὰρ ὁ θεὸς ἀγγέλων ἁμαρτησάντων
FOR~IF - GOD [2]ANGELS [3]HAVING SINNED

οὐκ ἐφείσατο ἀλλὰ ⌜σειραῖς⌝ ζόφου ταρταρώσας
[1]DID NOT SPARE BUT [2]TO CHAINS [3]OF GLOOM [4]HAVING BEEN SENT TO TARTARUS

παρέδωκεν εἰς κρίσιν τηρουμένους, **2.5** καὶ ἀρχαίου
[1]HE DELIVERED [THEM] [6]FOR [7]JUDGMENT [5]BEING KEPT, AND [THE] ANCIENT

κόσμου οὐκ ἐφείσατο ἀλλὰ ὄγδοον Νῶε
WORLD HE DID NOT SPARE BUT [3][THE] EIGHTH MAN [IN THE ARK] [2]NOAH

δικαιοσύνης κήρυκα ἐφύλαξεν κατακλυσμὸν κόσμῳ
[5]OF RIGHTEOUSNESS [4]A PREACHER [1]HE PRESERVED, [2]A FLOOD [UPON] [3][THE] WORLD

ἀσεβῶν ἐπάξας, **2.6** καὶ πόλεις Σοδόμων καὶ
[4]OF UNGODLY ONES [1]HAVING BROUGHT IN, AND [THE] CITIES OF SODOM AND

Γομόρρας τεφρώσας [καταστροφῇ] κατέκρινεν
GOMORRAH HAVING REDUCED TO ASHES, [BY] A CATASTROPHE JUDGED [THEM],

ὑπόδειγμα μελλόντων ἀσεβέ[σ]ιν τεθεικώς,
[2]AN EXAMPLE [3]OF THINGS TO COME [4]FOR [THE] UNGODLY [1]HAVING MADE [THEM],

2.7 καὶ δίκαιον Λὼτ καταπονούμενον ὑπὸ τῆς τῶν
AND RIGHTEOUS LOT, BEING DISTRESSED BY [1]THE [3]OF THE

ἀθέσμων ἐν ἀσελγείᾳ ἀναστροφῆς ἐρρύσατο·
[4]LAWLESS ONES [5]IN [6]LICENTIOUSNESS [2]CONDUCT, HE DELIVERED;

2.8 βλέμματι γὰρ καὶ ἀκοῇ ὁ δίκαιος
FOR~[BY] SEEING AND HEARING THE(THAT) RIGHTEOUS MAN

ἐγκατοικῶν ἐν αὐτοῖς ἡμέραν ἐξ ἡμέρας ψυχὴν
DWELLING AMONG THEM DAY BY DAY [3]SOUL

δικαίαν ἀνόμοις ἔργοις ἐβασάνιζεν·
[2][HIS] RIGHTEOUS [4]CONCERNING [THEIR] LAWLESS [5]WORKS [1]WAS BEING TORMENTED;

2.9 οἶδεν κύριος εὐσεβεῖς ἐκ πειρασμοῦ ῥύεσθαι,
[THE] LORD~KNOWS [2]GODLY ONES [3]FROM [4]TRIAL [1][HOW] TO RESCUE,

ἀδίκους δὲ εἰς ἡμέραν κρίσεως κολαζομένους
[3]UNRIGHTEOUS ONES [1]AND [5]FOR [6]A DAY [7]OF JUDGMENT [4]BEING PUNISHED

τηρεῖν, **2.10** μάλιστα δὲ τοὺς ὀπίσω σαρκὸς ἐν
[2]TO KEEP, ESPECIALLY - [1]THE ONES [3]AFTER [4][THE] FLESH [5]IN

ἐπιθυμίᾳ μιασμοῦ πορευομένους καὶ
[6]LUST [7]OF(PRODUCING) DEFILEMENT [2]GOING AND

κυριότητος καταφρονοῦντας.
LORDSHIP DESPISING.

Τολμηταὶ αὐθάδεις, δόξας οὐ τρέμουσιν
[THEY ARE] DARING, SELF-WILLED, GLORIOUS BEINGS THEY DO NOT TREMBLE [AT],

βλασφημοῦντες, **2.11** ὅπου ἄγγελοι ἰσχύϊ καὶ
REVILING [THEM], WHERE[AS] ANGELS [3]IN STRENGTH [4]AND

2:4 text: KJV ASVmg NIVmg NEBmg TEV (NJB) NRSV. var. σιροις (pits): ASV RSV NASB NIV NEB TEVmg NRSVmg.

δυνάμει μείζονες ὄντες οὐ φέρουσιν κατ' αὐτῶν παρὰ
5POWER 2GREATER 1BEING DO NOT BRING AGAINST THEM . FROM

κυρίου βλάσφημον κρίσιν. **2.12** οὗτοι δέ ὡς ἄλογα
[THE] LORD A SLANDEROUS JUDGMENT. BUT~THESE MEN AS IRRATIONAL

ζῷα γεγεννημένα φυσικὰ εἰς ἅλωσιν καὶ φθορὰν ἐν
ANIMALS HAVING BEEN BORN BY NATURE FOR CAPTURE AND DESTRUCTION, 2IN

οἷς ἀγνοοῦσιν βλασφημοῦντες, ἐν τῇ φθορᾷ
3MATTERS WHICH 4THEY ARE IGNORANT OF 1REVILING, IN THE CORRUPTION

αὐτῶν καὶ φθαρήσονται **2.13** ἀδικούμενοι μισθὸν
OF THEM INDEED THEY WILL BE CORRUPTED, SUFFERING HARM [AS] PAYMENT

ἀδικίας, ἡδονὴν ἡγούμενοι τὴν ἐν ἡμέρα τρυφήν,
[FOR] HARM [DONE], 5A PLEASURE 1CONSIDERING 3IN~THE 4DAY[TIME] 2INDULGENCE,

σπίλοι καὶ μῶμοι ἐντρυφῶντες ἐν ταῖς ⌐ἀπάταις⌐
SPOTS AND BLEMISHES REVELING IN THE DECEITS

αὐτῶν συνευωχούμενοι ὑμῖν, **2.14** ὀφθαλμοὺς ἔχοντες
OF THEM, [WHILE] FEASTING WITH YOU°, HAVING~EYES

μεστοὺς μοιχαλίδος καὶ ἀκαταπαύστους ἁμαρτίας,
FULL OF [DESIRE FOR] AN ADULTERESS AND NOT CEASING FROM SIN,

δελεάζοντες ψυχὰς ἀστηρίκτους, καρδίαν γεγυμνασμένην
ENTICING UNSTABLE~SOULS 2A HEART 3HAVING BEEN TRAINED

πλεονεξίας ἔχοντες, κατάρας τέκνα· **2.15** καταλείποντες
4OF(IN) GREED 1HAVING, ACCURSED CHILDREN!; FORSAKING

εὐθεῖαν ὁδὸν ἐπλανήθησαν, ἐξακολουθήσαντες τῇ ὁδῷ
A STRAIGHT WAY THEY WENT ASTRAY, HAVING FOLLOWED THE WAY

τοῦ Βαλαὰμ τοῦ Βοσόρ, ὃς μισθὸν ἀδικίας
- OF BALAAM, THE [SON] OF BOSOR, WHO 2[THE] WAGES 3OF UNRIGHTEOUSNESS

ἠγάπησεν **2.16** ἔλεγξιν δὲ ἔσχεν ἰδίας παρανομίας·
1LOVED, 3REPROOF 1BUT 2HE HAD OF HIS OWN TRANSGRESSION;

ὑποζύγιον ἄφωνον ἐν ἀνθρώπου φωνῇ φθεγξάμενον
A DUMB~DONKEY IN A MAN'S VOICE HAVING SPOKEN

ἐκώλυσεν τὴν τοῦ προφήτου παραφρονίαν.
HINDERED 1THE 3OF THE 4PROPHET 2MADNESS.

2.17 Οὗτοί εἰσιν πηγαὶ ἄνυδροι καὶ ὁμίχλαι ὑπὸ
THESE MEN ARE WATERLESS~FOUNTAINS AND MISTS 2BY

λαίλαπος ἐλαυνόμεναι, οἷς ὁ ζόφος τοῦ σκότους
3STORMS 1BEING DRIVEN, FOR WHOM THE GLOOM - OF DARKNESS

τετήρηται. **2.18** ὑπέρογκα γὰρ ματαιότητος
HAS BEEN KEPT. 3INFLATED [WORDS] 1FOR 4OF VANITY

φθεγγόμενοι δελεάζουσιν ἐν ἐπιθυμίαις σαρκὸς
2SPEAKING THEY ENTICE, BY [THE] LUSTS OF [THE] FLESH

ἀσελγείαις τοὺς ὀλίγως ἀποφεύγοντας τοὺς ἐν
IN LICENTIOUSNESS, THE ONES SCARCELY ESCAPING THE ONES 2IN

πλάνη ἀναστρεφομένους, **2.19** ἐλευθερίαν αὐτοῖς
3ERROR 1LIVING, 2FREEDOM 3TO THEM

ἐπαγγελλόμενοι, αὐτοὶ δοῦλοι ὑπάρχοντες τῆς
1PROMISING, THEMSELVES BEING~SLAVES -

might and power, do not bring against them a slanderous judgment from the Lord.*q* 12These people, however, are like irrational animals, mere creatures of instinct, born to be caught and killed. They slander what they do not under-stand, and when those creatures are destroyed,*r* they also will be destroyed, 13suffering*s* the penalty for doing wrong. They count it a pleasure to revel in the daytime. They are blots and blemishes, reveling in their dissipation*t* while they feast with you. 14They have eyes full of adultery, insatiable for sin. They entice unsteady souls. They have hearts trained in greed. Accursed children! 15They have left the straight road and have gone astray, following the road of Balaam son of Bosor,*u* who loved the wages of doing wrong, 16but was rebuked for his own transgression; a speechless donkey spoke with a human voice and restrained the prophet's madness.

17 These are waterless springs and mists driven by a storm; for them the deepest darkness has been reserved. 18For they speak bombastic nonsense, and with licentious desires of the flesh they entice people who have just*v* escaped from those who live in error. 19They promise them freedom, but they themselves are slaves

q Other ancient authorities read *before the Lord;* others lack the phrase
r Gk *in their destruction*
s Other ancient authorities read *receiving*
t Other ancient authorities read *love-feasts*
u Other ancient authorities read *Beor*
v Other ancient authorities read *actually*

2:13 text: KJV ASV RSV NASB NIV NEB NJBmg NRSV. var. αγαπαις (lovefeasts): ASVmg RSVmg NASBmg NIVmg NEBmg NJB NRSVmg.

of corruption; for people are slaves to whatever masters them. 20For if, after they have escaped the defilements of the world through the knowledge of our Lord and Savior Jesus Christ, they are again entangled in them and overpowered, the last state has become worse for them than the first. 21For it would have been better for them never to have known the way of righteousness than, after knowing it, to turn back from the holy commandment that was passed on to them. 22It has happened to them according to the true proverb,

"The dog turns back to
    its own vomit,"
and,
"The sow is washed only
    to wallow in the
    mud."

φθορᾶς· ᾧ γὰρ τις ἥττηται, τούτῳ
OF CORRUPTION; FOR~BY WHOM ANYONE HAS BEEN DEFEATED, TO THIS ONE

δεδούλωται. 2.20 εἰ γὰρ ἀποφυγόντες τὰ μιάσματα
HE HAS BECOME ENSLAVED. FOR~IF HAVING ESCAPED THE DEFILEMENTS

τοῦ κόσμου ἐν ἐπιγνώσει τοῦ κυρίου [ἡμῶν] καὶ
OF THE WORLD BY A KNOWLEDGE OF THE LORD OF US AND

σωτῆρος Ἰησοῦ Χριστοῦ, τούτοις δὲ πάλιν
SAVIOR, JESUS CHRIST, BUT~BY THESE AGAIN

ἐμπλακέντες ἥττῶνται, γέγονεν αὐτοῖς τὰ ἔσχατα
HAVING BEEN ENTANGLED, THEY ARE DEFEATED, 3HAS BECOME 4FOR THEM 1THE 2LAST [STATE]

χείρονα τῶν πρώτων. 2.21 κρεῖττον γὰρ ἦν αὐτοῖς μὴ
WORSE [THAN] THE FIRST. FOR~BETTER IT WAS FOR THEM NOT

ἐπεγνωκέναι τὴν ὁδὸν τῆς δικαιοσύνης ἢ ἐπιγνοῦσιν
TO HAVE KNOWN THE WAY - OF RIGHTEOUSNESS THAN HAVING KNOWN [IT]

ὑποστρέψαι ἐκ τῆς παραδοθείσης αὐτοῖς ἁγίας
TO TURN FROM 1THE 4HAVING BEEN PASSED ON 5TO THEM 2HOLY

ἐντολῆς. 2.22 συμβέβηκεν αὐτοῖς τὸ τῆς
3COMMANDMENT. HAS HAPPENED TO THEM THE [WORD] OF THE

ἀληθοῦς παροιμίας,
TRUE PROVERB,

Κύων ἐπιστρέψας ἐπὶ τὸ ἴδιον ἐξέραμα,
A DOG HAVING RETURNED TO - ITS OWN VOMIT,

καί,
AND,

Ὗς λουσαμένη εἰς κυλισμὸν βορβόρου.
A SOW HAVING BEEN WASHED TO WALLOWING OF(IN) [THE] MUD.

2:22 Prov. 26:11

CHAPTER 3

This is now, beloved, the second letter I am writing to you; in them I am trying to arouse your sincere intention by reminding you 2that you should remember the words spoken in the past by the holy prophets, and the commandment of the Lord and Savior spoken through your apostles. 3First of all you must understand this, that in the last days scoffers will come, scoffing and indulging their own lusts 4and saying, "Where is the

3.1 Ταύτην ἤδη, ἀγαπητοί, δευτέραν ὑμῖν γράφω
THIS NOW, BELOVED, [IS THE] 1SECOND 4TO YOU° 3I WRITE

ἐπιστολήν ἐν αἷς διεγείρω ὑμῶν ἐν ὑπομνήσει
2LETTER, IN [BOTH OF] WHICH 3I AROUSE 4YOUR° 1[AS] BY 2A REMINDER

τὴν εἰλικρινῆ διάνοιαν 3.2 μνησθῆναι τῶν
- 5SINCERE 6MIND[S] TO REMEMBER THE

προειρημένων ῥημάτων ὑπὸ τῶν ἁγίων προφητῶν καὶ
WORDS~HAVING BEEN PREVIOUSLY SPOKEN BY THE HOLY PROPHETS AND

τῆς τῶν ἀποστόλων ὑμῶν ἐντολῆς τοῦ κυρίου
1THE 7OF(BY) THE 8APOSTLES 9OF YOU° 2COMMANDMENT 3OF THE 4LORD

καὶ σωτῆρος. 3.3 τοῦτο πρῶτον γινώσκοντες ὅτι
5AND 6SAVIOR. 2THIS 3FIRSTLY 1KNOWING, THAT

ἐλεύσονται ἐπ' ἐσχάτων τῶν ἡμερῶν [ἐν]
THERE WILL COME DURING [THE] LAST OF THE DAYS 2[INVOLVED] IN

ἐμπαιγμονῇ ἐμπαῖκται κατὰ τὰς ἰδίας ἐπιθυμίας
3MOCKING 1MOCKERS, ACCORDING TO THE[IR] OWN LUSTS

αὐτῶν πορευόμενοι 3.4 καὶ λέγοντες, Ποῦ ἐστιν ἡ
- GOING ABOUT AND SAYING, WHERE IS THE

ἐπαγγελία τῆς παρουσίας αὐτοῦ; ἀφ᾽ ἧς   γὰρ
PROMISE   OF THE COMING   OF HIM? ²FROM ³[THE TIME] WHICH ¹FOR

οἱ πατέρες ἐκοιμήθησαν, πάντα οὕτως διαμένει ἀπ᾽
THE FATHERS FELL ASLEEP,   ALL THINGS SO   CONTINUE   FROM

ἀρχῆς   κτίσεως. 3.5 λανθάνει γὰρ αὐτοὺς τοῦτο
[THE] BEGINNING OF CREATION. ³IS HIDDEN ¹FOR ⁴[FROM] THEM ²THIS,

θέλοντας   ὅτι οὐρανοὶ ἦσαν ἔκπαλαι καὶ γῆ
[THEY] WANTING [IT SO], THAT HEAVENS EXISTED FROM LONG AGO AND EARTH

ἐξ   ὕδατος καὶ δι᾽   ὕδατος συνεστῶσα   τῷ
OUT FROM WATER AND THROUGH(IN) WATER HAVING BEEN FORMED BY THE

τοῦ θεοῦ λόγῳ, 3.6 δι᾽ ὧν   ὁ τότε κόσμος
-   WORD~OF GOD,   THROUGH WHICH [WATERS] THE THEN WORLD

ὕδατι κατακλυσθεὶς   ἀπώλετο· 3.7 οἱ δὲ νῦν
HAVING BEEN DELUGED~WITH WATER PERISHED;   BUT~THE NOW(PRESENT)

οὐρανοὶ καὶ ἡ γῆ   τῷ αὐτῷ λόγῳ
HEAVENS AND THE EARTH BY THE SAME WORD

τεθησαυρισμένοι εἰσὶν πυρὶ τηρούμενοι εἰς ἡμέραν
HAVE BEEN STORED UP;   BEING KEPT~FOR FIRE FOR A DAY

κρίσεως καὶ ἀπωλείας τῶν ἀσεβῶν ἀνθρώπων.
OF JUDGMENT AND DESTRUCTION -   OF UNGODLY MEN.

3.8 Ἐν   δὲ τοῦτο μὴ λανθανέτω ὑμᾶς,
³ONE THING ¹BUT ²THIS LET IT NOT ESCAPE YOU[R° NOTICE],

ἀγαπητοί, ὅτι μία ἡμέρα παρὰ κυρίῳ ὡς χίλια
BELOVED, THAT ONE DAY WITH [THE] LORD [IS] AS A THOUSAND

ἔτη καὶ χίλια ἔτη ὡς ἡμέρα μία. 3.9 οὐ βραδύνει
YEARS AND A THOUSAND YEARS AS ONE~DAY.   ²IS NOT SLOW

κύριος τῆς   ἐπαγγελίας, ὥς τινες
¹[THE] LORD [CONCERNING] THE(HIS) PROMISE,   AS SOME

βραδύτητα ἡγοῦνται, ἀλλὰ μακροθυμεῖ εἰς ὑμᾶς, μὴ
CONSIDER~SLOWNESS,   BUT IS LONGSUFFERING TOWARD YOU°, NOT

βουλόμενός τινας ἀπολέσθαι ἀλλὰ πάντας εἰς
WANTING   ANY TO PERISH   BUT ALL   ²TO

μετάνοιαν χωρῆσαι. 3.10 Ἥξει δὲ ἡμέρα κυρίου ὡς
³REPENTANCE ¹TO COME.   BUT~WILL COME [THE] DAY OF [THE] LORD AS

κλέπτης, ἐν ᾗ οἱ οὐρανοὶ ῥοιζηδὸν
A THIEF, IN WHICH THE HEAVENS WITH GREAT SUDDENNESS

παρελεύσονται στοιχεῖα δὲ καυσούμενα λυθήσεται
WILL PASS AWAY,   AND~[THE] ELEMENTS BURNING UP WILL BE DESTROYED

καὶ γῆ   καὶ τὰ ἐν αὐτῇ ἔργα ⸂εὑρεθήσεται.⸃
AND [THE] EARTH AND ¹THE ³IN ⁴IT ²WORKS WILL BE FOUND OUT.

3.11 τούτων   οὕτως πάντων λυομένων ποταποὺς
²THESE THINGS ³SO   ¹ALL ⁴BEING DESTROYED, WHAT KIND OF [PERSONS]

δεῖ   ὑπάρχειν [ὑμᾶς] ἐν ἁγίαις ἀναστροφαῖς
IT IS NECESSARY [FOR] YOU°~TO BE   IN HOLY   CONDUCT

καὶ εὐσεβείαις, 3.12 προσδοκῶντας καὶ σπεύδοντας τὴν
AND GODLINESS,   AWAITING   AND HASTENING THE

promise of his coming? For ever since our ancestors died,[w] all things continue as they were from the beginning of creation!" [5]They deliberately ignore this fact, that by the word of God heavens existed long ago and an earth was formed out of water and by means of water, [6]through which the world of that time was deluged with water and perished. [7]But by the same word the present heavens and earth have been reserved for fire, being kept until the day of judgment and destruction of the godless.

8 But do not ignore this one fact, beloved, that with the Lord one day is like a thousand years, and a thousand years are like one day. [9]The Lord is not slow about his promise, as some think of slowness, but is patient with you,[x] not wanting any to perish, but all to come to repentance. [10]But the day of the Lord will come like a thief, and then the heavens will pass away with a loud noise, and the elements will be dissolved with fire, and the earth and everything that is done on it will be disclosed.[y]

11 Since all these things are to be dissolved in this way, what sort of persons ought you to be in leading lives of holiness and godliness, [12]waiting for and hastening[z] the

w Gk *our fathers fell asleep*
x Other ancient authorities read *on your account*
y Other ancient authorities read *will be burned up*
z Or *earnestly desiring*

3:10 text: ASVmg NASBmg NIV NEB TEV NJBmg NRSV. var. κατακαησεται (will be burned up): KJV ASV RSV NASB NIVmg NEBmg TEVmg NJB NRSVmg. var. ευρεθησεται λυομενα (will be found destroyed): TEVmg.

coming of the day of God, because of which the heavens will be set ablaze and dissolved, and the elements will melt with fire? [13]But, in accordance with his promise, we wait for new heavens and a new earth, where righteousness is at home.

14 Therefore, beloved, while you are waiting for these things, strive to be found by him at peace, without spot or blemish; [15]and regard the patience of our Lord as salvation. So also our beloved brother Paul wrote to you according to the wisdom given him, [16]speaking of this as he does in all his letters. There are some things in them hard to understand, which the ignorant and unstable twist to their own destruction, as they do the other scriptures. [17]You therefore, beloved, since you are forewarned, beware that you are not carried away with the error of the lawless and lose your own stability. [18]But grow in the grace and knowledge of our Lord and Savior Jesus Christ. To him be the glory both now and to the day of eternity. Amen.[a]

[a] Other ancient authorities lack *Amen*

παρουσίαν τῆς τοῦ θεοῦ ἡμέρας δι᾿ ἣν οὐρανοὶ
COMING   OF THE - DAY~OF GOD,   BECAUSE OF WHICH [THE] HEAVENS

πυρούμενοι λυθήσονται καὶ στοιχεῖα καυσούμενα
BEING SET ON FIRE WILL BE DESTROYED AND [THE] ELEMENTS BURNING UP

τήκεται. **3.13** καινοὺς δὲ οὐρανοὺς καὶ γῆν καινὴν
ARE MELTED.   BUT~NEW   HEAVENS   AND   A NEW~EARTH

κατὰ τὸ ἐπάγγελμα αὐτοῦ προσδοκῶμεν, ἐν οἷς
ACCORDING TO THE PROMISE OF HIM WE AWAIT,   IN WHICH

δικαιοσύνη κατοικεῖ.
RIGHTEOUSNESS DWELLS.

3.14 Διό, ἀγαπητοί, ταῦτα προσδοκῶντες
WHEREFORE, BELOVED,   THESE THINGS AWAITING,

σπουδάσατε ἄσπιλοι καὶ ἀμώμητοι αὐτῷ εὑρεθῆναι
BE EAGER [5]SPOTLESS [6]AND [7]UNBLEMISHED [4]WITH HIM [1]TO BE FOUND

ἐν εἰρήνῃ **3.15** καὶ τὴν τοῦ κυρίου ἡμῶν μακροθυμίαν
[2]IN(AT) [3]PEACE,   AND [2]THE [4]OF THE [5]LORD [6]OF US [3]LONGSUFFERING

σωτηρίαν ἡγεῖσθε, καθὼς καὶ ὁ ἀγαπητὸς ἡμῶν
[7]SALVATION [1]CONSIDER, AS ALSO - OUR~BELOVED

ἀδελφὸς Παῦλος κατὰ τὴν δοθεῖσαν αὐτῷ
BROTHER   PAUL, ACCORDING TO [1]THE [3]HAVING BEEN GIVEN [4]TO HIM

σοφίαν ἔγραψεν ὑμῖν, **3.16** ὡς καὶ ἐν πάσαις
[2]WISDOM, WROTE TO YOU°,   AS ALSO IN ALL

ἐπιστολαῖς λαλῶν ἐν αὐταῖς περὶ τούτων, ἐν αἷς
[HIS] LETTERS SPEAKING IN THEM CONCERNING THESE THINGS, IN WHICH

ἐστιν δυσνόητά τινα, ἃ οἱ ἀμαθεῖς καὶ
IS(ARE) SOME THINGS~HARD TO BE UNDERSTOOD, WHICH THE IGNORANT AND

ἀστήρικτοι στρεβλοῦσιν ὡς καὶ τὰς λοιπὰς γραφὰς
UNSTABLE   TWIST   AS ALSO THE OTHER SCRIPTURES

πρὸς τὴν ἰδίαν αὐτῶν ἀπώλειαν. **3.17** Ὑμεῖς οὖν,
TO   -   THEIR~OWN DESTRUCTION.   YOU° THEREFORE,

ἀγαπητοί, προγινώσκοντες φυλάσσεσθε, ἵνα μὴ τῇ
BELOVED, KNOWING BEFOREHAND, GUARD YOURSELVES, LEST [1]WITH THE

τῶν ἀθέσμων πλάνῃ συναπαχθέντες ἐκπέσητε τοῦ
[3]OF THE [4]LAWLESS ONES [2]ERROR HAVING BEEN LED AWAY YOU° FALL FROM THE(YOUR°)

ἰδίου στηριγμοῦ, **3.18** αὐξάνετε δὲ ἐν χάριτι καὶ γνώσει
OWN   STABILITY;   BUT~GROW IN GRACE AND KNOWLEDGE

τοῦ κυρίου ἡμῶν καὶ σωτῆρος Ἰησοῦ Χριστοῦ. αὐτῷ
OF THE LORD OF US AND SAVIOR, JESUS CHRIST.   TO HIM

ἡ δόξα καὶ νῦν καὶ εἰς ἡμέραν αἰῶνος. [ἀμήν.]
[BE] THE GLORY BOTH NOW AND TO [THE] DAY OF [THE] AGE. AMEN.

THE FIRST LETTER OF
JOHN

ΙΩΑΝΝΟΥ Α
OF JOHN   1

1.1 Ὃ   ἦν ἀπ' ἀρχῆς, ὃ   ἀκηκόαμεν, ὃ
WHAT WAS FROM [THE] BEGINNING—WHICH WE HAVE HEARD, WHICH

ἑωράκαμεν τοῖς ὀφθαλμοῖς ἡμῶν, ὃ   ἐθεασάμεθα
WE HAVE SEEN WITH THE EYES   OF US, WHICH WE BEHELD

καὶ αἱ χεῖρες ἡμῶν ἐψηλάφησαν περὶ   τοῦ λόγου τῆς
AND THE HANDS OF US TOUCHED—WITH RESPECT TO THE WORD -

ζωῆς — **1.2** καὶ ἡ ζωὴ ἐφανερώθη, καὶ ἑωράκαμεν
OF LIFE —   INDEED THE LIFE WAS MANIFESTED, AND WE HAVE SEEN [IT]

καὶ μαρτυροῦμεν καὶ ἀπαγγέλλομεν ὑμῖν τὴν ζωὴν
AND WE GIVE TESTIMONY AND WE PROCLAIM   TO YOU° ¹THE ³LIFE

τὴν αἰώνιον ἥτις ἦν πρὸς τὸν πατέρα καὶ ἐφανερώθη
 - ²ETERNAL WHICH WAS WITH THE FATHER AND WAS MANIFESTED

ἡμῖν — **1.3** ὃ   ἑωράκαμεν καὶ ἀκηκόαμεν,.
TO US —   WHAT WE HAVE SEEN AND WE HAVE HEARD

ἀπαγγέλλομεν καὶ ὑμῖν, ἵνα καὶ ὑμεῖς κοινωνίαν
WE PROCLAIM   ALSO TO YOU°, THAT ²ALSO ¹YOU° ⁴FELLOWSHIP

ἔχητε μεθ' ἡμῶν. καὶ ἡ κοινωνία δὲ ἡ ἡμετέρα
³MAY HAVE WITH US. ²INDEED - ⁴FELLOWSHIP ¹AND - ³OUR

μετὰ τοῦ πατρὸς καὶ μετὰ τοῦ υἱοῦ αὐτοῦ Ἰησοῦ
[IS] WITH THE FATHER AND WITH THE SON OF HIM, JESUS

Χριστοῦ. **1.4** καὶ ταῦτα   γράφομεν ἡμεῖς, ἵνα ἡ
CHRIST.   AND THESE THINGS WRITE   WE,   THAT THE

χαρὰ ⌜ἡμῶν⌝ ᾖ πεπληρωμένη.
JOY   OF US   MAY BE MADE FULL.

1.5 Καὶ ἔστιν αὕτη ἡ ἀγγελία ἣν ἀκηκόαμεν ἀπ'
     AND THIS~IS   THE MESSAGE WHICH WE HAVE HEARD FROM

αὐτοῦ καὶ ἀναγγέλλομεν ὑμῖν, ὅτι ὁ θεὸς φῶς ἐστιν
HIM   AND WE PROCLAIM   TO YOU°, THAT - GOD IS~LIGHT

καὶ σκοτία ἐν αὐτῷ οὐκ ἔστιν οὐδεμία. **1.6** Ἐὰν
AND ⁴DARKNESS ⁵IN ⁶HIM ²NOT ¹THERE IS ³ANY.   IF

εἴπωμεν ὅτι κοινωνίαν ἔχομεν μετ' αὐτοῦ καὶ ἐν τῷ
WE SAY THAT WE HAVE~FELLOWSHIP WITH HIM AND IN THE

σκότει περιπατῶμεν, ψευδόμεθα καὶ οὐ ποιοῦμεν τὴν
DARKNESS WALK,   WE LIE   AND ARE NOT PRACTICING THE

ἀλήθειαν· **1.7** ἐὰν δὲ ἐν τῷ φωτὶ περιπατῶμεν ὡς
TRUTH.   BUT~IF IN THE LIGHT WE WALK   AS

αὐτός ἐστιν ἐν τῷ φωτί, κοινωνίαν ἔχομεν μετ'
HE   IS   IN THE LIGHT, WE HAVE~FELLOWSHIP WITH

We declare to you what was from the beginning, what we have heard, what we have seen with our eyes, what we have looked at and touched with our hands, concerning the word of life— ²this life was revealed, and we have seen it and testify to it, and declare to you the eternal life that was with the Father and was revealed to us— ³we declare to you what we have seen and heard so that you also may have fellowship with us; and truly our fellowship is with the Father and with his Son Jesus Christ. ⁴We are writing these things so that our[a] joy may be complete.

5 This is the message we have heard from him and proclaim to you, that God is light and in him there is no darkness at all. ⁶If we say that we have fellowship with him while we are walking in darkness, we lie and do not do what is true; ⁷but if we walk in the light as he himself is in the light, we have fellowship with

[a] Other ancient authorities read *your*

1:4 text: ASV RSV NASB NIV NEB TEV NJB NRSV. var. υμων (of you°): KJV ASVmg RSVmg NIVmg TEVmg NJBmg NRSVmg.

one another, and the blood of Jesus his Son cleanses us from all sin. [8]If we say that we have no sin, we deceive ourselves, and the truth is not in us. [9]If we confess our sins, he who is faithful and just will forgive us our sins and cleanse us from all unrighteousness. [10]If we say that we have not sinned, we make him a liar, and his word is not in us.

ἀλλήλων καὶ τὸ αἷμα Ἰησοῦ τοῦ υἱοῦ αὐτοῦ
ONE ANOTHER AND THE BLOOD OF JESUS, THE SON OF HIM,

καθαρίζει ἡμᾶς ἀπὸ πάσης ἁμαρτίας. **1.8** ἐὰν
CLEANSES US FROM EVERY SIN. IF

εἴπωμεν ὅτι ἁμαρτίαν οὐκ ἔχομεν, ἑαυτοὺς πλανῶμεν
WE SAY THAT [2]SIN [1]WE DO NOT HAVE, WE DECEIVE~OURSELVES

καὶ ἡ ἀλήθεια οὐκ ἔστιν ἐν ἡμῖν. **1.9** ἐὰν ὁμολογῶμεν
AND THE TRUTH IS~NOT IN US. IF WE CONFESS

τὰς ἁμαρτίας ἡμῶν, πιστός ἐστιν καὶ δίκαιος, ἵνα
THE SINS OF US, HE IS~FAITHFUL AND RIGHTEOUS, THAT

ἀφῇ ἡμῖν τὰς ἁμαρτίας καὶ καθαρίσῃ ἡμᾶς
HE MAY FORGIVE US THE(OUR) SINS AND MAY CLEANSE US

ἀπὸ πάσης ἀδικίας. **1.10** ἐὰν εἴπωμεν ὅτι
FROM ALL UNRIGHTEOUSNESS. IF WE SAY THAT

οὐχ ἡμαρτήκαμεν ψεύστην ποιοῦμεν αὐτὸν καὶ ὁ
WE HAVE NOT SINNED, A LIAR WE MAKE HIM AND THE

λόγος αὐτοῦ οὐκ ἔστιν ἐν ἡμῖν.
WORD OF HIM IS~NOT IN US.

CHAPTER 2

My little children, I am writing these things to you so that you may not sin. But if anyone does sin, we have an advocate with the Father, Jesus Christ the righteous; [2]and he is the atoning sacrifice for our sins, and not for ours only but also for the sins of the whole world.

3 Now by this we may be sure that we know him, if we obey his commandments. [4]Whoever says, "I have come to know him," but does not obey his commandments, is a liar, and in such a person the truth does not exist; [5]but whoever obeys his word, truly in this person the love of God has reached perfection. By this we may be sure that we are in him: [6]whoever says, "I abide in him," ought

2.1 Τεκνία μου, ταῦτα γράφω ὑμῖν ἵνα
LITTLE CHILDREN OF ME, THESE THINGS I WRITE TO YOU° SO THAT

μὴ ἁμάρτητε. καὶ ἐάν τις ἁμάρτῃ, παράκλητον
YOU° DO NOT SIN. AND IF ANYONE SINS, AN ADVOCATE

ἔχομεν πρὸς τὸν πατέρα Ἰησοῦν Χριστὸν δίκαιον·
WE HAVE WITH THE FATHER, JESUS CHRIST [THE] RIGHTEOUS;

2.2 καὶ αὐτὸς ἱλασμός ἐστιν περὶ τῶν ἁμαρτιῶν
AND HE IS~[THE] PROPITIATION(EXPIATION) FOR THE SINS

ἡμῶν, οὐ περὶ τῶν ἡμετέρων δὲ μόνον ἀλλὰ καὶ περὶ
OF US, [2]NOT [3]FOR - [4]OURS [1]YET ONLY BUT ALSO FOR

ὅλου τοῦ κόσμου. **2.3** Καὶ ἐν τούτῳ γινώσκομεν ὅτι
THE~WHOLE WORLD. AND IN(BY) THIS WE KNOW THAT

ἐγνώκαμεν αὐτόν, ἐὰν τὰς ἐντολὰς αὐτοῦ τηρῶμεν.
WE HAVE KNOWN HIM, IF THE COMMANDS OF HIM WE KEEP.

2.4 ὁ λέγων ὅτι Ἔγνωκα αὐτὸν καὶ τὰς ἐντολὰς
THE ONE SAYING, - I HAVE KNOWN HIM AND THE COMMANDS

αὐτοῦ μὴ τηρῶν, ψεύστης ἐστὶν καὶ ἐν τούτῳ ἡ
OF HIM NOT KEEPING, IS~A LIAR AND IN THIS ONE THE

ἀλήθεια οὐκ ἔστιν· **2.5** ὃς δ' ἂν τηρῇ αὐτοῦ τὸν λόγον,
TRUTH IS~NOT; BUT~WHOEVER KEEPS HIS - WORD,

ἀληθῶς ἐν τούτῳ ἡ ἀγάπη τοῦ θεοῦ τετελείωται,
TRULY IN THIS ONE THE LOVE - OF(FOR) GOD HAS BEEN PERFECTED,

ἐν τούτῳ γινώσκομεν ὅτι ἐν αὐτῷ ἐσμεν. **2.6** ὁ
IN(BY) THIS WE KNOW THAT IN HIM WE ARE. THE ONE

λέγων ἐν αὐτῷ μένειν ὀφείλει καθὼς ἐκεῖνος
CLAIMING [2]IN [3]HIM [1]TO ABIDE OUGHT AS THAT ONE

περιεπάτησεν καὶ αὐτὸς [οὕτως] περιπατεῖν.
WALKED   ALSO HIMSELF SO   TO WALK.

2.7 Ἀγαπητοί, οὐκ ἐντολὴν καινὴν γράφω ὑμῖν ἀλλ᾽
       BELOVED,   NOT A NEW~COMMAND   I WRITE TO YOU° BUT

ἐντολὴν παλαιὰν ἣν εἴχετε   ἀπ᾽ ἀρχῆς·   ἡ
AN OLD~COMMAND   WHICH YOU° WERE HAVING FROM [THE] BEGINNING; THE

ἐντολὴ ἡ παλαιά ἐστιν ὁ λόγος ὃν ἠκούσατε.
²COMMAND - ¹OLD   IS   THE WORD WHICH YOU° HEARD.

2.8 πάλιν ἐντολὴν καινὴν γράφω ὑμῖν, ὃ   ἐστιν
       AGAIN A NEW~COMMAND   I WRITE TO YOU°, WHICH IS

ἀληθὲς ἐν αὐτῷ καὶ ἐν ὑμῖν, ὅτι   ἡ σκοτία
TRUE   IN HIM AND IN YOU°, BECAUSE THE DARKNESS

παράγεται καὶ τὸ φῶς τὸ ἀληθινὸν ἤδη φαίνει.
IS PASSING AWAY AND THE ²LIGHT - ¹TRUE ALREADY IS SHINING.

2.9 ὁ   λέγων ἐν τῷ φωτὶ εἶναι καὶ τὸν ἀδελφὸν
       THE ONE CLAIMING ²IN ³THE ⁴LIGHT ¹TO BE AND THE BROTHER

αὐτοῦ μισῶν ἐν τῇ σκοτίᾳ ἐστὶν ἕως ἄρτι. **2.10** ὁ
OF HIM HATING ²IN ³THE ⁴DARKNESS ¹IS UNTIL NOW.   THE ONE

ἀγαπῶν τὸν ἀδελφὸν αὐτοῦ ἐν τῷ φωτὶ μένει   καὶ
LOVING   THE BROTHER OF HIM IN THE LIGHT ABIDES(REMAINS) AND

σκάνδαλον ἐν αὐτῷ οὐκ ἔστιν· **2.11** ὁ δὲ   μισῶν
A CAUSE FOR STUMBLING ³IN ⁴HIM ²NOT ¹IS;   BUT~THE ONE HATING

τὸν ἀδελφὸν αὐτοῦ ἐν τῇ σκοτίᾳ ἐστὶν καὶ ἐν τῇ
THE BROTHER OF HIM IN THE DARKNESS IS   AND IN THE

σκοτίᾳ περιπατεῖ καὶ οὐκ οἶδεν ποῦ ὑπάγει, ὅτι   ἡ
DARKNESS WALKS   AND DOES NOT KNOW WHERE HE GOES, BECAUSE THE

σκοτία ἐτύφλωσεν τοὺς ὀφθαλμοὺς αὐτοῦ.
DARKNESS BLINDED   THE   EYES   OF HIM.

2.12 Γράφω ὑμῖν, τεκνία,
       I WRITE TO YOU°, LITTLE CHILDREN,

       ὅτι   ἀφέωνται   ὑμῖν αἱ   ἁμαρτίαι
       BECAUSE HAVE BEEN FORGIVEN YOU° THE(YOUR°) SINS

       διὰ   τὸ ὄνομα αὐτοῦ.
       BECAUSE OF THE NAME OF HIM.

2.13 γράφω ὑμῖν, πατέρες,
       I WRITE TO YOU°, FATHERS,

       ὅτι   ἐγνώκατε   τὸν ἀπ᾽ ἀρχῆς.
       BECAUSE YOU° HAVE KNOWN THE ONE FROM [THE] BEGINNING.

       γράφω ὑμῖν, νεανίσκοι,
       I WRITE TO YOU°, YOUNG MEN,

       ὅτι   νενικήκατε   τὸν πονηρόν.
       BECAUSE YOU° HAVE OVERCOME THE EVIL ONE.

2.14 ἔγραψα ὑμῖν, παιδία,
       I WROTE TO YOU°, YOUNG CHILDREN,

       ὅτι   ἐγνώκατε   τὸν πατέρα.
       BECAUSE YOU° HAVE KNOWN THE FATHER.

       ἔγραψα ὑμῖν, πατέρες,
       I WROTE TO YOU°, FATHERS,

to walk just as he walked.

7 Beloved, I am writing you no new commandment, but an old commandment that you have had from the beginning; the old commandment is the word that you have heard. 8 Yet I am writing you a new commandment that is true in him and in you, because[b] the darkness is passing away and the true light is already shining. 9 Whoever says, "I am in the light," while hating a brother or sister,[c] is still in the darkness. 10 Whoever loves a brother or sister[d] lives in the light, and in such a person[e] there is no cause for stumbling. 11 But whoever hates another believer[f] is in the darkness, walks in the darkness, and does not know the way to go, because the darkness has brought on blindness.

12 I am writing to you, little children,
    because your sins are forgiven on account of his name.
13 I am writing to you, fathers,
    because you know him who is from the beginning.
I am writing to you, young people,
    because you have conquered the evil one.
14 I write to you, children, because you know the Father.
I write to you, fathers,

b Or that
c Gk hating a brother
d Gk loves a brother
e Or in it
f Gk hates a brother

because you know him
who is from the
beginning.
I write to you, young
people,
because you are strong
and the word of God
abides in you,
and you have
overcome the evil
one.
15 Do not love the world
or the things in the world.
The love of the Father is
not in those who love the
world; [16]for all that is in the
world—the desire of the
flesh, the desire of the eyes,
the pride in riches—comes
not from the Father but from
the world. [17]And the world
and its desire[g] are passing
away, but those who do the
will of God live forever.
18 Children, it is the last
hour! As you have heard that
antichrist is coming, so now
many antichrists have come.
From this we know that it is
the last hour. [19]They went
out from us, but they did not
belong to us; for if they had
belonged to us, they would
have remained with us. But
by going out they made it
plain that none of them
belongs to us. [20]But you
have been anointed by the
Holy One, and all of you
have knowledge.[h] [21]I write
to you, not because you do
not know the truth, but
because you know it, and

[g] Or *the desire for it*
[h] Other ancient authorities read *you know all things*

ὅτι ἐγνώκατε τὸν ἀπ' ἀρχῆς.
BECAUSE YOU° HAVE KNOWN THE ONE FROM [THE] BEGINNING.

ἔγραψα ὑμῖν, νεανίσκοι,
I WROTE TO YOU°, YOUNG MEN,

ὅτι ἰσχυροί ἐστε
BECAUSE YOU° ARE~STRONG

καὶ ὁ λόγος τοῦ θεοῦ ἐν ὑμῖν μένει
AND THE WORD - OF GOD IN YOU° ABIDES

καὶ νενικήκατε τὸν πονηρόν.
AND YOU° HAVE OVERCOME THE EVIL ONE.

2.15 Μὴ ἀγαπᾶτε τὸν κόσμον μηδὲ τὰ ἐν τῷ
DO NOT LOVE THE WORLD NEITHER THE THINGS IN THE

κόσμῳ. ἐάν τις ἀγαπᾷ τὸν κόσμον, οὐκ ἔστιν ἡ
WORLD. IF ANYONE LOVES THE WORLD, ⁵IS~NOT ¹THE

ἀγάπη τοῦ πατρὸς ἐν αὐτῷ· **2.16** ὅτι πᾶν τὸ
²LOVE ³OF(FOR) THE ⁴FATHER ⁶IN ⁷HIM; BECAUSE ALL THAT

ἐν τῷ κόσμῳ, ἡ ἐπιθυμία τῆς σαρκὸς καὶ ἡ
[IS] IN THE WORLD, THE LUST OF THE FLESH AND THE

ἐπιθυμία τῶν ὀφθαλμῶν καὶ ἡ ἀλαζονεία τοῦ
LUST OF THE EYES AND THE PRIDE [ABOUT] THE(THIS)

βίου, οὐκ ἔστιν ἐκ τοῦ πατρὸς ἀλλ' ἐκ τοῦ
LIFE'S POSSESSIONS, IS~NOT OF THE FATHER BUT OF THE

κόσμου ἐστίν. **2.17** καὶ ὁ κόσμος παράγεται καὶ ἡ
WORLD IS. AND THE WORLD IS PASSING AWAY AND THE

ἐπιθυμία αὐτοῦ, ὁ δὲ ποιῶν τὸ θέλημα τοῦ θεοῦ
LUST OF IT, BUT~THE ONE DOING THE WILL - OF GOD

μένει εἰς τὸν αἰῶνα.
REMAINS INTO THE AGE.

2.18 Παιδία, ἐσχάτη ὥρα ἐστίν, καὶ καθὼς ἠκούσατε
CHILDREN, [THE] LAST HOUR IT IS, AND AS YOU° HEARD

ὅτι ἀντίχριστος ἔρχεται, καὶ νῦν ἀντίχριστοι πολλοὶ
THAT AN ANTICHRIST IS COMING, EVEN NOW MANY~ANTICHRISTS

γεγόνασιν, ὅθεν γινώσκομεν ὅτι ἐσχάτη ὥρα ἐστίν.
HAVE COME, FROM WHICH WE KNOW THAT [THE] LAST HOUR IT IS.

2.19 ἐξ ἡμῶν ἐξῆλθαν ἀλλ' οὐκ ἦσαν ἐξ ἡμῶν·
FROM [AMONG] US THEY DEPARTED BUT THEY WERE~NOT OF US;

εἰ γὰρ ἐξ ἡμῶν ἦσαν, μεμενήκεισαν ἂν μεθ' ἡμῶν·
FOR~IF ²OF ³US ¹THEY WERE, THEY WOULD HAVE REMAINED WITH US;

ἀλλ' ἵνα φανερωθῶσιν ὅτι οὐκ εἰσὶν πάντες ἐξ ἡμῶν.
BUT THAT IT MAY BE MANIFESTED THAT ²ARE~NOT ¹ALL [OF THEM] ³OF ⁴US.

2.20 καὶ ὑμεῖς χρῖσμα ἔχετε ἀπὸ τοῦ ἁγίου καὶ
AND YOU° HAVE~AN ANOINTING FROM THE HOLY ONE AND

⌜οἴδατε πάντες.⌝ **2.21** οὐκ ἔγραψα ὑμῖν ὅτι
YOU° ²KNOW ¹ALL. I DID NOT WRITE TO YOU° BECAUSE

οὐκ οἴδατε τὴν ἀλήθειαν ἀλλ' ὅτι οἴδατε αὐτὴν καὶ
YOU° DO NOT KNOW THE TRUTH BUT BECAUSE YOU° KNOW IT, AND

2:20 text: ASVmg RSV NASB NIV NEB TEV NJB NRSV. var. οιδατε παντα (you° know all things): KJV ASV RSVmg NASBmg NIVmg NEBmg NJBmg NRSVmg.

ὅτι πᾶν ψεῦδος ἐκ τῆς ἀληθείας οὐκ ἔστιν. **2.22** Τίς
THAT EVERY LIE ²OF ³THE ⁴TRUTH ¹IS~NOT. WHO

ἐστιν ὁ ψεύστης εἰ μὴ ὁ ἀρνούμενος ὅτι Ἰησοῦς
IS THE LIAR EXCEPT THE ONE DENYING THAT JESUS

οὐκ ἔστιν ὁ Χριστός; οὗτός ἐστιν ὁ ἀντίχριστος,
- IS THE CHRIST? THIS ONE IS THE ANTICHRIST,

ὁ ἀρνούμενος τὸν πατέρα καὶ τὸν υἱόν. **2.23** πᾶς ὁ
THE ONE DENYING THE FATHER AND THE SON. EVERYONE

ἀρνούμενος τὸν υἱὸν οὐδὲ τὸν πατέρα ἔχει, ὁ
DENYING THE SON NEITHER ²THE ³FATHER ¹HAS; THE ONE

ὁμολογῶν τὸν υἱὸν καὶ τὸν πατέρα ἔχει. **2.24** ὑμεῖς ὃ
CONFESSING THE SON ALSO THE FATHER HAS. WHAT~YOU°

ἠκούσατε ἀπ' ἀρχῆς, ἐν ὑμῖν μενέτω. ἐὰν ἐν
HEARD FROM [THE] BEGINNING, IN YOU° LET IT REMAIN. IF ⁶IN

ὑμῖν μείνῃ ὃ ἀπ' ἀρχῆς ἠκούσατε, καὶ
⁷YOU° ⁵REMAINS(ABIDES) ¹WHAT ³FROM ⁴[THE] BEGINNING ²YOU° HEARD, ALSO

ὑμεῖς ἐν τῷ υἱῷ καὶ ἐν τῷ πατρὶ μενεῖτε.
YOU° IN THE SON AND IN THE FATHER WILL REMAIN(ABIDE).

2.25 καὶ αὕτη ἐστὶν ἡ ἐπαγγελία ἣν αὐτὸς
AND THIS IS THE PROMISE WHICH HE

ἐπηγγείλατο ἡμῖν, τὴν ζωὴν τὴν αἰώνιον.
PROMISED US, THE LIFE - ETERNAL.

2.26 Ταῦτα ἔγραψα ὑμῖν περὶ τῶν
THESE THINGS I WROTE TO YOU° CONCERNING THE ONES

πλανώντων ὑμᾶς. **2.27** καὶ ὑμεῖς τὸ χρῖσμα ὃ
DECEIVING YOU°. AND ⁴YOU° ¹THE ²ANOINTING ³WHICH

ἐλάβετε ἀπ' αὐτοῦ, μένει ἐν ὑμῖν καὶ οὐ χρείαν
⁵RECEIVED FROM HIM REMAINS IN YOU° AND ²NO ³NEED

ἔχετε ἵνα τις διδάσκῃ ὑμᾶς, ἀλλ' ὡς τὸ
¹YOU° HAVE THAT ANYONE SHOULD TEACH YOU°, BUT AS THE

αὐτοῦ χρῖσμα διδάσκει ὑμᾶς περὶ πάντων καὶ
SAME ANOINTING TEACHES YOU° CONCERNING EVERYTHING AND

ἀληθές ἐστιν καὶ οὐκ ἔστιν ψεῦδος, καὶ καθὼς ἐδίδαξεν
IS~TRUE AND IS~NOT A LIE, AND AS HE TAUGHT

ὑμᾶς, μένετε ἐν αὐτῷ.
YOU°, REMAIN(ABIDE) IN HIM.

2.28 Καὶ νῦν, τεκνία, μένετε ἐν αὐτῷ, ἵνα
AND NOW, LITTLE CHILDREN, REMAIN(ABIDE) IN HIM, THAT

ἐὰν φανερωθῇ σχῶμεν παρρησίαν καὶ μὴ
IF(WHEN) HE IS MANIFESTED WE MAY HAVE CONFIDENCE AND NOT

αἰσχυνθῶμεν ἀπ' αὐτοῦ ἐν τῇ παρουσίᾳ αὐτοῦ.
BE ASHAMED FROM(BEFORE) HIM AT THE COMING OF HIM.

2.29 ἐὰν εἰδῆτε ὅτι δίκαιός ἐστιν, γινώσκετε ὅτι καὶ
IF YOU° KNOW THAT HE IS~RIGHTEOUS, YOU° KNOW THAT ALSO

πᾶς ὁ ποιῶν τὴν δικαιοσύνην ἐξ αὐτοῦ γεγέννηται.
EVERYONE DOING - RIGHTEOUSNESS ²OF ³HIM ¹HAS BEEN BORN.

you know that no lie comes from the truth. ²²Who is the liar but the one who denies that Jesus is the Christ?ⁱ This is the antichrist, the one who denies the Father and the Son. ²³No one who denies the Son has the Father; everyone who confesses the Son has the Father also. ²⁴Let what you heard from the beginning abide in you. If what you heard from the beginning abides in you, then you will abide in the Son and in the Father. ²⁵And this is what he has promised us,ʲ eternal life.

26 I write these things to you concerning those who would deceive you. ²⁷As for you, the anointing that you received from him abides in you, and so you do not need anyone to teach you. But as his anointing teaches you about all things, and is true and is not a lie, and just as it has taught you, abide in him.ᵏ

28 And now, little children, abide in him, so that when he is revealed we may have confidence and not be put to shame before him at his coming.

29 If you know that he is righteous, you may be sure that everyone who does right has been born of him.

ⁱ Or the Messiah
ʲ Other ancient authorities read you
ᵏ Or it

CHAPTER 3

See what love the Father has given us, that we should be called children of God; and that is what we are. The reason the world does not know us is that it did not know him. [2]Beloved, we are God's children now; what we will be has not yet been revealed. What we do know is this: when he[l] is revealed, we will be like him, for we will see him as he is. [3]And all who have this hope in him purify themselves, just as he is pure.

[4]Everyone who commits sin is guilty of lawlessness; sin is lawlessness. [5]You know that he was revealed to take away sins, and in him there is no sin. [6]No one who abides in him sins; no one who sins has either seen him or known him. [7]Little children, let no one deceive you. Everyone who does what is right is righteous, just as he is righteous. [8]Everyone who commits sin is a child of the devil; for the devil has been sinning from the beginning. The Son of God was revealed for this purpose, to destroy the works of the devil. [9]Those who have been born of God do not sin, because God's seed abides in them;[m] they

[l] Or *it*

[m] Or *because the children of God abide in him*

3.1 ἴδετε ποταπὴν ἀγάπην δέδωκεν ἡμῖν ὁ πατὴρ,
SEE WHAT SORT OF LOVE [3]HAS GIVEN [4]TO US [1]THE [2]FATHER,

ἵνα τέκνα θεοῦ κληθῶμεν, καὶ ἐσμέν. διὰ τοῦτο
THAT CHILDREN OF GOD WE SHOULD BE CALLED, AND WE ARE. THEREFORE

ὁ κόσμος οὐ γινώσκει ἡμᾶς, ὅτι οὐκ ἔγνω αὐτόν.
THE WORLD DOES NOT KNOW US, BECAUSE IT DID NOT KNOW HIM.

3.2 Ἀγαπητοί, νῦν τέκνα θεοῦ ἐσμεν, καὶ οὔπω
BELOVED, NOW [2]CHILDREN [3]OF GOD [1]WE ARE, AND NOT YET

ἐφανερώθη τί ἐσόμεθα. οἴδαμεν ὅτι ἐὰν
IT WAS MANIFESTED WHAT WE WILL BE. WE KNOW THAT IF(WHEN)

φανερωθῇ, ὅμοιοι αὐτῷ ἐσόμεθα, ὅτι ὀψόμεθα αὐτὸν
HE IS MANIFESTED, LIKE HIM WE WILL BE, BECAUSE WE WILL SEE HIM

καθὼς ἐστιν. **3.3** καὶ πᾶς ὁ ἔχων τὴν ἐλπίδα ταύτην
AS HE IS. AND EVERYONE HAVING - THIS~HOPE

ἐπ' αὐτῷ ἁγνίζει ἑαυτόν, καθὼς ἐκεῖνος ἁγνός ἐστιν.
ON(IN) HIM PURIFIES HIMSELF, EVEN AS THAT ONE IS~PURE.

3.4 Πᾶς ὁ ποιῶν τὴν ἁμαρτίαν καὶ τὴν
EVERYONE PRACTICING - SIN ALSO -

ἀνομίαν ποιεῖ, καὶ ἡ ἁμαρτία ἐστὶν ἡ ἀνομία.
DOES~LAWLESSNESS, AND - SIN IS - LAWLESSNESS.

3.5 καὶ οἴδατε ὅτι ἐκεῖνος ἐφανερώθη, ἵνα τὰς
AND YOU° KNOW THAT THAT ONE WAS MANIFESTED THAT [2]THE

ἁμαρτίας ἄρη, καὶ ἁμαρτία ἐν αὐτῷ
[3]SINS [1]HE MIGHT TAKE AWAY, AND SIN IN HIM

οὐκ ἔστιν. **3.6** πᾶς ὁ ἐν αὐτῷ μένων οὐχ ἁμαρτάνει·
IS~NOT. EVERYONE IN HIM ABIDING IS NOT SINNING;

πᾶς ὁ ἁμαρτάνων οὐχ ἑώρακεν αὐτὸν οὐδὲ ἔγνωκεν
EVERYONE SINNING HAS NOT SEEN HIM NEITHER HAS KNOWN

αὐτόν. **3.7** Τεκνία, μηδεὶς πλανάτω ὑμᾶς· ὁ
HIM. LITTLE CHILDREN, LET NO ONE DECEIVE YOU°; THE ONE

ποιῶν τὴν δικαιοσύνην δίκαιός ἐστιν, καθὼς ἐκεῖνος
PRACTICING - RIGHTEOUSNESS IS~RIGHTEOUS, EVEN AS THAT ONE

δίκαιός ἐστιν· **3.8** ὁ ποιῶν τὴν ἁμαρτίαν ἐκ τοῦ
IS~RIGHTEOUS; THE ONE PRACTICING - SIN [2]OF [3]THE

διαβόλου ἐστίν, ὅτι ἀπ' ἀρχῆς ὁ διάβολος
[4]DEVIL [1]IS, BECAUSE FROM [THE] BEGINNING THE DEVIL

ἁμαρτάνει. εἰς τοῦτο ἐφανερώθη ὁ υἱὸς τοῦ θεοῦ,
SINS. FOR THIS [CAUSE] [4]WAS MANIFESTED [1]THE [2]SON - [3]OF GOD,

ἵνα λύσῃ τὰ ἔργα τοῦ διαβόλου. **3.9** Πᾶς ὁ
THAT HE MIGHT DESTROY THE WORKS OF THE DEVIL. EVERYONE

γεγεννημένος ἐκ τοῦ θεοῦ ἁμαρτίαν οὐ ποιεῖ, ὅτι
HAVING BEEN BORN OF - GOD [2]SIN [1]IS NOT PRACTICING, BECAUSE

σπέρμα αὐτοῦ ἐν αὐτῷ μένει, καὶ οὐ δύναται
[THE] SEED OF HIM IN HIM ABIDES, AND HE IS NOT ABLE

ἁμαρτάνειν, ὅτι   ἐκ τοῦ θεοῦ γεγέννηται. **3.10** ἐν
TO SIN,   BECAUSE OF - GOD   HE HAS BEEN BORN.   IN(BY)

τούτῳ φανερά ἐστιν τὰ τέκνα τοῦ θεοῦ καὶ τὰ τέκνα
THIS IS(ARE)~MANIFESTED THE CHILDREN - OF GOD AND THE CHILDREN

τοῦ διαβόλου· πᾶς ὁ μὴ ποιῶν   δικαιοσύνην
OF THE DEVIL;   EVERYONE NOT PRACTICING RIGHTEOUSNESS

οὐκ ἔστιν ἐκ τοῦ θεοῦ, καὶ ὁ   μὴ ἀγαπῶν τὸν
IS~NOT   OF - GOD, ALSO THE ONE NOT LOVING   THE

ἀδελφὸν αὐτοῦ.
BROTHER   OF HIM.

3.11 Ὅτι   αὕτη ἐστὶν ἡ ἀγγελία ἣν ἠκούσατε
         BECAUSE THIS IS   THE MESSAGE WHICH WE HEARD

ἀπ᾽ ἀρχῆς,   ἵνα ἀγαπῶμεν ἀλλήλους, **3.12** οὐ καθὼς
FROM [THE] BEGINNING, THAT WE LOVE ONE ANOTHER,   NOT AS

Κάϊν ἐκ τοῦ πονηροῦ ἦν καὶ ἔσφαξεν τὸν
CAIN 2OF 3THE 4EVIL ONE 1[WHO] WAS AND SLAUGHTERED THE

ἀδελφὸν αὐτοῦ· καὶ χάριν τίνος ἔσφαξεν   αὐτόν;
BROTHER OF HIM; AND [FOR] WHAT~CAUSE DID HE SLAUGHTER HIM?

ὅτι τὰ ἔργα αὐτοῦ πονηρὰ ἦν τὰ δὲ   τοῦ ἀδελφοῦ
BECAUSE THE WORKS OF HIM WERE~EVIL AND~THE ONES OF THE BROTHER

αὐτοῦ δίκαια. **3.13** [καὶ] μὴ θαυμάζετε, ἀδελφοί, εἰ
OF HIM RIGHTEOUS.   AND DO NOT MARVEL, BROTHERS, IF

μισεῖ ὑμᾶς ὁ κόσμος. **3.14** ἡμεῖς οἴδαμεν ὅτι
3HATES 4YOU° 1THE 2WORLD.   WE   KNOW   THAT

μεταβεβήκαμεν ἐκ τοῦ θανάτου εἰς τὴν ζωήν, ὅτι
WE HAVE PASSED OUT OF - DEATH INTO - LIFE BECAUSE

ἀγαπῶμεν τοὺς ἀδελφούς· ὁ   μὴ ἀγαπῶν μένει ἐν
WE LOVE THE BROTHERS; THE ONE NOT LOVING REMAINS IN

τῷ θανάτῳ. **3.15** πᾶς ὁ μισῶν τὸν ἀδελφὸν αὐτοῦ
- DEATH.   EVERYONE HATING THE BROTHER OF HIM

ἀνθρωποκτόνος ἐστίν, καὶ οἴδατε ὅτι πᾶς
IS~A MURDERER,   AND YOU° KNOW THAT EVERY

ἀνθρωποκτόνος οὐκ ἔχει ζωὴν αἰώνιον ἐν αὐτῷ
MURDERER   DOES NOT HAVE ETERNAL~LIFE 2IN 3HIM

μένουσαν. **3.16** ἐν τούτῳ ἐγνώκαμεν τὴν ἀγάπην, ὅτι
1ABIDING.   IN(BY) THIS WE HAVE KNOWN - LOVE, BECAUSE

ἐκεῖνος ὑπὲρ ἡμῶν τὴν ψυχὴν αὐτοῦ ἔθηκεν· καὶ
THAT ONE ON BEHALF OF US THE LIFE OF HIM LAID DOWN; AND

ἡμεῖς ὀφείλομεν ὑπὲρ τῶν ἀδελφῶν τὰς ψυχὰς
WE OUGHT,   ON BEHALF OF THE BROTHERS, THE(OUR) LIVES

θεῖναι. **3.17** ὃς δ᾽ ἂν ἔχῃ τὸν βίον   τοῦ
TO LAY DOWN. NOW WHOEVER HAS THE(THIS) LIFE'S POSSESSIONS OF THE

κόσμου καὶ θεωρῇ τὸν ἀδελφὸν αὐτοῦ χρείαν ἔχοντα
WORLD AND SEES THE BROTHER OF HIM HAVING~NEED

καὶ κλείσῃ τὰ σπλάγχνα αὐτοῦ ἀπ᾽ αὐτοῦ, πῶς ἡ
AND CLOSES - HIS~INNER AFFECTIONS FROM HIM, HOW [DOES] THE

cannot sin, because they have been born of God. [10]The children of God and the children of the devil are revealed in this way: all who do not do what is right are not from God, nor are those who do not love their brothers and sisters.[n]

11 For this is the message you have heard from the beginning, that we should love one another. [12]We must not be like Cain who was from the evil one and murdered his brother. And why did he murder him? Because his own deeds were evil and his brother's righteous. [13]Do not be astonished, brothers and sisters,[o] that the world hates you. [14]We know that we have passed from death to life because we love one another. Whoever does not love abides in death. [15]All who hate a brother or sister[n] are murderers, and you know that murderers do not have eternal life abiding in them. [16]We know love by this, that he laid down his life for us—and we ought to lay down our lives for one another. [17]How does God's love abide in anyone who has the world's goods and sees a brother or sister[p] in need and yet refuses help?

[n] Gk his brother
[o] Gk brothers
[p] Gk brother

18 Little children, let us love, not in word or speech, but in truth and action. [19]And by this we will know that we are from the truth and will reassure our hearts before him [20]whenever our hearts condemn us; for God is greater than our hearts, and he knows everything. [21]Beloved, if our hearts do not condemn us, we have boldness before God; [22]and we receive from him whatever we ask, because we obey his commandments and do what pleases him.

23 And this is his commandment, that we should believe in the name of his Son Jesus Christ and love one another, just as he has commanded us. [24]All who obey his commandments abide in him, and he abides in them. And by this we know that he abides in us, by the Spirit that he has given us.

ἀγάπη τοῦ θεοῦ μένει ἐν αὐτῷ;   **3.18** Τεκνία,
LOVE   -   OF GOD ABIDE   IN   HIM?   LITTLE CHILDREN,

μὴ ἀγαπῶμεν λόγῳ μηδὲ τῇ γλώσσῃ ἀλλὰ ἐν ἔργῳ καὶ
LET US NOT LOVE   IN WORD OR   -   IN TONGUE BUT   IN   DEED AND

ἀληθείᾳ.
IN REALITY.

3.19 [Καὶ] ἐν τούτῳ γνωσόμεθα ὅτι ἐκ τῆς ἀληθείας
AND   IN(BY) THIS WE WILL KNOW THAT [2]OF [3]THE [4]TRUTH

ἐσμέν, καὶ ἔμπροσθεν αὐτοῦ πείσομεν τὴν καρδίαν
[1]WE ARE, AND   BEFORE   HIM   WE WILL PERSUADE THE HEART

ἡμῶν, **3.20** ὅτι ἐὰν καταγινώσκῃ ἡμῶν ἡ καρδία, ὅτι
OF US,   THAT IF [3]CONDEMNS [US] [1]OUR - [2]HEART, BECAUSE

μείζων ἐστὶν ὁ θεὸς τῆς καρδίας ἡμῶν καὶ
GREATER IS   - GOD [THAN] THE HEART   OF US   AND

γινώσκει πάντα. **3.21** Ἀγαπητοί, ἐὰν ἡ καρδία [ἡμῶν]
HE KNOWS ALL THINGS.   BELOVED,   IF THE HEART   OF US

μὴ καταγινώσκῃ, παρρησίαν ἔχομεν πρὸς τὸν θεὸν
DOES NOT CONDEMN [US], WE HAVE~CONFIDENCE WITH - GOD

3.22 καὶ ὃ ἐὰν αἰτῶμεν λαμβάνομεν ἀπ᾽ αὐτοῦ, ὅτι
AND WHATEVER WE ASK WE RECEIVE   FROM HIM, BECAUSE

τὰς ἐντολὰς αὐτοῦ τηροῦμεν καὶ τὰ ἀρεστὰ
THE COMMANDS OF HIM WE KEEP   AND THE THINGS PLEASING

ἐνώπιον αὐτοῦ ποιοῦμεν. **3.23** καὶ αὕτη ἐστὶν ἡ
BEFORE   HIM   WE PRACTICE.   AND THIS IS   THE

ἐντολὴ αὐτοῦ, ἵνα πιστεύσωμεν τῷ ὀνόματι τοῦ υἱοῦ
COMMAND OF HIM,   THAT WE BELIEVE   IN THE NAME   OF THE SON

αὐτοῦ Ἰησοῦ Χριστοῦ καὶ ἀγαπῶμεν ἀλλήλους, καθὼς
OF HIM, JESUS   CHRIST,   AND WE LOVE   ONE ANOTHER,   AS

ἔδωκεν ἐντολὴν ἡμῖν. **3.24** καὶ ὁ τηρῶν τὰς
HE GAVE COMMAND TO US.   AND THE ONE KEEPING THE

ἐντολὰς αὐτοῦ ἐν αὐτῷ μένει καὶ αὐτὸς ἐν αὐτῷ·
COMMANDS OF HIM [2]IN [3]HIM [1]ABIDES AND HE   IN HIM;

καὶ ἐν τούτῳ γινώσκομεν ὅτι μένει ἐν ἡμῖν, ἐκ τοῦ
AND IN(BY) THIS WE KNOW   THAT HE ABIDES IN US,   BY THE

πνεύματος οὗ ἡμῖν ἔδωκεν.
SPIRIT   WHOM TO US HE GAVE.

CHAPTER 4

Beloved, do not believe every spirit, but test the spirits to see whether they are from God; for many false prophets have gone out into the world. [2]By this you know the Spirit of God: every

4.1 Ἀγαπητοί, μὴ παντὶ πνεύματι πιστεύετε ἀλλὰ
BELOVED,   [2]NOT [3]EVERY [4]SPIRIT [1]BELIEVE BUT

δοκιμάζετε τὰ πνεύματα εἰ ἐκ τοῦ θεοῦ ἐστιν, ὅτι
TEST   THE SPIRITS   IF OF - GOD THEY ARE, BECAUSE

πολλοὶ ψευδοπροφῆται ἐξεληλύθασιν εἰς τὸν κόσμον.
MANY   FALSE PROPHETS   HAVE GONE OUT INTO THE WORLD.

4.2 ἐν τούτῳ γινώσκετε τὸ πνεῦμα τοῦ θεοῦ· πᾶν
IN(BY) THIS WE KNOW   THE SPIRIT   - OF GOD; EVERY

πνεῦμα ὃ   ὁμολογεῖ Ἰησοῦν Χριστὸν ἐν σαρκὶ
SPIRIT   WHICH CONFESSES JESUS CHRIST   ²IN ³[THE] FLESH

ἐληλυθότα ἐκ τοῦ θεοῦ ἐστιν, **4.3** καὶ πᾶν πνεῦμα ὃ
¹HAVING COME ⁵OF - ⁶GOD ⁴IS,   AND EVERY SPIRIT WHICH

μὴ ὁμολογεῖ τὸν Ἰησοῦν ἐκ τοῦ θεοῦ οὐκ ἔστιν· καὶ
DOES NOT CONFESS - JESUS ²OF - ³GOD ¹IS~NOT.   AND

τοῦτό ἐστιν τὸ   τοῦ ἀντιχρίστου, ὃ   ἀκηκόατε
THIS   IS   THE [SPIRIT] OF THE ANTICHRIST, WHICH YOU° HAVE HEARD

ὅτι ἔρχεται, καὶ νῦν ἐν τῷ κόσμῳ ἐστὶν ἤδη.
THAT HE(IT) COMES AND NOW IN THE WORLD ALREADY~IS.

4.4 ὑμεῖς ἐκ τοῦ θεοῦ ἐστε, τεκνία,   καὶ νενικήκατε
YOU° OF - GOD ARE, LITTLE CHILDREN, AND YOU° HAVE OVERCOME

αὐτούς, ὅτι μείζων ἐστὶν ὁ   ἐν ὑμῖν ἢ ὁ   ἐν
THEM, BECAUSE GREATER IS THE ONE IN YOU° THAN THE ONE IN

τῷ κόσμῳ. **4.5** αὐτοὶ ἐκ τοῦ κόσμου εἰσίν, διὰ τοῦτο
THE WORLD.   THEY OF THE WORLD ARE, THEREFORE

ἐκ τοῦ κόσμου λαλοῦσιν καὶ ὁ κόσμος αὐτῶν ἀκούει.
OF THE WORLD THEY SPEAK AND THE WORLD HEARS~THEM.

4.6 ἡμεῖς ἐκ τοῦ θεοῦ ἐσμεν, ὁ   γινώσκων τὸν θεὸν
WE   OF - GOD ARE; THE ONE KNOWING - GOD

ἀκούει ἡμῶν, ὃς   οὐκ ἔστιν ἐκ τοῦ θεοῦ οὐκ ἀκούει
HEARS US; [HE] WHO IS~NOT OF - GOD DOES NOT HEAR

ἡμῶν. ἐκ τούτου γινώσκομεν τὸ πνεῦμα τῆς ἀληθείας
US. FROM THIS WE KNOW   THE SPIRIT - OF TRUTH

καὶ τὸ πνεῦμα τῆς πλάνης.
AND THE SPIRIT - OF ERROR.

4.7 Ἀγαπητοί, ἀγαπῶμεν ἀλλήλους, ὅτι   ἡ ἀγάπη
BELOVED,   LET US LOVE ONE ANOTHER, BECAUSE - LOVE

ἐκ τοῦ θεοῦ ἐστιν, καὶ πᾶς ὁ ἀγαπῶν ἐκ τοῦ θεοῦ
²OF - ³GOD ¹IS, AND EVERYONE LOVING ²OF - ³GOD

γεγέννηται καὶ γινώσκει τὸν θεόν. **4.8** ὁ   μὴ ἀγαπῶν
¹HAS BEEN BORN AND KNOWS - GOD.   THE ONE NOT LOVING

οὐκ ἔγνω τὸν θεόν, ὅτι ὁ θεὸς ἀγάπη ἐστίν. **4.9** ἐν
DID NOT KNOW - GOD, BECAUSE - GOD IS~LOVE.   IN(BY)

τούτῳ ἐφανερώθη ἡ ἀγάπη τοῦ θεοῦ ἐν ἡμῖν, ὅτι
THIS WAS MANIFESTED THE LOVE - OF GOD AMONG US, BECAUSE

τὸν υἱὸν αὐτοῦ τὸν μονογενῆ ἀπέσταλκεν ὁ θεὸς εἰς
- ⁵SON ³HIS - ⁴ONLY ²HAS SENT   - ¹GOD INTO

τὸν κόσμον ἵνα ζήσωμεν δι'   αὐτοῦ. **4.10** ἐν τούτῳ
THE WORLD THAT WE MAY LIVE THROUGH HIM.   IN THIS

ἐστὶν ἡ ἀγάπη, οὐχ ὅτι ἡμεῖς ἠγαπήκαμεν τὸν θεόν
IS - LOVE, NOT THAT WE HAVE LOVED   - GOD

ἀλλ' ὅτι αὐτὸς ἠγάπησεν ἡμᾶς καὶ ἀπέστειλεν τὸν
BUT THAT HE LOVED   US AND GAVE   THE

υἱὸν αὐτοῦ ἱλασμὸν   περὶ τῶν ἁμαρτιῶν ἡμῶν.
SON OF HIM [AS] A PROPITIATION(EXPIATION) FOR THE SINS OF US.

4.11 Ἀγαπητοί, εἰ οὕτως ὁ θεὸς ἠγάπησεν ἡμᾶς, καὶ
BELOVED, IF ²SO - ¹GOD LOVED   US, ALSO

spirit that confesses that Jesus Christ has come in the flesh is from God, [3]and every spirit that does not confess Jesus[q] is not from God. And this is the spirit of the antichrist, of which you have heard that it is coming; and now it is already in the world. [4]Little children, you are from God, and have conquered them; for the one who is in you is greater than the one who is in the world. [5]They are from the world; therefore what they say is from the world, and the world listens to them. [6]We are from God. Whoever knows God listens to us, and whoever is not from God does not listen to us. From this we know the spirit of truth and the spirit of error.

[7] Beloved, let us love one another, because love is from God; everyone who loves is born of God and knows God. [8]Whoever does not love does not know God, for God is love. [9]God's love was revealed among us in this way: God sent his only Son into the world so that we might live through him. [10]In this is love, not that we loved God but that he loved us and sent his Son to be the atoning sacrifice for our sins. [11]Beloved, since God loved us so much, we also

[q] Other ancient authorities read *does away with Jesus* (Gk *dissolves Jesus*)

ought to love one another. ¹²No one has ever seen God; if we love one another, God lives in us, and his love is perfected in us.

13 By this we know that we abide in him and he in us, because he has given us of his Spirit. ¹⁴And we have seen and do testify that the Father has sent his Son as the Savior of the world. ¹⁵God abides in those who confess that Jesus is the Son of God, and they abide in God. ¹⁶So we have known and believe the love that God has for us.

God is love, and those who abide in love abide in God, and God abides in them. ¹⁷Love has been perfected among us in this: that we may have boldness on the day of judgment, because as he is, so are we in this world. ¹⁸There is no fear in love, but perfect love casts out fear; for fear has to do with punishment, and whoever fears has not reached perfection in love. ¹⁹We love[r] because he first loved us. ²⁰Those who say, "I love God," and hate their brothers or sisters,[s]

[r] Other ancient authorities add him; others add God
[s] Gk brothers

ἡμεῖς ὀφείλομεν ἀλλήλους ἀγαπᾶν. **4.12** θεὸν οὐδεὶς
WE OUGHT TO LOVE~ONE ANOTHER. ⁴GOD ¹NO ONE

πώποτε τεθέαται. ἐὰν ἀγαπῶμεν ἀλλήλους, ὁ θεὸς ἐν
²EVER ³HAS BEHELD. IF WE LOVE ONE ANOTHER, - GOD IN

ἡμῖν μένει καὶ ἡ ἀγάπη αὐτοῦ ἐν ἡμῖν
US ABIDES AND THE LOVE OF(FOR) HIM IN US

τετελειωμένη ἐστιν.
HAS BEEN PERFECTED.

4.13 Ἐν τούτῳ γινώσκομεν ὅτι ἐν αὐτῷ μένομεν
IN(BY) THIS WE KNOW THAT IN HIM WE ABIDE

καὶ αὐτὸς ἐν ἡμῖν, ὅτι ἐκ τοῦ πνεύματος αὐτοῦ
AND HE IN US, BECAUSE ³OF ⁴THE ⁵SPIRIT ⁶OF HIM

δέδωκεν ἡμῖν. **4.14** καὶ ἡμεῖς τεθεάμεθα καὶ
¹HE HAS GIVEN ²US. AND WE HAVE BEHELD AND

μαρτυροῦμεν ὅτι ὁ πατὴρ ἀπέσταλκεν τὸν υἱὸν
WE TESTIFY THAT THE FATHER HAS SENT THE SON

σωτῆρα τοῦ κόσμου. **4.15** ὃς ἐὰν ὁμολογήσῃ ὅτι
[AS] SAVIOR OF THE WORLD. WHOEVER CONFESSES THAT

Ἰησοῦς ἐστιν ὁ υἱὸς τοῦ θεοῦ, ὁ θεὸς ἐν αὐτῷ μένει
JESUS IS THE SON - OF GOD, - GOD IN HIM ABIDES

καὶ αὐτὸς ἐν τῷ θεῷ. **4.16** καὶ ἡμεῖς ἐγνώκαμεν καὶ
AND HE IN - GOD. AND WE HAVE KNOWN AND

πεπιστεύκαμεν τὴν ἀγάπην ἣν ἔχει ὁ θεὸς ἐν ἡμῖν.
HAVE BELIEVED THE LOVE WHICH ²HAS - ¹GOD AS TO US.

Ὁ θεὸς ἀγάπη ἐστίν, καὶ ὁ μένων ἐν τῇ
- GOD IS~LOVE, AND THE ONE ABIDING IN THE(THIS)

ἀγάπῃ ἐν τῷ θεῷ μένει καὶ ὁ θεὸς ἐν αὐτῷ μένει.
LOVE IN - GOD ABIDES AND - GOD IN HIM ABIDES.

4.17 ἐν τούτῳ τετελείωται ἡ ἀγάπη μεθ' ἡμῶν, ἵνα
IN(BY) THIS ³HAS BEEN PERFECTED ¹THE ²LOVE WITH US, THAT

παρρησίαν ἔχωμεν ἐν τῇ ἡμέρᾳ τῆς κρίσεως, ὅτι
WE MAY HAVE~CONFIDENCE IN THE DAY - OF JUDGMENT, BECAUSE

καθὼς ἐκεῖνός ἐστιν καὶ ἡμεῖς ἐσμεν ἐν τῷ
AS THAT ONE IS ALSO WE ARE IN -

κόσμῳ τούτῳ. **4.18** φόβος οὐκ ἔστιν ἐν τῇ ἀγάπῃ
THIS~WORLD. FEAR IS~NOT IN THE(THIS) LOVE,

ἀλλ' ἡ τελεία ἀγάπη ἔξω βάλλει τὸν φόβον, ὅτι ὁ
BUT THE PERFECT LOVE CASTS~OUT THE FEAR, BECAUSE -

φόβος κόλασιν ἔχει, ὁ δὲ φοβούμενος
FEAR HAS [TO DO WITH]~PUNISHMENT, AND~THE ONE FEARING

οὐ τετελείωται ἐν τῇ ἀγάπῃ. **4.19** ἡμεῖς ἀγαπῶμεν,
HAS NOT BEEN PERFECTED IN - LOVE. WE LOVE,

ὅτι αὐτὸς πρῶτος ἠγάπησεν ἡμᾶς. **4.20** ἐάν τις
BECAUSE HE FIRST LOVED US. IF ANYONE

εἴπῃ ὅτι Ἀγαπῶ τὸν θεὸν καὶ τὸν ἀδελφὸν αὐτοῦ
SAYS, - I LOVE - GOD AND ²THE ³BROTHER ⁴OF HIM

μισῇ, ψεύστης ἐστίν·   ὁ γὰρ   μὴ ἀγαπῶν τὸν ἀδελφὸν
¹HATES, HE IS~A LIAR.   FOR~THE ONE NOT LOVING   THE BROTHER

αὐτοῦ ὃν   ἑώρακεν, τὸν θεὸν ὃν   οὐχ ἑώρακεν
OF HIM WHOM HE HAS SEEN, -   ³GOD ⁴WHOM ⁵HE HAS NOT SEEN

οὐ δύναται ἀγαπᾶν. 4.21 καὶ ταύτην τὴν ἐντολὴν
¹HE IS NOT ABLE ²TO LOVE.   AND THIS   -   COMMAND

ἔχομεν ἀπ᾽ αὐτοῦ, ἵνα ὁ   ἀγαπῶν τὸν θεὸν ἀγαπᾷ
WE HAVE FROM HIM,   THAT THE ONE LOVING - GOD SHOULD LOVE

καὶ τὸν ἀδελφὸν αὐτοῦ.
ALSO THE BROTHER OF HIM.

are liars; for those who do not love a brother or sister[t] whom they have seen, cannot love God whom they have not seen. 21The commandment we have from him is this: those who love God must love their brothers and sisters[u] also.

[t] Gk *brother*
[u] Gk *brothers*

5.1 Πᾶς ὁ   πιστεύων ὅτι Ἰησοῦς ἐστιν ὁ Χριστός,
EVERYONE BELIEVING THAT JESUS   IS   THE CHRIST,

ἐκ τοῦ θεοῦ γεγέννηται, καὶ πᾶς ὁ ἀγαπῶν τὸν
OF - GOD HAS BEEN BORN, AND EVERYONE LOVING THE ONE

γεννήσαντα ἀγαπᾷ [καὶ] τὸν γεγεννημένον ἐξ αὐτοῦ.
HAVING GIVEN BIRTH LOVES ALSO THE ONE HAVING BEEN BORN OF HIM.

5.2 ἐν τούτῳ γινώσκομεν ὅτι ἀγαπῶμεν τὰ τέκνα τοῦ
IN(BY) THIS WE KNOW   THAT WE LOVE   THE CHILDREN -

θεοῦ, ὅταν τὸν θεὸν ἀγαπῶμεν καὶ τὰς ἐντολὰς αὐτοῦ
OF GOD, WHEN - GOD WE LOVE   AND THE COMMANDS OF HIM

ποιῶμεν. **5.3** αὕτη γάρ ἐστιν ἡ ἀγάπη τοῦ θεοῦ,   ἵνα
WE DO.   FOR~THIS IS   THE LOVE   - OF(FOR) GOD, THAT

τὰς ἐντολὰς αὐτοῦ τηρῶμεν, καὶ αἱ ἐντολαὶ αὐτοῦ
THE COMMANDS OF HIM WE KEEP,   AND THE COMMANDS OF HIM

βαρεῖαι οὐκ εἰσίν. **5.4** ὅτι   πᾶν τὸ γεγεννημένον ἐκ
²BURDENSOME ¹ARE~NOT.   BECAUSE ALL THAT HAS BEEN BORN OF

τοῦ θεοῦ νικᾷ   τὸν κόσμον· καὶ αὕτη ἐστὶν ἡ
-   GOD OVERCOMES THE WORLD;   AND THIS IS   THE

νίκη ἡ νικήσασα τὸν κόσμον, ἡ πίστις ἡμῶν.
VICTORY, THE ONE HAVING OVERCOME THE WORLD, THE FAITH OF US.

5.5 τίς [δέ] ἐστιν ὁ   νικῶν   τὸν κόσμον εἰ μὴ ὁ
AND~WHO IS   THE ONE OVERCOMING THE WORLD EXCEPT THE ONE

πιστεύων ὅτι Ἰησοῦς ἐστιν ὁ υἱὸς τοῦ θεοῦ;
BELIEVING THAT JESUS   IS THE SON - OF GOD.

5.6 Οὗτός ἐστιν ὁ   ἐλθὼν δι᾽ ὕδατος καὶ
THIS ONE IS   THE ONE HAVING COME BY WATER   AND

αἵματος, Ἰησοῦς Χριστός, οὐκ ἐν τῷ ὕδατι μόνον
BLOOD, JESUS   CHRIST, NOT IN(BY) THE WATER ONLY

ἀλλ᾽ ἐν τῷ ὕδατι καὶ ἐν τῷ αἵματι· καὶ τὸ
BUT IN(BY) THE WATER AND IN(BY) THE BLOOD; AND THE

πνεῦμά ἐστιν τὸ   μαρτυροῦν, ὅτι τὸ πνεῦμά ἐστιν
SPIRIT   IS   THE ONE GIVING TESTIMONY, BECAUSE THE SPIRIT   IS

Everyone who believes that Jesus is the Christ[v] has been born of God, and everyone who loves the parent loves the child. 2By this we know that we love the children of God, when we love God and obey his commandments. 3For the love of God is this, that we obey his commandments. And his commandments are not burdensome, 4for whatever is born of God conquers the world. And this is the victory that conquers the world, our faith. 5Who is it that conquers the world but the one who believes that Jesus is the Son of God?

6 This is the one who came by water and blood, Jesus Christ, not with the water only but with the water and the blood. And the Spirit is the one that testifies, for the Spirit is

[v] Or *the Messiah*

the truth. [7]There are three that testify:[w] [8]the Spirit and the water and the blood, and these three agree. [9]If we receive human testimony, the testimony of God is greater; for this is the testimony of God that he has testified to his Son. [10]Those who believe in the Son of God have the testimony in their hearts. Those who do not believe in God[x] have made him a liar by not believing in the testimony that God has given concerning his Son. [11]And this is the testimony: God gave us eternal life, and this life is in his Son. [12]Whoever has the Son has life; whoever does not have the Son of God does not have life.

13 I write these things to you who believe in the name of the Son of God, so that you may know that you have eternal life.

14 And this is the boldness we have in him, that if we ask anything according to his will, he hears us. [15]And if we know that he hears us in whatever we ask, we know that we have obtained the requests made of him. [16]If you see your brother or sister[y] committing what is not a mortal sin, you will ask, and God[z] will give

[w] A few other authorities read (with variations) [7]There are three that testify in heaven, the Father, the Word, and the Holy Spirit, and these three are one. [8]And there are three that testify on earth:
[x] Other ancient authorities read in the Son
[y] Gk your brother
[z] Gk he

ἡ   ἀλήθεια.   **5.7** ὅτι   τρεῖς εἰσιν οἱ μαρτυροῦντες,[T]
THE   TRUTH.   BECAUSE   THERE ARE~THREE -   GIVING TESTIMONY,

5.8 τὸ   πνεῦμα   καὶ   τὸ   ὕδωρ   καὶ   τὸ   αἷμα,   καὶ   οἱ   τρεῖς
THE   SPIRIT   AND   THE   WATER   AND   THE   BLOOD,   AND   THE   THREE

εἰς   τὸ   ἕν   εἰσιν.   **5.9** εἰ   τὴν   μαρτυρίαν   τῶν
[2]FOR   [3]THE   [4]ONE [TESTIMONY]   [1]ARE.   IF   THE   WITNESS   -

ἀνθρώπων   λαμβάνομεν,   ἡ   μαρτυρία   τοῦ   θεοῦ
OF MEN   WE RECEIVE,   THE   TESTIMONY   -   OF GOD

μείζων ἐστίν·   ὅτι   αὕτη   ἐστὶν ἡ   μαρτυρία   τοῦ   θεοῦ
IS~GREATER;   BECAUSE   THIS   IS   THE   TESTIMONY   -   OF GOD

ὅτι   μεμαρτύρηκεν   περὶ   τοῦ   υἱοῦ αὐτοῦ.   **5.10** ὁ
THAT   HE HAS TESTIFIED   CONCERNING   THE   SON   OF HIM.   THE ONE

πιστεύων   εἰς   τὸν   υἱὸν   τοῦ   θεοῦ   ἔχει   τὴν   μαρτυρίαν   ἐν
BELIEVING   IN   THE   SON   -   OF GOD   HAS   THE   WITNESS   IN

ἑαυτῷ,   ὁ   μὴ   πιστεύων   τῷ   θεῷ   ψεύστην   πεποίηκεν
HIMSELF,   THE ONE   NOT   BELIEVING   -   GOD   [3]A LIAR   [1]HAS MADE

αὐτόν,   ὅτι   οὐ πεπίστευκεν   εἰς   τὴν   μαρτυρίαν   ἣν
[2]HIM,   BECAUSE   HE HAS NOT BELIEVED   IN   THE   TESTIMONY   WHICH

μεμαρτύρηκεν ὁ θεὸς περὶ   τοῦ   υἱοῦ αὐτοῦ.   **5.11** καὶ
[2]HAS TESTIFIED   -   [1]GOD   CONCERNING   THE   SON   OF HIM.   AND

αὕτη   ἐστὶν ἡ   μαρτυρία,   ὅτι   ζωὴν αἰώνιον ἔδωκεν ἡμῖν
THIS   IS   THE   TESTIMONY,   THAT   [5]LIFE   [4]ETERNAL   [2]GAVE   [3]TO US

ὁ ˙θεός,   καὶ   αὕτη ἡ ζωὴ ἐν τῷ   υἱῷ   αὐτοῦ ἐστιν.
-   [1]GOD,   AND   THIS   -   LIFE   [2]IN   [3]THE   [4]SON   [5]OF HIM   [1]IS.

5.12 ὁ   ἔχων   τὸν   υἱὸν   ἔχει   τὴν   ζωήν·   ὁ   μὴ
THE ONE HAVING   THE   SON   HAS   THE(THIS) LIFE;   THE ONE   NOT

ἔχων   τὸν   υἱὸν   τοῦ   θεοῦ   τὴν   ζωὴν οὐκ ἔχει.
HAVING   THE   SON   -   OF GOD   THE   LIFE   DOES NOT HAVE.

5.13 Ταῦτα   ἔγραψα   ὑμῖν ἵνα   εἰδῆτε   ὅτι   ζωὴν
THESE THINGS   I WROTE   TO YOU°   THAT   YOU° MAY KNOW   THAT   [3]LIFE

ἔχετε   αἰώνιον, τοῖς   πιστεύουσιν   εἰς τὸ ὄνομα   τοῦ
[1]YOU° HAVE   [2]ETERNAL,   TO THE ONES   BELIEVING   IN   THE   NAME   OF THE

υἱοῦ τοῦ θεοῦ.   **5.14** καὶ   αὕτη   ἐστὶν ἡ   παρρησία   ἣν
SON   OF GOD.   AND   THIS   IS   THE   CONFIDENCE   WHICH

ἔχομεν   πρὸς   αὐτὸν ὅτι   ἐάν   τι αἰτώμεθα κατὰ   τὸ
WE HAVE   TOWARD   HIM   THAT   IF   WE ASK~ANYTHING   ACCORDING TO   THE

θέλημα   αὐτοῦ   ἀκούει ἡμῶν.   **5.15** καὶ   ἐὰν   οἴδαμεν ὅτι
WILL   OF HIM   HE HEARS   US.   AND   IF   WE KNOW   THAT

ἀκούει ἡμῶν ὃ ἐὰν   αἰτώμεθα, οἴδαμεν ὅτι ἔχομεν   τὰ
HE HEARS   US,   WHATEVER   WE ASK,   WE KNOW   THAT   WE HAVE   THE

αἰτήματα   ἃ   ᾐτήκαμεν ἀπ᾽ αὐτοῦ.
REQUESTS   WHICH   WE HAVE ASKED   FROM   HIM.

5.16 Ἐάν   τις   ἴδῃ   τὸν   ἀδελφὸν αὐτοῦ ἁμαρτάνοντα
IF   ANYONE SEES   THE   BROTHER   OF HIM   SINNING

ἁμαρτίαν   μὴ πρὸς   θάνατον,   αἰτήσει   καὶ   δώσει
A SIN   NOT [LEADING] TO   DEATH,   HE WILL ASK   AND   HE WILL GIVE

5:7b-8a A few late MSS of the Latin Vulgate add the words here that could be translated, 'in heaven: the Father, the Word, and the Holy Spirit, and these three are one. And there are three that testify on earth:' (from NIVmg; see also KJV NJBmg NRSVmg).

αὐτῷ ζωήν, τοῖς ἁμαρτάνουσιν μὴ πρὸς θάνατον.
TO HIM LIFE, TO THE ONES SINNING NOT [LEADING] TO DEATH.

ἔστιν ἁμαρτία πρὸς θάνατον· οὐ περὶ ἐκείνης
THERE IS A SIN [LEADING] TO DEATH; NOT CONCERNING THAT [SIN]

λέγω ἵνα ἐρωτήσῃ. **5.17** πᾶσα ἀδικία
DO I SAY THAT YOU SHOULD ASK. EVERY UNRIGHTEOUSNESS

ἁμαρτία ἐστίν, καὶ ἔστιν ἁμαρτία οὐ πρὸς
IS~SIN, AND THERE IS SIN NOT [LEADING] TO

θάνατον.
DEATH.

5.18 Οἴδαμεν ὅτι πᾶς ὁ γεγεννημένος ἐκ τοῦ θεοῦ
WE KNOW THAT EVERYONE HAVING BEEN BORN OF - GOD

οὐχ ἁμαρτάνει, ἀλλ᾽ ὁ γεννηθεὶς ἐκ τοῦ θεοῦ
DOES NOT CONTINUALLY SIN, BUT THE ONE HAVING BEEN BORN OF - GOD

τηρεῖ αὐτὸν καὶ ὁ πονηρὸς οὐχ ἅπτεται αὐτοῦ.
KEEPS HIM AND THE EVIL ONE DOES NOT TOUCH HIM.

5.19 οἴδαμεν ὅτι ἐκ τοῦ θεοῦ ἐσμεν καὶ ὁ
WE KNOW THAT OF - GOD WE ARE AND THE

κόσμος ὅλος ἐν τῷ πονηρῷ κεῖται. **5.20** οἴδαμεν δὲ
WHOLE~WORLD IN THE EVIL ONE LIES. AND~WE KNOW

ὅτι ὁ υἱὸς τοῦ θεοῦ ἥκει καὶ δέδωκεν ἡμῖν
THAT THE SON - OF GOD HAS COME AND HAS GIVEN US

διάνοιαν ἵνα γινώσκωμεν τὸν ἀληθινόν, καὶ ἐσμὲν ἐν
UNDERSTANDING THAT WE MAY KNOW THE TRUE ONE, AND WE ARE IN

τῷ ἀληθινῷ, ἐν τῷ υἱῷ αὐτοῦ Ἰησοῦ Χριστῷ.
THE TRUE ONE, [EVEN] IN THE SON OF HIM, JESUS CHRIST.

οὗτός ἐστιν ὁ ἀληθινὸς θεὸς καὶ ζωὴ αἰώνιος.
THIS ONE IS THE TRUE GOD AND ETERNAL~LIFE.

5.21 Τεκνία, φυλάξατε ἑαυτὰ ἀπὸ τῶν εἰδώλων.
LITTLE CHILDREN, KEEP YOURSELVES FROM - IDOLS.

life to such a one—to those whose sin is not mortal. There is sin that is mortal; I do not say that you should pray about that. [17]All wrongdoing is sin, but there is sin that is not mortal.

18 We know that those who are born of God do not sin, but the one who was born of God protects them, and the evil one does not touch them. [19]We know that we are God's children, and that the whole world lies under the power of the evil one. [20]And we know that the Son of God has come and has given us understanding so that we may know him who is true;[a] and we are in him who is true, in his Son Jesus Christ. He is the true God and eternal life.

21 Little children, keep yourselves from idols.[b]

[a] Other ancient authorities read *know the true God*
[b] Other ancient authorities add *Amen*

THE SECOND LETTER OF
JOHN

ΙΩΑΝΝΟΥ Β
OF JOHN   2

1.1 Ὁ πρεσβύτερος ἐκλεκτῇ   κυρίᾳ καὶ τοῖς τέκνοις
THE ELDER   TO [THE] CHOSEN LADY AND TO THE CHILDREN

αὐτῆς, οὓς ἐγὼ ἀγαπῶ ἐν ἀληθείᾳ, καὶ οὐκ ἐγὼ μόνος
OF HER, WHOM I   LOVE IN [THE] TRUTH, AND NOT   ONLY~I

ἀλλὰ καὶ πάντες οἱ   ἐγνωκότες τὴν ἀλήθειαν,
BUT   ALSO ALL   THE ONES HAVING KNOWN THE   TRUTH,

1.2 διὰ   τὴν ἀλήθειαν τὴν μένουσαν ἐν ἡμῖν καὶ
BECAUSE OF THE   TRUTH   -   ABIDING   IN US,   AND

μεθ᾽ ἡμῶν ἔσται εἰς τὸν αἰῶνα. **1.3** ἔσται μεθ᾽ ἡμῶν
WITH US   IT WILL BE INTO THE   AGE.   [4]WILL BE [5]WITH [6]US

χάρις ἔλεος εἰρήνη παρὰ θεοῦ πατρὸς καὶ παρὰ
[1]GRACE, [2]MERCY, [3]PEACE FROM   GOD   [THE] FATHER AND FROM

Ἰησοῦ Χριστοῦ τοῦ υἱοῦ τοῦ   πατρὸς ἐν ἀληθείᾳ καὶ
JESUS   CHRIST,   THE SON OF THE FATHER,   IN TRUTH   AND

ἀγάπῃ.
LOVE.

1.4 Ἐχάρην λίαν   ὅτι εὕρηκα ἐκ   τῶν τέκνων
I REJOICED EXCEEDINGLY THAT I HAVE FOUND [SOME] OF THE CHILDREN

σου περιπατοῦντας ἐν ἀληθείᾳ, καθὼς ἐντολὴν
OF YOU WALKING   IN [THE] TRUTH, AS   A COMMAND [TO DO SO]

ἐλάβομεν παρὰ τοῦ πατρός. **1.5** καὶ νῦν ἐρωτῶ σε,
WE RECEIVED FROM THE   FATHER.   AND NOW I ASK YOU,

κυρία, οὐχ ὡς ἐντολὴν καινὴν γράφων σοι ἀλλὰ
LADY,   NOT AS [3]COMMAND [2]A NEW   [1]WRITING [4]TO YOU BUT

ἣν   εἴχομεν ἀπ᾽ ἀρχῆς,   ἵνα ἀγαπῶμεν
[THAT] WHICH WE HAD   FROM [THE] BEGINNING, THAT WE SHOULD LOVE

ἀλλήλους. **1.6** καὶ αὕτη ἐστὶν ἡ ἀγάπη, ἵνα
ONE ANOTHER.   AND THIS   IS   -   LOVE,   THAT

περιπατῶμεν κατὰ   τὰς ἐντολὰς αὐτοῦ· αὕτη ἡ
WE SHOULD WALK ACCORDING TO THE COMMANDS OF HIM; THIS [2]THE

ἐντολή ἐστιν, καθὼς ἠκούσατε ἀπ᾽ ἀρχῆς,   ἵνα ἐν
[3]COMMAND [1]IS,   AS   YOU[o] HEARD FROM [THE] BEGINNING, THAT IN

αὐτῇ περιπατῆτε. **1.7** ὅτι   πολλοὶ πλάνοι ἐξῆλθον εἰς
IT   WE SHOULD WALK.   BECAUSE MANY   DECEIVERS WENT OUT INTO

τὸν κόσμον, οἱ   μὴ ὁμολογοῦντες Ἰησοῦν Χριστὸν
THE   WORLD, THE ONES NOT CONFESSING   JESUS   CHRIST

ἐρχόμενον ἐν σαρκί· οὗτός ἐστιν ὁ πλάνος καὶ ὁ
[AS] COMING IN [THE] FLESH; THIS ONE IS   THE DECEIVER AND THE

1 The elder to the elect lady and her children, whom I love in the truth, and not only I but also all who know the truth, [2]because of the truth that abides in us and will be with us forever:

3 Grace, mercy, and peace will be with us from God the Father and from[a] Jesus Christ, the Father's Son, in truth and love.

4 I was overjoyed to find some of your children walking in the truth, just as we have been commanded by the Father. [5]But now, dear lady, I ask you, not as though I were writing you a new commandment, but one we have had from the beginning, let us love one another. [6]And this is love, that we walk according to his commandments; this is the commandment just as you have heard it from the beginning—you must walk in it.

7 Many deceivers have gone out into the world, those who do not confess that Jesus Christ has come in the flesh; any such person is the deceiver and the

[a] Other ancient authorities add the Lord

antichrist! ⁸Be on your guard, so that you do not lose what we*ᵇ* have worked for, but may receive a full reward. ⁹Everyone who does not abide in the teaching of Christ, but goes beyond it, does not have God; whoever abides in the teaching has both the Father and the Son. ¹⁰Do not receive into the house or welcome anyone who comes to you and does not bring this teaching; ¹¹for to welcome is to participate in the evil deeds of such a person.

12 Although I have much to write to you, I would rather not use paper and ink; instead I hope to come to you and talk with you face to face, so that our joy may be complete.

13 The children of your elect sister send you their greetings.*ᶜ*

ᵇ Other ancient authorities read *you*
ᶜ Other ancient authorities add *Amen*

ἀντίχριστος.　**1.8** βλέπετε ἑαυτούς,　ἵνα μὴ ἀπολέσητε
ANTICHRIST.　　　　　WATCH [OUT]　[FOR] YOURSELVES,　LEST　　YOU° LOSE

ἃ ⌜εἰργασάμεθα⌝ ἀλλὰ μισθὸν πλήρη ἀπολάβητε.
WHAT　WE WORKED [FOR],　BUT　³REWARD　²A FULL　¹YOU° MAY RECEIVE.

1.9 πᾶς ὁ προάγων　καὶ μὴ μένων ἐν τῇ διδαχῇ
EVERYONE　GOING AHEAD(BEYOND)　AND　NOT　REMAINING　IN　THE　TEACHING

τοῦ Χριστοῦ θεὸν οὐκ ἔχει·　ὁ　μένων ἐν τῇ
-　OF CHRIST　²GOD　¹DOES NOT HAVE;　THE ONE REMAINING IN　THE

διδαχῇ, οὗτος καὶ τὸν πατέρα καὶ τὸν υἱὸν ἔχει.
TEACHING,　THIS ONE BOTH　THE　FATHER　AND　THE　SON　HAS.

1.10 εἴ τις　ἔρχεται πρὸς ὑμᾶς καὶ ταύτην τὴν
IF　ANYONE　COMES　TO　YOU°　AND　THIS　-

διδαχὴν οὐ φέρει,　μὴ λαμβάνετε αὐτὸν εἰς οἰκίαν
TEACHING　DOES NOT BRING,　DO NOT RECEIVE　HIM　INTO [YOUR°] HOUSE

καὶ χαίρειν αὐτῷ μὴ λέγετε·　**1.11** ὁ　λέγων γὰρ
AND　³"GREETINGS"　²TO HIM　¹DO NOT SAY;　　　²THE ONE ³SAYING　¹FOR

αὐτῷ χαίρειν κοινωνεῖ τοῖς ἔργοις αὐτοῦ τοῖς
TO HIM　"GREETINGS"　PARTICIPATES　IN THE　²WORKS　³OF HIM　-

πονηροῖς.
¹EVIL.

1.12 Πολλὰ ἔχων ὑμῖν γράφειν οὐκ ἐβουλήθην διὰ
HAVING~MANY THINGS　TO WRITE~TO YOU°　I WANTED~NOT [TO DO SO]　WITH

χάρτου καὶ μέλανος, ἀλλὰ ἐλπίζω γενέσθαι πρὸς
PAPER　AND　INK,　　BUT　I HOPE　TO BE　WITH

ὑμᾶς καὶ στόμα πρὸς στόμα λαλῆσαι, ἵνα ἡ χαρὰ
YOU°　AND　²MOUTH　³TO　⁴MOUTH　¹TO SPEAK,　THAT　THE JOY

ἡμῶν πεπληρωμένη ᾖ.　**1.13** Ἀσπάζεταί σε τὰ τέκνα
OF US　MAY BE FULL.　　　⁷GREETS　⁸YOU ¹THE ²CHILDREN

τῆς ἀδελφῆς σου τῆς ἐκλεκτῆς.
³OF THE ⁵SISTER　⁶OF YOU　-　⁴CHOSEN.

v. 8 text: (KJV) ASV RSVmg NASB NEB TEV NJB NRSV. var. εἰργασασθε (you° worked [for]): ASVmg RSV NASBmg NIV TEVmg NJBmg NRSVmg.

THE THIRD LETTER OF
JOHN

ΙΩΑΝΝΟΥ Γ
OF JOHN   3

1.1 Ὁ πρεσβύτερος Γαΐῳ τῷ ἀγαπητῷ, ὃν ἐγὼ
THE ELDER   TO GAIUS, THE BELOVED,   WHOM I

ἀγαπῶ ἐν ἀληθείᾳ.
LOVE IN [THE] TRUTH.

1.2 Ἀγαπητέ, περὶ   πάντων εὔχομαί σε εὐοδοῦσθαι
BELOVED,   CONCERNING ALL THINGS I WISH   YOU TO DO WELL

καὶ ὑγιαίνειν, καθὼς εὐοδοῦταί σου ἡ ψυχή.
AND TO BE IN HEALTH, EVEN AS ³DOES WELL ¹YOUR - ²SOUL.

1.3 ἐχάρην γὰρ λίαν   ἐρχομένων ἀδελφῶν καὶ
FOR~I REJOICED EXCEEDINGLY [AFTER THE] COMING OF [THE] BROTHERS AND

μαρτυρούντων σου τῇ   ἀληθείᾳ, καθὼς σὺ ἐν
GIVING TESTIMONY OF YOU [BEING] IN THE TRUTH, AS YOU IN

ἀληθείᾳ περιπατεῖς. **1.4** μειζοτέραν τούτων
[THE] TRUTH WALK.   ²GREATER   ⁴[THAN] THESE THINGS

οὐκ ἔχω χαράν, ἵνα ἀκούω τὰ ἐμὰ τέκνα ἐν τῇ
¹I HAVE~NO ³JOY,   THAT I HEAR [OF] - MY CHILDREN ²IN ³THE

ἀληθείᾳ περιπατοῦντα.
⁴TRUTH   ¹WALKING.

1.5 Ἀγαπητέ, πιστὸν ποιεῖς ὃ ἐὰν ἐργάσῃ εἰς
BELOVED,   YOU DO~A FAITHFUL THING WHENEVER YOU DO A WORK FOR

τοὺς ἀδελφοὺς καὶ τοῦτο ξένους, **1.6** οἳ
THE BROTHERS, ESPECIALLY [WHEN THEY ARE] STRANGERS,   WHO

ἐμαρτύρησάν σου τῇ ἀγάπῃ ἐνώπιον ἐκκλησίας,
GAVE TESTIMONY OF YOU - IN LOVE BEFORE [THE] CHURCH,

οὓς   καλῶς ποιήσεις προπέμψας   ἀξίως
[AS TO] WHOM YOU WILL DO~WELL   HAVING SENT ON [THEIR] WAY [IN A MANNER] WORTHY

τοῦ θεοῦ· **1.7** ὑπὲρ γὰρ τοῦ ὀνόματος ἐξῆλθον
-    OF GOD;   FOR~ON BEHALF OF THE NAME   THEY WENT FORTH

μηδὲν λαμβάνοντες ἀπὸ τῶν ἐθνικῶν. **1.8** ἡμεῖς οὖν
TAKING~NOTHING   FROM THE GENTILES.   WE   THEREFORE

ὀφείλομεν ὑπολαμβάνειν τοὺς τοιούτους, ἵνα
OUGHT   TO GIVE HOSPITALITY -   TO SUCH MEN, THAT

συνεργοὶ γινώμεθα τῇ   ἀληθείᾳ.
WE MAY BE~CO-WORKERS   WITH THE TRUTH.

1.9 Ἔγραψά τι   τῇ ἐκκλησίᾳ· ἀλλ’ ὁ
I WROTE SOMETHING TO THE CHURCH;   BUT THE ONE

φιλοπρωτεύων αὐτῶν Διοτρέφης οὐκ ἐπιδέχεται ἡμᾶς.
LOVING TO BE FIRST [AMONG] THEM, DIOTREPHES, DOES NOT RECEIVE US.

1 The elder to the beloved Gaius, whom I love in truth.

2 Beloved, I pray that all may go well with you and that you may be in good health, just as it is well with your soul. ³I was overjoyed when some of the friends[a] arrived and testified to your faithfulness to the truth, namely how you walk in the truth. ⁴I have no greater joy than this, to hear that my children are walking in the truth.

5 Beloved, you do faithfully whatever you do for the friends,[a] even though they are strangers to you; ⁶they have testified to your love before the church. You will do well to send them on in a manner worthy of God; ⁷for they began their journey for the sake of Christ,[b] accepting no support from non-believers.[c] ⁸Therefore we ought to support such people, so that we may become co-workers with the truth.

9 I have written something to the church; but Diotrephes, who likes to put himself first, does not acknowledge our authority.

[a] Gk brothers
[b] Gk for the sake of the name
[c] Gk the Gentiles

¹⁰So if I come, I will call attention to what he is doing in spreading false charges against us. And not content with those charges, he refuses to welcome the friends,^d and even prevents those who want to do so and expels them from the church.

11 Beloved, do not imitate what is evil but imitate what is good. Whoever does good is from God; whoever does evil has not seen God. ¹²Everyone has testified favorably about Demetrius, and so has the truth itself. We also testify for him,^e and you know that our testimony is true.

13 I have much to write to you, but I would rather not write with pen and ink; ¹⁴instead I hope to see you soon, and we will talk together face to face.

15 Peace to you. The friends send you their greetings. Greet the friends there, each by name.

^d Gk *brothers*
^e Gk lacks *for him.*

1.10 διὰ τοῦτο, ἐὰν ἔλθω, ὑπομνήσω αὐτοῦ τὰ ἔργα
THEREFORE,   IF(WHEN) I COME, I WILL REMEMBER HIS - WORKS

ἃ ποιεῖ λόγοις πονηροῖς φλυαρῶν ἡμᾶς, καὶ
WHICH HE DOES, WITH MALICIOUS~WORDS TALKING NONSENSE [ABOUT] US, AND

μὴ ἀρκούμενος ἐπὶ τούτοις οὔτε αὐτὸς ἐπιδέχεται
NOT BEING SATISFIED WITH THESE (ACTIONS), HE~NEITHER RECEIVES

τοὺς ἀδελφοὺς καὶ τοὺς βουλομένους κωλύει καὶ
THE BROTHERS AND THE ONES INTENDING [TO DO SO] HE PREVENTS AND

ἐκ τῆς ἐκκλησίας ἐκβάλλει.
²OUT OF ³THE ⁴CHURCH ¹HE PUTS [THEM].

1.11 Ἀγαπητέ, μὴ μιμοῦ τὸ κακὸν ἀλλὰ τὸ ἀγαθόν.
BELOVED, DO NOT IMITATE THE BAD BUT THE GOOD.

ὁ ἀγαθοποιῶν ἐκ τοῦ θεοῦ ἐστιν· ὁ κακοποιῶν
THE ONE DOING GOOD ²OF - ³GOD ¹IS; THE ONE DOING BAD

οὐχ ἑώρακεν τὸν θεόν. **1.12** Δημητρίῳ μεμαρτύρηται
HAS NOT SEEN - GOD. TO DEMETRIUS TESTIMONY HAS BEEN GIVEN

ὑπὸ πάντων καὶ ὑπὸ αὐτῆς τῆς ἀληθείας· καὶ ἡμεῖς
BY ALL AND BY ³ITSELF ¹THE ²TRUTH; ³ALSO ²WE

δὲ μαρτυροῦμεν, καὶ οἶδας ὅτι ἡ μαρτυρία ἡμῶν
¹AND GIVE TESTIMONY, AND YOU KNOW THAT THE TESTIMONY OF US

ἀληθής ἐστιν.
IS~TRUE.

1.13 Πολλὰ εἶχον γράψαι σοι ἀλλ' οὐ θέλω διὰ
I HAD~MANY THINGS TO WRITE TO YOU BUT I DO NOT WANT ³WITH

μέλανος καὶ καλάμου σοι γράφειν· **1.14** ἐλπίζω δὲ
⁴INK ⁵AND ⁶PEN ²TO YOU ¹TO WRITE; BUT~I AM HOPING

εὐθέως σε ἰδεῖν, καὶ στόμα πρὸς στόμα λαλήσομεν.
³IMMEDIATELY ²YOU ¹TO SEE, AND MOUTH TO MOUTH WE WILL SPEAK.

1.15 εἰρήνη σοι. ἀσπάζονταί σε οἱ φίλοι.
PEACE TO YOU. ³GREET ⁴YOU ¹THE(OUR) ²FRIENDS.

ἀσπάζου τοὺς φίλους κατ' ὄνομα.
GREET THE(OUR) FRIENDS NAME(PERSON) BY NAME(PERSON).

THE LETTER OF
JUDE

ΙΟΥΔΑ
OF JUDE

1.1 Ἰούδας Ἰησοῦ Χριστοῦ δοῦλος, ἀδελφὸς δὲ
JUDE, OF JESUS CHRIST A SLAVE, AND~BROTHER

Ἰακώβου, τοῖς ἐν θεῷ πατρὶ ἠγαπημένοις καὶ
OF JAMES, ¹TO THE ⁴IN ⁵GOD ⁶[THE] FATHER ³HAVING BEEN LOVED ⁷AND

Ἰησοῦ Χριστῷ τετηρημένοις κλητοῖς· **1.2** ἔλεος ὑμῖν
⁹IN JESUS ¹⁰CHRIST ⁸HAVING BEEN KEPT ²CALLED ONES: MERCY TO YOU°

καὶ εἰρήνη καὶ ἀγάπη πληθυνθείη.
AND PEACE AND LOVE MAY IT BE MULTIPLIED.

1.3 Ἀγαπητοί, πᾶσαν σπουδὴν ποιούμενος γράφειν
BELOVED, ²EXTREMELY ³EAGER ¹BEING TO WRITE

ὑμῖν περὶ τῆς κοινῆς ἡμῶν σωτηρίας ἀνάγκην ἔσχον
TO YOU° CONCERNING - OUR~COMMON SALVATION I FOUND [IT]~NECESSARY

γράψαι ὑμῖν παρακαλῶν ἐπαγωνίζεσθαι τῇ ἅπαξ
TO WRITE TO YOU° ENCOURAGING [YOU°] TO CONTEND FOR ¹THE ³ONCE FOR ALL

παραδοθείσῃ τοῖς ἁγίοις πίστει. **1.4** παρεισέδυσαν γάρ
⁴DELIVERED ⁵TO THE ⁶SAINTS ²FAITH. FOR~CAME IN STEALTHILY

τινες ἄνθρωποι, οἱ πάλαι προγεγραμμένοι εἰς
CERTAIN MEN, THE ONES OF OLD HAVING BEEN WRITTEN ABOUT FOR

τοῦτο τὸ κρίμα, ἀσεβεῖς, τὴν τοῦ θεοῦ ἡμῶν χάριτα
THIS - JUDGMENT, UNGODLY [ONES], ²THE ⁴OF THE ⁵GOD ⁶OF US ³GRACE

μετατιθέντες εἰς ἀσέλγειαν καὶ τὸν μόνον δεσπότην
¹PERVERTING INTO LICENTIOUSNESS AND THE ONLY MASTER

καὶ κύριον ἡμῶν Ἰησοῦν Χριστὸν ἀρνούμενοι.
AND LORD OF US, JESUS CHRIST, DENYING.

1.5 Ὑπομνῆσαι δὲ ὑμᾶς βούλομαι, εἰδότας [ὑμᾶς]
³TO REMIND ¹BUT ⁴YOU° ²I WANT, YOU°~HAVING KNOWN

πάντα ὅτι ⌜[ὁ] κύριος⌝ ἅπαξ λαὸν ἐκ
ALL [THESE] THINGS THAT THE LORD ²ONCE ⁴[THE] PEOPLE ⁵OUT OF

γῆς Αἰγύπτου σώσας τὸ δεύτερον τοὺς
⁶[THE] LAND ⁷OF EGYPT ¹HAVING ³DELIVERED, [IN] THE SECOND PLACE ²THE ONES

μὴ πιστεύσαντας ἀπώλεσεν, **1.6** ἀγγέλους τε τοὺς μὴ
³NOT ⁴HAVING BELIEVED ¹DESTROYED, AND~ANGELS - NOT

τηρήσαντας τὴν ἑαυτῶν ἀρχὴν ἀλλὰ ἀπολιπόντας τὸ
HAVING KEPT - THEIR OWN DOMAIN BUT HAVING LEFT THE[IR]

ἴδιον οἰκητήριον εἰς κρίσιν μεγάλης ἡμέρας
OWN HABITATION ⁶FOR ⁷[THE] JUDGMENT ⁸OF [THE] GREAT ⁹DAY

δεσμοῖς ἀϊδίοις ὑπὸ ζόφον τετήρηκεν,
³BONDS ²IN ETERNAL ⁴UNDER ⁵DARKNESS ¹HE HAS KEPT,

1 Jude,[a] a servant[b] of Jesus Christ and brother of James,

To those who are called, who are beloved[c] in[d] God the Father and kept safe for[d] Jesus Christ:

2 May mercy, peace, and love be yours in abundance.

3 Beloved, while eagerly preparing to write to you about the salvation we share, I find it necessary to write and appeal to you to contend for the faith that was once for all entrusted to the saints. [4]For certain intruders have stolen in among you, people who long ago were designated for this condemnation as ungodly, who pervert the grace of our God into licentiousness and deny our only Master and Lord, Jesus Christ.[e]

5 Now I desire to remind you, though you are fully informed, that the Lord, who once for all saved[f] a people out of the land of Egypt, afterward destroyed those who did not believe. [6]And the angels who did not keep their own position, but left their proper dwelling, he has kept in eternal chains in deepest darkness for the judgment of the great day.

[a] Gk *Judas*
[b] Gk *slave*
[c] Other ancient authorities read *sanctified*
[d] Or *by*
[e] Or *the only Master and our Lord Jesus Christ*
[f] Other ancient authorities read *though you were once for all fully informed, that Jesus* (or *Joshua*) *who saved*

v. 5 text: KJV ASV RSVmg NASB NIV NEB TEV NJB NRSV. var. Ιησους (Jesus): ASVmg RSVmg NASBmg NIVmg NEBmg TEVmg NJBmg NRSVmg. var. θεος (God): RSVmg.

7Likewise, Sodom and Gomorrah and the surrounding cities, which, in the same manner as they, indulged in sexual immorality and pursued unnatural lust,g serve as an example by undergoing a punishment of eternal fire.

8 Yet in the same way these dreamers also defile the flesh, reject authority, and slander the glorious ones.h 9But when the archangel Michael contended with the devil and disputed about the body of Moses, he did not dare to bring a condemnation of slanderi against him, but said, "The Lord rebuke you!" 10But these people slander whatever they do not understand, and they are destroyed by those things that, like irrational animals, they know by instinct. 11Woe to them! For they go the way of Cain, and abandon themselves to Balaam's error for the sake of gain, and perish in Korah's rebellion. 12These are blemishesj on your love-feasts, while they feast with you without fear, feeding themselves.k They are waterless clouds carried along by the winds; autumn trees without fruit, twice dead, uprooted; 13wild waves of the sea, casting up the foam of their own shame; wandering stars, for whom the deepest darkness has been reserved forever.

g Gk went after other flesh
h Or angels; Gk glories
i Or condemnation for blasphemy
j Or reefs
k Or without fear. They are shepherds who care only for themselves

---

1.7 ὡς Σόδομα καὶ Γόμορρα καὶ αἱ περὶ αὐτὰς πόλεις
AS SODOM AND GOMORRAH AND ¹THE ³AROUND ⁴THEM ²CITIES

τὸν ὅμοιον τρόπον τούτοις ἐκπορνεύσασαι
IN THE LIKE MANNER TO THESE [ANGELS] HAVING INDULGED IN FORNICATION

καὶ ἀπελθοῦσαι ὀπίσω σαρκὸς ἑτέρας, πρόκεινται
AND HAVING GONE AFTER DIFFERENT~FLESH, ARE SET FORTH

δεῖγμα πυρὸς αἰωνίου δίκην ὑπέχουσαι.
[AS] AN EXAMPLE, ⁴FIRE ³ETERNAL ²[THE] PENALTY ¹UNDERGOING.

1.8 Ὁμοίως μέντοι καὶ οὗτοι ἐνυπνιαζόμενοι σάρκα
LIKEWISE INDEED ALSO THESE DREAMING ONES ³[THE] FLESH

μὲν μιαίνουσιν κυριότητα δὲ ἀθετοῦσιν
¹ON THE ONE HAND ²DEFILE, ³LORDSHIP ¹ON THE OTHER ²REJECT,

δόξας δὲ βλασφημοῦσιν. **1.9** ὁ δὲ Μιχαὴλ ὁ
³GLORIOUS BEINGS ¹AND ²BLASPHEME. - BUT MICHAEL THE

ἀρχάγγελος, ὅτε τῷ διαβόλῳ διακρινόμενος
ARCHANGEL, WHEN ²WITH THE ³DEVIL ¹DISPUTING

διελέγετο περὶ τοῦ Μωϋσέως σώματος, οὐκ ἐτόλμησεν
HE WAS ARGUING ABOUT - MOSES' BODY, DID NOT DARE

κρίσιν ἐπενεγκεῖν βλασφημίας ἀλλὰ εἶπεν,
³ACCUSATION ¹TO BRING ²A SLANDEROUS BUT SAID,

Ἐπιτιμήσαι σοι κύριος. **1.10** οὗτοι δὲ ὅσα μὲν
²REBUKE ³YOU ¹[THE] LORD. BUT~THESE ONES WHAT THINGS -

οὐκ οἴδασιν βλασφημοῦσιν, ὅσα δὲ φυσικῶς ὡς τὰ
THEY DO NOT KNOW THEY BLASPHEME, BUT~WHAT ²NATURALLY ³[IT IS] AS -

ἄλογα ζῷα ἐπίστανται, ἐν τούτοις φθείρονται.
⁴UNREASONING ⁵ANIMALS ¹THEY UNDERSTAND, IN THESE THINGS THEY ARE CORRUPTED.

1.11 οὐαὶ αὐτοῖς, ὅτι τῇ ὁδῷ τοῦ Κάϊν
WOE TO THEM, BECAUSE IN THE WAY - OF CAIN

ἐπορεύθησαν καὶ τῇ πλάνῃ τοῦ Βαλαὰμ μισθοῦ
THEY WENT AND ²[IN]TO THE ³ERROR - ⁴OF BALAAM ⁵OF(FOR) PAY

ἐξεχύθησαν καὶ τῇ ἀντιλογίᾳ τοῦ Κόρε ἀπώλοντο.
¹RUSHED AND ²IN THE ³REBELLION - ⁴OF KORAH ¹PERISHED.

1.12 οὗτοί εἰσιν οἱ ἐν ταῖς ἀγάπαις ὑμῶν σπιλάδες
THESE ONES ARE ¹THE ³IN ⁴THE ⁵LOVEFEASTS ⁶OF YOU° ²REEFS(SPOTS)

συνευωχούμενοι ἀφόβως, ἑαυτοὺς ποιμαίνοντες,
FEASTING TOGETHER WITH [YOU°] WITHOUT FEAR, TENDING TO~THEMSELVES,

νεφέλαι ἄνυδροι ὑπὸ ἀνέμων παραφερόμεναι,
WATERLESS~CLOUDS BY WINDS BEING CARRIED ABOUT,

δένδρα φθινοπωρινὰ ἄκαρπα δὶς ἀποθανόντα
LATE AUTUMN~TREES, WITHOUT FRUIT, HAVING DIED~TWICE,

ἐκριζωθέντα, **1.13** κύματα ἄγρια θαλάσσης ἐπαφρίζοντα
HAVING BEEN UPROOTED, WILD~WAVES OF [THE] SEA FOAMING OUT

τὰς ἑαυτῶν αἰσχύνας, ἀστέρες πλανῆται οἷς ὁ
- THEIR OWN SHAME[FUL ACTIONS], WANDERING~STARS, FOR WHOM THE

ζόφος τοῦ σκότους εἰς αἰῶνα τετήρηται.
BLACKNESS OF THE DARKNESS INTO [THE] AGE HAS BEEN KEPT.

1.14 Προεφήτευσεν δὲ καὶ τούτοις ἕβδομος ἀπὸ
⁶PROPHESIED ¹AND ⁷ALSO ⁸TO THESE ONES ³[THE] SEVENTH ⁴FROM

Ἀδὰμ Ἐνὼχ λέγων, Ἰδοὺ ἦλθεν κύριος ἐν
⁵ADAM ²ENOCH ⁹SAYING, BEHOLD, CAME [THE] LORD AMIDST(WITH)

ἁγίαις μυριάσιν αὐτοῦ **1.15** ποιῆσαι κρίσιν κατὰ
³HOLY ONES ¹MYRIADS ²OF HIS, TO MAKE JUDGMENT AGAINST

πάντων καὶ ἐλέγξαι πᾶσαν ψυχὴν περὶ πάντων τῶν
ALL AND TO CONVICT EVERY SOUL CONCERNING ALL THE

ἔργων ἀσεβείας αὐτῶν ὧν ἠσέβησαν καὶ περὶ
WORKS OF UNGODLINESS OF THEM WHICH THEY IMPIOUSLY DID AND CONCERNING

πάντων τῶν σκληρῶν ὧν ἐλάλησαν κατ' αὐτοῦ
ALL THE HARSH THINGS WHICH ³SPOKE ⁴AGAINST ⁵HIM

ἁμαρτωλοὶ ἀσεβεῖς. **1.16** Οὗτοί εἰσιν γογγυσταί
²SINNERS ¹UNGODLY. THESE ONES ARE GRUMBLERS,

μεμψίμοιροι κατὰ τὰς ἐπιθυμίας ἑαυτῶν
COMPLAINERS, ACCORDING TO - THEIR OWN~LUSTS

πορευόμενοι, καὶ τὸ στόμα αὐτῶν λαλεῖ ὑπέρογκα,
WALKING, AND THE MOUTH OF THEM SPEAKS HAUGHTY [WORDS],

θαυμάζοντες πρόσωπα ὠφελείας χάριν.
ADMIRING PERSONS FOR THE SAKE OF~ADVANTAGE.

1.17 Ὑμεῖς δέ, ἀγαπητοί, μνήσθητε τῶν ῥημάτων τῶν
BUT~YOU°, BELOVED, REMEMBER THE WORDS -

προειρημένων ὑπὸ τῶν ἀποστόλων τοῦ κυρίου
HAVING BEEN PREVIOUSLY SPOKEN BY THE APOSTLES OF THE LORD

ἡμῶν Ἰησοῦ Χριστοῦ **1.18** ὅτι ἔλεγον ὑμῖν [ὅτι]
OF US, JESUS CHRIST, THAT THEY WERE TELLING YOU°, -

Ἐπ' ἐσχάτου [τοῦ] χρόνου ἔσονται ἐμπαῖκται κατὰ
AT(IN) [THE] LAST OF THE TIME WILL BE MOCKERS ²ACCORDING TO

τὰς ἑαυτῶν ἐπιθυμίας πορευόμενοι τῶν ἀσεβειῶν.
- ³THEIR OWN ⁴LUSTS ¹WALKING - ⁵OF(FOR) UNGODLY THINGS.

1.19 Οὗτοί εἰσιν οἱ ἀποδιορίζοντες, ψυχικοί,
THESE ARE THE ONES CREATING DIVISIONS, NATURAL [MEN],

πνεῦμα μὴ ἔχοντες. **1.20** ὑμεῖς δέ, ἀγαπητοί,
³[THE] SPIRIT ¹NOT ²HAVING. BUT~YOU°, BELOVED,

ἐποικοδομοῦντες ἑαυτοὺς τῇ ἁγιωτάτῃ ὑμῶν πίστει, ἐν
BUILDING UP YOURSELVES - IN YOUR°~MOST HOLY FAITH, IN

πνεύματι ἁγίῳ προσευχόμενοι, **1.21** ἑαυτοὺς ἐν ἀγάπῃ
[THE] HOLY~SPIRIT PRAYING, ²YOURSELVES ³IN ⁴[THE] LOVE

θεοῦ τηρήσατε προσδεχόμενοι τὸ ἔλεος τοῦ κυρίου
⁵OF GOD ¹KEEP, ANTICIPATING THE MERCY OF THE LORD

ἡμῶν Ἰησοῦ Χριστοῦ εἰς ζωὴν αἰώνιον. ⌐**1.22** καὶ οὓς
OF US, JESUS CHRIST, FOR LIFE ETERNAL. AND ²SOME

μὲν ἐλεᾶτε διακρινομένους, **1.23** οὓς δὲ σῴζετε
- ¹HAVE MERCY [ON] ³[WHO ARE] WAVERING, AND~OTHERS SAVE

ἐκ πυρὸς ἁρπάζοντες, οὓς δὲ ἐλεᾶτε ἐν φόβῳ
²OUT OF ³[THE] FIRE ¹SNATCHING [THEM], ³OTHERS ¹AND ²HAVE MERCY [ON] WITH FEAR,

See textual note on vv. 22-23 on following page.

14 It was also about these that Enoch, in the seventh generation from Adam, prophesied, saying, "See, the Lord is coming[l] with ten thousands of his holy ones, 15to execute judgment on all, and to convict everyone of all the deeds of ungodliness that they have committed in such an ungodly way, and of all the harsh things that ungodly sinners have spoken against him." 16These are grumblers and malcontents; they indulge their own lusts; they are bombastic in speech, flattering people to their own advantage.

17 But you, beloved, must remember the predictions of the apostles of our Lord Jesus Christ; 18for they said to you, "In the last time there will be scoffers, indulging their own ungodly lusts." 19It is these worldly people, devoid of the Spirit, who are causing divisions. 20But you, beloved, build yourselves up on your most holy faith; pray in the Holy Spirit; 21keep yourselves in the love of God; look forward to the mercy of our Lord Jesus Christ that leads to[m] eternal life. 22And have mercy on some who are wavering; 23save others by snatching them out of the fire; and have mercy on still others with fear,

[l] Gk *came*
[m] Gk *Christ to*

hating even the tunic defiled by their bodies.[n]

24 Now to him who is able to keep you from falling, and to make you stand without blemish in the presence of his glory with rejoicing, [25]to the only God our Savior, through Jesus Christ our Lord, be glory, majesty, power, and authority, before all time and now and forever. Amen.

[n] Gk *by the flesh.* The Greek text of verses 22-23 is uncertain at several points

μισοῦντες καὶ τὸν ἀπὸ τῆς σαρκὸς ἐσπιλωμένον
HATING   EVEN   [1]THE [4]FROM(BY) [5]THE [6]FLESH [3]HAVING BEEN STAINED

χιτῶνα. ⌐
[2]GARMENT.

1.24 Τῷ δὲ   δυναμένῳ φυλάξαι ὑμᾶς ἀπταίστους
NOW~TO THE ONE BEING ABLE TO GUARD YOU° WITHOUT STUMBLING

καὶ στῆσαι κατενώπιον τῆς δόξης αὐτοῦ ἀμώμους ἐν
AND TO SET [YOU°] BEFORE   THE GLORY OF HIM BLAMELESS, WITH

ἀγαλλιάσει, **1.25** μόνῳ   θεῷ σωτῆρι ἡμῶν διὰ
EXULTATION,   TO [THE] ONLY GOD [THE] SAVIOR OF US THROUGH

Ἰησοῦ Χριστοῦ τοῦ κυρίου ἡμῶν δόξα   μεγαλωσύνη
JESUS   CHRIST   THE LORD OF US [BE] GLORY, MAJESTY,

κράτος καὶ ἐξουσία πρὸ παντὸς τοῦ αἰῶνος καὶ νῦν
DOMINION, AND AUTHORITY BEFORE ALL   THE AGE   AND NOW

καὶ εἰς πάντας τοὺς αἰῶνας, ἀμήν.
AND INTO ALL   THE AGES,   AMEN.

vv. 22-23 There are several textual variants in these verses. Some MSS indicate three classes of people, as follows:

(a) and show mercy to some who have doubts [or, who dispute]; and save some, snatching them from fire and to some show mercy with fear: ASV NASB NIV NEBmg TEV NJB NRSV. (b) and reprove some who have doubts [or, who dispute]; and save some, snatching them from fire; and to some show mercy with fear: RSV.

Some MSS indicate two classes of people, as follows:

(a) and show mercy to some who have doubts--save them by snatching them from fire; and to some show mercy with fear: (KJV) NEB NJBmg. (b) and reprove some who have doubts [or, who dispute], and in fear save some from fire: none. (c) and some snatch from fire, and show mercy with fear to others who have doubts: none.

THE
REVELATION
TO JOHN

ΑΠΟΚΑΛΥΨΙΣ ΙΩΑΝΝΟΥ
[THE] REVELATION   OF JOHN

1.1 Ἀποκάλυψις Ἰησοῦ Χριστοῦ ἣν ἔδωκεν αὐτῷ
[THE] REVELATION   OF JESUS   CHRIST   WHICH ²GAVE   ³TO HIM

ὁ θεὸς δεῖξαι τοῖς δούλοις αὐτοῦ ἃ   δεῖ
- ¹GOD TO SHOW TO THE SLAVES OF HIM THE THINGS WHICH HAVE

γενέσθαι ἐν τάχει, καὶ ἐσήμανεν ἀποστείλας διὰ
TO HAPPEN WITH SPEED, AND HE SIGNIFIED [IT] HAVING SENT [IT] THROUGH

τοῦ ἀγγέλου αὐτοῦ τῷ δούλῳ αὐτοῦ Ἰωάννῃ, **1.2** ὃς
THE ANGEL OF HIM TO THE SLAVE OF HIM,   JOHN,   WHO

ἐμαρτύρησεν τὸν λόγον τοῦ θεοῦ καὶ τὴν μαρτυρίαν
GAVE TESTIMONY TO THE WORD - OF GOD AND THE TESTIMONY

Ἰησοῦ Χριστοῦ ὅσα   εἶδεν. **1.3** μακάριος ὁ
OF JESUS CHRIST [OF] WHATSOEVER HE SAW. BLESSED   [IS] THE ONE

ἀναγινώσκων καὶ οἱ   ἀκούοντες τοὺς λόγους τῆς
READING   AND THE ONES HEARING   THE WORDS OF THE(THIS)

προφητείας καὶ τηροῦντες τὰ   ἐν αὐτῇ
PROPHECY   AND KEEPING   THE THINGS ²IN ³IT

γεγραμμένα, ὁ γὰρ καιρὸς ἐγγύς.
¹HAVING BEEN WRITTEN, FOR~THE TIME [IS] NEAR.

1.4 Ἰωάννης ταῖς ἑπτὰ ἐκκλησίαις ταῖς ἐν τῇ
JOHN   TO THE SEVEN CHURCHES   -   IN -

Ἀσίᾳ· χάρις ὑμῖν καὶ εἰρήνη ἀπὸ ὁ   ὢν καὶ
ASIA: GRACE TO YOU° AND PEACE FROM THE ONE BEING AND

ὁ   ἦν   καὶ ὁ   ἐρχόμενος καὶ ἀπὸ τῶν ἑπτὰ
THE ONE [WHO] WAS AND THE ONE COMING,   AND FROM THE SEVEN

πνευμάτων ἃ   ἐνώπιον τοῦ θρόνου αὐτοῦ **1.5** καὶ ἀπὸ
SPIRITS   WHICH [ARE] BEFORE THE THRONE OF HIM,   AND FROM

Ἰησοῦ Χριστοῦ, ὁ μάρτυς, ὁ πιστός, ὁ πρωτότοκος
JESUS   CHRIST,   THE ²WITNESS - ¹FAITHFUL, THE FIRSTBORN

τῶν νεκρῶν καὶ ὁ ἄρχων τῶν βασιλέων τῆς γῆς.
OF THE DEAD   AND THE RULER OF THE KINGS   OF THE EARTH.

Τῷ   ἀγαπῶντι ἡμᾶς καὶ ⌐λύσαντι⌐ ἡμᾶς ἐκ τῶν
TO THE ONE LOVING   US   AND HAVING FREED US   FROM THE

ἁμαρτιῶν ἡμῶν ἐν τῷ αἵματι αὐτοῦ, **1.6** καὶ ἐποίησεν
SINS   OF US BY THE BLOOD OF HIM,   AND MADE

ἡμᾶς βασιλείαν, ἱερεῖς τῷ θεῷ καὶ πατρὶ αὐτοῦ,
US   A KINGDOM,   PRIESTS - TO ²GOD ³AND ⁴FATHER ¹HIS,

The revelation of Jesus Christ, which God gave him to show his servants[a] what must soon take place; he made[b] it known by sending his angel to his servant[c] John, [2]who testified to the word of God and to the testimony of Jesus Christ, even to all that he saw.

3 Blessed is the one who reads aloud the words of the prophecy, and blessed are those who hear and who keep what is written in it; for the time is near.

4 John to the seven churches that are in Asia:

Grace to you and peace from him who is and who was and who is to come, and from the seven spirits who are before his throne, [5]and from Jesus Christ, the faithful witness, the first-born of the dead, and the ruler of the kings of the earth.

To him who loves us and freed[d] us from our sins by his blood, [6]and made[b] us to be a kingdom, priests serving[e] his God and Father,

[a] Gk slaves
[b] Gk and he made
[c] Gk slave
[d] Other ancient authorities read washed
[e] Gk priests to

1:5 text: ASV RSV NASB NIV NEB TEV NJBmg NRSV.   var. λουσαντι (wash): KJV ASVmg NJB NRSVmg.

to him be glory and dominion forever and ever. Amen.
⁷ Look! He is coming with
    the clouds;
    every eye will see him,
    even those who pierced
        him;
    and on his account all
        the tribes of the
        earth will wail.
So it is to be. Amen.
    8 "I am the Alpha and the
Omega," says the Lord God,
who is and who was and
who is to come, the
Almighty.
    9 I, John, your brother
who share with you in Jesus
the persecution and the
kingdom and the patient
endurance, was on the island
called Patmos because of
the word of God and the
testimony of Jesus.ᶠ ¹⁰I was
in the spiritᵍ on the Lord's
day, and I heard behind me a
loud voice like a trumpet
¹¹saying, "Write in a book
what you see and send it
to the seven churches, to
Ephesus, to Smyrna, to
Pergamum, to Thyatira, to
Sardis, to Philadelphia, and
to Laodicea."
    12 Then I turned to see
whose voice it was that
spoke to me, and on turn-
ing I saw seven golden
lampstands, ¹³and in the
midst of the lampstands
I saw one like the Son

ᶠ Or testimony to Jesus
ᵍ Or in the Spirit

αὐτῷ   ἡ   δόξα   καὶ   τὸ   κράτος   εἰς   τοὺς   αἰῶνας   [τῶν
TO HIM [BE] THE GLORY AND THE DOMINION INTO THE   AGE   OF THE

αἰώνων]·   ἀμήν.
AGES;   AMEN.

1.7 Ἰδοὺ   ἔρχεται   μετὰ   τῶν   νεφελῶν,
      LOOK,   HE COMES   WITH   THE   CLOUDS,

    καὶ   ὄψεται   αὐτὸν   πᾶς   ὀφθαλμὸς
    AND   ³WILL SEE   ⁴HIM   ¹EVERY ²EYE

καὶ   οἵτινες   αὐτὸν   ἐξεκέντησαν,
AND   THE ONES WHO PIERCED~HIM,

    καὶ   κόψονται   ἐπ'   αὐτὸν   πᾶσαι   αἱ
    AND   ⁶WILL MOURN ⁷FOR   ⁸HIM   ¹ALL   ²THE

        φυλαὶ   τῆς   γῆς.
        ³TRIBES   ⁴OF THE ⁵EARTH.

ναί,   ἀμήν.
YES,   AMEN.

1.8 Ἐγώ   εἰμι   τὸ   Ἄλφα   καὶ   τὸ   Ὦ,   λέγει   κύριος   ὁ
      I   AM   THE   ALPHA   AND THE OMEGA, SAYS   [THE] LORD -

θεός,   ὁ   ὢν   καὶ   ὁ   ἦν   καὶ   ὁ   ἐρχόμενος,
GOD,   THE ONE BEING AND THE ONE [WHO] WAS AND THE ONE COMING,

ὁ   παντοκράτωρ.
THE ALMIGHTY.

1.9 Ἐγὼ   Ἰωάννης,   ὁ   ἀδελφὸς   ὑμῶν   καὶ   συγκοινωνὸς
      I   JOHN,   THE BROTHER   OF YOU° AND   PARTNER

ἐν   τῇ   θλίψει   καὶ   βασιλείᾳ   καὶ   ὑπομονῇ   ἐν   Ἰησοῦ,
IN   THE AFFLICTION AND KINGDOM   AND ENDURANCE IN   JESUS,

ἐγενόμην   ἐν   τῇ   νήσῳ τῇ   καλουμένῃ   Πάτμῳ   διὰ
WAS   IN(ON) THE ISLAND - BEING CALLED   PATMOS   BECAUSE OF

τὸν   λόγον   τοῦ   θεοῦ   καὶ   τὴν   μαρτυρίαν   Ἰησοῦ.
THE   WORD   -   OF GOD AND   THE   TESTIMONY   OF(FOR) JESUS.

1.10 ἐγενόμην   ἐν   πνεύματι   ἐν   τῇ   κυριακῇ   ἡμέρᾳ   καὶ
        I WAS   IN   SPIRIT   IN(ON) THE LORD'S   DAY   AND

ἤκουσα   ὀπίσω   μου   φωνὴν   μεγάλην   ὡς   σάλπιγγος
I HEARD   BEHIND   ME   A GREAT~SOUND   AS   OF A TRUMPET

1.11 λεγούσης,   Ὃ   βλέπεις   γράψον   εἰς   βιβλίον   καὶ
        SAYING,   WHAT YOU SEE   WRITE   IN   A BOOK   AND

πέμψον   ταῖς   ἑπτὰ   ἐκκλησίαις,   εἰς   Ἔφεσον   καὶ   εἰς
SEND [IT] TO THE SEVEN   CHURCHES,   TO   EPHESUS   AND   TO

Σμύρναν   καὶ   εἰς   Πέργαμον   καὶ   εἰς   Θυάτειρα   καὶ   εἰς
SMYRNA   AND   TO   PERGAMUM   AND   TO   THYATIRA   AND   TO

Σάρδεις   καὶ   εἰς   Φιλαδέλφειαν   καὶ   εἰς   Λαοδίκειαν.
SARDIS   AND   TO   PHILADELPHIA   AND   TO   LAODICEA.

1.12 Καὶ   ἐπέστρεψα   βλέπειν   τὴν   φωνὴν   ἥτις   ἐλάλει
        AND   I TURNED   TO SEE   THE   VOICE   WHICH WAS SPEAKING

μετ'   ἐμοῦ,   καὶ   ἐπιστρέψας   εἶδον   ἑπτὰ   λυχνίας   χρυσᾶς
WITH   ME,   AND   HAVING TURNED I SAW   SEVEN   GOLDEN~LAMPSTANDS,

1.13 καὶ   ἐν   μέσῳ   τῶν   λυχνιῶν   ὅμοιον   υἱὸν
        AND   IN   [THE] MIDST OF THE LAMPSTANDS [ONE] LIKE [THE] SON

ἀνθρώπου ἐνδεδυμένον   ποδήρη   καὶ
OF MAN,   HAVING BEEN CLOTHED IN [A GARMENT]   [REACHING]TO THE FEET   AND

περιεζωσμένον   πρὸς τοῖς μαστοῖς ζώνην χρυσᾶν.
HAVING BEEN WRAPPED AROUND   AT   THE   BREASTS   WITH A GOLDEN~SASH.

1.14 ἡ δὲ   κεφαλὴ αὐτοῦ καὶ αἱ τρίχες λευκαὶ   ὡς
      AND~THE HEAD   OF HIM AND THE HAIRS [WERE] WHITE LIKE

ἔριον λευκὸν ὡς χιὼν καὶ οἱ ὀφθαλμοὶ αὐτοῦ ὡς
WHITE~WOOL,   LIKE SNOW, AND THE EYES   OF HIM LIKE

φλὸξ πυρὸς **1.15** καὶ οἱ   πόδες   αὐτοῦ ὅμοιοι
A FLAME OF FIRE,   AND THE FEET   OF HIM LIKE

χαλκολιβάνῳ ὡς ἐν καμίνῳ πεπυρωμένης   καὶ ἡ
BURNISHED BRONZE AS IF ²IN ³A FURNACE ¹HAVING BEEN MADE TO GLOW, AND THE

φωνὴ αὐτοῦ ὡς φωνὴ   ὑδάτων πολλῶν, **1.16** καὶ ἔχων
VOICE OF HIM AS   [THE] SOUND OF MANY~WATERS,   AND HAVING

ἐν τῇ δεξιᾷ χειρὶ αὐτοῦ ἀστέρας ἑπτὰ καὶ ἐκ   τοῦ
IN THE RIGHT HAND OF HIM SEVEN~STARS AND OUT OF THE

στόματος αὐτοῦ ῥομφαία δίστομος ὀξεῖα ἐκπορευομένη
MOUTH   OF HIM A ³SWORD ²TWO-EDGED ¹SHARP GOING FORTH

καὶ ἡ ὄψις αὐτοῦ ὡς ὁ ἥλιος φαίνει ἐν τῇ
AND THE FACE OF HIM LIKE THE SUN   SHINING IN   -

δυνάμει αὐτοῦ.
ITS~POWER.

1.17 Καὶ ὅτε εἶδον αὐτόν, ἔπεσα πρὸς τοὺς πόδας
      AND WHEN I SAW HIM,   I FELL   AT   THE   FEET

αὐτοῦ ὡς   νεκρός, καὶ ἔθηκεν τὴν δεξιὰν   αὐτοῦ
OF HIM AS [THOUGH] DEAD,   AND HE PLACED THE RIGHT [HAND] OF HIM

ἐπ' ἐμὲ λέγων, Μὴ φοβοῦ· ἐγώ εἰμι ὁ πρῶτος καὶ
UPON ME, SAYING, DO NOT FEAR;   I   AM   THE FIRST   AND

ὁ ἔσχατος **1.18** καὶ ὁ ζῶν,   καὶ ἐγενόμην νεκρὸς
THE LAST   AND THE LIVING ONE, AND I BECAME   DEAD

καὶ ἰδοὺ ζῶν εἰμι εἰς τοὺς αἰῶνας τῶν αἰώνων καὶ
AND BEHOLD I AM~LIVING INTO THE AGES   OF THE AGES   AND

ἔχω τὰς κλεῖς τοῦ θανάτου καὶ τοῦ ᾅδου.
I HAVE THE KEYS   -   OF DEATH AND   -   OF HADES.

1.19 γράψον οὖν   ἃ   εἶδες καὶ ἃ   εἰσὶν
      WRITE THEREFORE THE THINGS YOU SAW AND THE THINGS [WHICH] ARE

καὶ ἃ   μέλλει γενέσθαι μετὰ ταῦτα.
AND THE THINGS [WHICH] ARE ABOUT TO HAPPEN AFTER THESE THINGS.

1.20 τὸ μυστήριον τῶν ἑπτὰ ἀστέρων οὓς εἶδες ἐπὶ
      THE MYSTERY   OF THE SEVEN STARS   WHICH YOU SAW ON(IN)

τῆς δεξιᾶς   μου καὶ τὰς ἑπτὰ λυχνίας τὰς χρυσᾶς·
THE RIGHT [HAND] OF ME AND THE SEVEN ²LAMPSTANDS - ¹GOLDEN:

οἱ ἑπτὰ ἀστέρες ἄγγελοι   τῶν ἑπτὰ ἐκκλησιῶν
THE SEVEN STARS ²ANGELS(MESSENGERS) ³OF(FOR) THE ⁴CHURCHES

εἰσιν καὶ αἱ λυχνίαι αἱ ἑπτὰ ἑπτὰ ἐκκλησίαι εἰσίν.
¹ARE   AND THE ²LAMPSTANDS - ¹SEVEN ⁴SEVEN ⁵CHURCHES   ³ARE.

of Man, clothed with a long robe and with a golden sash across his chest. [14]His head and his hair were white as white wool, white as snow; his eyes were like a flame of fire, [15]his feet were like burnished bronze, refined as in a furnace, and his voice was like the sound of many waters. [16]In his right hand he held seven stars, and from his mouth came a sharp, two-edged sword, and his face was like the sun shining with full force.

[17]When I saw him, I fell at his feet as though dead. But he placed his right hand on me, saying, "Do not be afraid; I am the first and the last, [18]and the living one. I was dead, and see, I am alive forever and ever; and I have the keys of Death and of Hades. [19]Now write what you have seen, what is, and what is to take place after this. [20]As for the mystery of the seven stars that you saw in my right hand, and the seven golden lampstands: the seven stars are the angels of the seven churches, and the seven lampstands are the seven churches.

CHAPTER 2

"To the angel of the church in Ephesus write: These are the words of him who holds the seven stars in his right hand, who walks among the seven golden lampstands:

2 "I know your works, your toil and your patient endurance. I know that you cannot tolerate evildoers; you have tested those who claim to be apostles but are not, and have found them to be false. [3]I also know that you are enduring patiently and bearing up for the sake of my name, and that you have not grown weary. [4]But I have this against you, that you have abandoned the love you had at first. [5]Remember then from what you have fallen; repent, and do the works you did at first. If not, I will come to you and remove your lampstand from its place, unless you repent. [6]Yet this is to your credit: you hate the works of the Nicolaitans, which I also hate. [7]Let anyone who has an ear listen to what the Spirit is saying to the churches. To everyone who conquers, I will give permission to eat from the tree of life that is in the paradise of God.

8 "And to the angel of the church in Smyrna write: These are the words of the first and the last, who was dead and came to life:

9 "I know your affliction

2.1 Τῷ   ἀγγέλῳ τῆς   ἐν Ἐφέσῳ ἐκκλησίας γράψον·
TO THE ANGEL   OF THE [2]IN [3]EPHESUS [1]CHURCH   WRITE:

Τάδε   λέγει ὁ   κρατῶν τοὺς ἑπτὰ ἀστέρας ἐν τῇ
THESE THINGS SAYS   THE ONE HOLDING THE SEVEN STARS   IN THE

δεξιᾷ   αὐτοῦ, ὁ   περιπατῶν ἐν μέσῳ   τῶν ἑπτὰ
RIGHT [HAND] OF HIM, THE ONE WALKING   IN [THE] MIDST OF THE SEVEN

λυχνιῶν τῶν χρυσῶν· **2.2** Οἶδα τὰ ἔργα σου καὶ τὸν
[2]LAMPSTANDS -   [1]GOLDEN;   I KNOW THE WORKS OF YOU AND THE

κόπον καὶ τὴν ὑπομονήν σου καὶ ὅτι οὐ δύνῃ
LABOR AND THE ENDURANCE OF YOU AND THAT YOU CANNOT

βαστάσαι κακούς, καὶ ἐπείρασας τοὺς   λέγοντας
BEAR   EVIL MEN, AND TESTED   THE ONES CALLING

ἑαυτοὺς ἀποστόλους καὶ οὐκ εἰσὶν καὶ εὗρες αὐτοὺς
THEMSELVES APOSTLES   AND ARE~NOT,   AND FOUND THEM

ψευδεῖς, **2.3** καὶ ὑπομονὴν ἔχεις καὶ ἐβάστασας διὰ
LIARS,   AND YOU HAVE~ENDURANCE, AND PERSEVERED BECAUSE OF

τὸ ὄνομά μου καὶ οὐ κεκοπίακες. **2.4** ἀλλὰ ἔχω
THE NAME   OF ME AND HAVE NOT BECOME WEARY. BUT   I HAVE

κατὰ   σοῦ ὅτι τὴν ἀγάπην σου τὴν πρώτην
[THIS] AGAINST YOU, THAT - [3]LOVE   [1]YOUR - [2]FIRST

ἀφῆκες.   **2.5** μνημόνευε οὖν   πόθεν   πέπτωκας
YOU ABANDONED.   REMEMBER THEREFORE FROM WHERE YOU HAVE FALLEN

καὶ μετανόησον καὶ τὰ πρῶτα ἔργα ποίησον· εἰ δὲ
AND REPENT   AND THE FIRST WORKS DO;   BUT~IF

μή, ἔρχομαί σοι καὶ κινήσω τὴν λυχνίαν σου ἐκ
NOT, I AM COMING TO YOU AND I WILL REMOVE THE LAMPSTAND OF YOU FROM

τοῦ τόπου αὐτῆς, ἐὰν μὴ μετανοήσῃς. **2.6** ἀλλὰ τοῦτο
THE PLACE OF IT,   UNLESS   YOU REPENT.   BUT   THIS

ἔχεις, ὅτι μισεῖς τὰ ἔργα τῶν Νικολαϊτῶν ἃ   κἀγὼ
YOU HAVE, THAT YOU HATE THE WORKS OF THE NICOLAITANS, WHICH ALSO

μισῶ. **2.7** ὁ   ἔχων οὓς ἀκουσάτω τί   τὸ πνεῦμα
I HATE.   THE ONE HAVING AN EAR LET HIM HEAR WHAT THE SPIRIT

λέγει ταῖς ἐκκλησίαις. τῷ   νικῶντι δώσω αὐτῷ
SAYS TO THE CHURCHES.   TO THE ONE OVERCOMING I WILL GIVE TO HIM

φαγεῖν ἐκ τοῦ ξύλου τῆς ζωῆς, ὁ   ἐστιν ἐν τῷ
TO EAT OF THE TREE   - OF LIFE, WHICH IS   IN THE

παραδείσῳ τοῦ θεοῦ.
PARADISE   - OF GOD.

2.8 Καὶ τῷ   ἀγγέλῳ τῆς ἐν Σμύρνῃ ἐκκλησίας
AND   TO THE ANGEL   OF THE [2]IN [3]SMYRNA [1]CHURCH

γράψον·
WRITE:

Τάδε   λέγει ὁ   πρῶτος καὶ ὁ ἔσχατος, ὃς
THESE THINGS SAYS THE FIRST AND THE LAST,   WHO

ἐγένετο νεκρὸς καὶ ἔζησεν· **2.9** Οἶδά σου τὴν θλῖψιν
BECAME   DEAD   AND CAME TO LIFE;   I KNOW YOUR - AFFLICTION

καὶ τὴν πτωχείαν, ἀλλὰ πλούσιος εἶ, καὶ τὴν
AND - POVERTY, BUT YOU ARE~RICH, AND THE

βλασφημίαν ἐκ τῶν λεγόντων Ἰουδαίους εἶναι
SLANDER OF THE ONES DECLARING ³JEWS ²TO BE

ἑαυτοὺς καὶ οὐκ εἰσὶν ἀλλὰ συναγωγὴ τοῦ Σατανᾶ.
¹THEMSELVES, AND ARE~NOT BUT [ARE] A SYNAGOGUE - OF SATAN.

2.10 μηδὲν φοβοῦ ἃ μέλλεις πάσχειν. ἰδοὺ
FEAR~NOT AT ALL THE THINGS YOU ARE ABOUT TO SUFFER. BEHOLD

μέλλει βάλλειν ὁ διάβολος ἐξ ὑμῶν εἰς φυλακὴν
³IS ABOUT ⁴TO CAST ¹THE ²DEVIL [SOME] OF YOU° INTO PRISON

ἵνα πειρασθῆτε καὶ ἕξετε θλῖψιν ἡμερῶν δέκα.
THAT YOU° MAY BE TESTED AND YOU° WILL HAVE AFFLICTION TEN~DAYS.

γίνου πιστὸς ἄχρι θανάτου, καὶ δώσω σοι τὸν
BE FAITHFUL UNTO DEATH, AND I WILL GIVE YOU THE

στέφανον τῆς ζωῆς. 2.11 ὁ ἔχων οὓς ἀκουσάτω τί
CROWN - OF LIFE. THE ONE HAVING EARS LET HIM HEAR WHAT

τὸ πνεῦμα λέγει ταῖς ἐκκλησίαις. ὁ νικῶν
THE SPIRIT SAYS TO THE CHURCHES. THE ONE OVERCOMING

οὐ μὴ ἀδικηθῇ ἐκ τοῦ θανάτου τοῦ δευτέρου.
NEVER WILL BE HURT BY THE ²DEATH - ¹SECOND.

2.12 Καὶ τῷ ἀγγέλῳ τῆς ἐν Περγάμῳ ἐκκλησίας
AND TO THE ANGEL OF THE ²IN ³PERGAMUM ¹CHURCH

γράψον·
WRITE:

Τάδε λέγει ὁ ἔχων τὴν ῥομφαίαν τὴν
THESE THINGS SAYS THE ONE HAVING THE ³SWORD -

δίστομον τὴν ὀξεῖαν· 2.13 Οἶδα ποῦ κατοικεῖς, ὅπου
²TWO-EDGED - ¹SHARP; I KNOW WHERE YOU DWELL, WHERE

ὁ θρόνος τοῦ Σατανᾶ, καὶ κρατεῖς τὸ ὄνομά μου
THE THRONE - OF SATAN [IS], AND YOU HOLD FAST THE NAME OF ME

καὶ οὐκ ἠρνήσω τὴν πίστιν μου καὶ ἐν ταῖς
AND DID NOT DENY THE FAITH OF(IN) ME, EVEN IN THE

ἡμέραις Ἀντιπᾶς ὁ μάρτυς μου ὁ πιστός μου, ὃς
DAYS OF ANTIPAS THE ³WITNESS ¹MY - ²FAITHFUL -, WHO

ἀπεκτάνθη παρ᾽ ὑμῖν, ὅπου ὁ Σατανᾶς κατοικεῖ.
WAS KILLED AMONG YOU°, WHERE - SATAN DWELLS.

2.14 ἀλλ᾽ ἔχω κατὰ σοῦ ὀλίγα ὅτι ἔχεις ἐκεῖ
BUT I HAVE ²AGAINST ³YOU ¹A FEW THINGS BECAUSE YOU HAVE THERE

κρατοῦντας τὴν διδαχὴν Βαλαάμ, ὃς ἐδίδασκεν τῷ
ONES HOLDING THE TEACHING OF BALAAM, WHO WAS TEACHING -

Βαλὰκ βαλεῖν σκάνδαλον ἐνώπιον τῶν υἱῶν Ἰσραὴλ
BALAK TO PUT A SNARE BEFORE THE SONS OF ISRAEL

φαγεῖν εἰδωλόθυτα καὶ πορνεῦσαι. 2.15 οὕτως
TO EAT FOOD SACRIFICED TO IDOLS AND TO COMMIT FORNICATION. SO

ἔχεις καὶ σὺ κρατοῦντας τὴν διδαχὴν [τῶν] Νικολαϊτῶν
³HAVE ²ALSO ¹YOU ONES HOLDING THE TEACHING OF THE NICOLAITANS

ὁμοίως. 2.16 μετανόησον οὖν· εἰ δὲ μή,
LIKEWISE. REPENT THEREFORE; BUT~IF NOT,

and your poverty, even though you are rich. I know the slander on the part of those who say that they are Jews and are not, but are a synagogue of Satan. ¹⁰Do not fear what you are about to suffer. Beware, the devil is about to throw some of you into prison so that you may be tested, and for ten days you will have affliction. Be faithful until death, and I will give you the crown of life. ¹¹Let anyone who has an ear listen to what the Spirit is saying to the churches. Whoever conquers will not be harmed by the second death.

12 "And to the angel of the church in Pergamum write: These are the words of him who has the sharp two-edged sword:

13 "I know where you are living, where Satan's throne is. Yet you are holding fast to my name, and you did not deny your faith in me[h] even in the days of Antipas my witness, my faithful one, who was killed among you, where Satan lives. ¹⁴But I have a few things against you: you have some there who hold to the teaching of Balaam, who taught Balak to put a stumbling block before the people of Israel, so that they would eat food sacrificed to idols and practice fornication. ¹⁵So you also have some who hold to the teaching of the Nicolaitans. ¹⁶Repent then. If not,

[h] Or deny my faith

I will come to you soon and make war against them with the sword of my mouth. ¹⁷Let anyone who has an ear listen to what the Spirit is saying to the churches. To everyone who conquers I will give some of the hidden manna, and I will give a white stone, and on the white stone is written a new name that no one knows except the one who receives it.

18 "And to the angel of the church in Thyatira write: These are the words of the Son of God, who has eyes like a flame of fire, and whose feet are like burnished bronze:

19 "I know your works—your love, faith, service, and patient endurance. I know that your last works are greater than the first. ²⁰But I have this against you: you tolerate that woman Jezebel, who calls herself a prophet and is teaching and beguiling my servantsⁱ to practice fornication and to eat food sacrificed to idols. ²¹I gave her time to repent, but she refuses to repent of her fornication. ²²Beware, I am throwing her on a bed, and those who commit adultery with her I am throwing into great distress, unless they repent of her doings; ²³and I will strike her children dead. And all the churches will know that I

ⁱ Gk slaves

ἔρχομαί σοι ταχὺ καὶ πολεμήσω μετ᾽ αὐτῶν ἐν τῇ
I AM COMING TO YOU QUICKLY AND WILL WAR WITH THEM BY THE

ῥομφαίᾳ τοῦ στόματός μου. 2.17 ὁ ἔχων οὖς
SWORD OF THE MOUTH OF ME. THE ONE HAVING AN EAR

ἀκουσάτω τί τὸ πνεῦμα λέγει ταῖς ἐκκλησίαις.
LET HIM HEAR WHAT THE SPIRIT SAYS TO THE CHURCHES.

τῷ νικῶντι δώσω αὐτῷ τοῦ μάννα τοῦ
TO THE ONE OVERCOMING I WILL GIVE HIM [SOME] OF THE MANNA -

κεκρυμμένου καὶ δώσω αὐτῷ ψῆφον λευκήν, καὶ ἐπὶ
HAVING BEEN HIDDEN, AND I WILL GIVE HIM A WHITE~STONE, AND UPON

τὴν ψῆφον ὄνομα καινὸν γεγραμμένον ὃ οὐδεὶς
THE STONE A NEW~NAME HAVING BEEN WRITTEN, WHICH NO ONE

οἶδεν εἰ μὴ ὁ λαμβάνων.
KNOWS EXCEPT THE ONE RECEIVING [IT].

2.18 Καὶ τῷ ἀγγέλῳ τῆς ἐν Θυατείροις ἐκκλησίας
AND TO THE ANGEL OF THE ²IN ³THYATIRA ¹CHURCH

γράψον·
WRITE:

Τάδε λέγει ὁ υἱὸς τοῦ θεοῦ, ὁ ἔχων τοὺς
THESE THINGS SAYS THE SON - OF GOD, THE ONE HAVING THE

ὀφθαλμοὺς αὐτοῦ ὡς φλόγα πυρὸς καὶ οἱ πόδες αὐτοῦ
EYES OF HIM AS A FLAME OF FIRE AND THE FEET OF HIM

ὅμοιοι χαλκολιβάνῳ· 2.19 Οἶδά σου τὰ ἔργα καὶ τὴν
LIKE BURNISHED BRONZE. I KNOW YOUR - WORKS AND THE

ἀγάπην καὶ τὴν πίστιν καὶ τὴν διακονίαν καὶ τὴν
LOVE AND THE FAITH AND THE RIGHTEOUSNESS AND THE

ὑπομονήν σου, καὶ τὰ ἔργα σου τὰ ἔσχατα πλείονα
ENDURANCE OF YOU, AND THE ²WORKS ³OF YOU - ¹LAST MORE

τῶν πρώτων. 2.20 ἀλλὰ ἔχω κατὰ σοῦ ὅτι
[THAN] THE FIRST. BUT I HAVE [THIS] AGAINST YOU THAT

ἀφεὶς τὴν γυναῖκα Ἰεζάβελ, ἡ λέγουσα ἑαυτὴν
YOU PERMIT THE WOMAN JEZEBEL, THE ONE CALLING HERSELF

προφῆτιν καὶ διδάσκει καὶ πλανᾷ τοὺς ἐμοὺς δούλους
A PROPHETESS, AND SHE TEACHES AND DECEIVES - MY SLAVES

πορνεῦσαι καὶ φαγεῖν εἰδωλόθυτα. 2.21 καὶ
TO COMMIT FORNICATION AND TO EAT FOOD SACRIFICED TO IDOLS. AND I

ἔδωκα αὐτῇ χρόνον ἵνα μετανοήσῃ, καὶ οὐ θέλει
GAVE HER TIME THAT SHE MIGHT REPENT, AND SHE DOES NOT WISH

μετανοῆσαι ἐκ τῆς πορνείας αὐτῆς. 2.22 ἰδοὺ βάλλω
TO REPENT OF THE FORNICATION OF HER. BEHOLD, I AM THROWING

αὐτὴν εἰς κλίνην καὶ τοὺς μοιχεύοντας μετ᾽ αὐτῆς
HER INTO A BED, AND THE ONES COMMITTING ADULTERY WITH HER

εἰς θλῖψιν μεγάλην, ἐὰν μὴ μετανοήσωσιν ἐκ τῶν
INTO GREAT~AFFLICTION, UNLESS THEY REPENT OF THE

ἔργων αὐτῆς, 2.23 καὶ τὰ τέκνα αὐτῆς ἀποκτενῶ ἐν
WORKS OF HER, AND THE CHILDREN OF HER I WILL KILL WITH

θανάτῳ. καὶ γνώσονται πᾶσαι αἱ ἐκκλησίαι ὅτι ἐγώ
DEATH. AND ⁴WILL KNOW ¹ALL ²THE ³CHURCHES THAT I

εἰμι ὁ   ἐραυνῶν νεφροὺς καὶ καρδίας, καὶ δώσω
AM   THE ONE SEARCHING [THE] MINDS AND   HEARTS,   AND I WILL GIVE

ὑμῖν ἑκάστῳ κατὰ   τὰ ἔργα ὑμῶν. 2.24 ὑμῖν δὲ
TO YOU°, EACH ONE, ACCORDING TO THE WORKS OF YOU°.   ³TO YOU° ¹BUT

λέγω τοῖς λοιποῖς τοῖς   ἐν Θυατείροις, ὅσοι
²I SAY, THE REST,   TO THE ONES IN THYATIRA,   AS MANY AS

οὐκ ἔχουσιν τὴν διδαχὴν ταύτην, οἵτινες οὐκ ἔγνωσαν
HAVE~NOT   -   THIS~TEACHING,   WHO   DID NOT KNOW

τὰ βαθέα   τοῦ Σατανᾶ ὡς λέγουσιν· οὐ βάλλω ἐφ'
THE DEEP THINGS -   OF SATAN AS THEY SAY; I AM NOT PUTTING ON

ὑμᾶς ἄλλο βάρος, 2.25 πλὴν   ὃ   ἔχετε κρατήσατε
YOU° ANOTHER BURDEN,   NEVERTHELESS WHAT YOU° HAVE HOLD FAST

ἄχρι[ς] οὗ ἂν ἥξω. 2.26 καὶ ὁ   νικῶν   καὶ ὁ
UNTIL   I COME.   AND THE ONE OVERCOMING AND THE ONE

τηρῶν ἄχρι τέλους τὰ ἔργα μου,
KEEPING UNTIL [THE] END THE WORKS OF ME,

     δώσω αὐτῷ ἐξουσίαν ἐπὶ τῶν ἐθνῶν
     I WILL GIVE HIM AUTHORITY OVER THE NATIONS,

2.27 καὶ ποιμανεῖ αὐτοὺς ἐν ῥάβδῳ σιδηρᾷ
     AND HE WILL SHEPHERD THEM WITH A ROD OF IRON,

        ὡς τὰ σκεύη τὰ κεραμικὰ συντρίβεται,
        AS THE VESSELS - OF POTTERY ARE BROKEN,

2.28 ὡς κἀγὼ εἴληφα παρὰ τοῦ πατρός μου, καὶ
     AS I ALSO HAVE RECEIVED FROM THE FATHER OF ME, AND

δώσω αὐτῷ τὸν ἀστέρα τὸν πρωϊνόν. 2.29 ὁ
I WILL GIVE HIM THE ²STAR   -   ¹MORNING.   THE ONE

ἔχων οὖς ἀκουσάτω τί τὸ πνεῦμα λέγει ταῖς
HAVING AN EAR LET HIM HEAR WHAT THE SPIRIT SAYS TO THE

ἐκκλησίαις.
CHURCHES.

am the one who searches minds and hearts, and I will give to each of you as your works deserve. 24But to the rest of you in Thyatira, who do not hold this teaching, who have not learned what some call 'the deep things of Satan,' to you I say, I do not lay on you any other burden; 25only hold fast to what you have until I come. 26To everyone who conquers and continues to do my works to the end,

I will give authority over the nations;
27to rule[j] them with an iron rod,
as when clay pots are shattered—

28even as I also received authority from my Father. To the one who conquers I will also give the morning star. 29Let anyone who has an ear listen to what the Spirit is saying to the churches.

[j] Or to shepherd

3.1 Καὶ τῷ ἀγγέλῳ τῆς ἐν Σάρδεσιν ἐκκλησίας
    AND TO THE ANGEL OF THE ²IN ³SARDIS   ¹CHURCH

γράψον·
WRITE:

Τάδε   λέγει ὁ   ἔχων τὰ ἑπτὰ πνεύματα τοῦ
THESE THINGS SAYS THE ONE HAVING THE SEVEN SPIRITS   -

θεοῦ καὶ τοὺς ἑπτὰ ἀστέρας· Οἶδά σου τὰ ἔργα ὅτι
OF GOD AND THE SEVEN STARS; I KNOW YOUR - WORKS THAT

ὄνομα ἔχεις ὅτι ζῇς, καὶ νεκρὸς εἶ. 3.2 γίνου
YOU HAVE~A NAME THAT YOU LIVE, AND ARE~DEAD.   BE

γρηγορῶν καὶ στήρισον τὰ   λοιπὰ ἃ   ἔμελλον
WATCHING AND STRENGTHEN THE THINGS REMAINING WHICH ARE ABOUT

ἀποθανεῖν, οὐ γὰρ εὕρηκά σου τὰ ἔργα πεπληρωμένα
TO DIE,   FOR~NOT HAVE I FOUND YOUR - WORKS HAVING BEEN COMPLETED

"And to the angel of the church in Sardis write: These are the words of him who has the seven spirits of God and the seven stars:

"I know your works; you have a name of being alive, but you are dead. 2Wake up, and strengthen what remains and is on the point of death, for I have not found your works perfect in the sight of my God. ³Remember then what you received and heard; obey it, and repent. If you do not wake up, I will come like a thief, and you will not know at what hour I will come to you. ⁴Yet you have still a few persons in Sardis who have not soiled their clothes; they will walk with me, dressed in white, for they are worthy. ⁵If you conquer, you will be clothed like them in white robes, and I will not blot your name out of the book of life; I will confess your name before my Father and before his angels. ⁶Let anyone who has an ear listen to what the Spirit is saying to the churches.

7 "And to the angel of the church in Philadelphia write:
These are the words of the holy one, the true one,
who has the key of David,
who opens and no one will shut,
who shuts and no one opens:
8 "I know your works. Look, I have set before you an open door, which no one is able to shut. I know that you have but little power, and yet you have kept my word and have not denied my name. ⁹I will make those of the synagogue of Satan

ἐνώπιον τοῦ θεοῦ μου. **3.3** μνημόνευε οὖν πῶς
BEFORE THE GOD OF ME. REMEMBER THEREFORE HOW

εἴληφας καὶ ἤκουσας καὶ τήρει καὶ μετανόησον.
YOU HAVE RECEIVED AND HEARD, AND KEEP [IT] AND REPENT.

ἐὰν οὖν μὴ γρηγορήσῃς, ἥξω ὡς κλέπτης, καὶ
IF THEREFORE YOU DO NOT WATCH, I WILL COME AS A THIEF, AND

οὐ μὴ γνῷς ποίαν ὥραν ἥξω ἐπὶ σέ.
NEVER WOULD YOU KNOW AT WHAT HOUR I WILL COME UPON YOU.

3.4 ἀλλὰ ἔχεις ὀλίγα ὀνόματα ἐν Σάρδεσιν ἃ
BUT YOU HAVE A FEW NAMES(PERSONS) IN SARDIS WHICH

οὐκ ἐμόλυναν τὰ ἱμάτια αὐτῶν, καὶ περιπατήσουσιν
DID NOT SOIL THE GARMENTS OF THEM, AND THEY WILL WALK

μετ' ἐμοῦ ἐν λευκοῖς, ὅτι ἄξιοί εἰσιν. **3.5** ὁ
WITH ME IN WHITE, BECAUSE THEY ARE~WORTHY. THE ONE

νικῶν οὕτως περιβαλεῖται ἐν ἱματίοις λευκοῖς
OVERCOMING, IN SIMILAR MANNER, WILL BE CLOTHED IN WHITE~GARMENTS,

καὶ οὐ μὴ ἐξαλείψω τὸ ὄνομα αὐτοῦ ἐκ τῆς βίβλου
AND NEVER WILL I BLOT OUT THE NAME OF HIM FROM THE BOOK

τῆς ζωῆς καὶ ὁμολογήσω τὸ ὄνομα αὐτοῦ ἐνώπιον τοῦ
- OF LIFE AND I WILL CONFESS THE NAME OF HIM BEFORE THE

πατρός μου καὶ ἐνώπιον τῶν ἀγγέλων αὐτοῦ. **3.6** ὁ
FATHER OF ME AND BEFORE THE ANGELS OF HIM. THE ONE

ἔχων οὓς ἀκουσάτω τί τὸ πνεῦμα λέγει ταῖς
HAVING AN EAR LET HIM HEAR WHAT THE SPIRIT SAYS TO THE

ἐκκλησίαις.
CHURCHES.

3.7 Καὶ τῷ ἀγγέλῳ τῆς ἐν Φιλαδελφείᾳ ἐκκλησίας
AND TO THE ANGEL OF THE ²IN ³PHILADELPHIA ¹CHURCH

γράψον·
WRITE:

Τάδε λέγει ὁ ἅγιος, ὁ ἀληθινός,
THESE THINGS SAYS THE HOLY ONE, THE TRUE ONE,

ὁ ἔχων τὴν κλεῖν Δαυίδ,
THE ONE HAVING THE KEY OF DAVID,

ὁ ἀνοίγων καὶ οὐδεὶς κλείσει
THE ONE OPENING AND NO ONE WILL SHUT

καὶ κλείων καὶ οὐδεὶς ἀνοίγει·
AND SHUTTING AND NO ONE OPENS:

3.8 Οἶδά σου τὰ ἔργα, ἰδοὺ δέδωκα ἐνώπιόν σου
I KNOW YOUR - WORKS, BEHOLD, I HAVE GIVEN BEFORE YOU

θύραν ἠνεῳγμένην, ἣν οὐδεὶς δύναται κλεῖσαι αὐτήν,
A DOOR HAVING BEEN OPENED, WHICH NO ONE IS ABLE TO SHUT IT,

ὅτι μικρὰν ἔχεις δύναμιν καὶ ἐτήρησάς μου τὸν
BECAUSE YOU HAVE~A LITTLE POWER(STRENGTH) AND KEPT MY -

λόγον καὶ οὐκ ἠρνήσω τὸ ὄνομά μου. **3.9** ἰδοὺ
WORD AND DID NOT DENY THE NAME OF ME. BEHOLD,

διδῶ ἐκ τῆς συναγωγῆς τοῦ Σατανᾶ τῶν
I MAY GIVE(MAKE) [SOME] OF THE SYNAGOGUE - OF SATAN, THE ONES

λεγόντων ἑαυτοὺς Ἰουδαίους εἶναι, καὶ οὐκ εἰσὶν ἀλλὰ
DECLARING THEMSELVES TO BE~JEWS, AND ARE~NOT BUT

ψεύδονται. ἰδοὺ ποιήσω αὐτοὺς ἵνα ἥξουσιν καὶ
LIE; BEHOLD, I WILL MAKE THEM THAT THEY WILL COME AND

προσκυνήσουσιν ἐνώπιον τῶν ποδῶν σου καὶ
WILL WORSHIP BEFORE THE FEET OF YOU AND

γνῶσιν ὅτι ἐγὼ ἠγάπησά σε. **3.10** ὅτι ἐτήρησας
THEY WOULD KNOW THAT I LOVED YOU. BECAUSE YOU KEPT

τὸν λόγον τῆς ὑπομονῆς μου, κἀγώ
THE WORD OF(CONCERNING) THE ENDURANCE OF(FOR) ME, I ALSO

σε τηρήσω ἐκ τῆς ὥρας τοῦ πειρασμοῦ τῆς μελλούσης
WILL KEEP~YOU FROM THE HOUR - OF TRIAL - BEING ABOUT

ἔρχεσθαι ἐπὶ τῆς οἰκουμένης ὅλης πειράσαι τοὺς
TO COME UPON ²THE ³INHABITED [WORLD] ¹ALL TO TRY THE ONES

κατοικοῦντας ἐπὶ τῆς γῆς. **3.11** ἔρχομαι ταχύ· κράτει
DWELLING UPON THE EARTH. I AM COMING QUICKLY; HOLD

ὃ ἔχεις, ἵνα μηδεὶς λάβῃ τὸν στέφανόν σου.
WHAT YOU HAVE, THAT NO ONE TAKES THE CROWN OF YOU.

3.12 ὁ νικῶν ποιήσω αὐτὸν στῦλον ἐν τῷ ναῷ
THE ONE OVERCOMING I WILL MAKE HIM A PILLAR IN THE TEMPLE

τοῦ θεοῦ μου καὶ ἔξω οὐ μὴ ἐξέλθῃ ἔτι καὶ
OF THE GOD OF ME AND ³OUT ¹NEVER ²MAY HE GO ANY MORE AND

γράψω ἐπ᾽ αὐτὸν τὸ ὄνομα τοῦ θεοῦ μου καὶ τὸ
I WILL WRITE UPON HIM THE NAME OF THE GOD OF ME AND THE

ὄνομα τῆς πόλεως τοῦ θεοῦ μου, τῆς καινῆς
NAME OF THE CITY OF THE GOD OF ME, THE NEW

Ἰερουσαλὴμ ἡ καταβαίνουσα ἐκ τοῦ οὐρανοῦ ἀπὸ
JERUSALEM, - COMING DOWN OUT OF - HEAVEN FROM

τοῦ θεοῦ μου, καὶ τὸ ὄνομά μου τὸ καινόν. **3.13** ὁ
THE GOD OF ME, AND THE ²NAME ³OF ME - ¹NEW. THE ONE

ἔχων οὓς ἀκουσάτω τί τὸ πνεῦμα λέγει ταῖς
HAVING AN EAR LET HIM HEAR WHAT THE SPIRIT SAYS TO THE

ἐκκλησίαις.
CHURCHES.

3.14 Καὶ τῷ ἀγγέλῳ τῆς ἐν Λαοδικείᾳ ἐκκλησίας
AND TO THE ANGEL OF THE ²IN ³LAODICEA ¹CHURCH

γράψον·
WRITE:

Τάδε λέγει ὁ ἀμήν, ὁ μάρτυς ὁ πιστὸς καὶ
THESE THINGS SAYS THE AMEN, THE ⁴WITNESS - ¹FAITHFUL ²AND

ἀληθινός, ἡ ἀρχὴ τῆς κτίσεως τοῦ θεοῦ· **3.15** Οἶδά
³TRUE, THE ORIGIN OF THE CREATION - OF GOD; I KNOW

σου τὰ ἔργα ὅτι οὔτε ψυχρὸς εἶ οὔτε ζεστός.
YOUR - WORKS, THAT NEITHER COLD YOU ARE NOR HOT.

ὄφελον ψυχρὸς ἦς ἢ ζεστός. **3.16** οὕτως ὅτι
I WOULD [THAT] YOU WERE~COLD OR HOT. SO BECAUSE

χλιαρὸς εἶ καὶ οὔτε ζεστὸς οὔτε ψυχρός, μέλλω
YOU ARE~LUKEWARM AND NEITHER HOT NOR COLD, I AM ABOUT

who say that they are Jews and are not, but are lying—I will make them come and bow down before your feet, and they will learn that I have loved you. ¹⁰Because you have kept my word of patient endurance, I will keep you from the hour of trial that is coming on the whole world to test the inhabitants of the earth. ¹¹I am coming soon; hold fast to what you have, so that no one may seize your crown. ¹²If you conquer, I will make you a pillar in the temple of my God; you will never go out of it. I will write on you the name of my God, and the name of the city of my God, the new Jerusalem that comes down from my God out of heaven, and my own new name. ¹³Let anyone who has an ear listen to what the Spirit is saying to the churches.

14 "And to the angel of the church in Laodicea write: The words of the Amen, the faithful and true witness, the origin[k] of God's creation:

15 "I know your works; you are neither cold nor hot. I wish that you were either cold or hot. ¹⁶So, because you are lukewarm, and neither cold nor hot, I am

[k] Or *beginning*

about to spit you out of my mouth. [17]For you say, 'I am rich, I have prospered, and I need nothing.' You do not realize that you are wretched, pitiable, poor, blind, and naked. [18]Therefore I counsel you to buy from me gold refined by fire so that you may be rich; and white robes to clothe you and to keep the shame of your nakedness from being seen; and salve to anoint your eyes so that you may see. [19]I reprove and discipline those whom I love. Be earnest, therefore, and repent. [20]Listen! I am standing at the door, knocking; if you hear my voice and open the door, I will come in to you and eat with you, and you with me. [21]To the one who conquers I will give a place with me on my throne, just as I myself conquered and sat down with my Father on his throne. [22]Let anyone who has an ear listen to what the Spirit is saying to the churches."

σε ἐμέσαι ἐκ τοῦ στόματός μου. **3.17** ὅτι λέγεις
TO SPIT~YOU   OUT OF   THE   MOUTH   OF ME.   BECAUSE   YOU SAY,

ὅτι Πλούσιός εἰμι καὶ πεπλούτηκα καὶ οὐδὲν χρείαν
-    I AM~RICH   AND HAVE BECOME WEALTHY AND   ²NO   ³NEED

ἔχω, καὶ οὐκ οἶδας ὅτι σὺ εἶ ὁ ταλαίπωρος καὶ
¹HAVE, AND YOU DO NOT KNOW THAT YOU ARE THE ONE WRETCHED   AND

ἐλεεινὸς καὶ πτωχὸς καὶ τυφλὸς καὶ γυμνός,
PITIFUL   AND   POOR   AND   BLIND   AND   NAKED,

3.18 συμβουλεύω σοι ἀγοράσαι παρ' ἐμοῦ χρυσίον
          I COUNSEL   YOU   TO BUY   FROM   ME   GOLD

πεπυρωμένον ἐκ πυρὸς ἵνα πλουτήσῃς, καὶ
HAVING BEEN PURIFIED BY FIRE THAT YOU MAY BE RICH,   AND

ἱμάτια λευκὰ ἵνα περιβάλῃ καὶ μὴ φανερωθῇ ἡ
WHITE~GARMENTS THAT YOU MAY CLOTHED AND ⁶NOT ⁷BE MANIFESTED ¹THE

αἰσχύνη τῆς γυμνότητός σου, καὶ κολλ[ο]ύριον
²SHAME   ³OF THE ⁴NAKEDNESS   ⁵OF YOU, AND   SALVE

ἐγχρῖσαι τοὺς ὀφθαλμούς σου ἵνα βλέπῃς. **3.19** ἐγὼ
TO RUB ON   THE   EYES   OF YOU THAT YOU MAY SEE.   ²I

ὅσους ἐὰν φιλῶ ἐλέγχω καὶ παιδεύω· ζήλευε οὖν
¹AS MANY AS   AM FOND OF I REPROVE AND DISCIPLINE;   BE HOT   THEREFORE

καὶ μετανόησον. **3.20** ἰδοὺ ἔστηκα ἐπὶ τὴν θύραν
AND   REPENT.   BEHOLD, I HAVE STOOD AT   THE   DOOR

καὶ κρούω· ἐάν τις ἀκούσῃ τῆς φωνῆς μου καὶ
AND KNOCK;   IF ANYONE HEARS   THE   VOICE   OF ME AND

ἀνοίξῃ τὴν θύραν, [καὶ] εἰσελεύσομαι πρὸς αὐτὸν καὶ
OPENS   THE   DOOR,   INDEED   I WILL COME IN   TO   HIM   AND

δειπνήσω μετ' αὐτοῦ καὶ αὐτὸς μετ' ἐμοῦ. **3.21** ὁ
WILL DINE   WITH   HIM   AND   HE   WITH   ME.   THE ONE

νικῶν δώσω αὐτῷ καθίσαι μετ' ἐμοῦ ἐν τῷ
OVERCOMING, I WILL GIVE TO HIM TO SIT   WITH   ME   IN(ON) THE

θρόνῳ μου, ὡς κἀγὼ ἐνίκησα καὶ ἐκάθισα μετὰ τοῦ
THRONE OF ME, AS I ALSO OVERCAME AND   SAT   WITH   THE

πατρός μου ἐν τῷ θρόνῳ αὐτοῦ. **3.22** ὁ ἔχων οὖς
FATHER   OF ME IN(ON) THE THRONE OF HIM.   THE ONE HAVING AN EAR

ἀκουσάτω τί τὸ πνεῦμα λέγει ταῖς ἐκκλησίαις.
LET HIM HEAR WHAT THE SPIRIT   SAYS   TO THE CHURCHES.

CHAPTER 4

After this I looked, and there in heaven a door stood open! And the first voice, which I had heard speaking to me like a trumpet, said, "Come

4.1 Μετὰ ταῦτα εἶδον, καὶ ἰδοὺ θύρα ἠνεῳγμένη
        AFTER   THESE THINGS I SAW,   AND   BEHOLD A DOOR HAVING BEEN OPENED

ἐν τῷ οὐρανῷ, καὶ ἡ φωνὴ ἡ πρώτη ἣν ἤκουσα
IN - HEAVEN,   AND THE ²VOICE - ¹FIRST WHICH I HEARD

ὡς σάλπιγγος λαλούσης μετ' ἐμοῦ λέγων, Ἀνάβα
[WAS] AS OF A TRUMPET SPEAKING   WITH   ME   SAYING,   COME UP

ὧδε, καὶ   δείξω   σοι ἃ   δεῖ   γενέσθαι μετὰ
HERE, AND I WILL SHOW YOU THE THINGS WHICH NEED TO HAPPEN   AFTER

ταῦτα.   **4.2** εὐθέως ἐγενόμην ἐν πνεύματι, καὶ ἰδοὺ
THESE THINGS.   AT ONCE   I WAS   IN   SPIRIT,   AND BEHOLD,

θρόνος ἔκειτο   ἐν τῷ οὐρανῷ, καὶ ἐπὶ τὸν θρόνον
A THRONE WAS BEING SET IN -   HEAVEN,   AND UPON THE THRONE

καθήμενος, **4.3** καὶ ὁ   καθήμενος ὅμοιος ὁράσει
ONE SITTING,   AND THE ONE   SITTING   [WAS] LIKE IN APPEARANCE

λίθῳ   ἰάσπιδι καὶ σαρδίῳ, καὶ ἶρις   κυκλόθεν τοῦ
TO ⁴STONE ¹A JASPER ²AND ³CARNELIAN, AND A RAINBOW [WAS] AROUND THE

θρόνου ὅμοιος ὁράσει   σμαραγδίνῳ. **4.4** καὶ   κυκλόθεν
THRONE LIKE IN APPEARANCE TO AN EMERALD.   AND   AROUND

τοῦ θρόνου θρόνους εἴκοσι τέσσαρες, καὶ ἐπὶ τοὺς
THE THRONE ²THRONES ¹TWENTY-FOUR   AND ON   THE

θρόνους εἴκοσι τέσσαρας πρεσβυτέρους καθημένους
THRONES TWENTY-FOUR   ELDERS   SITTING,

περιβεβλημένους ἐν ἱματίοις λευκοῖς καὶ ἐπὶ τὰς
HAVING BEEN CLOTHED IN WHITE~GARMENTS AND ON   THE

κεφαλὰς αὐτῶν στεφάνους χρυσοῦς. **4.5** καὶ ἐκ   τοῦ
HEADS   OF THEM GOLDEN~CROWNS.   AND OUT OF THE

θρόνου ἐκπορεύονται ἀστραπαὶ καὶ φωναὶ καὶ
THRONE COMES FORTH   LIGHTNING AND SOUNDS AND

βρονταί, καὶ ἑπτὰ λαμπάδες πυρὸς καιόμεναι ἐνώπιον
THUNDERS, AND SEVEN TORCHES OF FIRE BURNING   BEFORE

τοῦ θρόνου, ἅ   εἰσιν τὰ ἑπτὰ πνεύματα τοῦ θεοῦ,
THE THRONE, WHICH ARE THE SEVEN SPIRITS   -   OF GOD,

4.6 καὶ ἐνώπιον τοῦ θρόνου ὡς   θάλασσα
       AND BEFORE   THE THRONE AS [IF THERE WERE] A SEA

ὑαλίνη ὁμοία κρυστάλλῳ.
OF GLASS, LIKE CRYSTAL.

Καὶ ἐν μέσῳ   τοῦ θρόνου καὶ κύκλῳ τοῦ θρόνου
AND IN [THE] MIDST OF THE THRONE AND AROUND THE THRONE

τέσσαρα ζῷα   γέμοντα ὀφθαλμῶν ἔμπροσθεν καὶ
FOUR   LIVING BEINGS BEING FULL OF EYES   IN FRONT   AND

ὄπισθεν. **4.7** καὶ τὸ ζῷον   τὸ πρῶτον ὅμοιον λέοντι
IN BACK.   AND THE ²LIVING BEING - ¹FIRST [WAS] LIKE A LION,

καὶ τὸ δεύτερον ζῷον   ὅμοιον μόσχῳ καὶ τὸ τρίτον
AND THE SECOND LIVING BEING LIKE A CALF, AND THE THIRD

ζῷον   ἔχων τὸ πρόσωπον ὡς ἀνθρώπου καὶ τὸ
LIVING BEING HAVING THE FACE AS OF A MAN,   AND THE

τέταρτον ζῷον   ὅμοιον ἀετῷ πετομένῳ. **4.8** καὶ τὰ
FOURTH   LIVING BEING LIKE A FLYING~EAGLE.   AND THE

τέσσαρα ζῷα,   ἓν καθ᾽ ἓν αὐτῶν ἔχων ἀνὰ
FOUR   LIVING BEINGS, EACH ONE OF THEM HAVING EACH

πτέρυγας ἕξ, κυκλόθεν καὶ ἔσωθεν γέμουσιν ὀφθαλμῶν,
SIX~WINGS, AROUND   AND WITHIN THEY ARE FULL OF EYES,

up here, and I will show you what must take place after this." [2] At once I was in the spirit,[l] and there in heaven stood a throne, with one seated on the throne! [3] And the one seated there looks like jasper and carnelian, and around the throne is a rainbow that looks like an emerald. [4] Around the throne are twenty-four thrones, and seated on the thrones are twenty-four elders, dressed in white robes, with golden crowns on their heads. [5] Coming from the throne are flashes of lightning, and rumblings and peals of thunder, and in front of the throne burn seven flaming torches, which are the seven spirits of God; [6] and in front of the throne there is something like a sea of glass, like crystal.

Around the throne, and on each side of the throne, are four living creatures, full of eyes in front and behind: [7] the first living creature like a lion, the second living creature like an ox, the third living creature with a face like a human face, and the fourth living creature like a flying eagle. [8] And the four living creatures, each of them with six wings, are full of eyes all around and inside.

[l] Or *in the Spirit*

Day and night without
ceasing they sing,
   "Holy, holy, holy,
    the Lord God the
     Almighty,
    who was and is and is
     to come."
9And whenever the living
creatures give glory and
honor and thanks to the one
who is seated on the throne,
who lives forever and ever,
10the twenty-four elders fall
before the one who is seated
on the throne and worship
the one who lives forever
and ever; they cast their
crowns before the throne,
singing,
 11"You are worthy, our
   Lord and God,
   to receive glory and
    honor and power,
  for you created all things,
  and by your will they
   existed and were
   created."

καὶ   ἀνάπαυσιν   οὐκ ἔχουσιν   ἡμέρας   καὶ   νυκτὸς
AND   REST(CESSATION)   THEY DO NOT HAVE   DAY   AND   NIGHT

λέγοντες,
SAYING,

   Ἅγιος   ἅγιος   ἅγιος
   HOLY,   HOLY,   HOLY,

   κύριος   ὁ θεὸς   ὁ   παντοκράτωρ,
   LORD   -   GOD   THE   ALMIGHTY,

     ὁ   ἦν   καὶ ὁ   ὢν   καὶ ὁ
     THE ONE   [WHO] WAS   AND   THE ONE BEING   AND   THE ONE

     ἐρχόμενος.
     COMING.

4.9 καὶ   ὅταν   δώσουσιν τὰ ζῷα   δόξαν καὶ
AND   WHENEVER   3WILL GIVE   1THE   2LIVING BEINGS   GLORY   AND

τιμὴν καὶ   εὐχαριστίαν   τῷ   καθημένῳ ἐπὶ   τῷ
HONOR   AND   THANKS   TO THE ONE SITTING   ON   THE

θρόνῳ   τῷ   ζῶντι εἰς   τοὺς   αἰῶνας τῶν   αἰώνων,
THRONE,   TO THE ONE LIVING   INTO   THE   AGES   OF THE AGES,

4.10 πεσοῦνται   οἱ   εἴκοσι τέσσαρες   πρεσβύτεροι ἐνώπιον
4WILL FALL   1THE   2TWENTY-FOUR   3ELDERS   BEFORE

τοῦ   καθημένου ἐπὶ   τοῦ θρόνου καὶ   προσκυνήσουσιν
THE ONE   SITTING   ON   THE   THRONE   AND   WILL WORSHIP

τῷ   ζῶντι εἰς τοὺς   αἰῶνας τῶν   αἰώνων καὶ   βαλοῦσιν
THE ONE LIVING   INTO THE   AGES   OF THE AGES   AND   WILL THROW

τοὺς στεφάνους αὐτῶν ἐνώπιον τοῦ θρόνου λέγοντες,
THE   CROWNS   OF THEM BEFORE   THE   THRONE   SAYING,

4.11 Ἄξιος εἶ,   ὁ   κύριος καὶ ὁ   θεὸς ἡμῶν,
WORTHY   YOU ARE,   THE LORD   AND   THE   GOD   OF US,

   λαβεῖν   τὴν δόξαν καὶ   τὴν τιμὴν καὶ   τὴν
   TO RECEIVE   THE   GLORY   AND   THE   HONOR   AND   THE

    δύναμιν,
    POWER,

  ὅτι   σὺ ἔκτισας τὰ πάντα
  BECAUSE   YOU   CREATED   -   ALL THINGS

   καὶ   διὰ   τὸ θέλημά σου   ἦσαν   καὶ
   AND   BECAUSE OF   THE   WILL   OF YOU   THEY EXISTED   AND

    ἐκτίσθησαν.
    WERE CREATED.

CHAPTER 5

Then I saw in the right hand
of the one seated on the throne
a scroll written on the inside
and on the back, sealed[m]
with seven seals; 2and

5.1 Καὶ   εἶδον ἐπὶ   τὴν δεξιὰν   τοῦ   καθημένου
AND   I SAW   ON   THE   RIGHT [HAND]   OF THE ONE   SITTING

ἐπὶ   τοῦ θρόνου βιβλίον   γεγραμμένον ἔσωθεν καὶ
ON   THE   THRONE   A SCROLL   HAVING BEEN WRITTEN   INSIDE   AND

ὄπισθεν κατεσφραγισμένον σφραγῖσιν ἑπτά.   **5.2** καὶ
ON BACK,   HAVING BEEN SEALED   WITH SEVEN~SEALS.   AND

*m Or written on the inside, and sealed
on the back*

εἶδον   ἄγγελον   ἰσχυρὸν   κηρύσσοντα   ἐν   φωνῇ   μεγάλῃ,
I SAW   A STRONG~ANGEL   PROCLAIMING   IN   A LOUD~VOICE,

Τίς   ἄξιος   ἀνοῖξαι   τὸ   βιβλίον   καὶ   λῦσαι   τὰς
WHO   [IS] WORTHY   TO OPEN   THE   SCROLL   AND   BREAK   THE

σφραγῖδας   αὐτοῦ;   **5.3** καὶ   οὐδεὶς   ἐδύνατο   ἐν   τῷ
SEALS   OF IT?   AND   NO ONE   WAS BEING ABLE   IN   -

οὐρανῷ   οὐδὲ   ἐπὶ   τῆς   γῆς   οὐδὲ   ὑποκάτω   τῆς   γῆς
HEAVEN   OR   ON   THE   EARTH   OR   UNDER   THE   EARTH

ἀνοῖξαι   τὸ   βιβλίον   οὔτε   βλέπειν   αὐτό.   **5.4** καὶ
TO OPEN   THE   SCROLL   OR   TO LOOK [INTO]   IT.   AND

ἔκλαιον   πολύ,   ὅτι   οὐδεὶς   ἄξιος   εὑρέθη   ἀνοῖξαι   τὸ
I WAS WEEPING GREATLY, BECAUSE NO ONE   WAS FOUND~WORTHY TO OPEN   THE

βιβλίον   οὔτε   βλέπειν   αὐτό.   **5.5** καὶ   εἷς   ἐκ   τῶν
SCROLL   OR   TO LOOK [INTO]   IT.   AND   ONE   OF   THE

πρεσβυτέρων   λέγει   μοι,   Μὴ   κλαῖε,   ἰδοὺ   ἐνίκησεν   ὁ
ELDERS   SAYS   TO ME,   DO NOT WEEP,   LOOK,   ¹⁰[HAS] CONQUERED   ¹THE

λέων   ὁ   ἐκ   τῆς   φυλῆς   Ἰούδα,   ἡ   ῥίζα   Δαυίδ,
²LION   -   ³OF   ⁴THE   ⁵TRIBE   ⁶OF JUDAH,   ⁷THE   ⁸ROOT   ⁹OF DAVID,

ἀνοῖξαι   τὸ   βιβλίον   καὶ   τὰς   ἑπτὰ   σφραγῖδας
[HE IS ABLE] TO OPEN   THE   SCROLL   AND   THE   SEVEN   SEALS

αὐτοῦ.
OF IT.

5.6 Καὶ   εἶδον   ἐν   μέσῳ   τοῦ   θρόνου   καὶ   τῶν
AND   I SAW   IN   [THE] MIDST   OF THE   THRONE   AND   OF THE

τεσσάρων   ζῴων   καὶ   ἐν   μέσῳ   τῶν   πρεσβυτέρων
FOUR   LIVING BEINGS   AND   IN   [THE] MIDST   OF THE   ELDERS

ἀρνίον   ἑστηκὸς   ὡς   ἐσφαγμένον   ἔχων   κέρατα   ἑπτὰ
A LAMB   HAVING STOOD   AS   HAVING BEEN SLAIN,   HAVING   SEVEN~HORNS

καὶ   ὀφθαλμοὺς   ἑπτά   οἵ   εἰσιν   τὰ   [ἑπτὰ]   πνεύματα
AND   SEVEN~EYES,   WHICH   ARE   THE   SEVEN   SPIRITS

τοῦ   θεοῦ   ἀπεσταλμένοι   εἰς   πᾶσαν   τὴν   γῆν.   **5.7** καὶ
-   OF GOD   HAVING BEEN SENT   INTO   ALL   THE   EARTH.   AND

ἦλθεν   καὶ   εἴληφεν   ἐκ   τῆς   δεξιᾶς   τοῦ
HE CAME   AND   HAS TAKEN [THE SCROLL]   OUT OF   THE   RIGHT [HAND]   OF THE ONE

καθημένου   ἐπὶ   τοῦ   θρόνου.   **5.8** καὶ   ὅτε   ἔλαβεν   τὸ
SITTING   ON   THE   THRONE.   AND   WHEN   HE RECEIVED   THE

βιβλίον,   τὰ   τέσσαρα   ζῷα   καὶ   οἱ   εἴκοσι   τέσσαρες
SCROLL,   THE   FOUR   LIVING BEINGS   AND   THE   TWENTY-FOUR

πρεσβύτεροι   ἔπεσαν   ἐνώπιον   τοῦ   ἀρνίου   ἔχοντες   ἕκαστος
ELDERS   FELL   BEFORE   THE   LAMB,   EACH ONE~HAVING

κιθάραν   καὶ   φιάλας   χρυσᾶς   γεμούσας   θυμιαμάτων,   αἵ
A HARP   AND   GOLDEN~BOWLS   BEING FULL   OF INCENSE,   WHICH

εἰσιν   αἱ   προσευχαὶ   τῶν   ἁγίων,   **5.9** καὶ   ᾄδουσιν
ARE   THE   PRAYERS   OF THE   SAINTS;   AND   THAT ARE SINGING

ᾠδὴν   καινὴν   λέγοντες,
A NEW~SONG   SAYING,

Ἄξιος   εἶ   λαβεῖν   τὸ   βιβλίον
WORTHY   ARE YOU   TO TAKE   THE   SCROLL

I saw a mighty angel proclaiming with a loud voice, "Who is worthy to open the scroll and break its seals?" ³And no one in heaven or on earth or under the earth was able to open the scroll or to look into it. ⁴And I began to weep bitterly because no one was found worthy to open the scroll or to look into it. ⁵Then one of the elders said to me, "Do not weep. See, the Lion of the tribe of Judah, the Root of David, has conquered, so that he can open the scroll and its seven seals."

6 Then I saw between the throne and the four living creatures and among the elders a Lamb standing as if it had been slaughtered, having seven horns and seven eyes, which are the seven spirits of God sent out into all the earth. ⁷He went and took the scroll from the right hand of the one who was seated on the throne. ⁸When he had taken the scroll, the four living creatures and the twenty-four elders fell before the Lamb, each holding a harp and golden bowls full of incense, which are the prayers of the saints. ⁹They sing a new song:

"You are worthy to take
the scroll

and to open its seals,
for you were slaughtered
and by your blood
you ransomed for
God
saints from[n] every tribe
and language and
people and nation;
[10] you have made them to
be a kingdom and
priests serving[o] our
God,
and they will reign on
earth."

11 Then I looked, and I
heard the voice of many
angels surrounding the
throne and the living creatures and the elders; they
numbered myriads of
myriads and thousands of
thousands, [12] singing with
full voice,
"Worthy is the Lamb that
was slaughtered
to receive power and
wealth and wisdom
and might
and honor and glory and
blessing!"
[13] Then I heard every creature in heaven and on earth
and under the earth and in
the sea, and all that is in
them, singing,
"To the one seated on the
throne and to the
Lamb
be blessing and honor
and glory and might
forever and ever!"

[n] Gk ransomed for God from
[o] Gk priests to

καὶ ἀνοῖξαι τὰς σφραγῖδας αὐτοῦ,
AND TO OPEN THE SEALS OF IT,

ὅτι ἐσφάγης καὶ ἠγόρασας τῷ θεῷ
BECAUSE YOU WERE SLAIN AND PURCHASED [ONES] - FOR GOD

ἐν τῷ αἵματί σου
WITH THE BLOOD OF YOU

ἐκ πάσης φυλῆς καὶ γλώσσης καὶ λαοῦ
FROM EVERY TRIBE AND TONGUE AND PEOPLE

καὶ ἔθνους
AND NATION

5.10 καὶ ἐποίησας αὐτοὺς τῷ θεῷ ἡμῶν βασιλείαν
AND MADE THEM FOR THE GOD OF US A KINGDOM

καὶ ἱερεῖς,
AND PRIESTS,

καὶ βασιλεύσουσιν ἐπὶ τῆς γῆς.
AND THEY WILL REIGN ON THE EARTH.

5.11 Καὶ εἶδον, καὶ ἤκουσα φωνὴν ἀγγέλων πολλῶν
AND I SAW, AND I HEARD [THE] VOICE OF MANY~ANGELS

κύκλῳ τοῦ θρόνου καὶ τῶν ζῴων καὶ τῶν
AROUND THE THRONE AND OF THE LIVING BEINGS AND OF THE

πρεσβυτέρων, καὶ ἦν ὁ ἀριθμὸς αὐτῶν μυριάδες
ELDERS, AND ⁴WAS ¹THE ²NUMBER ³OF THEM MYRIADS

μυριάδων καὶ χιλιάδες χιλιάδων **5.12** λέγοντες
OF MYRIADS AND THOUSANDS OF THOUSANDS, SAYING

φωνῇ μεγάλῃ,
WITH A LOUD~VOICE,

Ἄξιόν ἐστιν τὸ ἀρνίον τὸ ἐσφαγμένον λαβεῖν
WORTHY IS THE LAMB - HAVING BEEN SLAIN TO RECEIVE

τὴν δύναμιν καὶ πλοῦτον καὶ σοφίαν καὶ ἰσχὺν
THE POWER AND WEALTH AND WISDOM AND STRENGTH

καὶ τιμὴν καὶ δόξαν καὶ εὐλογίαν.
AND HONOR AND GLORY AND PRAISE.

5.13 καὶ πᾶν κτίσμα ὃ ἐν τῷ οὐρανῷ καὶ ἐπὶ
AND EVERY CREATURE WHICH [IS] IN - HEAVEN AND ON

τῆς γῆς καὶ ὑποκάτω τῆς γῆς καὶ ἐπὶ τῆς θαλάσσης
THE EARTH AND UNDER THE EARTH AND ON THE SEA

καὶ τὰ ἐν αὐτοῖς πάντα ἤκουσα λέγοντας,
AND - ²IN ³THEM ¹ALL THINGS I HEARD SAYING,

Τῷ καθημένῳ ἐπὶ τῷ θρόνῳ καὶ τῷ ἀρνίῳ
TO THE ONE SITTING ON THE THRONE AND TO THE LAMB

ἡ εὐλογία καὶ ἡ τιμὴ καὶ ἡ δόξα καὶ τὸ
[BE] THE PRAISE AND THE HONOR AND THE GLORY AND THE

κράτος
DOMINION

εἰς τοὺς αἰῶνας τῶν αἰώνων.
INTO THE AGES OF THE AGES.

5.14 καὶ τὰ τέσσαρα ζῷα ἔλεγον, Ἀμήν. καὶ
AND THE FOUR LIVING BEINGS WERE SAYING, AMEN. AND

οἱ πρεσβύτεροι ἔπεσαν καὶ προσεκύνησαν.
THE ELDERS FELL [DOWN] AND WORSHIPED.

[14]And the four living creatures said, "Amen!" And the elders fell down and worshiped.

6.1 Καὶ εἶδον ὅτε ἤνοιξεν τὸ ἀρνίον μίαν ἐκ τῶν
AND I SAW WHEN [3]OPENED [1]THE [2]LAMB ONE OF THE

ἑπτὰ σφραγίδων, καὶ ἤκουσα ἑνὸς ἐκ τῶν τεσσάρων
SEVEN SEALS, AND I HEARD ONE OF THE FOUR

ζῴων λέγοντος ὡς φωνὴ βροντῆς, Ἔρχου.
LIVING BEINGS SAYING AS WITH A SOUND OF THUNDER, COME.

6.2 καὶ εἶδον, καὶ ἰδοὺ ἵππος λευκός, καὶ ὁ
AND I SAW, AND BEHOLD, A WHITE~HORSE, AND THE ONE

καθήμενος ἐπ᾽ αὐτὸν ἔχων τόξον καὶ ἐδόθη αὐτῷ
SITTING ON IT HAVING A BOW AND [2]WAS GIVEN [3]TO HIM

στέφανος καὶ ἐξῆλθεν νικῶν καὶ ἵνα νικήσῃ
[1]A CROWN AND HE WENT FORTH CONQUERING AND THAT HE MIGHT CONQUER.

6.3 Καὶ ὅτε ἤνοιξεν τὴν σφραγίδα τὴν δευτέραν,
AND WHEN HE OPENED THE [2]SEAL - [1]SECOND,

ἤκουσα τοῦ δευτέρου ζῴου λέγοντος, Ἔρχου. **6.4** καὶ
I HEARD THE SECOND LIVING BEING SAYING, COME. AND

ἐξῆλθεν ἄλλος ἵππος πυρρός, καὶ τῷ καθημένῳ ἐπ᾽
WENT FORTH ANOTHER HORSE, A RED ONE, AND TO THE ONE SITTING ON

αὐτὸν ἐδόθη αὐτῷ λαβεῖν τὴν εἰρήνην ἐκ τῆς γῆς
IT WAS GIVEN TO HIM TO TAKE - PEACE FROM THE EARTH

καὶ ἵνα ἀλλήλους σφάξουσιν καὶ ἐδόθη αὐτῷ
AND THAT THEY WILL SLAY~ONE ANOTHER, AND WAS GIVEN TO HIM

μάχαιρα μεγάλη.
A GREAT~SWORD.

6.5 Καὶ ὅτε ἤνοιξεν τὴν σφραγῖδα τὴν τρίτην,
AND WHEN HE OPENED THE [2]SEAL - [1]THIRD,

ἤκουσα τοῦ τρίτου ζῴου λέγοντος, Ἔρχου. καὶ
I HEARD THE THIRD LIVING BEING SAYING, COME. AND

εἶδον, καὶ ἰδοὺ ἵππος μέλας, καὶ ὁ καθήμενος
I SAW, AND BEHOLD, A BLACK~HORSE, AND THE ONE SITTING

ἐπ᾽ αὐτὸν ἔχων ζυγὸν ἐν τῇ χειρὶ αὐτοῦ. **6.6** καὶ
ON IT HAVING A PAIR OF SCALES IN THE HAND OF HIM. AND

ἤκουσα ὡς φωνὴν ἐν μέσῳ τῶν τεσσάρων
I HEARD AS [IT WERE] A VOICE IN [THE] MIDST OF THE FOUR

ζῴων λέγουσαν, Χοῖνιξ σίτου δηναρίου καὶ
LIVING BEINGS SAYING, A CHOENIX OF WHEAT OF(FOR) A DENARIUS AND

Then I saw the Lamb open one of the seven seals, and I heard one of the four living creatures call out, as with a voice of thunder, "Come!"[p] [2]I looked, and there was a white horse! Its rider had a bow; a crown was given to him, and he came out conquering and to conquer.

3 When he opened the second seal, I heard the second living creature call out, "Come!"[p] [4]And out came[q] another horse, bright red; its rider was permitted to take peace from the earth, so that people would slaughter one another; and he was given a great sword.

5 When he opened the third seal, I heard the third living creature call out, "Come!"[p] I looked, and there was a black horse! Its rider held a pair of scales in his hand, [6]and I heard what seemed to be a voice in the midst of the four living creatures saying, "A quart of wheat for a day's pay,[r] and

[p] Or "Go!"
[q] Or went
[r] Gk a denarius

three quarts of barley for a day's pay,[s] but do not damage the olive oil and the wine!'"

7 When he opened the fourth seal, I heard the voice of the fourth living creature call out, "Come!"[t] 8I looked and there was a pale green horse! Its rider's name was Death, and Hades followed with him; they were given authority over a fourth of the earth, to kill with sword, famine, and pestilence, and by the wild animals of the earth.

9 When he opened the fifth seal, I saw under the altar the souls of those who had been slaughtered for the word of God and for the testimony they had given; 10they cried out with a loud voice, "Sovereign Lord, holy and true, how long will it be before you judge and avenge our blood on the inhabitants of the earth?" 11They were each given a white robe and told to rest a little longer, until the number would be complete both of their fellow servants[u] and of their brothers and sisters,[v] who were soon to be killed as they themselves had been killed.

12 When he opened the sixth seal, I looked, and there came a great earthquake; the sun became

[s] Gk *a denarius*
[t] Or *"Go!"*
[u] Gk *slaves*
[v] Gk *brothers*

τρεῖς χοίνικες κριθῶν δηναρίου, καὶ τὸ ἔλαιον καὶ
THREE CHOENIXES OF BARLEY OF(FOR) A DENARIUS, AND THE OIL AND

τὸν οἶνον μὴ ἀδικήσῃς.
THE WINE YOU MAY NOT HARM.

6.7 Καὶ ὅτε ἤνοιξεν τὴν σφραγῖδα τὴν τετάρτην,
AND WHEN HE OPENED THE ²SEAL - ¹FOURTH,

ἤκουσα φωνὴν τοῦ τετάρτου ζῴου λέγοντος, Ἔρχου.
I HEARD [THE] VOICE OF THE FOURTH LIVING BEING SAYING, COME.

6.8 καὶ εἶδον, καὶ ἰδοὺ ἵππος χλωρός, καὶ ὁ
AND I SAW, AND BEHOLD A PALE~HORSE, AND THE ONE

καθήμενος ἐπάνω αὐτοῦ ὄνομα αὐτῷ [ὁ] θάνατος, καὶ
SITTING UPON IT [THE] NAME FOR HIM, - DEATH, AND

ὁ ᾅδης ἠκολούθει μετ' αὐτοῦ καὶ ἐδόθη αὐτοῖς
- HADES WAS FOLLOWING WITH HIM, AND ²WAS GIVEN ³TO THEM

ἐξουσία ἐπὶ τὸ τέταρτον τῆς γῆς ἀποκτεῖναι ἐν
¹AUTHORITY OVER THE FOURTH [PART] OF THE EARTH TO KILL WITH

ῥομφαίᾳ καὶ ἐν λιμῷ καὶ ἐν θανάτῳ καὶ ὑπὸ τῶν
SWORD AND WITH FAMINE AND WITH DEATH AND BY THE

θηρίων τῆς γῆς.
WILD BEASTS OF THE EARTH.

6.9 Καὶ ὅτε ἤνοιξεν τὴν πέμπτην σφραγῖδα, εἶδον
AND WHEN HE OPENED THE FIFTH SEAL, I SAW

ὑποκάτω τοῦ θυσιαστηρίου τὰς ψυχὰς τῶν
UNDERNEATH THE ALTAR THE SOULS OF THE ONES

ἐσφαγμένων διὰ τὸν λόγον τοῦ θεοῦ καὶ διὰ
HAVING BEEN SLAIN BECAUSE OF THE WORD - OF GOD AND BECAUSE OF

τὴν μαρτυρίαν ἣν εἶχον. **6.10** καὶ ἔκραξαν
THE[IR] TESTIMONY WHICH THEY WERE KEEPING. AND THEY CRIED OUT

φωνῇ μεγάλῃ λέγοντες, Ἕως πότε, ὁ δεσπότης ὁ
WITH A LOUD~VOICE SAYING, UNTIL WHEN, - MASTER, THE

ἅγιος καὶ ἀληθινός, οὐ κρίνεις καὶ ἐκδικεῖς τὸ αἷμα
HOLY ONE AND TRUE, DO YOU NOT JUDGE AND AVENGE THE BLOOD

ἡμῶν ἐκ τῶν κατοικούντων ἐπὶ τῆς γῆς; **6.11** καὶ
OF US FROM THE ONES DWELLING ON THE EARTH? AND

ἐδόθη αὐτοῖς ἑκάστῳ στολὴ λευκὴ καὶ ἐρρέθη αὐτοῖς
³WAS GIVEN ⁴TO THEM ⁵EACH ONE ²ROBE ¹A WHITE AND IT WAS TOLD THEM

ἵνα ἀναπαύσονται ἔτι χρόνον μικρόν, ἕως
THAT THEY WILL REST YET A LITTLE~WHILE, UNTIL

πληρωθῶσιν καὶ οἱ σύνδουλοι αὐτῶν καὶ οἱ
[THE NUMBER] SHOULD BE COMPLETE ALSO - OF THEIR~FELLOW SLAVES AND -

ἀδελφοὶ αὐτῶν οἱ μέλλοντες ἀποκτέννεσθαι ὡς καὶ
THEIR~BROTHERS, THE ONES BEING ABOUT TO BE KILLED AS ALSO

αὐτοί.
THEY.

6.12 Καὶ εἶδον ὅτε ἤνοιξεν τὴν σφραγῖδα τὴν ἕκτην,
AND I SAW WHEN HE OPENED THE ²SEAL - ¹SIXTH,

καὶ σεισμὸς μέγας ἐγένετο καὶ ὁ ἥλιος ἐγένετο
AND A GREAT~EARTHQUAKE OCCURRED AND THE SUN BECAME

μέλας ὡς σάκκος τρίχινος καὶ ἡ σελήνη ὅλη ἐγένετο
BLACK AS SACKCLOTH MADE OF HAIR AND THE WHOLE~MOON BECAME

ὡς αἷμα **6.13** καὶ οἱ ἀστέρες τοῦ οὐρανοῦ ἔπεσαν εἰς
LIKE BLOOD AND THE STARS OF THE HEAVEN(SKY) FELL TO

τὴν γῆν, ὡς συκῆ βάλλει τοὺς ὀλύνθους αὐτῆς ὑπὸ
THE EARTH, AS A FIG TREE CASTS THE UNRIPE FIGS OF IT ²BY

ἀνέμου μεγάλου σειομένη, **6.14** καὶ ὁ οὐρανὸς
⁴WIND ³A GREAT ¹BEING SHAKEN, AND THE HEAVEN(SKY)

ἀπεχωρίσθη ὡς βιβλίον ἑλισσόμενον καὶ πᾶν ὄρος
WAS SPLIT APART AS A SCROLL BEING ROLLED UP AND EVERY MOUNTAIN

καὶ νῆσος ἐκ τῶν τόπων αὐτῶν ἐκινήθησαν. **6.15** καὶ
AND ISLAND OUT OF THE PLACES OF THEM WERE MOVED. AND

οἱ βασιλεῖς τῆς γῆς καὶ οἱ μεγιστᾶνες καὶ οἱ
THE KINGS OF THE EARTH AND THE GREAT MEN AND THE

χιλίαρχοι καὶ οἱ πλούσιοι καὶ οἱ ἰσχυροὶ καὶ πᾶς
MILITARY LEADERS AND THE RICH MEN AND THE STRONG MEN AND EVERY

δοῦλος καὶ ἐλεύθερος ἔκρυψαν ἑαυτοὺς εἰς τὰ σπήλαια
SLAVE AND FREE MAN HID THEMSELVES IN THE CAVES

καὶ εἰς τὰς πέτρας τῶν ὀρέων **6.16** καὶ λέγουσιν
AND IN THE ROCKS OF THE MOUNTAINS, AND THEY SAY

τοῖς ὄρεσιν καὶ ταῖς πέτραις, Πέσετε ἐφ᾽ ἡμᾶς καὶ
TO THE MOUNTAINS AND TO THE ROCKS, FALL ON US AND

κρύψατε ἡμᾶς ἀπὸ προσώπου τοῦ καθημένου ἐπὶ
HIDE US FROM [THE] FACE OF THE ONE SITTING ON

τοῦ θρόνου καὶ ἀπὸ τῆς ὀργῆς τοῦ ἀρνίου, **6.17** ὅτι
THE THRONE AND FROM THE WRATH OF THE LAMB, BECAUSE

ἦλθεν ἡ ἡμέρα ἡ μεγάλη τῆς ὀργῆς αὐτῶν, καὶ
⁵CAME(HAS COME) ¹THE ³DAY - ²GREAT - ⁴OF THEIR~WRATH, AND

τίς δύναται σταθῆναι;
WHO IS ABLE TO STAND?

black as sackcloth, the full moon became like blood, ¹³and the stars of the sky fell to the earth as the fig tree drops its winter fruit when shaken by a gale. ¹⁴The sky vanished like a scroll rolling itself up, and every mountain and island was removed from its place. ¹⁵Then the kings of the earth and the magnates and the generals and the rich and the powerful, and everyone, slave and free, hid in the caves and among the rocks of the mountains, ¹⁶calling to the mountains and rocks, "Fall on us and hide us from the face of the one seated on the throne and from the wrath of the Lamb; ¹⁷for the great day of their wrath has come, and who is able to stand?"

CHAPTER 7

7.1 Μετὰ τοῦτο εἶδον τέσσαρας ἀγγέλους
AFTER THIS I SAW FOUR ANGELS

ἑστῶτας ἐπὶ τὰς τέσσαρας γωνίας τῆς γῆς,
HAVING TAKEN [THEIR] STAND ON THE FOUR CORNERS OF THE EARTH,

κρατοῦντας τοὺς τέσσαρας ἀνέμους τῆς γῆς ἵνα
HOLDING THE FOUR WINDS OF THE EARTH SO THAT

μὴ πνέῃ ἄνεμος ἐπὶ τῆς γῆς μήτε ἐπὶ τῆς
²SHOULD NOT BLOW ¹WIND ON THE EARTH NOR ON THE

θαλάσσης μήτε ἐπὶ πᾶν δένδρον. **7.2** καὶ εἶδον ἄλλον
SEA NOR ON ANY TREE. AND I SAW ANOTHER

ἄγγελον ἀναβαίνοντα ἀπὸ ἀνατολῆς ἡλίου ἔχοντα
ANGEL COMING UP FROM [THE] RISING OF [THE] SUN, HAVING

σφραγῖδα θεοῦ ζῶντος, καὶ ἔκραξεν φωνῇ μεγάλῃ τοῖς
A SEAL OF [THE] LIVING~GOD, AND HE CRIED WITH A LOUD~VOICE TO THE

After this I saw four angels standing at the four corners of the earth, holding back the four winds of the earth so that no wind could blow on earth or sea or against any tree. ²I saw another angel ascending from the rising of the sun, having the seal of the living God, and he called with a loud voice to the

four angels who had been given power to damage earth and sea, ³saying, "Do not damage the earth or the sea or the trees, until we have marked the servantsʷ of our God with a seal on their foreheads."

4 And I heard the number of those who were sealed, one hundred forty-four thousand, sealed out of every tribe of the people of Israel:

5 From the tribe of Judah twelve thousand sealed,
from the tribe of Reuben twelve thousand,
from the tribe of Gad twelve thousand,
6 from the tribe of Asher twelve thousand,
from the tribe of Naphtali twelve thousand,
from the tribe of Manasseh twelve thousand,
7 from the tribe of Simeon twelve thousand,
from the tribe of Levi twelve thousand,
from the tribe of Issachar twelve thousand,
8 from the tribe of Zebulun twelve thousand,
from the tribe of Joseph twelve thousand,
from the tribe of Benjamin twelve thousand sealed.

9 After this I looked, and there was a great multitude that no one could count, from every nation, from all tribes and peoples and languages, standing before

ʷ Gk *slaves*

τέσσαρσιν ἀγγέλοις οἷς ἐδόθη αὐτοῖς ἀδικῆσαι τὴν
FOUR   ANGELS   TO WHOM IT WAS GIVEN TO THEM TO HARM   THE

γῆν καὶ τὴν θάλασσαν **7.3** λέγων, Μὴ ἀδικήσητε τὴν
EARTH AND THE SEA,   SAYING, DO NOT HARM   THE

γῆν μήτε τὴν θάλασσαν μήτε τὰ δένδρα, ἄχρι
EARTH NOR THE SEA   NOR THE TREES,   UNTIL

σφραγίσωμεν τοὺς δούλους τοῦ θεοῦ ἡμῶν ἐπὶ τῶν
WE SEAL   THE SLAVES   OF THE GOD OF US UPON THE

μετώπων αὐτῶν. **7.4** καὶ ἤκουσα τὸν ἀριθμὸν τῶν
FOREHEADS OF THEM.   AND I HEARD THE NUMBER   OF THE ONES

ἐσφραγισμένων, ἑκατὸν τεσσεράκοντα τέσσαρες
HAVING BEEN SEALED,   A HUNDRED FORTY-FOUR

χιλιάδες, ἐσφραγισμένοι ἐκ πάσης φυλῆς υἱῶν
THOUSAND, HAVING BEEN SEALED FROM EVERY TRIBE OF [THE] SONS

Ἰσραήλ·
OF ISRAEL.

7.5 ἐκ φυλῆς Ἰούδα δώδεκα χιλιάδες ἐσφραγισμένοι,
     OF [THE] TRIBE OF JUDAH TWELVE THOUSAND HAVING BEEN SEALED,

ἐκ φυλῆς Ῥουβὴν δώδεκα χιλιάδες,
OF [THE] TRIBE OF REUBEN TWELVE THOUSAND,

ἐκ φυλῆς Γὰδ δώδεκα χιλιάδες,
OF [THE] TRIBE OF GAD TWELVE THOUSAND,

7.6 ἐκ φυλῆς Ἀσὴρ δώδεκα χιλιάδες,
     OF [THE] TRIBE OF ASHER TWELVE THOUSAND,

ἐκ φυλῆς Νεφθαλὶμ δώδεκα χιλιάδες,
OF [THE] TRIBE OF NAPHTALI TWELVE THOUSAND,

ἐκ φυλῆς Μανασσῆ δώδεκα χιλιάδες,
OF [THE] TRIBE OF MANASSEH TWELVE THOUSAND,

7.7 ἐκ φυλῆς Συμεὼν δώδεκα χιλιάδες,
     OF [THE] TRIBE OF SIMEON TWELVE THOUSAND,

ἐκ φυλῆς Λευὶ δώδεκα χιλιάδες,
OF [THE] TRIBE OF LEVI TWELVE THOUSAND,

ἐκ φυλῆς Ἰσσαχὰρ δώδεκα χιλιάδες,
OF [THE] TRIBE OF ISSACHAR TWELVE THOUSAND,

7.8 ἐκ φυλῆς Ζαβουλὼν δώδεκα χιλιάδες,
     OF [THE] TRIBE OF ZEBULUN TWELVE THOUSAND,

ἐκ φυλῆς Ἰωσὴφ δώδεκα χιλιάδες,
OF [THE] TRIBE OF JOSEPH TWELVE THOUSAND,

ἐκ φυλῆς Βενιαμὶν δώδεκα χιλιάδες
OF [THE] TRIBE OF BENJAMIN TWELVE THOUSAND

ἐσφραγισμένοι.
HAVING BEEN SEALED.

7.9 Μετὰ ταῦτα εἶδον, καὶ ἰδοὺ ὄχλος πολύς, ὃν
     AFTER THESE THINGS I SAW, AND BEHOLD, A GREAT~CROWD, WHICH

ἀριθμῆσαι αὐτὸν οὐδεὶς ἐδύνατο, ἐκ παντὸς ἔθνους
³TO NUMBER   -   ¹NO ONE ²WAS BEING ABLE, OUT OF EVERY NATION

καὶ φυλῶν καὶ λαῶν καὶ γλωσσῶν ἑστῶτες ἐνώπιον
AND [FROM] TRIBES AND PEOPLES AND TONGUES STANDING BEFORE

τοῦ θρόνου καὶ ἐνώπιον τοῦ ἀρνίου περιβεβλημένους
THE THRONE AND BEFORE THE LAMB, HAVING BEEN CLOTHED WITH

στολὰς λευκὰς καὶ φοίνικες ἐν ταῖς χερσὶν αὐτῶν,
WHITE~ROBES AND PALM BRANCHES IN THE HANDS OF THEM,

7.10 καὶ κράζουσιν φωνῇ μεγάλῃ λέγοντες,
AND THEY CRY WITH A GREAT(LOUD)~VOICE SAYING,

Ἡ σωτηρία τῷ θεῷ ἡμῶν τῷ καθημένῳ
- SALVATION [BELONGS] TO THE GOD OF US, THE ONE SITTING

ἐπὶ τῷ θρόνῳ καὶ τῷ ἀρνίῳ.
ON THE THRONE, AND TO THE LAMB.

7.11 καὶ πάντες οἱ ἄγγελοι εἱστήκεισαν κύκλῳ τοῦ
AND ALL THE ANGELS STOOD AROUND THE

θρόνου καὶ τῶν πρεσβυτέρων καὶ τῶν τεσσάρων
THRONE AND THE ELDERS AND THE FOUR

ζῴων καὶ ἔπεσαν ἐνώπιον τοῦ θρόνου ἐπὶ τὰ
LIVING BEINGS AND FELL BEFORE THE THRONE ON THE

πρόσωπα αὐτῶν καὶ προσεκύνησαν τῷ θεῷ
FACES OF THEM AND THEY WORSHIPED - GOD

7.12 λέγοντες,
SAYING,

Ἀμήν, ἡ εὐλογία καὶ ἡ δόξα καὶ ἡ σοφία καὶ
AMEN, THE PRAISE AND THE GLORY AND THE WISDOM AND

ἡ εὐχαριστία καὶ ἡ τιμὴ καὶ ἡ δύναμις καὶ ἡ
THE THANKSGIVING AND THE HONOR AND THE POWER AND THE

ἰσχὺς τῷ θεῷ ἡμῶν εἰς τοὺς αἰῶνας τῶν αἰώνων·
STRENGTH TO THE GOD OF US INTO THE AGES OF THE AGES;

ἀμήν.
AMEN.

7.13 Καὶ ἀπεκρίθη εἷς ἐκ τῶν πρεσβυτέρων λέγων
AND 5ANSWERED 1ONE 2OF 3THE 4ELDERS SAYING

μοι, Οὗτοι οἱ περιβεβλημένοι τὰς στολὰς τὰς λευκὰς
TO ME, THESE ONES HAVING BEEN CLOTHED WITH THE 2ROBES - 1WHITE,

τίνες εἰσὶν καὶ πόθεν ἦλθον; **7.14** καὶ εἴρηκα
WHO ARE THEY AND FROM WHERE DID THEY COME? AND I HAVE SAID

αὐτῷ, Κύριέ μου, σὺ οἶδας. καὶ εἶπέν μοι, Οὗτοί
TO HIM, LORD OF ME, YOU KNOW. AND HE SAID TO ME, THESE

εἰσιν οἱ ἐρχόμενοι ἐκ τῆς θλίψεως τῆς μεγάλης
ARE THE ONES COMING OUT OF THE 2TRIBULATION - 1GREAT

καὶ ἔπλυναν τὰς στολὰς αὐτῶν καὶ ἐλεύκαναν αὐτὰς
AND THEY WASHED THE ROBES OF THEM AND WHITENED THEM

ἐν τῷ αἵματι τοῦ ἀρνίου.
IN THE BLOOD OF THE LAMB.

7.15 διὰ τοῦτό εἰσιν ἐνώπιον τοῦ θρόνου τοῦ θεοῦ
THEREFORE THEY ARE BEFORE THE THRONE - OF GOD

καὶ λατρεύουσιν αὐτῷ ἡμέρας καὶ νυκτὸς ἐν
AND SERVE HIM DAY AND NIGHT IN

τῷ ναῷ αὐτοῦ,
THE TEMPLE OF HIM,

the throne and before the Lamb, robed in white, with palm branches in their hands. [10]They cried out in a loud voice, saying,

"Salvation belongs to our God who is seated on the throne, and to the Lamb!"

[11]And all the angels stood around the throne and around the elders and the four living creatures, and they fell on their faces before the throne and worshiped God, [12]singing,

"Amen! Blessing and glory and wisdom and thanksgiving and honor and power and might be to our God forever and ever! Amen."

[13]Then one of the elders addressed me, saying, "Who are these, robed in white, and where have they come from?" [14]I said to him, "Sir, you are the one that knows." Then he said to me, "These are they who have come out of the great ordeal; they have washed their robes and made them white in the blood of the Lamb.

[15]For this reason they are before the throne of God, and worship him day and night within his temple,

and the one who is
seated on the throne
will shelter them.
¹⁶ They will hunger no
more, and thirst no
more;
the sun will not strike
them,
nor any scorching heat;
¹⁷ for the Lamb at the center
of the throne will be
their shepherd,
and he will guide them
to springs of the
water of life,
and God will wipe away
every tear from
their eyes."

καὶ ὁ   καθήμενος ἐπὶ τοῦ θρόνου
AND   THE ONE SITTING   ON   THE THRONE

σκηνώσει   ἐπ᾽ αὐτούς.
WILL SPREAD [HIS] TENT OVER THEM.

7.16 οὐ πεινάσουσιν ἔτι   οὐδὲ διψήσουσιν ἔτι
THEY WILL NOT HUNGER ANY MORE NOR THIRST   ANY MORE

οὐδὲ μὴ πέσῃ ἐπ᾽ αὐτοὺς ὁ ἥλιος
NEITHER - MAY FALL ON THEM THE SUN

οὐδὲ πᾶν καῦμα,
NOR ANY SCORCHING HEAT,

7.17 ὅτι   τὸ ἀρνίον τὸ ἀνὰ μέσον τοῦ θρόνου
BECAUSE THE LAMB - IN [THE] MIDST OF THE THRONE

ποιμανεῖ αὐτοὺς
WILL SHEPHERD THEM

καὶ ὁδηγήσει αὐτοὺς ἐπὶ ζωῆς πηγὰς
AND WILL LEAD THEM TO ³OF LIFE ¹FOUNTAINS

ὑδάτων,
²OF WATERS,

καὶ ἐξαλείψει ὁ θεὸς πᾶν δάκρυον
AND ²WILL WIPE AWAY - ¹GOD EVERY TEAR

ἐκ   τῶν ὀφθαλμῶν αὐτῶν.
FROM THE EYES   OF THEM.

CHAPTER 8

When the Lamb opened the
seventh seal, there was
silence in heaven for about
half an hour. ²And I saw the
seven angels who stand
before God, and seven
trumpets were given to
them.

3 Another angel with a
golden censer came and
stood at the altar; he was
given a great quantity of
incense to offer with the
prayers of all the saints
on the golden altar that is
before the throne. ⁴And the
smoke of the incense, with
the prayers of the saints,
rose before God from the
hand of the angel. ⁵Then

8.1 Καὶ ὅταν ἤνοιξεν τὴν σφραγίδα τὴν ἑβδόμην,
AND WHEN HE OPENED THE ²SEAL - ¹SEVENTH,

ἐγένετο σιγὴ ἐν τῷ οὐρανῷ ὡς ἡμιώριον. **8.2** καὶ
THERE WAS SILENCE IN - HEAVEN ABOUT HALF AN HOUR. AND

εἶδον τοὺς ἑπτὰ ἀγγέλους οἳ ἐνώπιον τοῦ θεοῦ
I SAW THE SEVEN ANGELS WHO ²BEFORE - ³GOD

ἑστήκασιν, καὶ ἐδόθησαν αὐτοῖς ἑπτὰ σάλπιγγες.
¹STOOD, AND THERE WERE GIVEN TO THEM SEVEN TRUMPETS.

8.3 Καὶ ἄλλος ἄγγελος ἦλθεν καὶ ἐστάθη ἐπὶ τοῦ
AND ANOTHER ANGEL CAME AND STOOD AT THE

θυσιαστηρίου ἔχων λιβανωτὸν χρυσοῦν, καὶ ἐδόθη
ALTAR,   HAVING A GOLDEN~CENSER, AND THERE WAS GIVEN

αὐτῷ θυμιάματα πολλά, ἵνα δώσει   ταῖς
TO HIM MUCH~INCENSE, THAT HE WILL GIVE [IT] WITH THE

προσευχαῖς τῶν ἁγίων πάντων ἐπὶ τὸ θυσιαστήριον
PRAYERS OF ²THE ³SAINTS ¹ALL AT THE ²ALTAR

τὸ χρυσοῦν τὸ ἐνώπιον τοῦ θρόνου. **8.4** καὶ ἀνέβη ὁ
- ¹GOLDEN - BEFORE THE THRONE. AND ASCENDED THE

καπνὸς τῶν θυμιαμάτων ταῖς προσευχαῖς τῶν ἁγίων
SMOKE OF THE INCENSES WITH THE PRAYERS OF THE SAINTS

ἐκ χειρὸς τοῦ ἀγγέλου ἐνώπιον τοῦ θεοῦ. **8.5** καὶ
OUT OF [THE] HAND OF THE ANGEL BEFORE - GOD. AND

εἴληφεν ὁ ἄγγελος τὸν λιβανωτὸν καὶ ἐγέμισεν
³HAS TAKEN ¹THE ²ANGEL THE CENSER AND FILLED

αὐτὸν ἐκ τοῦ πυρὸς τοῦ θυσιαστηρίου καὶ ἔβαλεν
IT FROM THE FIRE OF THE ALTAR AND HE THREW [IT]

εἰς τὴν γῆν, καὶ ἐγένοντο βρονταὶ καὶ φωναὶ καὶ
TO THE EARTH, AND THERE WERE THUNDERS AND SOUNDS AND

ἀστραπαὶ καὶ σεισμός.
LIGHTNING AND AN EARTHQUAKE.

8.6 Καὶ οἱ ἑπτὰ ἄγγελοι οἱ ἔχοντες τὰς ἑπτὰ
AND THE SEVEN ANGELS - HAVING THE SEVEN

σάλπιγγας ἡτοίμασαν αὐτοὺς ἵνα
TRUMPETS PREPARED THEMSELVES THAT

σαλπίσωσιν.
THEY MIGHT SOUND [THE] TRUMPETS.

8.7 Καὶ ὁ πρῶτος ἐσάλπισεν· καὶ ἐγένετο χάλαζα
AND THE FIRST TRUMPETED; AND THERE CAME HAIL

καὶ πῦρ μεμιγμένα ἐν αἵματι καὶ ἐβλήθη εἰς
AND FIRE HAVING BEEN MINGLED WITH BLOOD AND IT WAS THROWN TO

τὴν γῆν, καὶ τὸ τρίτον τῆς γῆς κατεκάη καὶ τὸ
THE EARTH, AND THE THIRD [PART] OF THE EARTH WAS BURNT UP, AND THE

τρίτον τῶν δένδρων κατεκάη καὶ πᾶς χόρτος χλωρὸς
THIRD [PART] OF THE TREES WAS BURNT UP AND ALL GREEN~GRASS

κατεκάη.
WAS BURNT UP.

8.8 Καὶ ὁ δεύτερος ἄγγελος ἐσάλπισεν· καὶ ὡς
AND THE SECOND ANGEL TRUMPETED; AND AS [IT WERE]

ὄρος μέγα πυρὶ καιόμενον ἐβλήθη εἰς τὴν
A GREAT~MOUNTAIN WITH FIRE BURNING WAS THROWN INTO THE

θάλασσαν, καὶ ἐγένετο τὸ τρίτον τῆς θαλάσσης
SEA, AND ⁵BECAME ¹THE ²THIRD [PART] ³OF THE ⁴SEA

αἷμα **8.9** καὶ ἀπέθανεν τὸ τρίτον τῶν κτισμάτων
⁶BLOOD AND ¹⁰DIED ¹THE ²THIRD [PART] ³OF THE ⁴CREATURES

τῶν ἐν τῇ θαλάσσῃ τὰ ἔχοντα ψυχὰς καὶ τὸ τρίτον
- ⁵IN ⁶THE ⁷SEA - ⁸HAVING ⁹LIFE, AND THE THIRD

τῶν πλοίων διεφθάρησαν.
OF THE SHIPS WERE DESTROYED.

8.10 Καὶ ὁ τρίτος ἄγγελος ἐσάλπισεν· καὶ ἔπεσεν
AND THE THIRD ANGEL TRUMPETED; AND FELL

ἐκ τοῦ οὐρανοῦ ἀστὴρ μέγας καιόμενος ὡς λαμπάς
OUT OF - HEAVEN A GREAT~STAR BLAZING AS A TORCH

καὶ ἔπεσεν ἐπὶ τὸ τρίτον τῶν ποταμῶν καὶ ἐπὶ τὰς
AND IT FELL ON THE THIRD [PART] OF THE RIVERS AND ON THE

πηγὰς τῶν ὑδάτων, **8.11** καὶ τὸ ὄνομα τοῦ ἀστέρος
FOUNTAINS OF THE WATERS, AND THE NAME OF THE STAR

λέγεται ὁ Ἄψινθος, καὶ ἐγένετο τὸ τρίτον τῶν
IS SAID [TO BE] - WORMWOOD, AND ⁵BECAME ¹THE ²THIRD [PART] ³OF THE

ὑδάτων εἰς ἄψινθον καὶ πολλοὶ τῶν ἀνθρώπων
⁴WATERS - WORMWOOD(BITTER) AND MANY OF THE MEN

the angel took the censer and filled it with fire from the altar and threw it on the earth; and there were peals of thunder, rumblings, flashes of lightning, and an earthquake.

6 Now the seven angels who had the seven trumpets made ready to blow them.

7 The first angel blew his trumpet, and there came hail and fire, mixed with blood, and they were hurled to the earth; and a third of the earth was burned up, and a third of the trees were burned up, and all green grass was burned up.

8 The second angel blew his trumpet, and something like a great mountain, burning with fire, was thrown into the sea. ⁹A third of the sea became blood, a third of the living creatures in the sea died, and a third of the ships were destroyed.

10 The third angel blew his trumpet, and a great star fell from heaven, blazing like a torch, and it fell on a third of the rivers and on the springs of water. ¹¹The name of the star is Wormwood. A third of the waters became wormwood, and many

died from the water, because it was made bitter.

12 The fourth angel blew his trumpet, and a third of the sun was struck, and a third of the moon, and a third of the stars, so that a third of their light was darkened; a third of the day was kept from shining, and likewise the night.

13 Then I looked, and I heard an eagle crying with a loud voice as it flew in midheaven, "Woe, woe, woe to the inhabitants of the earth, at the blasts of the other trumpets that the three angels are about to blow!"

ἀπέθανον ἐκ τῶν ὑδάτων ὅτι ἐπικράνθησαν.
DIED FROM THE WATERS BECAUSE THEY WERE MADE BITTER.

8.12 Καὶ ὁ τέταρτος ἄγγελος ἐσάλπισεν· καὶ
AND THE FOURTH ANGEL TRUMPETED; AND

ἐπλήγη τὸ τρίτον τοῦ ἡλίου καὶ τὸ τρίτον τῆς
5WAS STRUCK 1THE 2THIRD [PART] 3OF THE 4SUN AND THE THIRD [PART] OF THE

σελήνης καὶ τὸ τρίτον τῶν ἀστέρων, ἵνα
MOON AND THE THIRD [PART] OF THE STARS, THAT

σκοτισθῇ τὸ τρίτον αὐτῶν καὶ ἡ ἡμέρα
4MIGHT BE DARKENED 1THE 2THIRD [PART] 3OF THEM AND THE DAY

μὴ φάνῃ τὸ τρίτον αὐτῆς καὶ ἡ νὺξ ὁμοίως.
COULD NOT APPEAR [FOR] THE THIRD [PART] OF IT, AND THE NIGHT LIKEWISE.

8.13 Καὶ εἶδον, καὶ ἤκουσα ἑνὸς ἀετοῦ πετομένου ἐν
AND I SAW, AND I HEARD ONE EAGLE FLYING IN

μεσουρανήματι λέγοντος φωνῇ μεγάλῃ, Οὐαὶ οὐαὶ οὐαὶ
MIDHEAVEN(MIDAIR) SAYING WITH A LOUD~VOICE, WOE, WOE, WOE

τοὺς κατοικοῦντας ἐπὶ τῆς γῆς ἐκ τῶν λοιπῶν
TO THE ONES DWELLING ON - EARTH [BECAUSE] OF THE REMAINING

φωνῶν τῆς σάλπιγγος τῶν τριῶν ἀγγέλων τῶν
SOUNDS(BLASTS) OF THE TRUMPET OF THE THREE ANGELS -

μελλόντων σαλπίζειν.
BEING ABOUT TO TRUMPET.

CHAPTER 9

And the fifth angel blew his trumpet, and I saw a star that had fallen from heaven to earth, and he was given the key to the shaft of the bottomless pit; 2he opened the shaft of the bottomless pit, and from the shaft rose smoke like the smoke of a great furnace, and the sun and the air were darkened with the smoke from the shaft. 3Then from the smoke came locusts on the earth, and they were given authority like the authority of scorpions of the earth. 4They were told not to damage the grass of the earth or any green growth or any tree, but

9.1 Καὶ ὁ πέμπτος ἄγγελος ἐσάλπισεν· καὶ εἶδον
AND THE FIFTH ANGEL TRUMPETED; AND I SAW

ἀστέρα ἐκ τοῦ οὐρανοῦ πεπτωκότα εἰς τὴν γῆν, καὶ
A STAR OUT OF - HEAVEN HAVING FALLEN TO THE EARTH, AND

ἐδόθη αὐτῷ ἡ κλεὶς τοῦ φρέατος τῆς ἀβύσσου
WAS GIVEN TO IT THE KEY OF THE SHAFT OF THE ABYSS,

9.2 καὶ ἤνοιξεν τὸ φρέαρ τῆς ἀβύσσου, καὶ
AND HE OPENED THE SHAFT OF THE ABYSS, AND

ἀνέβη καπνὸς ἐκ τοῦ φρέατος ὡς καπνὸς
SMOKE~ROSE OUT OF THE SHAFT AS SMOKE

καμίνου μεγάλης, καὶ ἐσκοτώθη ὁ ἥλιος καὶ ὁ ἀὴρ
OF A GREAT~FURNACE, AND WAS DARKENED THE SUN AND THE AIR

ἐκ τοῦ καπνοῦ τοῦ φρέατος. **9.3** καὶ ἐκ τοῦ καπνοῦ
BY THE SMOKE OF THE SHAFT. AND OUT OF THE SMOKE

ἐξῆλθον ἀκρίδες εἰς τὴν γῆν, καὶ ἐδόθη αὐταῖς
CAME FORTH LOCUSTS TO THE EARTH, AND 2WAS GIVEN 3TO THEM

ἐξουσία ὡς ἔχουσιν ἐξουσίαν οἱ σκορπίοι τῆς γῆς.
1AUTHORITY AS 4HAVE 5AUTHORITY 1THE 2SCORPIONS - 3OF EARTH.

9.4 καὶ ἐρρέθη αὐταῖς ἵνα μὴ ἀδικήσουσιν τὸν χόρτον
AND IT WAS TOLD THEM THAT THEY SHOULD NOT HARM THE GRASS

τῆς γῆς οὐδὲ πᾶν χλωρὸν οὐδὲ πᾶν δένδρον, εἰ μὴ
OF THE EARTH NOR ANY GREENERY NOR ANY TREE, EXCEPT

τοὺς ἀνθρώπους οἵτινες   οὐκ ἔχουσι τὴν σφραγῖδα τοῦ
THE   MEN,   EVERYONE WHO DOES NOT HAVE THE   SEAL   -

θεοῦ ἐπὶ τῶν μετώπων. **9.5** καὶ ἐδόθη   αὐτοῖς ἵνα
OF GOD ON THE(IR) FOREHEADS.   AND IT WAS GIVEN TO THEM THAT

μὴ ἀποκτείνωσιν αὐτούς, ἀλλ' ἵνα βασανισθήσονται
THEY SHOULD NOT KILL   THEM,   BUT THAT THEY WILL BE TORMENTED

μῆνας πέντε, καὶ ὁ βασανισμὸς αὐτῶν ὡς βασανισμὸς
FIVE~MONTHS, AND - THEIR~TORMENT   [IS] AS [THE] TORMENT

σκορπίου ὅταν παίσῃ ἄνθρωπον. **9.6** καὶ ἐν ταῖς
OF A SCORPION WHEN IT STRIKES A MAN.   AND IN -

ἡμέραις ἐκείναις ζητήσουσιν οἱ ἄνθρωποι τὸν θάνατον
THOSE~DAYS   ²WILL SEEK   - ¹MEN   DEATH

καὶ οὐ μὴ   εὑρήσουσιν αὐτόν, καὶ ἐπιθυμήσουσιν
AND BY NO MEANS WILL FIND   IT,   AND THEY WILL DESIRE

ἀποθανεῖν καὶ φεύγει ὁ θάνατος ἀπ' αὐτῶν.
TO DIE   AND ²FLEES - ¹DEATH   FROM THEM.

9.7 Καὶ τὰ ὁμοιώματα τῶν ἀκρίδων ὅμοια ἵπποις
AND THE APPEARANCES OF THE LOCUSTS [WERE] LIKE HORSES

ἡτοιμασμένοις εἰς πόλεμον, καὶ ἐπὶ τὰς κεφαλὰς
HAVING BEEN PREPARED FOR WAR,   AND ON THE   HEADS

αὐτῶν ὡς στέφανοι ὅμοιοι χρυσῷ, καὶ τὰ πρόσωπα
OF THEM AS CROWNS LIKE GOLD   AND THE FACES

αὐτῶν ὡς πρόσωπα ἀνθρώπων, **9.8** καὶ εἶχον τρίχας
OF THEM AS FACES   OF MEN,   AND THEY HAD HAIR

ὡς τρίχας γυναικῶν, καὶ οἱ ὀδόντες αὐτῶν ὡς λεόντων
AS HAIR   OF WOMEN,   AND THE TEETH   OF THEM ²AS ³LIONS'

ἦσαν, **9.9** καὶ εἶχον θώρακας ὡς θώρακας σιδηροῦς,
¹WERE,   AND THEY HAD BREASTPLATES LIKE IRON~BREASTPLATES

καὶ ἡ φωνὴ τῶν πτερύγων αὐτῶν ὡς   φωνὴ
AND THE SOUND OF THE WINGS   OF THEM [WAS] AS [THE] SOUND

ἁρμάτων ἵππων   πολλῶν τρεχόντων εἰς πόλεμον,
²CHARIOTS ³[WITH] HORSES ¹OF MANY RUNNING   INTO BATTLE,

9.10 καὶ ἔχουσιν οὐρὰς ὁμοίας σκορπίοις καὶ κέντρα,
AND THEY HAVE TAILS LIKE   SCORPIONS, AND STINGS,

καὶ ἐν   ταῖς οὐραῖς αὐτῶν ἡ ἐξουσία   αὐτῶν
AND ⁴[IS] IN(WITH) ⁵THE ⁶TAILS ⁷OF THEM ¹THE ²AUTHORITY(POWER) ³OF THEM

ἀδικῆσαι τοὺς ἀνθρώπους μῆνας πέντε, **9.11** ἔχουσιν ἐπ'
TO HARM   -   MEN   FIVE~MONTHS;   THEY HAVE OVER

αὐτῶν βασιλέα τὸν ἄγγελον τῆς ἀβύσσου, ὄνομα
THEM A KING,   THE ANGEL   OF THE ABYSS,   [THE] NAME

αὐτῷ Ἑβραϊστὶ Ἀβαδδών, καὶ ἐν τῇ Ἑλληνικῇ
FOR HIM IN HEBREW,   ABADDON,   AND IN THE GREEK

ὄνομα ἔχει Ἀπολλύων.
HE HAS~[THE] NAME APOLLYON.

9.12 Ἡ οὐαὶ ἡ μία ἀπῆλθεν· ἰδοὺ ἔρχεται ἔτι δύο
THE ²WOE - ¹FIRST PASSED; BEHOLD, YET~COMES TWO

οὐαὶ μετὰ ταῦτα.
WOES AFTER THESE THINGS.

only those people who do
not have the seal of God on
their foreheads. [5]They were
allowed to torture them for
five months, but not to kill
them, and their torture was
like the torture of a scorpion
when it stings someone.
[6]And in those days people
will seek death but will not
find it; they will long to die,
but death will flee from
them.

7 In appearance the
locusts were like horses
equipped for battle. On their
heads were what looked like
crowns of gold; their faces
were like human faces,
[8]their hair like women's hair,
and their teeth like lions'
teeth; [9]they had scales like
iron breastplates, and the
noise of their wings was like
the noise of many chariots
with horses rushing into
battle. [10]They have tails like
scorpions, with stingers, and
in their tails is their power
to harm people for five
months. [11]They have as king
over them the angel of the
bottomless pit; his name
in Hebrew is Abaddon,[x]
and in Greek he is called
Apollyon.[y]

12 The first woe has
passed. There are still two
woes to come.

[x] That is, *Destruction*
[y] That is, *Destroyer*

13 Then the sixth angel blew his trumpet, and I heard a voice from the four[z] horns of the golden altar before God, [14]saying to the sixth angel who had the trumpet, "Release the four angels who are bound at the great river Euphrates." [15]So the four angels were released, who had been held ready for the hour, the day, the month, and the year, to kill a third of humankind. [16]The number of the troops of cavalry was two hundred million; I heard their number. [17]And this was how I saw the horses in my vision: the riders wore breastplates the color of fire and of sapphire[a] and of sulfur; the heads of the horses were like lions' heads, and fire and smoke and sulfur came out of their mouths. [18]By these three plagues a third of humankind was killed, by the fire and smoke and sulfur coming out of their mouths. [19]For the power of the horses is in their mouths and in their tails; their tails are like serpents, having heads; and with them they inflict harm.

20 The rest of humankind,

[z] Other ancient authorities lack four
[a] Gk hyacinth

9.13 Καὶ ὁ ἕκτος ἄγγελος ἐσάλπισεν· καὶ ἤκουσα
AND THE SIXTH ANGEL TRUMPETED; AND I HEARD

φωνὴν μίαν ἐκ τῶν [τεσσάρων] κεράτων τοῦ
ONE~VOICE FROM THE FOUR HORNS OF THE

θυσιαστηρίου τοῦ χρυσοῦ τοῦ ἐνώπιον τοῦ θεοῦ,
[2]ALTAR - [1]GOLDEN - BEFORE - GOD,

9.14 λέγοντα τῷ ἕκτῳ ἀγγέλῳ, ὁ ἔχων τὴν
SAYING TO THE SIXTH ANGEL, THE ONE HAVING THE

σάλπιγγα, Λῦσον τοὺς τέσσαρας ἀγγέλους τοὺς
TRUMPET, RELEASE THE FOUR ANGELS -

δεδεμένους ἐπὶ τῷ ποταμῷ τῷ μεγάλῳ Εὐφράτῃ.
HAVING BEEN BOUND AT THE [2]RIVER - [1]GREAT, EUPHRATES.

9.15 καὶ ἐλύθησαν οἱ τέσσαρες ἄγγελοι οἱ
AND WERE RELEASED THE FOUR ANGELS -

ἡτοιμασμένοι εἰς τὴν ὥραν καὶ ἡμέραν καὶ μῆνα καὶ
HAVING BEEN PREPARED FOR THE HOUR AND DAY AND MONTH AND

ἐνιαυτόν, ἵνα ἀποκτείνωσιν τὸ τρίτον τῶν ἀνθρώπων.
YEAR, THAT THEY SHOULD KILL THE THIRD [PART] - OF MEN.

9.16 καὶ ὁ ἀριθμὸς τῶν στρατευμάτων τοῦ ἱππικοῦ
AND THE NUMBER - OF TROOPS - OF CAVALRY

δισμυριάδες μυριάδων, ἤκουσα τὸν ἀριθμὸν αὐτῶν.
TWICE TEN THOUSAND [TIMES] TEN THOUSAND, I HEARD THE NUMBER OF THEM.

9.17 καὶ οὕτως εἶδον τοὺς ἵππους ἐν τῇ ὁράσει καὶ
AND THUS I SAW THE HORSES IN THE VISION AND

τοὺς καθημένους ἐπ᾽ αὐτῶν, ἔχοντας θώρακας
THE ONES SITTING ON THEM, HAVING BREASTPLATES

πυρίνους καὶ ὑακινθίνους καὶ θειώδεις, καὶ αἱ
FIERY [RED] AND HYACINTH [BLUE] AND SULFUR [YELLOW], AND THE

κεφαλαὶ τῶν ἵππων ὡς κεφαλαὶ λεόντων, καὶ ἐκ
HEADS OF THE HORSES LIKE HEADS OF LIONS, AND FROM

τῶν στομάτων αὐτῶν ἐκπορεύεται πῦρ καὶ καπνὸς καὶ
THE MOUTHS OF THEM GOES FORTH FIRE AND SMOKE AND

θεῖον. **9.18** ἀπὸ τῶν τριῶν πληγῶν τούτων ἀπεκτάνθησαν
SULFUR. FROM - [2]THREE [3]PLAGUES [1]THESE WERE KILLED

τὸ τρίτον τῶν ἀνθρώπων, ἐκ τοῦ πυρὸς καὶ τοῦ
THE THIRD [PART] - OF MEN, BY THE FIRE AND THE

καπνοῦ καὶ τοῦ θείου τοῦ ἐκπορευομένου ἐκ τῶν
SMOKE AND THE SULFUR - COMING OUT OF THE

στομάτων αὐτῶν. **9.19** ἡ γὰρ ἐξουσία τῶν ἵππων ἐν
MOUTH OF THEM. FOR~THE AUTHORITY(POWER) OF THE HORSES [2]IN

τῷ στόματι αὐτῶν ἐστιν καὶ ἐν ταῖς οὐραῖς αὐτῶν,
[3]THE [4]MOUTHS [5]OF THEM [1]IS AND IN THE TAILS OF THEM,

αἱ γὰρ οὐραὶ αὐτῶν ὅμοιαι ὄφεσιν, ἔχουσαι κεφαλὰς
FOR~THE TAILS OF THEM [ARE] LIKE SERPENTS, HAVING HEADS,

καὶ ἐν αὐταῖς ἀδικοῦσιν.
AND WITH THEM THEY DO INJURY.

9.20 Καὶ οἱ λοιποὶ τῶν ἀνθρώπων, οἳ οὐκ
AND THE REST OF THE MEN, THE ONES NOT

ἀπεκτάνθησαν ἐν ταῖς πληγαῖς ταύταις, οὐδὲ
KILLED BY - THESE~PLAGUES, NOT EVEN

μετενόησαν ἐκ τῶν ἔργων τῶν χειρῶν αὐτῶν, ἵνα
REPENTED OF THE WORKS OF THE HANDS OF THEM, THAT

μὴ προσκυνήσουσιν τὰ δαιμόνια καὶ τὰ εἴδωλα τὰ
THEY SHALL(SHOULD) NOT WORSHIP - DEMONS AND THE IDOLS -

χρυσᾶ καὶ τὰ ἀργυρᾶ καὶ τὰ χαλκᾶ καὶ τὰ λίθινα
GOLDEN AND - SILVER AND - BRONZE AND - STONE

καὶ τὰ ξύλινα, ἃ οὔτε βλέπειν δύνανται οὔτε
AND - WOODEN, WHICH NEITHER ARE ABLE~TO SEE NOR

ἀκούειν οὔτε περιπατεῖν, **9.21** καὶ οὐ μετενόησαν ἐκ τῶν
TO HEAR NOR TO WALK, AND THEY DID NOT REPENT OF THE

φόνων αὐτῶν οὔτε ἐκ τῶν φαρμάκων αὐτῶν οὔτε ἐκ τῆς
MURDERS OF THEM NOR OF THE SORCERIES OF THEM NOR OF THE

πορνείας αὐτῶν οὔτε ἐκ τῶν κλεμμάτων αὐτῶν.
FORNICATIONS OF THEM NOR OF THE THEFTS OF THEM.

who were not killed by these plagues, did not repent of the works of their hands or give up worshiping demons and idols of gold and silver and bronze and stone and wood, which cannot see or hear or walk. [21]And they did not repent of their murders or their sorceries or their fornication or their thefts.

CHAPTER 10

10.1 Καὶ εἶδον ἄλλον ἄγγελον ἰσχυρὸν καταβαίνοντα
AND I SAW ANOTHER STRONG~ANGEL COMING DOWN

ἐκ τοῦ οὐρανοῦ περιβεβλημένον νεφέλην, καὶ ἡ
OUT OF - HEAVEN HAVING BEEN WRAPPED IN A CLOUD, AND THE

ἶρις ἐπὶ τῆς κεφαλῆς αὐτοῦ καὶ τὸ πρόσωπον
RAINBOW [WAS] ON THE HEAD OF HIM AND THE FACE

αὐτοῦ ὡς ὁ ἥλιος καὶ οἱ πόδες αὐτοῦ ὡς στῦλοι
OF HIM [WAS] AS THE SUN AND THE FEET OF HIM AS PILLARS

πυρός, **10.2** καὶ ἔχων ἐν τῇ χειρὶ αὐτοῦ βιβλαρίδιον
OF FIRE, AND HAVING IN THE HAND OF HIM A LITTLE SCROLL

ἠνεῳγμένον. καὶ ἔθηκεν τὸν πόδα αὐτοῦ τὸν δεξιὸν
HAVING BEEN OPENED. AND HE PLACED - [3]FOOT [1]HIS - [2]RIGHT

ἐπὶ τῆς θαλάσσης, τὸν δὲ εὐώνυμον ἐπὶ τῆς γῆς,
ON THE SEA, AND~THE LEFT ON THE LAND,

10.3 καὶ ἔκραξεν φωνῇ μεγάλῃ ὥσπερ λέων μυκᾶται.
AND HE CRIED WITH A GREAT~VOICE AS A LION ROARS.

καὶ ὅτε ἔκραξεν, ἐλάλησαν αἱ ἑπτὰ βρονταὶ τὰς
AND WHEN HE CRIED OUT, [4]UTTERED [1]THE [2]SEVEN [3]THUNDERS -

ἑαυτῶν φωνάς. **10.4** καὶ ὅτε ἐλάλησαν αἱ ἑπτὰ
THEIR VOICES. AND WHEN [4]SPOKE [1]THE [2]SEVEN

βρονταί, ἤμελλον γράφειν, καὶ ἤκουσα φωνὴν ἐκ τοῦ
[3]THUNDERS, I WAS ABOUT TO WRITE, AND I HEARD A VOICE OUT OF -

οὐρανοῦ λέγουσαν, Σφράγισον ἃ ἐλάλησαν αἱ
HEAVEN SAYING, SEAL THE THINGS WHICH [4]SPOKE [1]THE

ἑπτὰ βρονταί, καὶ μὴ αὐτὰ γράψῃς. **10.5** Καὶ ὁ
[2]SEVEN [3]THUNDERS, AND [3]NOT [2]THEM [1]WRITE. AND THE

And I saw another mighty angel coming down from heaven, wrapped in a cloud, with a rainbow over his head; his face was like the sun, and his legs like pillars of fire. [2]He held a little scroll open in his hand. Setting his right foot on the sea and his left foot on the land, [3]he gave a great shout, like a lion roaring. And when he shouted, the seven thunders sounded. [4]And when the seven thunders had sounded, I was about to write, but I heard a voice from heaven saying, "Seal up what the seven thunders have said, and do not write it down." [5]Then the angel whom I saw standing on the sea and the land raised his right hand to heaven 6 and swore by him who lives forever and ever, who created heaven and what is in it, the earth and what is in it, and the sea and what is in it: "There will be no more delay, 7but in the days when the seventh angel is to blow his trumpet, the mystery of God will be fulfilled, as he announced to his servants*b* the prophets."

8 Then the voice that I had heard from heaven spoke to me again, saying, "Go, take the scroll that is open in the hand of the angel who is standing on the sea and on the land." 9So I went to the angel and told him to give me the little scroll; and he said to me, "Take it, and eat; it will be bitter to your stomach, but sweet as honey in your mouth." 10So I took the little scroll from the hand of the angel and ate it; it was sweet as honey in my mouth, but when I had eaten it, my stomach was made bitter.

11 Then they said

b Gk *slaves*

ἄγγελος, ὃν εἶδον ἑστῶτα ἐπὶ τῆς θαλάσσης
ANGEL, WHOM I SAW HAVING TAKEN [HIS] STAND ON THE SEA

καὶ ἐπὶ τῆς γῆς,
AND ON THE EARTH,

ἦρεν τὴν χεῖρα αὐτοῦ τὴν δεξιὰν εἰς τὸν οὐρανὸν
LIFTED - ³HAND ¹HIS - ²RIGHT TO - HEAVEN

10.6 καὶ ὤμοσεν ἐν τῷ ζῶντι εἰς
AND SWORE BY THE ONE LIVING INTO

τοὺς αἰῶνας τῶν αἰώνων,
THE AGES OF THE AGES,

ὃς ἔκτισεν τὸν οὐρανὸν καὶ τὰ ἐν αὐτῷ καὶ
WHO CREATED THE HEAVEN AND THE THINGS IN IT AND

τὴν γῆν καὶ τὰ ἐν αὐτῇ καὶ τὴν θάλασσαν καὶ
THE EARTH AND THE THINGS IN IT AND THE SEA AND

τὰ ἐν αὐτῇ, ὅτι χρόνος οὐκέτι ἔσται, **10.7** ἀλλ' ἐν
THE THINGS IN IT, THAT DELAY WILL BE~NO LONGER, BUT IN

ταῖς ἡμέραις τῆς φωνῆς τοῦ ἑβδόμου ἀγγέλου, ὅταν
THE DAYS OF THE SOUNDING OF THE SEVENTH ANGEL, WHEN

μέλλῃ σαλπίζειν, καὶ ἐτελέσθη τὸ μυστήριον τοῦ
HE IS ABOUT TO TRUMPET, ALSO WOULD BE COMPLETED THE MYSTERY -

θεοῦ, ὡς εὐηγγέλισεν τοὺς ἑαυτοῦ δούλους τοὺς
OF GOD, AS HE PROCLAIMED - TO HIS SLAVES, THE

προφήτας.
PROPHETS.

10.8 Καὶ ἡ φωνὴ ἣν ἤκουσα ἐκ τοῦ οὐρανοῦ
AND THE VOICE WHICH I HEARD FROM - HEAVEN

πάλιν λαλοῦσαν μετ' ἐμοῦ καὶ λέγουσαν, Ὕπαγε
[WAS] AGAIN SPEAKING WITH ME AND SAYING, GO

λάβε τὸ βιβλίον τὸ ἠνεῳγμένον ἐν τῇ χειρὶ τοῦ
TAKE THE SCROLL - HAVING BEEN OPENED, IN THE HAND OF THE

ἀγγέλου τοῦ ἑστῶτος ἐπὶ τῆς θαλάσσης καὶ
ANGEL - HAVING TAKEN [HIS] STAND ON THE SEA AND

ἐπὶ τῆς γῆς. **10.9** καὶ ἀπῆλθα πρὸς τὸν ἄγγελον
ON THE EARTH. AND I WENT TO THE ANGEL,

λέγων αὐτῷ δοῦναί μοι τὸ βιβλαρίδιον. καὶ λέγει
TELLING HIM TO GIVE ME THE LITTLE SCROLL. AND HE SAYS

μοι, Λάβε καὶ κατάφαγε αὐτό, καὶ πικρανεῖ σου
TO ME, TAKE AND EAT IT, AND IT WILL MAKE ³BITTER ¹YOUR

τὴν κοιλίαν, ἀλλ' ἐν τῷ στόματί σου ἔσται γλυκὺ
- ²STOMACH, BUT IN THE MOUTH OF YOU IT WILL BE SWEET

ὡς μέλι. **10.10** καὶ ἔλαβον τὸ βιβλαρίδιον ἐκ τῆς
AS HONEY. AND I TOOK THE LITTLE SCROLL OUT OF THE

χειρὸς τοῦ ἀγγέλου καὶ κατέφαγον αὐτό, καὶ ἦν ἐν
HAND OF THE ANGEL. AND ATE IT, AND IT WAS IN

τῷ στόματί μου ὡς μέλι γλυκὺ καὶ ὅτε ἔφαγον
THE MOUTH OF ME AS SWEET~HONEY, AND WHEN I ATE

αὐτό, ἐπικράνθη ἡ κοιλία μου. **10.11** καὶ λέγουσίν
IT, ⁴WAS MADE BITTER ¹THE ²STOMACH ³OF ME. AND THEY SAY

μοι, Δεῖ   σε πάλιν προφητεῦσαι ἐπὶ λαοῖς
TO ME, IT IS NECESSARY [FOR] YOU TO PROPHESY~AGAIN ABOUT PEOPLES

καὶ ἔθνεσιν καὶ γλώσσαις καὶ βασιλεῦσιν πολλοῖς.
AND NATIONS AND TONGUES AND MANY~KINGS.

to me, "You must prophesy again about many peoples and nations and languages and kings."

CHAPTER 11

11.1 Καὶ ἐδόθη μοι κάλαμος ὅμοιος ῥάβδῳ, λέγων,
AND WAS GIVEN TO ME A MEASURING ROD LIKE A STAFF, SAYING,

Ἔγειρε καὶ μέτρησον τὸν ναὸν τοῦ θεοῦ καὶ τὸ
RISE AND MEASURE THE TEMPLE - OF GOD AND THE

θυσιαστήριον καὶ τοὺς προσκυνοῦντας ἐν αὐτῷ.
ALTAR AND THE ONES WORSHIPING IN IT.

11.2 καὶ τὴν αὐλὴν τὴν ἔξωθεν τοῦ ναοῦ ἔκβαλε
AND THE ²COURT - ¹OUTER OF THE TEMPLE TAKE(LEAVE)

ἔξωθεν καὶ μὴ αὐτὴν μετρήσῃς, ὅτι ἐδόθη τοῖς
OUT AND ³NOT ²IT ¹MEASURE, BECAUSE IT WAS GIVEN TO THE

ἔθνεσιν, καὶ τὴν πόλιν τὴν ἁγίαν πατήσουσιν
NATIONS, AND THE ²CITY - ¹HOLY THEY WILL TRAMPLE [UPON]

μῆνας τεσσεράκοντα [καὶ] δύο. **11.3** καὶ δώσω
⁴MONTHS ¹FORTY ²AND ³TWO. AND I WILL GIVE [AUTHORITY]

τοῖς δυσὶν μάρτυσίν μου καὶ προφητεύσουσιν ἡμέρας
TO THE TWO WITNESSES OF ME, AND THEY WILL PROPHESY ⁴DAYS

χιλίας διακοσίας ἑξήκοντα περιβεβλημένοι σάκκους.
¹ONE THOUSAND ²TWO HUNDRED ³[AND] SIXTY, HAVING BEEN CLOTHED IN SACKCLOTH.

11.4 οὗτοί εἰσιν αἱ δύο ἐλαῖαι καὶ αἱ δύο λυχνίαι
THESE ONES ARE THE TWO OLIVE TREES AND THE TWO LAMPSTANDS

αἱ ἐνώπιον τοῦ κυρίου τῆς γῆς ἑστῶτες.
- ²BEFORE ³THE ⁴LORD ⁵OF THE ⁶EARTH ¹HAVING TAKEN [THEIR] STAND.

11.5 καὶ εἴ τις αὐτοὺς θέλει ἀδικῆσαι πῦρ
AND IF ANYONE ³THEM ¹WANTS ²TO INJURE FIRE

ἐκπορεύεται ἐκ τοῦ στόματος αὐτῶν καὶ κατεσθίει τοὺς
COMES OUT OF THE MOUTH OF THEM AND DESTROYS THE

ἐχθροὺς αὐτῶν· καὶ εἴ τις θελήσῃ αὐτοὺς ἀδικῆσαι,
ENEMIES OF THEM; AND IF ANYONE WANTS TO INJURE~THEM,

οὕτως δεῖ αὐτὸν ἀποκτανθῆναι. **11.6** οὗτοι
THUS IT IS NECESSARY [FOR] HIM TO BE KILLED. THESE ONES

ἔχουσιν τὴν ἐξουσίαν κλεῖσαι τὸν οὐρανόν, ἵνα μὴ
HAVE THE AUTHORITY TO SHUT THE HEAVEN(SKY), THAT NO

ὑετὸς βρέχῃ τὰς ἡμέρας τῆς προφητείας αὐτῶν,
RAIN MAY FALL [DURING] THE DAYS OF THE PROPHECY OF THEM,

καὶ ἐξουσίαν ἔχουσιν ἐπὶ τῶν ὑδάτων στρέφειν αὐτὰ
AND AUTHORITY THEY HAVE OVER THE WATERS TO TURN THEM

εἰς αἷμα καὶ πατάξαι τὴν γῆν ἐν πάσῃ πληγῇ
INTO BLOOD AND TO STRIKE THE EARTH WITH EVERY [SORT OF] PLAGUE

ὁσάκις ἐὰν θελήσωσιν. **11.7** καὶ ὅταν τελέσωσιν τὴν
AS OFTEN AS - THEY WANT. AND WHEN THEY COMPLETE THE

Then I was given a measuring rod like a staff, and I was told, "Come and measure the temple of God and the altar and those who worship there, ²but do not measure the court outside the temple; leave that out, for it is given over to the nations, and they will trample over the holy city for forty-two months. ³And I will grant my two witnesses authority to prophesy for one thousand two hundred sixty days, wearing sackcloth."

4 These are the two olive trees and the two lampstands that stand before the Lord of the earth. ⁵And if anyone wants to harm them, fire pours from their mouth and consumes their foes; anyone who wants to harm them must be killed in this manner. ⁶They have authority to shut the sky, so that no rain may fall during the days of their prophesying, and they have authority over the waters to turn them into blood, and to strike the earth with every kind of plague, as often as they desire.

7 When they have finished

their testimony, the beast that comes up from the bottomless pit will make war on them and conquer them and kill them, [8]and their dead bodies will lie in the street of the great city that is prophetically [c] called Sodom and Egypt, where also their Lord was crucified. [9]For three and a half days members of the peoples and tribes and languages and nations will gaze at their dead bodies and refuse to let them be placed in a tomb; [10]and the inhabitants of the earth will gloat over them and celebrate and exchange presents, because these two prophets had been a torment to the inhabitants of the earth.

11 But after the three and a half days, the breath[d] of life from God entered them, and they stood on their feet, and those who saw them were terrified. [12]Then they[e] heard a loud voice from heaven saying to them, "Come up here!" And they went up to heaven in a cloud while their enemies watched them. [13]At that moment there was a great earthquake, and a tenth of the city fell; seven thousand people were killed in the earthquake, and the rest

[c] Or *allegorically;* Gk *spiritually*
[d] Or *the spirit*
[e] Other ancient authorities read *I*

μαρτυρίαν αὐτῶν, τὸ θηρίον τὸ ἀναβαῖνον ἐκ τῆς
TESTIMONY OF THEM, THE BEAST - COMING UP FROM THE

ἀβύσσου ποιήσει μετ᾽ αὐτῶν πόλεμον καὶ νικήσει
ABYSS WILL MAKE [2]WITH [3]THEM [1]WAR AND WILL CONQUER

αὐτοὺς καὶ ἀποκτενεῖ αὐτούς. **11.8** καὶ τὸ πτῶμα αὐτῶν
THEM AND WILL KILL THEM. AND THE CORPSE OF THEM

ἐπὶ τῆς πλατείας τῆς πόλεως τῆς μεγάλης, ἥτις
[WILL BE] ON THE STREET OF THE [2]CITY - [1]GREAT, WHICH

καλεῖται πνευματικῶς Σόδομα καὶ Αἴγυπτος, ὅπου καὶ
IS CALLED SPIRITUALLY SODOM AND EGYPT, WHERE ALSO

ὁ κύριος αὐτῶν ἐσταυρώθη. **11.9** καὶ βλέπουσιν ἐκ
THE LORD OF THEM WAS CRUCIFIED. AND [10]SEE [1][SOME] OF

τῶν λαῶν καὶ φυλῶν καὶ γλωσσῶν καὶ ἐθνῶν τὸ
[2]THE [3]PEOPLES [4]AND [5]TRIBES [6]AND [7]TONGUES [8]AND [9]NATIONS THE

πτῶμα αὐτῶν ἡμέρας τρεῖς καὶ ἥμισυ καὶ τὰ πτώματα
CORPSE OF THEM [FOR] THREE~DAYS AND A HALF AND [2]THE [3]CORPSES

αὐτῶν οὐκ ἀφίουσιν τεθῆναι εἰς μνῆμα. **11.10** καὶ
[4]OF THEM [1]THEY DO NOT PERMIT TO BE PUT INTO A TOMB. AND

οἱ κατοικοῦντες ἐπὶ τῆς γῆς χαίρουσιν ἐπ᾽ αὐτοῖς
THE ONES DWELLING ON THE EARTH REJOICE OVER THEM

καὶ εὐφραίνονται καὶ δῶρα πέμψουσιν ἀλλήλοις, ὅτι
AND MAKE MERRY AND THEY WILL SEND~GIFTS TO ONE ANOTHER, BECAUSE

οὗτοι οἱ δύο προφῆται ἐβασάνισαν τοὺς κατοικοῦντας
THESE - TWO PROPHETS TORMENTED THE ONES DWELLING

ἐπὶ τῆς γῆς. **11.11** καὶ μετὰ τὰς τρεῖς ἡμέρας καὶ
ON THE EARTH. AND AFTER THE THREE DAYS AND

ἥμισυ πνεῦμα ζωῆς ἐκ τοῦ θεοῦ εἰσῆλθεν ἐν
A HALF A BREATH (SPIRIT) OF LIFE FROM - GOD ENTERED IN[TO]

αὐτοῖς, καὶ ἔστησαν ἐπὶ τοὺς πόδας αὐτῶν, καὶ
THEM, AND THEY STOOD UPON THE FEET OF THEM, AND

φόβος μέγας ἐπέπεσεν ἐπὶ τοὺς θεωροῦντας αὐτούς.
A GREAT~FEAR FELL UPON THE ONES SEEING THEM.

11.12 καὶ ἤκουσαν φωνῆς μεγάλης ἐκ τοῦ οὐρανοῦ
AND THEY HEARD A GREAT (LOUD)~VOICE OUT OF - HEAVEN

λεγούσης αὐτοῖς, Ἀνάβατε ὧδε. καὶ ἀνέβησαν εἰς τὸν
SAYING TO THEM, COME UP HERE. AND THEY WENT UP INTO -

οὐρανὸν ἐν τῇ νεφέλῃ, καὶ ἐθεώρησαν αὐτοὺς οἱ
HEAVEN IN THE CLOUD, AND [4]SAW [5]THEM [1]THE

ἐχθροὶ αὐτῶν. **11.13** Καὶ ἐν ἐκείνῃ τῇ ὥρᾳ ἐγένετο
[2]ENEMIES [3]OF THEM. AND IN THAT - HOUR OCCURRED

σεισμὸς μέγας καὶ τὸ δέκατον τῆς πόλεως ἔπεσεν
A GREAT~EARTHQUAKE AND THE TENTH [PART] OF THE CITY FELL

καὶ ἀπεκτάνθησαν ἐν τῷ σεισμῷ ὀνόματα
AND THERE WERE KILLED IN THE EARTHQUAKE [2]NAMES (PERSONS)

ἀνθρώπων χιλιάδες ἑπτὰ καὶ οἱ λοιποὶ
[3]AMONG MEN [1]SEVEN~THOUSAND AND THE REST

ἔμφοβοι ἐγένοντο καὶ ἔδωκαν δόξαν τῷ θεῷ τοῦ
BECAME~AFRAID   AND   GAVE   GLORY TO THE GOD   -

οὐρανοῦ.
OF HEAVEN.

11.14 Ἡ οὐαὶ ἡ δευτέρα ἀπῆλθεν· ἰδοὺ ἡ οὐαὶ ἡ
THE ²WOE - ¹SECOND PASSED;   BEHOLD, THE ²WOE -

τρίτη ἔρχεται ταχύ.
¹THIRD IS COMING QUICKLY.

11.15 Καὶ ὁ ἕβδομος ἄγγελος ἐσάλπισεν· καὶ
AND THE SEVENTH ANGEL   TRUMPETED;   AND

ἐγένοντο φωναὶ μεγάλαι ἐν τῷ οὐρανῷ λέγοντες,
THERE WERE LOUD~VOICES   IN -   HEAVEN   SAYING,

Ἐγένετο ἡ βασιλεία τοῦ κόσμου
⁵BECAME ¹THE ²KINGDOM ³OF THE ⁴WORLD

τοῦ κυρίου ἡμῶν
[THAT] OF THE LORD OF US

καὶ τοῦ Χριστοῦ αὐτοῦ,
AND THE CHRIST OF HIM,

καὶ βασιλεύσει εἰς τοὺς αἰῶνας τῶν αἰώνων.
AND HE WILL REIGN INTO THE AGES   OF THE AGES.

11.16 καὶ οἱ εἴκοσι τέσσαρες πρεσβύτεροι [οἱ]
AND THE TWENTY-FOUR   ELDERS

ἐνώπιον τοῦ θεοῦ καθήμενοι ἐπὶ τοὺς θρόνους αὐτῶν
²BEFORE - ³GOD ¹SITTING ON THE THRONES OF THEM

ἔπεσαν ἐπὶ τὰ πρόσωπα αὐτῶν καὶ προσεκύνησαν τῷ
FELL   ON THE FACES   OF THEM AND WORSHIPED   -

θεῷ **11.17** λέγοντες,
GOD,   SAYING,

Εὐχαριστοῦμέν σοι, κύριε ὁ θεὸς ὁ παντοκράτωρ,
WE THANK   YOU, LORD - GOD, THE ALMIGHTY,

ὁ ὢν καὶ ὁ ἦν,
THE ONE BEING AND THE ONE [WHO] WAS,

ὅτι εἴληφας τὴν δύναμίν σου τὴν μεγάλην
BECAUSE YOU HAVE TAKEN - ³POWER ¹YOUR - ²GREAT

καὶ ἐβασίλευσας.
AND REIGNED.

11.18 καὶ τὰ ἔθνη ὠργίσθησαν,
AND THE NATIONS WERE ANGRY,

καὶ ἦλθεν ἡ ὀργή σου
AND ²CAME - ¹YOUR~WRATH

καὶ ὁ καιρὸς τῶν νεκρῶν κριθῆναι
AND THE TIME OF(FOR) THE DEAD TO BE JUDGED

καὶ δοῦναι τὸν μισθὸν τοῖς δούλοις σου τοῖς
AND TO GIVE THE REWARD - TO YOUR~SLAVES, THE

προφήταις
PROPHETS

were terrified and gave glory
to the God of heaven.
    14 The second woe has
passed. The third woe is
coming very soon.
    15 Then the seventh angel
blew his trumpet, and there
were loud voices in heaven,
saying,
    "The kingdom of the
        world has become
        the kingdom of our
        Lord
    and of his Messiah,ᶠ
    and he will reign forever
        and ever."
16 Then the twenty-four
elders who sit on their
thrones before God fell on
their faces and worshiped
God, ¹⁷singing,
    "We give you thanks,
        Lord God
        Almighty,
    who are and who were,
    for you have taken your
        great power
    and begun to reign.
    ¹⁸ The nations raged,
        but your wrath has
            come,
        and the time for
            judging the dead,
    for rewarding your
        servants,ᵍ the
        prophets

ᶠ Gk *Christ*
ᵍ Gk *slaves*

and saints and all who
fear your name,
both small and great,
and for destroying those
who destroy the
earth."
19 Then God's temple in
heaven was opened, and the
ark of his covenant was seen
within his temple; and there
were flashes of lightning,
rumblings, peals of thunder,
an earthquake, and heavy
hail.

καὶ τοῖς ἁγίοις καὶ τοῖς φοβουμένοις τὸ
AND THE SAINTS AND THE ONES FEARING THE

ὄνομά σου,
NAME OF YOU,

τοὺς μικροὺς καὶ τοὺς μεγάλους,
THE SMALL ONES AND THE GREAT ONES,

καὶ διαφθεῖραι τοὺς διαφθείροντας τὴν γῆν.
AND TO DESTROY THE ONES DESTROYING THE EARTH.

11.19 καὶ ἠνοίγη ὁ ναὸς τοῦ θεοῦ ὁ ἐν τῷ οὐρανῷ
AND WAS OPENED THE TEMPLE - OF GOD - IN - HEAVEN,

καὶ ὤφθη ἡ κιβωτὸς τῆς διαθήκης αὐτοῦ ἐν τῷ
AND WAS SEEN THE ARK OF THE COVENANT OF HIM IN THE

ναῷ αὐτοῦ, καὶ ἐγένοντο ἀστραπαὶ καὶ φωναὶ
TEMPLE OF HIM, AND THERE WERE FLASHES OF LIGHTNING AND VOICES

καὶ βρονταὶ καὶ σεισμὸς καὶ χάλαζα μεγάλη.
AND THUNDERS AND AN EARTHQUAKE AND GREAT~HAIL.

CHAPTER 12

A great portent appeared in
heaven: a woman clothed
with the sun, with the moon
under her feet, and on her
head a crown of twelve stars.
²She was pregnant and was
crying out in birth pangs, in
the agony of giving birth.
³Then another portent
appeared in heaven: a great
red dragon, with seven
heads and ten horns, and
seven diadems on his heads.
⁴His tail swept down a third
of the stars of heaven and
threw them to the earth.
Then the dragon stood
before the woman who was
about to bear a child, so that
he might devour her child as
soon as it was born. ⁵And
she gave birth to a son, a
male child, who is to
rule ʰ all the nations with

ʰ Or to shepherd

12.1 Καὶ σημεῖον μέγα ὤφθη ἐν τῷ οὐρανῷ, γυνὴ
AND A GREAT~SIGN WAS SEEN IN - HEAVEN, A WOMAN

περιβεβλημένη τὸν ἥλιον, καὶ ἡ σελήνη ὑποκάτω
HAVING BEEN CLOTHED WITH THE SUN, AND THE MOON UNDERNEATH

τῶν ποδῶν αὐτῆς καὶ ἐπὶ τῆς κεφαλῆς αὐτῆς στέφανος
THE FEET OF HER AND ON THE HEAD OF HER A CROWN

ἀστέρων δώδεκα, **12.2** καὶ ἐν γαστρὶ ἔχουσα, καὶ
OF TWELVE~STARS, AND IN [HER] WOMB HAVING [A CHILD], AND

κράζει ὠδίνουσα καὶ βασανιζομένη τεκεῖν.
SHE CRIES SUFFERING BIRTH PANGS AND BEING IN PAIN TO GIVE BIRTH.

12.3 καὶ ὤφθη ἄλλο σημεῖον ἐν τῷ οὐρανῷ, καὶ
AND WAS SEEN ANOTHER SIGN IN - HEAVEN, AND

ἰδοὺ δράκων μέγας πυρρὸς ἔχων κεφαλὰς ἑπτὰ καὶ
BEHOLD, ³DRAGON ¹A GREAT ²RED HAVING SEVEN~HEADS AND

κέρατα δέκα καὶ ἐπὶ τὰς κεφαλὰς αὐτοῦ ἑπτὰ
TEN~HORNS AND ON THE HEADS OF IT SEVEN

διαδήματα, **12.4** καὶ ἡ οὐρὰ αὐτοῦ σύρει τὸ
DIADEMS, AND THE TAIL OF HIM DRAGS [DOWN] THE

τρίτον τῶν ἀστέρων τοῦ οὐρανοῦ καὶ ἔβαλεν αὐτοὺς
THIRD [PART] OF THE STARS - OF HEAVEN AND THREW THEM

εἰς τὴν γῆν. καὶ ὁ δράκων ἕστηκεν ἐνώπιον τῆς
TO THE EARTH. AND THE DRAGON WAS STANDING - BEFORE THE

γυναικὸς τῆς μελλούσης τεκεῖν, ἵνα ὅταν τέκῃ
WOMAN - BEING ABOUT TO GIVE BIRTH, THAT WHEN SHE GIVES BIRTH TO

τὸ τέκνον αὐτῆς καταφάγῃ. **12.5** καὶ ἔτεκεν
THE CHILD OF HER HE MIGHT DEVOUR [HIM]. AND SHE GAVE BIRTH TO

υἱὸν ἄρσεν, ὃς μέλλει ποιμαίνειν πάντα τὰ ἔθνη ἐν
A SON, A MALE, WHO IS ABOUT TO SHEPHERD ALL THE NATIONS WITH

ῥάβδῳ σιδηρᾷ.   καὶ   ἡρπάσθη   τὸ   τέκνον   αὐτῆς   πρὸς
A ROD   OF IRON.   AND ⁴WAS SNATCHED UP ¹THE ²CHILD   ³OF HER   TO

τὸν   θεὸν   καὶ   πρὸς   τὸν   θρόνον   αὐτοῦ.   **12.6** καὶ   ἡ   γυνὴ
-     GOD   AND   TO   THE   THRONE   OF HIM.   AND THE WOMAN

ἔφυγεν   εἰς   τὴν   ἔρημον,   ὅπου   ἔχει   ἐκεῖ   τόπον
FLED   INTO THE   WILDERNESS, WHERE SHE HAS THERE A PLACE

ἡτοιμασμένον   ἀπὸ   τοῦ   θεοῦ,   ἵνα   ἐκεῖ   τρέφωσιν
HAVING BEEN PREPARED FROM(BY) -   GOD,   THAT THERE THEY MIGHT NOURISH

αὐτὴν   ἡμέρας   χιλίας   διακοσίας   ἑξήκοντα.
HER   ⁴DAYS   ¹A THOUSAND ²TWO HUNDRED ³[AND] SIXTY.

12.7 Καὶ   ἐγένετο   πόλεμος   ἐν   τῷ   οὐρανῷ,   ὁ   Μιχαὴλ
        AND   THERE WAS   WAR   IN   -   HEAVEN,   -   MICHAEL

καὶ   οἱ   ἄγγελοι   αὐτοῦ   τοῦ   πολεμῆσαι   μετὰ   τοῦ
AND   THE ANGELS   OF HIM   -   [WENT] TO WAR WITH   THE

δράκοντος.   καὶ   ὁ   δράκων   ἐπολέμησεν   καὶ   οἱ   ἄγγελοι
DRAGON.   AND   THE DRAGON   WARRED   AND   THE ANGELS

αὐτοῦ,   **12.8** καὶ   οὐκ   ἴσχυσεν   οὐδὲ   τόπος   εὑρέθη
OF HIM,   AND   HE WAS NOT STRONG [ENOUGH] NOR   WAS FOUND~A PLACE

αὐτῶν   ἔτι   ἐν   τῷ   οὐρανῷ.   **12.9** καὶ   ἐβλήθη
[FOR] THEM ANY LONGER IN   -   HEAVEN.   AND   WAS THROWN [DOWN]

ὁ   δράκων   ὁ   μέγας,   ὁ   ὄφις   ὁ   ἀρχαῖος,   ὁ
THE ²DRAGON -   ¹GREAT,   THE ²SERPENT - ¹ANCIENT,   THE ONE

καλούμενος   Διάβολος   καὶ   ὁ   Σατανᾶς,   ὁ   πλανῶν   τὴν
BEING CALLED [THE] DEVIL   AND   - SATAN,   THE ONE DECEIVING THE

οἰκουμένην   ὅλην,   ἐβλήθη   εἰς   τὴν   γῆν,   καὶ   οἱ
WHOLE~INHABITED EARTH, HE WAS THROWN TO   THE   EARTH, AND   THE

ἄγγελοι   αὐτοῦ   μετ᾽   αὐτοῦ   ἐβλήθησαν.   **12.10** καὶ
ANGELS   OF HIM   WITH   HIM   WERE THROWN [DOWN].   AND

ἤκουσα   φωνὴν   μεγάλην   ἐν   τῷ   οὐρανῷ   λέγουσαν,
I HEARD   A LOUD~VOICE   IN   -   HEAVEN,   SAYING,

Ἄρτι   ἐγένετο   ἡ   σωτηρία   καὶ   ἡ   δύναμις
NOW   CAME(HAS COME) THE SALVATION AND   THE POWER

καὶ   ἡ   βασιλεία   τοῦ   θεοῦ   ἡμῶν
AND   THE KINGDOM   OF THE GOD   OF US

καὶ   ἡ   ἐξουσία   τοῦ   Χριστοῦ   αὐτοῦ,
AND   THE AUTHORITY OF THE CHRIST   OF HIM,

ὅτι   ἐβλήθη   ὁ   κατήγωρ   τῶν   ἀδελφῶν   ἡμῶν,
BECAUSE WAS THROWN [DOWN] THE ACCUSER   OF THE BROTHERS   OF US,

ὁ   κατηγορῶν   αὐτοὺς   ἐνώπιον   τοῦ   θεοῦ
THE ONE ACCUSING   THEM   BEFORE   THE   GOD

ἡμῶν
OF US

ἡμέρας   καὶ   νυκτός.
DAY   AND   NIGHT.

12.11 καὶ   αὐτοὶ   ἐνίκησαν   αὐτὸν   διὰ   τὸ   αἷμα   τοῦ
         AND   THEY   OVERCAME   HIM   BECAUSE OF THE BLOOD OF THE

ἀρνίου
LAMB

a rod of iron. But her child was snatched away and taken to God and to his throne; ⁶and the woman fled into the wilderness, where she has a place prepared by God, so that there she can be nourished for one thousand two hundred sixty days.

7 And war broke out in heaven; Michael and his angels fought against the dragon. The dragon and his angels fought back, ⁸but they were defeated, and there was no longer any place for them in heaven. ⁹The great dragon was thrown down, that ancient serpent, who is called the Devil and Satan, the deceiver of the whole world—he was thrown down to the earth, and his angels were thrown down with him.

10 Then I heard a loud voice in heaven, proclaiming,

"Now have come the
    salvation and the
    power
  and the kingdom of our
    God
  and the authority of his
    Messiah,ⁱ
for the accuser of our
    comradesʲ has been
    thrown down,
  who accuses them day
    and night before our
    God.
¹¹ But they have conquered
    him by the blood of
    the Lamb

ⁱ Gk *Christ*
ʲ Gk *brothers*

and by the word of their
testimony,
for they did not cling to
life even in the face
of death.
12 Rejoice then, you
heavens
and those who dwell in
them!
But woe to the earth and
the sea,
for the devil has come
down to you
with great wrath,
because he knows that
his time is short!"
13 So when the dragon
saw that he had been thrown
down to the earth, he
pursued[k] the woman who
had given birth to the male
child. 14 But the woman was
given the two wings of the
great eagle, so that she could
fly from the serpent into the
wilderness, to her place
where she is nourished for a
time, and times, and half a
time. 15 Then from his mouth
the serpent poured water like
a river after the woman, to
sweep her away with the
flood. 16 But the earth came
to the help of the woman; it
opened its mouth and
swallowed the river that the
dragon had poured from his
mouth. 17 Then the dragon
was angry with the woman,
and went off to make war on
the rest of her children, those
who keep the commandments

[k] Or *persecuted*

καὶ διὰ τὸν λόγον τῆς μαρτυρίας αὐτῶν
AND BECAUSE OF THE WORD OF THE TESTIMONY OF THEM

καὶ οὐκ ἠγάπησαν τὴν ψυχὴν αὐτῶν ἄχρι θανάτου.
AND THEY DID NOT LOVE THE SOUL(LIFE) OF THEM UNTO DEATH.

12.12 διὰ τοῦτο εὐφραίνεσθε, [οἱ] οὐρανοὶ
THEREFORE BE GLAD, - HEAVENS

καὶ οἱ ἐν αὐτοῖς σκηνοῦντες.
AND THE ONES [2]IN [3]THEM [1]TABERNACLING.

οὐαὶ τὴν γῆν καὶ τὴν θάλασσαν,
WOE [TO] THE EARTH AND THE SEA,

ὅτι κατέβη ὁ διάβολος πρὸς ὑμᾶς
BECAUSE [3]CAME DOWN [1]THE [2]DEVIL TO YOU°

ἔχων θυμὸν μέγαν,
HAVING GREAT~ANGER,

εἰδὼς ὅτι ὀλίγον καιρὸν ἔχει.
KNOWING THAT A SHORT TIME HE HAS.

12.13 Καὶ ὅτε εἶδεν ὁ δράκων ὅτι ἐβλήθη εἰς
AND WHEN [3]SAW [1]THE [2]DRAGON THAT HE WAS THROWN TO

τὴν γῆν, ἐδίωξεν τὴν γυναῖκα ἥτις ἔτεκεν τὸν
THE EARTH, HE PERSECUTED THE WOMAN WHO GAVE BIRTH TO THE

ἄρσενα. **12.14** καὶ ἐδόθησαν τῇ γυναικὶ αἱ δύο
MALE [CHILD]. AND WERE GIVEN TO THE WOMAN - TWO

πτέρυγες τοῦ ἀετοῦ τοῦ μεγάλου, ἵνα πέτηται εἰς τὴν
WINGS OF THE [2]EAGLE - [1]GREAT, THAT SHE MIGHT FLY INTO THE

ἔρημον εἰς τὸν τόπον αὐτῆς, ὅπου τρέφεται ἐκεῖ
WILDERNESS TO THE PLACE OF HER, WHERE SHE IS NOURISHED THERE

καιρὸν καὶ καιροὺς καὶ ἥμισυ καιροῦ ἀπὸ
[FOR] A TIME AND TIMES AND HALF A TIME, AWAY FROM

προσώπου τοῦ ὄφεως. **12.15** καὶ ἔβαλεν ὁ ὄφις ἐκ
[THE] PRESENCE OF THE SERPENT. AND [3]SPEWED [1]THE [2]SERPENT [4]FROM

τοῦ στόματος αὐτοῦ ὀπίσω τῆς γυναικὸς ὕδωρ ὡς
- [5]ITS~MOUTH [9]AFTER [10]THE [11]WOMAN [6]WATER [7]AS

ποταμόν, ἵνα αὐτὴν ποταμοφόρητον ποιήσῃ.
[8]A RIVER, THAT [2]HER [3]CARRIED AWAY BY A RIVER [1]HE MIGHT MAKE.

12.16 καὶ ἐβοήθησεν ἡ γῆ τῇ γυναικί καὶ ἤνοιξεν
AND [3]AIDED [1]THE [2]EARTH THE WOMAN AND [3]OPENED

ἡ γῆ τὸ στόμα αὐτῆς καὶ κατέπιεν τὸν ποταμὸν
[1]THE [2]EARTH - ITS~MOUTH AND SWALLOWED THE RIVER

ὃν ἔβαλεν ὁ δράκων ἐκ τοῦ στόματος αὐτοῦ.
WHICH [3]SPEWED [1]THE [2]DRAGON OUT OF THE MOUTH OF HIM.

12.17 καὶ ὠργίσθη ὁ δράκων ἐπὶ τῇ γυναικὶ καὶ
AND [3]WAS ANGRY [1]THE [2]DRAGON AT THE WOMAN AND

ἀπῆλθεν ποιῆσαι πόλεμον μετὰ τῶν λοιπῶν τοῦ
WENT AWAY TO MAKE WAR WITH THE REST OF THE

σπέρματος αὐτῆς τῶν τηρούντων τὰς ἐντολὰς τοῦ
SEED OF HER, THE ONES KEEPING THE COMMANDS -

θεοῦ καὶ ἐχόντων τὴν μαρτυρίαν Ἰησοῦ. **12.18** καὶ
OF GOD AND HAVING THE TESTIMONY OF JESUS. AND

⌜ἐστάθη⌝ ἐπὶ τὴν ἄμμον τῆς θαλάσσης.
HE STOOD ON THE SAND OF THE SEA.

12:18 text: ASV RSV NASB NIV TEV NJBmg NRSV. var. εσταθην (I stood): KJV ASVmg RSVmg NASBmg NIVmg NEBmg TEVmg NJB NRSVmg.

of God and hold the testimony of Jesus.

18 Then the dragon[l] took his stand on the sand of the seashore.

[l] Gk *Then he;* other ancient authorities read *Then I stood*

13.1 Καὶ εἶδον ἐκ τῆς θαλάσσης θηρίον ἀναβαῖνον,
AND I SAW ³OUT OF ⁴THE ⁵SEA ¹A BEAST ²COMING UP,

ἔχον κέρατα δέκα καὶ κεφαλὰς ἑπτὰ καὶ ἐπὶ τῶν
HAVING TEN~HORNS AND SEVEN~HEADS AND ON THE

κεράτων αὐτοῦ δέκα διαδήματα καὶ ἐπὶ τὰς κεφαλὰς
HORNS OF IT TEN DIADEMS AND ON THE HEADS

αὐτοῦ ὀνόμα[τα] βλασφημίας. **13.2** καὶ τὸ θηρίον ὃ
OF IT NAMES OF BLASPHEMY. AND THE BEAST WHICH

εἶδον ἦν ὅμοιον παρδάλει καὶ οἱ πόδες αὐτοῦ ὡς
I SAW WAS LIKE A LEOPARD AND THE FEET OF IT AS

ἄρκου καὶ τὸ στόμα αὐτοῦ ὡς στόμα λέοντος. καὶ
A BEAR AND THE MOUTH OF IT AS [THE] MOUTH OF A LION. AND

ἔδωκεν αὐτῷ ὁ δράκων τὴν δύναμιν αὐτοῦ καὶ τὸν
³GAVE ⁴TO IT ¹THE ²DRAGON THE POWER OF IT AND THE

θρόνον αὐτοῦ καὶ ἐξουσίαν μεγάλην. **13.3** καὶ μίαν ἐκ
THRONE OF IT AND GREAT~AUTHORITY. AND ONE OF

τῶν κεφαλῶν αὐτοῦ ὡς ἐσφαγμένην εἰς θάνατον, καὶ
THE HEADS OF IT AS HAVING BEEN SLAIN TO DEATH, AND

ἡ πληγὴ τοῦ θανάτου αὐτοῦ ἐθεραπεύθη. καὶ
THE WOUND [CAUSING]THE DEATH OF IT WAS HEALED. AND

ἐθαυμάσθη ὅλη ἡ γῆ ὀπίσω τοῦ θηρίου
⁴MARVELED ¹ALL ²THE ³EARTH, [FOLLOWING] AFTER THE BEAST,

13.4 καὶ προσεκύνησαν τῷ δράκοντι, ὅτι ἔδωκεν τὴν
AND THEY WORSHIPED THE DRAGON, BECAUSE HE GAVE THE

ἐξουσίαν τῷ θηρίῳ, καὶ προσεκύνησαν τῷ θηρίῳ
AUTHORITY TO THE BEAST, AND THEY WORSHIPED THE BEAST

λέγοντες, Τίς ὅμοιος τῷ θηρίῳ καὶ τίς δύναται
SAYING, WHO [IS] LIKE THE BEAST AND WHO IS ABLE

πολεμῆσαι μετ᾽ αὐτοῦ;
TO MAKE WAR WITH IT?

13.5 Καὶ ἐδόθη αὐτῷ στόμα λαλοῦν μεγάλα καὶ
AND WAS GIVEN TO IT A MOUTH SAYING GREAT THINGS AND

βλασφημίας καὶ ἐδόθη αὐτῷ ἐξουσία ποιῆσαι μῆνας
BLASPHEMIES, AND WAS GIVEN TO IT AUTHORITY TO ACT ⁴MONTHS

τεσσεράκοντα [καὶ] δύο. **13.6** καὶ ἤνοιξεν τὸ στόμα
¹[FOR] FORTY ²AND ³TWO. AND IT OPENED THE MOUTH

¹And I saw a beast rising out of the sea, having ten horns and seven heads; and on its horns were ten diadems, and on its heads were blasphemous names. ²And the beast that I saw was like a leopard, its feet were like a bear's, and its mouth was like a lion's mouth. And the dragon gave it his power and his throne and great authority. ³One of its heads seemed to have received a death-blow, but its mortal wound[m] had been healed. In amazement the whole earth followed the beast. ⁴They worshiped the dragon, for he had given his authority to the beast, and they worshiped the beast, saying, "Who is like the beast, and who can fight against it?"

5 The beast was given a mouth uttering haughty and blasphemous words, and it was allowed to exercise authority for forty-two months. ⁶It opened its mouth

[m] Gk *the plague of its death*

to utter blasphemies against God, blaspheming his name and his dwelling, that is, those who dwell in heaven. [7]Also it was allowed to make war on the saints and to conquer them.[n] It was given authority over every tribe and people and language and nation, [8]and all the inhabitants of the earth will worship it, everyone whose name has not been written from the foundation of the world in the book of life of the Lamb that was slaughtered.[o]

9 Let anyone who has an ear listen:
[10]If you are to be taken captive,
into captivity you go;
if you kill with the sword,
with the sword you must be killed.
Here is a call for the endurance and faith of the saints.

11 Then I saw another beast that rose out of the earth; it had two horns like a lamb and it spoke like a dragon. [12]It exercises all the authority of the first beast on its behalf, and it makes the earth and its inhabitants worship the first beast, whose mortal wound[p] had been healed. [13]It performs great signs, even making fire

[n] Other ancient authorities lack this sentence
[o] Or written in the book of life of the Lamb that was slaughtered from the foundation of the world
[p] Gk whose plague of its death

αὐτοῦ εἰς βλασφημίας πρὸς τὸν θεὸν βλασφημῆσαι τὸ
OF IT IN BLASPHEMIES AGAINST - GOD, TO BLASPHEME THE

ὄνομα αὐτοῦ καὶ ⌐τὴν σκηνὴν αὐτοῦ, τοὺς ἐν τῷ
NAME OF HIM AND THE TABERNACLE OF HIM, THE ONES [2]IN -

οὐρανῷ σκηνοῦντας⌐. 13.7 καὶ ἐδόθη αὐτῷ ποιῆσαι
[3]HEAVEN [1]TABERNACLING. AND WAS GIVEN TO IT TO MAKE

πόλεμον μετὰ τῶν ἁγίων καὶ νικῆσαι αὐτούς, καὶ
WAR WITH THE SAINTS AND TO OVERCOME THEM, AND

ἐδόθη αὐτῷ ἐξουσία ἐπὶ πᾶσαν φυλὴν καὶ λαὸν καὶ
WAS GIVEN TO IT AUTHORITY OVER EVERY TRIBE AND PEOPLE AND

γλῶσσαν καὶ ἔθνος. 13.8 καὶ προσκυνήσουσιν αὐτὸν
TONGUE AND NATION. AND WILL WORSHIP IT

πάντες οἱ κατοικοῦντες ἐπὶ τῆς γῆς, οὗ
ALL THE ONES DWELLING ON THE EARTH, [3]OF WHOM

οὐ γέγραπται τὸ ὄνομα αὐτοῦ ἐν τῷ βιβλίῳ τῆς ζωῆς
[4]HAS NOT BEEN WRITTEN [1]THE [2]NAME - IN THE BOOK - OF LIFE

τοῦ ἀρνίου τοῦ ἐσφαγμένου ἀπὸ καταβολῆς κόσμου.
OF THE LAMB - HAVING BEEN SLAIN FROM [THE] FOUNDATION OF [THE] WORLD.

13.9 Εἴ τις ἔχει οὖς ἀκουσάτω.
IF ANYONE HAS AN EAR LET HIM HEAR.

13.10 εἴ τις εἰς αἰχμαλωσίαν,
IF ANYONE [IS TO GO] INTO CAPTIVITY,

εἰς αἰχμαλωσίαν ὑπάγει·
INTO CAPTIVITY HE GOES.

εἴ τις ἐν μαχαίρῃ ἀποκτανθῆναι
IF ANYONE BY A SWORD [IS] TO BE KILLED,

αὐτὸν ἐν μαχαίρῃ ἀποκτανθῆναι.
HE BY A SWORD [IS] TO BE KILLED.

Ὧδέ ἐστιν ἡ ὑπομονὴ καὶ ἡ πίστις τῶν ἁγίων.
HERE IS THE ENDURANCE AND THE FAITH OF THE SAINTS.

13.11 Καὶ εἶδον ἄλλο θηρίον ἀναβαῖνον ἐκ τῆς
AND I SAW ANOTHER BEAST COMING UP OUT OF THE

γῆς, καὶ εἶχεν κέρατα δύο ὅμοια ἀρνίῳ καὶ ἐλάλει
EARTH, AND IT HAD TWO~HORNS LIKE A LAMB, AND IT WAS SPEAKING

ὡς δράκων. 13.12 καὶ τὴν ἐξουσίαν τοῦ πρώτου
LIKE A DRAGON. AND [2]THE [3]AUTHORITY [4]OF THE [5]FIRST

θηρίου πᾶσαν ποιεῖ ἐνώπιον αὐτοῦ, καὶ ποιεῖ
[6]BEAST [1]ALL IT EXERCISES BEFORE IT, AND IT MAKES

τὴν γῆν καὶ τοὺς ἐν αὐτῇ κατοικοῦντας ἵνα
THE EARTH AND THE ONES [2]IN [3]IT [1]DWELLING THAT

προσκυνήσουσιν τὸ θηρίον τὸ πρῶτον, οὗ ἐθεραπεύθη
THEY WILL WORSHIP THE [2]BEAST - [1]FIRST, WHOSE [3]WAS HEALED

ἡ πληγὴ τοῦ θανάτου αὐτοῦ. 13.13 καὶ ποιεῖ
- [1]WOUND - [2]OF DEATH - AND IT DOES

σημεῖα μεγάλα, ἵνα καὶ πῦρ ποιῇ ἐκ τοῦ
GREAT~SIGNS, THAT EVEN FIRE IT SHOULD CAUSE [2]OUT OF -

13:6 text: ASV RSV NASB NEBmg NRSV. var. την σκηνην αυτου, και τους εν τω ουρανω σκηνουντας (his tabernacle, and those tabernacling in heaven): KJV NIV TEV NJB. var. την σκηνην αυτου εν τω ουρανω (his tabernacle in heaven): NEB. 13:7 text: all. omit: ASVmg RSVmg NEBmg NRSVmg.

οὐρανοῦ καταβαίνειν εἰς τὴν γῆν ἐνώπιον τῶν
³HEAVEN ¹TO COME DOWN TO THE EARTH BEFORE -

ἀνθρώπων, **13.14** καὶ πλανᾷ τοὺς κατοικοῦντας ἐπὶ
MEN; AND IT DECEIVES THE ONES DWELLING ON

τῆς γῆς διὰ τὰ σημεῖα ἃ ἐδόθη αὐτῷ
THE EARTH BECAUSE OF THE SIGNS WHICH WAS(WERE) GIVEN TO IT

ποιῆσαι ἐνώπιον τοῦ θηρίου, λέγων τοῖς κατοικοῦσιν
TO PERFORM BEFORE THE BEAST, TELLING THE ONES DWELLING

ἐπὶ τῆς γῆς ποιῆσαι εἰκόνα τῷ θηρίῳ, ὃς ἔχει τὴν
ON THE EARTH TO MAKE AN IMAGE TO THE BEAST WHO HAS THE

πληγὴν τῆς μαχαίρης καὶ ἔζησεν. **13.15** καὶ
WOUND OF THE SWORD AND [YET] CAME TO LIFE. AND

ἐδόθη αὐτῷ δοῦναι πνεῦμα τῇ εἰκόνι τοῦ θηρίου,
IT WAS GIVEN TO IT TO GIVE SPIRIT(BREATH) TO THE IMAGE OF THE BEAST,

ἵνα καὶ λαλήσῃ ἡ εἰκὼν τοῦ θηρίου καὶ ποιήσῃ
THAT EVEN ⁵MIGHT SPEAK ¹THE ²IMAGE ³OF THE ⁴BEAST AND MIGHT CAUSE

[ἵνα] ὅσοι ἐὰν μὴ προσκυνήσωσιν τῇ εἰκόνι τοῦ
THAT AS MANY AS - WOULD NOT WORSHIP THE IMAGE OF THE

θηρίου ἀποκτανθῶσιν. **13.16** καὶ ποιεῖ πάντας, τοὺς
BEAST TO BE KILLED. AND IT CAUSES ALL, THE

μικροὺς καὶ τοὺς μεγάλους, καὶ τοὺς πλουσίους καὶ
SMALL AND THE GREAT, BOTH THE RICH AND

τοὺς πτωχούς, καὶ τοὺς ἐλευθέρους καὶ τοὺς δούλους,
THE POOR, AND THE FREE AND THE SLAVES,

ἵνα δῶσιν αὐτοῖς χάραγμα ἐπὶ τῆς χειρὸς αὐτῶν
THAT TO THEM~SHOULD [BE] GIVE[N] A MARK ON - ³HAND ¹THEIR

τῆς δεξιᾶς ἢ ἐπὶ τὸ μέτωπον αὐτῶν **13.17** καὶ ἵνα
- ²RIGHT OR ON THE FOREHEAD OF THEM, AND THAT

μή τις δύνηται ἀγοράσαι ἢ πωλῆσαι εἰ μὴ ὁ
NO ONE SHOULD BE ABLE TO BUY OR TO SELL EXCEPT THE ONE

ἔχων τὸ χάραγμα τὸ ὄνομα τοῦ θηρίου ἢ τὸν
HAVING THE MARK, THE NAME OF THE BEAST OR THE

ἀριθμὸν τοῦ ὀνόματος αὐτοῦ. **13.18** Ὧδε ἡ σοφία ἐστίν.
NUMBER OF THE NAME OF IT. HERE - IS~WISDOM.

ὁ ἔχων νοῦν ψηφισάτω τὸν ἀριθμὸν τοῦ
THE ONE HAVING UNDERSTANDING LET HIM CALCULATE THE NUMBER OF THE

θηρίου, ἀριθμὸς γὰρ ἀνθρώπου ἐστίν, καὶ ὁ ἀριθμὸς
BEAST, ⁴NUMBER ¹FOR ³A MAN'S ²IT IS, AND THE NUMBER

αὐτοῦ ⸀ἑξακόσιοι ἑξήκοντα ἕξ⸃.
OF IT [IS] SIX HUNDRED [AND] SIXTY-SIX.

13:18 text: all. var. εξακοιοι δεκα εξ (six hundred [and] sixteen): ASVmg RSVmg NASBmg NJBmg NRSVmg.

come down from heaven to earth in the sight of all; [14]and by the signs that it is allowed to perform on behalf of the beast, it deceives the inhabitants of earth, telling them to make an image for the beast that had been wounded by the sword[q] and yet lived; [15]and it was allowed to give breath[r] to the image of the beast so that the image of the beast could even speak and cause those who would not worship the image of the beast to be killed. [16]Also it causes all, both small and great, both rich and poor, both free and slave, to be marked on the right hand or the forehead, [17]so that no one can buy or sell who does not have the mark, that is, the name of the beast or the number of its name. [18]This calls for wisdom: let anyone with understanding calculate the number of the beast, for it is the number of a person. Its number is six hundred sixty-six.[s]

[q] Or *that had received the plague of the sword*
[r] Or *spirit*
[s] Other ancient authorities read *six hundred sixteen*

CHAPTER 14

Then I looked, and there was the Lamb, standing on Mount Zion! And with him were one hundred forty-four thousand who had his name and his Father's name written on their foreheads. [2]And I heard a voice from heaven like the sound of many waters and like the sound of loud thunder; the voice I heard was like the sound of harpists playing on their harps, [3]and they sing a new song before the throne and before the four living creatures and before the elders. No one could learn that song except the one hundred forty-four thousand who have been redeemed from the earth. [4]It is these who have not defiled themselves with women, for they are virgins; these follow the Lamb wherever he goes. They have been redeemed from humankind as first fruits for God and the Lamb, [5]and in their mouth no lie was found; they are blameless.

6 Then I saw another angel flying in midheaven, with an eternal gospel to proclaim to those who live[f] on the earth— to every nation and tribe and language and people. [7]He said in a loud voice, "Fear God and give him

[f] Gk *sit*

14.1 Καὶ εἶδον, καὶ ἰδοὺ τὸ ἀρνίον ἑστὸς
AND   I SAW,   AND   BEHOLD THE LAMB   HAVING TAKEN [HIS] STAND

ἐπὶ τὸ ὄρος Σιὼν καὶ μετ᾽ αὐτοῦ ἑκατὸν
ON - MOUNT ZION AND WITH HIM   ONE HUNDRED

τεσσεράκοντα τέσσαρες χιλιάδες ἔχουσαι τὸ ὄνομα
[AND] FORTY-FOUR   THOUSAND   HAVING   THE NAME

αὐτοῦ καὶ τὸ ὄνομα τοῦ πατρὸς αὐτοῦ γεγραμμένον
OF HIM AND THE NAME OF THE FATHER OF HIM HAVING BEEN WRITTEN

ἐπὶ τῶν μετώπων αὐτῶν. **14.2** καὶ ἤκουσα φωνὴν ἐκ
ON THE FOREHEADS OF THEM.   AND I HEARD A SOUND OUT OF

τοῦ οὐρανοῦ ὡς φωνὴν ὑδάτων πολλῶν καὶ ὡς φωνὴν
- HEAVEN   AS A SOUND OF MANY~WATERS AND AS A SOUND

βροντῆς μεγάλης, καὶ ἡ φωνὴ ἣν ἤκουσα ὡς
OF GREAT~THUNDER, AND THE SOUND WHICH I HEARD [WAS] AS

κιθαρῳδῶν κιθαριζόντων ἐν ταῖς κιθάραις αὐτῶν.
OF HARPISTS HARPING   WITH THE HARPS   OF THEM.

14.3 καὶ ᾄδουσιν [ὡς] ᾠδὴν καινὴν ἐνώπιον τοῦ
AND THEY SING AS [IT WERE] A NEW~SONG BEFORE   THE

θρόνου καὶ ἐνώπιον τῶν τεσσάρων ζῴων καὶ τῶν
THRONE AND BEFORE   THE FOUR   LIVING BEINGS AND THE

πρεσβυτέρων, καὶ οὐδεὶς ἐδύνατο μαθεῖν τὴν ᾠδὴν
ELDERS,   AND NO ONE WAS BEING ABLE TO LEARN THE SONG

εἰ μὴ αἱ ἑκατὸν τεσσεράκοντα τέσσαρες χιλιάδες,
EXCEPT THE ONE HUNDRED [AND] FORTY-FOUR   THOUSAND,

οἱ ἠγορασμένοι ἀπὸ τῆς γῆς. **14.4** οὗτοί εἰσιν
THE ONES HAVING BEEN PURCHASED FROM THE EARTH.   THESE ARE

οἳ μετὰ γυναικῶν οὐκ ἐμολύνθησαν, παρθένοι γάρ
[THOSE] WHO [2]WITH [3]WOMEN [1]WERE NOT DEFILED, [3]CELIBATES [1]FOR

εἰσιν, οὗτοι οἱ ἀκολουθοῦντες τῷ ἀρνίῳ ὅπου ἂν
[2]THEY ARE; THESE [ARE] THE ONES FOLLOWING THE LAMB WHEREVER

ὑπάγῃ. οὗτοι ἠγοράσθησαν ἀπὸ τῶν ἀνθρώπων
HE GOES. THESE ONES WERE PURCHASED FROM - MEN

ἀπαρχὴ τῷ θεῷ καὶ τῷ ἀρνίῳ, **14.5** καὶ ἐν τῷ
[AS] FIRSTFRUIT[S] - TO GOD AND TO THE LAMB,   AND IN THE

στόματι αὐτῶν οὐχ εὑρέθη ψεῦδος, ἄμωμοί εἰσιν.
MOUTH   OF THEM WAS NOT FOUND A LIE;   THEY ARE~UNBLEMISHED.

14.6 Καὶ εἶδον ἄλλον ἄγγελον πετόμενον ἐν
AND I SAW ANOTHER ANGEL FLYING   IN

μεσουρανήματι, ἔχοντα εὐαγγέλιον αἰώνιον εὐαγγελίσαι
MIDHEAVEN(MIDAIR), HAVING AN ETERNAL~GOSPEL   TO PREACH

ἐπὶ τοὺς καθημένους ἐπὶ τῆς γῆς καὶ ἐπὶ πᾶν
TO THE ONES SITTING   ON THE EARTH AND TO EVERY

ἔθνος καὶ φυλὴν καὶ γλῶσσαν καὶ λαόν, **14.7** λέγων ἐν
NATION AND TRIBE AND TONGUE   AND PEOPLE,   SAYING IN

φωνῇ μεγάλῃ, Φοβήθητε τὸν θεὸν καὶ δότε αὐτῷ
A LOUD~VOICE, FEAR   -   GOD AND GIVE HIM

δόξαν, ὅτι ἦλθεν ἡ ὥρα τῆς κρίσεως αὐτοῦ,
GLORY, BECAUSE CAME(HAS COME) THE HOUR OF THE JUDGMENT OF HIM,

καὶ προσκυνήσατε τῷ ποιήσαντι τὸν οὐρανὸν καὶ
AND WORSHIP THE ONE HAVING MADE THE HEAVEN AND

τὴν γῆν καὶ θάλασσαν καὶ πηγὰς ὑδάτων.
THE EARTH AND SEA AND FOUNTAINS OF WATERS.

14.8 Καὶ ἄλλος ἄγγελος δεύτερος ἠκολούθησεν
AND ANOTHER ANGEL, A SECOND [ONE] FOLLOWED

λέγων, Ἔπεσεν ἔπεσεν Βαβυλὼν ἡ μεγάλη ἣ ἐκ τοῦ
SAYING, FELL, FELL, BABYLON THE GREAT, WHO OF THE

οἴνου τοῦ θυμοῦ τῆς πορνείας αὐτῆς πεπότικεν
WINE OF THE PASSION - OF HER~FORNICATION ¹SHE HAS MADE ⁵TO DRINK

πάντα τὰ ἔθνη.
²ALL ³THE ⁴NATIONS.

14.9 Καὶ ἄλλος ἄγγελος τρίτος ἠκολούθησεν αὐτοῖς
AND ANOTHER ANGEL, A THIRD [ONE] FOLLOWED THEM

λέγων ἐν φωνῇ μεγάλῃ, Εἴ τις προσκυνεῖ τὸ θηρίον
SAYING IN A GREAT(LOUD)~VOICE, IF ANYONE WORSHIPS THE BEAST

καὶ τὴν εἰκόνα αὐτοῦ καὶ λαμβάνει χάραγμα ἐπὶ τοῦ
AND THE IMAGE OF IT AND RECEIVES A MARK ON THE

μετώπου αὐτοῦ ἢ ἐπὶ τὴν χεῖρα αὐτοῦ, **14.10** καὶ αὐτὸς
FOREHEAD OF HIM OR ON THE HAND OF HIM, EVEN HE

πίεται ἐκ τοῦ οἴνου τοῦ θυμοῦ τοῦ θεοῦ τοῦ
WILL DRINK OF THE WINE OF THE WRATH - OF GOD -

κεκερασμένου ἀκράτου ἐν τῷ ποτηρίῳ τῆς ὀργῆς
HAVING BEEN MIXED UNDILUTED IN THE CUP OF THE WRATH

αὐτοῦ καὶ βασανισθήσεται ἐν πυρὶ καὶ θείῳ ἐνώπιον
OF HIM, AND HE WILL BE TORMENTED IN(BY) FIRE AND SULFUR BEFORE

ἀγγέλων ἁγίων καὶ ἐνώπιον τοῦ ἀρνίου. **14.11** καὶ ὁ
HOLY~ANGELS AND BEFORE THE LAMB. AND THE

καπνὸς τοῦ βασανισμοῦ αὐτῶν εἰς αἰῶνας αἰώνων
SMOKE - OF THEIR~TORMENT FOR AGES OF AGES

ἀναβαίνει, καὶ οὐκ ἔχουσιν ἀνάπαυσιν ἡμέρας καὶ
ASCENDS, AND THEY DO NOT HAVE REST DAY AND

νυκτὸς οἱ προσκυνοῦντες τὸ θηρίον καὶ τὴν εἰκόνα
NIGHT, THE ONES WORSHIPING THE BEAST AND THE IMAGE

αὐτοῦ καὶ εἴ τις λαμβάνει τὸ χάραγμα τοῦ
OF IT AND IF ANYONE RECEIVES THE MARK OF THE

ὀνόματος αὐτοῦ. **14.12** Ὧδε ἡ ὑπομονὴ τῶν ἁγίων
NAME OF IT. HERE ²THE ³ENDURANCE ⁴OF THE ⁵SAINTS

ἐστίν, οἱ τηροῦντες τὰς ἐντολὰς τοῦ θεοῦ καὶ τὴν
¹IS, THE ONES KEEPING THE COMMANDS - OF GOD AND THE

πίστιν Ἰησοῦ.
FAITH OF(IN) JESUS.

14.13 Καὶ ἤκουσα φωνῆς ἐκ τοῦ οὐρανοῦ λεγούσης,
AND I HEARD A VOICE OUT OF - HEAVEN SAYING,

Γράψον· Μακάριοι οἱ νεκροὶ οἱ ἐν κυρίῳ
WRITE: BLESSED [ARE] THE DEAD, THE ONES IN [THE] LORD

glory, for the hour of his judgment has come; and worship him who made heaven and earth, the sea and the springs of water."

8 Then another angel, a second, followed, saying, "Fallen, fallen is Babylon the great! She has made all nations drink of the wine of the wrath of her fornication."

9 Then another angel, a third, followed them, crying with a loud voice, "Those who worship the beast and its image, and receive a mark on their foreheads or on their hands, ¹⁰they will also drink the wine of God's wrath, poured unmixed into the cup of his anger, and they will be tormented with fire and sulfur in the presence of the holy angels and in the presence of the Lamb. ¹¹And the smoke of their torment goes up forever and ever. There is no rest day or night for those who worship the beast and its image and for anyone who receives the mark of its name."

12 Here is a call for the endurance of the saints, those who keep the commandments of God and hold fast to the faith of ᵘ Jesus.

13 And I heard a voice from heaven saying, "Write this: Blessed are the dead

ᵘ Or *to their faith in*

who from now on die in the Lord." "Yes," says the Spirit, "they will rest from their labors, for their deeds follow them."

14 Then I looked, and there was a white cloud, and seated on the cloud was one like the Son of Man, with a golden crown on his head, and a sharp sickle in his hand! 15Another angel came out of the temple, calling with a loud voice to the one who sat on the cloud, "Use your sickle and reap, for the hour to reap has come, because the harvest of the earth is fully ripe." 16So the one who sat on the cloud swung his sickle over the earth, and the earth was reaped.

17 Then another angel came out of the temple in heaven, and he too had a sharp sickle. 18Then another angel came out from the altar, the angel who has authority over fire, and he called with a loud voice to him who had the sharp sickle, "Use your sharp sickle and gather the clusters of the vine of the earth, for its grapes are ripe." 19So the angel swung his sickle over the earth and gathered the vintage of the earth, and he threw it into the great winepress of the wrath of God. 20And the winepress was

ἀποθνήσκοντες	ἀπ'	ἄρτι.	ναί,	λέγει	τὸ	πνεῦμα,	ἵνα
DYING,	FROM	NOW [ON].	YES,	SAYS	THE	SPIRIT,	SO THAT

ἀναπαήσονται	ἐκ	τῶν	κόπων	αὐτῶν,	τὰ	γὰρ	ἔργα	αὐτῶν
THEY WILL REST	FROM	THE	LABORS	OF THEM,	FOR~THE		WORKS	OF THEM

ἀκολουθεῖ	μετ'	αὐτῶν.
FOLLOW	AFTER	THEM.

14.14 Καὶ εἶδον, καὶ ἰδοὺ νεφέλη λευκή, καὶ ἐπὶ
AND I SAW, AND BEHOLD A WHITE~CLOUD, AND ON

τὴν νεφέλην καθήμενον ὅμοιον υἱὸν ἀνθρώπου, ἔχων
THE CLOUD ONE SITTING LIKE [THE] SON OF MAN, HAVING

ἐπὶ τῆς κεφαλῆς αὐτοῦ στέφανον χρυσοῦν καὶ ἐν τῇ
ON THE HEAD OF HIM A GOLDEN~CROWN AND IN THE

χειρὶ αὐτοῦ δρέπανον ὀξύ. **14.15** καὶ ἄλλος ἄγγελος
HAND OF HIM A SHARP~SICKLE. AND ANOTHER ANGEL

ἐξῆλθεν ἐκ τοῦ ναοῦ κράζων ἐν φωνῇ μεγάλῃ τῷ
CAME OUT OF THE TEMPLE, CRYING WITH A LOUD~VOICE TO THE ONE

καθημένῳ ἐπὶ τῆς νεφέλης, Πέμψον τὸ δρέπανόν
SITTING ON THE CLOUD, SEND(PUT FORTH) THE SICKLE

σου καὶ θέρισον, ὅτι ἦλθεν ἡ ὥρα θερίσαι,
OF YOU AND REAP, BECAUSE CAME(HAS COME) THE HOUR TO REAP,

ὅτι ἐξηράνθη ὁ θερισμὸς τῆς γῆς. **14.16** καὶ
BECAUSE WAS DRIED(RIPE) THE HARVEST OF THE EARTH. AND

ἔβαλεν ὁ καθήμενος ἐπὶ τῆς νεφέλης τὸ δρέπανον
6PUT FORTH 1THE ONE 2SITTING 3ON 4THE 5CLOUD THE SICKLE

αὐτοῦ ἐπὶ τὴν γῆν καὶ ἐθερίσθη ἡ γῆ.
OF HIM ON THE EARTH AND 3WAS REAPED 1THE 2EARTH.

14.17 Καὶ ἄλλος ἄγγελος ἐξῆλθεν ἐκ τοῦ ναοῦ τοῦ
AND ANOTHER ANGEL CAME OUT OF THE TEMPLE -

ἐν τῷ οὐρανῷ ἔχων καὶ αὐτὸς δρέπανον ὀξύ. **14.18** Καὶ
IN - HEAVEN, 3HAVING 2ALSO 1HE A SHARP~SICKLE. AND

ἄλλος ἄγγελος [ἐξῆλθεν] ἐκ τοῦ θυσιαστηρίου [ὁ]
ANOTHER ANGEL CAME OUT OF THE ALTAR,

ἔχων ἐξουσίαν ἐπὶ τοῦ πυρός, καὶ ἐφώνησεν
HAVING AUTHORITY OVER THE FIRE, AND HE SPOKE

φωνῇ μεγάλῃ τῷ ἔχοντι τὸ δρέπανον τὸ ὀξὺ
WITH A LOUD~VOICE TO THE ONE HAVING THE 2SICKLE - 1SHARP

λέγων, Πέμψον σου τὸ δρέπανον τὸ ὀξὺ καὶ
SAYING, SEND(PUT FORTH) YOUR - 2SICKLE - 1SHARP AND

τρύγησον τοὺς βότρυας τῆς ἀμπέλου τῆς γῆς, ὅτι
GATHER THE CLUSTERS OF THE VINE OF THE EARTH, BECAUSE

ἤκμασαν αἱ σταφυλαὶ αὐτῆς. **14.19** καὶ ἔβαλεν ὁ
4RIPENED 1THE 2GRAPES 3OF IT. AND 3PUT FORTH 1THE

ἄγγελος τὸ δρέπανον αὐτοῦ εἰς τὴν γῆν καὶ ἐτρύγησεν
2ANGEL THE SICKLE OF HIM TO THE EARTH AND GATHERED

τὴν ἄμπελον τῆς γῆς καὶ ἔβαλεν εἰς τὴν ληνὸν
THE VINTAGE OF THE EARTH AND THREW [IT] INTO THE 2WINEPRESS

τοῦ θυμοῦ τοῦ θεοῦ τὸν μέγαν. **14.20** καὶ ἐπατήθη
3OF THE 4WRATH - 5OF GOD - 1GREAT. AND 3WAS TRODDEN

ἡ	λῆνὸς	ἔξωθεν	τῆς	πόλεως	καὶ	ἐξῆλθεν	αἷμα	ἐκ
¹THE	²WINEPRESS	OUTSIDE	THE	CITY	AND	BLOOD~CAME OUT		FROM

τῆς	ληνοῦ	ἄχρι	τῶν	χαλινῶν	τῶν	ἵππων	ἀπὸ
THE	WINEPRESS	UP TO	THE	BRIDLES	OF THE	HORSES,	FROM(FOR)

σταδίων	χιλίων	ἑξακοσίων.
³STADIA	¹ONE THOUSAND	²SIX HUNDRED.

trodden outside the city, and blood flowed from the winepress, as high as a horse's bridle, for a distance of about two hundred miles.ᵛ

ᵛ Gk *one thousand six hundred stadia*

15.1
Καὶ	εἶδον	ἄλλο	σημεῖον	ἐν	τῷ	οὐρανῷ	μέγα
AND	I SAW	ANOTHER	SIGN	IN	-	HEAVEN,	GREAT

καὶ	θαυμαστόν,	ἀγγέλους	ἑπτὰ	ἔχοντας	πληγὰς	ἑπτὰ
AND	MARVELOUS,	SEVEN~ANGELS		HAVING	SEVEN~PLAGUES,	

τὰς	ἐσχάτας,	ὅτι	ἐν	αὐταῖς	ἐτελέσθη	ὁ	θυμὸς
THE	LAST ONES,	BECAUSE	IN(BY)	THEM	WAS(IS) COMPLETED	THE	WRATH

τοῦ	θεοῦ.
-	OF GOD.

15.2
Καὶ	εἶδον	ὡς	θάλασσαν	ὑαλίνην
AND	I SAW	AS [IT WERE]	A GLASSY~SEA	

μεμιγμένην	πυρὶ	καὶ	τοὺς	νικῶντας	ἐκ	τοῦ	θηρίου
HAVING BEEN MINGLED	WITH FIRE	AND	THE	OVERCOMERS	OF	THE	BEAST

καὶ	ἐκ	τῆς	εἰκόνος	αὐτοῦ	καὶ	ἐκ	τοῦ	ἀριθμοῦ	τοῦ
AND	OF	THE	IMAGE	OF IT	AND	OF	THE	NUMBER	OF THE

ὀνόματος	αὐτοῦ	ἑστῶτας	ἐπὶ	τὴν	θάλασσαν	τὴν
NAME	OF IT	HAVING TAKEN [ITS] STAND	ON	THE	²SEA	-

ὑαλίνην	ἔχοντας	κιθάρας	τοῦ	θεοῦ.	**15.3**	καὶ	ᾄδουσιν
¹GLASSY	HAVING	HARPS	-	OF GOD.		AND	THEY SING

τὴν	ᾠδὴν	Μωϋσέως	τοῦ	δούλου	τοῦ	θεοῦ	καὶ	τὴν	ᾠδὴν
THE	SONG	OF MOSES,	THE	SLAVE	-	OF GOD,	AND	THE	SONG

τοῦ	ἀρνίου	λέγοντες,
OF THE	LAMB,	SAYING,

Μεγάλα	καὶ	θαυμαστὰ	τὰ	ἔργα	σου,
GREAT	AND	MARVELOUS	[ARE] THE	WORKS	OF YOU,

κύριε	ὁ	θεὸς	ὁ	παντοκράτωρ·
LORD	-	GOD,	THE	ALMIGHTY;

δίκαιαι	καὶ	ἀληθιναὶ	αἱ	ὁδοί	σου,
RIGHTEOUS	AND	TRUE	[ARE] THE	WAYS	OF YOU,

ὁ	βασιλεὺς	τῶν	⌜ἐθνῶν·⌝
THE	KING	OF THE	NATIONS;

15.4
τίς	οὐ	μὴ	φοβηθῇ,	κύριε,
WHO	WOULD NEVER FEAR [YOU],			LORD,

καὶ	δοξάσει	τὸ	ὄνομά	σου;
AND	WILL GLORIFY	THE	NAME	OF YOU?

ὅτι	μόνος	ὅσιος,
BECAUSE	[YOU] ONLY	[ARE] HOLY,

Then I saw another portent in heaven, great and amazing: seven angels with seven plagues, which are the last, for with them the wrath of God is ended.

2 And I saw what appeared to be a sea of glass mixed with fire, and those who had conquered the beast and its image and the number of its name, standing beside the sea of glass with harps of God in their hands. ³And they sing the song of Moses, the servantʷ of God, and the song of the Lamb:

"Great and amazing are your deeds,
Lord God the Almighty!
Just and true are your ways,
King of the nations!ˣ
4 Lord, who will not fear and glorify your name?
For you alone are holy.

ʷ Gk *slave*
ˣ Other ancient authorities read *the ages*

15:3 text: ASVmg RSVmg NASB NEBmg TEV NJB NRSV. var. αιωνων (ages): ASV RSV NASBmg NIV NEB TEVmg NRSVmg. var. αγιων (saints): KJV.

All nations will come and worship before you,
for your judgments have been revealed."

5 After this I looked, and the temple of the tent[y] of witness in heaven was opened, [6]and out of the temple came the seven angels with the seven plagues, robed in pure bright linen,[z] with golden sashes across their chests. [7]Then one of the four living creatures gave the seven angels seven golden bowls full of the wrath of God, who lives forever and ever; [8]and the temple was filled with smoke from the glory of God and from his power, and no one could enter the temple until the seven plagues of the seven angels were ended.

[y] Or *tabernacle*
[z] Other ancient authorities read *stone*

ὅτι πάντα τὰ ἔθνη ἥξουσιν
BECAUSE ALL THE NATIONS WILL COME

καὶ προσκυνήσουσιν ἐνώπιόν σου,
AND WILL WORSHIP BEFORE YOU,

ὅτι τὰ δικαιώματά σου ἐφανερώθησαν.
BECAUSE THE RIGHTEOUS ACTS OF YOU WERE MANIFESTED.

15.5 Καὶ μετὰ ταῦτα εἶδον, καὶ ἠνοίγη ὁ ναὸς
AND AFTER THESE THINGS I SAW, AND WAS OPENED THE TEMPLE,

τῆς σκηνῆς τοῦ μαρτυρίου ἐν τῷ οὐρανῷ,
[THAT IS,] THE TABERNACLE OF THE TESTIMONY IN - HEAVEN,

15.6 καὶ ἐξῆλθον οἱ ἑπτὰ ἄγγελοι [οἱ] ἔχοντες τὰς
AND [8]CAME [1]THE [2]SEVEN [3]ANGELS - [4]HAVING [5]THE

ἑπτὰ πληγὰς ἐκ τοῦ ναοῦ ἐνδεδυμένοι λίνον
[6]SEVEN [7]PLAGUES OUT OF THE TEMPLE, HAVING BEEN CLOTHED IN [3]LINEN

καθαρὸν λαμπρὸν καὶ περιεζωσμένοι περὶ τὰ στήθη
[1]CLEAN [2]BRIGHT AND HAVING BEEN WRAPPED AROUND THE BREASTS

ζώνας χρυσᾶς. **15.7** καὶ ἓν ἐκ τῶν τεσσάρων ζῴων
[WITH] GOLDEN~SASHES. AND ONE OF THE FOUR LIVING BEINGS

ἔδωκεν τοῖς ἑπτὰ ἀγγέλοις ἑπτὰ φιάλας χρυσᾶς
GAVE TO THE SEVEN ANGELS SEVEN GOLDEN~BOWLS

γεμούσας τοῦ θυμοῦ τοῦ θεοῦ τοῦ ζῶντος εἰς τοὺς
BEING FULL OF THE WRATH - OF GOD - LIVING INTO THE

αἰῶνας τῶν αἰώνων. **15.8** καὶ ἐγεμίσθη ὁ ναὸς
AGES OF THE AGES. AND WAS FILLED THE TEMPLE

καπνοῦ ἐκ τῆς δόξης τοῦ θεοῦ καὶ ἐκ τῆς δυνάμεως
WITH SMOKE FROM THE GLORY - OF GOD AND FROM THE POWER

αὐτοῦ, καὶ οὐδεὶς ἐδύνατο εἰσελθεῖν εἰς τὸν ναὸν
OF HIM, AND NO ONE WAS BEING ABLE TO ENTER INTO THE TEMPLE

ἄχρι τελεσθῶσιν αἱ ἑπτὰ πληγαὶ τῶν ἑπτὰ
UNTIL SHOULD BE COMPLETED THE SEVEN PLAGUES OF THE SEVEN

ἀγγέλων.
ANGELS.

CHAPTER 16

Then I heard a loud voice from the temple telling the seven angels, "Go and pour out on the earth the seven bowls of the wrath of God."

2 So the first angel went and poured his bowl on the earth, and a foul and painful sore came on those who had

16.1 Καὶ ἤκουσα μεγάλης φωνῆς ἐκ τοῦ ναοῦ
AND I HEARD A LOUD VOICE OUT OF THE TEMPLE

λεγούσης τοῖς ἑπτὰ ἀγγέλοις, Ὑπάγετε καὶ ἐκχέετε
SAYING TO THE SEVEN ANGELS, GO AND POUR OUT

τὰς ἑπτὰ φιάλας τοῦ θυμοῦ τοῦ θεοῦ εἰς τὴν γῆν.
THE SEVEN BOWLS OF THE WRATH - OF GOD ONTO THE EARTH.

16.2 Καὶ ἀπῆλθεν ὁ πρῶτος καὶ ἐξέχεεν τὴν φιάλην
AND [3]DEPARTED [1]THE [2]FIRST AND POURED OUT THE BOWL

αὐτοῦ εἰς τὴν γῆν, καὶ ἐγένετο ἕλκος κακὸν καὶ
OF HIM ONTO THE EARTH, AND [5]CAME [4]SORE [1]A BAD [2]AND

πονηρὸν ἐπὶ τοὺς ἀνθρώπους τοὺς ἔχοντας τὸ χάραγμα
[3]EVIL ON THE MEN - HAVING THE MARK

τοῦ θηρίου καὶ τοὺς προσκυνοῦντας τῇ εἰκόνι αὐτοῦ.
OF THE BEAST AND THE ONES WORSHIPING THE IMAGE OF IT.

16.3 Καὶ ὁ δεύτερος ἐξέχεεν τὴν φιάλην αὐτοῦ εἰς
AND THE SECOND POURED OUT THE BOWL OF HIM ONTO

τὴν θάλασσαν, καὶ ἐγένετο αἷμα ὡς νεκροῦ,
THE SEA, AND IT BECAME BLOOD LIKE [THAT] OF A DEAD MAN'S,

καὶ πᾶσα ψυχὴ ζωῆς ἀπέθανεν τὰ ἐν τῇ θαλάσσῃ.
AND EVERY LIVING~SOUL DIED, THE THINGS IN THE SEA.

16.4 Καὶ ὁ τρίτος ἐξέχεεν τὴν φιάλην αὐτοῦ εἰς
AND THE THIRD POURED OUT THE BOWL OF HIM ONTO

τοὺς ποταμοὺς καὶ τὰς πηγὰς τῶν ὑδάτων, καὶ
THE RIVERS AND THE FOUNTAINS OF THE WATERS, AND

ἐγένετο αἷμα. **16.5** καὶ ἤκουσα τοῦ ἀγγέλου τῶν
IT BECAME BLOOD. AND I HEARD THE ANGEL OF THE

ὑδάτων λέγοντος,
WATER SAYING,

Δίκαιος εἶ, ὁ ὢν καὶ ὁ ἦν, ὁ
RIGHTEOUS ARE YOU, THE ONE BEING AND THE ONE [WHO] WAS, THE

ὅσιος,
HOLY ONE,

ὅτι ταῦτα ἔκρινας,
BECAUSE THESE THINGS YOU JUDGED,

16.6 ὅτι αἷμα ἁγίων καὶ προφητῶν ἐξέχεαν
BECAUSE [THE] BLOOD OF SAINTS AND PROPHETS THEY SHED

καὶ αἷμα αὐτοῖς [δ]έδωκας πιεῖν,
AND ³BLOOD ²THEM ¹YOU HAVE GIVEN TO DRINK,

ἄξιοί εἰσιν.
THEY ARE~DESERVING [OF IT].

16.7 καὶ ἤκουσα τοῦ θυσιαστηρίου λέγοντος,
AND I HEARD THE ALTAR SAYING,

Ναί κύριε ὁ θεὸς ὁ παντοκράτωρ,
YES, LORD - GOD, THE ALMIGHTY,

ἀληθιναὶ καὶ δίκαιαι αἱ κρίσεις σου.
TRUE AND RIGHTEOUS [ARE] THE JUDGMENTS OF YOU.

16.8 Καὶ ὁ τέταρτος ἐξέχεεν τὴν φιάλην αὐτοῦ ἐπὶ
AND THE FOURTH POURED OUT THE BOWL OF HIM ONTO

τὸν ἥλιον, καὶ ἐδόθη αὐτῷ καυματίσαι τοὺς
THE SUN, AND IT WAS GIVEN TO IT TO SCORCH

ἀνθρώπους ἐν πυρί. **16.9** καὶ ἐκαυματίσθησαν οἱ
MEN WITH FIRE. AND ²WERE SCORCHED -

ἄνθρωποι καῦμα μέγα καὶ ἐβλασφήμησαν τὸ
¹MEN ⁴HEAT ³[WITH] GREAT, AND THEY BLASPHEMED THE

ὄνομα τοῦ θεοῦ τοῦ ἔχοντος τὴν ἐξουσίαν ἐπὶ τὰς
NAME - OF GOD, THE ONE HAVING THE AUTHORITY OVER -

πληγὰς ταύτας καὶ οὐ μετενόησαν δοῦναι αὐτῷ δόξαν.
THESE~PLAGUES AND DID NOT REPENT TO GIVE HIM GLORY.

16.10 Καὶ ὁ πέμπτος ἐξέχεεν τὴν φιάλην αὐτοῦ ἐπὶ
AND THE FIFTH POURED OUT THE BOWL OF HIM ON

the mark of the beast and who worshiped its image.

3 The second angel poured his bowl into the sea, and it became like the blood of a corpse, and every living thing in the sea died.

4 The third angel poured his bowl into the rivers and the springs of water, and they became blood. ⁵And I heard the angel of the waters say,

"You are just, O Holy One, who are and were,
for you have judged these things;
⁶ because they shed the blood of saints and prophets,
you have given them blood to drink.
It is what they deserve!"
⁷And I heard the altar respond,
"Yes, O Lord God, the Almighty,
your judgments are true and just!"

8 The fourth angel poured his bowl on the sun, and it was allowed to scorch people with fire; ⁹they were scorched by the fierce heat, but they cursed the name of God, who had authority over these plagues, and they did not repent and give him glory.

10 The fifth angel poured

his bowl on the throne of the beast, and its kingdom was plunged into darkness; people gnawed their tongues in agony, [11]and cursed the God of heaven because of their pains and sores, and they did not repent of their deeds.

12 The sixth angel poured his bowl on the great river Euphrates, and its water was dried up in order to prepare the way for the kings from the east. [13]And I saw three foul spirits like frogs coming from the mouth of the dragon, from the mouth of the beast, and from the mouth of the false prophet. [14]These are demonic spirits, performing signs, who go abroad to the kings of the whole world, to assemble them for battle on the great day of God the Almighty. [15]("See, I am coming like a thief! Blessed is the one who stays awake and is clothed,[a] not going about naked and exposed to shame.") [16]And they assembled them at the place that in Hebrew is called Harmagedon.

17 The seventh angel poured his bowl into the air, and a loud voice came out of the temple, from the throne, saying, "It is done!" [18]And

[a] Gk and keeps his robes

τὸν θρόνον τοῦ θηρίου, καὶ ἐγένετο ἡ βασιλεία αὐτοῦ
THE THRONE OF THE BEAST, AND [2]BECAME - [1]ITS~KINGDOM

ἐσκοτωμένη, καὶ ἐμασῶντο τὰς γλώσσας αὐτῶν
[3]DARKENED, AND THEY WERE BITING THE TONGUES OF THEM

ἐκ τοῦ πόνου, **16.11** καὶ ἐβλασφήμησαν τὸν θεὸν
[BECAUSE] OF THE PAIN, AND THEY BLASPHEMED THE GOD

τοῦ οὐρανοῦ ἐκ τῶν πόνων αὐτῶν καὶ ἐκ τῶν
- OF HEAVEN [BECAUSE] OF THE PAINS OF THEM AND [BECAUSE] OF THE

ἑλκῶν αὐτῶν καὶ οὐ μετενόησαν ἐκ τῶν ἔργων αὐτῶν.
SORES OF THEM AND THEY DID NOT REPENT FROM THE WORKS OF THEM.

16.12 Καὶ ὁ ἕκτος ἐξέχεεν τὴν φιάλην αὐτοῦ ἐπὶ
AND THE SIXTH POURED OUT THE BOWL OF HIM ON

τὸν ποταμὸν τὸν μέγαν τὸν Εὐφράτην, καὶ ἐξηράνθη
THE [2]RIVER - [1]GREAT, THE EUPHRATES, AND WAS DRIED UP

τὸ ὕδωρ αὐτοῦ, ἵνα ἑτοιμασθῇ ἡ ὁδὸς τῶν βασιλέων
THE WATER OF IT, THAT MIGHT BE PREPARED THE WAY OF THE KINGS

τῶν ἀπὸ ἀνατολῆς ἡλίου. **16.13** Καὶ εἶδον ἐκ
- FROM [THE] RISING OF [THE] SUN. AND I SAW [COMING] OUT OF

τοῦ στόματος τοῦ δράκοντος καὶ ἐκ τοῦ στόματος
THE MOUTH OF THE DRAGON AND OUT OF THE MOUTH

τοῦ θηρίου καὶ ἐκ τοῦ στόματος τοῦ ψευδοπροφήτου
OF THE BEAST AND OUT OF THE MOUTH OF THE FALSE PROPHET

πνεύματα τρία ἀκάθαρτα ὡς βάτραχοι· **16.14** εἰσὶν γὰρ
[3]SPIRITS [1]THREE [2]UNCLEAN LIKE FROGS; FOR~THEY ARE

πνεύματα δαιμονίων ποιοῦντα σημεῖα, ἃ
SPIRITS OF DEMONS PERFORMING SIGNS, WHICH

ἐκπορεύεται ἐπὶ τοὺς βασιλεῖς τῆς οἰκουμένης ὅλης
GO FORTH TO THE KINGS OF THE WHOLE~INHABITED [EARTH]

συναγαγεῖν αὐτοὺς εἰς τὸν πόλεμον τῆς ἡμέρας τῆς
TO GATHER THEM TO THE BATTLE OF THE [2]DAY -

μεγάλης τοῦ θεοῦ τοῦ παντοκράτορος. **16.15** Ἰδοὺ
[1]GREAT - OF GOD, THE ALMIGHTY. BEHOLD,

ἔρχομαι ὡς κλέπτης. μακάριος ὁ γρηγορῶν καὶ
I AM COMING AS A THIEF. BLESSED [IS] THE ONE WATCHING AND

τηρῶν τὰ ἱμάτια αὐτοῦ, ἵνα μὴ γυμνὸς περιπατῇ καὶ
KEEPING THE GARMENTS OF HIM, LEST HE WALK~NAKED AND

βλέπωσιν τὴν ἀσχημοσύνην αὐτοῦ. **16.16** καὶ
THEY SEE THE SHAME OF HIM. AND

συνήγαγεν αὐτοὺς εἰς τὸν τόπον τὸν καλούμενον
THEY GATHERED THEM INTO THE PLACE - BEING CALLED

Ἑβραϊστὶ Ἁρμαγεδών.
IN HEBREW, HARMAGEDON(ARMAGEDDON).

16.17 Καὶ ὁ ἕβδομος ἐξέχεεν τὴν φιάλην αὐτοῦ ἐπὶ
AND THE SEVENTH POURED OUT THE BOWL OF HIM ON

τὸν ἀέρα, καὶ ἐξῆλθεν φωνὴ μεγάλη ἐκ τοῦ ναοῦ
THE AIR, AND [3]CAME [2]VOICE [1]A GREAT(LOUD) OUT OF THE TEMPLE

ἀπὸ τοῦ θρόνου λέγουσα, Γέγονεν. **16.18** καὶ ἐγένοντο
FROM THE THRONE SAYING, IT HAS HAPPENED. AND THERE WERE

ἀστραπαὶ	καὶ	φωναὶ	καὶ	βρονταὶ	καὶ	σεισμὸς
FLASHES OF LIGHTNING	AND	SOUNDS	AND	THUNDER,	AND	²EARTHQUAKE

ἐγένετο	μέγας,	οἷος	οὐκ ἐγένετο	ἀφ' οὗ	ἄνθρωπος
³OCCURRED	¹A GREAT,	SUCH AS	DID NOT OCCUR	SINCE	MAN

ἐγένετο	ἐπὶ	τῆς	γῆς	τηλικοῦτος	σεισμὸς	οὕτω	μέγας.
WAS	ON	THE	EARTH,	SO MIGHTY	AN EARTHQUAKE,	SO	GREAT.

16.19 καὶ ἐγένετο ἡ πόλις ἡ μεγάλη εἰς τρία μέρη

AND	⁴BECAME [SPLIT]	¹THE ³CITY	-	²GREAT	INTO	THREE	PARTS

καὶ	αἱ	πόλεις	τῶν	ἐθνῶν ἔπεσαν.	καὶ	Βαβυλὼν	ἡ
AND	THE	CITIES	OF THE	NATIONS FELL.	AND	BABYLON	THE

μεγάλη	ἐμνήσθη	ἐνώπιον	τοῦ	θεοῦ	δοῦναι	αὐτῇ	τὸ
GREAT	WAS REMEMBERED	BEFORE	-	GOD,	TO GIVE	HER	THE

ποτήριον	τοῦ	οἴνου	τοῦ	θυμοῦ	τῆς	ὀργῆς	αὐτοῦ.
CUP	OF THE	WINE	OF THE	FURY	OF THE	WRATH	OF HIM.

16.20 καὶ πᾶσα νῆσος ἔφυγεν καὶ ὄρη

AND	EVERY	ISLAND	FLED,	AND	MOUNTAINS

οὐχ	εὑρέθησαν.	**16.21** καὶ	χάλαζα	μεγάλη	ὡς
WERE NOT FOUND.		AND	GREAT~HAIL		AS

ταλαντιαία	καταβαίνει	ἐκ	τοῦ	οὐρανοῦ	ἐπὶ	τοὺς
TALENT [IN WEIGHT]	COMES DOWN	FROM	-	HEAVEN	ON	-

ἀνθρώπους,	καὶ	ἐβλασφήμησαν	οἱ	ἄνθρωποι	τὸν	θεὸν
MEN,	AND	²BLASPHEMED	-	¹MEN	-	GOD

ἐκ	τῆς	πληγῆς	τῆς	χαλάζης,	ὅτι	μεγάλη	ἐστὶν
[BECAUSE] OF	THE	PLAGUE	OF THE	HAIL,	BECAUSE	⁶GREAT	⁴IS

ἡ	πληγὴ	αὐτῆς	σφόδρα.
¹THE	²PLAGUE	³OF IT	⁵EXTREMELY.

there came flashes of lightning, rumblings, peals of thunder, and a violent earthquake, such as had not occurred since people were upon the earth, so violent was that earthquake. ¹⁹The great city was split into three parts, and the cities of the nations fell. God remembered great Babylon and gave her the wine-cup of the fury of his wrath. ²⁰And every island fled away, and no mountains were to be found; ²¹and huge hailstones, each weighing about a hundred pounds,[b] dropped from heaven on people, until they cursed God for the plague of the hail, so fearful was that plague.

[b] Gk *weighing about a talent*

CHAPTER 17

17.1 Καὶ ἦλθεν εἷς ἐκ τῶν ἑπτὰ ἀγγέλων τῶν

AND	CAME	ONE	OF	THE	SEVEN	ANGELS	-

ἐχόντων	τὰς	ἑπτὰ	φιάλας	καὶ	ἐλάλησεν	μετ'	ἐμοῦ
HAVING	THE	SEVEN	BOWLS	AND	SPOKE	WITH	ME

λέγων,	Δεῦρο,	δείξω	σοι	τὸ	κρίμα	τῆς	πόρνης	τῆς
SAYING,	COME,	I WILL SHOW	YOU	THE	JUDGMENT	OF THE	²PROSTITUTE	-

μεγάλης	τῆς	καθημένης	ἐπὶ	ὑδάτων	πολλῶν,	**17.2** μεθ'
¹GREAT	-	SITTING	ON	MANY~WATERS,		WITH

ἧς	ἐπόρνευσαν	οἱ	βασιλεῖς	τῆς	γῆς	καὶ
WHOM	⁵COMMITTED FORNICATION	¹THE	²KINGS	³OF THE	⁴EARTH	AND

ἐμεθύσθησαν	οἱ	κατοικοῦντες	τὴν	γῆν	ἐκ	τοῦ
⁵BECAME DRUNK	¹THE ONES	²DWELLING ON	³THE	⁴EARTH	FROM	THE

οἴνου	τῆς	πορνείας	αὐτῆς	**17.3** καὶ	ἀπήνεγκέν	με	εἰς
WINE	OF THE	FORNICATION	OF HER;	AND	HE CARRIED ME AWAY		INTO

ἔρημον	ἐν	πνεύματι.	καὶ	εἶδον	γυναῖκα	καθημένην
A WILDERNESS	IN	SPIRIT.	AND	I SAW	A WOMAN	SITTING

ἐπὶ	θηρίον	κόκκινον,	γέμον[τα]	ὀνόματα
ON	A SCARLET~BEAST		BEING FILLED [WITH]	NAMES

Then one of the seven angels who had the seven bowls came and said to me, "Come, I will show you the judgment of the great whore who is seated on many waters, ²with whom the kings of the earth have committed fornication, and with the wine of whose fornication the inhabitants of the earth have become drunk." ³So he carried me away in the spirit[c] into a wilderness, and I saw a woman sitting on a scarlet beast that was full of

[c] Or *in the Spirit*

blasphemous names, and it had seven heads and ten horns. ⁴The woman was clothed in purple and scarlet, and adorned with gold and jewels and pearls, holding in her hand a golden cup full of abominations and the impurities of her fornication; ⁵and on her forehead was written a name, a mystery: "Babylon the great, mother of whores and of earth's abominations." ⁶And I saw that the woman was drunk with the blood of the saints and the blood of the witnesses to Jesus.

When I saw her, I was greatly amazed. ⁷But the angel said to me, "Why are you so amazed? I will tell you the mystery of the woman, and of the beast with seven heads and ten horns that carries her. ⁸The beast that you saw was, and is not, and is about to ascend from the bottomless pit and go to destruction. And the inhabitants of the earth, whose names have not been written in the book of life from the foundation of the world, will be amazed when they see the beast, because it was and is not and is to come.

9 "This calls for a mind that has wisdom: the seven heads are seven mountains on which the woman is seated; also, they are seven kings, ¹⁰of whom five have fallen, one is living, and the other has not yet come;

βλασφημίας, ἔχων κεφαλὰς ἑπτὰ καὶ κέρατα δέκα.
OF BLASPHEMY, HAVING SEVEN~HEADS AND TEN~HORNS.

17.4 καὶ ἡ γυνὴ ἦν περιβεβλημένη πορφυροῦν καὶ
AND THE WOMAN HAD BEEN CLOTHED IN PURPLE AND

κόκκινον καὶ κεχρυσωμένη χρυσίῳ καὶ λίθῳ τιμίῳ καὶ
SCARLET, AND GILDED WITH GOLD AND PRECIOUS~STONE AND

μαργαρίταις, ἔχουσα ποτήριον χρυσοῦν ἐν τῇ χειρὶ
PEARLS, HAVING A GOLDEN~CUP IN THE HAND

αὐτῆς γέμον βδελυγμάτων καὶ τὰ ἀκάθαρτα τῆς
OF HER BEING FULL OF ABOMINATIONS AND THE IMPURITIES OF THE

πορνείας αὐτῆς **17.5** καὶ ἐπὶ τὸ μέτωπον αὐτῆς ὄνομα
FORNICATION OF HER, AND ON THE FOREHEAD OF HER A NAME

γεγραμμένον, μυστήριον, Βαβυλὼν ἡ μεγάλη, ἡ μήτηρ
HAVING BEEN WRITTEN, MYSTERY, BABYLON THE GREAT, THE MOTHER

τῶν πορνῶν καὶ τῶν βδελυγμάτων τῆς γῆς. **17.6** καὶ
OF THE PROSTITUTES AND OF THE ABOMINATIONS OF THE EARTH. AND

εἶδον τὴν γυναῖκα μεθύουσαν ἐκ τοῦ αἵματος τῶν
I SAW THE WOMAN BEING DRUNK FROM THE BLOOD OF THE

ἁγίων καὶ ἐκ τοῦ αἵματος τῶν μαρτύρων Ἰησοῦ.
SAINTS AND FROM THE BLOOD OF THE WITNESSES OF JESUS.

Καὶ ἐθαύμασα ἰδὼν αὐτὴν θαῦμα μέγα.
AND ³I MARVELED ¹HAVING SEEN ²HER, ⁵WONDER ⁴[WITH] GREAT.

17.7 καὶ εἶπέν μοι ὁ ἄγγελος, Διὰ τί ἐθαύμασας; ἐγὼ
AND SAID TO ME THE ANGEL, WHY DID YOU MARVEL? I

ἐρῶ σοι τὸ μυστήριον τῆς γυναικὸς καὶ τοῦ θηρίου
WILL TELL YOU THE MYSTERY OF THE WOMAN AND OF THE BEAST

τοῦ βαστάζοντος αὐτὴν τοῦ ἔχοντος τὰς ἑπτὰ κεφαλὰς
- CARRYING HER, - HAVING THE SEVEN HEADS

καὶ τὰ δέκα κέρατα. **17.8** τὸ θηρίον ὃ εἶδες ἦν
AND THE TEN HORNS. THE BEAST WHICH YOU SAW WAS

καὶ οὐκ ἔστιν καὶ μέλλει ἀναβαίνειν ἐκ τῆς
AND IS~NOT, AND IS ABOUT TO COME UP OUT OF THE

ἀβύσσου καὶ εἰς ἀπώλειαν ὑπάγει, καὶ θαυμασθήσονται
ABYSS AND ²TO ³DESTRUCTION ¹GOES, AND ⁶WILL BE AMAZED

οἱ κατοικοῦντες ἐπὶ τῆς γῆς, ὧν οὐ γέγραπται
¹THE ONES ²DWELLING ³ON ⁴THE ⁵EARTH, WHOSE° ²HAS NOT BEEN WRITTEN

τὸ ὄνομα ἐπὶ τὸ βιβλίον τῆς ζωῆς ἀπὸ καταβολῆς
- ¹NAME ON(IN) THE BOOK - OF LIFE FROM [THE] FOUNDATION

κόσμου, βλεπόντων τὸ θηρίον ὅτι ἦν καὶ οὐκ ἔστιν
OF [THE] WORLD; SEEING THE BEAST THAT IT WAS AND IS~NOT

καὶ παρέσται **17.9** ὧδε ὁ νοῦς ὁ ἔχων σοφίαν. αἱ
AND WILL BE PRESENT, HERE [IS] THE MIND - HAVING WISDOM. THE

ἑπτὰ κεφαλαὶ ἑπτὰ ὄρη εἰσίν, ὅπου ἡ γυνὴ
SEVEN HEADS ²SEVEN ³MOUNTAINS ¹ARE, WHERE THE WOMAN

κάθηται ἐπ᾽ αὐτῶν. καὶ βασιλεῖς ἑπτά εἰσιν·
SITS ON THEM. ALSO ²SEVEN ³KINGS ¹THEY ARE;

17.10 οἱ πέντε ἔπεσαν, ὁ εἷς ἔστιν, ὁ ἄλλος
THE FIVE FELL, THE ONE IS, THE OTHER

οὔπω ἦλθεν,   καὶ   ὅταν   ἔλθῃ   ὀλίγον   αὐτὸν
DID NOT YET COME,   AND   WHEN   HE COMES   4A LITTLE WHILE   2HIM

δεῖ   μεῖναι.   **17.11** καὶ   τὸ   θηρίον   ὃ   ἦν   καὶ
1IT IS NECESSARY [FOR]   3TO REMAIN.   AND   THE   BEAST   WHICH   WAS   AND

οὐκ ἔστιν   καὶ   αὐτὸς   ὄγδοός ἐστιν   καὶ   ἐκ   τῶν ἑπτά
IS~NOT,   EVEN   HE   IS~AN EIGHTH,   AND   OF   THE   SEVEN

ἔστιν,   καὶ   εἰς   ἀπώλειαν   ὑπάγει.   **17.12** καὶ   τὰ   δέκα
IS,   AND   TO   DESTRUCTION   GOES.   AND   THE   TEN

κέρατα   ἃ   εἶδες   δέκα   βασιλεῖς   εἰσιν,   οἵτινες
HORNS   WHICH   YOU SAW   2TEN   3KINGS   1ARE,   WHO°

βασιλείαν   οὔπω ἔλαβον,   ἀλλὰ   ἐξουσίαν   ὡς   βασιλεῖς
A KINGDOM   DID NOT YET RECEIVE,   BUT   2AUTHORITY   3AS   4KINGS

μίαν   ὥραν   λαμβάνουσιν   μετὰ   τοῦ   θηρίου.   **17.13** οὗτοι
5[FOR] ONE   6HOUR   1WILL RECEIVE   WITH   THE   BEAST.   THESE

μίαν   γνώμην   ἔχουσιν,   καὶ   τὴν   δύναμιν   καὶ   ἐξουσίαν
2ONE   3MIND   1HAVE,   AND   THE   POWER   AND   AUTHORITY

αὐτῶν τῷ   θηρίῳ   διδόασιν.   **17.14** οὗτοι   μετὰ   τοῦ   ἀρνίου
OF THEM TO THE BEAST   THEY GIVE.   THESE   2WITH   3THE   4LAMB

πολεμήσουσιν   καὶ   τὸ   ἀρνίον   νικήσει   αὐτούς,   ὅτι
1WILL MAKE WAR,   AND   THE   LAMB   WILL CONQUER   THEM,   BECAUSE

κύριος   κυρίων   ἐστὶν   καὶ   βασιλεὺς   βασιλέων   καὶ
LORD   OF LORDS   HE IS   AND   KING   OF KINGS,   AND

οἱ   μετ᾽   αὐτοῦ   κλητοὶ   καὶ   ἐκλεκτοὶ   καὶ   πιστοί.
THE ONES   WITH   HIM   [ARE] CALLED   AND   CHOSEN   AND   FAITHFUL.

17.15 Καὶ   λέγει   μοι,   Τὰ   ὕδατα   ἃ   εἶδες   οὗ   ἡ
AND   HE SAYS   TO ME,   THE   WATERS   WHICH   YOU SAW,   WHERE   THE

πόρνη   κάθηται,   λαοὶ   καὶ   ὄχλοι   εἰσὶν   καὶ   ἔθνη   καὶ
PROSTITUTE   SITS,   PEOPLES   AND   CROWDS   ARE   AND   NATIONS   AND

γλῶσσαι.   **17.16** καὶ   τὰ   δέκα   κέρατα   ἃ   εἶδες   καὶ
TONGUES.   AND   THE   TEN   HORNS   WHICH   YOU SAW   AND

τὸ   θηρίον   οὗτοι   μισήσουσιν   τὴν   πόρνην   καὶ
THE   BEAST,   THESE   WILL HATE   THE   PROSTITUTE   AND

ἠρημωμένην   ποιήσουσιν   αὐτὴν   καὶ   γυμνὴν   καὶ
3HAVING BEEN MADE DESOLATE   1THEY WILL MAKE   2HER   AND   NAKED   AND

τὰς   σάρκας   αὐτῆς   φάγονται   καὶ   αὐτὴν   κατακαύσουσιν
2THE   3FLESH   4OF HER   1WILL EAT   AND   WILL BURN HER UP

ἐν   πυρί.   **17.17** ὁ   γὰρ   θεὸς   ἔδωκεν   εἰς   τὰς   καρδίας
IN(WITH)   FIRE.   -   FOR   GOD   GAVE(PUT)   INTO   THE   HEARTS

αὐτῶν   ποιῆσαι   τὴν   γνώμην   αὐτοῦ   καὶ   ποιῆσαι   μίαν
OF THEM   TO ACCOMPLISH   THE   DECISION   OF HIM   AND   TO ACT   [WITH] ONE

γνώμην   καὶ   δοῦναι   τὴν   βασιλείαν   αὐτῶν   τῷ   θηρίῳ
MIND   AND   TO GIVE   THE   KINGDOM   OF THEM   TO THE   BEAST,

ἄχρι   τελεσθήσονται   οἱ   λόγοι   τοῦ   θεοῦ.   **17.18** καὶ   ἡ
UNTIL   4WILL BE FULFILLED   1THE   2WORDS   -   3OF GOD.   AND   THE

γυνὴ   ἣν   εἶδες   ἔστιν   ἡ   πόλις   ἡ   μεγάλη   ἡ   ἔχουσα
WOMAN   WHOM   YOU SAW   IS   THE   2CITY   -   1GREAT   -   HAVING

βασιλείαν   ἐπὶ   τῶν   βασιλέων   τῆς   γῆς.
A KINGDOM   OVER   THE   KINGS   OF THE   EARTH.

and when he comes, he must remain only a little while. [11]As for the beast that was and is not, it is an eighth but it belongs to the seven, and it goes to destruction. [12]And the ten horns that you saw are ten kings who have not yet received a kingdom, but they are to receive authority as kings for one hour, together with the beast. [13]These are united in yielding their power and authority to the beast; [14]they will make war on the Lamb, and the Lamb will conquer them, for he is Lord of lords and King of kings, and those with him are called and chosen and faithful."

15 And he said to me, "The waters that you saw, where the whore is seated, are peoples and multitudes and nations and languages. [16]And the ten horns that you saw, they and the beast will hate the whore; they will make her desolate and naked; they will devour her flesh and burn her up with fire. [17]For God has put it into their hearts to carry out his purpose by agreeing to give their kingdom to the beast, until the words of God will be fulfilled. [18]The woman you saw is the great city that rules over the kings of the earth."

CHAPTER 18

After this I saw another angel coming down from heaven, having great authority; and the earth was made bright with his splendor. [2]He called out with a mighty voice,
"Fallen, fallen is
    Babylon the great!
It has become a
    dwelling place of
    demons,
a haunt of every foul
    spirit,
a haunt of every foul
    bird,
a haunt of every foul
    and hateful beast.[d]
[3] For all the nations have
    drunk[e]
of the wine of the wrath
    of her fornication,
and the kings of the earth
    have committed
    fornication with
    her,
and the merchants of
    the earth have
    grown rich from the
    power[f] of her
    luxury."
4 Then I heard another voice from heaven saying,
    "Come out of her, my
    people,

[d] Other ancient authorities lack the words *a haunt of every foul beast* and attach the words *and hateful* to the previous line so as to read *a haunt of every foul and hateful bird*
[e] Other ancient authorities read *She has made all nations drink*
[f] Or *resources*

18.1 Μετὰ   ταῦτα   εἶδον   ἄλλον   ἄγγελον·
AFTER   THESE THINGS   I SAW   ANOTHER   ANGEL

καταβαίνοντα   ἐκ   τοῦ   οὐρανοῦ   ἔχοντα
COMING DOWN   OUT OF   -   HEAVEN   HAVING

ἐξουσίαν μεγάλην,   καὶ   ἡ   γῆ   ἐφωτίσθη   ἐκ   τῆς
GREAT~AUTHORITY,   AND   THE   EARTH   WAS ILLUMINATED   BY   THE

δόξης   αὐτοῦ.   **18.2** καὶ   ἔκραξεν   ἐν   ἰσχυρᾷ   φωνῇ   λέγων,
SPLENDOR   OF HIM.   AND   HE CRIED   IN   A STRONG   VOICE   SAYING,

  Ἔπεσεν   ἔπεσεν   Βαβυλὼν   ἡ   μεγάλη,
  FELL,   FELL,   BABYLON   THE   GREAT,

    καὶ   ἐγένετο   κατοικητήριον   δαιμονίων
    AND   BECAME   A HABITATION   OF DEMONS

  καὶ   φυλακὴ   παντὸς   πνεύματος   ἀκαθάρτου
  AND   A PRISON   OF EVERY   UNCLEAN~SPIRIT

    καὶ   φυλακὴ   παντὸς   ὀρνέου   ἀκαθάρτου
    AND   A PRISON   OF EVERY   UNCLEAN~BIRD

  [καὶ   φυλακὴ   παντὸς   θηρίου   ἀκαθάρτου]
  AND   A PRISON   OF EVERY   [4]BEAST   [1]UNCLEAN

      καὶ   μεμισημένου,
      [2]AND   [3]HAVING BECOME DETESTABLE,

18.3 ὅτι   ἐκ   τοῦ   οἴνου   τοῦ   θυμοῦ   τῆς
BECAUSE   OF   THE   WINE   OF THE   PASSION   OF THE

        πορνείας   αὐτῆς
        FORNICATION   OF HER

  ⌜πέπωκαν⌝   πάντα   τὰ   ἔθνη
  [4]HAVE DRUNK   [1]ALL   [2]THE   [3]NATIONS,

  καὶ   οἱ   βασιλεῖς   τῆς   γῆς   μετ᾽   αὐτῆς
  AND   THE   KINGS   OF THE   EARTH   [2]WITH   [3]HER

      ἐπόρνευσαν
      [1]COMMITTED FORNICATION,

  καὶ   οἱ   ἔμποροι   τῆς   γῆς   ἐκ   τῆς
  AND   THE   MERCHANTS   OF THE   EARTH   [2]BY   [3]THE

        δυνάμεως   τοῦ
        [4]RESOURCES   [5]OF THE

      στρήνους   αὐτῆς   ἐπλούτησαν.
      [6]LUXURY   [7]OF HER   [1]BECAME RICH.

18.4 Καὶ   ἤκουσα   ἄλλην   φωνὴν   ἐκ   τοῦ οὐρανοῦ
AND   I HEARD   ANOTHER   VOICE   OUT OF   -   HEAVEN

λέγουσαν,
SAYING,

  Ἐξέλθατε   ὁ   λαός   μου   ἐξ   αὐτῆς
  COME OUT   -   [3]MY~PEOPLE   [1]OF   [2]HER,

18:3 text: KJV ASVmg RSV NASB NIV NEB TEV NJB NRSV.   var. πεπτωκασιν παντα τα εθνη (all nations have fallen by) ASV RSVmg NASBmg (NEBmg).

ἵνα   μὴ συγκοινωνήσητε ταῖς   ἁμαρτίαις
THAT   YOU° MAY NOT PARTICIPATE   IN THE   SINS

αὐτῆς,
OF HER,

καὶ ἐκ   τῶν πληγῶν αὐτῆς
AND   ³[SOME] OF ⁴THE ⁵PLAGUES   ⁶OF HER

ἵνα   μὴ λάβητε,
¹THAT ²YOU° MAY NOT RECEIVE,

18.5 ὅτι   ἐκολλήθησαν αὐτῆς αἱ ἁμαρτίαι ἄχρι
BECAUSE ³WERE PILED UP   ¹HER   -   ²SINS   [REACHING] UP TO

τοῦ οὐρανοῦ
-    HEAVEN,

καὶ ἐμνημόνευσεν ὁ θεὸς τὰ ἀδικήματα
AND   ²REMEMBERED   - ¹GOD THE UNRIGHTEOUSNESSES

αὐτῆς.
OF HER.

18.6 ἀπόδοτε αὐτῇ ὡς   καὶ αὐτὴ ἀπέδωκεν
RENDER   TO HER AS   ALSO SHE   RENDERED

καὶ διπλώσατε τὰ διπλᾶ κατὰ   τὰ ἔργα
AND   DOUBLE   THE DOUBLE ACCORDING TO THE WORKS

αὐτῆς,
OF HER,

ἐν τῷ   ποτηρίῳ ᾧ   ἐκέρασεν κεράσατε αὐτῇ
IN THE CUP   WHICH SHE MIXED,   MIX   FOR HER

διπλοῦν,
DOUBLE;

18.7 ὅσα   ἐδόξασεν αὐτὴν καὶ ἐστρηνίασεν,
SO MUCH AS SHE GLORIFIED HER[SELF] AND LIVED IN LUXURY,

τοσοῦτον δότε αὐτῇ βασανισμὸν καὶ πένθος.
GIVE~SO MUCH   ⁴TO HER ¹TORMENT   ²AND ³GRIEF.

ὅτι   ἐν τῇ καρδίᾳ αὐτῆς λέγει ὅτι
BECAUSE IN THE HEART   OF HER SHE SAYS, -

Κάθημαι βασίλισσα
I SIT   A QUEEN

καὶ χήρα οὐκ εἰμί
AND   A WIDOW I AM~NOT

καὶ πένθος οὐ μὴ ἴδω.
AND   GRIEF   NEVER MAY I SEE.

18.8 διὰ τοῦτο ἐν μιᾷ ἡμέρᾳ ἥξουσιν αἱ πληγαὶ
THEREFORE IN ONE DAY   WILL COME THE PLAGUES

αὐτῆς,
OF(ON) HER,

θάνατος καὶ πένθος καὶ λιμός,
DEATH   AND   GRIEF   AND   FAMINE,

καὶ ἐν πυρὶ κατακαυθήσεται,
AND   WITH FIRE SHE WILL BE BURNED UP,

so that you do not take
part in her sins,
and so that you do not
share in her plagues;
⁵ for her sins are heaped
high as heaven,
and God has
remembered her
iniquities.
⁶ Render to her as she
herself has
rendered,
and repay her double
for her deeds;
mix a double draught
for her in the cup
she mixed.
⁷ As she glorified herself
and lived
luxuriously,
so give her a like
measure of torment
and grief.
Since in her heart she
says,
'I rule as a queen;
I am no widow,
and I will never see
grief,'
⁸ therefore her plagues will
come in a single
day—
pestilence and
mourning and
famine—
and she will be burned
with fire;

for mighty is the Lord God who judges her."

9 And the kings of the earth, who committed fornication and lived in luxury with her, will weep and wail over her when they see the smoke of her burning; [10]they will stand far off, in fear of her torment, and say,

"Alas, alas, the great city,
Babylon, the mighty city!
For in one hour your judgment has come."

11 And the merchants of the earth weep and mourn for her, since no one buys their cargo anymore, [12]cargo of gold, silver, jewels and pearls, fine linen, purple, silk and scarlet, all kinds of scented wood, all articles of ivory, all articles of costly wood, bronze, iron, and marble, [13]cinnamon, spice, incense, myrrh, frankincense, wine, olive oil, choice flour and wheat, cattle and sheep, horses and chariots, slaves—and human lives.[g]

[g] Or chariots, and human bodies and souls

ὅτι   ἰσχυρὸς   κύριος   ὁ   θεὸς ὁ   κρίνας
BECAUSE STRONG   [IS THE] LORD - GOD, THE ONE HAVING JUDGED

αὐτήν.
HER.

18.9 Καὶ κλαύσουσιν καὶ κόψονται ἐπ' αὐτὴν οἱ
        AND WILL WEEP   AND WAIL   OVER HER   THE

βασιλεῖς τῆς   γῆς   οἱ   μετ'   αὐτῆς
KINGS   OF THE EARTH, THE ONES [2]WITH [3]HER

πορνεύσαντες   καὶ στρηνιάσαντες,   ὅταν βλέπωσιν
[1]HAVING COMMITTED FORNICATION AND HAVING LIVED IN LUXURY, WHEN THEY SEE

τὸν καπνὸν τῆς   πυρώσεως αὐτῆς, **18.10** ἀπὸ μακρόθεν
THE SMOKE   OF THE BURNING   OF HER,   [2]FROM [3]AFAR

ἑστηκότες   διὰ   τὸν φόβον τοῦ   βασανισμοῦ αὐτῆς,
[1]HAVING STOOD BECAUSE OF THE FEAR   OF THE TORMENT   OF HER,

λέγοντες,
SAYING,

Οὐαὶ οὐαί, ἡ   πόλις ἡ μεγάλη,
WOE,   WOE,   THE [2]CITY - [1]GREAT,

Βαβυλὼν ἡ   πόλις ἡ ἰσχυρά,
BABYLON   THE [2]CITY - [1]STRONG,

ὅτι   μιᾷ   ὥρᾳ   ἦλθεν ἡ   κρίσις   σου.
BECAUSE IN ONE HOUR CAME   THE JUDGMENT OF YOU.

18.11 Καὶ οἱ   ἔμποροι τῆς   γῆς   κλαίουσιν καὶ
        AND THE MERCHANTS OF THE EARTH CRY   AND

πενθοῦσιν ἐπ' αὐτήν, ὅτι   τὸν γόμον αὐτῶν   οὐδεὶς
GRIEVE   OVER HER,   BECAUSE THE CARGO OF THEM NO ONE

ἀγοράζει οὐκέτι   **18.12** γόμον χρυσοῦ καὶ ἀργύρου καὶ
BUYS   ANY MORE: CARGO OF GOLD AND OF SILVER AND

λίθου τιμίου   καὶ μαργαριτῶν καὶ βυσσίνου   καὶ
OF PRECIOUS~STONE AND OF PEARLS   AND OF FINE LINEN AND

πορφύρας καὶ σιρικοῦ καὶ κοκκίνου,   καὶ πᾶν
OF PURPLE AND OF SILK AND OF SCARLET, AND EVERY [KIND OF]

ξύλον θύϊνον καὶ πᾶν   σκεῦος ἐλεφάντινον καὶ
CITRON~WOOD   AND EVERY [KIND OF] IVORY~VESSEL   AND

πᾶν   σκεῦος ἐκ ξύλου τιμιωτάτου   καὶ χαλκοῦ   καὶ
EVERY [KIND OF] VESSEL OF VALUABLE~WOOD   AND OF BRONZE AND

σιδήρου καὶ μαρμάρου, **18.13** καὶ κιννάμωμον καὶ
OF IRON AND OF MARBLE,   AND CINNAMON   AND

ἄμωμον καὶ θυμιάματα καὶ μύρον καὶ λίβανον   καὶ
SPICE   AND INCENSE   AND MYRRH AND FRANKINCENSE AND

οἶνον καὶ ἔλαιον καὶ σεμίδαλιν καὶ σῖτον καὶ κτήνη
WINE   AND OIL   AND FINE FLOUR AND WHEAT AND CATTLE

καὶ πρόβατα, καὶ ἵππων   καὶ ῥεδῶν   καὶ σωμάτων,
AND SHEEP,   AND OF HORSES AND OF CHARIOTS AND OF BODIES

καὶ ψυχὰς ἀνθρώπων.
AND SOULS OF MEN(SLAVES).

18.14 καὶ ἡ ὀπώρα σου τῆς ἐπιθυμίας τῆς ψυχῆς
AND THE FRUIT ³OF YOUR ¹OF THE ²DESIRE - ⁴SOUL

ἀπῆλθεν ἀπὸ σοῦ,
DEPARTED FROM YOU,

καὶ πάντα τὰ λιπαρὰ καὶ τὰ λαμπρὰ
AND ALL THE LUXURIOUS THINGS AND THE SPLENDOROUS THINGS

ἀπώλετο ἀπὸ σοῦ
PERISHED FROM YOU,

καὶ οὐκέτι οὐ μὴ αὐτὰ εὑρήσουσιν.
AND NO MORE, NEVER, WILL THEY FIND~THEM.

18.15 οἱ ἔμποροι τούτων οἱ πλουτήσαντες ἀπ᾽
THE MERCHANTS OF THESE THINGS, THE ONES HAVING BECOME RICH FROM

αὐτῆς ἀπὸ μακρόθεν στήσονται διὰ τὸν φόβον τοῦ
HER, FROM AFAR WILL STAND BECAUSE OF THE FEAR OF THE

βασανισμοῦ αὐτῆς κλαίοντες καὶ πενθοῦντες
TORMENT OF HER, WEEPING AND GRIEVING,

18.16 λέγοντες,
SAYING,

Οὐαὶ οὐαί, ἡ πόλις ἡ μεγάλη,
WOE, WOE, THE ²CITY - ¹GREAT,

ἡ περιβεβλημένη βύσσινον
THE ONE HAVING CLOTHED HERSELF WITH FINE LINEN

καὶ πορφυροῦν καὶ κόκκινον
AND PURPLE AND SCARLET

καὶ κεχρυσωμένη [ἐν] χρυσίῳ
AND HAVING BEEN GILDED WITH GOLD

καὶ λίθῳ τιμίῳ καὶ μαργαρίτῃ,
AND PRECIOUS~STONE AND PEARL,

18.17 ὅτι μιᾷ ὥρᾳ ἠρημώθη ὁ τοσοῦτος πλοῦτος.
BECAUSE IN ONE HOUR ³WAS LAID WASTE - ¹SUCH GREAT ²WEALTH.

Καὶ πᾶς κυβερνήτης καὶ πᾶς ὁ ἐπὶ τόπον πλέων
AND EVERY STEERSMAN AND EVERYONE ²TO ³A PLACE ¹SAILING

καὶ ναῦται καὶ ὅσοι τὴν θάλασσαν ἐργάζονται, ἀπὸ
AND SAILORS AND AS MANY AS ²THE ³SEA ¹WORK, FROM

μακρόθεν ἔστησαν **18.18** καὶ ἔκραζον βλέποντες τὸν
AFAR STOOD AND WERE CRYING OUT, SEEING THE

καπνὸν τῆς πυρώσεως αὐτῆς λέγοντες, Τίς ὁμοία τῇ
SMOKE OF THE BURNING OF HER, SAYING, WHAT [IS] LIKE THE

πόλει τῇ μεγάλῃ; **18.19** καὶ ἔβαλον χοῦν ἐπὶ τὰς
²CITY - ¹GREAT? AND THEY THREW DUST ON THE

κεφαλὰς αὐτῶν καὶ ἔκραζον κλαίοντες καὶ
HEADS OF THEM AND WERE CRYING OUT, WEEPING AND

πενθοῦντες λέγοντες,
GRIEVING, SAYING,

Οὐαὶ οὐαί, ἡ πόλις ἡ μεγάλη,
WOE, WOE, THE ²CITY - ¹GREAT,

¹⁴"The fruit for which your soul longed has gone from you, and all your dainties and your splendor are lost to you, never to be found again!"

¹⁵The merchants of these wares, who gained wealth from her, will stand far off, in fear of her torment, weeping and mourning aloud,

¹⁶"Alas, alas, the great city, clothed in fine linen, in purple and scarlet, adorned with gold, with jewels, and with pearls!

¹⁷For in one hour all this wealth has been laid waste!"

And all shipmasters and seafarers, sailors and all whose trade is on the sea, stood far off ¹⁸and cried out as they saw the smoke of her burning,

"What city was like the great city?"

¹⁹And they threw dust on their heads, as they wept and mourned, crying out,

"Alas, alas, the great city,

where all who had
ships at sea
grew rich by her
wealth!
For in one hour she has
been laid waste."
20 Rejoice over her,
O heaven, you saints and
apostles and prophets! For
God has given judgment
for you against her.
21 Then a mighty angel
took up a stone like a great
millstone and threw it into
the sea, saying,
"With such violence
Babylon the great
city
will be thrown down,
and will be found no
more;
22 and the sound of harpists
and minstrels and of
flutists and
trumpeters
will be heard in you no
more;
and an artisan of any
trade
will be found in you no
more;
and the sound of the
millstone
will be heard in you no
more;
23 and the light of a lamp
will shine in you no
more;
and the voice of
bridegroom and
bride

ἐν ᾗ   ἐπλούτησαν πάντες οἱ   ἔχοντες τὰ
BY WHICH BECAME RICH   ALL   THE ONES HAVING   -

πλοῖα
SHIPS

ἐν τῇ θαλάσσῃ ἐκ τῆς τιμιότητος αὐτῆς,
IN THE SEA   BY THE COSTLINESS   OF HER,

ὅτι   μιᾷ   ὥρᾳ ἠρημώθη.
BECAUSE IN ONE HOUR SHE WAS LAID WASTE.

18.20 Εὐφραίνου ἐπ᾽ αὐτῇ, οὐρανὲ
REJOICE   OVER HER,   HEAVEN

καὶ οἱ ἅγιοι καὶ οἱ ἀπόστολοι καὶ οἱ
AND - SAINTS AND - APOSTLES   AND   -

προφῆται,
PROPHETS,

ὅτι   ἔκρινεν ὁ θεὸς τὸ   κρίμα   ὑμῶν
BECAUSE ²MADE JUDGMENT - ¹GOD ⁵[FOR] THE(HER) ⁶JUDGMENT ⁷OF YOU°

ἐξ   αὐτῆς.
³AGAINST ⁴HER.

18.21 Καὶ ἦρεν εἷς ἄγγελος ἰσχυρὸς λίθον ὡς
AND ⁴LIFTED ¹ONE ³ANGEL ²STRONG A STONE LIKE

μύλινον μέγαν καὶ ἔβαλεν εἰς τὴν θάλασσαν λέγων,
A GREAT~MILLSTONE AND THREW [IT] INTO THE SEA   SAYING,

Οὕτως ὁρμήματι βληθήσεται
THUS   WITH VIOLENCE WILL BE THROWN [DOWN]

Βαβυλὼν ἡ μεγάλη πόλις
BABYLON THE GREAT   CITY,

καὶ οὐ μὴ εὑρεθῇ   ἔτι.
AND NEVER WOULD IT BE FOUND ANY MORE.

18.22 καὶ φωνὴ   κιθαρῳδῶν καὶ μουσικῶν
AND [THE] SOUND OF HARPERS   AND   OF MUSICIANS

καὶ αὐλητῶν καὶ σαλπιστῶν
AND OF FLUTISTS AND OF TRUMPETERS

οὐ μὴ ἀκουσθῇ   ἐν σοὶ ἔτι,
NEVER WOULD BE HEARD IN YOU ANY MORE,

καὶ πᾶς τεχνίτης πάσης τέχνης
AND EVERY CRAFTSMAN OF EVERY CRAFT

οὐ μὴ εὑρεθῇ   ἐν σοὶ ἔτι,
NEVER WOULD BE FOUND IN YOU ANY MORE,

καὶ φωνὴ   μύλου
AND [THE] SOUND OF A MILL

οὐ μὴ ἀκουσθῇ   ἐν σοὶ ἔτι,
NEVER WOULD BE HEARD IN YOU ANY MORE,

18.23 καὶ φῶς   λύχνου
AND [THE] LIGHT OF A LAMP

οὐ μὴ φάνῃ   ἐν σοὶ ἔτι,
NEVER WOULD SHINE IN YOU ANY MORE,

καὶ φωνὴ   νυμφίου   καὶ νύμφης
AND [THE] VOICE OF A BRIDEGROOM AND OF A BRIDE

οὐ μὴ ἀκουσθῇ   ἐν σοὶ ἔτι·
NEVER   WOULD BE HEARD   IN   YOU   ANY MORE;

ὅτι   οἱ ἔμποροί σου   ἦσαν οἱ μεγιστᾶνες
BECAUSE   THE   MERCHANTS OF YOU   WERE   THE   GREAT ONES

τῆς   γῆς,
OF THE   EARTH,

ὅτι   ἐν τῇ φαρμακείᾳ   σου
BECAUSE   BY   THE   SORCERY   OF YOU

ἐπλανήθησαν πάντα τὰ ἔθνη,
WERE DECEIVED   ALL   THE   NATIONS,

18.24 καὶ ἐν αὐτῇ αἷμα   προφητῶν καὶ ἁγίων
AND   IN   HER   [THE] BLOOD   OF PROPHETS   AND   OF SAINTS

εὑρέθη
WAS FOUND

καὶ πάντων τῶν   ἐσφαγμένων ἐπὶ τῆς
AND   OF ALL   THE ONES   HAVING BEEN SLAIN   ON   THE

γῆς.
EARTH.

will be heard in you no
more;
for your merchants were
the magnates of the
earth,
and all nations were
deceived by your
sorcery.
²⁴ And in you[h] was found
the blood of
prophets and of
saints,
and of all who have
been slaughtered on
earth."

[h] Gk *her*

CHAPTER 19

19.1 Μετὰ ταῦτα   ἤκουσα ὡς   φωνὴν μεγάλην
AFTER   THESE THINGS   I HEARD   AS [IT WERE]   A LOUD~VOICE

ὄχλου πολλοῦ ἐν τῷ οὐρανῷ λεγόντων,
OF A GREAT~CROWD   IN   -   HEAVEN   SAYING,

ʼΑλληλουϊά·
ALLELUIA;

ἡ σωτηρία καὶ ἡ δόξα καὶ ἡ δύναμις
THE   SALVATION   AND   THE   GLORY   AND   THE   POWER

τοῦ   θεοῦ ἡμῶν,
[IS] OF THE   GOD   OF US,

19.2   ὅτι   ἀληθιναὶ καὶ δίκαιαι αἱ   κρίσεις
BECAUSE   TRUE   AND   RIGHTEOUS   [ARE] THE   JUDGMENTS

αὐτοῦ·
OF HIM;

ὅτι   ἔκρινεν τὴν πόρνην τὴν μεγάλην
BECAUSE   HE JUDGED   THE   ²PROSTITUTE   -   ¹GREAT

ἥτις ἔφθειρεν   τὴν γῆν ἐν τῇ πορνείᾳ
WHO   WAS CORRUPTING   THE   EARTH   WITH   THE   FORNICATION

αὐτῆς,
OF HER,

καὶ ἐξεδίκησεν τὸ αἷμα τῶν δούλων αὐτοῦ
AND   HE AVENGED   THE   BLOOD   OF THE   SLAVES   OF HIM

ἐκ   χειρὸς αὐτῆς.
AGAINST   [THE] HAND   OF HER.

After this I heard what
seemed to be the loud voice
of a great multitude in
heaven, saying,
"Hallelujah!
Salvation and glory and
power to our God,
² for his judgments are
true and just;
he has judged the great
whore
who corrupted the earth
with her
fornication,
and he has avenged on
her the blood of his
servants."[i]

[i] Gk *slaves*

³Once more they said,
"Hallelujah!
The smoke goes up from
her forever and
ever."
⁴And the twenty-four elders
and the four living creatures
fell down and worshiped
God who is seated on the
throne, saying,
"Amen. Hallelujah!"
5 And from the throne
came a voice saying,
"Praise our God,
all you his servants,ʲ
and all who fear him,
small and great."
⁶Then I heard what seemed
to be the voice of a great
multitude, like the sound of
many waters and like the
sound of mighty thunder-
peals, crying out,
"Hallelujah!
For the Lord our God
the Almighty reigns.
7 Let us rejoice and exult
and give him the glory,
for the marriage of the
Lamb has come,
and his bride has made
herself ready;

ʲ Gk *slaves*

19.3 καὶ   δεύτερον   εἴρηκαν,
AND   A SECOND [TIME]   THEY SAID,

᾽Αλληλουϊά·
ALLELUIA;

καὶ   ὁ   καπνὸς   αὐτῆς   ἀναβαίνει   εἰς   τοὺς
AND   THE   SMOKE   OF HER   ASCENDS   INTO   THE

αἰῶνας   τῶν   αἰώνων.
AGES   OF THE   AGES.

19.4 καὶ   ἔπεσαν   οἱ   πρεσβύτεροι   οἱ   εἴκοσι   τέσσαρες
AND   FELL [DOWN]   THE   ²ELDERS   -   ¹TWENTY-FOUR

καὶ   τὰ   τέσσαρα   ζῷα   καὶ   προσεκύνησαν   τῷ   θεῷ
AND   THE   FOUR   LIVING BEINGS   AND   WORSHIPED   -   GOD

τῷ   καθημένῳ ἐπὶ   τῷ   θρόνῳ λέγοντες,
-   SITTING   ON   THE   THRONE,   SAYING,

᾽Αμὴν   ᾽Αλληλουϊά,
AMEN,   ALLELUIA.

19.5 Καὶ   φωνὴ   ἀπὸ   τοῦ   θρόνου   ἐξῆλθεν   λέγουσα,
AND   A VOICE   FROM   THE   THRONE   CAME FORTH   SAYING,

Αἰνεῖτε   τῷ   θεῷ   ἡμῶν
PRAISE   THE   GOD   OF US

πάντες   οἱ   δοῦλοι   αὐτοῦ
ALL   THE   SLAVES   OF HIM

[καὶ]   οἱ   φοβούμενοι   αὐτόν,
AND   THE ONES   FEARING   HIM,

οἱ   μικροὶ   καὶ   οἱ   μεγάλοι.
THE   SMALL   AND   THE   GREAT.

19.6 καὶ   ἤκουσα   ὡς   φωνὴν   ὄχλου   πολλοῦ   καὶ   ὡς
AND   I HEARD   AS [IT WERE]   A SOUND   OF A GREAT~CROWD   AND   AS

φωνὴν   ὑδάτων   πολλῶν καὶ   ὡς   φωνὴν   βροντῶν ἰσχυρῶν
A SOUND   OF MANY~WATERS   AND   AS   A SOUND   OF MIGHTY~THUNDERPEALS,

λεγόντων,
SAYING,

᾽Αλληλουϊά,
ALLELUIA,

ὅτι   ἐβασίλευσεν   κύριος
BECAUSE   ⁶REIGNED   ¹[THE] LORD

ὁ   θεὸς   [ἡμῶν] ὁ   παντοκράτωρ.
-   ²GOD   ³OF US,   ⁴THE   ⁵ALMIGHTY.

19.7 χαίρωμεν   καὶ   ἀγαλλιῶμεν
LET US REJOICE   AND   EXULT,

καὶ   δώσωμεν   τὴν   δόξαν   αὐτῷ,
AND   GIVE   THE   GLORY   TO HIM,

ὅτι   ἦλθεν   ὁ   γάμος   τοῦ   ἀρνίου
BECAUSE   CAME(HAS COME)   THE   WEDDING   OF THE   LAMB

καὶ   ἡ   γυνὴ   αὐτοῦ   ἡτοίμασεν   ἑαυτὴν
AND   THE   WIFE   OF HIM   PREPARED   HERSELF,

19.8 καὶ   ἐδόθη   αὐτῇ   ἵνα   περιβάληται
AND   IT WAS GIVEN TO HER THAT SHE SHOULD BE CLOTHED [WITH]

βύσσινον   λαμπρὸν   καθαρόν·
FINE LINEN,   BRIGHT   [AND] CLEAN;

τὸ   γὰρ   βύσσινον   τὰ   δικαιώματα   τῶν   ἁγίων
FOR~THE FINE LINEN 2THE 3RIGHTEOUS ACTS 4OF THE 5SAINTS

ἐστίν.
1IS.

19.9 Καὶ   λέγει   μοι,   Γράψον·   Μακάριοι   οἱ   εἰς
AND   HE SAYS TO ME, WRITE: BLESSED   [ARE] THE ONES 2TO

τὸ   δεῖπνον   τοῦ   γάμου   τοῦ   ἀρνίου   κεκλημένοι.   καὶ
3THE 4SUPPER 5OF THE 6WEDDING 7OF THE 8LAMB   1HAVING BEEN CALLED. AND

λέγει   μοι,   Οὗτοι   οἱ   λόγοι   ἀληθινοὶ   τοῦ   θεοῦ   εἰσιν.
HE SAYS TO ME, THESE   2THE 4WORDS 3TRUE   -   5OF GOD 1ARE.

19.10 καὶ   ἔπεσα   ἔμπροσθεν   τῶν   ποδῶν   αὐτοῦ
AND   I FELL   BEFORE   THE   FEET   OF HIM

προσκυνῆσαι   αὐτῷ.   καὶ   λέγει   μοι,   Ὅρα   μή·
TO WORSHIP   HIM.   AND   HE SAYS TO ME, SEE [THAT] YOU [DO IT] NOT;

σύνδουλός   σού   εἰμι   καὶ   τῶν   ἀδελφῶν   σου   τῶν
A FELLOW SLAVE OF YOU I AM   AND   OF THE BROTHERS   OF YOU, THE ONES

ἐχόντων   τὴν   μαρτυρίαν   Ἰησοῦ·   τῷ   θεῷ   προσκύνησον.
HAVING   THE   TESTIMONY   OF JESUS;   -   WORSHIP~GOD.

ἡ   γὰρ   μαρτυρία   Ἰησοῦ   ἐστιν   τὸ   πνεῦμα   τῆς
FOR~THE TESTIMONY OF JESUS IS   THE   SPIRIT   -

προφητείας.
OF PROPHECY.

19.11 Καὶ   εἶδον   τὸν   οὐρανὸν   ἠνεῳγμένον,   καὶ   ἰδοὺ
AND   I SAW   -   HEAVEN   HAVING BEEN OPENED, AND   BEHOLD

ἵππος   λευκὸς   καὶ   ὁ   καθήμενος   ἐπ’   αὐτὸν
A WHITE~HORSE   AND   THE ONE SITTING   ON   IT

[καλούμενος]   πιστὸς   καὶ   ἀληθινός,   καὶ   ἐν   δικαιοσύνῃ
BEING CALLED   FAITHFUL AND   TRUE,   AND   IN   RIGHTEOUSNESS

κρίνει   καὶ   πολεμεῖ.   **19.12** οἱ   δὲ   ὀφθαλμοὶ   αὐτοῦ
HE JUDGES AND   MAKES WAR.   AND~THE   EYES   OF HIM

[ὡς]   φλὸξ   πυρός,   καὶ   ἐπὶ   τὴν   κεφαλὴν   αὐτοῦ
[ARE] AS A FLAME OF FIRE, AND   ON   THE   HEAD   OF HIM

διαδήματα   πολλά,   ἔχων   ὄνομα   γεγραμμένον   ὃ
MANY~DIADEMS,   HAVING A NAME HAVING BEEN WRITTEN WHICH

οὐδεὶς   οἶδεν   εἰ   μὴ   αὐτός,   **19.13** καὶ   περιβεβλημένος
NO ONE   KNOWS EXCEPT   HIMSELF,   AND   HAVING BEEN CLOTHED [WITH]

ἱμάτιον   βεβαμμένον   αἵματι,   καὶ   κέκληται   τὸ   ὄνομα
A GARMENT HAVING BEEN DIPPED IN BLOOD, AND   4HAS BEEN CALLED 1THE 2NAME

αὐτοῦ   ὁ   λόγος   τοῦ   θεοῦ.   **19.14** καὶ   τὰ   στρατεύματα
3OF HIM THE WORD   -   OF GOD.   AND   THE   ARMIES

[τὰ]   ἐν   τῷ   οὐρανῷ   ἠκολούθει   αὐτῷ   ἐφ’   ἵπποις   λευκοῖς,
-    IN   -   HEAVEN   WERE FOLLOWING HIM   ON   WHITE~HORSES,

8 to her it has been granted to be clothed with fine linen, bright and pure"— for the fine linen is the righteous deeds of the saints.

9 And the angel said[k] to me, "Write this: Blessed are those who are invited to the marriage supper of the Lamb." And he said to me, "These are true words of God." [10]Then I fell down at his feet to worship him, but he said to me, "You must not do that! I am a fellow servant[l] with you and your comrades[m] who hold the testimony of Jesus.[n] Worship God! For the testimony of Jesus[n] is the spirit of prophecy."

11 Then I saw heaven opened, and there was a white horse! Its rider is called Faithful and True, and in righteousness he judges and makes war. [12]His eyes are like a flame of fire, and on his head are many diadems; and he has a name inscribed that no one knows but himself. [13]He is clothed in a robe dipped in[o] blood, and his name is called The Word of God. [14]And the armies of heaven, wearing fine linen, white and pure, were following him on white horses.

[k] Gk *he said*
[l] Gk *slave*
[m] Gk *brothers*
[n] Or *to Jesus*
[o] Other ancient authorities read *sprinkled with*

15From his mouth comes a sharp sword with which to strike down the nations, and he will rule*p* them with a rod of iron; he will tread the wine press of the fury of the wrath of God the Almighty. 16On his robe and on his thigh he has a name inscribed, "King of kings and Lord of lords."

17 Then I saw an angel standing in the sun, and with a loud voice he called to all the birds that fly in midheaven, "Come, gather for the great supper of God, 18to eat the flesh of kings, the flesh of captains, the flesh of the mighty, the flesh of horses and their riders— flesh of all, both free and slave, both small and great." 19Then I saw the beast and the kings of the earth with their armies gathered to make war against the rider on the horse and against his army. 20And the beast was captured, and with it the false prophet who had performed in its presence the signs by which he deceived those who had received the mark of the beast and those who worshiped its image. These two were thrown alive

p Or *will shepherd*

ἐνδεδυμένοι   βύσσινον λευκὸν καθαρόν.   **19.15** καὶ
HAVING BEEN DRESSED IN   FINE LINEN,   WHITE   [AND] CLEAN.   AND

ἐκ   τοῦ στόματος αὐτοῦ ἐκπορεύεται ῥομφαία ὀξεῖα,
OUT OF   THE   MOUTH   OF HIM   GOES FORTH   A SHARP~SWORD,

ἵνα ἐν αὐτῇ πατάξῃ τὰ ἔθνη, καὶ αὐτὸς ποιμανεῖ
THAT WITH IT   HE MAY STRIKE THE NATIONS, AND HE   WILL SHEPHERD

αὐτοὺς ἐν ῥάβδῳ σιδηρᾷ, καὶ αὐτὸς πατεῖ τὴν ληνὸν
THEM   WITH A ROD   OF IRON,   AND HE   TREADS   THE PRESS

τοῦ οἴνου τοῦ θυμοῦ τῆς ὀργῆς τοῦ θεοῦ τοῦ
OF THE WINE OF THE FURY OF THE WRATH - OF GOD, THE

παντοκράτορος, **19.16** καὶ ἔχει ἐπὶ τὸ ἱμάτιον καὶ ἐπὶ
ALMIGHTY,   AND HE HAS ON THE GARMENT AND ON

τὸν μηρὸν αὐτοῦ ὄνομα γεγραμμένον· Βασιλεὺς
THE THIGH OF HIM A NAME HAVING BEEN WRITTEN: KING

βασιλέων καὶ κύριος κυρίων.
OF KINGS AND LORD OF LORDS.

19.17 Καὶ εἶδον ἕνα ἄγγελον ἑστῶτα   ἐν τῷ
AND I SAW ONE ANGEL HAVING TAKEN [HIS] STAND IN THE

ἡλίῳ καὶ ἔκραξεν [ἐν] φωνῇ μεγάλῃ λέγων πᾶσιν τοῖς
SUN AND HE CRIED OUT IN A LOUD~VOICE SAYING TO ALL THE

ὀρνέοις τοῖς πετομένοις ἐν μεσουρανήματι, Δεῦτε
BIRDS - FLYING IN MIDHEAVEN(MIDAIR), COME,

συνάχθητε εἰς τὸ δεῖπνον τὸ μέγα τοῦ θεοῦ **19.18** ἵνα
GATHER TO THE ²SUPPER - ¹GREAT - OF GOD, THAT

φάγητε σάρκας βασιλέων καὶ σάρκας χιλιάρχων καὶ
YOU° MAY EAT [THE] FLESH OF KINGS AND FLESH OF CAPTAINS AND

σάρκας ἰσχυρῶν καὶ σάρκας ἵππων καὶ τῶν
FLESH OF STRONG MEN AND FLESH OF HORSES AND OF THE ONES

καθημένων ἐπ' αὐτῶν καὶ σάρκας πάντων ἐλευθέρων τε
SITTING ON THEM AND FLESH OF ALL, BOTH~FREE MEN

καὶ δούλων καὶ μικρῶν καὶ μεγάλων. **19.19** Καὶ εἶδον
AND SLAVES AND SMALL AND GREAT.   AND I SAW

τὸ θηρίον καὶ τοὺς βασιλεῖς τῆς γῆς καὶ τὰ
THE BEAST AND THE KINGS OF THE EARTH AND THE

στρατεύματα αὐτῶν συνηγμένα   ποιῆσαι τὸν πόλεμον
ARMIES OF THEM HAVING BEEN GATHERED TO MAKE - WAR

μετὰ τοῦ   καθημένου ἐπὶ τοῦ ἵππου καὶ μετὰ τοῦ
WITH THE ONE SITTING ON THE HORSE AND WITH THE

στρατεύματος αὐτοῦ. **19.20** καὶ ἐπιάσθη τὸ θηρίον
ARMY OF HIM.   AND ³WAS CAPTURED ¹THE ²BEAST

καὶ μετ' αὐτοῦ ὁ ψευδοπροφήτης ὁ ποιήσας τὰ
AND WITH IT THE FALSE PROPHET, THE ONE HAVING PERFORMED THE

σημεῖα ἐνώπιον αὐτοῦ, ἐν οἷς ἐπλάνησεν τοὺς
SIGNS BEFORE IT, BY WHICH HE DECEIVED THE ONES

λαβόντας τὸ χάραγμα τοῦ θηρίου καὶ τοὺς
HAVING RECEIVED THE MARK OF THE BEAST AND THE ONES

προσκυνοῦντας τῇ εἰκόνι αὐτοῦ· ζῶντες ἐβλήθησαν
WORSHIPING THE IMAGE OF IT; ⁴LIVING(ALIVE) ³WERE THROWN

οἱ   δύο   εἰς   τὴν   λίμνην   τοῦ   πυρὸς   τῆς   καιομένης   ἐν
¹THE ²TWO INTO THE   LAKE   -   OF FIRE -   BURNING   WITH

θείῳ.   **19.21** καὶ   οἱ   λοιποὶ   ἀπεκτάνθησαν   ἐν   τῇ
SULFUR.   AND THE REST   WERE KILLED   WITH THE

ῥομφαίᾳ   τοῦ   καθημένου   ἐπὶ   τοῦ   ἵππου   τῇ
SWORD   OF THE ONE SITTING   ON   THE   HORSE, THE [SWORD]

ἐξελθούσῃ   ἐκ   τοῦ   στόματος   αὐτοῦ,   καὶ   πάντα   τὰ
HAVING PROCEEDED OUT OF THE MOUTH OF HIM,   AND   ALL   THE

ὄρνεα   ἐχορτάσθησαν   ἐκ   τῶν   σαρκῶν   αὐτῶν.
BIRDS   WERE FULLY FED BY   THE   FLESH   OF THEM.

into the lake of fire that burns with sulfur. ²¹And the rest were killed by the sword of the rider on the horse, the sword that came from his mouth; and all the birds were gorged with their flesh.

CHAPTER 20

20.1 Καὶ   εἶδον   ἄγγελον   καταβαίνοντα   ἐκ   τοῦ
        AND I SAW   AN ANGEL   COMING DOWN   OUT OF -

οὐρανοῦ   ἔχοντα   τὴν   κλεῖν   τῆς   ἀβύσσου   καὶ
HEAVEN   HAVING   THE   KEY   OF THE ABYSS   AND

ἄλυσιν   μεγάλην   ἐπὶ   τὴν   χεῖρα   αὐτοῦ.   **20.2** καὶ
A GREAT~CHAIN   ON   THE   HAND   OF HIM.   AND

ἐκράτησεν   τὸν   δράκοντα,   ὁ   ὄφις   ὁ   ἀρχαῖος,   ὅς
HE SEIZED   THE   DRAGON,   THE ²SERPENT - ¹ANCIENT,   WHO

ἐστιν   Διάβολος   καὶ   ὁ   Σατανᾶς,   καὶ   ἔδησεν   αὐτὸν
IS   [THE] DEVIL AND   -   SATAN,   AND   HE BOUND HIM

χίλια   ἔτη   **20.3** καὶ   ἔβαλεν   αὐτὸν   εἰς   τὴν   ἄβυσσον
A THOUSAND YEARS,   AND   THREW   HIM   INTO THE   ABYSS

καὶ   ἔκλεισεν   καὶ   ἐσφράγισεν   ἐπάνω   αὐτοῦ,   ἵνα
AND   SHUT   AND   SEALED [IT]   OVER   HIM,   THAT

μὴ   πλανήσῃ   ἔτι   τὰ   ἔθνη   ἄχρι   τελεσθῇ   τὰ
HE COULD NOT DECEIVE ANY MORE THE NATIONS UNTIL WERE COMPLETED THE

χίλια   ἔτη.   μετὰ   ταῦτα   δεῖ   λυθῆναι   αὐτὸν
THOUSAND YEARS. AFTER THESE THINGS IT IS NECESSARY [FOR] HIM~TO BE RELEASED

μικρὸν   χρόνον.
A SHORT   TIME.

20.4 Καὶ   εἶδον   θρόνους   καὶ   ἐκάθισαν   ἐπ᾽   αὐτοὺς   καὶ
        AND I SAW   THRONES   AND   THEY SAT   ON   THEM   AND

κρίμα   ἐδόθη   αὐτοῖς,   καὶ   τὰς   ψυχὰς   τῶν
JUDGMENT WAS GIVEN TO THEM, AND [I SAW] THE SOULS OF THE ONES

πεπελεκισμένων   διὰ   τὴν   μαρτυρίαν   Ἰησοῦ   καὶ
HAVING BEEN BEHEADED BECAUSE OF THE[IR] TESTIMONY OF(FOR) JESUS AND

διὰ   τὸν   λόγον   τοῦ   θεοῦ   καὶ   οἵτινες
BECAUSE OF THE WORD -   OF GOD AND   [THOSE] WHO

οὐ   προσεκύνησαν   τὸ   θηρίον   οὐδὲ   τὴν   εἰκόνα   αὐτοῦ   καὶ
DID NOT WORSHIP   THE BEAST   NOR   THE   IMAGE   OF IT   AND

οὐκ   ἔλαβον   τὸ   χάραγμα   ἐπὶ   τὸ   μέτωπον   καὶ   ἐπὶ   τὴν
DID NOT RECEIVE THE MARK   ON   THE FOREHEAD   AND   ON   THE

χεῖρα   αὐτῶν.   καὶ   ἔζησαν   καὶ   ἐβασίλευσαν   μετὰ
HAND   OF THEM. AND   THEY CAME TO LIFE AND REIGNED   WITH

Then I saw an angel coming down from heaven, holding in his hand the key to the bottomless pit and a great chain. ²He seized the dragon, that ancient serpent, who is the Devil and Satan, and bound him for a thousand years, ³and threw him into the pit, and locked and sealed it over him, so that he would deceive the nations no more, until the thousand years were ended. After that he must be let out for a little while.

4 Then I saw thrones, and those seated on them were given authority to judge. I also saw the souls of those who had been beheaded for their testimony to Jesus⁹ and for the word of God. They had not worshiped the beast or its image and had not received its mark on their foreheads or their hands. They came to life and reigned with

⁹ Or *for the testimony of Jesus*

Christ a thousand years.
⁵(The rest of the dead did
not come to life until the
thousand years were ended.)
This is the first resurrection.
⁶Blessed and holy are those
who share in the first resurrection. Over these the
second death has no power,
but they will be priests of
God and of Christ, and they
will reign with him a
thousand years.

7 When the thousand
years are ended, Satan will
be released from his prison
⁸and will come out to
deceive the nations at the
four corners of the earth,
Gog and Magog, in order to
gather them for battle; they
are as numerous as the sands
of the sea. ⁹They marched
up over the breadth of the
earth and surrounded the
camp of the saints and the
beloved city. And fire came
down from heavenʳ and
consumed them. ¹⁰And the
devil who had deceived
them was thrown into the
lake of fire and sulfur, where
the beast and the false
prophet were, and they will
be tormented day and night
forever and ever.

11 Then I saw a great
white throne and the one
who sat on it; the earth and
the heaven fled from his
presence, and no place was
found for them.

ʳ Other ancient authorities read *from
God, out of heaven,* or *out of
heaven from God*

τοῦ Χριστοῦ χίλια ἔτη. **20.5** οἱ λοιποὶ τῶν νεκρῶν
-        CHRIST   A THOUSAND YEARS.   THE REST   OF THE DEAD

οὐκ ἔζησαν ἄχρι τελεσθῇ τὰ χίλια ἔτη. αὕτη
DID NOT COME TO LIFE UNTIL SHOULD BE COMPLETED THE THOUSAND YEARS. THIS

ἡ   ἀνάστασις ἡ πρώτη. **20.6** μακάριος καὶ ἅγιος
[IS] THE ²RESURRECTION - ¹THE FIRST.   BLESSED   AND   HOLY

ὁ   ἔχων μέρος ἐν τῇ ἀναστάσει τῇ πρώτῃ· ἐπὶ
[IS] THE ONE HAVING PART IN   THE ²RESURRECTION - ¹FIRST;   ON

τούτων ὁ δεύτερος θάνατος οὐκ ἔχει ἐξουσίαν, ἀλλ᾽
THESE ONES THE SECOND DEATH DOES NOT HAVE AUTHORITY,   BUT

ἔσονται ἱερεῖς τοῦ θεοῦ καὶ τοῦ Χριστοῦ καὶ
THEY WILL BE PRIESTS - OF GOD AND - OF CHRIST   AND

βασιλεύσουσιν μετ᾽ αὐτοῦ [τὰ] χίλια ἔτη.
WILL REIGN   WITH HIM   THE THOUSAND YEARS.

20.7 Καὶ ὅταν τελεσθῇ τὰ χίλια ἔτη,
AND WHEN ⁴WOULD BE COMPLETED ¹THE ²THOUSAND ³YEARS,

λυθήσεται ὁ Σατανᾶς ἐκ τῆς φυλακῆς αὐτοῦ **20.8** καὶ
²WILL BE RELEASED - ¹SATAN FROM THE PRISON   OF HIM,   AND

ἐξελεύσεται πλανῆσαι τὰ ἔθνη τὰ ἐν ταῖς τέσσαρσιν
WILL GO FORTH TO DECEIVE THE NATIONS - IN THE   FOUR

γωνίαις τῆς γῆς, τὸν Γὼγ καὶ Μαγώγ,
CORNERS OF THE EARTH, - [THAT IS,] GOG AND MAGOG,

συναγαγεῖν αὐτοὺς εἰς τὸν πόλεμον, ὧν ὁ ἀριθμὸς
TO GATHER   THEM   TO THE WAR,   WHOSE° - NUMBER

αὐτῶν ὡς ἡ ἄμμος τῆς θαλάσσης. **20.9** καὶ
-       [IS] AS THE SAND OF THE SEA.   AND

ἀνέβησαν ἐπὶ τὸ πλάτος τῆς γῆς καὶ ἐκύκλευσαν
THEY WENT UP OVER THE BREADTH OF THE EARTH AND ENCIRCLED

τὴν παρεμβολὴν τῶν ἁγίων καὶ τὴν πόλιν τὴν
THE CAMP   OF THE SAINTS AND THE CITY -

ἠγαπημένην, καὶ κατέβη πῦρ ἐκ τοῦ οὐρανοῦ καὶ
HAVING BEEN LOVED, AND FIRE~CAME DOWN OUT OF - HEAVEN   AND

κατέφαγεν αὐτούς. **20.10** καὶ ὁ διάβολος ὁ πλανῶν
CONSUMED   THEM.   AND THE DEVIL,   THE ONE DECEIVING

αὐτοὺς ἐβλήθη εἰς τὴν λίμνην τοῦ πυρὸς καὶ θείου
THEM,   WAS THROWN INTO THE LAKE   - OF FIRE AND SULFUR,

ὅπου καὶ τὸ θηρίον καὶ ὁ ψευδοπροφήτης, καὶ
WHERE BOTH THE BEAST AND THE FALSE PROPHET [ARE],   AND

βασανισθήσονται ἡμέρας καὶ νυκτὸς εἰς τοὺς αἰῶνας
THEY WILL BE TORMENTED DAY AND NIGHT INTO THE AGES

τῶν αἰώνων.
OF THE AGES.

20.11 Καὶ εἶδον θρόνον μέγαν λευκὸν καὶ τὸν
AND I SAW ³THRONE ¹A GREAT ²WHITE AND THE ONE

καθήμενον ἐπ᾽ αὐτόν, οὗ ἀπὸ τοῦ προσώπου ἔφυγεν ἡ
SITTING   ON IT,   FROM~WHOSE - PRESENCE   FLED   THE

γῆ καὶ ὁ οὐρανὸς καὶ τόπος οὐχ εὑρέθη αὐτοῖς.
EARTH AND - HEAVEN, AND A PLACE WAS NOT FOUND FOR THEM.

20.12 καὶ   εἶδον   τοὺς   νεκρούς,   τοὺς   μεγάλους   καὶ   τοὺς
AND   I SAW   THE   DEAD,   THE   GREAT   AND   THE

μικρούς,   ἑστῶτας   ἐνώπιον τοῦ θρόνου.   καὶ
SMALL,   HAVING TAKEN [THEIR] STAND BEFORE   THE   THRONE.   AND

βιβλία   ἠνοίχθησαν,   καὶ   ἄλλο   βιβλίον   ἠνοίχθη,   ὅ
BOOKS   WERE OPENED,   AND   ANOTHER BOOK   WAS OPENED,   WHICH

ἐστιν   τῆς   ζωῆς,   καὶ   ἐκρίθησαν   οἱ   νεκροὶ   ἐκ
IS   THE [BOOK] OF LIFE, AND   ³WERE JUDGED ¹THE ²DEAD   BY

τῶν   γεγραμμένων   ἐν   τοῖς   βιβλίοις   κατὰ   τὰ
THE THINGS HAVING BEEN WRITTEN IN   THE   BOOKS   ACCORDING TO THE

ἔργα   αὐτῶν.   **20.13** καὶ   ἔδωκεν   ἡ   θάλασσα   τοὺς
WORKS   OF THEM.   AND   ³GAVE [UP] ¹THE ²SEA   THE

νεκροὺς   τοὺς   ἐν   αὐτῇ   καὶ   ὁ   θάνατος   καὶ   ὁ   ᾅδης
DEAD   -   IN   IT,   AND   -   DEATH,   AND   -   HADES

ἔδωκαν   τοὺς   νεκροὺς   τοὺς   ἐν   αὐτοῖς,   καὶ   ἐκρίθησαν
GAVE [UP] THE   DEAD   -   IN   THEM,   AND   THEY WERE JUDGED,

ἕκαστος   κατὰ   τὰ   ἔργα   αὐτῶν.   **20.14** καὶ   ὁ   θάνατος
EACH ONE, ACCORDING TO THE WORKS   OF THEM.   AND   -   DEATH

καὶ   ὁ   ᾅδης   ἐβλήθησαν   εἰς   τὴν   λίμνην   τοῦ   πυρός.
AND   - HADES   WERE THROWN   INTO THE   LAKE   -   OF FIRE.

οὗτος   ὁ   θάνατος   ὁ   δεύτερός   ἐστιν,   ἡ   λίμνη   τοῦ
THIS   ²THE ⁴DEATH   -   ³SECOND   ¹IS,   THE LAKE   -

πυρός.   **20.15** καὶ   εἴ   τις   οὐχ   εὑρέθη   ἐν   τῇ   βίβλῳ   τῆς
OF FIRE.   AND   IF ANYONE WAS NOT FOUND ²IN ³THE ⁴BOOK -

ζωῆς   γεγραμμένος,   ἐβλήθη   εἰς   τὴν   λίμνην   τοῦ
⁵OF LIFE ¹HAVING BEEN WRITTEN, HE WAS THROWN INTO THE   LAKE   -

πυρός.
OF FIRE.

[12]And I saw the dead, great and small, standing before the throne, and books were opened. Also another book was opened, the book of life. And the dead were judged according to their works, as recorded in the books. [13]And the sea gave up the dead that were in it, Death and Hades gave up the dead that were in them, and all were judged according to what they had done. [14]Then Death and Hades were thrown into the lake of fire. This is the second death, the lake of fire; [15]and anyone whose name was not found written in the book of life was thrown into the lake of fire.

21.1 Καὶ   εἶδον   οὐρανὸν   καινὸν   καὶ   γῆν   καινήν.
AND   I SAW   A NEW~HEAVEN   AND   A NEW~EARTH.

ὁ   γὰρ   πρῶτος   οὐρανὸς   καὶ   ἡ   πρώτη   γῆ   ἀπῆλθαν   καὶ
FOR~THE   FIRST   HEAVEN   AND   THE FIRST EARTH PASSED AWAY, AND

ἡ   θάλασσα   οὐκ   ἔστιν   ἔτι.   **21.2** καὶ   τὴν   πόλιν   τὴν
THE SEA   IS~NO   LONGER.   AND   THE   ²CITY   -

ἁγίαν   Ἰερουσαλὴμ   καινὴν   εἶδον   καταβαίνουσαν   ἐκ
¹HOLY,   NEW~JERUSALEM   I SAW   COMING DOWN   OUT OF

τοῦ   οὐρανοῦ   ἀπὸ   τοῦ   θεοῦ   ἡτοιμασμένην   ὡς   νύμφην
-    HEAVEN   FROM   -   GOD   HAVING BEEN PREPARED AS   A BRIDE

κεκοσμημένην   τῷ   ἀνδρὶ   αὐτῆς.   **21.3** καὶ   ἤκουσα
HAVING BEEN ADORNED FOR THE HUSBAND OF HER.   AND   I HEARD

φωνῆς   μεγάλης   ἐκ   τοῦ   θρόνου   λεγούσης,   Ἰδοὺ   ἡ
A LOUD~VOICE   FROM THE   THRONE   SAYING,   BEHOLD, THE

σκηνὴ   τοῦ   θεοῦ   μετὰ   τῶν   ἀνθρώπων,   καὶ   σκηνώσει
TABERNACLE -   OF GOD [IS] WITH -   MEN,   AND   HE WILL TABERNACLE

Then I saw a new heaven and a new earth; for the first heaven and the first earth had passed away, and the sea was no more. [2]And I saw the holy city, the new Jerusalem, coming down out of heaven from God, prepared as a bride adorned for her husband. [3]And I heard a loud voice from the throne saying,

"See, the home[s] of God
    is among mortals.
He will dwell[t]

[s] Gk *the tabernacle*
[t] Gk *will tabernacle*

with them;

they will be his peoples,ᵘ
and God himself will be
with them;ᵛ
4 he will wipe every tear
from their eyes.
Death will be no more;
mourning and crying and
pain will be no
more,
for the first things have
passed away."

5 And the one who was
seated on the throne said,
"See, I am making all things
new." Also he said, "Write
this, for these words are
trustworthy and true." 6Then
he said to me, "It is done!
I am the Alpha and the
Omega, the beginning and
the end. To the thirsty I will
give water as a gift from the
spring of the water of life.
7Those who conquer will
inherit these things, and I
will be their God and they
will be my children. 8But
as for the cowardly, the
faithless,ʷ the polluted, the
murderers, the fornicators,
the sorcerers, the idolaters,
and all liars, their place will
be in the lake that burns with
fire and sulfur, which is the
second death."

9 Then one of the seven
angels who had the seven
bowls full of the seven last
plagues came and said to
me, "Come, I will show you
the bride, the wife of the

ᵘ Other ancient authorities read *people*
ᵛ Other ancient authorities add *and be
their God*
ʷ Or *the unbelieving*

μετ᾽ αὐτῶν, καὶ αὐτοὶ λαοὶ αὐτοῦ ἔσονται, καὶ
WITH THEM, AND THEY ³PEOPLE ²HIS ¹WILL BE, AND

⌐αὐτὸς ὁ θεὸς μετ᾽ αὐτῶν ἔσται [αὐτῶν θεός]⌐, 21.4 καὶ
HE HIMSELF, - GOD-WITH-THEM, WILL BE THEIR GOD, AND

ἐξαλείψει πᾶν δάκρυον ἐκ τῶν ὀφθαλμῶν αὐτῶν, καὶ
HE WILL WIPE AWAY EVERY TEAR FROM THE EYES OF THEM, AND

ὁ θάνατος οὐκ ἔσται ἔτι οὔτε πένθος οὔτε κραυγὴ
- DEATH WILL BE~NO LONGER NOR GRIEF NOR CRYING

οὔτε πόνος οὐκ ἔσται ἔτι, [ὅτι] τὰ πρῶτα
NOR PAIN NO LONGER~WILL BE, BECAUSE THE FIRST(FORMER) THINGS

ἀπῆλθαν.
PASSED AWAY.

21.5 Καὶ εἶπεν ὁ καθήμενος ἐπὶ τῷ θρόνῳ, Ἰδοὺ
AND ⁶SAID ¹THE ONE ²SITTING ³ON ⁴THE ⁵THRONE, BEHOLD,

καινὰ ποιῶ πάντα, καὶ λέγει, Γράψον, ὅτι οὗτοι οἱ
³NEW ¹I MAKE ²ALL THINGS, AND HE SAYS, WRITE [THIS], BECAUSE THESE -

λόγοι πιστοὶ καὶ ἀληθινοί εἰσιν. 21.6 καὶ εἶπέν μοι,
WORDS ²FAITHFUL ³AND ⁴TRUE ¹ARE. AND HE SAID TO ME,

Γέγοναν. ἐγώ [εἰμι] τὸ Ἄλφα καὶ τὸ Ὦ, ἡ
THEY HAVE COME TO PASS. I AM THE ALPHA AND THE OMEGA, THE

ἀρχὴ καὶ τὸ τέλος. ἐγὼ τῷ διψῶντι δώσω ἐκ τῆς
BEGINNING AND THE END. I, TO THE ONE THIRSTING, WILL GIVE OF THE

πηγῆς τοῦ ὕδατος τῆς ζωῆς δωρεάν. 21.7 ὁ νικῶν
FOUNTAIN OF THE WATER - OF LIFE FREELY. THE ONE OVERCOMING

κληρονομήσει ταῦτα καὶ ἔσομαι αὐτῷ θεὸς καὶ
WILL INHERIT THESE THINGS AND I WILL BE TO HIM GOD AND

αὐτὸς ἔσται μοι υἱός. 21.8 τοῖς δὲ δειλοῖς καὶ
HE WILL BE TO ME A SON. BUT~FOR THE COWARDLY AND

ἀπίστοις καὶ ἐβδελυγμένοις καὶ φονεῦσιν καὶ
UNBELIEVING AND ONES HAVING BECOME VILE AND MURDERERS AND

πόρνοις καὶ φαρμάκοις καὶ εἰδωλολάτραις καὶ πᾶσιν
FORNICATORS AND SORCERERS AND IDOLATERS AND ALL

τοῖς ψευδέσιν τὸ μέρος αὐτῶν ἐν τῇ λίμνῃ τῇ
THE FALSE ONES, - THEIR~PART [WILL BE] IN THE LAKE -

καιομένῃ πυρὶ καὶ θείῳ, ὅ ἐστιν ὁ θάνατος ὁ
BURNING WITH FIRE AND SULFUR, WHICH IS THE ²DEATH -

δεύτερος.
¹SECOND.

21.9 Καὶ ἦλθεν εἷς ἐκ τῶν ἑπτὰ ἀγγέλων τῶν
AND CAME ONE OF THE SEVEN ANGELS -

ἐχόντων τὰς ἑπτὰ φιάλας τῶν γεμόντων τῶν ἑπτὰ
HAVING THE SEVEN BOWLS - BEING FULL OF THE SEVEN

πληγῶν τῶν ἐσχάτων καὶ ἐλάλησεν μετ᾽ ἐμοῦ λέγων,
²PLAGUES - ¹LAST AND SPOKE WITH ME SAYING,

Δεῦρο, δείξω σοι τὴν νύμφην τὴν γυναῖκα τοῦ
COME, I WILL SHOW YOU THE BRIDE, THE WIFE OF THE

21:3 text (which can also be rendered, 'God himself will be with them [and be] their God'): KJV ASV RSVmg NASBmg NIV NEBmg TEV NJB NRSVmg. var. αυτος ο θεος μετ᾽ αυτων εσται [with varying word order in different MSS] (God himself will be with them): RSV NASB NEB NRSV.

ἀρνίου. **21.10** καὶ ἀπήνεγκέν με ἐν πνεύματι ἐπὶ
LAMB.   AND   HE CARRIED AWAY ME IN   SPIRIT   ONTO

ὄρος μέγα καὶ ὑψηλόν, καὶ ἔδειξέν μοι τὴν πόλιν
A MOUNTAIN, GREAT AND HIGH,   AND SHOWED ME   THE ²CITY

τὴν ἁγίαν Ἰερουσαλὴμ καταβαίνουσαν ἐκ τοῦ
-    ¹HOLY,   JERUSALEM   COMING DOWN   OUT OF -

οὐρανοῦ ἀπὸ τοῦ θεοῦ **21.11** ἔχουσαν τὴν δόξαν τοῦ
HEAVEN FROM -   GOD,   HAVING   THE GLORY   -

θεοῦ, ὁ φωστὴρ αὐτῆς ὅμοιος λίθῳ τιμιωτάτῳ ὡς
OF GOD, THE RADIANCE OF IT [WAS] LIKE A PRECIOUS~STONE, AS

λίθῳ ἰάσπιδι κρυσταλλίζοντι. **21.12** ἔχουσα τεῖχος
A JASPER~STONE BEING CLEAR AS CRYSTAL;   HAVING   A WALL,

μέγα καὶ ὑψηλόν, ἔχουσα πυλῶνας δώδεκα καὶ ἐπὶ
GREAT AND HIGH, HAVING TWELVE~GATES   AND AT

τοῖς πυλῶσιν ἀγγέλους δώδεκα καὶ ὀνόματα
THE GATES   TWELVE~ANGELS   AND   NAMES

ἐπιγεγραμμένα, ἅ ἐστιν [τὰ ὀνόματα] τῶν
HAVING BEEN INSCRIBED ON [THEM], WHICH IS(ARE) THE NAMES OF THE

δώδεκα φυλῶν υἱῶν Ἰσραήλ· **21.13** ἀπὸ ἀνατολῆς
TWELVE TRIBES OF [THE] SONS OF ISRAEL;   FROM [THE] EAST

πυλῶνες τρεῖς καὶ ἀπὸ βορρᾶ πυλῶνες τρεῖς καὶ ἀπὸ
THREE~GATES   AND FROM [THE] NORTH THREE~GATES   AND FROM

νότου πυλῶνες τρεῖς καὶ ἀπὸ δυσμῶν πυλῶνες τρεῖς.
[THE] SOUTH THREE~GATES   AND FROM [THE] WEST THREE~GATES;

21.14 καὶ τὸ τεῖχος τῆς πόλεως ἔχων θεμελίους δώδεκα
AND THE WALL OF THE CITY HAVING TWELVE~FOUNDATIONS

καὶ ἐπ' αὐτῶν δώδεκα ὀνόματα τῶν δώδεκα ἀποστόλων
AND ON THEM TWELVE NAMES, OF THE TWELVE APOSTLES

τοῦ ἀρνίου.
OF THE LAMB.

21.15 Καὶ ὁ λαλῶν μετ' ἐμοῦ εἶχεν μέτρον
AND THE ONE SPEAKING WITH ME   HAD   ²MEASURING

κάλαμον χρυσοῦν, ἵνα μετρήσῃ τὴν πόλιν καὶ τοὺς
³ROD   ¹A GOLDEN, THAT HE MIGHT MEASURE THE CITY AND THE

πυλῶνας αὐτῆς καὶ τὸ τεῖχος αὐτῆς. **21.16** καὶ ἡ
GATES   OF IT AND THE WALLS OF IT.   AND THE

πόλις τετράγωνος κεῖται καὶ τὸ μῆκος αὐτῆς ὅσον
CITY LIES~SQUARE   AND THE LENGTH OF IT [IS] AS MUCH AS

[καὶ] τὸ πλάτος. καὶ ἐμέτρησεν τὴν πόλιν τῷ
ALSO THE BREADTH. AND HE MEASURED THE CITY WITH THE

καλάμῳ ἐπὶ σταδίων δώδεκα χιλιάδων, τὸ μῆκος
ROD   ACROSS ³STADIA ¹TWELVE ²THOUSAND, THE LENGTH

καὶ τὸ πλάτος καὶ τὸ ὕψος αὐτῆς ἴσα ἐστίν.
AND THE BREADTH AND THE HEIGHT OF IT IS(ARE)~EQUAL.

21.17 καὶ ἐμέτρησεν τὸ τεῖχος αὐτῆς ἑκατὸν
AND HE MEASURED THE WALL OF IT A HUNDRED

τεσσεράκοντα τεσσάρων πηχῶν μέτρον ἀνθρώπου, ὁ
FORTY-FOUR   CUBITS BY MAN'S~MEASUREMENT, WHICH

Lamb." [10]And in the spirit[x] he carried me away to a great, high mountain and showed me the holy city Jerusalem coming down out of heaven from God. [11]It has the glory of God and a radiance like a very rare jewel, like jasper, clear as crystal. [12]It has a great, high wall with twelve gates, and at the gates twelve angels, and on the gates are inscribed the names of the twelve tribes of the Israelites; [13]on the east three gates, on the north three gates, on the south three gates, and on the west three gates. [14]And the wall of the city has twelve foundations, and on them are the twelve names of the twelve apostles of the Lamb.

15 The angel[y] who talked to me had a measuring rod of gold to measure the city and its gates and walls. [16]The city lies foursquare, its length the same as its width; and he measured the city with his rod, fifteen hundred miles;[z] its length and width and height are equal. [17]He also measured its wall, one hundred forty-four cubits[a] by human measurement,

[x] Or in the Spirit
[y] Gk He
[z] Gk twelve thousand stadia
[a] That is, almost seventy-five yards

which the angel was using.
[18] The wall is built of jasper, while the city is pure gold, clear as glass. [19] The foundations of the wall of the city are adorned with every jewel; the first was jasper, the second sapphire, the third agate, the fourth emerald, [20] the fifth onyx, the sixth carnelian, the seventh chrysolite, the eighth beryl, the ninth topaz, the tenth chrysoprase, the eleventh jacinth, the twelfth amethyst. [21] And the twelve gates are twelve pearls, each of the gates is a single pearl, and the street of the city is pure gold, transparent as glass.

22 I saw no temple in the city, for its temple is the Lord God the Almighty and the Lamb. [23] And the city has no need of sun or moon to shine on it, for the glory of God is its light, and its lamp is the Lamb. [24] The nations will walk by its light, and the kings of the earth will bring their glory into it. [25] Its gates will never be shut by day— and there will be no night there. [26] People will bring into it the glory and the honor of the nations. [27] But nothing unclean will enter it,

ἐστιν ἀγγέλου. **21.18** καὶ ἡ ἐνδώμησις τοῦ τείχους
IS [ALSO] [THE] ANGEL'S.   AND   THE CONSTRUCTION OF THE WALL

αὐτῆς ἴασπις καὶ ἡ πόλις χρυσίον καθαρὸν ὅμοιον
OF IT [WAS OF] JASPER AND THE CITY [WAS] PURE~GOLD   LIKE

ὑάλῳ καθαρῷ. **21.19** οἱ θεμέλιοι τοῦ τείχους τῆς
PURE~GLASS;   THE FOUNDATIONS OF THE WALL   OF THE

πόλεως παντὶ καὶ λίθῳ τιμίῳ κεκοσμημένοι· ὁ
CITY   WITH   EVERY PRECIOUS~STONE HAVING BEEN ADORNED: THE

θεμέλιος ὁ πρῶτος ἴασπις, ὁ δεύτερος σάπφιρος, ὁ
[2]FOUNDATION - [1]FIRST JASPER,   THE SECOND   SAPPHIRE,   THE

τρίτος χαλκηδών, ὁ τέταρτος σμάραγδος, **21.20** ὁ
THIRD CHALCEDONY, THE FOURTH   EMERALD,   THE

πέμπτος σαρδόνυξ, ὁ ἕκτος σάρδιον, ὁ ἕβδομος
FIFTH   SARDONYX,   THE SIXTH CARNELIAN, THE SEVENTH

χρυσόλιθος, ὁ ὄγδοος βήρυλλος, ὁ ἔνατος τοπάζιον,
CHRYSOLITE, THE EIGHTH BERYL,   THE NINTH   TOPAZ,

ὁ δέκατος χρυσόπρασος, ὁ ἑνδέκατος ὑάκινθος, ὁ
THE TENTH   CHRYSOPRASE,   THE ELEVENTH JACINTH,   THE

δωδέκατος ἀμέθυστος, **21.21** καὶ οἱ δώδεκα πυλῶνες
TWELFTH   AMETHYST,   AND   THE TWELVE GATES

δώδεκα μαργαρῖται, ἀνὰ εἷς ἕκαστος τῶν
[WERE] TWELVE PEARLS,   [3]RESPECTIVELY [2]ONE [1]EACH   OF THE

πυλώνων ἦν ἐξ ἑνὸς μαργαρίτου. καὶ ἡ πλατεῖα
GATES   WAS OF ONE   PEARL.   AND   THE STREET

τῆς πόλεως χρυσίον καθαρὸν ὡς ὕαλος διαυγής.
OF THE CITY [WAS] PURE~GOLD   AS   TRANSPARENT~GLASS.

21.22 Καὶ ναὸν οὐκ εἶδον ἐν αὐτῇ, ὁ γὰρ κύριος ὁ
AND   A TEMPLE I DID NOT SEE IN IT,   FOR~THE LORD   -

θεὸς ὁ παντοκράτωρ ναὸς αὐτῆς ἐστιν καὶ τὸ
GOD,   THE ALMIGHTY   [2][THE] TEMPLE [3]OF IT [1]IS,   AND THE

ἀρνίον. **21.23** καὶ ἡ πόλις οὐ χρείαν ἔχει τοῦ ἡλίου
LAMB.   AND THE CITY [2]NO [3]NEED [1]HAS OF THE SUN

οὐδὲ τῆς σελήνης ἵνα φαίνωσιν αὐτῇ, ἡ γὰρ δόξα τοῦ
NOR   OF THE MOON   THAT THEY MAY SHINE IN IT,   FOR~THE GLORY -

θεοῦ ἐφώτισεν αὐτήν, καὶ ὁ λύχνος αὐτῆς τὸ
OF GOD ILLUMINED   IT,   AND THE LAMP   OF IT [IS] THE

ἀρνίον. **21.24** καὶ περιπατήσουσιν τὰ ἔθνη διὰ τοῦ
LAMB.   AND   [3]WILL WALK AROUND [1]THE [2]NATIONS BY THE

φωτὸς αὐτῆς, καὶ οἱ βασιλεῖς τῆς γῆς φέρουσιν τὴν
LIGHT   OF IT,   AND THE KINGS OF THE EARTH BRING   THE

δόξαν αὐτῶν εἰς αὐτήν, **21.25** καὶ οἱ πυλῶνες αὐτῆς
GLORY OF THEM INTO IT,   AND THE GATES OF IT

οὐ μὴ κλεισθῶσιν ἡμέρας, νὺξ γὰρ οὐκ ἔσται ἐκεῖ,
NEVER   WOULD BE SHUT BY DAY,   FOR~NIGHT WILL NOT BE THERE,

21.26 καὶ οἴσουσιν τὴν δόξαν καὶ τὴν τιμὴν τῶν
AND   THEY WILL BRING THE GLORY AND THE HONOR OF THE

ἐθνῶν εἰς αὐτήν. **21.27** καὶ οὐ μὴ εἰσέλθῃ εἰς αὐτὴν
NATIONS INTO IT.   AND   NEVER   MAY ENTER INTO IT

πᾶν   κοινὸν   καὶ [ὁ]   ποιῶν   βδέλυγμα καὶ
EVERY(ANY) PROFANE THING AND   THE ONE PRACTICING ABOMINATION AND

ψεῦδος εἰ μὴ οἱ   γεγραμμένοι ἐν τῷ βιβλίῳ τῆς
FALSEHOOD, BUT ONLY THE ONES HAVING BEEN WRITTEN IN   THE   BOOK   -

ζωῆς τοῦ   ἀρνίου.
OF LIFE OF THE LAMB.

nor anyone who practices
abomination or falsehood,
but only those who are
written in the Lamb's book
of life.

22.1 Καὶ ἔδειξέν μοι ποταμὸν ὕδατος ζωῆς λαμπρὸν
      AND   HE SHOWED ME A RIVER   OF WATER OF LIFE BRIGHT

ὡς κρύσταλλον, ἐκπορευόμενον ἐκ   τοῦ θρόνου τοῦ
AS   CRYSTAL,   GOING FORTH   OUT OF THE THRONE   -

θεοῦ καὶ τοῦ ἀρνίου. **22.2** ἐν μέσῳ   τῆς   πλατείας
OF GOD AND OF THE LAMB,   IN [THE] MIDDLE OF THE STREET

αὐτῆς καὶ τοῦ ποταμοῦ ἐντεῦθεν καὶ ἐκεῖθεν ξύλον
OF IT; AND ⁴OF THE RIVER ¹ON THIS [SIDE] ²AND ³ON THAT [SIDE] [THE] TREE

ζωῆς ποιοῦν καρποὺς δώδεκα, κατα   μῆνα ἕκαστον
OF LIFE PRODUCING TWELVE~FRUITS,   ACCORDING TO EACH~MONTH

ἀποδιδοῦν τὸν καρπὸν αὐτοῦ, καὶ τὰ φύλλα τοῦ ξύλου
YIELDING   THE FRUIT   OF IT,   AND THE LEAVES OF THE TREE

εἰς   θεραπείαν τῶν ἐθνῶν. **22.3** καὶ πᾶν κατάθεμα
[ARE] FOR [THE] HEALING OF THE NATIONS.   AND EVERY CURSE

οὐκ ἔσται ἔτι. καὶ ὁ θρόνος τοῦ θεοῦ καὶ τοῦ
NO LONGER~WILL BE. AND THE THRONE   - OF GOD AND OF THE

ἀρνίου ἐν αὐτῇ ἔσται, καὶ οἱ δοῦλοι αὐτοῦ
LAMB   IN IT   WILL BE, AND THE SLAVES OF HIM

λατρεύσουσιν αὐτῷ **22.4** καὶ ὄψονται τὸ πρόσωπον
WILL SERVE   HIM   AND WILL SEE   THE FACE

αὐτοῦ, καὶ τὸ ὄνομα αὐτοῦ ἐπὶ   τῶν μετώπων αὐτῶν.
OF HIM, AND THE NAME OF HIM [WILL BE] ON THE FOREHEADS OF THEM.

22.5 καὶ νὺξ οὐκ ἔσται ἔτι καὶ οὐκ ἔχουσιν χρείαν
      AND NIGHT NO LONGER~WILL BE AND THEY HAVE~NO   NEED

φωτὸς λύχνου καὶ φωτὸς ἡλίου, ὅτι κύριος ὁ
OF [THE] LIGHT OF A LAMP AND LIGHT OF [THE] SUN, BECAUSE [THE] LORD -

θεὸς φωτίσει   ἐπ' αὐτούς, καὶ βασιλεύσουσιν εἰς
GOD   WILL GIVE FORTH LIGHT ON THEM,   AND THEY WILL REIGN   INTO

τοὺς αἰῶνας τῶν αἰώνων.
THE   AGES   OF THE AGES.

22.6 Καὶ εἶπέν μοι, Οὗτοι οἱ λόγοι πιστοὶ   καὶ
      AND HE SAID TO ME, THESE - WORDS [ARE] FAITHFUL AND

ἀληθινοί, καὶ ὁ κύριος ὁ θεὸς τῶν πνευμάτων τῶν
TRUE,   AND THE LORD   - GOD OF THE SPIRITS   OF THE

προφητῶν ἀπέστειλεν τὸν ἄγγελον αὐτοῦ δεῖξαι τοῖς
PROPHETS SENT   THE ANGEL   OF HIM TO SHOW TO THE

δούλοις αὐτοῦ ἃ   δεῖ γενέσθαι ἐν τάχει.
SLAVES   OF HIM THINGS WHICH HAVE TO HAPPEN QUICKLY.

Then the angel[b] showed me
the river of the water of life,
bright as crystal, flowing
from the throne of God and
of the Lamb ²through the
middle of the street of the
city. On either side of the
river is the tree of life[c] with
its twelve kinds of fruit,
producing its fruit each
month; and the leaves of the
tree are for the healing of the
nations. ³Nothing accursed
will be found there any
more. But the throne of God
and of the Lamb will be in
it, and his servants[d] will
worship him; ⁴they will see
his face, and his name will
be on their foreheads. ⁵And
there will be no more night;
they need no light of lamp or
sun, for the Lord God will be
their light, and they will
reign forever and ever.

6 And he said to me,
"These words are trust-
worthy and true, for the
Lord, the God of the spirits
of the prophets, has sent his
angel to show his servants[d]
what must soon take place."

[b] Gk he
[c] Or the Lamb. ²In the middle of the
    street of the city, and on either side
    of the river, is the tree of life
[d] Gk slaves

7 "See, I am coming soon! Blessed is the one who keeps the words of the prophecy of this book."

8 I, John, am the one who heard and saw these things. And when I heard and saw them, I fell down to worship at the feet of the angel who showed them to me; 9but he said to me, "You must not do that! I am a fellow servant^e with you and your comrades^f the prophets, and with those who keep the words of this book. Worship God!"

10 And he said to me, "Do not seal up the words of the prophecy of this book, for the time is near. 11Let the evildoer still do evil, and the filthy still be filthy, and the righteous still do right, and the holy still be holy."

12 "See, I am coming soon; my reward is with me, to repay according to everyone's work. 13I am the Alpha and the Omega, the first and the last, the beginning and the end."

14 Blessed are those who wash their robes,^g so that they will have the right to the tree of life and may enter the city by the gates. 15Outside are the dogs and sorcerers and fornicators and

^e Gk *slave*
^f Gk *brothers*
^g Other ancient authorities read *do his commandments*

22.7 καὶ ἰδοὺ ἔρχομαι ταχύ. μακάριος ὁ τηρῶν
AND BEHOLD, I AM COMING QUICKLY. BLESSED [IS] THE ONE KEEPING

τοὺς λόγους τῆς προφητείας τοῦ βιβλίου τούτου.
THE WORDS OF THE PROPHECY - OF THIS~BOOK.

22.8 Κἀγὼ Ἰωάννης ὁ ἀκούων καὶ βλέπων
AND I JOHN [AM] THE ONE HEARING AND SEEING

ταῦτα. καὶ ὅτε ἤκουσα καὶ ἔβλεψα, ἔπεσα
THESE THINGS. AND WHEN I HEARD AND SAW, I FELL

προσκυνῆσαι ἔμπροσθεν τῶν ποδῶν τοῦ ἀγγέλου τοῦ
TO WORSHIP BEFORE THE FEET OF THE ANGEL -

δεικνύοντός μοι ταῦτα. **22.9** καὶ λέγει μοι, Ὅρα
SHOWING ME THESE THINGS. AND HE SAYS TO ME, SEE

μή· σύνδουλός σου εἰμι καὶ τῶν ἀδελφῶν
[THAT] YOU NOT [DO IT]; A FELLOW SLAVE OF YOU I AM AND OF THE BROTHERS

σου τῶν προφητῶν καὶ τῶν τηρούντων τοὺς λόγους
OF YOU, THE PROPHETS, AND OF THE ONES KEEPING THE WORDS

τοῦ βιβλίου τούτου· τῷ θεῷ προσκύνησον. **22.10** καὶ
- OF THIS~BOOK; WORSHIP~GOD. AND

λέγει μοι, Μὴ σφραγίσῃς τοὺς λόγους τῆς προφητείας
HE SAYS TO ME, DO NOT SEAL THE WORDS OF THE PROPHECY

τοῦ βιβλίου τούτου, ὁ καιρὸς γὰρ ἐγγύς ἐστιν.
- OF THIS~BOOK, ²THE ³TIME ¹FOR IS~NEAR.

22.11 ὁ ἀδικῶν ἀδικησάτω ἔτι καὶ ὁ
THE ONE BEING UNRIGHTEOUS LET HIM BE UNRIGHTEOUS STILL AND THE

ῥυπαρὸς ῥυπανθήτω ἔτι, καὶ ὁ δίκαιος
FILTHY ONE LET HIM BE FILTHY STILL, AND THE RIGHTEOUS ONE

δικαιοσύνην ποιησάτω ἔτι καὶ ὁ ἅγιος ἁγιασθήτω
LET HIM DO~RIGHTEOUSNESS STILL AND THE HOLY ONE LET HIM BE HOLY

ἔτι.
STILL.

22.12 Ἰδοὺ ἔρχομαι ταχύ, καὶ ὁ μισθός μου μετ'
BEHOLD, I AM COMING QUICKLY, AND - MY~REWARD [IS] WITH

ἐμοῦ ἀποδοῦναι ἑκάστῳ ὡς τὸ ἔργον ἐστὶν αὐτοῦ.
ME TO GIVE TO EACH ONE AS THE WORK OF HIM~IS.

22.13 ἐγὼ τὸ Ἄλφα καὶ τὸ Ὦ, ὁ πρῶτος καὶ ὁ
I [AM] THE ALPHA AND THE OMEGA, THE FIRST AND THE

ἔσχατος, ἡ ἀρχὴ καὶ τὸ τέλος.
LAST, THE BEGINNING AND THE END.

22.14 Μακάριοι οἱ πλύνοντες τὰς στολὰς αὐτῶν,
BLESSED [ARE] THE ONES WASHING THE ROBES OF THEM,

ἵνα ἔσται ἡ ἐξουσία αὐτῶν ἐπὶ τὸ ξύλον τῆς ζωῆς καὶ
THAT ³WILL BE - ²RIGHT ¹THEIR TO THE TREE - OF LIFE AND

τοῖς πυλῶσιν εἰσέλθωσιν εἰς τὴν πόλιν. **22.15** ἔξω
BY THE GATES THEY MAY ENTER INTO THE CITY. OUTSIDE

οἱ κύνες καὶ οἱ φάρμακοι καὶ οἱ πόρνοι καὶ οἱ
[ARE] THE DOGS AND THE SORCERERS AND THE FORNICATORS AND THE

φονεῖς καὶ οἱ εἰδωλολάτραι καὶ πᾶς φιλῶν καὶ
MURDERERS AND THE IDOLATERS AND EVERYONE LOVING AND

ποιῶν ψεῦδος.
PRACTICING FALSEHOOD.

22.16 Ἐγὼ Ἰησοῦς ἔπεμψα τὸν ἄγγελόν μου
I, JESUS, SENT THE ANGEL OF ME

μαρτυρῆσαι ὑμῖν ταῦτα ἐπὶ ταῖς ἐκκλησίαις. ἐγώ
TO TESTIFY TO YOU° THESE THINGS FOR THE CHURCHES. I

εἰμι ἡ ῥίζα καὶ τὸ γένος Δαυίδ, ὁ ἀστὴρ ὁ
AM THE ROOT AND THE OFFSPRING OF DAVID, THE ³STAR -

λαμπρὸς ὁ πρωϊνός. **22.17** Καὶ τὸ πνεῦμα καὶ ἡ
¹BRIGHT - ²MORNING. AND THE SPIRIT AND THE

νύμφη λέγουσιν, Ἔρχου. καὶ ὁ ἀκούων εἰπάτω,
BRIDE SAY, COME. AND THE ONE HEARING LET HIM SAY,

Ἔρχου. καὶ ὁ διψῶν ἐρχέσθω, ὁ θέλων
COME. AND THE ONE THIRSTING LET HIM COME, THE ONE DESIRING

λαβέτω ὕδωρ ζωῆς δωρεάν.
LET HIM TAKE [THE] WATER OF LIFE FREELY.

22.18 Μαρτυρῶ ἐγὼ παντὶ τῷ ἀκούοντι τοὺς λόγους
I~TESTIFY TO EVERYONE - HEARING THE WORDS

τῆς προφητείας τοῦ βιβλίου τούτου· ἐάν τις ἐπιθῇ
OF THE PROPHECY - OF THIS~BOOK; IF ANYONE ADDS

ἐπ᾽ αὐτά, ἐπιθήσει ὁ θεὸς ἐπ᾽ αὐτὸν τὰς πληγὰς τὰς
TO THEM, ²WILL ADD - ¹GOD TO HIM THE PLAGUES -

γεγραμμένας ἐν τῷ βιβλίῳ τούτῳ, **22.19** καὶ ἐάν
HAVING BEEN WRITTEN IN - THIS~BOOK, AND IF

τις ἀφέλῃ ἀπὸ τῶν λόγων τοῦ βιβλίου τῆς
ANYONE TAKES AWAY FROM THE WORDS OF THE BOOK -

προφητείας ταύτης, ἀφελεῖ ὁ θεὸς τὸ μέρος αὐτοῦ
OF THIS~PROPHECY, ²WILL TAKE AWAY - ¹GOD - HIS~PART

ἀπὸ τοῦ ξύλου τῆς ζωῆς καὶ ἐκ τῆς πόλεως τῆς ἁγίας
FROM THE TREE - OF LIFE AND FROM THE ²CITY - ¹HOLY,

τῶν γεγραμμένων ἐν τῷ βιβλίῳ τούτῳ.
OF THE THINGS HAVING BEEN WRITTEN IN - THIS~BOOK.

22.20 Λέγει ὁ μαρτυρῶν ταῦτα, Ναί, ἔρχομαι
SAYS THE ONE TESTIFYING THESE THINGS, YES, I AM COMING

ταχύ. Ἀμήν, ἔρχου κύριε Ἰησοῦ.
QUICKLY. AMEN, COME, LORD JESUS.

22.21 Ἡ χάρις τοῦ κυρίου Ἰησοῦ μετὰ πάντων.
THE GRACE OF THE LORD JESUS [BE] WITH ALL.

murderers and idolaters, and everyone who loves and practices falsehood.

16 "It is I, Jesus, who sent my angel to you with this testimony for the churches. I am the root and the descendant of David, the bright morning star."

17 The Spirit and the bride
say, "Come."
And let everyone who
hears say, "Come."
And let everyone who is
thirsty come.
Let anyone who wishes
take the water of life
as a gift.

18 I warn everyone who hears the words of the prophecy of this book: if anyone adds to them, God will add to that person the plagues described in this book; ¹⁹if anyone takes away from the words of the book of this prophecy, God will take away that person's share in the tree of life and in the holy city, which are described in this book.

20 The one who testifies to these things says, "Surely I am coming soon."
Amen. Come, Lord Jesus!

21 The grace of the Lord Jesus be with all the saints. Amen.ʰ

ʰ Other ancient authorities lack *all;* others lack *the saints;* others lack *Amen*